2 9 APR 2

KT-556-689

Eastern
Europe

Estonia
p337

Russia
p739

Latvia p449

Lithuania
p479

Russia (part) p739

Belarus
p79

Poland
p597

Ukraine p913

Czech Republic
p273

Slovakia
p827

Moldova
p545

Hungary
p377

Slovenia
p873

Romania
p677

Croatia
p209

Serbia
p799

**Bosnia &
Hercegovina**
p107

Bulgaria p151

Montenegro
p569

Kosovo p437

Macedonia
p515

Albania
p46

THIS EDITION WRITTEN AND RESEARCHED BY

Tom Masters

Caro   rc Di Duca,
Pete   inski, Anja
Mutić,   uke Waterson

C333434017

HVAR ISLAND, CROATIA
P250

OBROVSKÝ WATERFALL,
SLOVAKIA P850

HIROSHI HIGUCHI/GETTY IMAGES ©

LEE PENGELLY/GETTY IMAGES ©

Contents

ON THE ROAD

ANDY RAATZ/GETTY IMAGES ©

RUSSIAN *MATRYOSHKA* DOLLS

Contents

SURVIVAL GUIDE

welcome to Eastern Europe

Cultural Explosion

Eastern Europe is a warehouse of art, history and architecture, and its world-class museums, festivals and galleries will overwhelm even the most eager connoisseur. Star attractions Prague, Moscow, Kraków, St Petersburg and Budapest groan under the weight of their heritage: cross Prague's 14th-century Charles Bridge at dawn, marvel at Kraków's preserved Rynek Główny (Main Market Sq), see an unrivalled cross-section of art history at the Hermitage in St Petersburg and hear Liszt in his native Hungary. It's not all about high culture though – the people you'll meet are just as much of an attraction. Start a conversation with locals on a train and you'll likely end up sharing food and drinks with them, listening to folk songs, playing cards or even being invited home for dinner. Along the way you'll discover that myths about Eastern European cuisine are just that – delve into delicacies such as Croatian truffles and Hungarian *gulyás* (goulash) as well as delicious daily staples such as Polish *pierogi* (dumplings) and Russian bliny.

Spectacular Scenery

The variety of landscapes in Eastern Europe is simply mind-blowing. Take a boat ride on the blue Danube, discover that Eastern Europe means great beaches on the Croatian or Albanian riviera and hike your way through Poland and Slovakia's

Dramatically diverse, Eastern Europe remains a through-the-looking-glass experience after the certainties of the West. Head here for guaranteed adventure; it's surreal, exciting and surprising.

(left) Bled Island (p888), Slovenia
(below) Buskers near Charles Bridge (p283) in Prague, Czech Republic

High Tatras, Romania's Bucegi Mountains, Bulgaria's Rodopi Mountains and Albania's simply incredible 'Accursed Mountains'. Even less expected are the vast sand dunes of Curonian Spit in Lithuania, beautiful Lake Ohrid in Macedonia, the Great Masurian Lakes of Poland and the racing river gorges of Slovenia and Bosnia and Hercegovina. Those looking for an easier ride can take Eastern Europe's most impressive train journey from Belgrade to Bar through the spectacular canyons of Montenegro, or the Lake Koman ferry in Albania for astonishing mountain views. Whatever scenery you enjoy, you'll find exciting and unexpected landscapes in a region that is anything but grey and predictable.

Historic Overload

Eastern Europe's bleak past is present in its preserved palaces, haunting castles, magnificent churches and grandiose plazas. You can still stand in the room in the Livadia Palace where 'the big three' divided up Europe at the 1945 Yalta Conference, or feel the echo of the Romanian Revolution on Bucharest's Revolution Sq. Elsewhere you can see sights from more distant history – soak up the legacy of Ivan the Terrible's terrifying reign at St Basil's Cathedral on Moscow's Red Sq, cross the bridge where Archduke Ferdinand was assassinated in Sarajevo and take a stroll through the remains of Diocletian's Palace in Split, Croatia.

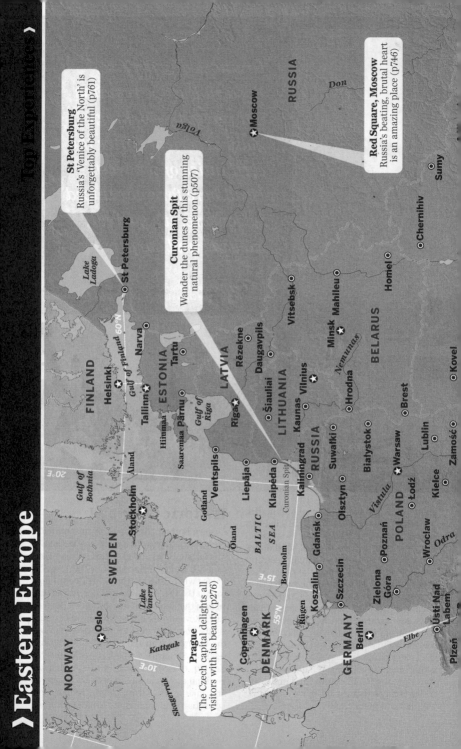

St Petersburg
Russia's 'Venice of the North' is unforgettably beautiful (p761)

Curonian Spit
Wander the dunes of this stunning natural phenomenon (p507)

Red Square, Moscow
Russia's beating, brutal heart is an amazing place (p746)

Prague
The Czech capital delights all visitors with its beauty (p276)

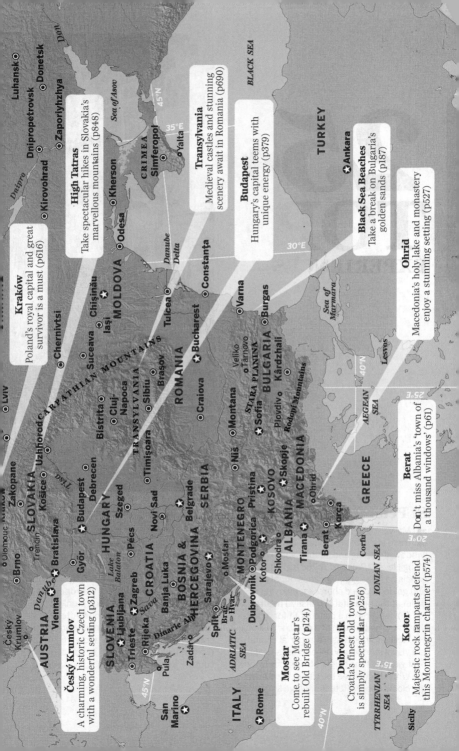

Český Krumlov
A charming, historic Czech town with a wonderful setting (p312)

Kraków
Poland's royal capital and great survivor is a must (p616)

High Tatras
Take spectacular hikes in Slovakia's marvellous mountains (p848)

Transylvania
Medieval castles and stunning scenery await in Romania (p690)

Budapest
Hungary's capital teems with unique energy (p379)

Black Sea Beaches
Take a break on Bulgaria's golden sands (p187)

Ohrid
Macedonia's holy lake and monastery enjoy a stunning setting (p527)

Berat
Don't miss Albania's 'town of a thousand windows' (p61)

Mostar
Come to see Mostar's rebuilt Old Bridge (p124)

Dubrovnik
Croatia's finest old town is simply spectacular (p256)

Kotor
Majestic rock ramparts defend this Montenegrin charmer (p574)

25 TOP EXPERIENCES

St Petersburg, Russia

1 Marvelling at how many masterpieces there are in the Hermitage (p761); window shopping and people-watching along Nevsky Prospekt (p768); gliding down canals past the grand facades of palaces and golden-domed churches; enjoying a ballet at the beautiful Mariinsky Theatre (p775); feasting on a banquet fit for a tsar then dancing till dawn at a dive bar in a crumbling ruin – Russia's imperial capital is a visual stunner and a hedonist's delight, best visited at the height of summer when the White Nights see the city party around the clock. Above: State Hermitage Museum

Prague, Czech Republic

2 The Czech capital is a near-perfectly preserved museum of European architecture through the ages. From the Old Town Sq (p277), across the Charles Bridge (p283) and up to Prague Castle (p276), it's almost as if a 14th-century metropolis has been transported in time and plunked down in the heart of modern Europe. After you've meandered the alleyways, neck sore from craning to spy the statues and gargoyles, retire to a local pub for some Czech beer – the country's pride and joy. Right: Old Town Sq

3

4

TIM MAKINS/GETTY IMAGES ©

Moscow's Red Square, Russia

3 Red Sq sucks in every visitor to Russia's capital, leaving them slack-jawed with wonder. Standing on the rectangular cobblestoned expanse – surrounded by the candy-coloured swirls of the cupolas atop St Basil's Cathedral (p746), the red-star-tipped towers of the Kremlin (p743), Lenin's squat granite mausoleum (p747), the handsome redbrick facade of the State History Museum (p747), and GUM (p757), a grand emporium of consumption – you are literally at the centre of Russia's modern history. Above: St Basil's Cathedral

Hiking the High Tatras, Slovakia

4 The rocky, alpine peaks of the High Tatras (p848) in Slovakia are the highest in the Carpathians, with 25 peaks soaring over 2500m. But hiking this impressive little range needn't require an Olympian effort. In the morning, ride a cable car up to 1800m and you can hike along mid-elevation trails (p850), stopping at a log-cabin hikers' hut with a restaurant for lunch. A few hours more and you're at the Hrebienok funicular terminus that will take you down to turn-of-the-20th-century Starý Smokovec below, well in time for dinner. Above: Funicular to Hrebienok (p850)

Kraków, Poland

5 As popular as it is, Poland's former royal capital (p616) never disappoints. It's hard to pinpoint why it's so special, but there's an aura of history radiating from the sloping stone buttresses of medieval buildings in the Old Town that makes its streets seem just right. Throw in the extremes of a spectacular castle and the low-key, oh-so-cool bar scene situated within the tiny worn buildings of the Kazimierz backstreets, and it's a city you want to seriously get to know. Above far right: Cafe in Kazimierz (p625)

Budapest, Hungary

6 Straddling both sides of the romantic Danube River, with the Buda Hills to the west and the start of the Great Plain to the east, Budapest (p379) is perhaps the most beautiful city in Eastern Europe. Parks brim with attractions, the architecture is second to none and museums are filled with treasures. Add to that pleasure boats sailing up and down the scenic Danube Bend, Turkish-era thermal baths belching steam and a nightlife throbbing till dawn most nights, and it's easy to see why the Hungarian capital is one of the continent's most delightful, fun cities to visit.
Left: Széchenyi Baths (p385)

Bay of Kotor, Montenegro

7 There's a sense of secrecy and mystery to the Bay of Kotor (p572). Grey mountain walls rise steeply from steely blue waters, getting higher and higher as you progress through their folds to the hidden reaches of the inner bay. Here, ancient stone settlements hug the shore line, with Kotor's old alleyways concealed in its innermost reaches behind hefty stone walls. Talk about drama! But you wouldn't expect anything else of the Balkans, where life is exuberantly Mediterranean and lived full of passion on these time-worn streets. Below: St George's Island (p574)

Black Sea Beaches, Bulgaria

8 Sun, sand and sea might not be what you associate with Eastern Europe, but Bulgaria's Black Sea coast (p187) has plenty of great beaches. Resorts such as Sunny Beach and Golden Sands attract international tourists with their pristine sand, nightlife and water sports, while resort towns Varna and Burgas have long stretches of beach on their doorsteps. If you want to escape the crowds, head south to Tsarevo or Sozopol or to the far north for peaceful, sandy Kavarna and remote Kamen Bryag. Below: Sozopol (p196)

Tallinn, Estonia

9 The Estonian capital is famous for its two-tiered chocolate-box Old Town (p340) with its landscapes of intertwining alleys, picturesque courtyards and rooftop views from medieval turrets. But step outside the Old Town walls and experience Tallinn's other treasures as well: no visit is complete without sampling the stylish restaurants plating up oh-so-fashionable New Nordic cuisine, its buzzing Scandinavian-influenced design community, its ever-growing number of museums, such as Kumu (p346), the city's award-winning modern-art repository, or its progressive contemporary architecture. Above: Raekoja plats (Town Hall Sq, p340)

Walking Dubrovnik's Old City Walls, Croatia

10 In Croatia, get up close and personal with Dubrovnik by walking its spectacular city walls (p256), as history is unfurled from the battlements. No visit is complete without a leisurely stroll along these ramparts, the finest in the world and Dubrovnik's main claim to fame. Built between the 13th and 16th centuries, they are still remarkably intact and the vistas over terracotta rooftops and the Adriatic Sea are sublime, especially at dusk when the sunset turns the hues dramatic and the panoramas unforgettable.

Taking an Overnight Train

11 With the windows down and the scenery racing past, there are few modes of transport more pleasurable than the overnight sleeper train – the best way to get about in Eastern Europe. Whether you're in *platzkart* (3rd class) playing cards and discussing life under communism with the locals or enjoying the more private *kupe* (2nd class) or even luxuriously private SV (1st class), this is an essential experience and a great way to avoid the cost of a hotel for a night.

Castles & Mountains of Transylvania, Romania

12 The Romanian region (p690) that so ghoulishly inspired Irish writer Bram Stoker to create his Dracula has some seriously spooky castles around. Monumental Bran Castle (p698), south of Braşov, is suitably vampiric, but our favourite haunt has to be the 13th-century Râşnov fortress (p698) just down the road. The castles are nestled high amid the Carpathians, a relatively under-explored mountain range that's ideal for all manner of outdoor activity, including hiking, trekking, mountain biking and skiing. Below: Bran Castle

Lviv, Ukraine

13 A sophisticated island in a post-Soviet sea, Ukraine's great hope for tourism (p925) is a moody city of arabica-scented coffee houses, verdant parks, trundling trams and Austro-Hungarian manners. Melodiously accented Ukrainian provides the soundtrack while incense billows through medieval churches that miraculously avoided their dates with Soviet dynamite, and violin-toting schoolchildren compete for seats on buses with smiling nuns and West Ukrainian hippies. Tourists now flock to Lviv, but the city seems determined not to do a Prague or a Kraków. Right: Latin Cathedral (p927)

12

Berat, Albania

14 This wine-producing region's town (p61) reigns supreme in terms of Ottoman-style wonder and magic. From the river, look up at the multiwindowed white and black Unesco-listed houses, then wander up the cobblestone paths to take a closer look. Meander through the town's living and breathing castle area, complete with a museum (p62) filled with stunning iconography by Onufri. Complete your visit with a stay in Berat's Ottoman-style hostel or one of two traditional-homes-turned-hotels and participate in the evening walk along the promenade for an enlivening experience. *Above right: Sheep below Church of the Holy Trinity (p62)*

Experiencing a Banya, Russia

15 The great Slavic tradition of the *banya*, or sauna (p789), is as Russian as things come. *Banyas* come in all shapes and sizes, from small wooden huts in back gardens to lavish and luxurious venues with hundreds of years of history. Don't be shy: get naked with your friends, expose yourself to brain-melting heat, enjoy a surprisingly pleasant whipping with birch twigs (to remove those toxins, you understand) and then plunge yourself into a pool of freezing water. Rinse, wash, repeat – unforgettable.

MIBIRD/GETTY IMAGES ©

Island Hopping in the Adriatic, Croatia

16 From short jaunts between nearby islands to overnight rides along the length of the Croatian coast (p239), travelling by sea is a great and inexpensive way to experience the Croatian side of the Adriatic. Take in the scenery of this stunning coastline as you whiz past some of Croatia's 1244 islands and if you have cash to splash, take it up a couple of notches and charter a sailboat to see the islands in style, propelled by winds and sea currents.

Art Nouveau Architecture in Rīga, Latvia

17 Latvia's impressive and surprising capital, Rīga (p452) boasts a superb architectural heritage known locally as *style moderne*, but better known to the world as art nouveau. Over 750 buildings (more than any other city in Europe) boast this style – a menagerie of mythical beasts, screaming masks, twisting flora, goddesses and goblins. Much of the city's personality can be gleaned through its architecture. Many of its elaborate apartments stand next to weathered, crumbling facades.

Ohrid, Macedonia

18 Whether you come to sublime, hilly Ohrid (p527) for its sturdy medieval castle, to wander the stone laneways of its Old Town or to gaze at its restored Plaošnik, every visitor pauses for a few moments at the Church of Sveti Jovan at Kaneo (p529), set high on a bluff overlooking Lake Ohrid and its popular beaches. It's the prime spot for absorbing the town's beautiful architecture, idling sunbathers and distant fishing skiffs – all framed by the rippling green of Mt Galičica to the southeast and the endless expanse of lake stretching out elsewhere.
Above: Church of Sveti Jovan at Kaneo

Mt Triglav & Vršič Pass, Slovenia

19 For such a small country, Slovenia has got it all: charming towns, great wines, a Venetian-inspired seashore and, most of all, mountains. The highest peak, Mt Triglav (p893), stands particularly tall in local lore. Indeed, the saying goes that you're not really Slovene until you've climbed to the top. If time is an issue and you're driving, head for the high-altitude Vršič Pass, which crosses the Julian Alps and leads down to the sunny coastal region in one hair-raising, spine-tingling hour.

Mostar, Bosnia & Hercegovina

20 If the 1993 bombardment of Mostar's iconic 16th-century stone bridge, Stari Most (p124), underlined the heartbreaking pointlessness of Yugoslavia's brutal civil war, its painstaking reconstruction is symbolic of a peaceful post-conflict era. The charming Ottoman quarter has been convincingly rebuilt and is once again a delightful patchwork of stone mosques, souvenir peddlers and inviting cafes. You can still find bombed-out buildings, but many of these seem to have become an almost organic part of the townscape. Below: Stari Most

Český Krumlov, Czech Republic

21 Showcasing possibly Europe's most glorious Old Town, for many travellers Český Krumlov (p312) is a popular day trip from Prague. But a rushed few hours navigating the town's meandering lanes and audacious clifftop castle sells it short. Stay at least one night to lose yourself in the Old Town's shape-shifting after-dark shadows and get cosy in riverside restaurants, cafes and pubs. The following morning get active with rafting or canoeing on the Vltava River, then explore the nearby Newcastle Mountains by horse or mountain bike.

Visegrád, Hungary

22 A lonely, abandoned fortress (p401) high atop the Danube River marks what was once the northern border of the Roman Empire. Long after the Romans decamped, the ancient Hungarian kings, the Ottoman Turks and the Austrian Habsburgs in turn all marked this turf as their own. Climb to the top for some soul-stirring vistas over the surrounding countryside and to ponder for a moment the kingdoms and peoples who have come and gone over the course of 16 centuries. Below: View from Visegrád Citadel

WITOLD SKRYPCZAK/GETTY IMAGES ©

CHRISTIAN KLEIN/ALAMY ©

KOCA SULEJMANOVIC/GETTY IMAGES ©

Toruń, Poland

23 This beautiful Gothic city offers just the right balance between sightseeing and relaxing. Grab a *zapiekanka* (a Polish snack consisting of a toasted roll topped with mushrooms, cheese and tomato sauce) from the window of the milk bar (p661) just off the main square, then saunter past the locals to check out the curious statuary around the square's edge, including a monument to local hero Copernicus. Finish the day at one of the fancy beer-garden decks perched on the cobblestones. Above: Rynek Staromiejski (Old Town Market Sq, p659)

Cycling Curonian Spit, Lithuania

24 Allegedly created by the sea goddess Neringa, the fragile, narrow sliver of land that is Curonian Spit (p507) juts out of the Baltic Sea, its celestial origins giving it a somewhat other-worldly ambience and its giant sand dunes earning it the nickname of 'Lithuania's Sahara'. The best way to explore it is by bicycle, riding through dense pine forest from one cheerful fishing village to the next, stopping to sample freshly smoked fish, or – if you're lucky – to glimpse the spit's elusive wildlife: elk, deer and wild boar.

Guča Trumpet Festival, Serbia

25 Otherwise a typical central Serbia village, the hamlet of Guča morphs into an orgiastic den of cacophonous revelry each August for the Dragačevo Trumpet Assembly of brass musicians (p818), who play their instruments in a fre-netic fashion unlike anywhere else on earth. Hundreds of mostly gypsy orchestras descend on Guča to show off their skills; appreciative crowds dance through the streets, gorge on spit roast and plaster money on the musicians' foreheads. This is Serbia personified: uninhib-ited, joyful, wild...and very, very loud.

need to know

Buses

» While often far from luxurious, buses cover almost all areas of Eastern Europe and are particularly useful for reaching more remote areas.

Trains

» The classic way to get around the region – comfortable trains connect nearly all major cities in the region and overnight trips are a fantastic experience.

When to Go

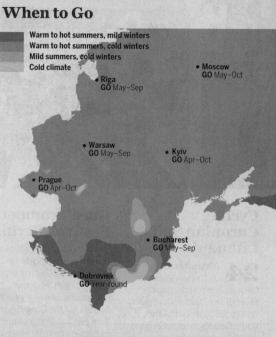

Warm to hot summers, mild winters
Warm to hot summers, cold winters
Mild summers, cold winters
Cold climate

Moscow
GO May–Oct

Rīga
GO May–Sep

Warsaw
GO May–Sep

Kyiv
GO Apr–Oct

Prague
GO Apr–Oct

Bucharest
GO May–Sep

Dubrovnik
GO Year-round

High Season (Jul & Aug)

» Expect high temperatures and long evenings.

» Hotels are up to 30% more expensive and you'll need to book in advance.

» Big draws such as Prague, Budapest and Kraków will be very crowded.

Shoulder (May & Jun, Sep & Oct)

» Crowds and prices drop off.

» The weather remains very pleasant.

» Overall the best time to travel in Eastern Europe.

Low Season (Nov–Apr)

» Hotel prices drop to their lowest.

» Weather can be decidedly cold and days short.

» Some places, such as resort towns, are like ghost towns.

Your Daily Budget

Budget less than €40

» Hostel beds for as little as €10

» Self-catering is easy throughout the region

» Take overnight train journeys to save on hotel costs

Midrange €40–150

» Midrange hotels are everywhere, averaging €40 a night

» Meals in decent restaurants are about €10 per person

» Travel comfortably by train in *kupe* (2nd class) or even 'soft' sleepers

Top end more than €150

» Top-end hotel rooms start at €100 per night

» In big cities top restaurant prices start at about €25 per person

» Hire cars start at about €30 per day

Driving

» Cars drive on the right. Roads are generally good, but be aware that many hire companies limit which countries their hire cars can be taken to.

Ferries

» Ferries connect the Balkans to Italy; Albania to Corfu; and Estonia and Russia to Finland. They aren't a common way to get around, however.

Bicycles

» Commonly hired in big cities where cycling is generally quite safe. Long-distance cycling is still something of a novelty.

Planes

» International air routes connect most capitals to neighbouring countries and Western European hubs. Internal flights are less common.

Websites

» **Deutsche Bahn** (www.bahn.de) The best online train timetable for the region.

» **Like a Local** (www.likealocalguide.com) Free online guides to the Baltic capitals, Tartu, Pärnu, Prague, Minsk and Brasov, written by locals.

» **Go East Europe** (www.goeasteurope.about.com) Great information and news stories.

» **Lonely Planet** (www.lonelyplanet.com/thorntree) Ask other travellers on this message board.

Money

» Countries using the euro: Estonia, Kosovo, Montenegro, Slovakia and Slovenia.

» Best currencies to take to countries not using the euro in order of preference: euro, US dollars, British pounds.

Visas

» EU, US, Canadian, Australian and New Zealand passport holders do not require a visa to visit the vast majority of Eastern Europe, though non-EU passport holders will need a visa if they plan to stay more than three months consecutively in the Schengen Area. South Africans often need visas in Eastern Europe.

» The following countries require some nationalities to have visas: Russia (everyone), Belarus (everyone), Moldova (Australians and New Zealanders), Ukraine (Australians and New Zealanders).

Arriving in Eastern Europe

Many travellers will also arrive by train, bus or car from other European transport hubs, such as Frankfurt, Berlin or İstanbul.

» **Moscow Domodedovo & Sheremetyevo Airports** Trains – R300, 7am to midnight, every 30 minutes. The journey takes 40 minutes. Taxi – R1000 to R1500, best booked in advance.

» **Václav Havel Airport Prague** Bus – Airport Express buses cost 50Kč to Prague's train station. Taxi – About 650Kč.

What to Take

» **Flip-flops (thongs)** Very useful on overnight train rides, in hostel bathrooms and for the beach.

» **Hiking boots** If you plan to take advantage of Eastern Europe's fantastic and easy walking.

» **Ear plugs** Helpful anywhere, but especially if you plan to sleep in hostels or on trains.

» **Car satnav system** Very useful if you plan on renting a car (be sure to download the right maps)

» **European plug adaptors** Brits, North Americans and Antipodeans will need these.

» **An unlocked mobile phone** Picking up a local SIM card to make cheap calls is a great way to save.

» **Mosquito repellent** Necessary near lakes and forests.

if you like...

Old Towns

With more cobbled squares, ancient churches and labyrinthine back streets than perhaps the rest of the world combined, there is simply nowhere better in the world to explore old towns than Eastern Europe.

Prague, Czech Republic It's hard not to fall instantly in love with the spires, churches and lanes of the incredibly preserved Staré Město (p277)

Kraków, Poland Arguably Eastern Europe's finest old town is to be found at the heart of Poland's royal capital and miraculous survivor (p617)

Dubrovnik, Croatia The marble-paved streets of the Stradun and the fantastical city walls are part of the finest old town in the Balkans (p256)

Vilnius, Lithuania Europe's largest baroque old town feels more 'real' than its Baltic neighbours and is a largely unsung draw to tiny Lithuania (p481)

Lviv, Ukraine Western Ukraine's repository of culture and its charmingly multicultural old town is a must-see on any Eastern European trip (p925)

Tallinn, Estonia The Estonian capital's old town is as chocolate box as they come, but it's nevertheless an utterly charming place to explore (p340)

Beaches

Don't associate Eastern Europe with beaches? You're certainly not alone, but you're definitely wrong – between the Adriatic, Baltic and Black Seas, not to mention pristine lakes and rivers across the region, definitely plan on being able to take it easy on a beautiful stretch of sand during your trip.

Beaches, Croatia Perhaps the most impressive beaches in Eastern Europe and certainly the best known, Croatia's coast and its thousand-odd islands are where the jet set now holiday (p239)

Curonian Spit, Lithuania & Russia Technically one long beach, this Unesco World Heritage Site of sand dunes and bracing waters is the best place to swim in the Baltic (p507, p787)

Drymades Beach, Albania The stuff of legend among backpackers, this white-sand beach on Albania's fast-disappearing undeveloped coastline remains the one to head for (p65)

Black Sea Coast, Bulgaria Bulgaria boasts the best beaches on the Black Sea, but we recommend avoiding the big resort towns and heading instead to Sozopol or Tsarevo (p196)

Castles

Transylvanian fortresses, Bohemian chateaux, Russian kremlins: Eastern Europe offers a huge range of royal dwellings and seats of political power that have survived the centuries amazingly intact.

Bran Castle, Romania Better known as Dracula's Castle despite having fairly tenuous associations with the man himself, this Transylvanian beauty is straight out of a horror movie (p698)

Spiš Castle, Slovakia This impressive site may now be a ruin, but its sheer size and situation make it one of the most popular sights in Slovakia (p857)

The Kremlin, Moscow, Russia The seat of power to medieval tsars and modern tyrants alike, Moscow's vast Kremlin is unlike anywhere else in the world – breathe in the power as you wander its incredible sights (p743)

Karlštejn Castle, Czech Republic A true piece of fairy-tale Gothic, this Bohemian beauty near Prague makes for a great day trip (p301)

PAUL POPLIS/GETTY IMAGES ©

» Hungarian goulash

Mountains & Hiking

Walkers and mountain lovers will be spoilt rotten in Eastern Europe; it's crisscrossed by mountain ranges, gentle rolling hills and thick forest, and hiking of all levels is never far away. Routes are generally well maintained and infrastructure in and around national parks has improved immensely in the past two decades.

Slovenský Raj National Park, Slovakia Waterfalls, gorges and thick forests decorate Slovakia's outstanding national park (p860)

Mountains, Bulgaria With no fewer than seven mountain ranges within its borders, Bulgaria is a hiker's dream; don't miss the trails around stunning Rila Monastery or the beautiful Rodopi Mountains (p164, p168)

Tatra Mountains, Poland There's great hiking to be had in Southern Poland's Tatra Mountains, including around wonderful emerald-green Lake Morskie Oko. Use Zakopane as as base for your walks (p637)

Zlatibor, Serbia The rolling hills and spectacular views in this corner of Southern Serbia are ideal for gentle hikes (p820)

Relics of Communism

While it may be dead and buried in almost all of the region, there's no denying that communism has more than left its mark on the countries of Eastern Europe. Anyone interested in the history of the 20th century's 'great experiment' will find plenty of monuments and statues to look at, and even the odd communist enclave apparently frozen in time.

Lenin's Mausoleum, Moscow, Russia Come and see communism's mecca, where a waxy Lenin lies in state on impressive Red Sq (p747)

Stalinist Minsk, Belarus Flattened during WWII, the capital city of Belarus was rebuilt in a monolithic Stalinist style during the 1950s and has barely changed since (p82)

Transdniestr, Moldova As relics go, a self-proclaimed country is pretty unbeatable, but that's what you get in this still-communist slice of Moldova (p557)

Grūto Parkas, Druskininka, Lithuania A privately run outdoor museum, this unique and controversial place displays hundreds of abandoned communist-era statues, in grounds that are designed to look like one of the Gulag concentration camps (p499)

Great Food & Drink

One of the hardest regional stereotypes to break is that going east of Berlin means nothing but cabbage-based delicacies and warm shots of vodka at dinnertime. Nothing could be further from the truth – dive in and enjoy Eastern Europe's surprisingly varied and delicious cuisine.

Hungarian Cuisine, Hungary Even its brand of communism was famously named after the national dish, goulash, and Hungary still has the best cuisine and wines in the region (p430)

Istrian delights, Croatia Istria is packed full of top eateries where slow food is a buzz word and truffles, wild asparagus and fresh seafood are on the menu. There's also a superb local wine scene (p226)

Nordic cuisine, Estonia Excellent dining scenes await in Tallinn, Tartu and Pärnu: don't miss cutting-edge Nordic cuisine at Ö in Tallinn, among others (p351)

Wine tasting, Moldova Hungary and the Balkans may be known for good wines, but for something totally different check out the great and largely undiscovered viniculture of plucky little Moldova (p556)

» Plitvice Lakes National Park (p226), Croatia

Extreme Sports

With its wide-open spaces, innovative tourism industries and relative affordability, Eastern Europe has fast become an extreme-sports playground.

Bovec and Bled, Slovenia The unrivalled capital of extreme sports in Eastern Europe is tiny Slovenia, where you can do everything from canyoning to hydrospeeding at Bovec and Bled (p895, p888)

Rafting and kayaking, Bosnia & Hercegovina Fast-flowing rivers provide world-class rafting and kayaking, especially in the Vrbas Canyons between Jajce and Banja Luka (p141)

Sigulda, Latvia The Baltic capital of extreme sports; come here to bobsleigh, bungee jump from a moving cable car and even try out 'aerodium' air blasting (p473)

Bridge diving, Mostar, Bosnia & Hercegovina You too can dive from Mostar's terrifyingly high bridge to the river below, after training from the locals (p124)

Spectacular Scenery

So dazzling is Eastern Europe's cultural heritage that many people don't realise how beautiful the region is, taking in everything from sand dunes to dramatic sea cliffs and magnificent national parks where you'll often not even see another visitor.

Plitvice Lakes National Park, Croatia With its shimmering turquoise waters, waterfalls and thick woods, this beautiful spot is one of the region's finest (p226)

Lake Koman Ferry, Albania See a part of the world few foreigners ever make it to on this beautiful ferry ride in Albania's remote and mountainous north (p59)

Cape Kolka, Latvia This desolate moonscape where the Gulf of Rīga meets the Baltic Sea is truly dramatic and hauntingly remote (p470)

Slovak Karst National Park, Slovakia See Central Europe's biggest cave system in this Unesco-listed national park in South East Slovakia (p865)

Danube Delta, Romania This sprawling, wild wetland where the Danube meets the Black Sea is all reeds and birds as far as the eye can see (p721)

Art Collections

Art lovers will be bowled over by the art of all forms on offer in this region, which is itself a kind of warehouse of art history – from the unparalleled wealth of the tsar's collection in St Petersburg to the more modest museums in the former Yugoslavia that miraculously survived the wars of the 1990s.

Hermitage, St Petersburg, Russia Housed in the Winter Palace, this is quite simply one of the world's greatest art collections, stuffed full of treasures from Egyptian mummies to a superb cache of Picassos (p761)

National Gallery, Prague, Czech Republic Inside the Šternberg Palace, this collection of 14th- to 18th-century art is one of the finest in Eastern Europe (p277)

PinchukArtCentre, Kyiv, Ukraine For a taste of something truly different visit this extraordinary centre for contemporary art, the pet project of one of Ukraine's wealthiest businessmen (p920)

State Tretyakov Gallery, Moscow, Russia This fabulous repository of Russian culture is Moscow's best collection of art, spanning an entire millennium, from religious icons to contemporary sculpture (p748)

If you like...newly independent countries
Make sure you include Kosovo on your trip – this controversial place is Europe's youngest state (p437)

Jewish Heritage

Despite the obliteration of centuries-old Jewish communities throughout Eastern Europe during the Holocaust, the imprint of Jewish culture and heritage remains strongly felt across the region, and many communities are now thriving again.

Prague's Jewish Sights, Czech Republic See Europe's oldest still-functioning synagogue, the 16th-century Jewish Town Hall and then wander the nearby Old Jewish Cemetry (p280)

Sugihara House, Kaunas, Lithuania The touching house museum of the erstwhile Japanese consul who saved some 6000 Jewish lives by issuing them Japanese visas (p499)

New Synagogue, Szeged, Hungary A refreshingly reborn synagogue being used as a place of worship rather than simply another museum, this spectacular building is testament to Szeged's multicultural heritage (p419)

Oświęcim, Poland Better known to the world as Auschwitz, this chilling site is still an absolute essential for any visitor to Eastern Europe (p627)

Contemporary Architecture

Eastern Europe's architectural heritage is world famous. Gothic Prague, neoclassical St Petersburg and art nouveau Rīga are all must-see destinations, but there's modern architecture too – from the sublime to the ridiculous, the following are some of our favourites.

Museum of Contemporary Art, Zagreb, Croatia Definitely one of the sleekest art museums in the world. This stunner, designed by local architect Igor Franić, is a stellar example of clever use of light and space (p218)

Kumu, Tallinn, Estonia A world-class concrete-and-glass building that holds an excellent art collection; it won the European Museum of the Year Award in 2008 (p346)

Košice, Slovakia As European Capital of Culture 2013, Košice has renovated existing buildings – including an art nouveau swimming pool and an old military base – into an arts and culture hub (p861)

National Library of Belarus, Minsk An example of what can only be called post-Soviet hubris, this spaceshiplike, glass-fronted rhombicuboctahedron has to be seen to be believed (p83)

Nightlife

It's not all stag parties and hen nights in Eastern Europe. Whether it's dancing to cutting-edge international DJs on the dance floors of Moscow or a rather more relaxed party on an Adriatic beach in mid-summer, this is a part of the world that knows how to party.

Budapest's Romkertek, Hungary So called 'ruin gardens' – essentially pop-up clubs in abandoned buildings – have put Budapest's nightlife on a par with that of Berlin or London (p393)

Moscow, Russia Once famed for its 'face control' (aggressively selective door policies) Moscow is now becoming an essential stop on the clubber's world map, with a slew of new democratically run bars and clubs (p755)

Belgrade, Serbia The Serbian capital is one of the most exciting and vibrant places to party the night away – and won't leave you too out of pocket either (p810)

Cluj-Napoca, Romania Cluj's historic backstreets house perhaps the friendliest bunch of student party animals anywhere in the world (p703)

Odesa, Ukraine Join the hordes and come to the Black Sea in the summer to party in this post-Soviet Petri dish of hedonism and debauchery (p938)

month by month

Top Events

1 **Budapest Spring Festival**, March

2 **St Petersburg White Nights**, June

3 **EXIT Festival**, July

4 **Dragačevo Trumpet Assembly**, August

5 **Terraneo Festival**, August

January

While it's cold across Eastern Europe, January is a great time to experience the region's winter-wonderland appearance, with everything under blankets of snow. You'll find most towns relatively tourist-free and hotel prices are rock-bottom.

Great-Value Skiing

Head to Eastern Europe's ski slopes for wallet-friendly prices. After the first week of January most hotels offer their lowest annual rates, making skiing affordable to all. Try the Bosnian slopes at Bjelašnica and Jahorina or Bulgaria's Mt Vitosha range or Bansko.

Küstendorf Film & Music Festival, Serbia

Created and curated by Serbian director Emir Kusturica, this international indie-fest (www.kustendorf-filmandmusicfestival.org) in the town of Drvengrad, near Zlatibor in Serbia, eschews traditional red-carpet glitz for oddball inclusions vying for the 'Golden Egg' prize.

February

Still cold, but with longer days and the promise of spring around the corner, February is when colourful carnivals are held across the region. Low hotel prices and the off-season feel also remain.

Carnivals, Croatia

For colourful costumes and nonstop revelry head to Rijeka, where Carnival is the pinnacle of the year's calendar. Zadar hosts colourful Carnival celebrations too, with street dancing, concerts and masked balls. This exciting rite of spring is also celebrated in Ptuj, Slovenia.

March

Spring arrives in the Balkans, while further north the remaining countries of Eastern Europe continue to freeze, though days are often bright and the sun shines.

Vitranc Cup, Slovenia

Anyone who enjoys watching thrilling acrobatics on the ski slopes should not miss the excitement of this men's slalom and giant slalom competition (www.pokal-vitranc.com) in Kranjska Gora.

Paganism, Poland

Head to Poland in March for the quirky rite of the Drowning of Marzanna, a surviving pagan ritual in which an effigy of the goddess of winter is immersed in water at the advent of spring. The festival, also celebrated as Maslenitsa in Russia, with variants in most other Slavic countries, features lots of delicious bliny to boot.

Waltzes, Hungary

One of Europe's top classical music events is the two-week Budapest Spring Festival (www.springfestival.hu) that takes place in late March each year. Concerts are held in a large number of beautiful venues including several stunning churches, the Hungarian State Opera House and the National Theatre.

Ski-Jumping World Cup, Slovenia

Held the third weekend in March, this exciting international competition (www.planica.si) in Planica was the site of a world-record jump of 239m in 2005 and is a must for all adrenalin junkies.

April

Spring has well and truly arrived by April – the Balkans are already enjoying warm, sunny days and, after months of snow, even Russia has finally seen a thaw. Hotel prices outside the Easter holiday period remain low.

★ Easter Festival of Sacred Music, Czech Republic

Six thematic concerts (www.mhf-brno.cz) with full orchestras take place in three of the oldest churches in Brno, Czech Republic, including the beautiful Cathedral of SS Peter & Paul, in the two weeks following Palm Sunday.

★ Music Biennale Zagreb, Croatia

Held since 1961, the Music Biennale Zagreb (www.mbz.hr/eng) is Croatia's most important contemporary music event. It takes place in various venues around the capital over 10 days during mid-April in odd years.

May

An excellent time to visit Eastern Europe. May is sunny and warm and full of things to do, while never too hot or too crowded, though you can still expect the big destinations to feel busy.

★ International Labour Day, Russia

Once bigger than Christmas in the communist world, International Labour Day may have dropped in status since the fall of the wall, but it's still a national holiday in Russia and several other former Soviet republics. You'll find fireworks, concerts and even the occasional military parade on Moscow's Red Sq.

★ Reliving History, Bulgaria

Military history fans should not miss the spectacular annual reenactment of the 1876 April Uprising against the Turks in the charming Bulgarian mountain village of Koprivshtitsa, which is bizarrely held on 1 or 2 May (presumably in the hopes of better weather).

🍷 Czech Beer Festival, Czech Republic

An event most travellers won't want to miss is the Czech Beer Festival (www.ceskypivnifestival.cz), where lots of food, music and – most importantly – some 70 beers from around the country are on offer in Prague from mid- to late May.

🏃 Rafting, Bosnia & Hercegovina

After the spring rains May is the time for experienced rafters to head to the fast-flowing river gorges of BiH, such as Foča, Bihać or Banja Luka. If you're a beginner, stay well away until summer, when conditions are more suitable.

★ Performances in Prague, Czech Republic

Three very different but equally excellent festivals make May a great time to visit the Czech capital, Prague. The three-week Prague Spring International Music Festival (www.festival.cz) sees international stars descend for major classical music events, while the Khamoro World Roma Festival (www.khamoro.cz/en) showcases the musical traditions of Europe's Roma people. Finally, the Prague Fringe Festival (www.prague-fringe.com) presents theatre, comedy and music with an irreverent tone, much of it in English.

June

The shoulder season is well under way – it's already summer in southeastern Europe and the sun is barely setting in the Baltic as the solstice approaches. This is definitely one of the best times to travel, if not the cheapest.

★ White Nights in the North, Russia

By mid-June the Baltic sun only just sinks behind the horizon at night, leaving the sky a grey-white colour and encouraging locals to forget their routines and party hard. The best place to join the fun is in the former Russian capital, St Petersburg, where balls, classical music concerts and other summer events keep spirits high.

Hartera Festival, Croatia

To hear some of the best young rock bands and top indie acts from around Europe, head to this three-day underground festival (www.hartera.com) in an abandoned paper factory in Rijeka – it's become the highlight of the year for some music fans. It's sometimes held in July.

St John's Eve & St John's Day, Baltic Countries

The Baltic region's biggest annual night out is a celebration of midsummer on 23 and 24 June. It's best experienced out in the country, where huge bonfires flare for all-night revellers.

July

The middle of summer sees Eastern Europe packed with both people and things to do. Temperatures and prices soar by the end of July, but hotel room rates remain reasonable early in the month.

EXIT Festival, Serbia

Eastern Europe's most talked-about music festival (www.exitfest.org) takes place each July within the walls of the Petrovaradin Fortress in Serbia's second city, Novi Sad. Book early for tickets as big international headlining acts attract music lovers from all over the continent.

Jewish Culture Festival, Poland

Kraków rediscovers its Jewish heritage during a packed week of music, art exhibitions and lectures (www.jewishfestival.pl) in late June/early July. Poland's festival is the biggest and most exciting Jewish festival in the region.

Baltica International Folklore Festival, Baltic Countries

This festival (www.festival-baltica.com) consists of five days of traditional Baltic folk music and dance. It rotates between the three capitals of the Baltic states; it will be in Tallinn (Estonia) in 2013, Vilnius (Lithuania) in 2014 and Rīga (Latvia) in 2015.

Slavyansky Bazaar, Belarus

Held in the old Russian city of Vitsebsk (in modern Belarus), this festival (www.festival.vitebsk.by/en) is one of the biggest cultural events in the former Soviet Union, featuring theatrical performances, music concerts and exhibits from all over the Slavic world.

Karlovy Vary International Film Festival, Czech Republic

The region's own version of Cannes is a far smaller affair than its French cousin, but its reputation grows each year. The festival (www.kviff.com) is held in one of the most beautiful spa towns in the Czech Republic, Karlovy Vary, and hundreds of new releases make up the program each year.

Bažant Pohoda, Slovakia

Slovakia's largest music festival (www.pohoda-festival.sk) represents all genres of music from rock to orchestral over eight different stages. It is firmly established now as one of Europe's biggest and best summer music festivals.

Ivana Kupala, Ukraine

On 7 July, Ukraine's exhilarating pagan celebration of midsummer involves fire jumping, maypole dancing, fortune telling, wreath floating and strong overtones of sex. Head for the countryside for the real deal.

Medieval Festival of the Arts, Romania

During July the beautiful Romanian city of Sighişoara hosts open-air concerts, parades and ceremonies, all glorifying medieval Transylvania and taking the town back to its fascinating 12th-century origins.

Ohrid Summer Festival, Macedonia

The month-long Ohrid Summer Festival (www.ohrid-summer.com.mk) comprises a wealth of performances ranging from classical, opera and rock acts to theatre and literature, all celebrating Macedonian culture. The best events are held in the town's magical open-air Roman Classical Amphitheatre.

Sarajevo Film Festival, Bosnia & Hercegovina

This globally acclaimed festival (www.sff.ba) that grew out of the ruins of the '90s civil war screens commercial and art-house movies side by side in the Bosnian capital. Usually in July or August.

Východná, Slovakia

Slovakia's top folk festival (www.festivalvychodna. sk) is held over the first weekend of July each year in the tiny Tatra Mountain village of Východná. Over a thousand performers descend here to celebrate traditional music, dance, arts and crafts.

August

It's easy enough to get away from the crowds and expense, even at summer's height. There's a huge amount to see and do in August, and the weather – from the Baltic coast to the Adriatic – is hot, hot, hot!

Trumpeting Insanity, Serbia

Guča's Dragačevo Trumpet Assembly (www.guca.rs) is one of the most exciting and bizarre events in all of Eastern Europe. Hundreds of thousands of revellers descend on the small Serbian town of Guča to damage their eardrums, livers and sanity over four cacophonous days of revelry.

International Music Festival, Czech Republic

Thousands of music lovers congregate in Český Krumlov for classical concerts, as well as jazz, rock and folk music, at this impressive month-long August festival (www.festivalkrumlov.cz),

which sometimes begins in July as well.

Terraneo Festival, Croatia

Croatia's newest festival (www.terraneofestival. com) has quickly become a summer highlight. This big five-day dance party, located in an old army barracks in Šibenik, draws in Croatian hipsters for its amazing line-up of international and local performers.

Sziget Music Festival, Hungary

A weeklong, great-value music festival (www.sziget. hu) held all over Budapest. Sziget features bands from around the world playing at more than 60 venues.

Don Cento Jazz Festival, Russia

A relatively new jazz event in Kaliningrad, Russia, that is already attracting jazz performers from across Europe, the Kaliningrad City Jazz Festival (www.jazzfestival.ru) is held over three days across the city, with nightclub jams, big concerts and even free open-air sessions.

September

The summer crowds have dropped off somewhat and prices are no longer sky high, but great weather remains across the entire region, making September a fantastic time to head for Eastern Europe.

Dance with Cows, Slovenia

This Slovenian mid-September weekend of folk

dancing, music, eating and drinking in Bohinj marks the return of the cows from their high pastures to the valleys in typically ebullient Balkan style.

Dvořák Autumn, Czech Republic

This festival (www.kso. kso.cz) of classical music honours the work of the Czech Republic's favourite composer, Antonín Dvořák. The event is held over three weeks in the spa town of Karlovy Vary.

Adventure Race, Montenegro

A one-day hiking, cycling and kayaking charity fundraising challenge (www. adventureracemontenegro. com) that is held within the beautiful confines of the Bay of Kotor in late September.

Lviv Coffee Festival, Ukraine

It's no surprise that Eastern Europe's first coffee festival (www.coffeefest.lviv. ua) takes place in charming Lviv, where the Central European coffee culture is really thriving. Come and taste coffees from all over the world as the city goes even more caffeine mad than usual.

October

October is still wonderfully warm in the Balkans but already getting cold in the north. Prices remain low and crowds lessen with each passing day, making it a good time to visit.

Wine Festival, Moldova

Winemakers, wine tasting, wine buying and wine-enriched folkloric performances (www.moldovawine-day.md) in and around Chişinău draw oenophiles and anyone that wants to take advantage of the 10-day visa-free arrangement (p567) Moldova introduces during the festival dates.

November

The days are short and the weather is cold, but you'll have most of Eastern Europe's attractions all to yourself and accommodation is cheap. If you want any chance of sunshine, you'll need to head south to the Balkans.

Sarajevo International Jazz Festival, Bosnia & Hercegovina

Held in Sarajevo in early November, this festival (www.jazzfest.ba) showcases local and international jazz musicians.

Martinje in Zagreb, Croatia

The Feast of St Martin is an annual wine festival held in Zagreb to celebrate the end of the grape harvest as Croatian wineries begin the crushing process. Expect lots of wine, good food and a generally upbeat mood.

December

December is a magical time to visit Eastern Europe: Christmas decorations brighten up the dark streets and, despite the cold across much of the region, as long as you avoid Christmas and New Year's Eve, prices remain surprisingly low.

Tirana International Film Festival, Albania

Each December Tirana holds its annual short- and feature-film festival (www.tiranafilmfest.com), the only one of its kind in tiny Albania. It's a great way to take stock of Eastern European film-making.

Christmas Markets

Throughout December Eastern Europe heaves with German-style Christmas markets. You'll find these in many cities in the region, though we recommend Bratislava's for its Slovakian charm and beautiful setting.

Christmas

Christmas is celebrated in different ways in Eastern Europe: most countries celebrate on Christmas Eve (24 December) with an evening meal and midnight mass. In Russia, Ukraine and Belarus, Christmas falls in January, as per the Gregorian calendar.

New Year's Eve

Even back when communist officials frowned on Christmas, New Year's Eve remained a big holiday in Eastern Europe. Join the party wherever you are and see in the new year with locals.

itineraries

Whether you've got six days or 60, these itineraries provide a starting point for the trip of a lifetime. Want more inspiration? Head online to lonelyplanet. com/thorntree to chat with other travellers.

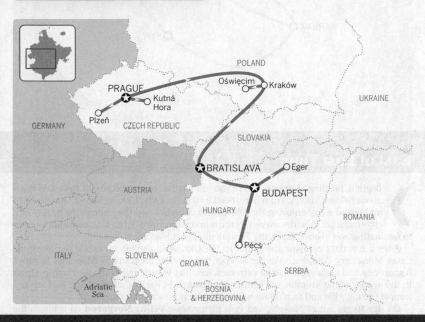

Two Weeks
Essential Eastern Europe

> Begin your trip in **Prague**, spending several days absorbing the Old Town, Malá Strana and the magnificent Prague Castle. Don't miss nearby towns such as beer lovers' mecca **Plzeň** and beautiful **Kutná Hora**.

On day five head by train into Poland and regal **Kraków**, with its gobsmacking Old Town and the vast Rynek Główny (Main Market Sq). Spending three nights here allows you to get to know the Wawel Castle complex, off-beat Kazimierz and a day trip to harrowing **Oświęcim** (Auschwitz).

On day eight head south to Slovakia, where you'll pass through magnificent scenery in the High Tatras before arriving in **Bratislava**, with its grand castle and wonderful Danube views.

On day 10 take a boat down the Danube to **Budapest**, where you can spend hours in luxurious sulphur baths, explore the famous coffee houses and take in the dazzling art and architecture of the forward-looking Hungarian capital. From here visit the Hungarian countryside – try the baroque city of **Eger**, or **Pécs**, full of relics from the Turkish occupation.

Three Weeks
East of East Tour

Begin in bustling **Warsaw**, where you can see the reconstructed Old Town and learn about its dark history. From here, head by train to **Lviv**, Ukraine's most beautiful city, and spend a day enjoying the Old Town's churches and the undeniable beauty of a city that is yet to be discovered by the tour-group crowd. From Lviv, continue by train to fascinating and historic **Kyiv**, the Jerusalem of East Slavonic culture.

After a few days enjoying the sights in the Ukrainian capital, including the awesome Caves Monastery Complex, take the sleeper train to the megalopolis **Moscow**, Europe's biggest city and a place of striking extremes, dazzling wealth and gridlocked traffic. Drink in the history of the Kremlin, see Lenin's Mausoleum, St Basil's Cathedral and Red Sq, and sample the nightlife and fashion for which the city is now rightly famous.

On day 10 get out of Moscow and visit picturesque **Veliky Novgorod** en route to the beautiful baroque and neoclassical architecture of mind-blowing **St Petersburg**. You can easily spend three or four days in the city itself, although there are abundant sights outside it as well, such as the tsarist palaces of Petrodvorets or Tsarskoe Selo.

From Russia take the train to Estonia's magical capital, **Tallinn**, where you can soak up the medieval Old Town and the rural delights of **Saaremaa** before heading south to Latvia. The Latvian capital **Rīga** boasts Europe's finest collection of art nouveau architecture and is a delightful place to spend a few days. Latvia has plenty of other highlights to offer though, such as the caves and medieval castles of **Sigulda** and the breathtaking Baltic coastline around **Ventspils**. Finally, cross into Lithuania, where a couple of nights in charming **Vilnius** will reveal the Baltic's least known and most underrated capital. From Vilnius make a trip to the huge sand dunes and fragile ecological environment of the amazing **Curonian Spit**. Those who have made the effort to get a visa can then take the train to the isolated republic of Belarus and its Stalinist-style capital **Minsk** before re-entering Poland and heading back to Warsaw.

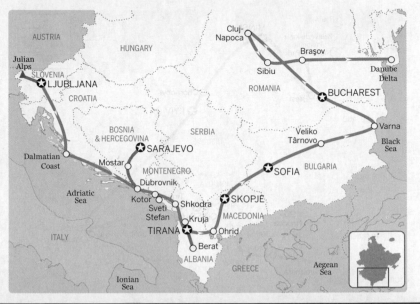

Four Weeks
The Balkans & Beyond

Begin in lively little Slovenia, with a cheap flight to charming **Ljubljana**. Indulge in superb scenery and adrenaline-rush mountain sports in the **Julian Alps** before heading south to the Croatian coast and working your way through the beaches along the **Dalmatian coast**. Stop in **Dubrovnik** to explore the Old Town, its vast ramparts and the surrounding islands, which shouldn't be missed. Take a side trip to Bosnia – perhaps a day trip to **Mostar** to see the legendary bridge and the interesting multiethnic community that has enjoyed rejuvenation since the Balkan War, or a night or two in the bustling capital of **Sarajevo**.

Continue south into Montenegro, one of Europe's youngest countries. Visit the historic walled city of **Kotor**, see the wonderful coastline and surrounding hills, and enjoy some of the country's beautiful beaches around **Sveti Stefan** before heading into Albania.

From the northern city of **Shkodra** take a bus straight on to **Tirana**, a mountain-shrouded ramshackle capital on the rise. Make an excursion to historic **Kruja** and the gorgeous Unesco-listed heritage town of **Berat** before taking a bus through the mountains into little-explored Macedonia, ending up in beautiful **Ohrid**. Spend at least two days here, enjoying the wonderful monastery and swimming in the eponymous lake. Make your way to **Skopje**, Macedonia's fun capital, from where you can head overland into Bulgaria.

Your obvious first stop is **Sofia**, one of Europe's best value capitals and a little-known gem. But there's more good stuff to come once you continue east to **Veliko Târnovo**, the awesome ancient capital and a university town with a dramatic setting over a fast-flowing river. From here it's an easy bus to the beach at **Varna**, complete with marvellous museums, Roman ruins and open-air nightclubs.

Finally plunge into Romania. Start off in **Bucharest** for excellent food and nightlife and a taste of megalomaniac architecture before heading to mythic Transylvania. Use **Cluj-Napoca** as your base for visiting the region of Maramureş, then head for the medieval superlatives of **Sibiu** and **Braşov** before reaching the **Danube Delta**, where you can ogle birds, dine on fish and enjoy some of the quietest beaches in Europe.

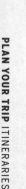

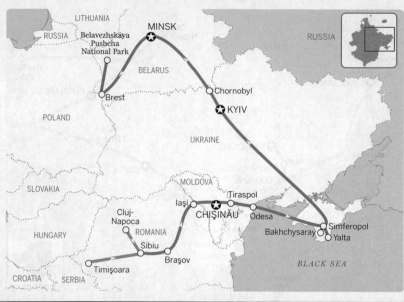

Four Weeks
On The Edge

Begin with a cheap flight from Western Europe to **Timişoara** or **Cluj-Napoca** in Romania before getting medieval in **Sibiu** and/or **Braşov** and making a run to lively **Iaşi**, near the Moldovan border.

Here the real adventure starts – cross into Moldova and head for the entertaining capital, **Chişinău**, where partying is a way of life and the excellent local wine is plentiful and cheap, including that from the must-visit vineyards of Cricova. Travel into Transdniestr, a country that doesn't officially exist and where the clock has resolutely stopped somewhere in the mid-1980s. In the fascinating 'capital' **Tiraspol** you'll feel as if time has stood still since the Soviet era, though change is slowly happening even here.

Entering Ukraine, make a beeline for the ethnic melting pot at **Odesa** and enjoy the relaxed pace of the Black Sea and its raucous nightlife during the summer months. If you want to check out the rest of the Crimea, head to **Simferopol**, the area's capital and transport hub. From here you can make a loop around the peninsula to admire the mountainous landscapes, the tsarist-era palaces near **Yalta**, and the fantastic Khan's Palace and monastery at **Bakhchysaray**.

When you have had your fill of sun and sea, head north to **Kyiv**, which demands several days' attention. This modern capital city is at once the ancient seat of Slavic and Orthodox culture and a modern, industrial Soviet city. Don't miss the Caves Monastery Complex and St Sophia's Cathedral. If you dare, book a tour to **Chornobyl** and become one of the few people in the world to visit the towns nearby to the ill-fated reactor No 4.

The final stop on this tour through the most remote parts of the region is Belarus, Europe's so-called 'last dictatorship'. Have a blast in monolithic **Minsk** and find a surprising amount going on in a city dominated by huge Stalinist avenues and Soviet memorials. Heading southwest, stop at **Brest** on the border and use it as a base to visit **Belavezhskaya Pushcha National Park**, where you'll be able to see Europe's largest mammal, the *zoobr* (European bison) as well as a host of other wild beauties before crossing back into the EU.

Four Weeks
The Ionian to the Baltic

> This trip takes you from Eastern Europe's south to its northern tip. Arrive in mountainous Albania by ferry from Corfu at the busy port of **Saranda**, then stay the night and try to see the glorious ruins of Butrint right on the Greek border. Afterwards, travel up through Albania to **Tirana** via either **Gjirokastra** or **Berat** – two of Albania's loveliest old towns. Spend a day or two exploring the Albanian capital before taking the bus to **Shkodra** and journeying on to Montenegro.

Don't miss lovely **Kotor** and its spectacular setting and old town, before picking up an overnight sleeper train to Belgrade from **Bar**, 60km southeast of Kotor. The scenery en route is spectacular, especially around the **Morača Canyon**.

Arriving the next morning in **Belgrade** you'll be struck by how vibrant and rejuvenated the Serbian capital is – it's definitely worth giving it a couple of days. Continue north to **Novi Sad** – if you come in July you might catch the EXIT Festival, held annually in the city's historic hilltop fortress.

Cross into Hungary at pretty **Szeged** and head for **Lake Balaton** for some sublime swimming. Keep surging north into Slovakia, aiming for plucky traveller favourite **Bratislava**, where it's perfectly acceptable to kick back and enjoy the good food and nightlife for a few days before going on to the incredible scenery of **Slovenský Raj National Park**.

Crossing the Tatra Mountains into Poland, travel via **Kraków** to unsung gem **Wrocław**, spending a few days in both before dropping in on beautifully restored **Poznań**. From here, the Baltic is yours. Try any of the towns along the coast: **Hel** and **Łeba** are both recommended for beaches, wildlife and water sports; **Malbork** is famed for Europe's biggest Gothic castle; while bustling Hanseatic **Gdańsk** (formerly the German Free City of Danzig) is the thriving port city where WWII broke out and the Solidarity social movement was born. Next up is the plucky Russian Baltic enclave of **Kaliningrad** – remember to have sorted your visa ahead of your arrival – spend some time in the decidedly German city and venture out to see the **Curonian Spit** as well. Fly on to **St Petersburg**, the most northern city in this book, for several days spent in Eastern Europe's most beautiful architectural ensemble.

Two Weeks
Baltic Blast

> This trip along the Baltic coast takes you through four very different countries and across a region that few travellers ever get to know beyond the universally loved capital cities of Tallinn, Rīga and Vilnius. Beginning in the gloriously beautiful Baltic city of **St Petersburg** for three nights, see the Hermitage, the Admiralty and vast Nevsky Prospekt's mansions and palatial residences. For a real palace, head to the superbly restored out-of-town **Petrodvorets**, which belonged to Peter the Great and is positioned with glorious views over the Baltic.

Travel across the border to **Narva**, walking across the long bridge connecting Russia and Estonia while soaking up great views of the castle. Carry on to the Estonian capital **Tallinn** for two days and wander the charmingly chocolate-box streets of the 14th- and 15th-century Old Town before heading to the beautiful, remote and pine-forest-clad island of **Saaremaa** for a day or two's exploration. From Saaremaa, head to the inviting Estonian beach resort of **Pärnu** for a slice of Eastern European holidaymaking (think mud baths, Bacchanalian youth and golden-sand beaches) before continuing south into Latvia.

Stop off in cheerful, castle-rich **Sigulda** and spend a day or two walking in tranquil landscapes and thick forests of the **Gauja National Park** before going to **Rīga** for a couple of nights. Latvia's delightful capital, where you can soak up the fantastic architecture, the Old Town and friendly atmosphere, has plenty to keep you interested for several days. Lithuania is next up – and it greets you straight away with its astounding hill of crosses in **Šiauliai**, a must-see even if there's no reason to dawdle. Charming university town **Kaunas** is Lithuania's second city and boasts a leafy old centre and friendly locals, as well as being just a short distance away from the chilling Ninth Fort concentration camp.

Finally, end your journey in beautiful **Vilnius**, the country's crowning glory, which boasts the biggest Old Town in the Baltic and is still relatively undiscovered by tour groups. To add to its quirky kudos, don't miss the Frank Zappa memorial or the wonderfully idiosyncratic Užupis Republic, a kernal of counter culture at the city's heart.

Two Weeks
Eastern Europe 101

Only got two weeks and want to see the most you can in such a limited time? This itinerary is for you. Start off by flying to the Polish capital **Warsaw** for one night, seeing the beautifully restored Old Town and eating delicious *pierogi* (dumplings) before taking the train south to **Kraków** for two nights, giving you time to see the Old Town, Wawel Castle and Kazimierz, and to do a day trip to **Oświęcim** (Auschwitz) before taking the overnight train to **Prague** for two days of intensive sightseeing – Prague Castle, Charles Bridge, wandering the Malá Strana and the Old Town and tasting genuine Czech Beer in a local brewery.

Take another overnight train to **Budapest** for two nights in Hungary. Soak in the city's glorious Gellért Baths, take a cruise on the Danube, see the magnificent Hungarian Parliament building and wander Castle Hill before yet another overnight train to Romania's much underrated capital, **Bucharest**. With a one-night stay you can cover the main sights, including the amazing Palace of Parliament, wander the small historic centre and pick up a sense of the city's energy in its bars and clubs.

Continue by train to wonderful and much-overlooked **Veliko Târnovo** in Northern Bulgaria for one night, a stunning and unusually located university town and a far more 'everyday' Eastern European town than most national capitals. While here, find the time to see the ancient Tsarevets Fortress (and stick around for the nightly summer light show) before finishing up your two weeks by taking the train to **Sofia** for two last nights that will give you a taste of the plucky Bulgarian capital, including the wonderful golden-domed Aleksander Nevski Church. On your last day take a day trip through the Rila Mountains to the unmissable **Rila Monastery**, the country's holiest site and one of the most important monasteries in Eastern Europe. From here you can fly out of Sofia or continue to bigger air hubs such as nearby Athens or İstanbul to get a flight home.

countries at a glance

Eastern Europe can appear overwhelming at first glance; after all, just two decades ago there were a mere eight countries in a region that today contains 21 independent nations. While the big hitters such as Russia, Croatia, the Czech Republic and Poland may need little introduction, here we've summed up each country in a few sentences to give you an initial idea of what there is to do there – although, of course, each place offers far more than we can mention here. Whether you spend your entire trip in one country or travel between a dozen, you'll be amazed by the sheer variety you'll encounter.

Albania

Beaches ✓✓
Scenery ✓✓✓
Culture ✓✓

Albania has some of the last undeveloped coastline on the Mediterranean, its mountains are some of Europe's most spectacular, and its mountain culture one of the most passionately traditional anywhere in the world.

p46

Belarus

History ✓✓
Architecture ✓✓
Nature ✓✓

If communist architecture is your thing, look no further than Minsk, which was rebuilt from rubble after WWII. Belarus also has two superb national parks – the Belavezhskaya Pushcha and the Pripyatsky National Park.

p79

Bosnia & Hercegovina

Scenery ✓✓
Adventure Holidays ✓✓✓
History ✓✓

One of the best Eastern European destinations for active holidays, BiH is a great place for kayaking, skiing, hiking and mountain biking. With its mixed Muslim and Christian heritage, it's also a fascinating blend of cultures.

p107

Bulgaria

Hiking ✓✓✓
Architecture ✓✓
Beaches ✓✓

With six mountain ranges within its borders, Bulgaria is a walker's fantasy, while you'll find the best Black Sea beaches on its sandy coastline and its ancient towns packed full of history.

p151

Croatia

Cuisine ✓✓
Architecture ✓✓✓
Beaches ✓✓✓

A dazzling coastline and thousands of islands, Dubrovnik's Old Town, Diocletian's Palace in Split, the extraordinary Plitvice Lakes National Park and Istria's foodie offerings – you're spoilt for choice in Croatia.

p209

Czech Republic

Old Towns ✓✓✓
Scenery ✓✓
Beer ✓✓✓

Prague's beautiful Old Town is just the tip of the iceberg – Bohemia enjoys spectacular scenery and nowhere else in the world has as much cachet among beer lovers as the breweries in the Czech Republic.

p273

Estonia

Islands & Coastline ✓✓
Architecture ✓✓✓
Culture ✓✓

Tallinn's Old Town is the medieval jewel of Estonia and walking its narrow streets is like strolling back to the 14th century. With an incredible 1521 islands studding its coastline, Estonia also offers great beaches.

p337

Hungary

Architecture ✓✓
Partying ✓✓✓
Wine ✓✓✓

Budapest is one of Eastern Europe's most happening party towns, while the architecture is to die for throughout the country. Oenophiles will love touring the vineyards of the Tokay region or tasting the famous Bull's Blood wine.

p377

Kosovo

Ottoman Architecture ✓✓
Monasteries ✓✓
Scenery ✓✓

Check out Europe's newest and most controversial country. Kosovo's Serbian monasteries date back to the 1300s and have outstanding frescos, while the impressive hills around Peja are ideal for hiking and skiing.

p437

Latvia

Architecture ✓✓✓
Castles ✓✓
History ✓✓

With over 750 *style moderne* buildings in Rīga alone, Latvia has the largest collection of art nouveau facades in the world. Crumbling castle ruins abound throughout the pine-peppered terrain, each a testament to a forgotten kingdom.

p449

Lithuania

Scenery ✓✓✓
Offbeat Attractions ✓✓
Castles ✓✓✓

The Curonian Spit is a wondrous mixture of pine forest and giant sand dunes: Norway meets the Sahara Desert. Don't miss Vilnius' Upper Castle, or Trakai Castle, which sits picturesquely in the middle of a lake.

p479

Macedonia

Cuisine ✓
Churches ✓✓✓
Lakes ✓

Macedonia grows arguably the finest sweet peppers in the world, its Byzantine churches contain some of the most important medieval art in the Balkans and its waters include Lake Ohrid, a beautiful spot for a dip.

p515

Moldova

Wine ✓✓
Cave Monasteries ✓✓✓
Breakaway Republics ✓✓

Among tiny Moldova's attractions are the breathtaking cave monasteries of Orheiul Vechi, an exceptional wine industry centred on the labyrinthine cellars at Cricova and Mileștii Mici, and the breakaway region of Soviet-inspired Transdniestr.

p545

Montenegro

Scenery ✓✓✓
Historic Sites ✓✓
Outdoor Pursuits ✓✓

Montenegro crams an awful lot into a very small space: jagged mountains, sheer-walled river canyons, historic sites, extreme sports, long sandy beaches and the spectacular Bay of Kotor.

p569

Poland

History ✓✓✓
Architecture ✓✓✓
Scenery ✓✓

From the southern Tatras to the Great Masurian Lakes of the north, Poland is one of Eastern Europe's most spectacular countries. History and architecture buffs will be similarly overwhelmed by the sheer variety here.

p597

Romania

Mountains ✓✓✓
Saxon Villages ✓✓
Monasteries ✓✓✓

The Carpathian Mountains offer some of Europe's finest hiking, Southern Transylvania's Saxon villages beckon with ancient churches, and the monasteries of Southern Bucovina are among Europe's most outstanding artistic achievements.

p677

Russia

History ✓✓✓
Architecture ✓✓
Art ✓✓✓

Brutal, fascinating, bizarre – there's no rivalling Russia for having a dramatic past. The medieval Kremlin, the Winter Palace and Lenin's Mausoleum all beg for your attention, while great art collections await you in both Moscow and St Petersburg.

p739

Serbia

People ✓✓✓
Food ✓✓
Partying ✓✓✓

Between Belgrade's legendary nightclubs and frenetic festivals such as Novi Sad's EXIT and Guča's Dragačevo Trumpet Assembly, Serbia is a land of rich hospitality, great food and passionate revelry. Ditch the calorie counting and dig in!

p799

Slovakia

Hiking ✓✓✓
Old Towns ✓✓
Castles ✓✓

From the rocky High Tatra peaks to its lower forested mountain ranges, Slovakia is riddled with hiking trails, hundreds of fortress ruins dot the countryside and medieval walls surround well-preserved Old Town centres.

p827

Slovenia

Scenery ✓✓✓
Outdoor Sports ✓✓✓
Wine ✓✓

Nearly all visitors are mesmerised by the sheer beauty of this tiny country. Don't miss the scenery of Mt Triglav, the Vršič Pass or Lake Bled. Wash it all down with a local wine

p873

Ukraine

Monasteries ✓✓
Scenery ✓✓
Extreme Tourism ✓✓✓

Kyiv overflows with ancient gold-domed churches and the fascinating Caves Monastery Complex. Elsewhere the Crimea's craggy mountain range and a visit to Chornobyl are Ukraine's biggest draws.

p913

Every listing is recommended by our authors, and their favourite places are listed first

Look out for these icons:

TOP CHOICE Our author's top recommendation

 A green or sustainable option

FREE No payment required

See the Index for a full list of destinations covered in this book.

On the Road

Albania

Includes »

Best Places to Eat

» Kujtimi (p70)
» Era (p53)
» Tradita G&T (p57)
» Oda (p53)

Best Places to Stay

» Tradita G&T (p57)
» Hotel Rilindja (p58)
» Hotel Mangalemi (p63)
» Hotel Kalemi (p69)

Why Go?

Albania has natural beauty in such abundance that you might wonder why it's taken 20 years for the country to take off as a tourist destination since the end of a particularly brutal strain of communism in 1991. So backward was Albania when it emerged blinking into the bright light of freedom that it needed two decades just to catch up with the rest of Eastern Europe. Now that it arguably has done so, Albania offers a remarkable array of unique attractions, not least due to this very isolation: ancient mountain codes of behaviour, forgotten archaeological sites and villages where time seems to have stood still are all on the menu. With its stunning mountain scenery, a thriving capital in Tirana and beaches to rival any elsewhere in the Mediterranean, Albania has become the sleeper hit of the Balkans. But hurry here, as word is well and truly out.

When to Go
Tirana

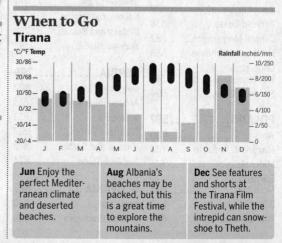

Jun Enjoy the perfect Mediterranean climate and deserted beaches.

Aug Albania's beaches may be packed, but this is a great time to explore the mountains.

Dec See features and shorts at the Tirana Film Festival, while the intrepid can snowshoe to Theth.

Connections

Albania has excellent connections in all directions: daily buses go to Kosovo, Montenegro, Macedonia and Greece. The southern seaport of Saranda is a short ferry trip from Greece's Corfu, while in summer ferries also connect Himara and Vlora to Corfu. Durrës has regular ferries to Italy. Travellers heading south from Croatia can pass through Montenegro to Shkodra (via Ulcinj), and loop through Albania before heading into Macedonia via Pogradec or Kosovo via the Lake Koman Ferry or new super-fast Albania–Kosovo highway. There are, however, no international train routes from Albania.

ITINERARIES

One Week

Spend a day in busy Tirana, checking out the various museums as well as the Blloku bars and nightclubs. On day two, head up the Dajti Express cable car and then make the two-hour trip to the Ottoman-era town of Berat. Spend a few nights in Berat, before continuing down the coast for a couple of days on the beach in Himara or Drymades. Loop around for one last night in charming Gjirokastra before returning to Tirana.

Two Weeks

Follow the first week itinerary and then head north into Albania's incredible 'Accursed Mountains'. Start in Shkodra, from where you can get transport to Koman for the stunning morning ferry ride to Fierzë. Continue the same day to the charming mountain village of Valbonë for a couple of nights, before trekking to Theth and spending your last couple of nights in the beautiful Theth National Park.

Essential Food & Drink

» **Byrek** Pastry with cheese or meat.
» **Fergesë** Baked peppers, egg and cheese, and occasionally meat.
» **Midhje** Wild or farmed mussels, often served fried.
» **Paçë koke** Sheep's head soup, usually served for breakfast.
» **Qofta** Flat or cylindrical minced-meat rissoles.
» **Sufllaqë** Doner kebab.
» **Tavë** Meat baked with cheese and egg.
» **Konjak** Local brandy.
» **Raki** Popular spirit made from grapes.
» **Raki mani** Spirit made from mulberries.

AT A GLANCE

» **Currency** lekë
» **Language** Albanian
» **Money** ATMs in most towns
» **Visas** Most visitors don't need one – a 90-day stamp is issued at the border

Fast Facts

» **Area** 28,748 sq km
» **Capital** Tirana
» **Country code** ✆355
» **Emergency** Ambulance ✆127, fire ✆128, police ✆129

Exchange Rates

Australia	A$1	114.59 lekë
Canada	C$1	107.95 lekë
Euro Zone	€1	140.19 lekë
Japan	¥100	116.24 lekë
New Zealand	NZ$1	91.85 lekë
UK	UK£1	165.99 lekë
USA	US$1	109.70 lekë

Set Your Budget

» **Budget hotel** €10–15 per person
» **Two-course meal** €8
» **Museum entrance** €1–3
» **Beer** €1.50
» **City transport ticket** 30 lekë

Resources

» **Albania-Hotel** (www.albania-hotel.com)
» **Balkanology** (www.balkanology.com/albania)
» **Journey to Valbona** (www.journeytovalbona.com)

Albania Highlights

1 Catch the **Lake Koman Ferry** (p59) through stunning mountain scenery, then continue to **Valbonë** and trek the 'Accursed Mountains'.

2 Explore the Unesco World Heritage–listed museum towns of dramatic **Berat** (p61), the so-called 'city of a thousand windows'.

3 Catch some sun at **Drymades** (p65), just one of the many beaches on the south's dramatic Ionian Coast.

4 Travel back in time to the ruins of **Butrint** (p68), hidden in the depths of a forest in a serene lakeside setting.

5 Feast your eyes on the wild colour schemes and experience the hip Blloku cafe culture in **Tirana** (p49).

6 Take a trip into the traditional Southern Albanian mountain town of **Gjirokastra** (p69), with is spectacular Ottoman-era mansions and impressive hilltop fortress.

TIRANA

📵 04 / POP 764,000

Lively, colourful Tirana is the beating heart of Albania, where this tiny nation's hopes and dreams coalesce into a vibrant whirl of traffic, brash consumerism and unfettered fun. Having undergone a transformation of extraordinary proportions since it awoke from its communist slumber in the early 1990s, Tirana is now unrecognisable, with its buildings painted in horizontal primary colours, and public squares and pedestrianised streets a pleasure to wander.

Trendy Blloku buzzes with well-dressed *nouvelle bourgeoisie* hanging out in bars or zipping between boutiques, while the city's grand boulevards are lined with fascinating relics of its Ottoman, Italian and communist past – from delicate minarets to loud socialist murals. Tirana's traffic does daily battle with both itself and pedestrians in a constant scene of unmitigated chaos. Loud, crazy, colourful and dusty – Tirana is never dull.

◉ Sights

The centre of Tirana is Skanderbeg Sq, a large traffic island with an equestrian statue of the Albanian national hero at its centre. Running through the square is Tirana's main avenue, Blvd Zogu I, which becomes Blvd Dëshmorët e Kombit (Martyrs of the Nation Blvd) south of the square. At the street's northern end is Tirana's train station; head to the other end and you're at the small Tirana University building.

NORTH OF THE RIVER

Sheshi Skënderbej   SQUARE

(Skanderbeg Sq) Skanderbeg Sq is the best place to start witnessing Tirana's daily goings-on. Until it was pulled down by an angry mob in 1991, a 10m-high bronze statue of Enver Hoxha stood here, watching over a mainly car-free square. Now only the **equestrian statue of Skanderbeg** remains, deaf to the cacophony of screeching horns as cars four lanes deep try to shove their way through the battlefield below.

TOP
CHOICE **National History Museum**   MUSEUM

(Muzeu Historik Kombëtar; Sheshi Skënderbej; adult/student 200/60 lekë; ⊙10am-5pm Tue-Sat, to 2pm Sun) The largest museum in Albania holds most of the country's archaeological treasures and a replica of Skanderbeg's massive sword (how he held it, rode his horse and fought at the same time is a mystery). The mosaic mural entitled *Albania* adorning the museum's facade shows Albanians victorious and proud from Illyrian times through to WWII. The collection is almost entirely signed in English and takes you chronologically from ancient Illyria to the postcommunist era. The highlight of the museum is a terrific exhibition of icons by Onufri, a renowned 16th-century Albanian master of colour. A disturbing and very important gallery devoted to those who suffered persecution under the communist regime is the most recent addition to the collection, though frustratingly almost none of this display is in English.

National Art Gallery   GALLERY

(Galeria Kombëtare e Arteve; www.gka.al; Blvd Dëshmorët e Kombit; admission 200 lekë; ⊙10am-6pm Mon-Sat) Tracing the relatively brief history of Albanian painting from the early 19th century to the present day, this beautiful space also has temporary exhibits that are worth a look. Downstairs there's a small but interesting collection of 19th-century paintings depicting scenes from daily Albanian life, while upstairs the art takes on a political dimension with some truly fabulous examples of Albanian socialist realism.

Et'hem Bey Mosque   MOSQUE

(Sheshi Skënderbej; ⊙8am-11am) To one side of Skanderbeg Sq, the 1789–1823 Et'hem

---

BUNKER LOVE

On the hillsides, beaches and generally most surfaces in Albania, you will notice small concrete domes (often in groups of three) with rectangular slits. Meet the bunkers: Enver Hoxha's concrete legacy, built from 1950 to 1985. Weighing in at 5 tonnes of concrete and iron, these little mushrooms are almost impossible to destroy. They were built to repel an invasion and can resist full tank assault – a fact proved by their chief engineer, who vouched for his creation's strength by standing inside one while it was bombarded by a tank. The shell-shocked engineer emerged unscathed, and tens of thousands were built. Today, some are creatively painted, one houses a tattoo artist, and some even house makeshift hostels.

Tirana

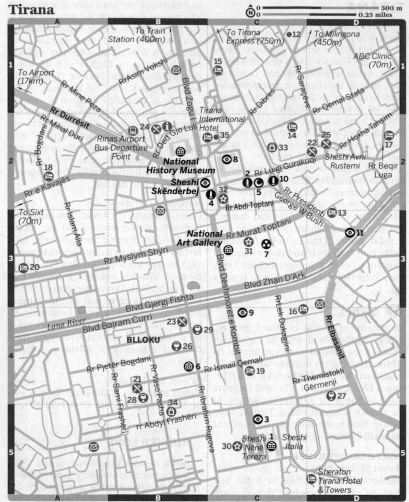

Bey Mosque was spared destruction during the atheism campaign of the late 1960s because of its status as a cultural monument. Small and elegant, it's one of the oldest buildings left in the city. Take your shoes off to look inside at the beautifully painted dome.

Clock Tower
TOWER

(Kulla e Sahatit; Rr Luigj Gurakuqi; admission 100 lekë; ☺9am-1pm Mon, 9am-1pm & 4-6pm Thu; ☎) Behind the mosque is the tall clock tower, which you can climb for impressive views of the square. Further on up the street, look for

the socialist realist **statue of the Unknown Partisan**.

Palace of Culture
NOTABLE BUILDING

(Pallate Kulturës; Sheshi Skënderbej) To the east of Sheshi Skënderbej is the white stone Palace of Culture, which has a theatre, shops and art galleries. Construction of the palace began as a gift from the Soviet people in 1960 and was completed in 1966, years after the 1961 Soviet–Albanian split.

Fortress of Justinian
RUINS

(Rr Murat Toptani) If you turn up Rr Murat Toptani, behind the National Art Gallery,

Tirana

you'll pass the 6m-high walls of the Fortress of Justinian, the last remnants of a Byzantine-era castle. These days half a cinema/nightclub overflows over the top. East from here, on the corner of Rr Presidenti George W Bush and the Lana River, is **Tanners' Bridge**, a small 19th-century slippery-when-wet stone bridge.

SOUTH OF THE RIVER

Pyramid   NOTABLE BUILDING
(Blvd Dëshmorët e Kombit) Designed by Enver Hoxha's daughter and son-in-law and completed in 1988, this monstrously unattractive building was formerly the Enver Hoxha Museum, and more recently a convention centre and nightclub. Today, covered in graffiti and surrounded by the encampments of Tirana's homeless, its once white marble walls are now crumbling but no decision on whether to demolish or restore it appears to have yet been reached.

Congress Building   NOTABLE BUILDING
(Blvd Dëshmorët e Kombit) Another creation of the former dictator's daughter and son-in-law is the square Congress Building, just a little down the boulevard from the Pyramid. Follow Rr Ismail Qemali two streets north of the Congress Building and enter the once totally forbidden but now totally trendy Blloku area. This former Communist Party elite hang-out was opened to the general public for the first time in 1991. Security still guards the **former residence of Enver Hoxha** (cnr Rr Dëshmorët e 4 Shkurtit & Rr Ismail Qemali).

Archaeological Museum   MUSEUM
(Muzeu Arkeologik; Sheshi Nënë Tereza; admission 100 lekë; ◎10.30am-2.30pm Mon-Fri) The collection here is comprehensive and impressive in parts, but there's no labelling in any language, nor tours in English offered, so unless this is your field, you may find yourself a little at a loss to get much out of the

museum. A total renovation is on the cards, but as one staff member pointed out to us, they've been waiting for this since 1985, so don't hold your breath.

Martyrs' Cemetery
CEMETERY

At the top of Rr Elbasanit is the Martyrs' Cemetery, where some 900 partisans who died in WWII are buried. The views over the city and surrounding mountains (including Mt Dajti to the east) are excellent, as is the sight of the immense, beautiful and strangely androgynous Mother Albania statue (1972). Hoxha was buried here in 1985 but in 1992 he was exhumed and interred in an ordinary graveyard elsewhere. Catch a municipal bus heading up Rr Elbasanit; the grand driveway is on your left.

☞ Tours

Get off the beaten track or discover Albania's tourist attractions with a Tirana-based tour company.

Albanian Experience
TOURS

(☑2272 055; www.albania-experience.al; Sheshi Italia, Sheraton Tirana Hotel) Organises tours of Albania with knowledgeable guides.

Outdoor Albania
TOURS

(☑2227 121; www.outdooralbania.com; Rr Sami Frasheri, Pallati Metropol) Excellent trailblazing adventure tour agency offering hiking, rafting, snowshoeing, sea and white-water kayaking and, in summer, hikes through the Alps.

★☆ Festivals & Events

Tirana International Film Festival
CINEMA

(www.tiranafilmfest.com) This festival is held each late November/early December and features both short and feature films from its international competition winners, as well as new cinematic work from Albanian filmmakers.

🛌 Sleeping

TOP CHOICE Brilant Antik
HOTEL €€

(☑2251 166; www.hotelbrilant.com; Rr Jeronim de Rada 79; s/d €50/60; ✳🔊) This charming house-cum-hotel has plenty of character, a central location and welcoming English-speaking staff to ease you into Tirana life. Rooms are spacious, decently furnished with the odd antique, and breakfast downstairs is a veritable feast each morning.

Rogner Hotel Europapark Tirana
HOTEL €€€

(☑2235 035; www.hotel-europapark.com; Blvd Dëshmorët e Kombit; s €150-180, d €170-210, ste €240-290; ✳@🔊🏊) With an unbeatable location in the heart of the city, the Rogner is a peaceful oasis with a huge garden, tennis court and facilities such as banks, travel and car-rental agencies. The rooms are spacious, extremely comfortable and come with flat-screen TVs.

Green House
BOUTIQUE HOTEL €€€

(☑068 2072 262, 4521 015; www.greenhouse.al; Rr Jul Variboba 6; s/d €80/90; ✳🔊) In a cool spot in Tirana sits this modern 10-room hotel with downlit, stylish rooms that might be the city's coolest. Its sprawling downstairs terrace restaurant is a friendly expat hang-out with a varied menu and a long wine list. It looks up at one of Tirana's quirkiest buildings.

TOP CHOICE Tirana Backpacker Hostel
HOSTEL €

(☑068 3133 451, 068 4682 353; www.tiranahostel. com; Rr Myslym Shyri, Vila 7, behind Alpet petrol station; dm €13, d €40, without bathroom €28; ✳🔊) Albania's first ever hostel now boasts very smart new premises in the centre of town, and looks more like a fancy restaurant than a hostel at first glance. There are three six-bed dorms, all with their own facilities, and several comfortable doubles, including one with a great balcony. All rooms are equipped with air-con, but you'll need to pay €3 extra per room per night to turn it on. The place is very social, with a busy bar-restaurant downstairs and plenty of atmosphere.

Capital Tirana Hotel
HOTEL €€

(☑2258 575, 069 2080 931; www.capitaltiranahotel. com; Rr Qemal Stafa; s/d €40/65; ℗✳🔊) Opened in 2012, this thoroughly modern 29-room hotel just a stone's throw from Skanderbeg Sq is a welcome addition to Tirana's accommodation scene. It may be a little sterile and businesslike, but the rooms are of good quality with flat-screen TVs and minibars, staff are very helpful and the location on a busy shopping street is great.

Hostel Albania
HOSTEL €

(☑067 2783 798; www.hostel-albania.com; Rr Beqir Luga 56; dm €11-12, d €30; @🔊) This hostel has small four- and six-person dorms, though the basement's 14-bed dorm (€11) is the coolest spot in summer and dividers hide the fact that there are so many bunks down there. Zen space is in the outdoor shoes-off oriental lounge, and a filling breakfast with filter coffee is included. The artist owners provide great information about the local art scene, and the location is central.

Freddy's Hostel
HOTEL €

(☎2266 077, 068 2035 261; www.freddyshostel.com; Rr Bardhok Biba 75; dm €12, r €32-56; 🅱@🛜) Freddy's is run by a friendly family whose knowledge of the city is second to none. The clean, basic bunk-free rooms have lockers and come in different configurations. Breakfast isn't included with the cheapest dorm places, but the central location is hard to beat. The owners can also arrange long-term apartment rentals.

Hotel Serenity
HOTEL €€

(☎2267 152; Rr Bogdani 4; s/d €25/40; 🅱@🛜) This villa-style hotel in a side street in central Tirana has a semi-boutique feel with stylish rooms and contemporary fittings. Despite the busy main road nearby, this is a quiet location. Rooms have tiled floors, minibars and TVs, and offer excellent value. Breakfast is not included.

Milingona
HOSTEL €

(☎069 2070 076, 069 2049 836; www.milingona-hostel.com; Rr Risa Cerova 197/2, off Rr Dibres; tent €7, dm €11-12, d €30; @🛜) Now in a new location a 15-minute walk from Skanderbeg Sq, 'the Ant' takes up a large house in a residential district and is cared for by multilingual sisters Zhujeta and Rozana. There are large dorms (sleeping six and eight people), each of which shares facilities with another dorm on the same floor. There's a large shared kitchen, a living room, a roof terrace and a garden. To get here from the centre, walk up Rr Dibres, and when it splits, bear right after the Medresa, and Rr Risa Cerova is the first street on the right.

✕ Eating

Most of Tirana's best eating is in and around Blloku, a square of some 10 blocks of shops, restaurants, cafes and hotels situated one block west of Dëshmorët and along the Lana River in south Tirana.

TOP CHOICE Era
ALBANIAN, ITALIAN €€

(☎2266 662; www.era.al; Rr Ismail Qemali; mains 300-700 lekë; ⊗11am-midnight; 🍴) This local institution serves traditional Albanian and Italian fare in the heart of Blloku. The inventive menu includes oven-baked veal and

eggs, stuffed eggplant, pizza, and pilau with chicken and pine nuts. Be warned: it's sometimes quite hard to get a seat as it's fearsomely popular, so you may have to wait. Delivery and takeaway are both available.

TOP CHOICE Oda
ALBANIAN €€

(Rr Luigj Gurakuqi; mains 350-550 lekë; ⊗noon-11pm) Bright flashing lights will guide you to this endearing little restaurant down a lane where you can choose from two brightly lit dining rooms or an atmospheric terrace. The place is stuffed full of traditional Albanian arts and crafts, and while its popularity with travellers means you won't feel like you've discovered a truly authentic slice of the country, the delicious menu and pleasant atmosphere make it well worth a visit.

Piazza
ITALIAN €€

(Rr Ded Gjo Luli; mains 400-700 lekë; ⊗noon-11pm) Behind the national museum, this restaurant consistently gets rave reviews from visitors who enjoy the formal service, the stylish interior and the fine Italian cuisine. The fish is the speciality here, and it's cooked to perfection, while the wine list has some excellent local vintages.

Green House
ITALIAN €€

(Rr Jul Variboba 6; mains 400-800 lekë) Downstairs from the small eponymous hotel, the Green House boasts an enviable terrace that hums with the buzz of the local Blloku crowds day and night. The menu is strongly Italian leaning, but there are Albanian and other international dishes too.

Patisserie Française
BAKERY €

(Rr Dëshmorët e 4 Shkurtit 1; pastries from 150 lekë; ⊗8am-10pm; 🛜) This popular Blloku cafe has has an array of sweet pastries, macaroons and sandwiches plus good coffee to boot. It's a good breakfast option.

Stephen Centre
CAFE €€

(Rr Hoxha Tahsim 1; mains 400-700 lekë; ⊗8am-8pm Mon-Sat; 🛜) If you like your fries thin, your wi-fi free and the spirit Christian, here's the cafe for you. A veritable institution in Tirana, the Stephen Centre also offers accommodation upstairs in single-bed configurations (single/double €35/50).

🍷 Drinking

Most of Tirana's nightspots are concentrated in the Blloku neighbourhood, and most will have you partying on to the wee hours.

Radio
BAR

(Rr Ismail Qemali 29/1) Set back from the street is this very cool yet understated and friendly bar. Check out the owner's collection of antique Albania-made radios while sipping cocktails with groovy locals.

Charl's
BAR

(Rr Pjetër Bogdani 36) Charl's is a consistently popular bar with Tirana's students because of its ever-varying live music on the weekends, and disco/dance crowd-pleasers the rest of the time. The relaxed vibe is enhanced by the bar's open-air garden.

Kaon Beer Garden
BEER HALL

(Rr Asim Zeneli; ⊙noon-1am) For those who hate the hassle of ordering beer after beer, here's Kaon. Its popular 'keg-on-the-table' approach means it can be hard to get a table in the evening (queuing is normal), but once you get in, it's a pleasant outdoor bar and restaurant in the fancy villa-filled part of town. You won't go hungry; Albanian meals start from 200 lekë. Locally brewed beer comes in standard glasses, or tabletop 2- and 3-litre 'roxys'.

Sky Club Bar
BAR

(Rr Dëshmorët e 4 Shkurtit, Sky Tower) Start your night here for spectacular city views from the revolving bar on top of one of the highest buildings in town.

☆ Entertainment

There is a good choice of entertainment options in Tirana, in the form of bars, clubs, cinema, performances, exhibitions and even 10-pin bowling. For the low-down on events and exhibitions, check posters around town. For alternative events, ask at Milingona hostel and Hostel Albania.

TOP CHOICE Tirana Express
GALLERY, MUSIC

(www.tiranaekspres.wordpress.com; Rr Karl Gega) This fantastic nonprofit arts project has converted a warehouse behind Tirana's semi-derelict train station into an arts space that hosts revolving temporary exhibits, concerts, installations and other events that appeal to Tirana's arty, alternative crowd. Go along and see what's on during your visit. Opening hours vary depending on what's on.

Folie
CLUB

(Rr Murat Toptani) This is where the big-name DJs come to play, and though the crowd can be a little more concerned with being seen than actually enjoying themselves, it's a great outdoor venue for a loud night out.

Kinema Millennium 2
CINEMA

(Rr Murat Toptani; tickets 300-500 lekë) Current-release movies that are cheaper the earlier in the day you go. At night it's a nightclub.

Theatre of Opera & Ballet
THEATRE

(☎2224 753; www.tkob.al; Sheshi Skënderbej; tickets from 350 lekë; ⊙performances from 7pm, from 6pm winter) Check the listings and posters outside the theatre for performances.

Academy of Arts
THEATRE

(☎2257 237; www.artacademy.al; Sheshi Nënë Tereza) Classical music and other performances take place throughout the year in either the large indoor theatre or the small open-air faux-classical amphitheatre; both are part of the university. Prices vary according to the program.

🛍 Shopping

Souvenir shops on Rr Durrësit and Blvd Zogu I sell red Albanian flags, red T-shirts, red lighters, bunker ashtrays and lively traditional textiles.

🍴 Natyral & Organik
FOOD & DRINK

(Rr Vaso Pasha) This tiny store in Blloku not only supports small village producers by stocking their organic olive oil, honey, herbs, tea, eggs, spices, raki and cognac (these make great gifts, but be aware of customs regulations in the countries you're travelling through), it's also a centre for environmental activism.

Market
FOOD & DRINK

(Sheshi Avni Rustemi) Buy fruit, vegetables and deli produce here; nearby Rr Qemal Stafa has secondhand stalls selling everything from bicycles to bedheads.

Adrion International Bookshop
BOOKS

(Sheshi Skënderbej, Palace of Culture; ⊙9am-9pm Mon-Sat) The place to head for maps, guides and English-language books.

ℹ Information

Tirana has plenty of ATMs linked to international networks.

ABC Clinic (☎2234 105; www.abchealth.org; Rr Qemal Stafa 260; ⊙9am-1pm Mon, Wed & Fri, to 5pm Tue & Thu) Has English-speaking Christian doctors and a range of services, including brief (600 lekë) and normal (1200 lekë) consultations.

Hygeia Hospital Tirana (☎2390 000; www. hygeia.al; Tirana-Durrës Hwy) This new Greek-owned private hospital has a 24-hour emergency department.

Post Office (Rr Çameria; ⊙8am-8pm) A shiny and clean oasis in a street jutting west from Sheshi Skënderbej. Smaller offices operate around the city.

Tirana in Your Pocket (www.inyourpocket. com) Has a local team of writers providing up-to-date coverage of Tirana. It can be downloaded free or bought at bookshops, hotels and some of the larger kiosks for 500 lekë.

Tirana Tourist Information Centre (☎2223 313; www.tirana.gov.al; Rr Ded Gjo Luli; ⊙9am-5pm Mon-Fri, to 2pm Sat) Friendly staff make getting information easy at this government-run initiative just off Skanderbeg Sq.

❶ Getting There & Around

There's now a good network of city buses running around Tirana costing 30 lekë per journey (payable to the conductor), although most of the sights can be covered easily on foot.

Air

The modern **Nënë Tereza International Airport** (Mother Teresa Airport; ☎2381 800; www. tirana-airport.com.al) is at Rinas, 17km northwest of Tirana. The Rinas Express airport bus operates an hourly (8am to 7pm) service from Rr Mine Peza on the western side of the National History Museum for 250 lekë one way. The going taxi rate is 2000 to 2500 lekë. The airport is about 20 minutes' drive away, but plan for possible traffic jams.

Bicycle

This was the main form of transport for Albanians until the early 1990s, and it's having a

comeback (cyclists seem to make more headway in Tirana's regular traffic snarls). Bike hire is available from several hostels.

Bus

You have the option of buses or *furgons* (minibuses). There is no official bus station in Tirana, though there's a makeshift bus station beside the train station where some buses drop passengers off and depart from. Confusingly, other buses and *furgons* depart from ever-changing places in and around the city, so check locally for the latest departure points. You can almost guarantee that taxi drivers will be in the know; however, you may have to dissuade them from taking you the whole way.

Furgons are usually slightly more expensive than buses and leave when full. Buses for Pristina in Kosovo (€20, five hours, three daily) leave from beside the museum on Blvd Zogu 1. To Macedonia, there are buses via Struga (€15, five hours) to Tetovo (€20, seven to eight hours) and Skopje (€20, eight hours) from the same spot. Buses to Ulcinj (€20) and Budva (€30) in Montenegro depart from 6am in front of the tourist information centre. If you're heading to Athens (€35, 15 hours), buses leave at around either 8am or 7pm from outside the travel agencies on Blvd Zogu 1. Most bus services are fairly casual; you turn up and pay the driver.

Car

Lumani Enterprise (☎04-2235 021; www. lumani-enterprise.com) is a local car-hire company. International companies in Tirana include the following (each also has an outlet at the airport):

Avis (☎2235 011; www.avis.al; Blvd Dëshmorët e Kombit, Rogner Hotel Europapark)

DOMESTIC BUSES FROM TIRANA

DESTINATION	PRICE (LEKË)	DURATION	DISTANCE (KM)
Berat	400	2½hr	122
Durrës	150	1hr	38
Elbasan	300	1½hr	54
Fier	400	2hr	113
Gjirokastra	800	7hr	232
Korça	600	4hr	181
Kruja	150	30min	32
Pogradec	500	3½hr	150
Saranda	1200	7hr	284
Shkodra	300	2hr	116
Vlora	500	4hr	147

Europcar (☑2227 888; www.europcar.com; Rr Durrësit 61)

Hertz (☑2262 511; www.hertzalbania.com; Sheshi Skënderbej, Tirana Hotel International)

Sixt (☑068 2068 500, 2259 020; Rr e Kavajës 116)

Taxi

Taxi stands dot the city, and taxis charge 300 to 400 lekë for a ride inside Tirana and 600 lekë at night and to destinations outside the city centre. Reach agreement on price with the driver before setting off. **Radio Taxi** (☑224 4444), with 24-hour service, is particularly reliable.

Train

The rundown train station is at the northern end of Blvd Zogu I. Albania's trains range from sort of OK to very decrepit, and as a result Albanians only tend to travel by train if they can't afford the bus. Seven trains daily go to Durrës (70 lekë, one hour). Trains also depart for Elbasan (190 lekë, four hours, 2.10pm), Pogradec (2km out of town; 295 lekë, eight hours, 5.30am), Shkodra (145 lekë, 3½ hours, 1.15pm) and Vlora (250 lekë, 5¾ hours, 4.25pm). Check timetables at the station the day before travelling. Purchase tickets before hopping on the train.

AROUND TIRANA

Just 25km east of Tirana is **Mt Dajti National Park** (1611m). It is the most accessible mountain in the country, and many Tiranans go there to escape the city rush and have a spit-roast lamb lunch. A sky-high, Austrian-made cable car, **Dajti Express** (www.dajtiekspres.com; return 700 lekë; ☺9am-9pm Tue-Sun), takes 15 minutes to rise to (almost) the top. It's a scenic trip over bunkers, forest, farms and hilltops. Once there, you can avoid all the touts and their minibuses and take the opportunity to stroll through lovely, shady beech and pine forests. There are grassy picnic spots along the road to the right, but if you didn't pack a picnic, try the lamb roast and spectacular views from the wide terrace of the **Panorama Restaurant** (mains 500 lekë).

To get to the Dajti Express departure point, take the public bus from outside Tirana's clock tower to 'Porcelain' (30 lekë). From here, it's a 1.5km walk uphill, or you can wait for a free bus transfer. Taxis seem to charge what they want to the Dajti Express drop-off point, but the trip from Tirana should only cost 600 lekë. It's also possible to drive or cycle to the top.

NORTHERN ALBANIA

Northern Albania is a scenic wonderland where the incredible landscape of the 'Accursed Mountains' dominates and the rich and independent mountain culture strongly flavours all journeys. The north also boasts rich wildlife around beautiful Lake Shkodra, not to mention the ancient city of the same name. This may be the Albania of blood feuds, but anyone visiting northern Albania will be amazed by how friendly and welcoming locals are.

Shkodra

☑022 / POP 95,000

Shkodra (Shkodër), the traditional centre of the Gheg cultural region, is one of the oldest cities in Europe. The ancient Rozafa Fortress has stunning views over the nearby lake, while a concerted effort to renovate the buildings in the Old Town has made wandering through Shkodra a treat for the eyes. Many travellers pass through here between Tirana and Montenegro, or en route to the Lake Koman Ferry and the villages of Theth and Valbonë, but it's worth spending a night to soak up this pleasant and welcoming place.

As the Ottoman Empire declined in the late 18th century, Shkodra became the centre of a semi-independent *pashalik* (region governed by a pasha, an Ottoman high official), which led to a blossoming of commerce and crafts. In 1913 Montenegro attempted to annex Shkodra (it succeeded in taking Ulcinj), a move not approved of by the international community, and the town changed hands often during WWI. Badly damaged by an earthquake in 1979, Shkodra was subsequently repaired and is Albania's fifth-largest town. The communist-era Hotel Rozafa in the town centre does little to welcome guests, but it makes a good landmark: restaurants, the information centre and most of the town's sights are close by.

◉ Sights

Rozafa Fortress   CASTLE

(admission 200 lekë; ☺8am-10pm) Three kilometres southwest of Shkodra, near the southern end of Lake Shkodra, the Rozafa Fortress was founded by the Illyrians in antiquity and rebuilt much later by the Venetians and then the Turks. The fortress derives its name from a woman named

Rozafa, who was allegedly walled into the ramparts as an offering to the gods so that the construction would stand. The story goes that Rozafa asked that two holes be left in the stonework so that she could continue to breastfeed her baby. There's a spectacular wall sculpture of her near the entrance of the castle's **museum** (admission 150 lekë; ⊘8am-7pm). Some nursing women come to the fortress to smear their breasts with the milky water that seeps from the wall during some months of the year. Municipal buses (30 lekë) stop near the turn-off to the castle, and it's a short walk up from there.

Marubi Permanent
Photo Exhibition
GALLERY

(Rr Muhamet Gjollesha; admission 100 lekë; ⊘8am-4pm Mon-Fri) Hidden behind a block of shops and flats, the Marubi Permanent Photo Exhibition has fantastic photography by the Marubi 'dynasty', Albania's first and foremost photographers. The first-ever photograph taken in Albania is here, taken by Pjetër Marubi in 1858. The exhibition shows fascinating portraits, places and events. Not only is this a rare insight into what things looked like in old Albania, it is also a small collection of mighty fine photographs. To get here, go northeast of the clock tower to Rr Çlirimi; Rr Muhamet Gjollesha darts off to the right. The exhibition is on the left in an unmarked building, but locals will help you find it if you ask.

🛏 Sleeping & Eating

TOP CHOICE **Tradita G&T**
BOUTIQUE HOTEL €€

(☏2240 537, 068 2086 056; www.traditagt.com; Rr Edith Durham; s/d/tr €35/50/55; 🅿🕸🛜) By far the best choice in town, this innovative, well-managed guesthouse is a delight. Housed in a painstakingly restored 17th-century mansion that once belonged to a famous Shkodran writer, the Tradita heaves with Albanian arts and crafts and has traditional yet very comfortable rooms with terracotta-roofed bathrooms and locally woven bed linen. A homemade, homegrown breakfast awaits guests in the morning and the restaurant serves excellent fish dishes in an ethnographic museum atmosphere. If you're heading Lake Koman way, the owner can arrange for the bus to pick you up from the hotel, and very happily shares a great deal of local knowledge with guests.

Hotel Kaduku
HOTEL €€

(HK; ☏069 2551 230, 42 216; www.hotel-kaduku.com; Sheshi 5 Heronjtë; s/d/tr/ste €23/32/48/50; 🕸🛜) This popular, modern hotel is behind Raiffeisen Bank on the roundabout near Hotel Rozafa. Its two wings have been renovated, but rooms are a little on the small side, and the bathrooms even more so. It's clean and friendly though, and the staff are able to provide information about getting to and from Theth.

Çoçja
ITALIAN €€

(Rr Hazan Riza; mains 300-800 lekë; ⊘10am-11pm) This classy place on a pleasant piazza a block north of the pedestrianised Rr Kolë Idromeno is all gleaming white tablecloths, timber floors and a refreshing lack of kitsch in the design choices. The menu encompasses great pizza as well as more exciting fare such as veal ribs and chicken fillet with mushrooms and cream. There's also a great little courtyard garden that's perfect for summer drinks.

Piazza Park
PIZZA €€

(Bul Skënderbeg; mains 300-900 lekë) Where the locals return to, night after night, day after day for people-watching and overloud music. The pizza is good though, and you've the choice of eating indoors in a smart dining room, or outside on the busy summer terrace. It's right next to the Mother Teresa monument on the main drag.

❶ Information

The information office (a stand-alone booth) at the intersection of Bul Skënderbeg and Rr Kolë Idromeno is open daily, and until 9pm in summer.

❶ Getting There & Away

BUS There are hourly *furgons* and buses to and from Tirana (300 lekë, two hours, 6am to 4pm). From Shkodra, *furgons* depart from outside Radio Shkodra near Hotel Rozafa. *Furgons* to Ulcinj in Montenegro leave at 9am and 4pm (600 lekë, two hours) from the other side of the park abutting Grand Hotel Europa. They fill quickly. From Ulcinj, buses leave for Shkodra at 6am and 12.30pm. Catch the 7am bus to Lake Koman (800 lekë, two hours) in time for the wonderful ferry trip along the lake to Fierzë near Kosovo. *Furgons* depart for Theth daily at 7am (700 lekë).

TAXI It costs between €40 and €45 for the trip from Shkodra to Uncinj in Montenegro, depending on your haggling skills.

TRAIN Trains depart Tirana daily at 1.15pm (145 lekë), and arrive in Shkodra at 4.50pm, but you'll need to be up early to catch the 5.40am train back. *Furgons* meet arriving trains.

Theth & Valbonë

These small villages deep in the 'Accursed Mountains' are all but deserted in winter (Theth locals head south to live in Shkodra), but come summer they're a magnet for those seeking beauty, isolation, mystery and adventure. From Theth, three circular hikes are very clearly marked out with red and white markers. It's possible to hike in the region without a guide, but they're helpful and charge between 3000 and 4000 lekë per day. Official guides charge €50.

The main hike is from Theth to Valbonë (or vice versa) and takes roughly six to seven hours. It takes around three hours to trek from Theth's centre (742m) to Valbonë pass (1812m), then a further two hours to the houses of Rragam and 1½ hours along a riverbed to near Bajram Curri. It's a spectacular hike and many visitors' highlight of Albania. If possible, combine it with the Koman Ferry for the ultimate Albanian mountain experience, though you're far better doing the circuit anticlockwise (ie going from Valbonë to Theth) if you choose to include the ferry.

⊙ Sights

Kulla   HISTORIC BUILDING
(Theth; admission €1) Visit this fascinating 'lock-in tower' in central Theth where men waited, protected, during a blood feud.

🛏 Sleeping & Eating

Many of Theth's traditional homes have become B&Bs (complete with Western-style bathrooms with hot showers), while in less developed Valbonë, hotels tend to be new builds specifically designed for the needs of travellers. Due to the absence of restaurants in both villages, hotels often include breakfast, lunch and dinner in the deal.

TOP CHOICE Hotel Rilindja   GUESTHOUSE €€
(Valbonë; ☑067 3014 638; www.journeytovalbona.com; per tent €6, r €30-34) Pioneering tourism in Valbonë since 2005, the Albanian-American run Rilindja is a real treat and garners rave reviews from travellers who love the comfortable accommodation and excellent food. A new 12-room building was due to open in 2013 1km up the road from the original building, which is located at the entrance to Valbonë. The five rooms in the old

building share a bathroom, except for one that has private facilities. With fluent English spoken, the helpful owners can organise hikes, picnics and transport.

Çarku Guesthouse   GUESTHOUSE €€
(Theth; ☑069 3164 211; www.guesthouse-thethicarku.com; per person €25; ☺Apr-Oct) Book in advance for a bed in this charming family home with thick stone walls, timber floors, a garden and farm. Food is all grown locally and meals are delicious. It's well signposted as you enter the village.

Guesthouse Tërthorja   GUESTHOUSE €€
(Theth; ☑069 3840 990; www.terthorja-guesthouse-tethi.com; per person incl full board €25) This renovated guesthouse has whitewashed walls, a sports field, sports equipment and a resident cow. Accommodation is in rooms sleeping up to five people and there are stunning views of the mountains all around.

Hotel & Camping Tradita   CHALET €€
(Valbonë; ☑067 301 4567, 067 383 800 14; s/d €25/50) This collection of five newly built chalets has a fantastic location in the middle of the village with extraordinary views in all directions. The pine cabins each come with hot water and private facilities, and the owner, Isa, also offers six further rooms in his adjacent stone house. There's a good restaurant on-site too.

❶ Getting There & Around

BUS Though Theth is only 70km from Shkodra, expect the occasionally hair-raising *furgon* trip to take four hours. The *furgon* leaves from Shkodra at 7am, and most hotels in town will be able to call ahead the night before and book you a seat on the bus, and sometimes, to have the bus pick you up from the hotel.

FERRY A popular route is to take the 7am *furgon* from Shkodra to the Koman Ferry, travel by ferry (two hours) then jump on a *furgon* from the ferry to Valbonë. If you're heading into Kosovo, it takes roughly 50 minutes to the border by car from the ferry terminal, but check that the car ferry is still running.

TAXI To get to Theth from Shkodra by taxi, expect to pay €100.

CENTRAL ALBANIA

Central Albania crams it all in. Travel an hour or two from Tirana and you can be Ottoman house-hopping in brilliant Berat, musing over ancient ruins in deserted Apol-

DON'T MISS

THE LAKE KOMAN FERRY

One of Albania's undisputed highlights is this superb three-hour ferry ride through the vast Lake Koman, connecting the towns of Koman and Fierzë. Lake Koman was created in 1978 when the River Drin was dammed, with the result that you can cruise through spectacular mountain scenery where many incredibly hardy peasants still live as they have for centuries, tucked away in tiny mountain villages.

The ferry is not set up for tourism, which makes the entire trip feel like a great adventure. The best way to experience the ride is to make a loop beginning and ending in Shkodra, and taking in Koman, Fierzë, Valbonë and Theth. Normally there are two ferries daily in the summer months – a passenger ferry that leaves Koman at 9am and a car ferry that leaves Koman at 10am. However, the car ferry didn't run in 2012 due to declining demand, and so it's likely that in future only the passenger ferry will run. Check www.journeytovalbona.com for the latest information.

The passenger ferry (500 lekë per person) arrives in Fierzë at around 1pm and is met by *furgons* that will take you to either Bajram Curri (200 lekë) or to Valbonë (400 lekë). There's no real reason to stay in Bajram Curri though, unless you plan to head to Kosovo. Hikers will want to head straight for Valbonë, where you can stay for a night or two before doing the stunning day hike to Theth, where you can stay for another night or two before taking a *furgon* back to Shkodra.

lonia or haggling for antiques in an Ottoman bazaar in Kruja.

Kruja

📞 0511 / POP 20,000

Kruja is Skanderbeg's town. Yes, Albania's hero was born here, and although it was over 500 years ago, there's still a great deal of pride in the fact that he and his forces defended Kruja from the Ottomans until his death. As soon as you get off the *furgon,* you're face to knee with a statue of Skanderbeg wielding his mighty sword with one hand, and it just gets more Skanderdelic after that.

From the road below, Kruja's houses appear to sit in the lap of a mountain. An ancient castle juts out to one side, and the massive Skanderbeg Museum juts out of the castle itself. The local plaster industry is going strong so expect visibility-reducing plumes of smoke to cloud views of the Adriatic Sea. Kruja's sights can be covered in a few hours, making this an ideal town to visit en route to Tirana's airport.

👁 Sights

Castle   CASTLE

(⊙24hr) Inside Kruja's sprawling castle grounds are Albania flag sellers, pizza restaurants and an array of mildly interesting sights, though few actually castle-related.

National Ethnographic Museum   MUSEUM

(admission 300 lekë; ⊙9am-1pm & 4-7pm Tue-Sun) This traditional home in the castle complex below the Skanderbeg Museum is one of the best in the country. Set in an original 19th-century Ottoman house that belonged to the affluent Toptani family, this museum shows the level of luxury and self-sufficiency the household maintained by producing its own food, drink, leather and weapons. They even had their very own mini *hammam* (Turkish bath) and watermill. The walls are lined with original frescos from 1764. The English-speaking guide's detailed explanations are excellent; offer a tip if you can.

Skanderbeg Museum   MUSEUM

(admission 200 lekë; ⊙9am-1pm & 4-7pm Tue-Sun) Designed by Enver Hoxha's daughter and son-in-law, this museum opened in 1982, and its spacious seven-level interior displays replicas of armour and paintings depicting Skanderbeg's struggle against the Ottomans. The museum is something of a secular shrine, and takes itself very seriously indeed, with giant statues and dramatic battle murals.

Teqe   MOSQUE

A short scramble down the cobblestone lane are the remains of a small *hammam* as well as a functioning *teqe* – a small place of worship for those practising the Bektashi branch of Islam. This beautifully decorated *teqe* has been maintained by

KRUJA: ENTERING SKANDERBEG'S TOWN

At a young age, Gjergj Kastrioti, the son of an Albanian prince, was handed over as a hostage to the Turks, who converted him to Islam and gave him a military education at Edirne in Turkey. There he became known as Iskander (after Alexander the Great) and Sultan Murat II promoted him to the rank of bey (governor), thus the name Skanderbeg.

In 1443 the Turks suffered a defeat at the hands of the Hungarians at Niš in present-day Serbia, and nationally minded Skanderbeg took the opportunity to abandon the Ottoman army and Islam and rally his fellow Albanians against the Turks. Skanderbeg made Kruja his seat of government between 1443 and 1468. Among the 13 Turkish invasions he subsequently repulsed was that led by his former commander, Murat II. Pope Calixtus III named Skanderbeg the 'captain general of the Holy See' and Venice formed an alliance with him. The Turks besieged Kruja four times. Though beaten back in 1450, 1466 and 1467, they finally took control of Kruja in 1478 (after Skanderbeg's death).

successive generations of the Dollma family since 1789. Skanderbeg himself reputedly planted the knotted olive tree at the front.

Bazaar
MARKET

This Ottoman-style bazaar is the country's best place for souvenir shopping and has WWII medical kits, antique gems and quality traditional ware, including beautifully embroidered tablecloths, copper coffee pots and plates. You can watch women using looms to make *kilims* (rugs) and purchase the results.

❶ Getting There & Away

Kruja is 32km from Tirana. Make sure your *furgon* from Tirana (150 lekë, 30 minutes) is going to Kruja, not just Fush Kruja, the modern town below. It is very easy to reach the airport (150 lekë, 15 minutes) by *furgon* or taxi from here, and it's en route to Shkodra, though you'll need to pull over a bus on the busy Tirana–Shkodra highway as they don't drive up the mountain into the town itself.

Durrës
☏052

Durrës was once – albeit briefly – Albania's capital. It's now virtually an extension of Tirana, joined to the capital by a ceaseless urban corridor full of hypermarkets and car dealerships. Blessed with a decent 10km stretch of beach, Durrës is sadly a lesson in unplanned development; hundreds of hotels stand side by side, and it's terribly crowded in the summer months. Despite this, there's an interesting amphitheatre

to see, although the famous archaeological museum on the seafront has been demolished and a new one is currently being built on the same site.

◉ Sights

Amphitheatre of Durrës
RUINS

(Rr e Kalasë; admission 300 lekë; ◷9am-7pm) The Amphitheatre of Durrës was built on the hillside inside the city walls in the early 2nd century AD. In its prime it had the capacity to seat 15,000 to 20,000 spectators, but these days a few inhabited houses occupy the stage, a reminder of its recent rediscovery (in 1966) and excavation. The Byzantine chapel in the amphitheatre has several beautiful mosaics. There are knowledgable English-speaking guides on site daily until 3pm; they work on a tipping basis.

▦ Sleeping

Hotel Ani
HOTEL €€

(☏224 228; anihoteldurres@yahoo.it; 1 Shëtitorja Taulantia; r from €60; ℗❋⊚) This very smart property faces the site of the new archaeological museum and backs onto the seafront. The smart and classy lobby gives way to spacious and comfortable rooms, and service is friendly and efficient.

Nais Hotel
HOTEL €€

(☏230 375, 052 224 940; hotelnais@hotmail.com; Rr Lagja 1, off Bul Epidamni; r €25-40; ❋⊚) Just a short wander from the amphitheatre in the centre of town, this friendly family-run place is a comfortable midrange option. Rooms are clean and modern, with a good breakfast served downstairs and the beachfront just moments away.

✕ Eating & Drinking

Palma ITALIAN €€
(Rr Taulantia; mains 400-1000 lekë) One of the better bets on the busy and commercial seafront, this smart place has a large menu of pizza, grills and fish dishes, and is a great spot to soak up the passing crowds.

Bar Torra BAR
(Sheshi Mujo Ulqinaku) This Venetian tower was opened by a team of local artists and was one of the first private cafes in Albania. There are art displays (and cosy nooks) downstairs, and in summer you can gaze around Durrës from the top of the tower.

❶ Getting There & Away

BOAT Agencies around the train station sell tickets for the many ferry lines plying the Durrës–Bari route (single deck €40, eight hours). **Venezia Lines** (☑052 383 83; www.venezialines.com) has the fastest boat to Bari (€60, 3½ hours). Ferries also depart Durrës for Ancona most days in summer (€65, 17 hours) and at least three days a week throughout the year.

BUS & FURGON *Furgons* (200 lekë, one hour) and buses (150 lekë, one hour) to Tirana leave from beside the train station when they're full. Buses leave for Shkodra at 7.30am and 1.30pm (400 lekë, three hours). In summer, long-distance buses and *furgons* going to and from Saranda, Gjirokastra, Fier and Berat (400 lekë, 1½ hours) bypass this station, picking up and dropping off passengers at the end of Plazhi i Durrësi, east of the harbour, which can be reached by the 'Plepa' orange municipal bus (30 lekë, 10 minutes). In July and August many buses connect Durrës with Pristina in Kosovo (€15, five hours).

TRAIN Seven trains a day head to Tirana (70 lekë, one hour, 6.15am, 8.45am, 9.20am, 1.05pm, 3.12pm, 4.45pm and 8.05pm). Trains also depart for Shkodra (1.05pm), Pogradec (6.45am), Elbasan (6.45am, 3.25pm) and Vlore (5.35pm). Check at the station for changes in departure times.

Apollonia

The ruined city of ancient **Apollonia** (admission 700 lekë; ☉9am-5pm) is 12km west of Fier, which is 90km south of Durrës. Set on rolling hills among olive groves, with impressive views all around, Apollonia (named after the god Apollo) was founded by Greeks from Corinth and Corfu in 588 BC and quickly grew into an important city-state, which minted its own currency and benefited from a robust slave trade. Under the Romans (from 229 BC), the city became a great cultural centre with a famous school of philosophy.

Julius Caesar rewarded Apollonia with the title 'free city' for supporting him against Gnaeus Pompeius Magnus (Pompey the Great) during the civil war in the 1st century BC, and sent his nephew Octavius, the future Emperor Augustus, to complete his studies here.

After a series of military and natural disasters (including an earthquake in the 3rd century AD that turned the river into a malarial swamp), the population moved southward into present-day Vlora, and by the 5th century only a small village with its own bishop remained at Apollonia.

There is far less to see at Apollonia than there is at Butrint, but there are some picturesque ruins within the 4km of city walls, including a small original theatre and the elegant pillars on the restored facade of the city's 2nd-century-AD administrative centre. You may be able to see the 3rd-century-BC **House of Mosaics** from a distance, though they're often covered up with sand for protection from the elements. Inside the **Museum of Apollonia** complex is the Byzantine monastery and Church of St Mary, which has gargoyles on the outside pillars. Much of the site remains to be excavated, but recent discoveries include a necropolis outside the castle walls with graves from the Bronze and Iron ages.

❶ Getting There & Away

Apollonia is best visited on a day trip from Tirana, Durrës, Vlora or Berat.

Furgons depart for the site (50 lekë) from Fier's '24th August Bar' (ask locals for directions). From Fier, *furgons* head to Durrës (200 lekë, 1½ hours), Tirana (400 lekë, two hours), Berat (300 lekë, one hour) and Vlora (200 lekë, 45 minutes).

If you'd prefer not to wait for the *furgon*, a taxi will charge approximately 500 lekë one way from Fier.

Berat

☑032 / POP 71,000
A highlight of any trip to Albania is a visit to beautiful Berat. Its most striking feature is the collection of white Ottoman houses climbing up the hill to its castle, earning it the title of 'town of a thousand windows' and helping it join Gjirokastra on the list

of Unesco World Heritage sites in 2008. Its rugged mountain setting is particularly evocative when the clouds swirl around the tops of the minarets, or break up to show the icy top of Mt Tomorri.

The old quarters are lovely ensembles of whitewashed walls, tiled roofs and cobblestone roads. Surrounding the town, olive and cherry trees decorate the gentler slopes, while pine woods stand on the steeper inclines. The modern town is dominated by the huge dome of the brand-new Berat University, while elsewhere the bridges over the Osumi River to the charmingly unchanged Gorics side include a 1780 seven-arched stone footbridge.

In the 3rd century BC an Illyrian fortress called Antipatrea was built here on the site of an earlier settlement. The Byzantines strengthened the hilltop fortifications in the 5th and 6th centuries, as did the Bulgarians 400 years later. The Serbs, who occupied the citadel in 1345, renamed it Beligrad, or 'White City'. In 1450 the Ottoman Turks took the town. After a period of decline, in the 18th and 19th centuries the town began to thrive as a crafts centre specialising in woodcarving. Berat today is now a big centre for tourism in Albania, though it has managed to retain its easygoing charm and friendly atmosphere.

◉ Sights

TOP CHOICE Kalasa
CASTLE

(admission 100 lekë, audio guide 500 lekë; ⊘24hr) The neighbourhood inside the castle's walls still lives and breathes; if you walk around this busy, ancient neighbourhood for long enough you'll invariably stumble into someone's courtyard thinking it's a church or ruin (no one seems to mind, though). In spring and summer the fragrance of chamomile is in the air (and underfoot), and wildflowers burst from every gap between the stones. The highest point is occupied by the Inner Fortress, where ruined stairs lead to a Tolkienesque water reservoir. Views are spectacular in all directions.

TOP CHOICE Onufri Museum
GALLERY

(admission 200 lekë; ⊘9am-1pm & 4-7pm May-Sep, 9am-4pm Oct-Apr, closed Mon) Kala was traditionally a Christian neighbourhood, but fewer than a dozen of the 20 churches remain. The quarter's biggest church, **Church of the Dormition of St Mary** (Kisha Fjetja e Shën Mërisë), is the site of the Onufri Museum. The church itself dates from 1797 and was built on the foundations of a 10th-century church. Onufri's spectacular 16th-century artworks are displayed on the ground level along with a beautifully gilded iconostasis.

Churches & Chapels
CHURCHES

Ask at the Onufri Museum if you can see the other churches and tiny chapels in Kala, including **St Theodore** (Shën Todher), close to the citadel gates; the substantial and picturesque **Church of the Holy Trinity** (Kisha Shën Triades), below the upper fortress; and the little chapels of **St Mary Blachernae** (Shën Mëri Vllaherna) and **St Nicholas** (Shënkolli). Some of the churches date back to the 13th century. Also keep an eye out for the **Red Mosque**, by the southern Kala walls, which was the first in Berat and dates back to the 15th century.

Chapel of St Michael
CHURCH

Perched on a cliff ledge below the citadel is the artfully positioned little chapel of St Michael (Shën Mihell), best viewed from the Gorica quarter.

Ethnographic Museum
MUSEUM

(admission 200 lekë; ⊘9am-1pm & 4-7pm May-Sep, 9am-4pm Oct-Apr, closed Mon) Down from the castle, this museum is in an 18th-century Ottoman house that's as interesting as the exhibits. The ground floor has displays of traditional clothes and the tools used by silversmiths and weavers, while the upper storey has kitchens, bedrooms and guest rooms decked out in traditional style. Check out the *mafil*, a kind of mezzanine looking into the lounge where the women of the house could keep an eye on male guests (and see when their cups needed to be filled). There are information sheets in Italian, French and English.

Mangalem Quarter
NEIGHBOURHOOD

Down in the traditionally Muslim Mangalem quarter, there are three grand mosques. The 16th-century **Sultan's Mosque** (Xhamia e Mbretit) is one of the oldest in Albania. The **Helveti teqe** behind the mosque has a beautiful carved ceiling and was specially designed with acoustic holes to improve the quality of sound during meetings. The Helveti, like the Bektashi, are a dervish order, or brotherhood, of Muslim mystics. The big mosque on the town square is the 16th-century **Lead Mosque** (Xhamia e Plumbit), so named because of the lead coating its sphere-shaped domes. The 19th-century **Bachelors' Mosque** (Xhamia e Beqarëvet) is down by the Osumi River; look for the enchanting paintings on its external walls. This mosque was built for unmarried shop assistants and junior craftsmen, and is perched between some fine Ottoman-era shopfronts along the river.

🏃 Activities

Bogove Waterfall
HIKING

Catch the 8am or 9am *furgon* to Bogove via Skrappar, or a later bus to Polican then transfer to a *furgon* to Bogove. Lunch at Taverna Dafinat above the bus stop, then follow the path along the river (starting on the Berat side) to this icy waterfall.

Çobo Winery
WINE TASTING

(☎122 088; www.cobowineryonline.com; ☻) The Çobo family winery is the best known in Albania, and it's worth checking out. Try its Shesh i Bardhe, Trebiano, Shesh i Izi and Kashmer wines, and, of course, its Raki me Arra. Any bus/*furgon* heading to Tirana can drop you off at the winery for 100 lekë.

Albania Rafting Group
TOURS

(☎2006 621; www.albrafting.com) This pioneering group runs rafting tours for all levels to some stunning gorges around Berat and Permet. Everyone from children to pensioners is welcome, and the various tours start at around €20 to €65 per person per day.

🛏 Sleeping & Eating

TOP CHOICE ### Hotel Mangalemi
HOTEL €€

(☎068 2323 238, 232 093; www.mangalemihotel.com; Rr Mihail Komneno; r from €35; ⓟ🛜) This hotel is housed in two sprawling Ottoman houses where all the rooms are beautifully furnished in traditional Berati style and balconies give superb views. Its terrace restaurant has great Albanian food with bonus views of Mt Tomorri. It's on the left side of the cobblestone road leading to the castle, just a short wander from the town centre.

TOP CHOICE ### Berat Backpackers
HOSTEL €

(☎069 474 8060, 069 3064 429; www.beratbackpackers.com; Gorica; tent/dm/r €7/12/28; ☻Apr-Nov; @🛜) Albania's best hostel is the brainchild of Englishman Scott; he's transformed a traditional house in the Gorica quarter (across the river from Mangalem)

into a vine-clad hostel with a basement bar, alfresco drinking area and a cheery, relaxed atmosphere that money can't buy. There's a shaded camping area on the terrace, cheap laundry available, two airy dorms with original ceilings, and one excellent-value double room that shares the bathroom facilities with the dorms.

Hotel Muzaka
HOTEL €€

(☎231 999; www.hotelmuzaka.com; Gorica; s/d from €40/50; ⓟ✳🛜) This superb new addition to Berat's hotel scene is a careful restoration of an old stone mansion on the riverfront in Gorica, just over the footbridge from the centre of town. Wooden floorboards, gorgeous bathrooms and beautifully chosen pieces of furniture in the 10 spacious rooms make this a good option for those looking for some style as well as tradition in their accommodation.

White House
ITALIAN €€

(Rr Santa Lucia; mains 200-1000 lekë; ☻8am-11pm) On the main road that runs north of the river, this smart place has a superb roof terrace with sweeping views over Berat, and serves up a mean pizza to boot. There's also a classier dining room downstairs with air-conditioning, perfect for a blowout meal.

Antigoni
ALBANIAN €€

(mains 600 lekë) This bustling restaurant may have an unusual style of service (some call it ignoring), but the Mangalem and Osumi River views from its upper levels are outstanding, and the food and local wine are both good.

ℹ Information

The town's **information centre** (www.bashkia-berat.com) is located in the council building, parallel to the Osumi River in new Berat.

ℹ Getting There & Away

Buses and *furgons* run between Tirana and Berat (400/500 lekë, 2½ hours) half-hourly until 3pm. From Tirana, buses leave from the 'Kombinati' station (catch the municipal bus from Sheshi Skënderbej to Kombinati for 30 lekë). In Berat, buses depart from and arrive in Sheshi Teodor Muzaka next to the Lead Mosque in the centre of town. There are buses to Vlora (350 lekë, 2½ hours, hourly until 2pm), Durrës (300 lekë, 1½ hours, five per day) and Saranda (1200 lekë, six hours, two daily at 8am and 2pm) via Gjirokastra (1000 lekë, four hours).

SOUTHERN COAST

With rough mountains falling head-first into bright blue seas, this area is wild and ready for exploration. The coastal drive between Vlora and Saranda is easily one of the most spectacular in Eastern Europe and shouldn't missed by any visitor to Albania. While beaches can be jam-packed in August, there's plenty of space, peace and happy-to-see-you faces in the low season. Sadly, the poorly planned development in the past decade has rather blighted many of the once-charming coastal villages, but there's still plenty of untouched beauty to be found here.

Vlora

033 / POP 184,000

It's here in sunny Vlora (the ancient Aulon) that the Adriatic Sea meets the Ionian, but the beaches are muddy and grubby, and the port town has really outgrown itself and is now a morass of overdevelopment. History buffs will still enjoy the museums and historic buildings, while beach lovers should hold out for the villages of Dhërmi, Drymades or Jal, all further south.

☉ Sights

Sheshi i Flamurit   SQUARE
At Sheshi i Flamurit (Flag Sq), near the top of Sadik Zotaj, a magnificent socialist-realist **Independence Monument** stands proud against the sky with the flag bearer hoisting the double-headed eagle into the blue. Near the base of the monument lies the grave of local Ismail Qemali, the country's first prime minister.

Ethnographic Museum   MUSEUM
(Sheshi i Flamurit; admission 100 lekë; ⊘9am-noon Mon-Sat) This ethnographic museum is jam-packed with relics of Albanian life. It's hidden behind an inconspicuous metal fence.

Muzeu Historik   MUSEUM
(Rr Ismail Qemali; ⊘8am-2pm daily, 5-8pm Tue-Thu in summer.) This antiquities museum opposite the ethnographic museum and just off Vlora's main square, Sheshi i Flamurit, has been renovated and has a good collection of ancient artefacts including Bronze Age relics and items from the Roman era. Labelling is spotty, however.

Muradi Mosque   MOSQUE
The 16th-century Muradi Mosque is a small elegant structure made of red and white stone, with a modest minaret; its exquisite design is attributed to one of the greatest Ottoman architects, Albanian-born Sinan Pasha.

National Museum of Independence   MUSEUM
(admission 100 lekë; ⊘9am-1pm & 5-8pm Tue-Sun) Down by the harbour, the National Museum of Independence is housed in the villa that became the headquarters of Albania's first government in 1912. The preserved offices, historic photographs and famous balcony make it an interesting place to learn about Albania's short-lived, but long-remembered, 1912 independence.

❶ Getting There & Away

BUS & FURGON Buses (500 lekë, four hours) and furgons (600 lekë, three hours) to Tirana and Durrës (500 lekë, 2½ hours) whiz back and forth from 4am until 7pm. Buses to Saranda (900 lekë, six hours) and on to Gjirokastra (1000 lekë, seven hours) leave at 7am and 12.30pm. There are nine buses a day to Berat (300 lekë, two hours). Buses leave from Rr Rakip Malilaj; departures to Athens (€25) and cities in Italy (from €70) depart from Muradi Mosque.

FERRY Vlora to Brindisi in Italy takes around six hours. From Monday to Saturday there are

---

LLOGARAJA PASS NATIONAL PARK

Reaching the pine-tree-clad Llogaraja Pass National Park (1025m) is a highlight of travels in Albania. If you've been soaking up the sun on the southern coast's beaches, it seems impossible that after a steep hairpin-bend climb you'll be up in the mountains tucking into spit-roasted lamb and homemade wine. There's great scenery up here, including the pisha flamur (flag pine) – a tree resembling the eagle design on the Albanian flag. Watch clouds descending onto the mountain, shepherds on the plains guiding their herds, and thick forests where deer, wild boar and wolves roam. Check out the resident deer at the Tourist Village before heading across the road to the cute family-run cabins at **Hotel Andoni** (☎068 240 0929; cabins 4000 lekë). The family does a wonderful lamb roast lunch (800 lekë) here.

departures from Brindisi at 11pm and Vlora at noon (deck €35). There are also ferries to Corfu during the summer months with Finikas Lines.

TRAIN The daily train departs Tirana for Vlora at 4.30pm and Vlora for Tirana at 4.30am (250 lekë, five hours).

Drymades

As you zigzag down the mountain from the Llogaraja Pass National Park, the white crescent-shape beaches and azure waters lure you from below. The first beach before the alluvial fan is Palasa, and it's one of the last bar/restaurant/hotel-free beaches around.

The next beach along is Drymades beach. Turn right just after the beginning of the walk down to Dhërmi beach and you'll be on the sealed road that twists through olive groves. After a 20-minute walk you'll be on its rocky white beach.

🛏 Sleeping & Eating

TOP CHOICE Sea Turtle CAMPGROUND €
(☏069 4016 057; per person incl half-board from 1000 lekë; ☺Jun-Sep) This great little set-up is run by two brothers. Each summer they turn the family orange orchard into a vibrant tent city, and the price includes the tent (with mattresses, sheets and pillows), breakfast and a family-cooked dinner (served up in true camp style). Hot showers are under the shade of old fig trees.

Drymades Inn Resort CABINS €€
(☏069 2074 004, 069 2074 000; www.drymades-inn.al; s/d €40/60; [P][❄][✳][🕸][🏊]) This attractive constellation of blue-painted timber cabins under the shade of pine trees is just a step away from the blue sea and the glorious beach. There's a bar, restaurant and shaded playground, plus a classic beach bar with a straw roof. Prices halve off-peak, which is by far the best time to come, as in high summer it's rammed.

Dhërmi

Dhërmi beach is well and truly under the tourist trance in summer: expect booked-out accommodation and an almost unbearable rubbish problem. Despite this, there is fun to be had, and, if techno isn't your style, there's peace and quiet to be had, too. It's made up of lovely rocky outcrops, Mediterranean-blue water and tiny coves.

The beach is 1.5km below the Vlora–Saranda road, so ask the driver to stop at the turn-off on the Llogaraja side of the village. From here it's an easy 10-minute walk downhill.

🛏 Sleeping & Eating

Blu Blu CABINS €€
(☏068 6090 485; r from €80; ☺May-Oct; [✳][🕸]) Hello? Whose stroke of genius is this? Turn left at the bottom of the road to Dhërmi, and follow the road almost to its end. Here you'll find one of the best 'no disco' beachside spots in Albania. Little white cabins with sea views sit among banana trees, and the bar/restaurant serves great food. Rooms start at €30 in May.

Hotel Greccia HOTEL €€
(☏069 6848 858, 069 5302 850; joanna_nino@hotmail.com; r from €60; [P][✳][🕸]) This smart five-floor place is on the hillside just above the village on the road down from the coastal highway. It's well set up for a comfortable stay, with balconies giving great views over the sea or back towards the mountains, and sleekly minimalist rooms that are kept spotlessly clean.

Hotel Luciano RESTAURANT €€
(mains 400-700 lekë) Sure, the mosaic on the wall of this waterfront pizza and pasta joint says 'no', but it's a resounding 'yes' to its wood-fired pizzas. It's the first place you'll find after walking down the hill from the main road.

Himara

☏0393 / POP 4500
This sleepy town has fine beaches, a couple of pleasant Greek seafood tavernas, some smart modern hotels and an interesting Old Town high on the hill. Most of the ethnic Greek population left in the 1990s, but many have returned – Greek remains the mother tongue of its people. The lower town comprises three easily accessible rocky beaches and the town's hotels and restaurants. The main Vlora–Saranda road passes the entrance to the hilltop castle, which, like Berat's, still houses many people. A taxi to the castle from Himara costs 300 lekë.

🛏 Sleeping

Rapo's Resort LUXURY HOTEL €€€
(☏22 856; www.raposresorthotel.com; s & d €120-130; [✳][🕸][🏊]) This top-end resort has smart

interior design, sparkling bathrooms and great service. It's near the beach, and also houses a massive swimming pool. For €9 anyone can relax by the pool for the day. Annoyingly at these high prices, wireless is limited to the lobby.

Kamping Himare CAMPGROUND €
(☑068 5298 940; www.himaracamping.com; tent per person 800 lekë; ۩Jun-Sep) Midnight movies in an open-air cinema add to the appeal of this camping ground across the road from the beach in an olive and orange grove. Tent rate includes mattresses, sheets and pillows. Try the restaurant's sublime pancakes (100 lekë) for breakfast.

Manolo BOUTIQUE HOTEL €€
(☑22 375; d €50) Right by the main beach in the centre of the village, Manolo is a cool bar downstairs with four contemporary and comfortable rooms that show good attention to detail and have sea views.

ⓘ Getting There & Away

Buses to Saranda and Vlora pass through Himara in the early morning; check with locals exactly when, as schedules change all the time.

Vuno & Jal

Less than 10 minutes' drive from Himara is Vuno, a tiny hillside village above a picturesque beach (Jal, pronounced Yal). Outdoor Albania renovated Vuno's primary school, and each summer its classrooms are filled with blow-up beds and it becomes **Shkolla Hostel** (☑068 4682 353, 068 3133 451; www.tiranahostel.com; tent/dm €4/7; ۩late Jun-Aug). What it lacks in infrastructure and privacy it makes up for with its goat-bell soundtrack and evening campfire. From Vuno, walk over the bridge and follow the rocky path to your right past the cemetery.

It's a challenging 40-minute signed walk through olive groves to picturesque Jal, or a 5km walk along the main beach road. Jal was a victim of the permit police a few years ago, and since then new structures have taken on a temporary tone. Jal has two beaches; one has free camping while the other has a **camping ground** (including tent 2000 lekë) set back from the sea. Fresh seafood is bountiful in Jal and there are plenty of beachside restaurants in summer.

Saranda

☑0852 / POP 37,700
Saranda has grown rapidly in the past decade; skeletal high-rises crowd around its horseshoe shape and hundreds more are being built in the outlying region. Saranda is bustling in summer – buses are crowded with people carrying swimming paraphernalia and the weather means it's almost obligatory to go for a swim. A daily stream of Corfu holidaymakers take the 45-minute ferry trip to Albania, add the Albanian stamp to their passports and hit Butrint or the Blue Eye Spring before heading back.

The town's name comes from Ayii Saranda, an early monastery dedicated to 40 saints; its bombed remains (including some preserved frescos) are still high on the hill above the town. The town was called Porto Edda for a period in the 1940s, after Mussolini's daughter.

Saranda's stony beaches are quite decent and there are plenty of sights in and around town, including the mesmerising ancient archaeological site of Butrint and the hypnotic Blue Eye Spring. Between Saranda and Butrint, the lovely beaches and islands of Ksamil are perfect for a dip after a day of exploring.

Four main streets arc around Saranda's bay, including the waterfront promenade that becomes prime *xhiro* (evening walk) territory in the evening.

ⓞ Sights

Synagogue RUINS
(Rr Skënderbeu; ۩24hr) This 5th-century synagogue is centrally located and is evidence of one of the earliest Balkan-Jewish communities.

Museum of Archaeology MUSEUM
(Rr Flamurit; ۩9am-2pm & 4-9pm) This office-like building houses a well-preserved 6th-century mosaic floor in its basement and has an interesting display about nearby Butrint. It's one block behind the harbour.

Castle of Lëkurësit CASTLE
This former castle is now a restaurant with superb views over Saranda and Butrint lagoon, especially at sunset. A taxi there costs about 1000 lekë return; arrange a time for the driver to pick you up, or it's a 15-minute walk up from the Saranda–Tirana road.

🛏 Sleeping

Hotel Porto Eda   HOTEL €€

(www.portoeda.com; Rr Jonianët; r €50; P☀️📶) Referencing the temporary name given to Saranda during the fascist occupation, this hotel is nevertheless a charming place and about as central as you can get, overlooking the harbour. The 24 rooms are comfortably and stylishly laid out, most with balconies, and the welcome is warm.

SR Backpackers   HOSTEL €

(📞069 4345 426; www.backpackerssr.hostel.com; Rr Mitat Hoxha 10; dm €11; @📶) The hostel with the most central location in Saranda, this is also the cheapest option. Housed in an apartment and hosted by the gregarious English-speaking Tomi, the 14 beds here are spread over three dorms, each with its own balcony. There's one shared bathroom, a communal kitchen and a friendly atmosphere.

Hairy Lemon   HOSTEL €

(📞069 3559 317; www.hairylemonhostel.com; cnr Mitat Hoxha & E Arberit; dm €12; 📶) With a prime 8th-floor location, a clean beach at its base and a friendly, helpful atmosphere, this Irish-run backpacker hostel is a good place to chill out. There's an open-plan kitchen and lounge, and two dorm rooms with fans and sea breezes. Follow the port road for around 10 minutes and continue when it becomes dirt; it's the orange-and-yellow apartment block on your right.

Hotel Palma   HOTEL €€

(📞22 929; Rr Mitat Hoxha; r from €30; ❄️🏊) Right next to the port, this hotel is good value and an easy walk into the town. Some rooms have great views with large balconies and all are super-clean. If you're up for it, guests get free entry into the on-site summer disco.

🍴 Eating

Veliani   ALBANIAN €€

(Bul Hasan Tahsini; mains 450-1100 lekë) Right in the heart of town, this upmarket place right on the waterfront isn't cheap, but does an excellent selection of Albanian dishes, including its signature octopus in red wine – a true local speciality.

Pizza Limani   PIZZA €€

(Bul Hasan Tahsini; pizza 400-800 lekë) The best pizza in town can be found on the seafront at this reliable and buzzing place with a giant terrace with superb harbour view and an excellent variety of tasty toppings on wood-fired oven-cooked dough.

Tani   SEAFOOD €

(mains 250-550 lekë) This portside seafood restaurant is run by chef Tani, who prides himself on serving dishes he's invented himself. The oven-baked filled mussels are a cheesy delight, and it's in a cool vine-draped location.

Dropulli   TRADITIONAL €

(cnr Rr Skënderbeu & Rr Mitro Dhmertika; mains 350 lekë) A local restaurant that has Albanian holidaymakers returning to it day after day has to be good, and vegetarians will love the melt-in-your-mouth stuffed peppers with tasty rice; ask for it to be served with potatoes.

ℹ Information

Banks with ATMs line the sea road (Rr 1 Maji) and the next street inland (Rr Skënderbeu).

Saranda's **ZIT information centre** (Rr Skënderbeu; ⏰8am-4pm Mon-Fri, 9am-2pm & 4-9pm Sat & Sun Oct-Jun, 8.30am-2pm & 4-10pm Jul-Sep) is the most established in Albania and provides information about transport and local sights. The newer, bigger tourist information centre on the promenade sells travel guides, souvenirs, Ismail Kadare novels and maps.

ℹ Getting There & Away

The ZIT information centre opposite the synagogue ruins has up-to-date bus timetables.

BUS The main bus station is uphill from the ruins on Rr Vangjel Pando. Municipal buses go to Butrint via Ksamil on the hour from 7am to 5pm (100 lekë, 30 minutes), leaving from the roundabout near the port and opposite ZIT. Buses to Tirana (1300 lekë, eight hours) via Gjirokastra (350 lekë) leave at 5am, 6.30am, 8.30am, 9.30am, 10.30am, 2pm and 10pm. The 5.30am and 9pm Tirana bus takes the coastal route (1300 lekë, eight hours) via Vlora (900 lekë). There are two buses and *furgons* an hour to Gjirokastra's new town (350 lekë, 1½ hours) – they all pass the turn-off to the Blue Eye Spring. Buses to Himara (400 lekë, two hours) leave around four times a day. Buses to the Greek border near Konispoli leave Saranda at 8am and 11am (200 lekë); otherwise you can reach the Greek border via Gjirokastra.

FERRY Finikas (📞067 2022 004, 260 57; www.finikas-lines.com; Rr Mithat Hoxha) at the port sells ferry tickets for Corfu with a daily departure at 10.30am (€19, 45 minutes). A slower boat departs daily at 4.30pm (€19, 90 minutes) and in summer a third ferry departs

Saranda at 4.30pm Thursdays, Saturdays and Sundays. From Corfu there are three ferries: one daily at 9am, one daily at 6.30pm and one at 9.15am Thursdays, Saturdays and Sundays. Note that Greek time is one hour ahead of Albanian time.

TAXI Taxis wait for customers at the bus stop and opposite Central Park on Rr Skënderbeu. A taxi to the Greek border at Kakavija costs 4000 lekë.

Around Saranda

BUTRINT

The ancient ruins of **Butrint** (www.butrint.org; admission 700 lekë; ⊙8am-dusk), 18km south of Saranda, are renowned for their size, beauty and tranquillity. They're in a fantastic natural setting and are part of a 29-sq-km national park. Set aside at least two hours to explore this fascinating place.

Although the site had been inhabited long before, Greeks from Corfu settled on the hill in Butrint (Buthrotum) in the 6th century BC. Within a century Butrint had become a fortified trading city with an acropolis. The lower town began to develop in the 3rd century BC, and many large stone buildings had already been built by the time the Romans took over in 167 BC. Butrint's prosperity continued throughout the Roman period, and the Byzantines made it an ecclesiastical centre. The city then went into a long decline and was abandoned until 1927, when Italian archaeologists arrived. These days Lord Rothschild's UK-based Butrint Foundation helps maintain the site.

As you enter the site the path leads to the right, to Butrint's 3rd-century-BC Greek theatre, secluded in the forest below the acropolis. Also in use during the Roman period, the theatre could seat about 2500 people. Close by are the small public baths, where geometric mosaics are buried under a layer of mesh and sand to protect them from the elements.

Deeper in the forest is a wall covered with crisp Greek inscriptions, and the 6th-century palaeo-Christian baptistry decorated with colourful mosaics of animals and birds, again under the sand. Beyond are the impressive arches of the 6th-century basilica, built over many years. A massive Cyclopean wall dating back to the 4th century BC is further on. Over one gate is a relief of a lion killing a bull, symbolic of a protective force vanquishing assailants.

The top of the hill is where the acropolis once was. There's now a castle here, housing an informative **museum** (⊙8am-4pm). The views from the museum's courtyard give you a good idea of the city's layout, and you can see the Vivari Channel connecting Lake Butrint to the Straits of Corfu. There are community-run stalls inside the gates where you can buy locally produced souvenirs.

ⓘ Getting There & Away

The municipal bus from Saranda to Butrint costs 100 lekë and leaves hourly from 7am to 5pm. It passes through Ksamil.

KSAMIL

Ksamil, 17km south of Saranda, has three small, dreamy islands within swimming distance and dozens of beachside bars and restaurants that open in the summer. The public Saranda–Butrint bus stops twice in the town (100 lekë; leaves hourly 1am to 5pm); either stop will get you to the pristine waters, though if you look closely you'll realise that the sand is trucked in.

Twenty-two kilometres east of Saranda, the **Blue Eye Spring** (Syri i Kaltër; per person/car 50/200 lekë) is a hypnotic pool of deep blue water surrounded by electric-blue edges like the iris of an eye. Bring your swimming gear and a towel, as it's a great spot for a dive into the cold water on a summer's day. It feeds the Bistrica River and its depth is unknown. It's a pleasant spot; blue dragonflies dash around the water, and the surrounding shady oak trees make a pleasant picnic spot, though it's often crowded in the summer months. There's a restaurant and cabins nearby. If you don't mind a 2km walk, any bus travelling between Saranda and Gjirokastra can drop you off at the spring's turn-off.

Hotel Joni (☏069 2091 554; s/d €20/25; ☏) is a clean hotel near the roundabout. There are plenty of 'rooms to rent' (averaging €20 per night) in private homes closer to the water, and seafood restaurants perch along the beachfront in summer.

EASTERN ALBANIA

Close to the Greek border and accessible from the Tirana–Saranda bus route is the Unesco World Heritage–listed town of Gjirokastra, surely one of Albania's most magical places and birthplace to two of its most famous sons. Expect bunker-covered mountains, winter-time snowfields and plenty of roads leading to Greece.

Gjirokastra

🖉 084 / POP 43,000

Defined by its castle, roads paved with chunky limestone and shale, imposing slate-roofed houses and views out to the Drina Valley, Gjirokastra is an intriguing hillside town described beautifully by Albania's most famous literary export and local-born author, Ismail Kadare (b 1936), in *Chronicles of Stone*. Archaeological evidence suggests there's been a settlement here for 2500 years, though these days it's the 600 'monumental' houses in town that attract visitors. Some of these magnificent houses, a blend of Ottoman and local architectural influence, have caved in on themselves, and Unesco funding is being spent to maintain them. Gjirokastra-born former dictator Enver Hoxha made sure his hometown was listed as a museum city, but after the fall of the communist regime the houses fell into disrepair.

◎ Sights

Gjirokastra Castle CASTLE
(admission 200 lekë; ⊙8am-8pm) The town's moody castle hosts an eerie collection of armoury and is the setting for Gjirokastra's folk festival (held every four or five years). There's been a fortress here since the 12th century, although much of what can be seen today dates to the early 19th century. It's definitely worth the steep walk up from the Old Town, as well as an extra 200 lekë to visit its interior Museum Kombetar and see prison cells and more armoury. One of the more quirky sights on display is that of a recovered US Air Force jet that was shot down during the communist era.

TOP CHOICE Zekate House HISTORIC BUILDING
(admission 200 lekë; ⊙9am-6pm) This incredible three-storey house dates from 1811 and has twin towers and a double-arched facade. It's fascinating to nose around the almost totally unchanged interiors of an Ottoman-era home, especially the upstairs galleries, which are the most impressive. The owners live next door and collect the payments; to get here, follow the signs past the Hotel Kalemi and keep zigzagging up the hill.

Skenduli House HISTORIC BUILDING
(Rr Ismail Kadare; admission 200 lekë; ⊙9am-7pm) The latest Ottoman-era mansion to receive a (partial) renovation, the Skenduli House is well worth a visit and desperately needs contributions to pay for the remaining restoration work. You'll most likely be shown around by Mr Skenduli himself, who speaks Italian and some basic French, but no English. The house dates from 1700 and has many fascinating features.

Ethnographic Museum MUSEUM
(admission 200 lekë; ⊙9am-6pm) This museum houses local homewares and was built on the site of Enver Hoxha's former house. Its collection is interesting if you're a fan of local arts and crafts, but don't come expecting anything about Hoxha himself.

Bazaar HISTORIC SITE
The 'Neck of the Bazaar' makes up the centre of the Old Town and contains artisan shops that support masters of the local stone- and wood-carving industries.

🛏 Sleeping

Definitely stay in the scenic Old Town, though there are accommodation options in the new town if you can't find a room.

TOP CHOICE Hotel Kalemi HOTEL €€
(🖉068 2234 373, 263 724; draguak@yahoo.com; Lagjia Palorto Gjirokastra; r €35; P🅿❄@🛜) This delightful, large Ottoman-style hotel has spacious rooms adorned with carved ceilings, antique furnishings and large communal areas, including a broad verandah with Drina Valley views. Some rooms even have fireplaces, though bathrooms can be on the cramped side. Breakfast (juice, tea, a boiled egg and bread with delicious fig jam) is an all-local affair.

Kotoni B&B B&B €
(🖉263 526, 069 2366 846; www.kotonihouse.com; Rr Bashkim Kokona 8; s/d from €20/25; P❄🛜) Hosts Haxhi and Vita look after you in true Albanian style here: they love Gjirokastra and are happy to pass on information, as well as pack picnics for guests' day trips. The fact that these rooms are 220 years old makes up for their small size, while the astonishing views and friendly cats further sweeten the deal. Laundry is available, and fishing trips and hikes can be arranged.

Hotel Çajupi HOTEL €€
(🖉269 010; www.cajupi.com; Sheshi Çerçiz Topulli; s/d/tr €30/40/55; ❄) Aside from its relatively gargantuan size, it's hard to tell

that this breezy and friendly place was once the default communist-era hotel for foreigners. Rooms are spacious, clean and pleasant. The hotel is located on the main square of the Old Town, perfectly situated for exploration. Breakfast is a fairly lame affair, but the rooftop restaurant affords great views.

Hotel Sopoti
HOSTEL €

(☑069 399 8922; Sheshi Çerçiz Topulli; per person 1000 lekë) The shared bathrooms here are extremely basic, but if you can get past that, this budget place is a steal. It boasts a great location in the heart of the Old Town, as well as clean rooms, many of which have gorgeous traditional floor tiles and balconies with superb valley views. If there's nobody at reception, go into the next-door cafe, where the owner works. Breakfast isn't included.

✖ Eating

TOP CHOICE Kujtimi
ALBANIAN €

(mains 200-600 lekë; ⊙11am-11pm) On the left-hand side of the path to Fantazia Restaurant is this wonderfully laid-back outdoor restaurant, run by the Dumi family. Try the delicious *trofte* (fried trout; 400 lekë), the *midhje* (fried mussels; 350 lekë) and *qifqi* (rice balls fried in herbs and egg, a local speciality). The terrace here is the perfect place to absorb the charms of the Old Town, and while it's popular with travellers, on a typical night it's still bustling with locals too.

Fantasia Restaurant
ALBANIAN €€

(mains 200-750 lekë; ⊙noon-11pm) This modern place doesn't exactly overflow with local colour or traditional charm, but it has a large menu ranging from pizza to Albanian dishes, pastas and meat grills that keeps tour groups happy. It's located by a viewpoint with great views across the valley.

ℹ Information

The new town (no slate roofs here) is on the main Saranda–Tirana road, and a taxi up to or back from the Old Town is 300 lekë.

Information Centre (⊙8am-4pm Mon-Fri, 9am-2pm & 4-9pm Sat & Sun Oct-Jun, 8.30am-2pm & 4-10pm Jul-Sep) Opposite Çajupi Hotel behind the statue of the partisans.

ℹ Getting There & Away

Buses pass through the new town on their way to Tirana and Saranda, and *furgons* also go to Saranda (300 lekë, one hour). It takes about an hour to get to the Blue Eye Spring from Gjirokastra; buses to and from Saranda pass by its entrance, which is 2km from the spring itself. Buses to Tirana (1200 lekë, seven hours) leave on the hour from 5am – the last one passes through after 11pm. There are also irregular *furgons* to Berat (1000 lekë, four hours). From the bottom of the hill leading from the Old Town, turn left and walk 800m to find the ad hoc bus station just after the Eida petrol station.

UNDERSTAND ALBANIA

Albania Today

Albania managed to manoeuvre itself around the crippling economic crisis that gripped other European countries in 2008, and economic growth has continued. Despite this, infrastucture deficiencies still plague the country. Albania joined NATO in 2009 and may well become an official EU membership candidate in 2013, if elections to be held then are deemed fair.

History

Albanians call their country Shqipëria, and trace their roots to the ancient Illyrian tribes. Their language is descended from Illyrian, making it a rare survivor of the Roman and Slavic influxes and a European linguistic oddity on a par with Basque. The Illyrians occupied the western Balkans during the 2nd millennium BC. They built substantial fortified cities, mastered silver and copper mining, and became adept at sailing the Mediterranean. The Greeks arrived in the 7th century BC to establish self-governing colonies at Epidamnos (now Durrës), Apollonia and Butrint. They traded peacefully with the Illyrians, who formed tribal states in the 4th century BC.

Roman, Byzantine & Ottoman Rule

Inevitably the expanding Illyrian kingdom of the Ardiaei, based at Shkodra, came into conflict with Rome, which sent a fleet of 200 vessels against Queen Teuta in 229 BC. A long war resulted in the extension of Roman control over the entire Balkan area by 167 BC.

Under the Romans, Illyria enjoyed peace and prosperity, though large agricultural estates were worked by slaves. The Illyrians preserved their own language and traditions despite Roman rule. Over time the populace slowly replaced their old gods with the new Christian faith championed by Emperor Constantine. The main trade route between Rome and Constantinople, the Via Egnatia, ran from the port at Durrës.

When the Roman Empire was divided in AD 395, Illyria fell within the Eastern Empire, later known as the Byzantine Empire. Three early Byzantine emperors (Anastasius I, Justin I and Justinian I) were of Illyrian origin. Invasions by migrating peoples (Visigoths, Huns, Ostrogoths and Slavs) continued through the 5th and 6th centuries.

In 1344 Albania was annexed by Serbia, but after the defeat of Serbia by the Turks in 1389 the whole region was open to Ottoman attack. The Venetians occupied some coastal towns, and from 1443 to 1468 the national hero Skanderbeg (Gjergj Kastrioti) led Albanian resistance to the Turks from his castle at Kruja. Skanderbeg won all 25 battles he fought against the Turks, and even Sultan Mehmet-Fatih, the conqueror of Constantinople, could not take Kruja. After Skanderbeg's death the Ottomans overwhelmed Albanian resistance, taking control of the country in 1479, 26 years after Constantinople fell.

Ottoman rule lasted 400 years. Muslim citizens were favoured and were exempted from the janissary system, whereby Christian households had to give up one of their sons to convert to Islam and serve in the army. Consequently, many Albanians embraced the new faith.

Independent Albania

In 1878 the Albanian League at Prizren (in present-day Kosovo) began a struggle for autonomy that the Turkish army put down in 1881. Further uprisings between 1910 and 1912 culminated in a proclamation of independence and the formation of a provisional government led by Ismail Qemali at Vlora in 1912. These achievements were severely compromised when Kosovo, roughly one-third of Albania, was ceded to Serbia in 1913. The Great Powers tried to install a young German prince, Wilhelm of Wied, as ruler, but he wasn't accepted and returned home after six months. With the outbreak of WWI, Albania was occupied in succession by the armies of Greece, Serbia, France, Italy and Austria-Hungary.

In 1920 the capital city was moved from Durrës to less vulnerable Tirana. A republican government under the Orthodox priest Fan Noli helped to stabilise the country, but in 1924 it was overthrown by the interior minister, Ahmed Bey Zogu. A northern warlord, he declared himself King Zogu I in 1928, but his close collaboration with Italy backfired in April 1939 when Mussolini ordered an invasion of Albania. Zogu fled to Britain with his young wife, Geraldine, and newborn son, Leka, and used gold looted from the Albanian treasury to rent a floor at London's Ritz Hotel.

On 8 November 1941 the Albanian Communist Party was founded with Enver Hoxha as first secretary, a position he held until his death in April 1985. The communists led

---

FAMILY FEUD WITH BLOOD AS THE PRIZE

The *Kanun* (Code) was formalised in the 15th century by powerful northern chieftain Lekë Dukagjin. It consists of 1262 articles covering every aspect of daily life: work, marriage, family, property, hospitality, economy and so on. Though the *Kanun* was suppressed by the communists, there has been a revival of its strict precepts in northern Albania.

According to the *Kanun*, the most important things in life are honour and hospitality. If a member of a family (or one of their guests) is murdered, it becomes the duty of the male members of that clan to claim their blood debt by murdering a male member of the murderer's clan. This sparks an endless cycle of killing that doesn't end until either all the male members of one of the families are dead, or reconciliation is brokered through respected village elders.

Hospitality is so important in these parts of Albania that the guest takes on a godlike status. There are 38 articles giving instructions on how to treat a guest – an abundance of food, drink and comfort is at his or her disposal, and it is also the host's duty to avenge the murder of his guest, should this happen during their visit. It's worth reading *Broken April*, by Ismail Kadare, a brilliant exploration of people living under the *Kanun*.

the resistance against the Italians and, after 1943, against the Germans.

Communist Albania

In January 1946 the People's Republic of Albania was proclaimed, with Hoxha as president and 'Supreme Comrade'.

In September 1948 Albania broke off relations with Yugoslavia, which had hoped to incorporate the country into the Yugoslav Federation. Instead, it allied itself with Stalin's USSR and put into effect a series of Soviet-style economic plans – raising the ire of the USA and Britain, which made an ill-fated attempt to overthrow the government.

Albania collaborated closely with the USSR until 1960, despite Krushchev's denunciation of Stalin in his 1954 'secret speech'. However, when a heavy-handed Khrushchev demanded that a submarine base be set up at Vlora in 1961, Albania broke off diplomatic relations with the USSR and reoriented itself towards Maoist China.

From 1966 to 1967 Albania experienced a Chinese-style cultural revolution. Administrative workers were suddenly transferred to remote areas and younger cadres were placed in leading positions. The collectivisation of agriculture was completed and organised religion was completely banned.

Following the Soviet invasion of Czechoslovakia in 1968, Albania left the Warsaw Pact and embarked on a self-reliant defence policy. Some 60,000 igloo-shaped concrete bunkers were built at this time, the crumbling remains of which can still be seen all over the country today. Under the communists, some malarial swamps were drained, hydroelectric schemes and railway lines were built, and the literacy level was raised. Albania's people, however, lived in fear of the Sigurimi (secret police) and were not permitted to leave the country. Many were tortured, jailed or murdered for misdemeanours such as listening to foreign radio stations.

With the death of Mao Zedong in 1976 and the changes that followed in China after 1978, Albania's unique relationship with China also came to an end, and the country was left totally isolated and without allies. The economy was devastated and food shortages became more common.

Post-Hoxha

Hoxha died in April 1985 and his associate Ramiz Alia took over the leadership. Res-

trictions loosened (Albania was opened up to tourists in organised groups) but people no longer bothered to work on the collective farms, leading to food shortages in the cities. Industries began to fail and Tirana's population tripled as people took advantage of being able to freely move to the city.

In June 1990, inspired by the changes that were occurring elsewhere in Eastern Europe, around 4500 Albanians took refuge in Western embassies in Tirana. After a brief confrontation with the police and the Sigurimi, these people were allowed to board ships for Brindisi in Italy, where they were granted political asylum.

Following student demonstrations in December 1990, the government agreed to allow opposition parties, and the Democratic Party, led by heart surgeon Sali Berisha, was formed.

The March 1992 elections ended 47 years of communist rule, with parliament electing Sali Berisha president. Former president Alia was later placed under house arrest for writing articles critical of the Democratic government, and the leader of the Socialist Party, Fatos Nano, was also arrested on corruption charges.

During this time Albania switched from a tightly controlled communist regime to a rambunctious free-market free-for-all. A huge smuggling racket sprang up in which stolen Mercedes-Benz cars were brought into the country, and the port of Vlora became a major crossing point for illegal immigrants from Asia and the Middle East into Italy.

In 1996, 70% of Albanians lost their savings when private pyramid-investment schemes, believed to have been supported by the government, collapsed. Riots ensued, elections were called, and the victorious Socialist Party under Nano – who had been freed from prison by a rampaging mob – was able to restore some degree of security and investor confidence.

In 1999 a different type of crisis struck when 465,000 Kosovars fled to Albania as a result of a Serbian ethnic-cleansing campaign. The influx had a positive effect on Albania's economy, and strengthened the relationship between Albania and Kosovo.

For the past decade Albania has found itself in a kind of mini-boom, with a lot of money being poured into construction projects and infrastructure renewal. The general election of 2005 saw a return of Berisha's Democratic Party to government, and in 2009 they narrowly won again, forming a coalition with the Socialist Movement for Intergration (LSI).

People

Albania's population is made up of approximately 95% Albanians, 3% Greeks and 2% 'other' – comprising Vlachs, Roma, Serbs, Macedonians and Bulgarians. The majority of young people speak some English, but speaking a few words of Albanian (or Italian, and, on the south coast, Greek) will be useful. Like most Balkan people, Albanians shake their heads sideways to say yes *(po)* and usually nod and 'tsk' to say no *(jo* – pronounced 'yo'*)*. Albanians familiar with foreigners often take on the nod-for-yes way, which increases confusion.

The Ghegs in the north and the Tosks in the south have different dialects, music, dress and the usual jokes about each other's weaknesses.

Albanians are nominally 70% Muslim, 20% Christian Orthodox and 10% Catholic, but more realistic statistics estimate that up to 75% of Albanians are nonreligious. Religion was ruthlessly stamped out by the 1967 cultural revolution, when all mosques and churches were taken over by the state. By 1990 only about 5% of Albania's religious buildings were left intact. The rest had been turned into cinemas or army stores, or were destroyed. Albania remains a very secular society.

The Muslim faith has a branch called Bektashism, similar to Sufism, and its world headquarters were in Albania from 1925 to 1945. Bektashi followers go to *teqe* (temple-like buildings without a minaret), which are found on hilltops in towns where those of the faith fled persecution. Most Bektashis live in the southern half of the country.

Arts

Literature

One Albanian writer who is widely read outside Albania is Ismail Kadare (b 1936). In 2005 he won the inaugural Man Booker International Prize for his body of work. His books are a great source of information on Albanian traditions, history and social events, and exquisitely capture the atmosphere of the country's towns, as in the lyrical descriptions of Kadare's birthplace, Gjirokastra, in *Chronicle in Stone* (1971). *Broken April* (1990), set in the northern highlands before the 1939 Italian invasion, describes the life of a village boy who is next in line in a desperate cycle of blood vendettas.

Cinema

During Albania's isolationist years the only Western actor approved by Hoxha was UK actor Sir Norman Wisdom (he became quite a cult hero). However, with so few international movies to choose from, the local film industry had a captive audience. While much of its output was propagandist, by the 1980s this little country was turning out an extraordinary 14 films a year. Despite a general lack of funds, two movies have gone on to win awards at international film festivals. Gjergj Xhuvani's comedy *Slogans* (2001) is a warm and touching account of life during communist times. This was followed in 2002 by *Tirana Year Zero*, Fatmir Koci's bleak look at the pressures on the young to emigrate. *Lorna's Silence* (2008), a film about Albanians living in Belgium, was awarded in the 2008 Cannes Film Festival.

Music

Blaring from cars, bars, restaurants and mobile phones – music is something you get plenty of in Albania. Most modern Albanian music has clarinet threaded through it and a goat-skin drum beat behind it. Polyphony, the blending of several independent vocal or instrumental parts, dates from ancient Illyrian times, and can still be heard, particularly in the south.

Visual Arts

One of the first signs of the Albanian arts scene are the multicoloured buildings of Tirana, a project organised by the capital's former mayor, Edi Rama, himself an artist. The building's residents don't get a say in the colour or design, and come home to find their homes daubed in spots, paintings of trees, or even paintings of laundry drying under their windowsills.

One of the most delicious Albanian art treats is to be found in Berat's Onufri Museum. Onufri was the most outstanding Albanian icon painter of the 16th and 17th centuries, and his work is noted for its unique intensity of colour, derived from natural dyes that are as fresh now as the day he painted with them.

Environment

Albania consists of 30% vast interior plains, 362km of coast and a mountainous spine that runs its length. Mt Korab, at 2764m, is Albania's highest peak.

The country's large and beautiful lakes include the Balkans' biggest, Lake Shkodra, which borders Montenegro in the north, and the ancient Lake Ohrid in the east (one-third Albanian, two-thirds Macedonian). Albania's longest river is the Drin (280km), which originates in Kosovo and is fed by melting snow from mountains in Albania's north and east. Hydroelectricity has changed Albania's landscape: Lake Koman was once a river, and the blue water from the Blue Eye Spring near Saranda travels to the coast in open concrete channels via a hydroelectricity plant. Agriculture makes up a small percentage of land use, and citrus and olive trees spice up the coastal plains. Most rural householders grow their own food.

National Parks & Wildlife

The number of national parks in Albania has risen from six to 15 since 1966 and include Dajti, Llogara, Tomorri, Butrint, Valbonë and Theth. Most are protected only by their remoteness, and tree-felling and hunting still take place. Hiking maps of the national parks are available, though they can be hard to find (try *Wanderkarte Nordalbanien* for Theth).

Albania's Alps have become a 'must-do' for hikers, and they're home to brown bear, wolf, otter, marten, wild cat, wild boar and deer. Falcons and grouse are also Alpine favourites, and birdwatchers can also flock to wetlands at Lake Butrint, Karavasta Lagoon and Lake Shkodra (though the wetlands aren't pristine).

Lake Ohrid's trout is endangered (but still eaten), and endangered loggerhead turtles nest on the Ionian coast and on the Karaburun Peninsula, where there have also been sightings of critically endangered Mediterranean monk seals.

Environmental Issues

During communism, there were around 2000 cars in the country. Now it seems everyone has one, with many of Albania's older cars being diesel Mercedes-Benzes stolen from Western Europe. As a consequence of the explosion, air-pollution levels in Tirana are five to 10 times higher than in Western European countries.

Illegal logging and fishing reached epidemic proportions during the 1990s, and there are signs of it today; fishing for the endangered *koran* trout in Lake Ohrid continues, as does fishing with dynamite along the coast.

Albania was practically litter-free until the early 1990s, as everything was reused or recycled, but today there's literally rubbish everywhere. Walk around the perimeter of a hotel in a picturesque location and you'll come across its very unpicturesque dumping ground. Some Albanians are doing their bit to improve these conditions, and a 'raising awareness' campaign against litter was started by well-known Albanians in 2010.

Food & Drink

In coastal areas the calamari, mussels and fish will knock your socks off, while high-altitude areas such as Llogaraja have roast lamb worth climbing a mountain for.

Offal is popular; *fërgesë Tiranë* is a traditional Tirana dish of offal, eggs and tomatoes cooked in an earthenware pot.

Italian influences mean vegetarians will probably become vegitalians, and many restaurants serve pizza, pasta or grilled and stuffed vegetables.

Local Drinks

Raki is very popular. The two main types are grape raki (the most common) and *mani* (mulberry) raki. Ask for homemade if possible *(raki ë bërë në shtëpi)*. If wine is more your cup of tea, seek out the Çobo winery near Berat and its Shesh i Bardhe white. Local beers include Tirana, Norga (from Vlora) and Korça. Coffee remains the standard drink of choice at any time of day.

SURVIVAL GUIDE

Directory A–Z
Accommodation

With almost every house, bar and petrol station doubling as a hotel, you might think you'll never have trouble finding a bed in Albania, and you're right, though seaside towns are often booked out in August.

Homestays abound in Theth, while the number of camping grounds is increasing; you'll find them at Himare, Livadhi, Dhërmi and Drymades (from €4 per person). Most have hot showers, on-site restaurants and entertainment.

All but the most basic places have free wireless internet for guests.

The following price categories for the cost of a double room in high season are used in the listings in this chapter.

€ less than €30

€€ €30 to €80

€€€ more than €80

Activities

Hiking and adventure sports are gaining popularity in Albania, and **Outdoor Albania** (☑2227 121; www.outdooralbania.com; Rr Sami Frasheri, Pallati Metropol) is an excellent organisation at the forefront of the industry. Smaller operatives are starting up: **Albania Rafting** (☑2006 621; www.albrafting.com) runs rafting tours of the Osumi River and canyons in Berat. Hiking in the Alps, particularly around Theth and Valbonë, is popular (with and without guides), as is mountain biking around the country.

Business Hours

Banks 9am to 3.30pm Monday to Friday

Cafes & Bars 8am to midnight

Offices 8am to 5pm Monday to Friday

Restaurants 8am to midnight

Shops 8am to 7pm; siesta time can be any time between noon and 4pm

Embassies & Consulates

There is no Australian, Canadian, New Zealand or Irish embassy in Albania. The following embassies and consulates are in Tirana:

French Embassy (☑04-238 9700; www.ambafrance-al.org; Rr Skënderbej 14)

German Embassy (☑04-2274 505; www.tirana.diplo.de; Rr Skënderbej 8)

Netherlands Embassy (☑04-2240 828; www.albanie.nlambassade.org; Rr Asim Zeneli 10)

UK Embassy (☑04-2234 973; www.ukinalbania.fco.gov.uk; Rr Skënderbej 12)

US Embassy (☑04-2247 285; http://tirana.usembassy.gov; Rr Elbasanit 103)

Food

The following price categories for the cost of a main course are used in the listings in this chapter.

€ less than 200 lekë

€€ 200 lekë to 500 lekë

€€€ more than 500 lekë

Gay & Lesbian Travellers

Extensive antidiscrimination legislation became law in 2010, but did not extend to legalising same-sex marriage. Gay and lesbian life in Albania is alive and well but is not yet organised into clubs or organisations. Gaydar will serve gay and lesbian visitors well here: you'll have to ask on the street or online where the parties are. The alternative music and party scene in Tirana is queer-friendly.

Internet Access

If you've brought your own smartphone or laptop you can access free wi-fi in most hotels and many restaurants around the country. Internet cafes (increasingly rare) cost around 100 lekë per hour.

Money

The lekë is the official currency, though the euro is widely accepted; you'll get a better rate in general if you use lekë. Accommodation is generally quoted in euros but can be paid in either currency. ATMs (found in most of Albania's towns, bar remote villages) usually offer to dispense cash in either currency.

Albanian banknotes come in denominations of 100, 200, 500, 1000, 2000 and 5000 lekë. There are five, 10, 20, 50 and 100 lekë coins.

Albanian lekë can't be exchanged outside the country, so exchange them or spend them before you leave.

Credit cards are accepted only in the larger hotels, shops and travel agencies, and few of these are outside Tirana.

It's polite to leave your change as a tip.

Post

The postal system is fairly rudimentary – there are no postcodes, for example – and it certainly does not enjoy a reputation for efficiency.

Public Holidays

New Year's Day 1 January

Summer Day 16 March

Nevruz 23 March

Catholic Easter March or April

Orthodox Easter March or April

May Day 1 May

Mother Teresa Day 19 October

Independence Day 28 November

Liberation Day 29 November

Christmas Day 25 December

Telephone

Albania's country phone code is ☑355 (dial ☑+ or ☑00 first from a mobile phone).

Three established mobile-phone providers are Vodafone, AMC and Eagle, and a fourth licence has been promised. Don't expect isolated areas to have coverage (though most do, including Theth). Prepaid SIM cards cost around 1000 lekë and include credit. Mobile numbers begin with ☑06. To call an Albanian mobile number from abroad, dial ☑+355 then either ☑67, ☑68 or ☑69 (ie drop the 0).

Tourist Information

Tourist information offices with some English-speaking staff operate in Tirana, Shkodra, Saranda, Gjirokastra (www.gjirokastra. org) and Berat (www.bashkia-berat.net).

Travellers with Disabilities

High footpaths and unannounced potholes make life difficult for mobility-impaired travellers. Tirana's top hotels do cater to people with disabilities, and some smaller hotels are making an effort to be more accessible. The roads and castle entrances in Gjirokastra, Berat and Kruja are cobblestone, although taxis can get reasonably close.

Visas

Visas are not required for citizens of EU countries or nationals of Australia, Canada, New Zealand, Japan, South Korea, Norway, South Africa or the USA. Travellers from other countries should check www.mfa.gov. al. Passports are stamped for a 90-day stay.

A €10 entry and exit fee was abolished some years ago; do not be conned into paying this by taxi drivers at border crossings.

Women Travellers

Albania is a safe country for women travellers, but outside Tirana it is mainly men who go out and sit in bars and cafes in the evenings. You may tire of being asked why you're travelling alone.

Getting There & Away

Air

Nënë Tereza International Airport is 17km northwest of Tirana and is a modern, well-run terminal. There are no domestic flights within Albania. The following airlines fly to and from Albania:

Adria Airways (☑04-2272 666; www.adria.si) Flies to Ljubljana.

Air One (☑04-2230 023; www.flyairone.it) Flies to Milan, Pisa and Venice.

Alitalia (☑04-2230 023; www.alitalia.com) Flies to Rome, Verona, Turin, Naples, Florence, Genoa, Milan, Catania and Venice.

Austrian Airlines (☑04-2235 029; www. austrian.com) Flies to Vienna.

BelleAir (☑04-2240 175; www.belleair.it) Flies to Pristina, Ancona, Rimini, Forli, Bari, Pescara, Naples, Trieste, Perugia, Milan, Treviso, Turin, Palma, Bologna, Pisa, Florence, Rome, Geneva, London, Prague, Brussels and Vienna.

British Airways (☑04-2381 991; www. britishairways.com) Flies to London.

Lufthansa (☑04-2258 010; www.lufthansa. com) Flies to Vienna and Munich.

Olympic Air (☑04-2228 960; www.olympicair. com) Flies to Athens.

Turkish Airlines (☑04-2258 459; www. turkishairlines.com) Flies to İstanbul.

Land

BORDER CROSSINGS

There are no passenger trains into Albania, so your border-crossing options are buses, *furgons*, taxis or walking to a border and picking up transport on the other side.

Montenegro The main crossings link Shkodra to Ulcinj (Muriqan) and to Podgorica (Hani i Hotit).

Kosovo The closest border crossing to the Koman Ferry terminal is Morina, and further south is Qafë Prush. Near Kukës use Morinë for the highway to Tirana.

Macedonia Use Blato to get to Debar, quiet Qafë e Thanës to the north of Lake Ohrid, or Sveti Naum, near Pogradec, to its south. There's also a crossing at Stenje.

Greece The main border crossing to and from Greece is Kakavija on the road from Athens to Tirana. It's about half an hour from Gjirokastra and 250km west of Tirana, and can take up to three hours to pass through during summer. Kapshtica (near Korça) also gets long lines in summer. Konispoli is near Butrint in Albania's south.

BUS

From Tirana, regular buses head to Pristina, Kosovo; to Struga, Tetovo and Skopje in Macedonia; to Budva and Ulcinj in Montenegro; and to Athens and Thessaloniki in Greece. *Furgons* and buses leave Shkodra for Montenegro, and buses head to Kosovo from Durrës. Buses travel to Greece from Albanian towns on the southern coast and buses to Italy leave from Vlora.

CAR & MOTORCYCLE

To enter, you'll need a Green Card (proof of third-party insurance, issued by your insurer); check that your insurance covers Albania.

TAXI

Heading to Macedonia, taxis from Pogradec will drop you off just before the border at Tushëmisht/Sveti Naum. Alternatively, it's an easy 4km walk to the border from Pogradec. It's possible to organise a taxi (or, more usually, a person with a car) from where the Koman Ferry stops in Fierzë to Gjakove in Kosovo. Taxis commonly charge €40 from Shkodra to Ulcinj in Montenegro.

Sea

Two or three ferries per day ply the route between Saranda and Corfu, in Greece, and there are plenty of ferry companies making the journey to Italy from Vlora and Durrës, as well as additional ferries from Vlora to Corfu.

Getting Around
Bicycle

Cycling in Albania is tough but certainly feasible. Expect lousy road conditions including open drains, some abysmal driving from fellow road users and roads that barely qualify for the title. Organised groups head north for mountain biking, and cyclists are even spotted cycling the long and tough Korça–Gjirokastra road. Shkodra, Durrës and Tirana are towns where you'll see locals embracing the bike, and Tirana even has bike lanes.

Bus

The first bus/*furgon* departure is often at 5am and things slow down around lunchtime. There are many buses catering for the crowds along the coast in July and August. Fares are low, and you either pay the conductor on board or when you hop off.

Municipal buses operate in Tirana, Durrës, Shkodra and Vlora, and trips cost 30 lekë.

Car & Motorcycle

Albania's drivers are not the best in the world, mostly due to the communist era, when car ownership required a permit from the government, and only two were issued to nonparty members. As a result, the government didn't invest in new roads, and most Albanians were inexperienced motorists. Nowadays the road infrastructure is improving; there's an excellent highway from Tirana to Kosovo, and the coastal route from the Montenegro border to Butrint, near Saranda, is in good condition.

Tourists are driving cars, motorbikes and mobile homes into the country in greater numbers, and, apart from bad roads and bad drivers, it's generally hassle-free.

Off the main routes a 4WD is a good idea. Driving at night is particularly hazardous; follow another car on the road as there's rarely any road markings or street lighting.

DRIVING LICENCE

Foreign driving licences are all that's required to drive a car in Albania.

CAR HIRE

There are lots of car-hire companies operating out of Tirana, including all the major international agencies. Hiring a small car costs from €35 per day.

ROAD RULES

Drinking and driving is forbidden, and there is zero tolerance for blood-alcohol readings. Both motorcyclists and passengers must wear helmets. Speed limits are as low as 30km/h in built-up areas and 35km/h on the edges, and there are plenty of speed cameras monitoring the roads. Keep your car's papers with you, as police are active checkers.

Hitching

Though never entirely safe, hitchhiking is quite a common way for travellers to get around – though it's rare to see locals doing it.

Train

Albanians prefer bus and *furgon* travel, and when you see the speed and the state of the (barely) existing trains, you'll know why. However, the trains are dirt cheap and travelling on them is an adventure. Daily passenger trains leave Tirana for Durrës, Shkodra, Fier, Vlora, Elbasan and a few kilometres out of Pogradec. Check time-tables at the station in person, and buy your ticket 10 minutes before departure. Albania is not connected to neighbouring countries by train.

Belarus

Includes »

Best Places to Eat

» Grand Cafe (p86)

» Bistro de Luxe (p86)

» Kukhmystr (p87)

» Strawnya Talaka (p87)

» Jules Verne (p95)

Best Places to Stay

» Crowne Plaza Minsk (p85)

» Hermitage Hotel (p94)

» Hotel Minsk (p85)

» Semashko (p91)

Why Go?

Eastern Europe's outcast, Belarus (Беларусь) lies at the edge of the region and seems determined to avoid integration with the rest of the continent at all costs. Taking its lead from the Soviet Union rather than the European Union, this little-visited dictatorship may seem like a strange choice for travellers, but its isolation is at the heart of its appeal.

While the rest of Eastern Europe has charged headlong into capitalism, Belarus allows the chance to visit a Europe with minimal advertising and no litter or graffiti. Outside the monumental Stalinist capital of Minsk, Belarus offers a simple yet pleasing landscape of cornflower fields, thick forests and picturesque villages. The country also offers two excellent national parks and is home to Europe's largest mammal, the zoobr (or European bison). While travellers will always be subject to curiosity, they'll also be on the receiving end of warm hospitality and genuine welcome.

When to Go
Minsk

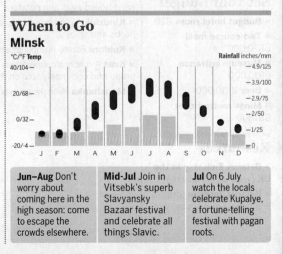

Jun–Aug Don't worry about coming here in the high season: come to escape the crowds elsewhere.	**Mid-Jul** Join in Vitsebsk's superb Slavyansky Bazaar festival and celebrate all things Slavic.	**Jul** On 6 July watch the locals celebrate Kupalye, a fortune-telling festival with pagan roots.

BELARUS

Fast Facts

» **Area** 207,600 sq km

» **Capital** Minsk

» **Country code** ☏375

» **Emergency** Ambulance ☏03, fire ☏01, police ☏02

Exchange Rates

Australia	A$1	BR9065
Canada	C$1	BR8525
Euro Zone	€1	BR11,072
Japan	¥100	BR9178
New Zealand	NZ$1	BR7253
UK	UK£1	BR13,122
USA	US$1	BR8677

Set Your Budget

» **Budget hotel room** €20

» **Two-course meal** BR70,000

» **Museum entrance** BR10,000

» **Beer** BR10,000

» **Minsk metro ticket** BR1800

Resources

» **Belarus Embassy in the UK** (www.uk.mfa.gov.by)

» **Belarus Tourism** (http:// eng.belarustourism.by)

Connections

Belarus has good overland links to all neighbouring countries. Daily trains from Minsk serve Moscow and St Petersburg in Russia, Vilnius in Lithuania, Warsaw in Poland (via Terespol) and Kyiv in Ukraine. Bus services, which tend to be less comfortable, connect Minsk to Moscow, St Petersburg, Kyiv, Warsaw and Vilnius; Vitsebsk to Moscow and St Petersburg; and Brest to Terespol in Poland.

ITINERARIES

Three Days

Spend two days getting to know Minsk – its Stalinist architecture belies a lively and friendly city – before taking a day trip to Dudutki and Mir to get a feel for the charming Belarusian countryside.

One Week

Begin with two nights in Brest, including a day trip to the Belavezhskaya Pushcha National Park, then take a train to Minsk, allowing yourself time for a day trip to Dudutki and Mir before continuing on to historic and charming Vitsebsk.

Essential Food & Drink

» **Belavezhskaya** A bitter herbal alcoholic drink.

» **Draniki** Potato pancakes, usually served with sour cream (*smetana*).

» **Kletsky** Dumplings stuffed with mushrooms, cheese or potato.

» **Khaladnik** A local variation on cold borsch, a soup made from beetroot and garnished with sour cream, chopped-up hard-boiled eggs and potatoes.

» **Kindziuk** A pig-stomach sausage filled with minced pork, herbs and spices.

» **Kolduni** Potato dumplings stuffed with meat.

» **Kvas** A mildly alcoholic drink made from black or rye bread and commonly sold on the streets in Belarus.

» **Manchanka** Pancakes served with a meaty gravy.

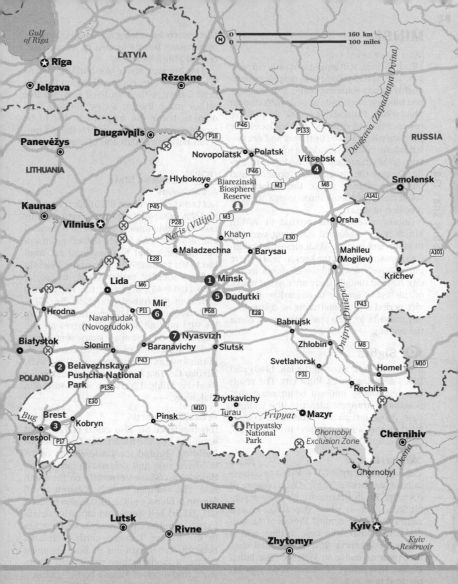

Belarus Highlights

❶ Get under the skin of **Minsk** (p82), the showpiece of Stalinist architecture and a friendly, accessible city.

❷ Spot a European bison, a brown bear or a wolf at **Belavezhskaya Pushcha National Park** (p96).

❸ Stroll through the mellow pedestrian streets of cosmopolitan Brest to the epic WWII memorial that is **Brest Fortress** (p92).

❹ Discover the childhood home of painter Marc Chagall in **Vitsebsk** (p96).

❺ Enjoy life at a slow pace while visiting the charming farm-museum in bucolic **Dudutki** (p91).

❻ See the fairy-tale 16th-century castle that presides over the tranquil town of **Mir** (p91).

❼ Explore one of the few historical complexes to have survived WWII at **Nyasvizh** (p91), amid beautiful lakes and the picturesque Radziwill Palace Fortress.

MINSK

☑017 / POP 1.9 MILLION

Minsk (Мінск) will almost certainly surprise you. The capital of Belarus is, despite its thoroughly dreary-sounding name, a progressive and modern place quite at odds with its own reputation. Fashionable cafes, impressive restaurants and crowded nightclubs vie for your attention, while sushi bars and art galleries have taken up residence in a city centre once totally remodelled to the tastes of Stalin. Despite the strong police presence and obedient citizenry, scrape the surface and you'll find that there's more than a whiff of rebellion in the air.

Totally razed to the ground in WWII, Minsk is an ideological statement wrought in stone and cement. With almost no buildings remaining from the prewar years, there are relatively few traditional sights in the city. Instead though, there are myriad places of interest to anyone fascinated by the Soviet period and a smattering of cosmopolitan pursuits to keep you entertained come the evening.

◉ Sights

Minsk was built anew in the late 1940s and 1950s as a flagship Stalinist city. The result is a remarkably uniform conurbation that is actually strangely attractive, the Stalinist style being far grander and more colourful than the later Soviet architecture of the 1960s and 1970s.

Oktyabrskaya pl   SQUARE
The city's main square is referred to universally by its Russian name, Oktyabrskaya pl (October Sq; in Belarusian, it's pl Kastrychnitskaya). This is where opposition groups gather to protest against President Alexander Lukashenko from time to time, and is where the infamous 2010 presidential election protests ended in violence. The failed Denim Revolution of March 2006 was attempted here as well.

Here you'll find the impressive, severe **Palats Respubliki** (Palace of the Republic), a concert hall. Also on this square is the classical, multicolumned **Trade Unions Culture Palace** and next to this is the **Museum of the Great Patriotic War** (☑277 5611; Oktyabrskaya pl; adult/student BR6000/4000, guided tour BR20,000; ◷10am-6pm Tue & Thu-Sat, 11am-7pm Wed & Sun), where Belarus' horrors and heroism during WWII are exhibited in photographs, huge dioramas and other media.

Particularly harrowing are the photographs of partisans being executed in recognisable central Minsk locations.

The big sign above the building means 'The feats of the people will live on for centuries', though the sign itself may not live on for much longer: a new building next door to house the museum is due to be completed in 2014, after which the old museum building is slated to become a luxury hotel.

TOP CHOICE Belarusian State Art Museum   MUSEUM
(vul Lenina 20; admission BR20,000; ◷11am-7pm Wed-Mon; ⓜKupalawskaja/Kastrychnitskaja) This excellent state museum has been renovated and now includes a light-bathed extension out the back that features local art from the 1940s to the 1970s. Don't miss Valentin Volkov's socialist realist *Minsk on July 3, 1944* (1944-45), depicting the Red Army's arrival in the ruined city. Yudel Pen, Chagall's teacher, is well represented, including his 1914 portrait of Chagall. There's also an impressive collection of icons, some great realist depictions of late-19th-century life in the Russian Empire and several works by Nikolai Ge, Ilya Repin, Isaak Levitan, Isaak Brodsky, Mikhail Nesterov and Konstantin Makovsky.

Pl Nezalezhnastsi   SQUARE
Independence Sq, also called pl Lenina, is dominated by the **Belarusian Government Building** (behind the Lenin statue) on its northern side and the equally proletarian **Belarusian State University** on the south side. The redbrick Catholic **Church of SS Simon & Elena**, built in 1910, is also here. Its tall, gabled bell tower and attractive detailing are reminiscent of many brick churches in the former Teutonic north of Poland. Beneath the square lies Stolitsa Shopping Centre, a modern three-storey mall where you'll find much of Minsk's best shopping.

Pr Nezalezhnastsi   AVENUE
Heading northeast from pl Nezalezhnastsi is the main part of pr Nezalezhnastsi and the bustling heart of Minsk, including the Soviet-era GUM department store. The KGB was never disbanded in Belarus after the collapse of the USSR, and continues to operate from the yellow **neoclassical building** with an ominous, templelike Corinthian portal at No 17. On the other side of the street is a long, narrow park with a

WHERE AM I?

Between the Soviet, post-Soviet, Russian and Belarusian names for streets and places in Belarus things can get confusing. We use Belarusian street and place names, as this is almost universally how they are written on signposts (in Cyrillic of course – so you'll still have to transliterate). However, almost everyone will tell you the Russian names for streets, so there's room for real confusion. When giving addresses we use the abbreviations vul (vulitsa), pr (praspekt) and pl (ploshcha) to denote street, avenue and square. Russian speakers will call these ulitsa, prospekt and ploshchad respectively.

Minsk is particularly confusing in this respect. To honour the great Belarusian renaissance man, the city's main thoroughfare was once called pr Francyska Skaryny, but in 2005 President Alexander Lukashenko changed it to 'Independence Avenue': pr Nezalezhnastsi (pr Nezavisimosti in Russian). Similarly pl Peramohi (Victory Sq) is often referred to as its Russian variant, pl Pobedy.

Metro stop and town square pl Lenina also goes by its post-Soviet name, which switches 'Lenin' for 'Independence': pl Nezalezhnastsi (pl Nezavisimosti in Russian). Metro change station and main town square Oktyabrskaya pl (its Russian name) is sometimes called pl Kastrychnitskaya (the Belarusian version of the same name). Enjoy!

bust of Felix Dzerzhinsky, the founder of the KGB's predecessor (the Cheka) and a native of Belarus.

Tsentralny Skver SQUARE
Across the street from Oktyabrskaya pl is Tsentralny Skver (Central Sq), a small park on the site of a 19th-century marketplace. The dark-grey building is **Dom Ofitserov** (Officer's Building), which has a tank memorial at the front, devoted to the soldiers who freed Minsk from the Nazis. Beyond this is the lifeless-looking, seriously guarded **Presidential Administrative Building**, from where Alexander Lukashenko rules.

Pl Peramohi SQUARE
North of the central part of pr Nezalezhnastsi, the thoroughfare crosses the Svislach River and then parkland on both sides, before coming into striking pl Peramohi (Victory Sq), marked by a giant **Victory Obelisk** and its eternal flame, which is directly beneath the obelisk underground.

Traetskae Pradmestse OLD TOWN
In lieu of any real remaining Old Town is Traetskae Pradmestse, a pleasant – if tiny – re-creation of Minsk's prewar buildings on a pretty bend of the river north of the centre. It's worth strolling through for its little cafes, restaurants and shops.

At the end of a little footbridge nearby is the evocative Afghan war memorial, **Island of Courage and Sorrow**, more commonly called the Island of Tears by locals. Standing on a small island connected by a walking bridge, it's built in the form of a tiny church, with four entrances, and is surrounded by towering gaunt statues of sorrowful mothers and sisters of Belarusian soldiers who perished in the war between the Soviet Union and Afghanistan (1979–89). Look for the small **statue of the crying angel**, off to the side – it is the guardian angel of Belarus.

Zaslavsky Jewish Monument MONUMENT
An extremely moving sight is the Zaslavsky Jewish Monument, rather hidden away in a sunken gully amid trees off vul Melnikayte. It commemorates the savage murder of 5000 Jews from Minsk at the hands of the Nazis on 2 March 1942. It is made up of sculptures of scared men, women and children lining up to be shot, one person even carrying their violin.

National Library of Belarus LIBRARY
(☑293 2853; old.nlb.by/en; pr Nezalezhnastsi 116; ◎10am-9pm Mon-Fri, 10am-6pm Sat & Sun, closed Sun Jun-Aug; ⓂVostok) For a taste of post-Soviet Belarus, head north of the centre to the new National Library of Belarus, a ghastly piece of Lukashenko-approved hubris. The building is a giant rhombicuboctahedron (look it up!) that is lit at night and contains more than two million records as well as art galleries and a **viewing platform** (admission BR3000; ◎1-9pm Tue-Fri, 10am-6pm Sat & Sun) on the 22nd floor.

Pl Svabody SQUARE
Between vul Internatsyanalnaya and the river is the charming pl Svabody, which

Minsk

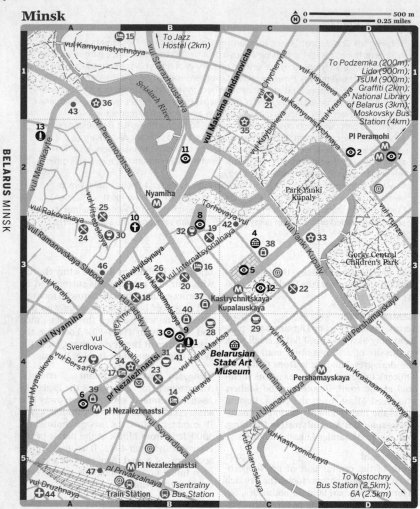

contains the baroque, twin-towered Orthodox **Holy Spirit Cathedral**, built in 1642. Standing confidently on a small hill, it was once part of a Polish Bernardine convent, along with the **former Bernardine Church** next door, which now houses city archives. The white medieval **ratusha** (town hall) is also on the square; this is a popular place for locals to come for wedding pictures, as you'll no doubt discover.

SS Peter & Paul Church CHURCH
(vul Rakovskaya 4) Off vul Lenina overpass is the attractively restored 17th-century Sts Pe-

ter & Paul Church, the city's oldest church (built in 1613, looted by Cossacks in 1707 and restored in 1871). Now it is awkwardly dwarfed by the surrounding morose concrete structures.

Church of St Aleksandr Nevsky CHURCH
(vul Kazlova 11) This red-brick church was built in 1898, was closed by the Bolsheviks, reopened by the Nazis, closed again by the Soviets and now it's open once more. It's said that during WWII, a bomb crashed through the roof and landed plum in front of the altar, but never detonated.

Minsk

Tours

Tours can be organised through travel agencies (p89), which also offer visa and accommodation booking services

Sleeping

Minsk's accommodation scene is generally limited to fusty old Soviet hotels or overpriced four- and five-star places geared to business travellers. A much better option if you're in the city for more than a few days is to rent an apartment. Several agencies offer this service, including **Belarus Rent** (www.belarusrent.com) and **Belarus Apartment** (www.belarusapartment.com). Rates range from €40 to €100 per night.

Crowne Plaza Minsk   LUXURY HOTEL €€€
(☎200 9353; www.cpminsk.com; vul Kirava 13; r incl breakfast from €185, ste from €256; ❄❊❀❂) Generally considered to be Minsk's finest hotel, the superb, central and sleek Crowne Plaza is the choice of business people and wealthier tourists. The rooms and bathrooms are large, well appointed and stylish, and the location can't be beaten.

Hotel Minsk   LUXURY HOTEL €€€
(☎209 9062; www.hotelminsk.by; vul Nezalezhnastsi 11; s/d incl breakfast €144/163, ste from €450; ❄❊) Excellently located, the city's long-standing hotel of choice has now arguably been eclipsed by newer five-star hotels, but it remains a solid option, with friendly

QUIRKY MINSK

Just across the bridge over the Svislach River, on the west bank, is the **former residence of Lee Harvey Oswald** (vul Kamyunistychnaya 4) – it's the bottom left apartment. The alleged assassin of former US president John F Kennedy lived here for a couple of years in his early 20s. He arrived in Minsk in January 1960 after leaving the US Marines and defecting to the USSR. Once here, he truly went native: he got a job in a radio factory, married a Minsk woman, had a child – and even changed his name to Alek. But soon he returned to the United States and...you know the rest.

Lovers of old coins should stop in at the train station's **left-luggage area**, where there are lockers that (surprise, surprise) date back to the Soviet days – and they still only work with Soviet coins. Pay BR550 and in exchange get two locker 'tokens' – 15-kopek coins from the USSR, some dating back to the 1960s.

and professional staff, pleasant and clean rooms and all the services you'd expect from a long-established top hotel.

Hotel Europe
LUXURY HOTEL €€€

(☎229 8333; www.hoteleurope.by; vul Internatsyanalnaya 28; s/d incl breakfast from €245/290, ste from €440; ❈🛜🐕) Some horrific crimes against taste may have been perpetrated in the lobby, but the spacious if flouncy rooms are of high quality, even if the hotel is now looking a little frayed around the edges. Service is excellent, and extras such as the small pool and central location are definite bonuses, though you'll get more bang for your buck at the Crowne Plaza.

40 Let Pobedy
HOTEL €

(☎294 7963; vul Azgura 3; s/d from €18/25; 🛜) This slightly out-of-the-way yet central place offers decent, good-value rooms and friendly service. The hotel has made a good effort to modernise itself (even if it is with cheap furnishings) and all the bathrooms have been redone.

Hotel Belarus
HOTEL €

(☎209 7337, 209 7537; www.hotel-belarus.com; vul Starazhouskaya 15; s/d incl breakfast from €16/20; 🛜🐕) Set in parkland amid plenty of open space a 15-minute amble from the city centre, this Soviet-era place has undergone little change since it was built, although a swimming pool with a waterslide sets it apart from other hotels of this standard. There's an enormous number of room categories, but at the lowest prices it's an OK deal.

Jazz Hostel
HOSTEL €

(☎03 3361 633; hostel.jazz@gmail.com; vul Mazyrskaya 37A; dm per person €10) Yes, there's finally a hostel in Minsk, and yes it's miles from anywhere and highly weird. What else did you expect? This large house has 43 beds spread over two floors, a large kitchen and even some double rooms for more privacy. The whole place is not really set up for foreigners and English isn't much spoken, but excursions and visa registration can be arranged. It's definitely an experience, as is getting here: take tram 4 from outside the main train station and get off at the Vozera stop.

🍴 Eating

Minsk has a decent eating scene and plenty of choice – don't believe the hype about food in Belarus; in the capital, at least, you'll eat well. Consider reserving tables at weekends.

TOP CHOICE Grand Cafe
ITALIAN €€€

(☎703 1111; vul Lenina 2; mains BR80,000-280,000) This classy place has great service from waiters in tuxedos and white-linen tablecloths starched enough to cause an injury. The interesting menu is big on seasonal Italian classics, with plenty of choice and a few non-Italian variations. Alternatively, just sit at the glamorous bar and drink sensational cocktails. Book for the evening and weekends.

TOP CHOICE Bistro de Luxe
BISTRO €€€

(Haradsky Val 10; mains BR75,000-150,000; ⏰8am-midnight; 🛜📶) Housed in a pleasant light-bathed space with chandeliers, sleek brasserie-style furnishings and aspirational toilets, Bistro de Luxe has an atmosphere that's hard to find elsewhere in Minsk. The food is excellent, leaning towards Italian, service is impeccable and the coffee service is efficient and friendly. Breakfast is served daily until midday.

Stolle
PIE SHOP €

(www.stolle.by; vul Rakovskaya 23; mains BR50,000-80,000, pies BR15,000; ⊗9am-11pm; ⊉) This St Petersburg institution has finally hit Minsk and very welcome it is too, with its delicious freshly baked sweet and savoury pies. The most central location of the three now open has a very pleasant upstairs dining room, as well as a takeaway counter downstairs. There's also a full non-pie menu serving up traditional Russian and Belarusian cuisine.

Kukhmystr
BELARUSIAN €€€

(⊉327 4848; vul Karla Marksa 40; mains BR60,000-200,000; ⊗noon-11pm, until 1am Fri-Sat) A stone's throw from the president's office, this charming Belarusian place boasts wooden beams, a tiled fireplace, wrought-iron light fittings and antique knick-knacks. Staff are equally pleasant and the menu is perhaps the most authentically Belarusian in town, though there's also a menu of Latvian cooking.

Strawnya Talaka
TRADITIONAL €€

(⊉203 2794; vul Rakovskaya 18; mains BR35,000-195,000; ⊗10am-6am; 🏠) This relaxed and cosy basement place is the best restaurant in Minsk for an authentic local meal and also has handy long opening hours. Try the hare in bilberry sauce, the mushroom soup served in a loaf of bread or just a bowl of their fantastic beer snacks and the fabulous *draniki* (potato pancakes). Staff are dressed in traditional peasant garb and the enormous wooden menus are fully pictorial and hilariously translated.

Vino y Comida
TAPAS BAR €

(vul Internatsyanalnaya 9/17; tapas BR15,000-35,000, mains BR30,000-80,000; ⊗11am-midnight) This stylish joint with olive-coloured walls, friendly service and bright dining areas serves up good tapas from a large menu. All the classics are present, as well as a range of meaty *platos calientes* (hot dishes) and excellent paella (BR60,000 to BR80,0000).

Pizza Tempo
PIZZA €€

(⊉292 1111; www.pizzatempo.by; vul Karla Marksa 9; mains BR16,000-100,000; ⊗9am-11pm; 🏠) This chain has seven pizzerias spread across the city, with each restaurant stylishly decorated and enjoying a relaxed vibe. Citywide delivery is available and the pizza is the best we've found in Minsk.

Gurman
RUSSIAN €

(⊉290 6774; vul Kamyunistychnaya 7; mains BR10,000-60,000; ⊗8am-11pm) This Minsk institution specialises in many varieties of delicious, freshly made *pelmeni* (Russian-style ravioli stuffed with meat) and also offers a wide selection of pastas, curries and other international cuisine. The light and airy premises and friendly staff make this well worth the wander from the metro. Try to book a table if you're going for dinner.

Byblos
LEBANESE €€

(vul Internatsyanalnaya 21; mains BR20,000-85,000; ⊗noon-midnight, until 2am Fri-Sat; 🏠🏠) What this Lebanese-style place lacks in authenticity it makes up for in value, quick service and an English menu. Great for an easy lunch; the kebabs and hummus are decent enough, given that you're in Belarus, and there's great people-watching from the enclosed terrace. There's wi-fi available until 5pm.

Lido
CANTEEN €

(pr Nezalezhnastsi 49/1; mains BR5000-20,000; ⊗8am-11pm Mon-Fri, 11am-11pm Sat & Sun; 🏠) This excellent place is a real lifesaver for a quick and filling meal. The large cafeteria has a huge array of food on display, so it's easy for non-Russian speakers: just point at what you want. Lunchtime is always packed, but it's usually easy to find a seat among the curious faux-medieval village decor.

🍷 Drinking

Bars

Drozhzhi United
IRISH PUB

(vul Sverdlova 2; ⊗9am-2am) Centrally located, Minsk's Irish pub is instantly recognisable to anyone who has ever been an expat, anywhere. There's good food, Guinness on tap and a friendly atmosphere though.

U Ratushi
PUB

(vul Gertsena 1, Pl Svabody; ⊗10am-2am) This multilevel pub-style restaurant, right across from the *ratusha* (town hall), is packed with a raucous, fun-loving crowd on weekends (there is often a small cover charge for live bands). Come early at the weekend to get a seat.

Rakovsky Brovar
MICROBREWERY

(vul Vitsebskaya 10; ⊗noon-midnight) Minsk's first microbrewery is housed in an enormous central venue and shows no sign of losing its popularity. There's a full menu here too (mains BR20,000 to BR70,000), although most people come here for after-work drinks and stay late amid the raucous atmosphere.

Cafes

The best cafes in Minsk include the sleek **News Café** (vul Karla Marksa 34; ⊙8am-midnight; 🛜), where free wi-fi (until 7pm), good coffee and full meals make for a great hang-out, and the bizarre **My English Granny** (vul Karla Marksa 36; ⊙9am-11pm; 🛜) next door, a cafe that has pulled off the incredible feat of making kitschy Victoriana look trendy, where you'll get a lovely pot of tea and some good cakes, as well as meals and a great breakfast selection. Two other slightly more bohemian options are sister cafes **Stary Mensk** (pr Nezalezhnastsi 14; ⊙10am-11pm) and **London** (pr Nezalezhnastsi 18; ⊙10am-midnight; 🛜), which both serve hot drinks and are favoured by Minsk's intellectual crowd.

☆ Entertainment

Performing Arts

A pleasant hangover from Soviet times is that performing arts are of very good quality and tickets are cheap.

To buy advance tickets or to find out what's on, head to the **central ticket office** (pr Nezalezhnastsi 13; ⊙9am-7pm). There are more places for tickets in the underpass at the junction of pr Nezalezhnastsi and vul Lenina in the centre. Same-day tickets are often available only from the performance venues.

Don't miss the highly respected **National Academic Opera & Ballet Theatre** (📞234 8074; pl Parizhskoy Kamunni 1; ⊙ticket office 9am-1pm & 2-6pm Mon-Fri), where there are several different operas performed each month; performances take place at 7pm on Thursday, Saturday and Sunday. The **Belarusian State Circus** (📞226 1008; pr Nezalezhnastsi 32) reopened in 2011 following a full refit and is now a modern and well-appointed venue.

Nightclubs

Minsk has a surprisingly good selection of nightlife and there's plenty going on in town to keep night owls busy.

Graffiti
UNDERGROUND BAR
(www.graffiti.by; pr Kalinina 16; cover BR20,000-40,000; ⊙11am-11pm, to 2am Fri & Sat) For something contemporary and underground, Graffiti offers nightly concerts from local bands and big weekend parties popular with an alternative and 'anti-Luka' crowd. It's a 10-minute walk from the Park Chelyuskintsev metro station: head up vul Tolbukhina, turn right onto vul Knorina and then left onto vul Belinskogo. Graffiti can be found in the unlikely looking industrial building on the corner.

Overtime
NIGHTCLUB
(pr Peremozhtsau 4; cover free-BR50,000; ⊙6pm-6am) Currently the hippest place in town despite its premises being better suited for use as a venue for a high-school disco. This club attracts a chic and monied crowd of local glitzy gals and their muscly boyfriends. Dress up to get in – face control can be tough.

6A
GAY CLUB
(pr Partizansky 6a; cover BR15,000; ⊙10pm-3am; Ⓜ Proletarskaya) The only gay club in Minsk is a curious but friendly Soviet throwback in a building where time appears to have stood still since Brezhnev's day. A unique experience, complete with old-school drag shows and a 1990s house soundtrack.

🔒 Shopping

Minsk's shopping scene is far from mind-blowing, but if you want a general browse a good place to start is the **Stolitsa Shopping Centre** (pl Nezalezhnastsi; ⊙10am-10pm), a three-level subterranean mall housing much of the capital's swankiest shops.

At many supermarkets you'll find candies with old-fashioned wrappers steeped in nostalgia for a Soviet childhood. Belarus is also known for its straw crafts, which include dolls and wooden boxes intricately ornamented with geometric patterns. Linens and other woven textiles unique to Belarus are also popular handicrafts. These are easily found in city department stores, hotel lobbies and at **Minsky Vernisazh** (Oktyabrskaya pl; ⊙8am-6pm Tue-Sun), a souvenir market next to the Museum of the Great Patriotic War where you can haggle for local art, folk crafts and other rather garish traditional items.

Other recommended shops include **Podzemka** (pr Nezalezhnastsi 43; ⊙10am-8pm Mon-Sat, 11am-6pm Sun), an underground bohemian shop-cum-art-gallery that sells all sorts of goodies you won't find anywhere else including an excellent range of DVDs, funky artistic pieces and handmade jewellery.

It's also worth browsing the department stores, such as **GUM** (pr Nezalezhnastsi 21) and **TsUM** (pr Nezalezhnastsi 54), or the **Tsentralnaya Kniharnya** (pr Nezalezhnastsi 19) bookshop for souvenirs.

ⓘ Information

Internet Access

Free wi-fi can be had in most top-end hotels (buy a coffee in the lobby and try to look like a guest) or go to My English Granny (p88), Bistro de Luxe (p86) and News Café (p88). The most accessible internet cafes include the following:

Internet Cafe (train station; ⊙9am-7am) Usefully located club on the 3rd floor of the city's railway station.

Soyuz Online (2nd fl, vul Krasnaarmeyskaya 3; ⊙24hr) Large internet cafe in the centre of town. Food and drinks available. Go up the steps to the Dom Ofitserov and enter the far door near the tank monument.

Tetris Internet Café (vul Frunze 3; ⊙8.30am-10pm)

Medical Services

24-hour Pharmacy (pr Nezalezhnastsi 16)

EcoMedservices (☑207 7474; www.ems. by; vul Tolstoho 4; ⊙8am-9pm) The closest thing to a reliable, Western-style clinic. Dental services are offered here too. Just south of the train station.

Money

ATMs can be found throughout the city. If for some reason you need foreign currency, many ATMs will dispense US dollars or euros (don't take out dollars or euros just to change them to roubles though – you'll pay the exchange rate twice). Big hotels all have exchange bureaux and a handful can cash travellers cheques.

Post

DHL and UPS have offices based in the major hotels.

Central Post Office (pr Nezalezhnastsi 10; ⊙7am-11pm) In the centre of town.

Tourist Information

Travel agencies generally provide the best information, but of course they want you to book tours or accommodation with them.

Minsk Tourist Information Centre (☑203 3995; www.minsk-tourism.by; vul Revalyutsiynaya 16-24; ⊙8.45am-1pm & 2-6pm Mon-Fri) Minsk finally has a tourist office, but unless you know where to look you'd be forgiven for missing it. The entrance is in the courtyard behind building 13 on vul Revalyutsiynaya. The well-meaning staff here speak some English and can help with hotel reservations and booking tours.

Travel Agencies

Alatan Tour (☑227 7417; www.welcomebelarus.com; vul Internatsionalnaya 33b) A reliable English-speaking outfit that offers visa support, hotel bookings, guide services and drivers.

Belarus Tour Service (☑200 5675; www.hotelsbelarus.com; vul Rozi Lyuksemburg 89) Visa support, hotel bookings and transfers.

Belintourist (☑226 9971; www.belintourist.by; pr Peramozhtsau 19) The state-run tourist agency does visa support, city tours and trips to Mir, Dudutki, Nyasvizh and Belavezhskaya Pushcha National Park – as well as offering all kinds of other tours including hunting trips, skiing trips and a 28-day 'Say Goodbye to Asthma' tour.

Top Tour (☑228 0205; www.en.toptour.by; vul Chkalova 22) Visa support, hotels, interpreters and tours.

Websites

Minsk in Your Pocket (www.inyourpocket.com/belarus) Has a free Minsk guide to download, which is updated annually; it's also available in hard copy from some hotels.

ⓘ Getting There & Away

Air

International flights entering and departing Belarus do so at the **Minsk-2 International Airport** (☑279 1300; www.airport.by), about 40km east of Minsk. Some flights to the former Soviet Union depart from the smaller **Minsk-1 Airport** (☑006; vul Chkalova 38), only a few kilometres south of the city centre.

Bus

There are three main bus stations and you can buy tickets for anywhere at any of them. To ask which station you're departing from in Russian is 'v ka-*kom* av-toh-vak-*za*-le ot-prav-*lye*-ni-ye'. The **MinskTrans** (www.minsktrans.by) website also gives full timetable information, though it's in Russian only. From Minsk, international services include buses to Vilnius in Lithuania, Warsaw in Poland, Kyiv in Ukraine, and Moscow and St Petersburg in Russia.

Tsentralny Bus Station (☑227 0473; vul Bobruyskaya 6) The main bus station is next to the train station in the centre of Minsk. Buses to Mir (Novgrorodok), Brest, Hrodna and Nyasvizh depart from here.

Moskovsky Bus Station (☑219 3622; vul Filimonava 63) Near Maskouskaya metro station, about 4km east of the city.

Vostochny Bus Station (☑247 4984; vul Vaneeva 34) To get here from the train station (or metro Pl Lenina), take bus 8 or trolley 20 or 30; get off at Avtovokzal Vostochny.

INTERNATIONAL TRAINS FROM MINSK

DESTINATION	PRICE PLATZKART/KUPE (3RD-/2ND-CLASS)	FREQUENCY	DURATION (HR)
Berlin (Germany)	€96 *kupe* only	1 daily	16
Kyiv (Ukraine)	€24/38	1 daily	12
Moscow (Russia)	€23/45	multiple daily	11
Prague (Czech Republic)	€110 *kupe* only	3 times a week	21
St Petersburg (Russia)	€25/48	1 daily	14
Vilnius (Lithuania)	€6/13	2 daily	4
Warsaw (Poland)	€47 *kupe* only	1 daily	10

Car & Motorcycle

You can hire cars from the following places:

Avis (☑334 7990; www.avis.by; Hotel Minsk, pr Nezalezhnastsi 11)

Europcar (☑209 9009; www.europcar.by; Hotel Minsk, pr Nezalezhnastsi 11)

Train

The busy and modern **Minsk train station** (☑225 7000, 105; Privakzalnaya pl; ☺24hr) is pretty easy to deal with. Very basic food is available here, as well as an **internet cafe** (☺24 hr; underground rail Ploshcha Nezalezhnastsi) on the 3rd floor, ATMs and exchange facilities. Buy domestic and CIS (Commonwealth of Independent States) tickets here.

Downstairs is a well-signed **left luggage office** (lockers BR1000, luggage room BR2000; ☺24hr), with a fiendishly complex system. To use the lockers, put your stuff in an empty one, select a code on the inside of the door, put a token in, shut the door. When you want it back, use your second token to reopen the locker. Ask staff to help if you're confused (you probably will be) – or pay a little extra to use the luggage room.

You can buy advance tickets for non-CIS destinations at the **international train ticket office** (☑213 1719; vul Bobruyskaya 4; ☺24hr), located to the right of the train station.

❶ Getting Around

To/From the Airport

From Minsk-2 airport, a 40-minute taxi ride into town should cost anywhere from €30, depending on your bargaining skills. There are buses and *marshrutki* (shared minibuses; BR10,000, 90 minutes, hourly) that bring you to the city centre, though you can get out at the first metro station (Uruchye) to get elsewhere in the city. From Minsk-1 airport, take bus 100 to the centre; it goes along pr Nezalezhnastsi.

Public Transport

Minsk's metro is simple: just two lines with one transfer point at the Kastrychnitskaya-Kupalauskaya interchange on pr Nezalezhnastsi. A third line is under construction, but at present the system isn't hugely useful to travellers. It's open daily from dawn until just after midnight. One token (*zheton*) costs BR1800.

Buses, trams, trolleybuses also cost BR1800 per ride. Many locals don't bother to buy tickets, as even the fines are miniscule. Private *marshrutky* cost far more, generally around BR8000 per ride and are usually much quicker than other overground transport methods. Popular bus 100 comes every five to 15 minutes and plies pr Nezalezhnastsi as far as Moskovsky Bus Station. You can buy a ticket from the person on board wearing a bright vest. Once you get the ticket, punch it at one of the red buttons placed on the poles.

Taxi

For taxis, ☑081 is the state service and almost always has cars available, while ☑007 is private, the cheapest and has the best service (less likely to rip off foreigners) but cars are sometimes not available during peak times. You can also hail one from the street. Unlike in Russia, private cars don't usually stop for passengers.

AROUND MINSK

Leave Minsk for an easy taste of the gently appealing Belarusian countryside, to a world where instead of mobile-phone shops and sushi bars, the few stores you'll see will have names like 'Bread' and 'Shoes', dating from a bygone era of no choice. Don't miss the fairy-tale castle at Mir or your chance to taste a slice of traditional village life at Dudutki.

To really immerse yourself in rural life, consider trying **Rural Belarus** (☎205 0465; www.ruralbelarus.by), a nonprofit association of B&Bs that offers dozens of homestays throughout the country.

Dudutki   Дудуткі

☎01713

Tasting delicious farm-made sausages, cheese and bread is only a small part of the experience of a visit to the **open-air interactive museum** (☎133 0747; www.dudutki.by; adult/child incl tastings BR25,000/7000; ☉10am-4pm Tue & Wed, 10am-5pm Thu-Sun) of Dudutki, located 40km south of Minsk. This completely self-sufficient farm offers horse riding, sleigh rides, demonstrations of ceramic making, blacksmithing and more. You'll be offered fresh *salo* (tallow) with garlic, salt and rye bread; pickles dipped in honey; and homemade moonshine – all scrumptious.

There are two daily buses (BR15,000 each way, one hour) to Dudutki from Minsk's Vostochny Bus Station at 9.40am and 12.55pm, with return buses at 2.20pm and 5.40pm. Otherwise, contact Valeria of **Dudutki Tur** (☎017-251 0076; dudutki@telecom.by), which can organise private transport.

Nyasvizh   Нясвіж

☎01770 / POP 15,000

The magical old buildings of Nyasvizh make it a great place to get in touch with Belarus' past – one that elsewhere has all too often been destroyed as military campaigns flattened the country. This quiet but green and attractive town 120km southwest of Minsk is one of the oldest in the country, dating from the 13th century. It reached its zenith in the mid-16th century while owned by the mighty Radziwill magnates.

The **Farny Polish Roman Catholic Church** was built between 1584 and 1593 in early baroque style and features a splendidly proportioned facade. Inside, the frescos have been restored to their former elaborate glory.

Just beyond the church is the red-brick arcaded **Castle Gate Tower**. Constructed in the 16th century, the tower was originally part of a wall and gateway controlling the passage between the palace and the town. Here there's an **excursion bureau** (vul Leninskaya 19; ☉8am-5pm Mon-Fri) where you pay to enter the fortress grounds (BR10,000). Guided tours (BR100,000) for one to 25 people last about 1½ hours and are available in either Russian or Belarusian.

Further on is a causeway leading to the beautiful **Radziwill Palace Fortress** (1583), the main sight in Nyasvizh. In Soviet times it was turned into a sanatorium but has since been fully restored and is looking superb. There are English and Japanese gardens to stroll in here, as well as an eternal flame in the attractive lakeside park, commemorating those who died in WWII.

From Minsk's Vostochny Bus Station, there are two daily buses to and from Nyasvizh (BR34,000, 2½ hours).

Mir   Мір

☎01596 / POP 2500

The charming small town of Mir, 85km southwest of Minsk, is dominated by the impossibly romantic 16th-century **Mir Castle** (☎23 035; admission BR25,000; ☉10am-5pm) that overlooks a small lake at one end of the town. It was once owned by the

---

HRODNA

If you're entering Belarus from northern Poland, or if you have extra time in the country, think about visiting Hrodna (Grodno in Russian). It was one of the few Belarusian cities that *wasn't* bombed during WWII, so it's rife with old wooden homes and, although it's a major city, it definitely has a 'big village' sort of feel to it. The city's best hotel by far is the privately run, super-friendly **Semashko** (☎0152-75 02 99; www.hotel-semashko.ru/en; vul Antonova 10; s/d incl breakfast from BR180,000/270,000; @❀), which you should reserve in advance due to its popularity. The room price includes use of the Oasis sauna and its small pool. Trains between Minsk and Hrodna leave five times a day (BR24,000, six hours), although *marshrutky* from Minsk's Vostochny Bus Station do the trip much faster and far more regularly (BR36,000, three hours).

powerful Radziwill princes and has been under Unesco protection since 1994. Sadly, today the exterior is the highlight of the castle as almost all the original contents have been removed. Even though it's worth a walk around the small areas open to visitors, there's little to see here. Guided tours in Russian are offered (BR140,000 for one to 10 people). The town of Mir itself is a delightful backwater.

The small, friendly **Hotel Mir** (☑23 851; pl 17ogo Sentyabrya 2; s/d €20/30) is the only place to stay in town. You'll find it on the charming town square, across the way from the bus station. Breakfast is not included, but there is a cafe here and a restaurant on the other side of the square.

From Minsk's Vostochny and Tsentralny Bus Stations, there are buses to Navahrudak (Novogrudok in Russian) that stop in Mir (BR28,000 to BR34,000, 2½ hours, hourly).

Khatyn   Хатынь

☑01774

The hamlet of Khatyn, 60km north of Minsk, was burned to the ground by the Nazis on 22 March 1943. Of a population of 149 (including 85 children), only one man, Yuzif Kaminsky, survived. The site is now a sobering **memorial** (☑55 787; ⊙9am-5pm Tue-Sat); tours are offered in Russian. More information can be found at www.khatyn.by. There's also an exhibit of photographs (admission BR5000).

There's no public transport to Khatyn from Minsk, but a taxi will cost around €35 for the return journey. Pricey trips are organised by Belintourist (p89).

SOUTHERN BELARUS

Leave Minsk and you're quickly in another world. The concrete landscape gives way to pastoral scenes and undulating flat green plains rich in simple bucolic beauty – a river wending its way gently past thick forests, fields of cornflowers in bloom and small villages populated entirely by pensioners. It's not dramatic, but this is the 'real' Belarus.

The south of Belarus is dominated by Brest, a lively and attractive border town with a more European feel than Minsk. The star attraction nearby is the wonderful Belavezhskaya Pushcha National Park,

which can be visited on a day trip from Brest, or – even better – on an overnight trip where you stay in the park itself. There's also the excellent Pripyatsky National Park for those *really* wanting to get off the beaten path.

Brest   Брэст

☑0162 / POP 312,000

If you've visited Minsk before arriving, you'd be forgiven for thinking you'd landed in another country when you get off the train in Brest. This prosperous and cosmopolitan border town looks far more to the neighbouring EU than to Minsk. It has plenty of charm and has performed a massive DIY job on itself over the past few years.

The city's main sight is the Brest Fortress, a moving WWII memorial where Soviet troops held out far longer than expected against the Nazi onslaught in the early days of Operation Barbarossa. But there are also several museums and this is the jumping-off point for the Belavezhskaya Pushcha National Park.

⊙ Sights

FREE **Brest Fortress**   MUSEUM COMPLEX
(Brestskaya krepost; pr Masherava) Very little remains of Brest Fortress. Certainly don't come here expecting a medieval turreted affair – this is a Soviet WWII memorial to the devastating battle that resulted when German troops advanced into the Soviet Union in the early days of Operation Barbarossa in 1941. The large complex occupies a beautiful spot at the confluence of the Buh and Mukhavets Rivers, a 20-minute walk from the town centre or a short hop on the hourly 17 bus from outside the Hotel Intourist.

The fortress was built between 1838 and 1842, but by WWII it was used mainly as a barracks. The two regiments bunking here when German troops launched a surprise attack in 1941 defended the fort for an astounding month and became venerated as national legends thanks to Stalin's propaganda machine.

The **Brest Fortress main entrance** is its most iconic building – a huge socialist star formed from concrete. Sombre music accompanies you through the tunnel and as you leave it, on the left and past a small hill, you'll see some **tanks**. Straight ahead is the

Brest

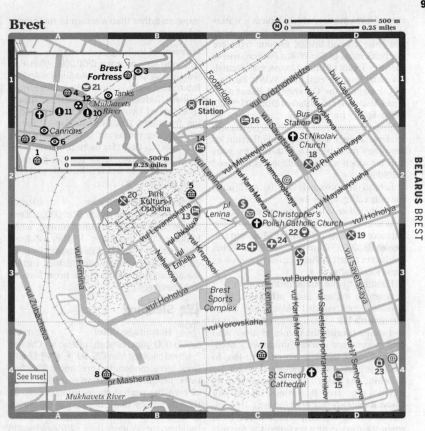

BELARUS BREST

Brest

stone **Thirst statue**, which depicts a water-starved soldier crawling for a drink. After you cross a small bridge, to your right are the brick ruins of the **White Palace**, where the 1918 Treaty of Brest-Litovsk was signed, marking Russia's exit from WWI. Further to the right is the **Defence of Brest Fortress Museum** (adult/student BR10,000/5000; ☺9am-6pm). Its extensive and dramatic exhibits demonstrate the plight of the defenders. There's also a small collection of weaponry from 18th- to 20th-century warfare for which a separate ticket is required (BR8000).

Behind the museum is Café Tsitadel (p95), the only eating option here.

On the other side of the fortress is a collection of **cannons**. Behind this area is the entrance to the new **Brest Art Museum** (admission BR5000; ☺10am-6pm Wed-Sun), which holds art created by Brest citizens, as well as some local crafts.

Heading to the **main monuments** – a large stone soldier's head projecting from a massive rock, entitled 'Valour', and a sky-scraping obelisk – you'll see an eternal flame and stones bearing the names of those who died (several are marked 'unknown'). Sombre orchestral music is played here too, to ensure you are suitably moved.

Behind the Valour rock is the attractive, recently renovated Byzantine **Nikalaivsky Church** (pr Masherava, Brest Fortress), the oldest church in the city, which dates from when the town centre occupied the fortress site. It holds regular services.

To the south is **Kholmskie Gate**; its bricks are decorated with crenulated turrets and its outer face is riddled with hundreds of bullet and shrapnel holes. Beyond the Kholmskie Gate is the **Bereste Archaeological Museum** (admission BR5000; ☺9am-6pm), a large covered archaeological site where peasant and artisan huts from the 12th to 14th centuries have been uncovered.

Museum of Confiscated Art   MUSEUM

(vul Lenina 39; admission BR10,000; ☺10am-5.30pm Tue-Sun) There are a couple of excellent museums in the city centre. The most interesting is the Museum of Confiscated Art, where there's an extraordinary display of icons, paintings, jewellery and other valuables that were seized from smugglers trying to get them across the border to Poland during the 1990s. Items on display are of unknown origin, hence their display in a museum rather than a return to their rightful owners.

Museum of Railway Technology   MUSEUM

(pr Masherava 2; admission BR10,000; ☺9am-6pm Wed-Sun May-Oct, 9am-5pm Wed-Sun Nov-Apr) An interesting sight is the outdoor Museum of Railway Technology, where there's a superb collection of locomotives and carriages dating from 1903 (the *Moscow-Brest Express* with shower rooms and a very comfy main bedroom) to 1988 (far more proletarian Soviet passenger carriages). You can go inside many of them, so train enthusiasts and children tend to love it here.

History of Brest Museum   MUSEUM

(vul Levaneiskaha 3; admission BR20,000; ☺10am-5.15pm Tue-Sat) In an unassuming white building, the two-storey History of Brest Museum has a small exhibit on the city in its different guises throughout history, including an excellent model of the Brest Fortress in its heyday.

🛏 Sleeping

TOP CHOICE **Hermitage Hotel**   HOTEL €€€

(☎276 000; www.hermitagehotel.by; vul Chkalova 7; s/d incl breakfast from €79/99; P❀⊛) Finally Brest has a modern top-end hotel! This fantastic new accommodation is streets ahead of even the nearest competition locally, although frankly that's not saying too much. Housed in a sensitively designed modern building, there's more than a little old-world style here, with spacious and grand well-appointed rooms and impressive public areas. Multilingual staff are charming and there's also good food available, including a great breakfast spread.

Hotel Molodyozhnaya   HOTEL €€

(☎216 376; vul Kamsamolskaya 6; s/d €20/32; ⊛) This small and very centrally located place is a short walk from the station. The rooms are comfortable and clean, all have private facilities and the welcome is almost warm.

Hotel Buh   HOTEL €

(☎236 417; vul Lenina 2; s/d €20/33, without bathroom €15/22; ⊛) The cheapest and oldest of Brest's hotels is also the best choice for some character – the brightly painted Stalin-era foyer is a highlight and service is friendly. The renovated rooms with private bathrooms are often booked up in advance though, leaving the older facility-free rooms as the only option.

Hotel Intourist
HOTEL €€

(📞200 510; www.brestintourist.com; pr Masherava 15; s/d incl breakfast from €37/54; 🖥) With notoriously frosty reception staff and a cavernous reception area that reminds you of the determinedly dark bygone days of Soviet travel, this old state behemoth is nobody's first choice. If you do stay here you'll find rooms are passable, though, with modernised facilities on almost every floor and a reasonably central location.

✖ Eating & Drinking

Brest has plenty of takeaways and fast food on offer, particularly around the pedestrianised area of vul Savetskaya. There's also a passable **supermarket** (vul Savetskaya 48; ⊗8am-11pm) in the centre. At the fortress itself there's only the decidedly mediocre **Café Tsitadel** (⊗9am-6pm) to cater for you – it's best to bring a packed lunch if you want to eat while you visit.

Jules Verne
FINE DINING €€€

(vul Hoholya 29; mains BR40,000-150,000; ⊗noon-midnight) It's almost a miracle that such a great restaurant exists in Brest. Decked out like a gentleman's club and with a travel theme, this dark, atmospheric joint manages to be refined without being stuffy. It serves up cracking dishes – from mouthwatering curries and a range of French cooking to sumptuous desserts and the best coffee in town. Don't miss it.

Traktir U Ozera
TRADITIONAL €€

(Park Kultury i Otdykha; mains BR30,000-130,000) This old-style *traktir* (Russian inn) by the lake in Brest's main park has plenty of charm, although it's perhaps better for an evening meal than a daytime one, as it rather squanders its lakeside position and is surprisingly dark inside. Dishes range from steaks and kebabs to sushi and grills. For something simpler in equally pleasant surroundings, there's an open-air cafe serving up kebabs and beer outside.

Pizzeria
PIZZA €

(vul Pushkinskaya 20; pizzas BR20,000-60,000) It's not well signed, but you can pretty much follow your nose into the building through a garish bakery and then down the stairs. Surprisingly good thin-crust pizzas are made to order and consumed in this basement place while dubbed Mexican soap operas entertain the diners.

Pub House
PUB

(vul Hoholya; ⊗10am-midnight) This friendly and rustic wooden bar offers up a selection of beers from all over Europe, as well as showing sports events and serving decent food. It's by far the most pleasant place for a drink in town.

🛍 Shopping

Souvenirs can be bought on the 1st floor of the city's **TsUM** (pr Masherava 17; ⊗9am-9pm Mon-Sat, 9am-7pm Sun), although the selection is fairly limited.

ℹ Information

24-hour Pharmacy (vul Hoholya 32)

Belarusbank (pl Lenina) Currency exchange, Western Union and a nearby ATM.

Beltelekom (pr Masherava 21; internet per hr BR1500; ⊗7am-10.30pm) You can make long-distance calls here, as well as use the internet cafe or the cheap wi-fi for those with laptops.

Brest Intourist (📞201 071, 225 571; www.brestintourist.com; pr Masherava 15; ⊗9am-6pm Mon-Fri) Inside Hotel Intourist; the superfriendly English-speaking staff can arrange city tours including 'Jewish Brest' and overpriced trips to the Belavezhskaya Pushcha National Park.

City Emergency Hospital (📞235 838; vul Lenina 15)

Cyber Brest (3rd fl, vul Kamsamolskaya 36; per hr BR10,000; ⊗9am-midnight) Internet access at your choice of 50 computers; follow the footprints to the top floor.

Post Office (pl Lenina)

ℹ Getting There & Around

BUS The **bus station** (📞114, 004; vul Mitskevicha) is in the centre of town and has left-luggage lockers and an internet cafe. There are five daily buses to Minsk (BR58,000 to BR70,000, five hours), 10 daily to Hrodna (BR60,000 to BR80,000, five hours) and a service to Vilnius in Lithuania on Friday and Sunday (BR110,000, eight hours).

TAXI For a taxi, call 📞061 or have your hotel call for you.

TRAIN The **train station** (📞005) has on-site customs. Trains leave for Minsk (BR35,000/65,000 *platzkart/kupe* – 3rd-/2nd-class– four hours) several times daily. When taking a train from Brest, note that the platform nearest the city centre is for eastbound trains (ie towards Minsk and Russia); the next one is for trains heading west (towards Poland). To get to the city from the train station, you'll have to

BELARUS BREST

mount a steep flight of steps from the platform; once you're up, go right on the overpass. It's a short walk, but a taxi into town should be no more than BR20,000.

Around Brest

BELAVEZHSKAYA PUSHCHA NATIONAL PARK

A Unesco World Heritage Site some 60km north of Brest, **Belavezhskaya Pushcha National Park** (☎01631 56 370) is the oldest wildlife refuge in Europe and is the pride of Belarus. Half the park's territory lies in Poland, where it's called Białowieża National Park.

Some 1300 sq km of primeval forest survives here. It's all that remains of a canopy that eight centuries ago covered northern Europe. Some oak trees here are more than 600 years old and some pines at least 300 years old.

At least 55 mammal species, including deer, lynx, boars, wild horses, wolves, elk, ermines, badgers, martens, otters, mink and beavers call this park home, but the area is most celebrated for its 300 or so European bison, the continent's largest land mammal. These free-range zoobr – slightly smaller than their American cousins – were driven to near extinction (the last one living in the wild was shot by a hunter in 1919) and then bred back from 52 animals that had survived in zoos. Now a total of about 3000 exist, of which more than 300 are wild in the Belavezhskaya Pushcha. Amazingly you can pay to shoot them – '300 is enough' according to park wardens, who want to control their numbers due to the vast amount of foliage these enormous beasts consume.

There's a **nature museum** (admission BR15,000; ⊙9am-5pm) that gives a great introduction to the species living in the park and *volerei* (enclosures; admission BR3000), where you can view bison, deer, bears, boars and other animals (including the rare hybrid Tarpan horse, a cross-breed of a species that was also shot into near extinction).

There are a few different options for overnight stays, all of which are best arranged through Brest Intourist. Camping requires permission and costs BR15,000 per person. The **Kamyanyuki Hotel Complex** (☎01631 56 497; s/d incl breakfast €15/20) includes a serviceable hotel next to the nature museum in the eponymous village just outside the national park. Rooms are remodelled and have bathrooms and balconies. Other options include **Dom Grafa Tushkevicha**, a guesthouse better for families or other small groups, and the historic **Viskuli Hotel**, where Lukashenko often stays. Book these through Brest Intourist as they aren't used to people just turning up. There's a restaurant in the Kamyanyuki Hotel Complex, as well as a couple of other cafes serving up simple *shashlyk* (meat kebabs) and bliny.

It's entirely possible (and a great deal cheaper) to see the national park without taking a guided tour, although if you don't speak Russian you may miss some interesting commentary on trips through the woods and in the museum. From Brest take one of the six daily *marshrutky* or buses to Kamyanyuki (BR38,000, one hour 20 minutes) and walk from the village to the clearly visible reserve buildings. Once there you can walk around the park yourself, or even better, hire a bike from the museum (BR18,000 per hour). On some days individuals with private cars or taxis are allowed to drive along the set route for tours in the reserve, although usually you'll have to join a tour bus, which runs one to three times a day from the museum (BR30,000, 1½ hours) depending on demand.

An altogether easier option is to book a day trip with Brest Intourist. This includes transport, the services of an English-speaking guide, and museum and park entry fees; it can be quite expensive unless you share the cost with a couple of other people.

NORTHERN BELARUS

In the north of the country, Vitsebsk is the most obviously appealing destination for travellers, with its dramatic river, a clutch of lovely churches and the artistic heritage bequeathed to it by Marc Chagall. Also of interest is lovely Hrodna, one of the few towns in the country not destroyed in WWII.

Vitsebsk   Віцебскі

☎0212 / POP 348,000

The historic city of Vitsebsk (known universally outside Belarus by its Russian name, Vitebsk) lies a short distance from the Russian border and almost 300km from Minsk. Vitsebsk was an important

PRIPYATSKY NATIONAL PARK

One of the best-kept secrets in Belarus is the excellent **Pripyatsky National Park** (☎02353 75 644, 02912 50 095; www.npp.by), a relatively untouched swathe of marshes, swampland and floodplains known locally as 'the lungs of Europe'. Flora and fauna particular to wetlands are found here, including more than 800 plant species, some 50 mammal species and more than 200 species of birds.

At the park headquarters and museum you can tour a great display of the flora and fauna specific to the area, and make all the arrangements you need. Excursions range from one day to a week and can include extended fishing, hunting and boating expeditions deep into the marshlands. Cruises on the river are particularly recommended.

Park staff can also put you up at one of their guest houses in town, arrange accommodation in a private home or, even better, put you up in the middle of the park itself. Several comfy cottages have been kitted out with kitchens and saunas and are set in sublimely peaceful settings. The park organises winter ice-fishing expeditions (followed by vodka and a sauna, of course) and many summer activities. Prices vary, but generally a person need only spend about €75 per day, including accommodation, three meals and guided tours.

From Minsk there are at least two daily buses to Turau (BR44,000, four to seven hours), plus one daily *marshrutka* (BR85,000, four hours) from Minsk's Vostochny Bus Station.

centre of Jewish culture when it was one of the major cities of the 'Pale of Settlement', where Jews were allowed to live in the Russian Empire. Indeed, the city was immortalised in the early work of Marc Chagall, the city's most famous son, who grew up and studied here before moving to St Petersburg, where his career began. With its relaxed atmosphere, attractive centre and diverting museums, Vitsebsk makes for a pleasant side trip or stopover on the way through to Russia.

The city was all but wiped off the face of the earth during WWII, with just 15 buildings still standing by the time of the Nazi withdrawal. Indeed, coming into Vitsebsk, you may be inclined to turn around and leave again, as the grey suburbs and heavy industry on the city's outskirts are particularly unappealing. The main drag, inventively named vul Lenina, runs parallel to the Dvina River, while the perpendicular Kirovsky Bridge crosses the river and leads via vul Kirova to the train and bus stations.

◉ Sights

Chagall Museum MUSEUM
(www.chagall.vitebsk.by; vul Punta 2; admission BR15,000, tours BR30,000; ☺11am-7pm Tue-Sun Mar-Sep, Wed-Sun Oct-Feb) The first museum on every itinerary should be the excellent Chagall Museum, which was established in 1992 and displays collections of Chagall lithographs – his illustrations for the Bible

(1956–60), designs to accompany Gogol's *Dead Souls* (1923–25) and graphic representations of the 12 tribes of Israel (1960). Downstairs there's a space for temporary exhibits. Sadly there aren't more Chagall painting in Belarus because his work was banned by the Soviet government, which even rejected a cache of paintings bequeathed to them by the artist himself.

Marc Chagall House Museum MUSEUM
(vul Pokrovskaya 11; admission BR12,000; ☺11am-7pm Tue-Sun) Across the town's river, a good 20-minute walk away from the Chagall Museum, is the Marc Chagall House Museum, where the artist lived as a child for 13 years between 1897 and 1910 – a period beautifully evoked in his autobiography, *My Life*. The simple, small house contains photographs of Chagall and his family, various Jewish knick-knacks and some period furniture. It leads out into a garden and is very evocative of a simple Jewish-Russian childhood.

Art Museum MUSEUM
(☎36 22 31; vul Lenina 32; admission BR10,000; ☺10am-6pm Tue-Sun) The grand halls of the Art Museum are decked with mainly local art, both old and new. There are numerous 18th- to 20th-century works, including those by Repin and Makovsky. A highlight is the collection of very moving realist scenes of early-20th-century Vitsebsk street life by Yudel Pen, Marc Chagall's first art teacher.

Of the 793 paintings Pen donated to the city before he died, only 200 have survived, most of them held here.

Churches
CHURCHES

While Vitsebsk does not have many churches of note, there is a pair of very different **Orthodox churches** on the eastern bank of the Dvina River, near the main bridge on vul Zamkovaya. Nearby too is the lovely **Svyato-Voskresensky Church**, on the corner of vul Lenina and vul Zamkovaya, a re-construction of a magnificent 18th-century church with gorgeous frescos on its facade and golden onion domes.

☆☆ Festivals & Events

Slavyansky Bazaar
FESTIVAL

(Slavic Bazaar; www.festival.vitebsk.by) This pop-ular festival is held in mid-July and brings in dozens of singers and performers from Slavic countries for a weeklong series of concerts. The annual event attracts tens of thousands of visitors, creating a huge party.

🛏 Sleeping

TOP CHOICE Hotel Eridan
HOTEL €€€

(☑36 24 56; www.eridan-vitebsk.com; vul Savet-skaya 21/17; s/d/ste incl breakfast €42/69/83; ❄) The best-value hotel in Vitsebsk is handy for the Chagall Museum and well lo-cated in the middle of the Old Town. With pleasant wooden furniture, high ceilings, cheap lobby wi-fi and rooms that are well equipped (albeit done out rather gaudily), this place has the charm so lacking in the standard-issue Soviet hotels you'll stay in elsewhere.

Hotel Luchesa
HOTEL €€

(☑29 85 00; www.luchesa.by; pr Stroiteley 1; s/d from €33/38; ❄@◎⊛) The top business hotel in town is the four-star Luchesa, housed in a modern building 2km south of the city centre. It's well run and has comfy – if fairly standard – modern rooms in varying shades of brown, with cheap wi-fi.

✕ Eating & Drinking

Zolotoy Lev
TRADITIONAL €€

(vul Suvorova 20/13; mains BR30,000-110,000; ⊗noon-midnight) The smartest place in town is the expansive 'Golden Lion'. There's a charming interior (when the TV is off), a large menu offering traditional Belarusian cuisine, and a spacious outdoor area serving up *shashlyk* and beer.

Vitebsky Traktir
INN €

(vul Suvorova 4; mains BR20,000-60,000; ⊗noon-midnight) What else would you expect to find in a dark cellar oozing centuries of Slavic tradition? Why, sushi of course. This decent place has lots of charm, even if it is a little too dark for its own good. A traditional Be-larusian menu and European dishes are also available.

Kofeynya
CAFE

(vul Suvorova 2) This small coffeehouse next door to the Vitebsky Traktir serves up the best coffee in town, as well as a large selec-tion of teas and cake.

ⓘ Information

There are ATMs on vul Lenina, although there always seems to be a queue for their services.

Internet Centre (vul Mayakovskaya 3; per hr BR5000; ⊗9am-10pm) On a small square off vul Lenina and behind the Svyato-Voskresensky Church.

Post Office (vul Lenina) Offers international phone calls and internet access.

ⓘ Getting There & Away

BUS There are approximately hourly to two-hourly buses or *marshrutky* to Minsk (BR65,000, four to five hours).

TRAIN Vitsebsk is on one of the major railway lines heading south from St Petersburg into Ukraine. There are two or three daily trains to Minsk (BR45,000 to BR79,000, 4½ to six hours) and one to St Petersburg (BR340,000, 13 hours). There's also a daily train to both Moscow (BR225,000, 11 hours) and Brest (BR135,000, 11 hours).

ⓘ Getting Around

While Vitsebsk is larger than most other regional centres, the city is pleasant to explore on foot. Buses ply the 1.5km main drag from the bus and train stations into town; get off just after cross-ing the Dvina River and you'll be only 500m from the Art Museum.

UNDERSTAND BELARUS

Belarus Today

The presidential elections of December 2010 followed a by-now-familiar pattern. Lukash-enko won a highly implausible 79% of the vote, all Organization for Security and Co-operation in Europe (OSCE) election monitors rejected the results out of hand, and protestors on the main square in Minsk were violently dispersed. The protests left more than 600 people in jail, including several of the opposition candidates, many of whom were allegedly beaten while the main opposition leader was reported as being forcibly abducted from the hospital where he was being treated. However, despite criticism from all sides, including once-loyal Russia, Lukashenko remains as entrenched in power as ever. Belarus is still a tightly controlled, repressive and sometimes violent police state at the time of writing and there's presently no end in sight to Lukashenko's iron grip on this nation.

History

Arrival of the Slavs

Evidence of a human presence in Belarus goes back to the early Stone Age. Eastern Slavs from the Krivichi, Dregovichi and Radimichi tribes arrived here in the 6th to 8th centuries AD. The principalities of Polatsk (first mentioned in 862), Turau (980), Pinsk and Minsk were formed, all falling under the suzerainty of Prince Vladimir's Kyivan Rus by the late 10th century. The economy was based on slash-and-burn agriculture, honey farming and river trade, particularly on the Dnjapro River (Dnepr in Russian), a vital link between Byzantium and the Nordic Varangians.

Lithuanian & Polish Control

Belarus means 'White Russia', a name derived from the fact that it is the one part of Rus that, while conquered by the Mongols in 1240, was never settled by them. The term 'white' refers therefore to the purity of the people, who unlike their Muscovite cousins, never intermarried.

In the 14th century, the territory of modern-day Belarus became part of the Grand Duchy of Lithuania. It was to be 400 years before Belarus came under Russian control, a period in which Belarusians became linguistically and culturally differentiated from the Russians to their east and the Ukrainians to their south.

After Lithuania became Roman Catholic following the uniting of its crown with Poland's in 1386, the Belarusian peasantry remained Orthodox but were reduced to serf status. Lithuania nonetheless permitted its subjects a fair degree of autonomy,

even using Belarusian as its state language during the early 15th century – an important fact for patriotic Belarusians today as proof of their historical legitimacy. All official correspondence, literature, doctrines and statutes at the time were written in Belarusian.

In 1596 the Polish authorities arranged the Union of Brest, which set up the Uniate Church (also known as Ukrainian Catholic or Greek Catholic), bringing much of the Orthodox Church in Belarus under the authority of the Vatican. The Uniate Church insisted on the pope's supremacy and Catholic doctrine, but permitted Orthodox forms of ritual.

Over the next two centuries of Polish rule, Poles and Jews controlled trade and most Belarusians remained peasants. Only after the three Partitions of Poland (1772, 1793 and 1795–96) was Belarus absorbed into Russia.

Tsarist Rule

Under Russian rule, a policy of Russification was pursued and in 1839 the Uniate Church was abolished, with most Belarusians returning to Orthodoxy. The Russian rulers and the Orthodox Church regarded Belarus as 'western Russia' and tried to obliterate any sense of a Belarusian nationality. Publishing in the Belarusian language was banned.

The economy slowly developed in the 19th century with the emergence of small industries such as timber milling, glassmaking and boat-building. However, industrial progress lagged behind that of Russia and poverty in the countryside remained at such a high level that 1.5 million people – largely the wealthy or educated – emigrated in the 50 years before the Russian Revolution in 1917, mostly to Siberia or the USA.

During the 19th century Belarus was part of the Pale of Settlement, the area where Jews in the Russian Empire were required to settle. The percentage of Jews in many Belarusian cities and towns before WWII was between 35% and 75%. The vast majority of Belarusians remained on the land, poor and illiterate. Due to their cultural stagnation, their absence from positions of influence and their historical domination by Poles and Russians, any sense among Belarusian speakers that they were a distinct nationality was very slow to emerge. Nonetheless, Belarusian intellectuals were part of a wave of nationalism across Europe and it was in the 19th century that the concept of Belarusians as a distinct people first emerged.

World Wars & the Soviet Union

In March 1918, under German occupation during WWI, a short-lived independent Belarusian Democratic Republic was declared, but the land was soon under the control of the Red Army and the Belarusian Soviet Socialist Republic (BSSR) was formed. The 1921 Treaty of Rīga allotted roughly the western half of modern Belarus to Poland, which launched a program of Polonisation that provoked armed resistance by Belarusians. The eastern half was left to the Bolsheviks and the redeclared BSSR was a founding member of the USSR in 1922.

In the 1920s the Soviet regime encouraged Belarusian literature and culture, but in the 1930s under Stalin, nationalism and the Belarusian language were discouraged and their proponents ruthlessly persecuted. The 1930s also saw industrialisation, agricultural collectivisation and purges in which hundreds of thousands were executed – most in the Kurapaty Forest, outside Minsk.

When Nazi Germany invaded Russia in 1941, Belarus was on the front line and suffered greatly. German occupation was savage and partisan resistance widespread until the Red Army drove the Germans out in 1944, with massive destruction on both sides. Hundreds of villages were destroyed and barely a stone was left standing in Minsk. At least 25% of the Belarusian population (over two million people) died between 1939 and 1945. Many of them, Jews and others, died in 200-plus concentration camps; the third-largest Nazi concentration camp was set up at Maly Trostenets, outside Minsk, where more than 200,000 people were executed.

Western Belarus remained in Soviet hands at the end of the war, with Minsk developing into the industrial hub of western USSR and Belarus becoming one of the Soviet Union's most prosperous republics.

The 1986 Chornobyl disaster, just over the border in Ukraine, was most profoundly felt by the people of Belarus. The radiation cloud released left about a quarter of the country seriously contaminated and its effects are still felt today, particularly in the southeastern regions of the country.

Post-Soviet Belarus

On 27 July 1990, the republic issued a declaration of sovereignty within the USSR. On 25 August 1991 a declaration of full national independence was issued. With no history whatsoever as a politically or economically independent entity, the country of Belarus was one of the oddest products of the disintegration of the USSR.

Since July 1994 Belarus has been governed by Alexander Lukashenko, a former collective-farm director. His nickname throughout the country and beyond is Bat'ka (Papa). His presidential style has been autocratic and authoritarian, and the country was declaimed an 'outpost of tyranny' by former US Secretary of State Condoleezza Rice. Lukashenko has on several occasions altered the constitution (the referenda were criticised by the EU and the OSCE), rendering the parliament essentially toothless and extending both his term and the number of times he can hold the presidency. Media distribution is handled by the state, so independently produced publications are easily quashed. Online publications are all that is left for independent Belarusian media and even those are on shaky ground as internet access is increasingly state controlled and antigovernment sites are routinely blocked.

On 19 March 2006, Lukashenko officially won another five-year term as president, with an apparent 83% of the vote and 98% voter turnout. On the night of the 19th, thousands of protesters turned out on the city's main square for what was being termed as the Denim Revolution – a 'mini-Maydan' echoing what happened in Kyiv 1½ years earlier. A peaceful tent city started and hundreds of people, mostly students, withstood freezing temperatures for almost a week. But once the international media left the scene to cover Ukrainian parliamentary elections, protesters were beaten and arrested by riot police.

People

There are approximately 9.4 million people in Belarus, of which 81.2% are Belarusian, 11.4% Russian, 4% Polish and 2.4% Ukrainian, with the remaining 1% consisting of other groups. This results in a rather homogeneous population. Prior to WWII, 10% of the national population was Jewish and in cities such as Minsk, Hrodna and Brest,

Jews made up between one-third and three-quarters of the population. They now make up about 0.3% of the country's population.

Generally speaking, Belarusians are quiet, polite and reserved people. Because they tend to be shy, they seem less approachable than Russians and Ukrainians, but they are just as friendly and generous (often more so) once introductions are made.

Atheism is widespread. Of believers, 80% are Eastern Orthodox and 20% are Roman Catholic (about 15% of the Catholics are ethnic Poles). During the early 1990s the Uniate Church (an Orthodox sect that looks to Rome, not Moscow) was re-established and now it has a following of over 100,000 members. There's also a small Protestant minority, the remnant of a once-large German population.

Arts

Assumed by many to be Russian or French, painter Marc Chagall (1887–1985) was actually born and grew up in Belarus and is by far the country's best-known artist. Born to a Jewish family in a village near Vitsebsk in 1887, Chagall lived and trained there before moving to St Petersburg aged 20 and then to Paris in the 1930s to set the world alight with his surrealist images and trademark flying people. His family home is now a small museum, although there are very few Chagalls in Belarus today – the Soviet government clearly didn't think much of his work, refusing multiple offers of canvases from the artist during his lifetime.

The hero of early Belarusian literary achievement was Francysk Skaryna. Born in Polatsk but educated in Poland and Italy, the scientist, doctor, writer and humanist became the first person to translate the Bible into Belarusian. He also built the first printing press in the country. In the late 16th century the philosopher and humanist Symon Budny printed a number of works in Belarusian. The 19th century saw the beginning of modern Belarusian literature with works by writers and poets such as Maxim Bohdanovich, Janka Kupala and Jakub Kolas.

Environment

It's safe to say that Belarus does not enjoy a wildly exciting geography. It's a flat country, consisting of low ridges dividing broad, often marshy lowlands with more than 11,000 small lakes. In the south are the Pripatsky National Park, Europe's largest marsh area, dubbed locally the 'lungs of Europe' because air currents passing over it are re-oxygenated and purified by the swamps. Around 6.4% of Belarusian land is protected.

Because of the vast expanses of primeval forests and marshes, Belarusian fauna abounds. The most celebrated animal is the zoobr (European bison), the continent's largest land mammal. It was hunted almost to extinction by 1919, but was fortunately bred back into existence from 52 animals that had survived in zoos. Now several hundred exist, mainly in the Belavezhskaya Pushcha National Park, a Unesco World Heritage Site. It is the oldest wildlife refuge in Europe, the pride of Belarus and the most famous of the country's five national parks.

The 1986 disaster at Chornobyl has been the defining event for the Belarusian environment. The dangers of exposure to radiation for travellers, particularly in the areas covered in this guide, are almost nonexistent. Ironically, the exclusion zone has proved a boon for nature – the absence of human habitation seems to have done more to improve biodiversity than a nuclear explosion appears to have done to damage it.

Food & Drink

Belarusian cuisine rarely differs from Russian cuisine, although there are a few uniquely Belarusian dishes. Although the cuisine is largely meat-based and the concept of vegetarianism is not exactly widespread, it is possible to find some dishes without meat; eating vegan will be considerably more difficult. *Draniki* and some versions of *kletsky* and *khaladnik* are all vegetarian-friendly local dishes.

Belarus is well known for several of its drinks. *Belavezhskaya* is a bitter herbal alcoholic drink, while of the Belarusian vodkas, Charodei is probably the most esteemed (but can be hard to find). Other popular souvenir-quality vodkas are Belarus Sineokaya and Minskaya. Beer is a much-loved drink in Belarus too. Local brews are decent, although most bars now serve imported lager from Western Europe.

Restaurants and bars usually open around 10am and, with few exceptions, close between 10pm and midnight. There is no nationwide ban on smoking, though most bars and restaurants have nonsmoking areas.

SURVIVAL GUIDE

Directory A–Z

Accommodation

While budget and midrange accommodation standards in Belarus tend to be lower than in Western Europe, they are still generally acceptable and often better than in Russia or Ukraine. Top-end places, of which there are a few in Minsk, are usually more expensive and of a lower standard than what you would expect from a top-end place in the West. Smoking in hotel rooms usually occurs in Belarus; only top-end hotels tend to offer nonsmoking rooms.

Rooms have private bathrooms unless otherwise indicated, but do not include breakfast. The standard practice for hotels due to the rapid fluctuation of exchange rates is to quote prices in euros and then charge for them in BR at the day's exchange rates. The following prices are for a double room in high season.

€ less than €25

€€ €25 to €60

€€€ more than €60

Farmers and villagers are usually generous about allowing campers to pitch a tent on their lot for an evening. Outside national parks you may camp pretty much anywhere, although camping in or near a city is asking for trouble from the police.

Activities

Belarus is flat, but visitors can still enjoy skiing. About 20km from Minsk is the Raubichy Olympic Sports Complex, where you can enjoy some great cross-country skiing, while downhill skiing and snowboarding are possible at **Logoisk** (www.logoisk.by) and the newer **Silichy** (www.silichy.by), both about 30km from Minsk.

Business Hours

Banks 9am to 5pm Monday to Friday

Offices hours 9am to 6pm Monday to Friday

Shops 9am or 10am to 9pm Monday to Saturday, to 6pm Sunday if open at all

Some businesses will close for lunch, which is usually for an hour and occurs any time between noon and 2pm. Restaurants and bars usually open between 10am and midday and close between 10pm and midnight.

Embassies & Consulates

There is no representation for Canada, Australia, New Zealand or the Netherlands in Belarus.

French Embassy (☑017 299 1800; www.ambafrance-by.org; pl Svabody 11)

German Embassy (☑017 217 5900; www.minsk.diplo.de; vul Zakharava 26)

Moldovan Embassy (☑017 289 1441; vul Belarusskaya 2)

Russian Embassy Minsk (☑017 222 4985; vul Novolvilenskaya 1a); Brest (☑0162 23 78 42; vul Pushkinskaya 10)

Romanian Embassy (☑017 203 8097; per Moskvina 4)

UK Embassy (☑017 229 8200; www.ukinbelarus.fco.gov.uk; vul Karla Marksa 37)

Ukrainian Embassy Minsk (☑017 283 1989; vul Staravilenskaya 51); Brest (☑0162 22 04 77; vul Vorovskaha 19)

US Embassy (☑017 210 1283; http://minsk.usembassy.gov; vul Staravilenskaya 46)

Food

Price ranges are based on the average cost of a main course.

€ less than BR50,000

€€ BR50,000 to BR100,000

€€€ more than BR100,000

Gay & Lesbian Travellers

Homophobia is rife in Belarus, even though gay sex acts were legalised in 1994. However, Slavic laissez-faire attitudes mean that you don't have to look hard to find gay life, which flourishes on the internet, at Minsk's one gay club, 6A, and at ever-changing venues that are gay-friendly or have gay nights.

As travellers, gay and lesbian couples are unlikely to horrify locals by asking for a double room, but otherwise discretion is advisable. Websites to check out include www.gaybelarus.by and www.gay.by (in Russian only) and the Russian site www.gay.ru, which has a section in English and includes information about Belarus.

Insurance

All visitors to Belarus are required to possess medical insurance to cover the entire period of their stay. It is unlikely you will ever be asked for it, but you may have to purchase the official policy at border posts if you don't have documentation to prove you're insured. Insurance is not required for holders of transit visas.

Internet Access

A new presidential decree introduced in 2010 made Belarusian internet laws by far the tightest in Europe. Legally, all internet cafes now need to make a note of your name and passport number before allowing you to surf, so bring your passport out with you if you plan to use the web. While some Minsk cafes and hotels offer free wi-fi, it's still far from the norm and most hotels offer wi-fi access via paid cards you buy at the lobby (usually requiring your passport and name as well). These cards are very cheap, however (around €1 per hour), and connections are generally good.

Language

Despite the fact that almost all official signage is in Belarusian, advertising and conversation on the street are both almost universally in Russian. This creates a rather strange dichotomy between what you see and hear; for example, if you ask somebody the name of the street you're on and are told it's ulitsa Krasnaya (Russian), you'll find that the street sign calls it vulitsa Chyrvonaya (Belarusian). Confused? You will be. For more information on navigating around Minsk, see p83. Where possible, we've used the Belarusian names for streets, to match the local signage. Some basic English is usually spoken by younger people, but learning the Cyrillic alphabet will be enormously helpful to any traveller.

Money

The Belarusian rouble (BR) is the national currency and the money's wide spectrum of bill denominations is overwhelming to the newcomer. There are BR10, BR20, BR50, BR100, BR500, BR1000, BR5000, BR10,000, BR20,000, BR50,000, BR100,000 and BR200,000 notes. There are no coins, so you'll quickly acquire a thick wad of largely worthless notes. Ensure you change any remaining roubles before leaving Belarus, as it's almost impossible to exchange the currency outside the country. Also check the exchange rates when you arrive, as the currency is far from stable.

ATMs and currency-exchange offices are not hard to find in Belarusian cities. Major credit cards are accepted at many of the nicer hotels, restaurants, and supermarkets in Minsk, but travellers cheques are not worth the effort.

Post

The word for post office is *pashtamt* in Belarusian, or *pochta* in Russian. You can mail important, time-sensitive items via the Express Mail Service (EMS), at most main post offices.

Public Holidays

New Year's Day 1 January

Orthodox Christmas 7 January

International Women's Day 8 March

Constitution Day 15 March

Catholic & Orthodox Easter March/April

Unity of Peoples of Russia and Belarus Day 2 April

International Labour Day (May Day) 1 May

Victory Day 9 May

Independence Day 3 July

Dzyady (Day of the Dead) 2 November

Catholic Christmas 25 December

Telephone

Landlines need to be dialled with the city or town's regional code before them if you're calling from another part of Belarus. The mobile-phone market is divided between four companies, of which **Velcom** (www.velcom.by) and **MTS** (www.mts.by) are the dominant players. Anyone with an unlocked mobile-phone handset can buy a SIM card for next to nothing (bring your passport and provide an address in Belarus).

To dial a Minsk landline number from a Minsk landline number, just dial the number;

from a local mobile phone, press ✆8 017 or ✆375 17 and then dial the number.

To make an intercity call from a land-line phone, dial ✆8 (wait for the tone), the city's area code (including the ✆0) and the number; from a mobile, do the same, and if it doesn't work, try dialling ✆+375 and the area code without the ✆0, then the number.

To make an international call from a landline phone, dial ✆8 (wait for the tone), ✆10, then the country code, area code and number; from a mobile, press +, then dial the country code, area code and number.

To phone Belarus from abroad, dial ✆375 followed by the city code (without the first zero) and number.

Visas

Belarusian visa regulations change frequently, so check by telephone with your nearest Belarusian embassy for the latest details. While most embassies have visa information on their websites, be aware that they are not always up to date.

Nearly all visitors require a visa and arranging one before you arrive is usually essential. Visas on arrival are only issued at the Minsk-2 international airport, but they are expensive and are just as much hassle, so it's well worth getting one in advance for peace of mind (it's rare but not unheard of for people to have problems getting visas at the airport).

APPLICATIONS

By far the simplest – although also the most expensive – way to get a visa is to apply through a visa agency. Alternatively, you can take a faxed or emailed confirmation from your hotel to the nearest Belarusian embassy and apply for one yourself.

Tallinn (Estonia), Rīga (Latvia) and Vilnius (Lithuania) have numerous travel agencies specialising in Belarusian visas.

Visa costs vary depending on the embassy you apply at and your citizenship. Americans pay more, but typically transit visas cost around €65, single-entry visas cost about €90 and to get either of those in 48 hours rather than five working days, count on paying double.

There are four main types of visa.

TOURIST VISA

Tourist visas are issued if you have an invitation from an accredited Belarusian travel agency or a hotel reservation voucher. Single-entry and double-entry visas are valid for 30 days.

PRIVATE VISA

The private visa is an excellent option if you're a citizen of the EU, Canada, South Africa, Australia or New Zealand. New regulations mean that you simply need to provide the name and address of a local friend or contact you'll be staying with (though in fact you can stay in a hotel or a rented apartment) and you can receive a visa. Guest visas are valid for 30 days and can only be single entry. The disadvantage is that many embassies are apparently unaware of these relatively new rules and are still demanding an official invitation from an individual.

BUSINESS VISA

Business visas are issued to those invited to Belarus by a business. Business visas are for a minimum of 90 days and can also be annual and allow for multiple entries.

TRANSIT VISA

If you are passing through Belarus and won't be in the country for more than 48 hours, you can apply for a transit visa, for which no invite or voucher is necessary. You simply have to show a train or air ticket to prove your need to transit through Belarus. The possession of a valid Russian visa is not enough to serve as a transit visa. Transit visas are not available at the border.

REGISTRATION

If you are staying in Belarus for more than five working days, you must have your visa officially registered. Hotels do this automatically and the service is included in the room price. They will stamp the back of your white landing card, which you will need to keep and show to immigration agents upon departure. In theory you'll be fined if you don't provide proof of registration for every day of your stay; in practice, proof of one day is good enough. If you're staying at a short-term let apartment, the owner will usually have a connection at a local hotel and will organise your registration for you. Note that if you're staying for fewer than five working days, there is no need to register.

If you've received a personal invitation, you'll need to find the nearest *passportno-vizovoye upravleniye* (passport and visa department; PVU, formerly OVIR), though this will be time-consuming and your host will need to come with you. The simplest place to register your visa in this case is at Minsk's **PVU main office** (☎017 231 9174; pr Nezalezhnastsi 8).

An easier way to get this done is to pay for one night's stay at a cheap hotel where the staff will register your visa – you don't even have to spend the night there if you have accommodation elsewhere, though don't make this clear to the staff.

Getting There & Away

Once you have your visa in your passport, the process of entering Belarus is relatively simple. Ensure you fill out one of the white migration cards in duplicate before presenting your passport to the immigration officer.

Air

Belarus' national airline is **Belavia** (☎017 220 2555; www.belavia.by; vul Nyamiha 14, Minsk), which has flights to London, Paris, Frankfurt, Berlin, Vienna, Rome, Milan, Barcelona, Istanbul, Tel Aviv, Warsaw, Prague, Rīga and many Russian cities, including Moscow and St Petersburg.

The following are the main international airlines that fly to Minsk:

Aeroflot (www.aeroflot.com)

Air Baltic (www.airbaltic.com)

Air Zena Georgian Airways (www.airzena.com)

Austrian Airlines (www.aua.com)

Czech Airlines (www.csa.cz)

El Al (www.elal.co.il)

Estonian Air (www.estonian-alr.ee)

Etihad Airways (www.etihad.com)

LOT Polish Airlines (www.lot.com)

Lufthansa (www.lufthansa.com)

Turkish Airlines (www.turkishairlines.com)

Land

BUS

Bus travel is a common and fast way to enter the country, although long queues at border crossings are not uncommon. Immigration and customs control will normally come aboard the bus and check all passengers and you may be asked to get off for luggage searches. The most frequently used international bus services are the quick four-hour trip between Vilnius (Lithuania) and Minsk, and the seven-hour trip between Minsk

and Białystok (Poland). Services also run to Białystok (Poland) from Brest.

CAR & MOTORCYCLE

If you're driving your own vehicle, there are 10 main-road routes into Belarus via border stations through which foreigners can pass. International Driving Permits are recognised in Belarus, as are most national licences. Roads in Belarus are generally very good and main motorways are wonderfully light on traffic, although the main M1/E30 motorway gets busy with long-distance trucks travelling between Russia and the EU in both directions. Signage is excellent throughout the country, although usually only in Cyrillic. On intercity road trips, fill up with fuel when exiting the city; fuel stations may be scant before you hit the next big town.

TRAIN

Trains are usually a more comfortable but slightly slower way to travel than bus. From Minsk there are services to Russia, Lithuania and Poland, plus connections to the rest of Europe via Brest. You can also get to Russia from Vitsebsk.

Getting Around
Bicycle

Belarus' flat landscape and generally good-quality roads make it perfect for cyclists, although it's not a common mode of transport for locals and drivers still have a long way to go before they could be called cycle-friendly. You can rent mountain bikes from several locations around the Svisloch River in Minsk.

Bus

Bus services cover much of the country and are generally a reliable, if crowded, means of transportation. You can always buy tickets on the day, usually before you board, at the bus station ticket desk. As in Russia, normal bus services are supplemented by *marshrutka* (shared minibus) routes.

Car & Motorcycle

It's perfectly possible to hire a car in Minsk, though cars are usually old and badly maintained. Look them over carefully and check the spare tyre before you drive off.

The Brest–Vitsebsk highway (Brestskoye shosse; E30/M1) is an excellent two-laner, but there are frequent tollbooths (they only charge cars with foreign licence plates).

Drivers from the US or EU can use their own country's driving licence for six months. Cars drive in the right-hand lane, children 12 and under must sit in a back seat and your blood-alcohol level should be 0%. Fuel is usually not hard to find, but try to keep your tank full; it would even be wise to keep some spare fuel as well.

You will be instructed by signs to slow down when approaching GAI (ДАІ; road po-lice) stations, and not doing so is a sure-fire way to get a substantial fine.

Train

Train is a popular and scenic way to travel between the major towns of Belarus, though the bus network is far more extensive and prices are similar. Travelling by train is an excellent way to meet locals, with whom you'll be sharing compartments. Bring along some food to share and you'll make friends in no time.

Bosnia & Hercegovina

Includes »

Best Places to Eat

» Mala Kuhinja (p117)

» Bridge-view restaurants, Mostar (p130)

» Riverside restaurants on the Una (p143)

» Vinoteka Vukuje (p134)

Best Places to Stay

» Muslibegović House (p128)

» Hotel Platani (p134)

» Želenkovac (p142)

» Kostelski Buk (p143)

Why Go?

This craggily beautiful land retains some lingering scars from the heartbreaking civil war in the 1990s. But today visitors will more likely remember Bosnia and Hercegovina (BiH) for its deep, unassuming human warmth and for the intriguing East-meets-West atmosphere born of fascinatingly blended Ottoman and Austro-Hungarian histories.

Major drawcards are the reincarnated antique centres of Sarajevo and Mostar, where rebuilt historical buildings counterpoint fashionable bars and wi-fi–equipped cafes. Elsewhere Socialist-era architectural monstrosities are surprisingly rare blots on predominantly rural landscapes. Many Bosnian towns are lovably small, wrapped around medieval castles and surrounded by mountain ridges or cascading river canyons. Few places in Europe offer better rafting or such accessible, inexpensive skiing.

When to Go
Sarajevo

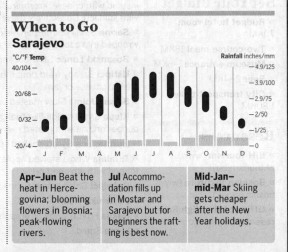

Apr–Jun Beat the heat in Hercegovina; blooming flowers in Bosnia; peak-flowing rivers.

Jul Accommodation fills up in Mostar and Sarajevo but for beginners the rafting is best now.

Mid-Jan–mid-Mar Skiing gets cheaper after the New Year holidays.

AT A GLANCE

» **Currency** Convertible mark (KM, BAM)

» **Language** Bosnian, Croatian, Serbian

» **Money** ATMs widely available in towns

» **Visas** Not required for most visitors

Fast Facts

» **Area** 51,129 sq km
» **Capital** Sarajevo
» **Country code** ☏387
» **Emergency** Ambulance ☏124, fire ☏123, police ☏122

Exchange Rates

Australia	A$1	1.59KM
Canada	C$1	1.51KM
Euro Zone	€1	1.96KM
Japan	¥100	1.62KM
New Zealand	NZ$1	1.28KM
UK	UK£1	2.32KM
USA	US$1	1.53KM

Set Your Budget

» **Budget hotel room** 70KM
» **Two-course meal** 18KM
» **Museum entrance** 1–5KM
» **Beer** 2–4KM
» **City transport ticket** 1.80KM

Resources

» **BiH Tourism** (www.bhtourism.ba)

» **Bosnian Institute** (www.bosnia.org.uk)

» **Office of the High Representative** (www.ohr.int)

Connections

Regular buses link the Croatian coast to Mostar and Sarajevo plus there's a little-publicised Trebinje–Dubrovnik service. Trains link Sarajevo to Zagreb, Belgrade and Budapest-Keleti, the only direct overland link to Hungary. There are numerous bus connections to Serbia and Montenegro from Sarajevo, Višegrad and Trebinje.

ITINERARIES

Six Days

Arriving from Dubrovnik (coastal Croatia), roam Mostar's Old Town and join a day tour visiting Počitelj, Blagaj and the Kravice waterfalls. After two days in Sarajevo head for Jajce then bus down to Split (Croatia). Or visit Višegrad en route to Mokra Gora and Belgrade (Serbia).

Two Weeks

Add Trebinje and (if driving) historic Stolac between Dubrovnik and Mostar. Ski or go cycling around Bjelašnica, visit the controversial Visoko pyramid and old-town Travnik en route to Jajce, and consider adding in some high-adrenaline rafting from Banja Luka, Bihać or Foča.

Essential Food & Drink

» **Ćevapi (Ćevapčići)** Minced meat formed into cylindrical pellets and served in fresh bread with melting *kajmak* (thick semi-soured cream).

» **Pljeskavica** Patty-shaped Ćevapi.

» **Burek** Bosnian *burek* are cylindrical lengths of filo-pastry filled with minced meat, often wound into spirals. *Buredici* is the same served with *kajmak* and garlic, *sirnica* is filled instead with cheese, *krompiruša* with potato and *zeljanica* with spinach. Collectively these pies are called *pita*.

» **Sarma** Small *dolma*-parcels of rice and minced meat wrapped in a cabbage or other green leaf.

» **Bosanski Lonac** Slow-cooked meat-and-veg hotpot.

» **Uštipci** Bready fried dough-balls often eaten with sour cream, cheese or jam.

» **Sogan Dolma** Slow roasted onions filled with minced meat.

» **Klepe** Small ravioli-like triangles served in a butter-pepper drizzle with grated raw garlic.

» **Hurmastica** Syrup-soaked sponge fingers.

» **Tufahija** Whole stewed apple with walnut-filling and topped with whipped cream.

» **Ražnjići** Shish kebab (ie meat barbequed on skewers).

» **Pastrmka** Trout.

» **Rakija** Fruit brandy or grappa.

» **Ligne** Squid.

Bosnia & Hercegovina Highlights

1 Nose about Mostar's atmospheric Old Town and admire the magnificently rebuilt **Stari Most** (p124).

2 Raft down one of BiH's fast-flowing rivers – whether from **Foča** (p135) **Bihać** (p143) or **Banja Luka** (p139).

3 Ski the 1984 Olympic pistes at **Jahorina** (p122) or **Bjelašnica** (p123) or explore the wild uplands behind them.

4 Potter around the timeless pedestrian lanes of **Sarajevo** (p110), and sample its fashionable cafes and eclectic nightlife.

5 Gaze through willow fronds at the Unesco-listed 16th-century bridge in **Višegrad** (p135) that inspired a Nobel Prize–winning novel.

6 Wine and dine in historic little **Trebinje** (p134) and wander the low-key, stone-flagged Old Town.

7 Tune in to the mystical energy of **Visoko** (p136), asking yourself if you're really climbing the world's biggest pyramid.

SARAJEVO

⌨033 / 436,000

In the 1990s Sarajevo was on the edge of annihilation. Today it's a vibrant yet very human city, notable for its attractive contours and East-meets-West ambience.

Beyond the stone-flagged alleys of central Baščaršija, 'Turkish Town', steep valley sides are fuzzed with red-roofed Bosnian houses and prickled with uncountable minarets, climbing towards green-topped mountain ridges. Westward, Sarajevo sprawls for over 10km through Novo Sarajevo and dreary Dobrinja past dismal ranks of bullet-scarred apartment blocks. At the westernmost end of the tramway spine, affluent Ilidža gives the city a final parkland flourish. In winter, Bjelašnica and Jahorina offer some of Europe's best-value skiing, barely 30km away.

History

Romans had bathed at Ilidža's sulphur springs a millennium earlier, but Sarajevo was officially 'founded' by 15th-century Turks. It rapidly grew wealthy as a silk-importing entrepôt and developed considerably during the 1530s when Ottoman governor Gazi-Husrevbey lavished the city with mosques and covered bazaars. In 1697 the city was burnt by Eugene of Savoy's Austrian army. When rebuilt, Sarajevo cautiously enclosed its upper flank in a large, fortified citadel, the remnants of which still dominate the Vratnik area.

The Austro-Hungarians were back more permanently in 1878 and erected many imposing central-European-style buildings. However, their rule was put on notice by Gavrilo Princip's fatal 1914 pistol shot that killed Archduke Franz Ferdinand, plunging the world into WWI.

Less than a decade after hosting the 1984 Winter Olympics, Sarajevo endured an infamous siege that horrified the world. Between 1992 and 1995, Sarajevo's heritage of six centuries was pounded into rubble and its only access to the outside world was via a metre-wide, 800m-long tunnel under the airport. Bosnian Serb shelling and sniper fire killed over 10,500 Sarajevans and wounded 50,000 more. Uncountable white-stoned graves on Kovači and up near Koševo Stadium are a moving testimony to those terrible years.

◉ Sights & Activities

The best way to really 'feel' the city is to stroll Old Sarajevo's pedestrian lanes and grand avenues and climb the gently picturesque slopes of Bjelave and Vratnik for sweeping views. Seeking out key museums is likely to take you into much more modern, businesslike Novo Sarajevo and on to park-filled Ilidža at the distant western end of the tram network.

OLD SARAJEVO

Baščaršija, the bustling old Turkish quarter is a warren of marble-flagged pedestrian courtyards and lanes full of mosques, copper workshops, jewellery shops and inviting restaurants. The riverbanks and avenues Ferhadija and Maršala Tita are well endowed with Austro-Hungarian architecture. And attesting to Sarajevo's traditional religious tolerance, you'll find within a couple of blocks several mosques, a synagogue, the artfully floodlit 1872 **Orthodox Cathedral** (Saborna Crkva Presvete Bogordice; Map p114; Trg Oslobođenja) and the **Catholic Cathedral** (Katedrala Srca Isusova; Map p114; Trg Fra Grge Martića 2; ⊘9am-4pm) where Pope John Paul II served mass in 1997. The area's charms are best discovered by wandering between the many street cafes.

Pigeon Square   NEIGHBOURHOOD
(Map p114) Nicknamed Pigeon Sq for all the birds, Baščaršija's central open space centres on the **Sebilj**, an ornate 1891 drinking fountain. It leads past the lively (if tourist-centric) coppersmith alley, **Kazandžiluk**, leading down to the garden-wrapped 16th-century **Baščaršija Džamija** (Baščaršija mosque; Map p114; Baščaršija 37).

Bursa Bezistan   MUSEUM
(Map p114; www.muzejsarajeva.ba; Abadžiluk 10; admission 3KM; ⊘10am-6pm Mon-Fri, 10am-3pm Sat) The six-domed 1551 Bursa Bezistan was

---

SARAJEVO IN TWO DAYS

Plunge into the pedestrianised 'Turkish' lanes of **Baščaršija** and the street cafes of **Ferhadija**. From the spot where a 1914 assassination kicked off WWI, cross the cute **Latin Bridge** for a beer at **Pivnica HS** or dinner overlooking the city rooftops at **Biban**.

Next day ponder the horrors of the 1990s siege era at the moving **History Museum** and unique **Tunnel Museum**. Recover with a drink at eccentrically Gothic **Zlatna Ribica** and a feisty gig at **Underground**.

originally a silk-trading bazaar. Today it's a small museum with bite-sized overviews of the city's history and a compelling model of Sarajevo as it looked in 1878.

Gazi-Husrevbey Mosque   MOSQUE

(Map p114; www.vakuf-gazi.ba; Saraći 18; admission 2KM; ☺9am-noon, 2.30-3.30pm & 5-6.15pm May-Sep, closed Ramadan) Ottoman governor Gazi-Husrevbey funded a series of splendid 16th-century buildings of which this mosque forms the greatest centrepiece. Its cylindrical minaret contrasts photogenically with the elegant stone clock tower off Mudželeti Veliki alley. The associated **madrassa** (Religious School; Saraći 33-49) across Saraći is used for occasional exhibitions and book sales, its time-worn stonework contrasting conspicuously with the brand new library next door.

Vijećnica   ARCHITECTURE

(Map p114) With its storybook neo-Moorish facades, the 1892 Vijećnica is Sarajevo's most beautiful Austro-Hungarian era building. Originally the City Hall, Franz Ferdinand was on the way back from here when shot by Princip in 1914. It later became the Bosnian National Library. However, during the 1990s siege it was deliberately hit by a Serb incendiary shell. Around 90% of its irreplaceable collection of manuscripts and Bosnian books was destroyed and for nearly two decades the building remained a sorry skeleton. Reconstruction is finally advancing and due for completion in April 2014.

Sarajevo 1878–1918   HISTORICAL MUSEUM

(Map p114; Zelenih Beretki 2; admission 2KM; ☺10am-6pm Mon-Fri, 10am-3pm Sat) This one-room exhibition examines the city's Austro-Hungarian–era history and the infamous 1914 assassination of Franz Ferdinand that happened right outside, ultimately triggering WWI.

Jewish Museum   MEDIEVAL SYNAGOGUE

(Muzej Jevreja BiH; Map p114; Mula Mustafe Bašeskije 40; admission 2KM; ☺10am-6pm Mon-Fri, 10am-1pm Sun) More religiously open-minded than most of Western Europe in its day, the 15th-century Ottoman Empire offered refuge to the Sephardic Jews who had been evicted en masse from Spain in 1492. While conditions varied, Bosnian Jews mostly prospered, until WWII that is, when most of the 14,000-strong community fled or were murdered by Nazis. The community's story is well told in this 1581 Sephardic synagogue that still sees active worship during Rosh Hashana (Jewish New Year).

Academy of Arts   ARCHITECTURE

(Likovna Akademija; Map p114; www.alu.unsa.ba; Obala Maka Dizdara 3) Originally built in 1899 as an evangelical church, the Gothic Revival–style Academy of Arts looks like a mini version of Budapest's magnificent national parliament building. Since August 2012 it has been fronted by Festina Lente ('Hurry Slowly'), an Escheresque new footbridge that 'loops-the-loop'.

BJELAVE & VRATNIK

TOP CHOICE Svrzo House   HOUSE MUSEUM

(Svrzina Kuća; Map p114; ☎535264; Glođina 8; admission 3KM; ☺10am-6pm Mon-Fri, 10am-3pm Sat) An oasis of white-washed walls, cobbled courtyards and partly vine-draped dark timbers, this 18th-century house museum is brilliantly restored and appropriately furnished, helping visitors imagine Sarajevo life in eras past. Notice the *čekme dolaf* (food hatch), designed to prevent inter-sex fratenization.

Izetbegović Museum   MUSEUM

(Map p112; www.muzejalijaizetbegovica.ba; Ploča bb; admission 2KM; ☺10am-6pm Mon-Fri, 10am-3pm Sat) Above the Kovaći cemetery where he's buried, there's a small but fascinating museum to Alija Izetbegović. Even if you're not interested in BiH's first president, the setting (in the historic Kula Ploče Tower) is interesting and the visit lets you walk along a last surviving section of city wall emerging at the Kula Širokac Tower.

Vratnik   NEIGHBOURHOOD

The once-vast Vratnik Citadel was built in the 1720s and reinforced in 1816. Not much remains but there are superb views from the grassy-topped **Yellow Bastion** (Žuta Tabija; Map p112; Jekovac bb). Minibus 55 gets you reasonably close.

NOVO SARAJEVO

During the 1992–95 siege, the wide road from the airport (Zmaja od Bosne) was dubbed 'sniper alley' because Serb gunmen in surrounding hills could pick off civilians as they tried to cross it. The distinctive, pudding-and-custard coloured **Holiday Inn** (Map p112; www.holidaysarajevo.com; Zmaja Od Bosne 4) famously housed most of the embattled journalists covering that conflict.

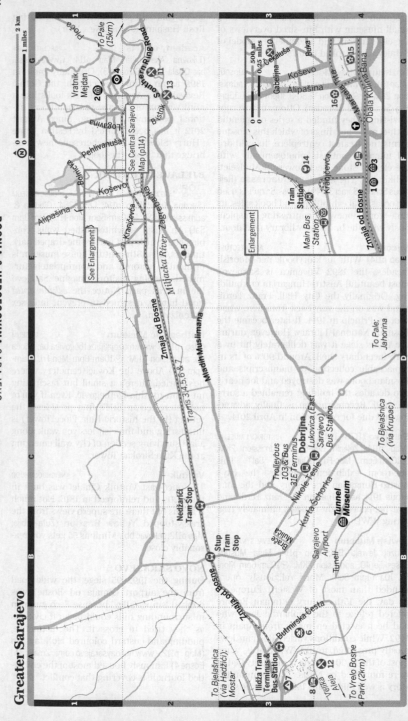

Greater Sarajevo

BOSNIA & HERCEGOVINA SARAJEVO

Greater Sarajevo

National Museum MUSEUM
(Zemaljski Muzej Bosne-i-Hercegovine; Map p112; www.zemaljskimuzej.ba; Zmaja od Bosne 3; ⊘temporarily closed) Bosnia's biggest and best endowed museum closed in October 2012 due to persistent funding problems. Ironically it had been a rare institution to have remained at least partly functioning throughout the siege era, and its impressive 1913 quadrangle of neo-classical 1913 buildings survived reasonably intact. Assuming it reopens, the greatest highlights are its Illyrian and Roman carvings and especially the world-famous **Sarajevo Haggadah**, a 14th-century Jewish codex said to be worth a billion US dollars. Geraldine Brooks' 2007 historical novel *People of the Book* is a part-fictionalised account of how the Nazis failed to grab it during WWII.

Outside at the front are some exceptional medieval *stečci* (carved grave slabs).

History Museum MUSEUM
(Map p112; Zmaja od Bosne 5; admission 4KM; ⊘9am-7pm Mon-Fri, 10am-2pm Sat-Sun) More than half of the small but engrossing History Museum 'non-ideologically' charts the course of the 1990s conflict. Affecting personal exhibits include examples of food aid, DIY guns, stacks of Monopoly-style 1990s dinars and a makeshift siege-time 'home'. The effect is emphasised by the building's miserable and still partly war-damaged 1970s architecture. Directly behind, the amusingly tongue-in-cheek **Tito Cafe** (www.caffetito. ba; ⊘24hr) has stormtrooper-helmet lampshades and garden seating surrounded by WWII artillery pieces.

ILIDŽA & BUTMIR

📦**TOP CHOICE** **Tunnel Museum** WAR MUSEUM
(Tunel Spasa; Map p112; www.tunelspasa.ba; Tuneli bb 1; admission 5KM; ⊘9.15am-5pm, last entry 4.30pm) For much of the 1990s war, Sarajevo was virtually surrounded by hostile Serb forces. Butmir was the last Bosniak-held part of the city still linked to the outside world. However, between Butmir and Sarajevo lies the airport runway. Although it was supposedly neutral and under tenuous UN control, crossing it would have been suicidal during the conflict. The solution was a hand-dug 800m tunnel beneath the runway. That was just enough to keep Sarajevo supplied with arms and food during the three-year siege. Most of the tunnel has since collapsed, but this museum retains a 20m section and gives visitors a glimpse of its hopes and horrors. Photos are displayed around the shell-pounded house that hides the tunnel entrance and there's a 20-minute video showing footage of the city bombardment and the wartime tunnel experience.

Joining a city tour that includes a visit here can often prove cheaper than coming by taxi and your guide can add a lot of useful insight. Alternatively take tram 3 to Ilidža (35 minutes, 11km from Baščaršija), then switch to Kotorac-bound bus 32 (10 minutes, twice hourly, 3km). Get off at the last stop, walk across the bridge, then turn immediately left down Tuneli for 500m.

Vrelo Bosne Park PARK
The focus of this extensive park is a patchwork of lush mini-islands at the cliff-mouth source of the Bosna River. While it's not worth a special trip from central Sarajevo, if you're staying in Ilidža the park makes

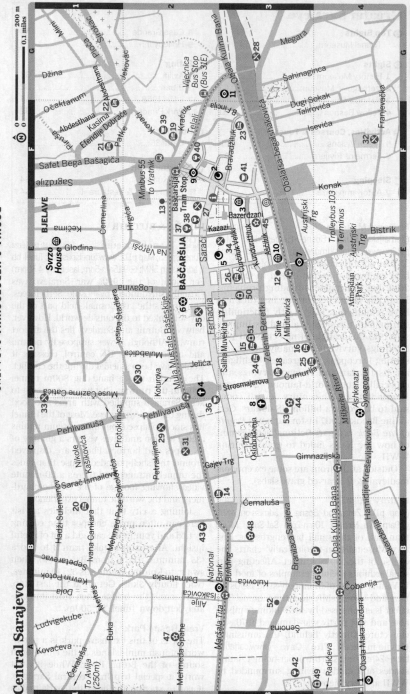

Central Sarajevo

BOSNIA & HERCEGOVINA SARAJEVO

Central Sarajevo

BOSNIA & HERCEGOVINA SARAJEVO

a pleasant outing accessible by horse-cart or on foot along Velika Aleja, an elegantly tree-lined pedestrian avenue stretching 3km from Ilidža's main hotel area.

Termalna Rivijera SWIMMING
(Map p112; www.terme-ilidza.ba/en; Butmirska Cesta 18; adult/child Mon-Fri 13/10KM, Sat & Sun 15/12KM; ⊙9am-10pm Sun-Fri, 9am-2am Sat) A complex of indoor and outdoor swimming pools 600m east of Ilidža tram terminus.

☞ Tours

Insider TOUR
(Map p114; ☎061-190591; www.sarajevoinsider.com; Zelenih Beretki 30; ⊙9am-6pm Mon-Fri, 9.30am-2pm Sat-Sun) Wide range of tours in and be-

yond Sarajevo. Popular daily offerings include the two-hour Tunnel Tour (€15, 2pm) and excellent three-hour 'Times of Misfortune' (€27, 11am), visiting sites related to the 1990s conflict. Tour customers get free entrance to Insider's two-room Siege 'museum' (otherwise 3KM), 17 photo-text panels explaining the Yugoslav conflict from Tito's death to Dayton.

Sarajevo Funky Tours TOUR
(Map p114; ☎062-910546; www.sarajevofunky-tours.com; Besarina Čikma 5) A similar range of tours to Insider.

Sarajevo Free Tour TOUR
Impressive 90-minute city walking tour starting 3pm from the tourist office or

4.30pm from Insider. Runs most days in summer. Pay through tips.

Green Visions
TOUR

(Map p112; ☎717290; www.greenvisions.ba; opposite Radnićka 66; ⊙9am-5pm Mon-Fri) Ecotourism specialist Green Visions offers a wide range of weekend and tailor-made hiking trips into the Bosnian mountains and villages with some fixed-day departures.

✯✯ Festivals & Events

Baščaršijske Noći
ARTS

(Baščaršija Nights; www.bascarsijskenoci.ba) Wide-ranging arts fest lasting all July.

Jazz Festival
MUSIC

(www.jazzfest.ba) Local and international jazz in early November.

Sarajevo Film Festival
FILM

(www.sff.ba) Globally acclaimed with commercial and art-house movies, most with English subtitles. Held in August or late July.

🛏 Sleeping

If you arrive without anywhere booked and everything seems full, there's still a chance of finding a bed through one of the three agencies on the north side of Mula Mustafe Bašeskije at Baščaršija tram stop.

CITY CENTRE

Hotel Michele
BOUTIQUE HOTEL €€€

(Map p114; ☎560310; www.hotelmichele.ba; Ivana Cankara 27; r €75-105, apt €120-150; ❈🅿🛜) Behind the exterior of an oversized contemporary townhouse, this offbeat guesthouse welcomes you into a lobby-lounge full of portraits, pinned butterflies and elegant fittings. Age-effect elements are in evidence in the 12 new standard rooms but what draws celebrity guests including Morgan Freeman and Kevin Spacey are the vast, indulgently furnished apartments with antique (if sometimes mismatching) furniture.

TOP CHOICE Villa Wien
GUESTHOUSE €€

(Map p114; Ćurčiluk Veliki 3; s/d 143/186KM; ❈🛜) Six well-equipped rooms decorated in opulent pseudo–belle époque style are hidden away above the Wiener Café. They are relatively good value perhaps because there's no reception – you have to check in a few blocks away at the less impressive yet more expensive **Hotel Art** (Map p114; ☎232855; www.hotelart.ba; Ferhadija 30a; s/d/ste 183/236/306KM; 🅿❈@🛜).

Hotel Central
HOTEL €€€

(Map p114; ☎033-561800; www.hotelcentral.ba; Cumurija 8; s/d/ste 200/240/300KM; ❈🛜🏊) Behind a grand Austro-Hungarian facade, most of this newly renovated 'hotel' is in fact an amazing three-floor gym complex with professional-standard weight rooms, saunas and big indoor pool manned by qualified sports training staff. The 15 huge, fashionably appointed guest rooms lead off corridors painted lugubriously deep purple.

TOP CHOICE Hostel Old City
HOSTEL €

(Map p114; ☎555355; www.hosteloldcity.ba; Sime Milutinovića 1; dm €15; ❈@🛜) One floor of a regal 1908 townhouse has been given a very impressive makeover in keeping with its heritage. Features include big lockers, well-constructed beds and a lounge with Latin Bridge balcony views.

Hotel Kovači
HOTEL €€

(Map p114; ☎573700; www.hotelkovaci.com; Kovači 12; s/d/tr/apt €50/70/90/100; ❈🛜) This wonderfully central family hotel blends a chic, understated modernism with a traditional design that incorporates overhanging ('doksat') windows. Its fresh white rooms are softened with photos of 19th-century Sarajevo on protruding panels.

City Boutique Hotel
BOUTIQUE HOTEL €€

(Map p114; ☎566850; www.cityhotel.ba; Mula Mustafe Bašekije 2; r Fri-Sat €76-91, Sun-Thu €94-114; ❈🛜) Contemporary, designer rooms in rectilinear modernist style feature striking colours and backlit ceiling panels. There's a 6th-floor self-serve lounge-cafe and rooftop terrace with limited views. Reception 24 hours.

Residence Rooms
HOSTEL €

(Map p114; ☎200157; www.residencerooms.ba; 1st fl, Saliha Muvekita 1; dm/s/d/tr €15/25/40/45; @🛜) High ceilings, ample common areas and widely spaced beds in the dorms all make for a convivial hostel experience. The lively bars directly outside can be a blessing or curse depending on your party plans.

HCC Sarajevo Hostel
HOSTEL €

(Map p114; ☎062-993330; www.hcc.ba; 3rd fl, Saliha Muvekita 1; dm €12-16, s €20-25, d €28-35; ❈@🛜) This sociable hostel has big lockers (padlock rental €1), a stylishly decorated kitchen/dining area and a bright lounge/lobby with DVDs to watch and a guitar to strum.

Pansion Divan PENSION €
(Map p114; ☑061420254; www.facebook.com/ pansion.divansarajevo; Brandžiluk 38; s €20-30, tw €30-35; 🛜) Above an Ali Baba's cave of a restaurant, these 10 neat, unfussy rooms with private bathrooms don't have reception or common room but at such bargain prices one can't complain. Wi-fi in five rooms.

Hotel Safir HOTEL €€
(Map p114; ☑475040; www.hotelsafir.ba; Jagodića 3; s/d €50/72; ❄🛜) Off stairways featuring vibrantly colour-suffused flower photos, rooms come with little mirror 'windows', conical basins and beam-me-up-Scotty shower booths. Six out of eight have a kitchenette.

Travellers Home HOSTEL €
(Map p114; ☑70 242 400; www.myhostel.ba; Ćumurija 4, 1st fl; dm 25-38KM, d 62-92KM; ⊘24hr; 🛜) One of Sarajevo's many high-ceilinged house-hostels, Travellers Home has outstandingly helpful, informative staff and a central yet peaceful locaton. Lockers are backpack-sized and power-points are accessible from each bunk.

Hotel Telal HOTEL €
(Map p114; ☑525125; www.hotel-telal.ba; Abdesthana 4; s/d/tr/apt €30/40/45/60; ❄) Reception feels a little claustrophobic and the walls are thin but the en suite rooms are comparatively smart and well tended for the rock-bottom price.

ILIDŽA & AIRPORT AREA
Several indulgent yet well-priced hotels lie in green, pleasant Ilidža. Parking is easier here than downtown but it's a 35-minute tram ride from Sarajevo's old centre.

TOP CHOICE **Casa Grande** HOTEL €€
(Map p112; ☑639280; www.casagrande-bih.com; Velika Aleja 2; s/d/tr/q 68/113/138/165KM; P❄🛜) Designed like an aristocratic 1920s villa, the Casa Grande sits amid the plane trees right at the start of Ilidža's classic avenue, Velika Aleja. Rooms range from spacious to huge and are remarkably luxurious for the price. Expect satellite TV, leather-padded doors, 30-nozzle full-body shower pods and framed imitations of 'classic' art.

AutoKamp Oaza CAMPING GROUND €
(Map p112; ☑636140; oaza@hotelilidza.ba; per person 10KM, plus per tent/car/campervan 7/10/15KM, bungalows 60-105KM) Tree-shaded camping and caravan hook-ups (electricity 3KM extra) tucked behind the Hotel Imzit, 1.5km west of Ilidža tram terminus.

✗ Eating

For inexpensive snack meals look along Bradžiluk or Kundurdžiluk: Bosna is a good place for cheap, fresh *burek*. Locals argue whether Hadžić, Mrkva or Željo is the best *ćevabdžinica* (ćevapi servery).

CITY CENTRE
Mala Kuhinja FUSION €€
(Map p114; ☑061 144741; www.malakuhinja.ba; Josipa Štadlera 6; meals 20-25KM; ⊘noon-4pm Mon-Sat) There's no menu at this tiny, fusion-food gem where the chefs simply ask you what you do/don't like and then set about making culinary magic. Sit at the three-seat 'bar' to watch the show in all its glory. Reservations advisable.

Dveri EUROPEAN €€
(Map p114; ☑537020; www.dveri.co.ba; Prote Bakovića 12; meals 11-18KM; ⊘8am-11pm; 🛜🍴) This tourist-friendly 'country cottage' eatery is densely hung with loops of garlic, corn cobs and gingham-curtained 'windows'. Classic European meat-based dishes are supplemented by inky risottos, vegie-stuffed eggplant and garlic-wine squid. There's a well-chosen wine list including some excellent Hercegovinian Blatinas.

To Be or Not to Be INTERNATIONAL €€
(Map p114; ☑233265; Čizmedžiluk 5; meals 10-22KM; ⊘11am-11pm; 🍴) Arched metal shutters creak open to reveal a tiny two-table room lovably decorated in traditional Bosnian style. Try the daring, tongue-tickling steak in chilli chocolate (22KM). The restaurant's name, with 'or Not' crossed out as a message of positivity, was originally a poster slogan for the 1994 Sarajevo Winter Festival, held against all odds during the siege.

Sushi San SUSHI €€
(Map p114; ☑833034; www.sarajevosushi.com; Muse Ćazima Ćatića 33 ; 2-piece sushi 5-6KM; ⊘11am-8pm Mon-Sat; 🍴) The sushi master at this tiny six-stool box restaurant learned his trade in San Fransisco and manages to produce salmon nigiri that will impress even salmon-haters. Caters to various embassies.

Pivnica HS INTERNATIONAL €€
(Map p114; sarajevska-pivara.ba/restaurant; Franjevačka 15; pasta 8-10KM, mains 13-25KM; ⊘10am-1am; 🍴) If Willy Wonka built a beer hall it might look like this – a giant festival of Las

BOSNIA & HERCEGOVINA SARAJEVO

Vegas vaudeville. Meals are well presented and satisfying and this is the only place you can be sure of finding Sarajevskaya full range of tap beers (brewed next door).

Karuzo
SEAFOOD €€

(Map p114; ✆444647; www.karuzorestaurant.com; Dženetića Čikma 2; pasta 13-18KM, mains 15-35KM; ⏰noon-3pm Mon-Fri, 6-11pm Mon-Sat; ✏🍴) This friendly little meat-free restaurant is styled vaguely like a yacht's interior. Along with fish dishes and sushi there are some imaginative vegetarian options including chard pockets with smoked tofu and basil sauce. The owner is both waiter and chef so don't be in a hurry.

Inat Kuća
BOSNIAN €€

(Spite House; Map p114; ✆447867; www.inatkuca.ba; Velika Alifakovac 1; mains 12-20KM, snacks 10KM; ⏰10am-10pm; 🍴) This Sarajevo institution occupies a classic Ottoman-era house that's a veritable museum piece with central fire-flue, antique decor and a great little riverside terrace. The menu tells the story of its odd name but some of the typical Bosnian fare (stews, *dolme*) can be slightly lacklustre.

Vegehana
VEGETARIAN €

(Map p114; www.vegehana.ba/; Ferhadija 39; mains 5-10KM; ⏰10am-9pm Mon-Fri, noon-9pm Sat; ✏🍴) The first fully vegetarian, organic eatery in Sarajevo uses plenty of Tahina, quinoa, tofu and seitan meat-substitute.

Markale
MARKET

(Map p114; Mula Mustafe Bašeskije; ⏰7am-5pm Mon-Sat, 7am-2pm Sun) Markale is an unassuming huddle of vegetable stalls. The massacre of marketgoers here in a 1995 Serb mortar attack proved a 'last straw', triggering NATO air strikes against the forces besieging Sarajevo.

GREATER SARAJEVO
Biban
BOSNIAN €€

(Map p112; ✆033-232026; Hošin Brijeg 95a; mains 7-16KM; ⏰10am-10pm Mon-Fri, 10am-9pm Sun; 🍴) Encompassing the whole Sarajevo Valley, Biban's panoramic city views trump even those of better-known Park Prinčeva, but the food is cheaper (and simpler) including typical meat dishes, squid and trout. The 10KM plates of *uštipci* (fist-size fried doughballs served with sour cream) are big enough to feed three people. Walk 600m uphill from Park Prinčeva, turning left after Nalina 15a.

Park Prinčeva
BALKAN, EUROPEAN €€€

(Map p112; ✆222708; www.parkprinceva.ba; Iza Hidra 7; meals 16-32KM; ⏰9am-11pm; 🍴) Like

Bono and Bill Clinton before you, gaze down across the city, the old city hall beautifully framed between rooftops, mosques and twinkling lights. Minibus 56 from Latin Bridge passes outside. Try the chicken in cherry sauce.

Avlija
BISTRO €€

(Map p112; ✆444 483; Sumbula Avde 2, opposite 53 Čekaluša; 9-20KM; ⏰8am-11pm; 🍴) Locals and in-the-know expats cosy up at painted wooden benches in this unpretentious covered yard, dangling with trailing potplants, strings of peppers and little witches. Generous portions of Central European pub food wash down merrily with local draft beers.

Ildžis 1968
ITALIAN €

(Map p112; Velika Aleja 3; mains 6-10KM, beer 2.50KM) Staying in Ilidža? Then consider drinking or dining at this rustic-effect wooden house filled with guitars, spinning wheels and giant model ships. At night it's very moodily lit and the woodland location is just as romantic by day. Pastas are copious, beautifully presented and served with oodles of Parmesan. It is two-minute stroll north of Casa Grande along tree-lined Velika Aleja.

🍷 Drinking

As chilly April melts into sunny May, terraces blossom and central Sarajevo becomes one giant street cafe.

Bars

📋 Zlatna Ribica
BAR

(Map p114; Kaptol 5; ⏰10am-2am) This inspiring little cafe-bar is loaded with eccentricities, including drink menus hidden away in old books that dangle from lampshades. Music swerves unpredictably between jazz, Parisian croons, opera, reggae and The Muppets. Wine might arrive with a free scallop-shell of grapes. And the uniquely stocked toilet will have you laughing out loud.

Pravda
COCKTAIL BAR

(Map p114; www.pravda.ba; Radićeva 4c; ⏰8am-midnight) Choose from marigold-patterned chill-out sofas or white-enamel perch-stools, then strike your pose amid Sarajevo's gilded youth. Oh no, don't say they've all gone next door to Cafe Nivea?! Or decamped to Dekanter?

Caffe 35
BAR

(Map p112; Avaz Twist Tower, 35th fl; coffee/cake/beer 2/3/4KM, sandwiches 3-5KM; ⏰9am-11pm) If you're waiting for a train, what better place to do so than admiring a full city panorama from the 35th floor of 'The Balkans' Tallest Tower'. Upstairs for 1KM you can see the same views in the open air with bars instead of windows. The glass elevator coming back down feels like it's freefalling.

Barhana
BAR

(Map p114; Đugalina 8; beer/rakija 2/3KM, mains 6-20KM; ⊙10am-midnight) Sample a selection of flavoured local shots in a hidden courtyard behind the equally enticing Babylon bar. A wide range of fair value meals is served.

Cafes

Kuća Sevdaha
CAFE

(Map p114; www.artkucasevdaha.ba/en/; Halači 5; ⊙9am-11pm) Sip Bosnian coffee, juniper sherbet or rose water while nibbling local sweets and listening to the lilting wails of *sevdah*, traditional Bosnian music. The ancient building that surrounds the cafe's glassed-in fountain courtyard is now used as a museum celebrating great 20th-century *sevdah* performers (admission 3KM, open 10am to 6pm Tuesday to Sunday).

Caffe Divan
CARAVANSERAI

(Map p114; Morića Han, Sarači 77; ⊙8am-midnight) Relax in wicker chairs beneath the wooden beams of a gorgeous, historic caravanserai courtyard whose stables now contain an alluring Iranian carpet shop. The restaurant section (kitchen till 10pm) serves good *klepe* (a kind of garlic ravioli).

Čajdžinica Džirlo
TEAHOUSE

(Map p114; www.facebook.com/CajdzinicaDzirlo; Kovači 16; ⊙8am-10pm) Miniscule but brimming with character, Džirlo offers 45 types of tea (per pot 4KM), many of them made from distinctive Bosnian herbs. Good coffee and local sherbets are also available. It's on a steeply sloping stretch of Kovači amid old workshops including metal beaters and a coffee roaster.

Dibek
BAR

(Map p114; Laledžina 3; ⊙8am-11pm) Smoking a hookah (*nargile* or water pipe; 5KM) is back in fashion as you'll see in this DJ-led bar that spreads colourful low stools beneath a central tree on a tiny Old Town square. Excellent coffee too.

Alfonso
CAFE

(Map p114; Trg Fra Grge Martica 4; ⊙8am-11pm) Great espressos served at open-air pavement seating that sprawls around the Catholic cathedral, or inside where a hip interior includes a catwalk between cushioned sunken seat spaces.

⭐ Entertainment

Nightclubs & Live Music

Within the old city, there are two small but ever-lively areas of late night music bars: around the Hacienda, and beneath HCC Sarajevo Hostel. Other clubs tend to be further west.

Underground
LIVE MUSIC

(Map p114; www.underground.ba; Maršala Tita 56; ⊙7pm-5am) Especially on Friday and Saturday nights, talented bands give classic rock songs a romping rework in this medium-sized basement venue. Free entry, tap beers 2.50KM.

FIS Kultura
LIVE MUSIC

(Bock; Map p112; Musala bb; ⊙6pm-2am) There's no sign so just follow the bass-beat to locate this tiny basement venue. Musical styles range wildly from grunge to punk to 'urban' party. Some nights private parties take over. It's on Musala, a north–south lane two blocks west of Radićeva.

Rooms Club & Restaurant
DJS, LIVE MUSIC

(Map p112; www.facebook.com/roomsclubsarajevo; Maršala Tita 7; ⊙9.30pm-4am Wed, Fri & Sat) This subterranean trio of stone cavern rooms includes a restaurant that serves till 3am, a sofa-dotted lounge and a contrastingly boisterous bar-performance area with live gigs that pull in crowds after midnight, especially on Wednesdays. The 5KM cover includes one drink.

Club Jež
CLUB

(Map p114; http://jez.nash.ba/v2; Zelenih Beretki 14b; ⊙9pm-late) This intimate stone-vaulted cavern club heaves with young local revellers overdosing on turbofolk. Cover charges (around 5KM) include one drink.

Sloga
CLUB

(Map p114; www.cinemas.ba; Seljo, Mehmeda Spahe 20; ⊙8pm-3am) This cavernous, blood-red club-disco-dance hall caters to an excitable, predominantly student crowd but dancing is oddly impeded by rows of tables. Cover charge 5KM at weekends. Occasional concerts.

Hacienda
DJ

(Map p114; Bazerdzani 3; ⊙10am-very late) The not-quite-Mexican food could be spicier. Not so the ambience, which by 2am has often morphed this cane-ceilinged cantina into one of the Old Town's most happening night spots. If it's quiet, try nearby alternatives **Pirates Pub** and **Caffe Red**.

Performing Arts

National Theatre   PERFORMING ARTS

(Narodno Pozorište; Map p114; ☑221682; www.nps.ba; Obala Kulina Bana 9; tickets from 10KM; ⊙box office 9am-noon & 4-7.30pm) Classically adorned with fiddly gilt mouldings, this proscenium-arched theatre hosts a ballet, opera, play or philharmonic concert virtually every night from mid-September to mid-June.

🛍 Shopping

Baščaršija's pedestrian lanes are full of jewellery stalls and wooden-shuttered souvenir shops flogging slippers, Bosnian flags, carpets, archetypal copperware and wooden spoons, though if you're heading to Mostar, you might find prices better there.

Some Sarajevo bookshops still stock the darkly humorous *Sarajevo Survival Guide*, originally published during the 1992–93 siege, as well as guidebooks, magazines and English-language books on ex-Yugoslavia.

Dugi Bezistan   COVERED BAZAAR

(Map p114; www.vakuf-gazi.ba; ⊙8am-8pm Mon-Fri, 9am-2pm Sat) Another of Gazi-Husrevbey's 16th-century architectural legacies, the stone-vaulted covered bazaar is little more than 100m long, but squint and you could be in Istanbul. Many of its 52 shops sell inexpensive souvenirs, cheap handbags and sunglasses (from 5KM).

BuyBook   BOOKSHOP

(Map p114; ☑716450; www.buybook.ba; Radićeva 4; ⊙9am-8pm Mon-Fri, 10am-6pm Sat)

Šahinpašić   BOOKSHOP

(Map p114; ☑667210; www.btcsahinpasic.com; Vladislava Skarića 8; ⊙9am-9pm Mon-Sat)

ℹ Information

ATMs are outside the bus station, inside the airport and sprinkled all over the city.

For currency exchanges, there's an airport **post-counter** (⊙9am-5pm Mon-Fri), **Postbank** (⊙8am-4pm Mon-Fri) branch hidden around the west side of the train station building and many banks along Ferhadija. At weekends try the Hotel Europe.

City.Ba (www.city.ba/en) Reviews of clubs, pubs, restaurants and more

Internet Caffe Baščaršija (Aščiluk bb; per hr 2KM; ⊙8am-midnight)

Klinički Centar Univerziteta Sarajevo (☑445522; www.kcus.ba; 1st fl, DIP Bldg, Stepana Tomića bb/Bolnička 25 ; ⊙8am-2pm Mon-Fri) English-speaking 'VIP Clinic' within the vast Koševo Hospital complex. Take bus 14 from Dom Armije to Hotel Belvedere and then walk 300m northwest.

Lonely Planet (www.lonelyplanet.com/bosnia-and-hercegovina/sarajevo)

Sarajevo Navigator Useful free maps and monthly guide pamphlets. Widely available.

Sonar (www.sonar.ba) Listings and information.

Tourist Office (Map p114; www.sarajevo-tourism.com; Sarači 58; ⊙9am-8pm Mon-Fri, 10am-6pm Sat-Sun)

ℹ Getting There & Away

Air

An hour is ample for check-in at Sarajevo's modern but very compact international **airport** (☑234841; www.sarajevo-airport.ba; Kurta Schorka 36; ⊙5am-11pm), about 12km southwest of Baščaršija.

Bus

Sarajevo's **main bus station** (Map p112; ☑213100; Put Života 8) primarily serves locations in the Federation, Croatia and Western Europe. Most services to the Republik Srpska (RS) and Serbia leave from **Lukovica (East Sarajevo) Bus Station** (Map p112; ☑057-317377; Nikole Tesle bb). The latter lies way out in the suburb of Dobrijna, 400m beyond the western terminus stop of trolleybus 103 and bus 31E. To some destinations, buses leave from both stations. For Jajce, take Banja Luka buses.

Train

From the **train station** (☑655330; Put Života 2) useful services include the following:

Belgrade (51.20KM, eight hours) Departs 11.49am.

Budapest (1st/2nd class 122.40KM, 11¼ hours) Departs 6.55am, routed via Osijek (Croatia, 55.40KM). Returns from Budapest-Keleti at 9.56am.

Mostar (9.90KM, 2¼ hours) Departs 7.05am, 8.05am and 6.18pm.

Zagreb (74.30KM, 9¼ hours) Trains depart 10.54am and 9.27pm. No couchette service.

ℹ Getting Around

To/From the Airport

Trolleybus 103 and bus 31E both run to the centre, picking up around 700m from the terminal. To find the stop turn right out of the airport following black-backed 'Hotel' signs. Take the first left, shimmy right-left-right past Hotel Octagon, then turn third right at the Panda car wash (Brače

BUSES FROM SARAJEVO

DESTINATION	DEPARTURE POINT	PRICE (KM)	DURATION	FREQUENCY
Banja Luka	Main bus station	32.90	5hr	5am, 7.45am, 9.15am, 2.30pm, 3.30pm, 4.30pm, 6.30pm
Banja Luka	East Sarajevo bus station	31	5hr	9.30am, 11.30am
Bihać	Main bus station	42	6½hr	7.30am, 1.30pm, 10pm
Belgrade (Serbia)	Main bus station	47	7½hr	6am
Belgrade (Serbia)	East Sarajevo bus station	40-55	8-11hr	8am, 9.45am, 12.30pm, 3pm, 10pm
Dubrovnik (Croatia)	Main bus station	47	7hr	7.15am, 10am, plus 2.30pm, 10.15pm summer
Foča	East Sarajevo bus station	9	1½hr	11.15am, 6.15pm, plus Trebinje, Podgorica & Herceg Novi services
Herceg Novi	East Sarajevo bus station	46	7½	9am plus summer specials
Jajce	Main bus station, East Sarajevo bus station	23.50	3½hr	Take Banja Luka buses
Ljubljana (Slovenia)	Main bus station	92	8½hr	8.40pm Tue, Fri, Sun
Mostar	Main bus station	18	2½hr	15 daily, 6.50am-7.55pm
Munich (Germany)	Main bus station	140	19hr	8am
Niš	East Sarajevo bus station	46	11hr	8.40am, 6pm
Novi Pazar	Main bus station	32	7-8hr	3pm, 9pm, 10pm
Pale	East Sarajevo bus station	3.50	40min	14 daily Mon-Fri, 6 on Sat & Sun
Pale	Main bus station	5.70	25min	7am, 10am, 2pm
Podgorica (Montenegro)	East Sarajevo bus station	36	6hr	8.15am, 2pm, 8pm, 10.30pm
Split (Croatia), via Mostar	Main bus station	53.50	7½hr	10am, 9pm, plus 7am in summer
Split (Croatia), via Livno	Main bus station	53.50	7¼hr	6am
Travnik	Main bus station	17	2hr	9 daily
Trebinje via Sutjeska National Park	East Sarajevo bus station	26	5hr	7.45am, 1pm, 4.05pm
Tuzla	Main bus station	21	3¼hr	9 daily
Visoko	Main bus station	6.30	50min	at least hourly by Kakanj bus
Vienna (Austria)	Main bus station	100	14½hr	11.15am
Zagreb (Croatia)	Main bus station	54	9½hr	6.30am, 12.30pm, 10pm
Zagreb (Croatia) via Bosanski Brod	Main bus station	54	8½hr	9.30am

Mulića 17). Before the Mercator Hypermarket (Mimar Sinana 1) cross the road and take the bus-trolleybus going back the way you've just come.

Metered taxis charge around 7KM to Ilidža, 16KM to Baščaršija. The airport closes 11pm to 5am.

Bicycle Rental

Gir (Map p114; ☑350 523; www.gir.ba; Zelenih Berekti 14a; city bike per hr/day/5-days 3/15/25KM, mountain bike 4/20/35KM; ☺10am-6pm) This cycle shop is 'hidden' within the commercial passageway that leads to Club Jež.

Car

Central Sarajevo isn't driver-friendly and hotel parking is very limited but a car makes it much easier to reach the surrounding mountain areas.

Public Transport

You can find timetables on www.gras.co.ba/hodnik.htm. Click 'Redove Voznje' then select mode of transport.

Single-ride tickets are 1.60/1.80KM from kiosks/drivers and must be stamped once aboard. Day tickets (5.60KM) are only sold from kiosks. They cover all trams and trolleybuses plus most buses (but not 31E).

Useful routes include the following. All service frequency reduces on Sunday.

Tram 3 (every four to seven minutes) From Ilidža passes the Holiday Inn then loops one way (anticlockwise) around Baščaršija. Last tram back to Ilidža departs Baščaršija at 12.10am.

Tram 1 (every 12 to 25 minutes) Starts at the train station then does the same loop as Tram 3. From the train station you could alternatively walk to the nearest Tram 3 stop in about seven minutes.

Trolleybus 103 (every six minutes till 11pm) Runs along the southern side of the city from Austrijski Trg passing near Green Visions en route to Dobrijna (35 minutes). Handy for Lukovica (East Sarajevo) bus station and the airport.

Bus 31E (three per hour, 6.30am to 10pm) Vijećnica to Dobrijna (for Lukovica bus station).

Taxi

Taxis from the central ranks (Latin Bridge, Hotel Kovači, etc) often want to fix a set fee. For reliable on-the-metre fares (2KM plus about 1KM per kilometre) call **Paja Taxis** (☑412555) .

AROUND SARAJEVO

Mountains rise directly behind the city, offering convenient access to winter skiing or summer rambles. Landmine dangers remain in some areas so stick to well-used paths especially in forests.

Jahorina
☑057

Of BiH's Olympic ski resorts, multi-piste **Jahorina** (www.oc-jahorina.com; ski pass per day/week 33/160KM, ski-set rentals per day 25-40KM) has by far the widest range of hotels, each within 300m of one of Jahorina's seven main ski lifts. In summer, Termag Hotel (p122) rents mountain bikes (per half-/full day 7/10KM) and quads (per hour for one/two people 50/70KM). There's an (over)heated indoor pool at **Hotel Board** (www.hotelboard-jahorina.com; guests/non-guests free/20KM; ☺10am-10pm year-round).

🛏 Sleeping & Eating

Hotels are strung out for 2.5km, starting from a small seasonal shopping 'village' where you'll find the cheaper *pansions* – all close out of season except Hotel Kristal. The Termag Hotel is 300m above, the Board is a little further then the road divides, passing the aging **Bistrica** one way, Dva Javora the other. Past the still-ruined Hotel Jahorina, the road tunnels beneath Rajska Vrata before dead-ending at the top of the Skočine Lift. Quoted ski-season rates are for mid-January to March with half-board; summer rates include breakfast only.

Termag Hotel   HOTEL **€€€**
(☑270422; www.termaghotel.com; s/d/ste 115/152/200KM, new block 55-100KM, ski season d/ste from 240/300KM, new block 65-110KM; P🅿🛜🛁) Within an oversized mansion built in Scooby Doo Gothic style, the Termag is a beautifully designed fashion statement where traditional ideas and open fireplaces are given a stylish, modernist twist. Note that guests booking the new, less exclusive rooms in a 2013 humbacked extension will not enjoy free access to the sauna, pool and underground parking.

Rajska Vrata   LODGE **€€**
(☑065 142244; www.jahorina-rajskavrata.com; d/tr €50/75; 🛜) Beside the longest piste in town, this perfect alpine ski-in cafe-restaurant has rustic sheepskin benches around a centrally flued real fire. The cosy pine-walled bedrooms are only available March to November.

Hotel Dva Javora   HOTEL **€€**
(☑270481; www.hoteldvajavora.com; per person B&B 40KM, ski season 65-90KM; 🛜) Upstairs above a row of seasonal sports shops, the

modern lobby bar has an attractive, open feel. Rooms are fairly plain but with new pine beds and clean checkerboard bathrooms. Wi-fi in the bar.

Pansion Sport LODGE €€
(☑270333; www.pansion-sport.com; d Sun-Fri 54-80KM, Sat 84-124KM; ⊙mid-Dec–early Apr) Pleasant Swiss chalet–style guesthouse in the resort's 'village area'. There's a spacious glass-fronted bar full of big wicker chairs.

❶ Getting There & Away

Jahorina is 6.5km off the newly improved road leading between Istochno Sarajevo (27km) and Pale (13km). Buses run in ski season only, departing from Pale (3KM, 25 minutes) at 7am, 3pm and 11.30pm, returning from Hotel Bistrica.

Bjelašnica
☑033

BiH's second Olympic ski field rises above the two-hotel resort of **Bjelašnica** (www. bjelasnica.ba; ski pass per day/night/week 27/15/180KM), around 30km south of Sarajevo. An attraction here is the floodlit night skiing (6pm to 9pm) and, in summer, the possibilities of exploring the magical mountain villages (p123) behind. You can rent bicycles (per hour/day 5/30KM) and quads (per hour 60KM to 100KM) from the excellent new **Hotel Han** (☑584150; www.hotelhan. ba; s/d summer 56.50/95KM, d mid-Dec–Mar 155-185KM; ☏), a stylish yet reasonably priced

construction directly facing the main piste. Fronted by what looks like a giant Plexiglas pencil, the friendly but older **Hotel Maršal** (☑584129, 584100; www.hotel-marsal.ba; s/d summer 71.50/96KM, Christmas-early Mar d 116-136KM; ☏) rents skis, boots and poles (guests/nonguests per day 15/20KM) in season and has a nightclub.

Aimed at cross-country enthusiasts (it's away 5km from the downhill pistes), the great-value **Hostel Feri** (☑775555; www.feri. ba; Veliko Polje; per person summer/winter/New Year 74.20/94.20/114.20KM, s 54.60-84.60KM; ☏) charges the same per person whether you're in a double or six-bedded room. It's luxurious for a 'hostel', with flat-screen TVs, gym and ski-season-only sauna included.

On weekends in season bus 44 runs from Sarajevo's National Museum at 9am, returning at 3.30pm from Hotel Maršal. In summer you'll need wheels.

HERCEGOVINA

Hercegovina is the part of BiH that no one in the West ever mentions, if only because they can't pronounce it. The arid, Mediterranean landscape has a distinctive beauty punctuated with barren mountain ridges and photogenic river valleys. Famed for its fine wines and sun-packed fruits, Hercegovina is sparsely populated, but it has some intriguing historic towns and the Adriatic coast is just a skip away.

BJELAŠNICA'S MOUNTAIN VILLAGES

If you're driving, don't miss exploring the web of rural lanes tucked away in the uplands above Bjelašnica. Most famous is timeless **Lukomir**, 19km by a manageable unpaved road starting to the right of Aurora 97 snack-shack near Bjelašnica's Hotel Maršal. From a knoll that's less than five minutes' obvious climb beyond the road end in Lukomir village, a 360-degree panorama is one of the best in Bosnia encompassing the layered stone hamlet, sloping stony sheep pastures behind and a plunging gorge backed by a far horizon of rocky-knobbed peaks. There's a seasonal house-cafe in Lukomir but for a little more 'civilisation' head for **Umoljani**. Tucked into a partly wooded cwm, 16km from Bjelašnica, Umoljani has three little restaurant-cafes and two *pansions*. The **Restoran Studeno Vrelo** (☑061 709540; coffee/snack 1.50/5KM), the only one to open year-round, charges just 20KM per person to sleep in the cute three-bedroom log house behind. **Koliba** seasonal cafe displays excellent hiking maps on its exterior wall. **Pansion Umoljani** (☑061 228142) has a big-view terrace. The asphalted approach road to Umoljani is beautiful and there are *stećci* just above the road around 2.5km before the village. There's a hiking trail from Lukomir down to Umoljani but by road you need to backtrack 8km then descend via **Milišići** (which has its own appeal and some further great views) and turn right at the sharp junction 1.2km from Šabići. Green Visions (p116) and other agencies organise a range of summer activities to get you to and around this lovely area.

Mostar

📷036 / POP 111,600

At dusk the lights of numerous millhouse restaurants twinkle across gushing streamlets. Narrow Kujundžiluk 'gold alley' bustles joyously with trinket sellers. And in between, the Balkans' most celebrated bridge forms a majestic stone arc between reincarnated medieval towers. It's an enchanting scene. Do stay into the evening to see it without the summer hoards of day trippers. Indeed stay longer to enjoy memorable attractions in the surrounding area as well as pondering the city's darker side – still vivid scars of the 1990s conflict that remain visible beyond the cobbled lanes of the attractively restored Ottoman quarter. Be aware that between November and April most tourist facilities will be in wholescale hibernation.

History

Mostar means 'bridge-keeper', and the crossing of the Neretva River here has always been its raison d'être. In the mid-16th century, Mostar boomed as a key transport gateway within the powerful, expanding Ottoman Empire. Some 30 *esnafi* (craft guilds) included tanners (for whom the Tabhana was built), and goldsmiths (hence Kujundžiluk, 'gold alley'). In 1557, Suleyman the Magnificent ordered a swooping stone arch to replace the suspension bridge whose wobbling had previously terrified tradesmen as they gingerly crossed the fast-flowing Neretva River. The beautiful Stari Most (Old Bridge) that resulted was finished in 1566 and came to be appreciated as one of the era's engineering marvels. It survived the Italian occupation of WWII, but after standing for 427 years the bridge was destroyed in November 1993 by Bosnian Croat artillery in one of the most poignant and depressingly pointless moments of the whole Yugoslav civil war.

Ironically Muslims and Croats had initially fought together against Serb and Montenegrin forces that had started bombarding Mostar in April 1992. However, on 9 May 1993, a bitter conflict erupted between the former allies. A de facto frontline emerged north–south along the Bulvar and Aleksi Šantiće street with Croats to the west, Bosniaks to the east. For two years both sides swapped artillery fire and by 1995 Mostar resembled Dresden after WWII, with all its bridges destroyed and all but one of its 27 Ottoman-era mosques utterly ruined. Vast international assistance efforts rebuilt almost all of the Unesco-listed old city core, including the classic bridge, painstakingly reconstructed using 16th-century-style building techniques and stone from the original quarry. However, nearly two decades after the conflict, significant numbers of shattered buildings remain as ghostlike reminders. The psychological scars will take generations to heal and the city remains oddly schizophrenic, with two bus stations and two postal systems – one Bosniak and the other Croat.

◉ Sights

Stari Most   BRIDGE

The world-famous Stari Most (Old Bridge) is the indisputable visual focus that gives Mostar its special magic. The medieval bridge's pale stone magnificently throws back the golden glow of sunset or the tasteful night-time floodlighting. Numerous well-positioned cafes and restaurants, notably behind the **Tabhana** (an Ottoman-era enclosed courtyard), tempt you to sit and savour the scene. If you wait long enough you are likely to see someone jump 21m off the parapet into the icy Neretva below. This is not an attempt at suicide but an age-old tradition maintained by an elite group of young men. There's even an annual bridge-diving competition (July). At other times, however, divers will only generally jump once their hustlers have collected enough photo money from onlookers. If you want to jump yourself (from €25), ask at the **Bridge-Divers' Clubhouse** beside the bridge's western end. They can organise a wetsuit, basic training and two divers who await beside the river below in case of emergencies.

At the bridge's eastern side, the **Old Bridge Museum** (adult/student 5/3KM; ⊙10am-6pm summer, 11am-2pm winter, closed Mon) has two parts, both offering relatively sparse exhibits. First you climb up a five-storey stone defence tower for partial views and interesting but limited displays about Stari Most's context and construction. Climb back down to walk through the bridge's archaeological bowels, and you'll emerge on Kujundžiluk.

Crooked Bridge   BRIDGE

(Kriva Ćuprija) Resembling Stari Most but in miniature, the pint-sized Crooked Bridge crosses the tiny Rabobolja creek amid a layered series of millhouse restaurants. The original bridge, weakened by wartime as-

IMAGES OF MOSTAR

At least four compelling videos of Mostar's demise and rebirth are on show around town. Each is subtly different but all include tragic footage of the moment the old bridge was blown apart. A decent free choice is within the **Old Hamam** (beside Tabhana; ⊘10am-4pm May-Oct) where an exhibition looks building-by-building at Mostar's destruction and reconstruction. Bookshop **Galerija Old Bridge** (Stari Most; ⊘9am-10pm), a former mosque right on the bridge's southwest parapet, plays and sells a similar DVD (€10). A 10-minute version concentrating more on bridge-diving is screened in a comfy cinema-style room at the Museum of Hercegovina. And there's a slow-moving 15-minute video shown at the Old Bridge Museum.

An **exhibition** (Helebija Kula, Stari Most; 6KM; ⊘9am-8.30pm Apr-Nov) of around 50 black-and-white still photos depicting city life during wartime is shown within the semi-circular Helebija Kula, a former gunpowder tower directly behind the Bridge Divers' Clubhouse. They're powerful images but there's no video and entry fees seem steep.

saults, was washed away by floods of 2000, but rebuilt a year later.

Koski Mehmed Paša Mosque   MOSQUE
(Mala Tepa 16; mosque/mosque & minaret 4/8KM; ⊘8am-8pm Apr-Sep, 9am-5pm Oct, closed Nov-Mar) Entered from a gated courtyard, the rebuilt 1618 Koski Mehmed Paša Mosque lacks a certain finess in its interior but climbing the claustrophobic minaret allows you to enjoy sweeping town views. The most attractive part of the mosque complex is the small courtyard outside with its fountain taps and garden area (access free).

Bišćevića Ćošak   HOUSE
(Turkish House; Bišćevića 13; admission 4KM; ⊘8.30am-6.30pm mid-Apr–Oct, closed winter except by tour) Bišćevića Ćošak is a slightly ramshackle 350-year-old Ottoman-Bosnian home with a colourfully furnished interior sporting a selection of traditional metalwork and carved wooden furniture. For interesting comparisons also visit the grander **Muslibegović House** (admission 4KM; ⊘10am-6pm mid-Apr–mid-Oct), which now doubles as a boutique hotel (p128).

Former Front Line   HISTORIC AREA
Nearly two decades after the conflict, many buildings remain as bullet-pocked skeletal wrecks, especially along Mostar's former 'front line'. Every year more are restored but you'll still see several tragic ruins around Spanski Trg, including the triangular nine-storey tower that was once **Ljubljanska Banka** (Kralja Zvonimira bb). Meanwhile Trg Musala, once the heart of Austro-Hungarian Mostar, is still scarred by the stumpy war-ruined shell of the once splendid **Hotel Neretva** (Trg Musala).

Museum of Hercegovina   MUSEUM
(http://muzejhercegovine.com; Bajatova 4; admission 5KM; ⊘8am-4pm Mon-Fri, 8am-1pm Sat) This small museum with archaeological and ethnographic sections, occupies the former house of Džemal Bijedić, former head of the Yugoslav government who died in mysterious circumstances in 1978. The unexplained plane wheels recall Mostar's Yugo-era aero-industry. Anton Zimlo's pre-WWI photos include a view of the Old Bridge carpet-decked for Austrian Emperor Franz Josef's 1910 visit.

Karađozbeg Mosque   MOSQUE
(Braće Fejića bb; mosque/mosque & minaret 4/8KM; ⊘times vary, closed during prayers) Mostar's most important mosque, built in 1557 but heavily damaged during the war, is now completely renovated with distinctive lead-roofed wooden verandah and four-domed madrassa annexe now used as a clinic.

Roznamedži Ibrahimefendi Mosque   MOSQUE
(Braće Fejića bb) This early-17th-century mosque was the only one to survive the 1993–35 shelling relatively unscathed. Its associated **madrassa**, demolished in 1960, has now also been rebuilt, the reincarnation hosting shops and a cafe.

⊆ Tours
Some homestays and hostels, including Majdas, Nina and **Miran's** (☏062 115333; www.hostelmiran-mostar.com; Pere Lažetića 13), offer walking tours around town and/or great-value full-day trips visiting Blagaj, Međugorje, Počitelj and the Kravice waterfalls for around 70KM. **Almira Travel** (☏551873; www.almira-travel.ba; Mala Tepa 9) offers alternative regional

Mostar

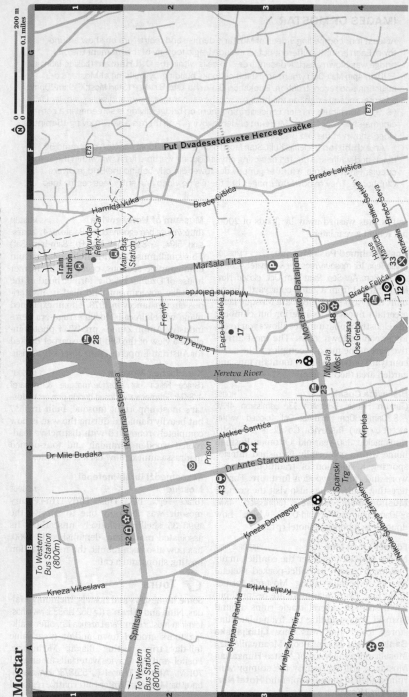

Put Dvadesetdevete Hercegovačke

Hamida Vuka

Braće Ćišića

Braće Lakišića

Salke Šahića

Braće Ševa

Hyundai
Rent-A-Car

Main Bus
Station

Train Station

Maršala Tita

Huse
Maslića

Rizkala

33

Mladena Balorde

Mostarskog Bataljona

Braće Fejića

25

11

12

Frenje

Pere Lažetića

17

48

Osmana
Ose Grebe

Lacina (Lace)

28

3

Musala
Most

Neretva River

23

Kardinala Stepinca

Alekse Šantića

44

Prison

Dr Mile Budaka

Dr Ante Starcevica

Krpića

43

Spanski
Trg

Nikole Subica Zrinskog

52

47

Kneza Domagoja

6

Kneza Višeslava

Splitska

Kralja Tvrtka

Stjepana Radića

Kralja Zvonimira

49

To Western
Bus Station
(800m)

To Western
Bus Station
(800m)

200 m
0.1 miles

0
0

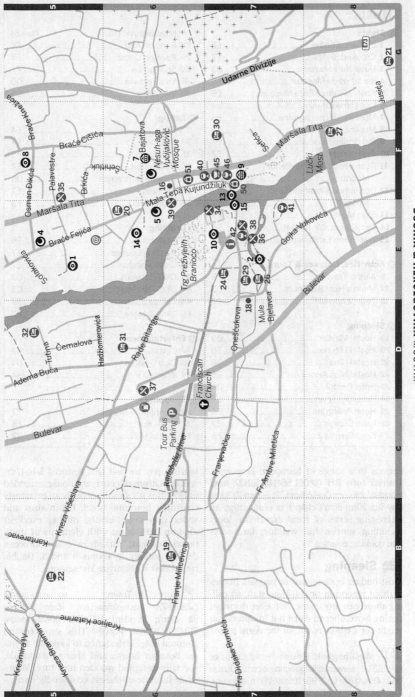

Mostar

options in a range of European languages. **Tourist Info BH** (☏061 564146 561127; www.tourist-infobh.com; Oneščukova 39; ⊙8am-10.30pm May-Sep, 10am-8pm Oct-Apr) is pioneering an interesting series of rural experience tours including sunrise hill walking, farm-stays and cooking courses.

🛏 Sleeping

Most budget options are in people's homes without reception or full-time staff, so calling ahead can prove wise. Some are dormant during November to April but in others you might get a whole room for the dorm price.

TOP CHOICE **Muslibegović House** HISTORIC HOTEL €€ (☏551379; www.muslibegovichouse.com; Osman Đikća 41; s/d/ste €60/90/105; ❄@) In summer, tourists pay to visit this restored late-17th-century Ottoman courtyard house, extended in 1871. But it's simultaneously an extremely charming boutique hotel. Room sizes and styles vary significantly, mixing excellent modern bathrooms with elements of traditional Bosnian, Turkish or even Moroccan design, notably in rooms 2 and 3. Double rooms cost €75 during low season.

🏷 **Hotel Old Town** BOUTIQUE HOTEL €€ (☏558877; www.oldtown.ba; Rade Bitange 9a; d/tr/q standard 180/250/300KM, deluxe 210/290/400KM; ⓟ❄@) This super-central 10-room hotel is designed to look like a typical Bosnian house and sports handmade, specially designed wooden furniture. Meanwhile its state-of-the-art ecofriendly energy-saving systems include waste-burning furnaces for water heating and air circulation to save on air-con wastage. Standard rooms are tucked into sloping roof eaves.

Kriva Ćuprija
MILLHOUSE €€

(📞550953; www.motel-mostar.ba; r 70-130KM, apt 100-180KM; ❄️🛎️) Set above the famous little Crooked Bridge, this delightful central getaway enjoys the soothing sounds of gushing streams and charming mill-styled stone architecture. Idyllic views from the suites' semi-private terraces cram together old rooftops, minarets and a mountain-ridge backdrop. Rooms are impeccably clean if not necessarily large. Co-owned **Kriva Ćuprija 2** (Maršala Tita 186) is more stylishly appointed and has two hot-tubs on a rear deck but lacks the quaint location of the original.

Shangri-La
B&B €€

(📞551819; www.shangrila.com.ba; Kalhanska 10; d €49-59; 🅿️❄️🛎️) Quiet yet central, a pseudo-19th-century facade hides rooms that are contemporary and better appointed than those of many Mostar hotels. The rooftop views are hard to beat and the English-speaking hosts are faultlessly welcoming without being intrusive.

Hostel Majdas
HOSTEL €

(📞062 265324, 061 382940; www.hostelmajdas.com; 1st fl, Franje Milicevica 39; dm/d without bathroom €12/27; ⊘closed Oct-Mar; ❄️@🛎️) By sheer force of personality, and a very human awareness of traveller needs, the host family has transformed this once dreary tower-block apartment into Mostar's cult hostel. Space is tight in the colour-coordinated bunk dorms and little communal areas, but it's a great place to meet fellow travellers; there are lockers, FAQ and cultural-tip sheets, inexpensive laundry, a book exchange and a taxi sign-up sheet. Sharp-witted Bata runs popular full-day regional tours several times weekly.

Hotel Pellegrino
HOTEL €€

(📞062 969000; www.hotel-pellegrino.ba; Faladžića 1c; s €50-80, d €80-120; ❄️🛎️) The big pluses here are the oversized, elegantly appointed studio rooms (many with kitchenette) and excellent anti-allergenic bedding. But there is no reception, just a door-bell, and despite the five floors there are neither views nor a lift.

Hotel Bristol
BUSINESS HOTEL €€

(📞500100; www.bristol.ba; Mostarskog Bataljona; s/d from €50.50/81.50; ❄️🛎️) Classier than you'd guess from the rectilinear concrete exterior, there's an expansive piano bar, riverside terrace and a lift accessing the typical business-style rooms. There are desks even in the poky little singles.

Villa Fortuna
B&B €€

(📞551888; www.villafortuna.ba; Rade Bitange 34; s/d/tr/apt €30/40/60/80, incl breakfast €35/50/70/100; 🅿️❄️🛎️) Behind the bland travel-agency facade, fresh if compact air-con rooms lead off a hallway with a museum-like collection of local tools and metalwork. Behind is a sweet little private courtyard area in mock farmhouse style.

Villa Mike
HOMESTAY €€

(📞062 661535, 580929; www.villamike-mostar.com; Tutina 15; s/d without bathroom €30/50; ❄️🛎️🏊) Villa Mike is a private house offering four sparklingly clean, brand new homestay rooms sharing two bathrooms. The obliging owner speaks good English, but most remarkably there's an excellent private swimming pool in the walled backyard.

Hostel Nina
HOSTEL €

(📞061 382743; www.hostelnina.ba; Čelebica 18; dm/d without bathroom €11/22; ❄️@) Popular homestay-hostel run by an obliging English-speaking lady whose husband, a war survivor and former bridge jumper, runs regional tours that often end up over bargain beers at his bar in the Tabhana. Sometimes when the main hostel has been full, guests have been relocated to an **annex** that lacks much charm and is far less central.

Pansion Aldi
HOSTEL €

(📞061 273457, 552185; www.pansion-aldi.com; Lačina 69a; dm €10; 🅿️❄️@🛎️) Handy for the bus station, 17 beds in five large, simple rooms share a kitchenette and three small toilet-shower cubicles. It's slightly austere but there's a river-facing terrace garden.

Pansion Oscar
PENSION €

(📞580237, 061 823649; Oneščukova 33; s/d €30/40/45, s/d/tr/q without bathroom €20/30/50/60; ❄️🛎️) Oskar is essentially a pair of family homes above a summer-only cocktail/shisha garden-bar slap bang in the historic centre. Standards vary somewhat between the nine rooms, with the best in the eaves of the newer back house. They're not bookable through hostel websites so this is a good punt if you're arriving without reservations.

Hostel Miturno
HOSTEL €

(📞552408; www.hostel-miturno.ba; Braće Felića 67; dm/d €10/20; ⊘closed Jan & Feb; 🚌❄️🛎️) Run by a youthful, music-loving crew, this central mini-hostel has a handful of rooms and small dorms above a main-street shop. The TV room-lobby is cramped but social and has a colourful graffiti-chic. Free coffee.

✗ Eating

Cafes and restaurants with divine views of the river cluster along the riverbank near Stari Most. Although unapologetically tourist-oriented, their meal prices are only a *maraka* or two more than any ordinary dive. Along Mala Tepa and Braće Fejića you'll find a morning **vegetable market** (☉6.30am-2pm), supermarkets and several inexpensive places for *ćevapi* and other Bosnian snacks.

Babilon
BALKAN €€

(Tabhana; mains 8-20KM; 🗋) Along with restaurants Bella Vista, Mlinica and Teatr next door, the Babilon has stupendous terrace views across the river to the Old Town and Stari Most. The food might be less impressive than the views, but some of the set 'tourist menus' are excellent value. Unlike several of its fellows, Babilon remains open in winter.

Hindin Han
BALKAN €€

(Jusovina bb; mains 7-20KM; ☉11am-11pm; 🛜🗋) Hindin Han is a rebuilt historic building with several layers of summer terrace perched pleasantly above a side stream. Locals rate its food as better than most other equivalent tourist restaurants, and the stuffed squid certainly passes muster. The highly quaffable house wine costs 3.75KM per glass.

Šadrvan
BALKAN €€

(Jusovina 11; mains 7-23KM; ☉closed Jan; 🗋) On a vine- and tree-shaded corner where the pedestrian lane from Stari Most divides, this tourist favourite has tables set around a trickling fountain made of old Turkish-style metalwork. The menu covers all bases and takes a stab at some vegetarian options. Meat-free *đuveč* (KM7) tastes like ratatouille on rice.

ABC
ITALIAN €

(☏061 194656; Braće Fejića 45; pizza & pasta 6-10KM, mains 13-17KM; ☉9am-10.30pm Mon-Fri, noon-10.30pm Sat & Sun; 🗋) Above a popular cakeshop-cafe, this relaxed pastel-toned Italian restaurant is decorated with photos of old Mostar and dotted with aspidistras. Pizzas are bready but the pastas come with an extra bucketful of parmesan. Try plate-lickingly creamy Aurora tortellini (9KM).

Urban Grill
BOSNIAN €

(Mala Tepa 26; mains 5-17KM; ☉8am-11pm Mon-Sat, 9am-11pm Sun) No longer limiting itself to *ćevapi*, this brightly modern take on Bosnian-rustic now serves a wider variety of local specialities but the secret trump card remains its little lower terrace with an unexpectedly excellent Old Bridge view.

Konoba Boncampo
BOSNIAN €€

(Husne Rebca 15 Bulevar; mains 8-18KM; ☉8am-10.30pm) You'll wonder why on earth we've sent you to this hard-to-find, visually ordinary locals' eatery at the base of a residential tower block. But try their *mučkalica* ('everything' dish) and shots of Bosnia's best *slivovice* (plum brandy from Goražde) and you might understand.

Eko-Eli
BOSNIAN €

(Maršala Tita 115; mains 2.50-3.50KM; ☉7am-11pm) Escape the tourists and watch typical Bosnian *pita* snacks (including *krompiraća*, *sirnica*, *burek* and *zeljanica*) being baked over hot coals. Take away, eat at the communal table, or dine in the almost comically uninspired bar next door.

🍷 Drinking

Ali Baba
BAR

(Kujundžiluk; ☉24hr Jun-Sep, 7am-7pm Oct, closed winter) Take a gaping cavern in the raw rock, add colourful low lighting, fat beats and Fashion TV and hey presto, you've got this one-off party bar. A dripping tunnel leads out to a second entrance on Maršala Tita.

OKC Abrašević
BAR

(☏561107; www.okcabrasevic.org; Alekse Šantića 25) This understatedly intellectual smoky box of a bar offers Mostar's most vibrantly alternative scene and has an attached venue for offbeat gigs. It's hidden away in an unsigned courtyard on the former front line. Draft beer from 2KM. Hours vary.

Terasa
CAFE

(Maršala Tita bb; ☉weather dependent) This spectacular open-air perch-terrace surveys Stari Most and the old city towers from altogether new angles. Enter through the little roof-garden of art studio Atelje Novalić.

Club Calamus
COCKTAIL BAR

(Integra Bldg, 5th fl, Dr Ante Starčevića bb; ☉10am-2am) DJs spin trancy beats after 10pm in this top-floor cocktail bar whose summer rooftop section affords fascinating if poignant views over some of Mostar's worst war ruins.

Caffe Marshall
BAR

(Oneščukova bb; ☺8am-1am) This minuscule box bar has a ceiling draped with musical instruments and is often the latest to be active in the Old Bridge area.

Wine & More
WINE BAR

(Mala Tepa; ☺9am-11pm; ☜) Play Bacchus, sampling Trebinje's famous Tvrdoš Monastery wines (per glass 5KM) at barrel tables on the Old Town's time-polished stone stairways.

Blasting Lounge
BAR

(Riverside; cocktails 5-10KM; ☺10am-late, closed mid-Nov–mid-May) Sip cocktails and fresh juice (no coffee machine) on a parasol-shaded bank of outdoor bag-cushions while gazing back at Stari Most.

☆ Entertainment

OKC Abrašević (p130) hosts occasional concerts and Ali Baba (p130) fills its summer cave with contemporary dance sounds, particularly on weekend party nights. There are several DJ cafes and nightclubs around the Rondo. Website www.bhclubbing.com gives upcoming listings.

Romana Inn
DISCO

(www.romanainn.com; ☺10.30pm-5am Thu-Sat) Large, somewhat generic weekend disco.

Club Oxygen
NIGHTCLUB

(www.biosphere.ba/biosfere-stranice-oxigen-en. html; Braće Fejića bb; ☺variable) Oxygen has DJ-parties and occasional live gigs.

Dom Herceg Stjepan Kosača
CULTURAL CENTRE

(http://kosaca-mostar.com/; Rondo; ☜) Diverse shows and concerts include occasional touring operas, ballets and theatre from Croatia.

Cinestar
CINEMA

(www.blitz-cinestar-bh.ba) Multiplex in the big new **Mepas Mall** (www.mepas-mall.com; Kardinala Stepinca bb).

🛍 Shopping

The stone-roofed shop-houses of Kujundžiluk throw open metal shutters to sell colourfully inexpensive Turkish and Indian souvenirs including glittery velveteen slippers, pashmina-style wraps, fezzes, *boncuk* (evil-eye) pendants and Russian-style nested dolls. You can still find pens fashioned from old bullets and shell casings hammered into works of art. However, as supplies of war debris are finally being exhausted, artisans such as coppersmith **Ismet Kurt** (Kujundžiluk 5; ☺9am-8pm) are increasingly using old cutlery and trays instead as starting materials.

ℹ Information

While no longer technically legal, in fact most businesses readily accept euros and Croatian

BOSNIA & HERCEGOVINA MOSTAR

BUSES FROM MOSTAR (MAIN BUS STATION)

DESTINATION	PRICE (KM)	DURATION	FREQUENCY
Banja Luka via Jajce	25	6hr	1.30pm
Belgrade (Serbia)	58	11 hr	7.30pm, 9pm
Čapljina	6	40min	11.15am, 1pm, 3.25pm
Dubrovnik (Croatia)	32	3-4hr	7am, 10am, 12.30pm
Herceg Novi via Kotor	71	4½hr	7am (plus 2.30pm Fridays)
Sarajevo	20	2½hr	6am, 6.30am, 7am, 9am, 10am, 11am, 3pm, 4pm, 5pm, 6.15pm
Split (Croatia)	33	4½hr	6.15am, 7am, 11.15am, 12.50pm
Stolac	6	1hr	roughly hourly
Trebinje via Nevesinje	21	3hr	6.15am Mon-Sat, 3.30pm, 5.30pm
Vienna (Austria) via Maribor	110	12hr	8.30am
Zagreb (Croatia)	43-52	9½hr	7am, 9am, 8.15pm

kuna as well as marakas. Braće Fejića, the main commercial street, has banks, ATMs, a pharmacy, supermarkets and an internet cafe. Mostar websites include **Grad Mostar** (www.turizam. mostar.ba), the **Hercegovina Tourist Board** (www.hercegovina.ba) and **Visit Mostar** (www. visitmostar.org).

Bosniak Post Office (Braće Fejića bb; ⊙8am-8pm Mon-Fri, 8am-6pm Sat)

Croat Post Office (Dr Ante Starčevića bb; ⊙7am-7pm Mon-Sat, 9am-noon Sun)

Tourist Information Centre (☑397350; Trg Preživjelih Branioco; ⊙9am-9pm Jun-Sep, closed Oct-May) See also Tourist Info BH (p128).

ⓘ Getting There & Around

AIR Mostar airport (OMO; ☑350992; www. mostar-airport.ba), 6km south of town off the Čapljina road, has no scheduled flights.

BICYCLE The souvenir stall beside the tourist info centre rents bicycles (per half-/full day €10/15) during the tourist season.

BUS Most long-distance buses use the **main bus station** (☑552025; Trg Ivana Krndelja) beside the train station. However, Renner buses to Stolac, a 4.30pm bus to Split (25KM) and seven weekday services to Međugorje (4KM, 45 minutes) start from the inconveniently located **western bus station** (☑348680; Autobusni Kolodvor; Vukovarska bb). It's around 800m from Mepas Mall, following Splitska west then the turning right at the third major junction. Yellow **Mostar Bus** (☑552250; www.mostarbus. ba/linije.asp) services to Blagaj start from opposite the train station and pick up passengers at Lučki Most stop.

CAR Hyundai Rent-A-Car (☑552404; www. hyundai.ba; main bus station; per day/week from 75/390KM; ⊙8am-11am & noon-4pm Mon-Fri, 9am-3pm Sat) offers good-value car hire including full insurance without deductible. Add 17% tax.

TRAIN Trains to Sarajevo (9.90KM, 2¼ hours) depart at 8.02am, 2.10pm and 6.43pm daily.

Around Mostar

By joining a tour or hiring a car you could visit Blagaj, Počitelj, Međugorje and the Kravice waterfalls all in one busy day.

BLAGAJ
☑036 / POP 4000

The signature sight in pretty Blagaj village is the half-timbered **Tekija** (Dervish House; www.fidantours.ba/tekke; ⊙8am-10pm summer, 8am-7pm winter) standing beside the surreally blue-green Buna River where it gushes out

of a cliff cave. Upstairs the Tekija's wobbly wooden interior entombs two 15th-century Tajik dervishes and attracts pious pilgrims. The best views are from across the river on a footpath leading behind the attractive riverside **Vrelo Restaurant** (☑572556; mains 8-27KM; ⊙9am-10pm).

Walking to the Tekija takes 10 minutes from the seasonal **tourist information booth** (⊙variable, closed Oct-Mar). En route you'll pass the **Ottoman Villa** (☑061 273459; www.velagomed.ba; Velagicevina bb; admission 2KM; ⊙10am-7pm, closed mid-Oct–Apr), an 18th-century Ottoman homestead with a unique set of island mill-meadow gardens. Out of hours the house's traditionally furnished little lounge transforms into the 'Oriental Nights' homestay room (€20 per person), by far the best of four guest rooms that share a single bathroom. There's a 'hanging garden' eating area outside and the French-speaking owner plans 'fair trade' tours. Alternatively, for accommodation try the friendly **Kayan Pansion** (☑061 241136, 572299; nevresaka-jan@yahoo.com; per person €10; ﹡), offering 11 beds in seven interconnected rooms above an ultra-friendly family home with sizeable gym. It's unmarked, set back across a side road from the octagonal 1892 **Sultan Sulejman Mosque**.

Mostar Bus (www.mostarbus.ba/linije.asp) routes 10, 11 and 12 from Mostar all run to (or very near) Blagaj (2.10KM, 30 minutes), with 16 services on weekdays but only a handful at weekends (last return 8pm).

MEĐUGORJE
☑036 / POP 4300

On 24 June 1981 a vision appeared to six local teenagers in Međugorje (www.med-jugorje.hr). What they believe they saw was a manifestation of the Holy Virgin. As a result, this formerly poor wine-making backwater has been utterly transformed into a bustling Catholic pilgrimage centre and continues to grow even though Rome has not officially acknowledged the visions' legitimacy. Today Međugorje has a blend of honest faith and cash-in tackiness that is reminiscent of Lourdes (France) or Fatima (Portugal) but there's little of beauty here and nonpilgrims generally find a one-hour visit ample to get the idea. The town's focus is double-towered 1969 **St James' Church** (Župna Crkva). In a garden 200m behind that, the mesmerising **Resurrected Saviour** (Uskrsli Spasitej) is a masterpiece of contemporary sculpture showing a 5m-tall metallic

Christ standing crucified yet cross-less, his manhood wrapped in scripture. At times the statue's right knee 'miraculously' weeps a colourless liquid that pilgrims queue to dab onto specially inscribed pads.

A 3km (5KM) taxi ride away at **Podbrdo** village, streams of the faithful climb **Brdo Ukazanja** (Apparition Hill) on red-earth paths studded with sharp stones. They're headed for a white statue of the Virgin Mary marking the site of the original 1981 visions. If you're fit you could nip up and back in 20 minutes but pilgrims spend an hour or more contemplating and praying at way stations, a few walking barefoot in deliberately painful acts of penitence.

For satelite mapped points of interest see www.medjugorjemap.com

POČITELJ
036 / POP 350

The stepped Ottoman-era fortress village of Počitelj is one of the most picture-perfect architectural ensembles in BiH. Cupped in a steep rocky amphitheatre, it's a warren of stairways climbing between ramshackle stone-roofed houses and pomegranate bushes. The large 1563 **Hadži Alijna Mosque** has been fully restored since the 1990s' destructions while the 16m **clock tower** (Sahat Kula) remains bell-less as it has been since 1917. The most iconic building is the climbable octagonal **Gavrakapetan Tower** in the still part-ruined **Utvrda** (Fort). But for even better panoramas climb to the uppermost rampart bastions. Breathtaking!

Accommodation is limited. Two new pine-walled **apartments** (d/tr €40/60; ❋) need to be pre-booked through English-speaking **Mediha Oruč** (✆062 481844), generally summer only. Year-round, simple **homestay rooms** (✆062 230023, 826468; per person €10) are rented by Razira Kajtaz who is often to be found hawking souvenirs at the gate-tower at the entrace to the Old Town. Three cafe-restaurants serve drinks and limited grill-meals.

Počitelj is right beside the main Split–Mostar road, 4km north of Čapljina. Mostar–Split, Mostar–Čapljina and some Mostar–Stolac buses pass by. By car, try to arrive an hour before sunset for perfect light and fewer Croatian tour groups.

KRAVICE WATERFALLS

In spring this stunning mini-Niagara of 25m **cascades** pounds itself into a dramatic, steamy fury. In summer the falls themselves are less impressive but surrounding pools

> ## WINE DIVINE
>
> Hercegovina's home-grown wines are a revelation. Local *živalka* grapes yield dry yet fruit-filled whites while suitably aged *blatina* and *vranac* reds can be velvety and complex. In restaurants, ordering *domaći* ('house') wine by the carafe (ie 'open') costs from just 15KM per litre. That's far less than by the bottle and ensures that you're drinking a really local drop. It's possible to visit a selection of rural wineries (see www.wineroute.ba) but it often pays to phone ahead.

become shallow enough for swimming. The site is 15 minutes' walk from a car park that's 4km down a dead-end road turning off the M6 (Čapljina–Ljubuški road). Turn at km42.5. There's no public transport.

Stolac
036 / POP 12,000

The attractive castle town of Stolac was the site of Roman Diluntum (3rd century AD) and became a prominent citadel from the 15th century. Stolac suffered serious conflict in 1993. The displaced population has long since returned and the town's greatest historical buildings have been painstakingly reconstructed. However, Stolac still hasn't fully recovered, war damage remains painfully evident and the only hotel has closed.

At the central junction, the large, mural-fronted 1519 **Čaršija Mosque** has been splendidly rebuilt. Following the Brevaga River upstream for 900m from here you'll pass the cute cubic **Ćuprija Mosque**, little stone-arched **Inat Ćuprija** (bridge) and three picturesque, if derelict, 17th-century stone **mill-races** before reaching unpretentious **Nota** (Kukovac bb; coffee/beer 1/2KM, pizza 4-7KM; ☺8am-11pm) cafe-pizzeria. It's unmarked but obvious with a terrace on stilts above the lip of a clogged horseshoe of waterfall.

Downstream from Čaršija Mosque, the tree-lined main street (Hrvatske-Brante, aka Ada) passes a diagonal switchback track that leads up to the hefty **castle ruins**. Around 300m further along Hrvatske-Brante is another group of historic buildings, some rebuilt. Across the bridges, views of the castle site are most memorable from near the Auro petrol station, 50m south of the graffiti-covered bus station.

Beside the Mostar road 3km west of Stolac is **Radimlja Necropolis** (admission free). At first glimpse it looks like a quarryman's yard. But on closer inspection the group of around 110 blocks prove to include some of Bosnia's most important *stećci* (carved grave-markers). Entry is free if you ignore the book-bearing beggar.

Buses run Mostar–Stolac (6KM) approximately hourly. There's no Stolac–Trebinje bus whatsoever but you might persuade locals to act as taxi and take you to Ljubinje (20km, 40KM), from where a 4.15pm minibus runs daily to Trebinje (8KM, one hour). The Stolac–Ljubinje road crosses a former wartime no-man's-land passing the still bombed-out hilltop hamlet of Žegulja at km33.2.

EASTERN BOSNIA & HERCEGOVINA

To get quickly yet relatively easily off the main tourist trail, try linking Sarajevo or Mostar to Dubrovnik via Trebinje, or head to Belgrade via Višegrad. Both journeys take you through the semi-autonomous Republika Srpska.

Trebinje

☑ 059 / POP 36,000

It's just 28km from Dubrovnik (28km), but in tourist terms a whole world away. Trebinje's small, walled **Old Town** (Stari Grad) is attractive but very much 'lived in', its unpretentious cafes offering a fascinating opportunity to meet friendly local residents and hear Serb viewpoints on divisive recent history. The Old Town ramparts back onto the riverside near a 19th-century former Austro-Hungarian barracks which now houses the **Hercegovina Museum** (www.muzejhercegovine.org; Stari Grad 59; admission 2KM; ☉8am-2pm Mon-Fri, 10am-2pm Sat).

Trebinje's 1574 **Arslanagić Bridge** (Perovića Most), 700m northeast of Hotel Leotar, is a unique double-backed structure but it's sadly let down by the unexotic suburban location to which it was moved in the 1970s.

For phenomenal views, take the 2km winding lane leading east behind the hospital to hilltop Hercegovacka Gracanica. The compact but eye-catching **Presvete Bogorodice Church** (Hercegovačka Gračanica) was erected here in 2000 to re-house the bones of local hero Jovan Dučić. Its design is based on the 1321 Gračanica monastery in Kosovo, a building that's symbolically sacred to many Serbs. The brand new **Arhangel Mihailo Church** on a second hilltop across town provides a certain sense of urban symmetry.

Siniša Kunić (☑065 645224; www.walkwithme.ba) offers small-group forest, hiking and pilgrimage trips.

🛌 Sleeping & Eating

Trebinje has half a dozen hotels including three motels across the river near the hospital. Within the Old Town, pizza windows sell slices for 1.50KM and there are many local-oriented cafe-bars including two at the river bank hidden behind the museum.

TOP CHOICE **Hotel Platani** BOUTIQUE HOTEL €€
(http://hotel-platani-trebinje.com; Trg Svobode; s/d/tr Platani-1 63/85/100KM, Platani-2 72/104/128KM; ✱☞) The Platani's two stone buildings both have distinctly Gallic-looking glass/wrought-iron overhangs and overlook the prettiest central square, shaded with chestnut and plane trees. Platini-1 is perfectly adequate but choose Platini-2 for its stylish contemporary rooms with virginal white sheets and Klimt-esque art. Some back rooms suffer road noise but it's fabulous value for money. So too is the excellent terrace restaurant where you can sip generous glasses of velvety Tvrdoš Vranac red wine for just 4KM.

TOP CHOICE **Vinoteka Vukoje 1982** WINE & CUISINE €€
(☑270370; www.podrum-vukoje.com; Mirna 28; mains 8-20KM; 🍴) Come for the free wine tasting (including Vukuje's irresistible Vranac Reserve) then stay for their imaginative cuisine employing a range of local herbs and meats. The two stylishly appointed new dining rooms have pale decor and sepia photos of the vineyards. From Hotel Platani it's 1.2km towards Bileća, 200m beyond the Niščić turn.

❶ Information

Tourist Office (☑273410; www.trebinjeturizam.com; Jovan Dučića bb; ☉8am-8pm Mon-Fri, 8am-3pm Sat May-Oct, 8am-4pm Mon-Fri, 9am-2pm Sat Nov-Apr) Diagonally opposite Hotel Platani-1 near the Old Town's western gate.

❶ Getting There & Away

The **bus station** (Autobusko Stajalište; Vojvode Stepe Stepanovića) is simply a shelter within a parking area, 200m west of the old town.

BUSES FROM TREBINJE

There are no buses to Stolac.

DESTINATION	PRICE (KM)	DURATION	FREQUENCY
Belgrade (Serbia) via Višegrad	52	11 hr	8am, 9.45pm
Dubrovnik (Croatia)	10	45min	10am Mon-Sat (returns at 1.30pm)
Foča	16	2½hr	take Belgrade, Novi Sad, Pale or Sarajevo buses
Ljubinje	8	1hr	3.05pm Mon-Fri, 7pm daily
Mostar via Nevesinje	24	3hr	6.15am, 10am, 2.30pm
Novi Sad	53	12hr	5.30pm
Pale	28.50	4½hr	5am
Podgorica via Nikšič	33	3½hr	8.30am, 3pm, 4.30pm
Sarajevo	26	4hr	5am, 7.30am, 11am

Trebinje To Višegrad

Trebinje–Belgrade and Trebinje–Sarajevo buses pass through the glorious **Sutjeska National Park** (www.npsutjeska.srbinje.net). Magnificent tree-dappled grey rock crags flank the Sutjeska canyon like scenes from classical Chinese paintings. A few kilometres further north the canyon opens out near an impressively vast concrete **Partizans' Memorial** commemorating the classic WWII battle of Tjentište. Mountaineers and hikers can explore more of the national park's scenic wonders with extreme-sports outfit **Encijan** (☑058-211150, 058-211220; www.pkencijan.com; Kraljapetra-I 1; ☺9am-5pm Mon-Sat), based in Foča (25km further north). Encijan also organises world-class rafting on the Tara River that cascades out of Europe's deepest canyon (across the Montenegrin border) then thunders over 21 rapids (class III to class IV in summer, class IV to class V in April).

Višegrad

☑058 / POP 20,000

A convenient stop between Sarajevo and Belgrade, Višegrad's main attraction is its 10-arch **Mehmet Paša Sokolović Bridge**. Built in 1571 it was immortalised in Ivo Andrić's Nobel Prize–winning classic *Bridge on the Drina*. To build on the connection, Višegrad is constructing **Andrićgrad** (www.andricgrad.com), a stone-walled mini 'old'

town that's due to open in 2014 as a historical fantasy cum cultural museum. Višegrad is otherwise architecturally unexciting but it's set between a series of impressive river canyons. On summer weekends there are usually **boat trips** (Sonja; ☑065-142742; per person incl lunch from 30KM) to explore them. Check booking details with the helpful **tourist office** (☑620950; www.visegradturizam.com; ul Kozachka; ☺8am-4pm Mon-Fri, 8am-3pm Sat) near the southern end of the old bridge. Their website has a town map.

A recently reconstructed narrow-gauge railway runs from Višegrad's decrepit station to Mokra Gora (Serbia), linking up with the popular Šargan 8 tourist train (p821). In 2012 the service departed Višegrad weekends only at 3pm (adult/child 800/400 Serbian Dinars) but frequency should increase. The train makes a sightseeing stop at the historic, if almost totally reconstructed, **Dobrun Monastery** (km11.5, Višegrad–Belgrade road), a resonant site for Serbs as Karađorđe hid here immediately before launching the 1804 Serb uprising.

🛏 Sleeping & Eating

Hotel Višegrad HOTEL €€
(☑620710; www.hotel.visegrad24.info; Trg Palih Boraca; s/d/tr 49/83/123KM; ☺7am-11pm; ☎) The facade is sickly yellow concrete, showers are feeble and decor's hardly stylish but friendly receptionists manage some English and the location is perfect, right at the riverside at the end of the historic bridge. The blandly

BUSES FROM VIŠEGRAD

DESTINATION	DEPARTURE POINT	PRICE (KM)	DURATION	FREQUENCY
Banja Luka	Hotel Višegrad	46	9hr	8am via Sarajevo
Belgrade (Serbia)	Hotel Višegrad	27	5½hr	5.15am
Belgrade (Serbia)	North side	27	5½hr	3.15am, 9.50am, 1.30pm
Foča	Hotel Višegrad	10	80min	7.15am, 9.30am
Mostar	North side	32	6hr	3.10am
Niš	North side	30	7hr	11.15am & alternate days 9.10pm
Sarajevo Lukavic	North side	19	3hr	12.45pm
Trebinje	North side	29	5hr	Overnight at 11.15pm
Užice	Hotel Višegrad	10	90min	11.30am, 6pm via Dobrun & Mokra Gora

boxlike restaurant (mains 6KM to 14KM) pumps out loud Europop, but its terrace frames bridge views between willow, pine and plane trees. And the inexpensive local fare is surprisingly well cooked. Wi-fi in restaurant only.

❶ Getting There & Away

Buses depart from outside the Hotel Višegrad as well as the north side of the old bridge and/or at Motel Okuka (1km northeast of the centre).

CENTRAL & WESTERN BOSNIA

West of Sarajevo lies a series of mildly interesting historic towns, green wooded hills, river canyons and rocky crags. The area offers ample opportunities for exploration and adrenaline-rush activities.

Visoko

♪ 032 / POP 17,000

Once the capital of medieval Bosnia and the spiritual centre of the controversial Bosnian Church, this unremarkable leather-tanning town had been largely forgotten during the 20th century. Then Bosnian archaeologist Semir Osmanagic hatched a bold theory that Visoko's 250m-high Visočica Hill is in fact the **World's Greatest Pyramid** (Piramida Sunca; www.piramidasunca.ba), built approximately 12,000 years ago by a long-disappeared superculture.

The mainly forested 'Sun Pyramid' does indeed have a seemingly perfect pyramidal shape when viewed from some angles (despite a long ridge at the back) and plates of bafflingly hard ancient 'concrete' found here are cited as having once covered the hill, creating an artificially smoothed surface. Visits to the archaeological excavations (without/with guide 3/5KM) start with a stiff 20-minute climb from a car park and info point-ticket booth near Bistro Vidikovac. To get there from Visoko bus station takes around 15 minutes' walk starting by crossing the river towards the Motel Piramida-Sunca. However, imediately across the bridge turn left down Visoko's patchily attractive main street, Alije Izetbegovića, at the start of which is an **information office** (Alije Izetbegovića 53; ☺8am-4pm Mon-Fri). Renamed Čaršijska, the street then curves to point directly towards the pyramid summit. After the bazaar veer left into Tvrtka/Mule Hodžić then turn right up the narrow asphalt lane directly beyond the church to find Bistro Vidikovac.

Other nearby hills are mooted to be lesser pyramids and archaeologists are busily investigating prehistoric subterranean labyrinths, notably the **Tunnel Ravne** (♪062 730299; admission 5KM; ☺call ahead), of which more is excavated every year. Guided hard-hat tours leave fairly regularly from an information booth outside (open 9am to 7pm) but you might have to wait a while. To find the site head 2km towards Kakanj from the Motel Piramida-Sunce. Turn left after the

Bingo Hypermarket and climb 500m up a tiny asphalt lane.

Young people come from across Europe to volunteer with the pyramids project and to soak up what many of them consider to be a potently spiritual earth energy that the valley exudes.

❶ Getting There & Away

Visoko is a stop for buses between Sarajevo (6.30KM, 50 minutes) and Kakanj (5KM, 35 minutes) running 18 times daily (seven times Sundays), last return to Sarajevo at 9.20pm. For Travnik and Jajce, direct buses depart Visoko at 8.10am, 9.50am, 2.10pm and 4.10pm or change in Zenica (14 buses on weekdays).

Travnik

☑030 / POP 27,500

Once the seat of Bosnia's Turkish viziers (Ottoman governors), Travnik is now best known for its sheep cheese – and as the birthplace of Nobel prize-winning author Ivo Andrić, who set his classic *Bosnian Chronicle* here. It's a pleasant place to spend a couple of hours when travelling between Sarajevo and Jajce.

For a basic walking tour exit the bus station to the south (down steps), cross a partly tree-shaded car park and turn left along Bosanska, Travnik's patchily interesting main street. You'll pass the distinctive **Sahat Kula** stone clocktower and 19th-century **Haji Alibey Mosque** before reaching the dreary Yugoslav-area **Hotel Lipa** (☑511604; Lažajeva 116/Bosanska 91; s/d/tr 52/84/111KM) in front of which the **Viziers' Turbe** is a pair of dome-sheltered collectons of Ottoman-era tombstones. At Bosanska's eastern end is Travnik's celebrated **Many Coloured Mosque** (Šasend Džamija; Bosanska 203) first built in 1757. Its fa-

mous murals have faded but it retains a little *bezistan* (mini-bazaar) built into the arches beneath its main prayer house.

Behind the mosque, take the pedestrian underpass beneath the M5 highway and follow Varoš steeply uphill to **Stari Grad** (☑518140; adult/student 2/1.50KM; ⊗8am-8pm Apr-Oct, by appointment Nov-Mar), Travnik's medieval grey-stone castle. Behind its extensively restored ramparts the multi-sided keep houses a modest museum of local history and costumes. Returning from the fortress, turn left on Musala beside the R&M store (Varoš 42) and immediately left again down the Hendek stairway. You'll emerge on Šumeća near Motel Aba. Turn left here to find Plava Voda (p138), a gaggle of restaurants flanking a merrily gurgling stream, criss-crossed by small bridges. Tucked behind here is the Moorish-styled **Elči-Ibrahimpaša Madrassa**.

🛏 Sleeping & Eating

Central hotels suffer from road rumble as do half a dozen other motels strung 10km along the eastbound M5. Travnik's better (but mostly winter-only) hotels are 27km northwest in the three-lift ski-resort of **Vlašić** (www.babanovac.net) above Babanovac village.

Motel Aba　　　　　　　　　　HOTEL €
(☑511462; www.aba.ba; Šumeća 166a; s 35-40KM, d/tr/q 50/70/80KM; 🛜) Handily near to Plava Voda, Aba provides highly acceptable, unfussy en suite rooms at unbelievably reasonable prices. The stairs and road noise are minor niggles, wi-fi works well and there's limited free parking. Breakfast costs 10KM extra.

Blanca　　　　　　　　RESORT & SPA €€€
(☑519900; www.blancaresort.com; s €52-165, d €74-242, tr €132-273; 🏊) If you don't mind driving

BOSNIA & HERCEGOVINA TRAVNIK

BUSES FROM TRAVNIK

DESTINATION	PRICE (KM)	DURATION	FREQUENCY
Babanovac	4	45min	10am, 3.10pm
Bihać	35.20	6hr	9.30am, 3.30pm, 4.20pm, 11.30pm
Jajce	8-12.70	1½hr	7.45am, 9.30am, 3pm, 4.20pm, 5.10pm, 5.30pm, 11.30pm
Sarajevo	15.50-17	2hr	6.50am, 8.05am, 9am, 10.40am, 12.15pm 3.40pm, 6.30pm, 7.30pm
Split (Croatia) via Bugojno	23-31	4½hr	6.50am, 8.20am, 11.10am, noon, 5.50pm
Zenica	5-7	1hr	25 daily

to Vlašić, the 2010 Blanca is a luxurious mountain getaway. Right at the base of the ski-jump, this complex uses wooden chalet elements to soften an overall sense of poised designer cool. Guests get free use of four different saunas, the indoor swimming pool has recliner chairs at view windows and unlike virtually every other Vlašić hotel it's open year-round. 'Classic' rooms have no view whatsoever while 'superior' rooms are huge. 'Premium' rooms strike the best balance.

Konoba Plava Voda　　　　BOSNIAN €€
(Šumeće bb; meals 4.50-20KM; ⊘7am-10pm; 🕾) This attractive warren of rooms is decked out like an ethnographic museum and has a tempting summer terrace in the attractive Plava Voda springs area. The menu is in English, portions generous and the kitchen stays open relatively late even off season.

Travnički Sir　　　　CHEESE SHOP
(Bosanska 157; ⊘8am-6pm Mon-Sat, 8am-3pm Sun) This small shop, overflowing with wooden churns, specialises in Travnik's trademark white cheese.

ⓘ Getting There & Away

Travnik's **bus station** (🗗792761) is off Sehida (the M5 highway) around 500m west of centre. Its ticket office has keys for a left-luggage room (garderob).

Jajce

🗗030 / POP 30,000

Above an impressive urban waterfall, Jajce's fortified Old Town climbs a steep rocky knoll to the powerful, ruined castle where Bosnia's medieval kings were once crowned.

The surrounding array of mountains, lakes and canyons make Jajce a potentially useful exploration base.

◉ Sights

Individually, none of old Jajce's attractions are major drawcards but together they make for an interesting two-hour exploration. Add in the surrounding lakes and canyons and you might want to stay for days.

For a quick visit, exit the bus station and walk anticlockwise around the bluff for views of the classic **waterfalls**. Before crossing the footbridge into town, you can visit the **AVNOJ Museum** (admission 2KM; ⊘9am-5pm) for five minutes to contemplate a gilded polystyrene statue of Tito in the hall where Yugoslavia's postwar socialist constitution was formulated in 1943. Across the river, past several cafes burrowed into the rock-face and through the city wall via the **Travnik Gate** (Sadije Softića 1; ⊘7am-11pm), you'll find Jajce's main shopping street. From the likeable Hotel Stari Grad you can escape the banal 20th-century architecture by climbing Svetog Luke past the new, if limited, **Ethno Museum** (Zavičajna Etno Zbinca; Svetog Luke bb; 1KM; ⊘8am-4pm Mon-Fri, 9am-4pm Sat & Sun) and a 15th-century **campanile tower**. Peep into the **Catacombs** (Svetog Luke bb; admission 1KM; ⊘9am-7pm May-Oct, 9am-5pm Nov-Apr), a small but imaginatively lit 15th-century crypt whose rough-carved sun-moon-cross centrepiece is a rare surviving memorial to the once independent Bosnian church. Up a stairway-street past the tiny, boxlike **Dizdar Džamija** (Women's Mosque) is the sturdy main **fortress** (adult/child 1/0.50KM; ⊘8am-7pm). Inside is mostly bald grass but there are sweeping views from the ramparts.

To return, backtrack to the Dizdar Džamija, turn left along Stari Grad and descend a section of the citadel wall to the **Midway Tower** (Mala Tabija) before retrieving the lane to the Hotel Stari Grad.

Just outside the old city, one block north then west of the conspicuous hypermarket and boxy **Hotel Turist** (☑658151; www.hotel-turist98.com; Kraljice Katerine bb; s/d/tr/q 58/86/109/138KM; 图) you'll find the **Mithraeum** (Mitrasova 12), a unique 4th-century sculpture featuring a bullfighting Mithras (the pre-Zoroastrian Persian sun god 'rediscovered' by mystical Romans). It's in a glass-sided enclosure at the end of Mitrasova.

The road on the south side of Hotel Turist, just before the bridge, leads west passing the good value Jajce Youth Hostel after 400m. Here guests can rent bicycles (per hour/day 4/10KM) and continue another 4km to the lovely **Pliva Lakes** (Plivsko Jezero) where wooded mountains reflect idyllically in calm, clear waters. Between the two main lakes, a collection of **17 miniature watermills** form one of Bosnia's most photographed scenes. And 800m beyond, passing the well-organised **Autokamp** (☑647210; campsite per person 8KM, bungalow from s/d 38/56KM; ☺Apr–mid-Oct), you'll find two lakeside hotels including the bargain-priced Plaža Motel at the jetty where pleasure boats are rented in summer.

🛏 Sleeping & Eating

Hotel Stari Grad CENTRAL HOTEL €€
(☑654006; www.jajcetours.com; Svetog Luke 3; s/d 57/84KM, apt 82-154KM; 图🕾) Although it's not actually old, beams, wood panelling and a heraldic fireplace give this comfortable little hotel a look of suavely modernised antiquity. Beneath the part-glass floor of the appealing lobby-restaurant (mains 10KM to 14KM) are the excavations of an Ottoman-era *hammam* (Turkish bath).

Jajce Youth Hostel HOSTEL €
(☑063 262168; www.jajce-youth-hostel.com; S Tomaševića 11; dm/d/tr 8/20/24KM; 🅿@🕾) Offering some of the cheapest formal accommodation in rural Bosnia, rooms are neater than you'd guess from the slightly unkempt public spaces and all have en suite bathrooms.

Plaža Motel LAKESIDE MOTEL €
(☑647200; www.motel-plaza.com; M5 (Bihać hwy) km91; s/d/tr/q 40/70/99/120KM, pizza 7-11KM, mains 9-14KM) Simple, inexpensive rooms above a large lakeside restaurant whose summer dining terrace serves trout, pizza or *ćevapi* right at the waterfront. Jezero-bound buses pass by.

Banja Luka

☑051 / POP 232,000
Since 1998 Banja Luka has been what's probably Europe's least-known 'capital' (of the Republika Srpska). The city is lively

BUSES FROM JAJCE			
DESTINATION	**PRICE (KM)**	**DURATION**	**FREQUENCY**
Banja Luka	8.50-12.80	1½hr	7.30am, 9.30am, 12.50pm, 4.20pm, 5.30pm, 6.50pm
Bihać	19-27.20	3½hr	7.30am, 11.30am, 12.30pm, 5.30pm
Jezero	2	15min	7.30am, 9.15am, 11.30am, 12.30pm, 4.40pm, 6.50pm
Mostar	18-18.50	5hr	1.25pm, 2.20pm
Sarajevo	23.50-27	3½hr	7.10am, 8.50am, 9.10am, 10.25am, 5.25pm, 12.30am
Split (Croatia)	31	4½hr	6am (from Split departs at 12.30pm)
Travnik	8-12.70	1¼hr	Take Zenica or Sarajevo buses
Zagreb (Croatia)	31-38	6½hr	7.30am, 8am, 10am, 11.15am, 12.30pm, 4pm, 6pm, 12.30am
Zenica	13.50-15	2¼hr	8.15am, 8.50am, 1.40pm, 3.15pm

more than lovely but it's a useful transport hub if you're planning rafting, canyoning or other adventure sports in the surrounding countryside. To organise any of the above contact **Guideline** (☑466411; www.guidelinebl. com; Kralja Petra 7; ⊘8am-8pm Mon-Fri, 9am-2pm Sat, cafe 8am-10pm daily) whose brand new information centre doubles as a traveller cafe with free internet (not just wi-fi). Alternatively discuss things with the enthusiastic **tourist office** (☑490308; www.banjaluka-tourism.com; Kralja Petra 87; ⊘8am-6pm Mon-Fri, 9am-2pm Sat). Both are conveniently found along the city's lengthy main drag, Kralja Petra.

Historic Banja Luka was ravaged by a 1969 earthquake then, late in the civil war, was flooded by Serb refugees from Croatia who dynamited over a dozen historic mosques. The most famous of these, the **Ferhadija Džamija** (Kralja Petra 42), is now being painstakingly reconstructed using traditional masonry techniques. On the riverside directly southeast, enclosing an area parkland, are the two-storey, 16th-century fortress walls of **Kastel Banja Luka**. Summer festivities held here include the famous **Demofest** (www.demofest.org; ⊘late July), a play-off competition between up-and-coming raw garage bands.

Otherwise, only two central city blocks offer much architectural appeal. These surround the memorable **Orthodox Cathedral of Christ Saviour** (Saborni Hram Hrista Spasitelja; www.hhsbl.org; Trg Srpskih Vladara 3), rebuilt between 2004 and 2009 using alternate layers of crab-pink and mustard-yellow stone. Its domes are eye-catchingly gilded and its brick belltower looks like a Moroccan minaret on Viagra.

The Republic Srpska's sizeable 'national' **museum** (www.muzejrs.com; Đure Daničića 1; admission 1KM; ⊘8am-7pm Mon-Fri, 10am-2pm Sat & Sun) has a scattering of stuffed birds but mainly walks visitors through the region's history from archaeological digs to horse worship to the horrors of the Ustashi concentration camps of WWII – which is a major culminating focus. Much is in English. The museum is entered from the east side of the large library/theatre building, a block east of the distinctive **1933 Hotel Palas** (Kralja Petra 60).

🛏 Sleeping & Eating

Running parallel to Kralja Petra, there are cheap snack bars in courtyards off Veselina Maslaše and many street cafes on its northern extension, Bana Milosavlevica. Close to the canoe club on Save Kovačevića, some 800m east of Ho(s)tel Hertz, are several characterful yet relatively inexpensive bars with tree-shaded riverside frontage: try **Monnet** (Save Kovačevića 42), **Deda Luka** (Save Kovačevića 32; beer/pizza from 1.20/3KM; ⊘7am-midnight) or **Castra** (Save Kovačevića 46).

Vila Vrbas   BOUTIQUE HOTEL €€
(☑433840; Brace Potkonjaka 1; s/d/ste 80/110/130KM; ꘎꘎꘎) Polished, excellent-value guest rooms are available above this relatively upmarket restaurant with a spacious terrace shaded by plane trees. From here there are glimpses of the castle ramparts across the river.

Hotel Talija   BOUTIQUE HOTEL €€
(☑327460; www.hoteltalija.com; Srpska 9; s/d/apt standard 123.50/157/147KM, superior 143.50/177/247KM; ꘎꘎) Above a classy pizzeria-cafe, the standard rooms are nothing exceptional but the brand new superior rooms are a whole level above with very elegant coffee-and-

BUSES FROM BANJA LUKA

DESTINATION	PRICE (KM)	DURATION (HR)	FREQUENCY
Belgrade (Serbia)	41.5	5¾-7½	many 5am-5pm plus 9pm & 11.30pm
Bihać	20	3	5.30am, 7.30am, 1pm, 2pm
Jajce	11.50	1½	6.40am, 7.45am, 1pm, 2pm, 4pm
Sarajevo	31	5	6.30am, 7.45am, 2.30pm, 4pm, 5pm, 12.30pm
Zagreb (Croatia)	31	7	3.15am, 6.30am, 8.45am, 9.10am, 11.30am, 4pm, 5.30pm

cream decor. Apartments give it all they've got with lashings of gilt and bold cubist-style artworks. It's 150m east of the cathedral on the road that passes **MacTire** (www.facebook.com/MacTire.Pub) Irish pub-restaurant.

Hotel Atina   BUSINESS HOTEL €€
(☑334800; www.atinahotel.com; Slobodana Kokanovica 5; 92/124/144KM; P❋❄🐾) Smart without undue extravagance; the main features are stylish rectilinear fittings and a helpfully central yet quiet location just east of the castle.

City Smile Hostel   HOSTEL €
(☑214187; www.citysmilehostel.com; Skendera Kulenovića 16; dm/d 22/54KM; 🐾) A large house turned into a friendly family-style hostel with a kitchen and small sitting area. Though officially on Skendera Kulenovića (the southwestern extension of Kralja Petra), the entrance is on Duška Koščige.

Ho(s)tel Herz   HOSTEL €
(☑066 617627; www.hostelherz.com; Milana Rakića 22; dm/d/tr 22/70/100KM) One of several new hostels, this bright, tailor-made place has tight-packed dorms but their four private rooms are hotelstandard en suite affairs. Triples add a fold-out sofa. Breakfast 5KM. It's 300m east of Hotel Atina.

❶ Getting There & Away

AIR The **airport** (☑535210; www.banjaluka-airport.com) is 22km north. The only commercial flight is a stop-off on BH Airlines' thrice-weekly Sarajevo–Zürich run.

BICYCLE Mountain bikes can be rented from **Cycling Shop** (www.cyclingshop-banjaluka.com; Gundulićeva 104; per hr/day 2/15KM), 1.3km northeast of central Banja Luka.

BUS The **main bus** and **train stations** (☑922000; Prote N Kostića 38) are together, 3km north. Access by buses 6, 8 or 10 from near Hotel Palas (opposite the tourist office).

TRAIN Destinations include Zagreb (27KM, 4¼ hours) at 3.49pm and 2.10am and Sarajevo (25KM, five hours) at 1.17pm and 1.49am.

Around Banja Luka
VRBAS CANYONS

Between Jajce and Banja Luka the Vrbas River descends through a series of lakes and gorges that together form one of BiH's foremost adventure-sport playgrounds. At Karanovac, 11km from Banja Luka by bus 8A, **Rafting Centar Kanjon** (☑065 882085;

CASTLE CAPERS

Dotted between the faceless postindustrial towns of utterly untouristed northeastern Bosnia are several very photogenic medieval castle ruins.

Srebrenik Truly dramatic crag-top setting 6km east of Srebrenik town.

Tešanj Powerful ruins rise above a loveable Old Town square.

Vranduk Small ruins set in BiH's most idyllic castle village, around 10km north of Zenica.

Gradačac Gradačac town centre is dominated by a partly reconstructed castle with a restaurant on top.

Doboj The city is a drab railway junction but the castle hosts costumed festivals and there's a great little cafe-tower.

www.guidelinebl.com; Karanovac; ⊙Apr-Oct) is a reliable, well-organised extreme-sports outfit offering guided canyoning (€25 including lunch), quad biking, hiking and especially top-class rafting. Rafting requires groups of at least four people but joining others is usually easy enough at short notice in summer. Some weekends there's a rare opportunity for floodlit night-rafting (with a week's advance reservation). Kanjon is building budget cottage accommodation and with its hypnotic river views, their splendid **Pastir Restaurant** (mains 7.50-15KM, uštipci 5KM) is one of the region's better dining spots.

Another decent stopping point if you're driving by is **Krupa na Vrbasu** (25km from Banja Luka). Set 700m off the main road here is a dainty set of cascades tumbling down between little wooden mill-huts. The tiny car park is overlooked by house-cafe **Krupski Slapovi** (coffee 1KM; ⊙8am-10pm).

The Jajce road winds steeply on past two dams. The higher one is overlooked by the stubby rock ruins of what was once **Bočac Citadel**.

Bihać
☑037 / POP 80,000

In central Bihać, a closely clumped **church tower, turbe** (tomb) and 16th-century stone **tower-museum** (☑223214; admission 2KM;

WORTH A TRIP

ŽELENKOVAC

Lost in relatively remote forests, the eccentric 'eco-village' of **Želenkovac** (☎030-278649; www.zelenkovac.org; John Lenon Sq; bed per person 10-25KM) is an inspirationally alternative retreat based around a ramshackle former watermill transformed into a gallery-bar-cafe. Half a dozen Tolkeinesque wooden cottages offer rustic accommodation, some with open fireplaces and indoor bathrooms. International voluntary camps meet here, and there's a July artist colony week. Hiking possibilities abound though many visitors simply hang out and strum guitars with like-minded locals. To find Želenkovac turn off the Jajce–Bihać road at Podbrdo's Eco petrol station, head 7km south towards Barači, then 500m (left) into the forest.

⊙call ahead) look very photogenic viewed through the trees across gushing rapids. But that's about all there is to see here apart from nearby **Fethija Mosque**, converted from a rose-windowed medieval church in 1595. Bihać could make a staging post for reaching Croatia's marvellous **Plitvice Lakes** (www.np-plitvicka-jezera.hr) just 30km away (p226). Otherwise visit the **Una National Park information office** (www.nationalpark-una.ba; Bosanska 1; ⊙8am-4.30pm Mon-Fri, 11am-3pm Sat, 11am-1pm Sun, closed weekends Nov-Apr) then head for the lovely Una Valley, preferably on a raft!

🍽 Sleeping & Eating

Opal Exclusive   RIVERSIDE HOTEL €€
(☎228586, 224182; www.hotelopalexclusive.net; Krupska bb; s/d/apt 89/138/196KM; P❀❀) Hidden away but only 300m north of the centre, the Opal's spacious rooms vary considerably in attractiveness but the best are appealing with paintings in gilt frames and lovely views over the river rapids. Similar views are shared by the tree-shaded terrace restaurant (mains 7KM to 25KM) and the top-floor fitness room.

Villa Una   GUEST HOUSE €€
(☎311393; villa.una@bih.net.ha; Bihaćkih Branilaca 20; s/d/tr 52/74/96KM; superior s/d 62/84KM; ⊙7-11am & 6-10pm; P❀❀) In this very friend-

ly *pansion*, homey standard rooms suffer some road noise but are every bit as comfortable as the rear 'superior' versions. It's very handy for the bus station with a frontage painted to look half-timbered.

ℹ Getting There & Away

Disguised as a mini-casino, Bihać's **bus station** (☎311939) is 1km west of the centre, just off Bihaćkih Branilaća towards Sarajevo. Destinations include the following:

Banja Luka (22KM, three hours) Departs 5.30am, 7.30am, 1pm and 3pm via Bosanska Krupa and Otoka Bosanska.

Ostražac (4.50KM, 25 minutes) via **Kostela** (2.50KM, 10 minutes) Use Cazin-bound buses, 10 times daily on weekdays, 8.50am, 11.30am and 3.30pm Saturday, 3.30pm only Sunday.

Plitvice Jezero The 4.45pm Zagreb bus passes Plitvice (8KM). Otherwise change at Grabovac (11KM, 45 minutes).

Sarajevo (46KM, six to seven hours) Departs 12.45am, 7.30am, 2.30pm and 10pm, via Travnik.

Zagreb (25KM, three hours) Departs 4.45am, 10.20am, 2pm and 4.45pm.

Around Bihać
UNA RIVER VALLEY

The adorable Una River goes through varying moods. In the lush green gorges northwest of Bihać, some sections are as calm as mirrored opal while others gush over widely fanned rapids. There are lovely **watermill restaurants** at Bosanska Krupa and near Otoka Bosanska. And up 4km of hairpins above the valley, spookily Gothic **Ostrožac Fortress** (☎061 236641; www.ostrozac.com) is the most inspiring of several castle ruins.

Southwest of Bihać there's a complex of cascades at **Martin Brod** while the river's single most dramatic falls are at glorious **Štrbački Buk** (5KM; ⊙8am-7pm May-Oct), which forms the centrepiece of the new **Una National Park** (www.nationalpark-una.ba). The easiest access is 8km along a good, largely flat unpaved lane from Orašac on the Kulen Vakuf road via National Park Gate 3. In dry conditions you can alternatively start from Gate 1 (Gorevac, 200m off the Bihać–Sarajevo road, 16km from Bihać) but that route uses 14km of woodland lanes that are rolling, very narrow and somewhat rocky (keep right then left at the only two turns en route).

The festive **Una Regatta** in late July sees hundreds of kayaks and rafts following a three-day course from Kulen-Vakuf to Bosanska Krupa via Bihać.

🏃 Activities

Various companies offer rafting (€25 to €55, six-person minimum), kayaking and a range of adventure sports. Each has its own campsite and provides transfers from Bihać since all are rurally based. Choices include the following:

Una Kiro Rafting   RAFTING
(☎037-361110; www.una-kiro-rafting.com) A big multisport outfit with extensive if over-manicured facilities at the southeast edge of greater Bihać.

Bjeli Una Rafting   RAFTING
(☎061 138853, 037-380222; www.una-rafting.ba; Klokot) At Klokot west of Bihać.

Una-Aqua   RAFTING
(☎061 604313; www.una-aqua.com; Račić) Across the river from Neron at Račić.

🛏 Sleeping & Eating

TOP CHOICE Kostelski Buk   RIVERSIDE HOTEL €€
(☎037-302340; www.kostelski-buk.com; M14, Kostela; s/d €40/59, superior €44/70.50; P❋🛜)
The Louis XVI chairs and leather-padded doors might be a little glitzy for some tastes but rooms are superbly equipped, amply sized and come with luxurious mattresses worthy of a five-star hotel. Superior rooms have river views surveying a set of waterfall rapids. The view is shared by the terrace seating of the very reliable lower restaurant (mains 8KM to 30KM) whose excellent seafood platters (40KM for two people) wash down well with the Hercegovinian Riesling (per litre 20KM). It's 9km from Bihać towards Banja Luka.

Neron Touristički Centar   RIVERSIDE ROOMS €
(☎061 142585; www.neronraft.com; Lohovo; per person without/with private bathroom 25/30KM; ☺May-Sep) Perched by the river at Lohovo where the Una's most testing rafting route ends (13km from Bihać, 5km southeast of Ripac), this museum-like cottage-restaurant (mains 7KM to 18KM)) and hotel is one of the most characterful dining/sleeping options on the Una. The three best rooms sleep three and come with kitchenette and views of the rapids.

Motel Estrada   FAMILY HOTEL €
(☎070-218933; Ostrožac; per person 20KM) Homestay-style en suite rooms in the fifth unmarked house on the left up the Pročići road; 300m southwest of Ostrožac castle.

UNDERSTAND BOSNIA & HERCEGOVINA

Bosnia & Hercegovina Today

Under EU and American pressure BiH has centralised considerably over the last decade in a movement away from the original Dayton 'separate powers' concept. BiH now has a unified army, common passports and a single currency though there remain three separate postal systems. Many, but by no means all, refugees have returned and rebuilt their prewar homes. Politicians running the RS are less radically nationalist these days though during the October 2012 elections the spectre of eventual RS independence was publically raised. Meanwhile in the Federation, the relative complexity of the canton system has proved unwieldy leading to funding log-jams, most notably for the National Gallery and National Museum. While deep post-conflict scars remain, today economics, job security and corruption are the greatest concern for most Bosnians. Non-payment of wages is a growing worry for those working in the 'grey' private economy while getting certain decent government jobs is rumoured to cost applicants a hefty bribe. When reports suggested that political parties were paying 50KM for votes in the 2012 election, one harried working mother told us 'I wish they'd asked me! I'd have taken 40KM'.

History

Be aware that much of BiH's history remains highly controversial and is seen very differently according to one's ethno-religious viewpoint.

In AD 9 ancient Illyrian Bosnia was conquered by the Romans. Slavs arrived from the late 6th century and were dominant by 1180, when Bosnia first emerged as an independent entity under former Byzantine governor Ban Kulina. BiH had a patchy golden age between 1180 and 1463, peaking in the

Entities of BiH

Republika Srpska (Serbs)

Federation of Bosnia & Hercegovina (Muslims & Croats)

late 1370s when Bosnia's King Tvtko gained Hum (future Hercegovina) and controlled much of Dalmatia.

Blurring the borderline between Europe's Catholic west and Orthodox east, medieval Bosnia had its own independent church. This remains the source of many historical myths, but the long-popular idea that it was 'infected' by the Bulgarian Bogomil heresy is now largely discounted.

Turkish Ascendancy

Turkish raids whittled away at the country throughout the 15th century and by the 1460s most of Bosnia was under Ottoman control. Within a few generations, easygoing Sufi-inspired Islam became dominant among townspeople and landowners, many Bosnians converting as much to gain civil privileges as for spiritual enlightenment. However, a sizeable proportion of the serfs *(rayah)* remained Christian. Bosnians also became particularly prized soldiers in the Ottoman army, many rising eventually to high rank within the imperial court. The early Ottoman era also produced great advances in infrastructure, with fine mosques and bridges built by charitable bequests. Later, however, the Ottomans failed to follow the West's industrial revolution. By the 19th century the empire's economy was archaic, and all attempts to modernise the feudal system in BiH were strenuously resisted by the entrenched Bosnian-Muslim elite. In 1873 İstanbul's banking system collapsed under the weight of the high-living sultan's debts. To pay these debts the sultan demanded added taxes. But in 1874 BiH's harvests failed, so paying those taxes would have meant starving. With nothing left to lose the mostly Christian Bosnian peasants revolted, leading eventually to a messy tangle of pan-Balkan wars.

Austro-Hungarian Rule

These wars ended with the farcical 1878 Congress of Berlin, at which the Western powers carved up the western Ottoman lands. Austria-Hungary was 'invited' to occupy BiH, which was treated like a colony even though it theoretically remained under Ottoman sovereignty. An unprecedented period of development followed. Roads, railways and bridges were built. Coal mining and forestry became booming industries. Education encouraged a new generation of Bosnians to look towards Vienna. But new nationalist feelings were simmering: Bosnian Catholics increasingly identified with neighbouring Croatia (itself within Austria-Hungary) while Orthodox Bosnians sympathised with recently independent Serbia's dreams of a greater Serbian homeland. In between lay Bosnia's Muslims (40%), who belatedly started to develop a distinct Bosniak consciousness.

While Turkey was busy with the 1908 Young Turk revolution Austria-Hungary annexed BiH, undermining the aspirations of those who had dreamed of a pan-Slavic or greater Serbian future. The resultant scramble for the last remainders of Ottoman Europe kicked off the Balkan Wars of 1912 and 1913. No sooner had these been (unsatisfactorily) resolved than the heir to the Austrian throne was shot dead while visiting Sarajevo. One month later Austria declared war on Serbia and WWI swiftly followed.

BiH in Yugoslavia

WWI killed an astonishing 15% of the Bosnian population. It also brought down both the Turkish and Austro-Hungarian empires, leaving BiH to be absorbed into proto-Yugoslavia.

During WWII, BiH was occupied partly by Italy and partly by Germany, then absorbed into the newly created fascist state of Croatia. Croatia's Ustaše decimated Bosnia's Jewish population, and they also persecuted Serbs and Muslims. Meanwhile a pro-Nazi group of Bosnian Muslims committed their own atrocities against Bosnian Serbs while Serb Četniks and Tito's Communist Partizans put up some stalwart resistance to the Germans (as well as fighting each other). The BiH mountains proved ideal territory for Tito's flexible guerrilla army, whose greatest victories are still locally commemorated with vast memorials. In 1943, Tito's antifascist council meeting at Jajce famously formulated a constitution for an inclusive postwar, socialist Yugoslavia. BiH was granted republic status within that Yugoslavia but up until 1971 (when *Muslim* was defined as a Yugoslav 'ethnic group'), Bosniaks were not considered a distinct community and in censuses had to register as Croat, Serb or 'Other/Yugoslav'. Despite considerable mining in the northeast and the boost of the 1984 Sarajevo Winter Olympics, BiH's economy remained relatively underdeveloped.

The 1990s Conflict

In the post-Tito era, as Yugoslavia imploded, religio-linguistic (often dubbed 'ethnic') tensions were ratcheted up by the ultra-nationalist Serb leader Slobodan Milošević and equally radical Croatian leader Franjo Tuđman. Although these two were at war by spring 1991, they reputedly came up with a de facto agreement in which they planned to divide BiH between breakaway Croatia and rump Yugoslavia.

Under president Alija Izetbegović, BiH declared independence from Yugoslavia on 15 October 1991. Bosnian Serb parliamentarians wanted none of this and withdrew to set up their own government at Pale, 20km east of Sarajevo. BiH was recognised internationally as an independent state on 6 April 1992 but Sarajevo was already under siege both by Serb paramilitaries and by parts of the Yugoslav army (JNA).

Over the next three years a brutal and extraordinarily complex civil war raged. Best known is the campaign of 'ethnic' cleansing in northern and eastern BiH creating the 300km 'pure'-Serb Republika Srpska (RS). But locals of each religion will readily admit that 'there were terrible criminals on our side too'. In western Hercegovina the Croat population armed itself with the help of neighbouring Croatia, eventually ejecting Serbs from their villages in a less reported but similarly brutal war.

Perhaps unaware of the secret Tuđman-Milošević understanding, Izetbegović had signed a formal military alliance with Croatia in June 1992. But by early 1993 fighting had broken out between Muslims and Croats, creating another war front. Croats attacked Muslims in Stolac and Mostar, bombarding their historic monuments and blasting Mostar's famous medieval bridge into the river. Muslim troops, including a small foreign *mujahedin* force, desecrated churches and attacked Croat villages, notably around Travnik.

UN Involvement

With atrocities on all sides, the West's reaction was confused and erratic. In August 1992, pictures of concentration-camp and rape-camp victims (mostly Muslim) found in northern Bosnia spurred the UN to create Unprofor, a protection force of 7500 peacekeeping troops. Unprofor secured the neutrality of Sarajevo airport well enough to allow the delivery of humanitarian aid, but overall proved notoriously impotent.

Ethnic cleansing of Muslims from Foča and Višegrad led the UN to declare 'safe zones' around the Muslim-majority towns of Srebrenica, Župa and Goražde. But rarely has the term 'safe' been so misused. When NATO belatedly authorised air strikes to protect these areas, the Serbs responded by capturing 300 Unprofor peacekeepers and chaining them to potential targets to keep the planes away.

WHAT'S IN A NAME?

Geographically Bosnia and Hercegovina (BiH) comprises Bosnia (in the north) and Hercegovina (Her-tse-GO-vina in the south), although the term 'Bosnian' refers to anyone from BiH, not just from Bosnia proper. Politically, BiH is divided into two entirely different entities. Southwest and central BiH falls mostly within the Federation of Bosnia and Hercegovina, usually shortened to 'the Federation'. Meanwhile most areas bordering Serbia, Montenegro and the northern arm of Croatia are within the Serb-dominated Republika Srpska (abbreviated RS). A few minor practicalities (stamps, phonecards) appear in different versions and the Cyrillic alphabet is more prominent in the RS, but these days casual visitors are unlikely to notice much immediately visible difference between the entities.

In July 1995 Dutch peacekeepers watched as the starving, supposedly 'safe' area of Srebrenica fell to a Bosnian Serb force led by the infamous Ratko Mladić. An estimated 8000 Muslim men were slaughtered in Europe's worst mass killings since WWII. Battered Goražde held out thanks to sporadically available UN food supplies. By this stage, Croatia had renewed its own internal offensive, expelling Serbs from the Krajina region of Croatia in August 1995. At least 150,000 of these dispossessed people then moved to the Serb-held areas of northern Bosnia.

Finally, another murderous Serb mortar attack on Sarajevo's main market (Markale) kick-started a shift in UN and NATO politics. An ultimatum to end the Serbs' siege of Sarajevo was made more persuasive through two weeks of NATO air strikes in September 1995. US president Bill Clinton's proposal for a peace conference in Dayton, Ohio, was accepted soon after.

The Dayton Agreement

While maintaining BiH's prewar external boundaries, Dayton divided the country into today's pair of roughly equally sized 'entities', each with limited autonomy. Finalising the border required considerable political and cartographic creativity and was only completed in 1999 when the last sticking point, Brčko, was belatedly given a self-governing status all of its own. Meanwhile BiH's curious rotating tripartite presidency has been kept in check by the EU's powerful High Representative (www.ohr.int).

For refugees (1.2 million abroad, and a million displaced within BiH), the Dayton Agreement emphasised the right to return to (or to sell) their prewar homes. International agencies donated very considerable funding to restore BiH's infrastructure, housing stock and historical monuments.

BOOKS

Bosnia: A Short History by Noel Malcolm is a very readable introduction to the complexities of Bosnian history. In *Not My Turn To Die,* by Savo Heleta, the memoirs of a besieged family at Goražde give insights into the strange mixture of terror, boredom and resignation of the 1990s conflict.

BuyBook (www.buybook.ba) produces several regional guidebooks.

People

Bosniaks (Bosnian Muslims, 48% of the population), Bosnian Serbs (Orthodox Christians, 37%) and Bosnian Croats (Catholics, 14%) differ by religion but are all Southern Slavs. Physically they are indistinguishable so the term 'ethnic cleansing', applied so often during the war, should more accurately have been called 'religio-linguistic forced expulsions'. The prewar population was mixed, with intermarriage common in the cities. Stronger divisions have inevitably appeared since the civil war of the 1990s which resulted in massive population shifts, changing the size and linguistic balance of many cities. Bosniaks now predominate in Sarajevo and central BiH, Bosnian Croats in western and southern Hercegovina, and Bosnian Serbs in the RS, which includes Istochno (East) Sarajevo and Banja Luka. Today social contact between members of the three groups remains somewhat limited. Religion is taken seriously as a badge of 'ethnicity' but spiritually most people are fairly secular.

Arts
Crafts

BiH crafts from *kilims* (woollen flat-weaves) to copperware and decoratively repurposed bullet casings are widely sold in Mostar's Kujundžiluk and Sarajevo's Baščaršija.

Stećci (singular *stećak*) are archetypal Bosnian forms of oversized medieval gravestones, best known at Radimlja near Stolac.

Literature

Bosnia's best-known writer, Ivo Andrić (1892–1975), won the 1961 Nobel Prize for Literature. With extraordinary psychological agility, his epic novel, the classic *Bridge on the Drina,* retells 350 years of Bosnian history as seen through the eyes of unsophisticated townsfolk in Višegrad. His *Travnik Chronicles* (aka *Bosnian Chronicle*) is also rich with human insight, portraying Bosnia through the eyes of jaded 19th-century foreign consuls in Travnik.

Many thought-provoking essays, short stories and poems explore the prickly subject of the 1990s conflict, often contrasting horrors against the victims' enduring humanity. Quality varies greatly but recommended collections include Miljenko and alpine valleys, most famously in the magnificent Sutjeska National Park. In the far northeast the peaks subside into rolling bucolic hills flattening out altogether in the far north.

Jergović's *Sarajevo Marlboro* and Semezdin Mehmedinović's *Sarajevo Blues*.

Movies

The relationship between two soldiers, one Muslim and one Serb, caught alone in the same trench during the Sarajevo siege was the theme for Danis Tanović's Oscar-winning 2002 film *No Man's Land*. The movie *Go West* takes on the deep taboo of homosexuality as a wartime Serb-Bosniak gay couple become a latter-day Romeo and Juliet. *Gori Vatra* (aka *Fuse*) is an irony-packed dark comedy set in the Bosnian castle town of Tešanj just after the war, parodying efforts to hide corruption and create a facade of ethnic reintegration for the sake of a proposed visit by US president Bill Clinton.

Music

Sevdah (traditional Bosnian music) typically uses heart-wrenching vocals to recount tales of unhappy amours, though singing it was once used as a subtle courting technique. Sarajevo has an annual **Jazz festival** (November) and a new October **Punkfest**. The post-industrial salt-mining city of Tuzla has vibrant rap and metal scenes.

Environment

BiH is predominantly mountainous. The mostly arid south (Hercegovina) dips one tiny toe of land into the Adriatic Sea at Neum then rises swiftly into bare limestone uplands carved with deep grey canyons. The central mountain core has some 30 peaks rising between 1700m and 2386m. Further north and east the landscape becomes increasingly forested with waterfalls

SURVIVAL GUIDE

Directory A–Z
Accommodation

Except in hostels, quoted room prices assume a private bathroom and breakfast unless otherwise indicated.

High season means June to September generally but late December to early March in ski resorts. In Mostar and Sarajevo summer prices rise 20% to 50% and touts appear at the bus stations. Our price ranges for a double room:

€ less than 80KM/€40

€€ 80KM/€40 to 190KM/€100

€€€ more than 190KM/€100

ACCOMMODATION TYPES

Hostels Usually bunk rooms in a semi-converted private home. Few have reception desks. Essentially Mostar, Sarajevo and Banja Luka only.

Hotels Anything from re-vamped Tito-era concrete monsters to elegantly restored Austro-Hungarian gems via modernist boxes and over-sized *pansions*.

Motels Generally new and suburban and ideal for those with cars. However, occasionally the term simply implies a lower midrange hotel so don't automatically assume there's much parking.

Pansions Anything from a glorified homestay to a little boutique hotel.

Ski hotels From Christmas to mid-January availability is stretched and prices rise up to 50%. Most close during April to November.

Activities

Skiing Inexpensive yet high quality at Jahorina, Bjelašnica or Vlašić.

Rafting Reaches terrifyingly difficult class V in April/May but is more suitable for beginners in summer. Top spots are around Foča, Bihać and Banja Luka.

Hiking and mountain biking Many upland areas and national parks have mine-safe, marked trails.

Business Hours

Office hours 8am to 4pm Monday to Friday.

Banks 8am to 6pm Monday to Friday, 8.30am to 1.30pm Saturday.

Shops 8am to 6pm daily.

Restaurants 11.30am to 10.30pm, often later in summer. Restaurant closing time depends on customer demand more than fixed schedules.

Embassies & Consulates

You can find a list of foreign embassies and consulates in Sarajevo on http://www.bosnia.org.uk/bosnia/viewtype.cfm?typeID=229.

Food

Average costs for restaurant main courses:

€ less than 10KM

€€ 10KM to 25KM

€€€ more than 25KM

Gay & Lesbian Travellers

Although homosexuality was decriminalised per se in 1998 (2000 in the RS), attitudes remain very conservative. **Association Q** (www.queer.ba) nonetheless attempts to empower the self-reliance of the gay community in BiH. **Gay Romeo** (www.gayromeo.com) chat site reportedly has several hundred Sarajevo members.

Internet Access

Most hotels and some cafes offer free wi-fi.

Money

» ATMs accepting Visa and MasterCard are ubiquitous.

» Bosnia's convertible mark (KM or BAM) is pronounced *kai-em* or *maraka* and divided into 100 fenig. It's tied to the euro at approximately €1=1.96KM. Though no longer officially sanctioned, many businesses still unblinkingly accept euros, for minor purchases using a slightly cutomer-favourable 1:2 rate. Exchanging euros is markedly better than changing other currencies as there's no rate-split.

» Exchanging travellers cheques usually requires the original purchase receipt.

Post

BiH fascinates philatelists by having three parallel postal organisations, each issuing their own stamps: **BH Pošta** (www.posta.ba; Federation), **Pošte Srpske** (www.postesrpske.com; RS) and **HP Post** (www.post.ba; Croat areas, western Mostar).

Public Holidays

NATIONWIDE HOLIDAYS

New Year's Day 1 January

Independence Day 1 March

May Day 1 May

National Statehood Day 25 November

ADDITIONAL HOLIDAYS IN THE FEDERATION

Kurban Bajram (Islamic Feast of Sacrifice)

Ramazanski Bajram (end of Ramadan)

Gregorian Easter March/April

Gregorian Christmas 25 December

ADDITIONAL HOLIDAYS IN THE RS

Orthodox Easter April/May

Orthodox Christmas 6 January

Safe Travel

Landmines and unexploded ordnance still affect 2.8% of BiH's area. There were six mine-deaths in 2010. BHMAC (www.bhmac.org) clears more every year but total clearance isn't envisaged before 2019. Stick to asphalt/concrete surfaces or well-worn paths in affected areas, avoiding war-damaged buildings.

Telephone

Mobile-phone companies BH Mobile (☎061- and ☎062-), HT/EroNet (☎063-) and M-Tel (☎065-) all have virtually nationwide coverage.

Country code ☎+387

International operator ☎1201

Local directory information ☎1188

Travellers with Disabilities

Bosnia's steep townscapes are full of stairways and rough streets that can prove very awkward if you're disabled. A few places have wheelchair ramps in response to all the war wounded, but smaller hotels won't have lifts and disabled toilets remain extremely rare.

Visas

Stays of under 90 days require no visa for citizens of most Europeans countries and Australia, Brunei, Canada, Japan, Malaysia, New Zealand, Singapore, South Korea, Turkey and the USA. Other nationals should see www.mfa.ba for visa details and where to apply: several of those nationalities can get a visa on arrival at Sarajevo airport. You might require a letter of invitation or a tourist-agency voucher. Visitors without 150KM per day's intended stay could technically be refused entry, though checks are very rare.

Getting There & Away

Air

All flights use Sarajevo airport, though BH Airlines Zurich flights stop at Banja Luka. Alternatively consider flying to Dubrovnik, Split or Zagreb (Croatia) and connecting to BiH by bus or train.

The following airlines fly to Bosnia & Hercegovina:

Adria (www.adria.si) Via Ljubljana

Austrian (www.austrian.com) Via Vienna.

BH Airlines (Map p114; ☑768335, 033-550125; www.bhairlines.ba; Branilaca Sarajeva 15; ⊗9am-5pm Mon-Fri, 9am-2pm Sat) Pronounced 'Bay-Ha', the national carrier flies a few time weekly from Sarajevo to Copenhagen, İstanbul and Zürich via Banja Luka.

Croatia Airlines (www.croatiaairlines.com) Via Zagreb.

Germanwings (www.germanwings.com) Köln-Bonn.

JAT (www.jat.com) Belgrade.

Lufthansa (www.lufthansa.com) Via Munich.

Norwegian (www.norwegian.no) Twice weekly to Stockholm and Oslo.

Turkish Airlines (www.thy.com) Via İstanbul.

Land

BUS

Buses to Zagreb and/or Split (Croatia) run at least daily from most towns in the Federation and to Serbia and/or Montenegro from many RS towns. Buses to Vienna and Germany run several times weekly from bigger BiH cities.

CAR & MOTORCYCLE

Drivers need Green Card insurance and an EU or International Driving Permit. Transiting Neum in a Croatian hire car is usually hassle-free.

TRAIN

The modest international network links Sarajevo to Belgrade, Zagreb (via Banja Luka), Budapest (via Osijek, Croatia) and to Ploče (coastal Croatia via Mostar).

Getting Around

Bicycle

Cyclists who can handle the hills will find BiH's secondary routes helpfully calm. There are off-road trails for mountain bikers but beware of straying from them in areas where landmines remain a danger.

Bus

Bus stations pre-sell tickets. Between towns it's normally easy enough to wave down any bus en route. Advance reservations are sometimes necessary for overnight routes or at peak holiday times. The biggest company, Centrotrans, has online timetables (click 'Red Vožnje').

Frequency drops drastically at weekends. Some shorter-hop routes stop altogether on Sundays.

Fares are around 7KM per hour travelled. Return tickets are often cheaper than two singles but are limited to one specific company. Expect to pay 2KM extra per stowed bag. Some bus-station ticket offices have a *garderob* for left luggage (from 2KM).

Car & Motorcycle

There's minimal public transport to BiH's most spectacular remote areas so having wheels can really transform your trip. Bosnia's winding roads are lightly trafficked and a delight for driving if you aren't in a hurry. **BIHAMK** (☑033 222210; www.bihamk.ba; Skenderija 23; annual membership 25KM; ⊗8am-4.30pm Mon-Fri, 9am-noon Sat) offers road assistance and towing services (call ☑1282 or ☑1288).

HIRE

International chains are represented while smaller local outfits are often based at hotels. Most companies add 17% VAT. A good deal is Hyundai.ba; its standard rates include full insurance, theft protection and CDW. Pick-up/drop-off is possible at Mostar train station, Novo Sarajevo or Sarajevo airport without extra charge for open-jaws. Prices drop October to April.

ROAD RULES

Drive on the right. First-aid kit, warning triangle, reflective vest and spare bulb kits are compulsory.

» The blood-alcohol limit is 0.03%.

» Headlights must be kept on day and night.

» LPG availability is very limited.

» Parking is awkward in Mostar, central Trebinje and Sarajevo, but contrastingly easy elsewhere. In town centres expect to pay 1KM per hour (attendant or meter) when marked *parking naplatu*.

» Petrol is typically around 2% cheaper in RS than Federation.

» Seat belts are compulsory.

» Snow chains are compulsory on some mountain roads (November to April) and wherever snow is over 5cm deep.

» Speed limits vary: 130km/h (Kakanj–Sarajevo motorway), 100km/h (other dual carriageways), 80km/h (rural), 60km/h or less (in town). Absurdly slow limits are often posted with no obvious logic but police spot-checks are common.

» Winter tyres are compulsory mid-November to mid-April.

Train

Trains are slower and less frequent than buses but generally around 30% cheaper. **RS Railways** (www.zrs-rs.com/red_voznje.php) has full, up-to-date rail timetables.

Bulgaria

Includes »

Best Places to Eat

» Manastirska Magernitsa (p159)

» Mehana Mencheva Kâshta (p166)

» Han Hadji Nikoli (p180)

» Di Wine (p190)

Best Places to Stay

» Hotel Niky (p155)

» Hotel Bolyarka (p166)

» Hotel Renaissance (p169)

» Hotel Bolyarski (p179)

» Hotel Tony (p193)

Why Go?

Bulgaria (България) may be best known for its long, sandy Black Sea beaches, but there's much more to see than that. Bulgaria boasts no fewer than seven mountain ranges and varied landscapes ideal for hiking, cycling, climbing and wildlife-watching. The country has some of Europe's most modern ski resorts as well. You'll find churches and monasteries full of vibrant icons, picturesque villages of timber-framed houses and cobbled lanes, and dramatic reminders of the country's ancient heritage, from Thracian tombs and Roman ruins to medieval fortresses, Ottoman mosques and communist monuments slowly crumbling away into history. Bulgaria's cities, too, reward visitors, with treasure-filled museums and galleries, and parks sprinkled with cafes and restaurants. Getting around is easy and still remarkably cheap so brush up on your Cyrillic, buy a bus ticket and get ready to explore.

When to Go
Sofia

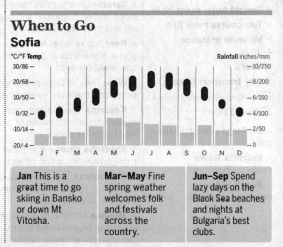

Jan This is a great time to go skiing in Bansko or down Mt Vitosha.

Mar–May Fine spring weather welcomes folk and festivals across the country.

Jun–Sep Spend lazy days on the Black Sea beaches and nights at Bulgaria's best clubs.

AT A GLANCE

» **Currency** Lev (lv)

» **Language** Bulgarian

» **Money** ATMs are everywhere

» **Visas** Not required for citizens of the EU, UK, USA, Canada, Australia and New Zealand

Fast Facts

» **Area** 110,910 sq km

» **Capital** Sofia

» **Country code** ☏359

» **Emergency** ☏112

Exchange Rates

Australia	A$1	1.60 lv
Canada	C$1	1.51 lv
Euro Zone	€1	1.96 lv
Japan	¥100	1.63 lv
New Zealand	NZ$1	1.28 lv
UK	UK£1	2.32 lv
USA	US$1	1.53 lv

Set Your Budget

» **Budget hotel room** 50 lv

» **Two-course meal** 10 lv

» **Museum entrance** 4–10 lv

» **Beer** 2 lv

» **City transport ticket** 1 lv

Resources

» **BG Maps** (www.bgmaps. com)

» **Bulgaria Travel** (www.bulgariatravel.com)

» **Beach Bulgaria** (www.beachbulgaria.com)

Connections

Although Sofia has international bus and train connections, it's not necessary to backtrack to the capital if you're heading to Bucharest or İstanbul. From central Veliko Târnovo, for example, there are daily trains both ways – and much of the country offers overnight buses to İstanbul. Heading to Greece or Belgrade by train means going through Sofia; for Skopje, you'll need to catch a bus from there, too.

ITINERARIES

One Week

Start with a day in Sofia, visiting the Archaeological Museum and Borisova Gradina, then take the bus to Veliko Târnovo for a few days of sightseeing and hiking. Next, head to Varna for some sea and sand. More adventurous travellers may want to head further south along the coast to prettier resorts closer to the Turkish border.

Two Weeks

After a couple of days in Sofia, catch a bus to Plovdiv and wander the cobbled lanes of the Old Town. From there, take a day trip to visit the Bachkovo Monastery. After a few days in Plovdiv, make for the coast, staying a couple of nights in ancient Sozopol. Head north to overnight in Varna then get a connection to Ruse for a glimpse of the Danube and some fine museums. Finish in Veliko Târnovo.

Essential Food & Drink

» **Banitsa** Flaky cheese pasty, often served fresh and hot.

» **Kebabche** Thin, grilled pork sausage, a staple of every *mehana* (tavern) in the country.

» **Tarator** On a hot day there's nothing better than this delicious chilled cucumber and yoghurt soup, served with garlic, dill and crushed walnuts.

» **Beer** You're never far from a cold beer in Bulgaria. Zagorka, Kamenitza and Shumensko are the most popular nationwide brands.

» **Wine** They've been producing wine here since Thracian times and there are some excellent varieties to try.

» **Kavarma** This 'claypot meal', or meat stew, is normally made with either chicken or pork and is one of the country's most popular dishes.

» **Shkembe chorba** Traditional stomach soup is one of the more adventurous and offbeat highlights of Bulgarian cuisine.

» **Shishcheta** This shish kebab, consisting of chunks of chicken or pork on wooden skewers with mushrooms and peppers, is widely available.

» **Musaka** Admittedly, Bulgarian moussaka bears more than a passing resemblance to its Greek cousin but it's a delicious staple of cheap cafeteria meals.

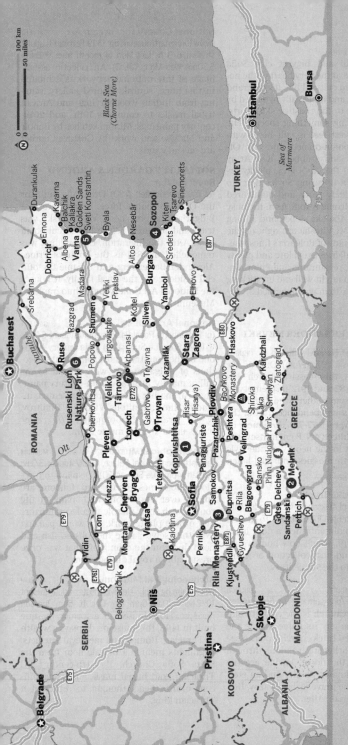

Bulgaria Highlights

① Go back in time through the National Revival houses in **Koprivshtitsa** (p175).

② Sip a glass or two of refreshing Bulgarian vino in the wine town of **Melnik** (p165).

③ Explore the luminous artistic and religious treasures of Bulgaria's revered **Rila Monastery** (p165).

④ Relax on the sands of the Black Sea at **Sozopol** (p196).

⑤ Go clubbing, take in the Summer Festival and stroll through Primorski Park in cosmopolitan **Varna** (p187).

⑥ Discover the wild landscapes and rich bird and animal life of the **Rusenski Lom Nature Park** (p186).

⑦ Visit the tsars' medieval stronghold in **Veliko Târnovo** (p177).

SOFIA

♫02 / POP 1.3 MILLION

Bulgaria's capital and biggest city, Sofia (София; *So*-fia) is at the very heart of the nation's political and cultural life. It's no grand metropolis, true, and it's usually bypassed by tourists heading to the coast or ski resorts, but they're missing something special. The old east-meets-west feel is still here, with a scattering of onion-domed churches, Ottoman mosques and stubborn Red Army monuments, and the city's grey, blocky architecture adds a lingering Soviet tinge to the place. Vast, leafy parks and manicured gardens offer welcome respite from the busy city streets and the ski slopes and hiking trails of mighty Mt Vitosha are right on the doorstep. With many of Bulgaria's finest museums and art galleries to explore and plenty of excellent bars, restaurants and entertainment venues, you might well end up sticking around for longer than you imagined.

⊙ Sights

PLOSHTAD ALEKSANDER NEVSKI

FREE **Aleksander Nevski Church**   CHURCH
(pl Aleksander Nevski; ⊙7am-7pm) One of *the* symbols of Sofia, this massive church was built between 1882 and 1912 in memory of the 200,000 Russian soldiers who died fighting for Bulgaria's independence during the Russo-Turkish War (1877–78). Designed by the Russian architect AN Pomerantsev, the church was built in the neo-Byzantine style and adorned with mosaics and gold-laden domes.

Aleksander Nevski Crypt   GALLERY
(Museum of Icons; pl Aleksander Nevski; adult/student 6/3 lv; ⊙10am-6pm Tue-Sun; ☐1) To the left of the church's main entrance, a door leads down to the crypt, which now houses Bulgaria's biggest and best collection of icons, stretching back to the 5th century.

Sveta Sofia Church   CHURCH
(ul Parizh; ⊙7am-7pm summer, to 6pm winter; ☐9) Sveta Sofia Church is the capital's oldest, and gave the city its name. Inside the much-restored red-brick church, you can see evidence of its earlier incarnations through glass panels in the floor. Outside are the Tomb of the Unknown Soldier and an eternal flame, and the grave of Ivan Vazov, Bulgaria's most revered writer.

National Gallery for Foreign Art   GALLERY
(www.foreignartmuseum.bg; ul 19 Fevruari 1; adult/student 6/3 lv, last Mon of month free; ⊙11am-6.30pm Wed-Mon; ☐1, 2) An eclectic assemblage of international artwork is exhibited in this huge, squeaky-floored gallery, ranging from Indian woodcarvings and African tribal masks to countless 19th- and 20th-century paintings. Minor sketches by Renoir and Matisse and works by Gustave Courbet are on show too.

SOFIA CITY GARDEN & AROUND

Royal Palace   PALACE
(ul Tsar Osvoboditel; ☐20) Originally built for the Ottoman police force, it was here that Bulgaria's national hero, Vasil Levski, was tried and tortured before his execution in 1873. After the liberation, the building was remodelled in 1887 as the home of Prince Alexander Battenberg and became the official residence of the royal family. It houses the National Art Gallery and Ethnographical Museum.

National Art Gallery   GALLERY
(pl Battenberg, Royal Palace; adult/student 6/3 lv; ⊙10am-6pm Tue-Sun; ☐20) This gallery holds one of the country's most important collections of Bulgarian art, with several rooms full of mainly 19th- and 20th-century paintings. All the big names are represented, including the ubiquitous Vladimir Dimitrov, whose orange, Madonna-like *Harvester* hangs in the former music room.

Ethnographical Museum   MUSEUM
(pl Battenberg, Royal Palace; adult/student 3/1 lv; ⊙10am-4pm Tue-Sun; ☐20) Displays on regional costumes, crafts and folklore are spread over two floors, and many of the rooms, with their marble fireplaces, mirrors and ornate plasterwork, are worth pausing over themselves; note the lobster, fish and dead duck on the ceiling of what was once presumably a royal dining room.

Archaeological Museum   MUSEUM
(www.naim.bg; pl Nezavisimost; adult/student 10/2 lv; ⊙10am-6pm May-Oct, to 5pm Tue-Sun Nov-Apr; ☐10) Housed in a former mosque built in 1496, this museum displays a wealth of Thracian, Roman and medieval artefacts. Highlights include a mosaic floor from the Sveta Sofia Church, the 4th-century BC Thracian gold burial mask, and a magnificent bronze head, thought to represent a Thracian king.

President's Building
NOTABLE BUILDING

(pl Nezavisimost; 🚇10) The Bulgarian president's office isn't open to the public, but the **changing of the guard** ceremony (on the hour) is a spectacle not to be missed, as soldiers in raffish Ruritanian uniforms stomp their way to their sentry boxes outside.

Party House
NOTABLE BUILDING

(pl Nezavisimost; 🚇20) This domineering Stalinist monolith, built in 1953, was once headquarters of the Bulgarian Communist Party. It is now used as government offices. The red star that perched on top of the building is in the **Museum of Socialist Art** (ul Lachezar Stanchev 7, Iztok; admission 6 lv; ⊙10am-5.30pm Tue-Sun; 🚇GM Dimitrov).

PLOSHTAD SVETA NEDELYA & AROUND

Sveta Nedelya Cathedral
CHURCH

(pl Sveta Nedelya; 🚇Serdika) Completed in 1863, this magnificent domed church is one of the city's major landmarks, noted for its rich, Byzantine-style murals. It was blown up by communists on 16 April 1925 in an attempt to assassinate Tsar Boris III. Over 120 people were killed in the attack, but Boris escaped unharmed.

Sveta Petka Samardzhiiska Church
CHURCH

(bul Maria Luisa; 🚇Serdika) Closed due to surrounding excavations at the time of research, this tiny church was built during the early years of Ottoman rule (late 14th century), which explains its sunken profile and inconspicuous exterior. Inside are some 16th-century murals. It's rumoured that the Bulgarian national hero Vasil Levski is buried here.

BULEVARD VITOSHA & PLOSHTAD BULGARIA

Bulevard Vitosha
NEIGHBOURHOOD

Extending south of pl Sveta Nedelya, towards its towering namesake, Mt Vitosha, this central section of bul Vitosha is now a car-free strip with Sofia's ritzlest shops, along with a few trendy coffee bars. After a kilometre it reaches **Ploshtad Bulgaria**, an elongated tree-lined plaza.

Monument to the Bulgarian State
MONUMENT

At the northern end of Ploshtad Bulgaria is the Monument to the Bulgarian State. Now fenced off, the socialist-era eyesore was erected in 1981 to celebrate the 1300th anniversary of the Bulgarian Empire, but it has been slowly falling apart for years.

BORISOVA GRADINA & AROUND

Monument to the Soviet Army
MONUMENT

(🚇Kliment Ohridski) Near the entrance to Borisova Gradina, this gigantic monument was built in 1954 and is a prime example of the forceful socialist-realism of the period. The place of honour goes to a Red Army soldier atop a column, surrounded by animated cast-iron sculptural groups depicting determined, gun-waving soldiers and grateful, child-caressing members of the proletariat.

Red House
GALLERY

(www.redhouse-sofia.bg; ul Lyuben Karavelov 15) The Red House is a lively cultural centre, with a busy program covering everything from heavyweight political debates and lectures to film screenings, concerts and dance performances. The house once belonged to the sculptor Andrey Nikolov (1878–1959) and some of his works are displayed in the **Nikolov Hall** (admission free; ⊙3-7pm Tue-Sat) here.

🛏 Sleeping

Accommodation in Sofia tends to be more expensive than anywhere else in Bulgaria, with prices comparable to those in Western European cities. Good-quality budget hotels are a rarity, and cheaper places that do exist are often either squalid dives or in awkward-to-reach locations; hostels are a better deal.

TOP CHOICE Hotel Niky
HOTEL €€

(☎953 0110; www.hotel-niky.com; ul Neofit Rilski 16; r/ste from 80/120 lv; 🅿⊜❄🛜🛗; 🚇1) Offering excellent value and a good central location, Niky has comfortable rooms and gleaming bathrooms, while the smart suites have kitchenettes with microwave ovens, fridges, and coffee and tea. It's a popular place and frequently full. Advance reservations are recommended.

Residence Oborishte
BOUTIQUE HOTEL €€€

(☎0885 006 810; www.residence-oborishte.com; ul Oborishte 63; s/d/ste from 180/200/220 lv; ⊜❄🛜; 🚇9, 72) A salmon-pink '30s-era home with its own bistro, the Residence has nine rooms and sumptuous suites with cherrywood flooring, antique-style furnishings and lots of space. The penthouse (260 lv) has a view over the Aleksander Nevski Church. Prices drop by 20% at weekends.

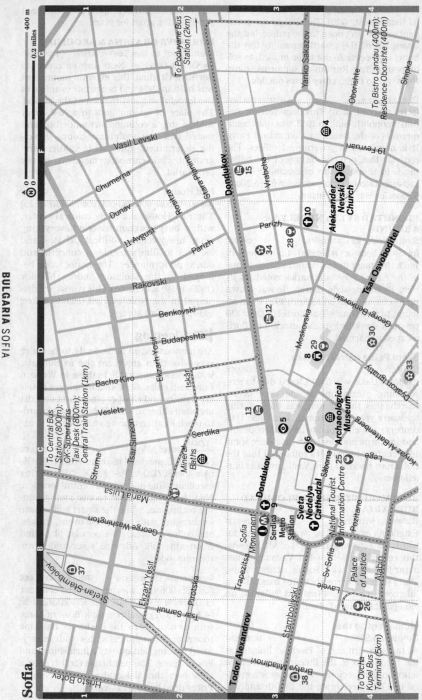

Sofia

To Central Bus
Station (800m);
OK-Supertrans
Taxi Desk (800m);
Central Train Station (1km)

To Poduyane Bus
Station (2km)

To Bistro Landau (400m);
Residence Oborishte (400m)

To Ovcha
Kupel Bus
Terminal (5km)

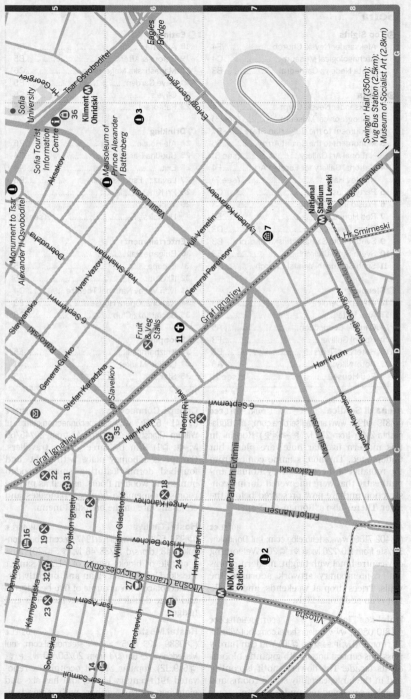

BULGARIA SOFIA

Swingin' Hall (350m);
Yug Bus Station (2.5km);
Museum of Socialist Art (2.8km)

Eagles
Bridge

Sofia
University

Sofia Tourist
Information
Centre

Kliment
Ohridski

Mausoleum of
Prince Alexander
Battenberg

Monument to Tsar
Alexander II Osvoboditel

National
Stadium
Vasil Levski

Hr Smirneski

Fruit
& Veg
Stalls

NDK Metro
Station

Vitosha (trams & bicycles only)

Sofia

◉ Top Sights

Aleksander Nevski Church	F4
Archaeological Museum	C4
Sveta Nedelya Cathedral	B3

◉ Sights

1	Aleksander Nevski Crypt	F4
	Ethnographical Museum	(see 8)
2	Monument to the Bulgarian State	B7
3	Monument to the Soviet Army	F6
	National Art Gallery	(see 8)
4	National Gallery for Foreign Art	F4
	Nikolov Hall	(see 7)
5	Party House	C3
6	President's Building	C3
7	Red House	E7
8	Royal Palace	D3
9	Sveta Petka Samardzhiiska Church	B3
10	Sveta Sofia Church	E3
11	Sveti Sedmochislenitsi Church	D6

◎ Sleeping

12	Arena di Serdica	D3
13	Arte Hotel	C3
14	Canapé Connection	A5
15	Hostel Gulliver	F3
16	Hotel Les Fleurs	B5
17	Hotel Niky	A6
	Red House	(see 7)

◎ Eating

18	Annette	C6
19	Before & After	B5
20	Manastirska Magernitsa	C6
21	Olive Garden	B5
22	Olive's	C5
23	Pastorant	A5

◎ Drinking

24	Ale House	B6
25	Buddha Bar	C4
26	Exit	A4
27	Lavazza Espression	B6
28	Pri Kmeta	E3
29	Toba & Co	D4
	Upstairs	(see 32)

◎ Entertainment

30	Bulgaria Hall	D4
31	Escape	C5
32	ID Club	B5
33	Ivan Vazov National Theatre	D4
34	National Opera House	E3
35	Social Jazz Club	C6

◎ Shopping

36	Knizharnitsa	F5
37	Ladies' Market	B1
38	Stenata	A3

Arena di Serdica
LUXURY HOTEL €€€

(☏819 9191; www.arenadiserdica.com; ul Buda-peshta 2-4; r from 220 lv; ⓟ⊜❄☎) Rooms in this modern five-star hotel are plush but understated. The hotel's name comes from the remains of the 4th-century Roman amphitheatre that were uncovered during construction and are now preserved below the foyer. There's also a 'Roman-style' spa.

Arte Hotel
HOTEL €€

(☏402 7100; www.artehotelbg.com; bul Dondukov 5; r/ste from 110/220 lv; ❄☎; ⓟ20) Welcoming city-centre hotel with bright, modern rooms and contemporary artwork adorning the walls. Prices drop at weekends, and breakfast is an additional 20 lv.

Hotel Les Fleurs
BOUTIQUE HOTEL €€€

(☏810 0800; www.lesfleurshotel.com; bul Vitosha 21; r from 270 lv; ⓟ⊜❄☎; ⓟ10) You can hardly miss this central hotel, with gigantic blooms on its facade. The flowery motif is continued in the large, carefully styled rooms and there's a very good restaurant on-site.

Canapé Connection
HOSTEL €

(☏441 6373; www.canapeconnection.com; ul William Gladstone 12a; dm/s/d from 20/46/60 lv; ⓐ; ⓟ1) Run by three young travellers, Canapé is a homey place with eight- and four-bed dorms featuring smart wooden bunks and wooden floors, as well as private rooms. Homemade *banitsa*, pancakes and croissants are on the breakfast menu.

Hostel Gulliver
HOSTEL €

(☏987 5210; www.gulliver1947-bg.com; bul Dondukov 48; dm/s/d 18/38/48 lv; ☎; ⓟ20) Just a couple of blocks north of pl Aleksander Nevski, Gulliver is a clean and brightly furnished place with a couple of five-bed dorms and three doubles. All rooms have TVs and fridges.

Hostel Mostel
HOSTEL €

(☏0889 223 296; www.hostelmostel.com; bul Makedoniya 2; dm/s/d from 20/50/60 lv; ⓟ☎; ⓟ6, 9, 12) Popular Mostel occupies a renovated 19th-century house, and has six- and eight-bed dorms, either with shared or private bathrooms, as well as a single and a couple of doubles. Guests have use of a kitchen and cosy lounge.

Red House
B&B €€

(📞988 8188; www.redbandb.com; ul Lyuben Karavelov 15; s/d from 50/80 lv; @; Ⓜ Vasil Levski; 🚌10) Attached to the Red House cultural centre, in an unusual Italianate building designed for the sculptor Andrei Nikolov. All rooms are individually decorated, though none have private bathrooms and some are a bit basic.

✕ Eating

Compared with the rest of Bulgaria, Sofia is gourmet heaven, with an unrivalled range of international cuisine and new, quality restaurants springing up all the time. It also has countless snack bars, fast-food outlets and cafes dotted across town. If you're on a budget, there are plenty of kiosks where you can buy fast food such as *banitsa* and *palachinki* (pancakes).

[TOP CHOICE] Manastirska Magernitsa
BULGARIAN €€

(📞980 3883; www.magernitsa.com; ul Han Asparuh 67; mains 5-10 lv; ⏱11am-2am; 🌱) This traditional *mehana* is among the best places in Sofia to sample authentic cuisine. The enormous menu features recipes collected from monasteries across the country, with dishes such as 'drunken rabbit' stewed in wine, as well as salads, fish, pork and game.

Pastorant
ITALIAN €€€

(📞981 4482; www.pastorant.eu; ul Tsar Assen 16; mains 11-26 lv; ⏱noon-10.30pm; 🌱🍴) This charming pea-green restaurant provides an intimate setting for high-quality Italian cuisine, including some inventive pasta and risotto dishes, and traditional favourites such as saltimbocca and pesto chicken.

Annette
MOROCCAN €€

(📞0885 139 676; www.annette.bg; ul Angel Kânchev 27; mains 8-18 lv; 🍴) With its cushion-filled couches, glowing candles, lanterns and spicy aromas, this is a great place for authentic Moroccan cooking, including a big selection of *mezze*, and tagine meals such as lamb with figs and apricots, and chicken in wine sauce.

Olive Garden
MEDITERRANEAN €€

(📞481 1214; www.olivegardensofia.com; ul Angel Kânchev 18; mains 10-22 lv; ⏱11am-11pm; 🍴🍴) Expertly cooked roast lamb, trout, salmon, pasta and risotto are served here. There's a

smart indoor dining room or you can sit in the little garden with its mulberry tree. A cheaper lunch menu is also offered.

Bistro Landau
BISTRO €€€

(📞814 4888; www.bistrolandau.com; ul Oborishte 63; mains 12-30 lv; ⏱7am-10.30pm; 🌱🍴; 🚌9, 72) Attached to the Residence Oborishte (p155), this romantic bistro offers an eclectic menu of interesting dishes such as beef entrecote, breaded tilapia, trout and sausages in curry sauce.

Before & After
CAFE €€

(📞981 6088; ul Hristo Belchev 12; mains 5-15 lv; ⏱10am-midnight; 🌱🍴; 🚌8) With its stylish art nouveau interior, this is an agreeable spot for light meals and drinks. Pasta, risotto, fish and steaks feature on the menu.

Olive's
INTERNATIONAL €€

(ul Graf Ignatiev 12; mains 7-18 lv; 🌱🍴🍴; 🚌10) Walls splashed with vintage advertising posters and mock newspapers for menus give Olive's a quirky twist, and the international cuisine is excellent, featuring dishes such as chicken skewers, pasta, steaks and burgers.

🍷 Drinking

There's a seemingly inexhaustible supply of watering holes all over Sofia. The cheapest places to grab a beer are the kiosks in the city's parks; if you're looking for more sophisticated ambience, the city centre has plenty of swish new bars.

Pri Kmeta
PUB

(At the Mayor's; www.prikmeta.com; ul Parizh 2; ⏱noon-4am; 🍴; 🚌20) Microbrewery serving its own Kmetsko beer. There are seats at ground level, but the cellar beer hall, with its gleaming copper vats, is more atmospheric, and hosts regular live-music events.

Ale House
BEER HALL

(www.alehouse.bg; ul Hristo Belchev 42; ⏱11am-midnight; 🚌9) No need to queue at the bar at this convivial beer hall – the tables have their own

---

SELF-CATERING

An abundance of fresh fruit and veg can be yours at the Ladies' Market (p161) and the stalls along ul Graf Ignatiev, outside the **Sveti Sedmochislenitsi Church** (Church of the Seven Saints; ul Graf Ignatiev; ⏱7am-7pm; 🚌10).

BULGARIA SOFIA

beer taps. Food is also served, and there's live music on Fridays and Saturdays.

Lavazza Espression
CAFE
(bul Vitosha 44; ☺8am-10pm; ☏) This trendy little cafe brings a touch of Italian style to the city centre, with a long list of coffees to choose from, and a brief menu of light meals and sandwiches.

Toba & Co
COCKTAIL BAR
(ul Moskovska 6; ☺8.30am-6am) Ensconced in what was once Tsar Ferdinand's butterfly house, in the gardens at the rear of the Royal Palace, this discreet cafe is a charming spot to indulge in a cocktail or two, as well as ice cream and cakes.

Upstairs
COCKTAIL BAR
(bul Vitosha 18; ☺10am-2am) Join the in crowd with a cocktail on the 1st-floor terrace stools, looking down on the shoppers and trams of bul Vitosha, or lounge on the sofas inside.

Buddha Bar
LOUNGE
(ul Lege 15a; ☺24hr; ☏; ☐10) Very hip, very trendy and very crowded, this Buddha-bedecked drinking spot also serves food, and has a nightly disco from around 9pm.

Exit
GAY
(☏0887 965 026; ul Lavele 16; ☺8am-2am; ☏; ☐8) This modern and fashionable bar/diner is a popular gay venue, with a DJ party every evening.

☆ Entertainment
If you read Bulgarian, or at least can decipher Cyrillic, *Programata* is the most comprehensive source of entertainment listings; otherwise check out its excellent English-language website, www.programata.bg. You can book tickets online at www.ticketpro.bg.

Nightclubs
Some clubs charge a cover of anywhere between 2 lv and 15 lv, mostly on weekends when live bands are playing.

Swingin' Hall
LIVE MUSIC
(☏963 0059; bul Dragan Tsankov 8; ☺9pm-4am; ☐10) Huge club offering an eclectic program of live music each night, ranging from jazz and blues to rock and folk pop.

Social Jazz Club
JAZZ
(☏0884 622 220; pl Slaveikov 4; ☺10pm-4am Mon-Sat; ☐10) The place to go to catch some quality live jazz, with leading international acts.

Escape
CLUB
(ul Angel Kânchev 1; cover 10 lv; ☺10pm-late Thu-Sun) Sofia's favourite central disco, Escape has various theme nights including Britpop parties, hip-hop and drum'n'bass night.

Avenue
CLUB
(☏0898 553 085; ul Atanas Manchev 1a, Studentski Grad; ☺24hr; ☐94) One of the more popular student joints, Avenue plays both Western songs and Bulgarian *chalga* (folk pop) music.

ID Club
GAY
(www.idclub.bg; ul Kârnigradska 19b; ☺9pm-5am Tue-Sat; ☏) ID is a big, glittering gay club with three bars, theme nights, cabaret and a playlist including everything from house to *chalga*.

Performing Arts
Ticket prices vary. For the Opera House or National Theatre, they may cost anything from 10 lv to 30 lv; shows at the National Palace of Culture can be much more expensive, with tickets running to 70 lv for international acts.

National Opera House
OPERA
(☏987 1366; www.operasofia.com; bul Dondukov 30, entrance on ul Vrabcha; ☺ticket office 9am-2pm & 2.30-7pm Mon-Fri, 11am-7pm Sat, 11am-4pm Sun; ☐9, ☐20) Opened in 1953, this monumental edifice is the venue for grand opera and ballet performances, as well as concerts.

National Palace of Culture
CONCERT VENUE
(NDK; ☏916 6368; www.ndk.bg; pl Bulgaria; ☺ticket office 9am-7pm; ☏; Ⓜ NDK) The NDK (as it's usually called) has 15 halls and is the country's largest cultural complex. It maintains a regular program of events throughout the year, ranging from film screenings and trade shows to big-name international music acts.

Bulgaria Hall
CLASSICAL MUSIC
(☏987 7656; ul Aksakov 1; ☺ticket office 9am-6pm; ☐9) The home of the excellent Sofia Philharmonic Orchestra, this is the place for classical music concerts.

Ivan Vazov National Theatre
THEATRE
(☏811 9219; www.nationaltheatre.bg; ul Dyakon Ignatiy 5; ☺ticket office 9.30am-7.30pm Mon-Fri, 11.30am-7.30pm Sat-Sun; ☐9) One of Sofia's most elegant buildings, the Viennese-style National Theatre opened in 1907, and is the city's main stage for Bulgarian drama.

🔒 Shopping

Bulevard Vitosha is Sofia's main shopping street, mostly featuring international brand-name boutiques interspersed with restaurants. More shops cluster along ul Graf Ignatiev, while ul Pirotska is a central pedestrian mall lined with cheaper shops selling clothes, shoes and household goods.

Knizharnitsa　　　　　　　　BOOKS
(Sofia University underpass; ⊙8.30am-8.30pm Mon-Fri, 9am-8.30pm Sat, 10am-8.30pm Sun; Ⓜ️Kliment Ohridski) One of the better selections of English, French and German-language novels, with a little cafe on-site.

Ladies' Market　　　　　　　　MARKET
(ul Stefan Stambolov; ⊙dawn-dusk; 🚌20) Stretching several blocks between ul Ekzarh Yosif and bul Slivnitsa, this is Sofia's biggest fresh-produce market. Fruit and vegetables, cheap clothes, shoes, car parts, kitchen utensils and pretty much anything else you can think of can be bought here. It does get very crowded, so watch your belongings.

Stenata　　　　　　OUTDOOR EQUIPMENT
(☎980 5491; www.stenata.com; ul Bratia Miladinovi 5; ⊙10am-8pm Mon-Fri, 10am-6pm Sat, 11am-6pm Sun; 🚌4) The best place in town to buy hiking, climbing and camping equipment, including backpacks, tents and sleeping bags.

ℹ️ Information

Dangers & Annoyances
The main danger you are likely to face comes from the dreadful traffic; pedestrian crossings and traffic lights don't mean much to many drivers, so be extra careful when crossing. Note that traffic lanes and pedestrian areas are marked only by faintly painted lines on the cobbles around pl Aleksander Nevski and pl Narodno Sabranie, and although a large section of bul Vitosha is now off-limits to private cars, you should still watch out for trams and for vehicles zipping out of the side streets.

Sofia has a large population of stray dogs – it is estimated that as many as 10,000 animals roam the city's streets, and there have been instances of people being attacked, seriously injured and even killed. You are unlikely to encounter packs of dogs in the centre, but exercise caution and do not approach feral dogs.

Medical Services
Neomed Pharmacy (☎951 5539; bul General Totleben 2b; ⊙24hr; 🚌4)

Pirogov Hospital (www.pirogov.bg; bul General Totleben 21; 🚌4)

Tokuda Hospital (☎403 4000; www.tokud-abolnica.bg; bul Nikola Vaptsarov 51b; ⊙24hr; 🚌88) Modern, Japanese-run private hospital with English-speaking staff.

Money
Unicredit Bulbank (cnr ul Lavele & ul Todor Alexandrov)

Post
Central Post Office (ul General Gurko 6; ⊙7.30am-8.30pm)

Tourist Information
National Tourist Information Centre (☎987 9778; www.bulgariatravel.org; ul Sveta Sofia; ⊙9am-5pm Mon-Fri; 🚌5) Helpful, English-speaking staff and glossy brochures for destinations around Bulgaria.

Sofia Tourist Information Centre (☎491 8345; Sofia University underpass; ⊙8am-8pm Mon-Fri, 10am-6pm Sat & Sun; Ⓜ️Kliment Ohridski) Lots of free leaflets and maps, and helpful English-speaking staff.

Websites
Programata (www.programata.bg) Comprehensive eating, drinking and clubbing information.

Sofia (www.sofia.bg) Official municipal website, with business information.

Sofia Life (www.sofia-life.com) Bar and restaurant reviews, as well as practical advice.

Sofia Traffic (www.sofiatraffic.bg) Information on public transport.

ℹ️ Getting There & Away

Air
The only domestic flights within Bulgaria are between Sofia and the Black Sea. Bulgaria Air flies daily to Varna, with two or three daily flights between July and September. Bulgaria Air also flies between the capital and Burgas.

Bus
Sofia's **Central Bus Station** (Tsentralna Avtogara; www.centralnaavtogara.bg; bul Maria Luisa 100; 24hr; 🚌7), right beside the train station, handles services to most big towns in Bulgaria as well as international destinations. There are dozens of counters for individual private companies, as well as an information desk and an **OK-Supertrans taxi desk** (⊙6am-10pm). Departures are less frequent between November and April.

From the far smaller **Ovcha Kupel bus station** (☎955 5362; bul Tsar Boris III, Zapad; 🚌5) – sometimes called Zapad (West) station – a few buses head south to Bansko, Blagoevgrad and Sandanski.

From tiny **Yug bus station** (☎872 2345; bul Dragan Tsankov 23; 🚌413, Ⓜ️Joliot-Curie),

TRANSPORT FROM SOFIA

Bus

DESTINATION	PRICE (LV)	DURATION (HR)	FREQUENCY (SUMMER)
Albena	36	8	4-5 daily
Bansko	16	3	5-6 daily
Burgas	30	7-8	6-10 daily
Kazanlâk	16	3½	4-5 daily
Nesebâr	37	7	5-10 daily
Plovdiv	14	2½	several hourly
Ruse	29	5	hourly
Shumen	31	6	7 daily
Sliven	24	5	8 daily
Smolyan	25	3½	6-7 daily
Sozopol	32	7	6-8 daily
Varna	33	7-8	every 30-45min
Veliko Târnovo	22	4	hourly
Vidin	20	5	6-7 daily

Train

DESTINATION	PRICE (LV) 1ST-/2ND-CLASS FARE	DURATION (HR)	FREQUENCY (DAILY)
Burgas	23.60/18.90 (fast), 28.80/23.10 (express)	7-8	4 fast & 2 express
Gorna Oryakhovitsa	18.30/14.60 (fast), 21.40/17.20 (express)	4-4½	6 fast & 2 express (for Veliko Târnovo)
Plovdiv	11.30/9 (fast), 14.30/11.50 (express)	2½-3	6 fast, 3 express & 4 slow
Ruse	23.60/18.90	6	3 fast
Varna	29.50/23.60 (fast), 36.90/29.60 (express)	7½-9	5 fast & 1 express
Vidin	17.30/13.30 (fast)	5	3 fast

buses and minibuses leave for Samokov (6 lv, one hour, every 30 minutes).

From the ramshackle **Poduyane bus station** (☑847 4262; ul Todorini Kukli; ☑79) – aka Iztok (East) station – buses leave infrequently for small towns in central Bulgaria, such as Troyan (15 lv, three hours, two daily).

Train

The **central train station** (bul Maria Luisa; ☑1, 7) is a massive, rather cheerless concrete hive, built in the 'Brutalist' style in the '70s.

Destinations for all domestic and international services are listed on timetables in Cyrillic, but departures (for the following two hours) and arrivals (for the previous two hours) are listed in English on a large screen on the ground floor. Other facilities include a post office, **left-luggage office** (per bag per day 2 lv; ☑6am-11pm), cafes, a supermarket and accommodation agencies.

Same-day tickets are sold at counters on the ground floor, while advance tickets are sold in the gloomy basement, accessed via an unsigned flight of stairs obscured by another set of stairs that heads up to some snack bars. Counters are open 24 hours, but normally only a few are staffed and queues are long. Don't turn up at the last moment to purchase your ticket, and allow extra time to work out the confusing system of platforms, indicated with Roman numerals, and tracks.

❶ Getting Around

To/From the Airport

Sofia airport (☏937 2211; www.sofia-airport. bg; off bul Brussels; minibus 30) is located 12km east of the city centre. Minibus 30 shuttles between the airport and pl Nezavisimost for a flat fare of 1.50 lv; you can catch it outside the Sheraton Hotel. Bus 84 from Terminal 1 and bus 284 from Terminal 2 (which handles the bulk of international flights) both take a slow and meandering route before depositing you opposite Sofia University.

When you emerge into the arrivals hall you will immediately be greeted by taxi drivers offering you a ride into town, at often ridiculously inflated rates; bypass these and instead head to the reputable OK-Supertrans taxi office counter, where you can book an official, meter-equipped taxi. They will give you a slip of paper with the three-digit code of your cab, which will normally be immediately available. A taxi (using the meter) from the airport to the city centre should cost no more than 15 lv.

Car & Motorcycle

Frequent public transport, cheap taxis and horrendous traffic all provide little or no incentive to drive a private or rented car around Sofia. If you wish to explore further afield, though, a car will come in handy.

Avis (☏945 9224; www.avis.bg; Sofia airport, Terminal 2; ◷9am-9pm)

Hertz (☏439 0222; www.hertz.bg; bul Nikola Vaptsarov 53; ◷9am-5.30pm Mon-Fri, 10am-2pm Sat; ☐88)

Sixt (☏945 9276; www.tsrentacar.com; Sofia Airport, Terminal 2; ◷8am-11pm)

Public Transport

Public transport – trams, buses, minibuses and trolleybuses, as well as the underground metro – run from 5.30am to 11pm every day.

Many buses, trams and trolleybuses are fitted with on-board ticket machines; tickets within Sofia cost 1 lv. However, it's far easier and quicker, especially during peak times, to buy tickets from kiosks at stops along the route before boarding.

If you plan to use public transport frequently, buy a one-day/five-day/one-month transit card (4/15/50 lv), which is valid for all trams, buses and trolleybuses (but not the metro). All tickets must be validated by inserting them in the small machine on-board; once punched, tickets are nontransferable. Inspectors will issue on-the-spot fines (10 lv) if you don't have a ticket; unwary foreigners are a favourite target.

Sofia's metro system (www.metropolitan.bg) is expanding and at the time of research much of the centre was being dug up for new lines. Tickets cost 1 lv but cannot be used on other forms of public transport. Useful central stations include Serdika, near pl Sveta Nedelya, Kliment Ohridski, close to Sofia University, and NDK, at the southern end of bulevard Vitosha.

Taxi

By law, taxis must use meters, but those that wait around the airport, luxury hotels and within 100m of pl Sveta Nedelya will often try to negotiate an unmetered fare – which, of course, will be considerably more. All official taxis are yellow, have fares per kilometre displayed in the window, and have obvious taxi signs (in English or Bulgarian) on top.

In the unlikely event you can't find a taxi, you can order one by ringing **OK-Supertrans** (☏973 2121; www.oktaxi.net) or **Yellow Taxi** (☏911 19). You will usually need to speak Bulgarian.

AROUND SOFIA

Boyana   Бояна
☏02

Boyana is a peaceful and prosperous suburb of Sofia, 8km south of the city centre. Once a favourite retreat for communist leaders and apparatchiks, these days it's home to Sofia's wealthy elite and two of the capital's major attractions.

◉ Sights

National Museum of History   MUSEUM
(www.historymuseum.org; ul Vitoshko Lale 16; admission 10 lv, with Boyana Church 12 lv; ◷9.30am-6pm; minibus 21) Housed in the former communist presidential palace, this museum occupies a stunning, if inconvenient, setting; unless a coach party turns up, you may have the place to yourself. The exhaustive collection includes Thracian gold treasures, Roman statuary, folk costumes, weaponry and icons, while outside you can see some Russian MiG fighters.

Boyana Church   CHURCH
(www.boyanachurch.org; ul Boyansko Ezero 3; adult/student 10/1 lv, combined ticket with National Historical Museum 12 lv, guide 10 lv; ◷9.30am-5.30pm Apr-Oct, 9am-5pm Nov-Mar; ☐64, minibus 21) The tiny, 13th-century Boyana Church is around 2km south of the museum. It's on Unesco's World Heritage list – its 90 murals are rare survivors from the 13th century and are among the very finest examples of Bulgarian medieval artwork. They include the oldest known portrait of St John of Rila,

along with representations of King Konstantin Asen and Queen Irina.

❶ Getting There & Away

Minibus 21 runs to Boyana from the city centre (pick it up on bul Vasil Levski). It will drop you right outside the gates of the museum and connects the museum with Boyana Church. You can also take bus 63 from pl Ruski Pametnik, or bus 64 from the Hladilnika terminal. Signs advertising the museum line the motorway, but it's not easy to spot the building, which is set back from the road behind a screen of trees. A taxi (about 8 lv one way) from the city centre to the museum is probably the easiest option of all; for the museum, ask for the 'Residentsia Boyana'.

Vitosha Nature Park

♩ 02

The Mt Vitosha range, 23km long and 13km wide, lies just south of the city. It's sometimes referred to as the 'lungs of Sofia' for the refreshing breezes it deflects onto the often-polluted capital. The mountain is part of the 227 sq km **Vitosha Nature Park** (www.park-vitosha.org), the oldest of its kind in Bulgaria (created in 1934). The highest point is Mt Cherni Vrâh (Black Peak; 2290m), the fourth-highest peak in Bulgaria, where temperatures in January can fall to -8°C.

As well as being a popular ski resort in winter, the nature park is popular with hikers, picnickers and sightseers on summer weekends, and receives around 1.5 million visitors a year. There are dozens of clearly marked hiking trails, a few hotels, cafes and restaurants, and numerous huts and chalets that can be booked through the Bulgarian Tourist Union.

🏃 Activities

The mountain has dozens of well-marked **hiking trails**. It's worth paying 5 lv for the Cyrillic trail map *Vitosha Turisticheska Karta* (1:50,000), available in Sofia. Popular trails include the steep 90-minute trip up Mt Cherni Vrâh (2290m) from Aleko; a three-hour trek east of Mt Sredets (1969m) from Aleko past Goli Vrâh (1837m) to Zlatni Mostove; and a three-hour hike from Boyana Church past a waterfall to Zlatni Mostove.

The **skiing**, from mid-December to April, covers 29km of the mountain; it's generally cheaper here than ski resorts (about 30 lv for a lift ticket) and you can ski higher (the peak is 1800m). Rental equipment is available; try to avoid busy weekends.

Most people reach the mountain by chairlift. **Dragalevtsi** has two chairlifts, located a few kilometres up from the village bus stop (walk via the creekside) – one lift goes to Bai Krâstyo, the second to Goli Vrâh (1837m). The other option is the six-person gondola at **Simeonovo**, which runs from Friday to Sunday (closed in April), and goes to Aleko, a popular hike/ski hub. It's possible to go up either Dragalevtsi or Simeonovo, hike 30 minutes, and return down the other.

❶ Getting There & Away

To Aleko, bus 66 departs from Sofia's Hladilnika terminal 10 times a day between 8am and 7.45pm on weekends, and four times a day on weekdays. Minibus 41 runs from Sofia city centre to Simeonovo (1.50 lv).

RILA & PIRIN MOUNTAINS

These two mountain chains snuggle up to the Greek border south of Sofia, and are made of serious Alps-like rocky-topped peaks full of rewarding hikes. It's here that one of Bulgaria's most famous sites, Rila Monastery, stands guarded by mountains, while Melnik is a favourite spot for wining weekends. For hiking, the monastery is a possible starting point, with several trails meeting others higher up. Pirin hikes are generally tougher than Rila ones, with more abrupt slopes. In summer it's better to end by walking down to Melnik.

Rila Monastery
Рилски Манастир

♩ 07054

Bulgaria's largest and most renowned monastery emerges abruptly out of a forested valley in the Rila Mountains. It's a major attraction for both Bulgarian pilgrims and foreign tourists. On summer weekends the monastery is especially busy, though at other times it provides more solitude. Stay at a nearby hotel or camping ground, or even at the monastery itself to experience Rila's photogenic early mornings and late evenings. You can also hike the surrounding mountains.

Rila Monastery was founded in AD 927 by hermit monk Ivan Rilski. Originally built 3km to the northeast, it got its current location in 1335. By the 14th century's end, it had become a powerful feudal fiefdom. While plundered early in the 15th century, the monastery was restored in 1469, when Rilski's relics were returned from Veliko Tärnovo. Rila Monastery was vital to the preservation of Bulgarian culture and religion under the Ottomans, who destroyed it several times.

An accident, however, caused Rila's greatest modern catastrophe: an 1833 fire nearly engulfed all monastic buildings. The inundation of funds from Bulgarian and foreign donors allowed reconstruction to commence within a year. In 1961 the Communist regime proclaimed Rila a national museum and 22 years later it became a Unesco World Heritage site.

⊙ Sights

FREE **Rila Monastery** MONASTERY
(⊙6am-9pm) Bulgaria's most famous monastery is set in a towering forested valley. The 300 monk cells span four levels of colourful balconies, overlooking a large misshapen courtyard, while the Nativity Church, built in the 1830s, contains 1200 magnificent murals.

Museum MUSEUM
(Rila Monastery; 8 lv; ⊙8am-5pm) The monastery's museum, in the compound's southeastern corner, contains 18th- and 19th-century ecclesiastical paraphernalia, prints and Bibles. The centrepiece is the astonishing Rila Cross – a double-sided crucifix carved by a certain Brother Raphael between 1790 and 1802. It's incised in miniature with 140 biblical scenes and inscriptions, and about 650 human figures.

Ethnographic Museum MUSEUM
(8 lv; ⊙8am-5pm) Beside the Samokov gate in the northeast of the monastic compound, this museum displays regional folk costumes, textiles and crafts.

Church of Rozhdestvo Bogorodichno CHURCH
(Church of the Nativity; Rila Monastery) This is Bulgaria's grandest monastery church. Built between 1834 and 1837, the structure is crowned by three domes. Its outside walls are covered with frescos both vivid and harrowing (or humorous, depending on your disposition).

They depict hell, where demons with whips, chains and pitchforks torture sinners in various states of woe and undress. The happier paintings depict the virtuous, accompanied by angels and saints.

🛏 Sleeping & Eating

Hotel Tsarev Vrah HOTEL €
(☑2280; www.tzarevvrah.com; s/d/tr 35/45/60 lv) On monastery-owned lands, the renovated Tsarev Vrah has clean, though not terribly well-lit rooms. Most balconies offer forest views, but you can request a monastery-view room. The hotel cooks decent renditions of Bulgarian cuisine (mains 6 lv to 11 lv), and the leafy garden tables are popular for a summer repast. It's signposted about 150m from Samokov gate.

Rila Monastery's Rooms MONASTERY €
(☑0896 872 010; www.rilamonastery.pmg-blg.com; r 30-60 lv) Rila Monastery offers older, dorm-style rooms (communal facilities have toilets, but no showers), and some nicer en suite rooms. In summer, the latter can be booked up by midday, so call ahead or arrive early. The reception office (in the southern wing) handles bookings.

Rila Restaurant BULGARIAN €
(mains 7-12 lv; ⊙8am-midnight) This restaurant, specialising in Bulgarian grills and local fish, is the area's most atmospheric, set in a traditionally decorated 19th-century building.

❶ Getting There & Away

Most travellers visit Rila Monastery from Sofia or Blagoevgrad. From Sofia's Ovcha Kupel bus station there is one daily morning bus (17 lv, 2½ hours) which returns in the afternoon. However, the monastery gets five daily buses from Rila village (4 lv), making the latter a better transport hub.

For monastery day trips by bus from Sofia you need to leave before 8am for Dupnitsa (1½ hours) from the central bus station or Ovcha Kupel bus station. Then grab the next bus to Rila village or monastery and repeat the process back to Dupnitsa, which also has train connections to Sofia.

Melnik   Мелник

☑07437 / POP 385

Officially Bulgaria's smallest town, tiny Melnik – hidden by jutting pyramid-style clay-sand mountains at the dramatic southwest end of the Pirins – is one of the country's most famous wine centres, and also has great day hikes. Family-run *mehanas* (taverns) boast their own barrels of blood-red Melnik, the unique local varietal, which is sold in plastic jugs on the dirt streets. A century ago, Melnik was home to 20,000

BULGARIA MELNIK

MELNIK'S RUINS

Of Melnik's original 70 churches only 40, mostly ruins, survive. The 10th-century **Bolyaskata Kâshta**, one of Bulgaria's oldest homes, is in ruin except for some partially standing walls. You can peer in and enjoy great views too. Nearby is the ruin of the 19th-century **Sveti Antoni Church** (also not signposted).

A signposted path leads to the **Sveti Nikolai Church** (1756), and to the Despot Slav's ruined **Slavova Krepost Fortress**. Both are visible from the Bolyaskata Kâshta ruins, or from near the Lumparova Kâshta Hotel. The trail veers east along the ridge about 300m to the **Sveta Zona Chapel**.

The **Turkish Baths** are difficult to recognise, standing just before the Mehana Mencheva Kâshta tavern. **Sveti Petâr and Pavel Church** (1840) is down from the Hotel Melnik's car park. Just below the Kordopulov House, the 15th-century **Sveta Varvara Church** has retained its walls and floor, and displays icons where visitors light candles. The caretaker at Sveti Nikolai Church can open the closed churches.

people – mostly Greeks – until much of it burned down during the 1912–13 Balkan Wars. The population never recovered and you can still see the ruins of many old family homes on the village outskirts. From the bus stop, roads run on either side of a largely dry creek into town.

☉ Sights

The major sights here, unsurprisingly, are wineries. Melnik's wines, celebrated for more than 600 years, include the signature dark red, *Shiroka Mehichka Loza*. Shops and stands dot Melnik's cobblestone paths, with reds and whites for 3 lv to 4 lv and up. Try to sample first and buy from the refrigerator; avoid bottles displayed in the sun all day.

Mitko Manolev Winery
WINERY

(incl tasting 2 lv; ☉9am-dusk) For the most atmospheric adventure in *degustatsia* (wine tasting), clamber up the slippery cobblestones to Mitko Manolev Winery. It's basically a cellar dug into the rocks, and a hut with tables and chairs outside, with both reds and whites available. It's along the hillside trail between the Bolyaskata Kâshta ruins and the Kordopulov House.

Kordopulov House
MUSEUM

(☎265; admission 2 lv; ☉8am-8pm) Built in 1754 and a former home of one of Melnik's foremost wine merchants, this is a truly impressive structure. The lovely sitting rooms have been carefully restored, and boast 19th-century murals, stained-glass windows and exquisite carved wooden ceilings, plus couches along the walls, bedecked with colourful pillows.

🛏 Sleeping

Private rooms (15 lv to 20 lv per person) usually come with shared bathrooms. Look for the 'Rooms to Sleep' signs.

TOP CHOICE Hotel Bolyarka
HOTEL €€

(☎2383; www.bolyarka.hit.bg; s/d/apt incl breakfast 40/60/130 lv; P ❉ 🛜) The spiffy Bolyarka has elegant and well-decorated rooms, and apartments with fireplaces. Sauna and massage treatments are available, but the authentic Ottoman-era *hammam* (Turkish bath) is for viewing only. The on-site restaurant is excellent. Bolyarka is about 300m straight down the main street on the right-hand side.

Hotel Bulgari
HOTEL €

(☎2215; www.hotelbulgari.net; s/d 30/50 lv; 🛜) This imposing new hotel, located after the square on the left, seems out of place. But the rooms are shiny, spacious and surprisingly good value. The cavernous restaurant is more suited to banquets than intimate dining, though.

🍴 Eating

Melnik's best eats are at hotel/pension restaurants, though other worthy spots abound. Aside from the local wine, try the traditional *banitsa*, a local speciality, and the mountain river trout.

TOP CHOICE Mehana Mencheva Kâshta
BULGARIAN €

(☎339; mains 6-11 lv; ☉10am-11.30pm) This tiny tavern, down towards the end of the village, has an atmospheric upper porch overlooking the main street. It's popular with locals and does the full run of Bulgarian dishes.

Chinarite Restaurant BULGARIAN €€
(📞0887 992 191; mains 5-8 lv; 🛜) Chinarite
and **Loznitsite Tavern** (📞283; mains 5-8 lv)
are next door midway up the main road, by
the bridge. The former also serves homemade Melnik *banitsa* and has a small wine
cellar for tasting, while the latter has an
inviting, vine-covered outdoor setting and
good Bulgarian fare.

❶ Getting There & Away

One daily direct bus connects Melnik with Sofia
(17 lv, four hours) though times vary. One daily
direct bus serves Blagoevgrad (9 lv, two hours).
Three daily minibuses go from Sandanski to
Melnik, continuing to Rozhen.

Bansko   Банско

📞0749 / POP 8562

Bansko is the big daddy of Bulgarian ski resorts. With trails from 900m to 2600m high,
and with more than 100 hotels and pensions, the once-quiet village has more beds
than permanent residents. In winter, Brits,
Russians, Bulgarians and others come to ski
(and party) in this sunny yet snow-filled resort. In summer things are quieter (except for
an August jazz festival), and the action shifts
to the leafy central square.

◎ Sights

**House Museum of
Nikola Vaptsarov** MUSEUM
(📞8304; pl Nikola Vaptsarov; admission 3 lv;
⊙8am-noon & 2-5.30pm) This house museum
was the birthplace of Nikola Vaptsarov
(1909–42), a respected antifascist poet and
activist. Influenced by communist ideology
while a student, his populist writings caused
his arrest and torture by the wartime fascist government; he wrote his most famous
poem while awaiting execution. Period decor, plus photographs, documents and Vaptsarov's personal belongings are exhibited.

Velyanov's House MUSEUM
(📞4181; ul Velyan Ognev 5; admission 3 lv; ⊙9am-
noon & 2-5pm Mon-Fri) Velyanov's House
features elaborately painted scenes and
woodcarvings from the 'Bansko School' of
carving, icon and fresco painting.

Sveta Troitsa Church CHURCH
(pl Vâzhrazhdane; ⊙7am-7pm) Sveta Troitsa
Church (1835) is surrounded by a 1m-thick
and 4m-high stone wall, and features magnificent wooden floors and faded murals.

It also hosts Bansko's major landmark: the
30m-high **clock tower** (1850). Until Sofia's
Alexander Nevsky Cathedral was completed
in 1912, it was Bulgaria's largest church.

✦ Activities

Bansko boasts Bulgaria's most reliable skiing conditions. The snow, often 2m thick
between mid-December and mid-April,
sometimes lasts until mid-May. Lifts and
slopes are modern and well-maintained,
while snow-making equipment works during above-freezing temperatures.

Bansko also boasts a state-of-the-art gondola (carrying eight people). The trip lasts
20 minutes and takes skiers directly from
town and onto the slopes at **Baderishka
Polyana**, with pubs, restaurants and ski
schools. At time of research, a second gondola was expected to open here in 2013.
From Baderishka Polyana, another chairlift
accesses more trails at Shiligarnika, which
has four chairlifts and five draglifts. Bansko
has 10 chairlifts and 16 draglifts.

Chalin Vrag I and II are the most famous
of Bansko's 15 (and counting) ski runs, which
total 67km, along with 8km of cross-country
trails. The total trail coverage comprises
35% for beginners, 40% for intermediates,
and 25% advanced.

An all-day Bansko lift pass costs 70 lv,
though prices rise yearly.

Pirin Sport (📞8537; ul Gen St Kovachev 8)
rents ski equipment (from about 55 lv per
day) and snowboarding gear, and provides
instructors for both sports. Similar services
are provided by **Intersport** (📞4876), and
some hotels near the gondola. Intersport
rents mountain bikes in summer.

⬛ Sleeping

Bansko accommodation ranges from simple private rooms to five-star luxury hotels.
Discreet camping is possible in the Pirin National Park. Most foreigners come on package tours, but independent bookings are
possible; the Bansko Tourist Information
Center recommends rooms for all budgets.
Book ahead for ski season, when rates are
25% higher.

Hotel Avalon HOTEL €€
(📞88 399; www.avalonhotel-bulgaria.com; ul Eltepe
4; s/d/tr/ste €20/30/40/55; 🅿@) A friendly,
British-run place popular with budget travellers, the Avalon has airy rooms, some with
spas, plus a restaurant serving French and
Italian fare. The owners also organise local

excursions. It's in the backstreets before the centre, to the left if coming from the bus/train stations (a five-minute walk).

Hadzhiradonova Kâshta   PENSION €
(☑8276; ul Buirov 7; s/d from 25/30 lv) An atmospheric house with large, traditionally furnished rooms with sheepskin bedspreads and spotless bathrooms. It overlooks a pretty courtyard, east of pl Vazrazhdane.

✖ Eating

Bansko's traditional *mehanas* offer regional delicacies and excellent local wine. Some close in summer.

Mehana Pri Dedo   BULGARIAN €€
(pl Nikola Vaptsarov; mains 6-9 lv; ☺8am-midnight; ☞) This main-square *mehana* serves good international and Bulgarian fare at prices half those of the bigger restaurants (rates don't increase in winter, either). There's an airy deck in summer and, in winter a cosy interior where a live guitarist croons pop classics. The laid-back owner will drive guests to their hotel for free if they've had too much to drink.

Mehana Tumbeva Kâshta   BULGARIAN €€
(☑0899 888 993; ul Pirin 7; mains 5-11 lv; ☺8am-midnight) This small and friendly bar-and-grill rests in a secluded garden (the cosy interior functions in winter) between the two central squares. It offers meat specialities and lighter fare.

❶ Information

Bansko Tourist Information Center (☑88 580; infocenter@bansko.bg; pl Nikola Vaptsarov 1; ☺9am-5pm) This centrally located tourist centre has friendly and informed staff who can advise on accommodation, cultural and outdoor activities, and upcoming events. They sell Bansko town maps (4 lv), with hotels, restaurants and banks listed on the front, and the Pirin National Park map on back; the similarly priced winter map features Bansko's ski trails, gondola and lifts too.

Pirin National Park Office (www.pirin-np.com; ul Bulgaria 4) Informs about long Pirin Mountain treks.

❶ Getting There & Away

Fifteen daily buses serve Bansko from Sofia (17 lv, three hours), most via Blagoevgrad. Buses from Blagoevgrad cost 6 lv. Several more buses travelling to Gotse Delchev stop at Bansko.

From Bansko, four or five daily buses serve Blagoevgrad (two hours). Two morning buses serve Plovdiv (16 lv, 3½ hours). Between mid-June and mid-September, three daily minibuses (4 lv) serve Hizha Banderitsa.

The coolest route to Bansko, however, is by narrow-gauge railway. This is the last such route in Bulgaria, from Bansko to Septemvri station in five hours (5 lv, four daily), from where you continue west to Sofia or east to Plovdiv and beyond.

Three daily trains depart Bansko for Septemvri. The ticket office only sells tickets 10 minutes before departure time, so ascertain these times ahead.

THRACIAN PLAIN & THE RODOPIS

Sitting in the wide-open Thracian plain, Plovdiv lies just within the cusp of the thickly forested Rodopi Mountains rising to the south. Like the Pirin and Rila, the Rodopis have good hikes and offer culturally rich villages. Smolyan is a key Rodopi hub from where you can travel further into the Rodopi range or east to out-of-the-way Kârdzhali to see the Thracian remains of Perperikon.

Plovdiv   Пловдив

☑032 / POP 338,184

With its art galleries, winding cobbled streets and bohemian cafes, Plovdiv (*Plovdiv*) equals Sofia in culture and is a determined rival in nightlife as well. Being a smaller and less stressful city, Plovdiv is also great for walking. As a major university town, Plovdiv has a lively, exuberant spirit.

Plovdiv's appeal derives from its lovely Old Town, largely restored to its mid-19th-century appearance and marked by winding cobblestone streets. It's literally packed with atmospheric house museums and art galleries and – unlike many other cities with 'Old Towns' – has eminent artists still living and working within its tranquil confines. The neighbourhood boasts Thracian, Roman, Byzantine and Bulgarian antiquities, most impressive being the Roman amphitheatres – the best preserved in the Balkans and still used for performances.

◉ Sights

Revival-era wooden-shuttered homes lean over narrow cobbled lanes in this hilly neighbourhood and about a dozen renovated *kâshta* (traditional homes) are now kept as museums. Also here are several art galleries, a couple of museums and some of Plovdiv's most interesting churches.

Roman Amphitheatre
HISTORIC SITE

(ul Hemus; 3 lv; ⊘8am-6pm) Plovdiv's magnificent 2nd-century AD Amphitheatre, built by Emperor Trajan was only uncovered during a freak landslide in 1972. It once held about 6000 spectators. Now largely restored, it again hosts large-scale special events and concerts. Visitors can admire the amphitheatre from several lookouts along ul Hemus, or from the cafes situated above.

Roman Stadium
HISTORIC STADIUM

This once huge stadium is mostly hidden under the pedestrian mall. However, in 2012 the subterranean southern back end was renovated and stairways from different sides now allow entrance into the gleaming rows. A small shop below provides some info and souvenirs.

Ethnographical Museum
MUSEUM

(🖉625 654; ul Dr Chomakov 2; adult/student 5/1 lv; ⊘9am-noon & 2-5.30pm Tue-Thu, Sat & Sun, 2-5.30pm Fri) This intriguing museum houses 40,000 exhibits, including folk costumes, musical instruments, jewellery and traditional crafts such as weaving, metalworking, winemaking and beekeeping. Tools displayed range from grape-crushers and wine-measures to apparatus used for distilling attar of roses.

Historical Museum
MUSEUM

(🖉623 378; ul Lavrenov 1; 2 lv; ⊘9am-noon & 1-5.30pm Mon-Sat) The Historical Museum concentrates on the 1876 April Uprising and the massacre of Bulgarians at Batak, which directly led to Russia declaring war on Turkey the next year. Built in 1848 by Dimitâr Georgiadi, it's also called the *Georgiadi Kâshta*.

Archaeological Museum
MUSEUM

(🖉624 339; pl Saedinenie 1; adult/child under 7yr 5 lv/free) Thracian and Roman pottery and jewellery, and ecclesiastical artefacts, icons and liturgical paraphernalia are on display here, along with a collection of 60,000 archaeological items.

Permanent Exhibition of Dimitar Kirov
GALLERY

(🖉635 381; Kiril Nektariev 17; adult/student 5/1 lv; ⊘9am-5pm Mon-Fri) This special place, housed in a grand Old Town mansion where Plovdiv's budding artists worked in the 1960s, celebrates the life and works of Dimitar Kirov, who died in 2008 at the age of 73. Arguably Plovdiv's most original artist, Kirov's works are marked by bold and vivid uses of colour, from mosaics to abstracts.

Church of Sveti Konstantin & Elena
CHURCH

(ul Sâborna 24; ⊘8am-7pm) Plovdiv's oldest church, this was built over a late Roman church. It's dedicated to Constantine the Great, the 4th-century emperor who made Orthodox Christianity the state religion, and his mother, Sveta Helena. The current church, however, dates to 1832. The wonderful iconostasis was painted by Zahari Zograf between 1836 and 1840. The covered portico features sumptuous frescoes.

Dzhumaya Mosque
MOSQUE

(pl Dzhumaya; ⊘6am-11pm) The largely renovated Dzhumaya Mosque, one of the Balkans' oldest, dates from the mid-15th century. With a 23m-high minaret, it was the largest of Plovdiv's more than 50 Ottoman-era mosques, though its thunder has slightly been stolen by the renovated Roman Stadium remains opposite.

🛏 Sleeping

🏆 Hotel Renaissance
BOUTIQUE HOTEL €€

(🖉266 966; www.renaissance-bg.com; pl Vâzhrazhdane 1; s/d incl breakfast from 115/145 lv; 🅿❄@🖝) This lovely boutique hotel between the Old Town and the main shopping streets aims to recreate a National Revival-era home through its intricate Plovdiv-style floral wall and ceiling paintings. Each room is unique, with handsome wood floors. Some boast period furniture. (Note the Arabic-language property document from 1878). Friendly, English-speaking owner Dimitar Vassilev is a fount of local knowledge.

Hikers Hostel
HOSTEL €

(🖉0896 764 854; www.hikers-hostel.org; ul Sâborna 53; incl breakfast tent/dm/s/d without bathroom 12/20/43/48 lv; @🖝) The ideal place for independent travellers to chill in Plovdiv's Old Town, Hikers has comfy couches, outside tables, and sleeping choices ranging from tents and dorms to lofts and private rooms. There's free wi-fi, a computer, lockers for luggage, and laundry service (5 lv). If full, they offer (less appealing) private rooms and dorms near Dzhumaya Mosque.

Hebros Hotel
BOUTIQUE HOTEL €€€

(🖉260 180; www.hebros-hotel.com; ul K Stoilov 51; s/apt incl breakfast 200/240 lv; ❄🖝) This two-century-old mansion in the Old Town has a subdued elegance in its 10 well-furnished, spacious rooms – it's a bit pricier than others, but tremendously atmospheric. There's

Plovdiv

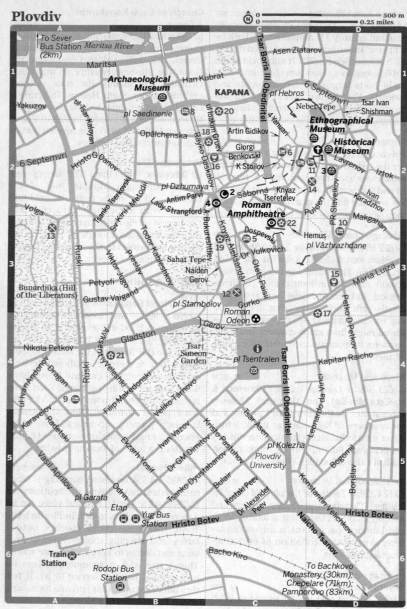

a back courtyard, spa and sauna (25 lv extra), plus a great restaurant.

Dali Art Hotel
BOUTIQUE HOTEL €€€

(☎621 530; ul Otets Paisii 11; d/ste/apt incl breakfast 100/130/150 lv; ❋❦) This intimate hotel off the mall has eight airy rooms, including two apartments, with appropriately minimalist decor. However, it's most distinguished by its friendly and relaxed staff – not to mention original works by Dali.

Plovdiv

Hotel Leipzig HOTEL €€

(☎654 000; www.leipzig.bg; bul Ruski 70; s/d/apt from 82/100/124 lv; [P][✱][@][🛜]) This sharply renovated old fixture has more than 60 appealing modern rooms and apartments designed with eclectic, colourful decor uncommon in a place that doubles as a business hotel and wedding banquet venue. Some rooms have great views of the Hill of the Liberators, and there's a restaurant, bar and casino.

Plovdiv Guest House HOSTEL €

(☎622 432; www.plovdivguest.com; ul Sâborna 20; dm/s/d/q €9/25/30/45; [✱][@][🛜]) Another backpacker option on Sâborna, this offers clean

and bright dorms with 10, eight and four beds, and there's one spacious attic double. Dorms feature their own self-contained and modern bathroom/shower. There's an outdoor cafe out the back, above the ancient Roman wall.

Hotel Elite HOTEL €€

(☎624 537; ul Rayko Daskalov 53; d/ste 60/100 lv; [✱]) The modern and reasonably priced hotel is on the corner of bul 6 Septemvri, just west of the Kapana bar district. Rooms are insulated from road noise, and it's clean and comfortable. The suites, however, are really glorified doubles.

✕ Eating

Puldin Restaurant INTERNATIONAL €€€

(☎631 720; ul Knyaz Tseretelev 8; mains 8-15 lv; ⊙9am-midnight; 🛜) The magical Puldin is one of Plovdiv's most atmospheric restaurants. In one dining room, the famous whirling dervishes of the Ottoman Empire once whirled themselves into ecstatic exhaustion, while in the cellar hall Byzantine-era walls and Roman artefacts predominate.

Hebros Hotel Restaurant BULGARIAN €€€

(☎625 929; ul K Stoilov 51; mains 11-22 lv; 🛜) The upscale restaurant of the eponymous hotel enjoys a secluded garden setting and does excellent and innovative Bulgarian cuisine, such as rabbit with plums, braised trout, and pork with blue cheese.

Restaurant Renaissance INTERNATIONAL €€

(pl Vâzhrazhdane 1; mains 9-17 lv; ⊙10am-10:30pm Tue-Sun) The restaurant of the Hotel Renaissance cooks up a wide range of inventive appetisers (duck lung stuffed with apple, anyone?), plus grills, risottos, and fresh fish from the Aegean. The local wine list is particularly strong, and the service is friendly and attentive.

Malâk Bunardzhik BULGARIAN €€

(☎446 140; ul Volga 1; mains 5-10 lv; 🛜) Quality Bulgarian cuisine is served at this popular place with garden dining and live music most nights.

♟ Drinking

Several good places occupy the district called Kapana, meaning 'the trap', referring to its tight streets (north of pl Dzhumaya, between ul Rayko Daskalov to the west and bul Tsar Boris Obedinitel to the east).

TOP CHOICE Naylona
BAR

(☑0889 496 750; ul Giorgi Benkovski 8, Kapana; ⊕noon-4am; ☎) They say the owners of this Kapana dive bar purposely didn't fix the roof so that the rain would trickle in; whatever the story, this damp, bare-bones place usually playing classic (and other) rock remains the unwashed, long-haired antithesis of Plovdiv style.

Art Bar Maria Luiza
BAR

(bul Maria Luiza 15; ⊕8am-4am; ☎) Too pretty to be just a dive bar, the Maria Luisa has dedicated owners who keep adapting the decor to suit their whims. The colourful downstairs is particularly stylish, vaguely reminiscent of 1920s Paris.

Dreams
CAFE €

(☑627 142; pl Stambolov; sandwiches around 2 lv; ⊕9am-11pm; ☎) This excellent and popular cafe is the perfect place to relax; sit before the giant, gushing fountain on a balmy summer's day. It serves good cakes, along with numerous alcoholic and nonalcoholic drinks.

☆ Entertainment

Much of the nightlife lingers around the Kapana district, around ul Benkovski north of Dzhumaya mosque.

Nightclubs

Petnoto
CLUB

(☑0898 542 787; ul Ioakim Gruev 36, Kapana; ⊕8am-6am; ☎) The pinstriped Petnoto combines a bar, small restaurant and a stage where Bulgarian bands and DJs perform.

City Place
CLUB

(☑0888 715 657; bul Maria Luiza 43; ⊕11pm-6am; ☎) Plovdiv's longest-running nightclub was formerly called Paparazzi. In its current incarnation it has seen some slick renovations though the DJ-driven house music, *chalga* (Bulgarian pop music) and hip-hop playlist remain the same.

Infinity
CLUB

(☑0888 281 431; Bratya Pulievi 4, Kapana; ⊕10am-late; ☎) Varied music, from pop to dance, is played at this club in Kapana favoured by students.

TRANSPORT FROM PLOVDIV

Bus

DESTINATION	PRICE (LV)	DURATION (HR)	FREQUENCY
Bansko	14	3½	2 daily
Blagoevgrad	13-15	3	3 daily
Burgas (private)	19	4	2 daily
Hisar	2.20	1	12 daily
Karlovo	8	1½	half-hourly
Ruse (private)	19	6	1 daily
Sliven	14	3	5 daily
Sofia	9	2½	half-hourly
Varna	22	7	2 daily
Veliko Tărnovo (private)	17	4½	3 daily

Train

DESTINATION	PRICE (LV)	DURATION (HR)	FREQUENCY
Burgas	14.60	6	6 daily
Karlovo	3.90	2	5 daily
Sofia	1st-/2nd-class 9/7 (express)	2½	14 daily

Theatre & Opera

Plovdiv Opera House   OPERA
(☑632 231; opera@thracia.net; ul Avksentiy Veleshki)
Classic and modern European operas are performed in Bulgarian at this venerable hall.

**Nikolai Masalitinov
Dramatic Theatre**   THEATRE
(☑224 867; ul Knyaz Aleksandâr 38) One of Bulgaria's top theatres, it features everything from Shakespeare to Ibsen (usually, in Bulgarian).

Roman Amphitheatre   THEATRE
(ul Hemus) The amphitheatre hosts Plovdiv's annual Verdi Festival (June), plus other summertime opera, ballet and music performances.

❶ Information

Exchange offices line ul Knyaz Aleksandâr and ul Ivan Vazov. Most close on Sunday. ATMs are widespread, including around pl Dzhumaya and ul Knyaz Aleksandâr, though not in the Old Town's upper reaches.

Internet Café Speed (2nd fl, bul Maria Luiza 1)

Main Post Office (pl Tsentralen; ☺7am-7pm Mon-Sat, to 11am Sun) Has several computers with online access.

Patrick Penov Personal Trips & Tours (☑0887 364 711; www.guide-bg.com) Licensed tour guide Svetlomir 'Patrick' Penov has two decades of experience leading individual and small group tours all over Bulgaria, covering everything from gastronomy and wine to churches and culture.

Tourist Information Centre (tic@plovdiv.bg; pl Tsentralen 1; ☺9am-7pm) This helpful centre by the post office provides maps, finds local accommodation and more.

❶ Getting There & Away

Bus

Plovdiv's main station is **Yug bus station** (☑626 937), with public and private buses operating. Yug is diagonally opposite the train station and a 15-minute walk from the centre (a taxi costs 5 lv to 7 lv). Alternatively, local buses (80 stotinki) stop across the main street outside the station, on bul Hristo Botev.

The **Sever bus station** (☑953 011), in the northern suburbs, has one daily bus to Pleven (23 lv), Ruse (12 lv), Koprivshtitsa (6 lv) and Veliko Târnovo (20 lv).

Etap (☑632 082; Yug bus station) sells bus tickets to İstanbul (40 lv), Athens (140 lv) and more.

Train

Plovdiv sits on the major Sofia–Burgas line and has many trains. Plovdiv's **train station** (bul Hristo Botev) is well organised, though the staff don't speak English. Computer screens at the station entrance and in the underpass leading to the platforms list recent arrivals and upcoming departures. The luggage storage (2 lv per bag for 24 hours) office is always open.

Smolyan   Смолян

☑0301 / POP 30,283

The longest (10km) and highest town in Bulgaria (1010m), Smolyan is actually an amalgamation of four villages, and the southern Rodopi Mountains' administrative centre. The steep and forested mountains rise abruptly on its southern flank, lending a lovely backdrop to a town that's otherwise rather gritty. As in most of the Rodopi region, there's a notable Pomak Muslim population here. It's an alternative place to stay for skiing Pamporovo and Chepelare, though certainly not the most beautiful one. Smolyan is also a base for exploring the seven **Smolyan Lakes**, the **caves** of Golubovitsa, partially underwater, and Uhlovitsa, with its bizarre rock formations.

◉ Sights

Planetarium   PLANETARIUM
(☑83 074; bul Bulgaria 20; 5 lv) Bulgaria's biggest planetarium, about 200m west of Hotel Smolyan, offers a spectacular show (35 to 40 minutes) with commentary in English, French or German at 2pm Monday to Saturday, and in Bulgarian at other times. The foreign-language shows are for groups of five or more; otherwise, you'll pay 25 lv for a solo viewing.

Historical Museum   MUSEUM
(☑62 727; Dicho Petrov 3; 5 lv; ☺9am-noon & 1-5pm Mon-Sat) Behind the civic centre, this museum's exhibits include Palaeolithic artefacts, Thracian armour and weaponry, Rodopi weaving and woodcarving, plus numerous traditional musical instruments and folk costumes (most notably the fantastical Kuker outfits worn at New Year celebrations). Upstairs has photos and models of traditional buildings.

⌯ Sleeping

The tourist office arranges private accommodation (about 20 lv per person). Ask about camping in the hills outside town.

Hotel Kiparis A   HOTEL €€
(☑64 040; www.hotelkiparis.eu; bul Bulgaria 3a; s/d/apt incl breakfast 50/75/110 lv; ❋☎) This

WORTH A TRIP

BACHKOVO MONASTERY

About 30km south of Plovdiv, the magnificent **Bachkovo Monastery** (Bachkovo; admission free; ⊙6am-10pm) was founded in 1083 by Georgian brothers Gregory and Abasius Bakuriani, aristocrats in Byzantine military service. The monastery flourished during the Second Bulgarian Empire (1185–1396), but was ransacked by Turks in the 15th and 16th centuries. Major reconstructions began in the mid-17th century. Bachkovo's now Bulgaria's second-largest monastery, after Rila.

In the courtyard, the **Church of Sveta Bogoroditsa** (1604) contains frescos by Zahari Zograf from the early 1850s. Other highlights include the 17th-century iconostasis, more 19th-century murals and a much-cherished icon of the Virgin, allegedly painted by St Luke, though actually dating from the 14th century. Pilgrims regularly pray before the silver-encased icon.

The monastery's southern side houses the former **refectory** (1601). The walls are filled with stunning frescos relating the monastery's history. A gate beside the refectory leads to a (rarely open) courtyard; this leads to the **Church of Sveti Nikolai** (1836). During the 1840s, Zograf painted the superb *Last Judgment* inside the chapel; note the condemned, nervous-looking Turks on the right and Zograf's self-portrait (no beard) in the upper-left corner.

Around 50m from the monastery entrance, the restored **Ossuary** features wonderful medieval murals, but remains closed.

A prominent explanation board provides monastic history (in English, French and German), and a map of **hiking trails** to nearby villages. A helpful guidebook (15 lv) is available too.

To get here, take any bus (3 lv) to Smolyan from Plovdiv's **Rodopi bus station** (⊉657 828), disembark at the turn-off about 1.2km south of Bachkovo village and walk about 500m uphill. There are also direct buses half-hourly.

comfortable hotel with an excellent spa centre has plush and light-toned rooms, plus all the mod cons.

Three Fir Trees House   PENSION €
(⊉81 028; www.trieli.hit.bg; ul Srednogorets 1; s/d/apt without bathroom 30/40/80 lv; @🕾) Some 200m east of the main bus station, this relaxed family-run place has well-maintained rooms. It's signposted, down the steps from bul Bulgaria. Bathrooms are shared. There's an excellent, varied breakfast (5 lv), and the helpful, multilingual owner arranges tours and rental cars, plus a cheap laundry service.

✕ Eating

Rodopski Kat   BULGARIAN €€
(bul Bulgaria 3; mains 5-8 lv; ⊙7am-2am) This nice restaurant, wedged between hotels in the centre, is excellent for traditional Rodopean fare.

Riben Dar   SEAFOOD €€
(⊉63 220; ul Snezhanka 16; mains 6-12 lv) In the western neighbourhood of Nevyasta, this is great for delicious fresh fish, such as Rodopi Mountain trout. Take a taxi (3 lv to 5 lv).

ℹ Getting There & Away

Most buses to/from Smolyan use the **main bus station** (⊉63 104; bul Bulgaria) at Smolyan's western end. Four daily buses serve Sofia (28 lv, 3½ hours) and hourly buses serve Plovdiv (17 lv, 2½ to three hours), via Chepelare (6 lv, one hour) and Pamporovo (4 lv, 30 minutes).

From near the station, local buses 2 and 3 (80 stotinki, every 20 minutes) serve the centre. Walk left out of the station and turn left up a double set of stairs; after 50m, you'll see the stop on the left. The taxi rank is further down the street. By taxi, it's around 3 lv to the tourist information centre.

CENTRAL BULGARIA

Bulgaria's central heartland is vital to the national consciousness for its role in the 18th- and 19th-century National Revival; this legacy lingers in the period architecture of Koprivshtitsa, and at battle sites such as the forested Shipka Pass. Central Bulgaria is ideal for hiking, climbing, caving, horseback riding and other outdoor activities in the Stara Planina mountains. The lowlands are famous too for the Valley of Roses, near Kazanlâk, an important producer of rose oil.

Most impressive, however, is Veliko Târnovo, once capital of the Bulgarian tsars. Built into steep hills and bisected by a river, its fortress is among Europe's most impressive.

Koprivshtitsa
Копривщица

📞07184 / POP 2900

This unique museum village, nestled between Karlovo and Sofia, is a perfectly preserved hamlet filled with Bulgarian National Revival-period architecture, cobblestone streets, and bridges that arc gently over a lovely brook. Nearly 400 buildings of architectural and historical significance are protected by government decree, some of them restored churches and house museums containing fascinating collections of decor and implements from yesteryear. Some of the traditional homes function as guesthouses or restaurants, most loaded with traditional ambience, making Koprivshtitsa a romantic getaway, too.

◉ Sights

Koprivshtitsa boasts six house museums. Some are closed either on Monday or Tuesday. To buy a combined ticket for all (adults/students 5/3 lv) visit the souvenir shop **Kupchinitsa**, near the Tourist Information Centre.

Oslekov House   HISTORIC BUILDING
(ul Gereniloto 4; ⊙closed Mon) Built between 1853 and 1856 by Oslekov, a rich merchant killed in the line of duty during the 1876 April Uprising, this is arguably the best example of Bulgarian National Revival–period architecture in Koprivshtitsa. It has a triple-arched entrance, spacious interior, stylish furniture and brightly coloured walls.

Kableshkov House   HISTORIC BUILDING
(ul Todor Kableshkov 8; ⊙closed Mon) A well-travelled wealthy local, Todor Kableshkov (1851–76) is revered as having (probably) been the person who fired the first shot in the 1876 uprising against the Turks. This, his glorious former home, dates back to 1845 and has exhibits about the April Uprising.

🛏 Sleeping

The tourist information centre can help arrange private rooms (40 lv to 50 lv).

Hotel Trayanov Kâshta   GUESTHOUSE €
(📞3750; ul Gereniloto 5; d/tr/apt 40/50/60 lv) Perhaps the most atmospheric place in

town, this house with a garden inside an enclosed courtyard has only a few rooms, all traditionally furnished and colourful. The upstairs balcony overlooking the back lawn is a great place for an evening drink.

Bonchova House   GUESTHOUSE €
(📞2614; ul Tumangelova Cheta 26; d/apt 30/50 lv) Close to the Kalachev Bridge, this cosy place has two bright, modern rooms and an apartment; the common room is relaxing and has a working fireplace. Breakfast is 5 lv extra.

✗ Eating

Traditional *kâshtas* can be found on side streets. They serve meaty meals, but some keep seasonal hours.

Dyado Liben   BULGARIAN €
(📞2109; ul Hadzhi Nencho Palaveev 47; mains 4-9 lv; ⊙11am-midnight; 📶) Astonishingly big, this traditional restaurant housed in a mansion dating from 1852 is a wonderfully atmospheric place for an evening meal. Management says it can seat 100 people, all in a warren of halls graced with ornately painted walls. Find it just across the bridge leading from the main square inside the facing courtyard.

❶ Information

There are ATMs and a post office/telephone centre inside the village centre.

Tourist Information Centre (www.koprivshtitsa.info; pl 20 April; ⊙10am-1pm & 2-7pm) This very helpful and friendly centre, in a small maroon building on the main square, provides local information and can organise private accommodation from 25 lv per person.

❶ Getting There & Away

Getting to Koprivshtitsa is a bit of a challenge. Being 9km north of the village, the train station requires a shuttle bus (2 lv, 15 minutes), which isn't always timed to meet incoming trains. Trains do come from Sofia (11 lv, 2½ hours, four daily) and connections can be made for Plovdiv and other points, such as Burgas, which gets a daily train (18 lv, five hours). Alternatively, Koprivshtitsa's bus stop is central and has more frequent connections, including five daily buses to Sofia (13 lv, two hours) and one to Plovdiv (12 lv, two hours).

Kazanlâk   Казанлък

📞0431 / POP 46,990

A bit rough around the edges, Kazanlâk is nevertheless a fascinating town where Bulgaria's various ethnic and religious groups commingle amicably. Life revolves around the loud central square, pl Sevtopolis. Most famous, however, are the archaeological remains from the area's ancient Thracian civilisation.

Kazanlâk is also the jumping-off point for journeys across the Valley of Roses (Rozovata Dolina), a wide plain blooming with roses, responsible for more than 60% of the world's supply of fragrant rose oil. Crossing the plain, one ascends to Shipka village and **Shipka Pass**, site of a decisive showdown in the 1877–78 Russo-Turkish War.

◉ Sights

Thracian Tomb of Kazanlâk   MUSEUM
(Tyulbe Park; admission 20 lv; ⊘10am-5pm) In hilly Tyulbe Park is a very large and very locked tomb. Built in the 4th century BC for a Thracian ruler, it was discovered in 1944 during a bomb shelter construction, and is now a Unesco World Heritage site. Along the dromos (vaulted entry corridor), a double frieze depicts battle scenes. The burial chamber is 12m in diameter and covered by a beehive dome typical of Thracian design in the 3rd to 5th centuries BC. The dome's murals depict events such as a funeral feast and chariot race. The tomb is a 15-minute walk northeast of the central square, across the small Stara Reka (Old River).

Museum   MUSEUM
(☏64 750; Tyulbe Park; admission 2 lv; ⊘10am-6pm) This museum has a full-scale Thracian Tomb replica. Most visitors choose not to spend the 20 lv required to see the real thing as the replica basically gives you the same experience. The staff guiding you around the faux tomb are friendly and speak good English.

Iskra Museum & Art Gallery   MUSEUM
(☏23 741; ul Sv Kiril i Metodii; adult/student 2/1 lv; ⊘9am-6pm Mon-Fri) This gallery displays extensive archaeological finds including pottery, jewellery and tools from excavations of Thracian tombs such as the one at Tyulbe Park. All explanations are in Bulgarian, so the brochure (2 lv) in English, French or German is helpful. Upstairs, numerous paintings are displayed, including some by renowned local artists such as Ivan Milev and Vasil Barakov. Purchase the printed catalogue (in English and French; 3 lv).

Kulata Ethnological Complex   MUSEUM
(☏621 733; ul Knyaz Mirski; admission 3 lv, with rose-liquor tasting 4 lv; ⊘8am-noon & 1-6pm) Just

down from Tyulbe Park and the Thracian Tomb, you'll find the appealing Kulata (Tower) district, site of the Kulata Ethnological Complex. A replica of a one-storey peasant's home and wooden sheds with agricultural implements and carts are among the rustic exhibits.

A courtyard leads to the two-storey House of Hadzhi Eno, built by a wealthy rose merchant in Bulgarian National Revival–period style. Some explanations in German and English are given, and you may be invited by the caretaker to sample some rose tea, liquor or jam.

[FREE] Museum of the Roses   MUSEUM
(☏23 741; ul Osvobozhdenie; ⊘9am-5pm summer) The grandly named Research Institute for Roses, Aromatic and Medicinal Plants houses this tiny museum. It's 3km north of centre up ul Osvobozhdenie; take a taxi (3 lv, one way), or bus 3 from Kazanlâk's main square. The photos and displays explain (in Bulgarian only) the 300-year-old method of cultivating the roses, picking their petals and processing the oil.

⨳ Sleeping & Eating

Hotel Palas   HOTEL €€
(☏62 311; www.hotel-palas.com; ul Petko Stajnov 9; s/d/ste incl breakfast 82/96/120 lv; P❋☷) This posh place opposite the post office and near the main square offers spacious, classy rooms. The suites are enticing and great value (prices can be negotiable for multinight stays). The restaurant is respectable though service is slow when busy. The buffet breakfast is better-than-average, though the 'spa centre' is only opened on request.

Hadzhi Eminova Kâshta   GUESTHOUSE €
(☏62 595; bul Nikola Petkov 22; s/d/apt 20/30/40 lv) This established guesthouse offers big, traditionally furnished rooms featuring woollen quilts and overlooking an authentic 19th-century walled compound. The one apartment is huge and worth booking ahead. All rooms feature bathrooms, though they tend to be small, and the restaurant is excellent.

Roza Hotel   HOTEL €€
(☏50 105; www.hotelrozabg.com; ul Rozova Dolina 2; s/d from 50/70 lv; ❋@☷) Set atop an office complex opposite the square, the Roza has a small collection of rooms and a giant,

astroturfed terrace with panoramic views. The rooms on the hall's right-hand side are smaller, with beds jammed in lengthways, whereas the slightly larger ones on the left are more normal (and slightly pricier).

New York Bar & Grill INTERNATIONAL €€
(pl Sevtopolis; mains 5-10 lv; 🛜) When in Kazanlåk... This eternally popular restaurant-pub on the square has a big menu (with pictures), serving everything from pizza to fish and grills. It's not gourmet, but the locals love it.

❶ Information

Internet Centre (ul Otets Paisii; per hour 1 lv; ⊘9am-11pm)
Post Office (ul 23 Pehoten Shipchenski Polk)
Tourist Information Centre (🖉62 817; ul Iskra 4; ⊘8am-1pm & 2-6pm Mon-Fri) Assists with hotels, excursions and general information about the town.

❶ Getting There & Away

From the bus and train stations, it's a 10-minute walk (or 2 lv cab ride) northwards to the square. Kazanlåk's **bus station** (🖉62 383; ul Kenali) has connections to Sofia (18 lv, 2½ hours, six daily), Veliko Tårnovo (17 lv, 2½ hours), and Plovdiv (13 lv, two hours).

The Kazanlåk **train station** (🖉662 012; ul Sofronii) serves Sofia (21 lv, 3½ hours, three daily) and Burgas (19 lv, three hours, four daily), via Karlovo (5 lv, one hour, six daily). Trains to or from Plovdiv often involve changing at the Tulovo station, just before Kazanlåk station.

Veliko Târnovo
Велико Търново

📞062 / POP 68,735

The evocative capital of the medieval Bulgarian tsars, sublime Veliko Târnovo is dramatically set amid an amphitheatre of forested hills, divided by the ribboning Yantra River. Commanding pride of place is the magisterial Tsarevets Fortress, citadel of the Second Bulgarian Empire. It's complemented by scores of churches and other ruins, many still being unearthed. As the site of Bulgaria's most prestigious university, Veliko Târnovo also boasts a revved-up nightlife that many larger towns would envy. There's great food and drink, too, in restaurants offering commanding views of the river and castle, or located in the Varosha quarter, with its terracotta rooftops and lounging cats.

❂ Sights

Tsarevets Fortress FORTRESS
(adult/student 6/2 lv, scenic elevator 2 lv; ⊘8am-7pm Apr-Sep, 9am-5pm Oct-Mar) This reconstructed fortress dominates the skyline and is one of Bulgaria's most beloved monuments. It features remains of more than 400 houses, 18 churches and numerous monasteries, dwellings, shops, gates and towers.

The fortress has a long history. Thracians and Romans used it as a defensive position, and the Byzantines built the first significant bulwark here between the 5th and 7th centuries. The fortress was rebuilt and fortified by the Slavs and Bulgars between the 8th and 10th centuries, and again by the Byzantines in the early 12th century. When Tårnovgrad became the Second Bulgarian Empire's capital, the fortress was truly magnificent, but with the Turkish invasion in 1393, it was sacked and destroyed.

The Patriarch's Complex and Baldwin Tower have received the most restoration, and considerable random rubble is lying about. Not much English-language information is provided, but guided English-language tours (10 lv) can be arranged by the Tourist Information Centre.

Sarafkina Kâshta MUSEUM
(ul General Gurko 88; adult/student 6/2 lv; ⊘9am-6pm Mon-Fri) Built in 1861 by a rich Turkish merchant, this fine five-storey National Revival–style house museum displays antique ceramics, metalwork, woodcarvings and jewellery, and has some fascinating exhibits about traditional costumes and breadmaking. Revival-period furniture fills the upper floor, along with vintage family photos.

Museum of National Revival & Constituent Assembly MUSEUM
(ul Ivan Vazov; adult/student 6/2 lv; ⊘9am-6pm Wed-Mon) This museum, in a former Turkish town hall built in 1872, was where Bulgaria's first National Assembly was held to write the country's first constitution in 1879. The ground floor contains costumes, books and photos about Veliko Tårnovo's history. The former assembly hall upstairs displays portraits of local personalities. The basement has classic old-town photos and some valuable icons.

Veliko Tårnovo Archaeological Museum MUSEUM
(ul Ivan Vazov; adult/student 6/2 lv; ⊘9am-6pm Tue-Sun) Housed in a grand old building

Veliko Tárnovo

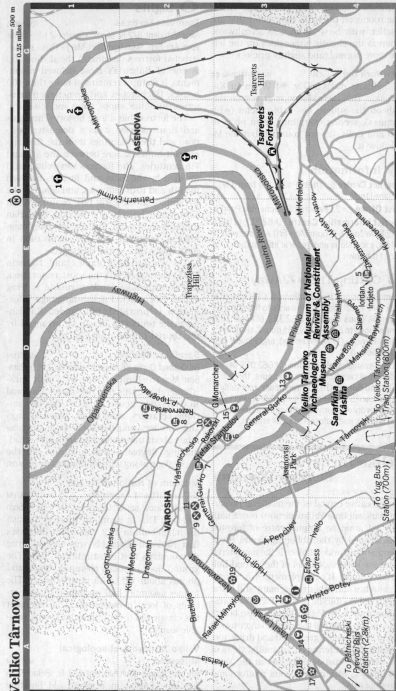

500 m
0.25 miles

ASENOVA

Mitropolska

Patriarh Evtimii

Tsarevets Hill

Tsarevets Fortress

Yantra River

Trapezitsa Hill

Highway

M Kefalov

Hristo Ivanov

Kraiłbreżna

Żeleznicharska

N Pikolo

Museum of National Revival & Constituent Assembly

Ivanka Boteva

Maksim Raykovich

Sheyni Iordan Indjeto

Chitalishtna

Veliko Tárnovo Archaeological Museum

Sarafkina Kāshta

T Tárnovski

To Veliko Tárnovo Train Station (800m)

Opalchenska

Rezervoarska

P Tipografov

G Momarchev

Vastamcheska

Stefan Stambolov

Stefan Rakovski

General Gurko

Asenovtsi Park

VAROSHA

General Gurko

A Penchev

Ivailo

Poborncheska

Kiril i Metodii

Dragoman

Hadji Dimitar

Nezavisimost

Buzludja

Rafael Mihaylov

Vasil Levski

Akatsia

Etap
Adress

Hristo Botev

To Yug Bus Station (700m)

To Bus Station (700m)

To Pātnicheski Prevozi Bus Station (2.8km)

Veliko Târnovo

with a colonnaded terrace and courtyard full of Roman sculptures, the archaeological museum contains Roman artefacts from Nikopolis-ad-Istrum, and more Roman pottery and statues from elsewhere. Medieval Bulgarian exhibits include huge murals of the tsars, while there's also some ancient gold from nearby Neolithic settlements.

Forty Martyrs Church CHURCH
(ul Mitropolska; adult/student 5/1 lv; ☺9am-5.30pm) This church, in the old Asenova quarter, was built in 1230 to celebrate Tsar Asen II's victory over the Byzantines. It was used as a royal mausoleum and then as a mosque by the Turks.

Church of Sveti Dimitâr CHURCH
(ul Patriarh Evtimii) Across the river, enclosed by a high wall, is Târnovo's oldest church.

During its 1185 consecration, Tsars Asen and Petâr proclaimed an uprising against Byzantine rule, which would create the Second Bulgarian Empire (1185–1396).

Church of Sveti Petr & Pavel CHURCH
(Church of St Peter & St Paul; ul Mitropolska; adult/student 4/2 lv; ☺9am-6pm) Located just past the bridge, this church contains fragments of murals from the 14th to 17th centuries.

🏃 Activities

Numerous local operators offer **hiking**, **mountain biking**, **horse riding** and **caving**; ask the Tourist Information Centre (p181) for hiking maps and contacts. The centre also offers the useful *Climbing Guide,* for serious rock climbers.

🛏 Sleeping

At time of writing, Veliko Târnovo's once-plentiful accommodation scene had been hit hard by the global economic crisis, with fewer tourists venturing to Bulgaria. This is not necessarily bad for travellers, however, as surviving hotels have stepped up services while keeping prices competitive.

The Tourist Information Centre (p181) finds private rooms (25 lv to 35 lv for a single/double). For atmosphere, stay near the Samovodska Charshiya Complex in the Varosha district, along the lower (southeastern) end of ul Gurko, or near Tsarevets Fortress.

TOP CHOICE Hotel Bolyarski HOTEL €€
(☎613 200; www.bolyarski.com; ul Stefan Stambolov 53a; s/d incl breakfast from 80/130 lv; P❄✳☎❄) One of the town's best hotels, the Bolyarski has a phenomenal location on the bluff on ul Stambolov, with magical views of the town and river from its long cafe patio and rooms, and close proximity to all the local restaurants and bars. Its modern, well-kept rooms are pitched at business travellers.

Hikers Hostel HOSTEL €
(☎0889 691 661; www.hikers-hostel.org; ul Rezevoarska 91; campsites/dm/d incl breakfast 14/20/52 lv; @❄) Still Târnovo's most laid-back hostel, Hikers has an unassuming location high in Varosha's old quarter (a 10-minute walk from downtown). Charismatic owner Toshe Hristov does free bus/train station pick-ups and also runs trips. The two dorms (one with four beds, the other with 10) are spartan but clean, and there's one double room, a kitchen and two shared bathrooms.

BULGARIA VELIKO TÂRNOVO

WORTH A TRIP

ARBANASI

Arbanasi is a historic village known for its monasteries and activities, such as horseback riding and hiking. Nearly 90 of the village's churches, homes and monasteries are state-protected cultural monuments. During the 16th century and after, it flourished under the Ottomans who, rather unusually, encouraged church-building here.

Arbanasi's three major sites, two churches and one house museum, are all covered by the same ticket (5 lv). Each opens 9.30am to 6pm daily, though they're usually closed between 1 October and 31 March.

The oldest surviving church here is the **Nativity Church** (adult/student 6/2 lv). It features a kaleidoscopic frescoed interior, with paintings (1632–49) covering its five chambers and a magnificent hand-carved central iconostasis. The 16th-century **Church of Sveti Arhangeli Mikhail and Gavril**, built over a ruined medieval church, also contains impressive frescoes.

The 17th-century **Konstantsalieva House** (admission 5 lv) was later rebuilt in National Revival style. It contains period furniture (and a souvenir shop). Arbanasi also hosts three 17th-century working monasteries: Sveti Georgi Church, the **Sveta Bogoroditsa Monastery** (☏620 322) and the **Sveti Nikolai Monastery** (☏650 345).

For equestrians, the **Arbanasi Horse Base** (☏623 668; Arbanasi), on the village's eastern edge, provides guided horseback-riding trips in the lush hills around Arbanasi. Phone for programs and prices, or consult Veliko Târnovo's Tourist Information Centre (p181).

There's no need to linger after seeing the sights, but should you seek some pampering the **Hotel Arbanassi Palace** (☏630 176; www.arbanassipalace.bg; s/d/ste from 90/125/170 lv; Ⓟ✳@ⓢⓈ) is the most venerable of several clifftop resorts. This grandly ageing structure (once Todor Zhivkov's local residence) has great views over the valley towards Veliko Târnovo from the restaurant balcony and from many of the rooms.

For humbler but still decent digs, the central **Rooms Mehana Arbat** (☏631 811; s/d incl breakfast 35/50 lv) offers doubles with weathered wood floors and traditional furnishings. Bathrooms are simple but modern. It's just above the similarly named **Mehana Arbat** (☏631 811; mains 6-12 lv), which does great Bulgarian fare at reasonable prices.

Arbanasi has always attracted moneyed visitors to its clifftop 'resort' hotels, but today it's mostly visited by tour buses on day trips. If based in Veliko Târnovo (4km away), it's easy to visit the main attractions, take in the views and have lunch, and still be back in town for dinner, whether you drive (taxis are 5 lv) or even hike (90 minutes).

Slavyanska Dusha GUESTHOUSE €
(☏625 182; www.slavianska-dusha.com; ul Nikola Zlatarski 21; s/d/tr/apt from 25/35/45/60 lv; ✳ⓢ) Very affordable and clean, this cheery guesthouse is run by a local couple who grow their own veg for the on-site restaurant. The place offers simple but nice rooms decked out in traditional decor.

Hostel Mostel HOSTEL €
(☏0897 859 359; www.hostelmostel.com; ul Iordan Indjeto 10; campsites/dm/s/d incl breakfast 18/20/46/60 lv; @ⓢ) The famous Sofia-based Hostel Mostel has become Târnovo's biggest, with clean, modern dorm rooms and doubles with sparkling bathrooms. It's just 150m from Tsarevets Fortress – good for exploring there, but a long walk from downtown (free bus/train pick-up is possible).

Hotel-Mehana Gurko HOTEL €€
(☏627 838; www.hotel-gurko.com; ul General Gurko 33; s/d/apt 80/110/135 lv; ✳@ⓢ) The Gurko is one of the best places to sleep (and eat) in town, located under the Old Town. Rooms are spacious and soothing, each individually decorated and with great views. There aren't any extras, but service is friendly.

✗ Eating

TOP
CHOICE **Han Hadji Nikoli** INTERNATIONAL €€€
(☏651 291; www.hanhadjinikoli.com; ul GS Rakovski 19; mains 25-30 lv; ⓢ) Without doubt Veliko Târnovo's finest restaurant. Start with escargots bourguignon, move on to roast chicken with cranberry and rose wine sauce, and finish with chocolate mousse flecked with raspberries and Cointreau.

Oh, and by the way, these are just from the 'regular' menu (there's also a discreet 'gourmet room' in the back, which has its own menu).

Shtastlivetsa BULGARIAN €€
(✆600 656; ul Stefan Stambolov 79; mains 7-14 lv; ⏱11am-1am; 🐾) A local institution, the 'Lucky Man' (as the impossible-to-pronounce name means in Bulgarian) has an ideal location overlooking the river's bend and a great menu of inventive meat dishes, baked-pot specials, nourishing pizzas and (at lunchtime) delicious soups.

Ego Pizza & Grill PIZZA €€
(✆601 804; ul Nezavisimost 17; mains 5-12 lv; ⏱9am-midnight; 🐾) Probably Tărnovo's best pizza, Ego has a new location overlooking the river's bend. It's a spacious restaurant with outdoor and indoor seating with excellent views. Service can be hit-or-miss.

🍷 Drinking

Dada Bar BAR
(ul Velcho Dzhamdzhiyata 12; ⏱10pm-4am) This funky place has a subterranean bar and outdoor enclosed courtyard beyond. Good prices, good music, and gets busy after midnight – just watch your head when going down the (rather low and steep) stairway.

Geronimo Bar BAR
(ul Vasil Levski 1; ⏱7am-2am) Coffee bar by day, drinks and cocktails by night, this stylish, popular place along the main road has a vaguely American-Southwest décor.

Tequila Bar BAR
(ul Stefan Stambolov 30; ⏱12pm-3am) Overlooking the main street and near the Samovodska Charshiya Compex, Tequila Bar is a festively painted student bar with good cocktails and cheap beer.

City Pub PUB
(ul Hristo Botev 15; ⏱noon-1am) This popular British-style pub near the post officee is somewhat gimmicky, but still a hit with local students and expats.

☆ Entertainment

Veliko Tărnovo's nightlife is buzzing year-round; in summer, backpackers and other foreign travellers pass through, while September summons back the town's 20,000 university students.

Konstantin Kisimov Dramatic Theatre THEATRE
(✆623 526; ul Vasil Levski) This theatre has regular performances from the international pantheon and Bulgarian plays. Ask the Tourist Information Centre (p181) what's on.

Melon Live Music Club CLUB
(✆0895 424 427; bul Nezavisnost 21; ⏱6pm-4am) This great spot for live music (ranging from rock to R&B and Latin jazz) is tucked halfway up the main street.

Jack CLUB
(✆0887 203 016; ul Magistraka 5; entry 3 lv; ⏱10pm-4am) This pumping student club is especially popular on weekends with house music and dancing.

Bally CLUB
(✆0885 565 666; ul Hristo Botev 2; ⏱10pm-5am Mon-Sat) This two-part club has rooms for Bulgarian folk-pop and more international pop fare. Monday is student night with special offers.

❶ Information

Hospital Stefan Cherkezov (✆626 841; ul Nish 1)

I-Net Internet Centre (off ul Hristo Botev; per hour 1.50 lv)

Main Post Office (ul Nezavisimost)

Tourist Information Centre (✆622 148; www.velikoturnovo.info; ul Hristo Botev 5; ⏱9am-6pm Mon-Fri, Mon-Sat summer) Helpful English-speaking staff can help book accommodation and rent cars.

❶ Getting There & Away

Bus

Two (non-central) bus stations serve Veliko Tărnovo. **Pătnicheski Prevozi bus station** (Zapad Bus Station; ✆640 908; ul Nikola Gabrovski 74), about 4km from centre, is the main intercity one. Local buses 10, 12, 14, 70 and 110 go there, along ul Vasil Levski. There's also a left-luggage office. From here, buses serve Kazanlăk (9 lv, 2½ hours, five daily), Ruse (8 lv, two hours, eight daily), Burgas (18 lv, four hours, four daily) and Plovdiv (19 lv, four hours, four daily).

The more central **Yug bus station** (✆620 014; ul Hristo Botev) has many daily buses to Sofia (21 lv, four hours), Varna (19 lv, four hours) and Burgas (23 lv, 3½ hours). From here, several daily buses also serve Shumen (13 lv, three hours) and Ruse (11 lv, two hours).

Etap Adress (✆630 564; ul Ivailo 2, Hotel Etăr) has hourly buses to Sofia (22 lv, 3½ hours) and Varna (18 lv, four hours), plus two daily buses to Dobrich (20 lv, four hours), one to Kavarna (21 lv, 4½ hours) via Albena and Balchik and one to Shumen (13 lv, two hours).

Train

The remarkably unhelpful **Veliko Târnovo train station** (☏620 065), 1.5km west of town, has been known to ask for a 'fee' to provide train information. Three daily trains serve Plovdiv (21 lv, five hours). Trains also serve Burgas (21 lv, five hours, three daily), Varna (20 lv, five hours, three daily) and Sofia (21 lv, 4½ hours, six daily). Regular trains serve Târnovo's other train station, at Gorna Oryakhovitsa. From the Veliko Târnovo station, buses 10, 12, 14, 70 and 110 go to the centre. Alternatively, take a taxi (3 lv to 6 lv).

Gorna Oryakhovitsa train station (☏826 118), 8.5km from town, is along the Sofia–Varna line. It has daily services to/from Sofia, via Pleven (18 lv, five hours, eight daily) and Varna (17 lv, four hours, three daily) and 11 trains to Ruse (9 lv, two hours).

Shumen   Шумен

☏054 / POP 80,510

There's an awful lot of concrete in Shumen, but it does make its own beer, the popular Shumensko. This somewhat faded but friendly industrial city full of communist memorials is crowned by a striking medieval fortress, and has tasty eateries and fun drinking spots. The town's offerings include several museums and a lengthy pedestrian mall, bul Slavyanski, which stretches from the city park to the main square, pl Osvobozhdenie.

◉ Sights

Shumen Fortress   FORTRESS
(adult/student 3/1 lv; ◷9am-5pm Mon-Fri) Towering over the city from a steep hillside, the Shumen Fortress dates to the early Iron Age. It was reinforced by the Thracians (5th century BC). Between the 2nd and 4th centuries AD, the Romans added towers and walls. It was refortified later by the Byzantines, who made it an important garrison.

During the Second Bulgarian Empire (1185–1396), the fortress was one of northeastern Bulgaria's most significant settlements, renowned for its pottery and metalwork. However, invading Ottomans in the late 14th century burnt and looted it. Placards are dotted around the site and a yellowing information booklet (2 lv) is available at the gate.

Creators of the Bulgarian State Monument   MONUMENT
This massive Soviet-era hilltop monument was built in 1981 to commemorate the First Bulgarian Empire's 1300th anniversary. Climb the staircase behind the **History Museum** (☏857 487; bul Slavyanski 17; admission 2 lv; ◷9am-5pm Mon-Fri) for the 3km path leading from the equally communist **Partisan's Monument**. The circuitous 5km road there starts along ul Sv Karel Shkorpil at the History Museum. Go by taxi (5 lv one way) and then just walk back down the steps to the centre.

The **Information Centre** (☏852 598; admission 3 lv; ◷8.30am-5pm winter, 8am-7pm summer), about 300m from the monument, has information about the structure and surrounding flora. A 3km path passes the Information Centre and car park, finishing at Shumen Fortress.

Tombul Mosque   MOSQUE
(☏802 875; ul Rakovski 21; admission 2 lv; ◷9am-6pm) Arguably Bulgaria's most beautiful mosque and definitely the largest still used, this 1744 mosque is also called the Sherif Halili Pasha Mosque. Its Turkish nickname, *tombul* (plump) refers to its 25m-high dome. The 40m-high minaret has 99 steps. Local Muslim belief says that the courtyard fountain gushes sacred water.

🛏 Sleeping

Hotel-Restaurant Minaliat Vek   HOTEL €€
(☏801 615; www.minaliatvek.com; bul Simeon Veliki 81; s/d/apt 58/70/95 lv; ✳🐾🛜) This hotel in the western part of town is remarkably popular with foreign travellers and represents good value. Rooms are clean and spacious (though not as terrific as the on-site restaurant). Staff are friendly and helpful.

Nirvana Art Hotel   HOTEL €€
(☏800 127; www.hotelnirvana.bg; ul Nezavisimost 25; s/d/apt from 75/85/130 lv; ✳🐾🛜) This relatively recent addition is set in a dusty residential part of south Shumen and boasts the city's most unique rooms. Each is painted in various soothing tones and with minimalist decor and the occasional canopy bed. Sauna, spa and massage (from 25 lv) are offered, and its gourmet restaurant (p183) is very good.

Hotel Zamaka   HOTEL €€
(☏800 409; www.zamakbg.eu; ul Vasil Levski 17; s/d/apt 40/60/85 lv; ✳🛜) This lovely hotel in

WORTH A TRIP

MADARA

Off the main highway between Shumen and Varna, Madara (Мадара) is a simple village that's home to the original, endlessly reproduced horseman figure that appears on Bulgaria's stotinki coins. The enigmatic 23m bas-relief on a sheer rock wall at the **Madara National Historical and Archaeological Reserve** (4 lv; ⊗8am-7.30pm summer, to 5pm winter) depicts a horseman spearing a lion. It's believed to date from the 8th century, though some argue it's much older. Afterwards follow a trail north and up 378 steps to a mountaintop fortress.

Public transport to Madara is limited, and the horseman is 3km up a steep road from the village. Several daily Shumen–Varna trains stop at Madara, but Shumen–Madara buses are infrequent; better to catch the bus from Shumen to Kaspichan (five daily), and then a minibus to Madara from there. A taxi from Shumen costs 30 lv return, including waiting time. Madara has no taxis.

a quiet residential neighbourhood just west of the main square has friendly staff and cosy rooms. It's set around a garden courtyard with a traditional restaurant.

✕ Eating

 Minaliat Vek

Restaurant BULGARIAN €€€
(☏801 615; bul Simeon Veliki 81; mains 9-17 lv; ☜) This local favourite, part of the Minaliat Vek hotel, seeks to recreate the 'old time' tastes its name suggests. There's a long (and colourfully described) list of Bulgarian specialities plus numerous Bulgarian wines.

Katmi PANCAKES €
(pl Osvobozhdenie 12; pancakes 2 lv; ⊗7.30am-8pm) This local takeaway institution, off a side entrance on the square, offers delicious *palachinki* (pancakes) – much better than the usual Balkan crepe – with a choice of 122 different combinations. Our favourite is the all-natural blueberry and strawberry jam filling.

Nirvana Gourmet

Restaurant INTERNATIONAL €€€
(☏300 127; ul Nezavisinost 25; mains 11-23 lv; ☜) For those seeking relatively elegant international dining, it's worth the 10-minute drive or cab ride to this gourmet restaurant, with grills and Italian fare more than a notch above the average for Shumen. There's a long wine list.

ℹ Getting There & Away

The bus and train stations are adjacent at Shumen's eastern end (3 lv to 5 lv by taxi). From the **bus station** (☏830 890; ul Rilski Pohod), buses serve Burgas (14 lv, three hours, four daily), Ruse (11 lv, two hours, three daily), Veliko Târnovo (11 lv, two hours, several daily), Madara (2 lv, 20 minutes, five daily), Sofia (31 lv, six hours, hourly) and Varna (11 lv, 1½ hours, nine daily). Private buses, such as those operated by **Etap Adress** (☏830 670), also stop in Shumen on the Sofia–Varna route.

From the **train station** (☏860 155; pl Garov) daily trains (including one express) serve Varna (7 lv, two hours, nine daily), and fast trains reach Sofia (19 lv, four to seven hours, two daily). Trains serve Ruse (12 lv, three hours, daily) and Plovdiv (18 lv, six hours, daily). Two trains stop at Madara. The station has a left-luggage office.

Ruse Pуce

☏082 / POP 182,500
One of Bulgaria's most elegant cities, Ruse (*roo*-seh), sometimes written 'Rousse', has more than a touch of *mitteleuropa* grandness not seen elsewhere in the country. It's a city of imposing belle époque architecture and neatly trimmed leafy squares, as if a little chunk of Vienna had broken off and floated down the Danube. Its past is abundantly displayed in several museums and in its ruined Roman fortress, standing guard high over the Danube. Ruse is also a base for visiting the nearby rock monasteries and other attractions at Rusenski Lom Nature Park.

⊙ Sights

Ruse Regional Museum of History MUSEUM
(www.museumruse.com; pl Aleksandar Battenberg 3; adult/student 4/1 lv; ⊗9am-6pm) The 5th-century-BC **Borovo Treasure**, consisting of silver cups and jugs adorned with Greek gods, is one of the highlights of Ruse's interesting museum. Other artefacts on display include Thracian helmets, Roman statues and 19th-century costumes.

BULGARIA RUSE

Ruse

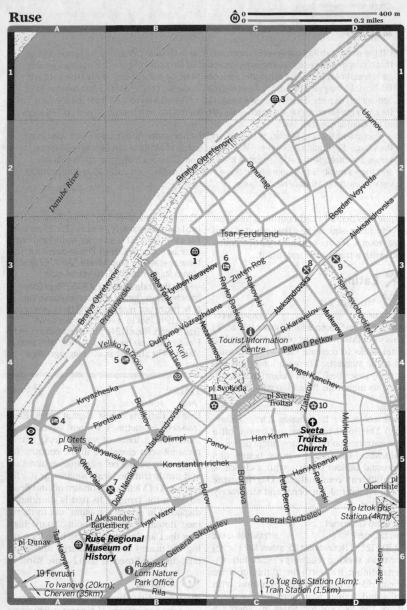

FREE **Sveta Troitsa Church** CHURCH
(ul Zlatarov; ☺7am-6pm) Built in 1632 below
ground level – according to the Turkish
stipulation that churches should be as un-
obtrusive as possible – Sveta Troitsa has a
fine gilt wood iconostasis and wooden pillars painted to look like marble, as well as
some well-preserved icons.

**Roman Fortress of
Sexaginta Prista** ARCHEOLOGICAL SITE
(ul Tsar Kaloyan 2; adult/student 2/1 lv; ☺9am-noon
& 12.30-5.30pm Tue-Sat) Closed for renovation

at the time of research, little remains today of what was once a mighty Roman fort, completed in 70 AD and housing some 600 soldiers at its peak. You can still see some barracks walls and columns, and the enthusiastic custodian will show you around and bring it all to life.

Transportation Museum MUSEUM
(ul Bratya Obretenovi 5; outside/indoor displays 4/2 lv; ☉10am-noon & 2-5pm Mon-Fri) Exhibits vintage locomotives from the late-19th and early-20th centuries, as well as carriages that once belonged to Tsar Boris III, Tsar Ferdinand and Turkish Sultan Abdul Aziz.

**Museum of the Urban
Lifestyle in Ruse** MUSEUM
(ul Tsar Ferdinand 36; adult/student 4/1 lv; ☉9am-noon & 12.30-5.30pm) Built in 1866, this elegant townhouse features some re-created period rooms, with 19th-century furniture, paintings and chandeliers upstairs. Downstairs there are changing exhibitions on social themes.

🛏 Sleeping

TOP CHOICE City Art Hotel BOUTIQUE HOTEL €€
(☎519 848; www.cityarthotel.com; ul Veliko Tărnovo 5; s/d 68/90 lv; ❄️🛜) Offers 19 artfully styled rooms with trendy colour schemes, giant headboards and upbeat philosophical quotations stencilled on the walls. The building is a renovated 19th-century hatmaker's shop on a quiet street near the centre, and guests receive a 10% discount at the Chinese restaurant in the back courtyard.

Anna Palace HOTEL €€
(☎825 005; www.annapalace.com; ul Knyazheska 4; s/d from 80/100 lv; P❄️@) In a bright yellow, neoclassical mansion by the river terminal, the luxurious Anna Palace has large, slightly chintzy rooms. There are smaller, discounted attic singles.

English Guest House B&B €
(☎875 577; vysachko@abv.bg; ul Rayko Daskalov 34; s/d/tr from 40/60/70 lv; P❄️@) A few blocks north of pl Svoboda, this British-run guesthouse has a selection of rooms in a renovated townhouse, including pricier en suite rooms. It's a sociable place where guests can mingle over some free tea in the garden.

✕ Eating

TOP CHOICE Chiflika BULGARIAN €€
(☎828 222; ul Otets Paisii 2; mains 6-25 lv; ☉11am-2am Mon-Sat, noon-1am Sun) Set in several rooms following an old-world *mehana* theme, with wooden benches, rugs, fleeces on the walls and waiters in pantaloons, Chiflika is the best place in town for hearty traditional food. On the big menu are clay-pot meals, including an excellent chicken *gyuvetch* (cooked in a clay-pot), soups, grills and more adventurous options such as stewed lamb intestines (10.90 lv).

Ostankino BULGARIAN €
(ul Aleksandrovska 76; mains 3-8 lv; ☉8.30am-midnight) Typical cheap and tasty Bulgarian food including sausages, grills, chicken steaks and fish are served at this busy cafe with outdoor tables. It's a good place to enjoy a couple of cold beers, too.

Hlebozavod Ruse FAST FOOD €
(ul Aleksandrovska; banitsa 70 stotinki; ☉6.30am-7pm Mon-Fri, to 2pm Sat) Ruse's best takeaway snack shop draws locals all day, who come for the hot, freshly baked *banitsa*.

☆ Entertainment

Ruse Opera House (☎825 037; pl Sveta Troitsa), open since about 1890 and one of the town's finest buildings, and the **Sava Ognyanov Drama Theatre** (pl Svoboda), are both well known for their quality productions.

BULGARIA RUSE

Buy tickets at the box offices, or through the Tourist Information Centre.

ⓘ Information

There are numerous banks with ATMs and foreign exchange offices along ul Aleksandrovska and pl Svoboda, including **Unicredit Bulbank** (cnr ul Alexandrovska & pl Svoboda) and **Banka DSK** (pl Sveta Troitsa).

Polyclinic (⌨834 200; ul Nezavisimost 2)

Post Office (pl Svoboda)

Rusenski Lom Nature Park Office (⌨872 397; www.lomea.org; ul General Skobelev 7; ☺9am-5pm Mon-Fri) Provides camping and hiking information and maps; can arrange trips to the Ivanovo Rock Monastery.

Tourist Information Centre (⌨824 704; www.tic.rousse.bg; ul Aleksandrovska 61; ☺9am-6pm Mon-Fri, 9.30am-6pm Sat & Sun) The helpful office hands out free city maps and leaflets.

ⓘ Getting There & Away

Bus

The **Yug bus station** (⌨828 151; ul Pristanishtna) has regular buses to Sofia (28 lv, five hours), Veliko Târnovo (10 lv, two hours), Shumen (6 lv, two hours), Burgas (27 lv, 4½ hours) and Varna (15 lv, four hours). To get to the station, take trolleybus 25 or bus 11 or 12 from ul Borisova. A taxi will cost about 4 lv.

The **Iztok bus station** (⌨844 064; ul Ivan Vedur 10), 4km east of the centre, has buses to nearby destinations such as Ivanovo and Cherven in the Rusenski Lom Nature Park. Take a taxi or city bus 2 or 13, which leave from ul Gen Skobelev, near the roundabout four blocks east of ul Borisova.

Ruse-based company **Ovonesovi** (⌨872 000) runs two daily minibuses to Bucharest, leaving from the Yug bus station and dropping you off in central Bucharest near the Piaţa Unirii metro station. Tickets are 20 lv one way or 30 lv return. Private taxis (90 lv one way) from Yug bus station also make the trip.

Train

From Ruse's grand **train station** (⌨820 222; ul Pristanishtna) there are seven daily trains to Sofia (18.90 lv, six to seven hours) and two to Varna (12.20 lv, four hours).

For Romania, three daily trains serve Bucharest (25 lv, 3½ hours). Show up at least 30 minutes before the train departure time for customs and passport checks.

In the station, the **Rila Bureau** (⌨828 016; ☺9am-5.30pm) sells international train tickets. It's best to buy a Bucharest ticket on the day of travel as there are sometimes delays. The train station's **left-luggage office** (☺6am-1.30pm & 2-8.30pm) is past the main buildings and in a smaller one up the hill. There's another branch of the **Rila Bureau** (⌨834 860; ul Knyazheska 33; ☺9am-noon & 1-5.30pm Mon-Fri) in the city centre.

Rusenski Lom Nature Park   Природен Парк Русенски Лом

This 32.6-sq-km nature park, sprawling south of Ruse around the Rusenski Lom, Beli Lom and Malki Lom Rivers, is a superb spot for birdwatching; 172 species are recorded here, including Egyptian vultures, lesser kestrels and eagle owls. It's also home to 67 species of mammals and 24 types of bats.

Most visitors are drawn first to the park's cliff churches. While around 40 medieval rock churches exist in and around some 300 local caves, only a handful are accessible, the most famous being those of Basarbovo and Ivanovo. The park also contains the second-longest cave in Bulgaria, the Orlova Chuka Peshtera (Eagle Peak Cave), between Tabachka and Pepelina villages. Thracian and Roman ruins have also been found here.

⊙ Sights

Basarbovo Rock Monastery   MONASTERY
(⌨082-800 765) Basarbovo is 8km south of Ruse near the Rusenski Lom River, on the road to the Ivanovo Monastery. Established sometime before the 15th century, the complex has been much restored and extended since. Visitors can see a rock-carved church with colourful icons and a little museum.

Ivanovo Rock Monastery   MONASTERY
(⌨0889 370 006; Sveti Archangel Michael; adult/student 4/1 lv; ☺9am-noon & 1-6pm) Around 4km east of Ivanovo, this Unesco World Heritage–listed monastery is built inside a cave 38m above ground. It's about a 10-minute walk on a good trail through a forest to get here. Built during the 13th century, it houses 14th-century murals regarded as some of the finest in Bulgaria, including a Last Supper scene.

Cherven Fortress   FORTRESS
(4 lv; ☺9am-noon & 1-6pm) Just outside the village of Cherven, 15km south of Ivanovo, are the remains of a remarkably intact 6th-century **citadel**. Several streets, towers and churches have also been discovered, and there are great views of the river valleys and hills from the top.

🛏 Sleeping

The nature park office in Ruse and Ivanovo's **information centre** (📞081-162 203; Ivanovo town hall) provide information on accommodation, such as private rooms in Cherven, Pisanets, Nisovo and Koshov (20 lv per person) as well as small village guesthouses (from 40 lv per person).

❶ Getting There & Away

From the Iztok bus station in Ruse, two or three buses leave daily for Cherven, via Ivanovo and Koshov, from Monday to Friday (3 lv, 40 minutes). The best way to get to Ivanovo, however, is by train (every 30 minutes), as there are only three daily buses to Ivanovo in summer and fewer in winter.

Ask at the Ruse Tourist Information Centre for details on getting to Basarbovo via local bus directly from the city centre. In summer, hourly buses go to Basarbovo, though in winter they are less frequent.

BLACK SEA COAST

The Black Sea coast is the country's summertime playground, attracting tourists from across Europe and beyond, as well as Bulgarians themselves. The big, purpose-built resorts here are serious rivals to Spain and Greece, while independent travellers will find plenty to explore away from the parasols and jet skis. Sparsely populated sandy beaches to the far south and north, the bird-filled Burgas Lakes and picturesque ancient towns such as Nesebâr and Sozopol are rewarding destinations, while the 'maritime capital' of Varna is one of Bulgaria's most vibrant cities.

Varna   Варна

📞052 / POP 335,000

Bulgaria's third city and maritime capital, Varna is by far the most interesting and cosmopolitan town on the Black Sea coast. A combination of port city, naval base and seaside resort, it's an appealing place to while away a few days, packed with history yet thoroughly modern, with an enormous park to amble around and a lengthy beach to lounge on. In the city centre you'll find Bulgaria's largest Roman baths complex and its finest archaeological museum, as well as a lively cultural and restaurant scene.

Dangers & Annoyances

Like elsewhere along the coast, some taxi drivers are prone to ripping off foreign visitors at the bus and train stations, so check the tariffs before getting in or, better still, pick up a cab on streets away from these places. Varna appears to be the last refuge in Bulgaria for black-market money changers, who lurk around pl Nezavisimost. Needless to say, it's illegal to change money on the street and you're sure to end up out of pocket.

◉ Sights

Archaeological Museum   MUSEUM

(ul Maria Luisa 41; adult/student 10/2 lv; ⊘10am-5pm Tue-Sun Apr-Sep, Tue-Sat Oct-Mar; 🚌3, 9, 109) Exhibits at this vast museum, the best of its kind in Bulgaria, include 6500-year-old bangles, necklaces and earrings (said to be the oldest worked gold found anywhere in the world), Roman surgical implements, Hellenistic tombstones and touching oddities such as a marble plaque listing, in Greek, the names of the city's school graduates for AD 221.

Roman Thermae   RUINS

(cnr ul Han Krum & ul San Stefano; adult/student 4/2 lv; ⊘10am-5pm Tue-Sun May-Oct, Tue-Sat Nov-Apr) The well-preserved ruins of Varna's 2nd-century-AD Roman Thermae are the largest in Bulgaria, although only a small part of the original complex still stands. You can just about make out individual bathing areas and the furnaces, where slaves kept the whole thing going.

History Museum   MUSEUM

(ul 8 Noemvri 3; adult/child 4/2 lv; ⊘10am-5pm Tue-Sun May-Oct, Mon-Fri Nov-Apr; 🚌20) Varna's ivy-covered History Museum is dedicated to city history between 1878 and 1939, with mock-ups of long-gone 1920s shops and offices, collections of photographs and postcards, and paraphernalia from local trades such as brewing and printing.

National Naval Museum   MUSEUM

(bul Primorski 2; 5 lv; ⊘10am-6pm Wed-Sun) The National Naval Museum hosts several galleries of model ships and uniforms. Anchors, artillery and helicopters can be seen rusting quietly in the grounds at the back, while the revered warship *Druzki,* which torpedoed a Turkish cruiser during the First Balkan War in 1912, is embedded in concrete outside.

Varna

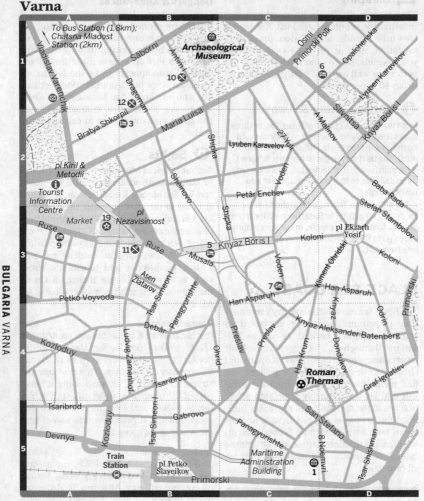

To Bus Station (1.8km);
Chatsna Mladost
Station (2km)

BULGARIA VARNA

Activities

The main activity here is **swimming** and the Varna **city beach** is 8km long. The **south beach** (with its pool complex, water slides and cafes) has a popular stretch. The central beach has thinner sand patches and is dominated by clubs. Beyond to the north is a rocky area lined with restaurants, and further north there are some wider and more attractive areas of sand, as well as an outdoor **thermal pool** with year-round hot water where locals take a daily dip.

The blue-flag **Bunite Beach** north of here is one of the better places to stretch out, al-though there's a big private section, with a beach bar and tacky plastic coconut trees, where you can get a sunbed for 7 lv, a double bed for 20 lv or a 'VIP pavilion' (a canvas tent) for 50 lv. Elsewhere, beach bars rent loungers and umbrellas for about 5 lv. Just in from the beach is **Primorski Park**, a vast expanse of greenery dotted with statues, open-air cafes and popcorn vendors.

Sleeping

Varna certainly has no shortage of accom-modation, although the better (or at least,

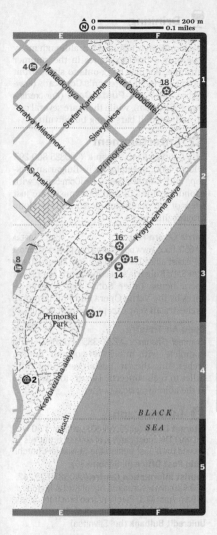

0 200 m
0 0.1 miles

Varna

BULGARIA VARNA

in 1912. Rooms are spacious and elegantly furnished, if a little chintzy, and the restaurant is especially good.

Modus Hotel   LUXURY HOTEL €€€
(☑660 910; www.modushotel.com; ul Stefan Stambolov 46; s/d from 180/200 lv; [P][☺][✳][✎][☎]; [✎]20) Just across the road from Primorski Park, Modus is a chic boutique with suitably stylish rooms and all the facilities you'd expect. Various discounts and package deals are offered, and there's also a gym, sauna and bistro.

Hotel Hi   HOTEL €€
(☑657 777; www.hotel-hi.com; ul Han Asparuh 11; s/d 80/112 lv; [P][✳][☎]) In a quiet neighbourhood south of the main thoroughfare, Hi is a friendly place featuring stylish, cosy rooms – some very small – with TVs and minibars.

Graffit Gallery Hotel   BOUTIQUE HOTEL €€€
(☑989 900; www.graffithotel.com; bul Knyaz Boris I 65; s/d/ste from 180/200/360 lv; [P][☺][✳][✎][☎]; [✎]9) With its own art gallery, this modern designer hotel is one of Varna's more colourful

the more central) places get busy during the summer months.

Private rooms are plentiful in Varna, and pensioners with spare rooms wait around the train station to greet new arrivals. Prices tend to be around 12 lv per person, but make sure you don't end up in some out-of-the-way suburb.

TOP CHOICE **Grand Hotel London**   LUXURY HOTEL €€€
(☑664 100; www.londonhotel.bg; ul Musala 3; s/d Mon-Thu from 170/210 lv, Fri-Sun from 150/190 lv; [P][☺][✳][☎]) Varna's grandest hotel is this five-star establishment, which originally opened

options. The large rooms on each of the four floors follow a different theme, and there's a spa and gym too.

Hotel Astra

HOTEL €€

(☑630 524; www.hotelastravarna.com; ul Opalchenska 9; s/d 50/60 lv; ❄❅; ☐9) A real bargain by Varna standards, this central, family-run hotel has 10 spacious and comfortable rooms, all with terraces, and basic but good-sized bathrooms.

Flag Hostel

HOSTEL €

(☑0897 408 115; www.varnahostel.com; ul Bratya Shkorpil 13a; dm incl breakfast 22 lv; ❏❅❄; ☐3, 9) The Flag is a long-established, sociable place with a young, international party atmosphere and three dorms with single beds only (no bunks), and breakfast included. Free pick-ups from the bus and train stations are offered.

Yo Ho Hostel

HOSTEL €

(☑0886 382 905; www.yohohostel.com; ul Ruse 23; dm/s/d incl breakfast from 14/30/40 lv; @; ☐109) Shiver your timbers at this pirate-themed place found just down the street from the Varna Opera House, with four- and 11-bed dorm rooms, two doubles and one single room. Free breakfast and pick-ups are offered, and staff also organise camping and rafting trips.

✗ Eating

TOP CHOICE Di Wine

MODERN EUROPEAN €€€

(☑606 050; www.diwine.bg; ul Bratya Shkorpil 2; mains 12-30 lv; ☐9) This formal but friendly restaurant is Varna's best fine-dining spot, with a big menu of tempting dishes including rack of lamb, T-bone steaks, guinea fowl, salmon and trout as well as cheaper barbecue dishes. There are plenty of good wines to try, too.

Tanasi

GREEK €€

(☑601 138; ul Bratya Shkorpil 16; mains 5-15 lv; ☐9) This welcoming Greek restaurant has fresh white linen indoors, plus less formal outdoor seating. Featured dishes include stuffed aubergines, roast lamb, rabbit and various fish, and they also offer an excellent value three-course set lunch for 5 lv.

Morsko Konche

PIZZERIA €€

(pl Nezavisimost; pizzas 5-10 lv; ❄✎) The 'Seahorse' is a cheap and cheerful pizza place with a big menu featuring all the standard varieties, as well as some inventive creations of its own: the 'exotic' pizza comes with bananas and blueberries.

♆ Drinking

Varna's trendiest bars are found along the beach on Kraybrezhna aleya, although many have only a brief existence in the summer sunshine. Popular hang-outs to sip seafront margaritas include **Pench's Cocktails** (Kraybrezhna aleya) and **Punta Cana** (Kraybrezhna aleya; ☺6am-4am), while there are several coffee and cocktail bars along bul Slivnitsa.

☆ Entertainment

Exit (☺10pm-6am), **4aspik** (☑0885 800 297; ☺10pm-4am), specialising in Bulgarian folk-pop, and **Copacabana** (☺10pm-5am), with a fondness for '70s and '80s music, are just a few of the many summertime clubs along Kraybrezhna aleya.

Varna Opera House

OPERA

(☑650 555; www.operavarna.bg; pl Nezavisimost 1; ☺ticket office 11am-1pm & 2-7pm Mon-Fri, 11am-6pm Sat) Bulgaria's second-most important opera house (after Sofia) hosts performances by the Varna Opera and Philharmonic Orchestra all year except July and August.

Open-Air Theatre

THEATRE

(Summer Theatre; ☑228 385; Primorski Park) Complete with mock ivy-covered Roman arches, this theatre hosts everything from ballet to rock concerts. Details are available at the adjoining ticket office.

❶ Information

Internet Doom (ul 27 Yuli 13; per hour 1.60 lv; ☺24hr) The most central of several branches around town, just behind the St Nikolai Church.

Main Post Office (ul Sâborni 36)

Tourist Information Centre (☑0887 703 242, 820 689; www.varnainfo.bg; pl Kiril & Metodii; ☺9am-7pm; ☐3) Plenty of free brochures and maps, and helpful multilingual staff.

Unicredit Bulbank (bul Slivnitsa)

❶ Getting There & Away

AIR Varna's international **airport** (☑573 323; www.varna-airport.bg; ☐409) has scheduled and charter flights from all over Europe, as well as regular flights to and from Sofia. From the centre, bus 409 goes to the airport.

BUS Varna has two bus stations – the scruffy **central bus station** (bul Vladislav Varenchik 158; ☐148) is about 2km northwest of the city centre. There are basic cafes and a **left-luggage office** (per hour 80 stotinki; ☺7am-7pm).

The **Chatsna Mladost Station** (☑500 039) is about 200m along a road that starts almost opposite the central bus station. From here,

TRANSPORT FROM VARNA

Bus

DESTINATION	PRICE (LV)	DURATION	FREQUENCY
Albena	5	45min	several daily
Balchik	5	1hr	16 daily
Burgas	14	2hr	4 daily
İstanbul	60	10hr	2 daily
Plovdiv	27	6hr	2 daily
Ruse	15	4hr	5 daily
Shumen	8	1½hr	3 daily
Sofia	32	7hr	20 daily
Veliko Târnovo	18	4hr	20 daily

Train

DESTINATION	PRICE (LV)	DURATION (HR)	FREQUENCY
Plovdiv	24.20	7	3 daily
Ruse	12.20	4	2 daily
Shumen	6.50	1½	10 daily
Sofia	23.60	7-8	7 daily

frequent minibuses go to destinations such as Balchik and Burgas. Ticket prices are the same as from the central bus station.

TRAIN Facilities at Varna's **train station** (☑630 414; pl Slaveikov) include a **left-luggage office** (⊗7.30am-8pm) and cafe.

The **Rila Bureau** (☑632 348; ul Preslav 13; ⊗8.30am-5.30pm Mon-Fri, 8am-3.30pm Sat) sells tickets for international services and advance tickets for domestic trains.

North Coast

BALCHIK   БАЛЧИК
☑0579 / POP 12,100

After the artificial resorts further down the coast, Balchik is a breath of fresh air. A pretty town and fishing port huddled below white-chalk cliffs, it's a low-key holiday spot that feels a world away from the likes of Albena, whose lights can be seen winking across the bay at night. The main attraction here is the Summer Palace of Romanian Queen Marie, with its lovely botanical gardens.

◉ Sights

Summer Palace of Queen Marie & Botanical Gardens   HISTORIC BUILDING, GARDENS
(Dvorets; 10 lv; ⊗8am-8pm May–mid-Oct, 8.30am-6.30pm mid-Oct–Apr) At the western end of the seafront, this little palace was completed in 1926 by King Ferdinand of Romania for his English wife, Queen Marie (Balchik was then part of Romania). It was rumoured that Marie entertained her much younger Turkish lover here. Size-wise, it's a relatively modest seaside villa, although the architecture – a blend of Bulgarian, Gothic and Islamic styles topped with a minaret – is unique. The half-dozen or so rooms on show contain original furnishings, including paintings by Marie, and several photographs of the queen striking dramatic poses in the grounds. Also here is a curious collection of local archaeological finds, including Roman pottery and mammoth bones.

Behind the palace are the extensive botanical gardens. Around 600 different species of flora are featured throughout a series of themed gardens, including an impressive collection of cacti. Also within the complex are a watermill, a classical-style nymphaeum, the tiny Chapel of Sveta Bogoroditsa and even a winery.

City Historical Museum   MUSEUM
(ul Vitosha 3; 2 lv; ⊗9am-noon & 1-5pm Mon-Fri) The diverse collection here includes Roman statuary, medieval pottery and vintage photographs of the town from the early 1900s.

SVETI KONSTANTIN, GOLDEN SANDS & ALBENA

North of Varna you'll find a succession of popular seaside resorts, starting with sedate Sveti Konstantin, famous for its spa treatments, before you hit the big beasts of Golden Sands and Albena, better known for their clubs, pubs and water sports.

The quiet beach resort **Sveti Konstantin** is about 9km northeast of Varna, with hotels attractively spaced out amid parkland. Established in 1946 under the name of Druzhba (Friendship), it's less commercial than other resorts and has long been popular with older holidaymakers. Indeed, it still has a number of 'rest homes' for retired civil servants and trade-union members. There are several new resort hotels geared towards young families, but this isn't the place for water sports or raucous nightlife

About 18km north of Varna, **Golden Sands** (Zlatni Pyasâtsi) was Bulgaria's original purpose-built resort, with the first hotel opening here in 1957. Today it's Bulgaria's second-largest coastal resort, with a 4km stretch of beach, and some of the best nightlife on the coast. Virtually everyone staying in the resort will be on a prebooked package, and it's not particularly friendly for walk-ins, but it's still a pretty beach for a day trip out to the coast.

Further up the road, **Albena** has a lovely, 4km-long beach and shallow water ideal for water sports. The downside are the high prices charged for just about everything and the fact that it's a package resort and not particularly user-friendly for independent travellers. That said, it's ideal to drop in for the day and swim and relax. Note that entry to the resort by private car costs 3 lv.

Ethnographic Museum   MUSEUM
(ul Vitosha; 1 lv; ⊙9am-5pm Mon-Fri) Opposite the Historical Museum, this museum features folk costumes and displays relating to traditional trades and crafts such as fishing, barrel making and woodcarving.

🛏 Sleeping

Hotel Mistral   HOTEL €€
(☑71 130; www.hotelmistralbg.com; ul Primorska 8b; s/d 92/112 lv; ⊝❋☎) One of the best waterfront hotels, the four-star Mistral is an upmarket place with large rooms, all with sea-facing balconies. Prices drop by up to half outside the summer season.

Hotel Regina Maria Spa   LUXURY HOTEL €€€
(☑460 065; www.reginamariaspa.com; r/ste 160/250 lv; ℙ❋☎☲) Near the palace, the four-star Regina Maria offers smart rooms in a variety of styles, all with sea views. Golfing packages and fishing trips can be arranged.

Hotel Helios   HOTEL €€
(☑76 970; www.heliosbg.com; d/apt 94/134 lv; ℙ❋@☲🐾) Helios is a modern, resort-style hotel and all rooms have balconies, many with superb sea views. Prices drop by up to 50% out of high season.

🍴 Eating

TOP CHOICE Tihoto Gnezdo   CAFE €
(mains from 3 lv; ⊙9am-11pm; 🖉) On the shore near the palace, this simple cafe serves light dishes such as salads and omelettes (from 3.50 lv) as well as fish. Prices are more reasonable than most seafront restaurants.

Francis Drake   SEAFOOD €€€
(mains 10-30 lv; ⊙8am-midnight; ☎) The restaurant of the Hotel Mistral is the place for some classier cuisine. Fried turbot, smoked salmon, and locally caught fish are among the offerings.

❶ Information
The post office and telephone centre are on the main square, pl Nezavisimost. You can change money at **SG Expressbank** (ul Cherno More).

❶ Getting There & Away
Balchik's **bus station** (☑74 069) is at the top of ul Cherno More, a steep 1km walk from the port. Minibuses travel from Balchik to Albena (3 lv, 20 minutes, every 30 minutes), Varna (5 lv, one hour, hourly) and Sofia (36 lv, 10 hours). Rather more conveniently, minibuses to Albena also call at the bus stop on ul Primorska, outside the supermarket.

Central Coast
Dominating the coastal strip between Varna and Burgas – often a mountainous ride, generally inland away from the water – is the huge, clubland resort of Sunny Beach (Slânchev Bryag) and its ancient, church-filled neighbour, Nesebâr. A few surprises can be found via out-of-the-way rough roads too.

VARNA TO BURGAS

Byala, about 54km south of Varna, is a basic town of 2100 people, set on the rising hills above the beach. Some 4km north – on a dirt road past rolling hills of vineyards – is the more attractive **Karadere beach**. Varna–Burgas buses pass by Byala.

About 13km south (past the small beach town of Ozbor, where buses stop), a road heads east a couple of kilometres towards the largely untouched **Irakli beach**, with a guesthouse and a couple of bungalows.

For the best views, a rough road rambles from Irakli for 8km up to hillside **Emona**. The trans-Bulgarian Mt Kom–Emine Cape hike (E3) ends here, and a very rough dirt road leads down to a small beach. The road curves inland, bypassing Sunny Beach and Nesebâr, and continues on 31km into Burgas.

NESEBÂR НЕСЕБЪР

📞 0554 / POP 10,300

On a small, rocky outcrop 37km northeast of Burgas, connected to the mainland by a narrow, artificial isthmus, pretty-as-a-postcard Nesebâr (Ne-*se*-bar) is famous for its surprisingly numerous, albeit mostly ruined, medieval churches. It has, inevitably, become heavily commercialised, and transforms into one huge, open-air souvenir market during the high season; outside summer, it's a ghost town. With Sunny Beach just across the bay, you have every conceivable water sport on hand. The New Town on the other side of the isthmus has the newest and biggest hotels and the main beach, but the sights are all in the Old Town.

◉ Sights & Activities

Nesebâr was once home to about 80 churches, but most are now in ruins. Characteristic of the Nesebâr style are the horizontal strips of white stone and red brick, and facades decorated with green ceramic discs.

Around 1.5km west of the Old Town is **South Beach**. All the usual water sports are available, including **jet skiing** and **waterskiing**. The longer sandy shores of Sunny Beach (Slânchev Bryag), just a few kilometres up the coast, are an alternative option.

Archaeological Museum MUSEUM
(www.ancient-nessebar.org; ul Mesembria 2; adult/child 5/3 lv; ☺9am-8pm Mon-Fri, 9.30am-1.30pm & 2-7pm Sat & Sun Jul & Aug) Greek and Roman pottery, statues and tombstones, as well as Thracian gold jewellery and ancient anchors

are displayed here. There's also a collection of icons recovered from Nesebâr's numerous churches.

Sveti Stefan Church CHURCH
(ul Ribarska; adult/student 5/2 lv; ☺9am-7pm Mon-Fri, 9am-1pm & 1.30-6pm Sat & Sun) Built in the 11th century and reconstructed 500 years later, this is the best preserved church in town, renowned for its beautiful 16th- to 18th-century murals, which cover virtually the entire interior. Try to come early, as it's popular with tour groups.

FREE **Sveta Sofia Church** CHURCH
(Old Metropolitan Church; ul Mitropolitska; ☺dawn-dusk) At the centre of town, the vast and impressive shell of this church is surrounded by cafes and artists' stalls.

FREE **St John Aliturgetos Church** CHURCH
(ul Mena; ☺dawn-dusk) Overlooking the harbour to the south, this earthquake-battered building is set on a cliff and provides a picturesque setting for summertime concerts.

FREE **Christ Pantokrator Church** CHURCH
(ul Mesembria; ☺dawn-dusk) This church has been converted into a commercial art gallery, selling the works of local painters, mainly seascapes and views of the Old Town.

⛁ Sleeping

In summer, you'll need to book accommodation in advance. Private rooms are the best option for budget travellers. Locals offering rooms often meet tourists off the bus.

TOP CHOICE **Hotel Tony** GUESTHOUSE €
(📞0889 268 004, 42 403; ul Kraybrezhna 20; r from 40 lv; ☺Jun-Sep; ✳) In a great spot overlooking the sea, Hotel Tony is reasonably priced and is regularly full in summer. Rooms are simple but clean and the chatty host is very helpful.

Hotel Trinity Sea Residence HOTEL €€
(📞46 600; www.trinity-nessebar.com; ul Venera 8; s/d/apt from 82/92/152 lv; ⓟ✳☎⏚) This pretty National Revival–style wooden villa has spacious rooms and apartments, many with stunning sea views, and half- and full-board deals are available. Children under eight stay free, and video games and baby cribs are available.

Prince Cyril Hotel HOTEL €
(☑42 220; hotelprincecyril@gmail.com; ul Slavyan-ska 9; d from 50 lv; ❋❅) Located on a quiet, cobbled, souvenir-stall-free lane, this is a friendly place with a variety of rooms, all with TV and fridge, but not all with air-con; check a few out first and try to avoid the cramped, top-floor fan-only rooms.

✖ Eating

All restaurants in Nesebâr are geared towards the passing tourist trade and prices are roughly twice what you'll pay away from the coastal resorts. Try to avoid those that employ touts.

Pri Shopite BULGARIAN €€
(ul Neptun 12; mains 7-15 lv; ☑) Set in a traditional, tavern-style courtyard around a twisted, 300-year-old fig tree, this is a welcoming place with great food, including freshly caught fish, grills, steaks and vegetarian options.

Old Nesebâr SEAFOOD €€
(☑42 070; ul Ivan Alexander 11; mains 8-15 lv) With two tiers of seating offering great sea views, this is a popular place for barbecues, grills and fish dishes, as well as salads and lighter meals.

Zlatnoto Runo BULGARIAN €€€
(☑45 602; ul Rusalka 6; mains 8-20 lv) Overlooking the sea on the southeastern end of the peninsula, the 'Golden Fleece' serves a varied menu, including roast lamb and rabbit plus some inventive seafood dishes, such as octopus with blueberry sauce.

❶ Information

Post Office (ul Mesembria; ❅8am-8pm Tue-Sat)

Tourist Information Centre (☑42 611; www.visitnessebar.org; ul Mesembria 10; ❅9am-5.30pm May-Oct)

Unicredit Bulbank (ul Mesembria; ❅8.30am-5pm Mon-Fri)

❶ Getting There & Away

Nesebâr is well connected to coastal destinations by public transport, and the town's bus station is on the small square just outside the city walls. The stop before this on the mainland is for the New Town. From the bus station, there are buses to nearby Sunny Beach (1 lv, 10 minutes, every 15 minutes), Burgas (6 lv, 40 minutes, every 30 minutes), Varna (15 lv, two hours, seven daily) and Sofia (30 lv, seven hours, several daily).

Fast Ferry (www.fastferry.bg) operates a summer-only high-speed hydrofoil service to

Sozopol (one way/return from 27/54 lv, 30 minutes, three to four daily).

Burgas ~~Бургас~~

☑056 / POP 229,000

For most visitors, the port city of Burgas (sometimes written as 'Bourgas') is no more than a transit point for the more obviously appealing resorts and historic towns further up and down the coast. If you do decide to stop over, you'll find a lively, well-kept city with a neat, pedestrianised centre, a long, uncrowded beach and some interesting museums. A clutch of reasonably priced hotels, as well as some decent restaurants, makes it a practical base for exploring the southern coast.

◎ Sights & Activities

Archaeological Museum MUSEUM
(bul Aleko Bogoridi 21; adult/student 4/2 lv; ❅10am-6pm Mon-Sat) This small museum houses a diverting collection of local finds, including neolithic flint tools, a wooden canoe from the 5th century BC, Greek statuary and the remarkably well-preserved wooden coffin of a Thracian chieftain.

Natural History Museum MUSEUM
(ul Konstantin Fotinov 20; adult/student 4/2 lv; ❅10am-6pm Mon-Sat) Old-fashioned but informative displays on local flora, fauna and geology are on view here. Exhibits of rocks, seashells, butterflies and beetles occupy the ground floor, while upstairs there's a collection of stuffed birds and animals.

Ethnographical Museum MUSEUM
(ul Slavyanska 69; adult/student 4/2 lv; ❅10am-6pm Mon-Sat) Regional folk costumes, jewellery and furniture are on show at this museum, as well as displays covering the local weaving and fishing industries. Everything is labelled in Bulgarian.

Soviet Army Monument MONUMENT
(pl Troikata) Standing sentinel over pl Troikata is this towering Red Army memorial, comprising a column surmounted by a saluting Russian soldier and figurative panels. It is a major city focal point.

Beach BEACH
(▣8, 12) Although it can't compare with beaches at the nearby resorts, Burgas beach still attracts plenty of locals on a hot summer day. It's a bit grubby at the southern

end, with its long concrete pier, used as a diving platform by teenage boys and a fishing station by old men, but further on there are beach bars and restaurants.

Sleeping

TOP CHOICE Hotel California
BOUTIQUE HOTEL €€

(☑531 000; www.burgashotel.com; ul Lyuben Karavelov 36; s/d 60/70 lv; P⊕✱❄; ☐4) This appealing boutique hotel on a quiet side street about five minutes' walk west of the centre is a winner, with large rooms featuring colourful wall prints and especially soft mattresses. Guests get a 20% reduction in the excellent restaurant.

Hotel Chiplakoff
BOUTIQUE HOTEL €€

(☑829 325; www.chiplakoff.com; ul Ferdinandova 88; s/d 50/60 lv; P✱@) A 10-minute walk west of the centre, this hotel occupies an attractively restored mansion, designed by the same architect who built the city's grand train station. Rooms are large and contemporary in style, and the original spiral staircases have been retained; there's no lift, however. There's a popular pizza restaurant downstairs.

Grand Hotel Primoretz
LUXURY HOTEL €€€

(☑812 345; www.hotelprimoretz.bg; ul Knyaz Al Battenberg 2; s/d/ste from 216/236/296 lv; P⊕✱❄≋; ☐12) This huge, five-star complex at the southern end of the city beach looks out of scale in Burgas, but excellent facilities include a spa and indoor and outdoor pools. Sea views cost a little extra, as does the wi-fi and parking, which seems a bit cheeky at these prices.

Fotinov Guest House
HOTEL €€

(☑0878 974 703; www.hotelfotinov.com; ul Konstantin Fotinov 22; s/d 72/82 lv; ✱❄) Conveniently located right in the city centre, with a selection of brightly coloured rooms, featuring fridges, kettles and cable TV. The multilingual staff are friendly and helpful, and there's even a small sauna.

Burgas Hostel
HOSTEL €

(☑825 854; hostelburgas@gmail.com; ul Slavyanska 14; dm incl breakfast 20 lv; @; ☐12) The only hostel in town didn't bother with a fancy name. It sports five- and eight-bed dorms, plus a small lounge and kitchen.

Eating & Drinking

Outlets along bul Aleko Bogoridi sell pizza, kebabs and ice cream, while there are several summertime bars along the beach, most of which also serve food.

Roma
ITALIAN €€

(☑825 467; bul Aleko Bogoridi 60; mains 6-20 lv; ☐8) This trendy Italian place has a wide menu ranging from simple pasta and risotto dishes (5 lv to 6 lv) up to pricier options such as grilled sea bass (20 lv). Steaks, grills and various fish dishes are available. Reservations are advisable in the evenings.

Vodenitsata
BULGARIAN €

(Water Mill; ☑0899 174 715; mains from 3 lv; ☺10am-2am; ☐12) Standing on the seafront overlooking the beach, this is a traditional wood-cabin affair, which is always packed out with locals. Specialities include grilled fish, barbecues, steaks and salads.

London Pub & Restaurant
BRITISH €€

(ul Tsar Simeon 4a; mains 8-20 lv; ☺10am-1am; ❄; ☐12) Catering to homesick British expats and visitors, come here for all-day English breakfasts, as well as mixed grills and steak-and-onion pie. The kitchen closes at 9pm, but drinks are served until 1am.

TOP CHOICE China Tea House
TEAHOUSE

(pl Troikata 4; tea from 2 lv; ☺8.30am-10pm Mon-Fri, 11am-10pm Sat; ❄) Oil paintings by local artists decorate this chilled-out teahouse, which offers a big menu of black, green and herbal teas, as well as a few freshly prepared vegetarian dishes.

Samba Lounge
BAR

(☺8am-midnight) One of the more attractive beach bars, set on decking over the sand and surrounded by potted flowers. It's a pleasant spot to relax with a beer (2 lv) and they also serve light meals such as salads and soups throughout the day.

Entertainment

In summer, nightclubs and bars materialise between the trees of Maritime Park; among the more reliable is Alibi (☑0897 962 262; Maritime Park; ☺11pm-late), offering 'retro nights', dance and Latino music. Live music, dance and drama performances often take place at the Summer Theatre, while the Sea Casino Cultural Centre (Maritime Park) hosts a varied program of concerts and exhibitions.

For something more sophisticated, find out what's on offer at the Adriana Boudevska Drama Theatre (☑842 266; ul Tsar Asen

TRANSPORT FROM BURGAS

Bus

DESTINATION	PRICE (LV)	DURATION	FREQUENCY
Sozopol	4.50	40min	every 30min
Nesebâr	6	40min	every 30-40min
Sunny Beach (Slânchev Bryag)	6	45min	every 30-40min
Primorsko	7	1hr	every 30min
Sofia	30	7-8hr	several daily
Plovdiv	17	4hr	several daily
Varna	14	2hr	every 30-40min

Train

DESTINATION	PRICE (LV)	DURATION (HR)	FREQUENCY
Sofia	23.10	7-8	6 daily
Plovdiv	19	5-6	7 daily
Kazanlâk	14.40	3	2 daily

I 36a) or the **Burgas Opera House** (☏840 762; www.operabourgas.com; ul Sv Kliment Ohridski 2).

ℹ Information

Numerous banks with ATMs can be found along ul Aleksandrovska and ul Aleko Bogorid, including **Unicredit Bulbank** (ul Aleksandrovska), **Central Cooperative Bank** (ul Aleksandrovska) and **Raffeisen Bank** (ul Ferdinandova).

Post Office (ul Tsar Petâr 2)

Tourist Information Centre (☏825 772; www.tic.burgas.bg; ul Hristo Botev; ⊗8.30am-5.30pm Mon-Fri; 🖥12) At the entrance to the underpass below ul Hristo Botev, the city's tourist office has English-speaking staff and plenty of brochures.

ℹ Getting There & Away

AIR Bulgaria Air links **Burgas Airport** (☏870 248; www.bourgas-airport.com; 🖥15), 10km north-east of town, with Sofia three times a day (April to October). In summer, **WizzAir** (www.wizzair.com) connects Burgas with London Luton, Budapest, Prague and Warsaw. Other carriers fly to destinations in Germany and Russia.

BUS Yug bus station (cnr ul Aleksandrovska & ul Bulair), outside the train station at the southern end of ul Aleksandrovska, is where most travellers arrive or leave. There are regular buses to coastal destinations. Departures are less frequent outside summer.

A number of agencies around Yug bus station, including **Union-Ivkoni** (☏840 986), run coaches to İstanbul each day (55 lv, seven hours). **Nışıklı Turızm** (☏841 261; ul Bulair) has several daily departures (55 lv to 60 lv) from outside its office. Union-Ivkoni also runs daily buses to destinations in Greece, including Thessaloniki (80 lv, 13 hours).

TRAIN The historic **train station** (ul Ivan Vazov) was built in 1902. Through the **ticket windows** (⊗8am-6pm) on the right, you can buy advance tickets for domestic and international services, while same-day tickets can be bought at the **windows** (⊗24hr) on the left. The **left-luggage office** (⊗6am-10.45pm) is outside the station.

International tickets are also available at the **Rila Bureau** (⊗8am-5.30pm Mon-Thu, to 4pm Fri, to 3.30pm Sat) inside the station.

South Coast

The finest sandy beaches dot the coast south from Sozopol to the Turkish border, though some come with less-appealing modern beach resorts. It helps to have wheels, but you can reach many rewarding spots by bus, too.

SOZOPOL   СОЗОПОЛ
☏0550 / POP 5000

Ancient Sozopol, with its charming Old Town of meandering cobbled streets and pretty wooden houses huddled together on a narrow peninsula, is one of the coast's real highlights. With two superb beaches, genial atmosphere, plentiful accommodation and good transport links, it has long been a popular seaside resort and makes an excellent base for exploring the area. Although not quite as crowded as Nesebâr, it is becoming ever more popular with international visitors. There's a lively cultural scene, too, with plenty of free concerts and other events in summer.

◉ Sights & Activities

The town's two beaches are attractive, though waves can be quite high. The 1km-long **Harmanite Beach** is wide and clean and offers a water slide, paddle boats, volleyball nets and beach bars. At the southern end, incongruously, archaeological excavations have uncovered stone sarcophagi on the site of the ancient **Apollonia necropolis**.

The **Town Beach** (or Northern Beach) is another pleasant curve of sand, but it's smaller, gets *very* crowded, and doesn't offer the same number of beachside cafes, restaurants and bars.

Archaeological Museum   MUSEUM
(ul Han Krum 2; 4 lv; ⊘9am-6pm, closed Sat & Sun winter) Housed in a drab concrete box near the port, this museum has a small collection of local finds. The high-quality Hellenic ceramics, dating from the 5th century BC, give an indication of the wealth and sophistication of early citizens, and there are lots of anchors and amphorae dredged up from ancient shipwrecks.

Southern Fortress Wall & Tower Museum   RUINS, MUSEUM
(ul Milet 40; adult/student 4/3 lv; ⊘9.30am-8pm Jul & Aug, to 5pm May, Jun, Sep & Oct) The reconstructed walls and walkways along the rocky coastline, and a 4th-century-BC well that was once part of a temple to Aphrodite here are free to explore – the few, mostly empty, rooms you get to see for your 4 lv are something of an anticlimax.

Church of Sveta Bogoroditsa   CHURCH
(ul Anaksimandâr 13; 1 lv; ⊘10am-1pm & 2-6pm) This 15th-century church was built below street level, as required at the time by the Ottoman rulers. Set in a courtyard with a giant fig tree, it is one of the most picturesque in town, with an exquisite wooden iconostasis and a pulpit carved with bunches of grapes.

Church of Sveti Georgi   CHURCH
(ul Apolonia; ⊘9am-1pm & 3-8pm Mon-Sat, 7am-1pm & 3-8pm Sun) This is another attractive church, with a fine painting of St George and the Dragon over the entrance and an impressive 19th-century iconostasis. The custodians here are rather keen to enforce the dress code (no shorts).

🛏 Sleeping

Sozopol has countless private homes offering rooms. Look for signs along Republikanska in the New Town and pretty much anywhere in the Old Town.

TOP CHOICE / Art Hotel   HOTEL €€
(☑24 081; www.arthotel-sbh.com; ul Kiril & Metodii 72; d Jul-Sep 75 lv, Oct-Jun from 40 lv; ❋❂) This peaceful Old Town house, belonging to the Union of Bulgarian Artists, is located within a walled courtyard towards the tip of the peninsula, away from the crowds. It has a small selection of bright and comfortable rooms with balconies, most with sea views, and breakfast is served on the terraces directly over the sea.

Hotel Villa List   HOTEL €€
(☑22 235; www.hotellist-bg.com; ul Yani Popov 5; s/d from 65/92 lv; ❋@❂❂) With a superb setting just off the town beach, big rooms with balconies and an outdoor pool with a view over the sea, Villa List is very popular and frequently fully booked in summer. There's even a 'nude terrace' for that all-over tan.

Hotel Diamanti   HOTEL €€
(☑22 640; www.hoteldiamanti.com; ul Morski Skali; d/apt 80/120 lv; ❂❋❂❂) Another Old Town hotel, Diamanti has a variety of rooms, some with sea views, including apartments with kitchenettes. Larger apartments are available in a second building nearby. There's also a terrace restaurant with live music in summer.

Sasha Khristov's Private Rooms   PENSION €
(☑23 434; ul Venets 17; s/d 20/30 lv) This lovely family home in the Old Town faces the art gallery at the end of the Sozopol peninsula. It comprises good-sized rooms and a large apartment. Book ahead in summer.

✖ Eating

Fish, naturally enough, is the local speciality, and several reasonably priced restaurants are strung out along the port area. The best restaurants in town are on ul Morksi Skali, and are large and traditional affairs with some spectacular views. The pedestrianised section of ul Ropotamo, alongside Harmanite Beach, is packed with cafes, restaurants and bars. They're all pretty much the same.

TOP CHOICE★ **Panorama** SEAFOOD €€€
(ul Morski Skali 21; mains 8-20 lv) As the name suggests, this place has an open terrace with a fantastic view towards Sveti Ivan island. Fresh, locally caught fish is a mainstay of the menu, and service is quick and friendly.

Bizhou SEAFOOD €€
(ul Kraybrezhna; mains 4-9 lv) This simple harbourside restaurant is good value, specialising in a variety of fresh fish dishes. Bulgarian staples such as *kebabcheta* (grilled minced meat with spices) and salads are also available.

ℹ Information

Many banks with ATMs can be found along the Old Town's main streets and around the New Town's main square.

Post Office (ul Apolonia; ⏰7am-8.30pm)
Unicredit Bulbank (ul Lazuren Bryag)

ℹ Getting There & Away

The small public **bus station** (ul Han Krum) is just south of the Old Town walls. Buses leave for Burgas (4.50 lv, 40 minutes) about every 30 minutes between 6am and 9pm in summer, and about once an hour in the low season.

In summer, hourly buses go to Primorsko (4.50 lv, 35 minutes). Public buses leave up to three times a day for Sofia.

Fast Ferry (☎0877 908 004; www.fastferry.bg; Fishing Harbour) runs ferries at least four days a week to Nesebâr (single/return from 27/54 lv, 30 minutes) between June and September.

SOZOPOL TO TSAREVO

Just south of Sozopol, an inland road rambles past undeveloped **Stork Beach** (Alepu), a protected beach backed by marsh that sees thousands of storks in August. The bustling resort towns of **Primorsko** (22km south of Sozopol) and **Kiten** (5km further south) attract mostly Bulgarian holidaymakers; neither is that atmospheric, but both have fine beaches and plenty of midrange hotels.

TSAREVO ЦАРЕВО
☎0590 / POP 5800

Spread lazily over two small peninsulas jutting out into the Black Sea, Tsarevo is a quiet, elegant little town, once a popular holiday spot for the Bulgarian royal family. Called Vasiliko until 1934, it was renamed Tsarevo ('royal place') in honour of Tsar Boris III; the communists then renamed it Michurin (after a Soviet botanist) in 1950, and it reverted once again in 1991. The centre, on the northern peninsula, has a calm, affluent atmosphere and feels more like a real town than some of Tsarevo's resort neighbours.

☉ Sights

Overlooking the rocky headland at the end of the main road, ul Han Asparuh, are the peaceful **Sea Gardens**, offering dramatic panoramic views across the Black Sea. Other sights of interest include the **Church of Sveti Tsar Boris-Mikhail**, dedicated to the former king, and the tiny **Church of the Holy Trinity**, built in 1810 above the beach, accessed by steps on the northern side of the headland. It's a small but picturesque scrap of sand with a couple of bars.

Across the wide bay, the southern peninsula is of less interest, dominated by modern apartments and holiday homes, although the headland, reached by scrambling over rocks, has Tsarevo's best **beach**. Sadly, this is no secret cove, as it's also occupied by the giant Serenity Bay hotel.

🛏 Sleeping & Eating

Hotel Zebra HOTEL €€
(☎55 111; www.hotel-zebra.com; ul Han Asparuh 10; s/d Jul & Aug 60/76 lv, s/d Sep-Jun from 46/56 lv; 🅿❄@❄) Near the Sea Gardens, this modern complex offers superb value. The large, comfortable rooms all have balconies and sparkling bathrooms, and there's an outdoor pool and restaurant.

Hotel Chaika HOTEL €
(☎0888 249 125; www.chaika.in; ul Han Asparuh 21; d 25-40 lv) In the centre of town, the Chaika is an older hotel which has been renovated. Most of the brightly painted rooms have balconies with sea views and are great value for this price.

Ribarska Sreshta SEAFOOD €€
(mains 5-12 lv; ⏰7am-midnight; 🐟) Fresh fish is on the menu at this harbourside restaurant, in a hotel of the same name.

ℹ Getting There & Away

Tsarevo's bus station is at the top of ul Mikhail Gerdzhikov, about 2km west of the centre. Minibuses to Burgas (9 lv, 50 minutes) run roughly every 30 minutes to one hour between 6am and 8pm via Kiten and Primorsko, and there are two daily buses to Sofia (37 lv, eight hours).

NORTHWEST BULGARIA

Bulgaria's little horn – jutting up between Romania and Serbia – is a bit of a backwater that's way off the usual tourist trail. Curved to the northeast by the Danube, it has seen plenty of military struggles, and prehistoric forces have forged stunning rock formations and gorges that make for great hiking and rock climbing. The train from Sofia goes past impressive **Iskâr Gorge**, south of Mezdra.

Vidin   Видин

☏094 / POP 48,000

Resting on a bend in the Danube in the far northwest of Bulgaria, Vidin feels a long way from anywhere, and unless you're crossing into Romania, there's little obvious reason for you to make your way up here. The population has shrunk dramatically over the last decade or so, and it can appear forlorn and eerily deserted. Having said all that, Vidin does enjoy some fine riverside views and its one major attraction, the majestic Baba Vida fortress, is one of the best preserved in the country.

◉ Sights

Baba Vida Museum-Fortress   FORTRESS
(adult/student 4/2 lv, combined ticket with Archaeological Museum 5 lv; ☺8.30am-5pm Mon-Fri, 9.30am-5pm Sat & Sun) About 1km north of the centre, the marvellously intact Baba Vida Museum-Fortress is largely a 17th-century Turkish upgrade of 10th-century Bulgarian fortifications, which in turn were built upon the ruins of the 3rd-century Roman fort of Bononia. There's little to see inside, but it's an atmospheric place. Watch out for uncovered holes and the sheer drops from the top.

Archaeological Museum   MUSEUM
(ul Tsar Simeon Veliki 12; adult/student 4/2 lv, combined ticket with Baba-Vida Fortress 5 lv; ☺9am-noon & 1.30-5.30pm Tue-Sat) Inside the former Turkish prison, this little museum holds a scrappy collection of neolithic flints, Roman statue fragments, medieval swords and 19th-century rifles. There's no English labelling and it's only worth a quick look.

⌂ Sleeping

Anna-Kristina Hotel   HOTEL €€
(☏606 038; www.annakristinahotel.com; ul Baba Vida 2; d from 84 lv; ᴘ❄@✦) Housed inside a century-old Turkish bathhouse set back from the river, the Anna-Kristina is a wel-

coming, if slightly formal, place with spacious rooms and smart modern bathrooms. There's a summer-only outdoor pool (10 lv extra) and a restaurant.

Old Town Hotel   BOUTIQUE HOTEL €€
(Hotel Staryat Grad; ☏600 023; www.oldtownhotel.dir.bg; ul Knyaz Boris I 2; s/d/tr 60/80/100 lv; ❄✦) Centrally located near the Old Town *Stambol Kapia* gateway, this charming boutique hotel has just eight rooms inside a renovated townhouse, fitted with antique-style furnishings and original works by local artists.

Hotel Bononia   HOTEL €
(☏606 031; www.hotelbononia.net; ul Bdin 2; s/d 36/39 lv; ❄) Just around the corner from the riverside park, the Bononia is an old-style hotel, though it offers acceptable rooms that are good value. It also has a decent restaurant.

✗ Eating & Drinking

Vidin has a few good restaurants and some cafes, though they're fairly subdued. The most popular are off the south side of the square before the Danube. There are no river views from most restaurants or cafes, thanks to the high river wall.

Classic Pizzeria   PIZZERIA €
(ul Aleksandar II 25; mains 5-15 lv) Opposite the Port Authority building on the riverbank, this is one of the better places in town, with a big menu of pizzas and pasta dishes, as well as locally caught fish.

ⓘ Information

Foreign exchange offices, banks and several ATMs line ul Tsar Simeon Veliki and pl Bdintsi.

ⓘ Getting There & Away

From Vidin's public **bus station** (ul Zhelezh-nicharska) there are two or three daily buses to Belogradchik (5 lv, 1½ hours). Nearby is the private Alexiev bus station, from where there are several daily buses to Sofia (20 lv, four hours) via Vratsa (10 lv).

   Three fast trains travel daily to Sofia (13.80 lv, five hours) via Vratsa (8 lv, three hours).

Belogradchik Белоградчик

☏0936 / POP 5150

The crisp mountain air and the weird and wonderful rock formations rising from a lonely hill are what draw visitors to little Belogradchik, on the eastern edge of the Stara Planina mountain range. Although rather remote, Belogradchik's charms are starting to attract more visitors.

⊙ Sights

Belogradchik Rocks
OUTDOORS

The massive Belogradchik limestone rock formations cover an area of around 90 sq km and tower over the town. They are accessible by road, about 2km west of town. The tall, oddly shaped and variously hued rocks have inspired many local legends.

Kaleto Fortress
FORTRESS

(admission 4 lv; ⊙9am-6pm Jun-Sep, to 5pm Oct-May) Almost blending in with the surrounding rocks is the Kaleto Fortress, originally built by the Romans and later expanded by the Byzantines, Bulgarians and Turks. Most of what you see today was completed in the 1830s. You can wander round three courtyards and explore the defensive bunkers, while accessing the highest rocks involves a precarious climb up steep ladders.

History Museum
MUSEUM

(pl 1850 Leto; 1 lv; ⊙9am-noon & 2-5pm Mon-Fri) The history museum, housed in a National Revival–era building built in 1810, displays folk costumes, jewellery and traditional local crafts such as woodcarving and pottery.

🛏 Sleeping & Eating

Hotel Madona
GUESTHOUSE €

(⌨65 546; www.madonainn-bg.com; ul Hristo Botev 26; s 20-30 lv, d 40-60 lv; ⊛) This cosy guesthouse has six traditional-style rooms, 600m up from the main square (it's signposted). The restaurant is one of the best in town, and guests can hire mountain bikes for 7 lv per day.

Hotel Castle Cottage
GUESTHOUSE €€

(⌨0898 623 727; www.castlecottage.eu; ul Tsolo Todorov 36; s/d 35/70 lv; P⊛) Standing not far from the fortress entrance, Castle Cottage is built in solid wood-and-stone traditional style. It offers one comfortable bedroom and two maisonettes, each individually designed, a log fire in winter and outdoor hottubs in summer.

Restaurant Elit
BULGARIAN €

(⌨64 558; ul Yuri Gagarin 2; mains 4-6 lv; ⊙9am-midnight) Elit is one of a handful of restaurants in town, offering a variety of traditional Bulgarian dishes. It's an uphill walk (600m) up steep ul Vasil Levski and then off to the left.

ℹ Information

Tourist Information Centre (⌨64 294; milena-tourist_centre@abv.bg; ul Poruchik Dvoryanov 5; ⊙9am-5pm Mon-Fri) Can help with accommodation and gives out maps.

ℹ Getting There & Away

From the **bus station** (⌨63 427), three or four daily buses serve Vidin (5 lv, 1½ hours). A 6am bus serves Sofia (16 lv, four hours). The three daily buses that serve the train station, 9km away at Gara Oreshets (2 lv, 20 minutes), are timed to meet the Sofia-bound train. Several daily trains from Gara Oreshets serve Vidin (5 lv, 30 minutes), Vratsa (7 lv, 20 minutes) and Sofia (10 lv, three hours, 30 minutes).

A taxi from Belogradchik to Gara Oreshets train station costs 5 lv. For very early morning trains, taxis wait in front of the bus depot.

UNDERSTAND BULGARIA

History
Becoming Bulgaria

Thracians moved into the area of modern Bulgaria in around 5000 BC and Greek colonists from the south began settling cities on the Black Sea coast from the 7th century BC. By AD 100 Bulgaria was part of the Roman Empire. The first Slavs migrated here from the north in the 5th century AD and the first Bulgarian state was formed in AD 681.

The fierce Bulgars first reached these areas from their expansive territories between the Caspian and Black Seas. By the time the Byzantine Empire conquered Bulgaria in 1014, the first state had created a language, the Cyrillic alphabet and a national church. Bulgaria gained independence from Constantinople in 1185, and this second kingdom, based in Veliko Târnovo, lasted until the Ottomans took control in 1396.

Under the Ottomans

The next 500 years were spent living 'under the yoke' of Ottoman rule. The Orthodox Church persevered by quietly holing up in monasteries. Higher taxes for Christians saw many convert to Islam.

During the 18th and 19th centuries, many 'awakeners' are credited with reviving Bulgarian culture. By the 1860s several revolutionaries (including Vasil Levski and Hristo Botev) organised *cheti* (rebel) bands for the unsuccessful April Uprising of 1876. With Russia stepping in, the Turks were defeated in 1878, and Bulgaria regained its independence.

War & Communism

With eyes on lost Macedonia, following a series of painful Balkan Wars (including WWI), Bulgaria aligned with Nazi Germany in WWII with hopes to expand its borders. Famously, however, Tsar Boris III said 'no' to Hitler, refusing to send Bulgaria's Jewish population to concentration camps, sparing up to 50,000 lives.

Towards the end of the war, the communist Fatherland Front gained control of Bulgaria, and Georgi Dimitrov became the first leader of the People's Republic in 1946. The royal family was exiled. A program of rapid industrialisation and collectivisation followed and under Todor Zhivkov, the country's leader from 1954–89, Bulgaria became one of the most repressive of the Eastern Bloc regimes, and the most loyal of Russia's client states, even proposing to join the USSR in 1973.

Modern Bulgaria

The communists were finally ousted in 1989, although reforming as the Socialist Party, they were re-elected into office the following year. In 2001, history was made when the former king, Simeon II, was elected as Bulgaria's prime minister; the first former monarch to return to power in Eastern Europe. Bulgaria joined NATO in 2004 and the EU in 2007, but low wages, organised crime and corruption are sources of continual complaint and anguish. That anguish came to a head in 2013, when the government of Prime Minister Boyko Borisov was forced to resign in the face of economic stagnation and rising energy prices.

People

The population of Bulgaria is about 7.3 million, and continues to shrink – it has been estimated that 1.4 million people have left the country over the last 20 years. Bulgarians and Slavs constitute roughly 85% of the population, with the largest minorities being Turks (9%) and Roma (4.5%).

There are around 200,000 Pomaks – Muslims of Slavic origin – in the villages of the Rodopi Mountains, although many consider themselves to be ethnic Turks and others claim to be descended from ancient Balkan tribes converted by Arab missionaries a thousand years ago, but nobody knows for sure. There's also a small Jewish population of about 5000, mostly living in Sofia. During the communist era Bulgaria was officially atheist. These days, about 83% of the population are Orthodox Christian and 12% are Muslim (almost all of these are Sunni).

Arts
Music
FOLK MUSIC

The vaguely oriental sounds of Bulgarian folk music offer an evocative aural impression of the country. Traditional instruments include the *gaida* (bagpipes), *gadulka* (a bowed stringed instrument) and *kaval* (flute). As in many peasant cultures, Bulgarian women were not given access to musical instruments, so they usually performed the vocal parts. Bulgarian female singing is polyphonic, featuring many voices and shifting melodies, and women from villages in the Pirin Mountains are renowned for their unique singing style. Regular folk music and

BULGARIA PEOPLE

VASIL LEVSKI

It's a name you'll see on street signs and public buildings in every Bulgarian town, and the matinee idol looks will soon become familiar from the countless moustachioed, gazing-into-the-distance statues across the country; a bit like Che Guevara but with neater hair. It's Vasil Levski, the 'Apostle of Freedom' and Bulgaria's undisputed national hero.

Born Vasil Ivanov Kunchev in Karlovo in 1837, Levski (a nickname meaning 'Lion') originally trained as a monk, but in 1862 fled to Belgrade to join the revolutionary fight against the Turks, led by Georgi Rakovski. A few years later he was back, travelling incognito around Bulgaria, setting up a network of revolutionary committees. Levski, who believed in the ideals of the French Revolution, was a charismatic and able leader of the independence movement, but he was captured in Lovech in December 1872 and hanged in Sofia in February 1873; the Levski Monument marks the spot where he died.

dance festivals are held around Bulgaria, and are great opportunities to experience the culture.

CONTEMPORARY SOUNDS

The most distinctive sound in Bulgarian contemporary music is the spirited, warbling, pop-folk idiom known as *chalga*. Influenced by Balkan, Turkish, Arabic and even flamenco rhythms, this is sexy, sweaty, repetitive dance music and is looked down on by many Bulgarians who consider it vulgar. Bands often feature a scantily clad female lead vocalist and play jazzed-up traditional Balkan tunes on instruments such as the electric guitar, clarinet and synthesiser. It's loud, brash and often self-consciously cheesy, and isn't to everyone's tastes, but there are plenty of clubs around Bulgaria that play little else, and it's hard to avoid on TV or radio. One of the biggest names in contemporary *chalga* is Azis, a gay, white-bearded, transvestite Roma.

Architecture

The most obvious product of the prodigious and creative Bulgarian National Revival era is the unique architectural style of homes seen throughout the country. These were either built side-by-side along narrow cobblestone streets, as in Plovdiv, or surrounded by pretty gardens, as in Arbanasi.

The wood-and-stone homes were usually painted brown and white (though some were more colourful), and featured bay windows and tiled roofs. Ceilings were often intricately carved and/or painted with bright murals and rooms would have several small fireplaces and low doors.

Architectural designs and styles of furniture differed from one region to another. The colour, shape and size of the typical home in Melnik contrasts significantly with those found in Arbanasi. Some of the most stunning examples of National Revival–period homes can also be appreciated in traditional villages such as Koprivshtitsa, Tryavna and Shiroka Lûka. There are also examples among the Old Towns of Plovdiv and Veliko Tårnovo, and at the re-created Etâr Ethnographic Village Museum near Gabrovo.

Visual Arts

Most of Bulgaria's earliest artists painted on the walls of homes, churches and monasteries. The works of these anonymous masters are considered national treasures, and rare surviving examples can be seen in churches and museums across the country, including the lovely Boyana Church, near Sofia.

Throughout the Ottoman occupation, the tradition of icon painting endured as a symbol of national culture and identity. The highpoint for Bulgarian icon painting came during the National Revival period, and the most famous artist of the time was Zahari Zograf (1810–53), who painted magnificent murals in the monasteries at Rila, Troyan and Bachkovo.

Environment

Bulgaria lies in the heart of the Balkan peninsula, stretching 502km from the Serbian border to the 378km-long Black Sea coast.

Bulgaria is one-third mountains. The Stara Planina (also known as the Balkan Mountains) stretch across central Bulgaria. In the southwest are three higher ranges: the Rila Mountains, south of Sofia (home to the country's highest point, Mt Musala, 2925m); the Pirin Mountains, just south towards Greece; and the Rodopi Mountains to the east.

Although Bulgaria has some 56,000 kinds of living creature – including 400 bird species and one of Europe's largest bear populations –

CHANTS & CHURCH MUSIC

Bulgarian ecclesiastic music dates back to the 9th century and conveys the mysticism of chronicles, fables and legends. To hear Orthodox chants sung by a choir of up to 100 people is a moving experience. Dobri Hristov (1875–1941) was one of Bulgaria's most celebrated composers of church and choral music, and wrote his major choral work, *Liturgy No 1*, for the Seven Saints ensemble, Bulgaria's best-known sacred-music vocal group, based in Sofia's Sveti Sedmochislenitsi Church.

The Sofia Boys' Choir, formed in 1968, brings together boys from various schools in the capital, aged eight to 15, and has performed around the world to great acclaim. As well as their traditional Easter and Christmas concerts, they are known for their Orthodox choral music and folk songs.

THE INIMITABLE CHRISTO

The most famous living Bulgarian artist is Christo Javacheff, known simply as Christo. Born in Gabrovo in 1935, he studied at Sofia's Fine Arts Academy in the 1950s and met his French-born wife, Jeanne-Claude, in Paris in 1958.

They have worked in collaboration since 1961, when they created their first outdoor temporary installation, *Stacked Oil Barrels*, at Cologne Harbour. Since then, the couple, who moved to New York in 1964, have made a name for themselves with their (usually) temporary, large-scale architectural artworks, often involving wrapping famous buildings in fabric or polypropylene sheeting to highlight their basic forms.

In 1985 they created *The Pont Neuf Wrapped*, covering the Parisian landmark in golden fabric for 14 days, while in 1995 the *Reichstag* in Berlin was covered entirely with silver fabric, and in 2005, *The Gates* was unveiled in New York's Central Park; an impressive installation consisting of 7503 vinyl gates spread over 32km of walkways.

Christo and Jeanne-Claude are still working on major projects around the world, and current schemes still in the planning stage include *The Mastaba*, a gigantic stack of 410,000 multicoloured oil barrels – first conceived in 1977 – to be built in the desert in Abu Dhabi. For the latest, see www.christojeanneclaude.net.

most visitors see little wildlife, unless venturing deep into the thickets and mountains. Popular birdwatching spots near the Black Sea include Burgas Lakes, west of Burgas, and Durankulak Lake, near the Romanian border.

Bulgaria has three national parks (Rila, Pirin and Central Balkan) and 10 nature parks, all of which offer some protection to the environment (and have tourist potential). The EU has funded a number of projects to offer more protection, particularly along the Black Sea Coast and the Rodopi Mountains. Also see www.bulgariannationalparks.org.

Food & Drink

Fresh fruit, vegetables, dairy produce and grilled meat form the basis of Bulgarian cuisine, which has been heavily influenced by Greek and Turkish cookery. Pork and chicken are the most popular meats, while tripe also features heavily on traditional menus. You will also find recipes including duck, rabbit and venison, and fish is plentiful along the Black Sea coast, but less common elsewhere.

Staples & Specialities

Skara (grilled meats) especially pork, are among the most popular dishes served in Bulgarian restaurants, *mehanas* and snack bars. You can't escape the omnipresent *kebabche* (grilled spicy pork sausages) and *kyufte* (a round and flat pork burger), which are tasty, filling and cheap staples of Bulgarian menus, usually served with chips/fried potatoes (*pârzheni kartofi*) or salad. The *kyufte tatarsko*, a seasoned pork burger filled with melted cheese, is another variant. The Greek-influenced *musaka* (moussaka), made with minced pork or veal and topped with potatoes, is a quick lunchtime staple of cafeterias.

Shishcheta (shish kebabs), consisting of chunks of chicken or pork on wooden skewers with mushrooms and peppers, and various steaks, fillets and chops are widely available.

Meat stews and 'claypot meals' (hot, sizzling stews served in clay bowls) are traditional favourites. *Kavarma*, normally made with either chicken or pork, is one of the most popular dishes. Exact recipes vary from one region to the next, but the meat is cooked in a pot with vegetables, cheese and sometimes egg, and is brought sizzling to your table.

Drinks

Coffee is the beverage of choice for most Bulgarians, though tea is also popular. Most common are the herbal (*bilkov*) and fruit (*plodov*) variety; if you want real, black tea, ask for *cheren chai* and if you'd like milk, ask for *chai s'mlyako*.

The national spirit is *rakia* (a clear and potent kind of brandy, usually made from grapes), and there are countless brands available. It's drunk as an aperitif, and served with ice in restaurants and bars, which often devote a whole page on their menus to list regional *rakias* on offer.

Bulgaria's excellent wines are a product of its varied climate zones, rich soil and proud tradition. Foreign interest and investment in recent years have made Bulgarian wines increasingly known and appreciated abroad. Wine-loving travellers can sample them at rustic wineries, in gourmet urban restaurants, and even at roadside stands.

SURVIVAL GUIDE

Directory A–Z
Accommodation

Bulgaria offers pretty much every kind of accommodation option you can think of, from spartan mountain huts to the most opulent five-star hotels. Accommodation is most expensive in Sofia and other big cities, notably Plovdiv and Varna. Elsewhere, prices are relatively cheap by Western European standards. If you're travelling independently around the country, one indispensable publication is the *Bulgaria B&B and Adventure Guidebook* (13.50 lv) published by the **Bulgarian Association for Alternative Tourism** (☑02-980 7685; www.baatbg.org; bul Stambolyiiski 20 B, Sofia), which lists sustainable, family-run guesthouses all over Bulgaria. You can buy it at **Zig Zag Holidays** (☑02-980 5102; www.zigzagbg.com; bul Stamboliyski 20-V; ⊙9.30am-6.30pm Mon-Fri) in Sofia.

As you would expect, prices are highest in the coastal resorts between July and August, and in the skiing resorts from December to March. Outside high season, many resort hotels close down. So if you're thinking of staying in, for example, Pamporovo in September or Nesebâr in February, phone ahead to see what the situation is.

Several useful websites offer acccomodation information or online booking facilities.

BgStay (www.bgstay.com)

BG Globe (www.bgglobe.net)

Bulgaria Hotels (www.bulgaria-hotels.com)

Hotels in Bulgaria (www.hotels.bg)

Sofia Hotels (www.sofiahotels.net)

PRICE RANGES

The following price ranges refer to a double room with bathroom in high season. Unless otherwise stated, breakfast is included in the price.

$ less than 60 lv

$$ 60 lv to 120 lv (200 lv in Sofia)

$$$ more than 120 lv (200 lv in Sofia)

CAMPING & HUTS

Camping grounds normally consist of wooden cabins in a patch of forest and are usually quite simple, but cheap. Camping outside camping grounds is technically illegal and potentially dangerous.

Hizhas (mountain huts) dot the high country and range in quality – they are shown on most Bulgaria maps. Most are basic places intended only for a one-night stopover. Many are now privately run (and cost about 10 lv to 30 lv per person); some more remote ones are free. In July and August, you may wish to reserve ahead at an agency.

PRIVATE ROOMS

Travellers on a budget can rent *stai pod naem* (private rooms), often offered by agencies or private individuals at train and bus stations. Rates range from 10 lv or 15 lv per person in smaller towns, to 35 lv or more in places such as Sofia, Plovdiv and Varna. Cheaper places tend to be far from the city centre.

Activities

All kinds of outdoor activities are catered for in Bulgaria, with hiking, biking, mountaineering, rock climbing, diving and skiing being just some of the sports available. The country is promoted as a growing ski destination, with new resorts in the Pirin mountains, while the country's unspoilt, mountainous terrain makes it ideal for trekking and hiking, with numerous well-marked trails and a system of mountain huts, or *hizhas*, for hikers to sleep in. Water sports are popular on the Black Sea coast, although these tend to be confined to the big package-holiday resorts. Windsurfing, paragliding, scuba diving and a host of other watery activities can be arranged during summer.

Cycling Bulgaria (www.cycling.bg) Multiday mountain-bike tours.

Hiking in Bulgaria (www.bghike.com) Guided hiking trips.

Neophron (www.birdwatchingbulgaria.net) Runs 10- to 14-day guided birdwatching trips across the country, which can be combined with botany and bearwatching tours.

Business Hours

Banks 9am to 4pm Monday to Friday

Bars 11am to midnight (or later)

Government offices 9am to 5pm Monday to Friday

Post offices 8am to 6pm Monday to Friday

Restaurants 11am to 11pm

Shops 9am to 6pm

Discount Cards

International Student (ISIC, www.isic.org), **Youth** (IYTC) and **Teacher** (ITIC) discount cards can be used in Bulgaria, offering a range of discounts on transport, accommodation, restaurants, shopping, entertainment venues and tourist attractions. Cards may be bought in Bulgaria at branches of the **Usit Colours travel agency** (www.usit-colours.bg). Check online for current details and for participating companies.

Embassies & Consulates

New Zealanders can turn to the British embassy for assistance or contact their consulate general in Athens. Embassies are located in Sofia.

Australian Embassy (☎02-946 1334; austcon@mail.orbitel.bg; ul Trakia 37; 🚍78)

Canadian Embassy (☎02-969 9710; general@canada-bg.org; ul Moskovska 9; 🚍20)

French Embassy (☎02-965 1100; www.ambafrance-bg.org; ul Oborishte 27-29; 🚍1)

German Embassy (☎02-918 380; www.sofia.diplo.de; ul Frederic Joliot-Curie 25; Ⓜ Joliot-Curie)

Irish Embassy (☎02-985 3425; www.embassyofireland.bg; ul Bacho Kiro 26-30; 🚍20)

Netherlands Embassy (☎02-816 0300; http://bulgaria.nlembassy.org; ul Oborishte 15; 20)

Turkish Embassy (☎02-935 5500; www.sofia.emb.mfa.gov.tr; bul Vasil Levski 80; 🚍94)

UK Embassy (☎02-933 9222; www.ukinbulgaria.fco.gov.uk; ul Moskovksa 9; 🚍20)

US Embassy (☎02-937 5100; http://bulgaria.usembassy.gov; ul Kozyak 16; 🚍88)

Food

Eating out in Bulgaria is remarkably cheap, and even if you're on a tight budget, you'll have no problem eating well. In this book, we've used the following price ranges (price of a typical main course):

€ less than 5 lv

€€ 5 lv to 10 lv

€€€ more than 10 lv

Gay & Lesbian Travellers

Homosexuality is legal in Bulgaria, though same-sex relationships have no legal recognition.

Bulgaria is conservative and opinion polls suggest a majority of Bulgarians have a negative opinion of homosexuality. Attitudes among younger people are slowly changing, and there are a few gay clubs and bars in Sofia and in other major cities.

Bulgayria (www.gay.bg)

Gay Bulgaria Ultimate Gay Guide (www.gay-bulgaria.info)

Gay Guide Bulgaria (www.gayguidebg.org)

Sofia Pride (www.sofiapride.info)

Internet Access

Wi-fi access is common in towns and cities, and is often free in hotels and restaurants. Hostels often have computers for guest use. Internet cafes have become less common in recent years, but most big towns will have at least one.

Legal Matters

Bulgaria is a member of the EU and follows the same legal system as the rest of Europe. You need to be 21 years old to rent a car and 18 or over to drink alcohol.

Money

The currency is the lev (plural: leva), comprised of 100 stotinki. It is usually abbreviated as lv. The lev is a stable currency. For major purchases such as organised tours, airfares, car rental, and midrange and top-end hotels, prices are often quoted in euros, though payment is usually made in leva. Bulgaria has no immediate plans to adopt the euro.

CASH

Bulgarian banknotes come in denominations of 2, 5, 10, 20, 50 and 100 leva. Coins come in 1, 2, 5, 10, 20 and 50 stotinki, and 1 lev.

CHANGING MONEY

Foreign-exchange offices can be found in all larger towns and current rates are always displayed prominently. Charging commission is no longer allowed, but that doesn't stop some from trying; always check the final amount you will be offered before handing over your cash. Avoid exchange offices at train stations, airports or tourist resorts as rates tend to be poor.

The best currencies to take to Bulgaria are euros, pounds sterling and US dollars. You may have trouble changing less-familiar currencies, such as Australian or Canadian dollars.

It's also easy to exchange cash at most of the larger banks in cities and major towns; the exchange rates listed on the electronic boards in bank windows may offer slightly higher rates than foreign exchange offices, but they may charge a commission.

CREDIT CARDS

Credit cards are commonly accepted in hotels, restaurants and shops in big cities, towns and tourist resorts, but acceptance is less widespread in rural areas. Some places, particularly the more expensive hotels, will add a 5% surcharge to your bill if you use a credit card.

TIPPING

In restaurants, round bills up to the nearest whole lev or tip 10% of the bill to reward good service. The same applies to taxi drivers.

Public Holidays

New Year's Day 1 January

Liberation Day (National Day) 3 March

Orthodox Easter Sunday & Monday March/April; one week after Catholic/Protestant Easter

May Day 1 May

St George's Day 6 May

Cyrillic Alphabet Day 24 May

Unification Day (National Day) 6 September

Bulgarian Independence Day 22 September

National Revival Day 1 November

Christmas 25 and 26 December

Safe Travel

You're unlikely to face major problems in Bulgaria. Pickpocketing or beach grab-and-runs can happen in summer, particularly on Varna's beach. There are plenty of rogue taxi drivers waiting to rip off foreigners; always use a reputable firm and if possible ask your hotel to call your cab.

Telephone

To call Bulgaria from abroad, dial the international access code, add ☎359 (the country code for Bulgaria), the area code (minus the first zero) and then the number.

MOBILE PHONES

Bulgarian mobile phones use the GSM 900/1800 network, the standard throughout Europe as well as in Australia and New Zealand, but not compatible with most mobile phones in North America or Japan. One possibility is to bring or buy an unlocked handset operating on this GSM band and purchase a local SIM card. Bulgaria has three mobile service providers which cover most of the country: **Globul** (www.globul.bg), **M-Tel** (www.mtel.bg) and **Vivacom** (www.vivacom.bg).

Mobile phone numbers can be identified by the prefixes ☎087, ☎088 or ☎089.

PHONECARDS

Prepaid phonecards for use in public telephones are available from newspaper kiosks and some shops in denominations ranging from 5 lv to 25 lv.

Travellers with Disabilities

Bulgaria is not an easy destination for travellers with disabilities. Uneven and broken footpaths are common in towns and wheelchair-accessible toilets and ramps are rare outside the more expensive hotels.

Visas

Citizens of other EU countries, as well as Australia, Canada, New Zealand, the USA and many other countries do not need a visa for stays of up to 90 days. Other nationals should contact the Bulgarian embassy in their home countries for current visa requirements.

Getting There & Away

Bulgaria is well connected by air, rail and road. Flights, tours and rail tickets can be booked online at lonelyplanet.com/bookings.

Entering the Country

Bulgaria is a member of the EU, though (as of this writing) not yet a member of the EU's common border and customs Schengen Zone. In practice, this means all border crossings, even with EU-member Romania, are subject to passport and customs inspection.

Air

AIRPORTS

The Bulgarian national carrier is **Bulgaria Air** (www.air.bg). It operates flights to destinations across Europe and the Middle East as well as domestic routes to the Black Sea coast.

Sofia Airport (☎02-937 2211; www.sofia-airport.bg) Main point of entry to the country.

Varna Airport (www.varna-airport.bg; ✈409) Domestic flights and seasonal flights to/from European destinations.

Burgas Airport (☎870 248; www.bourgas-airport.com; ✈15) Summer charter flights.

AIRLINES

Aegean Airlines (www.aegeanair.com)

Aeroflot (☎943 4489; www.aeroflot.ru)

Aerosvit (☎980 7880; www.aerosvit.com)

Air Berlin (www.airberlin.com)

Air France (☎939 7010; www.airfrance.com)

Alitalia (☎981 6702; www.alitalia.it)

British Airways (☎954 7000; www.britishairways.com)

Cyprus Airways (www.cyprusair.com)

easyJet (www.easyjet.com)

Lufthansa Airlines (☎930 4242; www.lufthansa.com)

Tarom (www.tarom.ro)

Turkish Airlines (☎988 3596; www.turkishairlines.com)

Wizz Air (☎960 3888; www.wizzair.com)

Land

BUS

Most international buses arrive in Sofia. You will have to get off the bus at the border and walk through customs to present your passport. When travelling out of Bulgaria by bus, the cost of entry visas for the countries concerned are not included in the prices of the bus tickets.

CAR & MOTORCYCLE

» In order to drive on Bulgarian roads, you will need to purchase a vignette, sold at all border crossings into Bulgaria, petrol stations and post offices. For a car, this costs 10/25 lv for one week/month.

» Your home driving licence is valid in Bulgaria for short-term stays.

» Petrol stations and car-repair shops are common around border crossing areas and along main roads.

TRAIN

There are a number of international trains from Bulgaria, including services to Romania, Greece and Turkey. Sofia is the main hub, although trains stop at other towns. The daily *TransBalkan,* running between Budapest and Thessaloniki, stops at Ruse, Gorna Oryakhovitsa (near Veliko Tárnovo) and Sofia. The *Balkan Express* normally goes daily between Belgrade and İstanbul, with stops in Sofia and Plovdiv. The *Bulgaria Express* to Bucharest leaves from Sofia.

Tickets for international trains can be bought at any government-run **Rila Bureau** (www.bdz-rila.com; ⊙closed most Sun) or at some dedicated ticket offices (most open daily) at larger stations with international connections.

River & Sea

International sea travel to/from Bulgaria is limited to commercial cargo vessels. The **UKR Shipping Company** (www.ukrferry.com) runs cargo ships between Varna and Ilyichevsk in Ukraine, and also accepts individual passengers. Check the website for current arrangements and prices. There are car-ferry crossings to Romania at Vidin, Oryahovo and Nikopol.

Getting Around
Air

The only scheduled domestic flights within Bulgaria are between Sofia and Varna and Sofia and Burgas. Both routes are operated by **Bulgaria Air** (www.air.bg).

Bicycle

» Many roads are in poor condition; some major roads are always choked with traffic and bikes aren't allowed on highways.

» Many trains will carry your bike for an extra 2 lv.

» Cycling is a more attractive option in the Black Sea resorts, where there are plenty of places renting out bikes. Spare parts are available in cities and major towns, but it's better to bring your own.

Bus

Buses link all cities and major towns and connect villages with the nearest transport hub. There are several private companies operating frequent modern, comfortable buses between the larger towns, while older, often cramped minibuses also run on routes between smaller towns.

DECODING YOUR TRAIN TICKET

All tickets are printed in Cyrillic. Other than the place of departure and destination, tickets also contain other important details:

» Клас *klas* – '1' (1st class) or '2' (2nd class)

» Категория *kategoriya* – type of train, ie T (express), 255 (fast) or G (slow passenger)

» Влак *vlak* – train number

» Час *chas* – departure time

» Дата *data* – date of departure

» Вагон *vagon* – carriage number

» Място *myasto* – seat number

Union-Ivkoni (☏02-989 0000; www.union-ivkoni.bg) Links most major towns and many smaller ones.

Biomet (☏02-868 8961; www.biomet.bg) Runs between Sofia and Veliko Tărnovo, Varna and Burgas.

Etap-Grup (☏02-813 3100; www.etapgroup.com) Buses between Sofia, Burgas, Varna, Ruse and Veliko Tărnovo, as well as routes between Sofia and Sozopol, Primorsko and Tsarevo.

Car & Motorcycle

Bulgaria's roads are among the most dangerous in Europe and the level of fatalities each year is high. The worst time is the holiday season (July to September), with drink-driving, speeding and poor road conditions contributing to accidents.

The **Union of Bulgarian Motorists** (☏02-935 7935, road assistance 02-980 3308; www.uab.org; pl Positano 3, Sofia) offers 24-hour road assistance and has some helpful basic information on its website.

ROAD RULES

» Drive on the right.

» Drivers and passengers in the front must wear seat belts; motorcyclists must wear helmets.

» Blood-alcohol limit is 0.05%.

» Children under 12 are not allowed to sit in front.

» From November to March, headlights must be on at all times.

» Speed limits are 50km/h in built-up areas, 90km/h on main roads and 120km/h om motorways.

CAR HIRE

To rent a car in Bulgaria you must be at least 21 years of age and have had a licence for at least one year. Rental outlets can be found all over Bulgaria, especially in the bigger cities, airports and Black Sea resorts. Prices start at around 50 lv to 60 lv per day. You'll need a valid credit card.

Train

Bălgarski Dârzhavni Zheleznitsi – the **Bulgarian State Railways** (BDZh; www.bdz.bg) – boasts an impressive 4278km of track across the country, linking most towns and cities.

Most trains tend to be antiquated and not especially comfortable, and journey times slower than buses. On the plus side you'll have more room in a train compartment and the scenery is likely to be more rewarding.

Trains are classified as *ekspresen* (express), *bârz* (fast) or *pâtnicheski* (slow passenger). Unless you absolutely thrive on train travel or want to visit a more remote town, use a fast or express train.

Two of the most spectacular train trips are along Iskâr Gorge, from Sofia to Mezdra, and on the narrow-gauge track between Septemvri and Bansko.

Croatia

Best Places to Eat

» Vinodol (p220)
» Konoba Batelina (p228)
» Foša (p241)
» Bajamonti (p247)

Best Places to Stay

» Studio Kairos (p219)
» Goli + Bosi (p246)
» Art Hotel Kalelarga (p241)
» Lešić Dimitri Palace (p253)

Why Go?

Croatia has been touted as the 'new this' and the 'new that' for years since its re-emergence on the tourism scene, but it's now clear that it's a unique destination that holds its own and then some: this is a country with a glorious 1778km-long coast and a staggering 1244 islands. The Adriatic coast is a knockout: its sapphire waters draw visitors to remote islands, hidden coves and traditional fishing villages, all while touting the glitzy beach and yacht scene. Istria captivates with its gastronomic delights and wines, and the bars, clubs and festivals of Zagreb, Zadar and Split remain little-explored gems. Eight national parks showcase primeval beauty with their forests, mountains, rivers, lakes and waterfalls. and you can finish up in dazzling Dubrovnik in the south – just the right finale. Best of all, Croatia hasn't given in to mass tourism: there are pockets of unique culture and plenty to discover off the grid.

When to Go
Zagreb

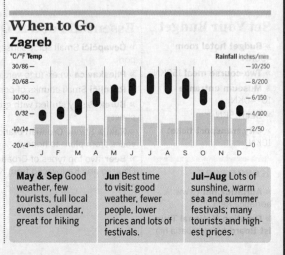

May & Sep Good weather, few tourists, full local events calendar, great for hiking

Jun Best time to visit: good weather, fewer people, lower prices and lots of festivals.

Jul–Aug Lots of sunshine, warm sea and summer festivals; many tourists and highest prices.

CROATIA

AT A GLANCE

» **Currency** Kuna (KN)

» **Language** Croatian

» **Money** ATMs available; credit cards accepted in most hotels and many restaurants

» **Visas** None for up to 90 days; South Africans and some other nationalities need them

Fast Facts

» **Area** 56,538 sq km

» **Capital** Zagreb

» **Country code** ☑385

» **Emergency** Ambulance ☑194, fire ☑193, police ☑192

Exchange Rates

Australia	A$1	6.21KN
Canada	C$1	5.85KN
Euro Zone	€1	7.60KN
Japan	¥100	6.30KN
New Zealand	NZ$1	4.97KN
UK	UK£1	8.99KN
USA	US$1	5.94KN

Set Your Budget

» **Budget hotel room** 450KN

» **Two-course meal** 150KN

» **Museum entrance** 10–40KN

» **Beer** 15KN

» **City transport ticket** 10KN

Resources

» **Adriatica.net** (www.adriatica.net)

» **Croatian National Tourist Board** (www.croatia.hr)

Connections

Croatia is a convenient transport hub for southeastern Europe and the Adriatic. Zagreb is connected by train and/or bus to Venice, Budapest, Belgrade, Ljubljana and Sarajevo in Bosnia and Hercegovina (BiH). Down south there are easy bus connections from Dubrovnik to Mostar and Sarajevo, and to Kotor (Montenegro). There are a number of ferries linking Croatia with Italy, including routes from Dubrovnik to Bari, and Split to Ancona.

ITINERARIES

One Week

After a day in dynamic Zagreb, delving into its simmering nightlife, fine restaurants and choice museums, head down to Split for a day and night at Diocletian's Palace, a living part of this exuberant seafront city. Then hop over to chic Hvar for a spot of partying and swimming off Pakleni Otoci. Next take it easy down the winding coastal road to magnificent Dubrovnik and take a day trip to Mljet for the final two days.

Two Weeks

After two days in Zagreb, head to Istria for a three-day stay, with Rovinj as the base, and day trips to Pula and Poreč. Go southeast next to the World Heritage–listed Plitvice Lakes National Park, a verdant maze of turquoise lakes and cascading waterfalls. After a quick visit, move on to Zadar, a real find of a city: historic, modern, active and packed with attractions. Then go on south to Split for a day or two. From here, take ferries to Hvar and then Korčula, spending a day or more on each island before ending with three days in Dubrovnik and an outing to Mljet.

Essential Food & Drink

» **Ćevapčići** Small spicy sausages of minced beef, lamb or pork.

» **Pljeskavica** An ex-Yugo version of a hamburger.

» **Ražnjići** Small chunks of pork grilled on a skewer.

» **Burek** Pastry stuffed with ground meat, spinach or cheese.

» **Rakija** Strong Croatian brandy comes in different flavours, from plum to honey.

» **Beer** Two top types of Croatian *pivo* (beer) are Zagreb's Ožujsko and Karlovačko from Karlovac.

ZAGREB

📌01 / POP 792,900

Everyone knows about Croatia's coast and islands, but a mention of the country's capital still draws the confused question: 'Is it worth visiting?' Here is the answer: Zagreb is a great destination, with lots of culture, arts, music, architecture, gastronomy and all the other things that make a quality capital.

Visually, Zagreb is a mixture of straight-laced Austro-Hungarian architecture and rough-around-the-edges socialist structures, its character a sometimes uneasy combination of these two elements. This mini metropolis is made for strolling the streets, drinking coffee in the permanently full cafes, popping into museums and galleries, and enjoying the theatres, concerts and cinema. It's a year-round outdoor city: in spring and summer everyone scurries to Jarun Lake in the southwest to swim, boat or dance the night away at lakeside discos, while in autumn and winter Zagrebians go skiing at Mt Medvednica, only a tram ride away, or hiking in nearby Samobor.

History

Zagreb's known history begins in medieval times with two hill settlements: Kaptol, now the site of Zagreb's cathedral, and Gradec. When the two merged in 1850, Zagreb was officially born.

The space now known as Trg Josipa Jelačića became the site of Zagreb's lucrative trade fairs, spurring construction around its edges. In the 19th century the economy expanded and cultural life blossomed with the development of a prosperous clothing trade and a rail link connecting Zagreb with Vienna and Budapest.

Between the two world wars, working-class neighbourhoods emerged in Zagreb between the railway and the Sava River, and new residential quarters were built on the southern slopes of Mt Medvednica. In April 1941, the Germans invaded Yugoslavia and entered Zagreb without resistance. Ante Pavelić and the Ustaše moved quickly to proclaim the establishment of the Independent State of Croatia (Nezavisna Država Hrvatska), with Zagreb as its capital.

In postwar Yugoslavia, Zagreb (to its chagrin) took second place to Belgrade but continued to expand. Zagreb was made the capital of Croatia in 1991, the same year that the country became independent.

💿 Sights

As the oldest part of Zagreb, the Upper Town (Gornji Grad) offers landmark buildings and churches from the earlier centuries of Zagreb's history. The Lower Town (Donji Grad) has the city's most interesting art museums and fine examples of 19th- and 20th-century architecture.

UPPER TOWN

Museum of Broken Relationships   MUSEUM
(http://brokenships.com; Ćirilometodska 2; adult/concession 25/20KN; ☺9am-10.30pm Jun–mid-Oct, 9am-9pm mid-Oct–May) Explore mementos that remain after a relationship ends at Zagreb's quirkiest museum. On display are donations from around the globe, in a string of all-white rooms with vaulted ceilings. Exhibits hit on a range of emotions, from a can of love incense from Indiana that 'doesn't work' to an iron from Norway once used to straighten a wedding suit. Check out the adjacent store and the cosy cafe with sidewalk tables.

Dolac Market   MARKET
(☺7am-3pm Mon-Fri, to 2pm Sat, to 1pm Sun) Zagreb's colourful Dolac is just north of Trg Josipa Jelačića. This buzzing centre of Zagreb's daily activity since the 1930s draws in traders from all over Croatia who flog their products here. The main part of the market is on an elevated square; the street level has indoor stalls selling meat and dairy products and, towards the square, flower stands.

Cathedral of the Assumption
of the Blessed Virgin Mary   CATHEDRAL
(Katedrala Marijina Uznešenja; Kaptol; ☺10am-5pm Mon-Sat, 1-5pm Sun) Kaptol Sq is dominated by the twin neo-Gothic spires of this 1899 cathedral, formerly known as St Stephen's. Elements of an earlier medieval cathedral, destroyed by an earthquake in 1880, can be seen inside, including 13th-century frescoes, Renaissance pews, marble altars and a baroque pulpit. Note that you might be turned away if you're not dressed appropriately: no bare legs or shoulders.

Lotrščak Tower   HISTORICAL BUILDING
(Kula Lotrščak; Strossmayerovo Šetalište 9; adult/concession 10/5KN; ☺9am-9pm) From Radićeva 5, off Trg Jelačića, a pedestrian walkway called Zakmardijeve Stube leads to this medieval tower, which can be climbed for a sweeping 360-degree view of the city.

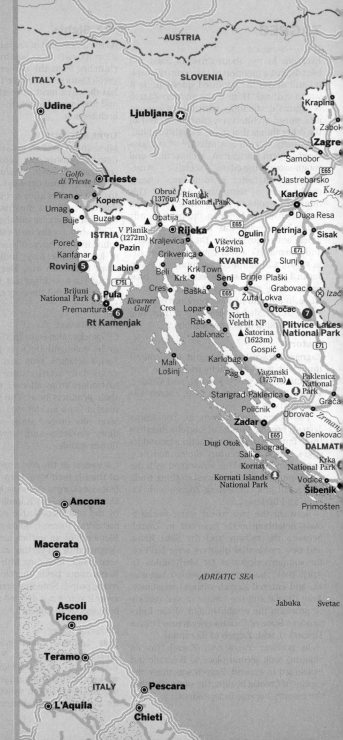

Croatia Highlights

1 Gape at the Old Town wall of **Dubrovnik** (p256), which surrounds luminous marble streets and finely ornamented buildings.

2 Admire the Venetian architecture and vibrant nightlife of **Hvar Town** (p250).

3 Indulge in the lively and historic delights of **Diocletian's Palace** (p242) in Split.

4 Explore the lakes, coves and island monastery of **Mljet** (p254).

5 Stroll the cobbled streets and unspoiled fishing port of **Rovinj** (p229).

6 Take in the wild landscapes of **Rt Kamenjak** (p227) cape near Pula.

7 Marvel at the turquoise lakes and waterfalls in **Plitvice Lakes National Park** (p226).

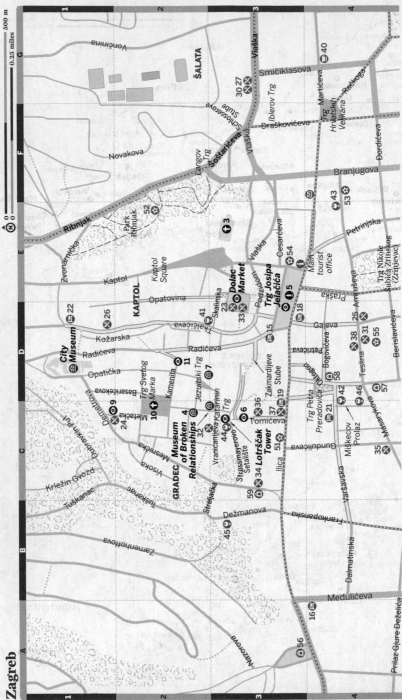

Zagreb

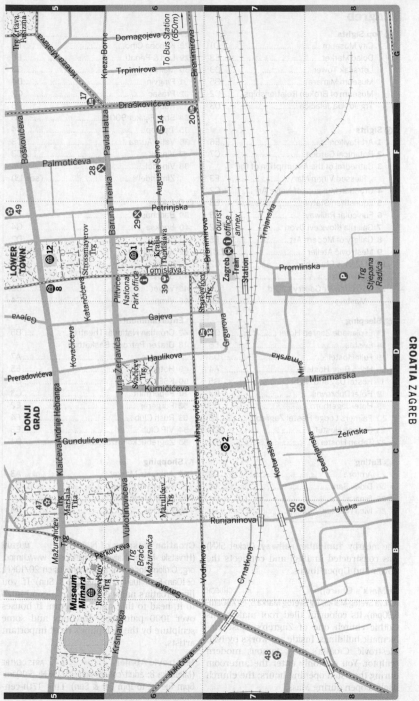

Map labels (Zagreb, Lower Town / Donji Grad):

- Trg Ortava Fašizna
- Kneza Mislava
- Kneza Borne
- Domagojeva
- Trpimirova
- Branimirova
- To Bus Station (650m)
- Draškovićeva
- 17
- Boškovićeva
- Pavla Hatza
- 14
- 20
- Palmotićeva
- 28
- Baruna Trenka
- Augusta Šenoe
- 49
- Petrinjska
- 29
- LOWER TOWN
- 12
- Strossmayerov Trg
- Trg Kralja Tomislava
- 1
- Branimirova
- Tourist office annex
- Zagreb Tram Station
- office annex
- Trnjanska
- Trnjanska
- Katančićeva
- 8
- Piltvice National Park office
- Tomislava
- 39
- Starčevićev Trg
- Promlinska
- Trg Stjepana Radića
- Gajeva
- Gajeva
- Kovačićeva
- Haulikova
- Grgurova
- e marska
- 13
- Jurja Žerjavića
- Soačićev Trg
- Kumičićeva
- Mihanovićeva
- Mihanova
- Miramarska
- Preradovićeva
- Klaićeva Andrije Hebranga
- DONJI GRAD
- Gundulićeva
- Zelinska
- Bednjanska
- Mažuranićev Trg
- Trg Maršala Tita
- 47
- Vukotinovićeva
- Marulićev Trg
- Runjaninova
- Koturaška
- 50
- Unska
- Museum Mimara
- Roosveltov Trg
- Perkovčeva
- Trg Braće Mažuranića
- Savska
- Vodnikova
- Crnatkova
- Krsnjavoga
- Kršnjavoga
- 2
- 48

Zagreb

The nearby **funicular railway** (ticket 5KN) was constructed in 1888 and connects the Lower and Upper Towns.

St Mark's Church CHURCH
(Crkva Svetog Marka; Trg Svetog Marka 5; ◷7.30am-6.30pm) Its colourful tiled roof makes this Gothic church one of Zagreb's most emblematic buildings. Inside are works by Ivan Meštrović, Croatia's most famous modern sculptor. You can only enter the anteroom during the listed opening hours; the church itself is open during Mass.

Croatian Museum of Naïve Art MUSEUM
(Hrvatski Muzej Naivne Umjetnosti; www.hmnu. org; Ćirilometodska 3; adult/concession 20/10KN; ◷10am-6pm Tue-Fri, to 1pm Sat & Sun) If you like Croatia's naïve art or want a good intro to it, head to this small museum. It houses over 1000 paintings, drawings and some sculpture by the discipline's most important artists.

Meštrović Atelier ARTS CENTRE
(Mletačka 8; adult/concession 30/15KN; ◷10am-6pm Tue-Fri, to 1pm Sat & Sun) This 17th-cen-

tury building, the former home of Croatia's most recognised artist, Ivan Meštrović, now houses an excellent collection of some 100 sculptures, drawings, lithographs and pieces of furniture created by the artist.

City Museum   MUSEUM
(Muzej Grada Zagreba; www.mgz.hr; Opatička 20; adult/concession 30/20KN; ☺10am-6pm Tue-Fri, 11am-7pm Sat, 10am-2pm Sun; ⓦ) Check out the scale model of old Gradec, atmospheric background music and interactive exhibits that fascinate kids. There are summaries in English in each room of the museum, which is in the former Convent of St Claire (1650).

Galerija Klovićevi Dvori   ART GALLERY
(www.galerijaklovic.hr; Jezuitski trg 4; adult/concession 30/20KN; ☺11am-7pm Tue-Sun) Housed in a former Jesuit monastery, this is the city's most prestigious space for exhibiting modern Croatian and international art. Note that the gallery closes in summer months.

Stone Gate   LANDMARK
Make sure you take a peek at this eastern gate to medieval Gradec Town, now a shrine. According to legend, a great fire in 1731 destroyed every part of the wooden gate except for the painting of the *Virgin and Child* by an unknown 17th-century artist.

LOWER TOWN
Trg Josipa Jelačića   SQUARE
Zagreb's main orientation point and the geographic heart of the city is Trg Josipa Jelačića. It has an **equestrian statue** of Jelačić, the 19th-century *ban* (viceroy or governor) who led Croatian troops into an unsuccessful battle with Hungary in the hope of winning more autonomy for his peo-

ple. The square is Zagreb's principal meeting point; sit in one of the cafes for quality people-watching.

Museum Mimara   MUSEUM
(Muzej Mimara; www.mimara.hr; Rooseveltov trg 5; adult/concession 40/30KN; ☺10am-7pm Tue-Fri, to 5pm Sat, to 2pm Sun Jul-Sep, 10am-5pm Tue-Wed & Fri-Sat, to 7pm Thu, to 2pm Sun Oct-Jun) Ante Topić Mimara donated his diverse collection to Croatia. Housed in a neo-Renaissance palace, it includes icons, glassware, sculpture, Oriental art and works by renowned painters such as Rembrandt, Velázquez, Raphael and Degas.

Strossmayer Gallery of
Old Masters   MUSEUM
(Strossmayerova Galerija Starih Majstora; Trg Nikole Šubića Zrinskog 11; adult/concession 30/10KN; ☺10am-7pm Tue, to 4pm Wed-Fri, to 1pm Sat & Sun) Inside the neo-Renaissance Croatian Academy of Arts and Sciences, this gallery showcases the impressive fine-art collection donated to Zagreb by Bishop Strossmayer in 1884. The interior courtyard has the **Baška Slab** (1102) from Krk Island, one of the oldest inscriptions in the Croatian language.

Art Pavilion   ART GALLERY
(Umjetnički Paviljon; www.umjetnicki-paviljon.hr; Trg Kralja Tomislava 22; adult/concession 30/15KN; ☺11am-7pm Tue-Sat, 10am-1pm Sun Sep–mid-Jul) The yellow Art Pavilion in a stunning 1897 art nouveau building presents changing exhibitions of contemporary art.

Gallery of Modern Art   ART GALLERY
(Moderna Galerija; www.moderna-galerija.hr; Andrije Hebranga 1; adult/concession 40/20KN; ☺11am-6pm Tue-Fri, to 1pm Sat & Sun) With a glorious

---

ZAGREB IN TWO DAYS

Start your day with a stroll through Strossmayerov trg, Zagreb's oasis of greenery. Take a look at the **Strossmayer Gallery of Old Masters** and then walk to **Trg Josipa Jelačića**, the city's centre.

Head up to Kaptol Square for a look at the **Cathedral**, the centre of Zagreb's religious life. While in the Upper Town, pick up some fruit at **Dolac market** or have lunch at **Amfora**. Then get to know the work of Croatia's best sculptor at **Meštrović Atelier** and see his naïve-art legacy at the **Croatian Museum of Naïve Art**, followed by a visit to the quirky **Museum of Broken Relationships**. See the lay of the city from the top of **Lotrščak Tower**, then spend the evening bar-crawling along Tkalčićeva.

On the second day, tour the Lower Town museums, reserving an hour for the **Museum Mimara** and as long for the **Museum of Contemporary Art**. Lunch at **Vinodol** and digest in the **Botanical Garden**. Early evening is best at Preradovićev trg before dining and sampling some of Zagreb's nightlife.

display of Croatian artists of the last 200 years, this gallery offers an excellent overview of Croatia's vibrant arts scene.

Botanical Garden
GARDENS

(Botanički Vrt; Mihanovićeva bb; ☺9am-2.30pm Mon & Tue, 9am-7pm Wed-Sun Apr-Oct) Laid out in 1890, the garden has 10,000 plant species, including 1800 tropical flora specimens. The landscaping has created restful corners and paths that seem a world away from bustling Zagreb.

OUTSIDE THE CENTRE

Museum of Contemporary Art
MUSEUM

(Muzej Suvremene Umjetnosti; www.msu.hr; Avenija Dubrovnik 17; adult/concession 30/15KN, 1st Wed of month free; ☺11am-6pm Tue-Fri & Sun, to 8pm Sat) Housed in a dazzling new city icon designed by local starchitect Igor Franić, this swanky museum in Novi Zagreb, across the Sava River, puts on solo and thematic group shows by Croatian and international artists. The year-round schedule is packed with film, theatre, concerts and performance art.

Mirogoj
CEMETERY

(☺6am-8pm Apr-Sep, 7am-6pm Oct-Mar) A 10-minute ride north of the city centre on bus 106 from the cathedral (or a half-mile walk through leafy streets) takes you to one of Europe's most beautiful cemeteries, a verdant resting place designed in 1876. The sculpted and artfully designed tombs lie beyond a majestic arcade topped by a string of cupolas.

FREE THRILLS

Though you'll have to pay to get into most of Zagreb's galleries and museums, there are some gorgeous parks and markets to be enjoyed for nowt – and there's always window shopping!

» Taste bits of food for free at Dolac (p211) – but don't be too cheeky!

» Smell the herbs at the Botanical Garden (p218).

» Enjoy the long walks around Maksimir Park (p218).

» See the magnificent Mirogoj cemetery (p218).

» Pop inside the ever-renovated cathedral (p211).

Maksimir Park
PARK

(www.park-maksimir.hr; Maksimirska bb; ☺park 9am-dusk, info centre 10am-4pm Tue-Fri, to 6pm Sat & Sun mid-Apr–mid-Oct, 10am-4pm Tue-Fri, 8am-4pm Sat & Sun mid-Oct–mid-Apr) Another green delight is Maksimir Park, a peaceful wooded enclave covering 18 hectares; it is easily accessible by trams 11 and 12 from Trg Josipa Jelačića. Opened to the public in 1794, it was the first public promenade in southeastern Europe. There's also a modest **zoo** (www.zoo.hr; adult/children 30/20KN; ☺9am-8pm) here.

Dražen Petrović Memorial Museum
MUSEUM

(☎48 43 146; Savska 30; tickets 10-20KN) Pay homage to Cibona's most famous player at this museum located south along Savska, on a small square just to the west.

☞ Tours

ZET
BUS TOUR

(www.zet.hr) Zagreb's public transportation network operates open-deck tour buses (70KN) departing from Kaptol on a hop-on, hop-off basis from April through September.

Funky Zagreb
GUIDED TOUR

(www.funky-zagreb.com) Personalised tours that range in theme from wine tasting (200KN for three hours) to hiking in Zagreb's surroundings (from 635KN per person).

Blue Bike Tours
CYCLING

(www.zagrebbybike.com) Has two-hour tours (170KN) departing daily. Reserve ahead.

Zagreb Talks
WALKING TOUR

(www.zagrebtalks.com) Tours include Do You Speak Croatian? on Saturday mornings, which teaches you basic language skills (95KN; 75KN for students). From May through September only; otherwise by appointment.

✯✯ Festivals & Events

For a complete listing of Zagreb events, see www.zagreb-touristinfo.hr.

Music Biennale Zagreb
MUSIC

(www.mbz.hr) Croatia's most important contemporary music event is held in April during odd-numbered years.

Subversive Festival
CULTURAL

(www.subversivefestival.com) Europe's activists and philosophers descend on Zagreb in droves for film screenings and lectures over two weeks in May.

INmusic Festival
MUSIC

(www.inmusicfestival.com) A three-day extravaganza every June, this is Zagreb's highest-profile music festival, with multiple stages by the Jarun Lake.

World Festival of Animated Film
FILM

(www.animafest.hr) This prestigious festival has been held in Zagreb annually in June since 1972.

Cest is D'Best
CULTURAL

(www.cestisdbest.com) In early June, it features five stages around the city centre, around 200 international performers and acts that include music, dance, theatre, art and sports.

Ljeto na Strossu
CULTURAL

(www.ljetonastrosu.com) From late May through late September, leafy Strossmayer Šetalište comes alive with free outdoor film screenings, concerts, art workshops and best-in-show mongrel dog competitions.

Eurokaz
THEATRE

(www.eurokaz.hr) Showcasing innovative theatre troupes and cutting-edge performances from all over the world in late June/early July.

Zagreb Summer Evenings
MUSIC

A cycle of concerts in the Upper Town each July, with the atrium of Galerija Klovićevi Dvori and the Gradec stage used for the performances of classical music, jazz, blues and world tunes.

World Theatre Festival
THEATRE

(www.zagrebtheatrefestival.hr) High-quality, contemporary theatre comes to Zagreb for a couple of weeks each September, often extending into early October.

🛏 Sleeping

Zagreb's accommodation scene has been undergoing a noticeable change, with many more budget options. Prices usually stay the same in all seasons, but be prepared for a 20% surcharge if you arrive during a festival or major event, in particular the autumn fair.

If you intend to stay in a private house or apartment – a good option if you want more privacy and a homey feel – try not to arrive on Sunday because most of the agencies will be closed, unless you've made prior arrangements. Prices for doubles run from about 300KN and studio apartments start at 400KN per night. There's usually a surcharge for staying only one night. Recommended agencies include **Evistas** (✆48 39 554; www.evistas.hr; Augusta Šenoe 28; s/d/apt from 240/290/340KN) and **InZagreb** (✆65 23 201; www.inzagreb.com; Remetinečka 13; apt 490-665KN).

🏆 TOP CHOICE Studio Kairos
B&B ₤₤

(✆46 40 680; www.studio-kairos.com; Vlaška 92; s 380-440KN, d 560-660KN; ❋❀) This adorable B&B has four well-appointed rooms in a street-level apartment. Rooms are decked out by theme and there's a cosy common space where breakfast is served. The main square (Trg Josipa Jelačića) is a 15-minute stroll away, a five-minute tram ride (take 11 or 12) or a five-minute bike ride (bikes are available for rent).

Esplanade Zagreb Hotel
HISTORIC HOTEL ₤₤₤

(✆45 66 666; www.esplanade.hr; Mihanovićeva 1; s/d 1385/1500KN; P❋@❀) Drenched in history, this six-storey hotel was built next to the train station in 1924 to welcome the *Orient Express* crowd in grand style. The art-deco masterpiece is replete with walls of swirling marble, immense staircases and wood-panelled lifts. Take a peek at the magnificent Emerald Ballroom and have a meal at superb **Zinfandel's restaurant** (Mihanovićeva 1; mains from 170KN).

Hotel Dubrovnik
HOTEL ₤₤

(✆48 63 555; www.hotel-dubrovnik.hr; Gajeva 1; s/d from 740/885KN; P❋❀) Smack on the main square, this glass city landmark has 245 elegant units with old-school classic style and, from some, great views of the square. Check out the great specials and packages.

Hobo Bear Hostel
HOSTEL ₤

(✆48 46 636; www.hobobearhostel.com; Medulićeva 4; dm 135-175KN; d from 400KN; ❋@❀) Inside a duplex apartment, this sparkling five-dorm hostel has exposed brick walls, hardwood floors, free lockers, a kitchen with free tea and coffee, a common room and book exchange. Take tram 1, 6 or 11 from Jelačića. The three doubles are across the street.

Hotel Jägerhorn
HOTEL ₤₤

(✆48 33 877; www.jaegerhorn.hr; Ilica 14; s/d/apt 598/749/1052KN; P❋@❀) A charming little hotel that sits right underneath Lotrščak Tower (p211), the 'Hunter's Horn' has friendly service and 18 spacious, classic rooms with good views (gaze over leafy Gradec from the top-floor attic rooms).

Funk Lounge Hostel HOSTEL €
(☑55 52 707; www.funkhostel.hr; Rendićeva 28b; dm 135-165KN, d 420KN; @☎) Located steps from Maksimir Park, this new outpost of the original Funk Hostel (southwest of the centre) has friendly staff, neat rooms and a range of freebies, including breakfast and a shot of *rakija* in the on-site restaurant and bar.

The budget end of the market has picked up greatly and various hostel options now abound. The following hostels are worth checking out: **Shappy Hostel** (☑48 30 179; www.hostel-shappy.com; Varšavska 8; dm 128-170, d from 420KN; P✳@☎), **Palmers Lodge Hostel Zagreb** (☑88 92 686; www.palmerslodge.com.hr; Branimirova 25; dm 120-150KN; @☎), **Chillout Hostel Zagreb Downtown** (☑48 49 605; www.chillout-hostel-zagreb.com; Kačićeva 3b; dm 135-180KN; ✳@☎), **Fulir Hostel** (☑48 30 882; www.fulir-hostel.com; Radićeva 3a; ✳@☎), **Hostel Day and Night** (www.hosteldayand-night.com; Kneza Mislava 1), **Buzz Hostel** (☑23 20 267; www.buzzbackpackers.com; Babukićeva 1b; ✳@☎) and **Taban Hostel** (www.tabanzagreb.com; Tkalčićeva 82).

✗ Eating

You'll have to love Croatian and Italian food to enjoy Zagreb's restaurants, but new places are branching out to include Japanese and other world cuisines. The biggest move is towards elegantly presented haute cuisine at haute prices.

You can pick up excellent fresh produce at Dolac market. The city centre's main streets, including Ilica, Teslina, Gajeva and Preradovićeva, are lined with fast-food joints and inexpensive snack bars.

Note that many restaurants close in August for their summer holiday, which typically lasts anywhere from two weeks to a month.

Vinodol CROATIAN €€
(Teslina 10; mains from 57KN) Well-prepared Central European fare much loved by local and overseas patrons. On warm days, eat on the covered patio entered through an ivy-clad passageway off Teslina. Highlights include the succulent lamb or veal and potatoes under *peka* (baked in a coal oven), as well as local mushrooms called *bukovače*.

Lari & Penati MODERN CROATIAN €
(Petrinjska 42a; mains from 40KN; ☺lunch & dinner Mon-Fri, lunch Sat) Small stylish bistro that serves up innovative lunch and dinner specials that change daily according to what's market fresh. The food is fab, the music cool and the few sidewalk tables lovely in warm weather. Closed for two weeks in August.

Tip Top SEAFOOD €
(Gundulićeva 18; mains from 55KN; ☺Mon-Sat) The excellent Dalmatian food is served by waitstaff sporting old socialist uniforms. Every day has its own set menu of mainstays.

Mali Bar TAPAS €€
(☑55 31 014; Vlaška 63; mains from 60KN; ☺closed Sun) This new spot by star chef Ana Ugarković shares the terraced space with Karijola (p220), hidden away in a *veža* (Zagreb alleyway). The cosy interior is earth-tone colourful and the food is focused on globally inspired tapas-style dishes. Book ahead.

Didov San DALMATIAN €€
(☑48 51 154; Mletačka 11; mains from 60KN) This Upper Town tavern features a rustic wooden interior with ceiling beams and tables on the streetside deck. Traditional fare hails from the Neretva River delta in Dalmatia's hinterland; try grilled frogs wrapped in proscuitto. Reserve ahead.

Karijola PIZZERIA €
(Vlaška 63; pizzas from 42KN; ☺Mon-Sat) Locals swear by the crispy thin-crust pizza churned out of a clay oven at this new location of Zagreb's best pizza joint. Expect high-quality toppings, such as smoked ham, olive oil, rich mozzarella, rocket and shiitake mushrooms.

Amfora SEAFOOD €
(Dolac 2; mains from 40KN; ☺lunch) This locals' lunch favourite serves super-fresh seafood straight from the market next door, paired with off-the-stalls veggies. This hole-in-the-wall has a few tables outside and an upstairs gallery with a nice market view.

Prasac MEDITERRANEAN €€
(☑48 51 411; Vranicanijeva 6; mains from 87KN; ☺Mon-Sat; ✋) Creative Mediterranean fare is conjured up by the Croatian-Sicilian chef at this intimate place with wooden beamed ceilings and a few alfresco tables. The market-fresh food is superb, but the service is slow and the portions small. Reserve ahead.

Stari Fijaker 900
TRADITIONAL CROATIAN €

(Mesnička 6; mains from 50KN) Tradition reigns in the kitchen of this restaurant–beer hall with a decor of banquettes and white linen, so try the homemade sausages, bean stews and *štrukli* (dumplings filled with cottage cheese), or one of the cheaper daily dishes.

Ivica i Marica
TRADITIONAL CROATIAN €€

(Tkalčićeva 70; mains from 70KN) Based on the Brothers Grimm story *Hansel and Gretel*, this restaurant–cake shop is made to look like the gingerbread house from the tale, with waiters clad in traditional costumes. It has veggie and fish dishes plus meatier fare. The cakes and *štrukli* are great.

Konoba Čiho
SEAFOOD €€

(Pavla Hatza 15; mains from 80KN) An old-school Dalmatian *konoba* (simple family-run establishment), where, downstairs, you can get fish (by the kilo) and seafood grilled or stewed. Try the wide range of *rakija* and house wines.

Vallis Aurea
TRADITIONAL CROATIAN €

(Tomićeva 4; mains from 37KN; ⊘Mon-Sat) This true local eatery has some of the best home cooking you'll find in town, so it's no wonder that it's chock-a-block at lunchtime for its *gableci* (traditional lunches). Right by the lower end of the funicular.

Pingvin
SANDWICH SHOP €

(Teslina 7; ⊘9am-4am Mon-Sat, 6pm-2am Sun) This quick-bite institution, around since 1987, offers tasty designer sandwiches and salads which locals savour perched on a couple of bar stools.

Rubelj
FAST FOOD €

(Dolac 2; mains from 25KN) One of the many Rubeljs across town, this Dolac branch is a great place for a quick portion of *ćevapčići* (small spicy sausage of minced beef, lamb or pork).

Vincek
PASTRIES, CAKES €

(Ilica 18) This institution of a *slastičarna* (pastry shop) serves some of Zagreb's creamiest cakes. They recently got some serious competition, however, with **Torte i To** (Nova Ves 11, 2nd fl, Kaptol Centar).

Dinara
BAKERY €

(Gajeva 8) The best bakery in town churns out an impressive variety of baked goodies. Try the *bučnica* (filo pie with pumpkin). It also has branches at **Ilica** (Ilica 71) and **Preradovićeva** (Preradovićeva 1).

🍷 Drinking

In the Upper Town, chic Tkalčićeva is throbbing with bars and cafes. In the Lower Town, there's bar-lined Bogovićeva and Trg Petra Preradovića (known locally as Cvjetni trg), the most popular spot in the Lower Town for street performers and occasional bands.

One of the nicest ways to see Zagreb is to join in on the *špica* – Saturday-morning prelunch coffee drinking on the terraces along Bogovićeva, Preradovićeva and Tkalčićeva.

TOP CHOICE Cica
BAR

(Tkalčićeva 18) This tiny storefront bar is as underground as it gets on Tkalčićeva. Sample one or – if you dare – all of the 25 kinds of *rakija* that the place is famous for.

Booksa
CAFE

(www.booksa.hr; Martićeva 14d; ⊘11am-8pm Tue-Sun; 🛜) Bookworms, poets and oddballs all come to chat and drink coffee, browse the library, surf with free wireless and hear readings at this book-themed cafe. There are English-language readings here, too. It's a 10-minute stroll east of the main square. It's closed for three weeks from late July.

Stross
OUTDOOR BAR

(Strossmayerovo Šetalište; ⊘Jun-Sep) From June to September, a makeshift bar is set up at the Strossmayer promenade in the Upper Town, with cheap drinks and live music most nights. Come for the mixed-bag crowd, great city views and leafy ambience.

Bacchus
BAR

(Trg Kralja Tomislava 16; ⊘closed Sun) You'll be lucky if you score a table at Zagreb's funkiest courtyard garden – lush and hidden in a passageway. After 10pm the action moves inside the artsy subterranean space, which hosts poetry readings and oldies' nights.

Kino Europa
CAFE-BAR

(www.kinoeuropa.hr; Varšavska 3; ⊘Mon-Sat; 🛜♿) Zagreb's oldest cinema, from the 1920s, now houses a glass-enclosed cafe, wine bar and *grapperia*, with an outdoor terrace and free wireless. The cinema hosts daily film screenings and occasional dance parties.

Velvet
CAFE-BAR

(Dežmanova 9; ⊘8am-10pm Mon-Fri, to 3pm Sat, to 2pm Sun) Stylish spot for a good, but pricey, cup of java and a quick bite amid the minimalist-chic interior decked out by owner Saša Šekoranja, Zagreb's hippest florist.

CROATIA ZAGREB

GAY & LESBIAN ZAGREB

The gay and lesbian scene in Zagreb is finally becoming more open than it has previously been, although free-wheeling it isn't.

For more information, browse www.zagrebgayguide.com.

Kolaž (Amruševa 11) This basement speakeasy-style bar behind an un-marked door caters to a primarily gay crowd.

Rush Club (Amruševa 10) A younger gay and lesbian crowd mixes at this fun club in the city centre, with themed nights such as karaoke.

Hotpot (Petrinjska 31) This new club in town has quickly become one of the favourites.

Vimpi (Miškecov Prolaz 3) Gathering spot for Zagreb's lady-loving ladies.

Velvet Gallery next door, known as 'Black Velvet', stays open till 11pm (except Sunday).

☆ Entertainment

Zagreb doesn't register high on the night-life Richter scale, but it does have an ever-developing art and music scene. Its theatres and concert halls present a variety of pro-grams throughout the year. Many are listed in the monthly brochure *Zagreb Events & Performances,* which is available from the main tourist office

Clubs

Club entry ranges from 20KN to 100KN. Clubs open around 10pm but most people show up around midnight. Most clubs open only from Thursday to Saturday.

VIP Club   CLUB
(www.vip-club.hr; Trg Josipa Jelačića 9; ⊙closed summer) This newcomer on the nightlife scene quickly became a favourite. A swank basement place on the main square, it offers a varied programme, from jazz to Balkan beats.

Tvornica   LIVE MUSIC
(www.tvornicakulture.com; Šubićeva 2) Excellent multimedia venue 20 minutes to the east of Trg Josipa Jelačića, showcasing live music performances, from Bosnian *sevdah* (Bos-nian blues) to alternative punk rock. Check out the website to see what's on.

Aquarius   CLUB
(www.aquarius.hr; Jarun Lake) Past its heyday but still a fun lakeside club with a series of rooms that opens onto a huge terrace. House and techno are the standard fare but there are also hip-hop and R&B nights. During summer, Aquarius sets up shop at Zrće on Pag (p234).

Pepermint   CLUB
(www.pepermint-zagreb.com; Ilica 24) Small and chic city-centre club clad in white wood, with two levels and a well-to-do older crowd. Programs change weekly but the vintage rockabilly, twist and swing night on Wednes-day is a definite hit.

Močvara   CLUB
(www.mochvara.hr; Trnjanski Nasip bb) In a former factory on the banks of the Sava River, 'Swamp' is one of Zagreb's best ven-ues for the cream of alternative music and attractively dingy charm. Live acts range from dub and dancehall to world music and heavy metal.

KSET   CLUB
(www.kset.org; Unska 3) Zagreb's top music venue, with anyone who's anyone perform-ing here – from ethno to hip-hop sounds. Saturday nights are dedicated to DJ music, when youngsters dance till late. You'll find gigs and events to suit most tastes.

Jabuka   CLUB
(Jabukovac 28) 'Apple' is an old-time fave, with 1980s hits played to a 30-something crowd that reminisces about the good old days when they were young and alternative. It's a taxi ride or a walk through the woods, set away in a posh area.

Medika   CLUB
(www.pierottijeva11.org; Pierottijeva 11) This artsy venue in an old pharmaceutical factory calls itself an 'autonomous cultural centre'. It's the city's first legalised squat with a program of concerts, art exhibits and parties fuelled by cheap beer and *rakija.*

Purgeraj   CLUB
(www.purgeraj.hr; Park Ribnjak 1) Live rock, blues and avant-garde jazz are on the music menu at this funky space that attracts a pretty young crowd. The brand-new Park just

merged with Purgeraj at the time of writing and started drawing in big-name bands.

Sport
Basketball is popular in Zagreb, home to the Cibona basketball team. There's a museum (p218) dedicated to Cibona star Dražen Petrović. Games take place frequently at the **Dražen Petrović Basketball Centre** (☑48 43 333; Savska 30; tickets from HRK35); tickets can be purchased at the door or online at www.cibona.com.

Performing Arts
Make the rounds of the theatres in person to check their programs. Tickets are usually available for even the best shows.

Zagrebačko Kazalište Mladih THEATRE
(☑48 72 554; www.zekaem.hr; Teslina 7) Zagreb Youth Theatre, better known as ZKM, is considered the cradle of Croatia's contemporary theatre. It hosts several festivals.

Croatian National Theatre THEATRE
(☑48 88 418; www.hnk.hr; Trg Maršala Tita 15) This neo-baroque theatre, established in 1895, stages opera and ballet performances.

🛍 Shopping
Ilica is Zagreb's main shopping street.

Prostor FASHION
(www.multiracionalnakompanija.com; Mesnička 5; ⏾noon-8pm Mon-Fri, 10am-3pm Sat) A fantastic little art gallery and clothes shop, featuring some of the city's best independent artists and young designers. In a courtyard off Mesnička.

Natura Croatica FOOD
(www.naturacroatica.com; Preradovićeva 8) Over 300 Croatian products and souvenirs are sold at this shop – from *rakija*, wines and chocolates to jams, spices and truffle spreads. A perfect pitstop for gifts.

Profil Megastore BOOKSTORE
(Bogovićeva 7) Inside an entryway, this most atmospheric of Zagreb bookstores has a great selection of books (many in English) and a nice cafe on the gallery.

ℹ Information

Discount Cards
Zagreb Card (www.zagrebcard.fivestars.hr; 24/72hr 60/90KN) Provides free travel on all public transport, a 50% discount on museum and gallery entries, plus discounts in some bars and restaurants, and on car rental. The card is sold at the main tourist office and many hostels, hotels, bars and shops.

Emergency
Police Station (☑45 63 311; Petrinjska 30)

Internet Access
Several cafes around town offer free wi-fi, including Booksa.

Sublink (☑48 19 993; www.sublink.hr; Teslina 12; per hr 15KN; ⏾9am-10pm Mon-Sat, 3-10pm Sun) The city's first cybercafe, still going strong.

Medical Services
Dental Emergency (☑48 28 488; Perkovčeva 3; ⏾10pm-6am)

KBC Rebro (☑23 88 888; Kišpatićeva 12; ⏾24hr) East of the city, provides emergency aid.

Pharmacy (☑48 16 198; Trg Josipa Jelačića 3; ⏾24hr)

Money
There are ATMs at the bus and train stations, the airport, and at numerous locations around town. Some banks in the train and bus stations accept travellers cheques. Exchange offices can be found in many locations around town.

MARKET DAYS

The Sunday **antiques market** (Britanski Trg; ⏾9am-2pm Sun) is one of central Zagreb's joys, but to see a flea market that's unmatched in the whole of Croatia, you have to head to **Hrelić** (⏾7am-3pm Wed & Sun). This huge open space is packed with anything – from car parts, cars and antique furniture to clothes, records, kitchenware, you name it. Shopping aside, it's also a great place to experience the truly Balkan part and chaotic fun of Zagreb – Roma music, bartering, grilled-meat smoke and general gusto. If you're going in the summer months, take a hat and slap on sunscreen – there's no shade.

By tram, take number 6 in the direction of Sopot, get off near the bridge and walk 15 minutes along the Sava to get to Hrelić; or take tram 14, get off at the last stop in Zaprude and do the 15-minute walk from there.

Post

Post Office (☎66 26 453; Jurišićeva 13;
⏰7am-8pm Mon-Fri, to 1pm Sat) Has a telephone centre.

Tourist Information

Main Tourist Office (☎info line 800 53 53,
office 48 14 051; www.zagreb-touristinfo.hr;
Trg Josipa Jelačića 11; ⏰8.30am-9pm Mon-Fri,
9am-6pm Sat & Sun) Distributes free city maps
and leaflets, and sells the Zagreb Card (p223).

Plitvice National Park Office (☎46 13 586;
Trg Kralja Tomislava 19; ⏰8am-4pm Mon-Fri)
Has details and brochures mainly on Plitvice
and Velebit but also on Croatia's other national
parks.

Tourist Office Airport (☎62 65 091;
⏰8.30am-9pm Mon-Fri, 9am-6pm Sat & Sun
Jun-Sep) Handy for airport arrivals.

Tourist Office Annex (train station; ⏰8.30am-
9pm Mon-Fri, 9am-6pm Sat & Sun Jun-Sep,
8.30am-8pm Mon-Fri, 12.30-6.30pm Sat & Sun
Oct-May) Same services as the main tourist
office.

Travel Agencies

Atlas Travel Agency (☎48 07 300; www.
atlas-croatia.com; Zrinjevac 17) Tours around
Croatia.

Croatia Express (☎49 22 237; Trg Kralja
Tomislava 17) Train reservations, car rental, air
and ferry tickets, hotell bookings and a daily
trip to the beach from June to September.

Zdenac Života (☎48 16 200; www.zdenac-
zivota.hr; 2nd fl, Vlaška 40) Thematic sightseeing tours of Zagreb plus active day trips
from the capital and multiday adventures
around Croatia.

Websites

Lonely Planet (www.lonelyplanet.com/croatia/
zagreb)

❶ Getting There & Away

AIR Zagreb Airport (☎45 62 222; www.
zagreb-airport.hr) Located 17km southeast of
Zagreb, this is Croatia's major airport, offering
a range of international and domestic services.

BUS Zagreb's **bus station** (☎060 313 333;
www.akz.hr; Avenija M Držića 4) is 1km east of
the train station. Trams 2, 3 and 6 run from the
bus station to the train station. Tram 6 goes
to Trg Josipa Jelačića. There's a **garderoba**
(left-luggage office; 1st 4hr 20KN, then per hr
2.50KN; ⏰24hr) at the bus station.

Before buying your ticket, ask about the arrival time – some of the buses take local roads
and stop in every town en route. Note that listed
schedules are somewhat reduced outside high
season.

TRAIN The **train station** (☎060 333 444;
www.hznet.hr; Trg Kralja Tomislava 12) is in the
southern part of the city. As you come out of it,
you'll see a series of parks and pavilions directly
in front of you, which lead into the town centre.
It's advisable to book train tickets in advance
because of limited seating. There's a **garderoba**
(Train station; lockers per 24hr 15KN; ⏰24hr)
left-luggage office at the station.

❶ Getting Around

Zagreb is a fairly easy city to navigate. Traffic is
bearable and the efficient tram system should
be a model for other polluted, traffic-clogged
European capitals.

To/From the Airport

The Croatia Airlines bus to the airport (30KN)
leaves from the bus station every half-hour or
hour from about 5am to 8pm, and returns from
the airport on the same schedule. Taxis cost
between 110KN and 300KN.

Car

Zagreb is a fairly easy city to navigate by car
(boulevards are wide and parking in the city
centre, although scarce, costs 10KN per hour).
Watch out for trams buzzing around.

Motorists can call **Hrvatski Autoklub** (HAK,
Croatian Auto Club; ☎46 40 800; www.hak.hr;
Avenija Dubrovnik 44) at ☎1987 for help on the
road.

International car-hire companies include
Budget Rent-a-Car (☎46 73 603; www.budget.
hr; Oreškovićeva 27) and **Hertz** (☎48 46 777;
www.hertz.hr; Vukotinovićeva 4). Local companies usually have lower rates; try **Oryx** (☎61
15 800; www.oryx-rent.hr; Grada Vukovara 74),
which has a desk at the airport.

Public Transport

Public transport is based on an efficient network
of trams, although the city centre is compact
enough to make them unnecessary. Buy tickets
at newspaper kiosks for 12KN. Tickets can be
used for transfers within 90 minutes, but only in
one direction.

A *dnevna karta* (day ticket), valid on all public
transport until 4am the next morning, is available for 40KN at most newspaper kiosks.

Make sure you validate your ticket when you
get on the tram by inserting it in the yellow box.

Taxi

Until recently, Zagreb had only one taxi company which charged astronomical fees for even
the shortest ride. That changed when other
companies joined the fray; all have meters now
and competitive rates. **Radio Taxi** (☎060 800
800, 1777) charges 10KN for a start and 5KN per
kilometre; waiting time is 40KN per hour.

TRANSPORT FROM ZAGREB

Domestic Bus

DESTINATION	PRICE (KN)	DURATION (HR)	FREQUENCY (DAILY)
Dubrovnik	205-250	9½-11	9-12
Korčula	264	11	1
Krk	113-219	3-4½	8-10
Mali Lošinj	287-312	5-6	3
Plitvice	92-106	2-3	11-15
Poreč	156-232	4-4½	11
Pula	105-196	3½-5½	17-20
Rijeka	91-155	2½-4	20-25
Rovinj	150-195	4-6	9-11
Split	115-205	5-8½	32-34
Zadar	105-139	3½-5	31

International Bus

DESTINATION	PRICE (KN)	DURATION (HR)	FREQUENCY (DAILY)
Belgrade (Serbia)	220	6	5
Munich (Germany)	375	9½	2
Sarajevo (Bosnia & Hercegovina)	160-210	7-8	4-5
Vienna (Austria)	250	5-6	3

Domestic Train

DESTINATION	PRICE (KN)	DURATION (HR)	FREQUENCY (DAILY)
Rijeka	97	4-6	6
Split	189	5-7	3

International Train

DESTINATION	PRICE (KN)	DURATION (HR)	FREQUENCY (DAILY)
Banja Luka (Bosnia & Hercegovina)	105	4½-5	2
Belgrade (Serbia)	169	6½	4
Budapest (Hungary)	230	6-7	2
Ljubljana (Slovenia)	130	2½	6
Mostar (Bosnia & Hercegovina)	292	11½	1
Munich (Germany)	674	8½-9	3
Ploče (Italy)	320	13½	1
Sarajevo (Bosnia & Hercegovina)	231	8-9½	2
Venice (Italy)	450	11½	2
Vienna (Austria)	465	6-7	2

PLITVICE LAKES NATIONAL PARK

Between Zagreb and Zadar, **Plitvice Lakes National Park** (🖉751 015; www.np-plitvicka-jezera.hr; adult/concession Apr-Oct 110/80KN, Nov-Mar 80/60KN; ⏰7am-8pm) comprises 19.5 hectares of wooded hills and 16 lakes, all connected by a series of waterfalls and cascades. The mineral-rich waters carve new paths through the rock, depositing tufa (new porous rock) in continually changing formations. Wooden footbridges follow the lakes and streams over, under and across the rumbling water for an exhilaratingly damp 18km. Swimming is not allowed. Your park admission also includes the boats and bus-trains you need to use to see the lakes. There is hotel accommodation onsite, and private accommodation just outside the park. Check the options with the Plitvice National Park Office (p224) in Zagreb.

Not all Zagreb–Zadar buses stop here as the quicker ones use the motorway, so check before boarding. You can check the schedules at www.akz.hr. The journey takes three hours from Zadar (95KN to 108KN) and 2½ hours from Zagreb (93KN to 106KN); there are 10 daily services.

Luggage can be left at the tourist information centre at the park's main entrance.

You'll have no trouble finding idle taxis, usually at blue-marked taxi signs; note that these are Radio Taxi stands.

For short city rides, **Taxi Cammeo** (🖉060 71 00, 1212) is typically the cheapest, as the 15KN start fare includes the first two kilometres (it's 6KN for every subsequent kilometre).

ISTRIA

🖉052

Continental Croatia meets the Adriatic in Istria (Istra to Croats), the heart-shaped 3600-sq-km peninsula just south of Trieste in Italy. While the bucolic interior of rolling hills and fertile plains attracts artsy visitors to its hilltop villages, rural hotels and farmhouse restaurants, the verdant indented coastline is enormously popular with the sun 'n sea set. Vast hotel complexes line much of the coast and its rocky beaches are not Croatia's best, but the facilities are wide-ranging, the sea is clean and secluded spots are still plentiful.

The coast, or 'Blue Istria', as the tourist board calls it, gets flooded with tourists in summer, but you can still feel alone in 'Green Istria' (the interior), even in mid-August. Add acclaimed gastronomy (starring fresh seafood, prime white truffles, wild asparagus, top-rated olive oils and award-winning wines), sprinkle it with historical charm and you have a little slice of heaven.

Pula

POP 57,800

The wealth of Roman architecture makes the otherwise workaday Pula (ancient Polensium) a standout among Croatia's larger cities. The star of the Roman show is the remarkably well-preserved Roman amphitheatre, which dominates the streetscape and doubles as a venue for summer concerts and festivals.

Historical attractions aside, Pula is a busy commercial city on the sea that has managed to retain a friendly small-town appeal. Just a short bus ride away, a series of beaches awaits at the resorts that occupy the Verudela Peninsula to the south. Although marred by residential and holiday developments, the coast is dotted with fragrant pine groves, seaside cafes and a clutch of fantastic restaurants. Further south along the indented shoreline, the Premantura Peninsula hides a spectacular nature park, the protected cape of Kamenjak.

◉ Sights

THE CITY

The oldest part of the city follows the ancient Roman plan of streets circling the central citadel. Most shops, agencies and businesses are clustered in and around the Old Town as well as on Giardini, Carrarina, Istarska and Riva, which runs along the harbour. The new Riva is currently being renovated, which makes the harbourfront one big construction site; the work is expected to finish in late 2013.

Roman Amphitheatre   HISTORIC BUILDING
(Arena; Flavijevska bb; adult/concession 40/20KN; ⏰8am-midnight Jul & Aug, around 8am-7pm Sep-Jun) Pula's most famous and imposing sight is this 1st-century amphitheatre, overlooking the harbour northeast of the Old Town. Built entirely from local limestone, the am-

phitheatre, known locally as the Arena, was designed to host gladiatorial contests, with seating for up to 20,000 spectators. In the chambers downstairs is a small **museum** with a display of ancient olive-oil equipment. **Pula Film Festival** (www.pulafilmfestival.hr) is held here every summer, as are pop and classical concerts.

Temple of Augustus   HISTORIC BUILDING

(Forum; adult/concession 20/10KN; ☉9am-8pm Mon-Fri, to 3pm Sat & Sun Apr-Oct) This is the only visible remnant from the Roman era on the Forum, Pula's central meeting place from antiquity through the Middle Ages. This temple, erected from 2 BC to AD 14, now houses a small historical **museum** with captions in English.

Archaeological Museum   MUSEUM

(Arheološki Muzej; Carrarina 3; adult/concession 20/10KN; ☉8am-8pm Mon-Fri, 9am-3pm Sat & Sun May-Sep, 9am-2pm Mon-Fri Oct-Apr) This museum presents archaeological finds from all over Istria. Even if you don't enter the museum, be sure to visit the large **sculpture garden** around it, and the **Roman theatre** behind. The garden, entered through 2nd-century twin gates, is the site of concerts in summer.

Zerostrasse   HISTORICAL SITE

(adult/concession 15/5KN; ☉10am-10pm Jun–mid-Sep) This underground system of tunnels was built before and during WWI to shelter the city's population and serve as storage for ammunition. Now you can walk through several of its sections, which all lead to the middle, where a photo exhibit shows early aviation in Pula. There are three entrances – inquire at the tourism office.

Triumphal Arch of Sergius   RUINS

Along Carrarina are Roman walls, which mark the eastern boundary of old Pula. Follow these walls south and continue down Giardini to this majestic arch erected in 27 BC to commemorate three members of the Sergius family who achieved distinction in Pula.

THE COAST

Pula is surrounded by a half-circle of rocky beaches, each one with its own fan club. The most tourist-packed are undoubtedly those surrounding the hotel complex on the **Verudela Peninsula**, although some locals will dare to be seen at the small turquoise-coloured **Hawaii Beach** near the Hotel Park.

Rt Kamenjak   NATURE PARK

(www.kamenjak.hr; pedestrians & cyclists free, per car/scooter 25/20KN; ☉7am-10pm) For seclusion, head out to the wild Rt Kamenjak on the Premantura Peninsula, 10km south of town. Istria's southernmost point, this gorgeous, entirely uninhabited cape has wildflowers (including 30 species of orchid), 30km of virgin beaches and coves, and a delightful beach bar, **Safari** (snacks 25-50KN; ☉Apr-Sep), half-hidden in the bushes near the beach, about 3.5km from the entrance to the park. For the wildest and least-discovered stretch of the cape, head to Gornji Kamenjak, which lies between the village of Volme and Premantura. Watch out for strong currents if swimming off the southern cape. **Windsurf Bar** (☎091 512 3646; www.windsurfing.hr; windsurfing equipment/courses per hr from 70/200KN) in Premantura rents bikes and windsurfing equipment and offers kayaking excursions. Take city bus 26 from Pula to Premantura (15KN), then rent a bike to get inside the park.

🏃 Activities

At the **Orca Diving Center** (☎098 409 850; www.orcadiving.hr; Hotel Histria) on the Verudela Peninsula, you can arrange boat and wreck dives. In addition to windsurfing, Windsurf Bar (p227) in Premantura offers cycling (250KN) and kayaking (300KN) excursions.

An easy 41km **cycling trail** from Pula to Medulin follows the path of Roman gladiators. Check out **Istria Bike** (www.istria-bike.com), a tourist board–run website outlining trails, packages and agencies that offer cycling trips.

🛏 Sleeping

Pula's peak tourist season runs from the second week of July to late August. During this period it's wise to make advance reservations. The tip of the Verudela Peninsula, 4km southwest of the city centre, has been turned into a vast tourist complex replete with hotels and apartments.

Any travel agency can give you information and book you into one of the hotels, or you can contact **Arenaturist** (☎529 400; www.arenaturist.hr; Splitska 1a).

The travel agencies in Pula can find you private accommodation, but there is little available in the town centre. Count on paying from 250KN to 490KN for a double room and from 300KN to 535KN for a two-person apartment. You can also browse the list of private accommodation at www.pulainfo.hr.

CROATIA PULA

Hotel Amfiteatar
HOTEL €€

(📞375 600; www.hotelamfiteatar.com; Amfiteatar-ska 6; s/d 475/658KN; P❄@🛜) The swankiest spot in town, right by the amphitheatre, is a new hotel with contemporary rooms with upscale trimmings such as flat-screen TVs. The restaurant is one of Pula's best. There's a surcharge for stays of less than two nights.

Hostel Pipištrelo
HOSTEL €

(📞393 568; www.hostel-pipistrelo.com; Flaciusova 6; dm/s/d 124/148/296KN; ❄@🛜) With its colourful facade, this recent addition to Pula's hostel scene sits right across the harbour. Its quirky thematic rooms were done up by young Pula designers. It is cash-only and closed Sundays, so call ahead.

Hotel Scaletta
HOTEL €€

(📞541 025; www.hotel-scaletta.com; Flavijevska 26; s/d 505/732KN; P❄🛜) There's a friendly family vibe at this cosy hotel. The rooms have tasteful decor and a bagful of trimmings (such as minibars). Plus it's just a hop and a skip from town, and a short walk from the Arena and the waterfront.

Riviera Guest House
HOTEL €€

(📞525 400; www.arenaturist.hr; Splitska 1; s/d 360/590KN; 🛜) This once-grand property in a Neo-Baroque 19th-century building is in dire need of a thorough overhaul. The saving grace: it's in the centre and the front rooms have water views.

Camping Stoja
CAMPING GROUND €

(📞387 144; www.arenacamps.com; Stoja 37; campsites per person/tent 58/37KN; ☺Apr-Oct) The closest camping ground to Pula, 3km southwest of the centre, has lots of space on the shady promontory, with a restaurant and a diving centre. Take bus 1 to Stoja.

✗ Eating

The centre of Pula is full of tourist traps, so for the best food and good value you'll have to head out of town. For cheap bites, browse around the central market, where you'll find excellent sandwiches at **Garfield** (Narodni Trg 9; sandwiches from 25KN; ☺9am-3pm Mon-Fri, to 2pm Sat) on the 1st floor. For a reliably good meal, head to the alfresco restaurant of Hotel Amfiteatar.

Vodnjanka
ISTRIAN €

(Vitezića 4; mains from 40KN; ☺closed Sat dinner & Sun winter) Locals swear by the real-deal home cooking at this no-frills spot. It's cheap, casual, cash-only and has a small menu that concentrates on simple Istrian dishes. To get here, walk south on Radićeva to Vitezića.

🏆 Konoba Batelina
SEAFOOD €€

(📞573 767; Čimulje 25, Banjole; mains from 85KN; ☺dinner) The superb food that awaits at this family-run tavern is worth a trek to Banjole village 3km east of Pula. The owner, fisherman and chef David Skoko, dishes out seafood that's some of the best and most creative you'll find in Istria. Reserve ahead.

Milan
MEDITERRANEAN €€

(www.milanpula.com; Stoja 4; mains from 85KN) An exclusive vibe, seasonal specialties, four sommeliers and an olive-oil expert on staff all create one of the city's best dining experiences. The five-course fish menu is well worth it.

Kantina
INTERNATIONAL €€

(Flanatička 16; mains from 70KN; ☺Mon-Sat; 🅿) The beamed stone cellar of this Habsburg building has been redone in a modern style. The ownership and culinary helm changed recently so the food quality is hit and miss.

🍷 Drinking & Entertainment

Try to catch a concert in the spectacular amphitheatre (p226); the tourist office has schedules. Although most of the nightlife is out of the town centre, in mild weather the cafes on the Forum and along the pedestrian streets Kandlerova, Flanatička and Sergijevaca are lively people-watching spots. For beach-bar action, head to Verudela or Medulin.

🏆 Cabahia
BAR

(Širolina 4) This artsy hideaway in Veruda has a cosy wood-beamed interior, eclectic decor of old objects, dim lighting, South American flair and a great garden terrace out the back. It hosts concerts and gets packed on weekends. If it's too full, try the more laid-back **Bass** (Širolina 3), just across the street.

Cvajner
CAFE

(Forum 2) Snag a prime alfresco table at this artsy cafe right on the buzzing Forum and check out rotating exhibits in the funky interior, which showcases works by up-and-coming local artists.

Rojc
CULTURAL CENTRE

(www.rojcnet.pula.org; Gajeva 3) For an arty underground experience, check the program at Rojc, a converted army barracks that houses a multimedia art centre and studios with occasional concerts, exhibitions and other events.

DOMESTIC BUSES FROM PULA

DESTINATION	PRICE (KN)	DURATION (HR)	FREQUENCY (DAILY)
Dubrovnik	580	15	1
Poreč	72	1	5
Rovinj	38	¾	12
Split	392	10	2
Zadar	255	7	3
Zagreb	190	4	12

Zeppelin BEACH BAR
(Saccorgiana Bay) Après-beach fun is on the menu at this new beach bar in Saccorgiana bay on Verudela, but it also does night parties ranging in theme from vodka to reggae and karaoke to martini.

ℹ️ Information

Active Travel Istra (☑215 497; www.activa-istra.com; Scalierova 1) Excursions around Istria, adventure trips and concert tickets.

Hospital (☑376 548; Zagrebačka 34)

IstrAction (☑383 369; www.istraction.com; Prilaz Monte Cappelletta 3) Offers fun half-day tours to Kamenjak and around Pula's fortifications, as well as medieval-themed full-day excursions around Istria.

Main post office (Danteov trg 4; ⊙7am-8pm Mon-Fri, to 1pm Sat) You can make long-distance calls here. Check out the cool staircase inside.

MMC Luka (Istarska 30; per hr 25KN; ⊙8am-midnight Mon-Fri, to 3pm Sat) Internet access. There's also free wi-fi all around town; inquire at the tourism office about specific locations.

Tourist Ambulance (Flanatička 27; ⊙8am-9.30pm Mon-Fri Jul & Aug) Medical clinic.

Tourist Information Centre (☑212 987; www.pulainfo.hr; Forum 3; ⊙8am-9pm Mon-Fri, 9am-9pm Sat & Sun summer, around 8am-7pm rest of yr) Knowledgeable and friendly staff provide maps, brochures and schedules of events in Pula and around Istria. Pick up two useful booklets: *Domus Bonus*, which lists the best-quality private accommodation in Istria, and *Istra Gourmet*, with a list of all restaurants.

ℹ️ Getting There & Away

BOAT Pula's harbour is located west of the bus station. **Jadroagent** (☑210 431; www.jadroagent.hr; Riva 14; ⊙7am-3pm Mon-Fri) has schedules and tickets for boats connecting Istria with the islands and south of Croatia.

Commodore Cruises (☑211 631; www.commodore-travel.hr; Riva 14) sells tickets for

a catamaran between Pula and Zadar (100KN, five hours), which runs five times weekly from July through early September and twice weekly in June and the rest of September. There's a Wednesday boat service to Venice (430KN, 3½ hours) between June and September.

BUS From the Pula **bus station** (☑060 304 091; Šijanska 4), located 500m northeast of the town centre, there are buses heading to Rijeka (97KN, 1½hr) almost hourly. In summer, reserve a seat a day in advance. There's also a **garderoba** (left-luggage office; per hr 2.50KN; ⊙24hr) here.

There are weekly buses to Frankfurt and twice-weekly buses to Munich.

TRAIN Less than 1km north of town, the train station is near the sea along Kolodvorska. There is one direct train daily to Ljubljana (144KN, 4½ hours) and three to Zagreb (140KN, nine hours), but you must board a bus for part of the trip, from Lupoglav to Rijeka.

ℹ️ Getting Around

The city buses of use to visitors are 1, which runs to Camping Stoja, and 2A and 3A to Verudela. The frequency varies from every 15 minutes to every half hour (from 5am to 11.30pm). Tickets are sold at *tisak* (news stands) for 6KN, or from the driver for 11KN.

Rovinj

POP 14,400

Rovinj (Rovigno in Italian) is coastal Istria's star attraction. It can get overrun with tourists in the summer months and residents are developing a sharp eye for maximising their profits (by upgrading hotels and restaurants to four-star status), but it remains one of the last true Mediterranean fishing ports. Fishermen haul their catch into the harbour in the early morning, followed by a horde of squawking gulls, and mend their nets before lunch.

The massive Church of St Euphemia, with its 60m-high tower, punctuates the peninsula.

CROATIA ROVINJ

Wooded hills and low-rise hotels surround the Old Town, which is webbed by steep, cobbled streets and piazzas. The 13 green, offshore islands of the Rovinj archipelago make for a pleasant afternoon away.

◎ Sights

The Old Town of Rovinj is contained within an egg-shaped peninsula. There are two harbours – the northern open harbour and the small, protected harbour to the south. About 1.5km south is the Punta Corrente Forest Park and the wooded cape of **Zlatni Rt** (Golden Cape).

Church of St Euphemia   CHURCH
(Sveta Eufemija; Petra Stankovića; ⊙10am-6pm Jun-Sep, 10am-4pm May, 10am-2pm Apr, by appointment Oct-Mar) The town's showcase is this imposing church, which dominates the Old Town from its hilltop location in the middle of the peninsula. Built in 1736, it's the largest baroque building in Istria, reflecting the period during the 18th century when Rovinj was its most populous town, an important fishing centre and the bulwark of the Venetian fleet.

Inside the church behind the right-hand altar, look for the marble **tomb of St Euphemia**, Rovinj's patron saint martyred in AD 304, whose body appeared in Rovinj one dark stormy night according to legend. The mighty 60m **bell tower** is topped by a copper statue of St Euphemia, which shows the direction of the wind by turning on a spindle. You can climb the tower (to the left of the altar) for 15KN.

Batana House   MUSEUM
(Pina Budicina 2; adult/child 10/5KN, with guide 15KN; ⊙10am-2pm & 7-11pm Jun-Sep, 10am-2pm & 4-6pm Tue-Sun Oct-Jan & Mar-May) On the harbour, Batana House is a museum dedicated to the *batana*, a flat-bottomed fishing boat that stands as a symbol of Rovinj's seafaring and fishing traditions.

Grisia
(🎨) Lined with galleries where local artists sell their work, this cobbled street leads uphill from behind the elaborate 1679 **Balbi Arch** to St Euphemia. The winding narrow backstreets that spread around Grisia are an attraction in themselves. Windows, balconies, portals and squares are a pleasant confusion of styles – Gothic, Renaissance, baroque and neoclassical. On the second Sunday in August each year, Grisia becomes

an open-air **art exhibition**, with anyone from children to professional painters displaying their work.

Punta Corrente Forest Park   PARK
Follow the waterfront on foot or by bike past Hotel Park to this verdant area, locally known as Zlatni Rat, about 1.5km south. It's covered in oak and pine groves and boasts 10 species of cypress. You can swim off the rocks or just sit and admire the offshore islands.

🏃 Activities

Most people hop aboard a boat for swimming, snorkelling and sunbathing. A trip to Crveni Otok or Sveta Katarina is easily arranged. In summer, there are hourly boats from 5.30am till midnight to the islands of **Sveta Katarina** (return 30KN, 10 minutes) and **Crveni Otok** (return 40KN, 15 minutes). They leave from just opposite Hotel Adriatic and also from the Delfin ferry dock near Hotel Park.

Nadi Scuba Diving Centar (☑813 290; www.scuba.hr) and **Petra** (☑812 880; www.divingpetra.hr) offer daily boat dives. The main attraction is the Baron Gautsch wreck, an Austrian passenger steamer sunk in 1914 by a sea mine in 40m of water.

Cycling around Rovinj and the Punta Corrente Forest Park is a superb way to spend an afternoon. You can rent bicycles at many agencies around town, for around 20KN per hour or 70KN per day.

There are other exciting options, such as kayaking; book a trip through **Adistra** (☑095 838 3797; Carera 69). Nine-kilometre jaunts around the Rovinj archipelago cost 270KN; a 14km outing to the Limska Draga Fjord is 290KN.

👉 Tours

Most travel agencies in Rovinj sell day trips to Venice (390KN to 520KN), Plitvice (500KN to 600KN) and Brijuni (380KN to 470KN). There are also fish picnics (250KN), panoramic cruises (100KN) and boat outings to Limska Draga Fjord (150KN). These can be slightly cheaper if booked through one of the independent operators that line the waterfront; **Delfin** (☑848 265) is reliable.

🛌 Sleeping

Rovinj has become Istria's destination of choice for hordes of summertime tourists, so reserving in advance is strongly recommended. Prices have been rising steadily and probably will continue to do so, as the city gears up to reach elite status.

If you want to stay in private accommodation, there is little available in the Old Town, where there's also no free parking and accommodation costs are higher. Double rooms start at 220KN in the high season, with a small discount for single occupancy; two-person apartments start at 330KN. Out of season, prices go down considerably.

The surcharge for a stay of less than three nights is up to 50%, and guests who stay only one night are sometimes punished with a 100% surcharge. Outside summer months, you should be able to bargain the surcharge away. You can book through one of the travel agencies.

Except for a few private options, most hotels and camping grounds in the area are managed by **Maistra** (www.maistra.com).

TOP CHOICE **Hotel Lone** DESIGN HOTEL €€€
(☏632 000; www.lonehotel.com; Luje Adamovića 31; s/d 1478/1847KN; [P][※][@][🤶]) Croatia's first design hotel, this 248-room powerhouse of style is a creation of Croatia's starchitects 3LHD. Rising over Lone bay, a 10-minute stroll from the Old Town, it has light-flooded rooms with private terraces, a restaurant and an extensive spa. Guests can use the pools at the next-door Monte Mulini.

Villa Valdibora HOTEL €€€
(☏845 040; www.valdibora.com; Silvano Chiurco 8; s/d 1080/1440KN; [※][🤶]) The 11 rooms, suites and apartments in this historic building come with cool stone floors and upscale trimmings such as hydromassage showers. There's a fitness room, massages and bikes for rent.

Villa Baron Gautsch GUESTHOUSE €€
(☏840 538; www.baron-gautsch.com; IM Ronjgova 7; s/d 293/586KN; [※][🤶]) This German-owned *pansion* (guesthouse), up the leafy street leading from Hotel Park, has 17 spick-and-span rooms, some with terraces and lovely views of the sea and the Old Town. It's cash (kuna) only.

Hotel Adriatic HOTEL €€€
(☏800 250; www.maistra.com; Pina Budicina bb; s/d 747/933KN; [P][※][🤶]) The location of this hotel, right on the harbour, is excellent and the rooms are well-equipped, albeit in need of renovation and on the kitschy side. The pricier sea-view rooms have more space and newer fittings.

Porton Biondi CAMPING GROUND €
(☏813 557; www.portonbiondi.hr; Aleja Porton Biondi 1; campsites per person/tent 42/26KN; ⊙mid-Mar–Oct; [🚽]) This beachside camping ground, which sleeps 1200, is about 700m from the Old Town.

🍴 Eating

Picnickers can get supplies at the supermarket next to the bus station or at one of the Konzum stores around town.

Most of the restaurants that line the harbour offer the standard fish and meat mainstays at similar prices. For a more gourmet experience, you'll need to bypass the water vistas. Note that many restaurants shut their doors between lunch and dinner.

TOP CHOICE **Male Madlene** TAPAS €
(Križa 28; snacks from 30KN; ⊙11am-2pm & 7-11pm May-Sep) Adorable spot in the owner's tiny living room hanging over the sea, where she serves up creative tapas with market-fresh ingredients, based on old Italian recipes, plus great Istrian wines by the glass.

Monte MEDITERRANEAN €€€
(☏830 203; Montalbano 75; mains from 190KN) Rovinj's top restaurant, right below St Euphemia Church, is worth the hefty cost for the pure enjoyment of its beautifully presented dishes served on the elegant glassed-in terrace. Reserve ahead in high season.

Da Sergio PIZZERIA €
(Grisia 11; pizzas 28-71KN) It's worth waiting in line to get a table at this old-fashioned two-floor pizzeria that dishes out Rovinj's best thin-crust pizza. The best is Gogo, with fresh tomato and arugula (rocket) and prosciutto.

Kantinon SEAFOOD €
(Alda Rismonda 18; mains from 30KN) A fishing theme runs through this high-ceilinged canteen, which specialises in fresh seafood at low prices. The Batana fish plate for two is great value, as are the set menus.

Ulika MEDITERRANEAN €€
(Porečka 6; mains from 100KN; [🍴]) Tucked away in an alleyway, this small, pretty tavern with streetside seating excludes the staples of Adriatic food kitsch (pizza, calamari) and instead features well-prepared, if pricey, Mediterranean fare.

Veli Jože FISH €
(Križa 3; mains from 50KN) Graze on good Istrian standards, either in the eclectic interior

BUSES FROM ROVINJ

DESTINATION	PRICE (KN)	DURATION	FREQUENCY (DAILY)
Dubrovnik	628	16hr	1
Labin	80	2hr	2
Poreč	35-50	50min	15
Pula	35-45	50min	20
Rijeka	93-127	1½-3hr	5
Split	444	11hr	1
Trieste (Italy)	100-120	1½hr	2
Zagreb	150-200	4-6hr	10

crammed with knick-knacks or at the clutch of outdoor tables with water views.

Drinking

Limbo CAFE-BAR
(Casale 22b; 🛜) Cosy cafe-bar with small candlelit tables and cushions laid out on the stairs leading to the Old Town's hilltop. It serves tasty snacks and good Prosecco.

Piassa Granda WINE BAR
(Veli trg 1) This stylish little wine bar with red walls and wood-beamed ceilings has 150 wine labels, mainly Istrian, 20 *rakija* varieties and delicious snacks.

Valentino COCKTAIL BAR
(Križa 28) Premium cocktail prices at this high-end spot include fantastic sunset views from cushions scattered on the water's edge.

Havana COCKTAIL BAR
(Aldo Negri bb) Tropical cocktails, Cuban cigars, straw parasols and the shade of tall pine trees make this open-air bar a popular spot.

Information

There are ATMs and banks all around town. Most travel agencies will change money.

Globtour (☎814 130; www.globtour-turizam.hr; Alda Rismonda 2) Excursions and private accommodation.

Medical Centre (☎813 004; Istarska bb)

Planet (☎840 494; www.planetrovinj.com; Križa 1) Good bargains on private accommodation. Doubles as an internet cafe (6KN per 10 minutes) and has a printer.

Main post office (Matteo Benussi 4; ⊙8am-9pm Mon-Sat summer, 8am-7pm Mon-Fri, to 1pm Sat winter) You can make phone calls here.

Tourist office (☎811 566; www.tzgrovinj.hr; Pina Budicina 12; ⊙8am-10pm Jun-Sep, 8am-

3pm Mon-Fri, to 1pm Sat Oct-May) Has plenty of brochures and maps. Just off Trg Maršala Tita.

Getting There & Around

The bus station is just to the southeast of the Old Town. There's a **garderoba** (left-luggage office; per day 10KN; ⊙6.30am-8pm).

Poreč

POP 20,600

Poreč (Parenzo in Italian) sits on a low, narrow peninsula halfway down the western coast of Istria. The ancient Roman town is the centrepiece of a vast system of resorts that stretch north and south, entirely devoted to summer tourism. While this is not the place for a quiet getaway (unless you come out of season), there is a World Heritage–listed basilica, a medley of Gothic, Romanesque and baroque buildings, well-developed tourist infrastructure and the pristine Istrian interior within easy reach.

Sights

The compact Old Town, called Parentium by the Romans, is based on a rectangular street plan. The ancient Decumanus with its polished stones is the main street running through the peninsula's middle, lined with shops and restaurants. Hotels, travel agencies and excursion boats are on the quayside Obala Maršala Tita, which runs from the small-boat harbour to the tip of the peninsula.

Euphrasian Basilica BASILICA
(Eufrazijeva bb; adult/concession 30/15KN; ⊙9am-6pm Mon-Sat, 2-6pm Sun Apr-Sep) The main reason to visit Poreč is to see the 6th-century Euphrasian Basilica, a World Heritage Site

and one of Europe's finest intact examples of Byzantine art. Built on the site of a 4th-century oratory, the sacral complex includes a church, an atrium and a baptistery. What packs in the crowds are the glittering wall mosaics in the apse, 6th-century master-pieces featuring biblical scenes, archangels and Istrian martyrs. The belfry affords an invigorating view of the Old Town.

Make sure to pop into the adjacent **Bishop's Palace**, which contains a display of ancient stone sculptures, religious paintings and 4th-century mosaics from the original oratory.

Sveti Nikola   ISLAND
There are pebble and concrete beaches to choose from here, as well as rocky breakwaters, shady pine forests and great views of the town across the way. From May to October there are passenger boats every 30 minutes (from 6.45am to 1am) from the wharf on Obala Maršala Tita.

🏃 Activities

Many recreational activities are to be found outside the town in either Plava Laguna or Zelena Laguna. For details, pick up the yearly *Poreč Info & Events* booklet from the tourist office.

From April to October, a **tourist train** operates regularly from Šetalište Antona Štifanića by the marina to Plava Laguna (20KN) and Zelena Laguna (20KN). There's a **passenger boat** (15KN) that makes the same run from the ferry landing every hour from 9am till just before midnight.

The gentle rolling hills of the interior and the well-marked paths make **cycling** and **hiking** prime ways to explore the region. The tourist office issues a free map of roads and trails. You can rent a bike at many agencies around town for 80KN per day.

There is good diving in and around shoals and sandbanks in the area, as well as at the nearby *Coriolanus*, a British Royal Navy warship that sank in 1945. At **Diving Centre Poreč** (☑433 606; www.divingcenter-porec.com), boat dives start at 135KN (more for caves or wrecks) it's 355KN with full equipment rental.

🛏 Sleeping

Accommodation in Poreč is plentiful but gets booked ahead of time, so advance reservations are essential if you come in July or August.

Many travel agencies can help you find private accommodation. Expect to pay between 200KN and 250KN for a double room with private bathroom in the high season, plus a 30% surcharge for stays shorter than three nights. There is a limited number of rooms available in the Old Town, which has no parking. Look for the *Domus Bonus* certificate of quality in private accommodation.

Valamar Riviera Hotel   HOTEL €€€
(☑400 800; www.valamar.com; Maršala Tita 15; s/d 1230/1455KN; 🅿✳@🛜) Rather swanky four-star incarnation right on the harbourfront, with a private beach on Sveti Nikola. Look out for online specials and packages.

Hotel Poreč   HOTEL €€
(☑451 811; www.hotelporec.com; Rade Končara 1; s/d 496/760KN; 🅿✳🛜) While the rooms inside this concrete box have uninspiring views over the bus station and the construction site for the shopping centre opposite, they're acceptable. They have balconies and it's an easy walk from the Old Town.

Camping Zelena Laguna   CAMPING GROUND €
(☑410 102; www.lagunaporec.com; Zelena Laguna; campsite per adult/site 62/117KN; ⊙mid-Apr–Sep; ✳@🛜🏊) Well-equipped for sports, this camping ground 5km from the Old Town can house up to 2700 people. It has access to many beaches, including a naturist one.

🍴 Eating

Gourmet   ITALIAN €€
(Eufrazijeva 26; mains from 60KN) Comforting Italian concoctions come in all shapes and forms here – penne, tagliatelle, fusilli, gnocchi and so on. There are also pizzas from a wood-fired oven as well as meat and seafood dishes. Tables spill out on the square.

TOP CHOICE Konoba Daniela   ISTRIAN €€
(☑460 519; Veleniki; mains from 65KN) In the sweet little village of Veleniki, 4.5km northeast of town, this rustic family-run tavern in an 1880s house is known for its steak tartare and seasonal Istrian mainstays. Taxis charge 80KN to 100KN one way.

Buffet Horizont   FAST FOOD €
(Eufrazijeva 8; mains from 30KN) For cheap and tasty seafood snacks such as sardines, shrimp and calamari, look out for this yellow house with wooden benches outside.

Drinking & Entertainment

In the last couple of years, Poreč has turned into Istria's party capital, with nightlife hawks coming from all parts of Europe to let loose in its late-night clubs.

Rakijarnica BAR
(Trg Marafor 10) Funky bar that specialises in *rakija*, serving up no less than 50 varieties. The vibe is boho and there are occasional live bands and DJs.

Torre Rotonda CAFE-BAR
(Narodni trg 3a) Take the steep stairs to the top of the historic Round Tower and grab a table at the open-air cafe to watch the action on the quays.

Byblos CLUB
(www.byblos.hr; Zelena Laguna 1) On weekends, celeb guest DJs such as David Morales crank out electro house tunes at this humongous open-air club, one of Croatia's hottest places to party.

❶ Information

You can change money at any of the many travel agencies or banks. There are ATMs all around town. There's free wi-fi on Trg Slobode and along the seafront.

Cold Fusion (K Huguesa 2; per hr 30KN; ☺9am-10pm) A computer centre at the bus station.

Main post office (Trg Slobode 14; ☺8am-8pm Mon-Sat) Has a telephone centre.

Poreč Medical Centre (☑426 400; Maura Gioseffija 2)

Sunny Way (☑452 021; sunnyway@pu.t-com. hr; Negrija 1) Specialises in boat tickets and excursions to Italy and around Croatia.

Tourist office (☑451 293; www.to-porec.com; Zagrebačka 9; ☺8am-9pm Mon-Sat, 9am-1pm & 5-9pm Sun May-Sep, 8am-4pm Mon-Fri, 9am-1pm Sat Oct-Apr) Gives out lots of brochures and useful info.

❶ Getting There & Away

The **bus station** (☑060 333 111; K Huguesa 2) is just outside the Old Town, behind Rade Končara, with a **garderoba** (left luggage; per hr 10KN; ☺6am-9pm). There are buses to Rovinj (42KN, 45 minutes, five daily), Zagreb (226KN, 4½ hours, five daily), Rijeka (89KN, 1½ hours, seven daily) and Pula (63KN, one to 1½ hours, five daily).

Ustica Line (www.usticalines.it) runs catamarans to Trieste every Saturday during the season (210KN, 1½ hours). There are four fast catamarans to Venice daily in high season (one way 250KN to 440KN, return 390KN to 880KN,

two hours), operated by **Venezia Lines** (www.venezialines.com) and **Commodore Cruises** (www.commodore-cruises.hr).

KVARNER REGION

🔊051

The Kvarner Gulf (Quarnero in Italian) covers 3300 sq km between Rijeka and Pag Island in the south, protected by the Velebit Range in the southeast, the Gorski Kotar in the east and the Učka massif in the northwest. Covered with luxuriant forests, lined with beaches and dotted with islands, the region has a mild gentle climate and a wealth of vegetation.

From the gateway city of Rijeka, Croatia's third-largest, you can easily connect to the foodie enclave of Volosko and the hiking trails inside the nature parks of Učka. The islands of Krk, Rab, Lošinj and Cres all have highly atmospheric old ports, and stretches of pristine coastline dotted with remote coves for superb swimming.

Rijeka

POP 128,700

Rijeka, Croatia's third-largest city, is an intriguing blend of gritty port and Hapsburg grandeur. Most people rush through en route to the islands or Dalmatia, but those who pause will discover charm and culture. Blend in with the coffee-sipping locals on the bustling Korzo pedestrian strip, take in the city museums and visit the imposing hilltop fortress of Trsat. Rijeka also boasts a good nightlife, intriguing festivals and Croatia's most colourful carnival.

Despite some regrettable architectural ventures in the outskirts, much of the centre is replete with ornate Austro-Hungarian–style buildings. It's a surprisingly verdant city once you've left its concrete core, which contains Croatia's largest port, with ships, cargo and cranes lining the waterfront.

Rijeka is a vital transport hub, but as there's no real beach in the city (and hotel options are few) most people base themselves in nearby Opatija.

◎ Sights

Trsat Castle CASTLE
(adult/concession 15/5KN; ☺9am-8pm May-Oct, to 5pm Nov-Apr) High on a hill above the city is this semi-ruined, 13th-century fortress that houses two galleries and has great vistas from the open-air cafe.

Church of Our Lady of Trsat CHURCH
(Crkva Gospe Trsatske; Frankopanski Trg; ⊗8am-5pm) Along with Trsat Castle, the other hill highlight is the Church of Our Lady of Trsat, a centuries-old magnet for believers that showcases an apparently miraculous icon of Virgin Mary.

City Monuments MONUMENTS
(Trg Ivana Koblera) One of the few buildings to have survived the earthquake, the distinctive yellow **City Tower** (Gradski Toranj; Korzo) was originally a gate from the seafront to the city. The still-functioning clock was mounted in 1873.

Pass under the City Tower to the **Roman Gate** (Stara Vrata), which marks the former entrance to Praetorium, an ancient military complex; you can see the remains in a small excavation area.

Maritime & History Museum MUSEUM
(Pomorski i Povijesni Muzej Hrvatskog Primorja; www.ppmhp.hr; Muzejski trg 1; adult/concession 10/5KN; ⊗9am-4pm Tue-Fri, to 1pm Sat) Housed in the Governor's Palace, this museum gives a vivid picture of life among seafarers, with model ships, sea charts, navigation instruments and portraits of captains.

Astronomical Centre OBSERVATORY
(Astronomski Centar; www.rijekasport.hr; Sveti Križ 33; ⊗8am-11pm Tue-Sat) High on a hill in the east of the city, Croatia's first astronomical centre is a striking modern complex encompassing an observatory, planetarium and study centre. To get here, catch bus 7A from the centre.

✦✦ Festivals & Events

Rijeka Carnival CARNIVAL
(www.ri-karneval.com.hr) This is the largest carnival in Croatia, with two weeks of pageants, street dances, concerts, masked balls, exhibitions and parades. It occurs between late January and early March, depending on when Easter falls.

Hartera MUSIC
(www.hartera.com) Hartera is an annual electronic music festival with DJs and artists from across Europe. It's held in a former paper factory on the banks of the Rječina River over three days in mid-June.

🛏 Sleeping

Prices in Rijeka hotels generally stay the same year-round, except at popular carnival time, when you can expect to pay a sur-charge. There are few private rooms in Rijeka itself; the tourist office (p236) lists these on its website. Nearby Opatija has a lot more accommodation.

Grand Hotel Bonavia HOTEL €€€
(☎357 100; www.bonavia.hr; Dolac 4; s/d from 800/977KN; P❀@🛜) Right in the heart of town, this striking glass-fronted modernist building is Rijeka's top hotel. The rooms are well-equipped and comfort levels are high. There's a well-regarded restaurant, a spa and a stylish pavement cafe.

Best Western Hotel Jadran HOTEL €€€
(☎216 600; www.jadran-hoteli.hr; Šetalište XIII Divizije 46; s/d from 706/833KN; P❀@🛜) Located 2km east of the centre, this attractive four-star hotel has seaview rooms where you can revel in the tremendous Adriatic vistas from your balcony right above the water. There's a tiny beach below.

Hotel Neboder HOTEL €€
(☎373 538; www.jadran-hoteli.hr; Strossmayerova 1; s/d from 462/578KN; P❀@) An iconic design, this modernist tower block offers small, neat and modish rooms, most with balconies and amazing views; however, only the superior rooms have air-conditioning.

Youth Hostel HOSTEL €
(☎406 420; www.hfhs.hr; Šetalište XIII Divizije 23; dm/s/d 130/236/314KN; @🛜) In the leafy residential area of Pečine, 2km east of the centre, this renovated 19th-century villa has clean, spacious (if plain) rooms and a communal TV area. Reserve ahead.

🍴 Eating

There's very little choice on Sundays, when most places are closed. Many cafes on Korzo serve light meals.

Foodies should consider heading to nearby Volosko, 2km east of Opatija, where there's a strip of really high-quality restaurants.

TOP CHOICE Na Kantunu SEAFOOD €€
(Demetrova 2; mains from 45KN) If you're lucky enough to grab a table at this tiny lunchtime spot on an industrial stretch of the port, you'll be treated to the superlative daily catch.

Kukuriku CROATIAN €€€
(☎691 519; www.kukuriku.hr; Trg Matka Laginje 1a, Kastav; 6-course meals 380-550KN; ⊗closed Mon Nov-Easter) This opulent yet modern hotel-restaurant is owned by slow-food pioneer

Nenad Kukurin, who has a reputation for his innovative take on traditional Croatian recipes. Located in historic Kastav, Rijeka's hilltop suburb, it's worth the splurge. Take bus 18 from Rijeka (33 and 37 from Opatija).

Restaurant Spagho ITALIAN €
(Ivana Zajca 24a; mains from 40KN) A stylish, modern Italian place with exposed brickwork, art and hip seating that offers delicious and filling portions of pasta, pizza, salads, and meat and fish dishes.

Zlatna Školjka SEAFOOD €€
(Kružna 12; mains from 65KN) Savour the superbly prepared seafood and choice Croatian wines at this formal maritime-themed restaurant. The adjacent **Bracera** (Kružna 12; mains from 60KN), by the same owners, serves crusty pizza, even on a Sunday.

Mlinar BAKERY €
(Frana Supila; items from 13KN; ☺6am-8pm Mon-Fri, 6.30am-3pm Sat, 7am-1pm Sun) The best bakery in town, with delicious filled baguettes, wholemeal bread, croissants and *burek*.

🍷 Drinking

The main drags of Riva and Korzo are the best bet for a drink, with everything from lounge bars to no-nonsense pubs.

TOP CHOICE Gradena CAFE
(www.bascinskiglasi.hr; Trsat; ☎) Set in the grounds of Trsat Castle, this happening cafe-bar with chillout music and friendly service would rate anywhere.

Filodrammatica Bookshop Cafe CAFE
(☎498 141; www.vbz.hr; Korzo 28) A cafe and bar with luxurious decor and a VBZ (Croatia's biggest publisher) bookshop at the back, Filodrammatica also prides itself on specialist coffees and fresh, single-source beans.

Caffe Jazz Tunel BAR
(☎327 116; www.jazztunel.com; Školjić 12; ☺9am-2am Mon-Fri, 5pm-2am Sat) One of the city's most popular bars, it's crowded all week long, but full to bursting on Friday and Saturday nights when you can find live music or DJs rocking the night.

ℹ Information

There are ATMs and exchange offices along Korzo and at the train station.

Hospital (☎658 111; Krešimirova 42)
Main post office (Korzo 13; ☺7am-8pm Mon-Fri, to 2pm Sat) Has a telephone centre and an exchange office.
Tourist Information Centre (☎335 882; www.tz-rijeka.hr; Korzo 33a; ☺8am-8pm Mon-Sat Apr-Sep, 8am-8pm Mon-Fri, to 2pm Sat Oct-Mar) Has good colour city maps, lots of brochures and private accommodation lists, though the staff can be aloof.

ℹ Getting There & Away

BOAT Jadroagent (☎211 626; www.jadroagent.hr; Trg Ivana Koblera 2) Has information on all boats around Croatia.
Jadrolinija (☎211 444; www.jadrolinija.hr; Riječki Lukobran bb; ☺8am-8pm Mon-Fri, 9am-5pm Sat & Sun) Sells tickets for the large coastal ferries that run all year between Rijeka and Dubrovnik on their way to Bari in Italy, via Split, Hvar, Korčula and Mljet. Check Jadrolinija's website for up-to-date schedules and prices. All ferries depart from the new ferry terminal.
BUS The **intercity bus station** (Trg Žabica) is west of the centre, at the western edge of Riva. The bus-station **garderoba** (left-luggage office; per day 15KN; ☺5.30am-10.30pm) is at the cafe next door to the ticket office.

If you fly into Zagreb, there is a Croatia Airlines van that goes directly from Zagreb airport to Rijeka daily (160KN, two hours, 3.30pm). It goes back to Zagreb from Rijeka at 5am. There are three daily buses to Trieste (60KN, 2½ hours)

DOMESTIC BUSES FROM RIJEKA

DESTINATION	PRICE (KN)	DURATION (HR)	FREQUENCY (DAILY)
Dubrovnik	362-503	12-13	3-4
Krk	59	1-2	14
Pula	97	2¼	8
Rovinj	90	1-2	4
Split	253-330	8	6-7
Zadar	161-210	4-5	6-7
Zagreb	137-160	2¼-3	13-15

and one daily bus to Ljubljana (175KN, five hours). To get to Plitvice (142KN, four hours), you have to change in Otočac.

CAR AMC (☎338 800; www.amcrentacar.hr; Lukobran 4) Based in the new ferry terminal building, has cars starting from 250KN per day.

TRAIN The **train station** (☎213 333; Krešimirova 5) is a 10-minute walk east of the city centre; ther's a **garderoba** (left-luggage office; per day 15KN; ⊙4.30am-10.30pm). Seven daily trains run to Zagreb (100KN, four to five hours). There's one daily connection to Split (170KN, eight hours), though it involves a change at Ogulin. Two direct daily services head to Ljubljana (98KN, three hours) and one daily train goes to Vienna (319KN to 525KN, nine hours).

ℹ Getting Around

Taxis are very reasonable in Rijeka (if you use the right firm). **Cammeo** (☎313 313) cabs are modern, inexpensive, have meters and are highly recommended; a ride in the central area costs 20KN.

Opatija

POP 7870

Opatija stretches along the coast, just 15km west of Rijeka, its forested hills sloping down to the sparkling sea. It was this breathtaking location and the agreeable all-year climate that made Opatija the most fashionable seaside resort for the Viennese elite during the days of the Austro-Hungarian empire. The grand residences of the wealthy have since been revamped and turned into upscale hotels, with a particular accent on spa and health holidays. Foodies have been flocking from afar too, for the clutch of terrific restaurants in the nearby fishing village of Volosko.

Opatija sits on a narrow strip of land sandwiched between the sea and the foothills of Mt Učka. Ulica Maršala Tita is the main road that runs through town; it's lined with travel agencies, ATMs, restaurants, shops and hotels.

◉ Sights & Activities

Lungomare PROMENADE
The pretty Lungomare is the region's showcase. Lined with plush villas and ample gardens, this shady promenade winds along the sea for 12km from Volosko to Lovran. Along the way are innumerable rocky outcrops – a better option than Opatija's concrete beach.

Villa Angiolina HISTORICAL BUILDING
(Park Angiolina 1; ⊙9am-1pm & 4.30-9.30pm Tue-Sun summer, shorter hours rest of year) The restored Villa Angiolina houses the **Croatian Museum of Tourism**, a grand title for a modest collection of old photographs, postcards, brochures and posters tracing the history of travel. Don't miss a stroll around the verdant gardens that surround the villa, replete with gingko trees, sequoias, holm oaks and Japanese camellia (Opatija's symbol).

Učka Nature Park NATURE RESERVE
Opatija and the surrounding region offer some wonderful opportunities for hiking and biking around the Učka mountain range; the **tourist office** (☎293 753; www.pp-ucka.hr; Liganj 42; ⊙8am-4.30pm Mon-Fri) has maps and information.

🛏 Sleeping & Eating

There are no real budget hotels in Opatija, but there's plenty of value in the midrange and top end. Private rooms are abundant but a little more expensive than in other areas; expect to pay around 170KN to 240KN per person.

Maršala Tita is lined with serviceable restaurants that offer pizza, grilled meat and fish, but don't expect anything outstanding. Head to nearby Volosko for fine dining and regional specialties.

Villa Ariston HISTORIC HOTEL €€
(☎271 379; www.villa-ariston.com; Ulica Maršala Tita 179; s/d 600/800KN; P❄@🖤🛜) With a gorgeous location beside a rocky cove, this historic hotel has period charm and celeb cachet in spades (Coco Chanel and the Kennedys are former guests).

Hotel Opatija HOTEL €€
(☎271 388; www.hotel-opatija.hr; Trg Vladimira Gortana 2/1; r from 486KN; P❄@🖤🛜) The setting in a Habsburg-era mansion is the forte of this large hilltop three-star hotel with comfortable rooms, an amazing terrace, a small indoor seawater pool and lovely gardens.

Medveja CAMPING GROUND €
(☎291 191; medveja@liburnia.hr; campsites per adult/tent 44/32KN; ⊙Easter–mid-Oct) On a pretty pebble cove 10km south of Opatija, this camping ground has apartments and mobile homes for rent too.

Istranka ISTRIAN €
(Bože Milanovića 2; mains from 55KN) Graze on flavourful Istrian mainstays like *maneštra* (vegetable and bean soup) at this rustic-themed tavern in a small street just up from Maršala Tita.

CROATIA OPATIJA

VOLOSKO

Volosko is one of the prettiest places on this coastline, a fishing village that has also become something of a restaurant mecca in recent years. This is not a tourist resort, and whether you're passing through for a drink or having a gourmet meal you'll enjoy the local ambience and wonderful setting.

Rijeka and Volosko are connected by bus, or you can walk along the coastal promenade from Opatija, a 30-minute stroll past bay trees, palms, figs and oaks and magnificent villas.

Tramerka (Andrije Mohorovičića 15; mains from 65KN; ⊗Tue-Sun) It doesn't have sea views but this wonderful place scores on every other level. Chef-patron Andrej Barbieri will expertly guide you through the short menu, chosen from the freshest available seafood (the *gregada* fish stew is just stupendous) and locally sourced meats.

Skalinada (www.skalinada.org; Put Uz Dol 17; meals from 80KN) An intimate, highly atmospheric little bistro-style place with sensitive lighting, exposed stone walls and a creative menu of Croatian food (small dishes or mains) using seasonal and local ingredients.

🍷 Drinking & Entertainment

Opatija is a pretty sedate place. Its Viennese-style coffee houses and hotel terraces are popular with the mature clientele, though there are a few stylish bars. Check out the slightly bohemian **Tantra** (Lido), which juts out into the Kvarner Gulf, and **Hemingway** (Zert 2), the original venue of what is now a nationwide chain of sleek cocktail bars.

ℹ Information

Da Riva (☑272 990; www.da-riva.hr; Ulica Maršala Tita 170) A good source for private accommodation, and runs excursions around Croatia.

Linea Verde (☑701 107; www.lineaverde-croatia.com; Andrije Štangera 42, Volosko) Specialist agency with trips to Risnjak and Učka Nature Park and gourmet tours around Istria.

Tourist office (☑271 310; www.opatija-tourism. hr; Ulica Maršala Tita 128; ⊗8am-10pm Mon-Sat, 5-9pm Sun Jul & Aug, shorter hours rest of year) This office has knowledgeable staff and lots of maps, leaflets and brochures.

ℹ Getting There & Away

Bus 32 runs through the centre of Rijeka along Adamićeva to the Opatija Riviera (20KN, 15km) as far as Lovran, every 20 minutes daily until late in the evening.

Krk Island

POP 16,400

Croatia's largest island, 409-sq-km Krk (Veglia in Italian) is also one of the busiest in the summer. It may not be the most beautiful or lush island in Croatia – in fact, it's overdeveloped – but its decades of experience in tourism make it an easy place to visit, with good transport connections and well-organised infrastructure.

ℹ Getting There & Around

The Krk toll bridge links the northern part of the island with the mainland, and a regular car ferry links Valbiska with Merag on Cres (passenger/car 18KN/115KN, 30 minutes) in summer.

Krk is also home to **Rijeka airport** (www. rijeka-airport.hr), the main hub for flights to the Kvarner region, which consist mostly of low-cost and charter flights during summer.

Rijeka and Krk Town are connected by nine to 13 daily bus services (56KN, one to two hours). Services are reduced on weekends.

Six daily buses run from Zagreb to Krk Town (179KN to 194KN, three to four hours). Note that some bus lines are more direct than others, which will stop in every village en route. **Autotrans** (www.autotrans.hr) has two quick daily buses.

KRK TOWN

POP 3370

The picturesque Krk Town makes a good base for exploring the island. It encompasses a medieval walled centre and, spreading out into the surrounding coves and hills, a modern development that includes a port, beaches, camping grounds and hotels.

☉ Sights

Highlights include the Romanesque **Cathedral of the Assumption** (Katedrala Uznešenja; Trg Svetog Kvirina; ⊗morning & evening Mass) and the fortified **Kaštel** (Trg Kamplin) facing the seafront on the northern edge of the Old

Town. The narrow cobbled streets that make up the pretty old quarter are worth a wander, although they're typically packed.

🛏 Sleeping & Eating

The Old Town only has one hotel; all the others are located in a large complex east of the centre and are very family orientated. Consult travel agencies for private accommodation. Note that the only hostel in town is pretty rundown.

TOP CHOICE Hotel Marina   BOUTIQUE HOTEL €€€
(☑221 357; www.hotelikrk.hr; Obala Hrvatske Mornarice 6; d 1460KN; P❄@🛜) The only hotel in the Old Town enjoys a prime waterfront location and has 10 deluxe contemporary units.

Bor   HOTEL €€
(☑220 200; www.hotelbor.hr; Šetalište Dražica 5; s/d from 480/960KN; ☉Apr-Oct; P🛜) The 22 rooms are modest and without trimmings at this low-key hotel, but the seafront location amid mature pines makes it a worthwhile place to stay.

Autocamp Ježevac   CAMPING GROUND €
(☑221 081; camping@valamar.com; Plavnička bb; campsite per adult/site 50/62KN; ☉mid-Apr–mid-Oct) Beachfront camping ground with shady pitches located on old farming terraces, with good swimming sites. It's a 10-minute walk southwest of town.

Konoba Nono   CROATIAN €
(Krčkih Iseljenika 8; mains from 40KN) Savour local specialties like *šurlice sa junećim* (pasta topped with goulash), just a hop and a skip from the Old Town.

Galija   PIZZERIA €
(www.galija-krk.com; Frankopanska 38; mains from 45KN) Munch your *margarita* or *vagabondo* pizza, grilled meat or fresh fish under beamed ceilings of this convivial part-*konoba*, part-pizzeria.

ℹ Information

The **main tourist office** (☑220 226; Vela Placa 1; ☉8am-3pm Mon-Fri) and **seasonal tourist office** (☑220 226; www.tz-krk.hr; Obala Hrvatske Mornarice bb; ☉8am-8pm Mon-Sat, 8am-2pm Sun Jun-Oct & Easter-May) distribute brochures and materials, including a map of hiking paths, and advice in many languages.

You can change money at any travel agency and there are numerous ATMs around town.

The bus from Rijeka stops at the station (no left-luggage office) by the harbour, a few minutes' walk from the Old Town.

DALMATIA

Roman ruins, spectacular beaches, old fishing ports, medieval architecture and unspoilt offshore islands make a trip to Dalmatia (Dalmacija) unforgettable. Occupying the central 375km of Croatia's Adriatic

LOŠINJ & CRES ISLANDS

Separated by an 11m-wide canal (with a bridge), these two highly scenic islands in the Kvarner archipelago are often treated as a single entity. On Lošinj, the more populated of the two, the pretty ports of Mali Lošinj and Veli Lošinj, ringed by pine forests and lush vegetation, attract plenty of summertime tourists. Consequently, there are varied sleeping and eating options. The waters around Lošinj are the first protected marine area for dolphins in the entire Mediterranean, watched over by the Mali Lošinj–based **Blue World** (www.blue-world.org) NGO.

Wilder, more barren Cres has a natural allure that's intoxicating and inspiring. Sparsely populated, it's covered in dense primeval forests and lined with a craggy coastline of soaring cliffs, hidden coves and ancient hilltop towns. The northern half of Cres, known as Tramuntana, is prime cruising terrain for the protected griffon vulture; see these giant birds at **Eco-Centre Caput Insulae** (☑840 525; www.supovi.hr; Beli 4; adult/concession 50/25KN; ☉9am-8pm, closed Nov-Mar), an excellent visitor centre in Beli on the eastern coast. The main seaside settlements lie on the western shore of Cres, while the highlands showcase the astounding medieval town of Lubenice.

The main maritime port of entry for the islands is Mali Lošinj, which is connected to Rijeka, Pula, Zadar and Venice in the summer. A variety of car ferries and catamaran boats are run by **Jadrolinija** (www.jadrolinija.hr), **Split Tours** (www.splittours.hr) and **Venezia Lines** (www.venezialines.com).

coast, Dalmatia offers a matchless combination of hedonism and historical discovery. The jagged coast is speckled with lush offshore islands and dotted with historic cities.

Split is the largest city in the region and a hub for bus and boat connections along the Adriatic, as well as home to the late-Roman Diocletian's Palace. Nearby are the early Roman ruins in Solin (Salona). Zadar has yet more Roman ruins and a wealth of churches. The architecture of Hvar and Korčula recalls the days when these islands were outposts of the Venetian empire. None can rival majestic Dubrovnik, a cultural and aesthetic jewel, while magical Mljet features isolated island beauty.

Zadar

023 / POP 73,400

Boasting a historic Old Town of Roman ruins and medieval churches, cosmopolitan cafes and quality museums, Zadar is an excellent city. It's not too crowded, it's not overrun with tourists and its two unique attractions – the sound-and-light spectacles of the Sea Organ and the Sun Salutation – need to be seen and heard to be believed.

It's not a picture-postcard kind of place, but the mix of beautiful Roman architecture, Hapsburg elegance, a wonderful seafront and some unsightly ordinary office blocks is what gives Zadar so much character – it's no Dubrovnik, but it's not a museum town either; this is a living, vibrant city, enjoyed by its residents and visitors alike.

The centre of town is not well blessed with hotels, though a few new places are springing up each year. Most visitors stay in the leafy resort area of Borik nearby. Zadar is a key transport hub with superb ferry connections to Croatia's Adriatic islands, Kvarner, southern Dalmatia and Italy.

⊙ Sights

Sea Organ   MONUMENT
Zadar's incredible Sea Organ, designed by architect Nikola Bašić, has a hypnotic effect. Set within the perforated stone stairs that descend into the sea is a system of pipes and whistles that exudes wistful sighs when the movement of the sea pushes air through it.

Sun Salutation   MONUMENT
(⊞) Right next to the Sea Organ is the Sun Salutation, another wacky and wonderful Bašić creation. It's a 22m circle cut into the pavement, filled with 300 multilayered glass

plates that collect the sun's energy during the day, and, together with the wave energy that makes the Sea Organ's sound, produce a trippy light show from sunset to sunrise that's meant to simulate the solar system.

Church of St Donat   CHURCH
(Crkva Svetog Donata; Šimuna Kožičića Benje; admission 15KN; ⊙9am-9pm May-Sep, to 4pm Oct-Apr) This circular 9th-century Byzantine structure was built over the Roman forum. A few architectural fragments are preserved inside. Notice the Latin inscriptions on the remains of the Roman sacrificial altars. Outside the church on the northwestern side is a pillar from the Roman era that served in the Middle Ages as a shame post, where wrongdoers were chained and publicly humiliated.

Museum of Ancient Glass   MUSEUM
(www.mas-zadar.hr; Poljana Zemaljskog Odbora 1; adult/concession 30/10KN; ⊙9am-9pm May-Sep, to 7pm Mon-Sat Oct-Apr) This is an impressive museum: its layout is superb, with giant lightboxes and ethereal music to make the experience special. The history and invention of glass is explained, through thousands of pieces on display: goblets, jars and vials; jewellery, rings and amulets.

Beaches   BEACHES
You can swim from the steps off the promenade and listen to the sound of the Sea Organ. There's a swimming area with diving boards, a small park and a cafe on the coastal promenade off Zvonimira. Bordered by pine trees and parks, the promenade takes you to a beach in front of Hotel Kolovare and then winds on for about a kilometre up the coast.

⌲ Tours

Travel agencies offer boat cruises to Telašćica Bay and the beautiful Kornati Islands, which include lunch and a swim in the sea or a salt lake. Aquarius Travel Agency (p242) charges 250–300KN per person for a full-day trip, or ask around on Liburnska Obala (where the excursion boats are moored).

Organised trips to the national parks of Paklenica, Krka and Plitvice Lakes are also popular.

✿ Festivals & Events

Between July and September, the Zadar region showcases some of the globe's most celebrated electronic artists, bands and DJs. The ringmaster for these festivals is the Zadar-based Garden (p241) bar, but the festivals are held in a gorgeous new location, in the small village of Tisno, 45km south of Zadar. The original event, the **Garden Festival** (www.thegardenfestival.eu), has been running every July since 2006. By 2010, four other festivals (Soundwave, Suncebeat, Electric Elephant and Stop Making Sense) had joined the party between July and September.

🛌 Sleeping

Most visitors stay in the 'tourist settlement' of Borik, which isn't as bad as it sounds as it has good swimming, a nice promenade and lots of greenery. Most hotels in Borik date from Yugo days (or before) and there's also a hostel, camping ground and *sobe* (rooms) here too. Many hotels are managed by the Austria-based **Falkensteiner** (www.falkensteiner.com) group.

Contact travel agencies for private accommodation; very little is available in the Old Town, though.

ZADAR

TOP CHOICE **Art Hotel Kalelarga** BOUTIQUE HOTEL €€€
(☑233 000; www.arthotel-kalelarga.com; Široka 23; s/d/ste 1225/1430/2300KN; P❋📶) Right in the heart of Zadar's Old Town, this 10-room boutique hotel is an understated beauty with a stylish cafe and spacious rooms in hues of sand and stone, with grand beds, elaborate lighting and cool lines. There is also a restaurant, which has tables on the main square.

Villa Hrešć HOTEL €€
(☑337 570; www.villa-hresc.hr; Obala Kneza Trpimira 28; s/d 670/850KN; P❋📶♨👪) This condo-style villa is about a 20-minute walk from Zadar's historic sights. There's a coastal garden with an Old Town vista, and good-value rooms and apartments benefit from subtle colours and attractive decor. Some have massive terraces.

Hotel Venera GUESTHOUSE €€
(☑214 098; www.hotel-venera-zd.hr; Šime Ljubića 4a; d 460KN) A modest guesthouse that has two things going for it: a good location on a quiet street in the Old Town and the friendly family owners. Breakfast not included.

Student Hostel HOSTEL €
(☑224 840; Obala Kneza Branimira bb; dm 153KN; ☉Jul & Aug) This student dormitory turns into a hostel in July and August. It's centrally located – right across the footbridge – and has no-frills three-bed rooms.

BORIK

Autocamp Borik CAMPING GROUND €
(☑332 074; per adult 56KN, per campsite 94-146KN; ☉May-Oct) A good option for those who want easy access to Zadar, this camping ground is steps away from the shore at Borik. Pitches are shaded by tall pines.

🍴 Eating

Dining options in Zadar are eclectic and generally good value. You'll find elegant restaurants specialising in Dalmatian cuisine and no-nonsense canteen-style places offering filling grub.

Zadar's **market** (☉6am-3pm), off Jurja Barakovica, is one of Croatia's best.

TOP CHOICE **Foša** MEDITERRANEAN €€
(www.fosa.hr; Kralja Dmitra Zvonimira 2; mains from 85KN) A classy place with a sleek interior and a gorgeous terrace that juts out into the harbour. Start by tasting the olive oils, and move on to a grilled Adriatic fish of your choice, though red-meat eaters won't be disappointed either.

Na po ure DALMATIAN €
(Špire Brusine 8; mains from 40KN) This unpretentious family-run *konoba* is the place to sate that appetite, with from-the-heart Dalmatian cooking: grilled lamb, calf's liver and fresh fish served with potatoes and vegetables.

Zalogajnica Ljepotica DALMATIAN €
(Obala Kneza Branimira 4b; mains from 35KN) The cheapest place in town prepares three to four dishes a day (think risotto, pasta and grilled meat) at knockout prices in a no-frills setting.

🍷 Drinking

Zadar has pavement cafes, lounge bars, boho bars and everything in between. Head to the district of Varoš on the southwest side of the Old Town for interesting little dive bars popular with students and arty types.

TOP CHOICE **Garden** BAR, RESTAURANT
(www.thegardenzadar.com; Bedemi Zadarskih Pobuna; ☉late May-Oct) If anywhere can claim to have put Zadar on the map it's this remarkable bar-club-garden-restaurant perched on top of the old city walls with jaw-dropping harbour views. It's very Ibiza-esque, with cushion mattresses, secluded alcoves, vast sail-like sunshades, purple-and-white decor and contemporary electronic music.

Arsenal   BAR, RESTAURANT
(www.arsenalzadar.com; Trg Tri Bunara 1) A huge renovated shipping warehouse that now contains a lounge bar, a restaurant, a gallery and a cultural centre and has a cool, cultured vibe. There are musical events, good food and even a tourist-info desk (which may or may not be staffed).

Caffe Bar Lovre   CAFE
(Narodni trg 1) With a huge terrace on Narodni Trg, gorgeous Lovre has plenty of atmosphere and a heart-of-the-city vibe.

ℹ Information

Aquarius Travel Agency (☏212 919; www.juresko.hr; Nova Vrata bb) Books accommodation and excursions.

Geris.net (Federica Grisogona 81; per hr 25KN) The city's best cybercafe.

Hospital (☏315 677; Bože Peričića 5)

Miatours (☏/fax 212 788; www.miatours.hr; Vrata Svetog Krševana) Arranges excursions and accommodation.

Post office (Poljana Pape Aleksandra III; ◷7.30am-9pm Mon-Sat, to 2pm Sun) You can make phone calls here and it has an ATM.

Tourist office (☏316 166; www.tzzadar.hr; ◷8am-10pm Mon-Fri, to 9pm Sat & Sun Jun-Sep, to 8pm daily Oct-May) Publishes a good colour map and the free *Zadar City Guide*.

ℹ Getting There & Away

AIR Zadar's airport, 12km east of the city, is served by **Croatia Airlines** (☏250 101; www.croatiaairlines.hr; Poljana Natka Nodila 7) and **Ryanair** (www.ryanair.com). A Croatia Airlines bus meets all flights and costs 23KN. For a taxi, call the very efficient and cheap **Lulić** (☏494 494).

BOAT On the harbour, **Jadrolinija** (☏254 800; www.jadrolinija.hr; Liburnska Obala 7) has tickets for all local ferries. Buy international tickets from **Jadroagent** (☏211 447; jadroagent-zadar@zd.t-com.hr; Poljana Natka Nodila 4), just inside the city walls.

BUS The **bus station** (☏211 035; www.liburnija-zadar.hr) is about 2km east of the Old Town and has daily buses to Zagreb (97KN to 147KN, 3½ to seven hours, every 30 minutes). Buses marked 'Poluotok' run from the bus station to the harbour and those marked 'Puntamika' (5 and 8) run to Borik every 20 minutes (hourly on Sunday). Tickets cost 10KN (15KN for two from a *tisak*).

TRAIN The **train station** (☏212 555; www.hznet.hr; Ante Starčevića 3) is adjacent to the bus station. There are six daily trains to Zagreb, but the journey time is very slow indeed; the fastest take over eight hours.

Split

☏021 / POP 178,200

The second-largest city in Croatia, Split (Spalato in Italian) is a great place to see Dalmatian life as it's really lived. Always buzzing, this exuberant city has just the right balance of tradition and modernity. Step inside Diocletian's Palace (a Unesco World Heritage site and one of the world's most impressive Roman monuments) and you'll see dozens of bars, restaurants and shops thriving amid the atmospheric old walls where Split life has been going on for thousands of years. To top it off, Split has a unique setting. Its dramatic coastal mountains act as the perfect backdrop to the turquoise waters of the Adriatic. You'll get a chance to appreciate this gorgeous cityscape when making a ferry journey to or from the city.

The Old Town is a vast open-air museum and the new information signs at the important sights explain a great deal of Split's history. The seafront promenade, Obala Hrvatskog Narodnog Preporoda, better known as Riva, is the best central reference point.

History

Split achieved fame when Roman emperor Diocletian (AD 245–313) had his retirement palace built here from 295 to 305. After his death the great stone palace continued to be used as a retreat by Roman rulers. When the neighbouring colony of Salona was abandoned in the 7th century, many of the Romanised inhabitants fled to Split and barricaded themselves behind the palace walls, where their descendants continue to live to this day.

◉ Sights

DIOCLETIAN'S PALACE
Facing the harbour, **Diocletian's Palace** is one of the most imposing Roman ruins in existence. Don't expect a palace though, nor a museum – this is the living heart of the city, its labyrinthine streets packed with people, bars, shops and restaurants.

It was built as a military fortress, imperial residence and fortified town, with walls reinforced by square corner towers.

Each wall has a gate named after a metal: at the northern end is the **Golden Gate** (Zlatna Vrata), while the southern end has the **Bronze Gate**; the eastern gate is the **Silver Gate** and to the west is the **Iron Gate**. Between the eastern and western gates there's a straight road (Krešimirova; also known as Decumanus), which separates the imperial residence on the southern side. The Bronze Gate, in the southern wall, led from the living quarters to the sea.

There are 220 buildings within the palace boundaries, home to about 3000 people.

Town Museum
MUSEUM

(Muzej Grada Splita; www.mgst.net; Papalićeva 1; adult/concession 10/5KN; ⊗9am-9pm Tue-Fri, to 4pm Sat-Mon Jun-Sep, 10am-5pm Tue-Fri, to 1pm Sat-Mon Oct-May) Built for one of the many noblemen who lived within the palace in the Middle Ages, the Papalić Palace that houses the museum is considered a fine example of late-Gothic style. Its three floors showcase a collection of drawings, coats of arms, 17th-century weaponry and fine furniture. Captions are in Croatian.

FREE Cathedral of St Domnius
CATHEDRAL

(Katedrala Svetog Duje; Svetog Duje 5; cathedral/treasury/belfry 15/15/10KN; ⊗8am-7pm Mon-Sat, 12.30-6.30pm Sun Jun-Sep, sporadic hours Oct-May) On the eastern side of the Peristil, Split's cathedral was built as Diocletian's mausoleum. The oldest remnants inside are the remarkable 13th-century scenes from the life of Christ carved on the wooden entrance doors. The choir is furnished with 13th-century Romanesque seats that are the oldest in Dalma-

tia. The treasury is rich in reliquaries, icons, church robes and illuminated manuscripts. You can climb the Romanesque belfry.

Note that admission to the cathedral also gets you free access to the Temple of Jupiter and its crypt. For 35KN, you can get a ticket that includes access to the cathedral, treasury and belfry.

Temple of Jupiter
TEMPLE

(temple/crypt 5/5KN; ⊗8am-7pm Mon-Sat, 12.30-6.30pm Sun May-Sep) The headless sphinx in black granite guarding the entrance to the temple was imported from Egypt at the time of the temple's construction in the 5th century. Take a look at the barrel-vaulted ceiling and a decorative frieze on the walls. You can also pop into the crypt.

Ethnographic Museum
MUSEUM

(Etnografski Muzej; www.etnografski-muzej-split.hr; Severova 1; adult/concession 10/5KN; ⊗9am-7pm Mon-Fri, to 1pm Sat Jun-Sep, 9am-4pm Mon-Fri, to 1pm Sat Oct-May) This mildly interesting museum has a collection of photos of old Split, traditional costumes and memorabilia of important citizens. For great Old Town views, make sure you climb the staircase that leads to the Renaissance terrace on the southern edge of the vestibule. These views are reason enough to visit.

CROATIA SPLIT

WORTH A TRIP

SOLIN (SALONA)

The ruin of the ancient city of Solin (known as Salona by the Romans), among the vineyards at the foot of mountains just northeast of Split, is the most interesting archaeological site in Croatia. Salona was the capital of the Roman province of Dalmatia from the time Julius Caesar elevated it to the status of colony. It held out against the barbarians and was only evacuated in AD 614 when the inhabitants fled to Split and neighbouring islands in the face of Avar and Slav attacks.

Begin your visit at the main entrance near Caffe Bar Salona, where you'll see an info-map of the complex. **Tusculum Museum** (admission 20KN; ⊗7am-7pm Mon-Fri, 8am-7pm Sat, 9am-1pm Sun Apr-Sep, shorter hours rest of year) is where you pay admission for the entire archaeological reserve (you'll get a brochure with a map) as well as for the small museum with interesting sculpture embedded in the walls and in the garden. Some of the highlights inside the complex include **Manastirine**, the fenced area behind the car park, a burial place for early Christian martyrs prior to the legalisation of Christianity; the excavated remains of **Kapljuč Basilica** – one of the early Christian cemeteries in Salona – and the 5th-century **Kapjinc Basilica** that sits inside it. Also look out for the **covered aqueduct** from the 1st century AD; the 5th-century **cathedral** with an octagonal baptistery; and the huge 2nd-century **amphitheatre**.

The ruins are easily accessible on Split city bus 1 (13KN), which goes all the way to the parking lot for Salona every half-hour from Trg Gaje Bulata. From Solin you can continue on to Trogir by catching westbound bus 37 (17KN) from the Širine crossroad. Take city bus 1 back to Širine and then walk for five minutes on the same road to get to the stop for bus 37 on the adjacent highway.

Central Split

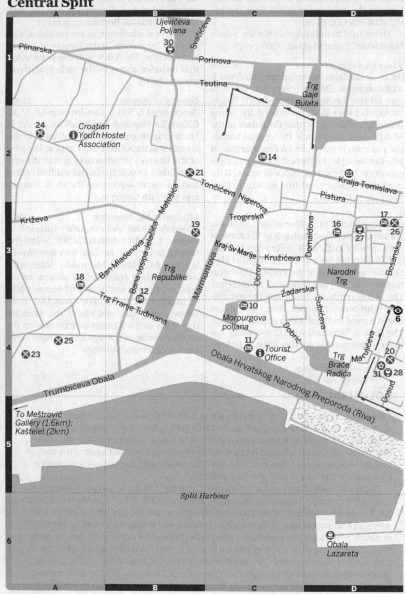

Peristil SQUARE

This picturesque colonnaded square, with a neo-Romanesque cathedral tower rising above, is a great place for a break in the sun. The **vestibule**, an open dome above the ground-floor passageway at the southern end of the Peristil, is overpoweringly grand and cavernous.

Basement Halls HISTORIC SITE

(adult/concession 35/15KN; ◷9am-9pm daily Jun-Sep, 9am-8pm Mon-Sat, to 6pm Sun Apr, May &

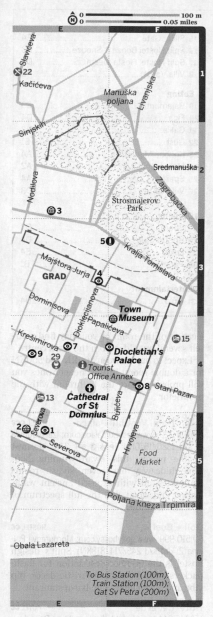

OUTSIDE THE PALACE WALLS

Gregorius of Nin — MONUMENT

(Grgur Ninski) This 10th-century statue is of the Croatian bishop who fought for the right to use old Croatian in liturgical services. Notice that his left big toe has been polished to a shine – it's said that rubbing the toe brings good luck.

Gallery of Fine Arts — GALLERY

(Galerija Umjetnina Split; www.galum.hr; Kralja Tomislava 15; adult/concession 20/10KN; ⊘11am-4pm Mon, to 7pm Tue-Fri, to 3pm Sat May-Sep, 9am-2pm Mon, to 5pm Tue-Fri, to 1pm Sat Oct-Apr) This gallery housed in a former hospital exhibits nearly 400 works of art spanning almost 700 years. Upstairs is the permanent collection; temporary exhibits downstairs change every few months. The pleasant cafe has a terrace overlooking the palace.

OUTSIDE CENTRAL SPLIT

Meštrović Gallery — GALLERY

(Galerija Meštrović; Šetalište Ivana Meštrovića 46; adult/concession 30/15KN; ⊘9am-7pm Tue-Sun May-Sep, shorter hours rest of year) At this stellar art museum, below Marjan to the west of the city centre, you'll see a comprehensive, nicely arranged collection of works by Ivan Meštrović, Croatia's premier modern sculptor. Don't miss the nearby **Kaštelet** (Šetalište Ivana Meštrovića 39; admission by Meštrović Gallery ticket; ⊘9am-7pm Tue-Sat, 10am-7pm Sun May-Sep, shorter hours rest of year), a fortress that Meštrović bought and restored to house his powerful Life of Christ wood reliefs.

Bačvice — BEACH

The most popular city beach is on the eponymous inlet. This biggish pebbly beach has good swimming, a lively ambience, a great cafe-bar and plenty of water games. There are showers and changing rooms at both ends of the beach.

🏃 Activities

Marjan — WALKING TRAIL

For an afternoon away from the city buzz, Marjan (178m) is the perfect destination. Considered the lungs of the city, this hilly nature reserve offers **trails** through fragrant pine forests, scenic **lookouts** and ancient **chapels**. There are different ways of reaching Marjan. Start from the stairway (Marjanske Skale) in Varoš, right behind the Church of Sveti Frane. It's a mild incline along old stone stairs and a scenic 10-minute trek to get to Vidilica (p248) cafe

Oct, shorter hours rest of year) Although mostly empty, save an exhibit or two, the rooms and corridors underneath the Diocletian's Palace exude a haunting timelessness that is well worth the price of a ticket.

Central Split

at the top. From here, right by the old Jewish cemetery, you can follow the marked trail, stopping en route to see the chapels, all the way to **Kašjuni cove**, a quieter beach option than the buzzing Bačvice.

✷ Festivals & Events

Carnival CULTURAL
This traditional February event sees locals dressing up and dancing in the streets for two very fun days.

Feast of St Duje RELIGIOUS
Otherwise known as Split Day, this 7 May feast involves much singing and dancing all around the city.

Split Summer Festival ARTS
(www.splitsko-ljeto.hr) From mid-July to mid-August, it features opera, drama, ballet and concerts on open-air stages.

⛺ Sleeping

Good budget accommodation has become more available in Split in the last couple of years but it's mostly comprised of hostels. Private accommodation is a great option and in summer you may be deluged at the bus station by women offering *sobe* (rooms available). You can also contact travel agencies. Make sure you are clear about the exact location of the room or you may find yourself several bus rides from the town centre.

Expect to pay between 300KN and 500KN for a double room; in the cheaper ones you will probably share the bathroom with the proprietor.

TOP CHOICE **Hotel Vestibul Palace** HOTEL €€€
(☑329 329; www.vestibulpalace.com; Iza Vestibula 4; s/d 1380/1670KN; P❋@☎) The poshest in the palace, this award-winning boutique hideaway has seven stylish rooms and suites, all with exposed ancient walls, leather and wood, and the full spectrum of upscale amenities.

Goli + Bosi HOSTEL €€
(☑510 999; www.gollybossy.com; Morpurgova Poljana 2; dm/s/d 245/714/818KN) Split's design hostel is the premier destination for flashpackers, with its sleek futuristic decor, hip vibe and a cool lobby cafe-bar-restaurant.

Hotel Bellevue HOTEL €€
(☑345 644; www.hotel-bellevue-split.hr; Bana Josipa Jelačića 2; s/d 620/865KN; P@) This atmospheric old classic has sure seen better days but it remains one of the more dreamy hotels in town, with regal-patterned wallpaper, art-deco elements, gauzy curtains and faded but well-kept rooms.

Villa Varoš   GUESTHOUSE €€
(☑483 469; www.villavaros.hr; Miljenka Smoje 1; d/
ste 600/900KN; ❈ 🛜) Owned by a New Yorker
Croat, Villa Varoš is central, the rooms are
simple, bright and airy, and the apartment
has a Jacuzzi and a small terrace.

Hotel Adriana   HOTEL €€€
(☑340 000; www.hotel-adriana.com; Hrvatskog
Narodnog Preporoda 8; s/d 750/1100KN; ❈🛜)
Good value, excellent location smack in the
middle of the Riva. The rooms are not mas-
sively exciting, with navy curtains and beige
furniture, but some have sea views.

CroParadise Split Hostels   HOSTEL €
(☑091 444 4194; www.croparadise.com; Čulića
Dvori 29; dm 180KN, d 400-500KN, apt from
500KN; ❈@🛜) A great collection of three
hostels – Blue, Green and Pink – inside converted apartments in the neighbourhood of
Manuš. Five apartments are also available.

Silver Central Hostel   HOSTEL €
(☑490 805; www.silvercentralhostel.com; Kralja
Tomislava 1; dm 167-190KN; ❈@🛜) In an upstairs apartment, this light-yellow-coloured
boutique hostel has four dorm rooms and a
pleasant lounge. It has a two-person apartment nearby and another hostel, **Silver
Gate** (☑322 857; www.silvergatehostel.com; Hr-
vojeva 6; dm per person 167KN), near the food
market.

Split Hostel Booze & Snooze   HOSTEL €
(☑342 787; www.splithostel.com; Narodni trg 8; dm
200-215KN; ❈@🛜) Run by a pair of Aussie
Croat women, this party place at the heart of
town has four dorms, a terrace, a book swap
and boat trips. Its newer outpost, **Split Hostel Fiesta Siesta** (Kružićeva 5; dm 200-215KN,
d 560KN; ❈@🛜) has five sparkling dorms
and one double above the popular Charlie's
Backpacker Bar.

✖️ Eating

Šperun   SEAFOOD €
(Šperun 3; mains from 65KN; 🍴) A sweet little
restaurant decked out with rustic details
and exposed stone walls, this favourite
among the foreigners churns out decent
Dalmatian classics. **Šperun Deva**, a corner
bistro across the street with a few tables outside, offers breakfasts, lighter summer fare
and a great daily menu.

TOP
CHOICE **Figa**
    INTERNATIONAL €
(Buvinina 1; mains from 50KN) Split's coolest lit-
tle restaurant and bar, with a funky interior

and tables on the stairs outside, Figa serves
nice breakfasts, innovative dishes and a
wide range of salads. There's live music
some nights and the kitchen stays open late.

Konoba Matejuška   DALMATIAN €
(Tomića Stine 3; mains from 50KN) Cosy, rustic
tavern in an alleyway minutes from the seafront, it specialises in well-prepared seafood
that also happens to be well priced.

Bajamonti   INTERNATIONAL €€
(Trg Republike 1; mains from 75KN) Sleek restaurant and cafe on Trg Republike (Prokurative
square), right off the Riva, with classic decor
and excellent international fare. Grab a table on the square or on the mezzanine level
inside.

TOP
CHOICE **Villa Spiza**
    DALMATIAN €
(Kružićeva 3; mains from 40KN; ⊙Mon-Sat) A locals' favourite within the palace walls, this
low-key joint offers Dalmatian mainstays
that change daily – think calamari, risotto,
stuffed peppers – at low prices, served at
the bar inside or at a couple of benches
outside.

Makrovega   VEGETARIAN €
(Leština 2; mains from 50KN; ⊙9am-8pm Mon-Fri,
to 5pm Sat) A meat-free haven with a stylish,
spacious interio, a delicious buffet and à la
carte food that alternates between macrobi-
otic and vegetarian.

Galija   PIZZERIA €
(Tončićeva 12; pizzas from 38KN) The go-to place
for pizza for several decades now, Galija is
the sort of joint where locals take you for a
good, simple meal. Die-hard pizza fans have
recently turned to the new favorite in town,
Gušt (Slavićeva 1; pizzas from 32KN).

🍷 Drinking & Entertainment

Split is great for nightlife, especially in the
spring and summer months. The palace
walls are generally throbbing with loud music on Friday and Saturday nights.

Žbirac   CAFE
(Bačvice bb) This beachfront cafe is like the
locals' open-air living room, a cult hang-out
with great sea views, swimming day and
night and occasional concerts.

Bifora   CAFE-BAR
(Bernardinova 5) A quirky crowd of locals
frequents this artsy spot on a lovely little
square, much loved for its intimate low-key
vibe.

CROATIA SPLIT

Ghetto Club
BAR

(Dosud 10) Split's most bohemian bar, in an intimate courtyard amid flowerbeds and a trickling fountain, with great music and a friendly atmosphere.

Luxor
CAFE-BAR

(Sveti Ivana 11) Touristy, yes, but it's great to have coffee and their delicious cake in the courtyard of the cathedral: cushions are laid out on the steps so you can watch the locals go about their business.

Vidilica
CAFE-BAR

(Nazorov Prilaz 1) Worth the climb up the stone stairs through the ancient Varoš quarter for a sunset drink at this hilltop cafe with amazing city and harbour views.

Paradox
WINE BAR

(Poljana Tina Ujevića 2) Stylish new wine bar with cool wine-glass chandeliers inside, alfresco tables and a great selection of well-priced Croatian wines and local cheeses.

Fluid
CLUB

(Dosud 1) This chic little spot is a jazzy party venue, pretty low-key and cool. Great for people-watching.

ⓘ Information

Internet Access

Several cafes around town, including Luxor offer free wi-fi access.

Backpackers Cafe (☏338 548; Kneza Domagoja bb; internet 30N; ☺7am-9pm) Also sells used books, offers luggage storage and provides information for backpackers. There's happy hour for internet use between 3pm and 5pm, when it's 50% off.

Medical Services

KBC Firule (☏556 111; Spinčićeva 1) Hospital.

Money

You can change money at travel agencies or the post office. There are ATMs around the bus and train stations and throughout the city.

Post

Main post office (Kralja Tomislava 9; ☺7.30am-7pm Mon-Fri, to 2.30pm Sat)

Tourist Information

Croatian Youth Hostel Association (☏396 031; www.hfhs.hr; Domilijina 8; ☺8am-4pm Mon-Fri) Sells HI cards and has information about youth hostels all over Croatia.

Tourist Office (☏360 066; www.visitsplit.com; Hrvatskog Narodnog Preporoda 9; ☺8am-9pm Mon-Sat, to 1pm Sun Apr–mid-Oct, 8am-8pm Mon-Fri, to 1pm Sat mid-Oct–Mar) Has Split info and sells the Split Card (35KN), which offers free and reduced prices to attractions and discounts on car rental, restaurants, shops and hotels.

Tourist Office Annex (☏345 606; www.visitsplit.com; Peristil bb; ☺9am-4pm Mon-Sat, 8am-1pm Sun Apr–mid-Oct, shorter hours rest of year) This tourist office annex on Peristil has shorter hours.

Travel Agencies

Daluma Travel (☏338 424; www.dalumatravel.hr; Kneza Domagoja 1) Arranges private accommodation, excursions and car rental.

Maestral (☏470 944; www.maestral.hr; Boškovića 13/15) Monastery stays, horseriding excursions, lighthouse holidays, trekking, sea kayaking and more.

Turist Biro (☏347 100; www.turistbiro-split.hr; Hrvatskog Narodnog Preporoda 12) Its forte is private accommodation and excursions.

ⓘ Getting There & Away

Air

Split airport (www.split-airport.hr) is 20km west of town, just 6km before Trogir. **Croatia Airlines** (☏362 997; www.croatiaairlines.hr; Hrvatskog Narodnog Preporoda 9; ☺8am-4pm Mon-Fri) operates one-hour flights to Zagreb several times a day and a weekly flight to Dubrovnik (during summer only).

A couple of low-cost airlines fly to Split, including **Easyjet** (www.easyjet.com), **germanwings** (www.germanwings.com) and **Norwegian** (www.norwegian.com).

Boat

Jadrolinija (☏338 333; www.jadrolinija.hr; Gat Sv Duje bb) handles most of the coastal ferry lines and catamarans that operate between Split and the islands. There is also a twice-weekly ferry service between Rijeka and Split (147KN, 7.30pm Thursday and Sunday, arriving at 6am). Three times weekly a car ferry goes from Split to Ancona in Italy (435KN, nine to 11 hours).

In addition to Jadrolinija's boats, there is a fast passenger boat, the **Krilo** (www.krilo.hr), that goes to Hvar Town (45KN, one hour) daily and on to Korčula (65KN, 2¾ hours).

SNAV (☏322 252; www.snav.it) has daily ferries to Ancona (Italy) from June through mid-September (660KN; five hours) and to Pescara (Italy) from late July through August (6½ hours). Also departing to Ancona from Split are **BlueLine** (www.blueline-ferries.com) car ferries (from 480KN per person, 540KN per car, 10 to 12 hours), on some days via Hvar Town and Vis.

Car ferries and passenger lines depart from separate docks; the passenger lines leave from Obala Lazareta and car ferries from Gat Sv Duje. You can buy tickets from either the main Jadro-

BUSES FROM SPLIT

DESTINATION	PRICE (KN)	DURATION (HR)	FREQUENCY
Dubrovnik	115-145	4½	25 daily
Ljubljana (Slovenia)	320	10	1 daily
Međugorje (Bosnia & Hercegovina)	100	3-4	4 daily
Mostar (Bosnia & Hercegovina)	105-128	3½-4½	9 daily
Pula	423	10-11	3 daily
Rijeka	330	8-8½	11 daily
Sarajevo (Bosnia & Hercegovina)	220	6½-8	4 daily
Triesta (Italy)	284	10½	2 daily
Vienna (Austria)	57	11½	2 weekly
Zadar	99-128	3-4	27 daily
Zagreb	114-204	5-8	40 daily

linija office in the large ferry terminal opposite the bus station, or at one of the two stalls near the docks. In summer it's necessary to reserve at least a day in advance for a car ferry and you are asked to appear several hours before departure.

Bus

Advance bus tickets with seat reservations are recommended. Most buses leave from the main **bus station** (☑060 327 777; www.ak-split.hr) beside the harbour, where there's a **garderoba** (left-luggage office; 1st hr 5KN, then 1.50KN per hr; ☺6am-10pm).

Bus 37 goes to Split airport and Trogir (21KN, every 20 minutes), also stopping at Solin; it leaves from a local bus station on Domovinskog Rata, 1km northeast of the city centre, but it's faster and more convenient to take an intercity bus heading north to Zadar or Rijeka.

Note that Split–Dubrovnik buses pass briefly through Bosnian territory, so keep your passport handy for border-crossing points.

Train

There are five daily trains between Split **train station** (☑338 525; www.hznet.hr; Kneza Domagoja 9) and Zagreb (189KN, six to eight hours), two of which are overnight. There are also two trains a day from Split to Zadar (111KN, five hours) via Knin. The station is just behind the bus station and there's a **garderoba** (left-luggage office; per day 15KN; ☺6am-10pm).

❶ Getting Around

Buses by **Pleso Prijevoz** (www.plesoprijevoz. hr) and **Promet Žele** (www.split-airport.com.hr) depart to Split airport (30KN) from Obala Lazareta several times daily. You can also take bus 37 from the local bus station on Domovinskog Rata (21KN, 50 minutes).

Buses run about every 15 minutes from 5.30am to 11.30pm. A one-zone ticket costs 11KN for one trip in central Split; it's 21KN to the surrounding districts.

Trogir

☑021 / POP 13,000

Gorgeous and tiny Trogir (formerly Trau) is beautifully set within medieval walls, its streets knotted and maze-like. It's fronted by a wide seaside promenade lined with bars and cafes and luxurious yachts docking in the summer. Trogir is unique among Dalmatian towns for its profuse collection of Romanesque and Renaissance architecture (which flourished under Venetian rule), and this, along with its magnificent cathedral, earned it World Heritage status in 1997.

Trogir is an easy day trip from Split and a relaxing place to spend a few days, taking a trip or two to nearby islands.

◉ Sights

The heart of the Old Town, which occupies a tiny island in the narrow channel between Čiovo Island and the mainland, is a few minutes' walk from the bus station. After crossing the small bridge near the station, go through the north gate. Most sights can be seen on a 15-minute walk around this island.

Cathedral of St Lovro CATHEDRAL
(Katedrala Svetog Lovre; Trg Ivana Pavla II; admission 25KN; ☺8am-8pm Mon-Sat, 2-6pm Sun Jun-Sep, shorter hours rest of year) The showcase of Trogir is this three-naved Venetian cathedral built from the 13th to 15th centuries. Its glory is

the **Romanesque portal** (1240) by Master Radovan, the earliest example of the nude in Dalmatian sculpture. Enter the building through an obscure back door to see the richly decorated Renaissance **Chapel of St Ivan**, choir stalls, pulpit and **treasury**, which contains an ivory triptych. You can even climb the 47m cathedral **tower** for a delightful view.

Kamerlengo Fortress
FORTRESS

(Tvrđava Kamerlengo; admission 20KN; ⊙9am-11pm May-Oct) Once connected to the city walls, the fortress was built around the 15th century. Today it hosts concerts during the **Trogir Summer** festival, which typically begins in mid-June and lasts through to late August.

Town Museum
MUSEUM

(Gradski Muzej; Gradska Vrata 4; admission 15KN; ⊙10am-5pm Jun-Sep, 9am-2pm Mon-Fri, to noon Sat Oct-May) Housed in the former Garagnin-Fanfogna palace, the museum has five rooms that exhibit books, documents, drawings and period costumes from Trogir's long history.

ℹ️ Information

Atlas Trogir (☑881 374; www.atlas-trogir.hr; Kralja Zvonimira 10) This travel agency arranges private accommodation and runs excursions.

Portal Trogir (☑885 016; www.portal-trogir. com; Bana Berislavića 3) Private accommodation; bike, scooter and kayak rental; excursions, including quad safaris, rafting and canyoning; and internet. The agency runs a 90-minute walking tour of the Old Town twice a day from May to October, departing from outside the agency. It also rents out two-person kayaks for 250KN per day, which you can use to kayak around the island and to Pantan beach.

ℹ️ Getting There & Away

Southbound intercity buses from Zadar (130km) and northbound buses from Split (28km) will drop you off in Trogir. Getting buses from Trogir to Zadar can be more difficult, as they often arrive full from Split.

City bus 37 from Split leaves every 20 minutes throughout the day, with a stop at Split airport en route to Trogir. You can buy the four-zone ticket (21KN) from the driver in either direction.

There are boats to and from Split four times daily (24KN) from Čiovo (150m to the left of the bridge).

Hvar Island

☑021 / POP 10,948

Hvar Island is the number-one carrier of Croatia's superlatives: it's the most luxurious island, the sunniest place in the country and, along with Dubrovnik, the most popular tourist destination. Hvar is also famed for its verdancy and its lavender fields, as well as other aromatic herbs such as rosemary.

The island's hub and busiest destination is Hvar Town. Visitors wander along the main square, explore the sights on the winding stone streets, swim on the numerous beaches or pop off to get into their birthday suits on the Pakleni Islands, but most of all they party at night. There are several good restaurants and a number of top hotels, as well as a couple of hostels.

Stari Grad (Old Town), on the island's north coast, is a more quiet, cultured and altogether sober affair than its stylish and stunning sister. If you're not after pulsating nightlife and thousands of people crushing each other along the streets in the high season, head for Stari Grad and enjoy Hvar at a more leisurely pace.

The interior of the island hides abandoned ancient hamlets, towering peaks and verdant, largely uncharted landscapes. It's worth exploring on a day trip, as is the southern end of the island, which has some of Hvar's most beautiful and isolated coves.

👁️ Sights

St Stephen's Square
SQUARE

(Trg Svetog Stjepana) The centre of town is this rectangular square, which was formed by filling in an inlet that once stretched out from the bay. Notice the 1520 **well** at the square's northern end, which has a wrought-iron grill dating from 1780.

Franciscan Monastery & Museum
MONASTERY

(admission 25KN; ⊙9am-1pm & 5-7pm Mon-Sat) At the southeastern end of Hvar Town you'll find this 15th-century Renaissance monastery, with a wonderful collection of Venetian paintings in the adjoining church and a cloister garden with a cypress tree said to be more than 300 years old.

Fortica
FORTRESS

(admission 25KN; ⊙8am-10pm Jun-Sep) On the hill high above Hvar Town, this Venetian fortress (1551) is worth the climb up to appreciate the sweeping panoramic views. The fort was built to defend Hvar from the Turks, who sacked it in 1539 and 1571. There's a lovely cafe at the top.

Arsenal
HISTORIC BUILDING

(Trg Svetog Stjepana; arsenal & theatre 20KN; ⏱9am-9pm) Smack in the middle of Hvar Town is the imposing Gothic arsenal, and upstairs is Hvar's prize, the **Renaissance theatre** (Trg Svetog Stjepana; admission 10KN; ⏱9am-9pm) built in 1612 – reported to be the first theatre in Europe open to plebs and aristocrats alike.

🏃 Tours

Secret Hvar
GUIDED TOURS

(📞717 615; www.secrethvar.com; Trg Svetog Stjepana 4a) Don't miss the great off-road tours, which take in hidden beauties of the island's interior. It's worth every lipa of 600KN, which includes lunch in a traditional tavern and a stop on the beach.

🛏 Sleeping

As Hvar is one of the Adriatic's most popular destinations, don't expect many bargains. Most Hvar hotels are managed by **Sunčani Hvar Hotels** (www.suncanihvar.com). Accommodation in Hvar is extremely tight in July and August; try the travel agencies for help. Expect to pay anywhere from 150KN to 300KN per person for a room with a private bathroom in the town centre.

Family-run, private-apartment options are so many in Hvar that the choice can be overwhelming. Here are a few reliable, good-value apartments: **Apartments Ukić** (www.hvar-apartments-center.com), **Apartments Komazin** (www.croatia-hvar-apartments.com) and **Apartments Bracanović** (www.hvar-jagoda.com).

Hotel Riva
HOTEL €€€

(📞750 100; www.suncanihvar.com; Riva bb; s/d 1390/2617KN; ❄@) The luxury veteran on Hvar's hotel scene, this 100-year-old hotel has 54 smallish contemporary rooms and a great location right on the harbourfront, perfect for watching the yachts glide up and away.

🔝 Hotel Croatia
TOP CHOICE
HOTEL €€€

(📞742 400; www.hotelcroatia.net; Majerovica bb; s/d 832/1110KN; P❄@⛱) Only a few steps from the sea, this medium-sized, rambling 1930s building sits among gorgeous, peaceful gardens. The rooms are simple and old-fashioned, many with balconies overlooking the gardens and the sea.

Hostel Marinero
HOSTEL €

(📞091 174 1601; Put Sv Marka 7; dm 200-240KN; ❄⛱) The location is the highlight at this six-dorm hostel right off the seafront. Dorms are basic but clean, and the restaurant downstairs is a good place to hang out. Be ready for some noise, as Kiva Bar is right next door.

Hvar Out Hostel
HOSTEL €

(📞717 375; hvarouthostel@gmail.com; Burak 23; dm 200-250KN; ❄@⛱) By the same owners as Split Hostel Booze & Snooze, this party place, steps from the harbour in the maze of the Old Town, has seven well-equipped dorms, a small shared kitchen and a terrace on the top floor.

Camping Vira
CAMPING GROUND €

(📞741 803; www.campingvira.com; campsite per adult/site 60/97KN; ⏱May–mid-Oct; P@⛱) This four-star camping ground on a beautiful wooded bay 4km from town is one of the best in Dalmatia. There's a gorgeous beach, a cafe and restaurant, and a volleyball pitch.

🍴 Eating

Hvar's eating scene is good and relatively varied, though, as with the hotels, restaurants often target affluent diners. Note that many restaurants close between lunch and dinner.

CROATIA HVAR ISLAND

WORTH A TRIP

PAKLENI ISLANDS

Most visitors to Hvar Town head to the Pakleni Islands (Pakleni Otoci), which got their name – 'Hell's Islands' in Croatian – from *paklina*, the resin that once coated boats and ships. This gorgeous chain of 21 wooded isles has crystal-clear seas, hidden beaches and deserted lagoons. Taxi boats leave regularly during the high season from in front of the Arsenal to the islands of **Jerolim** and **Stipanska** (35KN, 10 to 15 minutes), which are popular naturist islands (although nudity is not mandatory). They continue on to **Ždrilca** and **Mlini** (40KN) and, further out, **Palmižana** (60KN), which has a pebble beach and the **Meneghello Place** (www.palmizana.hr), a beautiful boutique complex of villas and bungalows scattered among lush tropical gardens. Run by the artsy Meneghello family, the estate holds music recitals, and features two excellent restaurants and an art gallery. Also on Palmižana are two top restaurant-cum-hang-out spots, Toto and Laganini.

Self-caterers can head to the supermarket next to the bus station, or pick up fresh supplies at the vegetable market next door.

Konoba Menego
DALMATIAN €€
(www.menego.hr; Groda bb; mains from 60KN) At this rustic old house, everything is decked out in Hvar antiques and the staff wear traditional outfits. Try the marinated meats, cheeses and vegetables, prepared the old-fashioned Dalmatian way.

Divino
MEDITERRANEAN €€€
(☑717 541; www.divino.com.hr; Put Križa 1 ; mains from 130KN; ☺dinner only) The fabulous location and the island's best wine list are reason enough to splurge at this swank restaurant. Add innovative food and dazzling views of the Pakleni Islands and there's a winning formula for a special night out.

Konoba Luviji
DALMATIAN €€
(☑091 519 8444; Jurja Novaka 6; mains from 50KN; ☺dinner) Food brought out of the wood oven at this tavern is simple, unfussy and tasty. Downstairs is the *konoba* where Dalmatian-style tapas are served; the upstairs restaurant has Old Town views.

Nonica
PASTRIES, CAKES €
(Burak 23; ☺8am-2pm & 5-11pm Mon-Sat, 8am-2pm Sun) Savour the best cakes in town, at this tiny storefront cafe right behind the Arsenal. Try the old-fashioned local biscuits such as *rafioli* and *forski koloc*.

Zlatna Školjka
MEDITERRANEAN €€€
(☑098 16 88 797; Petra Hektorovića 8; mains from 100KN; ☺dinner Sat & Sun) This slow-food, family-tun hideaway stands out for its creative fare conjured up by a local celebrity chef. Try the unbeatable *gregada* (fish stew) with lobster and sea snails; order in advance.

🍸 Drinking & Entertainment

Hvar has some of the best nightlife on the Adriatic coast.

Falko
BEACH BAR
(☺8am-10pm mid-May–mid-Sep) A 20-minute walk west from the town centre, past Hula-Hula and Hotel Amfora, brings you to this adorable hideaway in a pine forest just above the beach. Think low-key artsy vibe, homemade *rakija*, hammocks and a local crowd.

Carpe Diem
LOUNGE BAR
(www.carpe-diem-hvar.com; Riva) This swanky harbourfront spot is the mother of Croatia's coastal clubs, with house music spun nightly by resident DJs. The **Carpe Diem Beach** (www.carpe-diem-beach.com) on the island of Stipanska is the hottest place to party (from June to September), with daytime beach fun and all-night parties.

Hula-Hula
BEACH BAR
(www.hulahulahvar.com) *The* spot to catch the sunset to the sound of techno and house music, Hula-Hula is known for its après-beach party (4pm to 9pm), where all of young trendy Hvar seems to descend for cocktails. To find it, head west along the seafront.

Kiva Bar
BAR
(www.kivabarhvar.com; Fabrika bb) This happening alleyway spot is packed to the rafters most nights, with a DJ spinning old dance, pop and rock classics that really get the crowd going.

Veneranda
CLUB
(admission 100-150KN; ☺10pm-4am) A former fortress on the slope above the seafront, Veneranda is Hvar's only real club, with a great sound system and late-night parties fulled by famous DJs.

ℹ Information

Atlas Hvar (☑741 911; www.atlas-croatia.com) On the western side of the harbour, this travel agency finds private accommodation, rents bikes and boats, and books excursions to Vis, Bol and Dubrovnik.

Clinic (☑717 099; Biskupa Jurja Dubokovića 3) Medical clinic about 700m from the town centre, best for emergencies.

Del Primi (☑091 583 7864; www.delprimi-hvar.com; Burak 23) Travel agency specialising in private accommodation. Also rents jet skis.

Francesco (Burak bb; per hr 30KN; ☺8.30am-midnight) Internet cafe and call centre right behind the post office. Left luggage for 35KN per day and laundry service for 50KN per load.

Hvar Adventure (☑717 813; www.hvar-adventure.com; Obala bb) Adventure activities such as sailing, sea kayaking, cycling, hiking and rock climbing.

Pelegrini Tours (☑742 743; www.pelegrini-hvar.hr; Riva bb) Private accommodation, boat tickets to Italy with Blue Line, excursions (its daily trips to Pakleni Otoci are popular) and bike, scooter and boat rental.

Tourist office (☑741 059; www.tzhvar.hr; ☺8am-2pm & 3-9pm Jul & Aug, shorter hours rest of year) Right on Trg Svetog Stjepana.

ℹ Getting There & Away

The local Jadrolinija (p248) car ferry from Split calls at Stari Grad (47KN, two hours) six times a day in summer. Jadrolinija also has three to five catamarans daily to Hvar Town (47KN, one hour). Krilo (p248), the fast passenger boat, travels once a day between Split and Hvar Town (45KN, one hour) in summer; it also goes on to Korčula (50KN, 1½ hours). You can buy tickets at Pelegrini Tours.

Connections to Italy are available in the summer season. Two Jadrolinija ferries a week (on Saturday and Sunday night) go from Stari Grad to Ancona in Italy. Blue Line (p270) also runs regular boats to Ancona from Hvar Town. Pelegrini Tours sells these tickets.

ⓘ Getting Around

Buses meet most ferries that dock at Stari Grad and go to Hvar Town (27KN, 20 minutes). There are 10 buses a day between Stari Grad and Hvar Town in summer, but services are reduced on Sunday and in the low season.

A taxi costs from 300KN to 350KN. **Radio Taxi Tihi** (☑098 338 824) is cheaper if there are a number of passengers to fill up the minivan.

Korčula Island

☑020 / POP 16,438

Rich in vineyards and olive trees, the island of Korčula was named Korkyra Melaina (Black Korčula) by the original Greek settlers because of its dense woods and plant life. As the largest island in an archipelago of 48, it provides plenty of opportunities for scenic drives, particularly along the southern coast.

Swimming opportunities abound in the many quiet coves and secluded beaches, while the interior produces some of Croatia's finest wine, especially dessert wines made from the *grk* grape cultivated around Lumbarda. Local olive oil is another product worth seeking out.

On a hilly peninsula jutting into the Adriatic sits Korčula Town, a striking walled town of round defensive towers and red-roofed houses. Resembling a miniature Dubrovnik, the gated, walled Old Town is crisscrossed by narrow stone streets designed to protect its inhabitants from the winds swirling around the peninsula.

◉ Sights

Other than the circuit of the city walls or walking along the shore, sightseeing in Korčula centres on Trg Sv Marka (St Mark's Sq).

St Mark's Cathedral   CATHEDRAL

(Katedrala Svetog Marka; Statuta 1214; ⊙9am-9pm Jul & Aug, Mass only Sep-Jun) Dominating Trg Svetog Marka, the 15th-century Gothic-Renaissance cathedral features works by Tintoretto (*Three Saints* and *The Annunciation*). Check out the modern sculptures in the baptistery too, including a *pietà* by Ivan Meštrović.

Town Museum   MUSEUM

(Gradski Muze; Statuta 1214; admission 25KN; ⊙9am-9pm daily Jun-Aug, 9am-1pm Mon-Sat Sep-May) The 16th-century Gabriellis Palace opposite the cathedral houses the museum, with a stone-carving collection, prehistoric objects, and Korčulan traditional, and art, furniture, textiles and portraits.

Marco Polo Museum   MUSEUM

(De Polo; admission 20KN; ⊙9am-7pm Jun-Sep, 10am-4pm May & Oct) It's said that Marco Polo was born in Korčula in 1254; you can visit what is believed to be his birthplace and climb the very steep steps for an eagle's-eye vista over the Korčula Peninsula and Adriatic.

ⓕ Tours

Travel agencies, like Atlas Travel Agency and Kantun Tours (p254), can set you up on an island tour or a day trip to Mljet and offer mountain biking, and sea-kayaking and snorkelling trips. In the summer season water taxis offer trips to **Badija Island**, which features a 15th-century Franciscan monastery and a naturist beach, and the nearby village of **Lumbarda**, both of which have sandy beaches.

ⓛ Sleeping & Eating

Korčula's hotel scene is on the bulky and resort side. If you don't fancy staying in any of the big hotels, a more personal option is a guesthouse. Atlas Travel Agency (p254) and **Marko Polo Tours** (☑715 400; www.korcula. com; Biline 5; ⊙9am-9pm Mon-Fri, to 6pm Sat & Sun) arrange private rooms (from 250KN in high season).

ⓣᴏᴘ Lešić Dimitri Palace   APARTMENTS €€€
cʜᴏɪᴄᴇ

(☑715 560; www.lesic-dimitri.com; Don Pavla Poše 1-6; apt 3363-9752KN; ✴☞) Exceptional in every way (including its rates). Spread over several town mansions, the six 'residences' have been finished to an impeccable standard, while keeping original details. The restaurant is the best in town, too.

Villa DePolo   APARTMENT, RENTAL ROOMS €

(☑711 621; tereza.depolo@du.t-com.hr; Svetog Nikole bb; d 350KN; ✴☞) These small, simple but attractive modern rooms (and apartment) come

CROATIA KORČULA ISLAND

WORTH A TRIP

OREBIĆ

Orebić, on the southern coast of the Pelješac Peninsula, has the best beaches in southern Dalmatia – sandy coves bordered by groves of tamarisk and pine. Only 2.5km across the water from Korčula Town, it makes a perfect day trip or an alternative base. After lazing on the beach, you can take advantage of some excellent hiking up and around Mt Ilija (961m) or poke around a couple of churches and museums. The best beach in Orebić is Trstenica cove, a 15-minute walk east along the shore from the port.

In Orebić the ferry terminal and the bus station are adjacent to each other. Korčula buses to Dubrovnik, Zagreb and Sarajevo stop at Orebić (on the harbourfront by the ferry port).

with comfortable beds; one has a terrace with amazing views. The location is excellent, a short walk from the Old Town.

Hotel Bon Repos
RESORT €€

(☑726 800; www.korcula-hotels.com; d 596KN; P@🅰🐾) On the road to Lumbarda, this huge hotel has manicured grounds, a large pool overlooking a small beach and a water-taxi service to Korčula Town.

TOP CHOICE LD
MODERN MEDITERRANEAN €€

(☑715 560; www.lesic-dimitri.com; Don Pavla Poše 1-6; mains from 75KN) Korčula's finest restaurant, with tables right above the water, offers delectable combinations of Med ingredients and many wonderful Croatian choices.

TOP CHOICE Konoba Komin
DALMATIAN €

(☑716 508; Don Iva Matijace; mains from 45KN) This family-run *konoba* looks almost medieval, with its *komin* (roaring fire), roasting meat, ancient stone walls and solid wooden tables. The menu is simple and delicious and the space tight, so book ahead.

☆ Entertainment

Between June and September there's Moreška sword dancing (tickets 100KN; 9pm Monday and Thursday) by the Old Town gate. The clash of swords and the graceful movements of the dancers/fighters make an exciting show. Travel agencies sell tickets.

ⓘ Information

There are several ATMs around town, including one at HVB Splitska Banka. You can also change money at the post office or at any of the travel agencies.

Atlas Travel Agency (☑711 231; atlas-korcula@du.htnet.hr; Plokata 19 Travnja bb) Represents American Express, runs excursions and finds private accommodation.

Hospital (☑711 137; Kalac bb) About 1km past Hotel Marko Polo.

Kantun Tours (☑715 622; www.kantun-tours. com; Plokata 19 Travnja bb) Private accommodation, lots of excursions, car hire and boat tickets, plus internet access (25KN per hour) and luggage storage.

Tourist office (☑715 701; www.korcula.net; Obala Franje Tuđmana 4; ◷8am-3pm & 5-8pm Mon-Sat, 9am-1pm Sun Jul & Aug, 8am-2pm Mon-Sat Sep-Jun) On the west harbour; an excellent source of information.

ⓘ Getting There & Around

There are buses to Dubrovnik (95KN, three hours, one to three daily) and one to Zagreb (245KN, 11 hours). Book ahead in summer.

The island has two major entry ports – Korčula Town and Vela Luka. All the **Jadrolinija** (☑715 410) ferries between Split and Dubrovnik stop in Korčula Town. If you're travelling between Split and Korčula you have several options.

There's a daily fast boat, the **Krilo** (www.krilo. hr), which runs from Split to Korčula (65KN, 2¾ hours) all year round, stopping at Hvar en route. Jadrolinija runs a passenger catamaran daily from June to September from Split to Vela Luka (70KN, two hours), stopping at Hvar and continuing on to Lastavo. There's also a regular afternoon car ferry between Split and Vela Luka (60KN, three hours) that stops at Hvar most days (although cars may not disembark at Hvar).

From the Pelješac Peninsula you'll find very regular boats link Orebić and Korčula. Passenger launches (20KN, 10 minutes, 13 daily June to September, at least five daily the rest of year) sail to the heart of Korčula Town. Car ferries (22KN, 15 minutes, at least 14 daily all year round) also run this route, but use the deeper port of Dominče, 3km from Korčula Town.

Scooters (320KN for 24 hours) and boats (610KN per day) are available from **Rent a Đir** (☑711 908; www.korcula-rent.net; Biline 5).

Mljet Island

☑020 / POP 1232

Of all the Adriatic islands, Mljet (Meleda in Italian) may be the most seductive. Much of the island is covered by forests and the rest

---

is dotted with fields, vineyards and villages. The northwestern half of the island forms **Mljet National Park** (www.mljet.hr; adult/concession 100/50KN), where lush vegetation, pine forests and two saltwater lakes offer a scenic hideaway. It's an unspoiled oasis of tranquility that, according to legend, captivated Odysseus for seven years.

The island is 37km long, and has an average width of about 3km. The main points of entry are Pomena and Polače, two tiny towns about 5km apart.

Most people visit the island on excursions from Korčula or Dubrovnik (around 390KN and 245KN respectively), but it is possible to take a passenger boat from Dubrovnik or come on the regular ferry from Dubrovnik and stay a few days for hiking, cycling and boating.

◉ Sights & Activities

The highlights of the island are **Malo Jezero** and **Veliko Jezero**, the two lakes on the island's western end connected by a channel. In the middle of Veliko Jezero is an islet with a 12th-century **Benedictine monastery**, which contains a pricey but atmospheric restaurant.

There's a boat from Mali Most (about 1.5km from Pomena) on Malo Jezero that leaves for the island monastery every hour at 10 minutes past the hour. It's not possible to walk right around the larger lake as there's no bridge over the channel connecting the lakes to the sea. If you decide to swim it, keep in mind that the current can be strong.

Renting a **bicycle** (25/110KN per hour/day) is an excellent way to explore the national park. Several places including **Hotel Odisej** (744 022; www.hotelodisej.hr) in Pomena have bikes. Be aware that Pomena and Polače are separated by a steep hill. The bike path along the lake is an easier and very scenic pedal, but it doesn't link the two towns. You can rent a paddleboat and row over to the monastery but you'll need stamina.

The island offers some unusual opportunities for **diving**. There's a 3rd-century Roman wreck in relatively shallow water. The remains of the ship, including amphorae, have calcified over the centuries and this has protected them from pillaging. There's also a German torpedo boat from WWII and several walls to dive. Contact **Kronmar Diving** (744 022; Hotel Odisej).

🍴 Sleeping & Eating

The Polače tourist office arranges private accommodation (from around 250KN per double), but it's essential to make arrangements before peak season. You'll find more *sobe* signs around Pomena than Polače, and practically none at all in Sobra. Restaurants rent out rooms too.

Stermasi   APARTMENTS €€
TOP CHOICE
(098 93 90 362; www.stermasi.hr; Saplunara; apt 368-625KN; P✳) On the 'other' side of Mljet, these apartments are ideal if you want to enjoy the simple life and natural beauty of the island. Well-presented and bright, the nine modern units have terraces or private balconies. Sandy beaches are on your doorstep and guests get a 20% discount on meals at the amazing restaurant.

Soline 6   HOTEL €€
(744 024; www.soline6.com; Soline; d 598KN) This very green place is the only accommodation within the national park, with everything built from recycled products. Organic waste is composted, toilets are waterless and there's no electricity. The four studios are modern and equipped with private bathrooms, balconies and kitchens.

Camping Mungos   CAMPING GROUND €
(745 300; Babino Polje; campsite per person 54KN; ⊙May-Sep) Close to the beach and the lovely grotto of Odysseus, this camping ground has a restaurant, currency exchange and a minimart.

Melita   CROATIAN €€
(www.mljet-restoranmelita.com; St Mary's Island, Veliko Jezero; mains from 60KN) A more romantic spot can't be found on the island – this is the restaurant attached to the church on the little island in the middle of the big lake.

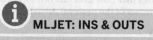

🛈 MLJET: INS & OUTS

Sightseeing boats from Korčula and the Dubrovnik catamarans arrive at Polače wharf in high season; Jadrolinija ferries use the Sobra port close to the centre of the island. The entry point for Mljet National Park is between Pomena and Polače. Your ticket includes bus and boat transfer to the Benedictine monastery. If you stay overnight on the island you only pay the park admission once.

ℹ️ Information

The **tourist office** (☎744 186; www.mljet.hr; ⏰8am-1pm & 5-7pm Mon-Sat, 9am-noon Sun Jun-Sep, 8am-1pm Mon-Fri Oct-May) is in Polače and there's an ATM next door (and another at Hotel Odisej in Pomena). There are free brochures and a good walking map for sale. There's another ATM at the Hotel Odisej in Pomena.

Babino Polje, 18km east of Polače, is the island capital. It's home to another **tourist office** (☎745 125; www.mljet.hr; ⏰9am-5pm Mon-Fri) and a post office.

ℹ️ Getting There & Away

Jadrolinija (p270) ferries stop only at Sobra (30KN, two hours) but the **G&V Line** (☎313 119; www.gv-line.hr) catamaran goes to Sobra (40KN, one hour) and Polače (54KN, 1½ hours) in the summer months, leaving Dubrovnik's Gruž harbour twice daily (9.15am and 7.10pm) and returning daily from Polače at 4.55pm, and twice daily from Sobra (6.15am and 5.35pm). You cannot reserve tickets in advance for this service; get to the harbour ticket office well in advance in high season to secure a seat (bicycles are not usually permitted either). In winter there's one daily catamaran. Tour boats from Korčula also run to Polače harbour in high season. Infrequent buses connect Sobra and Polače.

Dubrovnik

☎020 / POP 29,995

No matter whether you are visiting Dubrovnik for the first time or if you're returning again and again to this marvellous city, the sense of awe and beauty when you set eyes on the Stradun (the Old Town's main street) never fades. It's hard to imagine anyone, even the city's inhabitants, becoming jaded by its marble streets and baroque buildings, or failing to be inspired by a walk along the ancient city walls that protected a civilised, sophisticated republic for five centuries and that now look out onto the endless shimmer of the peaceful Adriatic.

History

Founded 1300 years ago by refugees from Epidaurus in Greece, medieval Dubrovnik (Ragusa until 1918) shook off Venetian control in the 14th century, becoming an independent republic and one of Venice's more important maritime rivals, trading with Egypt, Syria, Sicily, Spain, and later Turkey. The double blow of an earthquake in 1667 and the opening of new trade routes to the east sent Ragusa into a slow decline, ending with Napoleon's conquest of the town in 1808.

The deliberate shelling of Dubrovnik by the Yugoslav army in 1991 sent shockwaves through the international community but, when the smoke cleared in 1992, traumatised residents cleared the rubble and set about repairing the damage. Reconstruction has been extraordinarily skilful. All of the damaged buildings have now been restored.

After a steep postwar decline in tourism, Dubrovnik has bounced back. Today it is the most prosperous, elegant and expensive city in Croatia and a real tourism magnet.

◉ Sights

All the sights are in the Old Town, which is entirely closed to cars. Looming above the city is Mt Srđ, which is connected by cable car to Dubrovnik. Pile Gate is the main entrance to the Old Town; the main street is Placa (better known as Stradun).

OLD TOWN

TOP CHOICE City Walls & Forts CITY WALLS (Gradske Zidine; adult/concession 70/30KN; ⏰9am-6.30pm Apr-Oct, 10am-3pm Nov-Mar) No visit to Dubrovnik would be complete without a walk around the city walls, the finest in the world and Dubrovnik's main claim to fame. Built between the 13th and 16th centuries, they enclose the entire city in a protective veil more than 2km long and up to 25m high, with two round and 14 square towers, two corner fortifications and a large fortress. The views over the town and sea are great – this walk could be the highlight of your visit. The main entrance and ticket office to the walls is by the 1537 **Pile Gate**. You can also enter at the **Ploče Gate** in the east (wise at really busy times). The walls can only be walked clockwise.

TOP CHOICE War Photo Limited PHOTOGRAPHIC GALLERY (☎326 166; www.warphotoltd.com; Antuninska 6; admission 30KN; ⏰9am-9pm daily Jun-Sep, to 3pm Tue-Sat & to 1pm Sun May & Oct) A powerful experience, this state-of-the-art photographic gallery has beautifully displayed and reproduced exhibitions curated by the gallery owner and former photojournalist Wade Goddard, who worked in the Balkans in the 1990s. In addition to temporary shows, there's a permanent exhibition devoted to the war in Yugoslavia. It closes from November to April.

Franciscan Monastery & Museum MONASTERY
(Muzej Franjevačkog Samostana; Placa 2; adult/concession 30/15KN; ⏰9am-6pm) Inside this monas-

tery complex is a mid-14th-century **cloister**, one of the most beautiful late-Romanesque structures in Dalmatia. Further inside you'll find the third-oldest functioning **pharmacy** in Europe, in business since 1391. The small monastery **museum** has a collection of relics, liturgical objects including chalices, paintings and gold jewellery and pharmacy items.

Dominican Monastery
& Museum   MONASTERY
(Muzej Dominikanskog Samostana; off Ulica Svetog Dominika 4; adult/concession 20/10KN; ⊘9am-6pm May-Oct, to 5pm Nov-Apr) This imposing 14th-century structure in the northeastern corner of the city is a real architectural highlight, with a forbidding fortress-like exterior that shelters a rich trove of paintings from Dubrovnik's finest 15th- and 16th-century artists.

Rector's Palace   PALACE
(Pred Dvorom 3; adult/concession 35/15KN, audioguide 30KN; ⊘9am-6pm May-Oct, to 4pm Nov-Apr) This Gothic-Renaissance Rector's Palace built in the late 15th century houses a museum with artfully restored rooms, portraits, coats-of-arms and coins, evoking the glorious history of Dubrovnik. Today the atrium is often used for concerts during the Summer Festival (p259).

Cathedral of the Assumption
of the Virgin   CATHEDRAL
(Stolna Crkva Velike Gospe; Poljana M Držića; ⊘morning & late-afternoon Mass) Completed in 1713 in a baroque style, the cathedral is notable for its fine altars. The cathedral **treasury** (Riznica; adult/concession 10/5KN; ⊘8am-5.30pm Mon-Sat, 11am-5.30pm Sun May-Oct, 10am-noon & 3-5pm Nov-Apr) contains relics of St Blaise as well as 138 gold and silver reliquaries largely made in the workshops of Dubrovnik's goldsmiths between the 11th and 17th centuries.

Sponza Palace   PALACE
(Placa) The 16th-century Sponza Palace was originally a customs house, then a minting house, a state treasury and a bank. Now it houses the **State Archives** (Državni Arhiv u Dubrovniku; admission 20KN; ⊘8am-3pm Mon-Fri, to 1pm Sat) and the **Memorial Room of the Defenders of Dubrovnik** (⊘10am-10pm Mon-Fri, 8am-1pm Sat), a heartbreaking collection of portraits of young people who perished between 1991 and 1995.

Onofrio Fountain   FOUNTAIN
One of Dubrovnik's most famous landmarks, Onofrio Fountain was built in 1438 as part of a water-supply system that involved bringing water from a well 12km away.

Serbian Orthodox
Church & Museum   CHURCH, MUSEUM
(Muzej Pravoslavne Crkve; Od Puča 8; adult/concession 10/5KN; ⊘9am-2pm Mon-Sat) This 1877 Orthodox church has a fascinating collection of icons dating from the 15th to 19th centuries.

Synagogue   SYNAGOGUE
(Sinagoga; Žudioska 5; admission 20KN; ⊘10am-8pm Mon-Fri May-Oct, to 3pm Nov-Apr) The oldest Sephardic and second-oldest synagogue in the Balkans, dating back to the 15th century, has a small museum inside.

Orlando Column   MONUMENT
(Luža Sq) This popular meeting place used to be the spot where edicts, festivities and public verdicts were announced.

EAST OF THE OLD TOWN

TOP CHOICE **Cable Car**   CABLE CAR
(www.dubrovnikcablecar.com; Petra Krešimira IV; adult/concession 87/50KN; ⊘9am-10pm Tue-Sun May-Oct, shorter hours rest of year) Dubrovnik's cable car whisks you from just north of the city walls up to Mt Srđ in under four minutes, for a stupendous perspective of the city from a lofty 405m, down to the terracotta-tiled rooftops of the Old Town and the island of Lokrum, with the Adriatic and distant Elafiti Islands filling the horizon.

Homeland War Museum   MUSEUM
(www.tzdubrovnik.hr; admission 20KN; ⊘8am-6pm Apr-Oct, 9am-4pm Nov-Mar) Dedicated to the 'Homeland War' – as the 1990s war is dubbed in Croatia – this place inside a Napoleonic Fort, just above where the cable car drops you off, is interesting for those who want to learn more about Dubrovnik's wartime history.

THE COAST
The nicest beach that's walkable from the Old Town is below **Hotel Bellevue** (Petra Čingrije 7). In the Old Town, you can also swim below the two Buža bars.

Banje Beach   BEACH
(Outside Ploče Gate) Banje Beach is the most popular city beach, though it's even more crowded now that a section has been roped off for the exclusive EastWest Club (p261). Just southeast of here is **Sveti Jakov**, a good local beach that doesn't get rowdy and has showers, a bar and a restaurant. Buses 5 and 8 will get you there.

Dubrovnik

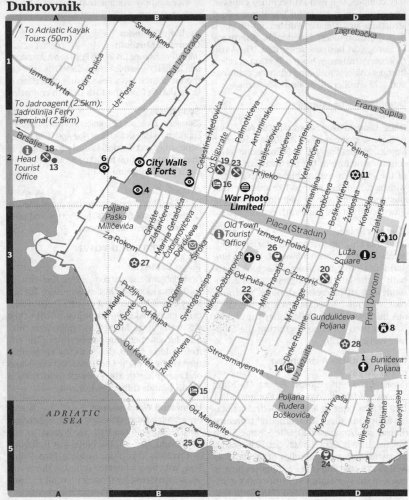

Lapad Bay BEACH
Lapad Bay is brimming with hotel beaches that you can use without a problem; try the bay by Hotel Kompas. A little further on is the good shallow **Copacabana Beach** on Babin Kuk Peninsula. If you're a naturist, head down to **Cava**, signposted near Copacabana Beach. In the Old Town, you can also swim below the two Buža bars.

Lokrum Island ISLAND
A better option than the mainland beaches is to take the **ferry** (return 40KN; ⊙last return boat 6pm) that shuttles roughly hourly in summer to lush Lokrum Island, a national park with a

rocky nudist beach (marked FKK), a botanical garden, the ruins of a medieval Benedictine monastery and an attractive cafe-restaurant.

🏃 Activities

Navis Underwater Explorers DIVING
(☏099 35 02 773; www.navisdubrovnik.com; Copacabana Beach; 🚹) Recreational dives (including the wreck of the *Taranto*) and courses.

**Adriatic Kayak
Tours** KAYAKING, WHITE-WATER RAFTING
(☏091 72 20 413; www.adriatickayaktours.com; Zrinsko Frankopanska 6) Kayak excursions (from a half-day paddle to a week-long trip);

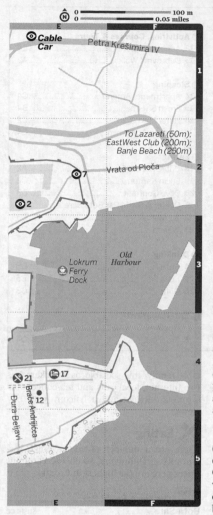

Cable Car

Petra Krešimira IV

To Lazareti (50m); EastWest Club (200m); Banje Beach (250m)

Vrata od Ploča

Lokrum Ferry Dock

Old Harbour

it also offers white-water rafting on the Tara River in Montenegro.

Tours

Dubrovnik Walks — WALKING

(095 80 64 526; www.dubrovnikwalks.com) Excellent guided walks in English. One-hour Old Town tours (90KN) run twice daily. The meeting place is the Fuego club just west of the Pile Gate. No reservation is necessary.

Adriatic Explore — BUS, BOAT

(323 400; www.adriatic-explore.com; Bandureva 4) Day trips to Mostar and Montenegro (both

360KN) are very popular. Excursions to Korčula and Pelješac (390KN) are offered, too.

Festivals & Events

The **Feast of St Blaise** is held on 3 February, and **Carnival** is also held in February.

Dubrovnik Summer Festival — CULTURAL

(326 100; www.dubrovnik-festival.hr; tickets 50-300KN) A major cultural event over five weeks in July and August, with theatre, music and dance performances at different venues in the Old Town.

Sleeping

Private accommodation is generally the best option in Dubrovnik, which is the most expensive destination in Croatia. Beware the scramble of private owners at the bus station and ferry terminal: some provide what they say they offer while others are scamming. Expect to pay from 300KN for a double room, and from 500KN for an apartment in high season.

OLD TOWN

TOP CHOICE **Karmen Apartments** — APARTMENTS €€

(098 619 282, 323 433; www.karmendu.com; Bandureva 1; apt 450-1200KN; ❄️🛜) Run by an Englishman who has lived in Dubrovnik for decades, these four inviting apartments with plenty of character enjoy a great location a stone's throw from Ploče harbour. Book well ahead.

TOP CHOICE **Fresh Sheets** — HOSTEL €

(091 79 92 086; www.igotfresh.com; Sv Šimuna 15; dm/d 210/554KN; @🛜) The only hostel in the Old Town is a warm place right by the city walls, with clean and simple dorms and a double with a sea view. It's run by a hospitable crew who organise imaginative outings, international dinners and other fun stuff.

Apartments Amoret — APARTMENTS €€

(091 53 04 910; www.dubrovnik-amoret.com; Dinke Ranjine 5; apt 755-1423KN; ❄️🛜) Spread over three historic buildings in the heart of the Old Town, Amoret offers 11 high-quality renovated studio apartments, all with bathrooms, a dash of art and parquetry flooring, and kitchenette-style cooking facilities.

Hotel Stari Grad — BOUTIQUE HOTEL €€€

(322 244; www.hotelstarigrad.com; Od Sigurate 4; s/d 1350/1800KN; ❄️🛜) This Old Town hotel is all about location – it's very close to the Pile Gate and just off the Stradun. Its eight

CROATIA DUBROVNIK

Dubrovnik

rooms are smallish but neat and attractive. Staff are sweet and views from the rooftop terrace dramatic.

OUTSIDE THE OLD TOWN
Begović Boarding House PRIVATE ACCOMMODATION €
(☑435 191; www.begovic-boarding-house.com; Primorska 17; dm/r/apt 150/320/385KN; P@) A steep walk uphill from Lapad harbourfront, this welcoming family-run place has smallish but clean pine-trimmed rooms, some opening out onto a communal garden with amazing views. There's free pick-up from the bus or ferry, free internet, a kitchen and excursions.

Hotel Ivka HOTEL €€
(☑362 600; www.hotel-ivka.com; Put Sv Mihajla 21; s/d 593/785KN; P✳@☎) Modern three-star hotel with pleasant, spacious rooms that have wooden floors (and most have a balcony). Comfort levels are high given the prices. It's closer to Lapad and the ferry terminal than the Old Town, but on a regular bus route.

Dubrovnik Backpackers Club HOSTEL €
(☑435 375; www.dubackpackers.com; Mostarska 2d; dm 120-170KN; @☎) Run by a very hospi-

table family, this sociable backpackers has free internet, local calls and tea/coffee, plus a guests' kitchen and a balcony with bay views.

✖ Eating

There are a number of very average restaurants in Dubrovnik, so choose carefully. Prices here are the highest in Croatia.

TOP CHOICE Oyster & Sushi Bar Bota Šare SUSHI €€
(☑324 034; www.bota-sare.hr; Od Pustijerne bb; oysters/sushi per piece from 12/15KN) Fresh Ston oysters and the best sushi this side of Dalmatia, plus an absolutely divine setting, with views of the cathedral from its terrace tables.

Lucin Kantun CROATIAN €€
(☑321 003; Od Sigurate bb; mains from 80KN) A modest-looking place with shabby-chic decor, a few pavement tables and some of the most creative food in Dubrovnik. Virtually everything on the short meze-style menu is freshly cooked from an open kitchen so you may have to wait a while at busy times.

Taj Mahal BOSNIAN, INTERNATIONAL €
(www.tajmahaldubrovnik.com; Nikole Gučetićeva 2; mains from 40KN) It's like an Aladdin's cave, with an interior loaded with Ottoman decorations and subdued lighting, and great Bosnian food. There are also three pavement tables.

Oliva Gourmet MEDITERRANEAN €€
(☏324 076; www.pizza-oliva.com; Cvijete Zuzorić 2; mains from 100KN;) A lovely little place with a terrace on a tiny street and a cute interior with vintage pieces, dishing out simple and local food. The **Oliva Pizzeria**, next door, has good pizza.

Wanda ITALIAN €€
(☏098 94 49 317; www.wandarestaurant.com; Prijeko 8; mains from 70KN) This is a very classy Italian, with good Croatian wines and dishes such as osso buco with saffron risotto and beautifully crafted pastas.

Dubravka 1836 INTERNATIONAL €
(www.dubravka1836.hr; Brsalje 1; mains from 49KN) This place has arguably Dubrovnik's best dining terrace, with stunning wall and sea views. Though it draws quite a touristy clientele, locals still rate the fresh fish, risotto and salads, pizza and pasta.

🍷 Drinking

TOP CHOICE **Buža** BAR
(Ilije Sarake) Finding this isolated bar-on-a-cliff feels like a real discovery as you duck and dive around the city walls and finally see the entrance tunnel. It showcases tasteful music and a mellow crowd soaking up the vibes, views and sunshine.

Buža II BAR
(Crijevićeva 9) Just a notch more upmarket than the original, this one is lower on the rocks and has a shaded terrace where you can snack on crisps, peanuts or sandwiches.

EastWest Club COCKTAIL BAR
(www.ew-dubrovnik.com; Frana Supila bb) By day this upmarket outfit on Banje Beach rents out sun loungers and umbrellas and serves drinks to the bathers. When the rays lengthen, the cocktail bar opens.

Gaffe IRISH PUB
(Miha Pracata bb) The busiest place in town, this huge pub has a homely interior and a long, covered side terrace.

☆ Entertainment

TOP CHOICE **Lazareti** CULTURAL CENTRE
(☏324 633; www.lazareti.com; Frana Supila 8) Dubrovnik's best cultural centre, Lazareti hosts cinema nights, club nights, live music, gigs and pretty much all the best things in town.

Troubadur LIVE MUSIC
(☏412 154; Bunićeva Poljana 2) Come to this corner bar, a legendary Dubrovnik venue, for live jazz concerts in the summer.

Open-Air Cinema CINEMA
(Kumičića, Lapad) In two locations, it's open nightly in July and August with screenings starting after sundown. Also in the **Old Town** (Za Rokom).

ℹ Information

There are numerous ATMs in town, in Lapad and at the ferry terminal and bus station. Travel agencies and post offices will also exchange cash.

Atlas Travel Agency (www.atlas-croatia.com) With offices in Gruž Harbour (☏418 001; Obala Papa Ivana Pavla II 1) and Pile Gate (☏442 574; Sv Đurđa 1, Pile Gate), this outfit organises excursions within Croatia and to Mostar and Montenegro. It also finds private accommodation.

Hospital (☏431 777; Dr Roka Mišetića) A kilometre south of Lapad Bay.

Lonely Planet (www.lonelyplanet.com/croatia/dubrovnik)

Main Post Office (cnr Široka & Od Puča)

Netcafé (www.netcafe.hr; Prijeko 21; per hr 30KN) A place to chill even if you're not surfing; has fast connections, CD burning, good drinks and coffee.

Tourist Office (www.tzdubrovnik.hr; ☺8am-8pm daily Jun-Sep, 8am-3pm Mon-Fri & 9am-2pm Sat Oct-May) Maps, information and the indispensable *Dubrovnik Riviera* guide. The smart new head office (☏020 312 011; Brsalje 5) that's under construction just west of the Pile Gate should open by the time you read this. There are also offices at Gruž Harbour (☏417 983; Obala Stjepana Radića 27), the bus station (☏417 581; Obala Pape Ivana Pavla II 44a), Lapad (☏437 460; Šetalište Kralja Zvonimira 25) and at Široka (☏323 587; www.tzdubrovnik.hr; Široka 1; ☺8am-8pm daily Jun-Sep, 8am-3pm Mon-Fri, 9am-2pm Sat Oct-May) in the Old Town.

ℹ Getting There & Away

Air

Daily flights to/from Zagreb are operated by **Croatia Airlines** (☏01 66 76 555; www.croatiaairlines.hr). Fares vary between 270KN

BUSES FROM DUBROVNIK

DESTINATION	PRICE (KN)	DURATION (HR)	FREQUENCY (DAILY)
Korčula	105	3	2
Kotor	130	2½	2-3
Mostar	130	3	3
Orebić	95	2½	2
Plitvice	350	10	1
Rijeka	370-510	13	4-5
Sarajevo	230	5	2
Split	140	4½	19
Zadar	190-230	8	8
Zagreb	270	11	7-8

for promo fares and around 760KN for flexi fares. The trip takes about an hour. Croatia Airlines also operate nonstop flights to Frankfurt and seasonal routes to cities such as Rome, Paris and Amsterdam.

Dubrovnik airport is served by over 20 other airlines from across Europe.

Boat

The **Jadrolinija ferry terminal** (☑418 000; www.jadrolinija.hr; Gruž Harbour) and the bus station are next to each other at Gruž, several kilometres northwest of the Old Town.

A twice-weekly Jadrolinija coastal ferry heads north to Korčula, Hvar, Split, Zadar and Rijeka. There's a local ferry that leaves Dubrovnik for So-bra and Polače on Mljet (60KN, 2½ hours) twice a week throughout the year; in summer there are also catamarans, which have a daily service to both Sobra and Polače (150KN, 1½ hours). Several daily ferries run year-round to the outlying Elafiti Islands of Koločep, Lopud and Šipan.

Ferries also go from Dubrovnik to Bari, in southern Italy; there are six a week in the summer season (300KN to 450KN, nine hours) and two in the winter months.

Jadroagent (☑419 000; Obala Stjepana Radića 32) books ferry tickets and has info.

Bus

Buses out of Dubrovnik **bus station** (☑060 305 070; Obala Pape Ivana Pavla II 44a) can be crowded, so book tickets ahead in summer. There's a **garderoba** (left-luggage office; 1st hr 7KN, then per hr 2KN; ☉4.30am-10pm) at the station.

Split–Dubrovnik buses pass briefly through Bosnian territory, so keep your passport handy for border-crossing points.

All bus schedules are detailed at www.libertas dubrovnik.hr.

ⓘ Getting Around

Čilipi international airport (www.airport-dubrovnik.hr) is 24km southeast of Dubrovnik. Atlas buses (35KN) leave from the main bus station irregularly, supposedly two hours before Croatia Airlines domestic flights, but it's best to check the latest schedule at the Atlas Travel Agency (p261) by the Pile Gate. These airport buses stop in Dubrovnik at Zagrebačka cesta, just north of the old town, en route out of the city (but not at the Pile Gate). Buses leave the airport for Dubrovnik bus station (via the Pile Gate in this direction) several times a day and are timed to coincide with arrivals; if your flight is late there's usually still one waiting.

Dubrovnik's buses run frequently and generally on time. The key tourist routes run until after 2am in summer, so if you're staying in Lapad there's no need to rush home. The fare is 15KN if you buy from the driver but only 12KN if you buy it at a kiosk.

UNDERSTAND CROATIA

Croatia Today

Croatia harbours a love-hate relationship with its own politicians, its political arena fuelled by constant drama. The pinnacle occurred in 2009, with the surprise resignation of then prime minister Ivo Sanader. In 2010 Sanader was arrested in Austria, in 2011 he was extradited to Croatia and later that year he was put on trial in Zagreb. The Sanader scandal remains the talk of the town; a fifth indictment on corruption charges was filed in September 2012.

Kukuriku Coalition

Croatian politics took a major turn in the 2011 parliamentary election, when the SDP joined three other centre-left parties to create the so-named Kukuriku coalition, an opposition bloc headed up by Zoran Milanović. Kukuriku won with an absolute majority, ousting Hrvatska Demokratska Zajednica (HDZ, Croatian Democratic Union), which had been in government for 16 of the 20 years since Croatia became independent in 1991.

Milanović took office as Croatia's prime minister in December 2011. But the slightly uplifted spirits quickly descended back into general discontent with politics, mainly due to the European debt crisis and the unpopular austerity measures that ensued.

EU Accession

In January 2012, about 44% of Croats turned up to vote in the referendum on European Union (EU) accession and supported the joining by a margin of two to one. But attitudes towards EU accession remain divided, in no small part due to the crisis. The divide aside, Croatia is slated to become the EU's 28th member state, which – on paper at least – will catapult it out of the Balkans and place it firmly in Central Europe. But the accession is no big bang; Croatia's inner strife remains.

Economic Woes

Croatia's economy has been in a shambles for several years, and the global downturn plus the EU crisis aren't helping. Unemployment is high, people's salaries are often months overdue, longstanding national companies are going bankrupt, pensions are ridiculously low and unemployment compensation isn't much better. Needless to say, from the point of view of the average Croat, life is tough and the global financial crisis has made itself clearly known. *Kriza* (crisis) is among the most uttered words in Croatia today; you'll hear it everywhere, all the time, like a mantra. Despite the double-dip recession, Croatia stands as a promising emerging market. It is compensating for the drastic drop in foreign investments by rapid growth in tourism revenue. It has, in fact, become the fastest-growing tourism market in the entire Mediterranean.

History

Since time immemorial, people have come and gone, invading, trading and settling. For long periods, the Croats have been ruled by and have fought off others – Venetians, Ottomans, Hungarians, Habsburgs, the French and the Germans. The creation of Yugoslavia after WWII brought some semblance of unity to the south Slavic nations. Yet it didn't last long. After the death of Yugoslav leader Tito in 1980, Yugoslavia slowly disintegrated, and a brutal civil war ensued.

Controversial Constituition

With political changes sweeping Eastern Europe, many Croats felt the time had come to separate from Yugoslavia, and the elections of April 1990 saw the victory of Franjo Tuđman's HDZ. On 22 December 1990, a new Croatian constitution changed the status of Serbs in Croatia from that of a 'constituent nation' to a national minority.

The constitution's failure to guarantee minority rights and mass dismissals of Serbs from the public service stimulated the 600,000-strong ethnic Serb community within Croatia to demand autonomy. In early 1991 Serb extremists within Croatia staged provocations designed to force federal military intervention. A May 1991 referendum (boycotted by the Serbs) produced a 93% vote in favour of independence, but when Croatia declared independence on 25 June 1991, the Serbian enclave of Krajina proclaimed its independence from Croatia.

War

Under pressure from the EC (now the EU), Croatia declared a three-month moratorium on its independence, but heavy fighting broke out in Krajina, Baranja (the area north of the Drava River opposite Osijek) and Slavonia. This initiated what Croats refer to as the Homeland War. The Serb-dominated Yugoslav People's Army intervened in support of Serbian irregulars, under the pretext of halting ethnic violence.

When the Croatian government ordered a shutdown of 32 federal military installations in the republic, the Yugoslav navy blockaded the Adriatic coast and laid siege to the strategic town of Vukovar on the Danube. During the summer of 1991, a quarter of Croatia fell to Serbian militias and the Yugoslav People's Army.

In late 1991, the federal army and the Montenegrin militia moved against Dubrovnik, and the presidential palace in Zagreb was hit by rockets from Yugoslav jets in an apparent assassination attempt on President Tuđman. When the three-month moratorium ended, Croatia declared full independence. Soon after, Vukovar finally fell when the Yugoslav army moved in, in one of the more bloodthirsty acts in all of the Yugoslav wars. During six months of fighting in Croatia, 10,000 people died, hundreds of thousands fled and tens of thousands of homes were destroyed.

Dayton Accord

Beginning on 3 January 1992, a UN-brokered ceasefire generally held. At the same time, the EU, succumbing to pressure from Germany, recognised Croatia. This was followed by US recognition, and in May 1992 Croatia was admitted to the UN.

The fighting continued until the Dayton Accord, signed in Paris in December 1995, recognised Croatia's traditional borders and provided for the return of eastern Slavonia. It was effected in January 1998. The transition proceeded relatively smoothly, but the two populations still regard each other with suspicion.

Postwar Politics

Franjo Tuđman's combination of authoritarianism and media control, and tendency to be influenced by the far right, no longer appealed to the postwar Croatian populace. By 1999 opposition parties united to work against Tuđman and the HDZ. Tuđman was hospitalised and died suddenly in late 1999, and planned elections were postponed until January 2000. Still, voters turned out in favour of a centre-left coalition, ousting the HDZ and voting in the centrist Stipe Mesić, who held the presidential throne for 10 years.

People

According to the 2011 census, Croatia has a population of roughly 4.3 million people, a decline from the prewar population of nearly five million. A discouraging economic outlook is largely responsible for a steady decline in Croatia's population, as educated young people leave in search of greater opportunities abroad. Then there was the still-recent war of the 1990s, during which about 50% of the Serbian population departed; less than half have returned. The post-independence economic crunch that followed sparked a mass exodus of Croats; some 120,000 emigrated. That was balanced out by the roughly equal number of ethnic Croat refugees who arrived from BiH and some 30,000 who came from the Vojvodina region of Serbia. These days, the recession-powered brain drain continues. It's not surprising: Croatia is right behind Spain and Greece when it comes to unemployment rates of young educated under-30s.

Religion

According to the most recent census, 87.8% of the population identifies as Catholic, 4.4% Orthodox, 1.3% Muslim, 0.3% Protestant and 6.2% other and unknown. Croats are overwhelmingly Roman Catholic, while Serbs belong to the Eastern Orthodox Church, a division that has its roots in the fall of the Roman Empire.

It would be difficult to overstate the extent to which Catholicism shapes the Croatian national identity. The Church is the most trusted institution in Croatia, rivalled only by the military. Religious holidays are celebrated with fervour and Sunday Mass is strongly attended.

Arts

Literature

Croatia's towering literary figure is 20th-century novelist and playwright Miroslav Krleža (1893–1981). His most popular novel is *The Return of Philip Latinovicz* (1932), which has been translated into English.

CROATIA PEOPLE

BOOKS

Lonely Planet's *Croatia* is a comprehensive guide to the country.

Interesting reads about Croatia include Rebecca West's *Black Lamb and Grey Falcon*, a classic travel book which recounts the writer's journeys through Croatia, Serbia, Bosnia, Macedonia and Montenegro in 1941. British writer Tony White retraced West's journey in *Another Fool in the Balkans* (2006), juxtaposing modern life in Serbia and Croatia with the region's political history. *Croatia: Travels in Undiscovered Country* (2003), by Tony Fabijančić, recounts the life of rural folks in a new Croatia. *Plum Brandy: Croatian Journeys* by Josip Novakovich is a sensitive exploration of his family's Croatian background.

Some contemporary writers worth reading include expat writer Dubravka Ugrešić, best known for her novels *The Culture of Lies* and *The Ministry of Pain*. Slavenka Drakulić's *Café Europa – Life After Communism* is an excellent read, while Miljenko Jergović's *Sarajevo Marlboro* and *Mama Leone* powerfully conjure up the atmosphere of life in pre-war Yugoslavia.

Music

Although Croatia has produced many fine classical musicians and composers, its most original musical contribution lies in its rich tradition of folk music. The instrument most often used in Croatian folk music is the *tamburica,* a three- or five-string mandolin that is plucked or strummed. Translated as 'group of people', *klapa* is an outgrowth of church-choir singing. The form is most popular in rural Dalmatia and can involve up to 10 voices singing in harmony.

There's a wealth of homegrown talent on Croatia's pop and rock music scene. Some of the most prominent pop, fusion and hip-hop bands are Hladno Pivo (Cold Beer), Pips Chips & Videoclips, TBF, Edo Maajka, Vještice (The Witches), Gustafi and the deliciously insane Let 3.

Visual Arts

Vlaho Bukovac (1855–1922) was the most notable Croatian painter in the late 19th century. Important early-20th-century painters include Miroslav Kraljević (1885–1913) and Josip Račić (1885–1908). Post-WWII artists experimented with abstract expressionism but this period is best remembered for the naive art that was typified by Ivan Generalić (1914–92). Recent trends have included minimalism, conceptual art and pop art. Contemporary Croatian artists worth checking out include Lovro Artuković, Sanja Iveković, Dalibor Martinis, Andreja Kulunčić, Sandra Sterle and Renata Poljak.

Environment

Croatia is shaped like a boomerang: from the Pannonian plains of Slavonia between the Sava, Drava and Danube Rivers, across hilly central Croatia to the Istrian peninsula, then south through Dalmatia along the rugged Adriatic coast.

The narrow Croatian coastal belt at the foot of the Dinaric Alps is only about 600km long as the crow flies, but it's so indented that the actual length is 1778km. If the 4012km of coastline around the offshore islands is added to the total, the length becomes 5790km. Most of the 'beaches' along this jagged coast consist of slabs of rock sprinkled with naturists. Don't come expecting to find sand, but the waters are sparkling clean, even around large towns.

Croatia's offshore islands are every bit as beautiful as those off the coast of Greece. There are 1244 islands and islets along the tectonically submerged Adriatic coastline, 50 of them inhabited. The largest are Cres, Krk, Mali Lošinj, Pag and Rab in the north; Dugi Otok in the middle; and Brač, Hvar, Korčula, Mljet and Vis in the south.

Wildlife

Deer are plentiful in the dense forests of Risnjak National Park, as are brown bears, wild cats and *ris* (lynx), from which the park gets its name. Occasionally a wolf or wild boar may appear but only rarely. Plitvice Lakes National Park, however, is an important refuge for wolves. The rare sea otter is also protected in Plitvice, as well as in Krka National Park. Two venomous snakes are endemic in Paklenica – the nose-horned viper and the European adder.

The griffon vulture, with a wingspan of 2.6m, has a permanent colony on Cres, and Paklenica National Park is rich in peregrine falcons, goshawks, sparrow hawks, buzzards and owls. Krka National Park is an important migration route and winter habitat for marsh birds as well as rare golden eagles and short-toed eagles. Kopački Rit Nature Park, near Osijek in eastern Croatia, is an extremely important bird refuge.

National Parks

When the Yugoslav federation collapsed, eight of its finest national parks ended up in Croatia. These have a total area of 96,135 sq km, of which 74,260 sq km is land and 21,875 sq km is water. Around 8% of Croatia is given over to its protected areas.

The dramatically formed karstic gorges and cliffs make Paklenica National Park along the coast a rock-climbing favourite. More rugged is the mountainous Northern Velebit National Park, a stunning patchwork of forests, peaks, ravines and ridges that backs northern Dalmatia and the Šibenik-Knin region. The abundant plant and animal life, including bears, wolves and deer, in the Plitvice Lakes National Park between Zagreb and Zadar has warranted its inclusion on Unesco's list of World Natural Heritage sites. Both Plitvice Lakes and Krka National Parks (near Šibenjk) feature a dramatic series of cascades and incredible turquoise lakes.

The Kornati Islands consist of 140 sparsely inhabited and vegetated islands, islets and reefs scattered over 300 sq km – an Adriatic showpiece easily accessible on an organised tour from Zadar. The northwestern half of the island of Mljet has been named a national park due to its two highly indented saltwater lakes surrounded by lush vegetation. The Brijuni Islands near Pula are the most cultivated national park since they were developed as a tourist resort in the late 19th century and were the getaway paradise for Tito.

Environmental Issues

The lack of heavy industry in Croatia has had the happy effect of leaving its forests, coasts, rivers and air generally fresh and unpolluted, but, as ever, an increase in investment and development brings forth problems and threats to the environment.

With the tourist boom, the demand for fresh fish and shellfish has risen exponentially. The production of farmed sea bass, sea bream and tuna (for export) is rising substantially, resulting in environmental pressure along the coast. Croatian tuna farms capture the young fish for fattening before they have a chance to reproduce and replenish the wild-fish population.

Coastal and island forests face particular problems. The dry summers and brisk *maestrals* (strong, steady westerly winds) also pose substantial fire hazards along the coast. In the last 20 years, fires have destroyed 7% of Croatia's forests.

Food & Drink

Croatian food is a savoury smorgasbord of taste, echoing the varied cultures that have influenced the country over the course of its history. You'll find a sharp divide between the Italian-style cuisine along the coast and the flavours of Hungary, Austria and Turkey in the continental parts.

Staples & Specialities

Zagreb and northwestern Croatia favour the kind of hearty meat dishes you might find in Vienna. Juicy spit-roasted and baked meat features *janjetina* (lamb), *svinjetina* (pork) and *patka* (duck), often accompanied by

mlinci (baked noodles) or *pečeni krumpir* (roast potatoes).

Coastal cuisine is typically Mediterranean, using a lot of olive oil, garlic, fresh fish and shellfish, and herbs. Along the coast, look for lightly breaded and fried *lignje* (squid) as a main course. For a special appetiser, try *paški sir,* a pungent, hard cheese from the island of Pag. Dalmatian *brodet* (stewed mixed fish served with polenta) is another regional treat.

Istrian cuisine has been attracting international foodies for its long gastronomic tradition, fresh foodstuffs and unique specialities. Typical dishes include *maneštra,* a thick vegetable-and-bean soup, *fuži,* hand-rolled pasta often served with truffles or game meat, and *fritaja* (omelette often served with seasonal veggies). Istrian wines and olive oil are highly rated.

Drinks

It's customary to have a small glass of brandy before a meal and to accompany the food with one of Croatia's many wines. Today winemaking is undergoing a renaissance in the hands of a new generation of winemakers with a focus on preserving indigenous varieties and revitalizing ancestral estates. Quality is rising, exports are increasing and the wines are garnering global awards and winning the affections of worldly wine lovers thirsty for authentic stories and unique terroirs. Croatians often mix their wine with water, calling it *bevanda. Rakija* (brandy) comes in different flavours. The most commonly drunk are *loza* (grape brandy), *šljivovica* (plum brandy) and *travarica* (herbal brandy).

The two top types of Croatian *pivo* (beer) are Zagreb's Ožujsko and Karlovačko from Karlovac. The small-distribution Velebitsko has a loyal following among in-the-know beer drinkers. You'll probably want to practise saying *živjeli!* (cheers!).

Where to Eat & Drink

Most restaurants cluster in the middle of the price spectrum – few are unbelievably cheap and few are exorbitantly expensive. A restaurant *(restoran)* is at the top of the food chain, generally presenting a more formal dining experience. A *gostionica* or *konoba* is usually a traditional family-run tavern. A *pivnica* is more like a pub, with a wide choice of beer. A *kavana* is a cafe. Self-service cafeterias are quick, easy and inexpensive, though the quality of the food tends to vary.

Restaurants are open long hours, often noon to 11pm (some midnight), but many close on Sunday out of peak season.

Vegetarians & Vegans

Outside of major cities like Zagreb, Rijeka, Split and Dubrovnik, vegetarian restaurants are few but Croatia's vegetables are usually locally grown and quite tasty. *Blitva* (swiss chard) is a nutritious side dish often served with potatoes. The hearty *štrukli* (baked cheese dumplings) are a good alternative too.

SURVIVAL GUIDE

Directory A–Z
Accommodation

Private accommodation is a lot more affordable in Croatia; it's very often great value if you don't mind foregoing hotel facilities.

Note that many establishments add a 30% charge for less than three-night stays and include 'residence tax', which is around 7KN per person per day. Prices quoted in this chapter do not include the residence tax.

The following price categories for the cost of double room with bathroom are used in the listings in this chapter.

€ less than 500KM

€€ 500KN to 900KN

€€€ more than 900KN

Breakfast is included in the prices for all hotels.

CAMPING

Nearly 100 camping grounds are scattered along the Croatian coast. Most operate from mid-April to mid-September, give or take a few weeks. The exact times change from year to year, so it's wise to call in advance if you're arriving at either end of the season.

Nudist camping grounds (marked FKK) are among the best, as their secluded locations ensure peace and quiet. Bear in mind that freelance camping is officially prohibited. A good site for camping information is www.camping.hr.

HOSTELS

The **Croatian YHA** (☑01-48 29 291; www.hfhs. hr; Savska 5/1, Zagreb) operates youth hostels

in Rijeka, Dubrovnik, Zadar, Zagreb and Pula. Nonmembers pay an additional 10KN per person per day for a stamp on a welcome card; six stamps entitle you to membership. The Croatian YHA can also provide information about private youth hostels in Zadar, Dubrovnik and Zagreb.

HOTELS

Hotels are ranked from one to five stars with most in the two- and three-star range. In August, some hotels may demand a surcharge for stays of less than three or four nights, but this is usually waived during the rest of the year, when prices drop steeply. In Zagreb prices are the same all year.

PRIVATE ROOMS

The best value for money in Croatia is a private room or apartment, often within or attached to a local home – the equivalent of small private guesthouses in other countries. Book private accommodation through travel agencies, by dealing directly with proprietors who meet you at the local bus or ferry station, or by knocking on the doors of houses with *sobe* or *zimmer* (rooms available) signs.

Whether you deal with the owner directly or book through an agency, you'll pay a 30% surcharge for stays of less than four or three nights and sometimes 50% or even 100% more for a one-night stay, although you may be able to get them to waive the surcharge if you arrive in the low season. Some will even insist on a seven-night minimum stay in the high season.

If you land in a room or apartment without a blue *sobe* or *apartmani* sign outside, the proprietor is renting to you illegally (ie not paying residence tax). They will probably be reluctant to provide their full name or phone number and you'll have absolutely no recourse in case of a problem.

Activities

There are numerous outdoorsy activities in Croatia.

Cycling Croatia has become a popular destination for cycle enthusiasts. See www.bicikl.hr and www.pedala.com.hr.

Diving Most coastal and island resorts have dive shops. For more info see the **Croatian Association of Diving Tourism** (www.croprodive.info), **Croatian Diving Federation** (www.diving-hrs.hr) and **Pro Diving Croatia** (www.diving.hr).

Hiking For information about hiking in Croatia, see the **Croatian Mountaineering Association** (www.plsavez.hr).

Kayaking and rafting Zagreb-based **Huck Finn** (www.huck-finn.hr) is a good contact for sea and river kayaking packages as well as rafting.

Rock climbing and caving For details, contact the Croatian Mountaineering Association or check its speleological department website at www.speleologija.hr.

Windsurfing For info about windsurfing in Croatia, see the **Croatian Windsurfing Association** (www.hukjd.hr) or www.windsurfing.hr.

Yachting A good source of information is the **Association of Nautical Tourism** (Udruženje Nautičkog Turizma; ☏ 051 209 147; www.croatiacharter.com; Bulevar Oslobođenja 23, Rijeka), which represents all Croatian marinas, and **Adriatic Croatia International Club** (www.aci-club.hr).

Business Hours

Hours can vary across the year.

Banks 9am to 7pm Monday to Friday, 8am to 1pm or 9am to 2pm Saturday

Bars and cafes 8am to midnight

Offices 8am to 4pm or 9am to 5pm Monday to Friday, 8am to 1pm or 9am to 2pm Saturday

Restaurants noon to 11pm or midnight, closed Sunday out of peak season

Shops 8am to 8pm Monday to Friday, to 2pm or 3pm Saturday

Embassies & Consulates

The following are all in Zagreb.

Albanian Embassy (☏01-48 10 679; Jurišićeva 2a)

Australian Embassy (☏01-48 91 200; Nova Ves 11, Kaptol Centar)

Bosnia & Hercegovina Embassy (☏01-45 01 070; Torbarova 9)

Bulgarian Embassy (☏01-46 46 609; Nike Grškovića 31)

Canadian Embassy (☏01-48 81 200; Prilaz Gjure Deželića 4)

Czech Embassy (☏01-61 77 246; Radnička Cesta 47/6)

French Embassy (☏01-48 93 600; Andrije Hebranga 2)

German Embassy (☏01-61 58 100; Ulica Grada Vukovara 64)

Hungarian Embassy (☏01-48 90 900; Pantovčak 257)

Irish Embassy (☏01-63 10 025; Miramarska 23)

Netherlands Embassy (☏01-46 42 200; Medveščak 56)

New Zealand Embassy (☏01-46 12 060; Vlaška 50a)

Polish Embassy (☏01-48 99 444; Krležin Gvozd 3)

Romanian Embassy (☏01-46 77 550; Mlinarska 43)

Serbian Embassy (☏01-45 79 067; Pantovčak 245)

Slovakian Embassy (☏01-48 77 070; Prilaz Gjure Deželića 10)

Slovenian Embassy (☏01-63 11 000; Savska cesta 41/annex)

UK Embassy (☏01-60 09 100; I Lučića 4)

US Embassy (☏01-66 12 200; Thomas Jefferson 2)

Food

Prices in this chapter are based on a main course.

€ less than 80KN

€€ 80KN to 150KN

€€€ more than 150KN

Gay & Lesbian Travellers

Homosexuality has been legal in Croatia since 1977 and is tolerated, but not welcomed with open arms. Public displays of affection between same-sex couples may be met with hostility, especially beyond the major cities.

Exclusively gay clubs are a rarity outside Zagreb, but many of the large discos attract a mixed crowd. On the coast, gay men gravitate to Rovinj, Hvar, Split and Dubrovnik, and tend to frequent naturist beaches.

In Zagreb, the last Saturday in June is Gay Pride Zagreb day.

Most Croatian websites devoted to the gay scene are in Croatian only, but a good starting point is www.travel.gay.hr.

Money

CREDIT CARDS

Amex, MasterCard, Visa and Diners Club cards are widely accepted in large hotels, stores and many restaurants, but don't count on cards to pay for private accommodation or meals in small restaurants. You'll find ATMs accepting MasterCard, Maestro, Cirrus, Plus and Visa in most bus and train stations, airports, all major cities and most small towns.

CURRENCY

Croatia uses the kuna (KN). Commonly circulated banknotes come in denominations of 500, 200, 100, 50, 20, 10 and five kuna. Each kuna is divided into 100 lipa. You'll find silver-coloured 50- and 20-lipa coins, and bronze-coloured 10-lipa coins.

TAX

Travellers who spend more than 740KN in one shop are entitled to a refund of the value-added tax (VAT), which is equivalent to 22% of the purchase price. In order to claim the refund, the merchant must fill out the Tax Cheque (required form), which you must present to the customs office upon leaving the country. Mail a stamped copy to the shop within six months, which will then credit your credit card with the appropriate sum.

TIPPING

If you're served well at a restaurant, you should round up the bill, but a service charge is always included. Bar bills and taxi fares can also be rounded up. Tour guides on day excursions expect to be tipped.

Public Holidays

New Year's Day 1 January

Epiphany 6 January

Easter Monday March/April

Labour Day 1 May

Corpus Christi 10 June

Day of Antifascist Resistance 22 June; marks the outbreak of resistance in 1941

Statehood Day 25 June

Homeland Thanksgiving Day 5 August

Feast of the Assumption 15 August

Independence Day 8 October

All Saints' Day 1 November

Christmas 25 and 26 December

Telephone

MOBILE PHONES

If you have an unlocked 3G phone, you can buy a SIM card for about 50KN. You can choose from four network providers: **VIP** (www.vip.hr), **T-Mobile** (www.t-mobile.hr), **Tomato** (www.tomato.com.hr) and **Tele2** (www.tele2.hr).

PHONE CODES

To call Croatia from abroad, dial your international access code, then ☎385 (the country code for Croatia), then the area code (without the initial ☎0) and the local number.

To call from region to region within Croatia, start with the area code (with the initial ☎0); drop it when dialling within the same code.

Phone numbers with the prefix ☎060 are either free or charged at a premium rate, so watch the small print. Phone numbers that begin with ☎09 are mobile phone numbers.

PHONECARDS

To make a phone call from Croatia, go to the town's main post office. You'll need a phone card to use public telephones. Phonecards are sold according to *impulsi* (units), and you can buy cards of 25 (15KN), 50 (30KN), 100 (50KN) and 200 (100KN) units. These can be purchased at any post office and most tobacco shops and newspaper kiosks.

Tourist Information

The **Croatian National Tourist Board** (www.croatia.hr) is a good source of info. There are regional tourist offices that supervise tourist development, and municipal tourist offices that have free brochures and information.

Travellers with Disabilities

Due to the number of wounded war veterans, more attention is being paid to the needs of disabled travellers in Croatia. Public toilets at bus stations, train stations, airports and large public venues are usually wheelchair accessible. Large hotels are wheelchair accessible, but very little private accommodation is. Bus and train stations in Zagreb, Zadar, Rijeka, Split and Dubrovnik are wheelchair accessible, but the local Jadrolinija ferries are not. For further information, get in touch with **Hrvatski Savez Udruga Tjelesnih Invalida** (☎01-48 12 004; www.hsuti.hr; Šoštarićeva 8, Zagreb), the Croatian union of associations for physically disabled persons.

Visas

Citizens of the EU, USA, Canada, Australia, New Zealand, Israel, Ireland, Singapore and the UK do not need a visa for stays of up to

90 days. South Africans must apply for a 90-day visa in Pretoria. Contact any Croatian embassy, consulate or travel agency abroad for information.

Getting There & Away

Getting to Croatia is becoming ever easier, especially if you're arriving in summer. Low-cost carriers are finally establishing routes to Croatia, and a plethora of bus and ferry routes shepherd holidaymakers to the coast.

Air

There are direct flights to Croatia from a number of European cities; however, there are no nonstop flights from North America to Croatia.

There are several major airports in Croatia.

Dubrovnik Airport (www.airport-dubrovnik. hr) Nonstop flights from Brussels, Cologne, Frankfurt, Hanover, London (Gatwick and Stansted), Manchester, Munich and Stuttgart.

Pula Airport (www.airport-pula.com) Nonstop flights from London (Gatwick) and Manchester.

Rijeka (www.rijeka-airport.hr) Nonstop flights from Cologne and Stuttgart.

Split Airport (www.split-airport.hr) Nonstop flights from Cologne, Frankfurt, London, Munich, Prague and Rome.

Zadar (www.zadar-airport.hr) Nonstop flights from Bari, Brussels, Dublin, London, Munich and more.

Zagreb Airport (www.zagreb-airport.hr) Direct flights from all European capitals, plus Cologne, Hamburg and Stuttgart.

Land

Croatia has border crossings with Hungary, Slovenia, BiH, Serbia and Montenegro.

Buses run to destinations throughout Europe.

From Austria, **Eurolines** (www.eurolines. com) operates buses from Vienna to several destinations in Croatia.

Bus services between Germany and Croatia are good, and fares are cheaper than the train. All buses are handled by **Deutsche Touring GmbH** (www.deutsche-touring. de); there are no Deutsche Touring offices in Croatia, but numerous travel agencies and bus stations sell its tickets.

Sea

Regular boats from the following companies connect Croatia with Italy:

Blue Line (www.blueline-ferries.com)

Commodore Cruises (www.commodore-cruises.hr)

Emilia Romagna Lines (www.emiliaromagnalines.it)

Jadrolinija (www.jadrolinija.hr)

Split Tours (www.splittours.hr)

SNAV (www.snav.com)

Termoli Jet (www.termolijet.it)

Ustica Lines (www.usticalines.it)

Venezia Lines (www.venezialines.com)

Getting Around
Air

Croatia Airlines (☑01-66 76 555; www. croatiaairlines.hr) Croatia Airlines is the only carrier for flights within Croatia. There are daily flights between Zagreb and Dubrovnik, Pula, Split and Zadar.

Bicycle

Cycling can be a great way to explore the islands. Relatively flat islands such as Pag and Mali Lošinj offer the most relaxed biking, but the winding, hilly roads on other islands offer spectacular views. Bicycles are easy to rent along the coast and on the islands. Some tourist offices, especially in the Kvarner and Istria regions, have maps of routes and can refer you to local bike-rental agencies. Even though it's not fully translated into English yet, www.pedala.hr is a great reference for cycling routes around Croatia.

Boat

JADROLINIJA FERRIES

Jadrolinija (www.jadrolinija.hr) operates an extensive network of car ferries and catamarans along the Adriatic coast. Ferries are a lot more comfortable than buses, though somewhat more expensive.

Services operate year-round, though they are less frequent in winter. Cabins should be booked a week ahead. Deck space is usually available on all sailings. You must buy tickets in advance at an agency or a Jadrolinija office. Tickets are not sold on board. In summer months, you need to check in two hours in advance if you bring a car.

Somewhat mediocre fixed-price menus in onboard restaurants cost about 100KN; the cafeteria only offers ham-and-cheese sandwiches for 30KN. Do as the Croats do: bring some food and drink with you.

LOCAL FERRIES

Local ferries connect the bigger offshore islands with each other and with the mainland, but you'll find many more ferries going from the mainland to the islands than from island to island.

On most lines, service is less frequent between October and April. Extra passenger boats are added in the summer; these are usually faster, more comfortable and more expensive. On some shorter routes, ferries run nonstop in summer and advance reservation is unnecessary.

Buy tickets at a Jadrolinija office or at a stall near the ferry (usually open 30 minutes prior to departure). There are no ticket sales on board. In summer, arrive one to two hours prior to departure, even if you've already bought your ticket.

Cars incur a charge; calculated according to the size of car and often very pricey. Reserve as far in advance as possible. Check in several hours in advance. Bicycles incur a small charge.

There is no meal service; you can buy drinks and snacks on board. Most locals bring their own food.

Bus

Bus services are excellent and relatively inexpensive. There are often a number of different companies handling each route so prices can vary substantially. Luggage stowed in the baggage compartment under the bus costs extra (7KN a piece, including insurance).

BUS COMPANIES

The companies listed here are among the largest.

Autotrans (✆060 30 20 10; www.autotrans. hr) Based in Rijeka. Connections to Istria, Zagreb, Varaždin and Kvarner.

Brioni Pula (✆052-535 155; www.brioni. hr) Based in Pula. Connections to Istria, Padua, Split, Trieste and Zagreb.

Contus (✆023-317 062) Based in Zadar. Connections to Split and Zagreb.

Croatiabus (✆01-61 13 073; www.croatiabus.hr) Connecting Zagreb with towns in Zagorje and Istria.

Samoborček (✆01-48 19 180; www. samoborcek.hr) Connecting Zagreb with towns in Dalmatia.

TICKETS & SCHEDULES

At large stations, bus tickets must be purchased at the office, not from drivers. Try to book ahead to be sure of a seat, especially in the summer.

Departure lists above the various windows at bus stations tell you which window sells tickets for your bus. On Croatian bus schedules, *vozi svaki dan* means 'every day' and *ne vozi nedjeljom i blagdanom* means 'no service Sunday and holidays'.

Some buses travel overnight, saving you a night's accommodation. Don't expect to get much sleep, though, as the inside lights will be on and music will be blasting the whole night. Take care not to be left behind at meal or rest stops, which usually occur about every two hours.

Car & Motorcycle

Croatia's motorway connecting Zagreb with Split is only a few years old and makes some routes much faster. Zagreb and Rijeka are now connected by motorway, and an Istrian motorway has shortened the travel time to Italy considerably.

Although the new roads are in excellent condition, there are stretches where service stations and facilities are few and far between. You can reach roadside assistance on ✆1987.

CAR HIRE

In order to rent a car you must be 21 or over, with a valid driving licence and a valid credit card.

Independent local companies are often much cheaper than the international chains, but the big companies offer one-way rentals. Sometimes you can get a lower car-rental rate by booking the car from abroad, or by booking a fly-drive package.

CAR INSURANCE

Third-party public liability insurance is included by law with car rentals, but make sure your quoted price includes full collision insurance, known as a collision damage waiver (CDW). Otherwise, your responsibility for damage done to the vehicle is usually determined as a percentage of the car's value, beginning at around 2000KN.

CROATIA GETTING AROUND

If you rent a car in Italy, many insurance companies will not insure you for a trip into Croatia. Border officials know this and may refuse you entry unless permission to drive into Croatia is clearly marked on the insurance documents.

Most car-rental companies in Trieste and Venice are familiar with this requirement and will furnish you with the correct stamp. Otherwise, you must make specific inquiries.

DRIVING LICENCE

Any valid driving licence is sufficient to drive legally and rent a car; an international driving licence is not necessary.

The **Hrvatski Autoklub** (HAK, Croatian Auto Club; ☎46 40 800; www.hak.hr; Avenija Dubrovnik 44) offers help and advice. For help on the road, you can contact the nationwide **HAK road assistance** (Vučna Služba; ☎987).

ON THE ROAD

Petrol stations are generally open from 7am to 7pm and often until 10pm in summer. Petrol is Eurosuper 95, Super 98, normal or diesel. See www.ina.hr for up-to-date fuel prices.

You have to pay tolls on all motorways, to use the Učka tunnel between Rijeka and Istria, to use the bridge to Krk Island, and on the road from Rijeka to Delnice.

For general news on Croatia's motorways and tolls, see www.hak.hr. The radio station HR2 broadcasts traffic reports in English every hour on the hour from July to early September.

ROAD RULES

In Croatia you drive on the right, and the use of seatbelts is mandatory. Unless otherwise posted, the speed limits for cars and motorcycles are 50km/h in built-up areas, 100km/h on main highways and 130km/h on motorways.

On two-lane highways, it's illegal to pass long military convoys or a line of cars caught behind a slow-moving truck.

It's illegal to drive with a blood alcohol content higher than 0.5%.

You are required to drive with your headlights on even during the day.

Local Transport

The main form of local transport is bus (although Zagreb and Osijek also have well-developed tram systems).

Buses in major cities such as Dubrovnik, Rijeka, Split and Zadar run about once every 20 minutes, less on Sunday. A ride is usually around 10KN, with a small discount if you buy tickets at a *tisak* (news stand).

Small medieval towns along the coast are generally closed to traffic and have infrequent links to outlying suburbs.

Bus transport within the islands is infrequent since most people have their own cars.

Train

Trains are less frequent than buses but more comfortable. For information about schedules, prices and services, contact **Croatian Railways** (Hrvatske Željeznice; ☎060 333 444; www.hznet.hr).

Zagreb is the hub for Croatia's less-than-extensive train system. No trains run along the coast and only a few coastal cities are connected with Zagreb. For travellers, the main lines of interest are the following:

Zagreb–Rijeka–Pula Via Lupoglava, where passengers switch to a bus.

Zagreb–Osijek

Zagreb–Split

Domestic trains are either 'express' or 'passenger' (local). Express trains have 1st- and 2nd-class cars, plus smoking and nonsmoking areas. A reservation is advisable for express trains.

Express trains are more expensive than passenger trains; any prices quoted in this chapter are for unreserved 2nd-class seating.

There are no couchettes on domestic services. There are sleeping cars on overnight trains between Zagreb and Split.

Baggage is free on trains; most stations have left-luggage services charging around 15KN a piece per day.

EU residents who hold an InterRail pass can use it in Croatia for free travel, but you're unlikely to take enough trains to justify the cost.

Czech Republic

Includes »

Why Go?

Since the fall of communism in 1989 and the opening of Central and Eastern Europe, Prague has evolved into one of Europe's most popular travel destinations. The city offers an intact medieval core that transports you back 500 years in time. The 14th-century Charles Bridge, traversing two historic riverside neighbourhoods, is one of the continent's most beautiful sights. The city is not just about history. It's a vital urban centre with a rich array of cultural offerings. Outside the capital, castles and palaces abound – including the audacious hilltop chateau at Český Krumlov – which illuminate the stories of powerful families and individuals whose influence was felt throughout Europe. Beautifully preserved Renaissance towns that withstood the ravages of the communist era link the centuries, and idiosyncratic landscapes provide a stage for active adventures.

Best Places to Eat

» Sansho (p292)

» Aberdeen Angus
Steakhouse (p309)

» Moritz (p323)

» Koishi (p318)

» Cukrkávalimonáda (p292)

Best Places to Stay

» Golden Well Hotel (p286)

» Fusion Hotel (p287)

» Hotel Templ (p327)

» Hostel Mitte (p317)

» Savic Hotel (p287)

When to Go
Prague

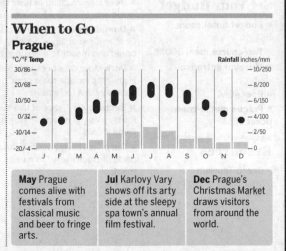

May Prague comes alive with festivals from classical music and beer to fringe arts.

Jul Karlovy Vary shows off its arty side at the sleepy spa town's annual film festival.

Dec Prague's Christmas Market draws visitors from around the world.

AT A GLANCE

» **Currency** Crown (Kč)

» **Language** Czech

» **Money** ATMs all over; banks open Monday to Friday

» **Visas** Schengen rules apply; visas not required for most nationalities

Fast Facts

» **Area** 78,864 sq km

» **Capital** Prague

» **Country code** ☏420

» **Emergency** ☏112

Exchange Rates

Australia	A$1	21.06Kč
Canada	C$1	19.84Kč
Euro Zone	€1	25.77Kč
Japan	¥100	21.37Kč
New Zealand	NZ$1	16.88Kč
UK	UK£1	30.51Kč
USA	US$1	20.17Kč

Set Your Budget

» **Budget hotel room** 1500Kč

» **Two-course meal** 300Kč

» **Museum entrance** 150Kč

» **Beer** 40Kč

» **Prague metro-tram ticket** 32Kč

Resources

» **Czech Tourism** (www.czechtourism.com)

Connections

The Czech Republic lies along major European road and rail lines and is a convenient hub for exploring neighbouring countries. Prague has excellent rail connections to Dresden and Berlin as well as Krakow, Bratislava, Budapest and Vienna. Major four-lane highways link Prague to German cities, Bratislava and Budapest.

ITINERARIES

One Week

Experience Prague's exciting combination of its tumultuous past and energetic present. Top experiences include the grandeur of Prague Castle, Josefov's Jewish Museum, and getting pleasantly lost amid the bewildering labyrinth of the Old Town. Take an essential day trip to Terezín, and then head south to Český Krumlov for a few days of riverside R&R.

Two Weeks

Begin in Prague before heading west for the spa scenes at Mariánské Lázně or Karlovy Vary. Balance the virtue and vice ledger with a few Bohemian brews in Plzeň before heading south for relaxation and rigour around Český Krumlov. Head east to the Renaissance grandeur of Telč and Brno's cosmopolitan galleries and museums. Use the Moravian capital as a base for exploring the Moravian Karst caves and Mikulov's wine country, before continuing to underrated Olomouc to admire the Holy Trinity Column.

Essential Food & Drink

» **Beer** Czechs claim to have the best *pivo* (beer) in the world and who are we to argue?

» **Dumplings** Every culture has its starchy side dish; for Czechs it's *knedliky* – big bread or potato balls sliced like bread and meant to mop up gravy.

» **Pork** Move over beef, *vepřové maso* (pork) is king here. Highlights include roast pork, pork *guláš* (goulash) or pork *vepřový řízek* (schnitzel).

» **Becherovka** A shot of this sweetish herbal liqueur from Karlovy Vary is a popular way to start (or end) a big meal. Drink it cold.

» **Carp** This lowly river fish, known locally as *kapr*, is given pride of place every Christmas at the centre of the family meal.

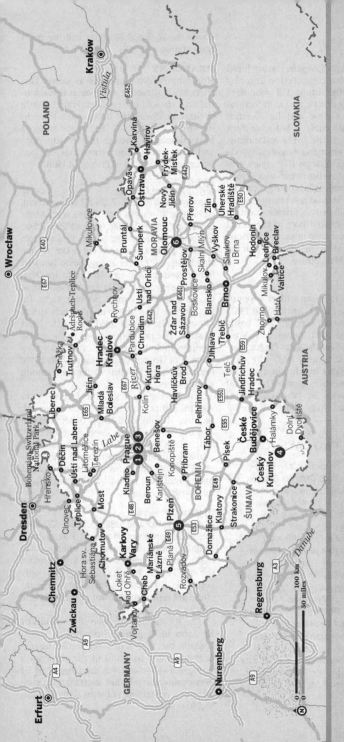

Czech Republic Highlights

① Stroll across the **Charles Bridge** (p283) in the early morning or late evening when the crowds thin out.

② Enjoy a beer in the open air on a warm summer evening at Prague's **Letná Beer Garden** (p293).

③ Join the appreciative throngs at Prague's **Astronomical Clock** (p277) at the top of the hour.

④ Repair to **Český Krumlov** (p312) to see the prettiest town in Central Europe.

⑤ Tour the **Pilsner Urquell Brewery** (p308) in Plzeň to see where it all started.

⑥ Amble through the stately town of **Olomouc** (p320), the most amazing place you've never heard of.

PRAGUE

POP 1.22 MILLION

It's the perfect irony of Prague: you are lured here by the past, but compelled to linger by the present and the future. Fill your days with its illustrious artistic and architectural heritage – from Gothic and Renaissance to art nouveau and cubist – but after dark move your focus to the lively restaurants, bars and clubs in emerging neighbourhoods like Vinohrady and Žižkov. If Prague's seasonal legions of tourists wear you down, that's okay. Just drink a glass of the country's legendary lager, relax and rest reassured that quiet moments still exist: a private dawn on Charles Bridge, a chilled beer in the Letná Beer Garden as you gaze upon the glorious cityscape of Staré Město or getting lost in the intimate lanes of Malá Strana.

◉ Sights

Prague nestles on the Vltava River, separating Hradčany (the Castle district) and Malá Strana (Lesser Quarter) on the west bank, from Staré Město (Old Town) and Nové Město (New Town) on the east. Prague Castle overlooks Malá Strana, while the twin Gothic spires of Týn Church dominate Old Town Sq (Staroměstské nám). The broad avenue of Wenceslas Sq (Václavské nám) stretches southeast from Staré Město towards the National Museum and the main train station.

HRADČANY

Hradčany (which translates as Castle District) is an attractive and peaceful residential area stretching west from Prague Castle to Strahov Monastery. It became a town in its own right in 1320, and twice suffered heavy damage – once in the Hussite Wars and again in the Great Fire of 1541 – before becoming a borough of Prague in 1598.

TOP CHOICE **Prague Castle**   CASTLE
(Pražský hrad; Map p282; ☑224 372 423; www.hrad. cz; Hradčanské náměstí; grounds free, sights adult/ concession full 350/175Kc, reduced 250/125Kc; ⊙grounds 5am-midnight Apr-Oct, 6am-11pm Nov-Mar; gardens 10am-6pm Apr & Oct, to 7pm May & Sep, to 9pm Jul & Aug, closed Nov-Mar; historic buildings 9am-6pm Apr-Oct, to 4pm Nov-Mar; ⓂMalostranská, ☒22) Immense Prague Castle is the city's most popular sight. Its has always been the seat of Czech rulers as well as the official residence of the head of state. The main attractions of the castle complex include the Old Royal Palace, Basilica of St George, **Golden Lane** (Zlatá ulička; Map p282), and St Vitus Cathedral, among many others.

Entry to the castle grounds is free, but to visit the sights, including St Vitus Cathedral, requires a combined-entry ticket. Several options are available, depending on how much time you have. Two main options are available: full-price and reduced-price tickets. The latter includes admission to most major sights and will satisfy the demands of most visitors.

St Vitus Cathedral
(Katedrála Sv Víta; Map p282; ☑257 531 622; www. katedralasvatehovita.cz; III nádvoří, Pražský hrad) Prague's principal cathedral anchors the castle grounds and is visible from around the city. Though it looks ancient, it was only completed in 1929. Its many treasures include **art nouveau stained glass** by Alfons Mucha.

The spectacular, baroque silver **tomb of St John of Nepomuk**, towards the back, contains two tonnes of silver in all. The biggest and most beautiful of the cathedral's numerous side chapels is the **Chapel of St Wenceslas**. Its walls are adorned with gilded panels containing polished slabs of semiprecious stones.

PRAGUE IN TWO DAYS

Beat the tourist hordes with an early-morning stroll across **Charles Bridge**, and continue uphill on Nerudova to Hradčany and the glories of **Prague Castle**. Don't miss also seeing the superb 'Princely Collections' at the **Lobkowicz Palace**. Cross the river again to the **Charles Bridge Museum**.

On day two, explore **Josefov**, Prague's original Jewish quarter, and then pack a hilltop picnic for the view-friendly fortress at **Vyšehrad**. Make time for a few Czech brews, either at the relaxed **Letná Beer Garden** or the excellent **Pivovarský Klub**, before kicking on for robust Czech food at **U Modré Kachničky** or some high-quality Asian-influenced fusion at **Sansho**. For a nightcap head to a cool late-night spot like **Čili Bar**.

Old Royal Palace

(Starý královský Palác; Map p282) The Old Royal Palace is one of the oldest parts of the castle, dating from 1135. At its heart is the grand **Vladislav Hall** (Map p282) and the **Bohemian Chancellery** (Map p282), scene of the famous Defenestration of Prague.

Basilica of St George

(Bazilika Sv Jiří; Map p282; Jiřské náměstí) The striking, brick-red, early-baroque facade that dominates St George Sq (Jiřské náměstí) conceals the Czech Republic's best-preserved Romanesque church, the Basilica of St George, established in the 10th century by Vratislav I. Next to the basilica is the **Convent of St George** (Klášter Sv Jiří; Map p282; ☑257 531 644; www.ngprague.cz; Jiřské náměstí 33; adult/concession 150/80Kč; ⊙10am-6pm Tue-Sun), the current home of the National Gallery's Museum of 19th-Century Czech Art.

Lobkowicz Palace

(Lobkovický Palác; Map p282; ☑233 312 925; www.lobkowicz.cz; Jiřská 3; adult/concession/family 275/200/690Kč; ⊙10.30am-6pm) This 16th-century palace houses a private museum known as the 'Princely Collections', which includes priceless paintings, furniture and musical memorabilia. You tour with an audio guide dictated by owner William Lobkowicz and his family – this personal connection really brings the displays to life, and makes the palace one of Prague Castle's most interesting attractions.

Šternberg Palace   GALLERY

(Šternberský palác; Map p282; ☑233 090 570; www.ngprague.cz; Hradčanské náměstí 15; adult/child 150/80Kč; ⊙10am-6pm Tue-Sun; ☐22) The baroque Šternberg Palace is home to the National Gallery's collection of 14th- to 18th-century European art, including works by Goya and Rembrandt. Fans of medieval altarpieces will be in heaven; there are also several Rubens, some Rembrandts and Breughels, and a large collection of Bohemian miniatures.

Sanctuary of Our Lady of Loreta   CHURCH

(Map p278; www.loreta.cz; Loretánské náměstí 7; adult/child 110/90Kč; ⊙9am-4.30pm Tue-Sun; ☐22, 23 to Pohořelec) The baroque Sanctuary of Our Lady of Loreta showcases precious religious artefacts, and the cloister houses a 17th-century replica of the Santa Casa from the Italian town of Loreta, reputedly the Virgin Mary's house in Nazareth, transported to Italy by angels in the 13th century.

> ℹ **MIND YOUR MANNERS**
>
> It's customary to say *dobrý den* (good day) when entering a shop, cafe or bar, and *na shledanou* (goodbye) when leaving.

Strahov Library   HISTORIC BUILDING

(Strahovská knihovna; Map p278; ☑233 107 718; www.strahovskyklaster.cz; Strahovské nádvoří 1; adult/concession 80/50Kč; ⊙9am-noon & 1-5pm; ☐22, 25) Strahov Library is the largest monastic library in the country, with two magnificent baroque halls dating from the 17th and 18th centuries. The main attractions are the two-storey-high **Philosophy Hall** (Filozofický sál; 1780–97) and the older but even more beautiful **Theology Hall** (Teologiský sál; 1679).

STARÉ MĚSTO

One of Europe's most beautiful urban spaces, the **Old Town Square** (Staroměstské náměstí; Map p288; Ⓜ Staroměstská), usually shortened in Czech to Staromák, has been Prague's principal public square since the 10th century, and was its main marketplace until the beginning of the 20th century. There are busking jazz bands and alfresco concerts, plus Christmas and Easter markets in season, all watched over by Ladislav Šaloun's brooding art nouveau **statue of Jan Hus** (Map p288; Ⓜ Staroměstská). It was unveiled on 6 July 1915, which was the 500th anniversary of Hus' death at the stake.

Old Town Hall   HISTORIC BUILDING

(Staroměstská radnice; Map p288; ☑12444; www.prazskeveze.cz; Staroměstské náměstí 1; guided tour adult/child 105/85Kč; ⊙11am-6pm Mon, 9am-6pm Tue-Sun; Ⓜ Staroměstská) Prague's Old Town Hall, founded in 1338, is a hotchpotch of medieval buildings acquired over centuries, presided over by a tall Gothic tower with its splendid Astronomical Clock. As well as housing the main tourist information office (p298), the town hall has several historic attractions, and hosts art exhibitions on the ground floor. The tower view is the best in town.

Astronomical Clock   HISTORIC SITE

(Map p288; Ⓜ Staroměstská) Ironically, if you wish to tell the time in Old Town Sq, it's easier to look at the clock above this, because the 1490 mechanical marvel is tricky to decipher. The clock's creator, Master Hanuš, was

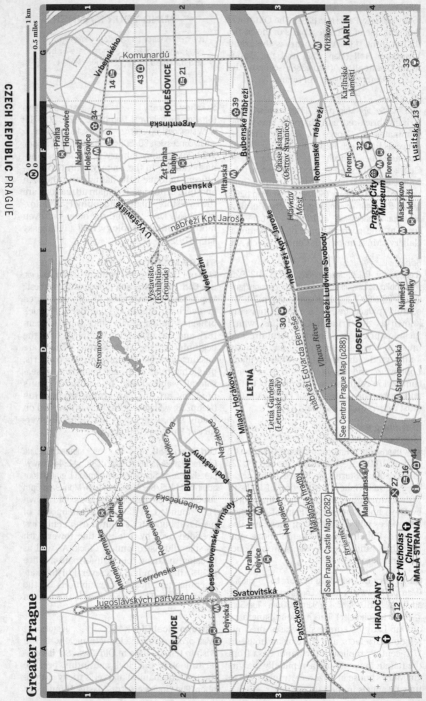

1 km
0.5 miles

See Central Prague Map (p288)

See Prague Castle Map (p282)

Prague City Museum

St Nicholas Church

DEJVICE

BUBENEČ

HRADČANY

MALÁ STRANA

LETNÁ

HOLEŠOVICE

KARLÍN

JOSEFOV

Stromovka

Vystaviště (Exhibition Grounds)

Letná Gardens (Letenské sady)

Vltava River

Chase Island (Ostrov Štvanice)

Vrbenského
Komunardů
Argentinská
Bubenské nábřeží
Rohanské nábřeží
nábřeží Ludvíka Svobody
nábřeží Edvarda Beneše
nábřeží Kpt Jaroše
Veletržní
Milady Horákové
Za Zátoří
Pod kaštany
Bubenečská
Wolkerova
Rooseveltova
Československé Armády
Terronská
Antonína Čermáka
Jugoslávských partyzánů
Svatovítská
Patočkova
Na valech
Mariánské hradby
Hradčanská
U Výstaviště
Vltavská
Bubenská
Žst Praha Bubny
Hlávkův Most
Husitská
Křižíkova
Karlínské náměstí

Praha Holešovice
Nádraží Holešovice
Praha Bubeneč
Praha Dejvice
Dejvická
Staroměstská
Náměstí Republiky
Florenc
Masarykovo nádraží
Malostranská

14
43
21
34
9
39
30
33
32
13
44
16
27
15
12
4

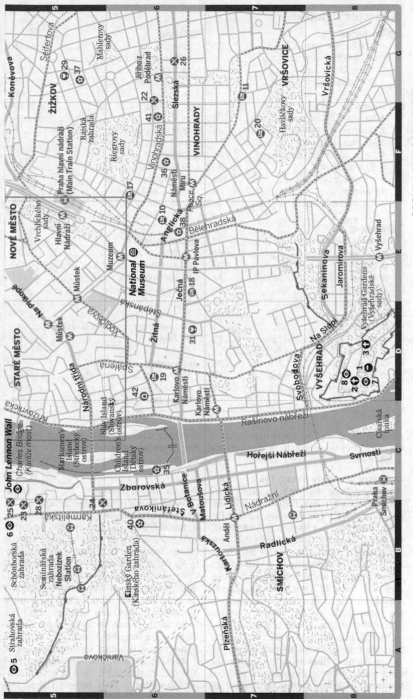

ŽIŽKOV

29
37

Konevova

Šeifertova

Mahlerovy
sady

Jiřího z
Poděbrad

26

Slezská

VRŠOVICE

Vršovická

22
41

Vinohradská

Riegrovy
sady

Rajská
zahrada

Praha hlavní nádraží
(Main Train Station)

Havlíčkovy
sady

11

20

Vršovická

36

VINOHRADY

Náměstí
Míru

17

NOVÉ MĚSTO

Vrchlického
sady

Hlavní
Nádraží

Muzeum

National
Museum

Štěpánská

Vodičkova

10

Anglická

38

Peace
Sq

Bělehradská

IP Pavlova

Sekaninova

Jaromírova

Vyšehrad

Vyšehrad Gardens
(Vyšehradské
sady)

Na přikopě

Můstek

Můstek

Můstek

STARÉ MĚSTO

Národní třída

Spálená

Žitná

Ječná

18

31

Na Slupi

Svobodova

VYŠEHRAD

4

3
1

8
6
2
7

Karlovo
Náměstí

Karlovo
Náměstí

19

42

Krizovnicka

Slav Island
(Slovanský
ostrov)

Marksmen's
Island
(Střelecký
ostrov)

Charles Bridge
(Karlův most)

John Lennon Wall

Rašínovo nábřeží

Otaňská
louka

Children's
Island
(Dětský
ostrov)

35

Hořejší Nábřeží

Svrnosti

Zborovská

Zborovská

6
25
23
28
24

Schönborská
zahrada

Seminářská
zahrada
Nebozízek

Strahovská
zahrada

5

Vaníčkova

Station

Kinský Garden
(Kinského zahrada)

40

N Botanice

Štefánikova

Matoušova

Lidická

Nádražní

Andel

Radlická

Praha
Smíchov

Karmelitská

Kartouzská

Plzeňská

SMÍCHOV

Greater Prague

allegedly blinded so he could not duplicate the clock elsewhere. Stop by on the hour for a little medieval marionette show.

Church of Our Lady Before Týn   CHURCH

(Kostel Panny Marie před Týnem; Map p288; ☎222 318 186; www.tyn.cz; Staroměstské náměstí; suggested donation 25Kč; ⊙10am-1pm & 3-5pm Tue-Sat, 10.30am-noon Sun Mar-Oct; Ⓜ Staroměstská) Its distinctive twin Gothic spires make the Týn church an unmistakable Old Town landmark. Like something out of a 15th-century – and probably slightly cruel – fairy tale, they loom over Old Town Sq, decorated with a golden image of the Virgin Mary made in the 1620s from the melted-down Hussite chalice that previously adorned the church.

Though impressively Gothic on the outside, the interior is smothered in baroque. Two of the most interesting features are the huge rococo **altar** on the northern wall and the **tomb of Tycho Brahe**, the Danish as-

tronomer who was one of Rudolf II's most illustrious 'consultants' (he died in 1601, allegedly of a burst bladder following a royal piss-up).

Prague Jewish Museum   MUSEUM

(Židovské muzeum Praha; Map p288; ☎222 317 191; www.jewishmuseum.cz; Reservation Centre, U starého hřbitova 3a; ordinary ticket adult/child 300/200Kč, combined ticket including entry to Old-New Synagogue 480/320Kč; ⊙9am-6pm Sun-Fri Apr-Oct, to 4.30pm Nov-Mar; Ⓜ Staroměstská) This museum consists of six Jewish monuments: the **Maisel Synagogue** (Maiselova synagóga; Map p288; Maiselova 10); the **Pinkas Synagogue** (Pinkasova synagóga; Map p288; Široká 3); the **Spanish Synagogue** (Španělská synagóga; Map p288; Vězeňská 1); the **Klaus Synagogue** (Klauzová synagóga; Map p288; U starého hřbitova 1); the **Ceremonial Hall** (Obřadní síň; Map p288); and the **Old Jewish Cemetery** (Starý židovský hřbitov; Map p288; Pinkas Synagogue, Široká 3); see p284 for a museum itinerary. The monuments are clustered together in **Josefov**, a small corner of the Old Town that was home to Prague's Jews for some 800 years before it was brought to an end by an urban renewal project at the start of the 20th century and the Nazi occupation during WWII.

The monuments cannot be visited separately but require a combined entry ticket which is good for all of the sights and available at ticket windows throughout Josefov. A fifth synagogue, the **Old-New Synagogue** (Staronová synagóga; Map p288; Červená 2; adult/ child 200/140Kč), is still used for religious services, and requires a separate ticket or additional fee.

The Jewish Museum was first established in 1906 to preserve objects from synagogues that were demolished during the slum clearance at the turn of the 20th century. The collection grew richer as a result of one of the most grotesquely ironic acts of WWII. During the Nazi occupation, the Germans took over management of the museum in order to create a 'museum of an extinct race'. To that end, they brought in objects from destroyed Jewish communities throughout Bohemia and Moravia.

Municipal House HISTORIC BUILDING
(Obecní dům; Map p288; ☑222 002 101; www.obec-nidum.cz; náměstí Republiky 5; guided tour adult/ child 290/240Kč; ☺public areas 7.30am-11pm, information centre 10am-8pm; Ⓜ Náměstí Republiky) Restored in the 1990s, Prague's most exuberant and sensual building is a labour of love, every detail of its design and decoration carefully considered, every painting loaded with symbolism. The restaurant and cafe flanking the entrance are like walk-in museums of art nouveau design; upstairs are half a dozen sumptuously decorated halls that you can visit by guided tour.

The Municipal House stands on the site of the Royal Court, seat of Bohemia's kings from 1383 to 1483 (when Vladislav II moved to Prague Castle), which was demolished at the end of the 19th century. Between 1906 and 1912 this magnificent art nouveau palace was built in its place – a lavish joint effort by around 30 leading artists of the day.

Convent of St Agnes GALLERY
(Klášter sv Anežky; Map p288; ☑224 810 628; www.ngprague.cz; U Milosrdných 17; adult/child 150/80Kč; ☺10am-6pm Tue-Sun; ☐5, 8, 14) In the northeastern corner of Staré Město is the former Convent of St Agnes, Prague's oldest surviving Gothic building. The 1st-floor rooms hold the National Gallery's permanent collection of medieval and early Renaissance art (1200–1550) from Bohemia and Central Europe, a treasure house of glowing Gothic altar paintings and polychrome religious sculptures.

Museum of Czech Cubism GALLERY
(Muzeum Českého Kubismu; Map p288; ☑224 211 746; www.ngprague.cz; Ovocný trh 19; adult/ child 100/50Kč; ☺10am-6pm Tue-Sun; Ⓜ Náměstí Republiky) Though dating from 1912, Josef Gočár's *dům U černé Matky Boží* (House of the Black Madonna) – Prague's first and finest example of cubist architecture – still looks modern and dynamic. It now houses three floors of remarkable cubist paintings and sculpture, as well as furniture, ceramics and glassware in cubist designs.

Estates Theatre HISTORIC BUILDING
(Stavovské divadlo; Map p288; ☑224 902 231; www.narodni-divadlo.cz; Ovocný trh 1; Ⓜ Můstek)

CHEAP THRILLS

Prague has become more expensive in recent years, but there are still some things you can do for free or to reduce your costs:

» Stroll through the gardens and courtyards at Prague Castle (p276).

» Visit Charles Bridge (p283) at dawn.

» Explore the fortress at Vyšehrad (p286).

» Catch tram 22 from Peace Sq in Vinohrady all the way to Prague Castle for a DIY city tour. It might be the best 32Kč you ever spend.

» Make lunch your main meal of the day to save money on eating out, taking advantage of restaurants' *denní menu* (daily menus).

» Combine people-watching and great river views while grabbing a cheap-as-chips sunset beer at the Letná Beer Garden (p293).

Prague Castle

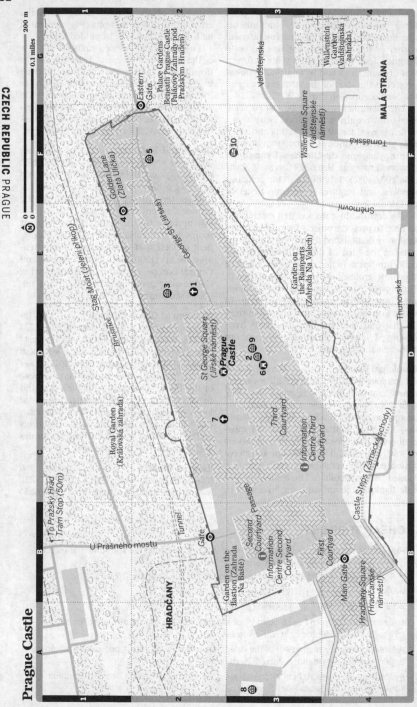

0 200 m
0 0.1 miles

G1
F3
G3

Palace Gardens Beneath Prague Castle (Palácové Zahrady pod Pražským Hradem)

Eastern Gate

Wallenstein Gardens (Valdštejnská zahrada)

Valdštejnská

MALÁ STRANA

Wallenstein Square (Valdštejnské náměstí)

Tomášská

Golden Lane (Zlatá Ulička)

5

10

George St (Jiřská)

Sněmovní

Stag Moat (Jelení příkop)

4

Garden on the Ramparts (Zahrada Na Valech)

Thunovská

E

Brusnice

3

1

St George Square (Jiřské náměstí)

Prague Castle

2 9

6

Royal Garden (Královská zahrada)

7

Third Courtyard

Information Centre Third Courtyard

Castle Steps (Zámecké schody)

To Pražský Hrad Tram Stop (50m)

Tunnel

Gate

U Prášného mostu

Garden on the Bastion (Zahrada Na Baště)

Second Courtyard Passage

Information Centre Second Courtyard

Second Courtyard

First Courtyard

Main Gate

Hradčany Square (Hradčanské náměstí)

HRADČANY

8

B3

B4

Prague Castle

◎ **Top Sights**

Prague Castle D2

◎ **Sights**

1 Basilica of St George E2
2 Bohemian Chancellery D3
3 Convent of St George E2
4 Golden Lane E1
5 Lobkowicz Palace F2
6 Old Royal Palace D3
7 St Vitus Cathedral C2
8 Šternberg Palace A3
9 Vladislav Hall D3

🛏 **Sleeping**

10 Golden Well Hotel F3

Prague's oldest theatre and finest neoclassical building, the Estates Theatre is where the premiere of Mozart's *Don Giovanni* was performed on 29 October 1787, with the maestro himself conducting. Opened in 1783 as the Nostitz Theatre (after its founder, Count Anton von Nostitz-Rieneck), it was patronised by upper-class German citizens and thus came to be called the Estates Theatre.

MALÁ STRANA

Across the river from the Old Town are the baroque backstreets of Malá Strana (Little Quarter), built in the 17th and 18th centuries by victorious Catholic clerics and nobles on the foundations of their Protestant predecessors' Renaissance palaces.

Charles Bridge   BRIDGE

(Karlův most; Map p288; Malostranské náměstí; 🚊17, 18 to Karlovy lázně) Strolling across the 14th-century Charles Bridge is everybody's favourite Prague activity. In 1357 Charles IV commissioned Peter Parler (the architect of St Vitus Cathedral) to replace the 12th-century Judith Bridge, which had been washed away by floods in 1342. The new bridge was completed in 1390, and took Charles' name only in the 19th century.

Despite occasional flood damage, it withstood wheeled traffic for 500-odd years – thanks, legend says, to eggs mixed into the mortar (though recent investigations have disproved this myth) – until it was made pedestrian-only in the decades after WWII.

St Nicholas Church   CHURCH

(Kostel sv Mikuláše; Map p278; 🕿257 534 215; Malostranské náměstí 38; adult/child 70/35Kč; ⏰9am-

5pm Mar-Oct, to 4pm Nov-Feb; 🚊12, 20, 22) Malá Strana is dominated by the huge green cupola of St Nicholas Church, one of Central Europe's finest baroque buildings. Don't confuse it with the other Church of St Nicholas, on Old Town Sq. It was begun by famed German baroque architect Kristof Dientzenhofer; his son Kilian continued the work and Anselmo Lurago finished the job in 1755.

On the ceiling, Johann Kracker's 1770 *Apotheosis of St Nicholas* is Europe's largest fresco (clever *trompe l'œil* technique has made the painting merge almost seamlessly with the architecture). In the first chapel on the left is a mural by Karel Škréta, which includes the church official who kept track of the artist as he worked; he is looking out through a window in the upper corner.

John Lennon Wall   HISTORIC SITE

(Map p278; Velkopřevorské náměstí; 🚊12, 20, 22) After his murder in New York on 8 December 1980, John Lennon became a pacifist hero for young Czechs. An image of Lennon was painted on a wall in a secluded square opposite the French Embassy (there is a niche on the wall that looks like a tombstone), along with political graffiti and Beatles lyrics.

Despite repeated coats of whitewash, the secret police never managed to keep it clean for long, and the Lennon Wall became a political focus for Prague youth. These days, it's still fun to take a look and scrawl something on the wall yourself.

Vrtbov Garden   GARDENS

(Vrtbovská zahrada; Map p278; 🚗257 531 480; www.vrtbovska.cz; Karmelitská 25; adult/concession 60/50Kč; ⏰10am-6pm Apr-Oct; 🚊12, 20, 22) This 'secret garden', hidden along an alley at the corner of Tržiště and Karmelitská, was built in 1720 for the Earl of Vrtba, the senior chancellor of Prague Castle. It's a formal baroque garden, climbing steeply up the hillside to a terrace graced with baroque statues of Roman mythological figures by Matthias Braun.

NOVÉ MĚSTO & VYŠEHRAD

Nové Město surrounds the Old Town on all sides and was originally laid out in the 14th century. Its main public area is Wenceslas Sq. This piece of Prague has witnessed a great deal of Czech history – a giant Mass was held here during the revolutionary upheavals of 1848; in 1918 the creation of the new Czechoslovak Republic was celebrated here; and in 1989 the fall of communism was announced here. At the southern end

A STROLL THROUGH PRAGUE'S JEWISH MUSEUM

The Prague Jewish Museum (p280), a collection of four synagogues, the former Ceremonial Hall and the Old Jewish Cemetery, is one of the city's treasures. Start your exploration at the **Pinkas Synagogue**, built in 1535 and used for worship until 1941. After WWII it was converted into a memorial, with walls inscribed with the names of the 77,297 Czech victims of the Nazis. It also has a collection of drawings by children held in the Terezín concentration camp during WWII.

The Pinkas Synagogue leads to the **Old Jewish Cemetery**, Europe's oldest surviving Jewish graveyard. Founded in the 15th century, it has a palpable atmosphere of mourning even after two centuries of disuse (it was closed in 1787). Around 12,000 crumbling stones are heaped together, but beneath them are tens of thousands of graves, piled in layers because of lack of space.

Exit through a gate between the **Klaus Synagogue** (Klausová Synagóga) and the **Ceremonial Hall** (Obřadní síň), both of which house exhibitions on Jewish forms of worship, family ceremonies and traditions.

A block southeast lies the neo-Gothic **Maisel Synagogue**, which replaced a Renaissance original built by Mordechai Maisel, the mayor of the Jewish community, in 1592. It houses an exhibit on the history of the Jews in Bohemia and Moravia from the 10th to 18th centuries.

East of the Maisel is the **Spanish Synagogue**. Named after its striking Moorish interior and dating from 1868, its exhibit continues the story of the Jews in the Czech lands from the 19th century to the present.

Separate from the Jewish Museum, the **Old-New Synagogue** dates from 1270 and is Europe's oldest working synagogue. Around the central chamber are an entry hall, a winter prayer hall and the room from which women watch the men-only services. The interior, with a pulpit surrounded by a 15th-century wrought-iron grill, looks much as it would have 500 years ago.

of the square is Josef Myslbek's muscular **equestrian statue of St Wenceslas** (sv Václav; Map p288; Václavské náměstí; Ⓜ Muzeum), the 10th-century pacifist Duke of Bohemia and the 'Good King Wenceslas' of Christmas-carol fame. Near the statue, a small **memorial to the victims of communism** bears photographs and handwritten epitaphs to anticommunist heroes.

National Museum   MUSEUM
(Národní muzeum; Map p278; ☎ 224 497 111; www.nm.cz; Václavské náměstí 68; ⊙ closed until 2015; Ⓜ Muzeum) Looming above Wenceslas Sq is the neo-Renaissance bulk of the National Museum, designed in the 1880s by Josef Schulz as an architectural symbol of the Czech National Revival. The museum mainly displays rocks, fossils and stuffed animals but was closed during our research for renovation and not expected to reopen until 2015. The museum's exterior is impressive and worth checking out.

Mucha Museum   GALLERY
(Muchovo muzeum; Map p288; ☎ 221 451 333; www.mucha.cz; Panská 7; adult/child 180/120Kč; ⊙ 10am-6pm; Ⓜ Můstek) This fascinating (and busy) museum features the sensuous art nouveau posters, paintings and decorative panels of Alfons Mucha (1860–1939), as well as many sketches, photographs and other memorabilia. The exhibits include countless artworks showing Mucha's trademark Slavic maidens with flowing hair and piercing blue eyes, bearing symbolic garlands and linden boughs.

Prague City Museum   MUSEUM
(Muzeum hlavního města Prahy; Map p278; ☎ 224 816 773; www.muzeumprahy.cz; Na Poříčí 52, Karlin; adult/child 120/50Kč; ⊙ 9am-6pm Tue-Sun; Ⓜ Florenc) This excellent museum, opened in 1898, is devoted to the history of Prague from prehistoric times to the 20th century. Among the many intriguing exhibits are the Astronomical Clock's original 1866 calendar wheel with Josef Mánes' beautiful painted panels representing the months – that's January at the top, toasting his toes by the fire.

What everybody comes to see is Antonín Langweil's astonishing 1:480 scale model of Prague as it looked between 1826 and 1834. The display is most rewarding after you get to know Prague a bit, as you can spot the changes – look at St Vitus Cathedral, for example, still only half-finished. Labels are in English as well as Czech.

Museum of Communism   MUSEUM
(Muzeum Komunismu; Map p288; ☎224 212 966; www.muzeumkomunismu.cz; Na Příkopě 10; adult/concession/child under 10 190/150Kč/free; ⊙9am-9pm; Ⓜ Můstek) It's difficult to think of a more ironic site for a museum of communism – an 18th-century aristocrat's palace, between a casino and a McDonald's. Put together by an American expat and his Czech partner, the museum tells the story of Czechoslovakia's years behind the Iron Curtain in photos, words and a fascinating collection of... well, stuff.

Charles Bridge Museum   MUSEUM
(Muzeum Karlova Mostu; Map p288; ☎776 776 779; www.charlesbridgemuseum.com; Křížovnické náměstí 3; adult/concession 150/70Kč; ⊙10am-8pm May-Sep, to 6pm Oct-Apr; ☒17, 18) Founded in the 13th century, the Order of the Knights of the Cross with the Red Star were the guardians of Judith Bridge (and its successor Charles Bridge), with their 'mother house' at the Church of St Francis Seraphinus on Křížovnické náměstí. This museum, housed in the order's headquarters, covers the history of Prague's most famous landmark.

☞ Tours

Amazing Walks of Prague   WALKING TOUR
(☎777 069 685; www.amazingwalks.com; per person 300-500Kč) Guide Roman Bílý is especially strong on WWII, the communist era and the Jewish Quarter.

Prague Walks   WALKING TOUR
(☎222 322 309; www.praguewalks.com; per person 220-990Kč) Runs interesting walking tours with themes such as Prague architecture, Žižkov pubs and the Velvet Revolution. Meet at the Astronomical Clock, or you can arrange to be met at your hotel.

Wittmann Tours   GUIDED TOUR
(Map p288; ☎222 252 472; www.wittmann-tours.com; Novotného lávka 5; per person 880Kč ; ⊙Josefov tours 10.30am & 2pm Sun-Fri mid-Mar-Dec; ☒17, 18) Offers a three-hour walking tour of Josefov, and seven-hour day trips to Terezín (1250Kč per person), daily May to October, four times a week April, November and December.

✯ Festivals & Events

Prague Spring   CLASSICAL MUSIC
(www.festival.cz; ⊙May) The Czech Republic's biggest annual cultural event, and one of Europe's most important festivals of classical music.

Khamoro   MUSIC & CULTURE
(www.khamoro.cz; ⊙late May) Annual celebration of Roma culture.

Prague Fringe Festival   ARTS
(www.praguefringe.com; ⊙late May-early Jun) Eclectic action.

Christmas Market   SEASONAL
(⊙1-24 Dec) In Old Town Sq.

🛏 Sleeping

At New Year, Christmas or Easter, and from May to September, book in advance. Prices quoted are for the high season: generally

---

THE STATUES OF CHARLES BRIDGE

The Charles Bridge is known best of all for its statues that line the bridge on both sides. The statues were not part of the original design but were added centuries later as part of the Austrian Habsburgs' efforts to convert sceptical Czechs to Catholicism.

The first monument erected on the bridge was the crucifix near the eastern end, in 1657. The first statue – the Jesuits' 1683 tribute to St John of Nepomuk – inspired other Catholic orders, and over the next 30 years a score more went up, like ecclesiastical billboards. New ones were added in the mid-19th century, and one (plus replacements for some lost to floods) was added in the 20th. As most of the statues were carved from soft sandstone, several weathered originals have been replaced with copies.

The most famous figure is the monument to **St John of Nepomuk**. According to the legend on the base of the statue, Wenceslas IV had him trussed up in armour and thrown off the bridge in 1393 for refusing to divulge the queen's confessions (he was her priest), though the real reason had to do with the bitter conflict between church and state; the stars in his halo allegedly followed his corpse down the river. Tradition says that if you rub the bronze plaque, you will one day return to Prague.

VYŠEHRAD: WHERE IT ALL BEGAN

Legend has it that **Vyšehrad** (Map p278; www.praha-vysehrad.cz; ☉9.30am-6pm Apr-Oct, to 5pm Nov-Mar; Ⓜ Vyšehrad) hill, south of Nové Město, is the place where Prague was born. According to myth, a wise chieftain named Krok built a castle here in the 7th century, and Libuše, the cleverest of his three daughters, prophesied that a great city would arise here. Taking as her king a ploughman named Přemysl, she founded both the city of Prague and the Přemysl dynasty.

While this is probably not entirely true, the site may have been permanently settled as early as the 9th century, and early ruler Boleslav II (r 972–99) lived here for a time. By the mid-11th century there was a fortified settlement, and Vratislav II (r 1061–92) moved his court here from Hradčany, beefing up the walls and adding a castle, the **Basilica of St Lawrence** (Map p278; admission 10Kč; ☉11am-5pm Mon-Fri, 11.30am-4pm Sat & Sun), the original **Church of SS Peter & Paul** (Kostel sv Petra a Pavla; Map p278; ☎249 113 353; www.praha-vysehrad.cz; K Rotundé 10, Vyšehrad; adult/child 30/10Kč; ☉9am-noon & 1-5pm Wed-Mon; Ⓜ Vyšehrad) and the **Rotunda of St Martin** (Rotunda sv Martina; Map p278; ☎241 410 348; www.praha-vysehrad.cz; V Pevnosti, Vyšehrad; ☉open only during mass; Ⓜ Vyšehrad). His successors stayed until 1140, when Vladislav II returned to Hradčany.

Charles IV was well aware of Vyšehrad's symbolic importance. In the 14th century, he repaired the walls and joined them to those of his new town, Nové Město. He built a small palace, no longer standing, and decreed that the coronations of Bohemian kings should begin with a procession from here to Hradčany.

Nearly everything was wiped out during the Hussite Wars of the 15th century. The fortress remained a ruin – except for a ramshackle township of artisans and traders – until after the Thirty Years' War, when Leopold I refortified it. Vyšehrad served as an Austrian fortress in the late 17th and18th centuries and was occupied for a time by both the French and the Prussians. These days it's peaceful park and a great spot to throw down a blanket and uncork a bottle of wine.

Don't miss **Vyšehrad Cemetery** (Vyšehradský hřbitov; Map p278; ☎249 198 815; www.praha-vysehrad.cz; K Rotundé 10, Vyšehrad ; ☉8am-7pm May-Sep, shorter hr rest of yr; Ⓜ Vyšehrad), the city's most prestigious burial ground and the final resting place of dozens of Czech luminaries, including composers Antonín Dvořák and Bedřich Smetana and artist Alfons Mucha.

April to October. For better value stay outside of the Old Town (Staré Město) and take advantage of Prague's excellent public transport network.

HRADČANY & MALÁ STRANA
Golden Well Hotel   HOTEL €€€
(Map p282; ☎257 011 213; www.goldenwell.cz; U Zlaté Studně 4; d/ste from 6250/12,500Kč; Ⓟ❄✳@☎; Ⓜ Malostranská) The Golden Well is one of Malá Strana's hidden secrets, tucked away at the end of a cobbled cul-de-sac – a Renaissance house that once belonged to Emperor Rudolf II, perched on the southern slope of the castle hill. The rooms are quiet and spacious, with polished wood floors, reproduction period furniture, and blue-and-white bathrooms with underfloor heating.

Domus Henrici   HOTEL €€
(Map p278; ☎220 511 369; www.domus-henrici. cz; Loretánská 11; d/ste from 3250/4000Kč; @☎)

🚌22, 25) This historic building in a quiet corner of Hradčany is intentionally nondescript out front, hinting that peace and privacy are top priorities here. There are eight spacious and stylish rooms, half with private fax, scanner/copier and internet access (via an ethernet port), and all with polished wood floors, large bathrooms, comfy beds and fluffy bathrobes.

Lokál Inn   INN €€
(Map p278; ☎257 014 800; www.lokalinn.cz; Míšeňská 12; d/ste from 3475/4475Kč; ⊖☎; 🚌12, 20, 22) Polished parquet floors and painted wooden ceilings abound in this 18th-century house designed by Prague's premier baroque architect, Kilian Dientzenhofer. The eight rooms and four suites are elegant and uncluttered, and the rustic, stone-vaulted cellars house a deservedly popular pub and restaurant run by the same folk as Lokál (p292).

Hotel Neruda
BOUTIQUE HOTEL €€

(Map p278; ☎257 535 557; www.hotelneruda.cz; Nerudova 44; r from 2225Kč; ☻❋☎; ☐12, 20, 22) Set in a tastefully renovated Gothic house dating from 1348, the Neruda has decor that is chic and minimalist in neutral tones enlivened by the odd splash of colour, with a lovely glass-roofed atrium and a sunny roof terrace. The bedrooms share the modern, minimalist decor and are mostly reasonably sized.

STARÉ MĚSTO

Residence Karolina
APARTMENT €€

(Map p288; ☎224 990 900; www.residence-karolina.com; Karoliny Světlé 4; 2-/4-person apt 3175/5475Kč; ☻@☎; ☐6, 9, 19, 21, 22) We're going to have to invent a new category of accommodation – boutique apartments – to cover this array of 20 beautifully furnished flats. Offering one- or two-bedroom options, all apartments have spacious seating areas with comfy sofas and flat-screen TVs, sleek modern kitchens and dining areas.

Savic Hotel
HOTEL €€€

(Map p288; ☎224 248 555; www.savic.eu; Jilská 7; r from 4125Kč; ❋@☎; Ⓜ Můstek) From the complimentary glass of wine when you arrive to the comfy king-size beds, the Savic certainly knows how to make you feel welcome. Housed in the former monastery of St Giles, the hotel is bursting with character and full of delightful period details including old stone fireplaces, beautiful painted timber ceilings and fragments of frescoes.

Perla Hotel
BOUTIQUE HOTEL €€

(Map p288; ☎221 667 707; www.perlahotel.cz; Perlová 1; s/d from 1975/2225Kč; ☻☎; Ⓜ Můstek) The 'Pearl' on Pearl St is typical of the slinky, appealing designer hotels that have sprung up all over central Prague. Here the designer has picked a – surprise, surprise – pearl motif that extends from the giant pearls that form the reception desk to the silky, lustrous bedspreads and huge screen prints on the bedroom walls.

Old Prague Hostel
HOSTEL €

(Map p288; ☎224 829 058; www.oldpraguehostel.com; Benediktská 2; dm/s/d from 375/1000/1200Kč; ☻@☎; Ⓜ Náměstí Republiky) Cheerful and welcoming, with colourful homemade murals brightening the walls, this is one of Prague's most sociable hostels, with a good mix of people from backpackers to families. Facilities are good, with lockers in the dorms, luggage storage and 24-hour reception, though the mattresses on the bunks are a bit on the thin side.

NOVÉ MĚSTO

Mosaic House
HOTEL, HOSTEL €€

(Map p288; ☎221 595 350; www.mosaichouse.com; Odboru 4; dm/s/d from 300/1840/2520Kč; ☻☎; Ⓜ Karlovo Náměstí) A blend of four-star hotel and boutique hostel, Mosaic House is a cornucopia of designer detail, from the original 1930s' mosaic in the entrance hall to the silver spray-painted tree branches used as clothes-hanging racks. The backpackers dorms are kept separate from the private rooms, but have the same high-quality decor and design.

Fusion Hotel
BOUTIQUE HOTEL, HOSTEL €

(Map p288; ☎226 222 800; www.fusionhotels.com; Panská 9; dm/d/tr 400/2000/2600Kč; @☎; ☐3, 9, 14, 24) Billing itself as an 'affordable design hotel', Fusion certainly has style in abundance. From the revolving bar and the funky sofas that litter the public areas, to the individually decorated bedrooms that resemble miniature modern-art galleries – all white walls and black trim with tiny splashes of colour – the place exudes 'cool'.

Icon Hotel
BOUTIQUE HOTEL €€€

(Map p288; ☎221 634 100; www.iconhotel.eu; V ámé 6; r from 3000Kč; ❋@☎; ☐3, 9, 14, 24) Staff clothes by Diesel, computers by Apple, beds by Hästens – pretty much everything in this gorgeous boutique hotel has a designer stamp on it. Appearing on Europe's trendiest hotels lists, the Icon's sleekly minimalist rooms are enlivened with a splash of purple from the silky bedspreads, while the curvy,

---

ACCOMMODATION AGENCIES

Useful accommodation agencies include the following:

Hostel.cz (☎415 658 580; www.hostel.cz) Website database of hostels and budget hotels, with a secure online booking system.

Mary's Travel & Tourist Service (Map p278; ☎222 254 007; www.marys.cz; Italská 31, Vinohrady; ⊙9am-7pm Mon-Fri, 10am-5pm Sat & Sun) Friendly, efficient agency offering private rooms, hostels, pensions, apartments and hotels in all price ranges in Prague and surrounding areas.

Central Prague

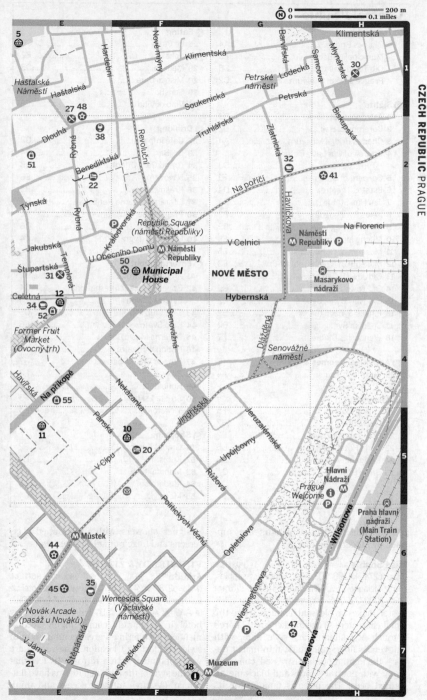

0 200 m
0 0.1 miles

E F G H

5

Klimentská

Haštalské
Náměstí
Haštalská

Nové mlýny

Klimentská

Barvířská

Samcova

Mlynářská

30

Petrské
náměstí

Lodecká

Petrská

Biskupská

27 48

Soukenická

Truhlářská

Dlouhá

Rybná

38

Revoluční

Zlatnická

32

41

Benediktská

Na poříčí

22

Týnská

Rybná

Havlíčkova

Králodvorská

Na Florenci

Republic Square
(náměstí Republiky)

Jakubská

Templová

U Obecního Domu

V Celnici

Náměstí
Republiky

Náměstí
Republiky

Štupartská

50

NOVÉ MĚSTO

31

Municipal
House

Masarykovo
nádraží

Celetná

12

34

Hybernská

52

Former Fruit
Market
(Ovocný trh)

Senovážná

Dlážděná

Senovážné
náměstí

Havířská

Na příkopě

Nekázanka

Jindřišská

55

Panská

11

10

Jeruzalémská

20

V Cípu

Spálená

Opletalova

Politických Vězňů

Růžová

Hlavní
Nádraží

Prague
Welcome

Praha hlavní
nádraží
(Main Train
Station)

Wilsonova

Můstek

44

45

35

Wenceslas Square
(Václavské
náměstí)

Novák Arcade
(pasáž u Nováků)

Štěpánská

Washingtonova

47

Legerova

V Jámě

21

Ve Smečkách

18

Muzeum

E F G H

Central Prague

⊙ Top Sights

⊙ Sights

✪ Activities, Courses & Tours

🛏 Sleeping

⊗ Eating

⊖ Drinking

✪ Entertainment

⊕ Shopping

reproduction art-deco armchairs are supplied by Modernista (p297).

Miss Sophie's
HOSTEL €

(Map p278; ☎296 303 530; www.miss-sophies. com; Melounova 3; dm from 410Kč, s/d/apt 1760/2000/2360Kč; ✉@☎; ⓂIP Pavlova) This hostel makes a pleasant change from the usual characterless backpacker hive. There's a touch of contemporary style here, with oak-veneer floors and stark, minimalist decor – the main motif is 'distressed' concrete, along with neutral colours and black metal-framed beds. The place is famous for its

'designer' showers, with autographed glass screens and huge rainfall shower heads.

VINOHRADY & ŽIŽKOV
Arkada
BOUTIQUE HOTEL €€

(Map p278; ☎242 429 111; www.arkadahotel.cz; Balbínova 8, Vinohrady; s/d from 1750/2250Kč; Ⓟ✉@☎; ⓂMuzeum, ☖11) This relatively new hotel in Vinohrady comes highly recommended for offering a great combination of style, comfort and location. The rooms are well appointed, with a retro-1930s feel that fits the style of the building. Rooms have flat-screen TVs, free internet access and minibars. Ask to see a couple before choosing, since the decor differs from room to room.

Czech Inn
HOSTEL, HOTEL €

(Map p278; ☑267 267 600; www.czech-inn.com; Francouzská 76, Vinohrady; dm 285-385Kč, s/d 1320/1540Kč, apt from 1650Kč; P🐾💬@🛜; 🚊4, 22) The Czech Inn calls itself a hostel, but the boutique label wouldn't be out of place. Everything seems sculpted by an industrial designer, from the iron beds to the brushed-steel flooring and minimalist square sinks. The Czech Inn offers a variety of accommodation, from standard hostel dorm rooms to good-value private doubles (with or without attached bathroom) and apartments.

Pension Královský Vinohrad
PENSION €

(Map p278; ☑222 515 093; www.kralovskyvinohrad. cz; Šmilovského 10, Vinohrady; d from 1500Kč, ste from 2100Kč; P🐾@; 🚊4, 22) This pension occupies a lovely 1910 apartment building in a leafy backstreet. The cheaper rooms are plain but functional, while the larger rooms and 'suites' (two-room apartments) are more stylishly decorated and furnished with antiques and stripped pine furniture. The suites also have minibars and tables and chairs. Offers steep discounts on the website.

Hostel Elf
HOSTEL €

(Map p278; ☑222 540 963; www.hostelelf. com; Husitská 11, Žižkov; dm from 340Kč, s/d 1230/1960Kč; @🛜; MFlorenc) Young, hip and sociable, Hostel Elf welcomes a steady stream of party-hearty backpackers from across the globe to its well-maintained dorms. The dorms are immaculately clean and brightly decorated with graffiti art and murals. There's a little beer-garden terrace and cosy lounge, with free tea and coffee and cheap beer, and Žižkov with its pubs is right on the doorstep.

HOLEŠOVICE
Absolutum Hotel
BOUTIQUE HOTEL €€

(Map p278; ☑222 541 406; www.absolutumhotel.cz; Jablonského 639/4; s/d 2500/3200Kč; P🐾❄@🛜; MNádraží Holešovice, 🚋Praha-Holešovice) A highly recommended, eye-catching boutique hotel, the Absolutum is located across from Nádraží Holešovice metro station. While the neighbourhood wouldn't win a beauty contest, the hotel compensates with a nice list of amenities, including beautifully designed rooms with exposed brickwork, well-appointed modern bathrooms (many rooms have a tub), air-conditioning, an excellent restaurant, a wellness centre and free parking.

Sir Toby's Hostel
HOSTEL €

(Map p278; ☑246 032 610; www.sirtobys.com; Dělnická 24; dm 200-400Kč, s/d 950/1200Kč; P🐾💬@🛜; 🚊1, 3, 5, 25) Set in a refurbished apartment building with a spacious kitchen and common room, Sir Toby's is only 10 minutes north of the city centre by tram. The dorms have between six and 10 bunks, including all-female rooms, and the bigger dorms are some of the cheapest in Prague. All rooms are light and clean, but don't expect anything fancy.

Hotel Leon
HOSTEL, HOTEL €

(Map p278; ☑220 941 351; www.antee.cz; Ortenovo náměstí 26; s/d from 940/1440Kč; P🐾💬; MNádraží Holešovice, 🚊5, 12, 15) The Hotel Leon advertises itself as something between a hostel and a small hotel. In truth, it's actually much nicer than a standard hostel and not much more expensive (especially if you share a three- or four-bed room). The rooms are basic, with no TV or much of anything else, but are quiet and clean, with adjoining bathrooms.

✖️ Eating

Eating in Prague's tourist areas is pricey, but cheaper eats are available just a block or two away. Regular lunch specials (look for *denní menu* in Czech) will stretch your travel budget. Most restaurants open from 11am to 11pm.

HRADČANY & MALÁ STRANA
Café Lounge
CAFE €

(Map p278; ☑257 404 020; www.cafe-lounge.cz; Plaská 8; mains 100-300Kč; ⏰7.30am-10pm Mon-Fri, 9am-1pm Sat, 9am-5pm Sun; 🐾🛜; 🚊6, 9, 12, 20, 22) Cosy and welcoming, Café Lounge sports an art-deco atmosphere, superb coffee, exquisite pastries and an extensive wine list. The all-day cafe menu offers freshly made salads and cornbread sandwiches, while lunch and dinner extends to dishes such as venison goulash or roast pike-perch with caraway seeds.

Lichfield
INTERNATIONAL €€

(Map p278; ☑266 112 284; www.theaugustine. com; Letenská 12; mains 270-460Kč; ⏰11am-11pm; 🛜; 🚊12, 20, 22) Named after society photographer Lord Lichfield, whose images of celebrities adorn the walls, this stylish yet relaxed restaurant is worth seeking out (it's hidden away in the Augustine Hotel). The menu ranges from down-to-earth but delicious dishes such as ox cheeks braised

WANT MORE?

For in-depth information, reviews and recommendations at your fingertips, head to the Apple App Store to purchase Lonely Planet's *Prague City Guide* and *Czech Phrasebook* iPhone apps.

Alternatively, head to www.lonelyplanet.com/czech-republic/prague for planning advice, author recommendations, traveller reviews and insider tips.

in the restaurant's own St Thomas beer, to top-end favourites such as grilled lobster and caviar.

Cukrkávalimonáda   INTERNATIONAL €

(CKL; Map p278; ☑257 225 396; www.cukrkavalimonada.com; Lázeňská 7; mains 100-180Kč; ◴9am-7pm; ▣12, 20, 22) A cute little cafe-cum-restaurant that combines minimalist modern styling with Renaissance-era painted timber roof-beams, CKL offers fresh pastas, frittatas, ciabattas, salads and pancakes (sweet and savoury) by day and a slightly more sophisticated bistro menu in the early evening. There's also a good breakfast menu offering ham and eggs, croissants, and yoghurt, and the hot chocolate is to die for.

U Modré Kachničky   CZECH €€€

(Map p278; ☑257 320 308; www.umodrekachnicky.cz; Nebovidská 6; mains 450-600Kč; ◴noon-4pm & 6.30pm-midnight; ▣12, 20, 22) A plush 1930s-style hunting lodge hidden away on a quiet side street, 'At the Blue Duckling' is a pleasantly old-fashioned place with quiet, candlelit nooks perfect for a romantic dinner. The menu is heavy on traditional Bohemian duck and game dishes, such as roast duck with *slivovice* (plum brandy), plum sauce and potato pancakes.

Café de Paris   FRENCH €€

(Map p278; ☑603 160 718; www.cafedeparis.cz; Maltézské náměstí 4; mains 230-290Kč; ◴noon-midnight; ▣12, 20, 22) A little corner of France tucked away on a quiet square, the Café de Paris is straightforward and unpretentious. So is the menu – just a couple of choices, onion soup or foie gras terrine to start, followed by entrecôte steak with chips, salad and a choice of sauces (they're very proud of the Café de Paris sauce, made to a 75-year-old recipe with 35 ingredients).

STARÉ MĚSTO

Mistral Café   BISTRO €

(Map p288; ☑222 317 737; www.mistralcafe.cz; Valentinská 11; mains 130-250Kč; ◴9am-11pm Mon-Fri, 10am-11pm Sat & Sun; ☎; ⓜStaroměstská) Is this the coolest bistro in the Old Town? Pale stone, bleached birchwood and potted shrubs make for a clean, crisp, modern look, and the clientele of local students and office workers clearly appreciate the competitively priced, well-prepared food. Fish and chips in crumpled brown paper with lemon and black-pepper mayo – yum!

Maitrea   VEGETARIAN €

(Map p288; ☑221 711 631; www.restaurace-maitrea.cz; Týnská ulička 6; mains 130-160Kč; ◴11.30am-11.30pm Mon-Fri, noon-11.30pm Sat & Sun; ☑; ⓜStaroměstská) Maitrea (a Buddhist term meaning 'the future Buddha') is a beautifully designed space full of flowing curves and organic shapes, from the sensuous polished-oak furniture and fittings to the blossom-like lampshades. The menu is inventive and wholly vegetarian, with dishes such as red bean chilli tortillas, beetroot cakes with sauerkraut and polenta, and pasta with smoked tofu, spinach and parmesan.

Vino di Vino   ITALIAN €€

(Map p288; ☑222 311 791; www.vinodivinopraha.cz; Štupartská 18; mains 250-300Kč; ◴noon-10pm; ⓜNáměstí Republiky) This Italian wine shop and delicatessen doubles as a restaurant, with a menu that makes the most of all those imported goodies – bresaola with smoked mozzarella, *spaghetti alla chitarra* (with squid and pecorino), and *saltimbocca alla Romana* (beef fillet with prosciutto and sage). Good list of Italian wines, too, including excellent Montepulciano d'Abbruzzo at 590Kč a bottle.

Lokál   CZECH €

(Map p288; ☑222 316 265; lokal-dlouha.ambi.cz; Dlouhá 33; mains 100-200Kč; ◴11am-1am Mon-Fri, noon-1am Sat, noon-10pm Sun; ☎; ▣5, 8, 14) Who'd have thought it possible? A classic Czech beer hall (albeit with slick modern decor); excellent *tankové pivo* (tanked Pilsner Urquell); a daily changing menu of traditional Bohemian dishes; smiling, efficient, friendly service; and a no-smoking area!

NOVÉ MĚSTO & VINOHRADY

Sansho   ASIAN, FUSION €€

(Map p288; ☑222 317 425; www.sansho.cz; Petrská 25; mains 120-300Kč, 6-course dinner

750Kč; ⏰11.30am-10.30pm Tue-Thu, to 11.30pm Fri, 6-11.30pm Sat; ☺; 🚇3, 8, 24) Friendly and informal best describes the atmosphere at this ground-breaking restaurant where British chef Paul Day champions Czech farmers by sourcing all his meat and vegetables locally. There's no menu – the waiter will explain what dishes are available, depending on market produce – typical dishes include salmon sashimi, pork belly with Asian spices, and 12-hour beef rendang.

Kofein   SPANISH €€
(Map p278; ☎273 132 145; www.ikofein.cz; Nitranská 9, Vinohrady; tapas plates 55-75Kč; ⏰11am-midnight Mon-Fri, 5pm-midnight Sat & Sun; 🕱⏰; Ⓜ Jiřího z Poděbrad, 🚇11) One of the hottest restaurants in town is this Spanish-style tapas place not far from the Jiřího z Poděbrad metro station. Descend into a lively space to see a red-faced chef minding the busy grill. Our faves include marinated trout with horseradish and pork belly confit with celeriac. Book ahead.

Mozaika   INTERNATIONAL €€
(Map p278; ☎224 253 011; www.restaurantmozaika. cz; Nitranská 13, Vinohrady; mains 180-450Kč; ☺🕱; Ⓜ Jiřího z Poděbrad) One of the most dependably good restaurants in the neighbourhood. The theme is an updated French bistro, with beef tournedos and *boeuf bourguignon* sharing the spotlight with international entrees such as stir-fries and BBQ pork ribs. Advance booking essential.

Le Patio   INTERNATIONAL €€
(Map p288; ☎224 934 375; www.lepatio.cz; Národní třída 22; mains 200-420Kč; ⏰8am-11pm Mon-Fri, 9am-11pm Sat & Sun; Ⓜ Můstek) It's easy to walk past this place on bustling Národní třída without noticing it, but it's well worth dropping in to sample its accomplished menu of local and international dishes in a relaxed atmosphere that hints of oriental travel – a ship's prow, lots of Asian-style lamps, paintings and textiles.

Aromi   ITALIAN €€€
(Map p278; ☎222 713 222; www.aromi.cz; Mánesova 78, Vinohrady; mains 400-600Kč; ⏰noon-11pm Mon-Sat, to 10pm Sun; 🕱; Ⓜ Jiřího z Poděbrad, 🚇11) Red brick, polished wood and country-style furniture create a rustic atmosphere in this gourmet Italian restaurant. Brisk and businesslike at lunchtime, romantic in the evening, Aromi has a reputation for authentic, excellent Italian cuisine. Advance booking essential.

🍷 Drinking

Czech beers are among the world's best. The most famous brands are Budvar, Plzeňský Prazdroj (Pilsner Urquell) and Prague's own Staropramen. Independent microbreweries and regional Czech beers are also becoming more popular in Prague.

Bars & Pubs
Prague Beer Museum   PUB
(Map p288; ☎732 330 912; www.praguebeermuseum.com; Dlouhá 46; ⏰noon-3am; 🚇5, 8, 14) Although the name seems aimed at the tourist market, this lively and always heaving pub is very popular with Praguers. There are no fewer than 31 beers on tap (plus an extensive beer menu with tasting notes to guide you).

TOP CHOICE Pivovarský Klub   BEER HALL
(Map p278; ☎222 315 777; www.gastroinfo.cz/pivoklub; Křižíkova 17, Karlín; ⏰11am-11.30pm; Ⓜ Florenc) This bar is to beer what the Bodleian Library is to books – wall-to-wall shelves lined with myriad varieties of bottled beer from all over the world, and six guest beers on tap. Perch on a bar stool or head downstairs to the snug cellar and order some of the pub's excellent grub (such as authentic *guláš* with bacon dumplings for 235Kč) to soak up the beer.

TOP CHOICE Letná Beer Garden   BEER GARDEN
(Letenský zámeček; Map p278; ☎233 378 208; www.letenskyzamecek.cz; Letenské sady 341, Bubeneč; ⏰11am-11pm summer only; 🚇1, 8, 15, 25, 26 to Letenské náměstí) No accounting of watering holes would be complete without a nod toward the city's best beer garden, situated at the eastern end of Letna park. Buy a takeaway beer from a small kiosk and grab a picnic table, or sit on a small terrace where you can order beer-by-the-glass and decent pizza.

Pivovarský Dům   BREWERY
(Map p278; ☎296 216 666; www.gastroinfo.cz/pivodum; cnr Ječná & Lipová; ⏰11am-11pm; 🚇4, 6, 10, 16, 22) While the tourists flock to U Fleků, locals gather here to sample the classic Czech lager (40Kč per 0.5L) that is produced on the premises, as well as wheat beer and a range of flavoured beers (including coffee, banana and cherry, 40Kč per 0.3L).

Bukowski's   COCKTAIL BAR
(Map p278; ☎222 212 676; Bořivojova 86, Žižkov; ⏰6pm-2am; 🚇5, 9, 26) Like many of the drinking dens that are popular among expats,

Bukowski's is more a cocktail dive than a cocktail bar. Named after hard-drinking American writer Charles Bukowski, it cultivates a dark and slightly debauched atmosphere – the decor is self-consciously 'interesting' (when you can see it through the smoke-befogged candlelight).

TOP CHOICE U Vystřeleného oka
PUB

(Map p278; ☑222 540 465; www.uvoka.cz; U Božích Bojovníků 3, Žižkov; ⊗4.30pm-1am Mon-Sat; ☐133, 207) You've got to love a pub that has vinyl pads on the wall above the gents' urinals to rest your forehead on. 'The Shot-Out Eye' – the name pays homage to the one-eyed Hussite hero atop the hill behind the pub – is a bohemian (with a small 'b') hostelry with a raucous Friday-night atmosphere where the cheap Pilsner Urquell pulls in a typically heterogeneous Žižkov crowd.

Čili Bar
COCKTAIL BAR

(Map p288; ☑777 945 848; www.cilibar.cz; Kožná 8; ⊗5pm-2am; MMůstek) This tiny cocktail bar could not be further removed in atmosphere from your typical Old Town drinking place. Cramped and smoky – there are Cuban cigars for sale – with battered leather armchairs competing for space with a handful of tables, it's friendly, relaxed and lively.

U Medvídků
BEER HALL

(At the Little Bear; Map p288; ☑224 211 916; www.umedvidku.cz; Na Perštýně 7; ⊗beer hall 11.30am-11pm, museum noon-10pm; ☎; MMůstek) The most micro of Prague's microbreweries, with a capacity of only 250L, U Medvídků started producing its own beer only in 2005, though its beer hall has been around for years. What it lacks in size, it makes up for in strength – the dark lager produced here is the strongest in the country, with an alcohol content of 11.8%.

U Zlatého Tygra
PUB

(Map p288; ☑222 221 111; www.uzlatehotygra.cz; Husova 17; ⊗3-11pm; MStaroměstská) The 'Golden Tiger' is one of the few Old Town drinking holes that has hung onto its soul, considering its location. It was novelist Bohumil Hrabal's favourite hostelry – there are photos of him on the walls – and the place that Václav Havel took Bill Clinton in 1994 to show him a real Czech pub.

Cafes
Krásný ztráty
CAFE

(Map p288; ☑775 755 143; www.krasnyztraty.cz; Náprstkova 10; ⊗9am-1am Mon-Fri, noon-1am Sat & Sun; ☎; ☐17, 18) This cool cafe doubles as an art gallery and occasional music venue, and is hugely popular with students from nearby Charles University. There are Czech newspapers and books to leaf through, chilled tunes on the sound system, and a menu of gourmet teas and coffees to choose from.

Kávovarna
CAFE

(Map p288; ☑296 236 233; Štěpánská 61, Pasáž Lucerna; ⊗8am-midnight; MMůstek) This retro-styled place has bentwood chairs and curved wooden benches in the smoky, dimly lit front room (there's a nonsmoking room beyond the bar), with exhibitions of arty black-and-white photography on the walls. The coffee is good and reasonably priced, and there's delicious Kout na Šumavě beer on tap at a very reasonable 37Kč per half litre.

Café Imperial
CAFE

(Map p288; ☑246 011 440; www.cafeimperial.cz; Na Poříčí 15; ⊗7am-11pm; MNáměstí Republiky) First opened in 1914, and given a complete facelift in 2007, the Imperial is a tour de force of art nouveau tiling – the walls and ceiling are covered in original ceramic tiles, mosaics, sculptured panels and bas-reliefs. The coffee is good, there are cocktails in the evening, and the Czech lunch and dinner offerings are first rate.

Literární Kavárna Řetězová
CAFE

(Map p288; ☑222 220 681; Řetězová 10; ⊗noon-11pm Mon-Fri, 5-11pm Sat & Sun; ☐17, 21) This is the kind of place where you can imagine yourself tapping out the Great Prague Novel on your laptop with a half-finished coffee on the table beside you. It's a plain, vaulted room with battered wooden furniture, a scatter of rugs on the floor and old black-and-white photos on the wall.

Grand Cafe Orient
CAFE

(Map p288; Ovocný trh 19, Nové Město; MNáměstí Republiky) Prague's only cubist café, the Orient was designed by Josef Gočár and is cubist down to the smallest detail, including the lampshades and coat-hooks. It was restored and reopened in 2005, having been closed since 1920. Decent coffee and inexpensive cocktails.

☆ Entertainment

From clubbing to classical music, puppetry to performance art, Prague offers plenty of entertainment. It's an established centre of classical music and jazz. For current listings see www.prague.tv. Try the following ticket agencies to see what might be on during your visit and to snag tickets online: **Bohemia Ticket International** (BTI; Map p288; ☑224 227 832; www.ticketsbti.cz; Malé náměstí 13; ⏱9am-5pm Mon-Fri), **Ticketpro** (Map p288; www.ticketpro.cz; Vodičkova 36, Pasáž Lucerna, Nové Město; ⏱noon-4pm & 4.30-8.30pm Mon-Fri) and **Ticketstream** (www.ticketstream.cz).

Performing Arts

Prague offers a nightly array of classic music, dance, opera and theatre in season (September to May). Buy tickets in advance at venue box offices or at the theatre an hour before the performance starts.

National Theatre
OPERA, BALLET

(Národní divadlo; Map p288; ☑224 901 377; www.narodni-divadlo.cz; Národní třída 2; tickets 30-1000Kč; ⏱box offices 10am-6pm; ☐6, 9, 18, 21, 22) The much-loved National Theatre provides a stage for traditional opera, drama and ballet by the likes of Smetana, Shakespeare and Tchaikovsky, sharing the program alongside more modern works by composers and playwrights such as Philip Glass and John Osborne. The box offices are in the Nový síň building next door, and in the Kolowrat Palace (opposite the Estates Theatre).

Prague State Opera
OPERA, BALLET

(Státní opera Praha; Map p288; ☑224 901 886; www.opera.cz; Wilsonova 4; opera tickets 100-1150Kč, ballet tickets 100-800Kč; ⏱box office 10am-5.30pm Mon-Fri, 10am-noon & 1-5.30pm Sat & Sun; Ⓜ Muzeum) The impressive neo-rococo home of the Prague State Opera provides a glorious setting for performances of classical, mostly Italian, opera and ballet.

Smetana Hall
CLASSICAL MUSIC

(Smetanova síň; Map p288; ☑222 002 101; www.obecnidum.cz; náměstí Republiky 5; tickets 250-600Kč; ⏱box office 10am-6pm; Ⓜ Náměstí Republiky) Smetana Hall is the home venue of the Prague Symphony Orchestra (Symfonický orchestr hlavního města Prahy), and also stages performances of folk dance and music.

Rudolfinum
LIVE MUSIC

(Map p288; ☑227 059 227; www.ceskafilharmonie.cz; náměstí Jana Palacha, Staré Město; ⏱box office 10am-6pm Mon-Fri; Ⓜ Staroměstska) One of Prague's main venues for classical music concerts is the Dvořák Hall in the neo-Renaissance Ruldolfinum, home to the Czech Philharmonic Orchestra.

Estates Theatre
OPERA, BALLET

(Stavovské divadlo; Map p288; ☑224 902 322; www.narodni-divadlo.cz; Ovocný trh 1; tickets 30-1260Kč; ⏱box office 10am-6pm; Ⓜ Můstek) The Estates Theatre (p281) is the oldest theatre in Prague, famed as the place where Mozart conducted the premiere of *Don Giovanni* on 29 October 1787. The repertoire includes various opera, ballet and drama productions.

Archa Theatre
THEATRE

(Divadlo Archa; Map p288; ☑221 716 111; www.archatheatre.cz; Na poříčí 26; tickets 150-880Kč; ⏱box office 10am-6pm Mon-Fri; ☐5, 8, 14) The Archa has been described as Prague's alternative National Theatre, a multifunctional venue for the avant garde and the experimental. As well as contemporary drama (occasionally in English), dance and performance art, the theatre also stages live music, from Indian classical to indie rock.

Švandovo Divadlo Na Smíchově
THEATRE

(Šandovo Theatre in Smíchov; Map p278; ☑257 318 666; www.svandovodivadlo.cz; Stefaníkova 57, Smíchov; tickets 150-300Kč; ⏱box office 11am-2pm & 2.30-7pm Mon-Fri, 5-7pm Sat & Sun; ☐6, 9, 12, 20) This experimental theatre space, performing Czech and international dramatic works, is admired for its commitment to staging 'English-friendly' performances. It also hosts occasional live music and dance, as well as regular 'Stage Talks' – unscripted discussions with noted personalities.

Nightclubs

Cross Club
CLUB

(Map p278; ☑736 535 053; www.crossclub.cz; Plynární 23, Holešovice; admission free-150Kč; ⏱cafe noon-2am, club 6pm-4am; ☎; Ⓜ Nádraží Holešovice) An industrial club in every sense of the word: the setting in an industrial zone; the thumping music (both DJs and live acts); and the interior, an absolute must-see jumble of gadgets, shafts, cranks and pipes, many of which move and pulsate with light to the music. The program includes occasional live music, theatre performances and art happenings.

Roxy
CLUB, PERFORMING ARTS

(Map p288; ☑224 826 296; www.roxy.cz; Dlouhá 33; admission Fri & Sat free-300Kč; ⏱7pm-midnight Mon-Thu, to 6am Fri & Sat; ☐5, 8, 14) Set in the ramshackle shell of an art-deco cinema, the legendary Roxy is the place to see the country's top DJs and frequent live acts. On the 1st floor is NoD, an 'experimental space' that stages drama, dance, performance art, cinema and live music.

TOP CHOICE **Sasazu** CLUB

(Map p278; ☎284 097 455; www.sasazu.com; block 25, Holešovice market, Bubenské nábřeží 306, Holešovice; admission 200-1000Kč; ⏱9pm-5am; ☜; ⓂVltavská, 🚋1, 3, 5, 25) One of the most popular dance clubs in the city, Sasazu attracts the fashionable elite and hangers-on in equal measure. If you're into big dance floors and long lines (hint: go early), this is your place.

Radost FX CLUB

(Map p278; ☎224 254 776; www.radostfx.cz; Bělehradská 120, Vinohrady; admission 100-250Kč; ⏱10pm-6am; ☜; ⓂIP Pavlova) Though not quite as trendy as it once was, slick and shiny Radost is still capable of pulling in the crowds, especially for its Thursday hip-hop and R&B night, **FXbounce** (www.fxbounce.com). The place has a chilled-out, bohemian atmosphere, with an excellent lounge and vegetarian restaurant that keeps serving into the small hours.

Live Music

Palác Akropolis LIVE MUSIC, CLUB

(Map p278; ☎296 330 911; www.palacakropolis.cz; Kubelikova 27, Žižkov; admission free-50Kč; ⏱club 7pm-5am; 🚋5, 9, 26 to Lipanska) The Akropolis is a Prague institution, a labyrinthine, sticky-floored shrine to alternative music and drama. Its various performance spaces host a smorgasbord of musical and cultural events, from DJs to string quartets to Macedonian Roma bands to local rock gods to visiting talent – Marianne Faithfull, the Flaming Lips and the Strokes have all played here.

Lucerna Music Bar LIVE MUSIC

(Map p288; ☎224 217 108; www.musicbar.cz; Palác Lucerna, Vodičkova 36; admission 100-500Kč; ⏱8pm-4am; ⓂMůstek, 🚋3, 9, 14, 24) Nostalgia reigns supreme at this atmospheric old theatre, now looking a little dog-eared, with anything from Beatles tribute bands to mainly Czech artists playing jazz, blues, pop, rock and more on midweek nights. But the most popular events are the regular 1980s and '90s video parties held every Friday and Saturday night.

JazzDock JAZZ

(Map p278; ☎774 058 838; www.jazzdock.cz; Janáčkovo nábřeží 2, Smíchov; admission 90-150Kč; ⏱4pm-3am; ⓂAnděl, 🚋7, 9, 12, 14) Most of Prague's jazz clubs are smoky cellar affairs. This riverside club is a definite step up, with a clean, modern decor and a decidedly romantic view out over the Vltava. This place draws some of the best local talent and oc-casional international acts. Go early or book to get a good table.

Jazz Club U Staré Paní JAZZ

(Map p288; ☎602 148 377; www.jazzstarapani.cz; Michalská 9; admission 250Kč; ⏱7pm-1am Wed-Sun, music from 9pm; ⓂMůstek) Located in the basement of the Hotel U Staré Paní, this long-established but recently revamped jazz club caters to all levels of musical appreciation. There's a varied program of modern jazz, soul, blues and Latin rhythms, and a dinner menu if you want to make a full evening of it.

Gay & Lesbian Venues

The neighbourhood of Vinohrady is developing as a gay quarter, and the city enjoys a relaxed scene.

FREE **Termix** CLUB

(Map p278; ☎222 710 462; www.club-termix.cz; Třebízckého 4a, Vinohrady; ⏱8pm-5am Wed-Sun; ⓂJiřího z Poděbrad) Termix is one of Prague's most popular gay dance clubs, with an industrial high-tech vibe (lots of shiny steel and glass and plush sofas) and a young crowd that contains as many tourists as locals. The smallish dance floor fills up fast and you may have to queue to get in.

ON Club CLUB, LIVE MUSIC

(Map p278; www.onclub.cz; Vinohradská 40, Vinohrady; ⏱10pm-5am; ⓂMuzeum, 🚋11) The ON Club is the latest incarnation in a series of gay and gay-friendly clubs to occupy the cavernous Radio Palác building. The crowd is mostly men, but there are some women, and everyone is welcome. Most nights there's a disco, but weekends usually bring big-name DJs and occasional live music.

Cinemas

Most films are screened in their original language with Czech subtitles (*české titulky*), but some Hollywood blockbusters, especially those aimed at kids, are dubbed into Czech (*dabing*).

Kino Světozor CINEMA

(Map p288; ☎608 330 088; www.kinosvetozor.cz; Vodičkova 41; tickets 90-120Kč; ☜; ⓂMůstek) The Světozor is under the same management as Kino Aero but is more central, and has the same emphasis on classic cinema and art-house films screened in their original language – everything from *Battleship Potemkin* and *Casablanca* to *Annie Hall* and *The Motorcycle Diaries*.

Kino Aero   CINEMA
(☑271 771 349; www.kinoaero.cz; Biskupcova 31, Žižkov; tickets 60-100Kč; ☒5, 9, 10, 16, 19) The Aero is Prague's best-loved art-house cinema, with themed programs, retrospectives and unusual films, often in English or with English subtitles. This is the place to catch reruns of classics from *Smrt v Benátkách (Death in Venice)* to *Život Briana (The Life of Brian)*.

🔒 Shopping

Near Old Town Sq, explore the antique shops of Týnská and Týnská ulička.

Granát Turnov   JEWELLERY
(Map p288; ☑222 315 612; www.granat.eu; Dlouhá 28-30; ☺10am-6pm Mon-Fri, to 1pm Sat; Ⓜ Náměstí Republiky) Part of the country's biggest jewellery chain, Granát Turnov specialises in Bohemian garnet, and has a huge range of gold and silver rings, brooches, cufflinks and necklaces featuring the small, dark, blood-red stones.

Kubista   HOMEWARES
(Map p288; ☑224 236 378; www.kubista.cz; Ovocný trh 19; ☺10am-6pm Tue-Sun; Ⓜ Náměstí Republiky) Appropriately located in the Museum of Czech Cubism in Prague's finest cubist building, this shop specialises in limited-edition reproductions of distinctive cubist furniture and ceramics, and designs by masters of the form such as Josef Gočár and Pavel Janák.

Manufaktura   ARTS & CRAFTS
(Map p288; ☑257 533 678; www.manufaktura.cz; Melantrichova 17; ☺10am-8pm; Ⓜ Můstek) There are several Manufaktura outlets across town, but this small branch near Old Town Sq seems to keep its inventory especially enticing.

Modernista   HOMEWARES
(Map p288; ☑224 241 300; www.modernista.cz; Celetná 12; ☺11am-7pm; Ⓜ Náměstí Republiky) Modernista is an elegant gallery specialising in reproduction 20th-century furniture in classic styles ranging from art deco and cubist to functionalist and Bauhaus. The shop is inside the arcade at Celetná 12 (not visible from the street).

Moser   GLASS
(Map p288; ☑224 211 293; www.moser-glass.com; Na Příkopě 12; ☺10am-8pm; Ⓜ Můstek) One of the most exclusive and respected of Bohemian glassmakers, Moser was founded in Karlovy Vary in 1857 and is famous for its rich and flamboyant designs. The shop on

Na Příkopě is worth a browse as much for the decor as for the goods.

Pivní Galerie   FOOD & DRINK
(Map p278; ☑220 870 613; www.pivnigalerie.cz; U Průhonu 9, Holešovice; ☺noon-7pm Tue-Fri; ☒1, 3, 5, 25) If you think Czech beer begins and ends with Pilsner Urquell, a visit to the tasting room at Pivní Galerie (the Beer Gallery) will lift the scales from your eyes. Here you can sample and purchase a huge range of Bohemian and Moravian beers – nearly 150 varieties from 30 different breweries.

Shakespeare & Sons   BOOKS
(Map p278; ☑257 531 894; www.shakes.cz; U Lužického Semináře 10; ☺11am-7pm; ☒12, 20, 22) Excellent English-language bookshop with heaps of books in several rooms on several levels.

Globe Bookstore & Café   BOOKS
(Map p278; ☑224 934 203; www.globebookstore. cz; Pštrossova 6; ☺9.30am-midnight Sun-Wed, 9.30am-1am Thu-Sat; 🛜; Ⓜ Karlovo Náměstí) A popular hangout for book-loving expats, the Globe is a cosy English-language bookshop with an excellent cafe.

ℹ️ Information

Dangers & Annoyances

Pickpockets work the crowds at the Astronomical Clock, Prague Castle and Charles Bridge, and on the central metro and tramlines, especially crowded trams 9 and 22.

Most taxi drivers are honest, but some operating from tourist areas overcharge their customers. Phone a reputable taxi company or look for the red and yellow signs for the 'Taxi Fair Place' scheme, indicating authorised taxi stands.

The park outside the main train station is a hangout for dodgy types and worth avoiding late at night.

Emergency

If your passport or valuables are stolen, obtain a police report and crime number. You'll need this for an insurance claim. There's usually an English-speaker on hand. The emergency phone number for the police is ☑158.

Internet Access

Many hotels, bars and fast-food restaurants provide wi-fi hotspots.

Globe Bookstore & Café (☑224 934 203; www.globebookstore.cz; Pštrossova 6; per min 1Kč; ☺9.30am-midnight; 🛜; Ⓜ Karlovo Náměstí) No minimum. Also has ethernet ports so you can connect your own laptop, and free wi-fi.

Relax Café-Bar (☑224 211 521; www.relaxcafe-bar.cz; Dlážděná 4; per 15min 20Kč; ☺8am-10pm Mon-Fri, 2-10pm Sat; ☎; MNáměstí Republiky) A conveniently located internet cafe. Wi-fi is free.

Medical Services

Canadian Medical Care (☑235 360 133, 724 300 301; www.cmcpraha.cz; Veleslavínská 1, Veleslavín; ☺8am-6pm Mon-Fri, to 8pm Tue & Thu; ☐20, 26) A pricey but professional private clinic with English-speaking doctors; an initial consultation will cost from 1500Kč to 2500Kč.

Na Homolce Hospital (☑257 271 111; www. homolka.cz; 5th fl, Foreign Pavilion, Roentgenova 2, Motol; ☐167, MAnděl) The best hospital in Prague, equipped and staffed to Western standards, with staff who speak English, French, German and Spanish.

Polyclinic at Národní (Poliklinika na Národní; ☑222 075 120, 24hr emergencies 777 942 270; www.poliklinika.narodni.cz; Národní třída 9, Nové Město; ☺8.30am-5pm Mon-Fri; MMůstek) A central clinic with staff who speak English, German, French and Russian. Expect to pay around 800Kč to 1500Kč for an initial consultation.

Money

The major banks are best for changing cash, but using a debit card in an ATM gives a better rate of exchange. Avoid *směnárna* (private exchange booths), which advertise misleading rates and have exorbitant charges.

Post

Main post office (☑221 131 111; www.cpost. cz; Jindřišská 14, Nové Město; ☺2am-midnight; MMůstek) Collect a ticket from the automated machines outside the main hall (press 1 for stamps and parcels, 4 for Express Mail Service – EMS).

Tourist Information

Prague Welcome (Map p288; ☑221 714 444; www.praguewelcome.cz; Old Town Hall, Staroměstské náměstí 5; ☺9am-7pm; MStaroměstská) is the city's tourist information office, with branches at **Staré Město** (Map p288; Rytířská 31, Staré Město; ☺10am-7pm Mon-Sat; MMůstek) and the **Malá Strana Bridge Tower** (Map p278; Mostecká ; ☺10am-6pm Apr-Oct; ☐12, 20, 22) as well as at Prague airport and the **main train station** (Map p288; Wilsonova 8, Nové Město; ☺10am-6pm Mon-Sat; MHlavní Nádraží). The offices stock maps and brochures, all free.

ℹ Getting There & Away

Bus

The main terminal for international and domestic buses is **Florenc bus station** (ÚAN Praha Florenc; Map p278; ☑900 144 444; www. florenc.cz; Křižíkova 4; ☺4am-midnight, information counter 6am-9.30pm; MFlorenc), 600m northeast of the main train station. Short-haul tickets are sold on the bus, and long-distance domestic tickets are sold in the newly renovated central hall.

For convenience, some regional buses arrive at and depart from outlying metro stations, including Dejvická, Černý Most, Nádraží Holešovice, Smíchovské nádraží, Roztyly and Haje. Check timetables and departure points at www.idos.cz. Recommended bus lines include the following:

Eurolines (☑245 005 245; www.elines.cz) Big international coach service that runs buses to all over Europe.

Student Agency (☑800 100 300; www.studentagency.cz) Links major Czech cities; also services throughout Europe.

Train

Prague is well integrated into European rail networks and if you're arriving from somewhere in Europe, chances are you're coming by train. The Czech rail network is operated by **České dráhy** (ČD; Czech Railways; ☑840 112 113; www. cd.cz). Timetable information is available online at www.vlak-bus.cz.

Most trains arrive at **Praha hlavní nádraží** (Main Train Station; ☑840 112 113; www.cd.cz; Wilsonova 8, Nové Město). Some trains, particularly from Berlin, Vienna and Budapest, also stop at **Praha-Holešovice** (☑840 112 113; www. cd.cz; Vrbenského, Holešovice), north of the city centre. Both stations have their own stops on the metro line C (red).

ℹ Getting Around

To/From the Airport

To get into town from the airport, buy a full-price public transport ticket (32Kč) from the Prague Public Transport Authority (p300) desk in the arrivals hall and take bus 119 (20 minutes, every 10 minutes, 4am to midnight) to the end of metro line A (Dejvická), then continue by metro into the city centre (another 10 to 15 minutes; no new ticket needed).

Note you'll need a half-fare (16Kč) ticket for your bag or suitcase (per piece) if it's larger than 25cm x 45cm x 70cm.

If you're heading to the southwestern part of the city, take bus 100, which goes to the Zličín metro station (line B).

There's also an **Airport Express** (tickets 50Kč; ☺5am-10pm) bus which takes 35 minutes and runs every 30 minutes. It goes to Praha hlavní nádraží (main train station), where you can connect to metro line C (buy a ticket from the driver; luggage goes free).

Alternatively, take a **Cedaz** (☑220 116 758; www.cedaz.cz; ticket 130Kč; ☺7.30am-7pm)

TRANSPORT FROM PRAGUE

Domestic Bus

DESTINATION	PRICE (KČ)	DURATION (HR)	FREQUENCY
Brno	165	2½	hourly
České Budějovice	150	2¾	several daily
Český Krumlov	180	3	7 daily
Karlovy Vary	150	2¼	8 daily
Kutná Hora	80	1¼	6 daily
Plzeň	100	1½	hourly

International Bus

DESTINATION	PRICE (KČ)	DURATION (HR)	FREQUENCY
Berlin (Germany)	1310	4½	daily
Budapest (Hungary)	1000	6	daily
Dresden (Germany)	840	2¼	daily
Munich (Germany)	1420	5¼	2 daily
Vienna (Vienna)	990	4½	several daily
Warsaw (Poland)	1590	12	3 weekly

Domestic Train

DESTINATION	PRICE (KČ)	DURATION (HR)	FREQUENCY
Brno	210	3	frequent
České Budějovice	220	2¾	several daily
Kutná Hora	100	1	4 daily
Olomouc	220	2¾	several daily
Plzeň	100	1½	hourly

International Train

DESTINATION	PRICE (KČ)	DURATION (HR)	FREQUENCY
Berlin (Germany)	737	5	daily
Bratislava (Slovakia)	381	4¼	several daily
Dresden (Germany)	483	2¼	several daily
Frankfurt (Germany)	1245	8	2 daily
Munich (Germany)	737	5	4 daily
Vienna (Austria)	483	4-5	several daily
Warsaw (Poland)	483	8½	2 daily

minibus from outside either arrival terminal to the Czech Airlines office near náměstí Republiky (20 minutes, every 30 minutes); buy a ticket from the driver. The minibus service also runs in the opposite direction for returning to the airport.

AAA Radio Taxi (p300) operates a 24-hour taxi service, charging around 500Kč to 700Kč to get to the centre of Prague. You'll find taxi stands outside both arrivals terminals. Drivers usually speak some English and accept credit cards.

Bicycle

Biking is gaining in popularity and several parts of the city now have marked bike lanes (look for yellow bike-path signage). Still, with its cobblestones, tram tracks and multitudes of pedestrians, Prague has a long way to go to catch up with far more bike-friendly cities like Vienna or Amsterdam.

The black market for stolen bikes is thriving, so don't leave bikes unattended for longer than a few minutes and always use the sturdiest lock money can buy.

City Bike (☑776 180 284; www.citybike-prague.com; Královdorská 5, Staré Město; rental per day 500Kč, tours per person 550-800Kč; ⊙9am-7pm Apr-Oct; Ⓜ Náměstí Republiky) Rental includes helmet, padlock and map; good-quality Trek mountain bikes are available for 750Kč per 24 hours.

Praha Bike (☑732 388 880; www.prahabike.cz; Dlouhá 24; rental per day 500Kč, tours per person 490Kč; ⊙9am-8pm; Ⓜ Náměstí Republiky) Hires out good, new bikes with lock, helmet and map, plus offers free luggage storage. It also offers student discounts and group bike tours.

Car & Motorcycle

Challenges to driving in Prague include cobblestones, trams and one-way streets. Try not to arrive or leave on a Friday or Sunday afternoon or evening, when Prague folk are travelling to and from their weekend houses.

Central Prague has many pedestrian-only streets, marked with *pěší zóna* (pedestrian zone) signs, where only service vehicles and taxis are allowed; parking can be a nightmare. Meter time limits range from two to six hours at around 50Kč per hour. Parking in one-way streets is normally only allowed on the right-hand side.

Public Transport

Prague's excellent public-transport system combines tram, metro and bus services. It's operated by the **Prague Public Transport Authority** (DPP; ☑800 191 817; www.dpp.cz) which has information desks at Prague airport (7am to 10pm) and in several metro stations, including Muzeum, Můstek, Anděl and Nádraží Holešovice. The metro operates daily from 5am to midnight.

The metro has three lines: line A (shown on transport maps in green) runs from the northwestern side of the city at Dejvická to the east at Depo Hostivař; line B (yellow) runs from the southwest at Zličín to the northeast at Černý Most; and line C (red) runs from the north at Letňany to the southeast at Háje. Convenient stops for visitors include Staroměstská (closest to Old Town Sq), Malostranská (Malá Strana), Můstek (Wenceslas Sq), Muzeum (National Museum) and Hlavní nádraží (main train station).

After the metro closes, night trams (51 to 58) rumble across the city about every 40 minutes through the night (only full-price 32Kč tickets are valid on these services). If you're planning a late evening, find out if one of these lines passes near where you are staying.

Tickets are sold from machines at metro stations and some tram stops (coins only), as well as at DPP information offices and many newsstands and kiosks. Tickets are valid on all metros, trams and buses.

Tickets can be purchased individually or as discounted day passes valid for one or three days. A full-price individual ticket costs 32/16Kč per adult/child aged six to 15 years and senior aged 65 to 70 (kids under six ride free) and is valid for 90 minutes of unlimited travel, including transfers. For shorter journeys, buy short-term tickets that are valid for 30 minutes of unlimited travel. These cost 24/12Kč per adult/child and senior. Bikes and prams travel free.

If you're planning on staying more than a few hours, it makes sense to buy either a one- or three-day pass. One-day passes cost 110/55Kč per adult/child and senior; three-day passes cost 310Kč (no discounts available for children or seniors).

Taxi

Taxis are frequent and relatively expensive. The official rate for licensed cabs is 40Kč flagfall plus 28Kč per kilometre and 6Kč per minute while waiting. On this basis, any trip within the city centre – say, from Wenceslas Sq to Malá Strana – should cost around 170Kč. A trip to the suburbs, depending on the distance, should run from around 200Kč to 400Kč, and to the airport between 500Kč and 700Kč.

While the number of dishonest drivers has fallen in recent years, taxi rip-offs are still an occasional problem, especially among drivers who congregate in popular tourist areas like Old Town Sq and Wenceslas Sq.

Instead of hailing cabs off the street, call a radio taxi, as they're better regulated and more responsible. From our experience the following companies have honest drivers and offer 24-hour service and English-speaking operators:

AAA Radio Taxi (☑222 333 222, 14014; www.aaataxi.cz)

City Taxi (☑257 257 257; www.citytaxi.cz)

ProfiTaxi (☑14015; www.profitaxi.cz)

AROUND PRAGUE

Karlštejn

Rising above the village of Karlštejn, 30km southwest of Prague, this medieval castle is in such good shape it wouldn't look out of place on Disneyworld's Main St. The crowds come in theme-park proportions as well, but the peaceful surrounding countryside offers views of Karlštejn's stunning exterior that rival anything you'll see on the inside.

Karlštejn Castle (Hrad Karlštejn; ☑311 681 617; www.hradkarlstejn.cz; adult/child Tour 1 270/180Kč, Tour 2 300/200Kč, Tour 3 120/60Kč; ⊙9am-6.30pm Jul & Aug, to 5.30pm Tue-Sun May, Jun & Sep, to 4.30pm Tue-Sun Apr & Oct, reduced hr Nov-Mar) was born of a grand pedigree, starting life in 1348 as a hideaway for the crown jewels and treasury of the Holy Roman Emperor, Charles IV. Run by an appointed burgrave, the castle was surrounded by a network of landowning knight-vassals, who came to the castle's aid whenever enemies moved against it.

Karlštejn again sheltered the Bohemian and the Holy Roman Empire crown jewels during the Hussite Wars of the 15th century, but fell into disrepair as its defences became outmoded. Considerable restoration work in the late-19th century returned the castle to its former glory.

There are three guided tours available. Tour 1 (50 minutes) passes through the Knight's Hall, still daubed with the coats-of-arms and names of the knight-vassals, Charles IV's bedchamber, the Audience Hall and the Jewel House, which includes treasures from the Chapel of the Holy Cross and a replica of the St Wenceslas Crown.

Tour 2 (70 minutes, May to October only) must be booked in advance and takes in the the Marian Tower, with the Church of the Virgin Mary and the Chapel of St Catherine, then moves on the Great Tower for the castle's star attraction, the exquisite Chapel of the Holy Cross.

Tour 3 (40 minutes, May to October only) visits the upper levels of the Great Tower, the highest point of the castle, which provides stunning views over the surrounding countryside.

❶ Getting There & Away

From Prague, there are frequent train departures daily from Prague's *hlavní nádraží* (main station). The journey takes about 40 minutes and costs around 50Kč.

Konopiště

Archduke Franz Ferdinand d'Este, heir to the Austro-Hungarian throne, is famous for being dead – after all, it was his assassination in 1914 in Sarajevo that sparked WWI. But the archduke was an enigmatic figure who avoided the intrigues of the Vienna court and for the last 20 years of his life hid away in what became his ideal country retreat.

Konopiště Chateau (Zámek Konopiště; ☑317 721 366; www.zamek-konopiste.cz; adult/child Tour 1 or 2 210/130Kč, Tour 3 310/210Kč; ⊙10am-noon & 1-5pm Tue-Sun Jun-Aug, to 4pm Apr, May & Sep, 10am-noon & 1-3pm Sat & Sun Oct & Nov, closed Dec-Mar), lying amid extensive grounds 3km west of the town of Benešov, is a testament to the archduke's twin obsessions – hunting and St George. Having renovated the massive Gothic and Renaissance building in the 1890s and installed all the latest technology – including electricity, central heating, flush toilets, showers and a luxurious lift – Franz Ferdinand decorated his home with his hunting trophies.

His game books record that he shot about 300,000 creatures in his lifetime, from foxes and deer to elephants and tigers. About 100,000 animal trophies adorn the walls, each marked with the date and place it met its end – the crowded Trophy Corridor (Tours 1 and 3), with a forest of mounted animal heads, and the antler-clad Chamois Room (Tour 3), with its 'chandelier' fashioned from a stuffed condor, are truly bizarre sights.

❶ Getting There & Away

To reach Konopiště from Prague, take any one of the frequent trains to Benešov (70Kč, 50 minutes) and hike along a marked trail for 30 minutes. Infrequent buses (60Kč, one hour) leave from a small bus station at the top of the Roztyly metro stop on Prague's line C (red).

Kutná Hora

In the 14th century, the silver-rich ore under Kutná Hora, 60km southeast of Prague, gave the now-sleepy town an importance in Bohemia second only to Prague. The local mines and mint turned out silver *groschen* for use as the hard currency of Central Europe. The silver ore ran out in 1726, leaving the medieval townscape largely unaltered. Now, with several fascinating and unusual historical attractions, the Unesco World Heritage–listed town is a popular day trip from Prague.

◉ Sights

Sedlec Ossuary   CHURCH
(Kostnice; ☑327 561 143; www.ossuary.eu; Zámecká 127; adult/concession 60/40Kč; ⊙8am-6pm Mon-Sat Apr-Sep, 9am-5pm Mar & Oct, 9am-4pm Nov-Feb) When the Schwarzenberg family

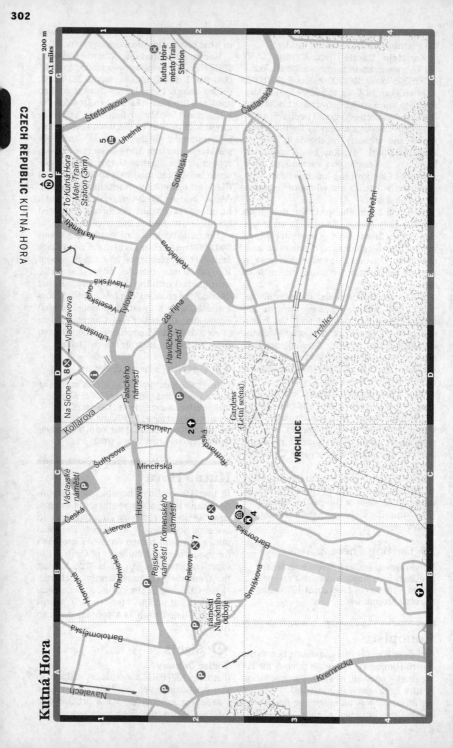

CZECH REPUBLIC KUTNÁ HORA

Kutná Hora

200 m
0.1 miles

Kutná Hora-
město Train
Station

Štefánikova

5 Uhelna

To Kutná Hora
Main Train
Station (3km)

Na náměstí

Sokolská

Roháčova

Pobřežní

Čáslavská

Vrchlice

Havlíčkovo
náměstí

28. října

Vladislavova

Libušina

Tylova

Veselská

Havlířská

Na Sione

8

f

Palackého
náměstí

Gardens
(Letní scéna)

VRCHLICE

Kollárova

Jakubská

2

Ruthardská

Šultysova

Mincířská

Václavské
náměstí

Česká

Husova

Lierova

Komenského
náměstí

6

3
4

Barborská

Rejskovo
náměstí

Rakova

7

Radnicka

Hornická

Smíškova

náměstí
Národního
odboje

Bartolomějská

Kremnická

Navalech

Kutná Hora

purchased Sedlec monastery in 1870 they allowed a local woodcarver to get creative with the bones that had been piled in the crypt for centuries. But this was no piddling little heap of bones: it was the remains of no fewer than 40,000 people. The result was the remarkable 'bone church' of Sedlec Ossuary.

Garlands of skulls and femurs are strung from the vaulted ceiling like Addams Family Christmas decorations, while in the centre dangles a vast chandelier containing at least one of each bone in the human body. Four giant pyramids of stacked bones squat in each of the corner chapels, and crosses, chalices and monstrances of bone adorn the altar. There's even a Schwarzenberg coat of arms made from bones – note the crow pecking the eyes from the Turk's head, a grisly motif of the Schwarzenberg family.

Cathedral of St Barbara   CHURCH
(Chrám sv Barbora; ☎327 512 115; Barborská; adult/concession 60/40Kč; ◉10am-4pm Mon, 9am-5.30pm Tue-Sun May-Sep, 10am-4pm daily Oct-Apr) Kutná Hora's greatest monument is the Gothic Cathedral of St Barbara. Rivalling Prague's St Vitus in size and magnificence, its soaring nave culminates in elegant, six-petalled ribbed vaulting, and the ambulatory chapels preserve original 15th-century frescoes, some of them showing miners at work.

Construction began in 1380, interrupted during the Hussite Wars and abandoned in 1558 when the silver began to run out. It was finally completed in neogothic style at the end of the 19th century. Take a walk around the outside of the church, too; the terrace at the east end enjoys the finest view in town.

Czech Silver Museum   MUSEUM
(České muzeum stříbra; ☎327 512 159; www. cms-kh.cz; Barborská 28; adult/concession Tour 1 70/40Kč, Tour 2 120/80Kč, combined 140/90Kč; ◉10am-6pm Jul & Aug, 9am-6pm May, Jun & Sep, 9am-5pm Apr & Oct) From the southern side of **St James Church**, a narrow cobbled lane (Ruthardská) leads down and then up to the **Hrádek** (Little Castle). Originally part of the town's fortifications, it was rebuilt in the 15th century as the residence of Jan Smíšek, administrator of the royal mines, who grew rich from silver he illegally mined right under the building. It now houses the Czech Silver Museum.

Visiting is by guided tour. Tour I (one hour) leads through the main part of the museum where the exhibits celebrate the mines that made Kutná Hora wealthy, including a huge wooden device once used to lift loads weighing as much as 1000kg from the 200m-deep shafts.

Tour II (90 minutes) allows you to don a miner's helmet and explore 500m of medieval mine shafts beneath the town. Kids need to be aged at least seven for this tour.

🛏 Sleeping

Penzión U Kata   PENSION €
(☎327 515 096; www.ukata.cz; Uhelná 596; s/d/tr 500/760/1140Kč; 🅿@🛜) You won't lose your head over the rates at this good-value family hotel called the 'Executioner'. Bikes can be hired for 200Kč per hour and it's a short stroll from the bus station. Downstairs is a welcoming Czech beer hall and restaurant.

🍴 Eating & Drinking

Pivnice Dačický   BEER HALL €
(☎327 512 248; www.dacicky.com; Rakova 8; mains 120-330Kč; ◉11am-11pm) Get some froth on your moustache at this old-fashioned, wood-panelled Bohemian beer hall, where you can dine on dumplings and choose from five different draught beers, including Pilsner Urquell, Budvar and Primátor Dark.

U Sňeka Pohodáře   ITALIAN €
(☎327 515 987; www.usneka.cz; Vladislavova 11; mains 100-235Kč; 🛜) Kutná Hora's best Italian flavours are found at this cosy local favourite that's very popular for takeaway or dine-in pizza and pasta. And no, we don't know why it's called 'The Contented Snail'.

Kavárna Mokate   CAFE
(Barborská 37; ◉8am-10pm Mon-Fri, 10am-10pm Sat, 10am-8pm Sun) This cosy little cafe, with

ancient earthenware floor tiles, timber beams, mismatched furniture and oriental rugs dishes up a wide range of freshly ground coffees and exotic teas, as well as iced tea and coffee in summer.

ℹ Information

The **Kutná Hora tourist office** (Informační centrum; ☎327 512 378; www.guide.kh.cz; Palackého náměstí 377; ☉9am-6pm Apr-Sep, 9am-5pm Mon-Fri, 10am-4pm Sat & Sun Oct-Mar) books accommodation, provides internet access (1Kč per minute) and rents out bicycles (220Kč per day).

ℹ Getting There & Away

Kutná Hora can be reached from Prague by either bus or train. The town's bus station is located on the Old Town's northeastern edge, which is convenient to the Old Town sites, but 3km from the Sedlec Ossuary. There's regular bus service throughout the day from Prague (68Kč, 1¼ hours). Some buses depart from the main Florenc bus station, while others leave from a small stop at the Haje metro station on line C (red).

Kutná Hora's main train station, by contrast, is just 800m from the ossuary, but about 3km from the Old Town. Sporadic trains throughtout the day leave from Prague's main station (101Kč, one hour).

Terezín

The military fortress at Terezín (*Theriesenstadt* in German), 60km north of Prague, was built by the Habsburgs in the 18th century to guard the empire's northern frontier against possible incursion by the Prussian army, but the place is better known as a notorious WWII prison and concentration camp.

Around 150,000 men, women and children, mostly Jews, were detained here en route to the Auschwitz-Birkenau extermination camps: 35,000 of them died here of hunger, disease or suicide, and only 4000 ultimately survived. From 1945 to 1948 the fortress served as an internment camp for the Sudeten Germans, who were expelled from Czechoslovakia after the war.

Terezín also played a tragic role in deceiving the world about the ultimate goals of the Nazi's 'Final Solution'. Official visitors were immersed in a charade, with Terezín being presented as a Jewish 'refuge', complete with shops, schools and cultural organisations – even an autonomous Jewish 'government'.

As late as April 1945, Red Cross visitors delivered positive reports.

The **Terezín Memorial** (www.pamatnik-terezin.cz) consists of the **Ghetto Museum** (muzeum ghetta; ☎416 782 225; adult/child 170/140Kč, combined with Lesser Fortress 210/160Kč; ☉9am-6pm Apr-Oct, to 5.30pm Nov-Mar) in the Main Fortress, the **Magdeburg Barracks** (cnr Tyršova & Vodárenská; ☉9am-6pm Apr-Oct, to 5.30pm Nov-Mar) and the **Lesser Fortress** (Malá pevnost; ☎416 782 576; Pražská; adult/child 170/140Kč, combined with Ghetto Museum 210/170Kč; ☉8am-6pm Apr-Oct, to 4.30pm Nov-Mar), a 10-minute walk east across the Ohře River.

The Ghetto Museum records daily life in the camp during WWII, through moving displays of paintings, letters and personal possessions. Displays at the Magdeburg Barracks highlight the rich cultural life – including music, theatre, fine arts and literature – that flourished against this backdrop of fear.

The Lesser Fortress was used to hold political prisoners, including anti-Nazi Czech partisans. Take the grimly fascinating self-guided tour through the prison barracks, workshops, morgues and mass graves, before arriving at the bleak execution grounds, where more than 250 prisoners were shot.

ℹ Getting There & Away

Direct buses from Prague to Litoměřice (165Kc return, one hour) normally stop at Terezín. Buses leave from outside the Praha-Holešovice train station.

BOHEMIA

The Czech Republic's western province boasts surprising variety. Český Krumlov, with its riverside setting and dramatic Renaissance castle, is in a class by itself, but lesser-known towns like Loket exude unexpected charm. Big cities like České Budějovice and Plzeň offer urban attractions like great museums and restaurants. The spa towns of western Bohemia were world famous in the 19th century and retain old-world lustre.

Karlovy Vary

POP 60,000

Karlovy Vary (KV) is the closest the Czech Republic has to a glam resort, but it is still only glam with a small 'g'. While the resort was famous across Europe in the 19th century as a *kurort* (health spa), these days the town attracts mostly day trippers, content to stroll the main colonnade area and sip on allegedly health-restoring sulphuric compounds from ceramic, spouted drinking cups. Despite the spa rep, Karlovy Vary is not entirely welcoming to walk-ins looking for high-end treatments like exotic massages and peelings; these services are available, but require advance bookings. Good bus services from Prague makes this an easy return day trip.

◉ Sights

FREE **Hot Spring Colonnade** SPRING
(Vřídelní Kolonáda; www.karlovyvary.cz; Vřídelní Kolonáda; ⊘Pramen Vřídlo 6am-7pm) The Hot Spring Colonnade houses the most impressive of the town's geysers, **Pramen Vřídlo**. The building itself is an incongruous, mid-'70s structure once dedicated to Soviet cosmonaut Yuri Gagarin. The geyser belches some 15m into the air; people lounge about inhaling the vapours or sampling the waters from a line of taps in the next room.

Church of Mary Magdalene CHURCH
(kostel sv Maří Magdaléná; www.karlovyvary.cz; náměstí Svobody 2; ⊘open during Mass) Whatever your thoughts on the excesses of baroque architecture, it's hard not to fall for this confection by Kilian Ignatz Dientzenhofer, dating from the 1730s. You can arrange a tour through a branch of the Infocentrum to see the baroque **crypt** and the unique **funeral chapel**.

Church of SS Peter & Paul CHURCH
(kostel Sv Petra a Pavla; Krále Jiřího; ⊘9am-6pm) The impressive Orthodox Church of SS Peter & Paul, with five polished onion domes and art nouveau exterior murals, was apparently modelled after a similar church near Moscow. One of the church's most prominent decorations is a relief depicting Tsar Peter the Great.

Karlovy Vary Museum MUSEUM
(Krajské muzeum Karlovy Vary; ☑353 226 252; www.kvmuz.cz; Nová Louka 23; adult/concession 60/30Kč; ⊘9am-noon & 1-5pm Wed-Sun) The Karlovy Vary Museum has extensive exhibits on the town's history as a spa resort, Czech glasswork and the area's natural history.

Moser Glass Museum MUSEUM
(Sklářské muzeum Moser; ☑353 416 132; www.moser-glass.com; Kpt Jaroše 19; adult/child 80/50Kč; glassworks 120/70Kč, combined ticket 180/100Kč;

⊘9am-5pm, glassworks to 2.30pm; 🚌1) The Moser Glass Museum has more than 2000 items on display. Tours of the adjacent **glassworks** and combined tickets are also available. There is a shop here, too, but the prices are not anything special, and there's another shop in town. To get here catch bus 1 from the Tržnice bus station.

FREE **Diana Lookout Tower** TOWER
(☑353 222 872; www.karlovy-vary.cz/en/diana-tower; ⊘9am-7pm Jun-Sep, to 6pm Apr, May & Oct, to 5pm Feb, Mar, Nov & Dec) This lookout tower, atop a wooded hill to the west of the historic spa area, is the perfect destination for a short afternoon hike.

🏃 Activities

Castle Spa SPA
(Zámecké Lázně; ☑353 225 502; www.castle-spa.com; Zámecký vrch 1; ⊘7.30am-7.30pm Mon-Fri, from 8.30am Sat & Sun) Most KV accommodation offers some kind of spa treatment for a fee, but if you're just a casual visitor or day tripper, consider Castle Spa, a modernised spa centre complete with a subterranean thermal pool. Consult the website for a full menu of treatments and prices.

Swimming Pool SWIMMING
(☑359 001 111; www.thermal.cz; IP Pavlova 11; adult/child 100/80Kč; ⊘8.30am-8pm) The Hotel Thermal's 50m pool is open to the public year-round. The waters are heated by thermal springs. To find it, follow the 'Bazén' signs up the hill behind the hotel to the pool.

🎊 Festivals & Events

Karlovy Vary International Film Festival FILM
(www.kviff.com; ⊘Jul) The Karlovy Vary Film Festival always features the year's top films as well as attracting plenty of (B-list) stars. It's rather behind the likes of Cannes, Venice and Berlin but is well worth the trip.

🛏 Sleeping

Accommodation prices in Karlovy Vary have risen steeply in recent years to be similar to those in Prague, especially in July during the film festival. Indeed, if you're planning a July arrival, make sure to book well in advance. Expect to pay an additional 'spa tax' (15Kč per bed per night). The city's Infocentrum offices can help out with hostel, pension and hotel bookings. Alternatively, consider staying in Loket and visiting Karlovy Vary as a day trip.

TOP CHOICE **Hotel Maltézský Kříž** HOTEL €€

(☑353 169 011; www.maltezskykriz.cz; Stará Louka 50; s/d 1650/2800Kč; @☎) Welcome to Karlovy Vary's best-value midrange hotel. Oriental rugs and wooden floors combine at this spiffy property, with cosy rooms and a more spacious double-storeyed apartment. The bathrooms are decked out in warm, earthy tones.

Carlsbad Plaza HOTEL €€€

(☑353 225 501; www.carlsbadplaza.cz; Mariánskolázeňská 23; s/d 4000/6000Kč; P❂✳@☎≋) Seriously stylish, this relatively new hotel has raised the bar in spa town, with soothingly modern treatment facilities, classy rooms and a vegetarian-friendly Asian restaurant.

Embassy Hotel HOTEL €€

(☑353 221 161; www.embassy.cz; Nová Luka 21; s/d from 2260/3130Kč; @☎) KV's not short of top-end hotels, but most lack the personal touch of the family-owned Embassy, with its riverside location and perfectly pitched heritage rooms. The hotel's pub and restaurant have seen visits from plenty of film-fest luminaries.

Grandhotel Pupp HOTEL €€€

(☑353 109 631; www.pupp.cz; Mírové náměstí 2; r 4000-7000Kč; P❂✳@☎≋) No accounting of KV's hotels would be complete without mentioning the granddaddy, the Pupp, whose history dates back to the 18th century. Take a look at a few rooms, as layouts and furnishings differ from wing to wing.

OPLÁTKY

To quote Monty Python, 'Do you get wafers with it?' The answer is a resounding 'yes' according to Karlovry Vary locals, who prescribe the following method of taking your spring water: have a sip from your *lázeňský pohárek* (spa cup), then dull the sulphurous taste with a big, round, sweet wafer called *oplatky*. *Oplatky* are sold for around 10Kč each at a few spa hotels and speciality shops, or you can pick them up at **Kolonada Oplatky** (cnr Nehrova & Masarykova). Steer clear of the fancy chocolate or hazelnut flavours, though; they're never as crunchily fresh and warm as the standard vanilla flavour.

Even if you're not staying here, take a peek inside; the restaurants are very good, and the period-piece atmosphere is perfect.

Hotel Romania HOTEL €€

(☑353 222 822; www.romania.cz; Zahradni 49; s/d 1200/1950Kč; ☎) Don't be put off by the ugly monolith of the Hotel Thermal dominating the views from this good-value, reader-recommended hotel (just squint a little). The spacious rooms are very tidy and the English-speaking staff very helpful.

Hotel Boston HOTEL €

(☑353 362 711; www.boston.cz; Luční vrch 9; s/d 1390/1570Kč; ☻☎) Tucked away down a quiet lane, this family-owned hotel has relatively spacious rooms decorated in bright colours with updated bathrooms. The flash cafes of Stará Louka are just around the corner.

✗ Eating & Drinking

Hospoda U Švejka CZECH €€

(☑353 232 276; www.svejk-kv.cz; Stará Louka 10; mains 160-370Kč; ☺11am-11pm; ☻) A great choice for lunch or dinner, right in the heart of the spa centre. Though the presentation borders on extreme kitsch, the food is actually very good and the atmosphere not unlike a classic Czech pub.

Embassy Restaurant CZECH €€€

(☑353 221 161; www.embassy.cz; Nová Louka 21; mains 200-500Kč) The in-house restaurant of the Embassy Hotel (p306) is a destination in its own right. The dining room is richly atmospheric and the food, mostly Czech standards like roast pork or duck, is top notch. There's an excellent wine list, and in nice weather they sometimes offer outdoor seating.

Tandoor INDIAN €€

(☑608 701 341; www.tandoor-kv.cz; IP Pavlova 25; mains 150-250Kč; ☺noon-10pm Mon-Sat, to 6pm Sun; ☑) Located under a block of flats, Tandoor turns out a winning combo of authentic Indian flavours, Gambrinus beer and smooth, creamy lassis. Vegetarian options abound, or if you're after a serious chilli hit, order the Chicken Phall.

Promenáda INTERNATIONAL €€€

(☑353 225 648; www.hotel-promenada.cz; Tržiště 31; mains 250-650Kč) The house restaurant of the Hotel Promenáda has appeared in some 'best of' lists for the Czech Republic and is a perennial favourite on online forums. The elegant dining area is conducive to a memorable evening, and the food is very good (though perhaps not always worth the steep prices).

Sklípek
CZECH €

(☏353 220 222; www.restaurantsklipek.com; Moskevská 2; meals 120-180Kč) Red-checked tablecloths and an emphasis on good steaks, fish and pasta give this place an honest, rustic ambience missing from the more expensive chi-chi spots down the hill in the spa district.

Café Elefant
CAFE

(☏353 223 406; Stará Louka 30; coffee 50Kč) Classy old-school spot for coffee and cake. A tad touristy, but still elegant and refined.

Retro Cafe Bar
BAR

(☏353 100 710; www.retrocafebar.cz; TG Masaryka 18; ⊙10am-midnight Sun-Thu, to 3am Fri & Sat) A retro-themed bar, cafe and restaurant that defies easy categorisation. A nice place to chill for coffee or a cocktail, and the food is not bad either. Retro Cafe Bar also has music in the evenings and retro-themed nights.

ℹ Information

Karlovy Vary has several tourist information offices scattered around town – the main office is at **Dolní nádraží** (☏353 232 838; www.karlovyvary.cz; Západní 2a, lower bus station; ⊙9am-6pm Mon-Fri, 10am-5pm Sat & Sun) and there are others at **Hotel Thermal** (☏355 321 171; www.karlovyvary.cz; IP Pavlova 11; ⊙9am-5pm Mon-Fri, 10am-5pm Sat & Sun) and **Hot Spring Colonnade** (☏773 291 243; www.karlovyvary.cz; Vřídelní kolonáda; ⊙9am-5pm Mon-Fri, 10am-5pm Sat & Sun). In addition to providing maps and helpful advice, the offices can help find accommodation in private rooms and apartments that are much cheaper than hotels.

ℹ Getting There & Away

Buses are the only practical way of reaching Karlovy Vary. **Student Agency** (www.studentagency.cz) runs frequent buses to/from Prague Florenc (from 155Kč, 2¼ hours, several daily) departing from the main bus station beside Dolní nádraží train station. Buses to nearby Loket (30Kč, 30 minutes) run throughout the day.

Loket

POP 3200

Surrounded by a wickedly serpentine loop in the Ohře River, the picturesque village of Loket may as well be on an island. According to the local tourist office, it was Goethe's favourite town and, after a lazily subdued stroll around the gorgeous main square and castle, it may be yours as well. Most people visit Loket as a day trip from Karlovy Vary, but it's also a sleepy place to ease off the travel accelerator for a few days, especially when the day trippers have departed. Loket also makes a good base for visiting Karlovy Vary.

⊙ Sights

Hrad Loket
CASTLE

(Loket Castle; ☏352 684 648; www.hradloket.cz; Hrad; adult/concession with English guide 110/90Kč, with English text 95/75Kč; ⊙9am-4.30pm Apr-Oct, 9am-3.30pm Nov-Mar) Built on the site of a Romanesque fort, of which the only surviving bits are the tall, square tower and fragments of a rotunda. Its present late-Gothic look dates from the late 14th century. From 1788 to 1947 it was used as a prison. Highlights include two rooms filled with the town's lustrous porcelain and views from the castle tower.

☆ Activities

Ask at the Infocentrum about **hiking** possibilities in the surrounding forests, including a semi-ambitious day hike to Karlovy Vary (around four hours) along a 17km blue-marked trail. Karlovy Vary is also the destination for **rafting** trips.

🛏 Sleeping & Eating

There are plenty of cafes and pizzerias that come and go with the season scattered around the main square.

Hotel Císař Ferdinand
HOTEL €€

(☏352 327 130; www.hotel-loket.cz; TG Masaryka 136; s/d 1060/1850Kč; P◉🐾🕸) Located in the centre of town, this former malt house of a local brewery has recently renovated rooms and the best little microbrewery and restaurant in town.

ℹ Information

Infocentrum Loket (Loket Information Centre; ☏352 684 123; www.loket.cz; TG Masaryka 12; ⊙10.30am-12.30pm & 1-5pm) Decent source of local info, though most brochures and maps are in German. Has internet access (10Kč per 15 minutes).

ℹ Getting There & Away

Frequent bus departures link Karlovy Vary to Loket (30Kč, 20 minutes). The bus arriving from Karlovy Vary stops across the bridge from the Old Town. Walk across the bridge to reach the castle, accommodation and tourist information.

Plzeň

POP 173,000

Plzeň, the regional capital of western Bohemia and the second-biggest city in Bohemia after Prague, is best known as the home of the Pilsner Urquell Brewery, but it has a handful of other interesting sights and enough good restaurants and night-time pursuits to justify an overnight stay. Most of the sights are located near the central square, but the brewery itself is about a 15-minute walk outside the centre. Try to arrive in the morning to tour the non-drinking attractions first, and save the brewery tour and inevitable post-tour beers for the late afternoon (which makes for a more natural progression to dinner, continuing the pub crawl after dark).

◉ Sights

Pilsner Urquell Brewery   BREWERY
(Prazdroj; ☑377 062 888; www.prazdroj.cz; U Prazdroje 7; guided tour adult/child 150/80Kč; ◷8.30am-6pm Apr-Sep, to 5pm Oct-Mar; tours in English 12.45pm, 2.15pm & 4.15pm) Plzeň's most popular attraction is the Pilsner Urquell Brewery, in operation since 1842 and arguably home to the world's best beer. Entry is by guided tour only, with three tours in English available daily. Tour highlights include a trip to the old cellars (dress warmly) and a glass of unpasteurised nectar at the end.

Brewery Museum   MUSEUM
(☑377 235 574; www.prazdroj.cz; Veleslavínova 6; adult/child guided tour 90/60Kč, English text 90/60Kč; ◷10am-6pm Apr-Dec, to 5pm Jan-Mar) The Brewery Museum offers an insight into how beer was made (and drunk) in the days before Prazdroj was founded. Highlights include a mock-up of a 19th-century pub, a huge wooden beer tankard from Siberia and a collection of beer mats. All have English captions and there's a good English written guide available.

Underground Plzeň   UNDERGROUND
(Plzeňské historické podzemí; ☑377 235 574; www.plzenskepodzemi.cz; Veleslavínova 6; adult/child

---

WORTH A TRIP

MARIÁNSKÉ LÁZNĚ & CHODOVÁ PLANÁ

Mariánské Lázně (known abroad as Marienbad) is smaller, less urban and arguably prettier than Karlovy Vary. In the resort's heyday, Mariánské Lázně drew such luminaries as Goethe, Thomas Edison, Britain's King Edward VII and even author Mark Twain.

These days most visitors seem to be day trippers from Germany, hauled in by coach to stroll the gardens and colonnades before repairing to a cafe for the inevitable *apfelstrudel* (apple strudel) then the ride back home.

The restored cast-iron **Colonnade** (Lázeňská kolonáda; Lázeňská kolonáda; ◷6am-6pm) is the spa's striking centrepiece, with a whitewashed pavilion that houses taps for the various springs. Do as others do and purchase a porcelain drinking mug for walking and sipping. Notices on the walls (in English too) describe the various properties of the spa waters.

The colonnade is the site of numerous classical and brass-band concerts throughout the day in high season. In the evening, there's a **singing fountain**, where lights and water sashay to the sounds of Bach and Chopin.

The centrally located **Infocentrum** (☑354 622 474; www.marianskelazne.cz; Hlavní třída 47; ◷9am-6pm) is a good place to turn for information on spa treatments and hiking possibilities in the ample forests surrounding the town.

Mariánské Lázně is easy to reach from both Prague and Plzeň. Half a dozen trains a day run from Prague (250Kč, three hours), passing through Plzeň en route. Regular (slow) trains link Mariánské Lázně and Karlovy Vary (63Kč, 1¾ hours).

If you prefer your spas with suds, so to speak, not far from Mariánské Lázně, in the village of **Planá**, you'll find a unique beer spa, **Beer Wellness Land**, at the **Chodovar Brewery** (☑374 617 100; www.chodovar.cz; Pivovarská 107; treatments from 660Kc). As the name implies, it's similar to a water bath, but here the liquid is heated beer, complete with confetti-sized fragments of hops. This may very well be the perfect spot to simultaneously sample both of Bohemia's claims to fame: world-class spas and beer.

90/70Kč; ⊙10am-6pm Apr-Dec, to 5pm Feb-Mar, closed Jan; English tour 1pm daily) This extraordinary tour explores the passageways below the old city. The earliest were probably dug in the 14th century, perhaps for beer production or defence; the latest date from the 19th century. Of an estimated 11km that have been excavated, some 500m of tunnels are open to the public. Bring extra clothing (it's a chilly 10°C underground).

St Bartholomew Church
CHURCH

(kostel Sv Bartoloměje; ☑377 226 098; www.katedralaplzen.org; náměstí Republiky; adult/concession church 20/10Kč, tower 35/25Kč; ⊙10am-6pm Wed-Sat Apr-Sep, Wed-Fri Oct-Dec) Gigantic Gothic St Bartholomew Church looms over the surrounding facades from the centre of náměstí Republiky. Ask at the City Information Centre (p310) about guided tours. Look inside at the delicate marble 'Pilsen Madonna' (dating from c 1390) on the main altar, or climb the 301 steps to the top of the tower (weather permitting) for serious views.

Puppet Museum
MUSEUM

(muzeum Loutek; ☑378 370 801; www.muzeumloutek.cz; náměstí Republiky 23; adult/concession 60/30Kč; ⊙10am-6pm Tue-Sun; ⊕) Since opening in 2011, this museum has been a hit with the younger set. The exhibitions are well done, and many are interactive, allowing visitors to indulge their inner puppeteers.

Great Synagogue
SYNAGOGUE

(Velká Synagoga; ☑377 223 346; www.zoplzen.cz; sady Pětatřicátníků 11; adult/child 60/40Kč; ⊙10am-6pm Sun-Fri Apr-Oct) The Great Synagogue, west of the Old Town, is the third-largest in the world – only those in Jerusalem and Budapest are bigger. It was built in the Moorish style in 1892 by the 2000 Jews who lived in Plzeň at the time. English guides cost 500Kč. The building is often used for concerts and art exhibitions.

Patton Memorial Pilsen
MUSEUM

(☑378 037 954; www.patton-memorial.cz; Podřežni 10; adult/concession 60/40Kč; ⊙9am-1pm & 2-5pm Tue-Sun) The Patton Memorial Pilsen details the liberation of Plzeň in May 1945 by the American army, under General George S Patton. Especially poignant are the handwritten memories of former American soldiers who have returned to Plzeň over the years, and the museum's response to the communist-era revisionist fabrications that claimed Soviet troops, not Americans, were responsible for the city's liberation.

🛏 Sleeping

Pension Stará Plzeň
PENSION €

(☑377 259 901; www.pension-sp.cz; Na Roudné 12; s 600-1000Kč, d 800-1200Kč; P⊕❀@⊛) The pension 'Old Pilsen' offers light-and-sunny rooms with skylights, wooden floors and comfy beds. The more expensive rooms offer antique-style beds, Persian rugs and exposed, wood-beam ceilings. To get here, walk north on Rooseveltova across the river, then turn right onto Na Roudné and continue for 300m.

Courtyard by Marriott
HOTEL €€

(☑373 370 100; www.marriott.com; sady 5 května 57; r 2000-2600Kč; P⊕❀@⊛) This handsome branch of the Marriott has a good location, near the Brewery Museum and central sights. The rooms are relatively spacious, clean and bright, with all of the conveniences you'd expect. The reception desk is particularly helpful and can arrange brewery tours and sightseeing options. Expect sizeable discounts on weekends.

U Salzmannů
PENSION €

(☑377 235 476; www.usalzmannu.cz; Pražská 8; s & d 950-1350Kč, ste 1500Kč; ⊜⊛) This pleasant pension, right in the heart of town, sits above a historic pub. The standard rooms are comfortable but basic; the more luxurious double 'suites' have antique beds and small sitting rooms, as well as kitchenettes. The pub location is convenient if you overdo it; to reach your bed, just climb the stairs.

Pension City
PENSION €

(☑377 326 069; www.pensioncityplzen.cz; sady 5 kvetna 52; s/d 1050/1450Kč; ⊜⊛) On a quiet street near the river, Pension City has comfortable rooms and friendly, English-speaking staff armed with lots of local information.

Hotel Central
HOTEL €€

(☑378 011 855; www.central-hotel.cz; náměstí Republiky 33; s/d 1800/2700Kč; ⊜@⊛) This rather modern building across from St Bartholomew Church has an excellent location, right on the main square. The renovated rooms are clean and inviting, with the best rooms being those that face the square.

🍴 Eating & Drinking

Aberdeen Angus Steakhouse
STEAKHOUSE €€

(☑725 555 631; www.angusfarm.cz; Pražská 23; mains 180-400Kč) For our money, this may be the best steakhouse in all of the Czech Republic. The meats hail from the nearby

Angus Farm, where the livestock is raised organically. There are several cuts and sizes on offer; lunch options include a tantalising cheeseburger. The downstairs dining room is cosy; there's also a creekside terrace. Book in advance.

Na Parkánu
CZECH €

(☑377 324 485; www.naparkanu.com; Veleslavínova 4; mains 80-180Kč; 🐕) Don't overlook this pleasant pub-restaurant, attached to the Brewery Museum. It may look a bit touristy, but the traditional Czech food is top rate, and the beer, naturally, could hardly be better. Try to snag a spot on the summer garden. Don't leave without trying the *nefiltrované pivo* (unfiltered beer).

U Mansfelda
CZECH, PUB €€

(☑377 333 844; www.umansfelda.cz; Dřevěná 9; mains 155-229Kč; 🐕) Sure, it's a pub – remember you're in Plzeň now – but it's also more refined and has more interesting food than many other places. Try Czech cuisine like wild boar *guláš* (spicy meat and potato soup). Downstairs from the beer-fuelled terrace is a more relaxed *vinárna* (wine bar).

Groll Pivovar
CZECH €€

(☑602 596 161; www.pivovargroll.cz; Truhlářska 10; mains 129-259Kč) If you've come to Plzeň on a beer pilgrimage, then another essential visit is for a beer-garden lunch at this spiffy microbrewery. Meals include well-priced steaks and salads. The highlight is the drinks menu: homemade light and dark beers, complemented by an excellent (and still relatively rare) yeast beer.

Na Spilce
CZECH €

(☑377 062 755; www.naspilce.com; U Prazdroje 7; mains 80-230Kč; ⊙11am-10pm Sun-Thu, to 11pm Fri & Sat) This excellent pub and restaurant within the confines of the Pilsner Urquell Brewery feels like a factory canteen. The traditional Czech cooking is above average, and the beer is fresh from tanks next door.

Slunečnice
VEGETARIAN €

(☑377 236 093; www.slunecniceplzen.cz; Jungmanova 4; baguettes 60Kč; ⊙7.30am-6pm; 🍴) For fresh sandwiches, self-service salads and vegetarian dishes. Around 100Kč will buy a plateful.

❶ Information

City Information Centre (Informační centrum města Plzně; ☑378 035 330; www.icpilsen.cz; náměstí Republiky 41; ⊙9am-7pm Apr-Sep, to 6pm Oct-Mar) Reserves accommodation, organises guides, sells maps and changes money.

American Center Plzeň (☑377 237 722; www.americancenter.cz; Dominikánská 9; ⊙9am-10pm) Mainly a business resource centre, with a restaurant-bar, internet access and CNN news.

❶ Getting There & Away

BUS From Prague, the bus service to Plzeň (100Kč, one hour) is frequent (hourly), relatively fast and inexpensive. The main bus station is west of the centre on Husova.

TRAIN From Prague, eight trains (150Kč, 1½ hours) leave daily from the main station, *hlavní nádraží*. It's on the eastern side of town, 10 minutes' walk from Old Town Sq (náměstí Republiky).

České Budějovice

POP 96,000

České Budějovice (chesky bood-yo-vit-zah) is the provincial capital of southern Bohemia and a natural base for exploring the region. Transport connections to nearby Český Krumlov are good, meaning you could easily spend the day there and evenings here. While České Budějovice lacks top sights, it does have one of Europe's largest main squares (the biggest in the Czech Republic) and a charming labyrinth of narrow lanes and winding alleyways. It's also the home of 'Budvar' beer (aka Czech 'Budweiser'), and a brewery tour usually tops the 'must-do' list.

◉ Sights

Budweiser Budvar Brewery
BREWERY

(www.budvar.cz; cnr Pražská & K Světlé; adult/child 100/50Kč; ⊙9am-5pm Mar-Dec, closed Sun & Mon Jan-Feb) The Budweiser Budvar Brewery is 3km north of the main square. Group tours run every day and the 2pm tour (Monday to Friday only) is open to individual travellers. The highlight is a glass of real-deal Budvar deep in the brewery's chilly cellars. Catch bus 2 to the Budvar stop.

Náměstí Přemysla Otakara II
SQUARE

(náměstí Přemysla Otakara II) This mix of arcaded buildings centred on **Samson's Fountain** (Samsonova kašna; 1727) is the broadest plaza in the country, spanning 133m. Among the architectural treats is the 1555 Renaissance **Town Hall** *(radnice)*, which received a baroque facelift in 1731. The figures on the balustrade – Justice, Wisdom, Courage and Prudence – are matched by an exotic quartet of bronze gargoyles.

WORTH A TRIP

BOHEMIAN ROOTS – TÁBOR

The Old Town of Tábor was a formidable natural defence against invasion. Six centuries ago, the Hussite religious sect founded Tábor as a military bastion in defiance of Catholic Europe.

Based on the biblical concept that 'nothing is mine and nothing is yours, because everyone owns the community equally', all Hussites participated in communal work, and possessions were allocated equally in the town's main square.

This exceptional nonconformism may have given the word 'bohemian' the connotations we associate it with today. Religious structures dating from the 15th century line the town square, and it's possible to visit a 650m stretch of **underground tunnels** the Hussites used for refuge in times of war.

There are also excellent hotels and a handful of clean, reasonably priced pensions. The **Hotel Nautilus** (☑380 900 900; www.hotelnautilus.cz; Žižkovo náměstí 20; s/d from 2250/2700Kč; P☺✳☏) on the central square is the cream of the crop. **Pension Jana** (☑381 254 667; www.bedandbreakfast.euweb.cz; Kostinická 161; s/d/tr from 700/1100/1350Kč; P☺) is a step down in price, but is friendly and also centrally located.

Tábor has excellent bus connections to Prague and neighbouring towns. Buses for Prague's Florenc station (93Kč) leave approximately every two hours. Train travel to Prague (140Kč, 1½ hours) is about as frequent but more expensive.

Black Tower
TOWER

(Černá věž; ☑386 801 413; U Černé věže 70/2; adult/concession 30/20Kč; ⊙10am-6pm Tue-Sun Apr-Oct) The dominating, 72m Gothic-Renaissance Black Tower was built in 1553. Climb its 225 steps (yes, we counted them) for fine views. The tower's two **bells** – the Marta (1723) and Budvar (1995), are a gift from the brewery and are rung daily at noon.

Museum of South Bohemia
MUSEUM

(Jihočeské muzeum; ☑387 929 311; www.muzeumcb.cz; Dukelská 1) The Museum of South Bohemia holds an enormous collection of historic books, coins and weapons. It was closed in 2012 for reconstruction and, during research for this book, it wasn't clear when it would reopen: check the website for the latest information.

South Bohemian Motorcycle Museum
MUSEUM

(Jihočeské Motocyklové muzeum; ☑723 247 104; www.motomuseum.cz; Piaristické náměstí; adult/concession 50/20Kč; ⊙10am-6pm) There are nearly 100 historic motorcycles on display here at this unlikely, ecclesiastical setting for a motorcycle museum. In addition to motorbikes, there are old-time bicycles and model airplanes on display.

🛏 Sleeping

Hotel Budweis
HOTEL €€

(☑389 822 111; www.hotelbudweis.cz; Mlýnská 6; s/d 2200-2800Kč; P☺✳@☏) The Hotel Budweis opened its doors in 2010, hived out of an old grain mill with a picturesque canalside setting. The owners have opted for a smart contemporary look. All of the rooms have airconditioning and are wheelchair accessible. There are two good restaurants in-house, and the central location puts other eating and drinking options a short walk away.

Grandhotel Zvon
HOTEL €€

(☑381 601 611; www.hotel-zvon.cz; náměstí Přemysla Otakara II 28; r 2600-4400Kč; ✳☏) 'Since 1533' says the sign, but we're pretty sure Zvon – one of the city's leading hotels – has been renovated since then. The ritzy facade across three main-square buildings is let down by standard rooms, but the executive rooms (add a whopping 80% to listed prices) would be classy in any town.

Hotel Bohemia
HOTEL €€

(☑386 360 691; www.bohemiacb.cz; Hradební 20; s/d 1490/1790Kč; ☏) Carved wooden doors open to a restful interior inside these two old burghers' houses in a quiet street. The restaurant comes recommended by the tourist information office.

Penzión Centrum
PENSION €€

(☑387 311 801; www.penzioncentrum.cz; Biskupská 130/3; s/d/tr 1000/1400/1800Kč; ☺☏) Huge rooms with satellite TV, queen-sized beds with crisp white linen, and thoroughly professional staff all make this a top reader-recommended spot near the main square.

Hotel Malý Pivovar
HOTEL €€

(☎386 360 471; www.malypivovar.cz; Karla IV 8-10; s/d 2000/2800Kč; P☀@) With a cabinet of sports trophies and sculpted leather sofas, the lobby resembles a gentlemen's club. However the elegant and traditionally furnished rooms will please both the men and the ladies, and it's just a short stroll to the cosy Budvarka beer hall downstairs.

Ubytovna U Nádraží
HOSTEL €

(☎972 544 648; www.ubytovna.vors.cz; Dvořákova 161/14; s 450-490Kč, d 660-730Kč; ☀@☎) Recently renovated, this tower block a few hundred metres from the bus and train stations has good-value accommodation with shared bathrooms (usually with just one other room). Shared kitchens are available; a good option for longer-stay students.

✖ Eating

Masné Kramý
CZECH €

(☎387 201 301; www.masne-kramy.cz; Krajinská 13; mains 129-239Kč) No visit to České Budějovice would be complete without stopping at this renovated 16th-century meat market (now a popular pub) for excellent Czech food and a cold Budvar. You'll find all the Czech staples, including the house 'brewer's goulash', on the food menu. The drinks menu is equally important: try the superb unfiltered yeast beer. Advance booking essential.

U Tří Sedláku
CZECH €

(☎387 222 303; www.utrisedlaku.cz; Hroznová 488; mains 100-170Kč) Locals celebrate that nothing much has changed at U Tři Sedláku since its opening in 1897. Tasty meaty dishes go with the Pilsner Urquell that's constantly being shuffled to busy tables.

Indická
INDIAN €€

(Gateway of India; ☎777 326 200; www.indickarestaurace.cz; Piaristická 22; mains 120-220Kč; ☀11am-11pm Mon-Sat; ☎✍) From Chennai to the Czech Republic comes respite for travellers wanting something different. Request spicy because they're used to dealing with more timid local palates. Daily lunch specials (85Kč to 100Kč) are good value.

Fresh Salad & Pizza
PIZZERIA €

(☎387 200 991; Hroznová 21; salads 70-100Kč, pizza 100-130Kč; ☀☎✍) This lunch spot with outdoor tables does exactly what it says on the tin: healthy salads and (slightly) less healthy pizza dished up by a fresh and funky, youthful crew.

☕ Drinking

Café Hostel
CAFE

(☎387 204 203; www.cafehostel.cz; Panská 13; ☀noon-10pm Mon-Fri, from 5pm Sat & Sun; ☎) This cosy cafe and bar features occasional DJ sets and live music. The scruffy rear garden could charitably be described as a work in progress. Upstairs are a couple of simple, but spotless, dorm rooms.

Singer Pub
PUB

(☎386 360 186; www.singerpub.cz; Česká 55) With Czech and Irish beers, and good cocktails, don't be surprised if you get the urge to rustle up something on the Singer sewing machines scattered around here. If not, challenge the regulars to a game of *foosball* with a soundtrack of noisy rock.

ℹ Information

Česká Spořitelna (☎956 744 630; www.csas. cz; FA Gerstnera 2151/6; ☀8.30am-4pm Mon-Fri) Change money at this bank.

Municipal Information Centre (Městské Informační Centrum; ☎386 801 413; www.c-budejovice.cz; náměstí Přemysla Otakara II 2; ☀8.30am-6pm Mon-Fri, to 5pm Sat, 10am-4pm Sun May-Sep, 9am-5pm Mon-Fri, to 1pm Sat, closed Sun Oct-Apr) Books tickets, tours and accommodation, and has free internet.

ℹ Getting There & Away

BUS From Prague, Student Agency (p298) yellow buses leave from Na Knížecí bus station (150Kč, 2½ hours) at the Anděl metro station (Line B). There are decent bus services from České Budějovice to Český Krumlov (35Kč, 45 minutes) and Tábor (70Kč, one hour). České Budějovice's bus station is 300m southeast of the train station above the Mercury Central shopping centre on Dvořákova.

TRAIN From Prague, there's a frequent train service (222Kč, 2½ hours, hourly). Regular (slow) trains trundle to Český Krumlov (32Kč, 45 minutes). From the train station it's a 10-minute walk west down Lannova třída, then Kanovnická, to nám Přemysla Otakara II, the main square.

Český Krumlov

POP 14,100

Outside of Prague, Český Krumlov is arguably the Czech Republic's only other world-class sight and must-see. From a distance, the town looks like any other in the Czech countryside, but once you get closer and see the Renaissance castle towering over the undisturbed 17th-century townscape, you'll feel the appeal; this really is that fairy-tale

WORTH A TRIP

HLUBOKÁ NAD VLTAVOU

The delightful confection known as **Hluboká Chateau** (☎387 843 911; www.zamek-hluboka.eu; Zámek; adult/concession Tour 1 250/160Kč, Tour 2 230/160Kč, Tour 3 170/80Kč; ☺9am-5pm Tue-Sun May & Jun, to 6pm Jul & Aug, shorter hr Sep-Feb, closed Mar) is one of the most popular day trips from České Budějovice. Built by the Přemysl rulers in the latter half of the 13th century, Hluboká was taken from the Protestant Malovec family in 1662 as punishment for supporting an anti-Habsburg rebellion, and then sold to the Bavarian Schwarzenbergs. Two centuries later, they gave the chateau the English Tudor/Gothic face it wears today, modelling its exterior on Britain's Windsor Castle.

Crowned with crenellations and surrounded by a dainty garden, Hluboká is too prissy for some, but this remains the second-most-visited chateau in Bohemia after Karlštejn, and for good reason.

There are three English-language tours available: Tour 1 (called the 'representation room' on the website) focuses on the castle's public areas; Tour 2 goes behind the scenes in the castle apartments; Tour 3 explores the kitchens. Tour 1 is all most visitors will need to get the flavour of the place.

The surrounding park is open throughout the year (admission free). Buses make the journey to the main square in Hluboká nad Vltavou every 30 to 60 minutes (20 minutes, 20Kč).

town the tourist brochures promised. Český Krumlov is best approached as an overnight destination; it's too far for a comfortable day trip from Prague. Consider staying two nights, and spend one of the days hiking or biking in the surrounding woods and fields.

⊙ Sights

Český Krumlov Castle — TOP CHOICE — CASTLE
(☎380 704 711; www.castle.ckrumlov.cz; Zámek; adult/concession Tour 1 250/160Kč, Tour 2 240/140Kč, Theatre Tour 380/220Kč, tower 50/30Kč; ☺9am-6pm Tue-Sun Jun-Aug, 9am-5pm Apr, May, Sep & Oct) Český Krumlov's striking Renaissance castle, occupying a promontory high above the town, began life in the 13th century. It acquired its present appearance in the 16th to 18th centuries under the stewardship of the noble Rožmberk and Schwarzenberg families. The interiors are accessible by guided tour only, though you can stroll the grounds and climb the tower on your own.

Three main tours are offered: Tour 1 takes in the opulent Renaissance rooms, including the chapel, baroque suite, picture gallery and masquerade hall, while Tour 2 visits the Schwarzenberg portrait galleries and their apartments used in the 19th century; and the Theatre Tour explores the chateau's remarkable rococo theatre, complete with original stage machinery.

Egon Schiele Art Centrum — MUSEUM
(☎380 704 011; www.schieleartcentrum.cz; Široká 71; adult/concession 120/70Kč; ☺10am-6pm Tue-Sun) This excellent private gallery houses a small retrospective of the controversial Viennese painter Egon Schiele (1890–1918), who lived in Krumlov in 1911 and raised the ire of townsfolk by hiring young girls as nude models. For this and other sins he was eventually driven out. The centre also houses interesting temporary exhibitions.

🏃 Activities

Maleček — CANOEING
(☎380 712 508; http://en.malecek.cz; Rooseveltova 28; 2-person canoe per 30min 390Kč; ☺9am-5pm) In summer, messing about on the river is a great way to keep cool. You can rent boats – a half-hour splash in a two-person canoe costs 390Kč, or you can rent a canoe for a full-day trip down the river from the town of Rožmberk (850Kč, six to eight hours).

Expedicion — ADVENTURE TOUR
(☎607 963 868; www.expedicion.cz; Soukenická 33; ☺9am-7pm) Expedicion rents out bikes (290Kč per day), arranges horse riding (250Kč per hour), and operates action-packed day trips (1680Kč including lunch) incorporating horse riding, fishing, mountain biking and rafting in the nearby Newcastle Mountains region.

Český Krumlov

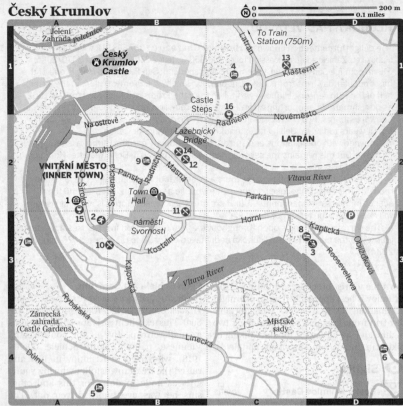

👉 Tours

Sebastian Tours
GUIDED TOUR

(📞607 100 234; www.sebastianck-tours.com; 5 Května Ul, Plešivec; day trip to Hluboká nad Vltavou per person 599Kč) Sebastian Tours can get you discovering South Bohemia on guided tours including stops at Hluboká nad Vltavou and České Budějovice. Also offers shuttle bus service to destinations further afield like Linz, Vienna and Salzburg in Austria.

🛏 Sleeping

Castle Apartments
APARTMENT €€

(📞380 725 110; www.zameckaapartma.cz; Latrán 45-47; apt 1800-3800Kč; ⊜🐾) Three adjoining houses near the castle district have been transformed into comfortable private apartments that offer wooden floors, and modern kitchenettes and bathrooms (no additional charge for the romantic views). Castle Apartments just may be Český Krumlov's best-value accommodation option.

🏆TOP CHOICE Dilettante's Hangout
GUESTHOUSE €

(📞728 280 033; www.dilettanteshangout.com; Plesivecke náměstí 93; r 790-990Kč; ⊜) Don't be fooled by the bland exterior. Inside this intimate homestay are three romantic, arty rooms decorated with mementos of the owner's global wanderings. Each room is unique, but they're all cosy and eclectic. There are kitchenettes for self-catering.

U Malého Vítka
HOTEL €€

(📞380 711 925; www.vitekhotel.cz; Radnični 27; d 1500Kč; 🅿⊜🐾) We really like this small hotel in the heart of the Old Town. The room furnishings are of high-quality, hand-crafted wood, and each room is named after a traditional Czech fairy-tale character. The downstairs restaurant and cafe are very good too.

Pension Kapr
PENSION €

(📞602 409 360; www.penzionkapr.cz; Rybářská 28; s 1000Kč; d 1200-1800Kč; @🐾) OK, it may be named after a fish (carp), but this river-

Český Krumlov

side pension, with exposed bricks and 500 years of history, has a quiet location and wonderful views of the Old Town. The lovely rooms, with whitewashed walls and wooden floors, are all named after the owners' children.

Krumlov House HOSTEL €
(☎380 711 935; www.krumlovhostel.com; Rooseveltova 68; dm/d/tr 300/750/1350Kč; ❄☎) Perched above the river, Krumlov House is friendly and comfortable, and has plenty of books, DVDs, and local information to feed your inner wanderer. Lots of day trips are on offer. The owners are English-speaking and traveller-friendly.

Pension Myší Díra PENSION €
(☎380 712 853; www.ceskykrumlov-info.cz; Rooseveltova 28; s/d from 1290/1590Kč; ℗❄@) This welcoming pension has a great location overlooking the river, and bright, beautiful rooms with lots of pale wood and quirky handmade furniture. Deluxe rooms and weekend accommodation (June to August) are 300Kč extra, but rates fall by 40% in winter. Breakfast is served in your room.

🍴 Eating

TOP CHOICE Laibon VEGETARIAN €€
(☎728 676 654; www.laibon.cz; Parkán 105; mains 90-180Kč; ❄☎☎) Candles and vaulted ceilings create a great boho ambience in the best little vegetarian teahouse in Bohemia. Just paging through the menu with seldom-seen words like guacamole and hummus can start the mouth watering. The riverside setting's pretty fine as well. Order the blueberry dumplings for dessert.

Nonna Gina ITALIAN €
(☎380 717 187; Klášterní 52; pizza 90-155Kč; ❄) Authentic Italian flavours from the authentic Italian Massaro family feature in this *pizzerie* down a quiet lane. Grab an outdoor table and pretend you're in Naples.

Krčma v Šatlavské CZECH €€
(☎380 713 344; www.satlava.cz; Horní 157; mains 150-260Kč) Nirvana for meat-lovers, this medieval barbecue cellar serves sizzling platters in a funky labyrinth illuminated by candles and the flickering flames of open grills. Booking ahead is essential. Be forewarned: summer months bring tour-bus crowds.

Hospoda Na Louži CZECH €
(☎380 711 280; www.nalouzi.cz; Kájovská 66; mains 90-170Kč; ❄) Nothing's changed in this wood-panelled *pivo* (beer) parlour for almost a century. Locals and tourists pack Na Louži for huge meals and tasty dark (and light) beer from the Eggenberg brewery.

U Dwau Maryí CZECH €
(☎380 717 228; www.2marie.cz; Parkán 104; mains 100-200Kč) This medieval tavern recreates old recipes and is your best chance to try dishes made with buckwheat and millet: all tastier than they sound. Wash the food down with a goblet of mead or choose a 21st-century Pilsner. In summer it's a tad touristy, but the stunning riverside castle views easily compensate.

🍷 Drinking

Café Schiele CAFE
(☎380 704 011; www.schieleartcentrum.cz; Široká 71; ⏱10am-7pm; ☎) A lovely cafe housed in the art gallery, with ancient oak floorboards, mismatched furniture and a grand piano with sawn-off legs serving as a coffee table. Excellent fair-trade coffee.

Zapa Cocktail Bar COCKTAIL BAR
(☎380 712 559; www.zapabar.cz; Latrán 15; ⏱6pm-1am) Český Krumlov empties out after dinner,

but Zapa keeps going most nights until after midnight. Expect great cocktails and a relaxed vibe.

❶ Information

Infocentrum (☑380 704 622; www.ckrumlov. info; náměstí Svornosti 1; ⊙9am-7pm Jun-Aug, to 6pm Apr, May, Sep & Oct, to 5pm Nov-Mar) Transport and accommodation info, maps, internet access (5Kč per five minutes) and audio guides (100Kč per hour). A guide for disabled visitors is available.

❶ Getting There & Away

BUS From Prague, Student Agency (p298) coaches (195Kč, three hours) leave regularly from the Na Knížecí bus station at Anděl metro station (Line B). Book in advance for weekends or in July and August.

TRAIN From Prague, the train journey (260Kč, 3½ hours) requires a change in České Budějovice. Buses are usually quicker and cheaper. There's a regular train service between České Budějovice and Český Krumlov (32Kč, 45 minutes).

MORAVIA

The Czech Republic's eastern province, Moravia, is yin to Bohemia's yang. If Bohemians love beer, Moravians love wine. If Bohemia is towns and cities, Moravia is rolling hills and pretty landscapes. Once you've seen the best of Bohemia, head east for a different side of the Czech Republic. The capital, Brno, has the museums, but the northern city of Olomouc has captivating architecture. The south is dominated by vineyards and, naturally, wine-drinking day-tipplers.

Brno

POP 387,200

Among Czechs, Moravia's capital has a dull rep: a likeable place where not much actually happens. There was even a hit movie a few years back called *Nuda v Brně (Boredom in Brno)*. The reality, though, is different. Tens of thousands of students ensure lively cafe and club scenes that easily rival Prague's. The museums are great too. Brno was one of the leading centres of experimental architecture in the early 20th century, and the Unesco-protected Vila Tugendhat is considered a masterwork of functionalist design.

◉ Sights

ŠPILBERK CASTLE & AROUND

Špilberk Castle CASTLE
(☑542 123 611; www.spilberk.cz; combined entry adult/concession 200/120Kč; ⊙9am-5pm Tue-Sun Oct-Apr, to 5pm daily May & Jun, 10am-6pm daily Jul-Sep) Brno's dramatic hilltop castle is considered the city's most important landmark, and is home to the **Brno City Museum** (muzeum města Brna; ☑542 123 611; www. spilberk.cz; Špilberk Castle; combined entry including admission to Špilberk Castle adult/concession 200/120Kč; ⊙9am-5pm Tue-Sun Oct-Apr, to 5pm daily May & Jun, 10am-6pm daily Jul-Sep). You can also visit the **casemates** (small rooms within the castle walls) and climb the lookout **tower**. Buy a combined entry ticket for all sights or purchase separate tickets; see the website for a full menu.

The two most popular exhibitions at the museum are **From Castle to Fortress**, on the castle's history, and **Prison of Nations**, on the role Špilberk played in the 18th and 19th centuries. Other exhibitions focus on the history, art and architecture of Brno. A combined ticket (adult/child 120/60Kč) gives access to all displays.

Cathedral of SS Peter & Paul CHURCH, TOWER
(katedrála sv Petra a Pavla; www.katedrala-petrov.cz; Petrov Hill; adult/concession tower 40/30Kč, crypts 20/10Kč; ⊙11am-6pm Mon-Sat, from 11.45am Sun) This 14th-century cathedral atop Petrov Hill was originally built on the site of a pagan temple to Venus, and has been reconstructed many times since. The highly decorated 11m-high main altar with figures of SS Peter and Paul was carved by Viennese sculptor Josef Leimer in 1891. You can also climb the **tower** for dramatic views, or visit the **crypts**.

The Renaissance **Bishop's palace** (closed to the public) adjoins the cathedral. To the left is the pleasant **Denisovy sady**, a verdant park sweeping around Petrov Hill.

HISTORIC CENTRE

Spacious **náměstí Svobody** is the city's bustling central hub. It dates from the early 13th century, when it was called Dolní trh (lower market). The **plague column** here dates from 1680, and the **House of the Lords of Lipá** (Dům Pánů z Lipé; nám Svobody 17) is a Renaissance palace (1589-96) with a 19th-century sgraffito facade and arcaded courtyard. On the eastern side of the square is the **House of the Four Mamlases** (Dům U čtyř mamlasů; nám Svobody 10). The facade here is supported by a quartet of well-muscled but clearly moronic 'Atlas' figures, each struggling to hold up the building and their loincloths at the same time.

FREE **Old Town Hall** HISTORIC BUILDING
(Stará radnice; Radnická 8; adult/concession tower 30/15Kč; ⊙9am-5pm) Brno's atmospheric Old Town Hall dates from the early 13th century. The tourist office (p320) is here, plus oddities including a crocodile hanging from the ceiling (known affectionately as the Brno 'dragon') and a wooden wagon wheel with a unique story. You can also climb the **tower**.

Capuchin Monastery CEMETERY
(Kapucínský klášter; www.kapucini.cz; adult/concession 60/30Kč; ⊙9am-noon & 1pm-4.30pm May-Sep, closed Mon mid-Feb–Apr & Oct–mid-Dec, closed mid-Dec–mid-Feb) One of the city's leading attractions is this ghoulish cellar crypt that holds the mummified remains of several city noblemen from the 18th century. Apparently the dry, well-ventilated crypt has the natural ability to turn dead bodies into mummies. Up to 150 cadavers were deposited here prior to 1784, the desiccated corpses including monks, abbots and local notables.

Brno Underground UNDERGROUND
(Brněnské podzemí; www.ticbrno.cz; Zelný trh 21; adult/concession 150/75Kč; ⊙9am-6pm Tue-Sun) In 2011 the city opened the first of what will be several opportunities to explore the underground passages of the medieval city. This tour takes around 40 minutes to explore several of the cellars situated 6m to 8m below the Cabbage Market. The cellars were built for two purposes: to store goods and to hide in during wars.

Church of St James CHURCH
(kostel sv Jakuba; ☎542 212 039; www.svatyjakub-brno.wz.cz; Jakubská 11; ⊙8am-6pm) This austere 15th-century church contains a baroque pulpit with reliefs of Christ dating from 1525. But the biggest drawcard is a small stone figure known as the 'Nehaňba' (The Shameless): above the 1st-floor window on the south side of the clock tower at the church's west end is the figure of a man baring his buttocks towards the cathedral. Local legend claims this was a disgruntled mason's parting shot to his rivals working on Petrov Hill.

OUTSIDE THE CENTRE

TOP CHOICE **Vila Tugendhat** ARCHITECTURE
(Villa Tugendhat; ☎515 511 015; www.tugendhat.eu; Černopolní 45; adult/concession 300/180Kč;

⊙10am-6pm Tue-Sun; ☐3, 5, 11) Brno had a reputation in the 1920s as a centre for modern architecture in the functionalist and Bauhaus styles. Arguably the finest example is this family villa, designed by modern master Mies van der Rohe in 1930. Entry is by guided tour, booked in advance by phone or via the website.

Mendel Museum MUSEUM
(Mendelianum; ☎543 424 043; www.mendel-museum.com; Mendlovo náměstí 1; adult/concession 60/30Kč; ⊙10am-6pm Tue-Sun Apr-Oct, to 5pm Nov-Mar) Gregor Mendel (1822–84), the Augustinian monk whose studies of peas and bees at Brno's Abbey of St Thomas established modern genetics, is commemorated here. In the garden are the foundations of Mendel's original greenhouse.

Museum of Romany Culture MUSEUM
(Muzeum romské kultury; ☎545 571 798; www.rommuz.cz; Bratislavská 67; adult/concession 40/20Kč; ⊙10am-6pm Mon-Fri, to 5pm Sun) This excellent museum provides an overdue positive showcase of Romany culture. Highlights include a couple of music-packed videos, period photographs from across Europe, and regular special exhibitions.

🛏 Sleeping

In February, April, August, September and October, Brno hosts major international trade fairs, and hotel rates increase by 40% to 100%. Book ahead if possible. For budget options, see the tourist information office for private rooms from around 400Kč. It can also help with accommodation in student dorms during July and August.

TOP CHOICE **Hostel Mitte** HOSTEL €
(☎734 622 340; www.hostelmitte.com; Panská 22; dm incl breakfast 490Kč, s/d 1000/1100Kč; ⊜@⊚) Set in the heart of the Old Town, this clean and stylish hostel opened in 2011 and still smells and looks brand new. The rooms are named after famous Moravians (like Milan Kundera) or famous events (Austerlitz) and decorated accordingly. There's a cute cafe on the ground floor with free wi-fi.

Hotel Europa HOTEL €€
(☎545 421 400; www.hotel-europa-brno.cz; třída kpt Jaroše 27; s/d 1375/1625Kč; ℙ⊜⊚) Set in a quiet neighbourhood a 10-minute walk from the centre, this self-proclaimed 'art' hotel (presumably for the wacky futuristic

lobby furniture) offers clean and tastefully furnished modern rooms in a historic 19th-century building. The lobby has free wi-fi, while the rooms have cable (ethernet) connections. There is free street parking out the front.

Hotel Pod Špilberkem
HOTEL €€

(☎543 235 003; www.hotelpodspilberkem.cz; Pekařská 10; s/d/tr 1400/1600/2500Kč; P✱@🖘) Tucked away near the castle are these quiet rooms, all clustered around a central courtyard. The secure car park is a good option for self-drive travellers.

Hotel & Pivnice Pegas
HOTEL €€

(☎542 210 104; www.hotelpegas.cz; Jakubská 4; s/d 2000/2500Kč; 🖘🖘) Centrally located, the Pegas has been refurbished to include huge beds, flat-screen TVs and updated bathrooms. Expect a friendly welcome at reception and the lure of the Pegas microbrewery and pub downstairs. The rooms are on the 4th floor, so there is no problem with noise from the bar.

Grandhotel
HOTEL €€

(☎542 518 111; www.grandhotelbrno.cz; Benešova 18-20; r from 2500Kč; P✱@🖘) Under Austrian ownership, Brno's oldest hotel has been refurbished to emerge as one of the city's most comfortable and characterful sleeping options. The building's heritage style now includes all modcons, including a gym and sauna. Rooms are spacious and quiet, despite the location opposite the train station. Check online for good discounts.

Hostel Fléda
HOSTEL €

(☎533 433 638; www.hostelfleda.com; Štefánikova 24; dm/d from 300/800Kč; 🖘🖘) A quick tram ride from the centre, one of Brno's best music clubs offers funky and colourful rooms. A nonsmoking cafe and good bar reinforce the social vibe. Catch tram 1 or 6 to the Hrnčirská stop.

✗ Eating

Koishi
ASIAN €€€

(☎777 564 744; www.koishi.cz; Údolní 11; mains 395-490Kč; ⊙11am-11pm Mon-Fri, 9am-11pm Sat

---

WORTH A TRIP

EXPLORING MORAVIA'S CAVES

The area to the immediate north of Brno has some of the Czech Republic's best caving in a region known as the Moravian Karst (Moravský kras). Carved with canyons and some 400 caves, the landscape is very pretty, with lots of woods and hills. See the excellent website www.cavemk.cz for information on the various caves in the area.

The karst formations here result from the seepage of faintly acidic rainwater through limestone, which over millions of years slowly dissolves it, creating hollows and fissures. In the caves themselves, the slow dripping of this water has produced extraordinary stalagmites and stalactites.

The organisational centre for any caving expedition is the town of **Blansko**, which has a good **tourist information office** (Blanenská Informační Kancelář; ☎516 410 470; www.blansko.cz; Rožmitálova 6, Blansko; ⊙9am-6pm Mon-Fri, to noon Sat) that sells maps and advance tickets to two of the main caves: the Punkva and Kateřinská Caves. The office can field transport questions and can help with accommodation. On weekends, particularly in July and August, cave-tour tickets sell out in advance, so try to book ahead with the tourist information office.

The most popular tour is through the **Punkva Cave** (Punkevní jeskyně; ☎516 418 602; www.smk.cz; adult/child 170/80Kč; ⊙8.40am-2pm Tue-Sun Jan-Mar, 8.20am-4pm Tue-Sun Apr-Sep, 8.40am-2pm Tue-Sun Oct-Dec). It involves a 1km walk through limestone caverns to the bottom of the Macocha Abyss, a 140m-deep sinkhole. Small, electric-powered boats then cruise along the underground river back to the entrance.

Another popular tour is to the **Kateřinská Cave** (Kateřinská jeskyně; ☎516 413 161; www.moravskykras.net; adult/child 80/60Kč; ⊙8.20am-4pm daily May-Aug, 9am-4pm Tue-Sun Apr & Sep, 9am-2pm Tue-Sun Oct, 10am-2pm Tue-Fri Mar & Nov, closed Dec-Feb). It's usually a little less crowded than the Punkva option. The 30-minute tour here explores two massive chambers.

Though it's easiest to explore the cave region with your own wheels, it is possible to see the caves on a day trip from Brno with public transport. Trains make the 30-minute run to Blansko hourly most days (37Kč): ask at Brno's tourist information office (p320).

& Sun; 😊🔊) Sushi master Tadayoshi Ebina and top seafood chef Petr Fučík have combined to bring award-winning cooking to Brno. Koishi has earned a reputation for excellent sushi, but it has since expanded its range to include more traditional European and Czech cooking, with an Asian touch. It has an excellent wine list as well. Reserve in advance.

Spolek CZECH €
(☑774 814 230; www.spolek.net; Orli 22; mains 60-140Kč; 😊9am-10pm Mon-Fri, 10am-10pm Sun; 🔊)
You'll get friendly, unpretentious service at this coolly 'bohemian' (yes, we're in Moravia) haven with interesting salads and soups, and a concise but diverse wine list. Photojournalism on the walls is complemented by a funky mezzanine bookshop. It has excellent coffee too.

Sabaidy ASIAN €
(☑545 428 310; www.sabaidy.cz; trída kpt Jaroše 29; mains 150-230Kč; 😊5-11pm Mon-Fri; 😊🔊)
With decor incorporating Buddhist statues and a talented Laotian chef delivering authentic flavours, Sabaidy delivers both 'om' and 'mmmm'. After lots of same-ish Czech food, this really is different. The easiest access is via Hotel Amphone at trída kpt Jaroše 29.

Špaliček CZECH €€
(☑542 215 526; Zelný trh 12; mains 160-310Kč; 😊)
Brno's oldest restaurant sits on the edge of the Cabbage Market. Ignore the irony and dig into huge Moravian meals, partnered with a local Starobrno beer or something from the decent local wine list.

Rebio VEGETARIAN €
(☑542 211 110; www.rebio.cz; Orli 26; mains 80-100Kč; 😊8am-7pm Mon-Fri, 10am-3pm Sat; 🔊)
Healthy risottos and vegie pies stand out in this self-service spot that changes its tasty menu every day. Organic beer and wine is available. There's another all-vegie branch at the **Velký Spaliček shopping centre** (Mečova 2, 1st fl; 😊9am-9pm Mon-Fri, 11am-8pm Sat & Sun).

 Drinking

U Richarda PUB
(☑775 027 918; www.uricharda2.cz; Údolní 7)
This microbrewery is highly popular with students, who come for the great housebrewed, unpasteurised yeast beers, including a rare cherry-flavoured lager, and good

traditional Czech cooking (mains 109Kč to 149Kč). Book in advance.

Pivnice Pegas PUB
(☑542 210 104; www.hotelpegas.cz; Jakubská 4)
Pivo melts that old Moravian reserve as the locals become pleasantly noisy. Don't miss the wheat beer with a slice of lemon. Try to book a table in advance, or grab a spot at one of Brno's longest bars. The food's pretty good too, but the interior can get smoky.

Avia CAFE
(☑739 822 215; www.aviacafe.cz; Botanická 1; 😊11am-10pm; 🔊) Popular student cafe-restaurant situated on the ground floor of the Jan Hus Congregational Church, a landmark functionalist building from 1929. The architecture and location, close to the university, lend an intellectual atmosphere. When you've tired of talking Proust, you can shoot pool in the adjoining billiard room.

Kavárna Vladimíra Menšíka CAFE
(☑777 001 411; Veselá 3; coffee 30-50Kč; 😊9am-11pm Mon-Sat, 11.30am-10pm Sun; 🔊) One of our favourite places to hide away in Brno is this corner cafe dedicated to late Czech film star Vladimír Menšík, a leading actor of the Czech New Wave. You'll find a relaxed space and good coffee, with pictures and film stills of Menšík all over the walls.

☆ **Entertainment**

Stará Pekárna CLUB, LIVE MUSIC
(☑541 210 040; www.starapekarna.cz; Štefánikova 8; 😊5pm-late Mon-Sat) Old and new music with blues, world beats, DJs and rock. Catch a 1, 6 or 7 tram to Pionýrská. Gigs usually kick off at 8pm.

Fléda LIVE MUSIC
(☑533 433 559; www.fleda.cz; Štefánikova 24; 😊to 2am) DJs, Brno's best up-and-coming bands and occasional touring performers all rock the stage at Brno's top music club. Catch tram 1 or 6 to the Hrnčírská stop.

Brno State Philharmonic Orchestra CLASSICAL MUSIC
(☑539 092 811; www.filharmonie-brno.cz; Komenského náměstí 8) City's main venue for classical music. Buy tickets at the **Philharmonic Orchestra Box Office** (Besedníul; 😊9am-2pm Mon & Wed, 1-6pm Tue, Thu & Fri).

Janáček Theatre OPERA, BALLET

(Janáčkovo divadlo; Rooseveltova 1-7, sady Osvobození) Hosts high-quality opera and ballet. Buy tickets at the **National Theatre Box Office** (Národní Divadlo v Brně Prodej Vstupnek; ☑542 158 120; www.ndbrno.cz; Dvořákova 11; ⏰8am-5.30pm Mon-Fri, to noon Sat).

Reduta Theatre CLASSICAL MUSIC, OPERA

(Reduta divadlo; www.ndbrno.cz; Zelný trh 4) Opera and classical music with an emphasis on Mozart (he played here in 1767). Buy tickets at the National Theatre Box Office.

Kino Art CINEMA

(☑541 213 542; www.kinoartbrno.cz; Cihlářská 19) Screens art-house films.

ℹ Information

Cyber Café (www.facebook.com/cybercafebrno; Mečova 2, Velký Spaliček shopping centre; per hr 60Kč; ⏰10am-10pm Mon-Sat; 📶) Has computers for surfing the web. There's also a free wi-fi hot spot in the Velký Spaliček shopping centre.

Tourist information office (☑542 211 090; www.ticbrno.cz; Radnická 8, Old Town Hall; ⏰8am-6pm Mon-Fri, 9am-6pm Sat & Sun) Sells maps and books accommodation. Free internet up to 15 minutes.

ℹ Getting There & Away

BUS Brno is well connected by bus; service to and from Prague (165Kč, 2½ hours) via the local coach service **Student Agency** (☑841 101 101; www.studentagency.cz) is especially good. The main bus station is behind the train station, though buses to Prague often leave from a small stop in front of the Grandhotel (p318). From Prague, buses depart from Florenc bus station hourly through the day.

TRAIN Express trains run between Brno's **train station** (☑541 171 111) and Prague's *hlavní nádraží* every couple of hours during the day (210Kč, 2½ hours). Brno is also a handy junction for onward train travel to Vienna (220Kč, two hours) and Bratislava (218Kč, 1½ hours).

ℹ Getting Around

Brno has a reliable system of trams and buses that hits most of the major spots (though you'll have to hike up to Špilberk (p316) on your own two legs). Buy public transport tickets from vending machines and newsstands. Tickets valid for 60 minutes cost 25Kč and allow unlimited transfers; 24-hour tickets are 70Kč. For taxis, try **City Taxis** (☑542 321 321).

Olomouc

POP 105,000

Olomouc is a sleeper. Practically unknown outside the Czech Republic and underappreciated at home, the city is surprisingly majestic. The main square is among the country's nicest, surrounded by historic buildings and blessed with a Unesco-protected trinity column. The evocative central streets are dotted with beautiful churches, testifying to the city's long history as a bastion of the Catholic Church. Explore the foundations of ancient Olomouc Castle at the must-see Archdiocesan Museum, then head for one of the city's many pubs or microbreweries. Don't forget to try the cheese, *Olomoucký sýr*, reputedly the smelliest in the country.

◎ Sights & Activities

HORNÍ NÁMĚSTÍ & AROUND

Olomouc's main square, Horní (or 'upper') náměstí, will be your first port of call. This is where the tourist office is, as well the city's most important sight: a gargantuan trinity column. The square also contains two of the city's six baroque fountains. The **Hercules Fountain** (Herkulova kašna) dates from 1688 and features the muscular Greek hero standing astride a pit of writhing serpents, while the **Caesar Fountain** (Caeserova kašna), east of the town hall, was built in 1724 and is Olomouc's biggest.

Holy Trinity Column MONUMENT

(Sousoší Nejsvětější trojice; Horní náměstí) The town's pride and joy is this 35m-high (115ft) baroque sculpture that dominates the square and is a popular meeting spot for local residents. The trinity column was built between 1716 and 1754 and is allegedly the biggest single baroque sculpture in Central Europe. In 2000, the column was awarded an inscription on Unesco's World Heritage list.

The individual statues depict a bewildering array of Catholic religious motifs, including the Holy Trinity, the 12 apostles, the assumption of Mary, and some of the best-known saints. There's a small **chapel** at the base of the column that's sometimes open during the day for you to poke your nose in.

FREE **Town Hall** TOWER

(Radnice; Horní náměstí; tower 15Kč) Olomouc's Town Hall dates from the 14th century and is home to one of the quirkier sights in town:

an astronomical clock from the 1950s, with a face in Socialist Realist style. The original was damaged in WWII. At noon the figures put on a little performance. The tower is open twice daily to climb, at 11pm and 3pm.

St Moritz Cathedral   CHURCH

(Chrám sv Mořice; www.moric-olomouc.cz; Opletalova 10; ⊘tower 9am-5pm Mon-Sat, noon-5pm Sun) This vast Gothic cathedral is Olomouc's original parish church, built between 1412 and 1540. The western tower is a remnant of its 13th-century predecessor. The cathedral's amazing sense of peace is shattered every September with an **International Organ Festival**; the cathedral's organ is Moravia's mightiest. The tower provides the best view in town.

DOLNÍ NÁMĚSTÍ & AROUND

Dolní náměstí (lower square), runs south of Horní náměstí and sports its own **Marian Plague Column** (Mariánský morový sloup) and baroque fountains dedicated to **Neptune** and **Jupiter**. The 1661 **Church of Annunciation of St Mary** stands out with its beautifully sober interior.

St Michael Church   CHURCH

(kostel sv Michala; www.svatymichal.cz; Žerotínovo náměstí 1; ⊘8am-6pm) This church on Žerotínovo náměstí has a green dome and a robust baroque interior with a rare painting of a pregnant Virgin Mary. Wrapped around the entire block is an active **Dominican seminary** (Dominikánský klášter).

NÁMĚSTÍ REPUBLIKY & AROUND

Olomouc Museum of Art   MUSEUM

(Olomoucký muzeum umění; ☑585 514 111; www.olmuart.cz; Denisova 47; adult/child 50/25Kč, Wed & Sun free; ⊘10am-6pm Tue-Sun) This popular museum houses an excellent collection of 20th-century Czech painting and sculpture. Admission includes entry to the Archdiocesan Museum (p321).

Archbishop's Palace   MUSEUM

(Arcibiskupský palác; ☑587 405 421; www.arcibiskupskypalac.ado.cz; Wurmova 9; adult/concession 60/30Kč; ⊘10am-5pm Tue-Sun May-Sep, 10am-5pm Sat & Sun Apr & Oct) This expansive former residence of the archbishop was built in 1685. Entry to see the lavish interiors is by guided tour only (free audioguide provided in English). It was here that Franz-Josef I was crowned Emperor of Austria in 1848 at the tender age of 18.

VÁCLAVSKÉ NÁMĚSTÍ & AROUND

It's hard to believe now, but this tiny square, northeast of the centre, was where Olomouc began. A thousand years ago this was the site of Olomouc Castle. You can still see the castle foundations in the lower levels of the Archdiocesan Museum. The area holds Olomouc's most venerable buildings and darkest secrets. Czech King Wenceslas III (Václav III) was murdered here in 1306 under circumstances that are still unclear to this day.

Archdiocesan Museum   MUSEUM

(Arcidiecézni muzeum; ☑585 514 111; www.olmuart.cz; Václavské náměstí 3; adult/concession 50/25Kč, Sun & Wed free; ⊘10am-6pm Tue-Sun) The impressive holdings of the Archdiocesan Museum trace the history of Olomouc back 1000 years. The thoughtful layout, with helpful English signage, takes you through the original Romanesque foundations of Olomouc Castle, and highlights the cultural and artistic development of the city during the Gothic and baroque periods.

St Wenceslas Cathedral   CHURCH

(dóm sv Václava; Václavské náměstí; ⊘8am-6pm) Adjacent to the museum, this cathedral, the seat of the Olomouc Archbishop, was originally a Romanesque basilica first consecrated back in 1131. It was rebuilt several times before having a neo-Gothic makeover in the 1880s. There's a crypt inside that you can enter.

🛏 Sleeping

Penzión Na Hradě   PENSION €€

(☑585 203 231; www.penzionnahrade.cz; Michalská 4; s/d 1390/1890Kč; ⊖🛜) Tucked away in the robust shadow of St Michael Church, this designer pension has sleek, cool rooms and professional service, creating a contemporary ambience in the heart of the Old Town.

Poet's Corner   HOSTEL €

(☑777 570 730; www.hostelolomouc.com; Sokolská 1, 3rd fl; dm/tw/tr/q 350/900/1200/1600Kč; ⊖🛜) The Australian-Czech couple who mind this friendly and exceptionally well-run hostel are a wealth of local information. Bicycles can be hired from 100Kč to 200Kč per day. In summer there's a two-night minimum stay, but Olomouc is definitely worth it, and there's plenty of day-trip information on offer.

Pension Angelus   PENSION €€

(☑776 206 936; www.pensionangelus.cz; Wurmova 1; s/d 1250/1850Kč; P⊖🛜) With antique

Olomouc

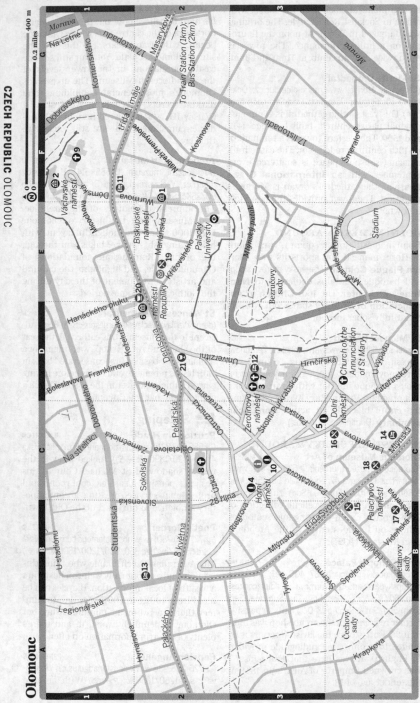

Morava

Na Letné

To Train Station (1km);
Bus Station (2km)

Moravě

Stadium

Michalské stromořadí

Masarykova

17. listopadu

17. listopadu

Šmeralova

Kosinova

Komenského

Dobrovského

třída 1. máje

Nábřeží Přemyslovců

⛪9

🏛2

Václavské
náměstí

Mlčochova

Dobrovská

Domská

11

Wurmova

1

Biskupské
náměstí

Mariánská

Palacký
University

Mlýnský potok

Bezručovy
sady

Hanáckého pluku

Koželužská

19

Křížkovského

20

6 🏛

náměstí
Republiky

Denisova

Univerzitní

12

Hrnčířská

Church of the
Annunciation
of St Mary

U Výpadu

Kateřinská

Boleslavova

Franklinova

Dobrovského

Na střelnici

Kateřní

Pekařská

Ostružnická

Zámečnická

21

Žerotínovo
náměstí

3 7

Školní

Pavelčákova

Purkrabská

panská

5

Dolní
náměstí

16

Lafayettova

14

Mlýnská

Studentská

Slovenská

Sokolská

Opletalova

Uhlíř

28. října

8

Horní
náměstí

4

10

třída Svobody

18

Palachovo
náměstí

Nešverova

Vídeňská

U stadiónu

8. května

Riegrova

Mlýnská

Havlíčkova

15

17

Sokolská

Smetanovy
sady

13

Tylova

Sokolská

Spojenců

Legionářská

Palackého

Hynaisova

Čechovy
sady

Krapkova

400 m

0.2 miles

Olomouc

furniture, crisp white duvets and oriental rugs on wooden floors, the Angelus is a spacious and splurge-worthy romantic getaway. To get here catch bus 2 or 6 from the train station or bus 4 from the bus station, jumping off at the U Domú stop.

Ubytovna Marie
GUESTHOUSE €

(🖉585 220 220; www.ubytovnamarie.cz; třída Svobody 41; per person 500Kč; 🖘🛜) Spick and span (if spartan) double and triple rooms with shared bathrooms and kitchens make this spot popular with long-stay overseas students. Significant discounts kick in after two nights.

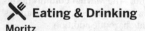

✕ Eating & Drinking

Moritz
CZECH €€

(🖉585 205 560; www.hostinec-moritz.cz; Nešverova 2; mains 120-260Kč; 🖘🛜) This microbrewery and restaurant is a firm local favourite. We reckon it's a combination of the terrific beers, good-value food and a praise-worthy 'no smoking' policy. In summer, the beer garden's the only place to be. Advance booking a must.

Nepal
NEPALESE €

(🖉585 208 428; www.nepalska.cz; Mlýnská 4; mains 110-150Kč; 🛜🖉) Located in a popular Irish pub, this Nepalese-Indian eatery is the place to go for something a little different. The 100Kč buffet lunch is the best deal, but loyal patrons say the quality of the food is better in the evening.

Drápal
CZECH €

(🖉585 225 818; www.restauracedrapal.cz; Havlíčkova 1; mains 110-150Kč; 🛜) It's hard to go wrong with this big, historic pub on a busy corner near the centre. The unpasteurised Pilsner Urquell is arguably the best beer in Olomouc. The smallish menu is loaded with Czech classics, like the ever-popular *Španělský ptáček* (literally 'Spanish bird'), a beef roulade stuffed with smoked sausage, parsley and a hard-boiled egg.

Svatováclavský Pivovar
CZECH €€

(🖉585 207 517; www.svatovaclavsky-pivovar.cz; Mariánská 4; mains 170-290Kč; 🖘) Another microbrewery (what's in the water in Olomouc?), this is a bit bigger than Moritz and it's easier to find a walk-in table here. The microbrewery produces several excellent versions of unpasteurised yeast beer. The menu features mostly Czech standards done well, plus a few dishes that experiment with Olomouc's signature stinky cheese.

Hanácacká Hospoda
CZECH €

(Dolní náměstí 38; mains 100-180Kč; 🖼) The menu lists everything in the local Haná dialect at this popular pub-restaurant. It's worth persevering though because the huge Moravian meals are tasty and supreme value. Don't worry – they've got an English menu if you're still getting up to speed with Haná.

🅃🄾🄿 Cafe 87
CAFE

(🖉585 202 593; Denisova 47; chocolate pie 35Kč, coffee 40Kč; 🕑7.30am-9pm Mon-Fri, 8am-9pm Sat & Sun; 🛜) Locals come in droves to this funky cafe beside the Olomouc Museum of Art for coffee and its famous chocolate pie. Some people still apparently prefer the dark chocolate to the white chocolate. When will they learn? It's a top spot for breakfast and toasted sandwiches too.

Vertigo
BAR

(www.klubvertigo.cz; Univerzitní 6; 🕑1pm-midnight Mon-Thu, 4pm-2am Fri-Sun) A dark, dank student bar that reeks of spilled beer and stale

CZECH BEER

There is an increasing number of excellent Czech regional beers worth investigating. Buy the *Good Beer Guide to Prague & the Czech Republic* by long-time Prague resident Evan Rail. In Prague it's available at Shakespeare & Sons (p297) or the Globe Bookstore & Cafe (p297). Here are our picks to get you started on your hoppy way:

» Pivovarský Klub (p293)
» Prague Beer Museum (p293)
» Na Parkánu (p310)
» U Richarda (p319)
» Svatováclavský Pivovar (p323)

smoke. In other words, a very popular drinking spot in a college town like Olomouc.

ℹ Information

Slam (www.slam.cz; Slovenská 12; per min 1Kč; ⏱9am-9pm Mon-Fri, from 10am Sat & Sun; 🛜) Internet.

Tourist information office (Olomoucká Informační Služba; ☎585 513 385; www. tourism.olomouc.eu; Horní náměstí ; ⏱9am-7pm) Sells maps and makes accommodation bookings.

ℹ Getting There & Away

BUS There are around 15 buses daily to/from Brno (92Kč, 1¼ hours), as well as dozens of other lines that service regional towns and cities; see www.jizdnirady.idnes.cz. The bus station is 1km east of the train station.

TRAIN Olomouc is on a main rail line, with regular services from both Prague (240Kč, three hours) and Brno (100Kč, 1½ hours). The train station (*hlavní nádraží*) is 2km east of the centre, over the Morava River and its tributary the Bystřice.

Telč

POP 6000

The Unesco-protected town of Telč, perched on the border between Bohemia and Moravia, possesses one of the country's prettiest and best-preserved historic town squares. Actually, we can't think of another that comes close. The main attraction is the beauty of the square itself, lined with Renaissance and baroque burgers' houses, with their brightly coloured yellow, pink and green facades.

Spend part of your visit simply ambling about, taking in the classic Renaissance chateau on the square's northwestern end and the parklands and ponds that surround the square on all sides. Telč empties out pretty quickly after the last tour bus leaves, so plan an overnight stay only if you're looking for some peace and quiet. In late July/early August the town holds the **Prázdniny v Telči** (www.prazdninyvtelci.cz) folk festival.

◉ Sights

Telč's sumptuous **Renaissance chateau** (Zámek; www.zamek-telc.cz; náměstí Zachariáše z Hradce; adult/concession Route A 110/70Kč, Route B 90/60Kč; ⏱9-11.45am & 1-6pm Tue-Sun Apr-Oct), part of which is known as the Water Chateau, guards the north end of the Telč peninsula. Entry is by guided tour only: Route A takes one hour, passing through the Renaissance halls; Route B takes 45 minutes, exploring the castle's apartment rooms.

The chateau was rebuilt from the original Gothic structure by Antonio Vlach (between 1553 and 1556) and Baldassare Maggi (from 1566 to 1568). The surviving structure remains in remarkably fine fettle, with immaculately tended lawns and beautifully kept interiors. In the ornate Chapel of St George (kaple sv Jiří), opposite the ticket office, are the remains of the castle's founder Zachariáš z Hradce.

Telč's stunning town square, **Náměstí Zachariáše z Hradce**, is a tourist attraction in its own right. Most houses here were built in Renaissance style in the 16th century after a fire levelled the town in 1530. Some facades were given baroque facelifts in the 17th and 18th centuries, but the overall effect is harmoniously Renaissance.

Some famous houses on the square include No 15, which shows the characteristic Renaissance sgraffito. The house at No 48 was given a baroque facade in the 18th century. No 61 has a lively Renaissance facade rich in sgraffito. The **Marian column** in the middle of the square dates from 1717, and is a relatively late baroque addition.

Dominating the town centre are the Gothic towers of the **Church of St James the Elderly** (kostel sv Jakuba Staršího; adult/concession 20/15Kč; ⏱10-11.30am & 1-6pm Tue-Sun Jun-Aug, 1-5pm Sat & Sun May & Sep). Also watching over the square is the baroque **Holy Name of Jesus Church** (kostel Jména Ježíšova; náměstí Zachariáše z Hradce 3; ⏱8am-6pm), completed in 1667 as part of a Jesuit college.

North of the square is a narrow lane leading to the old town's **Small Gate** (Malá brána), through which is a large English-style park surrounding the duck ponds (once the town's defensive moat). South along Palackého, toward the **Great Gate** (Velká brána), is the imposing Romanesque **Church of the Holy Spirit** (kostel sv Ducha; Palackého; ⊘7am-6pm) from the early 13th century. Outside the Great Gate you can walk along parts of Telč's remaining bastions.

Sleeping

Accommodation can be hard to get and expensive during the annual Prázdniny v Telči folk music festival in late July/early August, so book ahead. The tourist information office can book private rooms from 300Kč per night.

Pension Steidler PENSION €
(☑721 316 390; www.telc-accommodation.eu; náměstí Zachariáše z Hradce 52; s/d without breakfast 500/800Kč) Rooms reconstructed with skylights and wooden floors combine with an absolute town square location to deliver one of Telč's best-value places to stay. Some rooms have views of the lake. Breakfast costs 50Kč per person. Note there's a surcharge of 100Kč per room in summer (June to August) for stays of less than two nights.

Hotel Celerin HOTEL €€
(☑567 243 477; www.hotelcelerin.cz; náměstí Zachariáše z Hradce 43; s/d 980/1530Kč; ⊕❋🖭) Variety is king in the Celerin's 12 comfortable rooms, with decor ranging from cosy wood to white-wedding chintz (take a look first). Rooms 4, 5, 9 and 10 have views out onto the square. The hotel sometimes closes in winter.

Penzin Kamenné Slunce PENSION €
(☑732 193 510; www.kamenne-slunce.cz; Palackého 2; s/d 450/900Kč; 🅿🖭🖭) Lots of brick, exposed beams and warm wooden floors make this a very welcoming spot just off the main square. Hip bathrooms with colourful tiles are further proof that this is arguably Telč's coolest place to stay. Breakfast costs 70Kč.

Hotel Černý Orel HOTEL €€
(☑567 243 222; www.cernyorel.cz; náměstí Zachariáše z Hradce 7; s/d 1200/1800Kč; 🅿🖭🖭) Right on the main square, the 'Black Eagle' is just the ticket if you're into slightly faded, old-world ambience. While the rooms are comfortable, they don't rise to the level of the exquisite exterior. The ground-floor restaurant is one of the town's more popular lunch venues.

Eating & Drinking

U Marušky CZECH €
(☑602 432 904; Palackého 28; mains 90-170Kč) This simple pub caters more to locals than visitors, but offers decent home-cooked Czech meals with the added bonus of very good Ježek beer on tap. There's also a small beer garden open during summer. The daily lunch menu is a steal at 75Kč.

Švejk CZECH €
(www.svejk-telc.cz; náměstí Zachariáše z Hradce 1; mains 105-165Kč; 🖭) Classic Czech cooking in a publike setting next to the castle. The names of menu items, unsurprisingly, are taken from classic WWI comic novel *The Good Soldier Švejk*. 'Cadet Biegler' chicken, for example, turns out to be a schnitzel that's stuffed with ham and cheese. The outdoor terrace is popular in nice weather.

Pizzerie ITALIAN €
(☑567 223 246; náměstí Zachariáše z Hradce 32; pizza 80-130Kč) Right on the main square and right on the money for better-than-average pizza.

Kavarná Antoniana CAFE
(☑603 519 903; náměstí Zachariáše z Hradce 23; coffee 24-30Kč, cake 35Kč; ⊘8am-2am) The best coffee on the square, plus beer and alcoholic drinks, and inspirational black-and-white photos of Telč plastered on the wall. There are only limited food options, but the late opening hours mean it's one of the few places in the centre where you can get a drink in the evening.

Getting There & Around

BUS Around half a dozen buses make the run daily from Prague's Florenc bus station (170Kč, 2½ hours), with many connections requiring a change in Jihlava. Regional service is decent, with around five daily buses to and from Brno (100Kč, two hours). Check www.bus-vlak.cz for times and prices.

TRAIN Passenger train services have been greatly scaled back and are not recommended.

Mikulov

POP 7600

The 20th-century Czech poet Jan Skácel (1922–89) bequeathed Mikulov a tourist slogan for the ages when he penned that the town was a 'piece of Italy moved to Moravia by God's hand'. Mikulov is arguably the most attractive of the southern Moravian wine towns, surrounded by white, chalky hills and adorned with an amazing hill-top Renaissance chateau, visible for miles around. Mikulov was also once a thriving cultural centre for Moravia's Jewish community, and the former Jewish Quarter is slowly being rebuilt. Once you've tired of history, explore the surrounding countryside (on foot or bike) or relax with a glass of local wine.

◉ Sights & Activities

Mikulov Chateau CASTLE
(Zámek; ☎519 309 019; www.rmm.cz; Zámek 1; adult/concession 100/50Kč; ☺9am-5pm Tue-Sun May-Sep, to 4pm Apr & Oct) This chateau was the seat of the Dietrichstein family from 1575 to 1945, and played an important role in the 19th century, hosting on separate occasions French Emperor Napoleon, Russia's Tsar Alexander and Prussian King Frederick. Much of the castle was destroyed by German forces in February 1945: the lavish interiors are the result of a painstaking reconstruction.

The castle is accessible by guided tour only. The full history tour takes two hours and visits significant castle rooms as well as exhibitions on viticulture and archaeology. There are three more specialised, shorter tours also available.

Jewish Quarter NEIGHBOURHOOD
(Husova) Mikulov was a leading centre of Moravian Jewish culture for several centuries until WWII. The former **synagogue** (Synagóga; ☎519 510 255; Husova 11; ☺1-5pm Tue-Sun 15 May-30 Sep) has a small exhibition on the Jews of Mikulov. It was under reconstruction during our research and it wasn't clear when it would reopen.

The evocative **Jewish Cemetery** (Židovský hřbitov; Vinohrady; adult/concession 20/10Kč; ☺9am-5pm Mon-Fri Jul & Aug) is a 10-minute walk from the tourist office. To find it, walk out Brněnská and look for a sign leading off to the right. Additionally, an 'instructive trail' runs through the Jewish Quarter, with information plaques in English. You can pick it up at the end of Husova near Alfonse Muchy.

WORTH A TRIP

LEDNICE & VALTICE

A few kilometres east of Mikulov, the Unesco-protected historic landscape of Lednice and Valtice is a popular weekend destination for Czechs, who tour the historic architecture, hike and bike, and sample the region's wines. The two towns are about 10km apart, connected by regular buses. Neither offers much in terms of nightlife, so they're best visited as a day trip from either Mikulov or Brno.

If you've got more time, either town makes a perfect base for exploring the rolling hills of the southern Moravian wine country: hundreds of miles of walking and cycling trails criss-cross a mostly unspoiled landscape.

Owned by the Liechtenstein family from 1582 to 1945, **Lednice Chateau** (Zámek; ☎519 340 128; www.zamek-lednice.com; Zámek, Lednice; adult/child standard tour 1 150/100Kč, tour 2 150/100Kč; ☺9am-6pm Tue-Sun May-Aug, to 5pm Tue-Sun Sep, to 4pm Sat & Sun only Apr & Oct) is one of the country's most popular weekend destinations. The crowds come for the splendid interiors and extensive gardens, complete with an exotic-plant greenhouse, lakes with pleasure boats, and a mock Turkish minaret – architectural excess for the 19th-century nobility.

Valtice Chateau (Zámek; ☎519 352 423; www.zamek-valtice.cz; Zámek 1, Valtice; standard tour adult/concession 100/80Kč; ☺9am-noon & 1-6pm Tue-Sun May-Aug, to 5pm Sep, to 4pm Apr & Oct), dating originally from the 12th century before getting a baroque facelift, is one of the Czech Republic's finest baroque structures, the work of JB Fischer von Erlach and Italian architect Domenico Martinelli. Entry is by guided-tour only, with two different tours on offer (in Czech, with English text available). The grounds and gardens are free for you to explore during opening times.

Valtice has regular train service throughout the day to/from Mikulov (23Kč, 12 minutes) and Břeclav (25Kč, 15 minutes), which has excellent onward connections to Brno, Bratislava and Vienna.

Both Lednice and Valtice are easily reachable by bus from Brno or Mikulov. Regular buses shuttle the short distance between Lednice and Valtice (20Kč, 15 minutes).

Goat Hill
HILL, LOOKOUT

(Kozí hrádek; tower 20Kč; ☉tower 9am-6pm May-Sep) Goat Hill is topped with an abandoned 15th-century **lookout tower** offering stunning views over the Old Town. To find it, walk uphill from the Jewish Cemetery, following a red-marked trail. Note that the tower keeps irregular hours: it's only open when the flag is flying. But even if the tower is closed, the views from the hilltop are spectacular.

Holy Hill
HILL, CHURCH

(Svatý kopeček; Gernerála Svobody) Another uphill venture is to scale the 1km path up this 363m peak, through a nature reserve and past grottos depicting the Stations of the Cross, to the compact **Church of St Sebastian**. The blue-marked trail begins at the bottom of the main square on Svobody. The whitewashed church and the limestone on the hill give it a Mediterranean ambience.

Dietrichstein Burial Vault
MAUSOLEUM

(Dietrichštejnská hrobka; náměstí 5; adult/concession 50/25Kč; ☉10am-6pm daily Jun-Aug, 9am-5pm Tue-Sun Apr, May, Sep & Oct) The Dietrichstein family mausoleum occupies the former St Anne's Church. The front of the building features a remarkable baroque facade – the work of Austrian master Johann Bernhard Fischer von Erlach – dating from the early 18th century. The tombs, dating from 1617 to 1852, hold the remains of 45 family members.

Mikulov Wine Trail
HIKING, CYCLING

A pleasant way to visit smaller, local vineyards across the rolling countryside is by bicycle on the Mikulov Wine Trail. The tourist office can recommend a one-day ride that also takes in the nearby chateaux at Valtice and Lednice. Bicycles and additional cycle touring information are available from **RentBike** (☎737 750 105; www.rentbike.cz; Kostelní náměstí 1; rental per hr/day 110/330Kč).

🛏 Sleeping

TOP CHOICE **Hotel Templ**
HOTEL €€

(☎519 323 095; www.templ.cz; Husova 50; s/d from 1390/1650Kč; P🌀🕸) This beautifully reconstructed, family-run hotel comprises a main building and an annex, two doors down. The updated rooms are done out in cheerful tiles and stained glass. The baths are as stylish as the rooms. Some rooms, such as ours (No 11 in the annex), open onto a secluded patio with tables for relaxing in the evening.

Pension Baltazar
PENSION €€

(☎519 324 327; www.pensionbaltazar.cz; Husova 44; d 1200-1800Kč; P🌀🕸) You'll find this place a few doors up from the Hotel Templ. Beautifully resurrected rooms effortlessly combine modern furniture with exposed-brick walls and wooden floors.

Penzión Husa
PENSION €€

(☎731 103 283; www.penzionhusa.cz; Husova 30; d 1590Kč; P🌀🕸) Yet another beautiful pension on Husova, the 'Goose' boasts furnishings with period flare, like canopy beds and big oriental rugs on top of hardwood floors. This place is popular, so try to book well in advance.

🍴 Eating & Drinking

Restaurace Templ
CZECH €€

(☎519 323 095; www.templ.cz; Husova 50; mains 165-280Kč; 🌀🕸) The best restaurant in town is matched by a fine wine list specialising in local varietals. The menu features an appetising mix of duck, pork and chicken dishes. Choose from either the formal restaurant or relaxed wine garden. There's also a small terrace out the back for dining alfresco on warm evenings.

Hospůdka Pod Zámkem
CZECH €

(☎519 512 731; www.hospudkapodzamkem.cz; Husova 49; daily special 69Kč; 🕸) This funky combination of old-school pub and coffee bar serves simple but very good Czech meals, usually limited to a few daily specials like soup plus roast pork or chicken drumsticks. It's also the unlikely home of Mikulov's best coffee and serves very good Gambrinus beer to boot. Find it across the street from the Hotel Templ.

Restaurace Alfa
CZECH €

(☎519 510 877; náměstí 27; mains 130-200Kč) The Alfa's beautiful sgraffito building, just across the square from the tourist information office, hides what's basically an ordinary Czech pub on the inside. That said, the kitchen turns out well-done Czech cooking, and there are even a few game dishes on the menu.

Petit Café
CAFE

(☎733 378 264; náměstí 27; crepes 40-70Kč; 🕸) Tasty crepes and coffee are dished up in a hidden courtyard/herb-garden setting. Later at night, have a beer or a glass of wine.

Vinařské Centrum   WINE BAR
(☑519 510 368; www.vinarskecentrum.com; náměstí 11; ⊘9am-9pm Mon-Sat, 10am-9pm Sun) This drinking room has an excellent range of local wines available in small tasting glasses (15Kč to 50Kč), or whole bottles when you've finally made up your mind.

ⓘ Information

Tourist information office (☑519 510 855; www.mikulov.cz; náměstí 1; ⊘8am-6pm Mon-Fri, 9am-6pm Sat & Sun Jun-Sep, 8am-noon & 12.30-5pm Mon-Fri, 9am-4pm Sat & Sun Apr, May & Oct) Organises tours (including specialist outings for wine buffs) and accommodation, and has internet access (1Kč per minute).

ⓘ Getting There & Away

BUS Mikulov is easily reached by bus from Brno (65Kč, 1½ hours), with coaches leaving hourly. From Prague, there are few direct buses; the best approach is to catch a bus for Brno and change. Regional bus services are good, with frequent buses to/from Valtice and Lednice.

TRAIN There are several daily trains to and from Břeclav (39Kč, 30 minutes), an important junction for onward services to Brno, Bratislava and Vienna. See the online timetable at www.vlak-bus.cz.

UNDERSTAND CZECH REPUBLIC

History

Over the centuries, the Czechs have been invaded by the Habsburgs, the Nazis and the Soviets, and the country's location has meant domestic upheavals have not stayed local for long. Their rejection of Catholicism in 1418 resulted in the Hussite Wars. The 1618 revolt against Habsburg rule ignited the Thirty Years' War, and the German annexation of the Sudetenland in 1938 helped fuel WWII. The liberal reforms of 1968's Prague Spring led to tanks rolling in from across the Eastern Bloc, and the peaceful ousting of the government during 1989's Velvet Revolution was a model for freedom-seekers everywhere.

Bohemian Beginnings

Ringed by hills, the ancient Czech lands of Bohemia and Moravia have formed natural territories since the earliest times. Slavic tribes from the east settled and were united from 830 to 907 in the Great Moravian Empire. Christianity was adopted after the arrival in 863 of the Thessalonian missionaries Cyril and Methodius, who created the first Slavic (Cyrillic) alphabet.

In the 9th century, the first home-grown dynasty, the Přemysls, erected some huts in what was to become Prague. This dysfunctional clan gave the Czechs their first martyred saints – Ludmila, killed by her daughter-in-law in 874, and her grandson, the pious Prince Václav (or Good 'King' Wenceslas; r 921–29), murdered by his brother Boleslav the Cruel.

The Přemysls' rule ended in 1306, and in 1310 John of Luxembourg came to the Bohemian throne through marriage, and annexed the kingdom to the German empire. The reign of his son, Charles IV (1346–78), who became Holy Roman Emperor, saw the first of Bohemia's two 'Golden Ages'. Charles founded Prague's St Vitus Cathedral, built Charles Bridge and established Charles University. The second was the reign of Rudolf II (1576–1612), who made Prague the capital of the Habsburg Empire and attracted artists, scholars and scientists to his court. Bohemia and Moravia remained under Habsburg dominion for almost four centuries.

Under the Habsburg Thumb

In 1415 Protestant religious reformer Jan Hus, rector of Charles University, was burnt at the stake for heresy. He inspired the nationalist Hussite movement that plunged Bohemia into civil war (1419–34).

When the Austrian and Catholic Habsburg dynasty ascended the Bohemian throne in 1526, the fury of the Counter-Reformation was unleashed after Protestants threw two Habsburg councillors from a Prague Castle window. This escalated into the Catholic–Protestant Thirty Years' War (1618–48), which devastated much of Central Europe.

The defeat of the Protestants at the Battle of White Mountain in 1620 marked the start of a long period of rule from Vienna, including forced re-Catholicisation, Germanisation and oppression of Czech language and culture.

National Reawakening

The Czechs started to rediscover their linguistic and cultural roots at the start of the

19th century, during the so-called Národní obrození (National Revival). Overt political activity was banned, so the revival was culturally based. Important figures included historian Josef Palacký and composer Bedřich Smetana.

An independent Czech and Slovak state was realised after WWI, when the Habsburg empire's demise saw the creation of the Czechoslovak Republic in October 1918. Three-quarters of the Austro-Hungarian empire's industrial power was inherited by Czechoslovakia, as were three million Germans, mostly in the border areas of Bohemia (the *pohraniči*, known in German as the Sudetenland).

The Czechs' elation was to be short-lived. Under the Munich Pact of September 1938, Britain and France accepted the annexation of the Sudetenland by Nazi Germany, and in March 1939 the Germans occupied the rest of the country (calling it the Protectorate of Bohemia and Moravia).

Most of the Czech intelligentsia and 80,000 Jews died at the hands of the Nazis. When Czech paratroopers assassinated Nazi governor Reinhardt Heydrich in 1942, the entire town of Lidice was wiped out in revenge.

Communist Coup

After the war, the Czechoslovak government expelled 2.5 million Sudeten Germans – including antifascists who had fought the Nazis – from the Czech borderlands and confiscated their property. During the forced marches from Czechoslovakia many were interned in concentration camps and tens of thousands died.

In 1947 a power struggle began between the communist and democratic forces, and in early 1948 the Social Democrats withdrew from the postwar coalition. The result was the Soviet-backed coup d'état of 25 February 1948, known as Vítězný únor (Victorious February). The new communist-led government established a dictatorship, which resulted in years of oppression. In the 1950s thousands of noncommunists fled the country. Others were captured and imprisoned, and hundreds were executed or died in labour camps.

Prague Spring & Velvet Revolution

In April 1968 the new first secretary of the Communist Party, Alexander Dubček, introduced liberalising reforms to create 'socialism with a human face' – known as 'Prague Spring'. Censorship ended, political prisoners were released and economic decentralisation began. Moscow was not happy, but Dubček refused to buckle and Soviet tanks entered Prague on 20 August 1968, closely followed by 200,000 Soviet and Warsaw Pact soldiers.

Many pro-reform Communist Party functionaries were expelled and 500,000 party members lost their jobs after the dictatorship was re-established. Dissidents were summarily imprisoned and educated professionals were made manual labourers.

The 1977 trial of the underground rock group the Plastic People of the Universe (for disturbing the peace at an unauthorised music festival) inspired the formation of the human-rights group Charter 77. The communists saw the musicians as threatening the status quo, but others viewed the trial as an assault on human rights. Charter 77's group of Prague intellectuals, including late playwright–philosopher Václav Havel, continued their underground opposition throughout the 1980s.

By 1989 Gorbachev's reforms, called *perestroika*, and the fall of the Berlin Wall on 9 November raised expectations of change. On 17 November an official student march in Prague was smashed by police. Daily demonstrations followed, culminating in a general strike on 27 November. Dissidents led by Havel formed the Anti-Communist Civic Forum and negotiated the resignation of the Communist government on 3 December, less than a month after the fall of the Berlin Wall.

A 'Government of National Understanding' was formed, with Havel elected president on 29 December. With no casualties, the days after 17 November became known as Sametová revoluce (the Velvet Revolution).

Velvet Divorce

Following the end of communist central authority, antagonisms between Slovakia and Prague re-emerged. The federal parliament granted both the Czech and Slovak Republics full federal status within a Czech and Slovak Federated Republic (ČSFR), but this failed to satisfy Slovak nationalists.

Elections in June 1992 sealed Czechoslovakia's fate. Václav Klaus' Civic Democratic Party (ODS) took 48 seats in the 150-seat federal parliament, while 24 went to the Movement for a Democratic Slovakia (HZDS), a left-leaning Slovak nationalist party led by Vladimír Mečiar.

In July the Slovak parliament declared sovereignty, and on 1 January 1993 Czechoslovakia ceased to exist for the second time. Prague became capital of the new Czech Republic, and Havel was elected its first president.

A New Country

Thanks to booming tourism and a solid industrial base, the Czech Republic enjoyed negligible unemployment and by 2003 Prague enjoyed Eastern Europe's highest standard of living. However, capitalism also meant a lack of affordable housing, rising crime and a deteriorating health system.

The Czech Republic became a member of NATO in 1999, and joined the EU on 1 May 2004. With EU membership, greater numbers of younger Czechs are now working and studying abroad, seizing opportunities their parents didn't have.

The celebrated dissident and first president after the Velvet Revolution, Václav Havel, died in 2011 after a long battle with cancer. His death rallied Czechs of all political stripes and marked what many saw as a formal end to the post-communist transition period.

People

The population of the Czech Republic is 10.5 million (2012 estimate); 95% of the population are Czech and 3% are Slovak. Only 150,000 of the three million Sudeten Germans evicted after WWII remain. A significant Roma population (0.3%) is subject to hostility and racism, suffering from poverty and unemployment.

Most Czechs profess to be atheist (39.8%) or nominally Roman Catholic (39.2%), but church attendance is low. There are small Protestant (4.6%) and Orthodox (3%) congregations. The Jewish community (1% in 1918) today numbers only a few thousand.

Arts

Literature

The communist period produced two Czech writers of world standing, both of whom hail originally from Brno: Milan Kundera (b 1929) and Bohumil Hrabal (1914–97).

For many visitors, Kundera remains the undisputed champ. His wryly told stories weave elements of humour and sex along with liberal doses of music theory, poetry and philosophy to appeal to both our low- and high-brow literary selves. His best known book, *The Unbearable Lightness of Being* (also made into a successful film in 1988), is set in Prague in the uncertain days ahead of the 1968 Warsaw Pact invasion. Look out too for Kundera's *The Joke* and *The Book of Laughter and Forgetting*.

Ask any Czech who their favourite author is and chances are they'll say Hrabal, and it's not hard to see why. Hrabal's writing captures what Czechs like best about themselves, including a keen wit, a sense of the absurd and a fondness for beer. Hrabal is also a great storyteller, and novels such as *I Served the King of England* and *The Little Town Where Time Stood Still* are both entertaining and insightful. Hrabal died in 1997 in classic Czech fashion: falling from a window.

No discussion of Czech literature would be complete without mentioning Franz Kafka (1883–1924), easily the best-known writer to have ever lived in Prague and the author of modern classics *The Trial* and *The Castle*, among many others. Though Kafka was German-speaking and Jewish, he's as thoroughly connected to the city as any Czech writer could be.

Kafka's Czech contemporary, and polar opposite, was the pub scribe Jaroslav Hašek (1883–1923), author of *The Good Soldier Švejk*, a book that is loved and reviled in equal doses. For those who get the jokes, it is a comic masterpiece of a bumbling, likeable Czech named Švejk and his (intentional or not) efforts to avoid military service for Austria-Hungary during WWI. Czechs tend to bridle at the assertion that an idiot like Švejk could somehow embody any national characteristic.

Art & Music

Czechs have always been active contributors to the arts, and no trip to Prague would be complete without a stroll through the city's major museums and galleries to admire the work of local painters, photographers and sculptors. For evenings, you'll be spoiled for choice among offerings of classical music, jazz and rock.

Two Czechs, Antonín Dvořák (1841–1904) and Bedřich Smetana (1824–84), are household names in classical music. Dvořák was heavily influenced by the Czech National Revival, which inspired his two *Slavonic Dances* (1878 and 1881), the operas *Rusalka*

THE CHALLENGING MR ČERNÝ

Czech installation artist David Černý (b 1967) has cultivated a reputation as the enfant terrible of the Prague and European art scenes. He first made international headlines in 1991 when he painted a WWII memorial with a Soviet tank bright pink, and his installations (several around Prague) manage to amuse and provoke in equal measure.

In Prague's Lucerna pasáž, he's hung St Wenceslas and his horse upside down, and across the river outside the Kafka Museum, Černý's *Piss* sculpture invites contributions by SMS. Rising above the city, like a faded relic from *Star Wars*, is the Žižkov TV Tower with Černý's giant babies crawling up the exterior.

Černý's other recent project is **MeetFactory** (www.meetfactory.cz), a multipurpose gallery, artists' collective and performance space in a former factory in Smíchov.

and *Čert a Kača (The Devil and Kate)*, and his religious masterpiece, *Stabat Mater*. He spent four years in the USA, where he composed his famous *Symphony No 9, From the New World*. Smetana wrote several operas and symphonies, and his signature work remains his *Moldau (Vlatva)* symphony.

Alfons Mucha (1860–1939) is probably the most famous visual artist to come out of the Czech lands, though because he attained his fame mostly in Paris, and not in Prague, his reputation remains more exalted abroad than at home.

Film

The 1960s was a decade of relative artistic freedom, and talented young directors such as Miloš Forman and Jiří Menzel crafted bittersweet films that charmed moviegoers with their grit and wit, while at the same time poking critical fun at their communist overlords.

During that period, dubbed the 'Czech New Wave', Czechoslovak films twice won the Oscar for 'Best Foreign Film', for the *Little Shop on Main Street* in 1965 and *Closely Watched Trains* in 1967. Forman eventually left the country and went on to win 'Best Picture' Oscars for *One Flew Over the Cuckoo's Nest* and *Amadeus*, which was partly filmed in Prague.

Since the Velvet Revolution, directors have struggled to make meaningful films, given the tiny budgets and a constant flood of Hollywood blockbusters. At the same time, they've had to endure nonstop critical scrutiny that their output meet the high standards set during the New Wave.

In recent years historical films have made a comeback, particularly films that explore WWII and the Nazi occupation. The best include director Adam Dvořák's *Lidice* (2011), Jan Hřebejk's *Kawasaki Rose* (2009) and Tomáš Lunák's *Alois Nebel* (2010). The latter is an inventive interpretation of a graphic novel on the final days of WWII and the subsequent expulsion of Czech Germans.

Environment

The landlocked Czech Republic is bordered by Germany, Austria, Slovakia and Poland. The land is made up of two river basins: Bohemia in the west, drained by the Labe (Elbe) River flowing north into Germany; and Moravia in the east, drained by the Morava River flowing southeast into the Danube. Each basin is ringed by low, forest-clad hills, notably the Šumava range along the Bavarian–Austrian border in the southwest, the Krušné hory (Ore Mountains) along the northwestern border with Germany, and the Krkonoše mountains along the Polish border east of Liberec. The country's highest peak, Sněžka (1602m), is in the Krkonoše.

Food & Drink

The classic Bohemian dish is *vepřo-knedlo-zelo,* slang for a plate of roast pork, bread dumplings and sauerkraut. Also look out for *svíčková na smetaně* (braised beef in a cream sauce) and *kapr na kmíní* (fried or baked carp with caraway seed).

A *bufet* or *samoobsluha* is a self-service cafeteria with *chlebíčky* (open sandwiches), salads, *klobásy* (spicy sausages), *špekačky* (mild pork sausages), *párky* (frankfurters), *guláš* (goulash) and of course *knedlíky* (those ubiquitous dumplings).

A *pivnice* is a pub without food, while a *hospoda* or *hostinec* is a pub or beer hall serving basic meals. A *vinárna* (wine bar) has anything from snacks to a full-blown menu. The occasional *kavárna* (cafe) has a full menu, but most only serve snacks and desserts. A *restaurace* is any restaurant.

In Prague and other main cities you'll find an increasing number of excellent vegetarian restaurants, but smaller towns' choices remain limited. There are a few standard *bezmasá jídla* (meatless dishes) served by most restaurants. The most common are *smažený sýr* (fried cheese) and vegetables cooked with cheese sauce.

For nonsmoking premises, look out for signs saying *Kouření zakázano*.

Beer & Wine

One of the first words of Czech you'll learn is *pivo* (beer). Most famous are Budvar and Pilsner Urquell, but there are many other local brews to be discovered.

Most beer halls have a system of marking everything you eat or drink on a small piece of paper that is left on your table, then totted up when you pay (say *zaplatím, prosím* – I'd like to pay, please).

The South Moravian vineyards around the town of Mikulov produce improving *bílé víno* (white wines).

SURVIVAL GUIDE

Directory A–Z

Accommodation

Outside the peak summer season, hotel rates can fall by up to 40%. Booking ahead – especially in Prague – is recommended for summer and around Christmas and Easter. Many hotels are now completely or mostly nonsmoking.

Prices quoted here are for rooms with a private bathroom and a simple breakfast, unless otherwise stated. The following price indicators apply (for a high-season double room):

€ less than 1600Kč

€€ 1600Kč to 3700Kč

€€€ more than 3700Kč

CAMPING

Most campsites are open from May to September only and charge around 80Kč to 100Kč per person. Camping on public land is prohibited. See **Czech Camping** (www.czech-camping.com) and **Do Kempu** (www.czech-camping.com) for information and online booking.

HOSTELS

Prague and Český Krumlov are the only places with a choice of backpacker-oriented hostels. Dorm beds costs around 450Kč in Prague and 350Kč to 450Kč elsewhere. Booking ahead is recommended. **Czech Youth Hostel Association** (www.czechhostels.com) offers information and booking for Hostelling International (HI) hostels.

HOTELS

Hotels in central Prague, Český Krumlov and Brno can be expensive, but smaller towns are usually significantly cheaper. Two-star hotels offer reasonable comfort for 1000Kč to 1200Kč for a double, or 1200Kč to 1500Kč with private bathroom (around 50% higher in Prague). It's always worth asking for a weekend discount in provincial Czech cities and towns. See **Czech Hotels** (www.czechhotels.net) and **Discover Czech** (www.discoverczech.com).

PRIVATE ROOMS & PENSIONS

Look for signs advertising *privát* or *Zimmer frei* (private rooms). Most tourist information offices can book for you. Expect to pay from 450Kč to 550Kč per person outside Prague. Bathrooms are usually shared.

Penzióny (pensions) are small, often family-run, accommodation offering rooms with private bathroom and breakfast. Rates range from 1000Kč to 1500Kč for a double room (1900Kč to 2500Kč in Prague). See **Czech Pension** (www.czechpension.cz).

Business Hours

Banks 8.30am to 4.30pm Monday to Friday

Bars 11am to midnight

Museums & Castles Usually closed Monday year-round

Restaurants 11am to 11pm

Shops 8.30am to 6pm Monday to Friday, 8.30am to noon Saturday

Embassies & Consulates

Most embassies and consulates are open at least 9am to noon Monday to Friday. All of the following are in Prague.

Australian Consulate (☏221 729 260; www.dfat.gov.au/missions/countries/cz.html; 6th fl, Klimentská 10, Nové Město; ⬛5, 8, 14, 26) Honorary consulate for emergency assistance only (eg a stolen passport); the nearest Australian embassy is in Vienna.

Canadian Embassy (☏272 101 800; www.canadainternational.gc.ca; Muchova 6, Bubeneč; Ⓜ Hradčanská)

French Embassy (☏251 171 711; www.france. cz; Velkopřevorské náměstí 2, Malá Strana; 🚊12, 20, 22)

German Embassy (☏257 113 111; www. deutschland.cz; Vlašská 19, Malá Strana; 🚊12, 20, 22)

Irish Embassy (☏257 530 061; www.embassyofireland.cz; Tržiště 13, Malá Strana; 🚊12, 20, 22)

Netherlands Embassy (☏233 015 200; www.netherlandsembassy.cz; Gotthardská 6/27, Bubeneč; 🚊1, 8, 15, 25, 26 then walk)

New Zealand Consulate (☏222 514 672; egermayer@nzconsul.cz; Dykova 19, Vinohrady; Ⓜ️Jiřího z Poděbrad)

Russian Embassy (☏233 375 650; www. czech.mid.ru; Korunovační 34, Bubeneč; 🚊1, 8, 15, 25, 26)

UK Embassy (☏257 402 111; http://ukinczechrepublic.fco.gov.uk; Thunovská 14, Malá Strana; 🚊12, 20, 22)

US Embassy (☏257 022 000; http://czech. prague.usembassy.gov; Tržiště 15, Malá Strana; 🚊12, 20, 22)

Food

Restaurants open as early as 11am and carry on till midnight; some take a break between lunch and dinner. The following price indicators apply to a main meal.

€ less than 200Kč

€€ 200Kč to 500Kč

€€€ more than 500Kč

Gay & Lesbian Travellers

Homosexuality is legal in the Czech Republic, but Czechs are not yet used to seeing public displays of affection; it's best to be discreet. For online information including links to accommodation and bars, see the **Prague Gay Guide** (www.prague.gay guide.net).

Internet Access

Most Czech accommodation now offers wi-fi access, and internet cafes remain common throughout the country. An increasing number of Infocentrum (tourist information) offices also offer internet access. In this guide, we've used the 🛜 symbol to denote places that offer wi-fi and the @ symbol for places that allow access to a computer.

Money

ATMS

ATMS linked to the most common global banking networks can be easily located in all major cities, and smaller towns and villages.

CASH & CREDIT CARDS

Keep small change handy for use in public toilets, telephones and tram-ticket machines, and try to keep some small-denomination notes for shops, cafes and restaurants. Changing larger notes from ATMs can be a problem.

Credit cards are widely accepted in petrol stations, midrange and top-end hotels, restaurants and shops.

EXCHANGING MONEY

Change cash or get a cash advance on credit cards at the main banks. Beware of *směnárna* (private exchange offices), especially in Prague – they advertise misleading rates, and often charge exorbitant commissions or 'handling fees'. There is no black market for currency exchange, and anyone who offers to change money in the street is dodgy.

TIPPING

» In bars, leave small change as a tip.
» Tipping is optional in restaurants, but increasingly expected in Prague; round the bill up the next 20Kč or 30Kč (5% to 10%).
» Tip taxi drivers the same as you would in restaurants.

Public Holidays

New Year's Day 1 January

Easter Monday March/April

Labour Day 1 May

Liberation Day 8 May

SS Cyril and Methodius Day 5 July

Jan Hus Day 6 July

Czech Statehood Day 28 September

Republic Day 28 October

Freedom and Democracy Day 17 November

Christmas 24 to 26 December

Post

The Czech Republic has a reliable postal service. Mail can be held at Prague Poste Restante, Jindřišská 14, 11000 Praha 1, Czech Republic.

Telephone

All Czech phone numbers have nine digits; dial all nine for any call, local or long distance. Buy phonecards for public telephones from post offices and newsstands from 100Kč.

Mobile-phone coverage (GSM 900/1800) is excellent. If you're from Europe, Australia or New Zealand, your own mobile phone should be compatible. Purchase a Czech SIM card from any mobile-phone shop for around 500Kč (including 300Kč of calling credit). Local mobile phone numbers start with the following: ☑601–608 and ☑720–779. The Czech Republic's country code is ☑420.

Tourist Information

Czech Tourism (Map p288; www.czechtourism.com) Official tourist information.

IDOS (www.idos.cz) Train and bus timetables.

Mapy (www.mapy.cz) Online maps.

Travellers with Disabilities

Ramps for wheelchair users are becoming more common, but cobbled streets, steep hills and stairways often make getting around difficult. Public transport is still problematic, but a growing number of trains and trams have wheelchair access. Major tourist attractions such as Prague Castle also offer wheelchair access. Anything described as *bezbarierová* is 'barrier free'. Resouces including the following:

Prague Integrated Public Transport (www.dpp.cz) See the 'Barrier Free' information online.

Prague Wheelchair Users Organisation (Pražská organizace vozíčkářů; ☑224 827 210; www.pov.cz; Benediktská 6, Staré Město) This is a watchdog organisation for the disabled. While it's mostly geared toward local residents, it can help to organise a guide and transportation at about half the cost of a taxi, and has information on the barrier-free Prague in Czech, English and German.

Visas

The Czech Republic is part of the Schengen Agreement, and citizens of most countries can spend up to 90 days in the country in a six-month period without a visa. For travellers from some other countries, a Schengen Visa is required; you can only get this from your country of residence.

Getting There & Away

Located in the middle of Europe, the Czech Republic is easily reached by air from key European hubs or overland by road or train from neighbouring countries. Flights, tours and rail tickets can be booked online at www.lonelyplanet.com/travel_services.

Entering the Country

Entering the country is straightforward and you are not likely to encounter serious problems or delays. If arriving by air from outside the EU's common border and customs area, the Schengen zone (this includes arrivals from Ireland and the UK), you must go through passport control. If arriving from a European hub within the Schengen zone, such as Amsterdam or Frankfurt, you will not pass through passport control in Prague.

If arriving overland by train, bus or car, the Czech Republic is surrounded on all sides by EU Schengen countries and there are no passport or customs checks on the border.

Air

Nearly all international flights arrive at **Václav Havel Airport Prague** (Letiště Praha; ☑220 111 888; www.prg.aero). Flights to and from destinations outside the EU's Schengen zone use the airport's Terminal 1, which has standard passport and customs checks. Flights within the Schengen zone use Terminal 2 and are treated as domestic flights.

The national carrier **Czech Airlines** (www.czechairlines.com) has a good safety record and is a member of the Skyteam airline alliance.

Land

The Czech Republic has border crossings with Germany, Poland, Slovakia and Austria. These are all EU member states within the Schengen zone, meaning there are no longer any passport or customs checks.

BUS

The main international bus terminal is **Florenc** (ÚAN Praha Florenc; ☑900 144 444; www.florenc.cz; Křižíkova 4; ☉4am-midnight, information counter 6am-9.30pm; Ⓜ Florenc) bus station in Prague. The station is equipped with an information booth, a large announcements board, ticket windows, shops and a Burger King restaurant.

Several bus lines run long-haul coach services to and from destinations around Europe. The leaders on the local market are **Student Agency** (☑800 100 300; www.studentagency.cz) and **Eurolines** (www.elines.cz). Both have offices at the Prague bus station.

CAR & MOTORCYCLE

The Czech Republic lies along major European highways. On entering the country, motorists are required to display on their windscreen a special prepaid sticker (*dálniční známka*), purchased at petrol stations and kiosks near the border. A sticker valid for 10 days costs 310Kč, for 30 days 440Kč, and for a year 1500Kč.

TRAIN

Prague's **Praha hlavní nádraží** (main train station; ☑840 112 113; www.cd.cz; Wilsonova 8, Nové Město) is the country's international train gateway, with frequent service to and from Germany, Poland, Slovakia and Austria. Trains to/from the south and east, including from Bratislava, Vienna and Budapest, normally stop at Brno's main train station as well.

In Prague, buy international train tickets in advance from **ČD Travel** (☑972 241 861; www.cdtravel.cz; Wilsonova 8) agency, which has a large ticketing office on the lower level of Praha hlavní nádraží and a **city centre office** (☑972 233 930; V Celnici 6) not far from náměstí Republiky. Sales counters are divided into those selling domestic tickets (*vnitrostátní jízdenky*) and international tickets (*mezinárodní jízdenky*), so make sure you're in the right line. The windows also sell seat reservations. Credit cards are accepted.

Both InterRail and Eurail passes are valid on the Czech rail network.

Getting Around

Bus

Within the Czech Republic, buses are often faster, cheaper and more convenient than trains. Many bus routes have reduced frequency (or none) at weekends. Buses occasionally leave early so get to the station at least 15 minutes before the official departure time. Check bus timetables and prices at www.idos.cz. Main bus companies:

CSAD (☑information line 900 144 444) The national bus company links cities and smaller towns.

Student Agency (☑800 100 300; www.studentagency.cz) Popular, private bus company with several destinations, including Prague, Brno, České Budějovice, Český Krumlov, Karlovy Vary and Plzeň.

Car & Motorcycle

DRIVING LICENCE

Foreign driving licences are valid for up to 90 days. Strictly speaking, licences that do not include photo identification need an International Driving Permit as well, although this rule is rarely enforced.

FUEL

Unleaded petrol is available as *natural* (95 octane) or *natural plus* (98 octane). The Czech for diesel is *nafta* or just *diesel*. *Autoplyn* (LPG gas) is available in every major town but at very few outlets.

TYPES OF TRAINS

Several different categories of train run on Czech rails, differing mainly in speed and comfort.

EC (EuroCity) Fast, comfortable international trains, stopping at main stations only, with 1st- and 2nd-class coaches; supplementary charge of 60Kč; reservations recommended. Includes 1st-class only SC Pendolino trains that run from Prague to Olomouc, Brno and Ostrava, with links to Vienna and Bratislava.

IC (InterCity) Long-distance and international trains with 1st- and 2nd-class coaches; supplement of 40Kč; reservations recommended.

Ex (express) Similar to IC trains, but no supplementary charge.

R (*rychlík*) The main domestic network of fast trains with 1st- and 2nd-class coaches and sleeper services; no supplement except for sleepers; express and *rychlík* trains are usually marked in red on timetables.

Os (*osobní*) Slow trains using older rolling stock that stop in every one-horse town; 2nd class only.

CAR HIRE

Small local companies offer better prices, but are less likely to have fluent, English-speaking staff. It's often easier to book by email than by phone. Typical rates for a Škoda Fabia are around 800Kč a day, including unlimited kilometres, collision-damage waiver and value-added tax (VAT). Bring your credit card as a deposit. A motorway tax coupon is included with most rental cars. One reliable rental outfit is **Secco Car** (☑220 802 361; www.seccocar.cz; Přístavní 39, Holešovice).

ROAD RULES

The minimum driving age is 18. Traffic moves on the right. The use of seat belts is compulsory for front- and rear-seat passengers.

» Children under 12 or shorter than 1.5m (4ft 9in) are prohibited from sitting in the front seat and must use a child-safety seat.

» Headlights must always be on, even in bright daylight.

» The legal blood-alcohol limit is zero; if the police pull you over for any reason, they are required to administer a breathalyser.

Local Transport

Local transport is affordable, well organised and runs from around 4.30am to midnight daily. Purchase tickets in advance from newsstands and vending machines. Validate tickets in time-stamping machines on buses and trams and at the entrance to metro stations.

Tours

AVE Bicycle Tours (☑251 551 011; www.bicycle-tours.cz; guided tour 1190Kč, self-guided tour 600Kč; ☉Apr-Oct) Cycle touring specialists.

E-Tours (www.etours.cz) Nature, wildlife and photography tours.

Top Bicycle (www.topbicycle.com) Biking and multisport tours.

Train

Czech Railways provides efficient train services to almost every part of the country. See www.idos.cz and www.cd.cz for fares and timetables.

Estonia

Includes »

Best Places to Eat

- » nAnO (p350)
- » Ö (p351)
- » Altja Kõrts (p357)
- » F-hoone (p351)
- » Supelsaksad (p366)

Best Places to Stay

- » Pädaste Manor (p370)
- » Villa Hortensia (p349)
- » Toomarahva Turismitalu (p357)
- » Antonius Hotel (p361)
- » Georg Ots Spa Hotel (p369)

Why Go?

Estonia doesn't have to struggle to find a point of difference in Eastern Europe; it's completely unique. It shares a similar geography and history with Latvia and Lithuania, but it's culturally very different. Its closest ethnic and linguistic buddy is Finland, yet although they may love to get naked together in the sauna, 50 years of Soviet rule have separated the two. For the past 300 years Estonia's been linked to Russia, but the two states have as much in common as a barn swallow and a bear (their respective national symbols).

In recent decades, and with a new-found confidence, Estonia has crept from under the Soviet blanket and leapt into the arms of Europe. The love affair is mutual: Europe has fallen for the chocolate-box allure of Tallinn and its Unesco-protected Old Town, while travellers seeking something different are tapping into Estonia's captivating blend of Eastern European and Nordic appeal.

When to Go
Tallinn

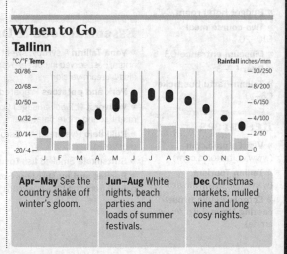

Apr–May See the country shake off winter's gloom.

Jun–Aug White nights, beach parties and loads of summer festivals.

Dec Christmas markets, mulled wine and long cosy nights.

AT A GLANCE

» **Currency** Euro (€)

» **Language** Estonian

» **Money** ATMs all over; banks open Monday to Friday

» **Visas** Not required for citizens of the EU, USA, Canada, New Zealand and Australia

Fast Facts

» **Area** 45,226 sq km

» **Capital** Tallinn

» **Country code** ☑372

» **Emergency** Ambulance & fire ☑112, police ☑110

Exchange Rates

Australia	A$1	€0.82
Canada	C$1	€0.77
Japan	¥100	€0.83
New Zealand	NZ$1	€0.65
UK	UK£1	€1.18
USA	US$1	€0.78

Set Your Budget

» **Budget hotel room** €45

» **Two-course meal** €10–20

» **Museum entrance** €3–5

» **Beer** €2–3

» **Tallinn–Tartu bus ticket** €8–10

Resources

» **VisitEstonia.com** (www.visitestonia.com)

» **Tallinn Tourism** (www.tourism.tallinn.ee)

» **Estonia Public Broadcasting News** (http://news.err.ee)

Connections

Estonia is well connected for travel to and from its neighbours. It's an easy northern addition to Eastern European roaming, as plenty of daily buses connect with destinations in Latvia and Lithuania. There's the option of following the white nights to Scandinavia – Tallinn has daily ferry connections to and from Stockholm and Helsinki. If you're hearing the siren call of Russia, daily trains connect Tallinn with Moscow or St Petersburg, and plenty of buses run between Tallinn or Tartu and St Petersburg.

ITINERARIES

Five Days

Hit Tallinn at a weekend to get in your sightseeing and partying. Get your bearings by heading to Raekoja plats to climb up the Town Hall Tower. Follow this with an in-depth exploration of the Old Town streets down below: museums, shops, churches, courtyards – whatever takes your fancy. That night treat yourself to a medieval feast at Olde Hansa or modern Estonian cuisine at Ö. The following day, do what most tourists don't – step out of Old Town. Explore Kadriorg Park for a first-rate greenery and art fix, and/or consider a cycling tour. Finish with a walk around Kalamaja district and dinner at F-hoone. After the weekend, head east to Lahemaa National Park or southwest to the island of Saaremaa – two (or four) wheels will offer the chance to really explore.

Two Weeks

In two weeks there'll be time to explore Tallinn more deeply. If the weather's fine, opt for fun in the sun in Pärnu, then get back to nature at Soomaa National Park, and finish with a pub crawl with local students in Tartu.

Essential Food & Drink

» **Vana Tallinn** A syrupy, sweet liqueur of indeterminate origin, best served in coffee, over ice or in champagne. There's also a cream version.

» **Pork and potatoes** Prepared a hundred different ways.

» **Verivorst** (blood sausage) Call it black pudding and it might sound more palatable.

» **Rukkileib** Rye bread, an Estonian staple, served with most meals.

» **Suitsukala** Smoked fish (usually trout or salmon).

» **Berries and mushrooms** Seasonal delights freshly picked from the forests in summer and autumn respectively.

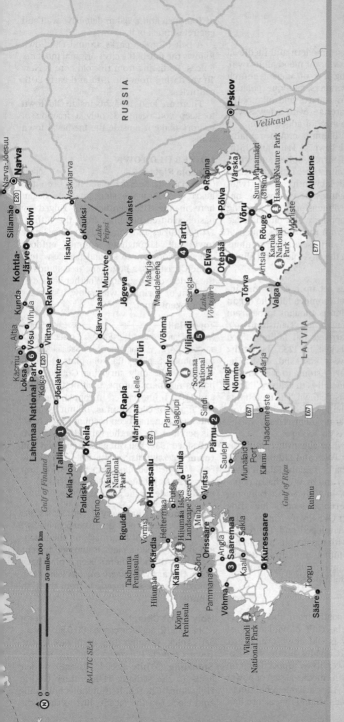

Estonia Highlights

1 Find medieval bliss exploring **Tallinn's Old Town** (p346), then unwind at leafy, lovely Kadriorg Park.

2 Get sand in your shorts in **Pärnu** (p363), Estonia's summertime mecca.

3 Escape to the island of **Saaremaa** (p368) for castles, coastlines and spas.

4 Further your local education among the bars and cafes of **Tartu** (p358), Estonia's premier university town and second city.

5 Let your hair down with 20,000 music lovers at **Viljandi Folk Music Festival** (p367).

6 Beat a retreat from Tallinn to chill out in the seaside villages and manor estates of **Lahemaa National Park** (p356).

7 Get back to nature, even if the snow's a no-show, at the 'winter capital' **Otepää** (p362).

TALLINN

POP 416,500

Today's Tallinn fuses modern and medieval to come up with a vibrant mood all its own. It's an intoxicating mix of ancient church spires, glass skyscrapers, baroque palaces, cafes set on sunny squares and bike paths to beaches and forests – with a few Soviet throwbacks in the mix, for added spice.

The jewel in Tallinn's crown remains its two-tiered Old Town, a 14th- and 15th-century jumble of turrets, spires and winding streets. Most tourists see little more than this cobblestoned labyrinth of intertwining alleys and picturesque courtyards, but Tallinn's modern dimension – its growing skyline, shiny shopping malls, cutting-edge art museum, the wi-fi that bathes much of the city – is a cool surprise and harmonious counterbalance to the city's old-world allure.

History

In 1219 the Danes set up a castle and installed a bishop on Toompea hill (the origin of the name Tallinn is thought to be from *Taani linn*, Estonian for 'Danish town'). German traders arrived and Tallinn joined the Hanseatic League in 1285, becoming a vital link between east and west. The Danes sold northern Estonia to the German knights and by the mid-14th century Tallinn was a major Hanseatic town. The merchants and artisans in the lower town built a fortified wall to separate themselves from the bishop and knights on Toompea.

Prosperity faded in the 16th century as Swedes, Russians, Poles and Lithuanians all fought over the Baltic region. Tallinn grew in the 19th century and by WWI had a population of 150,000. In 1944 Soviet bombing destroyed several central sectors, including a small section on Old Town's fringes. After WWII, industry developed and Tallinn expanded quickly, with much of its population growth due to immigration from Russia. Politically and economically, Tallinn is the driving force of modern Estonia.

◉ Sights

Tallinn spreads south from the edge of Tallinn Bay on the Gulf of Finland. Just south of the bay is Old Town (Vanalinn), the city's heart. It divides neatly into Upper Town and Lower Town. Upper Town on Toompea hill was the medieval seat of power and it still features the parliament buildings. Lower Town spreads around the eastern foot of Toompea and a 2.5km defensive wall still encircles much of it.

A belt of green parks around Old Town follows the line of the city's original moat defences. Radiating from this old core is New Town, dating from the 19th and early 20th centuries.

There are loads of sights inside Old Town to keep you occupied; only a fraction of visitors make it outside the medieval town walls.

LOWER OLD TOWN

Raekoja Plats   SQUARE

(Town Hall Sq) Raekoja plats has been the heart of Tallinn life since markets began here in the 11th century. It's ringed by pastel-coloured buildings from the 15th to 17th centuries and dominated by the Gothic town hall. Throughout summer, outdoor cafes implore you to sit and people-watch; come Christmas, a huge pine tree stands in the middle of the square. Whether bathed in sunlight or sprinkled with snow, it's always a photogenic spot.

Town Hall   HISTORIC BUILDING

(www.tallinn.ee/raekoda; Raekoja plats; adult/student €4/2; ⊘10am-4pm Mon-Sat Jul-Aug, by appointment Sep-Jun) Raekoja plats is dominated by the only surviving Gothic town hall in northern Europe, built between 1371 and 1404. Immortalised in copper, the warrior figure of **Old Thomas**, Tallinn's symbol and guardian, has been keeping watch from his perch on the weathervane atop the town hall since 1530. You can climb the **town hall tower** (Raekoja plats; adult/student €3/1; ⊘11am-6pm May–mid-Sep) for superb red-rooftop views. A tiny cafe, III Draakon (p352), is tucked inside on the ground level.

Town Council Pharmacy   HISTORIC BUILDING

(Raeapteek; Raekoja plats 11; ⊘10am-6pm Tue-Sat) The Town Council Pharmacy, on the northern side of Raekoja plats, is another ancient Tallinn institution; there's been a pharmacy or apothecary's shop here since at least 1422, though the present facade is from the 17th century.

Holy Spirit Church   CHURCH

(Pühavaimu 2; adult/concession €1/0.50; ⊘Mon-Sat) Duck through the arch beside the Town Council Pharmacy into the narrow **Saiakang** (White Bread Passage), which leads to the striking 14th-century Gothic Holy Spirit Church. Its luminous blue-and-gold clock (on the facade, just to the right

FANCY A VIEW?

Here's a run-down of some of Tallinn's best places for bird's-eye city views.

Fancy a freebie? Toompea hill has superb viewpoints onto Kohtu and off nearby Toom-Kooli.

Fancy a climb? Head up either the Town Hall Tower (p340) or the tower of St Olaf's church (p341).

Fancy a coffee? On the 4th floor of the Solaris centre, **Kohvik Komeet** (www.kohvik-komeet.ee; Estonia pst 9) has a dazzling array of cakes and a leafy view to Old Town. Its 5th-floor terrace is blissful when the sun is shining.

Fancy a cocktail? On the 30th floor of the Swissôtel, fancy-pants **Horisont Restaurant & Bar** (www.horisont-restoran.com; Tornimäe 3) offers outstanding panoramas (and prices to match).

Fancy a sweat? Book a sauna at Club 26 (p348) on the 26th floor of a hotel for first-class city vistas.

of the entry) is the oldest in Tallinn. The lavish carvings inside the church date from 1684.

Vene   STREET
Several 15th-century warehouses and merchant residences surround Raekoja plats, notably when heading towards the street of Vene (meaning 'Russian' in Estonian, and named for the Russian merchants who traded here). Lying off Vene are some gorgeous passageways and courtyards – the loveliest being **Katariina käik** (Vene 12), home to artisans' studios and a decent Italian restaurant, and **Masters' Courtyard** (Vene 6), a cobblestoned delight partially dating from the 13th century that's filled with craft stores and a sweet cafe-chocolaterie (p352).

Tallinn City Museum   MUSEUM
(www.linnamuuseum.ee; Vene 17; adult/student €3.20/1.90; ☺10am-5pm Wed-Mon) A medieval merchant's home houses the City Museum, which traces Tallinn's development from its early beginnings. The top floor presents an insightful portrait of life under Soviet rule.

Pikk   STREET
From the Holy Spirit Church you can stroll along Pikk (Long Street), which runs north to the **Great Coast Gate** – the medieval exit to Tallinn's port. Pikk is lined with the 15th-century houses of merchants and gentry, as well as the buildings of several old Tallinn guilds. Check out the fabulous sculpted facade of the 1911 **Draakoni Gallery** (Pikk 18), which hosts small exhibitions of contemporary art.

Estonian History Museum   MUSEUM
(www.ajaloomuuseum.ee; Pikk 17; adult/student €5/3; ☺10am-6pm, closed Wed Sep-Apr) This newly renovated museum has filled the striking 1410 Great Guild Hall with a series of ruminations on the Estonian psyche, presented through interactive and unusual displays. The major exhibition is the enthralling *Spirit of Survival – 11,000 years of Estonian History*.

St Olaf's Church   CHURCH
(entry at Lai 50) At the northern end of Pikk stands an important Tallinn landmark, the gargantuan St Olaf's Church. Anyone unafraid of a few stairs (258, to be precise) should head up to the **observation tower** (adult/student €2/1; ☺10am-6pm Apr-Oct, to 8pm Jul & Aug), halfway up the church's 124m structure; it offers the city's best views of Old Town. First built in the early 13th century, the church was once the world's tallest building (it measured 159m before several fires and reconstructions brought it down to its present size).

Former KGB Headquarters   HISTORIC SITE
(Pikk 59) Just south of St Olaf's Church is the former KGB headquarters, the basement windows of which were sealed to conceal the sounds of interrogations.

Fat Margaret   HISTORIC BUILDING
(Pikk 70) The Great Coast Gate is joined to Fat Margaret, a rotund 16th-century bastion that protected this entrance to Old Town. The **Maritime Museum** (www.meremuuseum.ee; adult/student €4/2; ☺10am-6pm daily May-Sep, closed Mon & Tue Oct-Apr) resides here,

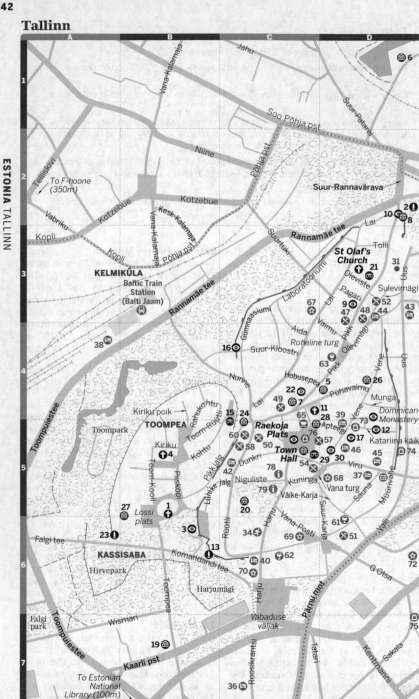

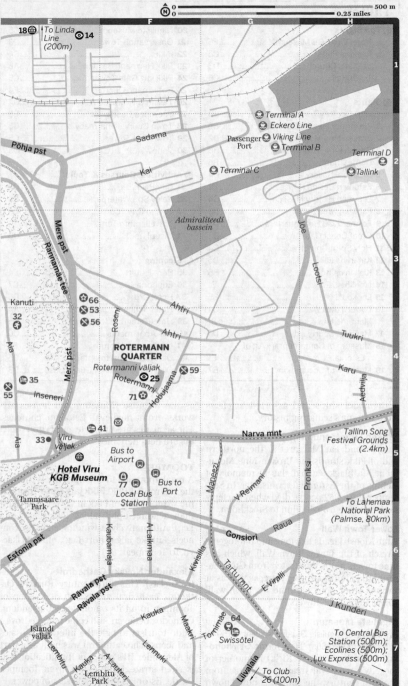

Tallinn

with model ships and assorted artefacts from Estonia's seafaring history.

Broken Line Monument   MONUMENT
Just beyond Fat Margaret at the northern end of Pikk stands the Broken Line Monument – a black, curved slab in memory of victims of the *Estonia* ferry disaster. In September 1994, 852 people died when the ferry sank en route from Tallinn to Stockholm.

Lower Town Wall   HISTORIC SITE
Suur-Kloostri leads to a long and photogenic stretch of the Lower Town Wall, which has nine towers along the stretch from Gumnaasiumi to Laboratooriumi. Here, as well as at various other points around the town wall, you can enter the towers.

Niguliste Museum   MUSEUM
(www.ekm.ee; Niguliste 3; adult/student €3.50/2; ◷10am-5pm Wed-Sun) The Gothic **St Nicholas' Church** (Niguliste Kirik) is another of the city's medieval treasures. Dating from the 13th century, the church is now known

as the Niguliste Museum and houses artworks from medieval Estonian churches. The acoustics are first-rate and **organ recitals** are held here most weekends.

TOOMPEA
A regal approach to Toompea hill is through the red-roofed 1380 **Pikk jalg Gate Tower** at the western end of Pikk in Lower Town, and then heading uphill along Pikk jalg (Long Leg). Alternatively, a winding stairway connects Lühike jalg (Short Leg), off Rataskaevu, to Toompea.

Alexander Nevsky Cathedral   CHURCH
(Lossi plats) This 19th-century Russian Orthodox cathedral greets you at the top of Toompea in all its onion-domed splendour. Orthodox believers still come here in droves, as do tourists to ogle the interior's mosaics and icons. The cathedral was built as a part of Alexander III's policy of Russification and is sited strategically across from Toompea Castle, Estonia's traditional seat of power.

Toompea Castle　　　HISTORIC BUILDING
(Lossi plats) The Riigikogu (Parliament) meets in the pink baroque-style building opposite the Orthodox cathedral; it was an 18th-century addition. Nothing remains of the original 1219 Danish castle but three of the four corner towers of its successor, the Knights of the Sword's Castle, are still standing. The finest of these towers is the 14th-century **Pikk Hermann** (Tall Hermann) at the southwestern corner, from which the Estonian flag flies.

A path leads down from Lossi plats through an opening in the wall to the **Danish King's Courtyard**, where in summer artists set up their easels.

Kiek in de Kök　　　TOWER, MUSEUM
(☎644 6686; www.linnamuuseum.ee/kok/en; Komandandi tee; adult/student €4.50/2.60; ☉10.30am-6pm Tue-Sun) Kiek in de Kök, a formidable cannon tower built around 1475, houses a museum that focuses mainly on the development of Tallinn's elaborate defences. Its kooky-sounding name is Low German for

'Peep into the Kitchen' – from the upper floors of the tower, medieval voyeurs could see into Old Town kitchens. Departing from the tower are tours that take in the **17th-century tunnels** (Kiek in de Kök; tours adult/student €5.80/3.20, bookings required) that connect the town's bastions, built by the Swedes to help protect the city.

Dome Church　　　CHURCH
(Toom-Kooli 6; ☉9am-5pm) Toompea is named after the Lutheran Dome Church (Toomkirik), founded in 1233. There is actually no dome – the nickname is a corruption of the Estonian word *toom*, itself borrowed from the German word *Dom*, meaning cathedral. The austere interior features finely carved tombs and coats of arms from Estonia's noble families. From the Dome Church, follow Kohtu to the city's favourite **lookout** over Lower Town.

Museum of Occupations　　　MUSEUM
(www.okupatsioon.ee; Toompea 8; adult/student €4/2; ☉10am-6pm Tue-Sun) This museum, just downhill from Toompea, has worthwhile

displays covering Estonia's 20th-century occupations. Photos and artefacts illustrate five decades of oppressive rule, under the Nazis, briefly, and the Soviets. Displays are good, but it's the videos (lengthy but enthralling) that leave the greatest impression – and the joy of a happy ending.

CITY CENTRE

TOP CHOICE Hotel Viru KGB Museum MUSEUM

(☑680 9300; www.sokoshotels.fi; Viru väljak 4; tour €8; ☺closed Mon Nov-Mar) When Hotel Viru was built in 1972 it was not only Estonia's first skyscraper, it was the only place for tourists to stay in Tallinn – and we mean that literally. Having all the foreigners in one place made it easier to keep tabs on them and the locals they had contact with, which is exactly what the KGB did from its 23rd-floor spy base. The hotel offers insightful and entertaining guided tours of the facility in Estonian, English, Finnish and Russian; call ahead for times and to book a place.

Rotermann Quarter NEIGHBOURHOOD

(Rotermanni Kvartal) One of Tallinn's recent developments has been the restoration and reinvigoration of the Rotermann Quarter, a former factory complex that sits between Old Town and the passenger port. It's now home to offices and apartments, shops and restaurants, and a quirky collection of studios and galleries.

KADRIORG

To reach the lovely wooded **Kadriorg Park**, 2km east of Old Town along Narva mnt, take tram 1 or 3 to the Kadriorg stop. There are a number of museums in the park, plus a playground and a fine cafe.

Kadriorg Palace PALACE, MUSEUM

(A Weizenbergi 37) Kadriorg Park and its centrepiece, Kadriorg Palace (1718–36), were designed for Peter the Great's wife Catherine I (Kadriorg means 'Catherine's Valley' in Estonian). Kadriorg Palace is now home to the **Kadriorg Art Museum** (www.ekm. ee; A Weizenbergi 37; adult/student €4.50/2.50; ☺10am-5pm Tue-Sun May-Sep, 10am-5pm Wed-Sun Oct-Apr). The 17th- and 18th-century foreign art is mainly unabashedly romantic, and the palace and its gardens are unashamedly splendid.

Kumu ART MUSEUM

(www.ekm.ee; Weizenbergi 34; adult/student €5.50/3.20; ☺11am-6pm Tue-Sun May-Sep, 11am-6pm Wed-Sun Oct-Apr) This futuristic seven-storey building is a spectacular structure of limestone, glass and copper, nicely integrated into the landscape. Kumu (the name is short for *kunstimuuseum* or art museum) contains the largest repository of Estonian art as well as constantly changing contemporary exhibits. There's a cafe, restaurant and gallery shop on-site.

TOWARDS PIRITA

Buses 1A, 8 and 34A run between the city centre and Pirita, stopping on Narva mnt near Kadriorg Park.

Pirita tee PROMENADE

Jutting north of Kadriorg alongside the sea coast towards Pirita is Pirita tee, Tallinn's seaside promenade. Summer sunsets around midnight are particularly romantic from here, and it's a popular cycling and rollerblading area.

Tallinn Song Festival Grounds AMPHITHEATRE

(Lauluväljak; www.lauluvaljak.ee; Narva mnt) North of Kadriorg is this impressive amphitheatre that hosts song festivals and big-name concerts. In 1988, 300,000 Estonians squeezed in for one songfest and publicly demanded independence during the 'Singing Revolution'.

Maarjamäe Palace MUSEUM

(www.ajaloomuuseum.ee; Pirita tee 56; adult/concession €3/1.50; ☺10am-5pm Wed-Sun) This 1870s neo-Gothic 'palace' (a rather grand title for what is more like a manor) is home to the second branch of the Estonian History Museum (the primary location is in Old Town). This branch does a particularly good job of detailing the twists and turns of 20th-century Estonian history. There's a park outside featuring old Soviet statues.

Pirita Yacht Club YACHT CLUB

Just before Pirita tee crosses the Pirita River, a side road leads to Pirita Yacht Club and the Tallinn Olympic Yachting Centre. This was the base for the sailing events of the 1980 Moscow Olympics. The facility built here for the Olympics (of dubious architectural appeal) is now home to a large hotel, and there are some good spots for an al fresco drink.

Pirita Beach BEACH

North of the bridge is 3km-long, white-sand Pirita beach, which is *the* place to shed your clothes in summertime Tallinn. It's easily the city's largest and most popular beach; it's backed by wooded parkland popular with walkers and cyclists.

WORTH A TRIP

EXPLORING KALAMAJA

Nothing says 'former Soviet' like a gigantic public building made of concrete and Tallinn's baffling **Linnahall** (City Hall; Mere pst 20) certainly fits the bill. It stands as a colossal barricade, cutting off the Old Town from the harbour. Built for the 1980 Moscow Olympics, it contains within its crumbling, much-graffitied hulk a vast concert hall. It's fair to say that the city doesn't know quite what to do with it since it closed its doors in 2009.

From here, you can take a leisurely walk along the 'Culture Kilometre' (actually a 2km path) to the Kalamaja neighbourhood, populated by distinctive wooden houses. Like all good working-class neighbourhoods, it's emerging as a cool hang-out for artists.

Heading west from the Linnahall, you'll pass the ramshackle **Museum of Contemporary Art** (www.ekkm.ee; admission free; ☉1-7pm Tue-Sun Apr-Oct), worth a stop for its sometimes-provocative exhibitions. A little further on you'll reach a tiny harbour and the **Estonian Design House** (www.estoniandesignhouse.ee; Kalasadama 8), a small showroom of locally designed objects that reveal strong Nordic influences. The cafe here, Café Klaus, is a treat.

As you continue along the trail, the most interesting of the area's attractions reveals itself: crumbling, eerie **Patarei** (www.patarei.org), built as a sea fortress under Tsar Nicholas, but serving as a prison from 1920 until, incredibly, 2005. Tours are possible (see the website), but you can also snoop around on your own. Behind the prison, at the waterfront, is a bizarre little strip of sand and a kiosk selling drinks. Concerts and parties are staged here in summer.

The final attraction along the trail is the vast and impressive new **Seaplane Harbour** (Lennusadam; www.lennusadam.eu; Vesilennuki 6; adult/child €10/5; ☉10am-7pm daily May-Sep, 11am-7pm Tue-Sun Oct-Apr), with a maritime museum that's home to an old submarine, an icebreaker and a British seaplane.

From here, a wander south through the residential streets will take you to the **market** behind the main train station (colourful in terms of scenery and characters), and from here you're just a short hop back in time (via Nunne) to the medieval magnificence of Old Town.

Pirita Convent
RUINS

(www.piritaklooster.ee; Kloostri tee; adult/student €2/1; ☉9am-7pm Jun-Aug, shorter hrs rest of yr) On the other side of Pirita tee from the beach are the ruins of the 15th-century Convent of St Birgitta, the perfect place for a ramble. During the 10-day **Birgitta Festival** (www.birgitta.ee) in August, atmospheric choral, opera and classical concerts are staged here.

TV Tower
VIEWPOINT

(Teletorn; www.teletorn.ee; Kloostrimetsa tee 58a; adult/child €7/4; ☉10am-7pm daily May-Sep, 11am-6pm Wed-Mon Oct-Apr) Tallinn's 314m TV Tower reopened to the public in 2012 after a futuristic refurb. From the viewing platform on the 22nd floor (at 175m) you get a great overview of the lay of the land, from offshore islets to parkland and ports, and the Soviet-era tower blocks of the suburbs. The tower is east of Pirita, 400m beyond the Botanic Gardens; take bus 34a, 38 or 49.

SOUTHWEST OF OLD TOWN

Tallinn Zoo
ZOO

(www.tallinnzoo.ee; Paldiski mnt 145; adult/child €5.80/2.90 May-Sep, €3.20/2 Oct-Apr; ☉9am-7pm May-Aug, shorter hrs rest of yr) About 4.5km southwest from Old Town, Tallinn Zoo boasts the world's largest collection of mountain goats and sheep (!), plus around 350 other species of feathered, furry and four-legged friends. Avoid Mondays, when some exhibits are closed. It's best reached by bus 22 or trolleybus 6 from the centre.

Estonian Open-Air Museum
MUSEUM

(www.evm.ee; Vabaõhumuuseumi tee 12; adult/child €6/3 May-Sep, €3/1.50 Oct-Apr; ☉buildings 10am-6pm May-Sep, grounds to 8pm May-Sep, 10am-5pm Oct-Apr) North of the zoo is the Rocca al Mare neighbourhood and its excellent open-air museum. Many of Estonia's oldest wooden structures, mainly farmhouses but also a chapel (1699) and a windmill, are preserved here. At 11am on Saturday and Sunday mornings from June to August there are folk song-and-dance shows; if you find yourself in Tallinn on Midsummer's Eve, come here to witness the traditional celebrations, bonfire and all. There's also an old wooden tavern serving traditional Estonian cuisine (open year-round). Bus 21 runs here from the train station.

🏃 Activities

Water Parks

Water parks are big business in Estonia; the biggest in Tallinn is the **Kalev Spa Waterpark** (www.kalevspa.ee; Aia 18; 2½hr visit adult/family €10.90/33; ⊘6.45am-9.30pm Mon-Fri, 8am-9.30pm Sat & Sun), just outside Old Town. For serious swimming there's an Olympic-size indoor pool, but there are plenty of other ways to wrinkle your skin, including waterslides, jacuzzis, saunas and a kids' pool. There's also a gym and day spa.

Saunas

Like their Finnish cousins, for Estonians, saunas come close to being a religious experience. If you're looking to convert, splurge at **Club 26** (☑631 5585; www.club26.ee; Liivalaia 33, Radisson Blu Hotel Olümpia; private sauna per hr €25-65), on the 26th floor of the Radisson Blu Hotel Olümpia, with correspondingly outstanding views. There are two private saunas here, each with plunge pool and tiny balcony. Food and drink can be ordered to complete the experience; book online.

Beaches

The most popular beaches are at Pirita (p346) and **Stroomi** (4km due west of the centre, or a 15-minute ride on bus 40).

Sea Kayaking

From June to August, **360° Adventures** (☑5645 6060; www.360.ee) offers daily kayaking trips giving paddlers three to four hours out on Tallinn Bay (€30) and a new perspective on Tallinn's sights. No previous kayaking experience is required. The company also offers bog-walking excursions and nature walks, plus snowshoeing in the winter (see the website).

Ice Skating

Rug up warm to join the locals at the scenic outdoor ice rink, **Uisuplats** (www.uisuplats.ee; Harju; per hr €3.50-4.50; ⊘10am-10pm Nov-Mar).

👉 Tours

Traveller Info Tent   WALKING, CYCLING
(☑5837 4800; www.traveller.ee; Niguliste) Runs entertaining, good-value walking and cy-

cling city tours – including a free, two-hour walking tour of the capital, departing at noon daily. Three-hour bike tours (€13) take in the town's well-known eastern attractions (Kadriorg, Pirita etc) or more offbeat areas to the west. There's also a pub crawl (€16, including drinks) and day trips to Lahemaa National Park (€49). From mid-May to mid-September, the tours run from the tent itself; the rest of the year they need to be booked in advance via the website or phone. Winter tours are weather dependent.

City Bike   CYCLING, WALKING
(☑511 1819; www.citybike.ee; Uus 33) Has a great range of Tallinn tours, by bike or on foot, as well as tours to Lahemaa National Park. Two-hour cycling tours (€16) of the capital run year-round and cover 16km, heading out towards Kadriorg and Pirita.

EstAdventures   WALKING, DAY TOURS
(☑5308 3731; www.estadventures.ee) A small company offering diverse, offbeat tours – four-hour walking tours of Tallinn (€32), plus full-day excursions further afield (€50) to Lahemaa National Park, Haapsalu or Tartu. Operates May to September.

Tallinn City Tour   BUS
(☑627 9080; www.citytour.ee; 24hr pass €16) Runs red double-decker buses that give you hop-on, hop-off access to the city's top sights on three different routes. Buses leave from Mere pst, just outside Old Town.

🎉 Festivals & Events

For a complete list of Tallinn's festivals, visit **Culture.ee** (www.culture.ee) and the events pages of **Tallinn Tourism** (www.tourism.tallinn.ee).

Big-ticket events include the following:

Jazzkaar   MUSIC
(www.jazzkaar.ee) Jazz greats from around the world converge on Tallinn in late April.

Old Town Days   ARTS, CULTURE
(www.vanalinnapaevad.ee) Week-long festival in late May/early June featuring dancing, concerts and plenty of medieval merrymaking.

Õllesummer   MUSIC
(Beer Summer; www.ollesummer.ee) Rock-music and beer-drinking extravaganza over four days in early July.

Black Nights Film Festival   FILM
(www.poff.ee) Films and animations bring life to cold nights for two weeks in late November.

Estonian Song & Dance Celebration
SONG, DANCE

(www.laulupidu.ee) Convenes every five years and culminates in a 30,000-strong traditional choir; due in Tallinn in 2014.

🛏 Sleeping

Old Town has the top lodgings, with plenty of atmospheric rooms set in beautifully refurbished medieval houses – though you'll pay a premium for them. Midrange and budget hotels are scarcer in Old Town; apartment-rental agencies have the best midrange deals and the capital has dozens of apartments for rent – a great alternative for those who prefer privacy and self-sufficiency.

In recent times there's been an explosion of hostels competing for the attention of backpackers. Most of them are small, friendly and laid-back; they're largely found in Old Town, but few offer private rooms.

The website **Tallinn** (www.tourism.tallinn.ee) has a full list of options. Whatever your preference, be sure to book in advance in summer. As ever, look for good deals on the internet.

OLD TOWN

TOP CHOICE Villa Hortensia
APARTMENTS €€

(☑504 6113; www.hoov.ee/villa-hortensia.html; Vene 6, Masters' Courtyard; studio s/d €40/55, apt s/d from €60/80; ☎) Villa Hortensia is a small collection of apartments in the Masters' Courtyard, off Vene. This sweet, cobblestoned courtyard has been a labour of love for Jaan Pärn, architect-turned-jeweller and the man responsible for the restoration of the ancient buildings. There are six apartments here (the website has pics). Four are compact, split-level studio ones, with private bathroom, kitchenette, table and chairs and access to a shared communal lounge. The two larger apartments are the real treats, with balcony, TV and kitchenette. This place offers great value in a winning location – book ahead.

Tallinn Backpackers
HOSTEL €

(☑644 0298; www.tallinnbackpackers.com; Olevimägi 11; dm with shared bathroom €12-15; @☎) In an ideal Old Town location, this 26-bed place has a global feel and a roll-call of traveller-happy features: happy hours, cheap dinners, free wi-fi and internet, lockers, free sauna, and day trips to nearby attractions. Staff organise pub crawls and city tours that anyone can join and a shuttle bus to Rīga. Private rooms

are available at the offshoot **Tallinn Boutique Hostel** (☑644 6050; www.tallinnboutiquehostel.com; Viru 5, 3rd fl; s/d with shared bathroom €25/40; @☎), also known as Viru Backpackers, which has less atmosphere but does boast a central location; its only downside is the shortage of shared bathrooms.

Hotel Telegraaf
HOTEL €€€

(☑600 0600; www.telegraafhotel.com; Vene 9; s/d/ste from €145/165/295; P@☎☈) This upmarket hotel, in a converted 19th-century former telegraph station, delivers style in spades. It boasts a spa and a small swimming pool, gorgeous black-and-white decor, a pretty courtyard, an acclaimed restaurant and smart, efficient service. Superior rooms are at the front of the house, with a little more historical detail (high ceilings, parquetry floors), but we prefer the marginally cheaper executive rooms, for their bigger proportions and sharper decor.

Old House Hostel & Guesthouse
GUESTHOUSE €

(☑641 1281; www.oldhouse.ee; Uus 22 & Uus 26; dm/s/d with shared bathroom €15/30/44; P@☎) Although one is called a hostel, these twin establishments feel much more like cosy guesthouses (antiques, plants, lamps and bedspreads, with minimal bunks), and they're a long way from earning the 'party hostel' tag. Dorms and private rooms are available at both (all bathrooms are shared); the guest kitchen, free wi-fi and parking are quality extras. The management also rents fantastic Old Town apartments at reasonable prices (see the website).

Old House Apartments
APARTMENTS €€

(☑641 1464; www.oldhouse.ee; Rataskaevu 16; per night €89-229; P🛜) 'Old House' is an understatement for this 14th-century merchant's house. It's been split into eight beautifully furnished apartments and there are a further 13 scattered around the Old Town in similar buildings. All have a kitchen; many have private sauna and laundry facilities.

Hotel Cru
HOTEL €€

(www.viruinn.ee; Viru 10; r from €130; 🛜) Behind its pretty powder-blue facade, this boutique 14th-century offering (formerly known as Viru Inn) has richly furnished rooms with plenty of original features (timber beams, stone walls) scattered along a rabbit warren of corridors. The cheapest are pretty snug.

Ites Apartments
APARTMENTS €€

(☑631 0637; www.ites.ee; Harju 6; per night €80-200; 🛜) Friendly and efficient bunch offering several well-appointed apartments in Old Town and its surrounds. There are significant discounts for stays of more than one night.

OUTSIDE OLD TOWN
The options listed here are all only minutes from the Old Town on foot.

Nordic Hotel Forum
HOTEL €€

(☑622 2900; www.nordichotels.eu; Viru väljak 3; r from €95; P@🛜🏊) The Forum shows surprising style and personality for a large, business-style hotel – witness the artwork on the hotel's facade and the trees on the roof. It stands out among its competitors for the facilities, laid on thick (including a lovely top-floor leisure centre with saunas and indoor pool), welcoming staff and prime location.

Bern Hotel
HOTEL €€

(☑680 6604; www.bern.ee; Aia 10; d €75-120; @🛜) One of a raft of newer hotels on the outskirts of Old Town, Bern is named after the Swiss city to indicate 'hospitality and high quality'. It's nothing special from the outside, but rooms are petite and modern, with great attention to detail for the price. Nice extras include robes and slippers, air-con, minibar, hairdryer and toiletries. Rooms can be had for around €60 if you get an online deal.

Hotel Schnelli
HOTEL €€

(☑631 0102; www.gohotels.ee; Toompuiestee 37; r from €55; P🅿🛜) This modern hotel at the train station isn't just for train travellers. The block-boring building is home to small but fresh and functional rooms, and offers decent value a short walk from Old Town; rates include buffet breakfast, parking and wi-fi. Non-trainspotters should opt for a room in the Green Wing, with views to the park opposite and Old Town beyond. Cheaper Blue Wing rooms overlook the station.

Euphoria
HOSTEL €

(☑5837 3602; www.euphoria.ee; Roosikrantsi 4; dm €11-18, d without bathroom €40; P@🛜) So laidback it's almost horizontal, this backpacker hostel just south of Old Town has adopted some very '60s hippie vibes and given them a modern twist. It's a fun place to stay, with a sense of traveller community – especially if you like hookah pipes, bongo drums, jugglers, musos, artists and impromptu late-night jam sessions (pack earplugs if you don't).

🍴 Eating

Quite simply, Tallinn is a wonderful city for food lovers. Global cuisines are well represented and prices are low compared with most other European capitals.

OLD TOWN

🏆 TOP CHOICE nAnO
CAFE €

(☑5552 2522; www.nanohouse.ee; Sulevimägi 5; meals around €6; ⏱12.30-4pm Tue-Fri) There's no real sign to indicate you've found this place, nor are there firm hours or a written menu. Instead, this is a whimsical world concocted by Beatrice, an Estonian model, and DJ partner Priit, who welcome guests into part of their colourful home and courtyard garden. Diners are offered fresh, affordable, homestyle meals along the lines of herb-filled borscht, Russian-style pastries and pasta with in-season chanterelles or salmon. It's a treat for all the senses. Wander past, or call ahead to check hours.

🏆 TOP CHOICE Must Puudel
CAFE €

(Müürivahe 20; mains under €5) From any angle, the Black Poodle is a near-perfect loungey cafe-bar: mismatched 1970s furniture, an eclectic soundtrack, courtyard seating, excellent coffee, cooked breakfasts, tasty light meals and long opening hours.

Olde Hansa
MEDIEVAL €€

(www.oldehansa.ee; Vana turg 1; mains €13-26)
Candlelit Olde Hansa is the place to indulge
in a gluttonous feast. And if the medieval
music, staff clad in ye-olde garb, and aromas of red wine and roast meats sound a bit
much, take heart – the chefs have done their
research in producing historically authentic
fare. It may be pitched heavily at tourists,
but even locals rate this place.

Von Krahli Aed
INTERNATIONAL €€

(www.vonkrahl.ee; Rataskaevu 8; mains €5-14; 🖋)
You'll find more greenery on your plate at
this rustic, plant-filled restaurant than at
other eateries in Tallinn (*aed* means garden).
The menu embraces fresh flavours and wins
fans by noting gluten-, lactose- and egg-free
options. There are creative vegetarian choices too.

Chedi
ASIAN €€€

(🖋646 1676; www.chedi.ee; Sulevimägi 1; dishes
€13-28) If you can't get a booking at top
Asian restaurants at home, console yourself
at sleek, sexy Chedi. UK restaurateur Alan
Yau (of London's Michelin-starred Hak-
kasan and Yauatcha) consulted on the menu
and some of his trademark dishes are featured here. The modern, pan-Asian food is
exemplary – try the delicious crispy duck
salad or sublime roasted silver cod.

Kompressor
PANCAKES €

(Rataskaevu 3; pancakes €3.50-4) Under an industrial ceiling you can plug any holes in
your stomach with cheap pancakes of the
sweet or savoury persuasion. By night, this
is a decent detour for a budget drink. It's low
on aesthetics but high on value.

Vanaema Juures
TRADITIONAL €€

(www.vonkrahl.ee; Rataskaevu 10/12; mains €7-
18.50) Food just like your grandma used to
make (if she was Estonian). 'Grandma's Place'
rates as a top choice for traditional, home-
style Estonian fare. The antique-furnished,
photograph-filled dining room has a formal
air and the menu stars plenty of roasted-meat
options (including elk and wild boar).

Troika
RUSSIAN €€

(www.troika.ee; Raekoja plats 15; bliny & pelmeni
€6-8, mains €11-19) Tallinn's most cheerful
Russian restaurant is an experience in itself.
Head to the *trahter,* the somewhat cheesy,
folksy country tavern (at ground level), for
a plate of delicious *pelmeni* (Russian-style
ravioli stuffed with meat), bliny or a bowl

of borsch, or stop in for an ice-cold shot of
vodka poured from on high.

OUTSIDE OLD TOWN

TOP CHOICE **F-hoone**
INTERNATIONAL €

(Telliskivi 60a; mains €5-8.50) If you suspected
there was probably a cool, casual eatery hidden away somewhere – where in-the-know
locals head for a quality, cheap feed – you
were right. Hidden in an old warehouse
complex on the wrong side of the tracks
(now used as artist studios, workshops and
band rehearsal spaces), this cavernous place
embraces industrial chic. We especially love
how the budget prices belie an excellent international menu.

Ö
MODERN ESTONIAN €€€

(🖋661 6150; www.restoran-o.ee; Mere pst 6e; mains
€14-28) With angelic chandelier sculptures
and charcoal-and-white overtones, the dining room at award-winning Ö is an understated work of art – as are the meals coming
out of the kitchen, showcasing winning
ways with seasonal local produce. Bookings
advised.

Sfäär
INTERNATIONAL €€

(www.sfaar.ee; Mere pst 6e; mains €8-18) Chic
Sfäär delivers an inventive menu highlighting the best Estonian produce (Otepää lamb,
Saaremaa beef and plenty of seafood) in a
warehouse-style setting that's like something
out of a Nordic design catalogue. But multipurpose Sfäär is not just a cafe-restaurant-
bar: it's also a store, selling wine and clothes.
It's found in an extensive warehouse bordering the Rotermann Quarter, now home to a
variety of restaurants.

Vapiano
ITALIAN €

(Hobujaama 10; pizza & pasta €5-8) Choose your
pasta or salad from the appropriate counter
and watch as it's prepared in front of you. If
it's pizza you're after, you'll receive a pager to

notify you when it's ready. This is 'fast' food done healthy, fresh and cheap. The restaurant itself is big, bright and buzzing, with huge windows, high tables and shelves of potted herbs. There's a second branch inside the Solaris Centre (p353).

🍷 Drinking

Bars & Pubs

Whether you seek a romantic wine cellar, a chic locals-only lounge or a raucous pub full of pint-wielding punters, you'll find plenty to choose from.

Hell Hunt   PUB
(www.hellhunt.ee; Pikk 39) See if you can score a few of the comfy armchairs out the back of this trouper of the pub circuit. It boasts an amiable air and reasonable prices for locally brewed beer and cider, plus decent pub grub. Don't let the menacing-sounding name put you off – it means 'Gentle Wolf'.

Drink Bar & Grill   PUB
(Väike-Karja 8) You know a bar means business when it calls itself Drink. This place takes its beer (and cider) seriously, and offers plenty of beer-friendly accompaniments: traditional pub grub, happy hour from 5pm to 7pm, big-screen sports, and comedy and quiz nights.

Gloria Wine Cellar   WINE BAR
(www.gloria.ee; Müürivahe 2; ⊙noon-11pm Mon-Sat) This romantic, mazelike cellar has a number of nooks and crannies where you can secrete yourself with a date and/or a good bottle of shiraz. The dark wood, antique furnishings and flickering candles add to the allure.

Clazz   LIVE MUSIC
(www.clazz.ee; Vana turg 2) Behind the cheesy name (a contraction of 'classy jazz') is a popular restaurant-bar, featuring live music every night (cover charge varies) and food served into the wee hours. Monday is the blues, Tuesday is Brazilian night; on other nights it could be DJs or bands – jazz, soul, disco etc (check the website).

Cafes

Tallinn's Old Town is so packed with absurdly cosy cafes that you can spend your whole trip wandering from one coffee house to the next. In most the focus is on coffee, tea, cakes and chocolates – there's usually considerably less effort put into savoury snacks.

These places often stay open until midnight, dispensing post-dinner sweets and treats.

Kehrwieder   CAFE
(www.kohvik.ee; Saiakang 1; ⊙8am-midnight) Sure, Kehrwieder has seating-with-a-view on Raekoja plats (and in a delightful garden oasis off Saiakang), but inside the city's cosiest cafe is where ambience is found in spades – you can stretch out on a couch, read by lamplight and bump your head on the arched ceilings.

III Draakon   CAFE
(Raekoja plats; ⊙8am-midnight) There's bucketloads of atmosphere at this lilliputian cafe below the Town Hall, and super-cheap elk soup or oven-hot pies (€1!). The historic setting is amped up – expect costumed wenches with a good line in tourist banter and beer served in ceramic steins.

Cafe-Chocolaterie de Pierre   CAFE
(www.pierre.ee; Vene 6, Masters' Courtyard; ⊙10am-11pm) Nestled inside the picturesque Masters' Courtyard, this snug, antique-filled cafe makes you feel like you're hiding away at your granny's place. It's renowned for its delectable handmade chocolates.

Park Café   CAFE
(www.park-cafe.ee; A Weizenbergi 22; ⊙10am-8pm Tue-Sun) At the western entrance to Kadriorg Park is this sweet slice of Viennese cafe culture. If the sun's shining, the alfresco tables by the pond might just be our favourite place in town.

☆ Entertainment

Tallinn is small as capitals go and the pace is accordingly slower than in other big cities, but there's lots to keep you stimulated – whether in a nightclub, laid-back bar or concert hall. Buy tickets for concerts and main events at **Piletilevi** (www.piletilevi.ee; Viru Keskus), which has a number of central locations. Events are posted on city centre walls and advertised on flyers found in shops and cafes.

Nightclubs

Club Hollywood   CLUB
(www.club-hollywood.ee; Vana-Posti 8; ⊙11pm-5am Wed-Sat) A multilevel emporium of mayhem, this is the nightclub that draws the largest crowds. Plenty of tourists and Tallinn's young party crowd mix it up to international and local DJs. Wednesday night is ladies'

night (free entry for women), so expect to see loads of guys looking to get lucky.

Bon Bon CLUB
(www.bonbon.ee; Mere pst 6e; ⊘11pm-5am Fri & Sat) With enormous chandeliers and a portrait of Bacchus overlooking the dance floor, Bon Bon is renowned for its chichi attitude. It attracts a 25- to 30-something A-list clientele who want to party in style. Frock up to fit in.

Club Privé CLUB
(www.clubprive.ee; Harju 6; ⊘11pm-6am Wed-Sat) Tallinn's most progressive club is at its busiest on Saturdays. Global DJs attract a club-savvy local and foreign crowd after something more cutting-edge than the likes of Club Hollywood. Minimum age is 20 on Friday and Saturday.

Performing Arts
Performances tend to be in Estonian only, save of course for modern dance shows or the rare show in English or other languages. *Tallinn in Your Pocket* (www.inyourpocket. com) lists major shows; other good sources of information are **Culture.ee** (www.culture.ee), **Eesti Kontsert** (www.concert.ee) and **Eesti Teatri Agentuur** (www.teater.ee).

Estonia Concert Hall & National Opera CONCERT HALL
(☑concert hall 614 7760, opera 683 1215; www. concert.ee; Estonia pst 4) The city's biggest concerts are held in this double-barrelled venue. It's Tallinn's main theatre and also houses the Estonian national opera and ballet.

City Theatre THEATRE
(Tallinna Linnateater; ☑665 0800; www.linnateater. ee; Lai 23) The most beloved theatre in town always stages memorable performances. Watch for its summer plays on an outdoor stage or in different Old Town venues.

Cinemas
Films are shown in their original language, subtitled in Estonian and Russian. Nighttime and weekend tickets cost about €5 to €6 (daytime sessions are slightly cheaper),

[TOP CHOICE] **Katusekino** OUTDOOR CINEMA
(www.katusekino.ee; Viru väljak, Viru Keskus; ⊘May-Sep) In the warmer months, a fun outdoor cinema is set up on the rooftop of Viru Keskus shopping centre. It screens an eclectic list (cult classics, as well as interesting new releases). Screen times depend on

sunset – anything from 9pm (September) to 11pm (July) – but food and drinks are available from midday. For booking information, see the website.

Artis ARTHOUSE CINEMA
(www.kino.ee; Estonia pst 9) Inside the Solaris Centre but somewhat tricky to find, this arthouse cinema shows European, local and independent productions.

Solaris Kino CINEMA
(www.solariskino.ee; Estonia pst 9) Also inside the Solaris Centre, with mostly mainstream offerings.

Coca-Cola Plaza CINEMA
(www.forumcinemas.ee; Hobujaama 5) Modern 11-screen cinema playing the latest Hollywood releases. Located behind the post office.

🛍 Shopping

Inside Old Town, dozens of small shops sell Estonian-made handicrafts. Linen, leather-bound books, ceramics, jewellery, silverware, stained glass and objects carved from limestone or made from juniper wood are all traditional Estonian souvenirs – as well as, of course, a bottle of Vana Tallinn. Look for signs for *käsitöö* (handicrafts). In summer a **souvenir market** is set up weekly (Wednesday) on Raekoja plats.

Katariina Gild HANDICRAFTS
(Katariina käik; Vene 12) This photogenic laneway is home to a number of artisans' studios where you can browse beautiful pieces, including stained glass, ceramics, textiles, patchwork quilts, hats, jewellery and leather-bound books.

Masters' Courtyard HANDICRAFTS
(Vene 6) Rich pickings here, with the courtyard home not only to a cosy cafe-chocolaterie (p352) but also small stores selling quality ceramics, jewellery, knitwear, candles, and wood and felt designs.

Knit Market KNITWEAR
(Müürivahe) Along the Old Town wall are vendors praying for cool weather and selling handmade linens, scarves, sweaters, mittens, beanies and socks.

Solaris Centre SHOPPING MALL
(www.solaris.ee; Estonia pst 9) Relative newcomer Solaris hosts a handful of boutiques, an excellent bookstore, popular restaurants, and both mainstream and art-house cinemas.

Viru Keskus
SHOPPING MALL

(www.virukeskus.com; Viru väljak) Tallinn's show-piece shopping mall, aka Viru Centre, lies just outside Old Town. It's home to mainstream fashion boutiques and a great bookstore (Rahva Raamat, with two quality on-site cafes). In summer there's a rooftop cinema. The bus terminal for local buses is in the basement.

ℹ Information

Discount Cards

Tallinn Card (www.tallinncard.ee; 1-/2-/3-day card €24/32/40) Offers free rides on public transport, admission to museums, free excursions and discounts at restaurants; cheaper children's cards are available. Buy online, from the tourist information centre, or from many hotels.

Internet Access

Tallinn is flooded with free wi-fi, but if you're not packing a laptop you'll find the city light on internet cafes. Most hostels and hotels offer a computer for guest use.

Estonian National Library (www.nlib.ee; Tõnismägi 2) Low-cost access at this behemoth, but there's a little paperwork involved to attain a one-day membership card.

Metro Internet (Viru väljak 4, basement, Viru Keskus; per hr €2.60; 8am-11pm) By the bus terminal under Viru Keskus shopping centre.

Media

Like a Local (www.likealocalguide.com/tallinn) Like a Local produces an invaluable map of Tallinn highlighting recommended spots. The website has great info too (download the app).

Lonely Planet (www.lonelyplanet.com/estonia/tallinn)

Tallinn In Your Pocket (www.inyourpocket.com) Full of useful listings. The booklets are on sale at bookshops, or can be downloaded free from its website.

Medical Services

Apteek 1 (Aia 7; 8.30am-8.30pm Mon-Fri, 9am-8pm Sat, 10am-6pm Sun) One of many well-stocked *apteek* (pharmacies).

East-Tallinn Central Hospital (622 7070, emergency department 620 7040; www.itk.ee; Ravi 18) Southeast of the city centre, has a full range of services plus 24-hour emergency room.

First-Aid Hotline (697 1145) English-language advice on treatment, hospitals and pharmacies.

Money

Foreign-currency exchange is available at any large bank (*pank*), transport terminals, exchange bureaux, the post office and major hotels, but check the rates. For better rates, steer clear of the small Old Town exchanges. Banks and ATMs are widespread.

Tavid (Aia 5; 24hr) Reliably good rates. Night-time rates aren't as good as those during business hours.

Post

Stamps can be purchased from any kiosk in town.

Central Post Office (Narva mnt 1; 8am-8pm Mon-Fri, 9am-3pm Sat) Entrance beside Nordic Hotel Forum.

Old Town Post Office (Viru 20; 10am-6pm Mon-Fri, to 3pm Sat & Sun) Small branch in Old Town. Open weekends in summer.

Telephone

Buy chip cards from news stands for local and international calls at the blue phone boxes scattered around town. Otherwise, post offices, supermarkets, phone-company stores (in the shopping centres) and some kiosks sell cheap mobile-phone starter kits with prepaid SIM cards (from €5).

Tourist Information

Tallinn Tourist Information Centre (www.tourism.tallinn.ee; cnr Kullassepa & Niguliste; 9am-8pm Mon-Fri, to 6pm Sat & Sun mid-Jun–Aug, shorter hrs daily Sep-mid-Jun) A block south of Raekoja plats, with maps and brochures for the capital and further afield. Note that it doesn't offer an accommodation-booking service.

Traveller Info Tent (www.traveller.ee; Niguliste; 9am-9pm mid-May–mid-Sep) Great source of information, set up by young local students in a tent opposite the official tourist information centre. Dispenses lots of local tips and maps, keeps a 'what's on' board, and operates entertaining, well-priced walking and cycling tours (p348).

Travel Agencies

Booking Estonia (557 7636; www.apartmentsestonia.com; Kullassepa 9) Agency booking bus and ferry tickets (no commission), and offering accommodation (including apartments in Old Town).

Union Travel (627 0621; Lembitu 14) Close to the Radisson Blu Hotel Olümpia and can help arrange visas to Russia although, due to changing regulations, it's best to arrange Russian visas in your home country prior to travelling.

ℹ Getting There & Away

Air

Tallinn airport (www.tallinn-airport.ee) is just 4km southeast of the city centre on Tartu mnt.

Avies Air flies from Tallinn to the islands of Hiiumaa and Saaremaa.

Boat

TO/FROM FINLAND

A fleet of ferries carries more than two million people annually across the 85km separating Helsinki and Tallinn. There are dozens of crossings made every day (ships two to 3½ hours; hydrofoils approximately 1½ hours). Note that in high winds or bad weather hydrofoils are often cancelled; they operate only when the sea is free from ice, while larger ferries sail year-round.

All companies provide concessions, allow pets and bikes (for a fee) and charge higher prices for peak services and weekend travel. Expect to pay about the price of an adult ticket extra to take a car. There's lots of competition, so check the companies for special offers and packages.

Operators include the following:

Eckerö Line (☑664 6000; www.eckeroline.ee; Terminal A; adult one way from €19; ☺year-round) Large new vessel sailing once or twice daily in both directions. Journey time is 2½ hours.

Linda Line (☑699 9333; www.lindaliini.ee; Linnahall Terminal; from €31; ☺late Mar-late Dec) Small, passenger-only hydrofoils sail up to seven times daily in season. Takes 1½ hours.

Tallink (☑640 9808; www.tallinksilja.com/en; Terminal D; adult from €19-54; ☺year-round) Up to seven services daily in each direction. The huge *Baltic Princess* takes 3½ hours; newer high-speed ferries take two hours.

Viking Line (☑666 3966; www.vikingline.com; Terminal A; adult €19-47; ☺year-round) Operates a giant car ferry, with two departures daily. Takes 2½ hours.

TO/FROM SWEDEN

Tallink (p355) sails every night between Tallinn's Terminal D and Stockholm, via the Åland islands (passage from €39, 16 hours). Book ahead.

Bus

For bus information and advance tickets for Estonian and international destinations, go to the **Central Bus Station** (Autobussijaam; ☑12550; Lastekodu 46), about 2km southeast of Old Town. Tram 2 or 4 will take you there, as will bus 17, 23 or 23A.

Ecolines (☑606 2217; www.ecolines.net) and **Lux Express** (☑680 0909; www.luxexpress.eu) have offices at the bus station, but you can easily book online, or Booking Estonia (p354) in Old Town will book and issue your bus tickets for no commission.

Ecolines connects Tallinn with several cities in Central and Eastern Europe. Lux Express has direct services connecting Tallinn with Rīga (€13 to €27, 4½ hours, up to eight daily) and Vilnius (€22 to €39, 8½ hours to nine hours, three direct buses daily, plus additional services via Rīga). Lux Express buses leave Tallinn for St Petersburg up to 10 times daily (€15 to €48, six to eight hours), passing through border town Narva en route. Handily, Lux Express can help arrange Russian visas (see the website); however, due to changing regulations, it's best to arrange Russian visas in your home country. Lux Express offers different travel classes – the most expensive buses have free hot drinks, wi-fi and plush leather seats.

The useful website www.tpilet.ee has times, prices and durations for all national bus services.

Car & Motorcycle

There are 24-hour fuel stations at strategic spots within the city and on major roads leading to and from Tallinn.

Your hotel can often arrange car rental. Many companies have a desk at the airport; some will deliver a car to you.

Advantec (☑520 3003; www.advantage.ee; Tallinn airport) Summer rates from €36 per day (cheaper for longer rentals).

Bulvar (☑503 0222; www.bulvar.ee; Regati pst 1) From €25 per day (good deals for longer rentals).

Hertz (☑611 6210; www.hertz.ee; Ahtri 12)

Train

The **Central Train Station** (Balti Jaam; www.baltijaam.ee; Toompuiestee 35) is on the northwestern edge of Old Town, a short walk from Raekoja plats via Nunne, or three stops on tram 1 or 2, heading north from the Mere pst stop.

Train travel is not as popular as bus travel in Estonia, so domestic routes are limited (as are international options).

There are no rail connections to Rīga or Vilnius, but there are daily services to and from Russia operated by **GO Rail** (☑631 0044; http://tickets.gorail.ee). An overnight train runs between Tallinn and Moscow (€129 in a four-berth compartment, 14½ hours). A daytime service has resumed between Tallinn and St Petersburg (from €22, 6½ hours).

ⓘ Getting Around

To & From the Airport

Public Bus Bus 2 runs every 20 to 30 minutes (6am to around 11pm) from A Laikmaa, next to Viru Keskus; the bus stop is opposite, not out front of, the Tallink Hotel. From the airport, bus 2 will take you to the centre. Buy tickets from the driver (€1.60); journey time depends on traffic but it rarely takes more than 20 minutes.

Taxi A taxi between the airport and the city centre should cost no more than €10.

To & From the Ferry Terminals

Tallinn's sea-passenger terminal is at the end of Sadama, a short 1km walk northeast of Old Town. Bus 2 runs every 20 to 30 minutes between the bus stop by Terminal A and A Laikmaa in the city centre; if you're heading to the terminal, the bus stop is out the front of the Tallink Hotel. Also from the heart of town (around the Viru Keskus transport hub), trams 1 and 2, and bus 3 go to the Linnahall stop, by the Statoil Petrol Station. From here you're a five-minute walk from terminals A, B and C, and the Linda Line terminal.

Terminal D is at the end of Lootsi, better accessed from Ahtri; bus 2 services the terminal (the same bus route that services terminal A and the airport).

A taxi between the city centre and any of the terminals will cost about €5.

Bicycle

As well as offering city cycling and walking tours, City Bike (p348) can take care of all you need to get around by bike, within Tallinn, around Estonia or throughout the Baltic region.

Public Transport

Tallinn has an excellent network of buses, trams and trolleybuses that usually run from 6am to 11pm. The major local bus station is on the basement level of Viru Keskus shopping centre; local buses may also terminate their route on the surrounding streets, just east of Old Town. Local public transport timetables are online at **Tallinn** (www.tallinn.ee).

In an innovative and generous move, public transport became free for all registered Tallinn residents as of January 2013. Visitors still need to pay, using the new e-ticketing system, which covers all three modes of local transport. Buy a plastic smartcard to top up with credit, then validate the card at the start of each journey using the orange card-readers. Fares using the e-ticketing system cost €1.10/3/5 for an hour/day/three days. Alternatively, you will still be able to buy a paper ticket (*piletid*) from the driver when you board (€1.60 for a single journey).

Note that the Tallinn Card gives free public transport.

Taxi

Taxis are plentiful in Tallinn. Oddly, taxi companies set their own rates, so flag fall and per-kilometre rates vary from cab to cab – prices should be posted in each taxi's right rear window. If you merely hail a taxi on the street, there's a chance you'll be overcharged. To save yourself the trouble, order a taxi by phone: try **Krooni Takso** (☎638 1212) and **Reval Takso** (☎601 4600).

NORTHEASTERN ESTONIA

This region has received considerably less attention from tourists than destinations such as Pärnu and Tartu, and shows a different side to Estonia. As you head east from Lahemaa, the vast majority of the population is Russian-speaking, which adds another flavour to the Estonian cultural mosaic; some places feel like Soviet relics.

Lahemaa National Park

The perfect country retreat from the capital, Lahemaa takes in a stretch of coast deeply indented with peninsulas and bays, plus 475 sq km of pine-fresh forested hinterland. Visitors are well looked after, with cosy guesthouses, restored manor houses, remote camping grounds along the sea and an extensive network of pine-scented forest trails.

◎ Sights & Activities

There is an abundance of sightseeing, hiking, cycling and boating to be done here; remote islands can also be explored. The park has several well-signposted nature trails and cycling paths winding through it. The small coastal towns of **Võsu**, **Käsmu** and (to a lesser extent) **Loksa** are popular seaside spots in summer. Käsmu is a particularly enchanting village, one of Estonia's prettiest.

Lahemaa also features historic manor houses. Park showpiece **Palmse Manor** (www.palmse.ee; adult/concession €4.80/3.20; ⊙10am-6pm or 7pm), next to the visitors centre (p357), was once a wholly self-contained Baltic German estate, while the pink-and-white neoclassical **Sagadi Manor** (www.sagadi.ee; adult/concession €2.60/1.30; ⊙10am-6pm May-Sep, by appointment Oct-Apr) was built in 1749. There are other manor houses at **Kolga** and **Vihula** – Vihula's is now part of a very picturesque 'country club' featuring activities, a spa, restaurants and pricey accommodation (www.vihulamanor.com).

🛏 Sleeping & Eating

Palmse Manor and Sagadi Manor have good sleeping and eating options on the estates, while the fishing village of Altja offers a rural seaside idyll.

ALTJA

TOP CHOICE Toomarahva Turismitalu CAMPING, GUESTHOUSE €

(☑505 0850; www.toomarahva.ee; Altja; campsite €10, d €40-60; ☜) A farmstead with thatch-roofed wooden outhouses, and a garden full of flowers and sculptures, this gem of a place offers an unforgettable taste of rural Estonia. There's a yard for camping, a barn full of beds serving as a summer dorm and usually accommodating small groups (€40, sleeps six), plus rooms in converted stables (the 'apartment' has kitchen facilities). There is a rustic sauna and bikes for rent. Ülle, the friendly owner, also offers catering. Signage is minimal – it's located opposite the yard of the Altja Kõrts.

Altja Kõrts TRADITIONAL ESTONIAN €€

(Altja; mains €5-12; ☉11am-9pm) Set in an old wooden farmhouse, this uber-rustic place serves delicious plates of home cooking. Don't be deterred by the menu's first page, listing pig's ears and black pudding as starters. Read on for more appetising options like juniper-grilled salmon, or pork roulade with horseradish. End on a high note with fresh blueberry pie (seasonal).

SAGADI

Sagadi Manor Hotel & Restaurant HOTEL €€

(☑676 7888; www.sagadi.ee; Sagadi; dm €15, s/d from €55/75, restaurant mains €7-15; @☜) With its whitewashed exterior and hanging flower baskets, the hotel on the Sagadi estate offers a cheerful welcome. On the ground floor are fresh rooms opening onto small patios and a courtyard. Upstairs rooms are older and marginally cheaper. Sagadi also has a 31-bed hostel in the old steward's house. The hotel's smart **restaurant** offers quality local flavours, from Baltic herring to wild boar.

ℹ Information

Lahemaa National Park visitor centre (☑329 5555; www.lahemaa.ee; ☉9am-6pm daily mid-Apr–mid-Oct, 9am-5pm Mon-Fri mid-Oct–mid-Apr) is in Palmse, 7km north of Viitna in the park's southeast, next door to Palmse Manor. Here you'll find the essential map of Lahemaa, as well as information on accommodation, hiking trails, island exploration and guide services.

ℹ Getting There & Away

Hiring a car is one way to reach and explore the areas inside the park; alternatively you can take a tour from Tallinn. A number of operators offer a day exploring the park highlights, costing around €50. If you feel like getting closer to nature, City Bike (p348) has packages that include transfer to the park plus bikes and maps for DIY touring, and guesthouse accommodation (€93/113 for one/two nights). Otherwise, for public transport exploration you'll need patience and plenty of time up your sleeve.

The best starting point for buses to destinations within the park is the town of Rakvere, about halfway between Tallinn and Narva. Regular buses connect Rakvere with Tallinn (€6.50, 1½ hours, 20 per day). From Rakvere buses run to the park year-round, but services are curtailed in winter. We highly recommend your own wheels or a tour.

Narva & Around

POP 67,000

Estonia's easternmost town is separated from Ivangorod in Russia only by the thin Narva River, and is almost entirely populated by Russians. Although the most outstanding architecture was destroyed in WWII, Estonia's third-largest city is an intriguing place to wander, as you'll find no other place in Estonia quite like it. The centre has a melancholy, downtrodden air; the prosperity evident in other parts of the country is harder to find here (though it does exist in some pockets, most notably the brash shopping centres along Tallinna mnt). Narva is a place that will have you scratching your head at times: is it a Russian city on the wrong side of the border?

◉ Sights

Narva Castle CASTLE

(Peterburi mnt) Restored after WWII, imposing Narva Castle, guarding the Friendship Bridge over the river to Russia, dates from Danish rule in the 13th century. It faces Russia's matching Ivangorod Fortress across the river, creating a picturesque face-off that's best captured from the park below the **Swedish Lion monument**, behind the Narva Hotel at Puškin 6. The castle houses the **Narva Museum** (www.narvamuuseum.ee; adult/concession €5/3.30; ☉10am-6pm, closed Mon & Tue Sep-May), with exhibits on the town and castle, and there's a restaurant (p358) in the grounds.

Narva-Jõesuu BEACH

About 13km north of Narva is the resort of Narva-Jõesuu, popular since the 19th century for its long golden-sand beach backed by pine forests. There are impressive early 20th-century wooden houses and villas here, as well as spa hotels. It's a popular spot for holidaying Russians.

🛏 Sleeping & Eating

King Hotel
HOTEL **€€**

(☎357 2404; www.hotelking.ee; Lavretsovi 9; s/d €48/60, restaurant mains €7-17; @🛜) Not far north of Narva's town centre (and with a few similarly priced hotels in the immediate vicinity), King has snug modern rooms and an excellent, atmospherically gloomy **restaurant** with a shady terrace. For something different, try the *lamprey* (a local fish from the Narva River).

Pansionaat Valentina
GUESTHOUSE **€€**

(☎357 7468; www.pansionaatvalentina.com; Aia 49, Narva- Jõesuu; s/d/f €30/50/90; @🛜) Behind the big Meresuu Spa & Hotel in Narva-Jõesuu, metres from the beach, is this handsome, salmon-coloured guesthouse offering rooms in immaculate grounds. It's family-friendly, with tennis courts, sauna, barbecue and cafe. Be sure to admire the breathtaking intricacy of the historic villa right next door.

Castell
RESTAURANT **€€**

(Peterburi mnt, Narva Castle; mains €14-24; ⊙11am-11pm) Inside the castle grounds, this medieval-styled restaurant-bar offers up a big menu of dubiously titled dishes ('Mystery of the River Depths', 'Bravery of the Military Field' etc).

ℹ Information

The efficient **tourist information centre** (☎359 9137; http://tourism.narva.ee; Peetri plats 3; ⊙10am-4pm) is beside the Estonia–Russia border crossing in the city centre.

ℹ Getting There & Away

The bus and train stations in Narva are located together at Vaksali 25, opposite the Russian Orthodox Voskresensky Cathedral. From there, walk north up Puškini to the castle (500m) and the centre. Narva is 210km east of Tallinn on the road to St Petersburg, which is a further 130km away. Transport to St Petersburg (buses from Tallinn and Tartu, train from Tallinn) stop in Narva to pick up passengers.

Around 20 daily buses travel between Tallinn and Narva (€10 to €12, three to four hours). There are also up to 10 daily Tartu-Narva buses (€7 to €11.40, 2½ to 3½ hours). Bus 31 runs about hourly to connect Narva with Narva-Jõesuu (€1, 20 minutes), as do numerous marshrutky (minibuses) without set timetables.

One train (€7.40, 3½ hours) runs daily between Tallinn and Narva.

SOUTHEASTERN ESTONIA

Set with rolling hills, picturesque lakes and vast woodlands, the southeast sings with some of Estonia's prettiest countryside. It also contains one of the country's most important cities: the vibrant university centre of Tartu.

Tartu

POP 102,000

If Tallinn is Estonia's head, Tartu may well be its heart (and possibly its university-educated brains, too). Tartu lays claim to being Estonia's spiritual capital – locals talk about a special Tartu *vaim* (spirit), created by the time-stands-still, 19th-century feel of many of its wooden-house-lined streets, and by the beauty of its parks and riverfront.

Small and provincial, with the Emajõgi River flowing through it, Tartu is Estonia's premier university town, with students comprising around one-fifth of the population. This injects a vitality into the leafy, historic setting and grants it a surprising sophistication for a city of its size.

Tartu was the cradle of Estonia's 19th-century national revival and it escaped Sovietisation to a greater degree than Tallinn. Today, visitors to Estonia's second city can get a more authentic depiction of the rhythm of Estonian life than in its glitzier cousin to the north (and accompanied by far fewer tourists, too). In addition to galleries and cafes, there are good museums here; the city is also a convenient gateway to exploring southern Estonia.

◉ Sights & Activities

As the major repository of Estonia's cultural heritage, Tartu has an abundance of first-rate museums. There are plenty more than those listed here (showcasing everything from brewing to sport to postal services to song festivals) – check with the tourist office.

Raekoja plats
SQUARE

At the centre on Raekoja plats is the **town hall** (1782–89), topped by a tower and weathervane, and fronted by a fountain and **statue** of students kissing under an umbrella – an apt, light-hearted symbol of Tartu. At the other end of the square is the wonderfully skew-whiff building housing the **Tartu Art Museum** (www.tartmus.ee; Raekoja plats 18; adult/

student €3/1.50; ☻noon-6pm Wed-Sun). In between are loads of cafes and alfresco terraces.

Tartu University
UNIVERSITY

(www.ut.ee; Ülikooli 18) The city's university was founded in 1632 by the Swedish king; the grand, neoclassical main university building dates from 1804. It houses the **University Art Museum** (admission €1; ☻11am-6pm Mon-Fri) and entertaining **Student's Lock-Up** (admission €1; ☻11am-5pm Mon-Fri), where 19th-century students were held for their misdeeds.

St John's Church
CHURCH

(Jaani 5; observation tower adult/child €1.60/1; ☻10am-6pm Tue-Sat) The magnificent Gothic St John's Church features elaborate brickwork and dates back to at least 1323. It's noteworthy for its rare terracotta sculptures in niches around the main portal. Climb the 135 steps of the 30m-high **observation tower** for a great bird's-eye view of Tartu.

TOP CHOICE Toy Museum
MUSEUM

(www.mm.ee; Lutsu 8; adult/child incl Theatre House €4/3; ☻11am-6pm Wed-Sun) The best place to pass a rainy few hours is in the enchanting Toy Museum, showcasing dolls, model trains, rocking horses, toy soldiers and tons of other desirables dating back a century or so. It's all geared to be nicely interactive – exhibits in pull-out drawers, toys to play with – and there's a kids' playroom too. The adjacent courtyard house is home to fun characters and props from Estonian animated films. Down the road is the affiliated **Theatre House** (www.teatrikodu.ee; Lutsu 2; ☻11am-6pm Wed-Sun), a newly restored children's theatre (performances are usually in Estonian). In the basement is a small, sweet museum showcasing theatre puppets of the world. While you're in the neighbourhood, check out the lovely artisan studios and workshops of **Antoniuse Gild** (Lutsu 5).

Estonian National Museum
MUSEUM

(www.erm.ee; Kuperjanovi 9; all/permanent collections €3/2, admission free Fri; ☻11am-6pm Tue-Sun) This absorbing museum is small, sweet and proud (much like the country itself), and does a fine job of tracing the history, life and traditions of the locals. There are ambitious plans afoot to create a massive new home for the museum at Raadi Manor (on the outskirts of town) by around 2015.

KGB Cells Museum
MUSEUM

(www.linnamuuseum.tartu.ee; Riia mnt 15b; adult/student €2/1; ☻11am-4pm Tue-Sat) The former KGB headquarters now houses this sombre and highly worthwhile museum. Chilling in parts, it gives a fascinating rundown of deportations during the Soviet era and life in the Gulag camps. Entrance is on Pepleri.

Toomemägi
PARK

(Cathedral Hill) Rising to the west of Raekoja plats is the splendid Toomemägi (Cathedral Hill), landscaped in the manner of a 19th-century English park and perfect for a stroll. The 13th-century Gothic **Tartu Cathedral** (Toomkirik; Cathedral Hill) at the top was rebuilt in the 15th century, despoiled during the Reformation in 1525 and partly rebuilt in 1804–07 to accommodate the university library, which is now the **Museum of University History** (museum & tower/museum only €2.60/1.60; ☻11am-5pm Wed-Sun).

✰✰ Festivals & Events

Tartu regularly dons its shiniest party gear and lets its hair down – good events to circle in your calendar include the following. Check out **Kultuuriaken** (http://kultuuriaken.tartu.ee) for more.

STUDENT LIFE IN TARTU

The world over, students gravitate to cheap meals and booze, and in Tartu it is no different. Many of the cafes on Raekoja plats cater to impoverished students with good-value weekday lunch deals – check out **Sõprade Juures** (Raekoja plats 12), with its soup/dish of the day for €1.85/3.30. In the evening, down cheap beer (a half-litre for about €2) alongside students at dive bars like tiny basement **Möku** (Rüütli 18) and industrial-chic **Zavood** (Lai 30). Other popular drinking spots include **Illegaard** (Ülikooli 5), a laid-back pub where you're likely to encounter foreign students studying in Tartu, and the seriously cool **Genialistide Klubi** (www.genklubi.ee; behind Lai 37, enter from Magasini), an all-purpose, grungy 'subcultural establishment' that manages to simultaneously be a bar, cafe, alternative nightclub, live-music venue, cinema and more – be sure to check it out.

Tartu

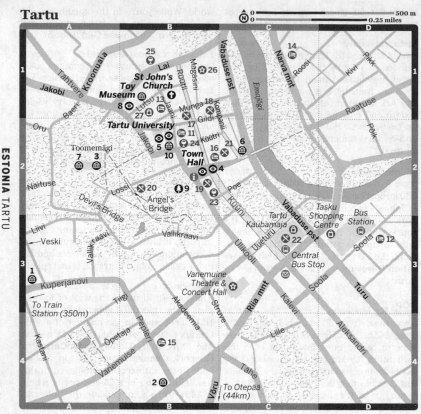

Tartu Ski Marathon

SPORT

(www.tartumaraton.ee) Tartu hosts this 63km race in mid-February, drawing around 4000 competitors to the region's cross-country tracks.

Tartu Student Days

STUDENT CELEBRATIONS

(www.studentdays.ee) Catch a glimpse of modern-day student misdeeds at the end of April, when they take to the streets to celebrate term's end. A second, smaller version occurs in mid-October.

Hansa Days Festival

HISTORY

(www.hansapaevad.ee) Crafts, markets, family-friendly performances and more to commemorate Tartu's Hanseatic past over three days in mid-July.

Tartuff

FILM

(www.tartuff.ee) For one week in August, a big outdoor cinema takes over Raekoja plats. Screenings (with arthouse leanings) are free, plus there are documentaries, poetry readings and concerts.

Sleeping

TOP CHOICE Antonius Hotel

HOTEL €€

(737 0377; www.hotelantonius.ee; Ülikooli 15; d €99-144;) Sitting plumb opposite the main university building, this first-class, 18-room boutique hotel is loaded with antiques and period features, from the library with fireplace to the suites with old-world stoves. Breakfast is served in the vaulted cellar (which by night is a romantic restaurant); the summertime terrace is delightful.

Terviseks

HOSTEL €

(565 5382; www.terviseksbbb.com; Raekoja plats 10, top fl; dm €15-17, s/d €22/44;) In a perfect, town-square location, this excellent 'backpackers bed & breakfast' (run by a Brit and a Canadian) offers dorms (maxi-

Tartu

mum four beds, no bunks), private rooms, shiny new facilities and lots of switched-on info about the cool places in town. You couldn't be better placed for a chilled-out good time.

Tartu Student Hostels STUDENT RESIDENCES €
(☎742 7608; www.tartuhostel.eu; s/d €25/40; @) Two student residences, Narva and Pepleri, offer outstanding value (but not much by way of character) in prime locations. **Pepleri** (Pepleri 14) is south of the river, and **Narva** (Narva mnt 27) is opposite parklands north of the city centre. The Narva apartments each have a living room, bathroom and kitchenette. Pepleri's standard rooms are smaller (there's no living room), but larger apartments are available (for €50). Advance reservations are a must.

Tampere Maja GUESTHOUSE €€
(☎738 6300; www.tamperemaja.ee; Jaani 4; s/d/tr/q from €44/66/88/110; @) With strong links to the Finnish city of Tampere (Tartu's sister city), this cosy guesthouse in the town's old quarter features six warm, light-filled guestrooms ranging in size. Breakfast is included and each room has cooking facilities; two-room suites sleep up to four. And it wouldn't be Finnish if it didn't offer an authentic sauna (open to non-guests).

Hotel Tartu HOTEL €€
(☎731 4300; www.tartuhotell.ee; Soola 3; hostel s/d/tr €32/44/56, s/d €45/65; @) In a handy location across from the bus station and Tasku shopping centre, this hotel offers rooms from the Ikea school of decoration – low-frills and contemporary. The 'hostel' portion of the hotel is actually six spotless, older-style hotel rooms (shared bathrooms in the corridor) sleeping three.

✗ Eating & Drinking

The most central **supermarket** (◷9am-10pm Mon-Sat, 10am-8pm Sun) is in the basement of the Tartu Kaubamaja shopping centre.

La Dolce Vita ITALIAN €€
(Kompanii 10; pizza & pasta €5-10, mains €8-19) Thin-crust pizzas come straight from the wood-burning oven at this cheerful, family-friendly pizzeria. It's the real deal, with a big Italian menu of bruschetta, pizza, pasta, gelati etc and classic casual decor (red-and-white checked tablecloths, Fellini posters – tick).

Noir INTERNATIONAL €€
(Ülikooli 7; mains €7-12) Definitely a place to impress a date, this sexy, black-walled restaurant-cum-vinoteque is a fine place for wining, dining and reclining. It's tucked

away in a flower-filled courtyard off Ülikooli, with outdoor tables and a well-priced fusion menu.

Crepp
CAFE €

(Rüütli 16; crepes €4; ⊙from 11am daily) Locals love this place. Its warm, stylish decor belies its bargain-priced crepes (of the sweet or savoury persuasion, with great combos like cherry-choc and almonds). They serve tasty salads too.

Püssirohukelder
PUB €€

(Lossi 28; mains €7-18) Set in a cavernous 18th-century gunpowder cellar under a soaring, 10m-high vaulted ceiling, this is both a boisterous pub and a good choice for beer-accompanying snacks and meaty meals (lots of pork options). There's regular live music too.

Tsink Plekk Pang
ASIAN

(Küütri 6; ⊙noon-11pm Sun-Wed, to midnight Thu-Sat) Behind Tartu's funkiest facade (look for the stripy paintwork) and set over three floors is this cool Asian-flavoured restaurant-lounge. Sadly the food is below-par, but the venue is great for cocktails or a beer on the roof terrace, with a DJ-spun soundtrack on weekends.

ⓘ Information

Tartu In Your Pocket (www.inyourpocket.com) There's great info in this listings guide; available in bookshops or online.

Tartu Tourist Information Centre (✆744 2111; www.visittartu.com; Raekoja plats, town hall; ⊙9am-6pm Mon-Fri, 10am-5pm Sat & Sun mid-May–mid-Sep, 9am-5pm Mon-Fri, 10am-2pm Sat & Sun mid-Sep–mid-May) This friendly office has local maps and brochures, and loads of other city info. It can also book accommodation and tour guides, sell you souvenirs and get you online (free internet access available).

ⓘ Getting There & Away

BUS Tartu is the main hub for destinations in south and southeastern Estonia. From the **bus station** (✆12550; Turu 2), daily buses run to and from Tallinn (€9 to €11, 2½ to three hours) about every 15 to 30 minutes from 6am to 9pm. At least 10 buses a day run to Pärnu (€10 to €11, 2½ to three hours). Four daily Lux Express buses connect Tartu with St Petersburg (€20 to €25, 6½ hours).

TRAIN Four or five daily trains make the journey between Tartu and Talllinn (€6.70, 2½ to three hours).

Otepää
POP 2100

The small hilltop town of Otepää, 44km south of Tartu, is the centre of a scenic area beloved by Estonians for its forests, hills and lakes, and hence for its nature-frollicking activities – hiking, cycling and swimming in summer and cross-country skiing in winter.

⊙ Sights

Pühajärv
LAKE

A blissful 12km nature trail and bike path encircle this 3.5km-long 'holy lake', which is rich in pagan legend. It was blessed by the Dalai Lama and a small monument on the eastern shore commemorates his visit in 1991.

It's a 30-minute (2.3km) walk from Otepää township (via Pühajärve tee) to the northern tip of the lake, where there's a short trail to a picturesque **beach park** that's popular with summer swimmers. Here you'll find waterslides, a swimming pontoon, a cafe and lifeguards; rowboats can be hired.

Winter Sports Museum
MUSEUM

(Tehvandi Stadium; adult/child €1.50/1; ⊙11am-4pm Wed-Sun) Just southeast of the town centre (off Rte 46), big, flash **Tehvandi Stadium**, used for football and ski events, is testimony to Otepää's obsession with sport. Within the bowels of the main stand, this two-room museum displays equipment, costumes and medals belonging to some of Estonia's most famous athletes.

St Mary's Church
CHURCH

Otepää's pretty 17th-century church is on a hilltop about 300m northeast of the bus station (off Rte 71). It was in this church in 1884 that the Estonian Students' Society consecrated its new blue, black and white flag, which later became the flag of independent Estonia.

The tree-covered hill south of the church is **Linnamägi** (Castle Hill), a major stronghold from the 10th to 12th centuries. There are traces of old fortifications on top and good views of the surrounding country.

⫶ Activities

It would be a shame to visit and not take advantage of the outdoor activities on offer. To rent bikes, rollerblades, skis and snowboards, contact **Fan Sport** (✆507 7537; www.fansport.ee), which has winter offices inside the larger hotels in Otepää. **VeeTee** (✆506

KIIKING – WHAT THE?

Is it only the Estonians who could turn the gentle pleasure of riding a swing into an extreme sport? (Frankly, we're surprised the New Zealanders didn't think of it first.) From the weird and wacky world of Estonian sport comes *kiiking*, invented in the mid-1990s (and adapted from an old Estonian tradition of wooden swings in most villages). *Kiiking* sees competitors stand on a swing and attempt to complete a 360-degree loop around the top bar (with their feet fastened to the swing base and their hands to the swing arms). The inventor of *kiiking*, Ado Kosk, observed that the longer the swing arms, the more difficult it is to complete a 360-degree loop. Kosk then designed swing arms that can gradually extend, for an increased challenge. In competition, the winner is the person who completes a loop with the longest swing arms – the current record stands at a fraction over 7m! If this concept has you scratching your head, head to the Kiiking.com website to get a visual picture, and find out where you can see it in action (or even give it a try yourself).

0987; www.veetee.ee) specialises in canoeing trips on the area's rivers and lakes (from €20). Ask at the tourist office for more options – there's everything from golf to snowtubing, sleigh rides and snowmobile safaris.

🛏 Sleeping & Eating

Low season here is April to May and September to November; at this time hotel prices are about 10% to 15% cheaper.

Pühajärve Spa Hotel   HOTEL €€
(☎766 5500; www.pyhajarve.com; Pühajärve tee; s/d weekdays €55/70, weekends €63/80; @🤶🏊) In a great lakeside location and with beautiful sprawling grounds, this is the best-equipped place in town: there's a day spa, indoor pool, bowling alley, gym, tennis courts and bike rental. Thankfully, rooms have recently been spruced up. There are also good eating options – best of all is the casual **pub** (mains €5-20). Check out the views from the tower **cafe**.

Edgari   GUESTHOUSE €
(☎766 6550; www.hot.ee/karnivoor; Lipuväljak 3; r per person €20-25; 🤶) A good-value place to stay in the heart of town, this guesthouse has a mix of hostel-style rooms (shared bathroom and kitchen, communal lounge), plus studio apartments with kitchenette and private bathroom. Downstairs is a tavern and small food shop.

I.u.m.i.   INTERNATIONAL €€
(Munamäe 8; mains €8.50-18) Mismatched furniture and cool cutlery lampshades create a groovy vibe at this big, bright newcomer. There's a fairly traditional list of fish, pork, beef and chicken dishes, rounded out with

some more creative items (interesting salads) and an excellent tapas platter. A great choice.

ℹ Information

The point where Valga mnt and Tartu mnt meet is the epicentre of the town, with the bus station here, alongside the **Otepää tourist information centre** (☎766 1200; www.otepaa.ee; Lipuväljak 13; ⏱10am-5pm Mon-Fri, to 4pm Sat & Sun mid-May–mid-Sep, closed Sun & Mon mid-Sep–mid-May).

Behind the tourist information centre is the triangular main 'square', Lipuväljak; in this area you'll find the town's main services, including a supermarket and ATM.

ℹ Getting There & Away

Frequent buses connect Otepää with Tartu (€3, one hour, 12 daily). One direct bus runs to and from Tallinn (€12, 3½ hours, daily).

WESTERN ESTONIA

As well as a tourist-magnet coastline come summer, the western half of the country houses Estonia's most popular resort town, sweet country villages, a vast national park and a handful of islands – developed or remote and windswept, take your pick.

Pärnu
POP 44,000

Local families, young party-goers, and German, Swedish and Finnish holidaymakers join together in a collective prayer for sunny weather while strolling the golden-sand beaches, sprawling parks and picturesque

Pärnu

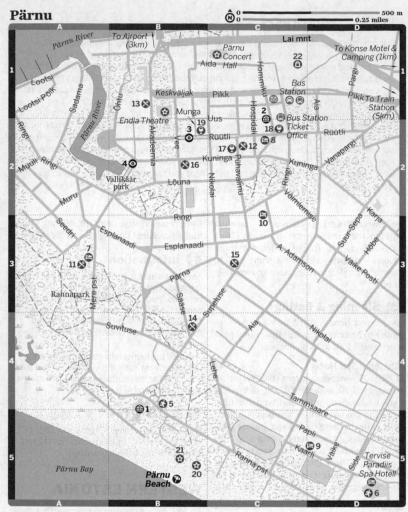

historic centre of Pärnu (*pair*-nu), Estonia's premier seaside resort.

In summer, the town acts as a magnet for party-loving Estonians – in these parts, its name is synonymous with fun in the sun. One hyperbolic local described it to us as 'Estonia's Miami', but it's usually called by its slightly more prosaic moniker, the nation's 'summer capital'.

In truth, most of Pärnu is quite docile, with leafy streets and expansive parks intermingling with turn-of-the-century villas that reflect the town's past as a resort capital of the Baltic region. Older visitors from Finland and the former Soviet Union still visit, seeking rest, rejuvenation and Pärnu's vaunted mud treatments.

◎ Sights & Activities

Pärnu Beach
BEACH

Pärnu's long, wide, golden-sand beach – sprinkled with volleyball courts, cafes and tiny changing cubicles – is easily the city's main drawcard. A curving path stretches along the sand, lined with fountains and park benches perfect for people-watching. Early-20th-century buildings are strung along Ranna pst, the avenue that runs par-

Pärnu

allel to the beach, including the handsome 1927 neoclassical **Mudaravila** (Ranna pst 1). The legendary mud baths that once operated in this historic building have been closed for years, awaiting restoration. Back from the sand, **Rannapark** holds picnic tables and plenty of kid-friendly draws (minigolf, trampolines, playgrounds).

From June to August **Tõruke Rattarent** (☎502 8269; www.bicyclerentalparnu.eu; cnr Ranna pst & Supeluse; bike per hr/day/week €2.50/10/43) rents out bikes by the beach. For €1 they'll deliver a bike to you year-round.

Rüütli　　　　　　　　　　　　　STREET
The main thoroughfare of the historic centre is Rüütli, lined with splendid buildings

dating back to the 17th century. Just off the main street is the **Red Tower** (Punane Torn; Hommiku 11), the city's oldest building, which dates from the 15th century; despite its name, it's actually white. Sadly at the time of research it was closed to the public.

Parts of the 17th-century Swedish moat and ramparts remain at the western end of Rüütli; the **Tallinn Gate** (Tallinna Värav), which once marked the main road to Tallinn, pierces the point where the rampart meets the western end of Kuninga.

Veekeskus　　　　　　　　　WATERPARK
(www.terviseparadiis.ee; Side 14; day ticket adult/concession €18/13; ◷10am-10pm) At the far end of the beach, Estonia's largest water park beckons with pools, slides, tubes and other slippery fun. It's a big family-focused draw, especially when bad weather ruins beach plans. It's part of the huge Tervise Paradiis spa hotel complex. Also here are fitness classes, ten-pin bowling and restaurants.

🛏 Sleeping

In summer it's well worth booking ahead; outside high season you should be able to snare yourself a good deal. Prices listed here are for high season (websites list off-season rates, which can be up to 50% lower).

Inge Villa　　　　　　　GUESTHOUSE €€
(☎443 8510; www.ingevilla.ee; Kaarli 20; s/d €75/92; 🖥) In a prime patch of real estate just back from the beach you'll find lovely Inge Villa, which calls itself a 'Swedish-Estonian villa hotel'. Its 11 rooms are simply decorated in muted tones with Nordic minimalism at the fore. The garden, lounge and sauna seal the deal. Closed November to February.

Netti　　　　　　　　　　GUESTHOUSE €€
(☎516 7958; www.nettihotel.ee; Hospidali 11-1; ste €77-107; 🖥) Anni, your host at Netti, is a ray of sunshine and her three-storey guesthouse, comprising four two-room suites, positively gleams under her care. The suites sleep two to four, have some kitchen facilities and are bright and breezy (reminiscent of the '80s). The downstairs sauna area is a lovely place to unwind after a hard day at the beach.

Hommiku Hostel　　　　　GUESTHOUSE €€
(☎445 1122; www.hommikuhostel.ee; Hommiku 17; dm/s/d €20/39/58; 🖥) Hommiku is more like a budget hotel than a hostel. This modern, year-round option is in a prime in-town position, offering handsome rooms with private

bathrooms, TV and kitchenettes (some also have old beamed ceilings).

Ammende Villa
HOTEL €€€

(☑447 3888; www.ammende.ee; Mere pst 7; r/ste from €179/243; ☎) Class and luxury abound in this exquisitely refurbished 1904 art nouveau mansion, which lords over handsomely manicured grounds. The gorgeous exterior is matched by an elegant lobby and individually antique-furnished rooms. Rooms in the gardener's house are more affordable but lack a little of the wow factor. Also houses a cafe and restaurant (p366).

Konse Motel & Camping
CAMPING, GUESTHOUSE €

(☑5343 5092; www.konse.ee; Suur-Jõe 44a; campsites €9-13, plus per person €2, d without/with bathroom €40/52; @☎) Perched on a spot by the river about 1km east of Old Town (off Lai), Konse offers camping and a variety of rooms (all with kitchen access). It's not an especially charming spot (and you're a couple of kilometres from the beach action) but there is a sauna, and bike and rowboat rental. Open year-round.

✗ Eating

The most central supermarket is **Port Artur Toidukaubad** (☺9am-10pm) inside the **Port Artur 2** complex, off Pikk and opposite the bus station.

⌜TOP⌝ Supelsaksad
⌞CHOICE⌟
CAFE €

(cnr Supeluse & Nikolai; mains €6-12) The street of Supeluse is lined with pretty wooden villas and this one houses a gorgeously colourful cafe, looking like it was designed by Barbara Cartland (bright pink and a riot of stripes and prints). The menu holds an appealing mix of wraps, salads and pastas, and, if you eat all your veggies, make a beeline for the bountiful cake display. Drop by in the evening for a glass of wine on the terrace.

Mahedik
CAFE €

(Pühavaimu 20; mains €5-13) Local, seasonal fare (organic where possible) is the glorious focus of this homey, plant-filled, all-day cafe. There are cooked breakfasts, locally caught fish and a divine array of cakes.

Si-si
ITALIAN €€

(www.si-si.ee; Supeluse 21; pizza & pasta €5-8, mains €11-18.50) Beachside dining in Pärnu is disappointingly bland, but a walk up Supeluse presents alluring options, including this

Italian restaurant-lounge. Inside is smart white-linen dining, outside is a stylishly relaxed terrace. There's a selection of gourmet pizzas and the all-important tiramisu.

Trahter Postipoiss
RUSSIAN €€

(www.trahterpostipoiss.ee; Vee 12; mains €8-20) This 19th-century postal building houses a rustic tavern with excellent Russian cuisine, a convivial crowd and imperial portraits watching over the proceedings. The spacious patio opens during summer and there's live music at weekends. Food ranges from simple (borsch and *pelmeni* – Russian-style ravioli stuffed with meat) to sophisticated (roasted duck breast with blackberry sauce).

Ammende Villa
RESTAURANT €€€

(☑447 3888; www.ammende.ee; Mere pst 7; cafe mains €7-8, restaurant mains €21; ☺cafe noon-4pm, restaurant 4-11pm) Nonguests can get a taste of life at this art nouveau gem by joining in the breakfast buffet (€15) – a splendid spread of salmon, fresh fruit and Champagne (bookings essential). Otherwise, various salons and the beautiful garden terrace are great spots to dine, or you can simply stop by for a coffee and cake. To help unleash your inner sophisticate, concerts are often held on the lawn in summer.

Mõnus Margarita
TEX-MEX €€

(Akadeemia 5; mains €4-16) Big, colourful and decidedly upbeat, as all good Tex-Mex places should be – but if you're looking for heavy-duty spice, you won't find it here. Fajitas, burritos and quesadillas all score goals, plus there are margaritas and tequilas for the grown-ups and a play area for the kids.

☕ Drinking & Entertainment

Piccadilly
CAFE-WINE BAR

(Pühavaimu 15) Piccadilly offers down-tempo bliss in plush surroundings, plus a top wine selection and an extensive range of coffee, tea and hot choc. Savoury food begins and ends with quiche – here it's all about the sweets, including moreish cheesecake and handmade chocolates.

Puhvet A.P.T.E.K.
BAR

(www.aptek.ee; Rüütli 40; ☺7pm-3am Tue-Thu, to 5am Fri & Sat) Drop by the old 1930s pharmacy to admire the clever restoration that has turned it into a smooth late-night haunt. Fabulous decor (including original cabinets, vials and bottles) compete for your attention with DJs and €5 cocktails.

Sweet Rosie PUB

(Munga 2) Revellers jam into the warm, dark-wood interior of this fun Irish pub for Guinness, pub grub, occasional live music and general good *craic*.

Sunset Club CLUB

(www.sunset.ee; Ranna pst 3; ⊘ 11pm-5am or later Fri & Sat Jun-Aug) Pärnu's biggest and most famous summertime nightclub has an outdoor beach terrace and a sleek multifloor interior with plenty of cosy nooks for when the dance floor gets crowded. Imported DJs and bands, plus a young crowd, keep things cranked until the early hours.

Rannakino OUTDOOR CINEMA

(www.rannakino.ee; Ranna pst 3a; tickets €6) From the people behind Tallinn's Katusekino comes this cool, summertime cinema, just back from the beach (next to Sunset Club). There's an eclectic mix of cult and classic films, plus a well-stocked bar. Check the website for programs and screening times.

ⓘ Information

Pärnu in Your Pocket (www.inyourpocket.com) Listings guide; available in bookshops or online.

Pärnu Tourist Information Centre (☑447 3000; www.visitparnu.com; Uus 4; ⊘9am-6pm daily mid-May–mid-Sep, 9am-5pm Mon-Fri, 10am-2pm Sat & Sun rest of yr) Pick up maps and brochures, or use the free internet. Staff will book accommodation or car hire for a €2 fee. There's useful information on summertime activities in the region, including guided walks, kayaking, horse riding and watersports.

ⓘ Getting There & Away

BUS About 25 daily buses connect Pärnu with Tallinn (€6 to €8.50, two hours) and about a dozen services connect Pärnu with Tartu (€7.50 to €10.60, 2½ to three hours). Tickets for a multitude of other destinations, including Rīga in Latvia and beyond, are available at the Pärnu **bus station ticket office** (Ringi), across from the bus station. **Lux Express** (www.luxexpress.eu) runs up to seven services daily to Riga (€8 to €20, 2½ hours).

TRAIN There are two daily Tallinn–Pärnu trains (€5.40, 2¾ hours), though the train station is an inconvenient 5km east of the town centre, down Riia mnt.

Viljandi

POP 20,000

One of Estonia's most charming towns, Viljandi, 90km east of Pärnu, is a relaxed place to stop for a day or more. It's a good base for exploring the country's largest flood plain and bog area (no laughing!) and the town itself, settled since the 12th century, has a gentle 19th-century flow to it. The **tourist information centre** (☑433 0442; www.viljandimaa.ee; Vabaduse plats 6; ⊘10am-6pm Mon-Fri, to 3pm Sat & Sun mid-May–mid-Sep, to 5pm Mon-Fri mid-Sep–mid-May) is one of Estonia's finest, with local maps and information in loads of languages. A town **walking tour** (€1) leaves from near the information centre at 1pm daily from June to August.

A highlight is **Castle Park** (Lossimäed), which sprawls out from behind the tourist centre. A picturesque green area with spectacular views over Lake Viljandi, the park contains the ruins of a 13th- to 15th-century **castle** founded by the German Knights of the Sword. Nearby, the excellent **Kondase Keskus** (www.kondas.ee; Pikk 8; adult/student €3.50/1; ⊘11am-6pm daily May-Sep, shorter hours rest of year) is the country's only art gallery devoted to naive art. The entry fee also includes admission to the modest local museum and **old water tower** offering fine vistas.

Easily the biggest event on the calendar is the hugely popular four-day **Viljandi Folk Music Festival** (www.folk.ee/festival), held in late July and renowned for its friendly relaxed vibe and impressive international line-up (incorporating traditional folk, folk rock and world music). It's the country's biggest music festival, with some 20,000-plus festival-goers. Pop into the **Estonian Traditional Music Centre** (www.folk.ee; Tasuja pst 6), in Castle Park, to see if there are any concerts being held during your visit.

On one of Viljandi's loveliest streets, the small, six-room **Hostel Ingeri** (☑433 4414; www.hostelingeri.ee; Pikk 2c; s €23, d €32-40; ☜) offers seriously good value with its bright, comfortable rooms, all with TV and bathroom. Plant life, sauna, a small gym and a kitchen for guest use make it a good home away from home, while the parkside location couldn't be better.

The outdoor terrace is one drawcard of the tavern-style **Tegelaste Tuba** (Pikk 2b; mains €2.50-6.50), but so are the comfy interiors on rainy days. Estonian handicrafts enliven the walls and a diverse crowd enjoys the wide-ranging menu of soups, pastas and meaty mains.

Inside the Traditional Music Centre, stylish **Aida** (Tasuja pst 6; mains €5-11) has views over Castle Park from its big windows or its roof terrace, and hearty, skilfully prepared Estonian food on offer.

Around 13 daily buses connect Viljandi with Tallinn (€8 to €10, 2½ hours). There are about 10 daily buses to and from Pärnu (€6 to €6.40, 1½ to two hours) and up to 13 to and from Tartu (€5 to €6, 1½ hours).

Soomaa National Park

Halfway between Pärnu and Viljandi is Soomaa National Park, a rich land of bogs, flood-plain meadows, waterside forests, wildlife and criss-crossing rivers. It's renowned for its 'fifth season' (around late March to April), when spring flooding sees waters rise up to 5m. Much more interesting than the word 'bog' implies, this 390 sq km park is full of quirky opportunities, from a walk through the swampland landscape to a single-trunk canoe trip down one of the rivers.

Park information is available from **Soomaa National Park visitor centre** (435 7164; www.soomaa.ee; 10am-6pm Apr-Sep, 10am-4pm Tue-Sat Oct-Mar) in Kõrtsi-Tõramaa. Tourist offices in Viljandi or Pärnu have maps and brochures – Viljandi has particularly comprehensive information, but for travellers without their own car Pärnu is a better access point for the park.

CLEAN & GREEN

Saaremaa is waking up to the potential of its clean, green image. Organic farms and cottage industries focusing on quality local produce are popping up, and many open their doors to the public. In summer you can make organic soap at **GoodKarma** (www.goodkarma.ee), sample local mustards at **Mustjala Mustard** (www.mustjalamustard.com), or pick your own fruit at various farms. Other places offer horse riding, farm activities and accommodation. Visits generally need to be arranged beforehand; pick up a copy of *Saare County Open Organic Farms* brochure and map, or download it from www.saaremahe.ee. A good source of information is Turuköök, a scrumptious bakery at the rear of the Kuressaare market (on Tallinna).

Soomaa.com (506 1896; www.soomaa.com) acts as a kind of umbrella organisation to help travellers access the wilderness, working in cooperation with local accommodation and service providers. The focus is on ecotourism and sustainable development, and there is a great range of year-round activities. The Wilderness day trip includes **river canoeing** and walking on peat bog (€50 from Soomaa, €70 from Pärnu, runs from May to September). There are also guided and self-guided canoeing, **beaver-watching**, **bog-shoeing** and **mushroom-picking** experiences and, in winter, **kick-sledding**, **cross-country-skiing** and **snowshoeing** excursions. You'll need to contact Soomaa.com in advance to arrange your itinerary; check the website for all the options.

Soomaa.com arranges transfers to the park from Pärnu. This is a better option than the twice-daily bus connection from Pärnu to the tiny village of Riisa (inside the park, but 5km north of the visitor centre).

Saaremaa

POP 33,000

For Estonians, Saaremaa (literally 'Island Land') is synonymous with space, spruce, peace and fresh air – and killer beer (there's a long history of beer home-brewing). Estonia's largest island (roughly the size of Luxembourg) still lies covered in thick pine and spruce forests and juniper groves, while old windmills, slender lighthouses and tiny villages appear unchanged by the passage of time.

During the Soviet era, the entire island was off limits (due to a radar system and rocket base). This unwittingly resulted in minimal industrial build-up and the protection of the island's rural charm.

To reach Saaremaa you must first cross Muhu, the small island where the ferry from the mainland docks; Muhu is connected to Saaremaa by a 2.5km causeway. Kuressaare, the capital of Saaremaa, is on the south coast (75km from the ferry terminal) and is a natural base for visitors – it's here, among the up-market hotels, that you'll understand where the island got its nickname, 'Spa-remaa'.

Sights & Activities

Bishop's Castle
CASTLE

The island's most distinctive landmark is the striking, fortress-style Bishop's Castle (1338–80), located at the southern end of

Kuressaare on an artificial island ringed by a moat. It looks like it was plucked from a fairy tale and now houses the **Saaremaa Museum** (www.saaremaamuuseum.ee; adult/ concession €5/2.50; ☺10am-7pm May-Aug, 11am-6pm Wed-Sun Sep-Apr), devoted to the island's nature and history. You can hire a rowboat at nearby cafes to float idly along the moat. Behind the castle area is the small town beach.

Angla
WINDMILLS

Angla is 40km north of Kuressaare, en route to the small harbour at Triigi. Just off the main road at the village is a photogenic group of five windmills. Two kilometres away, along the road opposite the windmills, is **Karja Church**, a striking 14th-century German Gothic church.

Kaali
METEORITE CRATER

At Kaali, 18km from Kuressaare, is a 110m-wide, water-filled **crater** formed by a meteorite at least 3000 years ago. In ancient Scandinavian mythology the site was known as the sun's grave. It's Europe's largest and most accessible meteorite crater, but looks mighty tiny up close!

Sõrve Peninsula
OUTDOORS

Saaremaa's magic can really be felt along the Sõrve Peninsula, jutting out south and west of Kuressaare. This sparsely populated strip of land saw some of the heaviest fighting in WWII and some bases and antitank defence lines still stand. A bike or car trip along the coastline provides some of the most spectacular vistas on the island; several daily buses from Kuressaare also head down the coast of the peninsula.

🛏 Sleeping

The tourist office can organise beds in private apartments and farms across the island. Hotel prices listed here are for summer – they're up to 50% cheaper from September to April. Spas are open to nonguests.

Georg Ots Spa Hotell
HOTEL €€

(✆455 0000; www.gospa.ee; Tori 2, Kuressaare; d €105-160; @🛜🏊🚲) The George Ots Spa Hotell (aka Gospa), named after a renowned Estonian singer, has fresh modern rooms with enormous king-size beds, CD players and a warm but minimal design. Most rooms have balconies and there's a pool, fitness centre and spa services, as well as top nosh at the hotel's restaurant. 'Residences' (ie, apartments) are also available (see the website) and families are very well catered to.

Karluti Hostel
GUESTHOUSE €

(✆501 4390; www.karluti.ee; Pärna 23, Kuressaare; tw/tr with shared bathroom €30/44; @🛜) Lovely Tiia is your host at this cheerful, mustard-yellow guesthouse, set in a large garden on a quiet residential street close to the centre. Three spotless rooms house seven beds (book ahead for summer) and there's kitchen access. Bike and car rental can also be arranged. For the price, it's excellent.

Kuursaal Guesthouse
GUESTHOUSE €€

(✆5192 8519; www.kuressaarekuursaal.ee; Lossipark 1, Kuressaare; r €90-130; 🛜) Alongside the newly renovated *kuursaal* (a beautiful, wooden resort hall dating from 1889) is this new guesthouse, with six bright rooms. With its castle views, room 1 is the top pick, but other rooms have leafy park vistas. Breakfast is downstairs in Ku-Kuu (p369) restaurant and guests get free use of the pool facilities at the George Ots Spa Hotell.

🍴 Eating & Drinking

RAE Supermarket (Raekoja 10, Kuressaare; ☺9am-10pm) is the best grocery store. It's behind the tourist information centre.

Sadhu Cafe
CAFE €

(Lossi 5, Kuressaare; mains €6-12) Kuressaare's best chill-out spot adds a touch of spice to the main street. It's decked out with hippy-chic textiles and trinkets from India and Asia, and the menu takes a few cues from there too. Other options include local fish dishes, hotpots and a wild-boar burger. Service runs from breakfast to late-night drinks on the garden terrace.

Veski Trahter
TRADITIONAL €€

(www.veskitrahter.ee; Pärna 19, Kuressaare; mains €8-12) Sure, it's a little touristy (the folk performances on summer evenings are a dead giveaway), but this tavern inside an 1899 windmill keeps quality and ambience at a premium, with plenty of hearty local fare such as Baltic herrings, roasted wild boar, home-brewed beers and Saaremaa cheeses.

Ku-Kuu
INTERNATIONAL €

(www.kuressaarekuursaal.ee; Lossipark 1, Kuressaare; mains €5.50-12) With a plumb location inside the *kuursaal* and a generous moatside terrace, new Ku-Kuu has much in its favour. The French-leaning menu highlights fresh, locally caught fish and the cake display is alluring. The *kuursaal* also hosts outdoor cinema and live-music events in

WORTH A TRIP

MUHU

Connected to Saaremaa by a 2.5km causeway, the island of Muhu (www.muhu.info) has the undeserved nickname of the 'doormat' for the bigger island – lots of people passing through on their way to and from the ferry, but few stopping. In fact, Estonia's third-biggest island offers plenty of excuses to hang around.

For quirk factor there's an ostrich farm open to visitors, but a true gem is **Koguva** in the island's west, a step-back-in-time, fairy-tale fishing village dating from at least the mid-16th century. It's still mainly inhabited by descendents of the original settlers, and a handful of buildings welcome visitors as part of an **open-air museum** (www.muhumuuseum.ee; Koguva; adult/concession €3/1.50; ⊗9am-6pm mid-May–mid-Sep, 10am-5pm Tue-Sat rest of yr). There is also a handful of B&Bs here, plus a gallery/cafe.

Vanatoa Turismitalu (☑454 8884; www.vanatoa.ee; Koguva; s/d in main house incl breakfast €39/51) provides good-value accommodation options right by Koguva – as well as en suite rooms in the main farmhouse, there are beds in atmospheric outhouses (per person €20), plus campsites, a sauna and on-site restaurant.

But for our money there's no finer place to bed down in Estonia than **Pädaste Manor** (☑454 8800; www.padaste.com; Muhu; d from €204; @☏). On a manicured bayside estate in Muhu's south, this luxurious boutique resort encompasses an exquisitely restored manor house, a fine-dining restaurant called **Alexander** (menus from €50; ⊗lunch Mar-May & Sep, dinner Mar-Sep), rated among Estonia's very best, a spa and a more-casual eatery. The hotel's attention to detail is second to none, from the private cinema to the decor featuring antiques and Muhu embroidery. Even if you're not staying at Pädaste, you can visit for a meal at Alexander (book ahead, online) or, in summer, at the beautifully sited **Sea House Terrace** (mains €8-14; ⊗noon-7pm Jun-Aug).

---

summer and you can hire bikes, boats (for moat-mooching) and petanque sets.

John Bull Pub

PUB

(Pärgi 4, Kuressaare) In the park surrounding the castle, this pub (not particularly English, despite its name) has a great moatside deck, a menu of cheap 'n' cheerful pub classics, and our favourite feature – a bar made from an old Russian bus.

❶ Information

Kuressaare's **tourist information office** (☑453 3120; www.visitsaaremaa.ee; Tallinna 2; ⊗9am-6pm Mon-Fri, 10am-4pm Sat & Sun Jun-Aug, shorter hrs rest of yr) can help you make the best of your stay. Pick up brochures outlining nature trails, cycling trails, spa holidays, craft and heritage excursions.

More information is online at **Saaremaa** (www.saaremaa.ee).

❶ Getting There & Around

AIR If time is short, consider flying. **Avies Air** (www.flyavies.ee) flies up to nine times a week year-round between Tallinn and Kuressaare (from €23, 45 minutes).

BOAT A year-round vehicle ferry runs throughout the day from Virtsu on the mainland to the island of Muhu, which is joined by causeway to Saare-

maa; see **Tuule Laevad** (☑452 4444; www.tuulelaevad.ee) for ferry schedules and prices.

BUS Around 15 direct buses travel daily between Tallinn and Kuressaare (€13 to €17, 3½ to 4¼ hours), via the ferry. Three buses run daily to and from Tartu (€16 to €18, 5½ to 6½ hours), and five to and from Pärnu (€12, three to 3½ hours).

UNDERSTAND ESTONIA

History

Early History

It's commonly held that in the mid-3rd millennium BC, Finno-Ugric tribes came from either the east or south to the territory of modern-day Estonia and parts of Latvia, and mixed with the tribes who had been there from the 8th millennium BC. They were little influenced from outside until German traders and missionaries, followed by knights, were unleashed by Pope Celestine III's 1193 crusade against the 'northern heathens'. In 1202 the bishop of Rīga established the Knights of the Sword to convert the region by conquest; southern Estonia was soon subjugated and the north fell to Denmark.

Foreign Rule

After a crushing battle with Russian prince and military leader Alexander Nevsky in 1242 on the border of present-day Estonia and Russia, the Knights of the Sword were subordinated to a second band of German crusaders, the Teutonic Order, which by 1290 ruled the eastern Baltic area as far north as southern Estonia, as well as most of the Estonian islands.

Denmark sold northern Estonia to the Livonian Order (a branch of the Teutonic Order) in 1346, placing Estonians under servitude to a German nobility that lasted till the early 20th century. Although Sweden and Russia would later rule the region, German nobles and land barons maintained great economic and political power. The Hanseatic League (a mercantile league of medieval German towns bound together by trade) encompassed many towns on the routes between Russia and the west, which prospered under the Germans, although many Estonians in rural areas were forced into serfdom.

By 1620 Estonia had fallen under Swedish control. The Swedes consolidated Estonian Protestantism and aimed to introduce universal education; however, frequent wars were devastating. After the Great Northern War (1700–21), Estonia became part of the Russian Empire. Repressive government from Moscow and economic control by German powers slowly forged a national self-awareness among native Estonians. Serfs were freed in the 19th century and their improved education and land-ownership rights also helped promote national culture and welfare.

Independence

With the Treaty of Brest-Litovsk, the Soviets abandoned the Baltic countries to Germany in March 1918, although Estonian nationalists had originally declared independence on 24 February. The resulting War of Independence led to the Tartu Peace Treaty on 2 February 1920, in which Russia renounced territorial claims to Estonia.

Damaged by the war and hampered by a world slump and disruptions to trade with the USSR, independent Estonia suffered economically even as it bloomed culturally. Prime Minister Konstantin Päts declared himself president in 1934 and ruled Estonia as a relatively benevolent dictator while also quietly safeguarding the USSR's interests.

Soviet Rule & WWII

The Molotov-Ribbentrop Pact of 23 August 1939, a nonaggression pact between the USSR and Nazi Germany, secretly divided Eastern Europe into Soviet and German spheres of influence. Estonia fell into the Soviet sphere and by August 1940 was under occupation. Estonia was 'accepted' into the USSR after fabricated elections and within a year more than 10,000 people in Estonia had been killed or deported. When Hitler invaded the USSR in 1941, many saw the Germans as liberators, but during their occupation about 5500 people died in concentration camps. Some 40,000 Estonians joined the German army to prevent the Red Army from reconquering Estonia; nearly twice that number fled abroad.

Russia annexed Estonia after WWII. Between 1945 and 1949 agriculture was collectivised, industry was nationalised and 60,000 more Estonians were killed or deported. An armed resistance led by the Metsavennad (Forest Brothers) fought Soviet rule until 1956.

With postwar industrialisation, Estonia received an influx of immigrant workers from Russia, Ukraine and Belarus, all looking for improved living conditions but having little interest in local language and customs. Resentment among Estonians grew as some of these immigrants received prized new housing and top job allocations. In the second half of the 20th century, within the USSR, Estonia developed the reputation of being the most modern and European of all the republics, mainly due to its proximity to Finland, and enjoyed a relatively high standard of living.

New Independence

On 23 August 1989, on the 50th anniversary of the Molotov-Ribbentrop Pact, an estimated two million people formed a human chain across Estonia, Latvia and Lithuania, calling for secession from the USSR. Independence came suddenly, however, in the aftermath of the Moscow putsch against Gorbachev. Estonia's declaration of complete independence on 20 August 1991 was recognised by the West immediately and by the USSR on 6 September.

In October 1992 Estonia held its first democratic elections, which brought to the presidency the much-loved Lennart Meri, who oversaw the removal of the last Russian troops in 1994. The decade after independence saw the government focusing on radical reform policies and on gaining membership to the EU and NATO. The sweeping transformations at all levels of society saw frequent changes of government, however, and no shortage of scandal and corruption charges. Yet despite this, the country came to be seen as *the* post-Soviet economic miracle. In 2004, Estonia officially entered both NATO and the EU, although an at-times troubled relationship with its big easterly neighbour occasionally rears its head.

The early 21st century saw the Estonian economy riding a huge boom; however, the brakes were slammed on by the global financial crisis, with the country falling sharply into recession in 2008. The government slashed public spending to counter the crisis. Economic recovery was strong in 2009–10, and in January 2011 Estonia took the euro as its official currency. It became only the third ex-communist state to make the switch (after Slovenia and Slovakia), and is the first former Soviet republic to have done so. This move highlights the country's resolve to look west, catch up with its Nordic neighbours and not to look back (nor east).

People

In the 1930s native Estonians made up 88% of the population. This began to change with the Soviet takeover; migration from other parts of the USSR occurred on a mass scale from 1945 to 1955. Today around 69% of the people living in Estonia are ethnic Estonians. Russians make up 26% of the population, with 2% Ukrainian, 1% Belarusian and 1% Finnish.

Ethnic Russians are concentrated in the industrial cities of the northeast, where in some places (such as Narva) they make up around 95% of the population. Russians also have a sizeable presence in Tallinn (39%). While much is made of tension between Estonians and Russians, the two communities live together in relative harmony, with only occasional flare-ups, such as the violence that followed the decision to move a Soviet war memorial from the centre of Tallinn in 2007.

Estonians are closely related to the Finns and more distantly to the Sami (indigenous Laplanders) and Hungarians; they're unrelated to the Latvians and Lithuanians, however, who are of Indo-European heritage.

Estonians are historically a rural people, wary of outsiders and stereotypically most comfortable when left alone. Women are less shy and more approachable than men. In general, the younger the Estonian, the more relaxed, open and friendly they'll be.

Historically Estonia was Lutheran from the early 17th century, though today only a minority of Estonians profess religious beliefs and there's little sense of Estonia as a religious society. The Russian community is largely Orthodox and brightly domed churches are sprinkled around eastern Estonia.

Land of Dreams

Estonia is a land of young talent and creative, dynamic entrepreneurs who have changed the world or are waiting to do so – usually, they're well under 25. The country's biggest success stories are Skype and Kazaa (the latter is file-sharing software), both developed by Estonians. They are among the planet's most downloaded programs – at peak times, there are 40 million Skype users online.

Environment

With an area of 45,226 sq km, Estonia is only slightly bigger than Denmark or Switzerland. It is part of the East European Plain and is extremely flat, and it's marked by extensive bogs and marshes. At a mere 318m, Suur Munamägi (Great Egg Hill) is the highest point in the country.

There are more than 1400 lakes, the largest of which is Lake Peipsi (3555 sq km), straddling the Estonia–Russia border. Swamps, wetlands and forests make up half of Estonia's territory. There are more than 1500 islands along the 3794km-long, heavily indented coastline; they make up nearly 10% of Estonian territory.

Estonia's islands and national parks boast some of the most unspoilt landscapes in Europe, and with the exception of the country's northeast (where Soviet-era industry is concentrated), Estonian levels of air pollution are low by European standards.

Almost 20% of Estonia's land (more than double the European average) is protected to some degree. These protected areas are home to beavers, otters, flying squirrels, lynxes, wolves and an estimated population of 800 brown bears. White and black storks are common in southern Estonia.

Food & Drink

Estonians have a close cultural affinity to the land and a traditional cuisine that prizes food that is both local and seasonal. So it's no great surprise to find the country's top chefs taking a number of cues from the fashionable New Nordic kitchens of their northern neighbours. You can eat amazingly well here, and at lower prices than you might expect.

Traditional Estonian gastronomy mixes Nordic, Russian and German influences. The hearty local diet relies on *sealiha* (pork), other red meat, *kana* (chicken), *vurst* (sausage) and *kapsa* (cabbage); potatoes add a generous dose of winter-warming carbs to a national cuisine often dismissed as bland, heavy and lacking in spice. Sour cream is served with everything but coffee, it seems. *Kala* (fish), most likely *forell* (trout) or *lõhe* (salmon), appears most often as a smoked or salted starter. *Sült* (jellied meat) is likely to be served as a delicacy as well. At Christmas time *verivorst* (blood sausage) is made from fresh blood and wrapped in pig intestine (joy to the world indeed!).

Õlu (beer) is the favourite alcoholic drink and the local product is very much in evidence. The best brands are Saku and A Le Coq, which come in a range of brews. *Viin* (vodka) and *konjak* (brandy) are also popular drinks. Vana Tallinn, a seductively pleasant, sweet and strong (40% to 50% alcohol) liqueur of unknown extraction, is an integral part of any Estonian gift pack.

When & Where to Eat

At mealtimes, seek out a *restoran* (restaurant) or *kohvik* (cafe); both are plentiful. In addition, a *pubi* (pub), *kõrts* (inn) or *trahter* (tavern) will usually serve hearty, traditional meals. Nearly every town has a *turg* (market) where you can buy fresh produce.

Estonian eating habits are similar to other parts of northern Europe. Either lunch or dinner may be the biggest meal of the day. Cooked breakfasts aren't always easy to find but many cafes serve pastries and cakes throughout the day. Tipping is fairly commonplace, with 10% the norm. For reviews of the country's culinary best, see www.eestimaitsed.com.

Smoking is not permitted in restaurants, bars, nightclubs and cafes, although it is permitted on outdoor terraces or in closed-off smoking rooms.

SURVIVAL GUIDE

Directory A–Z
Accommodation

In the budget category, you'll find backpackers' lodgings, hostels and basic guesthouses (many with shared bathrooms). A dorm bed generally costs €10 to €15. Midrange options run the gamut from family-run guesthouses to hotel rooms (private bathroom and breakfast generally included). Top-end accommodation comprises historic hotels, spa resorts and charming places offering something special (such as antique-filled rooms or ocean views).

There are a few *kämpingud* (camping grounds; open from mid-May to September) that allow you to pitch a tent, but most consist of permanent wooden huts or cabins, with communal showers and toilets. Farms and homestays offer more than a choice of rooms; in many cases meals, a sauna and a range of activities are available. There's a search engine at www.visitestonia.com for all types of accommodation.

The peak tourist season is June to August. If you're visiting during this time you should book well in advance – essential in Tallinn and in popular summertime destinations such as the islands and Pärnu. Note, too, that Tallinn is a popular weekend destination year-round.

The following price ranges are for a double room with private bathroom in high season.

€ less than €50

€€ €50 to €140

€€€ more than €140

Activities

Many travel agencies can arrange a variety of activity-based tours of Estonia. A detailed list of companies keeping tourists active can be found at **Turismiweb.ee** (www.turismiweb.ee).

For energetic, ecofriendly activities, contact **Reimann Retked** (☏511 4099; www.retked.ee). The company offers a range of sea-kayaking excursions (including overnight trips) exploring offshore islands. Other possibilities include diving, rafting, bog walking and snowshoeing, as well as kick sledding on sea ice, frozen lakes or in snowy forest; most arrangements need a minimum of eight to 10 people, but smaller groups should enquire as you may be able to tag along with another group.

City Bike (☑511 1819; www.citybike.ee; Uus 33) can take care of all you need to get around Tallinn, the rest of Estonia and the Baltic region by bike.

Business Hours

Banks 9am to 4pm Monday to Friday

Bars Noon to midnight Sunday to Thursday, to 2am Friday and Saturday

Cafes 8am or 9am to 10pm or later

Clubs 10pm to 4am Thursday to Saturday

Post offices 8am to 6pm Monday to Friday, 9am to 3pm Saturday

Restaurants noon to midnight

Shops 9am or 10am to 6pm or 7pm Monday to Friday, 10am to 4pm Saturday and Sunday

Supermarkets 9am or 10am to 10pm

Discount Cards

There are frequent student, pensioner and group discounts on transport, in museums and in some shops upon presentation of accredited ID.

Embassies & Consulates

For up-to-date contact details of Estonian diplomatic organisations, as well as foreign embassies and consulates in Estonia, check the website of the Estonian Ministry of Foreign Affairs (www.vm.ee).

All the following embassies and consulates are in Tallinn unless otherwise indicated.

Australian Consulate (☑650 9308; www.sweden.embassy.gov.au; Marja 9) Honorary consulate; embassy in Stockholm.

Canadian Embassy (☑627 3311; www.canada.ee; Toom-Kooli 13, 2nd fl)

Netherlands Embassy (☑680 5500; www.netherlandsembassy.ee; Rahukohtu 4-I)

Finnish Embassy (☑610 3200; www.finland.ee; Kohtu 4)

French Embassy (☑616 1610; www.ambafrance-ee.org; Toom-Kuninga 20)

German Embassy (☑627 5300; www.tallinn.diplo.de; Toom-Kuninga 11)

Irish Embassy (☑681 1888; www.embassyofireland.ee; Vene 2, 2nd fl)

Latvian Embassy (☑627 7850; embassy.estonia@mfa.gov.lv; Tõnismägi 10)

Lithuanian Embassy (☑616 4991; http://ee.mfa.lt; Uus 15)

New Zealand Consulate (☑667 1470; Liivalaia 13) Honorary consulate; embassy in Berlin.

Russian Embassy (☑646 4175; www.rusemb.ee; Pikk 19)

Russian Consulate (☑356 0652; narvacon@narvacon.neti.ee; Kiriku 8, Narva)

UK Embassy (☑667 4700; http://ukinestonia.fco.gov.uk; Wismari 6)

US Embassy (☑668 8100; http://estonia.usembassy.gov/; Kentmanni 20)

Festivals & Events

Estonia has a busy festival calendar celebrating everything from religion to music, art to film, beer to ghosts. Peak festival fun is in summer, with a highlight being midsummer festivities. A good list of upcoming major events nationwide can be found at www.culture.ee.

The biggest occasion in Estonia is Jaanipäev (24 June), a celebration of the pagan midsummer or summer solstice. Celebrations peak on the evening of 23 June and are best experienced far from the city along a stretch of beach, where huge bonfires are lit for all-night parties.

Food

These price ranges indicate the average cost of a main course.

€ less than €10

€€ €10 to €20

€€€ more than €20

Gay & Lesbian Travellers

Hand-in-hand with its relaxed attitude to religion, today's Estonia is a fairly tolerant and safe home for its gay and lesbian citizens – certainly more so than its Baltic neighbours or Russia. Unfortunately, that ambivalence hasn't translated into a wildly exciting scene. A good online reference is **GayMap Tallinn** (http://tallinn.gaymap.ee/).

Internet Access

There are approximately 1130 wi-fi areas throughout Estonia, with 344 in Tallinn alone; many of which are free. You'll find wi-fi hot spots in hotels, pubs, libraries, petrol stations, urban parks and elsewhere; visit **wifi.ee** (www.wifi.ee) for a list of locations.

Money

» Estonia joined the eurozone in January 2011, making the euro its official currency.

» Credit cards are widely accepted. Most banks (but not stores and restaurants) accept travellers cheques, but commissions can be high.

» Tipping in service industries has become the norm, but generally no more than 10% is expected.

Post

Mail service in and out of Estonia is highly efficient. To post a letter costs €1 to European destinations; €1.10 to the rest of the world.

Public Holidays

New Year's Day 1 January

Independence Day 24 February

Good Friday March/April

Easter Sunday March/April

May Day 1 May

Whitsunday Seventh Sunday after Easter; May/June

Victory Day (1919; Battle of Võnnu) 23 June

Jaanipäev (St John's Day; Midsummer's Day) 24 June

Day of Restoration of Independence 20 August

Christmas Eve 24 December

Christmas Day 25 December

Boxing Day 26 December

Telephone

There are no area codes. All landline numbers have seven digits; mobile numbers have seven or eight digits and begin with ☏5.

Estonia's country code is ☏372.

Visas

EU citizens can spend unlimited time in Estonia, while citizens of Australia, Canada, Japan, New Zealand, the USA and many other countries can enter visa-free for a maximum 90-day stay over a six-month period. Travellers holding a Schengen visa do not need an additional Estonian visa. For more information, check out the website of the **Estonian Ministry of Foreign Affairs** (www.vm.ee).

Getting There & Away

Air

The national carrier **Estonian Air** (www.estonian-air.ee) links Tallinn with more than 20 cities in Europe. Other airlines serving Tallinn airport include **airBaltic** (www.airbaltic.com), offering flights to Riga, and **Finnair** (www.finnair.com), with frequent links to Helsinki. Budget airlines serving Tallinn include **Ryanair** (www.ryanair.com) and **easyJet** (www.easyjet.com).

Land

BUS

Buses are the cheapest way of reaching the Baltics.

CAR & MOTORCYCLE

From Finland, put your vehicle on a Helsinki–Tallinn ferry. If approaching Estonia from the south or Western Europe, be sure to avoid crossing through Kaliningrad or Belarus – you'll need hard-to-get visas for these countries, and are likely to face hassles from traffic police and encounter roads in abominable condition.

TRAIN

There are international trains between Tallinn and Moscow, and a newly resurrected service connecting Tallinn and St Petersburg.

Sea

Ferries run to Finland and Sweden from Tallinn. See Tallinn Getting There & Away section (p355) for more information.

Getting Around

Air

Avies Air (www.flyavies.ee) provides domestic flights between Tallinn and the west-coast islands.

Bicycle

The flatness and small scale of Estonia, and the light traffic on most roads, make it good cycling territory. The islands are particularly popular cycling destinations in summer. Most cyclists bring their own bikes, but it's also possible to hire. Tallinn's **City Bike** (☏511 1819; www.citybike.ee; Uus 33; rental per hr/day/week €2.30/13/45) has good bikes for rent and plenty of useful cycling advice.

Bus

Buses are a good option, as they're more frequent and faster than trains, and cover many destinations not serviced by the limited rail network. For detailed bus information and advance tickets, contact Tallinn's **Central Bus Station** (Autobussijaam; ☑12550; Lastekodu 46). The useful website www.tpilet.ee has schedules and prices for all national bus services.

Car & Motorcycle

An International Driving Permit (IDP) is useful; otherwise, carry your national licence bearing a photograph. It's compulsory to carry your vehicle's registration papers and accident insurance, which can be bought at border crossings. Fuel and service stations are widely available.

Cars drive on the right-hand side of the road, and driving with any alcohol in your blood is illegal. Seatbelts are compulsory and headlights must be on at all times while driving. Speed limits in built-up areas are 50km/h; limits outside urban areas vary from 70km/h to 110km/h. Be on the lookout for signs, as these limits are often strictly enforced.

Train

Trains are slower and rarer than buses; the most frequent trains service the suburbs of Tallinn and aren't much use to travellers. Regional trains link the capital with Tartu, Viljandi, Narva and Pärnu a couple of times a day; schedules and prices can be found at **Edelaraudtee** (www.edel.ee).

Hungary

Includes »

Best Places to Eat

» Ikon (p426)

» Padlizsán (p403)

» Imola Udvarház Borétterem (p423)

» Kisbuda Gyöngye (p391)

» La Maréda (p404)

Best Places to Stay

» Four Seasons Gresham Palace Hotel (p390)

» Fábián Panzió (p416)

» Tisza Hotel (p419)

» Hotel Senator Ház (p423)

Why Go?

Hungary is just the place to kick off an Eastern European trip. A short hop from Vienna, this land of Franz Liszt and Béla Bartók, paprika-lashed dishes and the romantic Danube River continues to enchant visitors. The allure of Budapest, once an imperial city, is obvious at first sight, and it also boasts the hottest nightlife in the region. Other cities, too, like Pécs, the warm heart of the south, and Eger, the wine capital of the north, have much to offer travellers, as does the sprawling countryside, particularly the Great Plain, where cowboys ride and cattle roam. And where else can you laze about in an open-air thermal spa while snow patches glisten around you? In Hungary you'll find all the glamour, excitement and fun of Western Europe – at half the cost.

When to Go
Budapest

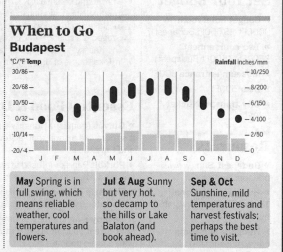

May Spring is in full swing, which means reliable weather, cool temperatures and flowers.

Jul & Aug Sunny but very hot, so decamp to the hills or Lake Balaton (and book ahead).

Sep & Oct Sunshine, mild temperatures and harvest festivals; perhaps the best time to visit.

AT A GLANCE

» **Currency** Forint (Ft)
» **Language** Hungarian
» **Money** ATMs abound
» **Visas** None for EU, USA, Canada, Australia & New Zealand

Fast Facts

» **Area** 93,030 sq km
» **Capital** Budapest
» **Country code** 36
» **Emergency** Ambulance ☑104, emergency assistance ☑112, fire ☑105, police ☑107

Exchange Rates

Australia	A$1	248Ft
Canada	C$1	234Ft
Euro Zone	€1	303Ft
Japan	¥100	252Ft
New Zealand	NZ$1	199Ft
UK	UK£1	359Ft
USA	US$1	238Ft

Set Your Budget

» **Budget hotel room** 9000Ft (15,000Ft Budapest)
» **Two-course meal** 3500Ft (4500Ft Budapest)
» **Museum entrance** 900Ft
» **Beer** 500Ft
» **City transport ticket** 320Ft

Resources

» **Budapest Sun** (www.budapestsun.com)
» **Hungarian National Tourist Office** (www.gotohungary.com)
» **Hungary Museums** (www.museum.hu)

Connections

Hungary lies at the heart of Central Europe and is easy to reach by rail, road or even boat. Rail connections are particularly good to and from Vienna; high-speed express trains cover the 260km between the Austrian capital and Budapest in just under three hours. Rail connections are also good to Bratislava and Prague, with continuing services to popular travel destinations like Berlin and Kraków. Rail connections to Croatia, Serbia and Romania are less frequent, though they're also reliable with some advance planning. Buses fan out in all directions from Budapest, and nearly all corners of Europe can be reached within 24 hours. Regular hydrofoil services link Budapest with Bratislava and Vienna. Budapest is the country's only practical destination by air but is well served by commercial and budget carriers.

ITINERARIES

One Week

Spend at least three days in Budapest, checking out the sights, museums, cafes and *romkertek* (outdoor clubs) On your fourth day take a day trip to a Danube Bend town: see the open-air museum in Szentendre or the cathedral at Esztergom. Day five can be spent on a day trip to Pécs to see the lovely Turkish remains and check out the many museums and galleries in town. If you've still got the travel bug, on day six try some local wine in Eger, a baroque town set in red-wine country. On your last day recuperate in one of Budapest's wonderful thermal baths.

Two Weeks

In summer spend some time exploring the towns and grassy beaches around Lake Balaton. Tihany is a rambling hillside village filled with craftsmen's houses set on a protected peninsula. Keszthely is an old town with a great palace in addition to a beach and Hévíz has a thermal lake. Try to see something of the Great Plain as well. Szeged is a splendid university town on the Tisza River, and Kecskemét is a centre of art nouveau. Finish your trip in Tokaj, home of Hungary's most famous sweet wine.

Essential Food & Drink

» **Gulyás** (goulash) Hungary's signature dish, though here it's more like a soup than a stew and made with beef, onions and tomatoes.
» **Pörkölt** Paprika-infused stew; closer to what we would call goulash.
» **Halászlé** Recommended fish soup made from poached freshwater fish, tomatoes, green peppers and paprika.
» **Savanyúság** Literally 'sourness'; anything from mildly sour-sweet cucumbers to almost acidic sauerkraut, eaten with a main course.

BUDAPEST

🎵1 / POP 1.75 MILLION

There's no other Hungarian city like Budapest in terms of size and importance. Home to almost 20% of the national population, Hungary's *főváros* (main city) is the nation's administrative, business and cultural cen-

tre; everything of importance starts, finishes or is taking place here.

But it's the beauty of Budapest – both natural and manmade – that makes it stand apart. Straddling a gentle curve in the Danube, the city is flanked by the Buda Hills on the west bank and the beginnings of the Great Plain to the east. Architecturally it is

Hungary Highlights

❶ Get lost in Hungary's best nightlife, especially the bars and pubs of **Budapest** (p393).

❷ Learn about the bravery of **Eger** (p421) while under Turkish attack, and how the city's Bull's Blood wine got its name.

❸ Watch the cowboys ride at Bugac in **Kiskunság**

National Park (p415), in the heart of the Great Plain.

❹ Absorb the Mediterranean-like climate and historic architecture of **Pécs** (p411), including its iconic Mosque Church.

❺ Take a pleasure cruise across **Lake Balaton** (p407), Central Europe's largest body of fresh water.

❻ Ease your aching muscles in the warm waters at the thermal lake in **Hévíz** (p410) and try one of the special treatments on offer.

❼ Mill about with artists, free thinkers and day-trippers at the too-cute-for-words artists' colony of **Szentendre** (p398).

a gem, with enough baroque, neoclassical, eclectic and art nouveau elements to satisfy anyone.

In recent years, Budapest has taken on the role of the region's party town. In the warmer months outdoor beer gardens called *romkertek* heave with partygoers, and the world-class Sziget music festival in August is a major magnet. Fun can always be found on your doorstep; indeed, the city's scores of new hostels offer some of the best facilities and most convivial company in Europe.

History

Strictly speaking, the story of Budapest begins only in 1873 with the administrative union of three cities: Buda, west of the Danube; the even older Óbuda to the north; and Pest on the eastern side of the river. But the area had already been occupied for thousands of years.

The Romans had a colony at Aquincum in Óbuda till the 5th century AD. In the 1500s the Turks arrived uninvited and stayed for almost 150 years. The Habsburg Austrians helped kick the occupiers out, but then made themselves at home for more than two centuries.

In the late 19th century, under the dual Austro-Hungarian monarchy, the population of Budapest soared; many notable buildings date from that boom period. The 20th century was less kind. Brutal fighting towards the end of WWII, with Hungary on the losing side, brought widespread destruction and new overlords, this time the Soviets. The futile 1956 revolution left thousands dead and buildings that to this day remain pockmarked with bullet holes.

Thankfully, those times are long gone. With Hungary a member of the European Union, Budapest is once again a sophisticated capital of a proud nation with a distinctive heritage.

WANT MORE?

For in-depth information, reviews and recommendations at your fingertips, head to the Apple App Store to purchase Lonely Planet's *Budapest City Guide* iPhone app.

Alternatively, head to www.lonelyplanet.com/hungary/budapest for planning advice, author recommendations, traveller reviews and insider tips.

◉ Sights & Activities

Budapest is an excellent city for sightseeing, especially on foot. The Castle District in Buda contains a number of museums, both major and minor, but the lion's share is in Pest. Think of Margaret Island as a green buffer between the two – short on things to see, but a great place for a breather.

BUDA

Castle Hill (Várhegy) is arguably Budapest's biggest tourist attraction and a first port of call for any visit to the city. Here, you'll find most of Budapest's remaining medieval buildings, the Royal Palace, some sweeping views over Pest across the river and a festive mood year-round.

You can walk to Castle Hill up the **Király lépcső**, the 'Royal Steps' that lead northwest off Clark Ádám tér, or else take the **Sikló** (Map p382; I Szent György tér; one way/return adult 900/1800Ft, child 550/1000Ft; ⊙7.30am-10pm, closed 1st & 3rd Mon of month; ⊟16, ⊟19, 41), a funicular railway built in 1870 that ascends from Clark Ádám tér to Szent György tér near the Royal Palace.

The 'other peak' overlooking the Danube, south of Castle Hill, is Gellért Hill.

Royal Palace   PALACE
(Királyi Palota; Map p382; I Szent György tér) The massive former Royal Palace, razed and rebuilt at least a half-dozen times over the past seven centuries, occupies the southern end of Castle Hill. Here you'll find atmospheric medieval streets as well as the **Hungarian National Gallery** (Nemzeti Galéria; Map p382; www.mng.hu; I Szent György tér 6; adult/concession 1200/600Ft; ⊙10am-6pm Tue-Sun; ⊟16, 16/a, 116, ⊟19, 41) and the **Budapest History Museum** (Budapesti Történeti Múzeum; Map p382; www.btm.hu; I Szent György tér 2; adult/concession 1500/750Ft; ⊙10am-6pm Tue-Sun Mar-Oct, reduced hours Nov-Feb; ⊟16, 16/a, 116, ⊟19, 41).

Matthias Church   CHURCH
(Mátyás Templom; Map p382; www.matyastemplom.hu; I Szentháromság tér 2; adult/concession 1000/700Ft; ⊙9am-5pm Mon-Fri, 9am-1pm Sat, 1-5pm Sun) The pointed spire and the colourful tiled roof make neo-Gothic Matthias Church (so named because King Matthias Corvinus held both his weddings here) a Castle Hill landmark. Parts date back some 500 years, notably the carvings above the southern entrance, but the rest of it was designed by architect Frigyes Schulek in 1896.

Budapest

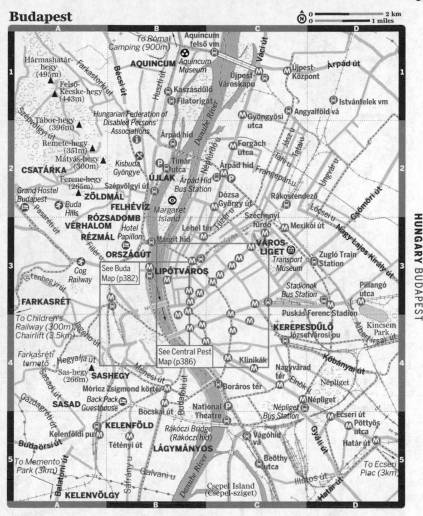

Fishermen's Bastion MONUMENT
(Halászbástya; Map p382; I Szentháromság tér; adult/concession 540/220Ft; ⊙9am-11pm mid-Mar–mid-Oct) Just east of Matthias Church, Fishermen's Bastion is another neo-Gothic folly built as a viewing platform in 1905. In front of it is the ornate equestrian **St Stephen statue** (Szent István szobor) by sculptor Alajos Stróbl.

Royal Wine House & Wine Cellar Museum MUSEUM
(Borház és Pincemúzeum; Map p382; ☎267 1100; www.kiralyiborok.com; I Szent György tér Nyugati sétány; adult/student & senior 990/750Ft; ⊙noon-8pm daily May-Sep, noon-8pm Tue-Sun Oct-Apr) Housed in what once were the royal cellars dating back to the 13th century, below Szent György tér, this place offers a crash course in Hungarian viticulture in the heart of the Castle District. Tastings cost 1990/2490/3790Ft for three/four/six wines.

FREE **Citadella** FORTRESS
(Map p382; www.citadella.hu; ⊙24hr) Built by the Habsburgs after the 1848–49 War of Independence to defend the city from further insurrection, the Citadella was obsolete by the time it was ready (1851) and the political

Buda

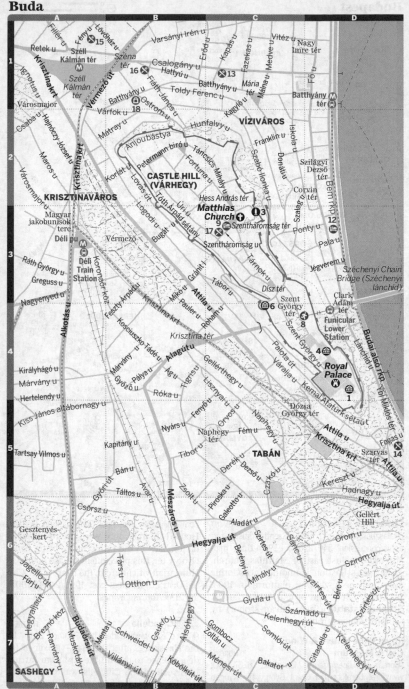

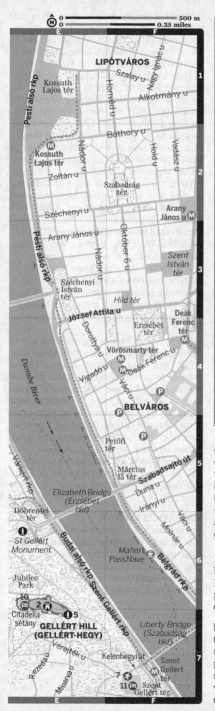

climate had changed. Today the Citadella contains some big guns and dusty displays in the central courtyard, the rather hokey **1944 Bunker Waxworks** (1944 Bunkér Panoptikum; Map p382; www.citadella.hu; admission 1200Ft; ⊙9am-8pm May-Sep, to 5pm Oct-Apr; ⊒27) inside a bunker used during WWII, and a hotel-cum-hostel (p390).

To reach here from Pest, cross Elizabeth Bridge and take the stairs leading up behind the statue of St Gellért, or cross Liberty Bridge and follow Verejték utca through the park starting opposite the entrance to the Gellért Baths.

Liberty Monument   MONUMENT
(Szabadság szobor; Map p382) The Liberty Monument – a lovely lady with a palm frond proclaiming freedom throughout the city – stands atop Gellért Hill. Some 14m high, she was raised in 1947 in tribute to the Soviet soldiers who died liberating Budapest in 1945,

but the victims' names in Cyrillic letters on the plinth and the statues of the Soviet soldiers were removed in 1992 and sent to Memento Park (p384).

TOP **CHOICE** **Memento Park** HISTORIC SITE
(off Map p381; www.mementopark.hu; XXII Balatoni út 16; adult/student 1500/1000Ft; ⊙10am-dusk) Home to almost four dozen statues, busts and plaques of Lenin, Marx and 'heroic' workers that once 'graced' the streets of Budapest and elsewhere, this socialist Disneyland 10km southwest of the city centre is a mind-blowing place to visit.

To get here, take tram 19 from Batthyány tér in Buda or tram 47 or 49 from Deák Ferenc tér in Pest to Kosztolány Dezsö tér in southern Buda and board city bus 150 (25 minutes, every 20 to 30 minutes) for the park. There's also a more expensive direct bus (with park admission adult/child return 4900/3500Ft), which departs from in front of the Le Meridien Budapest Hotel on Deák Ferenc tér at 11am year-round, with an extra departure at 3pm in July and August.

Aquincum Museum ARCHAEOLOGICAL SITE
(Aquincumi Múzeum; Map p381; www.aquincum. hu; III Szentendre út 139; adult/student & senior 1500/600Ft, archaeological park only 1000/300Ft; ⊙park 9am-6pm Tue-Sun May-Sep, reduced hours Apr & Oct; museum 10am-6pm Tue-Sun May-Sep, reduced hours Apr & Oct) Some 7km north of the centre is the Aquincum Museum, with the most complete ruins of a 2nd-century Roman civilian town in Hungary. Inside is a vast collection of coins and wall paintings. It can be reached by taking the HÉV from Batthyány tér in Buda to the Aquincum stop.

TOP **CHOICE** **Gellért Baths** BATHHOUSE
(Gellért Fürdő; Map p382; ✆466 6166; www. spasbudapest.com; XI Kelenhegyi út, Danubius Hotel Gellért; without/with private changing room 3200/4300Ft ; ⊙6am-8pm) Soaking in the art nouveau Gellért Baths, open to both men and women in separate sections but mixed on Sunday, has been likened to taking a bath in a cathedral. The eight thermal pools range in temperature from 26°C to 38°C.

Buda Hills HILL
(Map p381) With 'peaks' up to 500m, a comprehensive system of trails and no lack of unusual conveyances to get you around, the Buda Hills are the city's playground and a welcome respite from hot, dusty Pest in summer.

Heading for the hills is more than half the fun. From Széll Kálmán metro station on the M2 line in Buda, walk westward along Szilágyi Erzsébet fasor for 10 minutes (or take tram 18 or 56 for two stops) to the circular Hotel Budapest at Szilágyi Erzsébet fasor 47. Directly opposite is the terminus of the **Cog Railway** (Fogaskerekű vasút; Map p381; www.bkv.hu; Szilágyi Erzsébet fasor 14-16; admission 320Ft; ⊙5am-11pm). Built in 1874, the railway climbs 3.6km in 14 minutes three or four times an hour to Széchenyi-hegy (427m), one of the prettiest residential areas in Buda.

Here you can stop for a picnic in the attractive park south of the old-time station or board the narrow-gauge **Children's Railway** (Gyermekvasút; off Map p381; www. gyermekvasut.hu; adult/child 1 section 500/300Ft, entire line 700/350Ft; ⊙closed Mon Sep-Apr), two minutes to the south on Hegyhát út. The railway with eight stops was built in 1951 by Pioneers (socialist Scouts) and is now staffed entirely by schoolchildren aged 10 to 14 (the engineer excepted). The little train chugs along for 12km, terminating at Hűvösvölgy.

There are walks fanning out from any of the stops along the Children's Railway line, or you can return to Széll Kálmán tér on tram 61 from Hűvösvölgy. A more interesting way down, however, is to get off at Jánoshegy, the fourth stop and the highest point (527m) in the hills. About 700m to the east is the **chairlift** (Libegő; off Map p381; www.bkv. hu; adult/child 800/500Ft; ⊙9am-7pm Jul & Aug, 9.30am-5pm May, Jun & Sep, 10am-4pm Oct-Apr, closed 2nd & 4th Mon of every month), which will take you down 1040m to Zugligeti út. From here bus 291 returns to Szilágyi Erzsébet fasor.

MARGARET ISLAND

Neither Buda nor Pest, 2.5km-long **Margaret Island** (Margit-sziget; admission free; Map p381), in the middle of the Danube, was the domain of one religious order or another until the Turks came and turned what was then called the Island of Rabbits into – of all things – a harem. It's been a public park since the mid-19th century.

While not huge on unmissable sights, the island's gardens and shaded walkways are lovely places to stroll around. As the island is mostly off-limits to cars, cyclists also feel welcome here.

The easiest way to get to Margaret Island from Buda or Pest is via tram 4 or 6. Bus 26 covers the length of the island as it makes the run from Nyugati train station to Árpád Bridge. You can hire a bicycle from one of several stands on the island.

PEST

TOP CHOICE Great Synagogue
JEWISH

(Nagy zsinagóga; Map p386; ☎343 6756; www.dohanystreetsynagogue.hu; VII Dohány utca 2-8; adult/student & child 2750/2050Ft; ☉10am-5.30pm Sun-Thu, to 4pm Fri Apr-Oct, reduced hours Nov-Mar) Northeast of the Astoria metro stop is what remains of the Jewish quarter. The twin-towered, 1859 Great Synagogue, the largest Jewish house of worship in the world outside New York City and seating 3000, also contains the **Hungarian Jewish Museum** (Magyar Zsidó Múzeum; Map p386; ☎343 6756; www.zsidomuzeum.hu; VII Dohány utca 2; synagogue & museum adult/student & child 2750/2050Ft, call ahead for guided tours; ☉10am-6pm Sun-Thu, to 4pm Fri Mar-Oct, 10am-4pm Sun-Thu, to 2pm Fri Nov-Apr; Ⓜ M2 Astoria) with a harrowing exhibit on the Holocaust.

On the synagogue's north side, the **Holocaust Memorial** (Map p386; opp VII Wesselényi utca 6; Ⓜ M2 Astoria, ᎏ47, 49) stands over the mass graves of those murdered by the Nazis from 1944 to 1945. On the leaves of the metal 'tree of life' are the family names of some of the hundreds of thousands of victims.

Parliament
HISTORIC BUILDING

(Országház; Map p386; ☎441 4904; www.parlament.hu; V Kossuth Lajos tér 1-3; adult/concession/EU citizen 3500/1750Ft/free; ☉8am-4pm Mon-Sat, 8am-2pm Sun) The huge riverfront Parliament, dating back to 1902, dominates Kossuth Lajos tér. English-language tours are given at 10am, noon and 2pm (Hungarian tours depart continually). To avoid disappointment, book ahead (in person).

Hősök tere
SQUARE

(Heroes' Sq; Map p386) This public space holds a sprawling monument constructed to honour the millennium in 1896 of the Magyar conquest of the Carpathian Basin.

Museum of Fine Arts
MUSEUM

(Szépművészeti Múzeum; www.mfab.hu; XIV Dózsa György út 41; adult/concession 1800/900Ft, temporary exhibitions 3800/2000Ft; ☉10am-6pm Tue-Sun) On the northern side of the square, this gallery houses the city's outstanding collection of foreign artworks in a building dating from 1906. The Old Masters'

collection is the most complete, with thousands of works from the Dutch and Flemish, Spanish, Italian, German, French and British schools between the 13th and 18th centuries, including seven paintings by El Greco.

City Park
PARK

(Városliget; Map p386) City Park is Pest's green lung – an open space covering almost a square kilometre. It has boating on a small lake in summer, ice-skating in winter and duck-feeding year-round. The park's **Vajdahunyad Castle** (Map p386) was built in 1896 in various architectural styles from all over historic Hungary, including Gothic, Romanesque and baroque. It now contains the **Hungarian Agricultural Museum** (Magyar Mezőgazdasági Múzeum; Map p386; www.mmgm.hu; XIV Vajdahunyad sétány, Vajdahunyad Castle; adult/child 1100/550Ft; ☉10am-5pm Tue-Sun Apr-Oct, 10am-4pm Tue-Fri, to 5pm Sat & Sun Nov-Mar; Ⓜ M1 Hősök tere, ᎏ75, 79).

Further east the varied exhibits of the **Transport Museum** (Közlekedési Múzeum; Map p381; www.km.iif.hu; XIV Városligeti körút 11; adult/child 1400/700Ft; ☉10am-5pm Tue-Fri, to 6pm Sat & Sun May-Sep, reduced hours Oct-Apr; ☝) make it one of the most enjoyable spots in the city for children.

In the park's northern corner is the art nouveau **Széchenyi Baths** (Széchenyi Fürdő; off Map p386; ☎363 3210; www.spasbudapest.com; XIV Állatkerti út 1; ticket with locker/cabin weekdays 3400/3800Ft, weekends 3550/3950F; ☉6am-10pm; Ⓜ M1 Széchenyi fürdő), its cupola visible from anywhere in the park. Built in 1908 this place has a dozen thermal baths and five swimming pools.

Terror House
MUSEUM

(Terror Háza; Map p386; www.terrorhaza.hu; VI Andrássy út 60; adult/concession 2000/1000Ft; ☉10am-6pm Tue-Sun) The headquarters of the dreaded secret police has been turned into so-called Terror House, a museum focusing on the crimes and atrocities committed by both Hungary's fascist and Stalinist regimes. The years leading up to the 1956 uprising get the lion's share of the exhibition space. The excellent audio guide costs 1500Ft.

Hungarian State Opera House
CULTURAL BUILDING

(Magyar Állami Operaház; Map p386; ☎332 8197; www.operavisit.hu; VI Andrássy út 22; tours adult/concession 3000/2000Ft; ☉tours 3pm & 4pm) Designed by Miklós Ybl in 1884, the neo-

Central Pest

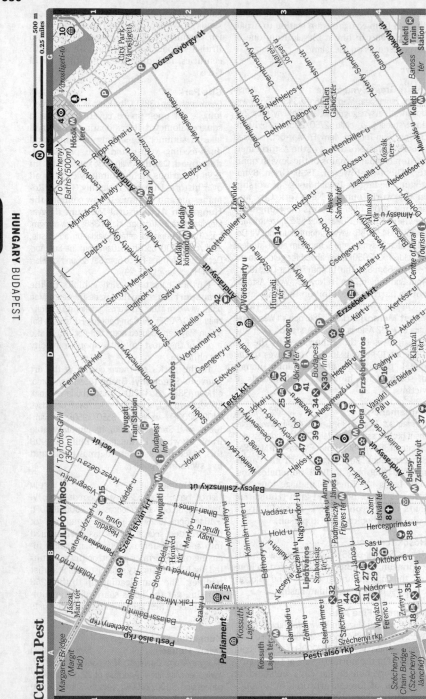

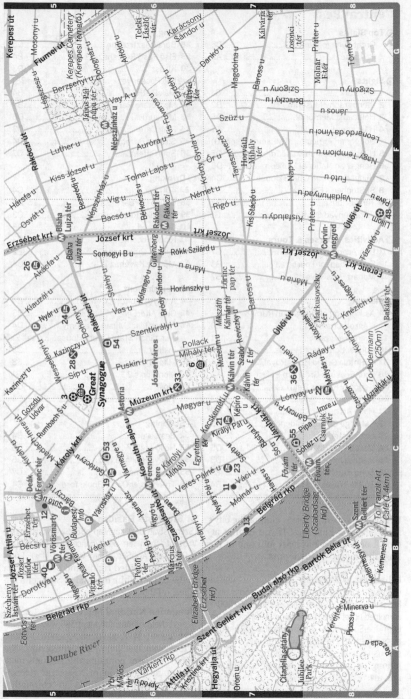

Central Pest

◎ Top Sights

◎ Sights

⊙ Activities, Courses & Tours

🛏 Sleeping

⊗ Eating

❸ Drinking

✪ Entertainment

🛍 Shopping

HUNGARY BUDAPEST

Renaissance opera house is among the city's most beautiful buildings. If you cannot attend a performance at least join one of the English-language guided tours.

Ethnography Museum MUSEUM
(Néprajzi Múzeum; Map p386; www.neprajz.hu; V Kossuth Lajos tér 12; adult/concession 1000/500Ft; combined ticket for all exhibitions 1400Ft; ⊙10am-6pm Tue-Sun) The Ethnography Museum, opposite the Parliament building, has an extensive collection of national costumes among its permanent displays on folk life and art.

St Stephen's Basilica CHURCH
(Szent István Bazilika; Map p386; www.basilica.hu; V Szent István tér; adult/concession 500/300Ft; ⊙9am-5pm Apr-Sep, 10am-4pm Oct-Mar) Look for the mummified right hand of St Stephen in the chapel of the colossal St Stephen's Basilica, off Bajcsy-Zsilinszky út.

Hungarian National Museum MUSEUM
(Magyar Nemzeti Múzeum; Map p386; www.mnm.hu; VIII Múzeum Q 14-16; adult/concession 1100/550Ft; ⊙10am-6pm Tue-Sun) The Hungarian National Museum contains the nation's most important collection of historical relics – from archaeological finds to coronation

regalia – in a large neoclassical building purpose-built in 1847.

☞ Tours

Free Budapest Tours WALKING TOUR
(Map p386; ☑06 20 534 5819; www.freebudapest-tours.eu; Deák Ferenc tér; ⊙10.30am & 2.30pm) Entertaining, knowledgeable guides offer two unique and highly professional tours of the city: 'Essential Pest', which takes in the highlights of Inner Town (1½ hours); and 'From Pest to Buda', which covers Inner Town's highlights, plus the banks of the Danube and the Castle District (2½ hours). The tours are free of charge; the guides work for tips only (be generous!) and departures are at 10.30am for 'From Pest to Buda' and 2.30pm for 'Essential Pest'. Meeting point is on Deák Ferenc tér (near the Deák tér metro) at the Budapest Sightseeing Bus stop. Evening thematic tours – 'Literary Walk' and 'Behind The Night' pub crawls – cost 3000Ft per person.

Mahart PassNave BOAT TOUR
(Map p386; ☑484 4013; www.mahartpassnave. hu; V Belgrád Rakpart, Landing Stage pier 3; adult/concession 2990/1490Ft; ⊙10am-10pm May-Sep, 11am-8pm Oct-Dec & Apr) Hour-long cruises between Margaret and Rákóczi bridges depart hourly in high season and at 1pm and 5pm in low season.

✸ Festivals & Events

Many festivals and events are held in and around Budapest. Look out for the tourist board's annual *Events Calendar* for a complete listing.

Budapest Spring Festival PERFORMING ARTS
(www.festivalcity.hu) The capital's largest and most important cultural event, with 200 events taking place over two weeks in late March/early April at dozens of venues.

Sziget Music Festival MUSIC
(www.sziget.hu) Now one of the biggest and most popular music festivals in Europe, this 10-day event is held in mid-August on Budapest's Óbuda Island.

Hungarian Formula One Grand Prix SPORT
(www.hungaroring.hu) Hungary's premier sporting event is held at Mogyoród, 24km northeast of Budapest, in early August.

Budapest International Wine Festival WINE
(www.winefestival.hu) Hungary's foremost wine-makers introduce their wines at this popular event held in mid-September in the Castle District.

Budapest International Marathon RUNNING
(www.budapestmarathon.com) Eastern Europe's most celebrated race goes along the Danube and across its bridges in early October.

🛏 Sleeping

Accommodation prices and standards are still quite reasonable in Budapest. Many year-round hostels occupy middle floors of old apartment buildings (with or without lift) in central Pest. Come summer (July to late August), student dormitories at colleges and universities open to travellers.

Private rooms in Budapest homes generally cost 6000Ft to 7500Ft for a single, 7000Ft to 8500Ft for a double and 10,000Ft to 13,000Ft for a small apartment. One centrally located broker is the **To-Ma Travel Agency** (Map p386; ☑353 0819; www.tomatour.hu; V Október 6 utca 22; ⊙9am-noon & 1-8pm Mon-Fri, 9am-5pm Sat & Sun).

BUDA

TOP CHOICE **Hotel Papillon** HOTEL **€€**
(☑212 4750; www.hotelpapillon.hu; II Rózsahegy utca 3/b; s/d/tr €60/75/95, apt €100-120; P✲@⏠≋) This small 20-room hotel in Rózsadomb has a delightful back garden with a small swimming pool, and several rooms have balconies. There are also four apartments available in the same building, one of which boasts a lovely roof terrace.

Back Pack Guesthouse HOSTEL **€**
(Map p381; ☑385 8946; www.backpackbudapest. hu; XI Takács Menyhért utca 33; beds in yurt 3000Ft, dm large/small 3800/4500Ft, d 11,000Ft; P@⏠) A friendly and very laid-back place, though relatively small with just 50 beds. There's a lush garden in the back with a hammock stretched invitingly between trees. Take bus 7 to Tétényi út (from Keleti train station) or tram 18 to Móricz Zsigmond körtér to catch bus 7.

Hotel Victoria HOTEL **€€**
(Map p382; ☑457 8080; www.victoria.hu; I Bem rakpart 11; s/d from €109/115; P✲@⏠) This rather elegant hotel has 27 comfortable and spacious rooms with larger-than-life views of Parliament and the Danube. Despite its small size it gets special mention for its friendly service and facilities, including the renovated 19th-century Jenő Hubay Music Hall, which now serves as a small theatre and function rooms.

Danubius Hotel Gellért
LUXURY HOTEL €€€

(Map p382; ☑889 5500; www.danubiusgroup.com/gellert; XI Szent Gellért tér 1; d/ste from €170/268; P❋❋@☞❀) Peek through the doors of this turn-of-the-20th-century *grand dame*, even if you don't choose to stay here. The 234-room, four-star hotel has loads of character and its famous thermal baths (p384) are free for guests. Prices depend on your room's view and the quality of its bathroom.

Burg Hotel
HOTEL €€

(Map p382; ☑212 0269; www.burghotelbudapest.com; I Szentháromság tér 7-8; s/d/ste from €105/115/134; P❋☞) This small hotel with all the mod cons is in the Castle District, just opposite Matthias Church. The 26 partly refurbished rooms look fresher than they once did but are not much more than just ordinary. But, as they say, location is everything and midrange options are as scarce as hen's teeth on Castle Hill.

Grand Hostel Budapest
HOSTEL €

(Map p381; www.grandhostel.hu; XII Hüvösvölgyi utca 69; dm 3600-4500Ft, s/d from 8400/13,500Ft; P@☞) 'Grand' might be tooting its own horn a bit, but this colourful hostel does come pretty close, with its cavernlike cocktail bar, tiled rooms, communal barbecues and DJ nights. To get here, take tram 61 from Széll Kálmán tér to the Kelemen László utca stop.

Citadella Hotel
HOSTEL €

(Map p382; ☑466 5794; www.citadella.hu; XI Citadella sétány; dm 3200Ft, s & d with shared shower/shower/bath tub 10,500/11,500/12,500Ft; @) This hostel in the fortress atop Gellért Hill is pretty threadbare, though the dozen guest rooms are extra large, retain some of their original features and have their own shower (toilets are on the circular corridor). The single dorm room has 14 beds and shared facilities.

Római Camping
CAMPGROUND €

(off Map p381; ☑388 7167; www.romaicamping.hu; III Szentendrei út 189; campsite for 1/2/van/caravan 4720/6000/5665/7220Ft; bungalow for 2/4 6000/12,000Ft; ☼year-round; P@☞) Located in a leafy park north of the city, opposite the popular **Rómaifürdő swimming pool** complex, this is the city's largest camping ground. To get here, take the HÉV suburban railway from the Batthyány tér metro station in Buda to the Rómaifürdő station about 900m out of the city, which is almost opposite the site.

PEST

TOP CHOICE Four Seasons
Gresham Palace Hotel
LUXURY HOTEL €€€

(Map p386; ☑268 6000; www.fourseasons.com/budapest; V Széchenyi István tér 5-6; r/ste from €325/1125; P❋❋@☞❀) Restored to its bygone elegance, with mushroom-shaped windows, whimsical ironwork and glittering gold decorative tiles on the exterior, the 179-room Four Seasons inhabits the art nouveau Gresham Palace (1907) and provides superb views of the Danube.

TOP CHOICE Gerlóczy Rooms
Delux
BOUTIQUE HOTEL €€

(Map p386; ☑501 4000; www.gerloczy.hu; V Gerlóczy utca 1; r €90; ❋@☞) Just 15 individually decorated rooms await you here, inside this revamped 1890s building. The rooms themselves are decked out in sombre shades (try to nab one of the two rooms with balconies) but it's details such as the stained glass, art-nouveau touches and original wrought-iron staircase that give the place character. Great cafe and restaurant downstairs, too.

Home-Made Hostel
HOSTEL €€

(Map p386; ☑302 2103; www.homemadehostel.com; VI Teréz körút 22; dm/d from 5500/15,000Ft; @☞) This cosy, extremely welcoming hostel with 20 beds in four rooms has unique decor, with recycled tables hanging upside down from the ceiling and old valises serving as lockers. The old-style kitchen is also a blast from the past.

Hotel Art
HOTEL €€€

(Map p386; ☑266 2166; www.hotelart.hu; V Király Pál utca 12; s €79-151, d €99-159; P❋☞) This Best Western property has art deco touches (including a pink facade) in the public areas, fitness centre and sauna, but the 32 guest rooms are, on the whole, quite ordinary except for the few that have separate sitting and sleeping areas. Rooms on the 5th floor have mansard roofs.

oKM Saga Guest Residence
GUESTHOUSE €

(Map p386; ☑215 6883, 217 1934; www.km-saga.hu; IX Lónyay utca 17, 3rd fl; s €25-63, d €28-80; ❋@) This unique place has five themed rooms, an eclectic mix of 19th-century furnishings and a hospitable, multilingual Hungarian-American owner, Shandor. It's essentially a gay B&B but everyone is welcome. Two rooms share a bathroom.

Corinthia Grand Hotel Royal
LUXURY HOTEL €€€

(Map p386; ☎479 4000; www.corinthia.hu; VII Erzsébet körút 43-49; r/ste from €140/347; P❋@☎☎) Decades in the remaking, this five-star beauty with 440 rooms has been carefully reconstructed in the Austro-Hungarian style of heavy drapes, sparkling chandeliers and large, luxurious ballrooms. Its restored Royal Spa, dating from 1886 but now as modern as tomorrow, is a legend reborn.

TOP CHOICE Connection Guest House
GUESTHOUSE €€

(Map p386; ☎267 7104; www.connectionguesthouse.com; VII Király utca 41; s/d from €45/60; @☎) This very central gay pension above a leafy courtyard attracts a young crowd due to its proximity to nightlife venues. Two of the nine rooms share facilities on the corridor and face partially pedestrianised Király utca.

Soho Hotel
BOUTIQUE HOTEL €€€

(Map p386; ☎872 8216; www.sohohotel.hu; VII Dohány utca 64; s/d/ste €189/199/249; P❋@☎) This delightfully stylish boutique 74-room hotel sports a foyer bar in eye-popping reds, blues and lime greens. The non-allergenic rooms have bamboo matting on the walls, parquet floors and a music/film theme throughout.

Aventura Hostel
HOSTEL €€

(Map p386; ☎239 0789; www.aventurahostel.com; XIII Visegrádi utca 12, 1st fl; dm/d/apt 4300/15,000/18,800Ft; @☎) This has got to be the most chilled hostel in Budapest, with four themed rooms (India, Japan, Africa and – our favourite – Space), run by two affable ladies. It's slightly out of the action, in Újlipótváros, but easily accessible by public transport.

Marco Polo Hostel
HOSTEL €

(Map p386; ☎1 413 2555; www.marcopolohostel.com; VII Nyár utca 6; dm/s/d/tr/q from 3500/12,000/15,000/19,000/24,000Ft; ☺@☎) The Mellow Mood Group's very central flagship hostel is a swish, powder-blue, 47-room place, with telephones and TVs in all the rooms, except the dorms, and a lovely courtyard.

Medosz Hotel
HOTEL €€

(Map p386; ☎374 3000; www.medoszhotel.hu; VI Jókai tér 9; s €49-59, d €59-69; P☎) Well priced for its central location, the Medosz is opposite the restaurants and bars of Liszt Ferenc tér. The 68 rooms are spare but comfortable and many have been renovated.

Loft Hostel
HOSTEL €

(Map p386; ☎328 0916; www.lofthostel.hu; V Veres Pálné utca 19; dm 4200-5000Ft, d 13,000Ft; @☎) This hostel may well succeed in its loft-y aspirations to be the hottest backpacker magnet in town. There are excellent Hungarian dishes on offer and there's a friendly atmosphere. The showers are among the best in town and it feels like staying at a friend's house. Bike rental and tours available.

✗ Eating

Very roughly, a cheap two-course sit-down meal for one person with a glass of wine or beer in Budapest costs 3500Ft, while the same meal in a midrange eatery would be 7000Ft. An expensive meal will cost up to 10,000Ft. Restaurants are generally open from 10am or 11am to 11pm or midnight. It's always best to arrive by 9pm or 10pm, though, to ensure being served. It is advisable to book tables at medium-priced to expensive restaurants, especially at the weekend.

Ráday utca and Liszt Ferenc tér are the two most popular traffic-free streets. The moment the weather warms up, tables, and umbrellas spring up on the pavements and the people of Budapest crowd the streets.

BUDA

For self-catering in Buda, visit the **Fény utca Market** (Map p382; II Fény utca; ☺6am-6pm Mon-Fri, to 2pm Sat), just next to the Mammut shopping mall.

Csalogány 26
HUNGARIAN €€€

(Map p382; ☎201 7892; www.csalogany26.hu; I Csalogány utca 26; 4-/8-course menus 8000/12,000Ft; ☺noon-3pm & 7-10pm Tue-Sat) One of the best restaurants in Budapest turns out superb Hungarian and international dishes at prices that, while no bargain, are considered good value for the quality of what's on offer. Reserve for the evenings.

Kisbuda Gyöngye
HUNGARIAN €€

(Map p381; ☎368 6402; www.remiz.hu; III Kenyeres utca 34; mains 2680-5220Ft; ☺closed Sun) This is a traditional and very elegant Hungarian restaurant in Óbuda; the antique-cluttered dining room and attentive service manage to create a *fin-de-siècle* atmosphere.

Éden
VEGETARIAN €

(Map p382; www.edenetterem.hu; I Iskola utca 31; mains 900-1200Ft; ☺8am-9pm Mon-Thu, to 6pm Fri, 11am-7pm Sun; ✐) Located in a town house just below Castle Hill, this self-service place offers solid but healthy vegan and vegetarian fare.

Nagyi Palacsintázója
HUNGARIAN €

(Granny's Palacsinta Place; Map p382; www.nagyipali.hu; I Hattyú utca 16; pancakes 160-680Ft; ⊗24hr; 🅙) This place serves Hungarian pancakes – both the savoury and sweet varieties – round the clock and is always packed. There are other 24-hour branches in **Buda** (I Batthyány tér 5), **Óbuda** (III Szentendrei út 131) and **Pest** (V Petőfi Sándor tér 17–19).

Ruszwurm Cukrászda
CAFE €

(Map p382; www.ruszwurm.hu; I Szentháromság utca 7; cakes 380-580Ft; ⊗10am-7pm) This is the perfect place for coffee and cakes in the Castle District, though it can get pretty crowded – especially in high season when it's almost always impossible to get a seat.

PEST

The **Nagycsarnok** (Great Market; Map p386; IX Vámház körút 1-3; ⊗9am-6pm Mon-Sat) is a vast historic market built of steel and glass. Head here for fruit, vegetables, deli items, fish and meat.

TOP CHOICE Mák Bistro
INTERNATIONAL €€

(Map p386; 🖉06 30 723 9383; www.makbistro.hu; V Vigyázó Ferenc utca 4; mains 3200-5600Ft; ⊗noon-3pm & 6pm-midnight Tue-Sat) With a new chef at the helm, Mák has gone from strength to strength. Try such ambitious pairings as scallops with grapefruit and sardine with mango, though you may be tempted by more traditional mains such as *mangalica* (a type of pork unique to Hungary) spare ribs and sirloin with polenta. The chocolate *millefeuille* really is to die for. Great wine selection too.

TOP CHOICE Klassz
INTERNATIONAL €€

(Map p386; www.klasszetterem.hu; VI Andrássy út 41; mains 1890-4390Ft; ⊗11.30am-11pm Mon-Sat, to 6pm Sun) Klassz is focused on wine, but the food is also of a very high standard. Varieties of foie gras and native *mangalica* are permanent stars on the menu, with dishes such as Burgundy-style leg of rabbit and lamb trotters with vegetable ragout playing cameo roles. Reservations not accepted; just show up and wait over a glass of wine.

Ring Cafe
BURGERS €

(Map p386; 🖉331 5790; www.ringcafe.hu; VI Andrássy út 38; burgers 1490-3290Ft; ⊗9am-late Mon-Fri, 10am-1am Sat, 10am-10pm Sun; 🛜) When

we tell you that these guys do the best burgers in town – bar none – we're not messing about. And with imaginative sandwiches, salads and egg-and-bacon power breakfasts to boot, it's little wonder that this place is always packed.

Első Pesti Rétesház
SWEETS €€

(Map p386; 🖉428 0135; www.reteshaz.com; V Október 6 utca 22; mains 2990-5990Ft; ⊗9am-11pm) It may be a bit overdone (think Magyar Disneyland, with old-world counters, painted plates on the walls and curios embedded in Plexiglas washbasins), but the 'First Strudel House of Pest' is just the place to taste Hungarian stretched pastry (360Ft) filled with apple, cheese, poppy seeds or sour cherry.

Momotaro Ramen
ASIAN €€

(Map p386; 🖉269 3802; www.momotaroramen.com; V Széchenyi utca 16; dumplings 600-1400Ft, noodles 1150-1800Ft, mains 1800-4750Ft; ⊗11am-10.30pm Tue-Sun; 🅙) This is a favourite pit stop for noodles – especially the soup variety – and dumplings when *pálinka* (fruit-flavoured brandy) and other lubricants have been a-flowing the night before. But it's also good for more substantial dishes.

LaciPecsenye
HUNGARIAN €€

(Map p386; 🖉333 1717; www.lacipecsenye.eu; V Sas utca 11; mains 2800-4700Ft; ⊗noon-midnight) Inside this minimalist chic bistro, the changing daily mains on black slate are largely for the carnivorous, though some are especially inspired, such as calamari stuffed with meat and anything with duck liver. Don't miss out on the pumpkin cake.

Soul Café
INTERNATIONAL €

(Map p386; 🖉217 6986; www.soulcafe.hu; IX Ráday utca 11-13; mains 1800-3700Ft) One of the more reliable choices along a street heaving with so-so restaurants and iffy cafes, the Soul has inventive continental dishes and decor and a great terrace on both sides of this pedestrian street.

Múzeum
HUNGARIAN €€

(Map p386; 🖉267 0375; www.muzeumkavehaz.hu; VIII Múzeum körút 12; mains 2800-6700Ft; ⊗6pm-midnight Mon-Sat) If you like to dine in old-world style, with a piano softly tinkling in the background, try this cafe-restaurant, still going strong after 125 years at the same location near the Hungarian National Museum. The goose liver dishes are above average and there's a good selection of Hungarian wines.

Trófea Grill
BUFFET €€

(off Map p386; ☎270 0366; www.trofeagrill.hu; XIII Visegrádi utca 50/a; lunch weekdays/weekends 3899/5499Ft, dinner 5499Ft; ☺noon-midnight Mon-Fri, 11.30am-midnight Sat, 11.30am-9pm Sun) This is the place to head when you *really* could eat a horse (which might be found sliced on one of the tables). It has an enormous buffet of more than 100 cold and hot dishes over which diners swarm like bees while being observed by the cooks from their kitchen. There's a half-dozen branches including one in **Buda** (II Margit körút 2).

Salaam Bombay
INDIAN €€

(Map p386; ☎411 1252; www.salaambombay.hu; V Mérleg utca 6; mains 1490-3900Ft; ☺noon-3pm & 6-11pm; ☒) If you hanker after a fix of authentic curry or tandoori in a bright, upbeat environment, look no further than this attractive eatery just east of Széchenyi István tér. As would be expected, there's a wide choice of vegetarian dishes too.

Bors Gasztro Bár
SANDWICHES €

(Map p386; www.facebook.com/BorsGasztroBar; VII Kazinczy utca 10; mains from 790Ft; ☺11.30am-9pm; ☒) We love this thimble-sized place, not just for its hearty imaginative soups but grilled baguettes too. Not really a sit-down kind of place; most people loiter by the doorway.

🍷 Drinking

Budapest is loaded with pubs and bars, and there's enough variation to satisfy all tastes. In summer, the preferred drinking venues are the *romkertek* – outdoor spaces, for the most part, in Pest that double as beer gardens and music clubs.

In the 19th century Budapest rivalled Vienna for cafe culture. The majority of the surviving traditional cafes are in Pest, but Buda can still lay claim to a handful of great ones.

BUDA
Tranzit Art Café
CAFE

(off Map p386; www.tranzitcafe.com; XI Kosztolányi Dezső tér 7; lunch 1200Ft; ☺9am-11pm Mon-Fri, 10am-10pm Sat & Sun) An abandoned bus station now houses a friendly cafe with artwork on walls, hammocks in the green courtyard for sipping your shake in, and good breakfasts and two-course lunches. Occasional events too.

PEST

For coffee in exquisite art nouveau surroundings, two places are particularly noteworthy. **Gerbeaud** (Map p386; ☎429 9000; www.gerbeaud.hu; V Vörösmarty tér 7; cakes from 750Ft; ☺9am-9pm; ⓜM1 Vörösmarty tér), Budapest's cake-and-coffee-culture king, has been at the same location since 1870. Or station yourself at the **Művész Kávéház** (Artist Coffeehouse; Map p386; ☎343 3544; www.muveszkavehaz.hu; VI Andrássy út 29; cakes 590-790Ft; ☺9am-10pm Mon-Sat, 10am-10pm Sun; ⓜM1 Opera) for some of the best pastries and people-watching in town.

DiVino Borbár
WINE BAR

(Map p386; ☎06 70 935 3980; www.divinoborbar. hu; V Szent István tér 3; ☺4pm-midnight Sun-Wed, to 2am Thu-Sat) Central, free-flowing and always heaving, DiVino is Budapest's most popular wine bar, and the crowds spilling out into the square in front of the basilica will immediately tell you that. The choice of wines (supposedly only from vintners aged under 35) at this self-service place is enormous.

400 Bar
BAR

(Map p386; www.400bar.hu; VII Kazinczy utca 52; ☺11am-3am Mon-Wed & Sun, to 5am Thu-Sat) This large cafe-bar with an attractive terrace is in a pedestrian zone in the heart of the city is great for coffee, cocktails, shooters and generally for meeting new people.

Kiadó Kocsma
PUB

(Map p386; VI Jókai tér 3; ☺10am-1am Mon-Fri, 11am-1am Sat & Sun) The 'Pub for Rent' on two levels is a great place for a swift pint and a quick bite. It's a stone's throw physically (but light years in attitude and presentation) from the places on Liszt Ferenc tér.

🍷 Lukács Cukrászda
CAFE

(Map p386; www.lukacscukraszda.com; VI Andrássy út 70; ☺9am-7.30pm) This cafe is dressed up in the finest of decadence – all mirrors and gold – with soft piano music in the background. The selection of cakes is pricey but superb.

☆ Entertainment

For a city of its size, Budapest has a huge choice of things to do and places to go after dark – from opera and (participatory) folk dancing to live jazz and pulsating clubs with some of the best DJs in the region.

Your best source of information in English for what's on in the city is the freebie **Budapest Funzine** (www.budapestfunzine.hu), available at hotels, bars, cinemas and wherever tourists congregate. The monthly freebie

Koncert Kalendárium has more serious of-ferings: classical concerts, opera, dance and the like.

Authentic *táncház*, literally 'dance house' but really folk-music workshops, are held at various locations throughout the week, but less frequently in summer. Very useful listings can be found on the **Dance House Guild** (www.tanchaz.hu) and **Folkrádió** (www. folkradio.hu) websites. The former also lists bands playing other types of traditional mu-sic, such as klezmer (Jewish folk music).

Performing Arts

You can book almost anything online at www. jegymester.hu and www.kulturinfo.hu. Anoth-er useful booking agency is **Ticket Express** (Map p386; ☎303 030 999; www.tex.hu; VI Andrássy út 18; ⊙10am-6.30pm Mon-Fri, to 3pm Sat), the largest ticket office network in the city.

Classical concerts are held regularly in the city's churches, including Matthias Church on Castle Hill in Buda.

Hungarian State Opera House   OPERA
(Magyar Állami Operaház; Map p386; ☎bookings 814 7225; www.opera.hu; VI Andrássy út 22) Take in a performance while admiring the incred-ibly rich interior decoration of this sublime building. The ballet company performs here as well.

Ferenc Liszt Music Academy   CLASSICAL MUSIC
(Liszt Ferenc Zeneakadémia; Map p386; ☎342 0179; www.zeneakademia.hu; VI Liszt Ferenc tér 8) Budapest's premier venue for classical con-certs is not just a place to hear music but to ogle at the wonderful, decorative Hungarian Zsolnay porcelain and frescos as well.

Live Music

Aranytíz Cultural Centre   TRADITIONAL MUSIC
(Aranytíz Művelődési Központ; Map p386; ☎354 3400; www.aranytiz.hu; V Arany János utca 10; ⊙bookings 2-9pm Mon & Wed, 9am-3pm Sat) At this cultural centre in the northern in-ner town in Pest, the wonderful Kalamajka Táncház, one of the best music and dance shows in town, has programs from 8.30pm on Saturday that run till about midnight.

Jedermann   LIVE MUSIC
(www.jedermannkavezo.blogspot.com; XI Ráday utca 58; ⊙8am-1am) This very mellow spot attached to the Goethe Institute and deco-rated with jazz posters fills up with students and intellectuals. Jazz gigs most nights and, in summer, the courtyard terrace is a pleas-ant refuge.

Most!   LIVE MUSIC
(Map p386; www.mostjelen.blogspot.com; VI Zichy Jenő utca 17; ⊙11am-2am Mon & Tue, to 4am Wed-Fri, 4pm-4am Sat, 4pm-2am Sun) This eclectic bar-cafe-performance space whose name means 'Now!' wears many hats. It's at its best when local pop and rock acts take to the stage, or when decent local DJs are spin-ning a set.

Nightclubs

Not all clubs and music bars in Budapest levy a cover charge, but those that do will ask for between 1500Ft and 3000Ft on the door. The trendier (and trashier) places usu-ally let women in for free. Nightclubs usually open from 4pm to 2am Sunday to Thursday and until 4am on Friday and Saturday; some open only at weekends.

Mappa Club   CLUB
(Map p386; http://mappaclub.com; IX Lilliom utca 41) An arty crowd and some of the best DJs in town makes the scene beneath the Trafó House of Contemporary Arts a must for lo-cals and visitors alike.

Morrison's 2   CLUB
(Map p386; ☎374 3329; www.morrisons.hu; V Szent István körút 11; ⊙5pm-4am Mon-Sat) Far and away Budapest's biggest party venue, this cellar club attracts a younger crowd with its four dance floors, half-dozen bars (including one in a covered courtyard) and enormous games room upstairs. Live bands from 9pm to 11pm in the week.

Instant   CLUB
(Map p386; ☎06 30 830 8747; www.instant.co.hu; VI Nagymező utca 38; ⊙1pm-3am) This cavern-ous space on Pest's most vibrant nightlife strip counts five bars on three levels with underground DJs and dance parties.

Gay & Lesbian Venues
Club AlterEgo   GAY
(Map p386; www.alteregoclub.hu; VI Dessewffy utca 33; ⊙10pm-6am Fri & Sat) Budapest's premier gay club, with the chicest (think attitude) crowd and the best dance music.

Eklektika Restolounge   LESBIAN
(Map p386; www.eklektika.hu; VI Nagymező utca 30; ⊙noon-midnight) There are no specifically lesbian bars in town, but this chilled-out eatery-bakery and lounge with a completely new look but the same ol' friendly vibe and gay-friendly crowd is probably the closest you'll find.

🛍 Shopping

As well as the usual folk arts, wines, spirits, food and music, Budapest has more distinctive items such as hand-blown glassware and antique books. But there are those who consider the city's flea markets their shopping highlight – and they certainly are a distinctive Budapest experience.

Shops are generally open from 9am or 10am to 6pm during the week, and till 1pm on Saturday.

TOP CHOICE Ecseri Piac   MARKET
(off Map p381; XIX Nagykőrösi út 156; ⏰6am-4pm Mon-Fri, to 3pm Sat, 8am-1pm Sun) The biggest flea market in Central Europe. Saturday is said to be the best day; dealers get here early for the diamonds amid the rust. Take bus 54 from Boráros tér in Pest or, for a quicker journey, the red-numbered express bus 84E, 89E or 94E from the Határ út stop on the M3 metro line and get off at the Fiume utca stop. Then follow the crowds over the pedestrian bridge.

Bestsellers   BOOKS
(Map p386; www.bestsellers.hu; V Október 6 utca 11; ⏰9am-6.30pm Mon-Fri, 10am-5pm Sat, 10am-4pm Sun) The best English-language bookshop in town, with lots of Hungarica too.

Holló Atelier   HANDICRAFTS
(Map p386; ☎317 8103; V Vitkovics Mihály utca 12; ⏰10am-6pm Mon-Fri, to 2pm Sat) Attractive folk art with a modern look. Everything handmade on site at the workshop.

Treehugger Dan's Bookstore   BOOKS
(Map p386; www.treehuggerdans.com; VI Lázár utca 16; ⏰10am-6pm Mon-Fri, to 4pm Sat) Tiny shop selling mostly secondhand English-language books; also does trade-ins and serves organic fairtrade coffee.

Bortársaság   WINE
(Map p382; ☎212 2569; www.bortarsasag.hu; I Batthyány utca 59; ⏰10am-7pm Mon-Fri, to 6pm Sat) Original shop of what's now a chain of 10 stores, this place has an exceptional selection of Hungarian wines.

Magyar Pálinka Háza   DRINK
(Hungarian Pálinka House; Map p386; ☎06 30 421 5463; www.magyarpalinkahaza.hu; VIII Rákóczi út 17; ⏰9am-7pm Mon-Sat) If *pálinka* (fruit-flavoured brandy) is your poison, this is the place for you.

ℹ Information

Dangers & Annoyances
No parts of Budapest are off limits to visitors, although some locals avoid Margaret Island after dark off-season, and both residents and visitors give the dodgier parts of the 8th and 9th districts (areas of prostitution) a wide berth.

Pickpocketing is most common in markets, the Castle District, Váci utca and Hősök tere, near major hotels and on certain popular buses (eg 7) and trams (2, 2A, 4, 6, 47 and 49).

Scams involving attractive young women, gullible guys, expensive drinks in nightclubs and a frog-marching to the nearest ATM by gorillas-in-residence have been all the rage in Budapest for nigh on two decades now. Guys, please: if it seems too good to be true, it certainly is. These scams have cost some would-be Lotharios hundreds, even thousands, of dollars and your embassy won't be able to help you. Trust us.

Discount Cards
Budapest Card (www.budapestinfo.hu; 24/48/72hr card 3900/7900/9900Ft) Offers access to many museums, unlimited public transport and discounts on tours and other services. You can buy it at hotels, travel agencies, large metro station kiosks and tourist offices, but it's cheaper online.

Medical Services
FirstMed Centers (☎24hr emergency hotline 224 9090; www.firstmedcenters.com; I Hattyú utca 14, 5th fl; ⏰8am-8pm Mon-Fri, to 2pm Sat) On call 24/7 for emergencies. Expensive.

SOS Dent (☎269 6010; www.smilistic.com; VI Király utca 14; ⏰24hr) Round-the-clock dental surgery.

Teréz Gyógyszertár (☎311 4439; VI Teréz körút 4; ⏰8am-8pm Mon-Fri, to 2pm Sat) Extended-hours pharmacy.

Money
There are ATMs everywhere, including in the train and bus stations and at the airport. ATMs at branches of OTP bank deliver difficult-to-break 20,000Ft notes. Moneychangers (particularly those along Váci utca) don't tend to give good rates, so go to a bank instead if possible.

Post
Main post office (Map p386; V Bajcsy-Zsilinsky út 16; ⏰8am-8pm Mon-Fri, to 2pm Sat) A few minutes' walk from central Deák Ferenc tér.

Tourist Information
Budapest Info (Map p386; ☎438 8080; V Sütő utca 2; ⏰8am-8pm) Also has an Oktogon **branch** (Map p386; VI Liszt Ferenc tér 11; ⏰10am-6pm Mon-Fri; Ⓜ M1 Oktogon, 🚋4, 6)

and desks in the arrivals sections of Ferenc Liszt International Airport's Terminals 1, 2A and 2B.

ⓘ Getting There & Away

Air

Ferenc Liszt International Airport (☎296 7000; www.bud.hu) has two modern terminals next to one another, 24km southeast of the city. Terminal 2A is served by flights from countries within the Schengen border, while other international flights and budget carriers use 2B.

Boat

Mahart PassNave (Map p382; ☎484 4000; www.mahartpassnave.hu; V Belgrád rakpart; ⊙8am-6pm Mon-Fri) runs hydrofoils to Bratislava and Vienna from May to late September, which arrive at and depart from the **International Ferry Pier** (Nemzetközi hajóállomás; ☎318 1223; V Belgrád rakpart). Hydrofoils depart Budapest on Mondays and Wednesdays at 9am, returning from Vienna at the same time on Tuesdays and Thursdays. Adult one-way/return fares to Vienna are €99/125. Transporting a bicycle costs €25.

For information on ferry services to the towns of the Danube Bend, see p398.

Bus

Volánbusz (☎382 0888; www.volanbusz.hu), the national bus line, has an extensive list of destinations from Budapest. All international buses and some buses to/from western Hungary use **Népliget Bus Station** (Map p381; ☎219 8030; IX Üllői út 131). **Stadionok Bus Station** (Map p381; ☎220 6227; XIV Hungária körút 48-52) generally serves places to the east of Budapest. Most buses to the Danube Bend arrive at and leave from the **Árpád Híd Bus Station** (Map p381; ☎412 2597; XIII Árbóc utca 1, off XIII Róbert Károly körút), though some leave from the small suburban bus terminal next to **Újpest-Városkapu train station** (XIII Arva utca, off Váci út), which is on the M3 blue metro line. In fact, all stations are on metro lines, and all are in Pest. If the ticket office is closed, you can buy your ticket on the bus.

Car & Motorcycle

Driving around Budapest is not for the faint-hearted. Dangerous manoeuvres, extensive roadworks and serious accidents abound and finding a place to park is next to impossible in some neighbourhoods. Use the public transport system instead.

If you want to venture into the countryside, travelling by car is an option. All major international rental firms, including **Avis** (☎318 4240; www.avis.hu; V Arany János utca 26-28; ⊙7am-6pm Mon-Sat, 8am-6pm Sun), **Budget**

(☎214 0420; www.budget.hu; VII Krisztina körút 41-43, Hotel Mercure Buda; ⊙8am-8pm Mon-Fri, to 6pm Sat & Sun) and **Europcar** (☎505 4400; www.europcar.hu; V Erzsébet tér 7-8; ⊙8am-6pm Mon & Fri, to 4.30pm Tue-Thu, to noon Sat), have offices in Budapest and at the airport. The best independent rental company with highly competitive rates is **Fox Autorent** (☎382 9000; www.foxautorent. com; VII Hársfa utca 53-55, Bldg I, ground fl; ⊙8am-6pm), which also has an office at the airport. Compact cars per day/week rent from €35/170.

Train

Hungarian State Railways (MÁV) runs the country's extensive rail network. Contact **MÁV-Start passenger service centre** (☎512 7921; www. mav-start.hu; V József Attila utca 16; ⊙9am-6pm Mon-Fri) for 24-hour information on domestic train departures and arrivals. Its website has a useful timetable in English for planning routes. Fares are usually noted for destinations within Hungary.

Buy tickets at one of Budapest's three main train stations. **Keleti train station** (Eastern Train Station; VIII Kerepesi út 2-4) handles most international trains as well as domestic ones from the north and northeast. For some international destinations (eg Romania), as well as domestic ones to/from the Danube Bend and Great Plain, head for **Nyugati train station** (Western Train Station; VI Nyugati tér). For trains bound for Lake Balaton and the south, go to **Déli train station** (Southern Train Station; I Krisztina körút 37). All three stations are on metro lines.

Always confirm your departure station when you buy your tickets, since stations can vary depending on the train.

ⓘ Getting Around

To/From the Airport

The cheapest (and slowest) way to get into the city centre from Ferenc Liszt International Airport is to take city bus 200E (320Ft) which terminates at the Kőbánya-Kispest metro station. From there, take the M3 metro into the city centre. Total cost: 640Ft to 720Ft.

The **Airport Shuttle Minibusz** (☎296 8555; www.airportshuttle.hu; one way/return 3200/5500Ft) ferries passengers in nine-seat vans from all three of the airport's terminals directly to the place you're staying. Tickets are available at a clearly marked desk in the arrivals hall, though you may have to wait while the van fills up.

Fő Taxi (☎222 2222; www.fotaxi.hu) has the monopoly on picking up taxi passengers at the airport. Fares to most locations in Pest are 5300Ft and in Buda 5500Ft to 6000Ft.

TRANSPORT FROM BUDAPEST

Bus

DESTINATION	PRICE (FT)	DURATION (HR)	FREQUENCY
Bratislava (Slovakia)	3400	3	1 daily
Prague (Czech Republic)	7900	7¼	1 daily
Rijeka (Croatia)	9900	8	1 weekly
Sofia (Bulgaria)	12,500	13½	1 daily
Subotica (Serbia)	3900	4½	2 daily
Vienna (Austria)	5900	3	5 daily

Train

DESTINATION	PRICE (€)	DURATION (HR)
Berlin (Germany)	95	12
Bratislava (Slovakia)	22	2½
Bucharest (Romania)	75	13-15
Frankfurt (Germany)	110	11
Lviv (Ukraine)	55	12
Ljubljana (Slovenia)	39	9
Munich (Germany)	95	10
Prague (Czech Republic)	45	7
Sofia (Bulgaria)	89	18
Zagreb (Croatia)	42	6½
Venice (Italy)	70	14
Vienna (Austria)	32	3
Warsaw (Poland)	72	12
Zürich (Switzerland)	94	12

HUNGARY BUDAPEST

Of course, you can take any taxi to the airport and several companies have a flat, discounted fare. **Rádió Taxi** (☏377 7777; www.radiotaxi.hu) charges from 4300Ft between Pest and the airport, and 4800Ft from Buda.

Public Transport

Public transport is run by **BKV** (Budapest Transport Company; ☏258 4636; www.bkv.hu). The three underground metro lines (M1 yellow, M2 red, M3 blue) meet at Deák tér in Pest; the long-awaited green M4 will open in 2014. The HÉV suburban railway runs north from Batthyány tér in Buda. Travel cards are only good on the HÉV within the city limits (south of the Békásmegyer stop).

There's also an extensive network of buses, trams and trolleybuses. Public transport operates from 4.30am until 11.30pm and some 40 night buses run along main roads. Tram 6 on the Big Ring Road now runs round the clock.

A single ticket for all forms of transport is 320Ft (60 minutes of uninterrupted travel on the same metro, bus, trolleybus or tram line *without* transferring/changing); a book of 10 tickets is 2800Ft. A transfer ticket (490Ft) is valid for one trip with one validated transfer within 90 minutes.

The three-day travel card (3850Ft) or the seven-day pass (4600Ft) make things easier, allowing unlimited travel inside the city limits. Keep your ticket or pass handy; the fine for 'riding black' is 8000Ft on the spot, or 16,000Ft if you pay later at the **BKV office** (☏461 6800; VII Akácfa utca 22; ☺6am-8pm Mon-Fri, 8am-1.45pm Sat).

Taxi

Taxi drivers overcharging foreigners in Budapest has been a problem since time immemorial. Never get into a taxi that lacks an official yellow licence plate, the logo of the taxi firm and a visible table of fares.

If you need a taxi, call one; this costs less than if you flag one down on the street. Make sure you know the number of the landline phone you're calling from, as that's how the dispatcher establishes your address (though you can call from a mobile as well). Dispatchers usually speak English.

Reliable companies include **City Taxi** (☏211 1111; www.citytaxi.hu), **Főtaxi** (☏222 2222; www.fotaxi.hu) and **Rádió Taxi** (☏377 7777; www.radiotaxi.hu). Note that rates are higher at night and in the early morning.

THE DANUBE BEND

North of Budapest, the Danube breaks through the Pilis and Börzsöny Hills in a sharp bend before continuing along the Slovak border. The Roman Empire had its northern border here and medieval kings ruled Hungary from majestic palaces overlooking the river at Esztergom and Visegrád. East of Visegrád the river divides, with Szentendre and Vác on different branches, separated by Szentendre Island. Today the easy access to historic monuments, rolling green scenery – and vast numbers of souvenir craft shops – lure many day trippers from Budapest.

❶ Getting There & Away

BUS Regular buses serve towns on the west bank of the Danube, but trains only go as far as Szentendre, with a separate line running to Esztergom; the east bank, including Vác, has excellent transport links.

BOAT The river itself is a perfect highway and regular boats ferry tourists to and from Budapest over the summer months. From May to September, a **Mahart PassNave** (www.mahartpassnave.hu) ferry departs Budapest's Vigadó tér at 10am Tuesday to Sunday bound for Szentendre (one way/return 1590/2390Ft, 1½ hours), returning at 5pm; the service runs on Saturday only in April.

Between May and late August there's a ferry from Vigadó tér at 9am, calling at Vác (one-way/return 1490/2240Ft, 11am) and Visegrád (1790/2690Ft, noon) before carrying on to Esztergom (1990/2990Ft, 1.45pm). It returns from Esztergom/Visegrád/Vác at 4.45/5.50/6.30pm, reaching Budapest at 8pm. The service is reduced to Saturday only in April and September.

Hydrofoils travel from Budapest to Visegrád (one way/return 2690/3990Ft, one hour) and Esztergom (one way/return 3990/5990Ft, 1½ hours) on Friday, Saturday and Sunday from early May to September; boats leave at 9.30am and return at 5pm from Esztergom and 5.30pm from Visegrád.

Szentendre

☏26 / POP 26,000

Once an artists' colony, now a popular day trip 19km north of Budapest, pretty little Szentendre (*sen*-ten-dreh) has narrow, winding streets and is a favourite with souvenir-shoppers. The charming old centre has plentiful cafes and galleries and there is a handful of noteworthy Serbian Orthodox churches, dating from the time when Christian worshippers fled here to escape the Turkish invaders. Expect things to get crowded in summer and at weekends. Outside town is Hungary's largest open-air village museum.

◉ Sights

Fő tér SQUARE
(Main Sq) Colourful Fő tér, the town's main square, is the best place to begin sightseeing in Szentendre. Here you'll find many buildings and monuments from the 18th and 19th centuries, including the **Memorial Cross** (1763) and the 1752 Serbian Orthodox **Blagoveštenska Church** (Blagoveštenska templom; ☏310 554; Fő tér; admission 300Ft; ◷10am-5pm Tue-Sun), with a stunning iconostasis. The pedestrian lanes surrounding the square are filled with shops sellings gift items and folkcraft.

Margit Kovács Ceramic Collection MUSEUM
(Kovács Margit Kerámiagyüjtemény; ☏310 244; www.pmmi.hu/hu/museum/6/intro; Vastagh György utca 1; adult/concession 1000/500Ft ; ◷10am-6pm) If you descend Görög utca from Fő tér and turn right onto Vastagh György utca you'll reach this museum in an 18th-century salt house, dedicated to the work of Szentendre's most famous artist. Kovács (1902–77) was a ceramicist who combined Hungarian folk, religious and modern themes to create Gothic-like figures.

Castle Hill VIEWPOINT
(Vár-domb) Castle Hill, reached via Váralja lépcső, the narrow steps between Fő tér 8 and 9, was the site of a fortress in the Middle Ages. All that's left of it today is the walled early Gothic **Church of St John the Baptist** (Keresztelő Szent János Templom; Templom tér, Vár-domb; admission free), from where you get splendid views of the town and river.

Hungarian Open-Air Ethnographical Museum MUSEUM
(Magyar Szabadtéri Néprajzi Múzeum; ☏502 500; www.skanzen.hu; Sztaravodai út; adult/student

1500/750Ft, on festival days 1600/800Ft; ⊙9am-5pm Tue-Sun Apr-Oct, 10am-4pm Sat & Sun Nov–early Dec, Feb & Mar) Just 5km northwest of Szentendre is Hungary's most ambitious *skanzen* (open-air folk museum), with farmhouses, churches, bell towers, mills and so on set up in eight regional divisions. Craftspeople and artisans do their thing on random days (generally at the weekend) from Easter to early December and the museum hosts festivals throughout the season. Reach it on bus 230 from bay/stop 7 at the bus station.

🛏 Sleeping & Eating

Seeing Szentendre on a day trip from Budapest is probably your best bet. For private rooms, visit the Tourinform (p399) office.

Mathias Rex   GUESTHOUSE **€€**
(Mathias Rex Panzió; ☑505 570; www.mathiasrexhotel.hu; Kossuth Lajos utca 16; s/d 10,000/15,000Ft, studio from 30,000Ft; ❄@) This very central *panzió* (pension or guesthouse) has a dozen rooms so clean they border on sterile, but they're of a good size. The decor is modern and minimalist, and there's a pretty courtyard and an inexpensive cellar-restaurant.

Pap-sziget Camping   CAMPGROUND **€**
(Pap-sziget Kemping; ☑310 697; www.pap-sziget.hu; small/large campsite for 2 4000/4400Ft, bungalows from 8600Ft; ⊙May–mid-Oct; @≋) This big leafy camping ground takes up most of Pap Island, some 2km north of Szentendre. Motel (6400Ft per double) and hostel (4800Ft per double) rooms are very basic, though the 'comfort bungalows' are slightly more, well, comfortable. Take bus 11 from the station.

TOP CHOICE **Promenade**   INTERNATIONAL **€€**
(☑312 626; www.promenade-szentendre.hu; Futó utca 4; mains 1850-4450Ft; ⊙11am-11pm Tue-Sun) Vaulted ceilings, whitewashed walls, a huge cellar for tasting wine and a wonderful terrace overlooking the Danube are all highlights at the Promenda, one of Szentendre's best restaurants serving 'enlightened' Hungarian and international dishes.

Erm's   HUNGARIAN **€€**
(☑303 388; www.erms.hu; Kossuth Lajos utca 22; mains 1590-3700Ft) Subtitled 'Csülök & Jazz', retro-style Erm's, with its walls festooned with early-20th-century memorabilia and simple wooden tables, is where to go for Hungarian-style pork knuckle in all its guises and live music at the weekend.

ℹ Information

Main post office (Kossuth Lajos utca 23-25)

OTP Bank (Dumtsa Jenő utca 6)

Tourinform (☑317 966; www.iranyszentendre.hu; Dumtsa Jenő utca 22; ⊙9.30am-4.30pm Mon-Fri, 10am-2pm Sat & Sun) Lots of information on Szentendre and the Bend.

DANUBE: THE DUSTLESS HIGHWAY

No other river in Europe is as evocative, or important, as the Danube. It has been immortalised in legends, tales, songs, paintings and films through the ages and has played an essential role in the cultural and economic life of millions of people since the earliest human populations settled along its banks.

Originating in Germany's Black Forest, the river cuts an unstoppable swathe through – or along the border of – 10 countries and, after more than 2800km, empties into the Black Sea in Romania. In Europe it is second only in length to the Volga (although, at 6400km, the Amazon dwarfs both) and, contrary to popular belief, is green-brown rather than blue (or 'blond', as the Hungarians say). About 2400km of its length is navigable, making it a major transport route across the continent.

Even though only 12% of the river's length is located in Hungary, the country is vastly affected by the Danube. The entire country lies within the Danube river basin and is highly prone to flooding. As early as the 16th century, large dyke systems were built for flood protection, but it's hard to stop water running where it wants to. The capital was devastated by flooding in 1775 and 1838; in 2006 the river burst its banks, threatening to fill Budapest's metro system and putting the homes of tens of thousands of people in danger. It came close to doing so again in 2009.

Despite the potential danger, the river is so loved that it actually has its own day. On 29 June every year cities along the river host festivals, family events and conferences on **Danube Day** (www.danubeday.org) in honour of the mighty river.

❶ Getting There & Away

The most convenient way to get to Szentendre is to take the HÉV suburban train from Buda's Batthyány tér metro station in central Budapest (630Ft, 40 minutes, every 10 to 20 minutes).

Vác

🎵 27 / POP 34,500

Lying on the eastern bank of the river, Vác (*vahts*) is a pretty town with interesting historic relics, from its collection of baroque town houses to its vault of 18th-century mummies. It's also the place to view glorious sunsets over the Börzsöny Hills reflected in the Danube.

Vác is an old town. Uvcenum – the town's Latin name – is mentioned in Ptolemy's 2nd-century *Geographia* as a river crossing on an important road. The town's medieval centre and Gothic cathedral were destroyed during the Turkish occupation; reconstruction under several bishops in the 18th century gave Vác its present baroque appearance.

◉ Sights

Március 15 tér   SQUARE

Vác's renovated main square has the town's most colourful buildings, including the **Town Hall** (Március 15 tér 11) from 1764, considered a baroque masterpiece. Note the statue of Justice and the seals held by the two figures on the gable – they represent Hungary and Bishop Kristóf Migazzi, the driving force behind Vác's reconstruction more than two centuries ago. In the square's centre, you'll see the entrance to a **crypt** (Március 15 tér; adult/concession 600/350Ft; ⊘2-6pm Wed-Fri, 10am-6pm Sat & Sun May-Oct), the only remnant of the medieval Church of St Michael. Tourinform (p400) holds the key.

Memento Mori   MUSEUM

(🎵500 750; Március 15 tér 19; adult/concession 1000/500Ft; ⊘10am-6pm Tue-Sun) This bizarre exhibit contains three mummies and assorted artefacts recovered from the crypt of the Dominican Church on Március 15 tér. The crypt functioned as a place of burial in the 18th century, but was later bricked up and forgotten. A cool temperature and minimal ventilation kept the bodies and clothes of the deceased in good condition for centuries. When it was rediscovered in 1994 and a total of 262 bodies were exhumed, it proved a gold mine for historians and helped to shed light on the burial practices and way of life in the 18th century.

Vác Cathedral   CHURCH

(Váci székesegyház; admission free; ⊘10am-noon & 1.30-5pm Mon-Sat, 7.30am-7pm Sun) Tree-lined Konstantin tér to the southeast of Március 15 tér is dominated by the town's colossal cathedral, which dates from 1775 and was one of the first examples of neoclassical architecture in Hungary. The frescos on the vaulted dome and the altarpiece are by celebrated artist Franz Anton Maulbertsch.

Triumphal Arch   MONUMENT

(Diadalív-kapu; Dózsa György út) North of the main square is the only such structure in Hungary. It was built by Bishop Migazzi in honour of a state visit by Empress Maria Theresa in 1764.

🛏 Sleeping & Eating

TOP CHOICE Tabán Panzió   GUESTHOUSE €€

(Alt Vendégház; 🎵06 30 910 3428, 316 860; altvendeghaz@invitel.hu; Tabán utca 25; s/d 5000/12,000Ft; ❄🛜) Staying at this small guesthouse above the Danube is like staying with nice relatives. The four rooms (No 3 has a balcony) are kitschy but cosy and there's a fully equipped kitchen and small garden for guests' use.

Fónagy & Walter   GUESTHOUSE €€

(🎵310 682; www.fonagy.hu; Budapesti főút 36; r 12,500Ft; @🛜) Fónagy & Walter is a homely little guesthouse 850m southeast of the main square. Its five suitelike rooms accommodating up to four people are overly decorated but comfortable and there's a well-stocked wine cellar.

Váci Remete Pince   HUNGARIAN €€

(🎵06 30 944 3538, 302 199; Fürdő lépcső 3; mains 1850-3290Ft) This wonderful eatery, with its covered terrace and views of the Danube, impresses with its top-notch wine selection, fine spread of Hungarian specialities and excellent service.

Duna Presszó   CAFE €

(🎵305 839; Március 15 tér 13; cakes 450Ft; ⊘9am-9pm Sun-Thu, to 10pm Fri & Sat) Duna is the quintessential cafe, with dark-wood furniture, chandeliers and excellent cake and ice cream. It's very central.

❶ Information

Main post office (Posta Park 2) Some 300m east of Március 15 tér.

OTP Bank (Széchenyi utca) In the Dunakanyar shopping centre.

Tourinform (☎316 160; www.tourinformvac. hu; Március 15 tér 17; ☺8am-5pm Mon-Fri, to 2pm Sat mid-Jun–Aug, 9am-5pm Mon-Fri, 10am-noon Sat Sep–mid-Jun) Overlooking the main square, Március 15 tér.

⊕ Getting There & Away

Car ferries (1500/430/430Ft per car/bicycle/ person, hourly 6am to 8pm) cross over to Szentendre Island; a bridge connects the island's west bank with the mainland at Tahitótfalu. From there hourly buses run to Szentendre (310Ft, 25 minutes). You can also catch half-hourly buses (560Ft, 50 minutes) and trains (650Ft, 45 minutes) from Vác to Budapest.

Visegrád

♪26 / POP 1860

The spectacular vista from what remains of the 13th-century hilltop citadel in Visegrád (*vish*-eh-grahd) is what pulls visitors to this sleepy town. The first fortress here was built by the Romans as a border defence in the 4th century. Hungarian kings constructed a mighty citadel on the hilltop, and a lower castle near the river, after the 13th-century Mongol invasions.

In the 14th century a royal palace was built on the flood plain at the foot of the hills and in 1323 King Charles Robert of Anjou, whose claim to the local throne was being fiercely contested in Buda, moved the royal household here. For nearly two centuries Hungarian royalty alternated between Visegrád and Buda.

Both the Turks and the Habsburgs played a role in the destruction of the citadel. All trace of the 350-room royal palace, situated close to the town centre, was lost until 1934 when archaeologists, by following descriptions in literary sources, uncovered the ruins that you can visit today.

The small town has two distinct areas: to the north around the Mahart PassNave ferry pier and another, the main town, about 1km to the south, near the Nagymaros ferry.

◉ Sights & Activities

Royal Palace PALACE
(Királyi Palota; ☎597 010; www.visegradmuzeum.hu; Fő utca 29; adult/concession 1100/550Ft) ☺9am-5pm Tue-Sun) The partial reconstruction of the royal palace, near the main town, only hints at the structure's former magnificence. The dozen or so rooms that can be visited are mostly the royal suites; the history of the palace and its reconstruction, along with ar-

chitectural finds such as richly carved stones dating from the 14th century, is told in an archaeological exhibition and lapidarium. To find the palace from the Mahart PassNave ferry, walk south for about 400m in the direction of the Nagymaros ferry and then turn left towards town to find Fő utca.

Solomon's Tower TOWER
(Salamon Torony; ☎398 026; adult/concession 700/350Ft; ☺9am-5pm Tue-Sun May-Sep) North of the main town and just a short walk up Görgey lépcső from the Mahart PassNave ferry port, 13th-century Solomon's Tower was once part of a lower castle used to control river traffic. These days, what's left of the stocky, hexagonal keep, with walls up to 8m thick, houses one of the palace's original Gothic fountains, along with exhibits related to town history.

Visegrád Citadel FORTRESS
(Visegrádi Fellegvár; ☎598 080; adult/child & student 1400/700Ft; ☺9am-5pm mid-Mar–Apr & Oct, to 6pm May-Sep, to 4pm Nov-Mar) Just north of Solomon's Tower, a trail marked 'Fellegvár' (Fortress) leads to Visegrád Citadel (1259) sitting atop a 350m hill and surrounded by moats hewn from solid rock. While the citadel ruins themselves are not as spectacular as their history, the **view** of the Danube Bend and the Börzsöny Hills from the walls is well worth the climb.

An alternative, less steep path leads to the citadel from the town centre area. Find the **trail** (Kálvária sétány) starting behind the Catholic church on Fő tér. You can also reach it by **City-Bus** (☎397 372; www.city-bus. hu; up to 6 people 2500Ft; ☺9am-6pm Apr-Sep) minibus in season.

⊨ Sleeping & Eating

Hotel Honti HOTEL €€
(☎398 120; www.hotelhonti.hu; Fő utca 66; hotel s/d €45/65, guesthouse s/d €40/55, campsites per person 1100Ft plus per tent/caravan 600/1200Ft; ✴@☎) This friendly establishment has seven homely rooms in its guesthouse on quiet Fő utca and 23 in the hotel facing Rte 11. The hotel's large garden and table-tennis table are for guest use, and bicycles are also available for rent (per day 2000Ft). There's now a camping ground next to the guesthouse as well.

Kovács-kert HUNGARIAN €€
(☎398 123; www.kovacs-kertetterem.hu; Rév utca 4; mains 1590-2490Ft) This adorable restaurant just up from the Nagymaros ferry pier has

a large photo menu covering a fine array of Hungarian standards and a lovely, leafy terrace.

Don Vito Pizzeria
PIZZERIA €

(☑397 230; www.donvitovisegrad.hu; Fő utca 83; pizza 990-1950Ft, pasta 1590-1890Ft; ☑) Don Vito is quite a joint for such a small town. Its collection of gangster memorabilia is impressive, as is its selection of pizzas, including vegetarian options.

❶ Getting There & Away

No train line reaches Visegrád but buses are very frequent (745Ft, 1¼ hours, hourly) to/from Budapest's Újpest-Városkapu train station, Szentendre (465Ft, 45 minutes, every 45 minutes) and Esztergom (560Ft, 45 minutes, hourly).

Esztergom

☑33 / POP 30,850

It's easy to see the attraction of Esztergom – especially from a distance. The city's massive basilica, sitting high above the town and Danube River, is an incredible sight rising magnificently from its rural setting.

But the significance of this town is even greater than its architectural appeal. The 2nd-century Roman emperor-to-be Marcus Aurelius wrote his famous *Meditations* while he camped here. In the 10th century, Stephen I, founder of the Hungarian state, was born here and crowned at the cathedral. From the late 10th to the mid-13th centuries Esztergom served as the Hungarian royal seat. In 1543 the Turks ravaged the town and much of it was destroyed, only to be rebuilt in the 18th and 19th centuries.

◉ Sights & Activities

Esztergom Basilica
CHURCH

(Esztergomi Bazilika; ☑402 354; www.bazilika-esztergom.hu; Szent István tér 1; admission free; ☺8am-6pm Apr-Sep, to 4pm Oct-Mar) The basilica, the largest church in Hungary, is on Castle Hill, and its 72m-high central dome can be seen for many kilometres around. The building of the present neoclassical church was begun in 1822 on the site of its 12th-century counterpart, which was destroyed by the Turks. The oldest part is the red-marble 1510 **Bakócz Chapel**, with splendid Italian Renaissance stone-carving and sculpture.

The **treasury** (kincstár; adult/child 800/400Ft; ☺9am-5pm Mar-Oct, 11am-4pm Tue-Sun Nov & Dec) is an Aladdin's cave of vestments and church plate in gold and silver studded with jewels. The door to the right as you enter the basilica leads to the **crypt** (altemplom; admission 200Ft; ☺9am-5pm Mar-Oct, 11am-2.45pm Nov-Feb), a series of eerie vaults down 50 steps. Among those at rest here is Cardinal József Mindszenty, who was imprisoned by the communists for refusing to allow Hungary's Catholic schools to be secularised. It's worth making the tortuous climb 400 steps up to the **cupola** (admission 600Ft; ☺9.30am-5.30pm Apr-Oct) for the outstanding views over the city.

Castle Museum
MUSEUM

(Vármúzeum; ☑415 986; www.mnmvarmuzeuma.hu; Szent István tér 1; adult/concession 1800/900Ft, courtyard only 500/250Ft; ☺10am-6pm Tue-Sun Apr-Sep, to 4pm Tue-Sun Oct-Mar) At the southern end of Castle Hill, the Castle Museum is housed in the former **Royal Palace**, which was built mostly by French architects in the 12th century during Esztergom's golden age. The museum concentrates on archaeological finds from the town and its surrounding area, the majority of which is pottery dating from the 11th century onwards.

Christian Museum
MUSEUM

(Keresztény Múzeum; ☑413 880; www.christianmuseum.hu; Berényi Zsigmond utca 2 ; adult/concession 900/450Ft; ☺10am-5pm Wed-Sun Mar-Nov)

Below Castle Hill in the picturesque riverbank Watertown (Víziváros) district is the former **Bishop's Palace**, today housing the Christian Museum with the finest collection of medieval religious art in Hungary. Don't miss the sublime Hungarian Gothic triptychs and altarpieces. From Castle Hill walk down steep Macskaút, which can be accessed from just behind the basilica.

Aquasziget
SPA

(☑511 100; www.aquasziget.hu; Táncsics Mihály utca 5; adult/child day pass 2950/1600Ft; ☺10am-8pm Mon-Fri, from 9am Sat & Sun) At the northern end of Primate Island south of Castle Hill is this enormous spa and water park with a plethora of indoor and outdoor pools, curly water slides and a full wellness centre.

🛏 Sleeping & Eating

Alabárdos Panzió
GUESTHOUSE €€

(☑312 640; www.alabardospanzio.hu; Bajcsy-Zsilinszky utca 49; s/d 8500/11,500Ft, apt from 20,100Ft; ✻☎) This mustard-yellow landmark up a small hill isn't flashy but does provide neat, tidy and sizeable accommodation in 23 rooms and apartments.

Ria Panzió
GUESTHOUSE €€

(☑06 20 938 3091, 313 115; www.riapanzio.com; Batthyány Lajos utca 11; s/d 9000/12,000Ft; ✳@중) This 11-room guesthouse in a converted town house just down from the basilica has quiet, cosy rooms, a tiny fitness centre in the wine cellar and bicycles for rent (1000Ft per day).

Gran Camping
CAMPGROUND €

(☑06 30 948 9563, 402 513; www.grancamping-fortanex.hu; Nagy-Duna sétány 3; campsites per adult/child/tent/tent & car 1400/800/1100/1400Ft, bungalows from 16,000Ft, dm/d/tr 3000/12,000/14,000Ft; ☺May-Sep; @✲) Small but centrally located on Primate Island, Gran Camping has space for 500 souls in various forms of accommodation (including a hostel with dormitory) as well as a good-sized swimming pool.

[TOP CHOICE] Padlizsán
HUNGARIAN €€

(☑311 212; Pázmány Péter utca 21; mains 1550-3000Ft) With a sheer rock face topped by a castle bastion as its courtyard backdrop, Padlizsán has a dramatic setting. And its menu doesn't let the show down either, featuring modern Hungarian dishes and imaginative salads. Soft live music most nights.

Csülök Csárda
HUNGARIAN €€€

(☑412 420; Batthyány Lajos utca 9; mains 1980-3890Ft) The 'Pork Knuckle Inn' – guess the speciality here – is a charming eatery that is popular with visitors and locals alike. It serves up good home cooking (try the bean soup, 1790Ft) and the portions are huge.

❶ Information

Cathedralis Tours (☑520 260; Bajcsy-Zsilinszky utca 26; ☺9am-6pm Mon-Fri, 9am-noon Sat (in summer)) Private travel agency can provide information.

Post office (Arany János utca 2) Enter from Széchenyi tér.

OTP Bank (Rákóczi tér 2-4)

❶ Getting There & Away

BUS Buses run to/from Budapest (930Ft, 1½ hours), Visegrád (560Ft, 45 minutes) and Szentendre (930Ft, 1½ hours) at least hourly.

TRAIN Trains depart from Budapest's Nyugati train station (1120Ft, 1½ hours) at least hourly. Cross the Mária Valéria Bridge into Štúrovo,

Slovakia, and you can catch a train to Bratislava, which is just 1½ hours away.

NORTHWESTERN HUNGARY

A visit to this region is a boon for anyone wishing to see remnants of Hungary's Roman legacy, medieval heritage and baroque splendour. Because it largely managed to avoid the Ottoman destruction of the 16th and 17th centuries, northwestern Hungary's main towns – Sopron and Győr – managed to retain their medieval cores; exploring their cobbled streets and hidden courtyards is a magical experience. Equally rewarding is the region's natural beauty.

Győr

☑96 / POP 131.300

Lying midway between Budapest and Vienna at the confluence of three rivers, Győr (*jyeur*) is a delightful city, with a medieval heart hidden behind a commercial facade. This was the site of a Roman town, Arrabona. In the 11th century, Stephen I established a bishopric here and in the 16th century a fortress was erected to hold back the Turks. The Ottomans captured Győr in 1594 but were able to hold on to it for only four years. For that reason Győr is known as the 'dear guard', watching over the nation through the centuries.

❂ Sights & Activities

Bécsi kapu tér
PUBLIC SQUARE

(Vienna Gate Square) The enchanting 1725 **Carmelite Church** (Karmelita Templom; Bécsí kapu tér) and many fine baroque palaces line riverfront Bécsí kapu tér. On the northwestern side of the square are the fortifications built in the 16th century to stop the Turks. A short distance to the east is **Napoleon House** (Király utca 4; adult/senior & student 800/400Ft; ☺10am-6pm Mon-Fri, 9am-1pm Sat), named after the French military leader.

[FREE] Basilica
CHURCH

(Bazilika; ☺8am-noon & 2-6pm) North up Káptalan-domb (Chapter Hill), in the oldest section of Győr, is the baroque Basilica. Situated on the hill, it was originally Romanesque, but most of what you see inside dates from the 17th and 18th centuries. Don't miss the Gothic **Héderváry Chapel** at the back of the cathedral, which contains the glittering 15th-century **Herm of László**, a gold bust of the eponymous king and saint.

Diocesan Treasury and Library   MUSEUM
(Egyházmegyei kincstár és könyvtár; Káptalandomb 26; adult/senior & student 800/400Ft; ☉10am-4pm Tue-Sun Mar-Oct) East of the Basilica is one of the richest collections of sacred objects in Hungary, containing Gothic chalices and Renaissance mitres embroidered with pearls. But the showstopper is the precious **library**, containing almost 70,000 volumes printed before 1850, including an 11th-century codex.

Raba Quelle   SPA
(☏514 900; www.gyortermal.hu; Fürdő tér 1; adult/child 2450/1900Ft; ☉thermal baths 9am-8.30pm Sun-Thu, to 9pm Fri & Sat year-round, pool 6am-8pm Mon-Sat year-round, open-air pool 8am-8pm May-Aug) The water temperature in the pools at this thermal spa ranges from 29°C to 38°C. You can also take advantage of its fitness and wellness centres, offering every treatment imaginable.

🛏 Sleeping & Eating

Hotel Klastrom   BOUTIQUE HOTEL €€€
(☏516 910; www.klastrom.hu; Zechmeister utca 1; s/d/tr 12,500/17,500/20,000Ft; ❀) This delightful three-star hotel occupies a 300-year-old Carmelite convent south of Bécsi kapu tér. Rooms are charming and bright, and extras include a sauna, solarium, pub with a vaulted ceiling, and a restaurant with seating in a leafy courtyard garden.

Kertész Pension   GUESTHOUSE €€
(☏317 461; www.kerteszpanzio.com; Iskola utca 11; s/d 8000/12,000Ft; ❀) The 'Gardener' has very simple rooms, but it's well located in central Győr, staff couldn't be more friendly and there's an attractive, wood-panelled bar.

Soho Café & Pension   PENSION €
(☏550 465; www.sohocafe.hu; Kenyér köz 7; s/d/tr 7000/10,000/13,000Ft; ❀) Győr's cheapest in-town pension has simple no-frills rooms and two big pluses: it's just a block from Széchenyi tér and has a ground-floor cafe with free wi-fi, friendly staff, and good coffee and beer.

TOP CHOICE La Maréda   INTERNATIONAL €€€
(☏510 982; www.lamareda.hu; Apáca utca 4; mains 2680-4850Ft) The most creative restaurant in town, La Maréda specialises in true fusion cuisine. Everything on the seasonal menu – from venison saddle with goat's cheese and spicy pumpkin cream to roast duck (pink and juicy in the middle!) with quince jelly – is expertly seasoned and presented beautifully enough to deserve the accolade 'food as art'. Yet the service is wonderfully unpretentious and attentive.

Matróz   SEAFOOD €€
(http://matroz-vendeglo.internettudakozo.hu; Dunakapu tér 3; mains 1200-2180Ft) Matróz makes the best fish dishes around, from warming carp soup to delicate pike-perch fillets. The handsome vaulted brick cellar, complete with dark-blue tiled oven and nautical memorabilia, completes this wonderful little eatery.

☆ Entertainment

A good source of information for what's on in Győr is the free magazine **Győri Est** (www.gyoriest.hu/).

Győr National Theatre   THEATRE
(Győri Nemzeti Színház; ☏box office 520 611; www.gyoriszinhaz.hu; Czuczor Gergely utca 7; ☉10am-1pm Mon-Fri, 2-6pm Tue-Fri) This modern venue is home to the celebrated **Győr Ballet** (www.gyoribalett.hu) as well as the city's opera company and philharmonic orchestra.

NAPOLEONIC PAUSE

Known only to pedants and Lonely Planet guidebook writers (until now) is the 'footnote fact' that France's Napoleon Bonaparte actually spent a night in Hungary – in Győr to be precise. The minuscule military commander slept over at Király utca 4, due east of Bécsi kapu tér, on 31 August 1809, in what is now called Napoleon-ház (Napoleon House). And why did NB choose Győr to make his grand entrée into Hungary? The city was near the site of the Battle of Raab (that's Győr in German), which had taken place just 11 weeks earlier between the Franco-Italian and Austrian-Hungarian armies. Bonaparte's side won and an inscription on the Arc de Triomphe in Paris still recalls 'la bataille de Raab'.

PANNONHALMA ABBEY

Take half a day and make the short, 20km trip from Győr to impressive **Pannonhalma Abbey** (Pannonhalmi főapátság; ☎570 191; www.bences.hu; Vár utca 1; foreign-language tours adult/student/family 2500/1500/6300Ft; ⊙9am-4pm Tue-Sun Apr & Oct–mid-Nov, 9am-5pm daily Jun-Sep, 10am-3pm Tue-Sun mid-Nov–Mar), a Unesco World Heritage Site since 1996. Most buildings in the complex date from the 13th to 19th centuries; highlights include the **Romanesque basilica and crypt** (1225), the **Gothic cloister** (1486) and the impressive collection of **ancient texts** in the library. Because it's an active monastery, the abbey must be visited with a guide. English and German tours leave at 11.20am and 1.20pm daily from May to September, with an extra tour at 3.20pm from June to September.

There are daily buses to the abbey from Győr (465Ft, 30 minutes) at 8am, 10.15am, 10.45am and noon.

❶ Information

Tourinform (☎311 771; www.gyortourism.hu; Baross Gábor utca 21-23; ⊙9am-6pm Mon-Fri, to 7pm Sat & Sun Jun-Aug, to 5pm Mon-Fri, to 1pm Sat Sep-May) Large new office with helpful staff and plenty of informative brochures.

OTP Bank (Baross Gábor utca 16)

Main post office (Bajcsy-Zsilinszky út 46; ⊙8am-6pm Mon-Fri) Opposite the Győr National Theatre.

❶ Getting There & Away

BUS Buses travel to Budapest (2520Ft, two hours, one to four daily), Pannonhalma (465Ft, 30 minutes, hourly), Esztergom (2200Ft, 2¼ hours, one daily) and Balatonfüred (2200Ft, 2½ hours, five daily).

TRAIN Győr is well connected by express train to Budapest's Keleti and Déli train stations (2520Ft, 1½ hours, half-hourly) and a dozen daily trains connect Győr with Vienna's Westbahnhof (3950Ft, 1½ hours).

Sopron

☎99 / POP 60,800

Sopron (*showp*-ron) is an attractive border town with a history that stretches back to Roman times. It boasts some well-preserved ancient ruins and a fetching medieval square, bounded by the original town walls, that invite an hour or two of aimless meandering.

The Mongols and Turks never got this far west so, unlike many Hungarian cities, numerous medieval buildings survived and are in use. The town's close history with nearby Austria goes back centuries and Sopron could easily have landed on the other side of the border if it weren't for a referendum

in 1921 in which town residents voted to remain part of Hungary. The rest of Bürgenland (the region to which Sopron used to belong) went to Austria. Once you've strolled through the quiet backstreets, have a glass or two of Kékfrancos, the local red wine.

◉ Sights & Activities

Fő tér SQUARE

Fő tér is the main square in Sopron; there are several museums, monuments and churches scattered around it, including the massive **Firewatch Tower** (Tűztorony; Fő tér), a 60m-high tower rising above the Old Town's **Fidelity Gate** (Fő tér, below Firewatch Tower) and under renovation at the time of research.

The building is a true architectural hybrid: the 2m-thick square base, built on a Roman gate, dates from the 12th century; the middle cylindrical and arcaded balcony was built in the 16th century; and the baroque spire was added in 1680. In the centre of the square is the **Trinity Column** (Szentháromság oszlop; Fő tér) from 1701, among the finest examples of a 'plague pillar' in Hungary.

Just off the square, along the town wall, are the small **open-air ruins** (Szabadtéri rom), with reconstructed Roman walls and 2nd-century houses dating from the time when Sopron was the tiny Roman outpost Scarbantia.

Storno House MUSEUM

(Storno Ház és Gyűjtemény; www.soprontourist.info/en/sopron//museums; adult/senior & student 1300/750Ft; ⊙10am-6pm Tue-Sun Apr-Sep, 2-6pm Oct-Mar) Storno House, built in 1417, was the residence of the Swiss–Italian family of Ferenc Storno, a chimney sweep turned art restorer, whose recarving of Romanesque and

Gothic monuments throughout Transdanubia divide opinions to this day. The wonderful **Storno Collection** of antiques and bric-a-brac on the 2nd floor includes much of their work. See what you think.

Fabricius House
MUSEUM

(www.soprontourist.info/en/sopron//museums; Fő tér 6; adult/senior & student 1000/500Ft; ☺10am-6pm Tue-Sun Apr-Sep, to 2pm Oct-Mar) Baroque Fabricius House was built on Roman foundations and contains an **archaeological exhibition** of Celtic, Roman and early Hungarian finds on its lower floors and a **lapidarium** of sarcophagi and reconstructed Scarbantia-era statues. Upstairs are the so-called **urban apartments**, where you can see how Sopron's burghers lived in the 17th and 18th centuries.

Goat Church
CHURCH

(Kecsketemplom; Templom utca 1; ☺7am-9pm May-Sep, 8am-6pm Mon-Sat Oct-Apr) Near the centre of Fő tér is this 13th-century Gothic church, whose name comes from the heraldic animal of its chief benefactor. Just off the main nave is the **Medieval Chapter Hall** (Középkori Káptalan Terem; ☑info 338 843; Templom utca 1; admission free; ☺10am-noon & 2-5pm mid-May–Sep), part of a 14th-century Franciscan monastery, with frescos and stone carvings.

Synagogues
JEWISH

The **Old Synagogue** (Ó Zsinagóga; Új utca 22; adult/student 700/350Ft; ☺10am-6pm Tue-Sun May-Oct) and the **New Synagogue** (Új Zsinagóga; Új utca 11), both built in the 14th century, are reminders of the town's once substantial Jewish population. The former contains a reconstructed *mikvah* (ritual bath) in the courtyard.

🛏 Sleeping & Eating

Wieden Panzió
GUESTHOUSE €€

(☑523 222; www.wieden.hu; Sas tér 13; s/d from 7000/9900Ft; 🖢) Sopron's cosiest pension is located in an attractive old town house within easy walking distance of the inner town. Rooms are spacious and bright, and the friendly staff will go out of its way to make you feel welcome.

Jégverem Fogadó
GUESTHOUSE €

(☑510 113; www.jegverem.hu; Jégverem utca 1; s/d 6900/8900Ft; 🖢) An excellent and central bet, with five suitelike rooms in an 18th-century ice cellar. Even if you're not staying here, try the terrace restaurant for enormous portions of pork, chicken and fish.

Graben
INTERNATIONAL €€

(☑340 256; www.grabenetterem.hu; Várkerület 8; mains 1690-3200Ft; ☺8am-10pm) Located in a cosy cellar near the old city walls, Graben attracts a largely Austrian clientele with its steaks, schnitzel and game dishes. Great flavours and friendly service. In summer its terrace spreads out over an inner courtyard.

Stubi
HUNGARIAN €

(Balfi utca 16; meals 600-1000Ft; ☺noon-9pm) This is very much a local place for local people. Stick with the Hungarian-style daily specials – *gulyás* (goulash), hearty cabbage and potato stew, noodles with crushed poppy seeds and so on. Portions are very large.

Liszt Salon
CAFE €

(Szent György utca 12; coffee 600Ft; ☺10am-10pm) This very stylish cafe attracts locals and tourists alike with a huge array of teas and coffees and two distinct areas – one with low, comfy couches and the other featuring upright chairs and tables. Occasional classical-music concerts.

☆ Entertainment

Ferenc Liszt Conference & Cultural Centre
PERFORMING ARTS

(☑517 517; www.prokultura.hu; Liszt Ferenc utca 1; ☺9am-5pm Mon-Fri, to noon Sat) A theatre, concert hall, casino and restaurant all rolled into one. The information desk has the latest on classical music and other cultural events in Sopron.

Petőfi Theatre
THEATRE

(☑517 517; www.prokultura.hu; Petőfi tér 1) This beautiful theatre with national Romantic-style mosaics on the front facade is Sopron's leading theatre.

❶ Information

Main post office (Széchenyi tér 7-8)

OTP Bank (Várkerület 96/a)

Tourinform (☑517 560; sopron@tourinform. hu; Liszt Ferenc utca 1, Ferenc Liszt Conference & Cultural Centre; ☺9am-6pm Mon-Fri, to 7pm Sat-Sun mid-Jun–Aug, shorter hours rest of year) Free internet access and a plethora of information on Sopron and the surrounding area, including local vintners.

❶ Getting There & Away

BUS Bus travel to/from Budapest involves lengthy transfers/changes in cities like Veszprém and Székesfehérvár and is not recommended. There are hourly buses to Győr

(1680Ft, 2½ hours) and two a day to Balaton-füred (3130Ft, four hours).

TRAIN Trains run to Budapest's Keleti train station (4200Ft, three hours, eight daily) via Győr. Local trains run to Wiener Neustadt (2800Ft, 40 minutes, hourly) in Austria, where you change for Vienna.

Lake Balaton

Central Europe's largest expanse of fresh water is Lake Balaton, covering 600 sq km. The main activities here include swimming, sailing and sunbathing, but the lake is also popular with cyclists lured here by more than 200km of marked bike paths that encircle the lake.

The southern shore is mostly a forgettable jumble of tacky resorts, with its centre at Siófok. The northern shore, however, is yin to the southern coast's yang. Here the pace of life is more refined and the forested hills of Balaton Uplands National Park create a wonderful backdrop. Historical towns such as Keszthely and Balatonfüred dot the landscape, while Tihany, a peninsula cutting the lake almost in half, is home to an important historical church.

BALATONFÜRED
🖉 87 / POP 13,600

Balatonfüred (*bal*-ah-ton fuhr-ed) is the oldest and most fashionable resort on the lake. In its glory days in the 19th century the wealthy and famous built large villas along its tree-lined streets, hoping to take advantage of the health benefits of the town's thermal waters. More recently, the lake frontage received a massive makeover and now sports the most stylish marina on Balaton. The hotels here are a bit cheaper than those on the neighbouring Tihany peninsula, making this a good base for exploring.

◉ Sights & Activities

Gyógy tér   SQUARE
(Cure Sq; Gyógy tér) This leafy square is the heart of the Balatonfüred spa. In the centre is **Kossuth Pump House** (1853), which dispenses slightly sulphuric, but drinkable, thermal water. This is as close as you'll get to the hot spring; the mineral baths are reserved for patients of the **State Hospital of Cardiology** on the eastern side of the square.

On the northern side is the **Balaton Pantheon** (Gyógy tér), with memorial plaques from those who took the cure at the hospital, while on the western side is the late

baroque **Horváth House** (Gyógy tér 3), the site of the first **Anna Ball** (www.annabal.hu; Anna Grand Hotel; tickets from Ft 25,000) – the town's red-letter annual event – in 1825. It's now held at the **Anna Grand Hotel** (🖉342 044; www.annagrandhotel.eu; Gyógy tér 1; s/d from 25,000/35,000Ft; ❀@✿☎⌂) every year on 26 July.

Public Beaches   BEACH
Balatonfüred's most accessible grassy beaches, measuring about a kilometre in length, are **Eszterházy Strand** (www.balatonfuredistrandok.hu; Tagore sétány; adult/child 900/540Ft; ⊘8.30am-7pm mid-Jun–mid-Aug, 8.30am-7pm mid-May–mid-Jun & mid-Aug–mid-Sep), with a water park right in town, and the more attractive **Kisfaludy Strand** (www.balatonfuredistrandok.hu; Aranyhíd sétány; adult/child 640/400Ft; ⊘8.30am-7pm mid-Jun–mid-Aug, 8.30am-7pm mid-May–mid-Jun & mid-Aug–mid-Sep) along the footpath about 800m northeast of the pier. Many beaches along the lake are `managed' – that is, keep opening hours and charge admission. Facilities almost always include changing rooms and showers.

Cruises   CRUISE
The park along the central shore, near the ferry pier, is worth a promenade. You can take a one-hour **pleasure cruise** (🖉342 230; www.balatonihajozas.hu; ferry pier; adult/concession 1500/6500Ft) four or five times a day, from late April to mid-September. The **retro disco boat** (Disco Hajo; 🖉342 230; www.balatonihajozas.hu; ferry pier; cruise 1900Ft), a two-hour cruise with music and drinks, leaves at 9pm Monday and Wednesday to Saturday.

🛏 Sleeping

Prices fluctuate throughout the year and usually peak between early July and late August. There are lots of houses with rooms for rent on the streets north of Kisfaludy Strand. Tourinform (p408) can help find private rooms from roughly 4000Ft per person per night.

Hotel Blaha Lujza   HOTEL €€
(🖉581 219; www.hotelblaha.hu; Blaha Lujza utca 4; s 11,000Ft, d 16,000-18,000Ft; ❀☎) This small hotel's 20 rooms are a little compact and very comfy. This was the summer home of the much-loved 19th-century actress-singer Lujza Blaha from 1893 to 1916.

Balaton Villa   HOTEL €€
(🖉788 290; www.balatonvilla.hu; Deák Ferenc utca 38; s/d 6400/13,000Ft; ❀☎) The nine rooms at

this pastel-yellow villa uphill from the lake are large and bright. Each has its own balcony overlooking a sunny garden and grape vines, and guests can make use of a well-equipped kitchen and grill area.

Füred Camping
CAMPGROUND €

(☏580 241; fured@balatontourist.hu; Széchenyi utca 24; campsite per adult/child/tent 1600/1200/5500Ft, bungalows/caravans from 17,000/23,000Ft; ☺mid-Apr–early Oct; @) This is one of the the largest camping grounds on the lake and has direct access to the water. Bungalows sleep up to four people.

✕ Eating & Drinking

La Riva
ITALIAN €€€

(☏06 20 391 4039; http://larivaristorante.hu; Zákonyi Ferenc sétány 4; mains 2000-4500Ft) Taking pride of place on the modern marina's waterfront is this imaginative restaurant. Pasta and pizza are the mainstays, but don't overlook the daily specials.

Balaton
HUNGARIAN €€

(Kisfaludy utca 5; mains 1800-3000Ft) This cool, leafy oasis amid all the hubbub is set back from the lake in the shaded park area. It serves generous portions and has an extensive fish selection.

Kedves
CAFE

(Blaha Lujza utca 7; cakes 400-650Ft) Join fans of Lujza Blaha and take coffee and cake at the cafe where the famous 19th-century actress-singer used to while away the hours. It's also appealing for its location, away from the madd(en)ing crowds.

① Information

Post office (Zsigmond utca 14)

OTP Bank (Petőfi Sándor utca 8)

Tourinform (☏580 480; balatonfured@ tourinform.hu; Blaha Lujza utca 5; ☺9am-7pm Mon-Fri, to 6pm Sat, to 1pm Sun Jul & Aug, 9am-5pm Mon-Fri, to 1pm Sat Jun & Sep, 9am-4pm Mon-Fri Oct-May) Well-stocked and well-run tourist office.

① Getting There & Around

The adjacent bus and train stations are on Dobó István utca, about 1km uphill from the lake. Buses to Tihany (310Ft, 30 minutes) leave every 30 minutes or so throughout the day. Several buses daily head to the northwestern lakeshore towns including Keszthely (1300Ft, 1½ hours, seven daily).

Buses and trains to Budapest (2520Ft, 2½ hours) are much of a muchness but the former are more frequent.

From April to October half a dozen daily ferries ply the water from Balatonfüred to Tihany (1100Ft, 30 minutes).

TIHANY
☑87 / POP 1350

The place with the greatest historical significance on Lake Balaton is Tihany (tee-haw-nee), a hilly peninsula jutting 5km into the lake. Activity here is centred on the tiny town of the same name, which is home to the celebrated Abbey Church. Contrasting with this are the hills and marshy meadows of the peninsula's nature reserve, which has an isolated, almost wild feel to it. It's ideal for hiking and birdwatching.

◉ Sights & Activities

ᴛᴏᴘ⌐CHOICE Abbey Church
CHURCH

(Bencés Apátság templom; http://tihany.osb. hu; András tér 1; adult/concession incl museum 1000/500Ft; ☺9am-6pm May-Sep, 10am-5pm Apr & Oct, 10am-3pm Nov-Mar) You can spot the twin-towered ochre-coloured Benedictine Abbey Church (1754) from a long way off. The nave is filled with fantastic altars, pulpits and screens carved in the mid-18th century by an Austrian lay brother and all are baroque-rococo masterpieces in their own right. Entombed in the **Romanesque crypt** is the abbey's founder, King Andrew I. Admission includes entry to the attached **Benedictine Abbey Museum** (Bencés Apátsági Múzeum; admission incl with Abbey Church entry fee; ☺9am-6pm May-Sep, 10am-5pm Apr & Oct, 10am-3pm Nov-Mar) Behind the church a path leads to a lookout with outstanding views.

Hiking
HIKING

Hiking is one of Tihany's main attractions; there's a good map outlining the colour-coded trails in the centre of the village at Kossuth Lajos utca and András tér. Following the Green Trail northeast of the village centre for an hour will bring you to the **Russian Well** (Oroszkút) and the ruins of the **Old Castle** (Óvár) at 219m, where Russian Orthodox monks, brought to Tihany by Andrew I, hollowed out cells in the soft basalt walls.

ᴋ Sleeping & Eating

Kántás Panzió
GUESTHOUSE €€

(☏448 072; www.kantas-panzio-tihany.hu; Csokonai út 49; r 13,000Ft; ※❀⊛) Kántás is a fine example of Tihany's cheaper accommodation. It's small and personal, with pleasant attic rooms (some with balcony) above a restaurant. Views are across the inner lake.

Adler
BOUTIQUE HOTEL €€€
(☑538 000; www.adler-tihany.hu; Felsőkopaszhegyi utca 1/a; r 14,700-16,900Ft, apt 29,700-32,400Ft; ✳🛜🌊) Adler counts 13 large, whitewashed rooms with balconies; good for families and also has a jacuzzi, sauna and restaurant.

【TOP CHOICE】 Ferenc Pince
HUNGARIAN €€
(☑448 575; Cserhegy 9; mains from 2500Ft; ⊙noon-11pm, closed Tue) About 2km south of the Abbey Church, Ferenc is a wine- and food-lover's dream. During the day, its terrace offers expansive views of the lake, while at night the lights of the southern shore are visible.

Rege Café
CAFE €
(Kossuth Lajos utca 22; cakes from 350Ft; ⊙10am-6pm) From its high vantage point near the Benedictine Abbey Museum, this modern cafe has an unsurpassed panoramic view of the Balaton.

❶ Information
Tihany Tourist (☑448 481; www.tihanytourist.hu; Kossuth Lajos utca 11; ⊙9am-5pm May-Sep, 10am-4pm Apr & Oct) Organises accommodation and local tours.
Tourinform (☑448 804; tihany@tourinform.hu; Kossuth Lajos utca 20; ⊙9am-7pm Mon-Fri, 10am-5pm Sat & Sun mid-Jun–mid-Sep, shorter hours rest of year) Central.

❶ Getting There & Away
Buses travel along the 14km of mostly lakeside road between Tihany village and Balatonfüred's train and bus stations (310Ft, 30 minutes) throughout the day.

From April to October, half a dozen daily ferries ply the water from Balatonfüred to Tihany (1100Ft, 30 minutes). You can follow a steep path up to the village from the pier to reach the Abbey Church.

KESZTHELY
☑83 / POP 21,000
At the very western end of the lake sits Keszthely (*kest*-hey), a place of grand town houses and a gentle ambience far removed from the lake's tourist hot spots. Its small, shallow beaches are well suited to families, and the lavish Festetics Palace is a must-see.

The beaches and the ferry pier lie to the southeast through a small park. The main commercial centre, where everything happens, is about 500m north of the bus and train stations uphill, along the main street, Kossuth Lajos utca.

◉ Sights & Activities

【TOP CHOICE】 Festetics Palace
PALACE
(Festetics Kastély; ☑312 190; www.helikonkastely.hu; Kastély utca 1; Palace & Coach Museum adult/concession 2300/1150Ft; ⊙9am-9pm Jul & Aug, 10am-4pm May, Jun & Sep, reduced hours & closed Mon Oct-Apr) The glimmering white, 100-room Festetics Palace was first built in 1745; the wings were extended out from the original building 150 years later. About a dozen rooms in the baroque south wing have been turned into the **Helikon Palace Museum** (Helikon Kastélymúzeum). Many of the decorative arts in the gilt salons were imported from England in the mid-1800s.

Also here is the palace's greatest treasure, the renowned **Helikon Library** (Helikon Könyvtár), with its 100,000 volumes and splendid carved furniture. Behind the palace in a separate building is the **Coach Museum** (Hintómúzeum; adult/concession 1000/500Ft; ⊙9am-9pm Jul & Aug, 10am-4pm May, Jun & Sep, reduced hours & closed Mon Oct-Apr), which is filled with coaches and sleighs fit for royalty.

Lakeside Area
BEACH
Keszthely's best beaches for swimming or sunbathing are **City Beach** (Városi Strand; adult/child 890/630Ft, 3 days 1800/1300Ft; ⊙8am-6pm mid-May–mid-Sept), which is close to the ferry pier and good for kids, and reedy **Helikon Beach** (Helikon Strand; adult/child 500/350Ft, 3 days 1050/840Ft; ⊙8am-6pm mid-May–mid-Sept) further south. There's windsurfing and kitesurfing rental at City Beach in summer. Many beaches keep opening hours and charge admission. Facilities almost always include changing rooms and showers.

You can take a one-hour **pleasure cruise** (☑312 093; www.balatonihajozas.hu; ferry pier; ⊙adult/concession 1500/650Ft) several times daily from late March to late October. In high season there are up to seven sailings a day.

🛏 Sleeping
Tourinform (p410) can help find private rooms (from 3500Ft per person). Otherwise, strike out on your own (particularly along Móra Ferenc utca) and keep an eye out for '*szoba kiadó*' or '*zimmer frei*' signs (Hungarian and German, respectively, for 'room for rent').

TOP CHOICE **Bacchus** HOTEL €€€

(☎510 450; www.bacchushotel.hu; Erzsébet királyné utca 18; s 13,500Fr, d 16,900-25,000Ft; apt 27,000Ft; ❋@🗣) Bacchus' central position and immaculate rooms make it a popular choice with travellers. Equally pleasing is its atmospheric cellar, which includes a lovely restaurant with wine tastings.

Tokajer GUESTHOUSE €€

(Tokaji Panzió Keszthely; ☎319 875; www. pensiontokajer.hu; Apát utca 21; s/d/apt from 9200/15,000/18,000Ft; ❋@🗣🏊) Spread over four buildings in a quiet part of town, the Tokajer – its German name – has slightly dated rooms, but they're spacious and some have a balcony. Extras include two pools, a wellness centre and fitness room, and free use of bicycles.

Ambient Hostel HOSTEL €

(☎06 30 460 3536; http://keszthely-szallas.fw.hu; Sopron utca 10; dm/d from 3600/7900Ft; @) Only a short walk north of Festetics Palace is this hostel with basic, cheap dorm rooms, each of which comes with its own bathroom. Ambient also has a colourful, modern roadside cafe.

✕ **Eating & Drinking**

TOP CHOICE **Margareta** HUNGARIAN €

(www.margaretaetterem.hu; Bercsényi utca 60; mains 1400-3200Ft; ⊙11am-10pm) Margareta is no beauty, but the wraparound porch and hidden backyard terrace is heaving in the warmer months and the small interior packs them in the rest of the year. Food sticks to the basic but hearty Hungarian staples, but be warned: portions are huge.

Pelso Café CAFE

(Fő tér; coffee & cake from 300Ft; ⊙10am-10pm; 🗣) This modern two-level cafe at the southern end of the main square does decent coffee and cake as well as cocktails. Wonderful terrace.

☆ **Entertainment**

Festetics Palace CLASSICAL MUSIC

(Festetics Kastély; ☎312 190; www.helikonkastely. hu; Kastély utca 1; ⊙8pm Thu) Classical-music concerts are held every Thursday throughout the year in the music hall of the palace.

🛈 **Information**

OTP Bank (Kossuth Lajos utca 38)

Tourinform (☎314 144; keszthely@tourinform. hu; Kossuth Lajos utca 28; ⊙9am-8pm Mon-Fri, to 6pm Sat mid-Jun–mid-Sep, 9am-5pm Mon-Fri, to 12.30pm Sat mid-Sep–mid-Jun) Excellent source of information on Keszthely and the lake.

🛈 **Getting There & Away**

BUS Buses from Keszthely run to destinations including Balatonfüred (1300Ft, 1½ hours, seven daily) and Budapest (3410Ft, three hours, seven daily).

TRAIN Keszthely is on a railway branch line linking the lake's southeastern shore with Budapest (3410Ft, four hours, six daily). To reach towns along Lake Balaton's northern shore by train, you have to change at Tapolca (465Ft, 30 minutes, hourly).

SOUTH CENTRAL HUNGARY

Southern Hungary is a region of calm; a place to savour life at a slower pace. It's only marginally touched by tourism, and touring

---

WORTH A TRIP

HÉVÍZ

Hévíz (population 4335), just 8km northwest of Keszthely, is the most famous of Hungary's spa towns because of the **Gyógy-tó** (Hévíz Thermal Lake; ☎501 700; www.spaheviz.hu; 3hr/5hr/whole day 2500/2800/3800Ft; ⊙8am-7pm Jun-Aug, 9am-6pm May & Sep, 9am-5pm Apr & Oct, 9am-4pm Mar & Nov-Feb) – Europe's largest 'thermal lake'. A dip into this water lily-filled lake is essential for anyone visiting the Lake Balaton region.

It's an astonishing sight: a surface of almost 4.5 hectares in the Park Wood, covered for most of the year in pink and white lotuses. The source is a spring spouting from a crater some 40m below ground that disgorges up to 80 million L of warm water a day, renewing itself every 48 hours or so. The surface temperature averages 33°C and never drops below 22°C in winter, allowing bathing throughout the year, even when there's ice on the fir trees. Do as the locals do and rent a rubber ring (600Ft) and just float.

A covered bridge leads to the thermal lake's *fin-de-siècle* central pavilion, which contains a small buffet, sun chairs, showers, changing rooms and steps down into the lake.

Buses link Hévíz with Keszthely (250Ft, 15 to 20 minutes) almost every half-hour.

through the countryside is like travelling back in time. Passing through the region, you'll spot whitewashed farmhouses whose thatched roofs and long colonnaded porticoes decorated with floral patterns seem unchanged over the centuries.

Historically, the area bordering Croatia and Serbia has often been 'shared' between Hungary and these countries, and is here that the remnants of the 150-year Turkish occupation can be most strongly felt.

The region is bounded by the Danube River to the east, the Dráva River to the south and west, and Lake Balaton to the north. It's generally flat, with the Mecsek and Villány Hills rising in isolation from the plain. The weather always seems to be a few degrees warmer here than in other parts of the country; the sunny clime is great for grape-growing and oak-aged Villány reds are well regarded.

Pécs

☑ 72 / POP 157,700

Blessed with a mild climate, an illustrious past and a number of fine museums and monuments, Pécs *(paich)* is one of the most pleasant and interesting cities to visit in Hungary. For those reasons and more – a handful of universities, the nearby Mecsek Hills, a lively nightlife and excellent wines – many travellers put it second only to Budapest on their Hungary must-see list.

The Roman settlement of Sopianae in what is now Pécs was the capital of the province of Lower Pannonia for 400 years. Christianity flourished here as early as the 4th century and in 1009 Stephen I made Pécs a bishopric. The Mongols swept through here in 1241, prompting the authorities to build massive city walls, parts of which are still standing. The Turkish occupation began in 1543 and lasted nearly a century and a half, lending Pécs an Ottoman patina that's immediately visible at the Mosque Church that stands at the heart of the city's main square.

◉ Sights & Activities

The city's main sights are clustered in three areas: Széchenyi tér, with the Mosque Church; Dóm tér (dominated by the Basilica of St Peter); and Káptalan utca, Pécs' 'museum street'.

TOP
CHOICE **Mosque Church** MOSQUE
(Mecset templom; Széchenyi tér; adult/concession 750/500Ft; ⊙10am-4pm mid-Apr–mid-Oct, to noon mid-Oct–mid-Apr, shorter hours Sun) The erstwhile Pasha Gazi Kassim Mosque is now the Inner Town Parish Church (Belvárosi plébánia templom), but it's more commonly referred to as the Mosque Church. It is the largest building still standing in Hungary from the time of the Turkish occupation and the very symbol of the city.

Synagogue SYNAGOGUE
(Zsinagóga; Kossuth tér; adult/concession 600/400Ft; ⊙10am-noon & 12.45-5pm Sun-Fri May-Oct) Pécs' beautifully preserved 1869 synagogue is south of Széchenyi tér.

Zsolnay Porcelain Museum MUSEUM
(Zsolnay Porcélan Múzeum; Káptalan utca 2; adult/concession 1200/600Ft; ⊙10am-5pm Tue-Sun) From the northern end of Széchenyi tér, climb Szepessy Ignéc utca and turn left (west) onto Káptalan utca, a street lined with museums and galleries. The Zsolnay Porcelain Museum is on the eastern end of this strip. English translations provide a good history of the artistic and functional ceramics produced from this local factory's illustrious early days in the mid-19th century to the present time. The museum was once the home of the Zsolnay family and contains many original furnishings and personal effects.

Basilica of St Peter CHURCH
(Szent Péter bazilika; Dóm tér; adult/concession 900/600Ft; ⊙9am-5pm Mon-Sat, 1-5pm Sun) The foundations of the four-towered basilica dedicated to St Peter date from the 11th century and the side chapels are from the 1300s. But most of what you see today of the neo-Romanesque structure is the result of renovations carried out in 1881. The 1770 **Bishop's Palace** (Püspöki palota; ☑ 513 030; Szent István tér 23; adult/child 1900/1000Ft; ⊙tours 2pm, 3pm & 4pm Thu late Jun–mid-Sep) is southwest of the cathedral. Also near the square is a 15th-century **barbican** (Barbakán; Esze Tamás utca 2; ⊙garden 7am-8pm May-Sep, 9am-5pm Oct-Apr), the only stone bastion to survive from the old city walls.

Cella Septichora
Visitors Centre RUINS
(Cella Septichora látogatóközpont; www.pecsorokseg.hu; Janus Pannonius utca; adult/concession 1200/600Ft; ⊙10am-6pm Tue-Sun) On the

Pécs

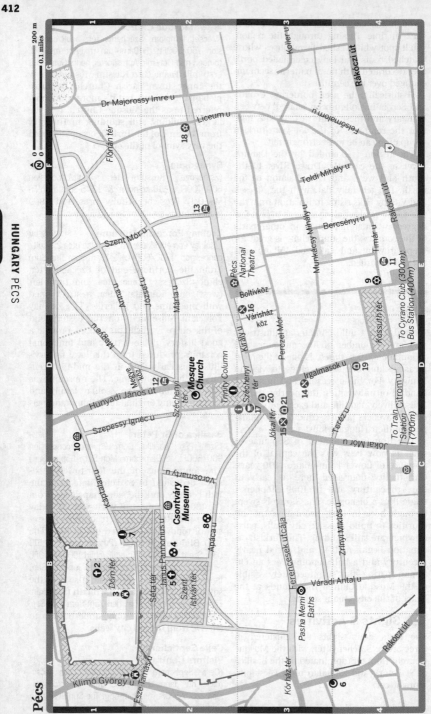

200 m
0.1 miles

Dr Majorossy Imre u

Liceum u

Flórián tér

18

Koller u

Rákóczi út

6

Felsőmalom u

Toldi Mihály u

Szent Mór u

13

Bercsényi u

Munkácsy Mihály u

Timár u

Rákóczi út

Anna u

József u

Mária u

Pécs National Theatre

Boltívköz

11

To Cyrano Club (300m);
Bus Station (400m)

Megye köz

12

Mosque Church

Trinity Column

Király u

Várisház köz

16

Perczel Mór u

9

Kossuth tér

Hunyadi János út

Széchenyi tér

Szepessy Ignác u

Irgalmasok u

14

20

19

Citrom u

10

Vörösmarty u

Jókai tér

17

21

15

Teréz u

To Train Station (700m)

Csontváry Museum

Apáca u

8

Jókai Mór u

Kaptalan u

Janus Pannonius u

Séta tér

Ferencesek utcája

Zrínyi Miklós u

Dóm tér

2

3

4

Szent István tér

5

7

Pasha Memi Baths

Váradi Antal u

Klimó György u

Esze Tamás u

Kórház tér

6

Rákóczi út

Pécs

southern side of Dom tér is the Cella Septichora Visitors Centre, which illuminates a series of early Christian burial sites that have been on Unesco's World Heritage list since 2000. The highlight is the so-called **Jug Mausoleum** (Korsós sírkamra; adult/child 300/150Ft; ☉10am-6pm Tue-Sun), a 4th-century Roman tomb whose name comes from a painting of a large drinking vessel with vines.

Early Christian Tomb Chapel   CHURCH
(Ókeresztény sírkápolna; Szent István tér 12; adult/concession 500/300Ft; ☉10am-6pm Tue-Sun) This early Christian tomb chapel dates from about AD 350 and has frescos of Adam and Eve and Daniel in the lion's den. Two **Roman tomb sites** (Apáca utca 8 & 14; adult/child/family 450/250/850Ft; ☉10am-5pm Tue-Sun) containing 110 graves from the same era are a little further south.

TOP CHOICE Csontváry Museum   MUSEUM
(☎310 544; Janus Pannonius utca 11; adult/child 1500/750Ft; ☉10am-6pm, closed Mon) The Csontváry Museum shows the major works of the 19th-century painter Tivadar Kosztka Csontváry (1853–1919), a unique symbolist artist whose tragic life is often compared with that of his great contemporary, Vincent Van Gogh.

Hassan Jakovali Mosque   MOSQUE
(Hassan Jakovali mecset; Rákóczi utca; adult/concession 600/300Ft; ☉9.30am-6pm Wed-Sun late Mar-Oct) Though wedged between two modern buildings, this 16th-century mosque is more intact than its larger cousin, the Mosque Church, and comes complete with a **minaret**. There's a small **exhibition** on the Ottomans in Hungary inside.

🛏 Sleeping

In July and August more than a dozen of the city's colleges open up their doors to travellers, and prices average 4000Ft to 6000Ft for a dorm bed; Tourinform (p414) has the complete list.

Hotel Fönix   HOTEL €€
(☎311 682; www.fonixhotel.hu; Hunyadi János út 2; s/d from 8200/14,000Ft; ✸@ 🖣) Fönix appears to be a hotel too large for the land it's built on and some of the 16 rooms and suites are not even big enough to swing a, well, phoenix in. Try to bag a room with a balcony; the Mosque Church is just within reach.

Hotel Diána   GUESTHOUSE €€
(☎328 594; www.hoteldiana.hu; Tímár utca 4/a; s/d/tr from 11,350/16,350/20,350Ft; ✸🖣) This very central hotel-cum-guesthouse offers 20 spotless rooms, comfortable kick-off-your-shoes decor and a warm welcome.

Nap Hostel   HOSTEL €
(☎950 684; www.naphostel.com; Király utca 23-25; dm/d from 2800/12,350Ft; @🖣) Clean, friendly hostel with dorms and a double room on the 1st floor of a former bank. There's also a large kitchen. Enter from Szent Mór utca.

✕ Eating & Drinking

Pubs, cafes and fast-food eateries line pedestrian-only Király utca. Another good bet is tiny and more intimate Jókai tér.

TOP CHOICE Enoteca & Bistro Corso
INTERNATIONAL €€€

(☑525 198; www.enotecapecs.hu; Király utca 14; mains 3200-5500Ft) One of Hungary's top restaurants, Corso offers dining on two levels: the top features refined Hungarian cooking with Italian and French influences, while the ground floor is slightly less expensive but equally good. The alfresco terrace is also a popular spot for snacks and drinks in the warmer months.

Áfium
BALKAN €

(☑511 434; Irgalmasok utca 2; mains 1500-2200Ft; ⊘11am-1am) With Croatia and Serbia so close, it's a wonder that more restaurants don't offer cuisine from south of the border. Don't miss the bean soup with trotters. Weekday set lunch is just 520Ft.

Az Elefánthoz
ITALIAN €€

(☑216 055; www.elefantos.hu; Jókai tér 6; mains 2600-4500Ft, pizza 1400-2600Ft) With its welcoming terrace overlooking Jókai tér and quality Italian dishes, this place is a sure bet for first-rate food in the centre. It has a wood-fired stove for pizzas, though the pasta dishes are also worth a try.

Coffein Café
CAFE

(Széchenyi tér 9; ⊘8am-midnight Mon-Thu, to 2am Fri & Sat, 10am-10pm Sun; ☏) For the best views across Széchenyi tér to the Mosque Church and Király utca, find a perch at this cool cafe, which is done up in the warmest of colours.

☆ Entertainment

Pécs has well-established opera and ballet companies as well as a symphony orchestra. Tourinform has schedule information. The free biweekly PécsiEst (www.pecsiest.hu) also lists what's on around town.

Cyrano Club
CLUB

(Czindery utca 6; men 800-1200Ft, women free; ⊘8pm-5am Fri & Sat) A big club, popular with a big-haired, big-nailed crowd that's been around for ages.

Varázskert
CLUB

(Király utca 65; ⊘6pm-3am summer) Big open-air beer garden and late-hours music club at the far end of Király utca.

🛍 Shopping

Pécs has been known for its leatherwork since Turkish times and you can pick up a few bargains in several shops around the city, including Blázek (☑332 460; Teréz utca 1), which deals mainly in handbags and wallets. Corvina Art Bookshop (☑310 427; Széchenyi tér 7-8) stocks English-language books and guides and Zsolnay (☑310 220; Jókai tér 2) has a porcelain outlet south of Széchenyi tér. About 3km southwest of town, a Sunday flea market (Vásártér; Megyeri út; ⊘8am-3pm Sun) attracts people from around the region.

ℹ Information

Tourinform (☑213 315; baranya-m@tourinform.hu; Széchenyi tér 9; ⊘9am-5pm Mon-Fri & 10am-3pm Sat & Sun Jun-Aug, closed Sun May, Sep & Oct, closed Sat & Sun Nov-Apr) Knowledgeable staff, copious information on Pécs and region.

Main post office (Jókai Mór utca 10) In a beautiful art nouveau building (1904) south of Széchenyi tér.

ℹ Getting There & Away

BUS Some five buses a day connect Pécs with Budapest (3010Ft, 4½ hours), eight with Szeged (3010Ft, 4½ hours) and two with Kecskemét (3010Ft, 4½ hours).

TRAIN Pécs is on a main rail line with Budapest's Déli train station (3950Ft, three hours, nine daily). One daily train runs from Pécs to Eszék in Croatia (the town is called Osijek in Croatia; two hours), with continuing service to the Bosnian capital, Sarajevo (nine hours).

SOUTHEASTERN HUNGARY

Like the outback for Australians or the Wild West for Americans, the Nagy Alföld (Great Plain) holds a romantic appeal for Hungarians. Many of these notions come as much from the collective imagination, paintings and poetry as they do from history, but there's no arguing the spellbinding potential of big-sky country – especially around Hortobágy and Kiskunság National Parks. The Great Plain is home to cities of graceful architecture and history. Szeged is a centre of art and culture, Kecskemét is full of art nouveau gems and Debrecen is 'the Calvinist Rome'.

Kecskemét

📱76 / POP 107,000

Located about halfway between Budapest and Szeged, Kecskemét (*kech*-kah-mate) is a green, pedestrian-friendly city with delightful art nouveau architecture, many fine museums and the region's excellent *barackpálinka* (apricot brandy). And Kiskunság National Park is right at the back door. Day-trip opportunities include hiking in the sandy, juniper-covered hills, a horse show at Bugac or a visit to one of the area's many horse farms.

◎ Sights

Kossuth tér SQUARE

(P) Kossuth tér is dominated by the massive 1897 art nouveau **City Hall** (📱513 513, ext 2263; Kossuth tér 1; admission free; ⊘by arrangement), which is flanked by the baroque **Great Church** (Nagytemplom; 📱487 501; Kossuth tér 2; ⊘9am-noon year-round plus 3-6pm May-Sep, closed Mon) and the earlier **Franciscan Church of St Nicholas** (Szent Miklós Ferences

Templom; 📱497 025; Lestár tér), parts of which date from the 13th century. Nearby is the magnificent 1896 **József Katona Theatre** (Katona József Színház; Katona József tér 5), a neobaroque venue with a statue of the **Holy Trinity** (1742) in front of it.

Ornamental Palace ARCHITECTURE

(Cifrapalota; Rákóczi út 1) The masterful art-nouveau-style Ornamental Palace, which dates from 1902, has multicoloured majolica tiles decorating its 'waving' walls. The palace contains the **Kecskemét Gallery** (Kecskeméti Képtár; 📱480 776; www.museum.hu/kecskemet/keptar; adult/concession 500/270Ft; ⊘10am-5pm Tue-Sun). Its collection of 20th-century Hungarian art is important, but visit mainly to see the aptly named **Decorative Hall** (Díszterem) and its amazing stuccowork and colourful tiles.

Hungarian Folk Craft Museum MUSEUM

(Népi Iparmüvészeti Múzeum; 📱327 203; www.nepiiparmuveszet.hu; Serfőző utca 19/a; adult/concession 500/250Ft; ⊘10am-5pm Tue-Sat Mar-Oct,

HUNGARY KECSKEMÉT

WORTH A TRIP

KISKUNSÁG NATIONAL PARK

Totalling more than 76,000 hectares, **Kiskunság National Park** (Kiskunsági Nemzeti Park; www.knp.hu) consists of nine 'islands' of protected land. Much of the park's alkaline ponds and sand dunes are off limits. Bugac (*boo*-gats) village (population 2850), 30km southwest of Kecskemét, is the most accessible part of the park.

The highlight of a trip here is a chance to see a popular **cowboy show** (csikósbemutató; www.bugacpuszta.hu; admission 1400Ft; ⊘12.15pm May-Oct), where the horse herders race one another bareback and ride 'five-in-hand', a breathtaking performance in which one *csikós* (cowboy) gallops five horses at full speed while standing on the backs of the back two.

There are also several nature and educational **hiking trails** in the vicinity, with explanatory sign-posting in English, where you can get out and see this amazing ecosystem of dunes, bluffs and swamps.

Getting to the show without your own vehicle is difficult. There's a morning bus from Kecskemét to Bugac (745Ft, one hour, 37km) but it won't get you there in time for the 12.15pm show. (Buses before that leave at an ungodly 5.25am weekdays and 6.30am at the weekend). An alternative but complicated way to go is to take the hourly train to Kiskunfélegyháza (465Ft, 16 minutes, 25km) at 9.11am and then the hourly bus to Bugac (370Ft, 30 minutes, 18km).

If you've got your own transportation, follow route 54 out of Kecskemét in the direction of Soltvadkert. Turn off the road at the 21km marker and follow a dirt track a couple of kilometres toward Bugacpuszta and then follow signs to the **Karikás Csárda** (📱575 112; www.bugacpuszta.hu/en/?pid=310; Nagybugac 135; mains 1600-3800Ft; ⊘10am-10pm May-Sep, to 8pm Apr & Oct), a kitschy but decent restaurant next to the park entrance that also doubles as a ticket and information booth to the show and small **Herder Museum** (Pásztormúzeum; 📱575 112; www.museum.hu/bugac/pasztormuzeum; admission free; ⊘10am-5pm May-Oct).

From there you can get to the show on foot or by **horse-driven carriage** (adult/child incl cowboy show 3500/2500Ft; ⊘11.30am May-Oct). Tourinform (p417) in Kecskemét can help plan an outing to the national park; the owners of the Fábián Panzió (p416) guesthouse in Kecskemét are another good source of information.

Kecskemét

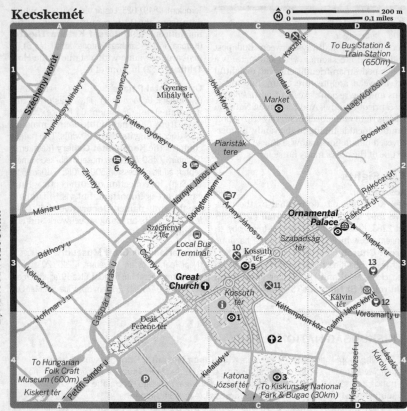

to 4pm Nov-Feb) A dozen rooms of a 200-year-old farm complex are crammed with embroidery, weaving, woodcarving, furniture, agricultural tools and textiles at the Hungarian Folk Craft Museum, the granddaddy of all Kecskemét museums.

🛏 Sleeping

Tourinform (p417) can help you locate the numerous colleges that offer dormitory accommodation in July and August.

TOP CHOICE Fábián Panzió GUESTHOUSE €€
(☎477 677; www.panziofabian.hu; Kápolna utca 14; s 9800-10,800Ft; d 11,000-12,800Ft; ❋@☎) The world-travelling family that owns this 10-room guesthouse seems to know exactly what their guests want: fridges and tea- and coffee-making facilities are room standards; there are local restaurant menus and tourist brochures to peruse; bikes are available for rent. Quiet street, garden coutyard.

Pálma HOTEL €€
(☎321 045; www.hotelpalma.hu; Arany János utca 3; s 6100-8500Ft; d 8900-10,900Ft; ❋☎) The central Pálma counts 40 simple guest rooms in two modern buildings. The more expensive ones are on the 1st floor and have TV, fridge and air-conditioning. Free self-service laundry facilities.

Teachers' College HOSTEL €
(Tanítóképző Főiskola; ☎486 977; www.kefo.hu; Piaristák tere 4; s/d 3500/7000Ft; ⊙mid-Jun–Aug; @👪) The most central and friendly of Kecskemét's summer college accommodation, this dormitory has basic rooms with twin beds and (mostly) en suite bathrooms.

🍴 Eating

TOP CHOICE Cézár ITALIAN €€
(☎328 849; www.clubcaruso.hu; Kaszap utca 4; mains 2200-4200Ft) As authentic a *ristorante italiano* as you'll find in the Hungarian

Kecskemét

provinces, Cézár serves dishes made with ingredients almost entirely sourced in Italy. The choice of pizza (980Ft to 1400Ft) and pasta dishes (1800Ft to 2700Ft) is huge and they do mains in half-portions.

Rozmaring HUNGARIAN €€€
(☑509 175; www.rozmaringbisztro.hu; Szabadság tér 2; mains 1800-4300Ft; ☑) Artistic presentations come standard at this silver-service restaurant on the city's pedestrian square. This is modern Hungarian done right.

Lordok CAFE €
(☑06 70 866 0223; Kossuth tér 6-7; mains 500-900Ft; ☺7am-midnight) This popular self-service canteen and adjoining trendier cafe-bar does triple duty as a cheap and tasty lunch option, a place for a midafternoon caffeine break and a spot for a sundowner.

☕ Drinking & Entertainment

For drinks, the Western-themed pub **Wanted Söröző** (☑415 923; Csányi János körút 4; ☺8am-midnight Mon-Thu, 10am-2am Fri & Sat, 10am-midnight Sun) sits handily just up the road from the more alternative **Black Cat Pub** (☑06 70 299 4040; Csányi János körút 6; ☺11am-midnight Sun-Thu, to 2am Fri & Sat).

Tourinform has a list of what concerts and performances are on, or check out the free weekly magazine *Kecskeméti Est*.

❶ Information

Main post office (Kálvin tér 10)

OTP Bank (Korona utca 2, Malom Centre) In central shopping centre.

Tourinform (☑481 065; www.kecskemet.hu; Kossuth tér 1; ☺8am-5pm Mon-Fri & 9am-1pm Sat & Sun Jun-Aug, 8am-6pm Mon-Fri Sep-May) In City Hall; rent out bikes and advises on excursions to Kiskunság National Park.

❶ Getting There & Away

The main bus and train stations are opposite each other, near József Katona Park. Frequent buses depart for Budapest (1680Ft, 1¼ hours, hourly) and for Szeged (1860Ft, two hours, hourly).

A direct rail line links Kecskemét to Budapest's Nyugati train station (1900Ft, 1½ hours, hourly), Pécs (3690Ft, 4½ hours, two daily) and Szeged (1650Ft, one hour, hourly).

Szeged

☑62 / POP 170,300

Busting border town Szeged (*seh*-ged) has a handful of historic sights that line the embankment along the Tisza River and a clutch of sumptuous art nouveau town palaces that are in varying states of repair. Importantly, it's also a big university town, which means lots of culture, lots of partying and an active festival scene that lasts throughout the year.

For centuries, the city's position at the confluence of the Maros and Tisza Rivers brought prosperity and growth. That happy relationship turned sour in 1879, when the Tisza overflowed its banks, wiping out much of the central city. Most of the historic buildings you see today date from the late 19th and early 20th centuries.

The **Szeged Open-Air Festival** (☑541 205; www.szegediszabadteri.hu), held in Dom tér in July and August, is the largest festival outside Budapest in Hungary. Main events include an opera, an operetta, a play, folk dancing, classical music, ballet and a rock opera.

◎ Sights & Activities

Dóm tér SQUARE
'Cathedral Square' contains Szeged's most important buildings and monuments and is the centre of events during the annual

Szeged

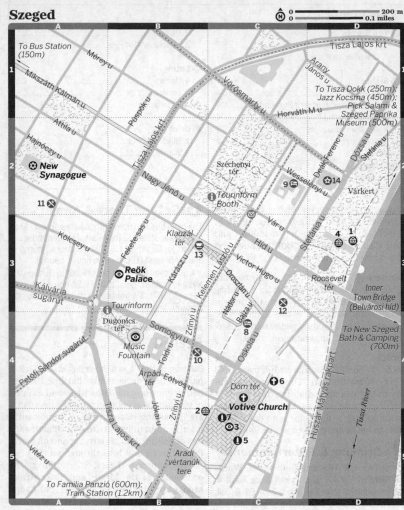

summer festival. Lording (as it were) above all else is the twin-towered **Votive Church** (Fogadalmi templom; ☑420 157; www.dom.szeged. hu; Dóm tér; admission free; ☺6.30am-7pm Mon-Sat, from 7.30am Sun), a disproportionate brick monstrosity that was pledged after the 1879 flood but built from 1913 to 1930. About the only things worth seeing inside are the organ, with more than 11,500 pipes, and dome covered with frescos.

Just in front is the Romanesque **St Demetrius Tower** (Dömötö-torony; Dóm tér), all that remains of a church erected here in the 12th century. At the northeastern end

of the square stands the **Serbian Orthodox church** (Görögkeleti Szerb ortodox templom; ☑424 246; Dóm tér; adult/child 400/300Ft; ☺8am-5pm), built in 1778. Take a peek inside at the fantastic iconostasis: a central gold 'tree', with 70 icons hanging from its 'branches'.

Back on Dóm tér, duck into the **Diocesan Museum & Treasury** (Egyházmegyei Múzeum és Kincstár; ☑420 932; www.museum.hu/ szeged/egyhazmegyei; Dom tér 5; adult/concession 100/50Ft; ☺10am-6pm Apr-Oct, closed Mon) and wade through the collection of monstrances, chalices and other liturgical objects. Running along three sides of the square is the

Szeged

National Pantheon (Nemzeti Emlékcsarnok; admission free; ⊙24hr), with statues and reliefs of 70 Hungarian notables.

New Synagogue SYNAGOGUE
(Új Zsinagóga; ☑423 849; www.zsinagoga.szeged. hu; Jósika utca 10; adult/concession 400/200Ft; ⊙10am-noon & 1-5pm Apr-Sep, 10am-2pm Oct-Mar, closed Sat) The art nouveau New Synagogue, which was designed by Lipót Baumhorn in 1903, is the most beautiful Jewish house of worship in Hungary and still in use, though the comunity has dwindled from 8000 before WWII to about 50 people. Dominating the enormous blue-and-gold interior is the cupola, decorated with stars and flowers and appearing to float skyward.

Reök Palace ARCHITECTURE
(Reök Palota; ☑541 205; www.reok.hu; Tisza Lajos körút 56) The Reök Palace (1907) is a mind-blowing green and lilac art nouveau structure that looks like an aquarium decoration. It's been polished up to its original lustre and now hosts regular photography and visual-arts exhibitions.

Ferenc Móra Museum MUSEUM
(☑549 040; www.mfm.u-szeged.hu; Roosevelt tér 1-3; adult/concession 900/600Ft; ⊙10am-6pm Tue, Wed & Fri-Sun, to 8pm Thu) The Palace of Education (1896) now houses this excellent museum containing a colourful collection of folk art from Csongrád County as well as traditional trades. After the 1879 flood claimed many of the walls of Szeged's riverfront castle, built around 1240, the city demolished the rest. For a closer look at the ancient subterranean walls, visit the nearby **Castle Museum & Lapidarium** (Varmuzéum

és kötár; ☑549 040; Stefánia sétány 15; adult/child 300/200Ft; ⊙10am-5pm, closed Mon).

Pick Salami & Szeged Paprika Museum MUSEUM
(Pick szalámi és Szegedi paprika múzeum; ☑06 20 989 8000; www.pickmuzeum.hu; Felső Tisza-part 10; adult/child incl salami tasting & paprika sample 980/740Ft; ⊙3-6pm, closed Mon) Between the two bridges spanning the Tisza is this museum, with two floors of exhibits showing the methods of salami production and the cultivating, processing and packaging of Szeged's 'red gold'. It's a lot more interesting than you might think and you even get samples.

🛏 Sleeping

TOP CHOICE Tisza Hotel HISTORIC HOTEL €€€
(☑478 278; www.tiszahotel.hu; Széchenyi tér 3; s/d classic 15,700/17,900Ft, superior 17,800/20,800Ft; ✳🅰🛈) Szeged's fine old-world hotel drips with crystal chandeliers and gilt mirrors, but many of its 49 rooms don't match up to the public elegance. All in all, it's a lovely (if somewhat frayed) place with large, bright and airy rooms.

Dóm Hotel BOUTIQUE HOTEL €€€
(☑423 750; www.domhotel.hu; Bajza utca 6; s/d/apt 26,500/30,500/47,000Ft; ✳@) A welcome addition to Szeged's top-end accommodation scene, this smart and extremely central 16-room hotel boasts a small wellness centre, popular in-house restaurant and multilingual staff for whom no request is too much.

Familia Panzió GUESTHOUSE €€
(☑441 122; www.familiapanzio.hu; Szentháromság utca 71; s/d/tr from 7000/9500/14,000Ft; ✳🛈) Budget travellers book up this family-run

guesthouse, which has two-dozen contemporary (if nondescript) rooms in a great old building close to the train station.

New Szeged Bath & Camping
CAMPGROUND €

(Újszegedi partfürdő és kemping; ☑430 843; www. szegedcamping.hu; Középkikötő sor 1-3; campsites per person 990Ft plus per tent 390Ft, bungalows 8000-11,500Ft; ⊗May-Sep; ☎☒) The large grassy camping ground with sites for 700 on the Tisza River looks a bit like a public park. Bungalows on stilts are also available. Adjoining spa open May to September.

✗ Eating & Drinking

Vendéglő A Régi Hídhoz
HUNGARIAN €€

(☑420 910; www.regihid.hu; Oskola utca 4; mains 1400-2400Ft) For an authentic meal that won't break the bank head for 'At the Old Bridge', a traditional Hungarian restaurant with all the favourites and a lovely terrace just a block back from the river. Great place to try *Szögedi halászlé* (2000Ft), Szeged's famous fish soup.

Taj Mahal
INDIAN €€

(☑452 131; www.tajmahalszeged.hu; Gutenberg utca 12; mains 1540-2290Ft; ☑) If you get a hankering for a curry or a spot of tandoor, this pleasantly authentic subcontinental restaurant just metres from the New Synagogue is the place to come. Lots of vegetarian options too.

Boci Tejivó
FAST FOOD €

(☑423 154; www.bocitejivo.hu; Zrínyi utca 2; mains 260-500Ft; ⊗24hr; ☑) This is a very modern take on an old-fashioned idea – the 'milk bar' so popular during socialist times. Order from among the dozens of meatless dishes – cheese and mushrooom omelettes, noodles with walnuts or poppyseed and anything with the ever-popular *túró* (curds), especially *túrógombóc* (curd dumplings; 590Ft).

A Cappella
CAFE

(☑559 966; Kárász utca 6; cakes 385-625Ft; ⊗7am-9pm) This giant sidewalk cafe overlooking Klauzál tér has a generous choice of cakes and ice creams.

☆ Entertainment

As a university town Szeged boasts a vast array of bars, clubs and other nightspots. Nightclub programs are listed in the free **Szegedi Est** (www.szegediest.hu) magazine.

Szeged National Theatre
THEATRE

(Szegedi Nemzeti Színház; ☑479 279; www.szinhaz. szeged.hu; Deák Ferenc utca 12-14) This theatre, where operas, ballet and classical concerts are staged, has been the centre of cultural life in Szeged since 1886.

Jazz Kocsma
LIVE MUSIC

(☑06 70 250 9279; jazzkocsma.blog.hu; Kálmány Lajos 14; ⊗5pm-midnight Mon-Thu, to 2am Fri & Sat) Small, ever-popular music club that gets pretty crowded during the academic year for live music on Friday and Saturday nights.

Tisza Dokk
CLUB

(www.tiszadokk.hu; Arany János utca 1; ⊗10am-1am Sun-Thu, to 5am Fri & Sat) This sophisticated bar-cum-dance-club on a dock on the Tisza attracts Szeged's beautiful people.

❶ Information

Main post office (Széchenyi tér 1)
OTP Bank (Klauzál tér 4)
Tourinform (☑488 690; http://tip.szeged-varos.hu; Dugonics tér 2; ⊗9am-5pm Mon-Fri, to 1pm Sat) Exceptionally helpful office tucked away in a quiet courtyard near the university. There's a seasonal Tourinform booth (Széchenyi tér; ⊗8am-8pm Mon-Fri, 9am-6pm Sat & Sun mid-Jun–mid-Sep) open in summer.

❶ Getting There & Around

The train station is south of the city centre on Indóház tér; from here, tram 1 or 2 will take you to the centre. The bus station is west of the centre in Mars tér and within easy walking distance via pedestrian Mikszáth Kálmán utca.

Buses run to Pécs (3410Ft, four hours, eight daily) and Debrecen (3950Ft, 4½ hours, up to three daily). Buses run to the Serbian city of Subotica (1200Ft, 1½ hours) up to four times daily.

Szeged is on the main rail line to Budapest's Nyugati train station (2420Ft, 2½ hours, hourly); trains also stop halfway along in Kecskemét (2100Ft, one hour). You have to change in Békéscsaba (1860Ft, two hours, half-hourly) to get to Arad in Romania.

NORTHEASTERN HUNGARY

If ever a Hungarian wine were world-famous, it would be tokaj (or tokay). And this is where it comes from, a region of Hungary containing microclimates conducive to wine production. The chain of wooded hills in the northeast constitutes the foothills of the Carpathian Mountains, which stretch along the Hungarian border with Slovakia. Though you'll definitely notice the rise in elevation, Hungary's highest peak of Kékes is, at 1014m, still just a bump in the road. The highlights here are the wine towns of Eger and Tokaj.

Eger

⟋36 / POP 56,500

Filled with wonderfully preserved baroque buildings, Eger (egg-air) is a jewelbox of a town. Learn about the Turkish conquest and defeat at its hilltop castle, climb an original minaret, hear an organ performance at the massive basilica and, best of all, go from cellar to cellar in the Valley of Beautiful Women, tasting the celebrated Bull's Blood wine from the region where it's made.

It was at Eger in 1552 that the Hungarians fended off the Turks for the first time during the 170 years of occupation. The Turks came back in 1596 and this time captured the city, turning it into a provincial capital and erecting several mosques and other buildings, until they were driven out at the end of the 17th century. Eger played a central role in Ferenc Rákóczi II's attempt to overthrow the Habsburgs early in the 18th century and it was then that a large part of the castle was razed by the Austrians. Eger flourished in the 18th and 19th centuries, when the city acquired most of its wonderful baroque architecture.

⊙ Sights & Activities

Eger Castle FORTRESS

(Egri Vár; www.egrivar.hu; Vár köz 1; castle grounds adult/child 800/400Ft, incl museum 1400/700Ft; ☺exhibits 9am-5pm Tue-Sun Mar-Oct, 10am-4pm Tue-Sun Nov-Feb, castle grounds 8am-8pm May-Aug, to 7pm Apr & Sep, to 6pm Mar & Oct, to 5pm Nov-Feb) The best view of the city can be had by climbing up cobblestone Vár köz from Dózsa György tér to Eger Castle, erected in the 13th century. Models and drawings in the **István Dobó Museum**, housed in the former Bishop's Palace (1470), painlessly explain the history of the castle.

The 19th-century building on the northwestern side of the courtyard houses the **Eger Art Gallery**, with works by Canaletto and Ceruti. The terrace of the renovated **Dobó Bastion** (Dobó Bástya; adult/concession 500/250Ft), which dates back to 1549 but collapsed in 1976, offers stunning views of the town; it now hosts changing exhibits.

Beneath the castle are **casemates** (Kazamata) hewn from solid rock, which you may tour with a Hungarian-speaking guide included in the price (English-language guide 800Ft extra). Other attractions, including the **Panoptikum** (Waxworks; waxworks adult/concession 500/350Ft) and a **3D film** (admission 400-600Ft), cost extra.

Minaret ISLAMIC

(⟋06 70 202 4353; Knézich Károly utca; admission 200Ft; ☺10am-6pm Apr-Oct) This 40m-tall minaret, topped incongruously with a cross, is the only reminder of the Ottoman occupation of Eger. Nonclaustrophobes can brave the 97 narrow spiral steps to the top for the awesome views.

Minorite Church of St Anthony of Padua CHURCH

(Páduai Szent Antal Minorita Templom; Dobó István tér 6; ☺9am-5pm Tue-Sun) On the southern side of Eger's main square stands the Minorite church (1771), one of the most glorious baroque buildings in Hungary. In front of the church are statues of national hero István Dobó and his comrades-in-arms routing the Turks in 1552.

AS STRONG AS A BULL

The story of the Turkish attempt to take Eger Castle is the stuff of legend. Under the command of István Dobó, a mixed bag of 2000 soldiers held out against more than 100,000 Turks for a month in 1552. As every Hungarian kid in short trousers can tell you, the women of Eger played a crucial role in the battle, pouring boiling oil and pitch on the invaders from the ramparts.

Eger's wine also played a significant role. Apparently Dobó sustained his troops with a ruby-red local wine. When they fought on with increased vigour – and stained beards – rumours began to circulate among the Turks that the defenders were drinking the blood of bulls. The invaders departed, for the time being, and the name Bikavér (Bull's Blood) was born.

View the mockup of the siege in miniature in the castle museum or read Géza Gárdonyi's *Eclipse of the Crescent Moon* (1901), which describes the siege in thrilling detail.

Eger

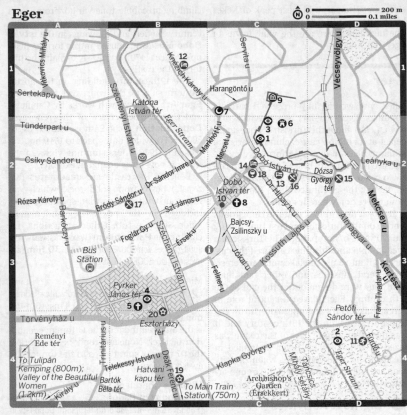

Eger Basilica CHURCH

(Egri Bazilika; Pyrker János tér 1; ⏱7.30am-6pm Mon-Sat, from 1pm Sun) The first thing you see as you come into town from the bus or train station is the mustard-coloured neoclassical basilica, with its gigantic pillars built in 1836. Try to time your visit with one of the half-hour **organ concerts** (800Ft; ⏱11.30am Mon-Sat, 12.45pm Sun mid-May–mid-Oct). You can tour the caverns below the basilica to see the archbishop's enormous former wine cellar at the **City under the City** (Pyrker János tér, Város a Város Alat; adult/concession 950/500Ft; ⏱9am-7pm Apr-Sep, 10am-5pm Oct-Mar) exhibition.

Turkish Bath SPA

(Török Fürdő; ☎510 552; www.egertermal.hu; Fürdő utca 3-4; 2½hr session adult/child 1900/1500Ft; ⏱4.30-9pm Mon & Tue, 3-9pm Wed-Fri, 9am-9pm Sat & Sun) A multimillion forint addition has added five pools, saunas, a steam room and a *hammam* (Turkish bath) to this historic spa dating back to 1617. Various kinds of massage and treatments are also available.

TOP CHOICE Valley of the Beautiful Women WINE TASTING

(Szépasszony-völgy) Wine tasting is popular in the wine cellars of the evocatively named Valley of the Women. This is the place to sample Bull's Blood – one of very few reds produced in Eger – or any of the whites: Leányka, Olaszrizling and Hárslevelű, from nearby Debrő. The choice of wine cellars – there are two dozen – can be a bit daunting and their characters can change, so walk around and have a look yourself. But be careful: those 1dL (100Ft) glasses go down pretty fast. The valley is a little over 1km southwest across Rte 25 and off Király utca. Walk, or board the **City Eye Bus Tour** (☎06 20 457 7871; Dobó István tér; tour 700Ft; ⏱8am-6.30pm Apr-Oct) in season from the west side of Dobó István tér. A taxi costs about 1000Ft.

Eger

🛏 Sleeping

TOP CHOICE Hotel Senator Ház
BOUTIQUE HOTEL €€

(Senator House; ☑411 711; www.senatorhaz.hu; Dobó István tér 11; s/d €50/70; ❋) Some 11 warm and cosy rooms with traditional white furnishings fill the upper floors of this delightful 18th-century inn on Eger's main square. The ground floor is shared between a quality restaurant and a reception area stuffed with antiques and curios.

Dobó Vendégház
HOTEL €€

(☑421 407; www.vendeghaz.hu; Dobó István utca 19; s/d 9000/13,500Ft; ☎) Tucked away along one of the old town's pedestrian streets just below the castle, this lovely little hotel has seven spick-and-span rooms, some with little balconies.

Agria Retur Panzió
GUESTHOUSE €

(☑416 650; http://agria.returvendeghaz.hu; Knézich Károly utca 18; s/d 3800/6400Ft; @☎) Walking up three flights of steps to this charming guesthouse near the Minaret, you enter a cheery communal kitchen/eating area central to four rooms. Out back is a huge garden with a barbecue at your disposal.

Tulipán Kemping
CAMPGROUND €

(☑311 542; www.tulipancamping.com; Szépasszony-völgy utca 71; campsites per person/tent/caravan 800/900/1600Ft, bungalows d/q 5000/6000Ft) Surrounded by vineyards, Tulipán Kemping is stumbling distance from the wine cellars of the Valley of the Beautiful Women. Bungalows are cabins, with no bath or kitchen.

🍴 Eating & Drinking

Lining the entry path to the Valley of the Beautiful Women are 10 food-stand eateries, with waiters that come to your covered picnic table with menus to point at (mains 850Ft to 1400Ft). There are also several *csárdák* (Hungarian-style inns) among the wine cellars to choose from.

TOP CHOICE Imola Udvarház Borétterem
HUNGARIAN €€

(☑516 180; www.imolaudvarhaz.hu; Dósza György tér 4; mains 1930-3970Ft) With its inventive menu and excellent wine list, this very stylish eatery at the foot of the castle has been named among the top dozen restaurants in Hungary. We'll come back in particular for the ever-changing four-course tasting menu (4570Ft).

Palacsintavár
CREPERIE €

(Pancake Castle; ☑413 986; www.palacsintavar.hu; Dobó István utca 9, enter from Fazola Henrik utca; mains 1490-1820Ft) Savoury *palacsinták* – pancakes, for want of a better word – are served at this eclectic eatery, with an abundance of fresh vegetables. Flavours range from Asian to Italian and there's a large choice of sweet ones too.

Szántófer Vendéglő
HUNGARIAN €€

(Plough; ☑517 298; www.szantofer.hu; Bródy Sándor utca 3; mains 1700-2400Ft) Choose the 'Plough' for hearty, home-style Hungarian fare. A covered courtyard out back is perfect for escaping the summer heat.

Bikavér Borház
WINE BAR

(📞413 262; Dobó István tér 10; ⏱9am-10pm) Try one or two of the region's wines at this central wine bar. The waiters can guide you through their selection, and bring along a plate of cheese or grapes to help you cleanse your palate.

☆ Entertainment

The Tourinform office can tell you what concerts and musicals are on. The free **Egri Est** (www.est.hu) magazine has nightlife listings.

Géza Gárdonyi Theatre
THEATRE

(Gárdonyi Géza Színház; 📞510 700; www.gardonyiszinhaz.hu; Hatvani kapu tér 4) Dance, opera and drama are staged at the town's theatre, due south of the basilica.

Gödör Kult Klub
CLUB

(Pyrker János tér 3; ⏱10pm-6am Wed, Fri & Sat) This bizarre cavelike DJ dance club, beneath the cathedral steps, parties hard on weekends.

ℹ Information

OTP Bank (Széchenyi István utca 2)

Post office (Széchenyi István utca 22)

Tourinform (📞517 715; http://mheger.hu; Bajcsy-Zsilinszky utca 9; ⏱9am-6pm Mon-Fri, to 1pm Sat & Sun mid-Jun–mid-Sep, 9am-5pm Mon-Fri, to 1pm Sat mid-Sep–mid-Jun) Covers Eger and surrounding areas.

ℹ Getting There & Away

BUS The bus station is west of Széchenyi István utca, near Pyrker János tér. From Eger, buses serve Kecskemét (3130Ft, 4½ hours, three daily) and Szeged (3950Ft, 5¾ hours, two daily). To get to Tokaj by bus, you have to go to Nyíregyháza (2520Ft, three hours, two daily) and catch another bus back.

TRAIN The main train station is on Vasút utca, south of the **Archbishop's Garden** (Érsek-kert; enter from Petőfi Sándor tér 2). To reach the city centre, walk north on Deák Ferenc utca and then head along pedestrian Széchenyi István utca.

Up to seven direct trains a day head to Budapest's Keleti train station (2830Ft, three hours). Otherwise, Eger is on a minor train line linking Putnok and Füzesabony, so you have to change at the latter for Debrecen (2230Ft, 2¾ hours).

Tokaj

📞47 / POP 4900

The world-renowned sweet wines of Tokaj (*toke*-eye) have been produced here since the 15th century. Today Tokaj is a pictur-

esque little town of old buildings, nesting storks and wine cellars, offering plenty of opportunity to sample its famous tipple. And lying at the confluence of the Bodrog and Tisza Rivers there are ample options for recreation too.

◉ Sights & Activities

Wine Tasting
WINE TASTING

Pincék (private cellars) and restaurants for wine tastings are scattered throughout Tokaj. The correct order is to move from dry to sweet: very dry Furmint, dry Szamorodni, sweet Szamorodni and then the honey-sweet Aszú wines. A basic flight of six Tokaj wines costs 2600Ft to 3200Ft; an all-Aszú tasting can run between 4200Ft and 6000Ft.

The granddaddy of tasting places is the 600-year-old **Rákóczi Cellar** (Rákóczi Pince; 📞352 408; www.rakoczipince.hu; Kossuth tér 15; ⏱11am-6pm), where bottles of wine mature in long corridors. **Erzsébet Cellar** (📞06 20 802 0137; www.erzsebetpince.hu; Bem utca 16; ⏱10am-6pm, by appointment) is a smaller, family-run affair that usually needs to be booked ahead. The most friendly of all is **Hímesudvar** (📞352 416; www.himesudvar.hu; Bem utca 2; ⏱10am-6pm), with an atmospheric 16th-century cellar and shop northwest of the town centre.

Tokaj Museum
MUSEUM

(Tokaji Múzeum; 📞352 636; www.tokaj.hu/tokaj/culture/museum/index; Bethlen Gábor utca 7; adult/concession 600/300Ft; ⏱10am-4pm Tue-Sun) The Tokay Museum, in an 18th-century mansion built by Greek wine traders, leaves nothing unsaid about the history of Tokaj and the production of its wines. There's also a superb collection of Christian liturgical art and Judaica from the 19th-century **Great Synagogue** (Nagy Zsinagóga; 📞552 000; Serház utca 55) just around the corner, which was used as a German barracks during WWII but is once again gleaming after a total renovation.

🛏 Sleeping & Eating

Huli-Bodrog Panzió
GUESTHOUSE €

(📞06 20 465 5903; www.hulipanzio.hu; Rákóczi út 16; s 4000-5000Ft; d 8000Ft; ❋🛜) The 19 down-to-earth rooms spread across the 1st floor of a popular counter-service restaurant aren't huge and decor is basic, but there are small fridges and the possibility of air-con (1500Ft).

Vaskó Panzió
GUESTHOUSE €

(☑352 107; http://vaskopanzio.hu; Rákóczi út 12; r 8000Ft; ❄️🐾📶) The very central Vaskó has 11 tidy rooms with window sills bedecked with flower pots. It's above a private wine cellar, and the proprietor can organise tastings.

Vízisport Turisztaház
HOSTEL €

(☑06 20 971 6564, 552 187; www.tokaj-info.hu; Horgász utca 3; campsites/dm 1000/2000Ft; @) Three- to four-bed rooms share a bathroom at this bare-bones hostel (beds only, no kitchen or common room) across the river from the centre. It rents out bikes, canoes and kayaks and organise canoe trips too.

Toldi Fogadó
HUNGARIAN €€

(☑353 403; www.toldifogado.hu; Hajdú köz 2; mains 1650-2590Ft; 🍴) Lovely restaurant offering quasi-fine dining down a small *köz* (lane) off the main drag, Toldi excels at fish dishes (try the catfish) but also has some excellent duck dishes (duck leg with *lecsó*, a kind of ratatouille) and a generous selection of vegetarian mains.

Fakapu
HUNGARIAN €

(Wooden Gate; ☑06 20 972 6307; Rákóczi út 27; mains 1200-1850Ft) Enter the 'Wooden Gate' through its impressive, well, wooden gate and you'll find a cute wine restaurant that offers simple Hungarian soups, stews and plates of smoked meats.

ℹ️ Information

OTP Bank (Rákóczi Ferenc út 35)

Post office (Rákóczi Ferenc út 24)

Tourinform (☑950 603; www.tokaj-turizmus. hu; Serház utca 1; ⏰9am-5pm Mon-Sat, 10am-3pm Sun Jun-Aug, 9am-4pm Mon-Fri Sep-May) Just off Rákóczi út. Hands out a useful booklet of wine cellars in the area and rents out bikes (2000/2400Ft per half-/full day).

ℹ️ Getting There & Away

BUS Buses arrive and depart from stops outside Serház utca 38, east of Kossuth tér. No direct buses link Tokaj with Budapest or Eger, though you can reach Debrecen (1680Ft, two hours) on two buses a day.

TRAIN Trains arrive 1.2km south of the town centre; from there, walk north on Baross Gábor utca and turn left on Bajcsy-Zsilinszky út, which turns into Rákóczi út, the main thoroughfare. Up to 16 trains a day head west to Budapest Keleti station (3950Ft, 2¾ hours) and east to Debrecen (2250Ft, 1¾ hours).

Debrecen
☑52 / POP 208,000

Debrecen (*deb*-re-tsen) is Hungary's second-largest city and its name has been synonymous with wealth and conservatism since the 16th century. Flanked by the golden Great Church and the historic Aranybika Hotel, Debrecen's central square sets the rather subdued tone for this city.

During summer frequent street festivals fill the pedestrian core with revellers, but old-town bars and nightclubs create a lively scene for night crawlers on weekends year-round. Debrecen's array of museums and thermal baths will keep you busy for a couple of days. The **Flower Carnival** (www.iranydebrecen.hu/info/flower-carnival) in mid-August is the event of the year.

The area around Debrecen has been settled for centuries. The city's wealth, based on salt, the fur trade and cattle-raising, grew steadily through the Middle Ages and increased during the Turkish occupation. Debrecen played a pivotal role in the 1848 nationalist revolt and it experienced a major building boom in the late 19th and early 20th centuries.

◉ Sights & Activities

Great Church
CHURCH

(Nagytemplom; ☑412 694; http://nagytemplom.hu; Piac tér 4-6; adult/concession 350/250Ft; ⏰9am-6pm Mon-Fri, to 2pm Sat, 10am-4pm Sun Apr-Oct, 10am-1pm daily Nov-Mar) Built in 1822, the iconic Great Church accommodates 3000 people and is Hungary's largest Protestant house of worship. The nave is rather austere apart from the magnificent organ; climb the 210 steps to the top of the west clock tower for grand views over the city.

Déri Museum
MUSEUM

(☑322 207; www.derimuz.hu; Déri tér 1; adult/child 500/300Ft; ⏰10am-6pm Apr-Oct, to 4pm Nov-Mar, closed Mon) Folklore exhibits at the Déri Museum, a short walk northwest of the Great Church, offer excellent insights into life on the plain and the bourgeois citizens of Debrecen up to the 19th century. Mihály Munkácsy's mythical artistic interpretations of the Hortobágy and his *Christ's Passion* trilogy usually take pride of place in a separate art gallery.

Aquaticum Debrecen
SPA

(☑514 174; www.aquaticum.hu; Nagyerdei Park; adult/concession 2350/1900Ft; ⏰11am-9pm Mon-Thu, 10am-9pm Fri-Sun) The main attraction in

Nagyerdei, a park 5km north of the centre, is Aquaticum, a complex of 'Mediterranean Enjoyment Baths' offering all manner of slides and waterfalls, spouts and grottoes within its pools. Rammed in summer.

🛏 Sleeping

TOP CHOICE Centrum Panzió GUESTHOUSE €

(☑442 843; www.panziocentrum.hu; Péterfia utca 37/a; s/d 6500/8500Ft; ❄@🅿️) A bit north of centre but every bit worth the extra half-kilometre, the Centrum looks a little like your grandmother's house, with flowery odds and ends. Some of the two-dozen large rooms (eg room 15) are in the back, facing a long garden that seems to go on forever. All have a minifridge and microwave. Bike rental is available.

Aranybika HOTEL €€

(☑508 600; www.hotelaranybika.com; Piac utca 11-15; s €46-88, d €56-106; ❄@🅿️🏊) This landmark art nouveau hotel has been *the* place to stay in Debrecen since 1915 but, alas, standards have fallen. Many of the 205 rooms retain their drab carpets and plain, proletarian furnishings of a different era. Superior rooms have a bit more space than standard, though, as well as antique reproduction furniture.

Stop Panzió GUESTHOUSE €

(☑420 302; www.stop.at.tf; Batthyányi utca 18; s/d/tr 6900/8900/11,900Ft; 📶) The dozen renovated rooms here fill up because they're the right price for the right location – in a courtyard off a cafe-filled pedestrian street.

György Maróthi College HOSTEL €

(Maróthi György Kollégium; ☑502 780; www.marothi kollegium.hu/; Blaháné utca 15; s/d 4130/6490Ft, without bathroom 2655/4550Ft; @) Just off the main pedestrian lanes, this central dormitory has fairly basic rooms, and bathroom facilities are shared. There's a kitchen on each floor.

🍴 Eating & Drinking

TOP CHOICE Ikon INTERNATIONAL €€€

(☑06 30 555 7766; www.ikonrestaurant.hu; Piac utca 23; mains 2900-6900Ft) Ikon comands a prominent position on the main square, but despite the postmodern decor and classily clad wait staff, is discreet and very upscale. The inventive dishes are some of the best in town.

Trattoria Trinacria ITALIAN €€

(☑416 988; http://dvklub.wix.com/trinacria; Batthyány utca 4; mains 1500-3500Ft) Charming Italian terrace eatery on a pedestrian side street. Serves well-prepared pasta dishes, including homemade ravioli, as well as very good wood-fired pizzas.

Csokonai Söröző HUNGARIAN €€

(☑410 802; http://www.csokonaisorozo.hu/eng; Kossuth utca 21; mains 1850-3490Ft) Medieval decor, sharp service and excellent Hungarian specialities all help to create one of Debrecen's most-recommended eating experiences. This cellar pub-restaurant also serves pasta and (go figure) Mexican dishes like *fajitas*.

Eve's Cofe & Lounge CAFE €

(☑322 222; http://hovamenjek.hu/debrecen/ eve-s-cofe-lounge; Simonffy utca 1/b; sandwiches 800-1000Ft; ⊙8am-midnight Mon-Thu, 8am-1am Fri & Sat, 9am-10pm Sun) Pleasantly upscale cafe (that's what we think 'cofe' means) that serves breakfasts as well as very good sandwiches and salads throughout the day.

🍷 Drinking & Entertainment

Pick up a copy of the biweekly entertainment freebie **Debreceni Est** (www.debreceniest.hu) for music listings. For bars and late-night cafes, check out Simonffy utca. For clubs, most of the action is along Bajcy-Zsilinszky.

B4 Gösser BAR

(☑06 70 943 7752; http://b4gosser.hu; Kálvin tér 4; ⊙10am-2am Sun-Thu, to 4am Fri & Sat) Tucked away in a courtyard just far enough east of the Great Church so as not to disturb the faithful, this pub/club/jazz bar is party central at the weekend.

Cool Music & Dance Club CLUB

(Bajcsy-Zsilinszky utca 1-3; cover charge 500-800Ft; ⊙11pm-5am Mon, Fri & Sat) DJs spin house and techno tunes here most weekends; Fridays (and sometimes Mondays) see frequent theme parties.

Csokonai Theatre THEATRE

(☑455 075; www.csokonaiszinhaz.hu; Kossuth utca 10) Three-tier gilt balconies, ornate ceiling frescos and elaborate chandeliers: the Csokonai is everything a 19th-century theatre should be. Musicals and operas are staged here.

ℹ Information

Main post office (Hatvan utca 5-9)

OTP Bank (Piac utca 45)

Tourinform (☑412 250; www.iranydebrecen. hu; Piac utca 20; ⊙9am-5pm year-round plus

9am-1pm Sat Jun-Sep) Helpful office in the central town hall. There's also a Tourinform **kiosk** (Kossuth tér; ◎10am-8pm Thu-Sun Jun-Sep) open in summer.

ℹ Getting There & Away

BUS The bus station is at the western end of Széchenyi utca. Buses are quickest if you're going directly to Eger (2520Ft, 2½ hours, six daily) or Szeged (3950Ft, 4½ hours, three daily).

TRAIN The train station is to the south on Petőfi tér; reach the centre by following Piac utca, which runs northward to Kálvin tér, site of the Great Church. Frequently departing trains will get you to Budapest (3950Ft, 3¼ hours) and Tokaj (2250Ft, 1¼ hours). The night train from Budapest to Moscow stops here at about 9.30pm.

UNDERSTAND HUNGARY

History
Hungary before the Magyars

The plains of the Carpathian Basin attracted waves of migration, from both east and west, long before the Magyar tribes settled here. The Celts occupied the area at the start of the 4th century BC, but the Romans conquered and expelled them just before the start of the Christian era. The lands west of the Danube (Transdanubia in today's Hungary) became part of the Roman province of Pannonia, where a Roman legion was stationed at the town of Aquincum (now Óbuda). The Romans brought writing, planted the first vineyards and built baths near some of the region's many thermal springs.

A new surge of nomadic tribespeople, the Huns, arrived on the scene in the 5th century AD led by a man who would become legendary in Hungarian history. By AD 441, Attila had conquered the Romans and his army acquired a reputation as great warriors. Many Hungarian boys and men bear the name Attila, even though the Huns have no connection with present-day Hungarians and the Huns' short-lived empire did not outlast Attila's death in AD 453.

Many tribes, including the Goths, the Longobards and the Avars – a powerful Turkic people who controlled parts of the area from the 5th to the 8th centuries – filled the vacuum left by the Huns and settled in the area. The Avars were subdued by Charlemagne in 796, leaving space for the Franks and Slavs to move in.

The Conquest

The Magyars, ancestors of modern-day Hungarians, are said to have moved into the Carpathian Basin at the very end of the 9th century. Legend has it that it was the *gyula* (supreme military commander) Árpád who led the alliance of seven tribes. The Magyars, a fierce warrior tribe, terrorised much of Europe with raids reaching as far as Spain and southern Italy. They were stopped at the Battle of Augsburg in 955 and subsequently converted to Christianity. Hungary's first king and its patron saint, Stephen (István), was crowned on Christmas Day in 1000, marking the foundation of the Hungarian state.

Medieval Hungary

Medieval Hungary was a powerful kingdom that included Transylvania (now in Romania), Transcarpathia (now in Ukraine), modern-day Slovakia and Croatia. Under King Matthias Corvinus (1458–90), Hungary experienced a brief flowering of Renaissance culture. However, in 1526 the Ottomans defeated the Hungarian army at Mohács in southern Hungary and by 1541 Buda Castle had been seized and Hungary sliced in three. The central part, including Buda, was controlled by the Ottomans, while Transdanubia, present-day Slovakia and parts of Transcarpathia were ruled by Hungarian nobility based in Pozsony (Bratislava) under the auspices of the Austrian House of Habsburg. The principality of Transylvania, east of the Tisza, prospered as a vassal state of the Ottoman Empire.

Habsburg Hegemony & War

After the Ottomans were evicted from Buda in 1686, the Habsburg domination of Hungary began. The 'enlightened absolutism' of the Habsburg monarchs Maria Theresa (r 1740–80) and her son Joseph II (r 1780–90) helped the country leap forward economically and culturally. Rumblings of Hungarian independence surfaced now and again, but it was the unsuccessful 1848 Hungarian revolution that really started to shake the Habsburg oligarchy. After Austria was defeated in war by France and then Prussia in 1859 and 1866, a weakened empire struck a compromise with Hungary in 1867, creating a dual monarchy. The two states would be self-governing in domestic affairs, but act jointly in matters of common interest, such as foreign relations. The Austro-Hungarian monarchy lasted until WWI.

After WWI and the collapse of the Habsburg Empire in November 1918, Hungary was proclaimed a republic. But Hungary had been on the losing side of the war; the 1920 Treaty of Trianon stripped the country of more than two-thirds of its territory – a hot topic of conversation to this very day.

In 1941 Hungary's attempts to recover lost territories saw the nation go to war on the side of Nazi Germany. When leftists tried to negotiate a separate peace in 1944, the Germans occupied Hungary and brought the fascist Arrow Cross Party to power. The Arrow Cross immediately began deporting hundreds of thousands of Jews to Auschwitz. By early April 1945 Hungary was defeated and occupied by the Soviet army.

Communism

By 1947 the communists assumed complete control of the government and began nationalising industry and dividing up large estates among the peasantry. On 23 October 1956, student demonstrators demanding the withdrawal of Soviet troops from Hungary were fired upon. The next day Imre Nagy, the reformist minister of agriculture, was named prime minister. On 28 October Nagy's government offered an amnesty to all those involved in the violence, promising to abolish the hated secret police, the ÁVH (known as ÁVO until 1949), and proclaim Hungary nonaligned. On 4 November Soviet tanks moved into Budapest, crushing the uprising. By the time the fighting ended on 11 November, thousands had been killed. Then the reprisals began: an estimated 20,000 people were arrested and 2000 executed, including Nagy. Another 250,000 fled to Austria.

After the revolt, the ruling party was reorganised as the Hungarian Socialist Workers' Party, which began a program to liberalise the social and economic structure, basing the reforms on compromise. By the 1970s Hungary had abandoned strict central economic control altogether in favour of a limited market system, often referred to as 'Goulash Communism'. In June 1987 Károly Grósz took over as premier and Hungary began moving towards full democracy. The huge number of East Germans who were able to slip through the Iron Curtain by leaving via Hungary was a major catalyst for the fall of the Berlin Wall in 1989.

The Republic

At their party congress in February 1989 the communists agreed to surrender their monopoly on power. The Republic of Hungary was proclaimed in October and democratic elections were scheduled for March 1990. Hungary changed its political system with scarcely a murmur and the last Soviet troops left the country in June 1991.

The painful transition to a full market economy resulted in declining living standards for most people and a recession in the early 1990s, but the early years of the 21st century saw astonishing growth. Hungary became a member of NATO in 1999 and joined the European Union (EU) in 2004.

Late in 2008, reeling from the fallout of the global financial crisis, Hungary was forced to approach the International Monetary Fund for economic assistance. Economic woes have plagued the nation ever since, but an even bigger concern to many Hungarians is the rise of the far-right Jobbik party, which garnered over 16% of the vote in the national elections of 2010.

Hungary's most recent appearance on the world stage came in 2011 when it assumed presidency of the EU Council. A new constitution went into effect at the start of 2012.

People

Just over 10 million people live within the national borders, and another five million Hungarians and their descendants are abroad. The estimated 1.44 million Hungarians in Transylvania constitute the largest ethnic minority in Europe and there are another 293,000 in Serbia, 520,500 in Slovakia, 156,600 in Ukraine, 40,500 in Austria, 16,500 in Croatia and 6250 in Slovenia.

Ethnic Magyars make up approximately 92% of the population. Many minority groups estimate their numbers to be significantly higher than official counts. There

---

HABITS & CUSTOMS

The Magyar are an especially polite people and their language is filled with courtesies. To toast someone's health before drinking, say egéségére (egg-eh-sheg-eh-ray), and to wish them a 'bon appetit' before eating, jo étvágyat (yo ate-vad-yaht). If you're invited to someone's home, always bring a bunch of flowers or a bottle of good local wine.

are 13 recognised minorities in the country, including Germans (2.6%), Serbs and other South Slavs (2%), Slovaks (0.8%) and Romanians (0.7%). The number of Roma is officially put at 1.9% of the population – just under 200,000 people – some sources place the figure as high as 4% (800,000).

Of those Hungarians declaring religious affiliation, just under 52% are Roman Catholic, 16% Reformed (Calvinist) Protestant, 3% Evangelical (Lutheran) Protestant, and 2.7% Greek Catholic and Orthodox. Hungary's Jewish people number around 80,000, down from a pre-WWII population of nearly 10 times that.

Arts

The history of Hungarian highbrow culture includes world-renowned composers such as Béla Bartók and Franz Liszt, and the Nobel Prize–winning writer Imre Kértesz. Hungary's insatiable appetite for music and dance means that opera, symphony and ballet are high on the entertainment agenda and even provincial towns have decent companies.

For the more contemporary branches of artistic life Budapest is the focus, containing many art galleries, theatre and dance companies. The capital is also a centre for folk music and dance, which have got a new lease of life in recent years.

Literature

Hungary has some excellent writers, both of poetry and prose. Sándor Petőfi (1823–49) is Hungary's most celebrated poet. A line from his work *National Song* became the rallying cry for the 1848 War of Independence, in which he fought and died.

Contemporary Hungarian writers whose work has been translated into English and are worth a read include Péter Esterházy and Sándor Márai. The most celebrated Hungarian writer is the 2002 Nobel Prize winner Imre Kertész. Among his novels available in English are *Fateless* (1975) and *Kaddish for an Unborn Child* (1990). Hungary's most prominent contemporary female writer, who died in 2007 at age 90, was Magda Szabó (*Katalin Street,* 1969; *The Door,* 1975).

Making a big splash in literary circles both at home and abroad these days is László Krasznahorka (1954-), whose demanding postmodernist novels (*Satantango,* 1985; *The Melancholy of Resistance,* 1988) are called 'forbidding', even in Hungarian.

Classical & Traditional Music

Hungary's most influential musician was composer Franz (Ferenc) Liszt (1811–86). The eccentric Liszt described himself as 'part Gypsy' and in his *Hungarian Rhapsodies,* as well as in other works, he does indeed weave motifs of the Roma people into his compositions.

Ferenc Erkel (1810–93) is the father of Hungarian opera and his stirringly nationalist *Bánk Bán* is a standard at the Hungarian State Opera House in Budapest. Béla Bartók (1881–1945) and Zoltán Kodály (1882–1967) made the first systematic study of Hungarian folk music; both integrated some of their findings into their compositions.

Hungarian folk musicians play violins, zithers, hurdy-gurdies, bagpipes and lutes on a five-tone diatonic scale. Look out for Muzsikás, Marta Sebestyén, Ghymes (a Hungarian folk band from Slovakia) and the Hungarian group Vujicsics, which mixes in elements of southern Slav music. Another folk musician with eclectic tastes is the Paris-trained Bea Pálya, who combines such sounds as traditional Bulgarian and Indian music with Hungarian folk.

Romani music – as opposed to the schmaltzy Gypsy fare played at touristy restaurants – has become fashionable among the young, with Romani bands playing 'the real thing' in trendy bars till the wee hours: it's a dynamic, hopping mix of fiddles, bass and cymbalom (a stringed instrument played with sticks). A Romani band would never be seen without the tin milk bottle used as a drum, which gives Hungarian Romani music its characteristic sound. Some modern Romani music groups – Kalyi Jag (Black Fire) from northeastern Hungary, Romano Drom (Gypsy Road) and Romani Rota (Gypsy Wheels) – have added guitars, percussion and even electronics to create a whole new sound.

Klezmer (traditional Eastern European Jewish music) has also made a comeback in playlists recently.

Pop music is as popular here as anywhere. Indeed, Hungary has one of Europe's biggest pop spectacles – the annual Sziget Music Festival (p389). It has more than 1000 performances over a week and attracts an audience of up to 400,000 people.

Visual Arts

Favourite painters from the 19th century include realist Mihály Munkácsy (1844–1900), the so-called painter of the *puszta* (Great Plain) and the Symbolist Tivadar Kosztka

Csontváry (1853–1919). Győző Vásárhelyi (1908–97), who changed his name to Victor Vasarely when he emigrated to Paris, is considered the 'father of op art'. Probably the most successful Hunagarian painter in history was the beloved József Rippl-Rónai (1861–1927).

In the 19th and early 20th centuries, the Zsolnay family created world-renowned decorative art in porcelain. Ceramic artist Margit Kovács (1902–77) produced a large number of statues and ceramic objects during her career. The traditional embroidery, weavings and ceramics of the nation's *népművészet* (folk art) endure, and there is usually at least one handicraft store in every town.

Environment

The Landscape

Hungary occupies the Carpathian Basin to the southwest of the Carpathian Mountains. Water dominates much of the country's geography. The Danube (Duna) River divides the Great Plain (Nagyalföld) in the east from Transdanubia (Dunántúl) in the west. The Tisza (596km in Hungary) is the country's longest river and historically has been prone to flooding. Hungary has hundreds of small lakes and is riddled with thermal springs. Lake Balaton (596 sq km), in the west, is the largest freshwater lake in Europe outside Scandinavia. Hungary's 'mountains' to the north are really hills, with the country's highest peak being Kékes (1014m) in the Mátra range.

Wildlife

There are a lot of common European animals in Hungary (deer, hares, wild boar and foxes), as well as some rare species (wild cat, lake bat and Pannonian lizard), but most of the country's wildlife comes from the avian family. Around 75% of the country's 480 known vertebrates are birds, for the most part waterfowl attracted by the rivers, lakes and wetlands. Some rare species include the saker falcon, eastern imperial eagle, great bustard and black stork.

National Parks

There are 10 *nemzeti park* (national parks) in Hungary. Bükk, north of Eger, is a mountainous limestone area of forest and caves. Kiskunság National Park (p415), near Kecskemét, and Hortobágy, outside Debrecen, protect the unique grassland environment of the plains.

Food & Drink

Hungary enjoys perhaps the most varied and interesting cuisine in all of Eastern Europe.

Hungarian Cuisine

The omnipresent seasoning in Hungarian cooking is paprika, a mild red pepper that appears on restaurant tables as a condiment beside the salt and black pepper, as well as in many recipes. *Pörkölt,* a paprika-infused stew, can be made from different meats, especially *borjúhús* (veal), and usually has no vegetables. *Galuska* (small, gnocchilike dumplings) are a good accompaniment to soak up the sauce. The well-known *csirke paprikás* (chicken paprika) is stewed chicken in a tomato, cream and paprika sauce. *Töltött káposzta/paprika* (cabbage/peppers stuffed with meat and rice) is cooked in a roux made with paprika, and topped with sour cream. Another local favourite is *halászlé* (fisherman's soup), a rich mix of several kinds of poached freshwater fish, tomatoes, green peppers and (you guessed it) paprika.

Leves (soup) is the start to any main meal in a Hungarian home. *Gulyás* (goulash), although served as a stew outside Hungary, is a soup here, cooked with beef, onions and tomatoes. Traditional cooking methods are far from health-conscious, but they are tasty. Frying is a nationwide obsession and you'll often find breaded and fried turkey, pork and veal schnitzels on the menu.

For dessert you might try *palincsinta* (crêpes filled with jam, sweet cheese or chocolate sauce). A good food-stand snack is *lángos,* fried dough that can be topped with cheese and/or *tejföl* (sour cream).

Vegetarians & Vegans

Traditional Hungarian cuisine and vegetarianism are definitely not a match made in heaven. However, things are changing and there are places even in the provinces that serve good vegetarian dishes or even full meals. Where there are no vegetarian restaurants, you'll have to make do with what's on the regular menu or shop for ingredients in the markets.

Cold *gyümölcs leves* (fruit soup) made with sour cherries and other berries is a summertime mainstay. Some not very light but widely available dishes for vegetarians to look for are *rántott sajt* (fried cheese), *gombafejek rántva* (fried mushroom caps), *gomba leves* (mushroom soup) and *túrós csusza* (short, wide pasta with cheese). Note, *bableves* (bean soup) almost always contains meat.

Where to Eat & Drink

An *étterem* is a restaurant with a large selection and formal service. A *vendéglő* is smaller and more casual, and serves home-style regional dishes. The overused term *csárda,* which originally meant a rustic country inn with Roma music, can now mean anything – including 'tourist trap'. To keep prices down, look for *étkezde* (a tiny eating place that may have a counter or sit-down service), *önkiszolgáló* (a self-service canteen), *grill* (which generally serves gyros or kebabs and other grilled meats from the counter) or a *szendvics bár* (which has open-faced sandwiches to go).

Wine has been produced in Hungary for hundreds of years and you'll find it available by the glass or bottle everywhere. There are plenty of pseudo-British/Irish/Belgian pubs, smoky *sörözők* (Hungarian pubs, often in a cellar, where drinking is taken very seriously), *borozók* (wine bars, usually dives) and nightclubs, but the most pleasant place to enjoy a cocktail or coffee may be in a cafe. A *kávéház* may primarily be an old-world dessert shop, or it may be a bar with an extensive drinks menu; either way they sell alcoholic beverages in addition to coffee. In spring, tables sprout up along the pavement.

SURVIVAL GUIDE

Directory A–Z

Accommodation

Hungary has a wide variety of accommodation options, ranging from hostels and camping grounds at the budget level, private rooms and guesthouses or *panziók* (pensions) at midrange, and hotels and luxury boutiques at the top end. The high season for lodging typically runs from April to October and over the Christmas and New Year holidays, and prices are highest in Budapest. We define price ranges for a double with private bathroom as the following:

€ less than 9000Ft/€30 (15,000Ft/€50 in Budapest)

€€ 9000Ft/€30 to 16,5000Ft/€55 (15,000Ft/ €50 to 33,500Ft/€110 in Budapest)

€€€ more than 16,500Ft/€55 (33,500Ft/€110 in Budapest)

Prices in shops and restaurants in Hungary are uniformly quoted in forint, but many hotels and guesthouses and even MÁV, the national rail company, give their rates in euros. In such cases, we have followed suit and you can usually pay in either euros or forint.

Hungary's camping grounds are listed in Tourinform's *Camping Hungary* map and brochure; also try the website of the **Hungarian Camping Association** (MKSZ; www.camping.hu). Facilities are generally open April or May to September or October and can sometimes be difficult to reach without a car.

The **Hungarian Youth Hostels Association** (MISZSZ; www.miszsz.hu) keeps a list of official year-round hostels throughout Hungary. In general, these hostels have a communal kitchen, laundry and internet service, and sometimes a lounge; a basic bread-and-jam breakfast may be included. Having an HI card is not required anywhere, but it may get you a 10% discount.

From July to August, students throughout Hungary vacate college and university dorms, and the administration opens them to travellers. Facilities are usually – but not always – pretty basic and shared. We list them under Sleeping; the local Tourinform office can help you find such places.

Renting a private room in a Hungarian home is a good budget option and can be a great opportunity to get up close and personal with the culture. Prices outside Budapest run from 4000Ft to 6500Ft per person per night. Tourinform offices can usually help with finding these too. Otherwise look for houses with signs reading *szoba kiadó* or *Zimmer frei* ('room available' in Hungarian and German) .

An engaging alternative is to stay in a rural village or farmhouse, but only if you have wheels: most of these places are truly remote. Contact **Tourinform** (☑ from abroad 36 1 438 80 80, within Hungary 800 36 000 000; www.tourinform.hu), the **Association of Hungarian Rural & Agrotourism** (FATOSZ; Map p386; ☑ 1-352 9804; www.fatozs.eu; VII Király utca 93; ☐ 73, 76) or the **Centre of Rural Tourism** (☑ 1-321 2426; www.falutur.hu; VII Dohány utca 86) in Budapest.

Activities

CANOEING

For canoeists, Ecotours leads week-long Danube River canoe and camping trips (tent rental and food extra) for about €500, as well as shorter Danube Bend and Tisza River trips.

CYCLING

Hungary's flat terrain makes it ideal for cycling. Velo-Touring, a large cycling travel agency, has a great selection of seven-night trips in all regions, from a senior-friendly Southern Transdanubia wine tour (€835) to a bike ride between spas on the Great Plain (€750). Lake Balaton is circled by a 200km-long cycling track that takes four to five days to complete at a leisurely pace.

HIKING/BIRDWATCHING

Hiking enthusiasts may enjoy the trails around Tihany at Lake Balaton, the Bükk Hills north of Eger or the plains at Bugac Puszta south of Kecskemét. The birdwatching expert in Hungary is Gerard Gorman, who owns and operates Probirder, an information website and guide service.

HORSEBACK RIDING

See the **Hungarian National Tourist Office** (HNTO; www.gotohungary.com) website and its *Hungary on Horseback* brochure. Equus Tours leads seven-night horseback tours (from €750) in the Hortobágy, Mátra Hills and Northeast Hungary.

SPAS

Hungary has more than 100 thermal baths open to the public. The HNTO puts out a booklet called *Hungary: A Garden of Well-Being* and has listings online. Also try the **Spas in Hungary** (www.spasinhungary.com) website.

Business Hours

Banks 8am or 9am to 4pm or 5pm Monday to Friday

Museums 9am or 10am to 5pm or 6pm Tuesday to Sunday

Restaurants Roughly 11am to midnight

Discount Cards

The **Hungary Card** (www.hungarycard.hu; basic/standard/plus 2550/5800/9300Ft) offers free entry to many museums; 50% off on six return train fares and some bus and boat travel; up to 20% off selected accommodation; and 50% off the price of the **Budapest Card** (www.buda-pestinfo.hu; 24/48/72hr card 3900/7900/9900Ft). It's available at Tourinform offices.

Embassies & Consulates

Embassies in Budapest (phone code ☏1) include the following:

Australian Embassy (☏457 9777; www.hungary.embassy.gov.au; XII Királyhágó tér 8-9, 4th fl; ⊙visas 9-11am, general enquiries 8.30am-4.30pm Mon-Fri)

Austrian Embassy (☏479 7010; www.austrian-embassy.hu; VI Benczúr utca 16; ⊙8-11am Mon-Fri)

Canadian Embassy (☏392 3360; www.hungary.gc.ca; II Ganz utca 12-14; ⊙8.30-11am & 2-3.30pm Mon-Thu)

Croatian Embassy (☏354 1315; veleposlanstvo.budimpesta@mvpei.hr; VI Munkácsy Mihály utca 15; ⊙9am-5pm Mon-Fri)

French Embassy (☏374 1100; www.ambafrance-hu.org; VI Lendvay utca 27; ⊙9am-12.30pm Mon-Fri)

German Embassy (☏488 3567; www.budapest.diplo.de; I Úri utca 64-66; ⊙9am-noon Mon-Fri)

Irish Embassy (☏301 4960; www.embassyofireland.hu; V Szabadság tér 7, Bank Center, Granit Tower, 5th fl; ⊙9.30am-12.30pm & 2.30-4.30pm Mon-Fri)

Netherlands Embassy (☏336 6300; www.netherlandsembassy.hu; II Füge utca 5-7; ⊙10am-noon Mon-Fri)

Romanian Embassy (☏384 0271; http://budapesta.mae.ro; XIV Thököly út 72; ⊙8.30am-12.30pm Mon-Fri; ▣5, 7, 173)

Serbian Embassy (☏322 9838; ambjubp@mail.datanet.hu; VI Dózsa György út 92/a; ⊙10am-1pm Mon-Fri)

Slovakian Embassy (☏273 3500; www.mzv.sk/Budapest; XIV Gervay út 44; ⊙9am-noon Mon-Fri)

Slovenian Embassy (☏438 5600; http://budimpesta.veleposlanstvo.si; II Csatárka köz 9; ⊙9am-noon Mon-Fri)

South African Embassy (☏392 0999; budapest.admin@foreign.gov.za; II Gárdonyi Géza út 17; ⊙9am-12.30pm Mon-Fri)

UK Embassy (☏266 2888; http://ukinhungary.fco.gov.uk/en; V Harmincad utca 6; ⊙9.30am-12.30pm & 2.30-4.30pm Mon-Fri)

Ukrainian Embassy (☏422 4122; www.mfa.gov.ua; XIV Stefánia út 77; ⊙9am-noon Mon-Wed)

US Embassy (☏475 4400; www.usembassy.hu; V Szabadság tér 12; ⊙8.30am-4.30pm Mon-Fri)

Food

Price ranges are as follows:

€ less than 2000Ft (3000Ft in Budapest)

€€ 2000Ft to 3500Ft (3000Ft to 6500Ft in Budapest)

€€€ more than 3500Ft (6500Ft in Budapest)

Gay & Lesbian Travellers

Budapest has a large and active gay scene, though there is virtually nothing 'out' in the rest of the country. The **Háttér Gay & Lesbian Association** (☑1-329 2670; www.hatter. hu; ☺6-11pm) in Budapest has an advice and help line operating daily. **Company** (www. companymedia.hu) is a monthly magazine featuring info on events, venues and parties (available at gay venues around Budapest). The **Labrisz Lesbian Association** (☑1-252 3566; www.labrisz.hu) has info on Hungary's cultural lesbian scene.

Internet Access

Most hostels and hotels offer internet access. Wi-fi is almost always free of charge. Use of a terminal will cost between 200Ft and 400Ft per hour.

Language Courses

Debreceni Nyári Egyetem (Debrecen Summer University; ☑52-532 595; www.nyariegyetem. hu; Egyetem tér 1, Debrecen) is the best-known school for studying Hungarian. It organises intensive two- and four-week courses during July and August and 80-hour, two-week advanced courses during the academic year. The **branch** (Map p386; ☑1-320 5751; www.nyariegyetem.hu/bp; V Váci utca 63, 2nd fl; Ⓜ M2 Kossuth Lajos tér) in Budapest also offers similar courses.

Media

Budapest has two English-language newspapers: the weekly **Budapest Times** (www. budapesttimes.hu; 750Ft), with interesting reviews and opinion pieces, and the business-oriented biweekly **Budapest Business Journal** (www.bbjonline.hu; 1250Ft). Both are available on newsstands. An excellent online newspaper is the **Budapest Sun** (www.budapestsun.com).

Money

The unit of currency is the Hungarian forint (Ft). Coins come in denominations of five,

10, 20, 50, 100 and 200Ft, and notes are denominated in 500, 1000, 2000, 5000, 10,000 and 20,000Ft. ATMs are everywhere, even in small villages. Tip waiters, hairdressers and taxi drivers approximately 10% of the total.

Post

Postcards and small letters mailed within Europe cost 220Ft. To addresses outside Europe, expect to pay 240Ft.

Public Holidays

New Year's Day 1 January

1848 Revolution Day 15 March

Easter Monday March/April

International Labour Day 1 May

Whit Monday (Pentecost) May/June

St Stephen's/Constitution Day 20 August

1956 Remembrance/Republic Day 23 October

All Saints' Day 1 November

Christmas Holidays 25 & 26 December

Telephone

Hungary's country code is ☑36. To make an outgoing international call, dial ☑00 first. To dial city-to-city within the country, first dial ☑06, wait for the second dial tone and then dial the city code and phone number. All localities in Hungary have a two-digit city code, except for Budapest, where the code is ☑1.

In Hungary you must always dial 06 when ringing mobile telephones, which have specific area codes depending on the telecom company. Telecom companies include **Telenor** (☑06 20; www.telenor.hu), **T-Mobile** (☑06 30; www.t-mobile.hu) and **Vodafone** (☑06 70; www.vodafone.hu).

Consider buying a rechargeable SIM chip, which will reduce the cost of making local calls. Vodafone, for example, sells prepaid vouchers for 1680Ft, with 500Ft worth of credit. Top-up cards cost from 2000Ft to 12,000Ft and are valid for from one month to a year.

There's also a plethora of phonecards for public phones on offer, including Magyar Telekom's **Barangoló** (www.t-home.hu) and **NeoPhone** (www.neophone.hu), with cards valued at between 1000Ft and 5000Ft.

Tourist Information

The **Hungarian National Tourist Office** (www.gotohungary.com) has a chain of more than 140 **Tourinform** (www.tourinform.hu) information offices across the country. These are the best places to ask general questions and pick up brochures across the country. In the capital, you can also visit **Budapest Info** (⏰1-438 8080; www.budapestinfo.hu).

Travellers with Disabilities

Wheelchair ramps and toilets fitted for people with disabilities do exist, though they are not as common as in Western Europe. Audible traffic signals are becoming more common in big cities. For more information, contact the Budapest-based **Hungarian Federation of Disabled Persons' Associations** (MEOSZ; ⏰1-250 9013; www.meoszinfo.hu; III San Marco utca 76).

Visas

Citizens of virtually all European countries, as well as Australia, Canada, Israel, Japan, New Zealand and the USA, do not require visas to visit Hungary for stays of up to 90 days. Check current visa requirements on the Consular Services page of the **Ministry for Foreign Affairs** (http://konzuliszolgalat.kormany.hu/en) website.

Getting There & Away

Air

The vast majority of international flights land at **Ferenc Liszt International Airport** (⏰296 7000; www.bud.hu) on the outskirts of Budapest. The national carrier, Malév Hungarian Airlines, went into liquidation at the start of 2012. Airlines now serving Hungary include the following:

Aeroflot (SU; ⏰1-318 5955; www.aeroflot.com; hub Moscow)

Air Berlin (AB; ⏰06 80 017 110; www.airberlin.com; hub Cologne)

Air France (AF; ⏰1-483 8800; www.airfrance.com; hub Paris)

Alitalia (AZ; ⏰1-483 2170; www.alitalia.it; hub Rome)

Austrian Airlines (OS; ⏰1-296 0660; www.aua.com; hub Vienna)

British Airways (BA; ⏰1-777 4747; www.ba.com; hub London)

CSA Czech Airlines (OK; ⏰1-318 3045; www.csa.cz; hub Prague)

EasyJet (U2; www.easyjet.com; hub London)

EgyptAir (MS; www.egyptair.com; hub Cairo)

El Al (LY; ⏰1-266 2970; www.elal.co.il; hub Tel Aviv)

Finnair (AY; ⏰1-296 5486; www.finnair.com; hub Helsinki)

German Wings (4U; ⏰1-526 7005; www.germanwings.com; hub Cologne)

LOT Polish Airlines (LO; ⏰1-266 4771; www.lot.com; hub Warsaw)

Lufthansa (LH; ⏰1-411 9900; www.lufthansa.com; hub Frankfurt)

Ryanair (FR; www.ryanair.com; hub London)

SAS (SK; www.flysas.com; hub Copenhagen)

Tarom Romanian Airlines (RO; www.tarom.ro; hub Bucharest)

Turkish Airlines (TK; ⏰1-266 4291; www.thy.com; hub Istanbul)

Wizz Air (W6; ⏰06 90 181 181; www.wizzair.com; hub Katowice (Poland))

Land

Hungary is well connected with all seven of its neighbours by road, rail and even ferry, though most transport begins or ends its journey in Budapest.

Border formalities with its EU neighbours – Austria, Romania, Slovenia and Slovakia – are virtually nonexistent. But Hungary must implement the strict Schengen border rules, so expect a somewhat closer inspection of your documents when travelling to/from Croatia, Ukraine and Serbia.

BUS

Most international buses arrive at the **Népliget bus station** (⏰219 8030; IX Üllői út 131) in Budapest and most services are run by **Eurolines** (www.eurolines.com) in conjunction with its Hungarian affiliate, Volánbusz. Useful international routes include buses from Budapest to Vienna in Austria, Bratislava in Slovakia, Subotica in Serbia, Rijeka in Croatia, Prague in the Czech Republic and Sofia in Bulgaria.

CAR & MOTORCYCLE

Foreign driving licences are valid for one year after entering Hungary. Drivers of cars and riders of motorbikes will need the vehicle's registration papers. Third-party insurance is compulsory for driving in Hungary; if your car is registered in the EU, it's assumed you have it. Other motorists must show a Green Card or buy insurance at the border.

Travel on Hungarian motorways requires pre-purchase of a *matrica* (highway pass) available from petrol stations and post offices. Your licence-plate/registration number will be entered into a computer database where it can be screened by highway-mounted surveillance cameras. Prices are 2975Ft for a week and 4780Ft for a month.

TRAIN
Magyar Államvasutak (MÁV; ☑06 40 494 949, 1-371 9449; http://elvira.mav-start.hu), the Hungarian State Railways, links up with international rail networks in all directions, and its schedule is available online.

Eurail passes are valid, but not sold, in Hungary. EuroCity (EC) and Intercity (IC) trains require a seat reservation and payment of a supplement. Most larger train stations in Hungary have left-luggage rooms open from at least 9am to 5pm. There are three main train stations in Budapest, so always note the station when checking a schedule online.

Some direct train connections from Budapest include Austria, Slovakia, Romania, Ukraine (continuing to Russia), Croatia, Serbia, Germany, Slovenia, Czech Republic, Poland, Switzerland, Italy, Bulgaria and Greece.

River
A hydrofoil service on the Danube River between Budapest and Vienna operates twice a week from May to late September.

Getting Around
Note that Hungary does not have any scheduled domestic flights.

Boat
In summer there are regular passenger ferries on the Danube from Budapest to Szentendre, Vác, Visegrád and Esztergom as well as on Lake Balaton.

Bus
Domestic buses, run by the **Volán** (www.volan.eu) association of coach operators, cover an extensive nationwide network.

Timetables are posted at all stations. Some footnotes you could come across include *naponta* (daily), *hétköznap* (weekdays), *munkanapokon* (on work days), *munkaszüneti napok kivételével naponta* (daily except holidays) and *szabad és munkaszüneti napokon* (on Saturday and holidays). A few large bus stations have luggage rooms, but these generally close by 6pm.

Car & Motorcycle
Most cities and towns require that you pay for street parking (usually 9am to 6pm workdays) by buying temporary parking passes from machines. Most machines take only coins (so keep a lot handy); place the time-stamped parking permit on the dashboard. The cost averages about 200Ft an hour in the countryside and up to 450Ft on central Budapest streets.

AUTOMOBILE ASSOCIATIONS
The so-called 'Yellow Angels' of the **Hungarian Automobile Club** (Magyar Autóklub; ☑1-345 1800; www.autoklub.hu; IV Berda József utca 15, Budapest; Ⓜ M3 Újpest Városkapu) do basic breakdown repairs for free if you belong to an affiliated organisation such as AAA in the USA or AA in the UK. You can call 24 hours a day on ☑188 nationwide.

FUEL & SPARE PARTS
Ólommentes benzin (unleaded petrol 95/98 octane) is available everywhere. Most stations also have *gázolaj* (diesel).

HIRE
In general, you must be at least 21 years old and have had your licence for at least a year to rent a car. Drivers under 25 sometimes have to pay a surcharge. Rental agencies are common in large cities and at Budapest airport. The competition is fierce but local rental rates can be high; your best bet is to book online before you travel.

ROAD RULES
The most important rule to remember is that there's a 100% ban on alcohol when you are driving, and this rule is strictly enforced.

Using a mobile phone while driving is prohibited in Hungary. *All* vehicles must have their headlights switched on throughout the day outside built-up areas. Motorcyclists must have their headlights on at all times.

Hitching
Hitching is never entirely safe in any country and we don't recommend it. Travellers

who decide to hitch are taking a small but potentially serious risk. Hitchhiking is legal everywhere in Hungary except on motorways. Though it isn't as popular as it once was, the road to Lake Balaton is always jammed with hitchhikers in the holiday season.

Local Transport

Public transport is efficient and extensive, with bus and, in many towns, trolleybus services. Budapest, Szeged and Debrecen also have trams, and there's an extensive metro and a suburban commuter railway in Budapest. Purchase tickets at newsstands before travelling and validate them once aboard. Inspectors do check tickets, especially on the metro lines in Budapest.

Train

MÁV (☑1-444 4499; www.mav-start.hu) operates reliable train services on its 7600km of tracks. Schedules are available online and computer information kiosks are popping up at rail stations around the country. Second-class domestic train fares range from 155Ft for a journey of less than 5km to about 4660Ft for a 300km trip.

First-class fares – where available – are usually 25% more. IC trains are express trains, the most comfortable and modern. *Gyorsvonat* (fast trains) take longer and use older cars; s*zemélyvonat* (passenger trains) stop at every village along the way. *Helyjegy* (seat reservations) cost extra and are required on IC and some fast trains; these are indicated on the timetable by an 'R' in a box or a circle (a plain 'R' means seat reservations are available but not required).

In all stations a yellow board indicates *indul* (departures) and a white board is for *érkezik* (arrivals). Express and fast trains are indicated in red, local trains in black.

On certain trains (look for the bicycle symbol on the schedule), bicycles can be transported in special carriages for 235Ft per 50km travelled. You can freight a bicycle for 25% of a full 2nd-class fare.

If you plan to travel extensively in Hungary consider purchasing the Hungary pass from **Eurail** (www.eurail.com), available to non-European residents only, before entering the country. It costs US$92/132 for five/10 days of 1st-class travel in a 15-day period, and US$80/101 for those under 26 years of age in 2nd class. Children aged six to 14 pay half price.

Kosovo

Includes »

Best Places to Eat

» Tiffany (p441)

» Home Bar & Restaurant (p441)

» De Rada Brasserie (p441)

Best Places to Stay

» Swiss Diamond Hotel (p440)

» Dukagjini Hotel (p444)

» Hotel Sara (p441)

» Hotel Prizreni (p445)

Why Go?

Kosovo may be Europe's newest country, but its long and dramatic history can be witnessed at every turn. Far from being the dangerous or depressing place most people imagine when they hear the name, Kosovo is a fascinating land at the heart of the Balkans and one of the last corners of Eastern Europe where tourism has yet to take off.

Barbs of its past are impossible to miss however: roads are dotted with memorials to those killed in 1999, when Serbia stripped Kosovo of its autonomy and initiated ethnic cleansing, while NATO forces still guard Serbian monasteries. But with independence has come stability, and Kosovo is now the latest word in getting off the beaten track in the Balkans. Visitors who make the journey here will be rewarded with welcoming smiles, charming mountain towns, incredible hiking opportunities and 13th-century domed Serbian monasteries just for starters.

When to Go
Pristina

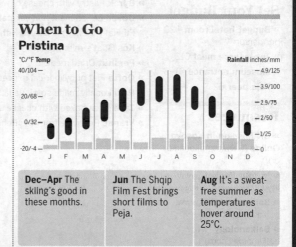

Dec–Apr The skiing's good in these months.

Jun The Shqip Film Fest brings short films to Peja.

Aug It's a sweat-free summer as temperatures hover around 25°C.

AT A GLANCE

» **Currency** Euro (€)

» **Language** Albanian, Serbian

» **Money** ATMs in larger towns; banks open Monday to Friday

» **Visas** Kosovo is visa-free for all nationalities. All passports are stamped on arrival for a 90-day stay.

Fast Facts

» **Area** 10,887 sq km

» **Capital** Pristina

» **Country code** ☏381

» **Emergency** Ambulance ☏94, fire ☏93, police ☏92

Exchange Rates

Australia	A$1	€0.82
Canada	C$1	€0.77
Japan	¥100	€0.83
New Zealand	NZ$1	€0.65
UK	UK£1	€1.18
USA	US$1	€0.78

Set Your Budget

» **Budget hotel room** €20 per person

» **Two-course meal** €12

» **Museum entrance** €1–3

» **Peja beer** €2

Resources

» **UN Mission in Kosovo Online** (www.unmikonline.org)

» **In Your Pocket** (www.inyourpocket.com/kosovo)

» **Balkan Insight** (www.balkaninsight.com)

» **Balkanology** (www.balkanology.com)

Connections

Kosovo has good bus connections between Albania, Montenegro and Macedonia, with regular services from Pristina, Peja and Prizren to Tirana (Albania), Skopje (Macedonia) and Podgorica (Montenegro). There's also a train line from Pristina to Macedonia's capital, Skopje.

Do note that Kosovo's independence is not recognised by Serbia, and so if you plan to continue to Serbia but entered Kosovo via Albania, Macedonia or Montenegro, officials at the Serbian border will deem that you entered Serbia illegally and you will not be let in. You'll need to exit Kosovo to a third country and then enter Serbia from there. If you entered Kosovo from Serbia, then there's no problem returning to Serbia.

ITINERARIES

Two to Three Days

Spend a day in cool little Pristina and get to know this burgeoning nation's charming capital. The next day, visit Gračanica Monastery and then curl through the mountains to Prizren's Ottoman sights, or make a beeline for mountainous Peja.

One Week

After a couple of days in the capital, and a visit to Gračanica Monastery, loop to Prizren for castle views and its Ethnological Museum, then Peja for monasteries and markets before taking a couple of days to hike in the beautiful Rugova Mountains.

Essential Food & Drink

» **Byrek** Pastry with cheese or meat.

» **Duvĕc** Baked meat and vegetables.

» **Fli** Flaky pastry pie served with honey.

» **Kos** Goat's-milk yoghurt.

» **Pershut** Dried meat.

» **Qofta** Flat or cylindrical minced-meat rissoles.

» **Raki** Locally made spirit, usually made from grapes.

» **Tavë** Meat baked with cheese and egg.

» **Vranac** Red wine from the Rahovec region of Kosovo.

Kosovo Highlights

1 See the sights in Pristina's charming **bazaar area** (p440) and discover this bustling new capital.

2 Breathe deep at Peja's Saturday **Cheese Market** (p444).

3 Buy local wine and cheese at the serene 14th-century **Visoki Dečani Monastery** (p444).

4 Wander the picturesque streets of **Prizren's** (p445) charming old town.

5 Trek around the **Rugova mountains** (p444).

6 Visit the important hub of Serbian cultural that is the **Gračanica Monastery** (p441).

PRISTINA

⏰038 / POP 198,000

Pristina (pronounced Prish-tEEna) is a city changing fast and one that feels full of the optimism and potential that you'd expect from Europe's newest capital city. Far more provincial town than great city, Pristina's vibe is laid back and frequently unpredictable: the UN and EU both have huge presences here and Pristina feels rich and more sophisticated as a result. But get out of the centre, with its international restaurants and smart cafes, and you'll find yourself in the quaint Turkic hillside neighbourhoods that have defined the city for centuries.

◉ Sights

BAZAAR AREA

To the north of the Vellusha district, around Rruga Agim Ramadani, are the narrow and twisting streets of the bazaar area, where you'll find many of Pristina's sights as well as the bustling market.

Ethnographic Museum   HISTORIC BUILDING

(Rr Iliaz Agushi; admission €2.50; ⏰10am-4pm) Follow the signs all around Pristina to locate this well-kept 'how we lived' Ottoman house.

Kosovo Museum   MUSEUM

(Sheshi Adam Jashari; admission €3; ⏰10am-4pm Tue-Sat) A written plea to have antiquities returned from Serbia greets visitors; while you're waiting, see modern exhibits upstairs (celebrating America's support for Kosovo when we visited) and delicate 6000-year-old statues on the ground floor. It was closed for a full renovation at the time of research.

Mosques   MOSQUES

Fronting the Kosovo Museum is the 15th-century **Carshi Mosque** (Agim Ramadani). Nearby, the **Sultan Mehmet Fatih Mosque** (Big Mosque; Rr Ilir Konushevci) was built by its namesake around 1461, converted to a Catholic church during the Austro-Hungarian era and refurbished again during WWII. **Jashar Pasha Mosque** (Rr Ylfete Humolli) has vibrant interiors that exemplify Turkish baroque style.

Clock Tower   LANDMARK

This 26m tower makes a good point of reference. The **Great Hamam** nearby is being renovated.

CENTRE

The centre of Pristina was being impressively spruced up in autumn 2012, based around the new Ibrahim Rugova Sq, the centrepiece of the city at the end of pedestrianised Bul Nenë Terezë.

National Library   LIBRARY

(www.biblioteka-ks.org; Agim Ramadani; ⏰7am-8pm Mon-Fri, 7am-2pm Sat) The National Library, completed in 1982 by Croatian Andrija Mutnjakovic, must be seen to be believed (think gelatinous eggs wearing armour).

FREE Kosovo Art Gallery   ART GALLERY

(Agim Ramadani 60; ⏰10am-6pm Tue & Fri-Sat) Behind the National Library, this gallery is a welcoming place featuring the works of local artists.

FREE Independence House of Kosovo   HISTORIC BUILDING

(⏰10am-5pm Mon-Sat) This small house opposite the stadium is devoted to former president Ibrahim Rugova and Kosovo's recent independence movement. English-speaking guides will show you around the small display, including video footage of Rugova's meetings with world leaders.

⏦ Sleeping

TOP CHOICE Swiss Diamond Hotel   LUXURY HOTEL €€€

(⏰220 000; www.swissdiamondhotelprishtina.com; Sheshi Nëna Terezë; s/d incl breakfast from €137/157; [P][⊛][❄][@][☎][≋]) This is the international standard five-star hotel that Pristina has been waiting for. Opened in 2012 right in the heart of the city, this place is all marble floors, obsequious staff and liveried bell boys. The rooms are lavish and the suites are immense, all decorated with expensive furnishings and many enjoying great city views. There's also a spa, restaurant, wine cellar and piano lounge.

TOP CHOICE Velania Guesthouse   PENSION €

(⏰044 167 455, 531 742; http://guesthouse-ks.net/eng/vlersimet.html; Velania 4/34; dm/s/d/apt €9/15/20/35; [@]) This bustling guesthouse is spread over two buildings in an affluent part of town. The jovial professor who runs it loves a chat and could double as your grandfather. The hike up to it is much more fun in a taxi (€1.50) – either way consult the website first and print out the map, as it's hard to find!

Hotel Begolli   HOTEL €€

(⏰244 277; www.hotelbegolli.com; Rr Maliq Pashë Gjinolli 8; s/d incl breakfast €40/50, ste €60; [❄][@][☎]) While it may have gone overboard with its '90s-style furniture, Begolli is a pleasant, rather sprawling place to stay. The suite

GRAČANICA MONASTERY & GADIMË CAVE

Explore beyond Pristina by heading southeast to Gračanica Monastery or south to Gadimë Cave. Dusty fingers of sunlight pierce the darkness of **Gračanica Monastery** (☉6am-5pm), completed in 1321 by Serbian King Milutin. It's an oasis in a town that is the cultural centre of Serbs in central Kosovo. Take a Gjilan-bound bus (€0.50, 15 minutes, every 30 minutes); the monastery's on your left. Rumours abound that bus drivers won't let you on or off if you tell them where you're going, so be discreet.

Famed for helictites, **Gadimë Cave** (Shpella Mermerit; admission €2.50; ☉9am-7pm) is visited with a guide who enthusiastically points out shapes like a hand, an elephant head and various body parts. Buses go to Gadimë (€1, 30 minutes, every half-hour) via Lipjan. Or take a Ferizaj-bound bus, get dropped at the Gadimë turn-off and walk the 3km to town.

has two bedrooms and is good value, while the normal rooms are a little on the small side, but comfy. Staff are friendly and a good breakfast is served in the ground-floor bar.

Hotel Sara
HOTEL €€

(☎236 203, 238 765; www.hotel-sara.com; Rr Maliq Pashë Gjinolli; s/d/tr/apt incl breakfast €30/40/50/70; ❄☎) In a tiny street filled with hotels by the bazaar, this 33-room hotel is rather garishly furnished in a style that suggests aspiration to boutique quality, but sadly rather misses the mark. That said, the rooms are good value at this price, and room 603 has a small balcony with great city views if you can cope with the colour scheme.

Hotel Afa
HOTEL €€

(☎227 722, 225 226; www.hotelafa.com; Ali Kelmendi 15; s/d/ste €45/65/69; ❄@) There's a classy lobby here (and a thank-you note from one former guest, Joe Biden) but the rooms are rather less grand, all featuring fairly bizarre assemblages of furniture and art, although many have jacuzzis and other such vice-presidential trimmings. It's a solid midrange option though, and staff are super helpful.

Hotel Xhema
HOTEL €

(☎719 716; Rr Maliq Pashë Gjinolli; s/d/ste incl breakfast €25/30/60; P❄☎) Behind two other hotels on this tiny side street by the bazaar, this is the best budget deal in the city centre. The suites are hilariously furnished and feature jacuzzis, kitchens and plush beds, while the cheaper rooms all smell rather musty and could use a refit, though they're ok for the price. The welcome is friendly and it's central.

 Eating

TOP CHOICE Tiffany
TRADITIONAL €€

(Fehmi Agani; mains €8; ☉8am-11pm Mon-Sat, to 6pm Sun) The oral menu here can be a little confusing (though the staff's English is not at fault), but other than that there's no problem to be found with this brilliant place, much prized by the foreign community in Pristina. Enjoy the day's grilled special (whatever's fresh that day), beautifully cooked seasonal vegetables and oven-baked bread on the sun-dappled terrace. The restaurant is unsigned, hidden behind a well-tended bush on Fehmi Agani.

De Rada Brasserie
INTERNATIONAL €€

(Rr UÇK 50; mains €5-8; ☉7.30am-7pm) A smart and atmospheric place right in the heart of town that serves up breakfasts, lunches and early dinners to an international clientele. The menu leans towards Italian, but there's plenty of choice. Grab a table outside on the street when the weather's good.

Home Bar & Restaurant
INTERNATIONAL €

(Luan Haradinaj; mains €4-9; ☉7am-11pm Mon-Sat, 11am-11pm Sun; ☎) Having been here since the dark days of 2001, this is the closest Pristina has to an ex-pat institution, and it lives up to its name, being exceptionally cosy and friendly, with scattered curios and antiques. The menu is international and eclectic and offers exactly what most travellers will be dreaming of: spring rolls, hummus, curries, wraps, burgers and even fajitas.

Osteria Basilico
ITALIAN €€

(Fehmi Agani 29/1; mains €5-11) This smart place is Pristina's most reliable Italian restaurant. There's a lovely terrace and a stylish interior where you can enjoy the wide-ranging menu, including plenty of regional classics as well as some more inventive dishes.

NOMNOM
INTERNATIONAL €€

(Rr Rexhep Luci 5; mains €7-12; ☉7am-midnight; ☎) Just off the main drag, this modern

Pristina

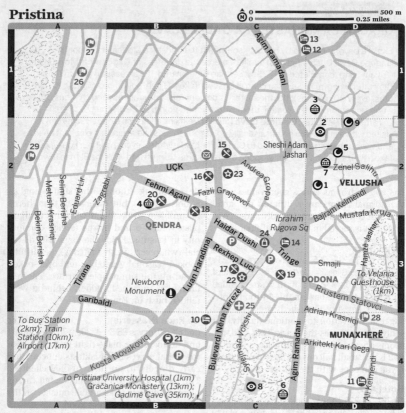

two-floor bar and restaurant caters to a smart local and foreign crowd. It has a huge summer terrace, and plenty of indoor seating too. The menu offers pizza, pasta, salad, grills and burgers. Sadly the place's overall style is compromised by terrible muzak.

Pishat TRADITIONAL €€

(Rr Qamil Hoxha 11; mains €4-11; ⊗8am-11pm Mon-Sat, noon-11pm Sun) It's not only the cuisine that is typically Albanian here, but the fug of smoke hovering over the entire space. Despite that, this is a great spot to sample Albanian dishes with a largely local crowd.

🍷 Drinking

There's a slight madness to Pristina's drinking scene; places are hip one minute and empty the next. Try the bars along 2 Korriko, Haidar Dushi and Rehep Luci for 'spill-out-in-the-street' summer drinking.

Publicco BAR

(Rr Garibaldi 7) A suave option for coffee and cocktail seekers.

☆ Entertainment

Kino ABC CINEMA

(www.kinoabc.info; Rr Rexhep Luci 1; ⊗8am-midnight) Two cinemas – the second is **ABC1** (www.kinoabc.info; R Luan Haradinaj) – usually show a couple of movies daily.

🔒 Shopping

Library Dukagjini BOOKS

(Bul Nëna Terezë 20; ⊗8am-8pm Mon-Sat) Sells maps, language and history books and novels, including many titles in English.

ℹ Information

Barnatore Pharmacy (Bul Nëna Terezë; ⊗8am-10pm)

Pristina University Hospital (Bul I Dëshmorët)

Pristina

KOSOVO PEJA (PEĆ)

PTK Post (Rr UÇK; 8am-10pm Mon-Sat) Post and phone services.

Getting There & Around

AIR Taxis charge €25 for the 20-minute, 18km trip to **Pristina International Airport** (958 123; www.airportpristina.com). There is a bus service between the **Grand Hotel** (Bul Nëna Terezë) in Pristina and the airport every two hours 24 hours a day (€2).

BUS The **bus station** (Stacioni i Autobusëve; Rr Lidja e Pejes) is 2km southwest of the centre off Bul Bil Klinton. Taxis to the centre should cost €2. International buses from Pristina include Serbia's Belgrade (€20, six hours, 11pm) and Novi Pazar (€5, three hours, 10am); Sarajevo (Bosnia and Hercegovina) via Novi Pazar (€23, 4pm); Durres and Tirana, Albania (€10, five hours); Skopje, Macedonia (€5, 1½ hours, every 30 minutes 5.30am to 5pm); Podgorica, Montenegro (€15, seven hours, 5.45pm, 7pm and 7.30pm).

TAXI Local taxi trips cost a few euro; the meter starts at €1.50. A good operator is **Radio Taxi Victory** (044 111 222, 555 333). Fares for unofficial taxis must be negotiated beforehand.

TRAIN Trains run from Pristina to Peja (€3, two hours, 8.01am and 4.41pm) and, internationally, to Skopje in Macedonia (€4, three hours, 7.22am).

AROUND PRISTINA

Kosovo is a small country, which can be crossed by car in any direction in around an hour. Not far in distance, but worlds away from the chaotic capital, the smaller towns of Peja and Prizren both offer a different pace and a new perspective on Kosovar life. The attractive countryside is dotted with historic sites and heavily guarded Serbian monasteries, whose presence remains an extremely emotive subject for all ethnic groups.

Peja (Peć)
039 / POP 170,000

Peja (known as Peć in Serbian) is Kosovo's third-largest city and one flanked by sites vital to Orthodox Serbians. With a Turkish-style bazaar at its heart and the beautiful Rugova Mountains all around it, it's a diverse and progressive place that's ripe for tourism

Peja is also home to the Shqip Short Film Festival (www.shqipfilmfest.com), which takes place in the last week of June each year and attracts international film makers.

◉ Sights

Patriachate of Peć MONASTERY

(☎044 15 07 55; ◷9am-6pm) This church and monastery are a slice of Serbian Orthodoxy. Multilingual Mrs Dobrilla may be able to show you around. It's guarded by NATO's Kosovo Force (KFOR) and you will need to hand in your passport for the duration of your visit. From the food stands around the main square, walk along Lekë Dukagjini with the river on your left for 15 minutes until you reach the monastery walls.

Cheese Market MARKET

(◷8am-4pm Sat) The town's bustling bazaar makes you feel like you've turned left into İstanbul. Farmers gather here on Saturday with wooden barrels of goat's cheese, so follow your nose.

Ethnological Museum MUSEUM

(Aquer Haxhi Zeka; admission €1; ◷9am-noon & 3-7pm Tue-Sat, 9am-4pm Sun) This Ottoman house is filled with local traditional crafts and the various displays illustrate life in Peja under the Ottomans.

🏃 Activities

Rugova Experience ADVENTURE TOUR

(☎044 137 734, 432 352; www.rugovaexperience.org; Mbretëreshë Teuta) This excellent, locally run company is championing the Rugova region for hikers and cultural tourists. It organises homestays in mountain villages, runs very good trekking tours, enjoys great local access and works with English-speaking guides. Its helpful office has maps and plenty of information about Peja's local trekking opportunities.

🛏 Sleeping & Eating

There are several good hotels in Peja, but by comparison a lack of decent places to eat. Both the Dukagjini and Cocktail hotels have recommended restaurants, and if you're looking for budget eats the pedestrianised Lekë Dukagjini, off the main square by the river, is lined with kebab shops and cafes.

TOP CHOICE **Dukagjini Hotel** HOTEL €€

(☎771 177; www.hoteldukagjini.com; Sheshi I Dëshmorëve 2; s/d incl breakfast €50/70; ⊕❄🎧🏊) What on earth is a hotel like this doing in Peja, you may well ask yourself as you step into the regal setting of the Dukagjini's lobby. The hotel has been totally remodelled and the entire place displays international standards you probably didn't expect in a small city in Kosovo. Rooms are large, grandly appointed and have supremely comfortable beds. Try for a 1st-floor room with access to an enormous balcony overlooking the town centre.

Cocktail Hotel HOTEL €€

(☎039 428 735, 044 159 011; Mbretëresha Teuta; s/d incl breakfast €40/60; 🎧) Opened in 2012, this new place contains both a pleasant hotel with spacious and clean rooms, and an expansive restaurant offering up a tasty menu of pizza, pasta, risotto, steak and other meat grills (mains €3–8).

Hotel Gold HOTEL €€

(☎434 571; Rr Eliot Engl 122/2; s/d incl breakfast €40/50; 🎧) 'Our experience, your relax' may

Vertical margin text: KOSOVO PEJA (PEĆ)

DON'T MISS

VISOKI DEČANI MONASTERY

This imposing whitewashed **monastery** (☎49-776 254; www.decani.org; ◷11am-1pm & 4-6pm), 15km south of Peja, is one of Kosovo's absolute highlights. Located in an incredibly beautiful spot beneath the mountains and surrounded by a forest of pine and chestnut trees, the monastery has been here since 1327 and is today heavily guarded by KFOR. Despite frequent attacks from locals who'd like to see the Serbs leave – most recently a grenade attack in 2007 – the 25 Serbian monks living here in total isolation from the local community have stayed. Here they get on with the serious business of making delicious wines, cheeses and honey (on sale at the small shop) and of slowly restoring the monastery's fabulous icons and frescoes.

Buses go to the town of Dečani from Peja (€1, 30 minutes, every 15 minutes) on their way to Gjakovë. It's a pleasant 1km walk to the monastery from the bus stop. From the roundabout in the middle of town, take the second exit if you're coming from Peja. Keep to the roads – KFOR warns of UXO (unexploded ordnance) in the area. You'll need to surrender your passport while visiting.

be their somewhat garbled slogan, but all the basics are covered here at this admittedly rather sterile establishment. The rooms are on the small side for the price, and the furniture choices questionable, but at least it's unlikely to be booked up.

ⓘ Getting There & Away

BUS Frequent buses run to Pristina (€5, 90 minutes, every 20 minutes) and Prizren (€4, 80 minutes, hourly). International buses link Peja with Ulclinj (€15, 10am, 8.30pm) and Podgorica in Montenegro (€12, 10am).

TRAIN Trains depart Peja for Pristina at 5.30am and 11.10am (two hours) and depart Pristina for Peja at 7.22am and 4.41pm.

Prizren

📞 029 / POP 178,000

Picturesque Prizren is Kosovo's second city and it shines with post-independence euphoria and enthusiasm that's infectious. If you're passing through between Albania and Pristina, the charming mosque-filled old town is well worth setting aside a few hours to wander about in.

◉ Sights

Prizren's 15th-century **Ottoman bridge** has been superbly restored. Nearby is **Sinan Pasha Mosque** (1561), which renovations are resurrecting as a central landmark in Prizren. Have a peek at the nonfunctioning **Gazi Mehmed Pasha Baths** nearby as well.

The **Orthodox Church of the Virgin of Leviša** is not exactly welcoming – it's heavily guarded, but at least it's no longer surrounded by barbed wire as it has been for the past decade.

The **Ethnological Museum** (admission €1; ⊙11am-7pm Tue-Sun) is where the Prizren League (for Albanian autonomy) organised itself in 1878.

There is not much of interest at the 11th-century **Kalaja** on top of the hill overlooking the old town, but the 180-degree views over Prizren from this fort are worth the walk. On the way, more barbed wire surrounds the heavily guarded **Saint Savior Church**, hinting at the fragility of Prizren's once-robust multiculturalism.

🛏 Sleeping & Eating

There are plenty of stylish new hotels in Prizren. There's also a vibrant strip of bars and eateries on the castle side of the river and around the old-town square.

TOP CHOICE **Hotel Prizreni**　　　HOTEL €€
(☑225 200; www.hotelprizreni.com; Rr Shën Flori 2; r incl breakfast €40-50; ❄️🛜) With an unbeatable location just behind the Sinan Pasha Mosque (though you may well disagree at dawn), the Prizreni is a brand new place with 10 stylish and contemporary rooms, great views and enthusiastic staff. There's a good restaurant downstairs (open 8am to 11pm).

Hotel Centrum　　　HOTEL €€
(☑230 530; www.centrumprizren.com; Rr Bujtinat 1; s/d €40/50; ❄️🛜) A great choice is this sleekly designed 23-room place, which is a little tricky to find, but well worth the effort of doing so. Coming from the main square of the Old Town, turn right after the Orthodox Church and you'll find this stylish bolthole on a small side street. Some rooms have great balconies and below it there's a good restaurant.

Ambient　　　TRADITIONAL €
(Rr Vatrat Shqiptare; mains €3-7; ⊙8am-midnight) With by far the most charming location in Prizren by a waterfall cascading down the cliffside by the river, and views over the old town, this is a place to come for a romantic dinner or sundowner. The menu includes a Pasha burger, steaks, seafood and a catch of the day cooked to your specification.

Arasta　　　TRADITIONAL €
(Sheshi Shadёrvan; mains €3-7; ⊙8am-midnight) On the riverside with a prime location and great outdoor seating, this traditional-style tavern also has a cosy interior perfect for an evening meal. The menu runs from meat grills to fresh fish, pizza and pasta.

ⓘ Getting There & Away

Prizren is well connected to Pristina (€4, 90 minutes, every 10 to 25 minutes), Peja (€4, 90 minutes, six daily) and Albania's Tirana (€12, four hours).

UNDERSTAND KOSOVO

History

Be aware that Kosovo's history is interpreted very differently depending on who you're talking to, with people of differing ethnic and religious backgrounds tending to be polarised along these lines.

In the 12th century Kosovo was the heart of the Orthodox Christian Serbian empire, until Turkish triumph at the pivotal 1389 Battle of Kosovo ushered in 500 years of Ottoman rule and Islam.

Serbia regained control in the 1912 Balkan War and the region became part of Yugoslavia upon its creation in 1918. In WWII the territory was incorporated into Italian-controlled Albania and was liberated and returned to Yugoslavia in October 1944 by Albanian partisans. Following decades of postwar neglect, Kosovo was granted de facto self-government status in 1974.

Kosovo War

In 1989 the autonomy Kosovo enjoyed under the 1974 constitution was suspended by Slobodan Milošević. Ethnic Albanian leaders declared independence from Serbia in 1990. War broke out in 1992 – that same year, Ibrahim Rugova was elected as the first president of the self-proclaimed Republic of Kosovo. Ethnic conflict heightened and the Kosovo Liberation Army (KLA) was formed in 1996.

In March 1999 a US-backed plan to return Kosovo's autonomy was rejected by Serbia, which moved to empty the province of its non-Serbian population. Nearly 850,000 Kosovo Albanians fled to Albania and Macedonia. After Serbia refused to desist, NATO unleashed a bombing campaign on 24 March 1999. In June, Milošević agreed to withdraw troops, air strikes ceased, the KLA disarmed and the NATO-led KFOR (Kosovo Force; the international force responsible for establishing security in Kosovo) took over. From June 1999, Kosovo was administered as a UN–NATO protectorate.

Kosovo caught the world's attention again in 2004 when violence broke out in Mitrovica between the ethnic Serbian and ethnic Albanian communities; 19 people were killed, 600 homes were burnt and 29 monasteries and churches were destroyed in the worst ethnic violence since 1999.

NEWSPAPERS

Prishtina Insight (www.prishtinainsight.com; €1), a newspaper run by the Balkan Investigative Reporting Network, gives exactly what its title says.

Independence

UN-sponsored talks on Kosovo's status began in February 2006 and Kosovo's parliament declared Kosovo independent on 17 February 2008. In June 2008 a new constitution transferred power from the UN to the government of Kosovo. Kosovo Serbs established their own assembly in Mitrovica.

In 2010 the International Court of Justice ruled that Kosovo's declaration of independence did not violate international law; however, Serbia's president reiterated that Serbia would 'never recognise the unilaterally proclaimed independence of Kosovo'. To date, Kosovo has been recognised as an independent country by 100 countries around the world, including most of the EU, the US and Canada.

New Leadership

Following a string of acting presidents after Ibrahim Rugova's death in 2006, Atifete Jahjaga became Kosovo's president in 2011. A non-partisan, female former police chief, Jahjaga has been a breath of fresh air for politics in Kosovo, even if controversy has never been far from Hashim Thaçi, the current prime minister and the position of real power in the country. Thaçi has been accused of everything from drug trafficking to selling the organs of Serbian prisoners during his time heading the KLA, although he denies all such charges.

People

The population was estimated at 1.8 million in 2010; 92% are Albanian and 8% are Serb (mostly living in enclaves), Bosniak, Gorani, Roma, Turks, Ashkali and Egyptians. The main religious groups are Muslims (mostly Albanians), Serbian Orthodox and Roman Catholic.

Arts

Former president Ibrahim Rugova was a significant figure in Kosovo's literary scene; his presidency of the Kosovo Writers' Association was a step towards presidency of the nation. Try Albanian writer Ismail Kadare's *Three Elegies for Kosovo* for a beautifully written taste of this land's sad history.

Kosovar music bears the imprint of five centuries of Turkish rule; high-whine flutes carry tunes above goat-skin drumbeats. Architecture also shows Islamic influence, mixed with Byzantine and vernacular styles.

The visual-arts scene is re-emerging after troubled times; visit Kosovo Art Gallery (p440) to check it out.

Environment

Kosovo is broadly flat but surrounded by impressive mountains, the highest being Đeravica (2656m). Most of Kosovo's protected area is in Šara National Park, created in 1986.

Among the estimated 46 species of mammal in Kosovo are bears, lynx, deer, weasels and the endangered river otter. Around 220 bird species live in or visit Kosovo, including eagles and falcons.

Pollutants emitted from infrastructure hit by NATO bombs have affected Kosovo's biodiversity. Industrial pollution, rapid urbanisation and overharvesting of wood threaten ecosystems.

Food & Drink

'Traditional' food is generally Albanian – most prominently, stewed and grilled meat and fish. *Kos* (goat's-cheese yoghurt) is eaten alone or with almost anything. Turkish kebabs and *đuveč* (baked meat and vegetables) are common. The local beer is Peja (from the town of the same name). The international presence has brought world cuisines to the capital. Outside Pristina, however, waiters respond to vegetarian requests with thigh-slapping laughter. Requests for nonsmoking areas will be met with the same reaction.

SURVIVAL GUIDE

Directory A–Z

Accommodation

Accommodation is booming in Kosovo, with most large towns now offering a good range of options.

Price ranges used in listings in this chapter are for a double room with bathroom.

€ less than €40

€€ €40 to €80

€€€ more than €80

Business Hours

Reviews include hours only if they differ significantly from these.

Banks 8am to 5pm Monday to Friday, until 2pm Saturday

Bars 8am to 11pm (on the dot if police are cracking down)

Shops 8am to 6pm Monday to Friday, until 3pm Saturday

Restaurants 8am to midnight

Embassies & Consulates

There are no embassies for Australia, Canada, New Zealand or Ireland in Kosovo, so consular issues are handled by the embassies in Belgrade. The following are all in Pristina:

French Embassy (✉2245 8800; www.ambafrance-kosovo.org; Ismail Qemali 67)

German Embassy (✉254 500; www.pristina.diplo.de; Azem Jashanica 17)

Netherlands Embassy (✉516 101; kosovo.nlembassy.org; Xhemajl Berisha 12)

Swiss Embassy (✉248 088; www.eda.admin.ch/pristina; Adrian Krasniqi 11)

UK Embassy (✉254 700; www.ukinkosovo.fco.gov.uk; Ismail Qemajli 6)

US Embassy (✉5959 3000; http://pristina.usembassy.gov; Nazim Hikmet 30)

Food

The following price categories for the average cost of a main course are used in this chapter.

€ less than €5

€€ €5 to €10

€€€ more than €10

Money

Kosovo's currency is the euro, despite not being part of the eurozone or the EU. It's best to arrive with small denominations and euro coins are particularly useful. ATMs are common and established businesses accept credit cards.

Post

PTK post and telecommunications offices operate in Kosovo's main towns.

Public Holidays

New Year's Day 1 January

Independence Day 17 February

Kosovo Constitution Day 9 April

Labour Day 1 May

Europe Holiday 9 May

Note that traditional Islamic holidays are also observed.

Safe Travel

Check government travel advisories before travelling to Kosovo. Sporadic violence occurs in North Mitrovica. Unexploded ordnance (UXO) has been cleared from roads and paths but you should seek KFOR (www.aco.nato.int/kfor.aspx) advice before venturing off beaten tracks.

Make sure your insurance covers you for travel in Kosovo. It's not a good idea to travel in Kosovo with Serbian plates on your car.

Telephone

Kosovo's country code is ☎381. Mobile phone numbers (starting with ☎044, ☎045, ☎043 or ☎049) are hosted by Monaco (☎377) and Slovenia (☎386). Various mobile phone operators have SIM cards that are effectively free; the €5 fee includes €5 worth of credit.

Visas

Visas are not required; check the **Ministry of Foreign Affairs** (www.mfa-ks.net) website for changes. Upon arrival, you get a 90-day entry stamp.

If you wish to travel between Serbia and Kosovo you'll need to enter Kosovo from Serbia first (see p438).

Getting There & Away

Air

Pristina International Airport (☎038-5958 123; www.airportpristina.com) is 18km from the centre of Pristina. The following airlines fly to Kosovo:

Adria Airways (www.adria.si)

Air Prishtina (☎038-222 099; info.airprishtina.com)

Austrian Airlines (☎038-548 435, 038-502 456; www.austrian.com)

Croatia Airways (☎038-233 833; www.croatiaairlines.com)

Germania Airlines (www.flygermania.de)

Germanwings (www.germanwings.com)

Kosova Airlines (☎038-220 220; www.kosovaairlines.com)

Swiss (☎038-243 446; www.swiss.com)

Turkish Airlines (☎038-247 696, 038-247 711; www.turkishairlines.com)

Land

You can take international bus trips to and from all neighbouring capital cities including Belgrade (the bus travels via Montenegro first) from Pristina. There's also a train to Skopje from Pristina (€4, three hours, 7.22am).

BORDER CROSSINGS

Albania To get to Albania's Koman Ferry use the Morina border crossing west of Gjakovë. A short distance further south is the Qafë Prush crossing, though the road continuing into Albania is bad here. The busiest border is at Vionica, where the excellent new motorway connects to Tirana.

Macedonia Blace from Pristina and Gllobocicë from Prizren.

Montenegro The main crossing is the Kulla/Rožaje crossing on the road between Rožaje and Peja.

Serbia Due to outbreaks of violence, travellers are advised to be extra vigilant if entering Kosovo at Jarinje or Bërnjak/Banja. There are a total of six border crossings between the countries in total. Note that it's not possible to leave Kosovo into Serbia unless you entered Kosovo from Serbia.

Getting Around

Bus

Buses stop at distinct blue signs, but can be flagged down anywhere. Bus journeys are generally cheap, but the going can be slow on Kosovo's single-lane roads.

Car

Serbian-plated cars have been attacked in Kosovo, and rental companies do not let cars hired in Kosovo travel to Serbia and vice versa. European Green Card vehicle insurance is not valid in the country. However, it's perfectly easy to hire cars here, and travel with them to neighbouring countries (with the exception of Serbia).

Train

The train system is something of a novelty, but routes inclue Pristina–Peja (€3, 1½ hours, 8.01am and 4.41pm) and Pristina–Skopje (€4, three hours, 7.22am). Locals generally catch buses.

Latvia

Includes »

Best Places to Eat

» Istaba (p464)

» Fish Restaurant (p463)

» Vincents (p464)

» 36.Line (p470)

Best Places to Stay

» Hotel Bergs (p462)

» Radisson Blu Hotel Elizabete (p462)

» Fontaine Royal (p472)

» Dome Hotel (p462)

Why Go?

Tucked between Estonia to the north and Lithuania to the south, Latvia is the meat of the Baltic sandwich. We're not implying that the neighbouring nations are slices of white bread, but Latvia is the savoury middle, loaded with colourful fillings. Thick greens take the form of Gauja Valley pines. Onion-domed cathedrals sprout above local towns. Cheesy Russian pop blares along coastal beaches. And spicy Rīga adds an extra zing as the country's cosmopolitan nexus and unofficial capital of the entire Baltic.

If that doesn't whet your appetite, hear this: the country's under-the-radar profile makes it the perfect pit stop for those seeking something a bit more authentic than the overrun tourist hubs further afield. So, consider altering your Eastern European itinerary and fill up on little Latvia instead of big-ticket destinations Prague, Vienna or – dare we say it – Hungary.

When to Go
Rīga

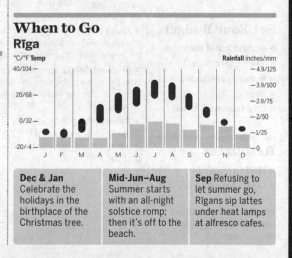

Dec & Jan
Celebrate the holidays in the birthplace of the Christmas tree.

Mid-Jun–Aug
Summer starts with an all-night solstice romp; then it's off to the beach.

Sep Refusing to let summer go, Rīgans sip lattes under heat lamps at alfresco cafes.

AT A GLANCE

» **Currency** Lats (Ls)

» **Language** Latvian, Russian

» **Money** ATMs all over Rīga and smaller cities; banks open Monday to Saturday

» **Visas** Not required for EU citizens, or for stays of up to 90 days for Australian, Canadian, New Zealand and US citizens

Fast Facts

» **Area** 64,589 sq km
» **Capital** Rīga
» **Country code** ☑371
» **Emergency** ☑112

Exchange Rates

Australia	A$1	0.57Ls
Canada	C$1	0.54Ls
Euro Zone	€1	0.70Ls
Japan	¥100	0.58Ls
New Zealand	NZ$1	0.46Ls
UK	UK£1	0.83Ls
USA	US$1	0.55Ls

Set Your Budget

» **Budget hotel room** 25Ls
» **Two-course meal** 10Ls
» **Museum entrance** 1.50Ls
» **Beer** 1.20Ls
» **City transport ticket** 0.70Ls

Resources

» **1188** (www.1188.lv)

» **Latvia Institute** (www.li.lv)

» **Latvia Tourism Development Agency** (www.latviatourism.lv)

Connections

Latvia is the link in the Baltic chain, making Rīga a convenient point between Tallinn and Vilnius. Long-distance buses and trains also connect the capital to St Petersburg, Moscow and Warsaw, and ferry services shuttle passengers to Sweden and Germany. Rīga is the hub of airBaltic, which offers direct service to dozens of major European cities.

ITINERARIES

Three Days

Fill your first two days with a feast of Rīga's architectural eye candy, and spend your third day hiking betwixt Sigulda's castles, sunbathing in scintillating Jūrmala or snapping photos of Rundāle's opulent palace.

One Week

After a few days in the capital, swing by Jūrmala on your way up the horn of Cape Kolka for saunas, sunsets and solitude. Glide through western Latvia comparing its ultrabucolic townships to Rundāle's majestic grounds, then blaze a trail across eastern Latvia for a rousing trip back in time spiced with adrenaline sports.

Essential Food & Drink

» **Black Balzām** Goethe called it 'the elixir of life'. The jet-black, 45% proof concoction is a secret recipe of more than a dozen fairy-tale ingredients including oak bark, wormwood and linden blossoms. A shot a day keeps the doctor away, so say most of Latvia's pensioners. Try mixing it with glass of cola to take the edge off.

» **Mushrooms** Not a sport but a national obsession; mushroom picking takes the country by storm during the first showers of autumn.

» **Alus** For such a tiny nation there's definitely no shortage of *alus* (beer) – each major town has its own brew. You can't go wrong with Užavas (Ventspils' contribution).

» **Smoked fish** Dozens of fish shacks dot the Kurzeme coast – look for the veritable smoke signals rising above the tree line. Grab 'em to go; they make the perfect afternoon snack.

» **Kvass** Single-handedly responsible for the decline of Coca-Cola at the turn of the 21st century, Kvass is a beloved beverage made from fermented rye bread. It's surprisingly popular with kids!

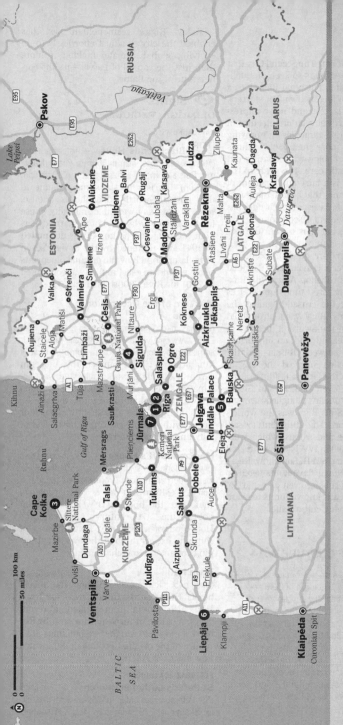

Latvia Highlights

1 Click your camera at the menagerie of gargoyles, beasts, goddesses and twisting vines that inhabits the surplus of **Riga's art nouveau architecture** (p461).

2 Lose yourself in the maze of cobblestones, church spires and gingerbread trim that is **Old Riga** (p452).

3 Listen to the waves pound the awesomely remote **Cape Kolka** (p470), which crowns the desolate Kurzeme coast.

4 Swing through **Sigulda** (p472) on a bungee cord.

5 Sneak away from the capital and indulge in aristocratic decadence at **Rundāle Palace** (p470).

6 Wander past gritty Soviet tenements and gilded cathedrals in the crumbling Karosta district of portly **Liepāja** (p472).

7 Hobnob with Russian jetsetters in the heart of **Jūrmala's swanky spa scene** (p469).

RĪGA

POP 700,000

'The Paris of the North', 'The Second City that Never Sleeps' – everyone's so keen on qualifying Latvia's capital, but regal Rīga does a hell of a job of holding its own. For starters, the city has the largest and most impressive showing of art nouveau architecture in Europe. Nightmarish gargoyles and praying goddesses adorn more than 750 buildings along the stately boulevards radiating out from the city's castle core. The heart of the city – Old Rīga – is a fairy-tale kingdom of winding wobbly lanes that beat to the sound of clicking stilettos, beer-garden brouhahas and rumbling basement discotheques.

Although some Latvians lament the fact that they are an ethnic minority in their own capital, others are quick to point out that Rīga was never a 'Latvian' city. Founded in 1201 by German Bishop Albert von Buxhoevden (say that three times quickly) as a bridgehead for the crusade against the northern 'heathens', Rīga was a stronghold for the Knights of the Sword, a member of the Hanseatic League and an important trading junction between Russia and the West. When Sweden snagged the city in 1621, it grew into the largest holding of the Swedish empire (even bigger than Stockholm). Soon the Russians ploughed through, and by the mid-1860s Rīga was the world's biggest timber port. The 20th century saw the birth of cafes and salons, which were bombed to high hell in WWI and suppressed by the Nazis during WWII. Somehow, Rīga's indelible international flavour managed to rise up from the rubble; even as a part of the USSR the city was known for its forward thinking and thriving cultural life.

CAPITAL OF CULTURE 2014

The European Union has declared Rīga the European Capital of Culture for 2014. Expect a full calendar year of exciting events, including the inauguration of the new national library across the river from Old Rīga, the World Choir Games featuring singers from over 90 countries, a celebration of the 500th anniversary of the printed book and more than 200 other cultural events. Check out www.riga2014.org for more information.

Today, Rīga's cosmopolitan past has enabled the city to adjust effortlessly to an evolving global climate, making it more than just the capital of Latvia – it's the cornerstone of the Baltic.

◉ Sights

OLD RĪGA (VECRĪGA)

RĀTSLAUKUMS

TOP CHOICE Blackheads' House HISTORIC BUILDING
(Melngalvju House; Map p456; http://nami.riga.lv/mn; Rātslaukums 7; admission 2Ls; ◷10am-5pm Tue-Sun) Touristy Rātslaukums is home to the postcard-worthy Blackheads' House, built in 1344 as a veritable fraternity house for the Blackheads' guild of unmarried German merchants. The house was decimated in 1941 and flattened by the Soviets seven years later. Somehow the original blueprints survived and an exact replica was completed in 2001 for Rīga's 800th birthday.

Museum of the Occupation of Latvia MUSEUM
(Latvijas okupācijas muzejs; Map p456; ☎6721 2715; www.omf.lv; Latviesu Strēlnieku laukums 1; admission by donation; ◷11am-6pm) Ironically inhabiting a Soviet bunker, this museum carefully details Latvia's Soviet and Nazi occupations between 1940 and 1991. Exhibits are well curated and intriguing, though the focus on minutia can be slightly tedious for those without pre-existing knowledge of Latvian political history.

Mentzendorff's House HISTORIC BUILDING
(Mencendorfa nams; Map p456; ☎6721 2951; www.mencendorfanams.com; Grēcinieku iela 18; admission 1Ls; ◷10am-5pm Wed & Fri-Sun, noon-7pm Thu) Once the home of a wealthy German noble, the 17th-century Mentzendorff's House offers insight into Rīga's history of shipping excess through the everyday trappings of an elite merchant family.

Town Hall HISTORIC BUILDING
(Map p456; Rātslaukums) Facing the Blackheads' House across the square is the Town Hall, also rebuilt from scratch in recent years. A statue of Rīga's patron saint **St Roland** stands between the two buildings. It's a replica of the original, erected in 1897, which now sits in St Peter's.

PĒTERBAZNĪCA LAUKUMS

St Peter's Lutheran Church CHURCH
(Sv Pēterabaznīca; Map p456; www.peterbaznic.lv; Skārņu iela 19; admission 4Ls; ◷11am-6pm

RĪGA IN TWO DAYS

Start your adventure in the heart of the city with a stop at the much-loved **Blackheads' House** in **Rātslaukums**. Pick up some handy brochures at the in-house information centre, then spend the rest of the morning wandering among the twisting cobbled lanes that snake through medieval **Old Rīga**. After a leisurely lunch, wander beyond the ancient walls, passing the **Freedom Monument** as you make your way to the grand boulevards that radiate away from the city's castle core. Head to the **Quiet Centre**, where you'll find some of Rīga's finest examples of **art nouveau architecture**. Don't miss the **Rīga Art Nouveau Centre**, then check out the neighbourhood's facades nearby.

On your second day, fine-tune your bargaining skills (and your Russian) during a visit to the **Central Market** where you can haggle for anything from wild berries to knock-off T-shirts. Take a relaxing boat ride along the **Daugava** and the city's inner canals. For a late lunch, wander up to the **Miera iela** area just north of the art nouveau district to enjoy the city's emerging hipster cafe culture near the sweet-smelling Laima chocolate factory. In the evening, if the **opera** is in season, treat yourself to some of the finest classical music in Europe.

Tue-Sun) Rīga's skyline centrepiece is Gothic St Peter's Lutheran Church, thought to be around 800 years old. Don't miss the view from the spire, which has been rebuilt three times in the same baroque form. Legend has it that in 1667 the builders threw glass from the top to see how long the spire would last. A greater number of shards meant a very long life. The glass ended up landing on a pile of straw and didn't break – a year later the tower was incinerated. When the spire was resurrected after a bombing during WWII, the ceremonial glass chucking was repeated, and this time it was a smash hit. The spire is 123.25m high, but the lift whisks you up only to 72m.

Museum of Decorative Arts & Design
MUSEUM

(Dekoratīvi lietišķās mākslas muzejs; Map p456; ☎6722 7833; www.dlmm.lv; Skārņu iela 10/20; admission 3Ls; ⊗11am-5pm Tue & Thu-Sun, to 7pm Wed) Behind St Peter's Church sits another impressive religious structure – the former **St George's Church** – that is now the Museum of Decorative Arts & Design, highlighting Latvia's impressive collection of woodcuts, textiles and ceramics. The building's stone foundations date back to 1204, when the Livonian Brothers of the Sword erected their castle here.

KALĒJU IELA & MĀRSTAĻU IELA

Zigzagging Kalēju iela and Mārstaļu iela are dotted with poignant reminders of the city's legacy as a wealthy northern European trading centre. Don't forget to look up at the curling vines and barking gargoyles adorning several art nouveau facades.

Latvian Photography Museum
MUSEUM

(Latvijas fotogrāfijas muzejs; Map p456; ☎6722 2713; www.fotomuzejs.lv; Mārstaļu iela 8; admission 1.50Ls; ⊗10am-5pm Wed & Fri-Sun, noon-7pm Thu) Several of the old merchants' manors have been transformed into museums such as this photography museum, which displays unique photographs from 1920s' Rīga.

Rīga Synagogue
SYNAGOGUE

(Map p456; Peitavas iela 6/8) Wander the area south of St Peter's square and you'll find the only Old Town synagogue to survive the war. It's the only active Jewish house of worship in the capital. The structure was restored in a 'sacral art nouveau' style at the end of 2009 after a generous infusion of money from the EU.

LIVU LAUKUMS

Great Guild
HISTORIC BUILDING

(Lielā ģilde; Map p456; Amatu iela 6) The 19th-century Gothic exterior of the Great Guild encloses a sumptuous merchants' meeting hall, built during the height of German power in the 1330s. It sits in the bustling square of Livu Laukums, which is lined by a colourful row of 18th-century buildings – most of which have been turned into rowdy restaurants and beer halls.

Small Guild
HISTORIC BUILDING

(Mazā ģilde; Map p456; Amatu iela 5) This fairytale castle was founded during the 14th century as the meeting place for local artisans.

Cat House
HISTORIC BUILDING

(Kaķu māja; Map p456; Miestaru iela 10/12) Don't miss the Cat House, named for the spooked

Rīga

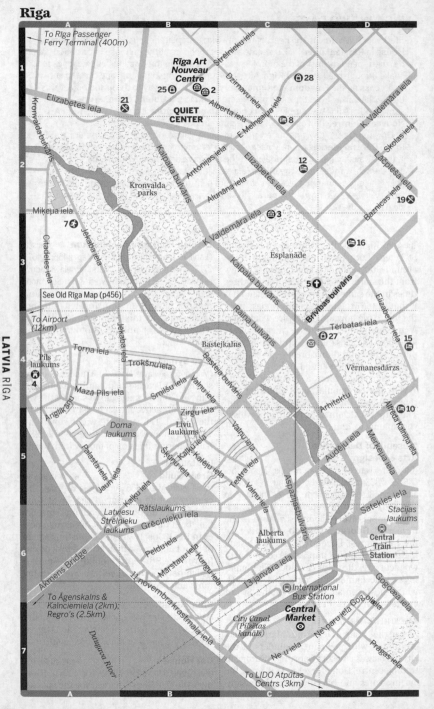

To Rīga Passenger Ferry Terminal (400m)

Strēlnieku iela

Rīga Art Nouveau Centre

25

2

Dzirnavu iela

28

Alberta iela

QUIET CENTER

Elizabetes iela

Kronvalda bulvāris

21

E Melngaiļa iela

8

Antonijas iela

12

Kronvalda parks

Kalpaka bulvāris

Alunāna iela

K Valdemāra iela

3

Elizabetes iela

Skolas iela

Lāčplēša iela

Baznīcas iela

K. Valdemāra iela

Mikeļa iela

Citadeles iela

Jēkaba iela

7

19

Esplanāde

5

16

Kalpaka bulvāris

See Old Rīga Map (p456)

Raiņa bulvāris

Brīvības bulvāris

To Airport (12km)

Tērbatas iela

27

15

Toŗņa iela

Jēkaba iela

Bastejkalns

Vērmanesdārzs

Trokšņu iela

Basteja bulvāris

Pils laukums

4

Maza Pils iela

Smilšu iela

Valņu iela

Zirgu iela

Anglikāņu

Doma laukums

Līvu laukums

Valņu iela

Arhitektu

Alfrēda Kalniņa iela

10

Palasta iela

Šķūņu iela

Kaļķu iela

Kalēju iela

Teātra iela

Valņu iela

Audēju iela

Merķeļa iela

Jauniela

Kaļķu iela

Rātslaukums

Aspazijas bulvāris

Satekles iela

Stacijas laukums

Latviešu Strēlnieku laukums

Grēcinieku iela

Peldu iela

Mārstaļu iela

Kungu iela

Alberta laukums

Central Train Station

To Āgenskalns & Kalnciemiela (2km); Regro's (2.5km)

Akmens Bridge

11. novembra krastmala iela

13 janvāra iela

International Bus Station

Central Market

City Canal (Pilsētas kanāls)

Gogoļa iela

Prāgas iela

Dugavas River

Neļaru iela

Gogoļa iela

Ne u iela

To LIDO Atpūtas Centrs (3km)

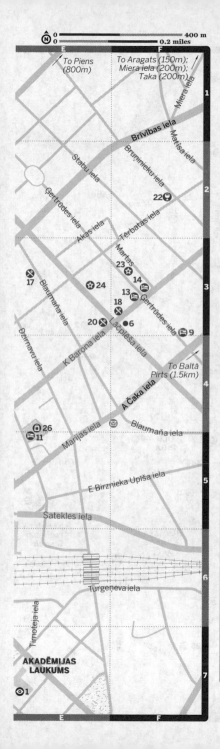

Rīga

LATVIA RĪGA

Old Rīga

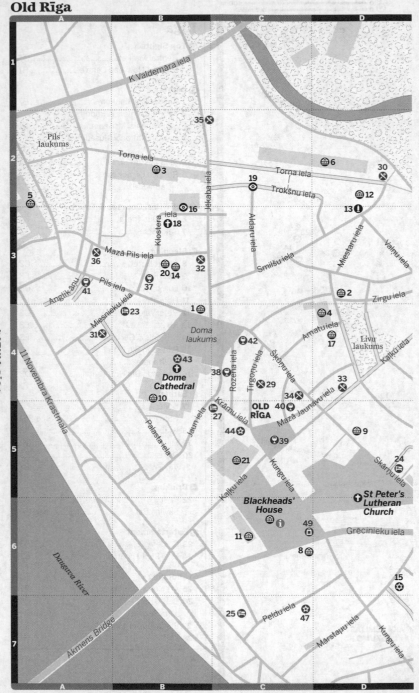

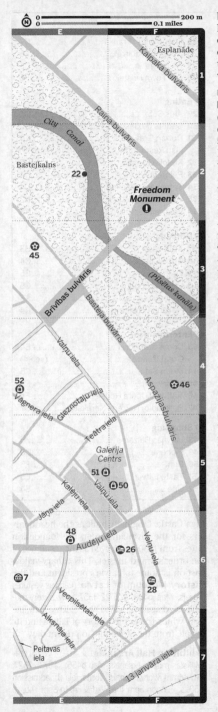

black cat sitting on the roof. According to legend, the owner was rejected from the local Merchants' Guild across the street, and exacted revenge by placing a black cat on the top of his turret with its tail raised towards the esteemed Great Guild hall.

DOMA LAUKUMS

Dome Cathedral
CHURCH

(Doma baznīca; Map p456; ☑6721 3213; www. doms.lv; Doma laukums 1; admission 2Ls; ☻9am-5pm) The centrepiece of expansive Doma Laukums is Rīga's enormous Dome Cathedral. Founded in 1211 as the seat of the Rīga diocese, it is still the largest church in the Baltics. The floor and walls of the huge interior are dotted with old stone tombs. In 1709, the cholera and typhoid outbreak that killed a third of Rīga's population was blamed on a flood that inundated the crypt. The cathedral's pulpit dates from 1641 and the huge, 6768-pipe organ was the world's largest when it was completed in 1884 (it's now the fourth largest). Mass is held at noon on Sundays and at 8am every other day.

Art Museum Rīga Bourse
MUSEUM

(Bīrzasnams; Map p456; ☑6722 6467; www.lnmm. lv; Doma laukums 6; admission 2Ls; ☻10am-6pm Tue-Sun) Rīga's newest museum houses the city's wealth of foreign art in a beautifully restored building that was once the city's stock market centre. The clay-tinged facade features an ornate coterie of deities that dance between the windows. Inside, visitors will uncover vaulted ceilings and gorgeous tilework.

Museum of the History of Rīga & Navigation
MUSEUM

(Rīgas vēstures un kuģniecības muzejs; Map p456; ☑6735 6676; www.rigamuz.lv; Palasta iela 4; admission 3Ls; ☻11am-5pm Fri-Tue, noon-7pm Thu) This is the Baltics' oldest museum, situated in the monastery's cloister at the back of the Dome Cathedral complex. Founded in 1773, the exhibition space features a permanent collection of artefacts from the Bronze Age all the way to WWII.

Three Brothers
HISTORIC BUILDING

(Trīs brāļi; Map p456; Mazā Pils iela 17, 19 & 21) Located behind Doma Laukums, the Three Brothers exemplifies Old Rīga's diverse collection of old architectural styles. Number 19 (built in the 17th century) is now the **Rīga Museum of Architecture** (Latvijas arhitektūras muzejs; Map p456; www.archmuseum. lv; admission by donation; ☻9am-5pm Mon-Fri).

LATVIA RĪGA

Old Rīga

Note the tiny windows on the upper levels – Rīga's property taxes during the Middle Ages were based on the size of one's windows.

St Jacob's Cathedral CHURCH

(Sv Jēkaba katedrāle; Map p456; Klostera iela) Latvia's first Lutheran services were held in St Jacob's Cathedral, which has an interior dating back to 1225. Today it is the seat of Rīga's Roman Catholic archbishopric.

PILS LAUKUMS

Rīga Castle CASTLE

(Rīgas pils; Map p454; Pils laukums 3) In the far corner of Old Rīga near the Vanšu bridge, verdant **Pils Laukums** sits at the doorstep of Rīga Castle. Originally built as the headquarters for the Livonian Order, the foundation dates from 1330 and served as the residence of the order's grand master. This canary-yellow bastion is home to Latvia's president and the **History Museum of Latvia** (Latvijas vēstures muzejs; Map p456; ☎6722 1357; www.history-museum.lv; admission 2Ls, Wed Wed; ☉10am-5pm Tue-Sun), which traces the history of Latvia and its people from the Stone Age to present day.

Exhibition Hall Arsenāls ART GALLERY

(Mākslas muzejs Arsenāls; Map p456; ☎6735 7527; www.lnmm.lv/en/arsenals; Torņa iela 1; admission 2.50Ls; ☉noon-6pm Tue, Wed & Fri, to 8pm Thu, to 5pm Sat & Sun) Constructed in 1832 in Russian

Late Empire style, the building was originally used as a warehouse. Today it features a variety of international art exhibitions and houses the finalists of the Purvītis Art Prize – most prestigious in Latvia, named for Vilhelms Purvītis (the 'father of Latvian Painting').

Saeima NOTABLE BUILDING
(Map p456; Jēkaba iela 11) Sharing a block with Arsenāls, Latvia's Parliament lives in a Florentine Renaissance structure originally commissioned as the Knights' House of the German landlords.

TORŅA IELA

Jacob's Barracks HISTORIC BUILDING
(Jēkaba Kazarmas; Map p456; Torņa iela 4) The entire north side of handsome Torņa iela is flanked by the custard-coloured Jacob's Barracks, built as an enormous warehouse in the 16th century. Tourist-friendly cafes and boutiques now inhabit the refurbished building.

Swedish Gate GATE
(Zviedru vārti; Map p456; Torņa iela 11) Towards the centre of Old Town, look for Trokšnu iela, Old Rīga's narrowest street. It leads to the Swedish Gate, which was built into the city walls in 1698 to celebrate Swedish occupation.

Powder Tower TOWER
(Pulvertornis; Map p456; Smilšu iela 20) The cylindrical Powder Tower dates back to the 14th century, and is the only survivor of the 18 original towers that punctuated the old city wall. In the past it served as a prison, torture chamber and frat house. Today it is the **Museum of War** (Kara muzejs; Map p456; www.karamuzejs.lv; Smilšu iela 20; admission free; ☺10am-6pm Tue, Wed & Fri-Sun, 11am-7pm Thu).

CENTRAL RĪGA (CENTRS)

ESPLANADE & AROUND

Freedom Monument MONUMENT
(Map p456; Brīvības bulvāris) Affectionately known as 'Milda', Rīga's Freedom Monument was erected in 1935 where a statue of Russian ruler Peter the Great once stood. A copper female Liberty tops the soaring monument, holding three gold stars representing the original cultural regions of Latvia: Kurzeme, Vidzeme and Latgale. Two soldiers stand guard at the monument throughout the day and perform a modest changing of the guard every hour on the hour from 9am to 6pm.

A second spire, the **Laima Clock** (Laimas pulkstenis), sits between Milda and the entrance to Old Rīga. Built in the 1920s as a gentle way to encourage Rīgans not to be late for work, the clock is now used as the preferred meeting place for young Latvians.

FREE Russian Orthodox Cathedral CHURCH
(Pareizticīgo katedrāle; Map p454; Brīvības bulvāris 23) At the far end of the Esplanāde, this stunning 19th-century cathedral majestically rises above the trees with its gilded cupolas. During the Soviet era the church was used as a planetarium.

Latvian National Museum of Art MUSEUM
(Latvijas Nacionālais mākslas muzejs; Map p454; ☑6732 5051; www.lnmm.lv; K Valdemāra iela 10a; admission 1.50Ls; ☺11am-6pm Tue-Sun) Sitting within the Esplanāde's leafy grounds, this impressive gallery features pre-WWII Russian and Latvian art displayed among the Soviet grandeur of ruched net curtains, marble columns and red carpets. The structure was purpose-built at the turn of the 20th century. At the time of research it was under extensive renovation and is due to properly reopen in 2014.

CENTRAL MARKET DISTRICT

TOP CHOICE Central Market MARKET
(Centrāl tirgus; Map p454; www.centraltirgus.lv; Nēģu iela 7; ☺7am-5pm Sun & Mon, to 6pm Tue-Sat) Haggle for your huckleberries at the Central Market, housed in a series of mammoth Zeppelin hangars constructed for the Germans during WWI. Check out the seafood pavilion for locally adored herring and smoked eel, or swing by the produce section for chilled sauerkraut juice – a traditional hangover remedy. It's a fantastic spot to assemble a picnic lunch and do some people-watching.

Akadēmijas Laukums SQUARE
(Zinātņu Akadēmija; Map p454; www.lza.lv; Akadēmijas laukums 1; ☺9am-8pm) Just beyond the soaring hangars of the Central Market lies Akadēmijas Laukums, home to the Academy of Science. Also called 'Stalin's Birthday Cake', this is Rīga's Russified Empire State Building. Those with an eagle eye will spot hammers and sickles hidden in the convoluted facade. A few lats grants you admission to the observation deck on the 17th floor.

QUIET CENTRE

Just when you thought that Old Rīga was the most beautiful neighbourhood in town, the city's audacious art nouveau district swoops in to vie for the prize.

TOP CHOICE **Rīga Art Nouveau Centre** MUSEUM
(Rīgas jūgemdstila muzejs; Map p454; ☎6718 1465; www.jugendstils.riga.lv; Alberta iela 12; admission 3.50Ls, English tour 10Ls; ☉10am-6pm Tue-Sun) If you're curious about what lurks behind Rīga's imaginative art nouveau facades, then it's definitely worth stopping here. Once the home of Constantīns Pēkšēns (a local architect responsible for more than 250 of the city's buildings), the centre has been completely restored to resemble a middle-class apartment from the 1920s. Note the geometric frescos, rounded furniture, original stained glass in the dining room, and the still-functioning stove in the kitchen. Don't miss the free 10-minute video detailing the city's distinct decor, and check out the centre's website for details about the art nouveau walking routes around town. Enter from Strēlnieku iela; push No 12 on the doorbell.

Janis Rozentāls & Rūdolfs Blaumanis' Museum
MUSEUM
(Map p454; ☎6733 1641; Alberta iela 12; admission 1Ls; ☉11am-6pm Wed-Sun) Follow the wonderfully lavish stairwell up to the 5th floor to find the former apartment of Janis Rozentāls, one of Latvia's most celebrated painters. Enter from Strēlnieku iela; push No 9 on the doorbell.

OUTLYING NEIGHBOURHOODS
Those who venture beyond Rīga's inner sphere of cobbled alleyways and over-the-top art nouveau will uncover a handful of other neighbourhoods that help paint a full picture of this cosmopolitan capital.

Miera iela
NEIGHBOURHOOD
(off Map p454) Old factory meets olfactory along Miera iela, an industrial district that's home to the Laima chocolate maker just beyond the scatter of stunning art nouveau facades in the Quiet Centre. Walk down the main street to find a charming assortment of cafes, craft shops and bookstores. Sadly there are no golden tickets available to visit the chocolate factory.

Āgenskalns & Kalnciemiela
NEIGHBOURHOOD
(off Map p454) Rīga's gritty working-class neighbourhood across the Daugava River is a serious throwback to earlier times, especially at Užaras Park. This sprawling green space (now mostly used as a soccer field) is home to the so-called **Victory Monument** (Užaras Piemineklis), which was built by the Soviets to commemorate the communist 'victory' over fascism.

Unlike many of Rīga's other districts, this area was not destroyed during WWII, and it thus makes for a great place to wander around by bicycle to get a feel for how life was here many decades ago. Don't miss **Kalnciemiela**, a lovingly restored courtyard with several wooden buildings. It has become the location of a very popular weekend market during the summer months (usually on Thursday evenings in the colder months), where Rīgans hawk their local produce – fresh meats, cheeses, vegetables and even local spirits.

Take tram 2 or 8 over the Akmens Bridge, and disembark at the 'Āgenskalna Tirgus' stop, or take tram 5 and get off at the second stop on the other side of the bridge.

Latvian Ethnographic Open-Air Museum
MUSEUM
(Latvijas etnogrāfiskais brīvdabas muzejs; www. brivdabasmuzejs.lv; Brīvības gatve 440; adult/child 2/1Ls; ☉10am-5pm) If you don't have time to visit the heart of the Latvian countryside, then a stop at the Latvian Ethnographic Open-Air Museum is recommended. This vast stretch of forest contains more than 100 wooden buildings from all over Latvia. Take bus 1 to the 'Brīvdabas muzejs' stop.

✗ Activities

Baltā Pirts
SPA
(off Map p454; ☎6727 1733; www.baltapirts.lv; Tallinas iela 71; sauna 7Ls; ☉8am-8pm Wed-Sun) Baltā Pirts combines traditional Latvian relaxation techniques (the name means 'white birch') with a subtle, oriental design scheme. In the 1980s the property had a seedy reputation but the original owners of the sauna have since reclaimed the building and turned it into quite a wonderful place.

Take a tram heading northalong A Čaka until you reach Tallinas iela.

Taka Spa
SPA
(Map p454; ☎6732 3150; www.takaspa.lv; Kronvalda bulvāris 3a; treatments from 15Ls; ☉10am-9pm Mon-Fri, to 7pm Sat & Sun) You don't have to run all the way to Jūrmala to see some serious spa action. Taka Spa is one of Rīga's standout spots to get pampered in the traditional Latvian style: being whipped by dried birch branches while sweating it out in temperatures beyond 40°C. Sounds relaxing.

Regro's
SHOOTING RANGE
(off Map p454; ☎6760 1705; Daugav-grīvas iela 31; bullets 0.80-2Ls; ☉10am-7pm Mon-Sat, by appoint-

ART NOUVEAU IN RĪGA

If you ask any Rīgan where to find the city's world-famous art nouveau architecture, you will always get the same answer: 'Look up!' More than 750 buildings in Rīga (more than any other city in Europe) boast this flamboyant and haunting style of decor, and the number continues to grow as myriad restoration projects get underway. Art nouveau is also known as Jugendstil, meaning 'youth style', named after a Munich-based magazine called *Die Jugend,* which popularised the design on its pages.

Art nouveau's early influence was Japanese print art disseminated throughout Western Europe, but as the movement gained momentum, the style became more ostentatious and free-form – design schemes started to feature mythical beasts, screaming masks, twisting flora, goddesses and goblins. The turn of the 20th century marked the height of the art nouveau movement, as it swept through every major European city from Porto to Petersburg.

The art nouveau district (known more formally as the 'Quiet Centre') is anchored around **Alberta iela** (check out 2a, 4 and 13 in particular), but you'll find fine examples all throughout the city. Don't miss the renovated facades of **Strēlnieku 4a** and **Elizabetes 10b** and **33**, and then check out the highly informative Rīga Art Nouveau Centre.

ment Sun) The ambience at Regro's is reason enough to visit: a dingy Soviet fallout shelter adorned with posters of rifle-toting models wearing fur bikinis. Choose from a large selection of retro firearms (including Kalashnikovs) to aim at your paper cut-out of James Bond. You pay by the bullet. Take the Vanšu bridge across the river, pass Kīpsala and take your first right until you hit a petrol station. Also accessible by tram 13. Don't forget your passport.

☞ Tours

Swarms of operators offer tours around Rīga and day trips to nearby attractions such as Rundāle Palace and Sigulda. Check out www.jugendstils.riga.lv for touring routes focusing on the city's clutch of art nouveau architecture. The tourist information centre in Rātslaukums can help organise any type of tour you desire, with guides who speak a multitude of languages.

E.A.T. Rīga HISTORY TOUR
(☏2246 9888; www.eatriga.lv; tours from 25Ls) Not a foodie's tour – these walking and bicycling jaunts give visitors a chance to sneak behind the (iron) curtain and see the 'real Rīga'.

Rīga By Canal CITY TOUR
(Map p456; ☏6750 9974; www.kmk.lv; adult/child 5/3Ls; ☉9am-11pm) Enjoy a different perspective of the city aboard the 100-year-old *Darling,* a charming wooden canal cruiser that runs on 15% solar energy (the rest diesel). There are three other boats in the fleet that

paddle along the same route and operate on electrical power.

Rīga Out There CULTURAL TOUR
(Map p454; ☏2938 9450; www.rigaoutthere.com) Organises tours, day trips and activities for tourists, from AK-47 shooting to late-night pub-crawls. It also runs funky apartment-style accommodation (30Ls) from its office.

★☆ Festivals & Events

Check out www.rigatourism.lv for a complete list of local events.

Rīga Opera Festival MUSIC
(www.opera.lv; ☉Jun) The National Opera's 10-day event featuring performances by local and world-renowned talent.

Baltā Nakts ART
(www.baltanakts.lv; ☉Sep) 'White Night' mirrors Paris' nightlong showcase of artists and culture around the city.

Arsenāls International Film Forum FILM
(www.arsenals.lv; ☉Sep) An annual film festival showcasing more than 100 movies relating to experiential and interactive themes.

⊨ Sleeping
OLD RĪGA (VECRĪGA)
Neiburgs BOUTIQUE HOTEL €€€
(Map p456; ☏6711 5522; www.neiburgs.com; Jauniela 25/27; s/d/ste incl breakfast from 100/130/170Ls; ✴@☎) Beautiful Neiburgs blends contemporary touches (think patterned accent walls and chrome in bathrooms) with carefully preserved details (like curling crown moulding)

LATVIA RĪGA

for its signature blend of boutique-chic style. Try for a room on one of the higher floors – you'll be treated to a colourful clutter of gabled roofs and twisting medieval spires. The in-house restaurant is exceptionally popular with locals. Go for the 'Business Lunch' – it's so well priced you'll think the waiter left a zero off the bill!

Dome Hotel
BOUTIQUE HOTEL €€€

(Map p456; ☑6750 9010; www.domehotel.lv; Miesnieku iela 4; d/ste from 190/280Ls) An exciting addition to Old Rīga's clutch of high-end accommodation options, Dome Hotel occupies an almost-ancient structure that was once part of a row of butcheries. Today, a gorgeous wooden staircase leads guests up to the charming assortment of uniquely decorated rooms that sport eaved ceilings, wooden panelling, upholstered furniture and picture-windows with city views.

Naughty Squirrel
HOSTEL €

(Map p456; ☑2646 1248; www.thenaughtysquirrel. com; Kalēju iela 50; dm/d 8/30Ls; @🛜) This has been the address of several hostel incarnations and the Naughty Squirrel is by far the best yet. Brilliant slashes of bright paint and cartoon graffiti have breathed new life into the city's capital of backpacker-dom, which buzzes as travellers rattle the foosball table and chill out in the TV room. Sign up for regular pub-crawls, adrenaline day trips to the countryside, or summer barbecues.

OH CHRISTMAS TREE

Rīga's Blackheads' House (p452) was known for its wild parties; it was, after all, a clubhouse for unmarried merchants. On a cold Christmas Eve in 1510, a squad of bachelors, full of holiday spirit (and other spirits, so to speak), hauled a great pine tree up to their clubhouse and smothered it with flowers. At the end of the evening, they burned the tree to the ground in an impressive blaze. From then on, decorating the 'Christmas Tree' became an annual tradition, which eventually spread across the globe (as you probably know, the burning part never really caught on).

An octagonal commemorative plaque, inlaid in cobbled Rātslaukums, marks the spot where the original tree once stood.

Ekes Konventas
HISTORIC HOTEL €€

(Map p456; ☑6735 8393; www.ekeskonvents.lv; Skārņu iela 22; d incl breakfast €57; 🛜) Not to be confused with Konventa Sēta next door, the 600-year-old Ekes Konventas oozes wobbly medieval charm from every crooked nook and cranny. Curl up with a book in the adorable stone alcoves on the landing of each storey. Breakfast is served in the mod cafe down the block.

Old Town Hostel
HOSTEL €

(Map p456; ☑6722 3406; www.rigaoldtownhostel. lv; Vaļņu iela 43; dm/d 7/30Ls; @🛜) The cosy English-style pub on the ground floor doubles as the hostel's hang-out space, and if you can manage to lug your suitcase past the faux bookshelf door and up the twisting staircase, you'll find spacious dorms with chandeliers and plenty of sunlight. Private rooms are located in another building near the train station.

Friendly Fun Franks
HOSTEL €

(Map p456; ☑2599 0612; www.franks.lv; 11 Novembra Krastmala 29; dm/d from 5.90/40Ls; @🛜) If you want to party, look no further than this bright orange stag-magnet, where every backpacker is greeted with a hearty hello and a complimentary pint of beer. The staff offer free 'What to Do' tours of Rīga, beach parties and Saturday trips to Sigulda. Accommodation must be booked in advance.

CENTRAL RĪGA (CENTRS)

[TOP CHOICE] Hotel Bergs
BOUTIQUE HOTEL €€€

(Map p454; ☑6777 0900; www.hotelbergs.lv; Elizabetes iela 83/85; ste from €164; [P]❄@🛜) A refurbished manor house embellished with Scandi-sleek design, Hotel Bergs embodies the term 'luxury' from the lobby's mix of sharp lines, rococo portraits and tribal reliefs to the spacious suites lavished with high-quality monochromatic furnishings worthy of a magazine spread. Other treats await, such as a custom-composed sleeping soundtrack in the room's CD player and an endless supply of complimentary Acqua Panna. Our favourite – the 'pillow service' – allows guests to choose from an array of different bed pillows. Be sure to check out the in-house restaurant – the menu of refined Latvian fare reads like an ode to your taste buds, and all seasonal items are locally sourced.

Radisson Blu Hotel Elizabete
HOTEL €€

(Map p454; ☑6778 5555; www.radissonblu.com/ elizabetehotel-riga; Elizabetes iela 73; d incl breakfast from €75; (P✳@❧) The newest link in the Radisson Blu chain is a flash address designed by an up-and-coming London architectural firm. The facade is an eye-catching mix of chrome, steel and giant sheets of glass, and the interior continues to impress: stylish furnishings and clever floor plans give the rooms a cosy-yet-trendy feel.

Europa Royale
HISTORIC HOTEL €€€

(Map p454; ✑6707 9444; www.europaroyale.com; K Barona iela 12; s/d/ste incl breakfast €79/89/189; ✳@❧) Once the home of media mogul Emīlija Benjamiņa (Latvia's version of Anna Wintour), this ornate manse retains much of its original opulence with sweeping staircases and stately bedrooms. In fact, when Latvia regained its independence, the house was initially chosen to be president's digs but the government didn't have enough funds for the restoration. There are 60 large rooms, yet guests will feel like they're staying at their posh aunt's estate.

Albert Hotel
HOTEL €€

(Map p454; ✑6733 1717; www.alberthotel.lv; Dzirnavu iela 33; s/d incl breakfast €64/69; P✳@❧) The boxy, metallic facade starkly contrasts with the surrounding art nouveau gargoyles, but the interior design is undeniably hip, paying tribute to the hotel's namesake, Albert Einstein. The patterned carpeting features rows of atomic energy symbols, and the 'do not disturb' doorknob danglers have been replaced with red tags that read 'I'm thinking'.

Radisson Blu Hotel Latvija
HOTEL €€€

(Map p454; ✑6777 2222; www.radissonblu.com/latvijahotel-riga; Elizabetes iela 55; d incl breakfast from €79; ✳@❧✺) During the height of the Soviet regime, the Hotel Latvija was a drab monstrosity in which several floors were devoted to monitoring the various goings-on of the hotel's guests. The room keys weighed several kilos, as they were outfitted with conspicuous listening devices. Today, after a much-needed facelift, the era of espionage is long gone; it's all swipe-cards and smiley service now. Don't miss the views from the Skyline Bar on the 26th floor.

Hotel Valdemārs
HOTEL €€

(Map p454; ✑6733 4462; www.valdemars.lv; Valdemāra iela 23; s/d incl half-board from €50/60; ✳@❧) Modern Hotel Valdemārs is a great find geared towards the Scandinavian market – rooms feel efficient yet homey, in an upmarket Ikea kind of way. Don't forget to give

away the flower adorning the bureau in your room – it's a Latvian tradition!

Krišjānis & Ģertrūde
B&B €€

(Map p454; ✑6750 6604; www.kg.lv; K Barona iela 39; s/d/tr incl breakfast €35/45/55; @❧) Step off the bustling intersection into this quaint, family-run B&B adorned with still-life pictures of fruit and flowers. It's best to book ahead since there are only six cosy rooms. Enter from Ģertrūdes iela.

B&B Rīga
APARTMENT €€

(Map p454; ✑6727 8505; www.bb-riga.lv; Ģertrūdes iela 43; s/d €39/49; @❧) Snug, apartment-style accommodation comes in different configurations (suites with lofted bedrooms are particularly charming) and are scattered throughout a residential block.

KB
B&B €

(Map p454; ✑6731 2323; www.kbhotel.lv; K Barona iela 37; s/d/tr 19/21/23Ls; @❧) This great find in the pinch-a-penny category is located up a rather opulent marble staircase. The rooms are simple but well appointed, and there's a modern communal kitchen.

✗ Eating

OLD RĪGA (VECRĪGA)

If you're self-catering, there's a branch of **Rimi** (Map p456; www.rimi.lv; Audēju iela 16), a reputable supermarket chain, in Old Rīga's Galerija Centrs shopping mall.

TOP CHOICE Fish Restaurant
SEAFOOD €€€

(Map p456; www.domehotel.lv; Miesnieku iela 4; mains 7-16Ls) The Dome Hotel's restaurant quickly reminds diners that Rīga sits near a body of water that's full of delicious fish. Service is impeccable and dishes are expertly prepared to reflect the eclectic assortment of recipes in the modern Latvian lexicon – this is not to be missed if you're looking to spend a little more on some high-end comfort food.

Dorian Gray
CAFE €€

(Map p456; www.doriangray.lv; Mazā Muzeja iela 1; mains 3.60-8Ls) With seating purchased from a car-boot sale, random pillows scattered about, and cracked crimson brick crumbling off the walls, Dorian Gray might just be (rather ironically) the least image-obsessed place in town. Down-to-earth wait staff serve curious concoctions such as chicken stuffed with shrimp and a strange carrot cake that could more appropriately be defined as a dessert salad. Swing by for weekly movie nights and brunch-time screenings of *Ugly Betty*.

Pelmeņi XL
FAST FOOD €

(Map p456; Kaļķu iela 7; dumpling bowls 0.86-2.50Ls; ☺9am-4am) A Rīga institution for backpackers and undiscerning drunkards, this extralarge cafeteria stays open extra late serving up huge bowls of *pelmeņi* (Russian-style ravioli stuffed with meat) amid Flintstonesmeets-Gaudí decor (you'll see). There's a second location in the central train station.

Alus Sēta
LATVIAN €

(Map p456; www.lido.lv; Tirgoņu iela 6; mains 2-7Ls) The pick of the LIDO litter in central Rīga, Alus Sēta feels like an old Latvian brewhouse. It's popular with locals as well as tourists – everyone flocks here for cheapas-chips grub and homemade beer. Seating floods the cobbled streets during the warmer months.

V. Ķuze
SWEETS €

(Map p456; www.kuze.lv; Jēkaba iela 20/22; coffee & cake from 1.20Ls) Vilhelms Ķuze was a prominent entrepreneur and chocolatier while Latvia flirted with freedom between the world wars. When the Soviets barged in he was promptly deported to Siberia where he met his demise. Today, Ķuze Chocolates is up and running once more, and this charming cafe-cum-confectioner functions not only as a memoriam to dear Vilhelms but also as a tribute to the colourful art nouveau era when arcing furniture and geometric nature motifs were en vogue.

Cadets de Gascogne
BAKERY €

(Franču Maiznīca; Map p456; Basteja bulvāris 8; baguette sandwich 2.20Ls; ☺7am-10am Mon-Sat) Got a tummy ache from one too many *pelmeņi*? Nurse your digestive system at this Frenchrun bakery – pick up a mug of hot chocolate and a baguette sandwich stuffed with ham and cornichons (gherkins). Additional seating is available on the roof promenade. There's a second location in Berga Bāzars.

Vecmeita ar kaki
LATVIAN €€

(Spinster & Her Cat; Map p456; Mazā Pils iela 1; mains 3.10-9.90Ls) This cosy spot across from the president's palace specialises in cheap Latvian grub and meaty mains. In warmer weather, patrons dine outside on converted sewing-machine tables.

Šefpavārs Vilhelms
FAST FOOD €

(Chef William; Map p456; Šķūņu iela 6; pancake rolls 0.65Ls) Customers of every ilk are constantly queuing for a quick nosh – three stuffed pancakes (blintzes) smothered in sour cream and jam equals the perfect backpacker's breakfast.

Ķiploku Krogs
INTERNATIONAL €€

(Garlic Bar; Map p456; Jēkaba iela 3/5; mains 3.40-9.80Ls) Vampires beware – *everything* at this joint contains garlic, even the ice cream. The menu is pretty hit-and-miss, but, no matter what, it's best to avoid the garlic-pesto spread – it'll taint your breath for days (trust us). Enter from Mazā Pils.

CENTRAL RĪGA (CENTRS)

Self-caterers should try **Rimi** (www.rimi.lv; K Barona iela 46) in the Barona Centrs shopping mall or check out the Central Market (p459).

⌇TOP CHOICE Istaba
CAFE €€

(Map p454; ☎6728 1141; K. Barona iela 31a; mains 3-10Ls; ☺Mon-Sat) Owned by local chef and TV personality Mārtiņš Sirmais, the 'Room' sits in the rafters above a like-named gallery space adorned with trendsetting bric-a-brac. In summer you can dine on the street-side veranda, though we prefer heading upstairs to grab a seat in the mob of discarded lamps and sofas. There's no set menu – you're subject to the cook's fancy – but it's all about flavourful and filling portions served on mismatched dishware. Reservations are recommended.

⬧Vincents
GOURMET €€€

(Map p454; ☎6733 2634; www.restorans.lv; Elizabetes iela 19; mains 13-20Ls; ☺6-11pm Mon-Sat) Ask any Rīgan – they'll all tell you that Vincents is the top spot in town. So it's no surprise that it's also the most expensive. Apparently when Queen Elizabeth spent a day in town, she ate both her lunch and dinner here, and other world figures have followed suit. The head chef is a stalwart of the Slow Food movement and crafts his ever-changing menu amid eye-catching van Gogh–inspired decor (hence the name).

Miit
CAFE €

(Map p454; www.miit.lv; Lāčplēša iela 10; mains from 2Ls) A bike-shop-cum-cafe that takes its cues from Berlin's hipster culture, Miit is a wonderful addition to Rīga's student scene with space to sip a latte and blog about Nietzsche amid toppled-over IKEA bookcases, comfy couches and discarded bicycle parts. The twocourse lunch is a fantastic deal for pennypinchers – expect a soup and a main course for under 3Ls (dishes change every day).

Aragats
GEORGIAN €€

(off Map p454; 📞6737 3445; Miera iela 15; mains 4-8Ls; ⊙Tue-Sun) Ignore the plastic shrubbery – this place is all about sampling some killer cuisine from the Caucasus. Start with an appetiser of pickled vegetables – the perfect chaser for your home-brewed *chacha* (Georgian vodka). Then make nice with the owner as she dices up fresh herbs at your table to mix with the savoury lamb stew. At the end of the meal men should pay for the women at the table, especially since the women's menus don't have any of the prices listed!

Bonēra
CAFE €€

(Map p454; www.bonera.lv; Blaumaņa iela 12a; mains 3-8Ls; ⊙Mon-Sat) Life is indeed good at Bonēra, whose name is a play on the word 'happiness'. The cafe doubles as a vintage clothing store, though these days most locals come for the 5Ls all-you-can-eat buffet dinner that's stocked with an unending assortment of delicious dishes such as Waldorf salads, homemade pâté, and scrumptious carbonara pasta.

Garage
CAFE €€

(Map p454; Elizabetes iela 83/85; mains 2-7Ls) Although it bills itself more as a wine bar attached to a Latvian handicrafts shop, Garage has transformed into a trendy cafe serving brilliant snacks and light dishes after legions of local fans have encouraged its expansion into some of the retail space. Friendly staff and an eclectic assortment of secondhand chairs give it that extra *je ne sais quoi*.

Osīriss
CAFE €€

(Map p454; K Barona iela 31; mains 3-9Ls; ⊙8am-midnight; 🛜) Despite Rīga's mercurial cafe culture, Osīriss continues to be a local mainstay. The green faux-marble tabletops haven't changed since the mid '90s and neither has the clientele: angsty artsy types scribbling in their Moleskines over a glass of red wine.

Taka
CAFE €

(off Map p454; Miera iela 10; mains 2.50-3.50Ls; ⊙Mon-Sat; 🛜) This stop on the underground music scene has a flock of origami cranes dangling in the front window. Inside you'll find bright murals on the walls, extra-comfy couches, and 20- to 30-somethings gathered around during mealtime to down some delicious vegetarian fare.

LIDO Atpūtas Centrs
LATVIAN €

(LIDO Recreation Centre; off Map p454; www.lido. lv; Krasta iela 76; mains 2-6.50Ls) If Latvia and Disneyworld had a love child it would be the LIDO Atpūtas Centrs – an enormous wooden palace dedicated to the country's coronary-inducing cuisine. Servers dressed like Baltic milkmaids bounce around as patrons hit the rows of buffets for classics such as pork tongue and cold beet soup. Take the free bus from Rātslaukums or tram 3, 7 or 9 and get off at the 'LIDO' stop. There are a handful of miniature LIDO restaurants dotted around the city centre for those who don't have time to make it out to the mothership.

🍷 Drinking

If you want to party like a Latvian, assemble a gang of friends and pub-crawl your way through the city, stopping at colourful haunts for rounds of shots, belly laughter and, of course, Black Balzāms. On summer evenings, nab a spot at one of the city's many beer gardens.

OLD RĪGA (VECRĪGA)

Nekādu Problēmu
BEER GARDEN

(No Problem; Map p456; www.nekaduproblemu. lv; Doma laukums) This sea of sturdy patio ware enlivens Doma laukums in the warmer months as the rousing fits of live music bounce off the cathedral walls. You can sample more than 20 types of draught beer and the food's pretty darn good too.

Egle
BEER GARDEN

(Map p456; www.spoguegle.lv; Kaļķu iela 1a) Old Rīga's second beer garden is a cosier addition to the city, with tables plunked closely together and folk music in the evenings.

La Belle Epoque
BAR

(French Bar; Map p456; Mazā Jaunavu iela 8) Students flock to this boisterous basement bar to power down its trademark 'apple pie' shots (1Ls). The Renoir mural and kitschy *Moulin Rouge* posters seem to successfully ward off stag parties.

Mojo
LOUNGE

(Map p456; www.mojocafe.lv; Pils iela 7) Oh Mojo, how you endear us with your retro wallpaper prints, shaggy rugs, and dozens of other throwbacks to the '70s like old radios and leather couches dyed in odd colours.

Aptieka
BAR

(Pharmacy Bar; Map p456; Mazā Miesnieku iela 1) Antique apothecary bottles confirm the subtle but stylish theme at this popular drinking haunt run by a Latvian–American.

Cuba Cafe
BAR

(Map p456; www.cubacafe.lv; Jaun iela 15; 🛜)
An authentic mojito and a table overlooking Doma laukums is just what the doctor ordered after a long day of sightseeing. On colder days, swig your caipirinha inside amid dangling Cuban flags, wobbly stained-glass lamps and the murmur of trumpet jazz.

CENTRAL RĪGA (CENTRS)

TOP CHOICE Piens
BAR, CLUB

(Milk; off Map p454; Brīana iela 9) Piens is, without a doubt, the most happening spot in town. Located up in the Miera iela area, this bar-club hybrid occupies a large chunk of industrial land and features a brilliant mix of decorative motifs – Soviet, I-Love-Lucy '50s, and geometric art nouveau. The neighbouring Delisnack – a beloved import from Liepāja – means that trips to the west coast are no longer necessary to devour its trademark hangover-curing hamburgers.

Pērle
BAR, CAFE

(Map p454; Tērbatas iela 65) Pērle is where outmoded technology goes to die a stylish rockstar death. It's everything you'd want in a neighbourhood hipster hang-out: discarded Game Boys, racks of vintage tweed, a massacre of mannequin parts and designer lattes... with Baileys. Oh, and everything's for sale. Naturally.

Skyline Bar
BAR

(Map p454; Elizabetes iela 55; 🛜) A must for every visitor, glitzy Skyline Bar sits on the 26th floor of the Reval Hotel Latvija. The sweeping views are the city's best, and the mix of glam spirit-sippers makes great people-watching under the retro purple lighting.

☆ Entertainment

Nightclubs

Pulkvedim Neviens Neraksta
CLUB

(No One Writes to the Colonel; Map p456; www.pulkvedis.lv; Peldu iela 26/28) There's no such thing as a dull night at this club. The atmosphere is 'warehouse chic', with pumping '80s tunes on the ground floor and trance beats down below.

Nabaklab
CLUB

(Map p456; www.nabaklab.lv; Meierovica bulvaris 12) Imagine if your favourite alternative radio station opened a nightspot that played its signature blend of experimental tunes and electronica. Well, you're in luck – Naba's (93.1FM) club space attracts the city's boho

hobos with its DJ beats, vintage clothes racks, art gallery and cheap beer in the quaint Soviet-style den.

Moon Safari
CLUB

(Map p456; www.moonsafari.lv; Krāmu iela 2) Beds in the 'VIP room' and a pet snake at the bar? It's all pretty suggestive, but the 2Ls cocktails and colourful karaoke booth lure a young Erasmus crowd for all-night shenanigans.

Golden
GAY, LESBIAN

(Map p454; www.mygoldenclub.com; Ģertrūdes iela 33/35; admission 3-5Ls) It's all about smoke and mirrors (literally) at Rīga's most 'open' venue. However, if you're looking for a thriving gay scene, better pick another city.

Performing Arts
National Opera House
OPERA

(Map p456; ☎6707 3777; www.opera.lv; Aspazijas bulvāris 3) The pride of Latvia, boasting some of the finest performing arts in all of Europe (and for the fraction of the price of other countries). Mikhail Baryshnikov got his start here. Note that Rīga's ballet, opera and theatre season breaks for summer holidays (between June and September).

Dome Cathedral
LIVE MUSIC

(Doma baznīca; Map p456; ☎6721 3213; www.doms.lv; Doma laukums 1) Twice-weekly short organ concerts (Wednesday and Saturday evenings) and lengthier Friday night performances are well worth attending.

Great Guild
LIVE MUSIC

(Map p456; ☎6722 4850; www.lnso.lv; Amatu iela 6) Home to the acclaimed Latvian National Symphonic Orchestra. Classical music and jazz scats are often heard from the window.

New Rīga Theatre
THEATRE

(Jaunais Rīgas Teātris; Map p454; ☎6728 0765; www.jrt.lv; Lačplēša iela 25) Contemporary repertory theatre.

🔒 Shopping

Latvians love their shopping malls – a palpable marker of globalisation, but tourists will be pleased to find a wide assortment of local shops that specialise in all sorts of Latvian items – knits, crafts, spirits and fashion. You'll find a wonderful assortment at **Berga Bazars** (Map p454; www.bergabazars.lv; Dzirnavu iela 84), a maze of upmarket boutiques orbiting the five-star Hotel Bergs. Street sellers peddle their wares – amber trinkets, paintings and Russian dolls – outside St Peter's Church and along the southern end of Valnu iela. Rīga's large crafts fair, the **Gadatirgus**, is held in Vermanes darzs on the first weekend in June. Keep an eye out for the beautiful Nameju rings worn by Latvians around the world as a way to recognise one another.

ZoFA
FASHION

(Map p454; www.zofa.eu; Antonijas iela 23) Uber-friendly Elīna greets customers with her uberslanty haircut in an uberchic black dress. Custom-made shoes range from 130Ls to 180Ls, which is a great deal considering that they are designed and assembled in the studio behind the storefront.

Pienene
ACCESSORIES

(Map p456; Kungu iela 7/9) 'The Dandelion' is an airy boutique in the heart of Old Rīga where visitors can sample some of the countryside's richest wellness products. Expect soaps, scarves and candles made from local wax and herbs.

Sakta Flower Market
MARKET

(Map p454; Tērbatas iela 2a) Open extra-late for those midnight mea culpas when you've gotta bring a gift home to your spouse after a long evening out with friends.

Upe
MUSIC

(Map p456; www.upett.lv; Vāgnera iela 5) Classical Latvian tunes play as customers peruse traditional instruments and CDs of local folk, rock and experimental sounds.

Latvijas Balzāms
FOOD, DRINK

(Map p456; www.lb.lv; Audēju iela 8) A popular chain of liquor stores selling the trademark Latvian Black Balzām. There's another branch on Blaumaņa iela and another on K Barona iela along with several others around town.

Taste Latvia
FASHION

(Map p456; www.tastelatvia.lv; Audejū iela 16) Hidden on the 4th floor of an otherwise corporate shopping centre, Taste Latvia is a stark white realm filled with the latest threads of local designers.

Jāņa Sēta
BOOKS

(Map p454; www.mapshop.lv; Elizabetes iela 83/85) The largest travel bookstore in the Baltic overflows with a bounty of maps, souvenir photo books and Lonely Planet guides.

Art Nouveau Rīga
SOUVENIRS

(Map p454; www.artnouveauriga.lv; Strēlnieku iela 9) Purchase a variety of art nouveau–related souvenirs, from guidebooks and postcards to stone gargoyles and bits of stained glass.

ℹ Information

Internet Access

Every hostel and hotel has some form of internet connection available to guests. Internet cafes are a dying breed in Rīga and they're usually filled with 12-year-olds blasting cybermonsters.

Elik Kafe (Merķeļa iela 1; per 30min/1hr 0.45/0.85Ls; ◷24hr) Conveniently located near the train station above McDonald's. Second location at Kaļķu iela 11.

Media

Lonely Planet (www.lonelyplanet.com/latvia/riga)

Rīga in Your Pocket (www.inyourpocket.com/latvia/riga) Handy city guide published every other month. Download a PDF version or pick up a copy at most midrange or top-end hotels (free). The tourist offices and several bookshops also have copies (2Ls).

Rīga This Week (www.rigathisweek.lv) An excellent (and free) city guide available at virtually every sleeping option in town. Published every second month.

Medical Services

ARS (☑6720 1003; www.ars-med.lv; Skolas iela 5) English-speaking doctors and 24-hour consultation available.

Money

There are scores of ATMs scattered around the capital. Withdrawing cash is easier than trying to exchange travellers cheques or foreign currencies; exchange bureaux often have lousy rates and most do not take travellers cheques.

Marika (Brīvības bulvāris 30) Offers 24-hour currency exchange services with reasonable rates. Second location at Dzirnavu 96.

Post

Those blue storefronts with 'Pasta' written on them aren't Italian restaurants – they're post offices. See www.pasts.lv for more info.

Central post office (Map p454; Brīvības bulvaris 32; ◷7.30am-8pm Mon-Fri, 8am-6pm Sat, 10am-4pm Sun) International calling and faxing services available.

Post office (Map p454; Elizabetes iela 41/43; ◷7.30am-9pm Mon-Fri, 8am-4pm Sat)

Tourist Information

Tourism Information Centre (Map p456; ☑6730 7900; www.rigatourism.com; Rātslaukums 6; ◷9am-6pm) Gives out excellent tourist maps and walking-tour brochures. Staff can arrange accommodation and book day trips. Sells concert and opera tickets in summer.

TRANSPORT FROM RĪGA

Bus

DESTINATION	PRICE (LS)	DURATION (HR)	FREQUENCY
Bauska	2.15	1¼	every 30min 6.30am-11pm
Cēsis	2.90	2	every 30min 8am-10.30pm
Kolka	4.40	3½-4½	5 daily 7.20am-5.15pm
Kuldīga	4.50	2½-3¼	hourly 7am-8pm
Liepāja	6	4	every 45min 6.45am-8.30pm
Sigulda	1.50	1	every 30min 8am-10pm
Ventspils	5.30	3-4	hourly 7am-10.30pm

Train

DESTINATION	PRICE (LS)	DURATION	FREQUENCY
Cēsis	2.45	1¾hr	5 daily
Jūrmala	1	30min	2 hourly
Sigulda	1.65	70min	Hourly

Satellite tourism offices can be found at the train station, bus station and airport. Buy the Rīga Card (www.rigacard.lv; 24hr card 10Ls), which offers discounts on sights and restaurants, and free rides on public transportation.

❶ Getting There & Away

Air

Rīga airport (p477) is in the suburb of Skulte, 13km southwest of the city centre.

Boat

See www.rigapt.lv for information about ferries and cruises to/from Rīga.

Bus

Buses depart from Rīga's **international bus station** (Rīgas starptautiskā autoosta; Map p454; www.autoosta.lv; Prāgas iela 1), located behind the railway embankment just beyond the southeastern edge of Old Town. International destinations include Tallinn, Vilnius, Warsaw, Pärnu, Kaunas, St Petersburg and Moscow.

Ecolines (✆6721 4512; www.ecolines.net)
Eurolines Lux Express (✆6778 1350; www.luxexpress.eu)
Nordeka (✆6746 4620; www.nordeka.lv)

Train

Rīga's **central train station** (centrālā stacija; Stacijas laukums) is convenient to Old Rīga and Centrs, and is housed in a conspicuous glass-encased shopping centre near the Central Market. Give yourself extra time to find the ticket booths, as they are scattered throughout the building and sometimes tricky to find.

The city's network of handy suburban train lines makes day tripping quite convenient. Purchase tickets to the suburban destinations at windows 7 to 12.

Rīga is directly linked by long-distance trains to Daugavpils (4¾ hours), Moscow (16½ hours), St Petersburg (13¼ hours) and Pskov (8½ hours). Visit www.ldz.lv to view the timetables and prices for long-haul international and domestic trains. Train service is not convenient to any destinations in western Latvia.

❶ Getting Around

To/From the Airport

There are three means of transport connecting the city centre to the airport. The cheapest option is bus 22 (0.70Ls), which runs every 15 minutes and stops at several points around town including the Stockmanns complex and the Daugava River (near Friendly Fun Franks hostel). Passengers who carry luggage onto public transportation (with the exception of bus 22) need a 'luggage ticket' (0.10Ls; available from the driver). AirBaltic runs lime-green minibuses (3Ls) from the airport to a selection of midrange hotels in Central Rīga. Lime-green taxis cost a flat rate of 10Ls from the airport; cabbies run the meter when heading to the airport (figure around 8Ls from Central Rīga with light traffic).

Bicycle

Zip around town with **Baltic Bikes** (☑6778 8333; www.balticbike.lv; per hour/day 0.70/6Ls). A handful of stands are conveniently positioned around Rīga and Jūrmala; simply choose your bike, call the rental service and receive the code to unlock your wheels.

Public Transport

Most of Rīga's main tourist attractions are within walking distance of one another, so you might never have to use the city's convoluted network of tramlines, trolleybus paths and bus routes. Tickets cost 0.70Ls (0.50Ls if you buy your ticket ahead of time from an automated machine or news stand). City transport runs daily from 5.30am to midnight. Some routes have an hourly night service. For Rīga public transport routes and schedules visit www.rigassatiksme.lv.

Taxi

Taxis charge 0.40Ls to 0.50Ls per kilometre (oftentimes 0.50Ls to 0.60Ls between 10pm and 6am). Insist on having the meter on before you set off. Meters usually start running at 1Ls to 1.50Ls. Don't pay more than 4Ls for a short journey (like crossing the Daugava for dinner in Ķīpsala). There are taxi ranks outside the bus and train stations, at the airport, and in front of a few major hotels in Central Rīga, such as Radisson Blu Hotel Latvija.

AROUND RĪGA

It's hard to believe that long stretches of flaxen beaches and shady pine forests lie just 20km from Rīga's metropolitan core. The highway connecting Rīga to Jūrmala (Latvia's only six-lane road) was known as '10 Minutes in America' during Soviet times, because locally produced films set in the USA were always filmed on this busy asphalt strip.

Jūrmala

POP 55,000

The Baltic's version of the French Riviera, Jūrmala is a long string of townships with stately wooden beach estates belonging to Russian oil tycoons and their supermodel trophy wives. Even during the height of communism, Jūrmala was always a place to see and be seen. Today, at summer weekends, vehicles clog the roads when jetsetters and day-tripping Rīgans flock to the resort town for some serious fun in the sun.

If you don't have a car or bicycle, you'll want to head straight to the heart of the action – the townships of Majori and Dzintari.

A 1km-long pedestrian street, **Jomas iela**, connects these two districts and is considered to be Jūrmala's main drag.

◉ Sights & Activities

Jūrmala's first spa opened in 1838, and since then, the area has been known far and wide as the spa capital of the Baltic countries. Treatments are available at a variety of big-name hotels and hulking Soviet sanatoriums further along the beach towards Ķemeri National Park. Many accommodation options offer combined spa and sleeping deals.

Wooden Houses   HISTORIC BUILDING

Besides the beach and spa scene, Jūrmala's main attraction is its colourful art nouveau wooden houses, distinguishable by frilly awnings, detailed facades and elaborate towers. There are more than 4000 fairy-tale-like structures (most are lavish summer cottages) found throughout Jūrmala, but you can get your fill of wood by taking a leisurely stroll along Jūras iela, which parallels Jomas iela between Majori and Dzintari. The houses are in various states of repair; some are dilapidated and abandoned, some are beautifully renovated and others are brand new. Download the detailed *Routes along the Historical Centres of Jurmala* brochure from www.jurmala.lv for more info.

Ķemeri National Park   PARK

(☑6714 6819; www.kemeri.gov.lv) Beyond Jūrmala's stretch of celebrity summer homes lies a verdant hinterland of sleepy fishing villages, quaking bogs and thick forests. At the end of the 19th century Ķemeri was known for its curative mud and spring water, attracting visitors from as far away as Moscow.

Baltic Beach Spa   SPA

(☑6777 1446; www.balticbeach.lv; Jūras iela 23/25; day-use & massages from 25Ls; ⊗8am-10pm) The Baltic Beach Spa is the largest treatment centre in the Baltic, with three rambling storeys full of massage rooms, saunas, yoga studios, swimming pools and spas. The 1st floor is themed like a country barn and features invigorating hot-and-cold treatments in which one takes regular breaks from the steam room by pouring buckets of ice water over one's head à la Jennifer Beals in *Flashdance*.

⏸ Sleeping & Eating

Jūrmala has a wide selection of lodging options – very few of them are good value. If penny-pinching's your game, do a day trip to

WORTH A TRIP

RUNDĀLE PALACE

If you only have time for one day trip out of Rīga, make it to **Rundāle Palace** (Rundāles pils; ☏6396 2274; www.rundale.net; short/long route 2.50/3.50Ls, photo permit 1Ls; ☉10am-7pm May-Oct, to 5pm Nov-Apr), 75km south of the capital near the tiny town of Bauska. The architect of this sprawling monument to aristocratic ostentation was Italian baroque genius Bartolomeo Rastrelli, best known for designing the Winter Palace in St Petersburg. About 40 of the palace's 138 rooms are open to visitors, as are the wonderfully landscaped gardens.

Most tour operators run frequent day trips to the palace (figure 20Ls per person); it's best to rent a car if you plan on reaching Rundāle under your own steam. You can also take a bus from Rīga to Bauska (2Ls, 70 minutes, twice hourly), then switch to one of the nine daily buses (0.35Ls) connecting Bauska to the palace (Pilsrundāle), 12km away.

Jūrmala and sleep in Rīga. Check out www.jurmala.lv for additional lodging options across a wider spectrum of wallet sizes.

Hotel MaMa　　　　　　BOUTIQUE HOTEL €€
(☏6776 1271; www.hotelmama.lv; Tirgonu iela 22; d from €75; P@☎) The bedroom doors have thick, mattresslike padding on the interior (psycho-chic?) and the suites themselves are a veritable blizzard of white drapery. A mix of silver paint and pixie dust accent the ultramodern furnishings and amenities. If heaven had a bordello, it would probably look something like this. The in-house restaurant has a special menu for dogs (no joke), and check out the 'Adam and Eve' bathrooms with a fun surprise on the ceiling.

TOP CHOICE 36.Line　　　MODERN LATVIAN €€€
(☏2201 0696; www.lauris-restaurant.lv; Līnija 36; mains 5-20Ls; ☉lunch & dinner) The brainchild of popular local chef Lauris Alekseyev, 36.Line has a private slice of sand in the corner of Jūrmala where diners can tailor an entire day around a meal. Enjoy the beach in the late afternoon and switch to casual attire while savouring modern twists on traditional Latvian dishes. In the evening it's not uncommon to find DJ beats spinning beats.

ⓘ Information

Tourism Information Centre (☏6714 7902; www.jurmala.lv; Lienes iela 5; ☉9am-7pm Mon-Fri, 10am-5pm Sat, 10am-3pm Sun) Located across from Majori train station. Staff can assist with accommodation bookings and bicycle rentals.

ⓘ Getting There & Away

Two to three trains per hour link central Rīga to the sandy shores of Jūrmala (1Ls). Take any train bound for Dubulti, Sloka or Tukums and disembark at Majori station (30 to 35 minutes). Minibuses (1.10Ls) are also a common mode of transportation. From Jūrmala catch a ride along the street at Majori train station. In Rīga, minibuses depart from the suburban minibus station across the street from the main entrance to the train station. Motorists driving the 15km into Jūrmala must pay a 1Ls toll per day, even if they are just passing through. Keep an eye out for the multilane self-service toll stations sitting at both ends of the resort town.

WESTERN LATVIA

Just when you thought Rīga was the only star of the show, in comes western Latvia from stage left, dazzling audiences with a whole different set of talents. While the capital wows the crowd with intricate architecture and metropolitan majesty, Kurzeme (Courland in English) takes things in the other direction: vast expanses of austere landscapes.

It's hard to believe that desolate Kurzeme was once the bustling Duchy of Courland. During the 17th century, Duke Jakob, Courland's ruler, flexed his imperial muscles by colonising Tobago and the Gambia. He even had plans to colonise Australia! (Needless to say, that didn't quite work out...)

Cape Kolka (Kolkasrags)

Enchantingly desolate and hauntingly beautiful, a journey to Cape Kolka (Kolkasrags) feels like a trip to the end of the earth. During Soviet times the entire peninsula was zoned off as a high-security military base – the dusty road between Ventspils and Kolka was a giant aircraft runway. The region's development was subsequently stunted, and today the string of desolate coastal villages has a distinct anachronistic feel as though they've been locked away in a time capsule.

Base yourself in the village of **Kolka**; it's here that the Gulf of Rīga meets the Baltic Sea in a very dramatic fashion. A monument to those claimed by treacherous waters marks the entrance to the beach near a small information booth. The poignant stone slab, with its haunting anthropomorphic silhouette, was erected in 2002. If you plan to stay the night, **Ūši** (✆2947 5692; www.kolka.info; s/d 16/22Ls, campsite per person 2.50Ls), across from the Russian Orthodox church, has two simple but prim rooms and a spot to pitch tents in the flower-filled garden.

❶ Getting There & Away

The easiest way to reach Cape Kolka is by private vehicle (adventurous types can bike), but buses are also available. To reach the town of Kolka, buses either follow the Gulf Coast Rd through Roja, or they ply the route through Talsi and Dundaga (inland). There are five daily buses that link Rīga and Kolka town (4.50Ls, three to four hours).

Kuldīga

POP 13,000

If Kuldīga were a tad closer to Rīga it would be crowded with day-tripping camera-clickers. Fortunately, the town is located deep in the heart of rural Kurzeme, making its quaint historic core the perfect reward for more intrepid travellers. In its heyday, Kuldīga served as the capital of the Duchy of Courland (1596–1616) and was known as the 'city where salmon fly' – during spawning season salmon would swim upstream and when they reached **Ventas Rumba** (the widest waterfall in Europe) they would jump through the air, attempting to surpass it.

Kuldīga was badly damaged during the Great Northern War and was never able to regain its former lustre. Today, this blast from the past is a favourite spot to shoot Latvian period-piece films – 30 movies and counting.

Kuldīga's best hotel, **Hotel Metropole** (✆6335 0588; Baznīcas iela 11; d/ste incl breakfast 44/50Ls; @), rolls out the red carpet up its mod concrete stairwell to charming double-decker bedrooms overlooking the town's main drag, pedestrian **Liepājas iela**. Long ago, guests used to receive a lady with their

room – needless to say, things have changed quite a bit since then.

At **Dārziņš Bakery** (Baznīcas iela 15; snacks 0.10-2Ls; ◷8am-6pm Mon-Fri, to 3pm Sat) the cashier calculates your bill with an amber abacus. Try the *sklandu rausis*, an ancient Cour carrot cake. **Pagrabiņš** (Baznīcas iela 5; mains 3-7Ls), with its charming brick alcoves and wafting '60s rock, lurks in the cellar beneath the information centre in what used to be the town's prison.

❶ Information

Tourist Information Centre (✆6332 2259; www.visit.kuldiga.lv; Baznīcas iela 5; ◷9am-6pm Mon-Sat, 10am-2pm Sun May-Aug, 9am-5pm Mon-Fri Sep-Apr) The helpful office in the Old Town hall provides brochures.

❶ Getting There & Away

Buses run to and from Rīga (4.50Ls, 2½ to 3½ hours, 12 daily), Liepāja (2.70Ls to 3.10Ls, 1¾ hours, seven daily) and Ventspils (1.90Ls to 2.10Ls, 1¼ hours, six daily).

Ventspils

POP 42,000

Fabulous amounts of oil and shipping money have turned Ventspils into one of Latvia's most beautiful and dynamic towns. And although locals coddle their Užavas beer and claim that there's not much to do, tourists will find a weekend's worth of fun in the form of brilliant beaches, interactive museums and winding Old Town lanes.

The city's biggest draws are the state-of-the-art museum in the 13th-century **Livonian Order Castle** (✆6362 2031; www.ventspilsmuzejs.lv; Jāņa iela 17; adult/child 1.50/0.75Ls; ◷10am-6pm Tue-Sun) and the **House of Crafts** (✆6362 0174; Skolas iela 3; admission 0.60Ls; ◷10am-6pm Tue-Fri, to 3pm Sat) where you can watch local artisans spin yarns (literally).

Our favourite spot to spend the night, **Kupfernams** (✆6362 6999; kupfernams@inbox.lv; Kārļa iela 5; s/d 26/37Ls), sits in an inviting wooden house at the centre of Old Town. The cheery rooms with slanted ceilings sit above a fantastic restaurant and a trendy hair salon (which doubles as the front desk).

❶ Information

Tourism Information Centre (✆6362 2263; www.tourism.ventspils.lv; Dārza iela 6; ◷8am-7pm Mon-Fri, 10am-5pm Sat, 10am-3pm Sun) Located in the ferry terminal. Pick up the handy

Walking Routes brochure detailing four scenic tours through town.

ⓘ Getting There & Away

Ventspils is served by buses to/from Rīga (5.30Ls, three to four hours, hourly), Liepāja (3.65Ls to 4.55Ls, two to three hours, six daily) and Kuldīga (1.90Ls to 2.10Ls, 1¼ hours, six daily). There is no train service.

See **Scandlines** (www.scandlines.com/en) and **Finnlines** (www.finnlines.de) for details about ferry services to Germany, Sweden and Russia.

Liepāja

POP 87,000

For the last decade Liepāja has been searching for its identity like an angsty teenager. The city's growing pains are evident in the visual clash of gritty warehouses and tricked-out nightclubs. The local tourist office calls Liepāja 'the place where wind is born', but we think the city's rough-around-the-edges vibe is undoubtedly its biggest attraction.

Start in the Karosta district, 4km north of the city centre, where you'll find a particularly dour collection of **Soviet tenements** mingling with the gilded cupolas of **St Nicholas Orthodox Maritime Cathedral**. Daily multilingual tours lead visitors through **Karosta Prison** (Karostas cietums; ☑2636 9470; www.karostascietums.lv; Invalīdu iela 4; tours 2.50Ls, 2hr shows 5.50Ls, sleepovers 8Ls; ⊙10am-6pm May-Sep, by appointment Oct-Apr), which was used to punish disobedient Russian soldiers. Sign up to be a prisoner for the night and subject yourself to regular bed checks and verbal abuse by guards in period garb. For those only wanting a pinch of masochism, there are abridged two-hour 'reality shows'.

Everything is gaudy and gilded at **Fontaine Royal** (☑6343 2005; www.fontaineroyal.lv; Stūrmaņu iela 1; s/d 18/25Ls, d with shared bathroom 15Ls; ☜). Strange knick-knacks and sculptures abound like an orphanage for unwanted objets d'arts, and the plethora of gold trimming and sparkly spray paint is blinding – as though guests were sleeping in a framed Renaissance painting. We much prefer staying here than at one of the drab cookie-cutter motels around town.

For a night out on the town, try **Latvia's 1st Rock Café** (www.pablo.lv; Stendera iela 18/20; mains 2.50-4.50Ls), a pseudo-industrial megacomplex, or **Fontaine Palace** (www.fontainepalace.lv; Dzirnavu iela 4), an always open rock house luring loads of live acts

and crowds of sweaty fanatics. The attached **Fontaine Delisnack** (mains 3-8Ls) was designed with the inebriated partier in mind: the burgers, nachos and pizzas are a foolproof way to sop up those vodka shots downed earlier in the evening.

ⓘ Information

Tourist Information Centre (☑6348 0808; www.liepaja.lv; Rožu laukums 5; ⊙9am-7pm Mon-Fri, 10am-6pm Sat, 10am-3pm Sun Jun–mid-Sep, 9am-5pm Mon-Fri, 10am-3pm mid-Sep–May) Offers walking-tour maps. Can help with accommodation bookings.

ⓘ Getting There & Away

Buses run to/from Kuldīga (2.70Ls to 3.10Ls, 1¾ hours, seven daily), Ventspils (3.65Ls to 4.55Ls, two to three hours, six daily) and Rīga (5.30Ls, four hours, every 45 minutes). Liepāja and Rīga are also connected by an infrequent train service (departing Liepāja on Monday and Saturday).

EASTERN LATVIA

When Rīga's urban hustle fades into a pulsing hum of chirping crickets, you've entered eastern Latvia. Known as Vidzeme, or 'the Middle Land', to locals, the country's largest region is an excellent sampler of what Latvia has to offer. Most tourists head to **Gauja National Park** (Gaujas nacionālais parks; www.gnp.gov.lv), the country's oldest preserve, where forest folks hike, bike or paddle through the thicketed terrain and history buffs ogle at the generous sprinkling of castles.

Sigulda

POP 10,400

With a name that sounds like a mythical ogress, it comes as no surprise that the gateway to the Gauja is an enchanting little spot with delightful surprises tucked behind every dappled tree. Locals proudly call their pine-peppered town the 'Switzerland of Latvia', but if you're expecting the majesty of a mountainous snowcapped realm, you'll be rather disappointed. Instead, Sigulda mixes its own exciting brew of scenic trails, extreme sports and 800-year-old castles steeped in colourful legends.

◉ Sights

If you've just arrived from the train or bus station, walk down Raina iela to linden-lined Pils iela until you reach **Sigulda New**

Castle (Pils iela 16), built in the 18th century during the reign of German aristocrats. Check out the ruins of **Sigulda Medieval Castle** (Pils iela 18) around back, which was constructed in 1207 by the Order of the Brethren of the Sword, but now lies mostly in ruins after being severely damaged during the Great Northern War.

Follow Ainas iela to the rocky precipice and take the **cable car** (☑6797 2531v; Poruka iela 14; 1-way weekday/weekend 2/2.50Ls; ⊙10am-7.30pm Jun-Aug, to 4pm Sep-May) over the scenic river valley to **Krimulda Manor** (www.krimuldapils.lv; Mednieku iela 3), an elegant estate currently used as a rehabilitation clinic. Visit the crumbling ruins of **Krimulda Medieval Castle** (Krimuldas iela) nearby, then follow the serpentine road down to **Gūtmaņa Cave** where you can read myriad inscriptions carved into the cavern walls.

Walk up the hill to find the **Turaida Museum Reserve** (☑6797 1402; www.turaida-muzejs.lv; Turaidas iela 10; admission 3Ls; ⊙10am-6pm May-Oct, to 5pm Nov-Apr), home to a beautiful 13th-century castle that was erected over an ancient Liv stronghold.

🏃 Activities

Extreme Sports

If you're looking to test your limits with a bevy of adrenaline-pumping activities, then you've come to the right place. Sigulda's 1200m artificial **bobsled track** (☑6797 3813; bobtrase@lis.lv; Šveices iela 13; ⊙noon-7pm Sat & Sun) was built for the former Soviet bobsleigh team. In winter you can fly down the 16-bend track at 80km/h in a five-person **Vučko tourist bob** (ride per person 7Ls), or try the real Olympian experience on the hair-raising **winter bob** (ride per person 35Ls). Summer speed fiends can try the wheeled **summer sled** (ride per person 7Ls) without booking in advance.

If the bobsled isn't enough to make you toss your cookies, take your daredevil shenanigans to the next level and try a 43m **bungee jump** (☑2921 2731; www.bungee.lv; Poruka iela 14; Thu/Fri-Sun jumps 20/25Ls; ⊙6.30pm to last jump Thu-Sun Apr-Nov) from the cable car that glides high over the Gauja River.

The one-of-a-kind **aerodium** (☑2838 4400; www.aerodium.lv; 2min weekday/weekend 15/18Ls; ⊙6-8pm Tue-Fri, noon-8pm Sat & Sun) is a giant wind tunnel that propels participants up into the sky as though they are flying.

Hiking, Cycling & Canoeing

Sigulda is prime hiking territory, so bring your *spieķis* (walking stick). Check out S!gulda (www.sigulda.lv) for a detailed list of trails and cycling routes.

Makars Tourism Agency (☑2924 4948; www.makars.lv; Peldu iela 1) runs a camping ground and arranges one- to three-day water tours around the park. Less intrepid paddlers can hire canoes and rubber boats seating between two and six people starting at 10Ls per day.

🛏 Sleeping & Eating

Click on www.sigulda.lv for additional lodging and dining options.

Līvkalns B&B €

(☑6797 0916; www.livkalns.lv; Pēteralas iela; s/d from 15/25Ls) No place is more romantically rustic than this idyllic retreat next to a pond on the forest's edge. The rooms are pine-fresh and sit among a campus of adorable thatch-roof manors. The cabin-in-the-woods-style restaurant is fantastic.

Kaķu Māja LATVIAN €

(www.cathouse.lv; Pils iela 8; bistro mains from 2Ls; apt d 30Ls) The 'Cat House' is the top spot around town for a cheap bite. In the bistro, point to the ready-made dishes that tickle your fancy, then hunker down on one of the inviting picnic tables outside. For dessert, visit the attached bakery to try out-of-this-world pastries and pies. On Friday and Saturday nights the restaurant at the back busts out the disco ball until the wee hours of the morning. Apartment-style accommodation is also available.

ℹ Information

Gauja National Park Visitors Centre (☑6780 0388; www.gnp.gov.lv; Baznīcas iela 7; ⊙9am-5pm) Can arrange tours, backcountry camping and other accommodation. Cycle and hiking-trail maps are also available.

Tourism Information Centre (☑6797 1335; www.sigulda.lv; Raiņa iela 3; ⊙10am-7pm May-Sep, to 5pm Oct-Apr) Has an internet kiosk and mountains of helpful information about activities and accommodation. Ask about the *Sigulda Spieķis* discount card.

ℹ Getting There & Around

Buses run between Sigulda and Cēsis (1.40Ls, 45 minutes).

Sigulda's attractions are quite spread out; bus 12 links all of the sights and plies the route seven times daily (more on weekends). Bus times are posted at the stations and on the info centre's official website (www.sigulda.lv).

Cēsis

POP 17,700

Cēsis' unofficial moniker, 'Latvia's most Latvian town', pretty much holds true and day trippers will be treated to a mosaic of quintessential country life – a stunning Livonian castle, soaring church spires, cobbled roads and a lazy lagoon – all wrapped up in a bow like an adorable adult Disneyland.

In 1209 the Knights of the Sword founded the fairy-tale-like **Cēsis Castle** (Cēsu pils) with its two stout towers at the western end. To enter, visit **Cēsis History and Art Museum** (Cēsu Vēstures un mākslas muzejs; Pils laukums 9; admission 3Ls; ☉10am-5pm Tue-Sun) in the adjoining 18th-century salmon-pink 'new castle'.

Province (☑6412 0849; www.provincecesis. viss.lv; Niniera iela 6; d from 30Ls) pops out from the surrounding Soviet-block housing with its cute, celery-green facade. The rooms are simple and spotless, and there's a cafe on the ground floor slinging a variety of international eats.

❶ Information

Tourist Information Centre (☑6412 1815; www.tourism.cesis.lv; Pils laukums 9; ☉10am-6pm Jun-Aug, to 5pm Sep-May) Pick up a map, check email or arrange bike rentals.

❶ Getting There & Away

Buses run between Cēsis and Sigulda (1.40Ls, 45 minutes).

UNDERSTAND LATVIA

History
The Beginning

The first signs of modern people in the region date back to the Stone Age, although Latvians descended from tribes that migrated to the region around 2000 BC. Eventually, four main Baltic groups evolved: the Selonians, the Letts (or Latgals), the Semigallians and the Cours. The latter three lent their names to Latvia's principal regions: Latgale, Zemgale and Kurzeme. The country's fourth region, Vidzeme (Livland), borrowed its name from the Livs, a Finno-Ugric people unrelated to the Balts.

A Piece of the European Puzzle

In 1201, at the behest of the Pope, German crusaders conquered Latvia and founded Rīga. They also founded the Knights of the Sword and made Rīga their base for subjugating Livonia. Colonists from northern Germany followed, and during the first period of German rule Rīga became the major city in the German Baltic, thriving from trade between Russia and the West and joining the Hanseatic League (a medieval merchant guild) in 1282.

The 15th, 16th and 17th centuries were marked with battles and disputes about how to divvy up what would one day become Latvia. After a 'golden' period of Swedish rule, the Russians conquered the area during the Great Northern War (1700–21) and held the former fiefdom for two centuries.

A Taste of Freedom

Out of the post-WWI confusion and turmoil arose an independent Latvian state, declared on 18 November 1918. By the 1930s, Latvia had achieved one of the highest standards of living in all of Europe. Initially, the Soviets were the first to recognise Latvia's independence, but the honeymoon didn't last long. Soviet occupation began in 1939 with the Molotov–Ribbentrop Pact. Nationalisation, killings and mass deportations to Siberia followed. Latvia was occupied partly or wholly by Nazi Germany from 1941 to 1945, during which time an estimated 175,000 Latvians were killed or deported.

Soviet Rule

When WWII ended, the Soviets marched back in claiming to 'save' Latvia from the Nazi invaders. A series of deportations and mass killings began anew as the nation was forced to adapt to communist ideology. The first public protest against Soviet occupation was on 14 June 1987, when 5000 people rallied at Rīga's Freedom Monument to commemorate the 1941 Siberia deportations. On 23 August 1989, two million Latvians, Lithuanians and Estonians formed a 650km human chain from Vilnius, through Rīga, to Tallinn, to mark the 50th anniversary of the Molotov–Ribbentrop Pact. Although an all-important Moscow coup failed in 1991, the attempt rocked the Soviet just enough for Latvia to finally break free.

Looking Towards Today

The country declared independence on 21 August 1991 and on 17 September 1991 Latvia, along with its Baltic brothers, joined the UN. After a game of prime minister roulette and a devastating crash of the country's economy, Latvia finally shook off its antiquated Soviet fetters, and on 1 May 2004 the EU opened its doors to the fledgling nation.

Latvia registered the highest economic growth in the EU from 2004 to 2007, which later proved to be a curse when the national bank imploded during the Global Economic Crisis. The nation is proudly (but slowly) marching back towards stability, but a recent shift in politics might be the prelude to a strengthening trade relationship with Russia rather than the EU. At the end of President Zatlers' term, he called for the dissolution of the Latvian parliament. This took place at the beginning of current president Andris Berzinš's term towards the end of 2011. The request to dissolve the parliament was an effort by the Latvian government to put a stop to the nation's unofficial oligarchical reign.

People

Casual hellos on the street aren't common, but Latvians are a friendly and welcoming bunch. Some will find that there is a bit of guardedness in the culture, but this caution, most likely a response to centuries of foreign rule, has helped preserve the unique language and culture through changing times. Today, Latvians readily embrace the changes in their globalising country – classic hipster trappings are worn like uniforms of some world-wise army; locals even have their own version of Facebook. Although you'll mostly hear either Latvian or Russian, most locals – especially the younger generations – do speak a fair bit of English.

Most Latvians are members of the Lutheran Church, although ancient pagan traditions still influence daily life. These pre-Christian beliefs are centred on nature-related superstition and although they seem incongruous when juxtaposed with Christian ideals, Latvians have done a good job of seamlessly uniting the two. Midsummer's Day, or Jani as it's commonly known, is the most popular holiday in Latvia. The solstice was once a sunlit night of magic and sorcery, and today everyone flocks to the countryside for an evening of revelry.

Of Latvia's two million citizens only around 60% are ethnically Latvian. Russians account for 29% of the total population and make up the ethnic majority in most major cities, including the capital. Unlike Latvians, they are mostly members of the Roman Catholic, Old Believer and Orthodox churches.

Arts

Latvians often wax poetic about their country, calling it 'the land that sings'. It seems to be in the genes; locals are blessed with unusually pleasant voices and their canon of traditional tunes is the power source for their indomitable spirit. Latvians (along with their Baltic brothers) literally sang for their freedom from the USSR in a series of dramatic protests known as the 'Singing Revolution', and today the nation holds the Song and Dance Festival, which unites thousands upon thousands of singers from across the land in splendid harmony.

In 2003 the Song and Dance Festival was inscribed on Unesco's list of 'Oral and Intangible Heritage of Humanity' masterpieces.

Food & Drink

For centuries in Latvia, food equalled fuel, energising peasants as they worked the fields and warming their bellies during bone-chilling Baltic winters. Today, the era of boiled potatoes and pork gristle has begun to fade, as food becomes more than a necessary evil. Although it will be a few more years before globetrotters stop qualifying local restaurants as being 'good by Latvia's standards', the cuisine scene has improved by leaps and bounds over the last couple of years.

Lately the Slow Food movement has taken the country by storm. Seasonal menus feature carefully prepared, environmentally conscious dishes using organic produce grown in Latvia's ample farmland. Beyond the sphere of upmarket eats, many joints still embrace the literal sense of the term 'slow food', with tortoise-speed service.

As the country's dining scene continues to draw its influence from a clash of other cultures, tipping is evolving from customary to obligatory. A 10% gratuity is common in the capital and many restaurants are now tacking the tip onto the bill.

SURVIVAL GUIDE

Directory A–Z

Accommodation

Prices quoted here are for rooms with a private bathroom unless otherwise stated. The following price indicators apply (for a high-season double room):

€ less than 25Ls (€35)

€€ 25Ls (€35) to 50Ls (€75)

€€€ more than 50Ls (€75)

We highly advise booking ahead during summer. Rates drop significantly in the colder months.

Most hotels in Latvia have a mix of smoking and nonsmoking accommodation.

Business Hours

Reviews don't list business hours unless they differ from those listed here.

Bars 11am to midnight daily, to 3am Friday and Saturday

Clubs 11pm to 6am Wednesday to Saturday, Tuesday to Sunday in summer

Restaurants 11am to 11pm daily

Shops 10am to 6pm Monday to Friday, to 5pm Saturday

Embassies & Consulates

Embassies and consulates are located in Rīga.

Australian Embassy (☑6722 4251; Tomsona iela 33-1)

Canadian Embassy (☑6781 3945; www.balticstates.gc.ca; Baznīcas iela 20/22)

Estonian Embassy (☑6781 2020; www.estemb.lv; Skolas iela 13)

French Embassy (☑6703 6600; www.ambafrance-lv.org; Raiņa bulvāris 9)

German Embassy (☑6722 9096; www.riga.diplo.de; Raiņa bulvāris 13)

Irish Embassy (☑6703 9370; www.embassyofireland.lv; Alberta iela 13)

Lithuanian Embassy (☑6732 1519; www.lv.mfa.lt; Rūpniecības iela 24)

Netherlands Embassy (☑6732 6147; www.netherlandsembassy.lv; Torņa iela 4)

Russian Embassy (☑6733 2151; www.latvia.mid.ru; Antonijas iela 2)

Swedish Embassy (☑6768 6600; www.swedenabroad.com/riga; Pumpura iela 8)

UK Embassy (☑6733 8126; www.ukinlatvia.fco.gov.uk/en; Alunāna iela 5)

US Embassy (☑6721 6571; http://riga.usembassy.gov; Raiņa bulvāris 7)

Festivals & Events

Latvians enjoy any excuse to party, especially during the summer months. Check out Kulture (www.culture.lv) for a yearly listing of festivals and events across the country. Latvia's biggest event, the **Song and Dance Festival**, is held every five years. It was last held in 2013.

Food

The following price ranges refer to a standard main course.

€ less than 5Ls

€€ 5Ls to 10Ls

€€€ more than 10Ls

Internet Access

Almost all accommodation in Rīga offers some form of internet access. Hotels in smaller cities have been doing a good job of following suit. Internet cafes are a dying breed, as many restaurants, cafes and bars now offer wireless connections.

Lattelecom (www.lattelecom.lv), Latvia's main communications service provider, has set up wi-fi beacons at every payphone around the city. Users can access the internet from within a 100m radius of these phone booths. To register for a Lattelecom password and username, call ☑9000 4111, or send an SMS with the word 'WiFi' to ☑1188.

Money

Latvia's currency, the lats, was introduced in March 1993. The lats (Ls) is divided into 100 santīms. The national bank, **Latvijas Bankas** (Latvian Bank; www.bank.lv), posts the lats' daily exchange rate on its website. Many of Rīga's hotels publish their rack rates in euros. Although Estonia has ascended to the euro, Latvia still has quite a way to go.

Post

Latvia's official postal service website (www.post.lv) can answer any of your mail-related questions, including shipping and stamp prices. Service is reliable; mail to North

America takes 10 days and within Europe it takes about a week.

Public Holidays

The website of the **Latvia Institute** (www.li.lv) has a page of special Latvian remembrance days.

New Year's Day 1 January

Easter In accordance with the Western Church calendar

Labour Day 1 May

Restoration of Independence of the Republic of Latvia 4 May

Mothers' Day Second Sunday in May

Whitsunday A Sunday in May or June in accordance with the Western Church

Līgo & Jāņi 23 & 24 June; St John's Day & Summer Solstice festival

National Day 18 November; anniversary of proclamation of Latvian Republic, 1918

Christmas Holiday 24–26 December

New Year's Eve 31 December

Telephone

Latvian telephone numbers have eight digits; landlines start with ☑6 and mobile numbers start with ☑2. To make any call within Latvia, simply dial the eight-digit number. To call a Latvian telephone number from abroad, dial the international access code, then the country code for Latvia (☑371) followed by the subscriber's eight-digit number.

Telephone rates are posted on the website of the partly state-owned Lattelecom (www.lattelecom.lv), which enjoys a monopoly on fixed-line telephone communications in Latvia.

Mobile phones are available for purchase at most shopping malls around Rīga and other major cities. If your own phone is GSM900-/1800-compatible, you can purchase a prepaid SIM-card package and top-up credit from any Narvesen superette or Rimi grocery store. The most popular plan is **ZZ by Tele2** (Tele-divi; www.tele2.lv; SIM card 0.99Ls).

Calls on a public phone are made using cardphones called *telekarte*, which come in different denominations and are sold at post offices, newspaper stands and superettes.

Visas

Holders of EU passports do not need a visa to enter Latvia; nor do Australian, Canadian, New Zealand and US citizens, if staying for less than 90 days. For information on obtaining visas (and seeing if you need one), visit www.mfa.gov.lv/en.

Getting There & Away

Most air, train and bus connections pass through Rīga. See the Rīga Getting There & Away section (p468) for more information.

Air

Rīga airport (Lidosta Rīga; ☑1187; www.riga-airport.com; Marupes pagast), about 13km southwest of the city centre, houses Latvia's national carrier, **airBaltic** (☑9000 1100; www.airbaltic.com), which offers direct flights to more than 30 destinations within Europe including Amsterdam, Berlin, Brussels, Copenhagen, Helsinki, Oslo, Rome, Stockholm and Vienna.

Other carriers with year-round direct flights to Rīga include the following:

Aeroflot (☑6724 0228; www.aeroflot.lv)

AMC Airlines (www.amcairlines.com)

Belavia (☑6732 0314; www.belavia.by)

Czech Airlines (☑6720 7636; www.czechairlines.lv)

Finnair (☑6720 7010; www.finnair.com)

LOT (☑6720 7113; www.lot.com)

Lufthansa (☑6750 7711; www.lufthansa.com)

Norwegian (www.norwegian.no)

Ryanair (www.ryanair.com)

Transaero (www.transaero.com)

Turkish Airlines (☑6721 0094; www.turkishairlines.com)

UTAir (☑6730 3077; www.utair.ru)

Uzebkistan Airways (☑6732 4563; www.uzairways.com)

Wizz Air (☑9020 0905; www.wizzair.com)

Land

In 2007 Latvia acceded to the Schengen Agreement, which removed all border control between Estonia and Lithuania. Carry your travel documents with you at all times, as random border checks do occur.

BUS

Updated timetables are available at www.1188.lv.

CAR

Rental cars are allowed to travel around the Baltic (Estonia and Lithuania) at no extra fee.

TRAIN

Several train routes link Rīga to destinations in other countries.

SEA

Latvia is connected to a number of destinations by sea. There are services to/from Rīga, and services to/from Ventspils.

Getting Around
Bus

Buses are much more convenient than trains if you're travelling beyond the capital's clutch of suburban rail lines. Updated timetables are available at www.1188.lv and www.autoosta.lv.

Car & Motorcycle

Driving is on the right-hand side. Headlights must be on at all times. Be sure to ask for *'benzene'* when looking for a petrol station – *gāze* means 'air'.

We recommend using an internationally recognised rental service for your vehicles – all major chains are represented here. Rentals range from €30 to €80 per day, depending on the type of car and time of year. The number of automatic cars in Latvia is limited. Companies usually allow you to drive in all three Baltic countries but not beyond.

Train

Most Latvians live in the large suburban ring around Rīga, hence the city's network of commuter rails makes it easy for tourists to reach day-tripping destinations. Latvia's further attractions are best explored by bus. All train schedule queries can be answered at www.1188.lv and www.ldz.lv.

Lithuania

Best Places to Eat

- » Holy Miko's (p491)
- » Moksha (p502)
- » Ararat (p506)
- » Lokys (p491)

Best Places to Stay

- » Palanga Hotel (p505)
- » Narutis (p487)
- » Miško Namas (p509)
- » Litinterp Guesthouse (p506)

Why Go?

A great little all-rounder, Lithuania has much to offer. Those with a passion for baroque architecture, ancient castles and archaeological treasures will find plenty in the capital and beyond. There are sculpture parks and interactive museums for travellers wishing to delve into the country's traumatic recent history; modern art spaces and exhibitions to titillate those whose interests are more contemporary and all-night clubbing in the cities and on the coast for those requiring something less cerebral. Throw in a whirlwind of great restaurants, beer gardens and bars, and you have urban entertainment aplenty.

Away from the cities, the giant sand dunes on the west coast and the southeast's lakes and forests beckon fresh-air fiends; they come alive in the summer with cyclists, berry pickers and campers.

Combine all that with Lithuania's pagan roots, boundless energy and rebellious spirit, and you're in for a heck of a ride.

When to Go
Vilnius

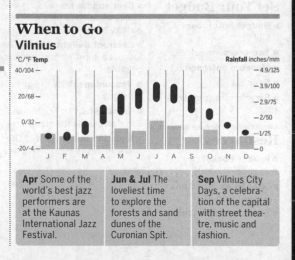

Apr Some of the world's best jazz performers are at the Kaunas International Jazz Festival.

Jun & Jul The loveliest time to explore the forests and sand dunes of the Curonian Spit.

Sep Vilnius City Days, a celebration of the capital with street theatre, music and fashion.

AT A GLANCE

» **Currency** Litas (Lt)

» **Language** Lithuanian

» **Money** ATMs all over

» **Visas** Not required for citizens of the EU, Australia, Canada, Israel, Japan, New Zealand, Switzerland or the US

Fast Facts

» **Area** 65,303 sq km
» **Capital** Vilnius
» **Country code** ⌕370
» **Emergency** ⌕112

Exchange Rates

Australia	A$1	2.82Lt
Canada	C$1	2.66Lt
Euro Zone	€1	3.45Lt
Japan	¥100	2.86Lt
New Zealand	NZ$1	2.26Lt
UK	UK£1	4.09Lt
USA	US$1	2.70Lt

Set Your Budget

» **Budget hotel room** 200Lt
» **Two-course meal** 55Lt
» **Museum entrance** 7Lt
» **Beer** 8Lt
» **Bicycle hire (per day)** 40Lt

Resources

» **In Your Pocket** (www.inyourpocket.com)

» **Lithuania's Museums** (www.muziejai.lt)

» **Tourism in Lithuania** (www.tourism.lt)

Connections

Buses, trains and ferries provide numerous travel options to Lithuania's neighbouring countries.

Vilnius is a hub for buses to Poland, Latvia, Estonia, Belarus and Russia's Kaliningrad; from Kaunas there are buses to Latvia, Estonia and Kaliningrad, and the latter may also be reached from Klaipėda and the Curonian Spit.

Trains serve Russia, Poland and Belarus from the capital. Sweden and Germany can be reached by ferry from Klaipėda, Lithuania's international port.

ITINERARIES

Three Days

Devote two days to exploring the baroque heart of Vilnius, then day trip to Trakai for its spectacular island castle and the homesteads of the Karaite people, stopping off at Paneriai on the way.

One Week

Spend four nights in Vilnius, with day trips to both Trakai and the Soviet sculpture park near Druskininkai. Travel cross-country to the Hill of Crosses, then explore some serious nature on the Curonian Spit for two or three days. Head back east via Klaipėda and Kaunas.

Essential Food & Drink

» **Potato creations** Try the *cepelinai* (potato-dough zeppelin stuffed with meat, mushrooms or cheese), *bulviniai blynai* (potato pancakes) or *žemaičių blynai* (heart-shaped mashed potato stuffed with meat and fried), or the *vedarai* (baked pig intestines stuffed with mashed potatoes).

» **Beer snacks** No drinking session is complete without a plate of smoked pigs' ears and *kepta duona* (deep-fried garlicky bread sticks).

» **Beetroot delight** Cold, creamy *šaltibarščiai* (beetroot soup) is a summer speciality, served with a side of fried potatoes.

» **Unusual meat** Try the game, such as beaver stew or bear sausages.

» **Smoked fish** The Curonian Spit is famous for its smoked fish, particularly the superb *rukytas unguris* (smoked eel).

» **Beer and mead** Šytutys, Utenos and Kalnapilis are top beers; *midus* (mead) is a honey-tinged nobleman's drink.

VILNIUS

POP 523,100

Vilnius, the baroque bombshell of the Baltics, is a city of immense allure. As beautiful as it is bizarre, it easily tops the country's best-attraction bill, drawing tourists to it with a confident charm and a warm, golden glow that makes one wish for long, midsummer evenings every day of the year.

At its heart is Europe's largest baroque Old Town, so precious that Unesco added it to its World Heritage list in 1994. Its skyline, pierced by (almost) countless Orthodox and Catholic church steeples, appears like a giant bed of nails from the basket of a hot-air balloon (p492). Adding to the intoxicating mix is a combination of cobbled alleys, hilltop views, breakaway states and traditional artists' workshops.

Lithuania Highlights

1 Explore beautiful baroque **Vilnius** (pCS) with its cobbled streets, skyline of church spires, and bars and bistros

2 Breathe the pure air within the fragrant pine forests and high sand dunes of the enchanting **Curonian Spit** (p507)

3 Hear the wind sigh between the thousands of crosses on the eerie **Hill of Crosses** (p503) near Šiauliai

4 Wander wonderful **Trakai** (p497), home of the Karaite people and a stunning island castle

5 Visit Lithuania's communist past at the **Grūtas sculpture park** (p499)

6 Marvel at the Horned One in many gulses at the Kaunas **Museum of Devils** (p499)

VILNIUS IN TWO DAYS

Spend your first day taking in the magic of the **Old Town**. Start off at the **Gate of Dawn**, then spend a few hours snaking your way towards **Cathedral Sq**. Climb **Gediminas Hill** for sunset, and crown the day with a meal at **Loky**.

On day two, devote some time to the **Museum of Genocide Victims**, explore the old **Jewish quarter** and bohemian **Užupis**, then finish off with dinner at **Holy Miko's**.

Vilnius feels tiny, but that's a bit deceptive because the suburban sprawl that surrounds the Old Town is a fairly typical Soviet-style mess of snarled traffic, car dealerships and concrete.

History

Legend has it that Vilnius was founded in the 1320s when Lithuanian Grand Duke Gediminas dreamed of an iron wolf that howled with the voices of 100 wolves – a sure sign to build a city as mighty as their cry. In fact, the site had already been settled for 1000 years.

Despite the threat of attacks from the Teutonic Knights and Tatars, Vilnius prospered during the Middle Ages and by the end of the 16th century it was among Eastern Europe's biggest cities. It became a key Jewish city by the 18th century and an isolated pocket of Poland after WWI, but WWII rang the death knell for its Jewish population.

Soviet rule scarred Vilnius' skyline with residential high-rises, but since independence it has fast become a modern European city. In 1994 its Old Town became a Unesco World Heritage site.

⊙ Sights

Vilnius is a compact city, and most sights are easily reached on foot. Those visiting for a couple of days will scarcely move out of the Old Town, where souvenir stalls and designer boutiques jostle for attention with a treasure trove of architectural gems. Stay a couple more days and the New Town – with its museums, shops and riverside action – beckons.

GEDIMINAS HILL & CATHEDRAL SQUARE

TOP CHOICE Cathedral Square   SQUARE

(Katedros aikštė; Map p488) At the base of Gediminas Hill sprawls Cathedral Square (Katedros aikštė), dominated by the splendid white neo-classical **Vilnius Cathedral** (Vilniaus Arkikatedra; Map p488; ☉7am-7.30pm, mass Sun 8am, 9am, 10am, 11.15am, 12.30pm, 5.30pm & 6.30pm) and its 57m-tall **belfry**, a Vilnius landmark. The square buzzes with local life, and the steps in front of the cathedral double as a skateboarding ramp on summer evenings. Amuse yourself by hunting for the secret **stebuklas (miracle) tile**; if found it can grant you a wish if you stand on it and turn around clockwise. It marks the spot where the 650km Tallinn–Vilnius human chain, protesting against Soviet rule, ended in 1989.

The first wooden cathedral, built here in 1387–88, was originally Gothic but has been rebuilt many times since then. Its outside was redone in today's classical style between 1783 and 1801. The showpiece of the airy, light interior is the baroque **St Casimir's Chapel** (Map p488), with white stucco sculptures and frescos depicting the life of St Casimir (Lithuania's patron saint), whose silver coffin lies within.

TOP CHOICE National Museum of Lithuania   MUSEUM

(Lietuvos Nacionalinis Muziejus; Map p488; www. lnm.lt; Arsenalo gatvė 1; adult/child 5/2Lt; ☉10am-5pm Tue-Sat, 10am-3pm Sun May-Sep, 10am-5pm Wed-Sun Oct-Apr) Lithuania's oldest museum is a stampede through the country's history from the 13th century to WWII, and standout objects include a scale model of the Battle of Grünwald, a hand print of Peter the Great, a box and spade used by Alexander II, a broken sword said to belong to Stanislaw Paniatorski – the last king of Poland and Grand Duke of Lithuania – and a flogging board for serfs. In the ethnography section, alongside the national costumes and recreations of rural dwellings there are some wonderfully ornate iron crosses – a traditional craft – and superb temporary exhibitions.

Gediminas Hill   HILL

(Map p488; funicular adult/child 3/2Lt; ☉funicular 10am-7pm) Vilnius was founded on 48m-high Gediminas Hill, topped since the 13th century by the oft-rebuilt **Gediminas Tower** (Map p488). There are spectacular views of the Old Town from the top of the tower, which houses the **Gediminas Castle & Museum** (Gedimino Pilis ir Muziejus; Map p488; on top of Gediminas Hill; adult/child 5/2Lt; ☉10am-7pm May-Sep, to 5pm Tue-Sun Oct-Apr), which contains medieval arms, models of castles and exhibits on Lithuania's 1990 proclamation of independence. It is reached by **funicular** (Map p488), located at the rear of the Museum of Applied Arts. From here you'll also see the white **Three Crosses** on a hill to the east, erected in memory of three crucified monks.

Museum of Applied Arts   MUSEUM

(Taikomosios Dailės Muziejus; Map p488; www.ldm.lt; Arsenalo gatvė 3a; adult/student 6/3Lt; ☺11am-6pm Tue-Sat, to 4pm Sun) Currently the keeper of Gediminas' treasure – tapestries, early Lithuanian coins, weaponry, jewellery – the Museum of Applied Arts houses a wealth of other exhibits, including a permanent collection showcasing 15th- to 19th-century Lithuanian sacred art and excellent temporary offerings, such as the recent 'Two centuries of fashion: haute couture up until the 1960s'. The treasure of Gediminas Palace was discovered in Vilnius cathedral only in 1985, after being hidden in the walls by Lithuanian soldiers in 1655 after Vilnius was about to be stormed by Russian soldiers, and is due to move to the restored palace in May 2013.

Gediminas Palace   PALACE

(Gedimino rumai; Map p488) Next door to the cathedral stands the *valdovǔ rumai* (royal palace), which buzzed with masked balls, gay banquets and tournaments in the 16th century. But in 1795 the Russians occupied Lithuania and demolished the palace along with the Lower Castle and city defence wall.

Having been rebuilt brick by brick, this palace has incredible dimensions and has risen from the ashes to mark the millennium anniversary of the first mention of Lithuania in writing. Renovations of the interior won't be completed until spring 2013, after which the palace will house Gediminas' treasure, currently on display at the Museum of Applied Arts.

St Peter & Paul Church   CHURCH

(Šv Apaštalų Petro ir Povilo Bažnycla; Map p484; Antakalnio gatvė 1; ☺6.30am-7pm) East of Cathedral Sq, magnificent St Peter & Paul Church is one of Vilnius' finest baroque churches. It's a treasure trove of over 2000 sparkling white stucco sculptures of real and mythical people, animals and plants, with touches of gilt, paintings and statues. The decoration was done by Italian sculptors between 1675 and 1704.

OLD TOWN

Eastern Europe's largest Old Town deserves its Unesco status. The area stretches 1.5km south from Cathedral Sq and the eastern end of Gedimino prospektas.

Vilnius University   HISTORIC BUILDING

(Vilniaus Universitetas; Map p488; www.vu.lt; Universiteto gatvė 3; adult/student 5/1Lt; ☺9am-6pm Mon-Sat) The students of Vilnius University attend classes on a spectacular campus featuring 12 or 13 courtyards (depending on one's definition) framed by 15th-century buildings and splashed with 300-year-old frescos.

Founded in 1579 during the Counter-Reformation, Eastern Europe's oldest university was run by Jesuits for two centuries and became one of the greatest centres of Polish learning before being closed by the Russians in 1832. It reopened in 1919.

The **library** here, with five million books, is Lithuania's oldest. The university also houses the world's first **Centre for Stateless Cultures** (Map p488; www.statelesscultures.lt/eng/apie.php), established for those cultures that lack statehood, such as Roma and Karaimic (Karaite) cultures, in its history faculty.

You need to go through the university entrance on Universiteto gatvė (and pay the

---

VILNIUS' MEMORABLE MONUMENTS

Frank Zappa Memorial (Map p488; Kalinausko gatvė 1) The first of its kind, erected in 1995 by the local Zappa fan club.

Heroic Soviet Figures (Map p484; Kalvarijų gatvė) Symbolising Youth, Labour and Military Glory along Green Bridge.

Užupis Angel (Map p488; Užupio gatvė) Born out of an oversized egg on April Fool's Day in 2002.

Mindaugas (Map p488; Arsenalo gatvė 1) Lithuania's only official king (1200–63); assassinated by his nephew.

Statue of Gediminas (Map p488; Katedros aikštė) The equestrian statue of Grand Duke Gediminas stands proud in Cathedral Sq, roughly on the spot where a howling iron wolf allegedly appeared in his dream and told him to build a city.

Vilnius

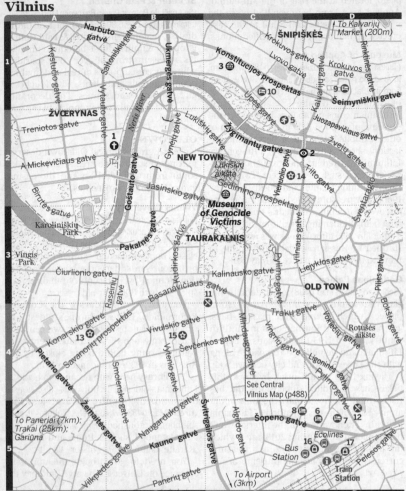

admission fee) to access **St John's Church** (Šv Jonų Bažnyčia; Map p488; Šv Jono gatvė 12; 11am-7.30pm Jun-Aug, 10am-6.30pm Sep-May), a baroque gem. It was founded in 1387 – well before the university arrived – and its 17th-century bell tower is the highest structure in the Old Town.

Gate of Dawn
HISTORIC BUILDING

(Aušros Vartai; Map p488; Aušros Vartų 12) Located at the southern border of the Old Town, the 16th-century Gate of Dawn is the only one of the town wall's original nine gates still intact. The gate houses the **Chapel of the Blessed**

Virgin Mary (Map p488; 6am-7pm, Mass 9am, 10am, 5.30pm & 6.30pm Mon-Sat, plus 9.30am Sun) and the black-and-gold 'miracle-working' **Virgin Mary icon** (enter through small door on the left). A gift from the Crimea by Grand Duke Algirdas in 1363, it is one of the holiest icons in Polish Catholicism, and the faithful arrive in droves to offer it whispered prayer. On Sundays, people gather for mass in the street facing the icon above the gate.

Pilies Gatvė
STREET

(Map p488) Cobbled Pilies gatvė – the hub of tourist action and the main entrance to the

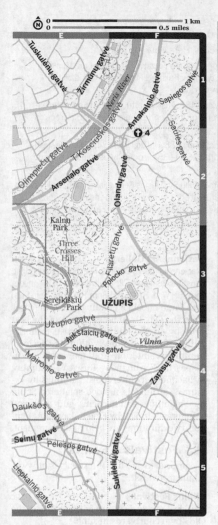

p488; Vilniaus gatvė 30), displaying Vilnius' trademark peach baroque style.

UŽUPIS

Lithuania's cheeky streak of rebellion flourishes in this district, located just east of the Old Town. In 1998 the resident artists, dreamers, squatters and vagabonds declared the district a breakaway state known as the Užupis Republic. The state has its own tongue-in-cheek president, anthem, flags and a 41-point **Užupis Republic constitution** (Map p488; Paupio gatvė) that, among other things, gives inhabitants the right to cry, the right to be misunderstood and the right to be a dog.

On April Fool's Day a huge party rages all day and all night. However, Užupis is worth visiting any time of year for its galleries, craft workshops and bohemian vibe.

Old Town from Cathedral Sq – buzzes with buskers, souvenir stalls and the odd beggar. At No 26 stands the **House of Signatories** (Signatarų Namai; Map p488; www.muziejai.lt; Pilies gatvė 26; admission 2Lt; ⊙10am-5pm Tue-Sat), where the Act granting Lithuania independence in 1918 was signed.

Vokiečių Gatvė STREET
(Map p488) Vokiečių gatvė, the Old Town's main commercial street, makes a good jumping-off point for explorations of the old Jewish quarter. Peering north from Vokiečių you'll spot **St Catherine's Church** (Map

BEST OF THE CHURCHES

The Old Town has a wealth of beautiful churches. Here's our top four:

St Anne's Church (Šv Onos Bažnyčia; Map p488; Maironio gatvė 8; ⊘Mass 6pm Mon-Sat, 9am & 11am Sun) Pint-sized red Gothic beauty that charmed Napoleon; fused to the baroque **Bernardine Church** (Map p488) next door.

St Teresa's Church (Šv Teresės Bažnyčia; Map p488; Aušros Vartų gatvė 14) Fantastic example of early baroque (1635–50), with an elaborate facade and a spectacular rococo interior.

St Casimir's Church (Šv Kazimiero Bažnyčia; Map p488; Didžioji gatvė 34) The oldest of Vilnius' baroque masterpieces, built by Jesuits (1604–35); ironically used as a museum of atheism under Soviet rule.

Orthodox Church of the Holy Spirit (Stačiatikių Šv Dvasios Cerkvė; Map p488; Aušros Vartų gatvė 10) Rococo stunner with a beautiful interior, packed with icons and frescos and sporting a magnificent cupola; the home of the supposedly incorruptible bodies of three saints.

NEW TOWN

TOP CHOICE Museum of Genocide Victims MUSEUM
(Genocido Aukų Muziejus; Map p484; www.genocid.lt/muziejus; Aukų gatvė 2a; adult/child 6/3Lt, audioguide 10Lt; ⊘10am-6pm Wed-Sat, to 5pm Sun) 'KGB Museum' to locals, this building used to be the notorious KGB headquarters and prison from 1940 to 1991. The detailed exhibits deal with Soviet oppression of the Lithuanian people, the post-WWII Lithuanian resistance movement (the 'Forest Brothers') and the mass deportation of locals to Siberia. Personal possessions of deportees include a rosary made of bread and a pinch of Lithuanian soil in a bag.

The museum's name is quite misleading, given that there is little mention of the fact that this was also the Gestapo headquarters between 1941 and 1944, or of the Gestapo's role in the genocide of much of the city's Jewish population (assisted by willing locals). The recent addition of a small Holocaust exhibition in one of the prison cells is welcome.

In the basement, peer into the water cell where prisoners had to balance on a tiny metal stool above ice-cold water (sometimes for days), the padded cell, and the execution chamber (in use between 1944 and the 1960s).

Gedimino Prospektas STREET
(Map p488) Vilnius' 19th-century New Town boasts a true European boulevard in Gedimino prospektas. It's a grand road with Vilnius Cathedral (p482) at one end and the silver-domed Russian Orthodox **Church of the Saint Virgin's Apparition** (Znamenskaya Tserkov; Map p484; A Mickevičiaus 1) at the other.

National Art Gallery GALLERY
(Nacionalinė Dailės Galerija; Map p484; www.ndg.lt; Konstitucijos gatvė 22; adult/child 6/3Lt; ⊘noon-7pm Tue, Wed, Fri & Sat, 1-8pm Thu, noon-5pm Sun) This large cubelike building across the river from the Old Town houses some of the best work by diverse Lithuanian artists from the 20th and 21st century within its spacious, minimalist interior. You may notice seascapes by Ferdinandos Ruščicas, sculpture by Jacques Lipchitz, cubist paintings by Vytautas Kairiiūkštis, a blood-splattered Stalin by Valentinas Antanavičius and a person submerged 'In Fat' by Eglė Rakaistaitė. Temporary exhibitions are held in the basement.

Festivals & Events

A comprehensive list of festivals is at www.vilniusfestivals.lt.

Vilnius Festival MUSIC
Classical music, jazz and folk concerts in the Old Town courtyards in June.

Vilnius City Days ARTS
Music, performing arts and fashion festival at the beginning of September.

Gaida MUSIC
The biggest and most important contemporary music festival in the Baltics, held in late October.

Sleeping

TOP CHOICE Domus Maria GUESTHOUSE €€
(Map p488; ☑5-264 4880; www.domusmaria.lt; Aušros Vartų gatvė 12; d/tr €93/114; 🅿@🛜) Unique and immensely popular, this guest-

house in a heavenly location within a 17th-century former monastery stays true to its monastic origins with wide-arched corridors and spartan white rooms, though you needn't adopt a monastic lifestyle: creature comforts are provided. And if you feel as if you're having breakfast in a chapel, that's because you are.

TOP CHOICE **Narutis** LUXURY HOTEL €€€

(Map p488; ☑5-212 2894; www.narutis.com; Pilies gatvė 24; r/ste from €112/650; P❀@🎧) Impossibly stylish and beautiful hotel with plenty of greenery in the atrium. It combines a you-can't-get-more-central-than-that location, 16th-century frescos and wooden beams with modern decadence, such as a spa and *hammam* (Turkish bath) in some suites and all mod cons. Impeccable service and a restaurant serving expertly prepared international dishes complete the experience.

TOP CHOICE **Jimmy Jumps House** HOSTEL €

(Map p488; ☑6078 8435; www.jimmyjumpshouse. com; Savičiaus gatvė 12-1; dm 37-42Lt, d 110Lt; @🎧) Sociable without being a stag-party magnet, this great Canadian-owned central hostel is for those who want to pack a lot into their stay – from themed pub crawls to machine gun tours and more. Free waffle breakfast, movie lounge and hookahs for those rainy days more than make up for the modest-sized dorms.

Litinterp B&B €

(Map p488; ☑5-212 3850; www.litinterp.lt; Bernardinų gatvė 7-2; s/d/tr 100/160/210Lt, without bathroom 80/140/180Lt, apt 280Lt; ☺office 8.30am-9pm Mon-Fri, 9am-3pm Sat; 🎧) This bright, clean and friendly budget-traveller favourite for over two decades is right in the heart of the Old Town and breakfast is delivered to your door in a little basket. Rooms with shared bathroom are only good for swinging a small cat, but those with en suite are generously large. Arrival time is required in advance, especially if checking in after office hours.

Dvaras BOUTIQUE HOTEL €€

(Map p488; ☑5-210 7370; www.dvaras.lt; Tilto gatvė 3-1; s/d/ste 301/342/494Lt; P❀@🎧) A mix of old-world grandeur and modern creature comforts, the Manor House has just eight beautifully appointed, individually decorated rooms. Extra touches include heated floors in bathrooms, and breakfast brought to your room on request. Ask for a room with a view of Gediminas Castle and the Cathedral.

JEWISH VILNIUS

Dubbed by Napoleon the 'Jerusalem of the north', Vilnius had one of Europe's most prominent Jewish communities until the Nazis brutality wiped it out (with assistance from some Lithuanians).

The old Jewish quarter lay in the streets west of Didžioji gatvė, including present-day Žydų gatvė (Jews St) and Gaono gatvė, named after Vilnius' most famous Jewish resident, Gaon Elijahu ben Shlomo Zalman (1720–97), a sage who could recite the entire Talmud by heart at the age of six.

A good place to start your tour is the **Centre for Tolerance** (Map p488; www.jmuseum. lt; Naugarduko gatvė 10; adult/child 5/2Lt; ☺11am-7pm Mon, 10am-6pm Tue-Thu, to 4pm Fri & Sun), a beautifully restored former Jewish theatre that houses thought-provoking displays on the history and culture of Jews in Lithuania before the Shoah (Holocaust) and beyond; occasional art exhibitions and concerts are also held. The **Holocaust Museum** (Holokausto Muziejus; Map p488; www.jmuseum.lt; Pamėnkalnio gatvė 12; adult/child 5/2Lt; ☺9am-5pm Mon-Thu, 9am-4pm Fri, 10am-4pm Sun), in the so-called Green House, is an unvarnished account detailing the horror suffered by Lithuanian Jews in an unedited display of horrific images and letters, put together by local Holocaust survivors. Nearby, the **Jewish Community of Lithuania** (Lietuvos Žydų Bendruomenė; Map p488; www.lzb.lt; Pylimo gatvė 4; admission free; ☺10am-5pm Mon-Fri) is an invaluable source of information on all things Jewish in Vilnius.

Vilnius' only remaining synagogue out of more than 100, the **Choral Synagogue** (Choralinė Sinagoga; Map p488; Pylimo gatvė 39; donations welcome; ☺10am-2pm Sun-Fri) was built in a Moorish style in 1903 and survived only because the Nazis used it as a medical store.

For a more casual glimpse of Jewish life, walk down Žydų gatvė to the **memorial bust of Gaon Elijahu** (Map p488; Žydų gatvė 3), imagining how life once was. There's a map of the two main Jewish ghettos during WWII on the spot that used to be the single **gate** (Map p488; Rūdninkų gatvė) to the largest ghetto.

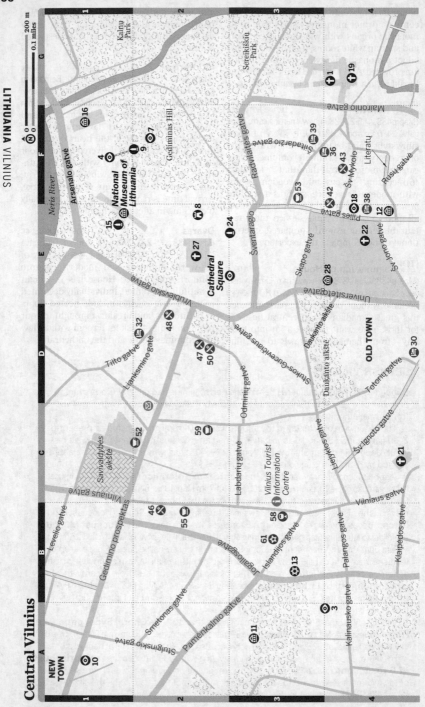

Central Vilnius

LITHUANIA VILNIUS

NEW TOWN

OLD TOWN

Cathedral Square

National Museum of Lithuania

Kalnų Park

Sereikiškių Park

Gediminas Hill

Nerís River

Vilnius Tourist Information Centre

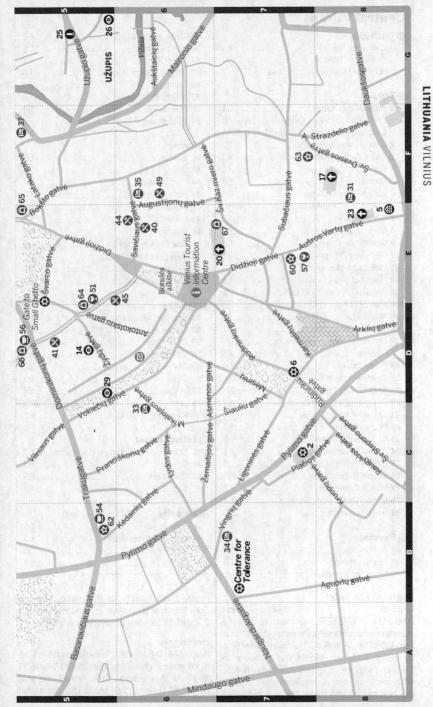

Central Vilnius

Radisson Blu Hotel Lietuva
BUSINESS HOTEL €€€

(Map p484; ☎5-272 6272; www.radissonblu.com/lietuvahotel-vilnius; Konstitucijos prospektas 20; r/ste from €109/269; P❄@🛜) The burly, bustling, 22-storey Radisson Blu is the antidote to Vilnius' plethora of quaint boutique hotels, with well appointed, business-class rooms, the best casino in Vilnius and a rare fitness centre that's worthy of the name. The top-floor **Sky Bar** (Map p484; ⊙5pm-1am Sun-Thu, to 2.30am Fri & Sat) has the city's best views.

Hostelgate
HOSTEL €

(Map p488; ☎6383 2818; www.hostelgate.lt; Mikalojaus gatvė 3; dm/d/tr/q from 38/110/141/180Lt; @🛜) At this central little hostel the staff go out of their way to make the guests feel welcome and the place attracts an international mix of backpackers. There's a lounge for socialising, free coffee and lockers, but no breakfast (there is a kitchen), and private rooms are in the building next door.

Come To Vilnius
HOSTEL €

(Map p484; ☑6560 5036; www.cometovilnius.eu; Šv Stepono gatvė 15; dm/d/d 55/120/150Lt; ☎) A great new addition to the hostel scene near the bus and train stations, with nice little touches, such as reading lights for every bed, good showers and compact, so-clean-you-can-eat-off-the-floor rooms. Alas, there's no real area for mingling apart from the kitchen and around, but the staff are ultra-helpful, making this a good reason to, erm, come to Vilnius.

Hotel Rinno
HOTEL €€

(Map p488; ☑5-262 2828; www.rinno.lt; Vingrių gatvė 25; s/d from 260/320Lt; P✳@☎) Rinno is tops – its staff are exceptionally helpful and polite; its rooms are first rate; its location, on a quiet central street between the Old Town and the train and bus stations, is handy; and its price is a bargain. Breakfast is served in the pleasant and private backyard, and though there's no lift, staff will assist with luggage.

Shakespeare
BOUTIQUE HOTEL €€€

(Map p488; ☑5-266 5885; www.shakespeare. lt; Bernardinų gatvė 8/8; s/d from €104/174; P✳@☎) To stay or not to stay, that is the question. Actually, it's a no-brainer: Shakespeare is a refined Old Town gem that evokes a cultured, literary feel with its abundance of books, antiques and flowers. Each room pays homage to a different writer – in name and design – and there's a quality restaurant on the premises serving international dishes.

Mabre Residence
HISTORIC HOTEL €€€

(Map p488; ☑5-212 2087; www.mabre.lt; Maironio gatvė 13; s/d/ste from €118/149/176; P✳@☎) With a splendid courtyard full of greenery, and quiet rooms enclosed within a 17th-century monastery on the edge of the Old Town, this is one of the more pleasant upmarket options. The spa is full of pampering options and the breakfast buffet ample, but some of the windows are too high to look out of and there is no lift.

Apia Hotel
HISTORIC HOTEL €€

(Map p488; ☑5-212 3426; www.apia.lt; Sv Ignoto gatvė 12; s/d/tr €60/75/90; P@☎) Pretty much next door to the Presidential Palace, this smart, friendly, family-run hotel may be housed in a restored 17th-century building in the heart of the Old Town, but its facilities are truly modern, with satellite TV in each of the nine rooms. Light sleepers should ask for a courtyard view. The breakfast is nothing to write home about.

AAA Hostel
HOSTEL €

(Map p484; ☑5-215 0270; www.ahostel.lt; Sodų gatvė 8; dm/s/d from 34/87/97Lt; @☎) This 16-bed dorm is modelled on Japan's capsule hotels, the walls between the beds giving some semblance of privacy. The decor stands out, with cavernlike kitchen, funky chairs in the lounge and blood-red carpets in the spacious rooms. Very near the train and bus stations, but not as noisy as you'd think, given the location. There's a less-nice **branch** (Map p484; ☑5-215 0270; www.ahostel.lt; Sodų gatvė 17) around the corner.

Ecotel
BUSINESS HOTEL €€

(Map p484; ☑5-210 2700; www.ecotel.lt; Slucko gatvė 8; s/d/tr 199/299/279Lt; P✳@☎) In a quiet part of town, Ecotel is a good bet, with simple but smart furnishings filling its squeaky-clean rooms, in which bathrooms have heated towel rails. Special provisions are made for disabled guests, those with allergies and extra-tall guests, too.

✗ Eating

Vilnius has an ever-growing mouth-watering selection of local and international cuisine.

TOP CHOICE Holy Miko's
INTERNATIONAL €€

(Map p488; ☑6681 2210; www.holymikos.lt; Šv Mykolo gatvė 4; mains 21-55Lt; ☎) This new family-run restaurant serves imaginative takes on Lithuanian and international dishes, complemented by an extensive wine list, in attractive cellarlike surroundings. The menu is succinct, with great attention to flavour and presentation. Do your taste buds a favour and go for the duck breast with sweet-potato souffle or the forest-mushroom risotto, and don't forget to leave room for the divine hazelnut and mascarpone cheesecake.

TOP CHOICE Lokys
LITHUANIAN €€

(Map p488; ☑5-262 9046; www.lokys.lt; Stiklių gatvė 8; mains 27-65Lt) Dine like a medieval noble at one of Vilnius's best-loved restaurants (ask to be seated in the atmospheric cellar). The game dishes range from the traditional – such as quail in blackberry sauce and venison with chanterelles – to

VILNIUS FROM ABOVE

Get some vertical perspective on Vilnius by either heading up the 326m-tall **TV Tower** (Televizijos Bokštas; www.lrtc.net; Sausio 13-osios gatvė 10; adult/child 21/9Lt; ⊙observation deck 10am-10pm; 🖳1, 3, 7 ,16), or – even better – take to the skies in a hot-air balloon courtesy of the **Oreivystės Centras** (Map p484; 🖉5-273 2703; www.ballooning.lt; Upės gatvė 5; per person €119-179). Finally, you can enjoy dizzying views of Vilnius from the 22nd floor Sky Bar (p490) while imbibing one of its seriously good cocktails.

the unusual (beaver stew, and 'cold noses': bilberry dumplings), but all are superbly prepared. The herbal wine and home-brewed *kvas* (a mildly alcoholic drink made from fermented bread) make a fine accompaniment.

TOP CHOICE Tres Mexicanos MEXICAN €€

(Map p488; www.tresmexicanos.lt; Tilto gatvė 2; mains 18-28Lt) All bright colours and Day of the Dead paintings, this cheerful little restaurant run by Mexican transplants packs some proper heat with a selection of authentically spicy enchiladas, tacos, burritos and more, and this may the best stop for *mole poblano* this side of the Atlantic. Daily lunch specials Monday to Thursday are a steal at around 10Lt.

Zoe's Bar & Grill INTERNATIONAL €€

(Map p488; www.zoesbargrill.com; Odminių gatvė 3; mains 21-49Lt) A restaurant can't always get away with trying to cover too many culinary bases. Bustling, friendly Zoe's, however, manages to pull it off, with the likes of African beef-and-pepper soup with citrus yoghurt, baby back ribs and fabulous meatballs. If you're not too hungry, there are sandwiches and salads aplenty and the crème brûlée is done just right.

Bistro 18 INTERNATIONAL €€

(Map p488; www.bistro18.lt; Stiklių gatvė 18; mains 19-66Lt; 🖱) The service is friendly, polite and attentive, the decor is minimalist, the food is imaginative and flavoursome, and the wine list features bottles from as far away as the Antipodes. Expect the likes of warm goat's cheese salad, duck with polenta and port-cranberry sauce and three-cheese risotto.

Sue's Indian Raja INDIAN €€

(Map p488; 🖉5-266 1887; www.suesindianraja.lt; Odminių gatvė 3; mains 22-48Lt; 🖉) Who said that you need to go to Britain (or India!) for a good curry? Loved by expats, Indian embassy staff and visitors alike, this eating establishment serves large portions of expertly flavoured Indian dishes, such as the sublime butter chicken, and a good range of veg options. If they tell you that a dish is spicy, trust them!

Osaka JAPANESE €€€

(Map p488; 🖉5-261 7176; www.osaka.lt; Vilniaus gatvė 19; sashimi per piece 8-12Lt; sushi rolls 15-39Lt; 🖘) Minimalist decor? Check. Extensive fish-based menu? Check. If it weren't for the Lithuanian waitresses in Japanese dress, the illusion would be complete. As it is, expect imaginative sushi rolls (*sakura* and *kaisen unagi* stand out), exquisite sashimi (try the *unagi* with fois gras or the *maguro* truffle), soups, noodles, tempura, and very professional service. The one concession to Western tastes is the matcha panna cotta.

Forto Dvaras LITHUANIAN €€

(Map p488; www.fortas.eu; Pilies gatvė 16; mains 12-38Lt; 🖘🖉) Perpetually popular folk-themed restaurant that's in danger of turning its patrons into something visually resembling its signature dish, the *cepelinai*. It's among the best in the city, as are the humongous beer snack platters and the vegie options – *šaltibarščiai*, potato pancakes and other potato-based creations.

Borsch UKRAINIAN €€

(Борщ!; Map p484; www.borsch.lt; Algirdo gatvė 5-2; mains 19-36Lt; 🖉) Combining traditional flavours with a minimum of stodge, everything at this Ukrainian restaurant – from the superb signature borsch to the sweet and savoury *pelmeni* and *vareniki* (dumplings) and meat dishes – is prepared with great attention to both taste and presentation. Wash it down with the sublime homemade *kvas*.

Vegafé VEGETARIAN €

(Map p488; Augustijonų gatvė 2/13; mains 11-15Lt; ⊙11am-9.30pm Mon-Sat; 🖉) This tiny place with an equally tiny terrace filled with greenery specialises in imaginative soups, smoothies (try the Vietnamese avocado smoothie), lassis (including the unusual spinach with cilantro and cumin) and flavourful mains that involve lentils, vegetables, tofu and whatever the chef happens to have to hand that day. Oh, and did we mention that all the dishes are vegetarian?

Balzac

FRENCH €€

(Map p488; ☑6148 9223; www.balzac.lt; Savičiaus gatvė 7; mains 29-49Lt) The menu at this bistro with exposed-brick walls and old movie posters reads like the pantheon of French classics: *boeuf tartare, fois gras, moûles marnière*, escargots...and it's all beautifully cooked and served without a hint of attitude (the only hint that this isn't as authentically French as could be!). Don't miss the *tarte tatin*.

Koldūnine

LITHUANIAN €

(Map p488; Savičiaus gatvė 6; mains 12-18Lt; 🕿🖉) You may have tasted them in other guises: *koldūninė* are Lithuanian dumplings akin to Polish *pierogi* and Russian *pelmeni*. At this informal eatery you'll find – count 'em! – 11 different varieties and they're all stomach-fillingly tasty. Not in a dumpling mood? There are pancakes and 'Caesarian salad', too.

Self-Catering

Iki (Map p484; Sodų gatvė 22, bus station; ⌚8am-10pm) and **Maxima** (Map p484; Geležinkelio gatvė, train station; ⌚8am-10pm) are leading supermarket chains; self-caterers may also want to stop by the **Kalvarijų Market** (Kalvarijų Turgus; off Map p484; Kalvarijų gatvė 61; ⌚7am-2pm Tue-Sun) or the **Halės Market** (Halės Turgus; Map p484; Pylimo gatvė 58/1; ⌚7am-5pm Tue-Sat, to 3pm Sun), which sells fresh fruit, vegetables, dairy, smoked meat and fish.

🍷 Drinking

Vilnius' riotous party culture centres on clubs in the cold months and outdoor cafes in the summer. At weekends, many cafes turn into clubs and many restaurants turn into raucous bars.

Cozy

CAFE

(Map p488; www.cozy.lt; Dominikonų gatvė 10; ⌚9am-2am Mon-Wed, to 4am Thu & Fri, 10am-4am Sat, to 2am Sun) Cozy wears many hats and we like all of them. It's a great spot for breakfast or leisurely coffee, the lunch and dinner mains are inexpensive and never disappointing and in the evenings (Thursday to Saturday) you can grab a drink or two to fuel you through the DJ sessions downstairs.

In Vino

WINE BAR

(Map p488; www.invino.lt; Aušros Vartų gatvė 7; ⌚4pm-2am Sun-Thu, to 4am Fri & Sat) Riding the crest of the current popularity of wine bars, this is among the best, with one of the loveliest courtyards in the city. Excellent wines,

good choice of tapas and a few meaty mains. Arrive early in summer to secure a table, then watch the place fill to overflowing.

Bambalynė

MICROBREWERY

(Map p488; www.bambalyne.lt; Stiklių gatvė 7; ⌚11am-10pm Sun & Mon, to midnight Tue-Sat; 🕿) When we say 'microbrewery', we actually mean that this brickseller watering hole collects microbrews from all over Lithuania. Its collection currently numbers around 80, ranging from dark to light – plenty to keep any real ale aficionado going.

Jackie

BAR

(Map p488; Vilniaus gatvė 31; ⌚6pm-1am Sun-Wed, to 3am Thu, to 5am Fri & Sat) This new whiskey bar, specialising in American whiskeys and bourbon, gets absolutely packed most nights, so if you wish to savour your poison, go early. Or go late on the weekend if you want to catch a DJ set.

Raw Raw

CAFE

(Map p488; www.rawraw.lt; Totorių gatvė 10) Minimalist decor, great fresh fruit and vegetable juices and an absence of grease and additives distinguish this cafe. It is supposed to be part of the raw food movement, ie nothing cooked over 42°C. We liked the Raw Raw couscous and the soups, but we're also taking bets on how long this place will last in a city of carnivores.

Coffee Inn

COFFEE HOUSE

(Map p488; www.coffee-inn.lt; Vilniaus gatvė 17; ⌚7am-10pm Mon-Thu, to midnight Fri, 9am-midnight Sat, to 11pm Sun; 🕿) The Lithuanian answer to Starbucks offers freshly made wraps, muffins, cookies and excellent grilled-vegetable sandwiches. Oh, and coffee – there's coffee too, from your basic espresso to frozen frappucino-style delights. There are also branches on **Traku gatvė** (Map p488; Trakų gatvė 7), **Gedimino prospektas 9** (Map p488; Gedimino prospektas 9) and **Pilies gatvė** (Map p488; Pilies gatvė 3).

⭐ Entertainment

In Your Pocket (www.inyourpocket.com) publishes a list of movie theatres as well as listings for opera, theatre, classical music and other big events. Most such venues close for the summer. The tourist offices also post events listings.

Clubs

Vilnius has a thriving nightlife. Expect cover charges on most nights and gorillas at the door.

Pabo Latino
CLUB

(Map p488; www.pabolatino.lt; Trakų gatvė 3; ⊙9pm-3am Thu, to 5am Fri & Sat) This sultry-red club specialises in live Latin music, good DJ sets and strong cocktails. Put on your dancing shoes, fortify your liver, and be prepared for a fun night out with some of the city's most beautiful people. Dress nicely.

Opium
DJ

(Map p488; Islandijos gatvė 4; cover 10-15Lt; ⊙10pm-6am Fri, 11pm-5am Sat) This compact venue – the playground of the city's best DJs – is for serious clubbers. Come here once, and there's a good chance you'll get addicted.

Tamsta
ROCK, JAZZ

(Map p488; www.tamstaclub.lt; Subačiaus gatvė 11a; ⊙7pm-midnight Wed & Thu, to 2am Fri & Sat) Live music by local musicians – ranging from rock to rock'n'roll to jazz. Inspired jamming some nights and the long bar get pretty packed most evenings.

Soho
GAY

(Map p484; www.sohoclub.lt; Švitrigailos gatvė 7/16; ⊙10pm-7am Fri & Sat) At the main haunt for Vilnius' gay community, you can leap into the limelight on the stage or the dance floor, or have a quiet-ish tête-à-tête with that attractive stranger you've just met in one of the mini halls or the mirrored VIP balcony.

Performing Arts

Lithuanian National Opera & Ballet Theatre
OPERA

(Lietuvos Nacionalinis Operos ir Baleto Teatras; Map p484; ☑5-262 0727; www.opera.lt; Vienuolio gatvė 1; ⊙Sep-Jun) Classical productions in a grand, gaudy building near the river.

Lithuanian National Philharmonic
CLASSICAL MUSIC

(Lietuvos Nacionalinė Filharmonija; Map p488; ☑5-266 5233; www.filharmonija.lt; Aušros Vartų gatvė 5; ⊙box office 10am-7pm Tue-Sat, to noon Sun) The country's most renowned orchestras perform here.

Cinemas

Forum Cinemas Vingis
CINEMA

(Map p484; www.forumcinemas.lt; Savanorių prospektas 7) Mostly popular Hollywood films are screened in English with Lithuanian subtitles at this 12-screen cinema.

🛍 Shopping

Linen & Amber Studio
SOUVENIRS

(Map p488; www.lgstudija.lt; Pilies gatvė 10; ⊙10am-7pm Mon-Sat, to 5pm Sun) One of the best places to purchase both amber and linen creations – the two things synonymous with Lithuania.

Ona
GIFTS

(Map p488; www.ona.lt; Šv Kazimiero gatvė 12; ⊙8am-6pm Mon-Fri) Stocks a range of original, ecofriendly jewellery, paintings and other crafts produced by small-scale local artists.

Julia Janus
FASHION

(Map p488; www.juliajanus.com; Stiklių gatvė 7; ⊙11am-7pm Mon-Fri, to 5pm Sat) Ready-to-wear, affordable fashion for women by prominent Lithuanian designer Julia Janus. Great accessories, too.

Mint Vinetu
BOOKS

(Map p488; www.mintvinetu.com; Šv Ignoto gatvė 16/10; ⊙11am-8pm) The largest selection of English-language titles in Vilnius.

ℹ Information

Internet Access

A growing number of cafes and restaurants offer free wi-fi, so internet cafes are rapidly becoming obsolete.

Collegium (Pilies gatvė 22-1; per hr 6Lt; ⊙10am-6pm Mon-Fri)

Medical Services

Baltic-American Medical & Surgical Clinic (☑6985 2655, 5-234 2020; www.bak.lt; Nemenčinės gatvė 54a; ⊙24hr) English-speaking health care inside Vilnius University's Antakalnis hospital, northeast of town.

Main Pharmacy (Gedimino Vaistinė; Gedimino prospektas 27; ⊙7.30am-8pm Mon-Fri, 10am-5pm Sat, to 4pm Sun)

Money

Vilnius is littered with ATMs and banks, and most offer the usual exchange, money transfer, travellers cheques and cash-advance services. Many are concentrated on Vokiečių gatvė.

Post

Central post office (Centrinis Paštas; Map p488; www.post.lt; Gedimino prospektas 7)

Post office (Map p488; Vokiečių gatvė 7)

Tourist Information

Vilnius Tourist Information Centres (www.vilnius-tourism.lt) Friendly centres operate at the **town hall** (Map p488; ☑5-262 6470; Didžioji gatvė 31, town hall; ⊙9am-6pm), **train station** (Map p484; ☑5-269 2091; Geležinkelio gatvė 16, train station; ⊙9am-1pm & 1.45-6pm) and **Vilniaus gatvė** (Map p488; ☑5-262 9660; Vilniaus gatvė 22; ⊙9am-6pm) with a wealth of glossy brochures and general information. They also give out the free *Vilnius Visitor's Guide*, arrange tour guides and book accommodation (a hotel reservation fee of 6Lt applies).

Websites
Lonely Planet (www.lonelyplanet.com/lithuania/vilnius)

ⓘ Getting There & Away

International bus services leave from the **bus station** (Autobusų Stotis; Map p484; ☏1661; www.toks.lt; Sodų gatvė 22), run by **Ecolines**

(☏5-262 0020; www.ecolines.net; bus station) or one of the affiliated carriers under **Eurolines** (www.eurolines.lt).

From the **train station** (Geležinkelio Stotis; ☏5-233 0088; www.litrail.lt; Geležinkelio gatvė 16), Vilnius is linked by regular direct trains to many international destinations. You'll need a Belarus visa for the Moscow train. For Warsaw, change in Kaunas.

There are left-luggage rooms at the **bus station** (per bag per 12hr 3Lt; ⏱5.25am-9pm Mon-Fri 7am-8.45pm Sat & Sun) and **train sta-**

TRANSPORT FROM VILNIUS

Domestic Bus

DESTINATION	PRICE (LT)	DURATION (HR)	FREQUENCY
Druskininkai	32	2-2¼	up to 12 daily
Kaunas	20	1½	2-3 hourly
Klaipėda	68	4-6½	15 daily
Palanga	68	4½-7½	7 daily
Šiauliai	47	3¼-5	up to 14 daily

International Bus

DESTINATION	PRICE (LT)	DURATION (HR)	FREQUENCY
Berlin (Germany)	130	13½	daily
Kaliningrad (Russia)	64	7½	1-2 daily
Rīga (Latvia)	35	3¾-4	up to 7 daily
St Petersburg (Russia)	155	24	2 daily
Tallinn (Estonia)	69	10½	daily
Warsaw (Poland)	65	8	1 daily

Domestic Train

DESTINATION	PRICE (LT)	DURATION	FREQUENCY (DAILY)
Ignalina	14	1¾-2hr	up to 7
Kaunas	16.30	1-1¾hr	up to 17
Klaipėda	51.20	4¾hr	3
Šiauliai	34.80	2½hr	3
Trakai	6.20	35-45min	up to 10

International Train

DESTINATION	PRICE (LT)	DURATION (HR)	FREQUENCY (DAILY)
Moscow (Russia)	From 317	14¾-15¾	up to 3
St Petersburg (Russia)	371	14-18½	2
Kaliningrad (Russia)	From 110	6¼-6½	up to 4
Minsk (Belarus)	From 30	3-4¾	up to 7
Warsaw (Poland)	From 85	10¾	1

tion (per bag per 12hr 3-6Lt; ⏲24hr); ask for the bagažinė.

The big international car-rental agencies such as **Avis** (☑5-230 6820; www.avis.lt; Laisvės gatvė 3; ⏲8am-5pm Mon-Fri, 9am-4pm Sat & Sun) and **Budget** (☑5-230 6708; www.budget. lt; at the airport; ⏲9am-7pm) are well represented at Vilnius airport.

ⓘ Getting Around

TO/FROM THE AIRPORT Vilnius international airport (Tarptautinis Vilniaus Oro Uostas; ☑5-230 6666; www.vno.lt; Rodūnios Kelias 2; ☎; ▣1, 2) lies 5km south of the centre. Bus 1 runs between the airport and the train station; bus 2 runs between the airport and the northwestern suburb of Šeškinė. A shuttle train service runs from the train station 17 times daily between 5.44am and 9.07pm (2.50Lt).

A taxi from the airport to the city centre should cost around 55Lt.

BICYCLE VeloCity (☑6741 2123; www.velo-city. lt; Aušros Vartų 12; ⏲9am-9pm) rents out bicycles for 10/40Lt per hour/day, provides information on cycling routes and arranges biking tours of the city. The one-hour city tour is free, while the four-hour city tour costs 50Lt. There's a 15% discount for ISIC card holders.

CAR & MOTORCYCLE There are numerous guarded paid car parks around town. Avoid parking on unlit streets overnight; car break-ins are common.

PUBLIC TRANSPORT The refillable electronic Vilniečio Kortelė (Vilnius Card) has been duly introduced; it can be purchased from news kiosks for 4Lt. A new pricing scheme ap-

plies: 30min/60min/24hr/72hr tickets cost 2.20/3.20/12/21Lt.

You're not obliged to get this electronic card; you can still purchase single-ride tickets from kiosks/ on board; but if you want to buy 24hr/72hr tickets, they cost 13/23Lt respectively, making them marginally pricier than the electronic card (unless you count the price of the electronic card as well).

TAXI Taxis (☑1409, ☑1411, ☑1818, ☑1445, no prefix needed; www.etaksi.lt) charge 1.50Lt to 3Lt per kilometre and they must have a meter. Drivers often try to rip off tourists, especially if flagged down on the street. You can phone a taxi using a Lithuanian SIM card, or queue up at one of the numerous taxi ranks. Popular spots are outside the train station and at the southern end of Vokiečių gatvė.

AROUND VILNIUS

A fairy-tale castle and ancient castle mounds lie within easy reach of the capital. Paneriai makes for a more sombre outing.

Paneriai

Between July 1941 and August 1944 the Nazis, aided by Lithuanian accomplices, exterminated 100,000 people, around 70,000 of whom were Jewish, at this site, 10km southwest of central Vilnius.

From the entrance a path leads to the small **Paneriai Museum** (☑Algys Karosas 6808 1278; Agrastų gatvė 17; ⏲10am-6pm Sun-Thu), with a graphic display of photographs and person-

---

WORTH A TRIP

BEYOND VILNIUS

There are two worthwhile jaunts out of town and they couldn't be more different in character. One is the **Europos Parkas sculpture park** (www.europosparkas.lt; Joneikiškės; adult/student/child 25/18/11Lt; guided tour 100Lt; ⏲10am-sunset; ▣146), 19km from Vilnius – an enormous open-air art gallery featuring close to 100 works from around the world by the likes of Sol LeWitt and Dennis Oppenheim, spread out across 55 hectares of woodland and hills. You can visit the exhibits either on foot or by bicycle, which you can rent at the entrance.

To get here, take trolleybus 5 from the Vilnius bus station (p495) towards Žirmūnai and alight at the Žalgirio bus stop on Kalvarijų gatvė. Then take the bus 146 marked 'Skirgiškės' (4Lt, 30 minutes, three to four daily) and tell the driver to drop you off at the entrance to the park.

More sobering is a visit to the **Underground Museum of Socialism** (Požeminis Socialismo Muziejus; ☑6984 4220; www.sovietbunker.com; 90min tour 25Lt), aka Soviet Bunker, where you're subjected to 90 minutes of role-playing, with yourself as a Soviet inmate, met by guards with dogs and escorted through a KGB interrogation room, Soviet school and typical Soviet apartment – half-kitsch, half-history. Transport to and from can be arranged at extra cost; call in advance for English-language tours.

al belongings of those who died here. Nearby are two monuments – one Jewish (marked with the Star of David), the other one Soviet (an obelisk topped with a Soviet star). Paths lead from here to grassed-over pits where the Nazis burnt the exhumed bodies of their victims to hide the evidence of their crimes.

There are hourly trains daily from Vilnius to Paneriai station (2Lt, eight to 11 minutes). From the station, it's a 1km walk southwest along Agrastų gatvė into the forest to reach the site.

Trakai

POP 4930

With its picturesque red-brick castle, Karaite culture, quaint wooden houses and pretty lakeside location, Trakai is within easy reach of the capital.

This area has protected status as the **Trakai Historical National Park** (www.seniejitrakai. lt). The **tourist information centre** (☎528-51934; www.trakai.lt; Vytauto gatvė 69; ☺9am-5pm Mon, to 6pm Tue-Fri, to 3pm Sat & Sun May-Aug) sells maps and has information on activities and accommodation in the area.

◎ Sights

[TOP CHOICE] **Trakai Castle**   CASTLE

(Trakų Pilis; www.trakaimuziejus.lt; adult/senior/ student & child 14/8/6Lt, camera 4Lt; ☺10am-7pm May-Sep, to 6pm Mar, Apr & Oct, to 5pm Nov-Feb; ⊕) Trakai's trophy piece is the fairy-tale island castle, occupying a small island in Lake Galvė. A footbridge links the island castle to the shore. The red-brick Gothic castle, painstakingly restored from original blueprints, dates from the late 14th century when Prince Kęstutis, father of Vytautas, once ruled the area. Vytautas completed what his father started in the early 1400s and died in the castle in 1430. In summer the castle courtyard stages concerts and plays and you can also put your children in the stocks or a medieval-style cage.

Trakai History Museum   MUSEUM

(Trakų Istorijos Muziejus; www.trakaimuziejus.lt; adult/senior/student & child 14/8/6Lt, camera 4Lt; ☺10am-7pm May-Sep, to 6pm Mar, Apr & Oct, to 5pm Nov-Feb) The exhibits inside Trakai Castle's cellars and tower tell the history of the building, and there's a bewildering variety of objects on show – hoards of coins, weaponry, pipes, porcelain – as well as interactive displays.

THE LAST OF THE KARAITE

The Karaite people are named after the term *kara*, which means 'to study the scriptures' in both Hebrew and Arabic. The sect originated in Baghdad and practises strict adherence to the *Torah* (rejecting the rabbinic Talmud). In around 1400 the grand duke of Lithuania, Vytautas, brought about 380 Karaite families to Trakai from Crimea to serve as bodyguards. Only a dozen families remain in Trakai today and their numbers are dwindling rapidly.

The museum has two other branches in town. The **Sacred Art Exhibition** (Sacralineo Meno Muziejus; Kestučio gatvė 4; adult/student & child 4/2Lt; ☺10am-6pm Wed-Sun) houses a small but very fine collection of precious reliquaries and monstrances. The **Karaite Ethnographic Exhibition** (Karaimų etnografinė paroda; Karaimų gatvė 22; adult/student & child 4/2Lt, camera 4Lt, guided tour 30Lt; ☺10am-6pm Wed-Sun) provides a good introduction to the fascinating Karaite culture.

✕ Eating

Try the *kibinai*, a Karaite speciality – meat-stuffed pastries that are similar to empanadas.

Kibininė   KARAITE €

(www.kibinas.lt; Karaimų gatvė 65; kibinai 4.50-7.50Lt; ☺10am-midnight) This place has a dreamy location right on the lake and features venison *kibinai* among others.

Kybynlar   KARAITE €€

(www.kybynlar.lt; Karaimų gatvė 29; mains 16-28Lt; ☺noon-9pm Mon, 11am-9pm Tue-Thu, to 10pm Fri & Sat, to 9pm Sun) This restaurant has a more Turkic feel and substantial meat dishes.

❶ Getting There & Away

Up to 10 daily trains (6.20Lt, 35 to 45 minutes) travel between Trakai and Vilnius. Trakai's bus station (closer to the castle) is served by Alytus-bound buses (6Lt, 40 minutes, twice hourly).

Kernavė

Inhabited for over 10,000 years and thought to have been the spot where Mindaugas (responsible for uniting Lithuania for the first time) celebrated his coronation in 1253, Kernavė comprises five old hill fort mounds – grassy hills that you can walk up – and the archaeological remains of a medieval town.

The fascinating heritage of the **Kernavė Cultural Reserve** (Kernavės kultūrinio rezervato; www.kernave.org; ⊗dawn-dusk) can be explored in the newly renovated, well-designed **Archaeological & Historical Museum** (Archeologijos ir Istorijos Muziejus; ☑info, tour 382-47385; Kerniaus gatvė 4a; admission 6Lt; ⊗10am-6pm Tue-Sat May-Oct, to 4pm Nov-Apr) which traces the history of the area from the first signs of human habitation in around 9000 BC to the growth of Kernavė as a major trade settlement from the 12th century AD. Guided tours are available by prior arrangement. Check with the museum on whether the **International Festival of Experimental Archaeology** will restart in 2013.

Kernavė, 35km northwest of Vilnius, is reached by regular buses (15Lt, one hour, up to seven daily).

EASTERN & SOUTHERN LITHUANIA

The mythical forests of eastern and southern Lithuania make easy day trips from Vilnius, as does the infamous sculpture park, although outdoor enthusiasts should not hesitate to spend more time here.

Aukštaitija National Park

Lithuania's first national park (founded in 1974) is a 400-sq-km wonderland of rivers, lakes, centuries-old forests and tiny villages still steeped in rural tradition. Around 70% of the park comprises pine, spruce and deciduous forests, inhabited by elk, deer, wild boar, storks and white-tailed and golden eagles. Its highlight is a network of 126 lakes, the deepest being Lake Tauragnas (60.5m deep).

The park is mainly for lovers of the outdoors, with nine fully equipped camping grounds located by the lakes, and biking, canoeing, kayaking and parachute jumping among the activities on offer. For those interested in getting deeper under the skin of this enchanting area, the **Aukštaitija National Park Office** (Aukštaitijos Nacionalinis Parkas; ☑386-53135; www.anp.lt; ⊗9am-6pm Mon-Sat) in Palūšė, 5km away from Ignalina, has everything you need to know, including park maps. The **tourist office** (☑386-52597; www.ignalinatic.lt; Ateites gatvė 23; ⊗9am-6pm

Mon-Fri, 10am-2pm Sat) in Ignalina, the main gateway town to the park, can also help.

To get here jump on a train from Vilnius to Ignalina (14Lt, 1½ to 1¾ hours, six daily); from there one bus travels to Palūšė at 2.55pm (3Lt, Friday to Monday).

CENTRAL LITHUANIA

Besides the lively historic town of Kaunas, the heart of the country boasts Lithuania's prime pilgrimage place – the eerie Hill of Crosses in Šiauliai.

Kaunas

POP 311,100

Kaunas has a compact Old Town, an array of museums – both entertaining and harrowing – and a rich history as Lithuania's sometime capital. Its sizeable student population provides it with plenty of vibrant, youthful energy, and its rough edges give it that extra bit of spice.

A great time to visit is in April, when the city comes alive during the four-day **International Jazz Festival** (www.kaunasjazz.lt).

⊙ Sights

OLD TOWN

Rotušės Aikštė   SQUARE

Surrounding the square are 15th- and 16th-century German merchants' houses. The 18th-century, white baroque former city hall, which served variously as a prison, palace and house of ill repute, is now the **Palace of Weddings** (Rotušės Aikštė). The southern side of the square is dominated by the 18th-century twin-towered **St Francis church** (Rotušės aikštė 7-9).

St Peter & Paul Cathedral   CHURCH

(Šventų Apaštalų Petro ir Povilo Arkekatedra Bazilika; Vilniaus gatvė 1; ⊗7am-7pm Mon-Sat, 8am-7pm Sun) St Peter and Paul Cathedral is Lithuania's largest Gothic house of worship (with Renaissance and baroque touches) and its interior is nothing short of splendid, the highlight being the baroque main altar. Outside the cathedral's south wall is the **tomb of Maironis**, one of Lithuania's most revered poets.

Presidential Palace of Lithuania   PALACE

(Istorinė Lietuvos Prezidentūra; www.istorineprezidentura.lt; Vilniaus gatvė 33; adult/student 4/2Lt; ⊗11am-5pm Tue-Sun, gardens 8am-9pm daily) This neo-baroque building, dating back to

WORTH A TRIP

GRŪTO PARKAS – COMMUNIST STATUE GRAVEYARD

Eight kilometres west of the southern spa town of Druskininkai, in the village of Grūtas, lies the infamous **Grūtas Park** (Grūto Parkas; www.grutoparkas.lt; adult/child 5-16yr 20/10Lt; ⊙9am-10pm summer, to 5pm rest of year; 🖶) – a cross between kitschy entertainment (the management stopped just short of bringing in visitors in cattle trucks à la deportation to Siberia) and an attempt at education about life in Soviet times. The sprawling grounds, designed to look like a concentration camp, contain the entire communist pantheon – 53 statues of Lenin, Stalin, Marx and local communist heroes, interspersed with wooden buildings containing exhibits on the Soviet oppression of Lithuania, propaganda posters and other assorted communist memorabilia – all to the tune of Soviet anthems blaring from the loudspeakers. These are all that's left of the socialist realism relics that once stood confidently in parks or squares across the country. There's even a small zoo for the kiddies and Soviet-style canteen where you can grab an inexpensive meat-and-potato lunch.

If coming by bus from Vilnius or Kaunas, ask the driver to let you off at Grūtas, then walk the final 1km to the park along a well signposted road. There are buses directly from Grūtas to Druskininkai at 12.26pm, 12.56pm and 1.16pm daily, so if you aim for a morning visit, you can then catch the bus either to Druskininkai for an overnight stay and a pamper at the one of the spas – consult the **tourist information centre** (☎313-51777; www.info.druskininkai.lt; Čiurlionio gatvė 65; ⊙10am-noon & 1-6.45pm Mon-Sat, 10am-5pm Sun) or else head back to the main road to catch a bus back to Vilnius or Kaunas.

1826, was the seat of power between 1920 and 1939 for three Lithuanian presidents. The ground floor is used for temporary exhibitions while upstairs you can view the room where President Antanas Smetona contemplated the Soviet ultimatum on 14 July 1940.

NEW TOWN

Kaunas expanded east from the Old Town in the 19th century, giving birth to the striking 1.7km-long pedestrian street, Laisvės alėja.

TOP CHOICE National MK Čiurlionis Art Museum
GALLERY

(MK Čiurlionio Valstybinis Dailės Muziejus; www.ciurlionis.lt; Putvinskio gatvė 55; adult/child 6/3Lt; ⊙11am-5pm Tue-Sun) Painter, composer and photographer Mikalojus Konstantinas Čiurlionis (1875–1911) is Lithuania's beloved artist and there's an extensive collection of his romantic symbolic paintings on display here. It's particularly worthwhile to sit in the little auditorium and listen to his joyful aural creations. There's a small, fascinating exhibition by his contemporaries, too.

TOP CHOICE Museum of Devils
MUSEUM

(Velnių Muziejus; Putvinskio gatvė 64; adult/child 6/3Lt; ⊙11am-5pm Tue-Sun) What started out as a peculiar collection of devil figurines by eccentric Antanas Žmuidzinavičius (1876–

1966) has turned into a superb exploration of the devil's role in mythology around the world. Amid the wood carvings, masks and clay figurines, see if you can spot a woven bespectacled devil with guitar, colourful Santeria devil from Cuba, and satanic figures of Hitler and Stalin, formed from tree roots and performing a deadly dance over Lithuania.

City Garden
GARDEN

(Miestos Sodas) Near the western end of Laisvės alėja you'll find the City Garden, where the **Romas Kalanta memorial** takes the form of several stone slabs. Kalanta was a Kaunas student who immolated himself on 14 May 1972 as a protest against communist rule. Nearby stands a **statue of Vytautas the Great** (Vytautas Didysis).

Sugihara House
MUSEUM

(Sugiharos Namas; www.sugiharahouse.lt; Valžganto gatvė 30; adult/child 10/5Lt; ⊙10am-5pm Mon-Fri, 11am-4pm Sat & Sun May-Oct) Chiune Sugihara, the Japanese consul to Lithuania (1939–40), saved around 6000 lives in collaboration with Dutch consul Jan Zwartendijk by issuing transit visas (against orders) to Polish and Lithuanian Jews who faced the advancing Nazi terror. The absorbing museum traces the life and work of 'Japan's Schindler' through a series of photos, artefacts and video recordings.

Kaunas

LITHUANIA KAUNAS

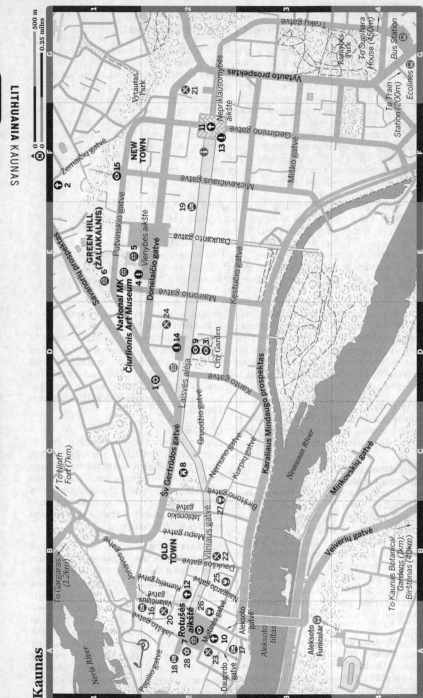

0 500 m
0 0.25 miles

OLD TOWN

NEW TOWN

GREEN HILL
(ŽALIAKALNIS)

National MK
Čiurlionis Art Museum

City Garden

Nemunas River

To Gargaras
(1.2km)

To Ninth
Fort (7km)

To Kaunas Botanical
Gardens (1km);
Birštonas (40km)

To Sugihara
House (450m)

To Train
Station (200m)

To Bus Station

Neris River

Vytauto prospektas
Savanorių prospektas
Jonavos gatvė
Papilio gatvė
Jakšto gatvė
Kumelių gatvė
Valančiaus gatvė
Rotušės aikštė
Muitinės gatvė
Aleksoto gatvė
Daugirdo gatvė
Naugardo gatvė
Vilniaus gatvė
Daukšos gatvė
Mapu gatvė
Jablonskio gatvė
Šv Gertrūdos gatvė
Nemuno gatvė
Kurpių gatvė
Birštono gatvė
Gruodžio gatvė
Laisvės alėja
Kanto gatvė
Griunvaldo gatvė
Donelaičio gatvė
Vienybės aikštė
Putvinskio gatvė
Žemaičių gatvė
Vytautas Park
Mickevičiaus gatvė
Maironio gatvė
Kęstučio gatvė
Daukanto gatvė
Miško gatvė
Gedimino gatvė
Nepriklausomybės aikštė
Neprikausomybės gatvė
Trakų gatvė
Ramybės Park
Karaliaus Mindaugo prospektas
Aleksoto tiltas
Aleksoto Funicular
Veiverių gatvė
Minkovskių gatvė

Kaunas

St Michael the Archangel Church
CHURCH

(Šv Archangelo Mykolo Rektoratas; Nepriklausomybės aikštė; ⊙9am-6pm) The white, neo-Byzantine St Michael the Archangel Church (1893) dominates the eastern end of Laisvės alėja. Originally built for Russian soldiers (hence the design), it did a brief spell as an art gallery during Soviet rule. On the same square, the **statue of Man** (Žmogus; Nepriklausomybės aikštė), modelled on Nike, the Greek god of victory, caused a storm of controversy when his glorious pose exposing his manhood was unveiled in 1991.

FREE Choral Synagogue
SYNAGOGUE

(Kauno Choralinė Sinagoga; ☑6140 3100; Ožeškienės gatvė 13; ⊙service 10am Sat) Near New Town's main artery is the pale-blue Choral Synagogue, a functioning house of worship with a striking altar. Next to it is a **memorial** to 50,000 or so Jewish children who perished in the Holocaust.

Military Museum of Vytautas the Great
MUSEUM

(Vytauto Didžiojo Karo Muziejus; Donelaičio gatvė 64; adult/child 4/2Lt; ⊙11am-5pm Tue-Sun) The highlight of this museum is the new 90th-anniversary exhibition in a grand, well-lit hall, decorated with suits of armour, machine guns and other tools of war. It features everything from Stone Age weaponry and Iron Age burial artefacts to a chess set handmade by a prisoner in a Soviet gulag, overlooked by enormous paintings of battle scenes, including that of the 1410 Battle of Grünwald in which the Grand Duke Vytautas laid waste to the Teutonic knights.

Freedom Monument
MONUMENT

(Laisvės Statula; Vienybės aikštė) The Freedom Monument, erected in 1928, honours 16 February 1918, the day Lithuania declared independence. It was destroyed during the Stalin era, and rebuilt and put back in place on 16 February 1989.

Christ's Resurrection Basilica
CHURCH

(Kauno paminklinė Kristhaus Prisikėlimo bašničia; www.prisikelimas.lt; Zemaicių gatvė 316; ⊙9.30am-7pm) Above the top funicular station at the **Žaliakalnio funikulierius** (Green Hill funicular; ☑200 883; Putvinskio gatvė 22; ticket 0.Lt50; ⊙7am-7pm) towers the white, angular Christ's Resurrection Basilica. A Nazi paper warehouse and radio factory under the Soviets, the church was finally consecrated in 2004 and is particularly striking when lit up at night.

NINTH FORT

The 19th-century **Ninth Fort** (IX Forto Muziejus; www.9fortomuziejus.lt; Žemaičių plentas 73; adult/child 6/3Lt, catacombs with guide 10Lt, tours 10-20Lt; ⊙10am-6pm Wed-Mon Apr-Oct, to 4pm Nov-Mar; ☒23), 7km north of Kaunas, used by the Russians in WWI to defend their western frontier against Germany, was the site of the Nazi massacre of an estimated 80,000 people (mostly Kaunas Jews) in WWII.

This excellent museum, immediately distinguishable by the massive stone memorial, comes in two parts. The bunkerlike church of the damned, its stained glass depicting the dead, displays personal possessions of Lithuanians deported to Siberia – including letters, crosses and a birch container. The old fort, nearby, has photographic exhibitions showing the consequences of the Molotov–Ribbentrop pact for Kaunas' Jews and displays on the fort's other uses.

Take bus 23 from Jonavos gatvė, alight at the '9-ojo Forto Muziejus' stop and take the pedestrian crossing under the motorway.

🛌 Sleeping

Apple Economy Hotel   HOTEL €
(☎37-321 404; www.applehotel.lt; Valančiaus gatvė 19; s/d from 100/135Lt; P@☎) Fans of minimalism (and Eve) will be tempted by the quirky, cheerful Apple. Spot the green-apple motif on your pillows and on the silk wall hangings that add a splash of colour to the otherwise spotless white rooms. Wi-fi only works in the lobby.

The Monk's Bunk   HOSTEL €
(☎6295 3870; www.hostels.com; Laisvės alėja 48-2; dm 34-38Lt, d 90Lt; ☎) Friendly hostel run by an ex-backpacker who knows what backpackers need: large common area, well-equipped kitchen with herbs for cooking, book exchange, large lockers, even a guitar if you fancy a strum. The only downside is the queue to the bathroom.

🏠 Kauno Arkivyskupijos Svečių Namai   GUESTHOUSE €
(☎37-322 597; kaunas.lcn.lt/sveciunamai; Rotušės aikštė 21; s/d/tr from 50/80/110Lt; P✳@) This charming guesthouse sits in a heavenly location between centuries-old churches overlooking the Old Town square and is one of very few places in town to employ eco-friendly practices, including energy-saving lightbulbs and recycling. Rooms are spartan but clean and spacious. No booze please: we're Catholic.

Daugirdas Hotel   BUSINESS HOTEL €€
(☎37-301 562; www.daugirdas.lt; Daugirdo gatvė 4; s/d from 260/320Lt; P@☎) This central hotel has spotless rooms large enough to fit a small bowling alley, an attractive cavernlike restaurant serving imaginative international cuisine, a rooftop bar and a summer terrace with great views over the Old Town. The downside? The staff: they're not likely to win any prizes for congeniality.

🍴 Eating

🏆 Moksha   INDIAN, THAI €€
TOP CHOICE
(☎6767 1649; Vasario 16-osios gatvė 6; mains 15-18Lt; ✎) The first of its kind in Kaunas, this tiny place with whitewashed brick walls and fresh flowers everywhere lures you in with exotic smells. Expect such daily specials as lamb kofta curry or crispy duck with persimmon salad and even vegan options such as dhal soup. On top of that, the service is super-friendly; a rarity in these parts!

Medžiotjų Užeiga   LITHUANIAN €€
(☎37-320 956; www.medziotojai.lt; Rotušės aikštė 10; mains 23-59Lt) The decor – stuffed deer heads and antique pistols – at this venerable hunting-lodge-themed restaurant gives the game (geddit?) away. This is the place in town to tuck into the likes of venison with cherry sauce, boar steak with chanterelles, roe-deer carpaccio and other temptations for the carnivorously inclined. Don't skip out on its hot cherry pie, either!

Bernelių Užeiga   LITHUANIAN €€
(☎37-200 913; www.berneliuuzeiga.lt; Valančiaus gatvė 9; mains 16-25Lt; ✎) If it's rustic Lithuanian cuisine served by fair maidens in traditional dress that you're after, then look no further than this place with such gut-busting delights as buckwheat pancakes with wild mushroom sauce and barbecued

pork shank. Plenty of options for vegetarians (provided you like potato and soup). Another branch is in **Donelaičio** (www.berneliuuzei-ga.lt; Donelaičio gatvė 11; mains 16-25Lt; ✐).

Le Rouge
FRENCH €€

(✐6066 2736; www.lerouge.lt; Vilniaus gatvė 26; mains 10-30Lt; ⊘4-11pm Tue-Thu, noon-midnight Fri & Sat, noon-9pm Sun; ✐) A slice of cosmopolitan France, Le Rouge, true to its name, has splashes of red in its decor and the likes of bouillabaisse de Marseille and *moules marinière* on the menu. Stop by for a Provence salad, stuffed crêpes, something more substantial or just a coffee. The service is efficient and pleasant and its crème brûlée ain't half bad.

🍷 Drinking

TOP CHOICE Whiskey Bar W1640
BAR

(www.viskiobaras.lt; Kurpių gatvė 29; ⊘5pm-1pm Tue-Thu, 5pm-5am Fri & Sat; 🛜) Tucked away down a side street, not only does this bar have a mind-boggling collection of whiskeys – mostly Scotch, but also some rarer Japanese ones – but the bar staff are the friendliest in town. If whiskey isn't your poison, then one of its ales just might be.

BO
BAR

(Muitinės gatvė 9) The laid-back 'Blue Orange' attracts an alternative student set and gets crammed to overflowing on weekends. Its own brew is a tasty but potent offering, there's live music some nights and it's a great place to meet locals.

Gyvas
MICROBREWERY

(Muitinės gatvė 1; ⊘noon-10pm Mon-Wed, to midnight Thu & Sun, to 2am Fri & Sat) If you consider yourself a beer connoisseur, you shouldn't miss the 30 or so microbrews from all over Lithuania on offer here, including some rather potent options. This may be a problem on weekends when it's pretty much standing room only.

☆ Entertainment

Gargaras
CONCERT VENUE

(www.gargaras.lt; Raudondvario plentas 101; ⊘9pm-5am Fri & Sat) This converted Soviet-era factory is one of the most happening places in town, with serious clubbing on weekends, as well as regular appearances by local and international bands and DJs. Gargaras also occasionally hosts exhibitions by up-and-coming artists. A great all-rounder.

WORTH A TRIP

THE HILL OF CROSSES

Lithuania's most awe-inspiring sight is the legendary **Hill of Crosses** (Kryžių kalnas). The sound of the myriad tiny crosses tinkling in the breeze, festooned upon the thousands of larger crosses which appear to grow on the hillock, is eerie, particularly if you have the place to yourself.

Legend says the tradition of planting crosses began in the 14th century. The crosses were bulldozed by the Soviets, but each night people crept past soldiers and barbed wire to plant more, risking their lives or freedom to express their national and spiritual fervour. Today the Hill of Crosses is a place of national pilgrimage. Some of the crosses are devotional, others are memorials (many for people deported to Siberia) and some are finely carved folk-art masterpieces.

The hill is 10km north of Šiauliai along highway A12, and another 2km east from a well-marked turn-off ('Kryžių kalnas 2').

With your own wheels, you can easily see it as a day trip from either Vilnius or Kaunas. Alternatively, from Šiauliai, take a Joniškis-bound bus (3Lt, 10 minutes, up to seven daily) to the 'Domantai' stop and then walk for 15 minutes along the signposted road. A round-trip taxi from Šiauliai with waiting time should cost around 60Lt. For accommodation, consult the **tourism information centre** (✐41-523 110; www.siauliai.lt/tic; Vilniaus gatvė 213; ⊘9am-1pm & 2-6pm Mon-Fri, 10am-4pm Sat) in Šiauliai.

From Šiauliai there are regular trains to Vilnius (35Lt, 2½ hours, three daily), Kaunas (22Lt, 2½ hours, one daily) and Klaipėda (from 23Lt, two to three hours, five daily). Regular buses run to Kaunas (35Lt, three hours, up to 21 daily), Klaipėda (35Lt, 3½ hours, up to six daily), Vilnius (47Lt, three hours, up to 12 daily) and Rīga (34Lt, 2½ hours, up to six daily).

BUSES FROM KAUNAS

Domestic Bus

DESTINATION	COST (LT)	DURATION (HR)	FREQUENCY
Druskininkai	30	2½-3	up to 13 daily
Klaipėda	51	2½-2¾	up to 16 daily
Palanga	57	3¼	up to 8 daily
Šiauliai	37	2½-3	up to 18 daily
Vilnius	20	1¾	up to 3 hourly

International Bus

DESTINATION	COST (LT)	DURATION (HR)	FREQUENCY
Rīga (Latvia)	65	5	3 daily
Tallinn (Estonia)	122	9½	daily
Warsaw (Poland)	55	6¼	daily

Kiemelis 837 CONCERT VENUE
(✆6553 3193; Rotušės aikštė 20; ⏱11am-midnight May-Sep) There's always something going on at this popular summer terrace inside the courtyard of the Communications Development Museum – from theatre performances and DJs to local live bands.

ℹ Information

Baitukas (Donelaičio gatvė 26; per hr 6Lt; ⏱8am-7pm Mon-Fri, 10am-6pm Sat) Internet access.

Kaunas in Your Pocket (www.inyourpocket. com) Annual city guide featuring detailed listings, sold at the tourist office and in some hotels for 6Lt. Extensive online listings.

Main post office (Laisvės alėja 102)

Tourist office (✆37-323 436; www.visit.kaunas.lt; Laisvės alėja 36; ⏱9am-5pm Mon-Fri, 10am-3pm Sat & Sun) Books accommodation, sells maps and guides, and arranges bicycle rental and guided tours of the Old Town.

ℹ Getting There & Around

AIR Kaunas international airport (✆37-399 307; www.kaunas-airport.lt; Vilniaus gatvė, Karmėlava) is 12km north of the Old Town in the suburb of Karmėlava. To get here, take bus 29 or 29E from the stop on Vytauto prospektas (2Lt).

BUS Major international services to/from Kaunas are operated by Lux Express (p513) and Kautra (p513) under the **Eurolines** (www.eurolines.lt) trademark, as well as **Ecolines** (www.ecolines.net). Buses to international destinations leave from the **long-distance bus station**

(Autobusų Stotis; ✆37-409 060; Vytauto prospektas 24).

TRAIN From the **train station** (Geležinkelio Stotis; ✆37-222 981; www.litrail.lt; Čiurlionio gatvė 16) there are trains to Vilnius (16Lt to 18Lt, 1¼ to 1¾ hours, up to 17 daily) and Šiauliai (20Lt, 2¾ hours, one daily).

WESTERN LITHUANIA

Lithuania's lively west coastline boasts a thriving port city, a thumping party town and its crown jewel, the starkly beautiful, sand dune–covered Curonian Spit.

Palanga

POP 15,500

Sleepy in winter, beachside Palanga becomes Lithuania's undisputed party capital in the summer months with all-night beach parties and clubbing.

The **tourist information centre** (✆460-48811; www.palangatic.lt; Kretingos gatvė 1; ⏱9am-7pm Mon-Fri, 10am-4pm Sat & Sun mid-Jun–Aug, 9am-5pm Mon-Fri, 10am-2pm Sat Sep–mid-Jun) adjoins the tiny bus station east of the main pedestrian Basanvičiaus gatvė.

◉ Sights

TOP CHOICE **Amber Museum** MUSEUM
(Gintaro Muziejus; www.pgm.lt; Vytauto gatvė 17; adult/student 8/4Lt; ⏱10am-8pm Tue-Sat, to 7pm Sun Jun-Aug) The highlight of the 1-sq-km

Botanical Park (Palangos Botanikos Parkas; S Dariaus ir S Gireno gatvė, Vytauto gatvė) area is the Amber Museum, inside a sweeping classical palace (1897). Upstairs, over 5000 exhibits focus on different aspects of amber – Baltic gold – how it's formed, its use throughout history, its different hues, amber with insects trapped inside, amber as ancient medicine, and finally – amber as innovative present-day jewellery.

Antanas Mončys House Museum   MUSEUM

(Antano Mončio Namai-Muziejus; Daukanto gatvė 16; adult/student 4/2Lt; ☉2-7pm Wed-Sun May-mid-Sep) Unlike in most museums, at this museum you can handle the Lithuanian sculptor's finest works in wood and stone as much as you like. Temporary art and photography exhibits also.

🛏 Sleeping & Eating

In summer, the cheapest digs consist of locals who stand at the eastern end of Kretingos gatvė touting *nuomojami kambariai* (rooms for rent).

TOP CHOICE Palanga Hotel   LUXURY HOTEL €€€

(☎460-41414; www.palangahotel.lt; Birutės gatvė 60; d/ste from €203/478, 1-room apt from €348; P❄@☎☒) Indulge in one of the many spa treatments and sample the restaurant's flambé dishes at this swish hotel of glass and wood surrounded by 80-year-old pine trees.

Žydroji Liepsna   HOTEL €€

(Blue Flame; ☎460-52441; www.zydrojiliepsna.lt; Gintaro 36; s/d/apt €43/73/116; @☎☒🚲) We really carry a torch for these guys – the carpeted rooms here are colourful and full of light, the service is friendly and the whole place is really good value in an overpriced town.

Vila Ramybė   BOUTIQUE HOTEL €€

(☎460-54124; www.vilaramybe.lt; Vytauto gatvė 54; s/d/apt 250/280/480Lt; @☎) Pristine little boutique hotel near the centre, with rooms

ranging from singles to two-bedroom apartments with their own terraces. The bar on the premises is one of the friendliest in town.

Žuvinė   SEAFOOD €€

(www.feliksas.lt; Basanavičiaus gatvė 37a; mains 22-45Lt; ☎) A quality restaurant-cum-library specialising in fresh fish and seafood dishes. A real stayer on a street of fly-by-night gimmicky eateries.

Cafe Floros Simfonija   CAFE €€

(Basanavičiaus gatvė; mains from 18Lt) Sip your coffee amid beautiful landscaped gardens across the little stream from the main pedestrian street, or else lounge in a wicker swing on the rooftop terrace.

❶ Getting There & Away

The bus station is located half a block from the main Vytauto gatvė.

Klaipėda

POP 160,400

Klaipėda, Lithuania's main port, is the gateway to the Curonian Spit, but it has enough attractions of its own to warrant lingering.

◉ Sights

Klaipėda Castle Museum   MUSEUM

(Klaipėda Pilies Muziejus; www.mlimuziejus.lt; Pilies gatvė 4; adult/child 6/3Lt; ☉10am-6pm Tue-Sat) Inside the atmospheric torch-lit tunnels of what remains of the town's old moat-protected castle, the exhibits here tell the castle's (and Klaipėda's) story through a wealth of period objects and black-and-white photos of the town during WWII. To get to the museum, walk through the Klaipėda State Sea Port Authority building and a ship repair yard.

Old Town   HISTORIC AREA

What little remains of Klaipėda's Old Town post-WWII is wedged between the Danė River and Turgaus gatvė. There are several

BUSES FROM PALANGA

DESTINATION	PRICE (LT)	DURATION	FREQUENCY
Kaunas	57	3¼-5½hr	up to 9 daily
Klaipėda	6	30min	every 30min
Liepaja	11	1¼hr	2 daily except Sun
Šiauliai	38	3hr	up to 5 daily
Vilnius	72	4½-6½hr	7 daily

well preserved old German half-timbered buildings in the vicinity of **Teatro aikštė** (Theatre Sq), including the **Drama Theatre** (Teatro aikštė 2), where in 1939 Hitler announced from the balcony the incorporation of Memel into Germany.

History Museum of Lithuania Minor

MUSEUM

(Mažosios Lietuvos Istorijos Muziejus; Didžioji Vandens gatvė 6; adult/child 5/2Lt; ⊙10am-6pm Tue-Sat) Engaging museum detailing the history of the area, with exhibits ranging from hoards of coins to nautical history to recreation of traditional dwellings, though with little English captioning. Excellent temporary exhibitions upstairs.

✸✸ Festivals

Sea Festival

NAUTICAL

(www.jurossvente.lt) The city celebrates its nautical heritage each July with a flamboyant Sea Festival that draws crowds for a weekend of concerts, parties, exhibitions and nautical manoeuvres.

⌨ Sleeping

TOP CHOICE Litinterp Guesthouse

B&B €€

(☎46-410 644; www.litinterp.lt; Puodžių gatvė 17; s/d/tr 100/160/210Lt, without bathroom 80/140/ 180Lt; ⊙8.30am-7pm Mon-Fri, 10am-3pm Sat; P @🛜) This accommodation agency arranges B&B stays in Klaipėda, Palanga and along the Curonian Spit. The 16 rooms in its own guesthouse are cheerful and comfortable, and breakfast is delivered in a basket.

Amberton Klaipėda

LUXURY HOTEL €€€

(☎46-404 372; www.ambertonhotel.com; Naujoji Sodo gatvė 1; r/ste from €94/350, older r from €54; P✳@🛜⊛) This 'City Within the City' has basic rooms in the old wing, and every imaginable creature comfort in the new. With three restaurants, casino, tennis court and bowling alley to keep you occupied, you need not even leave the hotel. But you should, really.

Friedrich Hotel

HOTEL €€

(☎46-391 020; www.pasazas.lt; Tiltų gatvė 26a; s/d/apt from 185/220/478Lt; P✳@🛜🍴) Great little hotel in the Old Town catering to all budgets. Everything from nicely furnished 'economy' rooms to swish, spacious apartments.

✕ Eating

TOP CHOICE Ararat

ARMENIAN €€

(www.ararat.lt; Liepų gatvė 48a; mains 21-34Lt; 🍴) This restaurant specialises in superbly flavoured Armenian dishes. Try the eggplant

---

BALTIC GOLD

The Baltic States, and Lithuania in particular, are synonymous with amber, known as 'Baltic gold'. The Baltic Sea is a particularly rich source of amber gathering and the hardened tree sap has been used to make jewellery in the region for millennia. In the past, amber creations tended to be largely limited to chunky bead jewellery favoured by older women, but contemporary amber design spans everything from delicate earrings and pendants to model ships, chess boards and mythological figures.

While amber is primarily yellow, colours can vary in shade from white to pale yellow, to orange, to what appears to be black (but is really a very dark red). The rarest are blue, violet and green specimens. The value of an amber piece also depends on the texture of the item, whether there are 'inclusions' within the stone, such as embedded plants or insects, and the quality of workmanship.

It's not uncommon for designers to work with raw chunks of amber that have just been fished out of the sea. They are sliced up and examined for colour and texture, and the designer usually has some idea in mind of how he or she intends to use the individual pieces, which may be cut, ground, drilled and carved as necessary, then polished and precisely fitted to pieces of jewellery or other items.

There's no shortage of amber outlets in Lithuania – from reputable shops, such as those along Aušros Vartų gatvė in Vilnius, and those inside the Amber Gallery in Nida and the Amber Museum in Palanga – to numerous street stalls claiming to offer a bargain. If you're not sure whether you're being offered the real thing, the simplest way to tell real amber from glass, plastic and other fakes is the smell test: if you rub a piece of amber vigorously, it will release the smell of pine (it will also do that if you hold a lighter to it, though street sellers may not let you near their wares with a naked flame).

BUSES FROM KLAIPĖDA

DESTINATION	PRICE (LT)	DURATION	FREQUENCY
Kaliningrad (Russia) via Nida	70	5½hr	daily
Kaunas	52	2¾-4½hr	up to 17 daily
Rīga (Latvia)	117	4½-5hr	up to 6 daily
Palanga	5.20	45min	every 20min
Šiauliai	40	3-3½hr	up to 6 daily
Vilnius	68	4-5½hr	up to 14 daily

with cottage cheese and the grilled meats, and finish off with a lump of hot, sweet *pakhlava* (baklava) washed down with traditional Armenian herbal tea.

Ferdinandas RUSSIAN €€
(Naujoji Uosto 10; mains 21-38Lt; 🍴) Whether you're after cabbage soup of Peter the Great, the czar's *pelmeni* (stuffed meat dumplings) or chicken shashlik, this place delivers. The Russian food is superb and it's hard to go wrong with anything involving eggplant.

Senoji Hansa LITHUANIAN €€
(Kurpių gatvė 1; mains 17-30Lt) If you're hankering after some filling potato pancakes or meat dishes, served by attentive staff, then this Old Town restaurant fits the bill perfectly. It's a shame that the lively summer terrace is squished into an alleyway, though.

🍷 Drinking

Memelis MICROBREWERY
(www.memelis.lt; Žvejų gatvė 4) This red-brick brewery and restaurant by the river, in operation since 1871, is popular with the city's expat community. Interior is old-style beer hall; outside is industrial-feel riverside terrace, and the beer is very good indeed.

🛈 Information

The **tourist office** (☑46-412 186; www.klaipedainfo.lt; Turgaus gatvė 7; ☺9am-7pm Mon-Fri, 10am-4pm Sat & Sun) is exceptionally efficient, selling maps, arranging accommodation and renting out bicycles.

🛈 Getting There & Away

BOAT The **International Ferry Port** (☑46-395 051; www.dfdsseaways.lt; Perkėlos gatvė 10) is 18km south of the city centre. **DFDS Seaways** (☑46-395 000; www.dfdsseaways.lt; Šaulių gatvė 19) runs passenger ferries to/from Kiel (from €56, 21 hours, six weekly) and Sassnitz (from €55, 18 hours, three weekly) in Germany and Karlshamn, Sweden (from €62, 13 to 14 hours, daily).

Krantas Travel (☑46-395 111; www.krantas.lt; Teatro gatvė 5; ☺8am-6pm Mon-Fri, 10am-3pm Sat) sells ferry tickets to Kiel, Karlshamn, and Sassnitz.

Passenger ferries to the Smiltynė ferry landing on the Curonian Spit leave from the **Old Castle Port** (Senasis Pilies Uostas; www.keltas.lt; Pilies gatvė 4; per passenger/bicycle 2.90Lt/free), near the castle, west of the Old Town. Ferries leave every half-hour in the high season (10 minutes). Vehicles must use the **New Port** (Naujasis Uostas; www.keltas.lt; Nemuno gatvė 8; per passenger/motorcycle/car 2.90/18/40Lt, bicycle free), 3km south of the passenger terminal. Services depart at least hourly.

Take bus 1 (2.40Lt) to both the New Port (10 minutes) and the International Ferry Port (30 minutes).

BUS Buses depart from Klaipėda **bus station** (Autobusų Stotis; ☑46-411 547; www.klap.lt; Butkų Juzės 9).

TRAIN From the **train station** (☑46-313 677; www.litrail.lt; Priestočio gatvė 1) there are trains to Vilnius (51Lt, 4¾ hours, three daily) and Šiauliai (from 23Lt, two to three hours, five daily).

Curonian Spit

POP 2640

This magical sliver of land, divided equally between Lithuania and Russia's Kaliningrad region, hosts some of Europe's most precious sand dunes and a menagerie of elk, deer and avian wildlife, with more than half its surface covered by pine forest.

Recognised by Unesco as a World Heritage site in 2000, and protected as **Curonian Spit National Park** (www.nerija.lt), the fragile spit is facing erosion, and tourism is exacerbating the problem.

WORTH A TRIP

LITHUANIAN SEA MUSEUM

Smiltynė's big attraction is the delightful **Lithuania Sea Museum** (Lietuvos Jūrų Muziejus; ☑46-490 754; www.juru.muziejus.lt; adult/student Jun-Aug 15/7Lt, Sep-May 12/6Lt; ☉10.30am-6.30pm Tue-Sun Jun-Aug, Wed-Sun Sep, 10.30am-5.30pm Sat & Sun Oct-Dec; ☒). Partaquarium, part history museum, this place hosts crowd-pleasing sea-lion shows. The brick tunnels of the 19th-century fort hold tanks of fish and engaging displays on the history of navigation and the history of Klaipėda port. To get here, walk 1.5km along the waterfront from the Smiltynė pier or hop aboard a tiny wheeled train (2Lt).

The Lithuania side is divided into two regions: Smiltynė village (part of Klaipėda); and Neringa (the villages of Juodkrantė, Pervalka, Preila and Nida).

❶ Getting There & Away

To get to the spit, take a ferry or bus from Klaipėda or take the Kaliningrad–Klaipėda bus.

From Smiltynė, buses and microbuses (9.50Lt, one hour, at least seven times daily) run regularly to/from the **Nida bus station** (☑469-54859; Naglių gatvė 18e) via Juodkrantė (4.50Lt, 15 to 20 minutes).

JUODKRANTĖ

Juodkrantė is a spread-out fishing village with a few guesthouses, restaurants and roadside kiosks selling superb *žuvis* (smoked fish).

Topping the strange sights' list in Juodkrantė is **Witches' Hill** (Raganų Kalnas; ☒), a collection of devils, witches and other fantastical and grotesque wooden carvings from Lithuanian folklore that skulk along wooded sculpture trails, ranging from fairy-tale playful to nightmare.

Less than 1km south is a massive **colony of grey herons and cormorants**. Steps lead from the road to a viewing platform where you can see thousands of nests amid pine trees – cormorants to the north, herons to the south. In March and April the air is thick with nesting birds, and in May the chicks are born.

For all manner of things fishy with an excellent view of the pier, try **Žuvelė** (☑6847 8707; www.jovila.lt/zuvele; L. Rēzos gatvė 1; mains 20-35Lt; ☉10am-10pm May-Sep). And if you wish to take away some local culture, stop by the **Weathervanes Gallery** (Vetrungių Galerija; ☑6982 7283; www.autentic.lt; Liudviko Rēzos gatvė 13; ☉9am-7pm May-Sep, 10am-5pm Apr & Oct).

Buses between Smiltyne and Nida all stop in Juodkrantė.

NIDA

Neringa's southernmost settlement is adorable Nida, which slumbers much of the year but in summer becomes Neringa's tourist nerve centre.

Bankas Snoras (Naglių gatvė 27) has a currency exchange and ATM opposite the bus station. The **tourist information centre** (☑469-52345; www.visitneringa.com; Taikos gatvė 4; ☉9am-7pm Jun-Aug, 9am-1pm & 2-6pm Mon-Sat Sep-May) stocks lots of useful information on walks, bike rides, fishing-boat trips and more.

◉ Sights & Activities

TOP CHOICE ❘ Parnidis Dune   LANDMARK

The Curonian Spit's sandscape is on full display from the restored granite sundial atop the 52m-high Parnidis Dune. The panorama of coastline, forests and the spit's most stunning dune extending towards Kaliningrad is unforgettable. Walk up here from town along a **nature trail** through the forest at the southern end of Naglių gatvė or drive via Taikos gatvė. Don't stray from the wooden boardwalk as the dune is very fragile.

Museums   MUSEUMS

Check out the restored 19th-century fisherman's cottage that is the **Ethnographic Museum** (Žvejo Etnografinė Sodyba; Naglių gatvė 4; adult/child 2/1Lt; ☉10am-6pm); the excellent little **Amber Gallery** (Gintaro Galerija; www.ambergallery.lt; Pamario gatvė 20; adult/child 4/2Lt; ☉9am-8pm Jun-Aug, 10am-7pm May, Sep & Oct), a combined museum and shop featuring some stunning amber pieces of all colours; and the **Neringa History Museum** (Neringos Istorijos Muziejus; Pamario gatvė 53; adult/child 2/1Lt; ☉10am-6pm), with its evocative displays on fishing, catching crows (biting their necks to kill them and washing away the taste with vodka), and wading into the surf after a storm, armed with a net, to trawl for amber.

Cycling   CYCLING

An excellent way to see the spit is by bicycle. A flat cycling trail runs all the way from Nida to Smiltynė, and you stand a good chance of seeing wild boar and other wildlife along the path. There are bicycles for hire (around 30/40Lt per 12/24 hours) on almost every street corner in Nida.

Sleeping & Eating

In winter expect steep discounts. Nida's eating scene explodes in summer, with plenty of open-air restaurants.

Miško Namas   GUESTHOUSE €€

(☑469-52290; www.miskonamas.com; Pamario gatvė 11-2; d 249Lt, 2-/4-person apt from 318/331Lt; @🛜♨) A beautiful wooden guesthouse with wonderfully friendly owners. Every room here has its own fridge, sink, kettle and satellite TV, and a couple have balconies. Self-cater in the cosy communal kitchen.

Nidos Kempingas   CAMPGROUND €€

(☑469-52045; www.kempingas.lt; Taikos gatvė 45a; campsite per tent/adult/child 11/17/9Lt, d from 250Lt, 4-/6-bed studios 350/490Lt; 🅿🛜♨) Set in pine forest, this is a popular catch-all option that provides everything from double rooms with satellite TV and fridge and self-catering apartments to a patch of earth to pitch your tent. Sauna, bike rental, swimming pool and tennis court at extra cost.

Kuršis   LITHUANIAN €€

(Naglių gatvė 29; mains 18-27Lt; ⊗9am-midnight; ⊝🛜♨) Open year-round, this popular bar-restaurant serves hearty Lithuanian staples, such as moreish *bulviniai blynai* (potato pancakes), excellent *šaltibarščiai* and ample meat and fish dishes.

Drinking

In Vino   BAR

(www.invino.lt; Taikos gatvė 32; ⊗10am-midnight) With a roof terrace with a fab view of Nida outside, this lively drinking joint draws crowds with its combination of good beer, friendly service and an ambitious menu featuring tapas and fusion dishes.

UNDERSTAND LITHUANIA

Lithuania Today

In 2004 Lithuania turned its sights to the West, joining both NATO and the European Union, just over a decade after its independence from the former Soviet Union. Relations with Russia have been rocky since independence and particularly since 2004 because Russia views the Baltic membership in the EU as the West's advance on Russian territory, especially since Lithuania shares an important border with the Russian enclave of Kaliningrad.

Lithuania's strong economic growth for much of the past decade or so came to a sudden halt in 2008, when the country became a victim of the global economic crisis, prompting austerity measures such as spending cuts and tax rises, as well as Lithuanian migration to other parts of the EU in search of work.

December 2012 saw the rise to power of the Social Democrat–led government that aims to ease some of these measures.

History

Lithuania's history started when ancient tribes fanned out across the Baltics to take advantage of the region's plentiful amber deposits. In 1009 those tribes were sufficiently assimilated for Lithuania to be mentioned for the first time in writing.

Birth & Death of the Lithuanian Empire

By the 12th century Lithuania's peoples had split into two tribal groups: the Samogitians (lowlanders) in the west and the Aukštaitiai (highlanders) in the east and southeast. In the mid-13th century Aukštaitiai leader Mindaugas unified Lithuanian tribes to create the Grand Duchy of Lithuania, of which he was crowned monarch in 1253 at Kernavė.

Lithuanian leader Gediminas pushed Lithuania's borders south and east between 1316 and 1341. In 1386 marriage forged an alliance with Poland against the Teutonic Order – Germanic crusaders – that lasted 400 years. The alliance defeated the German knights in 1410 at the battle of Grünwald in Poland, ushering in a golden period during which Vilnius was born and Lithuania became one of Europe's largest empires.

But in the 18th century, the Polish–Lithuanian state was so weakened by division that it was carved up by Russia, Austria and Prussia (successor to the Teutonic Order) in the partitions of Poland (1772, 1793 and 1795–96).

Lithuania in the 20th Century

Vilnius was a bastion of Polish culture in the 19th century and a focus of uprisings against Russia. It also became an important Jewish centre; Jews made up almost half of its 160,000-strong population by the early 20th century.

Lithuanian nationalists declared independence on 16 February 1918. Vilnius was to be the capital of independent Lithuania, but it was occupied by Polish forces between 1920 and 1938, so Kaunas became the seat of the Lithuanian government until Vilnius was liberated from Polish occupation. Lithuania's first president, Antanas Smetona, ruled the country with an iron fist during this time.

In 1940, after the Molotov–Ribbentrop Pact, Lithuania was forced into the USSR. Within a year, 40,000 Lithuanians were killed or deported. Up to 300,000 more people, mostly Jews, died in concentration camps and ghettos during the 1941–44 Nazi occupation.

The USSR ruled again between 1945 and 1991. An estimated 250,000 people were murdered or deported to Siberia while armed partisans resisted Soviet rule from the forests until around 1953.

The Push for Independence

In the late 1980s Lithuania led the Baltic push for independence. The popular front, Sajūdis, won 30 seats in the March 1989 elections for the USSR Congress of People's Deputies. Lithuania was the first Soviet republic to legalise noncommunist parties. In February 1990 Sajūdis was elected to form a majority in Lithuania's new Supreme Soviet (now the parliament), which on 11 March declared Lithuania independent.

Moscow marched troops into Vilnius and cut off Lithuania's fuel supplies. On 13 January 1991, Soviet troops stormed key buildings in Vilnius. Fourteen people were killed at Vilnius' TV tower and Lithuanians barricaded the Seimas (their parliament). In the wake of heavy condemnation from the West, the Soviets recognised Lithuanian independence on 6 September 1991, bringing about the first of the Baltic republics.

Life after the Soviet Union

The last Soviet troops left the country on 31 August 1993. Lithuania joined NATO in April 2004, and entered the EU a month later.

EU membership has its downside: members of the country's younger generation are leaving in droves for the greener pastures of the UK and Ireland. Yet Lithuania still remains a country of optimism.

People

Lithuania is ethnically homogeneous, with Lithuanians accounting for 83.7% of the total population. Poles form 6.6%, Russians 5.3% and Belorussians 1.3%. The remaining 3.1% comprises of various nationalities from Eastern Europe and beyond.

Some call Lithuanians the 'Italians of the Baltics', citing their fierce pride – a result of the many brutal attempts to eradicate their culture and the memories of their long-lost empire.

Lithuania was the last pagan country in Europe, and much of its religious art, national culture and traditions have raw pagan roots. Today the country is around 79% Roman Catholic, with a strong Russian Orthodox minority.

Arts

Lithuania's best-known national artist is Mikalojus Konstantinas Čiurlionis (1875–1911). The best collection of his paintings is in the National Čiurlionis Art Museum (p499) in Kaunas.

Lithuania has a thriving contemporary-art scene, and music is at the heart of the Lithuanian spirit, from traditional folk music to jazz, with an annual highlight being the Kaunas International Jazz Festival.

Lithuanian fiction began with the late-18th-century poem 'Metai' (The Seasons) by Kristijonas Donelaitis. Antanas Baranauskas' 1860 poem 'Anykščiai Pine Forest' uses the forest as a symbol of Lithuania.

Several major Polish writers grew up in Lithuania and regarded themselves as partly Lithuanian, most notably Adam Mickiewicz (1798–1855), the inspiration for 19th-century nationalists, whose great poem 'Pan Tadeusz' begins 'Lithuania, my fatherland..'

Environment

Lush forests and more than 4000 lakes mark the landscape of Lithuania, a country that is largely flat with a 100km-wide lowland centre. Forest covers a third of the country and contains creatures such as wild boar, wolves, deer and elk, but is under threat due to mismanagement and illegal logging.

For years the hot potato has been the Ignalina Nuclear Power Plant, 120km north of Vilnius. One of two reactors similar in design to Chernobyl was closed in December 2004, and the final shutdown of the plant took place in 2009, with the existing units of the plant in the process of being decommissioned (phase 1 to be completed in 2013).

To do your part for the environment, camp only in designated areas and keep to the marked trails on the sand dunes of the Curonian Spit and in other national parks.

Food & Drink

Lithuanian food is comfort eating rather than delicate morsels and vegetarian options are somewhat limited.

The national dish is the *cepelinai* (zeppelins): airship-shaped parcels of gluey potato dough stuffed with cheese, *mesa* (meat) or *grybai* (mushrooms). Another artery-hardening favourite is sour cream–topped *kugelis*, a dish that bakes grated potatoes and carrots in the oven. *Koldūnai* are ravioli stuffed with meat or mushrooms, and *virtiniai* are dumplings. *Šaltibarščiai* is a creamy cold beetroot soup.

The most popular brand of *alus* (beer) is Švyturys, but try Utenos, Kalnapilis and Gubernija as well. Beer is accompanied by *kepta duona* (deep-fried black bread with garlic) and smoked pigs' ears.

Midus (mead) is making a comeback these days. It's made of honey boiled with water, berries and spices, then fermented with hops.

SURVIVAL GUIDE

Directory A–Z
Accommodation

Book way ahead in the high season for Vilnius, Palanga and the Curonian Spit. Peak-season prices are around 30% higher than off-season prices. Prices are higher in Vilnius.

Price ranges used in listings in this chapter are for a double room with bathroom.

€ less than 150Lt/€45

€€ 150Lt/€45 to 350Lt/€100

€€€ more than 350Lt/€100

Business Hours

The opening hours here are for peak season. In the off season, museums, businesses and

---

---

tourist offices work reduced hours on weekends or are closed altogether.

Banks 8am to 3pm Monday to Friday

Bars 11am to midnight Sunday to Thursday, 11am-2am Friday and Saturday

Clubs 10pm to 5am Thursday to Saturday

Post offices 8am to 8pm Monday to Friday, 10am to 9pm Saturday, 10am to 5pm Sunday

Shops 9am or 10am to 7pm Monday to Saturday; some open on Sunday

Restaurants noon to 11pm; later on weekends

Embassies & Consulates

The following embassies and consulates are in Vilnius.

Australian Embassy (☑5-212 3369; australia@consulate.lt; Vilniaus gatvė 23; ☉10am-1pm Tue, 2-5pm Thu)

Belarusian Embassy (☑5-266 2200; www.lithuania.mfa.gov.by; Mindaugo gatvė 13)

Canadian Embassy (☑5-249 0950; www.canada.lt; Jogailos gatvė 4; ☉8.30am-5pm Mon-Fri)

Estonian Embassy (☑5-278 0200; www.estemb.lt; Mickevičiaus gatvė 4a; ☉8.30am-5pm Mon-Fri)

French Embassy (☑5-219 9600; www.ambafrance-lt.org; Švarco gatvė 1)

German Embassy (☑5-210 6400; www.wilna.diplo.de; Sierakausko gatvė 24)

Irish Embassy (☎5-262 9460; www.embassy-ofireland.lt; Gedimino prospektas 1; ☺10am-noon & 2-4pm Mon-Fri)

Latvian Embassy (☎5-213 1260; www.latvia.lt; Čiurlionio iela 76)

Netherlands Embassy (☎5-210 4620; www.lithuania.nlembassy.org; Kosciuskos gatvė 36; ☺8.30-12.30 Mon-Fri)

Polish Embassy (☎5-270 9001; www.wilno.msz.gov.pl/en; Smėlio gatvė 20a)

Russian Embassy (☎5-272 3893; www.lithuania.mid.ru; Latvių gatvė 53; ☺8am-noon & 1.30-4pm Mon-Fri)

UK Embassy (☎5-246 2900; www.ukinlithuania.fco.gov.uk; Antakalnio gatvė 2)

US Embassy (☎5-266 5500; www.vilnius.usembassy.gov; Akmenų gatvė 6)

Food

The following price categories for the average cost of a main course are used in this chapter:

€ less than 15Lt

€€ 15Lt to 40Lt

€€€ more than 40Lt

Internet Access

Lithuania is a wired country and free wi-fi hotspots are found all over Vilnius and other cities. All accommodation reviewed in this chapters offers internet and/or wi-fi, most of it free.

Money

The Lithuanian litas (the plural is litai; Lt) is divided into 100 centai. It is pegged to the euro at the rate of 3.45Lt per euro. If the euro stabilises, then Lithuania will exchange its litas for euros in 2015 at the earliest, but at the moment things are up in the air.

All but the smallest Lithuanian towns have at least one bank with a functional ATM. Most big banks cash travellers cheques and exchange most major currencies, and credit cards are widely accepted.

Public Holidays

New Year's Day 1 January

Independence Day 16 February

Lithuanian Independence Restoration Day 11 March

Easter Sunday March/April

Easter Monday March/April

International Labour Day 1 May

Mothers' Day First Sunday in May

Feast of St John (Midsummer) 24 June

Statehood Day 6 July

Assumption of Blessed Virgin 15 August

All Saints' Day 1 November

Christmas 25 and 26 December

Telephone

MOBILE PHONES

It's relatively inexpensive to call home using another European mobile in Lithuania. Local prepaid SIM cards can make it cheaper to call within the country. Mobile companies **Bitė** (www.bite.lt), **Omnitel** (www.omnitel.lt) and **Tele 2** (www.tele2.lt) sell prepaid SIM cards.

PHONE CODES

To call Lithuania from abroad, dial ☎370 then the city code, followed by the phone number. To call cities within Lithuania, dial ☎8 followed by the city code and phone number.

To make an international call, dial ☎00 before the country code. To call a mobile phone within Lithuania, dial ☎8 followed by the three-digit code and mobile number, and to call a mobile from abroad dial ☎370 instead of ☎8.

PHONECARDS

Public telephones are increasingly rare given the widespread use of mobiles and Skype. They only accept phonecards, which are sold at Lietuvos Spauda newspaper kiosks.

Visas

Citizens from the EU, Australia, Canada, Israel, Japan, New Zealand, Switzerland and the US do not require visas for entry into Lithuania if staying for less than 90 days. For information on other countries, visit www.migracija.lt.

Getting There & Away

Kaunas and Vilnius are both served by budget flights. Vilnius also receives numerous international flights. Plentiful rail, ferry and bus services make travel to neighbouring countries straightforward.

Since Lithuania's an EU member, entering the country is unlikely to present any problems for most visitors. However, those crossing overland from Russia or Belarus can expect delays at the border.

Air

There are direct flights to Lithuania from a number of European cities. There are three airports in Lithuania accepting international traffic:

Kaunas international airport (Kauno Oro Uostas; ☎37-399 307; www.kaunas-airport.lt) Nonstop flights to Bristol, London Stansted, Frankfurt, Reykjavik and Riga.

Palanga airport (Palangos Oro Uostas; ☎46-052 020; www.palanga-airport.lt) Nonstop flights to Copenhagen, Oslo, Riga and Moscow.

Vilnius international airport (Vilniaus Oro Uostas; ☎5-230 6666; www.vno.lt) Nonstop flights to London, Vienna, Moscow, Frankfurt, Paris, Milan, Copenhagen, Oslo, Warsaw, Kyiv, Dublin, Brussels and Prague, among others.

AIRLINES

Latvia's national airline, **airBaltic** (www.airbaltic.com), runs direct flights between Vilnius and about a dozen Western European destinations, as well as from Palanga to Riga.

Major international carriers with direct flights to Vilnius:

Aer Lingus (☎5-252 5010; www.aerlingus.com)

Austrian Airlines (☎5-210 5030; www.austrian.com)

Czech Airlines (☎5-215 1503; www.czechairlines.com)

Estonian Air (☎5-232 9300; www.estonian-air.com)

Finnair (☎5-252 5010; www.finnair.com)

LOT (☎5-273 9000; www.lot.com)

Lufthansa (☎5-232 9292; www.lufthansa.com)

Norwegian Air Shuttle (www.norwegian.no)

Ryanair (www.ryanair.com)

SAS (www.flysas.com)

WizzAir (www.wizzair.com)

Land

BORDER CROSSINGS

Lithuania borders Latvia, Poland, Belarus and Russia. You must have a valid visa for entering both Belarus and Russia (Kaliningrad).

BUS

The main international bus companies operating in Lithuania are **Lux Express** (www.luxexpress.eu) – under **Eurolines** (www.eurolines.com) – and **Ecolines** (www.ecolines.net).

CAR & MOTORCYCLE

Crossing into Russia (Kaliningrad) or Belarus in a rental car is forbidden by most rental companies.

TRAIN

Vilnius is linked by regular direct trains to Moscow, St Petersburg, Kaliningrad and Minsk; contact **Lithuanian Rail** (www.litrail.lt). You'll need a Belarus visa for the Moscow train.

Sea

International ferry services depart from Klaipėda. Destinations include Germany and Sweden.

Getting Around

Air

There are no domestic flights within Lithuania.

Bicycle

Two-wheeled exploration of certain parts of the country is rewarding as Lithuania is flat and its roads are mostly good.

Bicycles are easy to rent on the Curonian Spit and in all the major cities, where there are designated cycle lanes. Most tourist offices have maps of cycle routes.

Information about bike touring in Lithuania can be found on **BaltiCCycle.** (www.bicycle.lt)

Bus

Lithuania is covered by an extensive network of buses and minibuses. There are several different companies handling each route so prices vary. The most comfortable are Lux Express and Ecolines. See **Autobusbilietai** (www.autobusbilietai.lt) for bus timetables.

Ecolines (www.ecolines.net) Serves large cities and international destinations.

Eurolines (www.eurolines.com) Lux Express, Kautra and Toks operate under the Eurolines trademark in Lithuania.

Kautra (www.kautra.lt) Serves most destinations within Lithuania.

Lux Express (www.luxexpress.eu) Luxurious coaches connecting Vilnius with Riga, Tallinn, St Petersburg, Warsaw, Minsk and Berlin. Also stop in Kaunas and Šiauliai.

Toks (www.toks.lt) Serves most destinations within Lithuania.

Car & Motorcycle

Hiring a car is straightforward in Vilnius and Kaunas; international car-hire companies such as **Avis** (www.avis.lt), Hertz (www.hertz.lt) and **Europcar** (www.europcar.lt) are represented at the two airports, and a number of local rental companies such as **Fortuna** (www.rentacar.lt), **Aunela** (www.aunela.lt) and **Eura** (www.eura.lt) also offer competitive rates. Expect to pay around €170 per week for a compact.

You can drive from any point in Lithuania to another in a couple of hours. Modern four-lane highways link Vilnius with Klaipėda (via Kaunas) and Panevėžys.

The speed limit in Lithuania is 50km/h in cities and 70km/h to 90km/h on single carriageways and 110km/h to 130km/h on motorways. Dipped headlights must be on at all times, and winter tyres must be fitted between 1 November and 1 March.

You must have either an International Driving Permit (IDP) or your home-country licence with a photograph.

Local Transport

The main form of local transport is buses and minibuses; the bigger cities also have well-developed tram and trolleybus systems.

A ride costs around 2Lt, with a small discount if you buy tickets from a *Lietuvos Spauda* kiosk. Punch your ticket inside the vehicle or risk a fine.

Train

There are daily suburban train departures from Vilnius to Šiauliai, Kaunas, Ignalina, Klaipėda and Trakai. Trains are less frequent than buses.

For information about schedules, prices and services, contact **Lithuanian Rail** (www.litrail.lt).

Macedonia

Best Places to Eat

» Stara Gradska Kuča (p521)

» La Bodeguito Del Medio (p521)

» Letna Bavča Kaneo (p531)

» Restaurant Antiko (p531)

» El Greko (p534)

Best Places to Stay

» Hotel Radika (p527)

» Villa Dihovo (p535)

» Hi Skopje Hostel (p519)

» Vila Sveta Sofija (p530)

» Chola Guest House (p533)

» Hotel Pelister (p519)

Why Go?

Macedonia (Македонија) is hard to beat. Part Balkan and part Mediterranean, and offering impressive ancient sites and buzzing modern nightlife, the country packs in much more action, activities and natural beauty than would seem possible for a place its size.

Easygoing Skopje remains one of Europe's more unusual capitals, where constant urban renewal has made the city a continuous work in progress. With its hip cafes, restaurants, bars and clubs frequented by a large student population, Skopje is also emerging on the region's entertainment scene.

In summer try hiking, mountain biking and climbing in remote mountains, some concealing medieval monasteries. Visit Ohrid, noted for its summer festival, sublime Byzantine churches and a large lake. Winter offers skiing at resorts such as Mavrovo, and food-and-grog festivities in the villages. Meeting the locals and partaking in the country's living culture can be as memorable and rewarding as seeing the sights.

When to Go
Skopje

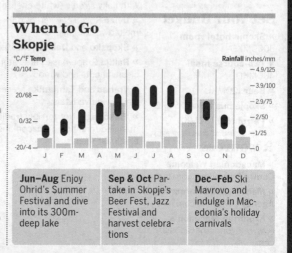

Jun–Aug Enjoy Ohrid's Summer Festival and dive into its 300m-deep lake

Sep & Oct Partake in Skopje's Beer Fest, Jazz Festival and harvest celebrations

Dec–Feb Ski Mavrovo and indulge in Macedonia's holiday carnivals

AT A GLANCE

» **Currency** Macedonian denar (MKD)

» **Language** Macedonian

» **Money** ATMs widespread in major towns

» **Visas** None for EU, US, Australian, Canadian or New Zealand citizens

Fast Facts

» **Area** 25,713 sq km

» **Capital** Skopje

» **Country code** ☏389

» **Emergency** Ambulance ☏194, fire ☏193, police ☏192

Exchange Rates

Australia	A$1	50.08MKD
Canada	C$1	47.18MKD
Euro Zone	€1	61.27MKD
Japan	¥100	50.81MKD
New Zealand	NZ$1	40.14MKD
UK	UK£1	72.54MKD
USA	US$1	47.94MKD

Set Your Budget

» **Skopje hotel room** 3000MKD

» **Two-course meal** 400MKD

» **Beer** 120MKD

» **Skopje bus ticket** 35MKD

» **Petrol (1L)** 100MKD

Resources

» **Macedonian Welcome Centre** (www.dmwc.org.mk)

» **Macedonian Information Agency** (www.mia.com.mk)

» **Exploring Macedonia** (www.exploringmacedonia.com)

Connections

Skopje's buses serve Sofia, Belgrade, Budapest, Pristina, Tirana, İstanbul, Thessaloniki and more. The train from Belgrade to Skopje reaches Gevgelija on the Greek border. The long-awaited arrival of budget airlines has improved Skopje's air connections.

ITINERARIES

One Week

Spend two nights in Skopje, marvelling at its bold new architecture on the square, and visiting its Čaršija (old quarter), with historic churches, mosques, museums and an Ottoman castle. Then travel southwest to Macedonia's most evocative and historic town, Ohrid, and its lake, via the lush forested mountains of Mavrovo and Bigorski Monastery, with its spectacular carved iconostasis. After two days, continue to cultured Bitola, the long-famed 'City of Consuls' known for its vibrant cafes and nearby ancient Heraclea and Pelister National Park.

Two Weeks

After Skopje, Ohrid and Bitola, visit Prilep, seeing its historic nearby monasteries. Before returning to Skopje, enjoy wines in the Tikveš wine region and see ancient Roman Stobi.

Essential Food & Drink

» **Ajvar** Sweet red-pepper sauce; accompanies meats and cheeses.

» **Šopska salata** Tomatoes, onions and cucumbers topped with flaky *sirenje* (white cheese).

» **Uviač** Rolled chicken or pork wrapped in bacon, filled with melted yellow cheese.

» **Skopsko** and **Dab lagers** Macedonia's favourite brews.

» **Rakija** Grape-based firewater, useful for toasts (and cleaning cuts and windows!).

» **Vranec** and **Temjanika** Macedonia's favourite red- and white-wine varietals.

» **'Bekonegs'** Not terribly traditional. but you will see this mangled rendition of 'bacon and eggs' on Macedonian breakfast menus.

SKOPJE

📋02 / POP 670,000

Skopje (Скопје) is among Europe's most entertaining and eclectic small capital cities. While a government construction spree has sparked controversy in recent years, Skopje's new abundance of statuary, bridges, museums and other structures has visitors' cameras snapping like never before and has defined the ever-changing city.

Yet plenty survives from earlier times – Skopje's Ottoman- and Byzantine-era wonders include the 15th-century Kameni Most (Stone Bridge), Čaršija (old Turkish bazaar), Sveti Spas Church, with its ornate, hand-carved iconostasis, and Tvrdina Kale Fortress, Skopje's guardian since the 5th century. And, with its bars, clubs and galleries, the city has modern culture too.

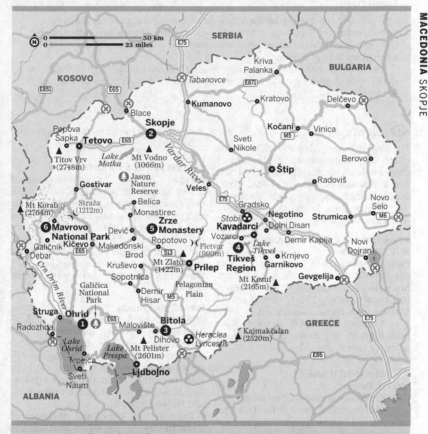

Macedonia Highlights

❶ Gaze out over Ohrid from the **Church of Sveti Jovan at Kaneo** (p529), immaculately set on a bluff above the lake.

❷ Dive into historic but still-changing **Skopje** (p517), a friendly, quintessentially Balkan capital.

❸ Enjoy the old-world ambience of **Bitola** (p533) and hike nearby Pelister National Park.

❹ Explore the **Tikveš wine region** (p536) and its ancient ruins and lake.

❺ Soak up the serenity at clifftop **Zrze Monastery** (p536), with sweeping views of the Pelagonian Plain and priceless Byzantine artworks.

❻ Ski **Mavrovo** (p526), Macedonia's premier winter resort.

SKOPJE IN...

One Day

After morning coffee on **Ploštad Makedonija**, cross this splendid, statue-studded square and the Vardar River via **Kameni Most** (Stone Bridge) into the **Čaršija**. Here peruse Turkish mosques, converted *hammam*s (turkish baths) and churches, and the **Holocaust Memorial Center**, before ascending **Tvrdina Kale Fortress**; the ramparts offer impressive views. Then enjoy dinner and drinks in the centre, the Čaršija or the leafy **Debar Maalo neighbourhood**.

Three Days

After seeing the centre and **Čaršija** sights, get another perspective from the forested **Mt Vodno**, flanking Skopje, and visit the 12th-century **Sveti Pantelejmon Monastery**. Along cafe-lined ul Makedonija see the **Memorial House of Mother Teresa** and **Museum of the City of Skopje**.

West of Skopje, **Lake Matka** occupies a deep canyon and its forests offer hiking trails and monastic grottoes. Later, enjoy great beer, wine and live music at the Čaršija's stylish nightspots.

◉ Sights

The Čaršija houses Skopje's main historic sights. Other museums are on the Vardar's southern shore, where cafes line pedestrianised ul Makedonija. Buzzing Ploštad Makedonija (Macedonia Sq) stands smack by the Ottoman stone bridge (Kameni Most), which accesses Čaršija.

PLOŠTAD MAKEDONIJA & THE SOUTH BANK

Ploštad Makedonija   SQUARE
(Macedonia Sq) Fronted by a Triumphal Arch, this square has audacious statues dedicated to national heroes. The towering, central 'Warrior on a Horse' is bedecked by fountains that are illuminated by night. From here, stroll or cycle along the riverbank, or relax in a river-facing cafe.

FREE Memorial House of Mother Teresa   MUSEUM
(☏3290 674; www.memorialhouseofmotherteresa. org; ul Makedonija bb; ⊙9am-8pm Mon-Fri, to 2pm Sat & Sun) This retro-futuristic structure has memorabilia of the famed Catholic nun of Calcutta, born in Skopje in 1910.

FREE Museum of the City of Skopje   MUSEUM
(Mito Hadživasilev Jasmin bb; ⊙9am-3pm Tue-Sat, to 1pm Sun) Occupying the old train station, this museum specialises in local ancient and Byzantine finds. The stone fingers of its clock remain frozen in time at 5.17am – the

moment Skopje's great earthquake struck on 27 July 1963.

NORTH BANK & ČARŠIJA

Čaršija   NEIGHBOURHOOD
Across Kameni Most, Čaršija evokes Skopje's Ottoman past – winding lanes filled with eateries, teahouses, craftsmen's stores and even good nightlife. It also boasts Skopje's best historic structures and museums. Čaršija runs from the Stone Bridge to Bit Pazar, a big, busy vegetable market purveying bric-a-brac, household goods and anything random.

Sveti Spas Church   CHURCH
(Makarie Frčkoski 8; admission 100MKD; ⊙8am-3pm Tue-Sun) Partially underground (the Turks banned churches from being taller than mosques), this church boasts a wood-carved iconostasis 10m wide and 6m high, built by early-19th-century master craftsmen Makarije Frčkovski and brothers Petar and Marko Filipovski.

Outside, the **Tomb and Museum of Goce Delčev** (Church of Sveti Spas) has the remains of Macedonia's foremost national hero. Leader of the VMRO (Internal Macedonian Revolutionary Organisation), Delčev was killed by Turks in 1903.

Museum of Macedonia   MUSEUM
(www.musmk.org.mk; Čurčiska bb; admision 50MKD; ⊙9am-5pm Tue-Sun) Documenting neolithic through communist times, this museum contains an ethnographic exhibition,

plus ancient jewellery and coins, icons and wood-carved iconostases.

Sultan Murat Mosque
MOSQUE

(bul K Misirkov) This 1436 mosque is among the Balkans' oldest and features a distinctive, red-tipped clock tower and Ottoman *madrasa* (Islamic school) remnants.

KALE & AROUND
Mustafa Paša Mosque
MOSQUE

(Samoilova bb) The 1492 Mustafa Paša Mosque exemplifies magnificent Ottoman architecture, with a lawn, garden and fountain.

FREE **Tvrdina Kale Fortress**
FORTRESS

(⊙daylight hours) This 6th-century AD Byzantine (and later, Ottoman) castle conceals archaeological finds from neolithic to Ottoman times. The ramparts offer great views over city and river.

Museum of Contemporary Art
MUSEUM

(☏3117 734; www.msuskopje.org.mk; Samoilova bb; ⊙10am-5pm Tue-Sat, 9am-1pm Sun) This elevated museum displays works by Macedonian and world-famous artists (there's even a Picasso).

MT VODNO & AROUND
Mt Vodno
MOUNTAIN

Framing Skopje to the south, Vodno's popular with hikers, though a gondola up the mountainside operates too. Two restaurants stand at Sredno (Middle) Vodno (taxis drive here for 200MKD). Hiking trails take you to the 66m-high **Millenium Cross** (2002), the world's largest and illuminated at night.

Sveti Pantelejmon Monastery
MONASTERY

(Gorno Nerezi village) Further west along Vodno, this 1164 monastery is among Macedonia's most significant churches. Its Byzantine frescos, such as the *Lamentation of Christ,* depict a pathos and realism predating the Renaissance by two centuries. It's 5km from the centre (by taxi, 300MKD) and offers great views.

✫✫ Festivals & Events

Skopsko Leto
ARTS

(www.dku.org.mk) Summer art exhibitions, performances and concerts.

Pivolend
BEER

(www.pivolend.com.mk) Held in September outside the Boris Trajkovski Sports Centre (p523), this event features rock acts and DJs, grilled meats and beer.

Skopje Jazz Festival
MUSIC

(☏3131 090; www.skopjejazzfest.com.mk) This October festival features artists from across the globe, and always a world-renowned player or group (Chick Corea, McCoy Tyner, Herbie Hancock and Tito Puente are some past headliners).

May Opera Evenings
OPERA

This event and **Off-Fest** (☏3131 090; www.offest.com.mk) combine world music and DJ events.

Taksirat Festival
MUSIC

(☏2775 430; www.taksirat.com.mk) Live rock music in November/December.

🛏 Sleeping

A few basic youth hostels lie between the bus/train stations and the Vardar River in the run-down (but safe enough) Madzar Maalo quarter. Better, but pricier, hotels are in the centre. The Debar Maalo neighbourhood (a 10-minute walk from centre towards the park) offers good midrange options amid cafes and restaurants.

TOP CHOICE **Hotel Pelister**
BOUTIQUE HOTEL €€

(☏3239 584; www.pelisterhotel.com.mk; Ploštad Makedonija; s/d/apt from €59/69/85; ❄@🛜) Located above Restaurant Pelister (p522; both formerly called 'Dal Met Fu'), this hotel enjoys an unbeatable location on the square, overlooking the city's new architectural wonders. The six rooms are spiffy, with somewhat standard decor though most come with a computer. The suites also have a spa, for the price of a smaller standard room elsewhere in the city.

TOP CHOICE **Urban Hostel**
HOSTEL €

(☏6142 785; www.urbanhostel.com.mk; Majka Teresa 22; dm/s/d/apt €13/24/34/75; ❄🛜) Skopje's best hostel is a short walk from the centre, opposite the leafy Debar Maalo neighbourhood, home to relaxed cafes and restaurants. Along with clean rooms, comfy beds and a fireplace, there's a piano, aquarium, computer room and friendly, helpful staff.

TOP CHOICE **Hi Skopje Hostel**
HOSTEL €

(☏6091-242; www.hiskopjehostel.com; Crniche 15; dm/s/d from 540/1200/2100MKD) In the cool shade of Mt Vodno, this cheerful new hostel offers dorms and two rooms (with a shared bathroom, however). There's a communal kitchen, and the relaxing back garden adds

Skopje

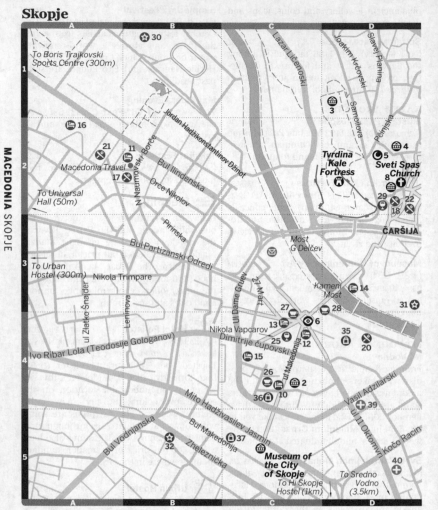

to the out-of-city vibe. The friendly young owners offer tons of info on city sights and events. It's located on a hilly street 2.5km from the bus/train stations (take a taxi for 150MKD).

Hotel City Park
HOTEL €€

(☑3290 860; www.hotelcitypark.com.mk; Mihail Cokov 8a, Gradski Park; s/d/ste from €75/90/105; ❄🞷) This sharp newcomer features bright, almost minimalist rooms with comfy beds and plenty of amenities. It's located opposite the park and its *fontana* (fountain) in the

Debar Maalo neighbourhood, a 10-minute walk from centre.

Hotel Square
BUDGET HOTEL €€

(☑3225 090; www.hotelsquare.com.mk; 6th fl, Nikola Vapcarov 2; s/d/tr €45/60/75; ❄@) Well situated six floors above the action, the Square offers cosy, well-kept and modern rooms. The balcony cafe offers great views and an optional breakfast (€5) is in Café Trend (p523) nearby. Look for the signposted business/apartment block off Ploštad Makedonija.

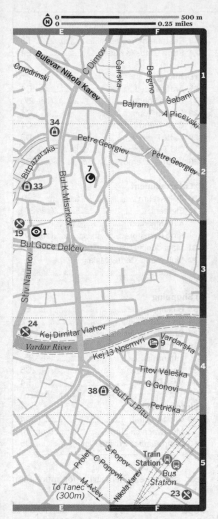

Best Western Hotel Turist
BUSINESS HOTEL €€€

(☎3289 111; www.bestwestern-ce.com/turist; ul Gjuro Strugar 11; s/d from €128/138; P❄✿) The Turist lies on pedestrianised ul Makedonija, though it's not particularly conspicuous by chain hotel standards. Service is professional and the business rooms come with all the mod cons.

Hotel Stone Bridge
LUXURY HOTEL €€€

(☎3244 900; www.stonebridge-hotel.com; Kej Dimitar Vlahov 1; s/d/apt from €138/159/299; P❄@✿) This Turkish-owned, five-star hotel sits across the Stone Bridge. The sophisticated rooms are graced with stylised Ottoman furnishings, and the restaurant is good. It's arguably overpriced (the grand 'Sultan Suite', certainly so, at a preposterous €549).

Art Hostel
HOSTEL €

(☎3223 789; www.art-hostel.com.mk; Ante Hadzimitkov 5; dm/s/d €12/25/40; ❄@✿) Near the train station in the Madjir Maalo neighbourhood, by the River Vardar, Art Hostel is a passable backpacker fallback, though the six-bed dorms and private rooms (all with shared bathrooms) are cramped.

✖ Eating

Restaurants open until midnight; nonsmoking laws are strictly enforced. *Skara* (grilled meat) is popular, but international flavours are well represented too. For breakfast, try *burek* (white cheese, spinach or ground meat in filo pastry) with drinking yoghurt.

The old town has more *skara* places, and *kebapčilnici* (beef-kebab restaurants) and doner-kebab shops – avoid the less-visited, less-hygienic ones.

⬛TOP CHOICE Stara Gradska Kuča
MACEDONIAN €€

(Pajko Maalo 14; mains 250-400MKD; ⏱8am-midnight) This restored traditional house has warm ambience, an excellent assortment of traditional Macedonian dishes and, sometimes, live Macedonian music. It's a bit touristy, but still a snug and cosy spot with its wood furnishings and traditional decor.

⬛TOP CHOICE La Bodeguito Del Medio
CUBAN €€

(Kej 13 Noemvri; mains 350-700MKD; ⏱9am-2am) Known to locals as 'the Cuban', this gregarious riverfront place has sizzling Cuban specialities, Latin cocktails and music, and a long bar lined with carousers by night. Borrow a magic marker to scrawl your message among hundreds of others on the walls and ceilings.

Tim's Apartments
APARTMENT €€

(☎3237 650; www.tims.com.mk; Orce Nikolov 120; s/d/apt €69/89/110; ❄@✿) Near the park, Tim's is a long-established and dependable option, with 10 classy rooms and seven en suite apartments.

Hotel TCC Plaza
LUXURY HOTEL €€€

(☎3111 807; www.tccplaza.com; Vasil Glavinov 12; s/d/ste from €84/110/145; P❄@✿✖) This five-star hotel offers spacious, well-lit rooms and suites, plus a spa centre with small swimming pool, and fitness and massage services. It lacks views or ambience, but it's very central.

Skopje

Restaurant Pelister INTERNATIONAL €€
(Dal Met Fu; Ploštad Makedonija; mains 280-350MKD; ⏱7.30am-midnight) This square-front place remains a local fixture – note the curious mix of pensioners debating politics over coffee, businessmen chatting up politicians, and random tourists. It does great pastas and offers a make-your-own-salad bar. The chocolate souffle with vanilla ice cream and spearmint sprig is worth the 10-minute wait.

Kebapčilnica Destan KEBAB €
(ul 104 6; 10 kebabs 120MKD) Skopje's best beef kebabs, accompanied by seasoned grilled bread, are served at this classic Čaršija place.

Idadija SKARA €€
(Rade Koncar 1; mains 180-250MKD) In Debar Maalo's *skara* corner, no-frills Idadija has

been serving excellent grills for more than 80 years.

Papu MACEDONIAN €€
(Djuro Djakovic 63; mains 250-400MKD) The tastes and decor of old Kruševo are preserved at this lovely place studded with stone arches and antiques, and filled with the sounds of cascading water.

Pivnica An MACEDONIAN, INTERNATIONAL €€
(mains 300-500MKD) You're paying for the ambience at this 'beerhouse' located in a restored Ottoman building's sumptuous courtyard as the tasty food is overpriced.

Restaurant Roulette SKARA €€
(Simeon Kavrakirov 9a; mains 150-350MKD) If you need a meal before a bus or train trip, this

local favourite on a residential street serves the best grills near the station.

K8
SWEETS €

(Gradište 7a; snacks 50-140 MKD; ☺9am-7pm) Established by an American expat baker, this fun little place is unique for its typical American soccer-mum snacks such as lemon bars, choc-chip brownies and apple pie.

🍷 Drinking

Čaršija has a couple of fun nightspots. Good bars sit around the square, while clubbers find open-air venues in the park by summer and indoors under the bus station by winter. Cafes and bars open until 1am, though nightclubs continue until later. Supermarkets sell alcohol until 7pm in winter and 9pm in summer.

TOP CHOICE Bistro London
PUB

(pl Makedonija; ☺8am-1am) Formerly 'London Pub,' this refurbished bar annex of neighbouring Café Trend (p523) has agreeable plaid-backed chairs, a decent pub ambience and friendly service. Along with a wide selection of beers, wines and cocktails it offers snacks and full meals. There's live music on weekends, including Sunday mid-morning jazz.

TOP CHOICE Vinoteka Temov
BAR

(Gradište 1a; ☺9am-midnight Mon-Thu, to 1am Fri-Sun) Skopje's best wine bar, in a restored wood building near Sveti Spas, is refined and atmospheric. A vast (and pricey) wine list presents the manifold flavours of Macedonia's vineyards, while live traditional and classical guitarists often play.

Old Town Brewery
BEER HALL

(Gradište 1; ☺10am-1am Sun-Thu, to 3am Fri & Sat) This beer bar above Vinoteka Temov is Skopje's only place for a yard of beer, and selection is good. In summer, the benches spill outside, where bands cover classic rock.

Café di Roma
CAFE

(ul Makedonija; ☺8am-1am) This stylish place does Skopje's best espresso and other caffeinated drinks, hot and cold, plus cakes.

Caffé Firenze
CAFE

(pl Makedonija; ☺8am-midnight) This sharp cafe on the square's southeastern edge is great for a relaxed espresso and also serves Italian fare (the pastas are more authentic than the desserts).

Arabesque
LOUNGE BAR

(☎072 304 304; www.arabesque.mk; Nikola Vapcarov 7) One of Skopje's newer nightspots, Arabesque has a long bar, big leather couches and eccentric orange lights but it aims for a swank, dressed-up clientele. Reservations suggested on weekends. Decent pastas are also served.

Café Trend
CAFE

(Ploštad Makedonija; ☺8am-1am) Aspiring socialites mix with (and gossip about) local celebrities at this long-established, slick place on the square. It also has a good restaurant.

☆ Entertainment

Skopje is a clubbing hot spot, hosting well-known international DJs; see www.skopjeclubbing.com.mk.

Colosseum
CLUB

(www.colosseum.com.mk; City Park in summer, under train station in winter) Skopje's biggest and most popular club, along with **Element** (www.element.com.mk; Gradski Park). When international DJs appear, tickets run from 250MKD to 500MKD.

Multimedia Center Mala Stanica
CAFE

(www.nationalgallery.mk; Zheleznička 18; ☺9am-midnight) Featuring arty, ornate decor, the National Art Gallery's cafe hosts temporary exhibitions and live music.

Universal Hall
LIVE MUSIC

(Univerzalna Sala; ☎3224 158; bul Partizanski Odredi bb) Hosts classical, jazz, pop and kids' performances.

Boris Trajkovski Sports Centre
SPORTS CENTRE

(Sportski Centar Boris Trajkovski; ☎3089 661; www.salaboristrajkovski.gov.mk; bul Ilindenska; ☺9am-11pm) Named for the late president, this big facility has everything from bowling, go-karts, ping pong and a kids' play land to cafes, an indoor pool and ice skating in winter. Sometimes international spectator sports (such as water polo) are held here.

Macedonian National Theatre
THEATRE

(☎3114 060; www.mnt.com.mk; Kej Dimitar Vlahov bb) Hosts opera, ballet and classical music in a communist-era building.

Kino Milenium
CINEMA

(☎3120 389; www.kinomilenium.mk; Gradski Trgovski Centar) Skopje's largest movie theatre.

Kino Ramstore CINEMA
(Ramstore Mall, Mito Hadživasilev Jasmin bb) This theatre gets second-rate Hollywood films but shows some popular kids' flicks.

🔒 Shopping

In Čaršija you can buy jewellery, traditional carpets, antiques, dresses and more but beware – most 'ancient' treasures on sale are fakes (and would be illegal to buy if they weren't). **Bit Pazar** sells fruit, vegetables, stolen phones and household items. The **Gradski Trgovski Centar** (11 Oktomvri), **Ramstore** (Mito Hadživasilev Jasmin bb) and

Vero Center (bul Jane Sandanski) are modern malls. Plenty of Macedonia-themed souvenir stalls are on or near the main square.

Balkan Corner JEWELLERY
(ul Bitpazarska; silver jewellery 600-4500MKD; ⏱9.30am-7.30pm) This tiny shop halfway down the old town's central street specialises in all kinds of handmade silver jewellery (and other gifts). Friendly owner Adnan is happy to give details on individual pieces.

Ikona HANDICRAFTS
(Luj Paster 19; ⏱9am-9pm Mon-Fri, to 4pm Sat) 'Traditional' souvenirs, including icons, ar-

TRANSPORT FROM SKOPJE

Domestic Bus

DESTINATION	PRICE (MKD)	DURATION (HR)	FREQUENCY
Bitola	480	3	12 daily
Gostivar	200	1	12 daily
Kavadarci	250	2	7 daily
Kruševo	380	3	3 daily
Makedonski Brod	330	3	5 daily
Mavrovo	330	2	7 Mon-Fri, 2 Sat-Sun
Negotino	210	2½	11 Mon-Fri, 9 Sat-Sun
Ohrid	520	3	11 daily
Prilep	390	2½	14 daily

International Bus

DESTINATION	PRICE (MKD)	DURATION (HR)	FREQUENCY
Belgrade	1400	10	12 daily
İstanbul	1900	12	5 daily
Ljubljana	3750	14	1 daily
Pristina	320	2	12 daily
Sofia	1040	5½	5 daily
Thessaloniki	1280	4	1 Mon, Wed & Fri
Zagreb	3150	12	1 daily

Domestic Train

DESTINATION	PRICE (MKD)	DURATION	FREQUENCY
Bitola	314	4hr	3 daily
Gevgelija	270	2½hr	3 daily
Kičevo	208	2hr	3 daily
Kumanovo	79	40min	4 daily
Negotino	198	2hr	3 daily
Prilep	250	3hr	3 daily

chaeological replicas, pottery, painted boxes and folk dolls.

Lithium
MUSIC
(www.lithiumrecords.com.mk; Gradski Trgovski Centar; ☺8.30am-8pm Mon-Sat) Buy Macedonian and international CDs, plus concert and festival tickets.

❶ Information

Dangers & Annoyances
Pensioners on bicycles constitute the gravest threat to public safety, whether you're walking on the sidewalk or driving a car. In general, Skopje drivers are reckless, and sidewalks are pock-marked by unexpected cracks and holes. Roma children's begging can be an irritant, though violent crime is rare.

Skopje's wild dogs are less troublesome than before, though joggers and cyclists are still fair game.

Internet Access
Free wi-fi is widespread in cafes, restaurants, hotels and even buses – few internet cafes remain.

Medical Services
City Hospital (☑3130 111; 11 Oktomvri 53; ☺24hr)
Neuromedica Private Clinic (☑3133 313; 11 Oktomvri 25; ☺24hr) Good private specialists.

Money
ATMs and *menuvačnici* (exchange offices) abound.

Menuvačnica Euro (Gradski Trgovski Centar; ☺9am-8.30pm Mon-Sat) Dependable exchange office near the southern end of the Gradski Trgovski Centar on the ground floor.

Post & Telephone
The **main post office** (☑3141 141; Orce Nikolov 1; ☺7am-7.30pm Mon-Sat, 7.30am-2.30pm Sun) is 75m northwest of Ploštad Makedonija. Others are opposite the train station, in the Gradski Trgovski Centar and in Ramstore.

Some kiosks (newsagents) have private telephones.

Travel Agencies
Go Macedonia (☑3071 265; www.gomacedonia.com; Ankarska 29a) Arranges hiking, cycling, caving and winery tours.
Macedonia Travel (www.macedoniatravel.com; Orce Nikolov 109/1, lok 3) Does tours, including trips to Jasen Nature Reserve, and air tickets.

Websites
Lonely Planet (www.lonelyplanet.com/macedonia/skopje)

Skopje Official Website (www.skopje.gov.com)
Skopje Online (www.skopjeonline.com.mk)
Tourist Association of Skopje (www.skopjetourism.org)

❶ Getting There & Away

Air
Skopje Alexander the Great Airport (☑3148 333; www.airports.com.mk; Petrovec), 21km east of Skopje, has had a long-awaited upgrade thanks to the Turkish company TAV, which also operates it. New budget carriers connect Skopje with the UK, Central Europe, Italy, Turkey and the Gulf. Nevertheless, airlines come and go so check the airport website first.

Adria Airways (www.adria.si; Dame Gruev 7)
Austrian Airlines (www.austrian.com)
Croatia Airlines (www.croatiaairlines.hr)
Fly Dubai (www.flydubai.com) Connects Skopje with Dubai and further east.
JAT (Yugoslav Airlines; ☑3118 306; www.jat.com; bul Partizanski Odredi 17) Has an office near the centre.
Pegasus Airlines (www.flypgs.com) Turkish budget carrier offers great fares to Turkey and elsewhere.
Turkish Airlines (www.thy.com)
WizzAir (www.wizzair.com) Good budget rates to London-Luton, Central Europe and Italy.

Bus
Skopje's **bus station** (www.sas.com.mk; bul Jane Sandanski), with ATM, exchange office and English-language info, adjoins the train station.

Buses to Ohrid go via Kičevo (three hours, 167km) or Bitola (four to five hours, 261km) – book ahead in summer. Most intercity buses are air-conditioned and are generally faster than trains, though more expensive.

Train
The **train station** (Zheleznička Stanica; bul Jane Sandanski) serves local and international destinations. Northbound trains pass through Kumanovo for Serbia. The southbound service transits Veles; from here, one line continues south through Gevgelija for Greece, while the other forks southwest through Prilep for Bitola.

Another line serves eastern Macedonian towns, while a lesser-used western line terminates at Kičevo.

At time of research, the Greek government had suspended international train routes, but hopefully the Skopje–Thessaloniki run will return someday (4½ hours). A train serves Belgrade (1300MKD, eight to 10 hours, two daily), and another reaches Pristina in Kosovo.

ⓘ Getting Around

TO/FROM THE AIRPORT An airport shuttle bus, Vardar Express, runs between the airport and the city. Buy tickets (100MKD) from the marked arrivals terminal booth. The bus leaves half-hourly or hourly, depending on passengers, and stops at several places including the bus/train station and central square. It returns via the same stops, though allow extra time as it is somewhat irregular. Otherwise, arrange a taxi to the airport (800MKD to 1000MKD) in advance. From the airport to centre, taxis cost 1200MKD.

BUS Skopje's public city buses (including London-style red double-deckers) cost 35MKD. Private ones cost 25MKD. Both follow the same stops and numbered routes. You can buy and validate tickets on board. Both congregate under the bus/train station (officially, 'Transporten Centar'), behind the enclosed area where intercity buses depart. Bus 22 is useful, cutting through the centre and down bul Partizanski Odredi.

CAR Daily rental prices start at 26,000MKD. Try Budget Car Rental. Free parking is hard to find in Skopje – even if you think you're safe, check again. Large white placards around the city instruct how to pay for parking via text message (otherwise, you may have to pay a 1200MKD fine).

TAXI Skopje's taxis are cheaper than in Western Europe. The base rate is 40MKD for the first kilometre and 25MKD for subsequent kilometres, and drivers use their meters. Central destinations cost 60MKD to 150MKD. Lotus has spiffy, air-conditioned cars, and In-Taxi is also good. Legit companies usually have the five-digit ordering phone number (starting with 15). Although various dubious cabs hover near Bit Pazar, the city has largely removed the shadier operators from the bus and train stations.

WESTERN MACEDONIA

Western Macedonia gets most of Macedonia's visitors, and no wonder: its mountain ranges provide a stunning backdrop, running south from Šar Planina to the gentler Jablanica range, ending with the 34km-long Lake Ohrid.

Lying outstretched southward, and flanked by Galičica National Park, the lake is dotted with coastal and upland villages. Ohrid itself boasts manifold historic sites, a lovely old quarter and summer cultural events and nightlife.

Mavrovo National Park
Маврово Национален Парк
♪042

Mavrovo's ski resort is Macedonia's biggest, comprising 730 sq km of birch and pine forest, gorges, karst fields and waterfalls, plus Macedonia's highest peak, **Mt Korab** (2764m). The rarefied air and stunning vistas are great year-round. Located up a winding road southwest of Gostivar, Mavrovo lies near Sveti Jovan Bigorski Monastery and Galičnik, famous for its traditional village wedding.

◉ Sights & Activities

Sveti Jovan Bigorski
Monastery MONASTERY
This revered 1020 Byzantine monastery is off the Debar road. Legend attests an icon of Sveti Jovan Bigorski (St John the Forerunner, ie St John the Baptist) miraculously

---

AROUND SKOPJE

A half-hour drive, or slightly longer city bus trip, accesses tranquil **Lake Matka** (NW Macedonia; 🚌60 from Bulevar Partizanski in Skopje). Although crowded at weekends, this idyllic spot beneath steep **Treska Canyon** is excellent, offering hiking, rock climbing, caving (€10) and ancient churches in its forested environs. On-site restaurants provide nourishment and lake views. Matka's underwater caverns are as deep, or maybe deeper, than any in Europe, at almost 218m.

Matka's traditional link with the Virgin Mary (Matka means 'womb' in Macedonian) is accentuated by grotto shrines such as **Sveta Bogorodica**. From here a steep path reaches **Sveti Spas**, **Sveta Trojca** and **Sveta Nedela** – the last, a 4km walk (around 1½ hours). These caves once sheltered ascetics and anti-Ottoman revolutionaries.

After the **Church of Sveti Nikola**, beyond the dam and across the bridge, visit the frescoed **Church of Sveti Andrej** (1389). The adjoining mountaineering hut **Matka** (✆3052 655) offers guides, climbing gear and accommodation.

From Skopje come by car, taxi (450MKD) or bus 60 along bul Partizanski Odredi (50MKD, 40 minutes, hourly).

appeared, and since then it's been rebuilt often – the icon occasionally reappearing too. The impressive church also houses Jovan's alleged forearm.

Bigorski's awe-inspiring iconostasis was the final of just three carved by local craftsmen Makarije Frčkovski and the brothers Filipovski between 1829 and 1835. This colossal work depicting biblical scenes is enlivened with 700 tiny human and animal figures. Gazing up at this enormous, intricate masterpiece is breathtaking. Upon finishing, the carvers allegedly flung their tools into the nearby Radika River – ensuring that the secret of their artistic genius would be washed away forever.

Galičnik
VILLAGE

Up a winding, tree-lined road ending in a rocky moonscape 17km southwest of Mavrovo, almost depopulated Galičnik features traditional houses along the mountainside. It's placid except for 12 and 13 July, when the **Galičnik Wedding** sees one or two lucky couples wed here. Visit, along with 3000 happy Macedonians, and enjoy eating, drinking, traditional folk dancing and music.

Zare Lazarevski Ski Centre
SKIING

(☑489 065; www.zarelaz.com; ☺8am-10pm) Macedonia's top ski resort, with average snow cover of 70cm and slopes from 1860m to 2255m. Zare Lazarevski offers ski rental (600MKD), lift tickets (800MKD/3500MKD per day/week) and ski school. Mavrovo's also good for summer hiking.

🛌 Sleeping & Eating

Go Macedonia (p525) arranges Galičnik Wedding trips including transport, guided activities, local accommodation and monastery tours. You will need to book ahead.

TOP CHOICE Hotel Radika
SPA HOTEL €€

(☑223 300; www.radika.com.mk; s/d/apt €43/60/69; P❄🐾) Just 5km from Mavrovo, this ultraposh spa hotel is perfect for pampering, with numerous massage treatments and excellent rooms. Prices fall considerably in summer. Nondrivers should take a taxi from Gostivar (650MKD), on the Skopje–Ohrid road.

Sveti Jovan Bigorski
MONASTERY €

(☑478 675; www.bigorski.org.mk; per person €5) The self-catering dormitories here are under reconstruction – check ahead.

Hotel Srna
SKI LODGE €€

(☑388 083; www.hotelsrnamavrovo.com; s/d/apt €25/40/60; ❄🐾) The small Srna, 400m from Mavrovo's chairlifts, has breezy, clean rooms.

Hotel Bistra
SKI LODGE €€

(☑489 002; www.bistra.com; s/d €45/70, d with spa €110; P❄🐾🏊) The Bistra has comfortable, clean rooms and amenities (restaurant, bar, pool, fitness centre, sauna) for cultivating that ski-lodge glow, plus spas in the deluxe rooms. Prices fall in summer. It also runs the simpler **Hotel Ski Škola** (s/d €20/40) and **Hotel Mavrovski** (s/d €20/40); guests can use the Bistra's facilities.

ℹ Getting There & Away

Southbound buses reach Mavrovo Anovi (2km away) en route to Debar (120MKD, seven daily), or while travelling north to Tetovo (140MKD, five daily) and Skopje (180MKD, three daily).

For Sveti Jovan Bigorski Monastery, drive; alternatively, buses transiting Debar for Ohrid or Struga will drop you off.

Ohrid
Охрид

☑046 / POP 55,700

Sublime Ohrid is Macedonia's prime destination, with its atmospheric old quarter with beautiful churches along a graceful hill, topped by a medieval castle overlooking serene, 34km-long Lake Ohrid. Nearby, mountainous Galičica National Park offers pristine nature, while secluded beaches dot the lake's eastern shore.

Ohrid and its beaches are packed from 15 July to 15 August, during the popular summer festival. June or September are quieter (and cleaner).

Lake Ohrid, 300m deep and three million years old, shared by Macedonia (two-thirds) and Albania (one-third), is among Europe's deepest and oldest. Although usually calm, during storms Ohrid seethes with steely-grey whitecaps evoking the sea.

History

Lychnidos ('city of light' in Greek, evincing the lake's clarity) hugged the Via Egnatia connecting Constantinople with the Adriatic in the 4th century BC. It became a Byzantine trade, cultural and ecclesiastical centre.

Slavic migrations created the name Ohrid (from *vo rid*, or 'city on the hill'). Bulgarian Slavs arrived in 867, and the Ohrid literary school – the first Slavic university – was

Ohrid

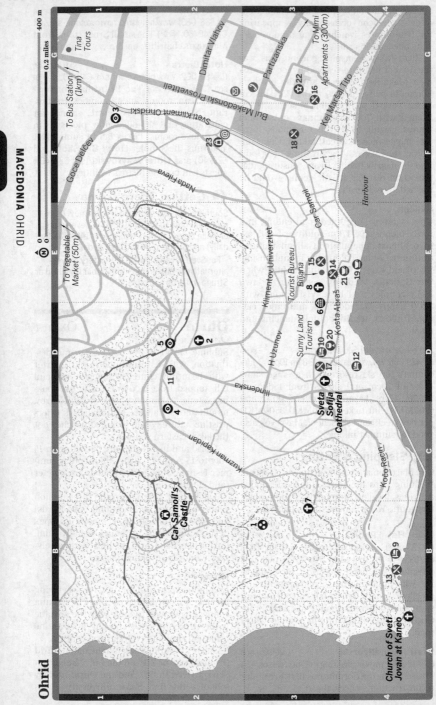

0.2 miles / 400 m

Church of Sveti Jovan at Kaneo

Car Samoil's Castle

Sveta Sofija Cathedral

Harbour

To Bus Station (1km)

To Vegetable Market (50m)

To Mimi Apartments (300m)

Tina Tours

Goce Delčev

Dimitar Vlahov

Bul Makedonski Prosvetiteli

Partizanska

Kej Maršal Tito

Sveti Kliment Ohridski

Nada Fileva

Car Samoil

Klimentov Univerzitet

Kuzman Kapidan

H Uzunov

Ilindenska

Kosta Abraš

Kočo Racin

Biljana

Tourist Bureau

Sunny Land Tourism

Ohrid

established by 9th-century Saints Kliment and Naum. Macedonia's Christianisation specifically and Slavic literacy in general were expedited when Kliment created the Cyrillic alphabet.

Bulgarian Cars Simeon (r 893–927) and Samoil (r 997–1014) ruled from here. When the Byzantines defeated Samoil, Ohrid was reclaimed. Ottoman Turks conquered Ohrid (and Macedonia), in the late 14th century. In 1767 Greek intrigue caused the abolition of Ohrid's archbishopric – a long-lasting grievance for both Macedonians and Bulgarians. Today, the restored archbishopric represents the Macedonian Orthodox Church's highest office.

⦿ Sights

Churches and museums are closed on Monday.

To see Ohrid's sights in the most efficient and least exhausting way, start at the **Gorna Porta** (Upper Gate), about 100MKD from centre by taxi, and walk down.

Church of Sveta Bogorodica Perivlepta
CHURCH
(Gorna Porta; admission 100MKD; ⊙9am-1pm & 4-8pm) Just inside the Gorna Porta, this 13th-century Byzantine church has vivid biblical frescos and an **icon gallery** (Gorna Porta; ⊙9am-2pm & 5-8pm, closed Mon) highlighting the founders' artistic achievements.

FREE Classical Amphitheatre
AMPHITHEATRE
Ohrid's impressive amphitheatre was built for theatre; the Romans later removed 10 rows to accommodate gladiators. It hosts Summer Festival performances.

Car Samoil's Castle
CASTLE
(admission 30MKD; ⊙9am-6pm Tue-Sun) The massive, turreted walls of the 10th-century castle indicate the power of the medieval Bulgarian state. Ascend the narrow stone stairways to the ramparts for fantastic views.

FREE Plaošnik
CHURCH
(⊙9am-6pm) Down a wooded path, Plaošnik boasts the Church of Sveti Kliment i Pantelejmon. This 5th-century basilica was restored in 2002 according to its Byzantine design. The multidomed church has glass floor segments revealing original foundations. It houses St Kliment's relics, with intricate 5th-century mosaics outside. Nearby are **4th-century church foundations**, replete with Early Christian flora and fauna mosaics.

Church of Sveti Jovan at Kaneo
CHURCH
(admission 50MKD; ⊙9am-6pm) This stunning 13th-century church is set on a cliff over the lake, and is possibly Macedonia's most photographed structure. Peer down into the azure waters and you'll see why medieval monks found spiritual inspiration

here. The small church has original frescos behind the altar.

Sveta Sofija Cathedral   CHURCH
(Car Samoil bb; admission 100MKD; ☺10am-8pm) Ohrid's grandest church, 11th-century Sveta Sofija is supported by columns and decorated with elaborate Byzantine frescoes. Its superb acoustics mean it's often used for concerts. Come by the road running down from Kaneo, past the Old Town's lovely houses, or along the new overwater walking bridge, beginning on the beach south of Kaneo.

National Museum   MUSEUM
(Car Samoil 62; admission 50MKD; ☺9am-4pm & 7-11pm Tue-Sun) Near Sveta Sofija, the 1827 National Museum features distinctive white-and-brown architecture. The **Robev Residence** houses ancient epigraphy and the **Urania Residence** opposite has an ethnographic display.

Sveta Bogorodica Bolnička & Sveti Nikola Bolnički   CHURCHES
Ohrid's minor frescoed 14th-century churches are open infrequently (ask at the museum). *Bolnica* means 'hospital' in Macedonian; during plagues visitors faced 40-day quarantines here.

Činar   TREE
Stroll ul Sveti Kliment Ohridski, lined with cafes and shops, to reach this enormous, 900-year-old plane tree – a likeable Ohrid landmark.

⮂ Courses

Macedonian Language Course   LANGUAGE COURSE
(www.ukim.edu.mk/smjlk; per person €850) This three-week course, run each August by the SS Cyril & Methodius University, attracts international students. It includes language lessons, cultural excursions and accommodation, and is, by all accounts, great fun.

✷ Festivals & Events

Balkan Festival of Folk Dances & Songs   CULTURAL
This July festival draws regional folkloric groups.

Ohrid Summer Festival   ARTS
(☎262 304; www.ohridsummer.com.mk) Features classical and opera concerts, theatre and dance.

Sveti Naum–Ohrid Swimming Marathon   SWIMMING
This 30km event is usually in August, and gets dozens of international competitors.

⮒ Sleeping

Private rooms or apartments (per person €5 to €10) are advertised by the sign '*sobi*' (rooms). Agencies also can book. Alternatively, good prices and central locations are offered by Apartmani Ohrid (www.apartmani-ohrid.com).

Avoid the touts waiting outside the bus station to pounce on arriving travellers.

TOP CHOICE ⮑ Vila Sveta Sofija   HOTEL €€
(☎254 370; www.vilasofija.com.mk; Kosta Abraš 64; s/d €40/65, ste €80-125; ❄@) This opulent getaway combines traditional furnishings with chic modern bathrooms in an old Ohrid mansion near Sveta Sofija.

Villa Lucija   GUESTHOUSE €€
(☎265 608; www.vilalucija.com.mk; Kosta Abraš 29; s/d/apt €20/30/50; ❄@) Lucija has Old Town ambience and lovingly decorated, breezy rooms with lake views.

Stefan Kanevče Rooms   RENTED ROOMS €
(☎234 813; apostolanet@yahoo.co.uk; Kočo Racin 47; per person €10) Atmospheric 19th-century house near Kaneo beach boasting carved wooden ceilings and good hospitality.

Hotel Millenium   HOTEL €€€
(☎263 361; www.milleniumpalace.com.mk; Kej Maršal Tito bb; s/d/ste/apt €49/70/99/149; ❄✿❄) Odd on the outside but nice inside, this southern hotel has business-class rooms, gym, sauna and indoor swimming pool with cocktail bar. Suites have lake-view terraces.

Mimi Apartments   APARTMENT €
(☎250 103; mimioh@mail.com.mk; Strašo Pinđur 2; r incl breakfast 800MKD) Spacious, centrally located private rooms with fridge.

Villa Forum   HOTEL €€
(☎251 340; www.villaforumohrid.com.mk; Kuzman Kapidan 1; s/d/apt €30/65/75; ❄@) This luxurious Gorna Porta hotel has well-furnished, comfortable rooms with sparkling bathrooms.

✗ Eating

Self-caterers have **Tinex supermarket** (bul Makedonski Prosvetiteli) and the **vegetable market** (Kliment Ohridski).

Ohrid's endemic trout is endangered and (supposedly) protected from fishing – order the equally tasty *mavrovska* and *kaliforniska* varieties instead.

TOP CHOICE Letna Bavča

Kaneo SEAFOOD €€
(Kočo Racin 43; fish 150-300MKD; ☉9am-11pm) This simple 'summer terrace' on Kaneo beach is inexpensive and great. A fry-up of diminutive *plasnica* fish, plus salad, feeds two. Swim from the restaurant's dock and soak up the sun.

TOP CHOICE Restaurant Antiko MACEDONIAN €€
(Car Samoil 30; mains 350-600MKD) In an old Ohrid mansion, the famous Antiko has great traditional ambience and pricey, but good, traditional dishes.

Restoran Belvedere SKARA €€
(Kej Maršal Tito 2; mains 300MKD) Try the excellent *skara* here, where outdoor tables extend under a leafy canopy.

Pizzeria Leonardo PIZZA €€
(Car Samoil 31; pizzas 200-350MKD) Ohrid's best pizza (it's popular with locals too).

Restoran Sveta Sofija MACEDONIAN €€€
(Car Samoil 88; mains 300-500MKD) This upscale restaurant opposite Sveta Sofija serves traditional fare and more than 100 Macedonian wines.

Drinking & Entertainment

TOP CHOICE Cuba Libre BAR
(Kosta Abraš; ☉10pm-4am) Perennially popular Old Town bar and club. After midnight in summer it is a standing-room-only party spilling out on the courtyard.

Aquarius CAFE
(Kosta Abraš bb; ☉10am-1am) Ohrid's original lake-terrace cafe, Aquarius remains cool for a midday coffee and is lively at night.

Liquid CAFE
(Kosta Abraš 17; ☉9am-1am) Hip and relaxed chill-out place with a lake-front patio.

Arena CLUB
(cnr Jane Sandanski & Karpoš Vojvoda; ☉10pm-4am) Sweaty, packed pop-and-rock nightclub, 1.5km from town.

Dom na Kultura EVENTS, CINEMA
(Grigor Prličev; admission 50-100MKD) Holds cultural events and houses Ohrid's movie theatre.

Shopping

Bisera JEWELLERY
(Sveti Kliment Ohridski 60; ☉9am-1pm & 6-10pm) From his little shop, friendly Vane Talev continues a family tradition started in 1924: making the unique Ohrid pearls. Prices range from 1500MKD for a simple piece to 36,000MKD for an elaborate necklace.

Information

Internet Café Inside (Amam Trgovski Centar, bul Makedonski Prosvetiteli; per hour 60MKD; ☉9am-1am) Located in a mall near Ploštad Sveti Kliment Ohridski.

Ohrid.com (www.ohrid.com.mk) Municipal website.

Post Office (bul Makedonski Prosvetiteli; ☉7am-8pm Mon-Sat) Also changes money.

Sunny Land Tourism (www.sunnylandtourism.com; Car Samoil, by the National Museum; ☉9am-7pm) Local expert Zoran Grozdanovski can find accommodation and arrange tours and activities.

Telephone Centre (bul Makedonski Prosvetiteli; ☉7am-8pm Mon-Sat) Round the corner from the post office.

Tina Tours (bul TuristIcka 66; ☉9am-6pm) Full-service central travel agency.

Tourist Bureau Biljana (www.beyondohrid.com; Car Samoil 38; ☉10am-midnight) Provides general info, accommodation and outdoor activities.

Getting There & Away

AIR Ohrid's **St Paul the Apostle Airport** (☎046 252 820; www.airports.com.mk), 10km north, handles summertime charter flights. Take a taxi (400MKD).

BUS From the **bus station** (7 Noemvri bb), 1.5km east of centre, buses serve Skopje, either via Kičevo (520MKD, three hours, 11 daily) or (the longer route) via Bitola; for Bitola itself, 10 daily buses run (200MKD, 1¼ hours). Buses to Struga (50MKD, 14km) leave every 30 minutes. In summer, reserve ahead for Skopje buses. Some *kombi* (minibuses) and taxis wait outside Tina Tours for intercity destinations.

International buses serve Belgrade (via Kičevo; 1800MKD, 15 hours, one daily). A 7pm bus serves Sofia (1450MKD, eight hours). For Albania, take a bus to Sveti Naum (110MKD, 29km). Cross the border and take a cab (€5, 6km) to Pogradeci. An Ohrid–Sveti Naum taxi costs 950MKD.

Around Ohrid

♪046

South of Ohrid, a long, wooded coast conceals pebble beaches, churches, villages and camping spots. In summer the big resort-style hotels and beaches are crowded and dirty (beyond them are better spots).

In summer, buses and *kombi* operate every 15 to 30 minutes until Gradište; further destinations such as Trpejca, Ljubaništa and Sveti Naum are served every hour or two.

◉ Sights & Activities

Beaches stretch down Ohrid's southern shore; unfortunately, in summer they're extremely overcrowded and unclean. Water clarity improves after overdeveloped **Peštani** (12km from Ohrid), which has an ATM and restaurants.

The wooded **Gradište camping ground**, 2km further, is popular with sunbathing students coming for beachside DJ parties at night. A fascinating **Neolithic Settlement Museum** here has artefacts from a 4000-year-old site where Ohrid's ancestors lived on stilt huts above the lake bed.

Trpejca　　　　　　　　　　VILLAGE
(Трпејца) Cupped between a sloping hill and tranquil bay, Ohrid's last traditional fishing village features clustered houses with terracotta roofs and a white-pebble beach. At night, the sounds of crickets and frogs are omnipresent.

Trpejca has limited services, though in midsummer its small beach gets very crowded. The superb waters offer excellent swimming, and forested Mt Galičica's just opposite.

From Trpejca, boats visit **Sveta Bogorodica Zahumska Church** (simply called Sveti Zaum), 2.5km south, on a wooded beach near the lake's deepest part (294m). Its unusual frescos date from 1361. Fishermen or Ohrid travel agencies organise trips.

Sveti Naum Monastery　　　MONASTERY
(Свети Наум) Sveti Naum is 29km south of Ohrid, before the border, above a sandy beach. Naum was a contemporary of St Kliment, and their monastery wasan educational centre. Naum's Church of the Holy Archangels (AD 900) became the 16th-century **Church of Sveti Naum**; this multidomed, Byzantine-style structure on a cliff, surrounded by roses and peacocks, boasts 16th- and 19th-century frescos.

Inside, drop an ear to the tomb of Sveti Naum to hear his muffled heartbeat. Outside, a wishing well collects spare denars. From the wall, lake views are excellent.

Sveti Naum has one of Ohrid's only sandy beaches, with good swimming and a hotel.

Galičica National Park　　NATIONAL PARK
The rippling, rock-crested Mt Galičica, over 200m in points, separates Lake Ohrid from Lake Prespa – a winding mountain road starting near the village of Trpejca connects the two lakes (at one point at the peak, you can see both lakes simultaneously). This national park comprises 228 sq km and features endemic plants and trees.

Try hiking or paragliding, which can be arranged by Ohrid tour operators.

🛏 Sleeping & Eating

Coastal accommodation and restaurants mostly open in summer only; private accommodation (per person 300 to 600MKD) is generally plentiful.

Hotel Sveti Naum　　　　HOTEL €€€
(☑283 080; www.hotel-stnaum.com.mk; Sveti Naum; s/d/ste from €37/74/116; ✳@) Fancy hotel with restaurant and luxurious, if dated, rooms. Lake-view rooms are €20 extra.

Vila De Niro　　　RENTED ROOMS €€
(☑070 212 518; d/apt €25/50; ✳@) Trpejca's only modern place, this yellow mansion is located where the walkway downhill diverges. It offers three doubles and an en suite apartment.

Camping Ljubaništa　　CAMPGROUND €
(☑283 240; per tent 800MKD; ⊙May-Oct) On a sandy beach, 27km from Ohrid. Good place for families and solitude-seekers, though facilities are dated.

Restoran Ribar　　　　SEAFOOD €€
(fish per person 300-750MKD; ⊙10am-midnight) Right on Trpejca's waterfront, Ribar serves local fish, meat and coffee.

❶ Getting There & Away

Frequent buses and *kombi* ply the Ohrid–Sveti Naum route in summer until Gradište. Services are less frequent to Trpejca, Ljubaništa and Sveti Naum. In Ohrid, wait for *kombi* by Tina Tours, opposite Ohridska Banka. These operate in summer until 2am.

Taxis are expensive; however, during summer some charge bus-ticket rates when filling up fast (check with the driver).

Boat tours from Ohrid to Sveti Naum (350MKD return) are regular in summer. Rates for village boat trips vary.

CENTRAL MACEDONIA

Macedonia's diverse central region is a wild, unexplored area flush with mountains, canyons, vineyards and caves. It also offers culture and significant historical sites.

Bitola · Битола

⏱ 047 / POP 95,400

With elegant buildings and beautiful people, elevated Bitola (660m) has a sophistication inherited from its Ottoman days as the 'City of Consuls'. Its 18th- and 19th-century colourful townhouses, Turkish mosques and cafe culture make it Macedonia's most intriguing and liveable major town. An essential experience is sipping a coffee and people-watching along the pedestrianised Širok Sokak ('Wide Street' in Turkish – still called ul Maršal Tito officially).

⊙ Sights & Activities

Širok Sokak STREET
(ul Maršal Tito) Bitola's Širok Sokak is the city's most representative and stylish street, with its multicoloured facades and European honorary consulates attesting to the city's Ottoman-era sophistication. Enjoying the cafe life here as the beautiful people promenade past is an essential Bitola experience.

Church of Sveti Dimitrija CHURCH
(11 Oktomvri bb; ⊙7am-6pm) This Orthodox church (1830) has rich frescos, ornate lamps and a huge iconostasis.

Mosques MOSQUES
Bitola's 16th-century **Yeni, Isak** and **Yahdar-Kadi Mosques**, all between the Dragor River and the Stara Čaršija (Old Bazaar), are Ottoman remnants, as is the enormous **Clock Tower** (Saat Kula).

Stara Čaršija BAZAAR
The Stara Čaršija boasted around 3000 clustered artisans' shops in Ottoman times; today, only about 70 different trades are conducted, but it's still worth a peek.

✨ Festivals & Events

The **Bit Fest** (⊙Jun-Aug) features concerts, literary readings and art exhibits. The **Ilinden Festival** (⊙2 Aug), honouring the Ilinden Uprising of 1903, is celebrated with food and music.

The **Manaki Brothers Film Festival** (www.manaki.com.mk; ⊙late Sep–early Oct) screens independent foreign films. It honours Milton and Ianachia Manaki, the Balkans' first film-makers (1905). The Inter Fest features classical-music performances in the cultural centre and Bitola Museum.

🛏 Sleeping & Eating

TOP CHOICE **Chola Guest House** GUESTHOUSE €
(⏱ 224 919; www.chola.mk; Stiv Naumov 80; s/d €12/20; ☎) Quiet place in an old mansion with clean, well-kept and pretty rooms and colourful modern bathrooms. Ask the taxi driver for Video Club Dju (opposite Chola).

Hotel De Niro HOTEL €€
(⏱ 229 656; www.hotel-deniro.com; Kiril i Metodij 5; s/d/ste from €25/50/80; ☀☎) Central yet discreet with lovely old-Bitola-style rooms (more expensive suites also have waterbeds and spas). There's an excellent pizza-and-pasta restaurant (mains 200MKD to 450MKD) attached.

Via Apartments APARTMENTS €
(⏱ 075 246 261; www.via.mk; Elpida Karamandi 4; s/d €12/24; ☀☎) These clean, well-designed central apartments share a kitchen, laundry, lounge and patio.

Hotel Rustiko HOTEL €
(⏱ 227 712; www.hotelrustiko.com.mk; s/d/ste €17/28/33) Opened in 2012, the Rustiko has fresh and well-maintained rooms in a quiet location. Breakfast (€2) is served in the onsite restaurant – tasty, but not particularly rustic.

Hotel Milenium HOTEL €€
(⏱ 241 001; h.milenium@t-home.mk; Marsal Tito 48; s/d/ste/apt €39/66/80/99; ☀☎) Atriums with stained glass, smooth marble opulence and historic relics channel old Bitola. The spacious rooms have sparkling bathrooms. Great value, and right on the Širok Sokak.

Hotel Epinal HOTEL €€
(⏱ 224 777; www.hotelepinal.com; Maršal Tito bb; s/d €49/69; P☀☎🏊) The big Epinal is old but quite nice – especially with its pool, spa and gym.

Premier Centar HOTEL €€
(⏱ 202 070; www.centar.premier.com.mk; Stiv Naumov 12; s/d/tr incl breakfast 1540/2580/3420

WORTH A TRIP

HERACLEA LYNCESTIS

Heraclea Lyncestis (admission 100MKD, photos 500MKD; ⊘9am-3pm winter, to 5pm summer), 1km south of Bitola (70MKD by taxi), is among Macedonia's best archaeological sites. Founded by Philip II of Macedon, Heraclea became commercially significant before Romans conquered (168 BC) and its position on the Via Egnatia kept it prosperous. In the 4th century Heraclea became an episcopal seat, but it was sacked by Goths and then Slavs.

See the Roman baths, portico and amphitheatre, and the striking Early Christian basilica and episcopal palace ruins, with beautiful, well-preserved floor mosaics. They're unique in depicting endemic trees and animals. Excavations continue, so you may see newer discoveries.

MKD; ✱🅿🛜) Set in a renovated period house on a residential street, it has 19 modern rooms (and one apartment) and a banquet-hall restaurant that's good for groups.

TOP CHOICE El Greko PIZZA €
(☑071 279 848; cnr Maršal Tito & Elipda Karamandi; mains 180-350MKD; ⊘10am-1am) This Sokak taverna and pizzeria has great beer-hall ambience and is popular with locals. At the time of research it was planning to also offer budget rooms.

🍷 Drinking & Entertainment

TOP CHOICE Porta Jazz BAR
(Kiril i Metodija; ⊘8am-midnight) Popular, funky place that's packed when live jazz and blues bands play. It's located near the Centar na Kultura.

Basa BAR
(⊘10pm-2am) This dark-lit bar on a side street off ul Leninova, behind Centar na Kultura, plays house music and local and Western pop.

Nightclub Rasčekor CLUB
(⊘10pm-4am) The slick Rasčekor, near the train station, is probably the town's poshest option, with leading DJs and dressed-up local partiers.

City Club CLUB
(Pelagonka 2) Relaxed nightclub popular with students.

Positive Summer Club CLUB
(City Park; ⊘9am-2am) Located by the city stadium and park, Positive is popular with locals for its swimming pool by day and open-air club by night.

ℹ Information

Širok Sokak has free wi-fi.

Baloyannis Tours (☑075 207 273, 220 204; Solunska 118; ⊘8am-6pm Mon-Sat) Provides city tours and outdoors trips (book ahead).

Tourist Information Centre (bitola-tourist-info@t-home.mk; Sterio Georgiev 1; ⊘9am-6pm Mon-Sat) Friendly info centre.

ℹ Getting There & Away

The **bus** and **train stations** (Nikola Tesla) are adjacent, 1km south of the centre. Buses serve Skopje (470MKD, 3½ hours, 12 daily) via Prilep (130MKD, one hour), Kavadarci (280MKD, two hours, five daily), Strumica (460MKD, four hours, two daily) and Ohrid (210MKD, 1¼ hours, 10 daily).

For Greece, go by taxi to the border (500MKD) and then find a cab to Florina. Some Bitola cab drivers will do the whole trip for about 3000MKD.

Three daily trains serve Skopje (210MKD) via Prilep (66MKD) and Veles (154MKD).

Pelister National Park

Macedonia's oldest national park (1948) covers 125 sq km on its third-highest mountain range, the quartz-filled Baba massif. Eight peaks top 2000m, crowned by Mt Pelister (2601m). Two glacial lakes, Pelisterski Oči (Pelister's Eyes), provide chilly refreshment.

Pelister's 88 tree species include the rare five-leafed Molika pine. It also hosts endemic Pelagonia trout, deer, wolves, chamois, wild boars, bears and eagles.

DIHOVO ДИХОВО

Only 5km from Bitola, the 830m-high mountainside hamlet of Dihovo is a base for Pelister hikes, with appealing stone houses and the icon-rich **Church of Sveti Dimitrije** (1830). Dihovo's **outdoor swimming pool** is basically a very large basin containing ice-cold mountain-spring waters, rushing from the boulder-filled Sapungica River.

For summer hiking trips or winter skiing, see Petar Cvetkovski of Villa Dihovo. From Bitola, a taxi costs 150MKD.

🛏 Sleeping & Eating

TOP CHOICE **Villa Dihovo** GUESTHOUSE €€
(☑070 544 744; www.villadihovo.com; rates negotiable; 🅿🛜) One of Macedonia's most remarkable guesthouses, Villa Dihovo comprises three traditionally decorated rooms in the 80-year-old home of Petar Cvetkovski and family, inside the first long driveway after Dihovo centre's restaurant. Its big flowering lawn is great for kids. The only fixed prices are for the homemade wine, beer and *rakija* (firewater); all else, room price included, is your choice.

Villa Patrice RENTED ROOMS €€
(☑075 466 878; s/d 900/1440MKD) Friendly family-run place with spacious, well-maintained rooms. A five-minute walk from the centre off the road towards the pool.

Restoran Idela SKARA €€
(mains 250-400MKD; ⊙6am-midnight) Idela has a hunting-lodge feel and does great *skara*.

Prilep   Прилеп

☑048 / POP 76,800

A hard-working, dusty, tobacco town, Prilep sits along the Pelagonian Plain, surrounded by weird, jagged-rock formations. It has some decent eating and drinking options along its smart new square, thronged by locals in the evening.

◎ Sights & Activities

Prilep's marketplace, the **Čaršija**, houses artisans' shops and is, along with the nearby **Clock Tower**, a relic of Ottoman times. Prilep's well-kept centre – flush with squares, fountains, statues (and a duck pond) – has become a national example. There's a robust cafe and bar scene, with live bands playing outdoors in summer.

The **theatre festival** (⊙Jun–Jul) has performances at the Dom na Kultura. The popular midsummer **Prilep beer festival** attracts thousands for prodigious consumption of beer and *skara* while being serenaded by well-known Balkan musical acts.

Some 2km from town, **King Marko's Towers** (Markovi Kuli) rise from a sharp cliff. Fortified since ancient times, this unique defensive position offers great views. It was famously commanded by King Marko (r 1371–95), a semiautonomous despot under the Turks, who ruled into today's northern Greece. Killed in battle while conscripted by Turks, King Marko is commemorated in Macedonian (and Serbian) folk songs, which celebrate his superhuman strength.

🛏 Sleeping

Hotel Sonce HOTEL €€
(☑401 800; www.makedonskosonce.com; Aleksandar Makedonski 4/3a; r incl breakfast 1240-2480MKD; 🅿❄🛜🏊) Decent rooms and restaurant, and a small outdoor swimming pool.

Hotel Crystal Palace HOTEL €€€
(☑418 000; www.kp.mk; Leninova 184; s/d/tr €35/59/83; 🅿❄🛜) Near the train station, Prilep's four-star institution has well-appointed rooms.

✗ Eating & Drinking

Pizzeria Leone PIZZA €€
(Goce Delcev 30; pizza 200-350MKD; ⊙11am-midnight) This central place does great pizzas.

Porta Club Restaurant RESTAURANT €€
(Republikanska 84; mains 300-450MKD; ⊙10am-midnight) A spacious, well-lit bistro, Porta Club does fancy grills and fish.

Virus BAR
(Borka Taleski bb) With weathered wooden stairs, ornate print wallpaper, old paintings and little balcony tables, Virus has character and sometimes live rock bands.

❶ Getting There & Away

From Prilep's **bus station** (Sotka Gorgioski) buses serve Skopje (380MKD) via Negotino and Veles, and Kavadarci (190MKD, 1½ hours, two daily). Buses head south to Bitola (130MKD, 10 daily), and some continue to Ohrid (360MKD).

Prilep is on the Bitola–Skopje train line (three daily trains).

Around Prilep

About 10km from Prilep, 13th-century **Treskavec Monastery** (Манастир Тресkавец) rises from Mt Zlato (1422m), a bare massif replete with twisted rock formations. Its frescos, including a rare depiction of Christ as a boy, line the 14th-century **Church of Sveta Bogorodica**, built over a 6th-century basilica. Earlier Roman remains are inside, along with graves, inscriptions and monks' skulls.

A paved road is being built, but a 4WD is best for the final rocky kilometres. Start from Prilep's cemetery and turn uphill at the sign marked 'Manastir Sveta Bogorodica, Treskavec'. Alternatively, to hike up, first drive or take a taxi to Dabnica, and then follow the cobbled track towards Mt Zlato; after the fountain, a path reaches Treskavec (two hours total; 4.5km).

Some 26km northwest of Prilep, towards Makedonski Brod, the 14th-century **Zrze Monastery** (Манастир Зрзе; ☑048 459 400; Manastir Sveto Preobrazhenije-Zrze; ☉8am-5pm) of the Holy Transfiguration rises like a revelation from a clifftop. The monastery's tranquil position around a spacious lawn, with views over the outstretched Pelagonian Plain, is stunning. At dawn, a low-lying fog sometimes shrouds the plain in marble.

During Ottoman times, Zrze underwent periods of abandonment, rebuilding and plunder but remained an important spiritual centre. Its 17th-century **Church of Saints Peter and Paul** contains important frescoes and icons.

At time of research, Zrze was planning accommodation. Visitors can enjoy coffee with the kind monks and a tour of the church, with its priceless frescos and icons. While today the museum in Skopje houses Zrze's most famous icon, the Holy Mother of God Pelagonitsa (1422), a large copy remains in the church.

On the adjacent hillside, excavations continue on Zrze's precursor: a 5th-century basilica.

Take the road towards Makedonski Brod and turn at Ropotovo village; several villages lie between it and the monastery (take the left-hand turn at Kostinci). Zrze is infrequently signposted. The dirt roads are well built but worsen at nearly deserted Zrze village, beneath the mountain. From here, walk 2km uphill to the monastery, or drive it with a 4WD vehicle.

Tikveš Wine Region

Macedonia's winery heartland, Tikveš, has produced wine since the 4th century BC. It features rolling vineyards, lakes, caves and mountains, plus archaeological sites and churches. It's especially beautiful at dusk, when the fading sunlight suffuses soft hills laden with millions of grapes. Tikveš' local grapes generally retain an ideal sugar concentration (17% to 26%).

Travel agencies arrange tastings; alternatively, prearrange with the wineries.

KAVADARCI КАВАДАРЦИ
☑043 / POP 38,700

West of the road and rail hub of Negotino, Kavadarci is fittingly dusty and agricultural, though it is improving its services. Attractions include wine tastings, monasteries, museums and Lake Tikveš, good for boating and birdwatching.

◉ Sights & Activities

FREE **Kavadarci Museum** MUSEUM
(7 Septembri 58; ☉8.30am-4.30pm Mon-Sat) Has ancient finds, some depicting wine bacchanalia.

Tikveš Winery WINERY
(☑414 304; www.tikves.com.mk; 29 Noemvri 5; ☉10am-5pm) Southeastern Europe's biggest winery (established 1885) offers tours and tastings of some of their 29 wines.

Vinoteka David WINERY
(cnr Cano Pop Ristov & Ilindenska; ☉8am-1pm & 5-7pm) This central winery offers regional wines.

✯ Festivals & Events

Kavadarci Wine Carnival WINE FESTIVAL
Costumed parade, public wine tasting and merrymaking from 5 to 7 September.

⌂ Sleeping & Eating

Hotel Uni Palas HOTEL €€
(☑419 600; Edvard Kardelj bb; s/d incl breakfast €36/56; ❄@) Comfortable, modern hotel by the bus station with well-appointed rooms, hydro-massage showers, and a popular cafe; a second location has similar rooms, but is less central.

Restoran Exclusive MACEDONIAN €€
(bul Makedonija 66; mains 250-450MKD; ☉9am-midnight) Kavadarci's best wine restaurant serves Macedonian and international dishes.

❶ Getting There & Away

From Kavadarci, buses serve Skopje (250MKD, seven daily), Prilep (190MKD, one hour, two daily) and Bitola (280MKD, five daily). For

OTHER WINERIES

Other wineries worth a visit include the following:

Bovin Winery (☏043 365 322; www.bovin.com.mk; Industriska bb; ⊘10am-5pm) Award-winning winery in Negotino. Tours include extensive tastings.

Elenov Winery (☏043 367 232; vinarija_elenov@t-home.com.mk; Ivo Lola Ribar bb) Elenov is at the southeastern edge of the wine region, by the magnificent **Demir Kapija Gorge**. It's visible on the western side of the north–south E75 highway. Dating from 1928, it was Serbian king Aleksandar's official wine cellar, and it organises tastings.

Popova Kula Winery (☏023 228 781; d/ste €60/120) In Demir Kapija, up an 800m dirt road past the cemetery, is possibly Macedonia's most aesthetically pleasing winery, with great views over vineyards and the gorge from a traditionally decorated tasting room. For overnights, call ahead to book one of the modern rooms.

Disan Hills Winery (☏070 384 325, 043 362 520; ristov@mt.net.mk) In the village of Dolni Disan, 5km south of Negotino, Disan Hills is set amid vineyards and is run by people who put heart and soul into crafting limited quantities of high-quality wine. Tastings can be arranged.

Negotino, use local buses (30MKD, 15 minutes, six daily) or take a taxi (200MKD).

AROUND KAVADARCI

Three kilometres southwest of Kavadarci, past **Vataša**, the **Monastery of Sveti Nikola** sits alongside a forested river and displays rare 16th-century frescos.

Created in 1968 by damming the Crna River, nearby **Lake Tikveš** is surrounded by scrubland and stark cliffs, dotted with medieval hermitage frescos and circled by eagles and hawks. Being artificial, it has no endemic species, though it seems the monster catfish – weighing up to 200kg – has become pretty territorial since Comrade Tito first dispatched them into the 100m depths.

The 32km-long lake lies 11km southwest of Kavadarci; turn south at **Vozarci** to reach the small beach.

To arrange half-day **boat trips** with skippers and an English-speaking guide, check in Kavadarci at the Hotel Uni Palas (p536) or the local municipality building. Some Skopje travel agencies also arrange tours. Large groups use the 40-seater boat (4000MKD per group) while small groups use a regular fishermen's caique (1800MKD).

The tour navigates the lake's widest stretches for 20km, visiting the 14th-century **Pološki Monastery** (Polog Monastery), inhabited by a single nun. The monastery's **Church of Sveti Gjiorgji** was built by Serbian emperor Stefan Dušan (r 1331–55), and

features expressive frescos of saints and the emperor.

Ringed by rugged cliffs, the lake offers **birdwatching** (look for the royal eagle, bearded vulture and white Egyptian vulture). Sometimes **fishing** is possible, though reeling in the obese catfish from the muddy depths might require a hydraulic lift. You can try **swimming**, but be mindful of the strong currents, steep drop-offs and rocks near the shore.

Stobi

The ruins of Roman **Stobi** (Стоби; www.stobi.mk; admission 100MKD; ⊘9am-5pm) occupy a valley beside the E75 highway, 9km northwest of Negotino. Discovered in 1861, Stobi's major ruins are signposted. A gift shop by the snack bar sells replicas and wines.

Established in the 7th century BC, Stobi grew under the Macedonians and Romans. Its ancient Jewish population is indicated by synagogue foundations, beneath Christian basilica remains.

Although important as a Byzantine archbishopric, Stobi was sacked by Goths in 479 and further doomed by an earthquake in 518.

Start at the Roman amphitheatre (on the left) and clamber up further for Stobi's best mosaics. The path continues past well-marked ruins, including ancient sanctuaries to gods. At the end, turn right to the enormous city walls. Excavations continue.

UNDERSTAND MACEDONIA

History

Historical or geographical Macedonia is divided between the Republic of Macedonia (38%), Greek Macedonia (51%) and Bulgaria's Pirin Macedonia (11%). For its people, their history is a source of great pride but also a heavy burden. The post-Yugoslav experience has seen existential pressure from neighbours constantly challenging the Macedonian identity. Macedonia's history is too complex for simple answers, but many have strong opinions.

Ancient Macedonians & Romans

The powerful Macedonian dynasty of King Philip II (r 359–336 BC) dominated the Greek city-states. Philip's son, Alexander the Great, spread Macedonian might to India. After his death (323 BC), the empire dissolved amid infighting. In 168 BC, Rome conquered Macedonia; its position on the Via Egnatia, from Byzantium to the Adriatic, and the Axios (Vardar River) from Thessaloniki up the Vardar Valley, kept cities prosperous.

Christianity reached Macedonia with the Apostle Paul. The Roman Empire's 395 AD division brought Macedonia under Byzantine Constantinople and Greek-influenced Orthodox Christianity.

The Coming of the Slavs & the Macedonian Cars

The 7th-century Slavic migrations intermingled Macedonia's peoples. In 862, two Thessaloniki-born monks, St Cyril and St Methodius, were dispatched to spread orthodoxy and literacy among Moravia's Slavs (in modern-day Czech Republic). Their disciple, St Kliment of Ohrid, helped create the Cyrillic alphabet. With St Naum, he propagated literacy in Ohrid (the first Slavic university).

Byzantium and the Slavs could share a religion, but not political power. Chronic wars unfolded between Constantinople and the expansionist Bulgarian state of Car Simeon (r 893–927) and Car Samoil (r 997–1014). After being defeated in today's Bulgaria, Prespa and Ohrid in Macedonia became their strongholds. Finally, Byzantine Emperor Basil II defeated Samoil at the Battle of Belasica (near today's Strumica, in eastern Macedonia) in 1014, and Byzantium retook Macedonia.

Later, the Serbian Nemanjid dynasty expanded into Macedonia. After Emperor Stefan Dušan (r 1331–55) died, Serbian power waned. The Ottoman Turks soon arrived, ruling until 1913.

Ottoman Rule & the Macedonian Question

The Ottomans introduced Islam and Turkish settlers. Skopje became a trade centre, and beautiful mosques, *hammams* (Turkish baths) and castles were built. However, Greeks still wielded considerable power. In 1767, Greek intriguing caused the abolition of the 700-year-old Ohrid archbishopric. Greek priests opened schools and built churches, to the resentment of locals. Bulgaria and Serbia also sought Macedonia. The lines were drawn.

In Macedonia, Western European ethnic nationalism collided with the Ottomans' civil organisation by religion (not ethnicity). Europe's powers intervened after the 1877–78 Russo-Turkish War, when the Treaty of San Stefano awarded Macedonia to Bulgaria. Fearing Russia, Western powers reversed this with the Treaty of Berlin, fuelling 40 years of further conflict.

Although Macedonia remained Ottoman, the 'Macedonian Question' persisted. Various Balkan powers sponsored revolutionary groups. In 1893, the Internal Macedonian Revolutionary Organisation (Vnatrešna Makedonska Revolucionerna Organizacija, or VMRO) formed. VMRO was divided between 'Macedonia for the Macedonians' propagandists and a pro-Bulgarian wing.

In the St Elijah's Day (Ilinden) Uprising (2 August 1903), Macedonian revolutionaries declared the Balkans' first democratic republic, in Kruševo; the Turks swiftly crushed it. Although leader Goce Delčev had died months earlier, he's considered Macedonia's national hero.

In 1912 the Balkan League (Greece, Serbia, Bulgaria and Montenegro) fought Turkey (the First Balkan War), with Macedonia a prime battleground. The Turks were expelled, but a dissatisfied Bulgaria turned on its allies in 1913 (the Second Balkan War). Defeated, Bulgaria allied with Germany in WWI, reoccupying Macedonia and prolonging local suffering.

The Yugoslav Experience

When Bulgaria withdrew after WWI, Macedonia was divided between Greece and the new Kingdom of Serbs, Croats and Slovenes (Royalist Yugoslavia). Belgrade banned the Macedonian name and language, and disgruntled VMRO elements helped Croat nationalists assassinate Serbian King Aleksandar in 1934.

During WWII, Josip Broz Tito's Partisans resisted the Bulgarian–German occupation. Tito promised Macedonians republican status within communist Yugoslavia but was disinterested in their aspirations; Partisans seeking to fight for Greek-controlled Macedonia were shot as an example to the others. Nevertheless, in the 1946–49 Greek Civil War, some ethnic Macedonians joined the communists fighting Royalists. The communist defeat forced thousands, including many children (known as the *begalci*, meaning 'refugees'), to flee Greece.

Tito's nationalisation of property and industry ruined villages, with farmers deprived of flocks. Concrete communist monstrosities sheltered a newly urbanised population. Nevertheless, some nation-building overtures were made, such as a Macedonian grammar in 1952 and the Macedonian Orthodox Church's creation in 1967 – the 200th anniversary of the Ohrid archbishopric's abolition.

Macedonia after Independence

In a 1991 referendum, 74% of Macedonians voted to secede becoming the only Yugoslav republic to do so peacefully. However, the withdrawing Yugoslav army took everything, leaving the country defenceless. Greece's fears of an invasion from the north thus seemed farcical to everyone but them; nevertheless Macedonia changed its first flag (with the ancient Macedonian Vergina star) to appease Athens, after it had already accepted a 'provisional' name, the Former Yugoslav Republic of Macedonia (FYROM) to join the UN in 1993. When the USA (following six EU countries) recognised 'FYROM' in 1994, Greece defiantly announced an economic embargo.

This crippling embargo coincided with wars in other former Yugoslav states, creating ideal conditions for high-level schemes for smuggling fuel and other goods. This 1990s 'transition' period created a political/business oligarchy amid shady privatisations, deliberate bankrupting of state-owned firms and dubious pyramid schemes.

Worse, Macedonia's ethnic Albanians understood the Kosovo crisis as a template for addressing their own grievances. During the 1999 NATO bombing of Serbia, Macedonia sheltered more than 400,000 Kosovo Albanian refugees. Nevertheless, diaspora Albanians (using Kosovo as a staging ground) created the Ushtria Člirimtare Kombetare (UČK; National Liberation Army; NLA). In Macedonia's ensuing 2001 conflict, the NLA were first denounced as 'terrorists' by NATO and various world powers, but were turned into a political party with Western backing after the war. The conflict-ending Ohrid Framework Agreement granted minority language and national symbol rights, along with quota-based public-sector hiring.

Macedonians found the conflict a humiliating defeat. Albanians saw it as the first step to a full ethnic federation. Foreign powers have argued that this may well occur, if Macedonia cannot join NATO and the EU.

Towards Europe?

Despite four successive recommendations by the European Commission, Macedonia in December 2012 was still blocked by Greece from starting EU accession negotiations.

With ethnic Albanian nationalism rising and a Bulgarian government threatening to veto Macedonia's EU ambitions too, Macedonia has felt increasingly alienated. Well aware of this, Turkey has become Macedonia's best regional ally. The shared history, political goodwill and significant Turkish investments have greatly increased Ankara's prominence here in recent years. Macedonia's future will likely see a return to the past mixture of East and West – which may be best for everyone.

People

The 2011 census was delayed indefinitely over ethnic Albanian complaints of unfairness. A true population figure may never be achievable, considering that many Macedonian citizens live abroad.

In 2004, the population of 2,022,547 was divided thus: Macedonians (66.6%), Albanians (22.7%), Turks (4%), Roma (2.2%), Serbs (2.1%) and others (2.4%), including Vlachs – alleged descendants of Roman frontier soldiers.

Religion

Most Macedonians are Orthodox Christians, with some Macedonian-speaking Muslims (the Torbeši and Gorani). Turks are Muslim, like Albanians and (nominally, at least) the impoverished Roma. In recent years, social and ethnic complexities relating to religion have caused concern over Islamic fundamentalism, as seen in protests and violent attacks on Christians.

A 200-strong Jewish community descends from Sephardic Jews who fled Spain after 1492. Sadly, 98% of their ancestors (more than 7200 people) were deported to Treblinkal by Bulgarian occupiers in WWII. The community holds a Holocaust commemoration ceremony every 11 March.

The Macedonian Orthodox Church isn't recognised by some neighbouring Orthodox countries, but it's active in church-building and restoration work. Although Macedonians don't attend church services often, they do stop to light candles, kiss icons and pray.

Arts

Macedonian folk instruments include the *gajda* (a single-bag bagpipe) and *zurla* (a double-reed horn) often accompanied by the *tapan* drum. Other instruments include the *kaval* (flute) and *tambura* (small lute with two pairs of strings). The *Čalgija* music form, involving clarinet, violin, *darabuk* (hourglass-shaped drum) and *đoumbuš* (banjolike instrument) is representative. Macedonian music employs the 7/8 time signature.

Traditional dancing includes the *oro* circle dance, the male-only *Teškoto oro* ('difficult dance'), *Komitsko oro* (symbolising the anti-Turkish struggle), and the *Tresenica* for women.

The **Ministry of Culture** (www.culture. in.mk) lists performance dates and venues. Folk-dance ensemble **Tanec** (☑2461 021; www.tanec.com.mk; Vinjamin Macukovski 7) tours worldwide.

Many Macedonian musicians have won international acclaim, including pianist Simon Trpčevski, opera singer Boris Trajanov, jazz guitarist Vladimir Četkar and percussionists the Tavitjan Brothers. Especially beloved is Toše Proeski, a charismatic singer admired for both his music and his humanitarian work. Proeski died tragically in 2007, aged just 26.

Environment

The Continental and Mediterranean climate zones converge in Macedonia (25,713 sq km). Although mostly plateau (600m to 900m above sea level), it features more than 50 mountain peaks topping 2500m. The Vardar River starts in the west, passes Skopje and runs into Greece's Aegean Sea. Lakes Ohrid and Prespa are among Europe's oldest tectonic lakes (three million years old); at 300m, Ohrid is the Balkans' deepest. International borders are largely mountainous, including Šar Planina, near Kosovo in the northwest; Mt Belasica, in the southeast, bordering Greece; and the Osogovski and Maleševski ranges near Bulgaria. Macedonia's highest peak, Mt Korab (Golem Korab; 2764m), borders Albania in the Mavrovo National Park.

Wildlife

Macedonia's eastern Mediterranean and Euro-Siberian vegetation contains pine-clad slopes. Lower mountains feature beech and oak. Vineyards dominate the central plains. Endemic fauna includes the *molika* tree, a subalpine pine unique to Mt Pelister, and the rare *foja* tree on Lake Prespa's Golem Grad island.

Macedonia's alpine and low Mediterranean valley zones have bears, wild boars, wolves, foxes, chamois and deer. The rare lynx inhabits Šar Planina and Jasen Nature Reserve. Blackcaps, grouse, white Egyptian vultures, royal eagles and forest owls inhabit woodlands. Lake birds include Dalmatian pelicans, herons and cormorants. Storks (and their huge nests) are prominent. Macedonia's national dog, the *šar planinec*, is a 60cm-tall sheepdog that bravely fights bears and wolves.

Lakes Ohrid, Prespa and Dojran are separate fauna zones, due to territorial and temporal isolation. With 146 endemic species, Ohrid is a living fossil-age museum – its endemic trout predates the last Ice Age. Ohrid also has whitefish, gudgeon and roach, plus a 30-million-year-old snail genus, and the mysterious Ohrid eel, which arrives from the Sargasso Sea to live for 10 years before returning to breed and die.

National Parks

Pelister (near Bitola) and Galičica (between Lakes Ohrid and Prespa) national parks are in a tri-border protected area involving Albania and Greece. Mavrovo (between Debar and Tetovo) offers great hiking in summer and skiing in winter. All parks are accessible by road and free.

Environmental Issues

Lake Ohrid's endemic trout is an endangered species. Do the right thing and choose from three other tasty and cheaper varieties (*mavrovska*, *kaliforniska* or *rekna*) instead.

Food & Drink

Macedonia's specialities are part Ottoman, part Central European. *Lutenica* is a hot-pepper-and-tomato sauce. The national salad, *šopska salata*, features tomatoes and cucumbers topped with *sirenje* (white cheese). *Čorba* (soup) and *tavče gravče* (oven-cooked white beans) are other specialities.

Skara (grilled meat) includes spare ribs, beef *kebapci* (kebabs) and *uviač* (rolled chicken or pork stuffed with yellow cheese). 'International' cuisine is also widespread.

For breakfast, try *burek* (cheese, spinach or minced meat in filo pastry) accompanied by drinking yoghurt or *kiselo mleko* ('sour milk', like yoghurt).

Bitter Skopsko Pivo is Macedonia's leading beer. The national firewater, *rakija*, is a strong grape spirit, delicious served hot with sugar in winter. *Mastika*, like ouzo, is also popular, as are homemade brandies made from cherries and plums.

SURVIVAL GUIDE

Directory A–Z

Accommodation

Skopje hotels are expensive; agencies find private rooms. Ohrid and villages have budget and midrange choices; book ahead for July and August, Orthodox Christmas (7 January), Orthodox Easter and during festivals or carnivals.

Prices quoted here are for rooms with a private bathroom unless otherwise stated.

The following price indicators apply (for a high-season double room):

€ less than 3000MKD/€50

€€ 3000MKD/€50 to 5000MKD/€80

€€€ more than 5000MKD/€80

Activities

Outdoor activities are endless. For skiing try Mavrovo's Zare Lazarevski. Mavrovo, Galičica and Pelister National Parks and Jasen Nature Reserve (www.jasen.com.mk) have great hiking and wildlife.

Enjoy wooded walks, boating and caving at Lake Matka, or swimming and boating at Lake Ohrid. Birdwatch on Lakes Prespa and Tikveš and paraglide on Mt Galičica.

Skopje, Ohrid and Bitola travel agencies run outdoors tours. Mountaineering association Korab Mountain Club (www.korab.org.mk/indexen.html) details mountain routes.

Macedonia is chronically affected by summer wildfires. Hikers should check conditions in advance – if you get stuck in the wrong patch of forest, not only could it be dangerous, it could also be illegal, if firemen or park wardens have closed the area.

Business Hours

Banks 7am to 5pm Monday to Friday

Businesses 8am to 8pm Monday to Friday, to 2pm Saturday

Cafes 10am to midnight

Post offices 6.30am to 8pm

Embassies & Consulates

All offices are in Skopje.

Australian Consulate (☑3061 114; www.serbia.embassy.gov.au/bgde/home.html; Londonska 11b)

Canadian Embassy (☑3225 630; www.canadianembassyinformation.com/embassy-in/republic-of-macedonia.html; bul Partizanski Odredi 17a)

French Embassy (☑3118 749; www.ambafrance-mk.org; Salvador Aljende 73)

German Embassy (☑3093 900; www.skopje.diplo.de/Vertretung/skopje/mk/Startseite.html; Lerinska 59)

Netherlands Embassy (☑023 129 319; www.nlembassy.org.mk; Leninova 69-71)

Russian Embassy (☑023 117 160; www.russia.org.mk; Pirinska 44)

UK Embassy (☑3299 299; www.ukinmacedonia.fco.gov.uk/en; Dimitrie Čupovski 26)

US Embassy (☑3102 000; http://macedonia.usembassy.gov; Samoilova bb)

Food

The following prices are for a main meal:

€ less than 150MKD

€€ 150MKD to 300MKD

€€€ more than 300MKD

Money

Macedonian denars (MKD) come in 10-, 50-, 100-, 500-, 1000- and 5000-denar notes, and one-, two-, five-, 10- and 50- denar coins. Taxi drivers hate it when you pay with a 1000-denar note, and may make you go into a shop to make change. Euros are generally accepted – some hotels quote euro rates, but denar payment is OK.

Macedonian *menuvačnici* (exchange offices) work commission-free. ATMs are widespread, except in villages, and using them is a good idea, considering that credit card fraud occasionally occurs. Avoid travellers cheques.

Post

Mail to Europe and North America takes seven to 10 days. *Preporačeno* (certified mail) is more expensive – fill out and keep the small green form. Letters to the USA cost 38MKD, to Australia 40MKD and to Europe 35MKD. Global-brand shipping companies operate.

Public Holidays

New Year's Day 1 January

Orthodox Christmas 7 January

Orthodox Easter Week March/April

Labour Day 1 May

Saints Cyril and Methodius Day 24 May

Ilinden Day 2 August

Republic Day 8 September

1941 Partisan Day 11 October

Safe Travel

The all-pervasive fear of a *promaja* (draft), which causes otherwise sane Macedonians to compulsively shut bus windows on swelteringly hot days, is undoubtedly the most incomprehensible and aggravating thing foreigners complain about – fight for your rights, or suffer in silence.

Roma children's begging and pickpocketing attempts can irritate. Littering remains problematic. Selling alcohol in shops after 7pm (9pm in summer) is prohibited.

Telephone & Fax

Macedonia's country code is ☑389. Internet cafes offer cheap international phone service. Public telephone cards sold in kiosks or post offices for 100 (200MKD), 200 (300MKD), 500 (650MKD) or 1000 (1250MKD) units offer good value for domestic landline calls. Drop the initial zero in city codes and mobile prefixes (☑07) when calling from abroad.

Macedonia's largest mobile provider is T-Mobile, followed by One and VIP – buying a local SIM card is good for longer stays.

Major post offices do international faxing (about 400MKD).

Tourist Information

Travel agencies are best, though some towns have information offices.

Travellers with Disabilities

Historic sites and old quarters aren't wheelchair-friendly. Expensive hotels may provide wheelchair ramps. Buses and trains lack disabled access.

Visas

Citizens of former Yugoslav republics, Australia, Canada, the EU, Iceland, Israel, New Zealand, Norway, Switzerland, Turkey and the USA can stay for three months, visa-free. Otherwise, visa fees average from US$30 for a single-entry visa and US$60 for a multiple-entry visa. Check the Ministry of Foreign Affairs website (www.mfa.gov.mk) if unsure of your status.

Getting There & Away

Air

Alexander the Great Airport (☑3148 333; www.airports.com.mk; Petrovec), 21km from Skopje, is Macedonia's main airport, with Ohrid's **St Paul the Apostle Airport** (☑046 252 820; www.airports.com.mk) mostly used for summer charters. See the **Airports of Mac-**

edonia website (www.airports.com.mk) for information, including timetables, carriers and weather conditions. Skopje airport has exchange offices, ATMs and hotel-booking and car-rental services.

Land

Macedonia and Albania have four border crossings, the busiest Kafasan–Qafa e Thanës, 12km southwest of Struga, and Sveti Naum–Tushëmishti, 29km south of Ohrid. Blato, 5km northwest of Debar, and Stenje, on Lake Prespa's southwestern shore, are the least used.

For Bulgaria, Deve Bair (90km from Skopje, after Kriva Palanka) accesses Sofia. The Delcevo crossing (110km from Skopje) leads to Blagoevgrad, while the southeastern Novo Selo crossing, 160km from Skopje beyond Strumica, reaches Petrich.

Blace, 20 minutes north from Skopje, reaches Pristina in Kosovo, while Tetovo's Jazince crossing is closer to Prizren.

Tabanovce is the major road/rail crossing for Belgrade, Serbia.

BUS
Buses serve European, Balkan and Turkish cities.

CAR & MOTORCYCLE
You need a Green Card endorsed for Macedonia.

TRAIN
Macedonian Railway (www.mz.com.mk) serves Serbia and Kosovo. These antiquated trains offer the cheapest and most iconic way to go, passing through wild terrain. There are currently no services between Greece and Macedonia.

Getting Around
Bicycle
Cycling is popular in Skopje. Traffic is light in rural areas, though mountains and reckless drivers are common.

Bus
Skopje serves most domestic destinations. Larger buses are new and air-conditioned; *kombi* (minibuses) are usually not. During summer, pre-book for Ohrid.

Car & Motorcycle
There are occasional police checkpoints; make sure you have the correct documentation. Call ☎196 for roadside assistance.

AUTOMOBILE ASSOCIATIONS
AMSM (Avto Moto Soyuz na Makedonija; ☎3181 181; www.art.com.mk; Ivo Ribar Lola 51) offers road assistance, towing and information (in German, English and Macedonian), with branches nationwide.

DRIVER'S LICENCE
Your national driver's licence is fine, though an International Driving Permit is best.

FUEL & SPARE PARTS
Petrol stations are omnipresent except in rural areas. Unleaded and regular petrol cost about 100MKD per litre, while diesel is around 70MKD per litre.

HIRE
Skopje's rental agencies include international biggies and local companies. Ohrid has many, other cities have fewer. Sedans average €60 daily, including insurance. Bring your passport, driver's licence and credit card.

INSURANCE
Rental agencies provide insurance (€15 to €25 a day, depending on vehicle type; the nonwaivable excess is €1000 to €2500). Green Card insurance is accepted and third-party insurance is compulsory.

ROAD RULES
» Drive on the right.
» Speed limits are 120km/h (motorways), 80km/h (open road) and 50km/h to 60km/h (in towns).
» Speeding fines start from 1500MKD.
» Seatbelt and headlight use is compulsory.
» Cars must carry replacement bulbs, two warning triangles and a first-aid kit (available at big petrol stations).
» From 15 November to 15 March snow tyres must be used, otherwise you can be fined, and chains should be on-board too.
» Motorcyclists and passengers must wear helmets.
» Police also fine for drink driving (blood alcohol limit 0.05%). Fines are payable immediately.

Taxi
Taxis are relatively inexpensive. Skopje cabs cost 40MKD for the first kilometre, and

20MKD per subsequent kilometre. Smaller cities are cheaper. Although police crackdowns have reduced the practice, some drivers will still *vozi za bilet* (drive for the price of a bus ticket) when four passengers are gathered.

Intercity taxis are expensive if travelling alone (it's 4000MKD from Skopje to Ohrid), but can be preferable for international travel. Skopje to Pristina in Kosovo is only 3000MKD, and twice as fast as public transport.

Train

Major lines are Tabanovce (on the Serbian border) to Gevgelija (on the Greek border), via Kumanovo, Skopje, Veles, Negotino and Demir Kapija; and Skopje to Bitola, via Veles and Prilep. Smaller Skopje–Kičevo and Skopje–Kočani lines exist.

Moldova

Includes »

Best Places to Eat

» Vatra Neamului (p551)

» Grill House (p551)

» Carmelo (p552)

» Symposium (p552)

» Oraşul Vechi (p552)

» Kumanyok (p560)

Best Places to Stay

» Adresa (p549)

» Chişinău Hostel (p549)

» Hotel Codru (p549)

» Orheiul Vechi Monastery (p557)

Why Go?

Only vaguely known in Europe and all but anonymous to the rest of the world, Moldova remains a mysterious and misunderstood land: part Romanian, part Russian, all Soviet. Once at the very edge of the USSR, Moldova has gone it alone since the early '90s. Independence has been economically painful and Moldova has been racked by civil war between the central government and the secessionist Russian-speaking region known as Transdniestr, which continues to exist as a state within a state today.

Moldova gets a tiny number of tourists and isn't much set up for travellers, but this is one of its greatest charms. Sights may be few and far between, but they are generally impressive, such as the dramatic and beautiful cave monasteries, Transdniestr's Soviet time-capsule feel, and the country's sophisticated and fascinating viniculture. Look no further for adventure: this is Eastern Europe's last unknown land.

When to Go

Chişinău

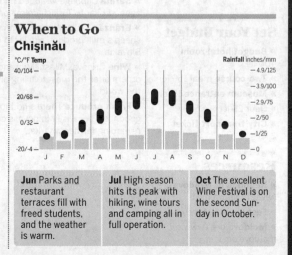

Jun Parks and restaurant terraces fill with freed students, and the weather is warm.

Jul High season hits its peak with hiking, wine tours and camping all in full operation.

Oct The excellent Wine Festival is on the second Sunday in October.

MOLDOVA

AT A GLANCE

» **Currency** Moldovan *leu* (plural *lei*)

» **Language** Moldovan

» **Money** ATMs abundant in Chişinău

» **Visas** None for the EU, USA, Canada and Japan – but required for Australians, New Zealanders and South Africans

Fast Facts

» **Area** 33,851 sq km

» **Capital** Chişinău

» **Country code** ☑373

» **Emergency** Ambulance ☑903, police ☑902

Exchange Rates

Australia	A$1	12.97 lei
Canada	C$1	12.22 lei
Euro Zone	€1	15.86 lei
Japan	¥100	13.16 lei
New Zealand	NZ$1	10.39 lei
UK	UK£1	18.78 lei
USA	US$1	12.41 lei

Set Your Budget

» **Budget hotel room** 400 lei

» **Two-course meal** 150 lei

» **Museum entrance** 15 lei

» **Beer** 25 lei

» **City transport ticket** 2 lei

Resources

» **Republic of Moldova** (www.moldova.md)

» **Fest** (www.fest.md)

» **Moldova.org** (www.moldova.org)

Connections

Despite its awkward geopolitical situation, Moldova has pretty decent overland links to its neighbouring countries. Daily buses and trains from Chişinău head to Iaşi and Bucharest in Romania, as well as to Odesa in Ukraine. Trains also serve Kyiv, Lviv, Minsk, Moscow and St Petersburg. Buses to Odesa avoid Transdniestr and thus the delays at the border. Trains between Chişinău and Odesa go via Tiraspol, but delays are minimal.

ITINERARIES

One Week

Use the capital Chişinău as your base and get to know this friendly and fast-changing town. Make day trips out to the stunning cave monastery at Orheiul Vechi and to one of the local big-name vineyards for a fascinating tour and tasting. Then spend a night or two in surreal Transdniestr before returning to Chişinău.

Ten Days

Follow the one-week itinerary at a leisurely pace before tacking on a few smaller vineyard tours around Chişinău, purchasing your customs limit, and taking a trip to Soroca to see the impressive fortress on the mighty Dniestr.

Essential Food & Drink

» **Muşchi de vacă/porc/miel** A cutlet of beef/pork/lamb.

» **Piept de pui** Chicken breast.

» **Mămăligă** A cornmeal porridge with a breadlike consistency that is a staple accompaniment to every Moldovan dish.

» **Sarma** Cabbage-wrapped minced meat or pilau rice packages, similar to Turkish dolma or Russian *goluptsy*.

» **Brânză** Moldova's most common cheese is a slightly sour sheep's milk product, similar to those made in Ukraine and Slovakia.

» **Wine** Cricova, Mileştii Mici and Cojuşna wineries and others offer the most fulfilling and inexpensive wine tours in the world.

» **Fresh produce** There's nothing else available, and thank goodness, because Moldova is essentially one big, very rewarding farmers market.

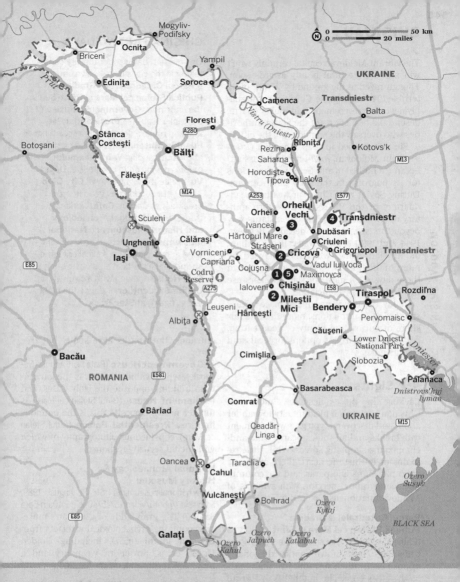

Moldova Highlights

1 Stroll the surprisingly pleasant streets and parks of the friendly capital **Chişinău** (p548).

2 Designate a driver for tours of the world-famous wine cellars at **Mileştii Mici** (p556) and **Cricova** (p556).

3 Detox at the fantastic cave monastery, burrowed by 13th-century monks, at **Orheiul Vechi** (p557).

4 Go *way* off the beaten path in the self-styled 'republic' of **Transdniestr** (p557), a surreal, living homage to the Soviet Union.

5 Gorge on the many excellent **dining options** (p551) found in Chişinău.

CHIŞINĂU

♪22 / POP 794,800

The vibrant Moldovan capital certainly won't win any architectural beauty awards soon. Though razed to the ground by WWII and a terrible 1940 earthquake, Chişinău has arguably never lost its cosmopolitan soul or charm, despite the best efforts of the Soviet authorities who oversaw the rebuilding of the city.

First chronicled in 1420, Chişinău (*kish*-i-now in Moldovan, *kish*-i-nyov in Russian) became a hotbed of anti-Semitism notorious for its pogroms in the early 20th century. During Soviet rule, Chişinău was the headquarters of the USSR's southwestern military operations, giving the city a status way beyond its size for many decades. Between 1944 and 1990 the city was called Kishinev, its Russian name, which is still used by many of the Russian-speaking locals, though these days even most Russian speakers use the Romanian pronunciation.

Today the city is an affable place with a smattering of attractions, more than its fair share of curios, and plenty of good eating, drinking and partying options for locals and visitors alike.

◉ Sights

Lacking in pulse-quickening 'must-sees', Chişinău is simply a pleasant city to wander about and discover as you go – with frequent cafe breaks and all-you-can-carry wine-and-champagne shopping sprees. While little remains of its historic heart, there are some good museums and parks, and the communist iconography merging with symbols of Moldovan nationalism is intriguing.

Parcul Catedralei & Grădina Publică Ştefan cel Mare şi Sfînt   PARKS
(Cathedral Park & Ştefan cel Mare Park; 🛜🚻) Chişinău's best-known parks diagonally oppose each other, forming two diamonds at the city's core. The highlights of **Parcul Catedralei** are the city's main **Orthodox Cathedral**, with its lovely bell tower (1836), and the Holy Gates (1841), also known as Chişinău's own **Arc de Triomphe**. On the northwestern side of the park is a colourful 24-hour **flower market**. **Grădina Publică Ştefan cel Mare şi Sfînt** is a first-rate strolling and people-watching area. Ştefan was Moldavia's greatest medieval prince and ubiquitous symbol of Moldova's brave past. His 1928 **statue** lords it over the

entrance. Both parks have spotty but free wi-fi.

Government House (Piaţa Marii Adunări Naţionale), where cabinet meets, is the gargantuan building opposite the Holy Gates, and **Parliament House** (B-dul Ştefan cel Mare) is further north. Opposite this is the ominous high-rise **Presidential Palace** (B-dul Ştefan cel Mare), conspicuous photography of which will elicit a security response.

National Archaeology & History Museum   MUSEUM
(www.nationalmuseum.md; Str 31 August 1989; admission/photo/video 15/15/40 lei; ⏰10am-6pm Sat-Thu) The grandaddy of Chişinău's museums contains archaeological artefacts from **Orheiul Vechi** (p557), including Golden Horde coins, Soviet-era weaponry and a huge WWII diorama on the 1st floor.

National Museum of Fine Arts   ART MUSEUM
(Muzeul de Arte Plastice; Str 31 August 1989, 115; adult/student 15/10 lei; ⏰10am-6pm Tue-Sun) Interesting collection of contemporary European (mostly Romanian and Moldovan) art, folk art, icons and medieval knick-knacks.

Pushkin Museum   MUSEUM
(Str Anton Pann 19; admission 15 lei, English-language tour 50 lei; ⏰10am-4pm Tue-Sun) Northeast of the central parks, this is where

Russia's national poet Alexander Pushkin (1799–1837) spent three years exiled between 1820 and 1823. It was here that he wrote *The Prisoner of the Caucasus* and other classics – that is, when he wasn't involved in the amorous intrigues, hard drinking and occasional violence of his social circles in what was then a distant rough-around-the-edges outpost of the Russian empire. You can view his tiny cottage, filled with original furnishings and personal items, including a portrait of his beloved Byron on his writing desk. There's also a three-room literary museum in the building facing the cottage, which documents Pushkin's dramatic life. If the gate is locked, knock on the nearby window.

National Ethnographic & Nature Museum
MUSEUM

(☑244 002; www.muzeu.md; Str M Kogălniceanu 82; adult/child 15/10 lei, English-language tour (arrange in advance) 100 lei; ☉10am-6pm Tue-Sun) The highlight of this massive and wonderful exhibition is a life-sized reconstruction of a dinothere (an elephantlike mammal that lived during the Pliocene Epoch – 5.3 million to 1.8 million years ago) skeleton, discovered in the Rezine region in 1966. Allow at least an hour to see the museum's pop art, taxidermied animals, and exhibits covering geology, botany and zoology.

National Army Museum
MUSEUM

(cnr Str 31 August 1989 & Str Tighina; admission/photo 2/3 lei; ☉9am-8pm Tue-Sun) This small open-air military exhibition displays a distinctly sorrylooking collection of Soviet-made tanks, fighter planes and other military toys inherited by Moldova's armed forces.

☞ Tours

Chişinău Brewery
BEER

(☑885 299; www.berechisinau.md; Str Uzinelor 167) Just east of the centre in Ciocana, the Chişinău Brewery offers free, one-hour tours that include a short video and a surprisingly generous tasting.

🛏 Sleeping

Chişinău has a fairly lamentable hotel selection, with few midrange options available. One popular alternative is to rent an apartment. Check out Marisha (p566) for cheap homestays and apartments.

🏆 Chişinău Hostel
HOSTEL €

(☑069-711 918; www.chishinau.ucoz.com; Str Arborilor 5/4, behind Malldova; dm/d incl breakfast €10/28; @🛜) Moldova's only proper hostel is about a 25-minute walk south from the centre. This comfortable, well-run place offers lockers, breakfast, shared kitchen, Wii and laundry (€2), and tours to wineries and Transdniestr. A number of maxitaxis stop here; ask for 'Malldova'. A taxi ride will cost 35 to 40 lei. It's a popular place, so book ahead.

Best Western Plus Flowers Hotel
HOTEL €€€

(☑260 202; www.hotelflowers.md; Str Anestiade 7; s/d incl breakfast from €100/116; P✦✳@🛜) This 40-room hotel is perhaps Chişinău's best top-end option. Enormous rooms boast minibars, orthopaedic mattresses and high ceilings and are tastefully decorated, with some rooms incorporating paintings by local artists. Since joining Best Western standards appear to have risen, with friendly English-speaking staff and gleaming public areas.

Adresa
APARTMENTS €€

(☑544 392; www.adresa.md; B-dul Negruzzi 1; apt €30-160; ☉24hr) For short- or long-term stays, this reliable agency offers a great alternative to hotels, renting out one- to three-room apartments throughout the city. It's a memorable way to live as the locals do, using rusty lifts or climbing disagreeable staircases. Still, they're safe, comfortable and clean. Most aren't right in the city centre but are a short taxi ride away.

Hotel Codru
HOTEL €€€

(☑208 104; www.codru.md; Str 31 August 1989, 127; s/d incl breakfast from €81/91; ✳🛜) Get through the ho-hum lobby and enjoy paradoxically nice rooms that become downright luxurious when you reach 'eurostandard' classification. The central location amid the government buildings, good balconies and immaculate bathrooms complete the package. There's also a good on-site restaurant.

Regency Hotel
HOTEL €€€

(☑999 100; www.regency.md; Str Sfatul Tării 17; s/d/ste incl breakfast from €80/100/150; P✳🛜) This brand new hotel in the heart of Chişinău's government quarter is a good midrange option with pretensions to top end. The 39 rooms are comfortable and spotlessly clean, with cable TV, minibar and unexciting beige-and-cream furnishings. The suites are extremely flouncy and aimed at local tastes, but, despite this, it's a good place to stay, with polite,

Central Chișinău

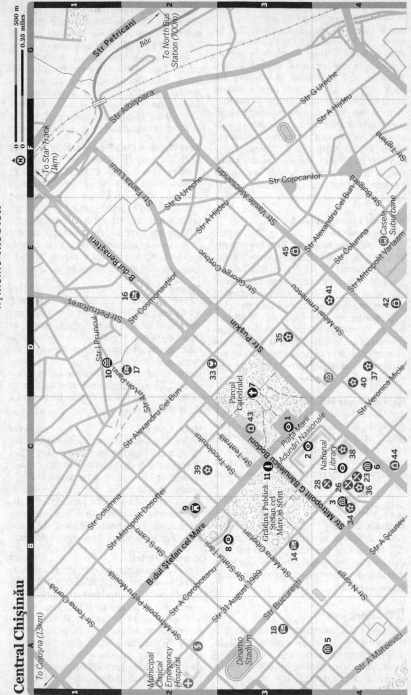

Map labels (as shown):

To Coliușna (13km)

Municipal Clinical Emergency Hospital

Str Toma Ciorbă

Str Mitropolit Petru Movilă

B-dul Stefan cel Mare

Str A Corobceanu

Str 31 August 1989

Str Stalui Lazri

Str Mare Ciobran

Grădina Publică Ștefan cel Mare și Sfânt

Dinamo Stadium

Str București

Str N Iorga

Str A Sciusev

Str A Mateevici

Str Columna

Str Mitropolit Dosoftei

Str S Lazo

Str Teatrolui

Str Theolorlui

Str Mitropolit G Bănulescu Bodoni

Piața Marii Adunări Naționale

National Library

Parcul Catedralei

Str A Pruncul

Str Anton Pann

Str Alexandru Cel Bun

Str Cosmonautilor

B-dul Renașterii

Str Petru Rareș

To Star Track (1km)

To Star Trac

Str Albișoara

Str Petricani

Bâc

To North Bus Station (700m)

Str Ianu Luini

Str G Ureche

Str Vasile Alexandri

Str George Coșbuc

Str Pușkin

Str A Hâjdeu

Str Cojocarilor

Str Alexandru Cel Bun

Str Columna

Str Mitropolit Varlaam

Str Mihai Eminescu

Str Veronica Micle

Str Bulgara

Str Trigoma

Casele Suburbane

500 m
0.25 miles

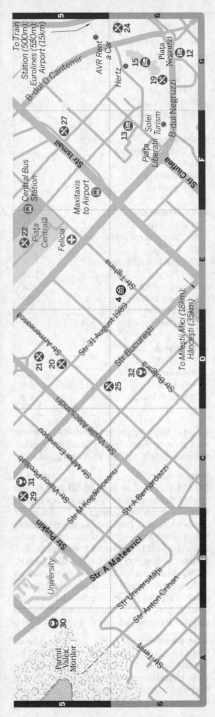

English-speaking staff, a gym and discounts available if you stay more than two nights.

Hotel Cosmos
HOTEL €€

(☏542 757; www.hotel-cosmos.com; Piaţa Negruzzi 2; s/d incl breakfast €29/39; ❈🛜) While its tagline 'you will come as a guest and you will leave as a friend' may be rather overstating the case, this concrete Soviet-era hulk of a hotel is certainly more welcoming than some of its counterparts. Rooms are reasonably priced and in various states of renovation. The economy rooms are studies in Soviet style – clearly untouched since the '80s and enjoying a certain character compared to the more sterile and pricier standards. Wi-fi is in the lobby and lower rooms only – ask for a room with wi-fi when you book.

Hotel Turist
HOTEL €

(☏220 637; B-dul Renaşterii 13; s 500-700 lei; d 450-560 lei; 🛜) For a kitsch blast of Soviet past, try this place, overlooking a Soviet memorial to communist youth. The socialist mural on its facade is prime photo material. The doubles are all unrenovated and spare, but just fine. More expensive rooms have refrigerators, air-con and balconies. Breakfast is 55 lei.

Hotel Zarea
HOTEL €

(☏227 625; Str Anton Pann 4; r without/with bathroom from 330/588 lei; ❈🛜) This drab high-rise has dour, smoky rooms that are appropriately priced and a bar-and-billiard club downstairs in the lobby. Higher-priced doubles have air-con and slightly more modern decor. English is limited.

✖ Eating

Chişinău has plenty of excellent dining options, although prices can be on the steep side in the best places.

TOP CHOICE Vatra Neamului
INTERNATIONAL €€

(Str Bucureşti 67; mains 90-200 lei; ⊜🍴📶) This superb place boasts charming old-world decor and unfailingly genial staff. A long menu of imaginatively dressed-up meats – think stewed pork with polenta, baked rabbit and salmon in pastry, not to mention copious vegetarian options – may prompt repeat visits. Enter via the door on Str Puşkin.

Grill House
INTERNATIONAL €€

(Str Armeneasca 24; mains 100-300 lei; ⊜🛜📶) It may not look like much from the street, but inside this sleek, low-lit place you'll find the best steaks in town served up by attentive staff from the glassed-in, fire-oven kitchen.

MOLDOVA CHIŞINĂU

Central Chişinău

Creative pasta dishes complement the array of hearty meat, seafood and fish and there's a great wine list to boot. Go down the atmospheric alley off the street.

Cactus Café　　　　　　　　　　CAFE €€
(Str Armenească 41; mains 100-200 lei; ⊙9am-11pm; ⊜🛜📶) What else would you expect to find in Moldova's capital? Yes, a wild-west theme bar, of course. While it sounds tacky, it's actually a smart place with good service and excellent food. There's a very pleasant summer terrace and a slightly over-styled interior. It's a great breakfast spot with a range of dishes to cater to all tastes.

Carmelo　　　　　　　　　　ITALIAN €€
(Str Veronica Micle 1/1; mains 150-350 lei, pizzas 75-150 lei; ⊜🛜📶) This Italian-run restaurant, *gelateria* and delicatessen has some of the best food in town and attracts a smart clientele of foreigners and business people. The real draws are the excellent pasta dishes and filling, thin crust pizzas, all served up on crisp white-linen tablecloths by attentive staff. The *secondi* (meat plates) are special-occasion prices, but are also very good.

Symposium　　　　　　　　　　FRENCH €€
(Str 31 August 1989, 78; mains 95-170 lei; 🛜📶) Regarded as one of the city's top dining experiences in terms of elegance and refinement, Symposium also has surprisingly reasonable prices. The French-style cuisine is sumptuous, including veal barbecue with vegetables, filet mignon with sherry sauce and grilled dorado, not to mention a long list of desserts such as chocolate crêpes and fried bananas in cognac sauce. There's a fabulous outside terrace with great atmosphere in the evenings when you can watch the city's political classes walk by.

Oraşul Vechi　　　　　　　　　　MOLDOVAN €
(Old City; Str Armenească 24; mains 40-100 lei; ⊙10am-3am; 🛜📶) This stylish restaurant with chandeliers, classic paintings and a fireplace has nightly live piano and a pleasant semi-outdoor terrace with vines creep-

ing around the wrought iron exterior. Dishes range from stewed rabbit in vegetables to grilled pike-perch and beef stroganoff. There's also an extensive local wine list.

Beer House   INTERNATIONAL €€
(B-dul Negruzzi 6/2; mains 75-250 lei; 🛜📶) This brewery-cum-restaurant has four delicious home-brewed beers and a superb menu, warming up with chicken wings and peaking at rabbit or chicken grilled in cognac. The relaxed ambience and good service add to the charm – summer evening meals outside on the terrace are a treat.

Pani Pit   MOLDOVAN €€
(31 August 1989, 115; mains 100-300 lei; 🛜📶) This charming courtyard restaurant with cushioned cast-iron chairs, vines and a small waterfall is set back from the main road. It features peasant-uniformed staff serving Moldovan dishes with a modern twist, such as pork and apples in teriyaki sauce, beef tartare and trout fried in almonds. There's also a classy inside dining room.

Delice d'Ange   CAFE €
(Str 31 August 117/2; 📶🍴) Dazzling pastries and great coffee (25 lei). There's a tree and a children's play area upstairs.

Pizza Mania   PIZZA €
(www.pizzamania.md; Str Ismail; pizza 40-100 lei; 🛜🚗📶) The most central of a cheap and well-run chain of pizza restaurants, Pizza Mania offers lots of choice, including salads, omelettes and grills as well as the eponymous pizza. There's also wireless and fast, efficient service.

Green Hills Market   SUPERMARKET €
(B-dul D Cantemir 6; 🕘9am-11pm) The most central location of the Green Hills Market chain, ideal for self-caterers with a wide range of products.

Central Market   MARKET €
(Piaţa Centrală; 🕘7am-5pm) Since 1825 this market in the very centre of the city has been the scene of lively price haggling for fresh meat and produce. Brave the crowds for its fresh food and singular ambience.

🍷 Drinking

Coliba Studenţilor   BAR
(Str A Mateevici; 🕘8am-11pm) This student hang-out, opposite the university, is quiet during summer, but during the school year the terrace is a good place to bump into eager English speakers.

Robin Pub   PUB
(Str Alexandru cel Bun 83; mains 70-250 lei; 🕘11am-midnight) A friendly, affordable local-pub feel reigns in this tastefully decorated hang-out. The menu includes omelettes, pastas, grills and desserts, all served up in the cosy interior or outside on the airy terrace.

Déjà Vu   COCKTAIL BAR
(Str Bucureşti 67; 🕘9pm-2am) A true cocktail bar, with a tantalising drinks menu, located in the centre of town and popular with a smart and cool young crowd. There's also a small dining hall serving meals.

Dublin Irish Pub   PUB
(Str Bulgară 27; 🕘noon-11pm) Rather expensive, but one of the few places in town where you can get a pint of Guinness (80 lei).

☆ Entertainment

Posters listing what's on are displayed on boards outside the city's various theatres.

Nightclubs

Chişinău parties in earnest every weekend, but in some of the larger clubs be prepared for body searches, metal detectors and tough-guy posturing from goonish doormen.

City Club   CLUB
(Str 31 August 1989, 121; 🕘10pm-6am) In the alley next to the Licurici Puppet Theatre, this 2nd-floor club consistently ranks as one of the hippest places in town. Tables are often 'reserved', but you can buy them for yourself and your party if you want better treatment (200 to 300 lei).

Star Track   CLUB
(Str Kiev 7; 🕘11pm-5am) About 1km northeast of the centre, Star Track's dark interior offers comfortable sofas and make-out booths where one can ogle dance performances by scantily clad men and women. Underneath is the less titillating but equally popular Military Pub.

Booz Time   BAR
(Str 31 August 1989, 117; 🕘9pm-3am) A popular bar attracting a young studenty crowd who certainly live up to the venue's name. There are regular theme nights such as salsa dancing, Latino and Retro Sundays.

Performing Arts
Opera & Ballet Theatre   BALLET
(www.nationalopera.md; B-dul Ştefan cel Mare 152; 🕘box office 10am-2pm & 5-7pm) Home to the

esteemed national opera and ballet company, which puts on productions from September to June.

Chekhov Drama Theatre
THEATRE

(Teatrul Dramatic A Cehov; www.chehov.md; Str Pârcălab 75) This is where Chişinău's choral synagogue was located until WWII. Plays in Russian are now performed at here.

Mihai Eminescu National Theatre
THEATRE

(B-dul Ştefan cel Mare 79; ⊘box office 11am-6.30pm) Contemporary Romanian productions can be seen at this theatre, founded in 1933.

Organ Hall
CLASSICAL MUSIC

(Sala cu Orgă; B-dul Ştefan cel Mare 79) Classical concerts and organ recitals are held here. Performances start at 6pm; tickets are sold at the door.

National Palace
THEATRE

(Palatul Naţional; Str Puşkin 21; ⊘box office 11am-5pm) Various cabarets, musicals and local-theatre-group productions are performed here.

Philharmonic Concert Hall
CONCERT VENUE

(Str Mitropolit Varlaam 78) Moldova's National Philharmonic is based here.

Sport

Moldovans are big football fans and Chişinău has three stadiums to prove it. The newest, the **Zimbru Stadium**, is the city's first European regulation football stadium, located in the Botanica district. **Dinamo Stadium** (Stadionul Dinamo; Str Bucureşti) is north of the city centre. Moldovans like football so much, in fact, that there's an American football team called the Chişinău Barbarians, who hold occasional matches in full gear.

🛍 Shopping

Cricova
WINE

(B-dul Ştefan cel Mare 126; ⊘10am-7pm Mon-Fri, to 6pm Sat, to 4pm Sun) One of several outlets for the Cricova wine factory. It stocks numerous types of shockingly affordable wine and champagne (25 to 80 lei each).

Mileştii Mici
WINE

(www.milestii-mici.md; Str Vasile Alecsandri 137; ⊘9am-7.30pm Mon-Fri, to 8pm Sat) The outlet store for the Mileştii Mici (p556) wine cellars. Table wine is sold in litre bottles for as little as 10 lei. There's another location at the airport.

Galeria L
ART

(Str Bucureşti 64; ⊘10am-6pm Mon-Fri, to 5pm Sat, to 4pm Sun) Holds temporary art exhibitions, and sells small works of art and souvenirs crafted by local artists.

ℹ Information

Medical Services

Contact the US embassy for a list of English-speaking doctors.

Municipal Clinical Emergency Hospital (✆emergency 903, info 248 435; Str Toma Ciorba 1; ⊘24hr) Has emergency services and there is a good likelihood of finding English-speaking staff.

Felicia (B-dul Ştefan cel Mare 62; ⊘24hr) Well-stocked pharmacy.

Money

Victoriabank (Str 31 August 1989, 141; ⊘9am-4pm Mon-Fri) Amex's representative in Moldova.

Post

Central post office (B-dul Ştefan cel Mare 134; ⊘8am-7pm Mon-Sat, to 6pm Sun) There is also a post office on Aleea Gării (open to 8pm).

Travel Agencies

There's no tourist information centre in Moldova, but there are plenty of travel agencies. Most offer discounted rates in some hotels.

Sometimes travel agencies take a while to reply to emails (if ever). A better bet for pre-trip contact are independent operators such as **West East** (✆06-006 06 06; www.moldova-travel.com) or **Natalia Raiscaia** (✆079-578 217; www.domasha.net) for apartment rentals, local information and assistance.

Solei Turism (✆271 314; www.solei.md; B-dul Negruzzi 5) A very efficient agency, Solei can book accommodation and transport tickets. Multiday excursions to monasteries and places of interest, incorporating rural homestays. Speaks English.

Valery Bradu (✆079-462 986, 227 850; valbradu@yahoo.com) A recommended tour guide and driver, English-speaking Valery has a 2011 Ford Focus with air-con and offers well-priced excursions throughout the country.

ℹ Getting There & Away

AIR Moldova's only international airport is the modern **Chişinău International Airport** (KIV; ✆525 111; www.airport.md), 15.5km southeast of the city centre. There are regular flights to many major European capitals. There are no internal flights within Moldova.

TRANSPORT FROM CHIŞINĂU

Bus

DESTINATION	DEPARTURE POINT	PRICE (LEI)	DURATION (HR)	FREQUENCY
Bălţi	North Bus Station	38	2	8 daily
Bendery	Central Bus Station	25	1½	every 20min 9am-3pm
Bucharest	Central Bus Station	225-250	12	4 daily
Iaşi	Southwestern Bus Station	118	4	2 daily
Kyiv	North Bus Station	284	11	1 daily
Moscow	North Bus Station	610	30	1 daily
Orhei	Casele Suburbane terminal	19	1	half-hourly 9.15am-10pm
Soroca	North Bus Station	46	2	12 daily
St Petersburg	North Bus Station	835	33-36	1 daily
Tiraspol	Central Bus Station	29	1½	every 20min 6am-7pm

Train

DESTINATION	PRICE (LEI)	DURATION (HOURS)	FREQUENCY
Bucharest (change here for Budapest)	398	14	1 daily
Kyiv	771	14	1 daily
Lviv	460	18	1 daily on odd dates
Minsk	878	25	1 daily on even dates
Moscow	1030	28-32	4 daily
St Petersburg	1030	40	1 daily

BUS Chişinău has three bus stations. Most domestic and international buses depart from the **north station** (Autogara Nord; www.autogara.md), except buses to Transdniestr, which depart from **central station** (Autogara Centrală; Str Mitropolit Varlaam). Avoid buses that go to Odesa via Transdniestr: opt instead for the longer, but less unpredictable, route through Palanca. You can buy advance tickets here or from a tiny office at the train station. The info booth charges 1 leu per question.

Bus services to/from Comrat, Hânceşti and other southern destinations use the **southwestern station** (Autogara Sud-vest; cnr Şoseaua Hânceşti & Str Spicului), around 2.2km from the city centre. **Eurolines** (☑222 827; www.eurolines.md), with an office at the train station, operates a few buses to other large cities, including once-weekly runs to Berlin, Warsaw, Braşov, Constanţa and Kyiv.

TRAIN International trains depart from the recently renovated station, Aleea Gării, south-east of Piaţa Negruzii, off B-dul Iurii Gagarin, **Left luggage** (per day 11 lei; ⊘5am-midnight) is available.

ⓘ Getting Around

TO/FROM THE AIRPORT Maxitaxi 165 departs every 20 minutes from Str Ismail, across from Eximbank near the corner of B-dul Ştefan cel Mare for the airport (3 lei). Coming from the airport, this is the last stop. A taxi costs around 80 lei to 100 lei.

BUS/MAXITAXI Route 45 runs from Central to Southwestern Bus Station, as does maxitaxi 117 from the train station. Bus 1 goes from the train station to B-dul Ştefan cel Mare. From the city centre, trolleybuses 1, 4, 5, 8, 18 and 22 go to the train station, buses 2, 10 and 16 go to Southwestern Bus Station, and maxitaxis 176 and 191 go to North Bus Station. Tickets are sold on board for buses (2 lei) and trolleybuses (1 leu). Nippy minitaxis (3 lei, pay the driver) serve most routes in town and to many outlying villages. Maxitaxis run regularly between 6am and 10pm, with reduced service until midnight.

CAR & MOTORCYCLE AVR Rent a Car (☎922 060; www.rentacar.md; B-dul D Cantemir 6) Locally run operation with cars for as little as €25 per day. Some English is spoken.

Hertz (☎274 097; www.hertz.md; Hotel Cosmos, Piaţa Negruzzi 2) Rents out a wide variety of vehicles, starting from €40 per day. English speaking.

TAXI Many official and unofficial taxis do not have meters or prices listed, and taxi-stand drivers may occasionally try to rip you off. Ordering a taxi (call ☎1448, ☎1433, ☎1422 or ☎1407) is best. Otherwise, agree on a price before you get in the car.

AROUND CHIŞINĂU

Even the furthest reaches of Moldova are a reasonable day trip from Chişinău, though that's not to say an overnight somewhere isn't a good idea. Get out of the capital and you'll find a far more tranquil atmosphere.

Cricova

Of Moldova's many fine vineyards, **Cricova** (☎022-453 659; www.cricova.md; Str Ungureanu 1; ⊗8am-4pm) is arguably the best known. Its underground wine kingdom, 15km north of Chişinău, is one of Europe's biggest. Some 60km of the 120km-long underground limestone tunnels – dating from the 15th century – are lined wall-to-wall with bottles. The most interesting part of the tour is the wineglass-shaped cellar of collectable bottles, including 19 bottles of Gerhing's wines, a 1902 bottle of Becherovka, a 1902 bottle of Evreiesc de Paşti from Jerusalem and pre-WWII French red wines.

Cricova wines and champagnes enjoy a high national and international reputation. Legend has it that in 1966 astronaut Yuri Gagarin entered the cellars, re-emerging (with assistance) two days later. Russian president Vladimir Putin celebrated his 50th birthday here.

You must have private transport and advance reservations to get into Cricova or you can arrange for staff to pick you up in Chişinău. Tours range from 45 minutes to 2½ hours (250 lei to 1350 lei per person), with increasing tastings and food as the price climbs.

Once you've finished at Cricova, head to the much-awarded **Acorex vineyard** (☎022-836 630; www.acorex.net; ⊗9am-6pm), just down the hill. There's no tour, but the shop sells limited lines not available in most stores or outside Moldova.

Mileştii Mici

While Cricova has the hype, **Mileştii Mici** (☎022-382 333; www.milestii-mici.md; 2hr tour 250 lei, tour, tasting & lunch per person 500-900 lei; ⊗9am-5pm Mon-Fri) has the goods. Housed in a limestone mine, these are *the* largest cellars in Europe (over 200km of tunnels). They were recognised by Guinness in 2005 for having the largest wine collection in the world (1.5 million bottles), though the collection has now surpassed the two-million-bottle mark.

Excellent-value tours by car wind down through the cellars with stops at notable collections and artistically executed tourist points, terminating at the elegantly decorated restaurant 60m below ground. The tours are striking, while refreshingly informal and hilarious. Tour groups must have a minimum of four people – though this is negotiable – while Saturday/Sunday tours require a minimum of 15 people.

Cojuşna

Just 13km northwest of Chişinău, **Cojuşna vineyard** (☎69-300 043, 022-615 329; Str Lomtadze 4; ⊗8am-6pm), in the village of the same name, offers spunky, friendly and affordable tours, though the setting is moribund in comparison to Cricova and Mileştii Mici.

You must ask in advance for English tours. Tours of one to three hours (250 lei to 390 lei per person) include a gift bottle, tastings and a hot meal at the top end. Prices rise significantly on weekends. Drop-ins are possible, but staff aren't always free to open the very worthwhile wine-tasting rooms, decorated with wooden furniture carved by a local boy and his father. However, you can always buy wine (20 lei to 280 lei per bottle) from the shop.

From Chişinău, catch one of the frequent maxitaxis leaving from Calea Eşilor (trolleybus 1, 5 or 11 up B-dul Ştefan cel Mare to the Ion Creangă university) and get off at Cojuşna. Ignore the fork on the left marked 'Cojuşna' and walk or hitch the remaining 2km along the main road to the vineyard entrance, marked again by a 'Cojuşna' sign and a whitewashed Jesus-on-the-cross. The vineyard is about 200m from the road.

DON'T MISS

ORHEIUL VECHI MONASTERY COMPLEX

The **Orheiul Vechi Monastery Complex** (Complexul Muzeistic Orheiul Vechi; ☏0235-34 242; admission 15 lei; ☉9am-6pm Tue-Sun) is unquestionably Moldova's most fantastic and picturesque sight, drawing visitors from around the globe. The complex is carved into a massive limestone cliff in a wild, rocky, remote spot, 10km southeast of Orhei in Orheiul Vechi ('Old Orhei', marked on maps as the village of Trebujeni).

The **Cave Monastery** (Mănăstire în Peşteră), inside a cliff overlooking the gently meandering Răut River, was dug by Orthodox monks in the 13th century. It remained inhabited until the 18th century, and in 1996 a handful of monks returned to this secluded place of worship and are slowly restoring it. You can enter the cave via an entrance on the cliff's plateau.

Ştefan cel Mare built a fortress here in the 14th century, but it was later destroyed by Tatars. In the 18th century the cave-church was taken over by villagers from neighbouring Butuceni. In 1905 they built a church above ground dedicated to the Ascension of St Mary. The church was shut down by the Soviets in 1944 and remained abandoned throughout the communist regime. Services resumed in 1996.

Ancillary attractions include remnants of a 15th-century defence wall surrounding the monastery complex, an **ethnographic museum** in the nearby village of Butuceni and newly opened caves across the valley.

You'll find the headquarters on the main road to the complex where you park and purchase your tickets for the complex. You can also arrange guides and get general information. It's forbidden to wear shorts and women must cover their heads while inside the monastery.

Orheiul Vechi Monastery Headquarters (☏0235-56 912; d 450 lei) has six pleasant rooms and a small restaurant. The rooms facing the monastery have spine-tingling balcony views. There are no proper meals served here, including breakfast, though meals can be arranged at the pensions in nearby Butuceni.

From Chişinău, daily buses depart from the Central Bus Station for Butuceni or Trebujeni (20 lei, about one hour) at 9.50am, 1.15pm and 5.15pm. Return trips run daily at 2.45pm and 6.45pm.

Soroca

POP 37,500

Soroca is the Roma 'capital' of Moldova, but people come here to see the outstanding **Soroca fortress** (☏069-323 734; adult/student/guided tour 3/2/100 lei; ☉9am-1pm & 2-6pm Wed-Sun May-Oct, low season by appt). Part of a medieval chain of military fortresses built by Moldavian princes between the 14th and 16th centuries to defend Moldavia's boundaries, the fortress was founded by Ştefan cel Mare and rebuilt by his son, Petru Rareş, in 1543-45.

The fortress is administered by the **Soroca Museum of History and Ethnography** (Str Independentei 68; adult/student 3/2 lei; ☉8am-1pm & 2-5pm Mon-Fri). This well-designed museum is a real treat; its 27,000 exhibits cover archaeological finds, weapons and ethnographic displays.

Hotel Central (☏0230-23 456; www.soroca-hotel.com; Str Kogâlniceanu 20; s/d incl breakfast 300/600 lei; ❇☏) is modern if simple, with bare, overwhelmingly blue rooms, glittery wallpaper, fridges and small, clean bathrooms. Signs point the way here from the centre. Across the plaza is the white, vaguely modern facade of the **Nistru Hotel** (☏0230-93 253, 0230-23 783; Str A Russo 12; r without/with bathroom 200/300 lei, ste 400 lei; ❇☏), with simple, bright rooms that are a sizeable step down, but fairly priced.

There are 12 daily buses to Soroca from Chişinău's North Bus Station (2½ hours).

TRANSDNIESTR

POP 518,700

The self-declared republic of Transdniestr (Pridnestrovskaya Moldavskaya Respublika, or PMR in Russian), a narrow strip of land on the eastern bank of the Dniestr River, is perhaps one of the strangest places in Eastern Europe, a ministate that doesn't officially exist in anyone's eyes but its own.

CROSSING INTO TRANSDNIESTR

We used to receive frequent reader feedback reporting disturbing hijinks at Transdniestran border crossings. Accusations of incomplete paperwork or invented transgressions led to ludicrous 'fines' of up to €200 and beyond. However, after several years of calm at the border, it seem as if the bribe-factory atmosphere has finally ended. That said, it's best not to carry ridiculous amounts of cash (in any currency), because if you are unlucky and a bribe is solicited, the less cash you have, the smaller the proposed bribe is likely to be.

Transiting the republic on a Moldova–Ukraine journey used to guarantee a bribe too, but at the time of writing the direct train service between Chişinău and Odesa was operating unmolested by the Moldovan border guards. Therefore, train is the best way to transit the country. Most buses, tired of the border hassles, circumnavigate Transdniestr altogether.

All that said, if you enter Transdniestr on public transport and are detained, often your best defence is calm and patience. Let the maxitaxi leave you behind. Another will be along shortly. Even the most persistent guards will eventually get tired of dealing with you, particularly if their tactics don't appear to be working. Worst-case scenario: you'll be stonewalled at a mirthfully small bribe offer (say €5 or 80 Moldovan lei) or you'll be sent back to where you came from.

Entry-permit prices/requirements change frequently. At the time of writing, there was no payment necessary to cross the border in either direction. However, if you're staying for more than 24 hours, you'll need to register with **OVIR** (☎533-55 047; ul Kotovskogo No 2a; ☺9am-noon Mon, 9am-noon & 1-4pm Tue & Thu, 1-3pm Fri). Registration is free and can be normally be handled by your hotel or whomever is organising your accommodation. If you do need to sort it out yourself, go down the alley and enquire at the rear white building with the red roof. Oh, and 'men must wear pants'! Seriously. Outside OVIR business hours go to the **Tiraspol Militia Office** (☎533-34 169; Roza Luxemburg 66; ☺24hr) where registration is possible, but you'll probably be asked to check in at the OVIR office the following working day anyway. Some hotels will register you automatically.

While on the one side Moldova maintains that Transdniestr was illegally grabbed from its sovereign territory with Russian support, Transdniestr proudly points to its having won its 'independence' during a bloody civil war in the early 1990s. However you look at it, a tenuous, bitter truce has ensued ever since.

Travellers will be stunned by this idiosyncratic region that has developed its own currency, police force, army and borders, controlled by Transdniestran border guards.

Until very recently, a visit to the area meant submitting to sometimes expensive, organised bribe shakedowns with border officials, but in recent years such instances have almost totally ceased and visiting this communist theme park is a relative breeze. Come and see one of Europe's strangest corners.

The Bank of the Republic of Transdniestr (www.cbpmr.net) has daily updated rates for the Transdniestran ruble against all major currencies.

History

Igor Smirnov was elected president of Transdniestr in 1991, following the region's declaration of independence four months earlier. During his two decades in power, Smirnov pushed for full independence from Moldova, as well as at times to join with Russia. With Transdniestr unrecognised by the Moldovan – or any other – government, the Russian 14th army, stationed in Tiraspol, provided the region with a sense of security despite its precarious legal existence. Alongside a number of agreements between Moldova and Transdniestr since 1991, there have been countless moves by both sides designed to antagonise or punish the other. In 2003, a piqued Smirnov slapped exorbitant tariffs on all Moldovan imports, instantly halting trade over the 'border' and making life more difficult for ordinary people on both sides. He later had phone connections severed between the two regions for a few weeks.

In 2011, having won no fewer than four elections, Smirnov was finally defeated at the ballot box by the reformist former speaker of Transdniestr's Supreme Soviet, Yevgeny Shevchuk. Smirnov had lost the support of Russia and alienated much of the electorate during his two decades in power. Significantly, however, the Kremlin's favoured candidate, Anatoly Kaminski, also lost out, and the young Shevchuk, who built his popularity on pledges to curtail endemic nepotism and corruption, is now faced with the task of bringing Transdniestr into the 21st century. While Shevchuk advocates independence for the region, he has also made it clear that he believes in compromise and good relations with neighbouring Moldova.

Tiraspol

♪ 533 / POP 159,000

The 'capital' of Transdniestr is also, officially at least, the second largest city in Moldova. But don't expect it to be anything like the chaotic Moldovan capital: here time seems to have stood still since the end of the Soviet Union. Eerily quiet streets, flower beds tended with military precision and old-school Soviet everything from street signs to litter-free parks named after communist grandees: Tiraspol (from the Greek, meaning 'town on the Nistru') will be one of the strangest places you'll ever visit.

This veritable Lenin-loving theme park may be starting to show capitalist cracks, as SUVs and wireless pizzerias become more and more common, and the divide between the haves and the have-nots continues to widen. But, for now, it's still a place to visit for anyone wanting a through-the-looking glass experience.

◉ Sights

Tiraspol National United Museum   MUSEUM
(ul 25 Oktober 42; admission 25 rubles; ⊙10am-5pm Sun-Fri) The closest thing to a local history museum, it features an exhibit focusing on poet Nikolay Zelinsky, who founded the first Soviet school of chemistry. Opposite is the **Presidential Palace**, from where newly minted leader Yevgeny Shevchuk rules the region. Loitering and/or photography here is likely to end in questioning and a guard-escorted trip off the property.

War Memorial   MEMORIAL
At the western end of ul 25 Oktober stands a Soviet armoured tank from which the Transdniestran flag flies. Behind is the War Memorial with its Tomb of the Unknown Soldier, flanked by an eternal flame in memory of those who died on 3 March

1992 during the first outbreak of fighting. On weekends, it's covered in flowers left by wedding-day brides.

Kvint Factory   BRANDY FACTORY
(☑96 577; www.kvint.biz; ul Lenina 38) The Kvint factory is one of Transdniestr's prides and joys – since 1897 it's been making some of Moldova's finest brandies. Buy the least expensive cognac in Europe (starting at less than €2!) either near the front entrance of the plant or at the **Kvint shop** (ul 25 Oktober 84; ⊙24hr). You can visit the factory on a tasting tour, which costs from €25 to €100 depending on the level of tour you select. All tours include a buffet.

House of Soviets   NOTABLE BUILDING
(ul 25 Oktober) The House of Soviets, towering over the eastern end of ul 25 Oktober, has Lenin's angry-looking bust peering out from its prime location. Inside is a **memorial** to those who died in the 1992 conflict. Close by is the military-themed **Museum of Headquarters** (ul Kommunisticheskaya 34; admission/photo 2/5 rubles; ⊙8.30am-5pm Mon-Sat), where you can see various displays about the defence of Tiraspol during the war.

Kirov Park   PARK
North along ul Lenina, towards the bus and train stations, is Kirov Park, with a **statue** of the Leningrad boss who was assassinated in 1934, conveniently sparking mass repressions throughout the USSR.

⌷ Sleeping

You must register at OVIR (p558) in central Tiraspol if staying more than 24 hours. Marisha (p566) can arrange a homestay.

Hotel Russia   LUXURY HOTEL €€€
(☑38 000; www.hotelrussia.md; ul Sverdlova 69; r incl breakfast 960 rubles; P❋☎) Opening to great fanfare in 2012, this large, luxurious and blandly furnished hotel is definitely the mainstay for business people and anyone wanting comfort. Rooms come with flat-screen TVs, smart bathrooms and comfortable beds, and security is tight. The hotel is located on a side street just by the House of Soviets. Its basement club is the hottest place in town at weekends.

City Club   HOTEL €€€
(☑59 000; www.cityclub.md; ul Gorkogo 18; s/d incl breakfast from 1015/1115 rubles; P❋☎) Spot the somewhat incongruous Pac-Man logo at this recently opened gated complex favoured

by wealthy out-of-towners and business people. The guest rooms upstairs are tastefully, if rather unexcitedly, furnished, with flat-screen TVs and all comforts. Downstairs you'll find a full gym, sauna and classy restaurant and bar. Staff are suitably obsequious and this is a good place to enjoy understated pampering.

Hotel Timoty
HOTEL €€

(☑73 742; ulitsa K Liebknechta 395A; s/d 550/855 rubles; ❖) The rooms at this quirky hotel are large but sparingly furnished with '90s flat-pack furniture and the kind of manmade fibres that only survive in hotel rooms of the former Soviet Union. It was once the hotel of choice before the luxury hotels opened. It's now one of the few midrange options in town. Call ahead as it's often full.

Tiraspol Hostel
HOSTEL €

(☑68-571 472; www.moldovahostels.com; ul Levanevskogo 31a; dm 218 rubles; ❖) Yes, as incredible as it may seem, Tiraspol has its own hostel. Run by Tim, an American ex-pat, this small country-style house has 11 beds strewn over three rooms, plus another small cottage with two beds. It's all pretty basic, but there's a simple kitchen and a pleasant patio. Prices include a free three-hour city tour. Call to arrange a free pick-up, as it's difficult to find on your own.

Stay at Lena's
APARTMENT €

(☑06-915 57 53; lena_lozinskiy@inbox.ru; ul Pravdy 6, apt 97; apt 290 rubles) Lena has a cosy, recently renovated one-room apartment near the Borodinka bus stop at the entrance to the town centre. There's 24-hour hot water and a basic kitchen. She can also arrange other rooms or full apartments around Tiraspol.

Hotel Aist
HOTEL €

(☑73 776; pereulok Naberezhny 3; r 150-800 rubles) Definitely an experience, from the gambling parlour in the lobby to the unique local art in the upstairs corridors. The Aist is a partially updated Soviet-era place and while the 'economy' rooms are beyond spartan, they're absolutely fine. The pricier 'upgraded' rooms smell musty and have lots of cheap flat-pack furniture. Some rooms have decent river views.

✕ Eating

You can eat surprisingly well in Tiraspol, as the middle class burgeons.

Kumanyok
UKRAINIAN €€

(ul Sverdlova 37; mains 50-125 rubles; ❖9am-11pm; ❖) Home from home for Transdniestr's ruling classes (as demonstrated by the rows of black Mercedes outside), this smart, traditional Ukrainian place is set in a kitsch faux-countryside home, where diners are attended to by a fleet of peasant-dressed waitresses. The menu is hearty Ukrainian fare; think dumplings, pancakes, fish, pork, mutton, chicken and veal.

Seven Fridays
CAFE €

(ul 25 Oktober 112; mains 30-80 rubles; ❖11am-midnight; ❖) A popular cafe in the centre of town serving all manner of meat, salads, soups, and, erm, sushi. It has a bustling brasserie feel and if you sit here long enough, you'll see most of Tiraspol drop by. Menus are in Russian, but there are pictures to point at.

Abazhur
RUSSIAN €

(ul Karla Liebknechta 385, cnr with ul Lenina; mains 20-90 rubles; ❖) As if you needed further communist nostalgia, here's Abazhur (from *abat-jour*, meaning lampshade in French), where you can dine under portraits of Yuri Gagarin, the USSR hockey team and other supreme Soviets. The style is refined '30s and '40s, and the menu takes in Russian classics such as bliny and fried perch, while pasta and escalopes can also be found representing more international taste.

Eilenburg
GERMAN €€

(pereulok Naberezhnyi 1; mains 50-125 rubles; ❖10.30am-midnight; ❖❖) A medieval-themed German restaurant, with girls in dirndl dresses, stone walls, a suit of armour and, coincidentally, decent food. Choose from beef stroganoff, fried quails' eggs, rabbit, ostrich, pork brisket, salmon, and a huge range of bliny (Russian pancakes), including one topped with red caviar. There's a short veg menu.

❶ Information

Antica Pharmacy (ul 25 October; ❖24hr)

Central telephone office (ul Karl Marx 149; phonecards 10-25 rubles; internet per hour 5.50 rubles; ❖8am-8pm, internet 10am-10pm) Go through the far-left door for phonecards and internet. You can also buy phone cards at any Sheriff Market.

Post office (ul Karl Marx 149; ❖7.30am-7pm Mon-Fri) Won't be of much use to you unless you want to send postcards to all your friends in Transdniestr.

GAGAUZIA

The region of Gagauzia (Gagauz Yeri) covers 1832 sq km of noncontiguous land in southern Moldova. This Turkic-influenced Christian ethnic minority (pop 171,500) forfeited full independence for autonomy, being subordinate to Moldova constitutionally and for foreign relations and defence. It comprises three towns and 27 villages.

Gagauzi Muslim antecedents fled here from the Russo-Turkish wars in the 18th century. They were allowed to settle in the region in exchange for their conversion to Christianity. Their language is a Turkish dialect, with its vocabulary influenced by Russian Orthodoxy, as opposed to the Islamic influences inherent in Turkish. Gagauz look to Turkey for cultural inspiration and heritage.

Comrat, Gagauzia's capital, is little more than an intriguing cultural and provincial oddity. In 1990 Comrat was the scene of clashes between Gagauz nationalists and Moldovan armed forces, preceded by calls from local leaders for the Moldovan government to hold a referendum on the issue of Gagauz sovereignty.

The captivating **Comrat Museum** (☑238-22 694; pr Lenina 164; admission 5 lei; ☺9am-4pm Tue-Sat) is a dizzying hotchpotch of mundane to fascinating items, seemingly collected from townspeoples' attics, including photos of noteworthy locals, books, historical newspaper clippings, costumes, tools, weapons, musical instruments, foreign currency, gifts from visiting dignitaries, furniture and models.

There are five daily return buses from Chişinău to Comrat (36 lei). From Comrat there is one daily direct bus via Bendery to Tiraspol, and others that make frequent stops.

MOLDOVA BENDERY

Transnistria Tour (☑694-27 502; www.transnistria-tour.com) This highly recommended new company is the first travel agency in Transdniestr to offer tours and travel services to foreign visitors. Its excellent English-language website is a great place to start planning your trip, and its wide variety of tours (with themes ranging from Soviet monuments and brandy to football and ecology) start at just €25 per day.

ⓘ Getting There & Away

BUS You can only pay for bus tickets with the local currency, but there are change facilities at the combined bus and train station. Buy tickets inside the left-hand door of the station. From Tiraspol there are eight daily buses to Odesa in Ukraine (47.10 rubles, three hours) and one daily to Kyiv (202 rubles, 14 hours). Buses/maxitaxis go to Chişinău (33.80 rubles) nearly every half-hour from 5am to 6pm. Trolleybus 19 (2.50 rubles) and quicker maxitaxis 19 and 20 (3 rubles) cross the bridge over the Dniestr to Bendery.

TRAIN There's a useful daily Chişinău to Odesa train, which calls at Tiraspol at 9.40am daily. Tickets to Odesa cost 100 rubles and the journey takes two hours. The train makes the return journey to Chişinău each evening, calling at Tiraspol at 7.15pm.

There's also one daily train to Moscow, via Kyiv, leaving at 2.03am (3rd/2nd class 835/1750 rubles, 26 hours).

Bendery
☑552 / POP 93,750

Bendery (sometimes called Bender, and previously known as Tighina), on the western banks of the Dniestr River, is the greener, more aesthetically agreeable counterpart to Tiraspol. Despite civil-war bullet holes still decorating several buildings – Bendery was hardest hit by the 1992 military conflict with Moldova – the city centre is a breezy, friendly place.

During the 16th century Moldavian prince Ştefan cel Mare built a large defensive fortress here on the ruins of a fortified Roman camp. In 1538 Ottoman sultan Suleiman the Magnificent conquered the fortress and transformed it into a Turkish *raia* (colony), renaming the city Bendery, meaning 'belonging to the Turks'. During the 18th century Bendery was seized from the Turks by Russian troops who then massacred Turkish Muslims in the city. In 1812 Bendery fell permanently into Russian hands. Russian peacekeeping forces remain here to this day.

◉ Sights

Tighina Fortress   FORTRESS
(admission/tour 20/35 rubles; ☺9am-6pm Tue-Sun) Bendery's main sight is this massive

Turkish fortress, built in the 1530s to replace a 12th-century fortress built by the Genovese. Until recently it was an off-limits Transdniestran military training ground (half the fortress is still closed), but the fortress can now be toured by private car. It's quite a walk from the centre of town; instead take trolleybus 1 or 5 one stop from outside the military base by the bridge towards Tiraspol, walk past the petrol station and follow the pathway around to your right.

Memorial Park   PARK

At the entrance to the city, close to the famous **Bendery-Tiraspol bridge**, is a memorial park dedicated to local 1992 war victims. An eternal flame burns in front of an armoured tank, from which flies the Transdniestran flag. Haunting memorials to those killed during the civil war are also scattered throughout many streets in the city centre.

🛏 Sleeping & Eating

There's currently only one hotel operating in Bendery, though there are plenty of eateries located around the town's main square and ul Lenina.

Prietenia Hotel   HOTEL €€

(✆29 622, 29 660; ul Tkachenko 18; d 260-800 rubles; ❈) Overlooking the Dniestr, this Soviet place is hard to find, as there's no sign – it's near the end of ul S Liazo on the embankment. At 300 rubles, the business-class rooms – essentially a renovated standard room – are the best deal. Some rooms have balconies with a river view and only the brand-new deluxe rooms have air-con.

Avenue   RUSSIAN, JAPANESE €€

(ul Lenina cnr ul Sovetskaya; mains 50-200 rubles; ⊙10am-midnight) Right on the central plaza, this friendly place has a slightly more sophisticated vibe than you'll find elsewhere and serves up a large number of dishes from its two menus: one of Russian classics and one of Japanese dishes to please the smart clientele.

Breeze   CAFE €

(cnr ul Kalinina & ul Lenina; mains 20-50 rubles; ⊙8am-11pm; 🛜) Located in the park across from the department store, this small restaurant has a popular shaded terrace, where grilled-meat dishes are the favourite. It also doubles as a hang-out and bar, with beer starting at 9 rubles.

ℹ Information

Central Department Store (cnr ul Lenina & ul Kalinina; per hour 4 rubles; ⊙9am-8pm) Tiraspol's main department store has internet access available from terminals for those without smart phones or laptops with them. It's on the town's central square.

Currency Exchange (ul Sovetskaya) Located next to the central market.

Pharmacy (cnr ul Suvorova & ul S Liazo; ⊙8am-9pm)

Telephone Office (cnr ul S Liazo & ul Suvorova; internet per hour 5.50 rubles; ⊙8am-12.30pm, 2-5.30pm & 7-9pm, internet 9am-12.20pm & 2-9pm) International phone calls can be booked here. It also has internet.

ℹ Getting There & Around

BUS There are buses and maxitaxis every half-hour or so to Chişinău (30.10 rubles, 1½ hours) from 6am to 11pm. Trolleybus 19 for Tiraspol (2.50 rubles) departs from the bus stop next to the main roundabout at the entrance to Bendery; maxitaxis also regularly make the 20-minute trip (3 rubles).

TRAIN One daily train goes to Moscow, via Kyiv, leaving at approximately 2am. Services also connect Bendery to Tiraspol, Odesa and Chişinău daily. The train station is at the far end of ul Lenina (in the opposite direction to the river).

UNDERSTAND MOLDOVA

History

As with so many countries in the region, Moldova's history consists of being continually sliced, diced, tossed and wrested by one invading force after another. A political and cultural tug-of-war between Russia and Romania continues to this day.

Bessarabia, part of the Romanian principality of Moldavia, was annexed in 1812 by the Russian empire. In 1918, after the October Revolution, Bessarabia declared its independence. Two months later the newly formed Democratic Moldavian Republic united with Romania. Russia never recognised this union.

Then in 1924 the Soviet Union created the Moldavian Autonomous Oblast on the eastern banks of the Dniestr River, and incorporated Transdniestr into the Ukrainian Soviet Socialist Republic (SSR). A few months later the Soviet government renamed the oblast the Moldavian Autonomous Soviet Socialist

Republic (Moldavian ASSR). During 1929 the capital was moved to Tiraspol from Balta (in present-day Ukraine).

In June 1940 the Soviet army, in accordance with the terms of the secret protocol associated with the Molotov–Ribbentrop Pact, occupied Romanian Bessarabia. The Soviet government immediately joined Bessarabia with the southern part of the Moldavian ASSR – specifically, Transdniestr – naming it the Moldavian Soviet Socialist Republic (Moldavian SSR). The remaining northern part of the Moldavian ASSR was returned to the Ukrainian SSR (present-day Ukraine). Bessarabia suffered terrifying Sovietisation, marked by the deportation of 300,000 Romanians.

World War II

During 1941 allied Romanian and German troops attacked the Soviet Union, and Bessarabia and Transdniestr fell into Romanian hands. Consequently, thousands of Bessarabian Jews were sent to labour camps and then deported to Auschwitz. In August 1944 the Soviet army reoccupied Transdniestr and Bessarabia. Under the terms of the Paris Peace Treaty of 1947, Romania had to relinquish the region and Soviet power was restored in the Moldavian SSR.

Once in control again the Soviets immediately enforced a Sovietisation program on the Moldavian SSR. The Cyrillic alphabet was imposed on the Moldovan language (a dialect of Romanian) and Russian became the official state language. Street names were changed to honour Soviet communist heroes, and Russian-style patronymics were included in people's names.

In July 1949, 25,000 Moldovans were deported to Siberia and Kazakhstan, and in 1950–52 Leonid Brezhnev, then first secretary of the central committee of the Moldovan Communist Party, is said to have personally supervised the deportation of a quarter of a million Moldovans.

Independence & Ethnic Tension

Mikhail Gorbachev's policies of *glasnost* (openness) and *perestroika* (restructuring) from 1986 paved the way for the creation of the nationalist Moldovan Popular Front in 1989. Moldovan written in the Latin alphabet was reintroduced as the official language in August 1989. In February and March 1990 the first democratic elections to the Supreme Soviet (parliament) were won by the Popular Front. Then in April 1990 the Moldovan national flag (the Romanian tricolour with the Moldavian coat of arms in its centre) was reinstated. Transdniestr, however, refused to adopt the new state symbols and stuck to the red banner.

In June 1990 the Moldovan Supreme Soviet passed a declaration of sovereignty. After the failed coup attempt against Gorbachev in Moscow in August 1991, Moldova declared its full independence and Mircea Snegur became the democratically elected president in December 1991. Moldova was granted 'most-favoured nation' status by the USA in 1992, qualifying for International Monetary Fund (IMF) and World Bank loans the same year.

Transdniestr's newly emerging desire for autonomy spawned the Yedinstivo-Unitatea (Unity) movement in 1988 to represent the interests of the Slavic minorities. This was followed in November 1989 by the creation of the Gagauz Halki political party in the south of Moldova, where the Turkic-speaking Gagauz minority was centred. Both ethnic groups' major fear was that an independent Moldova would reunite with Romania.

The Gagauz went on to declare the Gagauz Soviet Socialist Republic in August 1990. A month later the Transdniestrans declared independence, establishing the Dniestr Moldovan Republic. In presidential elections, Igor Smirnov came out as head of Transdniestr, Stepan Topal head of Gagauzia.

Whereas Gagauzia didn't press for more than autonomy within Moldova, Transdniestr settled for nothing less than outright independence.

Civil War

In March 1992 Moldovan president Mircea Snegur declared a state of emergency. Two months later full-scale civil war broke out in Transdniestr, when Moldovan police clashed with Transdniestran militia, backed by troops from Russia, in Bendery (then called Tighina). An estimated 500 to 700 people were killed and thousands wounded in events that shocked the former Soviet Union.

A ceasefire was signed by the Moldovan and Russian presidents, Snegur and Boris Yeltsin, in July 1992. Provisions were made for a Russian-led, tripartite peacekeeping force comprising Russian, Moldovan and Transdniestran troops to be stationed in the region. Troops remain there today, maintaining an uneasy peace. Transdniestr continues to aggravate Chişinău and generate the occasional statement of concern from the EU.

EU Aspirations

While Moldova is keen to join the ranks of the EU, two major obstacles still block its path: the country's mounting foreign debt and its inadequate economic growth.

Moldova is widely regarded as one of the most corrupt nations in Europe. Average household income remains low, and with roughly one-third of the country's GDP comprising monies sent home from emigrants working abroad, an unproductive economic dependency is developing, which will require long-term domestic cultivation to counteract. Even nationalists grudgingly admit that Moldova's economy may never flourish unless it's anchored to a stronger economic entity (ie Romania).

Romania's 2007 entrance into the EU transformed the Moldovan border into the EU's eastern frontier. After an initial period of isolated Moldovans waiting in demoralising lines to get Romanian visas, Romania eased border restrictions, ostensibly to alleviate visitation for cross-border relatives.

In early 2010 Moldova's newly elected Western-leaning government, led by Prime Minister Vlad Filat, signed an order to remove nearly 360km of the communist-era barbed-wire fence separating Moldova from Romania. Romania soon responded by promising €100 million in development aid and doubling the number of scholarships for Moldovan students wanting to study in Romania. With a newly elected reformist leader in Transdniestr elected in 2012, things are looking brighter for Moldova's future than they have at any time since independence.

People

With 4.3 million inhabitants, Moldova is the most densely populated region of the former Soviet Union. Moldovans make up 78.2% of the total population, Ukrainians constitute 8.4%, Russians 5.8%, Gagauz 4.4%, Bulgarians 1.9%, and other nationalities such as Belarusians, Poles and Roma comprise 1.3%.

Most Gagauz and Bulgarians inhabit southern Moldova. In Transdniestr, Ukrainians and Russians make up 58% of the region's population; Moldovans make up 34%. It is one of the least urbanised countries in Europe.

Moldova stays on course with the region's religious leanings; the vast majority are Eastern Orthodox (98%), with the recovering Jewish community (1.5%) at a distant second. Baptists and 'other' make up the remaining 0.5%.

Arts
Folk Art

There is a wealth of traditional folk art in Moldova, with carpet making, pottery, weaving and carving predominating.

Traditional dancing in Moldova is similar to the dances of other Eastern European countries. Couples dance in a circle, a semicircle or a line to the sounds of bagpipes, flutes, panpipes and violins.

Music & Art

Two of Moldova's most prolific modern composers are Arkady Luxemburg and Evgeny Doga, who have both scored films and multimedia projects, as well as written songs, concertos, suites and symphonies. Dimitrie Gagauz has for over three decades been the foremost composer of songs reflecting the folklore of the Turkic-influenced Gagauz population of southern Moldova.

The biggest name in Moldovan painting is Mihai Grecu (1916–98), who cofounded the National School of Painting and was also a poet and free-love advocate. In sculpture,

BOOKS

Playing the Moldovans at Tennis is Tony Hawks' dated but nevertheless hilarious account of his visit to a much bleaker Moldova in the mid-'90s to satisfy a drunken bet, challenging him to defeat the entire Moldovan football team at tennis. Moldova took a mild PR hit in *The Geography of Bliss* by Eric Weiner who recounts his visit to the alleged 'least happy nation on the planet'. *The Moldovans: Romania, Russia and the Politics of Culture* by Charles King is a more recent, textbook snapshot of this 'intriguing East Europe borderland'.

MAKE NEW FRIENDS

What with their friendly, outgoing disposition, you shouldn't have any trouble winning acquaintances in Moldova. However, if you want to be instantly embraced, and possibly kissed, steer the conversation towards music, then casually drop these names: Zdob şi Zdub and Gândul Mâţei.

Zdob şi Zdub (zdob-shee-zdoob; www.zdob-si-zdub.com) have been together since 1995, working Moldovan audiences into a lather with their Romanian-folk-meets-the-Red-Hot-Chilli-Peppers sound fusion. In 2005 the group achieved a stunning sixth-place finish in the Eurovision Song Contest. These days they tour so ferociously that poor Moldova hardly hears from them. You're more likely to catch a show in Romania.

Gândul Mâţei (Gun-dool muts-ehee; www.myspace.com/gandulmatei) nimbly run the gamut from lounge music to Coldplay-esque ballads to rocking *hard*. They're starting to break out of the Moldovan market, but still gig regularly in Chişinău.

Both bands have a very strong following in Moldova, and locals between the ages of 15 and 35 are guaranteed to become unwound with breathless reverence at the mere mention of their names. Moreover, their shows are fabulous and a highly recommended experience.

Anatol Coseac today produces some highly original woodworks.

Environment

Tiny and landlocked, Moldova is a country of gently rolling steppes, with a gradual sloping towards the Black Sea. With one of the highest percentages of arable land in the world, Moldova is blessed with rich soil. Fields of grains, fruits and sunflowers are characteristic of the countryside.

There are five scientific reserves (around 194 sq km) and 30 protected natural sites (around 223 sq km). The reserves protect areas of bird migration, old beech and oak forests, and important waterways. Codru Reserve, Moldova's oldest, boasts 924 plant species, 138 kinds of birds and 45 mammals; this is the most frequently visited reserve.

A great effort has been made by environmental groups to protect Moldova's wetland regions along the lower Prut and Dniestr Rivers.

Never heavily industrial, Moldova faces more issues of protection and conservation than pollution. The majority of its 3600 rivers and rivulets were drained, diverted or dammed, threatening ecosystems.

Food & Drink

In Moldova, some Russian influences have meant that pickled fruits and vegetables are popular, as are Russian meals such as *pelmeni* (Russian-style ravioli stuffed with meat). A Turkic influence has arguably been strong here; in the south you may find the delicious Gagauz *sorpa,* a spicy ram soup.

Though things have improved slightly in recent years, vegetarians will find their meals limited. Locally grown fresh fruit and veg is always a bonus, but expect to find few vegetarian choices.

Moldova produces excellent wines and brandies. Reds are called *negru* and *roşu,* white is *vin alb,* while *sec* means dry, *dulce* is sweet and *spumos* translates as sparkling.

Across the country, restaurants can be expected to stay open until at least 11pm nightly. Outside of Chişinău you'll be lucky to find a decent restaurant and may be stuck with hotel dining rooms, bars or cafeterias.

SURVIVAL GUIDE

Directory A–Z
Accommodation

Chişinău has a good range of hotels, but little in the midrange. Elsewhere, most towns have small hotels that have survived from communist days and have been somewhat done up. Some hotels may offer nonsmoking rooms, but in general smoking occurs everywhere.

You will be asked to briefly present your passport upon registration; they may keep it for several hours in order to register it.

Popas turistic (camping grounds) are practically nonexistent in Moldova. The good news is that wild camping is allowed anywhere unless otherwise prohibited.

The idea of homestays in Moldova is in its infancy. Check **Marisha** (☏06-915 57 53, 488 258; www.marisha.net) for a growing list of options.

Prices quoted are for rooms with private bathrooms. The following price indicators apply (based on a double room in the summer months):

€ less than 500 lei/€30

€€ 500 lei/€30 to 1000 lei/€60

€€€ more than 1000 lei/€60

Business Hours

Banks 9am to 3pm Monday to Friday

Businesses 8am to 7pm Monday to Friday, to 4pm Saturday

Shops 9am or 10am to 6pm or 7pm Monday to Saturday

Museums 9am to 5pm Tuesday to Sunday

Restaurants 10am to 11pm

Embassies & Consulates

French Embassy (☏22-200 400; www.ambafrance-md.org; Str Vlaicu Pircalab 6, Chişinău)

German Embassy (☏22-200 600; www.chisinau.diplo.de; Str Maria Cibotari 35, Chişinău)

Romanian Embassy (☏22-211 813; http://chisinau.mae.ro; Str Bucureşti 66/1, Chişinău)

Russian Embassy (☏22-235 110; www.moldova.mid.ru; B-dul Ştefan cel Mare 153, Chişinău)

Ministry of Foreign Affairs of Ukraine (☏22-582 151; www.mfa.gov.ua; Str V Lupu 17, Chişinău)

UK Embassy (☏22-225 902; www.ukinmoldova.fco.gov.uk; Str Nicolae Iorga 18, Chişinău)

US Embassy (☏22-851 705; http://moldova.usembassy.gov; Str A Mateevici 75, Chişinău, 2nd floor)

Food

The following price indicators apply for restaurants, based on the average cost of a main course.

€ less than 100 lei

€€ 100 lei to 200 lei

€€€ more than 200 lei

Gay & Lesbian Travellers

Before Moldova repealed its Soviet antigay law in 1995, it was one of only four European countries to still criminalise homosexuality. Now Moldova has among the most progressively liberal laws on the continent: homosexual activity is legal for both sexes at 14, the same age as for heterosexual sex.

Needless to say, homosexuality is still a hushed topic, and politicians still get away with antigay rhetoric. While most people take a laissez-faire attitude towards the notion of homosexuality, being visibly out is likely to attract unwanted attention. For more information, visit LGBT (www.lgbt.md).

Money

The currency of Moldova is the leu (plural lei), which comes in notes of 1, 5, 10, 20, 50, 100, 200, 500 and 1000 lei. Coins of 1, 5 and 10 lei exist, as well as 25 and 50 bani coins (100 bani makes up one leu). It's easy to find ATMs in Chişinău, but less so in other towns. Eximbank cashes travellers cheques and gives cash advances on major credit cards. While credit cards won't get you anywhere in rural areas, they are widely accepted in larger department stores, hotels and most restaurants in cities and towns.

The only legal tender in Transdniestr is the Transdniestran ruble (TR). Some taxi drivers, shopkeepers and market traders will accept payment in US dollars, eruos or even Moldovan lei – but generally you'll need to get your hands on some rubles to buy things there. Spend all your rubles before you leave, as no one honours or exchanges this currency outside Transdniestr. If you get stuck with a large amount, you might find takers with bad rates in Chişinău, from where maxitaxis bound for Transdniestr depart.

Public Holidays

New Year's Day 1 January

Orthodox Christmas 7 January

International Women's Day 8 March

Orthodox Easter April/May

Victory (1945) Day 9 May

Independence Day 27 August

National Language Day 31 August

Telephone

Locals tend to rely almost exclusively on mobile phones, as the rickety state landline network, run by the wonderfully named Moldtelecom, is notoriously unreliable.

Mobile-phone service in Moldova is provided by Moldcell (run by Moldtelecom) and Orange. It's straightforward to buy a local SIM card and use it in any unlocked handset. Moldova's country code is ☑373.

Visas

Citizens of EU member states, USA, Canada and Japan do not need visas. Everyone else is still on the hook, although Australians and New Zealanders no longer require an invitation. South Africans and some other nationalities require an invitation from a company, organisation or individual to get a visa. To obtain an invitation, contact a travel agency in Moldova or enquire with a hotel to see if they can send you one when you book. When acquiring a visa in advance, you usually need to pay the consulate via bank deposit at a specified bank.

Visas can be easily acquired on arrival at Chişinău airport or, if arriving by bus or car from Romania, at three border points: Sculeni (north of Iaşi); Leuşeni (main Bucharest–Chişinău border); and Cahul. Visas are not issued at any other border crossings, nor when entering by train. Citizens of countries requiring an invitation must present the original document (copies/faxes not accepted) at the border if buying a visa there.

Moldova allows visa-free visits for all foreigners wishing to partake in its Wine Festival (second Sunday in October). These visits cannot exceed 10 days. Nationalities ordinarily needing invitation letters must still acquire them, but they just need to present them on arrival in lieu of having a visa.

Check the **Ministry of Foreign Affairs** (www.mfa.gov.md) website and follow the link for Consular Affairs for the latest news on the visa situation.

Getting There & Away

Entering and leaving Moldova is usually a breeze. Moldovan border guards are no longer surprised to see foreign tourists – though they still haven't learned how to smile.

Air

Moldova's only airport of significance is in Chişinău.

Air Moldova (9U; ☑22-830 830; www.airmoldova.md; B-dul Negruzzi 10)

Austrian Airlines (OS; www.austrian.com)

Carpatair (V3; ☑22-549 339; www.carpatair.com)

Lufthansa (www.lufthansa.com)

Moldavian Airlines (2M; ☑22-549 339; www.mdv.md; B-dul Ştefan cel Mare 3)

S7 (www.s7.ru)

Tarom Romanian Air Transport (RO; ☑22-541 254; www.tarom.ro; B-dul Ştefan cel Mare 3; ☺9am-5pm) Flies to Bucharest once or twice daily.

Turkish Airlines (TK; ☑22-278 525; www.turkishairlines.com)

Land
BUS
Moldova is well linked by bus lines to central and Western Europe. While not as comfortable as the train, buses tend to be faster, though not always cheaper.

For bus journeys between Chişinău and Odesa, we advise taking the route going through the southeast Palanca border crossing, circumnavigating Transdniestr.

CAR & MOTORCYCLE
The Green Card (a routine extension of domestic motor insurance to cover most European countries) is valid in Moldova. Extra insurance can be bought at the borders.

TRAIN
From Chişinău, there are four daily trains to Moscow, daily trains to St Petersburg, Odesa, Tiraspol and Kyiv, and trains to Lviv (Ukraine) on all odd dates and trains to Minsk (Belarus) on all even dates.

There's an overnight service between Bucharest and Chişinău; at 12 hours, the journey is longer than taking a bus or maxitaxi (the train heads north to Iaşi, then south again), but is more comfortable if you want to sleep.

Getting Around
Bicycle
Moldova is mostly flat, making cycling an excellent way of getting around. That is, it would be if it weren't for the bad condition of most of the roads, and for the lack of infrastructure – outside of Chişinău, you'll have to rely on your own resources or sense of adventure (and trying to enlist help from friendly locals) if you run into mechanical trouble.

Bus & Maxitaxi

Moldova has a good network of buses running to most towns and villages. Maxitaxis, which follow the same routes as the buses, are quicker and more reliable. Buses cost 2 lei, trolleybuses 1 leu and city maxitaxis 3 lei.

Car & Motorcycle

In Chişinău, travel agencies can arrange car hire, or try **AVR Rent a Car** (☎22-922 060; www.rentacar.md; B-dul D Cantemir 6) or **Hertz** (☎22 274 097; www.hertz.md; Hotel Cosmos, Piaţa Negruzzi 2). Be wary, however, as the roads are in poor condition. EU and US driving licences are accepted here; otherwise, bring both your home country's driving licence and your International Driving Permit (IDP), which is recognised in Moldova.

The intercity speed limit is 90km/h and in built-up areas 60km/h; the legal blood alcohol limit is 0.03%. For road rescue, dial 901.

Taxi

In Moldova there are official (and unofficial) taxis, often without meters, which may try to rip you off. It's best to call a taxi. A taxi ride to anywhere inside Chişinău is unlikely to cost more than 60 lei, but you should agree upon a price before getting in the car.

Montenegro

Includes »

Best Places to Eat

» Konoba Ćatovića Mlini (p573)

» Konoba kod Rada Vlahovića (p589)

» Stari Most (p584)

» Blanche (p579)

» Miško (p582)

Best Places to Stay

» Old Town Hostel (p575)

» Palazzo Radomiri (p575)

» Vila Drago (p579)

» Eko-Oaza Suza Evrope (p590)

Why Go?

Imagine a place with sapphire beaches as spectacular as Croatia's, rugged peaks as dramatic as Switzerland's, canyons nearly as deep as Colorado's, *palazzi* as elegant as Venice's and towns as old as Greece's. Then wrap it up in a Mediterranean climate and squish it into an area two-thirds the size of Wales, and you start to get a picture of Montenegro (Црна Гора).

More adventurous travellers can easily sidestep the peak-season hordes on the coast by heading to the rugged mountains of the north. This is, after all, a country where wolves and bears still lurk in forgotten corners.

Montenegro, Crna Gora, Black Mountain: the name itself conjures up romance and drama. There are plenty of both on offer as you explore this perfumed land, bathed in the scent of wild herbs, conifers and Mediterranean blossoms. Yes, it really is as magical as it sounds.

When to Go
Podgorica

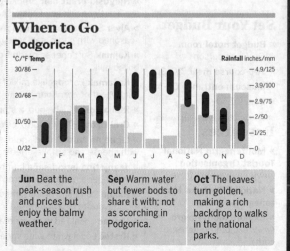

Jun Beat the peak-season rush and prices but enjoy the balmy weather.

Sep Warm water but fewer bods to share it with; not as scorching in Podgorica.

Oct The leaves turn golden, making a rich backdrop to walks in the national parks.

AT A GLANCE

» **Currency** Euro (€)

» **Language** Montenegrin

» **Money** ATMs in larger towns, banks open Monday to Friday and Saturday morning

» **Visas** None for citizens of EU, Canada, USA, Australia, New Zealand and many other countries

Fast Facts

» **Area** 13,812 sq km

» **Capital** Podgorica

» **Country code** ☎382

» **Emergency** Ambulance ☎124, fire ☎123, police ☎122

Exchange Rates

Australia	A$1	€0.82
Canada	C$1	€0.77
Japan	¥100	€0.83
New Zealand	NZ$1	€0.65
UK	UK£1	€1.18
USA	US$1	€0.78

Set Your Budget

» **Budget hotel room** €10–15 per person

» **Two-course meal** €10–30

» **Museum entrance** €1–5

» **Beer** €1.50

Resources

» **Montenegrin National Tourist Organisation** (www.montenegro.travel)

» **National Parks of Montenegro** (www.nparkovi.me)

» **Explore Montenegro** (www.exploremontenegro.com)

Connections

Many travellers make the most of the close proximity of Dubrovnik Airport to Herceg Novi to tie in a visit to Croatia with a Montenegrin sojourn. At the other end of the coast, Ulcinj is the perfect primer for exploring Albania and is connected by bus to Shkodra. Likewise, Rožaje captures elements of Kosovar culture and is well connected to Peja (Peć). A train line and frequent bus connections make a trip to Montenegro's closest cousins in Serbia a breeze. Montenegro shares a longer border with Bosnia and Hercegovina (BiH) than any of its neighbours. There are three main crossings for drivers, as well as regular bus services to Trebinje and Sarajevo. Ferries connect Bar to the Italian ports of Bari and Ancona.

ITINERARIES

One Week

Base yourself in the Bay of Kotor for two nights. Drive through Lovćen to Cetinje, then the next day continue to Šćepan Polje via Ostrog Monastery. Go rafting the following morning and spend the night in Podgorica. Head to Virpazar for a boat tour of Lake Skadar and then take the scenic lakeside road to Ulcinj. Finish in Sveti Stefan.

Two Weeks

Follow the itinerary above, but allow extra time in Kotor, Lake Skadar and Sveti Stefan. From Šćepan Polje, head instead to Žabljak and then to Biogradska Gora National Park before continuing to Podgorica.

Essential Food & Drink

» **Njeguški pršut i sir** Smoke-dried ham and cheese from the heartland village of Njeguši.

» **Ajvar** Spicy spread of fried red peppers and eggplant, seasoned with garlic, salt, vinegar and oil.

» **Kajmak** Soft cheese made from the salted cream from boiled milk.

» **Kačamak** Porridgelike mix of cream, cheese, potato and buckwheat or cornflour.

» **Riblja čorba** Fish soup, a staple of the coast.

» **Crni rižoto** Black risotto, coloured with squid ink.

» **Ligne na žaru** Grilled squid, sometimes stuffed (*punjene*) with cheese and smoke-dried ham.

» **Jagnjetina ispod sača** Lamb cooked (often with potatoes) under a metal lid covered with hot coals.

» **Rakija** Domestic brandy, made from nearly anything. The local favourite is grape-based *loza*.

» **Vranac** Local red wine varietal.

» **Krstač** Local white wine varietal.

Montenegro Highlights

1 Marvel at the majesty of the **Bay of Kotor** (p572) and exploring the historic towns hemmed in by the limestone cliffs.

2 Drive the vertiginous route from Kotor to the Njegoš Mausoleum at the top of **Lovćen National Park** (p582).

3 Enjoying the iconic island views while lazing on the sands of **Sveti Stefan** (p579).

4 Seeking the spiritual at peaceful **Ostrog Monastery** (p587).

5 Floating through paradise, rafting between the kilometre-plus walls of the **Tara Canyon** (p590).

6 Wandering through primeval forest mirrored in a tranquil alpine lake at **Biogradska Gora National Park** (p589).

7 Splashing through the floating meadows of water lilies garlanding vast **Lake Skadar** (p583).

BAY OF KOTOR

Coming from Croatia, the Bay of Kotor (Boka Kotorska) starts simply enough, but as you progress through fold upon fold of the bay and the surrounding mountains get steeper and steeper, the beauty meter gets close to bursting. It's often described as the Mediterranean's only fjord, and even though the geological label is not technically correct, the mental image that phrase conjures is spot on.

Herceg Novi   Херцег Нови

POP 12,700

It's easy to drive straight through Herceg Novi without noticing anything worth stopping for, especially if you've just come from Croatia with visions of Dubrovnik still dazzling your brain. However, just below the uninspiring roadside frontage hides an appealing Old Town with ancient walls, sunny squares and a lively atmosphere. The water's cleaner here, near the mouth of the bay, and while the town's pebbly coves and concrete swimming terraces aren't all that great, taxi boats do a brisk trade ferrying people to the secluded beaches on the Luštica Peninsula.

◉ Sights

Stari Grad   NEIGHBOURHOOD

Herceg Novi's Old Town is at its most impressive when approached from the pedestrian-only section of ul Njegoševa, which is paved in the same shiny marble as Dubrovnik and lined with elegant, mainly 19th-century buildings. The street terminates in cafe-ringed Trg Nikole Đurkovića, where steps lead up

---

ADVENTURE RACE MONTENEGRO

Started by a bunch of British expats operating outdoor-adventure businesses out of Herceg Novi, the **Adventure Race** (www.adventureracemontenegro.com) should be high on the agenda for anyone who fancies themselves an action man or wonder woman. Held in late September/early October, the Coastal Challenge is a day of kayaking, mountain biking, hiking and orienteering amid the exceptional scenery of the Bay of Kotor.

---

to an elegant crenulated **clock tower** (1667) which was once the main city gate.

Just inside the walls is Trg Herceg Stjepana (commonly called Belavista Sq), a gleaming white piazza that's perfect for relaxing, drinking and chatting in the shade. At its centre is the Orthodox **Archangel Michael's Church** (Crkva Sv Arhanđela Mihaila; ⊘7am-midnight Jun-Aug, to 9pm Sep-May). Built between 1883 and 1905, its lovely proportions are capped by a dome and flanked by palm trees. Its Catholic counterpart, **St Jerome's** (Crkva Sv Jeronima), is further down the hill, dominating Trg Mića Pavlovića.

Kanli-Kula   FORTRESS

(Bloody Tower; admission €1; ⊘8am-midnight) The big fort visible from the main road was a notorious prison during Turkish rule (roughly 1482–1687). You can walk around its sturdy walls and enjoy views over the town. In the dungeon below the lower set of flagpoles, former inmates have carved crosses and ships into the walls.

Savina Monastery   MONASTERY

(Braće Grakalić bb; ⊘6am-8pm) From its hillside location in the town's eastern fringes, this peaceful Orthodox monastery enjoys wonderful coastal views. It's dominated by the elegant 18th-century Church of the Dormition, carved from pinkish stone. Inside there's a beautiful gilded iconostasis, but you'll need to be demurely dressed to enter (no shorts, singlets or bikinis). The smaller church beside it has the same name but is considerably older (possibly 14th century) and has the remains of frescos.

The monastery is well signposted from the large roundabout on the highway at Meljine.

Regional Museum   MUSEUM

(Zavičajni muzej; www.rastko.rs/rastko-bo/muzej; Mirka Komnenovića 9; admission €1.50; ⊘9am-6pm Mon-Sat) Apart from the building itself (which is a fab bougainvillea-shrouded baroque palace with absolute sea views), the highlight of this little museum is its impressive icon gallery.

Španjola Fortress   FORTRESS

Situated high above the town, this fortress was started and finished by the Turks but named after the Spanish (yep, in 1538 they had a brief stint here as well). If the graffiti and empty bottles are anything to go by, it's now regularly invaded by local teenagers.

🏃 Activities

📍 Black Mountain
ADVENTURE TOURS

(☑067-640 869; www.montenegroholiday.com)
Can arrange pretty much anything, anywhere in the country, including mountain
biking, diving, rafting, hiking, paragliding,
canyoning, boat trips, wine tasting, accommodation, car hire and transfers.

📍 Kayak Montenegro
KAYAKING

(☑067-382 472; www.kayakmontenegro.com; hire
per 1/4/8hr from €5/15/25) Offers paddling
day tours across the bay to Rose and Dobreč
or Mamula and Mirišta (€45 including
equipment), as well as day trips to explore
Lake Skadar.

Yachting Club 32
OUTDOORS

(www.yachtingclub32.com; Šetalište Pet Danica 32)
Hires jet skis (€50 per 20 minutes), pedal
boats (€8 per hour) and mountain bikes
(€3/6/15 per one hour/three hours/day).

🛏 Sleeping

Private rooms start at about €15 per person.
Either look for signs saying 'sobe' or book
through a local agency such as **Trend Travel**
(☑031-321 639; www.trendtravelmontenegro.com;
Bus Station, Jadranski Put).

📍 Camp Full Monte
CAMPGROUND €

(☑067-899 208; www.full-monte.com; campsites
per person €10; ☺May-Sep) Hidden in the
mountains near the Croatian border, this
small British-run camping ground offers
solar-generated hot water, odourless composting toilets and a whole lot of seclusion.
If you hadn't guessed already, clothing is optional. Tents (with full bedding) can be hired
and meals can be arranged.

Hotel Perla
HOTEL €€€

(☑031-345 700; www.perla.me; Šetalište Pet Danica
98; s €84-112, d €104-140, apt €170-215; P❄🖥)
It's a 15-minute stroll from the centre but if
it's beach you're after, Perla's position is perfect. The front rooms of this medium-sized
modern block have private terraces and sea
views.

Izvor
HOSTEL €

(☑069-397 957; www.izvor.me; Jadranski Put bb,
Igalo; dm €12; P🖥) On the slopes above Igalo, this simple place consists of four basic
shared rooms which open on to a terrace
overlooking the bay. There's a traditional
restaurant downstairs (mains €4 to €9).

WORTH A TRIP

KONOBA ĆATOVIĆA MLINI

A crystalline stream flows around and
under this rustic former mill which
masquerades as a humble *konoba* (a
simple, family-run establishment) but in
reality is one of Montenegro's best **restaurants** (☑032-373 030; www.catovi-
camlini.me; mains €8-24; ☺11am-11pm).
Watch the geese idle by as you sample
the magical bread and olive oil, which
appears unbidden at the table. Fish is
the focus but traditional specialities
from the heartland village of Njeguši are
also offered. You'll find it in the village
of Morinj, in the western corner of the
inner section of the Bay of Kotor.

Vila Aleksandar
HOTEL €€

(☑031-345 806; www.hotelvilaaleksandar.com;
Save Kovačevića 64; s/d €51/82; ❄🖥🏊) The
decor's a little dated but almost all of the
rooms have balconies with sea views, and
the blue-tiled pool on the sunny terrace is
extremely enticing. The restaurant opens
onto the waterfront promenade.

🍴 Eating

If you want to take on the local women in a
tussle for the best fresh fruit and vegetables,
get to the **market** (Trg Nikole Đurkovića; ☺6am-
3pm Mon-Sat, to noon Sun) before 8am.

Konoba Feral
SEAFOOD €€

(Vasa Ćukovića 4; mains €7-17) A feral is a ship's
lantern, so it's seafood that takes pride
of place on the menu – not wild cat. The
grilled squid is excellent and comes with a
massive serving of seasonal vegetables and
salads.

ℹ Information

Tourist Information Kiosk (Šetalište Pet
Danica bb; ☺9am-11pm May-Sep)
Tourist Office (☑031-350 820; www.herceg-
novi.travel; Jova Dabovića 12; ☺9am-10pm
daily Jul & Aug, 9am-4pm Mon-Fri, 9am-2pm
Sat Sep-Jun)

ℹ Getting There & Around

BOAT Taxi boats ply the coast during summer,
charging about €10 to €15 to the beaches on the
Luštica Peninsula.
BUS Buses stop at the station just above the Old
Town. There are frequent buses to Kotor (€4,

one hour), Budva (€6, 1¾ hours), Cetinje (€7, 2½ hours) and Podgorica (€9, three hours). At least two buses head to Dubrovnik daily (€10, two hours).

CAR A tortuous, often gridlocked, one-way system runs through the town, so you're best to park in the parking building opposite the bus station. If you're driving to Tivat or Budva, it's usually quicker to take the **ferry** (car/motorcycle/passenger €4/1.50/free; ⊙24hr) from Kamenari (15km northeast of Herceg Novi) to Lepetane (north of Tivat). Queues can be long in summer.

Perast   Пераст

Looking like a chunk of Venice that has floated down the Adriatic and anchored itself onto the Bay of Kotor, Perast hums with melancholy memories of the days when it was rich and powerful. This tiny town boasts 16 churches and 17 formerly grand *palazzi*, one of which has been converted into **Perast Museum** (Muzej grada Perasta; ✆032-373 519; adult/child €2.50/1.50; ⊙9am-7pm) and showcases the town's proud seafaring history.

The 55m bell tower belongs to **St Nicholas' Church** (Crkva Sv Nikole; museum €1; ⊙museum 10am-6pm), which also has a museum containing relics and beautifully embroidered vestments.

Just offshore are two peculiarly picturesque islands. The smaller **St George's Island** (Sveti Đorđe) rises from a natural reef and houses a Benedictine monastery shaded by cypresses. Boats (€5 return) regularly head to its big sister, **Our-Lady-of-the-Rock Island** (Gospa od Škrpjela), which was artificially created in the 15th century. Every year on 22 July, the locals row over with stones to continue the task. Its magnificent church was erected in 1630.

Perast makes an atmospheric and peaceful base from which to explore the bay. Several houses rent rooms or you can try the **Hotel Conte** (✆032-373 687; www.hotel-conte. com; apt €100-160; ᴾ❋🛜), where options range from deluxe studios to two-bedroom seaview apartments in historic buildings around St Nicholas' Church. Its wonderful restaurant (mains €9 to €20) serves fresh fish with lashings of romance on a waterside terrace.

Not far from Perast, **Risan** is the oldest town on the bay, dating to at least the 3rd century BC. Signposts point to some superb Roman **mosaics** (admission €2; ⊙9am-7pm mid-May–mid-Oct), discovered in 1930.

Kotor   Котор

POP 13,500

Wedged between brooding mountains and a moody corner of the bay, this dramatically beautiful town is perfectly at one with its setting. Its sturdy walls – started in the 9th century and tweaked until the 18th – arch steeply up the slopes behind it. From a distance they're barely discernible from the mountain's grey hide but at night they're spectacularly lit, reflecting in the water to give the town a golden halo. Within those walls lie labyrinthine marbled lanes where churches, shops, bars and restaurants surprise you on hidden piazzas.

Kotor's funnel-shaped **Stari Grad** (Old Town) sits between the bay and the lower slopes of Mt Lovćen. Newer suburbs surround the town, linking up to the old settlement of **Dobrota** to the north. Continuing around the bay towards Tivat, the coastal road narrows to a single lane and passes cute villages such as **Prčanj**, **Stoliv** and **Lastva**.

WORTH A TRIP

BACK ROAD TO MT LOVĆEN

The journey from Kotor to Mt Lovćen, the ancient core of the country, is one of Montenegro's great drives. Take the road heading towards the Tivat tunnel and turn right just past the graveyard. After 5km, follow the sign to Cetinje on your left opposite the fort. From here there's 17km of narrow road snaking up 25 hairpin turns, each one revealing a vista more spectacular than the last. Take your time and keep your wits about you; you'll need to pull over and be prepared to reverse if you meet oncoming traffic. From the top, the views stretch over the entire bay to the Adriatic. At the entrance to Lovćen National Park you can continue straight ahead through Njeguši for the shortest route to Cetinje or turn right and continue on the scenic route through the park.

LUŠTICA PENINSULA

Reaching out to form the southern headland of the Bay of Kotor, this gorgeous peninsula hides secluded beaches such as **Dobreč**, **Žanjic** and **Mirišta**, and the pretty fishing village **Rose**. They're all popular destinations for day trippers travelling from Herceg Novi by taxi boat

At **Bjelila**, a cluster of old stone houses, **Villa Kristina** (☑032-679 739; www.villakristina.me; Bjelila bb; apt €60-80; 🌸🛜) has four apartments, each with its own little balcony gazing over the bay. It's terribly romantic, and there's a little private beach and a restaurant.

◉ Sights

The best thing to do in Kotor is to get lost and found again in the maze of streets. You'll soon know every corner, as the town is quite small, but there are plenty of churches to pop into and many coffees to be drunk in the shady squares.

Sea Gate GATE
(Vrata od Mora) The main entrance to the town was constructed in 1555 when the town was under Venetian rule. Stepping through onto Trg od Oružja (Weapons Square), you'll see a strange stone pyramid in front of a **clock tower** (1602); it was once used as a pillory to shame wayward citizens.

St Tryphon's Cathedral CHURCH
(Katedrala Sv Tripuna; Trg Sv Tripuna; admission €2; ⊙8am-7pm) Kotor's most impressive building is its Catholic Cathedral, which was originally built in the 12th century but reconstructed after several earthquakes. The gently hued interior is a masterpiece of Romanesque architecture, with slender Corinthian columns alternating with pillars of pink stone, thrusting upwards to support a series of vaulted roofs. Its gilded silver bas-relief altar screen is considered Kotor's most valuable treasure.

Town Walls FORTRESS
(admission €2; ⊙24hr, fees apply 8am-8pm May-Sep) The energetic can make a 1200m-long ascent up the fortifications via 1350 steps to a height of 260m, for unforgettable views and a huge sense of achievement. There are entry points near the **River Gate** (North Gate) and Trg od Salate.

Maritime Museum of Montenegro MUSEUM
(Pomorski muzej Crne Gore; www.museummaritimum.com; Trg Bokeljske Mornarice; adult/child €4/1; ⊙9am-6.30pm Mon-Sat, to 1pm Sun Apr-Oct, 9am-2pm daily Nov-Mar) Kotor's proud history as a naval power is celebrated in three storeys of displays housed in a wonderful early-18th-century palace.

🛏 Sleeping

Although the Stari Grad is a charming place to stay, you'd better pack earplugs. In summer the bars blast music onto the streets until 1am every night and rubbish collectors clank around at 6am. Some of the best options are just out of Kotor in quieter Dobrota. Enquire about private accommodation at the tourist information booth.

TOP CHOICE Old Town Hostel HOSTEL €
(☑032-325 317; www.hostel-kotor.me; near Trg od Salata; dm €12-14, r without bathroom €30, apt €40) Sympathetic renovations have brought this 13th-century *palazzo* back to life, and the ancient stone walls now echo with the chatter of happy travellers. Comfortable, sociable, reasonable, historical... exceptional.

TOP CHOICE Palazzo Radomiri HISTORIC HOTEL €€€
(☑032-333 172; www.palazzoradomiri.com; Dobrota; s €80-90, d €120-130, ste €150-220; ⊙Mar-Oct; 🅿🌸🛜🏊) Exquisitely beautiful, this honey-coloured early-18th-century *palazzo* in Dobrota has been transformed into a first-rate boutique hotel. Some rooms are bigger and grander than others, but all 10 have sea views and luxurious furnishings.

Forza Mare BOUTIQUE HOTEL €€€
(☑032-333 500; www.forzamare.com; Kriva bb, Dobrota; r €180-252; ⊙Apr-Oct; 🅿🌸🛜🏊) A bridge arches over a small pool before you even reach the front door of this opulent Dobrota

Kotor

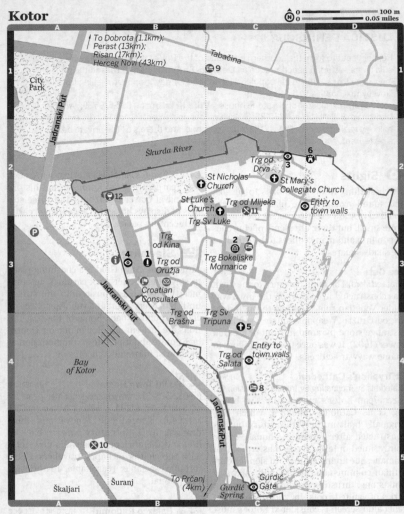

MONTENEGRO KOTOR

---

hotel. Downstairs there's a tiny private beach, restaurant and spa centre.

Hotel Monte Cristo
HOTEL €€

(☏032-322 458; www.montecristo.co.me; near Trg Bokeljske Mornarice; r €75-90, apt €115-150; P❄🛜) It's not going to win any hip design awards but this old stone place offers a cheerful welcome and clean, brightly tiled rooms in a supremely central (but potentially noisy) location.

Tianis
APARTMENT €€

(☏032-302 178; www.tianis.net; Tabačina 569; apt €60-120; P❄🛜) Well located without being

in the midst of the melee, this friendly establishment has a clutch of reasonably priced apartments, some of which have magical views of the Old Town.

🍴 Eating & Drinking

There are dozens of cafe-bars, restaurants, bakeries and takeaway joints on Kotor's cobbled lanes.

TOP CHOICE Galion
SEAFOOD €€€

(☏032-325 054; Šuranj bb; meals €10-21) With an achingly romantic setting, upmarket Galion gazes directly at the Old Town across the

Kotor

yachts in the marina. Fresh fish is the focus, served as traditional grills. It usually closes in winter.

Restoran Stari Mlini SEAFOOD €€€
(☏032-333 555; www.starimlini.com; Jadranski Put; meals €12-20) It's well worth making the trip to Ljuta, just north of Dobrota, to this romantic restaurant set in an 18th-century mill by the edge of the bay. It's pricier than most and the service is variable, but the food is excellent.

Stari Grad SEAFOOD €€
(☏032-322 025; www.restoranstarigrad.com; Trg od Mlijeka; mains €8-18) Head straight through to the stone-walled courtyard, grab a seat under the vines and prepare to get absolutely stuffed full of fabulous food – the serves are huge.

☆ Entertainment

Maximus CLUB
(☏067-216 767; www.discomaximus.com; near Trg od Oružja; admission free-€5; ⏰11pm-5am Thu-Sat, nightly in summer) Montenegro's most pumping club comes into its own in summer, hosting big-name international DJs and local starlets.

❶ Information

Tourist Information Booth (www.kotor.travel; ⏰8am-8pm)

❶ Getting There & Away

The **bus station** (☏032-325 809; ⏰6am-9pm) is to the south of town, just off the road leading to the Tivat tunnel. Buses to Herceg Novi (€4, one hour), Budva (€3.50, 40 minutes), Tivat (€2.20, 20 minutes) and Podgorica (€7, two hours) are at least hourly. Further-flung destinations include Kolašin (€12, four daily).

A taxi to Tivat airport should cost around €10.

Tivat Тиват

POP 9,450

In the throes of a major makeover, courtesy of the multimillion-dollar redevelopment of its old naval base into the **Porto Montenegro** (www.portomontenegro.com; ⏰7am-1am) super-yacht marina, Tivat is becoming noticeably more schmick each year. While it will never rival Kotor for charm, it makes a pleasant stop on a trip around the bay, and a useful base for exploring the sweet villages of the Vrmac and Luštica Peninsulas.

🛏 Sleeping & Eating

Hotel Villa Royal HOTEL €€
(☏032-675 310; www.rotortivat.com; Kalimanjska 18; s/d €42/68; ❄@?) It's not a villa and it's certainly not fit for a king, but this minihotel near the old marina has clean, bright rooms and friendly staff, making it our pick of Tivat's extremely limited accommodation options…at least until the Regent opens in 2014.

TOP **One** ITALIAN €€€
CHOICE
(☏067-486 045; Porto Montenegro; mains €10-20; ⏰8am-1am) Murals and sail-like flourishes on the ceiling invoke the yachtie lifestyle in this smart but informal brasserie, while the menu sails clear across the Adriatic for an authentic take on Italian cuisine.

Prova MEDITERRANEAN €€
(www.prova.co.me; Šetalište Iva Vizina 1; mains €8-18; ⏰8am-1am) Shaped like a boat with chandeliers that look like mutant alien jellyfish, this upmarket eatery is the very epitome of the new, increasingly chic Tivat. The pasta is excellent.

❶ Information

Tourist Office (☏032-671 324; www.tivat. travel; Palih Boraca 8; ⏰8am-8pm Mon-Fri,

MONTENEGRO TIVAT

8am-noon & 6-8pm Sat, 8am-noon Sun Jun-Aug, 8am-3pm Mon-Sat Sep-May)

❶ Getting There & Away

AIR Tivat airport is 3km south of town and 8km through the tunnel from Kotor. Major local and international rental-car companies have counters here. Taxis charge around €5 to €7 for Tivat, €10 for Kotor and €25 to Budva.

BUS Buses to Kotor (€2.20, 20 minutes) stop outside a silver kiosk on Palih Boraca. The main stop for longer trips is inconveniently located halfway between Tivat and the airport.

ADRIATIC COAST

Much of Montenegro's determination to re-invent itself as a tourist mecca has focused firmly on its gorgeous Adriatic coastline. In July and August it seems that the entire Serbian world and a fair chunk of its northern Orthodox brethren can be found crammed onto this scant 100km stretch. Avoid these months and you'll find a charismatic set of fortified towns and fishing villages to explore, set against clear Adriatic waters and Montenegro's mountainous backdrop.

Budva   Будва

POP 13,400

The poster child of Montenegrin tourism, Budva – with its atmospheric Old Town and numerous beaches – certainly has a lot to offer. Yet the child has moved into a difficult adolescence, fuelled by rampant development that has leeched much of the charm from the place. In the height of the season the sands are blanketed with package holidaymakers from Russia and the Ukraine, while the nouveau riche park their multimillion-dollar yachts in the town's guarded marina. By night you'll run a gauntlet of scantily clad women attempting to cajole you into the beachside bars. It's the buzziest place on the coast so if you're in the mood to party, this is the place to be.

◉ Sights & Activities

Stari Grad   HISTORIC AREA
Budva's best feature and star attraction is the Old Town – a mini-Dubrovnik with marbled streets and Venetian walls rising from the clear waters below. Much of it was ruined by two earthquakes in 1979 but it has since been completely rebuilt and now

houses more shops, bars and restaurants than residences. At its seaward end, the **Citadela** (admission €2; ⊙9am-midnight May-Oct, to 5pm Nov-Apr) offers striking views, a small museum and a library full of rare tomes and maps. In the square in front of the citadel is a cluster of interesting churches. Nearby is the entry to the **town walls** (admission €1).

Archaeological Museum   MUSEUM
(Arheološki muzej; ☑033-453 308; Petra I Petrovića 11; adult/child €2/1; ⊙9am-9pm Tue-Fri, 2-9pm Sat & Sun) This museum shows off the town's ancient and complicated history – dating back to at least 500 BC – over three floors of exhibits.

FREE **Modern Gallery**   GALLERY
(Moderna galerija; Cara Dušana 19; ⊙8am-2pm & 6-9pm Mon-Fri, 6-9pm Sat) An attractive gallery displaying temporary exhibitions.

Montenegro Adventure Centre   PARAGLIDING
(☑067-580 664; www.montenegrofly.com) Rafting, hiking, mountain biking, diving and accommodation can all be arranged, as well as paragliding from launch sites around the country. An unforgettable tandem flight landing 750m below at Bečići beach costs €65.

🛏 Sleeping

TOP CHOICE **Hotel Astoria**   HOTEL €€€
(☑033-451 110; www.astoriamontenegro.com; Njegoševa 4; s €90-105, d €110-130, ste €130-210; ❄@) Water shimmers down the corridor wall as you enter this chic boutique hotel hidden in the Old Town's fortifications. The rooms are on the small side but they're beautifully furnished.

Hotel Oliva   HOTEL €€
(☑033-459 429; olivai@t-com.me; Velji Vinogradi bb; s/d €30/58; P❄🅟🛜) Don't expect anything flashy, just a warm welcome, clean and comfortable rooms with balconies, and a nice garden studded with the olive trees that give this small hotel its name.

Saki Hostel & Apartmani   HOSTEL, APARTMENTS €
(☑067-368 065; www.saki-apartmani.com; IV Proleterska bb; dm €10, apt per person €25; P❄🛜) Not quite a hostel and not quite an apartment hotel, this friendly family-run block on the outskirts of town offers elements of both. Individual beds are rented, hostel-style, in a rambling set of rooms.

Eating

Porto
TOP CHOICE · SEAFOOD €€

(☎033-451 598; www.restoranporto.com; City Marina, Šetalište bb; mains €8-20; ☉10am-1am) From the waterfront promenade, a little bridge arches over a fish pond and into this romantic restaurant where jocular bow-tie-wearing waiters flit about with plates laden with fresh seafood.

Pizza 10 Maradona
PIZZERIA €

(Petra I Petrovića 10; pizza slice €2) A reader alerted us to this late-night hole-in-the-wall eatery selling pizza by the slice. We can confirm that after a hard night's hitting the city's night spots, Maradona's crispy-based pizza does indeed seem to come straight from the hand of God.

Drinking

Top Hill
CLUB

(www.tophill.me; Topliški Put; events €10-25; ☉11pm-5am Jul & Aug) The top cat of Montenegro's summer party scene attracts up to 5000 revellers to its open-air club atop Topliš hill, offering them top-notch sound and lighting, sea views, big-name touring DJs and performances by local pop stars.

Information

Tourist Office (☎033-452 750; www.budva. travel; Njegoševa 28; ☉9am-9pm Mon-Sat, 5-9pm Sun)

Getting There & Away

The **bus station** (☎033-456 000; Popa Jola Zeca bb) has frequent services to Herceg Novi (€6), Kotor (€3.50), Bar (€4.50) and Podgorica (€6).

Pržno & Sveti Stefan
Пржно И Свети Стефан

Gazing down on impossibly picturesque Sveti Stefan, 5km south of Budva, provides the biggest 'wow' moment on the entire coast. And gazing on it is all most people will get to do, as this tiny island – connected to the shore by a narrow isthmus and crammed full of terracotta-roofed dwellings dating from the 15th century – was nationalised in the 1950s and the whole thing is now a luxurious resort.

Sveti Stefan is also the name of the settlement that's sprung up onshore. From its steep slopes you get to look down at that iconic view all day – which some might suggest is even better than staying in the surreally glamorous enclave below.

The general public can access the main Sveti Stefan beach, which faces the island. From the beach there's a very pleasant walk north to the cute village of Pržno where there are some excellent restaurants and another attractive, often crowded beach.

Sleeping & Eating

Vila Drago
TOP CHOICE · GUESTHOUSE €€

(☎030-468 477; www.viladrago.com; Slobode 32; r €45-60, apt €120-130; ❋🏠) The only problem with this family-run place is that you may never want to leave your terrace, as the views are so sublime. Watch the sunset over Sveti Stefan island from the grapevine-covered terrace restaurant (mains €5 to €17).

Aman Sveti Stefan
TOP CHOICE · RESORT €€€

(☎033-420 000; www.amanresorts.com; ste €750-3000; P❋🏠🏊) Truly unique, this island resort offers 50 luxurious suites that showcase the stone walls and wooden beams of the ancient houses. Back on the shore, **Villa Miločer** has a further eight suites by the beach. Non-guests can avail themselves of three eateries: the **Olive Tree** at Sveti Stefan Beach, the **Beach Cafe** at Miločer and **Queen's Chair**, perched on a wooded hill facing Budva.

Vila Levantin
TOP CHOICE · APARTMENTS €

(☎033-468 206; www.villalevantin.com; Vukice Mitrović 3; r €30-50, apt €50-130; P❋🏠🏊) Levantin has a variety of modern rooms and apartments at extremely reasonable prices. The block is modern and well finished, with red stone walls, blue-tiled bathrooms and an attractive plunge pool on the terrace.

Hotel Residence Miločer
HOTEL €€

(☎033-427 100; www.residencemontenegro.com; Jadranski Put; s €69-99, d €79-119; P❋🏠🏊) The decor's fresh and modern, there's secure parking, the breakfast buffets are excellent, and the staff aren't afraid to smile. It's worth paying the additional €10 for a spacious junior suite.

Blanche
TOP CHOICE · EUROPEAN €€

(☎062-504 272; www.blanche-restaurant.com; Obala 11; mains €8-24; ☉10am-midnight) Higher than usual prices and upmarket decor don't necessary signal quality but in the case of this Pržno waterfront restaurant, you can breathe easy. Sharing the menu with Dalmatian seafood classics are succulent steaks and a wide selection of Italian dishes.

❶ Getting There & Away

Olimpia Express buses head to and from Budva (€1.50, 20 minutes) every 30 minutes in summer and hourly in winter.

Petrovac · Петровац
POP 1400

The Romans had the right idea, building their summer villas on this lovely bay. The pretty beachside promenade is perfumed with the scent of lush Mediterranean plants, and a picturesque 16th-century **Venetian fortress** guards a tiny stone harbour. This is one of the best places on the coast for families: the accommodation is reasonably priced, the water's clear and kids roam the esplanade at night with impunity.

In July and August you'll be lucky to find an inch of space on the town beach, but wander south and there's cypress- and oleander-lined **Lučice Beach** and, beyond it, the 2.5km-long sweep of **Buljarica Beach**.

🛏 Sleeping & Eating

Hotel Danica   HOTEL €€
(☏033-462 304; www.hoteldanica.net; s/d €55/60; P❄🅿😐) With a quiet location under the pine-covered hill immediately west of the town beach, this four-storey hotel is small enough to maintain a relaxed family ambience. There's a little pool on the terrace.

Camping Maslina   CAMPGROUND €
(☏033-461 215; akmaslina@t-com.me; Buljarica bb; per adult/child/tent/car/caravan €3/1.50/3/3/5; P🅿) Just off the road to Buljarica Beach, this well-kept campground has a tidy ablutions block with proper sit-down toilets and solar-powered hot water. As Montenegrin campsites go, this is one of the best.

Hotel Đurić   HOTEL €€
(☏033-462 005; www.hoteldjuric.com; Brežine bb; s/d €72/96; ⊗May-Sep; ❄🅿😐) There's a vaguely Spanish Mission feel to this smart boutique hotel. All rooms have kitchen facilities and there's a restaurant at the back under a canopy of kiwifruit and grapevines.

Konoba Bonaca   MONTENEGRIN, SEAFOOD €€
(☏069-084 735; mains €8-15) Set back slightly from the main beach drag, this traditional restaurant focuses mainly on seafood but

the local cheeses and olives are also excellent. Grab a table under the grapevines on the terrace.

❶ Getting There & Away

Petrovac's bus station is near the top of town. Regular services head to Budva and Bar (both €2.50, 30 minutes).

Bar · Бар
POP 13,500

Dominated by Montenegro's main port and a large industrial area, Bar is unlikely to be anyone's highlight, but it is a handy transport hub welcoming trains from Belgrade and ferries from Italy. More interesting are the ruins of Stari Bar (Old Bar) in the mountains behind.

◉ Sights

Stari Bar   TOP CHOICE   RUIN
(Old Bar; adult/child €2/1; ⊗8am-10pm) Bar's original settlements stands on a bluff 4km northeast, off the Ulcinj road. A steep cobbled hill takes you past a cluster of old houses and shops to the fortified entrance, where a short, dark passage pops you out into a large expanse of vine-clad ruins and abandoned streets overgrown with grass and wild flowers. A small museum just inside the entrance explains the site and its history.

The Illyrians founded the city in around 800 BC. It passed in and out of Slavic and Byzantine rule until Venice took it in 1443 and held it until the Ottoman conquest in 1571. Nearly all the 240 buildings now lie in ruins, a result of Montenegrin shelling when the town was captured in 1878.

Buses marked Stari Bar depart from the centre of new Bar every hour (€1).

King Nikola's Palace   MUSEUM
(Dvorac Kralja Nikole; ☏030-314 079; Šetalište Kralje Nikole; adult/child €1/.50; ⊗8am-2pm & 5-11pm) Presenting an elegant facade to the water, this former palace (1885) now houses a collection of antiquities, folk costumes and royal furniture. Its shady gardens contain plants cultivated from seeds and cuttings collected from around the world by Montenegro's sailors.

🛏 Sleeping & Eating

Hotel Princess   HOTEL €€€
(☏030-300 100; www.hotelprincess.me; Jovana Tomaševića 59; s €83-98, d €126-156, ste €205-275;

P✻@🛜🏊) The standards aren't what you'd expect for the price but this resort-style hotel is the best option in Bar by far. Get your money's worth at the private beach, swimming pool and spa centre.

🍴 Kaldrma
MONTENEGRIN €€

(📞030-341 744; kaldrmarestoran@t-com.me; mains €6-11; ⊙lunch & dinner; 🍴) Located on the steep road leading to Stari Bar's main gate, this wonderful little eatery manages to be simultaneously very traditional and slightly hippy-dippy. The focus is on the cuisine of Stari Bar itself, including tender lamb and seasonal vegetarian options. Accommodation is offered in a room upstairs with mattresses laid on woven rugs (€25).

ℹ️ Information

Tourist Information Centre (📞030-311 633; www.visitbar.org; Obala 13 Jula bb; ⊙8am-8pm Mon-Sat, to 2pm Sun Jul-Sep, 8am-4pm Mon-Fri Oct-Jun)

ℹ️ Getting There & Away

The bus station and adjacent train station are 1km southeast of the centre. Frequent buses head to Kotor (€6.50), Budva (€4.50), Ulcinj (€3) and Podgorica (€4.50). Trains head to Virpazar (€1.20, 23 minutes, seven daily), Podgorica (€2.40, one hour, nine daily) and Kolašin (€5.40, 2½ hours, four daily).

Montenegro Lines (📞030-311 164; www.montenegrolines.net) ferries to Italy (Bari and Ancona) leave from the ferry terminal near the centre of town.

Ulcinj
Улцињ

POP 10,700

If you want a feel for Albania without actually crossing the border, buzzy Ulcinj's the place to go. The population is 61% Albanian and in summer it swells with Kosovar holidaymakers for the simple reason that it's nicer than any of the Albanian seaside towns. The elegant minarets of numerous mosques give Ulcinj a distinctly Eastern feel, as does the music echoing out of the kebab stands.

For centuries Ulcinj had a reputation as a pirate's lair. By the end of the 16th century as many as 400 pirates, mainly from Malta, Tunisia and Algeria, made Ulcinj their main port of call – wreaking havoc on passing vessels and then returning to party up large on Mala Plaža. Ulcinj became the centre of a thriving slave trade, with people – mainly from North Africa – paraded for sale on the town's main square.

⊙ Sights & Activities

Beaches
BEACHES

Mala Plaža may be a fine grin of a cove but it's a little hard to see the beach under all that suntanned flesh in July and August. You are better off strolling southeast where a succession of rocky bays offers clear water and a little more room to breathe. **Lady Beach 'Dada'** (admission €1.50) has a women-only policy, while a section of the **Hotel Albatros Beach** is clothing-optional.

The appropriately named **Velika Plaža** (Big Beach) starts 4km southeast of the town and stretches for 12 sandy kilometres. Sections of it sprout deckchairs but there's still plenty of relatively empty space. To be frank, this large flat expanse isn't as picturesque as it sounds and the water is painfully shallow – great for kids but you'll need to walk a fair way for a decent swim.

On your way to Velika Plaža you'll pass the murky Milena canal, where local fishermen use nets suspended from long willow rods attached to wooden stilt houses. The effect is remarkably redolent of Southeast Asia. There are more of these contraptions on the banks of the Bojana River at the other end of Veliki Plaža.

Stari Grad
NEIGHBOURHOOD

The ancient Old Town is still largely residential and somewhat dilapidated – a legacy of the 1979 earthquake. A steep slope leads to the Upper Gate, where there's a small **museum** (admission €1; ⊙9am-8pm Tue-Sun) just inside the walls, containing Roman and Ottoman artefacts.

D'Olcinium Diving Club
DIVING

(📞067-319 100; www.uldiving.com; Detarët e Ulqinit bb) Local dive sites include various wrecks (this is pirate territory, after all) and the remains of a submerged town. If you've got up-to-date qualifications you can rent gear (€20), take a guided shore dive (€15) or head out on a boat for a day's diving (€50).

🛏️ Sleeping

[TOP CHOICE] Haus Freiburg
HOTEL €€

(📞030-403 008; www.hotelhausfreiburg.me; Kosovska bb; s/d/apt €50/65/85; P✻🛜🏊) High on the slopes above the town, this family-run hotel has well-kitted-out apartments and rooms, and a particularly attractive roof terrace with sea views, a swimming pool and small restaurant.

Dvori Balšića
HOTEL €€€

(☎030-421 609; www.hotel-dvoribalsica-montenegro.com; Stari Grad bb; s/d €65/100; ❄🏨) This stone *palazzo* and its equally grand sister, the **Palata Venecija**, are reached by the cobbled lanes and stairs of the Old Town. The sizeable rooms all have kitchenettes and sea views.

Real Estate Travel Agency
ACCOMMODATION SERVICES €

(☎030-421 609; www.realestate-travel.com; Hazif Ali Ulqinaku bb; per person from €15) Obliging English-speaking staff can help you find private rooms, apartments or hotel rooms. They also rent bikes (€10) and cars, run tours and sell maps of Ulcinj.

✕ Eating

TOP CHOICE Miško
SEAFOOD €€€

(Bojana River; mains €9-17) The most upmarket of the Bojana River restaurants (14km east of Ulcinj) is focused completely on seafood, including octopus, shrimps, shellfish, a big selection of fresh fish, and delicious *riblja čorba* (fish soup).

Restaurant Pizzeria Bazar
PIZZERIA, SEAFOOD €

(Hazif Ali Ulqinaku bb; mains €4-10; ⊙10am-1pm) An upstairs restaurant that's a great idling place when the streets below are heaving with tourists. People-watch in comfort as you enjoy a plate of *lignje na žaru* (grilled squid).

❶ Getting There & Away

The bus station is on the northeastern edge of town. Services head to Herceg Novi (€10, daily), Kotor (€9, daily), Budva (€7, eight daily), Podgorica (€6, 12 daily) and across the Albanian border to Shkodra (€6, two daily).

CENTRAL MONTENEGRO

The heart of Montenegro – physically, spiritually and politically – is easily accessed as a day trip from the coast but it's well deserving of a longer exploration. Two wonderful national parks separate it from the Adriatic and behind them lie the two capitals, the ancient current one and the newer former one.

Lovćen National Park
Ловћен

Directly behind Kotor is Mt Lovćen (1749m), the black mountain that gave *Crna Gora* (Montenegro) its name (*crna/negro* means 'black' and *gora/monte* means 'mountain' in Montenegrin and Italian respectively). This locale occupies a special place in the hearts of all Montenegrins. For most of its history it represented the entire nation – a rocky island of Slavic resistance in an Ottoman sea. The old capital of Cetinje nestles in its foothills.

Lovćen's star attraction is the magnificent **Njegoš Mausoleum** (Njegošev Mauzolej; admission €3; ⊙8am-6pm) at the top of its second-highest peak, Jezerski Vrh (1657m). Take the 461 steps up to the entry, where two granite giantesses guard the tomb. Inside, under a golden mosaic canopy, a 28-tonne Petar II Petrović Njegoš rests in the wings of an eagle, carved from a single block of black granite. The actual tomb lies below and a path at the rear leads to a dramatic circular viewing platform.

The national park's 6220 hectares are criss-crossed with well-marked hiking paths. The **National Park Visitor Centre** (www.nparkovi.me; ⊙9am-5pm) at Ivanova Korita offers accommodation in four-bedded bungalows (€40). If you're driving, the park can be approached from either Kotor or Cetinje (entry fee €2). Tour buses provide the only services into the park.

Cetinje
Цетиње

POP 14,000

Rising from a green vale surrounded by rough, grey mountains, Cetinje is an odd mix of former capital and overgrown village, where single-storey cottages and stately mansions share the same street. Pretty Njegoševa is a partly traffic-free thoroughfare lined with interesting buildings, including the **Blue Palace** (Plavi Dvorac), which houses the president, and various former embassies marked with plaques. Everything of significance is in the immediate vicinity.

◎ Sights

TOP CHOICE National Museum of Montenegro
MUSEUM

(www.mnmuseum.org; Narodni muzej Crne Gore; all museums adult/child €10/5; ⊙9am-4pm) The

National Museum is actually a collection of four museums and two galleries housed in a clump of important buildings. A joint ticket will get you into all of them or you can buy individual tickets.

Two are housed in the former parliament (1910), Cetinje's most imposing building. The fascinating **History Museum** (Istorijski muzej; ☏041-230 310; Novice Cerovića 7; adult/child €3/1.50) is very well laid out, following a timeline from the Stone Age to 1955. There are few English signs but the enthusiastic staff will walk you around and give you an overview before leaving you to your own devices.

Upstairs you'll find the equally excellent **Montenegrin Art Gallery** (Crnogorska galerija umjetnosti; adult/child €4/2). In 2012 an offshoot of the national gallery opened in a striking building on Cetinje's main street. The edgy **Miodrag Dado Đurić Gallery** (Galerija; Balšića Pazar; ☉10am-2pm & 6-9pm Tue-Sun) is devoted to 20th-century and contemporary Montenegrin art. The same ticket covers both galleries.

Entry to the **King Nikola Museum** (Muzej kralja Nikole; Dvorski Trg; adult/child €5/2.50) is by guided tour, which the staff will only give to a group, even if you've prepaid a ticket. Still, this 1871 palace of Nikola I, last sovereign of Montenegro, is worth the delay.

The castle-like **Njegoš Museum** (Njegošev muzej; Dvorski Trg; adult/child €3/1.50) was the residence of Montenegro's favourite son, prince-bishop and poet Petar II Petrović Njegoš. The palace was built in 1838 and housed the nation's first billiard table, hence the museum's alternative name, Biljarda. When you leave, turn right and follow the walls to the glass pavilion housing a fascinating large-scale **Relief Map** (admission €1) of Montenegro created by the Austrians in 1917.

Occupying the former Serbian Embassy, the **Ethnographic Museum** (Etnografski Muzej; Dvorski Trg; adult/child €2/1) is the least interesting of the six but if you've bought a joint ticket you may as well check it out. The collection of costumes and tools is well presented and has English notations.

Cetinje Monastery   MONASTERY
(Cetinjski Manastir; ☉8am-6pm) It's a case of four times lucky for the Cetinje Monastery, having been repeatedly destroyed during Ottoman attacks and rebuilt. This sturdy incarnation dates from 1786, with its only exterior ornamentation being the capitals of columns recycled from the original building, founded in 1484.

The chapel to the right of the courtyard holds what is said to be the mummified right hand of St John the Baptist. The casket's only occasionally opened for veneration, so if you miss out you can console yourself with the knowledge that it's not a very pleasant sight.

The monastery **treasury** (admission €2) is only open to groups but if you are persuasive enough and prepared to wait around, you may be able to get in (mornings are best). It holds a wealth of fascinating objects that form a blur as you're shunted around the rooms by one of the monks.

If your legs, shoulders or cleavage are on display you'll either be denied entry or given an unflattering smock to wear.

🛏 Sleeping & Eating

Pansion 22   GUESTHOUSE €€
(☏069-055 473; pansion22@mtel-cg.net; Ivana Crnojevića 22; s/d €22/40; 🛜) They may not be great at speaking English or answering emails, but the family that runs this central guesthouse offers a warm welcome nonetheless. The rooms are simply decorated yet clean and comfortable.

Kole   MONTENEGRIN, EUROPEAN €
(☏041-231 620; www.restaurantkole.me; Bul Crnogorskih Junaka 12; mains €3-12; ☉7am-11pm) Omelettes and pasta are served at this snazzy modern eatery, but what are really great are the local specialities. Try the *Njeguški ražanj*, smoky spit-roasted meat stuffed with *pršut* and cheese.

ℹ Information

Tourist Information (☏078-108 788; www.cetinje.travel; Novice Cerovića bb; ☉8am-6pm)

ℹ Getting There & Away

Cetinje is on the main Budva–Podgorica highway and can also be reached by a glorious back road from Kotor via Lovćen National Park. Buses stop at Trg Goloootočkih Žrtava, two blocks from the main street. There are regular services to Podgorica (€4) and Budva (€4).

Lake Skadar National Park   Скадарско Језеро

The Balkans' largest lake, dolphin-shaped Lake Skadar has its tail and two-thirds of its body in Montenegro and its nose in Albania.

Covering between 370 and 550 sq km (depending on the time of year), it's one of the most important reserves for wetland birds in the whole of Europe. The endangered Dalmatian pelican nests here, along with 256 other species, while 48 species of fish lurk beneath its smooth surface. On the Montenegrin side, an area of 400 sq km is protected by a national park. It's a blissfully pretty area, encompassing steep mountains, hidden villages, island monasteries, clear waters and floating meadows of waterlilies.

◉ Sights

Rijeka Crnojevića VILLAGE
The northwestern end of the lake thins into the serpentine loops of the Crnojević River and terminates near the pretty village of the same name. It's a charming, tucked-away kind of place, accessed by side roads that lead off the Cetinje–Podgorica highway. Taxi boats dock at the marble riverside promenade, near the photogenic arched stone bridge (1854).

Žabljak Crnojevića RUIN
For a brief time in the 15th century, this was the capital of Zetan ruler Ivan Crnojević. Now the enigmatic ruins stand forlornly on a hillside surrounded by green plains. The site's a little hard to find but well worth the effort. Heading towards Podgorica, turn left at the only set of traffic lights in Golubovci. After the railway bridge and the one-way bridge, turn left. Continue for about 4.5km until you see a bridge to your left. Cross the bridge and continue to the car park near the village. Take the stone stairs heading up from the path near the river and follow your nose along the overgrown path.

Virpazar TOWN
This little town, gathered around a square and a river blanketed with water lilies, serves as the main gateway to the national park. Most of the boat tours of the lake depart from here.

Murići BEACH
The southern edge of the lake is the most dramatic, with the Rumija Mountains rising precipitously from the water. From Virpazar there's a wonderful drive following the contours of the lake through the mountains towards the border before crossing the range and turning back towards Ulcinj. About halfway, a steep road descends to the village of Murići. This is one of the lake's best swimming spots. Local boatmen offer trips to the historic monasteries on the nearby islands for around €10 per hour.

🏃 Activities

Green Boats BOAT TOUR
(Zeleni Brodovi; ☑069-998 737; greenboats.me@gmail.com; per hr from Virpazar/Vranjina €25/40) Lake cruises are offered every two hours by this association of small local operators. Two-hour cruises are the norm, although longer trips can be arranged. We've heard glowing reports about one particular boat, the **Golden Frog** (☑069-413 307; www.skadar-lakecruise.blogspot.co.uk).

🌿Undiscovered Montenegro ADVENTURE TOURS
(☑069-402 374; www.lake-skadar.com; ☑Apr-Nov) Specialises in weeklong, all-inclusive, lake-based itineraries (per person €530 including accommodation at Villa Miela), but also offers an accommodation booking service and day tours. Options include guided hikes, kayaking, caving, boat tours, fishing, car safaris, wine tours and expert-led birdwatching.

🛏 Sleeping & Eating

Villa Miela GUESTHOUSE €€
(☑020-3287 0015; www.undiscoveredmontenegro.com; r €80; ☑Apr-Nov) Sitting pretty on the slopes near Virpazar, this lovingly renovated stone farmhouse has four rooms sharing a kitchen, BBQ area, orchard and lake views. In July and August it's reserved for Undiscovered Montenegro's seven-day activity holidays, but shorter stays are accepted at other times.

TOP CHOICE Stari Most SEAFOOD €€
(☑041-239 505; mains €8-25) You wouldn't expect it, but sleepy Rijeka Crnojevića is home to one of Montenegro's best restaurants. Freshwater fish – particularly eel, trout and carp – is the speciality.

Konoba Badanj MONTENEGRIN €€
(mains €6-12; ☑8am-midnight) Near the bridge in Virpazar, a cool stone-walled interior with solid wooden beams makes this an atmo_spheric eating option. The fish soup comes with big chunks of fish and delicious scone-like homemade bread.

ℹ Information

National Park Visitor Centre (☑020-879 103; www.nparkovi.me; admission €2, free with national park entry ticket; ☑8am-4pm, to 6pm summer) In Vranjina, this centre has excellent displays about all of Montenegro's national parks. A kiosk here and at Virpazar sells park entry tickets (per day €4) and fishing permits (per day summer/winter €10/5). In the busy months, tour operators have kiosks in the vicinity. Just across the busy highway and railway tracks are the remains of the 19th-century fortress Lesendro.

Virpazar Tourist Office (☑020-711 102; www.visitbar.org; ☺8am-5pm May-Sep, to 4pm Mon-Fri Oct-Apr; ☎) This big new office on the main square can assist you with arranging anything in the area, including boat trips, wine tastings and private accommodation. Upstairs there are displays about the national park, and the office operates as a storefront for the region's small wine producers.

ⓘ Getting There & Away

Buses on the Bar–Podgorica route stop on the highway. Virpazar's train station is off the main road, 800m south of town. There are seven trains to/from Bar (€1.20, 23 minutes) and Podgorica (€1.40, 30 minutes) every day.

Podgorica   Подгорица
POP 151,000

Podgorica's never going to be Europe's most happening capital, but if you can get past the sweltering summer temperatures and concrete apartment blocks, you'll find a pleasant little city with lots of green space and some excellent galleries and bars.

The city sits at the confluence of two rivers. West of the broad Morača is what passes for the business district. The smaller Ribnica River divides the eastern side in two. To the south is Stara Varoš, the heart of the former Ottoman town. North of the Ribnica is Nova Varoš, an attractive, mainly low-rise precinct of late-19th-century and early-20th-century buildings housing a lively mixture of shops and bars. At its centre is the main square, Trg Republika.

◉ Sights & Activities

FREE **Museums & Galleries of Podgorica**   MUSEUM
(Muzeji i Galerije Podgorice; ☑020-242 543; Marka Miljanova 4; ☺9am-8pm) Despite Cetinje nabbing most of the national endowment, the new capital is well served by this collection of art and artefacts. There's an interesting section on Podgorica's history which includes antiquities exhumed from its Roman incarnation, Doclea.

FREE **Petrović Palace**   PALACE, GALLERY
(Dvorac Petrovića; ☑020-243 513; www.csucg.co.me; Ljubljanska bb; ☺9am-2pm & 5-10pm Mon-Fri, 10am-2pm Sat) The Contemporary Art Centre operates two galleries in Podgorica. The bottom two floors of this former palace are given over to high-profile exhibitions, while the top floor has an oddball collection from its days as Yugoslavia's gallery devoted to art from Non-Aligned Movement countries.

Temporary exhibitions are also staged in the small **Galerija Centar** (☑020-665 409; Njegoševa 2; ☺10am-1pm & 6-pm Mon-Fri, 10am-1pm Sat).

Cathedral of Christ's Resurrection   CHURCH
(Saborni Hram Hristovog Vaskrsenja; www.hram-vaskrsenjapg.org; Bul Džordža Vašingtona) The large dome, white stone towers and gold crosses of this immense Serbian Orthodox cathedral are striking additions to Podgorica's skyline. Work commenced in 1993 and it's still a long way from completion, but you can usually enter and check out the glistening gold frescos inside.

Montenegro Adventures   ADVENTURE TOURS
(☑020-208 000; www.montenegro-adventures.com; Jovana Tomaševića 35) This well-respected and long-standing agency creates tailor-made adventure tours, country-wide. It can organise mountain guides, cycling logistics, kitesurfing, hiking, cultural activities, accommodation, flights...you name it.

🛏 Sleeping

Most visitors to Podgorica are here for business, either commerce or government-related. Hotels set their prices accordingly and private accommodation isn't really an option.

Hotel Podgorica   HOTEL €€€
(☑020-402 500; www.hotelpodgorica.co.me; Bul Sv Petra Cetinjskog 1; s €125-155, d €170-180, ste €190-200; P❉@☎) A wonderful showcase of 1960s Yugoslav architecture, the Podgorica has been luxuriously modernised yet retains its riverstone cladding and period charm. The best rooms have terraces facing the river.

Aria   HOTEL €€
(☑020-872 572; www.hotelaria.me; Mahala bb; s €56-76, d €93, apt €132-205; ❉☎) An oasis of green lawns in the scorched field surrounding the airport, this new hotel offers better

Podgorica

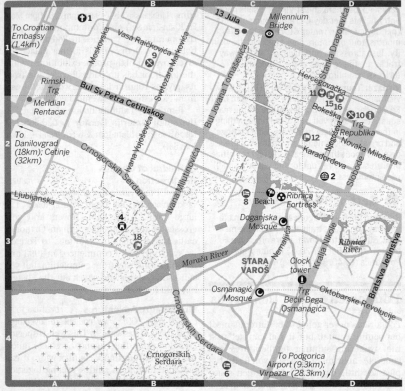

value than its city equivalents and is a great option if you've got a badly timed flight.

City Hotel
HOTEL €€€
(☎020-441 500; www.cityhotelmn.com; Crnogorskih serdara 5; s €75-95, d €100-120, apt €130-170; P❋@☎) A business-orientated makeover in 2008 has thankfully kept the 1970s exterior angularity of this city-fringe hotel, while the surrealist art of Dado Đurić has prevented a total beige-out inside.

Hotel Evropa
HOTEL €€
(☎020-623 444; www.hotelevropa.co.me; Orahovačka 16; s €40-55, d €70-90; P❋@☎) It's hardly a salubrious location, but Evropa is handy to the train and bus stations, and offers good clean rooms with comfortable beds, writing desks and decent showers.

✗ Eating & Drinking

Podgorica's nightlife is centred on Nova Varoš, particularly in the blocks west of ulica

Slobode. The hippest strip right now is ulica Bokeška.

TOP CHOICE / Lupo di Mare
SEAFOOD €€
(Trg Republika 22; mains €8-20; ☺8am-midnight) As you may have guessed from the name, there's a distinct Italian bent to this excellent seafood restaurant. Nautical knick-knacks hang from the pale stone walls and there's an interesting wine list.

Leonardo
ITALIAN €€
(☎020-242 902; www.leonardo-restoran.com; Svetozara Markovića bb; mains €5-17; ☺8am-midnight; ☎✗) Leonardo's unlikely position at the centre of a residential block makes it a little tricky to find but the effort's well rewarded by accomplished Italian cuisine. The pasta dishes are delicious and reasonably priced.

Buda Bar
BAR
(☎067-344 944; www.facebook.com/Budabarpg; Stanka Dragojevića 26; ☺8am-2am) A golden

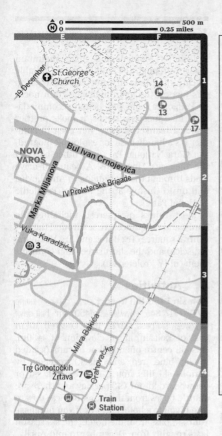

Podgorica

◉ Sights

1 Cathedral of Christ's Resurrection A1
2 Galerija Centar..................................D2
3 Museums & Galleries of Podgorica....E3
4 Petrović Palace................................B3

◎ Activities, Courses & Tours

5 Montenegro Adventures...................C1

⊜ Sleeping

6 City Hotel.......................................C4
7 Hotel Evropa E4
8 Hotel Podgorica...............................C3

⊗ Eating

9 Leonardo..B1
10 Lupo di Mare.................................D2

⊖ Drinking

11 Buda Bar.......................................D1

ⓘ Information

12 Albanian Embassy...........................D2
13 Bosnia & Hercegovinian Embassy F1
14 French Embassy..............................F1
15 German Embassy.............................D1
16 Serbian Embassy............................D2
17 UK Embassy...................................F1
18 USA Embassy B3

Buddha smiles serenely as you search for the eternal truth at the bottom of a cocktail glass. The semi-enclosed terrace is the place to be on balmy summer nights.

ⓘ Information

Tourist Organisation Podgorica (☑020-667 535; www.podgorica.travel; Slobode 47; ⊗8am-8pm Mon-Fri)

ⓘ Getting There & Around

AIR Podgorica airport is 9km south of the city. Airport taxis have a standard €15 fare to the centre.

BUS Podgorica's **bus station** (☑020-620 430; Trg Golootočkih Žrtava 1) has services to all major towns, including Herceg Novi (€9, three hours), Kotor (€7, 2¼ hours), Budva (€6, 1½ hours), Ulcinj (€6, one hour) and Cetinje (€3.50, 30 minutes)

TRAIN From Podgorica's **train station** (☑020-441 211; www.zpcg.me; Trg Golootočkih Žrtava

13) there are services to Bar (€2.40, one hour, nine daily), Virpazar (€1.40, 30 minutes, seven daily), Kolašin (€5.90, 1½ hours, five daily) and Belgrade (€20, 10 hours, three daily).

Ostrog Monastery
Манастир Острог

Resting in a cliff face 900m above the Zeta valley, the gleaming white Ostrog Monastery (Manastir Ostrog) is the most important site in Montenegro for Orthodox Christians. Even with its numerous pilgrims, tourists and trashy souvenir stands, it's a strangely affecting place.

The **Lower Monastery** (Donji manastir) is 2km below the main shrine. Stop here to admire the vivid frescos in the **Holy Trinity Church** (Crkva Sv Trojice; 1824). Behind it is a natural spring where you can fill your bottles with deliciously fresh water and potentially benefit from an internal blessing as you sup it. From here the faithful, some of them barefoot, plod up the steep road to the top. Nonpilgrims and the pure of heart may drive directly to the main car park and limit their penitance to just the final 200m.

The **Upper Monastery** (Gornji manastir; the really impressive one) is dubbed 'Sv Vasilije's miracle', because no one seems to understand how it was built. Constructed in 1665 within two large caves, it gives the impression that it has grown out of the very rock. Sv Vasilije (St Basil) brought his monks here after the Ottomans destroyed Tvrdoš Monastery near Trebinje. Pilgrims queue to enter the shrine where the saint's fabric-wrapped bones are kept. To enter you'll need to be wearing a long skirt or trousers (jeans are fine) and cover your shoulders. At the very top of the monastery is another cave-like chapel with faded frescos dating from 1667.

A **guesthouse** (☏020-811 133; dm €5) near the Lower Monastery offers tidy single-sex dorm rooms, while in summer sleeping mats are provided for free to pilgrims in front of the Upper Monastery.

NORTHERN MOUNTAINS

This really is the full Monte: soaring peaks, hidden monasteries, secluded villages, steep river canyons and a whole heap of 'wild beauty', to quote the tourist slogan. It's well worth hiring a car for a couple of days to get off the beaten track – some of the roads are truly spectacular.

Morača Canyon

Heading north from Podgorica, it doesn't take long before the scenery becomes breathtaking. The highway gets progressively more precarious as it follows the Morača River into a nearly perpendicular canyon, 300m to 400m deep. If you're driving, pull over into one of the viewing areas to enjoy it properly, as this is an extremely busy and unforgiving stretch of road.

Near the canyon's northern end is **Morača Monastery**. As you enter the walled compound it's like stepping back into the 13th century, when the monastery was founded. The larger of its two churches has faded external frescos by the celebrated master Đorđe Mitrofanović and a wealth of religious art inside.

Kolašin   Колашин

POP 2800

Kolašin is Montenegro's main mountain resort. Although the skiing's not as reliable as Durmitor, Kolašin's much easier to get to (it's just off the main highway, 71km north of Podgorica) and has better accommodation. Like most ski towns, it looks prettier under a blanket of snow but even in summer it's a handy base for exploring Biogradska Gora National Park and other parts of the Bjelasica Mountains. A beautiful drive leads through the mountains to Andrijevica and on to Gusinje at the base of Prokletije National Park.

Most things of interest, including the banks and post office, are set around the two central squares (Trg Borca and Trg Vukmana Kruščića) and the short street that connects them (ul IV Proleterske).

🏃 Activities

Kolašin 1450 Ski Resort   SKIING
(☏020-717 845; www.kolasin1450.com; half-day/day/week ski pass €12/20/104) Located 10km east of Kolašin, at an elevation of 1450m, this ski centre offers 30km of runs (graded green, blue, red and black) reached by various ski lifts. You can hire a full ski or snowboard kit for €13 per day and there are shuttle buses from the Hotel Bianca; they're free if you're a hotel guest or if you purchase your ski pass from the hotel. The ski season lasts roughly from December to mid-April.

Hiking   HIKING
Three marked hiking paths start from Trg Borca and head into the Bjelasica mountains. From the ski centre there's a 16km, five-hour loop route through the forest to Mt Ključ (1973m) and back.

Explorer Tourist Agency   ADVENTURE TOURS
(☏020-864 200; www.montenegroexplorer.co.me; Mojkovačka bb) Located near the bus station, this agency specialises in action-packed holidays, including hiking, skiing, rafting, mountain biking, canyoning, caving, mountain climbing, jeep safaris, horse riding, paragliding and fishing expeditions. It also hires mountain bikes.

🛏 Sleeping & Eating

TOP CHOICE **Bianca Resort & Spa**   RESORT €€€
(☏020-863 000; www.biancaresort.com; Mirka Vešovića bb; s/d from €79/108; P🛜🏊) Take one

large angular hotel with quirky hexagonal windows, completely gut it and give it a designer rustic look, and you end up with an atmospheric, idiosyncratic and first-rate ski resort.

Brile HOTEL, RESTAURANT €€
(☑020-865 021; www.montenegrohotelsonline.com/eng/hotel/46/brile.html; Buda Tomovića 2; s/d €35/70; 🛜) On the edge of the main square, this attractive family-run hotel has comfy rooms with polished wooden floors. There's a sauna for an après-ski defrost and a restaurant (mains €5 to €10) downstairs serving warming comfort food.

TOP CHOICE **Konoba kod Rada Vlahovića** MONTENEGRIN €€
(Trg Vukmana Kruščića; mains €6-8) Set on the square that was the heart of the old Turkish town, this rustic eatery is a standard-bearer for Montenegrin mountain cuisine, such as tender roast lamb which falls off the bone.

Vodenica MONTENEGRIN €€
(☑020-865 338; Dunje Dokić bb; mains €5-7) Set in a traditional watermill, Vodenica offers a taste of traditional stodgy mountain food designed to warm your belly on cold nights. Ease back and let your arteries clog.

Savardak MONTENEGRIN €€
(☑069-051 264; savardak@t-com.me; mains €8-9) Located 2.8km from Kolašin on the road to the ski centre, Savardak serves traditional food in what looks like a big haystack with a chimney attached. Four-person apartments (€40) are available in a thatch-roofed wooden chalet.

❶ Information

Bjelasica & Komovi Regional Tourism Organisation (☑020-865 110; www.bjelasica-komovi.com; Trg Borca 2; ☺9am-8pm Mon-Fri, 9am-noon & 4-8pm Sat & Sun)
Kolašin Tourist Office (☑020-864 254; www.kolasin.travel; Mirka Vešovića bb; ☺8am-8pm Mon-Fri, 9am-3pm Sat)

❶ Getting There & Away

BUS The **bus station** (☑020-864 033; Mojkovačka bb) is a shed set back from the road leading into town, about 200m from the centre. There are regular services to Podgorica (€5).
TRAIN Kolašin's train station is 1.5km from the centre. Trains head to Podgorica (€5, 90 minutes, five daily) and Bar (€5.48, 2½ hours, four daily). Buy your tickets onboard.

Biogradska Gora National Park Биоградска Гора

Nestled in the heart of the Bjelasica Mountain Range, this pretty national park has as its heart 16 sq km of virgin woodland – one of Europe's last primeval forests. The main entrance to the park is between Kolašin and Mojkovac on the Podgorica–Belgrade route. After paying a €2 entry fee you can drive the further 4km to the lake.

You can hire rowboats (per hour €8) and buy fishing permits (per day €20) from the **park office** (☑020-865 625; www.nparkovi.me; campsites per small tent/large tent/caravan €3/5/10, cabins €20; ☺7.30am-8.30pm) by the car park. Nearby there's a camping ground and a cluster of 12 windowless log cabins. The ablutions block for the cabins is much nicer than the campsite's basic squat toilets. **Restoran Biogradsko Jezero** (mains €5.70-9) has a terrace where you can steal glimpses of the lake through the trees as you tuck into a traditional lamb or veal dish.

The nearest bus stop is an hour's walk away, at Kraljevo Kolo, and the nearest train station is a 90-minute walk, at Štitarička Rijeka.

Durmitor National Park Дурмитор

Magnificent scenery ratchets up to the stupendous in this national park (€2 entry fee per day), where ice and water have carved a dramatic landscape from the limestone. Eighteen glacial lakes known as *gorske oči* (mountain eyes) dot the Durmitor range, with the largest, **Black Lake** (Crno jezero), a pleasant 3km walk from Žabljak. The rounded mass of **Meded** (The Bear; 2287m) rears up behind the lake flanked by others of the park's 48 peaks over 2000m, including the highest, **Bobotov Kuk** (2523m). From late December to March, Durmitor is Montenegro's main ski resort; in summer it's a popular place for hiking, rafting and other active pursuits.

Žabljak, at the eastern edge of the range, is the park's principal gateway and the only town within its boundaries. It's not very big and neither is it attractive, but it has a supermarket, post office, bank, hotels and restaurants, all gathered around the parking lot that masquerades as the main square.

⚡ Activities

Rafting

Slicing through the mountains at the northern edge of the national park like they were made from the local soft cheese, the Tara River forms a canyon that at its peak is 1300m deep. The best views are from the water, which explains why rafting along the river is one of the country's most popular tourist activities.

There are a few rapids but don't expect an adrenaline-fuelled white-water experience. You'll get the most excitement in April and May, when the last of the melting snow revs up the flow. Various operators run trips between April and October.

The 82km section that is raftable starts from Splavište, south of the Tara Bridge, and ends at Šćepan Polje on the Bosnian border. The classic two-day trip heads through the deepest part of the canyon on the first day, stopping overnight at Radovan Luka. **Summit Travel Agency** (☑052-360 082; www.summit.co.me; Njegoševa 12, Žabljak) offers trips, including transfers from Žabljak (half-/one-/two-day tour €50/110/200).

Most of the day tours from the coast traverse only the last 18km from Brstanovica – this is outside the national park and hence avoids hefty fees. You'll miss out on the canyon's depths but it's still a beautiful stretch, including most of the rapids. The buses follow a spectacular road along the Piva River, giving you a double dose of canyon action.

If you've got your own wheels you can save a few bucks and avoid a lengthy coach tour by heading directly to Šćepan Polje. It's important to use a reputable operator; in 2010, two people died in one day on a trip with inexperienced guides. At a minimum, make sure you're given a helmet and life-jacket – wear them and do them up.

One good operator is **Kamp Grab** (☑040-200 598; www.tara-grab.com; half-day incl lunch €44, 2-day all-inclusive €180), with lodgings blissfully located 8km upstream from Šćepan Polje. To get there, you'll need to cross the Montenegrin side of the border crossing and hang a right (tell the guards you're heading to Grab); the last 3.5km is unsealed. Accommodation is available, and Grab also offers guided riverboarding (hydrospeed), where you direct yourself down the river on what looks like a kick board (€35).

Tara Tour (☑069-086 106; www.tara-tour.com) offers an excellent half-day trip (€40, including two meals) and has a cute set of wooden chalets in Šćepan Polje; accommodation, three meals and a half-day's rafting costs €55.

Hiking

Durmitor has dozens of hiking trails, some of which traverse seriously high-altitude paths which are prone to fog and summer thunderstorms. Ask the staff at the visitors centre about tracks that suit your level of experience and fitness.

Skiing

On the slopes of Savin Kuk (2313m), you'll find Durmitor's main ski centre. Its 3.5km run starts from a height of 2010m and is best suited to advanced skiers. On the outskirts of Žabljak, near the bus station, **Javorovača Ski Centar** (☑067-800 971) has a gentle 300m slope that's good for kids and beginners. One of the big attractions for skiing in Durmitor is the cost: day passes are around €15, weekly passes €70, and ski lessons cost between €10 and €20.

🛏 Sleeping & Eating

TOP CHOICE Eko-Oaza Suza

Evrope   CABINS, CAMPGROUND €

(☑069-444 590; ekooazatara@gmail.com; Dobrilovina; campsites per tent/person/campervan €5/1/10, cabins €50; ☺Apr-Oct) Consisting of four comfortable wooden cottages (each sleeping five people) and a fine stretch of lawn, this magical family-run 'eco oasis' offers a genuine experience of Montenegrin hospitality. Home-cooked meals are provided on request.

Hotel Soa   HOTEL €€

(☑052-360 110; www.hotelsoa.com; Njegoševa bb, Žabljak; s €55-82, d €75-110, ste €130-160; ☎) Rooms are kitted out with monsoon shower heads, Etro toiletries, robes and slippers, and downstairs there's an appealing terrace restaurant. Best of all, the staff are genuinely friendly and the prices reasonable.

Zlatni Papagaj   PIZZERIA, CAFE €

(Vuka Karadžića 5, Žabljak; mains €4-13; ☎) The 'Golden Parrot' has the feel of a pirate lair, with wine-barrel tables and a thick fug of cigarette smoke in the air. The menu offers a crowd-pleasing selection of pizza and steaks.

ⓘ Information

Durmitor National Park Visitor Centre (www.nparkovi.co.me; Jovana Cvijića bb; ☺9am-5pm Mon-Fri)

PIVA CANYON

The highway to Šćepan Polje is a beautiful drive and quite a feat of engineering. It clings to the cliffs of the Piva Canyon and passes through 56 small tunnels carved out of the stone. The Piva River was blocked in 1975 by the building of a 220m-high hydroelectric dam at Plužine, flooding part of the canyon to create Lake Piva, which reaches depths of over 180m.

Great care was taken to move the **Piva Monastery** (Manastir Piva) to higher ground – a feat that took 12 years to complete. This Serbian Orthodox monastery has the distinction of being the only one to be built during the Turkish occupation.

Accommodation is available at the rafting camps around Šćepan Polje and in various *eko sela* (eco villages), scattered around Plužine and the back road to Žabljak. One excellent option is **Eko Selo Meadows** (☑069-718 078; www.meadows-eco.com; Donja Brezna bb; s/d/tr/q €20/30/42/50, mains €6-10; ℗), signposted from the highway, 17.5km south of Piva Monastery. Set on a flat plain edged by hills, the complex consists of a large restaurant serving local specialities and a collection of tidy wooden cabins.

ⓘ Getting There & Away

All of the approaches to Durmitor are spectacular. If you're coming from the coast, the quickest route is through Nikšić and Šavnik. There's a wonderful back road through the mountains leaving the highway near Plužine, but it's impassable as soon as the snows fall.

The bus station is at the southern edge of Žabljak, on the Šavnik road. Three buses head to Podgorica daily (€9.50).

UNDERSTAND MONTENEGRO

Montenegro Today

Going it alone was a brave move for a nation of this size but toughing it out is something this gutsy people have had plenty of experience in. Their national identity is built around resisting the Ottoman Empire for hundreds of years in a mountainous enclave much smaller than the nation's current borders.

The Never-Changing Government

In the 2012 general election, the Democratic Party of Socialists (DPS) fell two seats short of ruling in their own right but quickly formed a coalition with ethnic Bosniak, Albanian and Croat parties to form a government (ethnicity still plays a large role in political affiliation here). What's extraordinary about this is that the DPS has won every single vote since multiparty elections were established, marking the end of Communism in Yugoslavia.

Part of the party's continued popularity is the role they played in gaining Montenegro its independence. Several of the main opposition parties, especially the Serb-aligned parties, were strongly opposed to the break with Serbia, although most have publicly dropped their anti-independence stance.

The Đukanović Factor

Another factor in the DPS's success is the charismatic figure of returning Prime Minister Milo Đukanović. As a tall (198cm), handsome 26-year-old he was part of the 'antibureaucratic revolution' that took control of the Communist Party in 1989. At the age of 29 he became the first prime minister of post-Communist Montenegro and apart from a few years of 'retirement' he has been prime minister or president ever since.

However, Đukanović remains a controversial figure. While still president he was investigated by an Italian antimafia unit and charged for his alleged role in a multibillion-dollar cigarette-smuggling operation; the charges were dropped in 2009.

NATO and the EU

Shortly after independence, Montenegro applied to join both NATO and EU, and in June 2012 it opened formal EU accession negotiations. While most Montenegrins strongly favour EU membership, joining NATO is much more contentious. Memories of the NATO bombing of Serbia during the Kosovo conflict are still fresh. However, the

Montenegrin goverment has stood firm in its resolve, publicly stating that it expects to be invited to join the alliance in 2014.

History

Like all the modern states of the Balkan peninsula, Montenegro has a long, convoluted and eventful history. History is worn on the sleeve here and people discuss 600-year-old events (or their not-always-accurate versions of them) as if they happened yesterday. Events such as the split of the Roman Empire, the subsequent split in Christianity between Catholic and Orthodox, and the battles with the Ottoman Turks still have a direct bearing on the politics of today.

Before the Slavs

The Illyrians were the first known people to inhabit the region. By 1000 BC they had established a loose federation of tribes across much of the Balkans. By around 400 BC the Greeks had established some coastal colonies and by AD 10 the Romans had absorbed the entire region into their empire. In 395 the Roman Empire was split into two halves: the western half centred on Rome and the eastern half, which eventually became the Byzantine Empire, centred on Constantinople. Modern Montenegro lay on the fault line between the two entities.

In the early 7th century, the Slavs arrived from north of the Danube. Two main Slavic groups settled in the Balkans: the Croats along the Adriatic coast and the Serbs in the interior. With time most Serbs accepted the Orthodox faith, while the Croats accepted Catholicism.

First Serbian States

In the 9th century the first Serb kingdom, Raška, arose near Novi Pazar (in modern Serbia) followed shortly by another Serb state, Duklja, which sprang up on the site of present-day Podgorica. Raška eventually became known as Serbia and Duklja as Zeta. From the 12th century, Raška/Serbia became dominant over Zeta, which nonetheless remained a distinct area. At its greatest extent Serbia reached from the Adriatic to the Aegean and north to the Danube.

Expansion was halted in 1389 at the battle of Kosovo Polje, where the Serbs were defeated by the Ottoman Turks. By 1441 the Turks had rolled through Serbia and in the late 1470s they took on Zeta. The remnants of the Zetan nobility fled first to Žabljak Crnojevića, near Lake Skadar, and eventually into the mountains. In 1480 they established a stronghold at Cetinje on Mt Lovćen.

Montenegro & the Ottomans

This mountainous area became the last redoubt of Serbian Orthodox culture when all else fell to the Ottomans. It was during this time that the Venetians, who ruled Kotor, Budva and much of the Adriatic Coast, began calling Mt Lovćen the Monte Negro (Black Mountain). The Montenegrins, as they became known, built a reputation as fearsome warriors. The Ottomans opted for pragmatism, and largely left them to their own devices.

With the struggle against the Ottomans, the highly independent Montenegrin clans began to work collaboratively and the *vladika,* previously a metropolitan position within the Orthodox Church, began mediating between tribal chiefs. As such, the *vladika* assumed a political role, and *vladika* became a hereditary title: the prince-bishop.

In the late 18th century the Montenegrins under *vladika* Petar I Petrović began to expand their territory, doubling it within the space of a little over 50 years. Serbia achieved independence in 1835 and a similar rebellion against Ottoman control broke out in Bosnia in 1875. Montenegrins joined the insurgency and made significant territorial gains as a result. At the Congress of Berlin in 1878, Montenegro and Bosnia officially achieved independence.

In the early years of the 20th century there were increasing calls for union with Serbia and rising political opposition to Montenegro's autocratic Petrović dynasty. The Serbian king Petar Karadjordjević was suspected of involvement in an attempt to overthrow King Nikola Petrović, and Montenegrin–Serbian relations reached their historic low point.

The Balkan Wars of 1912–13 saw the Montenegrins joining the Serbs, Greeks and Bulgarians, and succeeding in throwing the Ottomans out of southeastern Europe. Now that Serbia and Montenegro were both independent and finally shared a border, the idea of a Serbian–Montenegrin union gained more currency. King Nikola pragmatically supported the idea on the stipulation that both the Serbian and Montenegrin royal houses be retained.

The Two Yugoslavias

Before the union could be realised WWI intervened. Serbia quickly entered the war and Montenegro followed in its footsteps. Austria-Hungary invaded Serbia shortly afterwards and swiftly captured Cetinje, with King Nikola escaping to France. In 1918 the Serbian army reclaimed Montenegro, and the French, keen to implement the Serbian–Montenegrin union, refused to allow Nikola to leave France. The following year Montenegro was incorporated in the Kingdom of the Serbs, Croats and Slovenes, the first Yugoslavia.

During WWII the Italians occupied Montenegro. Tito's Partisans and the Serbian Chetniks engaged the Italians, sometimes lapsing into fighting each other. Ultimately, the Partisans put up the best fight and with the support of the Allies, the Partisans entered Belgrade in October 1944 and Tito was made prime minister. Once the communist federation of Yugoslavia was established, Tito decreed that Montenegro have full republic status and the border of the modern Montenegrin state was set. Of all the Yugoslav states, Montenegro had the highest per-capita membership of the Communist Party and it was highly represented in the armed forces.

Union then Independence

In the decades following Tito's death in 1980, Slobodan Milošević used the issue of Kosovo to whip up a nationalist storm in Serbia and rode to power on a wave of nationalism. The Montenegrins largely supported their Orthodox coreligionists. In 1991 Montenegrin paramilitary groups were responsible for the shelling of Dubrovnik. In 1992, by which point Slovenia, Croatia and Bosnia and Hercegovina (BiH) had opted for independence, the Montenegrins voted overwhelmingly in support of a plebiscite to remain in Yugoslavia with Serbia.

In 1997 Montenegrin leader Milo Djukanović broke with an increasingly isolated Milošević and immediately became the darling of the West. As the Serbian regime became an international pariah, the Montenegrins increasingly wanted to re-establish their distinct identity.

In 2003 Yugoslavia was consigned to the dustbin of history, and Montenegro entered into a state union with Serbia. In theory this union was based on equality between the two republics; however, in practice Serbia was such a dominant partner that the union proved infeasible. In May 2006 the Montenegrins voted for independence.

People

In the last census (2011), 45% of the population identified as Montenegrin, 29% as Serb, 12% as Bosniak or Muslim, 5% as Albanian, 1% as Croat and 1% as Roma. Montenegrins are the majority along most of the coast and the centre of the country, while Albanians dominate in Ulcinj, Bosniaks in the far east (Rožaje and Plav), and Serbs in the north and Herceg Novi. Religion and ethnicity broadly go together in these parts. Over 72% of the population are Orthodox Christians (mainly Montenegrins and Serbs), 19% Muslim (mainly Bosniaks and Albanians) and 3% Roman Catholic (mainly Albanians and Croats).

Montenegrins traditionally considered themselves 'the best of the Serbs', and while most Montenegrins still feel a strong kinship to their closest siblings, this is coupled with a determination to maintain their distinct identity. After negotiating a reasonably amicable divorce from the unhappy state union in 2006, relations between the two countries took a turn for the worse. In 2008 Serbia expelled Montenegro's ambassador after Montenegro officially recognised the Serbian province of Kosovo as an independent country. Diplomatic relations have since resumed, but issues of ethnicity and identity remain thorny.

Food & Drink

Loosen your belt; you're in for a treat. Eating in Montenegro is generally an extremely pleasurable experience. By default, most of the food is local, fresh and organic, and hence very seasonal. The food on the coast is virtually indistinguishable from Dalmatian cuisine: lots of grilled seafood, garlic, olive oil and Italian dishes. Inland it's much more meaty and Serbian-influenced. The village of Njeguši in the Montenegrin heartland is famous for its *pršut* (dried ham) and cheese. Anything with Njeguški in its name is going to be a true Montenegrin dish and stuffed with these goodies.

Eating in Montenegro can be a trial for vegetarians and almost impossible for vegans. Pasta, pizza and salad are the best fallback options. Nonsmoking sections are a rumour from distant lands that have yet to trouble the citizens of Montenegro.

SURVIVAL GUIDE

Directory A–Z

Accommodation

Hotels and private accommodation (rooms and apartments for rent) form the bulk of the sleeping options, although hostels have been popping up in the more touristy areas in recent years. Camping grounds operate in summer and some of the mountainous areas have cabin accommodation in 'eco villages' or mountain huts.

In the peak summer season, some places require minimum stays (three days to a week). Many establishments on the coast, even some of the established hotels, close during winter.

An additional tourist tax (usually less than €1 per night) is added to the rate for all accommodation types. For private accommodation it's sometimes left up to the guest to pay it, but it can be nigh on impossible finding the right authority to pay it to (the procedure varies from area to area). Theoretically you could be asked to provide white accommodation receipt cards (or copies of invoices from hotels) when you leave the country, but in practice this is rarely required.

The following price categories for the cost of a room for a couple in the shoulder season (roughly June and September) are used in the listings in this chapter.

€ less than €20

€€ €30 to €90

€€€ more than €90

Business Hours

Business hours in Montenegro are a relative concept. Even if hours are posted on the doors of museums or shops, they may not be heeded.

Banks Usually 8am to 5pm Monday to Friday, 8am to noon Saturday

Cafes 10am to midnight (later in high season in busy areas)

Pubs 9pm to 2am

Restaurants 8am to midnight

Shops 8am to 7pm Monday to Friday, to 2pm Saturday; often closed in late afternoon

Supermarkets 8am to 8pm Monday to Friday, to 6pm Saturday, to 1pm Sunday

Embassies & Consulates

The following are all in Podgorica, unless otherwise stated. For a full list, see www. mip.gov.me.

Albanian Embassy (☑020-667 380; www. mfa.gov.al; Stanka Dragojevića 14)

Bosnia & Hercegovinia Embassy (☑020-618 105; www.mvp.gov.ba; Atinska 58)

Croatian Embassy (☑020-269 760; Vladimira Ćetkovića 2)

Croatian Consulate (☑032-323 127; Trg od Oružja bb, Kotor)

French Embassy (☑020-655 348; Atinska 35)

German Embassy (☑020-441 000; www. auswaertiges-amt.de; Hercegovačka 10)

Serbian Embassy (☑020-667 305; www. podgorica.mfa.gov.rs; Hercegovačka 18)

Serbian Consulate (☑031-350 320; www. hercegnovi.mfa.gov.rs; Njegoševa 40, Herceg Novi)

UK Embassy (☑020-618 010; www.ukinmontenegro.fco.gov.uk; Ulcinjska 8)

US Embassy (☑020-410 500; http://podgorica.usembassy.gov; Ljubljanska bb)

Food

The following price categories for the cost of a main course are used in the listings in this chapter.

€ less than €5

€€ €5 to €10

€€€ more than €10

Gay & Lesbian Travellers

Although homosexuality was decriminalised in 1977 and discrimination outlawed in 2010, attitudes to homosexuality remain hostile and life for gay people is extremely difficult. Many gay men resort to online connections (try www.gayromeo.com) or take their chances at a handful of cruisy beaches. Lesbians will find it even harder to access the local community.

Money

» Montenegro uses the euro (€). You'll find banks with ATMs in all the main towns, most of which accept Visa, MasterCard, Maestro and Cirrus. Don't rely on restaurants, shops or smaller hotels accepting credit cards.

» Tipping isn't expected, although it's common to round up to the nearest euro.

Public Holidays

New Year's Day 1 and 2 January

Orthodox Christmas 6, 7 and 8 January

Orthodox Good Friday & Easter Monday Usually April/May

Labour Day 1 May

Independence Day 21 May

Statehood Day 13 July

Telephone

» The international access prefix is ☎00 or ☎+ from a mobile.

» Mobile numbers start with ☎06.

» Local SIM cards are easy to find. The main providers are T-Mobile, Telenor and M:tel.

Women Travellers

Other than a cursory interest shown by men towards solo women travellers, travelling is hassle-free and easy. In Muslim areas some women wear a headscarf but most don't.

Getting There & Away

Air

Montenegro has two international airports – **Tivat** (TIV; ☎032-670 930; www.montenegroairports.com) and **Podgorica** (TGD; ☎020-444 244; www.montenegroairports.com) – although many visitors use Croatia's Dubrovnik Airport, which is very near the border. While various airlines run summer charter flights, the following airlines have regular scheduled flights to/from Montenegro.

Adria Airlines (www.adria.si) Ljubljana to Podgorica.

Austrian Airlines (www.austrian.com) Vienna to Podgorica.

Croatia Airlines (www.croatiaairlines.com) Zagreb to Podgorica.

Jat Airways (www.jat.com) Belgrade to Podgorica and Tivat.

Montenegro Airlines (www.montenegroairlines.com) Tivat to Belgrade and Moscow. Podgorica to Belgrade, Frankfurt, Ljubljana, Moscow, Niš, Paris, Rome, Vienna and Zurich.

Moskovia Airlines (www.ak3r.ru) Moscow to Tivat.

Rossiya Airlines (FV; www.rossiya-airlines.ru) St Petersburg to Tivat.

S7 Airlines (S7; www.s7.ru) Moscow to Tivat.

Turkish Airlines (www.turkishairlines.com) Istanbul to Podgorica.

Land

BORDER CROSSINGS

Albania The main crossings link Shkodra to Ulcinj (Sukobin) and to Podgorica (Hani i Hotit).

BiH The main checkpoints are at Dolovi and Šćepan Polje.

Croatia There's a busy checkpoint on the Adriatic highway between Herceg Novi and Dubrovnik; expect delays in summer.

Kosovo The only crossing is Kulina, between Rožaje and Peć.

Serbia The busiest crossing is Dobrakovo (north of Bijelo Polje), followed by Dračenovac (northeast of Rožaje) and Ranče (east of Pljevlja).

BUS

There's a well-developed bus network linking Montenegro with the major cities of the region.

Belgrade (Serbia) To Podgorica (€27, frequent), Budva (€26, 15 daily), Ulcinj (€33, four daily), Kotor (€32, seven daily) and Herceg Novi (€33, seven daily).

Dubrovnik (Croatia) To Herceg Novi (€10, two daily), Kotor (€14, two daily), Petrovac (€18, daily) and Podgorica (€19, daily).

Priština (Kosovo) To Podgorica (€17, daily) and Ulcinj (€18, six daily).

Sarajevo (BiH) To Podgorica (€19, six daily), Budva (€22, four daily), Herceg Novi (€24, two daily) and Ulcinj (€26, daily).

Shkodra (Albania) To Ulcinj (€6, two daily).

Trebinje (BiH) To Nikšić (€6.50, three daily).

CAR & MOTORCYCLE

Drivers are recommended to carry an International Driving Permit (IDP) as well as their home country's driving licence. Vehicles need Green Card insurance or insurance must be bought at the border.

TRAIN

At least two trains head between Bar and Belgrade daily (€21, 11 hours), with one continuing on to Novi Sad and Subotica.

Sea

Montenegro Lines (☎030-303 469; www.montenegrolines.net) has boats to Bar from the Italian ports of Bari and Ancona.

Getting Around
Bicycle

Cyclists are a rare species, even in the cities. Don't expect drivers to be considerate. Wherever possible, try to get off the main roads.

Bus

The local bus network is extensive and reliable. Buses are usually comfortable and air-conditioned, and are rarely full. It's slightly cheaper to buy your ticket on the bus rather than at the station, but a station-bought ticket theoretically guarantees you a seat. Luggage carried below the bus is charged at €1 per piece.

Car & Motorcycle

Independent travel by car or motorcycle is an ideal way to gad about and discover the country; some of the drives are breathtakingly beautiful. Traffic police are everywhere, so stick to speed limits and carry an IDP. Allow more time than you'd expect for the distances involved, as the terrain will slow you down.

The major international car-hire companies have a presence in various centres. **Meridian Rentacar** (☎020-234 944; www.meridian-rentacar.com), which has offices in Budva, Bar, Podgorica and the airports, is a reliable local option; one-day hire starts from €30.

Train

Montenegro Railways (Željeznica Crne Gore; www.zpcg.me) runs the passenger train service, heading north from Bar. The trains are old and can be hot in summer but they're priced accordingly and the route through the mountains is spectacular. Useful stops include Virpazar, Podgorica and Kolašin.

Poland

Includes »

Best Places to Eat

- » Glonojad (p624)
- » Warung Bali (p649)
- » Bernard (p644)
- » Sketch (p608)
- » Restauracja Pod Łososiem (p654)

Best Places to Stay

- » Hostel Mleczarnia (p643)
- » Castle Inn (p607)
- » Wielopole (p623)
- » Grand Hotel Lublinianka (p631)

Why Go?

If they were handing out prizes for 'most eventful history', Poland would be sure to get a medal. The nation has spent centuries at the pointy end, grappling with war and invasion. Nothing, however, has succeeded in suppressing the Poles' strong sense of nationhood and cultural identity. As a result, centres such as bustling Warsaw and cultured Kraków exude a sophisticated energy that's a heady mix of old and new.

Away from the cities, Poland is a diverse land, from its northern beaches to its magnificent southern mountains. In between are towns and cities dotted with ruined castles, picturesque squares and historic churches.

Although prices have steadily risen in the postcommunist era, Poland is still good value for travellers. As the Polish people work on combining their distinctive national identity with their place in the heart of Europe, it's a fascinating time to visit this beautiful country.

When to Go
Warsaw

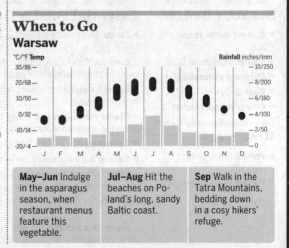

May–Jun Indulge in the asparagus season, when restaurant menus feature this vegetable.

Jul–Aug Hit the beaches on Poland's long, sandy Baltic coast.

Sep Walk in the Tatra Mountains, bedding down in a cosy hikers' refuge.

AT A GLANCE

» **Currency** Złoty (zł)

» **Language** Polish

» **Money** ATMs all over; banks open Monday to Friday

» **Visas** Not required for citizens of the EU, Canada, New Zealand and Australia

Fast Facts

» **Area** 312, 685 sq km

» **Capital** Warsaw

» **Country code** ☏48

» **Emergency** Ambulance ☏999, fire ☏998, police ☏997

Exchange rates

Australia	A$1	3.42zł
Canada	C$1	3.22zł
Euro Zone	€1	4.18zł
Japan	¥100	3.47zł
New Zealand	NZ$1	2.74zł
UK	UK£1	4.95zł
USA	US$1	3.27zł

Set Your Budget

» **Budget hotel room** 200zł

» **Two-course meal** 50zł

» **Museum entrance** 10zł

» **Beer** 6–9zł

» **City transport ticket** 3zł

Resources

» **Polska** (www.poland.travel)

» **Poland.pl** (www.poland.pl)

Connections

Poland offers plenty of possibilities for onward travel. The country is well connected by train: among its useful connections are direct services to Berlin from both Warsaw (via Poznań) and Kraków; to Prague from Warsaw and Kraków; and to Kyiv in Ukraine from Warsaw and Kraków (via Przemyśl and Lviv). Trains also link Warsaw to Minsk in Belarus and Moscow in Russia, and Gdańsk to Kaliningrad in Russia and Berlin in Germany. International buses head in all directions, including eastward to the Baltic States. From southern Zakopane, it's easy to hop to Slovakia via bus, or even minibus. And from the Baltic coast ports of Gdańsk, Gydnia and Świnoujscie, ferries head to various ports in Denmark and Sweden.

ITINERARIES

One Week

Spend a day exploring Warsaw with a stroll around the Old Town and a stop at the Warsaw Rising Museum for a glimpse of the city's wartime history. The next day, head to historic Kraków for three days, visiting the beautiful Old Town, striking Wawel Castle, the former Jewish district of Kazimierz and Wieliczka's impressive salt mine. Take a day trip to Auschwitz-Birkenau, the Nazi German concentration and extermination camp. Afterwards, head to Zakopane for two days for some mountain air.

Two Weeks

Follow the above itinerary, then travel to Wrocław for two days, visiting its unique Panorama. Progress north to Gothic Toruń for a day, then onward to Gdańsk for two days, exploring the attractive architecture and bars of the Old Town and visiting the monuments at Westerplatte. Wind down with a couple of days at the seaside in Sopot.

Essential Food & Drink

» **Żurek** This hearty sour soup includes sausage and hard-boiled egg.

» **Barszcz** This famous soup comes in two varieties: red (with beetroot) and white (with wheat flour and sausage).

» **Bigos** Extinguish hunger pangs with this thick sauerkraut and meat stew.

» **Placki ziemniaczane** These filling potato pancakes are often topped with a meaty sauce.

» **Szarlotka** Apple cake with cream is a Polish classic.

» **Sernik** Baked cheesecake – weighty but tasty.

» **Piwo** Poland's beer is good, cold and inexpensive, and often served in colourful beer gardens.

» **Wódka** Try it plain, or ask for *myśliwska* (flavoured with juniper berries).

» **Herbata z rumem** Tea with rum is the perfect pick-me-up after a heavy day of sightseeing.

Poland Highlights

1 Experience the beauty and history of Kraków's **Wawel Castle** (p616).

2 Encounter European bison and other magnificent fauna at **Białowieża National Park** (p614).

3 Hunt for **gnome statues** (p641) in the Old Town of Wrocław.

4 Remember the victims of Nazi German genocide at former extermination camp **Auschwitz-Birkenau** (p627).

5 Soak up the cosmopolitan vibe of **Gdańsk** (p650) and take a dip in the Baltic at nearby **Sopot** (p657).

6 Enjoy the skiing or hiking life of the **Tatra Mountains** (p637).

7 Discover Warsaw's tragic wartime history at the **Warsaw Rising Museum** (p606).

WARSAW

POP 1.7 MILLION

Warsaw (Warszawa in Polish, var-*shah*-va) may not be the prettiest of Poland's cities, but there's no mistaking its dynamism. As the bustling capital and business centre of the nation, Warsaw is home to an array of dining and nightlife that's the equal of any European city its size.

It's true, however, that Warsaw can be hard work. The city centre sprawls across a wide area, quite separate from the attractive but tourist-heavy Old Town, and its traffic-choked streets lined with massive concrete buildings can be less than enthralling.

However, look at Warsaw with a historic perspective and you'll see the capital in an entirely new light. As a city that's survived everything fate could throw at it – including the complete destruction of its historic heart in WWII – Warsaw is a place with an extraordinary backstory.

When you factor in its entertainment options; the beauty of its reconstructed Old Town, Royal Way and former Royal Parks; and the history represented by the Stalinist-era Palace of Culture and the Warsaw Rising Museum, what emerges is a complex city that well repays a visit.

History

The Mazovian dukes were the first rulers of Warsaw, establishing it as their stronghold in the 14th century. The city's strategic central location led to the capital being transferred from Kraków to Warsaw in 1596, following the earlier union of Poland and Lithuania.

Although the 18th century was a period of catastrophic decline for the Polish state, Warsaw underwent a period of prosperity during this period. Many magnificent churches, palaces and parks were built, and cultural and artistic life blossomed. The first (short-lived) constitution in Europe was instituted in Warsaw in 1791.

In the 19th century Warsaw declined in status to become a mere provincial city of the Russian Empire. Following WWI, the city was reinstated as the capital of a newly independent Poland and once more began to thrive. Following the Warsaw Rising of 1944, when the Poles revolted against German rule, the city centre was devastated and the entire surviving population forcibly evacuated. When the war ended, the people of Warsaw returned to the capital and set about rebuilding its historic heart.

Since the fall of communism, and particularly since Poland's entry into the EU, Warsaw has undergone a surge of economic development which has reshaped its commercial heart.

⊙ Sights

The Vistula River divides the city. The western left-bank sector is home to the city centre, including the Old Town – the historic nucleus of Warsaw. Almost all tourist attractions, as well as most tourist facilities, are on this side of the river.

OLD TOWN

Plac Zamkowy HISTORIC SQUARE
(Castle Square; Map p602) This square is the main gateway to the Old Town. All the buildings here were superbly rebuilt from their foundations after WWII, earning the Old Town a place on Unesco's World Heritage List. Within the square stands the **Monument to Sigismund III Vasa** (Map p602; Plac Zamkowy), who moved the capital from Kraków to Warsaw in 1596.

Royal Castle CASTLE
(Map p602; Plac Zamkowy 4; adult/concession 22/15zł; ⊙10am-4pm Mon-Sat, 11am-4pm Sun, closed

POLAND WARSAW

WARSAW IN TWO DAYS

Wander through the **Old Town** and tour the **Royal Castle**. Head along the **Royal Way**, checking out the impressive **Chopin Museum** en route, then have lunch at ever-so-cool **Sketch**. Take the lift to the top of the **Palace of Culture & Science** for views of the city, before promenading through the nearby **Saxon Gardens**.

The next day, visit the **Warsaw Rising Museum** in the morning, followed by lunch at one of the many restaurants along ul Nowy Świat. Spend the afternoon exploring **Łazienki Park**, before sipping a local brew at chilled bar **Relax**. Finish off the day with a visit to the nightclub district around **ul Mazowiecka**, or take in a concert at **Filharmonia Narodowa**.

Warsaw

N 0 ——— 2 km
  0 ——— 1 miles

Warsaw

⊙ Sights

1 Botanical Gardens	C4
2 Centre for Contemporary Art	C4
3 Ghetto Heroes Monument	B2
4 Jewish Cemetery	A2
5 Łazienki Park	C4
6 Museum of the History of Polish Jews	B2
7 Old Orangery	C4
8 Palace on the Water	C4
9 Pawiak Prison Museum	B2
10 Warsaw Rising Museum	A3

🛏 Sleeping

11 Hotel Premiere Classe	B3
12 Majawa Motor Inn & Camping 123	A4

Mon Oct-Apr) The dominant feature of Castle Square is this massive 13th-century castle, also reconstructed after the war. The highlight of the sumptuously decorated rooms is the Senators' Antechamber, where landscapes of 18th-century Warsaw by Bernardo Bellotto (Canaletto's nephew) are on show.

Historical Museum of Warsaw   MUSEUM
(Map p602; www.mhw.pl; Rynek Starego Miasta 42; adult/concession 8/4zł; ⊙11am-6pm Tue & Thu,

10am-3.30pm Wed & Fri, 10.30am-4.30pm Sat & Sun) Off the magnificent **Rynek Starego Miasta** (Old Town Market Sq) is this institution devoted to Warsaw's tumultuous history. At noon it shows an English-language film depicting the wartime destruction of the city (admission 6zł).

Barbican   FORTIFICATION
(Map p602; ul Nowomiejska) Northwest of the Rynek Starego Miasta along ul Nowomiejska

POLAND WARSAW

Warsaw Old Town

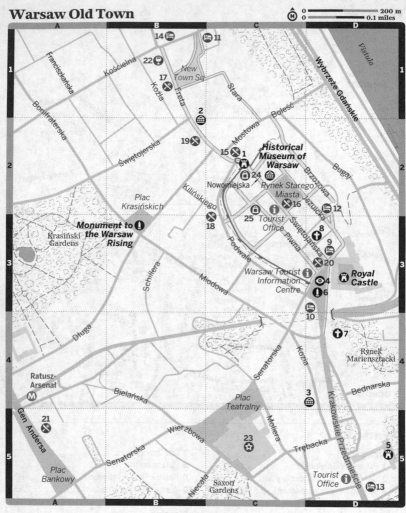

is this imposing fortified section of the medieval city walls. You can clamber onto the city walls via walkways here and get a feel for the height of the Old Town above the Vistula River.

Marie Skłodowska-Curie Museum
MUSEUM

(Map p602; ul Freta 16; adult/concession 11/6zł; ⊘10am-5pm) North of the Old Town along ul Freta, this museum features displays about Poland's great lady, Marie Curie, who, along with her husband Pierre, discovered radium and polonium, and laid the foundations for

radiography, nuclear physics and cancer therapy.

St John's Cathedral
CHURCH

(Map p602; ul Świętojańska 8; crypt 2zł; ⊘10am-1pm & 3-5.30pm Mon-Sat) Near the castle is this 15th-century Gothic cathedral, Warsaw's oldest church. Its relatively simple but elegant interior is worth a look.

Monument to the Warsaw Rising
MONUMENT

(Map p602; cnr ul Długa & ul Miodowa) West of the Old Town, this striking set of statuary honours the heroic Polish revolt against German rule in 1944.

Warsaw Old Town

ROYAL WAY

This 4km route (called Szlak Królewski in Polish) links the Royal Castle with Łazienki Park via ul Krakowskie Przedmieście, ul Nowy Świat and Al Ujazdowskie. Bus 180 runs along or near this route and continues south to Wilanów Park.

TOP CHOICE Chopin Museum   MUSEUM

(Map p604; www.chopin.museum; ul Okólnik 1; adult/concession 22/13zł, Tue free; ⊙11am-8pm Tue-Sun) To learn about Poland's most renowned composer, head to this institution. Renovated and expanded on the 200th anniversary of his birth in 2010, it presents an immersive audiovisual exhibition covering Chopin's work, possessions and his life in Paris. You're encouraged to take your time through four floors of displays, including stopping by the listening booths in the basement.

Saxon Gardens   GARDENS

(Map p604; ⊙24hr) West of the Royal Way are these attractive gardens, at whose entrance stands the small but poignant **Tomb of the Unknown Soldier** (Map p604; Saxon Gardens). It's housed within the only surviving remnant of the Saxon Palace that once stood here and was destroyed by the Germans during WWII. The ceremonial **changing of the guard** takes place at noon here on Sunday.

Church of the Holy Cross   CHURCH

(Map p604; ul Krakowskie Przedmieście 3) South of the Old Town is this prominent 17th-century church. **Chopin's heart** is preserved in the second pillar on the left-hand side of the main nave. It was brought from Paris, where he died of tuberculosis aged only 39.

National Museum   MUSEUM

(Map p604; www.mnw.art.pl; Al Jerozolimskie 3; adult/concession 15/10zł, Tue free; ⊙10am-6pm Tue-Sun) East of the junction of ul Nowy Świat and Al Jerozolimskie, the National Museum houses an impressive collection of Greek and Egyptian antiquities, Coptic frescos, medieval woodcarvings and Polish paintings. Look out for the surreal fantasies of Jacek Malczewski.

Łazienki Park   GARDENS

(Map p601; www.lazienki-krolewskie.pl; ul Agrykola; gardens free; ⊙dawn-dusk) This large, shady and popular park is best known for the 18th-century **Palace on the Water** (Map p601; ul Agrykola 1; adult/concession 15/10zł, Thu free; ⊙9am-4pm Tue-Sun). It was the summer residence of Stanisław August Poniatowski, the last king of Poland, who abdicated once the Third Partition of Poland dissolved his realm in 1795. The park was once a royal

POLAND WARSAW

Central Warsaw

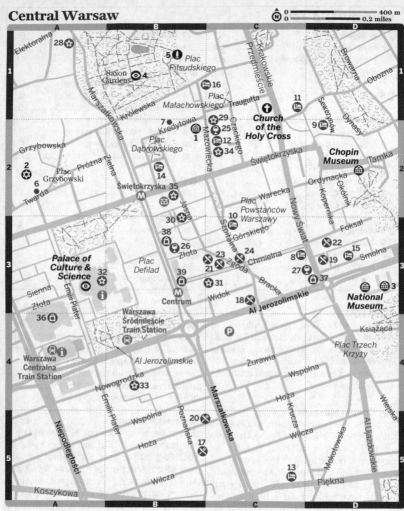

hunting ground attached to Ujazdów Castle.

Also within the park is the **Old Orangery** (Map p601; Łazienki Park; adult/student 10/5zł, Thu free; ⊙9am-4pm Tue-Fri), which contains a sculpture gallery and 18th-century theatre. **Piano recitals** are held among the nearby rose gardens between noon and 4pm every Saturday and Sunday from May to September.

St Anne's Church   CHURCH
(Map p602; ul Krakowskie Przedmieście 68) Just south of the Royal Castle, this ornate 15th-century church has impressive views from

its **tower** (ul Krakowskie Przedmieście 68; adult/concession 5/4zł; ⊙11am-9pm May-Oct).

Museum of Caricature   MUSEUM
(Map p602; www.muzeumkarykatury.pl; ul Kozia 11; adult/concession 5/3zł, Sat free; ⊙11am-6pm Tue-Sun) Along a side street off ul Krakowskie Przedmieście is this quirky museum, exhibiting numerous original works by Polish and foreign caricaturists, created from the 18th century onwards.

Radziwiłł Palace   PALACE
(Map p602; ul Krakowskie Przedmieście 48/50) This palace, off ul Krakowskie Przedmieście,

Central Warsaw

is the imposing residence of the Polish president. It's not open to the public.

Ethnographic Museum MUSEUM
(Map p604; www.ethnomuseum.website.pl; ul Kredytowa 1; adult/concession 12/6zł, Wed free; ◉10am-4pm Tue-Sat, noon-5pm Sun) South of the Saxon Gardens is the Ethnographic Museum. It displays Polish folk costumes, as well as regional arts and crafts.

Polish Army Museum MUSEUM
(Map p604; Al Jerozolimskie 3; adult/concession 10/5zł, Wed free; ◉10am-4pm Wed-Sun) Next door to the National Museum is this museum recording the history of the Polish army, with military vehicles outside and miscellaneous militaria within.

**Centre for
Contemporary Art** ART GALLERY
(Map p601; www.csw.art.pl; ul Jazdów 2; adult/concession 12/6zł, Thu free; ◉noon-7pm Tue-Sun) This cutting-edge gallery is housed in the

reconstructed **Ujazdów Castle**, originally built during the 1620s.

Botanical Gardens GARDENS
(Map p601; adult/concession 6/3zł; ◉10am-8pm Apr-Aug, 10am-5pm Sep-Oct) South of the Centre for Contemporary Art are these small but pleasant gardens, suitable for whiling away an idle hour on a sunny day.

WILANÓW

To reach Wilanów, take bus 116 or 180 from ul Nowy Świat or Al Ujazdowskie.

Wilanów Park GARDENS
(www.wilanow-palac.pl; ul Wisłostrada; adult/concession 5/3zł, Thu free; ◉9am-dusk) This magnificent park lies 6km southeast of Łazienki Park. Its centrepiece is the splendid **Wilanów Palace** (www.wilanow-palac.pl; adult/concession 20/15zł, Sun free; ◉9.30am-4.30pm Mon-Sat, 10.30am-6.30pm Sun), the summer residence of King Jan III Sobieski, who ended the Turkish threat to Central Europe by defeating the

Turks at Vienna in 1683. In summer, be prepared to wait for entry. The last tickets are sold one hour before closing time.

In the well-kept park behind the palace is the **Orangery** (ul Wisłostrada; admission varies with temporary exhibitions; ☉10am-6pm), which houses an art gallery with changing exhibitions. The **Poster Museum** (www.postermuseum.pl; ul Kostki Potockiego 10/16; adult/student 10/7zł, Mon free; ☉noon-4pm Mon, 10am-4pm Tue-Fri, 10am-6pm Sat & Sun; ☐116, 180) in the former royal stables is a repository of Poland's world-renowned poster art.

CITY CENTRE
Palace of Culture & Science   LANDMARK
(Map p604; www.pkin.pl; Plac Defilad 1; ☉9am-6pm) Massive, brooding and inescapable, this towering structure has become an emblem of the city, as it's slowly rehabilitated from its Stalinist past. It has a particularly sinister aspect at dusk, though it's also a handy landmark. The palace was built in the early 1950s as a 'gift of friendship' from the Soviet Union (the kind of unwanted gift that's hard to hide away), and is still one of Europe's tallest buildings (over 230m). The clock faces were added to the building in the postcommunist period.

The **observation terrace** (adult/concession 20/15zł) on the 30th floor provides a panoramic view, though it can be very cold and windy up there.

WEST OF THE CITY CENTRE
Warsaw Rising Museum   MUSEUM
(Map p601; www.1944.pl; ul Grzybowska 79; adult/concession 14/10zł, Sun free; ☉8am-6pm Mon, Wed & Fri, 8am-8pm Thu, 10am-6pm Sat & Sun) This impressive museum commemorates Warsaw's insurrection against its Nazi German occupiers in 1944, which ended in defeat and the destruction of much of the city and its population. The Rising was viciously suppressed by the Germans (while the Red Army stood by on the opposite bank of the Vistula River), with more than 200,000 Poles dying by its conclusion.

The moving story of the Rising is retold here via photographs, exhibits and audiovisual displays. The centrepiece is a massive **memorial wall** emitting a heartbeat and selected audio recordings. At the end of the journey there's a replica 1944 cafe, underlining the fact that life went on, even in the worst days of the struggle. Captions are in Polish and English. Catch trams 22 or 24 from Al Jerozolimskie, heading west.

FORMER JEWISH DISTRICT
The suburbs northwest of the Palace of Culture & Science were once predominantly inhabited by Jewish Poles. During WWII the Nazi German occupiers established a Jewish ghetto in the area, but razed it to the ground after crushing the Warsaw Ghetto Uprising in April 1943.

Jewish Cemetery   CEMETERY
(Map p601; ul Okopowa 49/51; admission 4zł; ☉10am-5pm Mon-Thu, 9am-1pm Fri, 11am-4pm Sun) The most poignant remainder of the wartime tragedy is Europe's largest Jewish resting place. Founded in 1806, it has more than 100,000 gravestones. Visitors must wear a head covering to enter. It's accessible from the Old Town on bus 180, heading north from ul Nowy Świat.

Ghetto Heroes Monument   MONUMENT
(Map p601; cnr ul Anielewicza & ul Zamenhofa) This monument was established to remember the victims of the Jewish ghetto, which was established here by the occupying Germans. It features pictorial plaques.

Museum of the History of Polish Jews   MUSEUM
(Map p601; www.jewishmuseum.org.pl; cnr ul Anielewicza & ul Zamenhofa; ☉10am-6pm Wed-Mon) Opposite the Ghetto Heroes Monument is this new multimedia and education centre, which opened on the 70th anniversary of the Ghetto Uprising in April 2013. Check with the tourist office for entry fees.

Pawiak Prison Museum   MUSEUM
(Map p601; ul Dzielna 24/26; adult/concession 6/4zł; ☉10am-4pm Wed-Sun) Once a Gestapo prison during the Nazi German occupation, this institution now contains moving exhibits, including letters and other personal items.

Nożyk Synagogue   SYNAGOGUE
(Map p604; ul Twarda 6; admission 6zł; ☉9am-8pm Mon-Fri, 11am-8pm Sun) This neo-Romanesque place of worship is the only Warsaw synagogue to survive WWII.

☞ Tours
Our Roots   TOUR
(Map p604; ☑22 620 0556; www.our-roots.jewish.org.pl; ul Twarda 6) Offers Jewish heritage tours.

Trakt   TOUR
(Map p604; ☑22 827 8068; www.trakt.com.pl; ul Kredytowa 6) Guided tours of Warsaw and beyond.

✯✯ Festivals & Events

Mozart Festival   MUSIC
(www.operakameralna.pl; ⊗Jun/Jul)

Warsaw Summer Jazz Days   MUSIC
(www.adamiakjazz.pl; ⊗Jul)

Street Art Festival   THEATRE
(www.sztukaulicy.pl; ⊗Jul)

**Warsaw Autumn International
Festival of Contemporary Music**   MUSIC
(www.warsaw-autumn.art.pl; ⊗Sep)

Warsaw Film Festival   FILM
(www.wff.pl; ⊗Oct)

🛏 Sleeping

Not surprisingly, Warsaw is the most expensive Polish city for accommodation, though there's a number of reasonably priced hostels around town. The tourist offices can help you find a room.

TOP CHOICE ⟋ Castle Inn   HOTEL €€
(Map p602; ☑22 425 0100; www.castleinn.eu; ul Świętojańska 2; s/d from 290/330zł; 🛜) Proceed up the stairs to the striking purple decor and shiny tiles of this Old Town hotel, situated in a 17th-century tenement house. All rooms overlook either Castle Sq or St John's Cathedral and come in a range of playful styles.

Oki Doki Hostel   HOSTEL €
(Map p604; ☑22 828 0122; www.okidoki.pl; Plac Dąbrowskiego 3; dm 39-93zł, s/d from 120/149zł; 🛜) There are no drab dorms here. Each is decorated thematically using the brightest paints available; try the communist (red with a big image of Lenin). Lower bunks have good head room and the shared bathrooms are clean and bright. The hostel also has a bar, free washing machine and a kitchen, as well as bikes for hire (28zł per day).

Nathan's Villa Hostel   HOSTEL €
(Map p604; ☑22 622 2946; www.nathansvilla.com; ul Piękna 24/26; dm 47-60zł, r 175-205zł; 🛜) Nathan's sunlit courtyard leads to well-organised dorms and comfortable private rooms. The kitchen is well set up and there's a laundry, book exchange and games to while away rainy days.

Hotel Le Regina   HOTEL €€€
(Map p602; ☑22 531 6000; www.mamaison.com/leregina; ul Kościelna 12; r/ste from €150/450; ❄🛜⊠) It's not cheap, but Le Regina is a jaw-dropping combination of traditional architecture and contemporary design. The enormous rooms feature king-size beds with headboards of dark, polished wood. Deluxe rooms also have timber floors and terraces with courtyard views. All rooms sport spectacular bathrooms with marble benchtops.

Apartments Apart   APARTMENTS €€
(Map p604; ☑22 351 2250; www.apartmentsapart.com; ul Nowy Świat 29/3; apt from €45; 🛜) Company offering a range of apartments dotted throughout the Old Town and the city centre. Most include a washing machine in addition to a kitchen. Check online first, as last-minute web specials can be great value.

Hotel Bristol   LUXURY HOTEL €€€
(Map p602; ☑22 551 1000; www.lemeridien.pl; ul Krakowskie Przedmieście 42/44; r from 750zł; ❄🛜⊠) Established in 1899 and restored to its former glory after a massive renovation, the Bristol is touted as Poland's most luxurious hotel. Its neoclassical exterior houses a feast of original art nouveau features and huge, traditionally decorated rooms. Attentive staff cater to your every whim.

Hotel Premiere Classe   HOTEL €€
(Map p601; ☑22 624 0800; www.premiere-classe-warszawa.pl; ul Towarowa 2; r 199zł; 🛜) If you're not bothered too much by room size, this modern hotel makes a good base. Rooms are small but bright, and neatly set up with modern furnishings. Guests can use the restaurants, bars and fitness centre in its neighbouring sister hotels. Catch tram 22 or 24 from Al Jerozolimskie.

Sofitel Victoria   HOTEL €€€
(Map p604; ☑22 657 8011; www.sofitel.com; ul Królewska 11; r from 400zł; 🛜⊠) The very model of a modern business hotel, with a spacious marble foyer and a lounge area housing a small library of books on Polish culture and history. The rooms are conservatively decorated, with gleaming bathrooms.

Hostel Helvetia   HOSTEL €
(Map p604; ☑22 826 7108; www.hostel-helvetia.pl; ul Kopernika 36/40; dm/r 59/220zł; 🛜) Bright hostel with an attractive combined lounge and kitchen. Dorms have lockers, and there's one small women-only dorm. Bike hire is 30zł per day. Enter from the street behind, ul Sewerynów.

Hostel Kanonia   HOSTEL €
(Map p602; ☑22 635 0676; www.kanonia.pl; ul Jezuicka 2; dm/s/d 45/90/160zł; 🛜) Housed in a historic building in the heart of the Old

Town, accommodation is mostly in dorms, with only one double and one triple. Some rooms have picturesque views onto the cobblestone streets. There's a dining room with basic kitchen facilities, and a washing machine.

Dom Literatury
HOTEL €€

(Map p602; ☑22 635 0404; www.fundacjadl.com; ul Krakowskie Przedmieście 87/89; s/d 220/370zł; 🛜) Within a grand historic building, this accommodation features rambling halls and staircases bedecked with pot plants and sizeable paintings. There's a maze of comfortable rooms, many of which have excellent views of the Old Town and the Vistula. You're paying for the location, however, rather than the standard of accommodation.

Hotel Harenda
HOTEL €€

(Map p604; ☑22 826 0071; www.hotelharenda. com.pl; ul Krakowskie Przedmieście 4/6; s/d from 310/340zł; 🛜) Boasting a great location just off the Royal Way, the Harenda's rooms are neat and clean, with solid timber furniture and an old-fashioned vibe. Breakfast is an additional 25zł.

Hotel Gromada Centrum
HOTEL €€

(Map p604; ☑22 582 9900; www.gromada.pl; Plac Powstańców Warszawy 2; s/d from 210/240zł; ✸🛜) Centrally located, the Gromada is a big concrete box but also a great launching pad for exploring the central city. Upstairs from the spacious foyer with folkloric decor, the corridors stretch out into the distance like an optical illusion. The rooms are plain, but clean and spacious.

Smolna Youth Hostel
HOSTEL €

(Map p604; ☑22 827 8952; www.hostelsmolna30. pl; ul Smolna 30; dm/s/d 50/85/150zł; 🛜) Very central and very popular, though there's a midnight curfew (2am in July and August) and reception is closed between 10am and 4pm. It's simple but clean, and there's a lounge and kitchen area. Note that guests are separated into dorms according to gender, and reception is up four flights of stairs.

Dom Przy Rynku Hostel
HOSTEL €

(Map p602; ☑22 831 5033; www.cityhostel.net; Rynek Nowego Miasta 4; dm 60zł; ⊙Jul-Sep; 🛜) Only open in summer and located in a quiet corner of the busy New Town, Przy Rynku is a neat, clean and friendly hostel occupying a 19th-century house. Its rooms accommodate two to five people, and there's a kitchen and laundry for guest use.

Majawa Motor Inn & Camping 123
CAMPING GROUND €

(Map p601; ☑22 823 3748; www.astur.waw.pl; ul Bitwy Warszawskiej 1920r 15/17; site per person/ tent 25/20zł, bungalows s/d from 50/80zł, hotel s/d from 70/120zł; 🛜🏊) Set in extensive grounds near the Dworzec Zachodnia bus station. The bungalows are available from mid-April to mid-October and there's a tennis court nearby. Catch tram 9 or 25 west from Al Jerozolimskie.

Hotel Mazowiecki
HOTEL €€

(Map p604; ☑22 827 2365; www.hotelewam.pl; ul Mazowiecka 10; s/d from 160/200zł; 🛜) One-star accommodation in a handy location on one of the city centre's nightlife strips. Most rooms have shared bathrooms, but a few have en suites.

✕ Eating

The most recent revolution in the Polish capital has been a gastronomic one. A good selection of restaurants can be found in the Old Town and New Town, and in the area between ul Nowy Świat and the Palace of Culture & Science.

Self-caterers can buy groceries at the **Carrefour Supermarket** (Map p604; ul Złota 59) in the Złote Tarasy shopping centre behind Warszawa Centralna train station; and at **ML Delikatesy** (Map p602; ul Piwna 47) in the Old Town.

⊡ TOP CHOICE Sketch
INTERNATIONAL €€

(Map p604; ul Foksal 19; mains 12-41zł; ⊙8am-1am) Shiny bright restaurant and bar with orange furniture and cool wait staff. There's lots of natural light and it's a great relaxed place for taking a break from sightseeing. Mains include baguettes, salads, pasta and grilled dishes. Sharing plates come in Polish, Spanish and Italian variants.

Bar Mleczny Pod Barbakanem
CAFETERIA €

(Map p602; ul Mostowa 27/29; mains 5-9zł; ⊙8am-5pm Mon-Fri, from 9am Sat & Sun; 🥢) Near the Barbican, this popular former milk bar that survived the fall of the Iron Curtain continues to serve cheap, unpretentious food in an interior dominated by tiles. Fill up while peering out through the lace curtains at the passing tourist hordes.

Podwale Piwna Kompania
GRILL €€

(Map p602; ul Podwale 25; mains 22-50zł; ⊙11am-1am Mon-Sat, noon-1am Sun) The restaurant's name (The Company of Beer) gives you an idea of the lively atmosphere in this eatery just outside the Old Town's moat. The menu features lots of grilled items and dishes such as roast duck, schnitzel, pork ribs and steak. There's a courtyard for outdoor dining.

Fret Á Porter
POLISH €€

(Map p602; ul Freta 37; mains 25-56zł; ⊙noon-11pm; ☎) Choose between the pavement terrace, with views of the New Town Sq, and the eccentric dining room with modern art on the walls. The menu indulges in similarly bold contrasts, ranging from traditional Polish dishes to exotic offerings such as kangaroo steaks.

Beirut
MIDDLE EASTERN €

(Map p604; ul Poznańska 12; mains 12-19zł; ☎ ☑) Very hip, the small Beirut 'Hummus and Music Bar' brings together two of the best things in life. The menu features hummus in several variations, as well as salads, falafel and pitta bread. There's a DJ turntable on hand for later in the evening, when the music part kicks in.

Cô tú
ASIAN €

(Map p604; Hadlowo-Usługowe 21; mains 12-18zł; ⊙10am-9pm Mon-Fri, 11am-7pm Sat & Sun) The wok at this simple Asian diner never rests, as hungry Poles can't get enough of the excellent dishes coming from the kitchen. The menu is enormous, covering seafood, vegetables, beef, chicken and pork. Duck through the archway at ul Nowy Świat 26 to find it.

Restauracja Pod Samsonem
JEWISH €€

(Map p602; ul Freta 3/5; mains 10-30zł) Situated in the New Town and frequented by locals looking for inexpensive and tasty meals with a Jewish flavour. Interesting appetisers include Russian pancakes with mushroom sauce, and 'Jewish caviar' (fried chopped liver). Spot the bas relief of Samson and the lion above the next door along from the entrance.

Tukan Salad Bar
VEGETARIAN €

(Map p602; Plac Bankowy 2; mains 5-19zł; ⊙8am-8pm Mon-Fri, 10am-6pm Sat; ☑) Vegetarian-friendly outlet offering a wide choice of salads. As the name suggests, look for the toucan on the door. It's hidden from the street in the arcade running parallel.

Restauracja Przy Zamku
POLISH €€€

(Map p602; Plac Zamkowy 15; mains 38-120zł) An attractive, old-world kind of place with hunting trophies on the walls and attentive, apron-wearing waiters. The top-notch Polish menu includes fish and game and a bewildering array of entrees – try the excellent hare pâté served with cranberry sauce.

Dżonka
ASIAN €€

(Map p604; ul Hoża 54; mains 15-31zł; ⊙11am-7pm Mon-Fri, noon-6pm Sat & Sun) This hidden gem serves a range of Asian dishes, covering Chinese, Japanese, Korean and Thai cuisine. Though small (just six tables), it has loads of personality, with dark timber surfaces and bamboo place mats. There's some spicy food on the menu, including Sichuan cuisine, though it's been toned down a little for Polish palates.

British Bulldog
BRITISH PUB €

(Map p604; Al Jerozolimskie 42; mains 9-27zł; ☎) If you must go to a faux-British pub, this is a good choice in the city centre. Serves steaks and fish and chips, along with an all-day breakfast. Happy hour runs from 4pm to 7pm.

Bazyliszek Restauracja
POLISH €€

(Map p602; Rynek Starego Miasta 1/3; mains 17-48zł) Step beneath the red-eyed basilisk into this restaurant in a prime spot on the Rynek Starego Miasta. It serves mainly Polish-style dishes, with forays into foreign cuisine such as Argentinian steak.

Taqueria Mexicana
MEXICAN €€

(Map p604; ul Zgoda 5; mains 24-50zł) Brightly hued place festooned with Mexican rugs and featuring a central bar. Varieties of tacos, enchiladas and fajitas adorn the menu; there's a 15zł set lunch from Monday to Friday.

Krokiecik
CAFETERIA €

(Map p604; ul Zgoda 1; mains 6-25zł) Attractive cafeteria serving a range of inexpensive and tasty dishes, including good soups. The house speciality is *krokiety* (filled savoury pancakes).

POLAND WARSAW

WANT MORE?

For in-depth information, reviews and recommendations at your fingertips, head to the Apple App Store to purchase Lonely Planet's *Warsaw City Guide* and *Polish Phrasebook* iPhone apps.

Alternatively, head to www.lonely-planet.com/poland/warsaw for planning advice, author recommendations, traveller reviews and insider tips.

Zgoda Grill Bar
POLISH €€

(Map p604; ul Zgoda 4; mains 24-69zł) A bright, informal place serving up a range of tasty Polish standards. There's also a decent salad selection.

Drinking

TOP CHOICE Polyester
CAFE-BAR

(Map p602; ul Freta 49/51; 🛜) Polyester, with its fashionably retro furnishings and vibe, is arguably the hippest cocktail bar in the vicinity of the Old Town. Serves excellent cocktails, as well as a full range of coffee variants and light food.

Relax
CAFE-BAR

(Map p604; ul Złota 8a; ⊙8am-11pm Mon-Fri, 10.30am-11pm Sat & Sun; 🛜) Compact, friendly place with retro-grungy charm at the back of a derelict cinema building. Serves a range of Polish microbrewery beers.

Sense
BAR

(Map p604; ul Nowy Świat 19; ⊙noon-late; 🛜) A very modern venue with a mellow atmosphere. Comfortable banquettes sit beneath strings of cube-shaped lights and there's an extensive wine and cocktail list. Try the house speciality – ginger rose vodka. There's also an impressive food menu if you're hungry.

Paparazzi
BAR

(Map p604; ul Mazowiecka 12; ⊙6pm-late; 🛜) This is one of Warsaw's flashest venues, where you can sip a bewildering array of cocktails under blown-up photos of Hollywood stars. It's big and roomy, with comfortable seating around the central bar.

☆ Entertainment

Nightclubs

There's no shortage of good clubs in Warsaw. Explore ul Mazowiecka, ul Sienkiewicza and the area around ul Nowy Świat for nightclub action. Free **jazz concerts** also take place in the Rynek Starego Miasta on Saturdays at 7pm in July and August.

Enklawa
CLUB

(Map p604; www.enklawa.com; ul Mazowiecka 12; ⊙9pm-4am Tue-Sat) Funky space with comfy plush seating, two bars and plenty of room to dance. Check out the long drinks list, hit the dance floor or observe the action from a stool on the upper balcony. Wednesday night is 'old school' night, with music from the '70s and '80s.

Tygmont
JAZZ CLUB

(Map p604; ☎22 828 3409; www.tygmont.com.pl; ul Mazowiecka 6/8; ⊙7pm-late) Hosting both local and international acts, the live jazz here is both varied and plentiful. Concerts start around 8pm but the place fills up early, so either reserve a table or turn up at opening time. Dinner is also available.

Capitol
CLUB

(Map p604; ul Marszałkowska 115; ⊙10pm-late Sat) If scarcity excites you, squeeze through the doors of this oh-so-cool club on the one night of the week it's open – Saturday. Low lighting gleams off pillars, retro decor and the shining faces of Warsaw's beautiful people as they gyrate within the dance-floor throng.

Underground Music Cafe
CLUB

(Map p604; www.under.pl; ul Marszałkowska 126/134; ⊙1pm-late) A swarm of students and backpackers pour into this basement club for its cheap beer, dark lighting and selection of music that varies from '70s and '80s to house, R & B and hip hop.

Performing Arts

Teatr Roma
MUSICAL THEATRE

(Map p604; ☎22 628 8998; www.teatrroma.pl; ul Nowogrodzka 49) Theatre staging big-budget musicals sung in Polish, such as the ever-popular *Deszczowa Piosenka* (aka *Singin' in the Rain*).

Teatr Wielki
OPERA

(Map p602; ☎22 692 0200; www.teatrwielki.pl; Plac Teatralny 1) The Grand Theatre hosts opera and ballet in its aptly grand premises.

Filharmonia Narodowa
CLASSICAL MUSIC

(Map p604; ☎22 551 7111; www.filharmonia.pl; ul Jasna 5) Classical-music concerts are held here.

Cinemas

To avoid watching Polish TV in your hotel room, catch a film at the central **Kino Atlantic** (Map p604; ul Chmielna 33) or enjoy a flick in socialist-era glory at **Kinoteka** (Map p604; Plac Defilad 1) within the Palace of Culture & Science. English-language movies are subtiled in Polish.

🔒 Shopping

There are also plentiful antique and arts and crafts shops around the Rynek Starego Miasta, so brandish your credit card and explore.

Wars & Sawa
MALL

(Map p604; ul Marszałkowska 104/122) A sprawling modern shopping mall in the city centre.

Lapidarium JEWELLERY
(Map p602; www.lapidarium.pl; ul Nowomiejska 15/7) One of the most interesting shops on the Rynek Starego Miasta; offers jewellery and communist-era collectables.

EMPiK BOOKS
Has several stores across Warsaw, including branches in the **Wars & Sawa shopping mall** (Map p604; ul Marszałkowska 116/122, Wars & Sawa shopping mall) and on **Royal Way** (Map p604; ul Nowy Świat 15/17). A good source of English-language books, newspapers and magazines.

ℹ Information

Discount Cards
Warsaw Tourist Card (www.warsawcard.com; 1/3 days 35/65zł) Free or discounted access to museums, public transport and some theatres, sports centres and restaurants. Available from tourist offices and some accommodation.

Internet Access
Expect to pay about 5zł per hour for internet access in Warsaw. Several convenient but dingy internet cafes are also located within Warszawa Centralna train station.

Verso Internet (ul Freta 17; ⊙8am-8pm Mon-Fri, 9am-5pm Sat, 9am-4pm Sun) Enter from the rear, off ul Świętojerska.

Warsaw Point Gallery (ul Złota 59, Złote Tarasy; ⊙9am-10pm) Pay at the information desk of this shopping mall.

Medical Services
Apteka Grabowskiego (Warszawa Centralna; ⊙24hr) At the train station.

Centrum Medyczne LIM (☑22 332 2888; www.cmlim.pl; Al Jerozolimskie 65/79, 3rd fl, Marriott Hotel) Offers specialist doctors, laboratory tests and house calls.

EuroDental (☑22 627 5888; www.eurodental. com.pl; ul Śniadeckich 12/16; ⊙8am-8pm Mon-Sat, 10am-2pm Sun) Private dental clinic with multilingual staff.

Money
Banks, *kantors* (foreign-exchange offices) and ATMs are easy to find around the city centre. *Kantors* that open 24 hours can be found at Warszawa Centralna train station and the airport, but exchange rates at these places are about 10% lower than in the city centre. Avoid changing money in the Old Town, where the rates can be even lower.

Post
Main Post Office (Map p604; ul Świętokrzyska 31/33; ⊙24hr)

Tourist Information
Each tourist office provides free city maps and free booklets, such as the handy *Warsaw in Short* and the *Visitor*, and sells maps of other Polish cities; offices can also help with booking hotel rooms.

Free monthly tourist magazines worth seeking out include the comprehensive *Warsaw Insider* (10zł) and *Warsaw in Your Pocket* (5zł).

Tourist Office (☑22 19431; www.warsaw-tour.pl) Old Town (Map p602; Rynek Starego Miasta 19; ⊙9am-9pm May-Sep, 9am-7pm Oct-Apr); Royal Way (Map p602; ul Krakowskie Przedmieście 15; ⊙11am-8pm Tue-Sun); Palace of Culture & Science (Map p604; Plac Defilad 1; ⊙8am-6pm); Warszawa Centralna train station (Map p604; Al Jana Pawła II; ⊙8am-8pm May-Sep, 8am-7pm Oct-Apr); Warsaw Frédéric Chopin Airport (ul Żwirki i Wigury 1; ⊙8am-8pm May-Sep, 8am-7pm Oct-Apr)

Warsaw Tourist Information Centre (Map p602; ☑22 635 1881; www.wcit.waw.pl; Plac Zamkowy 1/13; ⊙9am-6pm Mon-Fri, 10am-6pm Sat & Sun) Helpful privately run tourist office in the Old Town.

ℹ Getting There & Away

Air
The **Warsaw Frédéric Chopin Airport** (www.lotnisko-chopina.pl; ul Żwirki i Wigury 1), 7km from the city centre, is more commonly called Okęcie Airport.

There is a useful tourist office on the arrivals level, along with ATMs and several *kantors*. There are also car-hire companies, a left-luggage room and a newsagent where you can buy public transport tickets.

Domestic and international flights run by Poland's national carrier, LOT, can be booked at the **LOT office** (☑0801 703 703; Al Jerozolimskie 65/79) in town, or at any travel agency.

In July 2012, a new low-cost airport, **Warsaw Modlin** (www.modlinairport.pl; ul Generała Wiktora Thommée 1a, Nowy Dwór Mazowiecki), opened 35km north of the city. If you're flying on a budget carrier such as Ryanair or Wizz Air, you're likely to arrive here. It offers the usual services such as ATMs and car hire.

Bus
Warsaw's major bus station is **Dworzec Zachodnia** (Western Bus Station; www.pksbilety.pl; Al Jerozolimskie 144). This complex is southwest of the city centre and adjoins the Warszawa Zachodnia train station. To reach it, take the commuter train that leaves from Warszawa Śródmieście station. From here you can catch PKS buses in every direction.

Services run by the private company **Polski Bus** (www.polskibus.com) depart from the small bus station next to the Wilanowska metro station. Check its website for its timetable and fluctuating fares, as tickets must be purchased online.

International buses also depart from and arrive at Dworzec Zachodnia or, occasionally, outside Warszawa Centralna train station. Tickets are available from the bus offices at Dworzec Zachodnia, from agencies at Warszawa Centralna or from any of the major travel agencies in the city. **Eurolines Polska** (📞22 621 3469; www.eurolinespolska.pl) operates a huge number of buses to destinations throughout Europe; check its website for fares and special offers.

Train

Warsaw has several train stations, but the one that most travellers will use is **Warszawa Centralna** (Warsaw Central; Al Jerozolimskie 54). Opened in 1975 as a shining example of socialism, it became grimy and sinister in later years. It was impressively refurbished for the Euro 2012 football championships, but the shop-lined corridors beneath the main hall are still a confusing maze.

Warszawa Centralna is not always where trains start or finish, so make sure you get on or off promptly. Guard your belongings against pick-pocketing and theft at all times.

The station's main hall houses ticket counters, ATMs and snack bars, as well as a post office, newsagents and a tourist office. Along the underground mezzanine level leading to the platforms are several *kantors* (one of which is open 24 hours), a **left-luggage office** (🕒7am-midnight), lockers, eateries, outlets for local public transport tickets, internet cafes and bookshops.

Tickets for domestic and international trains are available from counters at the station (but allow at least an hour for possible queuing). Alternatively, automatic ticket machines are avail-

TRANSPORT FROM WARSAW

Bus

DESTINATION	COMPANY	PRICE (ZŁ)	DURATION (HR)	FREQUENCY
Berlin (Germany)	Polski Bus	Varies	10¼	2 daily
Gdańsk	PKS	56	6	Hourly
Gdańsk	Polski Bus	Varies	5¾	Hourly
Kraków	PKS	58	6	8 daily
Kraków	Polski Bus	Varies	5	4 daily
Lublin	Polski Bus	Varies	3	5 daily
Prague (Czech Republic)	Polski Bus	Varies	12	2 daily
Toruń	PKS	50	4	hourly
Vienna (Austria)	Polski Bus	Varies	12½	2 daily
Wrocław	PKS	63	7	6 daily
Wrocław	Polski Bus	Varies	7¼	2 daily
Zakopane	PKS	65	8	6 daily

Train

DESTINATION	DURATION (HR)	FREQUENCY
Berlin (Germany)	5	5 daily
Bratislava (Slovakia)	8	2 daily
Budapest (Hungary)	11½	1 daily
Kyiv (Ukraine)	15½	1 daily
Minsk (Belarus)	9½-12	2-3 daily
Moscow (Russia)	18-21	2-3 daily
Prague (Czech Republic)	8½-10½	2 daily
Vienna (Austria)	8	3 daily

able, displaying instructions in English. You can check prices and book international train tickets online via **PKP Intercity** (☑ 22 391 9757; www. intercity.pl). Tickets for immediate departures on domestic and international trains can also be bought at numerous, well-signed booths in the underpasses leading to Warszawa Centralna.

For train connections between Warsaw and other Polish locations, check the Getting There & Away section under each specific town or city in this chapter.

Some domestic trains also stop at Warszawa Śródmieście station, 300m east of Warszawa Centralna, and Warszawa Zachodnia, next to Dworzec Zachodnia bus station.

❶ Getting Around

To/From the Airport

In 2012 a train service began running from the new Okęcie airport station, Warszawa Lotnisko Chopina, stopping at either Warszawa Centralna or Warszawa Śródmieście stations in the city centre. Some services also stop at useful intermediate stations such as Warszawa Zachodnia. Trains depart approximately every 15 minutes from 4.30am to 11.30pm daily; the 20-minute journey costs 3.60zł on a regular one-trip public transport ticket.

Another way of getting from Warsaw's main airport to the city centre is bus 175 (3.60zł), which leaves every 10 to 15 minutes and travels via Warszawa Centralna train station and ul Nowy Świat, terminating at Plac Piłsudskiego, about a 500m walk from Castle Sq in the Old Town. If you arrive in the wee small hours, night bus N32 links the airport with Warszawa Centralna every 30 minutes.

The taxi fare between Okęcie airport and the city centre is about 45zł to 50zł. Official taxis displaying a name, telephone number and fares can be arranged at the official taxi counters at the international arrivals level.

From the new Warsaw Modlin airport, the easiest way to get to the city centre is aboard the regular **Modlin Bus** (☑ 503 558 148; www.modlin-bus.com; adult/child 33/23zł; ☺ 4am-midnight). Alternatively, a taxi to the centre will cost between 100zł and 130zł, depending on the time of day.

Car

Warsaw traffic isn't fun, but there are good reasons to hire a car for jaunts into the countryside. Major car-rental companies are listed in the local English-language publications. They include **Avis** (☑ 22 650 4872; www.avis.pl), **Hertz** (☑ 22 500 1620; www.hertz.pl) and **Sixt** (☑ 22 511 1550; www.sixt.pl).

Public Transport

Warsaw's public transport operates from 5am to 11pm daily. The standard fare (3.60zł) is valid for one ride only on a bus, tram or metro train travelling anywhere in the city.

Time-based tickets are available for 20/40/60 minutes (2.60/3.80/5.20zł), one day (12zł) and three days (24zł); with these you can transfer between vehicles within the time limit. Buy tickets from kiosks (including those marked 'RUCH') before boarding, and validate them on board.

Warsaw is the only place in Poland where ISIC cards get a public-transport discount (of 48%).

A metro line operates from the suburb of Ursynów (Kabaty station) at the southern city limits to Młociny in the north, via the city centre (Centrum), but is of limited use to visitors. Local commuter trains head out to the suburbs from the Warszawa Śródmieście station.

Taxi

Taxis are a quick and easy way to get around – as long as you use official taxis and drivers use their meters. Beware of unauthorised 'Mafia' taxis parked in front of top-end hotels, at the airport, outside Warszawa Centralna train station and in the vicinity of most tourist sights – they'll take you the long way round and overcharge for it.

MAZOVIA & PODLASIE

After being ruled as an independent state by a succession of dukes, Mazovia shot to prominence during the 16th century, when Warsaw became the national capital. The region has long been a base for industry, the traditional mainstay of Poland's third-largest city, Łódź. To the east of Mazovia, toward the Belarus border, lies Podlasie, which means 'land close to the forest'. The main attraction of this region is the impressive Białowieża National Park.

Łódź

POP 729,000

Little damaged in WWII, Łódź (pronounced 'woodge') is a lively, likeable place with a wealth of attractive art nouveau architecture and the added bonus of being off the usual tourist track. It's also an easy day trip from Warsaw. Łódź became a major industrial centre in the 19th century, attracting immigrants from across Europe. In the 20th century, it became the hub of Poland's cinema industry – giving rise to the nickname 'Holly-Woodge'. Though its textile industry slumped in the postcommunist years, the centrally located city has had some success in attracting new investment in more diverse commercial fields.

BIAŁOWIEŻA NATIONAL PARK

Once a centre for hunting and timber-felling, Białowieża (Byah-wo-*vyeh*-zhah) on Poland's eastern border is the nation's oldest national park. Its significance is underlined by Unesco's unusual recognition of the park as both a Biosphere Reserve *and* a World Heritage Site. The forest contains more than 100 species of birds, along with elk, wild boars and wolves. Its major drawcard is the magnificent European bison, which was once extinct outside zoos, but has been successfully reintroduced to its ancient home.

The main attraction is the **Strict Nature Reserve** (www.bpn.com.pl; adult/concession 6/3zł; ☉9am-5pm), which can only be visited on a three-hour tour with a licensed guide along an 8km trail (195zł for an English-speaking guide). The creatures can be shy of visitors and you may not see them at all. Even without bison for company, however, being immersed in one of Europe's last remnants of primeval forest is a special experience.

For a guarantee of spotting *żubry* (bison), visit the **European Bison Reserve** (Rezerwat Żubrów; www.bpn.com.pl; adult/concession 6/3zł; ☉9am-5pm May-Sep, 8am-4pm Tue-Sun Oct-Apr) on the Hajnówka–Białowieża road. It's an open-plan zoo containing many mighty bison, as well as wolves, strange horselike tarpans and the mammoth *żubroń* (a hybrid of bison and cow).

The logical visitor base is the charming village of Białowieża, with a range of accommodation from budget to top end. To arrange guides, bike hire or transport via horse-drawn cart, visit the **PTTK office** (☎85 681 2295; www.pttk.bialowieza.pl; ul Kolejowa 17; ☉8am-4pm) at the southern end of **Palace Park**, the former location of the Russian tsar's hunting lodge.

Białowieża can be a tricky place to reach by public transport. From Warsaw, the only direct option is a single daily bus to the village departing at 2.20pm from Dworzec Zachodnia (45zł, five hours). Alternatively, head first from Warsaw by train or bus to Białystok, from where you can catch buses to Białowieża either directly or by changing at Hajnówka.

For more details, check out Lonely Planet's *Poland* country guide or visit www.pttk.bialowieza.pl.

Many of the attractions are along ul Piotrkowska, the main thoroughfare. You'll find banks and *kantors* (foreign-exchange offices) here and on ul Kopernika, one street west. You can't miss the bronze statues of local celebrities along ul Piotrkowska, including director Roman Polański and pianist Artur Rubinstein, seated at a baby grand. The helpful **tourist office** (www.turystyczna.lodz.pl; ul Piotrkowska 87; ☉9am-5pm) hands out free brochures and advice.

◉ Sights & Activities

Cinematography Museum   MUSEUM
(www.kinomuzeum.pl; Plac Zwycięstwa 1; adult/concession 10/7zł, Tue free; ☉10am-4pm Tue, Wed & Fri, 11am-6pm Thu, Sat & Sun) Three blocks east of ul Piotrkowska's southern pedestrian zone. Worth a look both for its collection of old cinema gear and its mansion setting.

City Museum of Łódź   MUSEUM
(www.muzeum-lodz.pl; ul Ogrodowa 15; adult/concession 9/5zł, Sun free; ☉10am-2pm Mon, 2-6pm Wed, 11am-4pm Tue, Thu, Sat & Sun) Northwest of Plac Wolności, at the north end of the main drag, this splendid museum tells the lively story of the city from its 19th-century industrial heyday onwards.

Manufaktura   MALL
(www.manufaktura.com; ul Karskiego 5) Close by the City Museum is this fascinating shopping mall and entertainment centre, constructed within a massive complex of historic red-brick factory buildings.

Jewish Cemetery   CEMETERY
(www.jewishlodzcemetery.org; ul Bracka 40; admission 6zł, 1st Sun of month free; ☉9am-5pm Sun-Thu, 9am-3pm Fri Apr-Oct, 9am-3pm Sun-Fri Nov-Mar) One of the largest in Europe. It's 3km northeast of the city centre and accessible by tram 6 from a stop one block north of Plac Wolności to its terminus at Strykowska. Enter from ul Zmienna.

Dętka   TOUR
(Plac Wolności 2; adult/concession 5/3zł; ☉noon-7pm Thu-Sun May-Oct) Guided tours every half-hour through the old red-brick sewer system beneath the city's streets, demonstrating the city's industrial heritage via photographs

and documents exhibited along the route. Operated by the City Museum.

🛏 Sleeping & Eating

The tourist office can provide information about all kinds of accommodation.

Youth Hostel
HOSTEL €

(☑42 630 6680; www.yhlodz.pl; ul Legionów 27; dm 18-40zł, s/d from 65/80zł; 🛜) This place is excellent, so book ahead. It features nicely decorated rooms in a spacious old building, with free laundry and a kitchen. It's 250m west of Plac Wolności.

Hotel Savoy
HOTEL €€

(☑42 632 9360; www.centrumhotele.pl; ul Traugutta 6; s/d from 149/249zł; 🛜) Well positioned just off central ul Piotrkowska, with simple but spacious light-filled rooms with clean bathrooms.

Hotel Centrum
HOTEL €€

(☑42 632 8640; www.centrumhotele.pl; ul Kilińskiego 59; s/d from 207/308zł; ❄🛜) East of ul Piotrkowska, this communist-era behemoth offers neatly renovated rooms and will be handy for the Łódź Fabryczna train station once it reopens after reconstruction In 2014.

Chłopska Izba
POLISH €€

(☑42 630 8087; ul Piotrkowska 65; mains 11-28zł; ⊘noon-11pm) On ul Piotrkowska is this restaurant with folksy decor, serving up tasty versions of all the Polish standards.

Esplanada
EUROPEAN €€

(☑42 630 5989; ul Piotrkowska 100; mains 19-59zł) A vibrant eatery serving quality Polish and German cuisine in an attractive historic venue. Beware the enormous (if tasty) schnitzels.

ℹ Getting There & Around

AIR From **Łódź airport** (www.airport.lodz.pl; ul Maczka 35), which can be reached by city buses 55 and 65 (3.20zł, 20 minutes), there are flights to a number of British destinations including London (at least daily) via Ryanair and Wizz Air. Dublin has four Ryanair connections per week. There are no domestic flights.

TRAIN At time of research the most convenient train station to the city centre, Łódź Fabryczna, had closed for reconstruction and was expected to reopen in 2014. In the meantime, the best option for travellers is busy Łódź Kaliska station, 1.2km southwest of central Łódź and accessible by tram 12 from the city centre. Trains are generally a better option than bus services from Łódź.

POLAND ŁÓDŹ

TRANSPORT FROM ŁÓDŹ

Bus

DESTINATION	DURATION (HR)	FREQUENCY
Berlin (Germany)	7½	2 daily
Poznań	2¾	2 daily
Prague (Czech Republic)	9½	2 daily
Warsaw	2¾	5 daily
Wrocław	4½	3 daily

Train

DESTINATION	COST(ZŁ)	DURATION (HR)	FREQUENCY
Częstochowa	38	2	4 daily
Gdańsk	61	6½	6 daily
Kraków	52	4½	4 daily
Poznań	32	4½	5 daily
Toruń	34	3	10 Daily
Warsaw	36	2	at least hourly
Wrocław	48	4¼	5 daily

BUS Polski Bus (www.polskibus.com) has useful connections to some destinations from its stop at Łódź Kaliska station. Check fares and buy tickets online.

MAŁOPOLSKA

Małopolska (literally 'lesser Poland') is a stunning area within which the visitor can spot plentiful remnants of traditional life amid green farmland and historic cities. The region covers a large swathe of southeastern Poland, from the former royal capital Kraków, to the eastern Lublin Uplands.

Kraków

POP 758.000

While many Polish cities are centred on an attractive Old Town, none can compare with Kraków (*krak*-oof) for sheer, effortless beauty. With a charming origin involving the legendary defeat of a dragon by either Prince Krakus or a cobbler's apprentice (depending on which story you believe), and with a miraculous escape from destruction in WWII, the city seems to have led a lucky existence.

As a result, Kraków is blessed with magnificent buildings and streets dating back to medieval times, with a stunning historic centrepiece – Wawel Castle.

Just south of the castle lies Kazimierz, the former Jewish quarter, reflecting both new and old. Its silent synagogues are a reminder of the tragedy of WWII, while the district's tiny streets and low-rise architecture have become home in recent years to a lively nightlife scene.

Not that you'll have trouble finding nightlife anywhere in Kraków, or a place to sleep. As the nation's biggest tourist drawcard, the city has hundreds of restaurants, bars and other venues tucked away in its laneways and cellars. Though hotel prices are above the national average, and visitor numbers high in summer, this vibrant, cosmopolitan city is an essential part of any tour of Poland.

◉ Sights & Activities

WAWEL HILL

Kraków's main draw for tourists is Wawel Hill. South of the Old Town, this prominent mount is crowned with a castle containing a cathedral; both are enduring symbols of Poland.

Wawel Castle CASTLE
(☏12 422 5155; www.wawel.krakow.pl; grounds free; ☺6am-dusk) You can choose from several attractions within this magnificent structure, each requiring a separate ticket, valid for a specific time. There's a limited daily quota of tickets for some parts, so arrive early if you want to see everything.

Most popular are the splendid **State Rooms** (adult/concession 18/11zł, Sun Nov-Mar free; ☺9.30am-5pm Tue-Fri, from 10am Sat & Sun Apr-Oct, 9.30am-4pm Tue-Sun Nov-Mar) and the **Royal Private Apartments** (adult/concession 25/19zł; ☺9.30am-5pm Tue-Sun Apr-Oct, to 4pm Tue-Sat Nov-Mar). Entry to the latter is only allowed on a guided tour; you may have to accompany a Polish-language tour if it's the only one remaining for the day. If you want to hire a guide who speaks English or other languages, contact the on-site **guides office** (☏12 422 1697).

The 14th-century **Wawel Cathedral** (www.katedra-wawelska.pl; ☺9am-5pm Mon-Sat, from 12.30pm Sun) was the coronation and burial place of Polish royalty for four centuries. Ecclesiastical artefacts are displayed in its small **Cathedral Museum** (adult/concession 12/7zł; ☺9am-5pm Tue-Sun). Admission also gives access to the **Royal Tombs**, including that of King Kazimierz Wielki; and the **bell tower** of the golden-domed **Sigismund Chapel** (1539), which contains the country's largest bell (11 tonnes).

Other attractions within the castle grounds include the **Museum of Oriental Art** (adult/concession 8/5zł; ☺9.30am-5pm Tue-Sun Apr-Oct, to 4pm Tue-Sat Nov-Mar), the **Crown Treasury & Armoury** (adult/concession 18/11zł, Mon free; ☺9.30am-1pm Mon, to 5pm Tue-Sun Apr-Oct, 9.30am-4pm Tue-Sun Nov-Mar) and the **Lost Wawel** (adult/concession 8/5zł, Mon Apr-Oct & Sun Nov-Mar free; ☺9.30am-1pm Mon, to 5pm Tue-Sun Apr-Oct, 9.30am-4pm Tue-Sun Nov-Mar), a well-displayed set of intriguing archaeological exhibits.

In the warmer months there's also the **Former Buildings & Fortifications tour** (adult/concession 18/10zł; ☺1pm Sat-Mon May-Sep) of the grounds, and you can climb the 137-step **Sandomierska Tower** (admission 4zł; ☺10am-5pm May-Sep).

Finish your visit by entering the atmospheric cave known as the **Dragon's Den** (admission 3zł; ☺10am-5pm Apr-Oct), as its exit leads out onto the riverbank where you'll encounter a fire-spitting bronze dragon.

Hi-Flyer Balloon
BALLOON RIDE

(Rondo Grunwaldzkie; adult/concession 38/20zł; ◷9am-10pm) Located on the opposite bank of the Vistula River from Wawel Castle, this tethered balloon lifts its passengers 150m into the air, enabling great views of the city.

OLD TOWN

Kraków's Old Town is a harmonious collection of historic buildings dating back centuries, ringed by a linear park known as the Planty which replaced the old city walls in the 19th century. It's an eminently walkable area.

Rynek Główny
HISTORIC SQUARE

(Main Market Square) This vast square is the focus of the Old Town and is Europe's largest medieval town square at 200m by 200m. Its most prominent feature is the 15th-century **Town Hall tower** (Wieża Ratuszowa; Rynek Główny 1; adult/concession 7/5zł; ◷10.30am-6pm Apr-Oct), which you can climb.

Cloth Hall
HISTORIC BUILDING

(Sukiennice; Rynek Główny 1) At the centre of the square is this 16th-century Renaissance building, housing a large souvenir market (p626). Here you can enter **Rynek Underground** (www.podziemiarynku.com; Rynek Główny 1; adult/concession 17/14zł, Tue free; ◷10am-8pm Mon, to 4pm Tue, to 10pm Wed-Sun), a fascinating attraction beneath the market square, consisting of an underground route through medieval market stalls and other long-forgotten chambers. The experience is enhanced by holograms and other audiovisual wizardry.

Upstairs, the **Gallery of 19th-Century Polish Painting** (http://muzeum.krakow.pl; Rynek Główny 1; adult/concession 12/6zł; ◷10am-8pm Tue-Sat, to 6pm Sun) exhibits art from a range of genres, including Polish Impressionism.

On the west side of the Cloth Hall is the useful **Historical Museum Visitor Centre** (☑12 426 5060; Rynek Główny 1; ◷10am-7pm), where you can buy tickets for many of the city's museums.

St Mary's Church
CHURCH

(Rynek Główny 4; adult/concession 6/4zł; ◷11.30am-6pm Mon-Sat, 2-6pm Sun) This 14th-century place of worship fills the northeastern corner of the square. The huge main **altarpiece** by Wit Stwosz (Veit Stoss in German) of Nuremberg is the finest Gothic sculpture in Poland and is opened ceremoniously each day at 11.50am.

Every hour a *hejnał* (bugle call) is played from the highest tower of the church. The melody, played in medieval times as a warning call, breaks off abruptly to symbolise the moment when, according to legend, the throat of a 13th-century trumpeter was pierced by a Tatar arrow. In summer you can climb the church's highest **tower** (St Mary's Church; adult/concession 5/3zł; ◷9-11.30am & 1-5.30pm May-Aug).

Collegium Maius
HISTORIC BUILDING

(www.maius.uj.edu.pl; ul Jagiellońska 15; adult/concession 12/6zł; ◷10am-2.20pm Mon-Fri, to 1.20pm Sat) West of the Rynek Główny is the oldest surviving university building in Poland. Guided tours of its fascinating academic collection run half-hourly and there's usually a couple in English, at 11am and 1pm. Even if you don't go on a tour, step into the magnificent arcaded courtyard for a glimpse of the beautiful architecture.

Florian Gate
FORTIFICATION

(ul Floriańska) From St Mary's Church, walk up ul Floriańska to this 14th-century gate. It's a tourist hot spot, with crowds, buskers and artists selling their work along the remnant section of the old city walls. Beyond it is the **Barbican** (Barbakan; ul Basztowa; adult/concession 7/5zł; ◷10.30am-6pm May-Oct), a defensive bastion built in 1498.

Czartoryski Museum
MUSEUM

(www.czartoryski.org; ul Św Jana 19) Near the Florian Gate, this museum features an impressive collection of European art, including Leonardo da Vinci's *Lady with an Ermine*.

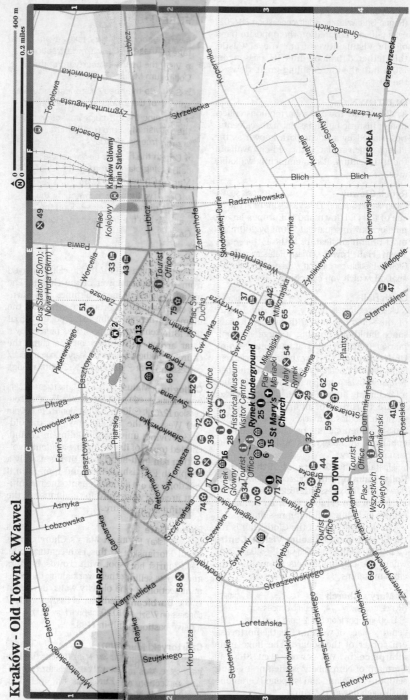

Kraków - Old Town & Wawel

POLAND KRAKÓW

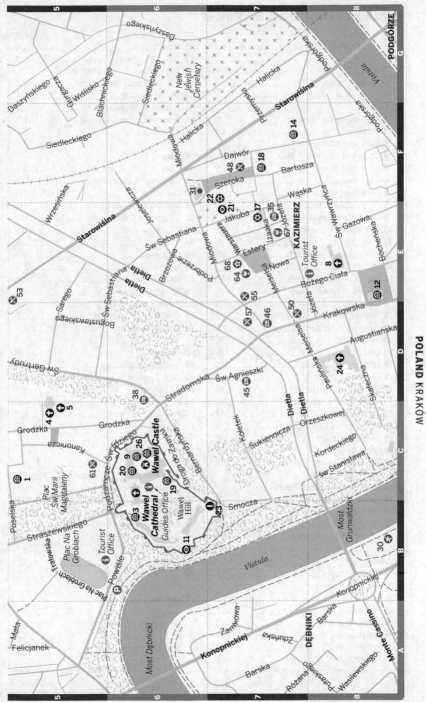

PODGÓRZE

Daszyńskiego

Daszyńskiego
Gułęcza
Wiślisko
Błachnickiego
Siedleckiego
New Jewish Cemetery
Halicka

Starowiślna

Podgórska
Przemyska
Halicka
Vistula

Siedleckiego

Wrzesińska

Miodowa
Halicka

Dajwór
48
18
Bartosza
Szeroka
31
22
21
Jakuba
17
35
Izaaka
67 Józefa
Józefa
Starowiślna

Starowiślna

Josefińska
Św Sebastiana

Brzozowa
Podbrzezie
Miodowa

Meiselsa
Estery
Nowa

Tourist Office
8
Bożego Ciała
12

Dietla
Dietl
Św Sebastiana

Bogusławskiego
Sarego
Bosucławskiego
53

68
64
55

Meiselsa
Józefa
Meiselsa
Krakowska

57
46
50

Augustiańska

24

Paulińska
Dietla
Dietla
Orzeszkowej
Skałeczna
Bochenska
Gazowa
Św Wawrzyńca

KAZIMIERZ

Św Gertrudy

Stradomska
Św Agnieszki
45
Koletek
Sukiennicza
Kordeckiego
Św Stanisława

Grodzka
38

4
5
Grodzka
Kanonicza

Podzamcze · Świętego Ducha
20 9
26
Wawel Castle

61
3
Wawel Cathedral
Guides Office
19
Wawel Hill
23
Smocza
11

Benedyktyńska
Droga do Zamku

Dietla
Dietl

Most Grunwaldzki
30

Poselska
Plac Św Marii Magdaleny
Straszewskiego
Plac Na Groblach
Groblach
Tourist Office
Powiśle

Plac Na Groblach
Tratowska

Vistula

Most Dębnicki

Zamkowa
Zduńska
Konopnickiej

DĘBNIKI

Barska
Konopnickiej
Barska
Różana
Wasilewskiego
Ptaśkiego
Monte Cassino

Mała
Felicjanek

Konopnickiej

Barska

Kraków - Old Town & Wawel

◎ Top Sights

Rynek Underground	C3
St Mary's Church	D3
Wawel Castle	C6
Wawel Cathedral	C6

◎ Sights

1	Archaeological Museum	C5
2	Barbican	D1
3	Cathedral Museum	B6
4	Church of SS Peter & Paul	C5
5	Church of St Andrew	C5
6	Cloth Hall	C3
7	Collegium Maius	B3
8	Corpus Christi Church	E8
9	Crown Treasury & Armoury	C6
10	Czartoryski Museum	D2
11	Dragon's Den	B6
12	Ethnographic Museum	E8
13	Florian Gate	D2
14	Galicia Jewish Museum	F7
15	Gallery of 19th-Century Polish Painting	C3
16	Historical Museum of Kraków	C3
17	Izaak's Synagogue	E7
18	Jewish Museum	F7
19	Lost Wawel	C6
20	Museum of Oriental Art	C6
21	Remuh Cemetery	E7
22	Remuh Synagogue	F7
	Royal Private Apartments	(see 26)
23	Sandomierska Tower	B7
24	St Catherine's Church	D8
25	St Mary's Tower	C3
26	State Rooms	C6
27	Town Hall tower	C3

◎ Activities, Courses & Tours

28	Cracow Tours	C3
29	English Language Club	D3
30	Hi-Flyer Balloon	B8
31	Jarden Tourist Agency	F6

◎ Sleeping

32	Cracow Hostel	C3
33	Greg & Tom Hostel	E1
34	Hostel Flamingo	C3
35	Hotel Abel	E7
36	Hotel Amadeus	D3
37	Hotel Campanile	E3
38	Hotel Royal	D6
39	Hotel Saski	C2
40	Hotel Stary	C2
41	Hotel Wawel	C4
42	Hotel Wit Stwosz	D3
43	Jordan Tourist Information & Accommodation Centre	E2
44	Mama's Hostel	C4
45	Nathan's Villa Hostel	D7
46	Tournet Pokoje Gościnne	D7
47	Wielopole	E4

◎ Eating

48	Ariel	F7
49	Carrefour Supermarket	E1
50	Deli Bar	D7
51	Glonojad	D1
52	Gruzińskie Chaczapuri	D2
53	Il Calzone	E5
54	Il Forno	D3
55	Manzana	E7
56	Milkbar	D3
57	Momo	D7
58	Nostalgia	B2
59	Pimiento	C4
60	Restauracja Pod Gruszką	C2
61	Smak Ukraiński	C5

◎ Drinking

62	Ambasada Śledzia	D4
63	Cafe Camelot	C3
64	Le Scandale	E7
65	Paparazzi	D3
66	Piwnica Pod Złotą Pipą	D2
67	Singer	E7

◎ Entertainment

68	Alchemia	E7
	Baccarat	(see 59)
69	Filharmonia Krakowska	B4
70	Harris Piano Jazz Bar	C3
71	Kino Pod Baranami	C3
72	Krakowskie Centrum Kinowe Ars	C2
73	Rdza	C3
74	Stary Teatr	C2
75	Teatr im Słowackiego	E2

◎ Shopping

76	Galeria Plakatu	D4
	Jarden Jewish Bookshop	(see 31)
77	Sklep Podróżnika	C2
	Souvenir Market	(see 6)

Also on display are Turkish weapons and artefacts, including a campaign tent from the 1683 Battle of Vienna. At the time of research it was closed for a major renovation, expected to take until 2013; check with the tourist office for an update.

Historic Churches   CHURCH
South of the Rynek Główny along ul Grodzka is the early-17th-century Jesuit **Church of SS Peter & Paul** (ul Grodzka 64; ☺dawn-dusk), Poland's first baroque church. The nearby Romanesque 11th-century **Church of St Andrew** (ul Grodzka 56; ☺9am-6pm Mon-Fri) was the only building in Kraków to withstand the Tatars' attack of 1241.

Archaeological Museum   MUSEUM
(ul Poselska 3; adult/concession 7/5zł, Sun free; ☺9am-3pm Mon-Wed, 2-6pm Thu, 10am-3pm Fri & Sun) Between the churches in the southern section of the Old Town you'll find this small but interesting museum, with displays on local prehistory and ancient Egyptian artefacts, including animal mummies.

Historical Museum of Kraków   MUSEUM
(www.mhk.pl; Rynek Główny 35; adult/concession 6/4zł, Sat free; ☺10am-5.30pm Wed-Sun) On the northwest corner of the Rynek Główny, this institution contains paintings, documents and oddments relating to the city's history.

English Language Club   SOCIAL GROUP
(ul Sienna 5; admission 2zł; ☺6-8pm Wed) Just south of St Mary's Church on the Rynek Główny, this social group has met weekly since the dying days of communism, when local students wanted to make contact with foreign visitors. Its weekly catch-ups are a fun way to meet a mixed bunch of Poles, expats and tourists in a relaxed setting.

KAZIMIERZ
Founded by King Kazimierz Wielki in 1335, Kazimierz was originally an independent town. In the 15th century, Jews were expelled from Kraków and forced to resettle in a small prescribed area in Kazimierz, separated from the rest of the town by a wall. The Jewish quarter later became home to Jews fleeing persecution throughout Europe.

By the outbreak of WWII there were 65,000 Jewish Poles in Kraków (around 30% of the city's population) and most lived in Kazimierz. Tragically, this thriving community was devastated in the Holocaust.

Nowadays the district's eastern quarter is dotted with synagogues and other reminders of Jewish culture and history, while the western half is home to a lively bar and dining scene. Kazimierz lies southeast of the Old Town.

Jewish Museum   MUSEUM
(www.mhk.pl; ul Szeroka 24; adult/concession 8/6zł, Mon free; ☺10am-2pm Mon & 9am-5pm Tue-Sun) This museum is housed within the 15th-century Old Synagogue, the oldest in Poland. Within its walls are exhibitions on Jewish traditions.

Galicia Jewish Museum   MUSEUM
(www.galiciajewishmuseum.org; ul Dajwór 18; adult/concession 15/10zł; ☺10am-6pm) South of the Old Synagogue, this fine museum features an impressive photographic exhibition, depicting modern-day traces of southeastern Poland's once thriving Jewish community.

Remuh Synagogue   SYNAGOGUE
(www.remuh.jewish.org.pl; ul Szeroka 40; adult/concession 5/2zł; ☺9am-6pm Sun-Fri) A short walk north from the Old Synagogue is this small 16th-century place of worship, still used for religious services. Behind it, the **Remuh Cemetery** (ul Szeroka 40; admission free; ☺9am-6pm Mon-Fri) boasts some extraordinary Renaissance gravestones.

Izaak's Synagogue   SYNAGOGUE
(ul Kupa 18; adult/concession 5/3zł; ☺9am-7pm Sun-Thu, to 3pm Fri) Heading west from ul Szeroka, you'll find this restored synagogue, decorated with impressive frescos from the 17th century.

Ethnographic Museum   MUSEUM
(www.etnomuzeum.eu; Plac Wolnica 1; adult/concession 9/5zł, Sun free; ☺11am-7pm Tue-Sat, to 3pm Sun May-Sep, 10am-6pm Mon, to 3pm Wed-Fri, to 2pm Sat & Sun Oct-Apr) Kazimierz's Old Town Hall contains this museum, displaying a collection of regional crafts and costumes.

Historic Churches   CHURCH
Kazimierz's western Catholic quarter includes the 14th-century Gothic **St Catherine's Church** (ul Augustiańska 7), with an imposing 17th-century gilded high altar, while the 14th-century **Corpus Christi Church** (ul Bożego Ciała 26) is crammed with baroque fittings.

PODGÓRZE
During the war the Germans relocated Jews to a walled ghetto in this district, just south of Kazimierz across the Vistula River. They were exterminated in the nearby Płaszów

WORTH A TRIP

NOWA HUTA

There's another side to Kraków that few tourists see. Catch tram 4 or 15 from Kraków Główny train station, or tram 22 from Kazimierz, east to Plac Centralny in Nowa Huta. This suburb was a 'workers' paradise' district built by the communist regime in the 1950s to counter the influence of the city's religious and intellectual traditions. Its immense, blocky concrete buildings stretch out along broad, straight streets; a fascinating contrast to the Old Town's delicate beauty.

Concentration Camp, as portrayed in Steven Spielberg's haunting film, *Schindler's List*.

TOP CHOICE **Schindler's Factory**   MUSEUM
(www.mhk.pl; ul Lipowa 4; adult/concession 17/14zł; ⊙10am-4pm Mon, 10am-8pm Tue-Sun) This impressive museum covering the German occupation of Kraków in WWII is housed in the former enamel factory of Oskar Schindler, which was immortalised in *Schindler's List*. Well-organised, innovative exhibits tell the moving story of the city from 1939 to 1945, recreating urban elements such as a tram carriage, a train station underpass and a crowded ghetto apartment within the factory's walls. It's an experience that shouldn't be missed.

From the main post office in the Old Town, catch any tram down ul Starowiślna and alight at the first stop over the river at Plac Bohaterów Getta. From here, follow the signs east along ul Kącik, under the railway line to the museum.

Museum of Contemporary Art in Kraków   GALLERY
(MOCAK; www.mocak.com.pl; ul Lipowa 4; adult/ concession 10/5zł, Tue free; ⊙11am-7pm Tue-Sun) Opened in 2011, MOCAK is a major museum of modern art and the first such building in Poland to be constructed from scratch. As it's right next to Schindler's Factory, the two attractions could be combined for an absorbing day out.

WIELICZKA
Wieliczka Salt Mine   UNDERGROUND MUSEUM
(www.kopalnia.pl; ul Daniłowicza 10; adult/concession 68/54zł; ⊙7.30am-7.30pm Apr-Oct, 8am-5pm Nov-Mar) Wieliczka (vyeh-*leech*-kah), 15km

southeast of the city centre, is famous for this former salt mine. It's an eerie but richly decorated world of pits and chambers, and every single element from chandeliers to altarpieces was hewn by hand from solid salt. The mine is included on Unesco's World Heritage List.

The highlight of a visit is the richly ornamented **Chapel of the Blessed Kinga**, a church measuring 54m by 17m and 12m high. Construction of this underground temple took more than 30 years (1895–1927), resulting in the removal of 20,000 tonnes of rock salt.

The obligatory guided tour through the mine takes about two hours (a 2km walk). Tours in English operate approximately hourly between 10am and 5pm, increasing to half-hourly from 8.30am to 6pm in July and August. If you're visiting independently, you must wait for a tour to start. Last admission to the mine is shortly before closing time.

To avoid queues at Wieliczka, buy your ticket in advance from the **Kopalnia Soli office** (ul Wiślna 12; ⊙9am-5pm Mon-Fri) in Kraków before setting out.

An easy way to get to Wieliczka is by minibus (3zł; look for the 'Salt Mine' sign on the windscreen), departing frequently between 6am and 8pm from ul Pawia near the Galeria Krakowska shopping mall next to Kraków Główny train station. Alternatively, bus 304 travels from the same area to the salt mine and requires a suburban ticket (3.40zł), which you can obtain from ticket vending machines. Get off at the 'Wieliczka Kopalnia Soli' stop.

☞ Tours
These companies operate tours of Kraków and surrounding areas.

Jarden Tourist Agency   JEWISH HERITAGE
(☑12 429 1374; www.jarden.pl; ul Szeroka 2) The best agency for tours of Polish Jewish heritage, based in Kazimierz. Its showpiece, 'Retracing Schindler's List' (two hours by car), costs 80zł per person. All tours require a minimum of three and must be booked in advance. Tours are in English, but other languages can be arranged.

Cracow Tours   GUIDED TOURS
(☑12 430 0726; www.cracowtours.pl; ul Krupnicza 3) This company runs various tours, including a four-hour general **bus tour of the city** (adult/concession 130/65zł).

Crazy Guides COMMUNIST HERITAGE
(☑50 009 1200; www.crazyguides.com) Offers entertaining tours of the city's communist-era suburbs, in restored cars of the socialist era. Guides collect tour members from their accommodation.

✹ Festivals & Events

**Krakow International
Film Festival** FILM
(www.kff.com.pl; ☺May/Jun)

Lajkonik Pageant HISTORIC
(☺May/June) Held seven days after Corpus Christi, this centuries-old parade is led by a man in a pointed hat riding a hobbyhorse, symbolising an ancient victory over invaders.

Jewish Culture Festival JEWISH
(www.jewishfestival.pl; ☺Jun/Jul)

**International Festival of
Street Theatre** THEATRE
(www.teatrkto.pl; ☺Jul)

Summer Jazz Festival MUSIC
(www.cracjazz.com; ☺Jul)

Organ Music Festival MUSIC
(☺Jul/Aug) A series of concerts held in churches each summer; check with the tourist office for the latest schedule.

Live Festival MUSIC
(www.livefestival.pl; ☺Aug) Big open-air music festival with a diverse range of performers.

**Kraków Christmas
Crib Competition** CHRISTMAS
(☺Dec) Competitive display of elaborate nativity scenes, exhibited in the Rynek each winter.

🛏 Sleeping

Kraków is unquestionably Poland's major tourist destination, with prices to match. Booking ahead in the busy summer months is recommended.

An agency offering decent rooms around town is **Jordan Tourist Information & Accommodation Centre** (☑12 422 6091; www.jordan.pl; ul Pawia 8; s/d around 150/250zł; ☺8am-6pm Mon-Fri, 9am-2pm Sat).

TOP CHOICE Wielopole HOTEL €€
(☑12 422 1475; www.wielopole.pl; ul Wielopole 3; s/d 299/359zł; ❈🕸) Smart and simple modern rooms in a renovated block on the eastern edge of the Old Town, with narrow beds but

spotless bathrooms. The tariff includes an impressive buffet breakfast.

Mama's Hostel HOSTEL €
(☑12 429 5940; www.mamashostel.com.pl; ul Bracka 4; dm 50-60zł, d 150zł; 🕸) Centrally located, brightly hued lodgings with a beautiful sunlit lounge overlooking a courtyard and the aroma of freshly roasted coffee drifting up from a cafe below in the mornings. There's a washing machine on-site.

Nathan's Villa Hostel HOSTEL €
(☑12 422 3545; www.nathansvilla.com; ul Św Agnieszki 1; dm from 42zł, d 184zł; 🕸) Comfy rooms, sparkling bathrooms, a laundry and a friendly atmosphere make this place a big hit with backpackers, and its cellar bar, minicinema, beer garden and pool table add to the appeal. Conveniently located between the Old Town and Kazimierz.

AAA Kraków Apartments APARTMENTS €€
(☑12 346 4670; www.krakow-apartments.biz; apt from 300zł; 🕸) Company renting out renovated apartments in the vicinity of the Old Town, with a smaller selection in Kazimierz. Cheaper rates are available for longer stays.

Hotel Amadeus HOTEL €€€
(☑12 429 6070; www.hotel-amadeus.pl; ul Mikołajska 20; s/d 540/620zł; 🕸) Everything about this hotel says 'class'. The rooms are tastefully furnished, though singles are rather small given the price. One room has wheelchair access, and there's a sauna, fitness centre and well-regarded restaurant. While hanging around the lobby, you can check out photos of famous guests.

Hotel Stary HOTEL €€€
(☑12 384 0808; www.stary.hotel.com.pl; ul Szczepańska 5; s/d 800/900zł; ❈🕸🏊) Setting a classy standard, the Stary is housed in an 18th-century aristocratic residence that exudes charm. The fabrics are all natural, the bathroom surfaces Italian marble, and there's a fitness centre, swimming pool and rooftop terrace to enjoy.

Hotel Abel HOTEL €€
(☑12 411 8736; www.hotelabel.pl; ul Józefa 30; s/d 160/220zł; 🕸) Reflecting the character of Kazimierz, this hotel has a distinctive personality, evident in its polished wooden staircase, arched brickwork and age-worn tiles. The comfortable rooms make a good base for exploring the historic Jewish neighbourhood.

Greg & Tom Hostel
HOSTEL €

(☑12 422 4100; www.gregtomhostel.com; ul Pawia 12; dm 57zł, d from 150zł; 🛜) This well-run hostel is in a handy location near the train station. There's a free Polish dinner served each Tuesday, the staff are friendly and laundry facilities are included.

Cracow Hostel
HOSTEL €

(☑12 429 1106; www.cracowhostel.com; Rynek Główny 18; dm 40-72zł, d 188zł; 🛜) This hostel spread over three floors may not be the best in town, with somewhat cramped dorms, but it's perched high above the Rynek Główny and has an amazing view from its comfortable lounge.

Hostel Flamingo
HOSTEL €

(☑12 422 0000; www.flamingo-hostel.com; ul Szewska 4; dm 55-85zł, d 190zł; 🛜) Colourful hostel with pink and lilac decor, a friendly attitude and a great location not far west of the Rynek Główny. Dorms have four to 10 beds.

Hotel Royal
HOTEL €€

(☑12 421 3500; www.hotelewam.pl; ul Św Gertrudy 26-29; s/d from 249/360zł; 🛜) Impressive art nouveau edifice with loads of old-world charm, just below Wawel Castle. It's split into two sections: the higher-priced rooms are cosy and far preferable to the fairly basic rooms at the back.

Tournet Pokoje Gościnne
HOTEL €€

(☑12 292 0088; www.accommodation.krakow.pl; ul Miodowa 7; s/d from 150/200zł; 🛜) This is a neat pension in Kazimierz, offering simple but comfortable and quiet rooms with compact bathrooms. The in-house restaurant serves Polish dishes.

Hotel Wit Stwosz
HOTEL €€€

(☑12 429 6026; www.wit-stwosz.com.pl; ul Mikołajska 28; s/d 330/420zł; 🛜) In a historic town house belonging to St Mary's Church, decorated in a suitably religious theme. Rooms are compact and simply furnished, but tasteful and attractive.

Hotel Wawel
HOTEL €€€

(☑12 424 1300; www.hotelwawel.pl; ul Poselska 22; s/d 340/480zł; ✳🛜) Ideally located just off busy ul Grodzka, this is a pleasant place offering tastefully decorated rooms with timber highlights. It's far enough from the main drag to minimise noise.

Hotel Saski
HOTEL €€

(☑12 421 4222; www.hotelsaski.com.pl; ul Sławkowska 3; s/d 295/395zł; 🛜) The Saski occupies a historic mansion, complete with a uniformed doorman, rattling old lift and ornate furnishings. The rooms themselves are comparatively plain.

Hotel Campanile
HOTEL €€

(☑12 424 2600; www.campanile.com.pl; ul Św Tomasza 34; r 369zł; 🛜) Straightforward modern hotel in a quiet corner of the Old Town, just a few blocks from the Rynek. It has attractive, bright rooms done out in corporate decor. Breakfast is 35zł extra.

Camping Smok
CAMPING GROUND €

(☑12 429 8300; www.smok.krakow.pl; ul Kamedulska 18; site per person/tent 25/15zł, r 180zł) It's small, quiet and pleasantly located 4km west of the Old Town, with both tent space and rooms. To get here from outside the Kraków Główny train station building, take tram 1, 2 or 6 to the end of the line in Zwierzyniec (destination marked 'Salwator') and change for any westbound bus (except bus 100).

✕ Eating

Kraków is a food paradise, tightly packed with restaurants serving a wide range of international cuisines.

One local speciality is *obwarzanki* (ring-shaped pretzels powdered with poppy seeds, sesame seeds or salt) available from street vendors who can often be found dozing next to their barrows throughout the city.

Self-caterers can stock up at the **Carrefour Supermarket** (ul Pawia 5, Galeria Krakowska; ⊙9am-10pm Mon-Sat, 10am-9pm Sun) within the Galeria Krakowska shopping mall, next to the Kraków Główny train station.

Glonojad
TOP CHOICE / VEGETARIAN €

(Plac Matejki 2; mains 8-14zł; ⊙8am-10pm; 🛜🍴) Attractive modern vegetarian restaurant with a great view onto Plac Matejki, just north of the Barbican. The diverse menu has a variety of tasty dishes including samosas, curries, potato pancakes, burritos, gnocchi and soups. There's also an all-day breakfast menu, so there's no need to jump out of your hotel bed too early.

Deli Bar
HUNGARIAN €€

(ul Meiselsa 5; mains 10-53zł; ⊙1-10pm) A Hungarian guy called László told us this was the best Magyar restaurant in Kraków, and he was right on the money. Its Hungarian owners turn out tasty paprika-laced classics such as goulash, *palacsinta* (crepes in Hungarian) and 'Budapest pork'.

Milkbar POLISH €
(ul Św Tomasza 24; mains 10-18zł; ☺9am-9pm)
Cleverly modernised version of the traditional *bar mleczny* (milk bar), serving affordable
dishes including breakfast in a pleasant dining area. The two-course set menu for 18zł is
great value.

Restauracja Pod Gruszką POLISH €€
(ul Szczepańska 1; mains 12-29zł; ☺noon-midnight)
A favourite haunt of writers and artists, this
upstairs establishment is the eatery that
time forgot, with its elaborate old-fashioned
decor featuring chandeliers, lace tablecloths, age-worn carpets and sepia portraits.
The menu covers a range of Polish dishes,
the most distinctive being the soups served
within small bread loaves.

Momo VEGETARIAN €
(ul Dietla 49; mains 10-16zł; ☺11am-8pm; 🖉) Vegans
will cross the doorstep of this Kazimierz restaurant with relief – the majority of the menu
is completely animal-free. The space is decorated with Indian craft pieces and serves up
subcontinental soups, stuffed pancakes and
rice dishes, with a great range of cakes. The
Tibetan dumplings are a treat worth ordering.

Il Calzone ITALIAN €€
(ul Starowiślna 15a; mains 16-44zł; ☺noon-11pm
Mon-Thu) This pleasant slice of Italy is a well-
kept secret, tucked away in a quiet nook set
back from the street. Considering its pleasant whitewashed decor and charming outdoor terrace, the food is excellent value.

Ariel JEWISH €€
(ul Szeroka 18; mains 19-78zł) Atmospheric Jewish restaurant packed with old-fashioned
timber furniture and portraits, serving a
range of kosher dishes. Try the Berdytchov
soup (beef, honey and cinnamon) for a tasty
starter. There's often live music here at night.

Nostalgia POLISH €€
(ul Karmelicka 10; mains 19-76zł; ☺noon-11pm) A
refined version of the traditional Polish eatery, Nostalgia features a fireplace, overhead
timber beams, uncrowded tables and courteous service. Wrap yourself around Russian
dumplings, a 'Hunter's Stew' of cabbage,
meat and mushrooms, or vegie options such
as potato pancakes. In warm weather diners
can enjoy the outdoor eating area.

Manzana MEXICAN €€
(ul Miodowa 11; mains 19-32zł; ☺7.30am-1am) Long
opening hours, a breakfast menu and some
impressively authentic dishes make this a

compelling dining choice. The interior is done
out in soothing burnt orange tones, with only
a minimum of sombreros as decoration.

Pimiento ARGENTINIAN €€€
(ul Stolarska 13; mains 44-159zł) This upmarket
grill serves a dizzying array of steaks to suit
both appetite and budget, and offers some
reasonable vegetarian alternatives for the
meat averse. Factor the South American
wine list into your calculations and you have
a classy night out.

Il Forno ITALIAN €€
(Mały Rynek 2; mains 21-79zł; ☺noon-late) This
place has an attractive view of the Mały
Rynek (Small Market Sq). It serves pizzas
and pasta, along with more ambitious meat
and fish dishes. The downstairs bar section
is the Arabian-styled **Shisha Club**, serving
Middle Eastern food.

Gruzińskie Chaczapuri GEORGIAN €€
(ul Floriańska 26; mains 16-29zł; ☺noon-11pm; 🖉)
Cheap and cheerful place serving up tasty
Georgian dishes. Grills, salads and steaks fill
the menu and there's a separate vegetarian
selection with items such as the traditional
Georgian cheese pie with stewed vegetables.

Smak Ukraiński UKRAINIAN €€
(ul Kanonicza 15; mains 18-30zł; ☺noon-10pm)
This Ukrainian restaurant presents authentic dishes in a cosy little cellar decorated
with provincial flair. Expect lots of dumplings, *borshch* (beetroot soup) and waiters
in waistcoats.

🍷 Drinking

There are hundreds of pubs and bars in
Kraków's Old Town, many housed in ancient
vaulted cellars. Kazimierz also has a lively
bar scene, centred on Plac Nowy and its surrounding streets.

Ambasada Śledzia BAR
(ul Stolarska 6; ☺8am-6am) The 'Herring Embassy' sits neatly, if cheekily, on this street
lined with consulates. It serves cheap beer
and vodka along with snack-sized servings
of *śledź* (herring), *kiełbasa* (sausage) or
golonka (pork knuckle) for around 10zł. It's
a good place to chow down if you're out late
clubbing.

Paparazzi BAR
(ul Mikołajska 9; ☺noon-1am Mon-Fri, 4pm-1am Sat
& Sun; 🖲) Bright, modern place, with B&W
press photos of celebrities covering the walls.
The drinks menu includes cocktails such as

WANT MORE?

For in-depth information, reviews and recommendations at your fingertips, head to the Apple App Store to purchase Lonely Planet's *Kraków City Guide* iPhone app.

Alternatively, head to www.lonelyplanet.com/poland/malopolska/krakow for planning advice, author recommendations, traveller reviews and insider tips.

the Polish martini, built around bison grass vodka. There's also inexpensive bar food.

Singer
CAFE-BAR

(ul Estery 20; ⊘9am-4am) Laid-back hang-out of the Kazimierz cognoscenti, this relaxed cafebar's moody candlelit interior is full of character. Alternatively, sit outside and converse over a sewing machine affixed to the table.

Piwnica Pod Złotą Pipą
PUB

(ul Floriańska 30; ⊘noon-midnight) Less claustrophobic than other cellar bars, with lots of tables for eating or drinking. Decent bar food and international beers on tap.

Le Scandale
BAR

(Plac Nowy 9; ⊘8am-3am; 🕏) Smooth Kazimierz drinking hole with low black-leather couches, ambient lighting and a gleaming well-stocked bar. Full of mellow drinkers sampling the extensive cocktail list.

Cafe Camelot
CAFE

(ul Św Tomasza 17; ⊘9am-midnight) For coffee and cake, try this genteel haven hidden around an obscure street corner in the Old Town. Its cosy rooms are cluttered with lacecovered candlelit tables and a quirky collection of wooden figurines featuring spiritual or folkloric scenes.

☆ Entertainment

The comprehensive Polish-English booklet *Karnet* (4zł), published by the city authorities' tourist office, lists almost every event in the city. In addition, the tourist office located at ul Św Jana 2 specialises in cultural events and can book tickets to many of them.

Nightclubs

TOP CHOICE Baccarat
CLUB

(ul Stolarska 13; ⊘8pm-late Thu-Sat) Luxuriously appointed nightclub playing a mix of house,

dance and disco sounds, via DJs and occasional live performers. Move your body beneath the shiny chandeliers and mirror balls.

Alchemia
BAR/CLUB

(ul Estery 5; ⊘9am-3am) This Kazimierz venue exudes a shabby-is-the-new-cool look with rough-hewn wooden benches, candlelit tables and a companionable gloom. It hosts regular live-music gigs and theatrical events through the week.

Harris Piano Jazz Bar
JAZZ

(Rynek Główny 28; ⊘9am-2am May-Oct, 1pm-2am Nov-Apr) Subterranean jazz haunt with one of Kraków's most varied programs. There's jazz, blues, big band, fusion or soul music every night, interspersed with free jam sessions. Ticketed events range from 15zł to 35zł.

Rdza
CLUB

(ul Bracka 3/5) This basement club attracts some of Kraków's more sophisticated clubbers, with its Polish house music bouncing off exposed brick walls and comfy sofas. Guest DJs start spinning at 9pm.

Performing Arts

Stary Teatr
THEATRE

(☎12 422 9080; www.stary.pl; ul Jagiellońska 5) Accomplished theatre company offering quality productions. To overcome the language barrier, pick a Shakespeare play you know well from the repertoire and take in the distinctive Polish interpretation.

Teatr im Słowackiego
OPERA, THEATRE

(☎12 424 4528; www.slowacki.krakow.pl; Plac Św Ducha 1) This grand place, built in 1893, focuses on Polish classics, large theatrical productions and opera.

Filharmonia Krakowska
CLASSICAL MUSIC

(☎12 619 8722; www.filharmonia.krakow.pl; ul Zwierzyniecka 1) Hosts one of the best orchestras in the country; concerts are usually held on Friday and Saturday.

Cinemas

Two convenient cinemas are **Krakowskie Centrum Kinowe Ars** (ul Św Jana 6) and **Kino Pod Baranami** (Rynek Główny 27), the latter located within a courtyard off the Rynek Główny. Films are in their original languages, with Polish subtitles.

🔒 Shopping

The place to start (or perhaps end) your Kraków shopping is at the large **souvenir**

market (Rynek Główny 3; ⊙10am-6pm) within the Cloth Hall (p617), selling everything from fine amber jewellery to tacky plush dragons.

Galeria Plakatu ART
(ul Stolarska 8; ⊙11am-6pm Mon-Fri, 11am-2pm Sat) Fascinating examples of Polish poster art can be purchased here.

Sklep Podróżnika BOOKS
(ul Jagiellońska 6; ⊙11am-7pm Mon-Fri, 10am-2pm Sat) For regional and city maps, as well as Lonely Planet titles.

Jarden Jewish Bookshop BOOKS
(ul Szeroka 2) Located in Kazimierz; well stocked with titles on Poland's Jewish heritage.

ℹ Information

Discount Cards

Kraków Tourist Card (www.krakowcard.com; 2/3 days 60/75zł) Available from tourist offices, the card includes travel on public transport and entry to many museums.

Internet Access

Centrum Internetowe (ul Stolarska 5; ⊙9am-midnight) Within the Pasaż Bielaka arcade.

Klub Garinet (ul Floriańska 18; per hr 4zł; ⊙9am-10pm)

Money

Kantors (foreign-exchange offices) and ATMs can be found all over the city centre. It's worth noting, however, that many *kantors* close on Sunday and some located near the Rynek Główny and Kraków Główny train station offer terrible exchange rates – check around before proffering your cash. There are also exchange facilities at the airport, with even less attractive rates.

Post

Main Post Office (ul Westerplatte 20; ⊙7.30am-8.30pm Mon-Fri, 8am-2pm Sat)

Tourist Information

Two free magazines, *Welcome to Cracow & Małopolska* and *Visitor: Kraków & Zakopane*, are available at upmarket hotels. The *Kraków in Your Pocket* booklet (5zł) is also very useful, packed with entertaining reviews of local sights and eateries.

DON'T MISS

AUSCHWITZ-BIRKENAU

Few place names have more impact than Auschwitz, which is seared into public consciousness as the location of history's most extensive experiment in genocide.

Established within disused army barracks in 1940, Auschwitz was initially designed to hold Polish prisoners, but was expanded by the German military occupiers into their largest centre for the extermination of European Jews.

Two more camps were subsequently established: Birkenau (Brzezinka, also known as Auschwitz II), 3km west of Auschwitz; and Monowitz (Monowice), several kilometres west of Oświęcim, the Polish town which contains the former death camp. In the course of their operation, between one and 1.5 million people were murdered by the Nazi Germany regime in these death factories – 90% of them Jews.

Auschwitz was only partially destroyed by the fleeing Nazis, so many of the original buildings remain as a bleak document of the camp's history. A dozen of the 30 surviving prison blocks house sections of the **State Museum Auschwitz-Birkenau** (☎33 844 8100; www.auschwitz.org.pl; ul Więźniów Oświęcimia 20; admission free; ⊙8am-7pm Jun-Aug, 8am-6pm May & Sep, 8am-5pm Apr & Oct, 8am-4pm Mar & Nov, 8am-3pm Dec-Feb).

Between May and October it's compulsory to join a tour if you arrive between 10am and 3pm. English-language tours of the Auschwitz-Birkenau complex (adult/concession 40/30zł, 3½ hours) leave at half-hourly intervals from 9.30am.

Auschwitz-Birkenau is an easy day trip from Kraków. Most convenient are the approximately hourly buses to Oświęcim (12zł, 1½ hours) departing from the bus station in Kraków, which either pass by or terminate at the museum. There are also numerous minibuses to Oświęcim (10zł, 1½ hours) from the minibus stands off ul Pawia, next to Galeria Krakowska.

Most travel agencies in Kraków offer organised tours of Auschwitz (including Birkenau), costing from 90zł to 130zł per person. Check with the operator for exactly how much time the tour allows you at each site, as some run to a very tight schedule.

For more about Oświęcim, including accommodation, check out Lonely Planet's *Poland* country guide or visit www.mpit-oswiecim.neostrada.pl.

TRANSPORT FROM KRAKÓW

Domestic Bus

DESTINATION	PRICE (ZŁ)	DURATION (HR)	FREQUENCY
Cieszyn (on the Czech border)	20	3	Hourly
Lublin	48	5½	6 daily
Oświęcim (Auschwitz)	12	1½	hourly
Zakopane	18	2	at least hourly
Zamość	52	8	9 daily

Domestic Train

DESTINATION	PRICE (ZŁ)	DURATION (HR)	FREQUENCY
Częstochowa	38	2¼	3 daily
Gdynia & Gdańsk	69	8-12	10 daily
Lublin	58	4½	2 daily
Poznań	61	8½	9 daily
Przemyśl	50	5	9 daily
Toruń	69	8½	3 daily
Warsaw	56	3	at least hourly
Wrocław	52	5½	hourly
Zakopane	24	3¾	8 daily

International Train

DESTINATION	DURATION (HR)	FREQUENCY
Berlin (Germany)	10	1 daily
Bratislava (Slovakia)	7½	1 daily
Budapest (Hungary)	10½	1 daily
Kyiv (Ukraine)	19½	1 daily
Lviv (Ukraine)	7½-9½	2 daily
Prague (Czech Republic)	10	1 daily
Vienna (Austria)	8	1 daily

Tourist Office ul Św Jana (☑12 421 7787; www. karnet.krakow.pl; ul Św Jana 2; ☺9am-7pm); Cloth Hall (☑12 433 7310; Rynek Główny 1; ☺9am-7pm May-Sep, 9am-5pm Oct-Apr); northeastern Old Town (☑12 432 0110; ul Szpitalna 25; ☺9am-7pm May-Sep, 9am-5pm Oct-Apr); southern Old Town (☑12 616 1886; Plac Wszystkich Świętych 2; ☺9am-5pm); Wawel Hill (ul Powiśle 11; ☺9am-7pm); Kazimierz (☑12 422 0471; ul Józefa 7; ☺9am-5pm); airport (☑12 285 5431; John Paul II International airport, Balice; ☺9am-7pm). Helpful city-run service; the office at ul Św Jana 2 specialises in cultural events.

ℹ Getting There & Away

Air

The **John Paul II International airport** (www. lotnisko-balice.pl; ul Medweckiego 1) is more often called Balice airport, after the suburb in which it's located, about 15km west of the Old Town. The airport terminal hosts car-hire desks, along with currency exchanges offering unappealing rates. To get to the Old Town by public transport, step aboard the free shuttle bus to the nearby train station. Buy a ticket (12zł) on board the train from a vending machine or the conductor for the 20-minute train journey to Kraków Główny station.

If you land instead at Katowice airport, catch the **Matuszek** (☑32 236 1111; www.matuszek.com. pl; one-way/return 44/88zł) shuttle bus to the Kraków bus station; the journey takes two hours.

LOT flies between Kraków and Warsaw several times a day and offers direct connections from Kraków to Frankfurt, Paris, Vienna and Athens. Bookings for all flights can be made at the **LOT office** (☎12 422 8989; ul Basztowa 15; ⊘9am-5pm Mon-Fri). There are also twice daily domestic flights via Eurolot to Gdańsk, Poznań and Szczecin.

A range of other airlines, including several budget operators, connect Kraków to cities in Europe, including an array of destinations across Britain and Ireland. There are direct flights daily to and from London via EasyJet and Ryanair. Dublin is serviced daily by Ryanair and Aer Lingus.

Bus

If you've been travelling by bus elsewhere in Poland, Kraków's modern main **bus station** (ul Bosacka 18) will seem like a palace compared with the usual facility. It's located on the other side of the main train station, northeast of the Old Town. Taking the train will generally be quicker, but several PKS buses head to places of interest; check fares and buy tickets online.

Two private bus companies, **Trans Frej** (www.trans-frej.com.pl) and **Szwagropol** (www.szwagropol.pl), also serve Zakopane frequently (19zł, two hours). **Polski Bus** (www.polskibus.com) departs from here to Warsaw (five hours, four daily) and Zakopane (2¼ hours, two daily).

Train

Kraków Główny train station (Plac Dworcowy), on the northeastern outskirts of the Old Town, handles all international trains and most domestic rail services. The railway platforms are about 150m north of the station building, and you can also reach them from the adjacent Galeria Krakowska shopping mall.

Lublin

POP 349,000

If the crowds are becoming too much in Kraków, you could do worse than jump on a train to Lublin. This attractive eastern city has many of the same attractions – a beautiful Old Town, a castle, and good bars and restaurants – but is less visited by international tourists.

Though today the city's beautifully preserved Old Town is a peaceful blend of Gothic, Renaissance and baroque architecture, Lublin has an eventful past. In 1569 the Lublin Union was signed here, uniting Poland and Lithuania; and at the end of WWII, the Soviet Union set up a communist government in Lublin, prior to the liberation of Warsaw.

⊙ Sights & Activities

OLD TOWN
Lublin Castle   CASTLE
(www.zamek-lublin.pl; ul Zamkowa; ⊘10am-5pm Tue-Sat, 10am-6pm Sun) This substantial forti-fication, standing on a hill at the northeastern edge of the Old Town, has a dark history. It was built in the 14th century, then rebuilt as a prison in the 1820s. During the occupation under Nazi Germany, more than 100,000 people passed through its doors before being deported to the death camps. The castle's major occupant is now the **Lublin Museum** (www.zamek-lublin.pl; ul Zamkowa 9; adult/concession 8.50/6.50zł; ⊘10am-5pm Wed-Sat, 9am-6pm Sun). On display are paintings, silverware, porcelain, woodcarvings and weaponry, mostly labelled in Polish. Check out the alleged 'devil's paw-print' on the 17th-century table in the foyer, linked to a local legend.

At the eastern end of the castle is the gorgeous 14th-century **Chapel of the Holy Trinity** (ul Zamkowa 9; adult/concession 8.50/6.50zł; ⊘10am-5pm Tue-Sat, 10am-6pm Sun), accessible via the museum. Its interior is covered with polychrome Russo-Byzantine frescos painted in 1418 – possibly the finest medieval wall paintings in Poland.

Historical Museum of Lublin   MUSEUM
(www.zamek.lublin.pl; Plac Łokietka 3; adult/concession 5.50/4.50zł; ⊘9am-4pm Wed-Sat, 9am-5pm Sun) Situated within the 14th-century **Kraków Gate**, a remnant of medieval fortifications, this institution displays documents and photos relating to the city's history. Daily at noon, a bugler plays a special tune atop the **New Town Hall** opposite the gate (if you like bugling, don't miss the annual National Bugle Contest here on 15 August).

Cathedral   CHURCH
(Plac Katedralny; ⊘dawn-dusk) A 16th-century place of worship that houses impressive baroque frescos. The painting of the Virgin Mary is said to have shed tears in 1949, so it's a source of pride and reverence for local believers.

Archdiocesan Museum   MUSEUM
(Plac Katedralny; adult/concession 7/5zł; ⊘10am-5pm) This museum of sacred art also offers expansive views of the Old Town, as it's housed within the lofty **Trinitarian Tower** (1819).

Underground Route   WALK
(Rynek 1; adult/concession 9/7zł; ⊘10am-4pm Tue-Fri, noon-5pm Sat & Sun) This guided tour winds its way through 280m of connected cellars beneath the Old Town, with historical exhibitions along the way. Entry is from the neoclassical **Old Town Hall** in the centre of the pleasant Rynek (Market Sq) at approximately

Lublin

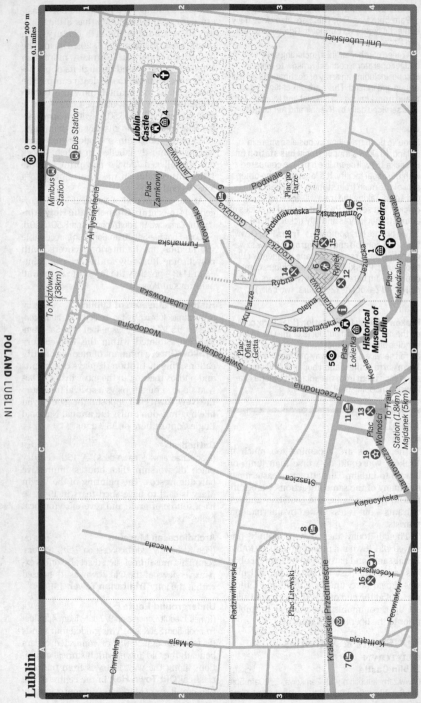

POLAND LUBLIN

200 m
0.1 miles

To Kozłówka
(38km)

To Train
Station (1.8km);
Majdanek (5km)

Lublin Castle

Plac Zamkowy

Bus Station

Minibus Station

Al Tysiąclecia

Furmańska

Kowalska

Lubartowska

Świętoduska

Wodopojna

Przechodnia

Zamkowa

Grodzka

Podwale

Plac po Farze

Archidiakońska

Dominikańska

Złota

Rynek

Jezuicka

Grodzka

Bramowa

Rybna

Ku Farze

Olejna

Szambelańska

Plac Łokietka

Kozia

Historical Museum of Lublin

Plac Katedralny

Cathedral

Podwale

Unii Lubelskiej

Plac Ofiar Getta

Niecała

Radziwiłłowska

3 Maja

Chmielna

Kołłątaja

Peowiaków

Kościuszki

Krakowskie Przedmieście

Plac Litewski

Kapucyńska

Staszica

Narutowicza

Plac Wolności

Swiętoduska

Lublin

two-hourly intervals; check with the tourist office for exact times.

MAJDANEK

FREE **Majdanek State Museum**   MEMORIAL
(www.majdanek.pl; ⊙9am-4pm) About 4km southeast of the Old Town is one of the largest Nazi German death camps, where some 235,000 people, including more than 100,000 Jews, were massacred. Barracks, guard towers and barbed-wire fences remain in place; even more chilling are the crematorium and gas chambers.

A short explanatory film (3zł) can be seen in the visitors centre, from which a marked 'visiting route' (5km) passes the massive stone **Monument of Fight & Martyrdom** and finishes at the domed **mausoleum** holding the ashes of many victims.

Trolleybus 156 and bus 23 depart from a stop on ul Królewska near Plac Katedralny, and travel to the entrance of Majdanek.

🛏 Sleeping

TOP CHOICE **Grand Hotel Lublinianka**   HOTEL €€
(✆81 446 6100; www.lublinianka.com; ul Krakowskie Przedmieście 56; s/d from 310/370zł; ❋🛜) The swankiest place in town includes free use of a sauna and spa. The cheaper (3rd-floor) rooms have skylights but are relatively small, while 'standard' rooms are spacious and have glitzy marble bathrooms. One room is designed for wheelchair access and there's a good restaurant on-site.

Vanilla Hotel   HOTEL €€
(✆81 536 6720; www.vanilla-hotel.pl; ul Krakowskie Przedmieście 12; s/d 330/370zł; 🛜) This beautiful boutique hotel is anything but vanilla. The rooms are filled with inspired styling, featuring vibrant colours, big headboards behind the beds and cool retro furniture. The attention to detail continues into the restaurant and coffee bar, which serves the best ice-cream concoctions in town.

Hotel Waksman   HOTEL €€
(✆81 532 5454; www.waksman.pl; ul Grodzka 19; s/d 210/230zł; 🛜) This small gem is excellent value for its quality and location. Just within the Grodzka Gate in the Old Town, it offers elegantly appointed rooms with different colour schemes and an attractive lounge with tapestries on the walls.

Hostel Lublin   HOSTEL €
(✆79 288 8632; www.hostellublin.pl; ul Lubartowska 60; dm/r 50/120zł; 🛜) The city's first modern hostel is situated within a former apartment building and contains neat, tidy dorms, a basic kitchenette and a cosy lounge. Take trolleybus 156 or 160 north from the Old Town.

Hotel Europa   HOTEL €€€
(✆81 535 0303; www.hoteleuropa.pl; ul Krakowskie Przedmieście 29; s/d from 410/450zł; ❋🛜) Central hotel offering smart, thoroughly modernised rooms with high ceilings and elegant furniture in a restored 19th-century building. Two rooms are designed for wheelchair access and there's a nightclub downstairs.

POLAND LUBLIN

TRANSPORT FROM LUBLIN

Bus

DESTINATION	PRICE (ZŁ)	DURATION (HR)	FREQUENCY
Kraków	48	5½	6 daily
Olsztyn	61	8¾	1 daily
Przemyśl	35		5 daily
Warsaw	30	3	at least hourly
Zakopane	70	8½	2 daily
Zamość	23	2	2 daily

Train

DESTINATION	PRICE (ZŁ)	DURATION (HR)	FREQUENCY
Gdańsk	69	9	2 daily
Kraków	58	4½	2 daily
Kyiv (Ukraine)		13-14	1 daily
Warsaw	40	2½	10 daily
Zamość	21	2¼	4 daily

Lubelskie Samorządowe Centrum
Doskonalenia Nauczycieli   HOSTEL €

(☎81 532 9241; ul Dominikańska 5; dm 66zł) This place is in an atmospheric Old Town building and has rooms with between two and five beds. It's good value and often busy, so book ahead.

✕ Eating & Drinking

There's a handy **Lux Supermarket** (Plac Wolności 1) located in the city centre, on Plac Wolności.

TOP
CHOICE Magia   INTERNATIONAL €€

(ul Grodzka 2; mains 16-65zł; ⊘noon-midnight) Charming, relaxed restaurant with numerous vibes to choose from within its warren of dining rooms and large outdoor courtyard. Dishes range from tiger prawns and snails to beef and duck, with every sort of pizza, pasta and pancake in between.

Mandragora   JEWISH €€€

(Rynek 9; mains 14-63zł) They're aiming for the *Fiddler on the Roof* effect here with lace tablecloths, knick-knacks and photos of old Lublin on the walls. The food is a hearty mix of Polish and Jewish.

Oregano   MEDITERRANEAN €€

(ul Kościuszki 7; mains 18-54zł; ⊘noon-11pm) This pleasant, upmarket restaurant specialises

in Mediterranean cuisine, featuring pasta, paella and seafood. There's a well-organised English-language menu and the chefs aren't scared of spice.

Biesy   POLISH €

(Rynek 18; mains 12-24zł) Atmospheric cellar eatery with multiple nooks and crannies. Its tasty speciality is large pizzalike baked tarts with a variety of toppings.

Złoty Osioł   PUB

(ul Grodzka 5a; ⊘noon-midnight; ☎) A classic example of the hidden Polish pub, the Golden Donkey is tucked away well back from the street. Its dimly lit but atmospheric rooms are a good place for a quiet drink.

Caram'bola Pub   PUB

(ul Kościuszki 8; ⊘10am-late Mon-Sat, noon-late Sun) This pub is a pleasant place for a beer or two. It also serves inexpensive bar food, including pizzas.

☆ Entertainment

Club Koyot   CLUB

(ul Krakowskie Przedmieście 26; ⊘5pm-late Wed-Sun) This club is concealed in a courtyard set way back from ul Krakowskie Przedmieście. Features live music or DJs most nights.

Filharmonia Lubelska CLASSICAL MUSIC

(☏81 531 5112; www.filharmonialubelska.pl; ul Skłodowskiej-Curie 5) Institution with a large auditorium that hosts classical and contemporary music concerts. To get here from the Old Town, head west on ul Krakowskie Przedmieście and then go south one block along ul Grottgera.

❶ Information

Main Post Office (ul Krakowskie Przedmieście 50; ⊗24hr)

Net Box (ul Krakowskie Przedmieście 52; per hr 10zł; ⊗10am-8pm Mon-Sat, 2-6pm Sun) Internet access in a courtyard off the street.

Tourist Office (☏81 532 4412; www.loitik. eu; ul Jezuicka 1/3; ⊗9am-7pm Mon-Fri, from 10am Sat & Sun May-Oct, 9am-5pm Mon-Fri, from 10am Sat & Sun Nov-Apr) Lots of free brochures, including the city walking-route guide *Tourist Routes of Lublin*, which includes a chapter outlining the *Heritage Trail of the Lublin Jews*.

❶ Getting There & Away

AIR The brand-new **Lublin airport** (www. airport.lublin.pl) is 10km east of Lublin, with budget airline flights from London and Dublin.

BUS From the **bus station** (Al Tysiąclecia), opposite the castle, PKS buses head to various national destinations and **Polski Bus** (www. polskibus.com) heads to Warsaw (three hours, five daily; book tickets online).

Private minibuses also run to various destinations, including Zamość (15zł, 1½ hours, half-hourly), from the **minibus station** north of the bus terminal.

TRAIN The **train station** (Plac Dworcowy) is 1.8km south of the Old Town and accessible by bus 1 or 13. When leaving the station, look for the bus stop on ul Gazowa, to the left of the station entrance as you walk down the steps (not the trolleybus stop).

Kozłówka

The hamlet of Kozłówka (koz-*woof*-kah), 38km north of Lublin, is famous for its sumptuous late-baroque **palace**, which houses the **Museum of the Zamoyski Family** (☏81 852 8310; www.muzeumzamoyskich.pl; adult/concession incl all sections 25/13zł; ⊗10am-4pm Apr-Nov). The collection in the **main palace** (adult/concession 17/8zł) features original furnishings, ceramic stoves and a large collection of paintings. You must see this area on a Polish-language guided tour, the start-

ing time for which will be noted at the top of your ticket. An English-language tour (best organised in advance) costs an extra 50zł. The entrance fee to this section also includes entry to the 1907 **chapel**.

Even more interesting is the incongruous **Socialist-Realist Art Gallery** (adult/concession 6/3zł), decked out with numerous portraits and statues of communist-era leaders. It also features many idealised scenes of farmers and factory workers striving for socialism. These stirring works were originally tucked away here in embarrassment by the communist authorities, after Stalin's death led to the decline of this all-encompassing artistic style.

You can pay the overall museum fee to see everything on the grounds, which also includes temporary exhibitions (5/2zł) and transport exhibitions within a coach-house (5/2zł); or if you prefer, just pay for each section you wish to view.

From Lublin, catch one of the frequent buses to Lubartów (7zł, 40 minutes, at least half-hourly), then change for Kozłówka by taking a PKS bus or private minibus (5zł, 10 minutes).

Zamość

POP 66,000

While most Polish cities' attractions centre on their medieval heart, Zamość (*zah-moshch*) is pure Renaissance. The streets of its attractive, compact Old Town are perfect for exploring and its central market square is a symmetrical delight, reflecting the city's glorious 16th-century origins.

Zamość was founded in 1580 by Jan Zamoyski, the nation's chancellor and commander-in-chief. Designed by an Italian architect, the city was intended as a prosperous trading settlement between Western Europe and the region stretching east to the Black Sea.

In WWII, the Nazis earmarked the city for German resettlement, sending the Polish population into slave labour or concentration camps. Most of the Jewish population of the renamed 'Himmlerstadt' was exterminated.

The splendid architecture of Zamość's Old Town was added to Unesco's World Heritage list in 1992. Since 2004, EU funds have been gradually restoring Zamość to its former glory.

◎ Sights

Rynek Wielki
HISTORIC SQUARE

(Great Market Square) The heart of Zamość's attractive Old Town, this impressive Italianate Renaissance square (exactly 100m by 100m) is dominated by the lofty, pink **Town Hall** and surrounded by colourful arcaded houses once owned by wealthy citizens.

The **Museum of Zamość** (ul Ormiańska 30; adult/concession 8/4zł; ⊙9am-5pm Tue-Sun) is based in two of the loveliest buildings on the square and houses interesting exhibits, including paintings, folk costumes, archaeological finds and a scale model of the 16th-century town.

Synagogue
SYNAGOGUE

(www.zamosc.fodz.pl; ul Pereca 14; admission 6zł; ⊙10am-6pm Tue-Sun) Before WWII, Jewish citizens accounted for 45% of the town's population and most lived in the area north and east of the palace. The most significant Jewish architectural relic is this Renaissance place of worship, built in the early 17th century. It was recently renovated and reopened to the public as a cultural centre, giving access to its beautiful interior decoration and an impressive digital presentation on the town's Jewish history.

Cathedral
CHURCH

(ul Kolegiacka; ⊙dawn-dusk) Southwest of the Rynek Wielki, this mighty 16th-century holy place hosts the tomb of Jan Zamoyski in the chapel to the right of the high altar. The **bell tower** (ul Kolegiacka; admission 2zł; ⊙10am-4pm Mon-Sat May-Sep) can be climbed for good views of the historic cathedral bells and the Old Town. In the grounds, the **Sacral Museum** (ul Kolegiacka 2; admission 2zł; ⊙10am-4pm Mon-Fri, 10am-1pm Sat & Sun May-Sep, 10am-1pm Sun Oct-Apr) features various robes, paintings and sculptures.

Bastion
FORTIFICATION

(ul Łukasińskiego) On the eastern edge of the Old Town is the best surviving bastion from the original city walls. You can take a **tour** (ul Łukasińskiego; adult/concession 7.50/4.50zł; ⊙8am-6pm) through the renovated fortifications, checking out displays of military gear and views over the city. Tickets can be bought from the souvenir shop next to the entrance and the tour only runs when a minimum of three people have gathered.

Zamoyski Palace
PALACE

This former palace directly west of the Old Town (closed to the public) lost much of its character when it was converted into a military hospital in the 1830s. To the north of the palace stretches a beautifully landscaped **park**. To its south is the **Arsenal Museum** (ul Zamkowa 2), though at the time of research this was closed for a major renovation. Check with the tourist office for an update.

⌨ Sleeping

⬛TOP⬛ CHOICE Hotel Senator
HOTEL €€

(☏84 638 9990; www.senatorhotel.pl; ul Rynek Solny 4; s/d from 164/229zł; ☏) Charming accommodation with tastefully furnished rooms, an on-site restaurant with its own fireplace and an unusual medieval vibe to its decor. The expansive breakfast buffet costs 25zł extra.

Hotel Zamojski
HOTEL €€

(☏84 639 2516; www.accorhotels.com; ul Kołłątaja 2/4/6; s/d from 191/253zł; ✷☏) This comfortable joint is situated within three connected old houses, just off the square. The rooms are modern and tastefully furnished, and there's a good restaurant and cocktail bar, along with a fitness centre.

Hotel Arkadia
HOTEL €

(☏84 638 6507; www.arkadia-zamosc.pl; Rynek Wielki 9; s/d from 100/140zł; ☏) With just nine rooms, this compact place offers a pool table and restaurant in addition to lodgings. It's charming but shabby, though its location right on the Rynek Wielki is hard to beat.

Hotel Renesans
HOTEL €€

(☏84 639 2001; www.hotelrenesans.pl; ul Grecka 6; s/d from 136/192zł; ☏) It's ironic that a hotel named after the Renaissance is housed in the Old Town's ugliest building. However, it's central and the rooms are surprisingly modern and pleasant.

Camping Duet
CAMPING GROUND €

(☏84 639 2499; www.duet.virgo.com.pl; ul Królowej Jadwigi 14; s/d 80/95zł, per tent/person 12zł/10zł; ✷) Only 600m west of the Old Town, Camping Duet has neat bungalows, tennis courts, a restaurant, sauna and spa. There's also a pleasant camping ground in a partly wooded area. Larger bungalows sleep up to six.

✕ Eating & Drinking

For self-caterers, there's a handy **Lux mini-supermarket** (ul Grodzka 16; ⊙6am-8pm Mon-Fri, 8am-6pm Sat & Sun) one block east of the Rynek Wielki.

Restauracja Muzealna   POLISH €€

(ul Ormiańska 30; mains 14-29zł; ⊙11am-10pm Mon-Sat, 11am-9pm Sun) Subterranean restaurant in an atmospheric cellar below the Rynek Wielki, bedecked with ornate timber furniture and portraits of nobles. It serves a good class of Polish cuisine at reasonable prices and has a well-stocked bar.

Bar Asia   POLISH €

(ul Staszica 10; mains 10-19zł; ⊙8am-5pm Mon-Fri, 8am-4pm Sat) For hungry but broke travellers, this old-style *bar mleczny* (milk bar) is ideal. It serves cheap and tasty Polish food, including several variants of *pierogi* (dumplings), in a minimally decorated space.

Corner Pub   PUB

(ul Żeromskiego 6) This cosy Irish-style pub is a good place to have a drink. It has comfy booths and the walls are ornamented with bric-a-brac such as antique clocks, swords and model cars.

ℹ Information

K@fejka Internetowa (Rynek Wielki 10; per hr 3zł; ⊙9am-5pm Mon-Fri, 10am-2pm Sat) Internet access.

Main Post Office (ul Kościuszki 9; ⊙7am-8pm Mon-Fri, 8am-3pm Sat)

Tourist Office (☑84 639 2292; Rynek Wielki 13; ⊙8am-6pm Mon-Fri, 10am-5pm Sat & Sun May-Sep, 8am-5pm Mon-Fri, 9am-2pm Sat & Sun Oct-Apr) Sells the glossy *Zamość – The Ideal City* (9.50zł).

ℹ Getting There & Away

Bus

The **bus station** (ul Hrubieszowska) is 2km east of the Old Town and linked by frequent city buses, primarily buses 0 and 3. From here, buses head to the following destinations:

Kraków (52zł, eight hours, three daily)
Lublin (23zł, two hours, two daily)
Warsaw (42zł, 5½ hours, two daily)

Two buses a day also travel to Jarosław (24zł, three hours), from where you can continue to Przemyśl near the Ukrainian border.

A quicker way to and from Lublin is via the minibuses that depart every 30 minutes (15zł, 1½ hours) from the minibus station opposite the bus station. Check the changeable timetable for departures to other destinations, including Warsaw and Kraków.

Train

From the **train station** (ul Szczebrzeska 11), 1km southwest of the Old Town, infrequent services run to Lublin (21zł, 2¼ hours, four daily) and Kraków (61zł, seven hours, one daily). The two trains per day to transport junction Jarosław (26zł, 3¾ hours) may be handy if you're heading to Przemyśl for Ukraine.

CARPATHIAN MOUNTAINS

The Carpathians (Karpaty) stretch from the southern border with Slovakia into Ukraine and their wooded hills and snowy mountains are a beacon for hikers, skiers and cyclists. The most popular destination here is the resort town of Zakopane in the heart of the Tatra Mountains (Tatry). Elsewhere, historic regional towns such as Przemyśl and Sanok offer a relaxed pace and unique insights into the past.

Zakopane

POP 27,900

Nestled at the foot of the Tatra Mountains, Zakopane is Poland's major winter sports centre, though it's a popular destination year-round. It may resemble a tourist trap, with its overcommercialised, overpriced exterior, but it also has a relaxed, laid-back vibe that makes it a great place to chill for a few days, even if you're not planning to ski or hike.

Zakopane also played an important role in sustaining Polish culture during the long period of foreign rule in the 19th century, thanks to the many artistic types who settled in the town during this period.

◎ Sights & Activities

Tatra Museum   MUSEUM
(www.muzeumtatrzanskie.pl; ul Krupówki 10; adult/ concession 7/5.50zł, Sun free; ⊙9am-5pm Tue-Sat, 9am-3pm Sun) Check out exhibits about regional history, ethnography and geology at this centrally located museum, along with displays on local flora and fauna.

Museum of Zakopane Style   MUSEUM
(www.muzeumtatrzanskie.pl; ul Kościeliska 18; adult/concession 7/5.50zł; ⊙9am-5pm Wed-Sat, 9am-3pm Sun) Fittingly housed in the 1892 Villa Koliba, which was the first house to be designed by artist and architect Stanisław Witkiewicz in the Zakopane style. This distinctive architectural style became the trademark of the town in the late 19th century

Szymanowksi Museum MUSEUM
(www.muzeum.krakow.pl; ul Kasprusie 19; adult/concession 6/3zł, Sun free; ⊘10am-4pm Tue-Sun) This institution within the Villa Atma is dedicated to the great composer Karol Szymanowski, who once lived here. It hosts piano recitals in summer.

Mt Gubałówka MOUNTAIN
Behind the township, this mountain (1120m) offers excellent views over the Tatras and is a popular destination for tourists who don't feel overly energetic. The **funicular** (ul Nowotarska; adult/concession one way 10/8zł, return 17/14zł; ⊘8am-9.45pm Jul & Aug, 9am-8pm Mar-Jun, Sep & Oct, 8.30am-6pm Nov & Dec) covers the 1388m-long route in less than five minutes, climbing 300m from the funicular station just north of ul Krupówki. You can also hike up or down if you like.

🛏 Sleeping

Given the abundance of private rooms and decent hostels, few travellers actually stay in hotels.

Some travel agencies in Zakopane can arrange private rooms, but in the high season they may not want to offer anything for less than three nights. Expect a double room (singles are rarely offered) to cost about 80zł in the high season in the town centre and about 60zł for somewhere further out.

Locals offering private rooms may approach you at the bus or train station; alternatively, just look out for signs posted in the front of private homes – *noclegi* and *pokoje* both mean 'rooms available'.

Like all seasonal resorts, accommodation prices fluctuate considerably between low season and high season (December to February and July to August). Always book accommodation in advance at peak times, especially on weekends.

TOP CHOICE Hotel Sabała HOTEL €€€
(☑18 201 5092; www.sabala.zakopane.pl; ul Krupówki 11; s/d from 340/460zł; 🐾🖳) Built in 1894 but thoroughly up to date, this striking timber building has a superb location overlooking the picturesque pedestrian thoroughfare. It offers cosy attic-style rooms and there's a sauna and solarium on the premises. A candlelit restaurant has views of street life.

Carlton HOTEL €€
(☑18 201 4415; www.carlton.pl; ul Grunwaldzka s/d 80/160zł; 🕾) Affordable pension in a grand old house away from the main drag, featuring light-filled rooms with modern furniture. There's an impressive shared balcony overlooking the road and a big comfy lounge lined with potted plants.

Youth Hostel Szarotka HOSTEL €
(☑18 201 3618; www.schroniskomlodziezowe.zakopane.org.pl; ul Nowotarska 45; dm/d 41/102zł) This friendly, homey place gets packed in the high season. There's a kitchen and washing machine on-site. It's on a noisy road about a 10-minute walk from the town centre.

🍴 Eating & Drinking

The main street, ul Krupówki, is lined with all sorts of eateries.

Czarny Staw GRILL €€
(ul Krupówki 2; mains 12-46zł; ⊘10am-1am) Offers a tasty range of Polish dishes, including a variety of dumplings, and much of the menu is cooked before your very eyes on the central grill. There's a good salad bar and live music most nights.

Pstrąg Górski SEAFOOD €€
(ul Krupówki 6; mains 15-33zł; ⊘9am-10pm) This self-service fish restaurant, done up in traditional style and overlooking a narrow stream, serves some of the freshest trout, salmon and sea fish in town. It's excellent value.

Stek Chałupa POLISH €€
(ul Krupówki 33; mains 17-44zł; ⊘8am-midnight) Big friendly barn of a place, with homey decor and waitresses in traditional garb. The menu features meat dishes, particularly steaks, though there are vegetarian choices among the salads and *pierogi* (dumplings).

Appendix CAFE-BAR
(ul Krupówki 6; ⊘3pm-midnight; 🕾) A mellow venue for an alcoholic or caffeine-laden drink, hidden away above the street with an ambient old-meets-new decor. It hosts live music most weekends.

ℹ Information

Centrum Przewodnictwa Tatrzańskiego (Tatra Guide Centre; ☑18 206 37 99; ul Chałubińskiego 42a; ⊘9am-3pm) Arranges English- and German-speaking mountain guides.

Księgarnia Górska (ul Zaruskiego 5) Bookshop in the reception area of the Dom Turysty PTTK hostel, sells regional hiking maps.

TRANSPORT FROM ZAKOPANE

Bus

DESTINATION	COST(ZŁ)	DURATION (HR)	FREQUENCY
Kraków	18	2	almost hourly
Lublin	70	8½	2 daily
Przemyśl	53	9	1 daily
Warsaw	65	8	6 daily

Train

DESTINATION	PRICE (ZŁ)	DURATION (HR)	FREQUENCY
Częstochowa	56	7	1 daily
Gdynia & Gdańsk	76	16	1 daily
Kraków	24	3¾	8 daily
Łódź	63	10½	1 daily
Poznań	65	11½	1 daily
Warsaw	63	9	3 daily

Main Post Office (ul Krupówki 20; ⊘7am-7.30pm Mon-Fri, 8am-2pm Sat)

PTTK Office (☑18 201 2429; www.pttkzakopane.pl; ul Krupówki 12) Provides handy info about hiking and mountain refuges.

Tourist Office (☑18 201 2211) Bus station (☑18 201 2211; ul Kościuszki 17; ⊘8am-8pm daily Jul-Aug, 9am-5pm Mon-Sat Sep-Jun); Town (ul Kościeliska 7; ⊘9am-5pm Mon-Sat) These offices offer advice, sell hiking and city maps, and provide information about rafting trips down the Dunajec River.

Widmo (ul Galicy 6; per hr 5zł; ⊘7.30am-11pm Mon-Fri, 9am-11pm Sat & Sun) Internet access.

ⓘ Getting There & Away

From the **bus station** (ul Chramcówki), PKS buses run to several destinations. Two private companies, **Trans Frej** (www.trans-frej.com.pl) and **Szwagropol** (www.szwagropol.pl) run comfortable Kraków-bound buses (19zł) every 45 minutes to an hour, and **Polski Bus** (www.polskibus.com) heads to Warsaw twice daily (seven hours) via Kraków (2¼ hours); book tickets online.

Locally, PKS buses – and minibuses from opposite the bus terminal – regularly travel to Lake Morskie Oko and on to Polana Palenica. To cross into Slovakia, get off this bus/minibus at Łysa Polana, cross the border on foot, and take another bus to Tatranská Lomnica and the other Slovak mountain towns.

Trains head to a number of destinations around Poland from Zakopane's **train station** (ul Chramcówki).

Tatra Mountains

The Tatras, 100km south of Kraków, are the highest range of the Carpathian Mountains, providing a dramatic range of rugged scenery that's a distinct contrast to the rest of Poland's flatness. Roughly 60km long and 15km wide, this mountain range stretches across the Polish–Slovak border. A quarter is in Poland and is mostly part of the Tatra National Park (about 212 sq km). The Polish Tatras contain more than 20 peaks over 2000m, the highest of which is Mt Rysy (2499m).

⊙ Sights & Activities

Lake Morskie Oko   LAKE

The emerald-green Lake Morskie Oko (Eye of the Sea) is among the loveliest lakes in the Tatras, completely surrounded by mountains and reached via a small pass. There's a restaurant and bar in the hostel by the lake. PKS buses and minibuses regularly depart from Zakopane for Polana Palenica (30 minutes), from where a road (9km) continues uphill to the lake. Cars, bikes and buses are not allowed up this road, so you'll have to walk, but it's not steep (allow about two hours one way). Alternatively, take a horse-drawn carriage (50/30zł per person uphill/downhill, but negotiable) to within 2km of the lake. In winter, transport is by horse-drawn four-seater sledge, which is mo expensive. The last minibus to Zakopane returns between 5pm and 6pm.

Mt Kasprowy Wierch Cable Car   CABLE CAR

(www.pkl.pl; adult/concession return 49/39zł; ⊙7.30am-4pm Jan-Mar, 7.30am-6pm Apr-Jun, Sep & Oct, 7am-9pm Jul & Aug, 9am-4pm Nov & Dec) The cable-car trip from Kuźnice (2km south of Zakopane) to the summit of Mt Kasprowy Wierch (1985m) is a classic tourist experience enjoyed by Poles and foreigners alike. At the end of the trip you can get off and stand with one foot in Poland and the other in Slovakia. The one-way journey takes 20 minutes and climbs 936m. The cable car normally shuts down for one week in May and won't operate if the snow or winds are dangerous.

The view from the top is spectacular (clouds permitting). Two chairlifts transport skiers to and from various slopes between December and April. A restaurant serves skiers and hikers alike. In summer, many people return to Zakopane on foot down the Gąsienicowa Valley, and the most intrepid walk the ridges all the way across to Lake Morskie Oko via Pięciu Stawów, a strenuous hike taking a full day in good weather.

If you buy a return ticket, your trip back is automatically reserved for two hours after your departure, so if you want to stay longer than that buy a one-way ticket to the top (39zł) and another one when you want to come down (25zł). Mt Kasprowy Wierch is popular; in summer, arrive early and expect to wait. PKS buses and minibuses to Kuźnice frequently leave from Zakopane.

Hiking   HIKING

If you're doing any hiking in the Tatras get a copy of the *Tatrzański Park Narodowy* map (1:25,000), which shows all hiking trails in the area. Better still, buy one or more of the 14 sheets of *Tatry Polskie*, available at Księgarnia Górska (p636) in Zakopane. In July and August these trails can be overrun by tourists, so late spring and early autumn are the best times. Theoretically you can expect better weather in autumn, when rainfall is lower.

Like all alpine regions, the Tatras can be dangerous, particularly during the snow season (November to May). Remember the weather can be unpredictable. Bring proper hiking boots, warm clothing and waterproof rain gear – and be prepared to use occasional ropes and chains (provided along the trails) to get up and down some rocky slopes.

Guides are not necessary because many the trails are marked, but they can be arranged in Zakopane for about 350zł per day.

There are several picturesque valleys south of Zakopane, including the **Dolina Strążyska**. You can continue from the Strążyska by the red trail up to **Mt Giewont** (1909m), 3½ hours from Zakopane, and then walk down the blue trail to Kuźnice in two hours.

Two long and beautiful forested valleys, the **Dolina Chochołowska** and the **Dolina Kościeliska**, are in the western part of the park, known as the Tatry Zachodnie (West Tatras). These valleys are ideal for cycling. Both are accessible by PKS buses and minibuses from Zakopane.

The Tatry Wysokie (High Tatras) to the east offer quite different scenery: bare granite peaks and glacial lakes. One way to get there is via cable car to **Mt Kasprowy Wierch**, then hike eastward along the red trail to Mt Świnica (2301m) and on to the Zawrat pass (2159m) – a tough three to four hours from Mt Kasprowy. From Zawrat, descend northwards to the Dolina Gąsienicowa along the blue trail and then back to Zakopane.

Alternatively, head south (also along the blue trail) to the wonderful **Dolina Pięciu Stawów** (Five Lakes Valley), where there is a mountain refuge 1¼ hours from Zawrat. The blue trail heading west from the refuge passes Lake Morskie Oko, 1½ hours from the refuge.

Skiing   SKIING

Zakopane boasts four major ski areas (and several smaller ones) with more than 50 ski lifts. Mt Kasprowy Wierch offers the best conditions and the most challenging slopes in the area, with its ski season extending until early May. Lift tickets cost 10zł for one ride at Mt Kasprowy Wierch. Alternatively, you can buy a day card (90zł), which allows you to skip the queues.

Another alternative is the **Harenda chairlift** (www.harendazakopane.pl; ul Harenda 63; 5zł; ⊙9am-6pm) just outside Zakopane, in the direction of Kraków.

Ski equipment rental is available at all ski areas except Mt Kasprowy Wierch. Outlets in Zakopane such as **Sport Shop & Service** (✆18 201 5871; ul Krupówki 52a) also rent ski gear.

🛏 Sleeping

Tourists are not allowed to take their own cars into the Tatra National Park; you must walk in, take the cable car or use an offial vehicle owned by the park or a hotel or hostel.

Camping is also not allowed in the park, but several PTTK mountain refuges/hostels provide simple accommodation. Most refuges are small and fill up fast; in midsummer and midwinter they're invariably packed beyond capacity. No one is ever turned away, however, though you may have to crash on the floor if all the beds are taken. Don't arrive too late in the day and remember to bring along your own bed mat and sleeping bag. All refuges serve simple hot meals, but the kitchens and dining rooms close early (sometimes at 7pm).

Most refuges are open all year but some may be temporarily closed for renovations or because of inclement weather. Check the current situation at the PTTK office (p637) in Zakopane. Its staff will be able to give you the location of all refuges and may be able to make bookings.

Kalatówki Mountain Hotel HOTEL €€
(☑18 206 3644; www.kalatowki.pl; dm/s/d from 66/89/170zł) This large and decent accommodation is the easiest to reach from Zakopane. It's a 40-minute walk from the Kuźnice cable-car station.

Dolinie Pięciu Stawów Hostel HOSTEL €
(☑781 055 555; www.piecstawow.pl; dm/d 45/120zł) This is the highest (1700m) and most scenically located refuge in the Polish Tatras. Breakfast is 14zł extra.

Morskie Oko Hostel HOSTEL €
(☑18 207 7609; www.schroniskomorskieoko.pl; dm 39-54zł) An early start from Zakopane would allow you to visit Morskie Oko in the morning and stay here at night.

Dunajec Gorge

An entertaining way to explore the Pieniny Mountains is to go rafting on craft piloted by the **Polish Association of Pieniny Oarsmen** (☑18 262 9721; www.flisacy.com.pl) along the Dunajec River, which traces the Polish–Slovak border through a spectacular and deep gorge. The rafts are large flat timber vessels which can hold a dozen or so passengers.

The trip starts at the wharf (Przystan Flisacka) in Sromowce Wyżne-Kąty, 46km northeast of Zakopane, and you can finish either at the spa town of Szczawnica (adult/concession 46/23zł, 2¼ hours, 18km), or further

on at Krościenko (adult/concession 55/28zł, 2¾ hours, 23km). The raft trip operates between April and October, but only starts when there's a minimum of 10 passengers.

The gorge is an easy day trip from Zakopane. Catch a regular bus to Nowy Targ (7zł, 30 minutes, hourly) from Zakopane to connect with one of five daily buses (10zł, 45 minutes) to Sromowce-Kąty. From Szczawnica or Krościenko, take the bus back to Nowy Targ (10zł, one hour, hourly) and change for Zakopane. You can also return to the Sromowce-Kąty car park by bus with the raftsmen.

To avoid waiting around in Sromowce-Kąty for a raft to fill up, reserve a place via any travel agency in Zakopane for around 50zł per person. You'll still have to make your own way to the wharf by car or bus.

Przemyśl
POP 65,000 / TRANSPORT HUB

Przemyśl (*psheh*-mishl) is a significant transport hub and a logical jumping-off point for the Ukrainian border about 15km east of the city.

The city has a selection of inexpensive accommodation, including the central **Dom Wycieczkowy PTTK Podzamcze** (☑16 678 5374; www.przemysl.pttk.pl; ul Waygarta 3; dm from 26zł, s/d 49/72zł; ☎) hostel on the western edge of the Old Town. More comfort is available at the two-star **Hotel Europejski** (☑16 675 7100; www.hotel-europejski.pl; ul Sowińskiego 4; s/d 110/140zł; ☎) in a renovated old building facing the train station. Another option is **Hotel Gromada** (☑16 676 1111; www.gromada.pl; ul Wybrzeże Piłsudskiego 4; s/d from 130/180zł; ☎), a big chain hotel west of the Old Town.

For restaurants and bars, head to the the sloping **Rynek** (Market Sq). The **tourist office** (☑16 675 2163; www.przemysl.pl; ul Grodzka 1; ◉10am-6pm Mon-Fri, 9am-5pm Sat & Sun) is situated above the southwest corner of the square.

From Przemyśl, buses run regularly to Lviv in Ukraine (25zł, two hours). Another option is to take a private minibus to the border (5zł, 15 minutes), then walk across to connect with Ukrainian transport on the other side. Buses also operate regularly to all towns in southeastern Poland, including Sanok (14zł, two hours, five daily).

Trains run to Kraków (50zł, five hours, nine daily) and Warsaw (61zł, eight hours

---

WORTH A TRIP

LAKE SOLINA & SANOK

In the far southeastern corner of Poland, wedged between the Ukrainian and Slovakian borders, lies Lake Solina. This sizeable reservoir (27km long and 60m deep) was created in 1968 when the San River was dammed. Today it's a popular centre for water sports and other recreational pursuits.

The best place to base yourself is **Polańczyk**. This pleasant town on the lake's western shore offers a range of attractions, including sailing, windsurfing, fishing and beaches. There are also numerous hotels and sanatoriums offering spa treatments.

On the route to the lake, the town of **Sanok** is noted for its unique **Museum of Folk Architecture** (www.skansen.mblsanok.pl; ul Rybickiego 3; adult/concession 12/8zł; ⊙8am-6pm May-Sep, 9am-2pm Oct-Apr), which features the buildings of regional ethnic groups.

Outside Sanok, the marked **Icon Trail** takes hikers or cyclists along a 70km loop, passing by 10 village churches as well as attractive mountain countryside.

There are regular buses from Przemyśl to Sanok (14zł, two hours, five daily), from where you can continue to Polańczyk (9zł, one hour, hourly). You can also reach Sanok directly by bus from Kraków (36zł, five hours, six daily). For more details about Sanok and its attractions, check out Lonely Planet's *Poland* country guide or step into the Sanok **tourist office** (☑13 464 4533; Rynek 14; ⊙9am-5pm Mon-Fri, 9am-1pm Sat & Sun).

---

twice daily); and international sleeper trains operate to Lviv (2¾ hours, twice daily) and Kyiv (13 hours, once daily) in Ukraine.

The bus terminal and adjacent train station in Przemyśl are about 1km northeast of the Rynek.

SILESIA

Silesia (Śląsk, *shlonsk*, in Polish) is a fascinating mix of landscapes. Though the industrial zone around Katowice has limited attraction for visitors, beautiful Wrocław is a historic city with lively nightlife, and the Sudeten Mountains draw hikers and other nature lovers.

The history of the region is similarly diverse, having been governed by Polish, Bohemian, Austrian and German rulers. After two centuries as part of Prussia and Germany, the territory was largely included within Poland's new borders after WWII.

Wrocław

POP 630,000

When citizens of beautiful Kraków enthusiastically encourage you to visit Wrocław (*vrots*-wahf), you know you're onto something good. The city's delightful Old Town is a gracious mix of Gothic and baroque styles and its large student population ensures a healthy number of restaurants, bars and nightclubs.

Wrocław has been traded back and forth between various rulers over the centuries, but began life in the year 1000 under the Polish Piast dynasty and developed into a prosperous trading and cultural centre. In the 1740s it passed to Prussia, under the German name of Breslau. Under Prussian rule, the city became a major textile manufacturing centre, greatly increasing its population.

Upon its return to Poland in 1945, Wrocław was a shell of its former self, having sustained massive damage in WWII. Though 70% of the city was destroyed, sensitive restoration has returned the historic centre to its former beauty.

◉ Sights

OLD TOWN

Rynek HISTORIC SQUARE

(Market Square) In the centre of the Old Town is Poland's second-largest old market square (after Kraków). It's an attractive, rambling space, lined by beautifully painted facades and with a complex of old buildings in the middle. The southwestern corner of the square opens into **Plac Solny** (Salt Place), once the site of the town's salt trade and now home to a 24-hour flower market.

City Museum of Art MUSEUM

(www.muzeum.miejskie.wroclaw.pl; Stary Ratusz; adult/concession 10/7zł; ⊙10am-5pm Wed-Sat, 10am-6pm Sun) The beautiful **Town Hall** (in Polish, Stary Ratusz), built 1327–1504, on the southern side of the square houses this mu-

...eum with stately rooms on show, including exhibits on the art of gold and the stories of famous Wrocław inhabitants.

Jaś i Małgosia
HISTORIC BUILDINGS
(ul Św Mikołaja) In the northwestern corner of the Rynek are these two attractive small houses linked by a baroque gate. Whimsically, they've been named after a couple better known to English speakers as Hansel and Gretel.

Gnomes of Wrocław
STATUES
See if you can spot the diminutive statue of a gnome at ground level, just to the west of the Jaś i Małgosia houses on the edge of the Rynek; he's one of more than 200, which are scattered through the city. Whimsical as they are, they're attributed to the symbol of the Orange Alternative – a communist-era dissident group that used ridicule as a weapon and often painted gnomes where graffiti had been removed by the authorities. You can buy a gnome map (6zł) from the tourist office and go gnome-spotting.

Church of St Elizabeth
CHURCH
(www.kosciolgarnizon.wroclaw.pl; ul Św Elżbiety 1; admission 5zł; ⊙10am-7pm Mon-Sat, noon-7pm Sun) Behind decorative houses and miniature gnome statues is this monumental 14th-century church with its 83m-high tower, which you can climb for city views.

Church of St Mary Magdalene
CHURCH
(ul Łaciarska; bridge adult/concession 4/3zł; ⊙10am-6pm Mon-Sat) One block east of the Rynek is this Gothic church with a Romanesque portal from 1280 incorporated into its southern external wall. Climb the 72m high tower and its connected bridge (⊙10am-6pm Apr-Oct) for a lofty view.

EAST OF THE OLD TOWN

TOP CHOICE **Panorama of Racławice**
MONUMENTAL ARTWORK
(www.panoramaraclawicka.pl; ul Purkyniego 11; adult/concession 25/18zł; ⊙9am-5pm) Wrocław's pride and joy (and major tourist attraction) is this giant 360-degree painting housed in a circular building east of the Old Town. The painting depicts the 1794 Battle of Racławice, in which a Polish peasant army led by Tadeusz Kościuszko defeated Russian forces intent on partitioning Poland. Created by Jan Styka and Wojciech Kossak for the centenary of the battle in 1894, it is an immense 114m long and 15m high and was brought here

by Polish immigrants displaced from Lviv (Ukraine) after WWII. Due to the communist government's uneasiness about glorifying a famous Russian defeat, however, the panorama wasn't re-erected until 1985.

Obligatory tours (with audio in English and other languages) run every 30 minutes between 9am and 4.30pm from April to November, and 10am and 3pm from December to March. The ticket also allows same-day entry to the nearby National Museum.

National Museum
MUSEUM
(www.mnwr.art.pl; Plac Powstańców Warszawy 5; adult/concession 15/10zł, Sat free; ⊙10am-5pm) Treasure trove of fine art on three floors, with extensive permanent collections and a stunning skylit atrium.

ECCLESIASTICAL DISTRICT

Cathedral of St John the Baptist
CHURCH
(Plac Katedralny; tower adult/concession 5/4zł; ⊙10am-4pm Mon-Sat, 2-4pm Sun) This Gothic cathedral has a unique lift to whisk you to the top of its tower for superb views. Next door to the cathedral is the **Archdiocesan Museum** (Plac Katedralny 16; adult/concession 4/3zł; ⊙9am-3pm Tue-Sun) featuring sacred art.

Church of Our Lady on the Sand
CHURCH
(ul Św Jadwigi) North of the river is Piasek Island (Sand Island), where you'll find this 14th-century place of worship with lofty Gothic vaults and a year-round nativity scene.

Church of the Holy Cross & St Bartholomew
CHURCH
(Plac Kościelny) Across a small bridge from Piasek Island lies Ostrów Tumski (Cathedral Island), a picturesque area full of churches. Admire this two-storey Gothic structure, which was built between 1288 and 1350.

Botanical Gardens
GARDENS
(ul Sienkiewicza 23; adult/concession 10/5zł; ⊙8am-6pm Apr-Nov) North of the Cathedral of St John the Baptist are these charming gardens, where you can chill out among the chestnut trees and tulips.

SOUTH OF THE OLD TOWN

Historical Museum
MUSEUM
(www.mmw.pl; ul Kazimierza Wielkiego 35; adult/concession 15/10zł; ⊙10am-5pm Tue-Sun) Housed in a grand former palace, this museum highlights the main events in Wrocław's thousand-year history and includes an art collection covering the past two centuries.

POLAND WROCŁAW

Wrocław

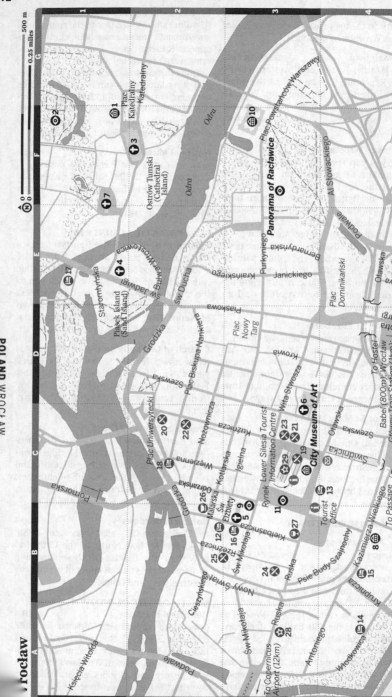

N
0 0

0.25 miles
500 m

G1 Plac Katedralny
Katedralny

Ostrów Tumski (Cathedral Island)

Odra

Piasek Island (Sand Island)

Staromłyńska

Św Jadwigi

Warmińska/osławiecka

Bulwar

Grodzka

Św Ducha

Piaskowa

Plac Biskupa Nankiera

Plac Nowy Targ

Krowia

Witta Stwosza

Purkyniego

Bernardyńska

Kraińskiego

Janickiego

Panorama of Racławice

Plac Powstańców Warszawy

Al Słowackiego

Podwale

Plac Dominikański

Oławska

Nowa

Piotra Skargi

City Museum of Art

Szewska

Kuźnicza

Nożownicza

Więzienna

Plac Uniwersytecki

Pomorska

Kotlarska

Odrzańska

Grodzka

Szewska

Oławska

Świdnicka

Igielna

Kiełbaśnicza

Św Mikołaja

Rzeźnicza

Nowy Świat

Cieszyńskiego

Św Elżbiety

Malarska

Ruska

Psie Budy Szajnochy

Kazimierza Wielkiego

Krupnicza

Antoniego

Włodkowica

Św Mikołaja

Rynek

Lower Silesia Tourist Information Centre

Tourist Office

To Hostel

Babel (800m); Wrocław Główny Train Station (1km); Bus Terminal (1.3km)

To Passage sculpture (700m)

To Copernicus Airport (12km)

Podwale

Księcia Witolda

Wrocław

Passage   PUBLIC ART
(cnr ul Świdnicka & ul Piłsudskiego) This fascinating sculpture depicts a group of pedestrians being swallowed by the pavement, only to re-emerge on the other side of the street.

🎎 Festivals & Events

Jazz on the Odra International Festival   MUSIC
(www.jazznadodra.pl; ☉Apr)

Musica Polonica Nova Festival   MUSIC
(www.musicapolonicanova.pl; ☉Apr) Celebrates new orchestral compositions, with a focus on Polish works.

Wratislavia Cantans   MUSIC
(www.wratislaviacantans.pl; ☉Sep) Features music with a vocal component, including opera and choral works.

Wrocław Marathon   SPORT
(www.wroclawmaraton.pl; ☉Sep)

🛏 Sleeping

TOP CHOICE Hostel Mleczarnia   HOSTEL €
(📞71 787 7570; www.mleczarniahostel.pl; ul Włodkowica 5; dm from 40zł, d 220zł; 🕸) This hostel, on a quiet road not far from the Rynek, has bags of charm: it has been decorated in a deliberately old-fashioned style

within a former residential building. There's a women-only dorm available, along with a kitchen and laundry facilities. Downstairs is a good cafe-bar.

Hotel Patio   HOTEL €€
(📞71 375 0400; www.hotelpatio.pl; ul Kiełbaśnicza 24; s/d from 300/360zł; 🕸🕸) Pleasant lodgings a short hop from the Rynek, housed within two buildings linked by a covered sunlit courtyard. Rooms are clean and light, sometimes small but with reasonably high ceilings. There's a restaurant and bar on-site.

Art Hotel   HOTEL €€
(📞71 787 7100; www.arthotel.pl; ul Kiełbaśnicza 20; s/d from 270/290zł; 🕸🕸) Elegant but affordable accommodation in a renovated apartment building. Rooms feature tastefully restrained decor, quality fittings and gleaming bathrooms. Within the hotel is a top-notch restaurant and there's a fitness room to work off the resultant kilojoules.

Hostel Babel   HOSTEL €
(📞71 342 0250; www.babelhostel.pl; ul Kołłątaja 16; dm from 45zł, d 140zł; 🕸) A tatty old staircase leads up to pleasant budget accommodation. Dorms are set in renovated apartment rooms with ornate lamps and decorative ceilings. Guests have access to a kitchen and washing machine.

POLAND WROCŁAW

Hotel Tumski
HOTEL €€

(☑71 322 6099; www.hotel-tumski.com.pl; Wyspa Słodowa 10; s/d from 260/380zł; 🕲) This is a neat hotel in a peaceful setting overlooking the river on Piasek Island, offering reasonable value for money. It's ideal for exploring the lovely ecclesiastical quarter and there's a good restaurant attached.

Hotel Zaułek
HOTEL €€

(☑71 341 0046; www.hotelzaulek.pl; ul Garbary 11; s/d from 270/380zł; 🕲) Run by the university, this guesthouse accommodates just 18 visitors in a dozen homey rooms. The 1pm checkout is a plus for heavy sleepers, and weekend prices are a steal. Breakfast is an additional 11zł; half and full board are also available.

Hotel Europejski
HOTEL €€

(☑71 772 1000; www.silfor.pl; ul Piłsudskiego 88; s/d from 200/250zł; ❋🕲) Pleasant hotel a stone's throw from the train station, with high ceilings, quality furniture and a cafe-bar and restaurant. Check its website for last-minute cheap deals.

AS Apartments
APARTMENTS €€

(☑71 341 8759; www.asapart.pl; Rynek 18; apt from €55; 🕲) Company offering a choice of apartments in the Old Town, many of them with a view of the Rynek. The fixtures and fittings can be old-fashioned, but the locations are fabulous for the price.

Hotel Europeum
HOTEL €€

(☑71 371 4500; www.europeum.pl; ul Kazimierza Wielkiego 27a; s/d 320/350zł; ❋🕲) Business-oriented hotel with stylish rooms in a great location near the Rynek. Rates drop dramatically at weekends.

✗ Eating & Drinking

TOP CHOICE Bernard
INTERNATIONAL €€

(Rynek 35; mains 27-77zł; ⊙10.30am-11pm) Bernard is one cool dude – this lively split-level bar-restaurant-brewery is a cut above its Rynek rivals. It serves a selection of upmarket comfort food including burgers, steak and fish dishes, along with a Polish choice or two; all washed down with the in-house lager. There's live music most nights and a breakfast menu from 10.30am to noon.

Restauracja Jadka
POLISH €€€

(ul Rzeźnicza 24/25; mains 58-83zł; ⊙1-11pm) One of the best restaurants in town, presenting impeccable modern versions of Polish classics amid elegant table settings in delightful Gothic surrounds. There's loads of character in the interior, with tables bearing lacy white tablecloths dotted beneath brick archways, illuminated by low-lit lamps.

Bazylia
CAFETERIA €

(Plac Uniwersytecki; mains per 100g 2.49zł; ⊙10am-6pm Mon-Fri, from 11am Sat & Sun) Inexpensive and bustling modern take on the classic *bar mleczny* (milk bar), set in a curved space with huge plate-glass windows overlooking the venerable university buildings. The menu has a lot of Polish standards such as *bigos* (thick sauerkraut and meat stew) and *gołąbki* (cabbage leaves stuffed with mince and rice), and a decent range of salads and other vegetable dishes. Everything is priced by weight at the same rate; order and pay at the till before receiving your food.

Darea
JAPANESE, KOREAN €€€

(ul Kuźnicza 43/45; mains 26-65zł; ⊙noon-11pm) Over time the menu at this place has become steadily more Japanese, but you'll still find authentic Korean dishes such as *bibimbab* and *bulgogi* on the list. It's all good Asian food in atmospheric surrounds.

La Scala
ITALIAN €€

(Rynek 38; mains 19-145zł) Offers authentic Italian food and particularly tasty desserts. Some dishes are pricey, but you're really paying for the location. The cheaper trattoria at ground level serves good pizza and pasta.

Mexico Bar
MEXICAN €€

(ul Rzeźnicza 34; mains 15-45zł; ⊙noon-11pm) Compact, warmly lit restaurant featuring sombreros, backlit masks and a chandelier made of beer bottles. There's a small bar to lean on while waiting for a table. All the Tex-Mex standards are on the menu.

Bar Wegetariański Vega
VEGETARIAN €

(Rynek 1/2; mains 4-11zł; ⊙8am-7pm Mon-Fri, 9am-5pm Sat & Sun; 🖉) This cheap cafeteria in the centre of the Rynek offers vegie dishes in a light green space, with a good choice of soups and crepes. Upstairs there's a vegan section, open from noon.

Pub Guinness
PUB

(Plac Solny 5; ⊙noon-2am) No prizes for guessing what this pub serves. A lively, fairly authentic Irish pub, spread over three levels on a busy corner. The ground-floor bar buzzes with student and traveller groups getting together, and there's a restaurant and beer cellar as well. A good place to wind down after a hard day's sightseeing.

TRAINS FROM WROCŁAW

DESTINATION	PRICE (ZŁ)	DURATION (HR)	FREQUENCY
Berlin (Germany)	Varies	5	1 daily
Częstochowa	40	3	6 daily
Kraków	52	5½	hourly
Łódź	48zł	4¼	5 daily
Poznań	46	3½	at least hourly
Szczecin	61	5	6 daily
Toruń	56	5	5 daily
Warsaw	61	6½	hourly

Cafe Artzat   CAFE
(ul Malarska 30; ☎) This low-key cafe just
north of the landmark Church of St Elizabeth is one of the best places in town to recharge the batteries over coffee or tea and a
good book.

☆ Entertainment

PRL   CLUB
(Rynek Ratusz 10; ☉noon-late) The dictatorship
of the proletariat is alive and well in this
tongue-in-cheek venue inspired by communist nostalgia. Disco lights play over a bust
of Lenin, propaganda posters line the walls
and red-menace memorabilia is scattered
through the maze of rooms. Descend to the
basement – beneath the portraits of Stalin
and Mao – if you'd like to hit the dance floor.

Bezsenność   CLUB
(ul Ruska 51; ☉7pm-late) With its alternative/
rock/dance line-up and distressed decor, 'In-
somnia' attracts a high-end clientele and is
one of the most popular clubs in town.

Filharmonia   CLASSICAL MUSIC
(☏71 342 2459; www.filharmonia.wroclaw.pl; ul
Piłsudskiego 19) Southwest of the Old Town,
across the river, this place hosts classical
music concerts.

ℹ Information

Internet Netvigator (ul Igielna 14; per hr 4zł;
☉9am-midnight)
Lower Silesia Tourist Information Centre
(☏71 342 2291; www.wroclaw-info.pl; ul Sukiennice 12; ☉10am-6pm)
Main Post Office (Rynek 28; ☉6.30am-
8.30pm Mon-Sat)
Tourist Office (☏71 344 3111; www.wroclaw-
info.pl; Rynek 14; ☉9am-9pm Apr-Oct, 9am-
7pm Nov-Mar)

ℹ Getting There & Away

AIR From **Copernicus Airport** (www.airport.
wroclaw.pl), national carrier LOT flies frequently between Wrocław and Warsaw. Internationally, it heads three times daily to Frankfurt
and four times daily to Munich. Tickets can be
bought at the **LOT office** (☏71 342 5151; ul
Piłsudskiego 36). Eurolot also links Wrocław
to Gdańsk.

A range of budget carriers connect Wrocław
with other European cities, including several
British and Irish regional destinations. Ryanair
and Wizz Air fly daily to London, while Ryanair
heads five times a week to Dublin.

The airport is in Strachowice, about 12km west
of the Old Town. The frequent bus 406 and infrequent night bus 249 link the airport with Wrocław
Główny train station and the bus terminal.

BUS The **bus station** (ul Sucha 11) is south of
the main train station, and offers five daily PKS
buses to Warsaw (60zł, six hours). For most
other destinations the train is a better choice,
though handy **Polski Bus** (www.polskibus.com)
services run from here to Łódź (4½ hours, twice
daily) and Prague (five hours, twice daily), as
well as Warsaw (7¼ hours, twice daily); check
fares and book tickets online.

TRAIN Wrocław Główny train station (ul
Piłsudskiego 105), formerly Breslau Hauptbahn-
hof, was opened in 1857 as a lavish architectural
confection resembling a castle with turrets
and Gothic arches. Extensively renovated and
restored for the UEFA football championship in
2012, it's easily Poland's most attractive railway
station and is worth visiting even if you're not
travelling by train.

Sudeten Mountains

The Sudeten Mountains (Sudety) run for
more than 250km along the Czech–Polish
border. The Sudetes feature dense forests

WORTH A TRIP

CZĘSTOCHOWA

This pilgrimage destination 114km northwest of Kraków and 150km east of Wrocław is dominated by the graceful **Paulite Monastery of Jasna Góra** (☑34 377 7408; www. bop.jasnagora.pl; admission free; ⊙dawn-dusk), sited atop a hill in the centre of town. Founded in 1382, it's the home of the *Black Madonna*, a portrait claimed to be the source of miracles. In recognition of these feats, in 1717 the painting was crowned Queen of Poland. It's well worth a trip to the monastery to check out its three museums, and of course to meet the *Black Madonna*.

Częstochowa has regular train connections with Kraków, Łódź, Warsaw, Zakopane and Wrocław. For more details, browse Lonely Planet's *Poland* country guide, visit www. info.czestochowa.pl, or step into the Częstochowa **tourist office** (☑34 368 2250; Al Najświętszej Marii Panny 65; ⊙9am-5pm Mon-Sat), which can assist with accommodation should you like to stay over.

amazing rock formations and deposits of semi-precious stones and can be explored along the extensive network of trails for **hiking** or **mountain biking**. The highest part of this old eroded chain is Mt Śnieżka (1602m).

Szklarska Poręba, at the northwestern end of the Sudetes, offers superior facilities for **hiking** and **skiing**. It's at the base of Mt Szrenica (1362m) and the town centre is at the upper end of ul Jedności Narodowej. The small **tourist office** (☑75 754 7740; www.szklarskaporeba.pl; ul Jedności Narodowej 1a; ⊙8am-4pm Mon-Fri, 9am-5pm Sat & Sun) can book accommodation and has info and maps. Nearby, several trails begin at the intersection of ul Jedności Narodowej and ul Wielki Sikorskiego. The red trail goes to **Mt Szrenica** (two hours) and offers a peek at **Wodospad Kamieńczyka**, a spectacular waterfall.

Karpacz to the southeast has more nightlife on offer, although it attracts fewer serious mountaineers. It's loosely clustered along a 3km road winding through Łomnica Valley at the base of Mt Śnieżka. The **tourist office** (☑75 761 8605; www.karpacz.pl; ul Konstytucji 3 Maja 25; ⊙9am-5pm Mon-Sat, 10am-2pm Sun) should be your first port of call. To reach the peak of Mt Śnieżka on foot, take one of the trails (three to four hours) from Hotel Biały Jar. Some of the trails pass by one of two splendid postglacial lakes: **Mały Staw** and **Wielki Staw**.

The bus is the fastest way of getting around the region. Every day from Szklarska Poręba, two buses head to Wrocław (31zł, three hours), as does one train (38zł, 3¾ hours). From Karpacz, get one of the frequent buses to Jelenia Góra (9zł, 30 minutes), from where buses and trains go in all directions, including to Wrocław. The two

mountain towns are also linked to each other by two buses each day (9zł, 45 minutes).

For the Czech Republic, at least three trains cross the border each day from Szklarska Poręba to Harrachov (5zł, 30 minutes). You can also take a bus from Szklarska Poręba to Jakuszyce (5zł, 15 minutes), cross the border on foot to Harrachov and take a Czech bus from there.

WIELKOPOLSKA

Wielkopolska (Greater Poland) is the region where Poland came to life in the Middle Ages and is referred to as the Cradle of the Polish State. As a result of this ancient eminence, its cities and towns are full of historic and cultural attractions.

The royal capital moved from Poznań to Kraków in 1038, though Wielkopolska remained an important province. Its historic significance didn't save it from international conflict, however, and the region became part of Prussia in 1793. Wielkopolska rose against German rule at the end of WWI and became part of the reborn Poland. The battles of WWII later caused widespread destruction in the area.

Poznań

POP 555,000

No one could accuse Poznań of being too sleepy. Between its regular trade fairs, student population and visiting travellers, it's a vibrant city with a wide choice of attractions. There's a beautiful Old Town at its centre, with a number of interesting museums and a range of lively bars, clubs and restaurants. The surrounding countryside is also good for cycling and hiking.

Poznań grew from humble beginnings, when 9th-century Polanian tribes built a wooden fort on the island of Ostrów Tumski. From 968 to 1038 Poznań was the de facto capital of Poland. Its position between Berlin and Warsaw has always underlined its importance as a trading town and in 1925 a modern version of its famous medieval trade fairs was instituted. The fairs, filling up the city's hotels for several days at a time, are the lynchpin of the city's economy.

As it's at the heart of Wielkopolska, Poznań makes a good transport hub from which to explore the region.

◉ Sights

OLD TOWN

Poznań's Old Town is centred on its attractive and ever-busy **Stary Rynek** (Old Market Sq), lined with restaurants and bars. There are several small museums of varying degrees of interest dotted around the square, in its central buildings and nearby; ask at the tourist office (p650) for the full list.

Historical Museum of Poznań   MUSEUM
(www.mnp.art.pl; Stary Rynek 1; adult/concession 7/5zł, Sat free; ⊙9am-3pm Tue-Thu, noon-9pm Fri, 11am-6pm Sat & Sun) Located within the Renaissance **Town Hall** (Stary Rynek), which was built 1550–60, this museum displays splendid period interiors. If you're outside the building at noon, look up. Every midday two mechanical metal goats above its clock butt their horns together 12 times, echoing an improbable centuries-old legend of two animals escaping a cook and fighting each other in the town hall tower.

Fish Sellers' Houses   HISTORIC BUILDINGS
(Stary Rynek) Located on the southeast side of the Stary Rynek, this endearing row of small arcaded buildings with colourful facades was built in the 16th century on the former site of fish stalls. It was later reconstructed after major damage in WWII.

Wielkopolska Military Museum   MUSEUM
(www.mnp.art.pl; Stary Rynek 9; adult/concession 7/5zł, Sat free; ⊙9am-3pm Tue-Thu, noon-9pm Fri, 11am-6pm Sat & Sun) Exhibits of arms from Poland's many conflicts over the centuries, dating from the 11th century to the present.

Museum of Musical Instruments   MUSEUM
(www.mnp.art.pl; Stary Rynek 45; adult/concession 5.50/3.50zł, Sat free; ⊙9am-3pm Tue-Thu, noon-9pm Fri, 11am-6pm Sat & Sun) Large though unimaginative collection of music-making devices, displayed over multiple levels.

Franciscan Church   CHURCH
(ul Franciszkańska 2) This 17th-century church, one block west of the square, has an ornate baroque interior, complete with wall paintings and rich stucco work.

Parish Church of St Stanislaus   CHURCH
(ul Gołębia 1) Two blocks south of Stary Rynek is this large, pink baroque place of worship with monumental altars dating from the mid-17th century.

Museum of Applied Arts   MUSEUM
(www.mnp.art.pl; Góra Przemysława 1) Collection of furniture, gold and silverware, glass, ceramics, weapons, clocks, watches and sundials from Europe and the Far East. At the time of research the museum was undergoing a major renovation as part of a restoration of the castle it's housed within, but should have reopened by the time you read this.

WEST OF THE OLD TOWN

Monument to the Victims of June 1956   MONUMENT
(Plac Mickiewicza) Emotive memorial to the dead and injured of the massive 1956 strike by the city's industrial workers, which was crushed by tanks. It's in a park west of the prominent Kaiserhaus building.

Palm House   GREENHOUSE
(Palmiarnia; www.palmiarnia.poznan.pl; ul Matejki 18; adult/concession 7/5zł; ⊙9am-5pm Tue-Sat, 9am-6pm Sun) This huge greenhouse (built in 1910) contains 17,000 species of tropical and subtropical plants. It's located in Park Wilsona, 1km southwest of the train station.

NORTH OF THE OLD TOWN

Museum of Armaments   MUSEUM
(Al Armii Poznań; adult/concession 4/2zł, Fri free; ⊙9am-4pm Tue-Sat, from 10am Sun) This museum of weaponry is located in Citadel Park about 1.5km north of the Old Town, within the remains of a 19th-century Prussian citadel. Some 20,000 German troops held out for a month here in February 1945, when the fortress was destroyed by artillery fire. Exhibits include Russian tanks and rocket launchers.

EAST OF THE OLD TOWN

Ostrów Tumski   HISTORIC AREA
This river island is dominated by the monumental, double-towered **Poznań Cathedral** (ul Ostrów Tumski 17; ⊙dawn-dusk), originally buil in 968. The Byzantine-style **Golden Cha**

POLAND POZNAŃ

GNIEZNO

If you're staying in Poznań, it's worth checking out historic Gniezno, one of Poland's oldest settlements. It was probably here that Poland's Duke Mieszko I was baptised in 966, the starting point of Catholicism's major role in the nation's story. In 1025, Bolesław Chrobry was crowned in the city's cathedral as the first Polish king. Gniezno probably also functioned as Poland's first capital before Poznań achieved that honour, though history is murky on this point.

Whatever the case, Gniezno makes a good day trip from Poznań, or a short stopover. Setting out from its attractive broad **market square** you can investigate its historic **cathedral**, dating from the 14th century, and a **museum** dedicated to Poland's origins, situated on the nearby lakeside.

An hour north of Gniezno is the Iron Age village of **Biskupin**, unearthed in the 1930s and partly reconstructed. Passing by it is a **tourist train** that links the towns of Żnin and Gąsawa, both of which have regular bus transport to Gniezno. Gniezno itself is linked to Poznań by frequent trains (45-minute trip) and buses (one-hour trip) throughout the day.

For more details, check out Lonely Planet's *Poland* country guide or drop into Gniezno's **tourist office** (☑61 428 4100; www.szlakpiastowski.com.pl; Rynek 14).

(1841) and the **mausoleums** of Mieszko I and Boleslaus the Brave are behind the high altar.

A new attraction under construction opposite the island's eastern shore is the **Cathedral Island Heritage Centre** (www.trakt.poznan.pl; ul Gdańska). A cutting-edge multimedia history museum, it should be open by mid-2013.

The island is 1km east of the Old Town (take any eastbound tram from Plac Wielkopolski).

Lake Malta   RECREATIONAL ZONE
Some 1.6km east of the Old Town is this body of water, a favourite weekend destination for Poles. It holds sailing regattas, outdoor concerts and other events in summer and in winter there's a ski slope in operation.

A fun way to visit the lake is to take tram 4, 8 or 17 from Plac Wielkopolski to the Rondo Śródka stop on the other side of Ostrów Tumski. From the nearby terminus, you can catch a miniature train along the **Malta Park Railway** (http://mpk.poznan.pl/maltanka; ul Jana Pawła II; adult/concession 6/4zł; ☺10am-6.30pm Apr-Oct), which follows the lake's shore to the **New Zoo** (www.zoo.poznan.pl; ul Krańcowa 81; adult/concession 20/10zł; ☺9am-7pm Apr-Sep, to 4pm Oct-Mar). This sprawling institution houses diverse species, including Baltic grey seals.

✦ Festivals & Events

St John's Fair   CULTURAL
(☺Jun) Held on the Stary Rynek, featuring craft items, local foods and street artist performances. The fair runs for two weeks.

**Malta International
Theatre Festival**   THEATRE
(www.malta-festival.pl; ☺Jul)

Ethno Port Poznań Festival   WORLD MUSIC
(www.ethnoport.pl; ☺Aug)

**Transatlantyk Poznań International
Film & Music Festival**   FILM, MUSIC
(www.transatlantyk.org; ☺Aug)

🛏 Sleeping

The largest trade fairs take place in January, June, September and October; during these times (and at other times when trade fairs are on), the rates of Poznań's accommodation dramatically increase. A room may also be difficult to find, so it pays to book ahead. Prices given here are for outside trade fair periods. You can check the dates of the fairs online at www.mtp.pl.

Rooms can also be found via **Biuro Zakwaterowania Przemysław** (☑61 866 3560; www.przemyslaw.com.pl; ul Głogowska 16; ☺10am-6pm Mon-Fri, to 2pm Sat), an accommodation agency with an office not far from the train station.

**TOP
CHOICE Hotel Stare Miasto**   HOTEL €€
(☑61 663 62 42; www.hotelstaremiasto.pl; ul Rybaki 36; s/d from 224/390zł; ▣🖤🔊) Elegant, value-for-money hotel with a tasteful chandeliered foyer and a spacious breakfast room. Rooms can be small, but are clean and bright with lovely starched white sheets. Some upper rooms have skylights in place of windows.

ezydencja Solei
HOTEL €€

📞61 855 7351; www.hotel-solei.pl; ul Szewska 2; s/d 199/299zł; 🛜) Temptingly close to Stary Rynek, this tiny hotel offers small but cosy rooms in an old-fashioned residential style, with wallpaper and timber furniture striking a homey note. The attic suite is amazingly large and can accommodate up to four people. Breakfast is 20zł extra.

Frolic Goats Hostel
HOSTEL €

(📞61 852 4411; www.frolicgoatshostel.com; ul Wrocławska 16/6; dm from 44zł, d 170zł; 🛜) Named after the feisty goats who fight above the Town Hall clock, this hostel is aimed squarely at the international backpacker. There's a washing machine on the premises, bike hire is available for 30zł per day and room rates are unaffected by trade fairs. Enter from ul Jaskółcza.

Brovaria
HOTEL €€

(📞61 858 6868; www.brovaria.pl; Stary Rynek 73/74; s/d from 250/290zł; 🛜) This multi-talented hotel also operates as a restaurant and bar, but most impressive is its in-house microbrewery. The elegant rooms have tasteful dark timber tones and some have views onto the Rynek.

Hostel Cameleon
HOSTEL €

(📞61 639 3041; www.hostel-cameleon.com; ul Świętosławska 12; dm 55zł, s/d from 120/165zł; 🛜) Centrally located hostel with contemporary decor and a spacious kitchen and lounge. The cheaper private rooms have shared bathrooms. Also has a washing machine.

Hotel Lech
HOTEL €€

(📞61 853 0151; www.hotel-lech.poznan.pl; ul Św Marcin 74; s/d 200/295zł; 🛜) Hotel Lech has standard two-star decor, but rooms are relatively spacious and the bathrooms are modern. Flash your ISIC card for a discount.

🍴 Eating & Drinking

TOP CHOICE Warung Bali
INDONESIAN €€€

(ul Żydowska 1; mains 36-62zł; 🕙noon-10pm) Excellent Indonesian restaurant not far from the main square, with a tastefully decorated interior. Indonesian music plays softly while you order *gado gado* (mixed vegetables with peanut sauce), satays, *nasi goreng* (fried rice) and other delicious classics.

Tapas Bar
SPANISH €€

(Stary Rynek 60; mains 19-88zł; 🕙9am-midnight) Atmospheric place dishing up authentic tapas and Spanish wine in a room lined with intriguing bric-a-brac. Most tapas dishes

cost about 26zł, so forget the mains and share with friends. Also serves breakfast.

Gospoda Pod Koziołkami
POLISH €€

(Stary Rynek 95; mains 13-78zł; 🕙11am-10pm) Homey bistro within Gothic arches on the ground floor and a grill in the cellar. The menu is crammed with tasty Polish standards, including some distinctively Wielkopolska specialities.

Bar Caritas
CAFETERIA €

(Plac Wolności 1; mains 6-12zł; 🕙8am-7pm Mon-Fri, 9am-5pm Sat, from 11am Sun) You can point at what you want without resorting to your phrasebook at this cheap and convenient milk bar. There are many variants of *naleśniki* (crepes) on the menu. Lunchtimes get crowded, so be prepared to share a table.

Ptasie Radio
CAFE-BAR

(ul Kościuszki 74; 🕙8am-midnight Mon-Fri, from 10am Sat & Sun; 🛜) This funky drinking hole, named after a famous Polish poem 'Bird Radio', is a retro riot of chipped wooden tables, pot plants and bird images everywhere along its shelves and walls. It's a mellow place for a coffee or something stronger.

Proletaryat
BAR

(ul Wrocławska 9; 🕙1pm-late Mon-Sat, 3pm-late Sun) Small, red communist nostalgia bar with an array of socialist-era gear on the walls, including the obligatory bust of Lenin in the window and various portraits of the great man and his comrades. Play 'spot the communist leader' while sipping a boutique beer.

⭐ Entertainment

Czarna Owca
CLUB

(ul Jaskółcza 13; 🕙6pm-late Wed-Sat) Literally 'Black Sheep', this is a popular club with nightly DJs playing a mix of genres including R & B, house, rock, Latin, soul and funk.

Teatr Wielki
THEATRE

(📞61 659 0280; www.opera.poznan.pl; ul Fredry 9) The main venue for opera and ballet.

Filharmonia
CLASSICAL MUSIC

(📞61 853 6935; www.filharmonia.poznan.pl; ul Św Marcin 81) Offers classical music concerts.

ℹ Information

Adax (ul Półwiejska 28; per hr 2.50zł; 🕙8am-9pm Mon-Fri, from 10am Sat, from noon Sun) Internet access south of Stary Rynek.

City Information Centre (📞61 851 9645; ul Ratajczaka 44; 🕙10am-7pm Mon-Fri, until 5pm Sat) Handles bookings for cultural events.

TRANSPORT FROM POZNAŃ

Domestic Train

DESTINATION	PRICE (ZŁ)	DURATION (HR)	FREQUENCY
Gdańsk & Gdynia	58	5	8 daily
Kraków	61	8½	9 daily
Szczecin	46	2¾	at least hourly
Toruń	24	2½	10 daily
Warsaw	56	3¼	at least hourly
Wrocław	46	3½	at least hourly
Zakopane	65	11½	1 daily

International Train

DESTINATION	DURATION (HR)	FREQUENCY
Berlin (Germany)	2½	6 daily
Kyiv (Ukraine)	19	1 daily
Moscow (Russia)	21	1 daily

Main Post Office (ul Kościuszki 77; ⊘7am-8pm Mon-Fri, 8am-3pm Sat)

Tourist Office (☑61 852 6156; www.poznan.pl; Stary Rynek 59; ⊘9am-8pm Mon-Sat, 10am-6pm Sun May-Sep, 10am-6pm Mon-Fri Oct-Apr)

❶ Getting There & Away

AIR From **Poznań Airport** (www.airport-poznan.com.pl; ul Bukowska 285), national carrier LOT flies up to three times a day to Warsaw, once daily to Frankfurt and twice daily to Munich. Tickets are available from the **LOT office** (☑61 849 2261; ul Bukowska 285) at the airport. There are also two domestic flights daily via Eurolot to Kraków.

A vast array of other European cities are serviced from Poznań, including London via Wizz Air and Ryanair (daily), and Dublin via Ryanair (four times a week). The airport is in the western suburb of Ławica, 7km from the Old Town and accessible by bus L from the main train station, or buses 48, 59 and night bus 242 from the Bałtyk stop near Rondo Kaponiera.

BUS The **bus station** (ul Towarowa 17) is a 10-minute walk east of the train station, though will eventually be integrated with the new Poznan Główny train station. In any case, most of its destinations can be reached more comfortably and frequently by train.

From the smaller Dworzec Górczyn bus station 5km southwest of the main train station along ul Głogowska, **Polski Bus** (www.polskibus.com) runs useful services to Warsaw (5¾ hours, three daily) and Berlin (4½ hours, twice daily) as well as other destinations around Poland; check fares and book online.

TRAIN The busy Poznań Główny train station was in two pieces at the time of research, with the partly opened new station building operating in conjuction with the old terminal next to it. The station is about 1.5km southwest of the Old Town.

POMERANIA

Pomerania (Pomorze in Polish) is an attractive region with diverse drawcards, from beautiful beaches to architecturally pleasing cities. It covers a large swathe of territory along the Baltic coast, from the German border in the west to the lower Vistula Valley in the east. A sandy coastline stretches from Gdańsk to western Szczecin and Toruń lies inland. Pomerania was fought over by Germanic and Slavic peoples for a millennium, before being incorporated almost fully within Poland after WWII.

Gdańsk

POP 460,000

Port cities are usually lively places with distinctive personalities, and Gdańsk is no exception. From its busy riverside waterfront to the Renaissance splendour of its charming narrow streets, there's plenty to like about this coastal city.

Few Polish cities occupy such a pivotal position in history as Gdańsk. Founded more than a millennium ago, it became the focus of territorial tensions when the Teutonic Knights seized it from Poland in 1308. The city joined the Hanseatic League in 1361 and became one of the richest ports in the Baltic through its membership of the trading organisation. Finally, the Thirteen Years' War ended in 1466 with the Knights' defeat and Gdańsk's return to Polish rule.

This to-and-fro between Germanic and Polish control didn't stop there, however – in 1793 Gdanśk was incorporated into Prussia and after the German loss in WWI it became the autonomous Free City of Danzig. The city's environs are where WWII began, when Nazi Germany bombarded Polish troops stationed at Westerplatte. Gdańsk suffered immense damage during the war, but upon its return to Poland in 1945 its historic centre was faithfully reconstructed.

In the 1980s, Gdańsk achieved international fame as the home of the Solidarity trade union, whose rise paralleled the fall of communism in Europe. Today it's a vibrant city and a great base for exploring the Baltic coast.

◉ Sights

MAIN TOWN
Royal Way   HISTORIC ROUTE
The historic parade route of Polish kings runs from the western **Upland Gate** (Brama Wyżynna), which was built in the 1770s on the site of a 15th-century gate, onward through the **Foregate** (Przedbramie), which once housed a torture chamber, and 1614 **Golden Gate** (Złota Brama), and east to the 1568 Renaissance **Green Gate** (Zielona Brama). Along the way it passes through beautiful **ul Długa** (Long Street) and **Długi Targ** (Long Market).

Central Maritime Museum   MUSEUM
(www.cmm.pl; ul Ołowianka 9; all sections 18/10zł; ☺10am-4pm Tue-Sun) On the waterfront north of the 14th-century **St Mary's Gate** you'll find the 15th-century **Gdańsk Crane** (ul Szeroka 67/68; adult/concession 8/5zł; ☺10am-4pm Tue-Sun), the largest of its kind in medieval Europe and capable of hoisting loads of up to 2000kg. It's part of this maritime history museum, which has a presence on both sides of the Motława River linked by its own regular ferry service.

On the west bank next to the crane is the spanking new **Maritime Cultural Centre** (ul Tokarska 21; adult/concession 12/8zł; ☺10am-6pm Tue-Sun), with an exhibition of boats

from around the world and an interactive section popular with kids. The branch on the east bank offers a fascinating insight into Gdańsk's seafaring past, including the **Sołdek Museum Ship** (ul Ołowianka 9; adult/concession 8/5zł; ☺10am-4pm Tue-Sun), built here just after WWII.

St Mary's Church   CHURCH
(ul Podkramarska 5; tower adult/concession 5/3zł; ☺8.30am-6pm, except during services) At the western end of picturesque **ul Mariacka**, with its gracious 17th-century burgher houses and amber shops, is this gigantic 14th-century place of worship. Watch little figures troop out at noon from its 14m-high **astronomical clock**, adorned with zodiacal signs. You can also climb the 405 steps of the **tower** for a giddy view over the town.

Amber Museum   MUSEUM
(www.mhmg.gda.pl; Targ Węglowy; adult/concession 10/5zł, Mon free; ☺11am-3pm Mon, 10am-7pm Tue-Sat, 11am-7pm Sun) Within the Foregate you can visit this museum, wherein you can marvel at the history of so-called 'Baltic gold'.

Historical Museum of Gdańsk   MUSEUM
(www.mhmg.gda.pl; ul Długa 47; adult/concession 10/5zł, Mon free; ☺11am-3pm Mon, 10am-7pm Tue-Sat, 11am-7pm Sun) Inside the towering Gothic Town Hall is this institution depicting photos of old Gdańsk and the damage caused to the city during WWII.

Neptune's Fountain   FOUNTAIN
(Długi Targ) Near the Town Hall, legend says this decorative fountain (1633) once gushed forth *goldwasser*, the iconic Gdańsk liqueur.

Artus Court Museum   MUSEUM
(www.mhmg.gda.pl; ul Długi Targ 43/44; adult/concession 10/5zł, free Mon; ☺11am-3pm Mon, 10am-7pm Tue-Sat, 11am-7pm Sun) Merchants used to congregate in this building, which boasts lavish interior decoration. Also note the adjacent **Golden House** (Złota Kamienica; Długi Targ), built in 1618, which has a strikingly rich facade.

Dom Uphagena   MUSEUM
(www.mhmg.gda.pl; ul Długa 12; adult/concession 10/5zł, Mon free; ☺11am-3pm Mon, 10am-7pm Tue-Sat, 11am-7pm Sun) This historic 18th-century residence features ornate furniture.

Free City of Danzig
Historical Zone   MUSEUM
(ul Piwna 19/21; admission 5zł; ☺11am-6pm) Small but intriguing display of items from

Gdańsk

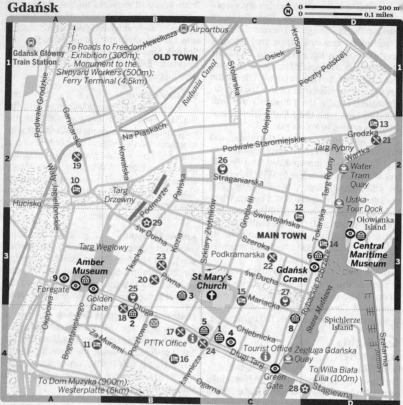

the interwar era when Gdańsk operated as a 'free city', independent of both Poland and Germany.

State Archaeological Museum
MUSEUM

(ul Mariacka 25/26; adult/concession 8/6zł; ◷10am-5pm Tue-Sun) Museum within St Mary's Gate, housing an overly generous number of formerly diseased ancient human skulls, displays of amber and river views from the adjacent **tower** (admission 5zł).

OLD TOWN

Almost totally destroyed in 1945, the Old Town has never been completely rebuilt, but contains some gems worth visiting.

TOP CHOICE Roads to Freedom Exhibition
MUSEUM

(ul Wały Piastowskie 24; adult/concession 6/4zł; ◷10am-6pm Tue-Sun) At the north end of the Old Town is this excellent museum. Its exhibits chart the decline and fall of Polish

communism and the rise of the Solidarity trade union. It's a place that anyone interested in Gdańsk's history should visit.

Monument to the Shipyard Workers
MONUMENT

(Plac Solidarności) A short walk further north, this soaring structure stands at the entrance to the Gdańsk Shipyards. It was erected in late 1980 in memory of 44 workers killed during the riots of December 1970 and was the first monument in a communist regime to commemorate the regime's victims.

OLIWA
Park Oliwski
GARDENS

(ul Cystersów; ◷8am-8pm) Some 9km northwest of the Main Town is the towering **Oliwa Cathedral** (ul Nowickiego 5; ◷9am-5pm), located within this lovely set of gardens. It was built in the 13th century with a Gothic facade and a long, narrow central nave. The famous baroque organ is used for recitals each hour

Gdańsk

between 10am and 3pm Monday to Saturday in July and August. There's an **Ethnographic Museum** (ul Cystersów 19; adult/concession 8/4zł, Fri free; ☺10am-5pm Tue-Sun) housed in the nearby Old Granary, and the **Modern Art Gallery** (ul Cystersów 18; adult/concession 10/6zł; ☺10am-5pm Tue-Sun) can be found in the former Abbots' Palace.

To reach the park, take the commuter train to the Gdańsk Oliwa station (3.60zł). From there, it's a 10-minute walk; head west up ul Poczty Gdańsk, turn right (north) along the highway and look for the signs to 'Ethnographic Museum' and 'Cathedral'.

WESTERPLATTE
Bus 106 (25 minutes) heads to Westerplatte every 15 minutes from a stop outside the Music Academy in Gdańsk. Alternatively, excursion boats sail from the Main Town to Westerplatte.

World War II Memorial   MEMORIAL
(ul Sucharskiego) WWII began at 4.45am on 1 September 1939, when the German battleship *Schleswig-Holstein* began shelling the Polish naval post at this location, 7km north of Gdańsk's Main Town. The 182-man Polish garrison held out against ferocious attacks for a week before surrendering.

The enormity of this event is marked by a hilltop **memorial**, a small **museum** (www. mhmg.gda.pl; ul Sucharskiego 1; adult/concession 3/2zł; ☺9am-7pm May-Sep) and **ruins** remaining from the Nazi German bombardment.

✦✦ Festivals & Events

**International Street &
Open-Air Theatre Festival**   THEATRE
(www.feta.pl; ☺Jul)

**International Organ
Music Festival**   MUSIC
(☺Jul/Aug)

Sounds of the North Festival   MUSIC
(www.nck.org.pl; ☺Jul/Aug) Folkloric music festival.

St Dominic's Fair   SHOPPING
(www.mtgsa.pl; ☺Jul/Aug) Annual shopping and cultural fair.

**International Shakespeare
Festival**   THEATRE
(www.shakespearefestival.pl; ☺Jul/Aug)

⌂ Sleeping

Accommodation can be tight in the warmer months. If you're having trouble finding a bed, check with the tourist office (p655).

Also consider staying in nearby Sopot or Gdynia; the tourist offices there can help.

TOP CHOICE **3 City Hostel** HOSTEL €
(☑58 354 5454; www.3city-hostel.pl; Targ Drzewny 12/14; dm from 50zł, r 180zł; ☏) Sparkling new hostel near the train station, with high ceilings, pleasant common areas, a kitchen and a lounge with a view. The cheapest beds are in Japanese-style capsules.

Kamienica Gotyk HOTEL €€
(☑58 301 8567; www.gotykhouse.eu; ul Mariacka 1; s/d 280/310zł; ☏) This Gothic guesthouse claims to be Gdańsk's oldest residence. Inside, the rooms are compact but neat, with clean bathrooms. The location is impressive, with St Mary's Church and the cafes and shops of ul Mariacka just outside the door.

Dom Muzyka HOTEL €€
(☑58 326 0600; www.dommuzyka.pl; ul Łąkowa 1/2; s/d 252/344zł; ✳☏) Gorgeous white rooms with arched ceilings and quality furniture, inside the Music Academy some 300m east of the city centre; trams 3, 8 and 9 will get you there from the train station. It's hard to spot from the street – head for the door on the city end of the courtyard within the big yellow-brick building.

Dom Zachariasza Zappio HOSTEL €
(☑58 322 0174; www.zappio.pl; ul Świętojańska 49; dm/s/d 50/99/158zł; ☏) This hostel is located in an atmospheric former convent next to St John's Church. Rooms are brightly furnished with contemporary furniture and there's a fantastic beer garden.

Happy Seven Hostel HOSTEL €
(☑58 320 8601; www.happyseven.com; ul Grodzka 16; dm from 45zł, d 230zł; ☏) Hostel in which each dorm has a light-hearted theme, including the 'Travel' dorm plastered with maps, and the 'Music', 'Sport' and 'Movie' dorms. The cool retro lounge contains a games console.

Kamienica Zacisze APARTMENTS €€
(☑69 627 4306; www.apartments.gdansk.pl; ul Ogarna 107; apt from 220zł; ☏) Set within a quiet courtyard off the street, this communist-era workers' dormitory building has been transformed into a set of light, airy apartments for up to nine people. Each apartment has high ceilings, a fully equipped kitchen and loads of space. Excellent value for the location and quality.

Apartments Poland APARTMENTS €€
(☑58 346 9864; www.apartmentpoland.com; apt €30-80) A company with renovated properties scattered through the Tri-City Area (Gdańsk–Sopot–Gdynia), including a number in central Gdańsk. Some are big enough for families or other groups.

Dom Harcerza HOTEL €
(☑58 301 3621; www.domharcerza.pl; ul Za Murami 2/10; dm 35zł, s/d from 60/120zł; ☏) The rooms are small but cosy at this place, which offers the best value and location for any budget-priced hotel. It's popular (so book ahead) and can get noisy when large groups are staying here. There's a charming old-fashioned restaurant on the ground floor.

Camping Nr 218 Stogi CAMPING GROUND €
(☑58 307 3915; www.kemping-gdansk.pl; ul Wydmy 9; site per person/tent 15/7zł, cabins 65-140zł; ☼May-Sep) This camping ground is only 200m from the beach in the seaside holiday centre of Stogi, about 5.5km northeast of the Main Town. Tidy cabins sleep between two and five people and facilities include a volleyball court and children's playground. Take tram 8 or 13 from the main train station in Gdańsk.

Willa Biała Lilia HOTEL €€
(☑58 301 7074; www.bialalilia.pl; ul Spichrzowa 16; s/d 260/340zł; ☏) The White Lily Villa is an attractive accommodation choice a short walk east of the Main Town on Spichlerze Island. Rooms are neat and clean; staff are helpful.

Hotel Hanza HOTEL €€€
(☑58 305 3427; www.hotelhanza.pl; ul Tokarska 6; s/d/ste from 450/530zł; ✳☏) The Hanza is attractively perched along the waterfront near the Gdańsk Crane and offers elegant, tasteful rooms in a modern building. Some rooms have enviable views over the river.

✗ Eating

For self-catering, visit **Kos Delikatesy** (ul Piwna 9/10; ☼24hr) in the Main Town.

Restauracja Pod Łososiem POLISH €€€
(ul Szeroka 52/54; mains 60-85zł; ☼noon-10pm) This is one of Gdańsk's oldest and most highly regarded restaurants. It is particularly famous for its salmon dishes and the gold-flecked liqueur *goldwasser*, which was invented here. Red-leather seats, brass chandeliers and a gathering of gas lamps fill out the posh interior.

elevetka KASHUBIAN €€€
(ul Długa 45; mains 20-69zł) This delightful eatery manages to evoke a rural theme without a single ancient agricultural knick-knack or trussed waitress in sight. Admire the heavy wooden furniture and soothing scenes of the Kashubian countryside, while munching through finely crafted regional dishes.

U Dzika POLISH €€
(ul Piwna 59/61; mains 15-77zł; ⊙11am-10pm) Pleasant eatery with a nice outdoor terrace, specialising in *pierogi* (dumplings). If you're feeling adventurous, try the Fantasy Dumplings, comprising cottage cheese, cinnamon, raisins and peach.

Bar Mleczny Neptun CAFETERIA €
(ul Długa 33/34; mains 2-16zł; ⊙7am-8pm Mon-Fri, 10am-6pm Sat & Sun; 🛜) This joint is a cut above your run-of-the-mill milk bar, with potted plants, lace curtains, decorative tiling and old lamps for decor.

Green Way VEGETARIAN €
(ul Garncarska 4/6; mains 4-12zł; ⊙11am-8pm Mon-Fri, noon-7pm Sat & Sun; 🖊) Popular with local vegetarians, this eatery serves everything from soy cutlets to Mexican goulash in an unfussy green-and-orange space. There's another, more central, **branch** (ul Długa 11; mains 4-12zł; ⊙10am-8pm; 🖊) on the Royal Way.

Przystań Gdańska POLISH €€
(ul Wartka 5; mains 17-43zł) An atmospheric place to enjoy outdoor dining, with a view along the river to the Gdańsk Crane. Serves Polish classics and a range of fish dishes.

🍷 Drinking

TOP CHOICE Cafe Lamus BAR
(ul Lawendowa 8; ⊙noon-late; 🛜) Achingly cool retro-themed bar serving a range of beers from small Polish breweries, set up by a couple of locals after they returned from working in pubs in the UK. Enter from ul Straganiarska.

Cafe Ferber CAFE-BAR
(ul Długa 77/78; ⊙9am-late; 🛜) It's startling to step from Gdańsk's historic main street into this modern cafe-bar, dominated by bright red panels, a suspended ceiling and boxy lighting. Partake of breakfast, well-made coffee, international wines and creative cocktails.

Kamienica CAFE-BAR
(ul Mariacka 37/39) The best of the bunch on ul Mariacka is this excellent two-level cafe with a calm, sophisticated atmosphere and a charming patio. It's as popular for daytime coffee and cakes as it is for a sociable evening beverage.

☆ Entertainment

Miasto Aniołów CLUB
(ul Chmielna 26) The City of Angels covers all the bases – late-night revellers can hit the spacious dance floor, crash in the chill-out area, or hang around the atmospheric deck overlooking the Motława River. Nightly DJs play disco and other dance-oriented sounds.

Parlament CLUB
(www.parlament.com.pl; ul Św Ducha 2; ⊙8pm-late Thu-Sat) Hardly a talking shop, this long-lived club plays host to big dance events. There's retro music on Thursday, electronica on Friday and disco on Saturday.

State Baltic Opera Theatre OPERA
(☎58 763 4906; www.operabaltycka.pl; Al Zwycięstwa 15) This venue is in the suburb of Wrzeszcz, not far from the train station at Gdańsk Politechnika.

ⓘ Information

Jazz 'n' Java (ul Tkacka 17/18; per hr 6zł; ⊙10am-10pm) Internet access.
Main Post Office (ul Długa 22; ⊙24hr)
PTTK Office (☎58 301 9151; www.pttk-gdansk.pl; ul Długa 45; ⊙10am-6pm) Provides tourist information, along with internet access for 10zł per hour.
Tourist Office (☎58 305 7080; www.gdansk4u.pl; Długi Targ 28/29; ⊙9am-7pm Jun-Aug, to 5pm Sep-May)

ⓘ Getting There & Away

Air
From **Lech Wałęsa Airport** (www.airport.gdansk.pl; ul Słowackiego 200), national carrier LOT has at least three daily flights to Warsaw and at least three daily to Frankfurt. Tickets can be bought at the **LOT office** (☎58 301 28 2223; ul Wały Jagiellońskie 2/4). Eurolot also flies twice daily to Wrocław and Kraków.

Gdańsk is also connected to a plethora of other European cities, including London via Ryanair and Wizz Air (three daily), and Dublin via Ryanair (four weekly).

The airport is accessible by bus 110 from the Gdańsk Wrzeszcz local commuter train station, or bus 210 or night bus N3 from outside the Gdańsk Główny train station. A private service, **Airportbus** (☎58 554 9393; www.airportbus.com.pl; ul Heweliusza 13; ticket 14.90zł), also runs from

TRAINS FROM GDAŃSK

Domestic Train

DESTINATION	PRICE (ZŁ)	DURATION	FREQUENCY
Białystok	63	7½hr	2 daily
Elbląg	16	1½hr	11 daily
Giżycko	56	5hr	2 daily
Kętrzyn	52	4¾hr	2 daily
Kraków	69	8-12hr	10 daily
Lublin	69	9hr	2 daily
Malbork	17	45min	at least hourly
Ostróda	24	3hr	2 daily
Olsztyn	40	3hr	6 daily
Poznań	58	5hr	8 daily
Szczecin	61	5½hr	3 daily
Toruń	46	3¾hr	9 daily
Warsaw	63	6¼hr	12 daily

International Train

DESTINATION	DURATION (HR)	FREQUENCY
Berlin (Germany)	6½	1 daily
Kaliningrad (Russia)	6	1 daily

the Mercure Hevelius hotel in the Old Town to the airport. Taxis cost 45zł to 55zł one way.

Boat

Polferries (☏22 830 0930; www.polferries.pl) offers daily services between Gdańsk and Nynäshamn (19 hours) in Sweden in summer (less frequently in the low season). The company uses the **Ferry Terminal** (ul Przemysłowa 1) in Nowy Port, about 5km north of the Main Town. The PTTK office in Gdańsk can provide information and sell tickets.

In the warmer months, **Żegluga Gdańska excursion boats** (www.zegluga.pl; ⊙10am-4pm Apr-Nov) leave regularly from the dock near the Green Gate in Gdańsk for Westerplatte (adult/concession return 45/22zł). From a quay further north along the dockside, **Ustka-Tour** (www.perlalew.pl; ⊙9am-7pm Apr-Oct) operates hourly cruises to Westerplatte (adult/concession return 40/22zł) aboard the *Czarna Perła* and *Galeon Lew*, replica 17th-century galleons. Just north of the galleon quay is the **Water Tram** (www.ztm.gda.pl; ⊙8.30am-7pm Jun-Aug), a ferry which heads to Hel (adult/concession 24/12zł, three daily) and Westerplatte (adult/concession 10/5zł, three daily). Bicycles cost an extra 5zł to transport.

Bus

The **bus station** (ul 3 Maja 12) is behind the main train station and connected to ul Podwale Grodzkie by an underground passageway. Useful PKS buses head to Frombork (18zł, 2¼ hours, three daily) and Warsaw (55zł, 5¾ hours, hourly). **Polski Bus** (www.polskibus.com) departs hourly to Ostróda (two hours) and Warsaw (5¾ hours); check fares and book online.

Train

The city's main train station, **Gdańsk Główny** (ul Podwale Grodzkie 1), is conveniently located on the western outskirts of the Old Town. Most long-distance trains actually start or finish at Gdynia, so make sure you get on/off quickly here.

ℹ Getting Around

The local commuter train – the SKM – runs every 15 minutes from 6am to 7.30pm, and less frequently thereafter, between Gdańsk Główny and Gdynia Główna train stations, via Sopot and Gdańsk Oliwa train stations. Buy tickets at any station and validate them in the yellow boxes at the platform entrance, or purchase them prevalidated from vending machines on the platform.

Around Gdańsk

Gdańsk is part of the so-called Tri-City Area including Gdynia and Sopot, which are easy day trips from Gdańsk.

SOPOT
POP 38,700

Since the 19th century, Sopot, 12km north of Gdańsk, has been one of the Baltic coast's most fashionable seaside resorts. It has an easygoing atmosphere, good nightlife and long stretches of sandy beach.

From the train station, head left to busy **ul Bohaterów Monte Cassino**, one of Poland's most attractive pedestrian streets. Here you can find plenty of restaurants and bars, and the surreal **Crooked House** (Krzywy Domek; ul Bohaterów Monte Cassino 53) shopping centre. At the eastern end of the street off Plac Zdrojowy is Poland's longest pier (515m), the famous **Molo** (www.molo.sopot.pl; adult/concession 7/3.50zł; ☉8am-11pm Jun-Aug, 8am-8pm May & Sep). Various attractions and cultural events can be found near and along the structure.

To the south, the **Sopot Museum** (www.muzeumsopotu.pl; ul Poniatowskiego 8; adult/concession 5/3zł, Thu free; ☉10am-5pm Tue-Fri, noon-6pm Sat & Sun) has displays recalling the town's 19th-century incarnation as the German resort of Zoppot.

For tourist information, including accommodation, check with the **tourist office** (☏58 550 3783; www.sts.sopot.pl; Plac Zdrojowy 2; ☉10am-8pm Jun-Sep, 10am-6pm Oct-May) in a modern building near the pier, which also houses a **mineral water pump room** and a **lookout** with a view of the Baltic.

From the Sopot train station, local SKM commuter trains run every 15 minutes to Gdańsk Główny (3.60zł, 15 minutes) and Gdynia Główna (3.60zł, 10 minutes) train stations. The Water Tram departs the pier in Sopot for Hel (adult/concession 22/11zł, three daily) from June to August.

GDYNIA
POP 249,000

As a young city with a busy port atmosphere, Gdynia, 9km north of Sopot, is less atmospheric than Gdańsk or Sopot. It was greatly expanded as a seaport after this coastal area (but not Gdańsk) became part of Poland following WWI.

From the southern end of Gdynia Główna train station, follow ul 10 Lutego east for about 1.5km to the **Southern Pier**. Here you'll find sights, shops and restaurants.

Moored on the pier's northern side are two interesting museum ships. First up is the curiously sky-blue destroyer **Błyskawica** (adult/concession 8/4zł; ☉10am-5pm Tue-Sun Jun-Oct), which escaped capture in 1939 and went on to serve successfully with Allied naval forces throughout WWII. Beyond it is the beautiful three-masted frigate **Dar Pomorza** (www.cmm.pl; adult/concession 8/4zł; ☉10am-4pm Feb-Nov), built in Hamburg in 1909 as a training ship for German sailors. There's information in English on the dockside.

For more information about Gdynia, including accommodation options, visit the **tourist office** (☏58 622 3766; www.gdyniaturystyczna.pl; ul 10 Lutego 24; ☉9am-6pm Mon-Fri, 9am-4pm Sat & Sun) near the train station.

Local commuter trains link Gdynia Główna train station with Sopot (3.60zł, 10 minutes) and Gdańsk (5.40zł, 25 minutes, every 15 minutes). Trains also run to Hel (16zł, 1¾ hours, nine daily) and Lębork (17zł, one hour, half-hourly), where you can change for Łeba.

Stena Line (☏58 660 9200; www.stenaline.pl) uses the **Terminal Promowy** (ul Kwiatkowskiego 60), about 5km northwest of Gdynia. It offers twice-daily services between Gdynia and Karlskrona (between 10½ and 12½ hours) in Sweden.

MALBORK
POP 39,400

The magnificent **Malbork Castle** (☏55 647 0978; www.zamek.malbork.pl; ul Starościńska 1; adult/concession 40/30zł; ☉9am-7pm 15 Apr-15 Sep, 10am-3pm 16 Sep-14 Apr) is the centrepiece of this town, 58km southeast of Gdańsk. It's the largest Gothic castle in Europe and was once known as Marienburg, headquarters of the Teutonic Knights. It was constructed by the order in 1276 and became the seat of their Grand Master in 1309. Damage sustained in WWII was repaired after the conflict's end and the castle was placed on the Unesco World Heritage List in 1997.

The entry fee includes a compulsory Polish-language tour, along with a free audio guide in English and other languages. Occasional English-language tours operate at a higher entry fee (adult/concession 48/38zł); otherwise, an English-speaking tour guide can be commissioned for 210zł. For one hour after the castle interiors have closed for the day, you can purchase a ticket to inspect the grounds for a bargain basement fee of adult/concession 7/4zł.

Malbork is an easy day trip from Gdańsk, but if you want to stay over, check with the

tourist office (📞55 647 4747; www.visitmalbork.
pl; ul Kościuszki 54; ⊙8am-4pm Mon-Fri) for accommodation details. Places to eat can be
found both at the castle and along the town's
main street, ul Kościuszki.

The castle is 1km west of the train and bus
stations. Leave the train station, turn right, cut
across the highway, head down ul Kościuszki
and follow the signs. Malbork is an easy day
trip by train from Gdańsk (17zł, 45 minutes,
at least hourly). Malbork is also connected to
Olsztyn (36zł, two hours, six daily) and Toruń
(22zł, 3¼ hours, seven daily including four operated by private company Arriva).

Toruń

POP 205,000

The first thing to strike you about Toruń,
south of Gdańsk, is its collection of massive
red-brick churches, looking more like fortresses than places of worship. The city is defined
by its striking Gothic architecture, which gives
its Old Town a distinctive appearance. Toruń
is a pleasant place to spend a few days, offering a nice balance between a relaxing slow
pace and engaging sights and entertainments.

Toruń is also famous as the birthplace of
Nicolaus Copernicus, a figure you cannot
escape as you walk the streets of his home
town – you can even buy gingerbread men
in his likeness. The renowned astronomer
spent his youth here and the local university
is named after him.

Historically, Toruń is intertwined with
the Teutonic Knights, who established an
outpost here in 1233. Following the Thirteen Years' War (1454–66), the Teutonic Order and Poland signed a peace treaty here,
which returned to Poland a large area of
land stretching from Toruń to Gdańsk.

Toruń was fortunate to escape major
damage in WWII and as a result is the best-
preserved Gothic town in Poland. The Old
Town was added to Unesco's World Heritage
List in 1997.

Toruń

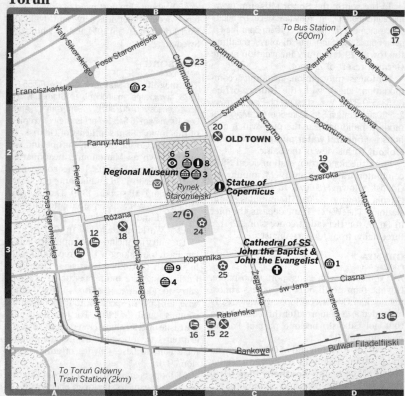

◉ Sights

Rynek Staromiejski
HISTORIC AREA

(Old Town Market Sq) The starting point for any exploration of Toruń is the Rynek Staromiejski. It's the focal point of the Old Town, lined by elegant facades and dominated by the massive 14th-century **Old Town Hall** (Ratusz Staromiejski).

In front of the Town Hall is an elegant **statue of Copernicus**. Look for other interesting items of statuary around the square, including a dog and umbrella from a famous Polish comic strip, a donkey that once served as a punishment device and a fabled violinist who saved Toruń from a plague of frogs.

Regional Museum
MUSEUM

(www.muzeum.torun.pl; Rynek Staromiejski 1; adult/concession 10/6zł; ⊘10am-6pm Tue-Sun May-Sep, to 4pm Tue-Sun Oct-Apr) Within the Town Hall, this institution features a fine collection of 19th- and 20th-century Polish art. Other displays recall the town's guilds and there's an exhibition of medieval stained glass and religious paintings. Climb the 40m-high **tower** (adult/concession 10/6zł; ⊘10am-4pm Tue-Sun Apr, to 8pm Tue-Sun May-Sep) for great views.

House of Copernicus
MUSEUM

(www.muzeum.torun.pl; ul Kopernika 15/17; adult/concession 10/7zł; ⊘10am-6pm Tue-Sun May-Sep, 10am-4pm Tue-Sun Oct-Apr) In 1473, Copernicus was allegedly born in the brick Gothic house that now contains this museum, presenting replicas of the great astronomer's instruments (though there's now some doubt he was really born here).

More engaging, if overpriced, is the museum's short **audiovisual presentation** (adult/concession 12/7zł) regarding Copernicus' life in Toruń, and the extravagantly titled **World of Toruń's Gingerbread** (adult/concession 10/6zł). In the latter, visitors are guided around the exhibition by a costumed medieval townswoman and given the chance to bake their own *pierniki* (gingerbread).

A combined ticket to all three attractions costs 20/15zł.

Cathedral of SS John the Baptist & John the Evangelist
CHURCH

(ul Żeglarska; adult/concession 3/2zł; ⊘9am-5.30pm Mon-Sat, 2-5.30pm Sun Apr-Oct) One block south of Rynek Staromiejski is this place of worship with its massive **tower** (adult/concession 6/4zł) and bell, founded in 1233 and completed more than 200 years later. A 3D movie about its history costs 2zł to view. No sightseeing is allowed during services.

Teutonic Knights' Castle Ruins
RUINS

(ul Przedzamcze; adult/concession 8/5zł, Mon free; ⊘10am-6pm) East of the remnants of the Old Town walls are the ruins of the Teutonic Castle, destroyed in 1454 by angry townsfolk protesting against the knights' oppressive regime. An occasional sound and light show (30zł) is staged here in summer.

Far Eastern Art Museum
MUSEUM

(www.muzeum.torun.pl; Rynek Staromiejski 35; adult/concession 7/4zł, Wed free; ⊘10am-6pm Tue-Sun May-Sep, to 4pm Tue-Sun Oct-Apr) The richly decorated, 15th-century **House Under the Star**, with its baroque facade and spiral wooden staircase, contains this collection of art from Asia.

POLAND TORUŃ

Explorers' Museum   MUSEUM

(www.muzeum.torun.pl; ul Franciszkańska 11) A street back from Rynek Staromiejski is this small but interesting display of artefacts from the collection of inveterate wanderer Antonio Halik and other travellers. At time of research it was closed pending renovation, but should have reopened by the time you read this – check with the tourist office for hours and entry fees.

Eskens' House   MUSEUM

(www.muzeum.torun.pl; ul Łazienna 16) This Gothic former residence houses city history displays, a collection of medieval weaponry and archaeological exhibits from the Iron and Bronze Ages, including a human skeleton buried in the distant past. At time of research it was closed for renovation, but should have now reopened.

🛏 Sleeping

Toruń is blessed with a generous number of hotels and hostels within converted historic buildings in its Old Town; but as they're fairly small, it pays to book ahead.

TOP CHOICE Hotel Karczma Spichrz   HOTEL €€

(✆56 657 1140; www.spichrz.pl; ul Mostowa 1; s/d 250/310zł, apt from 290zł; ❃🕏) Situated within a historic granary on the waterfront, this hotel's rooms are well supplied with personality, featuring massive exposed beams above elegant timber furniture. There's an excellent restaurant and bar within the establishment.

Green Hostel   HOSTEL €

(✆56 561 4000; www.greenhostel.eu; ul Małe Garbary 10; r from 100zł; 🕏) It may be labelled as a hostel, but there are no dorms. Instead, this budget accommodation boasts inexpensive rooms, a kitchen and a pleasant lounge. Note that most rooms share a bathroom and there's no breakfast.

Hotel Pod Czarną Różą   HOTEL €€

(✆56 621 9637; www.hotelczarnaroza.pl; ul Rabiańska 11; s/d 170/210zł; 🕏) 'Under the Black Rose' is spread between a historic inn and a newer wing facing the river, though its interiors present a uniformly clean, up-to-date look. Some doubles come with small but functional kitchens.

Orange Hostel   HOSTEL €

(✆56 652 0033; www.hostelorange.pl; ul Prosta 19; dm/s/d 30/50/90zł; 🕏) Orange is aimed at the international backpacker market. It's in a handy location, its decor is bright and cheerful, and its kitchen is an impressive place to practise the gentle art of self-catering.

POLAND TORUŃ

Toruń

TRAINS FROM TORUŃ

DESTINATION	PRICE (ZŁ)	DURATION (HR)	FREQUENCY
Gdańsk & Gdynia	46	3¾	9 daily
Kraków	69	8½	3 daily
Łódź	34	3	10 daily
Malbork	22	3¼	7 daily
Olsztyn	34	2¼	8 daily
Poznań	24	2½	10 daily
Warsaw	48	2¾	11 daily
Wrocław	56	5	5 daily

Hotel Petite Fleur
HOTEL €€
(☑56 621 5100; www.petitefleur.pl; ul Piekary 25; s/d 210/270zł; 🛜) The Petite Fleur offers fresh, airy rooms in a renovated old town house, some with exposed original brickwork and rafters. It also has a French cellar restaurant.

Hotel Gotyk
HOTEL €€
(☑56 658 4000; www.hotel-gotyk.com.pl; ul Piekary 20; s/d 170/230zł; 🛜) Housed in a modernised 14th-century building just off Rynek Staromiejski. Rooms are very neat, with ornate furniture and high ceilings, and all come with sparkling bathrooms.

Hotel Retman
HOTEL €€
(☑56 657 4460; www.hotelretman.pl; ul Rabiańska 15; s/d 180/240zł; 🛜) Attractively decorated accommodation offering spacious, atmospheric rooms with red carpet and solid timber furniture. Downstairs is a good pub and restaurant.

Camping Nr 33 Tramp
CAMPING GROUND €
(☑56 654 7187; www.mosir.torun.pl; ul Kujawska 14; camping per person/tent 9/7zł, s/d from 50/76zł; ⊙May-Sep) There's a choice of cabins or hotel-style rooms at this camping ground on the edge of the train line, along with an on-site snack bar. It's a five-minute walk west of the main train station.

Hotel 1231
HOTEL €€€
(☑56 619 0910; www.hotel1231.pl; ul Przedzamcze 6; s/d 340/400zł; ❄🛜) Elegant four-star accommodation in the shadow of the Old Town walls, with pleasantly appointed rooms and a cellar restaurant and bar.

🍴 Eating & Drinking

Toruń is famous for its *pierniki*, which come in a variety of shapes and can be bought at **Sklep Kopernik** (Rynek Staromiejski 6). There's a handy **Biedronka supermarket** (ul Szeroka 22) in the Old Town.

Masala
INDIAN, POLISH €€
(Rynek Nowomiejski 8; mains 19-45zł; ⊙10am-10pm; 🍴) Formerly known as Gospoda Pod Modrym Fartuchem, this 15th-century eatery on Rynek Nowomiejski (New Town Sq) has been visited by Polish kings and Napoleon. Polish dishes are joined by an array of Indian food, including a good vegetarian selection.

Bar Mleczny Pod Arkadami
CAFETERIA €
(ul Różana 1; mains 4-12zł; ⊙9am-7pm Mon-Fri, 9am-4pm Sat & Sun) This classic milk bar is just off Rynek Staromiejski, with a range of low-cost dishes. It also has a takeaway window serving a range of tasty *zapiekanki* (toasted rolls with cheese, mushrooms and tomato sauce) and sweet waffles.

Oberża
POLISH €
(ul Rabiańska 9; mains 8-15zł; ⊙11am-11pm Mon-Sat, to 9.30pm Sun; 🛜) This large self-service canteen stacks 'em high and sells 'em cheap for a hungry crowd of locals and tourists. Find your very own thatched mini-cottage among plentiful knick-knackery to enjoy *pierogi* (dumplings), soups, salads and other Polish mains.

Kuranty
POLISH, ITALIAN €€
(Rynek Staromiejski 29; mains 12-49zł; ⊙11am-2am; 🛜) The menu is firmly based on the three Ps: pizza, pasta and *pierogi* (including a rather tasty baked version). Random photos and extraordinary art nouveau lightshades add to the atmosphere. Be warned: TVs stuck on the sports channel hang off the walls.

Kona Coast Cafe
CAFE
(ul Chełmińska 18; ⊙9am-9pm Mon-Sat, 11am-6pm Sun; 🛜) Serves excellent freshly ground coffee,

along with homemade lemonade, chai and various cold drinks. There's also a light meal menu.

☆ Entertainment

Lizard King   CLUB
(ul Kopernika 3; ⊙7pm-late) Live-music venue with gigs ranging from local tribute bands to big rock acts from around Eastern and Central Europe.

Teatr Baj Pomorski   PUPPETRY
(⌖56 652 2029; www.bajpomorski.art.pl; ul Pienikarska 9) Puppet theatre shaped like a huge wooden cabinet, staging a variety of entertaining shows.

Dwór Artusa   CLASSICAL MUSIC
(⌖56 655 4929; Rynek Staromiejski 6) This place often presents classical music.

ⓘ Information

Ksero Uniwerek (ul Franciszkańska 5; per hr 4zł; ⊙8am-7pm Mon-Fri, 9am-2pm Sat) Internet access.

Main Post Office (Rynek Staromiejski; ⊙24hr)

Tourist Office (⌖56 621 0930; www.torun.pl; Rynek Staromiejski 25; ⊙9am-4pm Mon & Sat, to 6pm Tue-Fri, 11am-3pm Sun) Offers useful advice and hires out handheld MP3 players with English-language audio tours of the city (10zł per four hours).

ⓘ Getting There & Away

BUS The **bus station** (ul Dąbrowskiego) is a 10-minute walk north of the Old Town. From here, **Polski Bus** (www.polskibus.com) connects to Warsaw (3¾ hours, four daily) and Szczecin (6¼ hours, one daily); check fares and buy tickets online. However, most places can be reached more efficiently by train.

TRAIN The Toruń Główny train station is on the opposite side of the Vistula River and linked to the Old Town by bus 22 or 27 (get off at the first stop over the bridge). Some trains stop at the more convenient **Toruń Miasto train station** (Plac 18 Stycznia), about 500m east of the New Town.

Szczecin

POP 410,000 / TRANSPORT HUB

Szczecin (*shcheh*-cheen) is the major city and port of northwestern Poland. Though it's not the most beautiful of cities, it's a logical place to break a journey to or from Germany and has an international airport.

Decent midrange hotels handy for the train and bus stations include **Hotel Campanile** (⌖91 481 7700; www.campanile.com; ul Wyszyńskiego 30; r from 219zł; ❋🛜) and **Hotel Victoria** (⌖91 434 3855; Plac Batorego 2; s/d 160/220zł; 🛜). A budget option is **Hotelik Elka-Sen** (⌖91 433 5604; www.elkasen.szczecin. pl; Al 3 Maja 1a; s/d 120/150zł; 🛜), in the basement of an academic building.

WORTH A TRIP

BALTIC BEACHES

Between Gdańsk and the western city of Szczecin, there are numerous seaside towns with unpolluted waters and fine sandy beaches. Here are a few places for a sunbathing detour on your journey west along the Baltic coast towards the German border:

Hel Despite its name, this is an attractive place that's popular with windsurfers; it also houses a sanctuary for Baltic grey seals.

Łeba Pleasant holiday town with wide sandy beaches, the gateway to Słowiński National Park and its ever-shifting sand dunes.

Ustka Once the summer hang-out of German Chancellor Otto von Bismarck, this fishing port is full of atmosphere.

Darłowo A former medieval trading port with an impressive castle and two beaches linked by a pedestrian bridge over a river.

Kołobrzeg This coastal city offers historic attractions, spa treatments and Baltic cruises.

Międzyzdroje A popular seaside resort and the gateway to Wolin National Park.

Świnoujście On a Baltic island shared with Germany, this busy port town boasts a long sandy shore and pleasant parks.

For more details, check out Lonely Planet's *Poland* country guide, or www.poland.travel.

TRAINS FROM SZCZECIN

DESTINATION	PRICE (ZŁ)	DURATION (HR)	FREQUENCY
Berlin (Germany)	Varies	2	1 daily
Gdynia & Gdańsk	61	5½	3 daily
Poznań	46	2¾	at least hourly
Świnoujście	21	2	hourly
Warsaw	63	6½	7 daily
Wrocław	61	5	6 daily

You'll find plenty of restaurants and bars in the small but attractive **Old Town** northeast of the train station. There's a helpful **tourist office** (☑91 434 0440; www.szczecin. eu; Al Niepodległości 1; ⊘9am-5pm Mon-Fri, 10am-2pm Sat) in the city's nearby commercial heart, and a similarly useful **information centre** (☑91 489 1630; www.zamek.szczecin.pl/ cikit; ul Korsarzy 34; ⊘10am-6pm) in the imposing Castle of the Pomeranian Dukes next to the Old Town.

The **airport** (www.airport.com.pl) is in Goleniów, 45km northeast of the city. A shuttle bus (20zł) operated by **Interglobus** (☑91 485 0422; www.interglobus.pl) picks up from stops outside the LOT office and the train station before every flight, and meets all arrivals. Alternatively, a taxi should cost around 150zł to 200zł.

National carrier LOT flies between Szczecin and Warsaw three times a day. Book at the **LOT office** (☑91 488 3558; ul Wyzwolenia 17; ⊘9am-5pm Mon-Fri), about 200m past the northern end of Al Niepodegłości. There's also one or two flights daily to Kraków via Eurolot. International flights on Ryanair include London (four weekly) and Dublin (three weekly).

The **bus station** (Plac Grodnicki) and the nearby **Szczecin Główny train station** (ul Kolumba) are 600m southeast of the tourist office. Bus departures are of limited interest; however, from stand 3 in front of the train station Polski Bus heads once daily to Toruń (6¼ hours), continuing to Warsaw (10 hours).

Another way to reach Świnoujście is via the **Bosman Express ferry** (☑91 488 5564; http://www.wodolot.info.pl; ul Jana z Kolna 7; adult/ child 60/30zł; ⊘Apr-Oct), which travels twice daily from a quay northeast of the Old Town across the waters of the Szczeciński Lagoon (1¼ hours).

WARMIA & MASURIA

The most impressive feature of Warmia and Masuria is its beautiful postglacial landscape dominated by thousands of lakes, linked to rivers and canals, which host aquatic activities, including yachting and canoeing. This picturesque lake district has little industry and remains unpolluted and attractive, especially in summer. Like much of northern Poland, the region has changed hands between Germanic and Polish rulers over the centuries.

Elbląg-Ostróda Canal

The longest navigable canal still used in Poland stretches 82km between Elbląg and Ostróda. Constructed between 1848 and 1876, this waterway linked several lakes in order to transport timber from inland forests to the Baltic. To overcome the 99.5m difference in water levels, the canal utilises an unusual system of five water-powered slipways so that boats are sometimes carried across dry land on rail-mounted trolleys.

Nowadays excursion boats run along the route, operated by **Żegluga Ostródzka-Elbląska** (☑Elbląg 55 232 4307, Ostróda 89 646 3871; www.zegluga.com.pl). Various tours of different lengths are available, but the most interesting is the 10-hour **World of the Canal cruise** (adult/concession 149/139zł; ⊘May-Sep), which twice a week departs Elbląg at 8.30am, and in the other direction from Ostróda at 9am. The fare includes a bus transfer between boats in the middle of the trip, and a bus ride back to your starting point.

Along the way the canal boats pass beautiful green countryside replete with birdlife, navigating lakes and locks and the impressive 'inclined plane' slipways which raise or lower the vessels to the next section of canal.

POLAND ELBLĄG-OSTRÓDA CANAL

Boats each have a small cafe-bar that sells drinks and snacks.

Pensjonat Boss (☑55 239 3729; www.pensjonatboss.pl; ul Św Ducha 30; s/d 150/220zł) is a small hotel in Elbląg's Old Town, offering comfortable rooms above its own bar. **Camping Nr 61** (☑55 641 8666; www.camping61.com.pl; ul Panieńska 14; per person/tent 14/6zł, cabins 50-120zł; ☺May-Sep; ⊚), right at Elblag's boat dock, is a pleasant budget option. In Ostróda, try **Hotel Promenada** (☑89 642 8100; www.hotelpromenada.pl; ul Mickiewicza 3; s/d from 160/200zł), 500m east of the bus and train stations.

Elblag is accessible by frequent trains from Gdańsk (16zł, 1½ hours, 11 daily), Malbork (8zł, 30 minutes, hourly) and Olsztyn (19zł, 1¾ hours, 11 daily), and by bus from Frombork (7zł, 45 minutes, at least hourly).

Ostróda is reached by train from Olsztyn (10zł, 40 minutes, hourly), Toruń (28zł, two hours, eight daily) and Gdańsk (24zł, three hours, twice daily), and by hourly Polski Bus services directly from Warsaw (3¾ hours) and Gdańsk (two hours).

Buses also run regularly between Elblag and Ostróda (21zł, 1½ hours, hourly).

Frombork

POP 2500

It may look like the most uneventful town in history, but Frombork was once home to the famous astronomer Nicolaus Copernicus. It's where he wrote his ground-breaking *On the Revolutions of the Celestial Spheres,* which established the theory that the earth travelled around the sun. Beyond the memory of its famous resident, it's a charming, sleepy settlement that was founded on the shore of the Vistula Lagoon in the 13th century. It was later the site of a fortified ecclesiastical township, erected on Cathedral Hill.

The hill is now occupied by the extensive **Nicolaus Copernicus Museum** (www.frombork.art.pl; ul Katedralna 8; ☺9am-5.30pm), with several sections requiring separate tickets. The 14th-century **cathedral** (adult/concession 6/3zł; ☺9.30am-4.30pm) contains the tomb of Copernicus himself. The main exhibition area is within the **Bishops' Palace** (adult/concession 6/3zł; ☺9am-4.30pm Tue-Sun), while the **belfry** (adult/concession 6/3zł; ☺9.30am-5pm) is home to an example of Foucault's pendulum. A short distance from the main museum, the **Hospital of the Holy Ghost** (adult/concession 6/3zł; ☺9.30am-5pm Tue-Sat) exhibits historical medical instruments and manuscripts.

Hotel Kopernik (☑55 243 7285; www.hotel-kopernik.com.pl; ul Kościelna 2; s/d 150/220zł) is a comfortable modern hotel a short walk to the east of the museum bus stop. A budget option is **Camping Frombork** (☑506 803 151; www.campingfrombork.pl; ul Braniewska 14; per person/tent 10/5zł, d 50-140zł; ☺May-Sep), at the eastern end of town on the Braniewo road. It has basic cabins and a snack bar on the grounds.

The bus station is on the riverfront about 300m northwest of the museum. Frombork can be directly reached by bus from Elbląg (7zł, 45 minutes, at least hourly) and Gdańsk (18zł, 2¼ hours, three daily). The best place to get on and off is the bus stop directly below the museum on ul Kopernika.

Olsztyn

POP 175,000

Olsztyn (*ol-shtin*) is a pleasant, relaxed city whose rebuilt Old Town is home to cobblestone streets, art galleries, cafes, bars and restaurants. As a busy transport hub, it's also the logical base from which to explore the region, including the Great Masurian Lakes district.

It's also another city on the Copernicus trail, as the great astronomer once served as administrator of Warmia, commanding Olsztyn Castle from 1516 to 1520. From 1466 to 1772 the town belonged to the kingdom of Poland. With the first partition of the nation, Olsztyn became Prussian then German Allenstein, until it returned to Polish hands in 1945.

◉ Sights

Old Town   HISTORIC DISTRICT
Olsztyn's attractive historic centre was rebuilt after WWII destruction and centres on the **Rynek** (Market Sq). One of the Old Town's most striking features is the **High Gate** (ul Staromiejska, Old Town), a surviving fragment of the 14th-century city walls.

Museum of Warmia & Masuria   MUSEUM
(ul Zamkowa 2; adult/concession 9/7zł; ☺10am-4pm Tue-Sun) West of the main square, the 14th-century **Castle of the Chapter of Warmia** contains this historical museum. Its exhibits feature Copernicus, who made some astronomical observations here in the early 16th century, along with collections of coins, art and armour.

Cathedral of St James the Elder   CHURCH
(ul Długosza) This red-brick Gothic cathedral in the eastern Old Town dates from the

14th century and its 60m tower was added in 1596. The interior is an appealing blend of old and new decoration, including the bronze main doors that depict Pope John Paul II's visit in 1991.

🛏 Sleeping

TOP CHOICE Hotel Dyplomat
HOTEL €€
(☏89 512 4141; www.hoteldyplomat.com; ul Dąbrowszczaków 28; s/d from 199/390zł; ❄☎) Impressive new four-star hotel located midway between the train station and the Old Town. Its rooms are decked out with quality fittings and there's an excellent restaurant on the premises. Check the website for discounts.

Polsko-Niemieckie Centrum Młodzieży
HOTEL €€
(☏89 534 0780; www.pncm.olsztyn.pl; ul Okopowa 25; s/d from 175/240zł; ☎) This place devoted to Polish-German friendship is situated next to the castle. The rooms (some with views of the castle) are plain, but have gleaming bathrooms. There's a good sunlit restaurant off the foyer.

Hotel Wysoka Brama
HOTEL €
(☏89 527 3675; www.hotelwysokabrama.olsztyn.pl; ul Staromiejska 1; s/d from 100/120zł; ☎) Offers cheap but basic rooms in a very central location next to the Old Town's High Gate.

🍴 Eating & Drinking

TOP CHOICE Chilli
INTERNATIONAL €€
(ul Kołłątaja 1; mains 18-54zł; ☉9am-late; ☎) By day, this cool cafe-bar serves an international menu amid monochrome images of 20th-century America, to a background of chilled music. After dark it morphs into a smooth club with a lengthy cocktail menu.

Restauracja Staromiejska
POLISH €€
(ul Stare Miasto 4/6; mains 20-39zł; ☉10am-10pm) In classy premises on the Rynek, this restaurant serves quality Polish standards at reasonable prices. There's a range of *pierogi* (dumplings) and *naleśniki* (crepes) on the menu.

Bar Dziupla
POLISH €
(Rynek 9/10; mains 5-27zł; ☉8.30am-8.30pm) This small place is renowned among locals for its tasty Polish food, such as *pierogi*. It also does a good line in soups.

ℹ Information

The **tourist office** (☏89 535 3565; www.olsztyn.eu; ul Staromiejska 1; ☉8am-6pm Mon-Fri, 10am-3pm Sat & Sun May-Sep, 8am-4pm Mon-Fri Oct-Apr) is next to the High Gate in the Old Town and can help with finding accommodation. For snail mail, go to the **main post office** (ul Pieniężnego 21; ☉8am-8pm Mon-Fri, to 4pm Sat); for cybermail, visit the **library** (ul Stare

POLAND OLSZTYN

TRANSPORT FROM OLSZTYN

Bus

DESTINATIONT	PRICE (ZŁ)	DURATION (HR)	FREQUENCY
Białystok	46	5	6 daily
Lublin	61	8¾	1 daily
Warsaw	30	4	At least hourly

Train

DESTINATION	PRICE (ZŁ)	DURATION	FREQUENCY
Białystok	52	4½hr	2 daily
Elbląg	19	1¾hr	11 daily
Gdańsk & Gdynia	40	3hr	6 daily
Giżycko	21	2hr	5 daily
Kętrzyn	18	1½hr	5 daily
Malbork	36	2hr	6 daily
Ostróda	10	40min	hourly
Toruń	34	2¼hr	8 daily
Warsaw	48	4¾hr	3 daily

Miasto 33; internet free; ⊗9am-7pm Mon-Fri, to 2pm Sat) in the centre of the Rynek.

ℹ Getting There & Away

BUS Useful buses travel to destinations around Poland from the **bus station** (ul Partyzantów), attached to the train station building.

TRAIN Trains depart from **Olsztyn Główny train station** (ul Partyzantów). Note that a smaller train station, **Olsztyn Zachodni** (ul Konopnickiej), is located nearer to the Old Town, about 300m west of the castle along ul Nowowiejskiego and ul Konopnickiej; but you're unlikely to find services such as taxis here.

Great Masurian Lakes

This region east of Olsztyn has more than 2000 lakes, which are remnants of long-vanished glaciers, surrounded by green hilly landscape. The largest lake is Lake Śniardwy (110 sq km). About 200km of canals connect these bodies of water, so the area is a prime destination for yachties and canoeists, as well as those who love to hike, fish and mountain bike. There are also regular excursion boats along the lakes from May to September.

Two towns that make good bases for exploring this lake country are **Giżycko** and **Mikołajki**. Both the Giżycko **tourist office** (☑87 428 5265; www.gizycko.turystyka.pl; ul Wyzwolenia 2; ⊗9am-5pm Mon-Fri & 10am-2pm Sat May-Sep, 9am-5pm Mon-Fri Oct-Apr) and the Mikołajki **tourist office** (☑87 421 6850; www.mikolajki.pl; Plac Wolności 3; ⊗10am-6pm Jun-Aug, 10am-6pm Mon-Sat May & Sep) supply useful maps for sailing and hiking, provide excursion boat schedules and assist with finding accommodation.

Nature aside, there are some interesting fragments of history in this region. The village of **Święta Lipka** boasts a superb 17th-century **baroque church** (www.swlipka.org.pl; admission free; ⊗8am-6pm except during Mass), noted for its lavishly decorated organ which features dancing angels. This mechanism is demonstrated several times daily.

A grimmer reminder of the past is the **Wolf's Lair** (Wilczy Szaniec; www.wolfsschanze.pl; adult/concession 15/10zł; ⊗8am-dusk) and its museum. Located at **Gierłoż**, 8km east of Kętrzyn, this ruined complex was Hitler's wartime headquarters for his invasion of the Soviet Union. In 1944 a group of high-ranking German officers led by Claus von Stauffenberg tried to assassinate the Nazi leader here via a bomb concealed in a briefcase. Though the explosion killed and wounded several people,

Hitler suffered only minor injuries. Von Stauffenberg and some 5000 people allegedly involved in the plot were subsequently executed. These dramatic events were reprised in the 2008 Tom Cruise movie *Valkyrie*.

On 24 January 1945, as the Red Army approached, the Germans blew up Wolfsschanze (as it was known in German) and most bunkers were at least partly destroyed. However, huge concrete slabs – some 8.5m thick – and twisted metal remain. It's a fascinating if eerie place to visit.

Święta Lipka and the Wolf's Lair are both most easily accessed from **Kętrzyn**; contact the **tourist office** (☑89 751 4765; www.it.ketrzyn.pl; Plac Piłsudskiego 10; ⊗9am-6pm Mon-Fri, 10am-3pm Sat & Sun) there for transport details, or consult Lonely Planet's *Poland* country guide.

From Olsztyn, there are trains to Kętrzyn (18zł, 1½ hours, five daily) that continue to Giżycko (21zł, two hours, five daily). You can also catch trains from Gdańsk directly to Kętrzyn (52zł, 4¾ hours, two daily) and Giżycko (56zł, five hours, five daily).

From Olsztyn, buses head to Kętrzyn (19zł, two hours, hourly), Giżycko (21zł, 2¼ hours, nine daily) and Mikołajki (22zł, two hours, two daily). Buses also run between Giżycko and Mikołajki (17zł, 50 minutes, four daily).

UNDERSTAND POLAND

History
Early History

Poland's history started with the Polanians (People of the Plains). During the early Middle Ages, these Western Slavs moved into the flatlands between the Vistula and Odra Rivers. Mieszko I, Duke of the Polanians, adopted Christianity in 966 and embarked on a campaign of conquest. A papal edict in 1025 led to Mieszko's son Bolesław Chrobry (Boleslaus the Brave) being crowned Poland's first king.

Poland's early success proved fragile and encroachment from Germanic peoples led to the relocation of the royal capital from Poznań to Kraków in 1038. More trouble loomed in 1226 when the Prince of Mazovia invited the Teutonic Knights to help convert the pagan tribes of the north. These Germanic crusaders used the opportunity to create their own state along the Baltic coast. The south had its own invaders to contend with and Kraków was attacked by Tatars twice in the mid-13th century.

The kingdom prospered under Kazimierz III 'the Great' (1333–70). During this period, many new towns sprang up, while Kraków blossomed into one of Europe's leading cultural centres.

When the daughter of Kazimierz's nephew, Jadwiga, married the Grand Duke of Lithuania, Jagiełło, in 1386, Poland and Lithuania were united as the largest state in Europe, eventually stretching from the Baltic to the Black Sea.

The Renaissance was introduced to Poland by the enlightened King Zygmunt during the 16th century, as he lavishly patronised the arts and sciences. By asserting that the earth travelled around the sun, Nicolaus Copernicus revolutionised the field of astronomy in 1543.

Invasion & Partition

The 17th and 18th centuries produced disaster and decline for Poland. First it was subject to Swedish and Russian invasions, and eventually it faced partition by surrounding empires. In 1773 Russia, Prussia and Austria seized Polish territory in the First Partition; by the time the Third Partition was completed in 1795, Poland had vanished from the map of Europe.

Although the country remained divided through the entire 19th century, Poles steadfastly maintained their culture. Finally, upon the end of WWI, the old imperial powers dissolved and a sovereign Polish state was restored.

Very soon, however, Poland was immersed in the Polish-Soviet War (1919–21). Under the command of Marshal Józef Piłsudski, Poland had to defend its newly gained eastern borders from long-time enemy Russia, now transformed into the Soviet Union and determined to spread its revolution westward. After two years of impressive fighting by the outnumbered Poles, an armistice was signed, retaining Vilnius and Lviv within Poland.

WWII & Communist Rule

Though Polish institutions and national identity flourished during the interwar period, disaster soon struck again. On 1 September 1939, a Nazi German blitzkrieg rained down from the west; soon after, the Soviets invaded Poland from the east, dividing the country with Germany. This agreement didn't last long, as Hitler soon transformed Poland into a staging ground for the Nazi invasion of the Soviet Union. Six million Polish inhabitants died during WWII (including the country's three million Jews), brutally annihilated in death camps.

At the war's end, Poland's borders were redrawn yet again. The Soviet Union kept the eastern territories and extended the country's western boundary at the expense of Germany. These border changes were accompanied by the forced resettlement of more than a million Poles, Germans and Ukrainians.

Peacetime brought more repression. After WWII, Poland endured four decades of Soviet-dominated communist rule, punctuated by waves of protests, most notably the paralysing strikes of 1980–81, led by the Solidarity trade union. Finally, in the open elections of 1989, the communists fell from power and in 1990 Solidarity leader Lech Wałęsa became Poland's first democratically elected president.

Looking West

The postcommunist transition brought radical changes, which induced new social hardships and political crises. But within a decade Poland had built the foundations for a market economy and reoriented its foreign relations towards the West. In March 1999, Poland was granted full NATO membership and it joined the EU in May 2004.

A period of Eurosceptic policies put forward by the Law and Justice party's government, eccentrically headed by the twin Kaczyński brothers as president (Lech) and prime minister (Jarosław), came to an end after parliamentary elections in 2007. The new centrist government of prime minister Donald Tusk's Civic Platform set a pro-business, pro-EU course.

Shockingly, President Kaczyński and numerous senior military and government officials were killed in an air crash in April 2010, during an attempted landing at Smolensk, Russia. They had been en route to a commemoration of the Soviet massacre of Polish officers in the nearby Katyń forest in 1940. In the resulting election, Tusk's party ally Bronisław Komorowski was elected as president.

The 2011 parliamentary elections were relatively uneventful, confirming Civic Platform's hold on power. However, one remarkable element was the emergence of a strongly pro-secular party, Palikot's Movement, which came from nowhere to gain 10% of the vote. Among its elected representatives were Poland's first transsexual member of parliament and its first openly gay MP. Two Poles of black African descent were also elected as Civic Platform MPs, a reflection of the gradually changing nature of Polish society in the postcommunist era.

People

For centuries Poland was a multicultural country, home to Jewish, German and Ukrainian communities. Its Jewish population was particularly large and once numbered more than three million. However, after Nazi German genocide and the forced resettlements that followed WWII, the Jewish population declined to 10,000 and Poland became an ethnically homogeneous country, with some 98% of the population being ethnic Poles.

More than 60% of the citizens live in towns and cities. Warsaw is by far the largest urban settlement, followed by Kraków, Łódź, Wrocław, Poznań and Gdańsk. Upper Silesia (around Katowice) is the most densely inhabited area, while the northeastern border regions remain the least populated.

Between five and 10 million Poles live outside Poland. This émigré community, known as 'Polonia', is located mainly in the USA (particularly Chicago).

Poles are friendly and polite, but not overly formal. The way of life in large urban centres increasingly resembles Western styles and manners. However, Poles' sense of personal space may be a bit cosier than you are accustomed to – you may notice this trait when queuing for tickets or manoeuvring along city streets.

In the countryside, a more conservative culture dominates, evidenced by traditional gender roles and strong family ties. Both here and in urban settings, many Poles are devoutly religious. Roman Catholicism is the dominant Christian denomination, adhered to by more than 80% of Poles. The Orthodox church's followers constitute about 1% of the population, mostly living along a narrow strip on the eastern frontier.

The election of Karol Wojtyła, the archbishop of Kraków, as Pope John Paul II in 1978, and his triumphal visit to his homeland a year later, significantly enhanced the status of the church in Poland. The overthrow of communism was as much a victory for the Church as it was for democracy. The fine line between the Church and the state is often blurred in Poland and the Church is a powerful lobby on social issues.

Still, some Poles have grown wary of the Church's influence in society and politics, resulting in the success of outspokenly pro-secular candidates in recent parliamentary elections. However, Poland remains one of Europe's most religious countries and packed-out churches are not uncommon.

Arts
Literature

Poland has inherited a rich literary tradition dating from the 15th century, though its modern voice was shaped in the 19th century during the long period of foreign occupation. It was a time for nationalist writers such as the poet Adam Mickiewicz (1798–1855) and Henryk Sienkiewicz (1846–1916), who won a Nobel Prize in 1905 for *Quo Vadis?* This nationalist tradition was revived in the communist era when Czesław Miłosz was awarded a Nobel Prize in 1980 for *The Captive Mind*.

BOOKS

» *God's Playground: A History of Poland,* by Norman Davies. Offers an in-depth analysis of Polish history.

» *The Heart of Europe: A Short History of Poland* A condensed version of the above, also by Davies – has greater emphasis on the 20th century.

» *The Polish Way: A Thousand-Year History of the Poles and their Culture* by Adam Zamoyski. A superb cultural overview.

» *Rising '44* by Norman Davies. Vividly brings to life the wartime Warsaw Rising.

» *The Polish Revolution: Solidarity 1980–82* by Timothy Garton Ash. Entertaining and thorough.

» *Jews in Poland* by Iwo Cyprian Pogonowski. Provides a comprehensive record of half a millennium of Jewish life.

» Evocative works about rural life in interwar Poland include Bruno Schultz's *Street of Crocodiles* and Philip Marsden's *The Bronski House*.

At the turn of the 20th century, the avant-garde 'Young Poland' movement in art and literature developed in Kraków. The most notable representatives of this movement were writer Stanisław Wyspiański (1869–1907), also famous for his stained-glass work; playwright Stanisław Ignacy Witkiewicz (1885–1939), commonly known as Witkacy; and Nobel laureate Władysław Reymont (1867–1925). In 1996 Wisława Szymborska (b 1923) also received a Nobel Prize for her poetry.

Music

The most famous Polish musician was undoubtedly Frédéric Chopin (1810–49), whose music displays the melancholy and nostalgia that became hallmarks of the national style. Stanisław Moniuszko (1819–72) injected a Polish flavour into 19th-century Italian opera music by introducing folk songs and dances to the stage. His *Halka* (1858), about a peasant girl abandoned by a young noble, is a staple of the national opera houses.

Popular Polish musicians you might catch live in concert include the controversial Doda (pop singer); Andrzej Smolik (instrumentalist); Łzy (pop-rock band); Sofa (hip-hop/soul band); and Justyna Steczkowska (pop singer). Poland's equivalent of the Rolling Stones is Lady Pank, a rock band formed in 1982 and still going strong.

Visual Arts

Poland's most renowned painter was Jan Matejko (1838–93), whose monumental historical paintings hang in galleries throughout the country. Wojciech Kossak (1857–1942) is another artist who documented Polish history; he is best remembered for the colossal painting Panorama of Racławice (p641), on display in Wrocław.

A long-standing Polish craft is the fashioning of jewellery from amber. Amber is a fossil resin of vegetable origin that comes primarily from the Baltic region and appears in a variety of colours from pale yellow to reddish brown. The best places to buy it are Gdańsk, Kraków and Warsaw.

Polish poster art has received international recognition; the best selection of poster galleries is in Warsaw and Kraków.

Cinema

Poland has produced several world-famous film directors. The most notable is Andrzej Wajda, who received an Honorary Award at the 1999 Academy Awards. *Katyń*, his moving story of the Katyń massacre in WWII, was nominated for Best Foreign Language Film at the 2008 Oscars.

Western audiences are more familiar with the work of Roman Polański, who directed critically acclaimed films such as *Rosemary's Baby* and *Chinatown*. In 2002 Polański released the incredibly moving film *The Pianist*, which was filmed in Poland and set in the Warsaw Ghetto of WWII. The film went on to win three Oscars and the Cannes Palme d'Or.

The late Krzysztof Kieślowski is best known for the *Three Colours* trilogy. The centre of Poland's movie industry, and home to its prestigious National Film School, is Łódź.

Environment

Geography

Poland covers an area of 312,685 sq km – approximately as large as the UK and Ireland put together – and is bordered by seven nations and one sea.

The northern edge of Poland meets the Baltic Sea. This broad, 524km-long coastline is spotted with sand dunes and seaside lakes. Also concentrated in the northeast are many postglacial lakes – more than any country in Europe, except Finland.

The southern border is defined by the mountain ranges of the Sudetes and Carpathians. Poland's highest mountains are the rocky Tatras, a section of the Carpathian Range it shares with Slovakia. The highest peak of the Polish Tatras is Mt Rysy (2499m).

The area in between is a vast plain, sectioned by wide north-flowing rivers. Poland's longest river is the Vistula (Wisła), which winds 1047km from the Tatras to the Baltic.

About a quarter of Poland is covered by forest. Some 60% of the forests are pine trees, but the share of deciduous species, such as oak, beech and birch, is increasing.

National Parks & Animals

Poland's fauna includes hare, red deer, wild boar and, less abundantly, elk, brown bear and wildcat. European bison, which once inhabited Europe in large numbers, were brought to the brink of extinction early in the 20th century and a few hundred now live in Białowieża National Park. The Great Masurian Lakes district attracts a vast array of bird life, such as storks and cormorants. The eagle, though rarely seen today, is Poland's national bird and appears on the Polish emblem.

Poland has 23 national parks, but they cover less than 1% of the country. No permit is necessary to visit these parks, but most have small admission fees. Camping in the parks is sometimes allowed, but only at specified sites. Poland also has a network of less strictly preserved areas called 'landscape parks', scattered throughout the country.

Food & Drink
Staples & Specialities

Various cultures have influenced Polish cuisine, including Jewish, Ukrainian, Russian, Hungarian and German. Polish food is hearty and filling, abundant in potatoes and dumplings, and rich in meat.

Poland's most famous dishes are *bigos* (sauerkraut with a variety of meats), *pierogi* (ravioli-like dumplings stuffed with cottage cheese, minced meat, or cabbage and wild mushrooms) and *barszcz* (red beetroot soup, better known by the Russian word *borsch*).

Hearty soups such as *żurek* (sour soup with sausage and hard-boiled eggs) are a highlight of Polish cuisine. Main dishes are made with pork, including *golonka* (boiled pig's knuckle served with horseradish) and *schab pieczony* (roast loin of pork seasoned with prunes and herbs). *Gołąbki* (cabbage leaves stuffed with mince and rice) is a tasty alternative. *Placki ziemniaczane* (potato pancakes) and *naleśniki* (crepes) are also popular dishes.

Poles claim the national drink, *wódka* (vodka), was invented in their country. It's usually drunk neat and comes in a number of flavours, including *myśliwska* (flavoured with juniper berries), *wiśniówka* (with cherries) and *jarzębiak* (with rowanberries). The most famous variety is *żubrówka* (bison vodka), flavoured with grass from the Białowieża Forest. Other notable spirits include *krupnik* (honey liqueur), *śliwowica* (plum brandy) and *goldwasser* (sweet liqueur containing flakes of gold leaf).

Poles also appreciate the taste of *zimne piwo* (cold beer); the top brands, found everywhere, include Żywiec, Tyskie, Lech and Okocim, while regional brands are available in every city.

Where to Eat & Drink

The cheapest place to eat Polish food is a *bar mleczny* (milk bar), a survivor from the communist era. These no-frills, self-service cafeterias are popular with budget-conscious locals and backpackers alike, though they have been disappearing at an alarming rate since government subsidies were withdrawn. Up the scale, the number and variety of *restauracja* (restaurants) has ballooned in recent years, especially in the big cities. Pizzerias have also become phenomenally popular with Poles. And though Polish cuisine features plenty of meat, there are vegetarian restaurants to be found in most cities.

Menus usually have several sections: *zupy* (soups), *dania drugie* (main courses) and *dodatki* (accompaniments). The price of the main course may not include a side dish – such as potatoes and salads – which you choose (and pay extra for) from the *dodatki* section. Also note that the price for some dishes (particularly fish and poultry) may be listed per 100g, so the price will depend on the total weight of the fish or meat.

Poles start their day with *śniadanie* (breakfast); the most important and substantial meal of the day, *obiad*, is normally eaten between 2pm and 5pm. The third meal is *kolacja* (supper). Most restaurants, cafes and cafe-bars are open from 11am to 11pm. It's rare for Polish restaurants to serve breakfast, though milk bars and snack bars are open from early morning.

After much delay, in late 2010 smoking was banned in shared areas of bars and restaurants, though these establishments are allowed to set up separate smoking areas. Don't be surprised, however, if the smoking section in some places is actually bigger than the so-called main bar!

SURVIVAL GUIDE

Directory A–Z
Accommodation

In Poland, budget accommodation spans camping grounds, dorms and doubles; at midrange and top-end, our price breakdown is based on a double room. Unless otherwise noted, rooms have private bathrooms and the rate includes breakfast.

€ less than 150zł/€35

€€ 150zł/€35 to 400zł/€95

€€€ more than 400zł/€95

CAMPING

Poland has hundreds of camping grounds and many offer good-value cabins and bungalows. Most open May to September, but some only open their gates between June and August. A handy campsite resource is the website of the **Polish Federation of Camping and Caravanning** (☏22 810 6050; www.pfcc.eu).

HOSTELS

Schroniska młodzieżowe (youth hostels) in Poland are operated by the **Polish Youth Hostel Association** (Polskie Towarzystwo Schronisk Młodzieżowych; ☏22 849 8128; www.ptsm.org.pl), a member of Hostelling International. Most only open in July and August, and are often very busy with Polish students; the year-round hostels have more facilities. These youth hostels are open to all, with no age limit. Curfews are common and many hostels close between 10am and 5pm.

A large number of privately operated hostels operate in the main cities, geared towards international backpackers. They're open 24 hours and offer more modern facilities than the old youth hostels, though prices are higher. These hostels usually offer the use of washing machines (either free or paid), in response to the near-absence of laundromats in Poland.

A dorm bed can cost anything from 40zł to 80zł per person per night. Single and double rooms, if available, start at about 150zł a night.

HOTELS

Hotel prices often vary according to season, especially along the Baltic coast, and discounted weekend rates are common.

If possible, check the room before accepting. Don't be fooled by hotel reception areas, which may look great in contrast to the rest of the establishment. On the other hand, dreary scuffed corridors can sometimes open into clean, pleasant rooms.

Accommodation (sometimes with substantial discounts) can be reliably arranged via the internet through www.poland4u.com and www.hotelspoland.com.

MOUNTAIN REFUGES

PTTK (Polskie Towarzystwo Turystyczno-Krajoznawcze; ☏22 826 2251; www.pttk.pl) runs a chain of *schroniska górskie* (mountain refuges) for hikers. They're usually simple, with a welcoming atmosphere and serve cheap, hot meals. The more isolated refuges are obliged to accept everyone, so can be crowded in the high season. Refuges are normally open all year, but confirm with the nearest PTTK office before setting off.

PRIVATE ROOMS & APARTMENTS

Some destinations have agencies (usually called *biuro zakwaterowania* or *biuro kwater prywatnych*) that arrange accommodation in private homes. Rooms cost about 120/150zł per single/double. The most important factor to consider is location; if the home is in the suburbs, find out how far it is from reliable public transport.

During the high season, home owners also directly approach tourists. Also, private homes in smaller resorts and villages often have signs outside their gates or doors offering a *pokoje* (room) or *noclegi* (lodging).

In big cities such as Warsaw, Kraków, Wrocław and Gdańsk, some agencies offer self-contained apartments, which are an affordable alternative to hotels and allow for the washing of laundry.

Activities

CYCLING

As Poland is fairly flat, it's ideal for cyclists. Bicycle routes along the banks of the Vistula River are popular in Warsaw, Toruń and Kraków. Many of the national parks – including Tatra (near Zakopane) and Słowiński (near Łeba) – offer bicycle trails, as does the Great Masurian Lakes district. For more of a challenge, try cycling in the Bieszczady ranges around Sanok. Bikes can be rented at most resort towns and larger cities.

HIKING

Hikers can enjoy marked trails across the Tatra Mountains, where one of the most popular climbs is up the steep slopes of Mt Glewont (1894m). The Sudeten Mountains and the Great Masurian Lakes district also offer good walking opportunities. National parks worth hiking through include Białowieża National Park, Kampinos National Park just outside Warsaw, and Wielkopolska National Park outside Poznań. Trails are easy to follow and detailed maps are available at larger bookshops.

SKIING

Zakopane will delight skiers from December to March and facilities are cheaper than the ski resorts of Western Europe. Other sports on offer here include hang-gliding and paragliding. Another place to hit the snow is Szklarska Poręba in Silesia.

WATER SPORTS

Throngs of yachties, canoeists and kayakers enjoy the network of waterways in the Great

Masurian Lakes district every summer; boats are available for rent from lakeside towns and there are even diving excursions. Windsurfers can head to the beaches of the Hel peninsula.

Business Hours

Banks 8am to 5pm Monday to Friday, sometimes 8am to 2pm Saturday

Cafes & restaurants 11am to 11pm

Shops 10am to 6pm Monday to Friday, 10am to 2pm Saturday

Nightclubs 9pm to late

Embassies & Consulates

All diplomatic missions listed are located in Warsaw unless stated otherwise.

Australian Embassy (22 521 3444; www.australia.pl; ul Nowogrodzka 11)

Belarusian Embassy (22 742 0990; www.poland.mfa.gov.by; ul Wiertnicza 58)

Canadian Embassy (22 584 3100; www.canada.pl; ul Matejki 1/5)

French Embassy (22 529 3000; www.ambafrance-pl.org; ul Piękna 1)

French Consulate (12 424 5300; www.cracovie.org.pl; ul Stolarska 15, Kraków)

German Embassy (22 584 1700; www.warschau.diplo.de; ul Jazdów 12)

German Consulate (12 424 3000; www.krakau.diplo.de; ul Stolarska 7, Kraków)

Irish Embassy (22 849 6633; www.irlandia.pl; ul Mysia 5)

Netherlands Embassy (22 559 1200; www.nlembassy.pl; ul Kawalerii 10)

New Zealand Embassy (22 521 0500; www.nzembassy.com/poland; Al Ujazdowskie 51)

Russian Embassy (22 849 5111; http://warsaw.rusembassy.org; ul Belwederska 49)

South African Embassy (22 622 1031; warsaw.consular@dirco.gov.za; ul Koszykowa 54)

Ukrainian Embassy (22 622 4797; www.ukraine-emb.pl; Al Szucha 7)

UK Embassy (22 311 0000; www.ukinpoland.fco.gov.uk; ul Kawalerii 12)

UK Consulate (12 421 7030; ukconsul@sunley.pl; ul Św Anny 9, Kraków)

US Embassy (22 504 2000; http://poland.usembassy.gov; Al Ujazdowskie 29/31)

US Consulate (12 424 5100; http://krakow.usconsulate.gov; ul Stolarska 9, Kraków)

Food

Price ranges are based on the average cost of a main meal.

€ less than 20zł

€€ 20zł to 40zł

€€€ more than 40zł

Gay & Lesbian Travellers

Since the change of government in 2007, overt homophobia from state officials has declined; though with the Church remaining influential in social matters, gay acceptance in Poland is still a work in progress. The gay community is becoming more visible, however, and in 2010 Warsaw hosted **EuroPride** (www.europride.com), which was the first time this major event had been held in a former communist country. In late 2011 LGBT activist Robert Biedroń was elected as a member of the Polish parliament, its first openly gay representative.

In general though, the Polish gay and lesbian scene remains fairly discreet. Warsaw and Kraków are the best places to find gay-friendly bars, clubs and accommodation. The free tourist brochure, *The Visitor,* lists a few gay night spots, as do the **In Your Pocket** (www.inyourpocket.com) guides.

Another good source of information on gay Warsaw and Kraków is online at www.gayguide.net.

Internet Access

Internet access is near universal in Polish accommodation: either as wireless, via on-site computers, or both.

In the unlikely event that your lodgings are offline, you'll likely find an internet cafe nearby; expect to pay between 4zł and 5zł per hour. Also, some forward-thinking city councils have set up wireless access in their main market squares.

Media

The *Warsaw Business Journal* is aimed at the business community, while *Warsaw Insider* has more general-interest features, listings and reviews. *Warsaw Voice* is a weekly English-language news magazine with a business slant.

The free *Welcome to...* series of magazines covers Poznań, Kraków, Toruń, Zakopane and Warsaw monthly.

Recent newspapers and magazines from Western Europe and the USA are readily available at EMPiK bookshops and at news-stands in the foyers of upmarket hotels.

Poland has a mix of privately owned TV channels and state-owned nationwide channels. Foreign-language programs are painfully dubbed with one male voice covering all actors (that's men, women and children) and no lip-sync, so you can still hear the original language underneath. Most hotels offer English-language news channels.

Money

Poland is obliged by the terms of its accession to the EU to adopt the euro as its currency at some point in the future; but it's not likely to happen until at least 2016. In the meantime, the nation's currency is the złoty (*zwo*-ti), abbreviated to zł (international currency code PLN). It's divided into 100 groszy (gr). Denominations of notes are 10, 20, 50, 100 and 200 (rare) złoty; coins come in one, two, five, 10, 20 and 50 groszy and one, two and five złoty.

Bankomats (ATMs) accept most international credit cards and are easily found in the centre of all cities and most towns. Banks without an ATM may provide cash advances over the counter on credit cards.

Private *kantors* (foreign-exchange offices) are everywhere. They require no paperwork and charge no commission, though rates at *kantors* near tourist-friendly attractions or facilities can be poor.

Travellers cheques are more secure than cash, but *kantors* rarely change them and banks that do will charge a commission. A better option is a stored value cash card, which can be used in the same manner as a credit card; ask your bank about this before leaving home.

Post

Postal services are operated by Poczta Polska; the Poczta Główna (Main Post Office) in each city offers the widest range of services.

The cost of sending a normal-sized letter (up to 20g) or a postcard to other European countries is 2.40zł, rising to 3.20zł for North America and 4.50zł for Australia.

Public Holidays

New Year's Day 1 January

Epiphany 6 January

Easter Sunday March or April

Easter Monday March or April

State Holiday 1 May

Constitution Day 3 May

Pentecost Sunday Seventh Sunday after Easter

Corpus Christi Ninth Thursday after Easter

Assumption Day 15 August

All Saints' Day 1 November

Independence Day 11 November

Christmas 25 and 26 December

Safe Travel

Poland is a relatively safe country and crime has decreased significantly since the immediate postcommunism era. Be alert, however, for thieves and pickpockets around major train stations, such as Warszawa Centralna. Robberies have been a problem on night trains, especially on international routes. Try to share a compartment with other people if possible.

Theft from cars is a widespread problem, so keep your vehicle in a guarded car park whenever possible. Heavy drinking is common and drunks can be disturbing, though rarely dangerous.

As Poland is an ethnically homogeneous nation, travellers of a non-European appearance may attract curious glances from locals in outlying regions. Football (soccer) hooligans are not uncommon, so avoid travelling on public transport with them – especially if their team has lost!

Telephone

Polish telephone numbers have nine digits, with no area codes. To call Poland from abroad, dial the country code ☏48, then the Polish number. The international access code when dialling out of Poland is ☏00. For help, try the operators for local numbers (☏913), national numbers and codes (☏912), and international codes (☏908), but don't expect anyone to speak English.

The main mobile telephone providers are Plus, Orange, T-Mobile and Play, all of which offer prepaid SIM cards that come with call and data allowances. Such prepaid accounts are cheap by Western European standards and are easy to set up at local offices of these companies.

The cheapest way to make international calls from public telephones is via the prepaid international cards produced by various operators, which are available at post offices and kiosks. You can also buy magnetic phone cards from these places in order to make domestic calls.

Travellers with Disabilities

Poland is not set up well for people with disabilities, although there have been significant improvements in recent years. Wheelchair ramps are often only available at upmarket hotels and public transport will be a challenge for anyone with mobility problems. However, many hotels now have at least one room especially designed for disabled access – book ahead for these. There are also some low-floor trams running on bigger cities' public transport networks. Information on disability issues is available from **Integracja** (☎22 530 6570; www.integracja.org).

Visas

EU citizens do not need a visa to visit Poland and can stay indefinitely. Citizens of Australia, Canada, Israel, New Zealand, Switzerland and the USA can stay in Poland for up to 90 days without a visa.

However, since Poland's entry into the Schengen zone in December 2007, the 90-day visa-free entry period has been extended to all the Schengen countries; so if travelling from Poland through Germany and France, for example, you can't exceed 90 days in total. Once your 90 days is up, you must leave the Schengen zone for a minimum 90 days before you can once again enter it visa-free.

South African citizens do require a visa. Other nationals should check with Polish embassies or consulates in their countries for current visa requirements. Updates can be found at the website of the **Ministry of Foreign Affairs** (www.msz.gov.pl).

Websites

Commonwealth of Diverse Cultures (www.commonwealth.pl) Outlines Poland's cultural heritage.

Virtualtourist.com (www.virtualtourist. com) Poland section features postings by travellers.

Getting There & Away

Air

The majority of international flights to Poland arrive at Warsaw's Okęcie airport, while other important airports include Kraków, Gdańsk, Poznań and Wrocław. The national carrier **LOT** (☎801 703 703, 22 19572; www.lot. com) flies to all major European cities.

Other major airlines flying to/from Poland include the following:

Aeroflot (☎22 650 2511; www.aeroflot.com)

Air France (☎22 556 6400; www.airfrance. com)

Alitalia (☎22 556 6866; www.alitalia.it)

British Airways (☎00800 441 1592; www. ba.com)

EasyJet (☎703 103 988; www.easyjet.com)

Eurolot (☎22 574 0740; www.eurolot.com)

KLM (☎22 556 6444; www.klm.pl)

Lufthansa (☎22 338 1300; www.lufthansa.pl)

Ryanair (☎703 303 033; www.ryanair.com)

SAS (☎22 850 0500; www.flysas.com)

Wizz Air (☎703 603 993; www.wizzair.com)

Land

Since Poland is now within the Schengen zone, there are no border posts or border-crossing formalities between Poland and Germany, the Czech Republic, Slovakia and Lithuania. Below is a list of major road border crossings with Poland's non-Schengen neighbours that accept foreigners and are open 24 hours.

Belarus (South to north) Terespol, Kuźnica Białostocka

Russia (West to east) Gronowo, Bezledy

Ukraine (South to north) Medyka, Hrebenne, Dorohusk

If you're going to Russia or Lithuania and your train/bus passes through Belarus, you need a Belarusian transit visa and you must get it in advance.

BUS

International bus services are offered by dozens of Polish and international companies. One of the major operators is **Eurolines Polska** (☎22 621 3469; www.eurolinespolska.pl), which runs buses in all directions.

CAR & MOTORCYCLE

To drive a car into Poland, EU citizens need their driving licence from home, while other nationalities must obtain an International Drivers Permit in their home country. Also required are vehicle registration papers and liability insurance (Green Card).

TRAIN

Trains link Poland with every neighbouring country and beyond, but international train travel is not cheap. To save money on fares, investigate special train tickets and rail passes. Domestic trains in Poland are significantly cheaper, so you'll save money if you buy a ticket to a Polish border destination such as Szczecin or Prezmyśl, then take a local train.

You can search for international train connections and buy tickets from **PKP Intercity** (✆22 391 9757; www.intercity.pl). Another useful resource is the website of **Polrail Service** (www.polrail.com).

Do note that some international trains to/from Poland have been linked with theft. Keep an eye on your bags, particularly on the Prague–Warsaw and Prague–Kraków overnight trains.

Sea

Ferry services sail from Gdańsk (p656)and Gdynia (p657) to ports in Scandinavia. There are also car and passenger ferries from the Polish town of Świnoujście, operated by the following companies.

Polferries (www.polferries.pl) Offers daily services from Świnoujście to Ystad in Sweden (six hours), and to Copenhagen, Denmark (eight hours).

Unity Line (www.unityline.pl) Runs daily ferries between Świnoujście and the Swedish ports of Ystad (seven hours) and Trelleborg (eight hours).

Getting Around

Air

LOT (✆801 703 703, 22 19572; www.lot.com) flies several times a day from Warsaw to Gdańsk, Kraków, Poznań, Wrocław and Szczecin. A LOT subsidiary, **Eurolot** (✆22 574 0740; www.eurolot.com), serves the same airports.

Bicycle

Cycling is not great for getting around cities, but is often a good way to travel between villages. If you get tired, it's possible to place your bike in the luggage compartment at the front or rear of slow passenger trains (these are rarely found on faster services). You'll need a special ticket for your bike from the railway ticket office.

Bus

Buses can be useful on short routes and through the mountains in southern Poland; but usually trains are quicker and more comfortable, and private minibuses are quicker and more direct.

Most buses are operated by the state bus company, PKS. It provides two kinds of service from its bus terminals *(dworzec autobusowy PKS)*: ordinary buses (marked in black on timetables); and fast buses (marked in red), which ignore minor stops.

Timetables are posted on boards and additional symbols next to departure times may indicate the bus runs only on certain days or in certain seasons. You can also check timetables online at www.e-podroznik.pl. Terminals usually have an information desk, but it's rarely staffed with English speakers. Tickets for PKS buses can sometimes be bought at the terminal, but more often from drivers. Note that all bus frequencies quoted in this chapter relate to the summer schedule.

The price of PKS bus tickets is determined by the length, in kilometres, of the trip; a bus fare will usually work out cheaper than a comparable train ticket. Minibuses charge set prices for journeys and these are normally posted in their windows or at the bus stop.

A useful alternative to PKS is the private company **Polski Bus** (www.polskibus.com), which operates modern double-decker buses (with free wi-fi on board) to destinations throughout Poland and beyond including Warsaw, Kraków, Gdańsk, Lublin, Wrocław, Vienna, Prague and Berlin. Fares vary dynamically in the manner of a budget airline and must be purchased in advance via the company's website.

Car & Motorcycle

FUEL & SPARE PARTS
Petrol stations sell several kinds of petrol, including 94-octane leaded, 95-octane unleaded, 98-octane unleaded and diesel. Most petrol stations are open from 6am to 10pm (from 7am to 3pm Sunday), though some operate around the clock. Garages are plentiful. Roadside assistance can be summoned by dialling ✆19637.

HIRE
Major international car-rental companies, such as **Avis** (✆22 650 4872; www.avis.pl), **Hertz** (✆22 500 1620; www.hertz.pl) and **Europcar** (✆22 650 2564; www.europcar.com.pl), are represented in larger cities and have smaller offices at airports. Rates are comparable to full-price rental in Western Europe.

Rental agencies will need to see your passport, your home driving licence (which must have been held for at least one year) and a credit card (for the deposit). You need to be at least 21 years of age to rent a car; sometimes 25 for a more expensive car.

ROAD RULES

The speed limit is 130km/h on motorways, 100km/h on two- or four-lane highways, 90km/h on other open roads and 50km/h in built-up areas. If the background of the sign bearing the town's name is white you must reduce speed to 50km/h; if the background is green there's no need to reduce speed (unless road signs indicate otherwise). Radar-equipped police are very active, especially in villages with white signs.

Unless signs state otherwise, cars may park on pavements as long as a minimum 1.5m-wide walkway is left for pedestrians. Parking in the opposite direction to traffic flow is allowed. The permitted blood alcohol level is a low 0.02%, so it's best not to drink if you're driving. Seat belts are compulsory, as are helmets for motorcyclists. Between October and February, all drivers must use headlights during the day (and night!).

Train

Trains will be your main means of transport. They're cheap, reliable and rarely overcrowded (except for July and August peak times). **Polish State Railways** (PKP; www.pkp.pl) operates trains to almost every tourist destination; its online timetable is very helpful, providing routes, fares and intermediate stations in English. A private company, **Arriva** (www.arriva.pl), also operates local services in the eastern part of Pomerania.

TRAIN TYPES

» **Express InterCity trains** only stop at major cities and are the fastest way to travel by rail. These trains require seat reservations.

» Down the pecking order are the older but cheaper **TLK trains** (pociąg TLK). They're slower and more crowded, but are probably the type of train you'll most often catch. TLK trains also require seat reservations.

» **InterRegio trains** run between adjoining regions of Poland and often operate less frequently at weekends. No reservations are required.

» At the bottom of the hierarchy, slow **Regio trains**, also known as 'passenger trains' (pociąg osobowy) stop by every tree at the side of the track that could be imagined to be a station and are best used only for short trips. Seats can't be reserved.

CLASSES & FARES

Express InterCity and TLK trains carry two classes: *druga klasa* (2nd class) and *pierwsza klasa* (1st class), which is 50% more expensive.

Note that train fares quoted in this chapter are for a 2nd-class ticket on a TLK train, or the most likely alternative if the route is mainly served by a different type of train. Frequencies are as per the summer schedule.

In a couchette on an overnight train, compartments have four/six beds in 1st/2nd class. Sleepers have two/three people (1st/2nd class) in a compartment fitted with a washbasin, sheets and blankets. *Miejsca sypialne* (sleepers) and *kuszetki* (couchettes) can be booked at special counters in larger train stations; prebooking is recommended.

TIMETABLES

Train *odjazdy* (departures) are listed at train stations on a yellow board and *przyjazdy* (arrivals) on a white board. Ordinary trains are marked in black print, fast trains in red. The letter 'R' in a square indicates the train has compulsory seat reservation.

The timetables also show which *peron* (platform) it's using. The number applies to *both* sides of the platform. If in doubt, check the platform departure board or route cards on the side of carriages, or ask someone.

Full timetable and fare information in English can be found on the PKP website.

TICKETING

If a seat reservation is compulsory on your train, you will automatically be sold a *miejscówka* (reserved) seat ticket. If you do not make a seat reservation, you can travel on *any* train (of the type requested) to the destination indicated on your ticket on the date specified.

Your ticket will list the *klasa* (class); the *poc* (type) of train; where the train is travelling *od* (from) and *do* (to); the major town or junction the train is travelling *prez* (through); and the total *cena* (price). If more than one place is listed under the heading *prez* (via), ask the conductor *early* if you have to change trains at the junction listed or be in a specific carriage (the train may separate later).

If you get on a train without a ticket, you can buy one directly from the conductor for a small supplement (7zł) – but do it right away. If the conductor finds you first, you'll be fined for travelling without a ticket. You can always upgrade from 2nd to 1st class for a small extra fee (7zł), plus the additional fare.

Romania

Includes »

Best Places to Eat

- » Caru' cu Bere (p687)
- » Graf (p709)
- » Crama Sibiu Vechi (p701)
- » Chevalet (p728)
- » Bistro de l'Arte (p695)

Best Places to Stay

- » Doors (p686)
- » Hotel Elite (p709)
- » Hostel Costel (p707)
- » Felinarul Hostel (p700)
- » Casa Wagner (p695)

Why Go?

Beautiful and beguiling, Romania's rural landscape remains relatively untouched by the country's urban evolution. It's a land of aesthetically stirring hand-ploughed fields, sheep-instigated traffic jams, and lots and lots of homemade plum brandy. The Carpathian Mountains offer uncrowded hiking and skiing, while Transylvania's Saxon towns are time-warp strolling grounds for Gothic architecture, Austro-Hungarian legacies and, naturally, plenty of Vlad Ţepeş–inspired 'Dracula' shtick. Fish – and the birds that chomp them – thrive in the Danube Delta, bucolic Maramureş has the 'Merry Cemetery', and Unesco-listed painted monasteries dot southern Bucovina. And, for the record, the big cities are a blast too.

When to Go
Bucharest

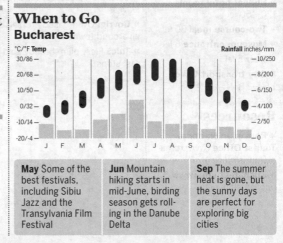

May Some of the best festivals, including Sibiu Jazz and the Transylvania Film Festival

Jun Mountain hiking starts in mid-June, birding season gets rolling in the Danube Delta

Sep The summer heat is gone, but the sunny days are perfect for exploring big cities

AT A GLANCE

» **Currency** Romanian leu

» **Language** Romanian

» **Money** ATMs abundant

» **Visas** Not required for citizens of the EU, USA, Canada, Australia, New Zealand

Fast Facts

» **Area** 237,500 sq km
» **Capital** Bucharest
» **Country code** ☑40
» **Emergency** ☑112

Exchange Rates

Australia	A$1	3.59 lei
Canada	C$1	3.39 lei
Euro Zone	€1	4.41 lei
Japan	¥100	3.66 lei
New Zealand	NZ$1	2.88 lei
UK	UK£1	5.23 lei
USA	US$1	3.44 lei

Set Your Budget

» **Budget hotel room** 120–150 lei
» **Two-course meal** 30 lei
» **Museum entrance** 6 lei
» **Beer** 5 lei
» **City transport ticket** 1.50–3 lei

Resources

» **Romanian National Tourist Office** (www.romaniatourism.com)

» **Bucharest Life** (www.bucharestlife.net)

Connections

The main train corridor to Romania from Western Europe passes through Budapest, and at least one train daily makes the overnight slog from here down to Bucharest, via Braşov, and back. The western city of Timişoara has excellent train, bus and air connections throughout Europe. By road, the main entry points from the west are at Arad and Oradea. There are international border crossings to/from Hungary, Serbia, Bulgaria, Ukraine and Moldova, and four ferry crossings into Bulgaria.

ITINERARIES

One Week

Spend a day viewing the parts of Bucharest that survived the Nicolae Ceauşescu dictatorship, then take a train to Braşov – Transylvania's main event – for castles, activities and beer at streetside cafes. Spend a day in Sighişoara's medieval citadel, then catch a train back to Bucharest or on to Budapest.

Two Weeks

Arrive in Bucharest by plane or Timişoara by train, then head into Transylvania, devoting a day or two each to Braşov, Sighişoara and Sibiu. Tour southern Bucovina's painted monasteries, then continue on to Bucharest.

Essential Food & Drink

» **Mămăligă** Cornmeal mush that's boiled or fried, sometimes topped with sour cream or cheese.

» **Ciorbă** Sour soup that's a mainstay of the Romanian diet and a powerful hangover remedy.

» **Sarmale** Spiced pork wrapped in cabbage or grape leaves.

» **Covrigi** Oven-baked pretzels served warm from windows all around town.

» **Ţuică** Fiery plum brandy sold in water bottles at roadside rest stops.

BUCHAREST

♩021 / POP 2.1 MILLION

Romania's capital gets a bad rap, but in fact it's dynamic, energetic and more than a little bit funky. It's where still-unreconstructed communism meets unbridled capitalism; where the soporific forces of the EU meet the passions of the Balkans and Middle East. Many travellers give the city just a night or two before heading off to Transylvania, but we think that's not enough. Budget at least a few days to take in the good museums, stroll the parks and hang out at trendy cafes.

◉ Sights

Bucharest teems with museums and attractions; all are fairly cheap and many are among the nation's best. The historic thoroughfare Calea Victoriei makes a nice walk, as it connects the two main squares of the city: Piaţa Victoriei in the north, and Piaţa Revoluţiei (Revolution Sq) in the centre. Continue south

Romania Highlights

❶ Ascend castles and mountains (and castles on top of mountains), using **Braşov** (p694) as a base.

❷ Follow the Unesco World Heritage line of painted monasteries in **southern Bucovina** (p718).

❸ Soak in **Sibiu** (p700), a beautifully restored Saxon town.

❹ Explore the medieval citadel of **Sighişoara** (p698), Dracula's birthplace.

❺ Rewind a few centuries in **Maramureş** (p709), Europe's last thriving peasant society.

❻ Row through the tributaries and the riot of nature in the **Danube Delta** (p721).

Bucharest

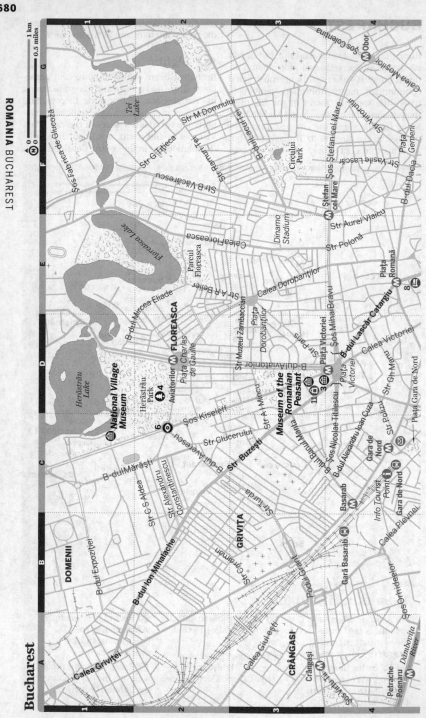

1 km
0.5 miles

Calea Griviței

DOMENII

B-dul Expoziției

B-dul Ion Mihalache

B-dul Mărăști

Str C-S Aldea

Str Alexandru Constantinescu

National Village Museum

Herăstrău Lake

Herăstrău Park

Șos Fabrica de Glucoză

Trei Lake

Floreasca Lake

B-dul Mircea Eliade

FLOREASCA

Aviatorilor

Piața Charles de Gaulle

Șos Kiseleff

Str Clucerului

Parcul Floreasca

Calea Floreasca

Str A R Belier

Str Muzeul Zambaccian

Piața Dorobanților

B-dul Aviatorilor

Calea Dorobanților

Str Paris

Dinamo Stadium

Str G Țițeica

Str B Văcărescu

Str M Domnului

Str Remuri Tei

B-dul Lacul Tei

Circului Park

Șos Colentina

Obor

Calea Moșilor

Piața Gemeni

B-dul Dacia

Str Vasile Lascăr

Str Vasile Lascăr

Șos Ștefan cel Mare

Str Viitorului

Ștefan cel Mare

Str Aurel Vlaicu

Str Polonă

Piața Romană

8

Str Mihai Bravu

B-dul Lascăr Catargiu

Piața Victoriei

Piața Victoriei

Museum of the Romanian Peasant

Str A I Mincu

B-dul Banu Manta

Șos Nicolae Titulescu

Str Nicolae Titulescu

Str Polizu

Str Gh Manu

Calea Victoriei

Piața Gara de Nord

Gara de Nord

Gara de Nord

Info Tourist Point

Calea Plevnei

Calea Plevnei

Basarab

Basarab

Gară Basarab

Str Buzești

Str Turda

Str Grădman

GRIVIȚA

B-dul Avrescu

Str Alexandru Ioan Cuza

Șos Orhideelor

Podul Grant

CRÂNGAȘI

Calea Giulești

Crângași

Petrache Poenaru

Șos Virtuți

Dâmbovița River

11

3

6

4

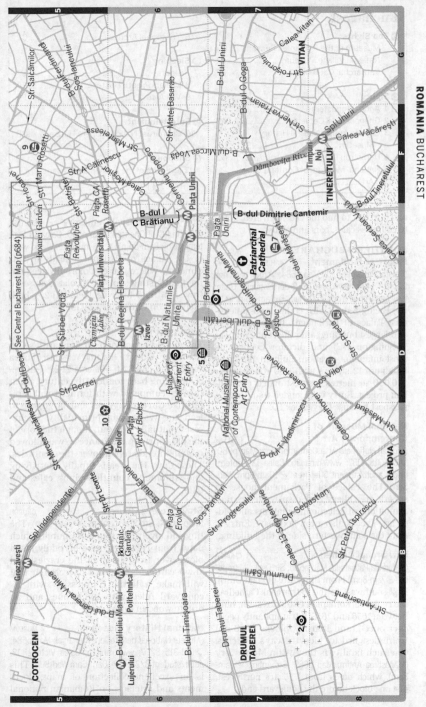

Bucharest

and turn east to find the Old Town area, home to countless cafes, bars and clubs.

SOUTHERN BUCHAREST

Palace of Parliament   HISTORIC BUILDING
(Palatul Parlamentului; Map p684; ✐tour bookings 021-414 1426; www.cdep.ro; B-dul Naţiunile Unite; tour adult/child from 25/13 lei; ⊙10am-4pm; Mizvor) Facing B-dul Unirii is the impossible-to-miss Palace of Parliament, the world's second-largest building (after the Pentagon near Washington DC) and dictator Ceauşescu's most infamous creation. Built in 1984, the building's 12 storeys and 3100 rooms cover 330,000 sq metres – an estimated €3.3 billion project. Entry is by guided tour. Bring a passport because they check ID.

National Museum of Contemporary Art   GALLERY

(Muzeul Naţionale Arta Contemporana; Map p680; ✐021-318 9137; www.mnac.ro; Calea 13 Septembrie 1; adult/student 5 lei/free; ⊙10am-6pm Wed-Sun) The Palace of Parliament houses a superb art gallery that displays temporary exhibitions of eclectic installations and video art. There's also a top-floor cafe. Entry is from the southwestern side of the building.

Patriarchal Cathedral   CHURCH

(Catedrala Patriahală; Map p680; Str Dealul Mitropoliei; ⊙7am-8pm) From the centre of Piaţa Unirii, look southwest to the Patriarchal Cathedral, the centre of Romanian Orthodox faith, built between 1656 and 1658. It triumphantly peeks over once-grand housing blocks on B-dul Unirii designed to 'hide' the city's churches. One such fatality is the **Antim Monastery** (Mânăstirea Antim; Map p680; Str Antim; ⊙7am-8pm), which dates from 1715. It's northwest, just one block before the boulevard ends.

FREE **Ghencea Civil Cemetery**   CEMETERY
(Cimitirul Civil Ghencea; Map p680; Calea 13 Septembrie; ⊙8am-8pm) A 45-minute walk west of the Palace of Parliament leads to this cemetery, where you can morbidly seek out the final resting spots of Nicolae Ceauşescu (row I-35) and his wife Elena (H-25), both executed on Christmas Day 1989.

OLD TOWN

The Old Town is home to Bucharest's **Old Princely Court** (Palatul Voievodal, Curtea Veche; Map p684; Str Franceză 21-23; ⊙10am-5pm) dating back to the 15th century, when the city competed with former royal capitals like Curtea de Argeş and Târgovişte to lead the Wallachian principality. Bucharest eventually won out, though the core of the old court, on Str Franceza, was allowed to fall into disrepair over the centuries. These days, the area is rapidly gentrifying and is home to countless clubs, cafes and bars.

Stavropoleos Church   CHURCH

(Map p684; Str Stavropoleos; ⊙7am-8pm) The tiny and lovely Stavropoleos Church, which dates from 1724, perches a bit oddly just a block over from some of the craziest Old Town carousing, but it's one church that will make a lasting impression with its courtyard filled with tombstones and an ornate wooden interior.

National History Museum   MUSEUM

(Muzeul National de Istorie a Romaniei; Map p684; ✐021-315 8207; www.mnir.ro; Calea Victoriei 12; adult/student 8/2 lei; ⊙10am-6pm Wed-Sun) This is an excellent collection of maps, documents and artefacts on Romanian national history. It's particularly strong on the country's Roman ties, including a replica of the 2nd-century Trajan's Column. Our favourite *piece*, though, is not inside the museum, but rather on the steps outside: a controversial **Statue of Emperor Trajan** (Map p684; Calea Victoriei 12) holding a Dacian wolf.

FREE **Jewish History Museum** MUSEUM
(Muzeul de Istorie al Comunitaţilor Evreieşti din România; Map p684; ✆021-311 0870; Str Mămulari 3; ⊙9am-2pm Mon-Thu, to 1pm Fri & Sun) The Jewish History Museum is housed in a colourful synagogue that dates from 1836 (rebuilt in 1910). Exhibits (in English and Romanian) outline Jewish contributions to Romanian history, which not all Romanians know about. You need your passport to enter.

PIAŢA REVOLUŢIEI

National Art Museum MUSEUM
(Muzeul Naţional de Artă; Map p684; ✆021-313 3030; www.mnar.arts.ro; Calea Victoriei 49-53; admission 15 lei; ⊙11am-7pm Wed-Sun) Housed in the 19th-century Royal Palace, this massive museum – signed in English – has three collections, including ancient and medieval Romanian art, modern Romanian painting, and European art. The ancient collection is strong on icons and religious art, while the Romanian painting section has an excellent survey of 19th-century masters.

Central Committee of the Communist Party Building HISTORIC BUILDING
(Map p684; www.mai.gov.ro; Piaţa Revoluţiei 1; ⊙closed to the public) The scene of Ceauşescu's infamous last speech was on the balcony of the former Central Committee of the Communist Party building on 22 December 1989. Amid cries of 'Down with Ceauşescu!' he escaped (briefly) by helicopter from the roof. Meanwhile, the crowds were riddled with bullets, and many died.

Rebirth Memorial MONUMENT
(Memorialul Renaşterii; Map p684; Calea Victoriei) This striking memorial of a white obelisk piercing a basketlike crown stands on an island in Calea Victoriei. It's meant to mark the dramatic events of 1989, when many people died for their opposition to the Ceauşescu regime. Local wags have dubbed it the 'potato of the revolution' (because of its shape).

FREE **Cişmigiu Garden** PARK
(Map p684) West of Calea Victoriei is the locally loved Cişmigiu Garden, with shady walks, a lake, cafes and a ridiculous number of benches on which to sit and stare at Bucharestians going by.

NORTHERN BUCHAREST

Bucharest's most luxurious villas and parks line the grand avenue Şos Kiseleff, which begins at Piaţa Victoriei. The major landmark here is the **Triumphal Arch** (Arcul de Triumf; Map p680; Piaţa Arcul de Triumf; ⊙occasionally open to the public), which stands halfway up Şos Kiseleff. The 27m arch was built in 1935 to commemorate the reunification of Romania in 1918. Heavy traffic makes it difficult to get close to the arch and the viewing platform is not always open to the public.

TOP **CHOICE** **Grigore Antipa**
Natural History Museum MUSEUM
(Muzeul de Istorie Naturală Grigore Antipa; Map p680; ✆021-312 8826; www.antipa.ro; Şos Kiseleff 1; adult/student/child 20/10/5 lei ; ⊡) One of the few attractions in Bucharest squarely aimed at kids, this natural history museum has been thoroughly renovated and features modern bells and whistles like video displays, games and interactive exhibits. Much of it is signed in English.

FREE THRILLS

Here are a few signature Bucharest activities that won't break the bank:

» Wander the Old Town (p682), admiring the jumble of recently renovated and still-crumbling buildings side by side.

» Take a break in the atmospheric courtyard at Stavropoleos Church (p682), central Bucharest's most serene spot.

» Escape the car-horn refrain of the centre in the exquisite grounds of Herăstrău Park (p686).

» Pay your disrespects to the final resting places of Nicolae and Elena Ceauşescu at Ghencea Civil Cemetery (p682).

» Enjoy a heat retreat in the heroically tended Cişmigiu Garden (p683).

Central Bucharest

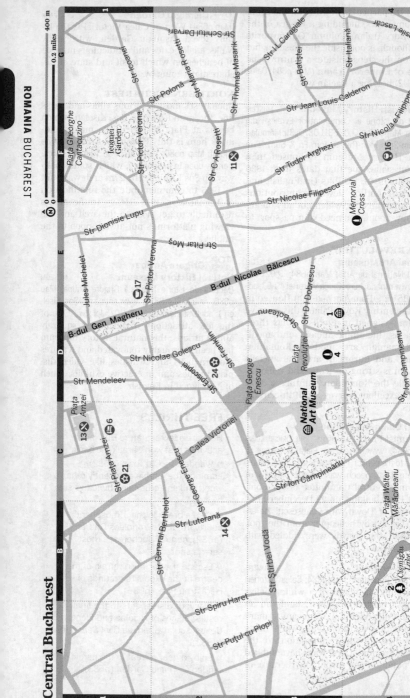

400 m
0.2 miles

Piata Gheorghe
Cantacuzino

Icoanei
Garden

Str Icoanei

Str Polonă

Str Pictor Verona

Str Dionisie Lupu

Str Schitul Darvari

Str Maria Rosetti

Str Thomas Masarik

Str Battiştei

Str I L Caragiale

Str Italiană

Str Vasile Lascăr

Str Jean Louis Calderon

Str Nicolae Filipescu

Str Tudor Arghezi

Str C A Rosetti

11 ✕

16

23

Memorial
Cross

Str Nicolae Filipescu

Str Pitar Moş

Jules Michelet

Str Pictor Verona

17

B-dul Nicolae Bălcescu

B-dul Gen Magheru

Str D I Dobrescu

Str Boteanu

Piaţa
Revoluţiei

1

Str Nicolae Golescu

Str Franklin

Str Episcopiei

24

Piaţa George
Enescu

4

Str Ion Câmpineanu

Str Matei Millo

Str Mendeleev

Piaţa
Amzei

13 ✕

6

Calea Victoriei

National
Art Museum

7

Str Piaţa Amzei

21

Str George Enescu

Str Ion Câmpineanu

Str General Berthelot

Str Luterană

14 ✕

Piaţa Walter
Mărăcineanu

Str Ştirbei Vodă

Cişmigiu
Lake

2

Str Spiru Haret

Str Puţul cu Plopi

A B C D E F G
1 2 3 4

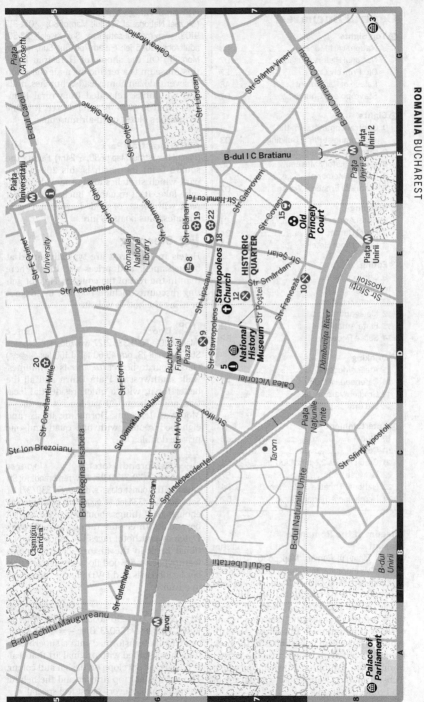

Central Bucharest

Museum of the Romanian Peasant
MUSEUM

(Muzeul Ţăranului Român; Map p680; ☎021-317 9661; www.muzeultaranuluiroman.ro; Şos Kiseleff 3; adult/child 8/2 lei; ⊙10am-6pm Tue-Sun) This collection of traditional peasant bric-a-brac, costumes, icons, artwork and partially restored houses and churches is one of the best museums in Bucharest. An 18th-century Transylvanian church is in the back lot, as is a gift shop. Don't miss the jarring communism exhibition downstairs, which focuses on the Ceauşescu-era program of land collectivisation.

National Village Museum
MUSEUM

(Muzeul Naţional al Satului; Map p680; ☎021-317 9103; www.muzeul-satului.ro; Şos Kiseleff 28-30; adult/child 10/5 lei; ⊙9am-7pm Tue-Sun, to 5pm Mon; ⊞) On the shores of Herăstrău Lake, this museum is a terrific open-air collection of several dozen homesteads, churches, mills and windmills, relocated from rural Romania. Built in 1936 by royal decree, it is one of Europe's oldest open-air museums.

FREE Herăstrău Park
PARK

(Parcul Herăstrău; Map p680; ⊙24hr) Facing the square from the north is this 200-hectare park which stretches along the wide namesake lake. It's (arguably) Bucharest's nicest park, with plenty of shaded strolls and open-air cafes, plus boats to hire.

🛏 Sleeping

Hotels in Bucharest are typically aimed at businessmen, and prices are higher here than in the rest of the country. Tips for getting discounts include booking in advance or using the hotel's website.

TOP CHOICE Doors
HOSTEL €

(Map p680; ☎021-336 2127; www.doorshostel.com; Str Olimpului 13; dm 45-60 lei, d 150 lei; ⊜@⊛) Our favourite hostel du jour is 15 minutes' walk southwest of Piaţa Unirii and all the better for it, with a quiet, residential location and a beautiful garden set up like a Moroccan tearoom. Dorms are in six- and eight-bed rooms, with one quad and one private double.

TOP CHOICE Rembrandt Hotel
HOTEL €€

(Map p684; ☎021-313 9315; www.rembrandt.ro; Str Smârdan 11; 'tourist class' s/d Mon-Fri 330/371 lei, Sat & Sun 294/334 lei; ⊜⊛@⊛) It's hard to say enough good things about this place. Stylish beyond its three-star rating, this 16-room, Dutch-owned hotel faces the landmark National Bank in the historic centre. Rooms feature polished wood floors, wall-sized timber headboards and DVD players. Book well in advance.

Vila Arte
BOUTIQUE HOTEL €€

(Map p680; ☎021-210 1035; www.vilaarte.ro; Str Vasile Lascăr 78; s/d 260/320 lei; ⊜⊛@⊛) A renovated villa transformed into a superb boutique hotel stuffed with original art that really pushes the envelope on design and colour. The services are top drawer and the helpful reception makes every guest feel special.

Hotel Amzei
HOTEL €€€

(Map p684; ☑021-313 9400; www.hotelamzei.ro; Piaţa Amzei 8; s/d 450/550 lei; ❃✳🖥📶) This tastefully reconstructed villa just off of Calea Victoriei has 22 rooms on four floors. The wrought-iron atrium in the lobby lends a refined feel. The rooms are in a more restrained contemporary style.

Midland Youth Hostel
HOSTEL €

(Map p680; ☑021-314 5323; www.themidland-hostel.com; Str Biserica Amzei 22; dm 35-60 lei; ❃✳@📶) This is a bright, cheerful, well-run hostel, with an excellent central location not far from Piaţa Romană. Accommodation is in six-, 10- or 14-bed dorms.

Hotel Carpaţi
HOTEL €€

(Map p684; ☑021-315 0140; www.hotelcarpatibucuresti.ro; Str Matei Millo 16; s/d 160/220 lei; 📶) This popular backpacker option in an old landmark hotel exudes a kind of communist-era charm; nevertheless, some of the 40 rooms have been renovated and offer good value. If you're on a strict budget, go for the cheaper rooms that don't have attached bathrooms.

Eating

Self-caterers will want to head to the daily **market** (Map p684) on Piaţa Amzei, with a good selection of fresh fruit and veg.

TOP CHOICE Caru' cu Bere
ROMANIAN €€

(Map p684; ☑021-313 7560; www.carucubere.ro; Str Stavropoleos 3-5; mains 15-40 lei; ⊙8am-midnight) Despite a decidedly touristy atmosphere, Bucharest's oldest beer house continues to draw a strong local crowd. The colourful belle époque interior and stained-glass windows dazzle, as does the classic Romanian food. Dinner reservations recommended.

Divan
MIDDLE EASTERN €€

(Map p684; ☑021-312 3034; www.thedivan.ro; Str Franceză 46-48; mains 20-30 lei; ⊙10am-1am; 📶) Deservedly popular Turkish and Middle Eastern place, where snagging a prized terrace table will take a mix of patience and good fortune.

Malagamba
ITALIAN €€

(Map p684; ☑021-313 3389; www.malagamba.ro; Str Sf Dumitru 2; mains 20-40 lei ; 📶📍) Creative Italian cooking, with an inventive mix of pasta dishes and delicious salads. On weekends there are babysitters on hand and special kiddie shows so that parents can take a break.

Sale e Pepe
ITALIAN €€

(Map p684; ☑021-315 8989; www.saleepepe.ro; Str Luterană 3; pizzas 15-30 lei; ⊙10am-midnight Mon-Fri, 3pm-midnight Sat & Sun) This tiny pizza/pasta place specialises in crunchy thin-crust pizzas – and for once in Romania, they don't undercook them. Pizza 'Pepperoni' comes topped with sliced red pepper and spicy sausage, and served with hot sauce on the side on request.

Lente & Cafea
INTERNATIONAL €€

(Map p684; ☑021-310 7424; www.lente.ro; Str Gen Praporgescu 31; mains 20-35 lei; ⊙11.30am-1am; 📶) Eclecticism is the theme at this trendy, in-the-know restaurant. The menu is an assortment of tempting fish and chicken concoctions (many with curry, wild rice, mushrooms etc) interspersed with pages of musical lyrics and musical '10 Best' lists, such as the best songs for a long road trip.

Drinking

Drinking options can be roughly broken down into cafes and bars, though there's little distinction in practice. Most of the popular places these days are in the Old Town.

TOP CHOICE Atelier Mecanic
CAFE

(Map p684; ☑0726-767 611; Str Covaci 12; ⊙11am-4am; 📶) The laid-back mood and the arty, mix-and-match junk-shop decor are a breath of fresh air compared with other Old Town cafes and pubs that are lined with corporate tat and tie-ins. They serve great coffee here, as well as wines and an impressive range of single-malt scotches.

Cafeneaua Actorilor
PUB

(Map p684; ☑0721-900 842; www.cafeneauaactorilor.ro; B-dul Nicolae Bălcescu 2; ⊙9am-3am; 📶) Located on the ground floor of the National Theatre (just behind the Inter-Continental Hotel). An oasis of good drink and good pizza in the middle of the centre. Drink (and breathe) on the open-air terrace in summer; in winter, the action shifts to the labyrinthine (and claustrophobic) rooms inside.

TOP CHOICE Grădina Verona
CAFE

(Map p684; ☑0732-003 061; Str Pictor Verona 13-15; ⊙9am-1am; 📶) A garden oasis hidden behind the Cărtureşti bookshop, serving standard-issue but excellent espresso drinks and some of the wackiest ice-tea infusions ever concocted in Romania, such as peony flower, mango and lime (it's not bad).

Old City
BAR

(Map p684; ☑0729-377 774; www.oldcity-lipscani. ro; Str Lipscani 45; ☺10am-5am; ☎) This remains one of our favourite go-to bars in the Old City, and most nights, especially weekends, bring big crowds and theme parties. There's a large, handsome bar area and a big garden out back.

☆ Entertainment

Bucharest has a lively night scene of concerts, theatre, and rock and jazz. Check the weekly guide **Şapte Seri** (www.sapteseri.ro) for entertainment listings. To buy tickets online, visit the websites of the leading ticketing agencies: www.myticket.ro and www.eventim.ro.

Performing Arts
Bucharest National
Opera House
OPERA

(Opera Naţională Bucureşti; Map p680; ☑021-314 6980, box office 021-313 1857; www.operanb.ro; B-dul Mihail Kogălniceanu 70-72; tickets 6-65 lei; ☺box office 9am-1pm & 3-7pm) The city's premier venue for classical opera and ballet. Buy tickets online or at the venue box office.

National Theatre of Bucharest
THEATRE

(Teatrul Naţional Bucureşti; Map p684; ☑box office 021-314 7171, theatre 021-313 9175; www.tnb.ro; B-dul Nicolae Bălcescu 2; ☺box office 10am-4pm Mon, to 7pm Tue-Sun) The National Theatre is the country's most prestigious dramatic stage. The building is a 1970s-era big box, but the facilities inside are excellent. Most dramatic works are performed in Romanian. Check the website for the program during your visit. Buy tickets at the box office.

Romanian Athenaeum
CLASSICAL MUSIC

(Ateneul Roman; Map p684; ☑box office 021-315 6875; www.fge.org.ro; Str Franklin 1-3; tickets 15-65 lei; ☺box office noon-7pm Tue-Fri, 4-7pm Sat, 10-11am Sun) The Athenaeum is home to the respected George Enescu Philharmonic and offers a wide array of classical music concerts from September to May, as well as a number of one-off musical shows and spectacles throughout the year. Buy tickets at the venue box office.

Nightclubs & Live Music
Club A
CLUB

(Map p684; ☑021-316 1667; www.cluba.ro; Str Blănari 14; ☺9pm-5am Thu-Sun) Run by students, this club is a classic and beloved by all who go there. Indie pop/rock tunes play until very late Friday and Saturday nights.

Control
CLUB

(Map p684; ☑0733-927 861; www.control-club.ro; Str Constantin Mille 4; ☺ 6pm-4am; ☎) This favourite among club-goers who like alternative, indie and garage sounds decamped to this new space not far from Calea Victoriei in 2012. Hosts both live acts and DJs, depending on the night.

Green Hours 22 Jazz Club
JAZZ

(Map p684; ☑0788-452 485; www.greenhours. ro; Calea Victoriei 120; ☺24hr) This old-school basement jazz club runs a lively program of jazz nights through the week and hosts an international jazz fest in June. Check the website for the schedule during your trip. Book a seat in advance.

La Muse
CLUB

(Map p684; ☑0734-000 236; www.lamuse.ro; Str Lipscani 53; ☺9am-3am Sun-Wed, to 6am Thu-Sat) Just about anything goes at this popular Old Town dance club. Try to arrive early, around 11pm, since it can get crowded later.

☐ Shopping

For beautifully made woven rugs, table runners, national Romanian costumes, ceramics and other local crafts, don't miss the folk-art shop at the **Museum of the Romanian Peasant**. (Map p680; www.muzeultaranuluiroman.ro; Şos Kiseleff 3; ☺10am-6pm Tue-Sun)

❶ Information
Dangers & Annoyances

The biggest day-to-day nuisance are packs of feral dogs who wander the streets. While the number of dogs has fallen in the past few years, you'll still see them limping down the street or more likely passed out under a shady tree or car. The best advice is to ignore them and they will ignore you. Bites are rare but be sure to go to a hospital for antirabies injections within 36 hours if you get bitten.

Dishonest taxi drivers constitute another annoyance. The worst offenders are those who park outside the Gara de Nord, in front of the Hotel Inter-Continental or at the airport. By law, drivers are required to post their rates on taxi doors, so look for vehicles that charge from 1.39 to 1.79 lei per kilometre. Anything higher is a rip-off.

Internet Access
Best Cafe (B-dul Mihail Kogălniceanu 19; per hr 5 lei; ☺24hr; ☎)

Medical Services
Emergency Clinic Hospital (☑021-9622, 021-599 2300; www.urgentafloreasca.ro; Calea Floreasca 8; ☺24hr)

Sensi-Blu (www.sensiblu.com; B-dul Nicolae Bălcescu 7; ☉8am-10pm Mon-Fri, 9am-9pm Sat & Sun) A highly recommended pharmacy chain with branches around town.

Money

You'll find hundreds of bank branches and ATMs in the centre. Most banks have a currency-exchange office and can provide cash advances against credit or debit cards. Always bring your passport, since you will have to show it to change money.

Outside of normal banking hours, you can change money at private *casa de schimb* (currency booths). There is a row of these along B-dul Gen Gheorghe Magheru, running north of Piaţa Universităţii. You'll have to show a passport here too.

Post

Central Post Office (Map p684; ☎021-315 9030; www.posta-romana.ro; Str Matei Millo 10; ☉7.30am-8pm Mon-Fri)

Tourist Information

Bucharest Tourist Information Center (Map p684; ☎021-305 5500, ext 1003; http://en.seebucharest.ro; Piaţa Universităţii; ☉10am-6pm Mon-Fri, to 2pm Sat & Sun) This small, poorly stocked tourist office is the best the city can offer for assisting visitors. Not much information on hand, but the English-speaking staff can field basic questions, make suggestions and help locate things on a map. It's in the underpass.

Info Tourist Point (Map p680; ☎0371-155 063; www.infotourist.ro; Gara de Nord; ☉10am-6pm Mon-Fri) This small booth, situated in the main terminal at the point where the rail tracks meet the station, can help with basic information and hotel booking.

Websites

Lonely Planet (www.lonelyplanet.com/romania/bucharest)

⊙ Getting There & Away

Air

All international and domestic flights use **Henri Coandă International Airport** (OTP,Otopeni; ☎021-204 1000; www.otp-airport.ro; Şos Bucureşti-Ploieşti). Henri Coandă is 17km north of Bucharest on the road to Braşov. Arrivals and departures use separate terminals. The airport is a modern facility, with restaurants, newsagents, currency exchange offices and ATMs. There are 24-hour information desks at both terminals.

The airport is the hub for the national carrier **Tarom** (Map p684; ☎call centre 021-204 6464, office 021-316 0220; www.tarom.ro; Spl Independenţei 17, City Centre; ☉8.30am-7.30pm Mon-Fri, 9am-1.30pm Sat). Tarom has a comprehensive network of internal flights to major Romanian cities as well to capitals and big cities around Europe and the Middle East.

Bus

It's possible to get just about anywhere in the country by bus from Bucharest, but figuring out where your bus or maxitaxi departs from can be tricky. Bucharest has several bus stations and they don't seem to follow any discernible logic. Even Bucharest residents have a hard time making sense of it.

The best bet is to consult the websites www.autogari.ro and www.cdy.ro. Both keep up-to-date timetables and are fairly easy to manage, though www.cdy.ro is only in Romanian. Be sure to follow up with a phone call just to make sure a particular bus is running on a particular day. Another option is to ask your hotel to help with arrangements or to book through a travel agency.

Car & Motorcycle

Driving in Bucharest is lunacy and you won't want to do it for more than a few minutes before you stow the car and use the metro. If you're travelling around the country by car and just want to visit Bucharest for the day, it's more sensible to park at a metro station on the outskirts and take the metro into the city.

In theory, hourly parking rates apply in the centre, particularly off Piaţa Victoriei and Piaţa Universităţii. Look for the wardens in yellow-and-blue uniforms or paid metered parking. In many places, though, you can just pull onto the sidewalk like everyone else. Petrol costs around 6 lei per litre.

Major rental agencies can be found at the Henri Coandă International Airport arrivals hall. Most large companies also have an in-town branch.

The cheapest rates available are from **Autonom** (☎airport branch 021-232 4325, call centre 0721-442 226; www.autonom.com; Henri Coandă International Airport), offering a Dacia Logan for around 140 lei per day (including unlimited mileage and insurance, minimum two days); rates drop if you rent for more than a week.

Train

Gara de Nord (☎021-319 9539, phone reservations 021-9522, phone reservations 021-9521; www.cfr.ro; Piaţa Gara de Nord 1) is the central station for most national and all international trains. The station is accessible by metro from the centre of the city.

Buy tickets at station ticket windows or in advance at **Agenţia de Voiaj CFR** (☎021-313 2642; www.cfr.ro; Str Domnita Anastasia 10-14; ☉7.30am-7.30pm Mon-Fri, 8am-noon Sat).

DOMESTIC TRAINS FROM BUCHAREST

DESTINATION	COST (LEI)	DURATION (HR)	FREQUENCY
Braşov	70	2½	frequent
Cluj-Napoca	90	7½	4 daily
Constanţa	60	2-4	5 daily
Iaşi	80	6	3 daily
Sibiu	70	5	3 daily
Sighişoara	80	4½	3 daily
Suceava	80	8	3 daily
Timişoara	100	8	2 daily

A seat reservation is compulsory if you are travelling with an InterRail or Eurail pass. For international tickets, the private travel agency **Wasteels** (☏021-317 0370; www.wasteels.ro; Gara de Nord; ⊙8am-7pm Mon-Fri, to 2pm Sat), located inside the train station, can help sort out complicated international connections.

Check the latest train schedules on either www.cfr.ro or the reliable German site www.bahn.de.

ⓘ Getting Around

To/From the Airport

BUS Express bus 783 leaves every 15 minutes between 5.37am and 11.23pm (every half-hour at weekends) from Piaţas Unirii and Piaţas Victoriei and points in between. The Piaţa Unirii stop is on the south side. Buy a ticket, valid for one round trip or two people one way, for 7 lei at any RATB bus and ticket booth near a bus stop.

To get to the centre from the airport, catch bus 783 from the downstairs ramp outside the arrivals hall; you'll need to buy a ticket from the stand at the northern end of the waiting platform (to the right as you exit).

TAXI A reputable taxi from the centre to the airport should cost no more than 70 to 80 lei. Negotiate the fare in advance with the driver.

TRAIN There's a regular shuttle train service (8 lei, 35 minutes) from Gara de Nord to the airport. Trains leave hourly at 10 minutes past the hour, starting at 8.10am and continuing until 7.10pm.

Public Transport

Bucharest's public transport system of metros, buses, trams and trolleybuses is operated by the tranport authority **RATB** (Regia Autonomă de Transport Bucureşti ; ☏info 021-9391; www.ratb.ro). The system runs daily from about 5am to approximately 11.30pm.

For buses, trams and trolleybuses, buy tickets at any RATB street kiosk, marked 'casa de bilete', located at major stops and public squares. Tickets for standard buses cost 1.30 lei per trip and are sold in two-ticket increments for 2.60 lei. Tickets for a small number of express buses, such as bus 783 which goes to the airport, cost 7 lei (good for two journeys). Punch your ticket on board or risk a 50 lei on-the-spot fine.

Metro stations are identified by a large letter 'M'. To use the metro, buy a magnetic-strip ticket available at ticketing machines inside station entrances (have small bills handy). Tickets valid for two journeys cost 4 lei. A 10-trip ticket costs 15 lei. The metro is a speedy way of moving up and down the central north–south corridor from Piaţa Victoriei to Piaţa Unirii, passing through the convenient stations of Piaţa Romană and Universitate. The metro is also useful for travelling from Gara de Nord to the centre and back.

TRANSYLVANIA

Transylvania conjures a vivid landscape of mountains, castles, fortified churches and superstitious old crones. The Carpathian Mountains are truly spectacular and outdoor enthusiasts can choose from caving in the Apuseni range, rock climbing at Piatra Craiului National Park, biking atop the flat Bucegi plateau or hiking the Făgăraş. The skiing scene, particularly in the Bucegi Mountains, is a great draw, while well-beaten paths up to Bran and Peleş castles are also worth the crowds.

A melange of architecture and chic sidewalk cafes punctuate the towns of Braşov, Sighişoara and Sibiu, while the vibrant student town Cluj-Napoca has the country's most vigorous nightlife. Many of southern Transylvania's Saxon villages are dotted with fortified churches that date back half a millennium. An hour north, in Székely Land, ethnic Hungarian communities are the majority. Throughout, you're likely to spot many Roma villagers – look out for black cowboy hats and rich red dresses.

Sinaia

POP 14,600

Nestled in a slender fir-clad valley, this pretty town teems with hikers in summer and skiers in winter. Backed by the imposing crags of the Bucegi Mountains, it's a dramatic place for a day's hike or, using the network of cabanas (mountain huts) open to walkers, several days.

The town itself is a melange of crayon-coloured wooden houses contrasted with the 'wedding-cake' style of its grander 19th-century buildings. Once home to Romanian King Carol I, who created a summer retreat here, Peleş Castle is a dream of hidden passages, fairy-tale turrets, vertiginous galleries and classical statues; it's so beguilingly imaginative, it could raise a swoon from the most hardened cynic.

⊙ Sights

Peleş Castle   CASTLE
(www.visit.peles.ro; tours adult/child from 20/5 lei, photots 3 lei; ⊙9am-5pm Tue-Sun; ⛟) The first European castle to have central heating, electricity and vacuuming(!), Peleş was intended as the summer residence of Romania's longest-serving monarch, King Carol I. Construction on the 3500-sq-metre edifice, built in neo-Renaissance style, began in 1875. Some 39 years later it was completed, just months before the king died in 1914.

The basic 40-minute tour takes in about 10 rooms, while two additional tours are available. In the first Armoury Hall (there's two), look for one of the 11 medieval knight suits with the long pointed boots. Rembrandt reproductions line the walls of the king's office, while real Gustav Klimt works are in the last stop, a theatre behind the entry.

Pelişor Palace   PALACE
(www.visit.peles.ro; compulsory tours adult/child 10/2.50 lei; ⊙noon-7pm Thu-Sun; ⛟) Heavily art nouveau in decor, and about 100m uphill from Peleş Castle, Pelişor Palace has a hard time competing with its neighbour. King Carol I planned this house for his nephew (and future king) Ferdinand (1865–1927) and wife Marie. Most of the furniture was imported from Vienna.

🏃 Activities

Skiing, hiking and biking are the main draws in the Bucegi Mountains, with a good range of basic, intermediate and advanced ski runs, and similarly challenging walking routes. A good source of ski equipment and information in town, **Snow** (Str Cuza Vodă 2a; ⊙9am-6pm), near the cable-car station, hires out skis (40 lei per day) and offers ski instruction services.

Bike, Ski and Rental Outlet (⌕0745-015 241; Str O Goga 1; skis per day 40 lei; ⊙8am-7pm) next to the park, rents out skis, boards (40 lei per day) and bikes (20 lei per hour).

🛏 Sleeping

Travel agencies around town can find you a room in one of the countless pensions, which start at 100 lei.

BEARS!

Thanks to its megalomaniacal dictator (under Ceauşescu no one but he was allowed to hunt), 60% of Europe's brown bears are today found in Romania (an estimated 6000).

The chances of you seeing one of these sizeable Yogis are high if you're trekking or going to a bear hide (where you're more or less guaranteed a sighting). A cousin of the grizzly, Romanian bears are smaller but have the same powerful hump of muscle on their back, and they can also move at 50km/h.

Hikers have been mauled and even killed by bears in recent years, usually because they've been surprised, so here's a few tips to be mindful of. Try to pitch your tent in an open spot so they can see you, keeping your food at least 4m off the ground in the branches of a tree. Also, any used sanitary material or trash should be kept in a Ziploc bag. Should you find yourself in the presence of a mother and cub, stand still to signify you're not afraid, and make yourself bigger by waving your arms. Similarly, when walking through dense forest, talk loudly to announce your presence; the last thing a bear wants is to engage with you.

Transylvania

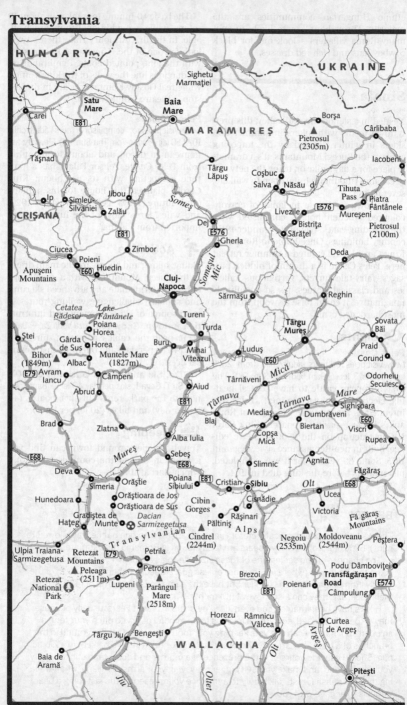

0 — 50 km
0 — 30 miles

Siret

Rădăuţi

Botoşani

Gura
Humorului
Suceava

Câmpulung
Moldovenesc

MOLDAVIA

Vatra
Dornei

Carpathian

*Lake Izvorul
Muntelui*

Topliţa
Toaca
(1904m)
Piatra-
Neamţ
Bicaz

Ditrău
Lacul Roşu

Bistriţa

Gheorgheni

Mountains

Harghitei
(1801m)

Siculeni
Miercurea
Ciuc
Armaseni
Comăneşti
Misentea

Târgu
Ocna

Tuşnad
Băile Tuşnad

Târgu
Seculesc
Breţcu
Vrancrei
Mountains

E574
Moacşa

Sfântu
Gheorghe
Covasna
Lăcăuţi
(1777m)

Chichis
Zagon
Comandă u

Härman

Poiana
Braşov
Braşov

Râşnov
Zărneşti
Predeal
Ciucaş
(1954m)

Bran Castle
Azuga
Cheia
Buşteni
Sinaia

Buzău

Bucegi
Mountains

E60

Câmpina

Vălenii
de Munte

Mizil

Prahova

Târgovişte

Ploieşti

Dâmboviţa

Ialomiţa

 Hotel Caraiman

HOTEL €€

(☎0244-311 542; palace@rdslink.ro; B-dul Carol I nr 4; s/d/ste 145/200/240 lei; 🅿😊📶) Built in 1880, this austere yet welcoming multi-gabled hotel has bags of atmosphere. Its stained-glass windows, chandeliers, sweeping stairways and wood-panelling hint at the affluent elite who used to patronise it. Fragrant rooms enjoy thick carpets, decent fittings, bathrooms and cable TV. Ask for one facing the park for the restful babble of the nearby fountain.

Hotel Economat

HOTEL €€

(☎0244-311 151; www.apps.ro; Aleea Peleşului 2; s/d/tr 90/150/180 lei; 🅿) Like a slice of Hansel and Gretel, this gingerbread-roofed hotel is a delight. Rooms are cosy with clean bathrooms. Head to the excellent Vanatoresc, its sister restaurant across the courtyard and up the hill. Festooned in bear furs and stag antlers, this ex-hunter's lodge is a fun place to take your complimentary breakfast.

Casa Noastra

HOTEL €

(☎0244-314 556; www.casanoastra.sinaia.ro; B-dul Carol I; s/d/tr 70/100/120 lei; 🅿📶) Some 500m south of the roundabout in the centre of town, this four-floored traditional-style hotel has clean rooms with sparkling bathrooms and fine views of the mountains. Outside of August there are decent discounts.

🍴 Eating

Irish House

INTERNATIONAL €€

(www.irishhouse.ro; B-dul Carol I nr 80; mains 15-25 lei; 🚼) Eat inside or out at this busy central watering hole, popular with families and après-skiers. Service is a little slow, but coffees are suitably frothy, and there's a menu spanning pizza, pasta and salads.

Bucegi Restaurant

ROMANIAN €€

(B-dul Carol I; mains 20 lei) Next to Irish House with an alpine ambience, this alfresco eatery dishes up specialities like venison, omelettes and pizza, as well as a range of salads.

ℹ️ Information

Central Post Office (Str Cuza Vodă; ⊙9am-7pm Mon-Fri, to noon Sat)

Salvamont (☎0244-313 131, 0-SALVAMONT; Primărie, B-dul Carol I) This 24-hour mountain-rescue service is located at the Cota 2000 chairlift station.

Sinaia Tourism Information Centre (☎0244-315 656; www.info-sinaia.ro; B-dul Carol I 47; ⊙8.30am-4.30pm Mon-Fri) This dinky office

WORTH A TRIP

DRACULA'S FINAL RESTING PLACE

Snagov Lake, 40km north of Bucharest, serves as the main weekend retreat for residents of the capital looking for a place to relax.

But the lake has an even bigger claim to fame: **Snagov Monastery** (Mănăstirea Snagov; ☎021-323 9905; www.snagov.ro; Snagov Island; adult/child 15/10 lei; ☺9am-6pm), on an island at the lake's northern end, just happens to be the reputed final resting place of none other than Vlad Ţepeş (aka 'Vlad the Impaler'), the legendarily brutal Wallachian prince who served as the inspiration for Bram Stoker's *Dracula*.

The monastery dates from the 15th century. Vlad Ţepeş' alleged grave is located inside towards the back.

As with many aspects of the 'Dracula' story, there's some debate as to whether the body buried here actually belongs to Ţepeş. The prince died in 1476 battling the Turks near Bucharest. His head was famously lopped off and carried back to İstanbul. What happened to the rest of the body was never clear.

The lake has a lovely rural setting, and there are plenty of opportunities for swimming, boating, fishing and sunbathing.

Though it's not far from Bucharest, it's not easy to get to Snagov without your own wheels. The best bet is to catch a maxitaxi (6 lei) from stands at Piaţa Presei Libera in the north of Bucharest. It will drop you at the centre of Snagov village, from where you can negotiate with a private boatsman to take you to the island (about 50 lei per person).

You can eat and stay the night at **Dolce Vita** (☎0723-580 780; www.dolcevitasnagov.ro; Snagov Parc; r 200 lei), across the lake from Snagov village. Once you arrive, give them a call and they will send a boatsman across the lake to fetch you.

packs a powerful punch, with free local maps, basic skiing and hiking maps, brochures, ideas for local activities and info on upcoming classical concerts.

ℹ Getting There & Away

BUS Buses and maxitaxis run every 45 minutes between 6am and 10pm from the train station to Azuga (4 lei) and Buşteni (3 lei, 10 minutes); some go all the way to Bucharest (25 lei, 1½ hours) or Braşov (16 lei, one hour).

TRAIN Sinaia is on the Bucharest–Braşov rail line – 126km from the former and 45km from the latter – so jumping on a train to Bucharest (38 lei, 1½ hours) or Braşov (13 lei, one hour) is a cinch.

Braşov

POP 274,400

Legend has it that the Pied Piper re-emerged from Hamelin in Braşov, and indeed there's something whimsically enchanting about the city, with its fairy-tale turrets and cobbled streets. Dramatically overlooked by Mt Tâmpa, her trees sporting a russet-gold coat (and cocky Hollywood-style sign), this is a remarkably relaxed city. Wander its maze of streets, stopping for caffeine injections at bohemian cafes, between losing yourself in a beguiling

coalescence of Austro-Hungarian gingerbread roofs, baroque gods, medieval spires and Soviet flat-tops. The city's centrepiece square is Piaţa Sfatului, a people-watcher's mecca. There are myriad things to see here, great restaurants and oodles of accommodation.

◉ Sights

Piaţa Sfatului   SQUARE

This wide square, chocka with cafes, was once the heart of medieval Braşov. In the centre stands the 1420 **council house** (Casa Sfatului), topped by a Trumpeter's Tower in which town councillors, known as centurions, would meet.

Black Church   CHURCH

(Biserica Neagră; adult/child 6/3 lei; ☺10am-5pm Tue-Sat, to noon Sun, closed Mon) Braşov's main landmark, the Black Church is the largest Gothic church between Vienna and İstanbul, and still used by German Lutherans today. Built between 1383 and 1480, it was named for its appearance after a fire in 1689. The original statues on the exterior of the apse are now displayed inside.

The church's 4000-pipe organ, built by Buchholz of Berlin in 1839, is believed to be the only Buchholz preserved in its original form.

Mt Tâmpa
MOUNTAIN

Towering above town from the east is Mt Tâmpa, where Braşov's original defensive fortress was built. Vlad Ţepeş attacked it in 1458, finally dismantling it two years later and – out of habit – impaling some 40 merchants atop the peak. These days it's an easy trip up by **cable car** (telecabina; one way/return 9/15 lei; ⊘9.30am-5pm Tue-Sun).

St Nicholas' Cathedral
CHURCH

(St Nicolae din Scheii; ⊘6am-9pm) The black-spired Orthodox Church of St Nicholas' Cathedral, on Piaţa Unirii, was first built in wood in 1392, replaced by a Gothic stone church in 1495, and later embellished in Byzantine style. Inside are murals of Romania's last king and queen, covered by plaster to protect them from communist leaders and uncovered in 2004.

☞ Tours

Roving Romania
TOUR

(☑0724-348 272; www.roving-romania.co.uk) Run by an Englishman based near Braşov, this is an out-of-home agency for personalised, usually small-scale tours – great for birding and 4WD trips. Email for sample itineraries.

Dan Marin
TOUR

(☑0744-319 708; www.transylvanian.ro) Run by a local Romanian and winner of the coveted Wanderlust World Guide Award in 2007 for Best Guide, this tour company specialises in wildlife, historical and cultural treks. Dan knows the forests well and is an expert tracker. For a group of four, a one-day hike costs €70.

🛏 Sleeping

TOP CHOICE Casa Wagner
HOTEL €€

(☑0268-411 253; www.casa-wagner.com; Piaţa Sfatului ; s/d incl breakfast 269/315 lei; @🖎) This former 15th-century German bank is now a boutique hotel with 24 well-appointed rooms. Right in the heart of the city, its exposed brick walls, tasteful furnishings, modern bathrooms, welcoming breakfast area and pleasant management make this an excellent choice.

Bella Muzica
HOTEL €€

(☑0268-477 956; www.bellamuzica.ro; Piaţa Sfatului 19; s/d 220/270 lei; 🖎) Within its wine-coloured corridors are 34 dark-wood and exposed-brick rooms. Very comfy beds, fans, bathrooms, friendly staff and cable TV all help make it a firm choice for aesthetes –

and we haven't even mentioned its dead central location or fabulous restaurant.

Rolling Stone Hostel
HOSTEL €

(☑0740-518 681, 0268-513 965; www.rollingstone.ro; Str Piatra Mare 2a; dm 38 lei, r from 115 lei; ⊜@🖎) Run by helpful sisters with unlimited reserves of energy, superfriendly Stone attracts a cosmopolitan mix of travellers. Dorms are a little crowded but the private double room without bathroom has elegant couches and an armoire. You'll be given a map and bags of info on arrival, plus there are personal lockers and organised tours. Breakfast is basic and laundry is 15 lei.

Casa Rozelor
BOUTIQUE HOTEL €€€

(☑0268-475 212; www.casarozelor.ro; Str Michael Weiss 20; s/d incl breakfast 315/380 lei; @🖎) This hidden courtyard oasis has five beautiful apartments, some with split-level floors adjoined by spiral staircases. Each is defiantly individual but all fuse contemporary chic with traditional Saxon; think antique furniture and modern art on brick walls.

✕ Eating

TOP CHOICE Bistro de l'Arte
BISTRO €€

(www.bistrodelarte.ro; Str Piaţa Enescu 11; mains 12-28 lei; 🖎📶) Tucked down a cobbled street straight out of a folk tale, this chi-chi joint

WORTH A TRIP

BUCEGI MOUNTAINS

These sandstone and limestone mountains rising 2505m are hugely popular. While some trails are poorly marked, there is a decent selection of cabanas and shelters, should your trek extend overnight or you get caught in inclement weather. Winter is severe and summer thunderstorms are common.

An added bonus is the hiker-friendly plateau above the horseshoe-shaped range that stands between Bran and Sinaia. The best walking map is Dimap's fold-out *Five Mountains from the Carpathian's Bend* (34 lei; www.dimap.hu) covering the Piatra Craiului, Bucegi, Postăvarul, Piatra Mare and Ciucaş ranges, plus a Braşov city map. A visit to the Sinaia Tourism Information Centre (p693) is essential before setting off on ambitious hikes.

Braşov

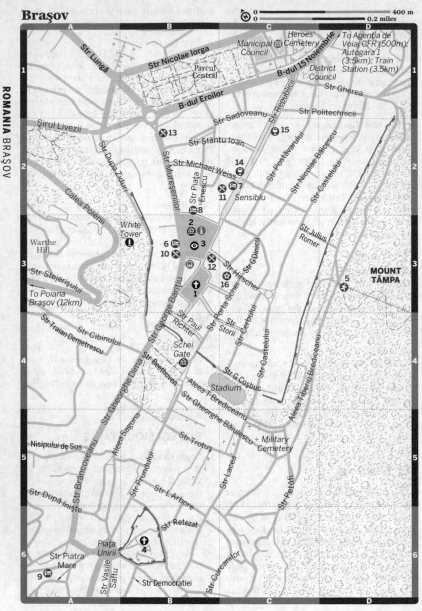

has decidedly boho genes, with sculpture and walls dotted with local artists' work. Gazpacho soup, shrimps and tomato gratin, snails...or just a croque monsieur. Perfect for nursing a cappucino and working on your laptop.

Bella Musica ROMANIAN, MEXICAN €€
(Str George Bariţiu 2; mains 20-30 lei; 🛜📱) In a vaulted grottolike cellar aflicker with candlelight, Musica offers intimate dining. Its menu spans Mexican fare like tasty fajitas, *ciorbă* (soup), pasta, foie gras, salads and

Braşov

schnitzel steak. Try the goulash beef stew with dumplings.

Sergiana   ROMANIAN €€
(Str Mureşenilor 28; mains 30 lei; ⊘10am-11pm) Authentically Saxon, this subterranean carnivore's heaven has two sections: the white room for nonsmokers, and the exposed brick vaults for *fumeurs*. Choose from a menu of venison, stag, boar, pork ribs, sirloin steak, and Transylvanian sour soup with smoked gammon and tarragon (11.50 lei). A hunter's dream.

Keller Steak House   STEAKHOUSE €€€
(www.kellersteakhouse.ro; Str Hirscher 2; mains 85 lei; ▣⋔) One of Brasov's premier steakhouses, where you can eat inside its ochre interior or tackle your sirloin outside on the terrace. Steak and Roquefort cheese, salad and boar...one thing is for certain, you won't leave here with an empty stomach.

🍷 Drinking

Deane's Irish Pub & Grill   PUB
(Str Republicii 19) As if transplanted from Donegal, this subterranean Irish pub, with its early-20th-century cloudy mirrored bar,

shadowy booths and old-world soundtracks, is a haven for Guinness-thirsty leprechauns. Live music some nights.

Festival 39   BAR
(Str Republicii 62; ⊘10am-1am) This romantic watering hole is an art deco dream of stained-glass ceilings, wrought-iron finery, candelabras and leather banquettes, and has a bar long enough to keep an army of barflies content.

☆ Entertainment

Gheorghe Dima State Philharmonic   CLASSICAL MUSIC
(Str Hirscher 10) Performs mainly between September and May.

ℹ Information

You'll find numerous ATMs, banks and currency exchange offices on and around Str Republicii and B-dul Eroilor.

County Hospital (☏0268-333 666; Calea Bucaresţi 25-27; ⊘24hr)

Red Net Internet (Str George Bariţiu 8; per hr 2.50 lei; ⊘7.30am-10pm)

Sensiblu (☏0268-411 248; Str Republicii 15; ⊘9am-6pm Mon-Fri, 8am-3pm Sat)

Tourist Information Centre (☏0268-419 078; www.brasovcity.ro; Piaţa Sfatului 30) Easily spotted in the gold city council building in the centre of the square, the English-speaking staff offer free maps and brochures, and track down hotel vacancies and train and bus times. The centre shares space with the history museum.

ℹ Getting There & Around

Bus

From 6am to 7.30pm, maxitaxis leave every half-hour for Bucharest (30 lei, 2½ hours), stopping in Buşteni and Sinaia. About four or five maxitaxis leave for Sibiu (35 lei, 2½ hours). Nine or 10 go daily to Sighişoara (30 lei). A handful of buses go to Constanţa (55 lei) and Iaşi (35 lei). The most accessible station is **Autogara 1** (Bus Station 1; ☏0268-427 267), next to the train station.

All European routes are handled by **Eurolines** (☏0268-475 219; www.eurolines.ro; Piaţa Sfatului 18; ⊘9am-8pm Mon-Fri, to 4pm Sat), which sells tickets for buses to Germany, Italy, Hungary and other European destinations.

Train

Advance tickets are sold at the **Agenţia de Voiaj CFR** (Str 15 de Noiembrie 43; ⊘8am-7.30pm Mon-Fri).

Daily domestic train services (prices are for 2nd-class seats on rapid trains) include at least hourly to Bucharest (42 lei, 3½ hours), a dozen to Sighişoara (36 lei, 2½ hours), two to Sibiu (50 lei, four hours) and 10 to Cluj-Napoca (65 lei, six hours). For Iaşi, transfer in Ploiesti or Bucharest (96 lei, nine hours).

Around Braşov

◉ Sights

Bran Castle
CASTLE
(☎0268-237 700; www.bran-castle.com; adult/student 25/5 lei, camera/video 20 lei; ☺9am-7pm Tue-Sun, noon-7pm Mon May-Sep, 9am-5pm Tue-Sun Oct-Apr) Facing the flatlands and backed by mountains, the 60m-tall Bran Castle is spectacular. If you can manage to avoid bottlenecks from tour groups that appear in waves, you may enjoy the largely renovated interiors and claustrophobic nooks and crannies.

Built by Saxons from Braşov in 1382 to defend the Bran Pass against Turks, the castle may have housed Vlad Ţepeş for a few nights on his flight from the Turks in 1462, following their attack on the Poienari fortress in the Argeş Valley. From 1920 Queen Marie lived in the castle, and it served as a summer royal residence until the forced abdication of King Michael in 1947.

Râşnov Fortress
FORTRESS
(Cetatea Râşnov; admission 10 lei; ☺9am-8pm May-Oct, to 6pm Nov-Apr) Râşnov, 12km from Bran towards Braşov, doubles the castle action with the tempting ruins of the 13th-century fortress. From the central square, steps lead up the hill where inclined alleys and a museum await.

⌂ Sleeping

Guesthouse
PENSION €
(☎0744-306 062; Str Principala ; r from 120-140 lei, tr 150 lei) With terrific views of Bran Castle, this guesthouse sits almost opposite Hanul Bran. It's clean and family-friendly with a kids' adventure playground and communal lounge and dining room.

Hanul Bran
HOTEL €
(☎0268-236 556; www.hanulbran.ro; Str Principala 384; s/d 100/120 lei) Probably the plushest option dead central ('scuse the pun), this ochre-coloured hotel with a bubbly adjoining restaurant enjoys a dramatic view of the castle. Large genial rooms with comfy beds, TV and bathroom.

ℹ Getting There & Away

Bran is an easy DIY day trip from Braşov. Buses marked 'Bran–Moieciu' (6 lei, one hour) depart every half-hour from Braşov's **Autogara 2** (Bus Station 2; ☎0268-426 332; Str Avram Iancu 114). Return buses to Braşov leave Bran every half-hour from roughly 7am to 6pm in winter, and 7am to 10pm in summer. All buses to Braşov stop each way at Râşnov.

Sighişoara
POP 26,400

So pretty it should be arrested, from the moment you enter Sighişoara's fortified walls, wending your way along cobblestones to its central square, the town burns itself into your memory. It's like stepping into a kid's fairy tale, the narrow streets aglow with lustrously coloured 16th-century houses, their gingerbread roofs tumbling down to pretty cafes. Horror fans won't be disappointed either, for this Unesco-protected citadel, the best preserved of its kind in Europe, was the birthplace of one of history's great monsters – Vlad Ţepeş (The Impaler).

◉ Sights

Most of Sighişoara's sights are conveniently clustered in the compact old town, the magical medieval **citadel** perched on a hillock and fortified with a 14th-century wall (to which 14 towers and five artillery bastions were later added). Today the citadel, which is on the Unesco World Heritage list, retains just nine of its original towers (named for the guilds in charge of their upkeep) and two of its bastions.

Entering the citadel, you pass under the massive **clock tower** (Turnul cu Ceas; Piata Muzeului) with its peacock-coloured roof tiles; it dates from 1280 and once housed the town council. Formerly the main entrance to the fortified city, the tower is 64m tall, with 2.35m-thick walls. Inside, the 1648 clock is a pageant of slowly revolving 80cm-high wooden figurines, each representing a character from the Greek–Roman pantheon: Peace bears an olive branch, Justice has a set of scales and Law wields a sword. The executioner is also present and the drum-player strikes the hour. Above stand seven figures, each representing a day of the week.

The diminutive **Piaţa Cetăţii** is the heart of old Sighişoara. It was here that markets, craft fairs, public executions, impalings and witch trials were held.

From the square, turn left up Str Şcolii to the 172 steps of the **covered stairway** (scara acoperită; Str Şcolii), which has tunnelled its way up the hill since 1642, to the 1345 Gothic **Church on the Hill** (Biserica din Deal; Bergkirche; ☉mid-Apr–Oct), a 429m Lutheran church and the town's highest point. Facing its entry – behind the church when approaching from the steps – is an atmospheric, overgrown German cemetery.

Also behind the church are the remains of the **Goldsmiths' Tower**. The guilds of the goldsmiths, tailors, carpenters and tinsmiths existed until 1875.

From the church, head back down the hill, cross Piaţa Cetăţii, then head down Str Bastionul. At its northern end are the 1896 **Roman Catholic church** (Str Bastionul) and the **Tailors' Tower** (Turnul Cizmarilor; Str Bastionul).

🛏 Sleeping

TOP CHOICE **Bed & Breakfast Kula** PENSION €
(☎0265-777 907; Str Tâmplarilor 40; r/apt per person 65/150 lei; ☺) Spilling with antique furniture, wood floors and rugs, this pension in a 400-year-old house feels like you're staying at a friend's...which you are by the time you've sat chatting with the owners in the pretty garden, as they ply you with homemade wine.

Pensiune Cristina & Pavel PENSION €
(☎0744-159 667, 0744-119 211; www.pensiuneafaur. ro; Str Cojocarilor 1; dm/s/d 45/80/125 lei; P) The floors are so clean at this four-room, onedorm guesthouse, you could eat your lunch off them. En suite rooms are spearmint white, plus there's an idyllic garden bursting with flowers.

Casa Wagner HOTEL €€
(☎0265-506 014; www.casa-wagner.com; Piaţa Cetăţii 7; s/d/ste €39/49/69; P☺☎) This appealing 16th-century hotel has 32 rooms spread across three buildings. Think peach walls, candelabras, dark-wood furniture and tasteful rugs. The rooms in the eaves are smaller but wood floored, cosy and very romantic for writing those *Harkeresque* diary entries.

Nathan's Villa HOSTEL €
(☎0265-772 546; www.nathansvilla.com; Str Libertăţii 8; dm 50 lei; @☎) Cramped dorms, but thoughtfully placed linen screens on bunks allow for a little more privacy. The purple dorm is cosy – check out the retro boiler. Another plus is a sofa and TV in dorms.

🍴 Eating

Café International & Family Centre CAFE €
(Piaţa Cetăţii 8; mains 13 lei; ☉8.30am-7.30pm Mon-Sat Jun-Sep, 9am-6pm Mon-Sat Oct-May; ☎☞) This delightful family-run cafe dishes up delicious pies, cookies, quiche and cakes. Inside it's a Gustavian-meets-rustic chic interior, while outside chairs and tables spill onto the cobbles come summer.

Cositorarului Casa RESTAURANT €
(Str Cositorarilor 9; mains 15-25 lei; ☉9am-10pm) Refresh yourself with beautiful views of the old town and homemade lemonade. They also rustle up toasted sandwiches and breakfast. Inside is cosy, and outside there's a small terrace.

Casa Dracula ROMANIAN €€
(Str Cositorarilor 5; mains 28 lei; ☝) Despite the ghoulish Dracula bust mounted on the wall, the house where Vlad was born could have been dealt a worse blow than this atmospheric, wood-panelled restaurant. The menu scuttles from tomato soup to salmon fillet – all with Dracula-related references.

SAXON LAND

Sighişoara, Sibiu and Braşov – the 'Saxon Triangle', if you will – enclose an area loaded with undulating hills and cinematic villages. These yesteryear villages, some sitting at the ends of rather nasty dirt roads, frequently have outstanding fortified churches dating from the 12th century. Even just a kilometre or two off the Braşov–Sibiu highway you'll find a world where horse carriages and walking are generally the only ways anyone gets around, and where a car – any car – gets stares.

Popular destinations include **Biertan** (28km southwest of Sighişoara) and **Viscri** (about 40km east).

Bus services are infrequent, but several guided tours cruise this area from either Braşov or Sibiu. You can also arrange a taxi for the day.

ℹ Information

Cultural Heritage Info Centre (☑0788-115 511; www.dordeduca.ro; Piaţa Muzeului; ☺10am-6pm Tue-Sun) Rents out bikes (5 lei per hour) and offers guided tours of Sighişoara and the fortified churches.

Farmacia Genţiana (Piaţa Hermann Oberth 45; ☺8am-8pm)

Post Office (☑0265-774 854; Str O Goga 12; ☺7.30am-7.30pm Mon-Fri)

Tourist Information (☑0265-770 415; Str O Goga; ☺10am-4pm Mon-Fri, 9am-1pm Sat) This useful English-speaking resource can book beds and check bus and train times, and has maps of the city.

ℹ Getting There & Away

BUS Next to the train station on Str Libertăţii, the **bus station** (☑0265-771 260) sends buses of various sizes and colours to Sibiu (20 lei, 2½ hours, four daily), among other destinations. Buses to Braşov (38 lei, 2½ hours) stop at the bus station a couple of times per day and require a reservation (☑0265-250 702).

TRAIN About a dozen trains connect Sighişoara with Braşov (21 lei, two hours), nine of which go on to Bucharest (65 lei, 4½ hours). Five daily trains go to Cluj-Napoca (59 lei, 3½ hours). You'll need to change trains in Mediaş to reach Sibiu (16 lei, 2½ hours), but the four daily trains are timed for easy transfers. Three daily trains go to Budapest (145 lei, nine hours), and the night train has a sleeper (from 200 lei). Buy tickets at the **train station** (☑0265-771 886).

Sibiu

POP 154,500

Instantly charming with her maze of cobbled streets and baroque squares undulating downhill, Romania's cultural first lady has a magic all of her own. Composers Franz Liszt and Johann Strauss were drawn here in the 19th century, and in 2007 the city was named the European Union's Capital of Culture. In fact, the country's first hospital, school, library and pharmacy were all established here, so there must be a spirit of enterprise in the air. Most months have myriad things going on, from festivals (with more festivals here than any other city in Romania) and exhibitions to theatre and opera. There are also plenty of cafes for people-watching in the city's three main squares.

◉ Sights

TOWN CENTRE
At the centre of the old walled city, the expansive Piaţa Mare is a good start for exploring Sibiu. Climb to the top of the former **Council Tower** (Turnul Sfatului; admission 2 lei; ☺10am-8pm), which links Piaţa Mare with its smaller sister square, Piaţa Mică.

Brukenthal Museum   MUSEUM
(www.brukenthalmuseum.ro; Piaţa Mare 5; adult/student 20/5 lei) The Brukenthal Museum is the oldest and possibly finest art gallery in Romania. Founded in 1817, the museum is in the baroque palace (1785) of former Austrian governor Baron Samuel Brukenthal (1721–1803), and hosts excellent collections of 16th- and 17th-century paintings.

History Museum   MUSEUM
(Str Mitropoliei 2; adult/child 20/5 lei) The History Museum displays Palaeolithic tools, ceramics, bronze, jewellery and life-sized home scenes, costumes and furniture. Other sections hold guild exhibits, an armoury, Roman artefacts and a treasury.

Biserica Evanghelică   CHURCH
(Evangelical Church; Piaţa Huet; church tower adult/child 3/2 lei) The Gothic Biserica Evanghelică, built from 1300 to 1520, is partially scaffolded due to renovation but you can still climb the church tower; ask for entry at Casa Luxemburg. Its 1772 organ features a staggering 6002 pipes (the largest in southeast Europe).

Pharmaceutical Museum   MUSEUM
(☑0269-218 191; www.brukenthalmuseum.ro; Piaţa Mică 26; adult/child 10/2.50 lei; ☺10am-6pm Tue-Sun Apr-Oct, 10am-6pm Wed-Sun Nov-Mar) Housed in the Piaţa Mică pharmacy (opened in 1600), the Pharmaceutical Museum is a three-room collection packed with pills and powders, old microscopes and scary medical instruments.

OUTSIDE THE CENTRE
Astra Museum of
Traditional Folk Civilisation   MUSEUM
(Muzeul Civilizaţiei Populare Tradiţionale Astra; Calea Răşinarilor 14; adult/child 15/3.50 lei; ☺museum 10am-6pm Tue-Sun, gift shop 9am-5pm Tue-Sun) Around 5km from the centre, this sprawling open-air museum has a dazzling 120 traditional dwellings, mills and churches brought from around the country and set among two small lakes and a tiny zoological garden. Many are signed in English, with maps showing where the structures came from.

🛏 Sleeping

TOP CHOICE **Felinarul Hostel**   HOSTEL €
(☑0269-235 260; www.felinarulhostelsibiu.ro; Str Felinarul 8; dm/r 55/140 lei; ❄@🖵) More *boutique*

than hostel, this labour of love is a wood-accented, courtyard oasis with one eight-berth and two six-berth dorms. There are also two homely private rooms with bathrooms, a book exchange, wine-coloured cafe, antique-style kitchen, posh coffees from the bar and wi-fi. Prepare to stay a while.

Am Ring
HOTEL €€
(📞0269-206 499; www.amringhotel.ro; Piața Mare 14; s/d/tr 250/290/420 lei; ❄🛜🖫) This 26-roomed centrally placed diva is lavish, with marble busts of Hadrian and Achilles, and at every turn antique furniture, velvet curtains and wood-raftered ceilings. There's a nice bar too. Rooms have Gustavian-period furniture, thick carpets and huge beds.

Old Town Hostel
HOSTEL €
(📞0728-184 959, 0269-216 445; www.hostelsibiu.ro; Piața Mică 26; dm/d 55/180 lei; 🛜) In a 450-year-old building with three dorms and two private rooms (one with bathroom), Old Town has sublime square views. It also has decidedly plush touches like parquet floors, fresh white walls, choice artwork, TV in dorms and considerably spaced beds (the antithesis of battery-hen mentality). It's a nice vibe too, from the communal kitchen room to the lounge.

Pensiunea Ela
PENSION €
(📞0269-215 197; www.ela-hotels.ro; Str Nouă 43; s/d/tr 100/120/160 lei; 🛜) Down a quiet street in the Lower Town, you might have to knock on the door a few times to get an answer. Within its flowery courtyard there are eight basic rooms with a rustic signature. Owner Ella is a welcoming host.

✖ Eating & Drinking

🔺 Crama Sibiu Vechi
TOP CHOICE   ROMANIAN €€
(Str P Ilarian; mains 25 lei; 🖫) Hidden in an old wine cellar with its staff dressed in trad garb, this is the most rustically evocative restaurant in Sibiu. It's certainly the most authentic place to explore Romanian fare like cheese croquettes, minced meatballs and peasant's stew with polenta.

Pardon Café and Bistro
INTERNATIONAL, ITALIAN €€
(Str Cetatii 14; mains 20 lei; 🕙9am-10pm; 🖫) Opposite the Philharmonic, this bijou treasure has walls stacked with old gramophones, clocks and antique telephones. Enjoy a pasta, steak, soup or salad in the cosy interior.

Zorba Greek Restaurant
GREEK €€
(Piața Mică 8; mains 25 lei; 🕙11am-2am; 🖫) Zorba dishes up Aegean-fresh fare: colossal Greek salads, souvlaki, calamari, pizza and pasta.

Imperium Club
BAR
(Str Nicolae Bălcescu 24; 🕙9am-dawn) Cosy bar-fly joint with vampish vaulted ceilings, dimly lit booths for canoodling, great cocktails – try the mojito – and live jazz some nights.

☆ Entertainment

Philharmonic
CLASSICAL MUSIC
(www.filarmonicasibiu.ro; Str Cetății 3-5; adult/child 10/7 lei) Founded in 1949, the Philharmonic has played a key role in maintaining Sibiu's prestige as a main cultural centre of Transylvania.

Radu Stancu State Theatre
THEATRE
(B-dul Spitelor 2-4; tickets 20 lei) Plays here are usually in Romanian, with occasional productions in German on Wednesday. It hosts the International Theatre Festival in May/June.

Agenția de Teatrală
BOOKING SERVICE
(Str Nicolae Bălcescu 17; 🕙11am-6pm Mon-Fri, to 3pm Sat) Tickets for major events are sold here.

ℹ Information

ATMs are located all over the centre.

Casa Luxemburg (📞0269-216 854; www.kultours.ro; Piața Mică 16) Travel agent offering loads of city tours (9 to 14 lei) and day trips (50 to 90 lei); has a useful free map of the centre too.

Farmasib (Str Nicolae Bălcescu 53; 🕙7am-11pm Mon-Fri, 8am-11pm Sat & Sun)

Hospital (📞0269-215 050; B-dul Corneliu Coposu 2-4)

Info Point (📞0269-244 442; www.kultours.ro; Piața Huet 1; 🕙9am-10pm) Info on local attractions, surrounding areas, booking bus tickets, car rental and bike hire (per day 35 lei). Also sells some decent souvenirs – books, bags and T-shirts.

Tourist Information Centre (📞0269-208 913; www.sibiu.ro; Piața Mare 2; 🕙9am-5pm Mon-Fri, to 1pm Sat & Sun) Based at the City Hall, staff here are fantastically helpful at guiding you to make the best of the city: cultural events, finding accommodation, and booking train and bus tickets.

ℹ Getting There & Around

BUS The **bus station** (Piața 1 Decembrie 1918) is opposite the train station. Bus and maxitaxi services include Brașov (25 lei, 2½ hours, two daily), Bucharest (40 lei, 5½ hours, six daily),

Cluj-Napoca (30 lei, 3½ hours, 16 daily) and Timişoara (51 lei, six hours, three daily).

TRAIN There are seven daily direct trains to Braşov (35.60 lei, 2½ hours), three daily trains to Bucharest (67 lei, five hours) and Timişoara (67 lei, five hours), and one early-morning run to Arad (55 lei, five hours). To get to/from Sighişoara (13 lei) or Cluj-Napoca (55 lei), you'll have to change at Copşa Mică or Mediaş (about nine or 10 trains daily). The **Agenţia de Voiaj CFR office** (✆0269-212 085; Str Nicolae Bălcescu 6; ⊙7am-8pm Mon-Fri) sells advance tickets and serves as agents for Blue Air and Eurolines.

Cluj-Napoca

POP 294,800

It may not be flanked by mountains or as instantly arresting as Braşov or Sibiu, but Cluj is big on charm. Romania's largest student population make this city their home, and with its boulevards, baroque architecture, bohemian cafe society and backstreets animated with bon viveurs and subterranean bars, you can see why. It's also the country's film capital and the **Transylvania International Film Festival** (www.tiff.ro), held each year in May, attracts plenty of international talent.

⊙ Sights

TOWN CENTRE

St Michael's Church   CHURCH

The vast 14th-century St Michael's Church dominates Piaţa Unirii. The neo-Gothic tower (1859) topping the Gothic hall church creates a great landmark, and the church is considered to be one of the finest examples of Gothic architecture in Romania.

Pharmaceutical Museum   MUSEUM

(Str Regele Ferdinand I; adult/child 5.20/3.10 lei; ⊙10am-4pm Mon-Wed & Fri, noon-6pm Thu) Tours are led by a hilarious pharmacist in a white lab coat, who points like a game-show model towards (seemingly ho-hum) glass cases of ground mummy dust, medieval alchemist symbols and painted 18th-century aphrodisiac bottles.

National Art Museum   MUSEUM

(Piaţa Unirii 30; adult/student 5/3 lei; ⊙10am-5pm Wed-Sun) On the eastern side of Piaţa Unirii is the National Art Museum, housed inside the baroque Banffy Palace (1791). The couple of dozen rooms are filled with paintings and artefacts, including a 16th-century church altar and many 20th-century paintings.

Ethnographic Museum of Transylvania   MUSEUM

(Muzeul Etnografic al Transilvaniei; www.muzeul-etnografic.ro; Str Memorandumului 21; adult/student 6/3 lei; ⊙9am-4pm Tue-Sat) The Ethnographic Museum of Transylvania has two floors of well-presented displays featuring tools, weapons, handcrafts, toys and household items with detailed descriptions in English.

OUTSIDE THE CENTRE

Museum of Zoology   MUSEUM

(Str Clinicilor 5-7; adult/student 3/1.50 lei; ⊙9am-3pm Mon-Fri, 10am-2pm Sat & Sun) In the 'student ghetto' west of the centre, inside the Biology and Geology Faculty you'll find the surprisingly rewarding Museum of Zoology, an L-shaped lab that looks like it hasn't changed in five decades. From Str Clinicilor, veer left through the brick gate.

Alexandru Borza Botanic Gardens   GARDENS

(Str Republicii 42; adult/student 5/3 lei) Through the campus housing, head past fast-food joints up Str Bogdan P Haşdeu to Str Pasteur to reach these fragrant 1930 gardens.

🏃 Activities

TOP CHOICE **Green Mountain Holidays**   HIKING

(✆0744-637 227; www.greenmountainholidays.ro) This terrific ecotourism organisation is recommended for its environmentally friendly, activity-filled week. Check the website for caving, hiking and biking tours in the Apuseni Mountains, with guides, transport, meals and accommodation, as well as self-guided trips.

🛏 Sleeping

TOP CHOICE **Retro Hostel**   HOSTEL €

(✆0264-450 452; www.retro.ro; Str Potaissa 13; dm/s/d/tr incl breakfast sandwich from 49/90/135/195 lei ; ⊝◉@⊚) Well organised, central and with helpful staff, Retro has clean dorms and decent double rooms (all with TV and shared bathrooms). There's also a pleasant cafe downstairs. The private rooms face the narrow road in which sit two noisy bars, so bring earplugs. Retro rents out a car for €35 per day, and lends out bikes for free.

TOP CHOICE **Fullton**   HOTEL €€

(✆0264-597 898; www.fullton.ro; Str Sextil Puşcariu 10; s 170-210 lei; d 196-236 lei; ⊛❄⊚) This boutique hotel with a pea-green facade has a great location in the old town and a couple of places to park. Rooms are fragrant and fresh, and have individual colour schemes (some, like room 101, have four-poster beds), bureaus and bathrooms. There's also a welcoming patio bar.

Piccola Italia   PENSION €

(☑0264-536 110; www.piccolaitalia.ro; Str Racoviţă 20; s/d/tr 115/130/150 lei; ℗🛜) Immediately left after you pass north over the river, Piccolo is a short haul uphill on a quiet road. It has nine clean, whitewashed rooms with reading lights, TV and bathroom. Add to this a garden dripping in vines, hearty breakfast and friendly management, and it's a winner.

Transylvania Hostel   HOSTEL €€

(☑0264-443 266; www.transylvaniahostel.com; Str Iuliu Maniu 26; dm/d 50/150 lei; ➌@🛜) Huddled around a leafy courtyard, this mercifully cool hostel has spacious dorms, private lockers and a lounge with comfy sofas that you may find hard to prise yourself off. There's also a games room, communal PC and flat-screen TV with plenty of DVDs.

✕ Eating

⭐ Camino   CAFE €

(Piaţa Muzeului 4; mains 15 lei; ⊘9am-midnight; 🛜) With jazz piping through its peeling arched interior decked in candelabras and threadbare rugs, this boho restaurant is perfect for a solo book-reading jaunt or romantic alfresco dinner. The homemade pasta is delicious, and the salads and tapas are full of zing.

Magyar Vendeglo   HUNGARIAN €€

(Str Iuliu Maniu 6; mains 25 lei) Based at the Hotel Agape, rustically painted wooden walls and finely carved furniture complement a menu spanning goulash, schnitzel, steak and, curiously, 'brain with egg'! Not sure whose brain.

Restaurant Matei Corvin   ROMANIAN €€

(Str Matei Corvin 3; mains 16-42 lei; 🍴) With its Romanesque arched ceilings and walls strung with oils, this old trusty delivers with a flavoursome menu of broths, soup, pork roulade and tortillas. Authentic.

🍷 Drinking

Many subterranean clubs and bars are spread throughout the centre: it pays to explore. The 'student ghetto', southwest of the centre (on and off Str Piezişă), teems with lively open-air bars.

Klausenberg Café   CAFE

(www.klausenburgcafe.ro; Str Universităţii 1; ⊘9am-midnight; 🍴) This swanky bar glitters with crystal.

Casa Tauffer Jazz Café   BAR, LIVE MUSIC

(Str Vasile Goldiş 2; ⊘24hr) With its oxblood walls ornamented with Rat Pack prints and antique trumpets, and Armstrong and Gillespie jumping on the speakers, this smoky joint is a slice of New Orleans. There are piano evenings and exhibitions too.

☆ Entertainment

Şapte Seri (www.sapteseri.ro) and 24-Fun are free biweekly booklets listing all the latest goings-on (in Romanian).

State Philharmonic   CLASSICAL MUSIC

(Filarmonica de Stat) The State had moved into the Student Culture House at research time. The improvised box office is just inside the front doors, on the right. Check with the

TRAINS FROM CLUJ

DESTINATION	PRICE (LEI)	DURATION (HR)	FREQUENCY (DAILY)
Braşov	67	5	8
Bucharest	82	9	5
Budapest (Hungary)	140	5	2
Iaşi	82	9	3
Oradea	39	2¼-4	12
Sibiu	48	5	2
Sighişoara	55	3½	5
Suceava	67	7	5
Timişoara	67	7	8

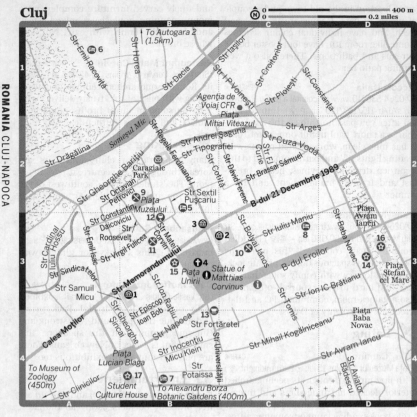

tourist information office to see where they are playing.

National Theatre Lucian Blaga   THEATRE
(Piaţa Ştefan cel Mare 2-4; tickets from 20 lei) National Theatre Lucian Blaga was designed by Viennese architects Fellner and Hellmer; performances are well attended. The **Opera** (☎0264-595 363; National Theatre Lucian Blaga) is in the same building. Tickets for both can be bought from the **Agenţia de Teatrală** (☎0264-595 363; Piaţa Ştefan cel Mare 14; ☺11am-5pm Tue-Fri), starting at 6.50 lei and 15 lei respectively.

Diesel   CLUB
(Piaţa Unirii 17; ☺6pm-dawn) Its outside terrace might look innocent enough but descend the stairway into the Sadean darkness and a dungeonlike interior awaits, complete with low-lit grotto bar, candelabras and a whole world of possibilities.

ℹ Information

Clematis (Piaţa Unirii 11; ☺8am-10pm) Pharmacy.

Pan Travel (☎0264-420 516; www.pantravel.ro; Str Grozavescu 13; ☺9am-5pm Mon-Fri) Books accommodation, car rentals, self-drive tours and multiday tours to the Apuseni Mountains, Saxon villages or around Maramureş.

Tourist Information Office (☎0264-452 244; www.visitcluj.ro; B-dul Eroilor 6-8; ☺8.30am-8pm Mon-Fri, 10am-6pm Sat) This super-friendly office has bags of info on trekking, train and bus times, eating, accommodation and cultural unmissables.

Transylvania Ecological Club (Clubul Ecologic Transilvania; ☎0264-431 626; www.greenagenda.org) One of Romania's most active grassroots environmental groups, operating since the mid-1990s. Can provide trail maps and find guides.

ℹ Getting There & Around

BUS Bus services from **Autogara 2** (Autogara Beta; ☎0264-455 249), 350m northwest of the

Cluj

⊙ Sights
1 Ethnographic Museum of
   Transylvania B3
2 National Art Museum C3
3 Pharmaceutical Museum...................B3
4 St Michael's Church B3

🛏 Sleeping
5 Fullton..B2
6 Piccola Italia A1
7 Retro Hostel..B4
8 Transylvania Hostel...........................C3

✖ Eating
9 Camino...B2
10 Magyar Vendeglo................................C3
11 Restaurant Matei Corvin....................B3

☕ Drinking
12 Casa Tauffer Jazz Café B3
13 Klausenberg Café B4

✪ Entertainment
14 Agenţia de Teatrală D3
15 Diesel...B3
16 National Theatre Lucian Blaga............D3
   Opera...(see 16)
17 State Philharmonic.............................B4

train station (take the overpass), include Braşov (50 lei, two daily), Bucharest (60 lei, 7½ hours, three daily), Budapest (75 lei, several daily) and Sibiu (28 lei, 3½ hours, eight daily).

TAXI Diesel Taxi (☎0264-946, 0264-953)

TRAIN The **Agenţia de Voiaj CFR** (☎0264-432 001; Piaţa Mihai Viteazul 20; ⊙8am-8pm Mon-Fri, 9am-1.30pm Sat) sells domestic and International train tickets in advance.

CRIŞANA & BANAT

Western Romania, with its geographic and cultural ties to neighbouring Hungary and Serbia, and historical links to the Austro-Hungarian Empire, enjoys an ethnic diversity that much of the rest of the country lacks. Timişoara, the regional hub, has a nationwide reputation as a beautiful and lively metropolis, and for a series of 'firsts'. It was the world's first city to adopt electric street lights (in 1884) and, more importantly, the first city to rise up against dictator Nicolae Ceauşescu in 1989. Outside the metropolitan areas, the remote and pristine Apuseni Mountains are littered with

dozens of amazing caves that cry out for exploration, and miles and miles of isolated hiking trails.

Timişoara
POP 312,000

Romania's third- or fourth-largest city (depending on the source) is also one of the country's most attractive urban areas, built around a series of beautiful public squares and lavish parks and gardens. It's known as Primul Oraş Liber (First Free Town), for it was here that anti-Ceauşescu protests first exceeded the Securitate's capacity for violent suppression in 1989, eventually sending Ceauşescu and his wife to their demise. With western Romania's nicest hotels and restaurants, it makes a perfect base for exploring the Banat region.

⊙ Sights

PIAŢA UNIRII

Piaţa Unirii is Timişoara's most picturesque square, featuring the imposing sight of the **Catholic cathedral** (Catedrală Episcopală Romano-Catolică; ☎0256-430 671; Piaţa Unirii 12; ⊙8am-6pm) and **Serbian church** (Biserica Ortodoxă Sârbă; Str Ungureanu 12) facing each other. A couple of blocks to the east, following Str Palanca, is the **Cetate** (Fortress), a classic 18th-century Austrian fortress that's been remodelled into a complex of shops and cafes.

[TOP CHOICE] **Permanent Exhibition of the 1989 Revolution**   MUSEUM
(☎0256-294 936; www.memorialulrevolutiei.ro; Str Popa Sapcă 3-5; admission by donation; ⊙8am-4pm Mon-Fri, 9am-1pm Sat) This work in progress is an ideal venue to brush up on the December 1989 anticommunist revolution that began in Timişoara. Displays include documentation, posters and photography from those fateful days, capped by a graphic, 20-minute video (not suitable for young children), with English subtitles.

Art Museum   MUSEUM
(Muzeul de Artă; ☎0256-491 592; www.muzeuldeartatm.ro; Old Prefecture Palace, Piaţa Unirii 1; admission 5 lei; ⊙10am-6pm Tue-Sun) The art museum displays a representative sample of paintings and visual arts over the centuries as well as regular, high-quality temporary exhibitions. It's housed in the baroque Old Prefecture Palace, built in 1754, and is worth a look inside for the graceful baroque interiors alone.

DON'T MESS WITH TIMIŞOARA

Even at the height of his power, Nicolea Ceauşescu never liked Romania's western-most metropolis. The dictator's visits to the city were few and brief, and required sur-reptitious, dread-fuelled travel and sleeping arrangements to allay his assassination concerns. So when the Romanian secret service, the Securitate, overplayed its hand in the already truculent city by trying to deport popular Hungarian pastor and outspo-ken Ceauşescu critic László Tőkés, the dictator should have sensed disaster looming. However, like most megalomaniacs, he didn't grasp the full scale of his folly until he was being shoved in front of a firing squad, looking genuinely stunned, a little more than a week later on Christmas Day 1989.

What started on 15 December 1989 as a human chain of Tőkés' parishioners protect-ing him from arrest mushroomed into a full-scale anticommunist revolt on 20 Decem-ber. Overconfident Ceauşescu actually left Romania during this time for a visit to Iran, leaving his wife Elena to cope with the escalating protests.

When Ceauşescu returned to Romania the next day, the situation was critical. Factory workers brought in by party officials to crush the demonstrations spontaneously joined the protesters in Piaţa Operei (today's Piaţa Victoriei), chanting antigovernment slogans and singing an old Romanian anthem ('Wake up, Romanians!') banned since the com-munists took power in 1947. The crowd, now over 100,000 strong, overpowered and then commandeered some of the tanks that had previously fired on demonstrators. Protests later ensued in Bucharest and around the country, and Ceauşescu's fate was sealed.

Learn more about the revolution and see video footage of the events at the excellent Permanent Exhibition of the 1989 Revolution.

PIAŢA VICTORIEI
Begging to be photographed with your widest lens is Piaţa Victoriei, a beautifully green pedestrian mall dotted with foun-tains in the middle and lined on both sides with shops and cafes. The square's northern end is marked by the 18th-century National Theatre & Opera House, where thousands of demonstrators gathered on 16 December 1989. A memorial on the front of the Opera House reads: 'So you, who pass by this build-ing, will dedicate a thought for free Rom-ania'. Towards the centre, there's a **statue of Romulus and Remus**.

Banat History Museum   MUSEUM
(Muzeul Banatului; Piaţa Huniades 1) The Ba-nat History Museum, housed in the his-toric Huniades Palace, was closed during our research for renovations expected to last until 2015. The exterior of the palace, though, is still worth a look. The origins of the building date to the 14th century and to Hungarian King Charles Robert, Prince of Anjou.

Metropolitan Cathedral   CHURCH
(Catedrala Ortodoxă; www.timisoara.org/catedrala; B-dul Regele Ferdinand I; ⊙10am-6pm) The Or-thodox Metropolitan Cathedral was built be-tween 1936 and 1946. Unique to the church are its electric bells cast from iron imported from Indonesia.

OUTSIDE THE CENTRE
Tőkés Reformed Church   CHURCH
(Biserica Reformată Tőkés; Str Timotei Cipariu 1) The 1989 revolution began at the Tőkés Re-formed Church, where Father László Tőkés spoke out against the dictator. You can sometimes peek in at the church, but Tőkés' small apartment is privately inhabited.

Banat Village Museum   MUSEUM
(Muzeul Satului Banaţean; ☑0256-225 588; www.muzeulsatuluibanatean.ro; Str Avram Imbroane 1; admission 4.50 lei; ⊙10am-6pm Tue-Sat, noon-8pm Sun) The museum exhibits more than 30 traditional peasant houses dating from the 19th century. The open-air display was created in 1917. Take tram 1 (black number) from the northern train station.

🛏 Sleeping
Pension Casa Leone   PENSION €
(☑0256-292 621; www.casaleone.ro; B-dul Eroilor 67; s/d/tr 125/150/200 lei; P❄✳🤖) This lovely seven-room pension offers exceptional serv-ice and individually decorated rooms. To find it, take tram 8 from the train station, alight at the 'Deliblata' station and walk

one block northeast to B-dul Eroilor (or call ahead to arrange transport).

Hostel Costel
HOSTEL €

(☏0726-240 223; www.hostel-costel.ro; Str Petru Sfetca 1; dm 40-45 lei, d 135 lei; ✎@🖥) Run by an affable guy named Vlad, this charming 1920s art nouveau villa is arguably the city's only real youth hostel. With three dorm rooms and one private double, the vibe is relaxed and congenial. There are lots of little rooms to relax in and a big garden out back.

Hotel Central
HOTEL €€

(☏0256-490 091; www.hotel-central.ro; Str N Lenau 6; s/d 160/180 lei; P✳🖥) It's not exactly the Taj Mahal, but this communist-era hotel has had a decent facelift, leaving the rooms clean, modern and comfortable. There's ample guarded parking out front (per day 10 lei) if you're travelling by car, and you can't beat the price for the location.

Hotel Cina Banatul
HOTEL €

(☏0256-490 130; www.hotelcina.ro; B-dul Republicii 7; s/d 120/140 lei; P✳🖥) One of the best-value places in the centre, though not quite as appealing as the Hotel Central. The hotel has clean, ultramodern rooms and a good restaurant.

 ## Eating

TOP CHOICE **Casa Bunicii**
ROMANIAN €€

(☏0356-100 870; www.casa-bunicii.ro; Str Virgil Onitiu 3; mains 18-30 lei; 🐸) The name translates to 'Granny's House' and indeed this casual, family-friendly restaurant specialises in home cooking and regional specialities from the Banat. We enjoyed the duck soup and the grilled chicken breast served in sour cherry sauce.

Casa cu Flori
ROMANIAN €€

(☏0256-435 080; www.casacuflori.ro; Str Alba Iulia 1; mains 18-28 lei) One of the best-known restaurants in the city and for good reason, serving excellent high-end Romanian cooking with refined service at moderate prices. In nice weather, climb three flights to the flower-lined rooftop terrace.

Intermezzo
ITALIAN €€

(☏0256-432 429; www.restaurant-intermezzo. ro; Piața Unirii 3; mains 22-36 lei, pizza 18-24 lei; ◷noon-midnight) This place has great pizzas and even better pastas. Dine on the terrace on Piața Unirii or in the cellar restaurant.

Restaurant Lloyd
ROMANIAN €€

(☏0256-294 949; http://restaurantlloyd.ro; Piața Victoriei 2; mains 15-50 lei; ◷9am-11pm; 🖥) A popular spot with visitors, located right on Piața Victoriei in front of the opera. The Romanian food is surprisingly good and the prices – given the terrace locale – are not as bad as you'd think.

Drinking

Aethernativ
CAFE

(☏0724-012 324; Str Mărăşeşti 14; ◷10am-1am Mon-Fri, noon-1am Sat, 5pm-1am Sun; 🖥) This informal art club, cafe and bar occupies a courtyard of a rundown building two blocks west of Piața Unirii. It resembles a Budapest ruin pub, with its eclectic furnishings and alternative, student vibe. There are no signs to let you know you're here; simply find the address, push open the door and walk up a flight of stairs.

Scarţ loc lejer
CAFE

(☏0751-892 340; Str Zoe 1; ◷10am-11pm Mon-Fri, 11am-11pm Sat, to 11pm Sun; 🖥) This is an old villa that's been retrofitted into a funky coffeehouse with albums pinned to the wall and chill tunes on the turntable. There are several cosy rooms in which to read, talk and relax, but our favourite is the lush garden out back.

Entertainment

State Philharmonic Theatre
CLASSICAL MUSIC

(Filharmonica de Stat Banatul; ☏0256-492 521; www.filarmonicabanatul.ro; B-dul CD Loga 2; ◷box office 2-7pm Wed, 9am-1pm Thu & Fri) Classical concerts are held most evenings here. Tickets (from 40 lei) can be bought at the box office inside the Philharmonic Theatre during limited opening hours or one hour before performances.

National Theatre & Opera House
THEATRE, OPERA

(Teatrul Naţional şi Opera Română; ☏opera 0256-201 286, theatre 0256-201 117; www.tntimisoara. com; Str Mărăşeşti 2) The National Theatre & Opera House features both dramatic works and classical opera, and is highly regarded. Buy tickets (from around 40 lei) in the nearby **Agenţia Teatrală** (☏0256-201 286; www.ort. ro; Str Mărăşeşti 2; ◷10am-1pm & 5-7pm Tue-Sun).

Club 30
CLUB

(☏0256-247 878; www.club30.ro; Piața Victoriei 7; admission 10 lei; ◷6pm-3am) This club has been a staple on the dance scene for years and shows no signs of slowing down, particularly on retro '80s and '90s dance nights. There's live music on some evenings.

Cinema Timiş
CINEMA

(☑0256-491 290; Piaţa Victoriei 7; tickets 6-8 lei) Centrally located cinema screens a mix of Hollywood blockbusters and popular European films. Movies are normally screened in their original language.

ℹ Information

Online Centers (B-dul Mihai Eminescu 5; per hr 5.40 lei; ⊙24hr; 🕾)

Sensi Blu Pharmacy (☑0256-201 21; www. sensiblu.com; Piaţa Victoriei 7; ⊙8am-8pm Mon-Fri, 9am-8pm Sat & Sun) One of at least half a dozen similar, modern pharmacies on or around Piaţa Victoriei

Timişoara County Hospital (Spitalul Clinic Judeţean de Urgenţă Timişoara; ☑0356-433 111; www.hosptm.ro; B-dul Iosif Bulbuca 10) Modern hospital with high-quality medical care and 24-hour emergency service.

Tourist Information Centre (Info Centru Turistic; ☑0256-437 973; www.timisoara-info.ro; Str Alba Iulia 2) This great tourism office can assist with accommodation and trains, and provide maps and Banat regional info.

ℹ Getting There & Away

BUS Timişoara lacks a centralised bus station for domestic services. Buses and minibuses are privately operated and depart from several points around the city, depending on the company. Consult the website www.autogari.ro for departure points. Bus service is extensive. Sample fares include Arad (15 lei), Cluj-Napoca (65 lei) and Sibiu (45 lei).

International buses leave from the **East bus station** (www.autogari.ro). The main international operators include **Atlassib** (☑0256-226 486; www.atlassib.ro; Calea Dorobantilor 59) and **Eurolines** (☑0256-288 132; www. eurolines.ro; Str M Kogălniceanu 20). Belgrade-based **Gea Tours** (www.geatours.rs) offers daily minibus service between Timişoara and Belgrade for one way/return 125/200 lei. Book over the website.

TRAIN Trains depart from **Gara Timişoara-Nord** (www.cfr.ro; Str Gării 2), the 'northern' station, though it's actually west of the centre. Daily express trains include two to Bucharest (100 lei, eight hours), two to Cluj-Napoca (127 lei, six hours) and five to Arad (20 lei, one hour). There's one daily train to Belgrade (70 lei, three hours), which leaves at 5.40am.

Oradea
POP 176.300

Fans of art nouveau and Secession architecture dating from the late 19th and early 20th centuries will want to make a special stopover in Oradea. While many of the once-elegant buildings here have been allowed to fall into disrepair, visitors with a sharp architectural eye will see Secession's signature lyric design elements and inlaid jewelwork on buildings up and down the main drag, Str Republicii, and across the Crişul Repede river at the **Black Eagle Arcade** (Pasajul Vulturul Negru; Str Independenţei 1).

◉ Sights

The best way to see the city is to stroll Str Republicii, lined on both sides with architectural gems from the early 20th century. Don't miss the **Moskovits Palace** (Palatul Moskovits; Str Republicii 13), a Secession masterwork from 1905.

Moon Orthodox Church
CHURCH

(Biserica cu Lună; www.bisericaculuna.ro; Piaţa Unirii; ⊙9am-5pm) The Orthodox Moon Church, built in 1784, has an unusual lunar mechanism on its tower that changes position in accordance with the moon's movement. Nearby, in the centre of Piaţa Unirii, stands an equestrian **statue of Mihai Viteazul**, the prince of Wallachia (r 1593–1601), who is said to have rested in Oradea in 1600.

Roman Catholic Cathedral
CHURCH

(Sirul Canonicilor; ⊙9am-6pm) This cathedral, 2km north of the centre, was built between 1752 and 1780 and is the largest baroque church in Romania. Organ concerts are occasionally held here. The adjacent **Bishop's Palace** (⊙closed to the public) from 1770 boasts 100 fresco-adorned rooms and 365 windows.

The street Sirul Canonicilor that runs just east of the cathedral includes a series of 57 arches that form part of the original baroque design as laid out by Austrian master architect FA Hillebrandt.

Orthodox Synagogue
SYNAGOGUE

(www.oradeajc.com; Str Mihai Viteazul 4; ⊙closed to the public) Oradea's Orthodox synagogue dates from 1890, and before WWII was the main house of worship for around a third of the city's residents. It survived the war intact but was badly neglected afterwards, and is now undergoing a thorough multiyear renovation. Though it is closed to the public, phone the **Jewish Community Centre** (0359-191 021; www.fcer.jewishfed.ro; Str Mihai Viteazul 4) to take a look inside.

🛏 Sleeping

TOP CHOICE Hotel Elite HOTEL €€
(0259-414 924; www.hotelelite.ro; Str IC Bratianu 26; s/d 250/280 lei; P❄🛜🏊♿) This beautiful hotel is worth the splurge, especially if you're travelling during the hot summer and have kids in tow. The rooms are spotless and well maintained, but the major drawcard is a gorgeous heated (and child-friendly) pool straight out of a Hollywood mansion.

Scorilo Hotel HOTEL €€
(0259-470 910; www.hotelscorilo.ro; Str Parcul Petőfi 16; s/d/apt 180/220/300 lei; P❄🛜) It's nearly impossible to book a room at this clean and way-too-popular family-run hotel, 10 minutes' walk from the train station. The rooms are small but tidy; some have balconies over the garden. The outdoor restaurant is the most festive place in town for an evening meal.

Hostel Felix HOSTEL €
(0259-437 011; tineret_bh@yahoo.com; Mihai Eminescu 11; dm 40 lei) This 'sometimes open, sometimes not' hostel, run by the local department for youth affairs, has four-bed dorms with seatless toilets and zero ambience, yet it's undeniably central and cheap.

🍴 Eating

TOP CHOICE Graf INTERNATIONAL €€€
(0259-421 421; www.restaurantgraf.ro; Str Barbu Stefanescu Delavrancea 3; mains 30-70 lei; ⏰11am-11pm; 🛜) Graf is Oradea's nicest restaurant and a perfect splurge option. The menu features wood-grilled steaks, fish and pork; on our visit, the caramelised duck leg was one of our best meals in Romania. The wine list is top notch.

Lactobar CAFE €
(www.lactobarretrobistro.ro; Calea Republicii 11; mains 8-15 lei; ⏰8am-11pm; 🛜♿) Even if you're not hungry, stop by this charming, very kid-friendly 'retro bistro' on the main street. The colourful decor of period-piece found objects is remarkable, topped off with an orange, ultracool Dacia automobile.

Cyrano ROMANIAN €€
(0740-163 943; Calea Republicii 7; mains 14-30 lei; ⏰8.30am-midnight Mon-Fri, 9.30am-midnight Sat, 11am-midnight Sun; 🛜) Popular hang-out ideal for people-watching from the coveted terrace tables. Though the menu teems with Romanian favourites, the incredible *ciorbă de vițel cu tarhon in chiflă* (beef and vegie stew in a bread bowl, 12.80 lei) is all the food you need.

ℹ Information

Alpha Bank (0259-457 834; Piața Unirii 24; ⏰9am-4pm Mon-Fri)

Internet Cafe (0359-454 566; Str George Enescu 24; per hr 3 lei; ⏰8.30am-midnight Mon-Fri, noon-midnight Sat & Sun; 🛜)

Post Office (0259-435 040; Str Roman Ciorogariu 12; ⏰8am-8pm Mon-Fri, to 2pm Sat)

ℹ Getting There & Away

BUS A small **bus station** (autogara; 0259-418 998; Str Războieni 81) is situated 2km south of the centre. From here you can catch frequent maxitaxis and regular buses to Băile Felix (4 lei, 10 minutes), Ştei (for access to Bear Cave; 13 lei, two hours) and Arieşeni (24 lei, three hours).

There's a small **maxitaxi** stand north of the train station for travelling to cities north of Oradea, such as Baia Mare (38 lei, three hours).

TRAIN Oradea's **train station** (0259-414 970; www.cfr.ro; Calea Republicii 114) is 2km north of the centre. Daily fast trains from Oradea include one to Budapest (150 lei, five hours), one slow overnight to Bucharest (about 105 lei, 12 hours), six to Cluj-Napoca (43 lei, three hours), two to Braşov (60 lei, nine hours) and five to Timişoara (47 lei, three hours).

MARAMUREŞ

This is widely regarded as Romania's most traditional region, scattered with steepled wooden churches and villagers' homes fronted by ornately carved gates. A visit to Maramureş is like climbing into a horse-drawn time machine and heading back 100 years. Smaller in scale and softer in contour than neighbouring Transylvania, Maramureş' tapestry of pastureland peopled by colourfully garbed peasants jumps straight from a Brothers Grimm story. But don't wait forever to visit – even here, the 21st century is making inroads.

Sighetu Marmaţiei

POP 44,200

Sleepy 'Sighet' (its shortened nickname) has a few sights for a morning's browsing, a pretty square bookended by a church, and the Ukrainian border crossing just a few minutes away; but your real reason for being in Maramureş is its rural charm, so you needn't linger long. For centuries Sighet formed a cultural and geographic border between Slav-dominated territories to the north and Hungary and Romania to the south. Its name is derived from the Thracian and Dacian word *seget* (fortress).

⊙ Sights

On Piaţa Libertăţii stands the **Hungarian Reformed church**, built during the 15th century. Close by is the 16th-century **Roman Catholic church**.

Maramureş Museum   MUSEUM

(Piaţa Libertăţii 15; adult/student 4/2 lei; ⊙10am-6pm Tue-Sun) The Maramureş Museum displays colourful folk costumes, rugs and carnival masks.

Elie Wiesel's House   HISTORIC BUILDING

Elie Wiesel, the Jewish writer and 1986 Nobel Peace Prize winner, was born in (and later deported from) Sighet. His house, on the corner of Str Dragoş Vodă and Str Tudor Vladimirescu, is open to visitors. Along Str Gheorghe Doja there is a **monument** (Str Mureşan) to the victims of the Holocaust.

Synagogue   SYNAGOGUE

(Str Bessarabia 10) Sighet's only remaining synagogue is found near Piaţa Libertăţii. You can look around for free, but it's customary to leave a donation (10 lei). Before

WWII the Jewish community was estimated at 50,000 – more than half of Sighet's pre-war population. Today the local Jewish community numbers around 200.

Most of the Jews perished at Auschwitz-Birkenau after being shipped there in 1944, when Hungary (which ruled over the area at the time) agreed to surrender its Jews to Nazi Germany.

Village Museum   MUSEUM

(Muzeul Satului; ☑0262-314 229; Str Dobăieş 40; adult/child/photo 4/2/4 lei) Allow two to three hours to wander through the incredible constructions at the open-air Village Museum, southeast of Sighet's centre. Children love the wooden dwellings, cobbled pathways and 'mini villages'. You can even stay overnight in tiny wooden cabins (20 lei) or pitch a tent (5 lei per person).

🛏 Sleeping

For homestays in the area, check out www.ruraltourism.ro and www.pensiuni.info.ro.

TOP CHOICE Casa Iurca   HOTEL €€

(☑0262-318 882; www.casaiurca.ro; Str Dragoş Vodă 14; r 150 lei, annexe s 92 lei, d 185-218 lei; ⊙🌬🛜) Rooms are elegant and cool in this fine wood-accented villa. Expect tasteful furniture, flat-screen TVs, tiled floors, leather chairs and spotless linen for your money. There's also in-room wi-fi, fridge, cable TV and fan. Hands down the best digs in town.

TOP CHOICE Cobwobs Hostel   PENSION €

(☑0745-635 673; www.cobwobs.com; Str 22 Decembrie 1989 nr; dm/d without bathroom 40/100 lei; ⊙@🛜) Friendly Cobwobs sits down a grassy lane in a pleasant house whose garden is so crowded with apple and plum

---

SIGHET PRISON: A SUFFERING NATION

In May 1947 the communist regime slaughtered, imprisoned or tortured thousands of Romanians who might oppose the new leadership. While many leading prewar figures were sent to hard-labour camps, the regime's most feared intellectual opponents were held in Sighet's maximum-security prison. Between 1948 and 1952 about 180 members of Romania's academic and government elite were imprisoned here and some 51 died.

The prison, housed in the old courthouse, was closed in 1974. In the early '90s it reopened as the **Memorial to the Victims of Communism and to the Resistance** (☑0262-319 424; www.memorialsighet.ro; Str Corneliu Coposu 4; admission 6 lei; ⊙9.30am-6.30pm Mon-Sun, to 4pm winter). Photographs and objects with short descriptions are displayed in the torture chambers and cells on two levels. There's also a small bookstore and gift shop. The emotional bronze statues in the courtyard, shielding themselves and covering their mouths in horror, are dedicated to those who died.

Maramureş

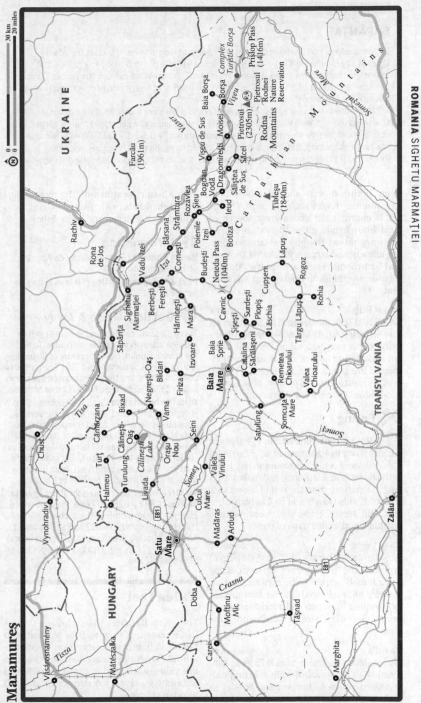

SĂPÂNŢA

Săpânţa village has a unique place in the hearts of Romanians. It boasts the **Merry Cemetery** (admission 4 lei), famous for the colourfully painted wooden crosses that adorn the tombstones in the village's graveyard. Shown in art exhibitions across Europe, the crosses attract coachloads of visitors who marvel at the gentle humour and human warmth that created them.

While most visitors stay just a couple of hours, there are a couple of nice pensions scattered around. With its traditional rooms nestled around a courtyard and its garden stacked with freshly shorn wool, **Pensiunea Ileana** (0262-372 137, 0745-491 756; sapantaileana@yahoo.com; d 80 lei) is old-school Maramureş. Ileana, the eponymous host, is lovely and has her own weaving workshop that she can show you. Opposite the cemetery.

trees, rioting flowers and talkative chickens, you may forget you're in town. Owner Lia is charm itself and a great source of local info (handy given there's no tourist office any more). Doubles and family rooms are homely and large, with shared showers and bathrooms. There are also two dorms. Outside are tables to read at and bikes for rent.

Motel Buţi HOTEL €
(0262-311 035; www.hotelbuti.ro; Str Ştefan cel Mare 6; s/d/tr 100/120/180 lei; ✳@✶) Admittedly rooms may be a bit on the small side, but considering how clean it is, and the high spec of the rooms with flat-screen TVs, decent furniture and crisp linen, this is very good value. There's a bar downstairs.

✗ Eating

TOP CHOICE Restaurant Tineretului ROMANIAN €
(Str Ioan Mihaly de Apşa; mains 10 lei; ✆7am-9pm) This rustic-accented restaurant is hung with cowbells and lanterns, and makes for a magic departure from the rest of Sighet's offerings. It's also lovely and cool in high summer, and serves gyros, cold meat platters, breakfast and grilled nape of pork.

Casa Veche ROMANIAN €€
(Str Iuliu Maniu 27; mains 14-30 lei; ✆8am-11pm) Probably the busiest joint in town, Casa has a bubbly terrace come evening, and an elegant, high-ceilinged interior besmirched by pumping Euro-pop and a stratosphere of smoke. Succulent steaks, salads and huge pizza.

David's ROMANIAN €€
(Str Ioan Mihaly de Apşa 1; mains 11-25 lei; ✆7am-10pm) With lime-washed walls sporting old-fashioned prints of London and booths to soak up the very smoky atmosphere, this is

an authentic local haunt. The menu offers up fresh salads with plenty of zing, and grilled pork, chicken and lamb dishes.

ℹ Information

Banca Română (Str Ioan Mihaly de Apşa 24; ✆9am-5pm Mon-Fri)
Post & Telephone Office (Str Ioan Mihaly de Apşa 39)

ℹ Getting There & Away

There's a small car/footbridge from Sighet to Ukraine about 2km outside the centre. To find the crossing point, from the centre of Sighet follow Str Titelescu north about 2km. The border is open 24 hours. The Ukrainian town on the other side is called Slatina and has a number of hotels.
BUS The **bus station** (Str Gării; ✆closed Sun) is opposite the train station. There are several local buses departing daily (except Sunday) to Baia Mare (12 lei, 65km) as well as Borşa (10 lei), Budeşti (7 lei), Călineşti (7 lei) and Vişeu de Sus (10 lei). There's also service to Bârsana, Botiza, Ieud and Mara (all around 6 lei). From Borşa, there are daily maxitaxi services to Moldavia.
TRAIN Advance tickets are sold at the **Agenţia de Voiaj CFR** (0262-312 666; Piaţa Libertăţii 25; ✆7am-8pm Mon-Fri). There's one daily fast train to Timişoara (93 lei, 12 hours), Bucharest (90 lei, 12 hours), Cluj-Napoca (60 lei, six hours) and Braşov (77 lei, eight hours). A sleeper train here costs 121 lei.

Valea Izei

POP 3000

The Valea Izei (Izei Valley) follows the Iza River eastwards from Sighetu Marmaţiei to Moisei. A tightly knit procession of quintessential Maramureş peasant villages nestle in the valley, all featuring the region's famed elaborately carved wooden gates and tall wooden churches.

Gradually developing tourism in the region provides visitors with the opportunity to sample traditional cuisine or try their hand at woodcarving, wool weaving and glass painting.

In mid-July Vadu Izei, together with the neighbouring villages of Botiza and Ieud, hosts the Maramuzical Festival, a lively four-day international folk-music festival.

VADU IZEI
Vadu Izei lies at the confluence of the Iza and Mara Rivers, 6km south of Sighetu Marmaţiei. Its museum is in the oldest house in the village (1750).

Casa Muntean (☑0766-755 267; www.casa-muntean.ro; Str Dumbrava 505; s/d without bathroom 40/80 lei; ❸@☎) offers colourful rooms enlivened by richly designed rugs, wood ceilings and wall hangings. The owner, Florin, can take you on a guided tour (60 lei) to local wooden churches or to the Merry Cemetery.

Nearby, the **Pensiunea Teodora Teleptean** (☑0742-492 240; Str Dumbrava 503; r 120 lei; ℗) has 10 rooms in a pretty wood-carved building (there are pots and pans hanging from a tree in the front garden – signifying there is a girl available for marriage in the house!). Rooms are spacious and fragrant with antique armoires, wood-raftered ceilings, TVs and bathrooms.

BÂRSANA
From Vadu Izei, continue for 12km through Onceşti to the village of Bârsana (formerly Bîrsana), dating from 1326. In 1720 it built its first church, the interior paintings of which were created by local artists Hodor Toador and Ion Plohod.

The famous Orthodox **Bârsana Monastery** (Mănăstirea Bârsana) is a popular pilgrimage spot in Maramureş; however, the church you see today was built in the 1990s. The 11am service is a magical experience among the rolling hills and wildflowers, and every 30 June the monastery celebrates the Twelve Apostles. Check out the beautiful church, shrine, museum and shop. Eleven nuns presently reside here.

ROZAVLEA
Continue south through Strâmtura to Rozavlea. Its fine church, dedicated to archangels Michael and Gabriel, was constructed between 1717 and 1720 in another village, then erected in Rozavlea on the site of an ancient church destroyed by the Tatars. The flower-strewn graveyard is a testament to the area's anarchic splendour.

BOTIZA
From Rozavlea, continue south to Şieu, then take the turn-off right for the sleepy village of Botiza, one of the prettiest in all of Maramureş and site of the some of the region's best homestays.

Botiza's old church, built in 1694, is overshadowed by the giant new church, constructed in 1974 to serve devout Orthodox families.

The 9am Sunday service is the major event of the week in Botiza. The *entire* village flocks to the church to partake in the religious activities, which continue well into the afternoon.

George Iurca (☑0722-942 140, 0262-334 110; botizavr@sintec.ro; Botiza 742; r per person 90 lei; @☎) is a friendly guide with a licence to conduct tours throughout Romania. He rents out clean, comfortable rooms as well as mountain bikes (25 lei per day) and vehicles with a driver/guide (300 lei per day for a group). You'll find his house four doors down from the new church.

Victoria Berbecaru (☑0262-334 107; r incl breakfast 80 lei) offers four rooms in her own home or, better yet, in the 19th-century wooden house just opposite. Downstairs there's a shop selling beautifully woven rugs.

IEUD
Packed with wooden houses and pensioners in traditional garb, the village of Ieud (6km off the road south from Şieu) has two beautiful churches, including what some consider to be the region's oldest wooden church.

Ieud was first documented in the 14th century, but evidence suggests the village was inhabited as early as the 11th century by Balc, Dragoş Vodă's grandson and later Prince of Moldavia.

Sometime in the 14th century, the town's fabulous Orthodox Church on the Hill (Biserica de Lemn din Deal) was built on castle ruins (though much of the current structure may date back only to the 17th century). Under its rooftop, the 'Ieud Codex' from 1391 was found, a document which is considered to be the oldest writing in Romanian language (today it is kept in the archives of the Romanian Academy in Bucharest).

Ieud's other church (Biserica de Lemn din Şes), today Greco-Catholic in denomination, was built in 1718. At the southern end of the village, it's unique to the region as it has no porch, and houses one of the largest collections of icons on glass found in Maramureş.

Cross the bridge to the modest **Ethnographic Museum** (adult/child 5/3 lei; ☺8am-noon & 1pm-8pm Mon-Sun) to see an old lady spinning thread on a wheel like Rumplestiltskin.

Vasile Chindris (☎0262-336 197, 0743-811 077; leud 201; r per person 90 lei; Ⓟ) offers rooms that are clean and homey, with shared bathrooms; meals cost 28 lei. The husband-and-wife team can drive you around.

MOISEI

About 9km southeast of the town of Vişeu de Sus, at the foot of the Rodna Massif (mountains), Moisei gained fame in 1944 when retreating Hungarian troops gunned down 31 people before setting fire to the entire village.

Only one house in Moisei survived the blaze – the one in which the prisoners were shot. Today, it houses a small **museum** (Expoziţia Documentar – Istorică Martirii de la Moisei 14 Octombrie 1944; admission 2 lei; ☺9.30am-4.30pm Tue-Sun), in tribute to those who died. Opposite the museum is a monument to the victims – 10 columns are decorated with a traditional carnival mask and two are decorated with human faces based on the features of the two survivors.

If the museum is locked, knock at the house next door and ask for the key.

Each year, on 15 August, the Feast of the Assumption shuts down the area. Villagers from around the county, walking in groups for two days or more, carry crosses and holy pictures to Moisei's monastery.

MOLDAVIA

Despite being among Romania's poorer regions, Moldavia is historically and culturally rich. Prince Ştefan cel Mare (r 1457–1504) defeated the Turks here, and built fortified painted monasteries which astonish with their kaleidoscopic ranges of colour and rich detail. Iaşi, a vibrant student city dotted with impressive architecture, parks and buzzing bars, has been Moldavia's capital for five centuries.

Iaşi

POP 263,400

Exuberant, cultured Iaşi (pronounced 'yash') clearly enjoys being one of the country's biggest cities. Once dubbed the 'city of the hundred churches', Iaşi is indeed bursting with centuries of architectural creations. Yet besides the monasteries, theatres and other historic buildings, this eclectic place has botanical parks, big squares and (for better or for worse) communist-era concrete and gleaming modern shopping malls.

☉ Sights

Union Museum   MUSEUM
(Muzeul Unirii; ☎0232-314 614; Str Alexandru Lăpuşneanu 14; adult/student 4/2 lei; ☺10am-5pm Tue-Sun) This small, neoclassical palace was Alexandru Cuza's home for three years (1859–62), and later housed King Ferdinand during his WWI retreat from Bucharest. It displays the Cuza family's opulent furniture, pictures and personal effects.

Moldavian Metropolitan Cathedral   CHURCH
(Mitropolia Moldovei; B-dul Ştefan cel Mare) Southeast of Piaţa Unirii, B-dul Ştefan cel Mare leads to this cavernous cathedral (1833–39), designed by architect Alexandru Orascu and decorated by painter Gheorghe Tattarescu.

Church of the Three Hierarchs   CHURCH
(Biserica Sfinţilor Trei Ierarhi; B-dul Ştefan cel Mare; ☺9.30am-noon & 1-5.30pm) Built by Prince Vasile Lupu between 1637 and 1639, and restored between 1882 and 1904, this is one of Iaşi's most beautiful churches. Its exterior stone pattern-work is exquisite, and reveals Turkish, Georgian and Armenian influences.

Palace of Culture   MUSEUM
(Palatul Culturii; B-dul Ştefan cel Mare) At B-dul Ştefan cel Mare's southern end stands the giant neo-Gothic Palace of Culture, built between 1906 and 1925 over Prince Alexandru cel Bun's ruined 15th-century princely court. At time of research, renovations were ongoing but set to conclude by 2014.

FREE **Golia Monastery**   MONASTERY
(Str Cuza Voda 51) This fortified late-Renaissance-style monastery is guarded by thick walls and the 30m Golia tower. The 17th-century church is notable for its vibrant Byzantine frescos and intricately carved doorways, and features wall bastions from 1667.

Copou Park   PARK
(Parcol Copou; B-dul Carol I) Designed between 1834 and 1848 under Prince Mihail Sturza, this 10-hectare park is allegedly where poet Mihai Eminescu (1850–89) wrote beneath a

linden tree. It still stands, behind the 13m-high Obelisk of Lions, supposedly modern Romania's oldest monument. A bronze **bust of Eminescu** sits in front.

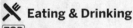 **Sleeping**

Pensiune Fiesta & Lavric   PENSION €
(☎0232-229 961; fiestalavric@yahoo.com; Str Horia 8; s/d 150/180 lei; ❄️🌐) Among Iaşi's better budget options, this popular place has six large and comfortable rooms, plus an on-site restaurant.

TOP CHOICE Hotel Unirea   HOTEL €€€
(☎0232-205 006; www.hotelunirea.ro; Piaţa Unirii 5; s/d/ste 225/295/395 lei; P❄️🌐🏊) Although several contenders vie for Iaşi's best hotel around the main square, an indoor pool, spa centre and 13th-floor Panoramic Restaurant (with its expansive views) set the Unirea apart. Rooms are bright and businessy, with comfortable beds and all amenities.

Grand Hotel Traian   HOTEL €€€
(☎0232-266 666; www.grandhoteltraian.ro; Piaţa Unirii 1; s/d 315/360 lei; P❄️🌐) Right in the centre, the elegant Traian was designed by Gustave Eiffel himself. The rooms are appropriately outfitted with billowing curtains, high ceilings and big baths, and a general old-world ambience pervades.

Hotel Eden   HOTEL €€
(☎0332-144 486; www.hotels-eden.ro; Str S Sava 1; s/d 160/170 lei; ❄️🌐) An excellent new three-star option, the Eden is central and has a restaurant. The fresh-smelling rooms are spacious, and some have balconies. Breakfast's 15 lei extra.

✗ **Eating & Drinking**

TOP CHOICE La Castel   INTERNATIONAL €€
(☎0232-225 225; www.lacastel.com; Str Aleea M Sadoveanu 54, Copou; mains 17-36 lei; 🍴) La Castel sprawls across breezy lawns on the Copou road (a 15-minute drive or cab ride from town). The varied cuisine, incorporating French and Bavarian flourishes, is complemented by a strong wine list and sinful desserts.

La Rustica   ITALIAN €€
(☎0735-522 405; www.larustica.ro; Str Anastasie Panu 30; mains 17-30 lei; ⏰8am-11pm) Run by an Italian chef and his Romanian wife, this classy subterranean restaurant is Iaşi's best Italian eatery. It's up Anastasie Panu, under a shopping and apartment complex.

Casa Lavric   ROMANIAN €€
(☎0232-229 960; Str Sf Atanasie 21; mains 10-40 lei) Good for Romanian cuisine, and decorated with classic musical instruments. Reserve ahead on weekends.

TOP CHOICE Cafeneaua Acaju   BAR
(☎0733-027 588; Str S Sava 15; ⏰9am-2am) Easy to miss and hard to forget, this hip but unpretentious bar is barely signposted on a street near the Armenian Church. Regulars include local artists, musicians and others of all ages.

La Baza   BAR
(B-dul Ştefan cel Mare, Cub; ⏰noon-3am) This festive indie fave has outlandish aquarium-green walls, saffron-curtain ceilings and what seem to be surrealist versions of Romanian monastic murals. But the beer is cheap.

Terasa Corso   PUB
(www.corsoterasa.ro; Str Alexandru Lăpuşneanu 11; mains 15-30 lei; ⏰9am-2am; 🌐) Well-trimmed hedges and gardens adorn the centre of this expansive, amphitheatre-shaped pub with overlapping rows of long tables. It's good for coffee by day and drinks by night.

☆ **Entertainment**

Vasile Alecsandri National Theatre   THEATRE, OPERA
(www.teatrulnationaliasi.ro; Str Agatha Bârsescu 18) Both the national theatre and opera are located in the same impressive neobaroque building. For advance bookings, go to the **Agenţia de Teatrala** (B-dul Ştefan cel Mare 8; ⏰10am-5pm Mon-Sat). Tickets cost 18 to 22 lei, with 50% student discounts.

Filarmonica   CLASSICAL MUSIC
(www.filarmonicais.ro; Str Cuza Vodă 29; tickets 20 lei; ⏰box office 10am-1pm & 5-7pm Mon-Fri) The Iaşi State Philharmonic Orchestra's home hall is excellent for classical music. Tickets start at 20 lei, with 50% student discounts.

Underground   CLUB
(B-dul Ştefan cel Mare, Cub; DJ nights admission 15 lei; ⏰8pm-3am) Slightly posher than neighbouring student bars, Underground does good live alternative music and DJ dance parties.

Dublin   CLUB
(☎0729-802 765; www.dublinpub.ro; Str Vasile Conta 30; ⏰noon-4am) A cross between a bar and a club, the Dublin is known for its weekend disco parties.

Iaşi

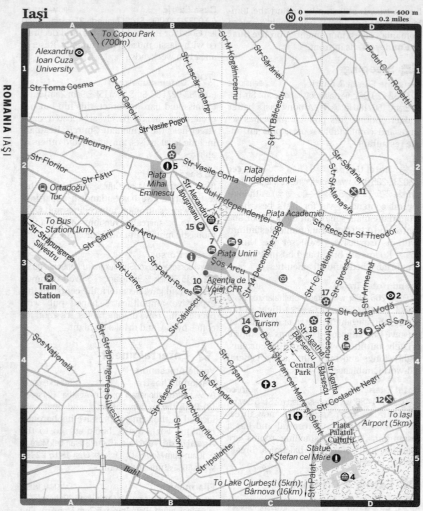

ℹ Information

Cliven Turism (☎0232-258 326; www.cliven.ro; B-dul Ştefan cel Mare 8-12; ☺9am-6pm Mon-Fri, to 2pm Sat)

Forte Cafe (B-dul Independenţei 27; per hr 4 lei; ☺24hr)

Post Office (Str Cuza Vodă 10; ☺9am-6pm Mon-Fri, to 1pm Sat)

Sfântu Spiridon University Hospital (☎ext 193 0232-240 822; B-dul Independenţei 1)

Tourist Information Centre (☎0232-261 990; www.turism-iasi.ro; Piaţa Unirii 12; ☺9am-6pm Mon-Fri, to 1pm Sat)

ℹ Getting There & Around

BUS The **bus station** (Str Moara de Foc 15a) has innumerable daily buses or maxitaxis, including for Suceava (30 lei, two hours, 12 daily), Cluj-Napoca (70 lei, nine hours, one daily) and Chişinău (30 lei, five hours, nine daily). Six daily buses serve Bucharest (60 lei).

Buy tickets for the daily İstanbul bus (170 lei, 16 hours), departing from Billa, at **Ortadoğu Tur** (☎0232-257 000; Str Bacinschi) across the street.

TRAIN Most trains use the Gara Centrală **train station** (Str Garii), also called Gara Mare and Gara du Nord. The **Agenţia de Voiaj CFR** (Piaţa

Iaşi

◉ Sights
1 Church of the Three Hierarchs C5
2 Golia Monastery..................................D3
3 Moldavian Metropolitan
    Cathedral C4
4 Palace of Culture D5
5 Statue of Mihai Eminescu..................B2
6 Union Museum...................................B3

⊜ Sleeping
7 Grand Hotel Traian B3
8 Hotel Eden..D4
9 Hotel Unirea......................................C3
10 Pensiune Fiesta & Lavric B3

⊗ Eating
11 Casa Lavric D2
12 La Rustica D4

⊖ Drinking
13 Cafeneaua Acaju...............................D4
14 La Baza...C4
15 Terasa Corso B3

⊕ Entertainment
16 Dublin B2
17 Filarmonica.......................................D3
    Underground...........................(see 14)
18 Vasile Alecsandri National
    Theatre..C4

Unirii 10; ⊘8am-8pm Mon-Fri, 9am-12.30pm Sat) sells advance tickets. A *bagaje de mana* (left-luggage office) is by the car park (6/8 lei for hand bag/large bag per 24 hours).

Six daily trains serve Bucharest (86 to 110 lei, seven hours), nine go to Suceava (21 lei to 39 lei, 2¾ hours), one to Braşov (86 lei, 8½ hours) and four to Cluj-Napoca (86 lei, nine hours) and on to Timişoara (78 lei, 16 hours) via Oradea.

For Chişinău (55 lei, six hours), one train leaves at 3.13am on Thursdays, Fridays and Saturdays only, crossing at Ungheni.

Suceava

POP 86,300

Suceava, the capital of Moldavia from 1388 to 1565, was a thriving commercial centre on the Lviv–İstanbul trading route. Today it's the seat of Suceava county with a handful of interesting sights, and makes for a decent gateway for exploring the painted churches of Bucovina.

◉ Sights

The unsightly **Casa de Cultură** (House of Culture) is at the western end of Piaţa 22 Decembrie, the city's main square. To the north is **St Dumitru's Church** (Biserica Sf Dumitru; Str Curtea Domnească) built by Petru Rareş in 1535.

Bucovina History Museum　　　MUSEUM
(Muzeul Naţional al Bucovinei; ☎0230-516 439; Str Ştefan cel Mare 33; adult/child 7/2 lei; ⊘10am-6pm Tue-Sun) Displays here range from the Bronze Age to the present but highlight Moldavia's famous rulers, particularly Ştefan cel Mare. While the numismatics, medieval armour and tools are interesting, Ştefan's 'Hall of Thrones' court recreation seems rather contrived.

Monastery of St John the New　　MONASTERY
(Mănăstirea Sfântu Ioan cel Nou; Str Ioan Voda Viteazul 2) This monastery off Str Mitropoliei (built 1514 to 1554) was an important pilgrimage destination: it houses, in a decorated silver casket, the relics of Saint John the New, which ruler Alexandru cel Bun had brought to Moldavia in 1415. The badly faded exterior paintings exemplify Bucovina style.

City of Residence Citadel　　FORTRESS
(Cetatea de Scaun; adult/child 5/2 lei, photography 10 lei; ⊘9am-6pm) Starting at McDonald's, follow the adjacent footpath along the stream, cross the little bridge and scale the 241 steps up to the equestrian statue of **Ştefan cel Mare** (1966). Follow the footpath to the left of the statue up to the City of Residence Citadel (p717), a fortress that held off Mehmed II, conqueror of Constantinople (İstanbul), in 1476. It's much more attractive from a distance than from the inside.

Ethnographic Museum　　MUSEUM
(☎0230-516 439; Str Ciprian Porumbescu 5; adult/child 6/3 lei; ⊘9am-5pm Tue-Sun) West of Piaţa 22 Decembrie, Hanul Domnesc is an 18th-century guesthouse housing the Ethnographic Museum. It displays Moldavian folk costumes and household items.

⌂ Sleeping

TOP CHOICE **Hotel Sonnenhof**　　HOTEL €€
(☎0230-220 033; www.hotelsonnenhof.ro; B-dul Sofia Vicoveanca 68 ; s/d from 220/265 lei; ✳☝) This fancy four-star place is good for drivers and those on a generous budget. It's 3km

from town on the Targu Neamt road (10 lei by taxi), but has excellent rooms loaded with amenities and is decorated in soothing tones (though the huge paintings above each bed are rather gauche).

Hotel Gloria
HOTEL €

(☑0230-521 209; www.hotelgloria.ro; Str Vasile Bumbac 4-8; s/d/ste incl breakfast from 85/140/260 lei; ❄❷❀) If Suceava is your base for local excursions, this three-star throwback is a good and central budget choice. It has fine, simple rooms with super-powered hot showers and cable internet. Although English is hit-or-miss, staff are unfailingly polite.

Union Apartment
APARTMENT €

(☑0741-477 047; www.union-apartments.ro; B-dul Ana Ipatescu 7; apt from 135-410 lei; ❄❀) Run by local tour guide extraordinaire Gigi Traciu, this central apartment sleeping up to seven people provides an excellent budget option and flexibility for self-caterers. Free airport pick-up is offered for stays of over three days.

✗ Eating & Drinking

TOP CHOICE Latino
ITALIAN €€

(Str Curtea Domnească 9; mains 12-45 lei, pizza 18-30 lei) Suceava's best Italian restaurant, this long-standing favourite has subdued class and prompt service. There are numerous pizzas, and the varied pasta starters (15 lei to 30 lei) are all excellent.

Restaurant Mozaik
INTERNATIONAL €€€

(B-dul Sofia Vicoveanca 68 , Hotel Sonnenhof; mains 25-45 lei) This upscale, gardened restaurant in the Hotel Sonnenhoff tries a bit too hard with its Romanian, French, Norwegian, German, Greek and Italian specialities, but, hey, the cooks were trained by a Michelin-starred French chef. Among the pricier dishes is beef in a doughy bread crust with mushrooms, pepper and cognac sauce.

Salzburg Cafe
CAFE

(Str Ştefan cel Mare 28; ⊗8am-10pm) This relaxing central cafe has a slightly Central European feel, and plays pop-rock and even live piano nights on Wednesdays. It's good for coffees, with a small desserts selection.

Oscar Wilde
PUB

(Str Ştefan cel Mare 26; ⊗8am-3am) Suceava's nearest thing to an Irish pub (look for the giant black Guinness canopies), Oscar Wilde's a big wood-floored bar with outdoor seating too.

ⓘ Information

There are several ATMs on Piaţa 22 Decembrie and along Str Ştefan cel Mare. Many restaurants, bars and cafes have free wi-fi.

AXA Travel (Str Sebastian Traciu; ☑0741-477 047; www.axatravel.ro) AXA is run by Sebastian 'Gigi' Traciu, an experienced local guide. One-day and multiday tours visit the Bucovina painted monasteries, Targu Neamt, Bicaz Gorge, Lacu Roşu and Maramureş. Rates depend on the number of participants.

Infoturism (☑0230-551 241; www.turism-suceava.ro; cnr B-dul Ana Ipătescu & Str Mitropoliei 4; ⊗8am-4pm Mon-Fri) Provides maps and information on local sites. It's located beside the park, between Str Ştefan Cel Mare and Bdul Ana Ipatescu.

Post Office (Str Dimitrie Onciul)

ⓘ Getting There & Away

BUS The central **bus station** (☑0230-524 340) is on Str Armenească. Bus and maxitaxi services include 19 daily to Gura Humorului (9 lei, one hour) and four to Bucharest (70 lei, eight hours). Maxitaxis to Iaşi (30 lei, 2½ hours, 12 daily) leave from a parking lot behind the bus station, dubbed 'Autogara Intertrans'.

One daily bus theoretically serves Chernivtsi in Ukraine (35 lei, three hours), though if it doesn't have enough passengers, the bus may not even come from Chernivtsi.

One daily bus at 6.30am serves Chişinău (60 lei, seven to eight hours).

TRAIN Suceava's two train stations, Gara Suceava and Gara Nord, are both roughly 5km north of centre. The **Agenţia de Voiaj CFR** (Str Nicolae Bălcescu 8; ⊗7.30am-8.30pm Mon-Fri) sells advance tickets. Most trains originate or terminate at Gara Suceava.

Train services include 10 to Gura Humorului (10 lei to 17 lei, 70 minutes), plus nine to Iaşi (39 lei, two hours), three to Timişoara (115 lei, 14 hours), four to Cluj-Napoca (71 lei, seven hours), one to Braşov (86 lei, 8½ hours) and six to Bucharest (86 lei to 107 lei, seven hours).

Southern Bucovina

Moldavian Prince Ştefan cel Mare and his successor Petru Rares endowed southern Bucovina with several spectacular monasteries, dating back to the 15th century. The best of these fortified structures, painted inside and out with exquisitely detailed frescos, are also Unesco World Heritage sites. Outside the monasteries, Bucovina is dotted with slant-roofed village houses and lovely groves of beech trees. As in

Southern Bucovina

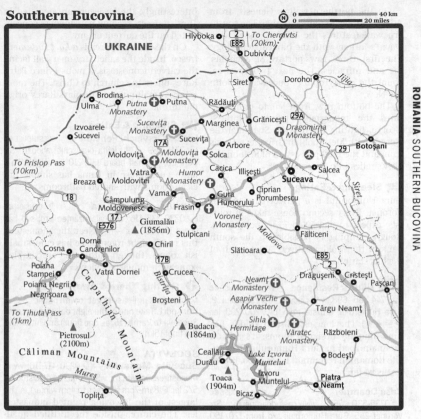

Maramureş, you'll encounter old women in traditional dress, fearless children riding bareback on horses and enterprising locals scouring the forest for truly massive mushrooms.

HUMOR

Of all the Bucovina monasteries, **Humor Monastery** (Mănăstirea Humorului; adult/student 5/2 lei; ☺8am-7pm summer, to 4pm winter) has the most impressive interior frescos.

On the southern exterior wall of the 1530 church, you can see the life of the Virgin Mary (on left), and St Nicholas and the parable of the prodigal son (on right). On the porch is the *Last Judgment* and, in the first chamber inside the church, scenes of martyrdom.

ⓘ Getting There & Away

Ten daily Suceava–Gura Humorului trains operate (10 lei to 17 lei, 50 minutes). Regular maxitaxis go the final 6km to the monastery,

VORONEŢ

Built in just three months and three weeks by Ştefan cel Mare following a key 1488 victory over the Turks, **Voroneţ Monastery** (adult/child 5/2 lei; ☺8am-7pm summer, to 4pm winter) is the only one to have a specific colour associated with it worldwide. 'Voroneţ Blue', a vibrant cerulean colour created from lapis lazuli and other ingredients, is prominent in its frescos. A 2011 restoration of frescos in the church's entryway revealed the incredible quality of these paintings even more clearly. Today Voroneţ is a nunnery.

The most famous Voroneţ painting, the *Last Judgment*, covers the western exterior wall. Angels at the top roll up the zodiac signs, indicating the end of time, while humanity is brought to judgment in the middle. On the left, St Paul escorts the believers, while a stern Moses takes the nonbelievers on the right.

On the northern wall is Genesis, from Adam and Eve to Cain and Abel. The southern wall features the Tree of Jesse (King David's father) with the biblical genealogy. The first three rows portray St Nicholas' life and miracles. The next two rows recount the martyrdom of Suceava's St John the New.

The bottom row, from left to right, features the monastery's patron saint, St George, fighting the dragon; St Daniel the Hermit with Metropolitan Grigorie; a Deisis icon; and the 1402 procession of St John the New's relics into Suceava.

🛏 Sleeping & Eating

Gura Humorului is a perfect base to visit Voroneţ. Every second house takes in tourists; expect to pay 50 to 75 lei per person. Rough camping is possible on the south bank of the Moldova River, 500m south of the bus station.

TOP CHOICE **Hilde's Residence** GUESTHOUSE €€
(📞0744-386 698; www.lucy.ro; Str Şipotului 2, Gura Humorului; s/d/ste from 180/200/290 lei; P⊖❋☎) The long-established Hilde's has nine uniquely designed rooms; it's just off the main road in Gura Humorului. The onsite Romanian restaurant is good too. Breakfast is 24 lei.

Casa Doamnei GUESTHOUSE €€
(📞0735-530 753; www.casa-doamnei.ro; Str Voroneţ 255, Gura Humorului; s/d from 120/150 lei) On the Voroneţ road (500m after the train tracks, 3.5km before the monastery), this guesthouse has stylish wood furniture, balconies and nice bathrooms. Breakfast is 20 lei.

ℹ Getting There & Away

Several buses and trains run daily from Suceava to Gura Humorului. A lovely option is to walk the 4km along a narrow village road to Voroneţ. The route is clearly marked and it's impossible to get lost.

MOLDOVIŢA

Moldoviţa Monastery (adult/student 5/2 lei; ⊙8am-7pm summer, to 4pm winter), built in 1532, occupies a fortified quadrangular enclosure with tower, gates and flowery lawns. The central painted church has been partly restored, and features impressive frescos from 1537. The southern exterior wall depicts the Siege of Constantinople in AD 626, under a combined Persian–Avar attack.

Interestingly, the besiegers are depicted in Turkish dress, keeping parishioners concentrated on the current enemy.

On the church's porch is *a Last Judgment* fresco. Inside the sanctuary, on a wall facing the carved iconostasis, a pious Prince Petru Rareş offers the church to Christ. The monastery's small museum displays Rareş' original throne.

🛏 Sleeping & Eating

Letitia Orsvischi Pension GUESTHOUSE €€
(📞0745-869 529; letita_orsvischi@yahoo.fr; Str Gării 20; s/d half board 130/210 lei; ❋☎) This large guesthouse in Vama has simple but clean rooms with shared bathrooms.

Pensiunea Crizantema PENSION €€
(📞0230-336 116; www.vilacrizantema.ro; s/d half board 140/180 lei; ⊖☎) Near the monastery, this rustic eight-room place has cute, smallish rooms (though bathrooms are simple), some with monastery views.

ℹ Getting There & Away

Moldoviţa is not easy to get to with public transport. Take one of the eight daily trains from Suceava to Vama (15 lei, one hour) and hitchhike the final 15km.

SUCEVIŢA

Suceviţa Monastery (📞0230 417-110; www. manastireasucevita.ro; Suceviţa; adult/student 5/2 lei; ⊙8am-7pm summer, to 4pm winter) is the largest of the Bucovina painted monasteries. The church inside the fortified quadrangular enclosure (built between 1582 and 1601) is almost completely covered in frescos. As you enter, you first see the *Ladder of Virtues* fresco covering most of the northern exterior wall, which depicts the 30 steps to paradise. On the southern exterior wall is Jesse's genealogical tree symbolising the continuity of the Old and New Testaments. The tree grows from the reclining figure of Jesse, who is flanked by a row of ancient Greek philosophers. To the left is the Virgin, with angels holding a red veil over her head. Mysteriously, the western wall remains blank. Legend has it that the artist fell off his scaffolding and died, leaving artists of the time too scared to follow in his footsteps.

🛏 Sleeping & Eating

It's worth spending a night here and doing a little hiking in the surrounding hills. The road from Marginea to Suceviţa is littered with *cazare* (room for rent) signs.

Pensiunea Emilia GUESTHOUSE €

(☎0743-117 827; Str Bercheza 173; r per person 80 lei) The most appealing local *pensiune* (pension), Emilia's has charming rooms and is 500m up the road opposite the monastery. Breakfast is 10 lei.

Ieremia Movilă GUESTHOUSE €

(☎0230-417 501; www.ieremiamovila.ro; Str Sucevita 459 ; r 110 lei; P🐕❄️🛜) This modern place has nice rooms with great bathrooms, balconies and wi-fi. Some rooms have monastery views. Good on-site restaurant.

❶ Getting There & Away

Take one of the hourly maxitaxis from Suceava to Rădăuţi (8 lei, 45 minutes), then switch to one of the southbound maxitaxis leaving hourly from an unmarked intersection about 300m east (towards Piaţa Unirii) from the bus station. Ask the driver to stop at Suceviţa.

DANUBE DELTA & BLACK SEA COAST

Danube Delta

After passing through several countries and absorbing countless lesser waterways, the Danube empties into the Black Sea just south of the Ukrainian border. The Danube Delta (Delta Dunării), included on Unesco's World Heritage list, is one of Romania's leading tourist attractions.

At the inland port of Tulcea, the river splits into three separate channels: the Chilia, Sulina and Sfântu Gheorghe arms, creating a constantly evolving 4187-sq-km wetland of marshes, floating reed islets and sandbars, providing sanctuary for 300 species of birds and 160 species of fish. Reed marshes cover 156,300 hectares, constituting one of the largest single expanses of reed beds in the world.

The delta is a haven for wildlife lovers, birdwatchers, anglers and anyone wanting to get away from it all for a few days. There are beautiful, secluded beaches at both Sulina and Sfântu Gheorghe, and the fish and seafood, particularly the fish soup, is the best in Romania

Much of the the delta is under the protection of the administration of the Danube Delta Biosphere Reserve Authority (DDBRA), headquartered in Tulcea, with branch offices throughout the delta, including in Sulina and Sfântu Gheorghe. There are around 20 strictly

Black Sea Coast

Danube Delta

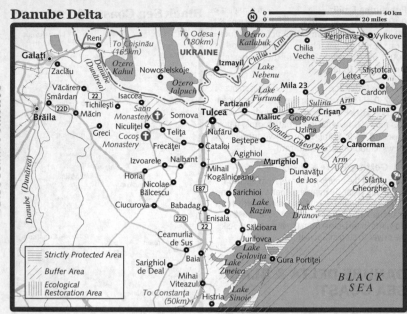

protected areas covering about 50,000 hectares that are off-limits to tourists, including the 500-year-old Leţea Forest and Europe's largest pelican colony. Visitation is limited in other areas. Note that visitors to the reserve are required to purchase an entry permit. Camping in the reserve is only allowed in official camping grounds.

ⓘ Getting Around

There is no rail service in the delta and few paved roads, meaning the primary mode of transport is by ferry. Regularly scheduled ferries, both traditional 'slow' ferries and faster (and more expensive) hydrofoils, leave from Tulcea's main port daily and access all major points in the delta. There are two main ferry operators and the ferry schedule can be bewildering on first glance. The helpful staff at the tourism information centre in Tulcea can help piece together a journey depending on your time and budget.

Ferries can get crowded in summer, so try to arrive at least an hour prior to departure to secure yourself a seat. Note that though the ferries run year-round, service is less reliable in winter.

PUBLIC FERRIES & HYDROFOILS

Two companies offer passenger-ferry service throughout the delta. State-run **Navrom** (☏0240-511 553; www.navromdelta.ro; Str Portului 26; ⏰ticket office 11.30am-1.30pm)

operates both slower, traditional ferries (referred to as 'classic ships' on timetables) as well as faster hyrdofoils (catamarans). A second company, **Nave Rapide** (☏0726-774 074, 0742-544 068; www.naverapide.ro), offers only hydrofoils.

For Navrom ferries, in Tulcea, buy tickets on the day of departure at the Navrom passenger ferry terminal (p724) daily from 11.30am to 1.30pm. Outside of Tulcea, buy tickets on departure at the entrance to the boat.

For Nave Rapide ferries, book at least a day in advance over the phone or turn to the tourism information centre for assistance

See p724 for details of ferries and hydrofoils from Tulcea.

TULCEA
POP 92,400

The Danube port of Tulcea (tool-*cha*) is the largest city in the delta and the main entry point for accessing the region. It has good bus and minibus connections to the rest of the country, and is home to the main passenger ferries. If you've only got a short amount of time (one to three days), base yourself here and explore the delta via boating day trips. If you have more time, you'll likely only transit through Tulcea on your way to deeper destinations like Sulina and Sfântu Gheorghe.

◎ Sights

TOP CHOICE **Central Eco-Tourism Museum of the Danube Delta** MUSEUM, AQUARIUM
(Centrul Muzeal Ecoturistic Delta Dunării; ☎0240-515 866; www.icemtl.ro; Str 14 Noiembrie 1; adult/student 15/5 lei; ☉10am-6pm Tue-Sun; ☝) This combined museum and aquarium is a good primer on the delta's varied flora and fauna. There are stuffed animals on the main floor and a small but fascinating aquarium on the lower level, with ample signage in English.

Folk Art & Ethnographic Museum MUSEUM
(☎0240-516 204; Str 9 Mai 4; adult/student 6/3 lei; ☉10am-6pm Tue-Sun) This modest museum displays the ethnic and cultural diversity of the delta region over the centuries, and the interaction of Romanians with Turks, Russians, Ukrainians and Bulgarians.

Independence Monument MONUMENT
As you stroll along the river you'll see the Independence Monument (1904) on Citadel Hill at the far eastern end of town. You can reach this by following Str Gloriei from behind the Egreta Hotel to its end.

History & Archaeology Museum MUSEUM
(☎0240-513 626; Str Gloriei; admission 5 lei; ☉10am-6pm Tue-Sun) Well worth visiting, this museum is presented on two levels, with the upper level given over to the extensive Roman findings and the lower level displaying even more fascinating artefacts of pre-Roman civilisations going back some 6000 years. The museum is situated at the Independence Monument.

☗ Activities

Tulcea's main activities are boating, fishing and birdwatching. The port is lined with private boat operators offering a variety of excursions on slow boats, speedboats and pontoon boats; these can be tailored to accommodate special pursuits. Excursions are generally priced per person, assuming a minimum number. If the minimum is not reached, prices go higher.

Safca TOUR
(☎0744-143 336; www.egretamica.ro) This small father-and-son company offers a variety of boat excursions for individuals or groups up to around eight persons. If offers a popular all-day 'hyper' trip to Sulina, including a visit to the beach, for 250 lei per person.

Ibis Tours TRAVEL AGENCY
(☎0722-381 398, 0240-512 787; www.ibis-tours.ro; Str Dimitrie Sturza 6; ☉9am-6pm Mon-Sat) Arranges wildlife and birdwatching tours in the delta and Dobrogea, led by professional ornithologists.

⌑ Sleeping

No camping is allowed within Tulcea's city limits. However, there are many areas where wild camping is permitted on the banks of the canal within a few kilometres of the city; ask at one of the tourist information offices for details.

TOP CHOICE **Hotel Select** HOTEL €€
(☎0240-506 180; www.calypsosrl.ro; Str Păcii 6; s/d 140/170 lei; P☺❅@☎) Though we normally shy away from these boxy high-rises, this is our favourite hotel in Tulcea. The rooms are plain but good value, with big and comfortable beds and light-blocking blinds on the windows. The restaurant is arguably the best in town.

Hotel Delta HOTEL €€
(☎0240-514 720; www.deltahotelro.com; Str Isaccei 2; s/d 3-star 220/280 lei, 4-star 280/360 lei; ☺❅☎☲) This landmark hotel towards the eastern end of the port offers both three- and four-star accommodation in adjoining separate buildings. The three-star rooms, with air-con and balcony views, are better value.

Insula Complex HOTEL €
(☎0240-530 908; Lake Ciuperca; s/d 80/100 lei; ☎) Minutes from the bus station on Lake Ciuperca, this two-star option has an onsite restaurant and large rooms. Turn right out of the train station and cross the small bridge to the island.

DELTA PERMITS

All visitors to the delta, including those on hiking or boating excursions from Tulcea, Sulina or Sfântu Gheorghe, are required to purchase an entry permit. Permits are available for one day (5 lei), one week (15 lei) or one year (30 lei) from Danube Delta Biosphere Reserve Authority offices in Tulcea (p724), Sulina (p725) or Sfântu Gheorghe (p725). Boats are subject to spot inspections and if you're caught without a permit you could be fined.

FERRIES & HYDROFOILS FROM TULCEA

DESTINATION	COMPANY	TYPE	PRICE (LEI)	DURATION (HR)	FREQUENCY
Sfântu Gheorghe (via Mahmudia)	Navrom	slow ferry	35	5-6	1.30pm Mon, Fri (return 7am Tue, Fri)
Sfântu Gheorghe (via Mahmudia)	Navrom	hydrofoil	46	3	1.30pm Wed, Thu (return 7am Thu, Fri)
Sfântu Gheorghe (via Mahmudia)	Nave Rapide	hydrofoil	60	1½	1.30pm (return 6.45am)
Sulina (via Crişan)	Navrom	slow ferry	34	4-5	1.30pm Mon, Wed, Fri (return 7am, Tue, Thu, Sun)
Sulina (via Crişan)	Navrom	hydrofoil	42	2-3	1.30pm Tue, Thu, Sat (return 7am Mon, Wed, Fri)
Sulina (via Crişan)	Nave Rapide	hydrofoil	60	1½	10am, 1pm (return 6.45am, noon)

Eating & Drinking

Restaurant Select ROMANIAN €€
(www.calypsosrl.ro; Str Păcii 6; mains 15-30 lei; ☎) The multilingual, varied menu offers fresh fish, pizza and the local speciality, *tochitura dobrogeana* (pan-fried meat with spicy sauce).

Trident Pizzeria PIZZA €
(Str Babadag; mains 13-20 lei; ☎) Excellent spot for good thin-crust pizza and fast pasta.

Istru PUB
(☑0740-075 330; Str Gării 12; ⊙10am-midnight; ☎) This is the best watering hole in the immediate port area, with great coffee drinks by day and Guinness and Skol wheat beer during the evening. Draws a mostly local student and arty (for Tulcea) crowd.

ℹ Information

The central area is filled with ATMs, pharmacies, and lots of shops and stores.

Danube Delta Biosphere Reserve Authority
(☑0240-518 945; www.ddbra.ro; Str Portului 34a; permits per day 5 lei; ⊙8am-4pm Mon-Fri) This office is run by the national group charged with managing the delta. It's a good source of information on what to see and do, and publishes and distributes the helpful pamphlet *Guide of the Touristic Routes*, which lays out 19 aquatic routes. Sells visitor permits.

Tourism Information Centre (☑0240-519 130; www.primariatulcea.ro; Str Gării 26; ⊙8am-7pm Mon-Fri, to noon Sat May-Sep) The helpful staff here can help sort through the confusing ferry schedules as well as advise on various travel agencies, hotels and restaurants. It's hidden slightly back from the river promenade, halfway between the main port administration and the Hotel Delta.

ℹ Getting There & Away

The **bus station** (☑0240-513 304; Str Portului 1) adjoins the **main ferry terminal** (Str Portului; ⊙11.30am-1.30pm). As many as 10 buses and maxitaxis head daily to Bucharest (55 lei, five hours); there are two daily buses to Iaşi (65 lei, four hours). Maxitaxis to Constanţa (30 lei, two hours) leave every half-hour from 5.30am to 8pm.

SULINA

The sleepy fishing port of Sulina is Romania's easternmost point and the highlight of any journey along the Danube's central arm. There's a beautiful, tranquil (during the day) beach here as well as a charming canal-side promenade. It's also an excellent base for forays deeper into the delta or onto the Black Sea.

🏃 Activities

Sulina is a quiet place. The main activities include strolling the main promenade (Str I), soaking in the sun at **Sulina Beach** (⊙May-Oct) or hiring the services of a local fisherman to take you around on the delta by small **boat** (☑0744-821 365; Str I; per person 30-50 lei). You'll find the boats lines up along Str I.

🛏 Sleeping & Eating

There are several *cazares* and pensions here: you can accept an offer from those who greet the boat, or ask around. Expect to pay around 100 lei per room. Wild camping is possible on the beach, but there are no services and two discos blast dance music into the night air in summer until 3am.

Pensiunea Ana
PENSION €

(☎0727-001 569, 0724-421 976; pensiuneana@ yahoo.com; Str IV 144; r 80 lei) This charming family-run affair has four rooms and a beautifully shaded garden. To find it, walk 200m west from the ferry port along the main promenade, bear left on Str Mihail Kogălniceanu, and walk four blocks inland.

Hotel Casa Coral
HOTEL €€

(☎0742-974 016; www.casacoralsulina.ro; Str I 195; r 150 lei; ❋ 🕸 🛜) This modern three-star property lacks character but is arguably the nicest hotel in Sulina centre. You'll have to book in advance in summer as it tends to fill up fast. You'll find it on the main passenger ferry port.

Restaurant Marea Neagră
ROMANIAN €€

(☎0240-543 130; Str I 178; mains 17-30 lei) This large and popular open-air terrace offers more than a dozen fish specialities.

ℹ Information

All of Sulina's services for visitors, including a pharmacy, supermarket and ATM, lie along Str I that stretches for about 1km west of the passenger ferry port.

Danube Delta Biosphere Reserve Authority (www.ddbra.ro; Str I; ⊘8am-4pm Tue-Fri, noon-8pm Sat & Sun May-Oct) Sparsely furnished and funded information centre has basic information on the delta. Buy delta visitors' permits here. Located 20m east of the Casa Coral Hotel.

ℹ Getting There & Away

Access to Sulina is by boat only. See p724 for details of passenger ferries from Tulcea.

SFÂNTU GHEORGHE

First recorded in the mid-14th century by Visconti, a traveller from Genoa, the remote seaside village of Sfântu Gheorghe retains an ever-so-slight alternative vibe fed by the town's lovely, lonely beach and its sleepy, noncommercial core. It's also one of the best places in the delta to sample traditional cooking (including some fabulous fish soup). Each August, the village hosts what just might be the world's most remote film festival, the **Anonimul Fest** (www.festival-anonimul.ro).

🏃 Activities

The sandy beach is 3km east of the centre. Hop the tractor-pulled **transport plaja** (Tro-

carici; ☎0740-572 269; Str Principala; per person 2 lei) that departs regularly during the day from the centre of the village. Several private **boat owners** (☎0755-415 219; Portul; per person 50 lei) offer hour-long excursions into the delta or to the Black Sea for around 75 lei per person. The Delta Marina hotel organises boat trips too.

🛏 Sleeping & Eating

There are several *cazares* and pensions here: you can accept an offer from those who greet the boat, or ask around. Wild camping is possible on the beach, but it gets very windy and it's a long 3km hike in the dark. There's a handy **supermarket** (Complex Comercial, Str Principala; ⊘8am-2pm & 4-10pm Mon-Sat, 8am-1pm Sun) in the centre of the village.

Delta Marina
PENSION €€

(☎0240-546 946; www.deltamarina.ro; Str Principala (Str I); r 130 lei; ❋ 🛜) This modern hotel is situated on the water about 200m west of the ferry port. The popular terrace resraurant is one of the few places in town to grab a sit-down meal (mains 17 to 20 lei).

Vila Petru & Marcela Stefanov
PENSION €

(☎0763-088 859, 0240-546 811; near Str Principala; s/d half board 120/150 lei) This family-run pension offers clean and comfortable accommodation just a few metres' walk from the town centre. Rates include half board, often a delicious fish soup followed up with more grilled fish. The street is unmarked, but the pension is three houses north (on the left-hand side) of the Complex Comercial and supermarket, just beyond Str Principala (Str I).

Bar Terasa
CAFE

(Str Principala ; ⊘7am-3am May-Sep; 🛜) When it comes to evening drinking, this centrally located open-air terrace (one door down from the BRD bank branch) is the only game in town.

ℹ Information

There's an **ATM** (☎0240-546 721; Str Principala, Complex Comercial; ⊘9am-5pm Mon-Fri) machine in the centre of the village.

Danube Delta Biosphere Reserve Authority (☎0240-518 926; www.ddbra.ro; Str Ia 39; permits per day/week 5/15 lei; ⊘7am-noon & 4-7pm Tue-Fri, 9am-1pm Sat & Sun May-Oct) Sells visitors' permits for one day or one week. The office is located on the harbour, about 50m from the entrance to the passenger ferry port.

ⓘ Getting There & Away

Access to Sfântu Gheorghe is by boat only. See p724 for details on passenger ferries from Tulcea.

Constanța

POP 260,000

Constanța is Romania's largest and most important port city on the Black Sea; in summer, it's also the gateway to the country's seaside resorts. Accommodation here is cheaper than Mamaia and maxitaxis cover the journey in about 15 minutes, so it may be worthwhile basing yourself here even if you're only coming for Mamaia's beaches and discos. While the city shows obvious signs of neglect, especially around the port area, there are some very good museums, and a pretty portside walk.

⊙ Sights

National History & Archaeological Museum
MUSEUM

(Muzeul de Istorie Nationala si Arheologie Constanța; ☏0241-618 763; www.minac.ro; Piața Ovidiu 12; adult/child 11/5 lei; ⊙9am-8pm Jun-Sep, to 5pm Tue-Sun Oct-May) The stunning ground-floor exhibits of vases, jewellery and statuary from the Greek and Roman periods, lasting until about AD 500, justify the admission price, but the upper floors on more recent times and Romanian national history are poorly lit and lack signage in English.

Art Museum
MUSEUM

(Muzeul de Artă; ☏0241-617 012; B-dul Tomis 82-84; adult/child 10/5 lei; ⊙9am-7pm Mon-Fri) This airy museum in an atrium is heavy on 19th-century realism and landscapes, including those by Nicolae Grigorescu, whose pointillist and impressionist paintings anticipated more modern movements.

Naval History Museum
MUSEUM

(Muzeul Marinei Române; ☏0241-619 035; Str Traian 53; adult/child 10/5 lei; ⊙9am-5pm Wed-Sun) Fascinating if slightly confusing stroll through 2000 years of maritime history on the Black Sea. The exhibit begins in the Greco-Roman period, with some intricate models of old Roman boats, but quickly moves to the 19th and 20th centuries.

Casino
HISTORIC BUILDING

(Faleza Casino Constanța; B-dul Elisabeta 1; admission free; ⊙10am-6pm Mon-Fri) Constanța's amazing art nouveau casino, dating from 1910, was awaiting a long overdue renovation at the time of research, but the city had opened the building to visitors to peek in and see some serious splendour.

Aquarium
AQUARIUM

(Acvariu; ☏0241-611 277; ww.delfinariu.ro; B-dul Elisabeta 1, Faleza Casino Constanța; adult/child 20/10 lei; ⊙9am-8pm Tue-Sun Jun–mid-Sep, 10am-6pm Tue-Sun mid-Sep–May; 🚼) This waterfront aquarium focuses on fish native to the Black Sea, including a large selection of endangered sturgeon, as well as local freshwater species. It's directly opposite the casino.

Dolphinarium
DOLPHIN SHOW

(Delfinariu; ☏0241-481 243; www.delfinariu.ro; B-dul Mamaia 255; adult/child 50/25 lei; ⊙shows at 11am, 3pm & 7pm Mon-Fri, 10am, 1pm, 4pm & 7pm Sat & Sun) The country's first Dolphinarium has been updated and modernised. Dolphin shows are held throughout the day in the large ampitheatre.

🛏 Sleeping

Hotel Ferdinand
HOTEL €€

(☏0241-617 974; www.hotelferdinand.ro; B-dul Ferdinand 12; s/d 220/260 lei; P🅿❄🖥) This is our favourite three-star hotel in town. Nothing fancy, just a very well run hotel in a smart, nicely restored 1930s town house. Rooms have big comfy beds and fridges.

Hotel Maria
HOTEL €€

(☏0241-611 711; www.hotelmaria-ct.ro; B-dul 1 Decembrie 1918 2d; s/d 160/200 lei; ❄🖥) This modern, spotless option, across from the park facing the train station, has lots of glass, chrome and deep blues to soothe your sun-withered nerves.

Hotel Class
HOTEL €€

(☏0241-660 766; www.hotelclass.ro; Str Răscoala din 1907 1; s/d/ste 200/220/265 lei; P❄🖥) Well-managed three-star option, with clean rooms and comfortable beds with thick mattresses. Ask for a quiet room away from busy Str Răscoala.

✗ Eating & Drinking

TOP CHOICE Irish Pub
INTERNATIONAL €€

(☏0241-550 400; www.irishpub.ro; Str Ștefan cel Mare 1; mains 20-40 lei; ⊙8am-midnight; 🖥) There are a couple of pub staples like burgers and fish and chips, but the menu has higher aspirations, with steaks and grilled fish. It's equally good for beer or coffee. Booking at meal times is essential.

Pizzico
INTERNATIONAL €€

(☎0241-615 555; www.newpizzico.ro; Piaţa Ovidiu 7; mains 15-40 lei; 🛜) Pizzico has expanded its range in the past couple of years, moving beyond wood-fired pizza to excellent grilled meats, seafood and chops. The location, on Ovid Sq, makes it easy to pair lunch here with a visit to a nearby museum.

On Plonge
FISH €€

(☎0241-601 905; Portul Turistic Tomis; mains 15-40 lei; ⊙9am-10pm) Brawny portside eatery with an informal, everyman vibe that specialises in fresh fish hauled in off the boat. Gets packed on summer nights and service suffers accordingly.

Friends & Co
CAFE

(Str Decebal 17; ⊙10am-midnight Mon-Thu, 11am-1am Fri & Sat, 2-11pm Sun; 🛜) Relaxed student cafe with an alternative, indie vibe and a pretty, secluded terrace.

☆ Entertainment

Oleg Danovski National Theatre
OPERA, BALLET

(Teatrul Naţional de Operă şi Balet 'Oleg Danovski'; ☎0241-481 460; www.opera-balet-constanta.ro; Str Mircea cel Bătrân 97; tickets 30 lei; ⊙box office 10am-5pm Mon-Fri) The city's premier venue for opera and dance. Buy tickets at the theatre box office or the central **ticket office** (www.opera-balet-constanta.ro; B-dul Tomis 97; ⊙10am-3pm Mon-Fri, to 1pm Sat).

❶ Information

Central Post Office (B-dul Tomis 79-81; ⊙7am-8pm Mon-Fri, 8am-1pm Sat)

Constanta Country Emergency Hospital (Spitalul Clinic Judeţean de Urgenţă Constanţa; ☎0241-662 222; www.spitalulconstanta.ro; B-dul Tomis 145)

Forte-Games (☎0241-551 251; www.forte-games.ro; B-dul Tomis 235; internet per hr 6 lei; ⊙24hr)

❶ Getting There & Away

BUS Constanţa has several bus stations, depending on which bus line is operating the route. Buses to Bucharest (55 lei, three to four hours) depart from outside the train station. Many other buses, including some travelling to the Black Sea resorts, use the large **southern bus station** (Autogara Sud; ☎0241-665 289; B-dul Ferdinand), about 200m north of the train station. Buses to Tulcea (30 lei, two to three hours) and points north often leave from other parts of town. Your best best is to check the website www.autogari. ro to see times and departure points.

TRAIN Constanţa's **train station** (☎0241-614 960; www.cfrcalatori.ro; B-dul Ferdinand 45) is near the southern bus station, 2km from the centre. There are two fast Inter-City trains a day to Bucharest (60 lei, three to four hours). There are also daily services to Suceava, Cluj-Napoca and Timişoara. In summer, several trains a day head from Constanţa south to Mangalia (7 lei, 1½ hours), with stops at resorts in between.

Mamaia

Mamaia, a thin strip of sand extending northwards from Constanţa, is Romania's most popular and expensive beach resort. In season, from early June to early September, the 8km-long beachfront is lined with sunbathers from around Romania who compete for that precious space of seaside real estate. By night, Mamaia morphs into party central, with dozens of high-adrenaline nightclubs and impromptu beach parties.

🏃 Activities

Mamaia's number-one attraction is its wide, golden beach, which stretches the length of the resort. The further north you go, the nicer it becomes.

Boats to Ovidiu Island
BOATING

(Insula Ovidiu; B-dul Mamaia; per person return 20 lei; ⊙boats 9am-midnight) In summer, boats ferry tourists across Lake Siutghiol to Insula Ovidiu (Ovidiu Island), with a good restaurant and where Ovid's tomb is said to be located. They depart every 30 minutes from the Tic-Tac wharf on the lake (not on the beach), at about the midpoint of the Mamaia resort.

Aqua Magic
WATER PARK

(www.aqua-magic.ro; adult/child Jun & Sep 40/20 lei, Jul & Aug 60/30 lei; ⊙10am-6pm Jun & Sep, 9am-7pm Jul & Aug; 🚼) This amazing water park has pools and slides and inner-tube rides galore.

🛏 Sleeping

Mamaia is lined with resort complexes that are more attuned to dealing with package tours than walk-ins. If you know your dates in advance and plan to stay at least three to four days, you're better off arranging a package through a travel agency like Mistral Tours (p728). Note that Mamaia pretty much shuts down in the off-season (September to May) and only the biggest hotels stay open.

Hotel Splendid   HOTEL €€€
(☎0341-412 541; www.splendidhotel.ro; B-dul Mamaia , Mamaia Nord ; s/d 480/560 lei; [P][⊛][✿][@][✿]) This five-storey modern hotel, built in 2007, is a quieter option since it's on the western side of main road (away from the beachfront, along Siutghiol Lake). You'll find it on the northern end of the resort.

Hotel Ovidiu   HOTEL €€
(☎0241-831 590; www.hotelovidiu.ro; d/tr 250/350 lei; [⊛][✿][✿]) This simple two-star hotel offers basic, clean rooms at a good price and not much else. Request an upper-floor room to get a better sea view.

GPM Campground   CAMPGROUND €
(☎0241-831 001; www.gpm.ro; B-dul Mamaia Nord, Navodari; campsite per person 20 lei, bungalows 140-460 lei; [✿]) Attractive camping ground at the far northern end of Mamaia. Call or arrive early to reserve a site near the beach. Excellent self-serve restaurant is open to campers and noncampers alike.

✗ Eating & Drinking

TOP CHOICE **Chevalet**   INTERNATIONAL €€€
(☎0721-421 501; www.restaurantchevalet.com; B-dul Mamaia; mains 50-80 lei; ☉11am-11pm; [✿]) Head chef Nelu Păucă trained around the world before opening this romantic terrace restaurant on Lake Siutghiol, near the southern end of Mamaia. Specialities include steak tartare, frog legs and a mouthwatering array of beef, pork and seafood. Book in advance and try to time your booking for sunset.

Crazy Beach   CLUB
(☎0726-779 292; www.crazybeach.ro; B-dul Mamaia Nord; ☉8am-1am) One of the hottest clubs in Mamaia is this open-air lounge and cocktail bar, situated in the extreme north of Mamaia, about 4km beyond the northern telegondola station. Take a taxi (about 10 lei from central Mamaia).

❶ Information

Asociatia de Promovare Litoral (☎0241-831 321; www.asociatia-litoral.ro; Telegondola base) Located inside the southern telegondola terminus, it can help with accommodation and tours of the region.

Mistral Tours (☎0241-557 007; www.mistraltours.ro; ☉9am-5pm Mon-Fri, to 1pm Sat) Located at the southern end of Mamaia's telegondola line, Mistral Tours can help find accommodation and plan day trips and excursions, including to the Danube Delta and Bulgarian Black Sea coast.

❶ Getting There & Around

Frequent maxitaxis (2 lei, 15 minutes) ply the route between central Constanţa and Mamaia from June to September. Maxitaxis 301 and 303 depart regularly from Constanţa's train station. You can wave them down conveniently on B-dul Ferdinand, across the street from both the Hotel Class and Hotel Ferdinand.

Once in Mamaia, stroll the boardwalk or take the **telegondola** (cable car; one way 10 lei; ☉9am-10pm Jun-Oct) that runs from the southern end of the resort to approximately the midway point.

Vama Veche

If you've got time for just one Romanian resort, make it Vama Veche, just north of the Bulgarian border. While it lacks the polish of Mamaia, it's smaller, more relaxed and more rustic. Under the communist regime, 'Vama' enjoyed a reputation as a haven for artists, hedonists and free-thinkers. While it's slowly moving towards the mainstream, there's still something of a counterculture vibe in the air.

✗ Activities

The main activities are swimming, sunbathing, drinking and partying, and not necessarily in that order. There's a 5km bike path to an adjoining seaside village called Doi Mai (2 Mai), that starts from the northern end of Vama Veche. The BazArt Hostel rents **bikes** (☎0241-858 009; www.bazarthostel.ro; Str Ion Creangă, BazArt Hostel ; per 2hr/day 10/30 lei).

🛏 Sleeping

There's wild camping at both the far southern and northern ends of the beach. Club d'Or offers **camping** (☎0743-335 114; www.clubdor.ro; Plaja Vama Veche; per tent 10 lei) on a wide strip of beach towards the northern end and has showers and toilets.

TOP CHOICE **Club d'Or**   HOTEL €€
(☎0743-335 114; www.clubdor.ro; Str Ion Creangă; r 160 lei; [P][⊛][✿][✿]) Clean, quiet and close enough to the beach to drift in and out when you want. The rooms resemble a motel and fan out around a gigantic, clean swimming pool. It's located 100m west of Hwy E87 at approximately the centre of the village.

Elga's Punk Rock Hotel
HOTEL €

(☏0722-366 711; www.punkrockhotel.com; Str Kogalniceanu, Hwy 87; r 80-100 lei; P⊖✳🛜) This welcoming family-run hotel offers small but ultraclean rooms with either double or twin beds in two price categories. 'A' level rooms are slightly larger and have air-conditioning, while category 'B' rooms are smaller and have fans.

BazArt
HOSTEL €

(☏0241-858 009; www.bazarthostel.ro; Str Ion Creangă; d 80-200 lei; q 150 lei; ⊖✳🛜) This popular student choice on Vama Veche's main drag offers a variety of rooms, including comfortable private doubles with bathrooms and air-conditioning, as well as budget twins and quads with shared facilities and no air-con.

✕ Eating & Drinking

TOP CHOICE **Cherhana**
FISH €€

(mains 15-25 lei; ⊙10am-11pm) This informal beachfront place with grill and picnic tables draws big crowds, particularly campers from the nearby wild camping grounds The fresh fish is grilled on the spot. It's situated on the northern edge of Vama Veche, beyond the Club d'Or camping area.

Molotov
BAR

(molotov_bar@yahoo.com; Str Falezel, Plaja Vama Veche; ⊙10am-3am) This scruffily charming cocktail bar is one of the best places in town to sip your drink while you listen to the roar of the surf. It's located on the beach on the southern end of Vama Veche.

❶ Getting There & Away

There are no trains to Vama Veche; instead take a maxitaxi from Constanţa (about 10 lei) or take a train to Mangalia and a maxitaxi for 8km (5 lei).

UNDERSTAND ROMANIA

Romania Today

Romania today finds itself in a strange place. The big picture view is mainly positive. Since independence, Romania has made great strides in developing a free market economy and parliamentary democracy. Many Romanians, however, see the situation differently. Corruption remains a serious problem and the transition to democracy has been marked by a series of crippling political crises, the most recent coming in 2012 when president Traian Băsescu narrowly escaped dismissal in a public referendum. The ongoing crises have clouded Romania's aim to join the European Union's common border Schengen Zone, which was hoped to take place in 2013 or 2014.

History
Ancient Romania & 'Dracula'

Ancient Romania was inhabited by Thracian tribes, more commonly known as Dacians. The Greeks established trading colonies along the Black Sea from the 7th century BC, and the Romans conquered in AD 105–06. The slave-owning Romans brought with them their civilisation and the Latin language.

From the 10th century the Magyars (Hungarians) expanded into Transylvania, and by the 13th century all of Transylvania was under the Hungarian crown.

The Romanian-speaking principalities of Wallachia and Moldavia offered strong resistance to the Ottomans' northern expansion in the 14th and 15th centuries. Mircea the Old, Vlad Ţepeş and Ştefan cel Mare (Stephen the Great) were legendary figures in this struggle.

Vlad Drăculea, ruling prince of Wallachia from 1456 to 1462 and 1476 to 1477, posthumously gained the moniker 'Ţepeş' (Impaler) after his favoured form of punishing his enemies – impaling. A dull wooden stake was carefully inserted into the anus, driven slowly through the body avoiding vital organs, until it emerged from the mouth, resulting in hours, even days, of agony before death. He is perhaps more legendary as the inspiration for 19th-century novelist Bram Stoker's Count Dracula. (Vlad's surname, Drăculea, means 'son of the dragon', after his father, Vlad Dracul, a knight of the Order of the Dragon.)

When the Turks conquered Hungary in the 16th century, Transylvania became a vassal of the Ottoman Empire. In 1600 the three Romanian states – Transylvania, Wallachia and Moldavia – were briefly united under Mihai Viteazul (Michael the Brave). In 1687 Transylvania fell under Habsburg rule.

In 1859 Alexandru Ioan Cuza was elected to the thrones of Moldavia and Wallachia, creating a national state, which in 1862 took the name Romania. The reformist

Cuza was forced to abdicate in 1866, and his place was taken by Prussian prince Karl of Hohenzollern, who took the name Carol I. Romania declared independence from the Ottoman Empire in 1877, and, after the 1877–78 War of Independence, Dobrogea became part of Romania.

Romania in WWI & WWII

In 1916 Romania entered WWI on the side of the Triple Entente (Britain, France and Russia), with one of the objectives being to retake Transylvania from Austria-Hungary. With the defeat of Austria-Hungary in 1918, the regions of the Banat and Transylvania went to independent Romania.

In the years leading to WWII, Romania sought security in a French alliance. This broke down, and on 30 August 1940 Romania was forced to cede northern Transylvania to Hungary by order of Nazi Germany and fascist Italy.

This loss of territory threw the political situation into turmoil. The result was a fascist dictatorship led by General Ion Antonescu and alleed to Nazi Germany. Antonescu forced King Carol II to abdicate and imposed a harsh, dictatorial regime, which mimicked Germany's brutal anti-Semitism. Some 400,000 Romanian Jews and 36,000 Roma, including those on Hungarian-occupied territories, were eventually murdered at Auschwitz and camps in Ukraine and Moldova.

On 23 August 1944 Romania suddenly changed sides and joined the Allies. The army captured some 53,000 German soldiers and declared war on Nazi Germany. By this act, Romania salvaged its independence and shortened the war.

The Communist Period

After the war, the Soviet-engineered return of Transylvania enhanced the prestige of left-wing parties, which won the parliamentary elections of November 1946. A year later the monarchy was abolished and the Soviet-backed Romanian People's Republic was proclaimed.

Soviet troops formally withdrew in 1958, and after 1960 Romania adopted a quasi-independent foreign policy within the Soviet bloc under two leaders: Gheorghe Gheorghiu-Dej (from 1952 to 1965) and his protégé, Nicolae Ceauşescu (1965 to 1989).

Ceauşescu's reign will forever be seen as misguided, chaotic and megalomaniacal.

The early years of the regime were relatively successful. Ceauşescu managed to defy the Soviet Union and keep Romanian troops out of the Warsaw Pact invasion of Czechoslovakia in 1968. In the late 1960s and early '70s, he positioned Romania as a nonaligned state and curried favour with the USA and UK in their cold war with the Soviet Union.

But following a trip to North Korea in 1971, Ceauşescu steadily lost his grip on reality and established what became the most hardline regime within the Eastern Bloc states. He placed his wife Elena, son Nicu and three brothers in important political positions, and embarked on expensive follies like building the Danube Canal and tearing down large swaths of Bucharest to build his humungous 'House of the People' (today's Palace of Parliament). Meantime, much of the country experienced severe food shortages.

Ceauşescu's Downfall

Ceauşescu managed to survive throughout the fateful year of 1989, when communist regimes around Eastern Europe fell like dominoes, but his luck ran out in December – approximately a month after the fall of the Berlin Wall. On 15 December 1989, in the western city of Timişoara, a Hungarian priest named László Tőkés publicly condemned the dictator from his church in Timişoara. Police attempts to arrest demonstrating parishioners failed and civil unrest quickly spread.

On 21 December in Bucharest, Ceauşescu addressed a rally that was cut short by demonstrators. They booed him, then retreated to the streets between Piaţa Universităţii and Piaţa Romană, only to be crushed later by police gunfire and armoured cars. The next morning thousands more demonstrators took to the streets. At midday Ceauşescu reappeared on the balcony of the Central Committee building to speak, only to be forced to flee by helicopter. Ceauşescu and his wife were soon arrested near Târgovişte, taken to a military base and, on 25 December, executed by firing squad.

The toppling of the dictator provoked widespread jubilation, but this initial enthusiasm was quashed when a former Ceauşescu confidante, Ion Iliescu, won the country's first 'democratic' elections in May 1990. Many felt betrayed by Iliescu's win and students launched large-scale protests in

Bucharest in June of that year. Iliescu called in some 20,000 coal miners from the Jiu Valley to bash student heads and to end the protests. Dozens of people were killed in this hideous phalanx of violence known today as the *mineriadă*.

The years since independence have not all been positive. Over the past two decades, Romania has had its share of scandal, corruption, investment-fund collapses and unstable governments. Nevertheless, the overall trend has been positive, as the country has tried hard to make up for lost time after four decades of communist misrule.

People

Romanians make up 89% of the population; Hungarians are the next largest ethnic group (7%), followed by Roma (2%) and smaller populations of Ukrainians, Germans, Russians and Turks. Germans and Hungarians live almost exclusively in Transylvania, while Ukrainians and Russians live mainly near the Danube Delta, and Turks along the Black Sea coast.

The government estimates that only 400,000 Roma live in Romania, although other sources estimate between 1.5 and 2.5 million. A good site to learn more about the Roma is the Budapest-based **European Roma Rights Centre** (http://errc.org).

Religion

The majority of Romania's population is Eastern Orthodox Christian (87%). The rest is made up of Protestants (6.8%), Catholics (5.6%) and Muslims (0.4%), along with some 39,000 Jehovah's Witnesses and 10,000 Jews.

Arts
Folk Art

Painting on glass and wood remains a popular folk art today. Considered to be of Byzantine origin, this traditional peasant art was widespread in Romania from the 17th century onwards. Superstition and strong religious beliefs surrounded these icons, painted to protect the household from evil spirits. Well-known 19th-century icon painters include Dionisie Iuga, Maria Chifor and Tudor Tocariu. The glass icons of contemporary artist Georgeta Maria Uiga (from Baia Mare) are exhibited worldwide.

Sculpture

Sculpture has been an active art form in the territory of modern Romania since the days of the ancient Greeks along the Black Sea, and the history and archaeology museums in Tulcea and Constanţa are filled with the works of antiquity.

In the 19th and 20th centuries, sculpture often took the form of statues of national heroes as a way of honouring these (usually) men or of fostering a nascent national identity.

This rigid, didactic statue-making, however, was blown away in the early 20th century by the abstract works of master Constantin Brâncuşi (1876–1957). Brâncuşi turned the world of modern sculpture on its head with his dictum of using sculpture not to focus on form, but on inner essence. His works are featured at Craiova's Museum of Art and Bucharest's National Museum of Art, as well as in a series of open-air public works at Târgu Jiu, not far from where he was born.

Contemporary Romanian sculpture got a boost – or perhaps a setback (depending on your point of view) – by a controversial work unveiled in 2012 at Bucharest's Museum of National History. The bronze statue, by Vasile Gorduz (1931–2008), depicts a fully nude (and anatomically correct but not particularly well endowed) Roman Emperor Trajan holding a wolf to symbolise the synthesis of Roman and Dacian cultures. It's provoked derision on all sides, but tellingly has emerged as the city's most-photographed work of art.

Literature

Few modern Romanian writers have managed to break through to a wider international public, but one notable exception is German-speaking author Herta Müller (b 1953), who won the Nobel Prize for Literature in 2009. Müller grew up in a German-speaking village in the Banat during a time when the German minority was subject to harsh oppression and deportation.

Unsurprisingly, her work centres on the severity of life in communist Romania. She left Romania in 1987 and lives in Berlin. Her books are anything but easy reads, but several are available in English, including *The Land of Green Plums* (1998), *The Appointment* (2002) and *The Hunger Angel* (2012).

Any discussion of Romanian Nobel laureates would not be complete without mention of Holocaust survivor and acclaimed writer Elie Wiesel, who was born in the northern city of Sighetu Marmaţiei in 1928 and who was awarded the Nobel Peace Prize in 1986. Wiesel has written some 57 books, but he's best known for *Night*, a moving depiction of his experiences as a prisoner at the Auschwitz-Birkenau and Buchenwald concentration camps during WWII.

Music

The Romanian classical music world is nearly synonymous with George Enescu (1881–1955), whose *Romanian Rhapsodies Nos 1 & 2* and opera *Odeipe* are considered classics. He was as accomplished a violinist as a composer, studied under Fauré in Paris and was also a conductor, cellist and pianist. Other figures of note include composer Ciprian Porumbescu (1853–83) and Paul Constantinescu (1909–63).

FOLK MUSIC
You won't travel far without hearing Romanian folk music, which is still common at family celebrations, holidays and weddings.

Traditional Romanian folk instruments include the *bucium* (alphorn), the *cimpoi* (bagpipes), the *cobză* (a pear-shaped lute) and the *nai* (a pan pipe of about 20 cane tubes). Many kinds of flute are used, including the ocarina (a ceramic flute) and the *tilinca* (a flute without finger holes).

Folk music can take many forms. A *doină* is a solo, improvised love song, a sort of Romanian blues with a social or romantic theme that is sung in a number of contexts (at home, at work or during wakes). The *doină* was added to the Unesco World Heritage list of intangible cultural elements in 2009. Another common form, the *baladă* (ballad), is a collective narrative song steeped in feeling.

Cinema

The so-called 'Romanian Wave' in cinema is red hot and showing no signs of abating. Hits like Nae Caranfil's comedy *Filantropica* (2002) and Cristi Puiu's *The Death of Mr Lăzărescu* (2005) started things off, then in 2007 director Cristian Mungiu won the Cannes Film Festival's top prize with *4 Months, 3 Weeks and 2 Days,* a disturbing tale of illegal abortion in communist-era Romania, while the late Cristian Nemescu's film *California Dreamin'* also took honours.

More recent buzz-worthy films include rare Romanian comedy *Tales from the Golden Age* (2009) by Cristian Mungiu and *Police, Adjective* by Corneliu Porumboiu, which won the Jury Prize in the Un Certain Regard section at Cannes in 2009. The 'wave' at Cannes continues, with Cristi Puiu's *Aurora* and Radu Muntean's *Tuesday, After Christmas* both being selected for Un Certain Regard.

Environment

When the gods were doling out unspoilt wildernesses they seem to have been extra generous with Romania; covering 237,500 sq km, this oval-shaped country offers a panorama of mountains, pristine forests, lakes and rolling meadows unparalleled in the rest of Europe. And thanks to traditional methods of farming, incursions into the habitats of wild animals have been relatively low.

Increasingly, travellers on the hunt for isolated locations abundant with nature and wildlife are coming to Romania – be it for birdwatching in the Danube Delta, wolf tracking in Transylvania, or even crouching in a hide looking for brown bears.

Still, there are significant threats to the environment. Two of the biggest problems, and key EU criticisms of Romania, include the way the country processes factory waste and water pollution.

A disastrous cyanide spill by a mine into the Someş River near Baia Mare in 2000 was a bellwether event that heightened public concern over the waste issue and led to stiffer regulations on what companies can discharge. Environmental groups say the measures do not go far enough and have expressed fears another calamity occuring that is only a matter of time.

Food & Drink

Romanian dishes have a delightful, home-made character to them, incorporating the fertile land's fresh, organic produce into relatively uncomplicated but delicious concoctions. Many dishes, perhaps even the majority, use pork in some form, paired with a staple like polenta, potatoes or cooked cabbage. The recipes derive from peasant cooking going back hundreds of years, with a liberal dose of borrowings from neighbouring (and occasionally occupying) cultures like Turkish, Hungarian, German and Slav.

STREET EATS

Romanians love to eat on the go, and in most towns and cities there are plenty of decent street food options. Look out especially for the following:

Covrigi Hot pretzels sprinkled with salt or sesame or poppy seeds

Gogosi Doughnuts, either dusted with sugar or stuffed with fruit

Placinte Sweet or savoury pastries, served warm and stuffed with fruit, curd cheese or meat

Mici Grilled rolls of spiced minced pork or beef, always served with mustard

Shoarma Like a shawarma, though usually made from chicken or pork, with unorthodox toppings like cabbage and ketchup

Comfort Food

Romanian food wasn't bred so much to dazzle but to satisfy, and menus are rich in 'comfort foods'. *Mămăligă*, a cornmeal mush (often translated as 'polenta' on English menus), seemingly was designed to warm and fill the stomach. You'll find it at restaurants, inns and family homes around the country. It can be disappointingly bland or stodgy in restaurants, but when homemade and served with fresh *smântână* (sour cream), it certainly hits the spot.

Mămăligă pairs beautifully with *sarmale*, the country's de facto national dish (though it's actually an import from the days of Ottoman rule) and comfort food extraordinaire. *Sarmale* are cabbage or vine leaves that are stuffed with spiced meat and rice; the *mămăligă* here provides an excellent backstop for soaking up the juices.

Wine, Beer & Moonshine

Romania is the 9th-biggest winemaker in the world and produces many wines that are world class. Wineries turn out both reds (*negru* and *roșu*) and whites (*alb*). Look for bottles from one of the five traditional wine-making regions: Târnave plateau (outside Alba Iulia; whites), Cotnari (outside Iași; whites), Murfatlar (near the Black Sea coast; whites and reds), Dealu Mare (south of the Carpathians; reds) and Odobești (in southern Moldavia; whites and reds).

For day-to-day tippling, Romanians are beer drinkers at heart. The quality of the beer ranges from passable to pretty good. Most Romanian breweries are owned by big international brewers and it's sometimes easier to find a Tuborg or a Heineken than a Romanian label. The better local brands to look for include Ciuc, Ursus, Silva and Timișoara's local favourite, Timișoreana.

When it comes to serious drinking, the only real contender is *țuică* (fruit brandy). Typically, *țuică* is made from plums (three-quarters of the nation's plums end up in a bottle). The best batches are from the backyard still, and nearly everyone has an uncle or grandfather who makes the 'best in Romania'. Unless you're a seasoned drinker, though, hold the line at one or two shots. Batches can run as high as 50% to 60% alcohol (100–120 proof).

SURVIVAL GUIDE

Directory A–Z

Accommodation

Romania has a wide choice of accommodation options to suit most budgets, including hotels, pensions and private rooms, hostels and camping grounds. Prices across these categories have risen in recent years, but are still generally lower than in Western Europe.

This book divides accommodation options into three categories based on price: budget, midrange and top end. Budget properties normally include hostels, camping grounds and some cheaper guesthouses. Midrange accommodation includes three-star hotels and pensions. Top end usually means four- and five-star hotels, corporate chains and boutiques.

» Watch for seasonal fluctuations on rates. Summer resorts, particularly on the Black Sea, have much higher prices in July and August.

» We've usually quoted prices in this guide in lei, though many hotels quote rates in euro. You'll still have to pay in lei and your credit card will be debited at the current exchange rate.

The following price categories for the cost of a double room are used in the listings in this chapter.

€ less than 130 lei

€€ 130 lei to 280 lei

€€€ more than 280 lei

Business Hours

Banks 9am to noon and 1pm to 5pm Monday to Friday

Clubs 8pm to 2am

Restaurants 10am to 11pm

Shops 10am to 6pm Monday to Friday, 10am to 5pm Saturday

Customs Regulations

» You're allowed to import hard currency up to a maximum of €10,000 or the equivalent.

» For foreigners, duty-free allowances for items purchased *outside* of the EU are 4L of wine, 2L of spirits and 200 cigarettes. For more information, go to www.customs.ro.

Embassies & Consulates

Embassies are located in Bucharest, while several countries maintain consulates at other cities around the country. There is no New Zealand embassy in Romania, so citizens should turn to the country's embassy in Brussels for consular matters.

Australian Consulate (☑021-206 2200; www.dfat.gov.au; Str Praga 3)

Canadian Embassy (☑021-307 5000; www.canadainternational.gc.ca/romania-roumanie; Str Tuberozelor 1-3)

French Embassy (☑021-303 1000; www.ambafrance-ro.org; Str Biserica Amzei 13-15)

Irish Embassy (☑021-310 2131; www.embassyofireland.ro; Str Buzeşti 50-52)

Netherlands Embassy (☑021-208 6030; http://romania.nlembassy.org; Aleea Alexandru 20)

UK Embassy (☑021-201 7200; www.ukinromania.fco.gov.uk; Str Jules Michelet 24)

Ukrainian Embassy (☑021-230 3660; www.mfa.gov.ua/romania; B-dul Aviatorilor 24)

US Embassy (☑consulate 021-270-6000, embassy 021-200 3300; http://romania.usembassy.gov; B-dul Dr Liviu Librescu 4-6)

Food

The following price categories for the cost of a main course are used in the listings in this chapter.

€ less than 13 lei

€€ 15 lei to 30 lei

€€€ more than 30 lei

Gay & Lesbian Travellers

Public attitudes towards homosexuality remain relatively negative. In spite of this, Romania has made significant legal progress in decriminalising homosexual acts and adopting antidiscrimination laws.

» Bucharest remains the most tolerant city in the country, though gay couples should refrain from open displays of affection.

» Bucharest-based **Accept Association** (☑021-252 9000; www.accept-romania.ro) organises a six-day GayFest in the capital in early summer, with films, parties, conferences and a parade.

Money

CASH

The currency is the leu (plural: lei), noted in this guide as 'lei' but listed in banks as RON. One leu is divided into 100 bani. Banknotes come in denominations of 1 leu, 5 lei, 10 lei, 50 lei, 100 lei, 200 lei and 500 lei. The coins come in 50 and 10 bani.

Romania is a member of the European Union, but the euro does not circulate. There is no point in converting your money into euro prior to arrival, since you will have to convert it to lei anyway.

ATMS

ATMs are nearly everywhere and give 24-hour withdrawals in lei on a variety of international bank cards, including Visa and MasterCard. Romanian ATMs require a four-digit PIN.

CHANGING MONEY

The best place to exchange money is at a bank. You'll pay a small commission, but get a decent rate. You can also change money at a private *casa de schimb* (exchange booth), but be wary of commission charges.

You will need to show a passport to change money, so have it handy.

Never change money on the street with strangers; it's always a rip-off.

CREDIT CARDS & TRAVELLERS CHEQUES

International credit and debit cards, including Visa and MasterCard, are widely accepted at hotels, restaurants and shops in cities. In rural areas, you'll usually need to pay cash.

» Credit card transactions may also require a PIN number, so it's best to work that out with your bank prior to departure.

» You will need a valid credit card to hire a car.

» Travellers cheques are increasingly difficult to change in Romania.

Post

The **Romanian Postal Service** (www.posta-romana.ro) is slow but reliable. Buy stamps in post offices, as letters must be weighed to determine correct postage. Delivery time within Europe is one week; overseas will take seven to 10 days.

Public Holidays

New Year 1 and 2 January

Orthodox Easter Monday April/May

Labour Day 1 May

Pentecost May/June, 50 days after Easter Sunday

Assumption of Mary 15 August

Feast of St Andrew 30 November

Romanian National Day 1 December

Christmas 25 and 26 December

Telephone

Romania has a modern telephone network of landlines and mobile phones. Romania's country code is ☑40.

All Romanian landlines have 10 digits, consisting of a zero, plus a city code and the number. This formula differs depending on whether the number is in Bucharest or outside of Bucharest. Bucharest numbers take the form ☑0 plus a two-digit city code (☑21 or ☑31) plus the seven-digit number. Outside of Bucharest, numbers take the form ☑0 plus the three-digit city code plus the six-digit number.

Mobile phone numbers are identified by a three-digit prefix starting with ☑7. All mobile numbers have 10 digits: ☑0 plus the three-digit prefix (☑7xx) and six-digit number.

TIPPING

Restaurants 10% of the bill

Hairdressers and other personal services 10%

Taxi drivers Round up to the nearest whole leu

Hotel cleaning staff 3 lei to 5 lei per night

CALLING FROM WITHIN ROMANIA & ABROAD

If you're calling from within Romania, to reach a landline, dial ☑0 plus the city code and the six-digit number. A landline in Bucharest would take the form ☑0 plus ☑21 (or ☑31) and the seven-digit number. To reach a mobile number, dial ☑0 plus the three-digit mobile prefix and the six-digit number.

» To call abroad from Romania, dial ☑00 plus the country code you want to call, the local area code and the number.

» To call a Romanian number from outside the country, dial your country's international access code plus ☑40 (Romania's country code), the city code (minus the zero) and the six- (or seven-) digit local number.

» To call a mobile number, dial your international access code plus ☑40, then ☑7xx and the six-digit number.

MOBILE PHONES & SMARTPHONES

Romanian mobile (cell) phones use the GSM 900/1800 network, the standard throughout Europe as well as in Australia and New Zealand, but it's not compatible with mobile phones in North America or Japan (though some multiband phones do work across regions). Ask your provider if you're uncertain whether or not your phone will work.

» To reduce expensive roaming fees, buy a prepaid Romanian SIM card, which gives you a temporary local number and charges local (cheaper) rates for calls, texts and data transfers.

» Prepaid SIM plans start at about 20 lei per card and include bonus minutes. They are offered by all three of Romania's main carriers: **Vodafone** (www.vodafone.ro), **Cosmote** (www.cosmote.ro) and **Orange** (www.orange.ro).

» The situation is more complicated if you have a smartphone like an iPhone, Android or Blackberry that cannot easily be unlocked. With these phones, it's best to contact your home provider to consider short-term international calling and data plans.

PAY PHONES & PHONECARDS

Public phones require a magnetic-stripe phonecard, which you can buy from post offices and newspaper kiosks. Phonecard rates start at about 10 lei.

Tourist Information

» The **Romanian National Tourist Office** (www.romaniatourism.com) maintains a wonderful website with a trove of useful information.

» Romania's national network of tourist offices has made strides in recent years. Nearly all big cities have decent tourist offices.

Travellers with Disabilities

» Romania is not well equipped for people with disabilities, even though there has been some improvement in recent years.

» Wheelchair ramps are available only at some upmarket hotels and restaurants, and public transport will be a challenge.

Visas

Citizens of EU countries do not need visas to visit Romania and can stay indefinitely. Citizens of the USA, Canada, Australia, New Zealand, Israel, Japan and many other countries can stay for up to 90 days without a visa. Other nationalities should check with the **Ministry of Foreign Affairs** (www.mae.ro).

Getting There & Away

Travellers entering Romania should not experience any trouble at customs and immigration.

Air

Romania has good air connections to Europe and the Middle East. At the time of research there were no direct flights to Romania from North America or Southeast Asia.

AIRPORTS

The majority of international flights to Romania arrive at Bucharest's **Henri Coandă International Airport** (OTP, Otopeni; ☎021-204 1000; www.otp-airport.ro; Şos Bucureşti-Ploieşti). Several other cities have international airports:

Cluj Airport (☎0264-416 702; www.airportcluj.ro; Str Traian Vuia 149)

Iaşi Airport (☎info 0733-261 111; www.aeroport.ro; Str Moara de Vant 34)

Sibiu Airport (☎0269-253 135; www.sibiuairport.ro; Sos Alba Iulia 73)

Târgu Mureş Airport (☎0265-328 259; www.targumuresairport.ro; Str Ludus, km14.5)

Timişoara Airport (Traian Vuia Timişoara Airport; ☎0256-493 639; www.aerotim.ro; Str Aeroport 2, Ghiroda)

AIRLINES

Air France (☎021-206 9200; www.airfrance.com)

Austrian Airlines (☎021-204 4560; www.austrian.com)

Blue Air (☎1499; www.blueairweb.com)

British Airways (☎reservations 021-303 2222; www.britishairways.com)

Carpatair (☎0256-300 900; www.carpatair.com)

ČSA (Czech Airlines/OK; ☎021-223 3205; www.csa.cz)

EasyJet (U2; www.easyjet.com)

Germanwings (☎toll 0903-760 101; www.germanwings.com)

KLM (KL; ☎021-206 9222; www.klm.com)

Ryan Air (☎in the UK 0871 246 0002; www.ryanair.com)

Swiss Airlines (☎021-312 0238; www.swiss.com)

Tarom (☎021-204 6464; www.tarom.ro) National carrier with good connections to major European and Middle Eastern cities.

WizzAir (☎toll 0903-760 160; www.wizzair.com)

Land

Romania shares a border with five countries: Bulgaria, Hungary, Moldova, Serbia and Ukraine. It has four car-ferry crossings with Bulgaria.

Highway border posts are normally open 24 hours, though smaller crossings may only be open from 8am to 8pm.

BORDER CROSSINGS

Bulgaria Road crossings at Giurgiu, Vama Veche, Calafat (planned for 2013). Ferry crossings at Calafat, Bechet, Turnu Măgerele, Călăraşi

Hungary Road crossings at Nădlac, Borş, Cenad, Valea lui Mihai, Urziceni

Moldova Road crossings at Rădăuţi-Prut, Albiţa, Galaţi, Ştefăneşti, Sculeni

Serbia Road crossings at Moraviţa, Comloşu Mare, Jimbolia, Porţile de Fier I

Ukraine Road crossings at Siret, Sighetu Marmaţiei

BUS

Long-haul bus service remains a popular way of travelling from Romania to Western Europe, as well as to parts of southeastern Europe and Turkey. Bus travel is comparable in price to train travel, but can be faster.

Bus services to and from Western Europe are dominated by two companies: **Eurolines** (www.eurolines.ro) and **Atlassib** (www.atlassib. ro; Soseaua Alexandriei 164). Both maintain vast networks from cities throughout Europe to destinations all around Romania. Check the websites for latest schedules, prices and departure points.

Bucharest is the hub for coach travel to Bulgaria, Greece and Turkey. One bus departs daily from Bucharest's **Filaret** (☑021-335 3290, info 021-336 0692; www.acfilaret.ro; Piaţa Gării Filaret 1) bus station to Sofia (seven hours, €18), and Bucharest-based **Murat Turism & Transport** (☑021-316 5520; www.muratturism.ro; Soseaua Viilor 33;) offers a daily bus service from Bucharest to İstanbul (14 hours, €40) and to Athens (18 hours, €50).

CAR & MOTORCYCLE

Ensure your documents (personal ID, insurance, registration and visas, if required) are in order before crossing into Romania.

TRAIN

Romania is integrated into the European rail grid, and there are decent connections to Western Europe and neighbouring countries. Nearly all of these arrive at and depart from Bucharest's main station, **Gara de Nord** (☑021-319 9539, phone reservations 021-9522, 021-9521; www.cfr.ro; Piaţa Gara de Nord 1).

» Budapest is the main rail gateway in and out of Romania from Western Europe. There are two daily direct trains between Budapest and Bucharest, with regular onward direct connections from Budapest to Prague, Munich and Vienna.

» Buy international train tickets at train stations or at CFR (Romanian State Railways) in-town ticket offices (identified by an Agenţia de Voiaj CFR sign).

Getting Around

Air

Given the distances and poor state of the roads, flying between cities is a feasible option if time is a primary concern.

The Romanian national carrier **Tarom** (☑021-204 6464; www.tarom.ro) operates a comprehensive network of domestic routes. The airline flies regularly between Bucharest and Cluj-Napoca, Iaşi, Oradea, Sibiu, Suceava and Timişoara.

Timişoara-based **Carpatair** (☑0256-300 900; www.carpatair.com) also runs many domestic flights. The carrier flies from Timişoara to Iaşi, Craiova and Bacau.

Bicycle

It's possible to hire bicycles in many cities and towns. The group **i'velo** (☑021-310 6397; www.ivelo.ro) is trying to popularise cycling and has opened bike-hire outlets in several cities, including Bucharest, Timişoara, Braşov, Constanţa, Iaşi and Sibiu. Rates average about 5 lei per hour or 30 to 50 lei per day.

Bus

A mix of buses, minibuses and 'maxitaxis' form the backbone of the Romanian national transport system. If you understand how the system works, you can move around regions and even across the country easily and cheaply.

Unfortunately, buses and maxitaxi routes change frequently and towns and cities will sometimes have a half-dozen different bus stations, depending on the bus company and destination.

In this chapter, we've identified bus stations and routes for towns and cities where possible. In other areas, we've directed readers to the website www.autogari.ro, an up-to-date timetable that is easy to use and lists routes, times, fares and departure points.

Car & Motorcycle

Roads are generally crowded and in poor condition. The country has only a few short stretches of *autostrada* (motorway), meaning that most of your travel will be along two-lane *drum naţional* (national highways) or *drum judeţean* (secondary roads).

When calculating arrival times, figure on about 50km per hour.

Western-style petrol stations are plentiful. A litre of unleaded 95 octane costs about 6 lei. Most stations accept credit cards, but you'll need a PIN to use them.

Local Transport

Romanian cities generally have good public transportation systems comprising buses, trams, trolleybuses and, in some cases, maxitaxis. Bucharest is the only city with a metro. The method for accessing the systems is broadly similar. Purchase bus or tram tickets at newsagents or street kiosks marked *bilete* or *casă de bilete* before boarding, and validate the ticket once aboard. For maxitaxis, you usually buy a ticket directly from the driver.

TAXIS

Taxis are cheap and a useful supplement to the public transport systems. Drivers are required by law to post their rates on their doors or windscreens. The going rate varies from city to city, but runs anywhere from 1.39 to 1.89 lei per kilometre. Any driver posting a much higher fare is likely a rip-off.

While it's usually okay to use a taxi parked at a taxi rank (provided the taxi is not at Bucharest's airport or main train station) or to hail one from the street, we recommend ordering taxis by phone from reputable companies.

Train

The extensive network covers much of the country, including most of the main tourist sights.

» The national rail system is run by **Căile Ferate Române** (CFR, Romanian State Railways; www.cfr.ro). The CFR website has a handy online timetable (*mersul trenurilor*).

» Buy tickets at train station windows, specialised Agenţia de Voiaj CFR ticket offices, private travel agencies or online at www.cfrcalatori.ro.

» *Sosire* means arrivals and *plecare* is departures. On posted timetables, the number of the platform from which the train departs is listed under *linia*.

TYPES OF TRAINS

Romania has three different types of trains that travel at different speeds, offer varying levels of comfort and charge different fares for the same destination:

» InterCity are listed in blue or green as 'IC' on timetables; the most expensive and most comfortable but not always faster than 'IR' trains.

» InterRegional are listed in red as 'IR' on timetables; cheaper and nearly as fast as 'IC' trains, but may not be as modern.

» Regional are listed in black as 'R' on timetables; typically the oldest and slowest trains in the system, often sporting (pre-) historic rolling stock.

Russia

Best Places to Eat

» Delicatessen (p753)

» Café Pushkin (p753)

» Khachapuri (p753)

» Teplo (p772)

» Botanika (p772)

Best Places to Stay

» Hotel Metropol (p751)

» Bulgakov Mini-Hotel (p751)

» Alexander House (p770)

» Soul Kitchen (p771)

» Radisson Hotel (p783)

Why Go?

Could there be a more iconic image of Eastern Europe than Moscow's awe-inspiring Red Square? Intimately associated with this vision is the lingering impression that Russia (Россия) remains a closed-off, difficult and unfriendly place in which to travel. Nothing could be further from the truth.

Two decades on from the demise of the Soviet Union, an economically and politically resurgent Russia is a brash, exciting and fascinating place to visit. All the fruits of capitalism, including good hotels, restaurants and fully stocked shops, stand alongside things that the country has long got right, such as beautiful architecture and a vibrant cultural scene of classical music, theatre and art.

Outside the major cities covered in this chapter – Moscow, St Petersburg, Veliky Novgorod and Kaliningrad – there are also the simple pleasures of a countryside dotted with timeless wooden cottages and deserted beaches. Don't let the matter of a little visa red tape deter you.

When to Go

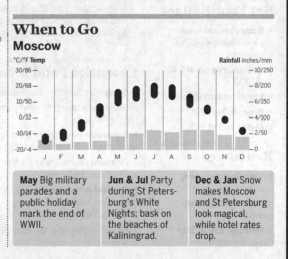

Moscow

May Big military parades and a public holiday mark the end of WWII.

Jun & Jul Party during St Petersburg's White Nights; bask on the beaches of Kaliningrad.

Dec & Jan Snow makes Moscow and St Petersburg look magical, while hotel rates drop.

AT A GLANCE

» **Currency** Ruble (R)

» **Language** Russian

» **Money** Plenty of ATMs, most accepting foreign cards

» **Visas** Required by all – apply at least a month in advance of your trip

Fast Facts

» **Area** 16,995,800 sq km

» **Capital** Moscow

» **Country code** ☑7

» **Emergency** Ambulance ☑03, emergency assistance ☑112, fire ☑01, police ☑02

Exchange Rates

Australia	A$1	R32.44
Canada	C$1	R30.58
Euro Zone	€1	R39.69
Japan	¥100	R32.91
New Zealand	NZ$1	R26.00
UK	UK£1	R46.99
USA	US$1	R31.06

Set Your Budget

» **Budget hotel room** R3000 Moscow (R1000 elsewhere)

» **Two-course meal** R400 to R1000

» **Museum entrance** R350

» **Beer** R50 to R120

» **Metro ticket** R28

Resources

» **Visit Russia** (www. visitrussia.org.uk)

» **Russia Made Easy** (www.redtape.ru)

» **Moscow Expat Site** (www.expat.ru)

Connections

Bordering Belarus, Estonia, Latvia, Lithuania, Poland and Ukraine, Russia has excellent train and bus connections with the rest of Europe. Be careful: many routes connecting St Petersburg and Moscow with points east – including Kaliningrad – go through Belarus, for which you'll need a transit visa. Buses are the best way to get from St Petersburg to Tallinn. St Petersburg to Helsinki can be done by boat, bus or train.

ITINERARIES

One Week

Spend three days in Moscow. See Red Sq, the Kremlin and the collections at the Tretyakov, New Tretyakov and Pushkin art museums. Journey to the magnificent Novodevichy Convent & Cemetery, and the revamped Gorky Park. Sweat it out in the Sanduny Baths or do a metro tour. Take the night train to Veliky Novgorod and spend a day exploring its ancient kremlin and churches. The last three days are reserved for splendid St Petersburg. Wander up Nevsky pr, see Dvortsovaya pl, and spend a half-day at the Hermitage. Tour the canals and the mighty Neva River by boat. Visit Peter & Paul Fortress, the Church of the Saviour on Spilled Blood and the wonderful Russian Museum.

Two Weeks

With two extra days in Moscow, explore Soviet landmarks like VDNKh (the All Russian Exhibition Centre), and take a day trip to charming Sergiev Posad. In St Petersburg, spend more time in the Hermitage and other museums, and tack on an excursion to Petrodvorets or Tsarskoe Selo. Then fly to Kaliningrad. Admire the capital's reconstructed Gothic Cathedral and wander along the river to the excellent World Ocean Museum. The Amber Museum is also impressive. Enjoy either the old Prussian charm of the spa town of Svetlogorsk or the sand dunes and forests of the Kurshskaya Kosa National Park.

Essential Food & Drink

» **Soups** Try lemony, meat *solyanka* or hearty fish *ukha*.

» **Bliny** (pancakes) Served with *ikra* (caviar) or *tvorog* (cottage cheese).

» **Salads** A wide variety usually slathered in mayonnaise, including the chopped potato one called Olivier.

» **Pelmeni** (dumplings) Stuffed with meat and eaten with sour cream and vinegar.

» **Central Asian dishes** Try *plov* (Uzbek pilaf), *shashlyk* (kebab) or *lagman* (noodles).

» **Vodka** The quintessential Russian tipple.

» **Kvas** A refreshing, beerlike drink, or the red berry juice mix *mors*.

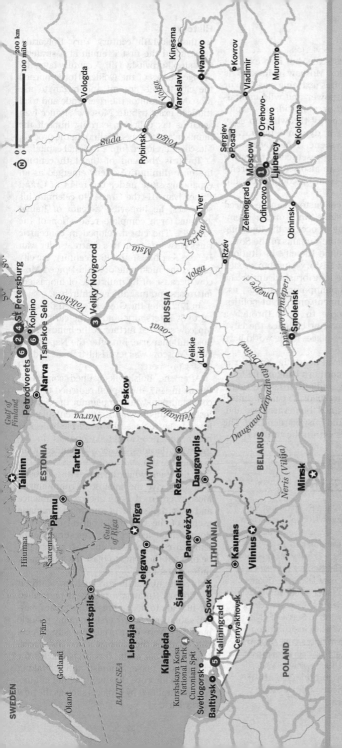

Russia Highlights

1 Be awe-inspired by the massive scale and riches of **Moscow** (p742), Russia's brash, energetic capital.

2 Take a walking, bike or boat tour of **St Petersburg** (p761).

an Italianate slice of Old Europe incongruously placed in Russia.

3 Trace Russia's roots back to **Veliky Novgorod** (p759), with its well-preserved kremlin and many picturesque churches.

4 Ogle the seemingly endless collection of masterpieces in St Petersburg's unrivalled **Hermitage** (p761).

5 Head to the quirky exclave of **Kaliningrad** (p779) to explore its brawny eponymous capital and the wind-swept Kurshskaya Kosa (Curonian Spit).

6 Day trip out of St Petersburg to see the tsars' country estates at **Petrodvorets** and **Tsarskoe Selo** (p777).

MOSCOW

📱495 & 📱499 / POP 11.5 MILLION

Intimidating in its scale, but also exciting and unforgettable, Moscow (Москва) is a place that inspires extreme passion or loathing. History, power and wild capitalism hang in the air alongside an explosion of creative energy throwing up edgy art galleries and a dynamic restaurant, bar and nightlife scene. Tchaikovsky and Chekhov are well represented at the city's theatres, but you can also see world premieres by up-and-coming composers and choreographers.

Russia's turbulent history can be traced from the sturdy stone walls of the Kremlin, which continue to occupy the founding site of Moscow, to the remains of the Soviet state scattered around the city. Institutions such as the Gulag History Museum broach subjects that were long brushed under the carpet, while contemporary artists use their work to comment on current politics. Whether you choose to stroll through a quiet neighbourhood or embrace the city's infectious buzz, few places in the world have so much to offer.

The city's medieval heart, the Kremlin, is a triangle on the northern bank of the Moscow River. The city radiates from the Kremlin in a series of ring roads. The most central rings are the tree-lined 'boulevard ring' and, beyond, the vast and busy 'garden ring'. The modern centre lies within the garden ring.

DON'T MISS

SERGIEV POSAD

The charming Golden Ring town of Sergiev Posad (Сергиев Посад), just 60km from central Moscow, is an easy day trip. The principal attraction here is the venerable 15th-century **Trinity Monastery of St Sergius** (Troitse-Sergieva Lavra; 📱496-544 5356; www.lavra.ru; ⊗10am-6pm), one of the most important and active monasteries in the Russian Orthodox religion. Bus 388 to Sergiev Posad from Moscow's VDNKh metro station departs every 15 minutes until 7.30pm (R145, 70 minutes), or take an express train (R320, one hour, twice daily) or more frequent *prigorodny* (suburban) train (R150, 1½ hours) from Moscow's Yaroslavsky vokzal.

History

In the mid-12th century Yury Dolgoruky constructed the first Kremlin at a strategic spot atop Borovitsky Hill. A century later, the Mongol forces of the Golden Horde burned the city to the ground and began to use Moscow to monitor the river trade and road traffic to exact tribute. Moscow's Prince Ivan acted as tax collector, earning himself the moniker 'Moneybags' (Kalita). In the process, Moscow developed into a regional capital.

Towards the end of the 15th century, the once diminutive duchy emerged as an expanding state under the reign of Grand Prince Ivan III (the Great). To celebrate his successes, he imported a team of Italian artisans for a complete renovation of the Kremlin. The city developed in concentric rings outwards from this centre. Under Ivan IV (the Terrible) in the 16th century, the city earned the nickname of 'Gold-Domed Moscow' because of its multitude of monastery fortresses and magnificent churches.

In 1712 Peter the Great relocated the capital to St Petersburg, and in the early 1800s Moscow suffered further at the hands of Napoleon Bonaparte. But after the Napoleonic Wars, Moscow was feverishly rebuilt and industry prospered.

After the Bolsheviks gained control of Russia in 1917, the capital returned to Moscow. Stalin's new urban plan for the city saw historic cathedrals and monuments demolished to be replaced by a marble-bedecked metro and neo-Gothic skyscrapers. In the following decades, Moscow expanded at an exponential rate.

In the 1990s while the rest of Russia struggled to survive the collapse of communism, Moscow emerged as an enclave of affluence and was the scene of the most dramatic events of the country's political transition. Boris Yeltsin led crowds protesting the attempted coup in 1991, and two years later he ordered the army to blast the parliament into submission.

In September 2010 Yuri Luzhkov was fired as Moscow's mayor, a role he'd performed for 18 years to his and his wife's great financial gain. Under his oversight, many historic buildings were destroyed, and skyscrapers shot up along the Moscow River. His successor, Sergey Sobyanin, has been praised for being more preservationist, and for taking strides to improve the quality of life in Moscow, exemplified by projects such as the new Gorky Park.

◉ Sights

The Kremlin   MUSEUM
(☑495-202 3776; www.kreml.ru; adult/student R350/100; ☺10am-5pm Fri-Wed, ticket office 9.30am-4.30pm; ⓜAleksandrovsky Sad) The apex of Russian political power and once the centre of the Orthodox Church, the Kremlin is not only the kernel of Moscow but of the whole country. It's from here that autocratic tsars, communist dictators and modern-day presidents have done their best – and worst – for Russia. Covering Borovitsky Hill on the north bank of the Moscow River, the Kremlin is enclosed by high walls 2.25km long, with Red Sq outside the east wall.

Before entering the Kremlin, deposit bags at the **left-luggage office** (per bag R60; ☺9am-6.30pm Fri-Wed), beneath the **Kutafya Tower** near the entrance. Ticket offices are in Kutafya Tower and nearby in **Alexandrovsky Garden** (Aleksandrovsky sad, Manezhnaya ul). The ticket to the 'Architectural Ensemble of Cathedral Square' covers entry to the grounds and to all four churches, as well as the Patriarch's Palace. It does not include Ivan the Great Bell Tower (which costs an additional R150), or the Armoury; you can buy tickets for those here, too.

Photography is not permitted inside the Armoury or any of the buildings on Sobornaya pl (Cathedral Sq). Visitors wearing shorts will be refused entry.

Southwest Buildings
From the Kutafya Tower, walk up the ramp and pass through the Kremlin walls beneath the **Trinity Gate Tower**. The lane to the right (south) passes the 17th-century **Poteshny Palace**, where Stalin lived. The horribly out-of-place glass-and-concrete **State Kremlin Palace** houses a concert and ballet auditorium, where many Western pop stars play when they are in Moscow.

Armoury
(adult/student R700/200; ☺entry 10am, noon, 2.30pm & 4.30pm) In the Kremlin's southwestern corner is this mind-numbingly opulent collection of treasures accumulated over time by the Russian state and church. Tickets specify entry times. Highlights include Fabergé eggs and reams of royal regalia.

Sobornaya Ploshchad
On the northern side of Sobornaya pl, with five golden helmet domes and four semicircular gables facing the square, is the **Assumption Cathedral** (Uspensky Sobor), built between 1475 and 1479. As the focal church

---

FREE THRILLS

Moscow can drain your wallet faster than an addiction to crack, but there are some things you can enjoy for free:

» March across Red Sq (p746) and pay your respects to Lenin.

» Head out to the 'burbs for epic Soviet creations like VDNKh (p749) and Izmaylovo (p749).

» Visit the graves of legendary Russian literary and other heroes at Novodevichy Cemetery (p750).

» Watch the changing of the guard in the Alexandrovsky Garden (p748).

» Wander around the newly revamped Gorky Park (p749) and the Garage Centre for Contemporary Culture (p749).

» Spend a morning browsing colourful covered bazaars such as Dorogomilovsky Market (p750).

---

of prerevolutionary Russia, it's the burial place of most heads of the Russian Orthodox Church from the 1320s to 1700. The iconostasis dates from 1652, but its lowest level contains some older icons, including the *Virgin of Vladimir,* an early-15th-century Rublyovschool copy of Russia's most revered image, the *Vladimir Icon of the Mother of God.*

The delicate little single-domed church beside the west door of the Assumption Cathedral is the **Church of the Deposition of the Robe** (Tserkov Rizpolozhenia), built between 1484 and 1486 by masons from Pskov.

With its two golden domes rising above the eastern side of Sobornaya pl, the 16th-century **Ivan the Great Bell Tower** (Kolokolnya Ivana Velikogo; special exhibits adult/student R150/100) offers wonderful views of Sobornaya pl and houses the Kremlin's newest exhibit, a multimedia presentation of the architectural history of the complex. Beside the bell tower stands the **Tsar Bell**, a 202-tonne monster that cracked before it ever rang. North of the bell tower is the mammoth **Tsar Cannon**, cast in 1586 but never shot.

The 1508 **Archangel Cathedral** (Arkhangelsky sobor), at the square's southeastern corner, was for centuries the coronation, wedding and burial church of tsars. The tombs of all of Russia's rulers from the 1320s to the 1690s are here bar one (Boris Godunov, who was buried at Sergiev Posad).

Central Moscow

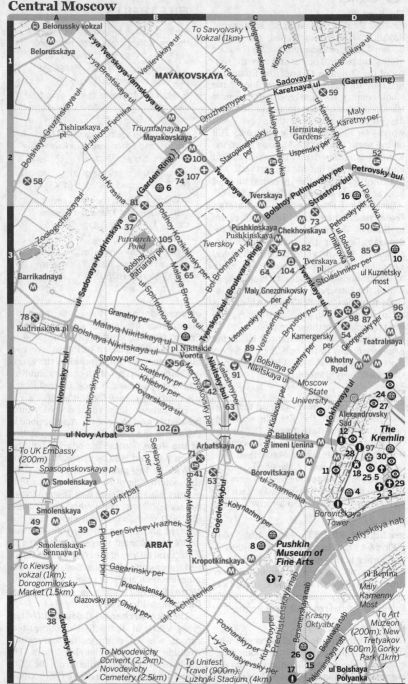

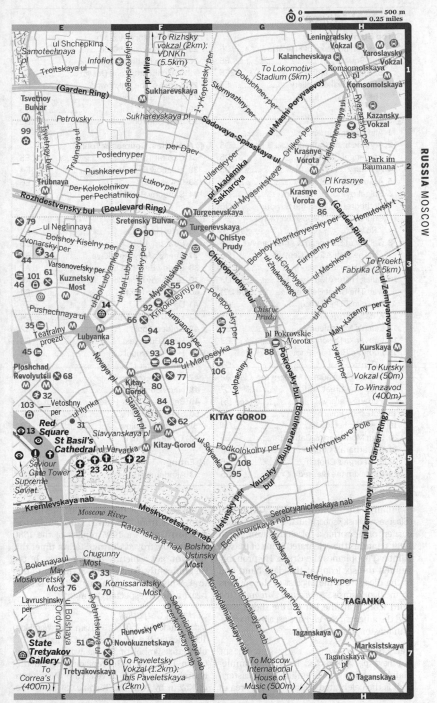

ul Shchepkina
Samotechnaya pl
Infoflot
Troitskaya ul
(Garden Ring)
To Rizhsky vokzal (2km); VDNKh (5.5km)
ul Gilyarovskogo
pr Mira
Sukharevskaya
Skornyazhny per
1-y Koptelsky per
Dokuchaev per
To Lokomotiv Stadium (5km)
Leningradsky Vokzal
Kalanchevskaya
Komsomolskaya pl
Yaroslavsky Vokzal
Komsomolskaya

Tsvetnoy Bulvar
99
Petrovsky
Trubnaya ul
Sukharevskaya pl
Sadovaya-Spasskaya ul
ul Mashi Poryvaevoy
Kazansky Vokzal
83
Komsomolskaya

Posledny per
per Daev
Ulansky per
Orlikov per
Krasnye Vorota
Park im Baumana

Pushkarev per
pr Akademika Sakharova
Krasnye Vorota
Pl Krasnye Vorota

Trubnaya
per Kolokolnikov
per Pechatnikov
Lukov per
ul Myasnitskaya
86
(Garden Ring)
Homutovsky t

Rozhdestvensky bul
(Boulevard Ring)
Turgenevskaya
Bolshoy Kharitonyevsky per
Furmanny per
ul Mashkova
To Proekt Fabrika (2.5km)

79
ul Neglinnaya
Bolshoy Kiselny per
Sretensky Bulvar
90
Turgenevskaya
Chistye Prudy
ul Chaplygina
ul Zhukovskogo
ul Pokrovka

Zvonarsky per
34
Varsonovefsky per
44
101
61
Kuznetsky Most
46
@
Myasnitskaya ul
Chistoprudny bul
Chistye Prudy
Maly Kazenny per
To Zemlyanoy val

14
Pushechnaya ul
35
Teatralny proezd
Lubyanka
45
55
92
Myasnitskaya
66
94
Krivokolenny per
Armyansky per
Potapovsky per
pl Pokrovskie Vorota
88
Pokrovsky bul
(Boulevard Ring)
Lyapin per
Kurskaya
To Kursky Vokzal (50m)
To Winzavod (400m)

Ploshchad Revolyutsii
68
48 109
93
106
47
ul Maroseyka
Kolpachny per
ul Solyanka
Podkolokolny per
ul Vorontsovo Pole
(Garden Ring)
To Zemlyanoy val

32
103
Vetoshny per
80
84
62
Staraya pl
Novaya pl
ul Ilynka
KITAY GOROD
108
95
Yauzsky bul
Ustinsky per

Red Square
13
31
St Basil's Cathedral
Slavyanskaya pl
Kitay-Gorod
ul Varvarka
Kitay-Gorod

Saviour Gate Tower
Supreme Soviet
21 23 20
22

Kremlevskaya nab
Moscow River
Rauzhskaya nab
Moskvoretskaya nab
Serebryanicheskaya nab
Bernikovskaya nab
Yauzskaya ul

Chugunny Most
33
Bolshoy Ustinsky Most
Kotelnicheskaya nab
Goncharnaya
Teterinsky per
TAGANKA

Bolotnaya ul
May Moskvoretsky Most 76
70
Komissariatsky Most
kosmodamianskaya nab
Sadovnicheskaya ul
Taganskaya

Lavrushinsky per
ul Bolshaya Ordynka
Pyatnitskaya ul
51
60
72
State Tretyakov Gallery
To Correa's (400m)
Tretyakovskaya
Novokuznetskaya
Runovsky per
Ozerkovskaya nab
To Paveletsky Vokzal (1.2km); Ibis Paveletskaya (2km)
To Moscow International House of Music (500m)
Taganskaya pl
Marksistskaya
Taganskaya

0 500 m
0 0.25 miles

Central Moscow

Finally, the **Annunciation Cathedral** (Blagoveshchensky sobor), at the southwestern corner of Sobornaya pl and dating from 1489, contains the celebrated icons of master painter Theophanes the Greek. He probably painted the six icons at the right-hand end of the diesis row, the biggest of the six tiers of the iconostasis. *Archangel Michael* (the third icon from the left on the diesis row) and the adjacent *St Peter* are ascribed to Russian master Andrei Rublyov.

Red Square   HISTORIC SITE
(Krasnaya pl; Ⓜ Ploshchad Revolyutsii) Immediately outside the Kremlin's northeastern wall is the celebrated 400m-by-150m area of cobbles that is at the very heart of Moscow. Approach from the north through **Resurrection Gate** – a 1995 replica of the 1680 original destroyed during Stalin's time: this way you get a picture-postcard view of the magnificently flamboyant St Basil's Cathedral. This panorama never fails to set the heart aflutter, especially at night.

St Basil's Cathedral
(adult/student R250/50; ⊙ 11am-5pm Wed-Mon) Technically the Intercession Cathedral, this ultimate symbol of Russia was created between 1555 and 1561 (replacing an existing church on the site) to celebrate the capture of Kazan by Ivan the Terrible. 'St Basil's' ac-

54	Akademiya	D4
	Akademiya	(see 26)
55	Art Lebedev Cafe Basmanny	F3
56	Art Lebedev Cafe Presnya	B4
57	Café Pushkin	C3
58	Correa's	A2
59	Delicatessen	D1
60	Grably	E7
61	Jagannath	E3
62	Jean-Jacques	F5
63	Jean-Jacques	C5
64	Khachapuri	C3
65	Mari Vanna	B3
66	Moo-Moo	F4
67	Moo-Moo	A6
68	Pelmeshka	E4
69	Prime Star	D3
70	Prime Star	E6
71	Prime Star	B5
72	Sok	E7
73	Starlite Diner	D3
74	Starlite Diner	B2
	Stolovaya 57	(see 103)
75	Teremok	D4
76	Teremok	E6
77	Teremok	F4
78	Tsentralny	A4
79	Uzbekistan	E3
80	Volkonsky	F4
81	Volkonsky	B2

⊙ Drinking

82	12 Volts	C3
	Bar Strelka	(see 26)
83	Central Station MSK	H2
84	Chinese Pilot Dzhao-Da	F4
	Gipsy	(see 15)

85	Gogol	D3
86	Hungry Duck	H2
87	Ketama Bar	D4
	Krasny Oktyabr	(see 26)
88	Krizis Zhanra	G4
89	Kvartira 44	C4
90	Liga Pap	F3
91	Mayak	C4
92	Papa's Place	F3
93	Pirogi on Maroseyka	F4
94	Propaganda	F4
	Rolling Stone	(see 15)
95	Solyanka	G5

⊙ Entertainment

96	Bolshoi Theatre	D4
97	Kremlin Ballet Theatre	D5
	Masterskaya	(see 35)
98	MKhAT	D4
99	Nikulin Circus on Tsvetnoy Bulvar	E2
100	Tchaikovsky Concert Hall	B2

⊙ Shopping

101	Atlas	E3
102	Dom Knigi	B5
103	GUM	E5
104	Ministerstvo Podarkov	C3
105	Podarky, Dekor & Podarky	B3

⊙ Information

106	36.6 Pokrovka	G4
107	36.6 Tverskaya	B2
108	Australian Embassy	G5
109	Belarusian Consulate	F4
	Maria Travel Agency	(see 109)

tually refers only to the northeastern chapel, which was added later. It was built over the grave of the barefoot holy fool Vasily (Basil) the Blessed, who predicted Ivan's damnation. Its design is the culmination of a wholly Russian style that had been developed through the building of wooden churches. Go inside to see the stark medieval wall paintings.

Lenin's Mausoleum
(⊙10am-1pm Tue-Thu, Sat & Sun) Before joining the queue at the northwestern corner of Red Sq to see Lenin's embalmed body, drop your camera and bag at the left-luggage office in the State History Museum, as you will not be allowed to take them with you. After troop-ing past the oddly waxy figure, emerge from his red-and-black granite tomb and inspect where Stalin, Brezhnev and many of communism's other heavy hitters are buried along the Kremlin wall.

State History Museum
(www.shm.ru; Krasnaya pl 1; adult/student R250/80, audioguide R200-350; ⊙10am-7pm Wed & Fri-Mon, 11am-9pm Thu; MOkhotny Ryad) At the northern end of Red Sq is this museum's enormous collection covering the Russian Empire from the Stone Age on. The building, dating from the late 19th century, is itself an attraction – each room is in the style of a different period or region.

Alexander Garden

(Aleksandrovsky sad; MAleksandrovsky Sad) The first public park in Moscow sits along the Kremlin's western wall. Colourful flower beds and impressive Kremlin views make it a favourite strolling spot. At the northern end is the **Tomb of the Unknown Soldier**, containing the remains of a soldier who died in December 1941 at km41 of Leningradskoe sh – the nearest the Nazis came to Moscow. The changing of the guard happens every hour.

State Tretyakov Gallery   MUSEUM

(www.tretyakovgallery.ru; Lavrushinsky per 10; adult/student R360/220; ⊘10am-7.30pm Tue-Sun; MTretyakovskaya) Nothing short of spectacular, the State Tretyakov Gallery holds the world's best collection of Russian icons and an outstanding collection of other prerevolutionary Russian art, particularly the works of the 19th-century *peredvizhniki* (wanderers) art movement. Andrei Rublyov's *Holy Trinity* (1420s) from Sergiev Posad, widely regarded as Russia's greatest icon, is on the ground floor in room 60. The collection is based on that of 19th-century industrialist brothers Pavel and Sergei Tretyakov (Pavel was a patron of the Peredvizhniki).

New Tretyakov   MUSEUM

(Krymsky val; adult/student R360/220, photos R200; ⊘10am-7.30pm Tue-Sun; MPark Kultury) This gargantuan edifice is the premier venue for 20th-century Russian art and shouldn't be missed. Besides perhaps the world's greatest collection of socialist realist art, the exhibits showcase avant-garde artists such as Malevich, Kandinsky, Chagall, Goncharova and Lyubov Popova. It's about 1km southwest of the main gallery, in Park Iskusstv. From Park Kultury metro, reach it by crossing the Moscow River.

FREE Art Muzeon   SCULPTURE PARK

(ul Krymsky val 10; MPark Kultury) This open-air sculpture park next to the New Tretyakov started as a collection of Soviet statues put out to pasture when they were ripped from their pedestals in the post-1991 wave of anti-Soviet feeling. They have now been joined by fascinating and diverse contemporary work. Zurab Tsereteli's monumental **Peter the Great statue** (Bersenevskaya nab; MPolyanka) stands on an artificial island overlooking the park. Dubbed 'Peter the Ugly', it's unclear whether the statue is meant to honour or mock the

mercurial tsar, who famously loathed Moscow and moved the capital to St Petersburg.

Pushkin Museum of Fine Arts   MUSEUM

(www.artsmuseum.ru; ul Volkhonka 12; admission R400; ⊘10am-7pm Tue-Sun; MKropotkinskaya) Moscow's premier foreign-art museum displays a broad selection of European works, mostly appropriated from private collections after the Revolution. They include Dutch and Flemish masterpieces from the 17th century, several Rembrandt portraits and the Ancient Civilisation exhibits, which include the impressive Treasures of Troy. The Pushkin's amazing collection of impressionist and post-impressionist paintings are next door at the **Gallery of European & American Art of the 19th & 20th Centuries** (www.newpaintart.ru; ul Volkhonka 14; admission R400, audioguide R250; ⊘10am-5pm Tue, Wed & Fri-Sun, to 9pm Thu; MKropotkinskaya).

Tverskoy District   NEIGHBOURHOOD

The streets around Tverskaya ul, Moscow's main avenue, comprise the vibrant Tverskoy district, characterised by old architecture and new commerce. Pedestrianised Kamergersky per and Stoleshnikov per are among Moscow's trendiest places to sip a coffee or a beer and watch the big-city bustle.

In the midst of the swanky shops on ul Petrovka, an archway leads to a courtyard strung with barbed wire and hung with portraits of famous political prisoners. This is the entrance to the grim but compelling **Gulag History Museum** (☑495-621 7346; www.gmig.ru; ul Petrovka 16; adult/student R100/20; ⊘11am-6pm Tue, Wed & Fri-Sun, noon-8pm Thu; MTeatralnaya). Guides dressed like guards describe the vast network of Soviet labour camps and recount the horrors of Gulag camp life.

Nearby is the permanent collection of the **Moscow Museum of Modern Art** (MMOMA; www.mmoma.ru; ul Petrovka 25; adult/student R150/100; ⊘noon-8pm Tue, Wed & Fri-Sun, 1-9pm Thu; MChekhovskaya), a pet project of the notorious Zurab Tsereteli. It contains 20th-century works by the likes of Chagall, Goncharova and Kandinsky, as well as a whimsical sculpture garden. The museum has four additional branches, mostly hosting temporary exhibitions; one ticket is good for all five.

Kitay Gorod   NEIGHBOURHOOD

This 13th-century neighbourhood was the first in Moscow to grow up outside the Kremlin walls. While its name means China Town in modern Russian, do not expect anything

Chinese – the name derives from an old Russian word meaning 'wattle', for the supports used for the walls that protected the suburb. This is the heart of medieval Moscow and parts of the suburb's walls are visible.

The main places of interest are Kitay Gorod's collection of churches. Look out for the charming, brightly painted Monastery of the Epiphany, opposite Ploshchad Revolyutsii metro station, and the small churches along ul Varvarka. These are **St Barbara's Church** (ul Varvarka 2; ☺11am-7pm; Ⓜ Kitay-Gorod), built in 1796–1804; the classic red-brick old Orthodox-style **Sign Monastery & Cathedral** (ul Varvarka 8; ☺noon-8pm; Ⓜ Kitay-Gorod), built in 1679–64; the 1698 **St Maxim the Blessed's Church** (ul Varvarka 4; Ⓜ Kitay-Gorod); and the colourful 1657 **St George's Church** (ul Varvarka 12; Ⓜ Kitay-Gorod) with its early-19th-century bell tower.

The one-time **Lubyanka Prison** (Lubyanskaya pl; Ⓜ Lubyanka) crowning Lubyanka Hill was once the headquarters of the dreaded KGB; today it's the nerve centre of its successor, the FSB (Federal Security Service), and is closed to the public.

FREE **Gorky Park**   PARK
(☎Ⓗ; Ⓜ Park Kultury) A massive facelift in 2012 turned Gorky Park from a hokey Soviet funfair into a refined urban oasis, complete with yoga and meditation zones, outdoor cinemas, beach volleyball courts, skate parks and anything else an outdoorsy urban hipster could want. Along the river is a trendy beach backed by trendy beach cafes, and in the winter a massive skating rink takes centre stage.

It gets better: Moscow's leading contemporary art space, the **Garage Centre for Contemporary Culture** (www.garageccc.com; Gorky Park; ☺9am-10pm Sun-Thu, to 11pm Fri & Sat ; Ⓜ Mendeleyevskaya/Novoslobodskaya), has relocated to Gorky Park. Pet project of Dasha Zhukova (supermodel and girlfriend of billionaire Roman Abramovich), Garage has made a name for itself by hosting top international artists and staging superb exhibitions of photography, art, multimedia, fashion, film – you name it.

Bits of the centre's ambitious Gorky Park project were just opening at the time of

---

WORTH A TRIP

SOVIET SIGHTS

While the Kremlin and the old churches are nice, let's not forget that Moscow spent 70 years as the quintessential Soviet city, and the Soviet stamp remains by far the capital's most predominant. Several impressive and/or bizarre Soviet creations warrant going a few extra stops out on the metro.

First and foremost on the list is **VDNKh** (All-Russia Exhibition Centre; Ⓜ VDNKh). The initials (ВДНХ) stand for Exhibition of Achievements of the National Economy, which sums up the conflict between Soviet dream and reality that the centre epitomises. Started in the 1930s, it consists of a series of grandiose pavilions – each representing a former Soviet republic – glorifying every aspect of socialist construction. Gargantuan statues, wide alleys and fountains, along with cheap amusement park rides and other trappings of downmarket post-Soviet consumerism, round out the effect. In the winter you'll find ice sculptures out here.

While you're out here, look for the gargantuan *Worker and Kolkhoz Woman* statue northeast of VDNKh. The famous 1937 World's Fair entry recently returned to its perch after an extensive restoration.

Close to VDNKh metro, the fantastic **Cosmonautics Museum** (www.space-museum.ru; admission R200; ☺10am-7pm Tue-Sun; Ⓜ VDNKh) is topped by a soaring 100m titanium obelisk built in 1964 to commemorate the launch of *Sputnik*.

A separate northbound metro branch takes you out to **Izmaylovo Market** (www.kremlin-izmailovo.com; Izmaylovskoye shosse 73; ☺10am-8pm; Ⓜ Partizanskaya), another notorious Soviet relic. It's a sprawling area of hotels and facilities built for the 1984 Olympics and then converted into Soviet Moscow's main tourist enclave. Today it still woos tourists with rows of midrange hotels and souvenir stands in a sprawling flea market. Emerging from the metro, look for the kitsch mock Kremlin (great for photos!) to find the market.

BULGAKOV'S MOSCOW

No country reveres their literary heroes quite like Russia. The slightest association with one of the Titans of Russian literature – a visit in 1896, a brief mention in *Crime and Punishment* – might lead a provincial town to erect a statue or rename a school.

All of the greats are suitably commemorated in Moscow, but perhaps no author epitomises Russia's capital quite like Mikhail Bulgakov, author of the beloved book *The Master and Margarita*. Some of the book's most famous scenes take place in the Tverskaya district around Patriarch's Pond, where the Devil appeared.

Nearby on the garden ring, the building where Bulgakov wrote the novel and lived until his death now contains a range of funky attractions, including the **Bulgakov House-Museum** (www.dombulgakova.ru; Bolshaya Sadovaya ul 10; admission R70; ⊙noon-7pm Tue, Wed & Fri-Sun, 5-9pm Thu; Ⓜ️Mayakovskaya), on the 4th floor in Bulgakov's apartment No 50. There's a smaller, free exhibition on the ground floor along with a groovy cafe and a large theatre where drama adaptations of *Margarita* and other plays are staged.

A black cat hangs out in the courtyard, where a maroon bus – No 302-bis, naturally – waits to take *Margarita* junkies on late-night (1am to 6am) tours dedicated to the novel (R1000). *Margarita* walking tours of the area happen on Sundays at 3pm (in Russian, R350).

research. A temporary outdoor exhibition area was hosting the travelling Museum of Everything (www.museumofeverything.com), while organisers had hired Dutch architect Rem Koolhaas to convert two mothballed Soviet structures – a 4500-sq-metre restaurant and a 9000-sq-metre exhibition pavilion – into cavernous galleries.

Until those are built, the main gallery space is a temporary pavilion made out of paper (life expectancy: four years) by noted Japanese architect Shegeru Ban.

Zhukova's Iris Foundation is behind both Garage and the similar Novaya Gollandiya (p768) project in St Petersburg.

Novodevichy Convent
CONVENT

(☎499-246 8526; adult/student R250/100, photos R100; ⊙grounds 8am-8pm, museums 9am-5pm Wed-Mon; Ⓜ️Sportivnaya) A cluster of sparkling domes behind turreted walls on the Moscow River about 3km southwest of the Kremlin, this convent was founded in 1524 to celebrate the taking of Smolensk from Lithuania. Peter the Great imprisoned his half-sister Sofia here for her part in the Streltsy Rebellion. The highlight is the Smolensk Cathedral, its interior covered in 16th-century frescos. You may be able to sneak into the grounds for free; a ticket is needed to enter the churches and museums.

FREE Novodevichy Cemetery
CEMETERY

(⊙9am-5pm; Ⓜ️Sportivnaya) Adjacent to Novodevichy Convent is Moscow's most famous cemetery. It's a veritable who's who

of Russian politics and culture – just walk around and see who you can find. Names to look out for include Chekhov, Gogol, Bulgakov, Stanislavsky, Krushchev, Eisenstein, Raisa Gorbachev and Yeltsin (whose grave is marked by an enormous Russian flag). Hint: most of the famous writers are near each other behind the wall in the northeast quadrant.

FREE Gorky House-Museum
MUSEUM

(Malaya Nikitskaya ul 6/2; ⊙11am-5.30pm Wed-Sun; Ⓜ️Pushkinskaya) Many of Moscow's writers' 'house museums' are worth visiting; we list this because it's particularly funky, and it's free.

FREE Cathedral of Christ the Saviour
CHURCH

(ul Volkhonka 15; ⊙10am-5.50pm; Ⓜ️Kropotkinskaya) Dominating the skyline along the Moscow River, this gargantuan cathedral, finished in 1997, sits on the site of an earlier and similar church of the same name. The original was built from 1839 to 1883 to commemorate Russia's victory over Napoleon, but was destroyed during Stalin's orgy of explosive secularism, after which the site served an important purpose: as the world's largest swimming pool.

Dorogomilovsky Market
MARKET

(ul Mozhaysky val 10; ⊙10am-8pm; Ⓜ️Kievskaya) Moscow markets *rynky* (markets) are busy, bustling places, full of activity and colour. Near Kievsky vokzal, this is probably the most colourful, with towering fruit stands, cherubic *babushka* vendors and rows of animal carcasses and dried fish just begging to be photographed.

Activities

Bathhouses

Don't leave Moscow without experiencing a good soak in a *banya* (sauna). See p789 for more on this quintessential Russian tradition.

TOP CHOICE Sanduny Baths   BATHHOUSE

(☑495-628 4633; www.sanduny.ru; Neglinnaya ul 14; general admission per 2hr R1100-2000, private cabins per hr R4000-8000; ☺8am-10pm, private rooms to midnight; MKuznetsky Most) This is Moscow's oldest and most luxurious *banya*.

Krasnopresnkiye Bani   BATHHOUSE

(☑495-253 8690; baninapresne.ru; Stolyarny per 7; general admission R750-850; ☺8am-10pm; MUlitsa 1905 Goda) Offers an excellent, segregated *banya* as well as spa services and on-site cafe.

Cycling

Bikes are an effective way to explore the city's spread-out sights and parks – just steer clear of the dangerous main roads. **Oliver Bikes** (☑8-926-431 4051; www.bikerentalmoscow. com; Pyatnitskaya ul 2; per day from R500; ☺10am-10pm; MNovokuznetskaya) rents out two-wheelers and also leads five-hour bike tours in the warm months (R800 including bike). Bike hire is also available in Gorky Park.

Tours

Capital Tours   BUS TOUR

(☑495-232 2442; www.capitaltours.ru; Gostiny Dvor, ul Ilyinka 4, entry 6; MKitay-Gorod) Offers a three-hour Kremlin tour (adult/child R1550/775), Moscow city bus tours (R950, 10.30am and usually 1.30pm daily), and an 'underground tour' of Moscow's famed metro on Sundays at 11am.

Moscow Free Tour   WALKING TOUR

(☑495-222 3466; http://moscowfreetour.com; Nikolskaya ul 4/5) Runs a daily free city walk as well as many other scheduled and tailored tours. Can also arrange 'hop-on, hop-off' bus tours.

Moscow Mania   WALKING TOUR

(☑8-903-713 0583; www.mosmania.com; tours per group R3500) Themed itineraries with young knowledgeable guides, including fun options such as a trip up Moscow's 340m Ostankino TV tower, the world's fourth-tallest tower.

Sleeping

Accommodation in Moscow is outrageously expensive. Staying in a hostel is the only way to avoid paying at least US$100 a night. The good news is that there are plenty of them so you shouldn't have trouble finding a bed, but book the popular hostels ahead in the summer months. See p792 for more on hostels and registration at hostels. Apartment rental is another way to save money – see p793 for a list of apartment rental agencies.

Hotels are overpriced, but weekend discounts can bring rates down substantially from Friday to Sunday. Rates are without breakfast unless otherwise indicated.

Hotel Metropol   HISTORIC HOTEL €€€

(☑499-501 7840/41; www.metmos.ru; Teatralny proezd 1/4; d weekend/weekday from R12,500/15,300; ☺✳@≋; MTeatralnaya) An art nouveau masterpiece dating back to 1907, the historic Metropol brings an artistic touch to every nook and cranny, from the spectacular exterior to the sumptuous restaurant to the individually decorated rooms.

TOP CHOICE Bulgakov Mini-Hotel   HOTEL €€

(☑495-229 8018; www.bulgakovhotel.com; ul Arbat 49; d R3300; ☺@≋; MSmolenskaya) The classy rooms, with high ceilings and *The Master and Margarita*–inspired art, are as good as it gets in Moscow for this price, especially considering the primo location. Just be careful not to accidentally book its woeful sister hostel, A La Russe. Request a fan when it's hot. There's also a 10-bed dorm here (dorm bed R500). Enter the courtyard from Plotnikov per and use entrance 2.

METRO TOUR

For just R27 you can spend the day touring Moscow's magnificent metro stations. Many of the stations are marble-faced, frescoed, gilded works of art. Among our favourites are **Komsomolskaya**, a huge stuccoed hall, its ceiling covered with mosaics depicting military heroes; **Novokuznetskaya**, featuring military bas-reliefs done in sober khaki, and colourful ceiling mosaics depicting pictures of the happy life; and **Mayakovskaya**, Grand Prize winner at the 1939 World's Fair in New York.

TOP CHOICE **Three Penguins** HOSTEL €

(www.3penguins.ru) The **Petrovsky** (📞8-910-446 17 78; www.3penguins.ru; 20-2 Petrovsky bul; dm R650-1100, s/d/tr without bathroom R1500/2200/2700; 🚌@🛜; Ⓜ Trubnaya) and **Pyatnitskaya** (📞8-985-238 6016; www.3penguins.ru; 17/1 ul Pyatnitskaya; dm R700, r without bathroom R2400; 🚌@🛜; Ⓜ Novokuznetskaya) branches of this friendly hostel are quiet, no-nonsense retreats. The two private rooms on Petrovsky are among Moscow's cheapest, while the slightly pricier Pyatnitskaya edition is steps from Novokuznetskaya metro, which links nicely to Paveletskaya and the trains to Domodedovo. Registration is mandatory and (bonus!) free. Laundry is free too.

TOP CHOICE **Golden Apple** BOUTIQUE HOTEL €€€

(📞495-980 7000; www.goldenapple.ru; ul Malaya Dmitrovka 11; d weekend/weekday from R6000/14,500; 🚌❄🛜; Ⓜ Pushkinskaya) An apple theme is worked into this sophisticated boutique hotel's rooms, decorated in a minimalist, modern style. Comfort is also paramount, with no skimping on luxuries such as heated bathroom floors and down-filled duvets.

Da! Hostel HOSTEL €

(📞495-691 5619; info@da-hostel.ru; ul Arbat 11; dm R500-1000; 🚌@🛜; Ⓜ Arbatskaya) Yes, Da is worthy of your rubles, with a open, spacious common/kitchen area, free coffee and porridge, and a nice mix of clean dorm rooms with sturdy wood bunk beds. It has about 100 spaces spread over two floors. No private rooms.

People Hostel & Hotel HOTEL €€

(📞495-363 4581; www.hostel-people.com; Novinsky bul 11; s/d R3590/3890, without bathroom R2490/3590; 🚌@🛜; Ⓜ Smolenskaya) More minihotel than hostel, it's spread across three floors of two buildings on the garden ring, each wing containing a lovely little kitchen and spiffy, exceptional-value rooms. Weekends bring further discounts. Request a fan in the summer.

Ibis Paveletskaya HOTEL €€

(📞495-661 8500; www.ibis.com; ul Shchipok 11; weekend/weekday from R3900/7000; 🚌❄🛜; Ⓜ Paveletskaya) This stellar business hotel is Moscow's best weekend deal. Standard rooms have comfy king-sized beds, flatscreen TVs, immaculate bathrooms and lovely muted tones. It's a 10-minute walk from Paveletsky train station and the trains to Domodedovo airport (but somewhat far from anything else).

TOP CHOICE **Artel Hotel** HOTEL €€

(📞495-626 9008; www.artelhotel.ru; Bldg 3, 3 Teatralny pr 3; s R2500-5200, d R3000-5700; 🛜) Wacky art abounds in this creative space where each room has a unique design – the cheapest are tiny and windowless. Not for the noise-averse: downstairs are the equally funky restaurant/bar/club/theatre space **Masterskaya** (www.mstrsk.ru; 🕐noon-6am; 🛜) and a nightclub.

Comrade Hostel HOSTEL €

(📞499-709 8760; www.comradehostel.com; ul Maroseyka 11; dm/s/d R650/1800/2200; 🚌@🛜; Ⓜ Kitay-Gorod) Wood bunk beds, a newly revamped common area/kitchen, and air-con in the rooms distinguish this peaceful, welcoming courtyard retreat. The four private rooms may be the best of any Moscow hostel and are decent value to boot.

Fresh Hostel Arbat HOSTEL €

(📞8-916-224 1212; www.freshhostel.ru; Merzlyakovsky per 16; dm R600-650) This quiet, well-hidden gem near the Arbat is clean and cosy with a great air-conditioned kitchen/hangout area. It offers exclusively eight- and 10-bed dorms: 50 beds in total. Look for the distinctive 'F' in the courtyard and get the door code before showing up.

Hotel Sverchkov 8 HOTEL €€

(📞495-625 4978; www.sverchkov-8.ru; Sverchkov per 8; s/d from R4800/5200; 🚌❄🛜; Ⓜ Chistye Prudy) A warm and intimate 12-room hotel in a graceful 18th-century building with hallways lined with plants, and paintings by local artists on the walls.

Shelter Hostel HOSTEL €

(📞8-926-338 4947; www.inshelter.ru; ul Petrovka 17; dm R600-1000, s/d without bathroom R2000/2600; 🚌@🛜) A hostel that forsakes communal fun for peace, quiet and a good mix of private rooms and four- to 14-bed dorms. Target the private rooms, which are good value. It's hidden in a courtyard a few blocks from the Bolshoi.

Hotel Budapest HOTEL €€

(📞495 925 3050; www.hotel-budapest.ru; Petrovskie linii 2/18; s/d from R5200/6200; 🚌❄🛜; Ⓜ Kuznetsky Most) The 19th-century neoclassical Budapest is the epitome of faded glory – think gold tones and liberal use of plush fabrics. But rooms are spacious and come at a big discount compared with other centrally located business hotels. For a fee you can use the pool, gym and other facilities of its more upscale adjoining sister, **Hotel Peter I** ([☎]495-925 3050; www.hotel-peter1.ru; ul Neglinnaya 17; r weekend/weekday from R10,000/14,000; [✦][❄][@][✆][❄]).

Napoleon Hostel
HOSTEL **€**

([☎]495-628 6695; www.napoleonhostel.com; Maly Zlatoustinsky per 2, 4th fl; dm R600-800; [✦][❄][@][✆]; [Ⓜ]Kitay-Gorod) If you want to meet and greet other travellers, look no further. The small common area is busy and buzzing with conversation in various tongues, and a full range of traveller services are on offer – tours, parties, transport, you name it. The spacious six- and eight-bed dorms all have air-con.

Buddy Bear Hostel
HOSTEL **€**

([☎]495-649 6736; www.bear-hostels.com; Smolensky bul 15; dm R750-950; d without bathroom R2500; [✦][❄][@][✆]; [Ⓜ]Smolenskaya) A smart, no-nonsense hostel with air-conditioned dorms (all co-ed) on the garden ring just west of the Arbat. The 50 wide bunk beds have guardrails to protect the young or inebriated. The Bear hostel chain also includes the run-of-the-mill **Bear on Mayakovskaya** ([☎]495-743 0876; www.bear-hostels.com; ul Sadovaya-Kudrinskaya 32; dm R500-1000; [✦][❄][@][✆]; [Ⓜ]Mayakovskaya) and the larger flagship **Bear on Arbatskaya** ([☎]495-649 6736; www.bear-hostels.com; ul Bolshaya Molchanovka 23; dm R450-1250; [✦][❄][@][✆]; [Ⓜ]Arbatskaya).

✗ Eating

Moscow has blossomed into a real culinary capital, but dining out doesn't come cheaply. If you're on any kind of budget, you'll find solace in the popular *stolovye* (canteens).

Discounted weekday 'business lunch' specials are a great way to sample some of the pricier restaurants.

Russians believe that one good thing deserves another, so many successful restaurants have several branches; don't be turned off by these 'chains', several of which we recommend here.

Pedestrian Kamergersky per east of Tverskaya ul is lined with cafes, bars and branches of many of the big Moscow chains, all with outdoor patios – perfect for summer strolling and grazing.

[TOP CHOICE] Delicatessen
INTERNATIONAL **€€**

(www.newdeli.ru; Savodovaya-Karetnaya ul 20; business lunch R270, mains R350-950; [◷]noon-midnight Tue-Sat; [✆][▣]; [Ⓜ]Tsvetnoy Bulvar) Juicy burgers (including those of the fish, duck and turkey variety), fish ceviche, cherry bourbon and friendly service – all great reasons for dropping by this stylish, well-hidden restaurant bar. Food is 20% off from noon to 5pm.

[TOP CHOICE] Café Pushkin
RUSSIAN **€€€**

([☎]495-739 0033; Tverskoy bul 26a; business lunch R750, mains R800-1800; [◷]24hr; [✆][▣]; [Ⓜ]Pushkinskaya) The queen mother of *haute russe* dining, with an exquisite blend of Russian and French cuisines. The lovely 19th-century building has a different atmosphere on each floor and a pleasant rooftop cafe.

Khachapuri
GEORGIAN **€€**

([☎]8-985-764 3118; Bolshoy Gnezdnikovsky per 10; dishes R250-550; [✆][▣]; [Ⓜ]Pushkinskaya) No over-the-top Georgian 'theme' here, just the capital's best Georgian food in a classy space,

---

THE EVOLUTION OF THE STOLOVAYA

In capitalist Moscow, Soviet-style *stolovye* (canteens) have been forced to modernise or close. Excellent contemporary versions of these serve-yourself cafes include **Grably** (Pyatnitskaya ul 27; meals R200-300; [◷]10am-11pm; [✦]; [Ⓜ]Novokuznetskaya) – this particular branch near the Tretyakov has an elaborate winter-garden seating area – and the ubiquitous Moo-Moo, instantly recognisable from its black-and-white Holstein-print decor and famous for its affordable and delicious borsch. Popular branches are in **Basmanny** (Myasnitskaya ul 14; meals R200-300; [◷]9am-11pm; [✦][✆]; [Ⓜ]Lubyanka) and on the **Arbat** (ul Arbat 45/24; meals R200-300; [◷]10am-11pm; [✆]; [Ⓜ]Smolenskaya).

Just a stumble away from Red Sq are two excellent *stolovye*, the cosy **Pelmeshka** (Bogoyavlensky per 1; meals R200-350; [◷]10am-midnight; [✆]; [Ⓜ]Ploshchad Revolyutsii), and **Stolovaya 57** (3rd fl, GUM, Red Sq; meals R300-400; [◷]10am-10pm; [Ⓜ]Okhotny Ryad), a rare oasis of affordability in the fancy-pants GUM department store.

For the real deal, drop by the grandly decorated **Tsentralny** (1 Kudrinskaya pl; meals R200-300; [◷]10am-10pm; [Ⓜ]Barrikadnaya) at the base of one of the Seven Sisters tower blocks.

WANT MORE?

For in-depth information, reviews and recommendations at your fingertips, head to the Apple App Store to purchase Lonely Planet's *Moscow City Guide* iPhone app.

Alternatively, head to www.lonelyplanet.com/russia/moscow for planning advice, author recommendations, traveller reviews and insider tips.

plus superb piano music most evenings. Try the namesake *khachapuri* (cheesy flatbread) or the wonderful *pkhali* (spinach balls). A second branch is near Kievsky vokzal.

Correa's
EUROPEAN €€

(www.correas.ru; meals R600-1000; ⊗8am-11pm; ⓘ) Bookings are essential for these restaurants in **Zamoskvorechie** (☑495-725 6035; ul Bolshaya Ordinka 40/2; ⊗8am-11pm; ⓘ; ⓜTretyakovskaya) and **Presnya** (☑495-933 4684; Bolshaya Gruzinskaya ul 32; ⓜBelorusskaya). The menu is simple – sandwiches (R200 to R300), pizzas and grills – but everything is prepared with the freshest ingredients and the utmost care. The outlet near the Tretyakov is roomier.

Uzbekistan
UZBEK €€€

(☑623 0585; Neglinnaya ul 29; mains R750-1900; ⊗noon-3am; ⓘ; ⓜTrubnaya) This legendary eatery was purportedly Stalin's favourite, which tells you how long it has been around. The food is excellent and the old Bukhara atmosphere lavish, with plush cushions, a huge outdoor garden seating area and a nightly belly-dancing show.

Sok
VEGETARIAN €

(Lavrushinsky per 15; mains R200-400; ⊗11am-11pm; ⊜ⓢⓟⓘ; ⓜTretyakovskaya) Cheerful cafe done up in bright yellow and orange and specialisng in vego fare with Italian and Middle Eastern flavours, plus freshly squeezed juices. A perfect pre- or post-Tretyakov stop.

Starlite Diner
AMERICAN €€

(Bolshaya Sadovaya ul 16; sandwiches R310-500; ⊗24hr; ⓢ; ⓜMayakovskaya) A Moscow institution, this 1950s-style diner was a refuge for expats in the 1990s, but today attracts at least as many locals. Bottomless coffee and suitably greasy breakfasts make it

Moscow's top spot for a caffeinated, wi-fi-enabled morning. The patty melt is absurdly good. This branch is the most pleasant; others include the original on the **Boulevard Ring** (Strastnoy bul 8a; ⓢ; ⓜChekhovskaya) and in **Zamoskvorechie** (Korovy val 9a; ⓢ; ⓜOktyabrskaya).

Jagannath
VEGETARIAN €

(jagannath.ru; Kuznetsky most 11; meals R200-350; ⊗10am-midnight; ⓟ; ⓜKuznetsky Most) Scrumptious vego/vegan *stolovaya*, new-age trinket store and health-food shop under one roof.

Art Lebedev Cafe
CAFE €€

(http://store.artlebedev.com/offline/lik; mains R300-600; ⊗9am-11pm Mon-Fri, 10am-11pm Sat & Sun; ⊜ⓢⓟ) Has a shabby chic vibe and a creative, compact menu of original home-cooked cuisine, good salads, and a countertop full of freshly baked sweet things. No booze at the **Presnya** (Bolshaya Nikitskaya ul 35b; ⓜArbatskaya) branch, but it's much cosier than the **Basmanny** (5 Bankovsky per; ⓜChistye Prudy) branch.

Mari Vanna
RUSSIAN €€€

(☑495-650 6500; Spiridonyevsky per 10; mains R550-1200; ⊗8am-midnight; ⊜ⓘ; ⓜPushkinskaya) Step back into the 1930s in this homey ground-floor apartment, with a menu of meaty old Russian favourites and homemade liqueurs. Reservations essential for dinner.

Volkonsky
BAKERY €

(www.wolkonsky.com; meals R200-400; ⊗8am-11pm) The queue often runs out the door, as loyal patrons wait their turn for the city's best fresh-baked breads, pastries and pies at branches in **Tverskoy** (Bolshaya Sadovaya ul 2/46, Tverskoy; ⓜMayakovskaya) and **Kitay Gorod** (ul Maroseyka 4/2; ⓜKitay Gorod).

Akademiya
ITALIAN €€

(☑495-771 7446; www.academiya.ru; business lunch R280, mains R400-1000; ⓢⓘ) Upscale pizza chain with all the best locations: **Kamergersky** (Kamergersky per 2; business lunch R280, meals R600-1000; ⊗8am-midnight; ⓜTeatralnaya), **Krasny Oktyabr** (☑495-771 7446; 6/3 Bersenevsky nab; ⊗noon-midnight Sun-Thu, to 6am Fri & Sat; ⓜKropotkinskaya) and **Arbat** (Gogolevsky bul 33/1; ⊗9am-midnight; ⓜArbatskaya). The massive contemporary art-packed and sofa-strewn edition in Krasny Oktyabr, dubbed Art Akademiya, is the coup de grâce.

Jean-Jacques
FRENCH €€

(mains R300-600; ⊘8am-6am; ☺🛜📶) A friendly and affordable chain of French bistros with attractive red-and-green decor and good wine and cheese lists. Branches in **Arbatskaya** (☎495-290 3886; Nikitsky bul 12; Ⓜ Arbatskaya) and **Kitay Gorod** (Lubyansky proezd 25; Ⓜ Kitay-Gorod).

Teremok
FAST FOOD €

(Kamergersky per; bliny R50-150; ⊘24hr; Ⓜ Teatralnaya) Award winning local snack stop serving all kinds of delicious *bliny* and cheap beer. Outlets everywhere, including **Pyatnitskaya** (Pyatnitskaya ul 2; ⊘9am-10pm) and **Pokrovka** (ul Pokrovka 4; ⊘9am-10pm).

Prime Star
FAST FOOD €

(ul Arbat 9; meals R200-300; ⊘8am-11pm; 🖊📶; Ⓜ Arbatskaya) Healthy quick eats with many additional outlets, including **Zamoskvorechie** (Pyatnitskaya ul 5; Ⓜ Novokuznetskaya) and **Tverskoy** (Kamergersky per 7/5; Ⓜ Teatralnaya).

🍷 Drinking

The line between cafe, bar and nightclub in Moscow is hazy, with many places serving all three functions. As such, we list them all in one place.

In an extremely welcome development, the best clubs in Moscow now dispense with cover charges and strict dress codes. But they still have strict *feis kontrol* (face control). One way to beat *feis kontrol* is to arrive early before the bouncers are posted. Barring that, speak English, as being a foreigner helps.

🔺TOP CHOICE Krasny Oktyabr
CLUB

(Red October; Zamoskvorechie; Ⓜ Kropotkinskaya) In the summer (and to a lesser extent in the cold months), there is one place to head if you only have one weekend night out: this converted chocolate factory on snakelike Bolotny island in the Moskva River. 'Red October' hosts a plethora of arty cafes that morph into blistering open-air rooftop nightclubs at weekends. The best is **Gipsy** (Bolotnaya nab 3; ⊘6pm-1am Sun-Thu, 2pm-6am Fri & Sat); 'if the world were to end tomorrow, tonight I'd be at Gipsy,' one punter quipped. While *feis kontrol* is strict, Gipsy lacks the uppitiness of so many Moscow clubs, as people lose the attitude and submit themselves to the singular thrill of open-air rooftop dancing in the Moscow dawn. Other happening openair clubs in the complex include **Rolling Stone** (Bolotnaya nab 3; ⊘10pm-7am Thu-Sat;

Ⓜ Kropotkinskaya) next door and **Bar Strelka** (www.artstrelka.ru; Bldg 5a, Bersenevskaya nab 14/5; ⊘9am-midnight Sun-Thu, noon-late Fri & Sat; 🛜; Ⓜ Kropotkinskaya) – also a great cafe, with dishes from R300 to R1000 – opposite the Cathedral of Christ the Saviour on the Moscow River. In the winter they cover the roof and turn on the heat.

Mayak
BAR

(www.clubmayak.ru; Bolshaya Nikitskaya ul 19; business lunch R270, mains R300-350; ⊘noon-6am; 🛜; Ⓜ Okhotny Ryad) Named for the Mayakovsky Theatre downstairs, this vintage 1930s-style bar, awash in dark wood, still attracts actors, artists and writers, who come to eat and drink into the night. Great rainy day/cold weather option. Food 20% off until 4pm.

Solyanka
CAFE, CLUB

(http://s-11.ru; ul Solyanka 11; cover R500 Fri & Sat; ⊘11am-6am; 🛜) An 18th-century merchant's house has been revamped into this hipster cafe-bar-club. The eclectic menu (mains R300 to R550) includes Thai and Mexican tastes. Thursday to Saturday nights the biggest room is cleared for dancing, starting around 11pm.

Kvartira 44
BAR

(www.kv44.ru; Bolshaya Nikitskaya ul 22/2; mains R300-500; ⊘noon to late; 🛜; Ⓜ Okhotny Ryad) An old ground-floor apartment has been converted into a cosy bar. It's a bit like a mini-Mayak. Great jazz and piano music kicks off Thursday to Saturday. There's another in **Zamoskvorechie** (ul Malaya Yakimanka 24/8; 🛜; Ⓜ Polyanka).

GAY & LESBIAN MOSCOW

Sunday is gay night at Propaganda (p756). For more information, see www.gay.ru/english.

Central Station MSK (www.centralclub.ru; Yuzhny proezd 4; ⊘restaurant from 7pm, club from 9pm; Ⓜ Komsomolskaya) Moscow's biggest and best gay dance club, with a gay cabaret, go-go boys, karaoke and a dance floor that can accommodate 800 sweaty bodies.

12 Volts (www.12voltclub.ru; Bldg 2, Tverskaya ul 12; ⊘6pm-6am; Ⓜ Mayakovskaya) Welcoming lesbian cafe-cum-social-club, tucked in the courtyard off Tverskaya.

Gogol
CLUB

(www.gogolclubs.ru; Stoleshnikov per 11; cover free; ◷noon-5am; Ⓜ Teatralnaya) Fun, informal and affordable (so surprising on swanky Stoleshnikov!), Gogol is great for food, drinks and music (live most nights, techno on weekends).

Propaganda
CAFE, CLUB

(www.propagandamoscow.com; Bolshoy Zlatoustinsky per 7; ◷noon-6am; 🕿; Ⓜ Kitay-Gorod) By day it's a cafe (meals R500 to R700) that sports exposed-brick walls and pipe ceilings; by night it's a happening club.

Krizis Zhanra
CAFE, BAR

(www.kriziszhanra.ru; ul Pokrovka 16/16; ◷11am-5am; Ⓜ Chistye Prudy) This was *the* place to go in Moscow circa 1997 (albeit in a different locale), and it's still kickin' it, with good cheap food, copious drinks and late-night live music or DJs Thursday to Saturday.

Papa's Place
BAR, CLUB

(http://papas.ru; Myasnitskaya ul 22; weekends cover R200-300; 🕿; Ⓜ Chistye Prudy) The theme varies from night to night (Beach Party, Ladies' Night) but the goal is the same: to get you inebriated quickly and cheaply. It's one of the few places in Moscow where you might find rowdy weeknight action. These are the same people behind the infamous **Hungry Duck** (Sadovaya-Chernogryazskaya 8/2; ◷noon-6am; 🕿; Ⓜ Krasnye Vorota), a raucous bar that epitomised the anything-goes 1990s Moscow. 'The Duck' has reopened after a long hiatus; as always bar-top dancing and naughty behaviour are encouraged.

Ketama Bar
BAR

(Kamergersky per 6; Ⓜ Teatralnaya) With a lively summer terrace right on colourful Kamergersky, this Moroccan-inspired bar is a great place to warm up for a night out.

Chinese Pilot Dzhao-Da
BAR

(www.jao-da.ru; Lubyansky proezd 25; concerts R300-500; 🕿; Ⓜ Kitay-Gorod) This divey, relaxed basement place hosts a mix of bands from around Europe and Russia. Concerts start around 11pm or midnight. Cheap food and beer too.

Pirogi on Maroseyka
CAFE, BAR

(www.ogipirogi.ru; ul Maroseyka 9/2; Ⓜ Kitay-Gorod) A dark place where the young, broke and beautiful flock to enjoy the centre's most affordable beer, coffee and food (mains R175 to R250), plus movies on Tuesdays and DJs most nights. Enter on Bolshoy Zlatoustinsky per.

Liga Pap
SPORTS BAR

(☎495-624 3636; www.ligapap.ru; ul Bolshaya Lubyanka 24; meals R500-1000; ◷24hr; Ⓜ Lubyanka) Big, trendy sports bar with plenty of screens.

☆ Entertainment

To find out what's on, see the weekly magazine *element* or the entertainment section in Thursday's *Moscow Times*. Most theatres, including the Bolshoi, are closed between late June and early September.

TOP CHOICE Bolshoi Theatre
BALLET, OPERA

(www.bolshoi.ru; Teatralnaya pl 1; tickets R200-4000; Ⓜ Teatralnaya) Dominating Teatralnaya

---

DON'T MISS

MOSCOW'S WHITE HOT ART SCENE

Garage (p749), which hosts the **Moscow Biennale of Contemporary Art** (www.moscowbiennale.ru), isn't the only place to take the pulse of the city's vibrant contemporary art scene. Apart from the following recommended spots, also see www.artguide.ru.

Proekt Fabrika (www.proektfabrika.ru; 18 Perevedenovsky per; ◷10am-8pm Tue-Sun; Ⓜ Baumanskaya), a still-functioning paper factory, is the location for a nonprofit set of gallery and performance spaces enlivened by arty graffiti and creative-industry offices.

The red-brick buildings of the former chocolate factory at Krasny Oktyabr Factory (p755) now host **Pobeda Gallery** (http://pobedagallery.com; Bldg 4, Bolotnaya nab 3; ◷1-8pm) and the **Lumiere Brothers Photography Centre** (www.lumiere.ru; Bldg 1, Bolotnaya nab 3; admission R250; ◷noon-9pm Tue-Sun; Ⓜ Kropotkinskaya) plus the centrepiece **Strelka Institute for Media, Architecture and Design** (www.strelkainstitute.ru; Bldg 5a, Bersenevskaya nab 14/5; Ⓜ Novokuznetskaya). Many trendy bars, clubs and restaurants are here too.

A former wine factory has morphed into **Winzavod** (www.winzavod.ru; 4 Siromyatnichesky per 1; admission free; ◷noon-8pm Tue-Sun; Ⓜ Chkalovskaya), a postindustrial complex of prestigious galleries, shops, a cinema and trendy cafe.

pl, the Bolshoi Theatre is where Tchaikovsky's *Swan Lake* premiered (to bad reviews) in 1877. An evening here is one of Moscow's most romantic options. Both the ballet and opera companies perform a range of Russian and foreign works. Productions take place on the main stage, now back in operation after a multiyear renovation, and on the smaller New Stage (Novaya Stsena). If you can't catch a performance (or it's closed for summer break) you might consider a tour of the Bolshoi.

Kremlin Ballet Theatre BALLET
(☑495-928 5232; www.kremlin-gkd.ru; ul Vozdvizhenka 1; Ⓜ Alexandrovsky Sad) The Bolshoi does not have a monopoly on ballet in Moscow. Leading dancers also appear with the Kremlin Ballet, which performs in the State Kremlin Palace (inside the Kremlin).

**Moscow International
House of Music** CLASSICAL MUSIC
(☑495-730 1011; www.mmdm.ru; Kosmodamianskaya nab 52/8; tickets R200-2000; Ⓜ Paveletskaya) This venue for the **National Philharmonic of Russia** (www.nfor.ru) towers over the Moscow River. It has three halls, including Svetlanov Hall, which has the largest organ in Russia.

Tchaikovsky Concert Hall CLASSICAL MUSIC
(www.meloman.ru; Triumfalnaya pl 4/31; tickets R300-2000; ☺ closed Jul & Aug; Ⓜ Mayakovskaya) Home to the State Symphony Orchestra, which specialises in the music of its namesake composer and other Russian classics.

MKhAT THEATRE
(http://art.theatre.ru; Kamergersky per 3; ☺ closed Jul & Aug; Ⓜ Teatralnaya) This is where method acting was founded over 100 years ago, by Stanislavsky and Nemirovich-Danchenko.

**Nikulin Circus on
Tsvetnoy Bulvar** CIRCUS
(☑495-625 8970; www.circusnikulin.ru; Tsvetnoy bul 13; tickets R400-2500; ☺ box office 11am-2pm & 3-7pm; Ⓜ Tsvetnoy Bulvar) Founded in 1880, this circus is named after beloved actor and clown Yury Nikulin (1921–97), who performed at the studio here for many years.

🛍 Shopping

Ul Arbat has always been a tourist attraction and is littered with souvenir shops and stalls. For a more Soviet experience, head out to Izmaylovo Market (p749).

FOOTBALL IN MOSCOW

Muscovites are avid football (soccer) fans. The city's top teams are **Spartak** (www.spartak.com), **Lokomotiv** (www.fclm.ru), **PFC CSKA** (www.pfc-cska.com), **Dynamo** (www.fcdynamo.ru) and **FK Moskva** (www.fcmoscow.ru). Buy tickets (R150 to R6000) online at the club websites, or immediately before games, which are played at **Lokomotiv Stadium** (Bolshaya Cherkizovskaya ul 125; Ⓜ Cherkizovskaya) and **Luzhniki Stadium** (☑495-785 9717; www.luzhniki.ru; Luzhnetskaya nab 24; Ⓜ Sportivnaya). A new stadium for Spartak was due to open in 2013.

Ministerstvo Podarkov GIFTS
(Ministry of Gifts; Maly Gnezdnikovsky per 12/27; Ⓜ Pushkinskaya) For clever souvenirs, stop by this artists' cooperative, which sells uniquely Russian gifts such as *tapki* (slippers), throwback Soviet notebooks and great mugs and T-shirts. There is another outlet – **Podarky, Dekor & Podarky** (Malaya Bronnaya ul 28/2; ☺11am-9pm Mon-Fri, noon-9pm Sat & Sun; Ⓜ Mayakovskaya) – near Patriarch's Ponds.

GUM MALL
(Krasnaya pl 3; ☺10am-10pm; Ⓜ Ploshchad Revolyutsii) Elegant heritage building on Red Sq, packed with designer labels and good souvenir shops including the glam grocery Gastronom No 1.

Dom Knigi BOOKS
(ul Novy Arbat 8; ☺9am-11pm Mon-Fri, 10am-11pm Sat & Sun; Ⓜ Arbatskaya) A huge bookshop with a full complement of LP and other guidebooks in English and Russian.

Atlas MAPS
(Kuznetsky most 9/10; ☺10am-8pm Mon-Fri, 11am-6pm Sat & Sun; Ⓜ Kuznetsky Most) Great map store thoroughly covers the whole country and the world.

ℹ Information
Dangers & Annoyances

Moscow is not as dangerous as paranoid locals may have you think, but, as in any big city, be on your guard against pickpockets and muggers, especially in metro stations.

Always be cautious about taking taxis late at night, especially near bars and clubs that are in isolated areas. Never get into a car that already has two or more people in it.

Internet Access

Wireless access is ubiquitous and almost always free.

Internet Club (Kuznetsky Most ul 12; per hr R90; ⊙9am-midnight; Ⓜ Kuznetsky Most)

Time Online (per hr R70-100; ⊙24hr) Okhotny Ryad (Manezhnaya pl; Ⓜ Okhotny Ryad); Komsomolskaya (Komsomolskaya pl 3; Ⓜ Komsomolskaya)

Media

Reliable listings magazines in Russian include *Afisha* and *Time Out*. The following English-language media are all free.

element (www.elementmoscow.ru) Weekly newsprint magazine with restaurant reviews and concert and art exhibition listings.

Moscow News (www.moscownews.ru) Long-standing weekly focuses on domestic and international politics and business.

Moscow Times (www.themoscowtimes.com) Undisputed king of the hill in locally published English-language news. The Thursday edition is a great source for what's happening at the weekend.

Medical Services

36.6 (www.366.ru; ⊙24hr) Tverskaya (Tverskaya ul 25/9); Pokrovka (ul Pokrovka 1/13; Ⓜ Kitay-Gorod) A chain of pharmacies with outlets all over the city.

American Medical Centre (✆ 495-933 7700; www.amcenter.ru; Grokholsky per 1; Ⓜ Pr Mira) Offers 24-hour emergency service, consultations and a full range of medical specialists.

Post

Main Post Office (Myasnitskaya ul 26; ⊙8am-8pm; Ⓜ Chistye Prudy)

Telephone & Fax

Two area codes function within Moscow: ✆ 495 and the nearly obsolete ✆ 499; if calling ✆ 499, dial ✆ 8 plus all 10 digits.

Payphones operate with cards that are available in the larger post offices. For more information on Russian mobile carriers, see p794.

Travel Agencies

Maria Travel Agency (✆ 495-777 8226; www.maria-travel.com; ul Maroseyka 13; Ⓜ Kitay-Gorod) Offers visa support, apartment rental and some local tours, including to the Golden Ring.

Unifest Travel (✆ 495-234 6555; http://unifest.ru; Komsomolsky pr 13; Ⓜ Park Kultury) About 500m south of the metro station, this is an on-the-ball travel company offering rail and air tickets, visa support and more.

❶ Getting There & Away

Air

Moscow is served by three main international airports:

Domodedovo (www.domodedovo.ru) Moscow's largest international airport is 48km south of the city.

Sheremetyevo 1&2 (http://svo.aero) Around 30km northwest of the city, Sheremetyevo 2 is the international terminal. The two terminals are connected by a free shuttle bus.

Vnukovo (www.vnukovo.ru/eng) Mostly domestic and CIS flights, 30km southwest of the city.

Boat

Moscow is a popular start or end point for cruises that ply the Volga River. Cruises to/from St Petersburg dock at the the **North River Station** (Severny Rechnoy Vokzal; Leningradskoe shosse 51; Ⓜ Rechnoy Vokzal), 10km northeast of the city.

Bus

Buses tend to be crowded but are usually faster and more convenient than *prigorodny* (suburban) trains to some Golden Ring destinations.

Shchyolkovsky bus station (Ⓜ Shchyolkovskaya), 8km east of the city centre, is the main long-distance bus station. Buses also depart from outside the various train stations, offering alternative transport to the destinations served by the train. These buses usually leave when full, not according to a schedule.

Train

It is more convenient to buy tickets from a centrally located travel agent or *zheleznodorozhnaya kassa* (railway ticket office) than at the train stations, but you'll pay at least a R200 service fee. Be careful of international travel agencies that may charge considerable mark-ups. For tips on booking tickets online, see p798. Moscow has nine main stations.

Belorussky Vokzal (Belarus Station; Tverskaya Zastava pl; Ⓜ Belorusskaya) For Smolensk, Kaliningrad, Minsk, Warsaw, Vilnius and Berlin; some trains to/from the Czech Republic; and suburban trains to/from the west. Also Aeroexpress to Sheremetyevo airport.

Kazansky Vokzal (Kazan Station; Komsomolskaya pl; Ⓜ Komsomolskaya) For Vladimir, Nizhny Novgorod, the Ural Mountains, Siberia; the Volga; and suburban trains to/from the southeast.

Kievsky Vokzal (Kyiv Station; Kievskaya pl; Ⓜ Kievskaya) Serves many Ukrainian cities including Kyiv (13 hours, frequent) and Odesa (19 hours, daily), as well as Budapest, Bucharest and Prague. Also Aeroexpress services to Vnukovo airport.

MOSCOW TO ST PETERSBURG

Dozens of trains travel daily between Russia's two main cities.

There are about six daily high-speed 'Sapsan' trains, which have airplane-style seating, take 3½ to four hours, and cost about R3000/5500 for a 1st-/2nd-class seat. Otherwise there are a dizzying array of slower trains, including several overnight options. These can take anywhere from seven to 11 hours and cost about R1000 for the lowest *platskart* (3rd-class) berth, or about twice that for more comfortable 4-bed *kupe* (2nd-class) berths.

Tickets often sell out in the high months, but keep your plans flexible and you should be able to find something, even at the last minute. If you are stuck and need to get to St Petersburg in a hurry, planes aplenty fly this route and they rarely sell out. An air ticket costs about the same as a 2nd-class Sapsan ticket.

Kursky Vokzal (Kursk Station; pl Kurskogo vokzala; Ⓜ Kurskaya) For the Caucasus, Crimea and eastern Ukraine including Kharkiv (12 hours, frequent). It also has some trains to/from Vladimir.

Leningradsky Vokzal (Leningrad Station; Komsomolskaya pl; Ⓜ Komsomolskaya) For Novgorod, Pskov, St Petersburg, Tallinn and Helsinki.

Paveletsky Vokzal (Pavelets Station; Paveletskaya pl; Ⓜ Paveletskaya) For trains heading south, including Aeroexpress to Domodedovo airport.

Rizhsky Vokzal (Rīga Station; Rizhskaya pl; Ⓜ Rizhskaya) For services to Latvia.

Savyolovsky Vokzal (Savyolov Station; pl Savyolovskogo vokzala; Ⓜ Savyolovskaya) Services to/from the north.

Yaroslavsky Vokzal (Yaroslavl Station; Komsomolskaya pl; Ⓜ Komsomolskaya) For trains to Siberia, the Far East, China and Mongolia.

❶ Getting Around

To/From the Airport

All airports are accessible by super-convenient **Aeroexpress** (www.aeroexpress.ru) trains, which leave from different stations depending on the airport they serve. They cost R320, take 35 minutes to 45 minutes, and run every 30 minutes from about 5am to 12.30am for Domodedovo and Sheremetyevo, and every hour from 6am to midnight for Vnukovo.

Penny-pinchers can take slower and more sporadic local trains from Domodedovo (R100, 1¼ hours) to Paveletsky vokzal. A cheap option from Sheremetyevo is the bus/metro combination (about R50). Take Bus 851 (frequent) to Rechnoy Vokzal metro.

Taxis from the official airport taxi stands cost R1500 to R2500, depending on where you want to go. Freelance cabbies might ask upwards of R3000.

Public Transport

The **Moscow metro** (www.mosmetro.ru) is a modern Soviet miracle. You will rarely wait on the platform for more than two minutes, and even late at night the average wait is less than four minutes. Stations are marked outside by 'M' signs. Magnetic tickets (R27) are sold at ticket booths. Save time by buying a multiple-ride ticket.

Buses, trolleybuses and trams are useful along a few radial or cross-town routes that the metro misses, and are necessary for reaching sights away from the city centre. Tickets (R28) are sold on the vehicle by a conductor.

Taxi

Unofficial taxis are still common in Moscow. Expect to pay R150 to R400 for a ride around the city centre, depending on your haggling skills.

Detskoe Taxi (☏ 495-765 1180; www.detskoetaxi.ru; per 10km R500) Has smoke-free cars and car seats for your children.

Taxi Blues (☏ 495-105 5115; www.taxi-blues.ru)

VELIKY NOVGOROD

☏ 8162 / POP 240,000

Between Moscow and St Petersburg, picturesque Veliky Novgord (Великий Новгород; 'Great New Town') spans the River Volkhov. In the 12th century it was Russia's biggest city, an independent quasidemocracy with a flourishing cultural life. Today it's a pleasant provincial town, with a magnificent historical legacy preserved in its numerous churches and museums, and the mighty walls of its kremlin.

The town's switched-on **tourist office** (☏ 773 074, 24hr hotline 8-905-290 8686; www.visitnovgorod.ru; Sennaya pl 5; ⊗ 9.30am-6pm) will help you get your bearings and can arrange city tours in a variety of languages.

◉ Sights & Activities

Bike rental (per hour/day R150/500) is available in Kremlevsky park, just north of the west entrance to the Kremlin.

Kremlin
HISTORIC SITE

(⊙6am-midnight) On the west bank of the Volkhov, and surrounded by a pleasant wooded park, the Kremlin was first built in the 9th century, then rebuilt with brick in the 14th century; this is the version that still stands today. It houses the city's most famous sites, including the handsome, Byzantine **Cathedral of St Sophia** (⊙8am-8pm, services 10am-noon daily & 6-8pm Wed-Sun). Finished in 1050, it is one of the oldest buildings in Russia. The onion domes were probably added during the 14th century – even so, they are perhaps the first example of this most Russian architectural detail.

Close by, the 15th-century belfry and a leaning 17th-century clock tower poke above the city walls. For panoramic views of Novgorod, climb the 41m-tall **Kokui Tower** (adult/student R100/80; ⊙noon-2.20pm & 3.30-8pm Tue, Wed & Fri-Sun, closed Nov-Apr), where telescopes await.

In the centre of the Kremlin stands the 16m-high, 300-tonne **Millennium of Russia Monument**. Unveiled in 1862, it's a who's who of Russian history, depicting some 127 figures – ranging from Mother Russia through to Catherine the Great.

Yaroslav's Court
HISTORIC SITE

Across a footbridge from the Kremlin are the remnants of an 18th-century market arcade. Beyond that is the market gatehouse, an array of churches sponsored by 13th- to 16th-century merchant guilds, and a 'road palace' built in the 18th century as a rest stop for Catherine the Great.

The 12th-century **Court Cathedral of St Nicholas** (adult/student R100/60; ⊙10am-noon & 1-6pm Wed-Sun, closed last Fri of month) is all that remains of the early palace complex of the Novgorod princes, from which Yaroslav's Court gets its name. The cathedral holds religious artefacts and temporary exhibitions of local interest. Downstairs you can see fragments from the church's original frescos.

Yuriyevo
HISTORIC BUILDINGS

Opposite the tourist office, hop on a cruise or bus 7 or 7A going southbound to the village of Yurievo, site of the the picturesque 12th-century **Yuriyev Monastery** (St George's Monastery; ⊙10am-8pm) with a beautiful waterside setting. About 600m up the road is the open-

air **Vitoslavlitsy Museum of Wooden Architecture** (adult/student R160/80; ⊙10am-8pm May-Aug, to 6pm Apr & Sep, to 5pm Oct-Mar) where you can explore some 20 or so attractive traditional timber buildings.

Boat Cruises
CRUISE

(per person R300-350) In the summer months, the *Mosckva* and *Vecher* boats run one- to 1½-hour cruises down the Volkhov River; some pass in view of Yuriyevo (R300). They depart from either side of the footbridge. These turn into fun disco boats on Friday and Saturday night.

🛏 Sleeping & Eating

The tourist office can recommend homestays (from R700 per person for a room).

Hotel Volkhov
HOTEL €€

(📞225 500; www.hotel-volkhov.ru; ul Predtechenskaya 24; s/d incl breakfast from R1900/2900; @🛜) Centrally located and offering modern, nicely furnished rooms with lots of amenities. Good value.

Hotel Akron
HOTEL €€

(📞736 906; www.hotel-akron.ru; ul Predtechenskaya 24; s/d incl breakfast from R1550/2200; 🛜) Similar to the Volkhov next door, but with lower prices and no elevator. Rooms have modern bathrooms, cable TV and minifridge. Friendly service is also a plus.

Park Inn Veliky Novgorod
HOTEL €€€

(📞940 910; www.parkinn.com/hotel-velikynovgorod; ul Studencheskaya 2a; s/d incl breakfast R4700/5400; ❄@🛜🏊) It's Novgorod's fanciest hotel but probably not fancy enough to overcome the poor location, especially at these prices. You'll need to cab it to the sights.

Nice People
CAFE €

(Khoroshie Lyudi; www.gonicepeople.ru; ul Meretskova-Volosova 1/1; mains R200-300; ⊙noon-midnight; ⊜🛜📱) Light floods into this appealing corner cafe-bar where there's a warm welcome from English-speaking staff. The menu details speciality DIY salads, and there's wine by the glass (R130). Super value.

Ilmen
CAFE €€

(ul Gazon 2; mains R300-500; ⊙noon-midnight; 🛜) The ground floor has a little deli for takeaway snacks, and a bistro for cheap sit-down eats and drinks (beer R70). Upstairs is more formal. The summer terrace in Kremlevsky park is reason enough to come here.

Café Le Chocolat CAFE, BAR €€
(☑739 009; www.cafelechocolate.ru; ul Lyudogosh-cha 8; mains R450-850; ☺9am-11pm) This stylish cafe-bar mixes French and Asian touches. A bit overpriced – breakfast is a better deal.

ⓘ Getting There & Around

The train and bus stations are next to each other on ul Oktyabrskaya, 1.5km northwest of the Kremlin. Take bus 9 or 101 (R15) into the centre, and 4, 19 or a host of others back. A taxi should cost about R100.

Trains between Moscow and St Petersburg do *not* pass through Novgorod. There's a single night train to/from Moscow (*platskartny/kupe* R1200/2550, eight hours). St Petersburg is served by *elektrichki* (suburban train; R355, three daily, three hours).

Buses serve St Petersburg (R370, four hours, 13 daily) and Rīga (R1080, 11 hours, Wednesday and Sunday), among other destinations.

ST PETERSBURG

☑812 / POP 4.8 MILLION

'St Petersburg (Санкт Петербург) is Russia, but it is not Russian.' The opinion of Nicholas II, the empire's last tsar, on his one-time capital still resonates. The city, affectionately known as Piter to locals, is a fascinating hybrid where one moment you can be clapping along to a fun Russian folk-music show in a baroque hall or sniffing incense inside a mosaic-covered Orthodox church, and in the next you can be grooving on the dance floor of an underground club or posing at a contemporary-art event in a renovated bakery.

Europe's fourth-largest city is also a visual delight. The Neva River and surrounding canals reflect unbroken facades of handsome 18th- and 19th-century buildings that house a spellbinding collection of cultural storehouses, culminating in the incomparable Hermitage. It's easy to imagine how such an environment, warts and all, was the inspiration for many of Russia's greatest artists, including the writers Pushkin, Gogol and Dostoevsky, and musical maestros such as Rachmaninoff, Tchaikovsky and Shostakovich. This giant warehouse of Russian culture has more to offer the traveller than perhaps anywhere else in the country.

History

Starting with the Peter and Paul Fortress, founded on the marshy estuary of the Neva River in 1703, Peter the Great and his successors commissioned a city built to grand design by mainly European architects. By the early 19th century, St Petersburg had firmly established itself as Russia's cultural heart. But at the same time as writers, artists and musicians – such as Pushkin, Turgenev and, later, Tchaikovsky and Dostoevsky – lived in and were inspired by the city, political and social problems were on the rise.

Industrialisation brought a flood of poor workers and associated urban squalor to St Petersburg, which became a hotbed of strikes and political violence. 'Bloody Sunday' on 9 January 1905 saw more than 100 people killed after troops fired on a crowd petitioning the tsar outside the Winter Palace, touching off an unsuccessful revolution. The tsar's government limped on, until Lenin and the Bolsheviks took advantage of Russia's disastrous involvement in WWI to instigate a successful revolution in 1917. Again, St Petersburg (renamed a more Russian-sounding Petrograd in 1914) was at the forefront of the action.

To break with the tsarist past, the seat of government was moved back to Moscow, and St Petersburg was renamed Leningrad after the first communist leader's death in 1924. The city – by virtue of its location, three million-plus population and industry – remained one of Russia's most important, thus putting it on the front line during WWII. For 872 days Leningrad was besieged by the Germans, and one million people perished in horrendous conditions.

During the 1960s, '70s and '80s Leningrad's bohemian spirit burned bright, fostering the likes of dissident poet Joseph Brodsky and underground rock groups such as Kino and Akvarium. In 1991, as the Soviet Union came tumbling down, the city reverted to calling itself St Petersburg.

Millions of rubles were spent on restoration for the city's tricentenary celebrations in 2003, and although the 2008 financial crash slowed down some big construction projects, St Petersburg probably looks better now than at any other time in its history.

◎ Sights

State Hermitage Museum MUSEUM
(Map p766; www.hermitagemuseum.org; Dvortsovaya pl 2; adult/student R400/free, 1st Thu of month free, photos R200; ☺10.30am-6pm Tue & Thu-Sun, to 9pm Wed, to 9pm Sat Jun-Sep; Ⓜ Admiralteyskaya) Mainly set in the magnificent

Central St Petersburg

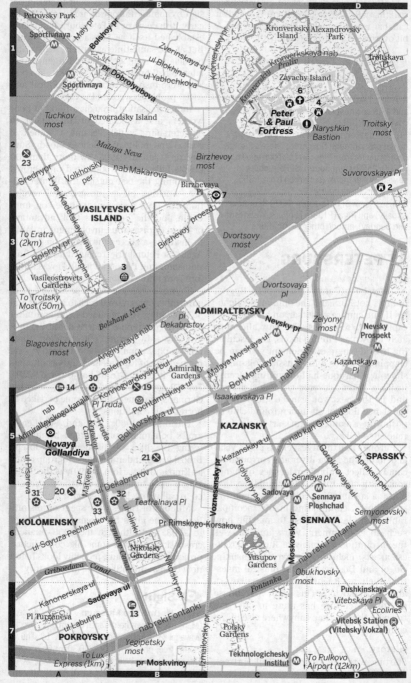

Petrovsky Park

Sportivnaya

Maly pr

Bolshoy pr

Zverinskaya ul

ul Blokhina
ul Yablochkova

pr Dobrolyubova

Sportivnaya

Tuchkov
most

Petrogradsky Island

Kronverksky pr

Kronverksky Alexandrovsky
Island Park

Kronverkskaya nab

Kronverksky Proliv

Zayachy Island

Troitskaya
Pl

**Peter
& Paul
Fortress**

6

4

Naryshkin
Bastion

Troitsky
most

Malaya Neva

nab Makarova

Birzhevoy
most

Suvorovskaya Pl

23

Srednypr

Volkhovsky
per

1-ya Kadetskaya linii

Birzhevaya
Pl

7

2

**VASILYEVSKY
ISLAND**

Birzhevoy proezd

Dvortsovy
most

To Eratra
(2km)

Bolshoy pr
ul Repina

3

Vasileostrovets
Gardens

To Troitsky
Most (50m)

Bolshaya Neva

Anglyskaya nab

Dvortsovaya
pl

ADMIRALTEYSKY

pl
Dekabristov

Nevsky pr

Zelyony
most

Nevsky
Prospekt

Blagoveshchensky
most

Galernaya ul

Admiralty
Gardens

Malaya Morskaya ul

Bol Morskaya ul

nab r Moyki

Kazanskaya
Pl

14

30

Konnogvardeysky bul

19

Pochtamtskaya ul

Isaakievskaya Pl

nab
Admiralteyskogo kanala

Pl Truda

ul Truda

Kryukov Canal

Bol Morskaya ul

KAZANSKY

nab kan Griboedova

**Novaya
Gollandiya**

21

Kazanskaya ul

Voznesensky pr

Stolyarny per

SPASSKY

Gorokhovaya ul

Apraksin per

ul Pisareva

20

per Matveeva

ul Dekabristov

32

Teatralnaya Pl

Sennaya pl

Sadovaya

Sennaya
Ploshchad

Semyonovsky
most

31

33

KOLOMENSKY

ul Soyuza Pechatnikov

ul Glinki

Pr Rimskogo-Korsakova

Moskovsky pr

SENNAYA

nab reki Fontanki

Kryukov Canal

Nikolsky
Gardens

Nikolsky per

Yusupov
Gardens

Obukhovsky
most

Pushkinskaya

Vitebskaya Pl

Ecolines

Griboedova Canal

Kanonerskaya ul

Sadovaya ul

Fontanka

Pl Turgeneva

ul Labutina

13

nabreki Fontanki

**Vitebsk Station
(Vitebsky Vokzal)**

POKROYSKY

Yegipetsky
most

Izmailovsky pr

Polsky
Gardens

To Lux
Express (1km)

pr Moskvinoy

**Tekhnologichesky
Institut**

To Pulkovo
Airport (12km)

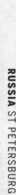

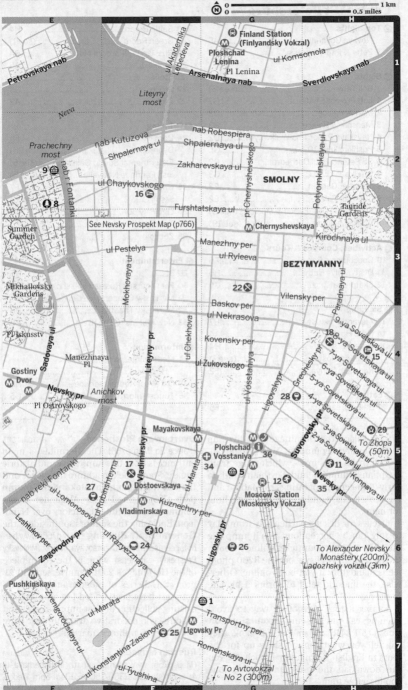

0 1 km
0 0.5 miles

Finland Station
(Finlyandsky Vokzal)
Ploshchad Lenina
Pl Lenina
ul Komsomola

Petrovskaya nab
Arsenalnaya nab
Sverdlovskaya nab

Neva
Liteyny most

nab Robespiera
nab Kutuzova
Shpalernaya ul
Shpalernaya ul
Zakharevskaya ul
SMOLNY

Prachechny most
nab r Fontanki
ul Chaykovskogo
16
Furshtatskaya ul

Tauride Gardens

Summer Garden
See Nevsky Prospekt Map (p766)
Chernyshevskaya
Kirochnaya ul

ul Pestelya
Manezhny per
ul Ryleeva
BEZYMYANNY

Mikhailovsky Gardens
22
Vilensky per

Pl Isknsstv
Baskov per
ul Nekrasova
Manezhnaya Pl
Kovensky per
ul Zukovskogo

Gostiny Dvor
Nevsky pr
Anichkov most
Pl Ostrovskogo
Mayakovskaya
Ploshchad Vosstaniya
36
34
5
To Zhopa (50m)

17
27
Dostoevskaya
Kuznechny per
12
Moscow Station (Moskovsky Vokzal)
35
11

Leshtukov per
nab reki Fontanki
Vladimirskaya
10
24
26
To Alexander Nevsky Monastery (200m); Ladozhsky vokzal (3km)

Pushkinskaya
ul Marata
1
Transportny per
25
Ligovsky Pr
Romenskaya ul
ul Tyushina
To Avtovokzal No 2 (300m)

Central St Petersburg

Winter Palace, the Hermitage fully lives up to its sterling reputation. You can be absorbed by its treasures – which range from Egyptian mummies and Scythian gold to early-20th-century paintings by Matisse and Picasso – for days and still come out wishing for more.

Queues for tickets, particularly from May to July, can be horrendous. You'll jump the queue by booking your ticket online through the Hermitage's website, but the R200 photo fee is mandatory if you book online. Otherwise, the lines do tend to shrink a bit late in the day.

Joining a tour is another way to avoid queuing: call the museum's **excursions office** (📞571 8446; ⊙11am-1pm & 2-4pm); they will tell you what time to show up for the tours in English, German or French. Or you can download the museum's smartphone app for a free tour.

Dvortsovaya Ploshchad   HISTORIC SITE
(Palace Sq; Map p766) The Hermitage's main entrance is from this impressive and historic square. Stand back to admire the palace and the central 47.5m-high **Alexander Column** (Map p766), named after Alexander I and commemorating the 1812 victory over Napoleon. Enclosing the square's south side is the **General Staff Building** (Map p766; www.hermitagemuseum.org; Dvortsovaya pl 6-8; ⓜNevsky Prospekt) – its east wing is the centrepiece of the Hermitage's 250th-anniversery '20/21' project. Galleries of modern and contemporary art have been added to an impressive existing collection of post-impressionist and Empire-style decorative art. The west wing still serves as military quarters.

Russian Museum   MUSEUM
(Map p766; www.rusmuseum.ru; Inzhenernaya ul 4; adult/student R300/150; ⊙10am-6pm Wed & Fri-Sun, to 5pm Mon, 1-9pm Thu; ⓜGostiny Dvor)

Facing onto the elegant pl Iskusstv (Arts Sq) is the handsome Mikhailovsky Palace, now housing one of the country's finest collections of Russian art. After the Hermitage you may feel you have had your fill of art, but try to make some time for this gem of a museum.

The museum owns three other city palaces, all worth visiting if you have time, where permanent and temporary exhibitions are held: the **Marble Palace** (Map p762; Millionnaya ul 5; adult/student R350/150; ⊙10am-6pm Wed & Fri-Sun, 10am-5pm Mon, 1-9pm Thu; ⓂNevsky Prospekt); the **Mikhailovsky Castle** (Mikhaylovsky Zamok; Map p766; Sadovaya ul 2; adult/student R300/150; ⊙10am-6pm Wed & Fri-Sun, 10am-5pm Mon, 1-9pm Thu; ⓂGostiny Dvor), also known as the Engineer's Castle; and the **Stroganov Palace** (Map p766; Nevsky pr 17; adult/student R300/150; ⊙10am-6pm Wed & Fri-Sun, 10am-5pm Mon, 1-9pm Thu; ⓂNevsky Prospekt). A combined ticket (adult/student R600/300), available at each palace, covers entrance to all four within a 24-hour period.

Church of the Saviour on Spilled Blood CHURCH

(Map p766; Konyushennaya pl; adult/student R250/150, audioguide R100; ⊙10am-6pm Thu-Tue; ⓂNevsky Prospekt) This multidomed dazzler, partly modelled on St Basil's in Moscow, was built between 1883 and 1907 on the spot where Alexander II was assassinated in 1881 (hence its gruesome name). The interior's 7000 sq metres of mosaics fully justify the entrance fee.

St Isaac's Cathedral CHURCH

(Isaakievsky Sobor; Map p766; www.cathedral.ru; Isaakievskaya pl; cathedral regular/evening R250/350, colonnade regular/evening R150/300; ⊙11am-6pm Thu-Tue, 6.15-10.30pm May-Sep; ⓂAdmiralteyskaya) The golden dome of this cathedral dominates the city skyline. Its lavish interior is open as a museum, but many visitors just buy the separate ticket to climb the 262 steps up to the colonnade to take in panoramic views. Behind the cathedral, Falconet's statue of Peter the Great, the **Bronze Horseman** (Map p766; pl Dekabristov; ⓂSadovaya), stands at the northern end of pl Dekabristov (Decembrists' Sq).

Peter & Paul Fortress FORTRESS

(Map p762; www.spbmuseum.ru; grounds free, exhibitions adult/student R370/190, per exhibit R130/70; ⊙grounds 6am-10pm Apr-Sep, to 9pm Oct-Mar, exhibitions 11am-7pm Thu-Tue, to 6pm Oct-Mar; ⓂGorkovskaya) Founded in 1703 on Zaychy Island as the original military base for the new city, this fortress was mainly used as a political prison up to 1917: famous residents include Peter's own son Alexei, as well as Dostoyevsky, Gorky and Trotsky.

Individual tickets are needed for each of the fortress' attractions, so the best deal is the combined entry ticket, which allows ac-

---

LOCAL KNOWLEDGE

DIMITRI OZERKOV, CHIEF CURATOR HERMITAGE 20/21 PROJECT

Dimitri Ozerkov, chief curator of the Hermitage 20/21 Project, recommends his favourite pieces from the museum's collection:

Egyptian mummies (Room 100) I first visited the Hermitage when I was five or six years old. At that time what I liked the most were these mummies displayed at a low height so I could see them well and read their names, such as Pa De Ist.

Raphael's Loggia (Room 227) Catherine the Great commissioned Giacomo Quarrengi in the 1780s to create this copy of a gallery she admired at the Vatican. It was made exactly to scale, so not only is it a great event of art but also of technique and design.

Perseus and Andromeda (Room 246) The Hermitage has lots of works by Rubens, many of them from his studio – he was like the Damien Hirst of his day, presiding over a factory of artists. One piece that undoubtedly was done by his hand, though, is this – it's a masterpiece. You look at Medusa's eyes and you feel afraid, and the horse looks so real you feel you could touch it.

Dance and Music (Room 344) From the 20th-century works, I recommend these magnificently vibrant pair of paintings by Matisse, commissioned by his patron Sergei Shchukin. Originally the genitalia of the nude male dancers were shown, but they were later painted over. If the light is right, it's possible to see the painting as Matisse intended. It's a dilemma for the Hermitage whether to restore it to the way it was.

Nevsky Prospekt

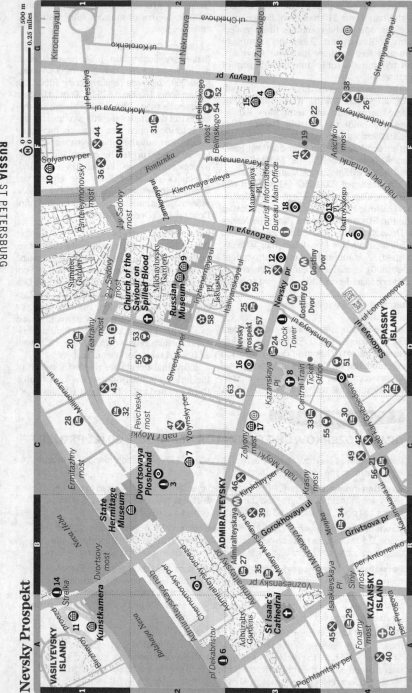

Nevsky Prospekt

RUSSIA ST PETERSBURG

cess to all of the exhibitions on the island except for the **bell tower** (Map p762; ☑498 0505; Peter & Paul Fortress, Zayachy Ostrov; adult/student R150/90; ⊙tours noon, 1.30pm, 3.30pm & 4pm May-Sep) and the **Nevskaya Panorama Walkway** (Map p762; Peter & Paul Fortress, Zay-achy Ostrov; adult/student R150/120) along part of the battlements.

It's worth heading into the **SS Peter & Paul Cathedral** (Map p762; adult/student R200/90), with its landmark needlelike golden spire and magnificent baroque interior. All

RUSSIA'S MOST FAMOUS STREET

Walking **Nevsky Prospekt** is an essential St Petersburg experience. Starting at Dvortsovaya pl, notice the gilded spire of the **Admiralty** (Map p766; Admiralteysky proezd 1; ⊘closed to the public; MNevsky Prospekt) to your right as you head southeast down Nevsky towards the Moyka River. Across the Moyka, Rastrelli's baroque Stroganov Palace (p765) houses a branch of the Russian Museum.

Opposite the Kazan Cathedral (p768) is the **Singer Building** (Map p766; Nevsky pr 28; MNevsky Prospekt), a Style Moderne (art deco) beauty restored to all its splendour when it was the headquarters of the sewing-machine company; inside is the bookshop Dom Knigi and **Café Singer** (Map p766; ⊘9am-11pm), serving good food and drinks with a great view over the street.

A short walk south of the cathedral, along Griboyedova Canal, sits one of St Petersburg's loveliest bridges, the **Bankovsky Most** (Map p766). The cables of this 25.2m-long bridge are supported by four cast-iron gryphons with golden wings.

View the lavish **Grand Hotel Europe** (Map p766; ☑329 6000; www.grandhoteleurope. com; Mikhailovskaya ul 1/7; ✳@☎☂; MNevsky Prospekt/Gostiny Dvor), built between 1873 and 1875, redone in Style Moderne in the 1910s and completely renovated in the early 1990s. Across Nevsky pr, the impressively restored Bolshoy Gostiny Dvor (p776) is another Rastrelli creation dating from 1757–85. Beside it stands the **clock tower** of the former Town Duma, seat of the prerevolutionary city government.

At 48 Nevsky pr, the **Passazh** (Map p766) department store has a beautiful arcade (note the glass ceilings), while on the corner of Sadovaya ul is the Style Moderne classic **Yeliseyevsky** (Map p766; Nevsky pr 56; MGostiny Dvor), once the city's most sumptuous grocery store and now reincarnated as a luxury confectionery.

An enormous **statue of Catherine the Great** (cnr Postovaya ul & Krasnaya ul) stands at the centre of **Ploshchad Ostrovskogo** (Map p766; MGostiny Dvor), commonly referred to as the Catherine Gardens; at the southern end of the gardens is **Aleksandrinksy Theatre** (Map p766; ☑710 4103; www.alexandrinsky.ru; pl Ostrovskogo 2; MGostiny Dvor), where Chekhov's The Seagull premiered (to tepid reviews) in 1896.

Nevsky pr crosses the Fontanka Canal on the Anichkov bridge, with its 1840s statues (sculpted by German Pyotr Klodt) of rearing horses at its four corners.

Russia's tsars since Peter the Great are buried here, including Nicholas II and his family – you'll find them in an anteroom to your right as you enter. Also look out for the famously ugly pinhead statue of Peter the Great in the centre of the fortress.

Kunstkamera
MUSEUM

(Museum of Anthropology & Ethnography; Map p766; www.kunstkamera.ru; Tamozhenny per; adult/child R250/50; ⊘11am-7pm Tue-Sun; MAdmiralteyskaya) Established in 1714 by Peter the Great, this museum is the city's oldest. Crowds still flock to see his ghoulish collection of monstrosities, notably preserved freaks, two-headed mutant foetuses and odd body parts, although the anthropological and ethnographic displays from around the world are pretty interesting, too.

Strelka
LANDMARK

(Map p762) Some of the best views of St Petersburg can be had from Vasilyevsky Island's eastern 'nose', known as the Strelka. The two **Rostral Columns** (Map p766) on

the point, studded with ships' prows, were oil-fired navigation beacons in the 1800s. Nearby the **Museum of Zoology** (Zoologichesky Muzey; Map p766; www.zin.ru/mus_e.htm; Universitetskaya nab 1; adult/student R200/70, Thu free; ⊘11am-6pm Wed-Mon; MAdmiralteyskaya) has some amazing exhibits, including a complete woolly mammoth, thawed out of the Siberian ice in 1902, and a live insect zoo.

FREE Kazan Cathedral
CHURCH

(Kazansky Sobor; Map p766; Kazanskaya pl 2; ⊘8.30am-7.30pm; MNevsky Prospekt) The great colonnaded arms of the Kazan Cathedral reach out towards Nevsky. Built between 1801 and 1811, its design by Andrei Voronikhin, a former serf, was influenced by St Peter's in Rome. This highly atmospheric church is well worth entering. Shorts are not allowed.

Novaya Gollandiya
ISLAND

(New Holland; Map p762; www.newhollandsp.ru; nab Admiralteyskogo kanala 2; ⊘11am-10pm Mon-Fri, to 11pm Fri & Sat, closed Oct-Apr; MAdmiralteyskaya) Closed to the public for centuries, this vast urban island is in the process of being turned into St Petersburg's most impressive public space, thanks to Dasha Zhukova's Iris Foundation – the brains and brawn behind the similar Garage Centre for Contemporary Culture (p749) in Moscow. Novaya Gollandiya's gaggle of mothballed 18th-century red-brick buildings will eventually house contemporary art. For now, it's more of a yuppie R&R zone. There's a grassy park strewn with cosy beanbag chairs, quirky shops, an awesome kids' zone, and facilities for volleyball, ping pong and other sporty diversions. At weekends DJs fill the air with chill-out music and many of the city's best restaurants set up booths, while concerts take place at night.

Sheremetyev Palace
MUSEUM

(Map p766; www.theatremuseum.ru; nab reki Fontanki 34; MGostiny Dvor) Facing the Fontanka Canal, the splendid Sheremetyev Palace (1750–55) houses two lovely museums. The **Museum of Music** (Map p766; admission R250; ⊙11am-7pm Wed-Sun) contains a collection of beautifully decorated instruments. The upstairs palace rooms have been wonderfully restored; you get a great sense of how cultured life must have been here.

In a separate wing of the palace, reached from Liteyny pr, is the charming **Anna Akhmatova Museum at the Fountain House** (Map p766; www.akhmatova.spb.ru; adult/child R80/40; ⊙10.30am-6.30pm Tue & Thu-Sun, 1-9pm Wed; MMayakovskaya), filled with mementos of the poet and her family, all persecuted during Soviet times.

Museum of the Defence & Blockade of Leningrad
MUSEUM

(Map p766; Solyarnoy per 9; adult/student R200/100, photos R100; ⊙10am-5pm Thu-Tue, closed last Thu of month; MChernyshevskaya) This engrossing museum is a required stop for anybody wishing to understand St Petersburg's darkest hour – the siege of Leningrad during WWII.

Menshikov Palace
MUSEUM

(Menshikovsky Dvorets; Map p762; www.hermitagemuseum.org; Universitetskaya nab 15; adult/student R60/free, 1st Thu of month free, audio tour R100, photos R200; ⊙10.30am-6pm Tue-Sat, to 5pm Sun; MVasileostrovskaya) This riverside palace was built in 1707 for Peter the Great's confidant Alexander Menshikov. Now a branch of the Hermitage, it has impressively restored interiors filled with period art and furniture.

FREE **Summer Garden**
PARK

(Map p762; ⊙10am-10pm May-Sep, to 8pm Oct-Mar, closed Tue; MGostiny Dvor) St Petersburg's prettiest park, dotted with fountains and classical statues, is a great place to relax. In its northeast corner is the modest, two-storey **Summer Palace** (Map p762; ☑314 0374; Muzey Letny Dvorets Petra 1; adult/student R300/150; ⊙10am-5pm Wed-Mon early May–early Nov), built for Peter from 1710 to 1714 and best viewed from its exterior.

Alexander Nevsky Monastery
MONASTERY

(off Map p762; Nevsky pr 179/2; suggested donation R130, cemeteries admission R200; ⊙grounds 6am-11pm, churches 6am-8.30pm, cemeteries 9.30am-6pm; MPloshchad Aleksandra Nevskogo) This working monastery southeast of the centre was founded in 1713 by Peter the Great, who wrongly thought this was the location where Alexander of Novgorod had beaten the Swedes in 1240. In 1797 it became a *lavra* (superior monastery).

The main reason for coming here is to see the graves of some of Russia's most famous artistic figures. The cemeteries are either side of the main entrance; tickets are sold in the booth on the right. The **Tikhvin Cemetery**, on the right, contains the biggest names, including the graves of Tchaikovsky, Rimsky-Korsakov (check out his wild tomb!), Borodin, Mussorgsky and Glinka. Turn right after entering to reach the tomb of Dostoevsky.

🏃 Activities

In winter, head down to Zaychy Island and watch the famous ice swimmers, or 'walruses', who start the day with a bracing dip in the water through a hole carved into the ice. In summer, the same spot sees sun worshippers out in force.

Cycling

Especially during White Nights, cycling is a brilliant and economical way to get around St Petersburg's spread-out sights, restaurants and bars. Off main drags like Nevsky pr (where you can ride on the sidewalk), St Petersburg's backstreets are quiet and sublime.

Skatprokat
CYCLING

(Map p762; ☑717 6838; www.skatprokat.ru; Goncharnaya ul 7; rental per day/24hr/week from

ST PETERSBURG'S CONTEMPORARY ART GALLERIES

St Petersburg has a thriving contemporary-art scene, with even the Hermitage diving into the 21st century with its ongoing 20/21 Project. With over 2000 works in its permanent collection, the superb museum and gallery **Erarta** (off Map p762; www.erarta.com; 29-ya Liniya 2; adult/student R300/150, audio tour R100; ⊙10am-10pm Wed-Mon; ☎; ⓂVasileostrovskaya), on Vasilyevsky Island, combines an exhibition over five floors tracing the post-WWII development of Russian art with a commercial gallery. To get here, catch bus 6 from the other side of the road from Vasileostrovskaya metro.

Other commercial galleries include the following:

Pushkinskaya 10 (Map p762; www.p-10.ru; Ligovsky pr 53; ⊙4-8pm Wed-Sun; ⓂPloshchad Vosstaniya) An artists' squat established in 1989, this legendary locale is home to several art galleries; a museum of nonconformist art; the Experimental Sound Gallery (p774) and its funky attached cafe, Gaz-21; and the quirky **Temple of Love, Peace & Music** (Map p762; Ligovsky pr 53; ⊙6-8pm Fri (sporadic at other times)), where collector Kolya Vasin (Russia's most famous Beatles fan) has amassed an amazing array of John Lennon paraphernalia.

Loft Project ETAGI (Map p762; ⓂLigovsky Prospekt) Hidden away off the main road in the former Smolninsky Bread Bakery, Loft Project consists of four large and industrial-looking gallery spaces, along with studio space, several shops and even a hostel.

R300/400/2100; ⊙1-8pm; ⓂPloshchad Vosstaniya) Besides renting out a wide variety of bikes, Skatprokat runs summer weekend and White Night bike tours, brought to you by the folks behind Peter's Walking Tours (p770).

Bathhouses

Degtyarniye Baths BATHHOUSE
(Map p762; www.d1a.ru; Degtyarnaya ul 1a; per hr R300-1000; ⊙9am-midnight; ⓂPloshchad Vosstaniya) A huge complex with a variety of rooms. Probably the most tourist-friendly *banya*: English is spoken and the website has a helpful English-language guide for *banya* novices.

Coachmen's Banya BATHHOUSE
(Yamskiye Bani; Map p762; ☎312 5836; www.yamskie.ru; ul Dostoevskogo 9; admission R150-500; ⊙men 8am-10.30pm Mon & Wed-Sun, women 8am-10.30pm daily; ⓂVladimirskaya) Traditional *banya* with both regular and luxe sections.

☞ Tours

Peter's Walking Tours WALKING
(☎943 1229; www.peterswalk.com; scheduled tours R650; ⊙scheduled tours Apr-Oct) Peter's guides give you insight into the city like no one else. The classic 4½-hour 'Original Walk' departs from Hostel Life at Nevsky pr 47; you tell your guide what you are interested in and they improvise a tour. Themed tours include a Friday-night pub crawl, a Rasputin Walk and a War & Peace tour. Peter's does great boat tours too.

Anglo Tourismo BOAT, WALKING
(Map p766; ☎8-921-989 4722; www.anglotourismo.com; nab reki Fontanki; adult/student R600/500; ⓂNevsky Prospekt) A boat tour of the canals is highly recommended, and from May to October there are plenty of boats for hire. This company's boat leaves from beside the Anichkov bridge and has English commentary. It also offers a range of walking tours.

✯ Festivals & Events

St Petersburg celebrates its founding on **City Day** (27 May) with mass festivities. During the **White Nights** (the last 10 days in June), the city parties all night. The **Scarlet Sails Festival** (around June 23) sees millions flock to the Neva embankment to watch midnight concerts, fireworks and fluvial battle reenactments.

⌶ Sleeping

High season is May to September, with some hotels increasing their rates even further in June and July. You can get great deals in the low season, when hotel prices drop 30% on average. Weekend discounts are less common than in Moscow, but do exist at business-oriented hotels.

TOP CHOICE **Alexander House** BOUTIQUE HOTEL €€€
(Map p762; ☎334 3540; www.a-house.ru; nab kanala Kryukova 27; s/d incl breakfast from R8300/9000; ❋☎; ⓂSadovaya/Sennaya Ploshchad) A real gem offering 19 extremely warm and comfortable rooms, each tastefully

styled after the world's top cities and decorated with high-quality art. Lovely common areas include a fireplace-warmed lounge and a vine-laden courtyard containing a guests-only restaurant.

TOP CHOICE **Soul Kitchen** HOSTEL €
(Map p766; ☑8-911-723 1032; www.soulkitchen-hostel.com; nab reki Moyki 62/2; dm R800, d from R3200, without bathroom from R2600; ☺@☺; Ⓜ Sadovaya/Sennaya Ploshchad) Russia's best hostel blends boho hipness and boutique-hotel comfort, scoring perfect 10s in many key categories: private rooms (chic), dorm beds (double-wide with privacy-protecting curtains), atmosphere (shabby chic, mellow), common areas (vast) and bathrooms (downright inviting). The common balcony overlooking the Moyka canal is just gravy.

TOP CHOICE **Andrey & Sasha's Homestay** APARTMENT €€
(Map p766; ☑315 3330, 8-921-409 6701; asamatuga@mail.ru; nab kanala Griboyedova 49; r €70-80; Ⓜ Sadovaya) Legendary hosts rent out rooms in two delightfully decorated vintage apartments; this one doubles as their home.

TOP CHOICE **W Hotel** LUXURY HOTEL €€€
(Map p766; ☑610 6161; www.wstpetersburg.com; Voznesensky pr 6; r from R13,000; ❋☺☀; Ⓜ Admiralteyskaya) Walk into the dazzling reception area of this 137-room property and you instantly know you're onto something special. The rooms are all spacious and very luxuriously appointed, with marble bathrooms, sumptuous king beds, a Nespresso coffeemaker and matching white flat-screen TVs and iPod docks.

TOP CHOICE **Hostel Life** HOSTEL €
(Map p766; ☑318 1808; www.hostel-life.ru; Nevsky pr 47; dm R800-1000, tw R2850; ☺; Ⓜ Mayakovskaya) You'll know you've made a good choice the minute you walk into the large and modern lounge/kitchen area. The dorms are cosy and the wide-open communal bathroom is immaculate. Access is from Zagorodny pr. Rates include a basic breakfast.

3MostA BOUTIQUE HOTEL €€
(Map p766; ☑332 3470; www.3mosta.com; nab reki Moyki 3a; economy s R3000, d from R5000; ❋☺; Ⓜ Nevsky Prospekt) 'Three Bridges' is a modern, classy inn in a beautiful old building with views of the Church on Spilled Blood.

The 26 rooms are surprisingly uncramped given its wonderful location. Just two economy singles. Breakfast is R300 extra.

Pushka Inn BOUTIQUE HOTEL €€
(Map p766; ☑312 0913; www.pushkainn.ru; nab reki Moyki 14; s/d incl breakfast from R5000/8300; ❋☺☂; Ⓜ Admiralteyskaya) Charming 33-room inn housed in a historic 18th-century building on a particularly picturesque stretch of the Moyka River. The beds are wonderful and the rooms are large (except for the two economy singles).

Location Hostel HOSTEL €
(Map p762; ☑329 1274; www.location-hostel.ru; Ligovsky pr 74; dm R600, d R1000-2900; ☺@☺; Ⓜ Ligovsky Prospekt) Part of the artsy Loft Project ETAGI, this is more a way of life than a hostel. The 200-plus beds are distribued among four- to 40-bed dorms, budget doubles (some windowless) and three much-in-demand 'design rooms'. The common area/kitchen, festooned with iMacs, feels like an architect's studio. Its other branch on **Admiralteysky pr** (Map p766; ☑812 490 6429; www.location-hostel.ru; Admiralteysky pr 8; dm/tw without bathroom R600/1200; ☺) is better located but more basic.

Rachmaninov Antique Hotel BOUTIQUE HOTEL €€
(Map p766; ☑327 7466; www.hotelrachmaninov.com; Kazanskaya ul 5; s/d incl breakfast from R4500/4900; ☺; Ⓜ Nevsky Prospekt) Superstylish minihotel, where minimalist decor is offset by antiques.

Hotel Vera BOUTIQUE HOTEL €€
(Map p762; ☑702 6190; www.hotelvera.ru; Suvorovsky pr 25/16; s/d incl breakfast from R3150/3950; ❋☺; Ⓜ Ploshchad Vosstaniya) This friendly 70-room boutique is awash in classic art deco flourishes yet maintains a contemporary feel. Shoot for the lovely, budget-friendly 'optima' rooms on the top floor. It's a 15-minute walk to the nearest metro.

Northern Lights HOTEL €€
(Map p766; ☑571 9199; www.nlightsrussia.com; Bolshaya Morskaya ul 50; r incl breakfast R2350-3430; ❋☺; Ⓜ Admiralteyskaya) There are just five rooms at this pleasant minihotel at the end of an impressive old staircase: three have their own bathrooms, while two share facilities. All have tons of space, sitting tables and closets. Breakfast is delivered to your room.

Radisson Sonya
HOTEL €€

(Map p762; http://radisson.ru/sonyahotel-stpetersburg; Liteyny pr 5/19; r weekend/weekday from R4850/8950; ☻❋@⦿; MⒸhernyshevskaya) Stupendous weekend discounts make this business hotel near the Summer Garden a fantastic choice for tourists from Friday to Sunday. Rates escalate during the week but the hotel's main attributes – good service, pleasing design and luscious king-sized beds – remain.

Diva Hostel
HOSTEL €

(Map p766; ☎579 0144; www.divahostel.ru; nab reki Fontanki 38-22; dm R600, s/d/tr/q without bathroom from R2000/2200/3000/4500; ❋⦿; MMayakovskaya) With just one 12-bed dorm and a tiny kitchen, this is not a hostel for socialising, but it's great if you seek a quiet, compact, clean private room at a great price. Pay R300 extra for a queen-sized bed.

Pio on Mokhovaya
B&B €€

(Map p766; ☎273 3585; www.hotelpio.ru; Mokhovaya ul 39; s/d/tr/q incl breakfast R3900/4700/5700/6400; ⦿⊞; MChernyshevskaya) The rooms at this appealing guesthouse are named after Italian towns. They're simply but elegantly furnished, with modern fixtures and dusky pastel-coloured walls. Sister property **Pio on Griboedov** (Map p766; ☎812 571 9476; ⦿; MNevsky Prospekt) has six rooms sharing bathrooms and canal views.

Hello Hostel
HOSTEL €

(Map p762; ☎643 2556; www.hellohostel.ru; Angliyskaya nab 50; dm including breakfast R550-1000, d without bathroom R2400; ⦿; MAdmiralteyskaya) An eclectic, arty hostel with a party vibe thanks to its popular lobby bar. The dorm rooms have extra-tall wooden bunk beds, some with privacy-protecting curtains. It occupies the bottom floors of a gorgeous art nouveau building, with bric-a-brac strewn everywhere.

Friends on Griboyedova
HOSTEL €

(Map p766; ☎571 0151; www.friendsplace.ru; nab kanala Griboyedova 20; dm R800-900, s/d/tr without bathroom R2300/2400/2900; ☻@⦿; MNevsky Prospekt) A sprawling hostel with bike rental and two foosball tables not far from the epicentre of St Pete's party scene around Dumskaya ul. The purple-toned private rooms are some of the best in the hostel business. Friends runs three other hostels, including the more party-oriented **Friends on Bankovsky** (Map p766; ☎310 4950; ⦿; MSadovaya) nearby.

Nauka
HOTEL €

(Map p766; ☎315 8696; www.nauka-hotel.ru; Millionnaya ul 27; 5-bed dm R700, s/d without bathroom from R1500/2000; ⦿; MAdmiralteyskaya) Soviet-era accommodation is an acquired taste, but if your budget is small, and you're happy to forgo bourgeois luxury, this no-frills hotel on the doorstep of the Hermitage fits the bill. It's on the 3rd floor of the Academy of Sciences building. No English, restaurant or services of any kind.

✖ Eating

St Petersburg has a fantastic selection of restaurants and cafes. Many successful Moscow chains such as Jean-Jacques (p755) have expanded into St Petersburg, and vice-versa.

TOP CHOICE Teplo
RUSSIAN €€

(Map p766; ☎570 1974; Bolshaya Morskaya ul 45; mains R250-550; ⊘9am-midnight; ☻⦿◿⌨; MAdmiralteyskaya) You'll instantly warm to this beloved restaurant's cosy living-room atmosphere, liberally scattered with cuddly soft toys. The food – roast veal with forest mushrooms, Finnish-style fish soup, savoury pies, plus delightful and affordable breakfasts – is equally comforting. Reservations essential at peak lunch and dinner hours.

TOP CHOICE Green Room
CAFE €

(Map p762; Ligivosky pr 74; mains R100-150; ⊘9am-11pm Sun-Thu, to 3am Fri & Sat; ⦿◿⌨; MLigovsky Prospekt) This bright cafe has a sprawling wooden rooftop terrace overlooking the graffiti-splashed courtyard of the funky Loft Project ETAGI artists' complex. Bask in the creativity of it all. Food leans towards Central Asian, and cocktails (R200) and half-litres of beer (R100) are affordable.

Botanika
VEGETARIAN €€

(Map p766; ☎272 7011; www.cafebotanika.ru; ul Pestelya 7; mains R220-500; ⊘11am-midnight; ☻⦿◿⌨; MChernyshevskaya) Enjoying perhaps the friendliest and most laid-back atmosphere in St Petersburg, this vegetarian charmer wins on all counts. The menu takes in Russian, Indian, Italian and Japanese dishes, all of which are delicious.

Soup Vino
MEDITERRANEAN €

(Map p766; ☎312 7690; Kazanskaya ul 24; mains R250-450; ⊘noon-11pm; ◿⌨; MNevsky Prospekt) This tiny place does exactly what it says on the label. The menu features Mediterranean-influenced soups, pasta and salads, perfect washed down with glasses of wine (R150 to R250).

Zoom Café
EUROPEAN €€

(Map p766; www.cafezoom.ru; Gorokhovaya ul 22; mains R200-400; ☺9am-midnight Mon-Sat, from 1pm Sun; 🔊🍴💻; MNevsky Prospekt) Perennially popular cafe with a funky feel and an interesting menu of hearty comfort food like potato pancakes with salmon and cream cheese. No reservations after 4pm – expect to wait.

Gogol
RUSSIAN €€

(Map p766; 🖉312 6097; Malaya Morskaya ul 8; meals R500-900; ☺noon-11pm; 🍴💻; MAdmiralteyskaya) An intimate place with piano music, chandeliers and antique furniture, Gogol specialises in meaty Russian comfort food – pork knuckles, venison, fiery borsch and homemade spicy horseradish vodka.

Idiot
VEGETARIAN €€

(Map p766; nab reki Moyki 82; mains R300-900; business lunch R250; ☺11am-1am; 🍴🔊🖉; MSennaya Ploshchad) This long-running cafe charms with its prerevolutionary atmosphere. The creative vego menu features great original salads, and sitting down earns you a free vodka shot.

Russian Vodkaroom No 1
RUSSIAN €€€

(Map p762; www.vodkaroom.ru; Konnogvardeysky bul 4; mains R450-900; 💻; MAdmiralteyskaya) Before dining in this elegant restaurant, it's worth taking the English guided tour of the attached small **Vodka Museum** (Map p762;

with/without guided excursion R300/150; ☺noon-7pm, to 10pm for restaurant patrons) and doing a tasting of three vodkas (R150). If that whets your appetite, there are some 140 vodkas on the menu to sample.

Pelmenya
RUSSIAN €€

(Map p766; nab reki Fontanki 25; meals R200-300; ☺11am-11pm; 🔊💻; MGostiny Dvor) All kinds of dumplings on the menu here – Georgian *khinkali*, Uzbek *manti*, Ukrainian *varenyky* and, of course, the namesake *pelmeni* – all prepared fresh in a delightful space near the main boat tour dock.

Troitsky Most
VEGETARIAN €

(☺9am-11pm; 🔊🍴💻) **Moyka** (Map p766; nab reki Moyki 27; dishes R75-125; ☺9am-11pm; 🔊🍴💻; MAdmiralteyskaya); **Vasilyevsky Island** (off Map p762; 6-ya liniya 27, Vasilyevsky Island; dishes R75-125; ☺9am-11pm; 🍴🖉💻; MVasileostrovskaya) This cheap and friendly chain of vegetarian cafes is great and the mushroom lasagne legendary. The salads are self-serve, *stolovaya* style.

Stolle
RUSSIAN €

(www.stolle.ru; small/large pie R35/70, mains R200-250; ☺9am-9pm; 🍴) **Konyushennaya per** (Map p766; www.stolle.ru; Konyushennaya per 1/6; pies R60-100; MNevsky Prospekt); **ul Dekabristov 19** (Map p762; ul Dekabristov 19; MSadovaya/Sennaya Ploshchad); **ul Dekabristov 33** (Map p762; www.stolle.ru; ul Dekabristov 33; pies R60-100; MSadovaya/Sennaya Ploshchad); **ul Vosstaniya** (Map p762; ul Vosstaniya 32; MChernyshevskaya); **Vasilyevsky Island** (Map p762; 1-ya linii 50, Va-

RUSSIA ST PETERSBURG

EATING ON THE CHEAP

Food in St Petersburg is a tad cheaper than in Moscow, but it's still expensive, and shoestring travellers will want to avoid sit-down restaurants.

As in Moscow, locals flock to the affordable Soviet-style cafeterias known as *stolovayas*. Unfortunately, St Pete lacks the slick, modernised versions found in Moscow, but many simpler, more authentic versions persist, such as **Stolovaya Lozhka.** (Map p766; ul Pestelya 15; meals R200-300; ☺9am-9pm; MChernyshevskaya). Look for the ubiquitous *stolovaya* signs – usually in lowercase cursive Cyrillic.

Quick-and-easy *bliny* (pancake) chain **Teremok** (Map p766; www.teremok.ru; Bolshaya Morskaya ul 11a; bliny R50-100; ☺8am-11pm; MAdmiralteyskaya) has a convenient outlet near the Hermitage; **Chaynaya Lozhka** (Tea Spoon; Map p766; www.teaspoon.ru; Nevsky pr 44; mains R30-100; ☺8am-11pm; MGostiny Dvor) is another popular chain for delicious *bliny*. More upmarket chain **Yolki-Palki** (Map p766; www.elki-palki.ru; Nevsky pr 88; meals R400-500; ☺24hr; 🍴💻; MMayakovskaya) is beloved for its country-cottage decor and all-you-can-eat salad bar stocked with Russian and Ukrainian favourites.

The Russian sushi obsession is alive and well in St Petersburg, with restaurants of any and all genres offering a sushi menu. **Dve Palochki** (Two Chopsticks; Map p766; www.dvepalochki.ru; Nevsky pr 22; sushi platter R400, dishes R150-200; ☺11am-6am; 🔊💻; MMayakovskaya) has several outlets that serve quality sushi quickly and relatively cheaply.

WANT MORE?

For in-depth information, reviews and recommendations at your fingertips, head to the Apple App Store to purchase Lonely Planet's *St Petersburg City Guide* iPhone app.

Alternatively, head to www.lonelyplanet.com/russia/st-petersburg for planning advice, author recommendations, traveller reviews and insider tips.

silevsky Island; Ⓜ Vasileostrovskaya) We can't get enough of the traditional Russian savoury and sweet pies at this chain of cafes. It's easy to make a meal of it with soups and other dishes that can be ordered at the counter.

Baltic Bread
BAKERY €€

(Baltiysky Khleb; Map p762; Vladimirsky pr 19; snacks R50-120; ⏰8.30am-10pm; ⊜🛜💳; Ⓜ Dostoevskaya) This British-run bakery in the Vladimirsky Passage shopping centre is a perfect spot for a quick coffee-fuelled breakfast, or for fresh bread, cakes and ready-made sandwiches any time of day. The elegant art deco **original restaurant** (Baltiisky Khleb; Map p762; Grechesky pr 25; snacks R50-120; ⏰10am-9pm; Ⓜ Ploshchad Vosstaniya) is more atmospheric but poorly located.

🍷 Drinking

St Petersburg is Russia's hub of alternative culture, and there is a wealth of undergound bars, 'trash' bars, artists' hang-outs and live music.

The club scene is also pulsating, but as in Moscow it's generally a weekend-only affair. The centre of the action is around Dumskaya ul, home to dozens of bars and clubs and a sea of drunken students after midnight at the weekends.

Many of the best clubs and live music bars are cafes by day, so we list them all in one place.

TOP CHOICE Hat
BAR

(Map p766; ul Belinskogo 9; ⏰8am-last customer; Ⓜ Mayakovskogo) Sit around the perfectly square bar, order a stiff drink and take in the superb live jazz jam sessions that take place nightly except Saturday. There's some real talent here and the atmosphere is boisterous. The Hat's sister bar, **Terminal Bar** (Map p762; ul Rubinshteyna 13a; ⏰4pm-last customer;

Ⓜ Dostoevskaya), is another slice of New York bohemia where regulars often bring the resident piano to life.

Ligovsky 50
BAR, CLUB

(Map p762; Ligovsky pr 50) If you don't care for the sloppy drunk-fest of Dumskaya ul, this complex of clubs is a good alternative. **Dyuni** (Dunes; Map p762; Ligovsky pr 50; ⏰24hr; 🛜; Ⓜ Ploshchad Vosstaniya) and more sophisticated **Jesus Club** (Map p762; Ligovsky pr 50; ⏰8pm-6am Thu-Sat; Ⓜ Ploshchad Vosstaniya) provide the most reliable fun. At Dyuni, they surround the outside of the club with sand and hold all-day-and-night beach parties in the warmer months.

Fish Fabrique Nouvelle
LIVE MUSIC

(Map p762; www.fishfabrique.spb.ru; Ligovsky pr 53; ⏰3pm-late; Ⓜ Ploshchad Vosstaniya) Here in the museum of boho known as Pushkinskaya 10 (p770), life artists, musicians and wannabes of all ages meet to drink beer and listen to music. Live bands kick up a storm after 10pm most nights outside August; other nights are reserved for underground movies. The **Experimental Sound Gallery** (GEZ-21; Map p762; www.gez21.ru; Ligovsky pr 53; cover free-R300; Ⓜ Ploshchad Vosstaniya) in the same complex also has bands almost nightly.

Griboedov
CLUB

(Map p762; www.griboedovclub.ru; Voronezhskaya ul 2a; cover R200-400; ⏰noon-6am; 🛜; Ⓜ Ligovsky Prospekt) Located in a bomb shelter, this is the longest-standing and still the most respected club in the city, founded by local ska collective Dva Samolyota. Above ground is the groovy cafe-bar Griboedov Hill, which hosts live music on many evenings.

FREE Radiobaby
BAR, CLUB

(Map p766; www.radiobaby.com; Kazanskaya ul 7; ⏰6pm-6am; Ⓜ Nevsky Prospekt) A laid-back club with cool lighting, a 'no techno, no house' music policy, table football and an atmosphere of eternal hedonism. Go through the arch at Kazanskaya ul 5, then turn left through a second arch to find it.

Dom Byta
CAFE, CLUB

(Map p762; www.dombeat.ru; Razyezzhaya ul 12; ⏰noon-6am; 🛜; Ⓜ Vladimirskaya) Funky '70s interior, a cool crowd, a worldly menu and tables cleared for dancing late night on weekends make this a great spot day or night. No cover charge but strict *feis kontrol* and expensive beer.

Mod Club   BAR, CLUB

(Map p766; www.modclub.info; nab kanala Griboyedova 5; cover R150-300; ☺6pm-6am; ⓂNevsky
Prospekt) There's a groovy mix of live and
spun music at this fun, invariably packed
place with two bars and a happening summer terrace.

Zoccolo   LIVE MUSIC

(Tsokol; Map p762; www.zoccolo.ru; 3-ya Sovetskaya
ul 2/3; cover R100-600; ☺noon-midnight Sun-Thu,
to 6am Fri & Sat, concerts 8pm; ⓂPloshchad Vosstaniya) This long-running punk and indie rock
institution (formerly Moloko) is the CBGBs
of St Petersburg. Entry is free before 5pm,
when the venue functions as an arty cafe.

Probka   BAR

(Map p766; ☎273 4904; www.probka.org; ul Belinskogo 5; ☺1pm-1am; ⓂGostiny Dvor) A sophisticated wine bar with a choice selection from
around the world. Several wines are available by the glass, and there's a menu of light
snacks.

Barackobamabar   BAR, CLUB

(Map p766; www.barakobamabar.ru; Konyushennaya pl 2; ☺6pm-6am; ⓂNevsky Prospket) This
cover charge–free dance club dedicated to
the US prez is choc-a-block full of beautiful
young things at wkeekends. The action spills
outdoors when it's warm. If it's dead, there
are two other clubs in the same courtyard.

Zhopa   BAR

(The Ass; off Map p762; pr Bakunina 6; ☺8pm-1am
Sun-Thu, to 8am Fri & Sat; ⓂPloshchad Vosstaniya)
You're liable to meet all manner of characters in this funky place, the most infamous
of Piter's 'trash bars'. Look for the letter Ж
on the front door.

Stirka   CAFE, BAR

(Laundry; Map p766; Kazanskaya ul 26; ☺10am-last
customer; ⓂSadovaya/Sennaya Ploshchad) Tiny,
quirky hipster hang-out with a nightly DJ
and three washing machines.

☆ Entertainment

From July to mid-September the big theatres like the Mariinsky and the Mikhaylovsky close but plenty of performances are
still staged. Check the *St Petersburg Times*
for comprehensive listings.

Mariinsky Theatre   OPERA, BALLET

(Map p762; ☎326 4141; www.mariinsky.ru; Teatralnaya pl 1; ☺performances 7pm; ⓂSadovaya/Sen-
naya Ploshchad) Home to the world-famous
Kirov Ballet and Opera Company. A visit

here is a must, if only to wallow in the sparkling glory of the interior. Use the website to
book and pay for tickets in advance – either
for the theatre or the acoustically splendid
concert hall (Map p762; www.mariinsky.ru; ul
Dekabristov 37; ☺closed mid-Jul–mid-Sep; ⓂSa-
dovaya/Sennaya Pl) nearby (entrance at ul
Dekabristov 37). The hulking **New Mariinsky Theatre** (Map p762; ul Dekabristov 34) is
being built across the Kryukova Canal.

Mikhaylovsky Opera &
Ballet Theatre   OPERA, BALLET

(Map p766; www.mikhailovsky.ru; pl Iskusstv 1;
☺box office 10am-9pm; ⓂNevsky Prospekt)
Challenging the Mariinksy in terms of the
standards and range of its performances is
this equally historic and beautifully restored
theatre.

Shostakovich Philharmonia
Bolshoy Zal   CLASSICAL MUSIC

(Big Hall; Map p766; www.philharmonia.spb.ru;
Mikhailovskaya ul 2; ⓂGostiny Dvor) This grand
hall is one of its two venues where the renowned St Petersburg Philharmonica Symphony Orchestra plays. The other is the
Maly Zal imeni Glinki (Small Hall; Map p766;
Nevsky pr 30; ⓂNevsky Pr).

Feel Yourself Russian Folkshow   DANCE

(Map p762; ☎312 5500; www.folkshow.ru; ul Truda
4, Nikolayevsky Palace; ticket incl drinks & snacks
R1600; ☺box office 11am-9pm, shows 6.30pm & in
high season 9.30pm; ⓂAdmiralteyskaya) Funny
name, but actually a very entertaining show
of traditional Russian folk dancing and

GAY & LESBIAN ST PETERSBURG

Check out **Excess** (www.xs.gay.ru) for
the latest city-specific information. The
main club is the large and mainstream
Central Station (Map p766; www.
centralstation.ru; ul Lomonosova 1/28;
cover after midnight R100-300; ☺6pm-
6am; ⓂGostiny Dvor). Some way out of
the city centre you'll find Russia's only
lesbian club, **3L** (Tri El; Map p762; www.
triel.spb.ru; 5-ya Sovetskaya ul 45; cover
free-R150; ☺5pm-midnight Tue, 10pm-6am
Wed-Sun; ⓂPloshchad Vosstaniya), as
well as the community-minded mixed
gay-lesbian club and social centre **Malevich** (www.malevich-club.ru; Moskovsky
pr 109/3; cover free-R300; ☺11pm-6am
Wed & Fri-Sun; ⓂMoskovskiye Vorota).

ZENIT

Petersburgers are fanatical about 2008 UEFA Cup–winning football team **Zenit** (www.fc-zenit.ru). Sponsored by oil and gas giant Gazprom, their light blue jerseys can be bought at shops across the city. Match tickets (R100 to R1000) can be purchased at theatre ticket booths or at the stadium, three days before a game.

music by enthusiastic, professional troupes, in the grand Nikolayevsky Palace.

🛍 Shopping

Bolshoy Gostiny Dvor   DEPARTMENT STORE
(Map p766; Nevsky pr 35; ⊙10am-10pm; ⓜGostiny Dvor) The granddaddy of all of St Pete's department stores. You'll find a great selection of nearly everything here, including fashion and souvenirs, at reasonably competitive prices.

Souvenir Market   SOUVENIRS
(Map p766; Konyushennaya pl; ⊙9am-dusk; ⓜNevsky Prospekt) With dozens of little stalls selling all kinds of arts, crafts and souvenirs, this is your best one-stop gift- and memento-shopping opportunity. Haggle here.

Dom Knigi   BOOKS
(Map p766; Nevsky pr 28; ⓜNevsky Prospekt) A good selection of guidebooks and maps are available in this bookshop in the elegant Singer Building.

❶ Information

Dangers & Annoyances

Mosquitoes are prevalent from May until October and can certainly keep you up at night. Bring repellent or a socket plug. Human pests include the ever-present pickpockets on Nevsky pr – be particularly vigilant around Griboyedova Canal.

Sadly, racist attacks are a reality in the city. Skinhead gangs have killed an unprecedented number of mainly Central Asian people from the Caucasus in the past few years, and there's a climate of fear among ethnic minorities. That said, attacks in the city centre are rare, so we still encourage nonwhite travellers to visit, but exercise caution. Avoid the suburbs whenever possible and try not to go out alone after dark.

Internet Access

Internet cafes and free wi-fi access are common across the city.

Cafe Max (www.cafemax.ru; Nevsky pr 90/92; per hr R120; ⊙24hr; ⓜMayakovskaya) Coffee (R90) and beer (R120) on offer too. Also has a branch in the Hermitage.

Russian Museum Internet Centre (Nevsky pr 17; per hr R70; ⊙10am-10pm; ⓜGostiny Dvor) Inside the courtyard of the Stroganov Palace.

Media

The following English-language publications are available free at many hotels, hostels, restaurants and bars across the city.

St Petersburg in Your Pocket (www.inyour-pocket.com/city/st_petersburg.html) Semi-monthly listings booklet with useful up-to-date information and short features.

St Petersburg Times (www.sptimes.ru) St Pete's fine English-language newspaper, published every Wednesday.

Medical Services

The clinics listed here are open 24 hours and have English-speaking staff.

Apteka Petrofarm (Map p766; Nevsky pr 22; ⊙24hr)

American Medical Clinic (Map p766; ☎740 2090; www.amclinic.ru; nab reki Moyki 78; ⓜAdmiralteyskaya)

Medem International Clinic & Hospital (Map p762; ☎336 3333; www.medem.ru; ul Marata 6; ⓜMayakovskaya)

Post

Post office branches are scattered throughout the city.

Central Post Office (Map p762; www.spbpost.ru; Pochtamtskaya ul 9; ⊙24hr; ⓜSadovaya/Sennaya Ploshchad) Worth visiting just to admire its elegant Style Moderne interior. The express mail service EMS Garantpost is available here.

Telephone

You can buy a local SIM card at any mobile-phone shop, such as **Euroset** (www.spb.euroset.ru), a chain with branches across the city, from as little as R150 including R100 of credit. **Megafon** (pl Vostanniya), with additional branches throughout the city, is a reliable operator.

Tourist Information

Tourist Information Bureau (☎300 3333, tourist helpline 0333; http://eng.ispb.info) Main Office (Map p766; ☎310 2822; http://eng.ispb.info; Sadovaya ul 14/52; ⊙10am-7pm Mon-Fri, noon-6pm Sat; ⓜGostiny Dvor); Hermitage Booth (http://eng.ispb.info; Dvortsovaya pl 12; ⊙10am-7pm; ⓜNevsky Prospekt); pl Vosstaniya (Map p762; pl Vosstaniya; ⊙10am-7pm; ⓜPloshchad Vosstaniya) These helpful offices are a rarity for Russia. Free city maps, brochures and transport advice.

Travel Agencies

The following agencies have English-speaking staff.

Express to Russia (✆570 6342; www.express-torussia.com; Muchnoi per 2) Visas, tours, hotel bookings, tickets – a little of everything.

Ost-West Kontaktservice (Map p762; ✆327 3416; www.ostwest.com; Nevsky pr 100; ⊙10am-6pm Mon-Fri; MPloshchad Vosstaniya) The multilingual staff here can find you an apartment to rent and organise tours and tickets.

ⓘ Getting There & Away

Air

St Petersburg's **Pulkovo Airport** (www.pulkovoairport.ru) is 17km south of the city centre. There are two terminals: **Pulkovo-1** (✆704 3822) handles domestic and CIS flights, plus all Rossiya Airlines international flights; **Pulkovo-2** (✆704 3444) handles all other international flights. International and local airline tickets can easily be purchased online or at any travel agent.

Boat

Linking Helsinki and St Petersburg three to four times weekly is the Finnish 11-hour overnight ferry **St Peter Line** (✆386 1147; www.stpeterline.com); coming from Helsinki, passengers are allowed to stay in St Petersburg visa-free for up to 72 hours. Trans-Exim (www.transexim.ru) runs twice-weekly car ferries to Baltiysk, Kaliningrad, from Ust-Luga, 150km west of St Petersburg.

Take bus 7 or trolleybus 10 from outside the Hermitage to the port (25 minutes).

Bus

The cheapest way to get to Helsinki is to take a *marshrutka* (fixed-route public van) from pl Vosstaniya (R500 to R800, seven to nine hours); they leave all day when full from the corner of Nevsky pr and Ligovsky pr, opposite the metro station. Daily **Sovavto** (www.sovavto.ru; MMoskovskaya) buses from the Grand Hotel Europe are another option (€40, eight hours).

Buses with **Ecolines** (Map p762; ✆325 2152; www.ecolines.ru; Podezdny per 3; MPushkinskaya) – five daily – and **Lux Express** (off Map p762; ✆441 3757; www.luxexpress.eu; Mitrofanievskoe sh 2, Admiral Business Centre; ⊙9am-9pm; MBaltiyskaya) – 11 daily – are the most convenient way to travel to Tallinn (from R600, 7½ hours); Lux Express also serves Riga (from R1080, 11 hours, four daily).

Additional international and European Russia services depart from St Petersburg's main bus station, **Avtovokzal No 2** (off Map p762; ✆766 5777; www.avokzal.ru; nab Obvodnogo kanala 36; MLigovsky Prospekt) – there isn't a No 1.

RUSSIA ST PETERSBURG

WORTH A TRIP

PETRODVORETS & TSARSKOE SELO

Among the several palace estates that the tsars built around St Petersburg as country retreats, the ones not to miss are **Petrodvorets** (Peterhof), 29km west of St Petersburg, and **Tsarskoe Selo**, 25km south of the city in the town of Pushkin.

If time is limited, Petrodvorets, Peter the Great's 'Russian Versailles', is the one to opt for, mainly because of its **Grand Cascade** (✆tel, info 427 7425; ul Razvodnaya 2; ⊙9am-8pm Mon-Fri, to 9pm Sat & Sun)and Water Avenue, a symphony of over 140 fountains and canals located in the **Lower Park** (Nizhny Park; adult/student R400/200; ⊙park 9am-8pm, fountains 10am-6pm). The fountains only work from mid-May to early October, but the gilded ensemble looks marvellous at any time of the year. There are several additional palaces, villas and parks here, each of which charges its own hefty admission price.

Tsarskoe Selo's big draw is the baroque **Catherine Palace** (http://eng.tzar.ru; adult/student R320/160; ⊙10am-6pm, closed Tue & last Mon of month), built between 1752 and 1756, but almost destroyed in WWII. The exterior and 20-odd rooms, including the dazzling Great Hall and Amber Room, have been expertly restored. From May to September individual visits to Catherine's Palace are limited to noon to 2pm and 4pm to 5pm, with other times being reserved for tour groups.

Buses and *marshrutky* (shared minibuses) to Petrodvorets (R70, 30 minutes) run frequently from outside metro stations Avtovo and Leninsky Prospekt. From May to September, hydrofoils (R1000 return, 30 minutes) leave from jetties behind the Hermitage and behind the Admiralty every 30 minutes from 10am to 6pm (last trip back 8pm).

The easiest way to get to Tsarskoe Tselo is by *marshrutka* from Moskovskaya metro station. Take the exit marked 'Buses for the airport', and pick up *marshrutka* 342 or K545 towards Pushkin (R70).

Train

You can get pretty much anywhere in Eastern Europe, Russia or the CIS from St Petersburg by train, but be aware that most westbound trains (including those serving Berlin, Budapest, Kaliningrad, Kyiv, Prague, Smolensk and Warsaw) pass through Belarus, for which you'll need a transit visa.

Apart from at stations, tickets can be purchased at the **Central Train Ticket Office** (Map p766; nab kanala Griboedova 24; ⏱8am-8pm Mon-Sat, to 6pm Sun; MNevsky Prospekt) and at many travel agencies (which charge a fee).

There are four main stations:

Finlyandsky Vokzal (Finland Station; pl Lenina 6; MPloshchad Lenina) For high-speed 'Alegro' trains to Helsinki (from R3500, four daily, 3½ hours).

Ladozhsky Vokzal (Ladoga Station; Zhanevsky pr 73; MLadozhskaya) For the far north of Russia, the Urals and the slow train to Helsinki (R3000, six hours, daily).

Moskovsky Vokzal (Moscow Station; pl Vosstaniya; MPloshchad Vosstaniya) Service to/from Moscow and Veliky Novgorod.

Vitebsky Vokzal (Vitebsk Station; Zagorodny pr 52; MPushkinskaya) The Baltics including Tallinn (from R1050, seven hours, daily), Kaliningrad, Belarus, the Czech Republic, Germany, Hungary, Poland and Ukraine.

THE RETURN OF THE CASTLE?

Königsberg's majestic castle, dating from 1255, once stood on Tsentralnaya pl. Left in ruins after WWII and dynamited out of existence in the late 1960s, it was replaced by the outstandingly ugly **Dom Sovetov** (House of Soviets; Tsentralnaya pl). During the eyesore's construction it was discovered that the land below it was hollow, with a (now flooded) four-level underground passage connecting to the cathedral. The decaying half-finished building has never been used.

If Kaliningrad's planners have their way, Dom Sovetov will eventually be masked by a rebuilt castle, part of a development that would also include a clutch of modern skyscrapers and a convention centre, but the estimated US$100 million needed for the proejct has yet to materialise.

ℹ Getting Around

To/From the Airport

Pulkovo Airport, 17km south of the centre, is easily and (very) cheaply accessed by metro and bus, but pay close attention to which terminal you are using, as Terminal 1 and Terminal 2 are not close to each other and a taxi between them costs at least R500.

From Moskovskaya metro station, bus 39 runs to Pulkovo-1, and buses 13 and 13b run to Pulkovo-2. Both trips take 15 to 20 minutes and cost R25 to R30, plus (sometimes) an extra R20 per big bag. Buy your ticket on the bus. All told it's about 50 minutes from the centre to the airport, including transfer and wait time.

By taxi it's R900 to the centre from official taxi booking kiosks located at both terminals.

Public Transport

The metro is usually the quickest way around the city. *Zhetony* (tokens) and credit-loaded cards can be bought from booths in the stations (R28).

Buses and trolleybuses (R23) and *marshrutky* (R35) often get you closer to the sights and are especially handy to cover long distances along main avenues like Nevsky pr.

Taxi

Unofficial taxis are common.

Peterburgskoe Taksi 068 (☑324 7777, 068; www.taxi068.spb.ru)

Taxi Blues (☑321 8888; www.taxiblues.ru)

KALININGRAD REGION

POP 937,900

One part German, two parts Russian and wedged inextricably between a Europe-thirsty Lithuanian rock and a proud Polish hard place, Kaliningrad (Калинингра Дская Область) is a region with an identity problem. Should it be resurrecting its German past, flaunting its undeniable Russianness, or forging ahead on a brave new path?

Brashly, Russia's smallest territory does all three. You'll definitely feel like you're in Russia, but it will seem a tad more liberal, a tad more open-minded, and a tad more Western-oriented than the rest of the country.

In this 'Little Russia' – only 15,100 sq km – you'll also find beautiful countryside, charming old Prussian seaside resorts and splendid beaches – including the pine forests and Sahara-style dunes of the Kurshskaya Kosa National Park, a Unesco World Heritage site.

Kaliningrad Region

Citizens of Japan and many European countries can visit Kaliningrad on a 72-hour visa. See p795 for details.

History

Ruled by Teutonic Knights since the 13th century, in 1525 the area became the Duchy of Prussia, Europe's first Protestant state, with Königsberg as its capital. The city's liberal atmosphere attracted scholars, artists and entrepreneurs from across Europe; in 1697 Peter the Great visited as part of Russia's Grand Embassy, and the 18th-century philosopher Immanuel Kant lived all his life here.

After WWI, East Prussia was separated from the rest of Germany when Poland regained statehood. The three-month campaign by which the Red Army took it in 1945 was one of the fiercest of WWII, leaving Königsberg in ruins.

In 1946 the region was renamed Kaliningrad in honour of Mikhail Kalinin, one of Stalin's more vicious henchmen. The Soviets proceeded to ship out all of the Germans, and out of the rubble of Königsberg rose Kaliningrad, which was meant to be the finest example of a Soviet planned city. The result was what you still see today: a blinding expanse of concrete that is extreme even by Soviet standards. Fortunately, traces of Germanic culture remain behind the brooding facades; the old cathedral has been rebuilt, and fragments of the medieval core of the city remain visible.

Kaliningrad
Калининград

📞 4012 / POP 423,000

Kaliningrad is an excellent introduction to Russia's most liberal region. Interesting museums and historical sights sprout in between the shiny new shopping centres and multitude of leafy parks that soften vast swaths of brutal Soviet architecture. Although little remains to indicate how Königsberg was once a Middle European architectural gem equal to Prague or Kraków, there are attractive residential suburbs and remnants of the city's old fortifications that evoke the Prussian past.

👁 Sights

Pl Pobedy is the modern heart of Kaliningrad, dominated by the Russo-Byzantine **Cathedral of Christ the Saviour** (Kafedralny Sobor Khrista Spasitelya), built in 2006.

Kaliningrad Cathedral   CHURCH
(www.sobor-kaliningrad.ru; Kant Island; adult/student R150/130, photos R50, concerts R250-300;

Kaliningrad

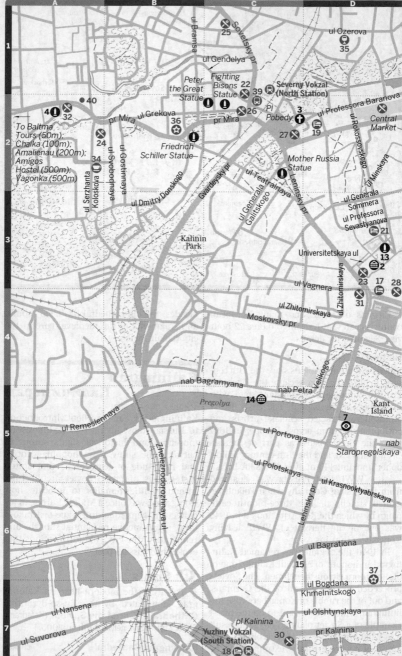

RUSSIA KALININGRAD

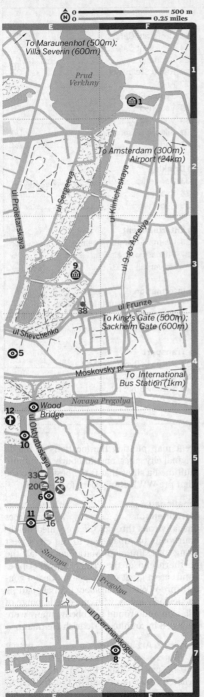

⊙10am-5pm) Photos displayed inside this Unesco World Heritage site attest to how thoroughly in ruins this cathedral was until the early 1990s, when German donations helped it to be rebuilt; the original dates back to 1333. The lofty interior is dominated by an ornate organ used for regular concerts that are worth attending; the Russian version of the website has the schedule. On the top floor is an austere room with the death mask of Immanuel Kant, whose rose-marble tomb lies outside on the outer north side.

Fish Village   NEIGHBOURHOOD
(Ribnaya Derevnya) From Kant's Island, cross the nearby **Honey Bridge**, the oldest of the city's bridges, and you'll arrive at the half-timber riverside development known as Fish Village. Disneyland-ish it may be, but this collection of hotels, shops, cafes and restaurants is a laudable attempt to reprise some of the city's destroyed architectural heritage.

The handsome **Jubilee Footbridge**, built in 2005 to celebrate the city's 750th birthday, will take you to the south bank of the river. Facing the cathedral here is the **Former Stock Exchange** (Leninsky pr 83), a fine Renaissance-style building built in the 1870s.

World Ocean Museum   MUSEUM
(www.world-ocean.ru; nab Petra Velikogo 1; combined adult/student R250/150, individual vessels R90/60; ⊙10am-6pm Wed-Sun) Two boats and a 1968 Foxtrot-class B413 submarine can be explored at this excellent museum, strung along the banks of the Pregolya River. The highlight is the handsome former expedition vessel *Vityaz*, which conducted many scientific studies around the world. Also here is a restored storehouse building with interesting displays on fishing and the sea-connected history of Kaliningrad, as well as a rare archaeological find: the remains of a 19th-century wooden fishing boat.

Amber Museum   MUSEUM
(www.ambermuseum.ru; pl Vasilevskogo 1; adult/student R170/110, photos R150; ⊙10am-7pm Tue-Sun) This museum has some 6000 examples of amber artworks, including enormous pieces of jewellery containing prehistoric insects suspended within, an amber flute and a four-panelled amber and ivory chalice depicting Columbus, the *Niña*, the *Pinta* and the *Santa Maria*.

Kaliningrad

City Fortifications & Gates
HISTORIC BUILDINGS

The Amber Museum is housed in the attractive **Dohna Tower** (pl Vasilevskogo), a bastion of the city's old defensive ring. It's adjacent to the **Rossgarten Gate**, one of Königsberg's city gates, which now contains a restaurant.

Several other bits of the fortifications and gates remain scattered around the city. The impressively renovated **King's Gate** (ul Frunze 112; adult/student R60/30; ◎11am-7pm Wed-Sun) houses a museum with cool models of old Königsberg and exhibits on the personalities who shaped the region's history. A little south of here is the twin-towered **Sackheim Gate** (cnr pr Moscovsky & Litovsky Val).

The **Friedland Gate** (www.fvmuseum.ru; pr Kalinina 6; adult/child R20/10, multimedia show R30; ◎10am-7pm May-Aug, to 6pm Sep-Apr, closed 1st Fri of month) contains a museum with a great map plotting the locations of the 13 original city gates, and an hourly 40-minute multimedia show that is the best way to see what pre-WWII Königsberg looked like.

Amalienau & Maraunenhof
NEIGHBOURHOODS

Casual strolls through the tree-lined neighbourhoods of Amalienau to the city's west along pr Mira and Maraunenhof at the northern end of the Prud Verkhny (Upper Pond) are a great way to get an idea of genteel pre-WWII Königsberg. Amalienau is particularly lovely, with an eclectic range of villas on and around pr Pobedy; many were designed by architect Friedrich Heitmann.

History & Art Museum
MUSEUM

(ul Klinicheskaya 21; adult/student R80/40; ◎10am-6pm Tue-Sun) Housed in a reconstructed 1912 concert hall by the Prud Nizhny (Lower Pond), the interesting exhibits here mainly focus on events since Russia's takeover of the region.

Bunker Museum
MUSEUM

(Muzei Blindazh; Universitetskaya ul 2; adult/student R80/40; ☺10am-6pm Tue-Sun, to 5pm Mon) The city's last German commander, Otto van Lasch, capitulated to the Soviets from this buried German command post in 1945. Now a WWII museum, it was closed for a major renovation at the time of research.

🏃 Activities

Planeta Sport
CYCLING

(Leninsky pr 133; bike rental per day R200-400; ☺10am-8pm Mon-Fri, to 6pm Sat, 11am-4pm Sun) A bicycle is not a bad way to get around sprawling Kaliningrad, and is especially pleasant around Fish Village and the Cathedral.

🛏 Sleeping

Kaliningrad is great value compared with Moscow and St Petersburg, although there's not much to choose from at the budget end. Hotel rates include breakfast unless otherwise noted.

TOP CHOICE Radisson Hotel
HOTEL €€€

(☏593 344; http://radisson-hotels.ru/kaliningrad; pl Pobedy 10; r from R6200; ✴@🖥) The uberstylish Radisson chain never fails to disappoint in Russia. Here you get soothing sea tones, amazing beds and cathedral views – perfect for business *or* romance. The rates drop by R2000 per night from Friday to Sunday.

TOP CHOICE Chaika
HOTEL €€€

(☏210 729; www.hotelchaika.ru; ul Pugacheva 13; s/d from R3500/4450; ☻✴@🖥) On a leafy street near the picturesque Amalienau area is this delightful 28-room property decorated with classy heritage touches. Has a restaurant, comfy lounge and fitness room.

Heliopark Kaiserhof
HOTEL €€€

(☏592 333; www.heliopark.ru; ul Oktyabrskaya 6a; s/d from R5700/6200; ✴@🖥) Can't quite match the style of the Radisson but not a bad back-up at the top end, with nice extras like comfy robes, marble-tiled bathrooms and a full-service spa. Location in Fish Village is a plus. Rates are almost halved at weekends.

Amigos Hostel
HOSTEL €

(☏8-911-485 2157; www.amigoshostel.ru; Epronovskaya ul 20-102; dm R550-650, tr/q without bathroom R2200/2900; 🖥) This was Kaliningrad's only viable hostel at the time of re-

search. It's a bit out of the way in a residential neighbourhood northeast of the centre, but quiet and perfectly adequate. Take the 3, 5 or 9 bus along pr Mira then walk.

Skipper Hotel
HOTEL €€

(Gostinitsa Skiperskaya; ☏307 237; www.skipperhotel.ru; ul Oktyabrskaya 4a; r R2500-2700; ☻✴🖥) Another Fish Village offering, the Skipper has characterless but functional rooms with river views and balconies; breakfast is taken in a cafe in the nearby lighthouse.

Villa Severin
PENSION €€

(☏365 373; www.villa-severin.ru; ul Leningradskaya 9a; r R1600-2800; ☻✴@🖥) There's a homely atmosphere at this pretty villa, with 10 comfortably furnished rooms including one simple student room (s/d R1000/1400 without breakfast). It rents out bikes (R400), which come in handy given the out-of-the-way location on Prud Verkhny.

Komnaty Otdykha
HOTEL €

(Resting Rooms; ☏586 447; Yuzhny vokzal; dm in d/tr R700/500, s/d R1000/1700) A great job has been made of renovating these rooms inside the south train station, turning them into en suite accommodation. Fantastic deal.

Ubileiniy Luks
HOTEL €€

(☏519 024; www.ubilejny-lux.ru; ul Universitetskaya 2; r from R2800; ✴🖥) Atop a business centre, this hotel's 13 rooms are all enormous, and most have kitchens. Breakfast not included.

STATUES & MONUMENTS

A statue of Königsberg's most famous son, **Immanuel Kant** (ul A Nevskogo, Kant State University), stands in front of the university named after him, tucked off Leninsky pr; the statue is a 1992 copy of the 1864 original by Christian Rauch.

A gem of Soviet iconography is the **Cosmonaut Monument** (pr Mira), celebrating the local guys who went into space, while in leafy Tsentralny Park a hulking statue of **Vladimir Vysotsky**, a legendary singer from the 1960s and '70s, overlooks the amphitheatre.

In the lobby of the nearby Scala cinema and Zarya cafe is a witty monument to **Woody Allen** (born Allen Konigsberg) – a pair of the film director's trademark glasses jutting from the wall.

KVARTIRA

Kvartira (Apartment; 216 736; ul Serzhanta Koloskova 13;) is tricky to classify but unquestionably one of the coolest hang-outs in Kaliningrad. Lined with a fascinating range of pop culture books, CDs, records and DVDs, all for sale or rent (as is everything else in the space, including the stylish furniture), Kvartira also serves drinks and snacks. Movies (including some in English) are screened for free on several nights, while on others there may be a party, an art event or – on Fridays – a DJ.

English-speaking owner Artyem, who inherited this wonderful apartment from his grandpa, a Soviet censor, is good fun and knows the K'grad arts scene inside and out. He organises a jazz festival and several film festivals in the nearby Scala theatre.

Kvartira is always open from 6pm to 10pm, but hours are erratic at other times so call before setting off.

Hotel Kaliningrad HOTEL €€
(350 500; www.hotel.kaliningrad.ru; Leninsky pr 81; s/d from R1950/2300;) Wears plenty of Soviet ant[i]charm, but it's reasonably renovated, and for guidebook writers or others who need to be in the centre of town, the location can't be beat. No such thing as a free breakfast (or free anything) here.

Eating & Drinking

Try the Prussian speciality *Königsberger klopse* – meatballs with capers in white wine sauce. Self-caterers should visit the lively central market on ul Chernyakhovskogo or the many outlets of the supermarket Viktoriya.

Kaputsin CAFE €
(ul Kirova 3/5; soups R150; 10am-10pm;) Looking like an art student's living room, plastered with books, maps and other knickknacks, this laid-back cafe plays classic rock and serves nicely brewed coffee and DIY noodle and rice dishes – choose your starch, topping and sauce. No booze.

Croissant Cafe CAFE €
(mains R200-300, croissants R40; 9am-11pm;) **pr Mira** (pr Mira 23); **pl Pobedy** (pl Pobedy); **Leninsky** (Leninsky pr 63;); **Prole-tarskaya 79** (ul Proletarsky 79) A chic baked-goods heaven. Indulge in flaky pastries, quiches, muffins, biscuits and cakes, as well as omelettes and bliny for breakfast.

Kmel RUSSIAN €
(pl Pobedy 10, Clover City Centre mall; meals R350-500; 10am-2am;) Four types of good beer are brewed at this appealing multilevel gastropub overlooking pl Pobedy. They're served alongside an interesting range of Russian and Siberian dishes such as reindeer, *omul* (a fish from Lake Baikal) and Kamchatka crab *pelmeni*.

Tyotka Fischer EUROPEAN €
(Auntie Fischer; ul Shevchenko 11a; mains R200-500; 11am-midnight) A homebrew specialist, this was the only place in town where we found *Königsberger klopse*. While not freshly prepared, it's still tasty and the location is central. Also has German sausages, pizza and plenty of Russian dishes on the menu.

Zarya CAFE €€
(pr Mira 43; mains R200-300; 9am-1am Mon-Wed, to 3am Thu-Sun;) Classic Russian menu in the classic Russian lobby of the Scala cinema. Great place to sip a drink.

KGTU Stolovaya CAFETERIA €
(Sovetsky pr 1; 9am-5pm Mon-Sat) They're not for everybody, but for those who appreciate a cheap meal and an authentic Soviet experience, *stolovye* are a fine choice. This one in the basement of Kaliningrad State Technical University keeps it real, down to the *kasha* (buckwheat)-slinging *babushki*.

Viktoriya SUPERMARKET €
(24hr) **pl Kalinina** (pl Kalinina); **Leninsky pr** (Leninsky pr 30); **Fish Village** (Oktyabrskaya ul) Large Western-style supermarket with branches all over the city.

TOP CHOICE **Reporter** BAR
(www.reporter-club.ru; ul Ozerova 18; mains R150-250, business lunch R140; noon-1am;) A great bar in a great industrial space, Reporter has something going on most nights, be it a movie, artist presentation or – on Mondays, Fridays and Saturdays – live music. Pub grub and pizza on the menu.

Bar Verf CAFE, BAR
(ul Oktyabrskaya 4a; snacks R100-300; 11am-midnight;) The ambience is pleasant at this self-styled wine bar in Fish Village that also has outdoor tables overlooking the ca-

thedral. It screens movies and provides coloured pencils and paper for doodling.

☆ Entertainment

Major DJs from Russia and Western Europe jet in for gigs at Kaliningrad's clubs, which open around 9pm but typically don't get going until well after midnight.

Drama & Comedy Theatre　　THEATRE
(pr Mira 4; tickets R150-200) Mostly plays, in Russian.

Philharmonic Hall　　CLASSICAL MUSIC
(www.kenigfil.ru; ul Bogdana Khmelnitskogo 61a; tickets from R200) This beautifully restored neo-Gothic church, which has excellent acoustics, hosts organ concerts, chamber-music recitals and the occasional symphony orchestra.

Universal　　CLUB
(www.club-universal.com; pr Mira 43; admission from R500; ☺from 9pm Fri & Sat) Kaliningrad's classiest club.

Vagonka　　CLUB
(www.vagonka.net; Stanochnaya ul 12; admission from R150; ☺Fri & Sat) This chilled-out club shuns face control and attracts a cool, alternative crowd with top DJs and live music, plus cheap drinks.

Amsterdam　　CLUB
(www.amsterdam-club.ru; 38/11 Litovsky Val; admission R1000; ☺9am-6am Fri & Sat) Long-running gay club hidden 200m down an unnamed side street off Litovsky Val.

❶ Information

Baltma Tours (☎931 931; www.baltma.ru; pr Mira 94) The efficient, multilingual staff here can arrange visas, accommodation and an array of local excursions including to Yantarny, home of what was once the world's largest amber mine. A private day tour to the Kurshskaya Kosa for two people is €100 for the car and another €100 if you want an English-speaking guide.

Branch Post Office (ul Chernyakhovskogo 32; ☺8am-8pm Mon-Fri, 9am-6pm Sat, 9am-2pm Sun)

Emergency Hospital (☎534 556; ul Nevskogo 90; ☺24hr)

King's Castle (☎350 782; www.kaliningrad info.ru; Leninsky pr 81, Hotel Kaliningrad; ☺9am-6pm Mon-Fri, to 4pm Sat, to 1pm Sun) Runs scheduled tours (in Russian) to the Kurshskaya Kosa on Wednesdays and Sundays in the summer (R980). Private tours to the

Kurshskaya Kosa and Yantarny are possible too (about R5000 for up to three people).

Königsberg.ru (www.konigsberg.ru) Web-based tour agency through which you can arrange visas, including the 72-hour express visa.

Regional Tourism Information Centre (☎555 200; www.visit-kaliningrad.ru; pr Mira 4; ☺9am-8pm Mon-Fri, 11am-6pm Sat) Multilingual staff here are a mine of information on the region, including info on transport, visas and the logistics of visiting the Kurshskaya Kosa.

UFMS Office (☎563 809; Sovetsky pr 13, room 9) For visa queries.

❶ Getting There & Away

There are three border crossings from Poland and four from Lithuania.

Air

Khrabrovo airport (☎459 426) is 24km north of the city. There are plenty of daily flights to Moscow, St Petersburg and Minsk, as well as a few weekly flights to Warsaw, Kyiv, Berlin and Copenhangen.

The cheapest way to get to Kaliningrad from Europe is usually to fly by budget airline to Gdansk, Poland, and then take a bus or (summer only) train.

Boat

Trans-Exim (www.transexim.ru) runs twice-weekly car ferries between Baltiysk and Ust-Luga, 150km west of St Petersburg.

Bus

There are two bus stations. The handiest is the **Yuzhny bus station** (ul Zheleznodorozhnaya 7) next to Yuzhny vokzal, which serves all domestic locations plus many international cities, including all buses to Gdansk and **Ecolines** (☎656 501; www.ecolines.net) buses to Warsaw and several German cities. **Zelenogradsk Trans** (☎656 501; http://atp-zt.ru) runs twice-daily buses departing at 6am and 3pm from Kaliningrad, and 6am and 5pm from Gdansk. Ecolines runs an additional trip on Thursday and Saturday.

Lots of buses depart for Svetlogorsk and Zelenogradsk from here, but it's more convenient to take a bus from the **bus stop** next to the Severny

---

TRAINS ON MOSCOW TIME

It's important to note that all long-distance trains from Kaliningrad run on Moscow time, so if a train is scheduled to depart at 10am it will leave at 9am Kaliningrad time. *Prigorodny* (suburban) trains run on local time.

TRANSPORT FROM KALININGRAD

Bus

DESTINATION	PRICE (R)	DURATION (HR)	FREQUENCY
Gdańsk (Poland)	500	2	daily
Klaipéda (Lithuania)	445	4	2 daily
Riga (Latvia)	950	9	2 daily
Vilnius (Lithuania)	920	6	daily
Warsaw (Poland)	750	9	daily

Train

DESTINATION	PRICE (R)	DURATION (HR)	FREQUENCY
Berlin (Germany)	4400	14	daily Jun-Sep
Gdańsk (Poland)	1000	6	daily Jun-Sep
Moscow	3000	23	3 daily
St Petersburg	2800	26	daily
Vilnius (Lithuania)	1650	6	4 daily

vokzal (north train station) on Sovetsky pr. They run about every 15 minutes until about 8pm (R55, one hour for Svetlogorsk; R50, 45 minutes for Zelenogradsk).

Additional international buses depart from the **international bus station** (Moskovsky pr 184).

Train

Kaliningrad's two stations are Severny vokzal and the larger Yuzhny vokzal (south station). All long-distance and many local trains go from Yuzhny vokzal, passing through but not always stopping at Severny vokzal.

Note that Moscow and St Petersburg trains go through Belarus so you'll need a Belarusian transit visa.

Local *prigorodny* (suburban) trains depart from the Prigorodny vokzal (next to the Yuzhny vokzal):

Svetlogorsk via Pereslavskoe (R60, one hour, 11 daily)

Zelenogradsk (R48, 45 minutes, seven daily)

❶ Getting Around

Bus 144 from the airport to/from the Yuzhny bus station runs on a schedule. There are 12 daily, the last one leaving the airport at 9.20pm (R30, 50 minutes).

A taxi from the airport to the centre is R400 if booked at the airport taxi booth. From the centre to the airport (R300), book through **Taxi Kaliningrad** (☑058, 585 858; www.taxi-kaliningrad.ru).

Trams, trolleybuses (both R10), buses (R12) and *marshrutky* (R15) will get you most places. Buy tickets on board. The useful 3, 5 and 9 buses travel the length of pr Leninsky and pr Mira from the Yuzhny vokzal area.

Car rental is available from **City-Rent** (☑509 191; www.city-rent39.ru; Moskovsky pr 182a), which also has a branch at the airport. Rates start at R1200 per day.

Svetlogorsk Светлогорск

☑40153 / POP 11,000

This sleepy beach town with some impressive Prussian-era half-timbered mansions makes an easy day trip from Kaliningrad. You can bag rays on the long, narrow beach or stroll along the promenade that separates the beach from the steep, sandy slopes that lead up to the town. Other favourite pastimes include amber shopping along the main drag (ul Lenina) and enjoying a lazy lunch with a view at one of several beachside eateries. Pick up a town map at any kiosk or the German-speaking **Tourist Information Centre** (☑22098; http://svetlogorsk-tourism.ru; ul Karl Marksa 7a; ☺10am-7pm).

◉ Sights

Walk around and check out the gallant wooden houses in the tranquil residential neighbourhood east of the town centre. After

WWII, the Soviets confiscated these houses from their original owners and many became dachas for elite apparatchiks.

Ul Oktyabrskaya
NEIGHBOURHOOD

This street is lined with handsome buildings, including the striking 25m-high water tower built in Jugendstil (art nouveau) style; take a peep inside the sanatorium beneath to see the colourful wall murals. Nearby, at the attractive half-timbered **Organ Hall** (Organniy Zal; organ-makarov.narod.ru; ul Kurortnaya 3; tickets R300), concerts are held throughout the week.

Promenade
PROMENADE

Steps or a rickety lift lead down to the seafront. Here you'll find Herman Brachert's *Nymph* statue in a mosaic-decorated shell, and at the eastern end is an impressive sundial, decorated with an eye-catching mosaic of the zodiac.

🛏 Sleeping

While Russians flock to Svetlogorsk's comfy hotels and renovated sanatoriums, few Western tourists stay for the night.

Lumiere Art Hotel
BOUTIQUE HOTEL €€€

(☎507 750; www.hotellumier.ru; per Lermontovsky 2a; d incl breakfast from R3700; ❀🛜) This playful boutique is Svetlogorsk's clear top choice. With the movies as the hotel's theme, the designer clearly had a lot of fun here. Even the standard rooms are stylish and come with cable TV and DVD players.

Stary Doktor
PENSION €

(☎21362; www.alterdoctor.ru; ul Gagarina 12; r incl breakfast from R2300; ⊜🍽🛜) In an old German home, this pension offers simple and cosy rooms.

🍴 Eating

If sitting in the sun munching on *shashlyk* (R200), drinking *pivo* (beer; R75) and listening to cheesy Russian pop doesn't make you happy, you're in the wrong country. You'll find open-air *shashlyk* stands all over during high season, particularly on the seafront promenade near the base of the lift.

Korvet
PIZZERIA, CAFE €€

(ul Oktyabrskaya 36; mains R200-400, pizzas R300-500) This pizzeria and cafe based in the 1901 Kurhaus is a lovely place for a meal. Lounge on comfy sofas; there are rugs to keep you warm if it gets too chilly.

❶ Getting There & Around

The frequent *marshrutky* from Kaliningrad let you off in the centre of town at the train station on ul Lenina. Buses terminate further out at the Svetlogorsk II train station.Trains to/from Kaliningrad are frequent; those that go via Pereslavskoe (R60, one hour, 11 daily) are much faster; others go via Zelenogradsk (two daily, 1½ hours). About four daily buses go to/from Zelenogrask (R55, 45 minutes).

Svetlogorsk is easy to navigate on foot or by bicycle; rent one from the stall along ul Oktyabrskaya for R100 per hour.

Kurshskaya Kosa National Park Куршская Коса

☑40150

The 98km-long Kurshskaya Kosa (Curonian Spit) is a remote and dramatic landscape with high sand dunes, pine forests, an exposed western coast and a calm lagoon that is shared by Russia and Lithuania. A Unesco World Heritage site, it's a paradise for elk, birds and travellers who like to get way off the beaten track. The 50km Russian half of the spit is protected within the **Kurshskaya Kosa National Park** (Park office in Rybachy; admission per person/car R30/250).

The spit has three tranquil fishing and holiday villages. From south to north they are: **Lesnoy**, **Rybachy** (the largest, with a population of 1200) and **Morskoe**, which has spectacular views of the dunes from raised platforms at nearby **Vistota Efa** (km42 mark).

A pretty smooth road runs the length of the spit, and you can access the unbroken beach at various points along the road via marked trails (do not stray from these).

To learn more about the park, drop by the **museum** (km14 Rybachy; admission R50; ⊙9am-5pm), where you can also see some deer and cute woodcarvings by a local artist.

A bit further down the road (km23) is the **Fringilla Field Station** (23km mark), a bird-ringing centre in operation since 1957, where enormous funnelled nets can trap an average of 1000 birds a day. In the peak season (spring), the avarian cacophony can reach epic heights. You can view the station from a platform near the road.

❶ Getting There & Around

Independent travellers should consider renting a bicycle. You'll save money, plus hear the wind and the birds better. The spit is pancake flat, but you'll want to be reasonably fit as it's a lengthy trip and headwinds can be vicious. You can rent a bike at various points on the spit itself or at **Rybak Sport** (ul Turgeneva 2a; per day R300; ⊙8am-6pm), less than a minute's walk from the train station in Zelenogradsk. You can overnight in one of the towns, which have plenty of reasonably priced hotels and rooms for rent – the regional tourism office (p785) in Kaliningrad has hotel info.

Your other options are a private tour or taxi from Kaliningrad (expensive), a taxi from Zelenogradsk (only slightly cheaper) or a public bus (cheap but sporadic). Four daily buses (two in winter) from Kaliningrad go via Zelenogradsk and terminate in Morskoe. Two others shuttle between Zelenogradsk and Morskoe (50 minutes).

UNDERSTAND RUSSIA

Russia Today

With no credible opponent, Putin rolled to victory in the March 2012 presidential elections, reclaiming the position after a four-year hiatus from his ally and predecessor, Dmitry Medvedev. Of course, during that hiatus Putin had served as Russia's prime minister and – many claimed – de facto leader. It all adds up to almost 15 years with Putin in charge or nominally in charge. And despite unprecedented opposition during the 2012 campaign, Putin remains genuinely popular among average Russians, who seem to prefer strong-armed, no-nonsense leaders in his mould.

He presides over a country that is on a roll both in terms of its economy and international standing. The country is preparing to host first the Winter Olympics in Sochi in 2014 and then, four years later, the soccer World Cup. While corruption remains a major problem (Transparency International says Russia is the world's most corrupt major economy), oil and gas revenues continue to generate great wealth. Economic growth is steady at 4% and Moscow is awash with billionaires. Just strolling any major Russian metropolis, it's impossible not to notice how much more affluent Russians look compared to a decade ago.

History

Russia's origins are rooted in countries it nowadays likes to think of as its satellites; it effectively sprang forth from Ukraine and Belarus in the Dark Ages, and took its alphabet from Bulgaria, from where Christianity also spread. The birth of the Russian state is usually identified with the founding of Novgorod in AD 862, although from the early 13th century until 1480 Russia was effectively a colony of the Mongols.

Ivan the Terrible

Russia's medieval period was a dark and brutal time, never more so than during the reign of Ivan the Terrible (r 1547–84), whose sobriquet was well earned through his fantastically cruel punishments such as boiling his enemies alive. He also killed his son and heir in a fit of rage and is said to have blinded the architects who built St Basil's Cathedral on Red Sq.

Despite Ivan the Terrible's conquest of the Volga basin and obsession with reaching the Baltic (at that time controlled by the Lithuanians and Swedes), it was not until the Romanov dynasty (1613–1917) that Russia began its massive territorial expansion. Between the 17th and 19th centuries, Siberia, the Far East, Central Asia and the Caucasus fell under Russia's sway, creating the huge country it is today.

Peter, Catherine & Later Tsars

Peter the Great (r 1689–1725) began to modernise Russia by setting up a navy and educational centres and beginning the construction of St Petersburg in 1703. Russia's capital moved north to St Petersburg from 1712, and remained there until the Bolsheviks moved it back more than two centuries later.

Catherine the Great (r 1762–96) continued Peter's legacy, in the process making Russia a world power by the mid-18th century. Feverish capitalist development in the 19th century was undermined by successively autocratic and backward-looking tsars. Alexander I (r 1801–25) was preoccupied with Napoleon, who invaded Russia and got as far as Moscow in 1812, but was eventually beaten by the Russian winter. Alexander II (r 1855–81) took the brave step of freeing the serfs in 1861, but baulked at political reform, thus sowing the seeds of a revolutionary movement.

The Bolsheviks & the USSR

Nicholas II, Russia's last tsar, ascended the throne in 1894. It was his refusal to countenance serious reform that precipitated the 1917 Revolution. What began as a liberal revolution was hijacked later the same year in a coup led by the Bolsheviks under

Vladimir Ulyanov, aka Lenin, which resulted in the establishment of the world's first communist state.

By the time Lenin died in 1924, Russia had become the principal member of the Union of Soviet Socialist Republics (USSR), a communist superpower absorbing some 14 neighbouring states between 1922 and 1945. Lenin's successor Josef Stalin, with single-minded brutality, forced the industrialisation of the country. Millions were killed or imprisoned under his watch. Stalin also saw Russia through the devastation of WWII, and by the time he died in 1953 the USSR had a full nuclear arsenal and half of Europe as satellite states.

The Collapse of Communism

Nikita Khrushchev (r 1957–64) began a cautious reform program and denounced Stalin before being removed and replaced by Leonid Brezhnev, whose rule (1964–82) was marked by economic stagnation and growing internal dissent. Mikhail Gorbachev's period of reform, known as perestroika, began in 1985, but it was too late to save the Soviet Union. Within six years the USSR had collapsed alongside communism, and reformer Boris Yeltsin was elected Russia's first-ever president in 1991.

Yeltsin led Russia into the roller-coaster world of cut-throat capitalism, which saw the creation of a new superclass of oligarchs – business people who made billions from buying once state-owned commodities and running them as private companies – while prices soared and the ruble crashed, wiping out the meagre savings of the vast majority of the population.

On New Year's Eve 1999, with his health on the wane, Yeltsin resigned, stepping aside for Vladimir Putin, a steely-faced ex-KGB officer who was prime minister at the time. Elected president the following year, Putin had a policy of steering a careful course between reform and centralisation that made him highly popular. Russia began to recover the confidence it had lost during the Yeltsin years, and the economy boomed off the back of oil and gas exports. However, Putin's tightening of control over the media and political opponents signalled his ruthless side, as did his ordering a brutal clampdown on the independence movement in Chechnya following terrorist attacks in the capital and elsewhere in 2002 and 2004.

People

There's some truth to the local saying 'scratch a Russian and you'll find a Tatar'. Over the centuries Russia has absorbed people from a huge number of nationalities, including the Mongols, the Tatars, Siberian peoples, Ukrainians, Jews and Caucasians. This means that while the vast majority of people you meet will describe themselves as Russian, ethnic homogeneity is not always that simple.

Russians have a reputation for being dour, depressed and unfriendly. In fact, most Russians are anything but, yet find constant smiling indicative of idiocy, and ridicule pointless displays of happiness commonly seen in Western culture. Even though Russians can appear to be unfriendly and even downright rude when you first meet them (especially those working behind glass windows of any kind),

RUSSIA PEOPLE

THE TRADITIONS OF THE BANYA

For centuries Russians have made it an important part of their week to visit a *banya* (hot bath), the focus of which is the *parilka* (steam room). Here, rocks are heated by a furnace, with water poured onto them using a long-handled ladle. Often, a few drops of eucalyptus or pine oils (sometimes even beer) are added to the water, creating a scent in the burst of scalding steam that's released into the room; people are naked in the *banya* but some wear *chapkas* (felt caps) to protect their hair from the effects of the heat, and *tapki* (sandals) to protect their feet.

As they sweat it out, some bathers grab hold of a *venik* (a tied bundle of birch branches) and beat themselves or each other with it. Though it can be painful, the effect can also be pleasant and cleansing: apparently, the birch leaves and their secretions help rid the skin of toxins. After the birch-branch thrashing, bathers run outside and, depending on their nerve, plunge into the *basseyn* (ice-cold pool) or take a cooling shower. The whole process is then repeated several times for anything up to two hours.

To take part, try the *bani* in Moscow or St Petersburg.

their warmth is quite astounding as soon as the ice is broken. Just keep working at it.

The vast majority of Russians identify themselves as Orthodox Christians (although the proportion of those who actually practise their faith is small). The church has become ever more vocal in recent years, virulently condemning homosexuality, contraception and abortion – even after the 2008 death of nationalistic-leaning Patriarch Alexy II. His successor, Kiril I, was at the forefront of the notorious Pussy Riot arrests in 2012. Kiril described the female punk rockers as 'doing the work of Satan'.

Arts

Literature

Russia's formal literary tradition sprung to life with the poetic genius of Alexander Pushkin (1799–1837), whose *Yevgeny Onegin* stands out as one of Russian literature's greatest achievements. Duels cut short the lives of both Pushkin and his literary heir, Mikhail Lermontov, who had the potential to equal or even surpass Pushkin's contribution – his novel *A Hero of Our Time* and his poetry spoke of incredible gifts.

By the late 19th century Leo Tolstoy and Fyodor Dostoyevsky were producing some of the world's great classics – the former penning epic tapestries of Russian life, the latter writing dark and troubled philosophical novels.

The early 20th century saw a continued literary flowering. From what was widely known as the Silver Age came the poetic talents of Alexander Blok, Anna Akhmatova and Osip Mandelstam. By the late 1920s, with Stalin's grip on power complete, all writers not spouting the party line were vilified. Dissenting writers were either shot, took their own lives, fled or were silenced as Stalin revealed his socialist-realist model of writing, which brought novels with titles such as *Cement* and *How the Steel was Tempered* to the toiling masses. Despite this, many writers wrote in secret, and novels such as Mikhail Bulgakov's *The Master and Margarita* and poems such as Akhmatova's 'Requiem' survived Stalinism to become classics.

Despite Khrushchev allowing some literary freedom (it was under his watch that Solzhenitsyn's *A Day in the Life of Ivan Denisovich*, a novella depicting life in one of Stalin's Gulag camps, was published), censorship continued until the mid-1980s when, thanks to Mikhail Gorbachev's policy of glasnost (openness), writers who had only been published through the illegal network of *samizdat* (the home printing presses), and were thus read only by the intelligentsia, suddenly had millions of readers.

Since the demise of the Soviet Union, Russian literature has bloomed and embraced the postmodernism that was prohibited by the Soviet authorities. Current literary big hitters, all of whose books have been trans-

---

RUSSIAN CINEMA

Russia has produced some of the world's most famous cinematic images – largely thanks to the father of the cinematic montage, Sergei Eisenstein, whose *Battleship Potemkin* (1925) and *Ivan the Terrible* (1944–46) are reference points for anyone serious about the history of film. Despite constant headaches with authority, Andrei Tarkovsky produced complex and iconoclastic films in the 1960s and 1970s; *The Mirror* and *Andrei Rublev* are generally considered to be his two greatest works.

In recent times Nikita Mikhalkov and Alexander Sokurov have established themselves as internationally renowned Russian directors. Mikhalkov's *Burnt by the Sun* won the Oscar for best foreign film in 1994; however, the first part of his follow-up *Burnt by the Sun 2: Exodus* – a $55 million production reputed to be Russia's most expensive movie since Soviet times – was a flop in cinemas in 2010.

Alexander Sokurov has made his name producing art-house historical dramas, including *Taurus*, *Molokh* and 2002's astonishing *Russian Ark* – the only full-length film ever made using one long tracking shot. The glossy vampire thriller *Night Watch* (2004), by Kazakhstan-born director Timur Bekmambetov, struck box-office gold both at home and abroad, leading to an equally successful sequel, *Day Watch* (2006), and to Bekmambetov being lured to Hollywood. He also directed a 2007 follow-up to the classic Soviet romantic comedy *Irony of Fate* (1975), one of Russia's all-time favourite movies.

lated into English, include mystery writer Boris Akunin; surrealist Viktor Pelevin; Tatyana Tolstaya, author of the symbolic sci-fi novel *The Slynx*; and Viktor Yerofeev.

Music

Mikhail Glinka, composer of the operas *A Life for the Tsar* (1836) and *Ruslan and Lyudmilla* (1842), is considered the father of Russian classical music. He was born in Smolensk, where an annual festival is held in his celebration.

Composers like Nikolai Rimsky-Korsakov and Modest Mussorgsky looked to Russia's folk past for inspiration, as did Igor Stravinsky, whose *The Rite of Spring* and *The Firebird* were both influenced by Russian folk music. Other composers such as Pyotr Tchaikovsky, Sergei Prokofiev and Sergei Rachmaninov embraced the romantic movements of Western classical music.

The ideological beliefs of Dmitry Shostakovich, who occasionally wrote brooding, bizarrely dissonant works, led to him being alternately praised and condemned by the Soviet government. Shostakovich's Symphony no 7 – the *Leningrad* – brought him honour and international standing when it was performed by the Leningrad Philharmonic during the Siege of Leningrad.

Progressive new music surfaced only slowly in the post-Stalin era. Symphony no 1 by Alfred Schnittke, probably the most important work of this major experimental modern Russian composer, had to be premiered by its champion, conductor Gennady Rozhdestvensky, in the city of Gorky (now Nizhny Novgorod) in 1974 and was not played in Moscow until 1986.

Visual Arts

Internationally, the best-known Russian artists are the avant-garde painters of the early 20th century, such as Natalia Goncharova, Vasily Kandinsky and Mikhail Larionov, who were at the centre of the Cézanne-influenced Jack of Diamonds group, and Kazimir Malevich, the founder of Suprematism, which employed abstract geometrical shapes.

However, most Russians will quite rightly point you towards the 'greats' of the 19th century, such as Ilya Repin and the *peredvizhniki* (wanderers) – the generation of painters who rejected the strict formalism of the St Petersburg Academy and painted realistic rural scenes with deep social messages.

RUSSIAN POP

Pretty-boy singer Dima Bilan, winner of 2008's Eurovision Song Contest, is the tame international face of Russia's contemporary music scene. More interesting music can be heard from groups Leningrad, Markscheider Kunst, Mumiy Troll and Deti Picasso, and the jazz-rock singer Zemfira. Legendary classic rockers Akvarium, DDT and Kino, whose revered lead singer Viktor Tsoi died in a 1990 car crash, are well worth listenting to.

Russia's contemporary art scene is beginning to flourish under the patronage of the country's wealthy elite. Artists worth looking out for include cheeky Siberian artists' collective Blue Noses, and the more luxurious works of Moscow-based quartet AES+F, as well as established talents such as Ilya Kabakov and Alexander Kosolapov.

Theatre & Ballet

Since Chekhov revolutionised Russian drama in the late 19th century, Russia has seen countless innovations, from Constantin Stanislavsky, who created method acting, to Vsevolod Meyerhold, the theatrical pioneer whom Stalin had arrested and murdered. Ballet in Russia evolved as an offshoot of French dance combined with Russian folk and peasant dance techniques. It stunned Western Europeans when it was first taken on tour during the late 19th century. Moscow's Bolshoi Theatre and St Petersburg's Mariinsky have worked hard to reinvent themselves since the end of the Soviet Union, and their productions regularly tour the world.

Environment

The disastrous environmental legacy of communism is enormous. As well as both Moscow and St Petersburg being polluted from traffic and heavy industry, the countryside is frequently blighted by crumbling and abandoned factories and other industrial plants. Environmental consciousness remains relatively low, although things are slowly changing with the emergence of a small but vocal Russian environmental movement.

For more details on the environmental problems being faced by Russia in the oil and gas and other sectors, see the sites of **Greenpeace Russia** (www.greenpeace.org/russia/en), Norway-based NGO **Bellona** (www.bellona.org) and **World Wide Fund for Nature in Russia** (www.wwf.ru/eng).

Food & Drink

Russian food, while very good, can be bland: spices are not widely used and dill is overwhelmingly the herb of choice. That said, you can eat extremely well in Russia – Caucasian food is popular throughout the country and is delicious. Moscow and St Petersburg overflow with restaurants serving cuisine from all over the world, as well as top-notch renditions of national dishes.

Staples & Specialities

Russian soups are excellent. Delicious borsch (beetroot soup), *solyanka* (a soup made from pickled vegetables) and *ukha* (fish soup) are always reliable. *Pelmeni* are Russian ravioli – meat or fish parcels wrapped in dough and served with *smetana* (sour cream) – and are available everywhere. Other, more interesting possibilities are *zharkoye* (literally 'hot' – meat stew in a pot), bliny, caviar, beef stroganoff, *goluptsy* (minced meat wrapped in cabbage leaves) and fish specialities, such as sturgeon, salmon and pikeperch.

Vegetarians & Vegans

Russia can be tough for vegetarians, and near impossible for vegans. Vegetarian possibilities include bliny with sour cream, mushrooms, cheese or savoury *tvorog* (whey), and mushroom julienne (mushrooms fried in garlic, cheese and cream). Note that Georgian restaurants generally contain a much wider selection of vegetarian dishes on their menus than the Russian menus.

Drinking Etiquette

Given its importance in Russian culture, it's drinking that is full of unspoken rules. First of all, never drink vodka without *zakuski* (snacks) – you'll get drunk otherwise, whereas (according to any Russian) that will *never* happen if you consume pickled herring or gherkins with your vodka. Once a bottle (vodka or otherwise) has been finished, it's considered rude to put it back on the table – always put it on the floor instead. Don't talk during toasts, and always appear to drink to the toast (even if you dribble it down your chin or drink nothing at all). Men should always down a vodka shot in one. Women are excused from this requirement, although being able to down a large shot will garner respect from all quarters.

SURVIVAL GUIDE

Directory A–Z
Accommodation

There has been a boom in budget-friendly hostels in both Moscow and St Petersburg, and if you're on a budget you'll want to consider these – even if you typically don't 'do' hostels. There are some very quiet and cosy hostels to choose from, and most offer a few private rooms; these book out fast in the summer so book them ahead if possible.

One question you'll have concerns registration. While most hotels register you automatically for free, hostels usually charge for it. Moreover, not all hostels insist on registering you.

Study the registration rules carefully – if you've already been registered, you may want to choose a hostel that does not insist on registering you again for a fee. Here is what to expect:

» In Moscow, the vast majority of hostels we surveyed will not register you unless you request it. If you want it, it costs R500 to R900. Others require you to register; it's required, it's free or less than R200.

» In St Petersburg, most hostels require you to register for R200 to R500; where it's not required, you must request it and it costs more than R500.

In hostels you're looking at R500 to R1000 for a dorm bed, and R2000 to R2600 for a private room with a shared bathroom. Elsewhere hotel rooms with a bathroom start at about R3300. At the other end of the spectrum the sky is the limit, but figure on at least R12,000 for top-end accommodation in Moscow and St Petersburg (quite a bit less elsewhere).

The following price categories for the cost of a double room are used in this chapter:

€ less than R1500 (R3000 in Moscow and St Petersburg)

€€ R1500 to R4000 (R3000 to R8000 in Moscow and St Petersburg)

€€€ more than R4000 (R8000 in Moscow and St Petersburg)

Business Hours

Restaurants and bars often stay open later than their stated hours if the establishment is full. In fact, many simply say that they work *do poslednnogo klienta* (until the last customer leaves).

Note that most museums close their ticket offices one hour (in some cases 30 minutes) before the official closing time.

Banks 9am to 6pm Monday to Friday, some open 9am to 5pm Saturday

Bars & Restaurants noon to midnight

Shops 10am to 9pm Monday to Friday, to 7pm Saturday and Sunday

Embassies & Consulates

See www.russianembassy.net for a full list of Russian embassies overseas.

Australian Embassy (☑495-956 6070; www.russia.embassy.gov.au; Podkolokolny per 10a/2, Moscow; ⓂKitay Gorod)

Australian Consulate (☑812-325 7334; Petrovsky pr 14, St Petersburg; ⓂNevsky pr)

Belarusian Embassy Kaliningrad (☑4012-214 412; ul Dm Donskogo 35a); St Petersburg (☑812-274 7212; ul Bonch-Bruevicha 3a; ⓂChernyshevskaya)

Belarusian Consulate (☑495-924 7031; www.embassybel.ru; Maroseyka ul 17/6, 101000, Moscow; ⓂKitay Gorod)

Canadian Embassy (☑495-925 6000; www.canadainternational.gc.ca/russia-russie/index.aspx; Starokonyushenny per 23, Moscow; ⓂKropotkinskaya)

French Embassy Moscow (☑495-937 1500; www.ambafrance-ru.org; ul Bolshaya Yakimanka 45; ⓂOktyabrskaya); St Petersburg (☑812-332 2270; nab reki Moyki 15; ⓂNevsky Pr)

German Embassy Kaliningrad (☑4012-920 230; www.kaliningrad.diplo.de; ul Leningradskaya 4); Moscow (☑495-937 9500; www.germania.diplo.de; Mosfilmovskaya ul 56; ⓂUniversitet, then bus 119); St Petersburg (☑812-320 2400; Furshtatskaya ul 39; ⓂChernyshevskaya)

Latvian Embassy Kaliningrad (☑4112-706 755; Englesa ul 52a); Moscow (☑495-232 9760; www.am.gov.lv/en/moscow; ul Chapligina 3; ⓂChistye Prudy)

Lithuanian Embassy Kaliningrad (☑4012-957 688; Proletarskaya ul 133); Moscow (☑495-785 8605; www.ru.mfa.lt; Borisoglebsky per 10; ⓂArbatskaya); St Petersburg (☑812-327 0230; ul Ryleyeva 37; ⓂChernyshevskaya)

Netherlands Embassy (☑495-797 2900; www.netherlands-embassy.ru; Kalashny per 6, Moscow; ⓂArbatskaya)

New Zealand Embassy (☑495-956 3579; www.nzembassy.com; Povarskaya ul 44, Moscow; ⓂArbatskaya)

Polish Embassy Kaliningrad (☑4012-976 44; www.kaliningradkg.polemb.net; Kashtanovaya Alleya 51); Moscow (☑495-231 1500; www.moskwa.polemb.net; Klimashkina ul 4; ⓂBelorusskaya)

UK Embassy Moscow (☑495-956 7200; www.ukinrussia.fco.gov.uk/en; Smolenskaya nab 10; ⓂSmolenskaya); St Petersburg (☑812-320 3200; pl Proletarskoy Diktatury 5; ⓂChernyshevskaya)

Ukrainian Embassy (☑495-629 9742; www.mfa.gov.ua; Leontevsky per 18, Moscow; ⓂPushkinskaya)

Ukrainian Consulate (☑812-331 5166; http://spb.mfa.gov.ua; ul Bonch-Bruevicha 1B, St Petersburg)

US Embassy Moscow (☑495-728 5000; www.moscow.usembassy.gov; Bol Devyatinsky per 8; ⓂBarrikadnaya); St Petersburg (☑812-331 2600; ul Furshtatskaya 15; ⓂChernyshevskaya)

Food

The following price categories for the cost of a main course are used in the listings in this chapter:

APARTMENT RENTAL

Booking an apartment is a good way to save money on accommodation, especially for small groups. They typically cost €100 to €200. The following have apartments in Moscow and/or St Petersburg. All travel agencies listed in both cities also arrange apartments.

City Realty (www.cityrealtyrussia.com)

Cheap Moscow (www.cheap-moscow.com)

HOFA (www.hofa.ru)

Moscow City Excursions Bureau (www.moscowapartments.net)

Ostwest (www.ostwest.com)

€ less than R500

€€ R500 to R1000

€€€ more than R1000

Gay & Lesbian Travellers

Homosexuality was legalised in Russia in the early 1990s but remains a divisive issue throughout the country. In general this is a conservative country and being gay is frowned upon. That said, there are active and relatively open gay and lesbian scenes in both Moscow and St Petersburg, although you shouldn't expect anything nearly as prominent as you might find in other major world centres. Away from these two major cities, the gay scene tends to be underground.

For a good overview, visit http://english. gay.ru, which has up-to-date information, good links and a resource for putting you in touch with personal guides for Moscow and St Petersburg. They're also involved in publishing the gay magazine *Kvir*. St Petersburg's **Krilija** (Wings; www.krilija.sp.ru) is Russia's oldest officially registered gay and lesbian community organisation.

Money

The Russian currency is the ruble, written as 'рубль' and abbreviated as 'руб' or 'р'. Rubles are divided into 100 almost worthless *kopeki* (kopecks). Coins come in amounts of R1, R2, R5 and R10 rubles, with banknotes in values of R10, R50, R100, R500, R1000 and R5000.

ATMs that accept all major credit and debit cards are everywhere, and most restaurants, shops and hotels in major cities gladly accept plastic. You can exchange dollars and euros (and some other currencies) at most banks; when they're closed, try the exchange counters at top-end hotels. You may need your passport. Note that crumpled or old banknotes are often refused. Many banks cash travellers cheques for a small commission.

Post

The Russian post service, Pochta Rossii, gets an unfair rap. Postcards, letters and parcels sent abroad usually arrive within a couple of weeks, but there are occasional lapses. To send a postcard or letter up to 20g anywhere in the world by air costs R25.

Public Holidays

Many businesses are closed from 1 to 7 January. Russia's main public holidays:

New Year's Day 1 January

Russian Orthodox Christmas Day 7 January

Defender of the Fatherland Day 23 February

International Women's Day 8 March

Easter Monday April

International Labour Day/Spring Festival 1 May

Victory Day 9 May

Russian Independence Day 12 June

Unity Day 4 November

Safe Travel

Travellers have nothing to fear from Russia's 'mafia' – the increasingly respectable gangster classes are not interested in such small fry. However, petty theft and pickpockets are prevalent in both Moscow and St Petersburg, so be vigilant with your belongings.

Some police officers can be bothersome, especially to dark-skinned or foreign-looking people. Other members of the police force target tourists, though reports of tourists being hassled about their documents and registration have declined. Still, you should always carry a photocopy of your passport, visa and registration stamp. If you are stopped for any reason – legitimate or illegitimate – you will surely be hassled if you don't have these.

Sadly, racism is a problem in Russia. Be vigilant on the streets around Hitler's birthday (20 April), when bands of right-wing thugs have been known to roam around spoiling for a fight with anyone who doesn't look Russian.

Telephone

The international code for Russia is ☏7. The international access code from landline phones in Russia is ☏8, followed by ☏10 after the second tone, followed by the country code.

The three main mobile-phone companies, all with prepaid and 4G internet options, are **Beeline** (www.beeline.ru), **Megafon** (www.megafon.ru) and **MTS** (www.mts.ru). Company offices are everywhere. It costs almost nothing to purchase a SIM card, but bring your passport.

In a quirk, mobile calls or texts from your 'home' city or region to another city or region are more expensive – essentially long-distance calls/texts. So active callers should consider purchasing a Moscow SIM card while in Moscow, and a St Petersburg SIM card while in St Petersburg.

To dial another area code (mobile or land line), dial ☑8 + 10 digits. Mobile numbers have 10 digits, always starting with ☑9 – often ☑915, ☑916 or ☑926. In this chapter, mobile numbers are written in the following format: ☑8-9xx-xxx xxxx.

Travellers with Disabilities

Travellers using wheelchairs aren't well catered for in Russia; there's a lack of access ramps and lifts. However, attitudes are becoming enlightened and things are slowly changing. Major museums, such as the Hermitage and the Russian Museum, offer good disabled access.

Visas

Everyone needs a visa to visit Russia. There are several types of visa, but most travellers will apply for a tourist visa, valid for 30 days from the date of entry. New visa rules for Americans (effective September 2012) mean that US citizens can now obtain three-year multiple-entry tourist visas.

Applying for a visa process is undeniably a headache, but the process is actually quite straightforward once you understand it. There are three stages: invitation, application and registration.

INVITATION

This is the easy part. Any travel agency, hostel or hotel will be only too happy to issue you a letter of invitation (LOI) for a fee – or free in the case of some hotels, provided you are staying with them; use any Russia-based hotel or travel agent listed in this chapter. Costs typically range from €20 to €35 for a tourist visa depending on whether you require a single- or double-entry type and how quickly you need the invitation, and €45 to €270 for the various types of business visas.

Under the new visa rules, US citizens no longer need an LOI, but they still need a 'sponsor'. Check with a travel agency on how this new rule is playing out on the ground.

APPLICATION

Invitation in hand, you can then apply for a visa. We highly recommended applying for your visa in your home country (or country of residence) rather than on the road. Indeed, the rule is that you're *supposed* to do this, although some embassies and consu-

lates are more flexible than others; it might be enough to have a business visa in the country where you apply.

If you can't go into the embassy in person, you'll have to send your passport to a visa-fixing agency in your home country. Even if you *can* get to your embassy, it's much easier to use a fixer. Fixers can usually handle LOIs too.

You'll pay three fees to a fixer: the visa-processing fee (anything from €35 to €350, depending on the type of visa applied for and how quickly you need it); the fixer's fee of €40 or so (again dependent on the type of visa applied for); and, if necessary, return postage to send your passport to the fixer.

If you are doing it on your own, you obviously just pay the visa-processing fee. Note that different Russian embassies charge different fees and have slightly different application rules. Avoid potential hassles by checking well in advance what these rules might be.

The website www.russianvisa.net has a list of fixers working in various countries. The www.waytorussia.com website also has information on fixers and on the entire visa process.

Reliable fixers:

For Australia (http://visalink.com.au)

For the UK (www.realrussia.co.uk, www.travel-direct.com)

For the US (www.gotorussia.com, www.travelvisapro.com)

REGISTRATION

Every visitor to Russia must have their visa registered within seven days of arrival, excluding weekends and public holidays. Registration is handled by your accommodat-

IMMIGRATION FORM

On arrival in Russia, you should fill out an immigration card – a long white form issued by passport control; often these are given out in advance on your flight. You surrender one half of the form immediately to the passport control, while the other you keep for the duration of your stay and give up only on leaving Russia. Take good care of this as you'll need it for registration and could face problems while travelling in Russia – and certainly will on leaving – if you cannot produce it.

ing party. If staying in a homestay or rental apartment, you'll either need to make arrangements with the landlord or a friend to register you through the post office. See http://waytorussia.net/RussianVisa/Registration.html for how this can be done.

Once registered, you'll receive a registration slip. Keep this safe – that's the document that any police who stop you will ask to see. Technically you do not need to register more than once unless you stay in additional cities for more than seven days, in which case you'll need additional registration slips.

Most hotels and some hostels will insist on registering you even if you've already been registered. There's no harm in having multiple registration slips.

72-HOUR VISA-FREE TRAVEL

If you take the St Peter Line ferry from Helsinki to St Petersburg it's possible to visit Russia without a visa as long as you stay less than 72 hours.

Citizens of Schengen countries, the UK, Switzerland and Japan can enter Kaliningrad with an on-demand 72-hour tourist visa. These need to be arranged via local tourist agencies (p785).

Women Travellers

The most common problem faced by foreign women in Russia is sexual harassment. It's not unusual to be propositioned in public, especially if you are walking alone at night. Unpleasant as it may be, this is rarely dangerous and a simple '*kak vam ne stydno*' ('you should be ashamed of yourself') delivered in a suitably stern manner should send anyone on their way.

That said, Russian men can also be extremely chivalrous, and will open doors, give up their seats and wherever possible help out any female to a far greater degree than their Western counterparts. Russian women are also very independent, and you won't attract attention by travelling alone as a female.

Getting There & Away
Air

Most major European carriers and a few US airlines serve one of Moscow's three airports and St Petersburg's Pulkovo-2 airport. The big Russian domestic carriers also have numerous direct flights to/from Europe, North America and Asia. International flights to Kaliningrad's Khrabrovo airport are rarer – Air Baltic and Aerosvit are among the few foreign carriers that serve Kaliningrad.

Land

Adjoining 13 countries, the Russian Federation has a huge number of border crossings. From Eastern Europe you are most likely to enter from Finland near Vyborg; from Estonia at Narva; from Latvia at Rēzekne; from Belarus at Krasnoye or Ezjaryshcha; and from Ukraine at Chernihiv. You can enter Kaliningrad from Lithuania and Poland at any of seven border posts.

Sea

Ferries connect St Petersburg with Helsinki. See p777 for details.

Getting Around
Air

Flying in Russia is not for the faint-hearted. Safety aside, flights can be delayed, often for hours and with little or no explanation.

That said, booking flights within Russia online is easier than ever, and domestic flights are relatively cheap. The big domestic carriers have effective booking sites with English interfaces, or you can use an online consolidater; www.skyscanner.net and anywayanyday.com have good coverage of Russian domestic routes, or try Russia-specialist booking sites like airtickets.ru, https://sindbad.ru and pososhok.ru.

Otherwise, it's no problem buying a ticket at ubiquitous *aviakassa* (ticket offices). These do collect a small fee, which makes them a tad pricer than what you might find online.

Major domestic carriers:

Aeroflot (www.aeroflot.ru)

Rossiya (http://eng.pulkovo.ru/en)

S7 Airlines (www.s7.ru)

Sky Express (www.skyexpress.ru/en) The closest thing Russia has to a low-cost carrier.

Transaero Airlines (www.transaero.com)

UT Air (www.utair.ru)

Boat

One of the most pleasant ways of travelling around Russia is by river. The season runs from late May through to mid-October. Numerous cruise boats ply the routes between Moscow and St Petersburg, many stopping at some of the Golden Ring cities on the way. Ferries also link Kaliningrad with Ust-Luga, near St Petersburg.

Some recommended boat operators and agencies:

Infoflot (☑495-684 9188; www.infoflot.com; ul Shchepkina 28, Moscow; ⓂPr Mira) The market leader with an office in St Petersburg.

Mosturflot (☑495-221 7222; www.mosturflot.ru)

Vodohod (☑495-223 96 09; www.bestrussian-cruises.com)

Bus

Buses and *marshrutky* (fixed-route vans or minibuses) are often more frequent, more convenient and faster than trains, especially on short-distance routes. There's almost no need to reserve a seat – just arrive a good 30 minutes before the scheduled departure and buy a ticket. Prices are comparable to 3nd-class train fares.

Marshrutky are quicker than the rusty old buses and often leave when full, rather than according to a schedule. Where roads are good and villages frequent, *marshrutky* can be twice as fast as buses, and are well worth the double fare.

Car & Motorcycle

You can bring your own vehicle into Russia, but expect delays, bureaucracy and the attention of the roundly hated GAI (traffic police), who take particular delight in stopping foreign cars for document checks.

To enter Russia with a vehicle you will need a valid International Driving Permit as well as the insurance and ownership documents for your car.

As you don't really need a car to get around big cities, hiring a car comes into its own for making trips out of town where public transport may not be so good. All the major agencies have offices in Moscow and St Petersburg.

Driving is on the right-hand side, and at an intersection traffic coming from the right generally (but not always) has the right of way. The maximum legal blood-alcohol content is 0.03%, a rule that is strictly enforced.

Hitching

Hitching for free is something of an alien concept in Russia, but in the countryside and remote areas not well served by pub-

lic transport it can work. In cities, hitching rides is called hailing a taxi. You'll be expected to pay.

Train

Russia's extensive train network is efficiently run by **Russian Railways** (www.eng.rzd.ru). *Prigorodny* (suburban) or short-distance trains – also known as *elektrichky* – do not require advance booking: you can buy your ticket at the *prigorodny poezd kassa* (suburban train ticket offices) at train stations.

For long-distance trains, unless otherwise specified we quote *kupe* (2nd-class sleeper) fares. Expect 1st-class (SV) fares to be double this, and *platskartny* (3rd class) to be about 40% less. Children under five travel free if they share a berth with an adult; otherwise, children under 10 pay a reduced fare for their own berth.

Reserve at least 24 hours in advance for any long-distance journey, although bookings cannot be made any earlier than 45 days before the date of departure. Over the busy summer months and holiday periods such as New Year and early May, securing berths at short notice on certain trains can be difficult.

You'll need your passport (or a photocopy) to buy tickets. You can buy tickets for others if you bring their passports or photocopies. Queues can be very long and move with interminable slowness. At train ticket offices (*Zh/D kassa*, short for *zheleznodorozhnaya kassa*), which are all over most cities, you can pay a surcharge of around R200 and avoid the queues. Alternatively, most travel agencies will organise

UNOFFICIAL TAXIS

In St Peterburg and Moscow few people think twice about flagging down any car to request a ride. A fare is negotiated for the journey – simply state your destination and ask '*skolko?*' (how much?), and off you go. Proceed with caution if you are alone and/or it's late at night, especially if you are a woman. While exceedingly rare, violent attacks on passengers have occurred. There are plenty of official taxis that charge about the same as unofficial taxis, although they can be harder to find.

TRAVEL AGENCIES

As internal air and train tickets become easier for foreigners to book online, travel agencies are less relevant for independent travellers than they once were.

However, travel agencies are still essential for predeparture visa support, and they can also make it easier to arrange tours and transport on the ground; without Russian-language skills, it can sometimes be tricky to organise more than a simple train or plane ticket. Although many foreign travel agents specialise in travel to Russia, they charge hefty premiums for everything. You'll save money with a local travel agent; reliable ones are listed in this chapter.

the reservation and delivery of train tickets at a substantial mark-up.

TICKETS

You can book train tickets online with RZD (rzd.ru) but its interface is in Russian. Otherwise, the following sites are in English (although you'll pay a significant premium):

Bilet.ru (www.bilet.ru)

Real Russia (www.realrussia.co.uk)

Russian Rails (www.russianrails.com)

TrainsRussia.com (www.trainsrussia.com/en/travels) Authorised US agent for RZD.

RZD has two types of electronic tickets:

e-tickets These are email vouchers that you print out and exchange for paper tickets at train stations in Russia. Moscow and St Petersburg stations have dedicated exchange points.

e-registration Only available for trains where you board at the initial station of the service, these are 'paperless' tickets; you'll still be sent an email confirmation but there's no need to exchange this for a regular ticket. You show the confirmation email and your passport to the *provodnitsa* (carriage attendent) on boarding the train.

Serbia

Includes »

Best Places to Eat

» Little Bay (p808)

» Dačo (p809)

» Šaran (p813)

» Hamam (p818)

Best Places to Stay

» Hotel Moskva (p807)

» Green Studio Hostel (p807)

» Hostel Sova (p814)

» Leopold I (p814)

Why Go?

Warm, welcoming and a hell of a lot of fun – everything you never heard about Serbia (Србија) is true. Exuding a feisty mix of élan and *inat* (Serbian trait of rebellious defiance), this country doesn't do 'mild': Belgrade is one of the world's wildest party destinations, the northern town of Novi Sad hosts the rocking EXIT festival, and even its hospitality is emphatic – expect to be greeted with *rakija* and a hearty three-kiss hello.

While political correctness is about as commonplace as a nonsmoking bar, Serbia is nevertheless a cultural crucible: the art nouveau town of Subotica revels in its proximity to Hungary, bohemian Niš echoes to the clip-clop of Roma horse carts, and minaret-studded Novi Pazar nudges some of the most sacred sites in Serbian Orthodoxy. And in the mountainous Kopaonik and Zlatibor regions, ancient traditions coexist with après-ski bling. Forget what you think you know: come and say *zdravo* (hello)...or better yet, *živeli* (cheers)!

When to Go

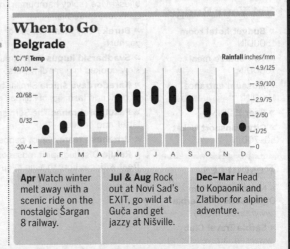

Belgrade

°C/°F Temp   Rainfall inches/mm

Apr Watch winter melt away with a scenic ride on the nostalgic Šargan 8 railway.

Jul & Aug Rock out at Novi Sad's EXIT, go wild at Guča and get jazzy at Nišville.

Dec–Mar Head to Kopaonik and Zlatibor for alpine adventure.

AT A GLANCE

» **Currency** Dinar (DIN)

» **Language** Serbian

» **Money** ATMs in all main and midsized towns

» **Visas** None for citizens of the EU, UK, Australia, New Zealand, Canada and the USA

Fast Facts

» **Area** 77,474 sq km

» **Capital** Belgrade

» **Country code** ☑381

» **Emergency** Ambulance ☑94, fire ☑93, police ☑92

Exchange Rates

Australia	A$1	91.56DIN
Canada	C$1	86.25DIN
Euro Zone	€1	112.03DIN
Japan	¥100	92.89DIN
New Zealand	NZ$1	73.38DIN
UK	UK£1	132.63DIN
USA	US$1	87.66DIN

Set Your Budget

» **Budget hotel room** 1500DIN

» **Two-course meal** 1000DIN

» **Museum entrance** 100DIN

» **Beer** 150DIN

» **City transport ticket** 50–70DIN

Resources

» **National Tourism Organisation of Serbia** (www.serbia.travel)

» **Serbia Travel Club** (www.serbiatravelers.org)

Connections

Serbia is landlocked by accessible neighbours. The northern town of Subotica is 10km from the Hungarian border, Vršac is the same distance from Romania, and Bulgaria is 45 minutes from Pirot. When things are calm on the Kosovo border, €5 and three hours get you from Novi Pazar to Priština. The Zlatibor region stretches to Bosnia and Hercegovina (BiH); travellers with wheels can take a day trip to the famous bridge on the Drina. All of Europe is accessible from Belgrade: Bucharest, Budapest, Ljubljana, Moscow, Sofia and Zagreb are a train ride away, and regular buses serve destinations including Vienna, Sarajevo and Podgorica.

ITINERARIES

One Week

Revel in three days of cultural and culinary exploration in Belgrade, allowing for at least one night of hitting the capital's legendary night spots. Carry on to Novi Sad for trips to the vineyards and monasteries of Fruška Gora and Sremski Karlovci.

Two Weeks

Follow the above itinerary then head north for the art nouveau architecture of Subotica, before slicing south to Zlatibor en route to Ottoman-influenced Novi Pazar and the lively city of Niš.

Essential Food & Drink

» **Kajmak** Along the lines of a salty clotted cream, this dairy delight is lashed on to everything from bread to burgers.

» **Ćevapčići** The ubiquitous skinless sausage and *pljeskavica* (spicy hamburger) make it very easy to be a carnivore in Serbia.

» **Burek** Flaky meat, cheese or vegetable pie eaten with yoghurt.

» **Svadbarski kupus** Sauerkraut and hunks of smoked pork slow-cooked in giant clay pots.

» **Karađorđeva šnicla** Similar to chicken Kiev, but with veal or pork and lashings of *kajmak* and tartar.

» **Pasulj prebranac** The Serbian take on baked beans, just fatter and porkier.

» **Urnebes** Creamy, spicy peppers-'n'-cheese spread.

» **Rakija** Distilled spirit most commonly made from plums. Treat with caution: this ain't your grandpa's brandy.

Serbia Highlights

① Marvel at Belgrade's mighty **Kalemegdan Citadel** (p802).

② Witness the laid-back town of **Novi Sad** (p814) as it morphs into the state of EXIT every July.

③ Ponder the exotic cultural fusions of Turkish-toned **Novi Pazar** (p819).

④ Steel your eardrums (and liver) at Guča's **Dragačevo Trumpet Assembly** (p818), one of the world's most frenetic music festivals.

⑤ Escape reality in the fantastic village of **Drvengrad** (p821), built by director Emir Kusturica for indie drama *Life is a Miracle*.

⑥ Goggle at splendid surprises bursting from the Vojvodinian plains, such as the art nouveau treasures of **Subotica** (p816).

⑦ Ski, hike or just take the mountain air in the magical villages of **Zlatibor** (p820).

BELGRADE

📋 011 / POP 1.6 MILLION

Outspoken, adventurous, proud and audacious: Belgrade (Београд) is by no means a 'pretty' capital, but its gritty exuberance makes it one of the most happening cities in Europe. While it hurtles towards a brighter future, its chaotic past unfolds before your eyes: socialist blocks are squeezed between art nouveau masterpieces, and remnants of the Habsburg legacy contrast with Ottoman relics.

It is here where the Sava River meets the Danube (Dunav), contemplative parkland nudges hectic urban sprawl, and old-world culture gives way to new-world nightlife.

Grandiose coffee houses, quirky sidewalk ice-creameries and smoky dens all find rightful place along Knez Mihailova, a lively pedestrian boulevard flanked by historical buildings all the way to the ancient Kalemegdan Citadel, crown of the city. Deeper in Belgrade's bowels are museums guarding the cultural, religious and military heritage of the country. Josip Broz Tito and other ghosts of the past have been laid to rest here.

'Belgrade' literally translates as 'White City', but Serbia's colourful capital is red hot.

History

Belgrade has been destroyed and rebuilt countless times in its 2300-year history. Celts first settled on the hill at the confluence of the Sava River and the Danube, the Romans came in the 1st century, and havoc was wreaked by Goths and Huns until the area was colonised by Slavic tribes in the 6th century.

In 1403 Hungary gave Belgrade to Despot Stefan Lazarević, making it the Serbian capital. The 1400s saw waves of Turkish attacks; it was conquered in 1521 and the city's population was shipped to İstanbul. The Karađorđević dynasty began in 1807 when Belgrade was liberated from the Turks, who finally relinquished control in 1867.

In 1914 the Austro-Hungarian empire captured Belgrade; they were soon driven out, only to return more triumphantly with German help in 1915, staying for three years. In 1918 Belgrade became the capital of Yugoslavia. The city was bombed by both Nazis and Allies during WWII.

In the 1990s Belgrade became the site of strong resistance against Slobodan Milošević. In 1999 NATO forces bombed Belgrade for three months after Milošević refused to end the repression of Albanians in Kosovo. The campaign killed dozens of Serbian civilians and destroyed not only military targets but also a hospital, residential buildings and, for still inexplicable reasons, the Chinese Embassy. In Belgrade's centre, the bombed building that housed the Yugoslavian Ministry of Defence has been left in ruins as a grim reminder of the city's darkest days.

⊙ Sights & Activities

KALEMGEDAN AREA

FREE **Kalemegdan Citadel** FORTRESS
(Kalemegdanska tvrđava) Some 115 battles have been fought over imposing, impressive Kalemegdan, and the citadel was destroyed more than 40 times throughout the centuries. Fortifications began in Celtic times, and the Romans extended it onto the flood plains during the settlement of 'Singidunum', Belgrade's Roman name. The fort's bloody history, discernible despite today's plethora of jolly cafes and funfairs, only makes Kalemegdan all the more fascinating.

Military Museum MUSEUM
(www.muzej.mod.gov.rs; adult/child 150/120DIN; ⏱10am-5pm Tue-Sun) Tucked away in Belgrade's sprawling Kalemegdan Citadel, this museum presents the complete military history of the former Yugoslavia. Gripping displays include captured Kosovo Liberation Army weapons, bombs and missiles (courtesy

---

BELGRADE IN TWO DAYS

Brunch at **Biblioteka** before exploring **Kalemegdan Citadel**. Take a stroll down **Knez Mihailova**, stopping at **Plato** for coffee and bookshelf browsing. People-watch at nearby **Trg Republike** and check whether the **National Museum** is open, or spend the afternoon in the **Ethnographic Museum**. When hunger sets in, drift down cobblestoned **Skadarska** to enjoy traditional Serbian fare and energetic Roma violins. Catch a live gig at the eclectic **Bitef Art Cafe** or join the retro revelry at **Kafana Pavle Korčagin**.

The next day, ponder the past at **Maršal Tito's Grave** before heading to **Zemun** for lunch. Back in the big smoke, hit a **Sava River barge-club** for a heady Belgrade nightlife experience. If clubbing's not for you, opt for a leisurely meal and live opera at **Little Bay**.

of NATO), rare guns and bits of the American stealth fighter that was shot down in 1999. You'll find the museum through the Stambol Gate, built by the Turks in the mid-1700s and used for public executions.

City Zoo
ZOO

(www.beozoovrt-izlog.org; Kalemegdan Citadel; adult/child 400/300DIN; ⊙8am-8pm summer, to 4.30pm winter) The City Zoo is home to about 2000 animals, the ancestors of whom escaped en masse when Nazi bombs destroyed enclosures in WWII: the resulting mayhem is captured brilliantly in the opening scenes of Serbian indie drama *Underground*.

STARI GRAD
Architecture
NOTABLE BUILDINGS

South of Kalemegdan is **Stari Grad** (Old Town; www.starigrad.org.rs). This jumble of architecture covers two centuries, from when Belgrade was snatched from the Ottoman Empire and given a boost by the Habsburgs. People stroll along pedestrian strip Knez Mihailova, where cafes spill onto pavements. Fine buildings include the elegant pink and white **School of Fine Arts** (cnr Knez Mihailova & Rajićeva). Further down is the Serbian Academy of Arts & Sciences (p811), an art nouveau building with the goddess Nike at its helm.

National Museum
MUSEUM

(Narodni Muzej; www.narodnimuzej.rs; Trg Republike 1a) Trg Republike (Republic Sq), a meeting point and outdoor exhibition space, is home to the National Museum, which will hopefully reopen soon; lack of funding for renovations has kept it shuttered for the last decade.

Ethnographic Museum
MUSEUM

(Etnografski Muzej; www.etnografskimuzej.rs; Studentski Trg 13; adult/student 150/60DIN; ⊙10am-5pm Tue-Sat, 9am-2pm Sun) This museum features traditional costumes, working utensils and folksy mountain-village interiors.

Palace of Princess Ljubica
PALACE

(Kneza Sime Markovića 8; adult/child 100/50DIN; ⊙10am-6pm Tue, Wed, Fri & Sat, noon-8pm Thu, 10am-2pm Sun) This preserved Balkan-style palace was built in 1831 for the wife of Prince Miloš. Take coffee with 'the princess' (actually the museum custodian in period dress) each Saturday from noon (250DIN) as she leads you through privileged 19th-century life.

Museum of the Serbian Orthodox Church
MUSEUM

(Kralja Petra 5; adult/child 50/20DIN; ⊙8am-4pm Mon-Fri, 9am-noon Sat, 11am-1pm Sun) The

FREE THRILLS

The best things in Belgrade are still free:

» Amble around Kalemegdan Citadel.

» Explore Stari Grad, the evocative Old Town.

» Have a splash at Ada Ciganlija (p807), an artificial island on the Sava.

» Gasp at the sheer scale of Sveti Sava (p807).

» Ramble along the Danube River to Zemun (p813).

Patriarchate (Patrijaršija) building houses this collection of ecclesiastical items, many of which were collected by St Sava, founder of the independent Serbian Orthodox church.

DORĆOL

Named from the Turkish words for 'four roads' *(dört yol)*, Dorćol stretches northeast from Stari Grad to the Danube. During the Ottoman occupation, Turks, Greeks, Jews, Germans, Armenians and Vlachs lived here side-by-side, bartering in a mix of languages. Today, Dorćol is a leafy, hip neighbourhood dotted with hidden *kafanas* (cafes) and cocktail bars.

Gallery of Frescos
GALLERY

(www.narodnimuzej.rs; Cara Uroša 20; admission 100DIN; ⊙10am-5pm Tue, Wed, Fri & Sat, noon-8pm Thu, 10am-2pm Sun) The gallery features full-size replicas (and the odd original) of Byzantine Serbian church art, right down to the last scratch. Unlike the sensitive originals, these frescos can be photographed to your heart's content.

Bajrakli Mosque
MOSQUE

(cnr Kralja Petra & Gospodar Jevremova) The last remaining – and functioning – mosque *(džamija)* in Belgrade was built around 1575. Damage caused by riots in 2004 (a backlash against anti-Serb pogroms in Kosovo) has since been repaired.

St Aleksandar Nevski Church
CHURCH

(Cara Dušana 63) Built during the Serbian-Ottoman War (1877), this is the oldest Christian church in Dorćol.

SKADARSKA

Skadarska or 'Skadarlija' is Belgrade's Montmartre. This cobblestoned strip east of Trg Republike was the bohemian heartland at the

Central Belgrade

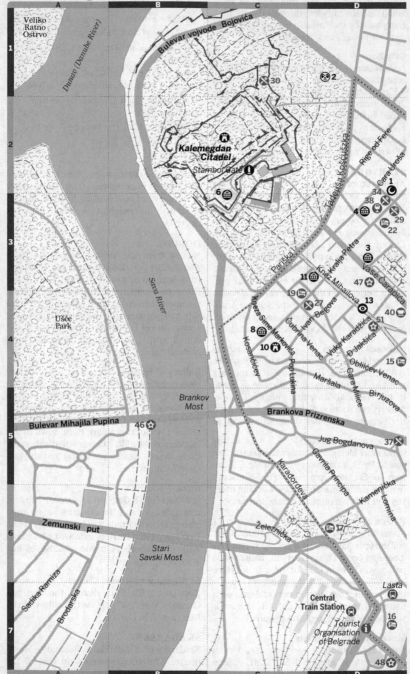

SERBIA BELGRADE

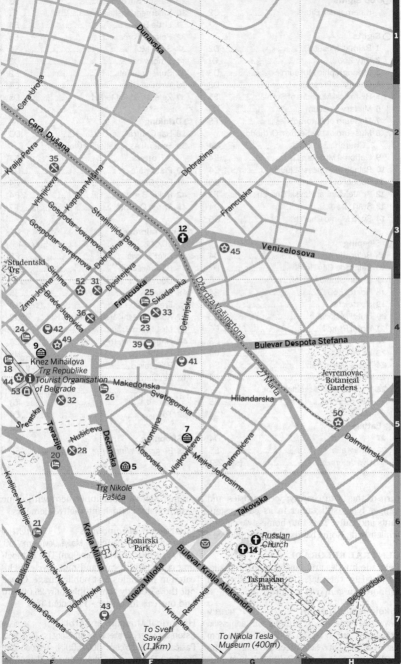

Central Belgrade

◉ Top Sights
Kalemegdan Citadel C2

◉ Sights
1 Bajrakli Mosque D2
2 City Zoo... D1
3 Ethnographic Museum......................... D3
4 Gallery of Frescos D3
5 Historical Museum of Serbia................F5
6 Military Museum C3
7 Museum of Automobiles........................F5
8 Museum of the Serbian Orthodox
  Church... C4
9 National Museum....................................E4
10 Palace of Princess Ljubica................... C4
11 School of Fine Arts D3
12 St Aleksandar Nevski Church F3
13 Stari Grad... D4
14 Sveti Marko Church...............................G6

⊜ Sleeping
15 Belgrade Art Hotel D4
16 Belgrade City Hotel D7
17 Green Studio Hostel D6
18 Hostel 360 ....E4
19 Hostelche.. C4
20 Hotel Moskva..E5
21 Hotel Prag..E6
22 Hotel Royal... D3
23 Le Petit Piaf..F4
24 Three Black Catz....................................E4
25 Travelling Actor......................................F4
26 Youth Hostel Association of
  Serbia F5

⊗ Eating
27 ?... D4
28 Biblioteka..E5
Dva Jelena....................................(see 23)

29 Kafana Suvobor...................................... D3
30 Kalemegdanska Terasa......................... C1
31 Little Bay...E4
32 Pekara Toma...E5
33 Šešir Moj..F4
34 Smokvica... D3
35 Supermarket...E2
36 Writers' Club E4
37 Zeleni Venac Market D5

⊖ Drinking
38 Bar Central... D3
39 Federal Association of Globe
  Trotters..F4
40 Plato Kafe... D4
41 Pub Brod..F4
42 Rakia Bar...E4
43 Three Carrots...F7

⊗ Entertainment
20/44...(see 46)
44 Bilet Servis E5
45 Bitef Art Cafe...G3
Dom Omladine.............................(see 26)
46 Exile...B5
Freestyler ....(see 46)
47 Kolarčev University Concert Hall D3
48 Mr Stefan Braun.................................... D7
49 National Theatre.....................................E4
50 Plastic...H5
Povetarac.....................................(see 46)
51 Serbian Academy of Arts &
  Sciences.. D4
Sound...(see 46)
52 Tube...E4

⊜ Shopping
53 Belgrade Window E5

---

turn of the 20th century; local artistes and dapper types still gather in its cute restaurants and cafes. Tuck into home-style cuisine while roving Roma bands provide ambience.

CENTRAL BELGRADE
Belgrade hustles and bustles along Terazije, crowned by the majestic Hotel Moskva, an art nouveau gem over a century old.

Nikola Tesla Museum   MUSEUM
(www.tesla-museum.org; Krunska 51; admission incl guided tour in English 300DIN; ☺10am-6pm Tue-Fri, to 3pm Sat & Sun) Meet the man on the 100DIN note at one of Belgrade's best mu-

seums. Release your inner nerd with some wondrously sci-fi-ish interactive elements.

Museum of Automobiles   MUSEUM
(www.automuseumbgd.com; Majke Jevrosime 30; adult/child 100/80DIN; ☺9am-9pm) This compelling collection of cars and motorcycles is located in Belgrade's first public garage. Check out the '57 Caddy convertible: only 25,000km and one careful owner – President Tito.

Historical Museum of Serbia   MUSEUM
(Istorijski Muzej Srbije; www.imus.org.rs; Trg Nikole Pašića 11; adult/child 100/50DIN; ☺noon-7pm Tue-Sun) Home to an absorbing wealth of ar-

chaeological, ethnographic and military collections. It's your best bet while the National Museum remains closed.

Sveti Marko Church
CHURCH

(Bul Kralja Aleksandra 17) This five-domed church, based on the design of Kosovo's Gračanica Monastery, houses priceless Serbian icons and the tomb of Emperor Dušan 'The Mighty' (1308–55). Behind is a tiny Russian Church erected by refugees who fled the October Revolution.

OUTER BELGRADE

Sveti Sava
CHURCH

(www.hramsvetogsave.com; Svetog Save) Sveti Sava is the world's biggest Orthodox church, a fact made entirely obvious when looking at the city skyline from a distance or standing under its dome. The church is built on the site where the Turks apparently burnt relics of St Sava. Work on the church interior (frequently interrupted by wars) continues today.

Maršal Tito's Grave
MONUMENT

(House of Flowers; www.mij.rs; Botićeva 6; incl entry to Museum of Yugoslav History 200DIN; ⊙10am-4pm Tue-Sun) A visit to Tito's mausoleum is obligatory. Also on display are thousands of elaborate relay batons presented to him by young 'Pioneers', plus gifts from political leaders and the voguish set of the era. Take trolleybus 40 or 41 at the south end of Parliament on Kneza Miloša. It's the second stop after turning into Bul Mira: ask the driver for Kuća Cveća.

Ada Ciganlija
BEACH

(www.adaciganlija.rs) In summertime, join the hordes of sea-starved locals (up to 250,000 a day) for sun and fun at this artificial island on the Sava. Cool down with a swim, kayak or windsurf after a leap from the 55m bungee tower. Take bus 53 or 56 from Zeleni Venac.

Aviation Museum
MUSEUM

(www.muzejvazduhoplovstva.org.rs; Nikola Tesla airport; admission 500DIN; ⊙8.30am-7pm Tue-Sun summer, 9am-3.30pm winter) This airport-based museum contains rare planes, a WWII collection and bits of the infamous American stealth fighter shot down in 1999.

Tours

TOP CHOICE Belgrade
Underground
HISTORICAL TOUR

(www.go2serbia.net; per person from €12) Delve into Belgrade's tumultuous past – from Roman times until the Cold War – on this fascinating two-hour tour of subterranean caves, bunkers and secret passageways. Bookings are a must.

iBikeBelgrade
BIKE TOUR

(www.ibikebelgrade.com; ⊙from 2pm May-Nov) Wheel around town on four-hour cycle tours that take in everywhere from Ada Ciganlija to Zemun.

Nightlife Academy
DRINKING TOUR

(☎669 008 386; www.nightlifeacademy.com; incl drinks & dinner €25) Take in Belgrade's (in)famous nightlife and learn how to party like a local during a 'kafana class'. Excellent value for money; reservations essential.

🛏 Sleeping

New hostels are popping up all the time, while some of the crumbling classics have had face (and price) lifts. Decent midrange options are few and far between. Private apartments (try www.bestbelgradeapartments.com) are a better bet for longer stays.

The **Youth Hostel Association of Serbia** (Ferijalni Savez Beograd; ☎322 0762; www.serbia-hostels.org; Makedonska 22/2; ⊙9am-5pm) does deals with local hotels. You need HI membership (under/over 26 years 500/800DIN) or an international student card.

Hotel Moskva
HISTORIC HOTEL €€€

(Hotel Moscow; ☎268 6255; www.hotelmoskva.rs; Balkanska 1; s €77-112, d €99-135, ste €130-330; ✳🛜) Art nouveau icon and proud symbol of the best of Belgrade, the majestic Moskva has been wowing guests – including Albert Einstein, Indira Gandhi and Alfred Hitchcock – since 1906. Laden with ye olde glamour, this is the place to write your memoirs at a big old desk.

TOP CHOICE **Green Studio Hostel**
HOSTEL €

(☎063-7562 357; www.greenstudiohostel.com; Karađorđeva 69, 6th floor; dm from €10, r €7-36, apt €40; ✳🛜) This sunny surprise goes down as one of the top budget options in Serbia. Clean, airy and staffed by your new best friends, it has a handy location near the bus and train stations, as well as Belgrade's main attractions. Free *rakija*!

Hostelche
HOSTEL €

(☎263 7793; www.hostelchehostel.com; Kralja Petra 8; dm from €14, s €25-27, tw €20-22; ✳🛜) A bend-over-backwards staff, homey atmosphere, free walking tours and a super location make this award-winner popular for all the right reasons.

Travelling Actor
PENSION €€€

(☎323 4156; www.travellingactor.rs; Gospodar Jevremova 65; s €62-69, d €88-98, apt €188; ❀⊚) Trip down the cobblestones and back in time at this Skadarlija boutique pension. True to its name, the gilded apartments are almost melodramatically over the top, but this luxe-campness only adds to the fun.

Three Black Catz
HOSTEL €

(☎262 9826; www.hostel.co.rs; Čika Ljubina 7; dm from €9, tw €16; ⊚) Never mind the 'catz': it's the night owls that will adore this convivial spot. While the atmosphere can border on merry chaos, the hostel doesn't completely forgo business for pleasure, offering heaps of info and advice.

Hostel 360
HOSTEL €

(☎263 4957; www.threesixtyhostel.com; Knez Mihailova 21; dm/s/tw/d €15/29/44/50, apt from €40; ❀⊚) Super-tidy rooms and a garden terrace are surpassed only by spirited staff on a mission to immerse guests in local life.

Le Petit Piaf
LUXURY HOTEL €€€

(☎303 5252; www.petitpiaf.com; Skadarska 34; s & d €84-92, ste €108; ❀⊚) Elegant loft rooms, refined decor and *soignée* service make this Skadarlija charmer a Parisian doppelgänger in all the right ways.

Arka Barka
HOSTEL €

(☎064-925 3507; www.arkabarka.net; Bul Nikole Tesle bb; dm €13; ❀⊚) Bobbing off Ušće Park, a mere stagger from the Danube barges, this 'floating house' offers sparkling rooms in 'wake-up!' colours, party nights and fresh river breezes. It's a moderate walk, or a short ride on bus 15 or 84 from the centre. Cash only.

Belgrade Art Hotel
BOUTIQUE HOTEL €€€

(☎331 2000; www.belgradearthotel.com; Knez Mihailova 27; s €115-135, d €130-150; ❀⊚) This Italian-designed hotel is everything its name suggests: stylish, refined and discerning. Soundproof windows are a godsend.

Hotel Royal
HOTEL €€

(☎263 4222; www.hotelroyal.rs; Kralja Petra 56; s 3680-4370DIN, d 5175-7820DIN; ❀⊚) Rooms are basic and far from sparkling, but this (very) central spot disarms with character and buzz.

Belgrade City Hotel
HOTEL €€

(☎360 0700; www.bgcityhotel.com; Savski Trg 7; s €49-65, d €65-95, tr €115, ste €89-109; ℗❀⊚) A convenient location (across the road from the train station), clean – if nondescript –

rooms and a decent continental breakfast make this a serviceable stopover.

Hotel Prag
HOTEL €€€

(☎321 4444; www.hotelprag.rs; Kraljice Natalije 27; s €79-92, d €106, ste €157-192; ❀⊚) Totally refurbished business hotel.

✖ Eating

From Slavic staples to fusion cuisine, Belgrade offers a diverse bill of fare. The choice is particularly overwhelming along Knez Mihailova, Kralja Petra and Makedonska.

SKADARSKA

Šešir Moj
SERBIAN €€

(My Hat; Skadarska 21; meals 400-1000DIN; ⊙9am-1am) Roma bands tug the heartstrings while traditional dishes like *punjena bela vešalica* (pork stuffed with *kajmak*) buoy up the belly.

Dva Jelena
SERBIAN €€

(Two Deer; www.dvajelena.com; Skadarska 32; meals 400-900DIN; ⊙11am-1am) A local icon, Dva Jelena has been dishing up hearty fare for over 180 years. Rustic, homespun and with the obligatory violin serenades, it ticks all the Skadarlija boxes.

Writers' Club
EUROPEAN €€€

(Klub Književnika; Francuska 7; meals 250-1500DIN; ⊙noon-1am Mon-Sat, to 6pm Sun) The former haunt of local literati and the visiting elite (think Simone de Beauvoir and Jean-Paul Sartre), this dignified spot is still a favourite for substantial steaks and stews.

CENTRAL BELGRADE

Indulge your post- or preclubbing munchies in cheap bakeries around Trg Republike. **Pekara Toma** (Kolarčeva 10; snacks 50-200DIN; ⊙24hr) is a favourite for fresh pizzas, sandwiches and salads. Forage through **Zeleni Venac Market** (cnr Brankova Prizrenska & Kraljice Natalije; ⊙6am-7pm) for DIY food – it's downhill from the Balkan Hotel towards the Sava River.

TOP CHOICE ▸ Little Bay
EUROPEAN €€

(www.little-bay.co.uk; Dositejeva 9a; meals 495-1295DIN) Little wonder locals and visitors have long been singing the praises of this gem: it's one of the best dining experiences in Belgrade. Tuck yourself into a private opera box and let the salmon in beer and tarragon sauce (645DIN) or a traditional English roast lunch (695DIN, Sundays only) melt in your mouth as a live opera singer does wonderful things to your ears.

? EASTERN EUROPEAN €€
(Znak Pitanja; Kralja Petra 6; meals 450-800DIN)
Belgrade's oldest *kafana* has been attracting the bohemian set since 1823 with dishes
such as stuffed chicken and 'lamb under the
iron pan'. Its quizzical name follows a dispute with the adjacent church, which object-
ed to the boozy tavern – originally called 'By
the Cathedral' – referring to a house of god.

Smokvica CAFE €€
(Kralja Petra 73; meals 200-1200DIN; ⊘9am-1am;
🛜) With its courtyard terrace, arty crowd and
gourmet menu, to stumble across Smokvica
('little fig') is to forget you're in hustling, bustling Belgrade. Graze on a blue cheese, rocket
and fig salad, snarf down a sanga with homemade ciabatta or just sip good coffee in an
atmosphere both rare and rarified.

Kafana Suvobor SERBIAN €€
(Kralja Petra 70; meals 500-1200DIN) Specialists
in Serbian cuisine, offering dishes such as
the to-die-for *rolovana pileća džigerica u
slanini* (rolled chicken liver wrapped in bacon). Lip-smackingly good.

Kalemegdanska Terasa EUROPEAN €€€
(📲328 3011; www.kalemegdanskaterasa.com; Mali
Kalemegdan bb; meals 870-1780DIN; ⊘noon-1am)
By the fortress, this is a literal bastion of refined dining, featuring sumptuous dishes
such as rolled steak and goose liver with truffle sauce. One for the romantics, and those
who packed a tie.

Supermarket INTERNATIONAL €€
(www.supermarket.rs; cnr Višnjićeva & Strahinjića
Bana; meals 575-1400DIN; ⊘9am-midnight Sun-
Thu, to 1am Fri & Sat) The burgeoning breed
of local hipsters descends on this slice of
Brooklyn in Belgrade, a designer eatery for
organic, oddball-on-purpose cuisine: ahem,
pickle-stuffed cannelloni with marmalade
sauce. Those with a plainer palate aren't left
out: the cafe-style breakfasts here are sublime. It's part of the Supermarket 'concept
store', with indie-label duds, cool trinkets
and exhibitions all under one spiffy roof.

Biblioteka INTERNATIONAL €€
(Terazije 27; meals 300-900DIN; ⊘7am-1am; ⊛)
Buzzing outside and aptly library-ambient
inside, Biblioteka is popular with locals for its
extensive breakfast menu, served until 1pm.

OUTER BELGRADE
Dačo SERBIAN €€
(📲278 1009; www.kafanadaco.com; Patrisa Lu-
mumbe 49; meals 500-1150DIN; ⊘noon-midnight

Tue-Sun) Making the haul out here is like visiting the Serbian granny you never knew you
had: the walls are cluttered with homey bits
and bobs, chequered tablecloths adorn rickety tables and chooks strut around in the garden. And you won't have to be told twice to
'Eat! Eat!' either. Reservations recommended.

Maharaja INDIAN €€
(www.maharaja.rs; Ljubićka 1b; meals 380-1450DIN;
⊘noon-midnight Tue-Sun) Craving curry in a
sea of *kajmak*? It's worth the trip out to one
of Belgrade's only Indian restaurants, serving all the staples from tikka to tandoori.
Vegetarians will find solace here.

🍷 Drinking

Quiet cafes morph into drinking dens at
night and then thumping clubs in the early
hours. In spring and summer, action spills
onto terraces and pavements.

Coffee chains abound: look out for Costa
Coffee, Greenet or Coffee Dream, or try your
luck at any of the independents along Knez
Mihailova.

TOP CHOICE **Kafana Pavle Korčagin** TAVERNA
(📲240 1980; Ćirila i Metodija 2a; ⊘8pm-1am)
Raise a glass to Tito at this frantic, festive
kafana. Lined with communist memorabilia
and packed to the rafters with revellers and
grinning accordionists, this table-thumping
throwback fills up nightly; reserve a table in
advance.

Federal Association of Globe Trotters BAR
(www.usp-aur.rs; Bul Despota Stefana 7/1; ⊘1pm-
midnight Mon-Fri, 3pm-late Sat & Sun; 🛜) Through
the big black gate and down into the basement lies one of Belgrade's coolest hang-outs.
Miscellaneous oddities clamour for wall
space while an equally motley clientele yaks
over cocktails.

Rakia Bar BAR
(www.rakiabar.com; Dobračina 5; ⊘9am-midnight
Sun-Thu, to 1am Fri & Sat) An ideal spot for *rakija* rookies to get their first taste of the spirit
of Serbia. English-speaking staff will gently guide you through the extensive drinks
menu, but beware: this stuff is strong.

Pub Brod BAR
(Bul Despota Stefana 36; ⊘noon-4am) This congenial student hang-out thumbs its nose at
dress codes, Top 40 and nouveau-Belgrade
bling. Small and smoky inside, in summertime indie music pumps over a whooping
sidewalk sprawl.

Bar Central
COCKTAIL BAR

(Kralja Petra 59; ⊘9am-1am) This is the HQ of Serbia's Association of Bartenders, a fact made evident after one sip of any of the sublime cocktails on offer. With an interior as polished as a bottle flip-pour, this ain't the place for tacky tikis and those little drink umbrellas.

Plato Kafe
CAFE

(1 Akademski Plato; ⊘9am-2am) Aptly located by 'Students' Square' off Knez Mihailova, Plato is a university bookshop-cafe offering fine coffees, booze, nibbles and smartypants live jazz and literary gigs.

Three Carrots
PUB

(Kneza Miloša 16; ⊘9am-2am) Dimly lit like any Irish bar worth its quirky ceiling-hangings should be, this place pulls both pints and a cosmopolitan crowd.

☆ Entertainment

Nightclubs

Belgrade has a reputation as one of the world's top party cities, with a wild club scene limited only by imagination and hours in the day. Check out www.serbianightlife.com for more pointers.

Plastic
NIGHTCLUB

(www.clubplastic.rs; cnr Dalmatinska & Takovska; ⊘Thu-Sat) A favourite among electro-heads and booty shakers, this slick venue is frequented by top local and international DJs. In summer, head to Plastic Light, the floating version of the club on the Sava River.

Bitef Art Cafe
LIVE MUSIC

(www.bitefartcafe.rs; Skver Mire Trailović 1; ⊘7pm-4am) There's something for everyone at this delightful hotchpotch of a cafe-club. Funk, soul and jazz get a good airing, as do rock and classical. Karaoke competitions pack in the punters.

Tube
NIGHTCLUB

(www.thetube.rs; Simina 21; ⊘Thu-Sat) Lovers of all music electronic will have a blast in this beautifully designed former nuclear bunker. Upmarket and oft-crowded, despite a whopping floor space, it's worth scrubbing up for.

Ona A Ne Neka Druga
NIGHTCLUB

(She and Not Some Other; ☏062-222 152; Grobljanska 9; ⊘9pm-4am Tue-Sun) As its unusual name suggests, this cosy club caters entirely to women...but in true Serbia style, it steers far from any PC aspects one might expect of such a distinction. Instead, women (and brave male friends) are encouraged to smash glasses, table dance and pinch waiters on the bum. In the Gardoš part of Zemun; take a taxi. Reservations suggested.

Mr Stefan Braun
NIGHTCLUB

(www.mrstefanbraun.rs; Nemanjina 4) Those who want to party like (and with) Serbian superstars will find their bliss at this 9th-storey den of decadence. Get your finest threads – and most model-like pout – on and get there before 1am to beat the queues.

River Barges

According to Michael Palin, Belgrade has so many nightclubs 'they can't fit them all on land'. Indeed: adjacent to Hotel Jugoslavija in Novi Belgrade is a 1km strip of some 20 Danube River barges, known collectively as *splavovi*. Most are closed in winter. Get there with bus 15 or 84 from Zeleni Venac or 68, 603 or 701 from Trg Republike; get out at Hotel Jugoslavija.

On the western bank of the Sava River is a 1.5km strip of *splavovi*. Most are only open in summer. Walk over Brankov Most or catch tram 7, 9 or 11.

Blaywatch
BARGE

(Danube River; ⊘midnight-late) This throbbing place gets crowded and dress codes may be enforced (scruffy bad on boys, skimpy good on girls). The crowd is a mix of local 'beautiful people' and foreigners, all occupied with each other and the turbo tunes.

Bahus
BARGE

(www.bahus.rs; Danube River; ⊘10am-1pm) This chic alternative attracts a refined crowd who'd rather sip cocktails than spill them down someone else's back.

Acapulco
BARGE

(Danube River; ⊘noon-late) Blinged-up boys come here to flaunt their (new) money and she-accessories. Got a low turbofolk threshold? Start swimming.

Freestyler
BARGE

(www.splavfree.rs; Brodarska bb, Sava River; ⊘11pm-5am Tue-Sun) The gigantic Freestyler has been a symbol of *splav* saturnalia for years, not least for its infamous foam parties.

Exile
BARGE

(Savski kej bb, Sava River; ⊘midnight-late) Exile pounds out techno.

Sound
BARGE

(Savski kej bb, Sava River; ⊘midnight-3am) Sound plays house and disco to a slightly older following.

Povetarac   BARGE
(Brodarska bb, Sava River; ⊗midnight-late, 8pm-late winter) This rusting cargo ship attracts an indie crowd.

20/44   BARGE
(Savski kej bb, Sava River; ⊗7pm-4am) Conga around a life-sized statue of John Cleese.

Performing Arts
For concert and theatre tickets, go to **Bilet Servis** (☑303 3311; www.biletservis.rs; Trg Republike 5; ⊗9am-8pm Mon-Fri, 10am-8pm Sat). Large venues for visiting acts include **Sava Centar** (☑220 6060; www.savacentar.net; Milentija Popovića 9; ⊗box office 10am-8pm Mon-Fri, to 3pm Sat) and **Belgrade Arena** (☑220 2222; www.arenabeograd.com; Bul Arsenija Čarnojevića 58; ⊗box office 10am-8pm Mon-Fri, to 3pm Sat).

National Theatre   THEATRE
(☑262 0946; www.narodnopozoriste.co.rs; Trg Republike; ⊗box office 10am-2pm Tue-Sun) Stages operas, dramas and ballets during winter.

Kolarčev University Concert Hall   LIVE MUSIC
(☑2630 550; www.kolarac.co.rs; Studentski Trg 5; ⊗box office 10am-7.30pm) Home to the Belgrade Philharmonica.

Dom Omladine   LIVE MUSIC, THEATRE
(www.domomladine.org; Makedonska 22; ⊗box office 10am-8pm Mon-Fri, 3pm-8pm Sat) Hosts a range of mostly youth-based cultural events.

Serbian Academy of Arts & Sciences   LIVE MUSIC
(☑202 7200; www.sanu.ac.rs; Knez Mihailova 35; ⊗concerts from 6pm Mon & Thu Oct-Jun) Stages free concerts and exhibitions.

DAY TRIPS FROM BELGRADE

It's easy to get stuck in Belgrade, but catching a glimpse of the country around the capital is a cinch if you get an early start. Hop a bus and have a gander at the following.

Smederevo (one hour)

Smederevo Fortress (www.tvrdjava.com; admission 50DIN; ⊗8am-8pm) is a huge, 25-tower fort constructed between 1427 and 1430. Once the temporary capital of Serbia, and one of the largest city-fortresses in Europe, it hosts a **theatre festival** (www.tvrdjavateatar.rs) each August and is home to the lovingly maintained **Smederevo Museum** (admission 70DIN; ⊗10am-5pm Tue-Fri, to 3pm Sat & Sun). Regular buses (500DIN) leave from Belgrade's Lasta station.

Topola (2.5 hours)

This is where Karađorđe plotted the Serbian insurrection against the Turks in 1804. One ticket (300DIN) grants access to all the park's impressive attractions, open daily from 8am to 6pm.

The complex includes a **museum** (ul Kraljice Marije), the Winegrower's House gallery and the white-marble, five-domed **Church of St George** (Avenija Kralja Petra I), where vibrant mosaics are magnificently rendered with over 40 million pieces of coloured glass. Millions more adorn the **Karađorđe mausoleum** under the church.

Frequent buses run to and from Belgrade (570DIN).

Despotovac (2.5 hours)

This little town is a gateway to attractions ranging from the sacred to the subterraneous.

Manasija Monastery was a refuge for artists and writers fleeing the Turkish invasion of Kosovo in the early 1400s. Many consider Manasija's vivid frescos to be predecessors to the Serbian equivalent of Renaissance art.

A winding 20km beyond Despotovac, the eight-million-year-old **Resavska Pećina** (Resava Cave; www.resavska pecina.rs; adult/child 300/250DIN; ⊗9am-5pm Apr-Nov) has guided tours through impressive underground halls, featuring natural formations with names like 'Hanged Sheep' and 'Thirst for Love'. Temperatures average just 7°C.

A taxi will take you to both sites from town; the return trip including waiting time should be around 2000DIN. Belgrade buses leave six times every weekday to Despotovac (1000DIN).

Shopping

Knez Mihailova is studded with global and luxury brands. Get souvenirs from Kalemegdan Park vendors or browse Zemun's Sunday-morning *buvljak* (flea market). Load up on Belgrade-themed art, clothes, books and fripperies at **Belgrade Window** (Knez Mihailova 6; 9am-9pm Mon-Sat), or get your fashion fix at Dorćol's Supermarket (p809).

Information

Internet Access

Net cafes come and go in Belgrade faster than you can click a mouse. Wireless is free at venues throughout the city and available at almost every hostel/hotel.

Belgrade City Library (Knez Mihailova 56; per min 2DIN; 8am-8pm Mon-Fri, to 2pm Sat)

Medical Services

Emergency Medical Assistance (94; www.beograd94.rs; Bul Franše D'Eperea 5; 24hr)

Klinički Centar (361 7777; www.klinicki-centar.rs; Pasterova 2; 24hr) Medical clinic.

Prima 1 (361 099; www.primax.rs; Nemanjina 2; 24hr) All-hours pharmacy.

Post

Central Post Office (8am-7pm Mon-Fri, to 3pm Sat)

Tourist Information

Tourist Organisation of Belgrade (www.tob.rs) Trg Republike 5 (328 1859; 9am-9pm Mon-Sat, 10am-3pm Sun); Train Station (361 2732; 7am-1.30pm Mon-Sat); Nikola Tesla Airport (209 7828; 9am-9.30pm) Helpful folk with a raft of brochures, city maps and all the info you could need.

Websites

Belgrade in Your Pocket (www.inyourpocket.com/serbia/belgrade)

Belgraded (www.belgraded.com)

Lonely Planet (www.lonelyplanet.com/serbia/belgrade)

Getting There & Away

Bus

Belgrade has two adjacent bus stations, near the eastern banks of the Sava River: **BAS** (263 6299; www.bas.rs; Železnička 4) serves the region, while **Lasta** (334 8555; www.lasta.rs; Železnička 2) deals with destinations around Belgrade.

TRANSPORT FROM BELGRADE

International Bus

DESTINATION	PRICE (DIN)	DURATION (HR)	FREQUENCY
Banja Luka (Bosnia & Hercegovina)	2530	7½	daily
Bratislava (Slovakia)	4180	12	Wed & Sun
Ljubljana (Slovenia)	4170	7½	daily
Podgorica (Montenegro)	2500	9	daily
Sarajevo (Bosnia & Hercegovina)	2510	8	daily
Skopje (Macedonia)	2750	7	daily
Split (Croatia)	5570	12½	Mon-Sat
Vienna (Austria)	4330	9½	daily

International Train

DESTINATION	PRICE (€)	DURATION (HR)
Bucharest (Romania)	48	14
Budapest (Hungary)	15	7
Ljubljana (Slovenia)	25	10
Moscow (Russia)	122	50
Munich (Germany)	145	17
Sofia (Bulgaria)	30	11
Vienna (Austria)	70	11
Zagreb (Croatia)	32	7

Frequent domestic services include Subotica (1280DIN, three hours), Novi Sad (600DIN, one hour), Niš (1420DIN, three hours) and Novi Pazar (1520DIN, three hours).

Car & Motorcycle

Several car-hire companies have offices at Nikola Tesla Airport:

Avaco (☑228 6434; www.avaco.rs; ☺8am-8pm)

Avis (☑209 7062; www.avis.rs; ☺8am-8pm)

Budget (☑228 6361; www.budget.rs; ☺8am-8pm Mon-Fri, 10am-6pm Sat, 10am-2pm Sun)

Train

The **central train station** (Savski Trg 2) has an information office on Platform 1, tourist information office, **exchange bureau** (☺6am-10pm) and **sales counter** (☺9am-4pm Mon-Sat).

Frequent trains go to Novi Sad (288DIN, 1½ hours), Subotica (480DIN, three hours) and Niš (784DIN, four hours).

❶ Getting Around

TO/FROM THE AIRPORT Nikola Tesla airport is 18km from Belgrade. Local bus 72 connects the airport with Zeleni Venac (65DIN to 120DIN, half-hourly, 5.20am to midnight from airport, 4.40am to 11.40pm from town); the cheapest tickets must be purchased from news stands. A minibus also runs between the airport and the central Slavija Sq (250DIN, 5am to 3.50am from airport, 4.20am to 3.20am from the square).

Don't get swallowed up by the airport taxi shark pit: ask the tourist office in the arrivals hall to call one for you. A taxi from the airport to Knez Mihailova should be around 1250DIN.

CAR & MOTORCYCLE Parking in Belgrade is regulated by three parking zones – red (one hour, 56DIN), yellow (two hours, 38DIN per hour) and green (three hours, 31DIN per hour). Tickets must be bought from kiosks or via SMS (in Serbian).

PUBLIC TRANSPORT Trams and trolleybuses ply limited routes but buses chug all over town. Rechargeable BusPlus cards can be bought and topped up (70DIN per ticket) at kiosks across the city; they're 140DIN if you buy from the driver.

Tram 2 connects Kalemegdan Citadel with Trg Slavija, bus stations and the central train station.

TAXI Move away from obvious taxi traps and flag down a distinctly labelled cruising cab, or get a local to call you one. A 5km trip costs around 415DIN. Flagfall is 140DIN, and reputable cabs should charge between 55DIN and 70DIN per kilometre.

AROUND BELGRADE

Zemun · Земун

Some 6km northwest of central Belgrade, Zemun was the most southerly point of the Austro-Hungarian empire when the Turks ruled Belgrade. Today it's known for its fish restaurants and quaint, nonurban ambience.

Up the narrow cobbled street of Grobljanska, remnants of the old village lead towards the 9th-century Gardoš fortress. Walls from the 15th century remain, as does the Tower of Sibinjanin Janko, built in 1896 to celebrate the millennial anniversary of the Hungarian state and to keep an eye on the Turks. Today you can enjoy the spectacular view. Descending from the tower, stop in at the 1731 **Nikolajevska Church** (Njegoševa 43) to goggle at its astounding baroque iconostasis.

Zemun is a laid-back accommodation alternative to Belgrade. Floating between Zemun and Belgrade is the Arka Barka (p808) barge-hostel. The lobby of the more upmarket **Hotel Skala** (☑011-307 5032; www.hotelskala.rs; Bežanijska 3; s/d/apt 6300/8100/9000DIN; ✳☜) has sunny, wi-fi-equipped rooms and a cavernous basement restaurant.

Among the many venues dishing up fish and fun along the Danube are **Šaran** (☑011-261 8235; www.saran.co.rs; Kej Oslobođenja 53; dishes from 1000DIN; ☺noon-1am), renowned as one of Zemun's best fish restaurants, **Reka** (☑011-261 1625; www.reka.co.rs; Kej Oslobođenja 73b; dishes from 690DIN; ☺noon-2am) and **Malevilla** (www.malevilla.rs; Kej Oslobođenja bb; dishes from 1000DIN; ☺10am-midnight).

Zemun is a 45-minute walk from Belgrade (across Brankov Most, along Nikole Tesle and the Kej Oslobođenja waterside walkway). Alternatively, take bus 15 or 84 from Zeleni Venac market, or bus 83 or 78 from the main train station.

VOJVODINA

Home to more than 25 ethnic groups, six languages and the best of Hungarian and Serbian traditions, Vojvodina's (Војводина) pancake plains mask a diversity unheard of in the rest of the country. Affable capital Novi Sad hosts the eclectic EXIT festival – the largest in southeast Europe – while the hilly region of Fruška Gora keeps the noise down in hushed monasteries and ancestral vineyards. Charming Subotica, 10km from Hungary, is an oasis of art nouveau delights.

Novi Sad   Нови Сад

♪ 021 / POP 335,700

As convivial as a *rakija* toast – and at times just as carousing – Novi Sad is a chipper town with all the spoils and none of the stress of the big smoke. Locals sprawl in parks and outdoor cafes, and laneway bars pack out nightly. The looming Petrovaradin Citadel keeps a stern eye on proceedings, loosening its tie each July to host Serbia's largest music festival. You can walk to all of Novi Sad's attractions from the happening pedestrian thoroughfare, Zmaj Jovina, which stretches from the town square (Trg Slobode) to Dunavska street.

◉ Sights

Petrovaradin Citadel   FORTRESS
Towering over the river on a 40m-high volcanic slab, this mighty citadel (*tvrđava*) is aptly nicknamed 'Gibraltar on the Danube'. Constructed with slave labour between 1692 and 1780, its dungeons have held notable prisoners including Karađorđe (leader of the first uprising against the Turks and founder of a dynasty) and Tito. Have a good gawk at the iconic clock tower: the size of the minute and hour hands are reversed so far-flung fishermen can tell the time.

Within the citadel walls, a **museum** (♪ 433 155; admission 200DIN; ◎ 9am-5pm Tue-Sun) offers insight (sans English explanations) into the site's history. The museum can also arrange tours of Petrovaradin's creepy – but cool – underground passageways.

Museum of Vojvodina   MUSEUM
(Muzej Vojvodine; www.muzejvojvodine.org.rs; Dunavska 35-7; admission 100DIN; ◎ 9am-7pm Tue-Fri, 10am-6pm Sat & Sun) This museum houses historical, archaeological and ethnological exhibits. Building 35 covers Vojvodinian history from Palaeolithic times to the late 19th century. Building 37 takes the story to 1945 with harrowing emphasis on WWI and WWII.

Štrand   BEACH
One of Europe's best by-the-Danube beaches, this 700m-long stretch of sand morphs into a city of its own come summertime, with bars, stalls and all manner of recreational diversions attracting thousands of sun-'n'-fun seekers from across the globe. It's also the ultimate Novi Sad party venue, hosting everything from local punk gigs to EXIT raves.

✶ Festivals & Events
Some festivals are worth sculpting a trip around (and booking accommodation in advance for). The biggest is the EXIT festival with blockbusting line-ups performing at the Petrovaradin Fortress each July.

June's **Cinema City Festival** (www.cinemacity.org) is a weeklong, city-wide film extravaganza, while each September Novi Sad morphs into an open-air stage for the **International Festival of Street Musicians** (www.ulicnisviraci.com). The city toots its own horn at the **Novi Sad Jazz Festival** (http://jazzns.eunet.rs) every November.

⏿ Sleeping
While Novi Sad is loaded with hotels and hostels, it fills up fast during EXIT season: book far ahead. Try www.novisadproperty.com for house/flat rentals.

TOP CHOICE Hostel Sova   HOSTEL €
(♪ 066-152 30; www.hostelsova.com; Ilije Ognjanovića 26; dm from €10, d €15; P ⊛) This cute spot is akin to a mini Novi Sad: super-friendly, attractive and given to laid-back socialising (not to mention the odd *rakija* or two). It's perched above a deceptively quiet street that's just around the corner from buzzy Zmaj Jovina and a couple of minutes' stagger from the best bars in town.

Leopold I   LUXURY HOTEL €€€
(♪ 488 7878; www.leopoldns.com; Petrovaradin Citadel; s/d from 7000/8200DIN; ste 12,100-26,600DIN; P ⊛ ⊛) This rock-top indulgence offers rooms in Gothic, Renaissance or the (slightly) more economical modern style. Warning: the regal Leopold I apartment may induce delusions of grandeur.

ENTERING THE STATE OF EXIT

Home to the epic **EXIT Festival** (www.exitfest.org), the Petrovaradin Fortress is stormed by thousands of revellers each July. The first festival in 2000 lasted 100 days and galvanised a generation of young Serbs against the Milošević regime, who 'exited' himself just weeks after the event. The festival has been attended by the likes of Faith No More, Chemical Brothers, Gogol Bordello, Gossip and Patti Smith, not to mention an annual tally of about 200,000 merrymakers from around the world.

Downtown   HOSTEL €

(☑69 139 7708; www.hostelnovisad.com; Njegoševa 2; dm from €10, s/d €25/30; @) Super-friendly staff and an 'in the thick of it' location off Trg Slobode make this rambunctious, slightly ramshackle hostel a Novi Sad experience in itself.

Hotel Vojvodina   HISTORIC HOTEL €€

(☑622 122; www.hotelvojvodina.rs; Trg Slobode 2; s/d from 2800/4200DIN) Reeking of communist-era retro, Novi Sad's oldest hotel (1854) isn't as slick as others, but its location overlooking the town square is unbeatable, as is the semi-faded splendour of its restaurant.

Hotel Fontana   HOTEL €€

(☑621 779; Pašićeva 27; s/d/tr incl breakfast 3200/4350/5700DIN; ❄) With its pink exterior and malapropos chandeliers, this hotel is peculiar but perky. Good-sized rooms overlook the leafy courtyard attached to the locally famous, eponymous restaurant.

✗ Eating

For dessert, lapse into a sugar coma at **Evropa** (Dunavska 6; cakes 100DIN) or **Poslastićarnica Šeherezada** (Zmaj Jovina 19; 2-scoop ice cream 80DIN).

TOP CHOICE Kod Lipe   SERBIAN €

(Svetozara Miletića 7; meals from 400DIN; ☉8am-11pm Mon-Fri, 7am-midnight Sat & Sun) This down-home eatery has been dishing up old-school ambience alongside traditional Vojvodinian fare since the 19th century.

Fish i Zeleniš   MEDITERRANEAN €€

(Fish and Greens; ☑452 000; Skerlićeva 2; mains from 700DIN; ☉noon-11pm Mon-Fri, to 1am Sat & Sun; ☑) This bright, snug little nook serves up the finest vegetarian/pescatarian meals in northern Serbia. Organic, locally sourced ingredients? Ambient? Ineffably delicious? Tick, tick, tick. A three-minute walk from Zmaj Jovina.

Lazina Bašta   SERBIAN €

(Laze Telečkog 5; meals from 450DIN) Replete with hay bales and knick-knackery, Lazina Bašta serves up country-mouse cuisine on the most happening street in town.

🍷 Drinking

Laze Telečkog (a car-free sidestreet running off Zmaj Jovina) is lined with bars to suit every whim. Squeeze into the frenetic **London Underground Club** (Laze Telečkog 15; ☉8am-3am) for good-timey tunes (and associated drunken sing-a-longs) or sidle next door to **Cuba Libre** (Laze Telečkog 13) and stake your spot on the narrow dance floor. The infinitely more calm **Atrium** (Laze Telečkog 2) serves drinks in a civilised (faux) library. Hang with local eccentrics at **Crni Bik** (Trg Mladenaca 8; ☉10am-late), a boisterous dive bar just a short stroll southeast from Laze Telečkog. During summer, check out any of the barefoot-bars along the Štrand (p814).

❶ Information

The centre of town is awash with free wi-fi: both the username and password are 'gost'.

Apoteka Novi Sad (www.apotekanovisad.co.rs; Mihajla Pupina 7; ☉24hr Mon-Sat) Art-deco pharmacy.

Main Post Office (Narodnih Heroja 2; ☉9am-7pm Mon-Fri, to 2pm Sat)

Tourist Information Centre (☑661 7343; www.turizamns.rs; Ul Modene 1; ☉7.30am-8pm Mon-Fri, 10am-3pm Sat) Ultra-helpful with maps and English info.

❶ Getting There & Away

The **bus station** (Bul Jaše Tomića; ☉information counter 6am-11pm) has regular departures to Belgrade (600DIN, one hour, every 10 minutes) and Subotica (600DIN, 1½ hours), plus services to Užice (1120DIN, five hours) and Zlatibor (1250DIN, six hours). From here, four stops on bus 4 will take you to the town centre: nip down the underpass and you'll see Trg Slobode on emerging.

NOVI SAD'S INDEX SANDWICH

New Orleans has the po'boy, England the chip butty, Philly the cheesesteak... and Novi Sad can proudly boast the *indeks sendvič* (index sandwich). Created in the early 1990s and named after a low-ranked local football team, the Index is an absurdly decadent take on the basic ham-'n'-cheese sanga: gooey cheese and mushrooms are melted between a thick fold of ham and shoved into a long toasted roll with *pavlaka* (sour cream), *urnebes*, tartar, mayonnaise, tomato slices and pickle, then dusted with chilli and curry powders. Too much? Trust us: it's never enough.

Sink your teeth into the local take on the sub sandwich at **Index House** (Bul Mihajla Pupina 5; sandwiches from 180DIN; ☉24hr), and order yours *veliki* (large)!

Frequent trains leave the **train station** (Bul Jaše Tomića 4), next door to the bus station, for Belgrade (288DIN, 1½ hours) and Subotica (384DIN, 1½ hours).

Another option for roadtrippers is the Novi Sad–based **Rent-a-Yugo** (☏065-526 5256; Mileve Marić 64; per day from €11) car-hire firm.

Subotica   Суботица

☏024 / POP 140,400

Sugar-spun art nouveau marvels, a laid-back populace and a delicious sprinkling of Serbian and Hungarian flavours make this quaint town a worthy day trip or stopover.

◎ Sights

Even the least architecturally inclined will fall for Subotica's art nouveau charms. Most sights are along the pedestrian strip of Korzo or on the main square, Trg Republike.

Town Hall   HISTORIC BUILDING
(Trg Republike) Built in 1910, this behemoth is a curious mix of art nouveau and something Gaudí may have had a playful dab at. The council chambers – with exquisite stained-glass windows and elaborate decor – are not to be missed.

Modern Art Gallery   HISTORIC BUILDING
(www.likovnisusret.rs; Park Ferenca Rajhla 5; admission 50DIN; ◎8am-2pm Mon, to 6pm Tue-Fri, 9am-noon Sat) This mansion was built in 1904 as an architect's design studio, and it shows. One of the most sumptuous buildings in Serbia, it's a vibrant flourish of mosaics, ceramic tiles, floral patterns and stained glass.

City Museum   MUSEUM
(www.gradskimuzej.subotica.rs; Trg Sinagoge 3; admission 100DIN; ◎10am-8pm Tue-Sat) Eclectic exhibitions are the go in this art nouveau residence designed by Budapest's Vago brothers.

Synagogue   SYNAGOGUE
(Trg Sinagoge 2) Alas, Subotica's first art nouveau building, remains shuttered and dilapidated as long-awaited renovations have failed to materialise. Grasp its former glory from the footpath.

⊨ Sleeping

Hotel Patria   HOTEL €€
(☏554 500; www.hotelpatria.rs; Đure Đakovića bb; s 3800-4400DIN; d 6400-7000DIN; apt 9000-14,000DIN; ❄🖳) The Patria has well-groomed, well-appointed rooms (the presidential suite

rocks a jacuzzi), a wellness centre and a great location a few hundred metres from the train station.

Hostel Incognito   HOSTEL €
(☏062-666 674; www.hostel-subotica.com; Hugo Badalića 3; s/d/tr/apt 1000/1800/2400/7000DIN; 🖳) This basic but clean hostel is a couple of minutes' walk from all the Subotica sights. Reception is in the restaurant downstairs: call ahead before lobbing up.

Hotel Galleria   HOTEL €€
(☏647 111; www.galleria-center.com; Matije Korvina 17; r 5675-7670DIN, apt 9355-11,350DIN, presidential ste 20,850-27,910DIN; ❄🖳🖳) These four-star rooms come over all 'gentleman's den', with warm mahogany-look fittings and beds lined with bookshelves. It's inside the Atrium shopping plaza.

Hostel Bosa Milićević   HOSTEL €
(☏548 290; Segedinski put 9-11; dm per person 1019DIN) Stay with the students at this cheapie tucked well away behind the Ekonomski Fakultet.

✗ Eating

Ravel   CAFE €
(Nušićeva 2; cakes 60-200DIN; ◎9am-10pm Mon-Sat, 11am-10pm Sun) Dainty nibbles at *gateaux* and twee tea-taking is the name of the game at this adorable art nouveau classic.

Boss Caffe   INTERNATIONAL €
(www.bosscaffe.com; Matije Korvina 7-8) Boss' offerings include a variety of tacos (285DIN to 510DIN) and pizza with sour cream (465DN to 780DIN). It's directly behind the Modern Art Gallery.

❶ Information

Tourist Information Office (☏670 350; www.visitsubotica.rs; Town Hall; ◎8am-6pm Mon-Fri, 9am-1pm Sat) Home to the Subotica Greeters, local volunteers only too thrilled to show you around their hometown (provided you book 10 working days before your arrival).

❶ Getting There & Away

From the **bus station** (www.sutrans.rs; Senćanski put 3) there are hourly services to Novi Sad (600DIN, two hours) and Belgrade (1280DIN, 3½ hours). See the website for updated prices and other destinations. Subotica's **train station** (Bose Milećević bb) has two trains to Szeged, Hungary (300DIN, 1¾ hours). Trains to Belgrade (480DIN, 3½ hours) stop at Novi Sad (384DIN, 1½ hours).

FRUŠKA GORA & SREMSKI KARLOVCI

Fruška Gora (Фрушка Гора) is an 80km stretch of rolling hills where monastic life has continued since 35 monasteries were built between the 15th and 18th centuries to safeguard Serbian culture and religion from the Turks. With your own vehicle you can flit freely between the 16 remaining monasteries; otherwise, ask about tours at tourist offices in Novi Sad and **Sremski Karlovci** (Сремски Карловци). Public transport gets you to villages within the park, from where you can walk between sights.

An easy outing is done with a bus from Novi Sad bound for Irig; ask to be let out at the **Novo Hopovo Monastery** (170DIN, 30 minutes). From here, walk or catch local buses to other points such as Vrdnik. Visit www.npfruskagora.co.rs for a rundown on the region; www.psdzeleznicarns.org.rs has detailed information on individual monasteries (click on 'manasija').

At the edge of Fruška Gora on the banks of the Danube is the photogenic village of **Sremski Karlovci**. Lined with stunning structures, including the Orthodox cathedral (1758–62), the baroque Four Lions fountain and the Chapel of Peace at the southern end of town (where the Turks and Austrians signed the 1699 Peace Treaty), Sremski Karlovci is also at the heart of a famed wine region. Visit the **Museum of Beekeeping & Wine Cellar** (www. muzejzivanovic.com; Mitropolita Stratimirovića 86) to try famous *bermet* wine, or drop in at any of the family-owned cellars around town. Buzzing during summer weekends with lively wedding parties, Sremski Karlovci also hosts a grape-harvesting festival every October.

Take frequent buses 61 or 62 from Novi Sad (140DIN, 30 minutes) and visit the **tourist organisation** (☑883 855; www.karlovci.org.rs; Patrijarha Rajačića 1; ⊙8am-6pm Mon-Fri, 10am-6pm Sat) just off the main square.

SOUTHERN SERBIA

Great adventures await south of Belgrade. Zlatibor's rolling hills are a peaceful privilege to explore any time of the year. Dramatic Kopaonik is a popular ski destination for Europeans in the know. Pressed against Balkan neighbours are the melding cultural heritages of the Raška region (known interchangeably by the Turkish 'Sandžak'), the last to be liberated from Ottoman rule in 1912.

Novi Pazar feels more Turkish than some pockets of İstanbul, with winding streets and an Ottoman skyline spiked by minarets, yet some of Serbia's most revered Orthodox monasteries are but a cab ride away.

Niš   Ниш

☑018 / POP 202,200

Niš is a lively city of curious contrasts, where Roma in horse-drawn carriages trot alongside new cars, and posh cocktails are sipped in antiquated alleyways.

Niš was settled in pre-Roman times and flourished during the time of local-boy-made-good Emperor Constantine (AD 280–337). Turkish rule lasted from 1386 until 1877 despite several Serb revolts; the Tower of Skulls and Niš Fortress are reminders of Ot-

toman dominion. The Nazis built one of Serbia's most notorious concentration camps here, ironically named 'the Red Cross'.

⦿ Sights

Niš Fortress   FORTRESS
(Niška tvrđava; Jadranska; ⊙24hr) While its current incarnation was built by the Turks in the 18th century, there have been forts on this site since ancient Roman times. Today it's a sprawling recreational area with restaurants, cafes, market stalls and ample space for moseying. It hosts the **Nišville International Jazz Festival** (www.nisville.com) each August and **Nišomnia** (www.facebook.com/festivalnisomnia), featuring rock and electro acts, in September. The city's main pedestrian boulevard, Obrenoviceva, stretches before the citadel.

Tower of Skulls   MONUMENT
(Ćele Kula; Bul Zoran Đinđić; adult/child 120/100DIN; ⊙8am-8pm Tue-Sun Apr-Oct, 9am-4pm Tue-Sat, 10am-4pm Sun Nov-Mar) With Serbian defeat imminent at the 1809 Battle of Čegar, the Duke of Resava kamikazeed towards the Turkish defences, firing at their gunpowder stores. In doing so, he killed himself, 4000 of his men, and 10,000 Turks. The Turks triumphed regardless, and to deter future acts of rebellion, they beheaded, scalped and

MADNESS, MADE IN SERBIA

On the surface, the **Dragačevo Trumpet Assembly** (an annual gathering of brass musicians) sounds harmless; nerdily endearing even. But band camp this ain't: it *is*, however, the most boisterous music festival in all of Europe, if not the world.

Known as 'Guča', after the western Serbian village that has hosted it each August since 1961, the six-day debauch is hedonism at its most rambunctious: tens of thousands of beer-and-brass-addled visitors dance wild *kola* through the streets, gorging on spit-meat and slapping dinar on the sweaty foreheads of the (mostly Roma) *trubači* performers. The music itself is relentless and frenzy-fast; even Miles Davis confessed, 'I didn't know you could play trumpet that way.' Sleep is a dubious proposition, but bring a tent or book ahead anyway: www.guca.rs has information on accommodation and transport.

embedded the skulls of the dead Serbs in this tower. Only 58 of the initial 952 skulls remain. Contrary to Turkish intention, the tower serves as a proud monument of Serbian resistance. Get there on any bus marked 'Niška Banja' from the stop opposite the Ambassador Hotel: ask to be let out at Ćele Kula.

Red Cross Concentration Camp   MUSEUM
(Crveni Krst; Bul 12 Februar; adult/child 120/100DIN; ⊙9am-4pm Tue-Sun Apr-Oct, 9am-4pm Tue-Fri, 10am-2pm Sat & Sun Nov-Mar) One of the best-preserved Nazi camps in Europe, the deceptively named Red Cross held about 30,000 Serbs, Roma, Jews and Partisans during the German occupation of Serbia (1941–45). Harrowing displays tell their stories, and those of the prisoners who attempted to flee in the biggest ever breakout from a concentration camp. A short walk north of the Niš bus station.

FREE Mediana   RUINS
(Bul Cara Konstantina; ⊙10am-6pm Tue-Sun) Mediana, on the eastern outskirts of Niš and a short walk from Ćele Kula, is what remains of Constantine's 4th-century Roman palace. Digging has revealed a palace, mosaics, forum and an expansive grain-storage area. There's an archaeology collection at the

small **museum** (Nikole Pašića 59; adult/child 120/100DIN; ⊙10am-6pm Tue-Sun).

🛏 Sleeping

Hostel Niš   HOSTEL €
(☑513 703; www.hostelnis.rs; Dobrička 3a; dm/d per person 1260/1780DIN; @) Perfectly central with outgoing, helpful staff, good-sized rooms and lockable storage? Winner. It's a five-minute walk (towards the river) from the bus station.

Hotel Niški Cvet   HOTEL €€
(☑297 700; www.niskicvet.com; Kej 29 Decembar 2; s/d €60/90, ste €78-120; P ❄ 🛜) Top views over the Nišava River and fortress from slick surrounds. Prices drop on weekends.

Hostel Sponsor   HOSTEL €
(www.hostel-sponsor.rs; Generala Milojka Lešjanina 18b; dm/s/d €11/19/22; P ❄ 🛜) Small, shiny and brand new, this amiable option is a mere 50m stroll from the centre of town. Prices are negotiable.

Hostel Sweet   HOSTEL €
(☑628-942 085; www.sweet-hostel.com; Milorad Veljkovića Špaje 11/4; dm/s/d/tr/q 1000/1500/2000/3000/4000DIN, apt 3000-10,000DIN; ❄ 🛜) This clean, genial spot has lockable storage in each room and a laid-back vibe.

Hotel Ambassador   HOTEL €€
(☑501 800; www.srbijaturist.com; Trg Kralja Milana bb; s €39-46, d €47-55, ste from €60; ❄ @) Elizabeth Taylor, a pal of Tito's, once stayed here… and not much has changed since. A communist relic, the rooms are stale but bearable.

🍴 Eating & Drinking

The cobblestoned Kopitareva (Tinkers' Alley) is chock-full of fast-paced eating and drinking options, including **Flo** (Kopitareva 11; ⊙7.30am-midnight Mon-Thu, to 2am Fri & Sat, 9am-midnight Sun) and **Tesla** (Kopitareva 8; ⊙8am-midnight; 🛜). Locals gather nightly to brown-bag it along the river.

Hamam   SERBIAN €€
(Tvrđava bb; meals 400-2200DIN; ⊙11am-midnight) A crumbling Turkish bath house outside, and an elegant multi-alcove dining space inside, the wonderful Hamam serves up mounds of meat worth salivating over (the Turkish-style grilled lamb is especially slobber-worthy).

Restoran Sindjelić   SERBIAN €
(Nikole Pasića 36; meals from 400DIN; ⊙8am-1am Sun-Fri, to 2am Sat) Hearty traditional fare.

Pekara Branković   BAKERY €

(Vožda Karađorđa 68; ⊘24hr) Niš fancies itself the *burek* capital of Serbia (no arguments there), and this *pekara* (bakery) cooks up some of the tastiest slabs in town.

Crazy Horse   BAR

(Davidova 8; ⊘8am-2am Sat-Thu, to 4am Fri; 📶) Guinness, darts, live Irish music, Champions League on TV...in the birthplace of Constantine the Great? Crazy – like the name says – but somehow, this Irish bar works.

Lo-Co Tropic Open Bar   CAFE

(Kej Kola Srpskih Sestara bb; ⊘8am-late Wed-Sat; 📶) Kick back in a porch swing with coffees or cocktails and watch the Nišava River trickle past. Under the bridge across from the fortress.

ℹ Information

Internet Cafe (Hotel Ambassador; per hr 50DIN; ⊘7am-11pm)

Post Office (Voždova Karađorđa 13a; ⊘8am-8pm) Internet access for 50DIN per hour.

Tourist Organisation of Niš (📞250 222; www.visitnis.com; Tvrđava; ⊘7.30am-7pm Mon-Fri, 9am-1pm Sat) Within the citadel gates.

ℹ Getting There & Away

The **bus station** (Bul 12 Februar) behind the fortress has frequent services to Belgrade (1420DIN, three hours) and Brus (714DIN, 1½ hours) for Kopaonik, and three daily to Novi Pazar (1120DIN, four hours).

From the **train station** (Dimitrija Tucovića), there are seven trains to Belgrade (784DIN, 4½ hours) and two to Sofia (702DIN, five hours).

Novi Pazar   Нови Пазар

📞020 / POP 60,600

Novi Pazar is the cultural centre of the Raška/Sandžak region, with a large Muslim population. Turkish coffee, cuisine and customs abound, yet some idyllic Orthodox sights are in the vicinity: this was the heartland of the Serbian medieval state.

⊙ Sights

The Old Town is lined with cafes and shops peddling Turkish goods, while just across the Raška River, cafes and restaurants flank 28 Novembar. Attempts to restore the ruined *hammam* (Turkish bath; off Maj street) have failed dismally, leaving it at the mercy of coffee-drinking men and picnickers.

Sopoćani Monastery, the Church of St Peter and St George Monastery are accessible by taxi; a return trip to a single site should cost around 900DIN.

Sopoćani Monastery   MONASTERY

Built in the mid-13th century by King Uroš (who is buried here), this was destroyed by the Turks in the late 1600s and restored in the 1920s. Frescos inside the Romanesque church are prime examples of medieval art that miraculously survived over two centuries exposed to the elements. The *Assumption of the Virgin Mary* fresco is one of Serbia's most renowned.

Church of St Peter   CHURCH

(Petrova Crkva) Three kilometres from town, this small stone building is the oldest intact church in Serbia; it was founded in the 4th century, with additions made between 600 and 800. The cemetery holds the grave of a 5th-century Illyrian prince. If it's locked, ask at the nearby house to be let in.

St George Monastery   MONASTERY

(Đurđev Stupovi) Near the Church of St Peter, this 1170 cloister is the result of a promise to God by Stefan Nemanja that he would endow a monastery to St George if he was released from captivity (his brothers had imprisoned him in a cave). Ongoing efforts to restore the complex after extensive WWII damage are resurrecting monastic life.

🛏 Sleeping

Hotel Vrbak   HOTEL €

(📞314 548; www.hotelvrbak.com; Maršala Tita bb; s/d/apt 2500/4500/5500DIN; 📶) The Vrbak is practically a destination in its own right: a motley mashup of architectural styles (think UFO-meets-magic-mushrooms, dolled up in nouveau-cement), it's an unmissable landmark in the centre of town. Though the lofty lobby atrium hints at Napoleonic delusions, the rooms are clean but basic. Still, it's worth staying just so you can say you did.

Hotel Tadž   HOTEL €€

(📞311 904; www.hoteltadz.rs; Rifata Burdževića 79; s/d/apt 4000/6000/8400DIN; ❇📶) This modern, upmarket hotel has working wi-fi and a high-quality restaurant.

Hotel Atlas   HOTEL €€

(📞316 352; Jošanički Kej bb; s/d/tr from €30/50/60; ❇📶) Modern, sprawling rooms that you'll be loathe to leave...though the

WORTH A TRIP

STUDENICA MONASTERY

One of the most sacred sites in Serbia, Studenica was established in the 1190s by founder of the Serbian empire (and future saint) Stefan Nemanja and developed by his sons Vukan, Stefan and Rastko (St Sava). Active monastic life was cultivated by Sava and continues today, though this thriving little community doesn't mind visitors.

Two well-preserved churches lie within impressive white-marble walls. **Bogorodičina Crkva** (Church of Our Lady), a royal funeral church, contains Stefan's tomb. Smaller **Kraljeva Crkva** (King's Church) houses the acclaimed *Birth of the Virgin* fresco and other masterpieces.

From Novi Pazar, catch a Kraljevo-bound bus to the village of Ušće (about one hour) and hop a local bus from there, or negotiate a return taxi journey.

free breakfast will lure you downstairs. Behind the marketplace (*pijaca*) near the river.

✕ Eating

Novi Pazar isn't a haven of haute cuisine, but there's plenty of local-style fast food to slaver over. The central 28 Novembar street is lined with no-frills eateries advertising *roštilj* (barbecue): you're in for a meaty treat at virtually any one of them. **Kod Jonuza** (28 Novembar 10; meals 100-300DIN; ⊙24hr) is a good choice.

ⓘ Getting There & Away

Frequent buses leave the bus station (a five-minute walk to Hotel Vrbak) for Belgrade (1520DIN, four hours). An overnight bus goes to Sarajevo (€16, seven hours) and there's one to Priština (€5, three hours).

Kopaonik   Копаоник
☑036

Situated around Pančićev Peak (Pančićev Vrh, 2017m) overlooking Kosovo, Serbia's prime ski resort has 44km of ski slopes and 23 lifts, and is a pleasant hiking base. Prices plummet off season, though many places open arbitrarily or close completely.

🛏 Sleeping & Eating

Large-scale hotels with restaurants, gym facilities, pizzerias, discos and shops are the go.

Hotel Grand   LUXURY HOTEL €€
(☑471 977; www.grand-kopaonik.com; s €60-170, d €82-240; ▣❄☎☍) Grand indeed, with a swimming pool, fitness centre, tennis courts and ski slopes on your doorstep.

Hostel Montana   HOSTEL €
(☑062-563 657; www.montana.rs; dm €13-25; ☐) Log-cabiny good times on the cheap.

JAT Apartments   APARTMENT €€
(☑547 1044; www.jatapartmani.com; apt per 1/2/3/4/5 persons from €30/34/36/50/58; ☎) Open year-round with spacious rooms and kitchenettes.

Komita Mountain House   SERBIAN €€
(Planinska kuća komita; ☑063-505 780; meals from 400DIN) A 3km cab ride from town, this endearing inn offers wholesome feasts (and blueberry pie!), plus a respite from Kop's relentlessly showy central choices.

ⓘ Information

The resort centre is amply equipped with ATMs, shops, restaurants and a post office.

Ski Centre Kopaonik (www.skis.rs; ⊙9am-5pm) Ski passes at the base of Hotel Grand.

Skiline (www.skiline.co.uk) Books ski holidays in 'Kop'.

Tourist Centre Kopaonik (Turistički Centar Kopaonik; www.tckopaonik.com) For assistance with tours, packages and accommodation.

ⓘ Getting There & Away

In season, there are three daily buses from Belgrade (1670DIN, five hours) and three from Niš to Brus (714DIN, 1½ hours). From Novi Pazar, pick up an infrequent connection in Raška; taxis cost around 2000DIN.

Zlatibor   Златибор
☑031 / POP 284,700

A romantic region of gentle mountains, traditions and hospitality, Zlatibor encompasses the Tara and Šargan mountains in the north and the Murtenica hills bordering BiH. The town centre (*tržni centar*) has everything you could need, but not far beyond are quaint villages where locals are oblivious to ski-bunny shenanigans.

🕴 Activities

Zlatibor's slopes are mild. Major skiing hills are Tornik (the highest peak in Zlatibor at 1496m) and Obudovica. The nordic skiing trail at the northern foothill of Šumatno Brdo is 1042m at its highest point.

Several walking trails start, end or pass the town centre. In easy reach is the monument in memory of local victims of German aggression in 1941; head south along Ul Sportova, cross the footbridge and follow the footpath to the monument and its wonderful views.

🛏 Sleeping & Eating

Private rooms and apartments offer more space and privacy for less money than resorts. In season they typically cost €25 to €80 for two to six people and €10 to €30 less out of season. Find them through Zlatibor Tours, travel agents or www.zlatibor.com. The best meals are found in local villages, but there are some decent options (and a trillion pizzerias) in the town centre.

Hotel Palisad HOTEL €€
(📞841 151; www.palisad.rs; Naselje Jezero bb; s/d/apt from 3300/5600/5800DIN; 🅿🌐🛜) With elegant, minimalistic room decor, modern art in the lobby and in-house bowling alley, this may seem like an unlikely hang-out for a communist honcho, but Tito adored this mountain retreat. You can even stay in his favourite suite (ask for 'Titov apartman'). Overlooking the lake in the town centre.

Hotel Mona Zlatibor HOTEL €€
(📞841 021; www.monazlatibor.com; Naselje Jezero 26; r 7700-9400DIN, apt from 8500DIN; 🛜) This well-groomed hotel opposite the bus station does its best to keep you indoors, with a wellness centre, two restaurants and a bar.

Konoba SERBIAN €€
(📞841 674; meals from 550DIN; ⏰8am-midnight) Serbian for 'tavern', Konoba delivers on its promise, with an atmosphere as full-blooded as its substantial meals. Rousing live *tamburaši* music adds to the knees-up feel.

Vendome NIGHTCLUB
(⏰8am-2am) Innocuous cafe by day, contender for the most-strobe-lights-in-a-club-ever award by night. Ditzy fun.

ℹ Information

Banka Intesa (Tržni Centar; ⏰8am-4pm Mon-Fri, to noon Sat) Has a 24-hour ATM inside.

Igraonica Internet Caffe (Tržni centar; per hr 200DIN; ⏰9am-11pm)

Post Office (Tržni centar; ⏰7am-7pm)

Zlatibor Tours (📞845 957; Tržni centar, bus station; ⏰8am-9pm) The scarily efficient Danijela will have your homestay and tours booked before you know what hit you.

WORTH A TRIP

ZLATIBOR EXCURSIONS

Tumble back in time to 19th-century Serbia at the **open-air museum** (www.sirogojno.org.rs; adult/child 150/100DIN; ⏰9am-4pm Nov-Apr, to 7pm Apr-Nov) in the village of Sirogojno. High-roofed, fully furnished wooden houses are spread across a pleasant mountainside and are open for your exploration.

Mokra Gora is home to the village of **Drvengrad** (Küstendorf; www.mecavnik.info; Mećavnik hill; adult/child 200/120DIN; ⏰9am-9pm), built by enigmatic filmmaker Emir Kusturica in 2002 for his film *Life is a Miracle*. Quirky, colourful flourishes give the village a fantastical feel: the Stanley Kubrick cinema shows Kusturica's films, there's a life-size statue of Johnny Depp, and Bruce Lee St is home to a restaurant where you can sip 'Che Guevara biorevolution juice' and goggle at prime panoramas. Drvengrad hosts the international Küstendorf Film and Music Festival each January.

The **Šargan 8 railway** (📞bookings 510 288; www.serbianrailways.com; adult/child 600/300DIN; ⏰10.30am & 1.25pm daily Apr-Oct, also 8am & 4.10pm depending on demand) tourist train was once part of a narrow-gauge railway linking Belgrade with Sarajevo and Dubrovnik. The joy of the 2½-hour journey is in its disorienting twists, turns and tunnels (all 22 of them).

Reach these sights via bus from Užice or on a tour with any of the agencies at Zlatibor bus station. Those with a smattering of Serbian should contact Toma of Mokra Gora's **Tomadija Tours** (📞060-0800 324; tomadija.tours@gmail.com). Born in a Šargan 8 tunnel, he's as local as it gets!

ⓘ Getting There & Around

Express buses leave the bus stand for Belgrade (1170DIN, four hours, hourly), Novi Sad (1250DIN, 6½ hours, four daily) and Užice (200DIN, 45 minutes, almost hourly 5.50am to 11.10pm), the nearest railhead.

Without your own wheels, the easiest way to go exploring is to join local tours. A return taxi to the edge of the region costs around 2400DIN.

UNDERSTAND SERBIA

Serbia Today

Serbia is a small but hugely misunderstood country. Artistic and passionate with a penchant for partying, it is also a fractious nation with many unresolved historical issues. Modern Serbs have an eye towards joining the EU; many others resist the changes such a move would bring to their fiercely independent country.

History

Events that took place centuries ago are as personal to many Serbs as if they happened last week. The country's history is extremely contentious and viewpoints differ between those of contrasting backgrounds.

Early Invasions

Serbian history has been punctuated by foreign invasions from the time the Celts supplanted the Illyrians in the 4th century BC through to the arrival of the Romans 100 years later, the Slavs in the 6th century AD, the Turks in the 14th century, the Austro-Hungarians in the late 19th and early 20th centuries, and the Germans briefly in WWII.

Enter the Ottomans

Independence briefly flowered from 1217 with a 'golden age' during Stefan Dušan's reign as emperor (1346–55). Serbia declined after his death, and the pivotal Battle of Kosovo in 1389, where the Turks defeated Serbia, ushered in 500 years of Islamic rule. Early revolts were crushed but an 1815 uprising led to de facto independence that became complete in 1878.

The Land of Southern Slavs

On 28 June 1914, Austria-Hungary used the assassination of Archduke Franz Ferdinand by a Bosnian Serb as cause to invade Serbia, sparking WWI: almost 60% of Serbia's male population perished. In 1918 Croatia, Slovenia, Bosnia & Hercegovina (BiH), Vojvodina, Serbia and its Kosovo province, Montenegro, and Macedonia were joined into the Kingdom of Serbs, Croats and Slovenes; these countries became Yugoslavia (Land of Southern Slavs) in 1929.

An anti-Axis coup in March 1941 led to the Nazi bombing of Belgrade. Royalist Četniks and communist Partisans fought the Germans, Croatia's pro-Nazi, genocidal Ustaše organisation and each other, with Josip Tito's Partisans finally gaining the upper hand. In 1945 they formed the government, abolished the monarchy and declared a federal republic including Serbia, Kosovo and Vojvodina.

Tito broke with former ally Stalin in 1948, and in 1961 founded the Non-Aligned Movement. Within Yugoslavia, growing regional inequalities and burgeoning Serbian expansionism fuelled demands for greater autonomy. Tito's death in1980 signalled the beginning of the rise of nationalism, stifled but long-simmering, within the republics.

A Turbulent Era

By 1986 Serbian nationalists were espousing a 'Greater Serbia', an ideology that would encompass Serbs from all republics into one state. Appropriated by Serbia's Communist Party leader Slobodan Milošević, the doctrine was fuelled by claims of the genocide of Serbs by Kosovo Albanians, leading to the abolishment of self-rule in Kosovo in 1990. Croatia, Slovenia, BiH and Macedonia seceded from the federation, sparking a series of violent conflicts known collectively as the Yugoslav Wars.

Bitter, bloody and monstrously complex, the wars – Slovenia's Ten-Day War, the Croatian War of Independence and the Bosnian War – were fought not just between breakaway forces and the majority-Serb Yugoslav Army, but along fractious ethnic and religious lines as well. Atrocities were committed on all sides: perhaps the most stunning display of savagery came with the Srebrenica massacre, in which 8000 Bosnian men and boys were allegedly killed under orders of Republika Srpska Army (RSA) commander Ratko Mladić and RS president Radovan Karadžić. Claims of rape camps, ethnic cleansing and other barbarisms saw Serbia assume the role of international pariah.

In April 1992 the remaining republics, Serbia and Montenegro, formed a 'third' Yugoslav federation without provision of autonomy for Kosovo, despite its Albanian majority. Violence erupted in January 1998.

In March 1999 peace talks failed when Serbia rejected the US-brokered Rambouillet Agreement. In response to organised resistance in Kosovo, Serbian forces attempted to empty the country of its Albanian population; hundreds of thousands fled into Macedonia and Albania, galvanising the US and NATO into a 78-day bombing campaign. On 12 June 1999 Serbian forces withdrew from Kosovo.

European Dawn

In the 2000 presidential elections, opposition parties led by Vojislav Koštunica declared victory, a claim denounced by Milošević. Opposition supporters from all over Serbia swarmed to Belgrade and stormed Parliament. When Russia recognised Koštunica's win, Milošević had to acknowledge defeat.

Koštunica restored ties with Europe, acknowledged Yugoslav atrocities in Kosovo and rejoined the UN. In April 2001 Milošević was arrested and extradited to the international war-crimes tribunal in The Hague.

In April 2002 a loose union of Serbia and Montenegro replaced Yugoslavia. In 2003 Serbia was shaken by the assassination of reformist Prime Minister Zoran Đinđić, who had been instrumental in handing Milošević to The Hague. In June 2004 Serbia gained a new president in pro-European Boris Tadić.

On 11 March 2006 Milošević was found dead in his cell. In May, 55% of Montenegrins voted for independence from Serbia. In February 2008 Kosovo declared its independence, a move that Serbia held to be illegal; later that year, Karadžić was arrested for war crimes after 12 years as a fugitive. Mladić was finally apprehended in 2011.

In the 2012 elections, Tadić lost to Tomislav Nikolić, a former member of the far-right Serbian Radical Party. Serbia is an official candidate for EU membership, but it remains unseen how Kosovo – and Nikolić – will affect these aspirations.

People

The population is estimated at 7.2 million people, made up of Serbs (83.3%), Hungarians (3.5%), Bosniaks (2%), Roma (2.1%) and others (5.1%). Around 85% of the population identify as Serbian Orthodox. The 5% Roman Catholic population are mostly Vojvodinian Hungarians. Muslims (Albanians and Slavic) comprise around 3% of the country's population.

Arts

The survival and active rebellion of artistic expression throughout dark periods in history is a source of pride. Today, creative juices flow thickly and freely, with films spawning idyllic villages, art sold in cocktail bars and eclectic music events.

Literature

Long-time Belgrade resident Ivo Andrić was awarded the Nobel prize for his epic (and very readable) *Bridge on the Drina*.

Internationally acclaimed word wizard Milorad Pavić writes in many dimensions: *The Inner Side of the Wind* can be read from the back or the front. Novelist Momo Kapor's *A Guide to the Serbian Mentality* is an amusing peek into the national psyche, while Vuk Drašković's *Knife* offers a harrowing introduction to inter-Balkan tensions.

Cinema

World-renowned director Emir Kusturica sets the bar on Serbian cinema with his raucous approach to storytelling. Check out *Underground* (1995), the surreal tale of seemingly never-ending Balkan conflicts, *Time of the Gypsies* (1989), *Black Cat, White Cat* (1998) and *Life is a Miracle* (2004), about an optimistic Serbian engineer working on the Mokra Gora railway. Serbian black humour gets a workout in Yugo-classics *Ko to Tamo Peva* (*Who's That Singing There?*, 1980) and *Balkanski Špijun* (*Balkan Spy*, 1984).

Music

Pleh muzika (wild, haunting brass sounds influenced by Turkish and Austrian military music), also called *trubači*, is the national music. Popular examples are the soundtrack to the film *Underground* and albums by trumpet player Boban Marković. *Trubači* gets an orgiastic outing at Guča's Dragačevo Trumpet Assembly each August.

Cross traditional folk with techno and you get 'turbofolk', controversial during the Milošević era for its nationalist overtones but now more mainstream fun.

'Ex-Yu' rock bands like Električni Orgazam and Partibrejkers offered a lively soundtrack to the fall of communism; these days, Novi

Sad punkers Athiest Rap serve up cheeky, if equally rebellious, ditties.

Architecture

Ottoman, Austro-Hungarian and Serbian-Byzantine styles have fought for dominance, often over the same buildings, which have been stripped, redressed and modified over the years depending on who was in charge. Layers of communist-era concrete aren't going anywhere in a hurry.

Environment

Serbia comprises 77,474 sq km. Midžor (2169m), on the Stara Planina range, is its highest peak. Zlatibor and Kopaonik are winter playgrounds.

Vojvodina is glass-flat agricultural land. South of the Danube (Dunav), the landscape rises through rolling green hills, which crest where the eastern outpost of the Dinaric Alps slices southeastwards across the country.

Major national parks are Kopaonik, Tara and Fruška Gora. Among Serbia's mammals are wild boars, wildcats, beavers, otters, susliks, lynx and mouflon. Around 40% of Serbia's 360 bird species are of European Conservation Concern.

Serbia faces air pollution around Belgrade and dumping of industrial waste into the Sava. Some remnants of the 1999 NATO bombings, such as factories outside Belgrade, are ecological hazards.

Food & Drink

The ubiquitous snack is *burek,* a filo-pastry pie made with *sir* (cheese), *meso* (meat), *krompir* (potato) or occasionally *pečurke* (mushrooms). Eat without yoghurt if you like the 'blasphemer' tag. Score *burek* and other snacks at shops labelled *pekara* (bakery).

Serbia is famous for grilled meats such as *ćevapčići* (rolled spicy mince), *pljeskavica* (spicy hamburger) and *ražnjići* (pork or veal shish kebabs).

Regional cuisines range from spicy Hungarian goulash in Vojvodina to Turkish kebabs in Novi Pazar, while the small central village of Ozrem takes extreme cuisine *do jaja* ('to the balls') at their annual Testicle Cooking Championships.

It's not an easy place for vegetarians. Try asking for *posna hrana* (meatless food); this is also suitable for vegans. Otherwise, there's always vegetarian pizza, *srpska salata* (raw peppers, onions and tomatoes, with oil, vinegar and occasionally chilli), *šopska salata* (tomatoes, cucumber and onion with grated white cheese), *gibanica* (cheese pie) or *zeljanica* (cheese pie with spinach).

Many people distil *rakija* (schnapps) from plums *(šljiva),* quince *(dunja)* or other fruits. The delicious – but deceptively potent – *medovača* is made from honey. Viscous Turkish coffee is omnipresent, but espresso is staging a takeover bid in larger towns.

SURVIVAL GUIDE

Directory A–Z

Accommodation

Private rooms and apartments offer superb value and can be organised through tourist offices. 'Wild' camping is possible outside national parks.

Tax is not always automatically included in hotel rates. If you depend on internet access, check that wireless actually works. Where a room is 'nonsmoking', it does not mean that the room has not been smoked in – only that you are free not to smoke in it.

The following price categories for the cost of a high-season double room are used in the listings in this chapter.

€ less than 3000DIN/€30

€€ 3000DIN/€30 to 70000DIN/€75

€€€ more than 7000DIN/€75

Activities

Serbia's national parks are havens for hikers looking for quiet paths; Tara National Park has almost 20 marked trails ranging from 2km to 18km. Climbers will enjoy the canyons of the Drina River.

It is possible to kayak and raft at Tara National Park along the Drina River; **Serbia Rafting** (www.serbiarafting.com/en) can organise rafting tours, as can the just-over-the-border, Bosnia-based **Drina-Tara Rafting Club** (www.raftingtara.com) and **Bodo** (www.tarabodo.com).

Several spots in Serbia have rich birdlife, including areas around Belgrade. Keen twitchers should contact the **League for Ornithological Action of Serbia** (www.ptica.org).

Business Hours

Banks 8am or 9am to 5pm Monday to Friday, 8am to 2pm Saturday

Bars 8am to 3am

Restaurants 8am to midnight or 1am

Shops 8am to 6pm Monday to Friday, some open Saturday evenings

Embassies & Consulates

A complete list of embassies and consulates in Serbia, as well as Serbian embassies around the world, is available at www.embassypages.com/serbia. New Zealand doesn't have an embassy in Serbia. It is represented through its embassy in The Hague. Countries represented in Belgrade (area code ☏011) include the following:

Australian Embassy (☏011-330 3400; www.serbia.embassy.gov.au; 7th fl, Vladimira Popovica 38-40)

Canadian Embassy (☏011-306 3000; bgrad@international.gc.ca; Kneza Miloša 75)

French Embassy (☏011-302 3500; www.ambafrance-srb.org; Pariska 11)

German Embassy (☏011-306 4300; www.belgrad.diplo.de; Neznanog Junaka 1)

Netherlands Embassy (☏011-2023 900; bel@minbuza.nl; Simina 29)

UK Embassy (☏011-264 5055; www.ukin-serbia.fco.gov.uk; Resavska 46)

US Embassy (☏011-361 9344; http://serbia.usembassy.gov; Kneza Miloša 50)

Food

The following price categories for the cost of a main course are used in the listings in this chapter.

€ less than 600DIN/€6

€€ 600DIN/€6 to 1000DIN/€10

€€€ more than 1000DIN/€10

Money

Serbia retains the dinar (DIN), though payment in euros for services and accommodation is commonplace.

ATMs are widespread and cards are accepted by established businesses. Exchange offices *(menjačnica)* are on every street corner. Exchange machines accept euros, US dollars and British pounds. Commission is charged for travellers cheques.

Post

Parcels should be taken unsealed to the main post office for inspection. You can receive mail, addressed poste restante, for a small charge.

Public Holidays

New Year 1 January

Orthodox Christmas 7 January

St Sava's Day 27 January

Statehood Day 15 February

Orthodox Good Friday April/May

Orthodox Easter Monday April/May

International Labour Days 1 and 2 May

Victory Day 9 May

St Vitus's Day (Vidovdan) 28 June

Safe Travel

Travelling around Serbia is generally safe for travellers who exercise the usual caution. The exceptions can be border areas, particularly the southeast Kosovo border where Serb–Albanian tensions remain. Check the situation before attempting to cross overland, and think thrice about driving there in Serbian-plated cars.

As evidenced by the neverending furore over Belgrade's Pride Parades (chronicled in the brilliant 2011 film *Parada*), life is not all rainbows for homosexuals in this conservative country. Discretion is highly advised.

Telephone

The country code is ☏381. Press the *i* button on public phones for dialling commands in English. Calls to Europe/Australia/North America cost around 50/100/80DIN per minute. Long-distance calls can also be made from booths in post offices.

Phonecards can be bought in post offices and tobacco kiosks for 300DIN (local cards) and 600DIN (international cards). Halo Plus cards allow longer calls locally, in the former Yugoslav Republic region or internationally, depending on which category you buy. Calls to Europe/Australia/USA cost from 15/40/40DIN per minute.

Mobile-phone SIM cards (around 200DIN) and recharge cards can be purchased at supermarkets and kiosks. All mobile numbers in Serbia start with ☏06.

Tourist Information

Tourist offices in Novi Sad and Belgrade have plenty of English material and friendly fonts of knowledge behind the desk.

In addition to the **National Tourism Organisation of Serbia** (www.serbia.travel), the **Tourist Organisation of Belgrade** (www.tob.rs) is loaded with useful information.

Visas

Tourist visas for stays of less than 90 days aren't required by citizens of EU countries, most other European countries, Australia, New Zealand, Canada and the USA. **The Ministry of Foreign Affairs** (www.mfa.gov. rs/Visas/Visas_en_how_to.htm) has full details.

Officially, all visitors must register with the police. Hotels and hostels will do this for you but if you're camping or staying in a private home, you are expected to register within 24 hours of arrival. Unofficially? This is rarely enforced, but being unable to produce registration documents upon leaving Serbia could result in a fine.

Getting There & Away
Air

Belgrade's **Nikola Tesla Beograd Airport** (☏011-209 4444; www.beg.aero) handles most international flights. The website has a full list of airlines.

Aeroflot (www.aeroflot.com)

Air France (www.airfrance.com)

Alitalia (www.alitalia.com)

Austrian Airlines (www.austrian.com)

JAT (www.jat.com)

Lufthansa (www.lufthansa.com)

Turkish Airlines (www.thy.com)

Land

Because Serbia does not acknowledge crossing points into Kosovo as international border crossings, it may not be possible to enter Serbia from Kosovo unless you first entered Kosovo from Serbia. Check with your embassy.

BUS

Bus services to both Western Europe and Turkey are well developed.

CAR & MOTORCYCLE

Drivers need International Driving Permits, and vehicles need either Green Card insurance or insurance purchased at the border (about €105 for a car, €66 for a motorbike).

Driving Serbian-plated cars into Kosovo isn't advised, and is often not permitted by rental agencies or insurers.

TRAIN

International rail connections leaving Serbia originate in Belgrade. Heading north and west, most call in at Novi Sad and Subotica. Heading east, they go via Niš.

Several trips from Serbia offer a nice slice of scenery, such as the route to Bar on the Montenegrin coast. For more information, visit **Serbian Railways** (www.serbianrailways. com).

Getting Around
Bicycle

Bicycle paths are improving in larger cities. Vojvodina is relatively flat, but main roads make for dull days. Mountainous regions such as Zlatibor offer mountain biking in summer months. Picturesque winding roads come with the downside of narrow shoulders.

Bus

Bus services are extensive, though outside major hubs sporadic connections may leave you in the lurch for a few hours. In southern Serbia particularly, you may have to double back to larger towns.

Reservations are only worthwhile for international buses and during festivals. Tickets can be purchased from the station before departure or on board.

Car & Motorcycle

The **Automobile & Motorcycle Association of Serbia** (Auto-Moto Savez Srbije; ☏011-333 1100, roadside assist 1987; www.amss.org.rs; Ruzveltova 18) provides roadside assistance and extensive information on its website.

Several car-hire companies (p813) have offices at Nikola Tesla Airport in Belgrade. Small-car hire typically costs €40 to €50 per day. Check where you are not able to take the car. In Belgrade and other large towns you may have to purchase parking tickets from machines, kiosks or via SMS (in Serbian only).

Traffic police are everywhere and accidents are workaday. The BAC limit is 0.03%.

Train

Serbian Railways (www.serbianrailways.com) serves Novi Sad, Subotica and Niš from Belgrade. Enthusiasts will enjoy the Šargan 8 railway in Mokra Gora.

Generally trains aren't as regular and reliable as buses, and can be murderously slow.

Slovakia

Why Go?

No, it isn't a province of the Czech Republic. Going strong over two decades as an independent state after the breakup of Czechoslovakia, Slovakia out-trumps the Czechs for ancient castles, and boasts nature far wilder than its western neighbours. It savours wine over beer and, in its bashful heartland amid mountains and forests, cradles an entrancing folk culture most European nations have lost.

Slovakia's small size is possibly its biggest attraction. You can hike woodsy waterfall-filled gorges one day and yodel from peaks soaring more than 2500m the next. Dinky capital Bratislava is awash with quirky museums and backed by thick forests. With its rabbit-warren Old Town, it might just win world prize for most cafes per city resident.

Don't leave without heading east, to where fortresses tower over tradition-rich medieval towns such as Levoča or Bardejov and hiking trails lace the hills. Down a *slivovica* (firewaterlike plum brandy) and drink a toast for us – *nazdravie!*

Best Places to Eat

» Café Verne (p835)
» Cactus (p866)
» Reštaurácia Bašta (p841)

Best Places to Stay

» Ginger Monkey Hostel (p854)
» Grand Hotel Kempinski (p852)
» Skaritz (p834)
» Hotel Marrol's (p834)

When to Go

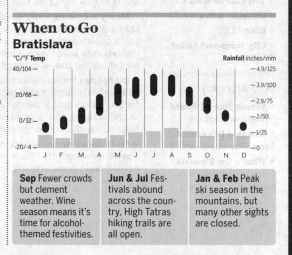

Bratislava

°C/°F Temp — 40/104 —, 20/68 —, 0/32 —, -20/-4 —
Rainfall inches/mm — 4.9/125, 3.9/100, 2.9/75, 2/50, 1/25, 0
J F M A M J J A S O N D

Sep Fewer crowds but clement weather. Wine season means it's time for alcohol-themed festivities.

Jun & Jul Festivals abound across the country, High Tatras hiking trails are all open.

Jan & Feb Peak ski season in the mountains, but many other sights are closed.

AT A GLANCE

» **Currency** Euro (€)

» **Language** Slovak

» **Money** ATMs widely available in cities

» **Visas** Not required for most visitors staying less than 90 days

Fast Facts

» **Area** 49,035 sq km

» **Capital** Bratislava

» **Country code** ☑02

» **Emergency** ♪112

Exchange Rates

Australia	A$1	€0.82
Canada	C$1	€0.77
Japan	¥100	€0.83
New Zealand	NZ$1	€0.65
UK	UK£1	€1.18
USA	US$1	€0.78

Set Your Budget

» **Budget hotel room** €30–60

» **Two-course meal** €15

» **Museum entrance** €3

» **Beer** €1.50

» **City transport ticket** €0.70

Resources

» **Slovak Tourist Board** (www.slovakia.travel)

» **Slovakia Document Store** (www.panorama.sk)

» **What's On Slovakia** (www.whatsonslovakia.com)

Connections

Though few airlines fly into Slovakia itself, Bratislava is just 60km from well-connected Vienna International Airport. By train from Bratislava, Budapest (three hours) and Prague (five hours) are easily reachable. Buses connect to Zakopane in Poland (two hours) from Poprad, and to Uzhhorod in Ukraine (2½ hours) via Košice.

ITINERARIES

Three Days

Two nights in Bratislava is enough to wander the Old Town streets and see some museums. The following day is best spent on a castle excursion, either to Devín or Trenčín. Or, better yet, spend all three days hiking in the rocky High Tatra mountains, staying central in the resort town of Starý Smokovec or in more off-beat Ždiar in the Belá Tatras.

One Week

After a day or two in Bratislava, venture east. Spend at least four nights around the Tatras so you have time to hike to a mountain hut as well as take day trips to the must-see Spiš Castle ruins, medieval Levoča, or to Slovenský Raj National Park for its highly rated Suchá Belá Gorge hike. For the last night or two, continue to Bardejov to marvel at its complete Renaissance town square, icon art and nearby wooden churches.

Essential Food & Drink

» **Sheep's cheese** *Bryndza* – sharp, soft and spreadable; *oštiepok* – solid and ball-shaped; *žinčina* – a traditional sheep's-whey drink (like sour milk).

» **Meaty moments** *Vývar* (chicken/beef broth served with *sližiky,* thin pasta strips, or liver dumplings); *kapustnica* (thick sauerkraut and meat soup, often with chorizo or mushrooms); baked duck/goose served in *lokše* (potato pancakes) and stewed cabbage.

» **Dumplings** Potato-based goodies in varieties such as *halušky* (mini-dumplings in cabbage or *bryndza* sauce topped with bacon) or *pirohy* (pocket-shaped dumplings stuffed with *bryndza* or smoked meat). For sweets, try *šulance* – walnut- or poppy-seed-topped dumplings.

» **Fruit firewater** Homemade or store-bought liquor, made from berries and pitted fruits, such as *borovička* (from juniper) and *slivovica* (from plums).

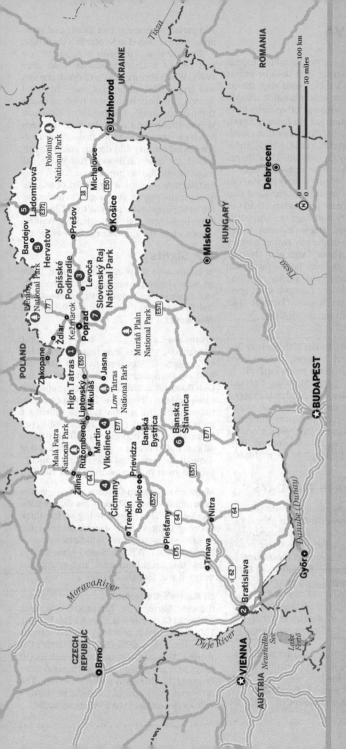

Slovakia Highlights

1 Hike between mountain huts in one of Europe's smallest alpine mountain ranges, the **High Tatras** (p848).

2 Linger over drinks at one of myriad sidewalk or riverfront cafes in Old Town **Bratislava** (p835).

3 Wander the ruins of **Spiš Castle** (p857), among the biggest in Europe.

4 Experience folk culture in traditional villages such as **Vlkolínec** (p842) and **Čičmany** (p842).

5 Seek out iconic, Unesco-listed wooden churches in isolated far-east Slovakia, such as **Hervatov** (p867) or **Ladomirová**.

6 Travel back in time at the spectacularly preserved ancient mining town of **Banská Štiavnica** (p846).

7 Climb creaking ladders past crashing waterfalls in the dramatic gorges of **Slovenský Raj National Park** (p860).

BRATISLAVA

♪02 / POP 432,800

Proximity to nature gives Slovakia's capital its strongest flavouring. The Danube wends through town and cycle paths through its verdant flood plain beginning just outside the centre. Meanwhile, a 30-minute walk from the train station are the densely forested Small Carpathians; the trailer to a mountainous extent that runs country-wide, virtually unimpeded by civilisation. Then there's ski runs and vineyards to amble among.

The charming – if tiny – Starý Mesto (Old Town) is the place to start appreciating Bratislava. Stroll narrow pedestrian streets of pastel 18th-century buildings or sample the nigh-on ubiquitous sidewalk cafes under the watchful gaze of the city castle, harking back to medieval times. Done with the old? In with the new: the city boasts intriguing Socialist-era architecture worth checking out and one of Eastern Europe's most spectacular modern art spaces. Contrasts like this are all part of Bratislava's allure.

History

Founded in AD 907, by the 12th century Bratislava (then called Poszony in Hungarian or Pressburg in German) was a large city in greater Hungary. King Matthias Corvinus founded a university here, Academia Istropolitana. Many of the imposing baroque palaces you see date to the reign of Austro-Hungarian empress Maria Theresa (1740–80), when the city flourished. From the 16th-century Turkish occupation of Budapest to the mid-1800s,

Hungarian parliament met locally and monarchs were crowned in St Martin's Cathedral.

'Bratislava' was officially born as the second city of a Czechoslovakian state after WWI. When Europe was redivided, the city was coveted by various nations – not least Austria (the population was predominantly German-speaking). US President Woodrow Wilson supported Czechoslovakian requests to have a Danube port included in their newly founded country and the city consequently almost got called Wilsonov. Post-WWII, the communists did a number on the town's architecture – razing a large part of the Old Town, including the synagogue, to make way for a highway. Bad architectural decisions have been reversed somewhat by positive ones, such as the Eurovea riverside complex.

◉ Sights

In addition to those mentioned here, there are several small museums and increasingly well-regarded galleries scattered about the Old Town: ask at the info centre for the *Art Plan* leaflet.

Bratislava Castle   CASTLE
(www.snm.sk; grounds free, museum adult/child €4/2; ⊘grounds 9am-9pm, museum 10am-6pm Tue-Sun) Dominating the southwest of the Old Town on a hill above the Danube, the castle today is largely a 1950s reconstruction; an 1811 fire left the fortress ruined for more than a century and renovations continue. Most buildings contain administrative offices, but there is a museum of Slovakia through the ages, and lawns and ramparts provide great vantage points for city viewing.

Museum of Jewish Culture   MUSEUM
(www.snm.sk; Židovská 17; adult/child €7/2; ⊘11am-5pm Sun-Fri) The most moving of the three floors of exhibits here focuses on the large Jewish community and buildings lost during and after WWII. Black-and-white photos show the neighbourhood and synagogue before it was ploughed under.

St Martin's Cathedral   CHURCH
(Dóm sv Martina; cnr Kapitulská/Starometská; adult/child €2/free; ⊘9-11.30am & 1-5pm Mon-Sat, 1.30-4.30pm Sun) A relatively modest interior belies the elaborate history of St Martin's Cathedral: 11 Austro-Hungarian monarchs (10 kings and one queen, Maria Theresa) were crowned in this 14th-century church. The busy motorway almost touching St Martin's follows the moat of the former city walls.

BRATISLAVA IN TWO DAYS

Start the morning climbing the ramparts of **Bratislava Castle** for views of the barrel-tile Old Town roofs and concrete kingdom Petržalka. On your way down, visit the excellent **Museum of Jewish Culture** and magnificent **St Martin's Cathedral**, coronation place of Hungarian monarchs. Spend the afternoon strolling through the Old Town, winding up with an atmospheric meal at **Cafe Verne** or a Slovak-style party at **Nu Spirit Club**.

On the second day, take a trip out to **Devín Castle** to see poignant ruins from the 9th to the 18th centuries, or jump aboard a boat to **Danubiana Meulensteen Art Museum**.

BRATISLAVA: QUEEN OF QUIRK

Bratislava deserves a crown for queen of quirkiness when it comes to sightseeing. The most photographed sight? Not a church or a castle, but the bronze statue called the **Watcher** (cnr Panská & Rybárska) peeping from an imaginary manhole. He's not alone: look out around the Old Town for other questionable statuesque characters, including the **Photographer** and a timepiece-toting monk. Other unusual attractions include the following:

Museum of Clocks (www.muzeum.bratislava.sk; Židovská 1; adult/child €2.30/1.50; ⊙10am-5pm Tue-Fri, 11am-6pm Sat-Sun) Random old clocks, but they're contained in an interestingly narrow building.

Blue Church (Kostol Svätej Alžbety; Bezručova 2; ⊙Services 7/9.30/11am & 6.30pm) Every surface of the 1911 Church of St Elizabeth, more commonly known as the Blue Church, is an art nouveau fantasy dressed in cool sky-blue and deeper royal blue.

Michael's Gate & Tower (www.muzeum.bratislava.sk; Michalská 24; adult/child €4.30/2.50; ⊙10am-6pm Tue-Sun) Climb past the five small storeys of medieval weaponry in Bratislava's only remaining gate for superior Old Town views from the top.

Hviezdoslavovo Námestie
SQUARE

Embassies, restaurants and bars are the mainstay of the long, tree-lined plaza that anchors the pedestrian zone's southern extremity. At Hviezdoslavovo's east end, the ornate 1886 Slovak National Theatre (p836), one of the city's opera houses, steals the show. The theatre is not open for tours, but ticket prices are not prohibitive. The nearby neo-baroque 1914 **Reduta Palace** (Eugena Suchoň nám; ⊙1-7pm Mon, Tue, Thu & Fri, 8am-2pm Wed) houses the Slovak Philharmonic: refurbishment included adding the impressive €1.5 million organ.

Hlavné Námestie
SQUARE

Cafe tables outline pretty Hlavné nám (Main Sq), the site of numerous festival performances. **Roland's Fountain**, at the square's heart, is thought to have been built in 1572 as a fire hydrant of sorts. Flanking the northeast side of the square is the 1421 **Old Town Hall** (www.muzeum.bratislava.sk; adult/child €5/2; ⊙10am-5pm Tue-Fri, 11am-6pm Sat & Sun), home to the city museum. You'll often find a musician in traditional costume playing a *fujira* on the steps of the **Jesuit Church**, on the edge of adjoining Františkánske nám.

Slovak National Gallery
ART MUSEUM

(Slovenská Národná Galéria; www.sng.sk; Rázusovo nábr 2; adult/child €3.50/2; ⊙10am-5pm Tue-Sun) A socialist modernist building and an 18th-century palace make interesting co-hosts for the Slovak National Gallery. The nation's eclectic art collection contained here ranges from Gothic to graphic design.

Apponyi Palace
WINE MUSEUM

(www.muzeum.bratislava.sk; Radničná 1; adult/child €6/3; ⊙10am-5pm Tue-Fri, 11am-6pm Sat & Sun) Explore the area's winemaking heritage in the cellar exhibits of this restored 1761 palace. There's an excellent, interactive English-language audio.

Slovak National Museum
MUSEUM

(www.snm.sk; Vajanského nábr 2; adult/child €3.50/1.50; ⊙9am-5pm Tue-Sun) Changing exhibits on the lower floors, natural history on top.

Bratislava Forest Park
FOREST

(Bratislavský Lesný Park; 🚌203) Marked by the Kamzik TV mast (complete with viewing platform and vista-endowed restaurant) and visible north of the city is this vast, hilly forest park. There's a **cable car** (Skiareál Mariánky, Dusíkova; €3; ⊙every 15min 10am-5pm) but you're up here for the superb, scenic hiking and biking. It's a 20-minute walk uphill from the Koliba trolleybus terminal to the park entrance.

🏃 Activities

From April through September, **Slovak Shipping & Ports** (☑5293 2226; www.lod.sk; Fajnorovo nábr 2) runs 45-minute Bratislava return boat trips (adult/child €5/3.50) on the Danube. Its Devín sightseeing cruise (adult/child return €7/5) plies the waters to the castle, stops for one to two hours and returns to Bratislava in 30 minutes.

You can rent bikes from **Bratislava Sightseeing** (☑0907683112; www.bratislavasightseeing. com; Fajnorovo nábr; per hr/day €6/18; ⊙10am-6pm

Central Bratislava

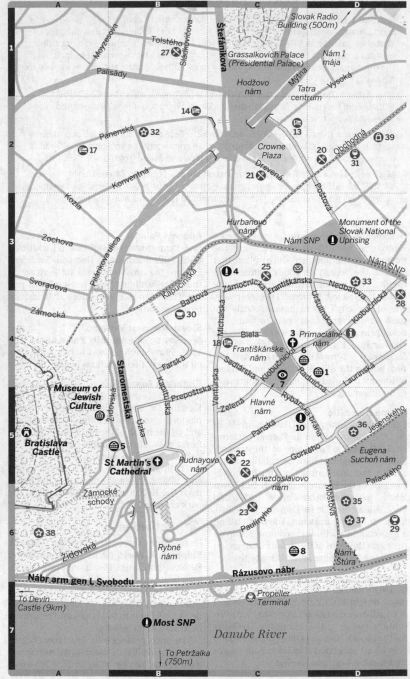

Slovak Radio Building (500m)

Tolstého

27

Štefánikova

Grassalkovich Palace (Presidential Palace)

Nám 1 mája

Moyzesova

Šancová

Palisády

Hodžovo nám

Mýtna

Tatra centrum

Vysoká

14

13

Panenská

32

Crowne Plaza

20

Obchodná

39

17

31

Konventná

Drevená

21

Poštová

Kozia

Hurbanovo nám

Monument of the Slovak National Uprising

Zochova

Nám SNP

Nám SNP

Svoradova

4

25

Františkánska

Nedbalova

33

Zámocká

Kapucínska

Zámočnícka

Ursulínska

Kloboučnícka

28

Pilárikova ulica

Baštová

Michalská

Biela

3

Primaciálne nám

30

18

Františkánske nám

6

1

Museum of Jewish Culture

Farská

Sedlárska

Kloboučnícka

Radničná

7

Laurinská

Staromestská

Kapitulská

Prepoštská

Ventúrska

Zelená

Hlavné nám

Rybárska brána

Žižkova

Úzka

Panská

10

36

Bratislava Castle

5

Rudnayovo nám

26

Gorkého

Eugena Suchoň nám

St Martin's Cathedral

22

Hviezdoslavovo nám

Mostová

Palackého

Žámocké schody

23

Paulínyho

35

37

38

Židovská

Rybné nám

8

29

Nábr arm gen L Svobodu

Rázusovo nábr

Nám L Štúra

To Devín Castle (9km)

Propeller Terminal

Most SNP

Danube River

To Petržalka (750m)

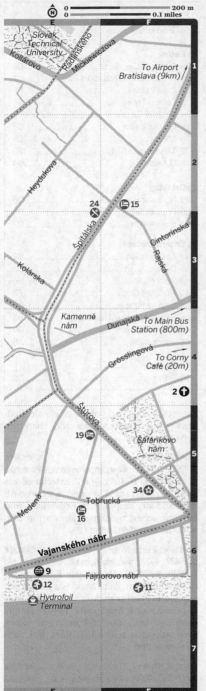

mid-May–mid-Sep), located in a children's playground along the waterfront.

Tours

Authentic Slovakia CULTURAL TOUR

TOP CHOICE
(☎908308234; www.authenticslovakia.com; per 2/4hr tour €25/39) Want to know about the Slovakia the other tours don't tell you about? Sign up with these guys for forays to weird Socialist-era buildings and typical *krčmy* (Slovak pubs): authentic (uncensored) Slovakia.

FREE Be Free Tours WALKING TOUR
(www.befreetours.com; ⊙11am & 4pm Tue-Sat, 4pm Sun & Mon) Lively, two-hour-plus English tour of the Old Town, leaving from the Hviezdoslav statue in Hviezdoslavovo nám. They also run pub crawls (Tuesdays, Thursdays and Saturdays).

Festivals & Events

Cultural Summer Festival CULTURE
(http://visit.bratislava.sk; ⊙Jun-Sep) A smorgasbord of plays and performances comes to the streets and venues around town in summer.

Bratislava Jazz Days MUSIC
(www.bjd.sk; ⊙Oct) World-class jazz takes centre stage for three days.

Christmas Market SHOPPING
(⊙Nov & Dec) From 26 November, Hlavné nám fills with food and drink, crafts for sale and staged performances.

International Film Festival FILM
(www.iffbratislava.sk; ⊙Nov) Showcases a great selection of offbeat worldwide cinema.

Fjúžn CULTURE
(www.fjuzn.sk; ⊙Apr) Dunaj (p837), which is an important venue for world music year-round, hosts this annual celebration of Slovak minorities and their cultures.

Sleeping

For a full accommodation list, see www.bkis.sk. Getting a short-term rental flat in the old town (€65 to €120 per night) is a great way to stay super-central without paying hotel prices, plus you can self-cater. Family-run and friendly, the modern units of **Apartments Bratislava** (www.apartmentsbratislava.com) are our top choice. Many hostels also have kitchens.

Central Bratislava

◉ Top Sights

◉ Sights

◉ Activities, Courses & Tours

◉ Sleeping

◉ Eating

◉ Drinking

◉ Entertainment

◉ Shopping

TOP CHOICE Skaritz BOUTIQUE HOTEL €€
(☑5920 9770; www.skaritz.com; Michalská 4; r €75-100; Ⓟ⊜⊛) Few other spots in the Old Town so effortlessly combine century-old elegance and contemporary design touches. Nor could you ask for a more central location. Choose from 20 rooms and six apartments.

TOP CHOICE Hotel Marrol's BOUTIQUE HOTEL €€
(☑5778 4600; www.hotelmarrols.sk; Tobrucká 4; s/d €120/150, ste from €500; ⊛⊜⊛) The sort of place where you could imagine Kaiser Wilhelm puffing contentedly on a cigar: no member of aristocracy would feel out of place in these 54 sumptuous rooms and suites, or in the Jasmine spa. Considering it's a regular in world's best luxury hotel lists, prices are very proletariat-friendly.

Downtown Backpackers HOSTEL €
(☑5464 1191; www.backpackers.sk; Panenská 31; dm €17-18, d €52; ⊜@⊛) The first hostel in Bratislava, Backpackers is still a boozy (you enter through a bar) bohemian classic. Red-brick walls and tapestries add character. Serves good food.

Penzión Virgo PENSION €€
(☑2092 1400; www.penzionvirgo.sk; Panenská 14; s/d/apt €61/74/85; ⊜@) Exterior-access rooms are arranged around a courtyard; light and airy despite dark-wood floors and baroque-accent wallpaper. Sip an espresso with the breakfast buffet (€5).

Penzión Zlatá Noha PENSION €
(☑5477 4922; ww.zlata-noha.sk; Bellova 2; s/d €39/49; ⊛; ⌨203) Up in leafy Koliba north of the Old Town, Zlatá Noha is a family-run enterprise offering some of the most decently priced rooms hereabouts. They're simply furnished but clean and the views down over vineyards across Bratislava will perk you up no end.

Hostel Blues HOSTEL €
(☑0905204020; www.hostelblues.sk; Špitálska 2; dm €15-20, d €52-63; ⊜@⊛) Choose from

five- to 10-bed single-sex or mixed dorms, or those with double bunk beds(!). Private rooms have their own bathrooms. Friendly staff also offer free sightseeing tours.

Tulip House Hotel BOUTIQUE HOTEL €€€
(☑3217 1819; www.tuliphouse.sk; Štúrova 10; ste incl breakfast €129-249; ☑☺❄@☎) Exquisite art nouveau property with a cafe-restaurant at street level.

Hotel-Penzión Arcus PENSION €€
(☑5557 2522; www.hotelarcus.sk; Moskovská 5; s/d incl breakfast €65/100; ☺☎) Family-run place with quite varied rooms (some with balcony, some with courtyard views). Pricey for what you get but sparkly clean. It's 500m northeast of Tesco, via Spitalska.

Austria Trend HOTEL €€
(☑5277 5800; www.austria-trend.sk; Vysoká 2a; r €90-150; ☑❄@) Newer business hotel on the edge of the Old Town.

🍴 Eating

The pedestrian centre is chock-a-block with overpriced samey dining options. Scour between the cracks, however, and you'll find great cafes and a few decent restaurants, but many of the most authentic and atmospheric have been pushed further out. Decent Slovak food isn't easy to find. Reasonable eateries, both sit-down and takeaway, line Obchodná. That Slovak fave, the set lunch menu, can be a real steal. Many restaurants in Bratislava do not have English-language menus.

TOP CHOICE **Café Verne** INTERNATIONAL €€
(Hviezdoslavovo nám 18; mains €4-11; ☺9am-midnight; ☑) Lively, friendly, good-value dining in the old town: the Czech beers flow and everyone from expats to students wolfs down hearty no-nonsense grub, including Slovak staples and decent English breakfasts.

Bistro St Germain BISTRO €
(Obchodná 17; mains €4; ☺10am-10pm) Big surprise in a little courtyard off Obchodná: a wonderfully decorated, relaxed place to gossip over homemade lemonade, cupcakes or light lunches (creative salads, baguettes and the like).

TOP CHOICE **Bratislavský Meštiansky Pivovar** SLOVAKIAN €€€
(☑0944512265; Drevená 8; mains €3-19; ☺11am-midnight Mon-Thu & Sat, to 1am Fri, to 11pm Sun) This stylish microbrewery serves Bratislava's freshest beer and offers creative Slovak cooking beneath vaulted ceilings and stylised Old Town artwork.

City Kebab TURKISH €
(Trnava Cesta & Tomašikova; kebabs & snacks €1-4; ☺7am-7pm Mon-Sat; ☑61) Bratislava's best Turkish food place. Behind it is the Freshmarket – stalls selling everything from *malokarpatské* (Small Carpathian) wine to myriad varieties of local mushrooms. It's 5km northeast of the city, towards the airport.

Lemon Tree THAI €€€
(☑5441 1244; www.lemontree.sk; Hviezdoslavovo nám 7; €5-15; ☑) Top-end Thai-Mediterranean restaurant with a 7th-floor upscale bar, Skybar, with great views. Reservations are a good idea.

Prašná Bašta SLOVAKIAN €€
(Zámočnicka 11; mains €6-15; ☺11am-11pm) This restaurant in the Old Town serves good Slovakian food in a charming round vaulted interior and one of the most private inner courtyards in the city.

Brasserie La Marine FRENCH €€€
(www.lamarine.sk; Pribinova; mains €11-21; ☺9am-11.30pm) A standout among the riverside eateries of the Eurovea mall, a 10-minute

---

SOCIALIST BRATISLAVA

The stint under socialism left its mark around town in bizarre and monumental ways.

Most SNP (New Bridge; www.u-f-o.sk; Viedenská cesta; observation deck adult/child €8/5; ☺10am-11pm) Colloquially called the UFO (pronounced 'ew-fo'), this Danube-spanning bridge is a modernist marvel from 1972 with a viewing platform and a restaurant with out-of-this-world prices.

Petržalka South of the Danube, this concrete jungle numbers among the largest Socialist housing developments in Eastern Europe.

Slavín War Memorial Huge memorial to the Soviets who fell in WWII, in a park of the same name yielding great city views.

Slovak Radio Building (Slovenský rozhlas; cnr Mýtna & Štefanovičova) A massive upside-down concrete pyramid; we'll leave the rest to your imagination.

walk east of the Old Town. It has one of the city's best wine lists and the food tastes just good enough to balance the high prices.

Traja Mušketieri
PUB €€

(☑5443 0019; Sládkovičova 7; mains €6-12) This way-upmarket version of a medieval tavern comes with a poetic menu ('Treacherous Lady de Winter' is a skewered chicken stuffed with Parma ham). Courteous service; reservations recommended.

U Jakubu
SLOVAKIAN €

(Nám SNP 24; mains €2-5; ☺8am-6pm Mon-Fri) Self-service cafeteria with Slovakian classics.

Pesto & Co
DELICATESSAN

(Špitálska 21; ☺Mon-Sat) Everything Italian you've ever wanted from grappa to espresso, with regional recommendations from the charismatic owner.

✒ Corny Café
CAFE €

(Grösslingová 20; ☺8am-10pm) As the cabinet inside showcases, this cosy, traditionally furnished joint offers coffee from almost anywhere you care to name (to buy and, on a rotational basis, to try). Then there's the delicious cakes, the tasty soups, the to-die-for quiches and a terrace by the Blue Church.

Shtoor
CAFE €

(Panská 23; light lunches €3-5; 🛜🖊🍴) Bursting onto the eating scene with tasty, cheap, healthy lunches, Shtoor has three locations in Bratislava but this, with two levels of seating, has the best (coffee- and cake-fuelled) atmosphere. Check the menus: written in old-fashioned Slovak as set down by Ľudovít Štúr, pioneer of Slovak literary language.

🍷 Drinking

From mid-April to October, sidewalk cafe tables sprout up in every corner of the pedestrian Old Town. Drinking without dining is normally fine. Hviezdoslavovo Nam has good options, as does Eurovea.

Prešporák
CAFE

(Baštova 9; ☺10am-11pm) Many are saying this does Bratislava's best coffee. Anyways, what with shelves of old books and more eccentric paraphernalia such as the huge model of a 16th-century sailing ship, it's a wonderful space to linger.

Slovak Pub
SLOVAKIAN

(Obchodná 62; mains €5-10; ☺10am-midnight Sun-Thu, 10am-2am Fri & Sat) It's touristy, but most beers are available and it serves every traditional national dish you can think of, albeit far from top quality.

Nu Spirit Bar
BAR

(Medená 16; ☺10am-2am Mon-Fri, 5pm-4am Sat & Sun) Deservedly popular cellar bar with regular live music as underground as its location: jazz, electronica, soul.

☆ Entertainment

Check **Slovak Spectator** (www.spectator.sme. sk), the **Bratislava Culture & Information Centre** (www.bkis.sk) and **Kam do Mesta** (www.kamdomesta.sk) for the latest.

Nightclubs & Live Music

Cover charges for Bratislava's music bars and clubs are usually quite low (free to €5).

Apollon Club
GAY & LESBIAN

(www.apollon-gay-club.sk; Panenská 24; ☺6pm-3am Mon-Thu, 8pm-5am Fri & Sat, 8pm-1am Sun) The gay disco in town has two bars and three stages. Tuesday is karaoke night.

Nu Spirit Club
NIGHTCLUB

(Šáfarikovo nám 7; ☺10pm-late, closed Sun & Mon) More of the same that Nu Spirit Bar offers, only in bigger, more danceable environs.

Hlava XXII
CLUB

(Bazová 9; ☺3pm-3am Tue-Sat) Jam sessions, blues and world beat – live. It's 1km northeast of centre, off Záhradnicka.

Subclub
NIGHCLUB

(Nábrežie arm gen L Svobudu; ☺10pm-4am Thu-Sat) An institution in the subterranean passageways under the castle. Techno, indie, hardcore dance etc pounds out to a younger, raucous crowd.

Sport

Bratislava's hallowed ice hockey team, HC Slovan, plays at the **Ondrej Nepela Stadium** (Odbojárov 9), which was revamped for the 2011 ice hockey world championship. Buy tickets at www.ticketportal.sk.

Performing Arts

Folk dance and music ensembles, like highly recommended **Lúcnica** (www.lucnica.sk), perform at venues around town; Dunaj caters to avant-garde tastes.

Slovak National Theatre
THEATRE

(Slovenské Národné Divadlo (SND); www.snd.sk; Hviezdoslavovo nám) The national theatre company stages quality operas (Slavic and international), ballets and dramas in two venues: the gilt decoration of the landmark **Historic SND** (Hviezdoslavovo nám, booking office cnr Jesenského & Komenského; ⊘8am-5.30pm Mon-Fri, 9am-1pm Sat) is a show in itself; the modern **New SND** (Pribinova 17; ⊘9am-5pm Mon- Fri) has a cafe.

Slovak Philharmonic   THEATRE
(www.filharm.sk; Eugena Suchoň nám; tickets €5-20; ⊘9am-2pm Mon, 1-6pm Tue-Fri & before performances)

Dunaj   PERFORMING ARTS
(www.kcdunaj.sk; Nedbalova 3; ⊘4pm-late) Cultural centre hosting some of Slovakia's most interesting drama and music performances. Something's on almost nightly. Also has a bar with Old Town panoramas from the terrace.

🛍 Shopping

There are several crystal, craft and jewellery stores, as well as souvenir booths, around Hlavné nám. Artisan galleries inhabit alleyways off Old Town streets.

Eurovea   MALL
(Pribinova) A 10-minute walk east from the Old Town, this has all the western chain stores abutted by fancy riverside restaurants and the new Slovak National Theatre (New SND).

Úľuv   HANDICRAFTS
(www.uluv.sk; Obchodná 64) For serious folk-art shopping head to the main outlet of Úľuv, the national handicraft cooperative, where a courtyard is filled with artisans' studios. Look for *šupolienky*: expressive figures made from painted corn husks.

ℹ Information

Most cafes have wi-fi access; Hlavné nám and Hviezdoslavovo nám are free wi-fi zones. Bratislava has numerous banks and ATMs in the Old Town, with several branches on Poštova. There are also ATMs/exchange booths in the train and bus stations, and at the airport.
Bratislava Culture & Information Centre (BKIS; ☑5443 3715, 16 186; www.bkis.sk; Klobučnícka 2; ⊘9am-6pm Mon-Fri, 9am-3pm Sat, 10am-3pm Sun) Amicable official tourist office. Brochures galore, including a small Bratislava guide.
Klar-i-net (Klariská 4; per hour €3.50; ⊘10am-10pm Mon-Fri, from 3pm Sat & Sun) Numerous well-equipped internet terminals.
Lonely Planet (www.lonelyplanet.com/slova-kia/bratislava)

Main Police Station (☑158; Hrobákova 44) Main police station for foreigners, in Petržalka.
Main Post Office (Nám SNP 34-35) In a beautiful building.
Poliklinika Ruzinov (☑4827 9111; www.ruzi-novskapoliklinika.sk, in Slovak; Ružinovská 10) Hospital with emergency services and 24-hour pharmacy.
Slovak Spectator (www.spectator.sme.sk) English-language weekly newspaper with current affairs and event listings.
Tatra Banka (Dunajská 4) English-speaking staff.
Visit Bratislava (http://visit.bratislava.sk) Comprehensive city tourist board site.

ℹ Getting There & Away

Bratislava is the main hub for trains, buses and the few planes that head in and out of the country.

Air
Keep in mind that Vienna's much busier international airport is only 60km west.
Airport Bratislava (BTS; www.airportbratis-lava.sk; Ivanská cesta) Nine kilometres northeast of the city centre. Flights connect to Italy, Spain, UK cities and more.
Danube Wings (www.danubewings.eu) The only airline with domestic services; has weekday flights (7am and 6pm) to Košice.

Boat
From April to October, plying the Danube is a cruisey way to get from Bratislava to Vienna.
Slovak Shipping & Ports (☑5293 2226; www.lod.sk; Fajnorova nábr 2, Hydrofoil Terminal) Several weekly hydrofoils to Vienna (€18 one way, 1¾ hours). Budapest services have been indefinitely cancelled.
Twin City Liner (☑0903 610 716; www.twincit-yliner.com; Rázusovo nábr, Propeller Terminal) Up to four boats daily to Vienna (€19 to €33 one way, 1½ hours).

SLOVAKIA BRATISLAVA

Bus

Direct destinations include cities throughout Slovakia and Europe, but the train is usually comparably priced and more convenient. The **Main Bus Station** (Mlynské Nivy; ☐Autobusová stanica, AS) is 1km east of the Old Town; locals call it 'Mlynské Nivy' (the street name). For schedules, see www.cp.atlas.sk.

Eurobus (www.eurobus.sk) Runs international routes.

Eurolines (☑5542 2734; www.slovaklines.sk) Contact for most international buses.

Slovenská Autobusová Doprava (SAD; www.sad.sk) National bus company.

Train

Rail is the main way to get around Slovakia and to neighbouring countries. Intercity and Euro-city (IC/EC) trains are quickest. *Ryclík* (R), or 'Fast' trains take slightly longer, but run more frequently and cost less. *Osobný* (Ob) trains are the milk runs. For schedules see www.cp.atlas.sk.

Main Train Station (Hlavná Stanica; www.slovakrail.sk; Predštanicné nám)

❶ Getting Around

To/From the Airport

City bus no 61 links Bratislava airport with the main train station (20 minutes).

Standing taxis (over)charge about €20 to town; ask the price before you get in.

A regular bus (€7.70) connects Vienna, Vienna airport, Bratislava bus station and Bratislava Airport.

Car

Numerous international car-hire companies such as Hertz and Sixt have offices at the airport. Good smaller agencies include the following.

Buchbinder (☑4363 7821; www.buchbinder.sk) In-town pick-up possible for a fee.

Car Rental 24 (☑903 582 400; www.carrental24.sk) Has an office at the airport.

Public Transport

Bratislava has an extensive tram, bus and trolleybus network; though the Old Town is small, so you won't often need it. **Dopravný Podnik Bratislava** (DPB; www.dpb.sk; Hodžovo nám;

TRANSPORT FROM BRATISLAVA

International Bus

DESTINATION	PRICE (€)	DURATION (HR)	FREQUENCY (DAILY)
Budapest (Hungary)	6-14	2½-4	4
London (Britain)	76	23-24	1
Prague (Czech Republic)	14	4¼	5
Vienna (Austria)	8	1¼	12

Domestic Train

DESTINATION	PRICE (€)	DURATION (HR)	FREQUENCY (DAILY)
Košice	19	5½	12
Poprad	15	4	12
Trenčín	6.50	1½	12
Žilina	9.50	2½	12

International Train

DESTINATION	PRICE (€)	DURATION (HR)	FREQUENCY (DAILY)
Budapest (Hungary)	15	2¾	7
Moscow (Russia)	132	41	1
Prague (Czech Republic)	27	4¼	6
Vienna (Austria)	11	1	hourly
Warsaw (Poland)	63	10½	1

6am-7pm Mon-Fri) is the public transport company; you'll find a route map online. The office is in the underground passage beneath Hodžovo nám. Check www.imhd.zoznam.sk for city-wide schedules.

Tickets cost €0.35/0.70/0.90 for 15/30/60 minutes. Buy at newsstands and validate on-board (or risk a legally enforceable €50 fine). Passes cost €4.50/8.30/10 for one/two/three days; buy at the DPB office, validate on board.

Important lines include the following:

Bus 93 Main Train Station to Hodžovo nám

Trolleybus 206 Main Bus Station to Hodžovo nám

Trolleybus 210 Main Bus Station to Main Train Station

Taxi

Standing cabs compulsively overcharge foreigners; an around-town trip should not cost above €10. To save, ask someone to help you order a taxi (not all operators speak English).

AA Euro Taxi (☎16 022)

Free Taxi (☎5596 9696) Cheap.

AROUND BRATISLAVA

Some of the best sights in Bratislava are actually way out of the centre. **Devín Castle** (www.muzeum.bratislava.sk; adult/child €3/1.50; ⊙10am-5pm Tue-Fri, to 7pm Sat & Sun May-Sep), 9km west, was once the military plaything of 9th-century warlord Prince Ratislav. The castle withstood the Turks but got blown up in 1809 by the French. Peer at older bits that have been unearthed and tour a reconstructed palace museum. Bus 29 links Devín with Bratislava's Nový Most (New Bridge) stop, under the bridge. Austria is just across the river from the castle.

Heading east out of the city you'll reach **Danubiana Meulensteen Art Museum** (www.danubiana.sk; Via Danubia, Čunovo; adult/child €6/3), Slovakia's most daring contemporary art museum, innovatively designed on a spit of sculpture-flanked land jutting into the Danube. Boat trips run from the city centre from June to October (€10/6 return, see website for details); otherwise take bus 91 from Nový Most to Čunovo and walk from the terminus (2.5km), or drive.

Hrad Červený Kameň (www.hradcervenykamen.sk; Slovak/foreign-language tour adult €6/7 child €3/3.50), aka the Red Stone Castle, is another member of Slovakia's fortified elite, exemplifying external Gothic resplendence along with interior baroque charm.

SMALL CARPATHIAN WINE ROUTE

Wine has been grown on Slovakian soil since at least the 6th century, when Celtic peoples exported their exotic-seeming drink to wine-deprived northern nations. Today there are six wine-growing regions. The Small Carpathians viticulture region extends northwest from Bratislava and is by far the most visitor-friendly, with many vineyards having open days. Twice a year (May and November) 80 wine cellars here open to visitors in the **Days of Open Wine Cellars**. For further information visit these websites:

Slovakwines.com (www.slovakwines.com) General information on Slovakia's wine-growing regions.

Small Carpathian Wine Route (www.mvc.sk) Focuses on this wine-growing region nearest Bratislava, with info on events (some in Slovak only).

The period-furnished rooms are interesting, but the vast cellar/dungeon complex is the highlight. The castle is not red at all, but white: the red refers to the stone it was built on. Two buses each hour connect Častá, the village below the castle, with Bratislava (€2, 1¼ hours).

WEST SLOVAKIA

Stupendous castles loom out of the crags of the Small Carpathians on the main trail northeast of Bratislava, with Trenčín's fortress one of the most magnificent along this heavily fortified stretch. The country's main spa, Piešťany, is en route, and vineyards cloak the fertile lower slopes.

Trenčín

☑032 / POP 56,400

High above the 18th- and 19th-century buildings of the Old Town, Trenčín's mighty castle has all the dark foreboding you'd want from a medieval fortress. Today's form dates from around the 15th century, but the city dates back much further. Roman legionnaires were stationed here (they called it Laugaricio) in the 2nd century AD: you can

WORTH A TRIP

PIEŠŤANY

Thermal waters bubble under much of the country, but it's Slovakia's premier spa site, **Piešťany** (www.spapiestany.sk), that attracts most visitors. Just across the river from Piešťany town, on **Kúpelne ostrov** (Spa Island) you can swim in thermal pools, breathe seasidelike air in a salt cave and be wrapped naked in hot mud. Many of the 19th-century buildings sport a new coat of Maria-Theresa-yellow paint; others are more modern. Reserve online for a stay, or head to the *kasa* (cashier) at **Napoleon 1** (☎033-775 7733; spa day package €36; ☺7.30am-7pm) to book day services. **Eva Pools** (adult/child €3/2; ☺11am-5pm) and **Balnea Esplanade Hotel** (per day adult/child €15/10, 3hr €10/7; ☺8am-10pm) have public swimming. Trains run from Bratislava (1¼ hours, €3.25, 12 daily, 87km) and you can continue on the same route to Trenčín (€2, 45 minutes) and the east.

read the inscription that's carved into a cliff in Trenčín to prove it! Afterwards, enjoy the sidewalk cafes and lively nightlife fuelled by the town's university population. The entire centre – including two large, interlocking pedestrian squares – is easily walkable.

◉ Sights & Activities

As well as the attractions listed here, there are other small museums around town that hold some interest, and historic buildings like the **Piarist Church** (Mierové nám) and the former 1913 **Synagogue** (Štúrovo nám) make for good exterior viewing.

Trenčín Castle
CASTLE

(www.muzeumtn.sk; adult/child €4.50/2.50; ☺9am-5.30pm) Spread-eagled domineeringly over a cliff above the Old Town, Trenčín's castle ranks as one of Slovakia's most impressive. Added to over virtually a millennium, much of what you see today is reconstruction – most recently from the 20th century – although there are remnants a-plenty dating to the earliest days. The lower echelons can be explored solo but to enter the keep and other furnished buildings you'll need a guide.

First noted in a Viennese chronicle of 1069, Trenčín Castle developed through the centuries until 1790 when it was damaged by fire.

From the town, climb stairs to reach the lowest level of fortifications and commanding views of the Váh River plain. Two levels higher, via a shop and eateries, you enter the towers and furnished palaces with one of the frequent tours (75 minutes, in Slovak only; call two days ahead to arrange English-speaking guides). The most evocative time to visit is during festivals or on

one of the castle's summer evening two-hour torchlight tours – complete with medieval sword fighting and staged frolics. Wonderful Brezina Forest Park – good for a stroll – lies alongside.

Roman Inscription
ANCIENT SITE

The town's unique claim to fame is a Roman inscription from AD 179; soldier's graffiti commemorating a battle against Germanic tribes. It's carved into the cliff behind the Hotel Elizabeth and can only be viewed through a window in the hotel's staircase; ask at reception.

Galéria Bazovského
MUSEUM

(www.gmab.sk; Palackého 27; adult/child €1.30/0.80; ☺9am-5pm Tue-Sun) Temporary exhibits represent leading 20th-century Slovakian and Czech art, while the permanent collection includes works by local painter Miloš Bazovský.

Town Gate Tower
LOOKOUT

(Mestská Veža; Sládkovičova; adult/child €1/0.50; ☺10am-8pm, closed Oct-May) An inconspicuous glass elevator and then six really steep flights of steps ascend to a 360-degree view of the Old Town.

Ostrov
BEACH

(off Mládežnícka) Floating in the middle of the Váh River, the Ostrov (island) is Trenčín's playground. A freely accessible, small, sandy beach, volleyball court and outdoor swimming pool are part of the attraction. It's just 200m north of the Old Town.

✸ Festivals & Events

World music, jazz, rock, techno, hip hop and alternative music are all represented in July's **Bažant Pohoda Festival** (www.pohodafestival.sk), the largest music festival in Slovakia.

🛏 Sleeping

Penzión Svorad HOSTEL €
(☑7430 322; www.svorad-trencin.sk; Palackého 4; dm €18-32, d €28-40; ☺) Peeling linoleum, thin mattresses – but oh, what castle views at this dormitorylike pension (with private bathrooms).

Hotel Pod Hradom HOTEL €€
(☑7481 701; www.podhradom.sk; Matúšova 12; s €65-75, d €76-116; ☻) A well-kept 10-room lodging with its own restaurant on a wee, winding street en route to the castle.

Autocamping na Ostrove CAMPING GROUND €
(☑7434 013; www.slovanet.sk/camping; Ostrov; campsite from €6, bungalow d €17) Riverside bungalow camping ground on the island; has central space for tents.

Hotel Elizabeth HISTORIC HOTEL €€
(☑6506 111; www.hotelelizabeth.sk; Ul gen MR Štefánika 2; s/d €99/115; ☎☻) Newly refurbished, neo-baroque hotel with one of the country's better spas, offering 78 rooms (five are suites). The famous Roman inscription of AD 179 is on the cliff behind: ask at reception to see it.

🍴 Eating & Drinking

Numerous restaurants and cafes line Mierové nám and Štúrovo nám; choose any one for imbibing al fresco.

TOP CHOICE Reštaurácia Bašta SLOVAK €€
(Ostrov; mains €3-11; ☺24hr) Some of the freshest, cooked-to-order Slovak faves we've ever tasted – pork stuffed with spicy *klobasa*, *bryndza* (sheep's cheese) cream soup... Breakfasts are tasty too. Well worth the walk to the Ostrov (island).

TOP CHOICE La Piazzetta BAR
(Mierové nám 20; ☺10am-late) Slovakia's best Italian wine selection, in an amospheric, meticulously run cellar bar. There's great coffee and delectable edible accompaniments.

Cinema Movie Club Restaurant & Bar INTERNATIONAL €
(Palackého 33; mains €3-7; ☺8am-11pm Sun-Thu, 8am-late Fri & Sat; ☎) Student haunt with hearty weekday set lunch menus for under €4. Also shows films.

Restaurant Lánius CZECH €€
(☑744 1978; Mierové nám 20; mains €6-12; ☺11am-midnight) The rustic set-up – creaking beams, wood fireplace – matches the hearty Slovakian fare. The dining room up at the rear of the courtyard is most fun.

Steps Bar BAR
(Sládkovičova 4-6; ☺10am-1am Mon-Thu, 10am-4am Fri & Sat, 4pm-midnight Sun) A sidewalk cafe and upstairs bar that attracts a hip, college-age crowd.

ℹ Information

Culture & Information Centre (☑6504 711; www.visittrencin.sk; Mierové nám 9; ☺8am-6pm Mon-Fri, to 4pm Sat May-Sep, 8am-5pm Mon-Fri Oct-Apr) Relocated to the main square, this is a helpful, well-informed tourist office. Good free map available.

Library of Trenčín (Palackého; ☺8am-6pm Mon, Tue, Thu & Fri, 10am-7pm Wed, to noon-Sat) Internet upstairs (€1 per hour).

Main Post Office (Mierové nám 21)

VUB Bank (Mierové nám 37)

ℹ Getting There & Away

IC and EC trains run regularly to Trenčín from Bratislava (€6.50, 1½ hours), Žilina (€4.50, 1¼ hours) and Poprad (€10, 2¾ hours), among others.

CENTRAL SLOVAKIA

The rolling hills and lolling, forested mountains of central Slovakia are home to the shepherding tradition that defines Slovak culture. This is where the nation's own Robin Hood, Juraj Jánošík, once roamed. Limited train routes means a car is helpful for exploring here. Look roadside for farmers selling local sheep's cheese before you lose yourself in a picturesque valley. Some of the nation's most fabled castles also beckon and, further south, there's the ancient mining town of Banska Štiavnica.

Žilina

☑041 / POP 85,100

Žilina is agreeable enough, but its main draw is as a jumping-off point for forays into the Malá Fatra National Park, surrounding fortresses and folksy villages. The cultural and culinary scene is livening up, though – watch this space.

From the train station in the northeast, a walk along Národná takes you through Nám A Hlinku up to Mariánské nám, the main pedestrian square.

🍽 Sleeping & Eating

The tourist information office can recommend student dorms that take travellers in July and August. Interchangeable cafe-bars lie around Mariánske nám and Hlinka nám: look for names like Café Le Jour, on Hlinka.

Hotel Dubna Skala   HOTEL €€
(📞5079 100; www.hoteldubnaskala.sk; Hurbanova 8; s/d €95/115; ❄️🛜) Modern boutique interiors fit surprisingly well within an ornately aged exterior. Within is a well-regarded wine-cellar restaurant and a cafe.

Penzion Central Park   GUESTHOUSE €€
(📞5622 021; www.penzioncentralpark.sk; s/d €55/75; 🛜♨️) Impressive art nouveau facade meets with slick modern rooms. This pension caters primarily to business travellers but its location is perfect. A spa/swimming pool is attached.

TOP CHOICE Voyage Voyage   SLOVAK €€
(Mariánske nám 191; mains about €5) A modernised Slovakian menu in elegant, animated surrounds, with inventive dishes such as chicken fillet stuffed with peaches and cheese.

Trattoria   ITALIAN €€
(📞5643 535; www.trattoria.sk; Jozefa Vuruma 5; pizzas €4-7) Cosy family-run Italian joint running the gamut of Italian foods and pleasing with most.

☆ Entertainment

TOP CHOICE Stanica   THEATRE
(www.stanica.sk; Závodská cesta 3) It's a theatre, arts centre, music venue and relaxed cafe-bar – but what's most incredible is how quickly this little oasis in the old train station has become Žilina's engine of bohemian creativity. May many follow its example.

ℹ Information

Main Post Office (Sládkovičova 1)
Tourist Information Office (TIK; 📞7233 186; www.tikzilina.eu; Andrej Hlinka nám 9; ⊙9am-5pm Mon-Fri, plus 9am-2pm Sat & Sun May-Sep) Town and surrounding-area information available.
Volksbank (Národná 28) Bank and ATM near the train station.

ℹ Getting There & Away

Žilina is on the main Bratislava–Košice railway line. Four daily IC (and many more, slower, 'fast') trains head to Bratislava (€9.50, 2¾ hours), Trenčín (€4.50, 1¼ hours), Poprad (€7, 1¾ hours) and Košice (€11, three hours).

Around Žilina

Besides nearby Malá Fatra National Park, a few folk-culture sights within an hour of Žilina are well worth exploring. Martin, and Ružomberok to the east, are key transport hubs.

MARTIN

On the southern side of Malá Fatra National Park, Martin is primarily an industrial town but it sports several small museums and the country's largest *skanzen* (open-air village museum). Traditional buildings (*krčma* – or village pub – included) from all over the region have been moved to the **Museum of the Slovak Village** (Múzeum Slovenskej Dediny; www.snm-em.sk; Malá Hora 2; adult/child €2/1; ⊙9am-4.30pm Tue-Sun). Contact the **Tourist Information Office** (📞4238 776; www.tikmartin.sk; A Kmeťa 22; ⊙9am-5pm Mon-Fri) for more details.

From Žilina it's easiest to take the bus the 35km to Martin (€1.75, 45 minutes, half-hourly). The village museum is 4km southeast of the town. Take local bus 10 from the main station to the last stop and walk the remaining 1km up through the forest (or hail a taxi in town). Martin is also the beginning of Slovakia's best train journey, around Velká Fatra National Park south to Banska Bystrica (€3, 1¼ hours, seven daily).

ČIČMANY

If you've seen a brochure or postcard of Slovakia, you've probably seen a photograph of Čičmany (www.cicmany.viapvt.sk); dark log homes painted with white geometric patterns fill this traditional village. This is no *skanzen;* most houses are private residences, but **Radenov House** (Čičmany 42; adult/child €2/1.30; ⊙9am-4.30pm Tue-Sun Jun-Aug, 8am-3.30pm Tue-Sun Sep-May) is a museum. There's a gift shop, a small restaurant and a pension in the long, narrow settlement. Buses run the 50 minutes south of Žilina (€2) five times a day; return times allow hours to wander and photograph. One of Slovakia's best campsites, **Slnečné Skaly** (📞904822692; http://camping-raj.sk; Rajecké Teplice; 2 adults & tent €7.50), awaits on the jaunt down near spa town Rajecké Teplice.

VLKOLÍNEC

The folksy mountain village of Vlkolínec, about 71km east and southeast of Žilina, is a Unesco-noted national treasure. The pastel paint and steep roofs on the 45 traditional plastered log cabins are remarkably well maintained. It's easy to imagine a *vlk* (wolf) wandering through this wooded mountainside settlement arranged along a small stream. You pay entry (adult/child €3/2, open 9am to 3pm) to walk around and one of the buildings has been turned into a small house museum, but this is still a living village – if just barely. Of the approximately 40 residents, almost half are schoolchildren. For more information, visit www.vlkolinec.sk.

Two weekday-only buses make the 25-minute (€0.50) journey to Vlkolínec from the Ružomberok train station; last return is at 3.15pm. Otherwise, driving or hiking the 6km uphill from Ružomberok is the only way to get to the village. Direct trains stop in Ružomberok en route to Bratislava (€11.50, 3½ hours, nine daily), Žilina (€3, 1¼ hours, hourly) and, in the other direction, to Poprad (€4.50, 1¼ hours, 17 daily).

Two kilometres west of Ružomberok, **Salaš Krajinka** (www.salaskrajinka.sk; E18; mains €3-9) is one of the country's best sheep dairy restaurants. Buy *bryndza* and other products on-site, or sit down for a full meal in the modern-rustic dining room with a glass wall looking into the barn.

ORAVSKÝ PODZÁMOK

Central Slovakia has numerous castles and ruins, but one of the most notorious is off the beaten track at the tiny community of Oravský Podzámok.

The classic 1922 vampire film *Nosferatu* featured the pointed towers of **Orava Castle** (Oravský hrad; www.oravamuzeum.sk; Oravský Podzámok; adult/child €5/3, with chapel €7/4; ☻8.30am-5pm, closed Apr), which rise from an impossibly narrow blade of rock above the village. This, one of Slovakia's most complete castles, dates from 1267. Later additions and reconstructions were made, most notably after a fire in 1800. The museum is chock full of weapons, folk art and period furniture. Legend has it the castle contains one mirror where the reflection will make you beautiful, and another that will make you ugly – make sure to ask the difference. Below the castle in the tiny village of Oravský Podzámok there's a pizza pub and a pension.

Buses run at least hourly between here and Ružomberok (€2, 45 minutes), where you can transfer to the Bratislava–Košice train line. Buses also run about every two hours to Žilina (€4, 1½ hours).

Malá Fatra National Park

♪041

Sentinel-like formations stand watch at the rocky gorge entrance to valleys filled with pine-clad slopes and wave after wave of crescendoing peaks. *Vitajte* (welcome) to the Malá Fatra National Park (Národný Park Malá Fatra), incorporating a chocolate-box-pretty, 200-sq-km swathe of its namesake mountain range. The Vrátna Valley (Vrátna dolina), 25km east of Žilina, lies at the heart of the park. From here you can access the trailheads, ski lifts and a cable car to start your exploration. The straggling, one-street town of Terchová at the lower end of the valley has most services; Chata Vrátna is at the top. The village of Štefanová lies east of the main valley road, 1km uphill from Terchová.

⊙ Sights & Activities

Statue of Juraj Jánošík MONUMENT

Above Terchová sits an immense aluminium statue of Juraj Jánošík, Slovakia's Robin Hood. In early August, much festivity goes on beneath his likeness during the **Jánošík Days** folk festival.

Považké Museum MUSEUM

(www.pmza.sk; Sv Cyrila a Metoda 96; adult/child €2/1; ☻9am-3.30pm Tue-Sun) Check out the exhibits (Slovak only) depicting the notorious highwayman Juraj Jánošík's exploits (and gruesome death) at this small museum in Terchová above the town info office.

Vrátna Valley PARK

(www.vratna.sk) The road to **Vrátna Valley** in Malá Fatra National Park runs south from Terchová through the crags of **Tiesňavy Gorge**, past picnic sites and scenic stops. The **cable car** (€8.50/10 one-way/return; ☻8am-6pm mid-Dec–Apr & Jun-Sep, Sat & Sun only Oct–mid-Dec & May) at Vratna Výťah carries you from the top of the valley to **Snilovské saddle** (1524m) below two peaks, **Chleb** (1647m) and **Velký Kriváň** (1709m). Both are on the red ridge trail, one of the most popular in the park. A hike northeast from Chleb over **Hromove** (1636m), **Poludňový grúň** (1636m) and **Stoh** (1608m) to **Medziholie saddle** (1185m) takes about 5½ hours. From there you can descend on the green trail to Štefanová village where there's a bus stop, accommodation and restaurants. Further east, the precipitous gorge of **Horné Diery** is known as Jánošíkové Diery (Jánošík's Holes) for its rock formations

Malá Fatra National Park

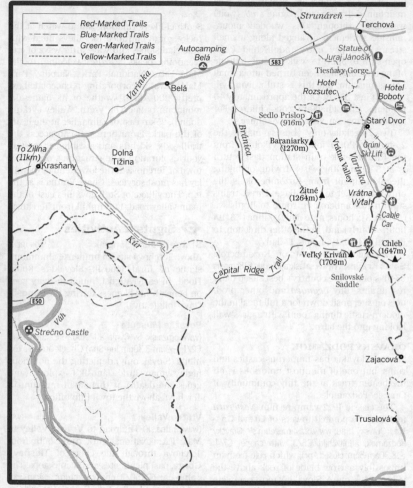

Map legend:
- Red-Marked Trails
- Blue-Marked Trails
- Green-Marked Trails
- Yellow-Marked Trails

Strunáreň
Terchová
Autocamping Belá
Statue of Juraj Jánošík
Tiesňavy Gorge
Hotel Rozsutec
Hotel Boboty
Belá
Varínka
Br.. nica
Sedlo Prislop (916m)
Starý Dvor
Baraniarky (1270m)
Grúni Ski Lift
Vrátna Valley
Varínka
To Žilina (11km)
Krasňany
Dolná Tižina
Žitné (1264m)
Vrátna Výtah
Cable Car
Kúr
Veľký Kriváň (1709m)
Chleb (1647m)
Capital Ridge Trail
Snilovské Saddle
Váh
Strečno Castle
Zajacová
Trusalová

SLOVAKIA MALÁ FATRA NATIONAL PARK

ravined by waterfalls. A challenging 2½-hour woodsy route, involving ascents by waterfall-splashed ladders, runs from Hotel Diery round to Hotel Boboty.

The main summer season is July and August; during other months businesses may close. For serious hiking, VKÚ's 1:50,000 Malá Fatra-Vrátna map (No 110) and Dajama's *Knapsacked Travel: Malá Fatra* are good. In summer, the **Organization for Sport Activities** (☎0903 546 600; www.splavovanie.sk; Starý Dvor; ◷9am-5pm Jul & Aug) rents mountain bikes (€8) and organises rafting trips (€13 per person).

Vrátna Valley's 14 ski tows and lifts (8am to 4pm) are open December to April. Shacks with **ski rental** (per day from €12) keep the same hours and are located at Starý Dvor, where **ski passes** (main season pass per day adult/child €25/18) are also available.

🛏 Sleeping & Eating

Numerous private cottages are available for rent in the Terchová area, many listed on the information office website (http://www.terchova-info.sk/en/ubytovanie.php). No camping is allowed in the park. Eating options in the valley are limited to restaurants at the

main lodgings and a few food stands near the chairlifts and cable car.

TOP CHOICE Hotel Diery
HOTEL €

(☎5695 323; www.hotel-diery.com; Biely Potok; s/d €35/59) Substantial, minimalist rooms in a voluminous, affably run hotel that is also the proud owner of the best restaurant in Malá Fatra, the Koliba. Cuisine isn't Slovak here: it's Central European fusion – and tasty.

Hotel Rozsutec
HOTEL €€

(☎5008 034; www.hotelrozsutec.sk; s/d €45/80; 🛜🌊) A relatively new addition to the hotel

scene: attentive service and gleaming facilities (spa/sauna and appealing restaurant) give it the edge over some of the other old stalwarts. Rooms with gorgeous balcony views cost more. It lies 1km west of Starý Dvor.

Penzión Sagan
PENSION €

(☎0903 744 302; www.penzionsagan.sk; Štefanová 553; s/d incl breakfast €30/50; 🛜🌊) Impeccably kept, pine-clad rooms plus a little restaurant at this guesthouse (with games room) in Štefanová village.

Hotel Boboty
HOTEL €€

(☎5695 228; www.hotelboboty.sk; Nový Dvor; s/d €45/85; @🛜🌊🌊) Services galore – sauna, massage, heated pool, billiards, free ski shuttle – are available at the valley's biggest lodging.

Chata na Grúni
MOUNTAIN HUT €

(☎5695 324; www.chatanagruni.sk; dm without/with breakfast €12/19) Hikers' hut at the top of Gruni Ski Lift; four- to six-bed dorms and self-service restaurant.

Autocamping Belá
CAMPING GROUND €

(☎5695 135; http://camping.bela.sk; 2 adults with tent €8.50; ☺May–mid-Oct; 🌊) Fine camping ground with 300 sites and a heated pool. There's a bus stop in front; 5km west of Terchová.

Vŕšky
SLOVAK €€

(☎5627 300; www.penzionvrsky.sk; Terchová; mains €6-14; 🛜🌊) Very popular restaurant with original takes on Slovak food and simple-but-spotless rooms in the **pension** (d €48). It's on the eastern edge of town on the road to Horné Diery.

Reštaurácia Starý Majer
SLOVAK €€

(☎5695 419; Starý Dvor; mains €5-10; ☺10am-7pm Sep-May, to 8pm Jun-Aug) Dig into well-done traditional shepherds' dishes at rough-hewn outdoor tables, or inside among rustic farm implements.

🛈 Information

Mountain Rescue Service (☎5695 232; www. hzs.sk) Also offers weather information.

Terchová Tourist Information Centre (☎5695 307; www.ztt.sk; Sv Cyrila a Metoda 96; ☺8am-4pm Mon-Fri, 10am-1pm Sat & Sun) Maps for sale; ATM in building.

Turistcko-Informačna Chalupa (☎0907534354; www.uteczmesta.sk; Vrátňanská cesta, Terchová; ☺8am-8pm) Private office that arranges lodgings and activities and provides information.

DON'T MISS

SLOVAKIA'S MOST-VISITED CASTLE

Bojnice Castle (www.bojnicecastle.sk; Bojnice zámok; adult/child €6.50/3; ⊙9am-5pm daily Jun-Sep, Tue-Sun May, 9am-3pm Tue-Sun Oct-Apr) is straight out of a fairy-tale dream, crowned with towers and turrets and crenulated mouldings. The original 12th-century fortification got an early-20th-century redo by the Pálffy family, who modelled it on French romantic castles. It's the country's most popular castle by visitor numbers. The time to visit is during the **International Festival of Ghosts & Ghouls** in May, when costumed guides put on shows. The palace also gets decked out for Christmas, Valentine's Day and various medieval events. The nearby city of Prievidza has bus connections to Žilina (€3.50, 1¼ hours, 10 daily) and Bratislava (€9.50, 3¼ hours, nine daily). From there take regular local buses 3 or 7 the 3km to Bojnice, a little town with lodging and restaurants.

ℹ️ Getting There & Around

Hourly buses link Žilina with Terchová (€1.80, 40 minutes) and valley stops, terminating near Chata Vrátna at Vrátna Výťah (€2, one hour). Otherwise change in Terchová for local buses. Check schedules at www.cp.atlas.sk.

Banská Bystrica & Around

This area was a mining centre for greater Hungary from the 14th to the 18th centuries. The ancient mining town of Banská Štiavnica, as well as Bojnice Castle, are gems from its lavish past.

BANSKÁ BYSTRICA

☑048 / POP 79,900

Slovakia's bustling, sixth-largest city, Banská Bystrica has attractions that combine handsome medieval architecture and a riveting insight into Slovakia's communist past. The excellent **tourist office** (☑415 5085; eng. ksibb.sk; Nám SNP 14; ⊙9am-6pm Mon-Fri, to 3pm Sat) is in the old town hall on the impressive main square. The key sight is arguably the country's best museum, the **SNP Museum** (www.muzeumsnp.sk; Kapitulská 23; adult/child €2/1; ⊙9am-6pm Tue-Sun May-Sep, to 4pm Tue-Sun Oct-Mar), documenting the Slovak national uprising and WWII Slovakia.

Direct trains serve Bratislava (€10, 3½ hours, every two hours) and, via a spectacular journey, Martin (€3.50, one hour, seven daily) near Malá Fatra National Park. Otherwise change at Zvolen or Vrútky. Destinations by bus include Liptovský Mikuláš (€4, 1¾ hours, hourly) near the High Tatras.

BANSKÁ ŠTIAVNICA

☑045 / POP 10,500

A time-trapped medieval delight, Banská Štiavnica enjoyed a 16th-century heyday as an internationally renowned architectural showcase and grew to become the old Hungarian Kingdom's third-largest city. As the minerals ran out and mines closed, progress stopped, leaving buildings wonderfully untouched. Meandering among the steeply terraced hillsides now you'll see many of the same Old Town burghers' houses, churches and alleys that you would have seen then. Unesco recognised the town in 1972. At a fraction of its peak population today, the town is primarily a holiday destination with numerous mining-related attractions and two castles facing each other across the steep valley.

⊙ Sights

Wandering the steep streets gazing at the buildings is the main attraction. In summer, the open-air pools high above town are a blessing.

Open-Air Mining Museum MUSEUM
(JK Hella 12; adult/child €5/2.50; ⊙8am-4pm Tue-Sun by tour) Take a trip down into a former working mine, 2km west of the centre. One of numerous affiliates of the **Slovak Mining Museum** (www.muzeumbs.sk).

Old Castle CASTLE
(Starozámocká 1; adult/child €4/2; ⊙9am-6pm daily May-Sep, 9am-4pm Tue-Sun Oct-Apr) Town history exhibits in a 16th-century stronghold.

New Castle CASTLE
(Novozámocká 1; adult/child €2/1; ⊙9am-4pm May-Sep, 9am-4pm Tue-Sun Oct-Apr) A former lookout tower during the Hungarian-Turkish wars, the town's 'new' castle was constructed only five years after the old one; inside are exhibits on the historical struggle against Turkish invasion.

FREE Kalvária   CHURCH

(Calvary; www.kalvaria.sk; end of Pod Kalvlánou; ◷9am-6pm daily May-Sep, 9am-4pm Tue-Sun Oct-Apr) A dramatic complex of 23 baroque religious buildings (19 chapels, three churches and a statue of the Virgin) cresting a hill 1km west of town.

🛏 Sleeping & Eating

Hostel 6   HOSTEL €

(☑0905106705; www.hostel6.sk; Andreja Sládkoviča 6; dm/tr €13/39; ☺@⑂) A hospitable little backpacker hostel with thoroughly modern amenities inside an old building. Choose from a private double, or five- or six-bed dorms. Great balcony views, full kitchen and laundry.

Penzión Príjemný Oddych   PENSION €

(☑6921 301; www.prijemnyoddych.sk; Starozámocká 3; r €43-49; ⑂) Distinctly *prijemný* (pleasing) hostelry below the Old Castle with a small on-site restaurant, playground and sauna.

Penzión Kachelman   SLOVAKIAN €

(☑6922 319; www.kachelman.sk; Kammerhofská 18; mains €5-10; ☎) Rustic Renaissance-era inn/restaurant with a long and varied Slovak menu and pizzas (€3 to €4). It's close to the bus stop, below the Old Town centre. Budget-friendly doubles here are €37.

Art Cafe   CAFE €

(Academická 2; €2-7; ◷8am-11pm) The best in town for wickedly strong coffee, fabulous cakes and lovingly prepared food, as well as beer and live music. Has an enticing terrace.

ℹ Information

City Tourist Information Office (☑6949 653; www.banskastiavnica.sk; Nám sv Trojice 6; ◷8am-6pm May-Sep, 8am-4pm Oct-Apr) Semiprecious stones for sale in addition to info; beside a branch of the mining museum. Two internet terminals (€1 per hour).

ℹ Getting There & Away

Banská Štiavnica is not the easiest place to get to. Only one direct bus departs from Bratislava daily (€8.50, 3½ hours), at 4.40pm. Otherwise, all bus and train arrivals require a change in Zvolen or Banská Bystrica, which has three direct buses (€3, one hour). Check schedules at www.cp.atlas.sk.

From the train/bus stations it's a 2/1.5km climb uphill through the outskirts to Nám sv Trojice, the main Old Town square. Local buses and taxis are available to take you up into town.

TATRA MOUNTAINS

Alpine peaks in Slovakia? As you look upon the snow-strewn jagged mountains rising like an apparition east of Liptovský Mikuláš, you may think you're imagining things. But there they are indeed. The High Tatras are undoubtedly where the adventure-junkies head, along with those who can afford the luxury mountain resorts, mostly located here. Tucked into the eastern end of the peaks is the Belá Tatras: the loveliest and least-discovered region.

Poprad

☑052 / POP 54,300 / TRANSPORT HUB

Poprad will likely be your first experience of mountain country, being the nearest sizeable city to the High Tatras and a major transport hub for the region. Most visitors just experience the so-so city centre but the 16th-century neighbourhood of Spišská Sobota and a popular thermal water park might make you linger. From the adjacent train and bus stations the central pedestrian square, Nám sv Egídia, is a five-minute walk south on Alžbetina.

💿 Sights & Activities

Spišská Sobota   NEIGHBOURHOOD

Sixteenth-century Spiš-style merchants' and artisans' houses line the Spišská Sobota town square. The suburb is 1.2km northeast of Poprad's train station.

Aqua City   SPA

(☑7851 111; www.aquacity.sk; Športová 1397; packages per day €16-29; ◷8am-9pm) Sauna, swim, bubble and slide zones are all part of Poprad's thermal water park. The park employs admirably green initiatives; the heat and electricity derive from geothermal and solar sources.

Adventoura   ADVENTURE SPORTS

(☑903641549; www.adventoura.eu; Uherova 33) Dog sledding, hut-to-hut hikes, snowboarding...this company can organise the works. Day prices for trips around the Tatras start at about €90.

🛏 Sleeping & Eating

There's a large Billa grocery store off Jiřho Wolera just east of the bus station.

TOP CHOICE **Penzión Sabato**   B&B **€€**

(☑7769 580; www.sabato.sk; Sobotské nám 6; r incl breakfast €90; ☏) Exposed stone arches, a cobblestone courtyard and open-hearth restaurant reveal this inn's 17th-century age – as do romantically decorated rooms.

Penzión Plesnivec   PENSION **€**

(☑911110410; www.penzion-plesnivec.sk; s/d €25/35; ☏) The friendliest welcome in Poprad. Rooms are bright, clean and simple and in the tribally decorated traveller-friendly bar/common room, these folks can help with High Tatras planning. English and Spanish spoken. It's between Aqua City and Spišská Sobota.

Hotel Cafe Razy   PENSION **€**

(☑7764 101; www.hotelcaferazy.sk; Nám Sv Egídia 58; s/d €29/39; ☏) Sane and simple rooms upstairs; semi-crazy pub and pizza cafe down. Breakfast is €5. On the modern main square.

ℹ Information

City Information Centre (☑7721 700; www.poprad.sk; Dom Kultúry Štefániková 72; ◷8am-5pm Mon-Fri, 9am-noon Sat) Town info only; lists private rooms.

ℹ Getting There & Away

AIR Poprad-Tatry International Airport (www.airport-poprad.sk; Na Letisko 100) is 5km west of the centre but doesn't receive any regular flights.

BUS Buses serve Levoča (€1.60, 45 minutes, hourly), Bardejov (€4.50, 2¼ hours, six daily) and Zakopane in Poland (€5, two hours, two daily April to October).

CAR Pick-up around town is available by pre-arrangement from **Car Rental Tatran** (☑0903 250 255; www.autopozicovnatatry.sk).

TRAIN Electric trains traverse the 14km or so to the High Tatras resorts. Mainline trains run directly to Bratislava (€16, four hours, hourly, four IC trains daily), Trenčín (€10, 2¾ hours, hourly, four IC trains daily) and Košice (€5, 1¼ hours, 24 daily).

High Tatras

☑052

The High Tatras (Vysoké Tatry), the tallest range in the Carpathian Mountains, tower over most of Eastern Europe. Some 25 peaks measure above 2500m. The massif is only 25km wide and 78km long, but photo opportunities are enough to get you fantasising about a National Geographic career – pristine snowfields, ultramarine mountain lakes, crashing waterfalls, undulating pine forests and shimmering alpine meadows. Most of this jagged range is part of the Tatra National Park (Tanap). Not that this fact has arrested development on the Slovakian ski slopes, much to the chagrin of watchdog groups like International Union for Conservation of Nature. The Tatra National Park complements a similar park across the peaks in Poland.

Midmountain, three main resort towns string west to east. Štrbské Pleso is the traditional ski centre and is most crowded, with construction galore. Eleven kilometres east, Smokovec is an amalgam of the Nový (New), Starý (Old), Dolný (lower) and Horný (upper) settlements. Here there's still a bit of a turn-of-the-20th-century heyday feel, plus numerous lodgings and the most services. Five kilometres further, Tatranská Lomnica is the quaintest, quietest village. All have mountain access by cable car, funicular or chairlift. Poprad is the closest city (with mainline train station and airport), 14km south of central Starý Smokovec.

When planning your trip, keep in mind that the highest trails are closed to snow from November to mid-June. June and July can be especially rainy. July and August are the warmest (and most crowded) months. Hotel prices and crowds are at their lowest from October to April.

◉ Sights & Activities

A 600km network of trails covers the alpine valleys and some peaks, with full-service mountain huts where hikers can stop for a meal or a rest along the way. Routes are colour coded and easy to follow. Pick up one of the numerous detailed maps and hiking guides available at bookstores and information offices. Park regulations require you to keep to trails and refrain from picking flowers. Be aware that many trails are rocky and uneven, watch for sudden thunderstorms on ridges where there's no protection, and know that the assistance of the Mountain Rescue Service is not free.

Distances for hikes in Slovakian national parks are officially given in hours rather than kilometres. For hikes here we have therefore given hikes in hours, as per official trail estimates. Depending on the gradient and terrain, in the High Tatras a reasonably fit person can expect to hike between 2km and 5km per hour.

High Tatras

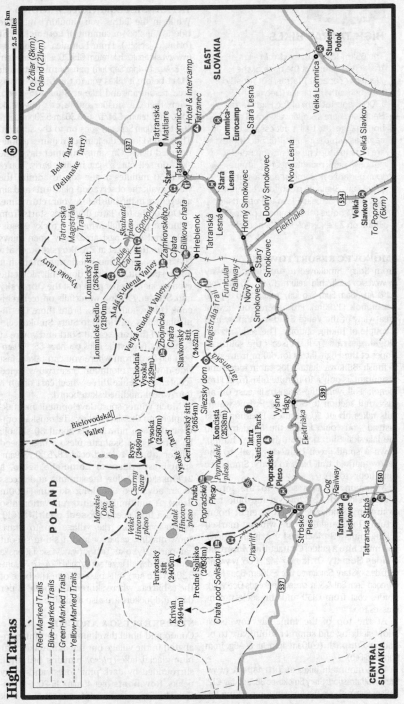

SLOVAKIA HIGH TATRAS

5 km
2.5 miles

To Ždiar (8km);
Poland (21km)

Red-Marked Trails
Blue-Marked Trails
Green-Marked Trails
Yellow-Marked Trails

EAST
SLOVAKIA

Studený
Potok

Tatranská
Matliare

Hotel & Intercamp
Tatranec

Tatranská Lomnica

Velká Lomnica

Lomnica-
Eurocamp

Stará Lesná

537

Belá Tatras
(Belianske Tatry)

Štart

Tatranská Lesná

Velká Slavkov

Skalnaté
pleso

Zamkovského
Chata

Stará
Lesná

Gondola

Bílikova chata

Tatranská Magistrála Trail

Cable
Car

Ski Lift

Hrebienok

Horný Smokovec

Dolný Smokovec

Nová Lesná

Velká
Slavkov

534

Cable

Lomnický štít
(2634m)

Skalnaté
pleso

Tatranská
Lesná

To Poprad
(6km)

Lomnické Sedlo
(2190m)

Malá Studená Valley

Tatranská Magistrála Trail

Vysoké Tatry

Velká Studená Valley

Zbojnícka
Chata

Slavkovský
štít
(2452m)

Funicular
Railway

Starý
Smokovec

Nový
Smokovec

Elektriáka

Východná
Vysoká
(2429m)

Magistrála Trail

Tatranská

Bielovodská
Valley

Vysoká
(2560m)

Gerlachovský štít
(2654m)

Koncistá
(2538m)

Sliezsky dom

Vyšné
Hágy

539

Tatra
National
Park

POLAND

Rysy
(2499m)

Vysoké Tatry

Elektriáka

Morskie
Oko
Lake

Czarny
Staw

Velké Hincovo
pleso

Popradské
pleso

Popradské
Chata

Popradské
Pleso

E50

Malé
Hincovo
pleso

Furkotský
štít
(2405m)

Cog
Railway

Predné Solisko
(2093m)

Štrbské
Pleso

Tatranská
Lieskovec

Tatranská Štrbá

Chairlift

Kriváň
(2494m)

Chata pod Soliskom

537

CENTRAL
SLOVAKIA

DON'T MISS

HIGH TATRAS HIKES

The 65km-long **Tatranská Magistrála Trail** starts at the base of the Western (Zapadné) Tatras, but mostly runs beneath the peaks (between 1300m and 1800m) of the High Tatras. Because there's a relatively small elevation change, the trail is accessible by cable-assisted cars and lifts, and there are huts to stop and eat at; you need not be in peak mountaineering shape to experience it. Some of our favourite routes are Skalnaté pleso to Hrebienok (2½ hours), Štrbské Pleso to Popradské pleso (1¼ hours) and Skalnaté pleso to Chata pri Zelenom plese (2¼ hours).

SMOKOVEC RESORT TOWNS

From Starý Smokovec a **funicular railway** (www.vt.sk; adult/child return €7/5; ☺7am-7pm Jul & Aug, 8am-5pm Sep-Jun) takes you up to **Hrebienok** (1280m). From here you have a great view of the **Velká Studená Valley** and a couple of hiking options. The red **Tatranská Magistrála Trail** transects the southern slopes of the High Tatras for 65km from start to finish. Bilíkova chata, a log-cabin lodge and restaurant, is only a 10-minute hike from Hrebienok. Following the Magistrála east on an easy trail section to **Studený Potok** waterfalls takes about 30 minutes. Heading west instead, you could follow the Magistrála to the lakeside **Sliezsky dom** hut (two hours), down a small green connector trail, to the yellow-marked trail back to Starý Smokovec (four hours total).

Mountain climbers scale to the top of **Slavkovský štít** (2452m) via the blue trail from Starý Smokovec (seven to eight hours return). To ascend the peaks without marked hiking trails (**Gerlachovský štít** included), you must hire a guide. Contact the **Mountain Guides Society Office** (☏4422 066; www.tatraguide.sk; Starý Smokovec 38; ☺10am-6pm Mon-Fri, noon-6pm Sat & Sun, closed weekends Oct-May); guides cost from €150 and the society runs classes too.

At the top of the funicular, tow-assist snow sledging and summer tubing are to be had at **Funpark** (☺10am-4pm Jul & Aug, from 9am Dec-Feb).

Rent mountain bikes at **Tatrasport** (www.tatry.net/tatrasport; Starý Smokovec 38; per day €12; ☺8am-6pm), above the bus-station parking lot.

TATRANSKÁ LOMNICA & AROUND

While in the Tatras, you shouldn't miss the ride to the 2634m summit of **Lomnický štít** (bring a jacket!). From Lomnica, a **gondola** (www.vt.sk; adult/child return €15/10; ☺8.30am-7pm Jul & Aug, to 4pm Sep-Jun) pauses midstation at **Štart** before it takes you to the winter-sports area, restaurant and lake at **Skalnaté pleso**. From there, a smaller **cable car** (www.vt.sk; adult/child return €24/17; ☺8.30am-5.30pm Jul & Aug, to 3.30pm Sep-Jun) goes on to the summit. The second leg of the journey requires a time-reserved ticket. On sunny summer days time slots do sell out, so get in line early. You're given 50 minutes at the top to admire the views, walk the observation platforms and sip a beverage in the cafe before your return time.

One of the top Tatra day hikes starts from Skalnaté pleso, following the rocky Magistrála Trail west past amazingly open views back into the forest at **Zamkovského chata** (1¼ hours), an atmospheric mountain hut and restaurant. Continue downhill, along the even rockier, steeper path past the **Obrovský** and **Studený Potok** waterfalls on to Hrebienok (three hours total). From there the funicular takes you down to Starý Smokovec.

Get off the cable car at Štart and you're at **Funtools** (www.vt.sk; rides per hour €5; ☺9am-6pm Jun-Sep), from where you can take a fast ride down the mountain on a two-wheeled scooter, a lugelike three-wheel cart or on a four-wheel modified skateboard.

Much winter-sport development has taken place on the slopes above Tatranská Lomnica; the area now counts about 30 skiable hectares. From Skalnaté pleso a high-speed winter **quadlift** (adult/child €8/5.50; ☺9am-4pm) hoists riders to **Lomnické sedlo**, a 2190m saddle below the summit, and access to an advanced 6km-long ski run (1300m drop). A multimillion-euro renovation also added a high-speed **six-seat chairlift** (€10; ☺9am-4pm) from the village up to Štart, snow-making capacity and a ski-in/ski-out car park. **Vysoké Tatry** (www.vt.sk; Tatranská Lomnica 7; day-lift ticket adult/child €24/17; ☺9am-3.30pm Dec-Apr) sells passes from the base of the cable car, where ski rental (from €15 per day) and lockers are also available.

ŠTRBSKÉ PLESO & AROUND

Condo and hotel development continue unabated in the village but the namesake clear blue glacial lake (*pleso*) remains beautiful, surrounded by dark pine forest and rocky peaks. **Row boats** (per 45min €15-20; ☺10am-6pm May-Sep) can be rented from the dock by Grand Hotel Kempinski: exorbitant, but you're on the water in front of Slovakia's most-photographed scenes.

In good weather the streets are overrun, as one of the most popular day hikes departs from here. Follow the red-marked **Magistrála Trail** uphill from the train station on a rocky forest trail for about 1¼ hours to **Popradské pleso**, an even more idyllic lake at 1494m. The busy mountain hut there has a large, self-service restaurant. You can return to the train line by following the paved road down to the Popradské pleso stop (45 minutes). Or the Magistrála zigzags dramatically up the mountainside from Popradské pleso and then traverses east towards Sliezsky dom and the Hrebienok funicular above Starý Smokovec (5¾ hours).

There is also a year-round **chairlift** (www.parksnow.sk; adult/child return €10/7; ⊙8am-3.30pm) up to **Chata pod Soliskom**, from where it's a one-hour walk north along a red trail to the 2093m summit of **Predné Solisko**.

Park Snow (www.parksnow.sk; day-lift ticket adult/child €19/13.50; ⊙8.30am-3.30pm), Štrbské Pleso's popular ski and snowboard resort, has two chairlifts, four tow lines, 12km of easy-to-moderate runs, one jump and a snow-tubing area.

🛌 Sleeping

For a full listing of Tatra lodgings, look online at www.tatryinfo.eu. Cheaper sleeps are available in small settlements like Nová Lesná down the hill or east over the ridge at Ždiar in the Belá Tatras. No wild/backcountry camping is permitted: there is a camping ground near Tatranská Lomnica. For the quintessential Slovak mountain experience, you can't beat hiking from one *chata* (a mountain hut; could be anything from a shack to a chalet) to the next, high up among the peaks. Food (optional meal service or restaurant) is always available. Beds fill up, so book ahead.

SMOKOVEC RESORT TOWNS

Look for reasonable, been-there-forever boarding houses with one-word names like 'Delta' just west of the Nový Smokovec electric train stop on the several no-name streets that run to the south.

TOP CHOICE Penzión Tatra PENSION €
(⌀0903650802; www.tatraski.sk; Starý Smokovec 66; s/d incl breakfast €23/46; @🛜) Big and colourful modern rooms fill this classic 1900 alpinesque building above the train station. It's super-central. Billiard table and ski storage available.

Villa Siesta HOTEL €€
(⌀4423 024; www.villasiesta.sk; Nový Smokovec 88; d €64, ste €83-113; 🛜) Light fills this airy, contemporary mountain villa furnished in natural hues. The full restaurant, sauna and jacuzzi are a bonus.

Grand Hotel HOTEL €€€
(⌀4870 000; www.grandhotel.sk; Starý Smokovec 38; r €99-179; 🛜🍽) More than 100 years of history are tied up in Starý Smokovec's *grande dame*. Rooms could use an update.

Penzion Vesna PENSION €
(⌀4422 774; www.penzionvesna.sk; Nový Smokovec 69; s/d €25/50) Rambling, good-value, family-run pension with some apartments available. Heading left over the electric railway tracks after the Palace Hotel, it's down a small road immediately to the left.

Bilíkova Chata MOUNTAIN HUT €
(⌀4422 439; www.bilikovachata.sk; s/d without bathroom €28/56) Basic log-cabin hotel with full-service restaurant among the clouds; only a seven-minute walk from Hrebienok funicular station.

Zbojnícka Chata MOUNTAIN HUT €
(⌀0903638000; www.zbojnickachata.sk; dm incl breakfast €20) Sixteen-bed dorm room, self-service eatery and small kitchen; at 1960m, a four-plus hours' hike up from Hrebienok.

TATRANSKÁ LOMNICA & AROUND

Look for private rooms (*privat* or *zimmer frei*), from €15 per person, on the back streets south and east of the train station. You can book ahead online at www.tatry.sk and www.tanap.sk/homes.html.

Grandhotel Praha HOTEL €€
(⌀4467 941; www.grandhotelpraha.sk; Tatranská Lomnica; r incl breakfast €85-175; @🍽) Remember when travel was elegant and you dressed for dinner? Well, the 1899 Grandhotel's sweeping marble staircase and crystal chandeliers do. Rooms are appropriately classic and there's a snazzy spa here, high above the village.

Penzión Encian PENSION €
(⌀4467 520; www.encian.eu; Tatranská Lomnica 32; s/d €30/47; @) Steep roofs, overflowing flowerboxes and a small restaurant hearth: Encian exudes mountain appeal. Breakfast buffet is €5.

MULTIRESORT SKI PASSES

Park Snow and Vysoký Tatry resorts, the ski concessions in Štrbské Pleso and Tatranská Lomnica have all joined forces to offer multiday, multiresort lift passes (three-day adult/child €93/65). The **Super Slovak Ski Pass** (www.vt.sk; 10-day adult €260) covers some of the main resorts as well as other smaller ski areas around Slovakia.

Penzion Daniela
PENSION €

(www.penziondaniela.sk; Tatranská Lomnica 40c; s/d €26/52) The five rooms are plainer than the rustic log chalet exterior suggests, but this is still Tatranská Lomnica's homeliest options.

Zamkovského Chata
MOUNTAIN HUT €

(✆4422 636; www.zamka.sk; per person €15-18) Atmospheric wood chalet with four-bed bunk rooms and restaurant; great hike stop midway between Skalnaté Pleso and Hrebienok.

Hotel & Intercamp Tatranec
CAMPING GROUND €

(✆4467 092; www.hoteltatranec.com; Tatranská Lomnica 202; campsite €7-10.50, d/cabin €85/96) Ageing six-person cabins, motel and restaurant – with an open tent field. North of the 'T Lomnica zast' stop on the train line to Studený Potok.

ŠTRBSKÉ PLESO & AROUND

Development and crowds make staying in this village our last choice, with one grand exception.

TOP CHOICE Grand Hotel Kempinski
LUXURY HOTEL €€€

(✆3262 554; www.kempinski.com/hightatras; Kupelna 6, Štrbské Pleso; r €400-450, ste €600-2800; ✳@≋) The swankiest Tatra accommodation is the classic, villalike Kempinski, enticing high-end travellers with evening turn-down service, heated marble bathroom floors and incredible lake views. See the mountains stretch before you through two-storey glass from the luxury spa.

Chata Pod Soliskom
MOUNTAIN HUT €

(✆0917 655 446; www.chatasolisko.sk; Štrbské Pleso; dm €16) Small log hostel (eight beds), nice terrace, no hiking required; next to the chairlift terminus at 1800m.

Chata Popradské Pleso
MOUNTAIN HUT €

(✆910948160; www.popradskepleso.sk; dm €14-18, s/d €23/46) Sizeable mountain hotel with restaurant and bar. It's a one-hour rugged hike up from the village or a paved hike up from Popradské pleso train stop.

Hotel Patria
HOTEL €€

(✆7848 999; s €81-121, d €110-164) This is where those Communist leaders holidayed back in the '70s...at least, that's the feel the gargantuan Hotel Patria gives. But somehow, we've got a soft spot for it. The rooms have views as good as the Kempinski and the restaurant's alright. It's on the other side of the lake from Štrbské Pleso, 1km from the village itself.

✗ Eating & Drinking

The resort towns are close enough that it's easy to sleep in one and eat in another. There's at least one grocery store per town. Nightlife is limited here.

SMOKOVEC RESORT TOWNS

A couple of oft-changing discos are scattered around; ask for the latest when you arrive.

TOP CHOICE Reštaurácia Svišť
SLOVAKIAN €€

(Nový Smokovec 30; mains €6-13; ⏱6-11pm) From hearty dumplings to beef fillet with wine reduction, this stylish Slovakian restaurant does it all well – and it's surprisingly reasonably priced.

Pizzeria La Montanara
ITALIAN €

(Starý Smokovec 22; mains €3.50-6; ⏱11am-9pm) A local favourite, La Montanara serves good pies, pastas, soups and vegetables. It's above a grocery store on the eastern edge of town.

Koliba Smokovec
SLOVAK €€

(Starý Smokovec 5; mains €7-15; ⏱3-10pm) A traditional rustic grill restaurant; some evening folk music. There's a **pension** (s/d €25/40) too.

Tatry Pub
PUB

(Tatra Komplex, Starý Smokovec; ⏱3pm-1am Sun-Thu, 3pm-3am Fri & Sat; ☎) The official watering hole of the Mountain Guide Club is a lively place to drink, with a full schedule of dart tournaments, concerts etc.

Cafe Hoepfner
CAFE

(Starý Smokovec 22, Hotel Smokovec; cakes €1-3) Friendly, local cafe with cakes and coffees; live jazz on summer Saturday evenings.

TATRANSKÁ LOMNICA & AROUND

Hikers can carb-load at predictable Slovakian eateries by the train station. The restaurant at Grandhotel Praha has the best food; for the chairlift-bound there's decent pizza up at Štart cable-car station.

Reštaurácia U Medveda CZECH, SLOVAKIAN €€
(Tatranská Lomnica 88; mains €5-12) A good, off-the-beaten-track choice (south by the post office) for traditional cooking. Grilled specialities are a highlight.

Humno BAR
(Tatranská Lomnica; ☺10am-midnight Sun-Thu, to 4am Fri & Sat) It's a club, it's cocktail bar, it's an après-ski... With capacity to hold 300, one of Lomnica's newest ventures can afford to be a little of everything. At the cable-car station base.

ŠTRBSKÉ PLESO & AROUND
Food stands line the road above the train station, on the way to the chair lift.

Reštaurácia Furkotka SLOVAKIAN €
(www.furkotka.sk; Štrbské Pleso; mains €3-6; ☺11am-midnight) Easy...right outside the Štrbské Pleso electric railway station, here's your snug one-stop-shop for good food, beer, coffee, cake and alright **accommodation** (r per person €10-24).

Koliba Patria SLOVAKIAN €€
(southern lake shore, Štrbské Pleso; mains €6-15) Come here for the lovely lakeside terrace and complex meat dishes. It's certainly more refined than a typical *koliba* (rustic mountain restaurant serving Slovak sheep-herder specialities).

ℹ Information

All three main resort towns have ATMs on the main street.

Emergency
Mountain Rescue Service (☎421-(0)52 7877 711, emergency 18 300; www.hzs.sk; Horný Smokovec 52) The main office of Slovakia.

Internet Access
U Michalka Café (Starý Smokovec 4; per hr €2; ☺10am-10pm; ☎) Pleasant cafe with four terminals, great tea and strudel.
Tatranská Lomnica Library (☺9am-3.30pm Mon, Thu & Fri)

Tourist Information
Note that information offices do not book rooms; they hand out a brochure that lists some – not all – accommodation.
Tatra Information Office Starý Smokovec (TIK; ☑4423 440; Starý Smokovec 23; ☺8am-8pm Mon-Fri, to 1pm Sat) Largest area info office, with the most brochures.
TIK Štrbské Pleso (☑4492 391; www.tatry-info.sk; Štrbské Pleso; ☺8am-4pm) Provides good trail Info especially; uphill north from the Hotel Toliar. Tiny museum (natural history mostly) to peruse.
TIK Tatranská Lomnica (☑4468 119; www.tatryinfo.sk; Cesta Slobody; ☺10am-6pm Mon-Fri, 9am-1pm Sat) Has the most helpful staff; opposite Penzión Encian on the main street.

Travel Agencies
T-Ski Travel (☑0905 350 810; www.slovakiatravel.sk; Starý Smokovec 46; ☺9am-4pm Mon-Thu, to 5pm Fri-Sun) Books lodgings, arranges

SLOVAKIA HIGH TATRAS

TRANSPORT FROM THE TATRAS

Bus

DESTINATION	DEPARTURE POINT	PRICE (€)	DURATION (MIN)	FREQUENCY
Starý Smokovec	Poprad	0.90	15	every 30 min
Štrbské Pleso	Poprad	1.60	60	every 45 min
Tatranská Lomnica	Poprad	1.20	35	hourly
Ždiar	Tatranská Lomnica	1	30	8 daily

Train

DESTINATION	DEPARTURE POINT	PRICE (€)	DURATION (MIN)
Starý Smokovec	Poprad	1.50	25
Starý Smokovec	Štrbské Pleso	1.50	40
Štrbské Pleso	Poprad	2	70
Tatranská Lomnica	Poprad	1.50	25-40
Tatranská Lomnica	Štrbské Pleso	2	60

ski and mountain-bike programs, offers rafting and other tours outside the Tatras. Located at the funicular station.

Websites

High Tatras Tourist Trade Association (www.tatryinfo.sk) Comprehensive overview of the area, including accommodation.

Tatra National Park (www.tanap.org) National park website.

Tatry.sk (www.tatry.sk) Official website of Tatra towns; look under 'Maps' for village layouts.

ⓘ Getting There & Around

To reach the Tatras by public transport, switch in Poprad. From there a narrow-gauge electric train makes numerous stops in the resort towns along the main road; buses go to smaller, downhill villages as well. Either way, to get between Štrbské Pleso and Tatranská Lomnica, change in Starý Smokovec. Check schedules at www.cp.atlas.sk.

TRAIN From 6am until 10pm, electric trains (TEZ) run more or less hourly. Buy individual TEZ tickets at stations and block tickets (one to three) at tourist offices. Validate all on-board.

Belá Tatras

☏052

Travel east over the High Tatra ridges and you start to hear Slovak spoken with a Polish accent. Goral folk culture is an intricate part of the experience in the small Belá Tatras (Belianské Tatry). Traditional wooden cottages, some with striking red-and-white graphic designs, are still being built today in the main village of Ždiar. A rustic, laid-back, more local-oriented atmosphere pervades here, from where it's an easy jaunt on to Poland (in peak season). Heck, it's almost close enough to walk.

ŽDIAR

Decorated timber cottages line Ždiar, the oldest Tatra settlement, inhabited since the 16th century. Goral traditions have been both bolstered and eroded by tourism. Several sections of the village are historical reservations, including the **Ždiar House Museum** (Ždiarsky Dom; €1; ⊙10am-4pm Tue-Fri, 10am-noon Sat & Sun), a tiny place with colourful local costumes and furnishings.

Cross over the main road from the museum and a green trail skirts the river through **Monkova Valley** (880m), a level hike with very little elevation change. After 45 minutes the trail climbs up over **Širkové saddle** (1826m) and gets you to **Kopské sad-**

dle (1750m) in about four hours total (seven hours return). Past this point you've crossed into the High Tatras; Chata pri Zelenom plese is an hour away and the cable car to Tatranská Lomnica is 2½ hours beyond that.

West of the main road are two ski areas; in summer one becomes **Bikepark Bachledova** (www.skibachledova.sk; ⊙9am-4pm mid-Jul–mid-Sep). Here you can rent mountain bikes (from €5 per hour), chairlift them up the hill (€5 per ride) and thunder down.

🛏 Sleeping & Eating

Ždiar has multiple pensions and *privaty* (here private rooms are sizeable lodgings with shared-facility rooms for rent, from €11 per person). Odds are pretty good if you just show up, or check www.zdiar.sk under *ubytovanie*. If everywhere else is shut for food, Buffet Livia serves beer and goulash, goulash, goulash.

TOP CHOICE **Ginger Monkey Hostel**　　　HOSTEL €

(☏52 4498 084; www.gingermonkey.eu; Ždiar 294; dm/d €13/32; @🛜📶) Sublime mountain views from a comfy Goral-style house, round-the-clock tea, laundry, free breakfast and an unexpected sense of traveller camaraderie. Clearly the world-travelling owner/managers have picked up some tips... The place has a full kitchen, where a communal dinner may be cooking (by donation), or the whole group might go out eating (and drinking!) together. Don't just book one night; you'll end up extending. Cat, dog and chickens on site.

Penzión Kamzík　　　PENSION €

(☏4498 226; www.penzionkamzik.sk; Ždiar 513; s/d €11/22; 📶) Cheerful staff, modern rooms, small restaurant, table tennis and sauna.

Goralska Karčma　　　SLOVAKIAN €

(Ždiar 460; mains €3-6) This *krčma* (traditional rural pub) serves all the regional specialities, like potato pancakes stuffed with a spicy sauté.

Rustika Pizzeria　　　ITALIAN €

(Ždiar 334; pizza €4-6; ⊙5-10pm) Wood-fired pizza in a rambling old log house midvillage.

Ždiarsky Dom　　　SLOVAK €

(Ždiar 55; mains €3-6) Rustic Slovakian cooking next door to the little museum.

ⓘ Information

PLP Shop (☏0903 642 492; Ždiar 333; ⊙9am-noon & 3-6pm) Souvenir shop, info office and bicycle rental (from €12 per day) by Rustika Pizzeria.

ⓘ Getting There & Away

Bus is the only way to get to the Belá Tatras. Poland (open EU border) is 14km north of Ždiar. For Slovak schedules, check www.cp.atlas.sk; for Polish, see also http://strama.eu. Buses from Ždiar connect directly with Poprad (€2, one hour, nine daily), Starý Smokovec (€1.60, 40 minutes, 11 daily) and Tatranská Lomnica (€1, 30 minutes, hourly). Between April and October, buses from Poprad stop in Zdiar en route to Zakopane in Poland (€2.20, 50 minutes, two daily).

EAST SLOVAKIA

Life gets, well, more laid-back the further east you venture. Somehow picturesque towns such as Levoča and Bardejov have avoided modern bustle and unfortunate 20th-century architectural decisions, while the national parks beckon with untrammelled wildernesses that are free from those Tatras-bound tourists.

Kežmarok

☑052 / POP 16,800

Snuggled beneath the broody High Tatras peaks, Kežmarok's pocket-sized Old Town square with distinctive churches and a small castle seems especially agreeable. The influence of original 13th-century Germanic settlers pervades the architecture even today. During July the **European Folk Craft Market** – one of the nation's largest – comes to town.

From the adjacent bus and train stations, 1km northwest of the pedestrian centre, follow Dr Alexandra street to the main square, Hlavné nám. The red-and-green, pseudo-Moorish **New Evangelical Church** (cnr Toporcerova & Hviezdoslavovo; admission €2; ☯10am-noon & 2-4pm Tue-Sat, closed Nov-Apr), c 1894, dominates the south end of town. Admission covers entry to the more evocative **Old Wooden Evangelical Church**, built in 1717 without a single nail. It has an amazing interior of carved and painted wood, as well as an original organ.

At the other end of the square, the stumpy, mansionlike 15th-century **Kežmarok Castle** (www.kezmarok.com; Hradné nám 45; adult/child €3/1.50; ☯9am-4pm by tour) is a museum with period furniture and archaeology exhibits.

You'll find cafes aplenty around pedestrianised Hlavné nám. If you're staying overnight, try the diminutive but elegant **Hotel Hviezdoslav** (Hlavne Nam; s/d €59/69) on this square, in the former house of the famed Slovak poet of the same name; it has a good restaurant. Bus connections also mean the town is a viable day trip from the High Tatras.

Kežmarok Information Agency (☑4492 135; www.kezmarok.net; Hlavné nám 46; ☯8.30am-4.15pm Mon-Fri, 8.30am-1pm Sat) has loads more information. Buses connect directly to Poprad (€1, 30 minutes, half-hourly), Tatranská Lomnica (€1, 30 minutes, hourly), Ždiar (€1.60, 40 minutes, four daily or change in Tatranská Lomnica) and Levoča (€1.30, one hour, four daily or change in Poprad).

Pieniny National Park

☑052

People hit 21-sq-km **Pieniny National Park** (www.pieniny.sk) to raft the river beneath impressive 500m-tall cliffs. Along with a Polish park on the north bank, Pieniny protects the Dunajec Gorge, east of the Slovak village of Červený Kláštor.

At the mouth of the gorge, rooms in the fortified 14th-century **Red Monastery** (Červený Kláštor; www.muzeumcervenyklastor.sk; adult/child €3/1; ☯8am-7pm Jul & Aug, 9am-5pm Apr-Jun, Sep & Oct, 10am-4pm Mon-Fri Nov-Mar) hold a diminutive museum, but the main reason why you're here is to float. There are two departure points for a **river float trip** (☑4282 840; www.pltnictvo.sk; adult/child €10/5; ☯9am-dusk May-Oct) on Rte 543: one opposite the monastery, another 1km upriver west of the village. Most visitors pile into one of the continually launching, traditional – and dry – *pltě* (shallow, flat-bottom wood rafts). But for €40 to €50 per person you can be outfitted for a wet, and slightly wilder, rubber-raft ride. Don't be expecting Class V thrills though. The Dunajec River is a fairly sedate 1½-hour experience terminating near the Slovak village of Lesnica.

To return to Červený Kláštor you can hike back the way you came, along an absorbing riverside trail through the 9km-long gorge, in two hours. Alternatively, 500m southeast of the river trip terminus is **Chata Pieniny** (☑4285 031; www.chatapieniny.sk; mains €3-10) in Lesnica. Here, rent a bicycle for a one-way ride (€4) back through the gorge, or board a minibus that will transport you the 22km back by road (€3). In summer, folk musicians often play at the log *chata* and its buzzing restaurant: touristy, but fun.

Overnighters can pitch tents in the field outside **Penzion Pltník** (☑4822 525; www.penzionpltnik.sk; Červený Kláštor 93; 2 adults & tent

€6.50, d €34) or check into one of the copious private rooms (usually signed *privaty*) on the road into Červený Kláštor.

Though Pieniny is only 42km north of Kežmarok, getting here is a challenge without your own vehicle. Travel agents in the High Tatras resorts can help arrange trips. Public buses run to Červený Kláštor from Poprad (€2.75, 1¾ hours), via Kežmarok (€2.25, 1¼ hour), once in the morning and twice in the afternoon. Several pedestrian bridges lead from here into Poland.

Levoča

♪ 053 / POP 14,900

So this is what Slovakia looked like in the 13th century... Unesco-listed Levoča is one of the few towns to still have its ancient defences largely intact. High medieval walls surround Old Town buildings and cobblestone alleyways. At the centre of it all stands the pride of the country's religious art and architecture collection, the Gothic Church of St Jacob. During the Middle Ages the king of Hungary invited Saxon Germans to colonise frontier lands. Levoča became central to the resulting Slavo-Germanic Spiš region, and became one of Slovakia's most important pilgrimage centres.

◉ Sights

Church of St Jacob   CHURCH
(Chrám Sv Jakuba; www.chramsvjakuba.sk; Nám Majstra Pavla; adult/child €2/1; ☺by hourly tour 8.40am-4pm Tue-Sat, 1-4pm Sun) The spindles-and-spires Church of St Jacob, built in the 14th and 15th centuries, elevates your spirit with its soaring arches, precious art and rare furnishings, where the main attraction is Slovakia's tallest altar, an impressive 18m high.

The splendid Gothic altar (1517), created by Master Pavol of Levoča, is the main reason why people flock to this church on Levoča's main square. Little is known about the alter's sculptor, but his work is much revered. Cherubic representations of the Last Supper and the Madonna and Child are carved into the wood-and-paint masterpiece.

Buy tickets from the cashier inside the Municipal Weights House across the street from the north door. Entry is generally on the hour, but admissions are more frequent in summer and more sporadic off-season. The adjacent 16th-century cage of shame was built to punish naughty boys and girls.

Nám Majstra Pavla   SQUARE
Gothic and Renaissance eye candy abound on the main square, Nám Majstra Pavla. The private **Thurzov House** (1517), at No 7, has a characteristically frenetic Spiš Renaissance roofline. No 20 is the **Master Pavol Museum**, dedicated to the works of the city's most celebrated son. The 15th-century **Historic Town Hall** (Radnica) building, centre square, is really more interesting than the limited exhibits within. Temporary, town-related displays are on show at No 40, **Creative Culture in Spiš** (Výtarná Kultura na Spiši). One ticket gets you into all of the last three, as they are branches of the **Spiš Museum** (www.spisskemuzeum.com; adult/child €3/1.50; ☺9.30am-3pm Tue-Fri).

Church of Mariánska Hora   CHURCH
From town you can see the Church of Mariánska Hora, 2km north, where the largest annual Catholic pilgrimage in Slovakia takes place in early July. You can walk or drive up for great views over Levoča: get directions in the tourist office.

🛏 Sleeping & Eating

Hotel U Leva   HOTEL €€
(♪4502 311; www.uleva.sk; Nám Majstra Pavla 24; s/d/apt €39/68/99; ☺⊚) Spread across two Old Town buildings, each of the 23 cleanly contemporary rooms is unique. All have muted jewel-tone walls enlivening them, and apartments come with kitchens. The fine restaurant (mains €7 to €13) combines atypical ingredients (brie, spinach) with time-honoured Slovak techniques.

Hotel Arkáda   HOTEL €
(♪4512 372; www.arkada.sk; Nám Majstra Pavla 26; s/d €36/52; ⊚⊚) Furnishings in this Old Town building are mostly uninspired, but you can upgrade to a suite with antiques and arched ceilings for just €65. The cellar restaurant (mains €5 to €11) is much more atmospheric, with ancient brick vaults. Traditional and grilled dishes here attract quite a local following.

Oáza   PENSION €
(♪4514 511; www.ubytovanieoaza.sk; Nová 65; dm incl breakfast from €10) Simple two-bed rooms with shared bathroom, and four-bed rooms with bath and kitchen, are just what the budget doctor ordered.

U Janusa   SLOVAK
(Klaštorská 22; mains €4-11) Cosy traditional restaurant that doubles as a pension. Try the many kinds of *pirohy* (dumplings).

ℹ Information

Everything you'll likely need, banks and post office included, is on the main square.

Levonet Internet Café (Nám Majstra Pavla 38; per hr €2; ⊙10am-10pm)

Tourist Information Office (☑4513 763; http://eng.levoca.sk; Nám Majstra Pavla 58; ⊙9am-4pm Mon-Fri year-round, plus 9am-4pm Sat & Sun May-Sep)

ℹ Getting There & Away

Levoča is on the main E50 motorway between Poprad (28km) and Košice (94km). Bus travel is the most feasible option here.

The local bus stop at Nám Štefana Kluberta is much closer to town than the bus station, which is 1km southeast of centre. From the bus stop, follow Košicka west two blocks and you'll hit the main square.

Frequent coach services take you to the following destinations:

Košice (€4.50, two hours, seven daily)

Poprad (€1.60, 45 minutes, hourly) Most convenient onward mainline train connections.

Spišská Nová Ves (€1, 20 minutes, half-hourly) For Slovenský Raj National Park.

Spišské Podhradie (€1, 20 minutes, half-hourly) For Spiš Castle.

Spišské Podhradie

☑053 / POP 4000

Sprawling for 4 hectares above the village of Spišské Podhradie, ruined Spiš Castle is undoubtedly one of the largest in Europe. Even if you've never been, you may have seen pictures: the fortress is one of Slovakia's most-photographed sights. Two kilometres west, the medieval Spiš Chapter ecclesiastical settlement is also a Unesco World Heritage Site. In between, the village itself has basic services.

◎ Sights

Spiš Castle   CASTLE

(Spišský hrad; www.spisskemuzeum.com; adult/child €5/3; ⊙9am-7pm, closed Nov-Mar) Heralding from at least as early as the 13th century, Spiš Castle and its vast complex of ruins crown a ridge above Spišské Podhradie. Its claim to fame as one of Europe's largest castle complexes will certainly seem accurate as you explore. Highlights include the climb up the central tower for spectacular panoramic views across the Spiš region.

From the E50 motorway you catch glimpses of eerie outlines and stony ruins atop the hill on the eastern side of Spišské Podhradie

village. Can it really be that big? Indeed, Spiš Castle seemingly rambles on forever. If the reconstructed ruins are this impressive, imagine what the fortress was once like. Be sure to get the English audio tour that brings the past into focus through story and legend.

Chronicles first mention Spiš Castle in 1209 and the remaining central residential tower is thought to date from then. From there defenders allegedly repulsed the Tatars in 1241. Rulers and noble families kept adding fortifications and palaces during the 15th and 16th centuries, but by 1780 the site had already lost military significance and much was destroyed by fire. It wasn't until the 1970s that efforts were made to restore what remained. Few structures are whole, but there's a cistern, a Romanesque palace that contains the very small **museum**, and the chapel adjacent to it. Night tours and medieval festivals take place some summer weekends.

Be sure to climb the steep spiral staircase of the central tower for great views, and imagine yourself as a patrolling medieval guard as you traipse around this colossal fortress's outer walls.

Spiš Castle is 1km east of Spišské Podhradie, a healthy, uphill hike above the spur rail station. The easiest approach to the castle by car is off the E50 highway on the east (Prešov) side.

Spiš Chapter   MONASTERY

(Spišská Kapitula; adult/child €2/1) On the west side of Spišské Podhradie, you'll find still-active Spiš Chapter, a 13th-century Catholic complex encircled by a 16th-century wall. The pièce de résistance is St Martin's Cathedral (1273), towering above the community of quirky Gothic houses and containing some arresting 15th-century altars.

The Romanesque cathedral features twin towers and an ornate sanctuary; the altars are impressive trifold-painted sights. Spiš Chapter is part of the wider Spiš Castle & Levoča Unesco World Heritage Site. Buy tickets for the cathedral and pick up a guide from the (often-closed) information office at Spišská Kapitula 4. If you're travelling to Spiš Chapter by bus from Levoča, get off one stop (and 1km) before Spišské Podhradie, at Kapitula.

🛏 Sleeping & Eating

This is potentially a day trip from Levoča, the High Tatras or Košice, so there's little reason to stay over. The castle has food stands and the village has a grocery store.

Penzión Podzámok   PENSION €

(☏4541 755; www.penzionpodzamok.sk; Podzámková 28; 2-4 bed r per person €13, without bathroom €8) Simple 42-bed guesthouse with a backyard view of the castle. It's in the village, north across the bridge. All meals are available: full board is an extra €13.50

TOP CHOICE **Spišsky Salaš**   MOUNTAIN HUT €

(☏4541 202; www.spisskysalas.sk; Levočská cesta 11; mains €3-5; 🐾) Dig into lamb stew in the folksy dining room or on the covered deck, and watch the kids romp on rough-hewn play sets. The rustic log complex also has three simple rooms for rent (per person

€13). It's 3km west of Spiš Chapter, on the road toward Levoča. It's a great hike from here to Spiš Chapter and Spiš Castle.

🛈 Getting There & Away

Spišské Podhradie is 15km east of Levoča and 78km northeast of Košice.

BUS Frequent buses connect with Levoča (€1, 20 minutes), Poprad (€2.15, 50 minutes) and Košice (€3.50, 1¾ hours).

TRAIN An inconvenient spur railway line heads to Spišské Podhradie from Spišské Vlachy (€0.75, 15 minutes, five daily), a station on the Bratislava–Košice main line. Check schedules at www.cp.atlas.sk.

Slovenský Raj & Around

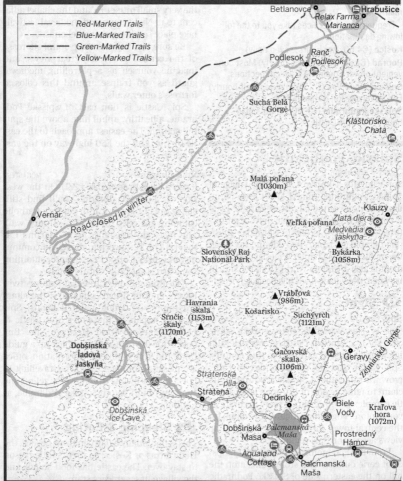

SLOVAKIA SPIŠSKÉ PODHRADIE

Slovenský Raj & Around

🎵 053

With rumbling waterfalls, sheer gorges and dense forests, Slovenský Raj lives up to the name of 'Slovak Paradise'. A few easier trails exist, but the one-way ladder-and-chain ascents make this a national park for the passionately outdoorsy. You cling to metal rungs headed up a precipice while an icy waterfall sprays you from a metre away: pure exhilaration.

The nearest major town is uninspiring Spišská Nová Ves, 23km southeast of Poprad. Of the three trailhead resort villages,

Podlesok, outside Hrabušice (16km south-west of Poprad), is our favourite – for its variety of hiking options and diverse lodging possibilities. Pretty Čingov, 5km west of Spišská Nová Ves, also has good lodgings. About 50km south, Dedinky is more a regular village with a pub and supermarket fronting a lake.

◉ Sights & Activities

Before you trek, pick up VKÚ's 1:25,000 *Slovenský Raj* hiking map (No 4) or Dajama's *Knapsacked Travel: The Slovak Paradise* hiking book, available at many tourist offices and bookshops countrywide. There

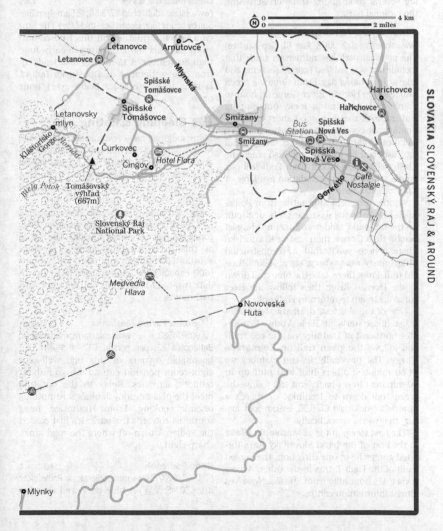

BUSES FROM SPISŠKA NOVÁ VES

DESTINATION	PRICE(€)	DURATION (MIN)	FREQUENCY
Čingov	0.50	15	1 direct Mon-Fri or change in Spišské Tomášovce
Dedinky	2	70	2 direct Mon-Fri or change in Poprad
Levoča	0.85	20	10 Mon-Fri
Podlesok via Spišský Štvrtok	1.20	30	2 Mon-Fri
Poprad via Spišský Štvrtok	1.70	40	12 Mon-Fri

are several good biking trails crisscrossing the national park.

Slovenský Raj National Park   PARK
(www.slovenskyraj.sk; Jul & Aug €1, Sep-Jun free) The national park has numerous trails that include one-way *roklina* (gorge) sections and take at least half a day. From Čingov a green trail leads up Hornád River Gorge an hour to **Tomašovský výhľad**, a rocky outcropping and overlook that is a good short-hike destination. Or continue to the green, one-way, technically aided **Kláštorisko Gorge** trail (at least eight hours). You can also reach the Kláštorisko Gorge ascent from Podlesok (six hours). There is accommodation available at **Kláštorisko Chata**.

Another excellent alternative from Podlesok is to hike on the six- to seven-hour circuit up the dramatic, ladder and technical-assist **Suchá Belá Gorge**, then east to Kláštorisko Chata, where you'll find a reconstructed 13th-century **monastery**, on a yellow then red trail. From there, take the blue trail down to the Hornád River, then follow the river gorge upstream to return to Podlesok.

One of the shortest, dramatic, technical-assist hikes starts at Biele Vody (15 minutes northeast of Dedinky via the red trail) and follows the green trail up **Zejmarská Gorge**. The physically fit can clamber up in 50 minutes; others huff and puff up in 90 minutes. To get back, you can follow the green trail down to Dedinky, or there's a **chairlift** (adult/child €1/0.50; ⏲9am-5pm Jun-Aug) that works sporadically.

The best viewpoint is at **Medvedia Hlava** in the east of the park. Slovenský Raj's forested gorges lie in one direction, the jagged teeth of the High Tatras in the other. Access it via a 4½ hour hike from Spišská Nová Ves tourist information centre.

Dobšinská Ice Cave   CAVE
(www.ssj.sk; adult/child €7/3.50; ⏲9am-4pm Tue-Sun by hourly tour, closed Oct–mid-May) The fanciful frozen formations in this Unesco-noted ice cave are more dazzling in early June than September. A 15-minute hike leads up from the settlement of Dobšinská ľadová jaskyňa to where tours begin every hour or so.

🛏 Sleeping & Eating

Many lodgings have restaurants. Numerous food stands and eateries and a small grocery are available in Podlesok. The biggest supermarket is next to the bus station in Spišská Nová Ves.

🏆 Autocamp Podlesok   CAMPING GROUND €
(☎4299 165; www.podlesok.sk; campsite €4-8, cottages & huts per person €10; 🕿) The office at this lively camping ground provides substantial trail info and wi-fi. Pitch a tent (600 capacity) or choose from fairly up-to-date two-to-12-bed cabins and cottages with bathrooms.

🏠 Relax Farma Marianka   PENSION
(☎905714583; www.relaxfarmamarianka.sk; Betlanovce 83; per person €17; P🕿📶) The hospitable owners of this big, well-kept eight-room pension can advise you about outdoor activities. Relax in the hot tub, meet the pigs or enjoy Janka's scrumptious organic cooking. From Hrabušice, head southeast towards the park: it's just passed the Podlesok turn-off where the road kinks sharp right.

Ranč Podlesok   PENSION €
(☎0918407077; www.rancpodlesok.sk; Podlesok 5; d/tr €30/45; 🕿📶) A blue park trail runs be-

hind this stone-and-log lodge and restaurant at the park's edge. There's sand volleyball too, if you fancy it. It's 1km past the Podlesok village area.

Penzión Lesnica　　　　PENSION €
(☑449 1518; www.stefani.sk; Čingov 113; s/d incl breakfast €30/40) Nine simple, sunny-coloured rooms close to the trail fill up fast, so book ahead. The attached restaurant is one of the best local places for a Slovakian repast (mains €3 to €10).

Hotel Flora　　　　HOTEL €
(☑449 1129; www.hotelfloraslovenskyraj.sk; Čingov 110; s/d incl breakfast €26/41; ☎) A certain mountain rusticity in the public areas but so-so rooms. The restaurant (mains €6 to €14) has a large, agreeable terrace.

Aqualand Cottage　　　　HOSTEL €
(☑0948007735; www.aqualand.sk; dm €13, s/d without bathroom €25/32) A sprawling cottage-hostel with common room, toasty fireplace and two kitchens across the lake from Dedinky proper.

Koliba Zuzana　　　　SLOVAKIAN €€
(☑0905278397; www.kolibazuzana.szm.sk; Dedinky 127; mains €3-10) Lakeside restaurant with terrace; two suites (€80) for rent upstairs.

Cafe Nostalgie　　　　INTERNATIONAL €€
(Letná 49, Spišska Nová Ves; mains €5-10; ☺10am-11pm) Next to the tourist information; probably the best thing in town. There's a quality international menu, including tasty Mexican options. If you've time to kill, kill it here.

❶ Information

Outside Spišská Nová Ves, lodgings are the best source of information; park info booths are open July through August. Get cash before you arrive in the park; there is an ATM and exchange at Spišská Nová Ves train station. Helpful websites include www.slovenskyraj.sk.

Mountain Rescue Service (☑emergency 183 00; http://his.hzs.sk)
Tourist Information Booth (Čingov; ☺9am-5pm, closed Sep-Jun)
Tourist Information Centre (☑4428 292; Letná 49, Spišská Nová Ves; ☺8am-6pm Mon-Fri, 9am-1pm Sat, 2-6pm Sun) Helps with accommodation.

❶ Getting There & Around

Off season especially, you may consider hiring a car in Košice; connections to the park can be a chore. You'll have to transfer at least once, likely in Spišská Nová Ves.

BUS Buses run infrequently on weekends, more often in July and August. No buses run directly between trailhead villages. Carefully check schedules at www.cp.atlas.sk.

TRAIN Trains run from Spišska Nová Ves to Poprad (€1, 20 minutes, 12 daily) and Košice (€3.80, one hour, 15 daily). The train station is 1½ blocks east of the bus station.

Košice

☑055 / POP 234,000
The world may now finally realise what Košice residents have long known: that East Slovakia's industrial powerhouse has cosmopolitan clout and a buoyant cultural scene plonking it firmly on Europe's city break map, fiercely independent of Bratislava. The reason: as 2013's European Capital of Culture, Košice has accordingly initiated a new string of attractions including major arts installations in a combination of impressively revamped buildings, and eclectic events to enliven city streets.

SLOVAKIA KOŠICE

ANDY WARHOL AND EAST SLOVAKIA

Andy Warhol wasn't born there, and took pains to disassociate himself from this area of Slovakia ('I come from nowhere', he once said) but Medzilaborce in far-eastern Slovakia is nevertheless where his parents grew up, before their move to the US. In 1991 the **Andy Warhol Museum** (☑421-57 7480 072; www.andywarhol.sk; Andyho Warhola 26, Medzilaborce; adult/child €3.50/1.75; ☺10am-4.30pm Tue-Fri, midday-4.30pm Sat & Sun) opened in this unlikely location as a shrine to pop art (alongside numerous Warhol originals are works from Basquiat, Lichtenstein and the like). Trains run from Košice, normally changing at un-delightful Humenné (€6.75, three hours, six daily). South of the station, Mierová becomes Andyho Warhola and the museum is 600m along this street.

The folks at Košice's **Muza Hotel** (www.hotelmuza.sk; Pri prachárni 5) have collected (and display) many Andy Warhol originals. It's 3km south of the Old Town near the Carrefour Shopping Centre in Lunik VIII.

Košice

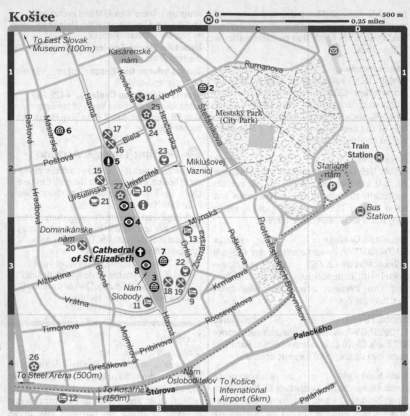

Košice

◎ Top Sights

◎ Sights

🛏 Sleeping

✗ Eating

◉ Drinking

✪ Entertainment

SLOVAKIA KOŠICE

Košice was always a medieval gem awaiting discovery. New enhancements build on an arts scene already home to the paintings of Andy Warhol and one of Europe's loveliest theatres. Its vast oval-shaped *námestie* (central square) contains the largest collection of historical monuments in Slovakia and when the buzzing cafes and restaurants open up here of a mellow evening, it's hard not to love the city or, at least, want a spirited affair. Out of town, nature encroaches spectacularly with the delights of Central Europe's grandest cave network. It's the base of choice, too, for forays deeper into the tradition-seeped east.

Košice received its city coat of arms in 1369 before any other city in Central Europe and for centuries was eastern stronghold of the Hungarian kingdom. On 5 April 1945 the Košice Government Program – which made communist dictatorship in Czechoslovakia a virtual certainty – got announced here.

◎ Sights

Hlavné Nám   SQUARE
Almost all of the sights are in or around the town's long plazalike main square, Hlavná. Landscaped flowerbeds surround the central **musical fountain**, across from the 1899 State Theatre (p865). To the north stands a large baroque **plague column** from 1723. Look for the turn-of-the-20th-century, art nouveau **Hotel Slávia** (☎622 4395; www.hotelslavia.sk; Hlavné Nám 63) at No 63. **Shire Hall** (1779), at No 27, is where the Košice Government Program was proclaimed in 1945; today there's a minor art gallery inside.

⌐TOP⌐ **Cathedral of St Elizabeth**   CHURCH
(Dóm Sv Alžbety; Hlavné Nám; church free, attractions €1; ⊙1-5pm Mon, 9am-5pm Tue-Fri, 9am-1pm Sat) The dark and brooding 14th-century Cathedral of St Elizabeth wins the prize for the sight most likely to grace your Košice postcard home. You can't miss Europe's easternmost Gothic cathedral, which dominates the square. Below the church, a **crypt** contains the tomb of Duke Ferenc Rákóczi, who was exiled to Turkey after the failed 18th-century Hungarian revolt against Austria.

Don't forget to ascend the 160 narrow, circular stone steps up the church's **tower** for city views. Climbing the **royal staircase** as the monarchs once did provides an interior perspective: note the rare interlocking flights of steps. Just to the south, the 14th-century **St Michael's Chapel** (Kaplinka sv Michala) has sporadic entry hours.

Lower Gate Underground Museum   MUSEUM
(Hlavné Nám; adult/child €1/0.50; ⊙10am-6pm Tue-Sun May-Sep) The underground remains of medieval Košice – lower gate, defence chambers, fortifications and waterways dating from the 13th to 15th centuries – were only uncovered during construction work in 1996. Get lost in the mazelike passages of the archaeological excavations at the south end of the square.

East Slovak Museum   MUSEUM
(Východoslovenské múzeum; ☎622 0309; www.vsmuzeum.sk; Hviezdoslavovo 3; per exhibition €1; ⊙9am-5pm Tue-Sat, 9am-1pm Sun) Hidden treasure can be found at the East Slovak Museum. Workers found the secret stash of 2920 gold coins, dating from the 15th to 18th centuries, while renovating a house on Hlavná in 1935. There's a romp through various aspects of regional history, too, showcased through a former prison and a metal foundry. In the museum yard there's a relocated 1741 wooden church.

⌐ Sleeping

The City Information Centre has an annual town booklet that lists local accommodation, including university dorms open to the public in July and August.

⌐TOP⌐ **Hotel Bankov**   HISTORIC HOTEL €€
(☎6324 522 ext 4; www.hotelbankov.sk; Dolný Bankov 2; s €85-135, d €95-145; P@☀) Going strong since 1869, Slovakia's oldest hotel lies 4km northwest of central Košice in a verdant location overlooking woodland. Rooms are surprisingly good value, oozing old-world charm (beams, period furniture). There's an elegant restaurant and a wellness centre. There's complimentary taxi service for guests.

Chrysso Penzión   BOUTIQUE HOTEL €€
(☎6230 450; www.penzionchrysso.sk; Zvonárska 3; s/d/apt €58/68/78; ❊☎) Think design-driven details such as silk throws and sleek leather chairs in chocolate and cream. A wine-cellar-bar, terrace and restaurant downstairs are similarly stylish.

⌐ **Ecohotel Dália**   BOUTIQUE HOTEL €€
(☎7994 321; www.hoteldalia.sk; Löfferova 1; s €59-89, d €74-109; P☎) One of Slovakia's

SLOVAKIA KOŠICE

NEW-LOOK KOŠICE

As 2013 European Capital of Culture, Košice has bolstered its appeal significantly. New/revamped attractions include the following:

Sándor Márai Memorial Room (☑625 8888; www.sandormarai.eu; Mäsiarska 35; ⊙1-3pm) House museum about the life of one of Slovakia's most famous writers, Sándor Márai, who was born in Košice (although he wrote in Hungarian).

Kunsthalle (Hall of Art; Mestský Park, cnr Rumanova & Štefánikova) Grandiose former swimming pool dating from the 1930s, transformed into a major exhibition centre.

Kosarné (Culture Park; ☑6854 299; www.kulturpark.sk; Kukučínova 2) The old military barracks, now a nationally renowned cultural centre for performing arts and a music venue, with ateliers and a cafe-bar. Just south of the Old Town.

first ecohotels, the Dália has the whole she-bang of green touches in its tucked-away location, including solar panelling, environmentally friendly toiletries and waste composting. Rooms have individual flourishes like hand-painted Chinese wallpaper. A wellness centre and a cafe-restaurant are on-site.

Hotel Zlatý Dukat
HOTEL €€
(☑7279 333; www.hotelzlatydukat.sk; Hlavná 16; s €75-79, d €85-89, ste €130-235; @🖭) Luxury main-square hotel with touches such as flat-screen TVs, flowers and room service.

Penzión Slovakia
PENSION €
(☑7289 820; www.penzionslovakia.sk; Orliá 6; s/d/ste €45/55/65; ✳🖭) Charming city guesthouse with grill restaurant downstairs.

K2
HOSTEL €
(☑6255 948; Štúrova 32; s/d without bathroom €16/27) These dowdy singles and doubles are the most centrally located budget option. No common room or kitchen; ask for a room away from the road.

✗ Eating

Med Malina
POLISH €€
(Hlavná 89; mains €7-11) The Polish owners cook up a variety of treats in this intimate little joint, like stuffed cabbage leaves or *zu-rek* (Polish potato soup).

TOP CHOICE Villa Regia
FINE DINING €€
(www.villaregia.sk; Dominikánske nám 3; mains €7-14; ▣) Steaks, seafood and vegetarian dishes get artistic treatment amid a rustic old-world atmosphere. The vaulted ceilings and stone walls extend to the upstairs pension rooms.

12 Apoštolov
SLOVAKIAN €€
(12 Apostles; Kováčska 51; mains €6-8) Košice's oldest restaurant has pulled its socks up to offer Slovakian-Hungarian cuisine as good as its surroundings are intense (stained-glass windows, church-pew seating).

Smelly Cat
CAFE €
(Zvonárska 6; ⊙9am-10pm Mon-Thu, 10am-1am Fri & Sat, 2-10pm Sun) Books, big ancient sofas, wicked coffee, delectable cakes: a refined boho hang-out on an amicable pedestrian street.

Nech Sa Páči
CAFE €
(Hlavná 27; snacks €1-5; ⊙10am-6pm Tue-Sun) Slickly designed cafe with a reputation for great breakfasts, coffees, desserts and cocktails. Has appealing outside seating; by the Cathedral of St Elizabeth.

Cafe Napoli
ITALIAN €€
(Hlavná 82; mains €4-11) Stylish young locals fill up this modern Italian restaurant, which does sublime pizza.

Cukráreň Aida
CAFE €
(Hlavná 81; cakes €1-3; ⊙8am-9pm) The most popular ice-cream and cake shop in town; several branches on the main square.

🍷 Drinking & Entertainment

For a city this small, options are plentiful. Any sidewalk cafe on the main square is great for a drink. Check free monthly publication *Kam do Mesta* (www.kamdomesta.sk) for entertainment listings.

Caffe Trieste
CAFE
(Uršulínska 2; ⊙7.30am-7.30pm) Original of the mini-chain now found in Bratislava. Knock-out espresso, in slurp-it-and-go Italian fashion.

Krčma Nositel Radu Prce
PUB

(Zvonárska 8) Return to the pre-1989 days: Lenin posters and oh-so-communist ambience and prices. It's authentic, mind – not a theme bar. Cheapest beer around.

Villa Cassa
BAR

(Vaznici 2; ⊙1pm-midnight Mon-Sat) Atmospheric wine bar offering more than 400 Slovak wines (plus others from across Europe).

Retro
CLUB

(Kováčska 49; ⊙7.30pm-2am) The place to get wild hereabouts, among beautiful people aplenty.

Jazz Club
CLUB

(http://jazzclub-ke.sk; Kováčska 39) DJs spin here most nights, but there are also occasional live concerts.

State Theatre
THEATRE

(Štátne Divadlo Košice; ☑6221 234; www.sdke.sk; Hlavné Nám 58; ⊙box office 9am-5.30pm Mon-Fri, 10am-1pm Sat) Local opera and ballet companies stage performances in this 1899 neo-baroque theatre.

State Philharmonic Košice
LIVE MUSIC

(Štátna Filharmónia Košice, House of the Arts; ☑6224 509; www.sfk.sk; Moyzesova 66) Concerts take place year-round but the spring musical festival is a good time to catch performances of the city's philharmonic.

Steel Aréna
SPORTS

(www.steelarena.sk; Nerudova 12) The hometown's revered ice-hockey team, HC Košice, plays here. Buy tickets at www.ticketportal.sk.

ⓘ Information

City Information Centre (☑6258 888; www.visitkosice.eu; Hlavná 59; ⊙9am-6pm Mon-Fri, 10am-4pm Sat & Sun) Ask for both the free annual town guide and the full-size colour brochure of historic sites. Good guided city tours can be arranged.

Internet Reading Room (Hlavná 48; per hr €1.60)

Ľudová Banka (Mlynská 29) Well-located ATM and exchange.

Police Station (☑159; Pribinova 6)

ⓘ Getting There & Away

Check bus and train schedules at www.cp.atlas.sk.

AIR Košice International Airport (p871) is 6km southwest of the centre. **Danube Wings** (V5; www.danubewings.eu) has two daily flights to Bratislava (weekdays only). Vienna and Prague are also served.

BUS You can book ahead on some Ukraine-bound buses through **Eurobus** (www.eurobus.sk). Getting to Poland is easier from Poprad. Destinations include Bardejov (€4, 1¾ hours, nine daily), Levoča (€4.80, two hours, eight daily) and Uzhhorod (Ukraine; €7, two to three hours, two daily).

CAR Several international car-hire companies such as Avis and Eurocar have representatives at the airport. **Buchbinder** (☑6832 397; www.buchbinder.sk) is a smaller company with good rates and gratis pick-up in the city.

ⓘ Getting Around

The Old Town is small, so you probably can walk everywhere. Transport tickets (€0.60 one zone) cover most buses and trams; buy them at newsstands and validate on board. Bus 23 between the airport and the train station requires a two-zone ticket (€1).

Around Košice

About 65km west of Košice lies Rožňava: the tourist office on the main square has information on how to visit the dramatic **Slovak Karst National Park** (Slovenský Kras; ☑58 7326 815; www.sopsr.sk/slovkras, in Slovak), undulating away outside town. Here more than 1000

TRAINS FROM KOŠICE

DESTINATION	PRICE (€)	DURATION (HR)	FREQUENCY (DAILY)
Bratislava	19	5-6	21
Lviv, Ukraine	60	13	1
Miskolc, Hungary	5	1¼	2
Poprad (High Tatras)	5	1¼	24
Spišská Nová Ves (Slovenský Raj)	4	1	23

caves, crevasses and abysses make up Central Europe's greatest karstic region. The subterranean highlight is **Domica Cave** (📞7882 010; tour with boat trip adult/child €7/3.50; ⏰9am-4pm Jun-Aug, 9.30am-2pm Feb-May & Sep-Dec) near Dlhá Ves, where cave systems over 1000m long beg to be explored. There are boat trips, and 16 bat species.

South of Košice on the approach to Hungary is Slovakia's best-known wine region, **Tokaj**. Wine tastings and tours are available in several villages hereabouts; ask at Košice's City Information Centre (p865).

Bardejov

📞054 / POP 33,400

It's tough competition in the medieval wonderland of East Slovakia, but Bardejov wins the award for our favourite Old Town square, which would look barely a brick out of place 400 years ago. Bardejov received its royal charter in 1376 and grew rich on trade between Poland and Russia into the 16th century. The steep roofs and flat fronts of the Unesco-listed burghers' houses here each have their own unique plaster details or inscriptions.

A clutch of museums shed light on this region's Eastern-facing art and culture and the town makes a good springboard for further exploration. The area's wooden churches reflect a Carpatho-Rusyn heritage, shared with neighbouring parts of Ukraine and Poland. Just north in Bardejovské Kúpele you can cure some ills at a thermal spa or see examples of these churches in a rewarding open-air village museum.

◉ Sights

The main square, **Radičné nám** is a sight in itself, and you can walk along the old **town walls and bastions** along Na Hradbách.

Šariš Museum
MUSEUM

(www.muzeumbardejov.sk; ⏰8am-noon & 12.30-4pm Tue-Sun) There are two local branches of the Šariš Museum worth seeing. Centre square, the **Town Hall** (Radničné nám 48; adult/child €1.50/1) contains altarpieces and a historical collection. Built in 1509, it was Slovakia's first Renaissance building. At the **Icon Exposition** (Radničné nám 27; adult/child €1.50/1), more than 130 dazzling icons and iconostases from the 16th to 19th centuries are displayed. This is an excellent opportunity to see the religious art that originally decorated Greek Catholic and Orthodox wooden churches east of Bardejov.

Basilica of St Egídius
CHURCH

(Bazilika Sv Egídia; Radničné nám; adult/child €1.50/1; ⏰9.30am-4pm Mon-Fri, 10am-3pm Sat, 11.30am-3pm Sun) The interior of this 15th-century basilica is packed with 11 Gothic altarpieces, built from 1460 to 1510. Each has thorough explanation in English.

🛏 Sleeping & Eating

Cafes can be found around Radničné nám.

el. Restaurant & Lodging
PENSION €

(📞4728 404; www.el-restaurant.sk; Stöcklova 43; s/d/apt incl breakfast €30/40/60; 📶) Three chirpy rooms up for grabs. It's very central and myriad chicken dishes are on the menu of the modern Slovakian restaurant downstairs.

Penzion Magura
PENSION €

(📞902374871; www.penzionmagura.sk; Andrasikova 31; s/d €27/39) There's oodles of space in these slickly finished rooms and a more traditional restaurant below.

Penzión Semafor
PENSION €

(📞0905830984; www.penzionsemafor.sk; Kellerova 13; s €26-33, d €39-43) Five bright doubles and an apartment in a family-run guesthouse. Nice and central.

[TOP CHOICE] Cactus
INTERNATIONAL €€

(www.cactus.sk; Štefánikova 61; mains €5-15; ⏰7am-10pm) Crisp salads, juicy steaks, stuffed trout...the food is flamboyant and with a glut of influences from the Scandinavian to the French – as modern as Bardejov is ancient. It's a light, enticing space with a snug whisky-cigar bar next door.

La Bello
ITALIAN €€

(Radničné nám 50; mains €6.50) An atmospheric, Italianesque restaurant dishing up wood-fired pizzas. The local fave.

Stadión
SLOVAK €

(www.penzionstadion.sk; Družstevná 1; mains €5; ⏰noon-8pm) No joke: this restaurant in the homonymous pension really is built into the football stadium – and it really does serve good food, in well-to-do sports-social-club-type environs. There are five rooms here (€28 to €48), including one apartment.

① Information

ČSOB (Radničné nám 7) Exchange and ATM.

Main Post Office (Dlhý rad 14)

WOODEN CHURCHES

Travelling east from Bardejov, you come to a crossroads of Western and Eastern Christianity. From the 17th to the 19th centuries, nearly 300 dark-wood, onion-domed churches were erected hereabouts. Of the 40-odd remaining, eight have been recognised by Unesco. A handful celebrate Roman Catholic or Protestant faiths, but most belong to the Eastern rites of Greek Catholicism and Orthodoxy.

Typically they honour the Holy Trinity with three domes, three architectural sections and three doors on the icon screen. Richly painted icons and venerated representations of Christ and the saints decorate the iconostases and invariably every inch of the churches' interiors have also been hand-painted. These can be quite a sight, but it's not easy to get inside. These rural churches are remote, with limited or non-existant bus connections to them, and doors are kept locked. Sometimes there's a map posted showing where the key-keeper lives; sometimes he's next door and sometimes you're out of luck.

The time-pressed can guarantee seeing icons and an interior at the Icon Exhibition in Bardejov and the *skanzen* in Bardejovské Kúpele, 3km north. The medieval Roman Catholic church in **Hervatov** (www.saris.eu.sk/hervatov; Hervartov) is one of the closest to Bardejov, while **Ladomirová** north of Svidník has an impressive Greek Catholic church. If you're up for a further adventure, the following resources can help:

Drevené Chrámy (www.drevenechramy.sk) Great online resource with detailed information on 39 wooden churches.

Cultural Heritage of Slovakia: Wooden Churches Comprehensive, full-colour book by Miloš Dudas with photos and church descriptions; for sale at bookstores.

Bardejov Tourist Information Centre A highly recommended first port of call for logistics on visiting the churches.

Tourist Information Centre (4744 003; www.bardejov.sk; Radničné nám 21; 9am-5.30pm Mon-Fri, 11.30am-3.30pm Sat & Sun, closed Sat & Sun Oct-Apr) Info, maps, souvenirs etc.

❶ Getting There & Away

Bardejov is on a spur train line, so buses are most convenient although it's way off the international bus routes.

Buses go to and from Košice (€3.75, 1¾ hours, eight daily), Poprad (€4.50, 2¼ hours, six daily) and Bardejovské Kúpele (€0.55, 10 minutes, 12 daily).

Bardejovské Kúpele

Three short kilometres to the north of Bardejov you'll find the leafy, promenade-filled spa town of Bardejovské Kúpele where the hot, sulfurous water fizzes as it spouts out the taps. Overall, it's somewhat dilapidated, but to book a service like a massage or a mineral bath (from €10), go directly to the **Spa House** (Kúpelny dom; 4774 225; www.kupele-bj. sk; 8am-noon & 1-5pm Mon-Sat) at the top of the main pedestrian street. The town also has Slovakia's oldest *skanzen*, the **Museum of Folk Architecture** (Múzeum Ľudovej Architektúry; adult/child €1.30/0.70; 9.30am-5pm Tue-Sun, to 3pm Oct-Apr) where you can see painted interiors and iconostases of the area's nail-less wooden churches. An ancient (Unesco-listed) example from Zboj has been moved here. Still, hunting out the churches themselves in the surrounding countryside is more fun.

Frequent buses connect with Bardejov. If you have a car, park in the lot by the bus station at the base of the town and walk uphill; the whole place is pedestrian-only. At the base near the colonnade is the **Tourist Information Office** (4774 477; www.bardejovske-kupele.sk; Kino Žriedlo; 8am-4pm Mon-Fri, 10.30am-4pm Sat & Sun).

UNDERSTAND SLOVAKIA

History

Slavic tribes wandered west into what would become Slovakia some time around the 5th century; in the 9th century, the territory was part of the short-lived Great Moravian empire. It was about this time that the Magyars (Hungarians) set up shop next door and subsequently laid claim to the whole territory. When in the early 16th century the Turks moved into Budapest, Hungarian monarchs took up residence in Bratislava (known then as Pozsony in Hungarian). Being Hungarian frontierland, many fortresses were constructed here during the Middle Ages and can still be seen today.

It wasn't until the 19th century that Slovakia, thanks to national hero Ľudovít Štúr, successfully forged its own literary language. In the early 1900s Slovak intellectuals cultivated the ties with neighbouring Czechs that would take their nation into the united Czechoslovakia post-WWI. The day before Hitler's troops invaded Czechoslovakia in March 1939, Slovak leaders declared Slovakia a German protectorate and a brief period of sovereignty ensued. This was not a popular move and in August 1944 Slovak partisans instigated the ill-fated Slovak National Uprising (Slovenské Národné Povstanie, or SNP), a source of ongoing national pride (and innumerable street names).

After the reunification and communist takeover in 1948, power was centralised in Prague until 1989 when the Velvet Revolution brought down the iron curtain here. Elections in 1992 saw the left-leaning nationalist Movement for a Democratic Slovakia (HZDS) come to power. Scarcely a year later, without referendum, the Czechoslovak federation dissolved peacefully (albeit with far from universal support among Slovaks) on 1 January 1993, bringing Slovakia its first true independence.

Slovakia was accepted into NATO and the EU by 2004, became a Schengen member state in 2007 and adopted the euro as the national currency in January 2009. Respective renaissances as a major stag-party and ski-break destination in the early 2000s were catalysts for getting wider attention from international tourism.

People

A deeply religious and familial people, Slovaks have strong family ties and a deep sense of folk traditions. Today Roman Catholics form the majority (about 69%), but evangelicals are also numerous and East Slovakia has many Greek Catholic and Orthodox believers. The young are warm and open, but there can be residual communist reserve within older generations. Friendliness lurks just behind this stoicism. If you make friends with a family, the hospitality (and free-flowing liquor) may just knock you out. Thankfully, in the tourist industry, surly service is now the exception rather than the rule.

Government statistics estimate that Slovakia's population is 86% Slovak, 10% Hungarian and 1.7% Roma. This last figure is in dispute: some groups estimate the Roma population, most of which are based in Eastern Slovakia, to be much higher. The Roma are viewed by the general populace with an uncompromising suspicion – at best.

ICE-HOCKEY OBSESSION

Slovakia's national ice-hockey team is usually deemed one of the world's 10 strongest. (Not bad, considering the team was only created when Czechoslovakia dissolved in 1993.) Local club rivalries are quite heated, with the most popular teams being HC Slovan (p836) in Bratislava and HC Košice (p865) in Košice. These teams' two stadiums co-hosted the IIHF world championships in 2011. Bratislava's Ondrej Nepela Arena got a big-money overhaul for the event, so it doesn't seem like the ice-hockey fever will cool down anytime soon. Puck-pushing season is September to April, when games seem to be on TVs everywhere.

Arts

Traditional folk arts – from music to architecture – are still celebrated across the country. Indeed, attending one of the many village folk festivals in summer can be the highlight of a visit: colourful costumes, upbeat traditional music, hearty *klobasa* and beer are all part of the fun. The biggest is Východná Folk Festival (www.obec-vychodna.sk), in the small namesake village 32km west of Poprad.

Traditional Slovak folk instruments include the *fujara* (a 2m-long flute), the *konkovka* (a shepherd's flute), drums and cimbalom. Today you'll likely still see a folk troupe accompanied by fiddle, bass, clarinet and sometimes trumpet or accordion. National folk companies like **Lučnica** (www.lucnica.sk) and **Sľuk** (www.sluk.sk) perform country-wide. But each microregion has its own particular melodies and costumes.

Outside of festivals, the best place to experience folk culture is at a *skanzen* – an open-air museum where examples of traditional wooden cottages and churches have been gathered in village form. The houses are fully furnished in traditional style and frequent activities, especially around holidays, focus on folk culture. The largest *skanzen* (p842), in Martin, represents several regions while Bardejovské Kúpele's open-air village museum (p867) has good examples of the nailless wooden churches for which the area is known.

Environment

A largely hilly, forested country, Slovakia sits at the heart of Europe (indeed Krahule, near Banska Bystricá, is one of several claimants to the title of 'geographical centre of Europe'). Straddling the northwestern end of the Carpathian Mountains, and with stupendous scenery, it's not surprising most Slovaks spend their weekends outdoors. National parks and protected areas comprise 20% of the territory and the entire country is laced with a network of trails.

Not to be missed is the High Tatras (Vysoké Tatry) National Park, protecting a 12km-long rocky mountain range that rises seemingly out of nowhere. The tallest peak, Gerlachovský štít, reaches an impressive 2654m. Then there are the lesser pine-clad ridges of Malá Fatra National Park, and Slovenský Raj National Park, where ladders and chain-assists make the challenging, narrow gorges accessible.

Unlike the mountainous north, southwestern Slovakia is a fertile lowland hugging the Danube River, which forms the border with Hungary. Slovak rivers are prone to serious flooding: watch for warnings.

Food & Drink

Slovakia isn't known for its 'cuisine' as much as for home cooking. Soups like *cesnaková polievka* (garlic soup), clear with croutons and cheese, start most meals. The national dish is *bryndzové halušky*, gnocchilike dumplings topped with sheep's cheese and bacon fat. You'll also find *bryndza* sheep cheese on potato pancakes, in *pirohy* (dumplings) and served as a *natierka* (spread) with bread and

SLOVAKIA'S MUSICAL HERITAGE

Slovakia has a surprisingly rich classical music pedigree. The career of **Franz Liszt** began in the De Pauli Palace in Ventúska street in Old Town Bratislava, while **Ludwig van Beethoven** lived in Hlohovec, north of Bratislava, gave concerts in the capital and even dedicated a sonata (Piano Opus 78) to Therese Brunsvik, member of one of the most influential city families at that time. Hungarian composer **Béla Bartók** also lived for a time in Bratislava (then Pressburg).

---

raw onions. Don't pass up an opportunity to eat in a *salaš* or a *koliba* (rustic eateries named for traditional parts of a sheep-herder's camp), where such traditional specialities abound.

Much of what you'll see on regular menus is basic Central European fare: various fried meat schnitzels, hearty pork dishes and paprika-infused stews. It's all very meaty, but most towns have at least one (vegetarian-friendly) pizza place. For dessert, try sweet *pirohy* filled with plum jam and poppy seeds (the signature secret dessert ingredient hereabouts) or *ovocné knedličky* (fruit dumplings).

Spirits of Slovakia

Expect to be served a shot of *slivovica* (plum-based firewater), *borovička* (a potent berry-based clear liquor), Demänovka (a herbal liquor related to Czech Becherovka) or something similar.

Unlike the Czech Republic, Slovakia is not known for its *pivo* (beer). But the full-bodied Zlatý Bažant and dark, sweet Martiner are decent.

Wine is big, however. The Modra region squeezes out dry medium-bodied reds, like frankovka and kláštorné. Slovak reisling and müller-uhurgau varietals are fruity but on the dry side. One of the best-regarded is Tokaj, an amber-hued dessert wine from the east similar to the homonymous, and neighbouring, Hungarian wine region. If money is no object, there's also *l'adové vino*: wine concocted with frozen grapes foraged after the first snows and thus extremely sweet.

SURVIVAL GUIDE

Directory A–Z
Accommodation

Bratislava has more hostels and five-star hotels than midrange accommodation. Outside the capital, you'll find plenty of reasonable *penzióny* (guesthouses). Breakfast is usually available (sometimes included) at all lodgings and wi-fi is common and usually free. Many lodgings offer nonsmoking rooms. Parking is only a problem in Bratislava. A recommended booking resource in the capital city is **Bratislava Hotels** (www.bratislavahotels.com).

The below ranges are based on the price of a double room with private bathroom in tourist season.

€ less than €60

€€ €60 to €150

€€€ more than €150

Activities

Hiking The **Mountain Rescue Service** (☑421-(0)52 7877 711, emergency 18 300; www.hzs.sk; Horný Smokovec 52) provides hiking and weather information in addition to aid: the main office is in Horný Smokovec in the High Tatras.

Skiing Check out the snow conditions at www.skiinfo.sk.

Business Hours

Sight and attraction hours vary throughout the year; standard opening times for the tourist season (May through September) are listed below. Schedules vary from October to April; check ahead.

Banks 8am to 5pm Monday to Friday

Bars 11am to midnight Monday to Thursday, 11am to 2am Friday and Saturday, 4pm to midnight Sunday

Grocery stores 6.30am to 6pm Monday to Friday, 7am to noon Saturday

Post offices 8am to 5pm Monday to Friday, 8am to 11am Saturday

Nightclubs 4pm to 4am Wednesday to Sunday

Restaurants 10.30am to 10pm

Shops 9am to 6pm Monday to Friday, 9am to noon Saturday

Embassies & Consulates

Australia and New Zealand do not have embassies in Slovakia; the nearest are in Vienna and Berlin respectively. The following are in Bratislava:

Canadian Embassy (☑5920 4031; www.canadainternational.gc.ca/czech-tcheque/; Mostová 2, Carlton-Savoy Building)

French Embassy (☑5934 7111; www.ambafrance-sk.org; Hlavné nám 7)

German Embassy (☑5920 4400; www.pressburg.diplo.de; Hviezdoslavovo nám 10)

Netherlands Embassy (☑5262 5081; www.holandskoweb.com; Frana Krála 5)

UK Embassy (☑5998 2000; http://ukinslovakia.fco.gov.uk; Panská 16)

US Embassy (☑5443 0861; http://slovakia.usembassy.gov; Hviezdoslavovo nám 4)

Food

Restaurant review price indicators are based on the cost of a main course.

€ less than €6

€€ €6 to €12

€€€ more than €12

Gay & Lesbian Travellers

Homosexuality has been legal in Slovakia since the 1960s but this is a conservative, mostly Catholic, country. The GLBT scene is small in Bratislava and all but nonexistent elsewhere. Check out www.gay.sk.

Internet Access

Wi-fi is widely available at lodgings and cafes across the country; so much so that internet cafes are becoming scarce. For the laptopless, lodgings also often have computers you can use.

Money

» ATMs are quite common even in smaller towns, but shouldn't be relied upon in villages.

» Visa and MasterCard are accepted at most hotels and the top-end, popular restaurants in main tourist zones.

» Since January 2009, Slovakia's legal tender has been the euro. But you'll still hear reference to the former currency, the Slovak crown, or Slovenská koruna (Sk).

» Tipping 10% is fairly standard, though some locals tip less.

Post

Post office service is reliable, but be sure to hand your outgoing mail to a clerk; your postcard may languish in a box for quite some time.

Public Holidays

New Year's and Independence Day 1 January

Three Kings Day 6 January

Good Friday and Easter Monday March/April

Labour Day 1 May

Victory over Fascism Day 8 May

SS Cyril and Methodius Day 5 July

SNP Day 29 August

Constitution Day 1 September

Our Lady of Sorrows Day 15 September

All Saints' Day 1 November

Christmas 24 to 26 December

Telephone

Landline numbers can have either seven or eight digits. Mobile phone numbers (10 digits) are often used for businesses; they start with ☑09. When dialling from abroad, you need to drop the zero from both city area codes and mobile phone numbers. Purchase local and international phone cards at newsagents. Dial ☑00 to call out of Slovakia.

MOBILE PHONES

The country has GSM (900/1800MHz) and 3G UMTS networks operated by providers Orange, T-Mobile and O_2.

Tourist Information

Association of Information Centres of Slovakia (AICES; ☑16 186; www.aices.sk) Runs an extensive network of city information centres.

Slovak Tourist Board (www.slovakia.travel) No Slovakia-wide information office exists; it's best to go online.

Travellers With Disabilities

Slovakia lags behind many EU states in accommodation for disabled travellers. **Slovak Union for the Disabled** (www.sztp.sk) works to change the status quo. Hotels and restaurants have few ramps or barrier-free rooms; pavements are far from universally smooth. There's some accessibility on public transport, including buses that lower, and special seating.

Visas

For a full list of visa requirements, see www.mzv.sk (under 'Ministry' and then 'Travel').

» No is visa required for EU citizens.

» Visitors from Australia, New Zealand, Canada, Japan and the US do not need a visa for up to 90 days.

» Visas are required for South African nationals, among others. For the full list see www.slovak-republic.org/visa-embassies.

Getting There & Away

Bratislava and Košice are the country's main entry/exit points. Flights, cars and tours can be booked online at lonelyplanet.com.

Entering Slovakia from the EU, indeed from most of Europe, is a breeze. Lengthy custom checks make arriving from the Ukraine more tedious.

Air

Bratislava's intra-European **airport** (BTS; www.airportbratislava.sk; Ivanská cesta), 9km northeast of the city centre, is small. Unless you're coming from the UK, which has several direct flights, your arrival will likely be by train. Vienna in Austria has the nearest international air hub.

AIRPORTS

Košice International Airport (KSC; www.airportkosice.sk)

Vienna International Airport (VIE; www.viennaairport.com) Austrian airport with regular buses that head the 60km east to Bratislava. Worldwide connections.

AIRLINES

The main airlines operating in Slovakia:

Austrian Airlines (www.aua.com) Connects Košice with Vienna.

Czech Airlines (www.czechairlines.com) Connects Košice with Prague.

Danube Wings (www.danubewings.eu) Connects Bratislava and Košice with Croatia.

Ryanair (www.ryanair.com) Connects Bratislava with numerous destinations across the UK and Italy, coastal Spain, Paris and Brussels.

Land

Border posts between Slovakia and fellow EU Schengen member states – Czech Republic, Hungary, Poland and Austria – are nonexistent. You can come and go at will. This makes checks at the Ukrainian border all the more strident, as you will be entering the EU. By bus expect one to two hours' wait; by car, much more.

BUS

Local buses connect Poprad and Ždiar with Poland. **Eurobus** (www.eurobus.sk)and **Eurolines** (www.slovaklines.sk) handle international routes across Europe from Bratislava and heading east to Ukraine from Košice.

CAR & MOTORCYCLE

Private vehicle requirements for driving in Slovakia are registration papers, a 'green card' (proof of third-party liability insurance), nationality sticker, first-aid kit and warning triangle.

TRAIN

See www.cp.atlas.sk for domestic and international train schedules. Direct trains connect Bratislava to Austria, the Czech Republic, Poland, Hungary and Russia; from Košice, trains connect to the Czech Republic, Poland, Ukraine and Russia. The fastest domestic trains are Intercity (IC) or Eurocity (EC). Rychlík (R), or 'fast' trains take slightly longer, but run more frequently and cost less. Osobný (Ob) trains are slowest (and cost least).

River

Danube riverboats offer an alternative way to get between Bratislava and Vienna.

Getting Around

Air

Danube Wings (V5; www.danubewings.eu) offers the only domestic air service: weekdays only, between Bratislava and Košice.

Bicycle

Roads are often narrow and potholed, and in towns cobblestones and tram tracks can prove dangerous for bike riders. Bike rental is uncommon outside mountain resorts. The cost of transporting a bike by rail is usually 10% of the train ticket.

Bus

Read timetables carefully; fewer buses operate on weekends and holidays. You can find up-to-date schedules online at www.cp.atlas. sk. The national bus company in Slovakia is **Slovenská Autobusová Doprava** (SAD; www.sad.sk).

Car & Motorcycle

» Foreign driving licences with photo ID are valid in Slovakia.
» *Nálepka* (toll stickers) are required on *all* green-signed motorways. Fines for not having them can be hefty. Buy at petrol stations (rental cars usually have them).
» City streetside parking restrictions are eagerly enforced. Always buy a ticket from a machine, attendant or newsagent in Old Town centres.
» Car hire is available in Bratislava and Košice primarily.

Local Transport

Towns all have good bus systems; villages have infrequent service. Bratislava also has trams and trolleybuses.
» Public transport generally operates from 4.30am to 11.30pm daily.
» City transport tickets are good for all local buses, trams and trolleybuses. Buy at newsstands and validate on board or risk serious fines (this is not a scam).

Train

Train is the way to travel in Slovakia; most tourist destinations are off the main Bratislava–Košice line. No online reservations; ticket machines are also rare. Reserve at train station offices. Visit www.cp.atlas.sk for up-to-date schedules. **Slovak Republic Railways** (ŽSR; ☑18 188; www.slovakrail. sk) has far-reaching, efficient national rail service.

Slovenia

Best Places to Eat

» Gostilna na Gradu (p882)

» Gostilna Ribič (p906)

» Gril Ranca (p905)

» Hiša Franko (p897)

» Gostilna Lectar (p889)

Best Places to Stay

» Antiq Palace Hotel & Spa (p881)

» Max Piran (p901)

» Hostel Pekarna (p905)

» Camping Bled (p889)

» Penzion Gasperin (p892)

Why Go?

It's a pint-sized place, with a surface area of just more than 20,000 sq km and two million people. But 'good things come in small packages', and never was that old chestnut more appropriate than in describing Slovenia. The country has everything from beaches, snowcapped mountains, hills awash in grape vines and wide plains blanketed in sunflowers to Gothic churches, baroque palaces and art nouveau buildings. Its incredible mixture of climates brings warm Mediterranean breezes up to the foothills of the Alps, where it can snow in summer.

The capital, Ljubljana, is a culturally rich city that values livability and sustainability over unfettered growth. This sensitivity towards the environment extends to rural and lesser-developed parts of the country as well. With more than half of its total area covered in forest, Slovenia really is one of the 'greenest' countries in the world.

When to Go
Ljubljana

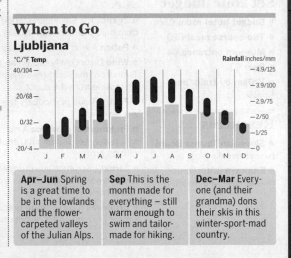

Apr–Jun Spring is a great time to be in the lowlands and the flower-carpeted valleys of the Julian Alps.

Sep This is the month made for everything – still warm enough to swim and tailor-made for hiking.

Dec–Mar Everyone (and their grandma) dons their skis in this winter-sport-mad country.

AT A GLANCE

» **Currency** Euro (€)

» **Language** Slovene

» **Money** ATMs are everywhere; banks open weekdays and Saturday morning

» **Visas** Not required for citizens of the EU, Australia, USA, Canada or New Zealand

Fast Facts

» **Area** 20,273 sq km

» **Capital** Ljubljana

» **Country code** ☑386

» **Emergency** Ambulance & fire ☑112, police ☑113

Exchange Rates

Australia	A$1	€0.82
Canada	C$1	€0.77
Japan	¥100	€0.83
New Zealand	NZ$1	€0.65
UK	UK£1	€1.18
USA	US$1	€0.78

Set Your Budget

» **Budget hotel room** €50

» **Two-course meal** €20

» **Museum entrance** €4

» **Beer** €3

» **100km by train/bus** €6/10

Resources

» **Slovenian Tourist Board** (www.slovenia.info)

» **E-uprava** (http://e-up-rava.gov.si/e-unprava/en)

Connections

Border formalities with Slovenia's three European Union neighbours – Italy, Austria and Hungary – are nonexistent and all are accessible by train and bus. Venice can also be reached by boat from Piran. Expect a somewhat closer inspection of your documents when travelling to/from non-EU Croatia.

ITINERARIES

One Week

Spend a couple of days in Ljubljana, then head north to unwind in Bohinj or romantic Bled beside idyllic mountain lakes. Depending on the season, take a bus or drive over the hair-raising Vršič Pass into the valley of the vivid blue Soča River and take part in some adventure sports in Bovec or Kobarid before returning to Ljubljana.

Two Weeks

Another week will allow you to see just about everything: all of the above as well as the Karst caves at Škocjan and Postojna and the Venetian ports of Koper and Piran on the Adriatic. The country is small, so even the far eastern region, particularly the historically rich and picturesque city of Ptuj, is just a few hours away by car or train.

Essential Food & Drink

» **Pršut** Air-dried, thinly sliced ham from the Karst region not unlike Italian prosciutto.

» **Žlikrofi** Ravioli-like parcels filled with cheese, bacon and chives.

» **Žganci** The Slovenian stodge of choice – groats made from barley or corn but usually *ajda* (buckwheat).

» **Potica** A kind of nut roll eaten at teatime or as a dessert.

» **Wine** Distinctively Slovenian tipples include peppery red Teran from the Karst region and Malvazija, a straw-colour white wine from the coast.

» **Postrv** Trout, particularly the variety from the Soča River, is a real treat.

» **Prekmurska gibanica** A rich concoction of pastry filled with poppy seeds, walnuts, apples, and cheese and topped with cream.

» **Štruklji** Scrumptious dumplings made with curd cheese and served either savoury as a main course or sweet as a dessert.

» **Brinjevec** A very strong brandy made from fermented juniper berries (and a decidedly acquired taste).

LJUBLJANA

🎵 01 / POP 280,607

Slovenia's capital and largest city also happens to be one of Europe's greenest and most livable capitals. Car traffic is restricted in the centre, leaving the leafy banks of the emerald-green Ljubljanica River, which flows through the city's heart, free for pedestrians and cyclists. In summer, cafes set up terrace seating along the river, lending the feel of a perpetual street party. Slovenia's master of early-Modern, minimalist design,

Jože Plečnik, graced Ljubljana with beautiful alabaster bridges and baubles, pylons and pyramids that are both elegant and playful. The museums, hotels and restaurants are among the best in the country.

History

Legacies of the Roman city of Emona – remnants of walls, dwellings, early churches, even a gilded statuette – can be seen everywhere. Ljubljana took its present form in the mid-12th century as Laibach under the Habsburgs, but it gained regional prominence in 1809,

SLOVENIA LJUBLJANA

Slovenia Highlights

❶ Enjoy a flight up on the funicular to **Ljubljana Castle** (p876).

❷ Consider the genius of architect Jože Plečnik at Ljubljana's **National & University Library** (p877).

❸ Gaze at the natural perfection that is **Lake Bled** (p888).

❹ Gawk in awe at the 100m high walls of the incredible **Škocjan Caves** (p898).

❺ Climb to the top of the country's tallest mountain, **Mt Triglav** (p893).

❻ Get lost wandering the Venice-inspired, narrow alleyways of **Piran** (p900).

LJUBLJANA IN TWO DAYS

Take the funicular to **Ljubljana Castle**, then come down and explore the **Central Market** area. After a seafood lunch at **Ribca**, walk around the **Old Town** then cross the Ljubljanica River and walk north along Vegova ulica to **Kongresni Trg** and **Prešernov Trg**. Plan your evening over a fortifying libation at one of the many cafes along the Ljubljanica: low key at **Jazz Club Gajo** or alternative at **Metelkova Mesto**.

On your second day check out the city's museums and galleries, and then stroll or cycle on a **Ljubljana Bike**, stopping for an oh-so-local horse burger at **Hot Horse** along the way. In the evening, take in a performance at the **Križanke** or **Cankarjev Dom** and then visit one of the clubs you missed last night.

when it became the capital of Napoleon's short-lived 'Illyrian Provinces'. Some fine art nouveau buildings filled up the holes left by a devastating earthquake in 1895, and architect Jože Plečnik continued the remake of the city up until WWII. In recent years the city's dynamic mayor, Zoran Janković, has doubled the number of pedestrian streets, extended a great swathe of the river embankment and spanned the Ljubljanica River with two new footbridges.

◉ Sights

The easiest way to see Ljubljana is on foot. The oldest part of town, with the most important historical buildings and sights (including Ljubljana Castle) lies on the right (east) bank of the Ljubljanica River. Center, which has the lion's share of the city's museums and galleries, is on the left (west) side of the river.

CASTLE AREA

Begin an exploration of the city by making the trek up to **Castle Hill** (Grajska Planota) to poke around grand Ljubljana Castle. The castle area offers a couple of worthwhile exhibitions, and the castle watchtower affords amazing views out over the city. The prospect of lunch at one of the city's best restaurants, Gostilna na Gradu (p882), provides an added inducement.

There are several ways to access the castle, with the easiest (and for kids, the most

fun) being a 70m-long **funicular** (vzpenjača; ☑reservations 306 42 00; www.ljubljanskigrad.si; Krekov trg 3-7; return adult/child €4/3; ☺9am-11pm Apr-Sep, 10am-9pm Oct-Mar) that leaves from Old Town not far from the market (p883) on Vodnikov trg. If you'd like to get some exercise, you can hike the hill in about 20 minutes. There are three main walking routes: Študentovska ulica, which runs south from Ciril Metodov trg; steep Reber ulica from Stari trg; and Ulica na Grad from Gornji trg.

TOP CHOICE **Ljubljana Castle** ⬛ CASTLE
(Ljubljanski Grad; ☑306 42 93; www.ljubljanskigrad.si; Grajska Planota 1; adult/child incl funicular and castle attractions €8/5, castle attractions only €6/3; with guided tour €10/8; ☺9am-11pm May-Sep, 10am-9pm Oct-Apr) There's been a human settlement here since at least Celtic times, but the oldest structures these days date from around the 16th-century, following an earthquake in 1511. It's free to ramble around the castle grounds, but you'll have to pay to enter the **Watchtower**, the **Chapel of St George** (Kapela Sv Jurija) and to see the worthwhile **Exhibition on Slovenian History**.

There are several admission options available; some include the price of the funicular ride, while others include a **castle tour**. Consult the castle website for details. The **Ljubljana Castle Information Centre** (☺9am-9pm Apr-Sep, 9am-6pm Oct-Mar) can advise on tours and events that might be on during your visit.

PREŠERNOV TRG & OLD TOWN
Prešernov Trg ⬛ SQUARE, PLAZA
This central and beautiful square forms the link between Center and the Old Town. Taking pride of place is the **Prešeren monument** (1905), designed by Maks Fabiani and Ivan Zajc and erected in honour of Slovenia's greatest poet, France Prešeren (1800–49). On the plinth are motifs from his poems.

Just south of the monument is the **Triple Bridge** (Tromostovje), called the Špital (Hospital) Bridge when it was built as a single span in 1842, which leads to the Old Town. The prolific architect Jože Plečnik added the two sides in 1931.

To the east of the monument at No 5 is the Italianate Central Pharmacy (Centralna Lekarna), an erstwhile cafe frequented by intellectuals in the 19th century. To the north, on the corner of Trubarjeva cesta and Miklošičeva cesta, is the delightful Secessionist **Palača Urbanc** (Urbanc Palace) building from 1903.

Mestni Trg
SQUARE

The first of the Old Town's three 'squares' (the other two – Stari trg and Gornji trg – are more like narrow cobbled streets), Mestni trg (Town Square) is dominated by the town hall, in front of which stands the **Robba Fountain** (the original is now in the National Gallery).

Town Hall
TOWN HALL

(Mestna Hiša; ☑306 30 00; Mestni trg; ⊘7.30am-4pm Mon-Fri) The seat of the city government and sometimes referred to as the *Magistrat* or *Rotovž*. It was erected in the late 15th century and rebuilt in 1718. The Gothic courtyard inside, arcaded on three levels, is where theatrical performances once took place and contains some lovely sgraffiti.

If you look above the south portal leading to a second courtyard you'll see a relief map of Ljubljana as it appeared in the second half of the 17th century.

Stari Trg
SQUARE

The 'Old Square' is the true heart of the Old Town. It is lined with 19th-century wooden shopfronts, quiet courtyards and cobblestone passageways. From behind the medieval houses on the eastern side, paths once led to Castle Hill, which was a source of water. The buildings fronting the river had large passageways built to allow drainage in case of flooding.

Gornji Trg
SQUARE

Upper Square is the eastern extension of Stari trg. The five **medieval houses** at Nos 7 to 15 have narrow side passages (some with doors) where rubbish was once deposited so that it could be washed down into the river.

FREE Botanical Garden
PUBLIC GARDEN

(Botanični Vrt; ☑427 12 80; www.botanicni-vrt.si; Ižanska cesta 15; ⊘7am-8pm Jul & Aug, 7am-7pm Apr-Jun, Sep & Oct, 7am-5pm Nov-Mar) About 800m southeast of the Old Town along Karlovška cesta and over the Ljubljanica River, this 2.5-hectare botanical garden was founded in 1810 as a sanctuary of native flora. It contains 4500 species of plants and trees, about a third of which are indigenous,

CENTER

This large district on the left bank of the Ljubljanica is the nerve centre of modern Ljubljana. It is filled with shops, commercial offices, government departments and embassies. The region is divided into several distinct neighbourhoods centred on town squares.

Trg Francoske Revolucije
SQUARE

'French Revolution Sq' was for centuries the headquarters of the Teutonic Knights of the Cross (Križniki). They built a commandery here in the early 13th century, which was transformed into the **Križanke** (☑241 60 00; Trg Francoske Revolucije 1-2) monastery complex in the early 18th century. Today it serves as the headquarters of the Ljubljana Festival (p881).

TOP CHOICE National & University Library
HISTORIC BUILDING

(☑200 11 09; Turjaška ulica 1; ⊘9am-6pm Mon-Fri, 9am-2pm Sat) This library is Plečnik's masterpiece, completed in 1941. To appreciate this great man's philosophy, enter through the main door (note the horse-head doorknobs) on Turjaška ulica – you'll find yourself in near darkness, entombed in black marble. As you ascend the steps, you'll emerge into a colonnade suffused with light – the light of knowledge, according to the architect's plans.

The **Main Reading Room** (Velika Čitalnica), now open to nonstudents only by group tour in summer, has huge glass walls and some stunning lamps, also designed by Plečnik.

City Museum
MUSEUM

(Mestni Muzej; ☑241 25 00; www.mestnimuzej.si; Gosposka ulica 15; adult/child €4/2.50; ⊘10am-6pm Tue & Wed, Fri-Sun, 10am-9pm Thu) The excellent city museum focuses on Ljubljana's history, culture and politics via imaginative multimedia and interactive displays. The reconstructed Roman street that linked the eastern gates of Emona to the Ljubljanica and the collection of well-preserved classical finds in the basement are worth a visit in themselves.

The permanent 'Faces of Ljubljana' exhibit of celebrated and lesser-known *žabarji* ('froggers', as natives of the capital are known) is memorable. They host some very good special exhibitions too.

National Museum of Slovenia
MUSEUM

(Narodni Muzej Slovenije; ☑241 44 00; www.nms.si; Prešernova cesta 20; adult/child €3/2.50, 1st Sun of month free; ⊘10am-6pm Fri-Wed, 10am-8pm Thu) Highlights include a highly embossed *Vače situla*, a Celtic pail from the late 6th century BC unearthed in a town east of Ljubljana, and a Stone Age bone flute discovered near Cerkno in western Slovenia in 1995. There are also examples of Roman glass and jewellery found in 6th-century Slavic graves, along with many other historical finds.

Ljubljana

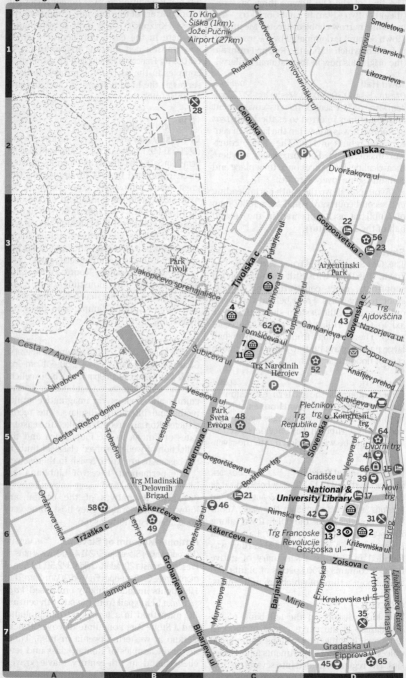

To Kino
Šiška (1km);
Jože Pučnik
Airport (27km)

Smoletova

Parmova

Livarska

Likozarjeva

Ruska ul

Medvedova c

Celovška c

Pivovarniška ul

28

Tivolska c

Dvoržakova ul

Gosposvetska c

22

56

23

Argentinski
Park

Park
Tivoli

Jakopičevo sprehajališče

Tivolska c

6

Puharjeva ul

Prešernova c

Slovenska c

Trg
Ajdovščina

Nazorjeva ul

4

Cankarjeva c

43

Županičeva ul

Čopova ul

62

Tomšičeva ul

Knafljev prehod

47

Šubičeva ul

7

52

11

Šubičeva ul

Trg Narodnih
Herojev

Cesta 27 Aprila

Škrabčeva

Veselova ul

Plečnikov
trg

Šubičeva ul

Cesta v Rožno dolino

Trobačna

Lestikova ul

Park
Sveta
Evropa

48

Trg
Republike

Kongresni
trg

64

Prešernova c

Gregorčičeva ul

19

Slovenska c

Dvorni trg

41

Vegova ul

15

Gradišče ul

39

Novi
trg

Oražnova ulica

Trg Mladinskih
Delovnih
Brigad

21

66

17

National &
University Library

Rimska c

42

31

58

Aškerčev c

46

Snežniška ul

13

3

2

Trg Francoske
Revolucije

Gosposka ul

Križevniška ul

49

Tržaška c

Aškerčeva c

Lepi pot

Zoisova c

Jamova c

Groharjeva c

Murnikova ul

Barjanska c

Mirje

Emonska c

Krakovska ul

Vrtna ul

Krakovski nasip

Ljubljanica River

35

Gradaška ul

Bibarjeva ul

Eipprova ul

45

65

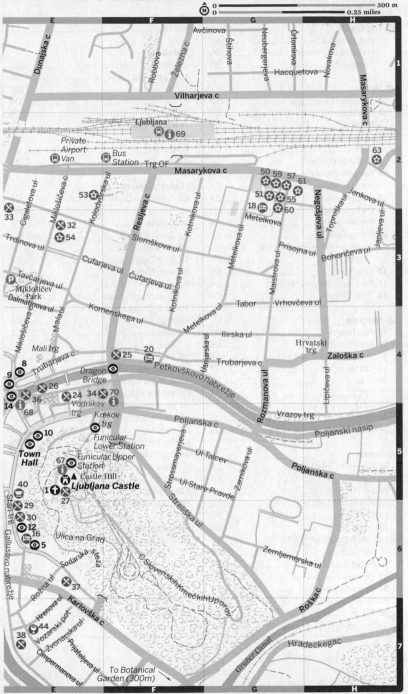

Ljubljana

Check out the ceiling fresco in the foyer, which features an allegorical Carniola surrounded by important Slovenes from the past and the statues of the Muses and Fates relaxing on the stairway banisters.

Slovenian Museum of Natural History
MUSEUM

(Prirodoslovni Muzej Slovenije; ☏241 09 40; www2.pms-lj.si; Prešernova cesta 20; adult/student €3/2.50, incl national museum €5/4; ☉10am-6pm Fri-Wed, 10am-8pm Thu; P) Housed in the same impressive building as the National Museum, the Natural History Museum contains the usual reassembled mammoth and whale skeletons, stuffed birds, reptiles and mammals. However, the mineral collections amassed by the philanthropic Baron Žiga Zois in the early 19th century and the display on Slovenia's unique salamander *Proteus anguinus* are worth a visit.

National Gallery
MUSEUM

(☏241 54 18; www.ng-slo.si; Prešernova cesta 24; adult/child €7/5, 1st Sun of month free; ☉10am-6pm Tue-Sun) Slovenia's foremost assembly of fine art is housed over two floors both in an old building dating to 1896 and an impressive modern wing.

Ljubljana Museum of Modern Art
MUSEUM

(☏241 68 00; www.mg-lj.si; Tomšičeva ulica 14; adult/student €5/2.50; ☉10am-6pm Tue-Sun) This museum houses the very best in Slovenian modern art. Keep an eye out for works by painters Tone Kralj *(Peasant Wedding)*, the expressionist France Mihelič *(The Quintet)* and the surrealist Štefan Planinc *(Primeval World series)* as well as sculptors such as Jakob Savinšek *(Protest)*.

The museum also owns works by the influential 1980s and 1990s multimedia group Neue Slowenische Kunst (NSK; *Suitcase for Spiritual Use: Baptism under Triglav*) and the artists' cooperative Irwin *(Kapital)*.

☞ Tours

Two-hour **walking tours** (adult/child €10/5; ☉10am, 2pm & 5pm Apr-Oct), combined with a ride on the funicular or the tourist train up to the castle or a cruise on the Ljubljanica, are organised by the TIC. They depart daily from the town hall on Mestni trg.

✻ Festivals & Events

Druga Godba
WORLD MUSIC

(http://festival.drugagodba.si; ☉May-Jun) This festival of alternative and world music, takes place in the Križanke from late May to early June.

Ljubljana Festival
MUSIC & THEATRE

(www.ljubljanafestival.si; ☉Jul & Aug) The number-one event on Ljubljana's social calendar is the Ljubljana Festival, a celebration from early July to late August of music, opera, theatre and dance held at venues throughout the city, but principally in the open-air theatre at the Križanke.

International Ljubljana Marathon
MARATHON

(www.ljubljanskimaraton.si; ☉Oct) Takes off on the last Saturday in October.

🛏 Sleeping

The TIC has comprehensive details of private rooms (from single/double €30/50) and apartments (from double/quad €55/80) though only a handful are central.

TOP CHOICE Antiq Palace Hotel & Spa
BOUTIQUE HOTEL €€€

(☏051 364 124; www.antiqpalace.com; Gosposka ulica 10 & Vegova ul 5a; s/d €180/210; P☜❄@☎) Easily the city's most luxurious sleeping option, the Antiq Palace occupies a 16th-century townhouse, about a block from the river. Accommodation is in 13 individually designed suites, each with several rooms and some stretching to 250 sq m in size. The list of amenities is a mile long. The target market is upscale honeymooners and businessmen on expenses.

Cubo
BOUTIQUE HOTEL €€€

(☏425 60 00; www.hotelcubo.com; Slovenska cesta 15; s/d €120/140) This sleek boutique hotel in the centre of town boasts high-end, minimalist design that could have stepped out of the pages of *Wallpaper* magazine. The owners have placed great emphasis on using the best construction materials and high-quality bedding to ensure a good night's sleep. The in-house restaurant is very good.

Celica Hostel
HOSTEL €€

(☏230 97 00; www.hostelcelica.com; Metelkova ulica 8; dm €19-25, s/d/tr cell €53/60/70; P@☎) This stylishly revamped former prison (1882) in Metelkova has 20 'cells', designed by different artists and architects and complete with original bars. There are nine rooms and apartments with three to seven beds and a packed, popular 12-bed dorm. The ground floor is home to a cafe and restaurant (set lunch €5 to €7, open 7.30am to midnight) and the hostel boasts its own gallery where everyone can show their work.

Slamič B&B PENSION €€

(☎433 82 33; www.slamic.si; Kersnikova ulica 1; s €65-75, d €95-100, ste from €135; P❋@☎) It's slightly away from the action but Slamič, a B&B above a famous cafe and teahouse, offers 11 bright rooms with antique(ish) furnishings and parquet floors. Choice rooms include the ones looking onto a back garden and the one just off an enormous terrace used by the cafe.

Penzion Pod Lipo PENSION €€

(☎031 809 893; www.penzion-podlipo.com; Borštnikov trg 3; d/tr/q/ste €65/75/100/125; @) Sitting atop one of Ljubljana's oldest *gostilna* (inn-like restaurant) and a 400-year-old linden tree, this 10-room inn offers plain rooms, but excellent value in a part of the city that is filling up with bars and restaurants. We love the communal kitchen, the original hardwood floors and the east-facing terrace with deck chairs that catch the morning sun.

H2O HOSTEL €

(☎041 662 266; www.h2ohostel.com; Petkovškovo nabrežje 47; dm €17-22, d €36-52, q €68-88; @☎) One of our favourite hostels in Ljubljana, this six-room place wraps around a tiny courtyard bordering the Ljubljanica River and one room has views of the castle. Private doubles are available and guests have access to a common kitchen.

Antiq Hotel BOUTIQUE HOTEL €€€

(☎421 35 60; www.antiqhotel.si; Gornji trg 3; s €75-120, d €85-150; ❋@☎) This attractive boutique has been cobbled together from several townhouses in the Old Town. There are 16 spacious rooms and a multitiered back garden. The decor is kitsch with a smirk and there are fabulous touches everywhere. Among our favourite rooms are enormous No 8, with views of the Hercules Fountain, and No 13, with glimpses of Ljubljana Castle.

Zeppelin Hostel HOSTEL €

(☎059 191 427; www.zeppelinhostel.com; 2 fl, Slovenska cesta 47; dm €18-24, d €49-60; @☎) Located in the historic Evropa building on the corner of Gosposvetska cesta, this hostel offers clean and bright dorm rooms (four to eight beds) and doubles and is run by a young team of international travellers who keep their guests informed on parties and happenings around town.

Alibi Hostel HOSTEL €

(☎251 12 44; www.alibi.si; Cankarjevo nabrežje 27; dm €15-18, d €40-50; ❋@) This very well-situated 106-bed hostel on the Ljubljanica has brightly painted, airy dorms with four to eight wooden bunks and a dozen doubles. There's a private suite at the top for six people.

✕ Eating

TOP CHOICE **Gostilna na Gradu** SLOVENIAN €

(☎031 523 760; www.nagradu.si; Grajska planota 1; mains €8-14; ⊙10am-midnight Mon-Sat, noon-6pm Sun) Be sure to plan a meal here at this marvelous traditional Slovenian restaurant during your visit to the castle. The chefs pride themselves on using only Slovenian-sourced breads, cheeses and meats, and age-old recipes to prepare a meal to remember. The castle setting is ideal. Book a table in advance to avoid disappointment.

Julija MEDITERRANEAN €€

(☎425 64 63; http://julijarestaurant.com; Stari trg 9; €10.90-18.90; ⊙noon-10pm) This is arguably the best of a trio of restaurants standing side by side on touristy Stari trg. We love the three-course set lunches served on the sidewalk terrace for €9. The cuisine here revolves around risottos and pastas, though the chicken breast special served in a spicy peanut sauce was one of the best meals on our trip.

Ribca SEAFOOD €

(☎425 15 44; www.ribca.si; Adamič-Lundrovo nabrežje 1; dishes €5-8; ⊙8am-4pm Mon-Fri, to 2pm Sat) One of the culinary joys of a visit to Ljubljana is the chance to sample inexpensive and well-prepared fish dishes. This basement seafood bar below the Plečnik Colonnade in Pogačarjev trg is one of the best for tasty fried squid, sardines and herrings. The setting is informal, though the cuisine is top notch. Set lunch on weekdays is €7.50.

Špajza SLOVENIAN €€

(☎425 30 94; www.spajza-restaurant.si; Gornji trg 28; mains €15-25; ⊙noon-11pm) This popular Old Town restaurant is the perfect spot for a splurge or romantic meal for two. The interior is decorated with rough-hewn tables and chairs, wooden floors, frescoed ceilings and nostalgic bits and pieces. The terrace in summer is a delight. The cooking is traditional Slovenian, with an emphasis on less-common mains like rabbit and veal.

Pri Škofu
SLOVENIAN €€

(📞426 45 08; Rečna ulica 8; mains €8-22; ⏱7am-11pm; 🛜) This wonderful little place in tranquil Krakovo, south of the centre, serves some of the best prepared local dishes and salads in Ljubljana, with an ever-changing menu. Weekday set lunches are good value at €8.

Lunch Café Marley & Me
INTERNATIONAL €€

(📞040 564 188; www.lunchcafe.si; Stari trg 9; mains from €7-20; ⏱11am-11pm; 🛜) The name couldn't be more misleading. It's more than a lunch cafe...and the 'Marley' bit? We just don't get it. Still, it's a very popular spot for lunch or dinner over salads, pastas and a variety of meats and seafood. There's sidewalk dining in nice weather.

Trta
ITALIAN €

(📞426 50 66; www.trta.si; Grudnovo nabrežje 21; pizza €8-10; ⏱11am-10pm Mon-Fri, noon-10.30pm Sat; 🛜) This award-winning pizzeria, with large pies cooked in a wood-fired oven, is slightly south of the centre, across the river opposite Trnovo.

Namasté
INDIAN €€

(📞425 01 59; www.restavracija-namaste.si; Breg 8; mains €10-20; ⏱11am-midnight Mon-Sat, to 10pm Sun; 🍴) Should you fancy a bit of Indian, head for this place on the left bank of the Ljubljanica. You won't get high-street-quality curry but the thalis and tandoori dishes are very good. The choice of vegetarian dishes is better than average and a set lunch costs between €6.50 €8.50. Eat along the river in nice weather.

Falafel
MIDDLE EASTERN €

(📞041 640 166; Trubarjeva cesta 40; sandwiches €4-6; ⏱11am-midnight Mon-Fri, noon-midnight Sat, 1-10pm Sun) Authentic Middle Eastern food, like falafel and hummus, served up to go or eat in at a few tables and chairs scattered about. Perfect choice for a quick meal on the run or the late-night munchies.

Hot Horse
BURGERS €

(📞521 14 27; www.hot-horse.si; Park Tivoli, Celovška cesta 25; snacks & burgers €3-6; ⏱9am-6pm Tue-Sun, 10am-6pm Mon) This little place in the city's biggest park supplies *Ljubljančani* (local people) with their favourite treat: horse burgers (€4). It's just down the hill from the Museum of Contemporary History.

Self-Catering
Self-caterers and those on a tight budget will want to head directly to Ljubljana's vast open-air market (Vodnikov trg; ⏱6am-6pm Mon-Fri, 6am-6pm Sat summer, 6am-6pm Mon-Sat winter) on Vodnikov trg, just across the Triple Bridge to the southeast of Prešernov trg. Here you'll find stalls selling everything from wild mushrooms and forest berries to honey and homemade cheeses. The **covered market** (Pogačarjev trg 1; ⏱7am-2pm Mon-Wed & Sat, 7am-4pm Thu & Fri) nearby sells meats and cheeses, and there's a **fish market** (Adamič-Lundrovo nabrežje 1; ⏱7am-4pm Mon-Fri, 7am-2pm Sat) too. You'll also find open-air **fish stands** selling plates of fried calamari for as low as €6. Another budget option is *burek*, pastry stuffed with cheese, meat or even apple. Reputedly the best places in town are **Olimpije** (Pražakova ulica 2; burek €2; ⏱24hr) southwest of the train and bus stations, and **Nobel Burek** (📞232 33 92; Miklošičeva cesta 30; burek €2, pizza slices €1.40; ⏱24hr).

🍷 Drinking

Few cities of this size have central Ljubljana's concentration of inviting cafes and bars, the vast majority with outdoor seating in the warmer months.

Bars & Pubs

TOP CHOICE **Žmavc**
BAR

(📞251 03 24; Rimska cesta 21; ⏱7.30am-1am Mon-Fri, from 10am Sat, from 6pm Sun; 🛜) A super-popular student hang-out west of Slovenska cesta, with *manga* comic-strip scenes and figures running halfway up the walls. There's a great garden terrace for summer-evening drinking, but try to arrive early to snag a table. Also excellent for morning coffee.

BiKoFe
BAR

(📞425 93 93; Židovska steza 2; ⏱7am-1am Mon-Fri, 10am-1pm Sat & Sun; 🛜) A favourite with the hipster crowd, this cupboard of a bar has mosaic tables, studenty art on the walls, soul and jazz on the stereo, and a giant water pipe on the menu for that long, lingering smoke outside. The shady outdoor patio is a great place to enjoy a recent purchase from the **Behemot** (📞251 13 92; www.behemot.si; Židovska steza 3; ⏱10am-8pm Mon-Fri, 10am-3pm Sat) bookshop across the street.

Dvorni Bar
WINE BAR

(📞251 12 57; www.dvornibar.net; Dvorni trg 2; ⏱8am-1am Mon-Sat, 9am-midnight Sun; 🛜) This wine bar is an excellent place to taste Slovenian vintages; it stocks more than 100 varieties and has wine tastings every month (usually the second Wednesday).

SLOVENIA LJUBLJANA

Šank Pub   PUB

(Eipprova ulica 19; ⊙7am-1am; 🛜) Down in studenty Trnovo, this raggedy little place with
brick ceiling and wooden floor is a relaxed
alternative to the nearby Sax. The Šank is
one of a number of inviting bars and cafes
along this stretch of Eipprova ulica.

Cafes & Teahouses

TOP CHOICE Nebotičnik   CAFE

(☑040 601 787; www.neboticnik.si; 12th fl,
Štefanova ulica 1; ⊙9am-1am Sun-Wed, 9am-3am
Thu-Sat; 🛜) After a decade-long hibernation this elegant cafe with its breathtaking
terrace atop Ljubljana's famed art deco
Skyscraper (1933) has reopened, and the
360-degree views are spectacular.

Le Petit Café   CAFE

(☑251 25 75; www.lepetit.si; Trg Francoske Revolucije 4; ⊙7.30am-1am; 🛜) Just opposite the
Križanke, this pleasant, boho place offers
great coffee and a wide range of breakfast
goodies, lunches and light meals, plus a
good restaurant on the 1st floor.

Čajna Hiša   TEAHOUSE

(☑421 24 40; Stari trg 3; ⊙9am-10.30pm Mon-Fri,
9am-3pm & 6-10pm Sat; 🛜) This elegant and
centrally located teahouse takes its teas very
seriously. They also serve light meals and
there's a tea shop next door.

Open Cafe   GAY & LESBIAN

(☑041 391 371; www.open.si; Hrenova ulica 19;
⊙4pm-midnight; 🛜) This very stylish gay-
owned-and-run cafe south of the Old Town
has become the meeting point for Ljubljana's
burgeoning queer culture. In June 2009 it
was attacked by fascist homophobes who attempted to torch the place and some patrons
fought back.

Zvezda   CAFE

(☑421 90 90; Wolfova ulica 14; ⊙7am-11pm Mon-
Sat, 10am-8pm Sun; 🛜) The 'Star' has all the
usual varieties of coffee and tea but is celebrated for its shop-made cakes, especially
skutina pečena (€3), an eggy cheesecake.

☆ Entertainment

Ljubljana in Your Pocket (www.inyourpocket.
com), which comes out every two months, is
a good English source for what's on in the
capital. Buy tickets for shows and events
at the venue box office, online through
Eventim (☑430 24 05; www.eventim.si), or
at Ljubljana Tourist Information Centre
(p886). Expect to pay around €10 to €20 for

tickets to live acts, and less for club entry
and DJ nights.

Nightclubs

Cirkus   CLUB

(Kinoklub Vič; ☑051 631 631; www.cirkusklub.si; Trg
Mladinskih Delovnih Brigad 7; €5; ⊙8pm-5am Tue-
Sat) This popular dance club, with DJs at the
weekends, occupies the former Kinoklub Vič.

Klub K4   CLUB

(☑040 212 292; www.klubk4.org; Kersnikova ulica
4; ⊙10pm-2am Tue, 11pm-4am Wed & Thu, 11pm-
6am Fri & Sat, 10pm-4am Sun) This evergreen
venue in the basement of the Student Organisation of Ljubljana University (ŠOU)
headquarters features rave-electronic music
Friday and Saturday, with other styles of
music on weeknights, and a popular gay and
lesbian night on Sunday.

KMŠ   CLUB

(☑425 74 80; www.klubkms.si; Tržaška cesta 2;
⊙8am-10pm Mon-Fri, 9pm-5am Sat) Located in
the deep recesses of a former tobacco factory complex, the Maribor Student Club stays
comatose till Saturday when it turns into a
raucous place with music and dancers all
over the shop.

Live Music

Kino Šiška   INDIE & ROCK

(☑box office 030 310 110; www.kinosiska.si; Trg Pre-
komorskih brigad 3; ⊙5-8pm Mon-Fri, 10am-1pm
Sat) This renovated old movie theatre has
been reopened as an urban cultural centre,
hosting mainly indie, rock and alternative
bands from around Slovenia and the rest of
Europe.

Orto Bar   ROCK

(☑232 16 74; www.orto-bar.com; Graboličeva
ulica 1; ⊙9pm-4am Tue & Wed, to 5am Thu-Sat) A
popular bar-club for late-night drinking and
dancing with occasional live music, Orto is
just five minutes' walk from Metelkova. Note
the program takes a two-month hiatus in
summer during July and August.

Jazz Club Gajo   JAZZ

(☑425 32 06; www.jazzclubgajo.com; Beethovnova
ulica 8; ⊙7pm-2am Mon-Sat) Now in its 18th
year, Gajo is the city's premier venue for
live jazz and attracts both local and international talent. Jam sessions are at 8.30pm
Monday.

Sax Pub   ROCK

(☑283 90 09; Eipprova ulica 7; ⊙noon-1am Mon,
10am-1am Tue-Sat, 4-10pm Sun) Two decades in

SOMETHING COMPLETELY DIFFERENT: METELKOVO MESTO

For a scruffy antidote to trendy clubs in Ljubljana, try **Metelkova Mesto** (Metelkova Town; www.metelkova.org; Masarykova cesta 24), an ex-army garrison taken over by squatters in the 1990s and converted into a free-living commune – a miniature version of Copenhagen's Christiania. In this two-courtyard block, a dozen idiosyncratic venues hide behind brightly tagged doorways, coming to life generally after midnight daily in summer and on Friday and Saturday the rest of the year. While it's certainly not for the genteel and the quality of the acts and performances varies with the night, there's usually a little of something for everyone on hand.

Entering the main 'city gate' from Masarykova cesta, the building to the right houses **Gala Hala** (☑431 70 63; www.galahala.com), with live bands and club nights, and **Klub Channel Zero** (www.ch0.org), with punk and hardcore. Above it on the 1st floor is **Galerija Mizzart** (www.mizzart.net) with a great exhibition space (the name is no comment on the quality of the creations – promise!).

Easy to miss in the first building to the left is the **Kulturni Center Q** (Q Cultural Centre) including **Tiffany** (www.kulturnicenterq.org/tiffany/klub) for gay men and **Klub Monokel** (www.klubmonokel.com) for lesbians. Due south is the ever-popular **Jalla Jalla Club** (www.metelkovamesto.org), a congenial pub with concerts. Beyond the first courtyard to the southwest, **Klub Gromka** (www.klubgromka.org) has folk concerts, theatre and lectures. Next door is **Menza pri Koritu** (☑434 03 45; www.menzaprikoritu.org), under the creepy ET-like figures, with performance and concerts. If you're staying at the Hostel Celica (p881), all of the action is just around the corner.

Trnovo and decorated with colourful murals and graffiti inside and out, the tiny Sax has live jazz at 9pm or 9.30pm on Thursday from late August to December and February to June. Canned stuff rules at other times.

Performing Arts

Cankarjev Dom OPERA, DANCE
(☑241 71 00, box office 241 72 99; www.cd-cc.si; Prešernova cesta 10; ☺box office 11am-1pm & 3-8pm Mon-Fri, 11am-1pm Sat, 1hr before performance) Ljubljana's premier cultural and conference centre has two large auditoriums (the Gallus Hall is said to have perfect acoustics) and a dozen smaller performance spaces offering a remarkable smorgasbord of performance arts. Buy tickets at the box office.

Opera & Ballet Ljubljana OPERA, DANCE
(☑box office 241 59 59; www.opera.si; Župančičeva ulica 1; ☺box office 10am-5pm Mon-Fri, 1hr before performance) Home to the Slovenian National Opera and Ballet companies, this historic neo-Renaissance theatre was fully renovated in 2011 and restored to its former luster.

Philharmonic Hall CLASSICAL
(Slovenska Filharmonija; ☑241 08 00; www.filharmonija.si; Kongresni trg 10; ☺7am-10pm) Home to the Slovenian Philharmonic Orchestra, this smaller but more atmospheric venue also stages concerts and hosts performances of the Slovenian Chamber Choir (Slovenski Komorni Zbor), which was founded in 1991.

Križanke CLASSICAL, THEATRE
(☑241 60 00, box office 241 60 26; www.ljubljanafestival.si; Trg Francoske Revolucije 1-2; ☺box office 10am-8pm Mon-Fri, 10am-1pm Sat Apr-Sep) The open-air theatre at this sprawling 18th-century monastery hosts the events of the Ljubljana Summer Festival. The smaller Knights Hall (Viteška Dvorana) is the venue for chamber concerts.

Cinema

Kinoteka CINEMA
(☑547 15 80; www.kinoteka.si; Miklošičeva cesta 28) Shows archival art and classic films in their original language (not always English).

Kino Dvor CINEMA
(Court Cinema; ☑239 22 13; www.kinodvor.org; Kolodvorska ulica 13) The sister cinema to Kinoteka nearby screens more contemporary films from around the world.

ℹ Information

Internet Access

Many cafes and restaurants offer free wi-fi for customers. Most hostels, and some hotels, maintain a public computer for guests to surf the internet. The Slovenia Tourist Information Centre has computers on-hand to check email (per 30 minutes €1).

Cyber Cafe Xplorer (☑430 19 91; Petkovškovo nabrežje 23; per 30min/1hr €2.50/4; ⏰10am-10pm Mon-Fri, 2-10pm Sat & Sun; 📶) Ljubljana's best internet cafe; also has wi-fi and offers discount international calling.

Medical Services
Central Pharmacy (Centralna Lekarna; ☑230 61 00; Prešernov trg 5; ⏰8am-7.30pm Mon-Fri, 8am-3pm Sat)

Health Centre Ljubljana (Zdravstveni Dom Ljubljana; ☑472 37 00; www.zd-lj.si; Metelkova ulica 9; ⏰7.30am-7pm) For non-emergencies.

University Medical Centre Ljubljana (Univerzitetni Klinični Center Ljubljana; ☑522 50 50, emergencies 522 84 08; www4.kclj.si; Zaloška cesta 2; ⏰24hr) University medical clinic with 24h accident and emergency service.

Money
There are ATMs at every turn, including a row of them outside the main Ljubljana Tourist Information Centre (TIC) office. At the train station you'll find a **bureau de change** (train station; ⏰7am-8pm) changing cash for no commission but not travellers cheques.

Abanka (☑300 15 00; www.abanka.si; Slovenska cesta 50; ⏰9am-1pm & 3pm-5pm Mon-Fri)

Nova Ljubljanska Banka (☑476 39 00; www.nlb.si; Trg Republike 2; ⏰8am-6pm Mon-Fri)

Post
Main Post Office (Slovenska cesta 32; ⏰8am-7pm Mon-Fri, to 1pm Sat) Holds poste restante for 30 days and changes money.

Tourist Information
Ljubljana Tourist Information Centre (TIC; ☑306 12 15; www.visitljubljana.si; Adamič-Lundrovo nabrežje 2; ⏰8am-9pm Jun-Sep, 8am-7pm Oct-May) Knowledgeable and enthusiastic staff dispense information, maps and useful literature and help with accommodation. Maintains an excellent website. Has a helpful **branch** (☑433 94 75; www.visitljubljana.si; Trg OF 6; ⏰8am-10pm Jun-Sep, 10am-7pm Mon-Fri, 8am-3pm Sat Oct-May) at the train station.

Slovenian Tourist Information Centre (STIC; ☑306 45 76; www.slovenia.info; Krekov trg 10; ⏰8am-9pm Jun-Sep, 8am-7pm Oct-May) Good source of information for the rest of Slovenia, with internet and bicycle rental also available.

Travel Agency
STA Ljubljana (☑439 16 90, 041 612 711; www.sta-lj.com; 1st fl, Trg Ajdovščina 1; ⏰10am-5pm Mon-Fri) Discount air fares for students and its cafe has internet access.

Trek Trek (☑425 13 92; www.trektrek.si; Bičevje ulica 5; ⏰10am-5pm Mon-Fri) Specialising in adventure travel in Slovenia, with emphasis on trekking and cycling holidays.

Websites
In addition to the websites of the Slovenian Tourist Information Centre and Ljubljana Tourist Information Centre the following sites might be useful:

City of Ljubljana (www.ljubljana.si) Comprehensive information portal on every aspect of life and tourism direct from city hall.

In Your Pocket (www.inyourpocket.com) Insider info on the capital updated regularly.

Lonely Planet (www.lonelyplanet.com/slovenia/ljubljana)

❶ Getting There & Away
Bus
Buses to destinations both within Slovenia and abroad leave from the **bus station** (Avtobusna Postaja Ljubljana; ☑234 46 00; www.ap-ljubljana.si; Trg Osvobodilne Fronte 4; ⏰5.30am-10.30pm Sun-Fri, 5am-10pm Sat) just next to train station. Next to the ticket windows are multilingual information phones and a touchscreen computer. You do not usually have to buy a ticket in advance; just pay as you board the bus. But for long-distance trips on Friday, just before the school break and public holidays, book the day before to be safe. There's a **left luggage** (Trg OF 4; per day €2; ⏰5.30am-10.30pm Sun-Fri, 5am-10pm Sat) area at window 3.

You can reach virtually anywhere in the country by bus.

Train
Domestic and international trains arrive at and depart from central Ljubljana's **train station** (Železniška Postaja; ☑291 33 32; www.slo-zeleznice.si; Trg Osvobodilne Fronte 6; ⏰6am-10pm) where you'll find a separate Info Center next to the Ljubljana Tourist Information Centre branch. Buy domestic tickets from window nos 1 to 8 and international ones from either window no 9 or the Info Center. There are **coin lockers** (Trg OF 6; per day €2-3; ⏰24hr) for left luggage on platform 1.

There's a surcharge of €1.55 on domestic InterCity (IC) and EuroCity (EC) train tickets.

❶ Getting Around
To/From the Airport
The cheapest way to Ljubljana's **Jože Pučnik Airport** (LJU/Aerodrom Ljubljana; ☑04-206 19 81; www.lju-airport.si/eng; Zgornji Brnik 130a, Brnik) is by public bus (€4.10, 45 minutes, 27km) from stop No 28 at the bus station. These run at 5.20am and hourly from 6.10am to 8.10pm

TRANSPORT FROM LJUBLJANA

Bus

DESTINATION	PRICE (€)	DURATION (HR)	DISTANCE (KM)	FREQUENCY
Bled	6.20	1½	57	hourly
Bohinj	9	2	91	hourly
Koper	12	2½	122	5 daily with more in season
Maribor	14	3	141	2-4 four daily
Piran	14	3	140	up to 7 daily
Postojna	7	1	53	up to 24 daily

Train

DESTINATION	PRICE (€)	DURATION	DISTANCE (KM)	FREQUENCY
Bled	6.20	55min	51	up to 21 daily
Koper	9	2½hr	153	up to 4 daily with more in summer
Maribor	15	1¾hr	156	up to 25 daily
Murska Sobota	14	3¼hr	216	up to 5 daily

Monday to Friday; at the weekend there's a bus at 6.10am and then one every two hours from 9.10am to 7.10pm. Buy tickets from the driver.

A **private airport van** (☑051 321 414; www. airport-shuttle.si) also links Trg OF, near the bus station, with the airport (€9) up to 11 times daily between 5.20am and 10.30pm, and is a 30-minute trip. It goes from the airport to Ljubljana 10 times a day between 5.45am and 11pm.

A taxi from the airport to Ljubljana will cost from €40 to €45.

Bicycle

Ljubljana is a pleasure for cyclists, and there are bike lanes and special traffic lights everywhere.

Ljubljana Bike (☑306 45 76; www.visitljubljana. si; Krekov trg 10; per 2hr/day €2/8; ☺8am-7pm or 9pm Apr-Oct) rents two-wheelers in two-hour or full-day increments from April through October from the Slovenia Tourist Information Centre.

For short rides, you can hire bikes as needed from **Bicike(lj)** (www.bicikelj.si; subscription weekly/yearly €1/€3 plus hourly rate; ☺24hr) bike stands located around the city. To rent a bike requires pre-registration and subscription over the company website plus a valid credit or debit card. After registration simply submit your card or an Urbana public-transport card plus a PIN number. The first hour of the rental is free, the second hour costs €1, the third hour €2, and each additional hour €4. Bikes must be returned within 24 hours.

Public Transport

Ljubljana's city buses operate every five to 15 minutes from 5am (6am on Sunday) to around 10.30pm. A flat fare of €1.20 (good for 90 minutes of unlimited travel, including transfers) is paid with a stored-value magnetic **Urbana** (☑430 51 74; www.lpp-lj.si/urbana) card, which can be purchased at newsstands, tourist offices and the **LPP Information Centre** (☑430 51 75; www.jhl.si; Slovenska cesta 56; ☺7am-7pm Mon-Fri) for €2; credit can then be added (from €1 to €50).

JULIAN ALPS

Slovenia's Julian Alps, part of the wider European Alpine range, is the epicentre for all things outdoors. If you're into adventure sports, head to this area. Much of the region, including the country's highest mountain, Mt Triglav, is protected as part of the Triglav National Park. The park has hiking and biking trails galore. The beautiful alpine lakes at Bled and Bohinj offer boating and swimming amid shimmering mountain backdrops. The region is not just about nature pursuits; you'll also find some of the country's most attractive and important historical towns, like Radovljica. These are unexpected treasure troves of Gothic, Renaissance and baroque architecture.

Lake Bled

⏺04 / POP 10900

With its emerald-green lake, picture-postcard church on an islet, a medieval castle clinging to a rocky cliff and some of the highest peaks of the Julian Alps and the Karavanke as backdrops, Bled is Slovenia's most popular resort, drawing everyone from honeymooners lured by the over-the-top romantic setting to backpackers, who come for the hiking, biking, boating and canyoning possibilities. Bled can be overpriced and swarming with tourists in mid-summer. But as is the case with many popular destinations around the world, people come in droves – and will continue to do so – because the place is special.

◉ Sights

Lake Bled
LAKE

(Blejsko jezero) Bled's greatest attraction is its crystal blue-green lake, measuring just 2km by 1380m. The lake is lovely to behold from almost any vantage point, and makes a beautiful backdrop for the 6km walk along the shore. Mild thermal springs warm the water to a swimmable 26°C from June through August. You can rent boats, go diving or simply snap countless photos.

Bled Castle
CASTLE, MUSEUM

(Blejski Grad; www.blejski-grad.si; Grajska cesta 25; adult/child €8/3.50; ⏺8am-8pm Apr-Oct, 8am-6pm Nov-Mar) Perched atop a steep cliff more than 100m above the lake, Bled Castle is how most people imagine a medieval fortress to be, with towers, ramparts, moats and a terrace offering magnificent views. The castle houses a museum collection that traces the lake's history from earliest times to the development of Bled as a resort in the 19th century.

The castle, built on two levels, dates back to the early 11th century, although most of what stands here now is from the 16th century. For 800 years, it was the seat of the Bishops of Brixen. Among the museum holdings, there's a large collection of armour and weapons (swords, halberds and firearms from the 16th to 18th centuries).

Bled Island
ISLAND

(Blejski Otok; www.blejskiotok.si) Tiny, tear-shaped Bled Island beckons from the shore. There's a church and small museum, but the real thrill is the ride out by gondola (*pletna*). The boat sets you down on the south side at the monumental South Staircase (Južno Stopnišče), built in 1655.

Vintgar Gorge
NATURE PARK

(Soteska Vintgar; adult/child/student €4/2/3; ⏺8am-7pm late Apr-Oct) One of the easiest and most satisfying day trips from Bled is to Vintgar Gorge, some 4km to the northwest. The highlight is a 1600m wooden walkway, built in 1893 and continually rebuilt since. It criss-crosses the swirling Radovna River four times over rapids, waterfalls and pools before reaching 13m-high Šum Waterfall.

🏃 Activities

Several local outfits organise a wide range of outdoor activities in and around Bled, including trekking, mountaineering, rock climbing, ski touring, cross-country skiing, mountain biking, rafting, kayaking, canyoning, caving, horse riding and paragliding.

3glav Adventures
ADVENTURE SPORTS

(⏺041 683 184; www.3glav-adventures.com; Ljubljanska cesta 1; ⏺9am-7pm Apr-Oct) The number-one adventure-sport specialists in Bled for warm-weather activities from 15 April to 15 October. The most popular trip is the Emerald River Adventure (€65), an 11-hour hiking and swimming foray into Triglav National Park. Also rents bikes (half-day/full day €8/15), conducts hot-air balloon flights (€150) and leads diving expeditions of Lake Bled (€70).

Gondola
BOATING

(Pletna; ⏺041 427 155; per person return €12) Riding a piloted gondola out to Bled Island is the archetypal tourist experience. There is a convenient jetty just below the TIC and another in Mlino on the south shore. You get about half an hour to explore the island. In all, the trip to the island and back takes about 1¼ hours.

Horse-drawn Carriages
CARRIAGE

(Fijaker; ⏺041 710 970; www.fijaker-bled.si) A romantic way to experience Bled is to take a horse-drawn carriage from the stand near the **Festival Hall** (Festivalna Dvorana; Cesta Svobode 11). A spin around the lake costs €40, and it's the same price to the castle; an extra 30 minutes inside costs €50. You can even get a carriage for four to **Vintgar** (adult/child €4/2; ⏺8am-7pm mid-May–Oct); the two-hour return trip costs €90.

🛏 Sleeping

Kompas has a list of private rooms and farmhouses, with singles/doubles starting at €24/38.

Hotel Triglav Bled　　HOTEL €€€
(☑575 26 10; www.hoteltriglavbled.si; Kolodvorska cesta 33; s €89-159, d €119-179, ste €139-209; P✳@🛜☷) This 22-room boutique hotel in a painstakingly restored caravanserai that opened in 1906 raises the bar of accommodation standards in Bled. The rooms have hardwood floors and oriental carpets and are furnished with antiques. There's an enormous sloped garden that grows the vegetables served in the terrace restaurants. The location is opposite Bled Jezero train station.

TOP CHOICE Camping Bled　　CAMPGROUND €
(☑575 20 00; www.camping-bled.com; Kidričeva cesta 10c; adult €10.90-12.90, child €7.60-9, glamping huts €60-80; ☺Apr–mid-Oct; P@🛜) Bled's upscale campground is one of the nicest in the country and one of the few places around to try 'glamping' – aka glamorous camping – in this case, ecofriendly, all-natural A-frame huts, some equipped with hot-tubs. The campground setting is a well-tended rural valley at the western end of the lake, about 2.5km from the bus station.

Garni Hotel Berc　　HOTEL €€
(☑576 56 58; www.berc-sp.si; Pod Stražo 13; s €45-50, d €70-80; P@🛜) This purpose-built place, reminiscent of a Swiss chalet, has 15 rooms on two floors in a quiet location above the lake.

Penzion Mayer　　PENSION €€
(☑576 57 40; www.mayer-sp.si; Želeška cesta 7; s €57, d €77-82, apt €120-150; P@🛜) This flower-bedecked 12-room inn in a renovated 19th-century house is in a quiet location above the lake. The larger apartment is in a delightful wooden cabin and the in-house restaurant is excellent.

Traveller's Haven　　HOSTEL €
(☑041 396 545; www.travellers-haven.si; Riklijeva cesta 1; dm/d €19/48; P@🛜) This is arguably the nicest of several hostels clustered on a hillside on the eastern shore of the lake, about 500m north of the centre. The setting is a renovated villa, with six rooms (including one private double), a great kitchen and free laundry. Note the upstairs rooms get hot in mid-summer.

✖️ Eating & Drinking

Vila Ajda　　SLOVENIAN €€
(☑576 83 20; www.vila-ajda.si; Cesta Svobode 27; mains €9-20; ☺11am-11pm; 🛜) Attractive destination restaurant with lovely views out over

---

WORTH A TRIP

RADOVLJICA

The town of Radovljica, an easy day trip from Bled, just 7km away, is filled with charming, historic buildings and blessed with stunning views of the Alps, including Mt Triglav. It was settled by the early Slavs and by the 14th century had grown into an important market town centred on a large rectangular square, today's **Linhartov trg**, and fortified with high stone walls. Much of the original architecture is still standing and looks remarkably unchanged from those early days.

Besides simply strolling historic Linhartov trg, don't miss the town's **Beekeeping Museum** (Čebelarski Muzej; www.muzeji-radovljica.si; Linhartov trg 1; adult/child €3/2; ☺10am-6pm Tue-Sun May-Oct, 8am-3pm Tue, Thu & Fri, 10am-noon & 3-5pm Wed, Sat & Sun Mar, Apr, Nov & Dec, 8am-3pm Tue-Fri Jan & Feb), which is more interesting than it sounds. The museum's collection of illustrated beehive panels from the 18th and 19th centuries, a folk art unique to Slovenia, is the largest in the country. Ask to see a short, instructive video in English.

Radovljica's other claim to fame is food, and the town is blessed with several excellent restaurants. Our favourite is the traditional **Gostilna Lectar** (☑537 48 00; www.lectar.com; Linhartov trg 2; mains €9-15; ☺noon-11pm; 🛜), an inviting guesthouse on the main square. Everything from relatively common dishes like veal goulash to harder to find items like 'beef tongue served with kohlrabi' are given a gourmet touch.

Across the street, **Gostilna Augustin** (☑531 41 63; Linhartov trg 15; mains €10-17; ☺10am-10pm) serves excellent Slovenian dishes to order. Don't miss the cellar dining room, which was once part of a prison (and may have seen an execution or two), and the wonderful back terrace with stunning views of Mt Triglav. Why not have lunch at one and dinner at the other?

Bled

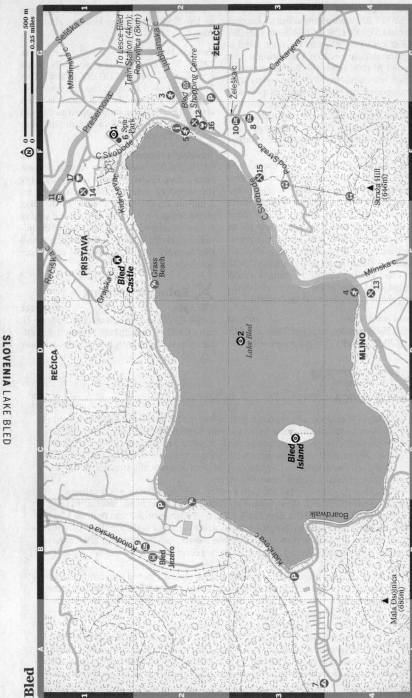

Bled

the lake and a menu that features traditional Slovenian cooking made from locally sourced ingredients. Eat outdoors in the garden in nice weather, or in the upscale dining room. Book in advance on warm evenings in summer.

Ostarija Peglez'n   SEAFOOD €€
(☏574 42 18; http://ostarija-peglezn.mestna-izlozba.com; Cesta Svobode 19a; mains €8-18; ☻11am-11pm) One of the better restaurants in Bled, the Iron Inn is just opposite the landmark Grand Hotel Toplice. It has fascinating retro decor with lots of old household antiques and curios (including the eponymous iron) and serves some of the best fish dishes in town.

Penzion Mlino   SLOVENIAN €€
(www.mlino.si; Cesta Svobode 45; mains €8-15; ☻noon-11pm; ☎) This is a wonderful choice for lunch along a quieter strip of the lake, about 3km outside the centre. The daily four-course set lunches (around €10) usually offer a fish choice, such as the unforgettable grilled trout we enjoyed on our stop.

Pizzeria Rustika   PIZZA €
(☏576 89 00; www.pizzeria-rustika.com; Riklijeva cesta 13; pizza €6-10; ☻noon-11pm; ☎) Conveniently located on the same hill as many of Bled's hostels, so the best pizza in town is just a couple of minutes' walk away.

Pub Bled   PUB
(Cesta Svobode 19a; ☻9am-2am Sun-Thu, 9am-3am Fri & Sat) This friendly pub above the Oštarija Peglez'n restaurant has great cocktails and, on some nights, a DJ.

Slaščičarna Šmon   CAFE
(http://slascicarna-smon.mestna-izlozba.com; Grajska cesta 3; ☻7.30am-10pm; ☎) Bled's culinary speciality is *kremna rezina* (€2.40), a layer of vanilla custard topped with whipped cream and sandwiched between two layers of flaky pastry, and while Šmon may not be its place of birth, it remains the best place in which to try it.

ⓘ Information

A Propos Bar (☏574 40 44; Bled Shopping Centre, Ljubljanska cesta 4; per 15/30/60min €1.25/2.10/4.20; ☻8am-midnight Sun-Thu, to 1am Fri & Sat; ☎) In Bled Shopping Centre, wireless connection as well.

Gorenjska Banka (Cesta Svobode 15) Just north of the Park Hotel.

Kompas (☏572 75 01; www.kompas-bled.si; Bled Shopping Centre, Ljubljanska cesta 4; ☻8am-7pm Mon-Sat, 8am-noon & 4-7pm Sun) Full-service travel agency, organises excursions to Bohinj and Radovljica, airport transfers and transport, rents bikes and skis, sells fishing licenses and arranges accommodation in private homes and apartments.

Post Office (Ljubljanska cesta 10)

Tourist Information Centre Bled (☏574 11 22; www.bled.si; Cesta Svobode 10; ☻8am-7pm Mon-Sat, 11am-5pm Sun) Occupies a small office behind the Casino at Cesta Svobode 10; sells maps and souvenirs, rents bikes (half day/full day €8/11); has a computer for checking email.

ⓘ Getting There & Around

BUS Bled is well connected by bus. There are buses every 30 minutes to Radovljica (€1.80, 15 minutes, 7km) and around 20 buses daily run from Bled to Lake Bohinj (€3.60, 45 minutes) via Bohinjska Bistrica, with the first bus leaving around 5am and the last about 9pm. Buses depart at least hourly for Ljubljana (€6.50, 1¼ hours, 57km).

TRAIN Bled has two train stations, though neither is close to the centre. Mainline trains for Ljubljana (€6.50, 55 minutes, 51km, up to 21 daily), via Škofja Loka and Radovljica, use

Lesce-Bled station, 4km to the east of town. Trains to Bohinjska Bistrica (€1.60, 20 minutes, 18km, eight daily), from where you can catch a bus to Lake Bohinj, use the smaller Bled Jezero station, which is 2km west of central Bled.

Lake Bohinj

🌊 04 / POP 5275

Many visitors to Slovenia say they've never seen a more beautiful lake than Bled...that is, until they've seen Lake Bohinj, just 26km to the southwest. We'll refrain from weighing in on the Bled vs Bohinj debate other than to say we see their point. Admittedly, Bohinj lacks Bled's glamour, but it's less crowded and in many ways more authentic. It's an ideal summer holiday destination. People come primarily to chill out or go for a swim in the crystal-clear, blue-green water. There are lots of outdoor pursuits like kayaking, cycling, climbing and horse riding if you've got the energy.

◉ Sights

Church of St John the Baptist   CHURCH
(Cerkev Sv Janeza Krstnika; Ribčev Laz; ⊙10am-noon & 4-7pm summer, by appointment other times) This church, on the northern side of the Sava Bohinjka river across the stone bridge, is what every medieval church should be: small, on a reflecting body of water and full of exquisite frescos. The nave is Romanesque, but the Gothic presbytery dates from about 1440.

Alpine Dairy Museum   MUSEUM
(Planšarski Muzej; www.bohinj.si; Stara Fužina 181; adult/child €3/2; ⊙11am-7pm Tue-Sun Jul & Aug, 10am-noon & 4-6pm Tue-Sun early Jan-Jun, Sep-late Oct) This museum in Stara Fužina, 1.5km north of Ribčev Laz, has a small collection related to Alpine dairy farming. The four rooms of the museum – once a cheese dairy itself – contain a mock-up of a mid-19th-century herder's cottage.

Savica Waterfall   WATERFALL
(Slap Savica; Ukanc; adult/child €2.50/1.25; ⊙9am-6pm Jul & Aug, 9am-5pm Apr-Jun, Sep & Oct; ℗) The magnificent Savica Waterfall, which cuts deep into a gorge 60m below, is 4km from the Hotel Zlatorog in Ukanc and can be reached by footpath from there.

🏃 Activities

While most people come to Bohinj to relax, there are more exhilarating pursuits available, including canyoning, caving, and para-gliding from the top of Mt Vogel, among others. Two companies, Alpinsport and Perfect Adventure Choice (PAC) Sports, specialise in these activities.

Alpinsport   ADVENTURE SPORTS
(✆572 34 86; www.alpinsport.si; Ribčev Laz 53; ⊙9am-8pm Jul-Sep, 9am-7pm Oct-Jun) Rents sporting equipment, canoes, kayaks and bikes; also operates guided rafting, canyoning and caving trips. Located in a kiosk at the stone bridge over the Sava Bohinjka river in Ribčev Laz.

Bohinj Cable Car   HIKING, SKIING
(adult/child one way €9/7 return €13/9; ⊙every 30min 8am-6pm) The Bohinj cable car operates year-round, hauling skiiers in winter and hikers in summer. There are several day hikes and longer treks that set out from Mt Vogel (1922m).

Mrcina Ranč   HORSE RIDING
(✆041 790 297; www.ranc-mrcina.com; Studor; per hr €20) Mrcina Ranč in Studor, 5km from Ribčev Laz, offers a range of guided tours on horseback, lasting one hour to three days on sturdy Icelandic ponies.

PAC Sports   ADVENTURE SPORTS
(Perfect Adventure Choice; ✆572 34 61; www.pac-sports.com; Hostel Pod Voglom, Ribčev Laz; ⊙7am-11pm Jul & Aug, 10am-6pm Sep-Jun) Popular youth-oriented sports and adventure company, located in the Hostel pod Voglom, 3km west of Ribcev Laz on the road to Ukanc. Rents bikes, canoes and kayaks, and operates guided canyoning, rafting, paragliding and caving trips. In winter, they rent sleds and offer winter rafting near Vogel (per person €15).

Tourist Boat   BOATING
(Turistična Ladja; ✆574 75 90; one way adult/child €9/6.50, return €10.50/7.50; ⊙half-hourly 9.30am-5.30pm Jun–mid-Sep, 10am, 11.30am, 1pm, 2.30pm, 4pm & 5.30pm early Apr-May, 11.30am, 1pm, 2.30pm & 4pm mid-Sep–Oct) An easy family-friendly sail from Ribčev Laz to Ukanc and back.

🛏 Sleeping

The tourist office can help arrange accommodation in private rooms and apartments. Expect to pay anywhere from €38 to €50 for a two-person apartment.

TOP CHOICE Penzion Gasperin   PENSION €€
(✆041 540 805; www.bohinj.si/gasperin; Ribčev Laz 36a; r €48-60; ℗❄✳@❋) This spotless

chalet-style guesthouse with 23 rooms is just 350m southeast of the TIC and run by a friendly British/Slovenian couple. Most rooms have balconies. The buffet breakfast is fresh and includes a sampling of local meats and cheeses.

Hotel Stare
PENSION €€
(☑040 558 669; www.bohinj-hotel.com; Ukanc 128; per person €42-50; P@☎) This beautifully appointed 10-room pension is situated on the Sava Bohinjka river in Ukanc and is surrounded by 3.5 hectares of lovely garden. If you really want to get away from it all without having to climb mountains, this is your place. Rates are half-board, including breakfast and dinner.

Hotel Jezero
HOTEL €€€
(☑572 91 00; www.bohinj.si/alpinum/jezero; Ribčev Laz 51; s €65-75, d €120-140; P@☎≋) Further renovations have raised the standards at this 76-room place just across from the lake. It has a lovely indoor swimming pool, two saunas and a fitness centre.

Hostel Pod Voglom
HOSTEL €
(☑572 34 61; www.hostel-podvoglom.com; Ribčev Laz 60; dm €18, r per person €23-26, without bathroom €20-22; P@) Bohinj's youth hostel, some 3km west of the centre of Ribčev Laz on the road to Ukanc, has 119 beds in 46 rooms in two buildings.

Autokamp Zlatorog
CAMPGROUND €
(☑577 80 00; www.hoteli-bohinj.si; Ukanc 2; per person €6-9; ☺May-Sep) This pleasant, pine-shaded 2.5-hectare camping ground accommodating 500 guests is at the lake's western end, 4.5km from Ribčev Laz. Prices vary according to site location, with the most expensive – and desirable – sites right on the lake.

✕ Eating

TOP CHOICE **Gostilna Rupa**
SLOVENIAN €€
(☑572 34 01; www.apartmajikatrnjek.com/rupa; Srednja Vas 87; mains €8-16; ☺10am-midnight Jul & Aug, Tue-Sun Sep-Jun) If you're under your own steam, head for this country-style restaurant in the next village over from Studor and about 5km from Ribčev Laz. Among the excellent home-cooked dishes are *ajdova krapi*, crescent-shaped dumplings made from buckwheat and cheese, various types of local *klobasa* (sausage) and Bohinj trout.

Gostilna Mihovc
SLOVENIAN €
(☑572 33 90; www.gostilna-mihovc.si; Stara Fužina 118; mains €7-10; ☺10am-midnight) This place in Stara Fužina is very popular – not least for its fiery homemade brandy. Try the *pasulj* (bean soup) with sausage (€6) or the beef *golač* (goulash; €5.20). Live music on Friday and Saturday evenings. In

---

SUMMITING MT TRIGLAV

The 2864m limestone peak called Mt Triglav (Mt Three Heads) has been a source of inspiration and an object of devotion for Slovenes for more than a millennium. Under the Habsburgs in the 19th century, the 'pilgrimage' to Triglav became, in effect, a confirmation of one's ethnic identity, and this tradition continues to this day: a Slovene is expected to climb Triglav at least once in his or her life.

You can climb Slovenia's highest peak too, but Triglav is not for the unfit or faint-hearted. We strongly recommend hiring a guide for the ascent, even if you have some mountain-climbing experience under your belt. A local guide will know the trails and conditions, and can prove invaluable in helping to arrange sleeping space in mountain huts and providing transport. Guides can be hired through 3glav (p888) in Bled or Alpinsport in Bohinj, or book in advance through the **Alpine Association of Slovenia** (PZS; www.pzs.si/).

Triglav is inaccessible from middle to late October to late May. June and the first half of July are the rainiest times in the summer months, so late July, August and particularly September and early October are the best times to make the climb.

There are many ways to reach the top, with the most popular approaches coming from the south, either starting from **Pokljuka**, near Bled, or from the Savica Waterfall, near Lake Bohinj. You can also climb Triglav from the north and the east (Mojstrana and the Vrata Valley). All of the approaches offer varying degrees of difficulty and have their pluses and minuses. Note that treks normally require one or two overnight stays in the mountains.

summer book in advance to secure a garden table.

ℹ Getting There & Away

Buses run regularly from Ljubljana (€9, two hours, 90km, hourly) to Bohinj Jezero and Ukanc – marked 'Bohinj Zlatorog' – via Bled and Bohinjska Bistrica. Around 20 buses daily run from Bled (€3.60, 45 minutes) to Bohinj Jezero (via Bohinjska Bistrica) and return, with the first bus leaving around 5am and the last about 9pm. From the end of June through August, **Alpetour** (☑532 04 45; www.alpetour.si) runs special tourist buses that leave from Ribčev Laz to Bohinjska Bistrica in one direction and to the Savica Waterfall (23 minutes) in the other.

Several trains daily make the run to Bohinjska Bistrica from Ljubljana (€6.70, two hours), though this route requires a change in Jesenice. There are also frequent trains between Bled's small Bled Jezero station (€1.60, 20 minutes, 18km, eight daily) and Bohinjska Bistrica.

Kranjska Gora

☑04 / POP 5510

Nestling in the Sava Dolinka Valley some 40km northwest of Bled, Kranjska Gora (Carniolan Mountain) is Slovenia's largest and best-equipped ski resort. It's at its most perfect under a blanket of snow, but its surroundings are wonderful to explore at other times as well. There are endless possibilities for hiking, cycling and mountaineering in Triglav National Park, which is right on the town's doorstep to the south, and few travellers will be unimpressed by a trip over Vršič Pass (1611m), the gateway to the Soča Valley.

◉ Sights & Activities

Most of the sights are situated along the main street, Borovška cesta, 400m south of where the buses stop. The endearing **Liznjek House** (Liznjekova Domačija; www.gornjesavskimuzej.si; Borovška 63; adult/child €2.50/1.70; ⊙10am-6pm Tue-Sat, 10am-5pm Sun), an 18th-century museum house, has a good collection of household objects and furnishings peculiar to the alpine region.

Kranjska Gora is best known as a winter resort, and chairlifts up to the **ski slopes** on Vitranc (1631m) are at the western end of town off Smerinje ulica. There are more ski slopes and a **ski-jumping facility** 6km to the west, near the villages of Rateče and Planica, which is home to the annual **Ski-Jumping World Cup Championships** (☑1 200 6241; www.planica.info; Planica; adult/child €20/3) in

mid-March. There are lots of places offering ski tuition and hiring out equipment, including **ASK Kranjska Gora Ski School** (☑588 53 02; www.ask-kg.com; Borovška c 99a; ⊙9am-4pm Mon-Sat, 10am-6pm Sun mid-Dec–mid-Mar, 9am-3pm Mon-Fri mid-Mar–mid-Dec).

In summer, the town is quieter, but there are still plenty of things to do. Kranjska Gora makes an excellent base for **hiking** in the Triglav National Park, and Jasna Lake, the gateway to the park, is 2km to the south. The 1:30,000-scale *Kranjska Gora* hiking map is available at the **Tourist Information Centre** (TIC; ☑580 94 40; www.kranjska -gora.si; Tičarjeva cesta 2; ⊙8am-7pm Mon-Sat, 9am-6pm Sun Jun-Sep & mid-Dec–Mar, 8am-3pm Mon-Sat Apr, May & Oct–mid-Dec) for €9.

The hiking map also marks out 15 **cycling routes** of varying difficulty. Most ski-rental outfits hire out bikes in summer, including **Intersport** (www.intersport-bernik.com; Borovška cesta 88a; ⊙8am-8pm mid-Dec–mid-Mar, 8am-8pm Mon-Sat, 8am-1pm Sun mid-Mar–mid-Dec). Expect to pay €10 for a full-day rental and helmet.

🛏 Sleeping & Eating

Accommodation costs peak from December to March and in mid-summer. Private rooms and apartments can be arranged through the Tourist Information Centre.

Hotel Kotnik　　　　　　　　　　　HOTEL €€
(☑588 15 64; www.hotel-kotnik.si; Borovška cesta 75; s €50-60, d €72-80; P@🛜) If you're not into big high-rise hotels with hundreds of rooms, choose this charming, bright-yellow, low-rise property. It has 15 cosy rooms, a great restaurant and pizzeria, and it couldn't be more central.

📷 Natura Eco Camp Kranjska Gora　　　　　　CAMPGROUND €
(☑064 121 966; www.naturacamp-kranjskagora. com; Borovška cesta 62; adult €8-10, child €5-7, cabin & tree tent €25-30) This wonderful site, some 300m from the main road on an isolated horse ranch in a forest clearing, is as close to paradise as we've been for awhile. Pitch a tent or stay in one of the little wooden cabins or the unique tree tents – great pouches with air mattresses suspended from the branches.

Hotel Miklič　　　　　　　　　　　HOTEL €€€
(☑588 16 35; www.hotelmiklic.com; Vitranška ulica 13; s €60-80, d €80-130; P@🛜) This pristine 15-room small hotel south of the centre is

surrounded by luxurious lawns and flower beds and boasts an excellent restaurant and a small fitness room with sauna (€12 per hour). It's definitely a cut above most other accommodation in Kranjska Gora.

Hotel Kotnik
SLOVENIAN €€

(☑588 15 64; www.hotel-kotnik.si; Borovška c 75; mains €8-18; ☏) One of Kranjska Gora's better eateries, the restaurant in this stylish inn, with bits of painted dowry chests on the walls, serves grilled meats – pepper steak is a speciality – that should keep you going for awhile. The adjoining pizzeria (pizza €6 to €9, open noon to 10.30pm) with the wood-burning stove is a great choice for something quicker.

Gostilna Pri Martinu
SLOVENIAN €

(☑582 03 00; Borovška c 61; mains €7-14; ⊘10am-11pm; ☏) This atmospheric tavern-restaurant in an old house opposite the fire station is one of the best places in town to try local specialities, such as *ješprenj* (barley soup), *telečja obara* (veal stew) and *ričet* (barley stew with smoked pork ribs). One of the few places to offer a full three-course luncheon menu (€7).

ℹ️ Getting There & Away

Buses run hourly to Ljubljana (€8.70, two hours, 91km) via Jesenice (€3.10, 30 minutes, 24km), where you should change for Bled (€2.70, 20 minutes, 19km). There's just one direct departure to Bled (€4.80, one hour, 40km) on weekdays at 9.15am and at 9.50am on weekends.

Alpetour (☑201 31 30; www.alpetour.si) runs regular buses to Trenta (€4.70, 70 minutes, 30km) and Bovec (€6.70, two hours,46km) from June through September via the Vršič Pass. Check the website for a timetable. There are normally about four departures daily (more at the weekend). Buy tickets from the driver.

Soča Valley

The Soča Valley region (Posočje) stretches from Triglav National Park to Nova Gorica, including the outdoor activity centres of Bovec and Kobarid. Threading through it is the magically aquamarine Soča River. Most people come here for the rafting, hiking and skiing, though there are plenty of historical sights and locations, particularly relating to WWI, when millions of troops fought on the mountainous battle front here.

BOVEC
☑05 / POP 1810

Soča Valley's de facto capital, Bovec, offers plenty to adventure-sports enthusiasts. With the Julian Alps above, the Soča River below and Triglav National Park all around, you could spend a week here hiking, kayaking, mountain biking and, in winter, skiing at Mt Kanin, Slovenia's highest ski station, without ever doing the same thing twice.

🏃 Activities

Rafting, **kayaking** and **canoeing** on the beautiful Soča River (10% to 40% gradient; Grades I to VI) are major draws. The season lasts from April to October.

Rafting trips of two to eight people over a distance of 8km to 10km (1½ hours) cost from €36 to €46 and for 21km (2½ hours) from €48 to €55, including neoprene long johns, windcheater, life jacket, helmet and paddle. Bring a swimsuit, T-shirt and towel. Canoes for two are €45 for the day; single kayaks €30. A number of beginners kayaking courses are also on offer (eg one-/two-days from €55/100). Longer guided kayak trips (up to 10km) are also available.

A 3km **canyoning** trip near the Soča, in which you descend through gorges and jump over falls attached to a rope, costs around €42.

Other popular activities include **cycling**, **hiking** and **fishing**. Visit the **Tourist Information Centre Bovec** (☑388 19 19; www.bovec.si; Trg Golobarskih Žrtev 8; ⊘8.30am-8.30pm summer, 9am-6pm winter) for specific information or check in with the following reputable agencies:

Soča Rafting
ADVENTURE SPORTS

(☑041-724 472, 389 62 00; www.socarafting.si; Trg Golobarskih Žrtev 14; ⊘9am-7pm year-round)

Top Extreme
ADVENTURE SPORTS

(☑041 620 636; www.top.si; Trg Golobarskih Žrtev 19; ⊘9am-7pm May-Sep)

Kanin Ski Centre
SKIING

(☑388 60 98; www.bovec.si; day pass adult/child/senior & student €22/16/18) The Kanin Ski Centre northwest of Bovec has skiing up to 2200m – the only real altitude alpine skiing in Slovenia. As a result, the season can be long, with good spring skiing in April and even May.

🛏️ Sleeping & Eating

Private rooms are easy to come by in Bovec through the TIC.

TOP CHOICE **Dobra Vila**
BOUTIQUE HOTEL €€€

(☑389 64 00; www.dobra-vila-bovec.si; Mala Vas 112; d €120-145, tr €160-180; P☀☏) This stunner of a 10-room boutique hotel is housed in an erstwhile telephone-exchange building dating to 1932. Peppered with interesting artefacts and objets d'art, it has its own library and wine cellar and a fabulous restaurant with a winter garden and outdoor terrace.

Martinov Hram
GUESTHOUSE €€

(☎388 62 14; www.martinov-hram.si; Trg Golobarskih Žrtev 27; s/d €33/54; P🖤) This lovely and very friendly guesthouse just 100m east of the centre has 14 beautifully furnished rooms and an excellent restaurant with an emphasis on specialities from the Bovec region.

Kamp Palovnik
CAMPGROUND €

(☎388 60 07; www.kamp-polovnik.com; Ledina 8; adult €6.50-7.50, child €5-5.75; ☉Apr–mid-Oct; P) About 500m southeast of the Hotel Kanin, this is the closest camping ground to Bovec. It is small (just over a hectare with 70 sites) but located in an attractive setting.

Gostišče Stari Kovač
PIZZA €

(☎388 66 99; Rupa 3; starters €6.50-7, mains €8-11, pizza €5-7.50; ☉noon-10pm Tue-Sun) The 'Old Blacksmith' is a good choice for pizza cooked in a wood-burning stove.

ⓘ Getting There & Away
Buses to Kobarid (€3.10, 30 minutes) depart up to six times a day. There are also buses to Ljubljana (€13.60, 3½ hours) via Kobarid and Idrija. From late June to August a service to Kranjska Gora (€6.70, two hours) via the Vršič Pass departs four times daily, continuing to Ljubljana.

KOBARID
☎05 / POP 1250

The charming town of Kobarid is quainter than nearby Bovec, and despite being surrounded by mountain peaks, Kobarid feels more Mediterranean than Alpine. On the surface not a whole lot has changed since Ernest Hemingway described Kobarid (then Caporetto) in *A Farewell to Arms* (1929) as 'a little white town with a campanile in a valley' with 'a fine fountain in the square'. Kobarid was a military settlement during Roman times, was hotly contested in the Middle Ages and was hit by a devastating earthquake in 1976, but the world will remember Kobarid as the site of the decisive battle of 1917 in which the combined forces of the Central Powers defeated the Italian army.

◉ Sights

Kobarid Museum
MUSEUM

(☎389 00 00; www.kobariski-muzej.si; Gregorčičeva ul 10; adult/child €5/2.50; ☉9am-6pm Mon-Fri,

9am-7pm Sat & Sun summer, 10am-5pm Mon-Fri, 9am-6pm Sat & Sun winter) This museum is devoted almost entirely to the Soča Front and WWI. There are many photographs documenting the horrors of the front, military charts, diaries and maps, and two large relief displays showing the front lines and offensives through the Krn Mountains and the positions in the Upper Soča Valley. Don't miss the 20-minute multimedia presentation.

🏃 Activities
A free pamphlet and map titled *The Kobarid Historical Trail* outlines a 5km-long route that will take you past remnants of WWI troop emplacements to the impressive **Kozjak Stream Waterfalls** (Slapovi Potoka Kozjak) and **Napoleon Bridge** (Napoleonov Most) built in 1750. More ambitious is the hike outlined in the free *Pot Miru/Walk of Peace* brochure.

Kobarid gives Bovec a run for its money in adventure sports, and you'll find several outfits on or off the town's main square that can organise rafting (from €34), canyoning (from €45), kayaking (€40) and paragliding (€110) between April and October. Two recommended agencies are listed below:

X Point
ADVENTURE SPORTS

(☎041 692 290, 388 53 08; www.xpoint.si; Trg Svobode 6)

Positive Sport
ADVENTURE SPORTS

(☎040 654 475; www.positive-sport.com; Markova ulica 2)

🛏 Sleeping

TOP CHOICE Hiša Franko
GUESTHOUSE €€€

(☎389 41 20; www.hisafranko.com; Staro Selo 1; r €80-135; P🖤) This guesthouse in an old farmhouse 3km west of Kobarid in Staro Selo, halfway to the Italian border, has 10 themed rooms – we love the Moja Afrika (My Africa) and Soba Zelenega Čaja (Green Tea Room) ones – some of which have terraces and jacuzzis. Eat in their excellent restaurant.

Hotel Hvala
HOTEL €€€

(☎389 93 00; wwww.hotelhvala.si; Trg Svobode 1; s €72-76, d €104-112; P🕸🖤) The delightful 'Hotel Thanks' (actually it's the family's name), has 31 rooms. A snazzy lift takes you on a vertical tour of Kobarid (don't miss both the Soča trout and Papa Hemingway at work); there's a bar, a Mediterranean-style cafe in the garden and a superb restaurant.

Kamp Koren CAMPGROUND €
(✆389 13 11; www.kamp-koren.si; Drežniške Ravne 33; per person pitch €11.50, chalets d/tr from €55/60; P🛈) The oldest camping ground in the valley, this 2-hectare site with 70 pitches is about 500m northeast of Kobarid on the left bank of the Soča River and just before the turn to Drežniške Ravne. In full view is the Napoleon Bridge.

✗ Eating

In the centre of Kobarid you'll find two of Slovenia's best restaurants.

TOP CHOICE **Hiša Franko** SLOVENIAN €€
(✆389 41 20; www.hisafranko.com; Staro Selo 1; mains €22-24; ☉noon-3pm & 6-11pm Tue-Sun) Foodies will love this superb gourmet restaurant in the guesthouse of the same name in Staro Selo, just west of town. Impeccable tasting menus, strong on locally sourced ingredients and which change according to the season, cost €50/75 for five/eight courses. It closes on Tuesday in winter.

Topli Val SEAFOOD €€
(Trg Svobode 1; starters €8-10, mains €9.50-25; ☉noon-10pm) Seafood is the speciality here, and it's excellent – from the carpaccio of sea bass to the Soča trout and signature lobster with pasta. Expect to pay about €30 to €60 per person with a decent bottle of wine. There's a lovely front terrace and back garden open in warmer months.

ℹ Information

Tourist Information Centre Kobarid (✆380 04 90; www.dolina-soce.com; Trg Svobode 16; ☉9am-1pm & 2-7pm Mon-Fri, 10am-1pm & 4-7pm Sat & Sun) Free internet.

ℹ Getting There & Around

There are half a dozen buses a day to Bovec (€3.10, 30 minutes). Other destinations include Ljubljana (€11.40 three hours) via Most na Soči train station (good for Bled and Bohinj). Daily in July and August, buses cross the spectacular Vršič Pass to Kranjska Gora (€6.70, three hours).

KARST & COAST

Slovenia's short coast (47km) is an area for both history and recreation. The southernmost resort town of Portorož has some decent beaches, but towns like Koper and Piran, famed for their Venetian Gothic architecture, are the main drawcards here. En route from Ljubljana or the Soča Valley, you'll cross the Karst, a huge limestone plateau and a land of olives, ruby-red Teran wine, *pršut* (air-dried ham), old stone churches and deep subterranean caves, including Postojna and Škocjan.

Postojna

✆05 / POP 8910
The karst cave at Postojna is one of the largest in the world and its stalagmite and stalactite formations are unequalled anywhere. It's a busy destination (visited by as many as a third of all tourists coming to Slovenia). The amazing thing is how the large crowds at the entrance seem to get swallowed whole by the size of the caves.

The small town of Postojna lies in the Pivka Valley at the foot of Sovič Hill (677m) with Titov trg at its centre. Postojna's bus station is at Titova cesta 36, about 250m southwest of Titov trg. The train station is on Kolodvorska cesta about 600m southeast of the square.

◉ Sights

Postojna Cave CAVE
(✆700 01 00; www.postojnska-jama.si; Jamska c 30; adult/child/student €22.90/13.70/18.30; ☉tours hourly 9am-6pm summer, 3 or 4 times from 10am daily winter) Slovenia's single most-popular tourist attraction, Postojna Cave is about 1.5km northwest of Postojna. The 5.7km-long cavern is visited on a 1½-hour tour – 4km of it by electric train and the rest on foot. Inside, impressive stalagmites and stalactites in familiar shapes stretch almost endlessly in all directions.

Proteus Vivarium MUSEUM
(www.turizem-kras.si; adult/child €8/4.80, with cave €27/16.20; ☉9am-5.30pm May-Sep, 10.30am-3.30pm Oct-Apr) Just steps south of the Postojna Cave's entrance is Proteus Vivarium, a spelio-biological research station with a video introduction to underground zoology. A 45-minute tour then leads you into a small, darkened cave to peep at some of the endemic Proteus anguinus, a shy (and miniscule) salamander unique to Slovenia.

🛏 Sleeping & Eating

Hotel Kras HOTEL €€
(✆700 23 00; www.hotel-kras.si; Tržaška cesta 1; s €68-74, d €84-96, apt €100-120; P🛈) This rather flash, modern hotel has risen, phoenix-like, from the ashes of a decrepit old caravanserai in the heart of town, and now boasts 27 comfortable rooms with all the mod cons. If you've got the dosh, choose one

PREDJAMA CASTLE

The tiny village of Predjama (population 85), 10km northwest of Postojna, is home to remarkable **Predjama Castle** (☎700 01 03; www.postojnska-jama.eu; Predjama 1; adult/child/student €9/5.40/7.20; ☉9am-7pm summer, 10am-4pm winter). The castle's lesson is clear: if you want to build an impregnable redoubt, put it in the gaping mouth of a cavern halfway up a 123m cliff. Its four storeys were built piece-meal over the years since 1202, but most of what you see today is 16th century. It looks simply unconquerable.

The castle holds great features for kids of any age – a drawbridge over a raging river, holes in the ceiling of the entrance tower for pouring boiling oil on intruders, a very dank dungeon, a 16th-century chest full of treasure (unearthed in the cellar in 1991), and a hiding place at the top called Erazem's Nook.

In mid-July, the castle hosts the **Erasmus Tournament**, a day of medieval duelling, jousting and archery.

The cave below Predjama Castle is a 6km network of galleries spread over four levels. Casual visitors can see about 900m of it; longer tours are available by prior arrangement only. **Gostilna Požar** (☎751 52 52; Predjama 2; meals from €11; ☉10am-10pm Thu-Tue, daily Aug) is a simple restaurant next to the ticket kiosk and in heart-stopping view of the castle.

of the apartments on the top (5th) floor with enormous terraces.

Hotel Sport
HOTEL, HOSTEL €€

(☎720 22 44; www.sport-hotel.si; Kolodvorska c 1; dm €25, s/d from €55/70; P@🛜) A hotel of some sort or another since 1880, the Sport offers reasonable value for money, with 37 spick-and-span and comfortable rooms, including five with nine dorm beds each. There's a kitchen with a small eating area. It's 300m north of the centre.

Jamski Dvorec
INTERNATIONAL €€

(☎700 01 81; starters €6.50-10, mains €13.50-22; ☉9am-6pm) Housed in a stunning 1920s-style building next to the entrance to the cave, the Cave Manor has fairly average international dishes but its set menus at €11 and €12 are a big attraction.

Čuk
PIZZA €

(☎720 13 00; Pot k Pivki 4; starters €5-7.50, pizza & pasta €6-9.50; ☉10am-11pm Mon-Fri, 11am-midnight Sat, noon-11pm Sun) Excellent restaurant southwest of Titov trg, just off Tržaška cesta, Čuk takes its pizza seriously but offers a wide range of Slovenian mains too.

❶ Getting There & Away

BUS Services from Ljubljana to the coast as well as Ajdovščina stop in Postojna (€6, one hour, 53km, hourly). Other destinations include Koper (€6.90, 1¼ hours, 68km, four to seven daily) and Piran (€8.30, 1½ hours, 86km, three or four a day).

TRAIN Postojna is on the main train line linking Ljubljana (€4.90, one hour, 67km) with Sežana and Trieste via Divača (€2.90 to €4.45, 40 minutes, 37km), and is an easy day trip from the capital. You can also reach here from Koper (€5.90 to €10.30, 1½ hours, 86km) on one of up to seven trains a day.

Škocjan Caves
☎05

The immense system of the **Škocjan Caves** (☎708 21 10; www.park-skocjanske-jame.si; Škocjan 2; adult/child €15/7; ☉10am-5pm), a Unesco World Heritage site, is more captivating than the larger one at Postojna, and for many travellers this will be the highlight of their trip to Slovenia.

Visitors walk in guided groups from the ticket office to the main entrance in the Globočak Valley. Through a tunnel built in 1933, you soon reach the head of the **Silent Cave**, a dry branch of the underground canyon that stretches for 500m. The first section, called **Paradise**, is filled with beautiful stalactites and stalagmites; the second part (called **Calvary**) was once the river bed. The Silent Cave ends at the **Great Hall**, a jungle of exotic dripstones and deposits; keep an eye out for the mighty stalagmites called the Giants and the Organ.

The sound of the Reka River heralds your entry into the **Murmuring Cave**, with walls 100m high. To get over the Reka and into Müller Hall, you must cross **Cerkevnik**

Bridge, some 45m high and surely the highlight of the trip.

Schmidl Hall, the final section, emerges into the Velika Dolina. From here you walk past **Tominč Cave**, where finds from a prehistoric settlement have been unearthed. A funicular takes you back to the entrance.

The temperature in the caves is constant at 12°C so bring along a light jacket or sweater. Good walking shoes, for the sometimes slippery paths, are recommended.

The nearest town with accommodation is **Divača**, 5km to the northwest. **Gostilna Malovec** (📞763 33 33; www.hotel-malovec.si; s/d €54/80; [P][@][奈]) has a half-dozen basic but renovated rooms in a building beside its traditional restaurant.The nearby **Orient Express** (📞763 30 10; pizza €4.60-14; ⊙11am-11pm Sun-Fri, 11am-2am Sat) is a popular pizzeria.

Buses from Ljubljana to Koper and the coast stop at Divača (€7.90, 1½ hours, half-hourly). Divača is also on the rail line to Ljubljana (€7.30, 1½ hours, hourly), with up to five trains a day to Koper (€4.05, 50 minutes) via Hrpelje-Kozina. The Škocjan Caves are about 5km by road southeast of the Divača train station – the route is signed. A courtesy van sometimes meets incoming Ljubljana trains.

Koper

📞05 / POP 24,725

Coastal Slovenia's largest town, Koper (Capodistria in Italian) at first glance appears to be a workaday city that scarcely gives tourism a second thought. Yet its central core is delightfully medieval and far less overrun than its ritzy cousin Piran, 18km down the coast. Known as Aegida to the ancient Greeks, Koper grew rich as a key port trading salt and was the capital of Istria under the Venetian republic during the 15th and 16th centuries. It remains Slovenia's most important port.

⊙ Sights

The easiest way to see Koper's Old Town is to walk from the marina on Ukmarjev trg east along Kidričeva ulica to Titov trg and then south down Čevljarska ulica, taking various detours along the way.

Koper Regional Museum MUSEUM
(📞663 35 70; www.pmk-kp.si; Kidričeva ul 19; adult/child €2/1.50; ⊙9am-7pm Tue-Fri, to 1pm Sat & Sun) The **Belgramoni-Tacco Palace** houses this museum with displays of old maps and photos of the port and coast, Italianate sculpture, and paintings dating from the 16th to 18th centuries. Note the wonderful bronze knocker on the door of Venus arising from a seashell.

Cathedral of the Assumption CATHEDRAL
(Stolnica Marijinega Vnebovzetja; ⊙7am-9pm) Opposite the Armoury in Titov trg is the Cathedral of the Assumption and its 36m-tall belfry, now called the **City Tower**. The cathedral, partly Romanesque and Gothic but mostly dating from the 18th century, has a white classical interior with a feeling of space and light that belies the sombre exterior.

[FREE] **Beach** BEACH
(Kopališko nabrežje 1; ⊙8am-7pm May-Sep) Koper's tiny beach, on the northwest edge of the Old Town, has a small bathhouse with toilets and showers, grassy areas for lying in the sun and a bar and cafe.

🛏 Sleeping

Hotel Koper HOTEL €€€
(📞610 05 00; www.terme-catez.si; Pristaniška ul 3; s €76-92, d €120-150; [※][@][奈]) This pleasant, 65-room property on the edge of the historic Old Town is the only really central hotel in town. Rates include entry to an aquapark. Choose a harbour-facing room.

Hotel Vodišek HOTEL €€
(📞639 24 68; www.hotel-vodisek.com; Kolodvorska c 2; s €48-60, d €72-90; [P][※][@][奈]) This small hotel with 35 reasonably priced rooms is in a shopping centre halfway between the Old Town and the train and bus stations. Guests get to use the hotel's bicycles for free.

Museum Hostel APARTMENTS €
(📞041 504 466, 626 18 70; bozic.doris@siol.net; Muzejski trg 6; per person €20-25; [奈]) This place is more a series of apartments with kitchens and bathrooms than a hostel. Reception is at Museum Bife, a cafe-bar on Muzejski trg; the rooms are scattered nearby.

🍴 Eating

Istrska Klet Slavček ISTRIAN, SLOVENIAN €
(📞627 67 29; Župančičeva ul 39; dishes €3-12; ⊙7am-10pm Mon-Fri) The Istrian Cellar, situated below the 18th-century Carli Palace, is one of the most colourful places for a meal in Koper's Old Town. Filling set lunches go for less than €8, and there's local Malvazija and Teran wine from the barrel.

SLOVENIA KOPER

LIPICA'S LIPIZZANER HORSES

The impact of Lipica has been far greater than its tiny size would suggest. It's here where the famed snow-white 'Lipizzaner' horses, made famous at Vienna's Spanish Riding School, were first bred in the late 16th century.

The breed got its start by pairing Andalusian horses from Spain with the local Karst breed the Romans once used to pull chariots. The white colour came two centuries later, when white Arabian horses got into the act.

The breed has subsequently become scattered – moved to Hungary and Austria after WWI, to the Sudetenland in Bohemia by the Germans during WWII, and then shipped off to Italy by the American army in 1945. Only 11 horses returned when operations resumed at Lipica in 1947.

Today, some 400 Lipizzaners remain at the **Lipica Stud Farm** (☑739 15 80; www.lipica.org; Lipica 5; tour adult/child €11/5.50, training/classical performance €13/18; ⊘training & classical performance Tue, Fri & Sun Apr-Oct), while Lipizzaners are also bred in various locations around the world, including Piber in Austria, which breeds the horses for the Spanish Riding School. The stud farm offers equestrian fans a large variety of tours and riding presentations as well as lessons and carriage rides. Tour times are complicated; see the website for details.

Most people visit Lipica as a day trip from Sežana, 4km to the north, or Divača, 13km to the northeast, both of which are on the Ljubljana–Koper rail line. There is no public transport from either train station; a taxi will cost between €10 and €20.

For overnights, try the 59-room **Hotel Maestoso** (☑739 15 80; s/d €80/120; P⊛☎), managed by the stud farm. It has many upscale amenities, including a restaurant, swimming pool, sauna and tennis courts.

La Storia ITALIAN €€
(☑626 20 18; www.lastoria.si; Pristaniška ul 3; mains €8.50-25) This Italian-style trattoria with sky-view ceiling frescos focuses on salads, pasta and fish dishes and has outside seating in the warmer months.

❶ Information

Banka Koper (Kidričeva ul 14)

Pina Internet Cafe (☑627 80 72; Kidričeva ul 43; per hr adult/student €4.20/1.20; ⊘noon-10pm Mon-Fri, from 4pm Sat & Sun)

Post Office (Muzejski trg 3)

Tourist Information Centre Koper (☑664 64 03; www.koper.si; Praetorian Palace, Titov trg 3; ⊘9am-8pm Jul & Aug, 9am-5pm Sep-Jun)

❶ Getting There & Away

BUS Services run to Izola, Strunjan, Piran (€2.70, 30 minutes and Portorož every half-hour on weekdays. There's a handy bus stop at the corner of Piranška ulica. Some five daily buses make the run to Ljubljana (€11.10, 1¾ to 2½ hours). Buses to Trieste (€3, one hour) run along the coast via Ankaran and Muggia from Monday to Saturday. Destinations in Croatia include Rijeka (€11.20, two hours) and Rovinj (€12, three hours) via Poreč (€10, two hours).

TRAIN Half a dozen trains a day link Koper to Ljubljana (€10.70, 2½ hours, 153km) via Postojna and Divača.

Piran

☑05 / POP 4470

Picturesque Piran, sitting at the tip of a narrow peninsula, is everyone's favourite town on the coast. Its Old Town – one of the best preserved historical towns anywhere on the Adriatic – is a gem of Venetian architecture, but it can be a mob scene at the height of summer. In April or October, though, it's hard not to fall in love with the winding alleyways and tempting seafood restaurants.

◉ Sights

Tartinijev Trg SQUARE
The **statue** of the nattily dressed gentleman in Tartinijev trg, an oval-shaped square that was the inner harbour until it was filled in 1894, is that of local boy-cum-composer Giuseppe Tartini (1692–1770). To the east is the **Church of St Peter** (Cerkev Sv Petra; Tartinijev trg), which contains the 14th-century **Piran Crucifix**. Across from the church is **Tartini House**, the composer's birthplace.

Sergej Mašera Maritime Museum
MUSEUM

(☑671 00 40; www.pommuz-pi.si; Cankarjevo nabrežje 3; adult/student & senior/child €3.50/ 2.50/2.10; ☺9am-noon & 5-9pm Tue-Sun summer, 9am-5pm Tue-Sun winter) Located in the lovely 19th-century Gabrielli Palace on the waterfront, this museum focuses on the sea, sailing and salt-making. There are some old photographs showing salt workers going about their duties, as well as a wind-powered salt pump and little wooden weights in the form of circles and diamonds that were used to weigh salt during the Venetian republic.

Cathedral of St George
CATHEDRAL

(Stolna Cerkev Sv Jurija; Adamičeva ul 2) Piran's hilltop cathedral was founded in 1344 and rebuilt in baroque style in 1637. It's undergoing a massive renovation, and visitors are allowed only into the choir to view the magnificent marble altar and star-vaulted ceiling. If time allows, visit the attached **Parish Museum of St George** (☑673 34 40; admission €1; ☺10am-1pm & 5-7pm Mon-Fri, 11am-7pm Sat & Sun), which contains paintings and a lapidary in the crypt.

Minorite Monastery
MONASTERY

(☑673 44 17; Bolniška ul 20) On your way up to Tartinijev trg are the Minorite Monastery with a wonderful cloister and the Church of St Francis Assisi, built originally in the early 14th century but enlarged and renovated over the centuries. Inside are ceiling frescos, a giant clam shell for donations and the Tartini family's burial plot.

🏃 Activities

The **Maona Tourist Agency** (☑673 45 20; www.maona.si; Cankarjevo nabrežje 7; ☺9am-8pm Mon-Sat, 10am-1pm & 5-7pm Sun) and several other agencies in Piran and Portorož can book you on any number of **cruises** – from a loop that takes in the towns along the coast to day-long excursions to Brioni National Park and Rovinj in Croatia, or Venice and Trieste in Italy.

For **swimming**, Piran has several 'beaches' – rocky areas along Prešernovo nabrežje – where you might get your feet wet. They are a little better on the north side near Punta, but as long as you've come this far keep walking eastward on the paved path for just under 1km to Fiesa, which has a small but clean beach.

🛌 Sleeping

TOP CHOICE **Max Piran**
B&B €€

(☑041 692 928, 673 34 36; www.maxpiran.com; Ul IX Korpusa 26; d €60-70; ✳@☎) Piran's most romantic accommodation has just six rooms, each bearing a woman's name rather than number, in a delightful coral-coloured 18th-century townhouse.

Miracolo di Mare
B&B €€

(☑051 445 511, 921 76 60; www.miracolodimare. si; Tomšičeva ul 23; s €50-55, d €60-70; @☎) A lovely B&B on the coast, the Wonder of the Sea has a dozen charming (though smallish) rooms, some of which (like No 3 and the breakfast room) look on to the most charming raised back garden in Piran. Floors and stairs are wooden (and original).

Val Hostel
HOSTEL €

(☑673 25 55; www.hostel-val.com; Gregorčičeva ul 38a; per person €22-27; @☎) This excellent central hostel on the corner of Vegova ulica has 22 rooms (including a few singles), with shared shower, kitchen and washing machine. It's a deserved favourite with backpackers, and prices include breakfast.

Kamp Fiesa
CAMPGROUND €

(☑674 62 30; autocamp.fiesa@siol.net; adult/child €12/4; ☺May-Sep; ℗) The closest camping ground to Piran is at Fiesa, 4km by road but less than 1km if you follow the coastal path (obalna pešpot) east from the Cathedral of St George. It's tiny and gets crowded in summer, but it's in a quiet valley by two small ponds and right by the beach.

🍴 Eating

There's an outdoor **fruit and vegetable market** (Zelenjavni trg; ☺7am-2pm Mon-Sat) in the small square behind the town hall.

TOP CHOICE **Pri Mari**
MEDITERRANEAN, SLOVENIAN €€

(☑041 616 488, 673 47 35; Dantejeva ul 17; mains €8.50-16; ☺noon-11pm Tue-Sun summer, noon-10pm Tue-Sat, noon-6pm Sun winter) This stylish and welcoming restaurant run by an Italian-Slovenian couple serves inventive Mediterranean and Slovenian dishes. Be sure to book ahead.

Riva Piran
SEAFOOD €€

(☑673 22 25; Gregorčičeva ul 46; mains €8-28; ☺11.30am-midnight) The best waterfront seafood restaurant, and worth patronising, is

Piran

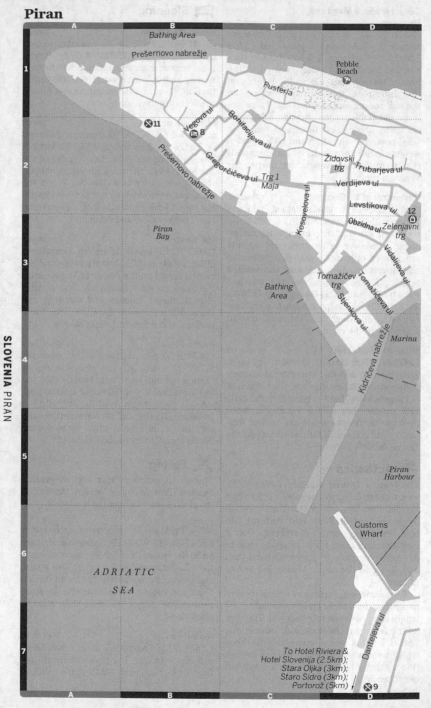

Bathing Area

Prešernovo nabrežje

Pebble Beach **7**

Pusterla

Vegova ul

11

8

Bonifacijeva ul

Gregorčičeva ul

Trg 1 Maja

Prešernovo nabrežje

Židovski trg

Trubarjeva ul

Verdijeva ul

Levstikova ul

12

Kosovelova ul

Obzidna ul

Zelenjavni trg

Piran Bay

Bathing Area

Tomažičev trg

Vidalijeva ul

Tomažičeva ul

Stjenkova ul

Marina

Kidričeva nabrežje

SLOVENIA PIRAN

Piran Harbour

ADRIATIC SEA

Customs Wharf

To Hotel Riviera & Hotel Slovenija (2.5km); Stara Oljka (3km); Staro Sidro (3km); Portorož (5km)

Dantejeva ul

9

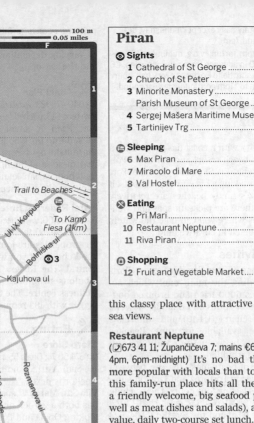

Piran

◉ Sights
1	Cathedral of St George E2
2	Church of St Peter...............................E3
3	Minorite Monastery F3
	Parish Museum of St George ....(see 1)
4	Sergej Mašera Maritime Museum E4
5	Tartinijev Trg E3

⬢ Sleeping
6	Max Piran...F2
7	Miracolo di Mare E6
8	Val Hostel...B2

⬢ Eating
9	Pri Mari...D7
10	Restaurant Neptune..........................E5
11	Riva Piran..B2

⬢ Shopping
12	Fruit and Vegetable Market...............D3

this classy place with attractive decor and sea views.

Restaurant Neptune SEAFOOD €
(☎673 41 11; Župančičeva 7; mains €6-12; ⊙noon-4pm, 6pm-midnight) It's no bad thing to be more popular with locals than tourists, and this family-run place hits all the buttons – a friendly welcome, big seafood platters (as well as meat dishes and salads), and a good-value, daily two-course set lunch.

❶ Information
Banka Koper (Tartinijev trg 12)

Caffe Neptun (☎041 724 237; www.caffeneptun.com; Dantejeva ul 4; per 20min €1; ⊙7am-1am; ⬢)

Post Office (Leninova ul 1)

Tourist Information Centre Piran (☎673 44 40, 673 02 20; www.portoroz.si; Tartinijev trg 2; ⊙9am-8pm summer, 9am-5pm winter)

❶ Getting There & Away
BUS Services run every 20 to 30 minutes to Koper (€2.70, 30 minutes). Other destinations include Ljubljana (€12, three hours) via Divača and Postojna, and Nova Gorica (€10.30, 2¾ hours).

Some five buses go daily to Trieste (€10, 1¾ hours) in Italy, except Sundays. One bus a day heads south for Croatian Istria from June to September, stopping at the coastal towns of Umag, Poreč and Rovinj (€10.30, 2¾ hours).

CATAMARAN There are catamarans from the harbour to Trieste (adult/child €8.30/4.75, 30

SLOVENIA PIRAN

minutes) in Italy daily except Wednesday, departing around 7pm.

MINIBUS From Tartinijev trg, minibuses (€1 on-board, €0.40 in advance from newsagencies, €6 for 20 rides) shuttle to Portorož every half-hour from 5.40am to 11pm continuously year-round.

Portorož

🕮 05 / POP 2900

Every country with a coast has got to have a honky-tonk beach resort and Portorož (Portorose in Italian) is Slovenia's. But the 'Port of Roses' is making a big effort to scrub itself up. Portorož's sandy beaches are relatively clean, and there are pleasant spas and wellness centres where you can take the waters or cover yourself in curative mud.

🏃 Activities

The **beaches** (🕗8am-8pm Apr-Sep) at Portorož, including the main one, which accommodates 6000 fried and bronzed bodies, have water slides and outside showers, and beach chairs (€4.10) and umbrellas (€4.10) are available for rent. Beaches are off-limits between 11pm and 6am and camping is forbidden.

A couple of boats make the run between the main pier in Portorož and Izola in summer on trips lasting four hours. They include the **Meja** (🕿041 664 132; adult/child €10/7; 🕗9.15am Tue & Fri) and the **Svetko** (🕿041 623 191; adult/child €15/10.50; 🕗2.30pm daily). The **Solinarka** (🕿031 653 682; www.solinarka.com; adult/child €12.50/6.25; 🕗varies) tour boat sails from Portorož to Piran and Strunjan and back.

Terme & Wellness Centre Portorož   SPA
(🕿692 80 60; www.lifeclass.net; Obala 43; swimming pool 2/4hr pass Mon-Fri €8/12, Sat & Sun €10/15; 🕗8am-9pm Jun-Sep, 7am-7pm Oct-May, swimming pool 1-8pm Mon-Wed & Fri-Sun, 2-8pm Thu) This place is famous for treatments using sea water and by-products like mud, as well as a host of other therapies and beauty treatments. And there's a pool too.

🛏 Sleeping

Portorož counts upwards of two dozen hotels, and very few fit into the budget category. Many properties close for the winter in October and do not reopen until April or even May. The **Maona Tourist Agency** (🕿674 03 63; Obala 14/b; 🕗9am-8pm Mon-Sat, 10am-1pm & 5-8pm Sun Jul & Aug, 9am-7pm Mon-Fri, 10am-7pm Sat, 10am-1pm Sun Sep-Jun) has

private rooms (s €18-21, d €26-40, tr €36-52) and **apartments** (apt for 2 €40-50), with prices varying depending on both the category and the season.

TOP CHOICE **Kaki Plac**   CAMPGROUND €
(🕿040 476 123; www.adrenaline-check/sea; Lucija; own tent €13, pitched tent €15, lean-to €20; 🕗Apr-Nov; ℗🚻) A small ecofriendly campsite tucked into the woods just outside Lucija on the outskirts of Portorož. Tents come with mattresses and linen, some sit snugly under thatched Istrian lean-tos, so you can sleep like a traditional shepherd (sort of).

Hotel Riviera & Hotel Slovenija   HOTEL €€€
(🕿692 00 00; www.lifeclass.net; Obala 33; s €142-185, d €184-250; ℗🌡@🏊) These four-star sister properties are joined at the hip and are good choices if you want to stay someplace central. The Riviera has 160 rooms, three fabulous swimming pools and an excellent wellness centre. The Slovenija is somewhat bigger with 183 rooms.

🍴 Eating

Staro Sidro   SEAFOOD €
(🕿674 50 74; Obala 55; mains €8-19; 🕗noon-11pm Tue-Sun) A tried-and-true favourite, the Old Anchor is next to the lovely (and landmark) Vila San Marco. It specialises in seafood and has both a garden and a lovely terrace overlooking Obala and Portorož Bay.

Stara Oljka   BALKAN €€
(🕿674 85 55; Obala 20; starters €5-9.60, mains €8.60-24; 🕗10am-midnight) The Old Olive Tree specialises in grills (Balkan, steaks etc), which you can watch being prepared in the open kitchen. There's a large and enticing sea-facing terrace.

ℹ Getting There & Away

BUS Buses leave Portorož for Koper (€2.30, 25 minutes) and Izola (€1.80, 15 minutes) about every 30 minutes throughout the year. Other destinations from Portorož and their daily frequencies are the same as those for Piran.

MINIBUS Minibuses make the loop from the Lucija camping grounds through central Portorož to Piran throughout the year.

EASTERN SLOVENIA

The rolling vine-covered hills of eastern Slovenia are attractive but less dramatic than the Julian Alps or, indeed, the coast. Two cities worth a detour include lively Maribor, Slovenia's second-largest city, and postcard-perfect Ptuj, less than 30km down the road.

Maribor

📞 02 / POP 88,350

Despite being the nation's second-largest city, Maribor has only about a third the population of Ljubljana and often feels more like an overgrown provincial town. It has no unmissable sights but oozes charm thanks to its delightfully patchy Old Town along the Drava River. Pedestrianised central streets buzz with cafes and student life and the riverside Lent district hosts major cultural events – indeed, Maribor was European Capital of Culture in 2012.

👁 Sights

Grajksi Trg   SQUARE

The centre of the Old Town, this square is graced with the 17th-century **Column of St Florian**, dedicated to the patron saint of fire fighters.

Maribor Castle   MUSEUM

(Grajski trg 2) On Grajski Trg, the centre of Maribor's Old Town, is Maribor's 15th-century castle. It contains a **Knights' Hall** (Viteška Dvorana) with a remarkable painted ceiling, the baroque **Loretska Chapel** and a magnificent **rococo staircase**.

Inside the castle, the **Maribor Regional Museum** (📞228 35 51; www.pmuzej-mb.si; Grajski trg; adult/child €3/2; ⊙9am-1pm & 4pm-7pm Mon-Fri, 9am-1pm Sat) has one of the richest collections in Slovenia. The building is undergoing renovation, so parts may be off-limits. On the ground floor there are archaeological, clothing and ethnographic exhibits, including florid, 19th-century beehive panels. Upstairs are rooms devoted to Maribor's history and guilds.

🛏 Sleeping

TOP
CHOICE **Hostel Pekarna**   HOSTEL €

(📞059 180 880; www.mkc-hostelpekarna.si; Ob železnici 16; dm/s/d €17/21/42; 📶🚻) This bright and welcoming hostel south of the river is a converted army bakery. Facilities, from the dorms to the cafe, are up to the minute, and there are several apartments with kitchens.

Hotel Lent   HOTEL €€

(📞250 67 69; www.hotel-lent.si; Dravska ulica 9; s/d €69/89; ❄🛜) Shiny riverside hotel in Lent, with a café out front. Rooms are stylishly decorated and comfortable, though the suites are tricked out in unexpected gangster bling.

🍴 Eating

TOP
CHOICE **Gril Ranca**   BALKAN €

(📞252 55 50; Dravska ul 10; dishes €4.80-7.50; ⊙8am-11pm Mon-Sat, noon-9pm Sun) This place serves simple but scrumptious Balkan grills such as *pljeskavica* (spicy meat patties) and *čevapčiči* (spicy meatballs of beef or pork) in full view of the Drava. It's cool on a hot night.

Pri Florjanu   MEDITERRANEAN €€

(📞059 084 850; Grajski trg 6; starters €5.50-7, mains €9-18; ⊙11am-10pm Mon-Thu, 11am-11pm Fri & Sat; 📷🍸) A great spot in full view of the Column of St Florian, this stylish place has both an open front and an enclosed back terrace and a huge minimalist restaurant in between. It serves inspired Mediterranean food, with a good supply of vegetarian options.

ℹ Information

Tourist Information Centre Maribor (📞234 66 11; www.maribor-pohorje.si; Partinzanska c 6a; ⊙9am-7pm Mon-Fri, 9am-6pm Sat & Sun) Very helpful TIC in kiosk opposite the Franciscan church.

ℹ Getting There & Away

BUS Services are frequent to Celje (€6.7, 1½ hours), Murska Sobota (€6.30, 1¼ hours), Ptuj (€3.60, 45 minutes) and Ljubljana (€12.40, three hours).

TRAIN From Ljubljana there is the ICS express service (€15.20, 1¾ hours), or more frequent slower trains (€9, 2½ hours). Both stop at Celje.

Ptuj

📞 02 / POP 19,010

Rising gently above a wide valley, Ptuj forms a symphony of red-tile roofs best viewed from across the Drava River. One of the oldest towns in Slovenia, Ptuj equals Ljubljana in terms of historical importance but the compact medieval core, with its castle, museums, monasteries and churches, can easily be seen in a day.

👁 Sights

Ptuj's Gothic centre, with its Renaissance and baroque additions, can be viewed on a 'walking tour' taking in Minoritski trg and Mestni trg, Slovenski trg, Prešernova ulica, Muzejski trg and Ptuj Castle.

Ptuj Castle
CASTLE

(Grad Ptuj; ☑787 92 45, 748 03 60; Na Gradu 1) Ptuj castle is an agglomeration of styles from the 14th to the 18th centuries. It houses the **Ptuj Regional Museum** (☑787 92 30; www. pok-muzej-ptuj.si; adult/child €4/2.50; ⊙9am-6pm Mon-Fri, 9am-8pm Sat & Sun summer, 9am-5pm daily winter) but is worth the trip for views of Ptuj and the Drava. The shortest way to the castle is to follow narrow Grajska ulica, which leads to a covered wooden stairway and the castle's Renaissance **Peruzzi Portal** (1570).

✦ Festivals

Kurentovanje
CARNIVAL

(www.kurentovanje.net) Kurentovanje is a rite of spring celebrated for 10 days in February leading up to Shrove Tuesday; it's the most popular and best-known folklore event in Slovenia.

🛏 Sleeping

TOP CHOICE MuziKafe
HOTEL €€

(☑787 88 60; www.muzikafe.si; Vrazov trg 1; 🛜) This quirky cracker of a place is tucked away off Jadranska ulica. Everything is bright, with each room idiosyncratically decorated by the hotel's artist owners. There's a terrace café, plus a vaulted brick cellar for musical and artistic events.

Hotel Mitra
HOTEL €€€

(☑051 603 069, 787 74 55; www.hotel-mitra.si; Prešernova ul 6; s €62-88, d €106; 🅿⚙@🛜) This pleasant hotel has 25 generous-sized guest rooms and four humongous suites, each with its own name and story and specially commissioned paintings on the wall. There are lovely Oriental carpets on the original wooden floors and a wellness centre in an old courtyard cellar.

Hostel Eva
HOSTEL €

(☑040 226 522, 771 24 41; www.hostel-ptuj.si; Jadranska ul 22; per person €12-20) This welcoming, up-to-date hostel connected to a bike shop (per-day rental €10) has six rooms containing two to six beds and a large light-filled kitchen.

✗ Eating

TOP CHOICE Gostilna Ribič
GOSTILNA €€

(☑749 06 35; Dravska ul 9; mains €9.50-20; ⊙10am-11pm Sun-Thu, 10am-midnight Fri & Sat) Arguably the best restaurant in Ptuj, the Angler Inn faces the river, with an enormous terrace, and the speciality here is – not surprisingly – fish, especially herbed and baked pike perch. The seafood soup served in a bread loaf bowl is exceptional.

Amadeus
GOSTILNA €€

(☑771 70 51; Prešernova ul 36; mains €6.50-20; ⊙noon-10pm Mon-Thu, noon-11pm Fri & Sat, noon-4pm Sun) This pleasant *gostilna* (inn-like restaurant) above a pub and near the foot of the road to the castle serves *štruklji* (dumplings with herbs and cheese), steak, pork and fish.

ℹ Information

Tourist Information Centre Ptuj (☑779 60 11; www.ptuj.info; Slovenski trg 5; ⊙8am-8pm summer, 9am-6pm winter)

ℹ Getting There & Away

BUS Services to Maribor (€3.60, 45 minutes) go every couple of hours, less frequently at weekends.

TRAIN Connections are better for trains than buses, with plentiful departures to Ljubljana (€8 to €13.60) direct or via Pragersko. Up to a dozen trains go to Maribor (€2.90 to €5.90, 50 minutes).

UNDERSTAND SLOVENIA

History

Early Years

Slovenes can make a credible claim to having invented democracy. By the early 7th century, their Slavic ancestors had founded the Duchy of Carantania (Karantanija), based at Krn Castle (now Karnburg in Austria). Ruling dukes were elected by enobled commoners and invested before ordinary citizens.

This unique model was noted by the 16th-century French political philosopher Jean Bodin, whose work was a reference for Thomas Jefferson when he wrote the American Declaration of Independence in 1776.

Carantania (later Carinthia) was fought over by the Franks and Magyars from the 8th to 10th centuries, and later divided up among Austro-Germanic nobles and bishops.

The Habsburgs & Napoleon

Between the late 13th and early 16th centuries, almost all the lands inhabited by Slovenes, with the exception of the Venetian-controlled coastal towns, came under the domination of the Habsburgs, ruled from Vienna.

Austrian rule continued until 1918, apart from a brief interlude between 1809 and 1813 when Napoleon created six so-called Illyrian Provinces from Slovenian and Croatian regions and made Ljubljana the capital.

Napoleon proved a popular conqueror as his relatively liberal regime de-Germanised the education system. Slovene was taught in schools for the first time, leading to an awakening of national consciousness. In tribute, Ljubljana still has a French Revolution Sq (Trg Francoske Revolucije) with a column bearing a likeness of the French emperor.

World Wars I & II

Fighting during WWI was particularly savage along the Soča Valley – the Isonzo Front– which was occupied by Italy then retaken by German-led Austro-Hungarian forces. The war ended with the collapse of Austria-Hungary, which handed western Slovenia to Italy as part of postwar reparations.

Northern Carinthia, including the towns of Beljak and Celovec (now Villach and Klagenfurt), voted to stay with Austria in a 1920 plebiscite. What remained of Slovenia joined fellow south (jug) Slavs in forming the Kingdom of Serbs, Croats and Slovenes, later Yugoslavia.

Nazi occupation in WWII was for the most part resisted by Slovenian partisans, though after Italy capitulated in 1943 the anti-partisan Slovenian Domobranci (Home Guards) were active in the west. To prevent their nemeses, the communists, from taking political control in liberated areas, the Domobranci threw their support behind the Germans.

The war ended with Slovenia regaining Italian-held areas from Piran to Bovec, but losing Trst (Trieste) and part of Gorica (Gorizia).

Tito's Yugoslavia

In Tito's Yugoslavia in the 1960s and '70s, Slovenia, with only 8% of the national population, was the economic powerhouse, creating up to 20% of the national GDP.

But by the 1980s the federation had become increasingly Serb-dominated, and Slovenes feared they would lose their political autonomy. In free elections, Slovenes voted overwhelmingly to break away from Yugoslavia and did so on 25 June 1991. A 10-day war that left 66 people dead followed; Yugoslavia swiftly signed a truce in order to concentrate on regaining control of coastal Croatia.

From Independence to Today

Shortly after the withdrawal of the federal army from Slovenian soil on 25 October 1991, Slovenia got a new constitution that provided for a bicameral parliamentary system of government.

The head of state, the president, is elected directly for a maximum of two five-year terms. Milan Kučan held that role from independence until 2002, when the late Janez Drnovšek (1950–2008), a former prime minister, was elected. Diplomat Danilo Türk has been president since 2007, having been re-elected in 2012.

Executive power is vested in the prime minister and his cabinet. The current premier is Janez Janša, who was returned to power in early 2012 after 3½ years in opposition.

Slovenia was admitted to the UN in 1992 as the 176th member-state. In May 2004, Slovenia entered the EU as a full member and less than three years later adopted the euro, replacing the tolar as the national currency.

People

The population of Slovenia is largely homogeneous. Just over 83% are ethnic Slovenes, with the remainder Serbs, Croats, Bosnians, Albanians and Roma; there are also small enclaves of Italians and Hungarians, who have special deputies looking after their interests in parliament.

Slovenes are ethnically Slavic, typically hardworking, multilingual and extrovert. Around 60% of Slovenes identify themselves as Catholics.

Arts

Slovenia's most cherished writer is the Romantic poet France Prešeren (1800–49). His patriotic yet humanistic verse was a driving force in raising Slovene national consciousness. Fittingly, a stanza of his poem 'Zdravljica' (A Toast) forms the lyrics of the national anthem.

Many of Ljubljana's most characteristic architectural features, including its recurring pyramid motif, were added by celebrated Slovenian architect Jože Plečnik (1872–1957), whose work fused classical building principles and folk-art traditions.

Postmodernist painting and sculpture were more or less dominated from the 1980s by the multimedia group NeueSlowenische Kunst (NSK) and the artists' cooperative Irwin. It also spawned the internationally known industrial-music group Laibach, whose leader, Tomaž Hostnik, died tragically in 1983 when he hanged himself from a *kozolec*, the traditional (and iconic) hayrack found only in Slovenia.

Slovenia's vibrant music scene embraces rave, techno, jazz, punk, thrash-metal and *chanson* (torch songs from the likes of Vita Mavrič); the most popular local rock group is Siddharta, formed in 1995 and still going strong. There's also been a folk-music revival: keep an ear out for the groups Katice and Katalena, who play traditional Slovenian music with a modern twist, and the vocalist Brina.

Films

Well-received Slovenian films in recent years include *Kruh in Mleko* (Bread & Milk, 2001), the tragic story by Jan Cvitkovič of a dysfunctional small-town family, and Damjan Kozole's *Rezerni Deli* (Spare Parts, 2003), about the trafficking of illegal immigrants through Slovenia from Croatia to Italy.

Much lighter fare is *Petelinji Zajtrk* (Rooster's Breakfast, 2007), a romance by Marko Naberšnik set on the Austrian border, and the bizarre US-made documentary *Big River Man* (John Maringouin, 2009) about an overweight marathon swimmer who takes on – wait for it – the Amazon and succeeds.

Environment

Slovenia is amazingly green; indeed, 58% of its total surface area is covered in forest and it's growing. Slovenia is home to almost 3200 plant species – some 70 of which are indigenous.

Triglav National Park is particularly rich in native flowering plants. Among the more peculiar endemic fauna in Slovenia is a blind salamander called *Proteus anguinus* that lives deep in Karst caves, can survive for years without eating and has been called a 'living fossil'.

Food & Drink

Slovenia boasts an incredibly diverse cuisine, but except for a few national favourites such as *žlikrofi* (pasta stuffed with cheese, bacon

and chives) and *jota* (hearty bean soup) and incredibly rich desserts like *gibanica* (a layer cake stuffed with nuts, cheese and apple), you're not likely to encounter many of these regional specialities on menus.

Dishes like *brodet* (fish soup) from the coast, *ajdovi žganci z ocvirki* (buckwheat 'porridge' with savoury pork crackling) and salad greens doused in *bučno olje* (pumpkin-seed oil) are generally eaten at home.

A *gostilna* or *gostišče* (inn) or *restavracija* (restaurant) more frequently serves *rižota* (risotto), *klobasa* (sausage), *zrezek* (cutlet/steak), *golaž* (goulash) and *paprikaš* (piquant chicken or beef 'stew'). *Riba* (fish) is excellent and usually priced by the *dag* (100g). Common in Slovenia are such Balkan favourites as *cevapčiči* (spicy meatballs of beef or pork) and *pljeskavica* (spicy meat patties), often served with *kajmak* (a type of clotted cream).

You can snack cheaply on takeaway pizza slices or pieces of *burek* (€2), flaky pastry stuffed with meat, cheese or apple. Alternatives include *štruklji* (cottage-cheese dumplings) and *palačinke* (thin sweet pancakes).

Wine, Beer & Brandy

Distinctively Slovenian wines include peppery red Teran (made from Refošk grapes in the Karst region), Cviček (a dry light red – almost rosé – wine from eastern Slovenia) and Malvazija (a straw-colour white from the coast that is light and dry). Slovenes are justly proud of their top vintages, but cheaper bar-standard *odprto vino* (open wine) sold by the decilitre (100mL) is just so-so.

Pivo (beer), whether *svetlo* (lager) or *temno* (porter), is best on *točeno* (draught) but always available in cans and bottles too.

There are dozens of kinds of *žganje* (fruit brandy) available, including *češnjevec* (made with cherries), *sadjevec* (mixed fruit), *brinjevec* (juniper), *hruška* (pears, also called *viljamovka*) and *slivovka* (plums).

SURVIVAL GUIDE

Directory A–Z
Accommodation

Accommodation runs the gamut from riverside camping grounds, hostels, mountain huts, cosy *gostišča* (inns) and farmhouses, to elegant castle hotels and five-star hotels in Ljubljana, so you'll usually have little trouble finding accommodation to fit your budget, except perhaps at the height of the season (July and August) on the coast, at Bled or Bohinj, or in Ljubljana.

The following price ranges refer to a double room, with en suite toilet and bath or shower and breakfast, unless otherwise indicated. Virtually every municipality in the land levies a tourist tax of between €0.50 and €1 per person per night.

€ less than €50

€€ €50 to €100

€€€ more than €100

FARMSTAYS

Hundreds of working farms in Slovenia offer accommodation to paying guests, either in private rooms in the farmhouse itself or in Alpine-style guesthouses. Many farms offer outdoor sport activities and allow you to help out with the farm chores if you feel so inclined.

Expect to pay about €15 per person in a room with shared bathroom and breakfast (from €20 for half-board) in the low season (September to mid-December and mid-January to June), rising in the high season (July and August) to a minimum €17 per person (from €25 for half-board).

For more information, contact the **Association of Tourist Farms of Slovenia** (Združenje Turističnih Kmetij Slovenije; ☑041 435 528, 03-425 55 11; www.farmtourism.si; Trnoveljska cesta 1) or check with the Slovenian Tourist Board.

Business Hours

The *delovni čas* (opening times) are usually posted on the door. *Odprto* is 'open', *zaprto* is 'closed'. The following hours are standard and reviews won't list business hours unless they differ from these.

Banks 9am to 5pm weekdays, and (rarely) from 8am until noon on Saturday.

Grocery stores 8am to 7pm weekdays and 8am until 1pm on Saturday.

Museums 10am to 6pm Tuesday to Sunday. Winter hours may be shorter.

Post offices 8am to 6pm or 7pm weekdays and until noon on Saturday.

Restaurant Hours vary but count on 11am to 10pm daily. Bars are usually open from 11am to midnight Sunday to Thursday and to 1am or 2am on Friday and Saturday.

Embassies & Consulates

All of the following are in Ljubljana:

Australian Consulate (☑01-234 86 75; Železna cesta 14; ☺9am-1pm Mon-Fri)

Canadian Consulate (☑01-252 44 44; 49a Linhartova cesta; ☺8am-noon Mon, Wed & Fri)

French Embassy (☑01-479 04 00; Barjanska cesta 1; ☺8.30am-12.30pm Mon-Fri)

German Embassy (☑01-479 03 00; Prešernova cesta 27; ☺9am-noon Mon-Thu, 9-11am Fri)

Irish Embassy (☑01-300 89 70; 1st fl, Palača Kapitelj, Poljanski nasip 6; ☺9.30am-12.30pm & 2.30-4pm Mon-Fri)

Netherlands Embassy (☑01-420 14 61; 1st fl, Palača Kapitelj, Poljanski nasip 6; ☺9am-noon Mon-Fri)

New Zealand Consulate (☑01-580 30 55; Verovškova ulica 57; ☺8am-3pm Mon-Fri)

UK Embassy (☑01-200 39 10; 4th fl, Trg Republike 3; ☺9am-noon Mon-Fri)

US Embassy (☑01-200 55 00; Prešernova cesta 31; ☺9-11.30am & 1-3pm Mon-Fri)

Festivals & Events

The official website of the **Slovenian Tourist Board** (www.slovenia.info), maintains a comprehensive list of major cultural events.

Food

The following price ranges are a rough approximation for a two-course sit-down meal for one person, with a drink. Many restaurants offer an excellent-value set menu of two or even three courses at lunch. These typically run from €5 to €9.

€ less than €15

€€ €16 to €30

€€€ over €30

Gay & Lesbian Travellers

National laws ban discrimination in employment and other areas on the basis of sexual preference. In recent years a highly visible campaign against homophobia has been put in place across the country. Outside Ljubljana, however, there is little evidence of a gay presence, much less a lifestyle.

Roza Klub (Klub K4 ; www.klubk4.org; Kersnikova ulica 4; ☺10pm-6am Sun Sep-Jun) in Ljubljana is made up of the gay and lesbian branches of **KUC** (www.skuc.org), which stands for Študentski Kulturni Center (Student Cultural

Centre) but is no longer student-orientated as such. It organises the gay and lesbian **Ljubljana Pride** (www.ljubljanapride.org) parade in late June and the **Gay & Lesbian Film Festival** (www.ljudmila.org/siqrd/fglf) in late November/early December. The gay male branch, **Magnus** (skucmagnus@hotmail.com), deals with AIDS prevention, networking and is behind the Kulturni Center Q (Q Cultural Centre) in Ljubljana's Metelkova Mesto, which includes Klub Tiffany for gay men and Klub Monokel for gay women.

A monthly publication called **Narobe** (Upside Down; www.narobe.si) is in Slovene only, though you might be able to at least glean some basic information from the listings.

Internet Access

Virtually every hotel and hostel now has internet access – a computer for guests' use (free or for a small fee), wi-fi – or both. Most of the country's tourist information centres offer free (or low-cost) access and many libraries in Slovenia have free terminals. Many cities and towns have at least one internet cafe (though they usually only have a handful of terminals), or even free wi-fi in town squares.

Money

The official currency is the euro. Exchanging cash is simple at banks, major post offices, travel agencies and *menjalnice* (bureaux de change), although many don't accept travellers cheques. Major credit and debit cards are accepted almost everywhere, and ATMs are ubiquitous.

Post

The Slovenian postal system (*Pošta Slovenije*), recognised by its bright yellow logo, offers a wide variety of services – from selling stamps and telephone cards to making photocopies and changing money. News stands also sell *znamke* (stamps). Post offices can sell you boxes.

Public Holidays

If a holiday falls on a Sunday, then the following Monday becomes the holiday.

New Year 1 and 2 January

Prešeren Day (Slovenian Culture Day) 8 February

Easter & Easter Monday March/April

Insurrection Day 27 April

Labour Day holidays 1 and 2 May

National Day 25 June

Assumption Day 15 August

Reformation Day 31 October

All Saints Day 1 November

Christmas Day 25 December

Independence Day 26 December

Telephone

Public telephones in Slovenia require a *telefonska kartica* or *telekartica* (telephone card) available at post offices and some newsstands. Phonecards cost €2.70/4/7.50/14.60 for 25/50/100/300 *impulzov* (impulses, or units).

To call Slovenia from abroad, dial the international access code, ☑386 (the country code for Slovenia), the area code (minus the initial zero) and the number. There are six area codes in Slovenia (☑01 to ☑05 and ☑07). To call abroad from Slovenia, dial ☑00 followed by the country and area codes and then the number. Numbers beginning with ☑80 in Slovenia are toll-free.

MOBILE PHONES

Network coverage amounts to more than 95% of the country. Mobile numbers carry the prefix ☑030 and ☑040 (SiMobil), ☑031, ☑041, ☑051 and ☑071 (Mobitel) and ☑070 (Tušmobil).

Slovenia uses GSM 900, which is compatible with the rest of Europe and Australia but not with the North American GSM 1900 or the totally different Japanese system. SIM cards with €5 credit are available for around €15 from **SiMobil** (www.simobil.si), **Mobitel** (www.mobitel.si) and **Tušmobil** (www.tusmobil.sil). Top-up scratch cards are available at post offices, news stands and petrol stations.

All three networks have outlets throughout Slovenia, including in Ljubljana.

Tourist Information

The **Slovenian Tourist Board** (Slovenska Turistična Organizacija, STO; ☑01-589 18 40; www.slovenia.info; Dunajska cesta 156), based in Ljubljana, is the umbrella organisation for tourist promotion in Slovenia, and produces a number of excellent brochures, pamphlets and booklets in English.

Walk-in visitors in Ljubljana can head to the **Slovenian Tourist Information Centre** (STIC; ☑306 45 76; www.slovenia.info; Krekov trg 10; ☉8am-9pm Jun-Sep, 8am-7pm Oct-May). In addition, the organisation oversees another five dozen or so local tourist offices and bureaus called 'tourist information centres' (TICs) across the country.

In the capital, the **Ljubljana Tourist Information Centre** (TIC; ☎306 12 15; www.visitljubljana.si; Adamič-Lundrovo nabrežje 2; ☑8am-9pm Jun-Sep, 8am-7pm Oct-May) knows just about everything there is to know about Ljubljana and almost as much about the rest of Slovenia. There's a branch at the train station.

Visas

Citizens of nearly all European countries, as well as Australia, Canada, Israel, Japan, New Zealand and the USA, do not require visas to visit Slovenia for stays of up to 90 days. Holders of EU and Swiss passports can enter using a national identity card.

Those who do require visas (including South Africans) can get them for up to 90 days at any Slovenian embassy or consulate – see the website of the **Ministry of Foreign Affairs** (www.mzz.gov.si) for a full listing. They cost €35 regardless of the type of visa or length of validity.

Getting There & Away

Border formalities with Slovenia's fellow European Union neighbours, Italy, Austria and Hungary, are virtually nonexistent. Croatia hopes to enter the EU in 2013 and plans to implement the Schengen border rules soon after. Until then expect a somewhat closer inspection of your documents – national ID (for EU citizens) or passport and, in some cases, visa when travelling to/from Croatia.

Air

Slovenia's only international airport is Ljubljana's **Jože Pučnik Airport** (LJU/Aerodrom Ljubljana; ☎04-206 19 81; www.lju-airport.si/eng; Zgornji Brnik 130a, Brnik) at Brnik, 27km north of Ljubljana. In the arrivals hall there's a **Slovenia Tourist Information Centre** (STIC; ☑11am-11pm Mon, Wed & Fri, 10am-10pm Tue & Thu, 10.30am-10.30pm Sat, 12.30pm-12.30am Sun) desk, a hotel-booking telephone and ATM. Car-rental agencies have outlets opposite the terminal.

From its base at Brnik, the Slovenian flag-carrier, **Adria Airways** (☎01-369 10 10, 080 13 00; www.adria-airways.com), serves some 20 European destinations on regularly scheduled flights.

Other airlines with regularly scheduled flights to and from Ljubljana include:

Air France (☎01-244 34 47; www.airfrance.com/si) Daily flights to Paris (CDG).

ČSA Czech Airlines (☎04-206 17 50; www.czechairlines.com) Flights to Prague.

EasyJet (☎04-206 16 77; www.easyjet.com) Low-cost daily flights to London Stansted.

JAT Airways (☎01-231 43 40; www.jat.com) Daily flights to Belgrade.

Lufthansa (☎01-434 72 46; www.lufthansa.com; Gosposvetska cesta 6) Code-shared flights with Adria.

Montenegro Airlines (☎04-259 42 52; www.montenegroairlines.com) Twice weekly flight to Podgorica.

Turkish Airlines (☎04-206 16 80; www.turkishairlines.com) Flights to Istanbul.

Land

BUS

International bus destinations from Ljubljana include Serbia, Germany, Croatia, Bosnia and Hercegovina, Macedonia, Italy and Scandinavia. You can also catch buses to Italy and Croatia from coastal towns, including Piran and Koper.

TRAIN

It is possible to travel to Italy, Austria, Germany, Croatia and Hungary by train; Ljubljana is the main hub, although you can, for example, hop on international trains in certain cities like Maribor and Ptuj. International train travel can be expensive. It is sometimes cheaper to travel as far as you can on domestic routes before crossing any borders.

Sea

Piran sends ferries to Trieste daily and catamarans to Venice at least once a week in season. There's also a catamaran between nearby Izola and Venice in summer months.

Getting Around

Bicycle

Cycling is a popular way of getting around. Bikes can be transported for €2.80 in the baggage compartments of some IC and regional trains. Larger buses can also carry bikes as luggage. Larger towns and cities have dedicated bicycle lanes and traffic lights.

ROAD RULES

» Drive on the right.

» Speed limits: 50km/h in town, 90km/h on secondary roads, 100km/h on highways; 130km/h on motorways.

» Seat belts are compulsory; motorcyclists must wear helmets.

» All motorists must illuminate their headlights throughout the day.

» Permitted blood-alcohol level for drivers is 0.05%.

Bus

Buy your ticket at the *avtobusna postaja* (bus station) or simply pay the driver as you board. In Ljubljana you should book your seat at least a day in advance if you're travelling on Friday, or to destinations in the mountains or on the coast on a public holiday. Bus services are restricted on Sunday and holidays.

A range of bus companies serve the country, but prices are uniform: €3.10/5.60/9.20/16.80 for 25/50/100/200km of travel.

Timetables in the bus station, or posted on a wall or column outside, list destinations and departure times. If you cannot find your bus listed or don't understand the schedule, get help from the *blagajna vozovnice* (information or ticket window), which are usually one and the same. *Odhodi* means 'departures' while *prihodi* is 'arrivals'.

Car & Motorcycle

Roads in Slovenia are generally good. There are two main motorway corridors – between Maribor and the coast (via the flyover at Črni Kal) and from the Karavanke Tunnel into Austria to Zagreb in Croatia – intersecting at the Ljubljana ring road, with a branch from Postojna to Nova Gorica. Motorways are numbered from A1 to A10 (for *avtocesta*).

Tolls are no longer paid separately on the motorways, instead all cars must display a *vinjeta* (road-toll sticker) on the windscreen. They cost €15/30/95 for a week/month/year for cars and €7.50/25/47.50 for motorbikes and are available at petrol stations, post offices and certain news stands and tourist information centres. These stickers will already be in place on a rental car; failure to display such a sticker risks a fine of up to €300.

Dial ☎1987 for roadside assistance.

HIRING A CAR

Renting a car in Slovenia allows access to cheaper out-of-centre hotels and farm or village homestays. Rentals from international firms such as Avis, Budget, Europcar and Hertz vary in price; expect to pay from €40/210 a day/week, including unlimited mileage, collision damage waiver (CDW), theft protection (TP), Personal Accident Insurance (PAI) and taxes. Some smaller agencies have somewhat more competitive rates; booking on the internet is always cheaper.

Train

Much of the country is accessible by rail, run by the national operator, **Slovenian Railways** (Slovenske Železnice, SŽ; ☎01-291 33 32; www.slo-zeleznice.si). The website has an easy-to-use timetable.

Figure on travelling at about 60km/h except on the fastest InterCity Slovenia (ICS) express trains that run between Ljubljana and Maribor (€13.60, 1¾ hours) at an average speed of 90km/h.

The provinces are served by *regionalni vlaki* (regional trains) and *primestni vlaki* (city trains), but the fastest are InterCity trains (IC).

An 'R' next to the train number on the timetable means seat reservations are available. If the 'R' is boxed, seat reservations are obligatory.

Purchase your ticket before travelling at the *železniška postaja* (train station); buying it from the conductor onboard costs an additional €2.50. Invalid tickets or fare dodging earn a €40 fine.

Ukraine

Includes »

Best Places to Eat

» Spotykach (p922)

» Pervak (p922)

» Gogol Mogol (p937)

» Masonic Restaurant (p929)

» Vegeteriya (p941)

Best Places to Stay

» Sunflower B&B (p921)

» Vintage (p929)

» Leopolis Hotel (p929)

» On the Corner (p931)

» Villa Sofia (p943)

Why Go?

Big, diverse and largely undiscovered, Ukraine (Україна) is one of Europe's last genuine travel frontiers, a poor nation rich in colour-splashed tradition, warm-hearted people and off-the-map travel experiences.

'Ukraine' means 'land on the edge', an apt title for this slab of Eurasia in many ways. This is the Slavic hinterland on Europe's periphery, a mere two decades into a troubled independence and dogged by Second World political anguish, ethnic divisions and deep-rooted corruption. But it's a country whose peoples can pull together when need arises, most recently for the remarkably successful Euro 2012 soccer championships which showed off the country at its hospitable best.

Most visitors head for capital Kyiv, but architecturally rich Lviv and hedonistic Odesa are attracting ever greater numbers. Add a spot of hiking or skiing in the Carpathians and the balmy beaches of Crimea, and Ukraine becomes a much more diverse destination than many might imagine.

When to Go
Kyiv

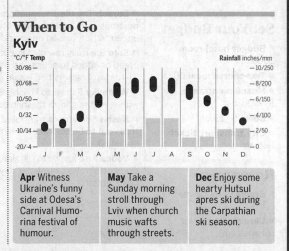

Apr Witness Ukraine's funny side at Odesa's Carnival Humorina festival of humour.

May Take a Sunday morning stroll through Lviv when church music wafts through streets.

Dec Enjoy some hearty Hutsul apres ski during the Carpathian ski season.

AT A GLANCE

» **Currency** Hryvnya (uah)

» **Language** Ukrainian, Russian

» **Money** ATMs widespread; credit cards accepted at most hotels

» **Visas** Not required for EU, UK, US and Canadian citizens for stays of up to 90 days

Fast Facts

» **Area** 603,628 sq km

» **Capital** Kyiv

» **Country code** ☎380

» **Emergency** ☎112

Exchange Rates

Australia	A$1	8.51uah
Canada	C$1	8.02uah
Euro Zone	€1	10.42uah
Japan	¥100	8.64uah
New Zealand	NZ$1	6.82uah
UK	UK£1	12.33uah
USA	US$1	8.15uah

Set Your Budget

» **Budget hotel room** 200uah

» **Two-course meal** 60uah

» **Museum entrance** 10–30uah

» **Beer** 15–25uah

» **City transport ticket** 1–2uah

Resources

» **Brama** (www.brama.com)

» **Ukraine.com** (www.ukraine.com)

Connections

Ukraine is well linked to its neighbours, particularly Russia and Belarus, with whom it shares the former Soviet rail system. Kyiv is connected by bus or train to Moscow, St Petersburg, Minsk, Warsaw and Budapest, as well as other Eastern European capitals. Odesa is the hub for travelling to the Moldovan capital Chişinău and Tiraspol in Transdniester, with several daily buses and one train a day making the trip. The city also has ferries to Bulgaria, Georgia and Turkey, though the service is erratic. From Uzhhorod it's a short journey to the international mainline into Europe at Chop, connecting Ukraine with Slovakia and Hungary. Lviv is the biggest city servicing the Polish border and an ever-increasing number of travellers are taking budget flights to Poland then crossing the border to Lviv by bus or train. It's also possible to take no-frills flights to Budapest or Bratislava, and continue to Ukraine from there by train.

ITINERARIES

One Week

Begin by sampling the charms of Kyiv before heading either south to party in Odesa or west for a more refined and relaxed time in Lviv. Alternatively, take in Kyiv and Lviv then trundle on down into the Carpathian mountains for a spot of skiing, hiking or mountain biking.

Two Weeks

Spend three days in Kyiv, two in Lviv, then pass through rocking Odesa to Crimea, making Yalta your base and being sure to visit Bakhchysaray.

Essential Food & Drink

» **Borsch** The Ukrainian national soup, which is made with beetroot, pork fat and herbs. There's also an aromatic 'green' variety, based on sorrel.

» **Salo** Basically raw pig fat, cut into slices and eaten with bread or added to soups and other dishes. Look out for the 'Ukrainian Snickers bar' – salo in chocolate.

» **Varenyky** Similar to Polish pierogi – pasta pockets filled with everything from mashed potato to sour cherries.

» **Kasha** Sometimes translated as 'porridge', but usually turns out to be buckwheat swimming in milk and served for breakfast.

» **Vodka** Also known in Ukraine as horilka, it accompanies every celebration, red-letter day and get-together – in copious amounts.

KYIV

☑044 / POP 2.8 MILLION

The local ancients must have been spoilt for choice when they needed a pretty spot to settle down – at least one can't help thinking this when in Kyiv (Київ), the birthplace of Eastern Slavic civilisation, which spread from here as far as Asia's Pacific coast. Its lovely forested hills overlook the Dnipro – a river so wide that birds fall down before reaching its middle, as writer Nikolay Gogol jokingly remarked.

Those hills, numbered seven as in Rome, cradle a wonderfully eclectic city that has preserved the legacy of its former possessors – Viking chieftains turned ancient Rus princes, plus Polish and Lithuanian kings, Russian tsars and Soviet dictators. Sometimes chaotic central Asia, other times quaint Central Europe, Kyiv (many agree) is the former USSR's most pleasant city, worth at least a week of any traveller's time.

◉ Sights

At last count, Kyiv had almost 50 museums documenting the history of everything from bread to film to decorative arts. The city's tourism website has the full list.

TOP CHOICE Caves Monastery   MONASTERY

(www.kplavra.kiev.ua; vul Lavrska 9; grounds 3uah, caves & exhibitions adult/child 50/25uah; ⊗8am-7pm Apr-Oct, 9am-6pm Nov-Mar; ⑤Arsenalna) Rolling across 28 hectares of wooded slopes above the Dnipro River, the Caves Monastery Complex, also known as the Kyiv-Pechersk Lavra, deserves at least half a day. It is the most popular tourist site in the city, a highlight of visiting Ukraine and arguably the spiritual heart of the Ukrainian nation. The site is divided into the Upper Lavra (a complex of churches and museums) and the Lower Lavra (the caves themselves).

Entering through the Upper Lavra's Trinity Gate takes you onto a square dominated by the Trinity Gate Church and the Dormition Cathedral. Further into the complex, there are several museums – many of which are of marginal interest – and the superb **Refectory Church of St Antoniy and St Feodosiy**, which contains beautifully painted frescos. There's a great view across the Dnipro from behind the church.

Continuing past the church and down under the flying buttresses will take you to the two sets of **caves** in the Lower Lavra, a few minutes' walk away; before you enter, buy a candle to light your way at a kiosk. Inside the caves, dozens of niches contain glass-topped coffins holding the blanketed bodies of the monks; believers kneel and pray at the coffins, and kiss the glass tops. It's all very spooky and it can be claustrophobic on busy days.

The **excursion bureau** (☑280 3071), just to the left past the main entrance to the Upper Lavra, sells two-hour guided tours in various languages (500uah per group of up to 10 people). Book in advance during peak periods. All tickets (even the 3uah pass to the grounds) can now be bought in advance through the website, but you'll have to have some knowledge of Ukrainian to do this.

St Sophia's Cathedral   CHURCH

(pl Sofiyska; grounds/cathedral/bell tower 3/53/13uah; ⊗grounds 9am-7pm, cathedral 10am-6pm Thu-Tue, 10am-5pm Wed; ⑤Maydan Nezalezhnosti) The city's oldest standing church is the magnificent St Sophia's Cathedral. Built from 1017 to 1031 and named after Hagia Sofia (Holy Wisdom) Cathedral in İstanbul, its Byzantine plan and decoration announced the new religious and political authority of Kyiv. Prince Yaroslav, the 10th-century prince under whom Kyiv reached the height of its cultural and military strength, is buried here. Perhaps the most memorable aspect of a visit is the cathedral's interior, where you'll find 11th-century mosaics and frescos.

Andriyivsky Uzviz   STREET

(⑤Kontraktova Pl) Kyiv's tourist epicentre is Andriyivsky Uzviz (Andrew's Descent) and no visit is complete without an amble up or down its steep, cobblestoned length, hemmed by a ribbon or craft and art stalls. One of Kyiv's oldest streets, it's named after Apostle Andrew who is believed to have climbed the hill here, affixed a cross to its summit and prophesied that this would be the site of a great Christian city. You can avoid the incline by taking the **funicular** (tickets 2uah; ⊗6.30am-11pm; ⑤Poshtova Pl) to the top of the hill, where you'll find **St Michael's Monastery**, with its seven-cupola, periwinkle cathedral. A little way down from the upper end of the street stands baroque **St Andrew's Church** (⊗10am-8pm), built in 1754 by Italian architect Bartelomeo Rastrelli, who also designed the Winter Palace in St Petersburg.

The Uzviz's unmissable sight is the **Museum of One Street** (Andriyivsky Uzviz 2b; admission 20uah; ⊗noon-6pm Tue-Sun), a jumble-sale nostalgia collection showcasing the lives of dressmakers, soldiers, shopkeepers,

Ukraine Highlights

1 Inspect Kyiv's collection of mummified monks by candlelight at the **Caves Monastery** (p915).

2 Make an ascent of **Andriyivsky Uzviz** (p915), Kyiv's most atmospheric street.

3 Do a spot of cobble-surfing in **Lviv's historical centre** (p925) packed with churches, museums and eccentric restaurants.

4 Climb to the top of Ukraine's highest peak, **Mt Hoverla** (p931).

5 Take a stroll through the island town of **Kamyanets-Podilsky** (p932) to its photogenic fortress.

6 See how the medieval Tatars lived at Bakhchysaray's **Khan's Palace** (p944).

7 Head south to Ukraine's capital of hedonism, **Odesa** (p934), with its thumping nightlife and balmy Black Sea beach scene.

Central Kyiv

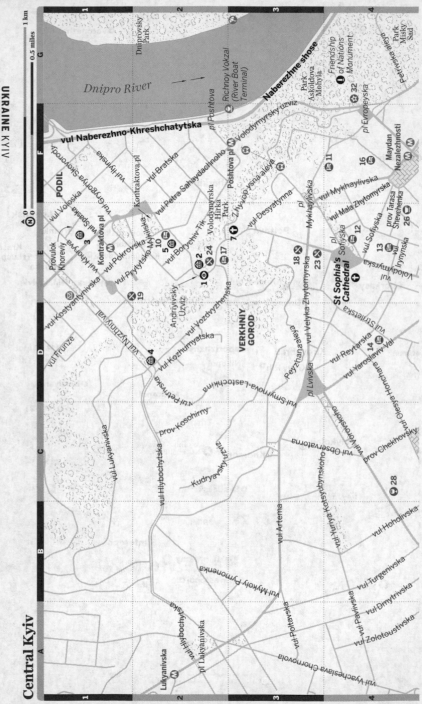

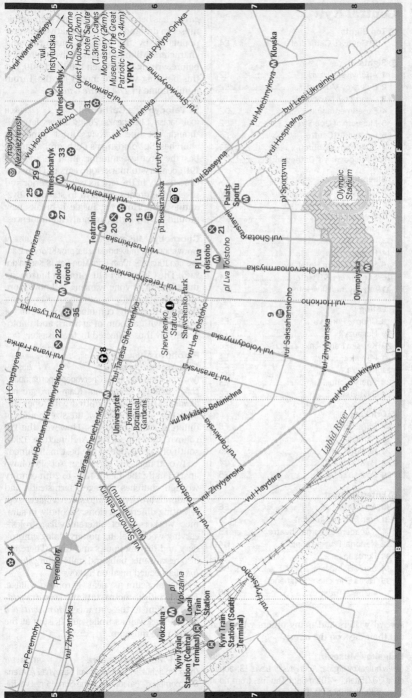

Map labels (left/bottom to right/top):

vul Ivana Mazepy
vul Instytutska

To Sherborne
Guest House (1.2km);
Hotel Salute
(1.3km); Caves
Monastery (2km);
Museum of the Great
Patriotic War (3.4km)
LYPKY

vul Pylypa Orlyka

Khreshchatyk
31
vul Horodetskoho

vul Bankova

vul Lyuteranska

vul Mechnykova Klovska

vul Hospitalna

maydan Nezalezhnosti
Khreshchatyk
33
29
Khreshchatyk
vul Khreshchatyk
Kruty uzviz

vul Baseyna

vul Pyrohova Sina

bul Lesi Ukrainky

25
27
30
15
20
Teatralna
vul Pushkinska
pl Beskrabska
6

Palats Sportu
21
vul Shota Rustaveli

pl Sportyvna

Olympic Stadium

vul Prorizna
Zoloti Vorota
35
vul Lysenka
vul Tereshchenkivska
Pl Lva Tolstoho
pl Lva Tolstoho
vul Chervonoarmiyska
Olympiyska

vul Horkoho

vul Ivana Franka
22
8
bul Tarasa Shevchenka
Shevchenko Statue
Shevchenko Park
vul Lva Tolstoho
vul Volodymyrska
vul Saksahanskoho
9
vul Zhylyanska
vul Zhytomyrska

vul Chapayeva
vul Bohdana Khmelnytskoho
vul Taraivska
vul Korolenkivska

Universytet
Fomin-Botanical Gardens
vul Mykilsko-Botanichna
vul Pankivska

Libid River

34
bul Tarasa Shevchenka
vul Symona Petlyury (vul Komintern)
vul Lva Tolstoho
vul Zhylyanska
vul Haydara

pl Peremohy
pr Peremohy
vul Zhylyanska

pl Vokzalna
Vokzalna
Kyiv Train Station (Central Terminal)
Local Train Station
Kyiv Train Station (South Terminal)
vul Urytskoho

Central Kyiv

several writers and many others who lived out their days on the *uzviz*.

Bulgakov Museum MUSEUM
(www.bulgakov.org.ua; Andriyivsky uzviz 13; adult/child 30/15uah; ◎10am-6pm Thu-Tue, from noon Mon; ⑤Kontraktova Pl) The early home of the much-loved author of *The Master and Margarita* has become a strange and memorable museum designed as an alternative universe populated by the author's memories and characters. Mikhail Bulgakov lived here long before writing it, between 1906 and 1919, but this building was the model for the Turbin family home in *The White Guard*.

St Volodymyr's Cathedral CHURCH
(bul Tarasa Shevchenka 20; ⑤Universytet) Although not one of Kyiv's most important churches, St Volodymyr's Cathedral arguably has the prettiest interior. Built in the late 19th century to mark 900 years of Orthodox Christianity in the city, its yellow exterior and seven blue domes conform to standard Byzantine style. However, inside it breaks new ground by displaying art nouveau influences.

Chornobyl Museum MUSEUM
(www.chornobylmuseum.kiev.ua; prov Khoryva 1; admission 10uah; ◎10am-6pm Mon-Sat; ⑤Kontraktova Pl) The Chornobyl Museum is a harrowing must-see for anyone wanting to know more about the world's worst nuclear accident. It very effectively combines two rooms of exhibits with a room of artwork and photography by those affected by the disaster.

Pyrohovo Museum of Folk Architecture MUSEUM
(www.nmnapu.org.ua; vul Chervonopraporna; adult/child 20/10uah; ◎museum 10am-5pm, grounds dawn-dusk) Ukraine is dotted with 'open-air' museums like this, full of life-size models of different rustic buildings. However, the Pyrohovo Museum of Folk Architecture, 12km south of Kyiv, is one of the best maintained.

Two things in particular set Pyrohovo apart. Firstly, the quaint 17th- to 20th-century wooden churches, cottages, farmsteads and windmills are divided into seven 'villages' representing different regions. Secondly, in summer, workers enact different village roles – carving wood, making pottery, doing embroidery and driving horses and carts. There are also restaurants, pubs and stalls selling *shashlyk* (barbecued meat on a skewer).

The museum is near Pyrohovo village. From Lybidska metro station take *marshrutka* 172 right to the entrance. *Marshrutka* 3 and 156, as well as trolleybus 11, stop at the turn to the museum.

FREE **PinchukArtCentre** ART GALLERY
(http://pinchukartcentre.org; vul Baseyna 2A, Arena City complex; ◎noon-9pm Tue-Sun; ⑤pl Lva Tol-

stoho or Teatralna) Located right opposite the Bessarabsky market, this world-class gallery of European contemporary art and design is a real unexpected bonus for most visitors to Kyiv. Financed by billionaire mogul Viktor Pinchuk, the visiting shows are always cutting edge and the space draws all kinds of curious Kyivites.

Museum of the Great
Patriotic War
MUSEUM

(www.warmuseum.kiev.ua; vul Lavrska 24; admission 10uah; ◉10am-5pm Tue-Sun; ⑤Druzhby Narodiv) This gloomy but atmospheric museum documents Ukrainian suffering during WWII and most memorably includes a gruesome pair of gloves made from human skin. Visible from miles around, the **Rodina Mat** (Defence of the Motherland Monument) stands right on top of the museum. Locals nickname the statue 'the Iron Lady' and 'Tin Tits'. Even if you don't like such Soviet pomposity, don't say too much: you'd be taking on a titanium woman carrying 12 tonnes of shield and sword. You can get right into her head – literally, via an elevator in the museum (200uah).

Experimentanium
MUSEUM

(www.experimentanium.com.ua; vul Verkhny Val 2a; adult/child 75/55uah; ◉9.30am-7pm Mon-Fri, 10am-8pm Sat & Sun; ⑤Kontraktova Pl) With kiddies in Kyiv? If so, this superb, brand-new science museum is just the ticket. Three floors of experiments shed light on basic scientific principles in an entertaining, hands-on way, plus there's a real Soviet-era fire engine to clamber around on, a baffling mirror maze and musical instruments to bash at. Loads of fun and a light-hearted break from Kyiv's sometimes solemn sights.

Babyn Yar
MONUMENT

(⑤Dorohozhychi) Not far from Dorohozhychi metro station, about 4km northwest of the city centre, is Babyn Yar, the location of a WWII execution site and mass grave used by the Nazis. Over 100,000 Kyiv citizens – mostly Jews – were murdered here between 1941 and 1943. The Soviet-era monument is in the wrong place. A small Jewish memorial, a menorah, better marks the spot.

🛏 Sleeping

TOP CHOICE **Sunflower B&B Hotel**
B&B €€€

(☑279 3846; www.sunflowerhotel.kiev.ua; vul Kostyolna 9/41; s/d from 930/1050uah; ✳@🛜; ⑤Maydan Nezalezhnosti) More a B&B than a hotel, the English-speaking staff make this super-central but quiet place a real cosy home away from home. Four of the five cheerily decorated rooms have baths. Very popular with foreigners so book ahead.

Dream House Hostel
HOSTEL €

(☑580 2169; www.dream-family.com; Andriyivsky Uzviz 2d; dm/d from 90/300uah; ✳@🛜; ⑤Kontraktova Pl) Kyiv's most happening hostel is this gleaming new 100-bed affair superbly located at the bottom of Andriyivsky Uzviz. An attached cafe-bar, a basement kitchen, a laundry room, keycards, bike hire (160uah per day) and daily events and tours make this a comfortable and entertaining base from which to explore the capital.

Hotel Oselya
BOUTIQUE HOTEL €€€

(☑258 8281; www.oselya.in.ua; vul Kamenyariv 11; s 640uah, d 840-940uah; ✳@🛜; ⑤Lybidska) Inconveniently located around 5km south of the city centre, just to the east of Zhulyany Airport, this superb seven-room family-run hotel has immaculately kept rooms in period style and receives encouraging reviews from travellers. The location feels almost rural and you'll need to arrange a pick-up from Lybidska metro station to find it (or grab a cab).

Gintama Hotel
LUXURY HOTEL €€€

(☑278 5092; www.gintama.com.ua; vul Tryokhsvyatytelska 9; s/d 1400/1600uah; ☕✳🛜✳; ⑤Maydan Nezalezhnosti) This friendly family-run hotel has an understated style, with smallish, individually decorated rooms tending towards the traditional, but with cleaner lines and fewer florals than usual. It's a three-minute walk from maydan Nezalezhnosti.

Radisson Blu
LUXURY HOTEL €€€

(☑492 2200; www.radissonsas.com; vul Yaroslaviv Val 22; r from 1750uah; ☕✳🛜; ⑤Zoloti Vorota) Before the Hyatt opened in 2007, Kyiv's first international hotel was well established as the city's best. Still, the building is an architectural gem, the sumptuous rooms have fluffy beds that invite entry via flying leap, and the open-all-hours health and fitness amenities are a welcome extra.

Vozdvyzhensky Hotel
BOUTIQUE HOTEL €€€

(☑531 9900; www.vozdvyzhensky.com; vul Vozdvyzhenska 60; standard s/d 1200/1400uah, superior r from 1500uah; ☕✳@; ⑤Kontraktova pl) Tucked away in a nook just off Andriyivsky Uzviz, the Vozdvyzhensky was one of Kyiv's first true boutique hotels. The 29 rooms are all individually designed and boast fine art and sumptuous fabrics.

KYIV'S APARTMENTS

Most reputable agencies have websites where you can browse their apartments. Bookings are best done online or by phone; only a few firms have offices. Prices start from 600uah for a studio apartment.

The following have English-speaking representatives and accept credit cards.

Grata Apartments (☑238 2603, 468 0757; www.accommodation.kiev.ua; prov Mykhaylivsky 9A, office 3) Service-oriented firm with a good range of apartments.

Uarent (☑278 8363; www.uarent.com) Offers some of the cheapest (though not very central) apartments.

Teren Plus (☑289 3949; www.teren.kiev. ua) Tried and true.

UKR Apartments (☑050 311 0309, 234 5637; www.ukr-apartments.kiev.ua) Has a wide selection of inexpensive apartments.

Chillout Hostel
HOSTEL €

(☑093 332 4306; www.chillouthostelkiev.com; vul Saksahanskoho 30b; dm 100uah, r without bathroom 300uah; @ ⑨; ⑤Olympiyska) With a touch of the psychedelic about it, this Polish- and Welsh-run place has two six-bed dorms and one double plus all the amenities you'd expect to find in a city-centre hostel. Enter through the arch at Gorkogo 22 and cross the courtyard diagonally, bearing left towards a yellow building.

St Petersburg Hotel
HOTEL €€

(☑279 7472; www.s-peter.com.ua; bul Tarasa Shevchenka 4; s/d without bathroom 325/514uah, with bathroom from 580/790uah; ⑨; ⑤Teatralna) Budget nomads should head for this once-grand old classic, slap bang in the city centre. Cheapo rooms are scuffed and populated with flimsy flatpack, but the shared showers and toilets are clean. A few hundred hryvnia more gets you a private bathroom but little else.

Hotel Bontiak
BOUTIQUE HOTEL €€€

(☑284 0475; http://bontiak.ru; vul Irynynska 5; d from 800uah; ✳@⑨; ⑤Zoloti Vorota) Flashy new 35-room boutique hotel within earshot of any future revolutions on maydan Nezalezhnosti. The stylishly minimalist rooms are generously cut and well equipped, and breakfast is served in your room.

Sherborne Guest House
BOUTIQUE HOTEL €€€

(☑490 9693; www.sherbornehotel.com.ua; prov Sichnevy 9, 1st entrance; apt from 1000uah; ✳@⑨; ⑤Arsenalna) A rare Ukrainian apartment-hotel, this is very salubrious both on the inside and out, with 12 internet-enabled apartments where you can cook for yourself and go about your business unhindered. The company also has other apartments throughout the centre. It's a short walk south of Arsenalna metro station along vul Lavrska.

Hotel Salute
HOTEL €€€

(☑494 1420; www.salute.kiev.ua; vul Ivana Mazepy 11b; s/d from 750/900uah; ⊖✳@⑨; ⑤Arsenalna) Affectionately dubbed 'the grenade', the Salute features psychedelic '70s furniture and a few rooms with exceptional views of the River Dnipro. For a converted Soviet hotel it has surprising benefits, like smiley receptionists and a 24-hour business centre. It's a short walk south of Arsenalna metro station along vul Lavrska.

✖ Eating

TOP CHOICE Spotykach
UKRAINIAN €€

(vul Volodymyrska 16; mains 80-150uah; ⊙11am-midnight; ⑤Maydan Nezalezhnosti) A tribute to the 1960s – a happier (and funnier) period of Soviet history – this discreetly stylish retro-Soviet place will make even a hardened dissident drop a nostalgic tear. The food is October Revolution Day banquet in the Kremlin, but with a Ukrainian twist. The eponymous *spotykach* is vodka-based liquor made with different flavours, from blackcurrant to horseradish.

Pervak
RUSSIAN, UKRAINIAN €€

(vul Rognidenska 2; mains 60-110uah; ⊙11am-midnight; ⓪; ⑤Pl Lva Tolstoho) Kyiv's best Ukrainian restaurant masterfully creates old Kyiv (c 1900) without falling into the schmaltzy trap that dogs many a Ukrainian theme-resto. The chefs boldly prepare original takes on Ukrainian classics, which are adroitly delivered to tables by waitresses in frilly, cleavage-baring country outfits.

Harbuzyk
UKRAINIAN €€

(Little Pumpkin; vul Khoryva 2v; mains 25-100uah; ⊙11am-11pm; ⑤Kontraktova pl) This fun, if slightly hokey, eatery offers a great introduction to Ukrainian food without breaking the bank. Pumpkin is not just in the name: it's all over the extensive menu, from the *mamalyha* porridge to fresh pumpkin juice. More unusual items on the drink list include birch tree sap and *kvas* (a gingery soft drink).

Svytlytsa
FRENCH/UKRAINIAN €€

(Andriyivsky Uzviz 136; mains 45-120uah; ☺11am-10pm; 🅿; ⓢKontraktova Pl) A survivor of times past and the *uzviz's* recent facelift, this ex-Soviet cafe in a wooden house reinvented itself as a French crêperie, though it keeps serving inexpensive Ukrainian fare. Yacht-themed decor and Russian pop music contribute to the overall schizophrenia, but most patrons avoid both by choosing tables on the summer terrace – a great place for *uzviz*-watching.

Tsarske Selo
UKRAINIAN €€

(vul Ivana Mazepy 42/1; mains 40-140uah; ☺11am-1am; ⓢArsenalna) A pure bodily delight that's well deserved by those who descend the spiritual heights of Kyivsko-Pecherska Lavra, this is Kyiv's quintessential Ukrainian theme restaurant, decorated in rustic style and filled with tour groups. Ukrainian staples are superbly done; go for *borshch* ((beetroot soup) or *varenyky* (filled pasta pockets) stuffed with cabbage.

Chorne Porosya
UKRAINIAN €€

(Black Piglet; vul Velyka Zhytomyrska 8/14; mains 30-100uah; ☺noon-midnight; ⓢMaydan Nezalezhnosti) Combining rural Ukrainian styling with 21st-century convenience, it's easy to guess what farmyard friend populates the menu at the Black Piglet, Kyiv's newest beer restaurant. If slabs of pork are not your thing, there are salads and fish dishes. Also a great place for those not initiated in the ways of *salo* to force down their first greasy chunk.

Barsuk
PUB €€

(prov Kutuzova 3a; mains 60-90uah; ⓢPecherska) Tucked away in a small lane opposite Pechersky market, 'The Badger' brings three nouvelle concepts to Kyiv – those of gastropub, organic food and open-view kitchen.

Kyivska Perepichka
FAST FOOD €

(vul Bohdana Khmelnytskoho 3; pastry 5.50uah; ☺9am-9pm Mon-Sat, from 11am Sun; ⓢTeatralna) The perpetually long queue moves with a lightning speed towards a window where two women hand out pieces of fried dough enclosing a mouth-watering sausage. Around for as long as anyone can remember and an essential Kyiv experience.

🍷 Drinking

Bars

Kupidon
PUB

(Cupid; vul Pushkinska 1-3/5; ☺10am-10pm; 🛜; ⓢKreshchatyk) Apocalyptically dubbing itself 'the last shelter for the Ukrainian intelligensia', this is in fact a missionary station spreading Ukrainian culture in the Russian-speaking capital. Siege mentality apart, Cupid is a lovely Lviv-styled *knaypa* (pub) with an attached secondhand bookshop – a favourite drinking den for nationalist-leaning and cosmopolitan bohemians alike.

Baraban
PUB

(The Drum; vul Prorizna 4a; mains 40-60uah; ☺11am-11pm; ⓢKhreshchatyk) This popular journo hang-out is *the* place to talk politics and plot revolutions, and it also has decent food at good prices. Located in a courtyard behind Prorizna 4 (next to the Radio and TV Ministry).

Palata No.6
BAR

(Ward No.6; vul Vorovskoho 31a; ☺noon-2am; ⓢUniversytet) For a healthy dose of insanity, sneak into this well-hidden dive bar named after Anton Chekhov's short story about life in a madhouse. Dressed in doctor's white robes, stern-looking waiters nurse you with excellent steaks and apply giant syringes to pour vodka into your glass.

Cafes

Kaffa
COFFEE HOUSE

(prov Tarasa Shevchenka 3; ⓢMaydan Nezalezhnosti) The onslaught of Ukrainian and Russian coffee chains has not changed one thing: long-standing Kaffa still serves the most heart-pumping, rich-tasting brew in town. Coffees and teas from all over the world are served in a pot sufficient for two or three punters in a blissfully smoke-free, white-washed, African-inspired interior.

Repriza
CAFE

(vul Bohdana Khmelnytskoho 40/25; ⓢZoloti Vorota) Not only does it have good coffee and delectable sandwiches, pastries and cakes, but Repriza also makes a fine, affordable lunch stop. There's also a branch in Podil at vul Sahaydachnoho 10.

Pasazh
COFFEE HOUSE

(off vul Khreshchatyk; ⓢKhreshchatyk) This Austrian-style coffee house is one of several cafes found on and around Pasazh, a hip street accessed through an ornate archway off vul Khreshchatyk. Great for people-watching as you tuck into its scrumptious cakes.

☆ Entertainment

Nightclubs

The club scene is constantly in flux, so check *What's On Kyiv* and the *Kyiv Post* for the latest big thing.

Art Club 44 LIVE MUSIC

(www.club44.com.ua; vul Khreshchatyk 44; ⑤Teatralna) A program packed with jazz, indie, rock and folk acts mean this venue remains a beacon for more sophisticated, alternative-minded night creatures.

Sorry Babushka CLUB

(www.sorrybabushka.com.ua; vul Dmytrivska 18/24; ⑤Universytet) Newcomer on the late-night scene and one of the capital's most popular with karaoke, '80s and '90s discos and big weekend acts.

Pomada GAY

(Lipstick; vul Zankovetskoyi 6; ⑤Khreshchatyk) You know Kyiv has come a long way when we can actually publish the names of gay clubs (they used to all be underground). This is lively and centrally located, but it's the one place in town where women might pay *more* to get in.

Performing Arts

Taras Shevchenko National Opera Theatre OPERA

(☑234 7165; www.opera.com.ua; vul Volodymyrska 50; ⑤Zoloti Vorota) This is a lavish theatre (1899–1901) and a performance here is a grandiose affair. True imbibers of Ukrainian culture should not miss a performance

of *Zaporozhets za Dunaem* (Zaporizhzhyans Beyond the Danube), a sort of operatic, purely Ukrainian version of *Fiddler on the Roof*. A New Year performance of *The Nutcracker* is also a magical experience.

Ivan Franko National Academic Drama Theatre THEATRE

(☑279 5991; pl Ivana Franka 3; ⑤Khreshchatyk) Kyiv's most respected theatre has been going strong since 1888.

National Philharmonic LIVE MUSIC

(☑278 1697; www.filarmonia.com.ua; Volodymyrsky uzviz 2; ⑤Maydan Nezalezhnosti) Originally the Kyiv Merchants' Assembly rooms, this beautiful building now houses the national orchestra.

❶ Information

Kyiv's authorities opened up no less than 12 tourist offices for the Euro 2012 soccer championships – and promptly closed every single one as soon as the fans had left.

Almost every cafe and restaurant offers free wi-fi these days and there are hot spots throughout the city centre.

American Medical Center (☑emergency hotline 490 7600; http://amcenters.com; vul Berdychivska 1; ☺24hr; ⑤Lukyanivska) Western-run medical centre with English-speaking doctors.

Central Post Office (vul Khreshchatyk 22; internet per hr 18uah; ☺8am-9pm Mon-Sat, 9am-7pm Sun, internet 24hr; ⑤Maydan Nezalezhnosti) Enter from maydan Nezalezhnosti.

Lonely Planet (www.lonelyplanet.com/ukraine/kyiv)

❶ Getting There & Away

Air

Most international flights use Boryspil International Airport (p954), about 35km east of the city. Some domestic airlines and Wizzair use **Zhulyany airport** (IEV; ☑585 7254; www.airport.kiev.ua), about 7km southwest of the centre. There's at least one flight a day to all major cities in Ukraine and international flights serve almost every European capital.

Plane tickets are sold at **Kiy Avia** (www.kiy-avia.com; pr Peremohy 2; ☺8am-9pm Mon-Fri, 8am-8pm Sat, 9am-6pm Sun).

Bus

One part of Kyiv not spruced up for Euro 2012 was the stubbornly Second World **Central Bus Station** (Tsentralny Avtovokzal; pl Moskovska 3), one stop from Lybidska metro station on trolleybus 1 or 12.

TRAVEL AGENCIES

SoloEast Travel (☑279 3505; www.tourkiev.com) Probably the most helpful, friendly travel service in Kyiv – offering tickets, apartments and tours, including to Chornobyl.

New Logic (☑206 3322; www.newlogic.com.ua; vul Mikhailivska 6a; ⑤Teatralna) Great deals on Chornobyl tours for individual tourists.

Sam (☑238 6020; www.sam.ua; vul Ivana Franka 40b; ⑤Universytet) The leading inbound operator organises sightseeing excursions, hotel bookings and trips to Chornobyl.

INTERNATIONAL TRAINS FROM KYIV

DESTINATION	DURATION (HR)	FREQUENCY
Bratislava	26	1 daily
Bucharest	25	1 daily
Budapest	24	1 daily
Chişinău	14-17	up to 5 daily
Minsk	13	1 or 2 daily
Moscow	10-16	Up to 20 daily
St Petersburg	25½	1 daily
Warsaw	17	1 daily

Long-distance express carriers Autolux (p956) and Gunsel (p956) run by far the fastest and most comfortable buses in the business. They have frequent services to most large regional centres (though not Lviv); many go via, or continue to, Boryspil airport. You can book on their websites or buy tickets at the Central Bus Station or Boryspil airport.

Train

You can get pretty much everywhere in the country from Kyiv's modern **train station.** (☑503 7005; pl Vokzalna 2; ⑤Vokzalna).

Heading west, the quickest way to Lviv is on the Intercity+ Hyundai express train (214uah, five hours, one daily) which leaves in the early evening. However, most plump for cheaper overnight passenger trains and there are a few daytime services (120uah to 180uah, eight to 10 hours).

Heading south, there are two daytime and two overnight services to Odesa (160uah, eight to 14½ hours) and four overnighters to Simferopol (150uah to 260uah, 14 to 18 hours).

You can buy tickets at the station or the **advance train ticket office** (bul Tarasa Shevchenka 38/40; ☺7am-9pm; ⑤Universytet), a five-minute walk from the station.

ⓘ Getting Around

To/From the Airport

There is a prepaid taxi booth near the exit in the arrivals zone (at Boryspil airport), which charges 250uah to the centre. When going to the airport try **Shuttle Taxi** (☑067-444 4864, 050-501 5811; www.shuttle-taxi.com.ua) who charge as little as 79uah for solo travellers.

Catching a SkyBus minibus (No 322) is the most common way to Boryspil airport (25uah, 45 minutes to one hour). They depart round the clock from behind the train station's South Terminal every 20 to 40 minutes. Buy tickets from the driver.

Trolleybus 22 runs to Zhulyany airport from Shulyavska metro station.

To/From the Train Station

The taxi drivers hanging out by the train station can be the biggest rip-off artists in Kyiv, typically charging 60uah to 100uah for what should be a 30uah ride into the centre. Avoid them by walking five minutes to bul Tarasa Shevchenka or take the metro.

Public Transport

Kyiv's metro is clean, efficient, reliable and now, thanks to Euro 2012, even sports English signage. Many of the stations are several dozen storeys underground, requiring escalator rides of seven to eight minutes! Trains run between around 6am and midnight on all three lines. Blue-green plastic tokens (*zhetony*; 2uah) are sold at windows and token dispensers at station entrances.

Buses, trolleybuses, trams and many quicker *marshrutky* serve most routes. Tickets for buses, trams and trolleybuses cost 1.50uah and are sold at kiosks or directly from the driver or conductor.

LVIV

☑032 / POP 756,000

If you've spent time in any other region of Ukraine, Lviv (Львів) will come as a shock. Mysterious and architecturally lovely, this Unesco World Heritage–listed city is the country's least Soviet and exudes the same Central European charm as pre-tourism Prague or Kraków once did. It's quaint cobbles, bean-perfumed coffeehouses and rattling trams are a continent away from the post-Soviet badlands to the east. It's also a place where the candle of Ukrainian national identity burns brightest and where Russian is definitely a minority language.

Lviv

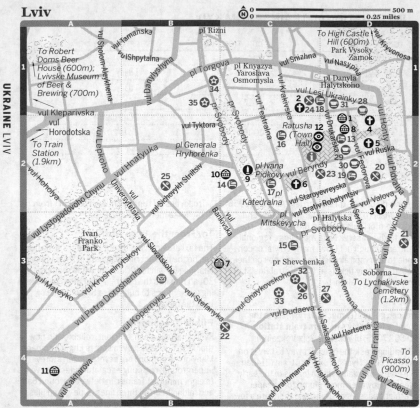

But the secret is out about Lviv, and those who foresaw a decade ago that the city would become Ukraine's premier tourist attraction are watching their prediction come true. No other place in the country is more geared up for visitors and no other attracts so many of them. The Euro 2012 soccer championships gave the world a taste of this Ukrainian treat; a successful bid for the 2022 Winter Olympics would be the icing on the cake.

◉ Sights

Ploshcha Rynok
SQUARE

Thanks to its splendid array of buildings Lviv was declared a Unesco World Heritage Site in 1998, and this old market square lies at its heart. The square was progressively rebuilt after a major fire in the early 16th century destroyed the original. The 19th-century **ratusha** stands in the middle of the plaza, with fountains featuring Greek gods at each of its corners. Vista junkies can climb the

65m-high neo-Renaissance **tower** (admission 5uah; ⊙9am-6pm), though it's a hard slog to the top. Multilingual signs point the way to the ticket booth on the 4th floor.

House No 4, the **Black Mansion**, has one of the most striking facades. Built for an Italian merchant in 1588–89, it features a relief of St Martin on a horse. The **Kornyakt House** at No 6 is named after its original owner, a Greek merchant. An interesting row of sculpted knights along the rooftop cornice makes it a local favourite.

Lychakivske Cemetery
CEMETERY

(www.lviv-lychakiv.ukrain.travel; vul Pekarska; admission 10uah; ⊙9am-6pm) Don't even think of leaving town until you've seen this amazing cemetery only a short tram ride east of the centre. This is the Père Lachaise of Eastern Europe, with the same sort of overgrown grounds and Gothic aura as the famous Parisian necropolis (but containing somewhat less well-known people). Laid out in the late

Lviv

18th century, when Austrian Emperor Josef II decreed that no more burials could take place in churchyards, it's still the place Lviv's great and good are laid to rest.

Many combine a trip to the cemetery with a visit to the Museum of Folk Architecture and Life. The cemetery is one stop further on tram 7.

**Museum of Folk Architecture
and Life**   MUSEUM
(www.skansen.lviv.ua; vul Chernecha Hora 1; admission 10uah; ◷9am-dusk Tue-Sun) This open-air museum displays different regional styles of farmsteads, windmills, churches and schools that dot a huge park east of the centre. Everything is pretty spread out here and a visit involves a lot of foot work. To get to the museum, take tram 7 from vul Pidvalna up vul Lychakivska and get off at the corner of vul Mechnykova. From the stop walk 10 minutes' north on vul Krupyarska, following the signs.

Latin Cathedral   CATHEDRAL
(Archcathedral Basilica of the Assumption of the Blessed Virgin Mary; pl Katedralna 1) With various chunks dating from between 1370 and 1480, this working cathedral is one of Lviv's most impressive churches. The exterior is most definitely Gothic while the heavily gilded interior, one of the city's highlights, has a more baroque feel with colourfully wreathed pillars hoisting frescoed vaulting, and mysterious side chapels glowing in candlelit half light. Services are in four languages including...wait for it...English! Entry by donation.

Dominican Cathedral   CHURCH
(pl Museyna) Dominating a small square to the east of pl Rynok is one of Lviv's signature sights, the large rococo dome of the Dominican Cathedral. Attached to the cathedral and to the left of the entrance is the **Museum of Religious History** (admission 5uah; ◷10am-6pm Tue-Sun), which was an atheist museum in Soviet times. The exhibition looks at all religions currently active in Ukraine and includes an Ostroh Bible, one of the first complete translations into Old Church Slavonic printed in 1580.

Armenian Cathedral   CHURCH
(vul Virmenska 7) Don't miss the elegant 1363 Armenian Cathedral. The placid cathedral courtyard is a maze of arched passageways and squat buildings festooned with intricate Caucasian detail. Stepping into the courtyard feels like entering another era. Outside,

quaint, cobbled vul Virmenska was once the heart of the old Armenian ('Virmenska' in Ukrainian) quarter.

Lviv History Museum
MUSEUM
(admission to each branch 10uah; ☉all branches 10am-5.30pm Thu-Tue) Lviv's main museum is split into four collections dotted around pl Rynok. The best branch is at **No 6**. Here you can enjoy the Italian Renaissance inner courtyard and slide around the exquisitely decorated interior in cloth slippers on the woodcut parquetry floor made from 14 kinds of hardwood. It was also here on 22 December 1686 that Poland and Russia signed the treaty that partitioned Ukraine. **No 2**, the Palazzo Bandinelli, focuses on jewellery, silver and glass while **No 24** expounds on the city's earlier history. **No 4** tells the story of Ukraine's western regions in the 19th and 20th centuries and has a section on the Ukrainian diaspora.

High Castle Hill
LANDMARK
Around 30 minutes' walk from pl Rynok, visiting the High Castle (Vysoky Zamok) on Castle Hill (Zamkova Hora) is a quintessential Lviv experience. There's little evidence of the 14th-century ruined stone fort that was Lviv's birthplace, but the summit mound sporting a mammoth Ukrainian flag thwacking in the wind offers 360-degree views of the city and the wooded hills between which it nestles.

Dormition Church
CHURCH
(Uspenska Tservka; vul Pidvalna 9; ☉8am-7pm) This Ukrainian Orthodox church is easily distinguished by the 65m-high, triple-tiered **Kornyakt bell tower** rising beside it. The tower was named after its Greek benefactor, a merchant who was also the original owner of Kornyakt House on pl Rynok. It's well worth going inside to see the beautifully gilt interior of the church, accessible through the gate to the right of the tower. Attached to the church is the diminutive **Three Saints Chapel** with its three, highly ornate mini-cupolas.

FREE National Museum and Memorial to the Victims of Occupation
MUSEUM
(www.lonckoho.lviv.ua; vul Bryullova; ☉10am-7pm) This infamous building on vul Bryullova was used as a prison by the Poles, Nazis and Communists, but the small and very moving ground-floor exhibition focuses on Stalinist atrocities in the early years of WWII.

Left exactly as it was when the KGB bailed out in 1991, the brutally bare cells, horrific statistics posted throughout and Nazi newsreel from summer 1941 will leave few untouched.

Lvivske Museum of Beer & Brewing
MUSEUM
(www.lvivske.com; vul Kleparivska 18; admission 15uah; ☉tours roughly every 90min 10.30am-6pm Wed-Mon) The oldest still-functioning brewery in Ukraine turns 300 in 2015, and a tasting tour through the mainly underground facilities is well worth the trek out of the centre. To reach the museum, take tram 6 or 7 to St Anne's Church, then walk north along vul Kleparivska for around 10 minutes.

Museum of Ethnography, Arts & Crafts
MUSEUM
(pr Svobody 15; admission 10uah; ☉11am-5.30pm Tue-Sun) Exhibits of furniture, clothing, woodcarvings, ceramics and farming implements give a basic introduction to Carpathian life.

Apteka Museum
MUSEUM
(Pharmacy Museum; vul Drukarska 2; admission 5uah; ☉9am-7pm Mon-Fri, 10am-5pm Sat & Sun) Ukraine's only pharmacy museum is located inside a still-functioning chemist's shop dating from 1735.

Lviv Art Gallery
GALLERY
(vul Kopernyka 15 & vul Stefanyka 3; admission to each 10uah; ☉11am-5pm Tue-Sat, noon-4pm Sun) Lviv's main art repository has two wings – one in the lavish **Pototsky Palace**, the other around the corner on **vul Stefanyka**. It has arguably the best collection of Polish art outside Poland with some works by Jan Matejko.

Bernardine Church and Monastery
CHURCH
(vul Vynnychenka) Lviv's most stunning baroque interior belongs to the 17th-century Bernadine Church.

Monument to Taras Shevchenko
MONUMENT
(pr Svobody) This statue of Taras Shevchenko, Ukraine's greatest nationalist writer, was a gift to the people of Lviv from the Ukrainian diaspora in Argentina.

🛏 Sleeping

Lviv must have the best selection of hotels outside Kyiv, with high standards inspired by an influx of visitors and the Euro 2012 soccer championships.

Vintage   BOUTIQUE HOTEL €€€

(📞235 6834; www.vintagehotel.com.ua; vul Serbska 11; s/d/ste from 760/960/1570uah; ❋🛜) Recently extended, Lviv's first real boutique hotel is this still delightfully intimate 29-room place, accessed through an inconspicuous entrance in the historical centre. Rooms ooze period style with hardwood floors, polished antique-style furniture and Victorian-style wallpaper, successfully blended with flat-screen TVs and 21st-century bathrooms. You'll be looking forward all night to the breakfast, cooked to order and served in the hotel's stylish restaurant.

Leopolis Hotel   LUXURY HOTEL €€€

(📞295 9500; www.leopolishotel.com; vul Teatralna 16; s/d from 1100/1300uah; ⊖❋@🛜) One of the historical centre's finest places to catch some Zs, the Leopolis comes from the same designer who fashioned Tallinn's Telegraaf Hotel. Every guest room in this 18th-century edifice is different, but all have a well-stocked minibar, elegant furniture and Italian marble bathrooms with underfloor heating. Wheelchair-friendly facilities, a new spa/fitness area in the cellars and a pretty decent brasserie are extras you won't find anywhere else.

Old City Hostel   HOSTEL €

(📞294 9644; www.oldcityhostel.lviv.ua; vul Beryndy 3; dm/d from 80/320uah; @🛜) Occupying two floors of an elegantly fading tenement just steps from pl Rynok, this expertly run hostel with period features and views of the Shevchenko statue from the wrap-around balcony has quickly established itself as the city's best. Fluff-free dorms hold four to 16 beds, shower queues are unheard of, sturdy lockers keep your stuff safe and there's a well-endowed kitchen.

Reikartz Medievale   HOTEL €€

(📞235 0890; www.reikartz.com; vul Drukarska 9; s/d from 595/680uah; ❋🛜) The Lviv link in this 100% Ukrainian chain limits the medieval theme to a few spired bedsteads, the odd tapestry and a bit of chunky furniture. There's also nothing of the Middle Ages about the huge bathrooms, crisp linens and exceptional service. More hryvnya get you a bigger room, but nothing else.

Grand Hotel   HOTEL €€€

(📞272 4042; www.grandhotel.lviv.ua; pr Svobody 13; s/d 880/1150uah; ⊖❋🛜≋) Having rested too long on its laurels as the only real luxury show in town, the Grand is no longer top dog in Lviv. The rooms, while still holding on to their old-world flavour, are beginning to age a bit and the service has been caught flat-footed by other more up-to-speed establishments. Fortunately its prime location on pr Svobody will never fade.

Hotel George   HOTEL €€

(📞232 6236; www.georgehotel.com.ua; pl Mitskevycha 1; s 330-780uah; d 400-850uah; 🛜) Seasoned travellers to Lviv will be saddened to learn that the George has been partially renovated and has lost its elusive 'Soviet chic' vibe. A prime candidate for a show-stopping five-star establishment, instead this gorgeous 1901 art nouveau building has received a crass, skin-deep makeover – plasticky, faux antique furniture clashes with the high-ceilinged period style in the rooms and cheapo carpets conceal the wonderfully creaky parquet floors.

Central Square Hostel   HOSTEL €

(📞095 225 6654; www.cshostel.com; pl Rynok 5; dm/d from 95/320; 🛜) This hostel may be small, but its location on pl Rynok puts you at the heart of the Lviv action. Free tea and coffee, a pint-sized kitchen and thief-proof lockers, but just one shower.

Eurohotel   BUSINESS HOTEL €€

(📞275 7214; www.eurohotel.lviv.ua; vul Tershakovtsiv 6A; s/d from 600/700uah; ⊖❋🛜) This unexciting place is a good example of just what you can do with a surplus Soviet lumpenhotel. The 90 bog-standard but comfortable rooms are for those who want to sleep, shower and access the net, but little else.

✖ Eating

Lviv is more famous for cafes than restaurants, but the food scene has seen dramatic developments in recent years with Ukraine's wackiest grouping of themed restaurants wowing and baffling diners in equal measure.

Masonic Restaurant   EUROPEAN €€€

(pl Rynok 14; mains before discount 300-500uah; ⏱11am-2am; 🏠) It's hard to know where to start with this place. Finding it is the first obstacle – head to the 2nd floor and open door of apartment 8 (they change the numbers around occasionally to throw people off the scent). You'll be accosted by an unshaven bachelor type, into whose Soviet-era kitchen you appear to have inadvertently wandered. Having barred your way for a few minutes he eventually opens the door to a fancy beamed restaurant full of Masonic symbols and portraits of bygone masons. The next shock is the menu – advertised as Galicia's most expensive restaurant, prices are 10 times higher than normal...so make sure you pick up a 90% discount card at Dim Lehend or Livy Bereh beforehand. The food, by the way, is great and the beer and *kvas* come in crystal vases. One of the loos is a candlelit Masonic throne. Ukraine's weirdest restaurant experience? Probably.

Dim Lehend UKRAINIAN €€

(vul Staroyevreyska 48; mains 30-65uah) Dedicated entirely to the city of Lviv, there's nothing dim about the 'House of Legends'. The five floors house a library stuffed with Lviv-themed volumes, a room showing live webcam footage of Lviv's underground river, rooms dedicated to lions and cobblestones, and another featuring the city in sounds. A GDR Trabant occupies the roof terrace, the views from which will have you reaching for your camera. From the limited menu, go for the pork chop in berry sauce or the *lavash* bread stuffed with roast chicken, followed by the delicious apple struddle. They also do a kick-starting breakfast.

Kupol CENTRAL EUROPEAN €€

(vul Chaykovskoho 37; mains 40-100uah; ⏰11am-9pm) One of the pre-tourism 'originals', this place is designed to feel like stepping back in time – to 1938 in particular, 'the year before civilisation ended' (ie before the Soviets rolled in). The olde-worlde interior is lined with framed letters, ocean-liner ads, antique cutlery, hampers and other memorabilia and the Polish/Austrian/Ukrainian food is tasty and beautifully garnished.

Livy Bereh INTERNATIONAL €€

(pr Svobody 28; mains 40-80uah; ⏰11am-2am; 📷) Buried deep beneath the Theatre of Opera and Ballet, this superb restaurant serves European fare, with a few Ukrainian and Hutsul favourites thrown in. The theme, not surprisingly, is opera, with live broadcasts from the stage above and props throughout, though this sits rather oddly with the wonky walls, crooked door frames and tottering walls. The name, meaning Left Bank, refers to Lviv's river which flows under the building, glassed in and crossed by wooden footbridges at the entrance to the restaurant.

Mons Pius UKRAINIAN/INTERNATIONAL €€

(www.monspius.lviv.ua; vul Lesi Ukrainky 14; mains 40-150uah; ⏰9am-11pm; 📷) Well-regimented serving staff dart across the polished brick floors and through the intimate courtyard of this former Armenian bank, a recent and top-quality addition to Lviv's dining scene. Meat dishes anchor the reassuringly brief menu though there are lots of salads and a few meat-free dishes for non-carnivores. Our only criticism is that the small portions, so beef up your beef with a couple of side dishes. Drinks include 'live' Mons Pius beer and lemonade like *babusya* used to make.

Kumpel PUB €€

(vul Vynnychenka 6; mains 25-80uah; ⏰24hr) Centred on two huge copper brewing vats cooking up Kumpel's own beer (1L for 32uah), this superb round-the-clock microbrewery-restaurant has a low-lit art deco theme. The menu is heavy on international meat-and-two-veg combos, with a few local elements included. Filling breakfast menu from 7am.

Veronika INTERNATIONAL €€€

(pr Shevchenka 21; mains 70-250uah; ⏰9am-11pm; 📷) This classy basement restaurant plates up an ambitiously multicultural menu of fish, beef steaks, *shashlyk*, crêpes, *vareniky* and pizzas in a cool, tranquil atmosphere. In addition there's a street-level *konditorei*, with criminally delicious desserts.

Puzata Khata CAFE €

(vul Sichovykh Striltsiv 12; mains 11-25uah; ⏰8am-11pm) This super-sized version of Ukraine's number-one restaurant chain stands out for its classy, Hutsul-themed interior and pure Ukrainian-rock soundtrack. There's another, more tranquil **branch** (⏰8am-11pm) at pr Shevchenka 10.

🍷 Drinking

Dzyga CAFE

(vul Virmenska 35; ⏰10am-midnight) This cafe-cum-art-gallery, in the shadow of the Dominican Cathedral, has a relaxed vibe. It's particularly popular with bohemian, alternative types, but seems to attract pretty much everyone, really. The summertime outdoor seating is gathered around the city's Monument to the Smile.

Lvivska Kopalnya Kavy CAFE

(pl Rynok 10; ⏰8am-11pm; 📶) Lviv is Ukraine's undisputed coffee capital and the 'Lviv Coffee Mine' is where the rich seam of Arabica is excavated by the local colliers from deep beneath pl Rynok. You can tour the mine or just sample the heart-pumping end product at tables as dark as the brews inside or out on the courtyard beneath old timber balconies.

Spizharka
CAFE

(Virmenska 27; ◷10am-8pm) The theme at this atmospherically intimate coffee halt is 19th-century apartment, equipped with tassled lamps, antique furniture and high-brow bookcases, an apt venue for meetings of Lviv's book club. To reach the cafe, pass through the attached deli selling traditional pickles and conserves.

Pid Synoyu Plyashkoyu
CAFE

(Under the Blue Bottle; vul Ruska 4; ◷10am-10pm) With its nostalgia for the Polish–Austrian past and dark interior, this tiny cafe at the back of a courtyard has a cosy, secretive atmosphere. It serves sandwiches and fondues, as well as wine and fine Lviv coffee. It's hard to find: look for the blue bottle.

Robert Doms Beer House
BEER HALL

(vul Kleparivska 18; ◷noon-midnight) This fantastic beer hall is located three storeys underground in a centuries-old beer-storage vault once used by the neighbouring Lvivske brewery.

☆ Entertainment

Nightclubs

Kult
LIVE MUSIC

(www.kult.lviv.ua; vul Chaykovskoho 7; ◷noon-2am) This superb basement venue next to the Philharmonia reverberates with live Ukrainian rock, jazz and blues music every night of the week from 9pm.

Picasso
CLUB

(www.picasso.lviv.ua; vul Zelena 88; ◷from 9pm) Lviv's most atmospheric club, inside a former theatre, has consistently good DJs and a festive crowd paying proper homage to them. Take trolleybus 11 or 24 to Vodohinna Stantsiya.

Opera, Theatre & Classical Music

Advance tickets for all Lviv's venues are sold at the **Teatralna Kasa** (Theatre Box Office; pr Svobody 37; ◷10am-5pm Mon-Sat).

Solomiya Krushelnytska Lviv Theatre of Opera & Ballet
THEATRE

(☎235 6586; www.opera.lviv.ua; pr Svobody 28) For an evening of high culture, and to enjoy the ornate building, take in a performance at this Lviv institution. The theatre shuts down for most of July and August.

Philharmonia
LIVE MUSIC

(☎235 8136; www.philharmonia.lviv.ua; vul Chaykovskoho 7) If classical music is your thing, let yourself be wooed by the sweet strains of Lviv's regional philharmonic orchestra. Things are very quiet here from July through to mid-September.

WORTH A TRIP

CARPATHIAN MOUNTAINS

One of the least-developed areas in Eastern Europe is the easternmost section of the Carpathian Mountains, which slice through the lower corner of Western Ukraine. Among the undulating ridges lives a cluster of various ethnic groups, including the Hutsuls, who, despite their clear Romanian ties, are a significant source of pride to the Ukrainian national identity.

The Carpathians are home to Ukraine's highest but easily climbable peak, **Mt Hoverla** (2062m), and its largest national park, the **Carpathian National Nature Park**. Opportunities abound for wild camping, homestays, hiking and mountain biking in some superbly rugged backcountry.

This is also one of Eastern Europe's premier skiing regions – see **Piligrim** (☎032-297 1899; www.piligrim.lviv.ua) and **SkiUkraine** (www.skiukraine.info) for information and bookings.

The town of **Yaremche** puts you at the heart of the mountains but has become crowded and touristy in recent years. Alternatives include **Kosiv**, **Rakhiv**, **Vorokhta** and **Kolomyya** where the unrivalled **On the Corner** (☎067 980 3326, 034 332 7437; www.onthecorner.info; vul Hetmanska 47A; d/dm 320/160uah) guesthouse is Ukraine's most foreigner-friendly digs, receiving rave reviews from travellers for it's warm welcome, scrumptious home-cooked food and excellent facilities. For accommodation across the region, **Karpaty Info** (www.karpaty.info) features hundreds of B&B, homestay and hotel listings in the region.

Lviv, Chernivtsi and Ivano-Frankivsk are gateways to the mountains with bus and train services into the main valleys.

INTERNATIONAL TRAINS FROM LVIV

DESTINATION	DURATION (HR)	FREQUENCY
Bratislava	18	1 daily
Budapest	14	1 daily
Kraków	6-10	2 daily
Minsk	13	1-2 daily
Moscow	24	up to 3 daily
Przemysl	3	2 daily
St Petersburg	30	2 weekly

ℹ️ Information

Central Post Office (vul Slovatskoho 1)

Chorna Medea (vul Petra Doroshenka 50; per hr 9uah; ⊙24hr) Lviv's only internet cafe.

Tourist Information Centre (📞254 6079; www.lviv.travel; pl Rynok 1, Ratusha; ⊙10am-8pm Mon-Fri, to 7pm Sat, to 6pm Sun) The excellent tourist office has branches at the **train station** (📞226 2005; Ticket Hall; ⊙9am-8pm) and the **airport** (📞067-673 9194; Terminal A; ⊙10am-8pm Mon-Sat, to 6pm Sun).

Visitlviv.net (www.visitlviv.net) One of the best sources of information on Lviv, updated on a daily basis.

ℹ️ Getting There & Away

Air

Lviv's shiny new **airport** (LWO; www.airport.lviv.ua) was bolted together for Euro 2012; it's about 7km southwest of the centre.

You can fly from Lviv to Kyiv (five daily). Book through **Kiy Avia** (📞272 7818; www.kiyavia.com; vul Hnyatuka 20-22; ⊙8am-8pm Mon-Sat, to 6pm Sun).

There are currently international flights to/from Vienna, Munich, Warsaw, Timişoara, İstanbul, Dortmund, Venice, Krakow, Naples, Tel Aviv and Moscow, and in late 2012 there were rumours 'flying' about that Ryanair was about to launch between Lviv and London Stansted.

Bus

The extremely inconveniently located **main bus station** (Holovny Avtovokzal; vul Stryska) is 8km south of the centre (take trolleybus 5).

From the main bus station, buses serve all major southern, eastern and central cities, including Kyiv (100uah to 180uah, nine hours, four daily), Kamyanets-Podilsky (110uah, five to eight hours, three daily) and Odesa (Lviv (200uah, 15 hours, two daily).

Some southbound buses depart from bus station no 8 in front of the train station. Destinations served include Odesa (daily) and Kyiv (twice daily).

Train

The quickest way to Kyiv is on the daily Intercity+ Hyudai express (238uah, five hours). There are also at least nine regular trains per day, most of them overnight services (110uah to 150uah, eight to 13 hours). Heading southwest to the border with Slovakia, there are trains to Chop (70uah to 100uah, five to seven hours, five daily).

Southern destinations include Odesa (160uah, 12 hours, three daily) and Simferopol (210uah, daily).

Buy tickets from the station or the centrally located **train ticket office** (vul Hnatyuka 20; ⊙8am-2pm & 3-8pm Mon-Sat, to 6pm Sun).

ℹ️ Getting Around

From the train station, take tram 1, 6 or 9 to the city centre. Trolleybus 9 goes to/from the university to the airport, which is also linked to the centre by bus 48 to/from pr Shevchenka.

KAMYANETS-PODILSKY

📞03849 / POP 103,000

In a country with no shortage of impressive fortresses, the unique town of Kamyanets-Podilsky (Кам'янець-Подільський) still stands out for its gorgeous castle and dramatic natural beauty. The name Kamyanets refers to the massive stone island created by a sharp bend in the river Smotrych, and the resulting verdant canyon rings a charming old town guarded by a fortress straight out of a fairy tale. If Český Krumlov in the Czech Republic or Bulgaria's Veliko Tărnovo were your thing, don't miss this equally stunning double-barrelled delight.

⊙ Sights

FORTRESS AREA

Kamyanets-Podilsky Fortress   FORTRESS
(admission 14uah; ⊙9am-7pm Tue-Sun, to 6pm Mon) Built of wood in the 10th to 13th cen-

turies, then redesigned and rebuilt in stone by Italian military engineers in the 16th century, KP's fortress is a complete mishmash of styles. But the overall impression is breathtaking, and if Ukraine ever gets its act together as a tourist destination, the view from the **Turkish Bridge** leading to the fortress will become one of the country's iconic, front-page vistas. The name of the bridge is slightly misleading, as it's essentially a medieval structure whose arches were filled in and fortified by Turks in the 17th century.

The fortress is in the shape of a polygon, with nine towers of all shapes and sizes linked by a sturdy wall. In the middle of it all is a vast courtyard. The **New East Tower** (1544) is directly to your right as you enter the fortress and contains a well and a huge winch stretching 40m deep through the cliff to bring up water.

Just beyond the New East Tower, an unmarked white building houses a fantastic **museum** that romps through the history of KP and Ukraine over the last century in a jumble of nostalgia-inducing exhibits. Two revolutions bookend the collections, with the blood-red silken flags of 1917 looking symbolically more potent than the limp orange banners of 2004.

POLISH QUARTER

Under the medieval Magdeburg Laws, each of the old town's four major ethnic groups – Poles, Ukrainians, Armenians and Jews – occupied a different quarter. The focus of the old Polish Quarter is the Polish Market Sq(Polsky rynok), the old town's main piazza.

Cathedral of SS Peter & Paul

CHURCH

(vul Starobulvarna) Through a small triumphal gate in the northwest corner of the square lies this fascinating cathedral, KP's busiest place of worship. One feature of the building perfectly illustrates how the Polish and Turkish empires collided in Kamyanets-Podilsky. Built in 1580 by the Catholic Poles, the cathedral was converted into a mosque when the Turks took over in the late 17th century; they even built an adjacent 42m-high minaret. When the town was handed back to the Poles by treaty in 1699, the Turks specifically stipulated that the minaret could not be dismantled. So the Poles topped it with its current 3.5m-tall golden statue of the Virgin Mary instead.

Ratusha

NOTABLE BUILDING

(Polsky rynok) The Polish Market Sq is lorded over by the tall 14th-century *ratusha* (town hall). The renovated peach-hued building now houses three single-room museums that are of limited interest unless you are into coins, medieval justice or the Magdeburg legal system, but there is a decent bar on the ground floor. In front of the *ratusha* stands the enclosed **Armenian well** (1638), which looks more like a baroque chapel than a well.

Dominican Monastery

MONASTERY

(vul Dominkanska) Vul Dominikanska cuts south from the Polish Market Sq, linking it with the Armenian Quarter. Here you'll find the Dominican Monastery complex, some parts of which date from the 14th century. The buildings suffered damage during WWII, but are now under constant restoration. The monastery **Church of St Nicholas** holds services in Ukrainian and Polish.

ARMENIAN QUARTER

The Armenian Quarter is centred on the quiet Armenian Market Sq, an elongated cobbled expanse to the south of the Polish Quarter.

Podillya Antiquities Museum

MUSEUM

(vul Ivano-Predtechynska 2; admission 5uah; ⊙10am-6pm Tue-Sun, to 5pm Mon) This imaginatively presented museum with English explanations takes visitors through the archaeology of Podillya in six easy steps. You'll begin in a Stone Age cave and end in a courtyard of sculpted Slavic gods, passing through Trypillian, Scythian and early Slav dwellings along the way.

🛏 Sleeping

Hotel 7 Days

HOTEL €€

(☑690 69; www.7dney.com; vul Soborna 4; s/d from 240/420uah; ❄❓✉) This constantly improving place in the new town impresses from the moment you enter the air-conditioned, designer-style lobby. Staff speak English, the service is professional and the room rate includes buffet breakfast and use of the swimming pool.

Hetman

HOTEL €€

(☑067 588 2215; www.hetman-hotel.com.ua; Polsky Rynok 8; r/ste from 385/450uah; ❄❓) The mammoth rooms, great location in a townhouse on the Polish Market Sq and easygoing staff make this atmospheric, 14-room themed hotel worth a little extra hryvnya. The walls are lined with paintings of all Ukraine's Hetmans (Cossack heads of state), an 11m-long tapestry bearing the words of the national anthem hangs in the stairwell and the Ukrainian restaurant serves five types of *borshch*.

🍴 Eating & Drinking

Kafe Pid Bramoyu
UKRAINIAN €

(vul Zamkova 1A; mains 20-35uah) Although the service at this *shashlyk* restaurant-cafe can be spotty, the view overlooking the fortress never takes a day off. The menu covers all the Ukrainian basics, including *deruny* (potato pancakes) and *varenyky* (dumplings), plus fresh fish that you can pick yourself.

Hostynny Dvir
RUSSIAN €

(vul Troitska 1; mains 15-40uah) If you can forgive the spread-eagled bearskin pinned to the far wall, this refined restaurant has the best food in the old town, although service can be glacially slow.

Stara Fortetsya
UKRAINIAN €

(vul Valy 1; mains 16-35uah) Unfortunately you can only take drinks on the balcony, perched dramatically on a 40m cliff over the gorge. Inside is where the Ukrainian food is served.

ℹ️ Information

Post, Internet & Telephone Office (vul Soborna 9; internet per hr 6uah; ⊘post 9am-6pm Mon-Fri, to 4pm Sat, internet 8.30am-9pm Mon-Fri, 10am-10pm Sat & Sun)

ℹ️ Getting There & Away

BUS There are two buses per day to Lviv (101uah, six to 7½ hours), one night bus to Odesa (232uah, 12 hours) and three day buses plus several overnighters to Kyiv (80uah to 220uah, seven to 11 hours).

TRAIN The express train 177 from Kyiv is the quickest way to reach Kamyanets-Podilsky. It departs Kyiv at 4.43pm (57uah, seven hours). The return leg (train 178) departs Kamyanets-Podilsky at 12.52am. There's also at least one overnight service to and from Kyiv (58uah, 6½ hours).

If coming from Lviv or Odesa, take a train to Khmelnytsky and continue by train or *marshrutka* from there. From Lviv you might also consider taking a train to Chernivtsi, and then a *marshrutka* to Kamyanets-Podilsky.

ℹ️ Getting Around

The bus station is within walking distance (two blocks east) of the new town centre. The train station is 1km north of the bus station. Take bus 1 into the new or old town.

ODESA

🗐 048 / POP ONE MILLION

Odesa (Одеса) is a city straight from literature – an energetic, chaotic boomtown. Its famous Potemkin Steps sweep down to the Black Sea and Ukraine's biggest commercial port. Behind them, a cosmopolitan cast of characters makes merry among pastel neo-classical buildings lining a geometrical grid of leafy streets.

But, it has to be said, few come to Ukraine's south coast for the sights – Odesa is definitely more about vibe, nightlife and the beach. Arkadia beach is backed by the best club scene outside Kyiv during the summer; in winter the action moves into the city centre.

Despite its position as the capital of Ukrainian hedonism, Barcelona or Brighton it ain't, and the city can have a distinctly seedy feel. Prostitutes, con artists, drug dealers and the mob have all found their niche here and the city is a magnet for sex tourists, wife hunters and general ne'er-do-wells from around the world. Odesa wasn't invited to the Euro 2012 soccer fest and it shows – there's little in English in Ukraine's most Russian city and some accommodation still has a whiff of the USSR about it.

History

Catherine the Great imagined Odesa as the St Petersburg of the South. Her lover, General Grygory Potemkin, laid the groundwork for her dream in 1789 by capturing the Turkish fortress of Hadjibey, which previously stood here. However, Potemkin died before work began on the city in 1794 and his senior commanders oversaw its construction instead. The Spanish–Neapolitan general José de Ribas, after whom the main street, vul Derybasivska, is named, built the harbour. The Duc de Richelieu (Armand Emmanuel du Plessis), an aristocrat fleeing the French Revolution, became the first governor from 1803 to 1814.

In 1815, when the city became a duty-free port, things really began to boom. Its huge appetite for more labour meant the city became a refuge ('Odesa Mama') for runaway serfs, criminals, renegades and dissidents.

It was the crucible of the 1905 workers' revolution, with a local uprising and the mutiny on the battleship *Potemkin Tavrichesky*. Between 1941 and 1944 Odesa sealed its reputation as one of Stalin's 'hero' cities, when partisans sheltering in the city's catacombs during WWII put up a legendary fight against the occupying Romanians (allies of the Nazis).

Odesa was once a very Jewish city, too, from which its famous sense of humour presumably derives. Jews initially came to Odesa to escape persecution, but tragically suffered the same fate here. In the early 20th century they accounted for one-third of the city's population, but after horrific pogroms in 1905 and 1941 hundreds of thousands emigrated.

◉ Sights & Activities

Potemkin Steps   LANDMARK
You've seen the steppe, now see the steps: the Potemkin Steps, the site of one of cinema's most famous scenes. Designed by Italian architect Franz Boffo, the last of the 192 granite steps was slotted into place in 1841. The lower steps are wider than those at the top creating an optical illusion – the steps seem to be the same width all the way up. If you don't fancy the climb back up to the top, take the free **funicular railway** (⊗8am-11pm) that runs parallel.

Vul Derybasivska   HISTORIC AREA
Odesa's main commercial street is jam-packed with restaurants, bars and, in the summer high season, tourists. At its quieter eastern end you'll discover the **De Ribas statue**, a bronze of the general who built Odesa's harbour and after whom the street is named. At the western end of the thoroughfare is the pleasant **City Garden** (Gorodskoy Sad), surrounded by several restaurants. You'll find various touristy knick-knacks for sale here and you can have your photo taken with a monkey or a snake, but the main draw is people-watching.

Across the street, the swanky **Passazh shopping arcade** (vul Derybasivska 33) is the best-preserved example of the neo-renaissance architectural style that permeated Odesa in the late 19th century.

Bul Prymorsky   STREET
Sooner or later everyone gravitates to this tree-lined pedestrian zone with replica 19th-century gas lamps, park benches and more photographers armed with a small zoo of animals. At the boulevard's eastern end, you'll spot the pink and white colonnaded **City Hall**, originally the stock exchange and later the Regional Soviet Headquarters. In the square in front of the City Hall is Odesa's most photographed monument, the **Pushkin statue**.

Continuing along the boulevard, at the top of the Potemkin Steps you'll reach the **statue** of the Duc de Richelieu, Odesa's first governor, looking like a Roman in a toga. The view from here is of the passenger port, the towering Hotel Odessa and the Black Sea.

Museum of Western & Eastern Art   GALLERY
(www.oweamuseum.odessa.ua; vul Pushkinska 9; admission 25uah; ⊗10.30am-6pm Thu-Tue) Housed in a beautifully renovated (at least on the outside) mid-19th-century palace, the museum's star turn used to be one of 12 known versions (most likely not the original) of Caravaggio's brilliant painting *The Taking of Christ*. However, in July 2008 the canvas was cut from its frame in Ukraine's biggest art heist and only recovered by police two years later. Updated on the outside a few years ago, inside the museum has been in a bit of a state in recent years with most of the Western and Eastern art off limits. However, it's still worth dropping by for the interesting temporary exhibitions that stop here.

Pushkin Museum   MUSEUM
(vul Pushkinska 13; admission 15uah; ⊗10am-5pm Mon-Fri) This is where Alexander Pushkin spent his first days in Odesa, after being exiled from Moscow by the tsar in 1823 for radical ideas. Governor Vorontsov subsequently humiliated the writer with petty administrative jobs, and it took only 13 months, an affair with Vorontsov's wife, a simultaneous affair with someone else's wife and more radical ideas for Pushkin to be thrown out of Odesa, too. Somehow, he still found time while in town to finish the poem *The Bakhchysaray Fountain,* write the first chapter of *Eugene Onegin* and scribble the notes and moaning letters found in this humble museum.

Arkadia Beach   BEACH
An evening at Arkadia is a must when in Odesa and this is definitely the city's best place to see and be seen. Here you can play old-school arcade games, dress up like a tsar or tsarina for a photo op, or hang out in a variety of cafes, bars and clubs.

Take tram 5 from the stop near the train station, in front of the McDonald's on vul Panteleymonivska, to the end of the line.

Opera & Ballet Theatre   THEATRE
(www.opera.odessa.ua; pereulok Chaykovskoho 1) The jewel in Odesa's architectural crown was designed in the 1880s by the architects who also designed the famous Vienna State Opera, namely Ferdinand Fellner and Herman Helmer.

🛏 Sleeping

Odesa is popular among Russians and Ukrainians, especially in July and August. Some of the city's cheap hotels are no more than knocking shops with hourly rates and thin walls. If booking ahead online, read reviews before committing!

Odesa

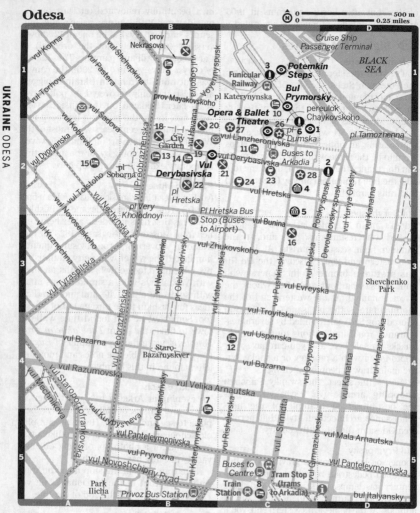

TOP CHOICE Mozart Hotel

HOTEL €€€

(☎377777; www.mozart-hotel.com; vul Lanzheronivska 13; s/tw from 1304/1635uah; ⊖❄☎✹) As the name suggests, this top choice epitomises European luxury, with elegant furnishings and a calm, light-filled interior lurking behind its refurbished neoclassical facade. The 40 rooms are individually decorated and the location across from the Opera and Ballet Theatre is perfect.

Frederic Koklen

BOUTIQUE HOTEL €€€

(☎737 5553; www.koklenhotel.com; per Nekrasova 7; d/ste from 975/1925uah; ❄☎) Odesa's most

sumptuous boutique hotel has guests gushing forth about exceptional service, luxurious period ambience and the great location. Rooms in this renovated mansion are studies in 18th- and 19th-century Imperial-era style and attention to detail – the quality of materials and standard of maintenance are outstanding for Ukraine.

Royal Street Hotel

HOTEL €€

(☎700 0068; www.royalstreet.com.ua; vul Derybasivska 27; s/d from 520/690uah; ❄☎) In the thick of the action at the busier end of vul Derybasivska, one of Odesa's best deals offers

Odesa

generously cut rooms done out in flock wallpaper and heavy drapes. There's no breakfast so hit the cafes on the main drag.

Hotel Londonskaya
HOTEL €€€

(☎738 0110; www.londred.com; bul Prymorsky 11; r 1100-1850uah; ❄✳🖥🛜) Last refurbished in the early 1990s, the rooms of Odesa's oldest luxury hotel are now slightly dated and a bit basic for the price, but with iron-lace balustrades, stained-glass windows, parquet flooring and an inner courtyard, the place still oozes period charm.

Babushka Grand Hostel
HOSTEL €

(☎063 070 5535; www.babushkagrand.com; vul Mala Arnautska 60; dm from 120uah; ✳@🛜) While Odessa's other hostels are decidedly for the young, day-sleeping crowd, the wonderfully named Babushka Grand, occupying a palatial apartment near the train station, has a more laid-back, traveller vibe. The stuccoed interiors and crystal chandeliers are stunning and the staff fun.

TIU Front Page Hostel
HOSTEL €

(☎050 172 8566, 096 834 4074; vul Koblevska 42, top fl; dm 120-130uah; @🛜) One of the few hostels to stay open year-round, this large apartment has 24 beds, three showers, a kitchen and a

friendly welcome. The current owners inherited the premises from a publishing company who had wallpapered the entire place in magazine front pages, hence the name.

Passazh Hotel
HOTEL €

(☎728 5500; www.passage-hotel.com.ua; vul Preobrazhenska 34; s/d from 190/265uah) The Passazh is the epitome of faded glory, but how glorious it must have been. The 132 rooms feature lots of Soviet antiques, awful wallpaper, cheapo furniture and shoddy tilework, but they are large and are fitted with old-world amenities such as full-length claw-footed bath tubs.

Bus Station Hotel
HOTEL €

(vul Kolontayivska 58, 3rd fl; d 200uah; ✳) On the 3rd floor of the slowly renovating bus station, this no-frills, characterless 20-room hotel is only attractive for the price and proximity to departing/arriving buses. All rooms are en suite and the staff are friendly enough. Tram 5 goes from outside direct to the train station and Arcadia beach.

✕ Eating

TOP CHOICE **Gogol Mogol**
EUROPEAN €€

(per Nekrasova 2; mains 60-130uah; ⏰9am-midnight; 🍴) From the multi-hued old bicycles and rainbow park benches bolted to the pavement outside to the jumble-sale decor of the quirky interior, this art cafe is an unmissable piece in the alternative city-centre jigsaw. The short menu doubles up as a visitor's book, they do a mean cappuccino and it's also a popular evening meeting spot.

Kompot
FRENCH €€

(vul Derybasivska 20; mains 40-90uah; ◷8am-11pm) Spilling out onto busy Derybasivska to a jolly Gallic soundtrack, this French-style eatery is good for any meal of the day. Fresh pastries and an early opening time are a godsend for caffeine-craving Westerners, light lunches can be devoured in the faux Parisian interior over a newspaper and you can dine out on the cobbles till late with a bottle of something nice. Service here can be *escargot*-paced when busy.

Bernadazzi
ITALIAN, UKRAINIAN €€

(vul Bunina 15, Philharmonic Hall; mains 60-160uah; ◷10am-last customer; 🖥) Few Ukrainian restaurants have truly authentic settings but the art nouveau dining room of this superb Italian job, part of the eye-catching Philharmonic Hall, is the real deal. In addition to well-crafted southern and Eastern European fare, there's an award-winning wine list, occasional live music and a secluded courtyard for summertime chilling.

Klarabara
INTERNATIONAL €€

(City Garden; mains 90-150uah; ◷9am-midnight) Tucked away in a quiet corner of the City Garden, this classy, cosy, ivy-covered cafe and restaurant is awash with antique furniture and fine art. The food is a mixed bag of *shashlyk*, salads, internationally flavoured starters such as frogs' legs and Czech-style fried cheese, Black Sea fish and steaks.

Kumanets
UKRAINIAN €€

(vul Havanna 7; mains 40-100uah; ◷noon-midnight) A kitsch little outpost of Ukraine in oh-so Russian Odesa, this veritable Ukrainian village produces affordable *holubtsy* (cabbage rolls), *varenyky* and *deruny* (potato pancakes), in addition to pricier mains.

Puzata Khata
CAFE €

(vul Derybasivska 21; mains 10-25uah; ◷9am-10pm; 🛜) Take the lift to the 6th floor of the Evropa shopping mall to find the Odesa branch of this national chain. The theme here is vaguely Greco-Black Sea, but the serving staff still look as though they've just stepped off the steppe. The cut-priced fare here is as tasty as at any other branch.

Tavriya
CAFE €

(pl Hretska, Galereya Afina mall; mains from around 10uah; ◷8am-10pm) This food mecca in the basement of a shopping mall has become the city's most popular quick eat. The *stolova* (cafeteria) has a larger choice of dishes than the city's other canteens, but can be a much more Ukrainian-style push-and-shove affair, and the service stinks.

Drinking

TOP CHOICE **Shkaf**
BAR

(vul Hretska 32; ◷7pm-late) This bar-cum-club is a sure-fire antidote to Odesa's pop-chick beach-club scene and pick-up bars. Recently moved to more findable premises, The Cupboard rocks most nights to live music, local DJs and the sounds of an alternative crowd of locals having fun.

Shuzz
LIVE MUSIC

(vul Uspenska 22; ◷5pm-3am, closed Jul & Aug) Occupying a former shoe factory, the vibe is laid-back here so grab a cloudy Chernihivske Bile and chill to whatever's playing – this is also the best alternative music venue in Odesa.

Friends and Beer
BAR

(vul Derybasivska 9; 🛜) This charming re-created USSR-era living room littered with photos of Russian film stars is proof that 'Retro Soviet' doesn't have to mean political posters and Constructivist art. The huge TV screen is possibly not authentic for the period, but it's great for sports.

☆ Entertainment

Nightclubs

Odesa's raucous club scene is divided into two seasons: summer (June to August) and the rest of the year. In summer, all the action is at Arkadia Beach, which boasts two huge, Ibiza-style nightclubs that produce heightened levels of madness seven days a week. At other times of the year, the action is closer to the city centre.

Ibiza
CLUB

(www.ibiza.ua; Arkadia Beach; ☺summer) This white, free-form, cavelike structure is Arkadia's most upmarket and most expensive club. European DJs and big-ticket Russian and Ukrainian pop bands often play here. Ticket prices can be high when a big act is in town.

Itaka
CLUB

(www.itaka-club.com.ua; Arkadia Beach; ☺summer) It's slightly more downmarket than Ibiza and consequently often rowdier (in a good way). The Greek columns and statues are a tad much, but you'll hardly care when it's 5am. Like Ibiza, it also draws big regional pop acts.

Shede
GAY

(www.shede-club.com.ua; vul Derybasivska 5) One of Ukraine's best openly gay nightclubs, it has Friday and Saturday night shows beginning at 1am.

Praetoria Music Club
LIVE MUSIC

(vul Lanzheronivska 26) One of the few city-centre clubs with a pulse in the summer.

Classical Music & Opera
Odessa Philharmonic Hall
LIVE MUSIC

(www.odessaphilharmonic.org; vul Bunina 15; ☺closed Jul & Aug) The best regional orchestra within the former Soviet Union is the Odessa Philharmonic Orchestra, which accounts for half the symphonies put on here.

Odesa Opera and Ballet Theatre
THEATRE

(www.opera.odessa.ua; pereulok Chaykovskoho 1) In addition to being architecturally magnificent Odesa's theatre is also known for its marvellous acoustics.

ℹ Information

Central Post Office (vul Sadova 10)

Kiy Avia (www.kiyavia.com; vul Preobrazhenska 15; ☺8am-8pm daily) Kiy Avia can sort you out with tickets and timetables.

Tourist Office (☎731 4808; www.go2odessa.ru; bul Italyansky 11; ☺9am-6pm Mon-Sat) One of Ukraine's best tourist offices, with dedicated staff, heaps of detailed info and lots of hands-on help for travellers.

ℹ Getting There & Away

Air

Odesa airport (www.odessa.aero) is better linked to Europe than most other regional Ukrainian airports. LOT, S7, Czech Airlines, Turkish Airlines and Aeroflot all have regular flights here, and various other carriers fly to Georgia, Israel and Egypt.

Domestic airlines UT Air and Aerosvit both fly to/from Kyiv up to five times a day. Kiy Avia will sort you out with tickets and timetables.

Bus

Odesa has two bus stations that are useful for travellers. The slightly chaotic **Privoz bus station** (vul Vodoprovodna), 300m west of the train station, is mainly for shorter trips.

Most international and long-haul domestic buses leave from the **long-distance bus station** (vul Kolontayivska 58), 3km west of the train station. Frequent **Gunsel** (☎702 2831; www.gunsel.com.ua) and **Autolux** (☎716 4612; www.autolux.ua) buses are the most comfortable and quickest way to travel to Kyiv (175uah to 260uah, six to seven hours). Otherwise speedy *marshrutky* leave from just in front of the station building (200uah, six hours). Other destinations include Simferopol (180uah, 12 hours, three daily), Yalta (200uah, 14 hours, two daily) and Lviv (200uah, 15 hours, two daily) via Kamyanets-Podilsky.

There are at least 13 buses a day to Chişinău (90uah to 105uah, five hours) some of which travel via Tiraspol in Transdnistr. **Ecollnes** (☎356 409; www.ecolines.net) operates coaches from Odesa to Moscow, Minsk and Riga.

Train

There are five trains to Kyiv (130uah to 180uah, 8½ to 12 hours), two of which are overnighters. Other destinations Include Lviv (130uah to 160uah, 12 hours, three daily) and Simferopol (120uah to 150uah, 11 hours, one or two daily). Longer-distance services go to Moscow, Minsk and St Petersburg. There's also one train per day to Chişinău (76uah, five hours) leaving at 4.48pm.

ℹ Getting Around

Odesa airport is about 12km southwest of the city centre, off Ovidiopilska doroha. Bus 129 goes to/from the train station; infrequent bus 117 runs to/from the pl Hretska stop.

To get to the centre from the train station (about a 20-minute walk), go to the stop near the McDonald's and take any bus marked with Площа Грецка (pl Hretska), such as the 148. Trolleybuses 4 and 10 trundle up vul Pushkinska before curving around to vul Prymorska past the passenger port and the foot of the Potemkin Steps.

Tram 5 goes from the train station to the long-distance bus station. From the Privoz bus station to pl Hretska take bus 220.

CRIMEA

Rip up what you think you know about Ukraine and start from scratch – Crimea (Крим) will confound any generalisations you've made about the country so far and take you into a new world of astonishing scenery, rich cultural ferment and a semitropical climate kept balmy by a warm breeze coming off the Black Sea. No wonder this peninsula has been fought over by the Greeks, Khazars, Tatars, Mongols, Huns, Genoese, Ottomans, Russians, French and British over the centuries.

The most attractive and interesting part of the peninsula is the so-called Russian Riviera – you'll understand the accuracy of the name if you're here in the summer months, when much of Moscow descends on the resorts here. In addition to the seedy resort towns of Yalta and Alupka, you'll find the fascinating palaces where modern European history was shaped in 1945 by the 'Big Three' (Stalin, Churchill and Roosevelt). But the highlight of the entire peninsula is without doubt tiny Bakhchysaray, the old Crimean Tatar capital with the dramatic setting and the perfectly preserved Khan's Palace.

History

While Crimea's early history is a palimpsest of cultural annexations from the Greeks and Scythians to the Genoese and Jews, the real crucible of the peninsula's history has been the conflict between Turkic and Slavic peoples for control.

The Mongols arrived in 1240 as they shattered Kyivan Rus, and their descendants, the Crimean Tatars, formed a khanate (subdivision of the Ottoman Empire ruled by a khan) here, which in later years became a vassal state of the Ottoman Empire.

While a Turkish vassal state, Crimea enjoyed much autonomy. The same was not true when the Russians arrived in 1783 and began a campaign of 'revenge' for the Tatars' slave-trading raids into Russia over the centuries. Most of the peninsula's four to five million Tatars fled to Turkey, while Russians, Ukrainians, Bulgarians and even some Germans were invited to resettle Crimea.

Much to the chagrin of its rival empires, Russia wanted to take over the faltering Ottoman Empire, and when Tsar Nicholas I sent troops into the Ottoman provinces of Moldavia and Wallachia (ostensibly to protect the Christians there) in 1854, the British and French assembled in Varna (now in Bulgaria) to protect İstanbul. Both sides lost about 250,000 soldiers in the ensuing Crimean War, many from bad medical care – to which British nurse Florence Nightingale drew attention.

By the 1860s, however, Crimea had become a chic leisure spot, thanks to Russia's imperial family building a summer estate at Livadia, on the outskirts of Yalta.

During the civil war that followed the Russian Revolution, Crimea was one of the last 'white' bastions. The Germans occupied the peninsula for three years during WWII and Crimea lost nearly half its inhabitants. In 1944 Stalin banished the entire Tatar population to Central Asia.

Throughout the Soviet era, millions came each year to Crimea, attracted by the warmth, beauty, beaches and mountain air. In 1954 Khrushchev transferred control of the peninsula to Ukraine, a sticking point today as the Crimean population still have more in common with Russia. Russia controversially uses Sevastopol as its Black Sea naval base.

Simferopol Сімферополь

📞 0652 / POP 344,000 / TRANSPORT HUB

If you're arriving in Crimea by rail or air, chances are you will spend a bit of time in the Crimean capital, a not unpleasant city, but one with few reasons to linger – everything else on the peninsula is much more exciting and only a short bus ride away. For those who do spend a night or two here, the city's quality restaurants and cafes are the definite highlight.

🛏 Sleeping

Simferopol's hostels tend to pop up for a few months over the summer, then close, only to reappear the next year in a new location. Check booking websites for the latest offerings.

Suvorovsky House Hotel HOTEL €
(www.gostinec.com.ua; Suvorovsky Spusk 9; s/d from 380-420uah; ✳ 🌐) For many the best deal in town, with immaculate, almost stylish rooms, 21st-century bathrooms and a quiet but central location. No breakfast.

Hotel Valencia
HOTEL €

(📞620 006; www.valencia.crimea.ua; vul Odeska 8; s/d from 250/350uah; ❄🛜) Fusing Crimea and Spain, this centrally located, friendly and well-run hotel is justifiably popular, so book ahead. Rooms won't win many awards for style but everything is kept clean and functional and the location puts you near edibles.

Hotel Ukraina
HOTEL €€

(📞532 253; www.ukraina-hotel.biz; vul Rozy Lyuxemburg 7; s/d from 530/690uah; ❄🛜) Admittedly, the baroque public areas of this central, forward-thinking hotel are a bit OTT, but rooms are restrained verging on spartan. Staff speak English, and there's a sauna and *hammam* (Turkish bath).

✗ Eating & Drinking

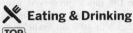

Vegeteriya
VEGETARIAN €

(vul Samokisha 18; mains 17-37uah; ⏰9am-9pm; 🛜📶📋) Crimea's first vegetarian eatery is also one of Ukraine's best and has been nationally recognised as such. With no gimmicks when it comes to decor, there's nothing to detract from the scrumptious organic fare which has a definite Indian and Italian theme. All the staff are vegetarian and there's an attached health-food shop.

Divan
CRIMEAN TATAR €

(vul Gorkoho 6; mains 16-55uah; ⏰9am-11pm; 📋) For an easily accessible, wallet-friendly and tasty introduction to Crimean Tatar tucker, head for this great cellar restaurant with its stained-glass lanterns and menu of local favourites such as *chebureki* (fried meat and onion turnovers), *plov* (rice stewed with carrot and lamb) and kebabs. As in most Tatar restuarants, there's no booze, just big pots of tea and glasses of *ayran* (fermented milk).

U Mamy
EASTERN EUROPEAN €

(vul Ushinskoho 1/48; mains 6-15uah; ⏰8am-9pm) A no-frills, half-circle cafeteria where ladle-wielding dinner ladies plate up belly-satisfying Eurasian comfort food such as *manty* (meat-filled dumplings), *borshch*, *tefteli* (meatballs), *pelmeni* (meat-filled pasta) and goulash. Located opposite the Simferopol Cinema.

Kofein
COFFEE HOUSE

(vul Pushkina 8; ⏰24hr; 🛜) The 'exoticism' at this trendy African-themed cafe overdoes its appreciation of the female form. But if you can position yourself where your eyes are not being poked out by a photographed nipple, you'll find it takes its coffee seriously and turns out a good brew.

Begemotobar
BAR

(vul Gorkoho 8) Biker-themed cellar pub, the decor of which looks like the scatterings of a particularly destructive RTA (think old tyres, battered number plates etc). Live music and Yalta beer, but things only get going here in the evenings.

ℹ Information

Central Post Office (vul Alexandra Nevskoho 1; internet per hr 7uah)

ℹ Getting There & Away

Air

Simferopol airport (www.airport.crimea.ua) is 15km northwest of the centre. Aerosvit, Turkish Airlines, Aeroflot and Air Onix all fly in from abroad. Budget carrier Wizzair connects Simferopol with London Luton via Kyiv.

Kiy Avia (📞272 167; www.kiyavia.crimea.ua; bul Lenina 1/7; ⏰9am-6pm Mon-Fri, 9am-5pm Sat) sells both international and domestic air tickets.

Bus

Buses to just about anywhere in Crimea depart from the Kurortnaya bus station, located next to McDonalds in front of the train station. There are frequent services to Yalta (28uah, 1½ hours, up to five hourly) and Bakhchysaray (10uah, one hour).

Simferopol is one end of the world's longest trolleybus route, the other end being Yalta (15uah, two hours, three hourly). Services depart from next to the Kurortnaya station.

Train

Simferopol is Crimea's main railway junction, with four trains daily to/from Kyiv (150uah to 260uah, 14 to 18 hours) and services to/from Lviv (190uah, 24 hours, daily) and Odesa (120uah to 150uah, 11 hours, one or two daily). There are also direct services to Moscow, St Petersburg, Ekaterinburg and Minsk.

Local *elektrychki* (local trains) run regularly along the Crimean peninsula to/from Yevpatoriya (two hours, seven a day in each direction) and Sevastopol (two hours, seven daily in each direction). The latter service stops en route in Bakhchysaray (40 minutes).

ℹ Getting Around

Trolleybus 9 (1.25uah, 30 minutes) runs from the airport to the train station and onwards to the centre. The hassle factor from taxi drivers at the airport is high – you're very likely to be ripped off if you take up their offers of transportation. From the train station you can also take trolleybus 5 or 7 into the centre, or a *marshrutka* or bus from near McDonald's with Сільпо (Silpo) on its side.

Yalta   Ялта

☑ 0654 / POP 79,500

Like dark matter, Yalta exerts a poorly understood yet irresistible force on people in Crimea, and it seems almost anyone you meet will be heading to or escaping from the peninsula's most famous and tackiest resort town, once the preserve of tsars and artists and now...well, not.

Yalta is best enjoyed in the shoulder seasons when temperatures are just about bearable and the tanned hordes of Slavic holidaymakers are thinner. Arrive during the Russian/Ukrainian summer holidays (July and August) and you only have yourself to blame.

◉ Sights

CITY CENTRE

Nab Lenina   SEAFRONT

The promenade, nab Lenina, stretches past numerous piers, palm trees, restaurants, boutiques and souvenir stalls to **Prymorsky Park**, where there are some carnival-type rides. The promenade starts at **ploscha Lenina** (Lenin Sq), the centre of activity. Here there are plenty of benches for people-watching under the shadow of a **statue of Lenin**. The former Soviet leader gawks at the McDonald's across the way as if Ronald were the red-haired devil himself.

Although swimming isn't an option along the promenade, you can descend to a few short lengths of beach, most of which are made up of rocks.

Chekhov House-Museum   MUSEUM

(www.chekhov.com.ua; vul Kirova 112; admission 30uah; ☉10am-5pm, last entry 4.30pm Tue-Sun Jun-Sep, Wed-Sun Sep-May) Anton Chekhov, Russia's greatest dramatist, wrote *The Cherry Orchard* and *Three Sisters* in what is now the Chekhov House-Museum. The small estate, where he entertained the likes of Chaliapin, Rachmaninov, Gorky and Tolstoy, is Yalta's only must-see sight. Take *marshrutka* 6 from Veshchevoy Rynok terminal or *marshrutka* 8 from the Spartak cinema to the Dom-Muzey Chekhova stop. It takes 15 to 20 minutes to walk from the Spartak Cinema.

OUTSIDE YALTA

Many travellers hang around in Yalta not because they're into the resorty vibe but be-

cause it makes an excellent base from which to see Crimea's spectacular historic and natural sights.

Massandra Winery   WINERY

(vul Vinodela Yegorova 9; tour prices vary; ☉4 tours per day) Memoirists claim that Tsar Nicholas II would always keep a flask of Massandra port hidden in his high boot during his daily walks, while his wife sipped the very same drink listening to Rasputin's prophesies. The imperial court's winery is now open to visitors. On a mandatory Russian-language excursion, you get to see the tsar's wine cellars, which contain over a million dust-covered bottles, including a 1775 Spanish Jerez de la Frontera, claimed to be the oldest preserved wine in the world. The visit ends with a tasting session. Take bus 3 or 40 from Veshchevoy Rynok.

Ay-Petri Cable Car   CABLE CAR

(one way 60uah; ☉ticket office 10am-4pm, services every 20min to 5pm) On the coastal road in Miskhor, behind a cluster of market stalls, is the cable car up the cliff of Mt Ay-Petri. It's a dizzying ride across the foothills and up the mountain's sheer face, during which you'll overlook the coast and the sea. Views from the top are stunning, while Mt Ay-Petri's dry plateau itself feels otherworldly, or at least Central Asian. There are also several Tatar eateries here. Buses 27 and 32 between Yalta and Alupka stop here.

Swallow's Nest   HISTORIC BUILDING

(Lastochkino Gnezdo; admission during exhibitions 35uah; ☉8am-6pm Tue-Sun) Like many movie stars, the Swallow's Nest is shorter in real life than it appears in pictures. This toy-town castle, 10km west of Yalta, is a favourite subject for Crimean postcards, calendars and a million other tacky souvenirs, though has little practical use other than as an occasional exhibition space.

It's the castle's precarious perch, overhanging the sheer cliff of Cape Ay-Todor, that gives a minor thrill as you traverse the surrounding walkway. Although the castle looks medieval in style, it was built in 1912 for German oil magnate Baron Steingel, as a gift for his mistress.

The most spectacular approach to the castle is by excursion boat (60uah to 80uah, up to 20 daily) that heads from Yalta pier to the beach and jetty just below. Buses 32, 26 and 27 also pass this way.

Livadia Palace   HISTORIC BUILDING

(admission 65uah; ⊗9am-6pm) It's not the most sumptuously furnished Crimean interior, but Livadia Palace reverberates with history. It's the site of the 1945 Yalta Conference, where dying US President Franklin Roosevelt and British Prime Minister Winston Churchill turned up to be bullied by Soviet leader Josef Stalin. While here, Churchill declared Crimea 'the Riviera of Hades' – and no wonder, given the company he was keeping. Stalin's insistent demands to keep Poland and other swaths of Eastern Europe shaped the face of postwar Europe.

In the enormous **White Hall**, the 'Big Three' and their staff met to tacitly carve up Europe. The crucial documents, dividing Germany and ceding parts of Poland to the USSR, were signed on 11 February in the English billiard room. The most famous Yalta photograph of Churchill, Roosevelt and Stalin is hung on a wall, along with the awkward outtakes, which bring history to life.

It's upstairs, however, that Livadia's other ghosts will genuinely move you. This Italian Renaissance-style building was designed as a summer residence for Russian Tsar Nicholas II in 1911. But he and his family spent just four seasons here before their arrest by Bolshevik troops in 1917 and murder in Yekaterinburg the following year. Photos and some poignant mementos of the doomed Romanovs remain in their private quarters.

Marshrutka 47a from Veshchevoy Rynok and *Marshrutka* 5 from the Spartak Cinema drop you in the palace grounds.

🛏 Sleeping

The entire city seems to be for rent in summer. Apartments come in all shapes from four walls and a bed for 250uah to fully furnished, multibedroom cottages that may cost up to 4000uah a night. Prices drop drastically off-season. Good agencies to try are **Travel 2 Sevastopol** (⊘050 649 8360; www.travel-2sevastopol.com) and **Black Sea Crimea** (⊘in UK 07808 160 621; www.blacksea-crimea.com). If turning up unannounced, look for signs saying Сдаётся квартира/жильё/комната (flat/accommodation/room for rent), usually followed by a mobile phone number to call.

TOP CHOICE **Villa Sofia**   BOUTIQUE HOTEL €€€

(⊘262 525; www.villasofia.com.ua; nab Lenina 31; d from 4000uah; ❊@☎) Just a few flip-flop thwacks from the seafront in a quiet(ish) spot on nab Lenina, this high-class boutique oasis is the latest addition to Yalta's sleeping scene. The seven gobsmacking rooms, occupying a restored mansion, are exquisitely designed, most exuding a cool Franco-Moorish ambience, but all boasting fittings and furnishings, the quality of which you'll be pushed to find anywhere else in Ukraine. Book well ahead as this place is always full.

Sobaka Hostel   HOSTEL €

(⊘063 317 0056; www.sobakahostel.com; vul Chernova 29a; d/tw 350/120uah; @☎) Located in a riddle of old streets around 800m up the hill from the seafront, this year-round hostel offers two dorms and three private rooms in a three-storey new-build. Clean rooms, fresh bunks, a kitchen and a washing machine make this a magnet for budget nomads. See the hostel website for directions.

Bristol   HISTORIC HOTEL €€€

(⊘234 560, 271 616; www.hotel-bristol.com.ua; vul Ruzvelta 10; r from 980uah; ❊☎⛱) Few of us ever really need more comfort than this central, three-star establishment provides. The town's oldest hotel occupies a 19th-century listed building, but rooms were thoughtfully renovated in 2003, many in yellow and blue hues. Throw in a good breakfast buffet and reasonable service, and a few nights here make a comfortable base from which to explore the area.

Vremena Goda   HOTEL €€€

(⊘237 935; www.hotel-seasons.com.ua; vul Rudanskoho 23; s/d from 680/950uah; ❊⛱) For something a little special, visit this spa hotel and medical centre for its chocolate massages and mud treatments. With clean, modern lines complemented by a few art nouveau stained-glass windows, the 'Four Seasons' is within fairly easy reach (a 10- to 15-minute walk) of the high-season action.

Otdykh   HOTEL €

(⊘276 027; www.otdyh-yalta.ru; vul Drazhinskoho 14; economy/standard d 300/640uah; ❊) Hotel 'Relaxation' was a 19th-century brothel; now it's a decent enough budget hotel. Some of the bathrooms are a bit whiffy and there's some street noise, but staff speak OK English and there's a cheap cafe on the premises.

🍴 Eating & Drinking

The waterfront and adjacent street are lined with restaurants offering standard 'European' (that is, post-Soviet) menus. Myriad Столовая signs mark cafeterias where you can choose from displayed dishes.

Khutorok La Mer
UKRAINIAN €€

(vul Sverdlova 9; mains 65-200uah; ⊙11am-2am)
Strange would be the *khutorok* (a traditional
Ukranian farm) with sea junk suspended
from its rafters, but this upmarket eatery is
random in other ways too. The cover-all-bases
menu is a geographically confused selection
of Ukrainian, Italian and marine items with
lots of grilled meat and Black Sea fish.

Apelsin
EUROPEAN, JAPANESE €€€

(nab Lenina 50b; mains 49-269uah; ⊙24hr) Won-
dering what the mammoth mock galleon
perched high on stilts at the southern end
of nab Lenina is? That's Apelsin, a huge restaurant with sweeping views of the promenade and a menu of sushi and international
mains. Come here for any meal of the day
at any time of day, though things only really
kick off after dark.

Smak
CRIMEAN TATAR €€

(vul Pushkinskaya 7a; mains 50-150uah) This
simple open-air eatery and takeaway makes
more than 10 different kinds of mouth-
watering *chebureki*, an impressive array of
other Crimean Tatar dishes, great *shash-
lyks* and Black Sea fish. There's also pizza
on the run served by a gang of 'real' Italian
chefs from Egypt.

Blinoteka
PANCAKES €

(vul Chekhova 9; mains 12-25uah; ⊙9am-11pm) This
cool, quiet, beige-brown-hued cafe specialises
in Russia's favourite comfort food – bliny (pancakes) – expertly filled with just about anything you might wish to find within a rolled
sheet of gently fried dough. Some Crimean
wines and decent coffees available, too.

Pinta
BEER HALL

(vul Pushkinskaya 7; ⊙10am-2am; 🛜) Low-lit
beer hall at the end of the promenade serving international beer brands, such as Bel-
gian Leffe and Czech Staropramen on tap
and a long meat-heavy menu.

❶ Information

Dozens of tourist booths line the waterfront
and around, selling reasonably priced Russian-
language day trips and, occasionally, maps.
Remember, some attractions don't need much
commentary.

Post Office (pl Lenina 1; ⊙7am-8pm Mon-Sat,
9am-4pm Sun)

Tourist office (☐3210; www.yalta-tic.com.ua;
nab Lenina 12; ⊙24hr) Open-all-hours office in
a yurt-shaped building at the end of the promenade. English spoken.

Travel2crimea.com (☐050 324 2350; www.
travel2crimea.com; vul Dzerzhinskoho 4;
⊙9.30am-5.30pm Mon-Fri, Sat & Sun in high
season) With years of experience, excellent
English and a helpful manner, owner Igor
Brudny runs a great travel service.

❶ Getting There & Away

Services depart on the world's longest trolleybus route from near Yalta's **main bus station**
(vul Moskovskaya 8) to Simferopol (15uah, two
hours, every 20 minutes). Otherwise ordinary
buses (28uah, two hours, up to five hourly) leave
from the station itself.

❶ Getting Around

There are several bus and *marshrutka* stations in
town. You'll arrive at the main bus station, which
is about 1.5km from the waterfront. From here,
trolleybuses 1, 2 and 3 (1.25uah) descend vul
Kyivska to the centre.

Behind the main bus station, on the lower level,
you'll find the buses and *marshrutky* going to the
sights around Yalta. But perhaps more useful
are Veshchevoy Rynok and Spartak cinema bus
stations.

Bakhchysaray
Бахчисарай

☑ 06554 / POP 33,800

A world away from the 'glamour' and clamour of the coastal resort towns, the former
capital of the Crimean khanate is an absolute
must-see on any trip to the peninsula. With
three stellar attractions: the Khans' Palace
(which dates back to the 16th century), the
still-working Uspensky Monastery built into
sheer cliff walls, and the 6th-century cave city
of Chufut-Kale. It's worth doing an overnight
trip here, not least because there are some
great accommodation options and plenty of
chances to taste Crimean Tatar cuisine.

◉ Sights

Khans' Palace
HISTORIC BUILDING

(www.hansaray.org.ua; vul Lenina 129; admission
50uah; ⊙9am-5.30pm) When she was busy
ordering the mass destruction of Bakhchysaray's mosques in the 18th and early 19th
centuries, Catherine the Great spared the
Khans' Palace as she thought the building
'romantic'. While it lacks the imposing grandeur of Islamic structures in, say, İstanbul,
this is a major landmark of Crimean culture
and history. Erected in the 16th century under the direction of Persian, Ottoman and
Italian architects, it was rebuilt a few times,
but the structure still resembles the original.

Passing through the back of the finely carved, Venetian Renaissance **Demir Qapi Portal** (also called Portal Alevizo after its Italian designer who also authored parts of Moscow's Kremlin), you'll enter the west wing and the dimly lit **Divan Hall**. This was the seat of government where the khan and his nobles discussed laws and wars.

Through the hall lies the inner courtyard, containing two fountains. With its white marble ornately inscribed with gold leaf, the **Golden Fountain** (1733) is probably the more beautiful. However, the neighbouring **Fountain of Tears** (1764) is more famous, thanks to Alexander Pushkin's poem *The Bakhchysaray Fountain*. It's tradition that two roses – one red for love and one yellow for chagrin – are placed atop the fountain; Pushkin was the first to do this.

Behind the palace is the only surviving **harem** of the four that were traditionally attached to the palace and belonged to the khans' wives. Across the yard you can see the **Falcon Tower**.

The tour route ends at the **museum** crammed full of ornate costumes, heeled sandals, musical instruments, mock-ups of furnished rooms and everyday items that were used by the Khans' household.

Uspensky Monastery
MONASTERY

Stop for a moment and say 'Aah!' at possibly the cutest little church in a country absolutely jam-packed with them. Part of the small Uspensky Monastery, the gold-domed church was built into the limestone rock of the surrounding hill, probably by Byzantine monks in the 8th or 9th century. Whitewashed monks' cells, a 'healing' fountain and tiled mosaics cling to the hillside, too.

Chufut-Kale
CAVES

(admission 40uah; ⊙9am-6pm) Rising 200m, this long plateau houses a honeycomb of caves and structures where for centuries people have taken refuge. It's wonderful to explore, especially the burial chambers and casemates with large open 'windows' in the vertiginous northern cliff.

First appearing in historical records as Kyrk-Or (Forty Fortifications), the city was settled between the 6th and 12th centuries by Christianised descendants of Sarmatian tribes. The last powerful ruler of the Golden Horde, Tokhtamysh, sheltered here after defeat in the 1390s, and the first Crimean khanate was established at Chufut-Kale in the 15th century, before moving to nearby

Bakhchysaray. After the Tatars left, Turkic–Jewish Karaites occupied the city until the mid-19th century, which won the mountain its current name of 'Jewish Fortress'.

Following the track from Uspensky, the best idea is to keep bearing right. The main entrance is not under the flat tin roof to the left of the Chufut-Kale sign, but further up the hill to the right. At this, the 14th-century main **South Gate**, you'll usually be hit for the entrance fee.

Soon after the gate, you enter a Swiss-cheese composition of carved-out rooms and steps. Behind this a stone path heads along the top of the plateau, past two locked **kenassas** (Karaite prayer houses) in a walled courtyard to the right. There is a **Karaite cultural centre and cafe** in the adjacent former house of the city's last resident, Karaite leader Avraam Firkovich.

To the left of the first intersection stands the red-tile roofed **Muslim mausoleum** (1437) of Dzhanike-Khanym, daughter of Tokhtamysh; to the right is an archway. Head left behind the mausoleum towards the cliff edge and enjoy the view of the valley below. To the right (east), a grassy track leads to two **burial chambers** in the northern side of the cliff.

From here it's hard to get lost; there are more caves until you reach the locked **East Gate**, where the road loops back on itself towards the main gate.

🛏 Sleeping & Eating

Dilara Hanum
B&B €

(☎063 227 3120, 050 930 4163; www.bahchisaray.net; vul Ostrovskoho 43; r from 320uah; @☎) Just 300m from the Khans' Palace but almost under the escarpment at the end of vul Ostrovskoho, a lane that climbs steeply from vul Lenina, this superb little unmarked guesthouse is managed by a friendly, English-speaking Crimean Tatar family with heaps of local knowledge. Rooms are modern and come with attached bathrooms and stupendous views of Bakhchysaray; communal facilities include a guest kitchen, a library with books in English, a TV and games room.

Hotel Meraba
GUESTHOUSE €

(☎067 731 5235; www.meraba.crimea.ua; vul Rechnaya 125b; r from 320uah; ☎) This nine-room guesthouse, just 200m from the Khans' Palace, is a long-time favourite among travellers, though it lacks the personal welcome of the town's homestays. Rooms are fairly austere, but bathrooms are post-millenium and there's a pleasant garden for summer barbeques.

Musafir
CRIMEAN TATAR €

(vul Gorkoho 21; mains 18-35uah; ⊗8am-11pm; 🛜🍴) A specially invited Uzbek *plov* master conjures up a magic stew in the *kazan* bowl, while patrons squatting on Turkish-styled rugs chill out to lilting oriental music. Apart from the usual Tatar dishes, they make excellent *yantyk* (pastry filled with minced meat or cheese) and Bakhchisaray's best Turkish coffee. Enter from vul Lenina. Also has rooms for overnighters.

Aliye
CRIMEAN TATAR €

(vul Lesi Ukrainki 1; mains 25-35uah; ⊗8am-10pm; 🍴) Popular with locals and tour groups, this superfriendly cafe on the main drag has Turkish-styled rugs on the upper terrace surrounded by a garden, and European tables on the lower terrace. Also has eight rooms to let (250uah to 300uah).

ℹ️ Information

Tourist office (📋066 100 6022; www.infocentre.crimea.ua; vul Lenina 102; ⊗9.30am-6pm daily May-Oct) USAID-funded office opposite the Khans' Palace.

ℹ️ Getting There & Away

BUS Bakhchysaray's bus station is just off the road linking Simferopol and Sevastopol, where you can catch a bus in either direction. Frequent direct buses originating in Bakhchysaray go to the inconveniently located Simferopol western bus station (10uah, 30 minutes). Buses originating in Sevastopol terminate at Simferopol's Kurortnaya station (10uah, 50 minutes).

ELEKTRYCHKA Local trains shuffle back and forth between Sevastopol (80 minutes) and Simferopol (50 minutes) seven times a day in each direction.

ℹ️ Getting Around

Marshrutka 2 (2.50uah per ride) shuttles constantly between the bus station, the train station, Khans' Palace and Uspensky Monastery.

UNDERSTAND UKRAINE

History

Kyivan Rus

In 882 Oleh of Novgorod – of the Varangians (a Scandinavian civilisation) – declared himself ruler of Kyiv. The city prospered and grew into a large, unified Varangian state that, during its peak, stretched between the Volga River, the Danube River and Baltic Sea. By the 11th and 12th centuries, the Varangian state began to splinter into 10 rival princedoms. When the prince of Suzdal, Andriy Bogolyubov, sacked Kyiv in 1169, the end of the Varangian era was complete.

Prince Roman Mstyslavych regained control of Kyiv in 1203 and united the regions of present-day western, central and northern Ukraine. There was a period of relative prosperity under his dynamic son, King Danylo, and grandson Lev. During this time, much of eastern and southern Ukraine came under the control of the Volga-based Mongol Golden Horde. Its empire was weakened, however, in the 14th century by the Black Death, as well as by the growing military strength of Russian, Polish and Lithuanian rulers.

Cossacks & Russian Control

By the turn of the 15th century, the uncontrolled steppe of southern Ukraine began to attract runaway serfs, criminals, Orthodox refugees and other outcasts from Poland and Lithuania. Along with a few semi-independent Tatars, the inhabitants formed self-governing militaristic communities and became known as *kazaki* (Cossacks), from the Turkic word meaning 'outlaw, adventurer or free person'. Ukrainian Cossacks eventually developed the self-ruling Cossack Hetmanate, which to some degree reasserted the concept of Ukrainian self-determination.

In 1648 Hetman Bogdan Khmelnytsky (aided by Tatar cavalry) overcame the Polish rulers at the battle of Pyliavtsi. He was forced to engage in a formal but controversial military alliance with Muscovy in 1654, but in 1660 a war broke out between Poland and Russia over control of Ukraine. This ended with treaties that granted control over Kyiv and northern Ukraine to Russia and territory to the west of the Dnipro River to the Poles.

During the course of the 18th century Russia expanded into southern Ukraine and also gained most of Western Ukraine from Poland, except for the far west, which went to the Habsburg Empire.

The 19th century saw a slow growth of nationalist sentiment, which became significant in Kyiv from the 1840s. When the tsarist authorities banned the use of Ukrainian as an official language in the capital, the movement's focus shifted to Austrian-controlled Lviv.

In 1854 Britain and France attacked Russia in the Crimean War, fearing the empire's creep to the Mediterranean Sea. The two-year war resulted in an estimated 250,000 dead on each side, but failed to check Russia's encroachment on the Mediterranean. In 1876 Russian influence over Ukraine was further cemented by Tsar Alexander II's banning of Ukrainian in print and on the stage.

The Early 20th Century

Following WWI and the collapse of tsarist power, Ukraine had a chance – but failed – to gain independence. Civil war broke out and exploded into anarchy: six different armies vied for power, and Kyiv changed hands many times within a year. Eventually Ukraine was again divided between Poland, Romania, Czechoslovakia and Russia. The Russian part became a founding member of the USSR in 1922, and later suffered immensely from a famine that killed millions in the years following Stalin's brutal collectivisation policies. Whether or not the famine was orchestrated by Stalin, who saw Ukrainian nationalism as a threat to Soviet power, remains a hotly contested matter in political and academic circles. What is in no doubt is that millions died of starvation between 1932 and 1933.

The Red Army rolled into Polish Ukraine in September 1939. The Germans attacked in 1941 and by the year's end controlled virtually all of Ukraine. However, Kharkiv and Kyiv were retaken two years later. An estimated six million Ukrainians died in WWII, which left most of the country's cities in ruin. After the war, the USSR kept the territory it had seized from Poland in 1939.

Independence

After the failed Soviet counter-coup in August 1991, which saw communist hardliners try to usurp power from a reform-minded Gorbachev, the Verkhovna Rada (Supreme Council) met, and speaker Stanyslav Hurenko's memorable announcement was recorded by the *Economist* for posterity: 'Today we will vote for Ukrainian independence, because if we don't, we're in the shit.' In December, some 84% of the population voted in a referendum to back the decision, and Leonid Kravchuk was elected president.

But the economy immediately hit the rocks, things seemed chaotic and people were largely dissatisfied with the results of their move for independence. Finally, the hryvnya, Ukraine's currency, was introduced in 1996, and a process of privatisation kick-started the economy. It wasn't until 1997, under President Leonid Kuchma, that inflation fell from an inconceivable 10,000% to 10%. The economy strengthened but not enough: the hryvnia felt the ripple effects hard from the 1998 Russian financial crisis, dipping 51% in value.

President Kuchma was returned to power in October 1999 after what were widely regarded as dubious elections. His credibility shrivelled further in November 2000 when a tape emerged of Kuchma having an alleged 'rid me of this turbulent priest' moment regarding Georgy Gongadze, a journalist highly critical of Kuchma's presidency, whose beheaded corpse had been discovered in a forest outside Kyiv a few months earlier.

The Orange Revolution

Kuchma was limited to two terms in power, and so he backed Viktor Yanukovych to run for office in the October 2004 presidential elections. But both the international press and the Ukrainian public were all about Viktor Yushchenko, who was poisoned (but not killed) a week before the elections, allegedly by political foes, turning his ruggedly handsome face into...well, just rugged.

Because no one carried more than 50% of the votes in the first round of elections, a run-off was scheduled for 21 November. The official results of this run-off had Yanukovych ahead by 3%, but exit polls showed Yushchenko ahead by 11%. Something wasn't quite right, and by the next day about 500,000 people had peacefully gathered on Kyiv's maydan Nezalezhnosti (Independence Sq), bearing flags, setting up tents, chanting, singing and generally having a good time. Kyiv citizens took complete strangers into their homes, and the media reported a marked drop in city crime during the span of the protest. The world was watching and officials had no choice but to annul the run-off results.

But the protesters stayed on, sometimes numbering more than one million and often withstanding freezing temperatures, until 26 December 2004, when a second run-off took place under intense international scrutiny. Yushchenko won with 52% and was inaugurated 23 January 2005, the climax to the peaceful 'Orange Revolution', so called as it was the colour of choice for the crowds supporting Yushchenko.

Post-Revolution Blues

Alas, the course of true reform never did run smooth in Ukraine and anyone hoping for a fairy-tale ending was swiftly disappointed. Less than a year after they had stood shoulder to shoulder on the maydan in Kyiv, the Orange Revolution's heroes had fallen out with each other.

Anyone who's been able to follow Ukraine's political scene since the Orange Revolution probably should get out more. In the late 2000s Ukraine's first female prime minister and gas oligarch Yulia Tymoshenko, a feeble president Yushenko and a resurgent Viktor Yanukovych engaged in an absurd political soap opera featuring snap elections, drawn-out coalition deals, fisticuffs in parliament and musical chairs in the prime minister's office. Russia turned off the gas at opportune moments and the West got bored and moved on. The upshot was disillusionment with the Orange Revolution among the population and victory for Viktor Yanukovych's Party of the Regions (whose party colour is blue) in the April 2010 presidential elections.

President Yanukovych has since been accused of wittling away at democracy, media freedom and the Ukrainian language, but the main cause of concern has been the imprisonment for abuse of office of his main political rival, Tymoshenko, a sentence many in the West feel was politically motivated. Alleged vote rigging, miscounting and manipulation in parliamentary elections in late 2012 only added to the feeling that Ukraine was firmly in the grip of a single party that had little intention of letting the electorate decide its fate.

People

The National Psyche

Having endured centuries of many different foreign rulers, Ukrainians are a long-suffering people. They're nothing if not survivors; historically they've had to be, but after suffering a kind of identity theft during centuries of Russian rule, this ancient nation which 'suddenly' emerged some 20 years ago is starting to forge a new personality.

Traditionally, many patriots would unite behind a vague sense of free-spirited Cossack culture and the national poet Taras Shevchenko. This is a religious society, a superstitious society and one in which strong family and community ties still bind, and traditional gender roles persist. It's a culture where people are sometimes friendly and more generous than they can really afford to be. Paradoxically, it's also one in which remnants remain of the Soviet mentality – such as unofficial unhelpfulness and a suspicion of saying too much. As in Russia, many people lead a kind of double life: snarling, elbowing *Homo sovieticus* outside the house but generous, kind and hospitable around the kitchen table.

In patchwork Ukraine, city dwellers and farmers, east and west, young and old, Russian-speaking and Ukrainian-speaking, Hutsul and Tatar – all have very different attitudes. Broadly speaking, Russian-speaking easterners look towards Russia, while Ukrainian-speaking westerners look towards a future in Europe.

Population

As a crossroads between Europe and Asia, Ukraine has been settled by numerous ethnic groups throughout history and has a fascinating underlying mix. However, most people still describe themselves as Ukrainians and, hence, of Slavic origin. According to the last census (2001), 78% of the country's population are ethnically Ukrainian, while 17% of the population, mainly concentrated in the south and east, describe their ethnicity as Russian.

MINORITIES

Ukraine's ethnic minority groups include, in order of size, Belarusians, Moldovans, Tatars, Bulgarians, Hungarians, Romanians, Poles and Jews. Almost all of the country's 260,000 Tatars live in Crimea.

DYING NATION

Since independence, Ukraine's population has fallen more dramatically than that of any other country not affected by war, famine or plague. The number of citizens plummeted from 52 million in 1993 to around 45.8 million (possibly as low as 39 million) in 2012, as birth rates and life expectancy dropped concomitantly.

Religion

As the sheer number of churches in Ukraine attests, religion in this country is pivotal. It has provided comfort during many hard times and even shaped Ukrainian identity: when Volodymyr the Great accepted Orthodox Christianity in 989, he cast Kyivan Rus as a European, rather than Islamic Asian, state.

UKRAINE'S MANY CHURCHES

Today the country's sizeable Christian population is confusingly splintered into three Orthodox churches and one major form of Catholicism.

In the 17th century, when Ukraine came under Russian rule, so did its Orthodox Church. Even now, nearly two decades after independence, the largest Orthodox congregation in the country belongs to the Ukrainian Orthodox Church (UOC-MP), the former Ukrainian section of the Russian Orthodox Church that pays allegiance to the Moscow patriarch. There are also two smaller, breakaway Orthodox churches, which are both more 'Ukrainian' in nature. A Ukrainian Orthodox Church (UOC-KP) was formed in 1992 after independence to pay allegiance to a local Kyiv patriarch. Meanwhile, the Ukrainian Autocephalous Orthodox Church (UAOC), formed during the 19th century in western Ukraine and suppressed by the Soviets, has bounced back since independence. The two main Orthodox churches – Moscow Patriarchate and Kyiv Patriarchate – are in constant conflict and divide the country along roughly the same lines as ethnic allegiance.

Five to six million Ukrainians follow another brand of Christianity. In 1596 the Union of Brest established the Uniate Church (often called the Ukrainian Catholic or Greek Catholic Church) that mixes Orthodox Christian practices with allegiance to the pope.

OTHER FAITHS

Minority faiths include Roman Catholicism, Judaism and, among Crimean Tatars, Sunni Islam. Evangelical, Buddhist, Jehovah's Witness and neo-pagan communities have also emerged since 1991.

Arts
Literature

The most celebrated Ukrainian writer is Taras Shevchenko (1814–61). Born a serf and orphaned as a teenager, Shevchenko studied painting at the Academy of Arts in St Petersburg, where in 1840 he published his first work, *Kobzar* (The Bard), a book of eight romantic poems. He was exiled in 1847 for his satirical poems about Russian oppression. Today every town across the land has a Shevchenko Square or Street.

Arguably the most talented and prolific Ukrainian writer of the early 20th century was Ivan Franko, whose scholarly and moving works shed light on the issues that plague Ukrainian society. He, too, was persecuted by the Russians. Lesya Ukrainka, a wealthy young woman whose frail health kept her indoors writing moody poetry, could be considered a Ukrainian Emily Dickinson.

Two internationally renowned authors usually claimed by Russia are Ukrainian-born. Mikhail Bulgakov's (1891–1940) first novel, *The White Guard,* is set in his native Kyiv. Nikolai Gogol's (1809–52) novels *Evenings on a Farm near Dikanka* and *Dead Souls* and short story *Taras Bulba* have links to his country of birth.

As far as contemporary writers go, Kyiv-based author Andrey Kurkov (b 1961) has been called Bulgakov's heir. His *Death and the Penguin, Penguin Lost* and *The President's Last Love* indulge in the same flights of fancy as Bulgakov's classic *The Master and Margarita.*

Cinema

Must-see pre-departure films include *Shadows of Forgotten Ancestors* (1964), a wonderfully shot (and subsequently banned) film full of shaggy Hutsul customs and symbolism from the Carpathians; and Sergei Eisenstein's *Battleship Potemkin* (1925), shot in Odesa.

Icons & Pysanky

Icons are small holy images painted on a lime-wood panel with a mix of tempera, egg

---

BOOKS

» *Death and the Penguin* (1996) by Andrey Kurkov

» *The White Guard* (1925) by Mikhail Bulgakov

» *Taras Bulba* (1835) by Nikolai Gogol

» *Everything is Illuminated* (2002) by Jonathan Safran Foer

» *Borderland* (1998) by Anna Reid

» *Complete Works* (reissued 2005) by Isaac Babel

» *A Short History of Tractors in Ukrainian* (2005) by Marina Lewycka

» *Street of Crocodiles* (1934) by Bruno Schulz

» *Dead Souls* (1842) by Nikolai Gogol

» *Recreations* (1998) by Yuri Andrukhovych

yolk and hot wax. Brought to Ukraine from Constantinople by Volodymyr the Great in the 10th century and remaining the key religious art until the 17th century, icons were attributed with healing and spiritual powers.

Painted Easter eggs (pysanky) are an ancient Slavonic art found across Eastern Europe. Designs are drawn in wax on the eggshell – the egg is dyed one colour and the process continually repeated until a complex pattern is built up.

Painting

Ukrainian-born Ilya Repin gained international fame. His famous Zaporizhsky Cossacks Writing a Letter to the Turkish Sultan and other Romantic paintings are found in the Art Museum in Kharkiv.

Ivan Ayvazosky is regarded as one of the world's best seascape painters. Ethnically Armenian, he was born and lived in Feodosiya, Crimea, where hundreds of his works can be found in the Ayvazosky Museum.

Some of Ukraine's oldest frescos are found in Kyiv's St Sophia's Cathedral.

Music

Ukrainian folk music developed as a form of storytelling. The guardians of Ukrainian folklore, kobzary were wandering minstrels who travelled from town to town spreading news through song while strumming their 65-string bandura.

The most famous Ukrainian songstress of the last 40 years bar none is Sofia Rotaru (b 1947), an ethnic Moldovan born near Chernivtsi. Most of what Ukraine produces today is porno chick pop, though cross-dressing comedian/singer Verka Serduchka occupies a category all his/her own. The same is true of NYC gypsy punk outfit Gogol Bordello, whose eccentric singer, Eugene Hutz, hails from Kyiv.

Food & Drink

Ukrainians admit theirs is a cuisine of comfort – full of hearty, mild dishes designed for fierce winters – rather than one of gastronomic zing. Yet, while it's suffered from negative stereotypes of Soviet-style cabbage slop and pernicious pickles, Ukrainian cooking isn't bad these days. In recent years chefs have rediscovered the wholesome appeal of the national cuisine. Plenty of Ukrainian-themed restaurants offer the chance to sample local specialities made with fresh ingredients.

If Ukraine has a culinary capital, it's probably Kyiv, but there are interesting regional sidelines, too. The Hutsul people of the Carpathians favour berries and mushrooms, plus their own speciality cheese brynza (sheep's milk cheese) and polenta-style banush (Carpathian polenta made with sour cream) or mamalyha (Ukrainian polenta). Central Asian–style Tatar cuisine adds spice to dining in Crimea.

Staples & Specialities

Borshch Locals would have you know that borshch (борщ) is Ukrainian – not Russian, not Polish, but Ukrainian – and there's nothing better than a steaming bowlful in winter. The main ingredients are beetroot, cabbage and herbs.

Bread Dark and white varieties of khlib (хліб) are available every day. Bread is often used in religious ceremonies and on special occasions. Visitors are traditionally greeted with bread and salt.

Cabbage rolls Holubtsy (голубці) are cabbage rolls stuffed with seasoned rice and meat then stewed in a tomato and soured cream sauce.

Kasha Pretty much any grain is called kasha (каша) in Ukrainian, and while the word might be used to describe what Westerners would call porridge, more commonly it turns out to be buckwheat. The latter appears as a side dish and as a filling breakfast gruel.

Pancakes Three types of pancake might land on your plate. Deruny (деруни) are potato pancakes, and are served with soured cream and vegetables or meat. Nalysnyky (налисники) are thin crepes, while mlyntsy (млинці) are thicker and smaller, like Russian blyny.

Varenyky Similar to Polish pierogi, varenyky (вареники) are to Ukraine what dim sum is to China and filled pasta to Italy. These small half-moon shaped dumplings have more than 50 different traditional vegetarian and meat fillings.

Drinks

Ukraine produces some very quaffable beers. In fact, the beer market is booming, with many young people turning their backs on vodka in favour of it. Chernihivske, Lvivske, Slavutych and Obolon are the most popular brands.

Wines are produced in Crimea and the Transcarpathian region, though, sadly, the best still come from neighbouring Moldova.

On street corners in summer, you'll see small drinks tankers selling *kvas* (квас), a gingery, beer-like soft drink, which is made from sugar and old black bread.

Where to Eat & Drink

Restaurant (ресторан) and cafe (кафе) sound similar in English and Ukrainian. Some Ukrainian restaurants specialise in a particular dish, such as a *varenychna* (варенична), which serves only *varenyky*. A *stolova* (столова) is a self-service canteen.

Be aware that prices for many meat and fish dishes are listed on the menu by weight. For example, *shashlyk* might look good value at 10uah, unless it's actually 10uah per 100g. Read menus carefully.

Chornobyl
The Accident

In perhaps the blackest of ironies ever known to history, the world's worst nuclear disaster was the result of an unnecessary safety test. On the night of 25 April 1986, reactor No 4 at the electricity-producing Chornobyl power plant in northern Ukraine was due to be shut down for regular maintenance. Workers decided to use the opportunity to see if, in the event of a shutdown, enough electricity remained in the grid to power the systems that cooled the reactor core, and turned off the emergency cooling system. For various reasons, including a design flaw in the type of RBMK reactor at Chornobyl, operational errors and flouted safety procedures, the result of the test was a power surge, a steam explosion and a full-blown nuclear explosion. At 1.26am on the morning of 26 April 1986, the reactor blew its 500-tonne top and spewed nearly nine tonnes of radioactive material into the sky in a fireball. Fallout blew north and west, dropping mainly over Belarus, but also over Ukraine, Russia, Poland and the Baltic region. Some material also wafted over Sweden, whose scientists were the first to alert the world.

Immediate Aftermath

The Soviets initially remained silent while the emergency unfolded. Two people died in the explosion and another 29 firemen – sent in to clean up without proper radiation protection – died in the following weeks. Some 135,000 people were evacuated from the satellite town of Prypyat and a 30km radius around the plant, but were told it was only 'temporary'. Six days after the disaster, with radioactive clouds blowing over Kyiv, May Day parades in the blissfully ignorant city went ahead.

Chornobyl Today

Today the long-term effects of the disaster are still being felt and assessed. The most obvious impact has been an upsurge of thyroid cancer in children, with nearly 2000 cases reported. Studies suggest that of the 600,000 'liquidators' brought in to clean up the site, more than 4000 have died from exposure and 170,000 suffer from terminal diseases. In addition, some 35,000 sq km of forest is contaminated, and the meat, milk, vegetables and fruit produced there have higher than normal levels of radioactivity. Silt carried down the Dnipro is radioactive, although the extent is still not fully known. Birth defects, suicides, deaths from heart disease and alcoholism are also unusually high in the region. It's estimated that by 2015 the disaster will have cost the economy US$200 billion, although, of course, all the figures surrounding the disaster and its toll are disputed.

The last working reactor at Chornobyl, No 3, was finally shut down in 2000. However, reactor No 4 remains 'a monster, a monster which is always near', according to one of the 8000 scientific staff and monitors who still work on-site, half of them commuting there daily from the new town of Slavutych.

After the accident, the damaged reactor and 180 tonnes of radioactive mess were hastily enclosed in a concrete-and-steel sarcophagus. However, no one really knows the state of the radioactive core inside the ruined reactor and that hastily built sarcophagus has long been crumbling. After several false starts, and a growing sense of outrage, a deal was finally signed in 2007 to begin building a secure new steel covering. Construction of this $1.4 billion shelter is being overseen by the European Bank for Reconstruction and Development (EBRD) and should be completed by 2015.

Unlikely Tourist Attraction

Chornobyl has become possibly the world's top 'dark tourism' destination, with tours becoming much easier to arrange and a little cheaper as they increase in popularity. If you're travelling alone or in a small group you'll save a lot of money by latching onto another group. Kyiv-based tour companies such as SoloEast Travel (p924), New Logic (p924) and Sam (p924) all run tours.

SURVIVAL GUIDE

Directory A–Z

Accommodation

Accommodation will be your single biggest expense in Ukraine, but with the value of the hryvnya low against most currencies, rooms are slightly more affordable than they once were.

The following price indicators apply for a high-season double room:

€ less than 400uah

€€ 400uah to 800uah

€€€ more than 800uah

HOMESTAYS

Crashing with a local isn't just cheap but also a great way to get to know individual cities. Perhaps surprisingly, hospitality clubs such as www.couchsurfing.com and www.hospitalityclub.org have thousands of members in Ukraine.

HOSTELS

Hostelling is now a well-established sector in Ukraine's accommodation market, especially in Kyiv, Lviv and Odesa.

Hostelling Ukraine International (www.hi-hostels.com.ua) gathers together all of Ukraine's hostels in one place. Online booking is possible.

HOTELS

Ukraine has a bewildering array of hotel and room types. At the bottom are Soviet-era budget crash pads for as little as 50uah; at the top are 'six-star' overpriced luxury in OTT surroundings. Everything in between can be hit and miss, and there are no national standards to follow, so forget any star ratings you might see.

It's only worth booking ahead in Odesa and Crimea in summer, in big cities in late December and early January, and in the Carpathians from November to March.

PRIVATE RENTALS

In Crimea and Odesa you'll find people standing outside train or bus stations offering rooms in their houses or private apartment rentals. Although the numbers of *babushky* (grannies) doing so are dwindling, it's also still possible in Kyiv. Expect to pay from 250uah per night for a one-room apartment (more in Kyiv). Alternatively contact an official rental agency.

Business Hours

Business hours can be hard to pin down in Ukraine. Lunch closures (1pm to 2pm or 2pm to 3pm) are an all-too-common throwback to Soviet days. Sunday closing is rare. Normal business hours are listed below.

Banks 9am to 5pm or 10am to 6pm

Restaurants noon to 11pm

Shops 9am to 6pm, to 8pm or 9pm in big cities

Sights 9am to 5pm or 6pm, closed at least one day a week

Customs Regulations

When entering Ukraine you are allowed to carry up to US$10,000, without having to sign any documentation. The following can also be imported duty-free: 1L of spirits, 2L of wine, 5L of beer, 200 cigarettes or 250g of tobacco, and gifts up to the value of €200.

If you exceed these limits, you'll have to sign a *deklaratsiya* (customs declaration).

Be careful not to lose this completed form – you will need to present it when departing the country.

Embassies & Consulates

The following are all in Kyiv:

Australian Consulate (☎246 4223; vul Kominterna 18, Apt 11; ⓢVokzalna)

Belarusian Embassy (☎537 5200; vul Mykhayla Kotsyubynskoho 3; ⓢUniversytet)

Canadian Embassy (☎590 3100; www.canadainternational.gc.ca/ukraine; Yaroslaviv Val 31; ⓢZoloti Vorota)

French Embassy (☎590 3600; www.ambafrance-ua.org; vul Reytarska 39; ⓢZoloti Vorota)

German Embassy (☎247 6800; www.kiew.diplo.de; vul Bohdana Khmelnytskoho 25; ⓢZoloti Vorota)

Hungarian Embassy (☎230 8000; vul Reytarska 33; ⓢZoloti Vorota)

Moldovian Embassy (☎044-521 2280; www.ucraina.mfa.md; vul Yagotinska 2; ⓢLybidska)

Netherlands Embassy (☎490 8200; www.netherlands-embassy.com.ua; pl Kontraktova 7; ⓢKontraktova pl)

Polish Embassy (☎230 0700; www.polska.com.ua; vul Yaroslaviv Val 12; ⓢZoloti Vorota)

Romanian Embassy (☎234 5261; http://kiev.mae.ro; vul Mykhayla Kotsyubynskoho 8; ⓢUniversytet)

Russian Embassy (☎244 0961; www.embrus.org.ua; pr Vozdukhoflotsky 27; ⓢVokzalna)

UK Embassy (☎490 3660; http://ukinukraine.fco.gov.uk/en; vul Desyatynna 9; ⓢMaydan Nezalezhnosti)

US Embassy (☎490 0000; http://kyiv.usembassy.gov; vul Yuriya Kotsyubynskoho 10; ⓢLukyanivska)

Food

The following price indicators are for a main meal:

€ less than 50uah

€€ 50uah to 150uah

€€€ more than 150uah

Gay & Lesbian Travellers

Ukraine is generally more tolerant of homosexuality than its neighbour Russia, but that's not saying much. Out-and-proud gay views mix badly with those of the Orthodox Church, hence most people's outwardly conservative attitudes. Homosexuality is legal in Ukraine, but attitudes vary across the country. Useful gay websites include www.gayua.com, www.gay.org.ua, www.ukrgay.com and www.gaylvov.at.ua.

Internet Access

Internet service in Ukraine has come on in leaps and bounds in recent years. Many upmarket and midrange hotels now offer free wi-fi internet access and free hot spots are much more common than in Western Europe.

Many restaurants and cafes have installed wi-fi technology. Upmarket hotels often have a business centre with a couple of terminals hooked up to the internet. Internet cafes are not as common as they once were but there's usually at least one in every town. Internet cafes often double up as noisy gaming centres. Prices for internet access range from about 6uah in smaller cities to up to 12uah in Kyiv.

Money

Coins come in denominations of one, five, 10, 25 and 50 kopecks, plus the rare one hryvnya. Notes come in one, two, five, 10, 20, 50, 100, 200 and 500 hryvnya. It's virtually impossible to buy hryvnya before you get to Ukraine.

ATMs are very common in cities, less widespread in smaller towns and nonexistent in rural areas. They accept all major cards and some issue dollars as well as hryvnya.

CASH

US dollars (post-1990 issue only), the euro and Russian roubles are the easiest currencies to exchange. Banks and currency exchange offices may not accept notes with rips or tears.

CREDIT CARDS

Credit cards are increasingly accepted by upmarket hotels, restaurants and shops both in and outside Kyiv. However, Ukraine remains primarily a cash economy.

Post

The national postal service is run by **Ukrposhta** (www.ukrposhta.com). Sending a postcard or a letter up to 20g costs 5.70uah to anywhere outside Ukraine.

Mail takes about a week or less to Europe, and two to three weeks to the USA or Australia.

Public Holidays

The main public holidays in Ukraine are listed here:

New Year's Day 1 January

Orthodox Christmas 7 January

International Women's Day 8 March

Orthodox Easter (Paskha) April

Labour Day 1 & 2 May

Victory Day (1945) 9 May

Orthodox Pentecost June

Constitution Day 28 June

Independence Day (1991) 24 August

Safe Travel

Despite what you may have heard, Ukraine is not a dangerous, crime-ridden place. The infamous mafia are not interested in tourists.

CRIME

Don't be overly worried about crime in Ukraine, which is normally as safe as most Western European countries. However, petty theft is a serious problem. Avoiding becoming a victim of theft is a matter of common sense: don't flash your money around and keep an eye on your wallet and belongings, particularly on public transport and in crowded situations.

Telephone

All numbers in Ukraine start with ☑0 and there are no pre-dialling codes like in Russia.

PHONE CODES

Ukraine's country code is ☑0038. To call Kyiv from overseas, dial ☑00 38 044 and the subscriber number.

To call internationally from Ukraine, dial ☑0, wait for a second tone, then dial ☑0 again, followed by the country code, city code and number.

MOBILE PHONES

European GSM phones usually work in Ukraine. If you intend making a few calls, it's more economical to get a prepaid SIM card locally.

Toilets

A women's toilet (*tualet*) is marked with an upwards-facing triangle or ж (for *zhinochy*); men's are marked with a downwards-facing triangle, ч or м (for *cholovichy* or *muzhcheny*).

Travellers With Disabilities

Even Kyiv, the best-equipped Ukrainian city, isn't that accessible to people with physical disabilities. The rest of the country is worse.

Visas

Tourist visas for stays of less than 90 days aren't required by citizens of the EU, Canada, the USA, Iceland, Japan, Norway, Switzerland and South Korea. Australians and New Zealanders need a visa.

Visas are required for citizens of most other countries and for anyone intending to work, study, take up permanent residency or stay for more than 90 days.

Getting There & Away

The majority of visitors fly to Ukraine – generally to Kyiv. However, low-cost flights to neighbouring countries mean a growing number of travellers are entering the country overland. Flights, tours and rail tickets can be booked online through Lonely Planet (www.lonelyplanet.com/bookings).

Entering the Country

Your passport must be valid for the duration of your intended stay in Ukraine (obviously). It must contain a visa if you need one. Border officials ask few questions these days and immigration cards were scrapped in September 2010.

Air

Low-cost airlines have struggled to find their way into Ukraine with only a couple of no-frills airlines (Ryanair and Wizzair) operating in Ukrainian airspace.

AIRPORTS & AIRLINES

Most international flights use Kyiv's main airport, **Boryspil International Airport** (KBP; ☑393 4371; www.kbp.aero). Other flights go to **Lviv International Airport** (LWO; www.lwo.aero) and **Odesa International Airport** (ODS; www.airport.odessa.ua).

Ukraine International Airlines (www.flyuia.com) is Ukraine's international airline carrier. Always check this airline's rates against your country's national carrier as UIA's ticket prices are often lower.

The following airlines also fly to/from Ukraine:

BUDGET FLIGHTS TO NEIGHBOURING COUNTRIES

A cheap way of getting to Ukraine is to take a budget flight to a neighbouring country, then cross the border by land. Poland has the most flights from Western Europe, but Hungary, Romania and Slovakia also provide a handful of options.

easyJet (www.easyjet.com) This no-frills airline links the UK, France and Germany with Budapest and Krakow.

Jet2.com (www.jet2.com) Links cities in northern England and Scotland with Krakow and Budapest.

Ryanair (www.ryanair.com) By the time you read this, Ireland's umatched budget airline shoud have launched direct flights from Stansted to Lviv. Otherwise connections between five cities in the UK and Rzeszow and between Liverpool/London Stansted and Lublin, the nearest Polish cities to the border with Ukraine, will continue. There are also daily flights to Budapest and Bratislava (Slovakia) from where you can continue by train.

Wizzair (www.wizzair.com) Wizzair has popular direct flights to Kyiv from London Luton, but also connects the UK with Lublin and Warsaw in Poland and Cluj-Napoca in northern Romania.

Check the websites www.flycheapo.com and www.skyscanner.net for the latest flight information.

Aeroflot (www.aeroflot.ru)

Air Baltic (www.airbaltic.com)

Air France (www.airfrance.com)

Austrian Airlines (www.austrian.com)

Belavia (www.belavia.by)

British Airways (www.ba.com)

Carpatair (www.carpatair.com)

Czech Airlines (www.czechairlines.com)

Delta (www.delta.com)

El Al (www.elal.co.il)

KLM (www.klm.com)

LOT (www.lot.com)

Lufthansa (www.lufthansa.com)

S7 (www.s7.ru)

Turkish Airlines (www.turkishairlines.com)

Land

BORDER CROSSINGS

Crossing the border into Ukraine is a fairly straightforward, if slightly drawn-out, affair. The Poland–Ukraine and Romania–Ukraine borders are popular cigarette-smuggling routes, hence the thorough customs checks. Expect customs personnel to scrutinise your papers and search your vehicle.

BUS

Buses are slower, less frequent and less comfortable than trains for long-distance travel.

CAR & MOTORCYCLE

To bring your own vehicle into the country, you'll need your original registration papers (photocopies not accepted) and a 'Green Card' International Motor Insurance Certificate. Your registration number will be noted, and you'll have to explain if leaving the country without your vehicle.

Sea

Some scheduled ferry services do exist, but as across the ex-USSR, boat services are erratic and sailings are cancelled without notice. Basing your travel plans around sea or river travel is not advisable.

Getting Around

Air

The national network mainly uses Kyiv as a hub. To fly between two Ukrainian cities you almost always have to go via the capital.

AIRLINES

Aerosvit (www.aerosvit.com) Part of the Ukrainian Aviation Group along with partner airlines Dniproavia and Donbassaero, Aerosvit hit financial turbulence in late 2012 and may not be around by the time you jet in.

Ukraine International Airlines (www.flyuia.com) Based at Boryspil international airport in Kyiv. Operates some domestic flights but is essentially an international airline.

UTair (www.utair.ru) Russian airline based at Kyiv Zhulyany airport and operating on several domestic routes in Ukraine.

Wizzair (www.wizzair.com) Not a Ukrainian airline, but does operate one handy domestic flight between Kyiv and Simferopol.

TICKETS

Kiy Avia (www.kiyavia.com) has branches across the country and you can book most flights with them. The website lists timetables, prices and the aircraft that are used – all in English.

Bicycle

Cycling is a terrific way to see the real Ukraine, despite the crazed drivers and potholed roads. The Carpathians and Crimea – in that order – are particularly pleasant cycling country. Volunteers involved in the **Bikeland** project in the Carpathians have marked out 1300km of mountain cycle trails.

Bus

Buses serve every city and small town, but are best for short trips (three hours or less) as vehicles are generally small, old and overcrowded. Tickets are sold at the bus station right up to departure and resemble shop-till receipts.

Autolux (www.autolux.ua), **Gunsel** (www.gunsel.com.ua) and **Ukrbus** (www.ukrbus.com) run main intercity routes using Western-standard coaches. While travelling anywhere in the former Soviet Union, you are likely to encounter the *marshrutka*. These are basically minibuses that ply bus routes but stop anywhere on request. They're most common in big cities but also serve intercity routes. Fares are usually higher than on buses but journey times shorter.

Hitching

You simply can't hitchhike around Ukraine for free. Hitching a ride is common, but it's necessary to pay drivers for the privilege. Stand at the roadside, hand up in the air, palm down.

Hitching is never entirely safe, and we don't recommend it. Travellers who hitch should understand that they are taking a small but potentially serious risk.

Local Transport

Ukrainian cities are navigable by trolleybus, tram, bus and metro in Kyiv. Urban public-transport systems are usually overworked and overcrowded. A ticket for one ride by bus, tram or trolleybus costs 1.25uah to 2uah. There are no return, transfer, timed or day tickets available anywhere, and tickets have to be punched on-board (or ripped by the conductor).

Metro barriers take plastic tokens *(zhetony)*, sold at counters inside stations.

Train

For long journeys, overnight train is the preferred method of travel in Ukraine. Services are incredibly punctual and you can save on accommodation costs by taking sleeper trains.

For schedules and even online bookings see the much improved **Ukrainian Railways** (www.uz.gov.ua), the official Ukrainian Railway website. A timetable for the entire ex-USSR (in English) can be found at **Poezda.net** (www.poezda.net).

All classes have assigned places. Carriage *(vahon)* and bunk *(mesto)* numbers are printed on tickets.

Lyuks or SV *Spalny vahon* (SV) – 1st-class couchette (sleeper) compartment for two people – costs two to three times more than *kupe*.

Kupe 2nd-class sleeper compartment for four people – about twice as costly as *platskart*. Any train prices quoted here are for *kupe*.

Platskart 3rd-class open-carriage sleeper with around 50 bunks.

C1 and C2 1st- and 2nd-class seats on the fast Intercity+ Hyundai services.

TICKETS

You no longer have to show your passport when buying tickets. Few Ukrainian Railways employees speak English so have a local write down your destination, date, time, train number etc on a piece of paper in Cyrillic. At Kyiv train station there are dedicated windows (8 and 9) for foreigners.

Survival Guide

Directory A–Z

Accommodation

There's accommodation to match every budget in Eastern Europe, from Soviet-era concrete behemoths, five-star luxury palaces and international hotel groups to rural campsites and homely grandmother-run private rooms.

Price Ranges

We divide our accommodation selections into the following three categories:

€ Bare-bones hostels and hotels, often with shared bathrooms and very limited amenities.

€€ Hotels and guesthouses with private facilities and more often than not, television and wi-fi.

€€€ Well-appointed, high-standard hotels with all the amenities and creature comforts you'd expect.

The price indicators used here refer to the cost of a double room in high season, including private bathroom (any combination of toilet, bath tub, shower and washbasin) and excluding breakfast unless otherwise noted. For more information, see individual country directories.

Price categories are broken down differently for each individual country, as in a region as large and diverse as Eastern Europe it's not been possible to come up with one price range for each category across all countries.

Reservations

Reservations are generally a good idea in high season and can usually be made by phone or, less regularly, online. Hostels and cheap hotels fill up very quickly, especially in popular backpacker destinations such as Prague, Budapest and Kraków. In most cities in East-ern Europe there's a shortage of good-value midrange accommodation options. Some tourist offices may be able to make reservations on your behalf (some charge a small fee for this service) but, in general, do not expect a Western European standard of service from tourist offices in Eastern Europe. Some countries, such as Belarus, Moldova, Ukraine and Kosovo, have no tourist offices and those that do exist offer very little in the way of service.

Seasons

» High season is typically in July and August.

» Rates often drop outside the high season – in some cases by as much as 50%.

» In business-oriented hotels in cities, rooms are most expensive from Monday to Friday and cheaper over the weekend.

Camping

The cheapest way to stay in Eastern Europe is to camp and there are many camping grounds throughout the region. That said, a large proportion of the region's attractions are found in cities, where there often simply aren't any camping grounds. Most camping grounds near urban areas are large sites, intended mainly for motorists, though they're usually accessible by public transport and there's almost always space for backpackers with tents. Many camping grounds in Eastern Europe rent small on-site cabins, bungalows or caravans for double or triple the regular camping fee; in the most popular resorts all the bungalows are usually full in July and August. Generally, camping grounds charge per tent, plus an extra fee per person.

The standard of camping grounds in Eastern Europe varies from country to country. They're unreliable in Romania, crowded in Slovenia and Hungary (especially on Lake Balaton),

---

BOOK YOUR STAY ONLINE

For more accommodation reviews by Lonely Planet authors, check out http://hotels.lonelyplanet.com. You'll find independent reviews, as well as recommendations on the best places to stay. Best of all, you can book online.

and variable in the Czech Republic, Poland, Slovakia and Bulgaria. Some countries, including Moldova and Belarus, have very few official camping grounds, but you can usually find somewhere to pitch your tent. Croatia's coast has nudist camping grounds galore (signposted FKK, the German acronym for 'naturist'); they're excellent places to stay because of their secluded locations, although they can be a bit far from other attractions.

» Camping grounds may be open from April to October, May to September, or perhaps only June to August, depending on the category of the facility, the location and demand.

» A few private camping grounds are open year-round.

» Camping in the wild is usually illegal; ask local people about the situation before you pitch your tent on a beach or in an open field.

» In Eastern Europe you are sometimes allowed to build a campfire; ask first, however.

Farmhouses

'Village tourism', which means staying at a farmhouse, is highly developed in Estonia, Latvia, Lithuania and Slovenia, and popular in Hungary. It's like staying in a private room or pension, except that the participating farms are in picturesque rural areas and may have activities nearby such as horse riding, kayaking, skiing and cycling. See **Worldwide Opportunities on Organic Farms** (www.wwoof.org) for information about working on organic farms in exchange for room and board.

Guesthouses & Pensions

Small private pensions are now very common in parts of Eastern Europe. Priced somewhere between hotels and private rooms, pensions typically have fewer than a dozen rooms and may sometimes have a small restaurant or bar on the premises. You'll get much more personal service at a pension than you would at a hotel, though there's a bit less privacy. Pensions can be a lifesaver if you arrive at night or on a weekend, when the travel agencies assigning private rooms are closed. Call ahead to check prices and ask about reservations – someone will usually speak some halting English, German or Russian.

Homestays & Private Rooms

It's perfectly legal to stay with someone in a private home, and homestays are often the best and most authentic way to see daily life in Eastern Europe. If you want to take advantage of this Eastern European hospitality, consider the following:

» In most Eastern European countries, travel agencies can arrange accommodation in private rooms in local homes. In Hungary you can get a private room almost anywhere, but in other countries only the main tourist centres have them. Some rooms are like mini-apartments, with cooking facilities and private bathrooms for the sole use of guests. Prices are low but there's often a 30% to 50% surcharge if you stay fewer than three nights. In Hungary, the Czech Republic and Croatia higher taxation has made staying in a private room less attractive than before, but it's still good value and cheaper than a hotel.

» People will frequently approach you at train or bus stations in Eastern Europe offering a private room or a hostel bed. This can be good or bad – it's impossible to generalise. Just make sure it's not in some cardboard-quality housing project in the outer suburbs and that you negotiate a clear price. Obviously, if you are staying with strangers, you shouldn't leave your valuables behind when you go out; certainly don't leave your money, credit cards or passport.

» You don't have to go through an agency or an intermediary on the street for a private room. Any house, cottage or farmhouse with *Zimmer Frei* (German), сниму комнату (Russian), *sobe* (Slovak) or *szoba kiadó* (Hungarian) displayed outside is advertising the availability of private rooms; just knock on the door and ask if any are available. However, in countries such as Russia or Belarus where visa registration is necessary, you'll probably have to pay a travel agency to register your visa with a hotel.

» Staying with Eastern European friends will almost certainly be a wonderful experience, thanks to the full hospitality the region is justly famous for. Make sure you bring some small gifts for your hosts – it's a deeply ingrained cultural tradition throughout the region.

Hostels

Hostels offer the cheapest roof over your head in Eastern Europe and you don't have to be young to take advantage of them. Most hostels are part of the national **Youth Hostel Association** (YHA), which is affiliated with the **Hostelling International** (HI; www.hihostels.com) umbrella organisation.

» Hostels affiliated with HI can be found in most Eastern European countries. A hostel card is seldom required, though you sometimes get a small discount if you have one.

» At a hostel, you get a bed for the night plus use of communal facilities; there's often a kitchen where you can prepare your own meals. You may be required to have a bed sheet or a sleeping bag; if you don't have one, you can usually hire one for a small fee.

» Hostels vary widely in their character and quality. The hostels in Poland tend to be extremely basic but they're inexpensive and friendly. In the Czech Republic and Slovakia, many hostels are actually fairly luxurious junior hotels with double rooms and are often fully occupied by groups.

» A number of privately run hostels in Prague and Budapest are serious party venues, while many Hungarian hostels outside Budapest are student dormitories that are open to travellers for six or seven weeks in summer only. Moscow and St Petersburg, once total deserts for cheap accommodaton, are now brimming with modern and friendly hostels to choose from. Hostels can even be found in places as far flung as Albania, Transdniestr and Moldova.

» There are many hostel guides and websites with listings, including the hostel bible, HI's *Europe*. Many hostels accept reservations by phone or email, but not always during peak periods (though they might hold a bed for you for a couple of hours if you call from the train or bus station). You can also book beds through national hostel offices.

Hotels

At the bottom end of the scale, cheap hotels may be no more expensive than private rooms or guesthouses, while at the other extreme you'll find beautifully designed boutique hotels and five-star hotels with price tags to match.

» Single rooms can be hard to find in Eastern Europe, as you are generally charged by the room and not by the number of people in it.

» The cheapest rooms sometimes have a washbasin but no bathroom, which means you'll have to go down the corridor to use the toilet and shower.

» Breakfast may be included in the price of a room, or it may be extra.

Rental Accommodation

In larger cities without a thriving hotel and hostel culture,

you may find the best option is to rent an apartment from a local agency. These can often be better value than a hotel, mean you can self-cater and give you far more independence, but they can also be of varying quality and some accommodation can be far flung. The agencies operate independently and sometimes quasi-legally, so you will have no recourse if you have a disagreement with them. The agencies we list have good reputations and we have generally used them ourselves.

» Cities where renting accommodation is a good idea include Prague, Budapest, Bratislava, Chişinău, Minsk, Kraków and Moscow.

» When dealing with agencies you've found online, never send money in advance unless you're sure they are genuine.

University Accommodation

Some universities rent out space in student halls in July and August. This is quite popular in the Baltic countries, Croatia, the Czech Republic, Hungary, Macedonia, Poland, Slovakia and Slovenia.

» Accommodation will sometimes be in single rooms (but is more commonly in doubles or triples) and will come with shared bathrooms. Basic cooking facilities may be available.

» Enquire at the college or university, at student-information services or at local tourist offices.

Activities

Birdwatching

The countries of Eastern Europe may not be the world's best destination for spotting our feathered friends, but birders will certainly get a look at some unusual species in Albania, the Danube Delta in Romania and several locations around Serbia.

Canoeing & Kayaking

Launch a kayak, raft or canoe at one of the following waterways:

» Poland's Great Masurian Lakes

» Slovenia's Soča River

» The Czech Republic's Vltava River

» Latvia's Gauja River

» Croatia's Elafiti and Kornati Islands

» Montenegro's Bay of Kotor

Cycling

The hills and mountains of Eastern Europe can be heavy going, but this is offset by the abundance of things to see. Physical fitness is *not* a major prerequisite for cycling on the plains of eastern Hungary, but the persistent wind might slow you down. Popular holiday cycling areas in Eastern Europe include the following:

» The Šumava region and the Moravian wine country in the Czech Republic.

» Various routes in Hungary and Poland, and the Curonian Spit in western Lithuania.

» Sinaia – a great place to go mountain biking across the plateau atop the Bucegi Mountains in Romania.

Diving

It's not the Caribbean, but the Adriatic offers its own rewards. Explore caves and shipwrecks along the coast in Croatia, Montenegro and Slovenia.

Extreme Sports

If medieval Old Towns, castle-topped peaks and communist monuments don't get your blood pumping, never fear – you can still get your adrenalin rush in Eastern Europe.

» In Sigulda, Latvia, you'll find bungee jumping, bob-sledding and skydiving.

» Bovec, Slovenia, is famous for hydrospeeding, canyoning and paragliding.

Hiking

Almost every country in Eastern Europe offers excellent hiking, with well-marked trails through forests, mountains and national parks. Chalets or mountain huts in Poland, Bulgaria, Slovakia, Romania and Slovenia offer dormitory accommodation and basic meals; public transport will often take you to the trailheads. The best months for hiking are from June to September, especially late August and early September, when the summer crowds will have largely disappeared. Popular destinations for hiking include the following:

» High Tatras of Poland and Slovakia
» Malá Fatra of Slovakia
» Rila Mountains of Bulgaria
» Julian Alps of Slovenia

There are also many other hiking areas that are less well known:

» Theth in Albania
» Various destinations in the Czech Republic
» A number of national parks in Macedonia
» The Bieszczady Mountains in Poland
» Tara National Park in Serbia
» Carpathian National Natural Park in Ukraine

Horse Riding

Though horse riding is possible throughout Eastern Europe, the sport is best organised – and cheapest – in Hungary, whose people, it's said locally, 'were created by God to sit on horseback'. The best horse-riding centres are on the Great Plain, though you'll also find riding schools in Transdanubia and northern Hungary. Horse riding is also very popular (and affordable) in the Baltic countries, the Czech Republic, Poland and Slovenia.

Rafting

Exciting white-water rafting is possible in spring and summer on some of Eastern Europe's most scenic rivers, including the following:

» Vrbas River and River Una in Bosnia and Hercegovina
» Tara River in Montenegro

» Drina in Serbia
» Soča River in Slovenia
» Rafting on the Dunajec River along the border of Poland and Slovakia is fun, but it's not a white-water experience.

Sailing

Eastern Europe's most famous yachting area is the passage between the long, rugged islands off Croatia's Dalmatian coast. Yacht tours and rentals are available, although this is certainly not for anyone on a budget. If your means are more limited try the following options:

» The Great Masurian Lakes of northeastern Poland, a good choice as small groups can rent sailing boats by the day for very reasonable rates; try the towns of Giżycko and Mikołajki.
» Hungary's Lake Balaton, also popular among sailing enthusiasts.

Skiing

The skiing season in Eastern Europe generally lasts from early December to late March, though at higher altitudes it may extend an extra month either way. Snow conditions can vary greatly from year to year and region to region, but January and February tend to be the best (and busiest) months. Snowboarding is especially popular in Slovakia, as is cross-country skiing in the Czech Republic and Ukraine. Eastern Europe's premier skiing areas include the following:

» High Tatras of Slovakia and Poland
» Carpathian Mountains in Romania and Ukraine
» Bankso in the Rila Mountains in Bulgaria
» Slovenia's Julian Alps
» Bosnian capital Sarajevo hosted the 1984 Winter Olympics and is a growing place for skiing; you'll find some of the best-value slopes in Europe within an hour of the city.
» Lesser-known ski areas in Belarus, Macedonia, Montenegro and Serbia

Thermal Baths & Saunas

There are hundreds of thermal baths in Eastern Europe open to the public. The most affordable are in the Czech Republic, Hungary and Slovenia, and along the Black Sea in Romania.

» Among the best are the Turkish baths of Budapest in Hungary and the fin de siècle spas of Karlovy Vary (Karlsbad) in the Czech Republic.
» The Baltic countries are famous for their proliferation of saunas – both the traditional 'smoke' variety and the clean and smokeless modern sauna. The traditionalist will find many opportunities to take in an old-style sauna in Lithuania.
» Another must for lovers of heat and sweat is the traditional Russian banya (p789), where you can be beaten into cleanliness with birch twigs!

Business Hours

Eastern Europe tends to have similar working patterns to Western Europe and North America.

Saturday and Sunday are official days off, although only banks and offices are shut; most shops, restaurants and cafes are open every day of the week.

Banks and offices are usually open from 9am to 5pm Monday to Friday, often with an hour or two off for lunch. They may also be open on Saturday mornings. Shops usually stay open until 7pm or later.

During the hot summer months, some enterprises will shut for two or three hours in the early afternoon, reopening at 3pm or 4pm and working into the evening.

Children

Travelling with your children in Eastern Europe will be a treat and a challenge for the whole family.

The number-one guideline for travelling with children is to avoid packing too much activity into the available time. (Actually, this should be the number-one guideline for travelling without children too.)

The second guideline is to allow your children to help plan the trip. Sure, they may not have an opinion about Macedonia versus Montenegro, but once you arrive, they will certainly have an opinion about how they would like to spend the day. Furthermore, if your kids have helped to plan the itinerary, they will know what to look forward to and will be more engaged upon arrival.

A good resource is Lonely Planet's *Travel with Children* by Cathy Lanigan and Maureen Wheeler.

Practicalities

» In Eastern Europe most car-rental firms have children's safety seats for hire at a small cost, but it is essential that you book them in advance.

» The same goes for high chairs and cots; they're standard in many restaurants and hotels but numbers are limited.

» The choice of baby food, infant formulas, soy and cows' milk, disposable nappies and the like is often as great in the Eastern European supermarkets as it is back home.

Discount Cards

Camping Card International

The Camping Card International (CCI) is a camping-ground ID valid for a year. It can be used instead of a passport when checking in to camping grounds and includes third-party insurance. As a result, many camping grounds will offer discounts of up to 25% for cardholders. CCIs are issued by automobile associations, camping federations and, sometimes, on the spot at camping grounds. Visit **Camping Card International** (www.campingcardinternational.org) for links to local organisations and lists of participating camping grounds.

Hostel Cards

No hostels in Eastern Europe require that you be a **Hostelling International** (HI; www.hihostels.com) member, but they sometimes charge less if you have a card. Some hostels will issue one on the spot or after a few days' stay, though this might cost a bit more than getting it at home.

Senior Cards

Many attractions offer reduced-price admission for people over 60 or 65 (or sometimes 55 for women). EU residents, especially, are eligible for discounts in many EU countries. Make sure you bring proof of age.

For a fee of about €20, European residents aged 60 and over can get a Railplus Card as an add-on to their national rail senior pass. It entitles the holder to train-fare reductions of about 25%.

Before leaving home, check with an agency that caters to senior travel – such as **Elderhostel** (www.roadscholar.org) – for age-related travel packages and discounts.

Student, Youth & Teacher Cards

An International Student Identity Card (ISIC) is a plastic ID-style card that provides discounts on many forms of transport (including airlines and local transport), cheap or free admission to museums and sights, and inexpensive meals in some student cafeterias and restaurants.

If you're under 26 but not a student, you are eligible to apply for an International Youth Travel Card (IYTC, formerly GO25), issued by the Federation of International Youth Travel Organisations, or the Euro26 card. The Euro26 card may not be recognised in Albania, Moldova, Romania, Serbia and Montenegro. Both cards go under different names in different countries and give much the same discounts and benefits as an ISIC.

An International Teacher Identity Card (ITIC) identifies the holder as an instructor and offers similar deals.

All these cards are issued by student unions, hostelling organisations or youth-oriented travel agencies; alternatively see the **International Student Travel Confederation** (www.isic.org).

Electricity

Plugs in Eastern Europe are the standard round two-pin variety, sometimes called the europlug. If your plugs are of a different design, you'll need an adapter.

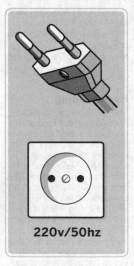

220v/50hz

Embassies & Consulates

It's important to realise what your embassy can and cannot do to help if you get into trouble while travelling abroad. Remember that you are bound by the laws of the country you are visiting.

Generally speaking, your embassy cannot help much if your emergency is of your own making. It will not post bail or otherwise act to get you out of jail.

If your documents are lost or stolen, your embassy can assist you in obtaining a new passport; this is greatly simplified if you have a photocopy or scan of your passport. Your embassy may refer you to a lawyer or a doctor, but it is highly unlikely to provide any financial assistance, no matter what your emergency.

Gay & Lesbian Travellers

Consensual homosexual sex is legal in all of the countries of Eastern Europe. The laws on the books do not signal an open-minded approach to sexual minorities, however.

» You are unlikely to raise any eyebrows by sharing a room (or a bed) with your same-sex partner. But in many countries, society frowns on overt displays of affection in any case – and even more so when it's between members of the same gender.

» Many countries have online forums and gay advocacy groups. Latvia, Hungary, Poland and Russia have all had gay-pride events in recent years. Unfortunately, on most occasions, marchers were outnumbered by antigay protesters, which often ended in arrests on both sides.

» Many gays and lesbians in Eastern Europe actually oppose such parades as they provoke the majority into taking an antigay stance when they would otherwise pay no heed to the gay and lesbian population.

» Despite this don't-ask-don't-tell situation, most Eastern European capitals have small, lively gay scenes, usually centred on one or two bars and clubs.

» Exceptions to this rule are Tirana in Albania, Pristina in Kosovo, Skopje in Macedonia and Sarajevo in Bosnia and Hercegovina, where there is nothing gay- or lesbian-specific that is accessible to visitors.

» Outside large towns, gay and lesbian life is almost nonexistent and the internet is the only realistic way to make contact with other gay people.

Health

Eastern Europe poses no big health risks to travellers, though as with anywhere else in the world there are several things you should be aware of.

Availability & Cost of Health Care

Good basic health care is readily available and pharmacists can give valuable advice and sell over-the-counter medication for minor illnesses. They can also advise when more specialised help is required and point you in the right direction.

The standard of dental care is usually good, but it is sensible to have a dental check-up before a long trip.

Medical care is not always readily available outside of major cities, but embassies, consulates and five-star hotels can usually recommend doctors or clinics. In some cases, medical supplies required in hospital may need to be bought from a pharmacy and nursing care may be limited. The usual precautions apply to help prevent transmission of hepatitis B and HIV/AIDS.

In general health-care costs are still relatively low in Eastern Europe and tend to be more expensive in EU member states than in non-EU member states; bear in mind, however, that in most non-EU states you'll probably want to go to a private clinic for anything more than a doctor's consultation

and therefore comprehensive health insurance is essential.

Potential Illnesses or Conditions
RABIES
Spread through bites or licks from an infected animal on broken skin, rabies is always fatal unless treated promptly and is present throughout Eastern Europe. To be vaccinated, three injections are needed over a month. If you are bitten and have not been vaccinated, you will need a course of five injections starting 24 hours, or as soon as possible, after the injury. If you have been vaccinated, you will need fewer injections and have more time to seek medical help.

TICK-BORNE ENCEPHALITIS
Spread by tick bites, tick-borne encephalitis is a serious infection of the brain. Vaccination is advised for those in risk areas who are unable to avoid tick bites (such as campers, forestry workers and walkers). Two doses of vaccine will provide protection for a year, while three doses provide up to three years' protection. Anyone hiking in the Baltics and Russia for any length of time should consider vaccination, as reported cases have been steadily rising.

TRAVELLER'S DIARRHOEA
If you develop diarrhoea, be sure to drink plenty of fluids, preferably an oral rehydration solution (eg Dioralyte). A few loose stools don't require treatment, but if you start having more than four or five stools a day, you should start taking an antibiotic (usually a quinolone drug) and an antidiarrhoeal agent (such as loperamide). If diarrhoea is bloody, persists for more than 72 hours or is accompanied by fever, shaking, chills or severe abdominal pain, you should seek medical attention.

EUROPEAN HEALTH INSURANCE CARD

Citizens of the EU, Switzerland, Iceland, Norway and Liechtenstein receive free or reduced-cost state-provided healthcare cover with the European Health Insurance Card (EHIC) for medical treatment that becomes necessary while in other EU countries. Every EU individual needs their own card. In the UK, get application forms from post offices, or download them from the **Department of Health** (www.dh.gov.uk), which has comprehensive information about the card's coverage.

The EHIC does not cover private healthcare, so make sure that you are treated by a state healthcare provider. In EU countries where state-provided healthcare isn't free, you will need to pay yourself and fill in a treatment form; keep the form to claim any refunds. In general, you can claim back around 70% of the standard treatment cost.

INSECT BITES & STINGS

Mosquitoes are found in most parts of Europe. They may not carry malaria but can cause irritation and infected bites. Use insect repellent, plug in antimosquito devices and cover up your arms and legs in the evening.

Water

Tap water may not be safe to drink, so it is best to stick to bottled water or boil water for 10 minutes, use water purification tablets or a filter. Do not drink water from rivers or lakes, as it may contain bacteria or viruses that can cause diarrhoea or vomiting. St Petersburg is a particular hot spot for dangerous water – *never* drink from the tap there. Brushing your teeth with tap water is very unlikely to lead to problems, but use bottled water if you want to be very safe.

Insurance

A travel-insurance policy to cover theft, loss and medical problems is always a good idea. The policies written by STA Travel and other student-travel organisations are usually good value.

» Some insurance policies will specifically exclude 'dangerous activities', which can include scuba diving, motorcycling and even hiking.

» Some policies even exclude certain countries, so read the fine print.

» Check that your policy covers ambulances and an emergency flight home.

» You may prefer a policy that pays doctors or hospitals directly rather than reimbursing your claims after the fact.

» Some policies ask you to call back (reverse charges) to a centre in your home country, where an immediate assessment of your problem is made.

» If you have to file a claim, make sure you keep all documentation.

» Worldwide travel insurance is available at www.lonely-planet.com/bookings. You can buy, extend and claim online at any time – even if you're already on the road.

Internet Access

With few exceptions, any decent-sized town in Eastern Europe has internet access in some shape or form.

Connections may be slow, there might not be coffee and you might be sitting in a smelly room full of teenage boys playing war games – but one way or another you'll never be far from the web, even in less developed nations such as Albania and Moldova. Indeed, in some cities, internet cafes can be a social hub and a great way to meet locals as well as other travellers.

In general, however, the internet cafe is a thing of the past and it's wireless all the way, even in the region's darkest corners. Laptops and smart phones can easily connect in many cafes, bars, libraries, hotels, hostels and even public places.

The Baltics are particularly good – Tallinn alone has more than 300 free wi-fi spots – but in general it's only in exceptional cases when you won't be able to get online easily and for free. It's now almost universal for high-standard or boutique hotels to have wi-fi in the rooms.

Sadly, some hotels still charge for this service (five-star international chains are the worst offenders), but nearly all boutique, midrange and budget hotels are more likely to offer it for free.

Maps

Bringing a good regional map will make things a great deal easier if you are planning a long trip taking in more than a couple of countries, although paper maps often feel redundant in the age of smart phones.

» If you do want to invest in one, there's a huge range available, but we recommend *Eastern Europe*, produced by Latvian publisher Jana Seta, and *Eastern Europe* from Freytag & Berndt.

» Buying city maps in advance is generally unnecessary, as nearly all large towns produce them locally for a fraction of the price you'll pay at home.

» Maps of Eastern European capitals and other major towns are widely available from travel bookshops if you want a particularly detailed map in advance.

Money

Things have simplified in Eastern Europe and there are no worries about 'soft' and 'hard' currencies for the most part.

The main problem you'll face is constant currency changes as you flit between the crown, złoty, rouble, lei, lev, lek, dinar and various other national currencies.

There is no longer any particular desire for 'hard' currency (the days when hoteliers would slash the rates if you paid in US dollars are long gone), and the convertibility of almost all Eastern European currencies makes them a stable and reliable way to carry cash.

The euro remains the easiest currency to change throughout the region. It can be used for everything in Estonia, Kosovo, Montenegro, Slovakia and Slovenia, where it is the national currency.

Most other countries in Eastern Europe are hoping to adopt the euro in the future, though the global financial downturn has tempered enthusiasm in many quarters. That said, it's often possible to pay for services such as hotels and tours in euro in countries where it's not the currency: Albania, Belarus, Moldova and Russia are all very euro-friendly, for example.

ATMs

Nearly all Eastern European countries have plenty of ATMs in their capitals and sizable towns. Check the specific situation in your destination before setting out from the big city – and never rely entirely on being able to find an ATM.

» Cash or debit cards can be used throughout Eastern Europe at ATMs linked to international networks such as Cirrus and Maestro.

» The major advantage of using ATMs is that you don't pay commission charges to exchange money, although you might pay a bank fee. The exchange rate is also usually better than that offered for travellers cheques or cash exchanges.

» If you choose to rely on plastic, go for two different cards – this allows one to be used as backup in the case of loss, or more commonly, if a bank does not accept one card.

» A combination of cards and travellers cheques, so you have something to fall back on if there are no ATMs in the area or they accept local cards only, is better still.

Cash

The two most favoured foreign currencies throughout Eastern Europe are the euro and the US dollar.

Although it's not difficult to exchange other major world currencies in big cities, you are at the mercy of the exchange office and its rates.

A far better option is to change your money into euros or US dollars before you leave home. Do note that in some places banks will not change damaged or worn notes. This is especially true in the former Soviet Union, so bring clean and newish notes from home, whenever possible.

Credit Cards

As purchase tools, credit cards are still not as commonly used as they are in Western Europe, but cards such as Amex, Visa and MasterCard are gaining ground. You'll be able to use them at upmarket restaurants, shops, hotels, car-rental firms, travel agencies and many petrol stations.

Bear in mind that if you use a credit card for purchases, exchange rates may have changed by the time your bill is processed, which can work out to your advantage or disadvantage.

Charge-card companies such as Amex have offices in most countries in Eastern Europe and, because they treat you as a customer of the company rather than of the bank that issued the card, they can generally replace a lost card within 24 hours.

The cards' major drawback is that they're not widely accepted off the beaten track. Credit cards such as Visa and MasterCard are more widely accepted because they tend to charge merchants lower commissions.

Moneychangers

Never exchange your hard-earned cash without first shopping around for a decent rate. If you happen to be in a tourist area, you will be offered crappy rates everywhere; for example around the Charles Bridge in Prague. In this case, don't bother shopping around – just leave for a less-touristy neighbourhood.

Border crossings, airports and train stations are typically places where rates aren't great, but many people change money here out of necessity.

Tipping

Tipping practices vary from country to country and often from place to place. In general, you can't go wrong if you add 10% onto your bill at a restaurant.

Porters at upmarket hotels will appreciate a few euros for their efforts. In fashionable venues in urban centres, the wait staff will expect this; in rural locations you might astonish your server.

Travellers Cheques

The benefit of using travellers cheques rather than cash is the protection they offer from theft. But this old-school travel tool has lost its once enormous popularity, as more and more travellers prefer to withdraw cash from ATMs as they go along.

Keep in mind that banks usually charge from 1% to 2% commission to change travellers cheques (up to 5% in Bulgaria, Estonia, Latvia, Lithuania and Romania) and opening hours are sometimes limited.

Always check the commission and rate before signing a travellers cheque or handing over any cash.

Amex and Thomas Cook representatives cash their own travellers cheques without commission, but both give poor rates of exchange. If you're changing more than US$20, you're usually better off going to a bank and paying the standard 1% to 2% commission to change there.

Western Union

If everything goes horribly wrong – your money, travellers cheques and credit cards are all stolen – don't despair. While it's a terrible (and highly unusual) situation, a friend or relative back home will be able to wire money to you anywhere in Eastern Europe via Western Union (WU). There are literally thousands of WU representatives; just look for the distinctive yellow and black sign. The sender is given a code that they communicate to you, then you take the code to the nearest office, along with your passport, to receive your cash.

Photography & Video

Eastern Europe was once notorious for its photographic restrictions – taking shots of anything 'strategic', such as bridges or train stations, was strictly forbidden. These days local officials are much less paranoid, but you need to use common sense when it comes to taking photos.

» Photographing military installations, for example, is never a good idea anywhere in the world. Most importantly, have the courtesy to ask permission before taking close-up photos of people.

Be aware that museums often demand that you buy permission to photograph or video their displays.

» Digital memory, film and camera equipment is available everywhere in Eastern Europe, though you'll have a better selection in larger towns. It's generally possible to download photos to dongles or CDs in internet cafes or any photo shop in Eastern Europe

» Lonely Planet's guide to *Travel Photography* covers all aspects of travel photography and shows you how to develop your skills to capture the perfect picture.

Post

Both the efficiency and cost of the national postal systems in Eastern Europe vary enormously. There seems to be no set rules, but EU countries are likely to be faster, more reliable and more expensive than the non-EU states.

» Postal service from Belarus, Moldova, Montenegro, Russia and Ukraine is slow, but the mail usually reaches its destination eventually. For added assurance and speed, most of these countries offer an express service.

» To send a parcel from Eastern Europe you usually have to take it unwrapped to a main post office; parcels weighing more than 2kg often must be taken to a special customs post office. The post-office staff will usually wrap the parcels for you. The staff may ask to see your passport and note the number on the form; if you don't have a return address within the country put the address of any large tourist hotel.

» If you desperately need something posted to you, do your research – find a friend of a friend who could receive the mail at their address, or ask nicely at a hotel you plan to stay at. You can also have

mail sent to you at Amex offices if you have an Amex card or are carrying its travellers cheques.

Public Holidays

Throughout Eastern Europe, children get the summer months (usually much of July and all of August) off from school, which is one reason why this is the busiest time to go to the beach and other resorts.

There are also usually breaks for Easter and Christmas; keep in mind that dates for Orthodox Christmas and Easter are different to those of their Catholic and Protestant counterparts (though Easter sometimes falls on the same date by both calendars).

Even in countries with a large Muslim population, such as Bosnia and Hercegovina, and Albania, school holidays generally follow these guidelines.

Safe Travel

Eastern Europe is as safe – or unsafe – as any other part of the developed world. If you can handle yourself in the big cities of Western Europe, North America or Australia, you'll have little trouble dealing with the less pleasant side of Eastern Europe. Look purposeful, keep alert and you'll be OK.

Some locals will regale you with tales of how dangerous their city is and recount various cases of muggings, break-ins, kidnappings etc, often involving Roma or other popular scapegoats (other Eastern Europeans will tell you horror stories about the Romanians and Albanians). Most of these stories are overblown and exaggerated and you are unlikely to have any threatening encounters.

Corruption

» Low-level corruption is disappearing fast and is

now rare for travellers to encounter. Do not pay bribes to people in official positions, such as police, border guards, train conductors and ticket inspectors.

» Be aware, however, that these anachronistic systems still exist in Belarus, Moldova, Russia and Transdniestr. If corrupt cops want to hold you up because some obscure stamp is missing from your documentation or on some other pretext, just let them and consider the experience an integral part of your trip. Insisting on calling your embassy is always a good move; officers are likely to receive some grief if their superiors learn they are harassing tourists.

» If you're taken to the police station for questioning, you'll have the opportunity to observe the quality of justice in that country from the inside. In most cases, the more senior officers will eventually let you go (assuming, of course, you haven't committed a real crime).

» If you do have to pay a fine or supplementary charge, insist on a proper receipt before turning over any money; this is now law in Hungary, for example, where traffic police were once notorious for demanding 'gifts' from motorists guilty of some alleged infraction. In all of this, try to maintain your cool, as any threats from you will only make matters worse.

Drugs

Always treat drugs with a great deal of caution. There are a lot of drugs available in the region, but that doesn't mean they are legal. The continual fighting in the former Yugoslavia in the 1990s forced drug traffickers to seek alternative routes from Asia to Western Europe, sometimes crossing through Hungary, Slovakia, the Czech Republic and Poland. Now EU members, these countries do not look lightly upon drug use.

SOLO TRAVELLERS

Eastern Europe is a great place to travel alone. Relatively low hostel and restaurant prices mean that it won't break the bank, and the entire region is unthreatening and well set up for lone travellers. If you want to take a break from going it alone, the best place to find some company is at hostels, which are set up to allow the guests to mix and mingle. Indeed, you may pick up a travelling companion who is heading in your direction. Other places to meet fellow travellers are internet cafes and expat bars (usually the ubiquitous Irish pubs).

Landmines

Bosnia and Hercegovina and Kosovo still have landmines in remote areas. Ask locals for the latest situation and stick to established roads and paths in places where mines are still a problem.

Scams

A word of warning about credit cards: fraudulent shopkeepers have been known to make several charge-slip imprints with your credit card when you're not looking and then simply copy your signature from the authorised slip.

There have also been reports of people making quick and very hi-tech duplicates of credit- or debit-card information with a machine. If your card leaves your possession for longer than you think necessary, consider cancelling it.

Now that most Eastern European currencies have reached convertibility, there is no longer a black market for currency exchange in this region. The days of getting five times the official rate for cash on the streets of Warsaw and Bucharest are well and truly over.

Anyone who approaches you offering such a deal (an uncommon occurrence these days) is an outright thief, trying to get their hands on your money, either by scamming you or by simply taking it.

Theft

Theft is definitely a problem in Eastern Europe and the threat comes from both local thieves and fellow travellers. The most important things to guard are your passport, other documents, tickets and money – in that order.

» It's always best to carry these items in a sturdy pouch on your belt or under your shirt. Train-station lockers or luggage-storage counters are useful to store your luggage (but not valuables) while you get your bearings in a new town. Be very suspicious of people who offer to help you operate your locker.

» Always be wary of snatch thieves and lessen your risk by taking simple precautions. Cameras and shoulder bags are great for these people, who sometimes operate from motorcycles or scooters, slashing the strap before you have a chance to react.

» A small daypack is more secure, but watch your rear and don't keep valuables in the outside pockets. Loop the strap around your leg while seated at bars or cafes.

» Pickpockets are most active in dense crowds, especially in busy train stations and on public transport during peak hours. A common ploy in the Budapest and Prague metros has been for a group of well-dressed young people to surround you, chattering away while one of the group zips through your pockets or purse.

» Be careful even in hotels: don't leave valuables lying around in your room. Carry your own padlock for hostel lockers and always use them.

» Parked cars containing luggage or other bags are prime targets for petty criminals in most cities, and cars with foreign number plates and/or rental-agency stickers attract particular attention. While driving in cities, beware of snatch thieves when you pull up at the lights – keep doors locked and windows rolled up.

» In the case of theft or loss, always report the incident to the police and ask for a statement; otherwise your travel-insurance company won't pay up.

Violence

It's unlikely that travellers will encounter any violence while in Eastern Europe. Be aware, however, that many countries in the region have thriving neo-Nazi movements, which tend to target local Roma populations as well as black and Asian travellers.

Russian neo-Nazis have been known to seek out fights with nonwhite people on Hitler's birthday (20 April); St Petersburg in particular has seen an extraordinary amount of violence against ethnic minorities – and not only on this date.

Telephone

Telephone services in Eastern Europe are generally excellent. The mobile phone is king across the region; most cities have call centres too, although they're used less and less. Call centres tend to be the domain of entrepreneurs who offer discounted rates, although there are also state-run call centres, which are often in the same building as the main post office. Here you can usually make your call from one of the booths inside an enclosed area, paying the cashier as you leave. Public telephones are almost always found at post offices.

Mobile Phones

The expansion of mobile-phone use in Eastern Europe has been phenomenal, and this can be great for travellers too. Mobile phones operate on the GSM standard. Compatible handsets will connect automatically with local providers, but watch for high roaming fees, particularly for data downloads.

» If you plan to spend more than a week or so in any one country, consider buying a SIM card to slip into your phone, although you'll need to check with your provider at home that your handset has been unlocked.

» SIM cards can cost as little as €5 and can be topped up with cards available at supermarkets, kiosks, newsagents

and mobile-phone dealers. With a smartphone, you can use a local SIM card for data as well.

» Alternatively, if you have roaming, your phone will usually switch automatically over to a local network. This can be expensive if you use the phone a great deal, but can be very useful for ad hoc and emergency use.

Phone Codes

» To call abroad from a landline you simply dial the international access code for the country you are calling from (most commonly 00 in Eastern Europe, but 8-10 in Belarus and Russia).

» From a mobile phone simply dial + followed by the country code, the city code and the local number.

» To make a domestic call to another city in the same country, you generally need to dial the area code (with the initial zero) and the number; however, in some countries the area code is an integral part of the phone number and must be dialled every time – even if you're just calling next door.

Phonecards

Local telephone cards – available from post offices, telephone centres, newsstands or retail outlets – are used everywhere in the region. In any given country, there's a wide range of local and international phonecards available. For local calls you're usually better off with a local phonecard.

Time

» Eastern Europe spans three time zones: Central European Time (GMT+1), Eastern European Time (GMT+2) and Moscow Time (GMT+3). At noon in New York, it's 6pm in Warsaw, 7pm in Minsk and 8pm in Moscow.

» All countries employ daylight savings. Clocks are put forward an hour at the start of daylight savings, usually on the last Sunday in March. They are set back one hour on the last Sunday in October.

» Note that the 24-hour clock is widely used in Eastern Europe, though not always conversationally.

Toilets

Toilets have improved enormously in the past decade across the region. The vast majority of toilets you use will be modern, sit down, flushing toilets.

» In Russia, Belarus, Ukraine and Moldova, however, you can expect to find smelly and rather unpleasant squat toilets in bus and train stations, though they are very rare in restaurants or hotels.

» Public toilets have improved too, though you'll need to pay a small fee to use most public toilets in Eastern Europe.

» Using hotel or restaurant facilities is nearly always free and one way to ensure you'll be using a clean bathroom.

Tourist Information

The provision of tourist information varies a huge amount. While countries that have successfully realised their potential as holiday destinations have developed a network of excellent tourist information centres (TICs), there are still many countries that take little or no interest in the economic benefits tourism can bring.

» Countries in the latter category are Ukraine, Belarus and Moldova. Russia is similarly badly organised, though there are unhelpful TICs in Moscow and St Petersburg.

» Among the best prepared are Slovakia, Slovenia, Croatia, the Czech Republic, Hungary, Poland and Bulgaria, many of which have tourist offices abroad as well as throughout the country.

» The Baltic countries of Montenegro, Romania, Albania and Macedonia fall in a middle category of places actively trying to encourage tourism, but whose efforts remain rather obscure at the moment.

Travellers with Disabilities

Eastern Europe is a real mixed bag for less-able travellers. While individual museums and hotels are slowly being brought up to Western European standards of accessibility, there is little coordinated effort to improve things regionally.

» In general, wheelchair-accessible rooms are available only at top-end hotels (and are limited, so be sure to book in advance). Rental cars and taxis may be accessible, but public transport rarely is. Most major museums and sites have disabled access, although there are many exceptions.

» If you have a physical disability, get in touch with your national support organisation (preferably the travel officer if there is one) and ask about the countries you plan to visit. The organisations often have libraries devoted to travel, including access guides, and staff can put you in touch with travel agencies who specialise in tours for the disabled.

» In the UK, the **Royal Association for Disability & Rehabilitation** (www.radar.org.uk) is a very helpful association and sells a number of publications for people with disabilities.

Visas

Visas have become a thing of the past for most travellers in Eastern Europe, though sadly they are still a reality for anyone wanting to explore the region's eastern extremities – all visitors to Russia and Belarus still require a visa, while several nationalities still require visas for Moldova and Ukraine.

» In line with the Schengen Agreement, there are no longer passport controls at the borders between most EU countries, but procedures between EU and non-EU countries can still be fairly thorough.

» If you do need to get a visa, it's important to remember that it has an expiration date and you'll be refused entry after that period has elapsed. Consulates sometimes issue visas on the spot, although some levy a 50% to 100% surcharge for 'express service'. If there's a choice between getting a visa in advance and on the border, go for the former option if you have the time. They're often cheaper in your home country and this

EASTERN EUROPE TIME ZONES

TIME ZONE	LOCATIONS
Central Europe (GMT+1 hour)	Albania, Bosnia & Hercegovina, Croatia, Czech Republic, Hungary, Kosovo, Macedonia, Montenegro, Poland, Serbia, Slovakia and Slovenia
Eastern Europe (GMT+2 hours)	Belarus, Bulgaria, Estonia, Kaliningrad, Latvia, Lithuania, Moldova, Romania and Ukraine
Moscow (GMT+3 hours)	Moscow and St Petersburg

can save on bureaucratic procedure.

» Decide in advance if you want a tourist or transit visa; transit visas, usually valid for just 48 or 72 hours, are often cheaper and issued faster, but it's usually not possible to extend a transit visa or change it to a tourist visa.

» Some countries require visitors to register with the local authorities within 48 hours of arrival, supposedly so they know where you are staying. If you're staying at a hotel or other official accommodation, the administration will take care of this registration for you.

» If you're staying with friends, relatives or in a private room, you're supposed to register with the police yourself. In some cases, this is a formality that is never enforced, so you can skip it. In other cases (such as Russia), you can be fined if you do not go through the motions.

» Obtaining registration through the proper channels is a hassle, often requiring fluent language skills, a pile of documents and several hours of negotiation. You are better off paying a local travel agency for the registration instead of trying to do it yourself.

» The hassles created by losing your passport and visa can be considerably reduced if you have a record of its number and issue date or, even better, photocopies of the relevant data pages. A photocopy of your birth certificate can also be useful.

Women Travellers

Women travellers will find that Eastern Europe is a safe and welcoming place to travel, whether you're in a group, with a mate, or on your own.

That is not to say that sexual harassment does not exist, however. It is not unusual for women to be propositioned by strangers on the street, which can be annoying and even feel threatening,

but rarely anything more. As a rule, foreigners are still a little exotic and therefore attract more attention, but this attention is rarely dangerous and is easily deflected with a shake of the head and a firm 'no'. Do remember that in much of the Balkans a nod of the head means no, not yes, though! Use the local language if you can, but English usually works fine too.

In Muslim countries, women travelling solo will certainly be of interest or curiosity to both local men and women. In Albania and Bosnia and Hercegovina, women may feel self-conscious in bars and cafes outside larger cities, which are usually populated only by men. Unmarried men rarely have contact with women outside their family unit and so may shower travelling women with too much attention. (In such areas, women travelling with a male companion will often experience the opposite and may need to pinch themselves as a reminder that yes, they actually exist.)

Work

The massive eastwards expansion of the EU in recent years has meant that EU citizens have free rein to work in many countries in the region. However, with unemployment still a problem, Eastern European countries aren't always keen on handing out jobs to foreigners.

If you're not an EU citizen, the paperwork involved in arranging a work permit can be almost impossible, especially for temporary work. That doesn't prevent enterprising travellers from topping up their funds occasionally – and they don't always have to do this illegally. If you do find a temporary job in Eastern Europe, though, the pay is often low. Do it for the experience, not to earn your fortune.

» Teaching English is the easiest way to make some extra cash, but the market is

saturated in places such as Prague and Budapest. You'll probably be much more successful in less popular places such as Sofia and Bucharest.

» If you play an instrument or have other artistic talents, you could try working the streets. As every Peruvian pipe player knows, busking is fairly common in major Eastern European cities such as Prague, Budapest and Warsaw. Some countries may require municipal permits for this sort of thing, so talk to other street artists before you start.

» *Work Your Way Around the World* by Susan Griffith gives good, practical advice on a wide range of issues. The publisher Vacation Work has some useful titles, including *The Directory of Summer Jobs Abroad,* edited by David Woodworth. *Working Holidays* by Ben Jupp (Central Bureau for Educational Visits & Exchanges in the UK) is another good source, as is *Now Hiring! Jobs in Eastern Europe* by Clarke Canfield (Perpetual Press).

» Organising a volunteer-work placement is another great way to gain a deeper insight into local culture. In some instances volunteers are paid a living allowance, sometimes they work for their keep, and sometimes they are required to pay to undertake the program. Lonely Planet's *Volunteer* is filled with practical information.

» Several websites can help you search for volunteer work opportunities in Eastern Europe. The **Coordinating Committee for International Voluntary Service** (www.ccivs.org) is an umbrella organisation, with more than 140 member organisations worldwide. It's useful if you want to find out about your country's national volunteer placement agency. Check the Transitions Abroad website and **Serve Your World** (www. serveyourworld.com) to search for vacancies and other volunteering opportunities in Eastern Europe.

Transport

GETTING THERE & AWAY

While not quite as well connected to the rest of the world as Western Europe, Eastern Europe is still a cinch to get to from almost anywhere, whether it be overland, by boat or by air.

Flights, tours and rail tickets can be booked online at www.lonelyplanet.com/bookings.

Entering Eastern Europe

All Eastern European countries require travellers to have a valid passport, preferably with at least six months between the time of departure and the passport's expiration date.

EU travellers from countries that issue national identity cards are increasingly using them to travel within the EU, although it's impossible to use them as sole travel documents outside the EU.

Visas are another thing to consider. Some countries require certain nationalities to buy a document allowing entry between certain dates. Specifically, Belarus and Russia require nearly all nationalities to obtain visas, while Aussie and Kiwi travellers also need visas to enter Moldova and Ukraine. Other nationalities may have additional requirements.

Air

Airports & Airlines

Moscow (Russia), Prague (Czech Republic), Budapest (Hungary) and Warsaw (Poland) are the region's best-connected air hubs. They all have transatlantic flights as well as plenty of flights from Western Europe; they are also well served by budget airlines. Other smaller hubs are St Petersburg (Russia), Rīga (Latvia), Timişoara (Romania), Zagreb (Croatia), Kyiv (Ukraine) and Bratislava (Slovakia), all of which have daily flights to many major European cities. Most of the small hubs also have budget-airline connections, although as a rule the further east you go the fewer there are.

NATIONAL AIRLINES

Almost every country in Eastern Europe has its own national carrier. Most of these airlines provide direct flights to major cities across Western Europe.

Adria Airways (www.adria-airways.com)

Aeroflot (www.aeroflot.ru)

Aerosvit Ukrainian Airline (www.aerosvit.com)

AirBaltic (www.airbaltic.com)

Belavia (www.belavia.by)

BH Airlines (www.bhairlines.ba)

Bulgaria Air (www.air.bg)

Croatia Airlines (www.croatiaairlines.hr)

Czech Airlines (www.csa.cz)

Estonian Air (www.estonian-air.ee)

Jat Airways (www.jat.com)

Kosova Airlines (www.kosovaairlines.com)

LOT Polish Airlines (www.lot.com)

Moldavian Airlines (www.mdv.md)

Tarom (www.tarom.ro)

Ukraine International Airlines (www.flyuia.com)

INTERNATIONAL AIRLINES

The invaluable travellers website **flycheapo** (www.flycheapo.com) is a great resource to see which budget airlines fly where.

Look out for some of the following airlines, which provide the biggest selection of flights to/from Eastern Europe:

Air Berlin (www.airberlin.com)

Air France (www.airfrance.com)

Alitalia (www.alitalia.com)

Austrian Airlines (www.austrian.com)

Belle Air (www.belleair.it)

Blue Air (www.blueair-web.com)

British Airways (www.ba.com)

Carpatair (www.carpatair.com)

EasyJet (www.easyjet.com)

El Al (www.elal.co.il)

Emirates (www.emirates.com)

Finnair (www.finnair.com)

Flybe.com (www.flybe.com)

Germanwings (www.german-wings.com)
Iberia (www.iberia.com)
KLM (www.klm.com)
Lufthansa (www.lufthansa.com)
Ryanair (www.ryanair.com)
SAS (www.flysas.com)
SmartWings (www.smartwings.net)
Swiss International Airlines (www.swiss.com)
Wizz Air (www.wizzair.com)

Land

Bus

Buses are always a useful fallback if there are no trains or flights to your destination. As a means for travelling from Western Europe they are also reliably cheap.

Eurolines (www.eurolines.com) has a vast network with member companies in many Eastern European countries and offers innumerable routes across the continent.

Ecolines (www.ecolines.net) also runs buses between Eastern and Western Europe.

Car & Motorcycle

Travelling by car or motorcycle into Eastern Europe gives travellers an immense amount of freedom and is generally worry-free.

If you're driving a car into Eastern Europe, keep in mind that some insurance packages, especially those covering rental cars, do not include all European countries. Be sure to ask the agency to insure the car in all the countries where you plan to travel. It's outright forbidden to take rental cars into certain countries.

Train

There are numerous routes into Eastern Europe by train. The big railway hubs in Eastern Europe are Prague (Czech Republic), Budapest (Hungary), Bucharest (Romania), Belgrade (Serbia) and Moscow (Russia).

Albania is unique in Eastern Europe, as it has no international train services at all.

From Asia, the Trans-Siberian, Trans-Mongolian and Trans-Manchurian Railways connect Moscow to the Russian Far East, China, North Korea and Mongolia. Central Asian cities such as Tashkent (Uzbekistan) and Almaty (Kazakhstan) are also regularly connected by long-distance trains to Moscow.

Sea

The expansion of budget airlines into Eastern Europe has made travelling in the region by sea far less financially attractive, but ferries are still an atmospheric way to travel.

Boats from several companies regularly connect Italy with Croatia, Slovenia, Montenegro and Albania; there are also services between Corfu (Greece) and Albania.

From Scandinavia, ferries ply the Gulf of Finland and the wide Baltic Sea, connecting Helsinki in Finland and Stockholm in Sweden with Tallinn (Estonia), St Petersburg (Russia) and Rīga (Latvia). In Poland, Gdańsk and Gdynia are linked to Sweden and Denmark.

GETTING AROUND

The Schengen Agreement, which allows for passport-free travel within a large chunk of Europe, includes Czech Republic, Slovakia, Hungary, Slovenia, Poland, Estonia, Latvia and Lithuania. Bulgaria and Romania are both likely to join the area at some point in the near future.

Air

The major Eastern European cities are connected by a full schedule of regular flights within the region. With the advent of low-cost airlines, prices are seriously competitive with trains and even buses.

Particularly well-connected regional airports include Moscow and St Petersburg (Russia), Prague (Czech Republic), Budapest (Hungary), Warsaw (Poland), Rīga (Latvia), Timişoara (Romania) and Zagreb (Croatia).

Many countries offer domestic flights, although there is rarely a need to fly internally unless you are in a particular rush. Russia is the exception; flying from either Moscow or St Petersburg to Kaliningrad saves the trouble of getting a double-entry Russian visa. If you travel to Kaliningrad by boat or land,

---

CLIMATE CHANGE & TRAVEL

Every form of transport that relies on carbon-based fuel generates CO_2, the main cause of human-induced climate change. Modern travel is dependent on aeroplanes, which might use less fuel per kilometre per person than most cars but travel much greater distances. The altitude at which aircraft emit gases (including CO_2) and particles also contributes to their climate change impact. Many websites offer 'carbon calculators' that allow people to estimate the carbon emissions generated by their journey and, for those who wish to do so, to offset the impact of the greenhouse gases emitted with contributions to portfolios of climate-friendly initiatives throughout the world. Lonely Planet offsets the carbon footprint of all staff and author travel.

you are given an exit stamp, making your single-entry visa invalid.

Bicycle

Eastern Europe is compact enough to make it ideal for a cycling trip and mountainous enough to ensure that it will be challenging.

If you are planning a tour of the region by bike, contact one of these helpful cycling clubs:

Cyclists' Touring Club (CTC; www.ctc.org.uk) Offers members an information service on all matters associated with cycling, including maps, cycling conditions, itineraries and detailed routes.

European Cyclists' Federation (www.ecf.com) Advocates bike-friendly policies and organises tours. Also manages EuroVelo, a project to create bike routes across the continent.

Hire

Except in a few of the more visited regions, it can be difficult to hire bikes in Eastern Europe. The best spots are often camping grounds and resort hotels during the summer months, or hostels in the major cities.

Transporting a Bicycle

You should be able to take your bicycle on plane trips. You can either take it apart and pack all the pieces in a bike bag or box, or simply wheel it to the check-in desk, where it should be treated as a piece of check-in luggage.

Within Western Europe, bikes can usually be transported on trains as luggage, subject to a fairly small supplementary fee. If it's possible, book tickets in advance.

Tours

Plenty of companies offer organised cycling tours of Eastern Europe. These specialist companies generally

---

AT YOUR OWN RISK

There is effectively no border between Russia and Belarus. In theory, it's possible to enter Belarus by train and leave it for Russia – or go to Russia and back from Belarus – without going through passport control, and therefore without needing a visa for the country you're entering. However, a hotel won't take you without a visa, so you'd have to stay with friends or rent an apartment, and if your visa-less documents are checked on the street, you will be deported.

If you do not receive a migration card when entering Russia, contact your embassy immediately upon arrival to find out how to get one. If you do not receive an entry stamp, go to the local OVIR (Visa and Registration) office in Russia – but bring a full supply of patience.

A much better option if you plan to travel from Belarus into Russia is to ensure you have a valid visa for Russia as well. This will be stamped by Belarusian control on entry to Belarus and, under the terms of the Russian-Belarusian 'one state' agreement, is valid as an entry stamp for Russia. Keep your immigration card from Belarus and use it when you leave Russia, as they are valid in both countries.

---

plan the itinerary, organise accommodation and transport luggage, making life a lot simpler for cyclists:

BaltiCCycle (www.balticcycle.eu) Promotes cycling in the Baltic countries and provides information on routes, maps and bike rental.

Experience Plus (www.experienceplus.com) Runs cycling tours throughout the region, including cycling Croatia, cycling the Danube from Budapest to the Black Sea, and cycling through the heart of the Balkans.

First Light Bicycle Tours (www.firstlightbicycletours.com) Offers several cycling tours in the Czech Republic, as well as one epic journey from Kraków to Budapest. Self-guided tours are also available.

Top Bicycle (www.topbicycle.com) This Czech company offers cycling tours of the Czech Republic and Slovakia, as well as more extensive tours around the region.

Velo Touring (www.velo-touring.hu) Based in Budapest, this company offers tours

of Hungary, as well as bike rentals for those who want to go it alone.

Boat

Eastern Europe's massive rivers and myriad canals, lakes and seas provide rich opportunities for boat travel, although in almost all cases these are very much pleasure cruises rather than particularly practical ways to get around. Boat travel is usually far more expensive than the equivalent bus or train journey, but that's not necessarily the point.

Bus

Buses are a viable alternative to the rail network in most Eastern European countries. Generally they tend to complement the rail system rather than duplicate it, though in some countries – notably Hungary, the Czech Republic and Slovakia – you'll almost always have a choice between the two options.

» Buses tend to be best for shorter hops, getting around cities and reaching remote rural villages. They are often the only option in mountainous regions.

» In general, buses are slightly cheaper and slower than trains. The ticketing system varies in each country, but advance reservations are rarely necessary. On long-distance buses you can usually pay upon boarding, although it's safest to buy your ticket in advance at the station.

» The only company covering the majority of the region is Eurolines.

Car & Motorcycle

Travelling with your own vehicle allows you increased flexibility and the option to get off the beaten track. However, cars can be inconvenient in city centres when you have to negotiate strange one-way systems or find somewhere to park in the narrow streets of old towns.

» Theft from vehicles is a problem in many parts of the region – never leave valuables in your car.

» Russia, Belarus and Ukraine still remain tediously difficult places to drive into – border controls can take a long time and bribes are often the order of the day.

» It is definitely not recommended to drive a rental car from Serbia into Kosovo, and vice versa.

Driving Licence & Documentation

Proof of ownership of a private vehicle should always be carried when driving in Eastern Europe.

An EU driving licence may be used throughout most of Eastern Europe, as may North American and Australian ones. If you want to be extra cautious – or if you have any other type of licence – you should obtain an International Driving Permit (IDP).

Always double-check which type of licence is required in your chosen destination before departure.

Fuel & Spare Parts

Fuel prices vary considerably from country to country, though they rarely bear any relation to the general cost of living. Relatively affluent Slovenia, for example, has very cheap fuel, while the opposite is true in inexpensive Hungary.

» Russia is the cheapest spot, followed by Romania, which has prices half those of neighbouring Hungary.

» Unleaded petrol of 95 or 98 octane is widely available throughout the region and it's slightly cheaper than super (premium grade). Look for the pump with green markings. Diesel is usually significantly cheaper than petrol in Eastern Europe.

» Spare parts for Western cars are widely available from garages and dealerships around the region, although this is less the case in Belarus, Moldova and Ukraine, and of course in more rural areas.

Hire

Hiring a car in Eastern Europe is now a totally straightforward procedure and can be done hassle-free, even in Moldova or Belarus, where you might imagine it to be somewhat problematic.

» The big international companies will give you reliable service and a good standard of vehicle. Prebooked rates are generally lower than walk-in rates at rental offices, but either way you'll pay about 20% to 40% more than in Western Europe.

» Local companies will usually offer lower prices than the multinationals, but it's best to only use local companies with good reputations – try asking at your hotel , or see the local agencies listed in each country chapter of this book.

» Bear in mind that many companies will not allow you to take cars into certain

countries. Russia, Belarus, Moldova and Kosovo all regularly feature on forbidden lists – there's usually a way around this, but check in advance with the car-hire company you're planning to use.

You should be able to make advance reservations online. See the following:

Avis (www.avis.com)

Budget (www.budget.com)

Europcar (www.europcar.com)

Hertz (www.hertz.com)

Insurance

Third-party motor insurance is compulsory throughout the EU. For non-EU countries make sure you check the requirements with your insurer. For more information contact the **Association of British Insurers** (www.abi.org.uk).

» You should get your insurer to issue a Green Card (which may cost extra), an internationally recognised proof of insurance, and check that it lists all the countries you intend to visit.

» If the Green Card doesn't list one of the countries you're visiting and your insurer cannot (or will not) add it, you will have to take out separate third-party cover at the border of the country in question. This may be the case for Bulgaria, Macedonia, Russia and the Baltic states. Allow extra time at borders to purchase insurance.

» The European Accident Statement is available from your insurance company and allows each party at an accident to record information for insurance purposes. The Association of British Insurers has more details. Never sign an accident statement you cannot understand – insist on a translation and sign only if it's acceptable.

» Taking out a European breakdown-assistance policy, such as the Five Star Service with **AA** (www.theaa.com) or the Eurocover Motoring Assistance with **RAC** (www.rac.co.uk), is a good investment.

» Non-Europeans might find it cheaper to arrange for international coverage with their own national motoring organisation before leaving home. Ask your motoring organisation for details about reciprocal services offered by affiliated organisations around Europe.

Road Rules

Motoring organisations can supply members with country-by-country information on motoring regulations, or they may produce motoring guidebooks for general sale.

Driving in Eastern Europe can be much more dangerous than in Western Europe. Driving at night can be particularly hazardous in rural areas as the roads are often narrow and winding, and you may encounter horse-drawn vehicles, cyclists, pedestrians and domestic animals. In the event of an accident, you're supposed to notify the police and file an insurance claim.

If your car has significant body damage from a previous accident, point this out to customs upon arrival in the country and have it noted somewhere. Damaged vehicles may only be allowed to leave the country with police permission.

Standard international road signs are used in Eastern Europe. When driving in the region, keep the following rules in mind:

» Drive on the right-hand side of the road and overtake on the left.

» Don't overtake more than one car at a time.

» Seat belts are mandatory for the driver and all passengers.

» Motorcyclists (and their passengers) must wear a helmet.

» Children under 12 and intoxicated passengers are not allowed to sit in the front seat in most countries.

» Drink-driving is a serious offence – most Eastern European countries have a 0% blood-alcohol concentration (BAC) limit.

» When two roads of equal importance intersect, the vehicle coming from the right has right of way unless signs indicate otherwise; in many countries this rule also applies to cyclists, so take care.

» Trams have priority at crossroads and when they are turning right.

» Don't pass a tram that's stopping to let off passengers until everyone is out and the doors have closed again.

» Never pass a tram on the left or stop within 1m of tram tracks. A police officer who sees you blocking a tram route by waiting to turn left will flag you over.

» It's usually illegal to stop or park at the top of slopes, in front of pedestrian crossings, at bus or tram stops, on bridges or at level crossings.

» Speed limits are posted, and are generally:

- 110km/h or 120km/h on motorways
- 100km/h on highways
- 80km/h on secondary and tertiary roads
- 50km/h or 60km/h in built-up areas

» Motorcycles are usually limited to 90km/h on motorways, and vehicles with trailers to 80km/h.

» Traffic police usually administer fines on the spot; always ask for a receipt.

» Almost everywhere in Europe it is compulsory to carry a red warning triangle, which you must use when parking on a highway in an emergency. If you don't use the triangle and another vehicle hits you from behind, you will be held responsible.

» A first-aid kit and a fire extinguisher are also required in most Eastern European countries, while a spare-bulb kit and headlamp converters are recommended. Contact the RAC or the AA for more information.

Hitching

Hitching is never entirely safe in any country and we don't recommend it. Travellers who decide to hitch should understand they are taking a small but potentially serious risk.

As long as public transport remains cheap in Eastern Europe, hitching is mostly for the adventure. In the former Soviet Union, Albania and Romania, drivers expect riders to pay the equivalent of a bus fare. In Romania, traffic is light, motorists are probably not going far and you'll often face small vehicles overloaded with passengers.

If you want to give it a try, remember the following key points:

» Hitch in pairs; it will be safer.

» Solo women should never hitch.

» Don't hitch from city centres; take public transport to suburban exit routes.

» Make a clearly written cardboard sign indicating your intended destination, remembering to use the local name for the town or city (Praha not Prague, or Warszawa not Warsaw).

» Don't let your luggage be put in the boot, only sit next to a door you can open and ask drivers where they are going before you say where you're going.

» Always let someone know where you're going before heading off.

Travellers considering hitching to get around can find destination-based information and ride-share options at the **Backpackers Ultimate Guide to Europe** (www.bugeurope.com) and the useful **Hitchhikers** (www.hitchhikers.org), which connects hitchhikers and drivers worldwide.

Local Transport

Public transport in Eastern Europe has been developed to a far greater extent than in Western Europe. There are excellent metro networks in Moscow and St Petersburg (Russia), Warsaw (Poland), Prague (Czech Republic), Kyiv (Ukraine), Minsk (Belarus), Budapest (Hungary) and Bucharest (Romania), as well as a rudimentary one in Sofia (Bulgaria).

One form of transport that doesn't exist in Western Europe is the shared minibus (*marshrutka* in the former Soviet Union, *furgon* in the Balkans). These quick but cramped minibuses are used throughout Eastern Europe as both inter- and intracity transport. St Petersburg would cease to function without them. It's also the most likely way you'll travel between mountain towns in Albania.

Trolleybuses are another phenomenon of Eastern Europe. Although slow, they are environmentally friendly (being powered by electricity) and can be found throughout the former Soviet Union. Check out the longest trolleybus route in the world in the Crimea, Ukraine.

Trams are also popular, though they vary greatly in speed and modernity. Those in Russia are often borderline antiques, which seem to derail on a daily basis, while Prague's fleet of sleek trams have electronic destination displays and automated announcements.

Tours

A package tour is generally worth considering only if your time is limited or you have a special interest such as skiing, canoeing, sailing, horse riding, cycling or spa treatments.

Cruises on the Danube are an exciting and romantic way to see Europe's most famous river, but they tend to be on the expensive side.

Most tour prices are for double occupancy, which means singles have to share a double room with someone of the same sex or pay a sup-plement to have the room to themselves.

Some experienced operators in Eastern Europe include the following:

Regent Holidays (www. regent-holidays.co.uk) UK-based company offers comprehensive individual and group tours, which take in everything from a two-week Hanseatic Baltic tour to city breaks in Minsk and tours of Albania.

Baltic Holidays (www.bal-ticholidays.com) Exclusively runs tours of the Baltic region and northwest Russia, including weekend city breaks, family holidays, spa breaks and activity tours. Custom itineraries follow themes such as Soviet or Jewish heritage.

Eastern Europe Russian Travel Centre (www.eetb-travel.com) Australia-based company offering dozens of upmarket tours to the whole region, but particularly Russia; it also offers river cruises.

Trans-Siberian Experience (www.trans-siberian. co.uk) This backpackers' travel organisation offers specialised trips in Russia.

Elder Hostel (www.elderhos-tel.org) Offers educational tours for people over 50 throughout Russia, the Baltic countries, the Balkans and Central Europe.

Train

Trains are the most atmospheric, comfortable and fun way to make long overland journeys in Eastern Europe. All major cities are on the rail network and it's perfectly feasible for train travel to be your only form of intercity transport. In general, trains run like clockwork and you can expect to arrive pretty much to the timetabled minute.

» If you're travelling overnight (which is often the case when you're going between countries), you'll get a bed reservation included in the price of your ticket, although you may have to pay a few euros extra for the bedding once on board.

» Each carriage is administered by a steward, who will look after your ticket and – crucially, if you arrive during the small hours – make sure that you get off at the correct stop.

» Each carriage has a toilet and washbasin at either end – the state of cleanliness varies. Be aware that toilets may be closed while the train is at a station and a good 30 minutes before you arrive in a big city.

» Overnight trains also have the benefit of saving you a night's accommodation. It's a great way to meet locals – and it's not unusual to be invited for dinner or even to stay for a night or two with people who shared your cabin.

Reservations

It's always advisable to buy a ticket in advance. Seat reservations are also recommended, but are only necessary if the timetable specifies one is required. On busy routes and during the summer, however, always try to reserve a seat several days in advance.

You can book most routes in the region from any main station in Eastern Europe.

For peace of mind, you may prefer to book tickets via travel agencies before you leave home, although this will be more expensive than booking on arrival.

Resources

If you plan to travel extensively by train, it might be worth checking the following resources:

Thomas Cook European Rail Timetable (www. thomascookpublishing.com) A complete listing of train schedules that indicates where supplements apply or where reservations are necessary; it's updated monthly and you can order it online from Thomas Cook Publishing.

Rail Europe (www.raileurope.com) Provides information on fares and passes as well as schedules for the most popular routes in Europe.

DB Bahn (www.reiseauskunft.bahn.de) A particularly useful resource of timetables and fares for trains all across Eastern Europe; the website is available in many languages, including English.

Safety

Trains, while generally safe, can attract petty criminals. Carry your valuables on you at all times – don't even go to the bathroom without taking your cash, wallet and passport.

» If you are sharing a compartment with others, you'll have to decide whether or not you trust them. If there's any doubt, be very cautious about leaving the compartment. At night, make sure your door is locked from the inside and your valuables are in your money belt or hidden in your luggage under the bed (which usually can't be accessed when someone is lying down), as sadly even the carriage attendants have been known to steal from trusting travellers.

» If you have a compartment to yourself, you can ask the steward to lock it while you go to the dining car or go for a wander outside when the train is stopped. However, be aware that most criminals strike when they can easily disembark from the train and on occasions the stewards are complicit.

» In the former Soviet Union, the open-plan 3rd-class accommodation is by far the most vulnerable to thieves.

Train Passes

Not all countries in Eastern Europe are covered by rail passes, but passes do include a number of destinations and so can be worthwhile if you are concentrating your travels on a particular part of the region. These are available online or through most travel agents. Check out the excellent summary of available passes, and their pros and cons, at **Man In Seat Sixty-one** (www.seat61.com/Railpass.htm).

Keep in mind that all passes offer discounted 'youth' prices for travellers who are under 26 years of age on the first day of travel. Those aged four to 11 are eligible for a child rate. Discounted fares are also available if you are travelling in a group of two to five people (although you must always travel together).

In the USA, you can buy passes through **Rail Europe** (www.raileurope.com); in Australia you can use either **Rail Plus** (www.railplus.com.au) or Rail Europe.

TRAIN CLASSES 101

The system of train classes in Eastern Europe is similar to that in Western Europe. Short trips, or longer ones that don't involve sleeping on the train, are usually seated like a normal train – benches (on suburban trains) or aeroplane-style seats (on smarter intercity services).

There are generally three classes of sleeping accommodation on trains – each country has a different name for them, but for the sake of simplicity we'll call them 3rd, 2nd and 1st class.

3rd class The cheapest option. Generally consists of six berths in each compartment; you may feel your privacy has been slightly invaded. In the former Soviet Union, 3rd class is called *platskartny* and does not have compartments; instead, there's just one open-plan carriage with beds everywhere. Third-class is not widely available.

2nd class Known as *kupe* in the former Soviet Union, 2nd class has four berths in a closed compartment. If there are two of you, you will share your accommodation with two others. However, if there are three of you, you'll often have the compartment to yourselves.

1st class SV or *myagky* in the former Soviet Union is a treat, although you are paying for space rather than decor. Here you'll find two berths in a compartment, usually adorned with plastic flowers to remind you what you've paid for.

While it's reasonably priced, train travel costs more than bus travel in some countries. First-class tickets are double the price of 2nd-class tickets, which are in turn approximately twice the price of 3rd-class tickets.

BALKAN FLEXIPASS

The Balkan Flexipass includes Bulgaria, Romania, Greece, Serbia, Montenegro, Macedonia and Turkey. This pass is not available to anyone who is a resident of Europe, Morocco, Turkey, or any of the countries of the former Soviet Union. It's valid for 1st-class travel only. In the USA, Rail Europe charges US$253/152/127 per adult/youth/child for five days of 1st-class travel within one month; passes for 10 or 15 days of travel are also available.

EURAIL GLOBAL

The famous **Eurail** (www.eurail.com) pass allows the greatest flexibility for 'overseas' visitors only – if you are a resident of Europe, check out the InterRail Pass. The Eurail Global pass allows unlimited travel in 21 countries, including Croatia, the Czech Republic, Hungary, Romania and Slovenia. The pass is valid for a set number of consecutive days or a set number of days within a period of time.

EURAIL SELECT

Again, only non-European residents can purchase this pass, which covers travel in three, four or five neighbouring countries, which you choose from the 18 available. Your Eastern European options include Bulgaria, Croatia, the Czech Republic, Hungary, Montenegro, Romania, Serbia and Slovenia. Note that Serbia and Montenegro count as one country for Eurail pass purposes, as do Croatia and Slovenia, so the clever travel-ler can get six countries for the price of three.

From Rail Europe this would be US$552/361/237 per adult/youth/child for five days of travel in four countries over two months; adult and child fares are for 1st class, while the youth fare is only for 2nd class. Additional countries and additional days of travel are available for a higher cost.

EUROPEAN EAST PASS

The European East Pass can be purchased by anyone not permanently resident in Europe and the former Soviet Union. The pass is valid for travel in Austria, the Czech Republic, Hungary, Slovakia and Poland, and offers five days of travel in a one-month period. It also includes bonuses such as Danube River cruises.

European East is sold in North America, Australia and the UK. Rail Europe charges US$307/214 for 1st-/2nd-class travel (half-price for children), with extra rail days available for purchase.

INTERRAIL GLOBAL

These passes are available to European residents of more than six months' standing (passport identification is required), although residents of Turkey and parts of North Africa can also buy them. Terms and conditions vary slightly from country to country, but the InterRail pass is not valid for travel within your country of residence. For complete information, check out the **InterRail** (www.interrail.eu) website.

InterRail Global allows unlimited travel in 30 European countries, including Bosnia and Hercegovina, Bulgaria, Croatia, the Czech Republic, Hungary, Macedonia, Montenegro, Poland, Romania, Serbia, Slovakia and Slovenia. The consecutive pass is valid for unlimited travel within a period of 22 days or one month. There is also a pass that allows for five or 10 rail days within a designated time period.

INTERRAIL & EURAIL COUNTRY PASSES

If you are intending to travel extensively within any one country, you might consider purchasing a Country Pass (InterRail if you are an EU resident, Eurail if not). The Eurail Country Pass is available for Bulgaria, Croatia, the Czech Republic, Hungary, Poland, Romania and Slovenia. The InterRail Country Pass is available for all of those countries, plus Serbia and Slovakia. The passes and prices vary for each country, so check out the websites for more information. You'll probably need to travel extensively to recoup your money, but the passes will save you the time and hassle of buying individual tickets that don't require reservations. Some of these countries also offer national rail passes.

RAIL PASS RATES

Eurail Global

AGE	CLASS	DURATION	PRICE (€)
12-25	2nd	1 month	586
12-25	2nd	15 days	369
over 26	1st	1 month	899
over 26	1st	15 days	567
12-25	2nd	10 days in 2 months	435
12-25	2nd	15 days in 2 months	571
over 26	1st	10 days in 2 months	668
over 26	1st	15 days in 2 months	876

InterRail Global

AGE	CLASS	DURATION	PRICE (€)
12-25	2nd	5 days in 10 days	181
12-25	2nd	10 days in 22 days	265
12-25	2nd	1 month	435
over 26	1st	5 days in 10 days	434
over 26	1st	10 days in 22 days	618
over 26	1st	1 month	1034
over 26	2nd	5 days in 10 days	276
over 26	2nd	10 days in 22 days	393
over 26	2nd	1 month	658

Language

This chapter offers basic vocabulary to help you get around Eastern Europe. Read our coloured pronunciation guides as if they were English and you'll be understood. The stressed syllables are indicated with italics.

Some phrases in this chapter have both polite and informal forms (indicated by the abbreviations 'pol' and 'inf' respectively). The abbreviations 'm' and 'f' indicate masculine and feminine gender respectively.

ALBANIAN

In Albanian – also understood in Kosovo – ew is pronounced as 'ee' with rounded lips, uh as the 'a' in 'ago', dh as the 'th' in 'that', dz as the 'ds' in 'adds', and zh as the 's' in 'pleasure'. Also, ll and rr are pronounced stronger than when they are written as single letters.

Basics

Hello.	Tungjatjeta.	toon·dya·tye·ta
Goodbye.	Mirupafshim.	mee·roo·paf·sheem
Excuse me.	Më falni.	muh fal·nee
Sorry.	Më vjen keq.	muh vyen kech
Please.	Ju lutem.	yoo loo·tem
Thank you.	Faleminderit.	fa·le·meen·de·reet
Yes.	Po.	po
No.	Jo.	yo

What's your name?
Si quheni?   see choo·he·nee

My name is ...
Unë quhem ...   oo·nuh choo·hem ...

WANT MORE?

For in-depth language information and handy phrases, check out Lonely Planet's *Eastern Europe Phrasebook*. You'll find it at **shop.lonelyplanet.com**, or you can buy Lonely Planet's iPhone phrasebooks at the Apple App Store.

Do you speak English?
A flisni anglisht?   a flees·nee ang·leesht

I don't understand.
Unë nuk kuptoj.   oo·nuh nook koop·toy

Accommodation

campsite	vend kampimi	vend kam·pee·mee
guesthouse	bujtinë	booy·tee·nuh
hotel	hotel	ho·tel
youth hostel	fjetore për të rinj	fye·to·re puhr tuh reeny

Do you have a single/double room?
A keni një dhomë teke/dopjo?   a ke·nee nyuh dho·muh te·ke/dop·yo

How much is it per night/person?
Sa kushton për një natë/njeri?   sa koosh·ton puhr nyuh na·tuh/nye·ree

Eating & Drinking

Is there a vegetarian restaurant near here?
A ka ndonjë restorant vegjetarian këtu afër?   a ka ndo·nyuh res·to·rant ve·dye·ta·ree·an kuh·too a·fuhr

What would you recommend?
Çfarë më rekomandoni?   chfa·ruh muh re·ko·man·do·nee

I'd like the bill/menu, please.
Më sillni faturën/ menunë, ju lutem.   muh seell·nee fa·too·ruhn/ me·noo·nuh yoo loo·tem

| I'll have ... | Dua ... | doo·a ... |
| Cheers! | Gëzuar! | guh·zoo·ar |

Emergencies

| Help! | Ndihmë! | ndeeh·muh |
| Go away! | Ik! | eek |

Call the doctor/police!
Thirrni doktorin/ — theerr·nee dok·to·reen/
policinë! — po·lee·tsee·nuh

I'm lost.
Kam humbur rrugën. — kam hoom·boor rroo·guhn

I'm ill.
Jam i/e sëmurë. (m/f) — yam ee/e suh·moo·ruh

Where are the toilets?
Ku janë banjat? — koo ya·nuh ba·nyat

Shopping & Services

I'm looking for ...
Po kërkoj për ... — po kuhr·koy puhr ...

How much is it?
Sa kushton? — sa koosh·ton

That's too expensive.
Është shumë — uhsh·tuh shoo·muh
shtrenjtë. — shtreny·tuh

market	treg	treg
post office	posta	pos·ta
tourist office	zyrë	zew·ra
	turistike	too·rees·tee·ke

Transport

boat	anija	a·nee·ya
bus	autobusi	a·oo·to·boo·see
plane	aeroplani	a·e·ro·pla·nee
train	treni	tre·nee

Numbers – Albanian

1	një	nyuh
2	dy	dew
3	tre	tre
4	katër	ka·tuhr
5	pesë	pe·suh
6	gjashtë	dyash·tuh
7	shtatë	shta·tuh
8	tetë	te·tuh
9	nëntë	nuhn·tuh
10	dhjetë	dhye·tuh

One ... ticket (to Shkodër), please.	Një biletë ... (për në Shkodër), ju lutem.	nyuh bee·le·tuh ... (puhr nuh shko·duhr) yoo loo·tem
one-way	për vajtje	puhr vai·tye
return	kthimi	kthee·mee

BULGARIAN

In Bulgarian, vowels in unstressed syllables are generally pronounced shorter and weaker than they are in stressed syllables. Note that uh is pronounced as the 'a' in 'ago' and zh as the 's' in 'pleasure'.

Basics

Hello.	Здравейте.	zdra·vey·te
Goodbye.	Довиждане.	do·veezh·da·ne
Excuse me.	Извинете.	iz·vee·ne·te
Sorry.	Съжалявам.	suh·zhal·ya·vam
Please.	Моля.	mol·ya
Thank you.	Благодаря.	bla·go·dar·ya
Yes.	Да.	da
No.	Не.	ne

What's your name?
Как се казвате/ — kak se kaz·va·te/
казваш? (pol/inf) — kaz·vash

My name is ...
Казвам се ... — kaz·vam se ...

Do you speak English?
Говорите ли — go·vo·ree·te lee
английски? — ang·lees·kee

I don't understand.
Не разбирам. — ne raz·bee·ram

Accommodation

campsite	къмпинг	kuhm·peeng
guesthouse	пансион	pan·see·on
hotel	хотел	ho·tel
youth hostel	общежитие	ob·shte·zhee·tee·ye

Do you have a ... room?
Имате ли — ee·ma·te lee
стая с ...? — sta·ya s ...

| single | едно легло | ed·no leg·lo |
| double | едно голямо легло | ed·no go·lya·mo leg·lo |

How much is it per night/person?
Колко е на вечер/ — kol·ko e na ve·cher/
човек? — cho·vek

Eating & Drinking

Do you have vegetarian food?

Имате ли	ee·ma·te lee
вегетерианска	ve·ge·te·ree·an·ska
храна?	hra·na

What would you recommend?

Какво ще	kak·vo shte
препоръчате?	pre·po·ruh·cha·te

I'd like the bill/menu, please.

Дайте ми сметката/	dai·te mee smet·ka·ta/
менюто, моля.	men·yoo·to mol·ya

I'll have ...	Ще взема ...	shte vze·ma ...
Cheers!	Наздраве!	na·zdra·ve

Emergencies

Help!	Помощ!	po·mosht
Go away!	Махайте се!	ma·hai·te se

Call the doctor/police!

Повикайте лекар/	po·vee·kai·te le·kar/
полицията!	po·lee·tsee·ya·ta

I'm lost.

Загубих се.	za·goo·beeh se

I'm ill.

Болен/Болна	bo·len/bol·na
съм. (m/f)	suhm

Where are the toilets?

Къде има тоалетни?	kuh·de ee·ma to·a·let·nee

Shopping & Services

I'm looking for ...

Търся ...	tuhr·sya ...

How much is it?

Колко струва?	kol·ko stroo·va

That's too expensive.

Скъпо е.	skuh·po e

bank	банка	ban·ka
post office	поща	po·shta
tourist office	бюро за	byoo·ro za
	туристическа	too·ree·stee·
	информация	ches·ka een·for·
		ma·tsee·ya

Transport

boat	корабът	ko·ra·buht
bus	автобусът	av·to·boo·suht
plane	самолетът	sa·mo·le·tuht
train	влакът	vla·kuht

Numbers – Bulgarian

1	един	ed·een
2	два	dva
3	три	tree
4	четири	che·tee·ree
5	пет	pet
6	шест	shest
7	седем	se·dem
8	осем	o·sem
9	девет	de·vet
10	десет	de·set

One ... ticket (to Varna), please.	Един билет ... (за Варна), моля.	e·deen bee·let ... (za var·na) mol·ya
one-way	в едната посока	v ed·na·ta po·so·ka
return	за отиване и връщане	za o·tee·va·ne ee vruhsh·ta·ne

CROATIAN & SERBIAN

Croatian and Serbian are very similar and mutually intelligible. Using them, you will also be fully understood in Bosnia & Hercegovina, and Montenegro, and in parts of Kosovo.

In this section, significant differences between Croatian and Serbian are indicated with (C) and (S) respectively. Note that r is rolled and that zh is pronounced as the 's' in 'pleasure'.

Basics

Hello.	Zdravo.	zdra·vo
Goodbye.	Zbogom.	zbo·gom
Excuse me.	Oprostite.	o·pro·sti·te
Sorry.	Žao mi je.	zha·o mi ye
Please.	Molim.	mo·lim
Thank you.	Hvala.	hva·la
Yes.	Da.	da
No.	Ne.	ne

What's your name?

Kako se zovete/	ka·ko se zo·ve·te/
zoveš? (pol/inf)	zo·vesh

My name is ...

Zovem se ...	zo·vem se ...

Do you speak English?

Govorite/Govoriš li	go·vo·ri·te/go·vo·rish
engleski? (pol/inf)	li en·gle·ski

I don't understand.

Ja ne razumijem.	ya ne ra·zu·mi·yem

Accommodation

campsite	kamp	kamp
guesthouse	privatni smještaj	pri·vat·ni smyesh·tai
hotel	hotel	ho·tel
youth hostel	prenoćište za mladež	pre·no·chish·te za mla·dezh

Do you have a single/double room?
Imate li jednokrevetnu/ i·ma·te li yed·no·kre·vet·nu/
dvokrevetnu sobu? dvo·kre·vet·nu so·bu

How much is it per night/person?
Koliko stoji po ko·li·ko sto·yi po
noći/osobi? no·chi/o·so·bi

Eating & Drinking

What would you recommend?
Što biste preporučili? shto bi·ste pre·po·ru·chi·li

Do you have vegetarian food?
Da li imate da li i·ma·te
vegetarijanski obrok? ve·ge·ta·ri·yan·ski o·brok

I'd like the bill/menu, please.
Mogu li dobiti račun/ mo·gu li do·bi·ti ra·chun/
jelovnik, molim? ye·lov·nik mo·lim

I'll have ...	Želim ...	zhe·lim ...
Cheers!	Živjeli!	zhi·vye·li

Emergencies

Help!	Upomoć!	u·po·moch
Go away!	Maknite se!	mak·ni·te se

Call the ...!	Zovite ...!	zo·vi·te ...
doctor	liječnika (C) lekara (S)	li·yech·ni·ka le·ka·ra
police	policiju	po·li·tsi·yu

I'm lost.
Izgubio/Izgubila iz·gu·bi·o/iz·gu·bi·la
sam se. (m/f) sam se

I'm ill.
Ja sam bolestan/ ya sam bo·le·stan/
bolesna. (m/f) bo·le·sna

Where are the toilets?
Gdje se nalaze gdye se na·la·ze
zahodi/toaleti? (C/S) za·ho·di/to·a·le·ti

Shopping & Services

I'm looking for ...
Tražim ... tra·zhim

Numbers – Croatian & Serbian

1	jedan	ye·dan
2	dva	dva
3	tri	tri
4	četiri	che·ti·ri
5	pet	pet
6	šest	shest
7	sedam	se·dam
8	osam	o·sam
9	devet	de·vet
10	deset	de·set

How much is it?
Koliko stoji/ ko·li·ko sto·yi/
košta? (C/S) kosh·ta

That's too expensive.
To je preskupo. to ye pre·sku·po

bank	banka	ban·ka
post office	poštanski ured	po·shtan·skee oo·red
tourist office	turistička agencija	tu·ris·tich·ka a·gen·tsi·ya

Transport

boat	brod	brod
bus	autobus	a·u·to·bus
plane	zrakoplov (C) avion (S)	zra·ko·plov a·vi·on
train	vlak/voz (C/S)	vlak/voz

One ... ticket (to Sarajevo), please.	Jednu ... kartu (do Sarajeva), molim.	yed·nu ... kar·tu (do sa·ra·ye·va) mo·lim
one-way	jedno-smjernu	yed·no-smyer·nu
return	povratnu	po·vrat·nu

CZECH

An accent mark over a vowel in written Czech indicates it's pronounced as a long sound. Note that air is pronounced as in 'hair', aw as in 'law', oh as the 'o' in 'note', ow as in 'how', uh as the 'a' in 'ago', kh as the 'ch' in the Scottish *loch*, and zh as the 's' in 'pleasure'. Also, r is rolled in Czech and the apostrophe (') indicates a slight y sound.

Basics

Hello.	Ahoj.	uh·hoy
Goodbye.	Na shledanou.	nuh·skhle·duh·noh

Excuse me.	Promiňte.	pro·min'·te
Sorry.	Promiňte.	pro·min'·te
Please.	Prosím.	pro·seem
Thank you.	Děkuji.	dye·ku·yi
Yes.	Ano.	uh·no
No.	Ne.	ne

What's your name?
| Jak se jmenujete/ | yuhk se yme·nu·ye·te/ |
| jmenuješ? (pol/inf) | yme·nu·yesh |

My name is ...
| Jmenuji se ... | yme·nu·yi se ... |

Do you speak English?
| Mluvíte anglicky? | mlu·vee·te uhn·glits·ki |

I don't understand.
| Nerozumím. | ne·ro·zu·meem |

Accommodation

campsite	tábořiště	ta·bo·rzhish·tye
guesthouse	penzion	pen·zi·on
hotel	hotel	ho·tel
youth hostel	mládežnická	mla·dezh·nyits·ka
	ubytovna	u·bi·tov·nuh

Do you have a ... room?
| Máte jednolůžkový/ | ma·te yed·no·loozh·ko·vee |
| dvoulůžkový pokoj? | dvoh·loozh·ko·vee po·koy |

How much is it per ...?	Kolik to stojí ...?	ko·lik to sto·yee ...
night	na noc	nuh nots
person	za osobu	zuh o·so·bu

Eating & Drinking

What would you recommend?
| Co byste doporučil/ | tso bis·te do·po·ru·chil/ |
| doporučila? (m/f) | do·po·ru·chi·luh |

Do you have vegetarian food?
| Máte vegetariánská | ma·te ve·ge·tuh·ri·ans·ka |
| jídla? | yeed·luh |

I'd like the bill/menu, please.
Chtěl/Chtěla bych	khtyel/khtye·luh bikh
účet/jídelníček,	oo·chet/yee·del·nyee·chek
prosím. (m/f)	... pro·seem

| I'll have ... | Dám si ... | dam si ... |
| Cheers! | Na zdraví! | nuh zdruh·vee |

Emergencies

| Help! | Pomoc! | po·mots |
| Go away! | Běžte pryč! | byezh·te prich |

Call the doctor/police!
| Zavolejte lékaře/ | zuh·vo·ley·te lair·kuh·rzhe/ |
| policii! | po·li·tsi·yi |

I'm lost.
| Zabloudil/ | zuh·bloh·dyil/ |
| Zabloudila jsem. (m/f) | zuh·bloh·dyi·luh ysem |

I'm ill.
| Jsem nemocný/ | ysem ne·mots·nee/ |
| nemocná. (m/f) | ne·mots·na |

Where are the toilets?
| Kde jsou toalety? | gde ysoh to·uh·le·ti |

Shopping & Services

I'm looking for ...
| Hledám ... | hle·dam ... |

How much is it?
| Kolik to stojí? | ko·lik to sto·yee |

That's too expensive.
| To je moc drahé. | to ye mots druh·hair |

bank	banka	buhn·kuh
post office	pošta	posh·tuh
tourist office	turistická	tu·ris·tits·ka
	informační	in·for·muhch·nyee
	kancelář	kuhn·tse·larzh

Transport

bus	autobus	ow·to·bus
plane	letadlo	le·tuhd·lo
train	vlak	vluhk

One ... ticket to (Telč), please.	... jízdenku do (Telče), prosím.	... yeez·den·ku do (tel·che) pro·seem
one-way	Jedno- směrnou	yed·no- smyer·noh
return	Zpátečni	zpa·tech·nyee

Numbers – Czech
1	jeden	ye·den
2	dva	dvuh
3	tři	trzhi
4	čtyři	chti·rzhi
5	pět	pyet
6	šest	shest
7	sedm	se·dm
8	osm	o·sm
9	devět	de·vyet
10	deset	de·set

ESTONIAN

Double vowels in written Estonian indicate they are pronounced as long sounds. Note that air is pronounced as in 'hair', aw as in 'law', ea as in 'ear', eu as the 'u' in 'nurse', ew as 'ee' with rounded lips, oh as the 'o' in 'note', ow as in 'how', uh as the 'a' in 'ago', kh as in the Scottish *loch*, and zh as the 's' in 'pleasure'.

Basics

Hello.	Tere.	te·re
Goodbye.	Nägemist.	nair·ge·mist
Excuse me.	Vabandage. (pol)	va·ban·da·ge
	Vabanda. (inf)	va·ban·da
Sorry.	Vabandust.	va·ban·dust
Please.	Palun.	pa·lun
Thank you.	Tänan.	tair·nan
Yes.	Jaa.	yaa
No.	Ei.	ay

What's your name?
Mis on teie nimi? mis on tay·e ni·mi

My name is ...
Minu nimi on ... mi·nu ni·mi on ...

Do you speak English?
Kas te räägite kas te rair·git·te
inglise keelt? ing·kli·se keylt

I don't understand.
Ma ei saa aru. ma ay saa a·ru

Eating & Drinking

What would you recommend?
Mida te soovitate? mi·da te saw·vit·tat·te

Do you have vegetarian food?
Kas teil on taimetoitu? kas tayl on tai·met·toyt·tu

I'd like the bill/menu, please.
Ma sooviksin ma saw·vik·sin
arvet/menüüd, palun. ar·vet/me·newt pa·lun

Numbers – Estonian

1	üks	ewks
2	kaks	kaks
3	kolm	kolm
4	neli	ne·li
5	viis	vees
6	kuus	koos
7	seitse	say·tse
8	kaheksa	ka·hek·sa
9	üheksa	ew·hek·sa
10	kümme	kewm·me

I'll have a ...	Ma tahaksin ...	ma ta·hak·sin ...
Cheers!	Terviseks!	tair·vi·seks

Emergencies

Help!	Appi!	ap·pi
Go away!	Minge ära!	ming·ke air·ra

Call the doctor/police!
Kutsuge arst/ ku·tsu·ge arst/
politsei! po·li·tsay

I'm lost.
Ma olen ära eksinud. ma o·len air·ra ek·si·nud

Where are the toilets?
Kus on WC? kus on ve·se

Shopping & Services

I'm looking for ...
Ma otsin ... ma o·tsin

How much is it?
Kui palju see maksab? ku·i pal·yu sey mak·sab

That's too expensive.
See on liiga kallis. sey on lee·ga kal·lis

bank	pank	pank
market	turg	turg
post office	postkontor	post·kont·tor

Transport

boat	laev	laiv
bus	buss	bus
plane	lennuk	len·nuk
train	rong	rongk

One ... ticket (to Pärnu), please.	Üks ... pilet (Pärnusse), palun.	ewks ... pi·let (pair·nus·se) pa·lun
one-way	ühe otsa	ew·he o·tsa
return	edasi-tagasi	e·da·si·ta·ga·si

HUNGARIAN

A symbol over a vowel in written Hungarian indicates it's pronounced as a long sound. Double consonants should be drawn out a little longer than in English. Note also that aw is pronounced as in 'law', eu as the 'u' in 'nurse', ew as 'ee' with rounded lips, and zh as the 's' in 'pleasure'. Finally, keep in mind that r is rolled in Hungarian and that the apostrophe (') indicates a slight y sound.

Basics

Hello.	Szervusz. (sg)	ser·vus
	Szervusztok. (pl)	ser·vus·tawk
Goodbye.	Viszlát.	vis·lat
Excuse me.	Elnézést	el·ney·zeysht
	kérek.	key·rek
Sorry.	Sajnálom.	shoy·na·lawm
Please.	Kérem. (pol)	key·rem
	Kérlek. (inf)	keyr·lek
Thank you.	Köszönöm.	keu·seu·neum
Yes.	Igen.	i·gen
No.	Nem.	nem

What's your name?
Mi a neve/   mi o ne·ve/
neved? (pol/inf)   ne·ved

My name is ...
A nevem ...   o ne·vem ...

Do you speak English?
Beszél/Beszélsz   be·seyl/be·seyls
angolul? (pol/inf)   on·gaw·lul

I don't understand.
Nem értem.   nem eyr·tem

Accommodation

campsite	kemping	kem·ping
guesthouse	panzió	pon·zi·āw
hotel	szálloda	sal·law·do
youth hostel	ifjúsági	if·yū·sha·gi
	szálló	sal·lāw

Do you have a single/double room?
Van Önnek kiadó egy   von eun·nek ki·o·dāw ed'
egyágyas/duplaágyas   ej·a·dyosh/dup·lo·a·dyosh
szobája?   saw·ba·yo

How much is it per night/person?
Mennyibe kerül egy   men'·nyi·be ke·rewl ej
éjszakára/főre?   ey·so·ka·ro/fēū·re

Eating & Drinking

What would you recommend?
Mit ajánlana?   mit o·yan·lo·no

Do you have vegetarian food?
Vannak Önöknél   von·nok eu·neuk·neyl
vegetáriánus ételek?   ve·ge·ta·ri·a·nush ey·te·lek

I'll have ...
... kérek.   ... key·rek

Cheers! (to one person)
Egészségedre!   e·geys·shey·ged·re

Cheers! (to more than one person)
Egészségetekre!   e·geys·shey·ge·tek·re

Numbers – Hungarian

1	egy	ej
2	kettő	ket·tēū
3	három	ha·rawm
4	négy	neyj
5	öt	eut
6	hat	hot
7	hét	heyt
8	nyolc	nyawlts
9	kilenc	ki·lents
10	tíz	teez

I'd like the ...	... szeretném.	... se·ret·neym
bill	A számlát	o sam·lat
menu	Az étlapot	oz eyt·lo·pawt

Emergencies

Help!	Segítség!	she·geet·sheyg
Go away!	Menjen innen!	men·yen in·nen

Call the doctor!
Hívjon orvost!   heev·yawn awr·vawsht

Call the police!
Hívja a   heev·yo o
rendőrséget!   rend·ēūr·shey·get

I'm lost.
Eltévedtem.   el·tey·ved·tem

I'm ill.
Rosszul vagyok.   raws·sul vo·dyawk

Where are the toilets?
Hol a vécé?   hawl o vey·tsey

Shopping & Services

I'm looking for ...
Keresem a ...   ke·re·shem o ...

How much is it?
Mennyibe kerül?   men'·nyi·be ke·rewl

That's too expensive.
Ez túl drága.   ez tūl dra·go

market	piac	pi·ots
post office	postahivatal	pawsh·to·hi·vo·tol
tourist office	turistairoda	tu·rish·to·i·raw·do

Transport

bus	busz	bus
plane	repülőgép	re·pew·lēū·geyp
train	vonat	vaw·not

One ... ticket to (Eger), please.	Egy ... jegy (Eger)be.	ej ... yej (e·ger)·be
one-way	csak oda	chok aw·do
return	oda-vissza	aw·do·vis·so

LATVIAN

A line over a vowel in written Latvian indicates it's pronounced as a long sound. Note that air is pronounced as in 'hair', aw as in 'law', ea as in 'ear', ow as in 'how', wa as in 'water', dz as the 'ds' in 'adds', and zh as the 's' in 'pleasure'. The apostrophe (') indicates a slight y sound.

Basics

Hello.	Sveiks.	svayks
Goodbye.	Atā.	a·taa
Excuse me.	Atvainojiet.	at·vai·nwa·yeat
Sorry.	Piedodiet.	pea·dwa·deat
Please.	Lūdzu.	loo·dzu
Thank you.	Paldies.	pal·deas
Yes.	Jā.	yaa
No.	Nē.	nair

What's your name?
Kā Jūs sauc? — kaa yoos sowts

My name is ...
Mani sauc ... — ma·ni sowts ...

Do you speak English?
Vai Jūs runājat angliski? — vai yoos ru·naa·yat ang·li·ski

I don't understand.
Es nesaprotu. — es ne·sa·prwa·tu

Eating & Drinking

What would you recommend?
Ko Jūs iesakat? — kwa yoos ea·sa·kat

Do you have vegetarian food?
Vai Jums ir veģetārie ēdieni? — vai yums ir ve·dye·taa·rea air·dea·ni

I'd like the bill/menu, please.
Es vēlos rēķinu/ ēdienkarti, lūdzu. — es vair·lwas rair·tyi·nu/ air·dean·kar·ti loo·dzu

I'll have a ...
Man lūdzu vienu ... — man loo·dzu vea·nu ...

Cheers!
Priekā! — prea·kaa

Emergencies

| Help! | Palīgā! | pa·lee·gaa |
| Go away! | Ej prom! | ay prwam |

Numbers – Latvian

1	viens	veans
2	divi	di·vi
3	trīs	trees
4	četri	che·tri
5	pieci	pea·tsi
6	seši	se·shi
7	septiņi	sep·ti·nyi
8	astoņi	as·twa·nyi
9	deviņi	de·vi·nyi
10	desmit	des·mit

Call the doctor/police!
Zvani ārstam/policijai! — zva·ni aar·stam/po·li·tsi·yai

I'm lost.
Esmu apmaldījies. — es·mu ap·mal·dee·yeas

Where are the toilets?
Kur ir tualetes? — kur ir tu·a·le·tes

Shopping & Services

I'm looking for ...
Es meklēju ... — es mek·lair·yu ...

How much is it?
Cik maksā? — tsik mak·saa

That's too expensive.
Tas ir par dārgu. — tas ir par daar·gu

bank	banka	ban·ka
market	tirgus	tir·gus
post office	pasts	pasts

Transport

boat	laiva	lai·va
bus	autobus	ow·to·bus
plane	lidmašīna	lid·ma·shee·na
train	vilciens	vil·tseans

One ... ticket (to Jūrmala), please.	Vienu ... biļeti (uz Jūrmalu), lūdzu.	vea·nu ... bi·lye·ti (uz yoor·ma·lu) loo·dzu
one-way	vienvirziena	vean·vir·zea·na
return	turp-atpakaļ	turp·at·pa·kal'

LITHUANIAN

Symbols on vowels in written Lithuanian indicate they are pronounced as long sounds. Note that aw is pronounced as in 'law', ea as in 'ear', ow as in 'how', wa as in 'water', dz as the 'ds' in 'adds', and zh as the 's' in 'pleasure'.

Basics

Hello.	*Sveiki.*	svay·*ki*
Goodbye.	*Viso gero.*	vi·so ge·ro
Excuse me.	*Atleiskite.*	at·*lays*·ki·te
Sorry.	*Atsiprašau.*	at·si·pra·*show*
Please.	*Prašau.*	pra·*show*
Thank you.	*Ačiū.*	aa·choo
Yes.	*Taip.*	taip
No.	*Ne.*	ne

What's your name?
Koks jūsų vardas? kawks *yoo*·soo *var*·das

My name is ...
Mano vardas ... ma·no var·das ...

Do you speak English?
Ar kalbate angliškai? ar kal·ba·te *aang*·lish·kai

I don't understand.
Aš nesuprantu. ash ne·su·pran·*tu*

Eating & Drinking

What would you recommend?
Ką jūs rekomenduotumėte? kaa yoos re·ko·men·*dwo*·tu·mey·te

Do you have vegetarian food?
Ar turite vegetariško maisto? ar tu·ri·te ve·ge·*taa*·rish·ko *mais*·to

I'd like the bill/menu, please.
Aš norėčiau sąskaitos/meniu ash no·rey·chyow saas·kai·taws/me·*nyu*

I'll have a ...
Aš užsisakysiu ... ash uzh·si·sa·*kee*·syu ...

Cheers!
Į sveikatą! ee svay·*kaa*·taa

Emergencies

Help!	*Padėkit!*	pa·*dey*·kit
Go away!	*Eikit iš čia!*	ay·kit ish chya

Call the doctor/police!
Iškvieskit gydytoją/policiją! ish·*kveas*·kit gee·dee·to·ya/po·*li*·tsi·ya

I'm lost.
Aš pasiklydau. ash pa·si·*klee*·dow

Where are the toilets?
Kur yra tualetai? kur ee·*ra* tu·a·le·tai

Shopping & Services

I'm looking for ...
Aš Ieškau ... ash *eash*·kow ...

Numbers – Lithuanian

1	*vienas*	vea·nas
2	*du*	du
3	*trys*	trees
4	*keturi*	ke·tu·ri
5	*penki*	pen·ki
6	*šeši*	she·shi
7	*septyni*	sep·tee·ni
8	*aštuoni*	ash·twa·ni
9	*devyni*	de·vee·ni
10	*dešimt*	de·shimt

How much is it?
Kiek kainuoja? keak kain·*wo*·ya

That's too expensive.
Per brangu. per *bran*·gu

bank	*bankas*	baan·kas
market	*turgus*	tur·gus
post office	*paštas*	paash·tas

Transport

boat	*laivas*	lai·vas
bus	*autobusas*	ow·to·bu·sas
plane	*lėktuvas*	leyk·tu·vas
train	*traukinys*	trow·ki·nees

One ... ticket (to Kaunas), please.	*Vieną bilietą ... (Į Kauną), prašau.*	vea·naa bi·lye·taa ... (ee kow·naa) pra·*show*
one-way	*į vieną pusę*	ee vea·naa pu·sey
return	*Į abi puses*	ee a·bi pu·ses

MACEDONIAN

Note that dz is pronounced as the 'ds' in 'adds', r is rolled, and zh as the 's' in 'pleasure'.

Basics

Hello.	Здраво.	zdra·vo
Goodbye.	До гледање.	do gle·da·nye
Excuse me.	Извинете.	iz·vi·ne·te
Sorry.	Простете.	pros·te·te
Please.	Молам.	mo·lam
Thank you.	Благодарам.	bla·go·da·ram
Yes.	Да.	da
No.	Не.	ne

What's your name?

Како се викате/
викаш? (pol/inf)
*ka·ko se vi·ka·te/
vi·kash*

My name is ...

Јас се викам ...
yas se vi·kam ...

Do you speak English?

Зборувате ли
англиски?
*zbo·ru·va·te li
an·glis·ki*

I don't understand.

Јас не разбирам.
yas ne raz·bi·ram

Accommodation

campsite	камп	kamp
guesthouse	приватно сместување	*pri·vat·no smes·tu·va·nye*
hotel	хотел	*ho·tel*
youth hostel	младинско преноќиште	*mla·din·sko pre·no·kyish·te*

Do you have a single/double room?

Дали имате
еднокреветна/
двокреветна соба?
*da·li i·ma·te
ed·no·kre·vet·na/
dvo·kre·vet·na so·ba*

How much is it per night/person?

Која е цената за
ноќ/еден?
*ko·ya e tse·na·ta za
noky/e·den*

Eating & Drinking

What would you recommend?

Што препорачувате
вие?
*shto pre·po·ra·chu·va·te
vi·e*

Do you have vegetarian food?

Дали имате
вегетаријанска храна?
*da·li i·ma·te
ve·ge·ta·ri·yan·ska hra·na*

I'd like the bill/menu, please.

Ве молам сметката/
мени.
*ve mo·lam smet·ka·ta/
me·ni*

I'll have ...

Јас ќе земам ...
yas kye ze·mam ...

Cheers!

На здравје!
na zdrav·ye

Emergencies

Help!

Помош!
po·mosh

Go away!

Одете си!
o·de·te si

Call the doctor/police!

Викнете лекар/
полиција!
*vik·ne·te le·kar/
po·li·tsi·ya*

I'm lost.

Се загубив.
se za·gu·biv

Numbers – Macedonian

1	еден	*e·den*
2	два	*dva*
3	три	*tri*
4	четири	*che·ti·ri*
5	пет	*pet*
6	шест	*shest*
7	седум	*se·dum*
8	осум	*o·sum*
9	девет	*de·vet*
10	десет	*de·set*

I'm ill.

Јас сум болен/
болна. (m/f)
*yas sum bo·len/
bol·na*

Where are the toilets?

Каде се тоалетите?
ka·de se to·a·le·ti·te

Shopping & Services

I'm looking for ...

Барам ...
ba·ram ...

How much is it?

Колку чини тоа?
kol·ku chi·ni to·a

That's too expensive.

Тоа е многу скапо.
to·a e mno·gu ska·po

market	пазар	*pa·zar*
post office	пошта	*posh·ta*
tourist office	туристичко биро	*tu·ris·tich·ko·to bi·ro*

Transport

boat	брод	brod
bus	автобус	*av·to·bus*
plane	авион	*a·vi·on*
train	воз	voz

One ... ticket (to Ohrid), please.	Еден ... (за Охрид), ве молам.	*e·den ... (za oh·rid) ve mo·lam*
one-way	билет во еден правец	*bi·let vo e·den pra·vets*
return	повратен билет	*pov·ra·ten bi·let*

POLISH

Polish vowels are generally pronounced short. Nasal vowels are pronounced as though you're trying to force the air through your nose, and are indicated with n or m following the vowel.

Note that ow is pronounced as in 'how', kh as the 'ch' in the Scottish *loch*, and zh as the 's' in 'pleasure'. Also, r is rolled in Polish and the apostrophe (') indicates a slight y sound.

Basics

Hello.	*Cześć.*	cheshch
Goodbye.	*Do widzenia.*	do vee·dze·nya
Excuse me.	*Przepraszam.*	pshe·*pra*·sham
Sorry.	*Przepraszam.*	pshe·*pra*·sham
Please.	*Proszę.*	*pro*·she
Thank you.	*Dziękuję.*	jyen·koo·ye
Yes.	*Tak.*	tak
No.	*Nie.*	nye

What's your name?
Jak się pan/pani   yak shye pan/*pa*·nee
nazywa? (m/f pol)   na·*zi*·va
Jakie się nazywasz? (inf)   yak shye na·*zi*·vash

My name is ...
Nazywam się ...   na·*zi*·vam shye ...

Do you speak English?
Czy pan/pani mówi   chi pan/*pa*·nee moo·vee
po angielsku? (m/f)   po an·*gyel*·skoo

I don't understand.
Nie rozumiem.   nye ro·*zoo*·myem

Accommodation

campsite	*kamping*	*kam*·peeng
guesthouse	*pokoje*	po·*ko*·ye
	gościnne	gosh·*chee*·ne
hotel	*hotel*	*ho*·tel
youth hostel	*schronisko*	skhro·*nees*·ko
	młodzieżowe	mwo·jye·*zho*·ve
Do you have	*Czy jest*	chi yest
a ... room?	*pokój ...?*	po·kooy ...
single	*jedno-*	yed·no·
	osobowy	o·so·*bo*·vi
double	*z podwójnym*	z pod·*vooy*·nim
	łóżkiem	woozh·kyem

How much is it per night/person?
Ile kosztuje   ee·le kosh·*too*·ye
za noc/osobę?   za nots/o·*so*·be

Eating & Drinking

What would you recommend?
Co by pan polecił? (m)   tso bi pan po·*le*·cheew
Co by pani poleciła? (f)   tso bi *pa*·nee po·le·*chee*·wa

Do you have vegetarian food?
Czy jest żywność   chi yest *zhiv*·noshch
wegetariańska?   ve·ge·tar·*yan'*·ska

I'd like the ..., please.
Proszę o rachunek/   pro·she o ra·*khoo*·nek/
jadłospis.   ya·*dwo*·spees

I'll have ...	*Proszę ...*	*pro*·she ...
Cheers!	*Na zdrowie!*	na *zdro*·vye

Emergencies

Help!	*Na pomoc!*	na *po*·mots
Go away!	*Odejdź!*	o·deyj

Call the doctor/police!
Zadzwoń po lekarza/   zad·zvon' po le·*ka*·zha/
policję!   po·*lee*·tsye

I'm lost.
Zgubiłem/   zgoo·bee·wem/
Zgubiłam się. (m/f)   zgoo·bee·wam shye

I'm ill.
Jestem chory/a. (m/f)   yes·tem kho·ri/a

Where are the toilets?
Gdzie są toalety?   gjye som to·a·*le*·ti

Shopping & Services

I'm looking for ...
Szukam ...   shoo·kam

How much is it?
Ile to kosztuje?   ee·le to kosh·*too*·ye

That's too expensive.
To jest za drogie.   to yest za *dro*·gye

market	*targ*	tark
post office	*urząd*	oo·zhond
	pocztowy	poch·*to*·vi
tourist office	*biuro*	*byoo*·ro
	turystyczne	too·ris·*tich*·ne

Numbers – Polish

1	*jeden*	ye·den
2	*dwa*	dva
3	*trzy*	tshi
4	*cztery*	*chte*·ri
5	*pięć*	pyench
6	*sześć*	sheshch
7	*siedem*	*shye*·dem
8	*osiem*	o·shyem
9	*dziewięć*	jye·vyench
10	*dziesięć*	jye·shench

Transport

boat	łódź	wooj
bus	autobus	ow·to·boos
plane	samolot	sa·mo·lot
train	pociąg	po·chonk

One ... ticket (to Katowice), please.	Proszę bilet ... (do Katowic).	pro·she bee·let ... (do ka·to·veets)
one-way	w jedną stronę	v yed·nom stro·ne
return	powrotny	po·vro·tni

ROMANIAN

Note that ew is pronounced as 'ee' with rounded lips, oh as the 'o' in 'note', ow as in 'how', uh as the 'a' in 'ago', and zh as the 's' in 'pleasure'. The apostrophe (') indicates a very short, unstressed i (almost silent).

Basics

Hello.	Bună ziua.	boo·nuh zee·wa
Goodbye.	La revedere.	la re·ve·de·re
Excuse me.	Scuzaţi-mă.	skoo·za·tsee·muh
Sorry.	Îmi pare rău.	ewm' pa·re ruh·oo
Please.	Vă rog.	vuh rog
Thank you.	Mulţumesc.	mool·tsoo·mesk
Yes.	Da.	da
No.	Nu.	noo

What's your name?
Cum vă numiţi?   koom vuh noo·meets'

My name is ...
Numele meu este ...   noo·me·le me·oo yes·te ...

Do you speak English?
Vorbiţi engleza?   vor·beets' en·gle·za

I don't understand.
Eu nu înţeleg.   ye·oo noo ewn·tse·leg

Accommodation

campsite	teren de camping	te·ren de kem·peeng
guesthouse	pensiune	pen·syoo·ne
hotel	hotel	ho·tel
youth hostel	hostel	hos·tel

Do you have a ... room?	Aveţi o cameră ...?	a·vets' o ka·me·ruh ...
single	de o persoană	de o per·so·a·nuh
double	dublă	doo·bluh

How much is it per ...?	Cît costă ...?	kewt kos·tuh ...
night	pe noapte	pe no·ap·te
person	de persoană	de per·so·a·nuh

Eating & Drinking

What would you recommend?
Ce recomandaţi?   che re·ko·man·dats'

Do you have vegetarian food?
Aveţi mâncare   a·ve·tsi mewn·ka·re
vegetariană?   ve·je·ta·rya·nuh

I'll have ...	Aş dori ...	ash do·ree ...
Cheers!	Noroc!	no·rok

I'd like the ..., please.	Vă rog, aş dori ...	vuh rog ash do·ree ...
bill	nota de plată	no·ta de pla·tuh
menu	meniul	me·nee·ool

Emergencies

Help!	Ajutor!	a·zhoo·tor
Go away!	Pleacă!	ple·a·kuh

Call the ...!	Chemaţi ...!	ke·mats' ...
doctor	un doctor	oon dok·tor
police	poliţia	po·lee·tsya

I'm lost.
M-am rătăcit.   mam ruh·tuh·cheet

I'm ill.
Mă simt rău.   muh seemt ruh·oo

Where are the toilets?
Unde este o toaletă?   oon·de yes·te o to·a·le·tuh

Shopping & Services

I'm looking for ...
Caut ...   kowt ...

How much is it?
Cât costă?   kewt kos·tuh

That's too expensive.
E prea scump.   ye pre·a skoomp

market	piaţă	pya·tsuh
post office	poşta	posh·ta
tourist office	biroul de informaţii turistice	bee·ro·ool de een·for·ma·tsee too·rees·tee·che

Numbers – Romanian		
1	*unu*	oo·noo
2	*doi*	doy
3	*trei*	trey
4	*patru*	pa·troo
5	*cinci*	cheench'
6	*şase*	sha·se
7	*şapte*	shap·te
8	*opt*	opt
9	*nouă*	no·wuh
10	*zece*	ze·che

Transport

boat	*vapor*	va·por
bus	*autobuz*	ow·to·booz
plane	*avion*	a·vyon
train	*tren*	tren

One ... ticket (to Cluj), please.	*Un bilet ... (până la Cluj), vă rog.*	oon bee·let ... (pew·nuh la kloozh) vuh rog
one-way	*dus*	doos
return	*dus-întors*	doos ewn·tors

RUSSIAN

In Russian – also widely used in Belarus – the kh is pronounced as the 'ch' in the Scottish *loch* and zh as the 's' in 'pleasure'. Also, r is rolled in Russian and the apostrophe (') indicates a slight y sound.

Basics

Hello.	Здравствуйте.	zdrast·vuyt·ye
Goodbye.	До свидания.	da svee·dan·ya
Excuse me./ Sorry.	Извините, пожалуйста.	eez·vee·neet·ye pa·zhal·sta
Please.	Пожалуйста.	pa·zhal·sta
Thank you.	Спасибо	spa·see·ba
Yes.	Да.	da
No.	Нет.	nyet

What's your name?
Как вас зовут? kak vaz za·vut

My name is ...
Меня зовут ... meen·ya za·vut ...

Do you speak English?
Вы говорите
по-английски? vi ga·va·reet·ye pa·an·glee·skee

I don't understand.
Я не понимаю. ya nye pa·nee·ma·yu

Accommodation

campsite	кемпинг	kyem·peeng
guesthouse	пансионат	pan·see·a·nat
hotel	гостиница	ga·stee·neet·sa
youth hostel	общежитие	ap·shee·zhi·tee·ye

Do you have a ... room?	У вас есть ...?	u vas yest' ...
single	одноместный номер	ad·nam·yes·ni no·meer
double	номер с двуспальней кроватью	no·meer z dvu·spaln·yey kra·vat·yu

How much is it ...?	Сколько стоит за ...?	skol'·ka sto·eet za ...
for two people	двоих	dva·eekh
per night	ночь	noch'

Eating & Drinking

What would you recommend?
Что вы
рекомендуете? shto vi ree·ka·meen·du·eet·ye

Do you have vegetarian food?
У вас есть
вегетарианские
блюда? u vas yest' vi·gi·ta·ri·an·ski·ye blyu·da

I'd like the bill/menu, please.
Я бы хотел/хотела
счёт/меню. (m/f) ya bi khat·yel/khat·ye·la shot/meon·yu

I'll have ...	..., пожалуйста.	... pa·zhal·sta
Cheers!	За здоровье!	za zda·rov·ye

Emergencies

Help!	Помогите!	pa·ma·gee·tye
Go away!	Идите отсюда!	ee·deet·ye at·syu·da

Call the doctor/police!
Вызовите врача/
милицию! vi·za·veet·ye vra·cha/mee·leet·si·yu

I'm lost.
Я потерялся/
потерялась. (m/f) ya pa·teer·yal·sa/ pa·teer·ya·las'

I'm ill.
Я болею. ya bal·ye·yu

Where are the toilets?
Где здесь туалет? gdye zdyes' tu·al·yet

Numbers – Russian

1	один	a·deen
2	два	dva
3	три	tree
4	четыре	chee·ti·ree
5	пять	pyat'
6	шесть	shest'
7	семь	syem'
8	восемь	vo·seem'
9	девять	dye·veet'
10	десять	dye·seet'

Shopping & Services

I'd like ...
Я бы хотел/ · ya bi khat·yel/
хотела ... (m/f) · khat·ye·la ...

How much is it?
Сколько стоит? · skol'·ka sto·eet

That's too expensive.
Это очень дорого. · e·ta o·cheen' do·ra·ga

bank	банк	bank
market	рынок	ri·nak
post office	почта	poch·ta
tourist office	туристическое	tu·rees·tee·
	бюро	chee·ska·ye
		byu·ro

Transport

boat	параход	pa·ra·khot
bus	автобус	af·to·bus
plane	самолёт	sa·mal·yot
train	поезд	po·yeest

One ... ticket · Билет ... · beel·yet ...
(to Novgorod), · (на Новгород). · (na nov·ga·rat)
please.

one-way · в один · v a·deen
 · конец · kan·yets

return · в оба конца · v o·ba kant·sa

SLOVAK

An accent mark over a vowel in written Slovak indicates it's pronounced as a long sound. Note that air is pronounced as in 'hair', aw as in 'law', oh as the 'o' in 'note', ow as in 'how', uh as the 'a' in 'ago', dz as the 'ds' in 'adds', kh as the 'ch' in the Scottish loch, and zh as the 's' in 'pleasure'. The apostrophe (') indicates a slight y sound.

Basics

Hello.	Dobrý deň.	do·bree dyen'
Goodbye.	Do videnia.	do vi·dye·ni·yuh
Excuse me.	Prepáčte.	pre·pach·tye
Sorry.	Prepáčte.	pre·pach·tye
Please.	Prosím.	pro·seem
Thank you.	Ďakujem	dyuh·ku·yem
Yes.	Áno.	a·no
No.	Nie.	ni·ye

What's your name?
Ako sa voláte? · uh·ko suh vo·la·tye

My name is ...
Volám sa ... · vo·lam suh ...

Do you speak English?
Hovoríte po · ho·vo·ree·tye po
anglicky? · uhng·lits·ki

I don't understand.
Nerozumiem. · nye·ro·zu·myem

Accommodation

campsite	táborisko	ta·bo·ris·ko
guesthouse	penzión	pen·zi·awn
hotel	hotel	ho·tel
youth hostel	nocľaháreň	nots·lyuh·ha·ren'
	pre mládež	pre mla·dyezh

Do you have a single room?
Máte jedno- · ma·tye yed·no-
posteľovú izbu? · pos·tye·lyo·voo iz·bu

Do you have a double room?
Máte izbu s · ma·tye iz·bu s
manželskou · muhn·zhels·koh
posteľou? · pos·tye·lyoh

How much is it per ...?
Koľko to stojí na · kol'·ko to sto·yee nuh
noc/osobu? · nots/o·so·bu

Eating & Drinking

What would you recommend?
Čo by ste mi · cho bi stye mi
odporučili? · od·po·ru·chi·li

Do you have vegetarian food?
Máte vegetariánske · ma·tye ve·ge·tuh·ri·yan·ske
jedlá? · yed·la

I'll have ... · Dám si ... · dam si ...
Cheers! · Nazdravie! · nuhz·druh·vi·ye

I'd like the ..., please.	Prosím si ...	pro·seem si ...
bill	účet	oo·chet
menu	jedálny lístok	ye·dal·ni lees·tok

Emergencies

| Help! | Pomoc! | po·mots |
| Go away! | Choďte preč! | khod'·tye prech |

Call ...!	Zavolajte ...!	zuh·vo·lai·tye ...
a doctor	lekára	le·ka·ruh
the police	políciu	po·lee·tsi·yu

I'm lost.
Stratil/Stratila som sa. (m/f) — struh·tyil/struh·tyi·luh som suh

I'm ill.
Som chorý/chorá. (m/f) — som kho·ree/kho·ra

Where are the toilets?
Kde sú tu záchody? — kdye soo tu za·kho·di

Shopping & Services

I'm looking for ...
Hľadám ... — hlyuh·dam ...

How much is it?
Koľko to stojí? — kol'·ko to sto·yee

That's too expensive.
To je príliš drahé. — to ye pree·lish druh·hair

market	trh	trh
post office	pošta	posh·tuh
tourist office	turistická kancelária	tu·ris·tits·ka kuhn·tse·la·ri·yuh

Numbers – Slovak		
1	jeden	ye·den
2	dva	dvuh
3	tri	tri
4	štyri	shti·ri
5	päť	pet'
6	šesť	shest'
7	sedem	se·dyem
8	osem	o·sem
9	deväť	dye·vet'
10	desať	dye·suht'

Transport

bus	autobus	ow·to·bus
plane	lietadlo	li·ye·tuhd·lo
train	vlak	vluhk

One ... ticket (to Poprad), please.	Jeden ... lístok (do Popradu), prosím.	ye·den ... lees·tok (do pop·ruh·du) pro·seem
one-way	jedno-smerný	yed·no-smer·nee
return	spiatočný	spyuh·toch·nee

SLOVENE

Note that uh is pronounced as the 'a' in 'ago', oh as the 'o' in 'note', ow as in 'how', zh as the 's' in 'pleasure', r is rolled, and the apostrophe (') indicates a slight y sound.

Basics

Hello.	Zdravo.	zdra·vo
Goodbye.	Na svidenje.	na svee·den·ye
Excuse me.	Dovolite.	do·vo·lee·te
Sorry.	Oprostite.	op·ros·tee·te
Please.	Prosim.	pro·seem
Thank you.	Hvala.	hva·la
Yes.	Da.	da
No.	Ne.	ne

What's your name?
Kako vam/ti je ime? (pol/inf) — ka·ko vam/tee ye ee·me

My name is ...
Ime mi je ... — ee·me mee ye ...

Do you speak English?
Ali govorite angleško? — a·lee go·vo·ree·te ang·lesh·ko

I don't understand.
Ne razumem. — ne ra·zoo·mem

Accommodation

campsite	kamp	kamp
guesthouse	gostišče	gos·teesh·che
hotel	hotel	ho·tel
youth hostel	mladinski hotel	mla·deen·skee ho·tel

Do you have a single/double room?
Ali imate enoposteljno/dvoposteljno sobo? — a·lee ee·ma·te e·no·pos·tel'·no/dvo·pos·tel'·no so·bo

How much is it per night/person?
Koliko stane na   ko·lee·ko sta·ne na
noč/osebo?   noch/o·se·bo

Eating & Drinking

What would you recommend?
Kaj priporočate?   kai pree·po·ro·cha·te

Do you have vegetarian food?
Ali imate   a·lee ee·ma·te
vegetarijansko hrano?   ve·ge·ta·ree·yan·sko hra·no

I'll have ...	*Jaz bom ...*	yaz bom ...
Cheers!	*Na zdravje!*	na zdrav·ye
I'd like the ...,	*Želim ...,*	zhe·*leem* ...
please.	*prosim.*	pro·seem
bill	*račun*	ra·*choon*
menu	*jedilni list*	ye·*deel*·nee leest

Emergencies

Help!	*Na pomoč!*	na po·*moch*
Go away!	*Pojdite stran!*	poy·*dee*·te stran

Call the doctor/police!
Pokličite zdravnika/   pok·*lee*·chee·te zdrav·*nee*·ka
policijo!   po·lee·*tsee*·yo

I'm lost.
Izgubil/   eez·*goo*·beew/
Izgubila sem se. (m/f)   eez·goo·*bee*·la sem se

I'm ill.
Bolan/Bolna sem. (m/f)   bo·*lan*/boh·na sem

Where are the toilets?
Kje je stranišče?   kye ye stra·*neesh*·che

Shopping & Services

I'm looking for ...
Iščem ...   *eesh*·chem ...

Numbers – Slovene

1	*en*	en
2	*dva*	dva
3	*trije*	*tree*·ye
4	*štirje*	*shtee*·rye
5	*pet*	pet
6	*šest*	shest
7	*sedem*	*se*·dem
8	*osem*	*o*·sem
9	*devet*	de·*vet*
10	*deset*	de·*set*

How much is this?
Koliko stane?   ko·lee·ko sta·ne

That's too expensive.
To je predrago.   to ye pre·dra·go

market	*tržnica*	*tuhrzh*·nee·tsa
post office	*pošta*	*posh*·ta
tourist office	*turistični urad*	too·rees·*teech*·nee oo·rad

Transport

boat	*ladja*	*lad*·ya
bus	*avtobus*	av·to·boos
plane	*letalo*	le·*ta*·lo
train	*vlak*	vlak
One ... ticket to (Koper), please.	*... vozovnico do (Kopra), prosim.*	... vo·*zov*·nee·tso do (ko·pra) pro·seem
one-way	*Enosmerno*	e·no·*smer*·no
return	*Povratno*	pov·*rat*·no

UKRAINIAN

Vowels in unstressed syllables are generally pronounced shorter and weaker than they are in stressed syllables. Note that kh is pronounced as the 'ch' in the Scottish *loch* and zh as the 's' in 'pleasure'. The apostrophe (') indicates a slight y sound.

Basics

Hello.	Добрий день.	*do*·bry den'
Goodbye.	До побачення.	do po·*ba*·chen·nya
Excuse me.	Вибачте.	*vy*·bach·te
Sorry.	Перепрошую.	pe·re·*pro*·shu·yu
Please.	Прошу.	*pro*·shu
Thank you.	Дякую.	*dya*·ku·yu
Yes.	Так.	tak
No.	Ні.	ni

What's your name?
Як вас звати?   yak vas zva·ty

My name is ...
Мене звати ...   me·*ne* zva·ti ...

Do you speak English?
Ви розмовляєте   vy roz·*mow*·lya·ye·te
англійською   an·*hliys*'·ko·yu
мовою?   *mo*·vo·yu

I don't understand.
Я не розумію.   ya ne ro·zu·*mi*·yu

Accommodation

campsite	кемпінг	*kem*·pinh
double room	номер на двох	*no*·mer na dvokh
hotel	готель	ho·*tel'*
single room	номер на одного	*no*·mer na o·*dno*·ho
youth hostel	молодіжний гуртожиток	mo·lo·*dizh*·ni hur·*to*·zhi·tok

Do you have any rooms available?
У вас є вільні номери?   u vas ye *vil'*·ni no·me·ri

How much is it per night/person?
Скільки коштує номер за ніч/особу?   *skil'*·ky ko·shtu·ye *no*·mer za nich/o·*so*·bu

Eating & Drinking

What do you recommend?
Що Ви порадите?   shcho vy po·*ra*·dy·te

I'm a vegetarian.
Я вегетаріанець/ вегетаріанка. (m/f)   ya ve·he·ta·ri·a·nets'/ ve·he·ta·ri·*an*·ka

Cheers!	Будьмо!	*bud'*·mo
I'd like ...	Я візьму ...	ya viz'·*mu* ...
bill	рахунок	ra·*khu*·nok
menu	меню	me·*nyu*

Emergencies

Help!
Допоможіть!   do·po·mo·*zhit'*

Go away!
Іди/Ідіть звідси! (pol/inf)   i·di/i·*dit'* *zvid*·si

Call the doctor/police!
Викличте лікаря/ міліцію!   *vi*·klich·te li·ka·rya/ mi·*li*·tsi·yu

I'm lost.
Я заблукав/ заблукала. (m/f)   ya za·blu·*kaw*/ za·blu·*ka*·la

I'm ill.
Мені погано.   me·*ni* po·*ha*·no

Where's the toilet?
Де туалети?   de tu·a·*le*·ti

Numbers – Ukrainian

1	один	o·*din*
2	два	dva
3	три	tri
4	чотири	cho·*ti*·ri
5	п'ять	pyat'
6	шість	shist'
7	сім	sim
8	вісім	*vi*·sim
9	дев'ять	de·*vyat'*
10	десять	de·*syat'*

Shopping & Services

I'd like to buy ...
Я б хотів/хотіла купити ... (m/f)   ya b kho·*tiw*/kho·*ti*·la ku·*pi*·ti ...

How much is this?
Скільки це він/вона коштує? (m/f)   *skil'*·ki tse vin/vo·*na* ko·shtu·ye?

That's too expensive.
Це надто дорого.   tse *nad*·to *do*·ro·ho

ATM	банкомат	ban·ko·*mat*
market	ринок	*ri*·nok
post office	пошта	*po*·shta
tourist office	туристичне бюро	tu·ri·*stich*·ne *byu*·ro

Transport

I want to go to ...
Мені треба їхати до ...   me·*ni* *tre*·ba yi·*kha*·ti do ...

bus	автобус	aw·*to*·bus
one-way ticket	квиток в один бік	kvi·*tok* v o·*din* bik
plane	літак	li·*tak*
return ticket	зворотний квиток	zvo·*ro*·tni kvi·*tok*
train	поїзд	*po*·yizd

Behind the Scenes

SEND US YOUR FEEDBACK

We love to hear from travellers – your comments keep us on our toes and help make our books better. Our well-travelled team reads every word on what you loved or loathed about this book. Although we cannot reply individually to postal submissions, we always guarantee that your feedback goes straight to the appropriate authors, in time for the next edition. Each person who sends us information is thanked in the next edition – the most useful submissions are rewarded with a selection of digital PDF chapters.

Visit **lonelyplanet.com/contact** to submit your updates and suggestions or to ask for help. Our award-winning website also features inspirational travel stories, news and discussions.

Note: We may edit, reproduce and incorporate your comments in Lonely Planet products such as guidebooks, websites and digital products, so let us know if you don't want your comments reproduced or your name acknowledged. For a copy of our privacy policy visit lonelyplanet.com/privacy.

OUR READERS

Many thanks to the travellers who used the last edition and wrote to us with helpful hints, useful advice and interesting anecdotes:
Ricardo A Ross, Jeroen Aalderink, Sophie Beckwith, Suzannah Conway, Nora Laufer, Yvan Lou, Christopher Mcdonald, Desi Mier, Nathan Pan, Alexandra Reese, Markus Schill, Nick Sweatman, Bas Van Opdorp, Dom Van Abbe, Pamela Wade, Sarah and Rob Waters, Emma White

AUTHOR THANKS

Tom Masters

An enormous debt of thanks to all my hard-working fellow authors on this book, and the teams in London and Melbourne who commissioned, edited and oversaw the project. Special thanks in Albania to Ardi Pulaj, Catherine Bohne, Tedi Sina and Bledi Strakosha; in Belrus to my friend Zhenya Artemyev; in Kosovo to Hekuran Avdyli and the folks at Libertas in Pristina; and in Moldova to Kostya Derenyov and Marina Waters in Chisinau and Lena Lozinsky in Tiraspol.

Carolyn Bain

Much love and thanks go to Graham Harris and Kate Johns for pre-Estonia fun and games, and to Brandon Presser for Nordic-Baltic inspiration (and for seeing the same Tallinn cafe from many different angles). In Tallinn, warmest thanks to Priit and Beatrice for excellent chats and food, Geli for her usual fine apartment assistance, Elina and Triin at Chado for their tips, and especially to Estonia's finest tea-meister, Steve Kokker.

Mark Baker

I met many helpful people all along the way in researching the countries for this guide and their names would be too numerous to mention. I've lived in Prague for two decades now and a very special thanks to my good friends here. In Slovenia, the staff of the Slovenia Tourist Board deserve special mention. Finally, a nod to Co-ordinating Author Tom Masters for putting this enormous guide together is definitely in order.

Greg Bloom

Pop was my wingman again, soaking up vodka shots and slogging around St Petersburg on trip one of three. *Spacibo* dad! A big *spacibo* to Lucy for joining on trip number three! Old Kyiv friends Jake Rudnitsky and Tim O'Brien helped me out big-time Moscow. Thanks to Mike Sito for letting me help the Pigs. Thanks to Peter and the gang in *Piter*; Kaz and (remotely) Aaron in Moscow, and the Petersburg ultimate frisbee crew.

Chris Deliso

As always a number of kind and helpful Macedonians (and other folks too) provided good tips, advice and assistance in the course of my research. Among them I can mention Pece, Patrice, Stevche, Emilija, Biljana, Dane, Stojko, Ace and Julija – you know who you are! Of course, this book couldn't have been completed without the work of my patient and devoted Lonely Planet colleagues, including Commissioning Editor Katie O'Connell, Coordinating Author Tom Masters and the mapmaking and production teams.

Marc Di Duca

A huge *dyakuju* to my Ukrainian parents-in-law for their support in Kyiv and their insights into the latest developments in Ukraine. Also many thanks to Yarema Dukh of Visitlviv.net for his invaluable support in Lviv; Mykola and Olya in Simferopol; Viktor in Odesa; all the dedicated staff at tourist offices in Lviv, Yalta and Bakhchysaray; Ostap in Lviv; Ukrainian Railways for finally realising that fast trains with seats that travel in the hours of daylight might be a good idea; and last but not least to my wife Tanya, for introducing me to Ukraine in the first place.

Peter Dragicevich

Many thanks to all the wonderful people who helped me in Montenegro, especially Ivica Erdelja, Hayley Wright and Jack Delf, Emma and Ben Heywood, Krstinja Petranović, Danica Ćeranić and Matthew Lane. Also, I owe a debt of gratitude to James and Lorraine Hedderman, Tim Benzie and Kerri Tyler for their contributions before and after the journey.

Mark Elliott

Many thanks to Snezhan, Vlaren, Semir, Nermen, Žlka, Sanila, Narmina and Branislav, the helpful folks at Travellers Home and New Age Hostel, and Jan Beran and Mišo Marić for such a wonderfully random *slivovice* (plum brandy) evening in Mostar. As ever my greatest thanks go to my endlessly inspiring family, notably my unbeatable parents who, nearly four decades ago, had the crazy idea of driving me to Bosnia in the first place.

Steve Fallon

Thanks to Bea Szirti and Ildikó Nagy Moran for their helpful suggestions. Péter Lengyel showed me the correct wine roads to follow again and Gerard Gorman where the birds are. For hospitality on the road I am indebted to Regina Bruckner (Budapest), András Cseh (Eger), Zsuzsi Fábián (Kecskemét) and Shandor Madachy (Budapest). *Nagyon szépen köszönöm mindenkinek!* As always, I'd like to dedicate my share of this to partner Michael Rothschild, with love and gratitude.

Anna Kaminski

Many people to thank, not least Katie for entrusting me with this task, Tom and the rest of the Eastern Europe team, and my friends and family who helped me along the way. A particularly big thank you to Gintaras and Viktor in Kaunas, to my adopted Lithuanian parents in Nida (you know who you are), Nikas, Simonas, Ben and Aleksandra in Vilnius, Tomas and Jacinta for the Palanga all-nighter, and Rasa Dooling.

Anja Mutić

Hvala, mama, for your home cooking and contagious laughter. *Obrigada,* Hoji, for being there before, during and after. A huge *hvala* to my friends in Croatia who gave me endless recommendations – this book wouldn't be the same without you. Special thanks go to

THIS BOOK

This 12th edition of Lonely Planet's Eastern Europe guidebook is part of Lonely Planet's Europe series. Other titles in this series include Western Europe, Mediterranean Europe, Central Europe, Southeastern Europe, Scandinavian Europe and Europe on a Shoestring. Lonely Planet also publishes phrasebooks for these regions. This guidebook was commissioned in Lonely Planet's London office, and produced by the following:

Commissioning Editors Lucy Monie Hall, Katie O'Connell, Helena Smith

Coordinating Editor Elin Berglund

Coordinating Cartographer Valentina Kremenchutskaya

Coordinating Layout Designer Katherine Marsh

Managing Editors Sasha Baskett, Angela Tinson

Managing Cartographers Adrian Persoglia, Anthony Phelan, Amanda Sierp

Managing Layout Designer Jane Hart

Assisting Editors Janet Austin, Kate Kiely, Helen Koehne, Kellie Langdon, Anne Mason, Joanne Newell, Lorna Parkes, Monique Perrin, Sam Trafford

Assisting Cartographers Xavier Di Toro, Julie Dodkins, Alex Leung, James Leversha

Cover Research Kylie McLaughlin

Internal Image Research Aude Vauconsant

Language Content Branislava Vladisavljevic

Thanks to Joe Bindloss, Laura Crawford, Ryan Evans, Samantha Forge, Larissa Frost, Chris Girdler, Genesys India, Jouve India, Andi Jones, Annelies Mertens, Darren O'Connell, Trent Paton, Dianne Schallmeiner, Rebecca Skinner, Kerrianne Southway, Navin Sushil, Gerard Walker

Lidija in Zagreb and Mila in Split, as well as the team at HTZ. Finally, to the inspiring memory of my father who travels with me still.

Brandon Presser

A massive thank you goes first and foremost to Aleksis Karlsons for your hospitality and friendship. Special thanks to Jānis Jenzis, Agnese Kleina, Live Rīga, TAVA and everyone else that had a hand in making this edition a great one. Thanks also to Joanne and my clever co-authors and editors at Lonely Planet, and a big shout out to Carolyn for letting me rediscover the black poodle twenty times over.

Tim Richards

As always, I'm indebted to the staff of Poland's tourist offices, and the national train company PKP. *Dziękuję* to my Polish friends – Ewa, Magda and Andrzej – for their companionship and insights regarding their mother country. I'm also grateful to the members of the English Language Club in Kraków, who supplied both friendly conversation and advice on new places of interest. Thanks also to the generous inhabitants of Twitter for their random and useful assistance, particularly Magda Rakita for music tips.

Tamara Sheward

To research here is to make a zillion friends, so in addition to thanking the population

of Serbia, I'd like to offer clinks of the *rakija* glass and *mnogo hvala na* to... the NS Kiosk Crew, Gagi of Niš, Toma of Mokra Gora, Zoran for saving us from snakes and wolves, all the helpful oddballs we met during our *medeni mesec/*research jaunt, Dragana Eremić, the Ljesević family, the Lučić clan, Pappa and Mumma, and as ever, to Dušan, *najbolje, najslađi čovek u svemiru*!

Luke Waterson

To Josef for the Spišské Podhradie adventure; to the HRL girls; to Michaela in the High Tatras; to the entire Košice 2013 team; to Michal for the ride round the east; to Peter and Brano for the 'authentic' ride round Bratislava; to Giovanni and his great wine; to Majo for his hospitality in Slovenský Raj; and to the old women who opened up the wooden churches: *d'akujem* for the wonderful insight into your little-in-size, big-at-heart country.

ACKNOWLEDGMENTS

Climate map data adapted from Peel MC, Finlayson BL & McMahon TA (2007) 'Updated World Map of the Köppen-Geiger Climate Classification', *Hydrology and Earth System Sciences*, 11, 1633–44.
Cover photograph: Parliament building, Budapest, Hungary, George Tsafos/Getty Images.

index

000 Map pages
000 Photo pages

how to use this book

These symbols will help you find the listings you want:

👁 Sights	👉 Tours	🍷 Drinking
🏊 Beaches	🎊 Festivals & Events	☆ Entertainment
🏃 Activities	🛏 Sleeping	🛍 Shopping
🐢 Courses	🍴 Eating	ℹ Information/Transport

These symbols give you the vital information for each listing:

☎ Telephone Numbers	🛜 Wi-Fi Access	🚌 Bus
⊙ Opening Hours	🏊 Swimming Pool	⛴ Ferry
P Parking	🥗 Vegetarian Selection	M Metro
⊖ Nonsmoking	🍴 English-Language Menu	S Subway
❄ Air-Conditioning	👪 Family-Friendly	🚊 Tram
@ Internet Access	🐾 Pet-Friendly	🚆 Train

Reviews are organised by author preference.

Map Legend

Sights
- 🏖 Beach
- 🛕 Buddhist
- 🏰 Castle
- ✝ Christian
- 🕉 Hindu
- ☪ Islamic
- ✡ Jewish
- 🗿 Monument
- 🏛 Museum/Gallery
- 🏚 Ruin
- 🍷 Winery/Vineyard
- 🐾 Zoo
- ● Other Sight

Activities, Courses & Tours
- 🤿 Diving/Snorkelling
- 🛶 Canoeing/Kayaking
- ⛷ Skiing
- 🏄 Surfing
- 🏊 Swimming/Pool
- 🚶 Walking
- 🏄 Windsurfing
- ⊕ Other Activity/Course/Tour

Sleeping
- 🛏 Sleeping
- ⛺ Camping

Eating
- 🍴 Eating

Drinking
- ☕ Drinking
- ☕ Cafe

Entertainment
- 🎭 Entertainment

Shopping
- 🛍 Shopping

Information
- 💲 Bank
- 🏛 Embassy/Consulate
- ➕ Hospital/Medical
- @ Internet
- 👮 Police
- ✉ Post Office
- ☎ Telephone
- 🚻 Toilet
- ℹ Tourist Information
- ● Other Information

Transport
- ✈ Airport
- ⊗ Border Crossing
- 🚌 Bus
- ⊞ Cable Car/Funicular
- Cycling
- ⊖ Ferry
- Monorail
- P Parking
- ⛽ Petrol Station
- 🚕 Taxi
- 🚉 Train/Railway
- 🚊 Tram
- Ⓜ Underground Train Station
- ● Other Transport

Routes
- Tollway
- Freeway
- Primary
- Secondary
- Tertiary
- Lane
- Unsealed Road
- Plaza/Mall
- Steps
-)==(Tunnel
- Pedestrian Overpass
- Walking Tour
- Walking Tour Detour
- Path

Geographic
- 🛖 Hut/Shelter
- 🗼 Lighthouse
- 👁 Lookout
- ▲ Mountain/Volcano
- 🌴 Oasis
- 🏞 Park
-)(Pass
- 🞣 Picnic Area
- 💧 Waterfall

Population
- ✪ Capital (National)
- ◉ Capital (State/Province)
- ● City/Large Town
- ● Town/Village

Boundaries
- International
- State/Province
- Disputed
- Regional/Suburb
- Marine Park
- Cliff
- Wall

Hydrography
- River, Creek
- Intermittent River
- Swamp/Mangrove
- Reef
- Canal
- Water
- Dry/Salt/Intermittent Lake
- Glacier

Areas
- Beach/Desert
- + + + Cemetery (Christian)
- × × × Cemetery (Other)
- Park/Forest
- Sportsground
- Sight (Building)
- Top Sight (Building)

Anja Mutić
Croatia It's been more than two decades since Anja left her native Croatia. The journey took her to several countries before she made New York City her base 13 years ago. But the roots are calling and she's been returning to Croatia frequently for work and play. She's happy that Croatia's beauties are appreciated worldwide but secretly longs for the time when you could head to Hvar and hear the sound of crickets instead of blasting music. Anja is online at www.everthenomad.com.

Brandon Presser
Latvia His wanderlust bigger than his wallet, Brandon earned his backpacker stripes after an epic overland adventure from Morocco to Finland. He then joined the glamourous ranks of eternal nomadism, and has since travelled to over 75 countries and has contributed to roughly 40 Lonely Planet titles. He is the lead author of the *Estonia, Latvia & Lithuania* series, and is always delighted to return to the Baltic where he puts his Harvard art history degree to good use while checking out Rīga's surplus of evocative art nouveau architecture. For more about Brandon, check out www.brandonpresser.com..

Tim Richards
Poland Tim taught English in Kraków in the 1990s, and was fascinated by Poland's post-communist transition. He's returned repeatedly for Lonely Planet, deepening his relationship with this beautiful, complex country. In 2011 Tim released a Kindle ebook collecting his media articles about Poland, *We Have Here the Homicide*. When he's not on the road for Lonely Planet, Tim is a freelance journalist in Melbourne, Australia, writing about travel and the arts. You can find his blog and social media contacts at www.iwriter.com.au.

Tamara Sheward
Serbia After years of freelance travel writing, rock'n'roll journalism and insalubrious authordom, Tamara joined the Lonely Planet ranks as the presenter of LPTV's *Roads Less Travelled: Cambodia* documentary. Since then, she's stuck to covering decidedly less leech-infested destinations, including arctic Russia and Serbia. She lives between northern Serbia, a mountain shack in Montenegro and Melbourne with her husband Dušan, whom she never would have met were it not for some late night 'researching' for the last edition of *Eastern Europe*.

Luke Waterson
Slovakia Dividing his love affair with Slovakia between the castles, the mountains, *pirohy* (potato dumplings) and (more unexplainably) Soviet architecture, Luke has, besides contributions to 15 Lonely Planet titles, written for BBC Travel, the *Guardian*, Avalon Travel Publishing and a clutch of in-flight magazines (thus keeping you entertained even in mid-air). He lives on the very edge of Bratislava, conveniently located for slurping Small Carpathian wine and his favourite (non-writing) weekend activity is hiking into the hills to a quirky *krčma* (rural pub).

Read more about Luke at:
lonelyplanet.com/memebers/lukewaterson

Chris Deliso

Macedonia Chris Deliso is an American travel writer and journalist who has been based in Macedonia for over a decade, writing considerably about the country since then in a range of world media. In addition to covering Macedonia for the current book, he has written for Lonely Planet guides to Greece, Crete, Turkey, Romania and Bulgaria. His original enthusiasm for the region and introduction to its cultures and history came with an MPhil in Byzantine Studies at Oxford University in 1999.

Marc Di Duca

Ukraine Driven by an urge to discover Eastern Europe's wilder side, Marc first hit Kyiv one dark, snow-flecked night in early 1998. Many prolonged stints, countless near misses with Kyiv's metro doors and a few too many overheated bus journeys later, he still never misses a chance to fine-tune his Russian while exploring far-flung nooks of this immense land. Marc has penned guides to Moscow, Siberia's Lake Baikal, Russia and the Trans-Siberian Railway; this is his 23rd Lonely Planet contribution.

Read more about Marc at:
lonelyplanet.com/memebers/madidu

Peter Dragicevich

Montenegro After a dozen years working for newspapers and magazines in both his native New Zealand and Australia, Peter ditched the desk and hit the road. While it was family ties that first drew him to the Balkans, it's the history, natural beauty and intriguing people that keep bringing him back. He wrote Lonely Planet's first guide to the newly independent Montenegro and has contributed to dozens of other Lonely Planet titles, including four successive editions of this book.

Mark Elliott

Bosnia & Hercegovina British-born travel writer Mark Elliott was only 11 when his family first dragged him to Sarajevo and stood him in the now defunct concrete footsteps of Gavrilo Princip. Fortunately no Austro-Hungarian emperors were passing at the time. He has since visited virtually every corner of Bosnia and Hercegovina, supping fine Hercegovinian wines with master vintners, talking philosophy with Serb monks and Sufi mystics, and drinking more Bosnian coffee than any healthy stomach should be subjected to.

Steve Fallon

Hungary Steve, who has written every edition of the Lonely Planet *Hungary* guidebook, first visited Magyarország in the early 1980s by chance. It was a brief visit but he immediately fell in love with thermal baths, Tokaj wine and *bableves* (bean soup). Not able to survive on the occasional fleeting fix, he moved to Budapest in 1992, where he could enjoy all three in abundance. Now based in London, Steve returns to Hungary regularly for all these things and more: *pálinka* (fruit-flavoured brandy), art nouveau and the haunting voice of Marta Sebestyén.

Anna Kaminski

Lithuania Having been going to Lithuania since it was still part of the Soviet Union, Anna finds a lot to appreciate about the country, from the familiar relics of Communism to the cold beetroot soup – a childhood favourite. Vilnius's cobbled streets aside, she particularly enjoys revisiting the fishing villages and sand dunes of Curonian Spit.

OUR STORY

A beat-up old car, a few dollars in the pocket and a sense of adventure. In 1972 that's all Tony and Maureen Wheeler needed for the trip of a lifetime – across Europe and Asia overland to Australia. It took several months, and at the end – broke but inspired – they sat at their kitchen table writing and stapling together their first travel guide, *Across Asia on the Cheap*. Within a week they'd sold 1500 copies. Lonely Planet was born.

Today, Lonely Planet has offices in Melbourne, London and Oakland, with more than 600 staff and writers. We share Tony's belief that 'a great guidebook should do three things: inform, educate and amuse'.

OUR WRITERS

Tom Masters

Coordinating Author, Albania, Belarus, Kosovo, Moldova Tom is a British writer and photographer whose work has taken him to some of the strangest and most challenging countries on earth. Having lived in Russia, travelled to all corners of Eastern Europe and currently residing in East Berlin, he has a good understanding of what makes the former communist world tick. You can find more of Tom's work at www.tommasters.net.

Carolyn Bain

Estonia Melbourne-born Carolyn got her first glimpse behind the Iron Curtain in Poland in early 1989, while a student in Denmark. It was the year communism unravelled throughout Eastern Europe, and thus began her fascination. Since then, on regular visits to the Baltic region she has applauded the renewed independence and flourishing creativity here. Among other destinations, she has covered Sweden, Denmark and Iceland for Lonely Planet. Estonia holds a special place in her heart for combining the best of Eastern Europe and Scandinavia and coming up with something heartwarmingly unique.

Mark Baker

Bulgaria, Czech Republic, Romania, Slovenia Based permanently in Prague, Mark has lived and worked in Eastern Europe for more than 20 years, first as a journalist for The Economist Group and then for Bloomberg News and Radio Free Europe/Radio Liberty. He travels frequently throughout the region and counts Bulgaria, Slovenia and Romania among his favourite countries in Europe. In addition to this book, Mark is co-author of the Lonely Planet guides to Prague, Slovenia, and Romania and Bulgaria.

Greg Bloom

Russia Greg cut his teeth in the former Soviet Union as a journalist and later editor-in-chief of the *Kyiv Post*. He left Ukraine in 2003, but returns frequently to the region. In the service of Lonely Planet, he has been detained in Uzbekistan, taken a *shlagbaum* to the head in Kyiv, swam in the dying Aral Sea, snowboarded down volcanoes in Kamchatka and hit 100km/h in a Latvian bobsled. These days Greg lives in Cambodia. Read about his trips at www.mytripjournal.com/bloomblogs.

Read more about Greg at:
lonelyplanet.com/memebers/gbloom4

OVER PAGE | MORE WRITERS

Published by Lonely Planet Publications Pty Ltd
ABN 36 005 607 983
12th edition – Oct 2013
ISBN 978 1 74220 416 1
© Lonely Planet 2013   Photographs © as indicated 2013
10 9 8 7 6 5 4 3 2 1
Printed in Singapore

Although the authors and Lonely Planet have taken all reasonable care in preparing this book, we make no warranty about the accuracy or completeness of its content and, to the maximum extent permitted, disclaim all liability arising from its use.